UNITED STATES CODE

2000 EDITION

CONTAINING THE GENERAL AND PERMANENT LAWS
OF THE UNITED STATES, IN FORCE
ON JANUARY 2, 2001

Prepared and published under authority of Title 2, U.S. Code, Section 285b,
by the Office of the Law Revision Counsel of the House of Representatives

VOLUME TWENTY-SEVEN

TITLE 50—WAR AND NATIONAL DEFENSE,
POPULAR NAMES, AND TABLES

Revised Titles, Revised Statutes 1878,
and Statutes at Large (1789–1899)

UNITED STATES
GOVERNMENT PRINTING OFFICE
WASHINGTON : 2001

70-027 D 1 : QL 3

For sale by the Superintendent of Documents, U.S. Government Printing Office
Internet: bookstore.gpo.gov Phone: (202) 512–1800 Fax: (202) 512–2250
Mail: Stop SSOP, Washington, DC 20402–0001

TITLES OF UNITED STATES CODE

*1. General Provisions.

2. The Congress.

*3. The President.

*4. Flag and Seal, Seat of Government, and the States.

*5. Government Organization and Employees; and Appendix.

†6. [Surety Bonds.]

7. Agriculture.

8. Aliens and Nationality.

*9. Arbitration.

*10. Armed Forces; and Appendix.

*11. Bankruptcy; and Appendix.

12. Banks and Banking.

*13. Census.

*14. Coast Guard.

15. Commerce and Trade.

16. Conservation.

*17. Copyrights.

*18. Crimes and Criminal Procedure; and Appendix.

19. Customs Duties.

20. Education.

21. Food and Drugs.

22. Foreign Relations and Intercourse.

*23. Highways.

24. Hospitals and Asylums.

25. Indians.

26. Internal Revenue Code; and Appendix.

27. Intoxicating Liquors.

*28. Judiciary and Judicial Procedure; and Appendix.

29. Labor.

30. Mineral Lands and Mining.

*31. Money and Finance.

*32. National Guard.

33. Navigation and Navigable Waters.

‡34. [Navy.]

*35. Patents.

*36. Patriotic and National Observances, Ceremonies, and Organizations.

*37. Pay and Allowances of the Uniformed Services.

*38. Veterans' Benefits; and Appendix.

*39. Postal Service.

40. Public Buildings, Property, and Works; and Appendix.

41. Public Contracts.

42. The Public Health and Welfare.

43. Public Lands.

*44. Public Printing and Documents.

45. Railroads.

*46. Shipping; and Appendix.

47. Telegraphs, Telephones, and Radiotelegraphs.

48. Territories and Insular Possessions.

*49. Transportation.

50. War and National Defense; and Appendix.

*This title has been enacted as positive law. However, any Appendix to this title has not been enacted as positive law.
†This title was repealed by the enactment of Title 31.
‡This title was eliminated by the enactment of Title 10.

CONTENTS

PREFACE—2000 EDITION

The 2000 edition of the United States Code represents the 75th anniversary of the Code. It is the thirteenth edition of the Code, first published in 1926 with a new edition published every six years since 1934. This edition is a consolidation and codification of the general and permanent laws of the United States in force on January 2, 2001. The only basic differences between this edition and the 1994 edition of the Code are the changes required to incorporate the legislation enacted subsequent to the 1994 edition. This edition was prepared and published under the supervision of John R. Miller, Law Revision Counsel of the House of Representatives, pursuant to section 285b of Title 2 of the Code, and may be cited "U.S.C. 2000 ed."

As adopted in 1926, the Code establishes prima facie the general and permanent laws of the United States. Since that time, the Office of the Law Revision Counsel and its predecessors have been engaged in an ongoing effort to revise and codify for enactment into positive law specific titles of the Code. Upon enactment into positive law, those titles became legal evidence of the law contained therein, and provide an updated statement of the law with the elimination of inconsistent, redundant, and obsolete provisions. As indicated in the table of titles, about half of the titles of the Code have been enacted into positive law. When the entire Code is enacted, there will be no need to resort to the numerous volumes of the United States Statutes at Large for general and permanent law.

Speaker of the House of Representatives

WASHINGTON, D.C., *January 2, 2001.*

TABLE OF TITLES AND CHAPTERS

TITLE 5—GOVERNMENT ORGANIZATION AND EMPLOYEES—Continued

PART II—CIVIL SERVICE FUNCTIONS AND RESPONSIBILITIES—CONTINUED

TITLE 6—SURETY BONDS [REPEALED]

TITLE 7—AGRICULTURE

TITLE 7—AGRICULTURE—Continued

TITLE 8—ALIENS AND NATIONALITY

TITLE 9—ARBITRATION

TITLE 10—ARMED FORCES

SUBTITLE A—GENERAL MILITARY LAW

PART I—ORGANIZATION AND GENERAL MILITARY POWERS

PART II—PERSONNEL

TITLE 10—ARMED FORCES—Continued

SUBTITLE A—GENERAL MILITARY LAW—CONTINUED

PART III—TRAINING AND EDUCATION

PART IV—SERVICE, SUPPLY, AND PROCUREMENT

SUBTITLE B—ARMY

PART I—ORGANIZATION

PART II—PERSONNEL

PART III—TRAINING

PART IV—SERVICE, SUPPLY, AND PROCUREMENT

TITLE 10—ARMED FORCES—Continued

SUBTITLE B—ARMY—CONTINUED

PART IV—SERVICE, SUPPLY, AND PROCUREMENT—CONTINUED

TITLE 15—COMMERCE AND TRADE—Continued

TITLE 18—CRIMES AND CRIMINAL PROCEDURE—Continued

PART I—CRIMES—CONTINUED

PART II—CRIMINAL PROCEDURE

PART III—PRISONS AND PRISONERS

PART IV—CORRECTION OF YOUTHFUL OFFENDERS

TITLE 20—EDUCATION—Continued

TITLE 21—FOOD AND DRUGS

TITLE 22—FOREIGN RELATIONS AND INTERCOURSE

TITLE 22—FOREIGN RELATIONS AND INTERCOURSE—Continued

TITLE 23—HIGHWAYS

TITLE 24—HOSPITALS AND ASYLUMS

TITLE 25—INDIANS

TITLE 26—INTERNAL REVENUE CODE

SUBTITLE A—INCOME TAXES

SUBTITLE B—ESTATE AND GIFT TAXES

SUBTITLE C—EMPLOYMENT TAXES

SUBTITLE D—MISCELLANEOUS EXCISE TAXES

TITLE 28—JUDICIARY AND JUDICIAL PROCEDURE—Continued

PART III—COURT OFFICERS AND EMPLOYEES—CONTINUED

TITLE 29—LABOR

TITLE 30—MINERAL LANDS AND MINING

TITLE 30—MINERAL LANDS AND MINING—Continued

TITLE 31—MONEY AND FINANCE

SUBTITLE I—GENERAL

SUBTITLE II—THE BUDGET PROCESS

SUBTITLE III—FINANCIAL MANAGEMENT

SUBTITLE IV—MONEY

SUBTITLE V—GENERAL ASSISTANCE ADMINISTRATION

SUBTITLE VI—MISCELLANEOUS

TITLE 32—NATIONAL GUARD

TITLE 33—NAVIGATION AND NAVIGABLE WATERS

TITLE 36—PATRIOTIC AND NATIONAL OBSERVANCES, CEREMONIES, AND ORGANIZATIONS—Continued

SUBTITLE I—PATRIOTIC AND NATIONAL OBSERVANCES AND CEREMONIES—CONTINUED

PART B—UNITED STATES GOVERNMENT ORGANIZATIONS INVOLVED WITH OBSERVANCES AND CEREMONIES—CONTINUED

TITLE 36—PATRIOTIC AND NATIONAL OBSERVANCES, CEREMONIES, AND ORGANIZATIONS—Continued

SUBTITLE I—PATRIOTIC AND NATIONAL OBSERVANCES AND CEREMONIES—CONTINUED

PART B—UNITED STATES GOVERNMENT ORGANIZATIONS INVOLVED WITH OBSERVANCES AND CEREMONIES—CONTINUED

TITLE 38—VETERANS' BENEFITS—Continued

PART VI—ACQUISITION AND DISPOSITION OF PROPERTY

TITLE 39—POSTAL SERVICE

PART I—GENERAL

PART II—PERSONNEL

PART III—MODERNIZATION AND FISCAL ADMINISTRATION

PART IV—MAIL MATTER

PART V—TRANSPORTATION OF MAIL

TITLE 40—PUBLIC BUILDINGS, PROPERTY, AND WORKS

TITLE 41—PUBLIC CONTRACTS

TITLE 42—THE PUBLIC HEALTH AND WELFARE

TITLE 42—THE PUBLIC HEALTH AND WELFARE—Continued

TITLE 42—THE PUBLIC HEALTH AND WELFARE—Continued

TITLE 50—WAR AND NATIONAL DEFENSE—Continued

TITLE 50, APPENDIX—WAR AND NATIONAL DEFENSE

TITLE 50—WAR AND NATIONAL DEFENSE

RATIFICATION OF JAPANESE TREATY

The Treaty of Peace with Japan, signed at San Francisco on Sept. 8, 1951, was ratified by the United States Senate on Mar. 20, 1952. For Resolution of Ratification, see Congressional Record, Vol. 98, No. 46, Thursday, Mar. 20, 1952, p. 2634. According to Proc. No. 2974, eff. Apr. 29, 1952, 17 F.R. 3813, 66 Stat. c31, terminating the national emergencies proclaimed on September 8, 1939, and May 27, 1941, and set out as a note preceding section 1 of the Appendix to this title, such treaty came into force on Apr. 28, 1952.

TITLE REFERRED TO IN OTHER SECTIONS

This title is referred to in title 49 section 40125.

CHAPTER 1—COUNCIL OF NATIONAL DEFENSE

§ 1. Creation, purpose, and composition of council

A Council of National Defense is established, for the coordination of industries and resources for the national security and welfare, to consist of the Secretary of the Army, the Secretary of the Navy, the Secretary of the Interior, the Secretary of Agriculture, the Secretary of Commerce, and the Secretary of Labor.

(Aug. 29, 1916, ch. 418, § 2, 39 Stat. 649; July 26, 1947, ch. 343, title II, § 205(a), 61 Stat. 501.)

CODIFICATION

Sections 1 to 5 of this title are from section 2 of act Aug. 29, 1916, popularly known as the Army Appropriation Act for the fiscal year 1916.

CHANGE OF NAME

Department of War designated Department of the Army and title of Secretary of War changed to Secretary of the Army by section 205(a) of act July 26, 1947, ch. 343, title II, 61 Stat. 501. Section 205(a) of act July 26, 1947, was repealed by section 53 of act Aug. 10, 1956, ch. 1041, 70A Stat. 641. Section 1 of act Aug. 10, 1956, enacted "Title 10, Armed Forces" which in sections 3010 to 3013 continued Department of the Army under administrative supervision of Secretary of the Army.

TRANSFER OF FUNCTIONS

For transfer of certain membership functions, insofar as they pertain to Air Force, which functions were not previously transferred from Secretary of the Army and Department of the Army to Secretary of the Air Force and Department of the Air Force, see Secretary of Defense Transfer Order No. 40 [App. C(11)], July 22, 1949.

§ 2. Advisory commission

The Council of National Defense shall nominate to the President, and the President shall appoint, an advisory commission, consisting of not more than seven persons, each of whom shall have special knowledge of some industry, public utility, or the development of some natural resource, or be otherwise specially qualified, in the opinion of the council, for the performance of the duties hereinafter provided. The members of the advisory commission shall serve without compensation, but shall be allowed actual expenses of travel and subsistence when attending meetings of the commission or engaged in investigations pertaining to its activities. The advisory commission shall hold such meetings as shall be called by the council or be provided by the rules and regulations adopted by the council for the conduct of its work.

(Aug. 29, 1916, ch. 418, § 2, 39 Stat. 649.)

TERMINATION OF ADVISORY COMMISSIONS

Advisory commissions in existence on Jan. 5, 1973, to terminate not later than the expiration of the 2-year period following Jan. 5, 1973, unless, in the case of a commission established by the President or an officer of the Federal Government, such commission is renewed by appropriate action prior to the expiration of such 2-year period, or in the case of a commission established by the Congress, its duration is otherwise provided by law. Advisory commissions established after Jan. 5, 1973, to terminate not later than the expiration of the 2-year period beginning on the date of their establishment, unless, in the case of a commission established by the President or an officer of the Federal Government, such commission is renewed by appropriate action prior to the expiration of such 2-year period, or in the case of a commission established by the Congress, its duration is otherwise provided by law. See sections 3(2) and 14 of Pub. L. 92–463, Oct. 6, 1972, 86 Stat. 770, 776, set out in the Appendix to Title 5, Government Organization and Employees.

§ 3. Duties of council

It shall be the duty of the Council of National Defense to supervise and direct investigations and make recommendations to the President and the heads of executive departments as to the location of railroads with reference to the frontier of the United States so as to render possible expeditious concentration of troops and supplies to points of defense; the coordination of military, industrial, and commercial purposes in the location of branch lines of railroad; the utilization of waterways; the mobilization of military and naval resources for defense; the increase of domestic production of articles and materials essential to the support of armies and of the people during the interruption of foreign commerce; the development of seagoing transportation; data as to amounts, location, method and means of production, and availability of military supplies; the giving of information to producers and manufacturers as to the class of supplies needed by the military and other services of the Government, the requirements relating thereto, and the creation of relations which will render possible in time of need the immediate concentration and utilization of the resources of the Nation.

(Aug. 29, 1916, ch. 418, § 2, 39 Stat. 649; Nov. 9, 1921, ch. 119, § 3, 42 Stat. 212.)

CODIFICATION

The words "extensive highways and" which preceded "branch lines of railroad" omitted on authority of act Nov. 9, 1921, which transferred powers and duties of Council relating to highways to Secretary of Commerce.

§ 4. Rules and regulations; subordinate bodies and committees

The Council of National Defense shall adopt rules and regulations for the conduct of its work, which rules and regulations shall be subject to the approval of the President, and shall provide for the work of the advisory commission to the end that the special knowledge of such commission may be developed by suitable investigation, research, and inquiry and made available in conference and report for the use of the council; and the council may organize subordinate bodies for its assistance in special investigations, either by the employment of experts or by the creation of committees of specially qualified persons to serve without compensation, but to direct the investigations of experts so employed.

(Aug. 29, 1916, ch. 418, § 2, 39 Stat. 650.)

TERMINATION OF ADVISORY COMMISSIONS

Advisory commissions in existence on Jan. 5, 1973, to terminate not later than the expiration of the 2-year period following Jan. 5, 1973, unless, in the case of a commission established by the President or an officer of the Federal Government, such commission is renewed by appropriate action prior to the expiration of such 2-year period, or in the case of a commission established by the Congress, its duration is otherwise provided by law. Advisory commissions established after Jan. 5, 1973, to terminate not later than the expiration of the 2-year period beginning on the date of their establishment, unless, in the case of a commission established by the President or an officer of the

Federal Government, such commission is renewed by appropriate action prior to the expiration of such 2-year period, or in the case of a commission established by the Congress, its duration is otherwise provided by law. See sections 3(2) and 14 of Pub. L. 92–463, Oct. 6, 1972, 86 Stat. 770, 776, set out in the Appendix to Title 5, Government Organization and Employees.

§5. Reports of subordinate bodies and committees; unvouchered expenditures

Reports shall be submitted by all subordinate bodies and by the advisory commission to the council, and from time to time the council shall report to the President or to the heads of executive departments upon special inquiries or subjects appropriate thereto. When deemed proper the President may authorize, in amounts stipulated by him, unvouchered expenditures.

(Aug. 29, 1916, ch. 418, §2, 39 Stat. 650; Aug. 7, 1946, ch. 770, §1(53), 60 Stat. 870.)

CODIFICATION

Second sentence was from a proviso to the first sentence, which was affected by act Aug. 7, 1946.

AMENDMENTS

1946—Act Aug. 7, 1946, repealed all provisions requiring annual reports to Congress of the Council's activities and expenditures.

TERMINATION OF ADVISORY COMMISSIONS

Advisory commissions in existence on Jan. 5, 1973, to terminate not later than the expiration of the 2-year period following Jan. 5, 1973, unless, in the case of a commission established by the President or an officer of the Federal Government, such commission is renewed by appropriate action prior to the expiration of such 2-year period, or in the case of a commission established by the Congress, its duration is otherwise provided by law. Advisory commissions established after Jan. 5, 1973, to terminate not later than the expiration of the 2-year period beginning on the date of their establishment, unless, in the case of a commission established by the President or an officer of the Federal Government, such commission is renewed by appropriate action prior to the expiration of such 2-year period, or in the case of a commission established by the Congress, its duration is otherwise provided by law. See sections 3(2) and 14 of Pub. L. 92–463, Oct. 6, 1972, 86 Stat. 770, 776, set out in the Appendix to Title 5, Government Organization and Employees.

§6. Repealed. Pub. L. 89–554, §8(a), Sept. 6, 1966, 80 Stat. 644

Section, act June 5, 1920, ch. 235, 41 Stat. 886, placed a limit on salaries of officers and employees of Council of National Defense.

CHAPTER 2—BOARD OF ORDNANCE AND FORTIFICATION

§§11 to 15. Repealed. Dec. 16, 1930, ch. 14, §1, 46 Stat. 1029

Section 11, act Sept. 22, 1888, ch. 1028, §1, 25 Stat. 489, related to composition and duties of Board of Ordnance and Fortification.

Section 12, act Feb. 24, 1891, ch. 283, 26 Stat. 769, provided for a civilian member of Board.

Section 13, act Mar. 2, 1901, ch. 803, 31 Stat. 910, provided for additional members of Board.

Section 14, act Feb. 18, 1893, ch. 136, 27 Stat. 461, related to qualifications of Board Members.

Section 15, act Sept. 22, 1888, ch. 1028, §6, 25 Stat. 490, related to purchases and tests.

CHAPTER 3—ALIEN ENEMIES

§21. Restraint, regulation, and removal

Whenever there is a declared war between the United States and any foreign nation or government, or any invasion or predatory incursion is perpetrated, attempted or threatened against the territory of the United States by any foreign nation or government, and the President makes public proclamation of the event, all natives, citizens, denizens, or subjects of the hostile nation or government, being of the age of fourteen years and upward, who shall be within the United States and not actually naturalized, shall be liable to be apprehended, restrained, secured, and removed as alien enemies. The President is authorized in any such event, by his proclamation thereof, or other public act, to direct the conduct to be observed on the part of the United States, toward the aliens who become so liable; the manner and degree of the restraint to which they shall be subject and in what cases, and upon what security their residence shall be permitted, and to provide for the removal of those who, not being permitted to reside within the United States, refuse or neglect to depart therefrom; and to establish any other regulations which are found necessary in the premises and for the public safety.

(R.S. §4067; Apr. 16, 1918, ch. 55, 40 Stat. 531.)

CODIFICATION

R.S. §4067 derived from act July 6, 1798, ch. 66, §1, 1 Stat. 577.

AMENDMENTS

1918—Act Apr. 16, 1918, struck out provision restricting this section to males.

WORLD WAR II PROCLAMATIONS

The following proclamations under this section were issued during World War II:

Proc. No. 2525, Dec. 7, 1941, 6 F.R. 6321, 55 Stat. Pt. 2, 1700.
Proc. No. 2526, Dec. 8, 1941, 6 F.R. 6323, 55 Stat. Pt. 2, 1705.
Proc. No. 2527, Dec. 8, 1941, 6 F.R. 6324, 55 Stat. Pt. 2, 1707.
Proc. No. 2533, Dec. 29, 1941, 7 F.R. 55, 55 Stat. Pt. 2, 1714.
Proc. No. 2537, Jan. 14, 1942, 7 F.R. 329, 56 Stat. Pt. 2, 1933, revoked by Proc. No. 2678, Dec. 29, 1945, 11 F.R. 221, 60 Stat. Pt. 2, 1336.
Proc. No. 2563, July 17, 1942, 7 F.R. 5535, 56 Stat. Pt. 2, 1970.
Proc. No. 2655, July 14, 1945, 10 F.R. 8947, 59 Stat. Pt. 2, 870.
Proc. No. 2674, Dec. 7, 1945, 10 F.R. 14945, 59 Stat. Pt. 2, 889.
Proc. No. 2685, Apr. 11, 1946, 11 F.R. 4079, 60 Stat. Pt. 2, 1342, set out as a note preceding section 1 of Appendix to this title.

WORLD WAR I PROCLAMATIONS

Proclamations issued under this chapter during the years 1917 and 1918 will be found in 40 Stat. 1651, 1716, 1730, and 1772.

SECTION REFERRED TO IN OTHER SECTIONS

This section is referred to in section 22 of this title; sections 9, 34, 1981, 1982 of Appendix to this title; title 5 section 8332.

§22. Time allowed to settle affairs and depart

When an alien who becomes liable as an enemy, in the manner prescribed in section 21 of this title, is not chargeable with actual hostility, or other crime against the public safety, he shall be allowed, for the recovery, disposal, and removal of his goods and effects, and for his departure, the full time which is or shall be stipulated by any treaty then in force between the United States and the hostile nation or government of which he is a native citizen, denizen, or subject; and where no such treaty exists, or is in force, the President may ascertain and declare such reasonable time as may be consistent with the public safety, and according to the dictates of humanity and national hospitality.

(R.S. §4068.)

CODIFICATION

R.S. §4068 derived from acts July 6, 1798, ch. 66, §1, 1 Stat. 577; July 6, 1812, ch. 130, 2 Stat. 781.

SECTION REFERRED TO IN OTHER SECTIONS

This section is referred to in sections 9, 34, 1981, 1982 of Appendix to this title; title 5 section 8332.

§23. Jurisdiction of United States courts and judges

After any such proclamation has been made, the several courts of the United States, having criminal jurisdiction, and the several justices and judges of the courts of the United States, are authorized and it shall be their duty, upon complaint against any alien enemy resident and at large within such jurisdiction or district, to the danger of the public peace or safety, and contrary to the tenor or intent of such proclamation, or other regulations which the President may have established, to cause such alien to be duly apprehended and conveyed before such court, judge, or justice; and after a full examination and hearing on such complaint, and sufficient cause appearing, to order such alien to be removed out of the territory of the United States, or to give sureties for his good behavior, or to be otherwise restrained, conformably to the proclamation or regulations established as aforesaid, and to imprison, or otherwise secure such alien, until the order which may be so made shall be performed.

(R.S. §4069.)

CODIFICATION

R.S. §4069 derived from act July 6, 1798, ch. 66, §2, 1 Stat. 577.

SECTION REFERRED TO IN OTHER SECTIONS

This section is referred to in sections 9, 34, 1981, 1982 of Appendix to this title; title 5 section 8332.

§24. Duties of marshals

When an alien enemy is required by the President, or by order of any court, judge, or justice, to depart and to be removed, it shall be the duty of the marshal of the district in which he shall be apprehended to provide therefor and to execute such order in person, or by his deputy or other discreet person to be employed by him, by causing a removal of such alien out of the territory of the United States; and for such removal the marshal shall have the warrant of the President, or of the court, judge, or justice ordering the same, as the case may be.

(R.S. §4070.)

CODIFICATION

R.S. §4070 derived from act July 6, 1798, ch. 66, §3, 1 Stat. 578.

SECTION REFERRED TO IN OTHER SECTIONS

This section is referred to in sections 9, 34, 1981, 1982 of Appendix to this title; title 5 section 8332.

CHAPTER 4—ESPIONAGE

§§31 to 39. Repealed. June 25, 1948, ch. 645, §21, 62 Stat. 862

Section 31, acts June 15, 1917, ch. 30, title I, §1, 40 Stat. 217; Mar. 28, 1940, ch. 72, title I, §1, 54 Stat. 79, related to unlawful obtaining or permitting to be obtained information affecting national defense. See section 793 of Title 18, Crimes and Criminal Procedure.

Section 32, act June 15, 1917, ch. 30, title I, §2, 40 Stat. 218, related to unlawful disclosures affecting national defense. See section 794 of Title 18.

Section 33, act June 15, 1917, ch. 30, title I, §3, 40 Stat. 219, related to seditious or disloyal acts or words in time of war. See section 2388 of Title 18. Section 33 was amended by act May 16, 1918, ch. 75, §1, 40 Stat. 553, which was repealed and the original section reenacted by act Mar. 3, 1921, ch. 136, 41 Stat. 1359.

Section 34, act June 15, 1917, ch. 30, title I, §4, 40 Stat. 219, related to conspiracy to violate sections 32 and 33 of this title. See sections 794 and 2388 of Title 18.

Section 35, acts June 15, 1917, ch. 30, title I, §5, 40 Stat. 219; Mar. 28, 1940, ch. 72, §2, 54 Stat. 79, related to the harboring or concealing of violators of the law. See sections 792 and 2388 of Title 18.

Section 36, act June 15, 1917, ch. 30, title I, §6, 40 Stat. 219, related to designation by proclamation of prohibited areas. See section 793 of Title 18.

Section 37, act June 15, 1917, ch. 30, title I, §8, 40 Stat. 219, related to places subject to provisions of sections 31 to 42 of this title. See section 2388 of Title 18.

Section 38, act June 15, 1917, ch. 30, title I, §7, 40 Stat. 219, related to jurisdiction of courts-martial and military commissions.

Section 39, act June 15, 1917, ch. 30, title XIII, §2, 40 Stat. 231; Proc. No. 2695, eff. July 4, 1946, 11 F.R. 7517, 60 Stat. 1352, related to jurisdiction of Canal Zone courts over offenses on high seas. See section 3241 of Title 18.

EFFECTIVE DATE OF REPEAL

Repeal of sections 31 to 39 effective Sept. 1, 1948, see section 38 of act June 25, 1948, set out as an Effective Date note preceding section 1 of Title 28, Judiciary and Judicial Procedure.

§40. Transferred

CODIFICATION

Section, act June 15, 1917, ch. 30, title XIII, §1, 40 Stat. 231, defined "United States" as used in act June 15, 1917, and was transferred to section 195 of this title.

§41. Repealed. June 25, 1948, ch. 645, §21, 62 Stat. 862

Section, act June 15, 1917, ch. 30, title VIII, §4, 40 Stat. 226, defined "Foreign government". See section 11 of Title 18, Crimes and Criminal Procedure.

EFFECTIVE DATE OF REPEAL

Repeal effective Sept. 1, 1948, see section 38 of act June 25, 1948, set out as an Effective Date note preceding section 1 of Title 28, Judiciary and Judicial Procedure.

§42. Transferred

CODIFICATION

Section, act June 15, 1917, ch. 30, title XIII, §4, 40 Stat. 231, related to savings provisions and is set out as a Separability note under section 191 of this title.

Section was formerly classified to section 536 of Title 18 prior to the general revision and enactment of Title 18, Crimes and Criminal Procedure, by act June 25, 1948, ch. 645, 62 Stat. 683.

CHAPTER 4A—PHOTOGRAPHING, SKETCHING, MAPPING, ETC., DEFENSIVE INSTALLATIONS

§§45 to 45d. Repealed. June 25, 1948, ch. 645, §21, 62 Stat. 862

Section 45, act Jan. 12, 1938, ch. 2, §1, 52 Stat. 3, related to photographing of defensive installations. See sections 795 to 797 of Title 18, Crimes and Criminal Procedure.

Section 45a, act Jan. 12, 1938, ch. 2, §2, 52 Stat. 3, related to photographing, etc., from aircraft. See section 796 of Title 18.

Section 45b, act Jan. 12, 1938, ch. 2, §3, 52 Stat. 3, related to reproducing, publishing, selling uncensored copies. See section 797 of Title 18.

Section 45c, act Jan. 12, 1938, ch. 2, §4, 52 Stat. 4, related to definitions of "aircraft", "post", "camp", and "station". See sections 795 and 796 of Title 18.

Section 45d, act Jan. 12, 1938, ch. 2, §5, 52 Stat. 4, related to geographical application of law.

EFFECTIVE DATE OF REPEAL

Repeal of sections 45 to 45d effective Sept. 1, 1948, see section 38 of act June 25, 1948, set out as an Effective Date note preceding section 1 of Title 28, Judiciary and Judicial Procedure.

CHAPTER 4B—DISCLOSURE OF CLASSIFIED INFORMATION

§§46 to 46b. Repealed. Oct. 31, 1951, ch. 655, §56(c), 65 Stat. 729

Section 46, act May 13, 1950, ch. 185, §2, 64 Stat. 159, related to unlawful disclosure of classified information. See section 798 of Title 18, Crimes and Criminal Procedure.

Section 46a, act May 13, 1950, ch. 185, §1, 64 Stat. 159, defined terms for use in this chapter.

Section 46b, act May 13, 1950, ch. 185, §3, 64 Stat. 160, related to penalties for improper disclosure.

SAVINGS PROVISION

Section 56(*l*) of act Oct. 31, 1951, provided that the repeal of sections 46 to 46b shall not affect any rights or liabilities existing hereunder on Oct. 31, 1951.

CHAPTER 4C—ATOMIC WEAPONS AND SPECIAL NUCLEAR MATERIALS INFORMATION REWARDS

§47a. Information concerning illegal introduction, manufacture, acquisition or export of special nuclear material or atomic weapons or conspiracies relating thereto; reward

Any person who furnishes original information to the United States—

(a) leading to the finding or other acquisition by the United States of special nuclear material or an atomic weapon which has been introduced into the United States or manufactured or acquired therein contrary to the laws of the United States, or

(b) with respect to the introduction or attempted introduction into the United States or the manufacture or acquisition or attempted manufacture or acquisition of, or a conspiracy to introduce into the United States or to manufacture or acquire, special nuclear material or an atomic weapon contrary to the laws of the United States, or

(c) with respect to the export or attempted export, or a conspiracy to export, special nuclear material or an atomic weapon from the United States contrary to the laws of the United States,

shall be rewarded by the payment of an amount not to exceed $500,000.

(July 15, 1955, ch. 372, §2, 69 Stat. 365; Pub. L. 93–377, §1(b), Aug. 17, 1974, 88 Stat. 472.)

AMENDMENTS

1974—Pub. L. 93–377 in par. (a) made minor changes in phraseology, in par. (b) included information relating to the actual introduction, manufacture and acquisition, or conspiring to introduce into the United States or to manufacture or acquire special nuclear material or an atomic weapon as within the information for which a reward would be given, and added par. (c).

SHORT TITLE

Section 1 of act July 15, 1955, as amended by section 1(a) of Pub. L. 93–377, provided: "That this Act [enacting this chapter] may be cited as the 'Atomic Weapons and Special Nuclear Materials Rewards Act'."

SECTION REFERRED TO IN OTHER SECTIONS

This section is referred to in section 47b of this title.

§47b. Determination by Attorney General of entitlement and amount of reward; consultation; Presidential approval

The Attorney General shall determine whether a person furnishing information to the United States is entitled to a reward and the amount to be paid pursuant to section 47a of this title. Before making a reward under this section the Attorney General shall advise and consult with the Atomic Energy Commission. A reward of $50,000 or more may not be made without the approval of the President.

(July 15, 1955, ch. 372, §3, 69 Stat. 365; Pub. L. 93–377, §1(b), Aug. 17, 1974, 88 Stat. 473.)

AMENDMENTS

1974—Pub. L. 93–377 substituted provisions authorizing the Attorney General, with the advice of the Atomic Energy Commission, to determine entitlement and the amount of reward for a person furnishing information to the United States, for provisions authorizing an Awards Board to determine entitlement and amount of such reward, setting forth the composition of the Board and criteria for reward.

TRANSFER OF FUNCTIONS

Atomic Energy Commission abolished and functions transferred by sections 5814 and 5841 of Title 42, The Public Health and Welfare. See also Transfer of Functions notes set out under those sections.

SECTION REFERRED TO IN OTHER SECTIONS

This section is referred to in sections 47c, 47d, 47e of this title.

§ 47c. Aliens; waiver of admission requirements

If the information leading to an award under section 47b of this title is furnished by an alien, the Secretary of State, the Attorney General, and the Director of Central Intelligence, acting jointly, may determine that the admission of such alien into the United States is in the public interest and, in that event, such alien and the members of his immediate family may receive immigrant visas and may be admitted to the United States for permanent residence, notwithstanding the requirements of the Immigration and Nationality Act [8 U.S.C. 1101 et seq.].

(July 15, 1955, ch. 372, § 4, 69 Stat. 366; Pub. L. 104–208, div. C, title III, § 308(f)(7), Sept. 30, 1996, 110 Stat. 3009–622.)

REFERENCES IN TEXT

The Immigration and Nationality Act, referred to in text, is act June 27, 1952, ch. 477, 66 Stat. 163, as amended, which is classified principally to chapter 12 (§ 1101 et seq.) of Title 8, Aliens and Nationality. For complete classification of this Act to the Code, see Short Title note set out under section 1101 of Title 8 and Tables.

AMENDMENTS

1996—Pub. L. 104–208 substituted "admission" for "entry".

EFFECTIVE DATE OF 1996 AMENDMENT

Amendment by Pub. L. 104–208 effective, with certain transitional provisions, on the first day of the first month beginning more than 180 days after Sept. 30, 1996, see section 309 of Pub. L. 104–208, set out as a note under section 1101 of Title 8, Aliens and Nationality.

SECTION REFERRED TO IN OTHER SECTIONS

This section is referred to in section 47f of this title.

§ 47d. Hearings; rules and regulations; conclusiveness of determinations of Attorney General

(a) The Attorney General is authorized to hold such hearings and make, promulgate, issue, rescind, and amend such rules and regulations as may be necessary to carry out the purposes of this chapter.

(b) A determination made by the Attorney General under section 47b of this title shall be final and conclusive and no court shall have power or jurisdiction to review it.

(July 15, 1955, ch. 372, § 5, 69 Stat. 366; Pub. L. 93–377, § 1(b), Aug. 17, 1974, 88 Stat. 473.)

AMENDMENTS

1974—Pub. L. 93–377 designated existing provisions as subsec. (a), substituted "Attorney General" for "Board as administering agent", and added subsec. (b).

§ 47e. Certification of award; approval; payment

Any awards granted under section 47b of this title shall be certified by the Attorney General and, together with the approval of the President in those cases where such approval is required, transmitted to the Director of Central Intelligence for payment out of funds appropriated or available for the administration of the National Security Act of 1947, as amended.

(July 15, 1955, ch. 372, § 6, 69 Stat. 366; Pub. L. 93–377, § 1(c), Aug. 17, 1974, 88 Stat. 473.)

REFERENCES IN TEXT

The National Security Act of 1947, as amended, referred to in text, is act July 26, 1947, ch. 343, 61 Stat. 495, as amended. For complete classification of this Act to the Code, see Short Title note set out under section 401 of this title and Tables.

AMENDMENTS

1974—Pub. L. 93–377 substituted "Attorney General" for "Awards Board".

§ 47f. Definitions

As used in this chapter—

(a) The term "atomic energy" means all forms of energy released in the course of nuclear fission or nuclear transformation.

(b) The term "atomic weapon" means any device utilizing atomic energy, exclusive of the means for transporting or propelling the device (where such means is a separable and divisible part of the device), the principal purpose of which is for use as, or for development of, a weapon, a weapon prototype, or a weapon test device.

(c) The term "special nuclear material" means plutonium, or uranium enriched in the isotope 233 or in the isotope 235, or any other material which is found to be special nuclear material pursuant to the provisions of the Atomic Energy Act of 1954 [42 U.S.C. 2011 et seq.].

(d) The term "United States," when used in a geographical sense, includes Puerto Rico, all Territories and possessions of the United States and the Canal Zone; except that in section 47c of this title, the term "United States" when so used shall have the meaning given to it in the Immigration and Nationality Act [8 U.S.C. 1101 et seq.].

(July 15, 1955, ch. 372, § 7, 69 Stat. 366.)

REFERENCES IN TEXT

The Atomic Energy Act of 1954, referred to in subsec. (c), is act Aug. 1, 1946, ch. 724, as added by act Aug. 30, 1954, ch. 1073, § 1, 68 Stat. 921, and amended, which is classified generally to chapter 23 (§ 2011 et seq.) of Title 42, The Public Health and Welfare. For complete classification of this Act to the Code, see Short Title note set out under section 2011 of Title 42 and Tables.

The Immigration and Nationality Act, referred to in subsec. (d), is act June 27, 1952, ch. 477, 66 Stat. 163, as amended, which is classified principally to chapter 12 (§ 1101 et seq.) of Title 8, Aliens and Nationality. For complete classification of this Act to the Code, see Short Title note set out under section 1101 of Title 8 and Tables.

CHAPTER 5—ARSENALS, ARMORIES, ARMS, AND WAR MATERIAL GENERALLY

SUBCHAPTER I—ARSENALS, ARMORIES, ARMS, AND WAR MATERIALS

SUBCHAPTER I—ARSENALS, ARMORIES, ARMS, AND WAR MATERIALS

§§51 to 57. Repealed. Aug. 10, 1956, ch. 1041, §53, 70A Stat. 641

Section 51, act Aug. 5, 1882, ch. 395, 22 Stat. 299, related to pay of master amorer at Springfield Armory.

Section 52, act June 23, 1874, ch. 486, 18 Stat. 282, related to pay of clerks at Springfield Armory.

Section 53, R.S. §1665, required an annual account of expenses of national armories, together with an account of arms made and repaired thereon.

Section 54, acts Aug. 18, 1890, ch. 797, §2, 26 Stat. 320; Aug. 7, 1946, ch. 770, §1(52), 60 Stat. 870, related to accounts of cost of type and experimental manufacture of guns and other articles.

Section 55, R.S. §1666, authorized Secretary of War to abolish useless or unnecessary arsenals. See section 4532 of Title 10, Armed Forces.

Section 56, R.S. §1669, provided for forfeitures by reason of misconduct of workmen in armories.

Section 57, R.S. §1671, exempted from jury duty all artificers and workmen employed in armories and arsenals, of the United States.

§58. Repealed. Sept. 1, 1954, ch. 1208, title III, §305(d), 68 Stat. 1114

Section, act July 17, 1912, ch. 236, 37 Stat. 193, related to awards. See section 4501 et seq. of Title 5, Government Organization and Employees.

EFFECTIVE DATE OF REPEAL

Repeal effective 90 days after Sept. 1, 1954, see section 307 of act Sept. 1, 1954.

§§ 59 to 66. Repealed. Aug. 10, 1956, ch. 1041, § 53, 70A Stat. 641

Section 59, act July 26, 1886, ch. 781, § 1, 24 Stat. 151, related to testing of rifled cannon for Navy.

Section 60, act July 8, 1918, ch. 137, 40 Stat. 817, authorized transfer of naval ordnance and ordnance material from Navy Department to Department of War.

Section 61, acts Mar. 3, 1879, ch. 183, 20 Stat. 412; Apr. 14, 1937, ch. 79, 50 Stat. 63, authorized issuance of arms and ammunition to protect public property, provided for reimbursement. See section 4655 of Title 10, Armed Forces.

Section 62, acts Feb. 10, 1920, ch. 64, 41 Stat. 403; June 5, 1920, ch. 240, 41 Stat. 976; May 26, 1952, ch. 334, 66 Stat. 94, authorized loan of rifles to organizations of honorably discharged soldiers. See section 4683 of Title 10.

Section 62a, act June 30, 1906, ch. 3938, 34 Stat. 817, authorized loan of ordnance to schools and State homes for veterans' orphans. See sections 4685 and 9685 of Title 10.

Section 62b, act Dec. 15, 1926, ch. 10, 44 Stat. 922, authorized Secretary of War to relieve posts or camps or organizations composed of honorably discharged soldiers, sailors, or marines, and sureties on bonds, from liability on account of loss or destruction of rifles, slings, and cartridge belts loaned to such organizations. See section 4683 of Title 10.

Section 62c, acts May 29, 1934, ch. 369, 48 Stat. 815; Aug. 30, 1935, ch. 826, 49 Stat. 1013, authorized Secretary of War to donate Army equipment loaned under authority of section 62 of this title.

Section 63, act May 11, 1908, ch. 163, 35 Stat. 125, authorized sales of ordnance property to schools and State homes for veterans' orphans. See sections 4625 and 9625 of Title 10, Armed Forces.

Section 64, acts May 28, 1908, ch. 215, § 14, 35 Stat. 443; June 28, 1950, ch. 383, title IV, § 402(g), 64 Stat. 273; Oct. 31, 1951, ch. 654, § 2(26), 65 Stat. 707, authorized sale of obsolete small arms to patriotic organizations. See sections 4684 and 9684 of Title 10.

Section 64a, act Mar. 3, 1875, ch. 130, 18 Stat. 388, provided for sale of useless ordnance materials, appropriated an amount equal to net proceeds of sale for purpose of procuring a supply of material, and limited expenditures to not more than $75,000 in any one year.

Section 65, acts Apr. 23, 1904, ch. 1485, 33 Stat. 276; Aug. 1, 1953, ch. 305, title VI, § 645, 67 Stat. 357, authorized sale of serviceable ordnance and ordnance stores to American designers.

Section 66, acts Feb. 8, 1889, ch. 116, 25 Stat. 657; Mar. 3, 1899, ch. 423, 30 Stat. 1073; May 26, 1900, ch. 586, 31 Stat. 216; June 28, 1950, ch. 383, title IV, § 402(e), 64 Stat. 273; Oct. 31, 1951, ch. 654, § 2(27), 65 Stat. 707, authorized issuance of condemned ordnance to State homes for soldiers and sailors. See sections 4686 and 9686 of Title 10.

§ 67. Transferred

CODIFICATION

Section, acts May 22, 1896, ch. 231, 29 Stat. 133; May 26, 1928, ch. 785, 45 Stat. 773; Feb. 28, 1933, ch. 137, 47 Stat. 1369; June 19, 1940, ch. 398, § 1, 54 Stat. 491; July 31, 1947, ch. 421, 61 Stat. 707; Feb. 27, 1948, ch. 76, § 1, 62 Stat. 37; Oct. 31, 1951, ch. 654, § 2(2), 65 Stat. 706, which authorized loans or gifts of condemned or obsolete equipment, was transferred to section 150p of former Title 5, Executive Departments and Government Officers and Employees, and subsequently repealed and reenacted as section 2572 of Title 10, Armed Forces, by act Aug. 10, 1956, ch. 1041, §§ 1, 53, 70A Stat. 143, 641.

§§ 68 to 71. Repealed. Aug. 10, 1956, ch. 1041, § 53, 70A Stat. 641

Section 68, acts Mar. 4, 1909, ch. 319, § 47, 35 Stat. 1075; June 28, 1950, ch. 383, title IV, § 402(i), 64 Stat. 273; Oct. 31, 1951, ch. 654, § 2(28), 65 Stat. 708, authorized sale of obsolete ordnance for public parks, public buildings and soldiers' monuments purposes. See sections 4684 and 9684 of Title 10, Armed Forces.

Section 69, act Mar. 2, 1905, ch. 1307, 33 Stat. 841, authorized sale of individual pieces of armament. See section 2574 of Title 10.

Section 70, acts Mar. 3, 1909, ch. 252, 35 Stat. 751; June 28, 1950, ch. 383, title IV, § 402(h), 64 Stat. 273, authorized sale of ordnance property to officers of the Navy and Marine Corps. See section 4625 and 9625 of Title 10.

Section 71, act Mar. 3, 1909, ch. 252, 35 Stat. 750, authorized sale of ordnance stores to civilian employees of Army and to American National Red Cross. See sections 4625 and 9625 of Title 10.

§ 72. Repealed. May 1, 1937, ch. 146, § 5(i), 50 Stat. 126

Section, act Aug. 29, 1916, ch. 418, § 1, 39 Stat. 643, related to sale of ordnance and stores to Cuba.

§ 73. Repealed. Aug. 1, 1953, ch. 305, title VI, § 645, 67 Stat. 357

Section, act Apr. 23, 1904, ch. 1485, 33 Stat. 276, related to disposition of proceeds from sales of serviceable ordnance and stores. See sections 2208 and 2210 of Title 10, Armed Forces.

§§ 74 to 81. Repealed. Aug. 10, 1956, ch. 1041, § 53, 70A Stat. 641

Section 74, act Jan. 22, 1923, ch. 28, 42 Stat. 1142, provided that net proceeds of sales of useless ordnance material by Navy Department should be covered into Treasury as "Miscellaneous receipts". See section 7543 of Title 10, Armed Forces.

Section 75, act Aug. 24, 1912, ch. 391, § 1, 37 Stat. 589, related to payment for transfers of ordnance or stores to bureaus or departments.

Section 76, act June 20, 1878, ch. 359, § 1, 20 Stat. 223, authorized private use of a machine for testing iron and steel.

Section 77, acts Mar. 3, 1885, ch. 360, 23 Stat. 502; May 29, 1928, ch. 901, par. 27, 45 Stat. 988, regulated tests of iron and steel and other materials for industrial purposes.

Section 78, act June 3, 1916, ch. 134, § 123, 39 Stat. 215, related to gauges, dies, and tools for manufacture of arms.

Section 79, act June 3, 1916, ch. 134, § 124, 39 Stat. 215, related to nitrate plants.

Section 80, act June 3, 1916, ch. 134, § 120, 39 Stat. 213, 214, related to procurement of war material and mobilization of industries. See sections 2538 to 2540 of Title 10.

Section 81, act May 14, 1928, ch. 544, 45 Stat. 509, authorized Secretary of War to secure assistance, whenever practicable, of Geological Survey, Coast and Geodetic Survey, or other mapping agencies of the Government in execution of military surveys and maps. Provisions similar to former section 81 were contained in the following appropriation acts:

Mar. 23, 1928, ch. 232, title I, 45 Stat. 342.
Feb. 23, 1927, ch. 167, title I, 44 Stat. 1123.
Apr. 15, 1926, ch. 146, title I, 44 Stat. 273.
Feb. 12, 1925, ch. 225, title I, 43 Stat. 911.
June 7, 1924, ch. 291, title I, 43, Stat. 496.
Mar. 2, 1923, ch. 178, title I, 42 Stat. 1402.
June 30, 1922, ch. 253, title I, 42 Stat. 741.

§ 82. Procurement of ships and material during war

(a) Definitions

The word "person" as used in subsections (b) and (c) of this section shall include any individual, trustee, firm, association, company, or corporation. The word "ship" shall include any boat, vessel, submarine, or any form of aircraft, and the parts thereof. The words "war material"

shall include arms, armament, ammunition, stores, supplies, and equipment for ships and airplanes, and everything required for or in connection with the production thereof. The word "factory" shall include any factory, workshop, engine works, building used for manufacture, assembling, construction, or any process, and any shipyard or dockyard. The words "United States" shall include the Canal Zone and all territory and waters, continental and insular, subject to the jurisdiction of the United States.

(b) Presidential powers

In time of war the President is authorized and empowered, in addition to all other existing provisions of law:

First. Within the limits of the amounts appropriated therefor, to place an order with any person for such ships or war material as the necessities of the Government, to be determined by the President, may require and which are of the nature, kind, and quantity usually produced or capable of being produced by such person. Compliance with all such orders shall be obligatory on any person to whom such order is given, and such order shall take precedence over all other orders and contracts theretofore placed with such person. If any person owning, leasing, or operating any factory equipped for the building or production of ships or war material for the Navy shall refuse or fail to give to the United States such preference in the execution of such an order, or shall refuse to build, supply, furnish, or manufacture the kind, quantity, or quality of ships or war material so ordered at such reasonable price as shall be determined by the President, the President may take immediate possession of any factory of such person, or of any part thereof without taking possession of the entire factory, and may use the same at such times and in such manner as he may consider necessary or expedient.

Second. Within the limit of the amounts appropriated therefor, to modify or cancel any existing contract for the building, production, or purchase of ships or war material; and if any contractor shall refuse or fail to comply with the contract as so modified the President may take immediate possession of any factory of such contractor, or any part thereof without taking possession of the entire factory, and may use the same at such times and in such manner as he may consider necessary or expedient.

Third. To require the owner or occupier of any factory in which ships or war material are built or produced to place at the disposal of the United States the whole or any part of the output of such factory, and, within the limit of the amounts appropriated therefor, to deliver such output or parts thereof in such quantities and at such times as may be specified in the order at such reasonable price as shall be determined by the President.

Fourth. To requisition and take over for use or operation by the Government any factory, or any part thereof without taking possession of the entire factory, whether the United States has or has not any contract or agreement with the owner or occupier of such factory.

(d)[1] Compensation for commandeered material

Whenever the United States shall cancel or modify any contract, make use of, assume, occupy, requisition, or take over any factory or part thereof, or any ships or war material, in accordance with the provisions of subsection (b) of this section, it shall make just compensation therefor, to be determined by the President, and if the amount thereof so determined by the President is unsatisfactory to the person entitled to receive the same, such person shall be paid fifty per centum of the amount so determined by the President and shall be entitled to sue the United States to recover such further sum as added to said fifty per centum shall make up such amount as will be just compensation therefor, in the manner provided for by section 1346 or section 1491 of title 28.

(Mar. 4, 1917, ch. 180, 39 Stat. 1192.)

REFERENCES IN TEXT

For definition of Canal Zone, referred to in subsec. (a), see section 3602(b) of Title 22, Foreign Relations and Intercourse.

CODIFICATION

In subsec. (d), "section 1346 or section 1491 of title 28" substituted for "section twenty-four, paragraph twenty, and section one hundred and forty-five of the Judicial Code" (those sections classified to sections 41(20) and 250 of former Title 28, Judicial Code and Judiciary) on authority of act June 25, 1948, ch. 646, 62 Stat. 869, section 1 of which enacted Title 28, Judiciary and Judicial Procedure. Section 1346 of Title 28 sets forth the basic jurisdiction of the district courts in cases in which the United States is defendant. Section 1491 of Title 28 sets forth the basic jurisdiction of the United States Court of Claims. Sections 24(20) and 145 of the Judicial Code were also classified to sections 1496, 1501, 1503, 2401, 2402, and 2501 of Title 28.

SIMILAR PROVISIONS

Provisions similar to those in this section were contained in the Naval Appropriation Act, 1918, act July 1, 1918, ch. 114, 40 Stat. 719, which terminated six months after the treaty of peace between the United States and Germany (Oct. 18, 1921).

TERMINATION OF WAR AND EMERGENCIES

Act July 25, 1947, ch. 327, §3, 61 Stat. 451, provided that in the interpretation of the provisions of this section, which authorized the President to acquire, through construction or conversion, ships, landing craft, and other vessels, the date July 25, 1947, shall be deemed to be the date of termination of any state of war theretofore declared by Congress and of the national emergencies proclaimed by the President on Sept. 8, 1939, and May 27, 1941.

EX. ORD. NO. 12742. NATIONAL SECURITY INDUSTRIAL RESPONSIVENESS

Ex. Ord. No. 12742, Jan. 8, 1991, 56 F.R. 1079, provided:

By the authority vested in me as President by the Constitution and the laws of the United States of America, including 50 U.S.C. App. 468, 10 U.S.C. 4501 and 9501 [former sections 4501 and 9501 of Title 10, Armed Forces], and 50 U.S.C. 82, it is hereby ordered as follows:

SECTION 101. *Policy*. The United States must have the capability to rapidly mobilize its resources in the interest of national security. Therefore, to achieve prompt delivery of articles, products, and materials to meet national security requirements, the Government

[1] So in original. No subsec. (c) has been enacted.

may place orders and require priority performance of these orders.

SEC. 102. *Delegation of Authority under*.

(a) Subject to paragraph (b) of this section, the authorities vested in the President, under, with respect to the placing of orders for prompt delivery of articles or materials, except for the taking authority under (c), are hereby delegated to:

(1) The Secretary of Agriculture with respect to all food resources;

(2) the Secretary of Energy with respect to all forms of energy;

(3) the Secretary of Transportation with respect to all forms of civil transportation; and

(4) the Secretary of Commerce with respect to all other articles and materials, including construction materials.

(b) The authorities delegated by paragraph (a) of this section shall be exercised only after:

(1) a determination by the Secretary of Defense that prompt delivery of the articles or materials for the exclusive use of the armed forces of the United States is in the interest of national security, or

(2) a determination by the Secretary of Energy that the prompt delivery of the articles or materials for the Department of Energy's atomic energy programs is in the interest of national security.

(c) All determinations of the type described in paragraph (b) of this section and all delegations—made prior to the effective date of this order under the Defense Production Act of 1950, as amended [50 App. U.S.C. 2061 et seq.], and under its implementing rules and regulations—shall be continued in effect, including but not limited to approved programs listed under the Defense Priorities and Allocations System (15 CFR Part 700).

SEC. 103. *Delegation of Authority under 10 U.S.C. 4501 and 9501, and 50 U.S.C. 82*.

(a) Subject to paragraph (b) of this section, the authorities vested in the President under 10 U.S.C. 4501 and 9501 [former sections 4501 and 9501 of Title 10] with respect to the placing of orders for necessary products or materials, and under 50 U.S.C. 82 with respect to the placing of orders for ships or war materials, except for the taking authority vested in the President by these acts, are hereby delegated to:

(1) the Secretary of Agriculture with respect to all food resources;

(2) the Secretary of Energy with respect to all forms of energy;

(3) the Secretary of Transportation with respect to all forms of civil transportation; and

(4) the Secretary of Commerce with respect to all other products and materials, including construction materials.

(b) The authorities delegated in paragraph (a) of this section may be exercised only after the President has made the statutorily required determination.

SEC. 104. *Implementation*. (a) The authorities delegated under sections 102 and 103 of this order shall include the power to redelegate such authorities, and the power of successive redelegation of such authorities, to departments and agencies, officers, and employees of the Government. The authorities delegated in this order may be implemented by regulations promulgated and administered by the Secretaries of Agriculture, Defense, Energy, Transportation, and Commerce, and the Director of the Federal Emergency Management Agency, as appropriate.

(b) All departments and agencies delegated authority under this order are hereby directed to amend their rules and regulations as necessary to reflect the new authorities delegated herein that are to be relied upon to carry out their functions. To the extent authorized by law, including 50 U.S.C. App. 486 [468], 10 U.S.C. 4501 and 9501 [former sections 4501 and 9501 of Title 10], and 50 U.S.C. 82, all rules and regulations issued under the Defense Production Act of 1950, as amended, with respect to the placing of priority orders for articles, products, ships, and materials, including war materials, shall be deemed, where appropriate, to implement the authorities delegated by sections 102 and 103 of this order, and shall remain in effect until amended or revoked by the respective Secretary. All orders, regulations, and other forms of administrative actions purported to have been issued, taken, or continued in effect pursuant to the Defense Production Act of 1950, as amended, shall, until amended or revoked by the respective Secretaries or the Director of the Federal Emergency Management Agency, as appropriate, remain in full force and effect, to the extent supported by any law or any authority delegated to the respective Secretary or the Director pursuant to this order.

(c) Upon the request of the Secretary of Defense with respect to particular articles, products, or materials that are determined to be needed to meet national security requirements, any other official receiving a delegation of authority under this Executive order to place orders or to enforce precedence of such orders, shall exercise such authority within 10 calendar days of the receipt of the request; provided, that if the head of any department or agency having delegated responsibilities hereunder disagrees with a request of the Secretary of Defense, such department or agency head shall, within 10 calendar days from the receipt of the request, refer the issue to the Assistant to the President for National Security Affairs, who shall ensure expeditious resolution of the issue.

(d) Proposed department and agency regulations and procedures to implement the delegated authority under this order, and any new determinations made under sections 102(b)(1) or (2), shall be coordinated by the Director of the Federal Emergency Management Agency with all appropriate departments and agencies.

SEC. 105. *Judicial Review*. This order is intended only to improve the internal management of the executive branch and is not intended to create any right or benefit, substantive or procedural, enforceable at law by a party against the United States, its agencies, its officers, or any person.

GEORGE BUSH.

§§ 83 to 85. Repealed. Aug. 10, 1956, ch. 1041, § 53, 70A Stat. 641

Section 83, act May 29, 1928, ch. 853, § 1, 45 Stat. 928, related to ammunition for use of Army and Navy, storage and dispersal, control by a joint board of officers. See section 172 of Title 10, Armed Forces.

Section 84, act Mar. 3, 1875, ch. 133, § 1, 18 Stat. 455, related to expenditure at armories for perfection of patentable inventions.

Section 85, act Mar. 3, 1921, ch. 128, § 6, 41 Stat. 1352, authorized Secretary of War to proceed with installation of guns and howitzers.

§§ 86 to 88. Omitted

CODIFICATION

Sections 86 to 88, act Feb. 15, 1936, ch. 74, §§ 1–3, 49 Stat. 1140, related to conservation of domestic sources of tin, and were superseded by the Export Control Act of 1949 (former sections 2021 to 2032 of the Appendix to this title) pursuant to section 10 of that Act (former section 2030 of the Appendix to this title). The act of Feb. 15, 1936 was subsequently superseded by the Export Administration Act of 1969 (former sections 2401 to 2413 of the Appendix to this title) pursuant to section 12 of that Act (former section 2411 of the Appendix to this title). See, also, the Export Administration Act of 1979, which is classified to section 2401 of the Appendix to this title.

Section 86, act Feb. 15, 1936, ch. 74, § 1, 49 Stat. 1140, related to conservation of domestic resources of tin.

Section 87, act Feb. 15, 1936, ch. 74, § 2, 49 Stat. 1140, related to prohibition of exportation except on license.

Section 88, act Feb. 15, 1936, ch. 74, § 3, 49 Stat. 1140, related to penalties for violations of sections 86 and 87 of this title.

SUBCHAPTER II—EDUCATION AND EXPERIMENTATION IN DEVELOPMENT OF MUNITIONS AND MATERIALS FOR NATIONAL DEFENSE

§§91 to 94. Repealed. Aug. 10, 1956, ch. 1041, §53, 70A Stat. 641

Section 91, act June 16, 1938, ch. 458, §1, 52 Stat. 707, authorized Secretary of War to place educational orders for munitions of special or technical design.

Section 92, act June 16, 1938, ch. 458, §2, 52 Stat. 708, related to production equipment.

Section 93, act June 16, 1938, ch. 458, §3, 52 Stat. 708, placed certain limitations on number of orders.

Section 94, acts June 16, 1938, ch. 458, §4, 52 Stat. 708; Apr. 3, 1939, ch. 35, §13, 53 Stat. 560, related to availability of appropriations for purposes of sections 91 to 94 of this title.

§95. Omitted

CODIFICATION

Section, act June 30, 1938, ch. 852, 52 Stat. 1255, authorized an appropriation of $2,000,000 to remain until expended for purpose of rotary-wing and other aircraft research, development, procurement, experimentation, and operation for service testing.

§96. Repealed. Aug. 10, 1956, ch. 1041, §53, 70A Stat. 641

Section, act July 15, 1939, ch. 283, 53 Stat. 1042, related to purchase by Secretary of War of equipment for experimental and test purposes. See section 2373 of Title 10, Armed Forces.

SUBCHAPTER III—ACQUISITION AND DEVELOPMENT OF STRATEGIC RAW MATERIALS

SUBCHAPTER REFERRED TO IN OTHER SECTIONS

This subchapter is referred to in section 2093 of Appendix to this title; title 7 sections 1301, 1743, 1745, 1856; title 15 section 714b; title 30 section 1604; title 31 sections 5112, 5116, 5132; title 40 section 474; title 42 section 5821.

§98. Short title

This subchapter may be cited as the "Strategic and Critical Materials Stock Piling Act".

(June 7, 1939, ch. 190, §1, as added Pub. L. 96–41, §2(a), July 30, 1979, 93 Stat. 319.)

PRIOR PROVISIONS

A prior section 98, acts June 7, 1939, ch. 190, §1, 53 Stat. 811; July 23, 1946, ch. 590, 60 Stat. 596, related to declaration of Congressional policy in enacting this subchapter, prior to repeal by section 2(a) of Pub. L. 96–41.

SHORT TITLE OF 1987 AMENDMENT

Pub. L. 100–180, div. C, title II, §3201, Dec. 4, 1987, 101 Stat. 1245, provided that: "This title [enacting section 98h–5 of this title, amending sections 98a, 98b, 98d, 98e–1, 98h, 98h–2, and 98h–4 of this title, enacting provisions set out as a note under section 98e–1 of this title, and repealing provisions set out as a note under this section] may be cited as the 'National Defense Stockpile Amendments of 1987'."

SHORT TITLE OF 1979 AMENDMENT

Section 1 of Pub. L. 96–41 provided: "That this Act [enacting this section and sections 98a to 98h–3 of this title, redesignating former section 98h–1 of this title as 98h–4 of this title, amending section 2093 of the Appendix to this title, sections 1743 and 1745 of Title 7, Agriculture, section 741b of Title 15, Commerce and Trade, and section 485 of Title 40, Public Buildings, Property, and Works, enacting a provision set out as a note under this section, and repealing a provision set out as a note under this section] may be cited as the 'Strategic and Critical Materials Stock Piling Revision Act of 1979'."

SHORT TITLE

Act June 7, 1939, ch. 190, §11, formerly §10, as added by act July 23, 1946, ch. 590, 60 Stat. 596; renumbered §11, Pub. L. 92–156, title V, §503(1), Nov. 17, 1971, 85 Stat. 427, provided that this Act, which enacted this subchapter, be cited as the "Strategic and Critical Materials Stock Piling Act", prior to repeal by Pub. L. 96–41, §2(b)(2), July 30, 1979, 93 Stat. 324.

NEW BUDGET AUTHORITY

Section 4 of Pub. L. 96–41 provided that: "Any provision authorizing the enactment of new budget authority contained in the amendments made by this Act [see Short Title of 1979 Amendment note above] shall be effective on October 1, 1979."

EXECUTIVE ORDER NO. 12155

Ex. Ord. No. 12155, Sept. 10, 1979, 44 F.R. 53071, as amended by Ex. Ord. No. 12417, May 2, 1983, 48 F.R. 20035, which related to delegation of functions vested in President by Strategic and Critical Materials Stock Piling Act, as amended [50 U.S.C. 98 et seq.], to various Federal agencies and officials, was revoked by Pub. L. 100–180, div. C, title II, §3203(b), Dec. 4, 1987, 101 Stat. 1247, effective 30 days after Dec. 4, 1987.

EX. ORD. NO. 12626. NATIONAL DEFENSE STOCKPILE MANAGER

Ex. Ord. No. 12626, Feb. 25, 1988, 53 F.R. 6114, provided:

By the authority vested in me as President by the Constitution and laws of the United States of America, including the Strategic and Critical Materials Stock Piling Act (50 U.S.C. 98 et seq.), as amended, section 3203 of the National Defense Authorization Act for Fiscal Year 1988 (Public Law 100–180) [amending section 98e–1 of this title and enacting a provision set out as a note under section 98e–1 of this title], and section 301 of Title 3 of the United States Code, it is hereby ordered as follows:

SECTION 1. The Secretary of Defense is designated National Defense Stockpile Manager. The functions vested in the President by the Strategic and Critical Materials Stock Piling Act [50 U.S.C. 98 et seq.], except the functions vested in the President by sections 7, 8, and 13 of the Act [50 U.S.C. 98f, 98g, 98h–4], are delegated to the Secretary of Defense. The functions vested in the President by section 8(a) of the Act [50 U.S.C. 98g(a)] are delegated to the Secretary of the Interior. The functions vested in the President by section 8(b) of the Act [50 U.S.C. 98g(b)] are delegated to the Secretary of Agriculture.

SEC. 2. The functions vested in the President by section 4(h) of the Commodity Credit Corporation Charter Act, as amended (15 U.S.C. 714b(h)), are delegated to the Secretary of Defense.

SEC. 3. The functions vested in the President by section 204(f) of the Federal Property and Administrative Services Act of 1949, as amended (40 U.S.C. 485(f)), are delegated to the Secretary of Defense.

SEC. 4. In executing the functions delegated to him by this Order, the Secretary of Defense may delegate such functions as he may deem appropriate, subject to his direction. The Secretary shall consult with the heads of affected agencies in performing the functions delegated to him by this Order.

RONALD REAGAN.

§98a. Congressional findings and declaration of purpose

(a) The Congress finds that the natural resources of the United States in certain strategic and critical materials are deficient or insufficiently developed to supply the military, industrial, and essential civilian needs of the United States for national defense.

(b) It is the purpose of this subchapter to provide for the acquisition and retention of stocks of certain strategic and critical materials and to encourage the conservation and development of sources of such materials within the United States and thereby to decrease and to preclude, when possible, a dangerous and costly dependence by the United States upon foreign sources for supplies of such materials in times of national emergency.

(c) The purpose of the National Defense Stockpile is to serve the interest of national defense only. The National Defense Stockpile is not to be used for economic or budgetary purposes.

(June 7, 1939, ch. 190, §2, as added Pub. L. 96–41, §2(a), July 30, 1979, 93 Stat. 319; amended Pub. L. 100–180, div. C, title II, §3202(b), Dec. 4, 1987, 101 Stat. 1245; Pub. L. 103–160, div. C, title XXXIII, §3311, Nov. 30, 1993, 107 Stat. 1961; Pub. L. 104–201, div. C, title XXXIII, §3311(b), Sept. 23, 1996, 110 Stat. 2857.)

PRIOR PROVISIONS

A prior section 98a, acts June 7, 1939, ch. 190, §2, 53 Stat. 811; July 23, 1946, ch. 590, 60 Stat. 596; 1953 Reorg. Plan No. 3, §2(b), eff. June 12, 1953, 18 F.R. 3375, 67 Stat. 634; 1958 Reorg. Plan No. 1, §2, eff. July 1, 1958, 23 F.R. 4991, 72 Stat. 1799; Oct. 21, 1968, Pub. L. 90–608, §402, 82 Stat. 1194; Ex. Ord. No. 11725, §3, eff. June 29, 1973, 38 F.R. 17175, related to determination of strategic and critical materials, the quantity and quality to be purchased, formation and functions of industry advisory committees, and the subsistence and traveling expenses of members of those committees, prior to repeal by section 2(a) of Pub. L. 96–41.

Provisions similar to those in this section were contained in former section 98 of this title prior to repeal by Pub. L. 96–41.

AMENDMENTS

1996—Subsec. (c). Pub. L. 104–201 added subsec. (c) and struck out former subsec. (c) which read as follows: "In providing for the National Defense Stockpile under this subchapter, Congress establishes the following principles:

"(1) The purpose of the National Defense Stockpile is to serve the interest of national defense only. The National Defense Stockpile is not to be used for economic or budgetary purposes.

"(2) Before October 1, 1994, the quantities of materials stockpiled under this subchapter should be sufficient to sustain the United States for a period of not less than three years during a national emergency situation that would necessitate total mobilization of the economy of the United States for a sustained conventional global war of indefinite duration.

"(3) On and after October 1, 1994, the quantities of materials stockpiled under this subchapter should be sufficient to meet the needs of the United States during a period of a national emergency that would necessitate an expansion of the Armed Forces together with a significant mobilization of the economy of the United States under planning guidance issued by the Secretary of Defense."

1993—Subsec. (c)(2). Pub. L. 103–160, §3311(1), substituted "Before October 1, 1994, the quantities" for "The quantities".

Subsec. (c)(3). Pub. L. 103–160, §3311(2), added par. (3).

1987—Subsec. (c). Pub. L. 100–180 added subsec. (c).

EFFECTIVE DATE OF 1996 AMENDMENT

Section 3311(c) of Pub. L. 104–201 provided that: "The amendments made by this section [amending this section and section 98h–5 of this title] shall take effect on October 1, 1996."

SECTION REFERRED TO IN OTHER SECTIONS

This section is referred to in sections 98b, 98h–2 of this title.

§98b. National Defense Stockpile

(a) Determination of materials; quantities

Subject to subsection (c) of this section, the President shall determine from time to time (1) which materials are strategic and critical materials for the purposes of this subchapter, and (2) the quality and quantity of each such material to be acquired for the purposes of this subchapter and the form in which each such material shall be acquired and stored. Such materials when acquired, together with the other materials described in section 98c of this title, shall constitute and be collectively known as the National Defense Stockpile (hereinafter in this subchapter referred to as the "stockpile").

(b) Guidelines for exercise of Presidential authority

The President shall make the determinations required to be made under subsection (a) of this section on the basis of the principles stated in section 98a(c) of this title.

(c) Quantity change; notification to Congress

(1) The quantity of any material to be stockpiled under this subchapter, as in effect on September 30, 1987, may be changed only as provided in this subsection or as otherwise provided by law enacted after December 4, 1987.

(2) The President shall notify Congress in writing of any change proposed to be made in the quantity of any material to be stockpiled. The President may make the change after the end of the 45-day period beginning on the date of the notification. The President shall include a full explanation and justification for the proposed change with the notification.

(June 7, 1939, ch. 190, §3, as added Pub. L. 96–41, §2(a), July 30, 1979, 93 Stat. 319; amended Pub. L. 100–180, div. C, title II, §3202(a), Dec. 4, 1987, 101 Stat. 1245; Pub. L. 100–456, div. A, title XII, §1233(b)(2), Sept. 29, 1988, 102 Stat. 2057; Pub. L. 102–484, div. C, title XXXIII, §3311, Oct. 23, 1992, 106 Stat. 2653; Pub. L. 104–201, div. C, title XXXIII, §3312(a), Sept. 23, 1996, 110 Stat. 2857.)

PRIOR PROVISIONS

A prior section 98b, acts June 7, 1939, ch. 190, §3, 53 Stat. 811; July 23, 1946, ch. 590, 60 Stat. 597; Aug. 2, 1946, ch. 753, title I, §§102, 121, 60 Stat. 815, 822; June 30, 1949, ch. 288, title I, §102(a), 63 Stat. 380; 1953 Reorg. Plan No. 3, §2(b), eff. June 12, 1953, 18 F.R. 3375, 67 Stat. 634; 1958 Reorg. Plan No. 1, §2, eff. July 1, 1958, 23 F.R. 4991, 72 Stat. 1799; Oct. 21, 1968, Pub. L. 90–608, §402, 82 Stat. 1194; Ex. Ord. No. 11725, §3, eff. June 29, 1973, 38 F.R. 17175, related to purchase, storage, refinement, rotation, and disposal of materials, prior to repeal by section 2(a) of Pub. L. 96–41. See section 98e of this title.

Provisions similar to those in this section were contained in former section 98a of this title prior to repeal by Pub. L. 96–41.

AMENDMENTS

1996—Subsec. (c)(2). Pub. L. 104–201 substituted "after the end of the 45-day period beginning on" for "effective on or after the 30th legislative day following" and struck out at end "For purposes of this paragraph, a legislative day is a day on which both Houses of Congress are in session."

1992—Subsec. (c)(2) to (5). Pub. L. 102–484 added par. (2) and struck out former pars. (2) to (5) which read as follows:

"(2) If the President proposes to change the quantity of any material to be stockpiled under this subchapter, the President shall include a full explanation and justification for the change in the next annual material plan submitted to Congress under section 98h–2(b) of this title.

"(3) If the proposed change in the case of any material would result in a new requirement for the quantity of such material different from the requirement for that material in effect on September 30, 1987, by less than 10 percent, the change may be made by the President effective on or after the first day of the first fiscal year beginning after the explanation and justification for the proposed change is submitted pursuant to paragraph (2).

"(4) In the case of a proposed change not covered by paragraph (3), the proposed change may be made only to the extent expressly authorized by law.

"(5) If in any year the reports required by sections 98h–2(b) and 98h–5 of this title are not submitted to Congress as required by law (including the time for such submission), then during the next fiscal year no change under paragraph (3) may be made in the quantity of any material to be stockpiled under this subchapter."

1988—Subsec. (c)(1). Pub. L. 100–456 substituted "December 4, 1987" for "the date of the enactment of the National Defense Stockpile Amendments of 1987", which for purposes of codification had been translated as "December 4, 1987", thus requiring no change in text.

1987—Subsec. (a). Pub. L. 100–180, §3202(a)(1), substituted "Subject to subsection (c) of this section, the" for "The".

Subsec. (b). Pub. L. 100–180, §3202(a)(2), substituted "the principles stated in section 98a(c) of this title." for "the following principles:" and struck out cls. (1) and (2) which related to purpose of National Defense Stockpile and quantities of materials stockpiled.

Subsec. (c). Pub. L. 100–180, §3202(a)(3), added subsec. (c) and struck out former subsec. (c) which read as follows: "The quantity of any material to be stockpiled under this subchapter, as determined under subsection (a) of this section, may not be revised unless the Committees on Armed Services of the Senate and House of Representatives are notified in writing of the proposed revision and the reasons for such revision at least thirty days before the effective date of such revision."

DELEGATION OF FUNCTIONS

Functions of the President under this section were delegated to the Secretary of Defense by section 1 of Ex. Ord. No. 12636, Feb. 25, 1988, 53 F.R. 6114, set out under section 98 of this title.

SECTION REFERRED TO IN OTHER SECTIONS

This section is referred to in sections 98e, 98g, 98h–6 of this title; title 15 section 714b; title 22 section 2796d.

§98c. Materials constituting the National Defense Stockpile

(a) Contents

The stockpile consists of the following materials:

(1) Materials acquired under this subchapter and contained in the national stockpile on July 29, 1979.

(2) Materials acquired under this subchapter after July 29, 1979.

(3) Materials in the supplemental stockpile established by section 1704(b) of title 7 (as in effect from September 21, 1959, through December 31, 1966) on July 29, 1979.

(4) Materials acquired by the United States under the provisions of section 2093 of the Appendix to this title and transferred to the stockpile by the President pursuant to subsection (f) of such section.

(5) Materials transferred to the United States under section 2423 of title 22 that have been determined to be strategic and critical materials for the purposes of this subchapter and that are allocated by the President under subsection (b) of such section for stockpiling in the stockpile.

(6) Materials acquired by the Commodity Credit Corporation and transferred to the stockpile under section 714b(h) of title 15.

(7) Materials acquired by the Commodity Credit Corporation under paragraph (2) of section 1743(a) of title 7, and transferred to the stockpile under the third sentence of such section.

(8) Materials transferred to the stockpile by the President under paragraph (4) of section 1743(a) of title 7.

(9) Materials transferred to the stockpile under subsection (b) of this section.

(10) Materials transferred to the stockpile under subsection (c) of this section.

(b) Transfer and reimbursement

Notwithstanding any other provision of law, any material that (1) is under the control of any department or agency of the United States, (2) is determined by the head of such department or agency to be excess to its needs and responsibilities, and (3) is required for the stockpile shall be transferred to the stockpile. Any such transfer shall be made without reimbursement to such department or agency, but all costs required to effect such transfer shall be paid or reimbursed from funds appropriated to carry out this subchapter.

(c) Transfer and disposal

(1) The Secretary of Energy, in consultation with the Secretary of Defense, shall transfer to the stockpile for disposal in accordance with this subchapter uncontaminated materials that are in the Department of Energy inventory of materials for the production of defense-related items, are excess to the requirements of the Department for that purpose, and are suitable for transfer to the stockpile and disposal through the stockpile.

(2) The Secretary of Defense shall determine whether materials are suitable for transfer to the stockpile under this subsection, are suitable for disposal through the stockpile, and are uncontaminated.

(June 7, 1939, ch. 190, §4, as added Pub. L. 96–41, §2(a), July 30, 1979, 93 Stat. 320; amended Pub. L. 99–661, div. C, title II, §3207(a)(1), Nov. 14, 1986, 100 Stat. 4069; Pub. L. 104–106, div. C, title XXXIII, §3311, Feb. 10, 1996, 110 Stat. 630.)

REFERENCES IN TEXT

Section 1704(b) of title 7, referred to in subsec. (a)(3), was amended generally by Pub. L. 101–624, title XV, §1512, Nov. 28, 1990, 104 Stat. 3635, and, as so amended, no longer contains provisions relating to a supplemental stockpile.

PRIOR PROVISIONS

A prior section 98c, acts June 7, 1939, ch. 190, §4, 53 Stat. 811; July 23, 1946, ch. 590, 60 Stat. 598; 1953 Reorg.

Plan No. 3, §2(b), eff. June 12, 1953, 18 F.R. 3375, 67 Stat. 634; 1958 Reorg. Plan No. 1, §2, eff. July 1, 1958, 23 F.R. 4991, 72 Stat. 1799; Oct. 21, 1968, Pub. L. 90–608, §402, 82 Stat. 1194; Ex. Ord. No. 11725, §3, eff. June 29, 1973, 38 F.R. 17175; Apr. 21, 1976, Pub. L. 94–273, §37, 90 Stat. 380, required reports to Congress, prior to repeal by section 2(a) of Pub. L. 96–41. See section 98h–2 of this title.

AMENDMENTS

1996—Subsec. (a)(10). Pub. L. 104–106, §3311(b), added par. (10).

Subsec. (c). Pub. L. 104–106, §3311(a), added subsec. (c).

1986—Pub. L. 99–661 substituted "on July 29, 1979" for "on the day before the date of the date of enactment of the Strategic and Critical Materials Stock Piling Revision Act of 1979" in pars. (1) and (3), and "after July 29, 1979" for "on or after the date of the enactment of the Strategic and Critical Materials Stock Piling Revision Act of 1979" in par. (2).

CLARIFICATION OF STOCKPILE STATUS OF CERTAIN MATERIALS

Pub. L. 102–484, div. C, title XXXIII, §3315, Oct. 23, 1992, 106 Stat. 2654, as amended by Pub. L. 103–337, div. A, title X, §1070(c)(4), Oct. 5, 1994, 108 Stat. 2858, provided that: "All materials purchased under section 303 of the Defense Production Act of 1950 (50 U.S.C. App. 2093) and held in the Defense Production Act inventory as of June 30, 1992, are hereby transferred to the National Defense Stockpile and shall be managed, controlled, and subject to disposal by the National Defense Stockpile Manager as provided in the Strategic and Critical Materials Stock Piling Act (50 U.S.C. 98a et seq.) [50 U.S.C. 98 et seq.]."

SECTION REFERRED TO IN OTHER SECTIONS

This section is referred to in section 98b of this title.

§ 98d. Authority for stockpile operations

(a) Funds appropriated for acquisitions; proposed stockpile transactions; significant changes therein

(1) Except for acquisitions made under the authority of paragraph (3) or (4) of section 98e(a) of this title, no funds may be obligated or appropriated for acquisition of any material under this subchapter unless funds for such acquisition have been authorized by law. Funds appropriated for such acquisition (and for transportation and other incidental expenses related to such acquisition) shall remain available until expended, unless otherwise provided in appropriation Acts.

(2) If for any fiscal year the President proposes certain stockpile transactions in the annual materials plan submitted to Congress for that year under section 98h–2(b) of this title and after that plan is submitted the President proposes (or Congress requires) a significant change in any such transaction, or a significant transaction not included in such plan, no amount may be obligated or expended for such transaction during such year until the President has submitted a full statement of the proposed transaction to the appropriate committees of Congress and a period of 45 days has passed from the date of the receipt of such statement by such committees.

(b) Disposal

Except for disposals made under the authority of paragraph (3), (4), or (5) of section 98e(a) of this title or under section 98f(a) of this title, no disposal may be made from the stockpile unless such disposal, including the quantity of the material to be disposed of, has been specifically authorized by law.

(c) Authorization of appropriations

There is authorized to be appropriated such sums as may be necessary to provide for the transportation, processing, refining, storage, security, maintenance, rotation, and disposal of materials contained in or acquired for the stockpile. Funds appropriated for such purposes shall remain available to carry out the purposes for which appropriated for a period of two fiscal years, if so provided in appropriation Acts.

(June 7, 1939, ch. 190, §5, as added Pub. L. 96–41, §2(a), July 30, 1979, 93 Stat. 321; amended Pub. L. 97–35, title II, §203(a), (b), Aug. 13, 1981, 95 Stat. 381, 382; Pub. L. 98–525, title IX, §903, Oct. 19, 1984, 98 Stat. 2573; Pub. L. 99–661, div. C, title II, §3207(a)(2), Nov. 14, 1986, 100 Stat. 4069; Pub. L. 100–180, div. C, title II, §3206(a), Dec. 4, 1987, 101 Stat. 1247; Pub. L. 102–484, div. C, title XXXIII, §3312, Oct. 23, 1992, 106 Stat. 2653; Pub. L. 103–160, div. C, title XXXIII, §3312, Nov. 30, 1993, 107 Stat. 1962.)

PRIOR PROVISIONS

A prior section 98d, acts June 7, 1939, ch. 190, §5, 53 Stat. 812; July 23, 1946, ch. 590, 60 Stat. 598, related to release of stock pile materials, prior to repeal by section 2(a) of Pub. L. 96–41. See section 98f of this title.

Provisions similar to those in this section were contained in former sections 98b and 98g of this title prior to repeal by Pub. L. 96–41.

AMENDMENTS

1993—Subsec. (a)(2). Pub. L. 103–160 substituted "and a period of 45 days has passed from the date of the receipt of such statement by such committees." for "and a period of 30 days has passed from the date of the receipt of such statement by such committees. In computing any 30-day period for the purpose of the preceding sentence, there shall be excluded any day on which either House of Congress is not in session because of an adjournment of more than three days to a day certain."

1992—Subsec. (b). Pub. L. 102–484 struck out "(1)" after "the stockpile" and ", or (2) if the disposal would result in there being an unobligated balance in the National Defense Stockpile Transaction Fund in excess of $100,000,000" after "authorized by law".

1987—Subsec. (a)(2). Pub. L. 100–180 struck out "or until each such committee, before the expiration of such period, notifies the President that it has no objection to the proposed transaction" before period at end of first sentence.

1986—Subsec. (b). Pub. L. 99–661 substituted "paragraph (3), (4), or (5)" for "paragraph (4) or (5)".

1984—Subsec. (b)(2). Pub. L. 98–525, §903(b), substituted "$100,000,000" for "$250,000,000".

Pub. L. 98–525, §903(a), substituted "an unobligated balance" for "a balance" where first appearing and "$250,000,000" for "$1,000,000,000 or, in the case of a disposal to be made after September 30, 1983, if the disposal would result in there being a balance in the fund in excess of $500,000,000".

1981—Subsec. (a). Pub. L. 97–35, §203(a), designated existing provisions as par. (1), inserted applicability to other incidental expenses, substituted "until expended, unless otherwise" for "for a period of five fiscal years, if so", and added par. (2).

Subsec. (b). Pub. L. 97–35, §203(b), inserted designation for cl. (1) and added cl. (2).

EFFECTIVE DATE OF 1984 AMENDMENT

Section 903(b) of Pub. L. 98–525, as amended by Pub. L. 99–145, title XVI, §1611(b), Nov. 8, 1985, 99 Stat. 776, provided in part that the amendment by section 903(b) of Pub. L. 98–525, is effective Oct. 1, 1987.

EFFECTIVE DATE OF 1981 AMENDMENT

Section 203(f) of Pub. L. 97–35 provided that: "The amendments made by subsection (a) [amending this section] shall apply with respect to funds appropriated for fiscal years beginning after September 30, 1981."

DELEGATION OF FUNCTIONS

Functions of President under this section delegated to Secretary of Defense by section 1 of Ex. Ord. No. 12636, Feb. 25, 1988, 53 F.R. 6114, set out under section 98 of this title.

PROHIBITION OF REDUCTIONS IN STOCKPILE GOALS

Pub. L. 99–145, title XVI, §1612, Nov. 8, 1985, 99 Stat. 776, as amended by Pub. L. 99–661, div. C, title II, §3201, Nov. 14, 1986, 100 Stat. 4067, prohibited action before Oct. 1, 1987, to implement or administer any change in a stockpile goal in effect on Oct. 1, 1984, that would result in a reduction in the quality or quantity of any strategic and critical material acquired for the National Defense Stockpile.

MATERIALS IN THE NATIONAL DEFENSE STOCKPILE

Provisions relating to certain materials in the National Defense Stockpile were contained in the following acts:

Pub. L. 106–398, §1 [div. C, title XXXIII, §3303], Oct. 30, 2000, 114 Stat. 1654, 1654A–483.

Pub. L. 106–65, div. C, title XXXIV, §3402(a)–(e), Oct. 5, 1999, 113 Stat. 972, 973.

Pub. L. 106–31, title I, §303, May 21, 1999, 113 Stat. 67.

Pub. L. 105–262, title VIII, §8109, Oct. 17, 1998, 112 Stat. 2322.

Pub. L. 105–261, div. C, title XXXIII, §§3301, 3303, Oct. 17, 1998, 112 Stat. 2262, 2263; Pub. L. 106–65, div. C, title XXXIV, §3403(a), Oct. 5, 1999, 113 Stat. 973; Pub. L. 106–398, §1 [div. C, title XXXIII, §3302], Oct. 30, 2000, 114 Stat. 1654, 1654A–483.

Pub. L. 105–85, div. A, title XXXIII, §§3301, 3303–3305, Nov. 18, 1997, 111 Stat. 2056, 2057; Pub. L. 106–65, div. C, title XXXIV, §§3402(f)(2), 3403(b), Oct. 5, 1999, 113 Stat. 973.

Pub. L. 104–201, div. C, title XXXIII, §§3301, 3303, Sept. 23, 1996, 110 Stat. 2854, 2855; Pub. L. 106–65, div. C, title XXXIV, §§3402(f)(1), 3403(c), Oct. 5, 1999, 113 Stat. 973, 974.

Pub. L. 103–337, div. C, title XXXIII, §3304, Oct. 5, 1994, 108 Stat. 3098.

Pub. L. 103–160, div. C, title XXXIII, §§3301, 3303(a), Nov. 30, 1993, 107 Stat. 1960, 1961.

Pub. L. 102–484, div. C, title XXXIII, §§3301–3303, Oct. 23, 1992, 106 Stat. 2649–2651; Pub. L. 103–160, div. C, title XXXIII, §3303(b), Nov. 30, 1993, 107 Stat. 1961; Pub. L. 103–337, div. A, title X, §1070(c)(3), div. C, title XXXIII, §3303, Oct. 5, 1994, 108 Stat. 2858, 3098.

Pub. L. 102–190, div. C, title XXXIII, §3301, Dec. 5, 1991, 105 Stat. 1583; Pub. L. 102–484, div. C, title XXXIII, §3308, Oct. 23, 1992, 106 Stat. 2653.

Pub. L. 102–172, title VIII, §8094, Nov. 26, 1991, 105 Stat. 1196.

Pub. L. 101–189, div. C, title XXXIII, §§3301, 3302, Nov. 29, 1989, 103 Stat. 1685.

Pub. L. 100–456, div. A, title XV, §1501, Sept. 29, 1988, 102 Stat. 2085.

Pub. L. 99–661, div. C, title II, §§3204, 3205, Nov. 14, 1986, 100 Stat. 4068.

Pub. L. 99–591, §101(c) [title IX, §9110], (m) [title V, §519], Oct. 30, 1986, 100 Stat. 3341–82, 3341–120, 3341–308, 3341–326.

Pub. L. 99–500, §101(c) [title IX, §9110], (m) [title V, §519], Oct. 18, 1986, 100 Stat. 1783–82, 1783–120, 1783–308, 1783–326.

Pub. L. 98–525, title IX, §§901, 902, Oct. 19, 1984, 98 Stat. 2573.

Pub. L. 97–377, title I, §101(c) [title VII, §799B], Dec. 21, 1982, 96 Stat. 1866.

Pub. L. 97–114, title VII, §788, Dec. 29, 1981, 95 Stat. 1592.

Pub. L. 97–35, title II, §201, Aug. 13, 1981, 95 Stat. 380.

AUTHORIZATION OF APPROPRIATIONS

Section 202 of Pub. L. 97–35 provided that:

"(a) Effective on October 1, 1981, there is authorized to be appropriated the sum of $535,000,000 for the acquisition of strategic and critical materials under section 6(a) of the Strategic and Critical Materials Stock Piling Act (50 U.S.C. 98e(a)).

"(b) Any acquisition using funds appropriated under the authorization of subsection (a) shall be carried out in accordance with the provisions of the Strategic and Critical Materials Stock Piling Act (50 U.S.C. 98 et seq.)."

DISPOSAL OF GOVERNMENT-OWNED TIN SMELTER AT TEXAS CITY, TEXAS

Act June 22, 1956, ch. 426, 70 Stat. 329, directed Federal Facilities Corporation immediately to sell or lease Government-owned tin smelter at Texas City, Texas, and waste acid plant and other assets of Government's tin program, prescribed corporate powers of Corporation in regard to sale or lease, established a Tin Advisory Committee to consult with Corporation, established periods for receipt and negotiation of purchase proposals, and provided that if no contract for sale or lease was effected prior to Jan. 31, 1957, then smelter and other assets be reported as excess property for transfer and disposal in accordance with provisions of Federal Property and Administrative Services Act of 1949.

MAINTENANCE OF DOMESTIC TIN-SMELTING INDUSTRY; TRANSFER OF FUNCTIONS, ETC.

Act June 28, 1947, ch. 159, 61 Stat. 190, as amended June 29, 1948, ch. 722, 62 Stat. 1101; June 30, 1949, ch. 284, 63 Stat. 350; Aug. 21, 1950, ch. 766, 64 Stat. 468; July 30, 1953, ch. 282, title I, §103, 67 Stat. 230; June 22, 1956, ch. 426, §5(a), 70 Stat. 329, declared tin to be a highly strategic and critical material in short supply, directed that it was in the public interest that Congress make a thorough investigation on the advisability of the maintenance of a permanent tin-smelting industry and study the availability of adequate tin supplies, provided that the powers, functions, duties, and authority of the United States exercised by the Reconstruction Finance Corporation to buy, sell, and transport tin, and tin ore and concentrates, to improve, develop, maintain, and operate by lease or otherwise the Government-owned tin smelter at Texas City, Texas, to finance research in tin smelting and processing, and to do all other things necessary to the accomplishment of the foregoing continue in effect until Jan. 31, 1957, or until such earlier time as the Congress shall otherwise provide, and be exercised and performed by such officer, agency, or instrumentality of the United States as the President may designate, authorized diversification of tin-recovery facilities in the United States, and required the Reconstruction Finance Corporation to report to Congress on its activities not later than Dec. 31, 1947, and at the end of each six months thereafter.

FEDERAL FACILITIES CORPORATION; ABOLITION AND DISSOLUTION OF RECONSTRUCTION FINANCE CORPORATION AND FEDERAL FACILITIES CORPORATION

Ex. Ord. No. 10539, eff. June 22, 1954, 19 F.R. 3827, designated the Federal Facilities Corporation to perform and exercise the functions formerly performed and exercised by the Reconstruction Finance Corporation under act June 28, 1947, set out as a note above. The Reconstruction Finance Corporation, which was created by the Reconstruction Finance Corporation Act, act Jan. 22, 1932, ch. 8, 47 Stat. 5, was subsequently abolished by section 6(a) of Reorg. Plan No. 1 of 1957, eff. June 30, 1957, 22 F.R. 4633, 71 Stat. 647, set out in the Appendix to Title 5, Government Organization and Employees. The Federal Facilities Corporation was, in turn, dissolved by Pub. L. 87–190, §6, Aug. 30, 1961, 75 Stat. 419, effective Sept. 30, 1961, set out as a note under sections 1921 to 1929 of the Appendix to this title.

DISPOSAL OF GOVERNMENT-OWNED TIN SMELTER AT TEXAS CITY, TEXAS; CANCELLATION OF OBLIGATIONS

Cancellation of obligation of General Services Administration to Federal Facilities Corporation existing by virtue of section 5(b) of act June 22, 1956, set out as a note above, see section 4(b) of Pub. L. 87–190, Aug. 30, 1961, 75 Stat. 418, set out as a note under sections 1921 to 1929 of the Appendix to this title.

SECTION REFERRED TO IN OTHER SECTIONS

This section is referred to in sections 98e, 98h, 98h–2, 98h–6 of this title.

§ 98e. Stockpile management

(a) Presidential powers

The President shall—

(1) acquire the materials determined under section 98b(a) of this title to be strategic and critical materials;

(2) provide for the proper storage, security, and maintenance of materials in the stockpile;

(3) provide for the upgrading, refining, or processing of any material in the stockpile (notwithstanding any intermediate stockpile quantity established for such material) when necessary to convert such material into a form more suitable for storage, subsequent disposition, and immediate use in a national emergency;

(4) provide for the rotation of any material in the stockpile when necessary to prevent deterioration or technological obsolescence of such material by replacement of such material with an equivalent quantity of substantially the same material or better material;

(5) subject to the notification required by subsection (d)(2) of this section, provide for the timely disposal of materials in the stockpile that (A) are excess to stockpile requirements, and (B) may cause a loss to the Government if allowed to deteriorate; and

(6) subject to the provisions of section 98d(b) of this title, dispose of materials in the stockpile the disposal of which is specifically authorized by law.

(b) Federal procurement practices

Except as provided in subsections (c) and (d) of this section, acquisition of strategic and critical materials under this subchapter shall be made in accordance with established Federal procurement practices, and, except as provided in subsections (c) and (d) of this section and in section 98f(a) of this title, disposal of strategic and critical materials from the stockpile shall be made in accordance with the next sentence. To the maximum extent feasible—

(1) competitive procedures shall be used in the acquisition and disposal of such materials; and

(2) efforts shall be made in the acquisition and disposal of such materials to avoid undue disruption of the usual markets of producers, processors, and consumers of such materials and to protect the United States against avoidable loss.

(c) Barter; use of stockpile materials as payment for expenses of acquiring, refining, processing, or rotating materials

(1) The President shall encourage the use of barter in the acquisition under subsection (a)(1) of this section of strategic and critical materials for, and the disposal under subsection (a)(5) or (a)(6) of this section of materials from, the stockpile when acquisition or disposal by barter is authorized by law and is practical and in the best interest of the United States.

(2) Materials in the stockpile (the disposition of which is authorized by paragraph (3) to finance the upgrading, refining, or processing of a material in the stockpile, or is otherwise authorized by law) shall be available for transfer at fair market value as payment for expenses (including transportation and other incidental expenses) of acquisition of materials, or of upgrading, refining, processing, or rotating materials, under this subchapter.

(3) Notwithstanding section 98b(c) of this title or any other provision of law, whenever the President provides under subsection (a)(3) of this section for the upgrading, refining, or processing of a material in the stockpile to convert that material into a form more suitable for storage, subsequent disposition, and immediate use in a national emergency, the President may barter a portion of the same material (or any other material in the stockpile that is authorized for disposal) to finance that upgrading, refining, or processing.

(4) To the extent otherwise authorized by law, property owned by the United States may be bartered for materials needed for the stockpile.

(d) Waiver; notification of proposed disposal of materials

(1) The President may waive the applicability of any provision of the first sentence of subsection (b) of this section to any acquisition of material for, or disposal of material from, the stockpile. Whenever the President waives any such provision with respect to any such acquisition or disposal, or whenever the President determines that the application of paragraph (1) or (2) of such subsection to a particular acquisition or disposal is not feasible, the President shall notify the Committee on Armed Services of the Senate and the Committee on Armed Services of the House of Representatives in writing of the proposed acquisition or disposal at least 45 days before any obligation of the United States is incurred in connection with such acquisition or disposal and shall include in such notification the reasons for not complying with any provision of such subsection.

(2) Materials in the stockpile may be disposed of under subsection (a)(5) of this section only if such congressional committees are notified in writing of the proposed disposal at least 45 days before any obligation of the United States is incurred in connection with such disposal.

(e) Leasehold interests in property

The President may acquire leasehold interests in property, for periods not in excess of twenty years, for storage, security, and maintenance of materials in the stockpile.

(June 7, 1939, ch. 190, § 6, as added Pub. L. 96–41, § 2(a), July 30, 1979, 93 Stat. 321; amended Pub. L. 97–35, title II, § 203(c), Aug. 13, 1981, 95 Stat. 382; Pub. L. 99–661, div. C, title II, § 3207(b), Nov. 14, 1986, 100 Stat. 4069; Pub. L. 101–189, div. C, title XXXIII, § 3314, Nov. 29, 1989, 103 Stat. 1688; Pub.

L. 101–510, div. C, title XXXIII, § 3301(a), (b), Nov. 5, 1990, 104 Stat. 1844; Pub. L. 102–190, div. C, title XXXIII, § 3312, Dec. 5, 1991, 105 Stat. 1584; Pub. L. 103–337, div. C, title XXXIII, § 3302, Oct. 5, 1994, 108 Stat. 3098; Pub. L. 104–106, div. A, title XV, § 1502(e)(1), Feb. 10, 1996, 110 Stat. 509; Pub. L. 104–201, div. C, title XXXIII, § 3312(b), (c), Sept. 23, 1996, 110 Stat. 2857; Pub. L. 105–85, div. C, title XXXIII, § 3306, Nov. 18, 1997, 111 Stat. 2058; Pub. L. 106–65, div. A, title X, § 1067(13), Oct. 5, 1999, 113 Stat. 775.)

PRIOR PROVISIONS

A prior section 98e, acts June 7, 1939, ch. 190, § 6, 53 Stat. 812; May 28, 1941, ch. 135, 55 Stat. 206; July 23, 1946, ch. 590, 60 Stat. 598; Ex. Ord. No. 9809, eff. Dec. 12, 1946, 11 F.R. 14281; Ex. Ord. No. 9841, eff. Apr. 23, 1947, 12 F.R. 2645; June 30, 1949, ch. 288, title I, § 105, 63 Stat. 381; 1953 Reorg. Plan No. 3, § 2(b), eff. June 12, 1953, 18 F.R. 3375, 67 Stat. 634; 1958 Reorg. Plan No. 1, § 2, eff. July 1, 1958, 23 F.R. 4991, 72 Stat. 1799; Oct. 21, 1968, Pub. L. 90–608, § 402, 82 Stat. 1194; Ex. Ord. No. 11725, § 3, eff. June 29, 1973, 38 F.R. 17175, related to transfer of surplus materials to stock piles, prior to repeal by section 2(a) of Pub. L. 96–41. See section 98c(b) of this title.

Provisions similar to those in this section were contained in former section 98b of this title prior to repeal by Pub. L. 96–41.

AMENDMENTS

1999—Subsec. (d)(1). Pub. L. 106–65 substituted "and the Committee on Armed Services" for "and the Committee on National Security".

1997—Subsec. (b). Pub. L. 105–85, in first sentence, substituted "strategic and critical materials from the stockpile shall be made in accordance with the next sentence" for "materials from the stockpile shall be made by formal advertising or competitive negotiation procedures".

1996—Subsec. (d)(1). Pub. L. 104–201, § 3312(b), substituted "45 days" for "thirty days".

Pub. L. 104–106, § 1502(e)(1)(A), substituted "Committee on Armed Services of the Senate and the Committee on National Security of the House of Representatives" for "Committees on Armed Services of the Senate and House of Representatives".

Subsec. (d)(2). Pub. L. 104–201, § 3312(c), substituted "45 days" for "thirty days".

Pub. L. 104–106, § 1502(e)(1)(B), substituted "such congressional committees" for "the Committees on Armed Services of the Senate and House of Representatives".

1994—Subsec. (a)(4). Pub. L. 103–337 inserted "or technological obsolescence" after "deterioration".

1991—Subsec. (a)(4). Pub. L. 102–190 inserted before semicolon "or better material".

1990—Subsec. (a)(3). Pub. L. 101–510, § 3301(b)(1), substituted "upgrading, refining," for "refining", inserted "(notwithstanding any intermediate stockpile quantity established for such material)" after "stockpile", and substituted "storage, subsequent disposition, and immediate use in a national emergency" for "storage and subsequent disposition".

Subsec. (c)(1). Pub. L. 101–510, § 3301(b)(2), inserted "under subsection (a)(1) of this section" after "the acquisition" and "under subsection (a)(5) or (a)(6) of this section" after "the disposal".

Subsec. (c)(2). Pub. L. 101–510, § 3301(b)(3), substituted "(the disposition of which is authorized by paragraph (3) to finance the upgrading, refining, or processing of a material in the stockpile, or is otherwise authorized by law)" for ", the disposition of which is authorized by law," and "of upgrading, refining" for "of refining".

Subsec. (c)(3), (4). Pub. L. 101–510, § 3301(a), added par. (3) and redesignated former par. (3) as (4).

1989—Subsec. (b). Pub. L. 101–189, § 3314(1), inserted "and" at end of par. (1), substituted a period for "; and" at end of par. (2), and struck out par. (3) which read as follows: "disposal of such materials shall be made for domestic consumption."

Subsec. (d)(1). Pub. L. 101–189, § 3314(2), substituted "paragraph (1) or (2)" for "paragraph (1), (2), or (3)".

1986—Subsec. (a)(3). Pub. L. 99–661 substituted "a form more" for "the form most".

1981—Subsec. (a)(6). Pub. L. 97–35 inserted reference to section 98d(b) of this title.

DELEGATION OF FUNCTIONS

Functions of President under this section delegated to Secretary of Defense by section 1 of Ex. Ord. No. 12636, Feb. 25, 1988, 53 F.R. 6114, set out under section 98 of this title.

ACQUISITION OF DEPLETED URANIUM FOR NATIONAL DEFENSE STOCKPILE

Pub. L. 101–511, title VIII, § 8095, Nov. 5, 1990, 104 Stat. 1896, directed President, using funds available in National Defense Stockpile Transaction Fund, to acquire over a period of ten years from current domestic sources not less than thirty-six million pounds of depleted uranium to be held in National Defense Stockpile, prior to repeal by Pub. L. 102–172, title VIII, § 8027A, Nov. 26, 1991, 105 Stat. 1177.

SECTION REFERRED TO IN OTHER SECTIONS

This section is referred to in sections 98d, 98h, 98h–2 of this title.

§ 98e–1. Transferred

CODIFICATION

Section, act June 7, 1939, ch. 190, § 6A, as added Nov. 14, 1986, Pub. L. 99–661, div. C, title II, § 3202(a), 100 Stat. 4067; amended Dec. 4, 1987, Pub. L. 100–180, div. C, title II, § 3203(a), 101 Stat. 1246, which related to National Defense Stockpile Manager, was transferred to section 98h–7 of this title.

§ 98f. Special Presidential disposal authority

(a) Materials in the stockpile may be released for use, sale, or other disposition—

(1) on the order of the President, at any time the President determines the release of such materials is required for purposes of the national defense; and

(2) in time of war declared by the Congress or during a national emergency, on the order of any officer or employee of the United States designated by the President to have authority to issue disposal orders under this subsection, if such officer or employee determines that the release of such materials is required for purposes of the national defense.

(b) Any order issued under subsection (a) of this section shall be promptly reported by the President, or by the officer or employee issuing such order, in writing, to the Committee on Armed Services of the Senate and the Committee on Armed Services of the House of Representatives.

(June 7, 1939, ch. 190, § 7, as added Pub. L. 96–41, § 2(a), July 30, 1979, 93 Stat. 322; amended Pub. L. 104–106, div. A, title XV, § 1502(e)(2), Feb. 10, 1996, 110 Stat. 509; Pub. L. 106–65, div. A, title X, § 1067(13), Oct. 5, 1999, 113 Stat. 775.)

PRIOR PROVISIONS

A prior section 98f, acts June 7, 1939, ch. 190, § 7, 53 Stat. 812; July 23, 1946, ch. 590, 60 Stat. 599, related to investigations of domestic ores, minerals, and agriculture resources for purposes of development, etc., prior to repeal by section 2(a) of Pub. L. 96–41.

Provisions similar to those in this section were contained in former section 98d of this title prior to repeal by Pub. L. 96–41.

AMENDMENTS

1999—Subsec. (b). Pub. L. 106–65 substituted "and the Committee on Armed Services" for "and the Committee on National Security".

1996—Subsec. (b). Pub. L. 104–106 substituted "Committee on Armed Services of the Senate and the Committee on National Security of the House of Representatives" for "Committees on Armed Services of the Senate and House of Representatives".

SECTION REFERRED TO IN OTHER SECTIONS

This section is referred to in sections 98d, 98e, 98h, 98h–7 of this title.

§ 98g. Materials development and research

(a) Development, mining, preparation, treatment, and utilization of ores and other mineral substances

(1) The President shall make scientific, technologic, and economic investigations concerning the development, mining, preparation, treatment, and utilization of ores and other mineral substances that (A) are found in the United States, or in its territories or possessions, (B) are essential to the national defense, industrial, and essential civilian needs of the United States, and (C) are found in known domestic sources in inadequate quantities or grades.

(2) Such investigations shall be carried out in order to—

(A) determine and develop new domestic sources of supply of such ores and mineral substances;

(B) devise new methods for the treatment and utilization of lower grade reserves of such ores and mineral substances; and

(C) develop substitutes for such essential ores and mineral products.

(3) Investigations under paragraph (1) may be carried out on public lands and, with the consent of the owner, on privately owned lands for the purpose of exploring and determining the extent and quality of deposits of such minerals, the most suitable methods of mining and beneficiating such minerals, and the cost at which the minerals or metals may be produced.

(b) Development of sources of supplies of agricultural materials; use of agricultural commodities for manufacture of materials

The President shall make scientific, technologic, and economic investigations of the feasibility of developing domestic sources of supplies of any agricultural material or for using agricultural commodities for the manufacture of any material determined pursuant to section 98b(a) of this title to be a strategic and critical material or substitutes therefor.

(c) Development of sources of supply of other materials; development or use of alternative methods for refining or processing materials in stockpile

The President shall make scientific, technologic, and economic investigations concerning the feasibility of—

(1) developing domestic sources of supply of materials (other than materials referred to in subsections (a) and (b) of this section) determined pursuant to section 98b(a) of this title to be strategic and critical materials; and

(2) developing or using alternative methods for the refining or processing of a material in the stockpile so as to convert such material into a form more suitable for use during an emergency or for storage.

(d) Grants and contracts to encourage conservation of strategic and critical materials

The President shall encourage the conservation of domestic sources of any material determined pursuant to section 98b(a) of this title to be a strategic and critical material by making grants or awarding contracts for research regarding the development of—

(1) substitutes for such material; or

(2) more efficient methods of production or use of such material.

(June 7, 1939, ch. 190, § 8, as added Pub. L. 96–41, § 2(a), July 30, 1979, 93 Stat. 322; amended Pub. L. 101–189, div. C, title XXXIII, § 3311, Nov. 29, 1989, 103 Stat. 1686.)

PRIOR PROVISIONS

A prior section 98g, act June 7, 1939, ch. 190, § 8, as added July 23, 1946, ch. 590, 60 Stat. 600; amended 1953 Reorg. Plan No. 3, § 2(b), eff. June 12, 1953, 18 F.R. 3375, 67 Stat. 634; 1958 Reorg. Plan No. 1, § 2, eff. July 1, 1958, 23 F.R. 4991, 72 Stat. 1799; Oct. 21, 1968, Pub. L. 90–608, § 402, 82 Stat. 1194; Ex. Ord. No. 11725, § 3, eff. June 29, 1973, 38 F.R. 17175, authorized appropriations for procurement, transportation, maintenance, rotation, storage, and refining or processing of materials acquired under this subchapter, prior to repeal by section 2(a) of Pub. L. 96–41. See section 98d(c) of this title.

Provisions similar to those in this section were contained in former section 98f of this title prior to repeal by Pub. L. 96–41.

AMENDMENTS

1989—Subsecs. (c), (d). Pub. L. 101–189 added subsecs. (c) and (d).

DELEGATION OF FUNCTIONS

Functions of President under subsec. (a) of this section delegated to Secretary of the Interior and functions of President under subsec. (b) of this section delegated to Secretary of Agriculture by section 1 of Ex. Ord. No. 12636, Feb. 25, 1988, 53 F.R. 6114, set out under section 98 of this title.

SECTION REFERRED TO IN OTHER SECTIONS

This section is referred to in section 98h–2 of this title.

§ 98h. National Defense Stockpile Transaction Fund

(a) Establishment

There is established in the Treasury of the United States a separate fund to be known as the National Defense Stockpile Transaction Fund (hereinafter in this section referred to as the "fund").

(b) Fund operations

(1) All moneys received from the sale of materials in the stockpile under paragraphs (5) and (6) of section 98e(a) of this title shall be covered into the fund.

(2) Subject to section 98d(a)(1) of this title, moneys covered into the fund under paragraph (1) are hereby made available (subject to such limitations as may be provided in appropriation Acts) for the following purposes:

(A) The acquisition, maintenance, and disposal of strategic and critical materials under section 98e(a) of this title.

(B) Transportation, storage, and other incidental expenses related to such acquisition, maintenance, and disposal.

(C) Development of current specifications of stockpile materials and the upgrading of existing stockpile materials to meet current specifications (including transportation, when economical, related to such upgrading).

(D) Testing and quality studies of stockpile materials.

(E) Studying future material and mobilization requirements for the stockpile.

(F) Activities authorized under section 98h–6 of this title.

(G) Contracting under competitive procedures for materials development and research to—

(i) improve the quality and availability of materials stockpiled from time to time in the stockpile; and

(ii) develop new materials for the stockpile.

(H) Improvement or rehabilitation of facilities, structures, and infrastructure needed to maintain the integrity of stockpile materials.

(I) Disposal of hazardous materials that are stored in the stockpile and authorized for disposal by law.

(J) Performance of environmental remediation, restoration, waste management, or compliance activities at locations of the stockpile that are required under a Federal law or are undertaken by the Government under an administrative decision or negotiated agreement.

(K) Pay of employees of the National Defense Stockpile program.

(L) Other expenses of the National Defense Stockpile program.

(3) Moneys in the fund shall remain available until expended.

(c) Moneys received from sale of materials being rotated or disposed of

All moneys received from the sale of materials being rotated under the provisions of section 98e(a)(4) of this title or disposed of under section 98f(a) of this title shall be covered into the fund and shall be available only for the acquisition of replacement materials.

(d) Effect of bartering

If, during a fiscal year, the National Defense Stockpile Manager barters materials in the stockpile for the purpose of acquiring, upgrading, refining, or processing other materials (or for services directly related to that purpose), the contract value of the materials so bartered shall—

(1) be applied toward the total value of materials that are authorized to be disposed of from the stockpile during that fiscal year;

(2) be treated as an acquisition for purposes of satisfying any requirement imposed on the National Defense Stockpile Manager to enter into obligations during that fiscal year under subsection (b)(2) of this section; and

(3) not increase or decrease the balance in the fund.

(June 7, 1939, ch. 190, § 9, as added Pub. L. 96–41, § 2(a), July 30, 1979, 93 Stat. 323; amended Pub. L. 97–35, title II, § 203(d), Aug. 13, 1981, 95 Stat. 382; Pub. L. 99–661, div. C, title II, § 3203(a), Nov. 14, 1986, 100 Stat. 4067; Pub. L. 100–180, div. C, title II, § 3204, Dec. 4, 1987, 101 Stat. 1247; Pub. L. 101–189, div. C, title XXXIII, § 3312(b), Nov. 29, 1989, 103 Stat. 1688; Pub. L. 101–510, div. C, title XXXIII, § 3301(c), Nov. 5, 1990, 104 Stat. 1845; Pub. L. 102–190, div. C, title XXXIII, § 3311(a), Dec. 5, 1991, 105 Stat. 1584; Pub. L. 102–484, div. C, title XXXIII, § 3313, Oct. 23, 1992, 106 Stat. 2653; Pub. L. 103–160, div. C, title XXXIII, § 3313, Nov. 30, 1993, 107 Stat. 1962; Pub. L. 105–261, div. C, title XXXIII, § 3304, Oct. 17, 1998, 112 Stat. 2264.)

PRIOR PROVISIONS

A prior section 98h, act June 7, 1939, ch. 190, § 9, as added July 23, 1946, ch. 590, 60 Stat. 600, related to disposition of receipts, prior to repeal by section 2(a) of Pub. L. 96–41. See section 98h(b)(1) of this title.

AMENDMENTS

1998—Subsec. (b)(2)(J) to (L). Pub. L. 105–261 added subpar. (J) and redesignated former subpars. (J) and (K) as (K) and (L), respectively.

1993—Subsec. (b)(2)(J), (K). Pub. L. 103–160, § 3313(a), added subpars. (J) and (K).

Subsec. (b)(4). Pub. L. 103–160, § 3313(b), struck out par. (4) which read as follows: "Notwithstanding paragraph (2), moneys in the fund may not be used to pay salaries and expenses of stockpile employees."

1992—Subsec. (b)(2)(A). Pub. L. 102–484, § 3313(a)(1), inserted ", maintenance, and disposal" after "acquisition" and substituted "section 98e(a)" for "section 98e(a)(1)".

Subsec. (b)(2)(B). Pub. L. 102–484, § 3313(a)(2), substituted "such acquisition, maintenance, and disposal" for "such acquisition".

Subsec. (b)(2)(H), (I). Pub. L. 102–484, § 3313(b), added subpars. (H) and (I).

Subsec. (b)(4). Pub. L. 102–484, § 3313(c), added par. (4).

1991—Subsec. (b)(2)(G). Pub. L. 102–190 added subpar. (G).

1990—Subsec. (d). Pub. L. 101–510 added subsec. (d).

1989—Subsec. (b)(2)(F). Pub. L. 101–189 added subpar. (F).

1987—Subsec. (b)(2)(F). Pub. L. 100–180 struck out subpar. (F) which related to other reasonable requirements for management of stockpile.

1986—Subsec. (b)(1). Pub. L. 99–661, § 3203(a)(1), struck out "Such moneys shall remain in the fund until appropriated." after "covered into the fund."

Subsec. (b)(2), (3). Pub. L. 99–661, § 3203(a)(2), added pars. (2) and (3) and struck out former pars. (2) and (3) which read as follows:

"(2) Moneys covered into the fund under paragraph (1) shall be available, when appropriated therefor, only for the acquisition of strategic and critical materials under section 98e(a)(1) of this title (and for transportation related to such acquisition).

"(3) Moneys in the fund, when appropriated, shall remain available until expended, unless otherwise provided in appropriation Acts."

1981—Subsec. (b). Pub. L. 97–35 in par. (1) struck out provisions relating to moneys remaining in the fund at the end of the third fiscal year following the fiscal year in which received, and in par. (3) substituted provisions respecting funds remaining available until expended, for provisions relating to funds remaining available for a period of five fiscal years.

USE OF FUNDS FROM NATIONAL DEFENSE STOCKPILE TRANSACTION FUND TO MEET NATIONAL DEFENSE STOCKPILE GOALS AND SPECIFICATIONS IN EFFECT ON OCTOBER 1, 1984

Pub. L. 100–440, title V, § 518, Sept. 22, 1988, 102 Stat. 1748, directed that, no later than Oct. 1, 1989, Administrator of General Services, or any Federal officer assuming Administrator's responsibilities with respect to management of the stockpile, to use all funds authorized and appropriated before Jan. 1, 1985, from National Defense Stockpile Transaction Fund to evaluate, test, relocate, upgrade or purchase stockpile materials to meet National Defense Stockpile goals and specifications in effect on Oct. 1, 1984. Similar provisions were contained in the following prior appropriation acts:

Pub. L. 100–202, § 101(m) [title V, § 519], Dec. 22, 1987, 101 Stat. 1329–390, 1329–417.

Pub. L. 99–500, § 101(m) [title V, § 520], Oct. 18, 1986, 100 Stat. 1783–308, 1783–326, and Pub. L. 99–591, § 101(m) [title V, § 520], Oct. 30, 1986, 100 Stat. 3341–308, 3341–326.

DEPOSIT OF FUNDS ACCRUING FROM NAVAL PETROLEUM RESERVES

Pub. L. 98–525, title IX, § 905, Oct. 19, 1984, 98 Stat. 2574, as amended by Pub. L. 99–145, title XVI, § 1611(a), Nov. 8, 1985, 99 Stat. 776, provided that: "There shall be deposited into the National Defense Stockpile Transaction Fund established under section 9 of the Act (50 U.S.C. 98h) 30 percent of all money accruing to the United States during fiscal years 1985 and 1986 from lands in the naval petroleum and oil shale reserves (less amounts spent for exploration, development and operation of those reserves and related expenses during that period). Moneys deposited into the Fund under this subsection shall be deemed to have been covered into the Fund under section 9(b) of the Act."

SECTION REFERRED TO IN OTHER SECTIONS

This section is referred to in section 98h–2 of this title.

§ 98h–1. Advisory committees

(a) Membership

The President may appoint advisory committees composed of individuals with expertise relating to materials in the stockpile or with expertise in stockpile management to advise the President with respect to the acquisition, transportation, processing, refining, storage, security, maintenance, rotation, and disposal of such materials under this subchapter.

(b) Expenses

Each member of an advisory committee established under subsection (a) of this section while serving on the business of the advisory committee away from such member's home or regular place of business shall be allowed travel expenses, including per diem in lieu of subsistence, as authorized by section 5703 of title 5 for persons intermittently employed in the Government service.

(c) Market Impact Committee

(1) The President shall appoint a Market Impact Committee composed of representatives from the Department of Agriculture, the Department of Commerce, the Department of Defense, the Department of Energy, the Department of the Interior, the Department of State, the Department of the Treasury, and the Federal Emergency Management Agency, and such other persons as the President considers appropriate. The representatives from the Department of Commerce and the Department of State shall be Cochairmen of the Committee.

(2) The Committee shall advise the National Defense Stockpile Manager on the projected domestic and foreign economic effects of all acquisitions and disposals of materials from the stockpile that are proposed to be included in the annual materials plan submitted to Congress under section 98h–2(b) of this title, or in any revision of such plan, and shall submit to the manager the Committee's recommendations regarding those acquisitions and disposals.

(3) The annual materials plan or the revision of such plan, as the case may be, shall contain—

(A) the views of the Committee on the projected domestic and foreign economic effects of all acquisitions and disposals of materials from the stockpile;

(B) the recommendations submitted by the Committee under paragraph (2); and

(C) for each acquisition or disposal provided for in the plan or revision that is inconsistent with a recommendation of the Committee, a justification for the acquisition or disposal.

(4) In developing recommendations for the National Defense Stockpile Manager under paragraph (2), the Committee shall consult from time to time with representatives of producers, processors, and consumers of the types of materials stored in the stockpile.

(June 7, 1939, ch. 190, § 10, as added Pub. L. 96–41, § 2(a), July 30, 1979, 93 Stat. 323; amended Pub. L. 102–484, div. C, title XXXIII, § 3314, Oct. 23, 1992, 106 Stat. 2654.)

PRIOR PROVISIONS

A prior section 10 of act June 7, 1939, ch. 190, § 10, was renumbered section 13 and is classified to section 98h–4 of this title.

Provisions similar to those in this section were contained in former section 98a(b) of this title prior to repeal by Pub. L. 96–41.

AMENDMENTS

1992—Subsec. (c). Pub. L. 102–484 added subsec. (c).

DELEGATION OF FUNCTIONS

Functions of President under this section delegated to Secretary of Defense by section 1 of Ex. Ord. No. 12636, Feb. 25, 1988, 53 F.R. 6114, set out under section 98 of this title.

TERMINATION OF ADVISORY COMMITTEES

Advisory committees established after Jan. 5, 1973, to terminate not later than the expiration of the 2-year period beginning on the date of their establishment, unless, in the case of a committee established by the President or an officer of the Federal Government, such committee is renewed by appropriate action prior to the expiration of such 2-year period, or in the case of a committee established by the Congress, its duration is otherwise provided for by law. See section 14 of Pub. L. 92–463, Oct. 6, 1972, 86 Stat. 776, set out in the Appendix to Title 5, Government Organization and Employees.

ADVISORY COMMITTEE REGARDING OPERATION AND MODERNIZATION OF STOCKPILE

Section 3306 of Pub. L. 102–484 provided that:

"(a) APPOINTMENT.—Not later than March 15, 1993, the President shall appoint an advisory committee under section 10(a) of the Strategic and Critical Materials Stock Piling Act (50 U.S.C. 98h–1(a)) to make recommendations to the President concerning the operation and modernization of the National Defense Stockpile.

"(b) MEMBERSHIP.—The committee shall consist of members who have expertise regarding strategic and critical materials, including—

"(1) employees of Federal agencies (including the Department of Defense, the Department of State, the Department of Commerce, the Department of Energy, the Department of the Treasury, the Department of the Interior, and the Federal Emergency Management Agency);

"(2) representatives of mining, processing, and fabricating industries and consumers that would be affected by the acquisition of materials for the stockpile or the disposal of materials from the stockpile; and

"(3) other interested persons or representatives of interested organizations."

§ 98h–2. Reports to Congress

(a) Not later than January 15 of each year, the President shall submit to the Congress an annual written report detailing operations under this subchapter. Each such report shall include—

(1) information with respect to foreign and domestic purchases of materials during the preceding fiscal year;

(2) information with respect to the acquisition and disposal of materials under this subchapter by barter, as provided for in section 98e(c) of this title, during such fiscal year;

(3) information with respect to the activities by the Stockpile Manager to encourage the conservation, substitution, and development of strategic and critical materials within the United States;

(4) information with respect to the research and development activities conducted under sections 98a and 98g of this title;

(5) a statement and explanation of the financial status of the National Defense Stockpile Transaction Fund and the anticipated appropriations to be made to the fund, and obligations to be made from the fund, during the current fiscal year; and

(6) such other pertinent information on the administration of this subchapter as will enable the Congress to evaluate the effectiveness of the program provided for under this subchapter and to determine the need for additional legislation.

(b)(1) Not later than February 15 of each year, the President shall submit to the appropriate committees of the Congress a report containing an annual materials plan for the operation of the stockpile during the next fiscal year and the succeeding four fiscal years.

(2) Each such report shall include details of all planned expenditures from the National Defense Stockpile Transaction Fund during such period (including expenditures to be made from appropriations from the general fund of the Treasury) and of anticipated receipts from proposed disposals of stockpile materials during such period. Each such report shall also contain details regarding the materials development and research projects to be conducted under section 98h(b)(2)(G) of this title during the fiscal years covered by the report. With respect to each development and research project, the report shall specify the amount planned to be expended from the fund, the material intended to be developed, the potential military or defense industrial applications for that material, and the development and research methodologies to be used.

(3) Any proposed expenditure or disposal detailed in the annual materials plan for any such fiscal year, and any expenditure or disposal proposed in connection with any transaction submitted for such fiscal year to the appropriate committees of Congress pursuant to section 98d(a)(2) of this title, that is not obligated or executed in that fiscal year may not be obligated or executed until such proposed expenditure or disposal is resubmitted in a subsequent annual materials plan or is resubmitted to the appropriate committees of Congress in accordance with section 98d(a)(2) of this title, as appropriate.

(June 7, 1939, ch. 190, § 11, as added Pub. L. 96–41, § 2(a), July 30, 1979, 93 Stat. 324; amended Pub. L. 97–35, title II, § 203(e), Aug. 13, 1981, 95 Stat. 382; Pub. L. 99–661, div. C, title II, § 3207(a)(3), Nov. 14, 1986, 100 Stat. 4069; Pub. L. 100–180, div. C, title II, § 3205, Dec. 4, 1987, 101 Stat. 1247; Pub. L. 100–456, div. A, title XV, § 1503, Sept. 29, 1988, 102 Stat. 2086; Pub. L. 101–189, div. C, title XXXIII, § 3315, Nov. 29, 1989, 103 Stat. 1688; Pub. L. 102–190, div. C, title XXXIII, §§ 3311(b), 3313(a), Dec. 5, 1991, 105 Stat. 1584; Pub. L. 103–35, title II, § 204(d), May 31, 1993, 107 Stat. 103.)

Prior Provisions

A prior section 11 of act June 7, 1939, ch. 190, formerly § 10, as added July 23, 1946, ch. 590, 60 Stat. 596; renumbered § 11, Pub. L. 92–156, title V, § 503(1), Nov. 17, 1971, 85 Stat. 427, was set out as a Short Title note under section 98 of this title, prior to repeal by section 2(b)(2) of Pub. L. 96–41.

Provisions similar to those in this section were contained in former section 98c of this title prior to repeal by Pub. L. 96–41.

Amendments

1993—Subsec. (a)(1). Pub. L. 103–35 substituted "fiscal year" for "six-month period".

1991—Subsec. (a). Pub. L. 102–190, § 3313(a)(1), substituted "Not later than January 15 of each year, the President" for "The President" and "an annual" for "every six months a".

Subsec. (a)(1). Pub. L. 102–190, § 3313(a)(2), which directed the substitution of "fiscal year" for "6-month period", could not be executed because the words "6-month period" did not appear in text.

Subsec. (a)(2). Pub. L. 102–190, § 3313(a)(3), substituted "fiscal year" for "period".

Subsec. (a)(5). Pub. L. 102–190, § 3313(a)(4), substituted "current fiscal year" for "next fiscal year".

Subsec. (b)(1). Pub. L. 102–190, § 3311(b)(1), designated first sentence of subsec. (b) relating to submission of report as par. (1).

Subsec. (b)(2). Pub. L. 102–190, § 3311(b), designated second sentence of subsec. (b) relating to contents of report as par. (2) and inserted at end "Each such report shall also contain details regarding the materials development and research projects to be conducted under section 98h(b)(2)(G) of this title during the fiscal years covered by the report. With respect to each development and research project, the report shall specify the amount planned to be expended from the fund, the material intended to be developed, the potential military or defense industrial applications for that material, and the development and research methodologies to be used."

Subsec. (b)(3). Pub. L. 102–190, § 3311(b)(1), designated third sentence of subsec. (b) relating to resubmission of proposed expenditures and disposals not obligated or executed as par. (3).

1989—Subsec. (a)(5). Pub. L. 101–189 substituted "made to the fund, and obligations to be made from the fund," for "made from the fund".

1988—Subsec. (a)(3) to (6). Pub. L. 100–456, § 1503(a), added pars. (3) and (4) and redesignated former pars. (3) and (4) as (5) and (6), respectively.

Subsec. (b). Pub. L. 100–456, § 1503(b), substituted "the next fiscal year" for "such fiscal year" and "all planned expenditures from the National Defense Stockpile Transaction Fund" for "planned expenditures for acquisition of strategic and critical materials" and inserted at end "Any proposed expenditure or disposal detailed in the annual materials plan for any such fiscal year, and any expenditure or disposal proposed in connection with any transaction submitted for such fiscal year to the appropriate committees of Congress pursuant to section 98d(a)(2) of this title, that is not obligated or executed in that fiscal year may not be obligated or executed until such proposed expenditure or disposal is resubmitted in a subsequent annual materials plan or is resubmitted to the appropriate committees of Congress in accordance with section 98d(a)(2) of this title, as appropriate."

1987—Subsec. (b). Pub. L. 100–180 substituted "Not later than February 15 of each year, the President" for "The President" and struck out "each year, at the time that the Budget is submitted to Congress pursuant to section 1105 of title 31 for the next fiscal year," after "Congress".

1986—Subsec. (b). Pub. L. 99–661 substituted "each year, at the time that the Budget is submitted to Congress pursuant to section 1105 of title 31 for the next fiscal year," for each year with the Budget submitted to Congress pursuant to section 201a of the Budget and Accounting Act, 1921 (31 U.S.C. 11(a)), for the next fiscal year".

1981—Pub. L. 97–35 designated existing provisions as subsec. (a) and added subsec. (b).

DELEGATION OF FUNCTIONS

Functions of President under this section delegated to Secretary of Defense by section 1 of Ex. Ord. No. 12636, Feb. 25, 1988, 53 F.R. 6114, set out under section 98 of this title.

SECTION REFERRED TO IN OTHER SECTIONS

This section is referred to in sections 98d, 98h–1, 98h–6 of this title.

§ 98h–3. Definitions

For the purposes of this subchapter:

(1) The term "strategic and critical materials" means materials that (A) would be needed to supply the military, industrial, and essential civilian needs of the United States during a national emergency, and (B) are not found or produced in the United States in sufficient quantities to meet such need.

(2) The term "national emergency" means a general declaration of emergency with respect to the national defense made by the President or by the Congress.

(June 7, 1939, ch. 190, § 12, as added Pub. L. 96–41, § 2(a), July 30, 1979, 93 Stat. 324.)

§ 98h–4. Importation of strategic and critical materials

The President may not prohibit or regulate the importation into the United States of any material determined to be strategic and critical pursuant to the provisions of this subchapter, if such material is the product of any foreign country or area not listed in general note 3(b) of the Harmonized Tariff Schedule of the United States (19 U.S.C. 1202), for so long as the importation into the United States of material of that kind which is the product of a country or area listed in such general note is not prohibited by any provision of law.

(June 7, 1939, ch. 190, § 13, formerly § 10, as added Pub. L. 92–156, title V, § 503(2), Nov. 17, 1971, 85 Stat. 427; renumbered § 13, Pub. L. 96–41, § 2(b)(1), July 30, 1979, 93 Stat. 324; amended Pub. L. 100–180, div. C, title II, § 3206(b), (c), Dec. 4, 1987, 101 Stat. 1247; Pub. L. 100–418, title I, § 1214(*o*), Aug. 23, 1988, 102 Stat. 1159; Pub. L. 104–201, div. C, title XXXIII, § 3313, Sept. 23, 1996, 110 Stat. 2857.)

REFERENCES IN TEXT

The Harmonized Tariff Schedule of the United States, referred to in text, is not set out in the Code. See Publication of Harmonized Tariff Schedule note set out under section 1202 of Title 19, Customs Duties.

CODIFICATION

Section was formerly classified to section 98h–1 of this title.

AMENDMENTS

1996—Pub. L. 104–201 substituted "not listed in general note" for "not listed as a Communist-dominated country or area in general note" and "product of a country or area listed in such general note" for "product of such Communist-dominated countries or areas".

1988—Pub. L. 100–418 substituted "general note 3(b) of the Harmonized Tariff Schedule of the United States" for "general headnote 3(d) of the Tariff Schedules of the United States".

1987—Pub. L. 100–180 inserted section catchline and, in text, substituted "The President" for "Notwithstanding any other provision of law, on and after January 1, 1972, the President".

EFFECTIVE DATE OF 1988 AMENDMENT

Amendment by Pub. L. 100–418 effective Jan. 1, 1989, and applicable with respect to articles entered on or after such date, see section 1217(b)(1) of Pub. L. 100–418, set out as an Effective Date note under section 3001 of Title 19, Customs Duties.

SECTION REFERRED TO IN OTHER SECTIONS

This section is referred to in section 98h–7 of this title.

§ 98h–5. Biennial report on stockpile requirements

(a) In general

Not later than January 15 of every other year, the Secretary of Defense shall submit to Congress a report on stockpile requirements. Each such report shall include—

(1) the Secretary's recommendations with respect to stockpile requirements; and

(2) the matters required under subsection (b) of this section.

(b) National emergency planning assumptions

Each report under this section shall set forth the national emergency planning assumptions used by the Secretary in making the Secretary's recommendations under subsection (a)(1) of this section with respect to stockpile requirements. The Secretary shall base the national emergency planning assumptions on a military conflict scenario consistent with the scenario used by the Secretary in budgeting and defense planning purposes. The assumptions to be set forth include assumptions relating to each of the following:

(1) The length and intensity of the assumed military conflict.

(2) The military force structure to be mobilized.

(3) The losses anticipated from enemy action.

(4) The military, industrial, and essential civilian requirements to support the national emergency.

(5) The availability of supplies of strategic and critical materials from foreign sources during the mobilization period, the military conflict, and the subsequent period of replenishment, taking into consideration possible shipping losses.

(6) The domestic production of strategic and critical materials during the mobilization period, the military conflict, and the subsequent period of replenishment, taking into consideration possible shipping losses.

(7) Civilian austerity measures required during the mobilization period and military conflict.

(c) Period within which to replace or replenish materials

The stockpile requirements shall be based on those strategic and critical materials necessary for the United States to replenish or replace, within three years of the end of the military conflict scenario required under subsection (b) of this section, all munitions, combat support items, and weapons systems that would be required after such a military conflict.

(d) Effect of alternative mobilization periods

The Secretary shall also include in each report under this section an examination of the effect that alternative mobilization periods under the military conflict scenario required under subsection (b) of this section, as well as a range of other military conflict scenarios addressing potentially more serious threats to national security, would have on the Secretary's recommendations under subsection (a)(1) of this section with respect to stockpile requirements.

(e) Plans of President

The President shall submit with each report under this section a statement of the plans of the President for meeting the recommendations of the Secretary set forth in the report.

(June 7, 1939, ch. 190, § 14, as added Pub. L. 100–180, div. C, title II, § 3202(c), Dec. 4, 1987, 101 Stat. 1246; amended Pub. L. 102–190, div. C, title XXXIII, § 3313(b)(1), (2), Dec. 5, 1991, 105 Stat. 1585; Pub. L. 103–160, div. C, title XXXIII, § 3314, Nov. 30, 1993, 107 Stat. 1962; Pub. L. 104–201, div. C, title XXXIII, § 3313(a), Sept. 23, 1996, 110 Stat. 2856.)

AMENDMENTS

1996—Subsecs. (b) to (e). Pub. L. 104–201 added subsecs. (b) to (d), redesignated former subsec. (c) as (e), and struck out former subsec. (b) which related to national emergency planning assumptions set forth in reports required under this section.

1993—Subsec. (b). Pub. L. 103–160 struck out before period at end of first sentence ", based upon total mobilization of the economy of the United States for a sustained conventional global war for a period of not less than three years" and inserted after first sentence "Before October 1, 1994, such assumptions shall be based upon the total mobilization of the economy of the United States for a sustained conventional global war for a period of not less than three years. On and after October 1, 1994, such assumptions shall be based on an assumed national emergency involving military conflict that necessitates an expansion of the Armed Forces together with a significant mobilization of the economy of the United States."

1991—Pub. L. 102–190, § 3313(b)(2), substituted "Biennial" for "Annual" in section catchline.

Subsec. (a). Pub. L. 102–190, § 3313(b)(1), in introductory provisions, substituted "Not later than January 15 of every other year, the Secretary" for "The Secretary" and "a report" for "an annual report" and struck out "shall be submitted with the annual report submitted under section 98h–2(b) of this title and" before "shall include".

EFFECTIVE DATE OF 1996 AMENDMENT

Amendment by Pub. L. 104–201 effective Oct. 1, 1996, see section 3311(c) of Pub. L. 104–201, set out as a note under section 98a of this title.

INITIAL REPORT DUE DATE

Section 3313(b)(3) of Pub. L. 102–190 provided that: "The first report required by section 14(a) of the Strategic and Critical Materials Stock Piling Act (50 U.S.C. 98h–5(a)), as amended by paragraph (1) shall be submitted not later than January 15, 1993."

§ 98h–6. Development of domestic sources

(a) Purchase of materials of domestic origin; processing of materials in domestic facilities

Subject to subsection (c) of this section and to the extent the President determines such action is required for the national defense, the President shall encourage the development of domestic sources for materials determined pursuant to section 98b(a) of this title to be strategic and critical materials—

(1) by purchasing, or making a commitment to purchase, strategic and critical materials of domestic origin when such materials are needed for the stockpile; and

(2) by contracting with domestic facilities, or making a commitment to contract with domestic facilities, for the processing or refining of strategic and critical materials in the stockpile when processing or refining is necessary to convert such materials into a form more suitable for storage and subsequent disposition.

(b) Terms and conditions of contracts and commitments

A contract or commitment made under subsection (a) of this section may not exceed five years from the date of the contract or commitment. Such purchases and commitments to purchase may be made for such quantities and on such terms and conditions, including advance payments, as the President considers to be necessary.

(c) Proposed transactions included in annual materials plan; availability of funds

(1) Descriptions of proposed transactions under subsection (a) of this section shall be included in the appropriate annual materials plan submitted to Congress under section 98h–2(b) of this title. Changes to any such transaction, or the addition of a transaction not included in such plan, shall be made in the manner provided by section 98d(a)(2) of this title.

(2) The authority of the President to enter into obligations under this section is effective for any fiscal year only to the extent that funds in the National Defense Stockpile Transaction Fund are adequate to meet such obligations.

Payments required to be as a result of obligations incurred under this section shall be made from amounts in the fund.

(d) Transportation and incidental expenses

The authority of the President under subsection (a) of this section includes the authority to pay—

(1) the expenses of transporting materials; and

(2) other incidental expenses related to carrying out such subsection.

(e) Reports

The President shall include in the reports required under section 98h–2(a) of this title information with respect to activities conducted under this section.

(June 7, 1939, ch. 190, § 15, as added Pub. L. 101–189, div. C, title XXXIII, § 3312(a), Nov. 29, 1989, 103 Stat. 1687.)

SECTION REFERRED TO IN OTHER SECTIONS

This section is referred to in section 98h of this title.

§ 98h–7. National Defense Stockpile Manager

(a) Appointment

The President shall designate a single Federal office to have responsibility for performing the functions of the President under this subchapter, other than under sections 98f and 98h–4 of this title. The office designated shall be one to which appointment is made by the President, by and with the advice and consent of the Senate.

(b) Title of designated officer

The individual holding the office designated by the President under subsection (a) of this section shall be known for purposes of functions under this subchapter as the "National Defense Stockpile Manager".

(c) Delegation of functions

The President may delegate functions of the President under this subchapter (other than under sections 98f and 98h–4 of this title) only to the National Defense Stockpile Manager. Any such delegation made by the President shall remain in effect until specifically revoked by law or Executive order. The President may not delegate functions of the President under sections 98f and 98h–4 of this title.

(June 7, 1939, ch. 190, § 16, formerly § 6A, as added Pub. L. 99–661, div. C, title II, § 3202(a), Nov. 14, 1986, 100 Stat. 4067; amended Pub. L. 100–180, div. C, title II, § 3203(a), Dec. 4, 1987, 101 Stat. 1246; renumbered § 16 and amended Pub. L. 101–189, div. C, title XXXIII, § 3313, Nov. 29, 1989, 103 Stat. 1688; Pub. L. 102–190, div. C, title XXXIII, § 3314, Dec. 5, 1991, 105 Stat. 1585.)

CODIFICATION

Section was classified to section 98e–1 of this title prior to its renumbering by Pub. L. 101–189.

AMENDMENTS

1991—Subsec. (d). Pub. L. 102–190 struck out subsec. (d) which read as follows: "During any period during which there is no officer appointed by the President, by and with the advice and consent of the Senate, serving in the position designated by the President under subsection (a) of this section or during which the authority of the President under this subchapter (other than under sections 98f and 98h–4 of this title) has not been delegated to that position, no action may be taken under section 98e(a)(6) of this title."

1989—Subsec. (a). Pub. L. 101–189, § 3313(b)(1), substituted "sections 98f and 98h–4" for "sections 98f, 98g, and 98h–4".

Subsec. (c). Pub. L. 101–189, § 3313(b)(1), (2), substituted "sections 98f and 98h–4" for "sections 98f, 98g, and 98h–4" and inserted at end "The President may not delegate functions of the President under sections 98f and 98h–4 of this title." after "Executive order."

Subsec. (d). Pub. L. 101–189, § 3313(b)(1), (3), substituted "sections 98f and 98h–4" for "sections 98f, 98g, and 98h–4" and "section 98e(a)(6)" for "section 98e(b) or 98e(d)".

1987—Pub. L. 100–180 amended section generally, revising and restating provisions of subsecs. (a) and (b) and adding subsecs. (c) and (d).

SAVINGS PROVISION

Section 3203(c) of Pub. L. 100–180 provided that: "Unless otherwise directed by the President under section 6A [renumbered § 16] of the Strategic and Critical Materials Stock Piling Act [this section], as amended by subsection (a), the designation of a National Defense Stockpile Manager in effect on the day before the date of the enactment of this Act [Dec. 4, 1987] shall remain in effect until the individual so designated ceases to hold the office held by the individual at the time of the designation."

DESIGNATION OF NATIONAL DEFENSE STOCKPILE MANAGER; DELEGATION OF FUNCTIONS

The Secretary of Defense was designated National Defense Stockpile Manager and functions of the President under this section were delegated to the Secretary of Defense by section 1 of Ex. Ord. No. 12636, Feb. 25, 1988, 53 F.R. 6114, set out under section 98 of this title.

DEADLINE FOR DESIGNATION OF MANAGER

Section 3202(b) of Pub. L. 99–661 directed President, not later than Feb. 15, 1987, to designate an official as National Defense Stockpile Manager, as required by this section.

§ 98i. Repealed. Pub. L. 85–861, § 36A, Sept. 2, 1958, 72 Stat. 1570

Section, act Aug. 3, 1956, ch. 939, title IV, § 416, 70 Stat. 1018, related to contracts for storage, handling, and distribution of liquid fuels. See section 2388 of Title 10, Armed Forces.

Section was not enacted as part of the Strategic and Critical Materials Stock Piling Act which comprises this subchapter.

§ 99. Transferred

CODIFICATION

Section, act July 2, 1940, ch. 508, § 6, 54 Stat. 714, was transferred to section 701 of Appendix to this title and subsequently repealed by act Aug. 10, 1956, ch. 1041, § 53, 70A Stat. 641.

§ 100. Nitrate plants

(a) Investigations; designation of sites; construction and operation of dams, locks, improvements to navigation, etc.

The President of the United States may make, or cause to be made, such investigation as in his judgment is necessary to determine the best, cheapest, and most available means for the production of nitrates and other products for munitions of war and useful in the manufacture of fertilizers and other useful products by water power or any other power as in his judgment is the best and cheapest to use; and is also authorized to designate for the exclusive use of the United States, if in his judgment such means is best and cheapest, such site or sites, upon any navigable or nonnavigable river or rivers or upon the public lands, as in his opinion will be necessary for national defense; and is further authorized to construct, maintain, and operate, at or on any site or sites so designated, dams, locks, improvements to navigation, power houses, and other plants and equipment or other means than water power as in his judgment is the best and cheapest, necessary or convenient for the generation of electrical or other power and for the production of nitrates or other products needed for munitions of war and useful in the manufacture of fertilizers and other useful products.

(b) Lease, purchase, or acquisition of lands and rights of way; purchase or acquisition of materials, minerals, and processes

The President is authorized to lease, buy, or acquire, by condemnation, gift, grant, or devise, such lands and rights of way as may be necessary for the construction and operation of such plants and to take from any lands of the United States, or to buy or acquire by condemnation materials, minerals, and processes, patented or otherwise, necessary for the construction and operation of such plants and for the manufacture of such products.

(c) Use of products of plants; disposal of surplus

The products of such plants shall be used by the President for military and naval purposes to the extent that he may deem necessary, and any surplus which he shall determine is not required shall be sold and disposed of by him under such regulations as he may prescribe.

(d) Employment of officers, agents, or agencies

The President is authorized to employ such officers, agents, or agencies as may in his discretion be necessary to enable him to carry out the purposes herein specified, and to authorize and require such officers, agents, or agencies to perform any and all of the duties imposed upon him by the provisions hereof.

(e) Government construction and operation

The plant or plants provided for under this section shall be constructed and operated solely by the Government and not in conjunction with any other industry or enterprise carried on by private capital.

(Aug. 10, 1956, ch. 1041, §37, 70A Stat. 634.)

CODIFICATION

Section was not enacted as part of the Strategic and Critical Materials Stock Piling Act which comprises this subchapter.

§100a. Omitted

CODIFICATION

Section, which was from the Department of Defense Appropriation Act, 1983, Pub. L. 97–377, title I, §101(c) [title VII, §712], Dec. 21, 1982, 96 Stat. 1833, 1851, prohibited use of funds available to Department of Defense agencies for acquisition, construction, or operation of certain scrap-processing facilities, and was not repeated in subsequent appropriation acts. Similar provisions were contained in the following prior appropriation acts:

Dec. 29, 1981, Pub. L. 97–114, title VII, §712, 95 Stat. 1580.

Dec. 15, 1980, Pub. L. 96–527, title VII, §713, 94 Stat. 3082.

Dec. 21, 1979, Pub. L. 96–154, title VII, §713, 93 Stat. 1154.

Oct. 13, 1978, Pub. L. 95–457, title VIII, §813, 92 Stat. 1246.

Sept. 21, 1977, Pub. L. 95–111, title VIII, §812, 91 Stat. 901.

Sept. 22, 1976, Pub. L. 94–419, title VII, §712, 90 Stat. 1293.

Feb. 9, 1976, Pub. L. 94–212, title VII, §712, 90 Stat. 170.

Oct. 8, 1974, Pub. L. 93–437, title VIII, §812, 88 Stat. 1226.

Jan. 2, 1974, Pub. L. 93–238, title VII, §712, 87 Stat. 1040.

Oct. 26, 1972, Pub. L. 92–570, title VII, §712, 86 Stat. 1198.

Dec. 18, 1971, Pub. L. 92–204, title VII, §712, 85 Stat. 729.

Jan. 11, 1971, Pub. L. 91–668, title VIII, §812, 84 Stat. 2032.

Dec. 29, 1969, Pub. L. 91–171, title VI, §612, 83 Stat. 481.

Oct. 17, 1968, Pub. L. 90–580, title V, §511, 82 Stat. 1131.

Sept. 29, 1967, Pub. L. 90–96, title VI, §611, 81 Stat. 244.

Oct. 15, 1966, Pub. L. 89–687, title VI, §611, 80 Stat. 992.

Sept. 29, 1965, Pub. L. 89–213, title VI, §611, 79 Stat. 875.

Aug. 19, 1964, Pub. L. 88–446, title V, §511, 78 Stat. 476.

Oct. 17, 1963, Pub. L. 88–149, title V, §511, 77 Stat. 265.

Aug. 9, 1962, Pub. L. 87–577, title V, §511, 76 Stat. 329.

Aug. 17, 1961, Pub. L. 87–144, title VI, §611, 75 Stat. 377.

July 7, 1960, Pub. L. 86–601, title V, §511, 74 Stat. 351.

Aug. 18, 1959, Pub. L. 86–166, title V, §611, 73 Stat. 380.

Aug. 22, 1958, Pub. L. 85–724, title VI, §611, 72 Stat. 725.

Aug. 2, 1957, Pub. L. 85–117, title VI, §612, 71 Stat. 325.

July 2, 1956, ch. 488, title VI, §612, 70 Stat. 469.

July 13, 1955, ch. 358, title VI, §615, 69 Stat. 317.

June 30, 1954, ch. 432, title VII, §715, 68 Stat. 352.

CHAPTER 6—WILLFUL DESTRUCTION, ETC., OF WAR OR NATIONAL-DEFENSE MATERIAL

§§101 to 106. Repealed. June 25, 1948, ch. 645, §21, 62 Stat. 862

Section 101, acts Apr. 20, 1918, ch. 59, §1, 40 Stat. 533; Nov. 30, 1940, ch. 926, 54 Stat. 1220; Dec. 24, 1942, ch. 824, 56 Stat. 1087; 1946 Proc. No. 2695, eff. July 4, 1946, 11 F.R. 7517, 60 Stat. 1352, related to definition of war terms. See section 2151 of Title 18, Crimes and Criminal Procedure.

Section 102, act Apr. 20, 1918, ch. 59, §2, 40 Stat. 534, related to destruction or injury of war material in time of war. See section 2153 of Title 18.

Section 103, act Apr. 20, 1918, ch. 59, §3, 40 Stat. 534, related to making or causing to be made defective war material. See section 2154 of Title 18.

Section 104, act Apr. 20, 1918, ch. 59, §4, as added Nov. 30, 1940, ch. 926, 54 Stat. 1220; amended Aug. 21, 1941, ch. 388, 55 Stat. 655, related to definition of national-defense terms. See section 2151 of Title 18.

Section 105, act Apr. 20, 1918, ch. 59, §5, as added Nov. 30, 1940, ch. 926, 54 Stat. 1220, related to destruction or injury of national-defense materials. See section 2155 of Title 18.

Section 106, act Apr. 20, 1918, ch. 59, §6, as added Nov. 30, 1940, ch. 926, 54 Stat. 1220, related to making or causing to be made defective national-defense material. See section 2156 of Title 18.

EFFECTIVE DATE OF REPEAL

Repeal of sections 101 to 106 effective Sept. 1, 1948, see section 38 of act June 25, 1948, set out as an Effective Date note preceding section 1 of Title 28, Judiciary and Judicial Procedure.

70-027 D 3 : QL 3

CHAPTER 7—INTERFERENCE WITH HOMING PIGEONS OWNED BY UNITED STATES

§§111 to 113. Repealed. June 25, 1948, ch. 645, §21, 62 Stat. 862

Section 111, act Apr. 19, 1918, ch. 58, §1, 40 Stat. 533, related to prohibited acts affecting homing pigeons owned by United States. See section 45 of Title 18, Crimes and Criminal Procedure.

Section 112, act Apr. 19, 1918, ch. 58, §2, 40 Stat. 533, related to possession of pigeons as evidence of violation of law. See section 45 of Title 18.

Section 113, act Apr. 19, 1918, ch. 58, §3, 40 Stat. 533, related to punishment. See section 45 of Title 18.

EFFECTIVE DATE OF REPEAL

Repeal of sections 111 to 113 effective Sept. 1, 1948, see section 38 of act June 25, 1948, set out as an Effective Date note preceding section 1 of Title 28, Judiciary and Judicial Procedure.

CHAPTER 8—EXPLOSIVES; MANUFACTURE, DISTRIBUTION, STORAGE, USE, AND POSSESSION REGULATED

§§121 to 144. Repealed. Pub. L. 91–452, title XI, §1106(a), Oct. 15, 1970, 84 Stat. 960

Section 121, acts Oct. 6, 1917, ch. 83, §1, 40 Stat. 385; Dec. 26, 1941, ch. 633, §2, 55 Stat. 863, defined "explosive", "explosives", "ingredients", "person", and "Director". See section 841 of Title 18, Crimes and Criminal Procedure.

Section 122, acts Oct. 6, 1917, ch. 83, §2, 40 Stat. 385; Dec. 26, 1941, ch. 633, §2, 55 Stat. 864, related to unauthorized manufacture, distribution, possession, acquisition, etc., of explosives or ingredients. See section 842 of Title 18.

Section 123, acts Oct. 6, 1917, ch. 83, §3, 40 Stat. 386; Dec. 26, 1941, ch. 633, §2, 55 Stat. 864; Nov. 24, 1942, ch. 641, 56 Stat. 1022; Aug. 23, 1958, Pub. L. 85–726, title XIV, §1405, 72 Stat. 808; Oct. 15, 1966, Pub. L. 89–670, §8(f), 80 Stat. 943, excepted from provisions of this chapter purchase or possession of ingredients when purchased or held in small quantities and not used or intended to be used in manufacture of explosives, explosives or ingredients in transit in conformity with applicable law, explosives manufactured under authority of the United States for armed forces or the F.B.I., and arsenals, etc., owned by, or operated by or on behalf of, the United States. See section 845 of Title 18.

Section 124, acts Oct. 6, 1917, ch. 83, §4, 40 Stat. 386; Dec. 26, 1941, ch. 633, §2, 55 Stat. 864, authorized a superintendent, foreman, or other duly authorized employee at a mine, quarry, or other work, when licensed, to sell or issue to any employee under him such amount of explosives or ingredients required by that employee in performance of his duties. See section 843 of Title 18.

Section 125, acts Oct. 6, 1917, ch. 83, §2, 40 Stat. 385; Dec. 26, 1941, ch. 633, §2, 55 Stat. 863, related to applicability of prohibitory provisions of this chapter.

Section 126, acts Oct. 6, 1917, ch. 83, §5, 40 Stat. 386; Dec. 26, 1941, ch. 633, §2, 55 Stat. 864, required licensees to keep records of disposition of explosives or ingredients. See section 843 of Title 18.

Section 127, acts Oct. 6, 1917, ch. 83, §6, 40 Stat. 386; Dec. 26, 1941, ch. 633, §2, 55 Stat. 865, authorized issuance of licenses. See section 843 of Title 18.

Section 128, acts Oct. 6, 1917, ch. 83, §7, 40 Stat. 386; Dec. 26, 1941, ch. 633, §2, 55 Stat. 865, set forth procedure for issuance of licenses and fees for such licenses.

Section 129, acts Oct. 6, 1917, ch. 83, §8, 40 Stat. 386; Dec. 26, 1941, ch. 633, §2, 55 Stat. 865; Ex. Ord. No. 9287, eff. Dec. 24, 1942, 7 F.R. 10897, provided for term of license, qualifications of applicants for licenses, and revocation of license. See section 843 of Title 18.

Section 130, acts Oct. 6, 1917, ch. 83, §9, 40 Stat. 386; Dec. 26, 1941, ch. 633, §2, 55 Stat. 866, set forth contents of applications for licenses. See section 843 of Title 18.

Section 131, acts Oct. 6, 1917, ch. 83, §10, 40 Stat. 387; Dec. 26, 1941, ch. 633, §2, 55 Stat. 866, required licensee or applicant to furnish information on request of Director or his authorized representative. See section 843 of Title 18.

Section 132, acts Oct. 6, 1917, ch. 83, §11, 40 Stat. 387; Dec. 26, 1941, ch. 633, §2, 55 Stat. 867, related to false representations as to required license.

Section 133, acts Oct. 6, 1917, ch. 83, §12, 40 Stat. 387; Dec. 26, 1941, ch. 633, §2, 55 Stat. 867, related to markings on manufacturing or storage premises for explosives.

Section 134, act July 1, 1918, ch. 113, 40 Stat. 671, related to cancellation of licenses for violations of law. See section 844 of Title 18.

Section 135, acts Oct. 6, 1917, ch. 83, §13, 40 Stat. 388; Dec. 26, 1941, ch. 633, §2, 55 Stat. 867, related to exclusion of public from manufacturing or storage premises for explosives and discharge of firearms, etc., on such premises.

Section 136, acts Oct. 6, 1917, ch. 83, §14, 40 Stat. 388; Dec. 26, 1941, ch. 633, §2, 55 Stat. 867, authorized investigations by Director of explosions and fires involving explosives or ingredients of explosives.

Section 137, acts Oct. 6, 1917, ch. 83, §15, 40 Stat. 388; Dec. 26, 1941, ch. 633, §2, 55 Stat. 867, authorized Director to exercise authority conferred upon him by this chapter under supervision of Secretary of the Interior and cooperation of other agencies with Director in administration and enforcement of this chapter.

Section 138, acts Oct. 6, 1917, ch. 83, §16, 40 Stat. 388; Dec. 26, 1941, ch. 633, §2, 55 Stat. 868; Oct. 28, 1949, ch. 782, title XI, §1106(a), 63 Stat. 972, authorized employment of personnel for administration of this chapter.

Section 139, acts Oct. 6, 1917, ch. 83, §17, 40 Stat. 388; Dec. 26, 1941, ch. 633, §2, 55 Stat. 868, prohibited any officer, employee, or licensing agent from divulging any information obtained in course of his duties under this chapter.

Section 140, acts Oct. 6, 1917, ch. 83, §18, 40 Stat. 388; Dec. 26, 1941, ch. 633, §2, 55 Stat. 868, authorized Director to issue rules and regulations. See section 847 of Title 18.

Section 141, acts Oct. 6, 1917, ch. 83, §19, 40 Stat. 388; Dec. 26, 1941, ch. 633, §2, 55 Stat. 868, set forth penalties for violations of this chapter. See section 844 of Title 18.

Section 142, acts Oct. 6, 1917, ch. 83, §20, 40 Stat. 388; Dec. 26, 1941, ch. 633, §2, 55 Stat. 868, provided that this chapter and regulations issued pursuant to it were to become operative only during war or national emergency.

Section 143, act Oct. 6, 1917, ch. 83, §21, 40 Stat. 389, related to agencies available for enforcement of provisions of this chapter.

Section 144, act July 1, 1918, ch. 113, 40 Stat. 671, subjected platinum, iridium, and palladium and compounds thereof to provisions of this chapter.

CHAPTER 9—AIRCRAFT

§§151 to 151f. Omitted

CODIFICATION

Sections 151 to 151f which related to a National Advisory Committee for Aeronautics were omitted pursuant to section 301(a) of Pub. L. 85–568, title III, July 29, 1958, 72 Stat. 432, set out as a note under section 2472 of Title 42, The Public Health and Welfare, which terminated the Committee and transferred all its functions, powers, duties, and obligations to the National Aeronautics and Space Administration. See section 2451 et seq. of Title 42.

Section 151, acts Mar. 3, 1915, ch. 83, 38 Stat. 930; Mar. 2, 1929, ch. 482, 45 Stat. 1451; June 23, 1938, ch. 601, §1107(e), 52 Stat. 1027; 1940 Reorg. Plan No. IV, §7, eff. June 30, 1940, 5 F.R. 2421, 54 Stat. 1235; July 26, 1947, ch. 343, title II, §205(a), 61 Stat. 501; May 25, 1948, ch. 335, §1, 62 Stat. 266; Aug. 10, 1949, ch. 412, §12(a), 63 Stat. 591; Aug. 8, 1950, ch. 645, §4, 64 Stat. 419; June 3, 1954, ch. 254,

68 Stat. 170, established National Advisory Committee for Aeronautics, provided for its composition, prescribed compensation of members and duties of Committee, and required reports to Congress.

Section 151a, act Mar. 2, 1929, ch. 482, 45 Stat. 1451, was incorporated in section 151 of this title.

Section 151b, act Aug. 8, 1950, ch. 645, §1, 64 Stat. 418, related to functions of Committee.

Section 151c, act Aug. 8, 1950, ch. 645, §2, 64 Stat. 418, related to transfer of supplies to Committee.

Section 151d, act Aug. 8, 1950, ch. 645, §3, 64 Stat. 418, related to employment of aliens.

Section 151e, act Aug. 8, 1950, ch. 645, §6, 64 Stat. 419, related to availability of appropriations.

Section 151f, act Aug. 8, 1950, ch. 645, §7, 64 Stat. 419, related to prosecution of projects.

§§152, 153. Repealed. May 25, 1948, ch. 335, §3(a), (b), 62 Stat. 267

Section 152, act July 1, 1918, ch. 113, 40 Stat. 650, as amended July 26, 1947, ch. 343, title II, §205(a), 61 Stat. 501, related to office space for Advisory Committee.

Section 153, act Mar. 3, 1915, ch. 83, 38 Stat. 930, related to annual reports.

§154. Repealed. Oct. 10, 1940, ch. 851, §4, 54 Stat. 1114

Section, act Apr. 22, 1926, ch. 171, 44 Stat. 314, related to purchases and services.

§155. Repealed. May 25, 1948, ch. 335, §3(c), 62 Stat. 267

Section, act Apr. 22, 1926, ch. 171, 44 Stat. 314, related to Langley Memorial Aeronautical Laboratory.

§§156, 157. Omitted

Codification

Section 156, acts Apr. 18, 1940, ch. 107, §1, 54 Stat. 134; Oct. 28, 1949, ch. 782, title XI, §1106(a), 63 Stat. 972, authorized National Advisory Committee for Aeronautics to pay compensation of a retired officer of the Army or Navy performing service for Committee. See note set out under sections 151 to 151f of this title.

Section 157, which related to transfer of aircraft, supplies, and equipment by Army and Navy to National Advisory Committee for Aeronautics, was from appropriation acts July 30, 1947, ch. 359, title I, §101, 61 Stat. 599; Apr. 20, 1948, ch. 219, title I, §101, 62 Stat. 188; Aug. 24, 1949, ch. 506, title I, §101, 63 Stat. 646; Sept. 6, 1950, ch. 896, ch. VIII, title I, §101, 64 Stat. 711, and was not repeated in the Independent Offices Appropriation Act, 1952, act Aug. 31, 1951, ch. 376, 65 Stat. 268. Section was formerly classified to section 246 of former Title 49, Transportation.

§§158 to 159. Transferred

Codification

Section 158, act Aug. 1, 1947, ch. 433, §1(b), (c), as added July 13, 1949, ch. 332, §1, 63 Stat. 410, related to professional and scientific service on the Committee and was transferred to section 1161 of former Title 5, Executive Departments and Government Officers and Employees, prior to repeal by Pub. L. 89–554, Sept. 6, 1966, 80 Stat. 378.

Section 158a, act Aug. 1, 1947, ch. 433, §2, 61 Stat. 715, related to classification of positions and appointments and was transferred to section 1162 of former Title 5, Executive Departments and Government Officers and Employees, prior to repeal by Pub. L. 89–554, Sept. 6, 1966, 80 Stat. 378, and reenacted as section 3104(b) of Title 5, Government Organization and Employees.

Section 159, acts Aug. 1, 1947, ch. 433, §3, 61 Stat. 715; July 13, 1949, ch. 332, §2, 63 Stat. 411, related to reports to Congress and confidential information and was transferred to section 1163 of former Title 5, Executive Departments and Government Officers and Employees, prior to repeal by Pub. L. 89–554, Sept. 6, 1966, 80 Stat. 378, and reenacted as section 3104(c) of Title 5, Government Organization and Employees.

§160. Omitted

Codification

Section, which was from acts Aug. 24, 1949, ch. 506, title I, §101, 63 Stat. 646; Sept. 6, 1950, ch. 896, ch. VIII, title I, §101, 64 Stat. 711, and prior appropriation acts, related to employment of aliens, and was not repeated in the Independent Offices Appropriation Act, 1952, act Aug. 31, 1951, ch. 376, 65 Stat. 268.

§§160a to 160f. Repealed. Pub. L. 85–707, §21(b)(5), July 7, 1958, 72 Stat. 337

Section 160a, act Apr. 11, 1950, ch. 86, §1, 64 Stat. 43, related to employees pursuing graduate study or research.

Section 160b, act Apr. 11, 1950, ch. 86, §2, 64 Stat. 43, related to acceptable types of graduate study and research.

Section 160c, act Apr. 11, 1950, ch. 86, §3, 64 Stat. 43, related to duration of leaves of absence available.

Section 160d, act Apr. 11, 1950, ch. 86, §4, 64 Stat. 43, related to payment of tuition and expenses.

Section 160e, act Apr. 11, 1950, ch. 86, §5, 64 Stat. 43, related to continuation of salary and leave benefits.

Section 160f, acts Apr. 11, 1950, ch. 86, §6, 64 Stat. 43; May 6, 1954, ch. 183, 68 Stat. 78; Mar. 17, 1958, Pub. L. 85–349, 72 Stat. 48, related to limitation on government expenditure.

Effective Date of Repeal

For effective date of repeal, see section 21(a) of Pub. L. 85–507.

CHAPTER 10—HELIUM GAS

§§161 to 164. Omitted

CODIFICATION

Act Mar. 3, 1925, ch. 426, 43 Stat. 1110, as completely amended, renumbered, and revised by Pub. L. 86–777, Sept. 13, 1960, 74 Stat. 918, is classified to section 167 et seq. of this title.

Section 161, acts Mar. 3, 1925, ch. 426, §1, 43 Stat. 1110; Mar. 3, 1927, ch. 355, 44 Stat. 1387; Sept. 1, 1937, ch. 895, 50 Stat. 885, authorized Secretary of the Interior to acquire and reserve helium-gas lands and to produce and store helium gas. See section 3 of act Mar. 3, 1925, as amended by Pub. L. 86–777, which is classified to section 167a of this title.

Section 162, acts Feb. 12, 1925, ch. 225, title I, 43 Stat. 908; July 26, 1947, ch. 343, title II, §205(a), 61 Stat. 501, authorized Navy Department to acquire helium-gas lands and to produce and experiment with helium gas.

Section 163, acts Mar. 3, 1925, ch. 426, §2, 43 Stat. 1111; Mar. 3, 1927, ch. 355, 44 Stat. 1387; Sept. 1, 1937, ch. 895, 50 Stat. 886, authorized Bureau of Mines to produce helium gas. See section 4 of act Mar. 3, 1925, as amended by Pub. L. 86–777, which is classified to section 167b of this title.

Section 164, acts Mar. 3, 1925, ch. 426, §3, 43 Stat. 1111; Mar. 3, 1927, ch. 355, 44 Stat. 1387; Sept. 1, 1937, ch. 895, 50 Stat. 886, related to disposal of helium by sale, upon request of Army or Navy or other Federal Government agencies, or for medicinal, scientific or commercial use, to deposit and use of funds obtained by sale of gas, and to an annual report to Congress by Secretary of the Interior on said funds. See section 6 of act Mar. 3, 1925, as amended by Pub. L. 86–777, which is classified to section 167d of this title.

§165. Repealed. Aug. 26, 1954, ch. 937, title V, §542(a)(13), 68 Stat. 861

Section, acts Mar. 3, 1925, ch. 426, §4, 43 Stat. 1111; Mar. 3, 1927, ch. 355, 44 Stat. 1388; Sept. 1, 1937, ch. 895, 50 Stat. 887, related to exportation of helium gas. See section 2778 of Title 22, Foreign Relations and Intercourse.

§166. Omitted

Section, acts Mar. 3, 1925, ch. 426, §5, 43 Stat. 1111; Mar. 3, 1927, ch. 355, 44 Stat. 1388; Sept. 1, 1937, ch. 895, 50 Stat. 887; July 26, 1947, ch. 343, title II, §205(a), 61 Stat. 501, authorized Secretaries of Army and Navy to designate representatives to cooperate with Department of the Interior to effectuate the purposes of this chapter, and gave them the right of access to plants, data, and accounts. See section 7 of act Mar. 3, 1925, as amended by Pub. L. 86–777, which is classified to section 167e of this title.

§167. Definitions

As used in this chapter:

(1) The term "Secretary" means the Secretary of the Interior;

(2) The term "person" means any individual, corporation, partnership, firm, association, trust, estate, public or private institution, or State or political subdivision thereof; and

(3) The terms "helium-bearing natural gas" and "helium-gas mixture" mean, respectively, natural gas and gas mixtures containing three-tenths of 1 per centum or more of helium by volume.

(Mar. 3, 1925, ch. 426, §2, as added Pub. L. 86–777, §2, Sept. 13, 1960, 74 Stat. 918.)

PRIOR PROVISIONS

A prior section 2 of act Mar. 3, 1925, authorized Bureau of Mines to produce helium gas and was classified to section 163 of this title, prior to the general amendment of this chapter by Pub. L. 86–777.

EFFECTIVE DATE OF 1960 AMENDMENT

Section 3 of Pub. L. 86–777 provided that: "The amendment made by this Act [enacting this section and sections 167a to 167n of this title] shall become effective on March 1, 1961."

SHORT TITLE OF 1996 AMENDMENT

Pub. L. 104–273, §1, Oct. 9, 1996, 110 Stat. 3315, provided that: "This Act [amending sections 167a to 167d, 167f, 167j, and 167m of this title] may be cited as the 'Helium Privatization Act of 1996'."

SHORT TITLE OF 1960 AMENDMENT

Section 1 of Pub. L. 86–777 provided that: "This Act [enacting this section, sections 167a to 167n of this title, and provisions set out as notes below] may be cited as the 'Helium Act Amendments of 1960'."

SHORT TITLE

Section 1 of act Mar. 3, 1925, as added by Pub. L. 86–777, §2, provided that: "This Act [enacting this section, sections 167a to 167n of this title, and provision set out as a note below] may be cited as the 'Helium Act'."

SEPARABILITY

Section 17 of act Mar. 3, 1925, as added by Pub. L. 86–777, §2, provided that: "If any provision of this Act [enacting this section, sections 167a to 167n of this title, and provisions set out as a note above], or the application of such provision to any person or circumstance, is held invalid, the remainder of this Act or the application of such provision to persons or circumstances other than those as to which it is held invalid, shall not be affected thereby."

SEVERANCE PACKAGE FOR HELIUM OPERATIONS EMPLOYEES

Pub. L. 106–113, div. B, §1000(a)(3) [title I, §112], Nov. 29, 1999, 113 Stat. 1535, 1501A–157, provided that:

"(a) Employees of Helium Operations, Bureau of Land Management, entitled to severance pay under 5 U.S.C. 5595, may apply for, and the Secretary of the Interior may pay, the total amount of the severance pay to the employee in a lump sum. Employees paid severance pay in a lump sum and subsequently reemployed by the Federal Government shall be subject to the repayment provisions of 5 U.S.C. 5595(i)(2) and (3), except that any repayment shall be made to the Helium Fund.

"(b) Helium Operations employees who elect to continue health benefits after separation shall be liable for not more than the required employee contribution under 5 U.S.C. 8905a(d)(1)(A). The Helium Fund shall pay for 18 months the remaining portion of required contributions.

"(c) The Secretary of the Interior may provide for training to assist Helium Operations employees in the transition to other Federal or private sector jobs during the facility shut-down and disposition process and for up to 12 months following separation from Federal employment, including retraining and relocation incentives on the same terms and conditions as authorized for employees of the Department of Defense in section 348 of the National Defense Authorization Act for Fiscal Year 1995 [Pub. L. 103–337, 10 U.S.C. 1597 note].

"(d) For purposes of the annual leave restoration provisions of 5 U.S.C. 6304(d)(1)(B), the cessation of helium production and sales, and other related Helium Program activities shall be deemed to create an exigency of public business under, and annual leave that is lost during leave years 1997 through 2001 because of 5 U.S.C. 6304 (regardless of whether such leave was scheduled in advance) shall be restored to the employee and shall be credited and available in accordance with 5 U.S.C. 6304(d)(2). Annual leave so restored and remaining unused upon the transfer of a Helium Program employee to a position of the executive branch outside of the Helium Program shall be liquidated by payment to the employee of a lump sum from the Helium Fund for such leave.

"(e) Benefits under this section shall be paid from the Helium Fund in accordance with section 4(c)(4) of the Helium Privatization Act of 1996 [probably means the Helium Act, which is classified to section 167b(c)(4) of this title]. Funds may be made available to Helium Program employees who are or will be separated before October 1, 2002 because of the cessation of helium production and sales and other related activities. Retraining benefits, including retraining and relocation incentives, may be paid for retraining commencing on or before September 30, 2002.

"(f) This section shall remain in effect through fiscal year 2002."

Similar provisions were contained in the following prior appropriation acts:

Pub. L. 105–277, div. A, § 101(e) [title I, § 112], Oct. 21, 1998, 112 Stat. 2681–231, 2681–254.

Pub. L. 105–83, title I, § 113, Nov. 14, 1997, 111 Stat. 1562.

§ 167a. Authority of Secretary

(a) Extraction and disposal of helium on Federal lands

(1) In general

The Secretary may enter into agreements with private parties for the recovery and disposal of helium on Federal lands upon such terms and conditions as the Secretary deems fair, reasonable, and necessary.

(2) Leasehold rights

The Secretary may grant leasehold rights to any such helium.

(3) Limitation

The Secretary may not enter into any agreement by which the Secretary sells such helium other than to a private party with whom the Secretary has an agreement for recovery and disposal of helium.

(4) Regulations

Agreements under paragraph (1) may be subject to such regulations as may be prescribed by the Secretary.

(5) Existing rights

An agreement under paragraph (1) shall be subject to any rights of any affected Federal oil and gas lessee that may be in existence prior to the date of the agreement.

(6) Terms and conditions

An agreement under paragraph (1) (and any extension or renewal of an agreement) shall contain such terms and conditions as the Secretary may consider appropriate.

(7) Prior agreements

This subsection shall not in any manner affect or diminish the rights and obligations of the Secretary and private parties under agreements to dispose of helium produced from Federal lands in existence on October 9, 1996, except to the extent that such agreements are renewed or extended after October 9, 1996.

(b) Storage, transportation, and sale

The Secretary may store, transport, and sell helium only in accordance with this chapter.

(Mar. 3, 1925, ch. 426, § 3, as added Pub. L. 86–777, § 2, Sept. 13, 1960, 74 Stat. 918; amended Pub. L. 104–273, § 3, Oct. 9, 1996, 110 Stat. 3315.)

PRIOR PROVISIONS

A prior section 3 of act Mar. 3, 1925, related to disposal of helium by sale, use of funds so obtained, and reports to Congress on such uses and was classified to section 164 of this title, prior to the general amendment of this chapter by Pub. L. 86–777.

AMENDMENTS

1996—Pub. L. 104–273 amended section generally. Prior to amendment, section enumerated various aspects of Secretary's authority, including provisions in subsec. (a) relating to conserving, producing, buying, and selling helium, in subsec. (b) relating to helium on public domain, and in subsec. (c) relating to contract price for helium.

§ 167b. Storage, transportation, and withdrawal of crude helium

(a) Storage, transportation, and withdrawal

The Secretary may store, transport, and withdraw crude helium and maintain and operate crude helium storage facilities, in existence on October 9, 1996, at the Bureau of Mines Cliffside Field, and related helium transportation and withdrawal facilities.

(b) Cessation of production, refining, and marketing

Not later than 18 months after October 9, 1996, the Secretary shall cease producing, refining, and marketing refined helium and shall cease carrying out all other activities relating to helium which the Secretary was authorized to carry out under this chapter before October 9, 1996, except activities described in subsection (a) of this section.

(c) Disposal of facilities

(1) In general

Subject to paragraph (5), not later than 24 months after the cessation of activities referred to in subsection (b) of this section, the Secretary shall designate as excess property and dispose of all facilities, equipment, and other real and personal property, and all interests therein, held by the United States for the purpose of producing, refining and marketing refined helium.

(2) Applicable law

The disposal of such property shall be in accordance with the Federal Property and Administrative Services Act of 1949 [40 U.S.C. 471 et seq.].

(3) Proceeds

All proceeds accruing to the United States by reason of the sale or other disposal of such property shall be treated as moneys received under this chapter for purposes of section 167d(f) of this title.

(4) Costs

All costs associated with such sale and disposal (including costs associated with termination of personnel) and with the cessation of activities under subsection (b) of this section shall be paid from amounts available in the helium production fund established under section 167d(f) of this title.

(5) Exception

Paragraph (1) shall not apply to any facilities, equipment, or other real or personal property, or any interest therein, necessary for the storage, transportation, and withdrawal of crude helium or any equipment, facilities, or other real or personal property, required to maintain the purity, quality control, and quality assurance of crude helium in the Bureau of Mines Cliffside Field.

(d) Existing contracts

(1) In general

All contracts that were entered into by any person with the Secretary for the purchase by the person from the Secretary of refined helium and that are in effect on October 9, 1996, shall remain in force and effect until the date on which the refining operations cease, as described in subsection (b) of this section.

(2) Costs

Any costs associated with the termination of contracts described in paragraph (1) shall be paid from the helium production fund established under section 167d(f) of this title.

(Mar. 3, 1925, ch. 426, §4, as added Pub. L. 86–777, §2, Sept. 13, 1960, 74 Stat. 920; amended Pub. L. 104–273, §3, Oct. 9, 1996, 110 Stat. 3316.)

REFERENCES IN TEXT

The Federal Property and Administrative Services Act of 1949, referred to in subsec. (c)(2), is act June 30, 1949, ch. 288, 63 Stat. 377, as amended. Provisions of that Act relating to disposal of government property are classified to chapter 10 (§471 et seq.) of Title 40, Public Buildings, Property, and Works. For complete classification of this Act to the Code, see Short Title note set out under section 471 of Title 40 and Tables.

PRIOR PROVISIONS

A prior section 4 of act Mar. 3, 1925, related to exportation of helium gas and was classified to section 165 of this title, prior to repeal by act Aug. 26, 1954, ch. 937, title V, §542(a)(13), 68 Stat. 861.

AMENDMENTS

1996—Pub. L. 104–273 amended section generally. Prior to amendment, section consisted of single par. authorizing Secretary to maintain and operate helium production and purification plants and to conduct or contract for research as to helium production, purification, transportation, liquefaction, storage, and utilization.

SECTION REFERRED TO IN OTHER SECTIONS

This section is referred to in section 167d of this title; title 35 section 210.

§167c. Fees for storage, transportation, and withdrawal

(a) In general

Whenever the Secretary provides helium storage withdrawal or transportation services to any person, the Secretary shall impose a fee on the person to reimburse the Secretary for the full costs of providing such storage, transportation, and withdrawal.

(b) Treatment

All fees received by the Secretary under subsection (a) of this section shall be treated as moneys received under this chapter for purposes of section 167d(f) of this title.

(Mar. 3, 1925, ch. 426, §5, as added Pub. L. 86–777, §2, Sept. 13, 1960, 74 Stat. 920; amended Pub. L. 104–273, §3, Oct. 9, 1996, 110 Stat. 3317.)

PRIOR PROVISIONS

A prior section 5 of act Mar. 3, 1925, authorized governmental cooperation with Department of the Interior to effectuate the purposes of this chapter and was classified to section 166 of this title, prior to the general amendment of this chapter by Pub. L. 86–777.

AMENDMENTS

1996—Pub. L. 104–273 amended section generally. Prior to amendment, section related to licensing for extraction, transportation, and sale of helium under Federal helium refining program, including provisions in subsec. (a) relating to rules and regulations, in subsec. (b) relating to terms, assignments, and revocations of licenses, in subsec. (c) relating to purpose of licenses, and in subsec. (d) relating to suspension of licenses and reacquisition of helium supplies in times of war or national emergency.

§167d. Sale of helium

(a) Purchase by Government agencies

The Department of Defense, the Atomic Energy Commission, and other agencies of the Federal Government, to the extent that supplies are readily available, shall purchase all major requirements of helium from persons who have entered into enforceable contracts to purchase an equivalent amount of crude helium from the Secretary.

(b) Sales by Secretary

The Secretary is authorized to sell crude helium for Federal, medical, scientific, and commercial uses in such quantities and under such terms and conditions as he determines. Except as may be required by reason of subsection (a) of this section, sales of crude helium under this section shall be in amounts as the Secretary determines, in consultation with the helium industry, necessary to carry out this subsection with minimum market disruption.

(c) Prices and determinations; repayable amounts

Sales of crude helium by the Secretary shall be at prices established by him which shall be adequate to cover all costs incurred in carrying out the provisions of this chapter and to repay to the United States by deposit in the Treasury, all funds required to be repaid to the United States as of October 1, 1995 under this section (referred to in this subsection as "repayable amounts"). The price at which crude helium is sold by the Secretary shall not be less than the amount determined by the Secretary by—

(1) dividing the outstanding amount of such repayable amounts by the volume (in million cubic feet) of crude helium owned by the United States and stored in the Bureau of Mines Cliffside Field at the time of the sale concerned, and

(2) adjusting the amount determined under paragraph (1) by the Consumer Price Index for years beginning after December 31, 1995.

(d) Extraction of helium from deposits on Federal lands

.All moneys received by the Secretary from the sale or disposition of helium on Federal lands shall be paid to the Treasury and credited against the amounts required to be repaid to the Treasury under subsection (c) of this section.

(e) Helium production fund

(1) All moneys received under this chapter, including moneys from sale of helium or other products resulting from helium operations and from the sale of excess property shall be credited to the helium production fund, which shall be available without fiscal year limitation, for carrying out the provisions of this chapter, including any research relating to helium carried out by the Department of the Interior. Amounts accumulating in said fund in excess of amounts the Secretary deems necessary to carry out this chapter and contracts negotiated hereunder shall be paid to the Treasury and credited against the amounts required to be repaid to the Treasury under subsection (c) of this section.

(2)(A) Within 7 days after the commencement of each fiscal year after the disposal of the facilities referred to in section 167b(c) of this title, all amounts in such fund in excess of $2,000,000 (or such lesser sum as the Secretary deems necessary to carry out this chapter during such fiscal year) shall be paid to the Treasury and credited as provided in paragraph (1).

(B) On repayment of all amounts referred to in subsection (c) of this section, the fund established under this section shall be terminated and all moneys received under this chapter shall be deposited in the general fund of the Treasury.

(Mar. 3, 1925, ch. 426, §6, as added Pub. L. 86–777, §2, Sept. 13, 1960, 74 Stat. 921; amended Pub. L. 104–273, §4, Oct. 9, 1996, 110 Stat. 3317.)

AMENDMENTS

1996—Subsec. (a). Pub. L. 104–273, §4(a), substituted "from persons who have entered into enforceable contracts to purchase an equivalent amount of crude helium from the Secretary" for "from the Secretary".

Subsec. (b). Pub. L. 104–273, §4(b), inserted "crude" before "helium" and inserted at end "Except as may be required by reason of subsection (a) of this section, sales of crude helium under this section shall be in amounts as the Secretary determines, in consultation with the helium industry, necessary to carry out this subsection with minimum market disruption."

Subsec. (c). Pub. L. 104–273, §4(c)(2), which directed the amendment of subsec. (c) by substituting "all funds required to be repaid to the United States as of October 1, 1995 under this section (referred to in this subsection as 'repayable amounts'). The price at which crude helium is sold by the Secretary shall not be less than the amount determined by the Secretary by—" and pars. (1) and (2) for "together with interest as provided in this subsection" and all that followed through the end of the subsec., was executed by making the substitution for language which read "together with interest as provided in subsection (d) of this section, the following:" along with former pars. (1) to (3), to reflect the probable intent of Congress. Prior to amendment, pars. (1) to (3) read as follows:

"(1) Within twenty-five years from September 13, 1960, the net capital and retained earnings of the helium production fund (established under section 164 of this title prior to amendment by the Helium Act Amendments of 1960), determined by the Secretary as of September 13, 1960, plus any moneys expended thereafter by the Department of the Interior from funds provided in the Supplemental Appropriation Act, 1959, for construction of a helium plant at Keyes, Oklahoma;

"(2) Within twenty-five years from the date of borrowing, all funds borrowed, as provided in section 167j of this chapter, to acquire and construct helium plants and facilities; and

"(3) Within twenty-five years from September 13, 1960, unless the Secretary determines that said period should be extended for not more than ten years, all funds borrowed, as provided in section 167j of this title for all purposes other than those specified in clause (2) above."

Pub. L. 104–273, §4(c)(1), inserted "crude" after "Sales of".

Subsec. (d). Pub. L. 104–273, §4(d), inserted heading and amended text generally. Prior to amendment, text read as follows: "Compound interest on the amounts specified in clauses (1), (2), and (3) of subsection (c) of this section which have not been paid to the Treasury shall be calculated annually at rates determined by the Secretary of the Treasury taking into consideration the current average market yields of outstanding marketable obligations of the United States having maturities comparable to the investments authorized by this chapter, except that the interest rate on the amounts specified in clause (1) of subsection (c) of this section shall be determined as of Sept. 13, 1960, and the interest rate on the obligations specified in clauses (2) and (3) of subsection (c) of this section as of the time of each borrowing."

Subsecs. (e), (f). Pub. L. 104–273, §4(e), (f), redesignated subsec. (f) as (e)(1), added par. (2), and struck out former subsec. (e) which read as follows: "Helium shall be sold for medical purposes at prices which will permit its general use therefor; and all sales of helium to non-Federal purchasers shall be upon condition that the Federal Government shall have a right to repurchase helium so sold that has not been lost or dissipated, when needed for Government use, under terms and at prices established by regulations."

TRANSFER OF FUNCTIONS

Atomic Energy Commission abolished and functions transferred by sections 5814 and 5841 of Title 42, The Public Health and Welfare. See also Transfer of Functions notes set out under those sections.

SECTION REFERRED TO IN OTHER SECTIONS

This section is referred to in sections 167b, 167c, 167f of this title.

§167e. Intragovernmental cooperation

The Secretary of Defense and the Chairman of the Atomic Energy Commission may each designate representatives to cooperate with the Secretary in carrying out the purposes of this chapter, and shall have complete right of access to plants, data, and accounts.

(Mar. 3, 1925, ch. 426, §7, as added Pub. L. 86–777, §2, Sept. 13, 1960, 74 Stat. 921.)

TRANSFER OF FUNCTIONS

Atomic Energy Commission abolished and functions transferred by sections 5814 and 5841 of Title 42, The Public Health and Welfare. See also Transfer of Functions notes set out under those sections.

§167f. Elimination of stockpile

(a) Stockpile sales

(1) Commencement

Not later than January 1, 2005, the Secretary shall commence offering for sale crude helium from helium reserves owned by the United States in such amounts as would be necessary to dispose of all such helium reserves in excess of 600,000,000 cubic feet on a straight-line basis between such date and January 1, 2015.

(2) Times of sale

The sales shall be at such times during each year and in such lots as the Secretary determines, in consultation with the helium industry, to be necessary to carry out this subsection with minimum market disruption.

(3) Price

The price for all sales under paragraph (1), as determined by the Secretary in consultation with the helium industry, shall be such price as will ensure repayment of the amounts required to be repaid to the Treasury under section 167d(c) of this title.

(b) Discovery of additional reserves

The discovery of additional helium reserves shall not affect the duty of the Secretary to make sales of helium under subsection (a) of this section.

(Mar. 3, 1925, ch. 426, §8, as added Pub. L. 86–777, §2, Sept. 13, 1960, 74 Stat. 922; amended Pub. L. 104–273, §5, Oct. 9, 1996, 110 Stat. 3318.)

AMENDMENTS

1996—Pub. L. 104–273 amended section generally. Prior to amendment, section related to condemnation proceedings under Federal helium refining program.

SECTION REFERRED TO IN OTHER SECTIONS

This section is referred to in section 167m of this title.

§167g. Promulgation of rules and regulations

The Secretary is authorized to establish and promulgate such rules and regulations, as are consistent with the directions of this chapter and are necessary to carry out the provisions hereof.

(Mar. 3, 1925, ch. 426, §9, as added Pub. L. 86–777, §2, Sept. 13, 1960, 74 Stat. 922.)

§167h. Administrative procedure

(a) The provisions of subchapter II of chapter 5 of title 5 shall apply to any agency proceeding and any agency action taken under this chapter, including the issuance of rules and regulations, and the terms "agency proceeding" and "agency action" shall have the meaning specified in subchapter II of chapter 5 of title 5.

(b) In any proceeding under this chapter for the granting, suspending, revoking, or amending of any license, or application to transfer control thereof, and in any proceeding for the issuance or modification of rules and regulations dealing with the activities of licensees, the Secretary shall grant a hearing upon the request of any person whose interest may be affected by the proceeding, and shall admit any such person as a party to such proceeding. Any final order entered in any such proceeding shall be subject to judicial review in the manner prescribed in chapter 158 of title 28, and to the provisions of chapter 7 of title 5.

(Mar. 3, 1925, ch. 426, §10, as added Pub. L. 86–777, §2, Sept. 13, 1960, 74 Stat. 922.)

CODIFICATION

In subsecs. (a) and (b), "subchapter II of chapter 5 of title 5" and "chapter 7 of title 5" substituted for "the Administrative Procedure Act of June 11, 1946 (60 Stat. 637; 5 U.S.C. 1001–1011), as amended", "the Administrative Procedure Act", and "section 10 of the Administrative Procedure Act", respectively, on authority of Pub. L. 89–554, §7(b), Sept. 6, 1966, 80 Stat. 631, the first section of which enacted Title 5, Government Organization and Employees.

In subsec. (b), "chapter 158 of title 28" substituted for "the Act of December 29, 1950 (64 Stat. 1129; 5 U.S.C. 1031–1042), as amended" on authority of Pub. L. 89–554, §7(b), Sept. 6, 1966, 80 Stat. 631, section 4(e) of which enacted chapter 158 of Title 28, Judiciary and Judicial Procedure.

§167i. Exclusion from Natural Gas Act provisions

The provisions of the Natural Gas Act of June 21, 1938, as amended [15 U.S.C. 717 et seq.], shall not be applicable to the sale, extraction, processing, transportation, or storage of helium either prior to or subsequent to the separation of such helium from the natural gas with which it is commingled, whether or not the provisions of such Act apply to such natural gas, and in determining the rates of a natural gas company under sections 4 and 5 of the Natural Gas Act, as amended [15 U.S.C. 717c, 717d], whenever helium is extracted from helium-bearing natural gas, there shall be excluded (1) all income received from the sale of helium; (2) all direct costs incurred in the extraction, processing, compression, transportation or storage of helium; and (3) that portion of joint costs of exploration, production, gathering, extraction, processing, compression, transportation or storage divided and allocated to helium on a volumetric basis.

(Mar. 3, 1925, ch. 426, §11, as added Pub. L. 86–777, §2, Sept. 13, 1960, 74 Stat. 922.)

REFERENCES IN TEXT

The Natural Gas Act of June 21, 1938, as amended, referred to in text, means act June 21, 1938, ch. 556, 52 Stat. 821, as amended, known as the Natural Gas Act, which is classified generally to chapter 15B (§717 et seq.) of Title 15, Commerce and Trade. For complete classification of this Act to the Code, see section 717w of Title 15 and Tables.

§167j. Land conveyance in Potter County, Texas

(a) In general

The Secretary of the Interior shall transfer all right, title, and interest of the United States in and to the parcel of land described in subsection (b) of this section to the Texas Plains Girl Scout Council for consideration of $1, reserving to the United States such easements as may be necessary for pipeline rights-of-way.

(b) Land description

The parcel of land referred to in subsection (a) of this section is all those certain lots, tracts or parcels of land lying and being situated in the County of Potter and State of Texas, and being the East Three Hundred Thirty-One (E331) acres out of Section Seventy-eight (78) in Block Nine (9), B.S. & F. Survey, (some times known as the G.D. Landis pasture) Potter County, Texas, located by certificate No. 1/39 and evidenced by letters patents Nos. 411 and 412 issued by the State of Texas under date of November 23, 1937, and of record in Vol. 66A of the Patent Records of the State of Texas. The metes and bounds description of such lands is as follows:

(1) First tract

One Hundred Seventy-one (171) acres of land known as the North part of the East part of said survey Seventy-eight (78) aforesaid, described by metes and bounds as follows:

Beginning at a stone 20 x 12 x 3 inches marked X, set by W.D. Twichell in 1905, for the Northeast corner of this survey and the Northwest corner of Section 59;

Thence, South 0 degrees 12 minutes East with the West line of said Section 59, 999.4 varas to the Northeast corner of the South 160 acres of East half of Section 78;

Thence, North 89 degrees 47 minutes West with the North line of the South 150 acres of the East half, 956.8 varas to a point in the East line of the West half Section 78;

Thence, North 0 degrees 10 minutes West with the East line of the West half 999.4 varas to a stone 18 x 14 x 3 inches in the middle of the South line of Section 79;

Thence, South 89 degrees 47 minutes East 965 varas to the place of beginning.

(2) Second tract

One Hundred Sixty (160) acres of land known as the South part of the East part of said survey No. Seventy-eight (78) described by metes and bounds as follows:

Beginning at the Southwest corner of Section 59, a stone marked X and a pile of stones; Thence, North 89 degrees 47 minutes West with the North line of Section 77, 966.5 varas to the Southeast corner of the West half of Section 78; Thence, North 0 degrees 10 minutes West with the East line of the West half of Section 78;

Thence, South 89 degrees 47 minutes East 965.8 varas to a point in the East line of Section 78;

Thence, South 0 degrees 12 minutes East 934.6 varas to the place of beginning.

Containing an area of 331 acres, more or less.

(Mar. 3, 1925, ch. 426, §12, as added Pub. L. 86–777, §2, Sept. 13, 1960, 74 Stat. 923; amended Pub. L. 104–273, §6, Oct. 9, 1996, 110 Stat. 3318.)

AMENDMENTS

1996—Pub. L. 104–273 amended section generally. Prior to amendment, section related to Secretary's authority under Federal helium refining program to obtain loans and issue obligations to carry out program.

§ 167k. Violations; penalties

Whoever willfully violates, attempts to violate, or conspires to violate, any provision of this chapter or any regulation or order issued or any terms of a license granted thereunder shall, upon conviction thereof, be punished by a fine of not more than $5,000 or by imprisonment for not more than two years, or both, except that whoever commits such an offense with intent to injure the United States or with intent to secure an advantage to any foreign nation, shall upon conviction thereof, be punished by a fine of not more than $20,000 or by imprisonment for not more than twenty years, or both.

(Mar. 3, 1925, ch. 426, §13, as added Pub. L. 86–777, §2, Sept. 13, 1960, 74 Stat. 923.)

§ 167*l*. Injunctions

Whenever in the judgment of the Secretary any person has engaged or is about to engage in any act or practice which constitutes or will constitute a violation of any provision of this chapter, or any regulation or order issued or any term of a license granted thereunder, any such act or practice may be enjoined by any district court having jurisdiction of such person, and proper proceedings to this end may be instituted under the direction of the Attorney General of the United States.

(Mar. 3, 1925, ch. 426, §14, as added Pub. L. 86–777, §2, Sept. 13, 1960, 74 Stat. 923.)

§ 167m. Report on helium

(a) NAS study and report

Not later than three years before the date on which the Secretary commences offering for sale crude helium under section 167f of this title, the Secretary shall enter into appropriate arrangements with the National Academy of Sciences to study and report on whether such disposal of helium reserves will have a substantial adverse effect on United States scientific, technical, biomedical, or national security interests.

(b) Transmission to Congress

Not later than 18 months before the date on which the Secretary commences offering for sale crude helium under section 167f of this title, the Secretary shall transmit to the Congress—

(1) the report of the National Academy under subsection (a) of this section;

(2) the findings of the Secretary, after consideration of the conclusions of the National Academy under subsection (a) of this section and after consultation with the United States helium industry and with heads of affected Federal agencies, as to whether the disposal of the helium reserve under section 167f of this title will have a substantial adverse effect on the United States helium industry, United States,[1] helium market or United States,[1] scientific, technological, biomedical, or national security interests; and

(3) if the Secretary determines that selling the crude helium reserves under the formula established in section 167f of this title will have a substantial adverse effect on the United States helium industry, the United States helium market or United States scientific, technological, biomedical, or national security interest, the Secretary shall make recommendations, including recommendations for proposed legislation, as may be necessary to avoid such adverse effects.

(Mar. 3, 1925, ch. 426, §15, as added Pub. L. 86–777, §2, Sept. 13, 1960, 74 Stat. 923; amended Pub. L. 104–273, §7, Oct. 9, 1996, 110 Stat. 3319.)

AMENDMENTS

1996—Pub. L. 104–273 amended section generally. Prior to amendment, section related to individual enterprise in developing helium.

§ 167n. Repealed. Pub. L. 105–362, title IX, § 901(q), Nov. 10, 1998, 112 Stat. 3291

Section, act Mar. 3, 1925, ch. 426, §16, as added Pub. L. 86–777, §2, Sept. 13, 1960, 74 Stat. 923, directed Secretary of the Interior to make annual reports to Congress.

[1] So in original. The comma probably should not appear.

CHAPTER 11—ACQUISITION OF AND EXPENDITURES ON LAND FOR NATIONAL-DEFENSE PURPOSES

§§171, 171–1. Repealed. Aug. 10, 1956, ch. 1041, §53, 70A Stat. 641

Section 171, acts Aug. 18, 1890, ch. 797, §1, 26 Stat. 316; July 2, 1917, ch. 35, 40 Stat. 241; Apr. 11, 1918, ch. 51, 40 Stat. 518, authorized Secretary of War to institute condemnation proceedings for acquisition of land, to purchase land, and to accept donations of land. See section 2663 of Title 10, Armed Forces.

Section 171–1, act Oct. 25, 1951, ch. 563, §101, 65 Stat. 641, granted certain condemnation authority to Secretary of Navy. See sections 2663 and 2668 of Title 10.

§171a. Omitted

CODIFICATION

Section, act July 2, 1917, ch. 35, §2, as added Mar. 27, 1942, ch. 199, title II, §201, 56 Stat. 177, related to acquisition of real property during war, and terminated on Dec. 28, 1945 by act Mar. 27, 1942, ch. 199, title II, §202, as added Dec. 28, 1945, ch. 590, §1(a), 59 Stat. 658.

§171b. Repealed. Pub. L. 85–861, §36A, Sept. 2, 1958, 72 Stat. 1570

Section, acts Aug. 3, 1956, ch. 939, title IV, §406, 70 Stat. 1015; Aug. 20, 1958, Pub. L. 85–685, title V, §510, 72 Stat. 662, related to acquisition of land not exceeding $5,000 in cost. See section 2672 of Title 10, Armed Forces.

§§172, 173. Repealed. Aug. 10, 1956, ch. 1041, §53, 70A Stat. 641

Section 172, act July 9, 1918, ch. 143, subch. XV §8, 40 Stat. 888, related to acquisition of property for production of lumber. See sections 2664 and 2665 of Title 10, Armed Forces.

Section 173, act Apr. 28, 1904, ch. 1762, §1, 33 Stat. 497, related to purchase of land for quarters and barracks in addition to sites for fortifications.

§174. Omitted

CODIFICATION

Section, act Aug. 18, 1890, ch. 797, §1, 26 Stat. 316, provided that nothing contained in former section 171 of this title should be construed to authorize an expenditure or involve the Government in any contract for future payment of money in excess of sums appropriated therefor.

§175. Transferred

CODIFICATION

Section, R.S. §355; June 28, 1930, ch. 710, 46 Stat. 828; Feb. 1, 1940, ch. 18, 54 Stat. 19; Oct. 9, 1940, ch. 793, 54 Stat. 1083; Sept. 1, 1970, Pub. L. 91–393, §1, 84 Stat. 835, which related to approval of title prior to Federal land purchases, payment of title expenses, application to Tennessee Valley Authority, and Federal jurisdiction over acquisitions, was transferred to section 255 of Title 40, Public Buildings, Property, and Works.

§176. Omitted

CODIFICATION

Section, act Mar. 28, 1918, ch. 28, §1, 40 Stat. 460, authorized acquisition of property on Hudson River owned by North German Lloyd Dock Company and Hamburg-American Line Terminal & Navigation Company and provided that section 175 of this title did not apply to expenditures authorized in connection with such property. The President, by proclamation dated June 28, 1918, took possession of such property.

§§177 to 179. Repealed. Aug. 10, 1956, ch. 1041, §53, 70A Stat 641

Section 177, act June 25, 1906, ch. 3540, 34 Stat. 463, related to contracts for construction of fortifications and other works of defense.

Section 178, act Apr. 11, 1898, No. 21, 30 Stat. 737, provided for erection of forts in emergency. See sections 4776 and 9776 of Title 10, Armed Forces.

Section 179, act June 30, 1921, ch. 33, §1, 42 Stat. 81, related to chargeability of appropriations with respect to transportation cost incident to construction and maintenance of seacoast fortifications.

CHAPTER 12—VESSELS IN TERRITORIAL WATERS OF UNITED STATES

§191. Regulation of anchorage and movement of vessels during national emergency

Whenever the President by proclamation or Executive order declares a national emergency to exist by reason of actual or threatened war, insurrection, or invasion, or disturbance or threatened disturbance of the international relations of the United States, or whenever the Attorney General determines that an actual or anticipated mass migration of aliens en route to, or arriving off the coast of, the United States presents urgent circumstances requiring an immediate Federal response, the Secretary of Transportation may make, subject to the approval of the President, rules and regulations governing the anchorage and movement of any vessel, foreign or domestic, in the territorial waters of the United States, may inspect such vessel at any time, place guards thereon, and, if necessary in his opinion in order to secure such vessels from damage or injury, or to prevent damage or injury to any harbor or waters of the United States, or to secure the observance of the rights and obligations of the United States, may take, by and with the consent of the President, for such purposes, full possession and control of such vessel and remove therefrom the officers and crew thereof and all other persons not specially authorized by him to go or remain on board thereof.

Whenever the President finds that the security of the United States is endangered by reason of actual or threatened war, or invasion, or insurrection, or subversive activity, or of disturbances or threatened disturbances of the international relations of the United States, the President is authorized to institute such measures and issue such rules and regulations—

(a) to govern the anchorage and movement of any foreign-flag vessels in the territorial waters of the United States, to inspect such vessels at any time, to place guards thereon, and, if necessary in his opinion in order to secure such vessels from damage or injury, or to prevent damage or injury to any harbor or waters of the United States, or to secure the observance of rights and obligations of the United States, may take for such purposes full possession and control of such vessels and remove therefrom the officers and crew thereof, and all other persons not especially authorized by him to go or remain on board thereof;

(b) to safeguard against destruction, loss, or injury from sabotage or other subversive acts, accidents, or other causes of similar nature, vessels, harbors, ports, and waterfront facilities in the United States and all territory and water, continental or insular, subject to the jurisdiction of the United States.

Any appropriation available to any of the Executive Departments shall be available to carry out the provisions of this title.[1]

(June 15, 1917, ch. 30, title II, §1, 40 Stat. 220; Aug. 9, 1950, ch. 656, §1, 64 Stat. 427; Sept. 26, 1950, ch. 1049, §2(b), 64 Stat. 1038; Pub. L. 89–670, §6(b)(1), Oct. 15, 1966, 80 Stat. 938; Pub. L. 96–70, title III, §3302(a), Sept. 27, 1979, 93 Stat. 498; Pub. L. 104–208, div. C, title VI, §649, Sept. 30, 1996, 110 Stat. 3009–711.)

REFERENCES IN TEXT

This title, referred to in text, means title II of act June 15, 1917, ch. 30, 40 Stat. 220, as amended, which enacted sections 191 and 192 to 194 of this title. For complete classification of this Act to the Code, see Tables.

AMENDMENTS

1996—Pub. L. 104–208, in first par., inserted "or whenever the Attorney General determines that an actual or anticipated mass migration of aliens en route to, or arriving off the coast of, the United States presents urgent circumstances requiring an immediate Federal response," after "international relations of the United States,".

1979—Pub. L. 96–70 struck out second par., providing that within the territory and waters of the Canal Zone the Governor of the Canal Zone, with the approval of the President, shall exercise all the powers conferred by this section on the Secretary of the Treasury, and in cl. (b) of third par., struck out "the Canal Zone," after "facilities in the United States,".

1950—Act Sept. 26, 1950, substituted "Governor of the Canal Zone" for "Governor of the Panama Canal" in second par.

Act Aug. 9, 1950, authorized the President to institute such rules and regulations to control anchorage and movement of foreign-flag vessels in United States waters when the national security is endangered.

EFFECTIVE DATE OF 1979 AMENDMENT

Amendment by Pub. L. 96–70 effective Oct. 1, 1979, see section 3304 of Pub. L. 96–70, set out as an Effective Date note under section 3601 of Title 22, Foreign Relations and Intercourse.

[1] See References in Text note below.

TERMINATION DATE OF 1950 AMENDMENT

Section 4 of act Aug. 9, 1950, provided that: "The provisions of this Act [amending this section and sections 192 and 194 of this title] shall expire on such date as may be specified by concurrent resolution of the two Houses of Congress."

TERMINATION OF WAR AND EMERGENCIES

Act July 25, 1947, ch. 327, §3, 61 Stat. 451, provided that in the interpretation of this section, the date July 25, 1947, shall be deemed to be the date of termination of any state of war theretofore declared by Congress and of the national emergencies proclaimed by the President on Sept. 8, 1939, and May 27, 1941.

REGULATIONS—POST-WAR GENERALLY

For regulations relating to safeguarding of vessels, harbors, ports, and waterfront facilities, under a finding that the security of the United States is endangered by reason of subversive activity, see Ex. Ord. No. 10173, Oct. 18, 1950, 15 F.R. 7005.

REGULATIONS—WORLD WAR II

Proc. No. 2732, June 2, 1947, 12 F.R. 3583, 61 Stat. 1069, revoked Proc. No. 2412, June 27, 1940, 5 F.R. 2419, 54 Stat. 2711, which granted consent of President to the exercise of certain powers under this section by the Secretary of the Treasury and the Governor of the Canal Zone.

REGULATIONS—WORLD WAR I

A proclamation was issued under this section on December 3, 1917.

SEPARABILITY

Section 4 of title XIII of act June 15, 1917, provided: "If any clause, sentence, paragraph, or part of this Act [see Tables for classification] shall for any reason be adjudged by any court of competent jurisdiction to be invalid, such judgment shall not affect, impair, or invalidate the remainder thereof but shall be confined in its operation to the clause, sentence, paragraph, or part thereof directly involved in the controversy in which such judgment shall have been rendered."

TRANSFER OF FUNCTIONS

"Secretary of Transportation" substituted for "Secretary of the Treasury" in first paragraph of text pursuant to section 6(b)(1) of Pub. L. 89–670, which transferred Coast Guard to Department of Transportation and transferred to and vested in Secretary of Transportation functions, powers, and duties, relating to Coast Guard, of Secretary of the Treasury and of other officers and offices of Department of the Treasury. See section 108 of Title 49, Transportation.

DELEGATION OF FUNCTIONS

For delegation to Secretary of the Treasury of authority vested in President by this section, see section 2(e) of Ex. Ord. No. 10289, Sept. 17, 1951, 16 F.R. 9499, as amended, and section 1(r) of Ex. Ord. No. 10637, Sept. 16, 1955, 20 F.R. 7025, set out as notes under section 301 of Title 3, The President.

PROC. NO. 6867. DECLARATION OF NATIONAL EMERGENCY AND INVOCATION OF EMERGENCY AUTHORITY RELATING TO REGULATION OF ANCHORAGE AND MOVEMENT OF VESSELS

Proc. No. 6867, Mar. 1, 1996, 61 F.R. 8843, provided:

WHEREAS, on February 24, 1996, Cuban military aircraft intercepted and destroyed two unarmed U.S.-registered civilian aircraft in international airspace north of Cuba;

WHEREAS the Government of Cuba has demonstrated a ready and reckless willingness to use excessive force, including deadly force, in the ostensible enforcement of its sovereignty;

WHEREAS, on July 13, 1995, persons in U.S.-registered vessels who entered into Cuban territorial waters suffered injury as a result of the reckless use of force against them by the Cuban military; and

WHEREAS the entry of U.S.-registered vessels into Cuban territorial waters could again result in injury to, or loss of life of, persons engaged in that conduct, due to the potential use of excessive force, including deadly force, against them by the Cuban military, and could threaten a disturbance in international relations;

NOW, THEREFORE, I, WILLIAM J. CLINTON, President of the United States of America, by the authority vested in me by the Constitution and the laws of the United States of America, including section 1 of title II of Public Law 65-24, ch. 30, June 15, 1917, as amended (50 U.S.C. 191), sections 201 and 301 of the National Emergencies Act (50 U.S.C. 1601 *et seq.*) [50 U.S.C. 1621, 1631], and section 301 of title 3, United States Code, find and do hereby proclaim that a national emergency does exist by reason of a disturbance or threatened disturbance of international relations. In order to address this national emergency and to secure the observance of the rights and obligations of the United States, I hereby authorize and direct the Secretary of Transportation (the "Secretary") to make and issue such rules and regulations as the Secretary may find appropriate to regulate the anchorage and movement of vessels, and delegate to the Secretary my authority to approve such rules and regulations, as authorized by the Act of June 15, 1917 [see Tables for classification].

SECTION 1. The Secretary may make rules and regulations governing the anchorage and movement of any vessel, foreign or domestic, in the territorial waters of the United States, which may be used, or is susceptible of being used, for voyage into Cuban territorial waters and that may create unsafe conditions and threaten a disturbance of international relations. Any rule or regulation issued pursuant to this proclamation may be effective immediately upon issuance as such rule or regulation shall involve a foreign affairs function of the United States.

SEC. 2. The Secretary is authorized to inspect any vessel, foreign or domestic, in the territorial waters of the United States, at any time; to place guards on any such vessel; and, with my consent expressly hereby granted, take full possession and control of any such vessel and remove the officers and crew, and all other persons not specifically authorized by the Secretary to go or remain on board the vessel when necessary to secure the rights and obligations of the United States.

SEC. 3. The Secretary may request assistance from such departments, agencies, officers, or instrumentalities of the United States as the Secretary deems necessary to carry out the purposes of this proclamation. Such departments, agencies, officers, or instrumentalities shall, consistent with other provisions of law and to the extent practicable, provide requested assistance.

SEC. 4. The Secretary may seek assistance from State and local authorities in carrying out the purposes of this proclamation. Because State and local assistance may be essential for an effective response to this emergency, I urge all State and local officials to cooperate with Federal authorities and to take all actions within their lawful authority necessary to prevent the unauthorized departure of vessels intending to enter Cuban territorial waters.

SEC. 5. All powers and authorities delegated by this proclamation to the Secretary may be delegated by the Secretary to other officers and agents of the United States Government unless otherwise prohibited by law.

SEC. 6. This proclamation shall be immediately transmitted to the Congress and published in the Federal Register.

IN WITNESS WHEREOF, I have hereunto set my hand this first day of March, in the year of our Lord nineteen hundred and ninety-six, and of the Independence of the United States of America the two hundred and twentieth.

WILLIAM J. CLINTON.

CONTINUATION OF NATIONAL EMERGENCY DECLARED BY PROC. NO. 6867

Notice of President of the United States, dated Feb. 25, 2000, 65 F.R. 10929, provided:

On March 1, 1996, by Proclamation 6867 [set out above], I declared a national emergency to address the disturbance or threatened disturbance of international relations caused by the February 24, 1996, destruction by the Government of Cuba of two unarmed U.S.-registered civilian aircraft in international airspace north of Cuba. In July 1996 and on subsequent occasions, the Government of Cuba stated its intent to forcefully defend its sovereignty against any U.S.-registered vessels or aircraft that might enter Cuban territorial waters or airspace while involved in a memorial flotilla and peaceful protest. Since these events, the Government of Cuba has not demonstrated that it will refrain from the future use of reckless and excessive force against U.S. vessels or aircraft that may engage in memorial activities or peaceful protest north of Cuba. Therefore, in accordance with section 202(d) of the National Emergencies Act (50 U.S.C. 1622(d)), I am continuing the national emergency with respect to Cuba and the emergency authority relating to the regulation of the anchorage and movement of vessels set out in Proclamation 6867.

This notice shall be published in the Federal Register and transmitted to the Congress.

WILLIAM J. CLINTON.

Prior continuations of national emergency declared by Proc. No. 6867 were contained in the following:

Notice of President of the United States, dated Feb. 24, 1999, 64 F.R. 9903.

Notice of President of the United States, dated Feb. 25, 1998, 63 F.R. 9923.

Notice of President of the United States, dated Feb. 27, 1997, 62 F.R. 9347.

SECTION REFERRED TO IN OTHER SECTIONS

This section is referred to in section 191a of this title; title 18 section 2277; title 42 section 267.

§ 191a. Transfer of Secretary of Transportation's powers to Secretary of Navy when Coast Guard operates as part of Navy

When the Coast Guard operates as a part of the Navy pursuant to section 3 of title 14, the powers conferred on the Secretary of Transportation by section 191 of this title, shall vest in and be exercised by the Secretary of the Navy.

(Nov. 15, 1941, ch. 471, § 2, 55 Stat. 763; Pub. L. 87–845, § 11, Oct. 18, 1962, 76A Stat. 699; Pub. L. 89–670, § 6(b)(1), Oct. 15, 1966, 80 Stat. 938.)

AMENDMENTS

1962—Pub. L. 87–845 substituted "section 3 of title 14" for "section 1 of title 14".

EFFECTIVE DATE OF 1962 AMENDMENT

Amendment by Pub. L. 87–845 effective Jan. 2, 1963, see section 25 of Pub. L. 87–845, set out as a note under section 14 of Title 18, Crimes and Criminal Procedure.

TRANSFER OF FUNCTIONS

"Secretary of Transportation" substituted in text for "Secretary of the Treasury" pursuant to section 6(b)(1) of Pub. L. 89–670, which transferred Coast Guard to Department of Transportation and transferred to and vested in Secretary of Transportation functions, powers, and duties, relating to Coast Guard, of Secretary of the Treasury and of other officers and offices of Department of the Treasury. See section 108 of Title 49, Transportation.

§191b. Repealed. Pub. L. 96–70, title III, §3303(a)(5), Sept. 27, 1979, 93 Stat. 499

Section, acts Nov. 15, 1941, ch. 471, §4, 55 Stat. 763; Sept. 26, 1950, ch. 1049, §2(b), 64 Stat. 1038; Oct. 18, 1962, Pub. L. 87–845, §12, 76A Stat. 699, provided that this section, section 191a of this title, and section 91 of title 14 not affect the authority of the Governor of the Canal Zone conferred by section 191 of this title or section 34 of Title 2, Canal Zone Code.

EFFECTIVE DATE OF REPEAL

Repeal effective Oct. 1, 1979, see section 3304 of Pub. L. 96–70, set out as an Effective Date note under section 3601 of Title 22, Foreign Relations and Intercourse.

§191c. Repealed. Aug. 4, 1949, ch. 393, §20, 63 Stat. 561

Section, act Nov. 15, 1941, ch. 471, §1, 55 Stat. 763, related to control of anchorage and movement of vessels to insure safety of naval vessels. See section 91 of Title 14, Coast Guard.

§192. Seizure and forfeiture of vessel; fine and imprisonment

If any owner, agent, master, officer, or person in charge, or any member of the crew of any such vessel fails to comply with any regulation or rule issued or order given under the provisions of this title,[1] or obstructs or interferes with the exercise of any power conferred by this title,[1] the vessel, together with her tackle, apparel, furniture, and equipment, shall be subject to seizure and forfeiture to the United States in the same manner as merchandise is forfeited for violation of the customs revenue laws; and the person guilty of such failure, obstruction, or interference shall be punished by imprisonment for not more than ten years and may, in the discretion of the court, be fined not more than $10,000.

(a) If any other person knowingly fails to comply with any regulation or rule issued or order given under the provisions of this title,[1] or knowingly obstructs or interferes with the exercise of any power conferred by this title,[1] he shall be punished by imprisonment for not more than ten years and may, at the discretion of the court, be fined not more than $10,000.

(June 15, 1917, ch. 30, title II, §2, 40 Stat. 220; Mar. 28, 1940, ch. 72, §3(a), 54 Stat. 79; Nov. 15, 1941, ch. 471, §3, 55 Stat. 763; Aug. 9, 1950, ch. 656, §3, 64 Stat. 428.)

REFERENCES IN TEXT

This title, referred to in text, means title II of act June 15, 1917, ch. 30, 40 Stat. 220, as amended, which enacted sections 191 and 192 to 194 of this title. For complete classification of this Act to the Code, see Tables.

AMENDMENTS

1950—Subsec. (a). Act Aug. 9, 1950, added subsec. (a).

1941—Act Nov. 15, 1941, struck out "by the Secretary of the Treasury or the Governor of the Panama Canal" before "under the provisions of this title".

1940—Act Mar. 28, 1940, increased term of imprisonment.

TERMINATION DATE OF 1950 AMENDMENT

For termination of amendment by act Aug. 9, 1950, see section 4 of act Aug. 9, 1950, set out as a note under section 191 of this title.

SECTION REFERRED TO IN OTHER SECTIONS

This section is referred to in title 42 section 267.

[1] See References in Text note below.

§193. Repealed. June 25, 1948, ch. 645, §21, 62 Stat. 862

Section, acts June 15, 1917, ch. 30, title II, §3, 40 Stat. 220; Mar. 28, 1940, ch. 72, §3(b), 54 Stat. 79, related to destruction of, injury to, or improper use of vessels. See section 2274 of Title 18, Crimes and Criminal Procedure.

EFFECTIVE DATE OF REPEAL

Repeal effective Sept. 1, 1948, see section 38 of act June 25, 1948, set out as an Effective Date note preceding section 1 of Title 28, Judiciary and Judicial Procedure.

§194. Enforcement provisions

The President may employ such departments, agencies, officers, or instrumentalities of the United States as he may deem necessary to carry out the purpose of this title.[1]

(June 15, 1917, ch. 30, title II, §4, 40 Stat. 220; Aug. 9, 1950, ch. 656, §2, 64 Stat. 428.)

REFERENCES IN TEXT

This title, referred to in text, means title II of act June 15, 1917, ch. 30, 40 Stat. 220, as amended, which enacted sections 191 and 192 to 194 of this title. For complete classification of this Act to the Code, see Tables.

AMENDMENTS

1950—Act Aug. 9, 1950, authorized President to employ such departments, agencies, etc., as he may deem necessary to carry out title II of act June 15, 1917.

TERMINATION DATE OF 1950 AMENDMENT

For termination of amendment by act Aug. 9, 1950, see section 4 of act Aug. 9, 1950, set out as a note under section 191 of this title.

SECTION REFERRED TO IN OTHER SECTIONS

This section is referred to in title 42 section 267.

§195. "United States" defined

The term "United States" as used in this Act includes all territory and waters, continental or insular, subject to the jurisdiction of the United States.

(June 15, 1917, ch. 30, title XIII, §1, 40 Stat. 231; Pub. L. 96–70, title III, §3302(b), Sept. 27, 1979, 93 Stat. 498.)

REFERENCES IN TEXT

This Act, referred to in text, means act June 15, 1917, ch. 30, 40 Stat. 217, as amended. For complete classification of this Act to the Code, see Tables.

CODIFICATION

Section was formerly classified to section 40 of this title. In the original this section defined "United States" as used in act June 15, 1917. Other provisions of that act were contained in sections 31 to 42 of this title and certain sections of former Title 18, Criminal Code and Criminal Procedure. The definition of "United States" as used in present provisions derived from those former sections is covered by sections 5 and 14 of Title 18, Crimes and Criminal Procedure.

AMENDMENTS

1979—Pub. L. 96–70 struck out "the Canal Zone and" after "this Act includes".

[1] See References in Text note below.

EFFECTIVE DATE OF 1979 AMENDMENT

Amendment by Pub. L. 96–70 effective Oct. 1, 1979, see section 3304 of Pub. L. 96–70, set out as an Effective Date note under section 3601 of Title 22, Foreign Relations and Intercourse.

§ 196. Emergency foreign vessel acquisition; purchase or requisition of vessels lying idle in United States waters

During any period in which vessels may be requisitioned under section 1242 of title 46, Appendix, the President is authorized and empowered through the Secretary of Transportation to purchase, or to requisition, or for any part of such period to charter or requisition the use of, or to take over the title to or possession of, for such use or disposition as he shall direct, any merchant vessel not owned by citizens of the United States which is lying idle in waters within the jurisdiction of the United States and which the President finds to be necessary to the national defense. Just compensation shall be determined and made to the owner or owners of any such vessel in accordance with the applicable provisions of section 1242 of title 46, Appendix. Such compensation hereunder, or advances on account thereof, shall be deposited with the Treasurer of the United States in a separate deposit fund. Payments for such compensation and also for payment of any valid claim upon such vessel in accord with the provisions of the second paragraph of subsection (d) of section 1242 of title 46, Appendix, shall be made from such fund upon the certificate of the Secretary of Transportation.

(Aug. 9, 1954, ch. 659, § 1, 68 Stat. 675; Pub. L. 96–70, title III, § 3302(c), Sept. 27, 1979, 93 Stat. 498; Pub. L. 97–31, § 12(152), Aug. 6, 1981, 95 Stat. 167.)

AMENDMENTS

1981—Pub. L. 97–31 substituted references to Secretary of Transportation for references to Secretary of Commerce wherever appearing.

1979—Pub. L. 96–70 struck out ", including the Canal Zone," after "jurisdiction of the United States".

EFFECTIVE DATE OF 1979 AMENDMENT

Amendment by Pub. L. 96–70 effective Oct. 1, 1979, see section 3304 of Pub. L. 96–70, set out as an Effective Date note under section 3601 of Title 22, Foreign Relations and Intercourse.

SECTION REFERRED TO IN OTHER SECTIONS

This section is referred to in section 198 of this title.

§ 197. Voluntary purchase or charter agreements

During any period in which vessels may be requisitioned under section 1242 of title 46, Appendix, the President is authorized through the Secretary of Transportation to acquire by voluntary agreement of purchase or charter the ownership or use of any merchant vessel not owned by citizens of the United States.

(Aug. 9, 1954, ch. 659, § 2, 68 Stat. 675; Pub. L. 97–31, § 12(152), Aug. 6, 1981, 95 Stat. 167.)

AMENDMENTS

1981—Pub. L. 97–31 substituted "Secretary of Transportation" for "Secretary of Commerce".

SECTION REFERRED TO IN OTHER SECTIONS

This section is referred to in section 198 of this title.

§ 198. Requisitioned vessels

(a) Documentation of vessels

Any vessel not documented under the laws of the United States, acquired by or made available to the Secretary of Transportation under sections 196 to 198 of this title, or otherwise, may, notwithstanding any other provision of law, in the discretion of the Secretary of the department in which the Coast Guard is operating be documented as a vessel of the United States under such rules and regulations or orders, and with such limitations, as the Secretary of the department in which the Coast Guard is operating may prescribe or issue as necessary or appropriate to carry out the purposes and provisions of sections 196 to 198 of this title, and in accordance with the provisions of subsection (c) of this section, engage in the coastwise trade when so documented. Any document issued to a vessel under the provisions of this subsection shall be surrendered at any time that such surrender may be ordered by the Secretary of the department in which the Coast Guard is operating. No vessel, the surrender of the documents of which has been so ordered, shall, after the effective date of such order, have the status of a vessel of the United States unless documented anew.

(b) Waiver of compliance

The President may, notwithstanding any other provisions of law, by rules and regulations or orders, waive compliance with any provision of law relating to masters, officers, members of the crew, or crew accommodations on any vessel documented under authority of this section to such extent and upon such terms as he finds necessary because of the lack of physical facilities on such vessels, and because of the need to employ aliens for their operation. No vessel shall cease to enjoy the benefits and privileges of a vessel of the United States by reason of the employment of any person in accordance with the provisions of this subsection.

(c) Coastwise trade; inspection

Any vessel while documented under the provisions of this section, when chartered under sections 196 to 198 of this title by the Secretary of Transportation to Government agencies or departments or to private operators, may engage in the coastwise trade under permits issued by the Secretary of Transportation, who is authorized to issue permits for such purpose pursuant to such rules and regulations as he may prescribe. The Secretary of Transportation is authorized to prescribe such rules and regulations as he may deem necessary or appropriate to carry out the purposes and provisions of this section. The second paragraph of section 9 of the Shipping Act, 1916, as amended [46 App. U.S.C. 808], shall not apply with respect to vessels chartered to Government agencies or departments or to private operators or otherwise used or disposed of under sections 196 to 198 of this title. Existing laws covering the inspection of steam vessels are made applicable to vessels documented under this section only to such extent and upon such conditions as may be required by regulations of the Secretary of the department in which the Coast Guard is operating: *Provided*,

That in determining to what extent those laws should be made applicable, due consideration shall be given to the primary purpose of transporting commodities essential to the national defense.

(d) Reconditioning of vessels

The Secretary of Transportation without regard to the provisions of section 5 of title 41 may repair, reconstruct, or recondition any vessels to be utilized under sections 196 to 198 of this title. The Secretary of Transportation and any other Government department or agency by which any vessel is acquired or chartered, or to which any vessel is transferred or made available under sections 196 to 198 of this title may, with the aid of any funds available and without regard to the provisions of said section 5 of title 41, repair, reconstruct, or recondition any such vessels to meet the needs of the services intended, or provide facilities for such repair, reconstruction, or reconditioning. The Secretary of Transportation may operate or charter for operation any vessel to be utilized under sections 196 to 198 of this title to private operators, citizens of the United States, or to any department or agency of the United States Government, without regard to the provisions of title VII of the Merchant Marine Act, 1936 [46 App. U.S.C. 1191 et seq.], and any department or agency of the United States Government is authorized to enter into such charters.

(e) Effective period

In case of any voyage of a vessel documented under the provisions of this section begun before the date of termination of an effective period of section 196 of this title, but is completed after such date, the provisions of this section shall continue in effect with respect to such vessel until such voyage is completed.

(f) "Documented" defined

When used in sections 196 to 198 of this title, the term "documented" means "registered", "enrolled and licensed", or "licensed".

(Aug. 9, 1954, ch. 659, §3, 68 Stat. 675; Pub. L. 89–670, §6(b)(1), (2), Oct. 15, 1966, 80 Stat. 938; Pub. L. 97–31, §12(152), Aug. 6, 1981, 95 Stat. 167.)

REFERENCES IN TEXT

The Merchant Marine Act, 1936, referred to in subsec. (d), is act June 29, 1936, ch. 858, 49 Stat. 1985, as amended. Title VII of the Merchant Marine Act, 1936 is classified generally to subchapter VII (§1191 et seq.) of chapter 27 of Title 46, Appendix, Shipping. For complete classification of this Act to the Code, see section 1245 of Title 46, Appendix, and Tables.

AMENDMENTS

1981—Subsecs. (a), (c), (d). Pub. L. 97–31 substituted references to Secretary of Transportation for references to Secretary of Commerce wherever appearing.

TRANSFER OF FUNCTIONS

"Secretary of the department in which the Coast Guard is operating" substituted in subsec. (a) for "Secretary of the Treasury" pursuant to section 6(b)(1), (2) of Pub. L. 89–670, which transferred Coast Guard to Department of Transportation and transferred to and vested in Secretary of Transportation functions, powers, and duties, relating to Coast Guard, of Secretary of the Treasury and of all other officers and offices of Department of the Treasury, and which provided that notwithstanding such transfer Coast Guard shall operate as part of Navy in time of war or when President directs as provided in section 3 of Title 14, Coast Guard. See section 108 of Title 49, Transportation.

DELEGATION OF FUNCTIONS

For delegation to Secretary of the Treasury of authority vested in President by subsec. (a) of this section, see Ex. Ord. No. 10289, eff. Sept. 17, 1951, 16 F.R. 9499, set out as a note under section 301 of Title 3, The President.

ADMINISTRATIVE DELEGATION OF FUNCTIONS BY SECRETARY OF THE TREASURY

Administrative delegation of functions by Secretary of the Treasury, see note set out preceding section 3 of the Appendix to Title 46, Shipping.

CHAPTER 13—INSURRECTION

§§ 201 to 204. Repealed. Aug. 10, 1956, ch. 1041, § 53, 70A Stat. 641

Section 201, R.S. §5297, provided for Federal aid for State Governments in case of an insurrection in any State. See section 331 of Title 10, Armed Forces.

Section 202, R.S. §5298, related to use of military and naval forces to enforce authority of Federal Government. See section 332 of Title 10.

Section 203, R.S. §5299, related to denial by State of equal protection of laws and authorized the President to take measures for the suppression of any insurrection, domestic violence, or combinations. See section 333 of Title 10.

Section 204, R.S. §5300, authorized the President to issue a proclamation commanding insurgents to disperse. See section 334 of Title 10.

§ 205. Suspension of commercial intercourse with State in insurrection

Whenever the President, in pursuance of the provisions of this chapter, has called forth the militia to suppress combinations against the laws of the United States, and to cause the laws to be duly executed, and the insurgents shall have failed to disperse by the time directed by the President, and when the insurgents claim to act under the authority of any State or States, and such claim is not disclaimed or repudiated by the persons exercising the functions of government in such State or States, or in the part or parts thereof in which such combination exists, and such insurrection is not suppressed by such State or States, or whenever the inhabitants of any State or part thereof are at any time found by the President to be in insurrection against the United States, the President may, by proclamation, declare that the inhabitants of such State, or of any section or part thereof where such insurrection exists, are in a state of insurrection against the United States; and thereupon all commercial intercourse by and between the same and the citizens thereof and the citizens of the rest of the United States shall cease and be unlawful so long as such condition of hostility shall continue; and all goods and chattels, wares and merchandise, coming from such State or section into the other parts of the United States, or proceeding from other parts of the United States to such State or section, by land or water, shall, together with the vessel or vehicle conveying the same, or conveying persons to or from such State or section, be forfeited to the United States.

(R.S. § 5301.)

CODIFICATION

R.S. § 5301 derived from acts July 13, 1861, ch. 3, § 5, 12 Stat. 257; July 31, 1861, ch. 32, 12 Stat. 284.

SECTION REFERRED TO IN OTHER SECTIONS

This section is referred to in sections 206, 223 of this title.

§ 206. Suspension of commercial intercourse with part of State in insurrection

Whenever any part of a State not declared to be in insurrection is under the control of insurgents, or is in dangerous proximity to places under their control, all commercial intercourse therein and therewith shall be subject to the prohibitions and conditions of section 205 of this title for such time and to such extent as shall become necessary to protect the public interests, and be directed by the Secretary of the Treasury, with the approval of the President.

(R.S. § 5302.)

CODIFICATION

R.S. § 5302 derived from act July 2, 1864, ch. 225, § 5, 13 Stat. 376.

§ 207. Persons affected by suspension of commercial intercourse

The provisions of this chapter in relation to commercial intercourse shall apply to all commercial intercourse by and between persons residing or being within districts within the lines of national military occupation in the States or parts of States declared in insurrection, whether with each other or with persons residing or being within districts declared in insurrection and not within those lines; and all persons within the United States, not native or naturalized citizens thereof, shall be subject to the same prohibitions, in all commercial intercourse with inhabitants of States or parts of States declared in insurrection, as citizens of States not declared to be in insurrection.

(R.S. § 5303.)

CODIFICATION

R.S. § 5303 derived from act July 2, 1864, ch. 225, § 4, 13 Stat. 376.

§ 208. Licensing or permitting commercial intercourse with State or region in insurrection

The President may, in his discretion, license and permit commercial intercourse with any part of such State or section, the inhabitants of which are so declared in a state of insurrection, so far as may be necessary to authorize supplying the necessities of loyal persons residing in insurrectionary States, within the lines of actual occupation by the military forces of the United States, as indicated by published order of the commanding general of the department or district so occupied; and, also, so far as may be necessary to authorize persons residing within such lines to bring or send to market in the loyal States any products which they shall have produced with their own labor or the labor of freedmen, or others employed and paid by them, pursuant to rules relating thereto, which may be established under proper authority. And no goods, wares, or merchandise shall be taken into a State declared in insurrection, or transported therein, except to and from such places and to such monthly amounts as shall have been previously agreed upon, in writing, by the commanding general of the department in which such places are situated, and an officer designated by the Secretary of the Treasury for that purpose. Such commercial intercourse shall be in such articles and for such time and by such persons as the President, in his discretion, may think most conducive to the public interest; and, so far as by him licensed, shall be conducted and carried on only in pursuance of rules and regulations prescribed by the Secretary of the Treasury.

(R.S. § 5304.)

CODIFICATION

R.S. § 5304 derived from acts July 13, 1861, ch. 3, § 5, 12 Stat. 257; July 2, 1864, ch. 225, § 9, 13 Stat. 377.

§ 209. Repealed. Pub. L. 89–554, § 8(a), Sept. 6, 1966, 80 Stat. 632

Section, R.S. § 5305, related to appointment of officers to carry into effect licenses to trade in State or region in an insurrection.

§ 210. Penalties for unauthorized trading, etc.; jurisdiction of prosecutions

Every officer of the United States, civil, military, or naval, and every sutler, soldier, marine, or other person, who takes, or causes to be taken into a State declared to be in insurrection, or to any other point to be thence taken into such State, or who transports or sells, or otherwise disposes of therein, any goods, wares, or merchandise whatsoever, except in pursuance of license and authority of the President, as provided in this chapter, or who makes any false statement or representation upon which license and authority is granted for such transportation, sale, or other disposition, or who, under any license or authority obtained, willfully and knowingly transports, sells, or otherwise disposes of any other goods, wares, or merchandise than such as are in good faith so licensed and authorized, or who willfully and knowingly transports, sells, or disposes of the same, or any portion thereof, in violation of the terms of such license or authority, or of any rule or regulation prescribed by the Secretary of the Treasury concerning the same, or who is guilty of any act of embezzlement, of willful misappropriation of public or private money or property, of keeping false accounts, or of willfully making any false returns, shall be deemed guilty of a misdemeanor, and shall be fined not more than $5,000, and imprisoned in the penitentiary not more than three years. Violations of this section shall be cognizable before any court, civil or military, competent to try the same.

(R.S. §5306.)

CODIFICATION

R.S. §5306 derived from act July 2, 1864, ch. 225, §10, 13 Stat. 377.

§211. Investigations to detect and prevent frauds and abuses

It shall be the duty of the Secretary of the Treasury, from time to time, to institute such investigations as may be necessary to detect and prevent frauds and abuses in any trade or transactions which may be licensed between inhabitants of loyal States and of States in insurrection. And the agents making such investigations shall have power to compel the attendance of witnesses, and to make examinations on oath.

(R.S. §5307.)

CODIFICATION

R.S. §5307 derived from act July 2, 1864, ch. 225, §10, 13 Stat. 377.

§212. Confiscation of property employed to aid insurrection

Whenever during any insurrection against the Government of the United States, after the President shall have declared by proclamation that the laws of the United States are opposed, and the execution thereof obstructed, by combinations too powerful to be suppressed by the ordinary course of judicial proceedings, or by the power vested in the marshals by law, any person, or his agent, attorney, or employee, purchases or acquires, sells or gives, any property of whatsoever kind or description, with intent to use or employ the same, or suffers the same to be used or employed in aiding, abetting, or promoting such insurrection or resistance to the laws, or any person engaged therein; or being the owner of any such property, knowingly uses or employs, or consents to such use or employment of the same, all such property shall be lawful subject of prize and capture wherever found; and it shall be the duty of the President to cause the same to be seized, confiscated, and condemned.

(R.S. §5308.)

CODIFICATION

R.S. §5308 derived from act Aug. 6, 1861, ch. 60, §1, 12 Stat. 319.

§213. Jurisdiction of confiscation proceedings

Such prizes and capture shall be condemned in the district court of the United States having jurisdiction of the amount, or in admiralty in any district in which the same may be seized, or into which they may be taken and proceedings first instituted.

(R.S. §5309; Feb. 27, 1877, ch. 69, §1, 19 Stat. 253; Mar. 3, 1911, ch. 231, §291, 36 Stat. 1167.)

CODIFICATION

R.S. §5309 derived derived from act Aug. 6, 1861, ch. 60, §2, 12 Stat. 319.

Act Mar. 3, 1911, conferred the powers and duties of the former circuit courts upon the district courts.

AMENDMENTS

1877—Act Feb. 27, 1877, inserted "may" after "any district in which the same".

§214. Repealed. Aug. 10, 1956, ch. 1041, §53, 70A Stat. 641

Section, R.S. §5310, provided that property taken on inland waters of the United States was not a maritime prize. See section 7651 of Title 10, Armed Forces.

§215. Institution of confiscation proceedings

The Attorney General, or the United States attorney for any judicial district in which such property may at the time be, may institute the proceedings of condemnation, and in such case they shall be wholly for the benefit of the United States; or any person may file an information with such attorney, in which case the proceedings shall be for the use of such informer and the United States in equal parts.

(R.S. §5311; June 25, 1948, ch. 646, §1, 62 Stat. 909.)

CODIFICATION

R.S. §5311 derived from act Aug. 6, 1861, ch. 60, §3, 12 Stat. 319.

CHANGE OF NAME

Act June 25, 1948, eff. Sept. 1, 1948, substituted "United States attorney" for "attorney of the United States". See section 541 of Title 28, Judiciary and Judicial Procedure, and Historical and Revision Notes thereunder.

§216. Preventing transportation of goods to aid insurrection

The Secretary of the Treasury is authorized to prohibit and prevent the transportation in any vessel, or upon any railroad, turnpike, or other road or means of transportation within the United States, of any property, whatever may be the ostensible destination of the same, in all cases where there are satisfactory reasons to believe that such property is intended for any place in the possession or under the control of insurgents against the United States, or that there is imminent danger that such property will fall into the possession or under the control of such insurgents; and he is further authorized, in all cases where he deems it expedient so to do, to require reasonable security to be given that property shall not be transported to any place under insurrectionary control, and shall not, in any way, be used to give aid or comfort to such insurgents; and he may establish all such general or special regulations as may be necessary or proper to carry into effect the purposes of this section; and if any property is transported in violation of this chapter, or of any regulation of the Secretary of the Treasury, established in pursuance thereof, or if any attempt shall be made so to transport any, it shall be forfeited.

(R.S. §5312.)

CODIFICATION

R.S. §5312 derived from act May 20, 1862, ch. 81, §3, 12 Stat. 404.

§217. Trading in captured or abandoned property

All persons in the military or naval service of the United States are prohibited from buying or selling, trading, or in any way dealing in captured or abandoned property, whereby they shall receive or expect any profit, benefit, or advantage to themselves, or any other person, directly or indirectly connected with them; and it shall be the duty of such person whenever such property comes into his possession or custody, or within his control, to give notice thereof to some agent, appointed by virtue of this chapter, and to turn the same over to such agent without delay. Any officer of the United States, civil, military, or naval, or any sutler, soldier, or marine, or other person who shall violate any provision of this section, shall be deemed guilty of a misdemeanor, and shall be fined not more than $5,000, and imprisoned in the penitentiary not more than three years. Violations of this section shall be cognizable before any court, civil or military, competent to try the same.

(R.S. §5313.)

CODIFICATION

R.S. §5313 derived from act July 2, 1864, ch. 225, §10, 13 Stat. 377.

§218. Repealed. Pub. L. 89–554, §8(a), Sept. 6, 1966, 80 Stat. 632

Section, R.S. §5314; act Mar. 2, 1929, ch. 510, §1, 45 Stat. 1496, related to authority of President in collection of duties to change ports of entry in case of insurrection.

§219. Removal of customhouse and detention of vessels thereat

Whenever, at any port of entry, the duties on imports cannot, in the judgment of the President, be collected in the ordinary way, or by the course provided in section 218[1] of this title, by reason of the cause mentioned in said section, he may direct that the customhouse for the district be established in any secure place within the district, either on land or on board any vessel in the district, or at sea near the coast; and in such case the collector shall reside at such place, or on shipboard, as the case may be, and there detain all vessels and cargoes arriving within or approaching the district, until the duties imposed by law on such vessels and their cargoes are paid in cash. But if the owner or consignee of the cargo on board any vessel thus detained, or the master of the vessel, desires to enter a port of entry in any other district where no such obstructions to the execution of the laws exist, the master may be permitted so to change the destination of the vessel and cargo in his manifest; whereupon the collector shall deliver him a written permit to proceed to the port so designated. And the Secretary of the Treasury, with the approval of the President, shall make proper regulations for the enforcement on shipboard of such provisions of the laws regulating the assessment and collection of duties as in his judgment may be necessary and practicable.

(R.S. §5315.)

REFERENCES IN TEXT

Section 218 of this title, referred to in text, was repealed by Pub. L. 89–554, §8(a), Sept. 6, 1966, 80 Stat. 632.

CODIFICATION

R.S. §5315 derived from acts July 13, 1861, ch. 3, §2, 12 Stat. 256; Mar. 3, 1875, ch. 136, §2, 18 Stat. 469.

TRANSFER OF FUNCTIONS

All offices of collector of customs, comptroller of customs, surveyor of customs, and appraiser of merchandise of the Bureau of Customs of Department of the Treasury to which appointments were required to be made by President with advice and consent of Senate ordered abolished, with such offices to be terminated not later than Dec. 31, 1966, by Reorg. Plan No. 1, of 1965, eff. May 25, 1965, 30 F.R. 7035, 79 Stat. 1317, set out in the Appendix to Title 5, Government Organization and Employees. All functions of offices eliminated were already vested in Secretary of the Treasury by Reorg. Plan No. 26 of 1950, eff. July 31, 1950, 15 F.R. 4935, 64 Stat. 1280, set out in the Appendix to Title 5.

SECTION REFERRED TO IN OTHER SECTIONS

This section is referred to in sections 220, 221 of this title.

§220. Enforcement of section 219

It shall be unlawful to take any vessel or cargo detained under section 219 of this title from the custody of the proper officers of the customs, unless by process of some court of the United States; and in case of any attempt otherwise to take such vessel or cargo by any force, or combination, or assemblage of persons, too great to be overcome by the officers of the customs, the President, or such person as he shall have empowered for that purpose, may employ such part of the Army or Navy or militia of the United States, or such force of citizen volunteers as may be necessary, to prevent the removal of such vessel or cargo, and to protect the officers of the customs in retaining the custody thereof.

(R.S. §5316.)

CODIFICATION

R.S. §5316 derived from act July 12, 1861, ch. 3, §3, 12 Stat. 256.

[1] See References in Text note below.

TRANSFER OF FUNCTIONS

All offices of collector of customs, comptroller of customs, surveyor of customs, and appraiser of merchandise of Bureau of Customs of Department of the Treasury to which appointments were required to be made by President with advice and consent of Senate ordered abolished, with such offices to be terminated not later than Dec. 31, 1966, by Reorg. Plan No. 1, of 1965, eff. May 25, 1965, 30 F.R. 7035, 79 Stat. 1317, set out in the Appendix to Title 5, Government Organization and Employees. All functions of offices eliminated were already vested in Secretary of the Treasury by Reorg. Plan No. 26 of 1950, eff. July 31, 1950, 15 F.R. 4935, 64 Stat. 1280, set out in the Appendix to Title 5.

SECTION REFERRED TO IN OTHER SECTIONS

This section is referred to in section 221 of this title.

§221. Closing ports of entry; forfeiture of vessels seeking to enter closed port

Whenever, in any collection district, the duties on imports can not, in the judgment of the President, be collected in the ordinary way, nor in the manner provided by sections 218[1] to 220 of this title, by reason of the cause mentioned in section 218 of this title, the President may close the port of entry in that district; and shall in such case give notice thereof by proclamation. And thereupon all right of importation, warehousing, and other privileges incident to ports of entry shall cease and be discontinued at such port so closed until it is opened by the order of the President on the cessation of such obstructions. Every vessel from beyond the United States, or having on board any merchandise liable to duty, which attempts to enter any port which has been closed under this section, shall, with her tackle, apparel, furniture, and cargo, be forfeited.

(R.S. §5317.)

REFERENCES IN TEXT

Section 218 of this title, referred to in text, was repealed by Pub. L. 89–554, §8(a), Sept. 6, 1966, 80 Stat. 632.

CODIFICATION

R.S. §5317 derived from act July 12, 1861, ch. 3, §4, 12 Stat. 256.

TRANSFER OF FUNCTIONS

All offices of collector of customs, comptroller of customs, surveyor of customs, and appraiser of merchandise of Bureau of Customs of Department of the Treasury to which appointments were required to be made by President with advice and consent of Senate ordered abolished, with such offices to be terminated not later than Dec. 31, 1966, by Reorg. Plan No. 1, of 1965, eff. May 25, 1965, 30 F.R. 7035, 79 Stat. 1317, set out in the Appendix to Title 5, Government Organization and Employees. All functions of offices eliminated were already vested in Secretary of the Treasury by Reorg. Plan No. 26 of 1950, eff. July 31, 1950, 15 F.R. 4935, 64 Stat. 1280, set out in the Appendix to Title 5.

§222. Transferred

CODIFICATION

Section, R.S. §5318; act Jan. 28, 1915, ch. 20, §1, 38 Stat. 800, related to use of auxiliary vessels to enforce this chapter and was transferred to section 540 of Title 19, Customs Duties.

[1] See References in Text note below.

§223. Forfeiture of vessels owned by citizens of insurrectionary States

From and after fifteen days after the issuing of the proclamation, as provided in section 205 of this title, any vessel belonging in whole or in part to any citizen or inhabitant of such State or part of a State whose inhabitants are so declared in a state of insurrection, found at sea, or in any port of the rest of the United States, shall be forfeited.

(R.S. §5319.)

CODIFICATION

R.S. §5319 derived from act July 12, 1861, ch. 3, §7, 12 Stat. 257.

§224. Refusing clearance to vessels with suspected cargoes; forfeiture for departing without clearance

The Secretary of the Treasury is authorized to refuse a clearance to any vessel or other vehicle laden with merchandise, destined for a foreign or domestic port, whenever he shall have satisfactory reason to believe that such merchandise, or any part thereof, whatever may be its ostensible destination, is intended for ports in possession or under control of insurgents against the United States; and if any vessel for which a clearance or permit has been refused by the Secretary of the Treasury, or by his order, shall depart or attempt to depart for a foreign or domestic port without being duly cleared or permitted, such vessel, with her tackle, apparel, furniture, and cargo, shall be forfeited.

(R.S. §5320.)

CODIFICATION

R.S. §5320 derived from act May 20, 1862, ch. 81, §1, 12 Stat. 404.

§225. Bond to deliver cargo at destination named in clearance

Whenever a permit or clearance is granted for either a foreign or domestic port, it shall be lawful for the collector of the customs granting the same, if he deems it necessary, under the circumstances of the case, to require a bond to be executed by the master or the owner of the vessel, in a penalty equal to the value of the cargo, and with sureties to the satisfaction of such collector, that the cargo shall be delivered at the destination for which it is cleared or permitted, and that no part thereof shall be used in affording aid or comfort to any person or parties in insurrection against the authority of the United States.

(R.S. §5321.)

CODIFICATION

R.S. §5321 derived from act May 20, 1862, ch. 81, §2, 12 Stat. 404.

TRANSFER OF FUNCTIONS

All offices of collector of customs, comptroller of customs, surveyor of customs, and appraiser of merchandise of Bureau of Customs of Department of the Treasury to which appointments were required to be made by President with advice and consent of Senate ordered abolished, with such offices to be terminated not later than December 31, 1966, by Reorg. Plan No. 1, of 1965, eff. May 25, 1965, 30 F.R. 7035, 79 Stat. 1317, set out in the Appendix to Title 5, Government Organization and Employees. All functions of offices eliminated were already vested in Secretary of the Treasury by Reorg. Plan No. 26 of 1950, eff. July 31, 1950, 15 F.R. 4935, 64 Stat. 1280, set out in the Appendix to Title 5.

§ 226. Protection of liens on condemned vessels

In all cases wherein any vessel, or other property, is condemned in any proceeding by virtue of any laws relating to insurrection or rebellion, the court rendering judgment of condemnation shall, notwithstanding such condemnation, and before awarding such vessel, or other property, or the proceeds thereof, to the United States, or to any informer, first provide for the payment, out of the proceeds of such vessel, or other property, of any bona fide claims which shall be filed by any loyal citizen of the United States, or of any foreign state or power at peace and amity with the United States, intervening in such proceeding, and which shall be duly established by evidence, as a valid claim against such vessel, or other property, under the laws of the United States or of any State thereof not declared to be in insurrection. No such claim shall be allowed in any case where the claimant has knowingly participated in the illegal use of such ship, vessel, or other property. This section shall extend to such claims only as might have been enforced specifically against such vessel, or other property, in any State not declared to be in insurrection, wherein such claim arose.

(R.S. § 5322.)

CODIFICATION

R.S. § 5322 derived from act Mar. 3, 1863, ch. 90, 12 Stat. 762.

CHAPTER 14—WARTIME VOTING BY LAND AND NAVAL FORCES

§§ 301 to 303. Repealed. Aug. 9, 1955, ch. 656, title III, § 307, 69 Stat. 589

Section 301, acts Sept. 16, 1942, ch. 561, title I, § 1, 56 Stat. 753; July 1, 1943, ch. 187, §§ 1, 5, 57 Stat. 371, granted absentee members of land or naval forces of the United States the right to vote in Presidential, Vice Presidential, and Congressional elections. See section 1973ff et seq. of Title 42, The Public Health and Welfare.

Section 302, act Sept. 16, 1942, ch. 561, title I, § 2, 56 Stat. 753, exempted persons in military service in time of war from paying poll taxes or other taxes as a condition of voting in any election for President, Vice President, electors for President or Vice President, or for Senator or Member of the House of Representatives.

Section 303, acts Sept. 16, 1942, ch. 561, title I, § 3, 56 Stat. 753; Apr. 1, 1944, ch. 150, 58 Stat. 136, provided for voting in accordance with State law.

ADDITIONAL REPEAL

Sections 301 to 303 were also repealed by act Aug. 10, 1956, ch. 1041, § 53, 70 Stat. 641.

§§ 304 to 315. Repealed. Apr. 1, 1944, ch. 150, 58 Stat. 136

Section 304, act Sept. 16, 1942, ch. 561, § 4, 56 Stat. 754, related to a public list of applicants.

Section 305, act Sept. 16, 1942, ch. 561, § 5, 56 Stat. 754, related to form of ballots and booklets.

Section 306, act Sept. 16, 1942, ch. 561, § 6, 56 Stat. 755, related to use of official envelopes.

Section 307, act Sept. 16, 1942, ch. 561, § 7, 56 Stat. 756, related to transmission of ballots.

Section 308, act Sept. 16, 1942, ch. 561, § 8, 56 Stat. 756, related to return of ballots.

Section 309, act Sept. 16, 1942, ch. 561, § 9, 56 Stat. 756, related to certification of votes.

Section 310, act Sept. 16, 1942, ch. 561, § 10, 56 Stat. 756, related to payment of expenses.

Section 311, act Sept. 16, 1942, ch. 561, § 11, 56 Stat. 757, related to utilization of services of local agencies.

Section 312, act Sept. 16, 1942, ch. 561, § 12, 56 Stat. 757, related to voting under State law.

Section 313, act Sept. 16, 1942, ch. 561, § 13, 56 Stat. 757, related to primary elections.

Section 314, act Sept. 16, 1942, ch. 561, § 14, 56 Stat. 757, related to offenses against elective franchise.

Section 315, act Sept. 16, 1942, ch. 561, § 15, 56 Stat. 757, related to formality of compliance.

§§ 321 to 331. Repealed. Aug. 9, 1955, ch. 656, title III, § 307, 69 Stat. 589

Section 321, act Sept. 16, 1942, ch. 561, title II, § 201, as added Apr. 1, 1944, ch. 150, 58 Stat. 136; amended Apr. 19, 1946, ch. 142, 60 Stat. 96, related to State absentee voting legislation.

Section 322, act Sept. 16, 1942, ch. 561, title II, § 202, as added Apr. 1, 1944, ch. 150, 58 Stat. 137; amended Apr. 19, 1946, ch. 142, 60 Stat. 96, related to use of post cards.

Section 323, act Sept. 16, 1942, ch. 561, title II, § 203, as added Apr. 1, 1944, ch. 150, 58 Stat. 137; amended Apr. 19, 1946, ch. 142, 60 Stat. 97, related to distribution of ballots.

Section 324, act Sept. 16, 1942, ch. 561, title II, § 204, as added Apr. 1, 1944, ch. 150, 58 Stat. 138; amended Apr. 19, 1946, ch. 142, 60 Stat. 97; Sept. 29, 1950, ch. 1112, § 1, 64 Stat. 1082, provided for style and markings of envelopes, protective inserts, return envelopes, and size and weight of ballots and envelopes.

Section 325, act Sept. 16, 1942, ch. 561, title II, § 205, as added Apr. 1, 1944, ch. 150, 58 Stat. 138; amended Apr. 19, 1946, ch. 142, 60 Stat. 97, related to signature and oath of voter.

Section 326, act Sept. 16, 1942, ch. 561, title II, § 206, as added Apr. 1, 1944, ch. 150, 58 Stat. 139; amended Apr. 19, 1946, ch. 142, 60 Stat. 98, related to instructions for marking ballots.

Section 327, act Sept. 16, 1942, ch. 561, title II, § 207, as added Apr. 1, 1944, ch. 150, 58 Stat. 139; amended Apr. 19, 1946, ch. 142, 60 Stat. 99, related to extension of State's time limits.

Section 328, act Sept. 16, 1942, ch. 561, title II, § 208, as added Apr. 19, 1946, ch. 142, 60 Stat. 99, provided for notification of forthcoming elections by secretaries of states.

Section 329, act Sept. 16, 1942, ch. 561, title II, § 209, as added Apr. 19, 1946, ch. 142, 60 Stat. 99; amended Sept. 29, 1950, ch. 1111, 64 Stat. 1082, provided for cooperation with States, printing and transmitting of post cards, and content of post cards.

Section 330, act Sept. 16, 1942, ch. 561, title II, § 210, as added Apr. 19, 1946, ch. 142, 60 Stat. 101; amended July 26, 1947, ch. 343, title II, § 205(a), 61 Stat. 501, related to transmission of post cards.

Section 331, act Sept. 16, 1942, ch. 561, title II, § 211, as added Apr. 19, 1946, ch. 142, 60 Stat. 101; amended July 26, 1947, ch. 343, title II, § 205(a), 61 Stat. 501, related to distribution of information.

A prior section 331, act Sept. 16, 1942, ch. 561, title III, § 301, as added Apr. 1, 1944, ch. 150, 58 Stat. 140, related to establishment of United States War Ballot Commission and was repealed by act Apr. 19, 1946, ch. 142, 60 Stat. 96.

ADDITIONAL REPEAL

Sections 321 to 331 were also repealed by act Aug. 10, 1956, ch. 1041, § 53, 70A Stat. 641.

§§ 332 to 340. Repealed. Apr. 19, 1946, ch. 142, 60 Stat. 96

Section 332, act Sept. 16, 1942, ch. 561, title III, § 302, as added Apr. 1, 1944, ch. 150, 58 Stat. 140, related to persons subject to this subchapter.

Section 333, act Sept. 16, 1942, ch. 561, title III, §303, as added Apr. 1, 1944, ch. 150, 58 Stat. 141, related to Federal war ballots.

Section 334, act Sept. 16, 1942, ch. 561, title III, §304, as added Apr. 1, 1944, ch. 150, 58 Stat. 143, related to administration of oaths.

Section 335, act Sept. 16, 1942, ch. 561, title III, §305, as added Apr. 1, 1944, ch. 150, 58 Stat. 143, related to administration of this subchapter.

Section 336, act Sept. 16, 1942, ch. 561, title III, §306, as added Apr. 1, 1944, ch. 150, 58 Stat. 144, related to lists of candidates.

Section 337, act Sept. 16, 1942, ch. 561, title III, §307, as added Apr. 1, 1944, ch. 150, 58 Stat. 144, related to distribution and collection of ballots.

Section 338, act Sept. 16, 1942, ch. 561, title III, §308, as added Apr. 1, 1944, ch. 150, 58 Stat. 145, related to merchant marine ballots.

Section 339, act Sept. 16, 1942, ch. 561, title III, §309, as added Apr. 1, 1944, ch. 150, 58 Stat. 145, related to transmission of ballots.

Section 340, act Sept. 16, 1942, ch. 561, title III, §310, as added Apr. 1, 1944, ch. 150, 58 Stat. 145, related to reports on balloting.

§341. Repealed. Aug. 9, 1955, ch. 656, title III, §307, 69 Stat. 589

Section, act Sept. 16, 1942, ch. 561, title III, §301, as added Apr. 19, 1946, ch. 142, 60 Stat. 101, provided for prevention of fraud, coercion, and undue influence; free discussion, and acts done in good faith.

A prior section 341, act Sept. 16, 1942, ch. 561, title III, §311, as added Apr. 1, 1944, ch. 150, 58 Stat. 146, related to validity of ballots and was repealed by act Apr. 19, 1946, ch. 142, 60 Stat. 96.

ADDITIONAL REPEAL

Section was also repealed by act Aug. 10, 1956, ch. 1041, §53, 70A Stat. 641.

§342. Repealed. May 24, 1949, ch. 139, §142, 63 Stat. 109

Section, act Sept. 16, 1942, ch. 561, title III, §302, as added Apr. 19, 1946, ch. 142, 60 Stat. 102, related to prohibition against taking of polls. See section 596 of Title 18, Crimes and Criminal Procedure.

A prior section 342, act Sept. 16, 1942, ch. 561, title III, §312, as added Apr. 1, 1944, ch. 150, 58 Stat. 146, which provided for safeguards and secrecy of ballots and prevention of fraud and coercion as to voting, was repealed by act Apr. 19, 1946, ch. 142, 60 Stat. 102.

§§343 to 347. Repealed. Apr. 19, 1946, ch. 142, 60 Stat. 96

Section 343, act Sept. 16, 1942, ch. 561, title III, §313, as added Apr. 1, 1944, ch. 150, 58 Stat. 146, related to penalties under sections 341 to 347 of this title.

Section 344, act Sept. 16, 1942, ch. 561, title III, §314, as added Apr. 1, 1944, ch. 150, 58 Stat. 146, related to prohibition on taking polls. See section 596 of Title 18, Crimes and Criminal Procedure.

Section 344 was also repealed by act June 25, 1948, ch. 645, §21, 62 Stat. 862.

Section 345, act Sept. 16, 1942, ch. 561, title III, §315, as added Apr. 1, 1944, ch. 150, 58 Stat. 147, related to certain State officials.

Section 346, act Sept. 16, 1942, ch. 561, title III, §316, as added Apr. 1, 1944, ch. 150, 58 Stat. 147, related to agencies acting for the Secretary of State.

Section 347, act Sept. 16, 1942, ch. 561, title III, §317, as added Apr. 1, 1944, ch. 150, 58 Stat. 147, related to construction of chapter.

§§351 to 355. Repealed. Aug. 9, 1955, ch. 656, title III, §307, 69 Stat. 589

Section 351, act Sept. 16, 1942, ch. 561, title IV, §401, as added Apr. 19, 1946, ch. 142, 60 Stat. 102, defined terms for purposes of this chapter.

A prior section 351, act Sept. 16, 1942, ch. 561, title IV, §401, as added Apr. 1, 1944, ch. 150, 58 Stat. 147, authorized appropriations for purposes of this chapter and was repealed by act Apr. 19, 1946, ch. 142, 60 Stat. 96.

Section 352, act Sept. 16, 1942, ch. 561, title IV, §402, as added Apr. 19, 1946, ch. 142, 60 Stat. 102; amended Sept. 29, 1950, ch. 1112, §2, 64 Stat. 1083, related to free postage.

A prior section 352, act Sept. 16, 1942, ch. 561, title IV, §402, as added Apr. 1, 1944, ch. 150, 58 Stat. 147, related to free postage and was repealed by act Apr. 19, 1946, ch. 142, 60 Stat. 96.

Section 353, act Sept. 16, 1942, ch. 561, title IV, §403, as added Apr. 19, 1946, ch. 142, 60 Stat. 103, related to administration of this chapter.

A prior section 353, act Sept. 16, 1942, ch. 561, title IV, §403, as added Apr. 1, 1944, ch. 150, 58 Stat. 148, defined terms for purposes of this chapter and was repealed by act Apr. 19, 1946, ch. 142, 60 Stat. 96.

Section 354, act Sept. 16, 1942, ch. 561, title IV, §404, as added Apr. 19, 1946, ch. 142, 60 Stat. 103, related to separability of provisions.

A prior section 354, act Sept. 16, 1942, ch. 561, title IV, §404, as added Apr. 1, 1944, ch. 150, 58 Stat. 148, related to separability of provisions and was repealed by act Apr. 19, 1946, ch. 142, 60 Stat. 96.

Section 355, act Sept. 16, 1942, ch. 561, title IV, §405, as added Apr. 19, 1946, ch. 142, 60 Stat. 103, related to construction of this chapter.

ADDITIONAL REPEAL

Sections 351 to 355 were also repealed by act Aug. 10, 1956, ch. 1041, §53, 70A Stat. 641.

CHAPTER 15—NATIONAL SECURITY

§ 401. Congressional declaration of purpose

In enacting this legislation, it is the intent of Congress to provide a comprehensive program for the future security of the United States; to provide for the establishment of integrated policies and procedures for the departments, agencies, and functions of the Government relating to the national security; to provide a Department of Defense, including the three military Departments of the Army, the Navy (including naval aviation and the United States Marine Corps), and the Air Force under the direction, authority, and control of the Secretary of Defense; to provide that each military department shall be separately organized under its own Secretary and shall function under the direction, authority, and control of the Secretary of Defense; to provide for their unified direction under civilian control of the Secretary of Defense but not to merge these departments or services; to provide for the establishment of unified or specified combatant commands, and a clear and direct line of command to such commands; to eliminate unnecessary duplication in the Department of Defense, and particularly in the field of research and engineering by vesting its overall direction and control in the Secretary of Defense; to provide more effective, efficient, and economical administration in the Department of Defense; to provide for the unified strategic direction of the combatant forces, for their operation under unified command, and for their integration into an efficient team of land, naval, and air forces but not to establish a single Chief of Staff over the armed forces nor an overall armed forces general staff.

(July 26, 1947, ch. 343, §2, 61 Stat. 496; Aug. 10, 1949, ch. 412, §2, 63 Stat. 579; Pub. L. 85–599, §2, Aug. 6, 1958, 72 Stat. 514.)

REFERENCES IN TEXT

This legislation, referred to in text, means act July 26, 1947, ch. 343, 61 Stat. 495, as amended, known as the National Security Act of 1947. For complete classification of this Act to the Code, see Short Title note set out below and Tables.

AMENDMENTS

1958—Pub. L. 85–599 amended section generally, and, among other changes, provided that each military department shall be separately organized, instead of separately administered, under its own Secretary and shall function under the direction, authority, and control of the Secretary of Defense, and inserted provisions relating to establishment of unified or specified combatant commands and for elimination of unnecessary duplication.

1949—Act Aug. 10, 1949, provided that the military departments shall be separately administered but be under the direction of the Secretary of Defense, and that there shall not be a single Chief of Staff over the armed forces nor an armed forces general staff.

EFFECTIVE DATE

Section 310 of act July 26, 1947, provided:

"(a) The first sentence of section 202(a) [section 171a of former Title 5, Executive Departments and Government Officers and Employees] and sections 1, 2, 307, 308, 309, and 310 [section 171 note of former Title 5, section 361 of this title, and sections 171m and 171n of former Title 5] shall take effect immediately upon the enactment of this Act [July 26, 1947].

"(b) Except as provided in subsection (a), the provisions of this Act [sections 171 to 171*l*, 181–1, 181–2, 411a, 411b, 626 to 626d of former Title 5, section 24 of Title 3, The President, and sections 401 to 405 of this title] shall take effect on whichever of the following days is the earlier: The day after the day upon which the Secretary of Defense first appointed takes office, or the sixtieth day after the date of the enactment of this Act [July 26, 1947]."

SHORT TITLE OF 1996 AMENDMENT

Pub. L. 104–293, title VIII, §801, Oct. 11, 1996, 110 Stat. 3474, provided that: "This title [enacting sections 403, 403–1, 403–5a, and 403t of this title, amending sections 402, 403, 403–3 to 403–6, and 404d of this title and sections 5314 and 5315 of Title 5, Government Organization and Employees, repealing former section 403 of this title, and enacting provisions set out as notes under sections 403–3, 403–4, and 403t of this title] may be cited as the 'Intelligence Renewal and Reform Act of 1996'."

SHORT TITLE OF 1994 AMENDMENT

Pub. L. 103–359, title VIII, §801, Oct. 14, 1994, 108 Stat. 3434, provided that: "This title [enacting sections 402a, 435 to 438, and 1821 to 1829 of this title, section 2170b of the Appendix to this title, section 1599 [now 1611] of Title 10, Armed Forces, and section 1924 of Title 18, Crimes and Criminal Procedure, amending section 783 of this title, section 2170 of the Appendix to this title, section 8312 of Title 5, Government Organization and Employees, section 1604 of Title 10, and sections 793, 794, 798, 3071, and 3077 of Title 18, enacting provisions set out as notes under sections 435 and 1821 of this title, and amending provisions set out as notes under sections 402 and 1801 of this title] may be cited as the 'Counterintelligence and Security Enhancements Act of 1994'."

SHORT TITLE OF 1992 AMENDMENT

Pub. L. 102–496, title VII, §701, Oct. 24, 1992, 106 Stat. 3188, provided that: "This title [enacting sections 401a and 403–3 to 403–6 of this title, amending sections 402, 403, 404, and 404a of this title, and repealing section 403–1 of this title] may be cited as the 'Intelligence Organization Act of 1992'."

SHORT TITLE OF 1984 AMENDMENT

Pub. L. 98–477, §1, Oct. 15, 1984, 98 Stat. 2209, provided: "That this Act [enacting sections 431 and 432 of this title, amending section 552a of Title 5, Government Organization and Employees, and enacting provisions set out as notes under sections 431 and 432 of this title] may be cited as the 'Central Intelligence Agency Information Act'."

SHORT TITLE OF 1982 AMENDMENT

Pub. L. 97–200, §1, June 23, 1982, 96 Stat. 122, provided: "That this Act [enacting subchapter IV of this chapter] may be cited as the 'Intelligence Identities Protection Act of 1982'."

SHORT TITLE OF 1949 AMENDMENT

Section 1 of act Aug. 10, 1949, provided that: "This Act [enacting sections 408 and 412 of this title and sections 171–1, 171t, 172, 172a to 172d, and 172f to 172j of former Title 5, Executive Departments and Government Officers and Employees, amending this section, sections 151, 402, 403d, 405, 410, 459, 481, and 494 of this title, sections 171, 171a, 171b to 171d, 171e to 171j, 171n, 171r, 172e, 411b, and 626c of former Title 5, section 1748b of Title 12, Banks and Banking, section 1517 of Title 15, Commerce and Trade, sections 474, 481 to 484, and 487 of Title 40, Public Buildings, Property, and Works, section 364a of Title 43, Public Lands, sections 1156 and 1157 of former Title 49, Transportation, and section 1193 of the Appendix to this title, and enacting provisions set out as notes under this section and sections 171 and 171c of former Title 5] may be cited as the 'National Security Act Amendments of 1949'."

SHORT TITLE

Section 1 of act July 26, 1947, provided: "That this Act [enacting this section, sections 401a to 403, 404, 405, and 408 to 412 of this title, and sections 171, 171–1, 171–2, 171a, 171b to 171d, 171e to 171j, 171k to 171m, 171n, 172, 172a to 172d, 172f to 172j, 181–1, 181–2, 411a, 411b, 626, 626a to 626c, and 626d of former Title 5, Executive Departments and Government Officers and Employees, amending sections 1, 11, and 172e of former Title 5, section 1517 of Title 15, Commerce and Trade, and section 72 of former Title 31, Money and Finance, and enacting provisions set out as notes under this section and section 135 of Title 10, Armed Forces] may be cited as the 'National Security Act of 1947'."

Sections of National Security Act of 1947, which were classified to former Title 5, were repealed and restated in Title 10, Armed Forces, except as noted, as follows:

Section of former Title 5	*Section of Title 10*
171	131, 133.
171a(a), (b)	133.
171a(c)	125, 136, 141, 3010, 3012, 5011, 5031, 8010, 8012.
171a(d)	133.
171a(e)	132.
171a(f)	133.
171a(g)–(i)	[Omitted].
171a(j)	124.
171c	134, 135, 136, 718, 2358.
171c–1, 171c–2	[Repealed].
171d	1580.

Section of former Title 5	Section of Title 10
171e	171.
171f	141, 142.
171g	143.
171h	2201.
171i	2351.
171j	173.
172	136.
172a	3014, 5061, 8014.
172b	2203.
172c	2204.
172d	2208.
172e	2209.
172f	126.
172g	2205.
172h	2206.
172i	2701.
181–1	101, 3011, 3012, 3062, T. 50 § 409.
181–2	3012.
411a(a)	101; T. 50 § 409.
411a(b)	5012.
411a(c)	5013, 5402.
626(a)	8012.
626(b)	[Repealed].
626(c)	101; T. 50 § 409.
626(d)	8013.
626(e)	8012.
626(f)	8033.
626(g)	8011.
626a	8012.
626b	8013.
626c	743, 8062.

SAVINGS PROVISION

Section 12(g) of act Aug. 10, 1949, provided: "All laws, orders, regulations, and other actions relating to the National Military Establishment, the Departments of the Army, the Navy, or the Air Force, or to any officer or activity of such establishment or such departments, shall, except to the extent inconsistent with the provisions of this Act [see Short Title of 1949 Amendment note above], have the same effect as if this Act had not been enacted; but, after the effective date of this Act [Aug. 10, 1949], any such law, order, regulation, or other action which vested functions in or otherwise related to any officer, department, or establishment, shall be deemed to have vested such function in or relate to the officer or department, executive or military, succeeding the officer, department, or establishment in which such function was vested. For purposes of this subsection the Department of Defense shall be deemed the department succeeding the National Military Establishment, and the military departments of Army, Navy, and Air Force shall be deemed the departments succeeding the Executive Departments of Army, Navy, and Air Force."

SEPARABILITY

Section 309 of act July 26, 1947, provided: "If any provision of this Act [see Short Title note above] or the application thereof to any person or circumstances is held invalid, the validity of the remainder of the Act and of the application of such provision to other persons and circumstances shall not be affected thereby."

[Section 310(a) of act July 26, 1947, set out as an Effective Date note above, provided that section 309 of act July 26, 1947, is effective July 26, 1947.]

NATIONAL COMMISSION FOR THE REVIEW OF THE NATIONAL RECONNAISSANCE OFFICE

Pub. L. 106–120, title VII, Dec. 3, 1999, 113 Stat. 1620, provided that:

"SEC. 701. FINDINGS.

"Congress makes the following findings:

"(1) Imagery and signals intelligence satellites are vitally important to the security of the Nation.

"(2) The National Reconnaissance Office (in this title referred to as the 'NRO') and its predecessor organizations have helped protect and defend the United States for more than 30 years.

"(3) The end of the Cold War and the enormous growth in usage of information technology have changed the environment in which the intelligence community must operate. At the same time, the intelligence community has undergone significant changes in response to dynamic developments in strategy and in budgetary matters. The acquisition and maintenance of satellite systems are essential to providing timely intelligence to national policymakers and achieving information superiority for military leaders.

"(4) There is a need to evaluate the roles and mission, organizational structure, technical skills, contractor relationships, use of commercial imagery, acquisition of launch vehicles, launch services, and launch infrastructure, mission assurance, acquisition authorities, and relationship to other agencies and departments of the Federal Government of the NRO in order to assure continuing success in satellite reconnaissance in the new millennium.

"SEC. 702. NATIONAL COMMISSION FOR THE REVIEW OF THE NATIONAL RECONNAISSANCE OFFICE.

"(a) ESTABLISHMENT.—There is established a commission to be known as the 'National Commission for the Review of the National Reconnaissance Office' (in this title referred to as the 'Commission').

"(b) COMPOSITION.—The Commission shall be composed of 11 members, as follows:

"(1) The Deputy Director of Central Intelligence for Community Management.

"(2) Three members appointed by the Majority Leader of the Senate, in consultation with the Chairman of the Select Committee on Intelligence of the Senate, one from Members of the Senate and two from private life.

"(3) Two members appointed by the Minority Leader of the Senate, in consultation with the Vice Chairman of the Select Committee on Intelligence of the Senate, one from Members of the Senate and one from private life.

"(4) Three members appointed by the Speaker of the House of Representatives, in consultation with the Chairman of the Permanent Select Committee on Intelligence of the House of Representatives, one from Members of the House of Representatives and two from private life.

"(5) Two members appointed by the Minority Leader of the House of Representatives, in consultation with the ranking member of the Permanent Select Committee on Intelligence of the House of Representatives, one from Members of the House of Representatives and one from private life.

The Director of the National Reconnaissance Office shall be an ex officio member of the Commission.

"(c) MEMBERSHIP.—(1) The individuals appointed as members of the Commission shall be individuals who are nationally recognized for expertise, knowledge, or experience in—

"(A) technical intelligence collection systems and methods;

"(B) research and development programs;

"(C) acquisition management;

"(D) use of intelligence information by national policymakers and military leaders; or

"(E) the implementation, funding, or oversight of the national security policies of the United States.

"(2) An official who appoints members of the Commission may not appoint an individual as a member of the Commission if, in the judgment of the official, such individual possesses any personal or financial interest in the discharge of any of the duties of the Commission.

"(3) All members of the Commission appointed from private life shall possess an appropriate security clearance in accordance with applicable laws and regulations concerning the handling of classified information.

"(d) CO-CHAIRS.—(1) The Commission shall have two co-chairs, selected from among the members of the Commission.

"(2) One co-chair of the Commission shall be a member of the Democratic Party, and one co-chair shall be a member of the Republican Party.

"(3) The individuals who serve as the co-chairs of the Commission shall be jointly agreed upon by the President, the Majority Leader of the Senate, the Minority Leader of the Senate, and Speaker of the House of Representatives, and the Minority Leader of the House of Representatives.

"(e) APPOINTMENT; INITIAL MEETING.—(1) Members of the Commission shall be appointed not later than 45 days after the date of the enactment of this Act [Dec. 3, 1999].

"(2) The Commission shall hold its initial meeting on the date that is 60 days after the date of the enactment of this Act.

"(f) MEETINGS; QUORUM; VACANCIES.—(1) After its initial meeting, the Commission shall meet upon the call of the co-chairs of the Commission.

"(2) Six members of the Commission shall constitute a quorum for purposes of conducting business, except that two members of the Commission shall constitute a quorum for purposes of receiving testimony.

"(3) Any vacancy in the Commission shall not affect its powers, but shall be filled in the same manner in which the original appointment was made.

"(4) If vacancies in the Commission occur on any day after 45 days after the date of the enactment of this Act, a quorum shall consist of a majority of the members of the Commission as of such day.

"(g) ACTIONS OF COMMISSION.—(1) The Commission shall act by resolution agreed to by a majority of the members of the Commission voting and present.

"(2) The Commission may establish panels composed of less than the full membership of the Commission for purposes of carrying out the duties of the Commission under this title. The actions of any such panel shall be subject to the review and control of the Commission. Any findings and determinations made by such a panel shall not be considered the findings and determinations of the Commission unless approved by the Commission.

"(3) Any member, agent, or staff of the Commission may, if authorized by the co-chairs of the Commission, take any action which the Commission is authorized to take pursuant to this title.

"SEC. 703. DUTIES OF COMMISSION.

"(a) IN GENERAL.—The duties of the Commission shall be—

"(1) to conduct, until not later than the date on which the Commission submits the report under section 708(a), the review described in subsection (b); and

"(2) to submit to the congressional intelligence committees, the Director of Central Intelligence, and the Secretary of Defense a final report on the results of the review.

"(b) REVIEW.—The Commission shall review the current organization, practices, and authorities of the NRO, in particular with respect to—

"(1) roles and mission;

"(2) organizational structure;

"(3) technical skills;

"(4) contractor relationships;

"(5) use of commercial imagery;

"(6) acquisition of launch vehicles, launch services, and launch infrastructure, and mission assurance;

"(7) acquisition authorities; and

"(8) relationships with other agencies and departments of the Federal Government.

"SEC. 704. POWERS OF COMMISSION.

"(a) IN GENERAL.—(1) The Commission or, on the authorization of the Commission, any subcommittee or member thereof, may, for the purpose of carrying out the provisions of this title—

"(A) hold such hearings and sit and act at such times and places, take such testimony, receive such evidence, and administer such oaths; and

"(B) require, by subpoena or otherwise, the attendance and testimony of such witnesses and the production of such books, records, correspondence, memoranda, papers, and documents,

as the Commission or such designated subcommittee or designated member considers necessary.

"(2) Subpoenas may be issued under paragraph (1)(B) under the signature of the co-chairs of the Commission, and may be served by any person designated by such co-chairs.

"(3) The provisions of sections 102 through 104 of the Revised Statutes of the United States (2 U.S.C. 192–194) shall apply in the case of any failure of a witness to comply with any subpoena or to testify when summoned under authority of this section.

"(b) CONTRACTING.—The Commission may, to such extent and in such amounts as are provided in advance in appropriation Acts, enter into contracts to enable the Commission to discharge its duties under this title.

"(c) INFORMATION FROM FEDERAL AGENCIES.—The Commission may secure directly from any executive department, agency, bureau, board, commission, office, independent establishment, or instrumentality of the Government information, suggestions, estimates, and statistics for the purposes of this title. Each such department, agency, bureau, board, commission, office, establishment, or instrumentality shall, to the extent authorized by law, furnish such information, suggestions, estimates, and statistics directly to the Commission, upon request of the co-chairs of the Commission. The Commission shall handle and protect all classified information provided to it under this section in accordance with applicable statutes and regulations.

"(d) ASSISTANCE FROM FEDERAL AGENCIES.—(1) The Director of Central Intelligence shall provide to the Commission, on a nonreimbursable basis, such administrative services, funds, staff, facilities, and other support services as are necessary for the performance of the Commission's duties under this title.

"(2) The Secretary of Defense may provide the Commission, on a nonreimbursable basis, with such administrative services, staff, and other support services as the Commission may request.

"(3) In addition to the assistance set forth in paragraphs (1) and (2), other departments and agencies of the United States may provide the Commission such services, funds, facilities, staff, and other support as such departments and agencies consider advisable and as may be authorized by law.

"(4) The Commission shall receive the full and timely cooperation of any official, department, or agency of the United States Government whose assistance is necessary for the fulfillment of the duties of the Commission under this title, including the provision of full and current briefings and analyses.

"(e) PROHIBITION ON WITHHOLDING INFORMATION.—No department or agency of the Government may withhold information from the Commission on the grounds that providing the information to the Commission would constitute the unauthorized disclosure of classified information or information relating to intelligence sources or methods.

"(f) POSTAL SERVICES.—The Commission may use the United States mails in the same manner and under the same conditions as the departments and agencies of the United States.

"(g) GIFTS.—The Commission may accept, use, and dispose of gifts or donations of services or property in carrying out its duties under this title.

"SEC. 705. STAFF OF COMMISSION.

"(a) IN GENERAL.—(1) The co-chairs of the Commission, in accordance with rules agreed upon by the Commission, shall appoint and fix the compensation of a staff director and such other personnel as may be necessary to enable the Commission to carry out its duties, without regard to the provisions of title 5, United States Code, governing appointments in the competitive service, and without regard to the provisions of chapter 51 and subchapter III or [of] chapter 53 of such title relating to classification and General Schedule pay rates, except that no rate of pay fixed under this subsection may exceed the equivalent of that payable to a person occupying a position at level V of the Executive Schedule under section 5316 of such title.

"(2) Any Federal Government employee may be detailed to the Commission without reimbursement from the Commission, and such detailee shall retain the rights, status, and privileges of his or her regular employment without interruption.

"(3) All staff of the Commission shall possess a security clearance in accordance with applicable laws and regulations concerning the handling of classified information.

"(b) CONSULTANT SERVICES.—(1) The Commission may procure the services of experts and consultants in accordance with section 3109 of title 5, United States Code, but at rates not to exceed the daily rate paid a person occupying a position at level IV of the Executive Schedule under section 5315 of such title.

"(2) All experts and consultants employed by the Commission shall possess a security clearance in accordance with applicable laws and regulations concerning the handling of classified information.

"SEC. 706. COMPENSATION AND TRAVEL EXPENSES.

"(a) COMPENSATION.—(1) Except as provided in paragraph (2), each member of the Commission may be compensated at not to exceed the daily equivalent of the annual rate of basic pay in effect for a position at level IV of the Executive Schedule under section 5315 of title 5, United States Code, for each day during which that member is engaged in the actual performance of the duties of the Commission under this title.

"(2) Members of the Commission who are officers or employees of the United States or Members of Congress shall receive no additional pay by reason of their service on the Commission.

"(b) TRAVEL EXPENSES.—While away from their homes or regular places of business in the performance of services for the Commission, members of the Commission may be allowed travel expenses, including per diem in lieu of subsistence, in the same manner as persons employed intermittently in the Government service are allowed expenses under section 5703(b) of title 5, United States Code.

"SEC. 707. TREATMENT OF INFORMATION RELATING TO NATIONAL SECURITY.

"(a) IN GENERAL.—(1) The Director of Central Intelligence shall assume responsibility for the handling and disposition of any information related to the national security of the United States that is received, considered, or used by the Commission under this title.

"(2) Any information related to the national security of the United States that is provided to the Commission by a congressional intelligence committee may not be further provided or released without the approval of the chairman of such committee.

"(b) ACCESS AFTER TERMINATION OF COMMISSION.—Notwithstanding any other provision of law, after the termination of the Commission under section 708, only the Members and designated staff of the congressional intelligence committees, the Director of Central Intelligence and the designees of the Director, and such other officials of the executive branch as the President may designate shall have access to information related to the national security of the United States that is received, considered, or used by the Commission.

"SEC. 708. FINAL REPORT; TERMINATION.

"(a) FINAL REPORT.—Not later than November 1, 2000, the Commission shall submit to the congressional intelligence committees, the Director of Central Intelligence, and the Secretary of Defense a final report as required by section 703(a).

"(b) TERMINATION.—(1) The Commission, and all the authorities of this title, shall terminate at the end of the 120-day period beginning on the date on which the final report under subsection (a) is transmitted to the congressional intelligence committees.

"(2) The Commission may use the 120-day period referred to in paragraph (1) for the purposes of concluding its activities, including providing testimony to committees of Congress concerning the final report referred to in that paragraph and disseminating the report.

"SEC. 709. ASSESSMENTS OF FINAL REPORT.

"Not later than 60 days after receipt of the final report under section 708(a), the Director of Central Intelligence and the Secretary of Defense shall each submit to the congressional intelligence committees an assessment by the Director or the Secretary, as the case may be, of the final report. Each assessment shall include such comments on the findings and recommendations contained in the final report as the Director or Secretary, as the case may be, considers appropriate.

"SEC. 710. INAPPLICABILITY OF CERTAIN ADMINISTRATIVE PROVISIONS.

"(a) FEDERAL ADVISORY COMMITTEE ACT.—The provisions of the Federal Advisory Committee Act (5 U.S.C. App.) shall not apply to the activities of the Commission under this title.

"(b) FREEDOM OF INFORMATION ACT.—The provisions of section 552 of title 5, United States Code (commonly referred to as the Freedom of Information Act), shall not apply to the activities, records, and proceedings of the Commission under this title.

"SEC. 711. FUNDING.

"(a) TRANSFER FROM NRO.—Of the amounts authorized to be appropriated by this Act [see Tables for classification] for the National Reconnaissance Office, the Director of the National Reconnaissance Office shall transfer to the Director of Central Intelligence $5,000,000 for purposes of the activities of the Commission under this title.

"(b) AVAILABILITY IN GENERAL.—The Director of Central Intelligence shall make available to the Commission, from the amount transferred to the Director under subsection (a), such amounts as the Commission may require for purposes of the activities of the Commission under this title.

"(c) DURATION OF AVAILABILITY.—Amounts made available to the Commission under subsection (b) shall remain available until expended.

"SEC. 712. CONGRESSIONAL INTELLIGENCE COMMITTEES DEFINED.

"In this title, the term 'congressional intelligence committees' means the following:

"(1) The Select Committee on Intelligence of the Senate.

"(2) The Permanent Select Committee on Intelligence of the House of Representatives."

COMMISSION ON ROLES AND CAPABILITIES OF UNITED STATES INTELLIGENCE COMMUNITY

Pub. L. 103–359, title IX, Oct. 14, 1994, 108 Stat. 3456, provided that:

"SEC. 901. ESTABLISHMENT.

"There is established a commission to be known as the Commission on the Roles and Capabilities of the United States Intelligence Community (hereafter in this title referred to as the 'Commission').

"SEC. 902. COMPOSITION AND QUALIFICATIONS.

"(a) MEMBERSHIP.—(1) The Commission shall be composed of 17 members, as follows:

"(A) Nine members shall be appointed by the President from private life, no more than four of whom shall have previously held senior leadership positions in the intelligence community and no more than five of whom shall be members of the same political party.

"(B) Two members shall be appointed by the majority leader of the Senate, of whom one shall be a Member of the Senate and one shall be from private life.

"(C) Two members shall be appointed by the minority leader of the Senate, of whom one shall be a Member of the Senate and one shall be from private life.

"(D) Two members shall be appointed by the Speaker of the House of Representatives, of whom one shall be a Member of the House and one shall be from private life.

"(E) Two members shall be appointed by the Minority Leader of the House of Representatives, of whom one shall be a Member of the House and one shall be from private life.

"(2) The members of the Commission appointed from private life under paragraph (1) shall be persons of demonstrated ability and accomplishment in government, business, law, academe, journalism, or other profession, who have a substantial background in national security matters.

"(b) CHAIRMAN AND VICE CHAIRMAN.—The President shall designate two of the members appointed from private life to serve as Chairman and Vice Chairman, respectively, of the Commission.

"(c) PERIOD OF APPOINTMENT; VACANCIES.—Members shall be appointed for the life of the Commission. Any vacancy in the Commission shall not affect its powers but shall be filled in the same manner as the original appointment.

"(d) DEADLINE FOR APPOINTMENTS.—The appointments required by subsection (a) shall be made within 45 days after the date of enactment of this Act [Oct. 14, 1994].

"(e) MEETINGS.—(1) The Commission shall meet at the call of the Chairman.

"(2) The Commission shall hold its first meeting not later than four months after the date of enactment of this Act.

"(f) QUORUM.—Nine members of the Commission shall constitute a quorum, but a lesser number of members may hold hearings, take testimony, or receive evidence.

"(g) SECURITY CLEARANCES.—Appropriate security clearances shall be required for members of the Commission who are private United States citizens. Such clearances shall be processed and completed on an expedited basis by appropriate elements of the executive branch of Government and shall, in any case, be completed within 90 days of the date such members are appointed.

"(h) APPLICATION OF CERTAIN PROVISIONS OF LAW.—In light of the extraordinary and sensitive nature of its deliberations, the provisions of the Federal Advisory Committee Act (5 U.S.C. App.), and the regulations prescribed by the Administrator of General Services pursuant to that Act, shall not apply to the Commission. Further, the provisions of section 552 of title 5, United States Code (commonly known as the 'Freedom of Information Act'), shall not apply to the Commission; however, records of the Commission shall be subject to the Federal Records Act [probably means chapters 21 to 31 of Title 44, Public Printing and Documents] and, when transferred to the National Archives and Records Agency, shall no longer be exempt from the provisions of such section 552.

"SEC. 903. DUTIES OF THE COMMISSION.

"(a) IN GENERAL.—It shall be the duty of the Commission—

"(1) to review the efficacy and appropriateness of the activities of the United States intelligence community in the post-cold war global environment; and

"(2) to prepare and transmit the reports described in section 904.

"(b) IMPLEMENTATION.—In carrying out subsection (a), the Commission shall specifically consider the following:

"(1) What should be the roles and missions of the intelligence community in terms of providing support to the defense and foreign policy establishments and how should these relate to tactical intelligence activities.

"(2) Whether the roles and missions of the intelligence community should extend beyond the traditional areas of providing support to the defense and foreign policy establishments, and, if so, what areas should be considered legitimate for intelligence collection and analysis, and whether such areas should include, for example, economic issues, environmental issues, and health issues.

"(3) What functions, if any, should continue to be assigned to the organizations of the intelligence community, including the Central Intelligence Agency, and what capabilities should these organizations retain for the future.

"(4) Whether the existing organization and management framework of the organizations of the intelligence community, including the Central Intelligence Agency, provide the optimal structure for the accomplishment of their missions.

"(5) Whether existing principles and strategies governing the acquisition and maintenance of intelligence collection capabilities should be retained and what collection capabilities should the Government retain to meet future contingencies.

"(6) Whether intelligence analysis, as it is currently structured and executed, adds sufficient value to information otherwise available to the Government to justify its continuation, and, if so, at what level of resources.

"(7) Whether the existing decentralized system of intelligence analysis results in significant waste or duplication, and, if so, what can be done to correct these deficiencies.

"(8) Whether the existing arrangements for allocating available resources to accomplish the roles and missions assigned to intelligence agencies are adequate.

"(9) Whether the existing framework for coordinating among intelligence agencies with respect to intelligence collection and analysis and other activities, including training and operational activities, provides an optimal structure for such coordination.

"(10) Whether current personnel policies and practices of intelligence agencies provide an optimal work force to satisfy the needs of intelligence consumers.

"(11) Whether resources for intelligence activities should continue to be allocated as part of the defense budget or be treated by the President and Congress as a separate budgetary program.

"(12) Whether the existing levels of resources allocated for intelligence collection or intelligence analysis, or to provide a capability to conduct covert actions, are seriously at variance with United States needs.

"(13) Whether there are areas of redundant or overlapping activity or areas where there is evidence of serious waste, duplication, or mismanagement.

"(14) To what extent, if any, should the budget for United States intelligence activities be publicly disclosed.

"(15) To what extent, if any, should the United States intelligence community collect information bearing upon private commercial activity and the manner in which such information should be controlled and disseminated.

"(16) Whether counterintelligence policies and practices are adequate to ensure that employees of intelligence agencies are sensitive to security problems, and whether intelligence agencies themselves have adequate authority and capability to address perceived security problems.

"(17) The manner in which the size, missions, capabilities, and resources of the United States intelligence community compare to those of other countries.

"(18) Whether existing collaborative arrangements between the United States and other countries in the area of intelligence cooperation should be maintained and whether such arrangements should be expanded to provide for increased burdensharing.

"(19) Whether existing arrangements for sharing intelligence with multinational organizations in support of mutually shared objectives are adequate.

"SEC. 904. REPORTS.

"(a) INITIAL REPORT.—Not later than two months after the first meeting of the Commission, the Commission shall transmit to the congressional intelligence committees a report setting forth its plan for the work of the Commission.

"(b) INTERIM REPORTS.—Prior to the submission of the report required by subsection (c), the Commission may issue such interim reports as it finds necessary and desirable.

"(c) FINAL REPORT.—No later than March 1, 1996, the Commission shall submit to the President and to the congressional intelligence committees a report setting forth the activities, findings, and recommendations of the Commission, including any recommendations for the enactment of legislation that the Commission considers advisable. To the extent feasible, such report shall be unclassified and made available to the public. Such report shall be supplemented as necessary by a classified report or annex, which shall be provided separately to the President and the congressional intelligence committees.

"SEC. 905. POWERS.

"(a) HEARINGS.—The Commission or, at its direction, any panel or member of the Commission, may, for the purpose of carrying out the provisions of this title, hold hearings, sit and act at times and places, take testimony, receive evidence, and administer oaths to the extent that the Commission or any panel or member considers advisable.

"(b) INFORMATION FROM FEDERAL AGENCIES.—The Commission may secure directly from any intelligence agency or from any other Federal department or agency any information that the Commission considers necessary to enable the Commission to carry out its responsibilities under this section. Upon request of the Chairman of the Commission, the head of any such department or agency shall furnish such information expeditiously to the Commission.

"(c) POSTAL, PRINTING AND BINDING SERVICES.—The Commission may use the United States mails and obtain printing and binding services in the same manner and under the same conditions as other departments and agencies of the Federal Government.

"(d) SUBCOMMITTEES.—The Commission may establish panels composed of less than the full membership of the Commission for the purpose of carrying out the Commission's duties. The actions of each such panel shall be subject to the review and control of the Commission. Any findings and determinations made by such a panel shall not be considered the findings and determinations of the Commission unless approved by the Commission.

"(e) AUTHORITY OF INDIVIDUALS TO ACT FOR COMMISSION.—Any member or agent of the Commission may, if authorized by the Commission, take any action which the Commission is authorized to take under this title.

"SEC. 906. PERSONNEL MATTERS.

"(a) COMPENSATION OF MEMBERS.—Each member of the Commission who is a private United States citizen shall be paid, if requested, at a rate equal to the daily equivalent of the annual rate of basic pay payable for level V of the Executive Schedule under section 5316 of title 5, United States Code, for each day (including travel time) during which the member is engaged in the performance of the duties of the Commission. All members of the Commission who are Members of Congress shall serve without compensation in addition to that received for their services as Members of Congress.

"(b) TRAVEL EXPENSES.—Each member of the Commission shall be allowed travel expenses, including per diem in lieu of subsistence, at rates authorized for employees of agencies under subchapter I of chapter 57 of title 5, United States Code, while away from their homes or regular places of business in the performance of services for the Commission.

"(c) STAFF.—

"(1) IN GENERAL.—The Chairman of the Commission may, without regard to the provisions of title 5, United States Code, governing appointments in the competitive service, appoint a staff director and such additional personnel as may be necessary to enable the Commission to perform its duties. The staff director of the Commission shall be appointed from private life, and such appointment shall be subject to the approval of the Commission as a whole. No member of the professional staff may be a current officer or employee of an intelligence agency, except that up to three current employees of intelligence agencies who are on rotational assignment to the Executive Office of the President may serve on the Commission staff, subject to the approval of the Commission as a whole.

"(2) COMPENSATION.—The Chairman of the Commission may fix the pay of the staff director and other personnel without regard to the provisions of chapter 51 and subchapter III of chapter 53 of title 5, United States Code, relating to classification of positions and General Schedule pay rates, except that the rate of pay fixed under this paragraph for the staff director may not exceed the rate payable for level V of the Executive Schedule under section 5316 of such title and the rate of pay for other personnel may not exceed the maximum rate payable for grade GS-15 of the General Schedule.

"(d) DETAIL OF GOVERNMENT EMPLOYEES.—Upon request of the Chairman of the Commission, the head of any Federal department or agency may detail, on a nonreimbursable basis, any personnel of that department or agency to the Commission to assist it in carrying out its administrative and clerical functions.

"(e) PROCUREMENT OF TEMPORARY AND INTERMITTENT SERVICES.—The Chairman of the Commission may procure temporary and intermittent services under section 3109(b) of title 5, United States Code, at rates for individuals which do not exceed the daily equivalent of the annual rate of basic pay payable for level V of the Executive Schedule under section 5316 of such title.

"(f) ADMINISTRATIVE AND SUPPORT SERVICES.—The Director of Central Intelligence shall furnish the Commission, on a non-reimbursable basis, any administrative and support services requested by the Commission consistent with this title.

"SEC. 907. PAYMENT OF COMMISSION EXPENSES.

"The compensation, travel expenses, per diem allowances of members and employees of the Commission, and other expenses of the Commission shall be paid out of funds available to the Director of Central Intelligence for the payment of compensation, travel allowances, and per diem allowances, respectively, of employees of the Central Intelligence Agency.

"SEC. 908. TERMINATION OF THE COMMISSION.

"The Commission shall terminate one month after the date of the submission of the report required by section 904(c).

"SEC. 909. DEFINITIONS.

"For purposes of this title—

"(1) the term 'intelligence agency' means any agency, office, or element of the intelligence community;

"(2) the term 'intelligence community' shall have the same meaning as set forth in section 3(4) of the National Security Act of 1947 (50 U.S.C. 401a(4)); and

"(3) the term 'congressional intelligence committees' refers to the Select Committee on Intelligence of the Senate and the Permanent Select Committee on Intelligence of the House of Representatives."

NATIONAL COMMISSION ON DEFENSE AND NATIONAL SECURITY

Pub. L. 101–511, title VIII, §8104, Nov. 5, 1990, 104 Stat. 1898, as amended by Pub. L. 102–172, title VIII, §8078, Nov. 26, 1991, 105 Stat. 1189, provided that:

"SECTION 1. This section establishes the National Commission on Defense and National Security.

"SEC. 2. FINDINGS.

"The Congress makes the following findings:

"(1) Recent revolutionary world events require a fundamental reassessment of the defense and national security policies of the United States.

"(2) Emerging democracies around the world will require political, technical, and economic assistance, as well as military assistance, from the developed free nations in order to thrive and to become productive members of the world community.

"(3) Real and potential military threats to the United States and its allies will continue to exist for the foreseeable future from not just the Soviet Union but also from terrorism and from Third World nations.

"(4) Proliferation of both sophisticated conventional weapons and of nuclear weapons could produce a world more dangerous than we have faced in the past.

"(5) Ethnic rivalries as well as economic inequalities may produce instabilities that could spark serious conflict.

"(6) In order to formulate coherent national policies to meet these challenges of a new world environment, it is essential for the United States to achieve a bipartisan consensus such as that which emerged following World War II.

"(7) Such a consensus can be fostered by the development of policy recommendations from a highly respected group of individuals who do not bear a partisan label and who possess critical expertise and experience.

"SEC. 3. ESTABLISHMENT.

"There is established a commission to be known as [the] National Commission on Defense and National Security (hereinafter in this Act referred to as the 'Commission'). The Commission is established until 30 days following submission of the final report required by section 6 of this section.

"SEC. 4. DUTIES OF COMMISSION.

"(a) IN GENERAL.—The Commission shall analyze and make recommendations to the President and Congress concerning the national security and national defense policies of the United States.

"(b) MATTERS TO BE ANALYZED.—Matters to be analyzed by the Commission shall include the following:

"(1) The world-wide interests, goals, and objectives of the United States that are vital to the national security of the United States.

"(2) The political, economic, and military developments around the world and the implications of those developments for United States national security interests, including—

"(A) the developments in Eastern Europe and the Soviet Union;

"(B) the question of German unification;

"(C) the future of NATO and European economic integration;

"(D) the future of the Pacific Basin; and

"(E) potential instability resulting from regional conflicts or economic problems in the developing world.

"(3) The foreign policy, world-wide commitments, and national defense capabilities of the United States necessary to deter aggression and implement the national security strategy of the United States, including the contribution that can be made by bilateral and multilateral political and economic associations in promoting interests that the United States shares with other members of the world community.

"(4) The proposed short-term uses of the political, economic, military, and other elements of national power for the United States to protect or promote the interests and to achieve the goals and objectives referred to in paragraph (1).

"(5) Long-term options that should be considered further for a number of potential courses of world events over the remainder of the century and into the next century.

"SEC. 5. MEMBERSHIP.

"(a) NUMBER AND APPOINTMENT.—The Commission shall be composed of 10 members, as follows:

"(1) Three appointed by the President.

"(2) Three appointed by the Speaker of the House of Representatives.

"(3) One appointed by the minority leader of the House of Representatives.

"(4) Two appointed by the majority leader of the Senate.

"(5) One appointed by the minority leader of the Senate.

"(b) QUALIFICATIONS.—Persons appointed to the Commission shall be persons who are not officers or employees of the Federal Government (including Members of Congress) and who are specially qualified to serve on the Commission by virtue of their education, training, or experience.

"(c) TERMS.—Members shall be appointed for the life of the Commission. A vacancy in the Commission shall be filled in the manner in which the original appointment was made.

"(d) BASIC PAY.—Members of the Commission shall serve without pay.

"(e) QUORUM.—A majority of the members of the Commission shall constitute a quorum, but a lesser number may hold hearings.

"(f) CHAIRMAN AND VICE CHAIRMAN.—The Chairman of the Commission shall be designated by the President from among the members appointed by the President. The Vice Chairman of the Commission shall be designated by the Speaker of the House of Representatives from among the members appointed by the Speaker.

"(g) MEETINGS.—The Commission shall meet at the call of the Chairman or a majority of its members.

"(h) DEADLINE FOR APPOINTMENTS. Members of the Commission shall be appointed not later than the end of the 30-day period beginning on the date of the enactment of this Act [Nov. 5, 1990].

"SEC. 6. REPORTS.

"(a) INITIAL REPORT.—The Commission shall transmit to the President and to Congress an initial report not later than six months after the date on which the Commission is first constituted with a quorum.

"(b) FINAL REPORT.—The Commission shall transmit to the President and to Congress a final report one year following submission of the initial report under subsection (a).

"(c) CONTENTS OF REPORTS.—The report under subsection (b) shall contain a detailed statement of the findings and conclusions of the Commission concerning the matters to be studied by the Commission under section 4, together with its recommendations for such legislation and administrative actions as it considers appropriate. Such report shall include a comprehensive description and discussion of the matters set forth in section 4.

"(d) REPORTS TO BE UNCLASSIFIED.—Each such report shall be submitted in unclassified form.

"(e) ADDITIONAL AND MINORITY VIEWS.—Each report may include such additional and minority views as individual members of the Commission may request be included.

"SEC. 7. DIRECTOR AND STAFF OF COMMISSION; EXPERTS AND CONSULTANTS.

"(a) DIRECTOR.—The Commission shall, without regard to section 5311(b) of title 5, United States Code, have a Director who shall be appointed by the Chairman and who shall be paid at a rate not to exceed the maximum rate of basic pay payable for GS–18 of the General Schedule.

"(b) STAFF.—The Chairman may appoint and fix the pay of such additional personnel as the Chairman considers appropriate.

"(c) APPLICABILITY OF CERTAIN CIVIL SERVICE LAWS.—The Director and staff of the Commission may be appointed without regard to the provisions of title 5, United States Code, governing appointments in the competitive service, and may be paid without regard to the provisions of chapter 51 and subchapter III of chapter 53 of such title relating to classification and General Schedule pay rates, except that no individual so appointed may receive pay in excess of the annual rate of basic pay payable for GS–18 of the General Schedule.

"(d) EXPERTS AND CONSULTANTS.—Subject to such rules as may be prescribed by the Commission, the Chairman may procure temporary and intermittent services under section 3109(b) of title 5 of the United States Code, but at rates for individuals not to exceed the daily equivalent of the maximum annual rate of basic pay payable for GS–18 of the General Schedule.

"(e) STAFF OF FEDERAL AGENCIES.—Upon request of the Commission, the head of any Federal agency may detail, on a reimbursable basis, any of the personnel of such agency to the Commission to assist the Commission in carrying out its duties under this Act.

"SEC. 8. POWERS OF COMMISSION

"(a) HEARINGS AND SESSIONS.—The Commission may, for the purpose of carrying out this Act, hold such hearings, sit and act at such times and places, take such testimony, and receive such evidence, as the Commission considers appropriate.

"(b) POWERS OF MEMBERS AND AGENTS.—Any member or agent of the Commission may, if so authorized by the Commission, take any action which the Commission is authorized to take by this section.

"(c) OBTAINING OFFICIAL DATA.—The Chairman or a designee on behalf of the Chairman may request information necessary to enable the Commission to carry out this Act directly from any department or agency of the United States.

"(d) GIFTS.—The Commission may accept, use, and dispose of gifts or donations of services or property.

"(e) MAILS.—The Commission may use the United States mails in the same manner and under the same conditions as other departments and agencies of the United States.

"(f) ADMINISTRATIVE SUPPORT SERVICES.—The Administrator of General Services shall provide to the Commission on a reimbursable basis such administrative support services as the Commission may request.

"SEC. 9. INITIAL FUNDING OF COMMISSION.

"If funds are not otherwise available for the necessary expenses of the Commission for fiscal year 1991, the Secretary of Defense shall make available to the Commission, from funds available to the Secretary for the fiscal year concerned, such funds as the Commission requires. When funds are specifically appropriated for the expenses of the Commission, the Commission shall reimburse the Secretary from such funds for any funds provided to it under the preceding sentence."

[References in laws to the rates of pay for GS–16, 17, or 18, or to maximum rates of pay under the General Schedule, to be considered references to rates payable under specified sections of Title 5, Government Organization and Employees, see section 529 [title I, §101(c)(1)] of Pub. L. 101–509, set out in a note under section 5376 of Title 5.]

INTELLIGENCE PRIORITIES AND REORGANIZATION

Pub. L. 101–510, div. A, title IX, §907, Nov. 5, 1990, 104 Stat. 1622, provided that:

"(a) REVISION OF PRIORITIES AND CONSOLIDATION OF FUNCTIONS.—The Secretary of Defense, together with the Director of Central Intelligence, shall conduct a joint review of all intelligence and intelligence-related activities in the Tactical Intelligence and Related Activities (TIARA) programs and the National Foreign Intelligence Program (NFIP). The Secretary, together with the Director, shall take the following actions with respect to those activities:

"(1) In cases in which redundancy or fragmentation exist, consolidate functions, programs, organizations, and operations to improve the efficiency and effectiveness of the conduct of those intelligence activities or programs.

"(2) Revise intelligence collection and analysis priorities and resource allocations to reflect changes in the international security environment.

"(3) Strengthen joint intelligence functions, operations, and organizations.

"(4) Improve the quality and independence of intelligence support to the weapons acquisition process.

"(5) Improve the responsiveness and utility of national intelligence systems and organizations to the needs of the combatant commanders.

"(b) PERSONNEL REDUCTIONS.—(1) The number of personnel assigned or detailed to the National Foreign Intelligence Program and related Tactical Intelligence and Related Activities programs shall be reduced by not less than 5 percent of the number of such personnel described in paragraph (2) during each of fiscal years 1992 through 1996.

"(2) The number of personnel referred to in paragraph (1) is the number of personnel assigned or detailed to such programs on September 30, 1990."

FOREIGN INTELLIGENCE ELECTRONIC SURVEILLANCE

For provisions relating to the exercise of certain authority respecting foreign intelligence electronic surveillance, see Ex. Ord. No. 12139, May 23, 1979, 44 F.R. 30311, set out under section 1802 of this title.

CHANGE OF TITLES OF SECRETARY OF DEFENSE, ET AL.; REAPPOINTMENT

Section 12(f) of act Aug. 10, 1949, provided in part that: "The titles of the Secretary of Defense, the Secretary of the Army, the Secretary of the Navy, the Secretary of the Air Force, the Under Secretaries and the Assistant Secretaries of the Departments of the Army, Navy, and Air Force, the Chairman of the Munitions Board, and the Chairman of the Research and Development Board, shall not be changed by virtue of this Act [see Short Title of 1949 Amendment note set out above] and the reappointment of the officials holding such titles on the effective date of this Act [Aug. 10, 1949] shall not be required."

REORGANIZATION PLAN NO. 8 OF 1949

Section 12(i) of act Aug. 10, 1949, provided that: "Reorganization Plan Numbered 8 of 1949, which was transmitted to the Congress by the President on July 18, 1949 [set out in Appendix to Title 5, Government Organization and Employees] pursuant to the provisions of the Reorganization Act of 1949, shall not take effect, notwithstanding the provisions of section 6 of such Reorganization Act of 1949."

EX. ORD. NO. 10431. NATIONAL SECURITY MEDAL

Ex. Ord. No. 10431, Jan. 19, 1953, 18 F.R. 437, provided:

1. There is hereby established a medal to be known as the National Security Medal with accompanying ribbons and appurtenances. The medal and its appurtenances shall be of appropriate design, approved by the Executive Secretary of the National Security Council.

2. The National Security Medal may be awarded to any person, without regard to nationality, including members of the armed forces of the United States, for distinguished achievement or outstanding contribution on or after July 26, 1947, in the field of intelligence relating to the national security.

3. The decoration established by this order shall be awarded by the President of the United States or, under regulations approved by him, by such person or persons as he may designate.

4. No more than one National Security Medal shall be awarded to any one person, but for subsequent services justifying an award, a suitable device may be awarded to be worn with the Medal.

5. Members of the armed forces of the United States who are awarded the decoration established by this order are authorized to wear the medal and the ribbon symbolic of the award, as may be authorized by uniform regulations approved by the Secretary of Defense.

6. The decoration established by this order may be awarded posthumously.

REGULATIONS GOVERNING THE AWARD OF THE NATIONAL SECURITY MEDAL

Pursuant to Paragraph 2 of Executive Order 10431, the following regulations are hereby issued to govern the award of the National Security Medal:

1. The National Security Medal may be awarded to any person without regard to nationality, including a member of the Armed Forces of the United States, who, on or after 26 July 1947, has made an outstanding contribution to the National intelligence effort. This contribution may consist of either exceptionally meritorious service performed in a position of high responsibility or of an act of valor requiring personal courage of a high degree and complete disregard of personal safety.

2. The National Security Medal with accompanying ribbon and appurtenances, shall be of appropriate design to be approved by the Executive Secretary of the National Security Council.

3. The National Security Medal shall be awarded only by the President or his designee for that purpose.

4. Recommendations may be submitted to the Executive Secretary of the National Security Council by any individual having personal knowledge of the facts of the exceptionally meritorious conduct or act of valor of the candidate in the performance of outstanding services, either as an eyewitness or from the testimony of others who have personal knowledge or were eyewitnesses. Any recommendations shall be accompanied by complete documentation, including where necessary, certificates, affidavits or sworn transcripts of testimony. Each recommendation for an award shall show the exact status, at the time of the rendition of the service on which the recommendation is based, with respect to citizenship, employment, and all other material factors, of the person who is being recommended for the National Security Medal.

5. Each recommendation shall contain a draft of an appropriate citation to accompany the award of the National Security Medal.

EXECUTIVE ORDER NO. 11905

Ex. Ord. No. 11905, Feb. 18, 1976, 41 F.R. 7703, as amended by Ex. Ord. No. 11985, May 13, 1977, 42 F.R. 25487; Ex. Ord. No. 11994, June 1, 1977, 42 F.R. 28869, which related to United States foreign intelligence activities, was superseded by Ex. Ord. No. 12036, Jan. 24, 1978, 43 F.R. 3674, formerly set out below.

EXECUTIVE ORDER NO. 12036

Ex. Ord. No. 12036, Jan. 24, 1978, 43 F.R. 3674, as amended by Ex. Ord. No. 12139, May 23, 1979, 44 F.R. 30311, which related to United States foreign intelligence activities, was revoked by Ex. Ord. No. 12333, Dec. 4, 1981, 46 F.R. 59941, set out below.

EX. ORD. NO. 12333. UNITED STATES INTELLIGENCE ACTIVITIES

Ex. Ord. No. 12333, Dec. 4, 1981, 46 F.R. 59941, provided:

TABLE OF CONTENTS

TABLE OF CONTENTS—Continued

Timely and accurate information about the activities, capabilities, plans, and intentions of foreign powers, organizations, and persons, and their agents, is essential to the national security of the United States. All reasonable and lawful means must be used to ensure that the United States will receive the best intelligence available. For that purpose, by virtue of the authority vested in me by the Constitution and statutes of the United States of America, including the National Security Act of 1947, as amended [see Short Title note above], and as President of the United States of America, in order to provide for the effective conduct of United States intelligence activities and the protection of constitutional rights, it is hereby ordered as follows:

PART 1—GOALS, DIRECTION, DUTIES AND RESPONSIBILITIES WITH RESPECT TO THE NATIONAL INTELLIGENCE EFFORT

1.1 GOALS

The United States intelligence effort shall provide the President and the National Security Council with the necessary information on which to base decisions concerning the conduct and development of foreign, defense and economic policy, and the protection of United States national interests from foreign security threats. All departments and agencies shall cooperate fully to fulfill this goal.

(a) Maximum emphasis should be given to fostering analytical competition among appropriate elements of the Intelligence Community.

(b) All means, consistent with applicable United States law and this Order, and with full consideration of the rights of United States persons, shall be used to develop intelligence information for the President and the National Security Council. A balanced approach between technical collection efforts and other means should be maintained and encouraged.

(c) Special emphasis should be given to detecting and countering espionage and other threats and activities directed by foreign intelligence services against the United States Government, or United States corporations, establishments, or persons.

(d) To the greatest extent possible consistent with applicable United States law and this Order, and with full consideration of the rights of United States persons, all agencies and departments should seek to ensure full and free exchange of information in order to derive maximum benefit from the United States intelligence effort.

1.2 THE NATIONAL SECURITY COUNCIL

(a) *Purpose*. The National Security Council (NSC) was established by the National Security Act of 1947 [see Short Title note above] to advise the President with respect to the integration of domestic, foreign and military policies relating to the national security. The NSC shall act as the highest Executive Branch entity that provides review of, guidance for and direction to the conduct of all national foreign intelligence, counterintelligence, and special activities, and attendant policies and programs.

(b) *Committees*. The NSC shall establish such committees as may be necessary to carry out its functions and responsibilities under this Order. The NSC, or a committee established by it, shall consider and submit to the President a policy recommendation, including all dissents, on each special activity and shall review proposals for other sensitive intelligence operations.

1.3 NATIONAL FOREIGN INTELLIGENCE ADVISORY GROUPS

(a) *Establishment and Duties.* The Director of Central Intelligence shall establish such boards, councils, or groups as required for the purpose of obtaining advice from within the Intelligence Community concerning:

(1) Production, review and coordination of national foreign intelligence;

(2) Priorities for the National Foreign Intelligence Program budget;

(3) Interagency exchanges of foreign intelligence information;

(4) Arrangements with foreign governments on intelligence matters;

(5) Protection of intelligence sources and methods;

(6) Activities of common concern; and

(7) Such other matters as may be referred by the Director of Central Intelligence.

(b) *Membership.* Advisory groups established pursuant to this section shall be chaired by the Director of Central Intelligence or his designated representative and shall consist of senior representatives from organizations within the Intelligence Community and from departments or agencies containing such organizations, as designated by the Director of Central Intelligence. Groups for consideration of substantive intelligence matters will include representatives of organizations involved in the collection, processing and analysis of intelligence. A senior representative of the Secretary of Commerce, the Attorney General, the Assistant to the President for National Security Affairs, and the Office of the Secretary of Defense shall be invited to participate in any group which deals with other than substantive intelligence matters.

1.4 THE INTELLIGENCE COMMUNITY

The agencies within the Intelligence Community shall, in accordance with applicable United States law and with the other provisions of this Order, conduct intelligence activities necessary for the conduct of foreign relations and the protection of the national security of the United States, including:

(a) Collection of information needed by the President, the National Security Council, the Secretaries of State and Defense, and other Executive Branch officials for the performance of their duties and responsibilities;

(b) Production and dissemination of intelligence;

(c) Collection of information concerning, and the conduct of activities to protect against, intelligence activities directed against the United States, international terrorist and international narcotics activities, and other hostile activities directed against the United States by foreign powers, organizations, persons, and their agents;

(d) Special activities;

(e) Administrative and support activities within the United States and abroad necessary for the performance of authorized activities; and

(f) Such other intelligence activities as the President may direct from time to time.

1.5 DIRECTOR OF CENTRAL INTELLIGENCE

In order to discharge the duties and responsibilities prescribed by law, the Director of Central Intelligence shall be responsible directly to the President and the NSC and shall:

(a) Act as the primary adviser to the President and the NSC on national foreign intelligence and provide the President and other officials in the Executive Branch with national foreign intelligence;

(b) Develop such objectives and guidance for the Intelligence Community as will enhance capabilities for responding to expected future needs for national foreign intelligence;

(c) Promote the development and maintenance of services of common concern by designated intelligence organizations on behalf of the Intelligence Community;

(d) Ensure implementation of special activities;

(e) Formulate policies concerning foreign intelligence and counterintelligence arrangements with foreign governments, coordinate foreign intelligence and counterintelligence relationships between agencies of the Intelligence Community and the intelligence or internal security services of foreign governments, and establish procedures governing the conduct of liaison by any department or agency with such services on narcotics activities;

(f) Participate in the development of procedures approved by the Attorney General governing criminal narcotics intelligence activities abroad to ensure that these activities are consistent with foreign intelligence programs;

(g) Ensure the establishment by the Intelligence Community of common security and access standards for managing and handling foreign intelligence systems, information, and products;

(h) Ensure that programs are developed which protect intelligence sources, methods, and analytical procedures;

(i) Establish uniform criteria for the determination of relative priorities for the transmission of critical national foreign intelligence, and advise the Secretary of Defense concerning the communications requirements of the Intelligence Community for the transmission of such intelligence;

(j) Establish appropriate staffs, committees, or other advisory groups to assist in the execution of the Director's responsibilities;

(k) Have full responsibility for production and dissemination of national foreign intelligence, and authority to levy analytic tasks on departmental intelligence production organizations, in consultation with those organizations, ensuring that appropriate mechanisms for competitive analysis are developed so that diverse points of view are considered fully and differences of judgment within the Intelligence Community are brought to the attention of national policymakers;

(*l*) Ensure the timely exploitation and dissemination of data gathered by national foreign intelligence collection means, and ensure that the resulting intelligence is disseminated immediately to appropriate government entities and military commands;

(m) Establish mechanisms which translate national foreign intelligence objectives and priorities approved by the NSC into specific guidance for the Intelligence Community, resolve conflicts in tasking priority, provide to departments and agencies having information collection capabilities that are not part of the National Foreign Intelligence Program advisory tasking concerning collection of national foreign intelligence, and provide for the development of plans and arrangements for transfer of required collection tasking authority to the Secretary of Defense when directed by the President;

(n) Develop, with the advice of the program managers and departments and agencies concerned, the consolidated National Foreign Intelligence Program budget, and present it to the President and the Congress;

(*o*) Review and approve all requests for reprogramming National Foreign Intelligence Program funds, in accordance with guidelines established by the Office of Management and Budget;

(p) Monitor National Foreign Intelligence Program implementation, and, as necessary, conduct program and performance audits and evaluations;

(q) Together with the Secretary of Defense, ensure that there is no unnecessary overlap between national foreign intelligence programs and Department of Defense intelligence programs consistent with the requirement to develop competitive analysis, and provide to and obtain from the Secretary of Defense all information necessary for this purpose;

(r) In accordance with law and relevant procedures approved by the Attorney General under this Order, give the heads of the departments and agencies access to all intelligence, developed by the CIA or the staff elements of the Director of Central Intelligence, relevant to the national intelligence needs of the departments and agencies; and

(s) Facilitate the use of national foreign intelligence products by Congress in a secure manner.

1.6 Duties and Responsibilities of the Heads of Executive Branch Departments and Agencies

(a) The heads of all Executive Branch departments and agencies shall, in accordance with law and relevant procedures approved by the Attorney General under this Order, give the Director of Central Intelligence access to all information relevant to the national intelligence needs of the United States, and shall give due consideration to the requests from the Director of Central Intelligence for appropriate support for Intelligence Community activities.

(b) The heads of departments and agencies involved in the National Foreign Intelligence Program shall ensure timely development and submission to the Director of Central Intelligence by the program managers and heads of component activities of proposed national programs and budgets in the format designated by the Director of Central Intelligence, and shall also ensure that the Director of Central Intelligence is provided, in a timely and responsive manner, all information necessary to perform the Director's program and budget responsibilities.

(c) The heads of departments and agencies involved in the National Foreign Intelligence Program may appeal to the President decisions by the Director of Central Intelligence on budget or reprogramming matters of the National Foreign Intelligence Program.

1.7 Senior Officials of the Intelligence Community

The heads of departments and agencies with organizations in the Intelligence Community or the heads of such organizations, as appropriate, shall:

(a) Report to the Attorney General possible violations of federal criminal laws by employees and of specified federal criminal laws by any other person as provided in procedures agreed upon by the Attorney General and the head of the department or agency concerned, in a manner consistent with the protection of intelligence sources and methods, as specified in those procedures;

(b) In any case involving serious or continuing breaches of security, recommend to the Attorney General that the case be referred to the FBI for further investigation;

(c) Furnish the Director of Central Intelligence and the NSC, in accordance with applicable law and procedures approved by the Attorney General under this Order, the information required for the performance of their respective duties;

(d) Report to the Intelligence Oversight Board, and keep the Director of Central Intelligence appropriately informed, concerning any intelligence activities of their organizations that they have reason to believe may be unlawful or contrary to Executive order or Presidential directive;

(e) Protect intelligence and intelligence sources and methods from unauthorized disclosure consistent with guidance from the Director of Central Intelligence;

(f) Disseminate intelligence to cooperating foreign governments under arrangements established or agreed to by the Director of Central Intelligence;

(g) Participate in the development of procedures approved by the Attorney General governing production and dissemination of intelligence resulting from criminal narcotics intelligence activities abroad if their departments, agencies, or organizations have intelligence responsibilities for foreign or domestic narcotics production and trafficking;

(h) Instruct their employees to cooperate fully with the Intelligence Oversight Board; and

(i) Ensure that the Inspectors General and General Counsels for their organizations have access to any information necessary to perform their duties assigned by this Order.

1.8 The Central Intelligence Agency

All duties and responsibilities of the CIA shall be related to the intelligence functions set out below. As authorized by this Order; the National Security Act of 1947, as amended [see Short Title note above]; the CIA Act of 1949, as amended [see Short Title of 1949 Amendment note above]; appropriate directives or other applicable law, the CIA shall:

(a) Collect, produce and disseminate foreign intelligence and counterintelligence, including information not otherwise obtainable. The collection of foreign intelligence or counterintelligence within the United States shall be coordinated with the FBI as required by procedures agreed upon by the Director of Central Intelligence and the Attorney General;

(b) Collect, produce and disseminate intelligence on foreign aspects of narcotics production and trafficking;

(c) Conduct counterintelligence activities outside the United States and, without assuming or performing any internal security functions, conduct counterintelligence activities within the United States in coordination with the FBI as required by procedures agreed upon [by] the Director of Central Intelligence and the Attorney General;

(d) Coordinate counterintelligence activities and the collection of information not otherwise obtainable when conducted outside the United States by other departments and agencies;

(e) Conduct special activities approved by the President. No agency except the CIA (or the Armed Forces of the United States in time of war declared by Congress or during any period covered by a report from the President to the Congress under the War Powers Resolution (87 Stat. 855) [50 U.S.C. 1541 et seq.]) may conduct any special activity unless the President determines that another agency is more likely to achieve a particular objective;

(f) Conduct services of common concern for the Intelligence Community as directed by the NSC;

(g) Carry out or contract for research, development and procurement of technical systems and devices relating to authorized functions;

(h) Protect the security of its installations, activities, information, property, and employees by appropriate means, including such investigations of applicants, employees, contractors, and other persons with similar associations with the CIA as are necessary; and

(i) Conduct such administrative and technical support activities within and outside the United States as are necessary to perform the functions described in sections (a) and [sic] through (h) above, including procurement and essential cover and proprietary arrangements.

1.9 The Department of State

The Secretary of State shall:

(a) Overtly collect information relevant to United States foreign policy concerns;

(b) Produce and disseminate foreign intelligence relating to United States foreign policy as required for the execution of the Secretary's responsibilities;

(c) Disseminate, as appropriate, reports received from United States diplomatic and consular posts;

(d) Transmit reporting requirements of the Intelligence Community to the Chiefs of United States Missions abroad; and

(e) Support Chiefs of Missions in discharging their statutory responsibilities for direction and coordination of mission activities.

1.10 The Department of the Treasury

The Secretary of the Treasury shall:

(a) Overtly collect foreign financial and monetary information;

(b) Participate with the Department of State in the overt collection of general foreign economic information;

(c) Produce and disseminate foreign intelligence relating to United States economic policy as required for the execution of the Secretary's responsibilities; and

(d) Conduct, through the United States Secret Service, activities to determine the existence and capability of surveillance equipment being used against the President of the United States, the Executive Office of the President, and, as authorized by the Secretary of the Treasury or the President, other Secret Service protectees and United States officials. No information shall be acquired intentionally through such activities except to protect against such surveillance, and those activities shall be conducted pursuant to procedures agreed upon by the Secretary of the Treasury and the Attorney General.

1.11 The Department of Defense

The Secretary of Defense shall:

(a) Collect national foreign intelligence and be responsive to collection tasking by the Director of Central Intelligence;

(b) Collect, produce and disseminate military and military-related foreign intelligence and counterintelligence as required for execution of the Secretary's responsibilities;

(c) Conduct programs and missions necessary to fulfill national, departmental and tactical foreign intelligence requirements;

(d) Conduct counterintelligence activities in support of Department of Defense components outside the United States in coordination with the CIA, and within the United States in coordination with the FBI pursuant to procedures agreed upon by the Secretary of Defense and the Attorney General;

(e) Conduct, as the executive agent of the United States Government, signals intelligence and communications security activities, except as otherwise directed by the NSC;

(f) Provide for the timely transmission of critical intelligence, as defined by the Director of Central Intelligence, within the United States Government;

(g) Carry out or contract for research, development and procurement of technical systems and devices relating to authorized intelligence functions;

(h) Protect the security of Department of Defense installations, activities, property, information, and employees by appropriate means, including such investigations of applicants, employees, contractors, and other persons with similar associations with the Department of Defense as are necessary;

(i) Establish and maintain military intelligence relationships and military intelligence exchange programs with selected cooperative foreign defense establishments and international organizations, and ensure that such relationships and programs are in accordance with policies formulated by the Director of Central Intelligence;

(j) Direct, operate, control and provide fiscal management for the National Security Agency and for defense and military intelligence and national reconnaissance entities; and

(k) Conduct such administrative and technical support activities within and outside the United States as are necessary to perform the functions described in sections (a) through (j) above.

1.12 Intelligence Components Utilized by the Secretary of Defense

In carrying out the responsibilities assigned in section 1.11, the Secretary of Defense is authorized to utilize the following:

(a) *Defense Intelligence Agency*, whose responsibilities shall include:

(1) Collection, production, or, through tasking and coordination, provision of military and military-related intelligence for the Secretary of Defense, the Joint Chiefs of Staff, other Defense components, and, as appropriate, non-Defense agencies;

(2) Collection and provision of military intelligence for national foreign intelligence and counterintelligence products;

(3) Coordination of all Department of Defense intelligence collection requirements;

(4) Management of the Defense Attache system; and

(5) Provision of foreign intelligence and counterintelligence staff support as directed by the Joint Chiefs of Staff.

(b) *National Security Agency*, whose responsibilities shall include:

(1) Establishment and operation of an effective unified organization for signals intelligence activities, except for the delegation of operational control over certain operations that are conducted through other elements of the Intelligence Community. No other department or agency may engage in signals intelligence activities except pursuant to a delegation by the Secretary of Defense;

(2) Control of signals intelligence collection and processing activities, including assignment of resources to an appropriate agent for such periods and tasks as required for the direct support of military commanders;

(3) Collection of signals intelligence information for national foreign intelligence purposes in accordance with guidance from the Director of Central Intelligence;

(4) Processing of signals intelligence data for national foreign intelligence purposes in accordance with guidance from the Director of Central Intelligence;

(5) Dissemination of signals intelligence information for national foreign intelligence purposes to authorized elements of the Government, including the military services, in accordance with guidance from the Director of Central Intelligence;

(6) Collection, processing and dissemination of signals intelligence information for counterintelligence purposes;

(7) Provision of signals intelligence support for the conduct of military operations in accordance with tasking, priorities, and standards of timeliness assigned by the Secretary of Defense. If provision of such support requires use of national collection systems, these systems will be tasked within existing guidance from the Director of Central Intelligence;

(8) Executing the responsibilities of the Secretary of Defense as executive agent for the communications security of the United States Government;

(9) Conduct of research and development to meet the needs of the United States for signals intelligence and communications security;

(10) Protection of the security of its installations, activities, property, information, and employees by appropriate means, including such investigations of applicants, employees, contractors, and other persons with similar associations with the NSA as are necessary;

(11) Prescribing, within its field of authorized operations, security regulations covering operating practices, including the transmission, handling and distribution of signals intelligence and communications security material within and among the elements under control of the Director of the NSA, and exercising the necessary supervisory control to ensure compliance with the regulations;

(12) Conduct of foreign cryptologic liaison relationships, with liaison for intelligence purposes conducted in accordance with policies formulated by the Director of Central Intelligence; and

(13) Conduct of such administrative and technical support activities within and outside the United States as are necessary to perform the functions described in sections (1) through (12) above, including procurement.

(c) *Offices for the collection of specialized intelligence through reconnaissance programs*, whose responsibilities shall include:

(1) Carrying out consolidated reconnaissance programs for specialized intelligence;

(2) Responding to tasking in accordance with procedures established by the Director of Central Intelligence; and

(3) Delegating authority to the various departments and agencies for research, development, procurement, and operation of designated means of collection.

(d) *The foreign intelligence and counterintelligence elements of the Army, Navy, Air Force, and Marine Corps,* whose responsibilities shall include:

(1) Collection, production and dissemination of military and military-related foreign intelligence and counterintelligence, and information on the foreign aspects of narcotics production and trafficking. When collection is conducted in response to national foreign intelligence requirements, it will be conducted in accordance with guidance from the Director of Central Intelligence. Collection of national foreign intelligence, not otherwise obtainable, outside the United States shall be coordinated with the CIA, and such collection within the United States shall be coordinated with the FBI;

(2) Conduct of counterintelligence activities outside the United States in coordination with the CIA, and within the United States in coordination with the FBI; and

(3) Monitoring of the development, procurement and management of tactical intelligence systems and equipment and conducting related research, development, and test and evaluation activities.

(e) *Other offices within the Department of Defense appropriate for conduct of the intelligence missions and responsibilities assigned to the Secretary of Defense.* If such other offices are used for intelligence purposes, the provisions of Part 2 of this Order shall apply to those offices when used for those purposes.

1.13 THE DEPARTMENT OF ENERGY

The Secretary of Energy shall:

(a) Participate with the Department of State in overtly collecting information with respect to foreign energy matters;

(b) Produce and disseminate foreign intelligence necessary for the Secretary's responsibilities;

(c) Participate in formulating intelligence collection and analysis requirements where the special expert capability of the Department can contribute; and

(d) Provide expert technical, analytical and research capability to other agencies within the Intelligence Community.

1.14 THE FEDERAL BUREAU OF INVESTIGATION

Under the supervision of the Attorney General and pursuant to such regulations as the Attorney General may establish, the Director of the FBI shall:

(a) Within the United States conduct counterintelligence and coordinate counterintelligence activities of other agencies within the Intelligence Community. When a counterintelligence activity of the FBI involves military or civilian personnel of the Department of Defense, the FBI shall coordinate with the Department of Defense;

(b) Conduct counterintelligence activities outside the United States in coordination with the CIA as required by procedures agreed upon by the Director of Central Intelligence and the Attorney General;

(c) Conduct within the United States, when requested by officials of the Intelligence Community designated by the President, activities undertaken to collect foreign intelligence or support foreign intelligence collection requirements of other agencies within the Intelligence Community, or, when requested by the Director of the National Security Agency, to support the communications security activities of the United States Government;

(d) Produce and disseminate foreign intelligence and counterintelligence; and

(e) Carry out or contract for research, development and procurement of technical systems and devices relating to the functions authorized above.

PART 2—CONDUCT OF INTELLIGENCE ACTIVITIES

2.1 NEED

Accurate and timely information about the capabilities, intentions and activities of foreign powers, organizations, or persons and their agents is essential to informed decisionmaking in the areas of national defense and foreign relations. Collection of such information is a priority objective and will be pursued in a vigorous, innovative and responsible manner that is consistent with the Constitution and applicable law and respectful of the principles upon which the United States was founded.

2.2 PURPOSE

This Order is intended to enhance human and technical collection techniques, especially those undertaken abroad, and the acquisition of significant foreign intelligence, as well as the detection and countering of international terrorist activities and espionage conducted by foreign powers. Set forth below are certain general principles that, in addition to and consistent with applicable laws, are intended to achieve the proper balance between the acquisition of essential information and protection of individual interests. Nothing in this Order shall be construed to apply to or interfere with any authorized civil or criminal law enforcement responsibility of any department or agency.

2.3 COLLECTION OF INFORMATION

Agencies within the Intelligence Community are authorized to collect, retain or disseminate information concerning United States persons only in accordance with procedures established by the head of the agency concerned and approved by the Attorney General, consistent with the authorities provided by Part 1 of this Order. Those procedures shall permit collection, retention and dissemination of the following types of information:

(a) Information that is publicly available or collected with the consent of the person concerned;

(b) Information constituting foreign intelligence or counterintelligence, including such information concerning corporations or other commercial organizations. Collection within the United States of foreign intelligence not otherwise obtainable shall be undertaken by the FBI or, when significant foreign intelligence is sought, by other authorized agencies of the Intelligence Community, provided that no foreign intelligence collection by such agencies may be undertaken for the purpose of acquiring information concerning the domestic activities of United States persons;

(c) Information obtained in the course of a lawful foreign intelligence, counterintelligence, international narcotics or international terrorism investigation;

(d) Information needed to protect the safety of any persons or organizations, including those who are targets, victims or hostages of international terrorist organizations;

(e) Information needed to protect foreign intelligence or counterintelligence sources or methods from unauthorized disclosure. Collection within the United States shall be undertaken by the FBI except that other agencies of the Intelligence Community may also collect such information concerning present or former employees, present or former intelligence agency contractors or their present or former employees, or applicants for any such employment or contracting;

(f) Information concerning persons who are reasonably believed to be potential sources or contacts for the purpose of determining their suitability or credibility;

(g) Information arising out of a lawful personnel, physical or communications security investigation;

(h) Information acquired by overhead reconnaissance not directed at specific United States persons;

(i) Incidentally obtained information that may indicate involvement in activities that may violate federal, state, local or foreign laws; and

(j) Information necessary for administrative purposes.

In addition, agencies within the Intelligence Community may disseminate information, other than information derived from signals intelligence, to each appropriate agency within the Intelligence Community for purposes of allowing the recipient agency to determine whether the information is relevant to its responsibilities and can be retained by it.

2.4 COLLECTION TECHNIQUES

Agencies within the Intelligence Community shall use the least intrusive collection techniques feasible within the United States or directed against United States persons abroad. Agencies are not authorized to use such techniques as electronic surveillance, unconsented physical search, mail surveillance, physical surveillance, or monitoring devices unless they are in accordance with procedures established by the head of the agency concerned and approved by the Attorney General. Such procedures shall protect constitutional and other legal rights and limit use of such information to lawful governmental purposes. These procedures shall not authorize:

(a) The CIA to engage in electronic surveillance within the United States except for the purpose of training, testing, or conducting countermeasures to hostile electronic surveillance;

(b) Unconsented physical searches in the United States by agencies other than the FBI, except for:

(1) Searches by counterintelligence elements of the military services directed against military personnel within the United States or abroad for intelligence purposes, when authorized by a military commander empowered to approve physical searches for law enforcement purposes, based upon a finding of probable cause to believe that such persons are acting as agents of foreign powers; and

(2) Searches by CIA of personal property of non-United States persons lawfully in its possession.

(c) Physical surveillance of a United States person in the United States by agencies other than the FBI, except for:

(1) Physical surveillance of present or former employees, present or former intelligence agency contractors or their present or former employees, or applicants for any such employment or contracting; and

(2) Physical surveillance of a military person employed by a nonintelligence element of a military service.

(d) Physical surveillance of a United States person abroad to collect foreign intelligence, except to obtain significant information that cannot reasonably be acquired by other means.

2.5 ATTORNEY GENERAL APPROVAL

The Attorney General hereby is delegated the power to approve the use for intelligence purposes, within the United States or against a United States person abroad, of any technique for which a warrant would be required if undertaken for law enforcement purposes, provided that such techniques shall not be undertaken unless the Attorney General has determined in each case that there is probable cause to believe that the technique is directed against a foreign power or an agent of a foreign power. Electronic surveillance, as defined in the Foreign Intelligence Surveillance Act of 1978 [50 U.S.C. 1801 et seq.], shall be conducted in accordance with that Act, as well as this Order.

2.6 ASSISTANCE TO LAW ENFORCEMENT AUTHORITIES

Agencies within the Intelligence Community are authorized to:

(a) Cooperate with appropriate law enforcement agencies for the purpose of protecting the employees, information, property and facilities of any agency within the Intelligence Community;

(b) Unless otherwise precluded by law or this Order, participate in law enforcement activities to investigate or prevent clandestine intelligence activities by foreign powers, or international terrorist or narcotics activities;

(c) Provide specialized equipment, technical knowledge, or assistance of expert personnel for use by any department or agency, or, when lives are endangered, to support local law enforcement agencies. Provision of assistance by expert personnel shall be approved in each case by the General Counsel of the providing agency; and

(d) Render any other assistance and cooperation to law enforcement authorities not precluded by applicable law.

2.7 CONTRACTING

Agencies within the Intelligence Community are authorized to enter into contracts or arrangements for the provision of goods or services with private companies or institutions in the United States and need not reveal the sponsorship of such contracts or arrangements for authorized intelligence purposes. Contracts or arrangements with academic institutions may be undertaken only with the consent of appropriate officials of the institution.

2.8 CONSISTENCY WITH OTHER LAWS

Nothing in this Order shall be construed to authorize any activity in violation of the Constitution or statutes of the United States.

2.9 UNDISCLOSED PARTICIPATION IN ORGANIZATIONS WITHIN THE UNITED STATES

No one acting on behalf of agencies within the Intelligence Community may join or otherwise participate in any organization in the United States on behalf of any agency within the Intelligence Community without disclosing his intelligence affiliation to appropriate officials of the organization, except in accordance with procedures established by the head of the agency concerned and approved by the Attorney General. Such participation shall be authorized only if it is essential to achieving lawful purposes as determined by the agency head or designee. No such participation may be undertaken for the purpose of influencing the activity of the organization or its members except in cases where:

(a) The participation is undertaken on behalf of the FBI in the course of a lawful investigation; or

(b) The organization concerned is composed primarily of individuals who are not United States persons and is reasonably believed to be acting on behalf of a foreign power.

2.10 HUMAN EXPERIMENTATION

No agency within the Intelligence Community shall sponsor, contract for or conduct research on human subjects except in accordance with guidelines issued by the Department of Health and Human Services. The subject's informed consent shall be documented as required by those guidelines.

2.11 PROHIBITION ON ASSASSINATION

No person employed by or acting on behalf of the United States Government shall engage in, or conspire to engage in, assassination.

2.12 INDIRECT PARTICIPATION

No agency of the Intelligence Community shall participate in or request any person to undertake activities forbidden by this Order.

PART 3—GENERAL PROVISIONS

3.1 CONGRESSIONAL OVERSIGHT

The duties and responsibilities of the Director of Central Intelligence and the heads of other departments, agencies, and entities engaged in intelligence activities to cooperate with the Congress in the conduct of its responsibilities for oversight of intelligence activities shall be as provided in title 50, United States Code, section 413. The requirements of section 662 of the Foreign Assistance Act of 1961, as amended (22 U.S.C. 2422), and section 501 of the National Security Act of 1947, as amended (50 U.S.C. 413), shall apply to all special activities as defined in this Order.

3.2 IMPLEMENTATION

The NSC, the Secretary of Defense, the Attorney General, and the Director of Central Intelligence shall issue such appropriate directives and procedures as are necessary to implement this Order. Heads of agencies within the Intelligence Community shall issue appropriate supplementary directives and procedures consistent with this Order. The Attorney General shall provide a statement of reasons for not approving any procedures established by the head of an agency in the Intelligence Community other than the FBI. The National Security Council may establish procedures in instances where the agency head and the Attorney General are unable to reach agreement on other than constitutional or other legal grounds.

3.3 PROCEDURES

Until the procedures required by this Order have been established, the activities herein authorized which require procedures shall be conducted in accordance with existing procedures or requirements established under Executive Order No. 12036 [formerly set out above]. Procedures required by this Order shall be established as expeditiously as possible. All procedures promulgated pursuant to this Order shall be made available to the congressional intelligence committees.

3.4 DEFINITIONS

For the purposes of this Order, the following terms shall have these meanings:

(a) *Counterintelligence* means information gathered and activities conducted to protect against espionage, other intelligence activities, sabotage, or assassinations conducted for or on behalf of foreign powers, organizations or persons, or international terrorist activities, but not including personnel, physical, document or communications security programs.

(b) *Electronic surveillance* means acquisition of a nonpublic communication by electronic means without the consent of a person who is a party to an electronic communication or, in the case of a nonelectronic communication, without the consent of a person who is visably [sic] present at the place of communication, but not including the use of radio direction-finding equipment solely to determine the location of a transmitter.

(c) *Employee* means a person employed by, assigned to or acting for an agency within the Intelligence Community.

(d) *Foreign intelligence* means information relating to the capabilities, intentions and activities of foreign powers, organizations or persons, but not including counterintelligence except for information on international terrorist activities.

(e) *Intelligence activities* means all activities that agencies within the Intelligence Community are authorized to conduct pursuant to this Order.

(f) *Intelligence Community* and *agencies within the Intelligence Community* refer to the following agencies or organizations:

(1) The Central Intelligence Agency (CIA);

(2) The National Security Agency (NSA);

(3) The Defense Intelligence Agency (DIA);

(4) The offices within the Department of Defense for the collection of specialized national foreign intelligence through reconnaissance programs;

(5) The Bureau of Intelligence and Research of the Department of State;

(6) The intelligence elements of the Army, Navy, Air Force, and Marine Corps, the Federal Bureau of Investigation (FBI), the Department of the Treasury, and the Department of Energy; and

(7) The staff elements of the Director of Central Intelligence.

(g) *The National Foreign Intelligence Program* includes the programs listed below, but its composition shall be subject to review by the National Security Council and modification by the President:

(1) The programs of the CIA;

(2) The Consolidated Cryptologic Program, the General Defense Intelligence Program, and the programs of the offices within the Department of Defense for the collection of specialized national foreign intelligence through reconnaissance, except such elements as the Director of Central Intelligence and the Secretary of Defense agree should be excluded;

(3) Other programs of agencies within the Intelligence Community designated jointly by the Director of Central Intelligence and the head of the department or by the President as national foreign intelligence or counterintelligence activities;

(4) Activities of the staff elements of the Director of Central Intelligence;

(5) Activities to acquire the intelligence required for the planning and conduct of tactical operations by the United States military forces are not included in the National Foreign Intelligence Program.

(h) *Special activities* means activities conducted in support of national foreign policy objectives abroad which are planned and executed so that the role of the United States Government is not apparent or acknowledged publicly, and functions in support of such activities, but which are not intended to influence United States political processes, public opinion, policies, or media and do not include diplomatic activities or the collection and production of intelligence or related support functions.

(i) *United States person* means a United States citizen, an alien known by the intelligence agency concerned to be a permanent resident alien, an unincorporated association substantially composed of United States citizens or permanent resident aliens, or a corporation incorporated in the United States, except for a corporation directed and controlled by a foreign government or governments.

3.5 PURPOSE AND EFFECT

This Order is intended to control and provide direction and guidance to the Intelligence Community. Nothing contained herein or in any procedures promulgated hereunder is intended to confer any substantive or procedural right or privilege on any person or organization.

3.6 REVOCATION

Executive Order No. 12036 of January 24, 1978, as amended, entitled "United States Intelligence Activities," is revoked.

RONALD REAGAN.

EXECUTIVE ORDER NO. 12334

Ex. Ord. No. 12334, Dec. 4, 1981, 46 F.R. 59955, as amended by Ex. Ord. No. 12701, Feb. 14, 1990, 55 F.R. 5953, which established the President's Intelligence Oversight Board, was revoked by Ex. Ord. No. 12863, §3.3, Sept. 13, 1993, 58 F.R. 48441, set out below.

EX. ORD. NO. 12863. PRESIDENT'S FOREIGN INTELLIGENCE ADVISORY BOARD

Ex. Ord. No. 12863, Sept. 13, 1993, 58 F.R. 48441, as amended by Ex. Ord. No. 13070, Dec. 15, 1997, 62 F.R. 66493, provided:

By the authority vested in me as President by the Constitution and the laws of the United States of America, and in order to enhance the security of the United States by improving the quality and effectiveness of intelligence available to the United States, and to assure the legality of activities of the Intelligence Community, it is ordered as follows:

PART I. ASSESSMENT OF INTELLIGENCE ACTIVITIES

SECTION 1.1. There is hereby established within the White House Office, Executive Office of the President, the President's Foreign Intelligence Advisory Board (PFIAB). The PFIAB shall consist of not more than 16 members, who shall serve at the pleasure of the President and shall be appointed by the President from among trustworthy and distinguished citizens outside the Government who are qualified on the basis of achievement, experience and independence. The President shall establish the terms of the members upon their appointment. To the extent practicable, one-third of the PFIAB at any one time shall be comprised of members whose term of service does not exceed 2 years. The President shall designate a Chairman and Vice Chairman from among the members. The PFIAB shall utilize full-time staff and consultants as authorized by the President. Such staff shall be headed by an Executive Director, appointed by the President.

SEC. 1.2. The PFIAB shall assess the quality, quantity, and adequacy of intelligence collection, of analysis and estimates, and of counterintelligence and other intelligence activities. The PFIAB shall have the authority to review continually the performance of all agencies of the Federal Government that are engaged in the collection, evaluation, or production of intelligence or the execution of intelligence policy. The PFIAB shall further be authorized to assess the adequacy of management, personnel and organization in the intelligence agencies. The heads of departments and agencies of the Federal Government, to the extent permitted by law, shall provide the PFIAB with access to all information that the PFIAB deems necessary to carry out its responsibilities.

SEC. 1.3. The PFIAB shall report directly to the President and advise him concerning the objectives, conduct, management and coordination of the various activities of the agencies of the Intelligence Community. The PFIAB shall report periodically, but at least semiannually, concerning its findings and appraisals and shall make appropriate recommendations for the improvement and enhancement of the intelligence efforts of the United States.

SEC. 1.4. The PFIAB shall consider and recommend appropriate action with respect to matters, identified to the PFIAB by the Director of Central Intelligence, the Central Intelligence Agency, or other Government agencies engaged in intelligence or related activities, in which the advice of the PFIAB will further the effectiveness of the national intelligence effort. With respect to matters deemed appropriate by the President, the PFIAB shall advise and make recommendations to the Director of Central Intelligence, the Central Intelligence Agency, and other Government agencies engaged in intelligence and related activities, concerning ways to achieve increased effectiveness in meeting national intelligence needs.

PART II. OVERSIGHT OF INTELLIGENCE ACTIVITIES

SEC. 2.1. The Intelligence Oversight Board (IOB) is hereby established as a standing committee of the PFIAB. The IOB shall consist of no more than four members designated by the President from among the membership of the PFIAB. The Chairman of the PFIAB may also serve as the Chairman or a member of the IOB if so designated by the President. The IOB shall utilize such full-time staff and consultants as authorized by the Chairman of the IOB with the concurrence of the Chairman of the PFIAB.

SEC. 2.2. The IOB shall:

(a) prepare for the President reports of intelligence activities that the IOB believes may be unlawful or contrary to Executive order or Presidential directive;

(b) forward to the Attorney General reports received concerning intelligence activities that the IOB believes may be unlawful or contrary to Executive order or Presidential directive;

(c) review the internal guidelines of each agency within the Intelligence Community that concern the lawfulness of intelligence activities;

(d) review the practices and procedures of the Inspectors General and General Counsel of the Intelligence Community for discovering and reporting intelligence activities that may be unlawful or contrary to Executive order or Presidential directive; and

(e) conduct such investigations as the IOB deems necessary to carry out its functions under this order.

SEC. 2.3. The IOB shall report to the President. The IOB shall consider and take appropriate action with respect to matters identified by the Director of Central Intelligence, the Central Intelligence Agency or other agencies of the Intelligence Community. With respect to matters deemed appropriate by the President, the IOB shall advise and make appropriate recommendations to the Director of Central Intelligence, the Central Intelligence Agency and other agencies of the Intelligence Community.

SEC. 2.4. The heads of departments and agencies of the Intelligence Community, to the extent permitted by law, shall provide the IOB with all information that the IOB deems necessary to carry out its responsibilities. Inspectors General and General Counsel of the Intelligence Community, to the extent permitted by law, shall report to the IOB, at least on a quarterly basis and from time to time as necessary or appropriate, concerning intelligence activities that they have reason to believe may be unlawful or contrary to Executive order or Presidential directive.

PART III. GENERAL PROVISIONS

SEC. 3.1. Information made available to the PFIAB, or members of the PFIAB acting in their IOB capacity, shall be given all necessary security protection in accordance with applicable laws and regulations. Each member of the PFIAB, each member of the PFIAB's staff and each of the PFIAB's consultants shall execute an agreement never to reveal any classified information obtained by virtue of his or her services with the PFIAB except to the President or to such persons as the President may designate.

SEC. 3.2. Members of the PFIAB shall serve without compensation but may receive transportation expenses and per diem allowance as authorized by law. Staff and consultants to the PFIAB shall receive pay and allowances as authorized by the President.

SEC. 3.3. Executive Order No. 12334 of December 4, 1981, as amended, and Executive Order No. 12537 of October 28, 1985, as amended [50 U.S.C. 403 note], are revoked.

WILLIAM J. CLINTON.

ACT REFERRED TO IN OTHER SECTIONS

The National Security Act of 1947 is referred to in section 47e of this title; section 469 of Appendix to this title; title 21 sections 1704, 1903.

SECTION REFERRED TO IN OTHER SECTIONS

This section is referred to in title 10 sections 113, 125, 155.

§ 401a. Definitions

As used in this Act:

(1) The term "intelligence" includes foreign intelligence and counterintelligence.

(2) The term "foreign intelligence" means information relating to the capabilities, intentions, or activities of foreign governments or elements thereof, foreign organizations, or foreign persons.

(3) The term "counterintelligence" means information gathered and activities conducted to protect against espionage, other intelligence activities, sabotage, or assassinations conducted by or on behalf of foreign governments or elements thereof, foreign organizations, or foreign persons, or international terrorist activities.

(4) The term "intelligence community" includes—

(A) the Office of the Director of Central Intelligence, which shall include the Office of the Deputy Director of Central Intelligence, the National Intelligence Council (as provided for in section 403–5(b)(3)[1] of this title), and such other offices as the Director may designate;

(B) the Central Intelligence Agency;

(C) the National Security Agency;

(D) the Defense Intelligence Agency;

(E) the National Imagery and Mapping Agency;

(F) the National Reconnaissance Office;

(G) other offices within the Department of Defense for the collection of specialized national intelligence through reconnaissance programs;

(H) the intelligence elements of the Army, the Navy, the Air Force, the Marine Corps, the Federal Bureau of Investigation, the Department of the Treasury, and the Department of Energy;

(I) the Bureau of Intelligence and Research of the Department of State; and

(J) such other elements of any other department or agency as may be designated by the President, or designated jointly by the Director of Central Intelligence and the head of the department or agency concerned, as an element of the intelligence community.

(5) The terms "national intelligence" and "intelligence related to the national security"—

(A) each refer to intelligence which pertains to the interests of more than one department or agency of the Government; and

(B) do not refer to counterintelligence or law enforcement activities conducted by the Federal Bureau of Investigation except to the extent provided for in procedures agreed to by the Director of Central Intelligence and the Attorney General, or otherwise as expressly provided for in this title.[2]

(6) The term "National Foreign Intelligence Program" refers to all programs, projects, and activities of the intelligence community, as well as any other programs of the intelligence community designated jointly by the Director of Central Intelligence and the head of a United States department or agency or by the President. Such term does not include programs, projects, or activities of the military departments to acquire intelligence solely for the planning and conduct of tactical military operations by United States Armed Forces.

(July 26, 1947, ch. 343, §3, as added Pub. L. 102–496, title VII, §702, Oct. 24, 1992, 106 Stat. 3188; amended Pub. L. 103–359, title V, §501(a)(1), Oct. 14, 1994, 108 Stat. 3428; Pub. L. 104–201, div. A, title XI, §1122(b)(1), Sept. 23, 1996, 110 Stat. 2687.)

REFERENCES IN TEXT

This Act, referred to in text, means act July 26, 1947, ch. 343, 61 Stat. 495, as amended, known as the National Security Act of 1947. For complete classification of this Act to the Code, see Short Title note set out under section 401 of this title and Tables.

This title, referred to in par. (5)(B), probably should be "this Act", meaning act July 26, 1947, see above, because this section is not a part of any title of act of July 26, 1947.

[1] So in original. Probably should be section "403–3(b)(3)".

[2] See References in Text note below.

AMENDMENTS

1996—Par. (4)(E). Pub. L. 104–201 substituted "National Imagery and Mapping Agency" for "Central Imagery Office".

1994—Par. (4)(E). Pub. L. 103–359 substituted "the Central Imagery Office" for "the central imagery authority within the Department of Defense".

EFFECTIVE DATE OF 1996 AMENDMENT

Amendment by Pub. L. 104–201 effective Oct. 1, 1996, see section 1124 of Pub. L. 104–201, set out as a note under section 193 of Title 10, Armed Forces.

AUTHORITY OF SECRETARY OF STATE

Except as otherwise provided, Secretary of State to have and exercise any authority vested by law in any official or office of Department of State and references to such officials or offices deemed to refer to Secretary of State or Department of State, as appropriate, see section 2651a of Title 22, Foreign Relations and Intercourse, and section 161(d) of Pub. L. 103–236, set out as a note under section 2651a of Title 22.

SECTION REFERRED TO IN OTHER SECTIONS

This section is referred to in sections 403–2a, 403–8, 404j of this title; title 22 section 1442a.

SUBCHAPTER I—COORDINATION FOR NATIONAL SECURITY

§402. National Security Council

(a) Establishment; presiding officer; functions; composition

There is established a council to be known as the National Security Council (hereinafter in this section referred to as the "Council").

The President of the United States shall preside over meetings of the Council: *Provided*, That in his absence he may designate a member of the Council to preside in his place.

The function of the Council shall be to advise the President with respect to the integration of domestic, foreign, and military policies relating to the national security so as to enable the military services and the other departments and agencies of the Government to cooperate more effectively in matters involving the national security.

The Council shall be composed of—

(1) the President;

(2) the Vice President;

(3) the Secretary of State;

(4) the Secretary of Defense;

(5) the Director for Mutual Security;

(6) the Chairman of the National Security Resources Board; and

(7) the Secretaries and Under Secretaries of other executive departments and of the military departments, the Chairman of the Munitions Board, and the Chairman of the Research and Development Board, when appointed by the President by and with the advice and consent of the Senate, to serve at his pleasure.

(b) Additional functions

In addition to performing such other functions as the President may direct, for the purpose of more effectively coordinating the policies and functions of the departments and agencies of the Government relating to the national security, it shall, subject to the direction of the President, be the duty of the Council—

(1) to assess and appraise the objectives, commitments, and risks of the United States

in relation to our actual and potential military power, in the interest of national security, for the purpose of making recommendations to the President in connection therewith; and

(2) to consider policies on matters of common interest to the departments and agencies of the Government concerned with the national security, and to make recommendations to the President in connection therewith.

(c) Executive secretary; appointment; staff employees

The Council shall have a staff to be headed by a civilian executive secretary who shall be appointed by the President. The executive secretary, subject to the direction of the Council, is authorized, subject to the civil-service laws and chapter 51 and subchapter III of chapter 53 of title 5, to appoint and fix the compensation of such personnel as may be necessary to perform such duties as may be prescribed by the Council in connection with the performance of its functions.

(d) Recommendations and reports

The Council shall, from time to time, make such recommendations, and such other reports to the President as it deems appropriate or as the President may require.

(e) Participation of Chairman or Vice Chairman of Joint Chiefs of Staff

The Chairman (or in his absence the Vice Chairman) of the Joint Chiefs of Staff may, in his role as principal military adviser to the National Security Council and subject to the direction of the President, attend and participate in meetings of the National Security Council.

(f) Participation by Director of National Drug Control Policy

The Director of National Drug Control Policy may, in the role of the Director as principal adviser to the National Security Council on national drug control policy, and subject to the direction of the President, attend and participate in meetings of the National Security Council.

(g) Board for Low Intensity Conflict

The President shall establish within the National Security Council a board to be known as the "Board for Low Intensity Conflict". The principal function of the board shall be to coordinate the policies of the United States for low intensity conflict.

(h) Committee on Foreign Intelligence

(1) There is established within the National Security Council a committee to be known as the Committee on Foreign Intelligence (in this subsection referred to as the "Committee").

(2) The Committee shall be composed of the following:

(A) The Director of Central Intelligence.

(B) The Secretary of State.

(C) The Secretary of Defense.

(D) The Assistant to the President for National Security Affairs, who shall serve as the chairperson of the Committee.

(E) Such other members as the President may designate.

(3) The function of the Committee shall be to assist the Council in its activities by—

(A) identifying the intelligence required to address the national security interests of the United States as specified by the President;

(B) establishing priorities (including funding priorities) among the programs, projects, and activities that address such interests and requirements; and

(C) establishing policies relating to the conduct of intelligence activities of the United States, including appropriate roles and missions for the elements of the intelligence community and appropriate targets of intelligence collection activities.

(4) In carrying out its function, the Committee shall—

(A) conduct an annual review of the national security interests of the United States;

(B) identify on an annual basis, and at such other times as the Council may require, the intelligence required to meet such interests and establish an order of priority for the collection and analysis of such intelligence; and

(C) conduct an annual review of the elements of the intelligence community in order to determine the success of such elements in collecting, analyzing, and disseminating the intelligence identified under subparagraph (B).

(5) The Committee shall submit each year to the Council and to the Director of Central Intelligence a comprehensive report on its activities during the preceding year, including its activities under paragraphs (3) and (4).

(i)[1] Committee on Transnational Threats

(1) There is established within the National Security Council a committee to be known as the Committee on Transnational Threats (in this subsection referred to as the "Committee").

(2) The Committee shall include the following members:

(A) The Director of Central Intelligence.

(B) The Secretary of State.

(C) The Secretary of Defense.

(D) The Attorney General.

(E) The Assistant to the President for National Security Affairs, who shall serve as the chairperson of the Committee.

(F) Such other members as the President may designate.

(3) The function of the Committee shall be to coordinate and direct the activities of the United States Government relating to combatting transnational threats.

(4) In carrying out its function, the Committee shall—

(A) identify transnational threats;

(B) develop strategies to enable the United States Government to respond to transnational threats identified under subparagraph (A);

(C) monitor implementation of such strategies;

(D) make recommendations as to appropriate responses to specific transnational threats;

(E) assist in the resolution of operational and policy differences among Federal departments and agencies in their responses to transnational threats;

[1] So in original. Another subsec. (i) is set out after subsec. (j).

(F) develop policies and procedures to ensure the effective sharing of information about transnational threats among Federal departments and agencies, including law enforcement agencies and the elements of the intelligence community; and

(G) develop guidelines to enhance and improve the coordination of activities of Federal law enforcement agencies and elements of the intelligence community outside the United States with respect to transnational threats.

(5) For purposes of this subsection, the term "transnational threat" means the following:

(A) Any transnational activity (including international terrorism, narcotics trafficking, the proliferation of weapons of mass destruction and the delivery systems for such weapons, and organized crime) that threatens the national security of the United States.

(B) Any individual or group that engages in an activity referred to in subparagraph (A).

(j) Participation of Director of Central Intelligence

The Director of Central Intelligence (or, in the Director's absence, the Deputy Director of Central Intelligence) may, in the performance of the Director's duties under this Act and subject to the direction of the President, attend and participate in meetings of the National Security Council.

(i)[2] Special Adviser to the President on International Religious Freedom

It is the sense of the Congress that there should be within the staff of the National Security Council a Special Adviser to the President on International Religious Freedom, whose position should be comparable to that of a director within the Executive Office of the President. The Special Adviser should serve as a resource for executive branch officials, compiling and maintaining information on the facts and circumstances of violations of religious freedom (as defined in section 6402 of title 22), and making policy recommendations. The Special Adviser should serve as liaison with the Ambassador at Large for International Religious Freedom, the United States Commission on International Religious Freedom, Congress and, as advisable, religious nongovernmental organizations.

(July 26, 1947, ch. 343, title I, §101, 61 Stat. 496; Aug. 10, 1949, ch. 412, §3, 63 Stat. 579; Oct. 28, 1949, ch. 782, title XI, §1106(a), 63 Stat. 972; Oct. 10, 1951, ch. 479, title V, §501(e)(1), 65 Stat. 378; Pub. L. 99–433, title II, §203, Oct. 1, 1986, 100 Stat. 1011; Pub. L. 99–500, §101(c) [title IX, §9115(f)], Oct. 18, 1986, 100 Stat. 1783–82, 1783–125, and Pub. L. 99–591, §101(c) [title IX, §9115(f)], Oct. 30, 1986, 100 Stat. 3341–82, 3341–125; Pub. L. 99–661, div. A, title XIII, §1311(f), Nov. 14, 1986, 100 Stat. 3986; Pub. L. 100–690, title I, §1003(a)(3), Nov. 18, 1988, 102 Stat. 4182; Pub. L. 102–496, title VII, §703, Oct. 24, 1992, 106 Stat. 3189; Pub. L. 104–293, title VIII, §§802, 804, Oct. 11, 1996, 110 Stat. 3474, 3476; Pub. L. 105–277, div. C, title VII, §713(b), Oct. 21, 1998, 112 Stat. 2681–693; Pub. L. 105–292, title III, §301, Oct. 27, 1998, 112 Stat. 2800.)

[2] So in original. Probably should be "(k)".

REFERENCES IN TEXT

The civil-service laws, referred to in subsec. (c), are set forth in Title 5, Government Organization and Employees. See, particularly, section 3301 et seq. of Title 5.

This Act, referred to in subsec. (j), means act July 26, 1947, ch. 343, 61 Stat. 495, as amended, known as the National Security Act of 1947. For complete classification of this Act to the Code, see Short Title note set out under section 401 of this title and Tables.

CODIFICATION

Pub. L. 99–591 is a corrected version of Pub. L. 99–500.

In subsec. (c), provisions that specified compensation of $10,000 per year for the executive secretary to the Council were omitted. Section 304(b) of Pub. L. 88–426 amended section 105 of Title 3, The President, to include the executive secretary of the Council among those whose compensation was authorized to be fixed by the President. Section 1(a) of Pub. L. 95–570 further amended section 105 of Title 3 to authorize the President to appoint and fix the pay of the employees of the White House Office subject to certain provisions.

In subsec. (c), "chapter 51 and subchapter III of chapter 53 of title 5" substituted for "the Classification Act of 1949, as amended" on authority of Pub. L. 89–554, §7(b), Sept. 6, 1966, 80 Stat. 631, the first section of which enacted Title 5, Government Organization and Employees.

AMENDMENTS

1998—Subsecs. (f), (g). Pub. L. 105–277 added subsec. (f) and redesignated former subsec. (f) as (g).

Subsec. (i). Pub. L. 105–292 added subsec. (i) relating to Special Adviser to the President on International Religious Freedom.

1996—Subsec. (h). Pub. L. 104–293, §802(2), added subsec. (h). Former subsec. (h) redesignated (j).

Subsec. (i). Pub. L. 104–293, §804, added subsec. (i).

Subsec. (j). Pub. L. 104–293, §802(1), redesignated subsec. (h) as (j).

1992—Subsec. (h). Pub. L. 102–496 added subsec. (h).

1988—Subsecs. (f), (g). Pub. L. 100–690, §§1003(a)(3), 1009, temporarily added subsec. (f), relating to participation by Director of National Drug Control Policy in meetings of National Security Council, and redesignated former subsec. (f) as (g). See Effective and Termination Dates of 1988 Amendment note below.

1986—Subsec. (e). Pub. L. 99–433 added subsec. (e).

Subsec. (f). Pub. L. 99–500, Pub. L. 99–591, and Pub. L. 99–661 amended section identically adding subsec. (f).

1951—Subsec. (a). Act Oct. 10, 1951, inserted cl. (5) relating to Director for Mutual Security, in fourth paragraph, and renumbered former cls. (5) and (6) thereof as cls. (6) and (7), respectively.

1949—Subsec. (a). Act Aug. 10, 1949, added the Vice President to the Council, removed the Secretaries of the military departments, to authorize the President to add, with the consent of the Senate, Secretaries and Under Secretaries of other executive departments and of the military department, and the Chairmen of the Munitions Board and the Research and Development Board.

Subsec. (c). Act Oct. 28, 1949, substituted "Classification Act of 1949" for "Classification Act of 1923, as amended".

EFFECTIVE AND TERMINATION DATES OF 1988 AMENDMENT

Amendment by Pub. L. 100–690 effective Jan. 21, 1989, and repealed on Sept. 30, 1997, see sections 1012 and 1009, respectively, of Pub. L. 100–690.

REPEALS

Act Oct. 28, 1949, ch. 782, cited as a credit to this section, was repealed (subject to a savings clause) by Pub. L. 89–554, Sept. 6, 1966, §8, 80 Stat. 632, 655.

TRANSFER OF FUNCTIONS

Office of Director for Mutual Security abolished and functions of Director, including those as a member of

National Security Council, transferred to Director of Foreign Operations Administration by Reorg. Plan No. 7 of 1953, eff. Aug. 1, 1953, 18 F.R. 4541, set out in the Appendix to Title 5, Government Organization and Employees. Foreign Operations Administration abolished by Ex. Ord. No. 10610, May 9, 1955, 20 F.R. 3179, and its functions and offices transferred to Department of State to be administered by International Cooperation Administration. For later transfer, see section 2381 of Title 22, Foreign Relations and Intercourse, and notes set out under that section.

National Security Resources Board, together with Office of Chairman, abolished by section 6 of Reorg. Plan No. 3 of 1953, eff. June 12, 1953, 18 F.R. 3375, 67 Stat. 634, set out under section 404 of this title. Functions of Chairman with limited exception, including his functions as a member of National Security Council transferred to Office of Defense Mobilization by section 2(a) of Reorg. Plan No. 3 of 1953. Functions of Director of Office of Defense Mobilization with respect to being a member of National Security Council transferred to Director of Office of Civil and Defense Mobilization by Reorg. Plan No. 1 of 1958, §4, eff. July 1, 1958, 23 F.R. 4991, 72 Stat. 1799, as amended by Pub. L. 85–763, Aug. 26, 1958, 72 Stat. 861, set out as a note under section 5195 of Title 42, The Public Health and Welfare. For subsequent transfers to Office of Emergency Planning, Office of Emergency Preparedness, and President, see Transfer of Functions notes set out under section 404 of this title.

Munitions Board, together with office of Chairman, abolished by section 2 of Reorg. Plan No. 6 of 1953, eff. June 30, 1953, 18 F.R. 3743, 67 Stat. 638, set out in the Appendix to Title 5, Government Organization and Employees. All functions vested in Munitions Board transferred to Secretary of Defense by section 1(a) of Reorg. Plan No. 6 of 1953.

Research and Development Board, together with office of Chairman, abolished by section 2 of Reorg. Plan No. 6 of 1953, eff. June 30, 1953, 18 F.R. 3743, 67 Stat. 638, set out in the Appendix to Title 5, Government Organization and Employees. Functions vested in Board transferred to Secretary of Defense by section 1(a) of Reorg. Plan No. 6 of 1953.

National Security Council, together with its functions, records, property, personnel, and unexpended balances of appropriations, allocations, and other funds (available or to be made available) transferred to Executive Office of President by Reorg. Plan No. 4 of 1949, eff. Aug. 20, 1949, 14 F.R. 5227, 63 Stat. 1067, set out in the Appendix to Title 5, Government Organization and Employees.

Rule of Construction for Duplicate Authorization and Appropriation Provisions of Public Laws 99–500, 99–591, and 99–661

For rule of construction for certain duplicate provisions of Public Laws 99–500, 99–591, and 99–661, see section 6 of Pub. L. 100–26, set out as a note under section 2302 of Title 10, Armed Forces.

Section as Unaffected by Repeals

Repeals by section 542(a) of Mutual Security Act of 1954 did not repeal amendment to this section by act Oct. 10, 1951.

National Security Agency Act of 1959

Pub. L. 86–36, May 29, 1959, 73 Stat. 63, as amended by Pub. L. 87–367, title II, §§201, 204, Oct. 4, 1961, 75 Stat. 789, 791; Pub. L. 87–793, §1001(c), Oct. 11, 1962, 76 Stat. 864; Sept. 23, 1950, ch. 1024, title III, §306(a), as added Mar. 26, 1964, Pub. L. 88–290, 78 Stat. 170; Aug. 14, 1964, Pub. L. 88–426, title III, §306(h), 78 Stat. 430; Oct. 6, 1964, Pub. L. 88–631, §3(d), 78 Stat. 1008; Sept. 6, 1966, Pub. L. 89–554, §8(a), 80 Stat. 660; Oct. 8, 1966, Pub. L. 89–632, §1(e), 80 Stat. 878; Pub. L. 91–187, §2, Dec. 30, 1969, 83 Stat. 850; Pub. L. 96–450, title IV, §402(a), Oct. 14, 1980, 94 Stat. 1977; Pub. L. 97–89, title VI, §§601–603, Dec. 4, 1981, 95 Stat. 1154–1156, eff. Oct. 1, 1981; Pub. L. 99–335, title V, §507(a), June 6, 1986, 100 Stat. 628; Pub. L. 99–569, title V, §505, Oct. 27, 1986, 100 Stat. 3200; Pub. L. 101–193, title V, §505(b), Nov. 30, 1989, 103 Stat. 1709; Pub. L. 101–194, title V, §506(c)(2), Nov. 30, 1989, 103 Stat. 1759; Pub. L. 102–88, title V, §503, Aug. 14, 1991, 105 Stat. 436; Pub. L. 102–183, title IV, §405, Dec. 4, 1991, 105 Stat. 1267; Pub. L. 102–496, title III, §304(a), title IV, §405, title VIII, §803(b), Oct. 24, 1992, 106 Stat. 3183, 3186, 3253; Pub. L. 103–359, title VIII, §806(b)(2), Oct. 14, 1994, 108 Stat. 3442; Pub. L. 104–106, div. A, title X, §1064(b), Feb. 10, 1996, 110 Stat. 445; Pub. L. 104–201, div. A, title XVI, §1633(b)(1), Sept. 23, 1996, 110 Stat. 2751, provided: "That this Act [this note] may be cited as the 'National Security Agency Act of 1959'. [Amended Pub. L. 89–554, §8(a), Sept. 6, 1966, 80 Stat. 660; Pub. L. 96–450, title IV, §402(a)(2), Oct. 14, 1980, 94 Stat. 1978.]

"[Sec. 2. Repealed. Pub. L. 104–201, div. A, title XVI, §1633(b)(1), Sept. 23, 1996, 110 Stat. 2751.]

"Sec. 3. [Amended section 1581(a) of Title 10, Armed Forces.]

"[Sec. 4. Repealed. Pub. L. 104–201, div. A, title XVI, §1633(b)(1), Sept. 23, 1996, 110 Stat. 2751.]

"Sec. 5. Officers and employees of the National Security Agency who are citizens or nationals of the United States may be granted additional compensation, in accordance with regulations which shall be prescribed by the Secretary of Defense, not in excess of additional compensation authorized by section 207 of the Independent Offices Appropriation Act, 1949, as amended (5 U.S.C. 118h) [see 5 U.S.C. 5941], for employees whose rates of basic compensation are fixed by statute.

"Sec. 6. (a) Except as provided in subsection (b) of this section, nothing in this Act or any other law (including, but not limited to, the first section and section 2 of the Act of August 28, 1935 (5 U.S.C. 654) [repealed by Pub. L. 86–626, title I, §101, July 12, 1960, 74 Stat. 427]) shall be construed to require the disclosure of the organization or any function of the National Security Agency, or any information with respect to the activities thereof, or of the names, titles, salaries, or number of the persons employed by such agency.

"(b) The reporting requirements of section 1582 of title 10, United States Code, shall apply to positions established in the National Security Agency in the manner provided by section 4 of this Act.

"[Sec. 7. Repealed. Pub. L. 89–554, §8(a), Sept. 6, 1966, 80 Stat. 660.]

"Sec. 8. The foregoing provisions of this Act shall take effect on the first day of the first pay period which begins later than the thirtieth day following the date of enactment of this Act [May 29, 1959].

"Sec. 9. (a) Notwithstanding section 322 of the Act of June 30, 1932 (40 U.S.C. 278a), section 5536 of title 5, United States Code, and section 2675 of title 10, United States Code, the Director of the National Security Agency, on behalf of the Secretary of Defense, may lease real property outside the United States, for periods not exceeding ten years, for the use of the National Security Agency for special cryptologic activities and for housing for personnel assigned to such activities.

"(b) The Director of the National Security Agency, on behalf of the Secretary of Defense, may provide to certain civilian and military personnel of the Department of Defense who are assigned to special cryptologic activities outside the United States and who are designated by the Secretary of Defense for the purposes of this subsection—

"(1) allowances and benefits—

"(A) comparable to those provided by the Secretary of State to members of the Foreign Service under chapter 9 of title I of the Foreign Service Act of 1980 (22 U.S.C. 4081 et seq.) or any other provision of law; and

"(B) in the case of selected personnel serving in circumstances similar to those in which personnel of the Central Intelligence Agency serve, comparable to those provided by the Director of Central Intelligence to personnel of the Central Intelligence Agency;

"(2) housing (including heat, light, and household equipment) without cost to such personnel, if the Director of the National Security Agency, on behalf of the Secretary of Defense determines that it would be in the public interest to provide such housing; and

"(3) special retirement accrual in the same manner provided in section 303 of the Central Intelligence Agency Retirement Act (50 U.S.C. 403 note) [50 U.S.C. 2001 et seq.] and in section 18 of the Central Intelligence Agency Act of 1949 [50 U.S.C. 403r].

"(c) The authority of the Director of the National Security Agency, on behalf of the Secretary of Defense, to make payments under subsections (a) and (b), and under contracts for leases entered into under subsection (a), is effective for any fiscal year only to the extent that appropriated funds are available for such purpose.

"(d) Members of the Armed Forces may not receive benefits under both subsection (b)(1) and title 37, United States Code, for the same purpose. The Secretary of Defense shall prescribe such regulations as may be necessary to carry out this subsection.

"(e) Regulations issued pursuant to subsection (b)(1) shall be submitted to the Permanent Select Committee on Intelligence of the House of Representatives and the Select Committee on Intelligence of the Senate before such regulations take effect.

[Amended Pub. L. 102–496, title VIII, §803(b), Oct. 24, 1992, 106 Stat. 3253. Amendment by Pub. L. 102–496 effective on first day of fourth month beginning after Oct. 24, 1992, see section 805 of Pub. L. 102–496, set out as an Effective Date note under section 2001 of this title.]

[Amended Pub. L. 101–193, title V, §505(b), Nov. 30, 1989, 103 Stat. 1709.]

[Amended Pub. L. 99–335, title V, §507(a), June 6, 1986, 100 Stat. 628. Amendment by Pub. L. 99–335 effective Jan. 1, 1987, see section 702(a) of Pub. L. 99–335, set out as an Effective Date note under section 8401 of Title 5, Government Organization and Employees.]

[Amended Pub. L. 97–89, title VI, §601, Dec. 4, 1981, 95 Stat. 1154.]

[Added Pub. L. 96–450, title IV, §401(a)(1), Oct. 14, 1980, 94 Stat. 1977.]

"SEC. 10. (a) The Director of the National Security Agency shall arrange for, and shall prescribe regulations concerning, language and language-related training programs for military and civilian cryptologic personnel. In establishing programs under this section for language and language-related training, the Director—

"(1) may provide for the training and instruction to be furnished, including functional and geographic area specializations;

"(2) may arrange for training and instruction through other Government agencies and, in any case in which appropriate training or instruction is unavailable through Government facilities, through nongovernmental facilities that furnish training and instruction useful in the fields of language and foreign affairs;

"(3) may support programs that furnish necessary language and language-related skills, including, in any case in which appropriate programs are unavailable at Government facilities, support through contracts, grants, or cooperation with nongovernmental educational institutions; and

"(4) may obtain by appointment or contract the services of individuals to serve as language instructors, linguists, or special language project personnel.

"(b)(1) In order to maintain necessary capability in foreign language skills and related abilities needed by the National Security Agency, the Director, without regard to subchapter IV of chapter 55 of title 5, United States Code, may provide special monetary or other incentives to encourage civilian cryptologic personnel of the Agency to acquire or retain proficiency in foreign languages or special related abilities needed by the Agency.

"(2) In order to provide linguistic training and support for cryptologic personnel, the Director—

"(A) may pay all or part of the tuition and other expenses related to the training of personnel who are assigned or detailed for language and language-related training, orientation, or instruction; and

"(B) may pay benefits and allowances to civilian personnel in accordance with chapters 57 and 59 of title 5, United States Code, and to military personnel in accordance with chapter 7 of title 37, United States Code, and applicable provisions of title 10, United States Code, when such personnel are assigned to training at sites away from their designated duty station.

"(c)(1) To the extent not inconsistent, in the opinion of the Secretary of Defense, with the operation of military cryptologic reserve units and in order to maintain necessary capability in foreign language skills and related abilities needed by the National Security Agency, the Director may establish a cryptologic linguist reserve. The cryptologic linguist reserve may consist of former or retired civilian or military cryptologic personnel of the National Security Agency and of other qualified individuals, as determined by the Director of the Agency. Each member of the cryptologic linguist reserve shall agree that, during any period of emergency (as determined by the Director), the member shall return to active civilian status with the National Security Agency and shall perform such linguistic or linguistic-related duties as the Director may assign.

"(2) In order to attract individuals to become members of the cryptologic linguist reserve, the Director, without regard to subchapter IV of chapter 55 of title 5, United States Code, may provide special monetary incentives to individuals eligible to become members of the reserve who agree to become members of the cryptologic linguist reserve and to acquire or retain proficiency in foreign languages or special related abilities.

"(3) In order to provide training and support for members of the cryptologic linguist reserve, the Director—

"(A) may pay all or part of the tuition and other expenses related to the training of individuals in the cryptologic linguist reserve who are assigned or detailed for language and language-related training, orientation, or instruction; and

"(B) may pay benefits and allowances in accordance with chapters 57 and 59 of title 5, United States Code, to individuals in the cryptologic linguist reserve who are assigned to training at sites away from their homes or regular places of business.

"(d)(1) The Director, before providing training under this section to any individual, may obtain an agreement with that individual that—

"(A) in the case of current employees, pertains to continuation of service of the employee, and repayment of the expenses of such training for failure to fulfill the agreement, consistent with the provisions of section 4108 of title 5, United States Code; and

"(B) in the case of individuals accepted for membership in the cryptologic linguist reserve, pertains to return to service when requested, and repayment of the expenses of such training for failure to fulfill the agreement, consistent with the provisions of section 4108 of title 5, United States Code.

"(2) The Director, under regulations prescribed under this section, may waive, in whole or in part, a right of recovery under an agreement made under this subsection if it is shown that the recovery would be against equity and good conscience or against the public interest.

"(e)(1) Subject to paragraph (2), the Director may provide to family members of military and civilian cryptologic personnel assigned to representational duties outside the United States, in anticipation of the assignment of such personnel outside the United States or while outside the United States, appropriate orientation and language training that is directly related to the assignment abroad.

"(2) Language training under paragraph (1) may not be provided to any individual through payment of the expenses of tuition or other cost of instruction at a non-Government educational institution unless appropriate instruction is not available at a Government facility.

"(f) The Director may waive the applicability of any provision of chapter 41 of title 5, United States Code, to any provision of this section if he finds that such waiver is important to the performance of cryptologic functions.

"(g) The authority of the Director to enter into contracts or to make grants under this section is effective for any fiscal year only to the extent that appropriated funds are available for such purpose.

"(h) Regulations issued pursuant to this section shall be submitted to the Permanent Select Committee on Intelligence of the House of Representatives and the Select Committee on Intelligence of the Senate before such regulations take effect.

"(i) The Director of the National Security Agency, on behalf of the Secretary of Defense, may, without regard to section 4109(a)(2)(B) of title 5, United States Code, pay travel, transportation, storage, and subsistence expenses under chapter 57 of such title to civilian and military personnel of the Department of Defense who are assigned to duty outside the United States for a period of one year or longer which involves cryptologic training, language training, or related disciplines. [Added Pub. L. 96–450, title IV, §402(a)(1), Oct. 14, 1980, 94 Stat. 1978, and amended Pub. L. 97–89, title VI, §602, Dec. 4, 1981, 95 Stat. 1154.]

"SEC. 11. The Administrator of General Services, upon the application of the Director of the National Security Agency, may provide for the protection in accordance with section 3 of the Act of June 1, 1948 (40 U.S.C. 318b), of certain facilities (as designated by the Director of such Agency) which are under the administration and control of, or are used by, the National Security Agency in the same manner as if such facilities were property of the United States over which the United States has acquired exclusive or concurrent criminal jurisdiction. [Added Pub. L. 96–450, title IV, §402(a)(1), Oct. 14, 1980, 94 Stat. 1978.]

"SEC. 12. (a)(1) The Secretary of Defense (or his designee) may by regulation establish a personnel system for senior civilian cryptologic personnel in the National Security Agency to be known as the Senior Cryptologic Executive Service. The regulations establishing the Senior Cryptologic Executive Service shall—

"(A) meet the requirements set forth in section 3131 of title 5, United States Code, for the Senior Executive Service;

"(B) provide that positions in the Senior Cryptologic Executive Service meet requirements that are consistent with the provisions of section 3132(a)(2) of such title;

"(C) provide, without regard to section 2, rates of pay for the Senior Cryptologic Executive Service that are not in excess of the maximum rate or less than the minimum rate of basic pay established for the Senior Executive Service under section 5382 of such title, and that are adjusted at the same time and to the same extent as rates of basic pay for the Senior Executive Service are adjusted;

"(D) provide a performance appraisal system for the Senior Cryptologic Executive Service that conforms to the provisions of subchapter II of chapter 43 of such title;

"(E) provide for removal consistent with section 3592 of such title, and removal or suspension consistent with subsections (a), (b), and (c) of section 7543 of such title (except that any hearing or appeal to which a member of the Senior Cryptologic Executive Service is entitled shall be held or decided pursuant to procedures established by regulations of the Secretary of Defense or his designee);

"(F) permit the payment of performance awards to members of the Senior Cryptologic Executive Service consistent with the provisions applicable to performance awards under section 5384 of such title;

"(G) provide that members of the Senior Cryptologic Executive Service may be granted sabbatical leaves consistent with the provisions of section 3396(c) of such title.[;] and

"(H) provide for the recertification of members of the Senior Cryptologic Executive Service consistent with the provisions of section 3393a of such title.

"(2) Except as otherwise provided in subsection (a), the Secretary of Defense (or his designee) may—

"(A) make applicable to the Senior Cryptologic Executive Service any of the provisions of title 5, United States Code, applicable to applicants for or members of the Senior Executive Service; and

"(B) appoint, promote, and assign individuals to positions established within the Senior Cryptologic Executive Service without regard to the provisions of title 5, United States Code, governing appointments and other personnel actions in the competitive service.

"(3) The President, based on the recommendations of the Secretary of Defense, may award ranks to members of the Senior Cryptologic Executive Service in a manner consistent with the provisions of section 4507 of title 5, United States Code.

"(4) Notwithstanding any other provision of this section, the Director of the National Security Agency may detail or assign any member of the Senior Cryptologic Executive Service to serve in a position outside the National Security Agency in which the member's expertise and experience may be of benefit to the National Security Agency or another Government agency. Any such member shall not by reason of such detail or assignment lose any entitlement or status associated with membership in the Senior Cryptologic Executive Service.

[Amended Pub. L. 104–106, div. A, title X, §1064(b), Feb. 10, 1996, 110 Stat. 445.]

[Amended Pub. L. 101–194, title V, §506(c)(2), Nov. 30, 1989, 103 Stat. 1759. Amendment by Pub. L. 101–194 effective Jan. 1, 1991, see section 506(d) of Pub. L. 101–194, set out as an Effective Date of 1989 Amendment note under section 3151 of Title 5, Government Organization and Employees.]

"SEC. 13. (a) The Director of the National Security Agency may make grants to private individuals and institutions for the conduct of cryptologic research. An application for a grant under this section may not be approved unless the Director determines that the award of the grant would be clearly consistent with the national security.

"(b) The grant program established by subsection (a) shall be conducted in accordance with the Federal Grant and Cooperative Agreement Act of 1977 (41 U.S.C. 501 et seq.) [31 U.S.C. 6301 et seq.] to the extent that such Act is consistent with and in accordance with section 6 of this Act.

"(c) The authority of the Director to make grants under this section is effective for any fiscal year only to the extent that appropriated funds are available for such purpose. [Added Pub. L. 97–89, title VI, §603, Dec. 4, 1981, 95 Stat. 1156.]

"SEC. 14. Funds appropriated to an entity of the Federal Government other than an element of the Department of Defense that have been specifically appropriated for the purchase of cryptologic equipment, materials, or services with respect to which the National Security Agency has been designated as the central source of procurement for the Government shall remain available for a period of three fiscal years. [Added Pub. L. 97–89, title VI, §603, Dec. 4, 1981, 95 Stat. 1156.]

"SEC. 15. (a) No person may, except with the written permission of the Director of the National Security Agency, knowingly use the words 'National Security Agency', the initials 'NSA', the seal of the National Security Agency, or any colorable imitation of such words, initials, or seal in connection with any merchandise, impersonation, solicitation, or commercial activity in a manner reasonably calculated to convey the impression that such use is approved, endorsed, or authorized by the National Security Agency.

"(b) Whenever it appears to the Attorney General that any person is engaged or is about to engage in an act or practice which constitutes or will constitute conduct prohibited by subsection (a), the Attorney

General may initiate a civil proceeding in a district court of the United States to enjoin such act or practice. Such court shall proceed as soon as practicable to the hearing and determination of such action and may, at any time before final determination, enter such restraining orders or prohibitions, or take such other action as is warranted, to prevent injury to the United States or to any person or class of persons for whose protection the action is brought. [Added Pub. L. 97–89, title VI, §603, Dec. 4, 1981, 95 Stat. 1156.]

"SEC. 16. (a) The purpose of this section is to establish an undergraduate training program, which may lead to the baccalaureate degree, to facilitate the recruitment of individuals, particularly minority high school students, with a demonstrated capability to develop skills critical to the mission of the National Security Agency, including mathematics, computer science, engineering, and foreign languages.

"(b) The Secretary of Defense is authorized, in his discretion, to assign civilian employees of the National Security Agency as students at accredited professional, technical, and other institutions of higher learning for training at the undergraduate level in skills critical to effective performance of the mission of the Agency.

"(c) The National Security Agency may pay, directly or by reimbursement to employees, expenses incident to assignments under subsection (b), in any fiscal year only to the extent that appropriated funds are available for such purpose.

"(d)(1) To be eligible for assignment under subsection (b), an employee of the Agency must agree in writing—

"(A) to continue in the service of the Agency for the period of the assignment and to complete the educational course of training for which the employee is assigned;

"(B) to continue in the service of the Agency following completion of the assignment for a period of one-and-a-half years for each year of the assignment or part thereof;

"(C) to reimburse the United States for the total cost of education (excluding the employee's pay and allowances) provided under this section to the employee if, prior to the employee's completing the educational course of training for which the employee is assigned, the assignment or the employee's employment with the Agency is terminated either by the Agency due to misconduct by the employee or by the employee voluntarily; and

"(D) to reimburse the United States if, after completing the educational course of training for which the employee is assigned, the employee's employment with the Agency is terminated either by the Agency due to misconduct by the employee or by the employee voluntarily, prior to the employee's completion of the service obligation period described in subparagraph (B), in an amount that bears the same ratio to the total cost of the education (excluding the employee's pay and allowances) provided to the employee as the unserved portion of the service obligation period described in subparagraph (B) bears to the total period of the service obligation described in subparagraph (B).

"(2) Subject to paragraph (3), the obligation to reimburse the United States under an agreement described in paragraph (1), including interest due on such obligation, is for all purposes a debt owing the United States.

"(3)(A) A discharge in bankruptcy under title 11, United States Code, shall not release a person from an obligation to reimburse the United States required under an agreement described in paragraph (1) if the final decree of the discharge in bankruptcy is issued within five years after the last day of the combined period of service obligation described in subparagraphs (A) and (B) of paragraph (1).

"(B) The Secretary of Defense may release a person, in whole or in part, from the obligation to reimburse the United States under an agreement described in paragraph (1) when, in his discretion, the Secretary determines that equity or the interests of the United States so require.

"(C) The Secretary of Defense shall permit an employee assigned under this section who, prior to commencing a second academic year of such assignment, voluntarily terminates the assignment or the employee's employment with the Agency, to satisfy his obligation under an agreement described in paragraph (1) to reimburse the United States by reimbursement according to a schedule of monthly payments which results in completion of reimbursement by a date five years after the date of termination of the assignment or employment or earlier at the option of the employee.

"(e)(1) When an employee is assigned under this section to an institution, the Agency shall disclose to the institution to which the employee is assigned that the Agency employs the employee and that the Agency funds the employee's education.

"(2) Agency efforts to recruit individuals at educational institutions for participation in the undergraduate training program established by this section shall be made openly and according to the common practices of universities and employers recruiting at such institutions.

"(f) Chapter 41 of title 5 and subsections (a) and (b) of section 3324 of title 31, United States Code, shall not apply with respect to this section.

"(g) The Secretary of Defense may issue such regulations as may be necessary to implement this section. [Added Pub. L. 99–569, title V, §505, Oct. 27, 1986, 100 Stat. 3200.]

"[SEC. 17. Repealed. Pub. L. 103–359, title VIII, §806(b)(2), Oct. 14, 1994, 108 Stat. 3442.]

"SEC. 18. (a) The Secretary of Defense may pay the expenses referred to in section 5742(b) of title 5, United States Code, in the case of any employee of the National Security Agency who dies while on a rotational tour of duty within the United States or while in transit to or from such tour of duty.

"(b) For the purposes of this section, the term 'rotational tour of duty', with respect to an employee, means a permanent change of station involving the transfer of the employee from the National Security Agency headquarters to another post of duty for a fixed period established by regulation to be followed at the end of such period by a permanent change of station involving a transfer of the employee back to such headquarters." [Added Pub. L. 102–183, title IV, §405, Dec. 4, 1991, 105 Stat. 1267; amended Pub. L. 102–496, title III, §304(a), Oct. 24, 1992, 106 Stat. 3183.]

EXECUTIVE ORDER NO. 10483

Ex. Ord. No. 10483, Sept. 2, 1953, 18 F.R. 5379, as amended by Ex. Ord. No. 10598, Feb. 28, 1955, 20 F.R. 1237, which provided for an Operations Coordinating Board, was superseded by Ex. Ord. No. 10700, Feb. 25, 1957, formerly set out below.

EXECUTIVE ORDER NO. 10700

Ex. Ord. No. 10700, Feb. 25, 1957, 22 F.R. 1111, as amended by Ex. Ord. No. 10773, July 1, 1958, 23 F.R. 5061; Ex. Ord. No. 10782, Sept. 6, 1958, 23 F.R. 6971; Ex. Ord. 10838, Sept. 16, 1959, 24 F.R. 7519, which provided for the Operations Coordinating Board, was revoked by Ex. Ord. No. 10920, Feb. 18, 1961, 26 F.R. 1463.

SECTION REFERRED TO IN OTHER SECTIONS

This section is referred to in title 22 section 6402.

§402a. Coordination of counterintelligence activities

(a) Establishment of Counterintelligence Policy Board

There is established within the executive branch of Government a National Counterintelligence Policy Board (in this section referred to as the "Board"). The Board shall report to the President through the National Security Council.

(b) Function of Board

The Board shall serve as the principal mechanism for—

(1) developing policies and procedures for the approval of the President to govern the conduct of counterintelligence activities; and

(2) resolving conflicts, as directed by the President, which may arise between elements of the Government which carry out such activities.

(c) Coordination of counterintelligence matters with Federal Bureau of Investigation

(1) Except as provided in paragraph (5), the head of each department or agency within the executive branch shall ensure that—

(A) the Federal Bureau of Investigation is advised immediately of any information, regardless of its origin, which indicates that classified information is being, or may have been, disclosed in an unauthorized manner to a foreign power or an agent of a foreign power;

(B) following a report made pursuant to subparagraph (A), the Federal Bureau of Investigation is consulted with respect to all subsequent actions which may be undertaken by the department or agency concerned to determine the source of such loss or compromise; and

(C) where, after appropriate consultation with the department or agency concerned, the Federal Bureau of Investigation undertakes investigative activities to determine the source of the loss or compromise, the Federal Bureau of Investigation is given complete and timely access to the employees and records of the department or agency concerned for purposes of such investigative activities.

(2) Except as provided in paragraph (5), the Director of the Federal Bureau of Investigation shall ensure that espionage information obtained by the Federal Bureau of Investigation pertaining to the personnel, operations, or information of departments or agencies of the executive branch, is provided through appropriate channels in a timely manner to the department or agency concerned, and that such departments or agencies are consulted in a timely manner with respect to espionage investigations undertaken by the Federal Bureau of Investigation which involve the personnel, operations, or information of such department or agency.

(3)(A) The Director of the Federal Bureau of Investigation shall submit to the head of the department or agency concerned a written assessment of the potential impact of the actions of the department or agency on a counterintelligence investigation.

(B) The head of the department or agency concerned shall—

(i) use an assessment under subparagraph (A) as an aid in determining whether, and under what circumstances, the subject of an investigation under paragraph (1) should be left in place for investigative purposes; and

(ii) notify in writing the Director of the Federal Bureau of Investigation of such determination.

(C) The Director of the Federal Bureau of Investigation and the head of the department or agency concerned shall continue to consult, as appropriate, to review the status of an investigation covered by this paragraph, and to reassess, as appropriate, a determination of the head of the department or agency concerned to leave a subject in place for investigative purposes.

(4)(A) The Federal Bureau of Investigation shall notify appropriate officials within the executive branch, including the head of the department or agency concerned, of the commencement of a full field espionage investigation with respect to an employee within the executive branch.

(B) A department or agency may not conduct a polygraph examination, interrogate, or otherwise take any action that is likely to alert an employee covered by a notice under subparagraph (A) of an investigation described in that subparagraph without prior coordination and consultation with the Federal Bureau of Investigation.

(5) Where essential to meet extraordinary circumstances affecting vital national security interests of the United States, the President may on a case-by-case basis waive the requirements of paragraph (1), (2), or (3), as they apply to the head of a particular department or agency, or the Director of the Federal Bureau of Investigation. Such waiver shall be in writing and shall fully state the justification for such waiver. Within thirty days, the President shall notify the Select Committee on Intelligence of the Senate and the Permanent Select Committee on Intelligence of the House of Representatives that such waiver has been issued, and at that time or as soon as national security considerations permit, provide these committees with a complete explanation of the circumstances which necessitated such waiver.

(6) The Director of the Federal Bureau of Investigation shall, in consultation with the Director of Central Intelligence and the Secretary of Defense, report annually, beginning on February 1, 1995, and continuing each year thereafter, to the Select Committee on Intelligence of the Senate and to the Permanent Select Committee on Intelligence of the House of Representatives and, in accordance with applicable security procedures, the Committees on the Judiciary of the House of Representatives and the Senate with respect to compliance with paragraphs (1) and (2) during the previous calendar year.

(7) Nothing in this section may be construed to alter the existing jurisdictional arrangements between the Federal Bureau of Investigation and the Department of Defense with respect to investigations of persons subject to the Uniform Code of Military Justice, nor to impose additional reporting requirements upon the Department of Defense with respect to such investigations beyond those required by existing law and executive branch policy.

(8) As used in this section, the terms "foreign power" and "agent of a foreign power" have the same meanings as set forth in sections[1] 1801(a) and (b), respectively, of this title.

(Pub. L. 103–359, title VIII, § 811, Oct. 14, 1994, 108 Stat. 3455; Pub. L. 106–120, title VI, § 602, Dec. 3,

[1] So in original. Probably should be "section".

1999, 113 Stat. 1620; Pub. L. 106–567, title VI, §605, Dec. 27, 2000, 114 Stat. 2853.)

CODIFICATION

Section was enacted as part of the Counterintelligence and Security Enhancements Act of 1994 and also as part of the Intelligence Authorization Act for Fiscal Year 1995, and not as part of the National Security Act of 1947 which comprises this chapter.

AMENDMENTS

2000—Subsec. (c)(1). Pub. L. 106–567, §605(a)(1), substituted "paragraph (5)" for "paragraph (3)".

Subsec. (c)(2). Pub. L. 106–567, §605(a)(1), (b), substituted "paragraph (5)" for "paragraph (3)" and inserted "in a timely manner" after "through appropriate channels" and "are consulted".

Subsec. (c)(3). Pub. L. 106–567, §605(a)(3), added par. (3). Former par. (3) redesignated (5).

Subsec. (c)(4). Pub. L. 106–567, §605(a), (c), added par. (4). Former par. (4) redesignated (6).

Subsec. (c)(5). Pub. L. 106–567, §605(a)(2), (4), redesignated par. (3) as (5) and substituted "paragraph (1), (2), or (3)" for "paragraph (1) or (2)". Former par. (5) redesignated (7).

Subsec. (c)(6) to (8). Pub. L. 106–567, §605(a)(2), redesignated pars. (4) to (6) as (6) to (8), respectively.

1999—Subsec. (c)(2). Pub. L. 106–120 struck out "after a report has been provided pursuant to paragraph (1)(A)" before period at end.

ANNUAL REPORTS ON INTELLIGENCE ACTIVITIES OF THE PEOPLE'S REPUBLIC OF CHINA

Pub. L. 105–107, title III, §308, Nov. 20, 1997, 111 Stat. 2253, provided that:

"(a) REPORT TO CONGRESS.—Not later than 90 days after the date of enactment of this Act [Nov. 20, 1997] and annually thereafter, the Director of Central Intelligence and the Director of the Federal Bureau of Investigation, jointly and in consultation with the heads of other appropriate Federal agencies, including the National Security Agency and the Departments of Defense, Justice, Treasury, and State, shall prepare and transmit to Congress a report on intelligence activities of the People's Republic of China directed against or affecting the interests of the United States.

"(b) DELIVERY OF REPORT.—The Director of Central Intelligence and the Director of the Federal Bureau of Investigation shall jointly transmit classified and unclassified versions of the report to the Speaker and Minority leader of the House of Representatives, the Majority and Minority leaders of the Senate, the Chairman and Ranking Member of the Permanent Select Committee on Intelligence of the House of Representatives, and the Chairman and Vice-Chairman of the Select Committee on Intelligence of the Senate."

§403. Office of the Director of Central Intelligence

(a) Director of Central Intelligence

There is a Director of Central Intelligence who shall be appointed by the President, by and with the advice and consent of the Senate. The Director shall—

(1) serve as head of the United States intelligence community;

(2) act as the principal adviser to the President for intelligence matters related to the national security; and

(3) serve as head of the Central Intelligence Agency.

(b) Deputy Directors of Central Intelligence

(1) There is a Deputy Director of Central Intelligence who shall be appointed by the President, by and with the advice and consent of the Senate.

(2) There is a Deputy Director of Central Intelligence for Community Management who shall be appointed by the President, by and with the advice and consent of the Senate.

(3) Each Deputy Director of Central Intelligence shall have extensive national security expertise.

(c) Military status of Director and Deputy Directors

(1)(A) Not more than one of the individuals serving in the positions specified in subparagraph (B) may be a commissioned officer of the Armed Forces, whether in active or retired status.

(B) The positions referred to in subparagraph (A) are the following:

(i) The Director of Central Intelligence.

(ii) The Deputy Director of Central Intelligence.

(iii) The Deputy Director of Central Intelligence for Community Management.

(2) It is the sense of Congress that, under ordinary circumstances, it is desirable that one of the individuals serving in the positions specified in paragraph (1)(B)—

(A) be a commissioned officer of the Armed Forces, whether in active or retired status; or

(B) have, by training or experience, an appreciation of military intelligence activities and requirements.

(3) A commissioned officer of the Armed Forces, while serving in a position specified in paragraph (1)(B)—

(A) shall not be subject to supervision or control by the Secretary of Defense or by any officer or employee of the Department of Defense;

(B) shall not exercise, by reason of the officer's status as a commissioned officer, any supervision or control with respect to any of the military or civilian personnel of the Department of Defense except as otherwise authorized by law; and

(C) shall not be counted against the numbers and percentages of commissioned officers of the rank and grade of such officer authorized for the military department of that officer.

(4) Except as provided in subparagraph (A) or (B) of paragraph (3), the appointment of an officer of the Armed Forces to a position specified in paragraph (1)(B) shall not affect the status, position, rank, or grade of such officer in the Armed Forces, or any emolument, perquisite, right, privilege, or benefit incident to or arising out of any such status, position, rank, or grade.

(5) A commissioned officer of the Armed Forces on active duty who is appointed to a position specified in paragraph (1)(B), while serving in such position and while remaining on active duty, shall continue to receive military pay and allowances and shall not receive the pay prescribed for such position. Funds from which such pay and allowances are paid shall be reimbursed from funds available to the Director of Central Intelligence.

(d) Duties of Deputy Directors

(1)(A) The Deputy Director of Central Intelligence shall assist the Director of Central Intelligence in carrying out the Director's responsibilities under this Act.

(B) The Deputy Director of Central Intelligence shall act for, and exercise the powers of, the Director of Central Intelligence during the Director's absence or disability or during a vacancy in the position of the Director of Central Intelligence.

(2) The Deputy Director of Central Intelligence for Community Management shall, subject to the direction of the Director of Central Intelligence, be responsible for the following:

(A) Directing the operations of the Community Management Staff.

(B) Through the Assistant Director of Central Intelligence for Collection, ensuring the efficient and effective collection of national intelligence using technical means and human sources.

(C) Through the Assistant Director of Central Intelligence for Analysis and Production, conducting oversight of the analysis and production of intelligence by elements of the intelligence community.

(D) Through the Assistant Director of Central Intelligence for Administration, performing community-wide management functions of the intelligence community, including the management of personnel and resources.

(3)(A) The Deputy Director of Central Intelligence takes precedence in the Office of the Director of Central Intelligence immediately after the Director of Central Intelligence.

(B) The Deputy Director of Central Intelligence for Community Management takes precedence in the Office of the Director of Central Intelligence immediately after the Deputy Director of Central Intelligence.

(e) Office of the Director of Central Intelligence

(1) There is an Office of the Director of Central Intelligence. The function of the Office is to assist the Director of Central Intelligence in carrying out the duties and responsibilities of the Director under this Act and to carry out such other duties as may be prescribed by law.

(2) The Office of the Director of Central Intelligence is composed of the following:

(A) The Director of Central Intelligence.

(B) The Deputy Director of Central Intelligence.

(C) The Deputy Director of Central Intelligence for Community Management.

(D) The National Intelligence Council.

(E) The Assistant Director of Central Intelligence for Collection.

(F) The Assistant Director of Central Intelligence for Analysis and Production.

(G) The Assistant Director of Central Intelligence for Administration.

(H) Such other offices and officials as may be established by law or the Director of Central Intelligence may establish or designate in the Office.

(3) To assist the Director in fulfilling the responsibilities of the Director as head of the intelligence community, the Director shall employ and utilize in the Office of the Director of Central Intelligence a professional staff having an expertise in matters relating to such responsibilities and may establish permanent positions and appropriate rates of pay with respect to that staff.

(4) The Office of the Director of Central Intelligence shall, for administrative purposes, be within the Central Intelligence Agency.

(f) Assistant Director of Central Intelligence for Collection

(1) To assist the Director of Central Intelligence in carrying out the Director's responsibilities under this Act, there shall be an Assistant Director of Central Intelligence for Collection who shall be appointed by the President, by and with the advice and consent of the Senate.

(2) The Assistant Director for Collection shall assist the Director of Central Intelligence in carrying out the Director's collection responsibilities in order to ensure the efficient and effective collection of national intelligence.

(g) Assistant Director of Central Intelligence for Analysis and Production

(1) To assist the Director of Central Intelligence in carrying out the Director's responsibilities under this Act, there shall be an Assistant Director of Central Intelligence for Analysis and Production who shall be appointed by the President, by and with the advice and consent of the Senate.

(2) The Assistant Director for Analysis and Production shall—

(A) oversee the analysis and production of intelligence by the elements of the intelligence community;

(B) establish standards and priorities relating to such analysis and production;

(C) monitor the allocation of resources for the analysis and production of intelligence in order to identify unnecessary duplication in the analysis and production of intelligence;

(D) direct competitive analysis of analytical products having National[1] importance;

(E) identify intelligence to be collected for purposes of the Assistant Director of Central Intelligence for Collection; and

(F) provide such additional analysis and production of intelligence as the President and the National Security Council may require.

(h) Assistant Director of Central Intelligence for Administration

(1) To assist the Director of Central Intelligence in carrying out the Director's responsibilities under this Act, there shall be an Assistant Director of Central Intelligence for Administration who shall be appointed by the President, by and with the advice and consent of the Senate.

(2) The Assistant Director for Administration shall manage such activities relating to the administration of the intelligence community as the Director of Central Intelligence shall require.

(July 26, 1947, ch. 343, title I, § 102, as added and amended Pub. L. 104–293, title VIII, §§ 805(a), 809(a), 810, 811, Oct. 11, 1996, 110 Stat. 3477, 3481, 3482; Pub. L. 105–107, title IV, § 405, Nov. 20, 1997,

[1] So in original. Probably should not be capitalized.

111 Stat. 2261; Pub. L. 105–272, title III, §306, Oct. 20, 1998, 112 Stat. 2401.)

REFERENCES IN TEXT

This Act, referred to in subsecs. (d)(1)(A), (e)(1), (f)(1), (g)(1), and (h)(1), means act July 26, 1947, ch. 343, 61 Stat. 495, as amended, known as the National Security Act of 1947. For complete classification of this Act to the Code, see Short Title note set out under section 401 of this title and Tables.

PRIOR PROVISIONS

A prior section 403, acts July 26, 1947, ch. 343, title I, §102, 61 Stat. 497; Apr. 4, 1953, ch. 16, 67 Stat. 19; Oct. 24, 1992, Pub. L. 102–496, title VII, §704, 106 Stat. 3189; Jan. 6, 1996, Pub. L. 104–93, title VII, §701, 109 Stat. 977; Feb. 10, 1996, Pub. L. 104–106, div. A, title V, §570, 110 Stat. 353, related to establishment of Central Intelligence Agency and appointment and functions of its Director and Deputy Director prior to repeal by Pub. L. 104–293, title VIII, §805(a), Oct. 11, 1996, 110 Stat. 3477.

AMENDMENTS

1998—Subsec. (g)(2)(D) to (F). Pub. L. 105–272 added subpar. (D) and redesignated former subpars. (D) and (E) as (E) and (F), respectively.

1997—Subsec. (e)(4). Pub. L. 105–107 added par. (4).

1996—Subsec. (f). Pub. L. 104–293, §809(a), added subsec. (f).

Subsec. (g). Pub. L. 104–293, §810, added subsec. (g).

Subsec. (h). Pub. L. 104–293, §811, added subsec. (h).

TRANSFER OF FUNCTIONS

Missions and functions of elements of Central Intelligence Agency as specified in classified annex to Pub. L. 104–201, and related personnel, assets, and balances of appropriations and authorizations of appropriations, transferred to National Imagery and Mapping Agency, see sections 1111 and 1113 of Pub. L. 104–201, set out as notes under section 441 of Title 10, Armed Forces.

SUPPORT FOR SCIENCE, MATHEMATICS, AND ENGINEERING EDUCATION

Pub. L. 103–178, title IV, §401, Dec. 3, 1993, 107 Stat. 2037, authorized Director of Central Intelligence to carry out a program in fiscal years 1994 and 1995 to award cash prizes and visits to the Central Intelligence Agency (including the payment of costs associated with such visits) for students who participate in high school science fairs within the United States.

CENTRAL INTELLIGENCE AGENCY CONSOLIDATION PLAN

Pub. L. 102–183, title VI, §601, Dec. 4, 1991, 105 Stat. 1269, authorized funding in fiscal year 1992 for costs associated with the land acquisition and related expenditures necessary to implement a plan for consolidation of Central Intelligence Agency facilities. Similar provisions were contained in Pub. L. 102–172, title VIII, §8083A, Nov. 26, 1991, 105 Stat. 1191.

EQUAL EMPLOYMENT OPPORTUNITY PLAN

Pub. L. 100–453, title IV, §403, Sept. 29, 1988, 102 Stat. 1908, directed Director of Central Intelligence and Secretary of Defense, 90 days after Sept. 29, 1988, to submit to Congress a report setting forth an analysis of each equal employment opportunity group's representation in Central Intelligence Agency and National Security Agency respectively and proposing a plan for rectifying any underrepresentation of any such equal employment opportunity group by Sept. 30, 1991, and further directed submission of interim reports on Feb. 1, 1989, 1990, and 1991 concerning Central Intelligence Agency and National Security Agency respectively detailing efforts made, and progress realized, by each such agency in achieving objectives of each such plan, including, but not limited to, number of applications from, and hiring, promotion, and training of, members of each equal employment opportunity group.

STUDY OF INTELLIGENCE PERSONNEL SYSTEMS

Pub. L. 100–178, title VII, §701, Dec. 2, 1987, 101 Stat. 1016, provided for submission, no later than Jan. 20, 1989, to Congress by Director of Central Intelligence Agency, of classified objective study to consist of a comprehensive review and comparative analysis of all personnel management and compensation systems affecting civilian personnel of agencies and entities of intelligence community, accompanied by such recommendations for legislative, regulative or other changes as determined advisable.

COMPENSATION OF DIRECTOR AND DEPUTY DIRECTOR OF CENTRAL INTELLIGENCE

Compensation of Director and Deputy Director, see sections 5313 and 5314 of Title 5, Government Organization and Employees.

CENTRAL INTELLIGENCE AGENCY RETIREMENT AND DISABILITY SYSTEM

Pub. L. 88–643, Oct. 13, 1964, 78 Stat. 1043, as amended by Pub. L. 90–539, Sept. 30, 1968, 82 Stat. 902; Pub. L. 91–185, Dec. 30, 1969, 83 Stat. 847; Pub. L. 91–626, §§1–6, Dec. 31, 1970, 84 Stat. 1872–1874; Pub. L. 93–31, May 8, 1973, 87 Stat. 65; Pub. L. 93–210, §1(a), Dec. 28, 1973, 87 Stat. 908; Pub. L. 94–361, title VIII, §801(b), July 14, 1976, 90 Stat. 929; Pub. L. 94–522, title I, §§101, 102, title II, §§201–213, Oct. 17, 1976, 90 Stat. 2467–2471; Ex. Ord. No. 12273, Jan. 16, 1981, 46 F.R. 5854; Ex. Ord. No. 12326, Sept. 30, 1981, 46 F.R. 48889; Pub. L. 97–269, title VI, §§602–611, Sept. 27, 1982, 96 Stat. 1145–1148, 1152–1153; Ex. Ord. No. 12443, Sept. 27, 1983, 48 F.R. 44751; Ex. Ord. No. 12485, July 13, 1984, 49 F.R. 28827; Pub. L. 98–618, title III, §302, Nov. 8, 1984, 98 Stat. 3300; Pub. L. 99–169, title VII, §702, Dec. 4, 1985, 99 Stat. 1008; Pub. L. 99–335, title V, §§501–506, June 6, 1986, 100 Stat. 622–624; Pub. L. 99–514, §2, Oct. 22, 1986, 100 Stat. 2095; Pub. L. 99–569, title III, §302(a), Oct. 27, 1986, 100 Stat. 3192; Pub. L. 100–178, title IV, §§401(a), 402(a), (b)(1), (2), Dec. 2, 1987, 101 Stat. 1012–1014; Pub. L. 100–453, title III, §302(a), (b)(1), (c)(1), (d)(1), (2), title V, §502, Sept. 29, 1988, 102 Stat. 1906, 1907, 1909; Pub. L. 101–193, title III, §§302–304(a), 307(b), Nov. 30, 1989, 103 Stat. 1703, 1707; Pub. L. 102–83, §5(c)(2), Aug. 6, 1991, 105 Stat. 406; Pub. L. 102–88, title III, §§302–305(a), 306–307(b), Aug. 14, 1991, 105 Stat. 431–433; Pub. L. 102–183, title III, §§302(a)–(c), 303(a), 304–306(b), 307, 309(a), 310(a), Dec. 4, 1991, 105 Stat. 1262–1266; Pub. L. 102–496, title III, §304(b), Oct. 24, 1992, 106 Stat. 3183, known as the Central Intelligence Agency Retirement Act of 1964 for Certain Employees, was revised generally by Pub. L. 102–496, title VIII, §802, Oct. 24, 1992, 106 Stat. 3196. As so revised, Pub. L. 88–643, now known as the Central Intelligence Agency Retirement Act, has been transferred to chapter 38 (§2001 et seq.) of this title. All notes, Executive orders, and other provisions relating to this Act have been transferred to section 2001 of this title.

COMMUNICATION OF RESTRICTED DATA

Authorization for the communication of Restricted Data by the Central Intelligence Agency, see Ex. Ord. No. 10899, eff. Dec. 9, 1960, 25 F.R. 12729, set out as a note under section 2162 of Title 42, The Public Health and Welfare.

EXECUTIVE ORDER NO. 10656

Ex. Ord. No. 10656, Feb. 6, 1956, 21 F.R. 859, which established the President's Board of Consultants on Foreign Intelligence Activities, was revoked by Ex. Ord. No. 10938, May 4, 1961, 26 F.R. 3951, formerly set out below.

EXECUTIVE ORDER NO. 10938

Ex. Ord. No. 10938, May 4, 1961, 26 F.R. 3951, which established the President's Foreign Intelligence Advisory Board, was revoked by Ex. Ord. No. 11460, Mar. 20, 1969, 34 F.R. 5535, formerly set out below.

EXECUTIVE ORDER NO. 11460

Ex. Ord. No. 11460, Mar. 20, 1969, 34 F.R. 5535, which established the President's Foreign Intelligence Advisory Board, was revoked by Ex. Ord. No. 11984, May 4, 1977, 42 F.R. 23129, set out below.

EX. ORD. NO. 11984. ABOLITION OF PRESIDENT'S FOREIGN INTELLIGENCE ADVISORY BOARD

Ex. Ord. No. 11984, May 4, 1977, 42 F.R. 23129, provided:
By virtue of the authority vested in me by the Constitution and statutes of the United States of America, and as President of the United States of America, in order to abolish the President's Foreign Intelligence Advisory Board, Executive Order No. 11460 of March 20, 1969, is hereby revoked.

JIMMY CARTER.

EXECUTIVE ORDER NO. 12331

Ex. Ord. No. 12331, Oct. 20, 1981, 46 F.R. 51705, which established the President's Foreign Intelligence Advisory Board, was revoked by Ex. Ord. No. 12537, Oct. 28, 1985, 50 F.R. 45083, formerly set out below.

EXECUTIVE ORDER NO. 12537

Ex. Ord. No. 12537, Oct. 28, 1985, 50 F.R. 45083, as amended by Ex. Ord. No. 12624, Jan. 6, 1988, 53 F.R. 489, which established the President's Foreign Intelligence Advisory Board, was revoked by Ex. Ord. No. 12863, § 3.3, Sept. 13, 1993, 58 F.R. 48441, set out as a note under section 401 of this title.

SECTION REFERRED TO IN OTHER SECTIONS

This section is referred to in sections 403f, 411 of this title; title 5 section 2305; title 42 section 2162.

§ 403–1. Central Intelligence Agency

There is a Central Intelligence Agency. The function of the Agency shall be to assist the Director of Central Intelligence in carrying out the responsibilities referred to in paragraphs (1) through (5) of section 403–3(d) of this title.

(July 26, 1947, ch. 343, title I, § 102A, as added Pub. L. 104–293, title VIII, § 805(b), Oct. 11, 1996, 110 Stat. 3479.)

PRIOR PROVISIONS

A prior section 403–1, act July 26, 1947, ch. 343, title I, § 102a, as added Dec. 9, 1983, Pub. L. 98–215, title IV, § 403, 97 Stat. 1477, related to appointment of Director of the Intelligence Community Staff prior to repeal by Pub. L. 102–496, title VII, § 705(a)(1), Oct. 24, 1992, 106 Stat. 3190.

DESIGNATION OF HEADQUARTERS COMPOUND OF CENTRAL INTELLIGENCE AGENCY AS THE GEORGE BUSH CENTER FOR INTELLIGENCE

Pub. L. 105–272, title III, § 309, Oct. 20, 1998, 112 Stat. 2403, provided that:
"(a) DESIGNATION.—The headquarters compound of the Central Intelligence Agency located in Langley, Virginia, shall be known and designated as the 'George Bush Center for Intelligence'.
"(b) REFERENCES.—Any reference in a law, map, regulation, document, paper, or other record of the United States to the headquarters compound referred to in subsection (a) shall be deemed to be a reference to the 'George Bush Center for Intelligence'."

§ 403–2. Intelligence Community contracting

The Director of Central Intelligence shall direct that elements of the Intelligence Community, whenever compatible with the national security interests of the United States and consistent with the operational and security concerns related to the conduct of intelligence activities, and where fiscally sound, shall award contracts in a manner that would maximize the procurement of products in the United States. For purposes of this provision, the term "Intelligence Community" has the same meaning as set forth in paragraph 3.4(f) of Executive Order 12333, dated December 4, 1981, or successor orders.

(Pub. L. 102–183, title IV, § 403, Dec. 4, 1991, 105 Stat. 1267.)

REFERENCES IN TEXT

Executive Order 12333, referred to in text, is set out as a note under section 401 of this title.

CODIFICATION

Section was enacted as part of the authorization act cited as the credit to this section, and not as part of the National Security Act of 1947 which comprises this chapter.

PRIOR PROVISIONS

Provisions similar to those in this section were contained in the following prior authorization act: Pub. L. 102–88, title IV, § 404, Aug. 14, 1991, 105 Stat. 434.

§ 403–2a. Construction of intelligence community facilities; Presidential authorization

(a) No project for the construction of any facility, or improvement to any facility, having an estimated Federal cost in excess of $300,000, may be undertaken in any fiscal year unless specifically identified as a separate item in the President's annual fiscal year budget request or otherwise specifically authorized and appropriated if such facility or improvement would be used primarily by personnel of the intelligence community.

(b) As used in this section, the term "intelligence community" has the same meaning given that term in section 401a(4) of this title.

(Pub. L. 103–335, title VIII, § 8131, Sept. 30, 1994, 108 Stat. 2653.)

CODIFICATION

Section was enacted as part of the Department of Defense Appropriations Act, 1995, and not as part of the National Security Act of 1947 which comprises this chapter.

§ 403–2b. Limitation on construction of facilities to be used primarily by intelligence community

(a) In general

(1) In general

Except as provided in subsection (b) of this section, no project for the construction of any facility to be used primarily by personnel of any component of the intelligence community which has an estimated Federal cost in excess of $750,000 may be undertaken in any fiscal year unless such project is specifically identified as a separate item in the President's annual fiscal year budget request and is specifically authorized by the Congress.

(2) Notification

In the case of a project for the construction of any facility to be used primarily by personnel of any component of the intelligence community which has an estimated Federal cost greater than $500,000 but less than $750,000, or where any improvement project to such a facility has an estimated Federal cost greater than $500,000, the Director of Central Intelligence shall submit a notification to the intelligence committees specifically identifying such project.

(b) Exception

(1) In general

Notwithstanding subsection (a) of this section but subject to paragraphs (2) and (3), a project for the construction of a facility to be used primarily by personnel of any component of the intelligence community may be carried out if the Secretary of Defense and the Director of Central Intelligence jointly determine—

(A) that the project is vital to the national security or to the protection of health, safety, or the quality of the environment, and

(B) that the requirement for the project is so urgent that deferral of the project for inclusion in the next Act authorizing appropriations for the intelligence community would be inconsistent with national security or the protection of health, safety, or environmental quality, as the case may be.

(2) Report

When a decision is made to carry out a construction project under this subsection, the Secretary of Defense and the Director of Central Intelligence jointly shall submit a report in writing to the appropriate committees of Congress on that decision. Each such report shall include (A) the justification for the project and the current estimate of the cost of the project, (B) the justification for carrying out the project under this subsection, and (C) a statement of the source of the funds to be used to carry out the project. The project may then be carried out only after the end of the 21-day period beginning on the date the notification is received by such committees.

(3) Projects primarily for CIA

If a project referred to in paragraph (1) is primarily for the Central Intelligence Agency, the Director of Central Intelligence shall make the determination and submit the report required by paragraphs (1) and (2).

(4) Limitation

A project carried out under this subsection shall be carried out within the total amount of funds appropriated for intelligence and intelligence-related activities that have not been obligated.

(c) Application

This section shall not apply to any project which is subject to subsection (a)(1)(A) or (c) of section 601.

(Pub. L. 103–359, title VI, § 602, Oct. 14, 1994, 108 Stat. 3432.)

REFERENCES IN TEXT

Section 601, referred to in subsec. (c), means section 601 of Pub. L. 103–359, title VI, Oct. 14, 1994, 108 Stat. 3431, which is not classified to the Code.

CODIFICATION

Section was enacted as part of the Intelligence Authorization Act for Fiscal Year 1995, and not as part of the National Security Act of 1947 which comprises this chapter.

DEFINITIONS

Section 604 of title VI of Pub. L. 103–359 provided that: ''As used in this title [enacting this section and provisions set out as a note under section 403–3 of this title]:

''(1) INTELLIGENCE COMMITTEES.—The term 'intelligence committees' means the Permanent Select Committee on Intelligence of the House of Representatives and the Select Committee on Intelligence of the Senate.

''(2) INTELLIGENCE COMMUNITY.—The term 'intelligence community' has the same meaning given that term in section 3(4) of the National Security Act of 1947 (50 U.S.C. 401a(4)).''

§ 403–3. Responsibilities of Director of Central Intelligence

(a) Provision of intelligence

(1) Under the direction of the National Security Council, the Director of Central Intelligence shall be responsible for providing national intelligence—

(A) to the President;

(B) to the heads of departments and agencies of the executive branch;

(C) to the Chairman of the Joint Chiefs of Staff and senior military commanders; and

(D) where appropriate, to the Senate and House of Representatives and the committees thereof.

(2) Such national intelligence should be timely, objective, independent of political considerations, and based upon all sources available to the intelligence community.

(b) National Intelligence Council

(1)(A) There is established within the Office of the Director of Central Intelligence the National Intelligence Council (hereafter in this section referred to as the ''Council''). The Council shall be composed of senior analysts within the intelligence community and substantive experts from the public and private sector, who shall be appointed by, report to, and serve at the pleasure of, the Director of Central Intelligence.

(B) The Director shall prescribe appropriate security requirements for personnel appointed from the private sector as a condition of service on the Council, or as contractors of the Council or employees of such contractors, to ensure the protection of intelligence sources and methods while avoiding, wherever possible, unduly intrusive requirements which the Director considers to be unnecessary for this purpose.

(2) The Council shall—

(A) produce national intelligence estimates for the Government, including, whenever the Council considers appropriate, alternative views held by elements of the intelligence community;

(B) evaluate community-wide collection and production of intelligence by the intelligence community and the requirements and resources of such collection and production; and

(C) otherwise assist the Director in carrying out the responsibilities described in subsection (a) of this section.

(3) Within their respective areas of expertise and under the direction of the Director, the

members of the Council shall constitute the senior intelligence advisers of the intelligence community for purposes of representing the views of the intelligence community within the Government.

(4) Subject to the direction and control of the Director of Central Intelligence, the Council may carry out its responsibilities under this subsection by contract, including contracts for substantive experts necessary to assist the Council with particular assessments under this subsection.

(5) The Director shall make available to the Council such staff as may be necessary to permit the Council to carry out its responsibilities under this subsection and shall take appropriate measures to ensure that the Council and its staff satisfy the needs of policymaking officials and other consumers of intelligence. The Council shall also be readily accessible to policymaking officials and other appropriate individuals not otherwise associated with the intelligence community.

(6) The heads of elements within the intelligence community shall, as appropriate, furnish such support to the Council, including the preparation of intelligence analyses, as may be required by the Director.

(c) Head of intelligence community

In the Director's capacity as head of the intelligence community, the Director shall—

(1) facilitate the development of an annual budget for intelligence and intelligence-related activities of the United States by—

(A) developing and presenting to the President an annual budget for the National Foreign Intelligence Program; and

(B) participating in the development by the Secretary of Defense of the annual budgets for the Joint Military Intelligence Program and the Tactical Intelligence and Related Activities Program;

(2) establish the requirements and priorities to govern the collection of national intelligence by elements of the intelligence community;

(3) approve collection requirements, determine collection priorities, and resolve conflicts in collection priorities levied on national collection assets, except as otherwise agreed with the Secretary of Defense pursuant to the direction of the President;

(4) promote and evaluate the utility of national intelligence to consumers within the Government;

(5) eliminate waste and unnecessary duplication within the intelligence community;

(6) protect intelligence sources and methods from unauthorized disclosure; and

(7) perform such other functions as the President or the National Security Council may direct.

(d) Head of Central Intelligence Agency

In the Director's capacity as head of the Central Intelligence Agency, the Director shall—

(1) collect intelligence through human sources and by other appropriate means, except that the Agency shall have no police, subpoena, or law enforcement powers or internal security functions;

(2) provide overall direction for the collection of national intelligence through human sources by elements of the intelligence community authorized to undertake such collection and, in coordination with other agencies of the Government which are authorized to undertake such collection, ensure that the most effective use is made of resources and that the risks to the United States and those involved in such collection are minimized;

(3) correlate and evaluate intelligence related to the national security and provide appropriate dissemination of such intelligence;

(4) perform such additional services as are of common concern to the elements of the intelligence community, which services the Director of Central Intelligence determines can be more efficiently accomplished centrally; and

(5) perform such other functions and duties related to intelligence affecting the national security as the President or the National Security Council may direct.

(July 26, 1947, ch. 343, title I, § 103, as added Pub. L. 102–496, title VII, § 705(a)(3), Oct. 24, 1992, 106 Stat. 3190; amended Pub. L. 103–178, title V, § 502, Dec. 3, 1993, 107 Stat. 2038; Pub. L. 104–293, title VIII, §§ 806, 807(a), Oct. 11, 1996, 110 Stat. 3479, 3480.)

PRIOR PROVISIONS

A prior section 103 of act July 26, 1947, was renumbered section 107 and is classified to section 404 of this title.

AMENDMENTS

1996—Subsec. (b)(1)(B). Pub. L. 104–293, § 806(1), inserted ", or as contractors of the Council or employees of such contractors," after "on the Council".

Subsec. (b)(2). Pub. L. 104–293, § 806(2), added subpar. (B) and redesignated former subpar. (B) as (C).

Subsec. (b)(4). Pub. L. 104–293, § 806(3), added par. (4). Former par. (4) redesignated (5).

Subsec. (b)(5). Pub. L. 104–293, § 806(3), (5), redesignated par. (4) as (5) and inserted at end "The Council shall also be readily accessible to policymaking officials and other appropriate individuals not otherwise associated with the intelligence community." Former par. (5) redesignated (6).

Subsec. (b)(6). Pub. L. 104–293, § 806(3), redesignated par. (5) as (6).

Subsec. (c)(1). Pub. L. 104–293, § 807(a)(1), added par. (1) and struck out former par. (1) which read as follows: "develop and present to the President an annual budget for the National Foreign Intelligence Program of the United States;".

Subsec. (c)(3) to (7). Pub. L. 104–293, § 807(a)(2), (3), added par. (3) and redesignated former pars. (3) to (6) as (4) to (7), respectively.

1993—Subsec. (d)(3). Pub. L. 103–178 substituted "provide" for "providing".

STANDARDS FOR SPELLING OF FOREIGN NAMES AND PLACES AND FOR USE OF GEOGRAPHIC COORDINATES

Pub. L. 105–107, title III, § 309, Nov. 20, 1997, 111 Stat. 2253, provided that:

"(a) SURVEY OF CURRENT STANDARDS.—

"(1) SURVEY.—The Director of Central Intelligence shall carry out a survey of current standards for the spelling of foreign names and places, and the use of geographic coordinates for such places, among the elements of the intelligence community.

"(2) REPORT.—Not later than 90 days after the date of enactment of this Act [Nov. 20, 1997], the Director shall submit to the congressional intelligence committees a report on the survey carried out under paragraph (1). The report shall be submitted in unclassified form, but may include a classified annex.

"(b) GUIDELINES.—

"(1) ISSUANCE.—Not later than 180 days after the date of enactment of this Act, the Director shall issue guidelines to ensure the use of uniform spelling of foreign names and places and the uniform use of geographic coordinates for such places. The guidelines shall apply to all intelligence reports, intelligence products, and intelligence databases prepared and utilized by the elements of the intelligence community.

"(2) BASIS.—The guidelines under paragraph (1) shall, to the maximum extent practicable, be based on current United States Government standards for the transliteration of foreign names, standards for foreign place names developed by the Board on Geographic Names, and a standard set of geographic coordinates.

"(3) SUBMITTAL TO CONGRESS.—The Director shall submit a copy of the guidelines to the congressional intelligence committees.

"(c) CONGRESSIONAL INTELLIGENCE COMMITTEES DEFINED.—In this section, the term 'congressional intelligence committees' means the following:

"(1) The Select Committee on Intelligence of the Senate.

"(2) The Permanent Select Committee on Intelligence of the House of Representatives."

PERIODIC REPORTS ON EXPENDITURES

Section 807(c) of Pub. L. 104–293 provided that: "Not later than January 1, 1997, the Director of Central Intelligence and the Secretary of Defense shall prescribe guidelines to ensure prompt reporting to the Director and the Secretary on a periodic basis of budget execution data for all national, defense-wide, and tactical intelligence activities."

DATABASE PROGRAM TRACKING

Section 807(d) of Pub. L. 104–293 provided that: "Not later than January 1, 1999, the Director of Central Intelligence and the Secretary of Defense shall develop and implement a database to provide timely and accurate information on the amounts, purposes, and status of the resources, including periodic budget execution updates, for all national, defense-wide, and tactical intelligence activities."

IDENTIFICATION OF CONSTITUENT COMPONENTS OF BASE INTELLIGENCE BUDGET

Pub. L. 103–359, title VI, §603, Oct. 14, 1994, 108 Stat. 3433, provided that: "The Director of Central Intelligence shall include the same level of budgetary detail for the Base Budget that is provided for Ongoing Initiatives and New Initiatives to the Permanent Select Committee on Intelligence of the House of Representatives and the Select Committee on Intelligence of the Senate in the congressional justification materials for the annual submission of the National Foreign Intelligence Program of each fiscal year."

SECTION REFERRED TO IN OTHER SECTIONS

This section is referred to in sections 401a, 403–1, 403–5, 403f, 403g, 404g, 411, 2011 of this title.

§403–4. Authorities of Director of Central Intelligence

(a) Access to intelligence

To the extent recommended by the National Security Council and approved by the President, the Director of Central Intelligence shall have access to all intelligence related to the national security which is collected by any department, agency, or other entity of the United States.

(b) Approval of budgets

The Director of Central Intelligence shall provide guidance to elements of the intelligence community for the preparation of their annual budgets and shall approve such budgets before their incorporation in the National Foreign Intelligence Program.

(c) Role of DCI in reprogramming

No funds made available under the National Foreign Intelligence Program may be reprogrammed by any element of the intelligence community without the prior approval of the Director of Central Intelligence except in accordance with procedures issued by the Director. The Secretary of Defense shall consult with the Director of Central Intelligence before reprogramming funds made available under the Joint Military Intelligence Program.

(d) Transfer of funds or personnel within National Foreign Intelligence Program

(1)(A) In addition to any other authorities available under law for such purposes, the Director of Central Intelligence, with the approval of the Director of the Office of Management and Budget, may transfer funds appropriated for a program within the National Foreign Intelligence Program to another such program and, in accordance with procedures to be developed by the Director and the heads of affected departments and agencies, may transfer personnel authorized for an element of the intelligence community to another such element for periods up to a year.

(B) The Director may only delegate any duty or authority given the Director under this subsection to the Deputy Director of Central Intelligence for Community Management.

(2)(A) A transfer of funds or personnel may be made under this subsection only if—

(i) the funds or personnel are being transferred to an activity that is a higher priority intelligence activity;

(ii) the need for funds or personnel for such activity is based on unforeseen requirements;

(iii) the transfer does not involve a transfer of funds to the Reserve for Contingencies of the Central Intelligence Agency;

(iv) the transfer does not involve a transfer of funds or personnel from the Federal Bureau of Investigation; and

(v) subject to subparagraph (B), the Secretary or head of the department which contains the affected element or elements of the intelligence community does not object to such transfer.

(B)(i) Except as provided in clause (ii), the authority to object to a transfer under subparagraph (A)(v) may not be delegated by the Secretary or head of the department involved.

(ii) With respect to the Department of Defense, the authority to object to such a transfer may be delegated by the Secretary of Defense, but only to the Deputy Secretary of Defense.

(iii) An objection to a transfer under subparagraph (A)(v) shall have no effect unless submitted to the Director of Central Intelligence in writing.

(3) Funds transferred under this subsection shall remain available for the same period as the appropriations account to which transferred.

(4) Any transfer of funds under this subsection shall be carried out in accordance with existing

procedures applicable to reprogramming notifications for the appropriate congressional committees. Any proposed transfer for which notice is given to the appropriate congressional committees shall be accompanied by a report explaining the nature of the proposed transfer and how it satisfies the requirements of this subsection. In addition, the Select Committee on Intelligence of the Senate and the Permanent Select Committee on Intelligence of the House of Representatives shall be promptly notified of any transfer of funds made pursuant to this subsection in any case in which the transfer would not have otherwise required reprogramming notification under procedures in effect as of October 24, 1992.

(5) The Director shall promptly submit to the Select Committee on Intelligence of the Senate and to the Permanent Select Committee on Intelligence of the House of Representatives and, in the case of the transfer of personnel to or from the Department of Defense, the Committee on Armed Services of the Senate and the Committee on Armed Services of the House of Representatives, a report on any transfer of personnel made pursuant to this subsection. The Director shall include in any such report an explanation of the nature of the transfer and how it satisfies the requirements of this subsection.

(e) Coordination with foreign governments

Under the direction of the National Security Council and in a manner consistent with section 3927 of title 22, the Director shall coordinate the relationships between elements of the intelligence community and the intelligence or security services of foreign governments on all matters involving intelligence related to the national security or involving intelligence acquired through clandestine means.

(f) Use of personnel

The Director shall, in coordination with the heads of departments and agencies with elements in the intelligence community, institute policies and programs within the intelligence community—

(1) to provide for the rotation of personnel between the elements of the intelligence community, where appropriate, and to make such rotated service a factor to be considered for promotion to senior positions; and

(2) to consolidate, wherever possible, personnel, administrative, and security programs to reduce the overall costs of these activities within the intelligence community.

(g) Termination of employment of CIA employees

Notwithstanding the provisions of any other law, the Director may, in the Director's discretion, terminate the employment of any officer or employee of the Central Intelligence Agency whenever the Director shall deem such termination necessary or advisable in the interests of the United States. Any such termination shall not affect the right of the officer or employee terminated to seek or accept employment in any other department or agency of the Government if declared eligible for such employment by the Office of Personnel Management.

(July 26, 1947, ch. 343, title I, §104, as added Pub. L. 102–496, title VII, §705(a)(3), Oct. 24, 1992, 106 Stat. 3192; amended Pub. L. 104–106, div. A, title XV, §1502(f)(5), Feb. 10, 1996, 110 Stat. 510; Pub. L. 104–293, title VIII, §807(b), Oct. 11, 1996, 110 Stat. 3480; Pub. L. 106–65, div. A, title X, §1067(16), Oct. 5, 1999, 113 Stat. 775; Pub. L. 106–567, title I, §105, Dec. 27, 2000, 114 Stat. 2834.)

PRIOR PROVISIONS

A prior section 104 of act July 26, 1947, was renumbered section 108 and is classified to section 404a of this title.

AMENDMENTS

2000—Subsec. (d)(1). Pub. L. 106–567, §105(b), designated existing provisions as subpar. (A) and added subpar. (B).

Subsec. (d)(2). Pub. L. 106–567, §105(a), designated existing provisions as subpar. (A), redesignated former subpars. (A) to (E) as cls. (i) to (v), respectively, of subpar. (A), in cl. (v) substituted "subject to subparagraph (B), the Secretary or head" for "the Secretary or head", and added subpar. (B).

1999—Subsec. (d)(5). Pub. L. 106–65 substituted "and the Committee on Armed Services" for "and the Committee on National Security".

1996—Subsec. (c). Pub. L. 104–293 inserted at end "The Secretary of Defense shall consult with the Director of Central Intelligence before reprogramming funds made available under the Joint Military Intelligence Program."

Subsec. (d)(5). Pub. L. 104–106 substituted "Committee on Armed Services of the Senate and the Committee on National Security of the House of Representatives" for "Committees on Armed Services of the Senate and House of Representatives".

POST-EMPLOYMENT RESTRICTIONS

Section 402 of Pub. L. 104–293 provided that:

"(a) IN GENERAL.—Not later than 90 days after the date of enactment of this Act [Oct. 11, 1996], the Director of Central Intelligence shall prescribe regulations requiring each employee of the Central Intelligence Agency designated by the Director for such purpose to sign a written agreement restricting the activities of the employee upon ceasing employment with the Central Intelligence Agency. The Director may designate a group or class of employees for such purpose.

"(b) AGREEMENT ELEMENTS.—The regulations shall provide that an agreement contain provisions specifying that the employee concerned not represent or advise the government, or any political party, of any foreign country during the three-year period beginning on the cessation of the employee's employment with the Central Intelligence Agency unless the Director determines that such representation or advice would be in the best interests of the United States.

"(c) DISCIPLINARY ACTIONS.—The regulations shall specify appropriate disciplinary actions (including loss of retirement benefits) to be taken against any employee determined by the Director of Central Intelligence to have violated the agreement of the employee under this section."

PERSONNEL, TRAINING, AND ADMINISTRATIVE ACTIVITIES

Section 807(e) of Pub. L. 104–293 provided that: "Not later than January 31 of each year through 1999, the Director of Central Intelligence shall submit to the Select Committee on Intelligence of the Senate and the Permanent Select Committee on Intelligence of the House of Representatives a report on the policies and programs the Director has instituted under subsection (f) of section 104 of the National Security Act of 1947 [50 U.S.C. 403–4(f)]."

SEPARATION PAY PROGRAM FOR VOLUNTARY SEPARATION FROM SERVICE

Pub. L. 103–36, §2, June 8, 1993, 107 Stat. 104, as amended by Pub. L. 103–226, §8(b), Mar. 30, 1994, 108

Stat. 118; Pub. L. 104–93, title IV, § 401, Jan. 6, 1996, 109 Stat. 968; Pub. L. 104–293, title IV, § 401, Oct. 11, 1996, 110 Stat. 3468; Pub. L. 106–120, title IV, § 402, Dec. 3, 1999, 113 Stat. 1616, provided that:

"(a) DEFINITIONS.—For purposes of this section—

"(1) the term 'Director' means the Director of Central Intelligence; and

"(2) the term 'employee' means an employee of the Central Intelligence Agency, serving under an appointment without time limitation, who has been currently employed for a continuous period of at least 12 months, except that such term does not include—

"(A) a reemployed annuitant under subchapter III of chapter 83 or chapter 84 of title 5, United States Code, or another retirement system for employees of the Government; or

"(B) an employee having a disability on the basis of which such employee is or would be eligible for disability retirement under any of the retirement systems referred to in subparagraph (A).

"(b) ESTABLISHMENT OF PROGRAM.—In order to avoid or minimize the need for involuntary separations due to downsizing, reorganization, transfer of function, or other similar action, the Director may establish a program under which employees may be offered separation pay to separate from service voluntarily (whether by retirement or resignation). An employee who receives separation pay under such program may not be reemployed by the Central Intelligence Agency for the 12-month period beginning on the effective date of the employee's separation. An employee who receives separation pay under this section on the basis of a separation occurring on or after the date of the enactment of the Federal Workforce Restructuring Act of 1994 [Mar. 30, 1994] and accepts employment with the Government of the United States within 5 years after the date of the separation on which payment of the separation pay is based shall be required to repay the entire amount of the separation pay to the Central Intelligence Agency. If the employment is with an Executive agency (as defined by section 105 of title 5, United States Code), the Director of the Office of Personnel Management may, at the request of the head of the agency, waive the repayment if the individual involved possesses unique abilities and is the only qualified applicant available for the position. If the employment is with an entity in the legislative branch, the head of the entity or the appointing official may waive the repayment if the individual involved possesses unique abilities and is the only qualified applicant available for the position. If the employment is with the judicial branch, the Director of the Administrative Office of the United States Courts may waive the repayment if the individual involved possesses unique abilities and is the only qualified applicant available for the position.

"(c) BAR ON CERTAIN EMPLOYMENT.—

"(1) BAR.—An employee may not be separated from service under this section unless the employee agrees that the employee will not—

"(A) act as agent or attorney for, or otherwise represent, any other person (except the United States) in any formal or informal appearance before, or, with the intent to influence, make any oral or written communication on behalf of any other person (except the United States) to the Central Intelligence Agency; or

"(B) participate in any manner in the award, modification, extension, or performance of any contract for property or services with the Central Intelligence Agency,

during the 12-month period beginning on the effective date of the employee's separation from service.

"(2) PENALTY.—An employee who violates an agreement under this subsection shall be liable to the United States in the amount of the separation pay paid to the employee pursuant to this section times the proportion of the 12-month period during which the employee was in violation of the agreement.

"(d) LIMITATIONS.—Under this program, separation pay may be offered only—

"(1) with the prior approval of the Director; and

"(2) to employees within such occupational groups or geographic locations, or subject to such other similar limitations or conditions, as the Director may require.

"(e) AMOUNT AND TREATMENT FOR OTHER PURPOSES.—Such separation pay—

"(1) shall be paid in a lump sum;

"(2) shall be equal to the lesser of—

"(A) an amount equal to the amount the employee would be entitled to receive under section 5595(c) of title 5, United States Code, if the employee were entitled to payment under such section; or

"(B) $25,000;

"(3) shall not be a basis for payment, and shall not be included in the computation, of any other type of Government benefit; and

"(4) shall not be taken into account for the purpose of determining the amount of any severance pay to which an individual may be entitled under section 5595 of title 5, United States Code, based on any other separation.

"(f) TERMINATION.—No amount shall be payable under this section based on any separation occurring after September 30, 2002.

"(g) REGULATIONS.—The Director shall prescribe such regulations as may be necessary to carry out this section.

"(h) REPORTING REQUIREMENTS.—

"(1) OFFERING NOTIFICATION.—The Director may not make an offering of voluntary separation pay pursuant to this section until 30 days after submitting to the Permanent Select Committee on Intelligence of the House of Representatives and the Select Committee on Intelligence of the Senate a report describing the occupational groups or geographic locations, or other similar limitations or conditions, required by the Director under subsection (d).

"(2) ANNUAL REPORT.—At the end of each of the fiscal years 1993 through 1997, the Director shall submit to the President and the Permanent Select Committee on Intelligence of the House of Representatives and the Select Committee on Intelligence of the Senate a report on the effectiveness and costs of carrying out this section.

"(i) REMITTANCE OF FUNDS.—The Director shall remit to the Office of Personnel Management for deposit in the Treasury of the United States to the credit of the Civil Service Retirement and Disability Fund (in addition to any other payments which the Director is required to make under subchapter III of chapter 83 and subchapter II of chapter 84 of title 5, United States Code), an amount equal to 15 percent of the final basic pay of each employee who, in fiscal year 1998, 1999, 2000, 2001, or 2002, retires voluntarily under section 8336, 8412, or 8414 of such title or resigns and to whom a voluntary separation incentive payment has been or is to be paid under this section. The remittance required by this subsection shall be in lieu of any remittance required by section 4(a) of the Federal Workforce Restructuring Act of 1994 (5 U.S.C. 8331 note)."

SECTION REFERRED TO IN OTHER SECTIONS

This section is referred to in sections 403–5, 403f, 411 of this title; title 21 section 1703.

§ 403–5. Responsibilities of Secretary of Defense pertaining to National Foreign Intelligence Program

(a) In general

The Secretary of Defense, in consultation with the Director of Central Intelligence, shall—

(1) ensure that the budgets of the elements of the intelligence community within the Department of Defense are adequate to satisfy the overall intelligence needs of the Depart-

ment of Defense, including the needs of the chairman[1] of the Joint Chiefs of Staff and the commanders of the unified and specified commands and, wherever such elements are performing governmentwide functions, the needs of other departments and agencies;

(2) ensure appropriate implementation of the policies and resource decisions of the Director of Central Intelligence by elements of the Department of Defense within the National Foreign Intelligence Program;

(3) ensure that the tactical intelligence activities of the Department of Defense complement and are compatible with intelligence activities under the National Foreign Intelligence Program;

(4) ensure that the elements of the intelligence community within the Department of Defense are responsive and timely with respect to satisfying the needs of operational military forces;

(5) eliminate waste and unnecessary duplication among the intelligence activities of the Department of Defense; and

(6) ensure that intelligence activities of the Department of Defense are conducted jointly where appropriate.

(b) Responsibility for performance of specific functions

Consistent with sections 403–3 and 403–4 of this title, the Secretary of Defense shall ensure—

(1) through the National Security Agency (except as otherwise directed by the President or the National Security Council), the continued operation of an effective unified organization for the conduct of signals intelligence activities and shall ensure that the product is disseminated in a timely manner to authorized recipients;

(2) through the National Imagery and Mapping Agency (except as otherwise directed by the President or the National Security Council), with appropriate representation from the intelligence community, the continued operation of an effective unified organization within the Department of Defense—

(A) for carrying out tasking of imagery collection;

(B) for the coordination of imagery processing and exploitation activities;

(C) for ensuring the dissemination of imagery in a timely manner to authorized recipients; and

(D) notwithstanding any other provision of law, for—

(i) prescribing technical architecture and standards related to imagery intelligence and geospatial information and ensuring compliance with such architecture and standards; and

(ii) developing and fielding systems of common concern related to imagery intelligence and geospatial information;

(3) through the National Reconnaissance Office (except as otherwise directed by the President or the National Security Council), the continued operation of an effective unified organization for the research and development, acquisition, and operation of overhead reconnaissance systems necessary to satisfy the requirements of all elements of the intelligence community;

(4) through the Defense Intelligence Agency (except as otherwise directed by the President or the National Security Council), the continued operation of an effective unified system within the Department of Defense for the production of timely, objective military and military-related intelligence, based upon all sources available to the intelligence community, and shall ensure the appropriate dissemination of such intelligence to authorized recipients;

(5) through the Defense Intelligence Agency (except as otherwise directed by the President or the National Security Council), effective management of Department of Defense human intelligence activities, including defense attaches; and

(6) that the military departments maintain sufficient capabilities to collect and produce intelligence to meet—

(A) the requirements of the Director of Central Intelligence;

(B) the requirements of the Secretary of Defense or the Chairman of the Joint Chiefs of Staff;

(C) the requirements of the unified and specified combatant commands and of joint operations; and

(D) the specialized requirements of the military departments for intelligence necessary to support tactical commanders, military planners, the research and development process, the acquisition of military equipment, and training and doctrine.

(c) Use of elements of Department of Defense

The Secretary of Defense, in carrying out the functions described in this section, may use such elements of the Department of Defense as may be appropriate for the execution of those functions, in addition to, or in lieu of, the elements identified in this section.

(d) Annual evaluation of Director of Central Intelligence

The Director of Central Intelligence, in consultation with the Secretary of Defense and the Chairman of the Joint Chiefs of Staff, shall submit each year to the Committee on Foreign Intelligence of the National Security Council and the appropriate congressional committees (as defined in section 404d(c) of this title) an evaluation of the performance and the responsiveness of the National Security Agency, the National Reconnaissance Office, and the National Imagery and Mapping Agency in meeting their national missions.

(July 26, 1947, ch. 343, title I, § 105, as added Pub. L. 102–496, title VII, § 706(a), Oct. 24, 1992, 106 Stat. 3194; amended Pub. L. 103–359, title V, § 501(a)(2), Oct. 14, 1994, 108 Stat. 3428; Pub. L. 104–201, div. A, title XI, § 1114(a), Sept. 23, 1996, 110 Stat. 2684; Pub. L. 104–293, title VIII, § 808, Oct. 11, 1996, 110 Stat. 3481.)

AMENDMENTS

1996—Subsec. (a). Pub. L. 104–293, § 808(1), inserted ", in consultation with the Director of Central Intel-

[1] So in original. Probably should be capitalized.

ligence,'' after ''Secretary of Defense'' in introductory provisions.

Subsec. (b)(2). Pub. L. 104–201 amended par. (2) generally. Prior to amendment, par. (2) read as follows: ''through the Central Imagery Office (except as otherwise directed by the President or the National Security Council), with appropriate representation from the intelligence community, the continued operation of an effective unified organization within the Department of Defense for carrying out tasking of imagery collection, for the coordination of imagery processing and exploitation activities, and for ensuring the dissemination of imagery in a timely manner to authorized recipients;''.

Subsec. (d). Pub. L. 104–293, § 808(2), added subsec. (d).

1994—Subsec. (b)(2). Pub. L. 103–359 substituted ''the Central Imagery Office'' for ''a central imagery authority''.

EFFECTIVE DATE OF 1996 AMENDMENT

Amendment by Pub. L. 104–201 effective Oct. 1, 1996, see section 1124 of Pub. L. 104–201, set out as a note under section 193 of Title 10, Armed Forces.

ROLE OF DIRECTOR OF CENTRAL INTELLIGENCE IN EXPERIMENTAL PERSONNEL PROGRAM FOR CERTAIN SCIENTIFIC AND TECHNICAL PERSONNEL

Pub. L. 106–567, title V, § 501, Dec. 27, 2000, 114 Stat. 2850, provided that: ''If the Director of Central Intelligence requests that the Secretary of Defense exercise any authority available to the Secretary under section 1101(b) of the Strom Thurmond National Defense Authorization Act for Fiscal Year 1999 (Public Law 105–261; 5 U.S.C. 3104 note) to carry out a program of special personnel management authority at the National Imagery and Mapping Agency and the National Security Agency in order to facilitate recruitment of eminent experts in science and engineering at such agencies, the Secretary shall respond to such request not later than 30 days after the date of such request.''

SECTION REFERRED TO IN OTHER SECTIONS

This section is referred to in section 411 of this title.

§ 403–5a. Assistance to United States law enforcement agencies

(a) Authority to provide assistance

Subject to subsection (b) of this section, elements of the intelligence community may, upon the request of a United States law enforcement agency, collect information outside the United States about individuals who are not United States persons. Such elements may collect such information notwithstanding that the law enforcement agency intends to use the information collected for purposes of a law enforcement investigation or counterintelligence investigation.

(b) Limitation on assistance by elements of Department of Defense

(1) With respect to elements within the Department of Defense, the authority in subsection (a) of this section applies only to the following:

(A) The National Security Agency.

(B) The National Reconnaissance Office.

(C) The National Imagery and Mapping Agency.

(D) The Defense Intelligence Agency.

(2) Assistance provided under this section by elements of the Department of Defense may not include the direct participation of a member of the Army, Navy, Air Force, or Marine Corps in an arrest or similar activity.

(3) Assistance may not be provided under this section by an element of the Department of Defense if the provision of such assistance will adversely affect the military preparedness of the United States.

(4) The Secretary of Defense shall prescribe regulations governing the exercise of authority under this section by elements of the Department of Defense, including regulations relating to the protection of sources and methods in the exercise of such authority.

(c) Definitions

For purposes of subsection (a) of this section:

(1) The term ''United States law enforcement agency'' means any department or agency of the Federal Government that the Attorney General designates as law enforcement agency for purposes of this section.

(2) The term ''United States person'' means the following:

(A) A United States citizen.

(B) An alien known by the intelligence agency concerned to be a permanent resident alien.

(C) An unincorporated association substantially composed of United States citizens or permanent resident aliens.

(D) A corporation incorporated in the United States, except for a corporation directed and controlled by a foreign government or governments.

(July 26, 1947, ch. 343, title I, § 105A, as added Pub. L. 104–293, title VIII, § 814(a), Oct. 11, 1996, 110 Stat. 3483.)

§ 403–5b. Protection of operational files of the National Imagery and Mapping Agency

(a) Exemption of certain operational files from search, review, publication, or disclosure

(1) The Director of the National Imagery and Mapping Agency, with the coordination of the Director of Central Intelligence, may exempt operational files of the National Imagery and Mapping Agency from the provisions of section 552 of title 5 which require publication, disclosure, search, or review in connection therewith.

(2)(A) Subject to subparagraph (B), for the purposes of this section, the term ''operational files'' means files of the National Imagery and Mapping Agency (hereafter in this section referred to as ''NIMA'') concerning the activities of NIMA that before the establishment of NIMA were performed by the National Photographic Interpretation Center of the Central Intelligence Agency (NPIC), that document the means by which foreign intelligence or counterintelligence is collected through scientific and technical systems.

(B) Files which are the sole repository of disseminated intelligence are not operational files.

(3) Notwithstanding paragraph (1), exempted operational files shall continue to be subject to search and review for information concerning—

(A) United States citizens or aliens lawfully admitted for permanent residence who have requested information on themselves pursuant to the provisions of section 552 or 552a of title 5;

(B) any special activity the existence of which is not exempt from disclosure under the provisions of section 552 of title 5; or

(C) the specific subject matter of an investigation by any of the following for any impropriety, or violation of law, Executive order, or Presidential directive, in the conduct of an intelligence activity:

(i) The Permanent Select Committee on Intelligence of the House of Representatives.

(ii) The Select Committee on Intelligence of the Senate.

(iii) The Intelligence Oversight Board.

(iv) The Department of Justice.

(v) The Office of General Counsel of NIMA.

(vi) The Office of the Director of NIMA.

(4)(A) Files that are not exempted under paragraph (1) which contain information derived or disseminated from exempted operational files shall be subject to search and review.

(B) The inclusion of information from exempted operational files in files that are not exempted under paragraph (1) shall not affect the exemption under paragraph (1) of the originating operational files from search, review, publication, or disclosure.

(C) Records from exempted operational files which have been disseminated to and referenced in files that are not exempted under paragraph (1) and which have been returned to exempted operational files for sole retention shall be subject to search and review.

(5) The provisions of paragraph (1) may not be superseded except by a provision of law which is enacted after December 3, 1999, and which specifically cites and repeals or modifies its provisions.

(6)(A) Except as provided in subparagraph (B), whenever any person who has requested agency records under section 552 of title 5 alleges that NIMA has withheld records improperly because of failure to comply with any provision of this section, judicial review shall be available under the terms set forth in section 552(a)(4)(B) of title 5.

(B) Judicial review shall not be available in the manner provided for under subparagraph (A) as follows:

(i) In any case in which information specifically authorized under criteria established by an Executive order to be kept secret in the interests of national defense or foreign relations is filed with, or produced for, the court by NIMA, such information shall be examined ex parte, in camera by the court.

(ii) The court shall, to the fullest extent practicable, determine the issues of fact based on sworn written submissions of the parties.

(iii) When a complainant alleges that requested records are improperly withheld because of improper placement solely in exempted operational files, the complainant shall support such allegation with a sworn written submission based upon personal knowledge or otherwise admissible evidence.

(iv)(I) When a complainant alleges that requested records were improperly withheld because of improper exemption of operational files, NIMA shall meet its burden under section 552(a)(4)(B) of title 5 by demonstrating to the court by sworn written submission that exempted operational files likely to contain responsible records currently perform the functions set forth in paragraph (2).

(II) The court may not order NIMA to review the content of any exempted operational file or files in order to make the demonstration required under subclause (I), unless the complainant disputes NIMA's showing with a sworn written submission based on personal knowledge or otherwise admissible evidence.

(v) In proceedings under clauses (iii) and (iv), the parties may not obtain discovery pursuant to rules 26 through 36 of the Federal Rules of Civil Procedure, except that requests for admissions may be made pursuant to rules 26 and 36.

(vi) If the court finds under this paragraph that NIMA has improperly withheld requested records because of failure to comply with any provision of this subsection, the court shall order NIMA to search and review the appropriate exempted operational file or files for the requested records and make such records, or portions thereof, available in accordance with the provisions of section 552 of title 5, and such order shall be the exclusive remedy for failure to comply with this subsection.

(vii) If at any time following the filing of a complaint pursuant to this paragraph NIMA agrees to search the appropriate exempted operational file or files for the requested records, the court shall dismiss the claim based upon such complaint.

(viii) Any information filed with, or produced for the court pursuant to clauses (i) and (iv) shall be coordinated with the Director of Central Intelligence prior to submission to the court.

(b) Decennial review of exempted operational files

(1) Not less than once every 10 years, the Director of the National Imagery and Mapping Agency and the Director of Central Intelligence shall review the exemptions in force under subsection (a)(1) of this section to determine whether such exemptions may be removed from the category of exempted files or any portion thereof. The Director of Central Intelligence must approve any determination to remove such exemptions.

(2) The review required by paragraph (1) shall include consideration of the historical value or other public interest in the subject matter of the particular category of files or portions thereof and the potential for declassifying a significant part of the information contained therein.

(3) A complainant that alleges that NIMA has improperly withheld records because of failure to comply with this subsection may seek judicial review in the district court of the United States of the district in which any of the parties reside, or in the District of Columbia. In such a proceeding, the court's review shall be limited to determining the following:

(A) Whether NIMA has conducted the review required by paragraph (1) before the expiration of the 10-year period beginning on December 3, 1999, or before the expiration of the 10-year period beginning on the date of the most recent review.

(B) Whether NIMA, in fact, considered the criteria set forth in paragraph (2) in conducting the required review.

(July 26, 1947, ch. 343, title I, § 105B, as added Pub. L. 106–120, title V, § 501(a)(1), Dec. 3, 1999, 113 Stat. 1616.)

REFERENCES IN TEXT

The Federal Rules of Civil Procedure, referred to in subsec. (a)(6)(B)(v), are set out in the Appendix to Title 28, Judiciary and Judicial Procedure.

TREATMENT OF CERTAIN TRANSFERRED RECORDS

Pub. L. 106–120, title V, § 501(b), Dec. 3, 1999, 113 Stat. 1619, provided that: "Any record transferred to the National Imagery and Mapping Agency from exempted operational files of the Central Intelligence Agency covered by section 701(a) of the National Security Act of 1947 (50 U.S.C. 431(a)) shall be placed in the operational files of the National Imagery and Mapping Agency that are established pursuant to section 105B of the National Security Act of 1947 [50 U.S.C. 403–5b], as added by subsection (a)."

§ 403–6. Appointment of officials responsible for intelligence-related activities

(a) Concurrence of DCI in certain appointments

(1) In the event of a vacancy in a position referred to in paragraph (2), the Secretary of Defense shall obtain the concurrence of the Director of Central Intelligence before recommending to the President an individual for appointment to the position. If the Director does not concur in the recommendation, the Secretary may make the recommendation to the President without the Director's concurrence, but shall include in the recommendation a statement that the Director does not concur in the recommendation.

(2) Paragraph (1) applies to the following positions:

(A) The Director of the National Security Agency.

(B) The Director of the National Reconnaissance Office.

(C) The Director of the National Imagery and Mapping Agency.

(b) Consultation with DCI in certain appointments

(1) In the event of a vacancy in a position referred to in paragraph (2), the head of the department or agency having jurisdiction over the position shall consult with the Director of Central Intelligence before appointing an individual to fill the vacancy or recommending to the President an individual to be nominated to fill the vacancy.

(2) Paragraph (1) applies to the following positions:

(A) The Director of the Defense Intelligence Agency.

(B) The Assistant Secretary of State for Intelligence and Research.

(C) The Director of the Office of Nonproliferation and National Security of the Department of Energy.

(3) In the event of a vacancy in the position of the Assistant Director, National Security Division of the Federal Bureau of Investigation, the Director of the Federal Bureau of Investigation shall provide timely notice to the Director of Central Intelligence of the recommendation of the Director of the Federal Bureau of Investigation of an individual to fill the position in order that the Director of Central Intelligence may consult with the Director of the Federal Bureau of Investigation before the Attorney General appoints an individual to fill the vacancy.

(July 26, 1947, ch. 343, title I, § 106, as added Pub. L. 102–496, title VII, § 706(a), Oct. 24, 1992, 106 Stat. 3195; amended Pub. L. 103–359, title V, § 501(a)(3), Oct. 14, 1994, 108 Stat. 3428; Pub. L. 104–293, title VIII, § 815(a), Oct. 11, 1996, 110 Stat. 3484.)

AMENDMENTS

1996—Pub. L. 104–293 amended section generally, substituting provisions relating to appointment of individuals responsible for intelligence-related activities for provisions relating to administrative provisions pertaining to defense elements within the intelligence community.

1994—Subsec. (b). Pub. L. 103–359 substituted "Central Imagery Office" for "central imagery authority" in heading and text.

SIMILAR PROVISIONS

Provisions similar to those in subsecs. (a) and (b) of this section are contained in section 201(a) and (b) of Title 10, Armed Forces.

§ 403–7. Prohibition on using journalists as agents or assets

(a) Policy

It is the policy of the United States that an element of the Intelligence Community may not use as an agent or asset for the purposes of collecting intelligence any individual who—

(1) is authorized by contract or by the issuance of press credentials to represent himself or herself, either in the United States or abroad, as a correspondent of a United States news media organization; or

(2) is officially recognized by a foreign government as a representative of a United States media organization.

(b) Waiver

Pursuant to such procedures as the President may prescribe, the President or the Director of Central Intelligence may waive subsection (a) of this section in the case of an individual if the President or the Director, as the case may be, makes a written determination that the waiver is necessary to address the overriding national security interest of the United States. The Permanent Select Committee on Intelligence of the House of Representatives and the Select Committee on Intelligence of the Senate shall be notified of any waiver under this subsection.

(c) Voluntary cooperation

Subsection (a) of this section shall not be construed to prohibit the voluntary cooperation of any person who is aware that the cooperation is being provided to an element of the United States Intelligence Community.

(Pub. L. 104–293, title III, § 309, Oct. 11, 1996, 110 Stat. 3467.)

CODIFICATION

Section was enacted as part of the Intelligence Authorization Act for Fiscal Year 1997, and not as part of the National Security Act of 1947 which comprises this chapter.

§ 403–8. Reaffirmation of longstanding prohibition against drug trafficking by employees of the intelligence community

(a) Finding

Congress finds that longstanding statutes, regulations, and policies of the United States prohibit employees, agents, and assets of the elements of the intelligence community, and of every other Federal department and agency, from engaging in the illegal manufacture, purchase, sale, transport, and distribution of drugs.

(b) Obligation of employees of intelligence community

Any employee of the intelligence community having knowledge of a fact or circumstance that reasonably indicates that an employee, agent, or asset of an element of the intelligence community is involved in any activity that violates a statute, regulation, or policy described in subsection (a) of this section shall report such knowledge to an appropriate official.

(c) Intelligence community defined

In this section, the term "intelligence community" has the meaning given that term in section 401a(4) of this title.

(Pub. L. 106–120, title III, § 313, Dec. 3, 1999, 113 Stat. 1615.)

CODIFICATION

Section was enacted as part of the Intelligence Authorization Act for Fiscal Year 2000, and not as part of the National Security Act of 1947 which comprises this chapter.

§ 403a. Definitions relating to Central Intelligence Agency

When used in sections 403a to 403s of this title, the term—

(a) "Agency" means the Central Intelligence Agency;

(b) "Director" means the Director of Central Intelligence;

(c) "Government agency" means any executive department, commission, council, independent establishment, corporation wholly or partly owned by the United States which is an instrumentality of the United States, board, bureau, division, service, office, officer, authority, administration, or other establishment, in the executive branch of the Government.

(June 20, 1949, ch. 227, § 1, 63 Stat. 208; Pub. L. 86–707, title V, § 511(a)(3), (c)(1), Sept. 6, 1960, 74 Stat. 800, 801.)

CODIFICATION

Section was enacted as part of the Central Intelligence Agency Act of 1949, and not as part of the National Security Act of 1947 which comprises this chapter.

AMENDMENTS

1960—Subsec. (c). Pub. L. 86–707, § 511(c)(1), substituted "Government." for "Government; and".

Subsec. (d). Pub. L. 86–707, § 511(a)(3), repealed subsec. (d) which defined "continental United States". See section 5921 of Title 5, Government Organization and Employees.

SHORT TITLE

Act June 20, 1949, ch. 227, § 10, formerly § 12, 63 Stat. 212; renumbered § 10, July 7, 1958, Pub. L. 85–507, § 21(b)(2), 72 Stat. 337, provided that: "This Act [enacting section 403a et seq. of this title] may be cited as the 'Central Intelligence Agency Act of 1949'."

SEPARABILITY

Act June 20, 1949, § 9, formerly § 11, 63 Stat. 212; renumbered § 9, July 7, 1958, Pub. L. 85–507, § 21(b)(2), 72 Stat. 337, provided that: "If any provision of this Act [enacting sections 403a et seq. of this title], or the application of such provision to any person or circumstances, is held invalid, the remainder of this Act or the application of such provision to persons or circumstances other than those as to which it is held invalid, shall not be affected thereby."

ACT REFERRED TO IN OTHER SECTIONS

The Central Intelligence Agency Act of 1949 is referred to in title 5 sections 2305, 5373; title 10 section 444.

SECTION REFERRED TO IN OTHER SECTIONS

This section is referred to in sections 403e, 403f of this title.

§ 403b. Seal of office of Central Intelligence Agency

The Director of Central Intelligence shall cause a seal of office to be made for the Central Intelligence Agency, of such design as the President shall approve, and judicial notice shall be taken thereof.

(June 20, 1949, ch. 227, § 2, 63 Stat. 208.)

CODIFICATION

Section was enacted as part of the Central Intelligence Agency Act of 1949, and not as part of the National Security Act of 1947 which comprises this chapter.

SECTION REFERRED TO IN OTHER SECTIONS

This section is referred to in sections 403a, 403e, 403f of this title.

§ 403c. Procurement authority of Central Intelligence Agency

(a) Purchases and contracts for supplies and services

In the performance of its functions the Central Intelligence Agency is authorized to exercise the authorities contained in sections 2304(a)(1) to (6), (10), (12), (15), (17), and sections 2305(a) to (c), 2306, 2307, 2308, 2309, 2312, and 2313 of title 10.[1]

(b) "Agency head" defined

In the exercise of the authorities granted in subsection (a) of this section, the term "Agency head" shall mean the Director, the Deputy Director, or the Executive of the Agency.

(c) Classes of purchases and contracts; finality of decision; powers delegable

The determinations and decisions provided in subsection (a) of this section to be made by the Agency head may be made with respect to individual purchases and contracts or with respect to classes of purchases or contracts, and shall be final. Except as provided in subsection (d) of this section, the Agency head is authorized to delegate his powers provided in this section, including the making of such determinations and decisions, in his discretion and subject to his direc-

[1] See Codification note below.

tion, to any other officer or officers or officials of the Agency.

(d) Powers not delegable; written findings

The power of the Agency head to make the determinations or decisions specified in paragraphs (12) and (15) of section 2304(a) and section 2307(a) of title 10[1] shall not be delegable. Each determination or decision required by paragraphs (12) and (15) of section 2304(a), by sections 2306 and 2313, or by section 2307(a) of title 10,[1] shall be based upon written findings made by the official making such determinations, which findings shall be final and shall be available within the Agency for a period of at least six years following the date of the determination.

(June 20, 1949, ch. 227, §3, 63 Stat. 208; Pub. L. 97–269, title V, §502(a), Sept. 27, 1982, 96 Stat. 1145; Pub. L. 104–106, div. E, title LVI, §5607(f), Feb. 10, 1996, 110 Stat. 702.)

CODIFICATION

Section was enacted as part of the Central Intelligence Agency Act of 1949, and not as part of the National Security Act of 1947 which comprises this chapter.

In subsecs. (a) and (d), references to the appropriate sections of title 10 were substituted for references to sections 2(c)(1) to (6), (10), (12), (15), (17), 3, 4, 5, 6, and 10 of the Armed Services Procurement Act of 1947 (Public Law 413, 80th Congress), on authority of section 49(b) of act Aug. 10, 1956, ch. 1041, 70A Stat. 640, section 1 of which enacted Title 10, Armed Forces. Prior to the enactment of Title 10, sections 2 to 6 and 10 of the Armed Services Procurement Act of 1947 were classified to sections 151 to 155 and 159 of Title 41, Public Contracts. Cited sections of the Act were restated in sections of Title 10 as follows:

Act	*Title 10*
2(c)	2304(a)
3	2305(a)–(c)
4	2306, 2313
5	2307
5(a)	2307(a)
6	2312
10	2308, 2309

Sections 2304 and 2305 of title 10 were amended generally by Pub. L. 98–369, and as so amended contain provisions differing from those referred to in subsecs. (a) and (d). Section 2308 of title 10 was repealed by Pub. L. 103–355, title I, §1503(b)(1), Oct. 13, 1994, 108 Stat. 3297. For similar provisions, see section 2311 of title 10.

AMENDMENTS

1996—Subsec. (e). Pub. L. 104–106 struck out subsec. (e) which read as follows: "Notwithstanding subsection (e) of section 759 of title 40, the provisions of section 759 of title 40 relating to the procurement of automatic data processing equipment or services shall not apply with respect to such procurement by the Central Intelligence Agency."

1982—Subsec. (e). Pub. L. 97–269 added subsec. (e).

EFFECTIVE DATE OF 1996 AMENDMENT

Amendment by Pub. L. 104–106 effective 180 days after Feb. 10, 1996, see section 5701 of Pub. L. 104–106, set out as an Effective Date note under section 1401 of Title 40, Public Buildings, Property, and Works.

EFFECTIVE DATE OF 1982 AMENDMENT

Section 703 of title VII of Pub. L. 97–269 provided that: "The provisions of titles IV and V [enacting former section 202 of Title 10, Armed Forces, and amending this section] and of this title [which, except for enacting this note was not classified to the Code] shall become effective upon the date of the enactment of this Act [Sept. 27, 1982]."

PROCUREMENT OF AUTOMATIC DATA PROCESSING EQUIPMENT OR SERVICES; CONTRACTS MADE BEFORE SEPTEMBER 27, 1982

Section 502(b) of Pub. L. 97–269 provided that: "Subsection (e) of section 3 of the Central Intelligence Agency Act of 1949 (50 U.S.C. 403c(e)), as added by subsection (a) of this section, does not apply to a contract made before the date of the enactment of this Act [Sept. 27, 1982]."

SECTION REFERRED TO IN OTHER SECTIONS

This section is referred to in sections 403a, 403e, 403f of this title.

§ 403d. Repealed. Pub. L. 85–507, § 21(b)(2), July 7, 1958, 72 Stat. 337

Section, act June 20, 1949, ch. 227, §4, 63 Stat. 208, related to education and training of officers and employees. See section 4101 et seq. of Title 5, Government Organization and Employees.

Section was enacted as part of the Central Intelligence Agency Act of 1949, and not as part of the National Security Act of 1947 which comprises this chapter.

§ 403e. Central Intelligence Agency personnel; allowances and benefits

(a) Travel, allowances, and related expenses for officers and employees assigned to duty stations outside United States

Under such regulations as the Director may prescribe, the Agency, with respect to its officers and employees assigned to duty stations outside the several States of the United States of America, excluding Alaska and Hawaii, but including the District of Columbia, shall—

(1)(A) pay the travel expenses of officers and employees of the Agency, including expenses incurred while traveling pursuant to authorized home leave;

(B) pay the travel expenses of members of the family of an officer or employee of the Agency when proceeding to or returning from his post of duty; accompanying him on authorized home leave; or otherwise traveling in accordance with authority granted pursuant to the terms of sections 403a to 403s of this title or any other Act;

(C) pay the cost of transporting the furniture and household and personal effects of an officer or employee of the Agency to his successive posts of duty and, on the termination of his services, to his residence at time of appointment or to a point not more distant, or, upon retirement, to the place where he will reside;

(D) pay the cost of packing and unpacking, transporting to and from a place of storage, and storing the furniture and household and personal effects of an officer or employee of the Agency, when he is absent from his post of assignment under orders, or when he is assigned to a post to which he cannot take or at which he is unable to use such furniture and household and personal effects, or when it is in the public interest or more economical to authorize storage; but in no instance shall the weight or volume of the effects stored together with the weight or volume of the effects transported exceed the maximum limitations fixed by regulations, when not otherwise fixed by law;

(E) pay the cost of packing and unpacking, transporting to and from a place of storage, and storing the furniture and household and personal effects of an officer or employee of the Agency in connection with assignment or transfer to a new post, from the date of his departure from his last post or from the date of his departure, from his place of residence in the case of a new officer or employee and for not to exceed three months after arrival at the new post, or until the establishment of residence quarters, whichever shall be shorter; and in connection with separation of an officer or employee of the Agency, the cost of packing and unpacking, transporting to and from a place of storage, and storing for a period not to exceed three months, his furniture and household and personal effects; but in no instance shall the weight or volume of the effects stored together with the weight or volume of the effects transported exceed the maximum limitations fixed by regulations, when not otherwise fixed by law.[1]

(F) pay the travel expenses and transportation costs incident to the removal of the members of the family of an officer or employee of the Agency and his furniture and household and personal effects, including automobiles, from a post at which, because of the prevalence of disturbed conditions, there is imminent danger to life and property, and the return of such persons, furniture, and effects to such post upon the cessation of such conditions; or to such other post as may in the meantime have become the post to which such officer or employee has been assigned.

(2) Charge expenses in connection with travel of personnel, their dependents, and transportation of their household goods and personal effects, involving a change of permanent station, to the appropriation for the fiscal year current when any part of either the travel or transportation pertaining to the transfer begins pursuant to previously issued travel and transfer orders, notwithstanding the fact that such travel or transportation may not all be effected during such fiscal year, or the travel and transfer orders may have been issued during the prior fiscal year.

(3)(A) Order to any of the several States of the United States of America (including the District of Columbia, the Commonwealth of Puerto Rico, and any territory or possession of the United States) on leave of absence each officer or employee of the Agency who was a resident of the United States (as described above) at time of employment, upon completion of two years' continuous service abroad, or as soon as possible thereafter.

(B) While in the United States (as described in paragraph (3)(A) of this subsection)[2] on leave, the service of any officer or employee shall be available for work or duties in the Agency or elsewhere as the Director may prescribe; and the time of such work or duty shall not be counted as leave.

(C) Where an officer or employee on leave returns to the United States (as described in paragraph (3)(A) of this subsection),[2] leave of absence granted shall be exclusive of the time actually and necessarily occupied in going to and from the United States (as so described) and such time as may be necessarily occupied in awaiting transportation.

(4) Notwithstanding the provisions of any other law, transport for or on behalf of an officer or employee of the Agency, a privately owned motor vehicle in any case in which it shall be determined that water, rail, or air transportation of the motor vehicle is necessary or expedient for all or any part of the distance between points of origin and destination, and pay the costs of such transportation. Not more than one motor vehicle of any officer or employee of the Agency may be transported under authority of this paragraph during any four-year period, except that, as a replacement for such motor vehicle, one additional motor vehicle of any such officer or employee may be so transported during such period upon approval, in advance, by the Director and upon a determination, in advance, by the Director that such replacement is necessary for reasons beyond the control of the officer or employee and is in the interest of the Government. After the expiration of a period of four years following the date of transportation under authority of this paragraph of a privately owned motor vehicle of any officer or employee who has remained in continuous service outside the several States of the United States of America, excluding Alaska and Hawaii, but including the District of Columbia, during such period, the transportation of a replacement for such motor vehicle for such officer or employee may be authorized by the Director in accordance with this paragraph.

(5)(A) In the event of illness or injury requiring the hospitalization of an officer or full time employee of the Agency incurred while on assignment abroad, in a locality where there does not exist a suitable hospital or clinic, pay the travel expenses of such officer or employee by whatever means the Director deems appropriate and without regard to the Standardized Government Travel Regulations and section 5731 of title 5, to the nearest locality where a suitable hospital or clinic exists and on the recovery of such officer or employee pay for the travel expenses of the return to the post of duty of such officer or employee. If the officer or employee is too ill to travel unattended, the Director may also pay the travel expenses of an attendant;

(B) Establish a first-aid station and provide for the services of a nurse at a post at which, in the opinion of the Director, sufficient personnel is employed to warrant such a station: *Provided*, That, in the opinion of the Director, it is not feasible to utilize an existing facility;

(C) In the event of illness or injury requiring hospitalization of an officer or full time employee of the Agency incurred in the line of duty while such person is assigned abroad, pay

[1] So in original. The period probably should be a semicolon.

[2] See Codification note below.

for the cost of the treatment of such illness or injury at a suitable hospital or clinic;

(D) Provide for the periodic physical examination of officers and employees of the Agency and for the cost of administering inoculation or vaccinations to such officers or employees.

(6) Pay the costs of preparing and transporting the remains of an officer or employee of the Agency or a member of his family who may die while in travel status or abroad, to his home or official station, or to such other place as the Director may determine to be the appropriate place of interment, provided that in no case shall the expense payable be greater than the amount which would have been payable had the destination been the home or official station.

(7) Pay the costs of travel of new appointees and their dependents, and the transportation of their household goods and personal effects, from places of actual residence in foreign countries at time of appointment to places of employment and return to their actual residences at the time of appointment or a point not more distant: *Provided*, That such appointees agree in writing to remain with the United States Government for a period of not less than twelve months from the time of appointment.

Violation of such agreement for personal convenience of an employee or because of separation for misconduct will bar such return payments and, if determined by the Director or his designee to be in the best interests of the United States, any money expended by the United States on account of such travel and transportation shall be considered as a debt due by the individual concerned to the United States.

(b) Allowances and benefits comparable to those paid members of Foreign Service; special requirements; persons detailed or assigned from other agencies; regulations

(1) The Director may pay to officers and employees of the Agency, and to persons detailed or assigned to the Agency from other agencies of the Government or from the Armed Forces, allowances and benefits comparable to the allowances and benefits authorized to be paid to members of the Foreign Service under chapter 9 of title I of the Foreign Service Act of 1980 (22 U.S.C. 4081 et seq.) or any other provision of law.

(2) The Director may pay allowances and benefits related to officially authorized travel, personnel and physical security activities, operational activities, and cover-related activities (whether or not such allowances and benefits are otherwise authorized under this section or any other provision of law) when payment of such allowances and benefits is necessary to meet the special requirements of work related to such activities. Payment of allowances and benefits under this paragraph shall be in accordance with regulations prescribed by the Director. Rates for allowances and benefits under this paragraph may not be set at rates in excess of those authorized by section 5724 and 5724a of title 5 when reimbursement is provided for relocation attributable, in whole or in part, to relocation within the United States.

(3) Notwithstanding any other provision of this section or any other provision of law relating to the officially authorized travel of Government employees, the Director, in order to reflect Agency requirements not taken into account in the formulation of Government-wide travel procedures, may by regulation—

(A) authorize the travel of officers and employees of the Agency, and of persons detailed or assigned to the Agency from other agencies of the Government or from the Armed Forces who are engaged in the performance of intelligence functions, and

(B) provide for payment for such travel, in classes of cases, as determined by the Director, in which such travel is important to the performance of intelligence functions.

(4) Members of the Armed Forces may not receive benefits under both this section and title 37 for the same purpose. The Director and Secretary of Defense shall prescribe joint regulations to carry out the preceding sentence.

(5) Regulations issued pursuant to this subsection shall be submitted to the Permanent Select Committee on Intelligence of the House of Representatives and the Select Committee on Intelligence of the Senate before such regulations take effect.

(June 20, 1949, ch. 227, §4, formerly §5, 63 Stat. 209; renumbered §4, Pub. L. 85–507, §21(b)(2), July 7, 1958, 72 Stat. 337; amended Pub. L. 86–707, title III, §§301(b), 323, title V, §511(a)(3), (c)(2)–(5), Sept. 6, 1960, 74 Stat. 795, 798, 800, 801; Pub. L. 97–89, title V, §501, Dec. 4, 1981, 95 Stat. 1152; Pub. L. 103–359, title IV, §401, Oct. 14, 1994, 108 Stat. 3427.)

REFERENCES IN TEXT

The Foreign Service Act of 1980, referred to in subsec. (b)(1), is Pub. L. 96–465, Oct. 17, 1980, 94 Stat. 2071, as amended. Chapter 9 of title I of the Foreign Service Act of 1980 is classified generally to subchapter IX (§4081 et seq.) of chapter 52 of Title 22, Foreign Relations and Intercourse. For complete classification of this Act to the Code, see Short Title note set out under section 3901 of Title 22 and Tables.

CODIFICATION

In subsec. (a)(3)(B), (C), "this subsection" substituted for "this section" as the probable intent of Congress in view of the designation of the existing provisions of this section as subsec. (a) and the addition of subsec. (b) by Pub. L. 97–89, title V, §501, Dec. 4, 1981, 95 Stat. 1152.

Section was enacted as part of the Central Intelligence Agency Act of 1949, and not as part of the National Security Act of 1947 which comprises this chapter.

AMENDMENTS

1994—Subsec. (a)(5)(A). Pub. L. 103–359, §401(1)(A)–(D), struck out ", not the result of vicious habits, intemperance, or misconduct on his part," after "the Agency" and substituted "the Director deems" for "he shall deem", "section 5731 of title 5" for "section 10 of the Act of March 3, 1933 (47 Stat. 1516; 5 U.S.C. 73b)", and "the recovery of such officer or employee" for "his recovery".

Pub. L. 103–359, §401(1)(E), which directed the substitution of "the return to the post of duty of such officer or employee" for "his return to his post", was executed by making the substitution for "his return to his post of duty" to reflect the probable intent of Congress.

Subsec. (a)(5)(B). Pub. L. 103–359, §401(2), substituted "the opinion of the Director" for "his opinion" in two places.

Subsec. (a)(5)(C). Pub. L. 103–359, §401(3), struck out ", not the result of vicious habits, intemperance, or misconduct on his part," after "the Agency".

1981—Pub. L. 97–89 designated existing provisions as subsec. (a) and added subsec. (b).

1960—Pub. L. 86–707, §323(a), substituted "duty stations outside the several States of the United States of America, excluding Alaska and Hawaii, but including the District of Columbia" for "permanent-duty stations outside the continental United States, its territories, and possessions" in opening provisions, and struck out subsec. (a) designation.

Par. (1)(A). Pub. L. 86–707, §511(c)(2), substituted "pursuant to authorized home leave" for "pursuant to orders issued by the Director in accordance with the provisions of subsection (a)(3) of this section with regard to the granting of home leave".

Par. (1)(D). Pub. L. 86–707, §301(b), authorized payment of cost of packing and unpacking and transporting to and from a place of storage, extended authority to pay storage costs for an officer or employee assigned to a post to which he cannot take or at which he is unable to use his furniture and household personal effects by striking out provisions which restricted such payment only to cases where an emergency exists, empowered Director to pay storage costs when it is in the public interest or more economical to authorize storage, and limited weight or volume of effects stored or weight or volume of effects transported to not more than maximum limitations fixed by regulations, when not otherwise fixed by law.

Par. (1)(E). Pub. L. 86–707, §301(b), authorized payment of cost of packing and unpacking and transporting to and from a place of storage, permitted payment from date of departure from officer's or employee's last post or from date of departure from place of residence in the case of a new officer or employee, empowered Director to pay storage costs in connection with separation of an officer or employee from the Agency, and limited weight or volume of effects stored or weight or volume of effects transported to not more than maximum limitations fixed by regulations, when not otherwise fixed by law.

Par. (3)(A). Pub. L. 86–707, §511(c)(3), substituted "to any of the several States of the United States of America (including the District of Columbia, the Commonwealth of Puerto Rico, and any territory or possession of the United States) on leave of absence each officer or employee of the Agency who was a resident of the United States (as described above) at time of employment, upon completion of two years' continuous service abroad, or as soon as possible thereafter" for "to the United States or its Territories and possessions on leave provided for in sections 30–30b of Title 5 [former Title 5, Executive Departments and Government Officers and Employees], or as such sections may hereafter be amended, every officer and employee of the agency who was a resident of the United States or its Territories and possessions at time of employment, upon completion of two years' continuous service abroad, or as soon as possible thereafter: Provided, That such officer or employee has accrued to his credit at the time of such order, annual leave sufficient to carry him in a pay status while in the United States for at least a thirty-day period".

Par. (3)(B). Pub. L. 86–707, §511(c)(4), substituted "United States (as described in paragraph (3)(A) of this section) on leave, the service of any officer or employee shall be available for work or duties in the Agency or elsewhere as the Director may prescribe" for "continental United States on leave, the service of any officer or employee shall not be available for work or duties except in the agency or for training or for reorientation for work".

Par. (3)(C). Pub. L. 86–707, §511(c)(5), substituted "returns to the United States (as described in paragraph (3)(A) of this section)" for "returns to the United States or its Territories and possessions", and "from the United States (as so described)" for "from the United States or its Territories and possessions".

Par. (4). Pub. L. 86–707, §323(b), limited transportation of motor vehicles to one for any officer or employee during any four-year period, and empowered Director to approve transportation of one additional motor vehicle for replacement either during the four-year period or after expiration of four years following date of transportation of a motor vehicle of any officer or employee who has remained in continuous service outside the several States, excluding Alaska and Hawaii, but including the District of Columbia, for such period.

Pub. L. 86–707, §511(a)(3), repealed subsec. (b) which authorized Director to grant allowances in accordance with provisions of section 1131(1), (2) of Title 22, Foreign Relations and Intercourse. See pars. (1)(D) and (1)(E) of this section.

EFFECTIVE DATE OF 1981 AMENDMENT

Amendment by Pub. L. 97–89 effective Oct. 1, 1981, see section 806 of Pub. L. 97–89, set out as an Effective Date note under section 1621 of Title 10, Armed Forces.

CLARIFICATION OF TERMS APPLIED TO FURNITURE, HOUSEHOLD GOODS, AND PERSONAL EFFECTS IN 1960 AMENDMENT

Section 301(d) of Pub. L. 86–707 provided that: "The term 'furniture and household and personal effects', as used in the amendments made by this part to the Foreign Service Act of 1946, as amended [amending section 1136 of Title 22, Foreign Relations and Intercourse], and the Central Intelligence Agency Act of 1949, as amended [amending this section], and the term 'household goods and personal effects', as used in the amendments made by this part to the Administrative Expenses Act of 1946, as amended [amending section 73b–1 of former Title 5, Executive Departments and Government Officers and Employees], mean such personal property of an employee and the dependents of such employee as the Secretary of State and the Director of Central Intelligence, as the case may be, with respect to the term 'furniture and household and personal effects', and the President, with respect to the term 'household goods and personal effects', shall by regulation authorize to be transported or stored under the amendments made by this part to such Acts (including, in emergencies, motor vehicles authorized to be shipped at Government expense). Such motor vehicle shall be excluded from the weight and volume limitations prescribed by the laws set forth in this part."

Section 301(d) of Pub. L. 86–707 was repealed by Pub. L. 89–554, §8(a), Sept. 6, 1966, 80 Stat. 661, insofar as it is applicable to the Administrative Expenses Act of 1946, as amended.

EXECUTIVE ORDER NO. 10100

Ex. Ord. No. 10100, Jan. 28, 1950, 15 F.R. 499, which provided for regulations governing the granting of allowances by the Director of the Central Intelligence Agency under this section, was revoked by section 5(a) of Ex. Ord. No. 10903, Jan. 9, 1961, 26 F.R. 217, set out under section 5921 of Title 5, Government Organization and Employees.

SECTION REFERRED TO IN OTHER SECTIONS

This section is referred to in sections 403a, 403f of this title.

§403e–1. Eligibility for incentive awards

(a) Scope of authority with respect to Federal employees and members of Armed Forces

The Director of Central Intelligence may exercise the authority granted in section 4503 of title 5, with respect to Federal employees and members of the Armed Forces detailed or assigned to the Central Intelligence Agency or to the Intelligence Community Staff, in the same manner as such authority may be exercised with respect to the personnel of the Central Intelligence Agency and the Intelligence Community Staff.

(b) Time for exercise of authority

The authority granted by subsection (a) of this section may be exercised with respect to Federal employees or members of the Armed Forces detailed or assigned to the Central Intelligence Agency or to the Intelligence Community Staff on or after a date five years before December 9, 1983.

(c) Exercise of authority with respect to members of Armed Forces assigned to foreign intelligence duties

During fiscal year 1987, the Director of Central Intelligence may exercise the authority granted in section 4503(2) of title 5 with respect to members of the Armed Forces who are assigned to foreign intelligence duties at the time of the conduct which gives rise to the exercise of such authority.

(d) Payment and acceptance of award

An award made by the Director of Central Intelligence to an employee or member of the Armed Forces under the authority of section 4503 of title 5 or this section may be paid and accepted notwithstanding—

(1) section 5536 of title 5; and

(2) the death, separation, or retirement of the employee or the member of the Armed Forces whose conduct gave rise to the award, or the assignment of such member to duties other than foreign intelligence duties.

(Pub. L. 98–215, title IV, §402, Dec. 9, 1983, 97 Stat. 1477; Pub. L. 99–569, title V, §503, Oct. 27, 1986, 100 Stat. 3198.)

CODIFICATION

Section was enacted as part of the Intelligence Authorization Act for Fiscal Year 1984, and not as part of the Central Intelligence Agency Act of 1949 which is classified to section 403a et seq. of this title, nor as part of the National Security Act of 1947 which comprises this chapter.

AMENDMENTS

1986—Subsecs. (c), (d). Pub. L. 99–569 added subsecs. (c) and (d).

§403f. General authorities of Agency

(a) In general

In the performance of its functions, the Central Intelligence Agency is authorized to—

(1) Transfer to and receive from other Government agencies such sums as may be approved by the Office of Management and Budget, for the performance of any of the functions or activities authorized under paragraphs (2) and (3) of section 403(a) of this title, subsections (c)(6) and (d) of section 403–3 of this title, subsections (a) and (g) of section 403–4 of this title, and section 405 of this title, and any other Government agency is authorized to transfer to or receive from the Agency such sums without regard to any provisions of law limiting or prohibiting transfers between appropriations. Sums transferred to the Agency in accordance with this paragraph may be expended for the purposes and under the authority of sections 403a to 403s of this title without regard to limitations of appropriations from which transferred;

(2) Exchange funds without regard to section 3651 of the Revised Statutes;

(3) Reimburse other Government agencies for services of personnel assigned to the Agency, and such other Government agencies are authorized, without regard to provisions of law to the contrary, so to assign or detail any officer or employee for duty with the Agency;

(4) Authorize personnel designated by the Director to carry firearms to the extent necessary for the performance of the Agency's authorized functions, except that, within the United States, such authority shall be limited to the purposes of protection of classified materials and information, the training of Agency personnel and other authorized persons in the use of firearms, the protection of Agency installations and property, and the protection of current and former Agency personnel and their immediate families, defectors and their immediate families, and other persons in the United States under Agency auspices;

(5) Make alterations, improvements, and repairs on premises rented by the Agency, and pay rent therefor;

(6) Determine and fix the minimum and maximum limits of age within which an original appointment may be made to an operational position within the Agency, notwithstanding the provision of any other law, in accordance with such criteria as the Director, in his discretion, may prescribe; and

(7) Notwithstanding section 1341(a)(1) of title 31, enter into multiyear leases for up to 15 years.

(b) Scope of authority for expenditure

(1) The authority to enter into a multiyear lease under subsection (a)(7) of this section shall be subject to appropriations provided in advance for—

(A) the entire lease; or

(B) the first 12 months of the lease and the Government's estimated termination liability.

(2) In the case of any such lease entered into under subparagraph (B) of paragraph (1)—

(A) such lease shall include a clause that provides that the contract shall be terminated if budget authority (as defined by section 622(2) of title 2) is not provided specifically for that project in an appropriations Act in advance of an obligation of funds in respect thereto;

(B) notwithstanding section 1552 of title 31, amounts obligated for paying termination costs with respect to such lease shall remain available until the costs associated with termination of such lease are paid;

(C) funds available for termination liability shall remain available to satisfy rental obligations with respect to such lease in subsequent fiscal years in the event such lease is not terminated early, but only to the extent those funds are in excess of the amount of termination liability at the time of their use to satisfy such rental obligations; and

(D) funds appropriated for a fiscal year may be used to make payments on such lease, for a maximum of 12 months, beginning any time during such fiscal year.

(c) Transfers for acquisition of land

(1) Sums appropriated or otherwise made available to the Agency for the acquisition of land that are transferred to another department or agency for that purpose shall remain available for 3 years.

(2) The Director shall submit to the Select Committee on Intelligence of the Senate and the Permanent Select Committee on Intelligence of the House of Representatives an annual report on the transfers of sums described in paragraph (1).

(June 20, 1949, ch. 227, § 5, formerly § 6, 63 Stat. 211; June 26, 1951, ch. 151, 65 Stat. 89; renumbered § 5, Pub. L. 85–507, § 21(b)(2), July 7, 1958, 72 Stat. 337; amended Pub. L. 88–448, title IV, § 402(a)(28), Aug. 19, 1964, 78 Stat. 494; Pub. L. 97–89, title V, § 502, Dec. 4, 1981, 95 Stat. 1153; Pub. L. 98–215, title IV, § 401, Dec. 9, 1983, 97 Stat. 1477; Pub. L. 103–178, title V, § 501(1), Dec. 3, 1993, 107 Stat. 2038; Pub. L. 105–107, title IV, § 401(a), Nov. 20, 1997, 111 Stat. 2257; Pub. L. 105–272, title IV, §§ 401, 403(a)(1), Oct. 20, 1998, 112 Stat. 2403, 2404; Pub. L. 106–567, title IV, § 405(a), (b), Dec. 27, 2000, 114 Stat. 2849.)

REFERENCES IN TEXT

Section 3651 of the Revised Statutes, referred to in subsec. (a)(2), was classified to section 543 of former Title 31, and was repealed by Pub. L. 97–258, § 5(b), Sept. 13, 1982, 96 Stat. 1084, the first section of which enacted Title 31, Money and Finance.

CODIFICATION

Section was enacted as part of the Central Intelligence Agency Act of 1949, and not as part of the National Security Act of 1947 which comprises this chapter.

AMENDMENTS

2000—Pub. L. 106–567 added subsec. (a) and (b) headings and subsec. (c).

1998—Subsec. (a)(1). Pub. L. 105–272, § 403(a)(1), substituted "paragraphs (2) and (3) of section 403(a)" for "subparagraphs (B) and (C) of section 403(a)(2)" and "(c)(6)" for "(c)(5)" and made technical amendments to references in original act which appear in text as references to sections 403, 403–3, 403–4 of this title.

Subsec. (a)(4). Pub. L. 105–272, § 401, substituted "and the protection of current and former Agency personnel and their immediate families, defectors and their immediate families," for "and the protection of Agency personnel and of defectors, their families,".

1997—Pub. L. 105–107 designated existing provisions as subsec. (a), redesignated former subsecs. (a) to (f) as pars. (1) to (6), respectively, of subsec. (a), in par. (5) substituted semicolon for "without regard to limitations on expenditures contained in the Act of June 30, 1932, as amended: *Provided*, That in each case the Director shall certify that exception from such limitations is necessary to the successful performance of the Agency's functions or to the security of its activities; and", and added par. (7) and subsec. (b).

1993—Subsec. (a). Pub. L. 103–178 substituted "Office of Management and Budget" for "Bureau of the Budget" and "subparagraphs (B) and (C) of section 403(a)(2) of this title, subsections (c)(5) and (d) of section 403–3 of this title, subsections (a) and (g) of section 403–4 of this title, and section 405 of this title" for "sections 403 and 405 of this title".

1983—Subsec. (f). Pub. L. 98–215 added subsec. (f).

1981—Subsec. (d). Pub. L. 97–89 substituted "Authorize personnel designated by the Director to carry firearms to the extent necessary for the performance of the Agency's authorized functions, except that, within the United States, such authority shall be limited to the purposes of protection of classified materials and information, the training of Agency personnel and other authorized persons in the use of firearms, the protection of Agency installations and property, and the protection of Agency personnel and of defectors, their families, and other persons in the United States under Agency auspices; and" for "Authorize couriers and guards designated by the Director to carry firearms when engaged in transportation of confidential documents and materials affecting the national defense and security;".

1964—Subsec. (f). Pub. L. 88–448 repealed subsec. (f) which authorized employment of not more than fifteen retired officers who must elect between civilian salary and retired pay. See section 3101 et seq. of Title 5, Government Organization and Employees.

1951—Subsec. (f). Act June 26, 1951, added subsec. (f).

EFFECTIVE DATE OF 2000 AMENDMENT

Pub. L. 106–567, title IV, § 405(c), Dec. 27, 2000, 114 Stat. 2849, provided that: "Subsection (c) of section 5 of the Central Intelligence Agency Act of 1949 [50 U.S.C. 403f(c)], as added by subsection (a) of this section, shall apply with respect to amounts appropriated or otherwise made available for the Central Intelligence Agency for fiscal years after fiscal year 2000."

EFFECTIVE DATE OF 1997 AMENDMENT

Pub. L. 105–107, title IV, § 401(b), Nov. 20, 1997, 111 Stat. 2257, provided that: "The amendments made by subsection (a) [amending this section] apply to multiyear leases entered into under section 5 of the Central Intelligence Agency Act of 1949 [this section], as so amended, on or after October 1, 1997."

EFFECTIVE DATE OF 1981 AMENDMENT

Amendment by Pub. L. 97–89 effective Oct. 1, 1981, see section 806 of Pub. L. 97–89, set out as an Effective Date note under section 1621 of Title 10, Armed Forces.

EFFECTIVE DATE OF 1964 AMENDMENT

Amendment by Pub. L. 88–448 effective on first day of first month which begins later than the ninetieth day following Aug. 19, 1964, see section 403 of Pub. L. 88–448.

RESTRICTION ON TRANSFER OF FUNDS AVAILABLE TO CENTRAL INTELLIGENCE AGENCY FOR DRUG INTERDICTION AND COUNTER-DRUG ACTIVITIES

Pub. L. 106–259, title VIII, § 8062(b), Aug. 9, 2000, 114 Stat. 688, provided that: "None of the funds available to the Central Intelligence Agency for any fiscal year for drug interdiction and counter-drug activities may be transferred to any other department or agency of the United States except as specifically provided in an appropriations law."

Similar provisions were contained in the following prior appropriation acts:

Pub. L. 106–79, title VIII, § 8065(b), Oct. 25, 1999, 113 Stat. 1244.

Pub. L. 105–262, title VIII, § 8065(b), Oct. 17, 1998, 112 Stat. 2312.

Pub. L. 105–56, title VIII, § 8071(b), Oct. 8, 1997, 111 Stat. 1235.

Pub. L. 104–208, div. A, title I, § 101(b) [title VIII, § 8080(b)], Sept. 30, 1996, 110 Stat. 3009–71, 3009–104.

Pub. L. 104–61, title VIII, § 8096(b), Dec. 1, 1995, 109 Stat. 671.

Pub. L. 103–335, title VIII, § 8154(b), Sept. 30, 1994, 108 Stat. 2658.

SECTION REFERRED TO IN OTHER SECTIONS

This section is referred to in sections 403a, 403e of this title.

§ 403g. Protection of nature of Agency's functions

In the interests of the security of the foreign intelligence activities of the United States and in order further to implement section 403–3(c)(6) of this title that the Director of Central Intelligence shall be responsible for protecting intelligence sources and methods from unauthorized disclosure, the Agency shall be exempted from the provisions of sections 1 and 2 of the Act of August 28, 1935 (49 Stat. 956, 957; 5 U.S.C. 654), and the provisions of any other law which require the publication or disclosure of the organization, functions, names, official titles, salaries, or numbers of personnel employed by the Agency: *Provided*, That in furtherance of this section, the Director of the Office of Management and Budget shall make no reports to the Congress in connection with the Agency under section 607 of the Act of June 30, 1945, as amended (5 U.S.C. 947(b)).

(June 20, 1949, ch. 227, § 6, formerly § 7, 63 Stat. 211; renumbered § 6, Pub. L. 85–507, § 21(b)(2), July 7, 1958, 72 Stat. 337; amended Pub. L. 103–178, title V, § 501(2), Dec. 3, 1993, 107 Stat. 2038; Pub. L. 105–272, title IV, § 403(a)(2), Oct. 20, 1998, 112 Stat. 2404.)

REFERENCES IN TEXT

Act of August 28, 1935, referred to in text, which provided for the yearly publication of the Official Register of the United States, was repealed by Pub. L. 86–626, title I, § 101, July 12, 1960, 74 Stat. 427.

Section 607 of the Act of June 30, 1945, as amended, referred to in text, was repealed by act Sept. 12, 1950, ch. 946, title III, § 301(85), 64 Stat. 843.

CODIFICATION

Section was enacted as part of the Central Intelligence Agency Act of 1949, and not as part of the National Security Act of 1947 which comprises this chapter.

AMENDMENTS

1998—Pub. L. 105–272 substituted ''403–3(c)(6)'' for ''403–3(c)(5)''.

1993—Pub. L. 103–178 substituted ''section 403–3(c)(5) of this title'' for ''the proviso of section 403(d)(3) of this title'' and ''Office of Management and Budget'' for ''Bureau of the Budget''.

SECTION REFERRED TO IN OTHER SECTIONS

This section is referred to in sections 403a, 403e, 403f of this title.

§ 403h. Admission of essential aliens; limitation on number

Whenever the Director, the Attorney General, and the Commissioner of Immigration and Naturalization shall determine that the admission of a particular alien into the United States for permanent residence is in the interest of national security or essential to the furtherance of the national intelligence mission, such alien and his immediate family shall be admitted to the United States for permanent residence without regard to their inadmissibility under the immigration or any other laws and regulations, or to the failure to comply with such laws and regulations pertaining to admissibility: *Provided*, That the number of aliens and members of their immediate families admitted to the United States under the authority of this section shall in no case exceed one hundred persons in any one fiscal year.

(June 20, 1949, ch. 227, § 7, formerly § 8, 63 Stat. 212; renumbered § 7, Pub. L. 85–507, § 21(b)(2), July 7, 1958, 72 Stat. 337; Pub. L. 104–208, div. C, title III, § 308(f)(6), Sept. 30, 1996, 110 Stat. 3009–622.)

REFERENCES IN TEXT

The immigration laws, referred to in text, are classified generally to Title 8, Aliens and Nationality. See also section 1101(a)(17) of Title 8.

CODIFICATION

Section was enacted as part of the Central Intelligence Agency Act of 1949, and not as part of the National Security Act of 1947 which comprises this chapter.

AMENDMENTS

1996—Pub. L. 104–208 substituted ''that the admission'' for ''that the entry'', ''shall be admitted to'' for ''shall be given entry into'', and ''families admitted to'' for ''families entering''.

CHANGE OF NAME

Ex. Ord. No. 6166, § 14, June 10, 1933, set out as a note under section 901 of Title 5, Government Organization and Employees, consolidated Bureaus of Immigration and Naturalization of Department of Labor to form an Immigration and Naturalization Service in Department of Labor, to be administered by a Commissioner of Immigration and Naturalization, which was then transferred from Department of Labor to Department of Justice by Reorg. Plan No. V of 1940, eff. June 14, 1940, 5 F.R. 2223, 54 Stat. 1238, set out in the Appendix to Title 5. Accordingly, ''Commissioner of Immigration and Naturalization'' was substituted for ''Commissioner of Immigration''.

EFFECTIVE DATE OF 1996 AMENDMENT

Amendment by Pub. L. 104–208 effective, with certain transitional provisions, on the first day of the first month beginning more than 180 days after Sept. 30, 1996, see section 309 of Pub. L. 104–208, set out as a note under section 1101 of Title 8, Aliens and Nationality.

TRANSFER OF FUNCTIONS

Functions of all other officers of Department of Justice and functions of all agencies and employees of such Department, with a few exceptions, transferred to Attorney General, with power vested in him to authorize their performance or performance of any of his functions by any of such officers, agencies, and employees, by Reorg. Plan No. 2 of 1950, §§ 1, 2, eff. May 24, 1950, 15 F.R. 3173, 64 Stat. 1261, set out in the Appendix to Title 5, Government Organization and Employees.

SECTION REFERRED TO IN OTHER SECTIONS

This section is referred to in sections 403a, 403e, 403f of this title.

§ 403i. Repealed. Sept. 1, 1954, ch. 1208, title VI, § 601(b), 68 Stat. 1115

Section, acts June 20, 1949, ch. 227, § 9, 63 Stat. 212; Aug. 16, 1950, ch. 719, 64 Stat. 450, related to establishment of positions in the professional and scientific field.

Section was enacted as part of the Central Intelligence Agency Act of 1949, and not as part of the National Security Act of 1947 which comprises this chapter.

§ 403j. Central Intelligence Agency; appropriations; expenditures

(a) Notwithstanding any other provisions of law, sums made available to the Agency by appropriation or otherwise may be expended for purposes necessary to carry out its functions, including—

(1) personal services, including personal services without regard to limitations on

types of persons to be employed, and rent at the seat of government and elsewhere; health-service program as authorized by law (5 U.S.C. 7901); rental of news-reporting services; purchase or rental and operation of photographic, reproduction, cryptographic, duplication, and printing machines, equipment, and devices, and radio-receiving and radio-sending equipment and devices, including telegraph and teletype equipment; purchase, maintenance, operation, repair, and hire of passenger motor vehicles, and aircraft, and vessels of all kinds; subject to policies established by the Director, transportation of officers and employees of the Agency in Government-owned automotive equipment between their domiciles and places of employment, where such personnel are engaged in work which makes such transportation necessary, and transportation in such equipment, to and from school, of children of Agency personnel who have quarters for themselves and their families at isolated stations outside the continental United States where adequate public or private transportation is not available; printing and binding; purchase, maintenance, and cleaning of firearms, including purchase, storage, and maintenance of ammunition; subject to policies established by the Director, expenses of travel in connection with, and expenses incident to attendance at meetings of professional, technical, scientific, and other similar organizations when such attendance would be a benefit in the conduct of the work of the Agency; association and library dues; payment of premiums or costs of surety bonds for officers or employees without regard to the provisions of section 14[1] of title 6; payment of claims pursuant to title 28; acquisition of necessary land and the clearing of such land; construction of buildings and facilities without regard to sections 259 and 267[1] of title 40; repair, rental, operation, and maintenance of buildings, utilities, facilities, and appurtenances; and

(2) supplies, equipment, and personnel and contractual services otherwise authorized by law and regulations, when approved by the Director.

(b) The sums made available to the Agency may be expended without regard to the provisions of law and regulations relating to the expenditure of Government funds; and for objects of a confidential, extraordinary, or emergency nature, such expenditures to be accounted for solely on the certificate of the Director and every such certificate shall be deemed a sufficient voucher for the amount therein certified.

(June 20, 1949, ch. 227, § 8, formerly § 10, 63 Stat. 212; renumbered § 8, Pub. L. 85–507, § 21(b)(2), July 7, 1958, 72 Stat. 337.)

REFERENCES IN TEXT

Section 14 of title 6, referred to in subsec. (a)(1), was repealed by Pub. L. 93–310, title II, § 203(1), June 6, 1972, 86 Stat. 202.

Sections 259 and 267 of title 40, referred to in subsec. (a)(1), were repealed by Pub. L. 86–249, § 17(12), Sept. 9, 1959, 73 Stat. 485. See section 601 et seq. of Title 40, Public Buildings, Property, and Works.

CODIFICATION

In subsec. (a)(1), "(5 U.S.C. 7901)" substituted for "(5 U.S.C. 150)" on authority of Pub. L. 89–554, § 7(b), Sept. 6, 1966, 80 Stat. 631, the first section of which enacted Title 5, Government Organization and Employees.

Section was enacted as part of the Central Intelligence Agency Act of 1949, and not as part of the National Security Act of 1947 which comprises this chapter.

AVAILABILITY OF APPROPRIATIONS FOR CONSTRUCTION PROJECTS

Pub. L. 103–139, title VIII, § 8104, Nov. 11, 1993, 107 Stat. 1463, provided that: "During the current fiscal year and thereafter, funds appropriated for construction projects of the Central Intelligence Agency, which are transferred to another Agency for execution, shall remain available until expended." Similar provisions were contained in the following prior appropriation acts:

Pub. L. 102–396, title IX, § 9030, Oct. 6, 1992, 106 Stat. 1907.

Pub. L. 102–172, title VIII, § 8030, Nov. 26, 1991, 105 Stat. 1177.

Pub. L. 101–511, title VIII, § 8031, Nov. 5, 1990, 104 Stat. 1881.

Pub. L. 101–165, title IX, § 9042, Nov. 21, 1989, 103 Stat. 1137.

Pub. L. 100–463, title VIII, § 8074, Oct. 1, 1988, 102 Stat. 2270–29.

Pub. L. 100–202, § 101(b) [title VIII, § 8095], Dec. 22, 1987, 101 Stat. 1329–43, 1329–79.

Pub. L. 99–500, § 101(c) [title IX, § 9130], Oct. 18, 1986, 100 Stat. 1783–82, 1783–128; Pub. L. 99–591, § 101(c) [title IX, § 9130], Oct. 30, 1986, 100 Stat. 3341–82, 3341–128.

ACQUISITION OF CRITICAL SKILLS

Pub. L. 99–569, title V, § 506, Oct. 27, 1986, 100 Stat. 3202, provided that: "Pursuant to the authority granted in section 8 of the Central Intelligence Agency Act of 1949 (50 U.S.C. 403j), the Director of Central Intelligence shall establish an undergraduate training program with respect to civilian employees of the Central Intelligence Agency similar in purpose, conditions, content, and administration to the program which the Secretary of Defense is authorized to establish under section 16 of the National Security Act of 1959 (50 U.S.C. 402 note) for civilian employees of the National Security Agency."

SECTION REFERRED TO IN OTHER SECTIONS

This section is referred to in sections 403a, 403e, 403f of this title; title 5 section 5948; title 31 sections 1344, 3524.

§ 403k. Authority to pay death gratuities

(a)(1) The Director may pay a gratuity to the surviving dependents of any officer or employee of the Agency who dies as a result of injuries (other than from disease) sustained outside the United States and whose death—

(A) resulted from hostile or terrorist activities; or

(B) occurred in connection with an intelligence activity having a substantial element of risk.

(2) The provisions of this subsection shall apply with respect to deaths occurring after June 30, 1974.

(b) Any payment under subsection (a) of this section—

(1) shall be in an amount equal to the amount of the annual salary of the officer or employee concerned at the time of death;

(2) shall be considered a gift and shall be in lieu of payment of any lesser death gratuity authorized by any other Federal law; and

[1] See References in Text note below.

(3) shall be made under the same conditions as apply to payments authorized by section 3973 of title 22.

(June 20, 1949, ch. 227, § 11, as added Pub. L. 96–450, title IV, § 403(a), Oct. 14, 1980, 94 Stat. 1978.)

CODIFICATION

In subsec. (b)(3), "section 3973 of title 22" substituted for "section 14 of the Act of August 1, 1956 (22 U.S.C. 2679a)" on authority of section 2401(c) of the Foreign Service Act of 1980 (22 U.S.C. 4172(c)), section 2205(10) of which repealed section 14 of the 1956 Act (22 U.S.C. 2679a).

Section was enacted as part of the Central Intelligence Agency Act of 1949, and not as part of the National Security Act of 1947 which comprises this chapter.

SECTION REFERRED TO IN OTHER SECTIONS

This section is referred to in sections 403a, 403e, 403f of this title.

§ 403*l*. Authority to accept gifts, devises and bequests

(a) Use for operational purposes prohibited

Subject to the provisions of this section, the Director may accept, hold, administer, and use gifts of money, securities, or other property whenever the Director determines it would be in the interest of the United States to do so. Any gift accepted under this section (and any income produced by any such gift) may be used only for artistic display or for purposes relating to the general welfare, education, or recreation of employees or dependents of employees of the Agency or for similar purposes, and under no circumstances may such a gift (or any income produced by any such gift) be used for operational purposes. The Director may not accept any gift under this section which is expressly conditioned upon any expenditure not to be met from the gift itself or from income produced by the gift unless such expenditure has been authorized by law.

(b) Sale, exchange and investment of gifts

Unless otherwise restricted by the terms of the gift, the Director may sell or exchange, or invest or reinvest, any property which is accepted under this section, but any such investment may only be in interest-bearing obligations of the United States or in obligations guaranteed as to both principal and interest by the United States.

(c) Deposit of gifts into special fund

There is hereby created on the books of the Treasury of the United States a fund into which gifts of money, securities, and other intangible property accepted under the authority of this section, and the earnings and proceeds thereof, shall be deposited. The assets of such fund shall be disbursed upon the order of the Director for the purposes specified in subsection (a) or (b) of this section.

(d) Taxation of gifts

For purposes of Federal income, estate, and gift taxes, gifts accepted by the Director under this section shall be considered to be to or for the use of the United States.

(e) "Gift" defined

For the purposes of this section, the term "gift" includes a bequest or devise.

(June 20, 1949, ch. 227, § 12, as added Pub. L. 96–450, title IV, § 404, Oct. 14, 1980, 94 Stat. 1979.)

CODIFICATION

Section was enacted as part of the Central Intelligence Agency Act of 1949, and not as part of the National Security Act of 1947 which comprises this chapter.

SECTION REFERRED TO IN OTHER SECTIONS

This section is referred to in sections 403a, 403e, 403f of this title.

§ 403m. Misuse of Agency name, initials, or seal

(a) Prohibited acts

No person may, except with the written permission of the Director, knowingly use the words "Central Intelligence Agency", the initials "CIA", the seal of the Central Intelligence Agency, or any colorable imitation of such words, initials, or seal in connection with any merchandise, impersonation, solicitation, or commercial activity in a manner reasonably calculated to convey the impression that such use is approved, endorsed, or authorized by the Central Intelligence Agency.

(b) Injunction

Whenever it appears to the Attorney General that any person is engaged or is about to engage in an act or practice which constitutes or will constitute conduct prohibited by subsection (a) of this section, the Attorney General may initiate a civil proceeding in a district court of the United States to enjoin such act or practice. Such court shall proceed as soon as practicable to the hearing and determination of such action and may, at any time before final determination, enter such restraining orders or prohibitions, or take such other action as is warranted, to prevent injury to the United States or to any person or class of persons for whose protection the action is brought.

(June 20, 1949, ch. 227, § 13, as added Pub. L. 97–89, title V, § 503, Dec. 4, 1981, 95 Stat. 1153.)

CODIFICATION

Section was enacted as part of the Central Intelligence Agency Act of 1949, and not as part of the National Security Act of 1947 which comprises this chapter.

EFFECTIVE DATE

Section effective Oct. 1, 1981, see section 806 of Pub. L. 97–89, set out as a note under section 1621 of Title 10, Armed Forces.

SECTION REFERRED TO IN OTHER SECTIONS

This section is referred to in sections 403a, 403e, 403f of this title.

§ 403n. Special provisions for spouses of Central Intelligence Agency employees applicable to Agency participants in Civil Service Retirement and Disability System

(a) Manner and extent of applicability

The provisions of sections 2002, 2031(b)(1)–(3), 2031(f), 2031(g), 2031(h)(2), 2031(i), 2031(*l*), 2032,

2033, 2034, 2035, 2052(b), 2071(b), 2071(d), and 2094(b) of this title establishing certain requirements, limitations, rights, entitlements, and benefits relating to retirement annuities, survivor benefits, and lump-sum payments for a spouse or former spouse of an Agency employee who is a participant in the Central Intelligence Agency Retirement and Disability System shall apply in the same manner and to the same extent in the case of an Agency employee who is a participant in the Civil Service Retirement and Disability System.

(b) Regulations

The Director of the Office of Personnel Management, in consultation with the Director of Central Intelligence, shall prescribe such regulations as may be necessary to implement the provisions of this section.

(June 20, 1949, ch. 227, § 14, as added Pub. L. 97–269, title VI, § 612, Sept. 27, 1982, 96 Stat. 1154; amended Pub. L. 99–569, title III, § 302(b), Oct. 27, 1986, 100 Stat. 3194; Pub. L. 100–178, title IV, §§ 401(b), 402(b)(3), Dec. 2, 1987, 101 Stat. 1013, 1014; Pub. L. 102–496, title VIII, § 803(a)(1), Oct. 24, 1992, 106 Stat. 3251.)

CODIFICATION

Section was enacted as part of the Central Intelligence Agency Act of 1949, and not as part of the National Security Act of 1947 which comprises this chapter.

AMENDMENTS

1992—Subsec. (a). Pub. L. 102–496 substituted references to sections 2002, 2031 to 2035, 2052, 2071, and 2094 of this title for references in original to sections 204, 221 to 225, 232, 234 and 263 of the Central Intelligence Agency Retirement Act of 1964 for Certain Employees which were formerly set out in a note under section 403 of this title.

1987—Subsec. (a). Pub. L. 100–178, § 402(b)(3), inserted "232(b)," before "234(c), 234(d),".

Pub. L. 100–178, § 401(b), inserted "225," after "223, 224,".

1986—Subsec. (a). Pub. L. 99–569 inserted "224," after "223,".

EFFECTIVE DATE OF 1992 AMENDMENT

Amendment by Pub. L. 102–496 effective on first day of fourth month beginning after Oct. 24, 1992, see section 805 of Pub. L. 102–496, set out as an Effective Date note under section 2001 of this title.

EFFECTIVE DATE OF 1987 AMENDMENT

Amendment by Pub. L. 100–178 effective Nov. 15, 1982, but not to be construed to require forfeiture by any individual of benefits received before Dec. 2, 1987, nor to require reduction in level of benefits received by any individual who was receiving benefits under section 232 of Pub. L. 88–643 before Dec. 2, 1987, see section 402(c)–(e) of Pub. L. 100–178, set out as an Effective Date of Amendments to Pub. L. 88–643 Prior to Enactment of Pub. L. 102–496 note under section 2001 of this title.

EFFECTIVE DATE OF 1986 AMENDMENT

Section 302(d) of Pub. L. 99–569 provided that: "The amendments made by this section [amending this section and provisions formerly set out as a note under section 403 of this title] shall take effect on October 1, 1986."

EFFECTIVE DATE

Section effective Nov. 15, 1982, see section 613 of Pub. L. 97–269 set out as an Effective Date of Amendments to Pub. L. 88–643 Prior to Enactment of Pub. L. 102–496 note under section 2001 of this title.

SECTION REFERRED TO IN OTHER SECTIONS

This section is referred to in sections 403a, 403e, 403f of this title.

§ 403*o*. Security personnel at Agency installations

(a) Special policemen: functions and powers; regulations: promulgation and enforcement

(1) The Director may authorize Agency personnel within the United States to perform the same functions as special policemen of the General Services Administration perform under section 318 of title 40, with the powers set forth in that section, except that such personnel shall perform such functions and exercise such powers—

(A) within the Agency Headquarters Compound and the property controlled and occupied by the Federal Highway Administration located immediately adjacent to such Compound;

(B) in the streets, sidewalks, and the open areas within the zone beginning at the outside boundary of such Compound and property and extending outward 500 feet;

(C) within any other Agency installation and protected property; and

(D) in the streets, sidewalks, and open areas within the zone beginning at the outside boundary of any installation or property referred to in subparagraph (C) and extending outward 500 feet.

(2) The performance of functions and exercise of powers under subparagraph (B) or (D) of paragraph (1) shall be limited to those circumstances where such personnel can identify specific and articulable facts giving such personnel reason to believe that the performance of such functions and exercise of such powers is reasonable to protect against physical damage or injury, or threats of physical damage or injury, to Agency installations, property, or employees.

(3) Nothing in this subsection shall be construed to preclude, or limit in any way, the authority of any Federal, State, or local law enforcement agency, or any other Federal police or Federal protective service.

(4) The rules and regulations enforced by such personnel shall be the rules and regulations prescribed by the Director and shall only be applicable to the areas referred to in subparagraph (A) or (C) of paragraph (1).

(5) Not later than December 1, 1998, and annually thereafter, the Director shall submit a report to the Permanent Select Committee on Intelligence of the House of Representatives and the Select Committee on Intelligence of the Senate that describes in detail the exercise of the authority granted by this subsection, and the underlying facts supporting the exercise of such authority, during the preceding fiscal year. The Director shall make such report available to the Inspector General of the Central Intelligence Agency.

(b) Penalties for violations of regulations

The Director is authorized to establish penalties for violations of the rules or regulations promulgated by the Director under subsection

(a) of this section. Such penalties shall not exceed those specified in section 318c of title 40.

(c) Identification

Agency personnel designated by the Director under subsection (a) of this section shall be clearly identifiable as United States Government security personnel while engaged in the performance of the functions to which subsection (a) of this section refers.

(June 20, 1949, ch. 227, § 15, as added Pub. L. 98–473, title I, § 140, Oct. 12, 1984, 98 Stat. 1973, as added Pub. L. 98–618, title IV, § 401, Nov. 8, 1984, 98 Stat. 3301; amended Pub. L. 105–107, title IV, § 404, Nov. 20, 1997, 111 Stat. 2260.)

CODIFICATION

Section was enacted as part of the Central Intelligence Agency Act of 1949, and not as part of the National Security Act of 1947 which comprises this chapter.

Provisions of this section were also enacted by the Intelligence Authorization Act for fiscal year 1985, Pub. L. 98–618, title IV, § 401, Nov. 8, 1984, 98 Stat. 3301.

AMENDMENTS

1997—Subsec. (a)(1). Pub. L. 105–107, § 404(1), (2), inserted "(1)" after "(a)", substituted "powers—" for "powers only within Agency installations, and the rules and regulations enforced by such personnel shall be rules and regulations promulgated by the Director.", and added subpars. (A) to (D).

Subsec. (a)(2) to (5). Pub. L. 105–107, § 404(3), added pars. (2) to (5).

DESIGNATION OF HEADQUARTERS COMPOUND OF CENTRAL INTELLIGENCE AGENCY AS THE GEORGE BUSH CENTER FOR INTELLIGENCE

Reference to the headquarters compound of the Central Intelligence Agency deemed to be a reference to the George Bush Center for Intelligence, see section 309 of Pub. L. 105–272, set out as a note under section 403–1 of this title.

SECTION REFERRED TO IN OTHER SECTIONS

This section is referred to in sections 403a, 403e, 403f of this title; title 10 section 444.

§ 403p. Health benefits for certain former spouses of Central Intelligence Agency employees

(a) Persons eligible

Except as provided in subsection (e) of this section, any individual—

(1) formerly married to an employee or former employee of the Agency, whose marriage was dissolved by divorce or annulment before May 7, 1985;

(2) who, at any time during the eighteen-month period before the divorce or annulment became final, was covered under a health benefits plan as a member of the family of such employee or former employee; and

(3) who was married to such employee for not less than ten years during periods of service by such employee with the Agency, at least five years of which were spent outside the United States by both the employee and the former spouse,

is eligible for coverage under a health benefits plan in accordance with the provisions of this section.

(b) Enrollment for health benefits

(1) Any individual eligible for coverage under subsection (a) of this section may enroll in a health benefits plan for self alone or for self and family if, before the expiration of the six-month period beginning on October 1, 1986, and in accordance with such procedures as the Director of the Office of Personnel Management shall by regulation prescribe, such individual—

(A) files an election for such enrollment; and

(B) arranges to pay currently into the Employees Health Benefits Fund under section 8909 of title 5 an amount equal to the sum of the employee and agency contributions payable in the case of an employee enrolled under chapter 89 of such title in the same health benefits plan and with the same level of benefits.

(2) The Director of Central Intelligence shall, as soon as possible, take all steps practicable—

(A) to determine the identity and current address of each former spouse eligible for coverage under subsection (a) of this section; and

(B) to notify each such former spouse of that individual's rights under this section.

(3) The Director of the Office of Personnel Management, upon notification by the Director of Central Intelligence, shall waive the six-month limitation set forth in paragraph (1) in any case in which the Director of Central Intelligence determines that the circumstances so warrant.

(c) Eligibility of former wives or husbands

(1) Notwithstanding subsections (a) and (b) of this section and except as provided in subsections (d), (e), and (f) of this section, an individual—

(A) who was divorced on or before December 4, 1991, from a participant or retired participant in the Central Intelligence Agency Retirement and Disability System or the Federal Employees Retirement System Special Category;

(B) who was married to such participant for not less than ten years during the participant's creditable service, at least five years of which were spent by the participant during the participant's service as an employee of the Agency outside the United States, or otherwise in a position the duties of which qualified the participant for designation by the Director of Central Intelligence as a participant under section 2013 of this title; and

(C) who was enrolled in a health benefits plan as a family member at any time during the 18-month period before the date of dissolution of the marriage to such participant;

is eligible for coverage under a health benefits plan.

(2) A former spouse eligible for coverage under paragraph (1) may enroll in a health benefits plan in accordance with subsection (b)(1) of this section, except that the election for such enrollment must be submitted within 60 days after the date on which the Director notifies the former spouse of such individual's eligibility for health insurance coverage under this subsection.

(d) Continuation of eligibility

Notwithstanding subsections (a), (b), and (c) of this section and except as provided in subsections (e) and (f) of this section, an individual divorced on or before December 4, 1991, from a participant or retired participant in the Central Intelligence Agency Retirement and Disability System or Federal Employees' Retirement System Special Category who enrolled in a health benefits plan following the dissolution of the marriage to such participant may continue enrollment following the death of such participant notwithstanding the termination of the retirement annuity of such individual.

(e) Remarriage before age fifty-five; continued enrollment; restored eligibility

(1) Any former spouse who remarries before age fifty-five is not eligible to make an election under subsection (b)(1) of this section.

(2) Any former spouse enrolled in a health benefits plan pursuant to an election under subsection (b)(1) of this section or to subsection (d) of this section may continue the enrollment under the conditions of eligibility which the Director of the Office of Personnel Management shall by regulation prescribe, except that any former spouse who remarries before age fifty-five shall not be eligible for continued enrollment under this section after the end of the thirty-one-day period beginning on the date of remarriage.

(3)(A) A former spouse who is not eligible to enroll or to continue enrollment in a health benefits plan under this section solely because of remarriage before age fifty-five shall be restored to such eligibility on the date such remarriage is dissolved by death, annulment, or divorce.

(B) A former spouse whose eligibility is restored under subparagraph (A) may, under regulations which the Director of the Office of Personnel Management shall prescribe, enroll in a health benefits plan if such former spouse—

(i) was an individual referred to in paragraph (1) and was an individual covered under a benefits plan as a family member at any time during the 18-month period before the date of dissolution of the marriage to the Agency employee or annuitant; or

(ii) was an individual referred to in paragraph (2) and was an individual covered under a benefits plan immediately before the remarriage ended the enrollment.

(f) Enrollment in health benefits plan under other authority

No individual may be covered by a health benefits plan under this section during any period in which such individual is enrolled in a health benefits plan under any other authority, nor may any individual be covered under more than one enrollment under this section.

(g) "Health benefits plan" defined

For purposes of this section the term "health benefits plan" means an approved health benefits plan under chapter 89 of title 5.

(June 20, 1949, ch. 227, § 16, as added Pub. L. 99–569, title III, § 303(a), Oct. 27, 1986, 100 Stat. 3194; amended Pub. L. 102–88, title III, § 307(c), Aug. 14, 1991, 105 Stat. 433; Pub. L. 103–178, title II, § 203(c), Dec. 3, 1993, 107 Stat. 2031.)

CODIFICATION

Section was enacted as part of the Central Intelligence Agency Act of 1949, and not as part of the National Security Act of 1947 which comprises this chapter.

AMENDMENTS

1993—Subsec. (a). Pub. L. 103–178, § 203(c)(2)(A), substituted "subsection (e)" for "subsection (c)(1)" in introductory provisions.

Subsecs. (c), (d). Pub. L. 103–178, § 203(c)(1), added subsecs. (c) and (d). Former subsecs. (c) and (d) redesignated (e) and (f), respectively.

Subsec. (e). Pub. L. 103–178, § 203(c)(2)(B), inserted "or to subsection (d) of this section" after "subsection (b)(1) of this section" in par. (2).

Pub. L. 103–178, § 203(c)(1)(A), redesignated subsec. (c) as (e). Former subsec. (e) redesignated (g).

Subsecs. (f), (g). Pub. L. 103–178, § 203(c)(1)(A), redesignated subsecs. (d) and (e) as (f) and (g), respectively.

1991—Subsec. (c)(3). Pub. L. 102–88 added par. (3).

EFFECTIVE DATE OF 1993 AMENDMENT

Amendment by section 203(c) of Pub. L. 103–178 applicable to individuals on and after Oct. 1, 1994, with no benefits provided pursuant to section 203(c) payable with respect to any period before Oct. 1, 1994, except that subsec. (d) of this section applicable to individuals beginning Dec. 3, 1993, see section 203(e) of Pub. L. 103–178, set out as a Survivor Annuity, Retirement Annuity, and Health Benefits for Certain Ex-Spouses of Central Intelligence Agency Employees; Effective Date note under section 2032 of this title.

EFFECTIVE DATE OF 1991 AMENDMENT

Section 307(d) of Pub. L. 102–88 provided that: "The amendments made by this section [amending this section and provisions formerly set out as a note under section 403 of this title] shall take effect as of October 1, 1990. No benefits provided pursuant to the amendments made by this section shall be payable with respect to any period before such date."

EFFECTIVE DATE

Section 303(b) of Pub. L. 99–569 provided that: "The amendment made by this section [enacting this section] shall take effect on October 1, 1986."

COMPLIANCE WITH BUDGET ACT

Section 307(e) of Pub. L. 102–88 provided that: "Any new spending authority (within the meaning of section 401(c) of the Congressional Budget Act of 1974 [2 U.S.C. 651(c)]) provided pursuant to the amendments made by this section [amending this section and provisions formerly set out as a note under section 403 of this title] shall be effective for any fiscal year only to such extent or in such amounts as are provided in advance in appropriation Acts."

SECTION REFERRED TO IN OTHER SECTIONS

This section is referred to in sections 403a, 403e, 403f of this title.

§ 403q. Inspector General for Agency

(a) Purpose; establishment

In order to—

(1) create an objective and effective office, appropriately accountable to Congress, to initiate and conduct independently inspections, investigations, and audits relating to programs and operations of the Agency;

(2) provide leadership and recommend policies designed to promote economy, efficiency, and effectiveness in the administration of such programs and operations, and detect fraud and abuse in such programs and operations;

(3) provide a means for keeping the Director fully and currently informed about problems and deficiencies relating to the administration

of such programs and operations, and the necessity for and the progress of corrective actions; and

(4) in the manner prescribed by this section, ensure that the Senate Select Committee on Intelligence and the House Permanent Select Committee on Intelligence (hereafter in this section referred to collectively as the "intelligence committees") are kept similarly informed of significant problems and deficiencies as well as the necessity for and the progress of corrective actions,

there is hereby established in the Agency an Office of Inspector General (hereafter in this section referred to as the "Office").

(b) Appointment; supervision; removal

(1) There shall be at the head of the Office an Inspector General who shall be appointed by the President, by and with the advice and consent of the Senate. This appointment shall be made without regard to political affiliation and shall be solely on the basis of integrity, compliance with the security standards of the Agency, and prior experience in the field of foreign intelligence. Such appointment shall also be made on the basis of demonstrated ability in accounting, financial analysis, law, management analysis, public administration, or auditing.

(2) The Inspector General shall report directly to and be under the general supervision of the Director.

(3) The Director may prohibit the Inspector General from initiating, carrying out, or completing any audit, inspection, or investigation, or from issuing any subpoena, after the Inspector General has decided to initiate, carry out, or complete such audit, inspection, or investigation or to issue such subpoena, if the Director determines that such prohibition is necessary to protect vital national security interests of the United States.

(4) If the Director exercises any power under paragraph (3), he shall submit an appropriately classified statement of the reasons for the exercise of such power within seven days to the intelligence committees. The Director shall advise the Inspector General at the time such report is submitted, and, to the extent consistent with the protection of intelligence sources and methods, provide the Inspector General with a copy of any such report. In such cases, the Inspector General may submit such comments to the intelligence committees that he considers appropriate.

(5) In accordance with section 535 of title 28, the Inspector General shall report to the Attorney General any information, allegation, or complaint received by the Inspector General relating to violations of Federal criminal law that involve a program or operation of the Agency, consistent with such guidelines as may be issued by the Attorney General pursuant to subsection (b)(2) of such section. A copy of all such reports shall be furnished to the Director.

(6) The Inspector General may be removed from office only by the President. The President shall immediately communicate in writing to the intelligence committees the reasons for any such removal.

(c) Duties and responsibilities

It shall be the duty and responsibility of the Inspector General appointed under this section—

(1) to provide policy direction for, and to plan, conduct, supervise, and coordinate independently, the inspections, investigations, and audits relating to the programs and operations of the Agency to ensure they are conducted efficiently and in accordance with applicable law and regulations;

(2) to keep the Director fully and currently informed concerning violations of law and regulations, fraud and other serious problems, abuses and deficiencies that may occur in such programs and operations, and to report the progress made in implementing corrective action;

(3) to take due regard for the protection of intelligence sources and methods in the preparation of all reports issued by the Office, and, to the extent consistent with the purpose and objective of such reports, take such measures as may be appropriate to minimize the disclosure of intelligence sources and methods described in such reports; and

(4) in the execution of his responsibilities, to comply with generally accepted government auditing standards.

(d) Semiannual reports; immediate reports of serious or flagrant problems; reports of functional problems; reports to Congress on urgent concerns

(1) The Inspector General shall, not later than January 31 and July 31 of each year, prepare and submit to the Director of Central Intelligence a classified semiannual report summarizing the activities of the Office during the immediately preceding six-month periods ending December 31 (of the preceding year) and June 30, respectively. Within thirty days of receipt of such reports, the Director shall transmit such reports to the intelligence committees with any comments he may deem appropriate. Such reports shall, at a minimum, include a list of the title or subject of each inspection, investigation, or audit conducted during the reporting period and—

(A) a description of significant problems, abuses, and deficiencies relating to the administration of programs and operations of the Agency identified by the Office during the reporting period;

(B) a description of the recommendations for corrective action made by the Office during the reporting period with respect to significant problems, abuses, or deficiencies identified in subparagraph (A);

(C) a statement of whether corrective action has been completed on each significant recommendation described in previous semiannual reports, and, in a case where corrective action has been completed, a description of such corrective action;

(D) a certification that the Inspector General has had full and direct access to all information relevant to the performance of his functions;

(E) a description of the exercise of the subpoena authority under subsection (e)(5) of this section by the Inspector General during the reporting period; and

(F) such recommendations as the Inspector General may wish to make concerning legislation to promote economy and efficiency in the administration of programs and operations undertaken by the Agency, and to detect and eliminate fraud and abuse in such programs and operations.

(2) The Inspector General shall report immediately to the Director whenever he becomes aware of particularly serious or flagrant problems, abuses, or deficiencies relating to the administration of programs or operations. The Director shall transmit such report to the intelligence committees within seven calendar days, together with any comments he considers appropriate.

(3) In the event that—

(A) the Inspector General is unable to resolve any differences with the Director affecting the execution of the Inspector General's duties or responsibilities;

(B) an investigation, inspection, or audit carried out by the Inspector General should focus on any current or former Agency official who—

(i) holds or held a position in the Agency that is subject to appointment by the President, by and with the advise[1] and consent of the Senate, including such a position held on an acting basis; or

(ii) holds or held the position in the Agency, including such a position held on an acting basis, of—

(I) Executive Director;

(II) Deputy Director for Operations;

(III) Deputy Director for Intelligence;

(IV) Deputy Director for Administration; or

(V) Deputy Director for Science and Technology;

(C) a matter requires a report by the Inspector General to the Department of Justice on possible criminal conduct by a current or former Agency official described or referred to in subparagraph (B);

(D) the Inspector General receives notice from the Department of Justice declining or approving prosecution of possible criminal conduct of any of the officials described in subparagraph (B); or

(E) the Inspector General, after exhausting all possible alternatives, is unable to obtain significant documentary information in the course of an investigation, inspection, or audit,

the Inspector General shall immediately notify and submit a report on such matter to the intelligence committees.

(4) Pursuant to Title V of the National Security Act of 1947 [50 U.S.C. 413 et seq.], the Director shall submit to the intelligence committees any report or findings and recommendations of an inspection, investigation, or audit conducted by the office which has been requested by the Chairman or Ranking Minority Member of either committee.

(5)(A) An employee of the Agency, or of a contractor to the Agency, who intends to report to Congress a complaint or information with respect to an urgent concern may report such complaint or information to the Inspector General.

(B) Not later than the end of the 14-calendar day period beginning on the date of receipt from an employee of a complaint or information under subparagraph (A), the Inspector General shall determine whether the complaint or information appears credible. If the Inspector General determines that the complaint or information appears credible, the Inspector General shall, before the end of such period, transmit the complaint or information to the Director.

(C) Upon receipt of a transmittal from the Inspector General under subparagraph (B), the Director shall, within 7 calendar days of such receipt, forward such transmittal to the intelligence committees, together with any comments the Director considers appropriate.

(D)(i) If the Inspector General does not transmit, or does not transmit in an accurate form, the complaint or information described in subparagraph (B), the employee (subject to clause (ii)) may submit the complaint or information to Congress by contacting either or both of the intelligence committees directly.

(ii) The employee may contact the intelligence committees directly as described in clause (i) only if the employee—

(I) before making such a contact, furnishes to the Director, through the Inspector General, a statement of the employee's complaint or information and notice of the employee's intent to contact the intelligence committees directly; and

(II) obtains and follows from the Director, through the Inspector General, direction on how to contact the intelligence committees in accordance with appropriate security practices.

(iii) A member or employee of one of the intelligence committees who receives a complaint or information under clause (i) does so in that member or employee's official capacity as a member or employee of that committee.

(E) The Inspector General shall notify an employee who reports a complaint or information to the Inspector General under this paragraph of each action taken under this paragraph with respect to the complaint or information. Such notice shall be provided not later than 3 days after any such action is taken.

(F) An action taken by the Director or the Inspector General under this paragraph shall not be subject to judicial review.

(G) In this paragraph:

(i) The term "urgent concern" means any of the following:

(I) A serious or flagrant problem, abuse, violation of law or Executive order, or deficiency relating to the funding, administration, or operations of an intelligence activity involving classified information, but does not include differences of opinions concerning public policy matters.

(II) A false statement to Congress, or a willful withholding from Congress, on an issue of material fact relating to the funding, administration, or operation of an intelligence activity.

---

[1] So in original. Probably should be "advice".

(III) An action, including a personnel action described in section 2302(a)(2)(A) of title 5, constituting reprisal or threat of reprisal prohibited under subsection (e)(3)(B) of this section in response to an employee's reporting an urgent concern in accordance with this paragraph.

(ii) The term "intelligence committees" means the Permanent Select Committee on Intelligence of the House of Representatives and the Select Committee on Intelligence of the Senate.

(e) Authorities of Inspector General

(1) The Inspector General shall have direct and prompt access to the Director when necessary for any purpose pertaining to the performance of his duties.

(2) The Inspector General shall have access to any employee or any employee of a contractor of the Agency whose testimony is needed for the performance of his duties. In addition, he shall have direct access to all records, reports, audits, reviews, documents, papers, recommendations, or other material which relate to the programs and operations with respect to which the Inspector General has responsibilities under this section. Failure on the part of any employee or contractor to cooperate with the Inspector General shall be grounds for appropriate administrative actions by the Director, to include loss of employment or the termination of an existing contractual relationship.

(3) The Inspector General is authorized to receive and investigate complaints or information from any person concerning the existence of an activity constituting a violation of laws, rules, or regulations, or mismanagement, gross waste of funds, abuse of authority, or a substantial and specific danger to the public health and safety. Once such complaint or information has been received from an employee of the Agency—

(A) the Inspector General shall not disclose the identity of the employee without the consent of the employee, unless the Inspector General determines that such disclosure is unavoidable during the course of the investigation or the disclosure is made to an official of the Department of Justice responsible for determining whether a prosecution should be undertaken; and

(B) no action constituting a reprisal, or threat of reprisal, for making such complaint may be taken by any employee of the Agency in a position to take such actions, unless the complaint was made or the information was disclosed with the knowledge that it was false or with willful disregard for its truth or falsity.

(4) The Inspector General shall have authority to administer to or take from any person an oath, affirmation, or affidavit, whenever necessary in the performance of his duties, which oath[2] affirmation, or affidavit when administered or taken by or before an employee of the Office designated by the Inspector General shall have the same force and effect as if administered or taken by or before an officer having a seal.

(5)(A) Except as provided in subparagraph (B), the Inspector General is authorized to require by subpoena the production of all information, documents, reports, answers, records, accounts, papers, and other data and documentary evidence necessary in the performance of the duties and responsibilities of the Inspector General.

(B) In the case of Government agencies, the Inspector General shall obtain information, documents, reports, answers, records, accounts, papers, and other data and evidence for the purpose specified in subparagraph (A) using procedures other than by subpoenas.

(C) The Inspector General may not issue a subpoena for or on behalf of any other element or component of the Agency.

(D) In the case of contumacy or refusal to obey a subpoena issued under this paragraph, the subpoena shall be enforceable by order of any appropriate district court of the United States.

(6) The Inspector General shall be provided with appropriate and adequate office space at central and field office locations, together with such equipment, office supplies, maintenance services, and communications facilities and services as may be necessary for the operation of such offices.

(7) Subject to applicable law and the policies of the Director, the Inspector General shall select, appoint and employ such officers and employees as may be necessary to carry out his functions. In making such selections, the Inspector General shall ensure that such officers and employees have the requisite training and experience to enable him to carry out his duties effectively. In this regard, the Inspector General shall create within his organization a career cadre of sufficient size to provide appropriate continuity and objectivity needed for the effective performance of his duties.

(8) Subject to the concurrence of the Director, the Inspector General may request such information or assistance as may be necessary for carrying out his duties and responsibilities from any Government agency. Upon request of the Inspector General for such information or assistance, the head of the Government agency involved shall, insofar as is practicable and not in contravention of any existing statutory restriction or regulation of the Government agency concerned, furnish to the Inspector General, or to an authorized designee, such information or assistance.

(f) Separate budget account

Beginning with fiscal year 1991, and in accordance with procedures to be issued by the Director of Central Intelligence in consultation with the intelligence committees, the Director of Central Intelligence shall include in the National Foreign Intelligence Program budget a separate account for the Office of Inspector General established pursuant to this section.

(g) Transfer

There shall be transferred to the Office the office of the Agency referred to as the "Office of Inspector General." The personnel, assets, liabilities, contracts, property, records, and unexpended balances of appropriations, authorizations, allocations, and other funds employed, held, used, arising from, or available to such "Office of Inspector General" are hereby trans-

[2] So in original. Probably should be followed by a comma.

ferred to the Office established pursuant to this section.

(June 20, 1949, ch. 227, §17, as added Pub. L. 100–453, title V, §504, Sept. 29, 1988, 102 Stat. 1910; amended Pub. L. 101–193, title VIII, §801, Nov. 30, 1989, 103 Stat. 1711; Pub. L. 102–496, title VI, §601, Oct. 24, 1992, 106 Stat. 3187; Pub. L. 103–359, title IV, §402, Oct. 14, 1994, 108 Stat. 3427; Pub. L. 104–93, title IV, §403, Jan. 6, 1996, 109 Stat. 969; Pub. L. 105–107, title IV, §402, Nov. 20, 1997, 111 Stat. 2257; Pub. L. 105–272, title VII, §702(a), Oct. 20, 1998, 112 Stat. 2414; Pub. L. 106–567, title IV, §§402, 403, Dec. 27, 2000, 114 Stat. 2847, 2848.)

REFERENCES IN TEXT

The National Security Act of 1947, referred to in subsec. (d)(4), is act July 26, 1947, ch. 343, 61 Stat. 495, as amended. Title V of the Act is classified generally to subchapter III (§413 et seq.) of this chapter. For complete classification of this Act to the Code, see Short Title note set out under section 401 of this title and Tables.

CODIFICATION

Section was enacted as part of the Central Intelligence Agency Act of 1949, and not as part of the National Security Act of 1947 which comprises this chapter.

AMENDMENTS

2000—Subsec. (d)(1)(E). Pub. L. 106–567, §402(a)(1), added subpar. (E) and struck out former subpar. (E) which read as follows: "a description of all cases occurring during the reporting period where the Inspector General could not obtain documentary evidence relevant to any inspection, audit, or investigation due to his lack of authority to subpoena such information; and".

Subsec. (d)(3). Pub. L. 106–567, §403, added subpars. (B) to (E) and concluding provisions and struck out former subpars. (B) and (C) which read as follows:

"(B) an investigation, inspection, or audit carried out by the Inspector General should focus upon the Director or Acting Director; or

"(C) the Inspector General, after exhausting all possible alternatives, is unable to obtain significant documentary information in the course of an investigation, inspection, or audit, the Inspector General shall immediately report such matter to the intelligence committees."

Subsec. (e)(5)(E). Pub. L. 106–567, §402(a)(2), struck out subpar. (E) which read as follows: "Not later than January 31 and July 31 of each year, the Inspector General shall submit to the Select Committee on Intelligence of the Senate and the Permanent Select Committee on Intelligence of the House of Representatives a report of the Inspector General's exercise of authority under this paragraph during the preceding six months."

Subsec. (e)(8). Pub. L. 106–567, §402(b), substituted "Government" for "Federal" wherever appearing.

1998—Subsec. (d). Pub. L. 105–272 inserted "; reports to Congress on urgent concerns" after "functional problems" in heading and added par. (5).

1997—Subsec. (b)(3). Pub. L. 105–107, §402(b), inserted ", or from issuing any subpoena, after the Inspector General has decided to initiate, carry out, or complete such audit, inspection, or investigation or to issue such subpoena," after "or investigation".

Subsec. (e)(5) to (8). Pub. L. 105–107, §402(a), added par. (5) and redesignated former pars. (5) to (7) as (6) to (8), respectively.

1996—Subsec. (b)(5). Pub. L. 104–93, §403(a), amended par. (5) generally. Prior to amendment, par. (5) read as follows: "In accordance with section 535 of title 28, the Director shall report to the Attorney General any information, allegation, or complaint received from the Inspector General, relating to violations of Federal criminal law involving any officer or employee of the Agency, consistent with such guidelines as may be issued by the Attorney General pursuant to subsection (b)(2) of such section. A copy of all such reports shall be furnished to the Inspector General."

Subsec. (e)(3)(A). Pub. L. 104–93, §403(b), inserted "or the disclosure is made to an official of the Department of Justice responsible for determining whether a prosecution should be undertaken" after "investigation".

1994—Subsec. (b)(1). Pub. L. 103–359, §402(1), substituted "analysis, public administration, or auditing" for "analysis, or public administration".

Subsec. (c)(1). Pub. L. 103–359, §402(2), substituted "to plan, conduct" for "to conduct".

Subsec. (d)(1). Pub. L. 103–359, §402(3), in introductory provisions, substituted "January 31 and July 31" for "June 30 and December 31" and "periods ending December 31 (of the preceding year) and June 30, respectively" for "period" and inserted "of receipt of such reports" after "thirty days".

Subsec. (d)(3)(C). Pub. L. 103–359, §402(4), substituted "investigation, inspection, or audit," for "investigation,".

Subsec. (d)(4). Pub. L. 103–359, §402(5), inserted "or findings and recommendations" after "report".

Subsec. (e)(6). Pub. L. 103–359, §402(6), substituted "the Inspector General shall" for "it is the sense of Congress that the Inspector General should".

1992—Subsec. (e)(3). Pub. L. 102–496, in introductory provisions, substituted "any person" for "an employee of the Agency" and inserted "from an employee of the Agency" after "received".

1989—Pub. L. 101–193 amended section generally, substituting subsecs. (a) to (g) relating to establishment of the Office of Inspector General and appointment, duties, and authority of Inspector General for introductory par. and subsecs. (a) to (e) relating to various reports to be filed with the intelligence committees by Director of Central Intelligence concerning selection and activities of Inspector General.

TERMINATION OF REPORTING REQUIREMENTS

For termination, effective May 15, 2000, of provisions of law requiring submittal to Congress of any annual, semiannual, or other regular periodic report listed in House Document No. 103–7 (in which the 4th item on page 156, relating to the transmittal of semiannual reports to the intelligence committees, identifies a reporting provision which, as subsequently amended, is contained in subsec. (d)(1) of this section), see section 3003 of Pub. L. 104–66, as amended, set out as a note under section 1113 of Title 31, Money and Finance.

SECTION REFERRED TO IN OTHER SECTIONS

This section is referred to in sections 403a, 403e, 403f of this title.

§403r. Special annuity computation rules for certain employees' service abroad

(a) Officers and employees to whom rules apply

Notwithstanding any provision of chapter 83 of title 5, the annuity under subchapter III of such chapter of an officer or employee of the Central Intelligence Agency who retires on or after October 1, 1989, is not designated under section 2013 of this title, and has served abroad as an officer or employee of the Agency on or after January 1, 1987, shall be computed as provided in subsection (b) of this section.

(b) Computation rules

(1) The portion of the annuity relating to such service abroad that is actually performed at any time during the officer's or employee's first ten years of total service shall be computed at the rate and using the percent of average pay speci-

fied in section 8339(a)(3) of title 5 that is normally applicable only to so much of an employee's total service as exceeds ten years.

(2) The portion of the annuity relating to service abroad as described in subsection (a) of this section but that is actually performed at any time after the officer's or employee's first ten years of total service shall be computed as provided in section 8339(a)(3) of title 5; but, in addition, the officer or employee shall be deemed for annuity computation purposes to have actually performed an equivalent period of service abroad during his or her first ten years of total service, and in calculating the portion of the officer's or employee's annuity for his or her first ten years of total service, the computation rate and percent of average pay specified in paragraph (1) shall also be applied to the period of such deemed or equivalent service abroad.

(3) The portion of the annuity relating to other service by an officer or employee as described in subsection (a) of this section shall be computed as provided in the provisions of section 8339(a) of title 5 that would otherwise be applicable to such service.

(4) For purposes of this subsection, the term "total service" has the meaning given such term under chapter 83 of title 5.

(c) Annuities deemed annuities under section 8339 of title 5

For purposes of subsections (f) through (m) of section 8339 of title 5, an annuity computed under this section shall be deemed to be an annuity computed under subsections (a) and (*o*)[1] of section 8339 of title 5.

(d) Officers and employees entitled to greater annuities under section 8339 of title 5

The provisions of subsection (a) of this section shall not apply to an officer or employee of the Central Intelligence Agency who would otherwise be entitled to a greater annuity computed under an otherwise applicable subsection of section 8339 of title 5.

(June 20, 1949, ch. 227, §18, as added Pub. L. 101–193, title III, §305, Nov. 30, 1989, 103 Stat. 1704; amended Pub. L. 102–496, title VIII, §803(a)(2), Oct. 24, 1992, 106 Stat. 3252.)

REFERENCES IN TEXT

Subsection (*o*) of section 8339 of title 5, referred to in subsec. (c), was redesignated subsec. (p) of that section by Pub. L. 102–378, §2(62), Oct. 2, 1992, 106 Stat. 1354.

CODIFICATION

Section was enacted as part of the Central Intelligence Agency Act of 1949, and not as part of the National Security Act of 1947 which comprises this chapter.

AMENDMENTS

1992—Subsec. (a). Pub. L. 102–496 substituted reference to section 2013 of this title for reference in original to section 203 of the Central Intelligence Agency Retirement Act of 1964 for Certain Employees which was formerly set out as a note under section 403 of this title.

EFFECTIVE DATE OF 1992 AMENDMENT

Amendment by Pub. L. 102–496 effective on first day of fourth month beginning after Oct. 24, 1992, see section 805 of Pub. L. 102–496, set out as an Effective Date note under section 2001 of this title.

SECTION REFERRED TO IN OTHER SECTIONS

This section is referred to in sections 403a, 403e, 403f, 403r–1, 2144 of this title; title 10 section 1605.

§403r–1. Portability of overseas service retirement benefit

The special accrual rates provided by section 2153 of this title and by section 403r of this title for computation of the annuity of an individual who has served abroad as an officer or employee of the Central Intelligence Agency shall be used to compute that portion of the annuity of such individual relating to such service abroad whether or not the individual is employed by the Central Intelligence Agency at the time of retirement from Federal service.

(Pub. L. 101–193, title III, §306, Nov. 30, 1989, 103 Stat. 1704; Pub. L. 103–178, title II, §204(a), Dec. 3, 1993, 107 Stat. 2033.)

CODIFICATION

Section was enacted as part of the Intelligence Authorization Act, Fiscal Year 1990, and not as part of the Central Intelligence Agency Act of 1949 which is classified to section 403a et seq. of this title, nor as part of the National Security Act of 1947 which comprises this chapter.

AMENDMENTS

1993—Pub. L. 103–178 substituted reference to section 2153 of this title for reference in original to section 303 of the Central Intelligence Agency Retirement Act of 1964 for Certain Employees.

§403s. Special rules for disability retirement and death-in-service benefits with respect to certain employees

(a) Officers and employees to whom section 2051 rules apply

Notwithstanding any other provision of law, an officer or employee of the Central Intelligence Agency subject to retirement system coverage under subchapter III of chapter 83 of title 5 who—

(1) has five years of civilian service credit toward retirement under such subchapter III of chapter 83, title 5;

(2) has not been designated under section 2013 of this title,[1] as a participant in the Central Intelligence Agency Retirement and Disability System;

(3) has become disabled during a period of assignment to the performance of duties that are qualifying toward such designation under such section 2013 of this title; and

(4) satisfies the requirements for disability retirement under section 8337 of title 5—

shall, upon his own application or upon order of the Director, be retired on an annuity computed in accordance with the rules prescribed in section 2051 of this title, in lieu of an annuity computed as provided by section 8337 of title 5.

(b) Survivors of officers and employees to whom section 2052 rules apply

Notwithstanding any other provision of law, in the case of an officer or employee of the Central

[1] See References in Text note below.

[1] So in original. The comma probably should not appear.

Intelligence Agency subject to retirement system coverage under subchapter III of chapter 83, title 5, who—

(1) has at least eighteen months of civilian service credit toward retirement under such subchapter III of chapter 83, title 5;

(2) has not been designated under section 2013 of this title,[2] as a participant in the Central Intelligence Agency Retirement and Disability System;

(3) prior to separation or retirement from the Agency, dies during a period of assignment to the performance of duties that are qualifying toward such designation under such section 2013 of this title; and

(4) is survived by a surviving spouse, former spouse, or child as defined in section 2002 of this title, who would otherwise be entitled to an annuity under section 8341 of title 5—

such surviving spouse, former spouse, or child of such officer or employee shall be entitled to an annuity computed in accordance with section 2052 of this title, in lieu of an annuity computed in accordance with section 8341 of title 5.

(c) Annuities under this section deemed annuities under chapter 83 of title 5

The annuities provided under subsections (a) and (b) of this section shall be deemed to be annuities under chapter 83 of title 5 for purposes of the other provisions of such chapter and other laws (including title 26) relating to such annuities, and shall be payable from the Central Intelligence Agency Retirement and Disability Fund maintained pursuant to section 2012 of this title.

(June 20, 1949, ch. 227, § 19, as added Pub. L. 101–193, title III, § 307(a), Nov. 30, 1989, 103 Stat. 1705; amended Pub. L. 102–496, title VIII, § 803(a)(3), Oct. 24, 1992, 106 Stat. 3252; Pub. L. 103–178, title V, § 501(3), Dec. 3, 1993, 107 Stat. 2038.)

Codification

Section was enacted as part of the Central Intelligence Agency Act of 1949, and not as part of the National Security Act of 1947 which comprises this chapter.

Amendments

1993—Subsec. (b). Pub. L. 103–178, § 501(3)(A), (C), substituted "section 2052" for "section 2051" in heading and closing provisions.

Subsec. (b)(2). Pub. L. 103–178, § 501(3)(B), made technical amendment to reference to section 2013 of this title to update reference to corresponding section of original act.

1992—Subsec. (a). Pub. L. 102–496, § 803(a)(3)(A), inserted heading, redesignated cl. (i) as par. (1), in cl. (ii), substituted reference to section 2013 of this title for reference in original to section 203 of the Central Intelligence Agency Retirement Act of 1964 for Certain Employees, as amended, which was formerly set out as a note under section 403 of this title, and redesignated such cl. as par. (2), in cl. (iii), inserted "such" before reference to section 2013 of this title and redesignated such cl. as par. (3), redesignated cl. (iv) as par. (4), and substituted reference to section 2051 of this title for "such section 231" in concluding provisions.

Subsec. (b). Pub. L. 102–496, § 803(a)(3)(B)(i), (ii), (iv)–(vi), inserted heading, redesignated cl. (i) as par. (1), in cl. (ii), substituted reference to section 2013 of this title for reference in original to section 203 of the Central Intelligence Agency Retirement Act of 1964 for Certain Employees, as amended, which was formerly set out as a note under section 403 of this title, and redesignated cl. (ii) as par. (2), redesignated cls. (iii) and (iv) as pars. (3) and (4), respectively, and in concluding provisions, substituted "surviving spouse, former spouse, or child" for "widow or widower, former spouse, and/or child or children" and substituted reference to section 2051 of this title for "such section 232".

Pub. L. 102–496, § 803(a)(3)(B)(iii), which directed the substitution of "surviving spouse, former spouse, or child as defined in section 2002 of this title" in cl. (iv) for "widow or widower, former spouse, and/or child or children as defined in section 204 and section 232 of such the Central Intelligence Agency Retirement Act of 1964 for Certain Employees", was executed by making the substitution for "widow or widower, former spouse, and/or a child or children as defined in section 204 and section 232 of the Central Intelligence Agency Retirement Act of 1964 for Certain Employees", to reflect the probable intent of Congress.

Subsec. (c). Pub. L. 102–496, § 803(a)(3)(D)(i)–(iii), inserted heading, struck out par. (1) designation before "The annuities provided", substituted "maintained pursuant to section 2012 of this title" for "established by section 202 of the Central Intelligence Agency Retirement Act of 1964 for Certain Employees", and struck out par. (2) which read as follows: "The annuities and/or other benefits provided under subsections (c) and (d) of this section shall be deemed to be annuities and/or benefits under chapter 84 of title 5 for purposes of the other provisions of such chapter and other laws (including title 26) relating to such annuities and/or benefits, but shall be payable from the Central Intelligence Agency Retirement and Disability Fund established by section 202 of the Central Intelligence Agency Retirement Act of 1964 for Certain Employees."

Pub. L. 102–496, § 803(a)(3)(C), (D), redesignated subsec. (e) as (c) and struck out former subsec. (c) which provided for retirement of officers and employees of the Central Intelligence Agency as though designated pursuant to section 302(a) of Pub. L. 88–643 which was formerly set out as a note under section 403 of this title.

Subsec. (d). Pub. L. 102–496, § 803(a)(3)(C), struck out subsec. (d) which provided that survivors of officers and employees of the Central Intelligence Agency were to receive benefits as though deceased had been designated pursuant to section 302(a) of Pub. L. 88–643, which was formerly set out as a note under section 403 of this title.

Subsec. (e). Pub. L. 102–496, § 803(a)(3)(D), redesignated subsec. (e) as (c).

Effective Date of 1992 Amendment

Amendment by Pub. L. 102–496 effective on first day of fourth month beginning after Oct. 24, 1992, see section 805 of Pub. L. 102–496, set out as an Effective Date note under section 2001 of this title.

Section Referred to in Other Sections

This section is referred to in sections 403a, 403e, 403f of this title.

§ 403t. General Counsel of Central Intelligence Agency

(a) Appointment

There is a General Counsel of the Central Intelligence Agency, appointed from civilian life by the President, by and with the advice and consent of the Senate.

(b) Chief legal officer

The General Counsel is the chief legal officer of the Central Intelligence Agency.

(c) Functions

The General Counsel of the Central Intelligence Agency shall perform such functions as

[2] So in original. The comma probably should not appear.

the Director of Central Intelligence may prescribe.

(June 20, 1949, ch. 227, § 20, as added Pub. L. 104–293, title VIII, § 813(a), Oct. 11, 1996, 110 Stat. 3483.)

CODIFICATION

Section was enacted as part of the Central Intelligence Agency Act of 1949, and not as part of the National Security Act of 1947 which comprises this chapter.

APPLICABILITY OF APPOINTMENT REQUIREMENTS

Section 813(b) of Pub. L. 104–293 provided that: "The requirement established by section 20 of the Central Intelligence Agency Act of 1949 [50 U.S.C. 403t], as added by subsection (a), for the appointment by the President, by and with the advice and consent of the Senate, of an individual to the position of General Counsel of the Central Intelligence Agency shall apply as follows:

"(1) To any vacancy in such position that occurs after the date of the enactment of this Act [Oct. 11, 1996].

"(2) To the incumbent serving in such position on the date of the enactment of this Act as of the date that is six months after such date of enactment, if such incumbent has served in such position continuously between such date of enactment and the date that is six months after such date of enactment."

§ 403u. Central services program

(a) In general

The Director may carry out a program under which elements of the Agency provide items and services on a reimbursable basis to other elements of the Agency, nonappropriated fund entities or instrumentalities associated or affiliated with the Agency, and other Government agencies. The Director shall carry out the program in accordance with the provisions of this section.

(b) Participation of Agency elements

(1) In order to carry out the program, the Director shall—

(A) designate the elements of the Agency that are to provide items or services under the program (in this section referred to as "central service providers");

(B) specify the items or services to be provided under the program by such providers; and

(C) assign to such providers for purposes of the program such inventories, equipment, and other assets (including equipment on order) as the Director determines necessary to permit such providers to provide items or services under the program.

(2) The designation of elements and the specification of items and services under paragraph (1) shall be subject to the approval of the Director of the Office of Management and Budget.

(c) Central Services Working Capital Fund

(1) There is established a fund to be known as the Central Services Working Capital Fund (in this section referred to as the "Fund"). The purpose of the Fund is to provide sums for activities under the program.

(2) There shall be deposited in the Fund the following:

(A) Amounts appropriated to the Fund.

(B) Amounts credited to the Fund from payments received by central service providers under subsection (e) of this section.

(C) Fees imposed and collected under subsection (f)(1) of this section.

(D) Amounts received in payment for loss or damage to equipment or property of a central service provider as a result of activities under the program.

(E) Other receipts from the sale or exchange of equipment or property of a central service provider as a result of activities under the program.

(F) Receipts from individuals in reimbursement for utility services and meals provided under the program.

(G) Receipts from individuals for the rental of property and equipment under the program.

(H) Such other amounts as the Director is authorized to deposit in or transfer to the Fund.

(3) Amounts in the Fund shall be available, without fiscal year limitation, for the following purposes:

(A) To pay the costs of providing items or services under the program.

(B) To pay the costs of carrying out activities under subsection (f)(2) of this section.

(d) Limitation on amount of orders

The total value of all orders for items or services to be provided under the program in any fiscal year may not exceed an amount specified in advance by the Director of the Office of Management and Budget.

(e) Payment for items and services

(1) A Government agency provided items or services under the program shall pay the central service provider concerned for such items or services an amount equal to the costs incurred by the provider in providing such items or services plus any fee imposed under subsection (f) of this section. In calculating such costs, the Director shall take into account personnel costs (including costs associated with salaries, annual leave, and workers' compensation), plant and equipment costs (including depreciation of plant and equipment other than structures owned by the Agency), operation and maintenance expenses, amortized costs, and other expenses.

(2) Payment for items or services under paragraph (1) may take the form of an advanced payment by an agency from appropriations available to such agency for the procurement of such items or services.

(f) Fees

(1) The Director may permit a central service provider to impose and collect a fee with respect to the provision of an item or service under the program. The amount of the fee may not exceed an amount equal to four percent of the payment received by the provider for the item or service.

(2)(A) Subject to subparagraph (B), the Director may obligate and expend amounts in the Fund that are attributable to the fees imposed and collected under paragraph (1) to acquire equipment or systems for, or to improve the equipment or systems of, central service providers and any elements of the Agency that are not designated for participation in the program in order to facilitate the designation of such elements for future participation in the program.

(B) The Director may not expend amounts in the Fund for purposes specified in subparagraph (A) in fiscal year 1998, 1999, or 2000 unless the Director—

(i) secures the prior approval of the Director of the Office of Management and Budget; and

(ii) submits notice of the proposed expenditure to the Permanent Select Committee on Intelligence of the House of Representatives and the Select Committee on Intelligence of the Senate.

(g) Audit

(1) Not later than December 31 each year, the Inspector General of the Central Intelligence Agency shall conduct an audit of the activities under the program during the preceding fiscal year.

(2) The Director of the Office of Management and Budget shall determine the form and content of financial statements to be prepared with respect to the program. Office of Management and Budget guidance shall also determine the procedures for conducting annual audits under paragraph (1)..[1] Such audits shall include an itemized accounting of the items or services provided, the costs associated with the items or services provided, the payments and any fees received for the items or services provided, and the agencies provided items or services.

(3) Not later than 30 days after the completion of an audit under paragraph (1), the Inspector General shall submit a copy of the audit to the following:

(A) The Director of the Office of Management and Budget.

(B) The Director of Central Intelligence.

(C) The Permanent Select Committee on Intelligence of the House of Representatives.

(D) The Select Committee on Intelligence of the Senate.

(h) Termination

(1) The authority of the Director to carry out the program under this section shall terminate on March 31, 2002.

(2) Subject to paragraph (3), the Director of Central Intelligence and the Director of the Office of Management and Budget, acting jointly—

(A) may terminate the program under this section and the Fund at any time; and

(B) upon such termination, shall provide for the disposition of the personnel, assets, liabilities, grants, contracts, property, records, and unexpended balances of appropriations, authorizations, allocations, and other funds held, used, arising from, available to, or to be made available in connection with the program or the Fund.

(3) The Director of Central Intelligence and the Director of the Office of Management and Budget may not undertake any action under paragraph (2) until 60 days after the date on which the Directors jointly submit notice of such action to the Permanent Select Committee on Intelligence of the House of Representatives and the Select Committee on Intelligence of the Senate.

[1] So in original.

(June 20, 1949, ch. 227, § 21, as added Pub. L. 105–107, title IV, § 403(a), Nov. 20, 1997, 111 Stat. 2258; amended Pub. L. 106–120, title IV, § 401, Dec. 3, 1999, 113 Stat. 1615; Pub. L. 106–567, title IV, § 401, Dec. 27, 2000, 114 Stat. 2847.)

CODIFICATION

Section was enacted as part of the Central Intelligence Agency Act of 1949, and not as part of the National Security Act of 1947 which comprises this chapter.

AMENDMENTS

2000—Subsec. (c)(2)(F) to (H). Pub. L. 106–567, § 401(a), added subpars. (F) and (G) and redesignated former subpar. (F) as (H).

Subsec. (e)(1). Pub. L. 106–567, § 401(b), in second sentence, inserted "other than structures owned by the Agency" after "depreciation of plant and equipment".

Subsec. (g)(2). Pub. L. 106–567, § 401(c), substituted "financial statements to be prepared with respect to the program. Office of Management and Budget guidance shall also determine the procedures for conducting annual audits under paragraph (1)." for "annual audits under paragraph (1)".

1999—Subsec. (a). Pub. L. 106–120, § 401(a), substituted ", nonappropriated fund entities or instrumentalities associated or affiliated with the Agency, and other" for "and to other".

Subsec. (c)(2)(D). Pub. L. 106–120, § 401(b)(1), amended subpar. (D) generally. Prior to amendment, subpar. (D) read as follows: "Amounts collected in payment for loss or damage to equipment or other property of a central service provider as a result of activities under the program."

Subsec. (c)(2)(E), (F). Pub. L. 106–120, § 401(b)(2), (3), added subpar. (E) and redesignated former subpar. (E) as (F).

Subsec. (f)(2)(A). Pub. L. 106–120, § 401(c), inserted "central service providers and any" before "elements of the Agency".

Subsec. (h)(1). Pub. L. 106–120, § 401(d), substituted "2002" for "2000".

AVAILABILITY OF FUNDS CREDITED TO CENTRAL SERVICES WORKING CAPITAL FUND

Pub. L. 106–259, title VIII, § 8045, Aug. 9, 2000, 114 Stat. 684, provided in part: "That funds appropriated, transferred, or otherwise credited to the Central Intelligence Agency Central Services Working Capital Fund during this or any prior or subsequent fiscal year shall remain available until expended."

Similar provisions were contained in the following prior appropriation acts:

Pub. L. 106–79, title VIII, § 8048, Oct. 25, 1999, 113 Stat. 1241.

Pub. L. 105–262, title VIII, § 8048, Oct. 17, 1998, 112 Stat. 2307.

§ 403v. Detail of employees

The Director may—

(1) detail any personnel of the Agency on a reimbursable basis indefinitely to the National Reconnaissance Office without regard to any limitation under law on the duration of details of Federal Government personnel; and

(2) hire personnel for the purpose of any detail under paragraph (1).

(June 20, 1949, ch. 227, § 22, as added Pub. L. 106–567, title IV, § 404, Dec. 27, 2000, 114 Stat. 2848.)

CODIFICATION

Section was enacted as part of the Central Intelligence Agency Act of 1949, and not as part of the National Security Act of 1947 which comprises this chapter.

§ 404. Emergency preparedness

(a) Employment of personnel

The Director of the Federal Emergency Management Agency, subject to the direction of the President, is authorized, subject to the civil-service laws and chapter 51 and subchapter III of chapter 53 of title 5, to appoint and fix the compensation of such personnel as may be necessary to assist him in carrying out his functions.

(b) Functions

It shall be the function of the Director of the Federal Emergency Management Agency to advise the President concerning the coordination of military, industrial, and civilian mobilization, including—

(1) policies concerning industrial and civilian mobilization in order to assure the most effective mobilization and maximum utilization of the Nation's manpower in the event of war;

(2) programs for the effective use in time of war of the Nation's natural and industrial resources for military and civilian needs, for the maintenance and stabilization of the civilian economy in time of war, and for the adjustment of such economy to war needs and conditions;

(3) policies for unifying, in time of war, the activities of Federal agencies and departments engaged in or concerned with production, procurement, distribution, or transportation of military or civilian supplies, materials, and products;

(4) the relationship between potential supplies of, and potential requirements for, manpower, resources, and productive facilities in time of war;

(5) policies for establishing adequate reserves of strategic and critical material, and for the conservation of these reserves;

(6) the strategic relocation of industries, services, government, and economic activities, the continuous operation of which is essential to the Nation's security.

(c) Utilization of Government resources and facilities

In performing his functions, the Director of the Federal Emergency Management Agency shall utilize to the maximum extent the facilities and resources of the departments and agencies of the Government.

(July 26, 1947, ch. 343, title I, § 107, formerly § 103, 61 Stat. 499; Oct. 28, 1949, ch. 782, title IX, § 1106(a), 63 Stat. 972; 1950 Reorg. Plan No. 25, § 1, eff. July 9, 1950, 15 F.R. 4366, 64 Stat. 1280; 1953 Reorg. Plan No. 3, § 2(a), eff. June 12, 1953, 18 F.R. 3375, 67 Stat. 634; Sept. 3, 1954, ch. 1263, § 50, 68 Stat. 1244; 1958 Reorg. Plan No. 1, § 2, eff. July 1, 1958, 23 F.R. 4991, 72 Stat. 1799; Pub. L. 90–608, ch. IV, § 402, Oct. 21, 1968, 82 Stat. 1194; Ex. Ord. No. 11725, § 3, eff. June 29, 1973, 38 F.R. 17175; Ex. Ord. No. 12148, §§ 1–103, 4–102, July 20, 1979, 44 F.R. 43239; renumbered § 107, Pub. L. 102–496, title VII, § 705(a)(2), Oct. 24, 1992, 106 Stat. 3190.)

References in Text

The civil-service laws, referred to in subsec. (a), are set forth in Title 5, Government Organization and Employees. See, particularly, section 3301 et seq. of Title 5.

Codification

In subsec. (a), "chapter 51 and subchapter III of chapter 53 of title 5" substituted for "the Classification Act of 1949" on authority of Pub. L. 89–554, § 7(b), Sept. 6, 1966, 80 Stat. 631, the first section of which enacted Title 5, Government Organization and Employees.

Amendments

1954—Act Sept. 3, 1954, struck out subsec. (a) relating to establishment of National Security Resources Board, and redesignated subsecs. (b) to (d) as subsecs. (a) to (c), respectively.

1949—Subsec. (b). Act Oct. 28, 1949, substituted "Classification Act of 1949" for "Classification Act of 1923".

Repeals

Act Oct. 28, 1949, ch. 782, cited as a credit to this section, was repealed (subject to a savings clause) by Pub. L. 89–554, Sept. 6, 1966, § 8, 80 Stat. 632, 655.

Transfer of Functions

"Director of the Federal Emergency Management Agency" substituted for "Chairman of the Board" in subsec. (a), and for "Board" in subsecs. (b) and (c), on authority of the following:

"Chairman of the Board", meaning Chairman of National Security Resources Board, substituted in subsecs. (b) and (c) for "Board", meaning National Security Resources Board, on authority of section 1 of Reorg. Plan No. 25 of 1950, set out below.

"Director of the Office of Defense Mobilization" substituted in text for "Chairman of Board" meaning National Security Resources Board, pursuant to Reorg. Plan No. 3 of 1953, §§ 1(a), 2(a), and 6, eff. June 12, 1953, 18 F.R. 3375, 67 Stat. 634, set out below, which established Office of Defense Mobilization, as an agency within Executive Office of President, abolished National Security Resources Board, and transferred to Director of Office of Defense Mobilization functions, records, property, personnel, and funds of Board.

Office of Defense Mobilization and Federal Civil Defense Administration consolidated to form Office of Emergency Planning, an agency within Executive Office of President, by section 2 of Reorg. Plan No. 1 of 1958, eff. July 1, 1958, 23 F.R. 4991, 72 Stat. 1799, as amended, set out in the Appendix to Title 5, Government Organization and Employees, and functions vested by law in Office of Defense Mobilization and Director thereof transferred to President, with power to delegate, by section 1 of Reorg. Plan No. 1 of 1958.

Office of Emergency Planning changed to Office of Emergency Preparedness pursuant to section 402 of Pub. L. 90–608, Oct. 21, 1968, 82 Stat. 1194, which provided that references in laws to Office of Emergency Planning after Oct. 21, 1968, should be deemed references to Office of Emergency Preparedness.

Office of Emergency Preparedness, including offices of Director, Deputy Director, Assistant Directors, and Regional Directors, abolished and functions vested by law in Office of Emergency Preparedness transferred to President of United States by sections 1 and 3(a)(1) of Reorg. Plan No. 1 of 1973, eff. July 1, 1973, 38 F.R. 9579, 87 Stat. 1089, set out in the Appendix to Title 5, Government Organization and Employees.

Functions vested in Director of Office of Emergency Preparedness as of June 30, 1973, by Executive Order, proclamation, or other directive issued by or on behalf of President or otherwise under this section and Ex. Ord. No. 10421, formerly set out below, with certain exceptions, transferred to Administrator of General Services by Ex. Ord. No. 11725, § 3, June 27, 1973, 38 F.R. 17175, formerly set out under section 2271 of the Appendix to this title, to be exercised in conformance with such guidance as provided by National Security Council and, with respect to economic and disposal aspects of stockpiling of strategic and critical materials by Council on Economic Policy. Functions of Administrator of General Services under this chapter performed by Federal Preparedness Agency within General Services Administration.

Functions of Director of Office of Defense Mobilization under this section, which were previously transferred to President, delegated to Director of Federal Emergency Management Agency by sections 1–103 and 4–102 of Ex. Ord. No. 12148, July 20, 1979, 44 F.R. 43239, set out as a note under section 5195 of Title 42, The Public Health and Welfare.

EMERGENCY PREPAREDNESS FUNCTIONS

For assignment of certain emergency preparedness functions to Director of Federal Emergency Management Agency, see parts 1, 2, and 17 of Ex. Ord. No. 12656, Nov. 18, 1988, 53 F.R. 47491, set out as a note under section 5195 of Title 42, The Public Health and Welfare.

OFFICE OF EMERGENCY PLANNING

Pub. L. 87–296, §2, Sept. 22, 1961, 75 Stat. 630, provided that: "Any reference in any other law to the Office of Civil and Defense Mobilization shall, after the date of this Act [Sept. 22, 1961], be deemed to refer to the Office of Emergency Planning."

REORGANIZATION PLAN NO. 25 OF 1950

Eff. July 9, 1950, 15 F.R. 4366, 64 Stat. 1280

Prepared by the President and transmitted to the Senate and the House of Representatives in Congress assembled, May 9, 1950, pursuant to the provisions of the Reorganization Act of 1949, approved June 20, 1949 [see 5 U.S.C. 901 et seq.].

NATIONAL SECURITY RESOURCES BOARD

SECTION 1. FUNCTIONS OF CHAIRMAN AND OF BOARD

The functions of the National Security Resources Board are hereby transferred to the Chairman of the National Security Resources Board, and the Board shall hereafter advise and consult with the Chairman with respect to such matters within his jurisdiction as he may request.

SEC. 2. VICE CHAIRMAN

There is hereby established the office of Vice Chairman of the National Security Resources Board. Such Vice Chairman shall (1) be an additional member of the National Security Resources Board, (2) be appointed from civilian life by the President, by and with the advice and consent of the Senate, (3) receive compensation at the rate of $16,000 per annum, and (4) perform such of the duties of the Chairman as the Chairman shall designate.

SEC. 3. PERFORMANCE OF FUNCTIONS OF CHAIRMAN

The Chairman may from time to time make such provisions as he shall deem appropriate authorizing the performance by any other officer, or by any agency or employee, of the National Security Resources Board of any function of the Chairman.

MESSAGE OF THE PRESIDENT

To the Congress of the United States:

I transmit herewith Reorganization Plan No. 25 of 1950, prepared in accordance with the provisions of the Reorganization Act of 1949. The plan transfers the function of the National Security Resources Board from the Board to the Chairman of the Board and makes the Board advisory to the Chairman. The plan also provides for a Vice Chairman, appointed by the President and confirmed by the Senate.

The function assigned to the National Security Resources Board by the National Security Act of 1947 is "to advise the President concerning the coordination of military, industrial and civilian mobilization." Proper performance of this function requires action by the Board and its staff in two broad areas:

(1) The conduct of advance mobilization planning which identifies the problems which will arise and the measures necessary to meet these problems if and when the Nation moves from a peacetime into a wartime situation.

(2) The formulation of current policies and programs which will help the Nation achieve an adequate state of readiness against the eventuality of a future war.

The role assigned the National Security Resources Board is clearly one of staff assistance to the President. The Congress recently recognized this fact in its approval of Reorganization Plan No. 4 of 1949 which, pursuant to the specific recommendation of the Hoover Commission, placed the National Security Resources Board in the Executive Office of the President.

The accompanying reorganization plan is designed to make the National Security Resources Board a more effective instrument. Successful performance of the Board's mission requires a wide range of detailed study and analysis to cover all the major aspects of national mobilization. A committee of department heads or departmental representatives encounters some natural difficulties in providing supervision and leadership in such an extensive and detailed activity. The Chairman has the difficult task of exercising discretion as to which matters shall be submitted for Board approval. The departmental members of the Board cannot possibly supervise or approve the Board's extensive and detailed activities and yet, as Board members, must accept ultimate responsibility for all such activities. Likewise, the departmental members are encumbered by the difficulty of having to reach collective and speedy decisions on a great many matters for which they, as Board members, are responsible.

By vesting the functions of the Board in the Chairman, the difficulties of Board operation will be overcome. At the same time, the reorganization plan provides for the continued participation of the several departments and agencies in the task of mobilization planning. This is not only a matter of established policy but also a requirement of the National Security Act. The departments will continue to have representation on the Board. The Board, in an advisory relationship to the Chairman, will be a useful arrangement for obtaining the necessary participation of departments in mobilization planning and for coordination of their activity. It will enable the departments to keep abreast of the total range of security resources planning. Without reliance on the departments for the execution of much of the actual job of mobilization planning, coordination with the total range of governmental policies and objectives would be lost.

The Congress in passing the National Security Act Amendments of 1949 recognized the difficulty which exists when functions of staff advice and assistance are placed in a board-type agency. The National Security Act Amendments of 1949, in clarifying the role of the Chairman of the Munitions Board and the Research and Development Board, strengthened and increased the effectiveness of these staff agencies of the Secretary of Defense by providing for the exclusive exercise of responsibilities by the Chairman. This plan achieves the same objective for the National Security Resources Board.

The accompanying reorganization plan provides for a Vice Chairman appointed by the President and confirmed by the Senate. The tremendous responsibilities of the National Security Resources Board and the heavy workload on the Chairman fully warrant this. Providing the Chairman with a principal associate for the exercise of his responsibilities is consistent with the usual practice in other agencies of the executive branch.

After investigation I have found and hereby declare that each reorganization included in Reorganization Plan No. 25 of 1950 is necessary to accomplish one or more of the purposes set forth in section 2(a) of the Reorganization Act of 1949.

I have found and hereby declare that it is necessary to include in the accompanying reorganization plan, by reason of reorganizations made thereby, provisions for the appointment and compensation of a Vice Chairman of the National Security Resources Board. The rate of compensation fixed for this officer is that which I have found to prevail in respect of comparable officers in the executive branch of the Government.

The taking effect of the reorganizations included in Reorganization Plan No. 25 may not in itself result in substantial immediate savings. However, the important objective is maximum effectiveness in security resources planning.

The security of this Nation requires that these steps be taken to enable security resources planning to move forward more effectively. It is for that reason that Reorganization Plan No. 25 is today submitted to the Congress. It is for that reason, and that reason alone, that I strongly urge congressional acceptance of Reorganization Plan No. 25.

HARRY S. TRUMAN.

THE WHITE HOUSE, May 9, 1950.

REORGANIZATION PLAN NO. 3 OF 1953

Eff. June 12, 1953, 18 F.R. 3375, 67 Stat. 634

Prepared by the President and transmitted to the Senate and the House of Representatives in Congress assembled, April 2, 1953, pursuant to the provisions of the Reorganization Act of 1949, approved June 20, 1949, as amended [see 5 U.S.C. 901 et seq.].

OFFICE OF DEFENSE MOBILIZATION

SECTION 1. ESTABLISHMENT OF OFFICE

(a) There is hereby established in the Executive Office of the President a new agency which shall be known as the Office of Defense Mobilization, hereinafter referred to as the "Office."

(b) There shall be at the head of the Office a Director of the Office of Defense Mobilization, hereinafter referred to as the "Director," who shall be appointed by the President by and with the advice and consent of the Senate and shall receive compensation at the rate of $22,500 per annum.

(c) There shall be in the Office a Deputy Director of the Office of Defense Mobilization, who shall be appointed by the President, by and with the advice and consent of the Senate, shall receive compensation at the rate of $17,500 per annum, shall perform such functions as the Director shall designate, and shall act as Director during the absence or disability of the Director or in the event of a vacancy in the office of the Director.

SEC. 2. TRANSFER OF FUNCTIONS

There are hereby transferred to the Director:

(a) All functions of the Chairman of the National Security Resources Board, including his functions as a member of the National Security Council, but excluding the functions abolished by section 5(a) of this reorganization plan.

(b) All functions under the Strategic and Critical Materials Stock Piling Act, as amended (50 U.S.C. 98 et seq.), vested in the Secretaries of the Army, Navy, Air Force, and Interior or in any of them or in any combination of them, including the functions which were vested in the Army and Navy Munitions Board by the item No. (2) in section 6(a) of the said Act (60 Stat. 598) [former section 98e(a)(2) of this title], but excluding functions vested in the Secretary of the Interior by section 7 of said Act [former section 98f of this title].

(c) The functions vested in the Munitions Board by section 4(h) of the Commodity Credit Corporation Charter Act, as amended (15 U.S.C. 714b(h)), and by section 204(e) of the Federal Property and Administrative Services Act of 1949 (40 U.S.C. 485(e)).

(d) All functions now vested by any statute in the Director of Defense Mobilization or in the Office of Defense Mobilization provided for in Executive Order Numbered 10193 (15 F.R. 9031) [revoked by Ex. Ord. No. 10480, 18 F.R. 4939, formerly set out as a note under section 2153 of Appendix to this title].

SEC. 3. PERFORMANCE OF TRANSFERRED FUNCTIONS

(a) The Director may from time to time make such provisions as he shall deem appropriate authorizing the performance by any other officer, or by any agency or employee, of the Office, of any function of the Director, exclusive of the function of being a member of the National Security Council.

(b) When authorized by the Director, any function transferred to him by the provisions of this reorganization plan (exclusive of the function of being a member of the National Security Council) may be performed by the head of any agency of the executive branch of the Government or, subject to the direction and control of any such agency head, by such officers, employees, and organizational units under the jurisdiction of such agency head as such agency head may designate.

(c) In addition to the representatives who by virtue of the last sentence of section 2(a) of the Strategic and Critical Materials Stock Piling Act, as amended [former section 98a(a) of this title], and section 2 of this reorganization plan are designated to cooperate with the Director, the Secretary of Defense, the Secretary of the Interior, and the heads of such other agencies having functions regarding strategic or critical materials as the Director shall from time to time designate, shall each designate representatives who shall similarly cooperate with the Director.

SEC. 4. RECORDS, PROPERTY, PERSONNEL, AND FUNDS

There shall be transferred with the functions transferred by this reorganization plan from the Chairman of the National Security Resources Board and the Department of Defense, respectively, so much of the records, property, personnel, and unexpended balances of appropriations, allocations, and other funds, used, held, employed, available, or to be made available in connection with the said functions, as the Director shall determine to be required for the performance of the transferred functions by the Office, but all transfers from the Department of Defense under the foregoing provisions of this section shall be subject to the approval of the Secretary of Defense.

SEC. 5. ABOLITION OF FUNCTIONS

(a) The functions of the Chairman of the National Security Resources Board under section 18 of the Universal Military Training and Service Act (50 U.S.C. App. 468), as affected by Reorganization Plan Numbered 25 of 1950 (64 Stat. 1280) [set out above], with respect to being consulted by and furnishing advice to the President as required by that section, are hereby abolished.

(b) So much of the functions of the Secretary of Defense under section 202(b) of the National Security Act of 1947, as amended [see 10 U.S.C. 113(b)], as consists of direction, authority, and control over functions transferred by this reorganization plan is hereby abolished.

(c) Any functions which were vested in the Army and Navy Munitions Board or which are vested in the Munitions Board with respect to serving as agent through which the Secretaries of the Army, Navy, Air Force, and Interior jointly act, under section 2(a) of the Strategic and Critical Materials Stock Piling Act, as amended [former section 98a of this title], are hereby abolished.

SEC. 6. ABOLITION OF NATIONAL SECURITY RESOURCES BOARD

The National Security Resources Board (established by the National Security Act of 1947, 61 Stat. 499 [this section]), including the offices of Chairman and Vice Chairman of the National Security Resources Board, is hereby abolished, and the Director shall provide for winding up any outstanding affairs of the said Board or offices not otherwise provided for in this reorganization plan.

[For subsequent history relating to Office of Defense Mobilization, see notes set out under this section.]

MESSAGE OF THE PRESIDENT

To the Congress of the United States:

I transmit herewith Reorganization Plan No. 4 of 1953, prepared in accordance with the provisions of the Reorganization Act of 1949, as amended.

The reorganization plan is designed to achieve two primary objectives: The first is to improve the organization of the Executive Office of the President; the second is to enable one Executive Office agency to exercise strong leadership in our national mobilization effort, including both current defense activities and readiness for any future national emergency.

The National Security Resources Board was established by the National Security Act of 1947 to advise the President concerning various aspects of future military, industrial, and civilian mobilization. The areas of responsibility assigned to the Board included the use of national and industrial resources for military and civilian needs; the sufficiency of productive facilities; the strategic relocation of industries; the mobilization and maximum utilization of manpower; and the maintenance and stabilization of the civilian economy.

The vigorous and efficient discharge of these vital functions is not well served by the simultaneous existence in the Executive Office of the President of the National Security Resources Board (charged with planning for the future) and the present Office of Defense Mobilization (charged with programs of the present). The progress of the current mobilization effort has made plain how artificial is the present separation of these functions.

Both functions should now be combined into one defense mobilization agency. Accordingly, the reorganization plan would create in the Executive Office of the President a new agency, to be known as the Office of Defense Mobilization. It would transfer to the new Office the functions of the Chairman of the National Security Resources Board and abolish that Board, including the offices of Chairman and Vice Chairman.

The reorganization plan also transfers to the new agency the statutory functions of the present Office of Defense Mobilization. These are of a minor nature, the major functions of the present Office of Defense Mobilization having been delegated to it by the President, principally under the Defense Production Act of 1950, as amended. It is my intention to transfer the latter functions to the new agency by Executive order, and to abolish the Office of Defense Mobilization established by Executive Order No. 10193. There will thus result a new agency which combines the activities of the National Security Resources Board and both the statutory and delegated functions of the heretofore existing Office of Defense Mobilization.

The proposed plan would also reorganize various activities relating to the stockpiling of strategic and critical materials. Those activities are principally provided for in the Strategic and Critical Materials Stock Piling Act, as amended. It has become increasingly apparent that the policy and program aspects of stockpiling are an integral part of mobilization planning. They should not be administered separately from plant expansion, conservation of materials, and materials procurement under the Defense Production Act of 1950, or from the duties placed in the National Security Resources Board by the National Security Act of 1947. Therefore, the reorganization plan would transfer to the Director of the new Office of Defense Mobilization responsibility for major stockpiling actions, including the determination of the nature and quantities of materials to be stockpiled. In the main, these functions are transferred from the Secretaries of the Army, Navy, and Air Force (acting jointly through the agency of the Munitions Board) and the Secretary of the Interior. The duties of the Administrator of General Services regarding the purchase of strategic and critical materials and the management of stockpiles are not affected by the reorganization plan, except that he will receive his directions, under the plan, from the Director of the Office of Defense Mobilization instead of from the Department of Defense.

This transfer of stockpiling functions will correct the present undesirable confusion of responsibilities. The functions of the heads of the military departments of the Department of Defense and the Secretary of the Interior under the Strategic and Critical Materials Stock Piling Act, as amended, are at present in considerable measure subject to other authority of delegates of the President springing from the Defense Production Act of 1950, as amended. The allocation and distribution of scarce materials among essential civilian and military activities and the continued maintenance of adequate stockpiles of strategic and critical materials are of major current importance. The reorganization plan will make possible more effective coordination and close control over the Government's whole stockpile program. It will speed decisions. It can result in significant economies.

The Department of Defense will, of course, continue to be responsible for presenting the needs of the military services. That Department and the Department of the Interior are specifically designated in the plan as additional agencies which shall appoint representatives to cooperate with the Director of the Office of Defense Mobilization in determining which materials are strategic and critical and how much of them is to be purchased. Final authority with regard to such determination will, however, be in the Director of the Office of Defense Mobilization.

Section 5(a) of the reorganization plan withholds from transfer to the Director and abolishes the functions of the Chairman of the National Security Resources Board with regard to being consulted by and furnishing advice to the President concerning the placing of orders of mandatory precedence for articles or materials for the use of the armed forces of the United States or for the use of the Atomic Energy Commission, and with regard to determining that a plant, mine, or other facility can be readily converted to the production or furnishing of such articles or materials. These abolished functions were vested in the National Security Resources Board by section 18 of the Selective Service Act of 1948 (later renamed as the Universal Military Training and Service Act) and were transferred to the Chairman of that Board by Reorganization Plan No. 25 of 1950. The practical effect of this abolition is to obviate a statutory mandate that the President consult and advise with another officer of the executive branch of the Government.

Section 5(b) of the reorganization plan abolishes the direction, authority, and control of the Secretary of Defense over functions transferred from the Department of Defense by the reorganization plan. The Secretary's functions in this regard are provided for in section 202(b) of the National Security Act of 1947, as amended (5 U.S.C. 171a(b)) [see 10 U.S.C. 113(b)].

Section 5(c) of the reorganization plan abolishes any functions which were vested in the Army and Navy Munitions Board or which are vested in the Munitions Board with respect to serving as the agent through which the Secretaries of the Army, Navy, Air Force, and the Interior jointly act in determining which materials are strategic and critical under the provisions of the Strategic and Critical Materials Stock Piling Act, as amended, and the quality and quantities of such materials to be stockpiled. These abolished functions are provided for in section 2(a) of the Strategic and Critical Materials Stock Piling Act, as amended.

After investigation I have found and hereby declare that each reorganization included in Reorganization Plan No. 3 of 1953 is necessary to accomplish one or more of the purposes set forth in section 2(a) of the Reorganization Act of 1949, as amended. I have also found and hereby declare that by reason of these reorganizations it is necessary to include in the reorganization plan provisions for the appointment and compensation of a Director and a Deputy Director of the Office of Defense Mobilization. The rates of compensation fixed for these officers are, respectively, those which I have found to prevail in respect of comparable officers of the executive branch of the Government.

The reorganization plan will permit better organization and management of the Federal programs relating to materials and requirements and will thus help to achieve the maximum degree of mobilization readiness at the least possible cost. It is not practicable, however, to itemize, in advance of actual experience, the reductions of expenditures to be brought about by the taking effect of the reorganizations included in Reorganization Plan No. 3 of 1953.

I urge that the Congress allow the proposed reorganization plan to become effective.

DWIGHT D. EISENHOWER.

THE WHITE HOUSE, April 2, 1953.

EXECUTIVE ORDER NO. 9905

Ex. Ord. No. 9905, Nov. 13, 1947, 12 F.R. 7613, as amended by Ex. Ord. No. 9931, Feb. 19, 1948, 13 F.R. 763, provided for membership of National Security Resources Board and defined functions, duties and authority of Chairman of Board.

EXECUTIVE ORDER NO. 10169

Ex. Ord. No. 10169, Oct. 11, 1950, 15 F.R. 6901, which provided for a National Advisory Committee on Mobilization Policy, was revoked by Ex. Ord. No. 10480, Aug. 14, 1953, 18 F.R. 4939, formerly set out under section 2153 of the Appendix to this title.

EXECUTIVE ORDER NO. 10421

Ex. Ord. No. 10421, Dec. 31, 1952, 18 F.R. 57, as amended by Ex. Ord. No. 10438, Mar. 13, 1953, 18 F.R. 1491; Ex. Ord. No. 10773, July 1, 1958, 23 F.R. 5061; Ex. Ord. No. 10782, Sept. 6, 1958, 23 F.R. 6971; Ex. Ord. No. 11051, Sept. 27, 1962, 27 F.R. 9683; Ex. Ord. No. 12148, July 20, 1979, 44 F.R. 43239, which related to physical security of defense facilities, was revoked by Ex. Ord. No. 12656, Nov. 18, 1988, 53 F.R. 47491, set out under section 5195 of Title 42, The Public Health and Welfare.

EXECUTIVE ORDER NO. 10438

Ex. Ord. No. 10438, Mar. 13, 1953, 18 F.R. 1491, which related to transfer of functions to Director of Defense Mobilization, was superseded by Ex. Ord. No. 11051, Sept. 27, 1962, 27 F.R. 9683, formerly set out under section 5195 of Title 42, The Public Health and Welfare.

§ 404a. Annual national security strategy report

(a) Transmittal to Congress

(1) The President shall transmit to Congress each year a comprehensive report on the national security strategy of the United States (hereinafter in this section referred to as a "national security strategy report").

(2) The national security strategy report for any year shall be transmitted on the date on which the President submits to Congress the budget for the next fiscal year under section 1105 of title 31.

(3) Not later than 150 days after the date on which a new President takes office, the President shall transmit to Congress a national security strategy report under this section. That report shall be in addition to the report for that year transmitted at the time specified in paragraph (2).

(b) Contents

Each national security strategy report shall set forth the national security strategy of the United States and shall include a comprehensive description and discussion of the following:

(1) The worldwide interests, goals, and objectives of the United States that are vital to the national security of the United States.

(2) The foreign policy, worldwide commitments, and national defense capabilities of the United States necessary to deter aggression and to implement the national security strategy of the United States.

(3) The proposed short-term and long-term uses of the political, economic, military, and other elements of the national power of the United States to protect or promote the interests and achieve the goals and objectives referred to in paragraph (1).

(4) The adequacy of the capabilities of the United States to carry out the national security strategy of the United States, including an evaluation of the balance among the capabilities of all elements of the national power of the United States to support the implementation of the national security strategy.

(5) Such other information as may be necessary to help inform Congress on matters relating to the national security strategy of the United States.

(c) Classified and unclassified form

Each national security strategy report shall be transmitted in both a classified and an unclassified form.

(July 26, 1947, ch. 343, title I, §108, formerly §104, as added Pub. L. 99–433, title VI, §603(a)(1), Oct. 1, 1986, 100 Stat. 1074; renumbered §108, Pub. L. 102–496, title VII, §705(a)(2), Oct. 24, 1992, 106 Stat. 3190; amended Pub. L. 106–65, div. A, title IX, §901(b), Oct. 5, 1999, 113 Stat. 717.)

AMENDMENTS

1999—Subsec. (a)(3). Pub. L. 106–65 added par. (3).

NATIONAL COMMISSION ON THE FUTURE ROLE OF UNITED STATES NUCLEAR WEAPONS, PROBLEMS OF COMMAND, CONTROL, AND SAFETY OF SOVIET NUCLEAR WEAPONS, AND REDUCTION OF NUCLEAR WEAPONS

Pub. L. 102–172, title VIII, §8132, Nov. 26, 1991, 105 Stat. 1208, provided for establishment of a National Commission which was to submit to Congress, not later than May 1, 1993, a final report containing an assessment and recommendations regarding role of, and requirements for, nuclear weapons in security strategy of United States as result of significant changes in former Warsaw Pact, former Soviet Union, and Third World, including possibilities for international cooperation with former Soviet Union regarding such problems, and safeguards to protect against accidental or unauthorized use of nuclear weapons, further directed Commission to obtain study from National Academy of Sciences on these matters, further authorized establishment of joint working group comprised of experts from governments of United States and former Soviet Union which was to meet on regular basis and provide recommendations regarding these matters, and further provided for composition of Commission as well as powers, procedures, personnel matters, appropriations, and termination of Commission upon submission of its final report.

SECTION REFERRED TO IN OTHER SECTIONS

This section is referred to in title 10 sections 113, 117, 118, 2501.

§ 404b. Multiyear national foreign intelligence program

(a) Annual submission of multiyear national foreign intelligence program

The Director of Central Intelligence shall submit to the congressional committees specified in subsection (d) of this section each year a multiyear national foreign intelligence program plan reflecting the estimated expenditures and proposed appropriations required to support that program. Any such multiyear national foreign intelligence program plan shall cover the fiscal year with respect to which the budget is submitted and at least four succeeding fiscal years.

(b) Time of submission

The Director shall submit the report required by subsection (a) of this section each year at or about the same time that the budget is submitted to Congress pursuant to section 1105(a) of title 31.

(c) Consistency with budget estimates

The Director of Central Intelligence and the Secretary of Defense shall ensure that the estimates referred to in subsection (a) of this section are consistent with the budget estimates submitted to Congress pursuant to section 1105(a) of title 31 for the fiscal year concerned and with the estimated expenditures and proposed appropriations for the multiyear defense program submitted pursuant to section 114a[1] of title 10.

(d) Specified congressional committees

The congressional committees referred to in subsection (a) of this section are the following:

(1) The Committee on Armed Services, the Committee on Appropriations, and the Select Committee on Intelligence of the Senate.

(2) The Committee on Armed Services, the Committee on Appropriations, and the Permanent Select Committee on Intelligence of the House of Representatives.

(Pub. L. 101–510, div. A, title XIV, § 1403, Nov. 5, 1990, 104 Stat. 1675; Pub. L. 104–106, div. A, title XV, § 1502(c)(4)(B), Feb. 10, 1996, 110 Stat. 507; Pub. L. 106–65, div. A, title X, § 1067(10), Oct. 5, 1999, 113 Stat. 774.)

REFERENCES IN TEXT

Section 114a of title 10, referred to in subsec. (c), was renumbered section 221 of title 10 by Pub. L. 102–484, div. A, title X, § 1002(c)(1), Oct. 23, 1992, 106 Stat. 2480.

CODIFICATION

Section was enacted as part of the National Defense Authorization Act for Fiscal Year 1991, and not as part of the National Security Act of 1947 which comprises this chapter.

AMENDMENTS

1999—Subsec. (d)(2). Pub. L. 106–65 substituted "Committee on Armed Services" for "Committee on National Security".

1996—Subsec. (a). Pub. L. 104–106, § 1502(c)(4)(B)(i), substituted "the congressional committees specified in subsection (d) of this section each year" for "the Committees on Armed Services and Appropriations of the Senate and the House of Representatives and the Select Committee on Intelligence of the Senate and the Permanent Select Committee on Intelligence of the House of Representatives each year".

Subsec. (d). Pub. L. 104–106, § 1502(c)(4)(B)(ii), added subsec. (d).

§ 404c. Annual report on United States security arrangements and commitments with other nations

(a) Report requirements

The President shall submit to the congressional committees specified in subsection (d) of this section each year a report (in both classified and unclassified form) on United States security arrangements with, and commitments to, other nations.

(b) Matters to be included

The President shall include in each such report the following:

(1) A description of—

(A) each security arrangement with, or commitment to, other nations, whether based upon (i) a formal document (including a mutual defense treaty, a pre-positioning arrangement or agreement, or an access agreement), or (ii) an expressed policy; and

(B) the historical origins of each such arrangement or commitment.

(2) An evaluation of the ability of the United States to meet its commitments based on the projected reductions in the defense structure of the United States.

(3) A plan for meeting each of those commitments with the force structure projected for the future.

(4) An assessment of the need to continue, modify, or discontinue each of those arrangements and commitments in view of the changing international security situation.

(c) Deadline for report

The President shall submit the report required by subsection (a) of this section not later than February 1 of each year.

(d) Specified congressional committees

The congressional committees referred to in subsection (a) of this section are the following:

(1) The Committee on Armed Services and the Committee on Foreign Relations of the Senate.

(2) The Committee on Armed Services and the Committee on International Relations of the House of Representatives.

(Pub. L. 101–510, div. A, title XIV, § 1457, Nov. 5, 1990, 104 Stat. 1696; Pub. L. 104–106, div. A, title XV, § 1502(c)(4)(C), Feb. 10, 1996, 110 Stat. 507; Pub. L. 106–65, div. A, title X, § 1067(10), Oct. 5, 1999, 113 Stat. 774.)

CODIFICATION

Section was enacted as part of the National Defense Authorization Act for Fiscal Year 1991, and not as part of the National Security Act of 1947 which comprises this chapter.

AMENDMENTS

1999—Subsec. (d)(2). Pub. L. 106–65 substituted "Committee on Armed Services" for "Committee on National Security".

1996—Subsec. (a). Pub. L. 104–106, § 1502(c)(4)(C)(i), substituted "shall submit to the congressional committees specified in subsection (d) of this section each year" for "shall submit to the Committees on Armed Services and on Foreign Affairs of the House of Representatives and the Committees on Armed Services and Foreign Relations of the Senate each year".

Subsec. (c). Pub. L. 104–106, § 1502(c)(4)(C)(ii), substituted "The President" for "(1) Except as provided in paragraph (2), the President" and struck out par. (2) which read as follows: "In the case of the report required to be submitted in 1991, the evaluation, plan, and assessment referred to in paragraphs (2), (3), and (4) of subsection (b) of this section may be submitted not later than May 1, 1991."

[1] See References in Text note below.

Subsec. (d). Pub. L. 104–106, §1502(c)(4)(C)(iii), added subsec. (d).

§404d. Annual report on intelligence

(a) In general

(1) Not later than January 31 each year, the President shall submit to the appropriate congressional committees a report on the requirements of the United States for intelligence and the activities of the intelligence community.

(2) The purpose of the report is to facilitate an assessment of the activities of the intelligence community during the preceding fiscal year and to assist in the development of a mission and a budget for the intelligence community for the fiscal year beginning in the year in which the report is submitted.

(3) The report shall be submitted in unclassified form, but may include a classified annex.

(b) Matters covered

(1) Each report under subsection (a) of this section shall—

(A) specify the intelligence required to meet the national security interests of the United States, and set forth an order of priority for the collection and analysis of intelligence required to meet such interests, for the fiscal year beginning in the year in which the report is submitted; and

(B) evaluate the performance of the intelligence community in collecting and analyzing intelligence required to meet such interests during the fiscal year ending in the year preceding the year in which the report is submitted, including a description of the significant successes and significant failures of the intelligence community in such collection and analysis during that fiscal year.

(2) The report shall specify matters under paragraph (1)(A) in sufficient detail to assist Congress in making decisions with respect to the allocation of resources for the matters specified.

(c)[1] "Appropriate congressional committees" defined

In this section, the term "appropriate congressional committees" means the following:

(1) The Select Committee on Intelligence, the Committee on Appropriations, and the Committee on Armed Services of the Senate.

(2) The Permanent Select Committee on Intelligence, the Committee on Appropriations, and the Committee on Armed Services of the House of Representatives.

(c)[1] Time for submission

The report under this section for any year shall be submitted at the same time that the President submits the budget for the next fiscal year pursuant to section 1105 of title 31.

(July 26, 1947, ch. 343, title I, §109, as added Pub. L. 103–178, title III, §304(a), Dec. 3, 1993, 107 Stat. 2034; amended Pub. L. 104–293, title VIII, §803(a), (b)(1), Oct. 11, 1996, 110 Stat. 3475, 3476; Pub. L. 106–65, div. A, title X, §1067(16), Oct. 5, 1999, 113 Stat. 775.)

[1] So in original. Two subsecs. (c) have been enacted.

AMENDMENTS

1999—Subsec. (c)(2). Pub. L. 106–65 substituted "Committee on Armed Services" for "Committee on National Security".

1996—Pub. L. 104–293, §803(b)(1), substituted "intelligence" for "intelligence community activities" in section catchline.

Subsecs. (a), (b). Pub. L. 104–293, §803(a), added subsecs. (a) and (b) and struck out former subsecs. (a) and (b), which read as follows:

"(a) IN GENERAL.—The Director of Central Intelligence shall submit to Congress an annual report on the activities of the intelligence community. The annual report under this section shall be unclassified.

"(b) MATTERS TO BE COVERED IN ANNUAL REPORT.—Each report under this section shall describe—

"(1) the activities of the intelligence community during the preceding fiscal year, including significant successes and failures that can be described in an unclassified manner; and

"(2) the areas of the world and the issues that the Director expects will require increased or unusual attention from the intelligence community during the next fiscal year."

Subsec. (c). Pub. L. 104–293, §803(a), added subsec. (c) providing definition.

DELEGATION OF AUTHORITY

Memorandum of President of the United States, Aug. 5, 1997, 62 F.R. 51367, provided:

Memorandum for Director of Central Intelligence

By virtue of the authority vested in me by the Constitution and laws of the United States of America, including section 301 of title 3 of the United States Code, I hereby delegate the functions conferred upon the President by section 803(a) of the Intelligence Authorization Act for Fiscal Year 1997, 50 U.S.C. section 404d, to the Director of Central Intelligence.

You are authorized and directed to publish this memorandum in the Federal Register.

WILLIAM J. CLINTON.

SECTION REFERRED TO IN OTHER SECTIONS

This section is referred to in section 403–5 of this title.

§404d–1. Transferred

CODIFICATION

Section 404d–1 of this title, act July 26, 1947, ch. 343, title I, §110, as added Oct. 11, 1996, Pub. L. 104–293, title III, §308(a), 110 Stat. 3466, which related to restrictions on intelligence sharing with United Nations, was renumbered section 112 of act July 26, 1947, by Pub. L. 105–107, title III, §303(b), Nov. 20, 1997, 111 Stat. 2252, and was transferred to section 404g of this title.

§404e. National mission of National Imagery and Mapping Agency

(a) In general

In addition to the Department of Defense missions set forth in section 442 of title 10, the National Imagery and Mapping Agency shall support the imagery requirements of the Department of State and other departments and agencies of the United States outside the Department of Defense.

(b) Requirements and priorities

The Director of Central Intelligence shall establish requirements and priorities governing the collection of national intelligence by the National Imagery and Mapping Agency under subsection (a) of this section.

(c) Correction of deficiencies

The Director of Central Intelligence shall develop and implement such programs and policies as the Director and the Secretary of Defense jointly determine necessary to review and correct deficiencies identified in the capabilities of the National Imagery and Mapping Agency to accomplish assigned national missions, including support to the all-source analysis and production process. The Director shall consult with the Secretary of Defense on the development and implementation of such programs and policies. The Secretary shall obtain the advice of the Chairman of the Joint Chiefs of Staff regarding the matters on which the Director and the Secretary are to consult under the preceding sentence.

(July 26, 1947, ch. 343, title I, § 110, formerly § 120, as added Pub. L. 104–201, div. A, title XI, § 1114(b), Sept. 23, 1996, 110 Stat. 2685; renumbered § 110, Pub. L. 105–107, title III, § 303(b), Nov. 20, 1997, 111 Stat. 2252.)

SECTION REFERRED TO IN OTHER SECTIONS

This section is referred to in title 10 section 442.

§ 404f. Collection tasking authority

Unless otherwise directed by the President, the Director of Central Intelligence shall have authority (except as otherwise agreed by the Director and the Secretary of Defense) to—

(1) approve collection requirements levied on national imagery collection assets;

(2) determine priorities for such requirements; and

(3) resolve conflicts in such priorities.

(July 26, 1947, ch. 343, title I, § 111, formerly § 121, as added Pub. L. 104–201, div. A, title XI, § 1114(c), Sept. 23, 1996, 110 Stat. 2685; renumbered § 111, Pub. L. 105–107, title III, § 303(b), Nov. 20, 1997, 111 Stat. 2252.)

§ 404g. Restrictions on intelligence sharing with United Nations

(a) Provision of intelligence information to United Nations

(1) No United States intelligence information may be provided to the United Nations or any organization affiliated with the United Nations, or to any officials or employees thereof, unless the President certifies to the appropriate committees of Congress that the Director of Central Intelligence, in consultation with the Secretary of State and the Secretary of Defense, has established and implemented procedures, and has worked with the United Nations to ensure implementation of procedures, for protecting from unauthorized disclosure United States intelligence sources and methods connected to such information.

(2) Paragraph (1) may be waived upon written certification by the President to the appropriate committees of Congress that providing such information to the United Nations or an organization affiliated with the United Nations, or to any officials or employees thereof, is in the national security interests of the United States.

(b) Periodic and special reports

(1) The President shall report semiannually to the appropriate committees of Congress on the types and volume of intelligence provided to the United Nations and the purposes for which it was provided during the period covered by the report. The President shall also report to the appropriate committees of Congress within 15 days after it has become known to the United States Government that there has been an unauthorized disclosure of intelligence provided by the United States to the United Nations.

(2) The requirement for periodic reports under the first sentence of paragraph (1) shall not apply to the provision of intelligence that is provided only to, and for the use of, appropriately cleared United States Government personnel serving with the United Nations.

(c) Delegation of duties

The President may not delegate or assign the duties of the President under this section.

(d) Relationship to existing law

Nothing in this section shall be construed to—

(1) impair or otherwise affect the authority of the Director of Central Intelligence to protect intelligence sources and methods from unauthorized disclosure pursuant to section 403–3(c)(6) of this title; or

(2) supersede or otherwise affect the provisions of subchapter III of this chapter.

(e) "Appropriate committees of Congress" defined

As used in this section, the term ''appropriate committees of Congress'' means the Committee on Foreign Relations and the Select Committee on Intelligence of the Senate and the Committee on Foreign Relations and the Permanent Select Committee on Intelligence of the House of Representatives.

(July 26, 1947, ch. 343, title I, § 112, formerly § 110, as added Pub. L. 104–293, title III, § 308(a), Oct. 11, 1996, 110 Stat. 3466; renumbered § 112, Pub. L. 105–107, title III, § 303(b), Nov. 20, 1997, 111 Stat. 2252.)

CODIFICATION

Section was formerly classified to section 404d–1 of this title prior to renumbering by Pub. L. 105–107.

§ 404h. Detail of intelligence community personnel—Intelligence Community Assignment Program

(a) Detail

(1) Notwithstanding any other provision of law, the head of a department with an element in the intelligence community or the head of an intelligence community agency or element may detail any employee within that department, agency, or element to serve in any position in the Intelligence Community Assignment Program on a reimbursable or a nonreimbursable basis.

(2) Nonreimbursable details may be for such periods as are agreed to between the heads of the parent and host agencies, up to a maximum of three years, except that such details may be extended for a period not to exceed one year when the heads of the parent and host agencies determine that such extension is in the public interest.

(b) Benefits, allowances, travel, incentives

An employee detailed under subsection (a) of this section may be authorized any benefit, allowance, travel, or incentive otherwise provided to enhance staffing by the organization from which the employee is detailed.

(c) Annual report

Not later than March 1, 1999, and annually thereafter, the Director of Central Intelligence shall submit to the Permanent Select Committee on Intelligence of the House of Representatives and the Select Committee on Intelligence of the Senate a report describing the detail of intelligence community personnel pursuant to subsection (a) of this section during the 12-month period ending on the date of the report. The report shall set forth the number of personnel detailed, the identity of parent and host agencies or elements, and an analysis of the benefits of the details.

(July 26, 1947, ch. 343, title I, § 113, as added Pub. L. 105–107, title III, § 303(a), Nov. 20, 1997, 111 Stat. 2251.)

EFFECTIVE DATE

Pub. L. 105–107, title III, § 303(d), Nov. 20, 1997, 111 Stat. 2252, provided that: "The amendment made by subsection (a) [enacting this section] shall apply to an employee on detail on or after January 1, 1997."

§ 404i. Additional annual reports from the Director of Central Intelligence

(a) Report on intelligence community cooperation with Federal law enforcement agencies

(1) Not later than December 31 of each year, the Director of Central Intelligence shall submit to the congressional intelligence committees and the congressional leadership a report describing the nature and extent of cooperation and assistance provided by the intelligence community to Federal law enforcement agencies with respect to efforts to stop the illegal importation into the United States of controlled substances (as that term is defined in section 102(6) of the Controlled Substances Act (21 U.S.C. 802(6)) that are included in schedule I or II under part B of such Act [21 U.S.C. 811 et seq.].

(2) Each such report shall include a discussion of the following:

(A) Illegal importation of such controlled substances through transit zones such as the Caribbean Sea and across the Southwest and northern borders of the United States.

(B) Methodologies used for such illegal importation.

(C) Additional routes used for such illegal importation.

(D) Quantities of such controlled substances transported through each route.

(3) Each such report may be prepared in classified form, unclassified form, or unclassified form with a classified annex.

(b) Annual report on the safety and security of Russian nuclear facilities and nuclear military forces

(1) The Director of Central Intelligence shall, on an annual basis, submit to the congressional intelligence committees and the congressional leadership an intelligence report assessing the safety and security of the nuclear facilities and nuclear military forces in Russia.

(2) Each such report shall include a discussion of the following:

(A) The ability of the Government of Russia to maintain its nuclear military forces.

(B) The security arrangements at civilian and military nuclear facilities in Russia.

(C) The reliability of controls and safety systems at civilian nuclear facilities in Russia.

(D) The reliability of command and control systems and procedures of the nuclear military forces in Russia.

(3) Each such report shall be submitted in unclassified form, but may contain a classified annex.

(c) Definitions

In this section:

(1) The term "congressional intelligence committees" means the Permanent Select Committee on Intelligence of the House of Representatives and the Select Committee on Intelligence of the Senate.

(2) The term "congressional leadership" means the Speaker and the minority leader of the House of Representatives and the majority leader and the minority leader of the Senate.

(July 26, 1947, ch. 343, title I, § 114, as added Pub. L. 105–272, title III, § 307(a), Oct. 20, 1998, 112 Stat. 2401.)

REFERENCES IN TEXT

The Controlled Substances Act, referred to in subsec. (a)(1), is title II of Pub. L. 91–513, Oct. 27, 1970, 84 Stat. 1242, as amended. Part B of the Act is classified generally to part B (§ 811 et seq.) of subchapter I of chapter 13 of Title 21, Food and Drugs. Schedules I and II are set out in section 812(c) of Title 21. For complete classification of this Act to the Code, see Short Title note set out under section 801 of Title 21 and Tables.

DATE FOR FIRST REPORT ON COOPERATION WITH CIVILIAN LAW ENFORCEMENT AGENCIES

Pub. L. 105–272, title III, § 307(c), Oct. 20, 1998, 112 Stat. 2402, provided that: "The first report under section 114(a) of the National Security Act of 1947 [50 U.S.C. 404i(a)], as added by subsection (a), shall be submitted not later than December 31, 1999."

§ 404j. Limitation on establishment or operation of diplomatic intelligence support centers

(a) In general

(1) A diplomatic intelligence support center may not be established, operated, or maintained without the prior approval of the Director of Central Intelligence.

(2) The Director may only approve the establishment, operation, or maintenance of a diplomatic intelligence support center if the Director determines that the establishment, operation, or maintenance of such center is required to provide necessary intelligence support in furtherance of the national security interests of the United States.

(b) Prohibition of use of appropriations

Amounts appropriated pursuant to authorizations by law for intelligence and intelligence-related activities may not be obligated or expended for the establishment, operation, or maintenance of a diplomatic intelligence support center that is not approved by the Director of Central Intelligence.

(c) Definitions

In this section:

(1) The term "diplomatic intelligence support center" means an entity to which employees of the various elements of the intelligence community (as defined in section 401a(4) of this title) are detailed for the purpose of providing analytical intelligence support that—

(A) consists of intelligence analyses on military or political matters and expertise to conduct limited assessments and dynamic taskings for a chief of mission; and

(B) is not intelligence support traditionally provided to a chief of mission by the Director of Central Intelligence.

(2) The term "chief of mission" has the meaning given that term by section 3902(3) of title 22, and includes ambassadors at large and ministers of diplomatic missions of the United States, or persons appointed to lead United States offices abroad designated by the Secretary of State as diplomatic in nature.

(d) Termination

This section shall cease to be effective on October 1, 2000.

(July 26, 1947, ch. 343, title I, §115, as added Pub. L. 106–120, title III, §303(a), Dec. 3, 1999, 113 Stat. 1610.)

§404k. Travel on any common carrier for certain intelligence collection personnel

(a) In general

Notwithstanding any other provision of law, the Director of Central Intelligence may authorize travel on any common carrier when such travel, in the discretion of the Director—

(1) is consistent with intelligence community mission requirements, or

(2) is required for cover purposes, operational needs, or other exceptional circumstances necessary for the successful performance of an intelligence community mission.

(b) Authorized delegation of duty

The Director may only delegate the authority granted by this section to the Deputy Director of Central Intelligence, or with respect to employees of the Central Intelligence Agency the Director may delegate such authority to the Deputy Director for Operations.

(July 26, 1947, ch. 343, title I, §116, as added Pub. L. 106–567, title III, §305(a), Dec. 27, 2000, 114 Stat. 2838.)

§404*l*. POW/MIA analytic capability

(a) Requirement

(1) The Director of Central Intelligence shall, in consultation with the Secretary of Defense, establish and maintain in the intelligence community an analytic capability with responsibility for intelligence in support of the activities of the United States relating to individuals who, after December 31, 1990, are unaccounted for United States personnel.

(2) The analytic capability maintained under paragraph (1) shall be known as the "POW/MIA analytic capability of the intelligence community".

(b) Unaccounted for United States personnel

In this section, the term "unaccounted for United States personnel" means the following:

(1) Any missing person (as that term is defined in section 1513(1) of title 10).

(2) Any United States national who was killed while engaged in activities on behalf of the United States and whose remains have not been repatriated to the United States.

(July 26, 1947, ch. 343, title I, §117, as added Pub. L. 106–567, title III, §307(a), Dec. 27, 2000, 114 Stat. 2839.)

SUBCHAPTER II—MISCELLANEOUS AND CONFORMING PROVISIONS

§405. Advisory committees; appointment; compensation of part-time personnel; applicability of other laws

(a) The Director of the Federal Emergency Management Agency, the Director of Central Intelligence, and the National Security Council, acting through its Executive Secretary, are authorized to appoint such advisory committees and to employ, consistent with other provisions of this Act, such part-time advisory personnel as they may deem necessary in carrying out their respective functions and the functions of agencies under their control. Persons holding other offices or positions under the United States for which they receive compensation, while serving as members of such committees, shall receive no additional compensation for such service. Retired members of the uniformed services employed by the Director of Central Intelligence who hold no other office or position under the United States for which they receive compensation, other members of such committees and other part-time advisory personnel so employed may serve without compensation or may receive compensation at a daily rate not to exceed the daily equivalent of the rate of pay in effect for grade GS–18 of the General Schedule established by section 5332 of title 5, as determined by the appointing authority.

(b) Service of an individual as a member of any such advisory committee, or in any other part-time capacity for a department or agency hereunder, shall not be considered as service bringing such individual within the provisions of section 203, 205, or 207 of title 18, unless the act of such individual, which by such section is made unlawful when performed by an individual referred to in such section, is with respect to any particular matter which directly involves a department or agency which such person is advising or in which such department or agency is directly interested.

(July 26, 1947, ch. 343, title III, §303, 61 Stat. 507; Aug. 10, 1949, ch. 412, §10(c), 63 Stat. 585; Sept. 3, 1954, ch. 1263, §8, 68 Stat. 1228; Aug. 10, 1956, ch. 1041, §53(b), 68A Stat. 676, 684; 1958 Reorg. Plan No. 1, §2, eff. July 1, 1958, 23 F.R. 4991, 72 Stat. 1799; Pub. L. 90–608, ch. IV, §402, Oct. 21, 1968, 82 Stat. 1194; Ex. Ord. No. 11725, §3, eff. June 29, 1973, 38 F.R. 17175; Ex. Ord. No. 12148, §§1–103, 4–102, July 20, 1979, 44 F.R. 43239; Pub. L. 97–89, title V, §504, Dec. 4, 1981, 95 Stat. 1153; Pub. L. 100–453, title V, §503, Sept. 29, 1988, 102 Stat. 1910.)

REFERENCES IN TEXT

This Act, referred to in subsec. (a), means act July 26, 1947, ch. 343, 61 Stat. 495, as amended, known as the National Security Act of 1947. For complete classification of this Act to the Code, see Short Title note set out under section 401 of this title and Tables.

AMENDMENTS

1988—Subsec. (a). Pub. L. 100–453 substituted "Retired members of the uniformed services employed by the Director of Central Intelligence who hold no other office or position under the United States for which they receive compensation, other" for "Other" in last sentence.

1981—Subsec. (a). Pub. L. 97–89, §504(a), substituted "at a daily rate not to exceed the daily equivalent of the rate of pay in effect for grade GS–18 of the General Schedule established by section 5332 of title 5" for "at a rate not to exceed $50 for each day of service".

Subsec. (b). Pub. L. 97–89, §504(b), substituted "section 203, 205, or 207 of title 18" for "section 281, 283, or 284 of title 18".

1956—Subsec. (a). Act Aug. 10, 1956, struck out "Secretary of Defense, the" after "The".

1954—Act Sept. 3, 1954, amended section generally, substituting the "Director of the Office of Defense Mobilization" for "Chairman of the National Security Resources Board" in subsec. (a), and substituting "sections 281, 283, or 284 of title 18" for "sections 198 or 203 of title 18 or section 119(e) of title 41".

1949—Subsec. (a). Act Aug. 10, 1949, inserted reference to National Security Council, and increased per diem payable to consultants from $35 to $50.

EFFECTIVE DATE OF 1981 AMENDMENT

Amendment by Pub. L. 97–89 effective Oct. 1, 1981, see section 806 of Pub. L. 97–89, set out as an Effective Date note under section 1621 of Title 10, Armed Forces.

TRANSFER OF FUNCTIONS

"Director of the Federal Emergency Management Agency" substituted in subsec. (a) for "Director of the Office of Defense Mobilization". See note set out under section 404 of this title.

National Security Council transferred to Executive Office of President by Reorg. Plan No. 4 of 1949, eff. Aug. 19, 1949, 14 F.R. 5227, 63 Stat. 1067. See note set out under section 402 of this title.

TERMINATION OF ADVISORY COMMITTEES

Advisory committees in existence on Jan. 5, 1973, to terminate not later than the expiration of the 2-year period following Jan. 5, 1973, unless, in the case of a committee established by the President or an officer of the Federal Government, such committee is renewed by appropriate action prior to the expiration of such 2-year period, or in the case of a committee established by the Congress, its duration is otherwise provided by law. Advisory committees established after Jan. 5, 1973, to terminate not later than the expiration of the 2-year period beginning on the date of their establishment, unless, in the case of a committee established by the President or an officer of the Federal Government, such committee is renewed by appropriate action prior to the expiration of such 2-year period, or in the case of a committee established by the Congress, its duration is otherwise provided by law. See section 14 of Pub. L. 92–463, Oct. 6, 1972, 86 Stat. 776, set out in the Appendix to Title 5, Government Organization and Employees.

REFERENCES IN OTHER LAWS TO GS–16, 17, OR 18 PAY RATES

References in laws to the rates of pay for GS–16, 17, or 18, or to maximum rates of pay under the General Schedule, to be considered references to rates payable under specified sections of Title 5, Government Organization and Employees, see section 529 [title I, §101(c)(1)] of Pub. L. 101–509, set out in a note under section 5376 of Title 5.

SECTION REFERRED TO IN OTHER SECTIONS

This section is referred to in section 403f of this title.

§406. Omitted

CODIFICATION

Section, act June 24, 1948, ch. 632, 62 Stat. 648, which related to authority of former Chairman of National Security Resources Board to appoint advisory committee members and part-time advisory personnel at rates up to $50 per day, has been superseded by section 405(a) of this title.

§407. Study or plan of surrender; use of appropriations

No part of the funds appropriated in any act shall be used to pay (1) any person, firm, or corporation, or any combinations of persons, firms, or corporations, to conduct a study or to plan when and how or in what circumstances the Government of the United States should surrender this country and its people to any foreign power, (2) the salary or compensation of any employee or official of the Government of the United States who proposes or contracts or who has entered into contracts for the making of studies or plans for the surrender by the Government of the United States of this country and its people to any foreign power in any event or under any circumstances.

(Pub. L. 85–766, ch. XVI, §1602, Aug. 27, 1958, 72 Stat. 884.)

CODIFICATION

Section was enacted as part of the Supplemental Appropriation Act, 1959, and not as part of the National Security Act of 1947 which comprises this chapter.

§408. Applicable laws

Except to the extent inconsistent with the provisions of this Act, the provisions of title 4 of the Revised Statutes as now or hereafter amended shall be applicable to the Department of Defense.

(July 26, 1947, ch. 343, title II, §201(d), as added Aug. 10, 1949, ch. 412, §4, 63 Stat. 579.)

REFERENCES IN TEXT

This Act, referred to in text, means act July 26, 1947, ch. 343, 61 Stat. 495, as amended, known as the National Security Act of 1947. For complete classification of this Act to the Code, see Short Title note set out under section 401 of this title and Tables.

Title 4 of the Revised Statutes, referred to in text, was entitled "Provisions Applicable to All Executive Departments", and consisted of R.S. §§158 to 198. For provisions of the Code derived from such title 4, see sections 101, 301, 303, 304, 503, 2952, 3101, 3106, 3341, 3345 to 3349, 5535, and 5536 of Title 5, Government Organization and Employees; section 207 of Title 18, Crimes and Criminal Procedure; sections 514 and 520 of Title 28, Judiciary and Judicial Procedure; section 3321 of Title 31, Money and Finance.

CODIFICATION

Section was formerly classified to section 171–1 of Title 5 prior to the general revision and enactment of Title 5, Government Organization and Employees, by Pub. L. 89–554, §1, Sept. 6, 1966, 80 Stat. 378.

§409. Definitions of military departments

(a) The term "Department of the Army" as used in this Act shall be construed to mean the

Department of the Army at the seat of the government and all field headquarters, forces, reserve components, installations, activities, and functions under the control or supervision of the Department of the Army.

(b) The term "Department of the Navy" as used in this Act shall be construed to mean the Department of the Navy at the seat of the government; the headquarters, United States Marine Corps; the entire operating forces of the United States Navy, including naval aviation, and of the United States Marine Corps, including the reserve components of such forces; all field activities, headquarters, forces, bases, installations, activities, and functions under the control or supervision of the Department of the Navy; and the United States Coast Guard when operating as a part of the Navy pursuant to law.

(c) The term "Department of the Air Force" as used in this Act shall be construed to mean the Department of the Air Force at the seat of the government and all field headquarters, forces, reserve components, installations, activities, and functions under the control or supervision of the Department of the Air Force.

(July 26, 1947, ch. 343, title II, §§205(c), 206(a), 207(c), 61 Stat. 501, 502.)

REFERENCES IN TEXT

This Act, referred to in text, means act July 26, 1947, ch. 343, 61 Stat. 495, as amended, known as the National Security Act of 1947. For complete classification of this Act to the Code, see Short Title note set out under section 401 of this title and Tables.

CODIFICATION

Section was formerly classified to section 171–2 of Title 5 prior to the general revision and enactment of Title 5, Government Organization and Employees, by Pub. L. 89–554, §1, Sept. 6, 1966, 80 Stat. 378.

Prior to the enactment of Title 10, Armed Forces, by act Aug. 10, 1956, subsecs. (a), (b), and (c) of this section were classified to sections 181–1(c), 411a(a), and 626(c), respectively, of former Title 5.

§409a. National Security Agency voluntary separation

(a) Short title

This section may be cited as the "National Security Agency Voluntary Separation Act".

(b) Definitions

For purposes of this section—

(1) the term "Director" means the Director of the National Security Agency; and

(2) the term "employee" means an employee of the National Security Agency, serving under an appointment without time limitation, who has been currently employed by the National Security Agency for a continuous period of at least 12 months prior to the effective date of the program established under subsection (c) of this section, except that such term does not include—

(A) a reemployed annuitant under subchapter III of chapter 83 or chapter 84 of title 5 or another retirement system for employees of the Government; or

(B) an employee having a disability on the basis of which such employee is or would be eligible for disability retirement under any of the retirement systems referred to in subparagraph (A).

(c) Establishment of program

Notwithstanding any other provision of law, the Director, in his sole discretion, may establish a program under which employees may, after October 1, 2000, be eligible for early retirement, offered separation pay to separate from service voluntarily, or both.

(d) Early retirement

An employee who—

(1) is at least 50 years of age and has completed 20 years of service; or

(2) has at least 25 years of service,

may, pursuant to regulations promulgated under this section, apply and be retired from the National Security Agency and receive benefits in accordance with chapter 83 or 84 of title 5 if the employee has not less than 10 years of service with the National Security Agency.

(e) Amount of separation pay and treatment for other purposes

(1) Amount

Separation pay shall be paid in a lump sum and shall be equal to the lesser of—

(A) an amount equal to the amount the employee would be entitled to receive under section 5595(c) of title 5 if the employee were entitled to payment under such section; or

(B) $25,000.

(2) Treatment

Separation pay shall not—

(A) be a basis for payment, and shall not be included in the computation, of any other type of Government benefit; and

(B) be taken into account for the purpose of determining the amount of any severance pay to which an individual may be entitled under section 5595 of title 5 based on any other separation.

(f) Reemployment restrictions

An employee who receives separation pay under such program may not be reemployed by the National Security Agency for the 12-month period beginning on the effective date of the employee's separation. An employee who receives separation pay under this section on the basis of a separation occurring on or after March 30, 1994, and accepts employment with the Government of the United States within 5 years after the date of the separation on which payment of the separation pay is based shall be required to repay the entire amount of the separation pay to the National Security Agency. If the employment is with an Executive agency (as defined by section 105 of title 5), the Director of the Office of Personnel Management may, at the request of the head of the agency, waive the repayment if the individual involved possesses unique abilities and is the only qualified applicant available for the position. If the employment is with an entity in the legislative branch, the head of the entity or the appointing official may waive the repayment if the individual involved possesses unique abilities and is the only qualified applicant available for the position. If the employment is with the judicial branch, the Director of the Administrative Office of the United States Courts may waive the repayment if the individual involved possesses unique abilities and is the only qualified applicant available for the position.

(g) Bar on certain employment

(1) Bar

An employee may not be separated from service under this section unless the employee agrees that the employee will not—

(A) act as agent or attorney for, or otherwise represent, any other person (except the United States) in any formal or informal appearance before, or, with the intent to influence, make any oral or written communication on behalf of any other person (except the United States) to the National Security Agency; or

(B) participate in any manner in the award, modification, or extension of any contract for property or services with the National Security Agency,

during the 12-month period beginning on the effective date of the employee's separation from service.

(2) Penalty

An employee who violates an agreement under this subsection shall be liable to the United States in the amount of the separation pay paid to the employee pursuant to this section multiplied by the proportion of the 12-month period during which the employee was in violation of the agreement.

(h) Limitations

Under this program, early retirement and separation pay may be offered only—

(1) with the prior approval of the Director;

(2) for the period specified by the Director; and

(3) to employees within such occupational groups or geographic locations, or subject to such other similar limitations or conditions, as the Director may require.

(i) Regulations

Before an employee may be eligible for early retirement, separation pay, or both, under this section, the Director shall prescribe such regulations as may be necessary to carry out this section.

(j) Reporting requirements

(1) Notification

The Director may not make an offer of early retirement, separation pay, or both, pursuant to this section until 15 days after submitting to the Permanent Select Committee on Intelligence of the House of Representatives and the Select Committee on Intelligence of the Senate a report describing the occupational groups or geographic locations, or other similar limitations or conditions, required by the Director under subsection (h) of this section, and includes[1] the proposed regulations issued pursuant to subsection (i) of this section.

(2) Annual report

The Director shall submit to the President and the Permanent Select Committee on Intelligence of the House of Representatives and the Select Committee on Intelligence of the Senate an annual report on the effectiveness and costs of carrying out this section.

(k) Remittance of funds

In addition to any other payment that is required to be made under subchapter III of chapter 83 or chapter 84 of title 5, the National Security Agency shall remit to the Office of Personnel Management for deposit in the Treasury of the United States to the credit of the Civil Service Retirement and Disability Fund, an amount equal to 15 percent of the final basic pay of each employee to whom a voluntary separation payment has been or is to be paid under this section. The remittance required by this subsection shall be in lieu of any remittance required by section 4(a) of the Federal Workforce Restructuring Act of 1994 (5 U.S.C. 8331 note).

(July 26, 1947, ch. 343, title III, §301, as added Pub. L. 106–567, title III, §304(a), Dec. 27, 2000, 114 Stat. 2836.)

REFERENCES IN TEXT

Section 4(a) of the Federal Workforce Restructuring Act of 1994, referred to in subsec. (k), is section 4(a) of Pub. L. 103–226, which is set out as a note under section 8331 of Title 5, Government Organization and Employees.

PRIOR PROVISIONS

A prior section 301 of act July 26, 1947, ch. 343, 61 Stat. 507, was classified to sections 171b and 171c–1 of former Title 5, Executive Departments and Government Officers and Employees, prior to repeal by Pub. L. 89–554, §8(a), Sept. 6, 1966, 80 Stat. 632.

§410. "Function" and "Department of Defense" defined

(a) As used in this Act, the term "function" includes functions, powers, and duties.

(b) As used in this Act, the term "Department of Defense" shall be deemed to include the military departments of the Army, the Navy, and the Air Force, and all agencies created under title II of this Act.

(July 26, 1947, ch. 343, title III, §308, 61 Stat. 509; Aug. 10, 1949, ch. 412, §12(e), 63 Stat. 591.)

PARTIAL REPEAL

Section 307 of Pub. L. 87–651, title III, Sept. 7, 1962, 76 Stat. 526, repealed subsection (a) of this section less its applicability to sections 401, 402, 403, 404, and 405 of this title.

REFERENCES IN TEXT

This Act, referred to in text, means act July 26, 1947, ch. 343, 61 Stat. 495, as amended, known as the National Security Act of 1947. For complete classification of this Act to the Code, see Short Title note set out under section 401 of this title and Tables.

Title II of this Act, referred to in subsec. (b), means title II of the National Security Act of 1947, act July 26, 1947, ch. 343, 61 Stat. 499, as amended, which enacted sections 408 and 409 of this title and sections 171, 171–1, 171–2, 171a, 171c, 171d, and 171e to 171i of former Title 5, Executive Department and Government Officers and Employees, amended sections 1 and 11 of former Title 5 and section 1517 of Title 15, Commerce and Trade, and enacted a provision formerly set out as a note under section 135 [now 137] of Title 10, Armed Forces. Section 171 of former Title 5 was repealed by Pub. L. 87–651,

[1] So in original. Probably should be "including".

title III, § 307, Sept. 7, 1962, and reenacted in part as section 131 of Title 10. Sections 171e, 171f, and 171g of former Title 5 were repealed by act Aug. 10, 1956, ch. 1041, § 53, 70A Stat. 641, and reenacted as sections 171, 141, 142, and 143 of Title 10, respectively. Sections 171–1 and 171–2 of former Title 5 were transferred to sections 408 and 409 of this title, respectively. For complete classification of title II to the Code, see Tables.

CODIFICATION

Section was formerly classified to section 171n of Title 5 prior to the general revision and enactment of Title 5, Government Organization and Employees, by Pub. L. 89–554, § 1, Sept. 6, 1966, 80 Stat. 378.

AMENDMENTS

1949—Subsec. (b). Act Aug. 10, 1949, substituted definition of "Department of Defense" for definition of "budget program".

§ 411. Authorization of appropriations

There are authorized to be appropriated such sums as may be necessary and appropriate to carry out the provisions and purposes of this Act (other than the provisions and purposes of sections 102, 103, 104, 105 [50 U.S.C. 403, 403–3, 403–4, 403–5] and titles V, VI, and VII [50 U.S.C. 413 et seq., 421 et seq., 431 et seq.]).

(July 26, 1947, ch. 343, title III, § 307, 61 Stat. 509; Pub. L. 103–178, title III, § 309, Dec. 3, 1993, 107 Stat. 2036.)

REFERENCES IN TEXT

This Act, referred to in text, means act July 26, 1947, ch. 343, 61 Stat. 495, as amended, known as the National Security Act of 1947. Titles V, VI, and VII of the Act are classified generally to subchapters III (§ 413 et seq.), IV (§ 421 et seq.), and V (§ 431 et seq.) of this chapter, respectively. For complete classification of this Act to the Code, see Short Title note set out under section 401 of this title and Tables.

CODIFICATION

Section was formerly classified to section 171m of Title 5 prior to the general revision and enactment of Title 5, Government Organization and Employees, by Pub. L. 89–554, § 1, Sept. 6, 1966, 80 Stat. 378.

AMENDMENTS

1993—Pub. L. 103–178 substituted "provisions and purposes of this Act (other than the provisions and purposes of sections 102, 103, 104, 105 and titles V, VI, and VII)" for "provisions and purposes of this Act".

§ 412. Repealing and savings provisions

All laws, orders, and regulations inconsistent with the provisions of this title are repealed insofar as they are inconsistent with the powers, duties, and responsibilities enacted hereby: *Provided*, That the powers, duties, and responsibilities of the Secretary of Defense under this title shall be administered in conformance with the policy and requirements for administration of budgetary and fiscal matters in the Government generally, including accounting and financial reporting, and that nothing in this title shall be construed as eliminating or modifying the powers, duties, and responsibilities of any other department, agency, or officer of the Government in connection with such matters, but no such department, agency, or officer shall exercise any such powers, duties, or responsibilities in a manner that will render ineffective the provisions of this title.

(July 26, 1947, ch. 343, title IV, § 411, as added Aug. 10, 1949, ch. 412, § 11, 63 Stat. 585.)

REFERENCES IN TEXT

This title, referred to in text, means title IV of act July 26, 1947, ch. 343, as added Aug. 10, 1949, ch. 412, § 11, 63 Stat. 585, which enacted section 412 of this title and sections 172, 172a to 172d, and 172f to 172j of former Title 5, Executive Departments and Government Officers and Employees, and amended section 172e of former Title 5 and section 72 of former Title 31, Money and Finance. Section 172 of former Title 5 was repealed by Pub. L. 87–651, title III, § 307, Sept. 7, 1962, 76 Stat. 526, and reenacted as section 136 [now 138] of Title 10, Armed Forces. Section 172a of former Title 5 was repealed by act Aug. 10, 1956, ch. 1041, § 53, 70A Stat. 641, and reenacted as sections 3014, 5061, and 8014 of Title 10. Sections 172b to 172d and 172f to 172h of former Title 5 were repealed by Pub. L. 87–651, title III, § 307, Sept. 7, 1962, 76 Stat. 526, and reenacted as sections 2203, 2204, 2208, 2207, 126, and 2206 of Title 10, respectively. Section 172i of former Title 5 was repealed by act Aug. 10, 1956, ch. 1041, § 53, 70A Stat. 641, and reenacted as section 2701 of Title 10. Section 172j, of former Title 5 was transferred to section 412 of this title. For complete classification of title IV to the Code, see Tables.

CODIFICATION

Section was formerly classified to section 172j of Title 5 prior to the general revision and enactment of Title 5, Government Organization and Employees, by Pub. L. 89–554, § 1, Sept. 6, 1966, 80 Stat. 378.

SUBCHAPTER III—ACCOUNTABILITY FOR INTELLIGENCE ACTIVITIES

SUBCHAPTER REFERRED TO IN OTHER SECTIONS

This subchapter is referred to in sections 403q, 404g, 411, 1526 of this title; title 10 sections 167, 421, 437, 2557; title 22 sections 287b, 2415, 2776, 2780, 2799aa–1.

§ 413. General Congressional oversight provisions

(a) Reports to Congressional committees of intelligence activities and anticipated activities

(1) The President shall ensure that the intelligence committees are kept fully and currently informed of the intelligence activities of the United States, including any significant anticipated intelligence activity as required by this subchapter.

(2) As used in this subchapter, the term "intelligence committees" means the Select Committee on Intelligence of the Senate and the Permanent Select Committee on Intelligence of the House of Representatives.

(3) Nothing in this subchapter shall be construed as requiring the approval of the intelligence committees as a condition precedent to the initiation of any significant anticipated intelligence activity.

(b) Reports concerning illegal intelligence activities

The President shall ensure that any illegal intelligence activity is reported promptly to the intelligence committees, as well as any corrective action that has been taken or is planned in connection with such illegal activity.

(c) Procedures for reporting information

The President and the intelligence committees shall each establish such procedures as may be necessary to carry out the provisions of this subchapter.

(d) Procedures to protect from unauthorized disclosure

The House of Representatives and the Senate shall each establish, by rule or resolution of such House, procedures to protect from unauthorized disclosure all classified information, and all information relating to intelligence sources and methods, that is furnished to the intelligence committees or to Members of Congress under this subchapter. Such procedures shall be established in consultation with the Director of Central Intelligence. In accordance with such procedures, each of the intelligence committees shall promptly call to the attention of its respective House, or to any appropriate committee or committees of its respective House, any matter relating to intelligence activities requiring the attention of such House or such committee or committees.

(e) Construction of authority conferred

Nothing in this Act shall be construed as authority to withhold information from the intelligence committees on the grounds that providing the information to the intelligence committees would constitute the unauthorized disclosure of classified information or information relating to intelligence sources and methods.

(f) "Intelligence activities" defined

As used in this section, the term ''intelligence activities'' includes covert actions as defined in section 413b(e) of this title.

(July 26, 1947, ch. 343, title V, §501, as added Pub. L. 102–88, title VI, §602(a)(2), Aug. 14, 1991, 105 Stat. 441.)

REFERENCES IN TEXT

This Act, referred to in subsec. (e), means act July 26, 1947, ch. 343, 61 Stat. 495, as amended, known as the National Security Act of 1947. For complete classification of this Act to the Code, see Short Title note set out under section 401 of this title and Tables.

PRIOR PROVISIONS

A prior section 413, act July 26, 1947, ch. 343, title V, §501, as added Oct. 14, 1980, Pub. L. 96–450, title IV, §407(b)(1), 94 Stat. 1981, related to Congressional oversight of intelligence activities, prior to repeal by Pub. L. 102–88, §602(a)(2).

SECTION REFERRED TO IN OTHER SECTIONS

This section is referred to in title 10 section 2723; title 42 section 7383d.

§413a. Reporting of intelligence activities other than covert actions

To the extent consistent with due regard for the protection from unauthorized disclosure of classified information relating to sensitive intelligence sources and methods or other exceptionally sensitive matters, the Director of Central Intelligence and the heads of all departments, agencies, and other entities of the United States Government involved in intelligence activities shall—

(1) keep the intelligence committees fully and currently informed of all intelligence activities, other than a covert action (as defined in section 413b(e) of this title), which are the responsibility of, are engaged in by, or are carried out for or on behalf of, any department, agency, or entity of the United States Government, including any significant anticipated intelligence activity and any significant intelligence failure; and

(2) furnish the intelligence committees any information or material concerning intelligence activities, other than covert actions, which is within their custody or control, and which is requested by either of the intelligence committees in order to carry out its authorized responsibilities.

(July 26, 1947, ch. 343, title V, §502, as added Pub. L. 102–88, title VI, §602(a)(2), Aug. 14, 1991, 105 Stat. 442.)

PRIOR PROVISIONS

A prior section 502 of act July 26, 1947, ch. 343, was renumbered section 504 and is classified to section 414 of this title.

FURNISHING OF INTELLIGENCE INFORMATION TO SENATE AND HOUSE SELECT COMMITTEES ON INTELLIGENCE

Section 405 of Pub. L. 102–88 provided that:

''(a) FURNISHING OF SPECIFIC INFORMATION.—In accordance with title V of the National Security Act of 1947 [50 U.S.C. 413 et seq.], the head of any department or agency of the United States involved in any intelligence activities which may pertain to United States military personnel listed as prisoner, missing, or unaccounted for in military actions shall furnish any information or documents in the possession, custody, or control of the department or agency, or person paid by such department or agency, whenever requested by the Permanent Select Committee on Intelligence of the House of Representatives or the Select Committee on Intelligence of the Senate.

''(b) ACCESS BY COMMITTEES AND MEMBERS OF CONGRESS.—In accordance with Senate Resolution 400, Ninety-Fourth Congress, and House Resolution 658, Ninety-Fifth Congress, the committees named in subsection (a) shall, upon request and under such regulations as the committees have prescribed to protect the classification of such information, make any information described in subsection (a) available to any other committee or any other Member of Congress and appropriately cleared staff.''

SECTION REFERRED TO IN OTHER SECTIONS

This section is referred to in title 22 section 7304.

§413b. Presidential approval and reporting of covert actions

(a) Presidential findings

The President may not authorize the conduct of a covert action by departments, agencies, or entities of the United States Government unless the President determines such an action is necessary to support identifiable foreign policy objectives of the United States and is important to the national security of the United States, which determination shall be set forth in a finding that shall meet each of the following conditions:

(1) Each finding shall be in writing, unless immediate action by the United States is required and time does not permit the preparation of a written finding, in which case a written record of the President's decision shall be contemporaneously made and shall be reduced to a written finding as soon as possible but in no event more than 48 hours after the decision is made.

(2) Except as permitted by paragraph (1), a finding may not authorize or sanction a covert

action, or any aspect of any such action, which already has occurred.

(3) Each finding shall specify each department, agency, or entity of the United States Government authorized to fund or otherwise participate in any significant way in such action. Any employee, contractor, or contract agent of a department, agency, or entity of the United States Government other than the Central Intelligence Agency directed to participate in any way in a covert action shall be subject either to the policies and regulations of the Central Intelligence Agency, or to written policies or regulations adopted by such department, agency, or entity, to govern such participation.

(4) Each finding shall specify whether it is contemplated that any third party which is not an element of, or a contractor or contract agent of, the United States Government, or is not otherwise subject to United States Government policies and regulations, will be used to fund or otherwise participate in any significant way in the covert action concerned, or be used to undertake the covert action concerned on behalf of the United States.

(5) A finding may not authorize any action that would violate the Constitution or any statute of the United States.

(b) Reports to intelligence committees; production of information

To the extent consistent with due regard for the protection from unauthorized disclosure of classified information relating to sensitive intelligence sources and methods or other exceptionally sensitive matters, the Director of Central Intelligence and the heads of all departments, agencies, and entities of the United States Government involved in a covert action—

(1) shall keep the intelligence committees fully and currently informed of all covert actions which are the responsibility of, are engaged in by, or are carried out for or on behalf of, any department, agency, or entity of the United States Government, including significant failures; and

(2) shall furnish to the intelligence committees any information or material concerning covert actions which is in the possession, custody, or control of any department, agency, or entity of the United States Government and which is requested by either of the intelligence committees in order to carry out its authorized responsibilities.

(c) Timing of reports; access to finding

(1) The President shall ensure that any finding approved pursuant to subsection (a) of this section shall be reported to the intelligence committees as soon as possible after such approval and before the initiation of the covert action authorized by the finding, except as otherwise provided in paragraph (2) and paragraph (3).

(2) If the President determines that it is essential to limit access to the finding to meet extraordinary circumstances affecting vital interests of the United States, the finding may be reported to the chairmen and ranking minority members of the intelligence committees, the Speaker and minority leader of the House of Representatives, the majority and minority leaders of the Senate, and such other member or members of the congressional leadership as may be included by the President.

(3) Whenever a finding is not reported pursuant to paragraph (1) or (2) of this section,[1] the President shall fully inform the intelligence committees in a timely fashion and shall provide a statement of the reasons for not giving prior notice.

(4) In a case under paragraph (1), (2), or (3), a copy of the finding, signed by the President, shall be provided to the chairman of each intelligence committee. When access to a finding is limited to the Members of Congress specified in paragraph (2), a statement of the reasons for limiting such access shall also be provided.

(d) Changes in previously approved actions

The President shall ensure that the intelligence committees, or, if applicable, the Members of Congress specified in subsection (c)(2) of this section, are notified of any significant change in a previously approved covert action, or any significant undertaking pursuant to a previously approved finding, in the same manner as findings are reported pursuant to subsection (c) of this section.

(e) "Covert action" defined

As used in this subchapter, the term "covert action" means an activity or activities of the United States Government to influence political, economic, or military conditions abroad, where it is intended that the role of the United States Government will not be apparent or acknowledged publicly, but does not include—

(1) activities the primary purpose of which is to acquire intelligence, traditional counterintelligence activities, traditional activities to improve or maintain the operational security of United States Government programs, or administrative activities;

(2) traditional diplomatic or military activities or routine support to such activities;

(3) traditional law enforcement activities conducted by United States Government law enforcement agencies or routine support to such activities; or

(4) activities to provide routine support to the overt activities (other than activities described in paragraph (1), (2), or (3)) of other United States Government agencies abroad.

(f) Prohibition on covert actions intended to influence United States political processes, etc.

No covert action may be conducted which is intended to influence United States political processes, public opinion, policies, or media.

(July 26, 1947, ch. 343, title V, §503, as added Pub. L. 102–88, title VI, §602(a)(2), Aug. 14, 1991, 105 Stat. 442.)

PRIOR PROVISIONS

A prior section 503 of act July 26, 1947, ch. 343, was renumbered section 505 and is classified to section 415 of this title.

SECTION REFERRED TO IN OTHER SECTIONS

This section is referred to in sections 413, 413a, 414 of this title.

[1] So in original. Probably should be "subsection,".

§414. Funding of intelligence activities

(a) Obligations and expenditures for intelligence or intelligence-related activity; prerequisites

Appropriated funds available to an intelligence agency may be obligated or expended for an intelligence or intelligence-related activity only if—

(1) those funds were specifically authorized by the Congress for use for such activities; or

(2) in the case of funds from the Reserve for Contingencies of the Central Intelligence Agency and consistent with the provisions of section 413b of this title concerning any significant anticipated intelligence activity, the Director of Central Intelligence has notified the appropriate congressional committees of the intent to make such funds available for such activity; or

(3) in the case of funds specifically authorized by the Congress for a different activity—

(A) the activity to be funded is a higher priority intelligence or intelligence-related activity;

(B) the need for funds for such activity is based on unforseen[1] requirements; and

(C) the Director of Central Intelligence, the Secretary of Defense, or the Attorney General, as appropriate, has notified the appropriate congressional committees of the intent to make such funds available for such activity;

(4) nothing in this subsection prohibits obligation or expenditure of funds available to an intelligence agency in accordance with sections 1535 and 1536 of title 31.

(b) Activities denied funding by Congress

Funds available to an intelligence agency may not be made available for any intelligence or intelligence-related activity for which funds were denied by the Congress.

(c) Presidential finding required for expenditure of funds on covert action

No funds appropriated for, or otherwise available to, any department, agency, or entity of the United States Government may be expended, or may be directed to be expended, for any covert action, as defined in section 413b(e) of this title, unless and until a Presidential finding required by subsection (a) of section 413b of this title has been signed or otherwise issued in accordance with that subsection.

(d) Report to Congressional committees required for expenditure of nonappropriated funds for intelligence activity

(1) Except as otherwise specifically provided by law, funds available to an intelligence agency that are not appropriated funds may be obligated or expended for an intelligence or intelligence-related activity only if those funds are used for activities reported to the appropriate congressional committees pursuant to procedures which identify—

(A) the types of activities for which nonappropriated funds may be expended; and

(B) the circumstances under which an activity must be reported as a significant anticipated intelligence activity before such funds can be expended.

(2) Procedures for purposes of paragraph (1) shall be jointly agreed upon by the intelligence committees and, as appropriate, the Director of Central Intelligence or the Secretary of Defense.

(e) Definitions

As used in this section—

(1) the term "intelligence agency" means any department, agency, or other entity of the United States involved in intelligence or intelligence-related activities;

(2) the term "appropriate congressional committees" means the Permanent Select Committee on Intelligence and the Committee on Appropriations of the House of Representatives and the Select Committee on Intelligence and the Committee on Appropriations of the Senate; and

(3) the term "specifically authorized by the Congress" means that—

(A) the activity and the amount of funds proposed to be used for that activity were identified in a formal budget request to the Congress, but funds shall be deemed to be specifically authorized for that activity only to the extent that the Congress both authorized the funds to be appropriated for that activity and appropriated the funds for that activity; or

(B) although the funds were not formally requested, the Congress both specifically authorized the appropriation of the funds for the activity and appropriated the funds for the activity.

(July 26, 1947, ch. 343, title V, §504, formerly §502, as added Pub. L. 99–169, title IV, §401(a), Dec. 4, 1985, 99 Stat. 1004; renumbered §504 and amended Pub. L. 102–88, title VI, §§602(a)(1), (c)(1), 603, Aug. 14, 1991, 105 Stat. 441, 444.)

Amendments

1991—Subsec. (a)(2). Pub. L. 102–88, §602(c)(1), substituted "section 413b" for "section 413".

Subsecs. (c) to (e). Pub. L. 102–88, §603, added subsecs. (c) and (d) and redesignated former subsec. (c) as (e).

Limitation on Transfer of Funds Between CIA and Department of Defense; Congressional Notification Required

Pub. L. 103–139, title VIII, §8107, Nov. 11, 1993, 107 Stat. 1464, provided that: "During the current fiscal year and thereafter, no funds may be made available through transfer, reprogramming, or other means between the Central Intelligence Agency and the Department of Defense for any intelligence or special activity different from that previously justified to the Congress unless the Director of Central Intelligence or the Secretary of Defense has notified the House and Senate Appropriations Committees of the intent to make such funds available for such activity." Similar provisions were contained in the following prior appropriation acts:

Pub. L. 102–396, title IX, §9014, Oct. 6, 1992, 106 Stat. 1903.

Pub. L. 102–172, title VIII, §8014, Nov. 26, 1991, 105 Stat. 1174.

Pub. L. 101–511, title VIII, §8015, Nov. 5, 1990, 104 Stat. 1878.

Pub. L. 101–165, title IX, §9022, Nov. 21, 1989, 103 Stat. 1134.

Pub. L. 100–463, title VIII, §8035, Oct. 1, 1988, 102 Stat. 2270–23.

[1] So in original. Probably should be "unforeseen".

Pub. L. 100–202, §101(b) [title VIII, §8037], Dec. 22, 1987, 101 Stat. 1329–43, 1329–68.

SENSE OF CONGRESS REGARDING DISCLOSURE OF ANNUAL INTELLIGENCE BUDGET

Pub. L. 102–496, title III, §303, Oct. 24, 1992, 106 Stat. 3183, provided that: "It is the sense of Congress that, beginning in 1993, and in each year thereafter, the aggregate amount requested and authorized for, and spent on, intelligence and intelligence-related activities should be disclosed to the public in an appropriate manner." Similar provisions were contained in the following prior appropriation act: Pub. L. 102–183, title VII, §701, Dec. 4, 1991, 105 Stat. 1270.

LIMITATION OF EXPENDITURE OF FUNDS APPROPRIATED FOR DEPARTMENT OF DEFENSE INTELLIGENCE PROGRAMS

Pub. L. 102–172, title VIII, §8089, Nov. 26, 1991, 105 Stat. 1193, provided that: "During the current fiscal year and hereafter, none of the funds appropriated for intelligence programs to the Department of Defense which are transferred to another Federal agency for execution shall be expended by the Department of Defense in any fiscal year in excess of amounts required for expenditure during such fiscal year by the Federal agency to which such funds are transferred."

ENHANCED SECURITY COUNTERMEASURES CAPABILITIES; APPLICATION OF SECTION

Section 401(c) of Pub. L. 99–169 provided that: "The amendment made by section 401(a) of this Act [enacting this section] shall not apply with respect to funds appropriated to the Director of Central Intelligence under the heading 'ENHANCED SECURITY COUNTERMEASURES CAPABILITIES' in the Supplemental Appropriations Act, 1985 (Public Law 99–88) [Aug. 15, 1985, 99 Stat. 311]."

SECTION REFERRED TO IN OTHER SECTIONS

This section is referred to in title 21 section 1703.

§415. Notice to Congress of certain transfers of defense articles and defense services

(a)(1) The transfer of a defense article or defense service, or the anticipated transfer in any fiscal year of any aggregation of defense articles or defense services, exceeding $1,000,000 in value by an intelligence agency to a recipient outside that agency shall be considered a significant anticipated intelligence activity for the purpose of this subchapter.

(2) Paragraph (1) does not apply if—

(A) the transfer is being made to a department, agency, or other entity of the United States (so long as there will not be a subsequent retransfer of the defense articles or defense services outside the United States Government in conjunction with an intelligence or intelligence-related activity); or

(B) the transfer—

(i) is being made pursuant to authorities contained in part II of the Foreign Assistance Act of 1961 [22 U.S.C. 2301 et seq.], the Arms Export Control Act [22 U.S.C. 2751 et seq.], title 10 (including a law enacted pursuant to section 7307(a) of that title), or the Federal Property and Administrative Services Act of 1949 [40 U.S.C. 471 et seq.], and

(ii) is not being made in conjunction with an intelligence or intelligence-related activity.

(3) An intelligence agency may not transfer any defense articles or defense services outside the agency in conjunction with any intelligence or intelligence-related activity for which funds were denied by the Congress.

(b) As used in this section—

(1) the term "intelligence agency" means any department, agency, or other entity of the United States involved in intelligence or intelligence-related activities;

(2) the terms "defense articles" and "defense services" mean the items on the United States Munitions List pursuant to section 38 of the Arms Export Control Act [22 U.S.C. 2778] (22 CFR part 121);

(3) the term "transfer" means—

(A) in the case of defense articles, the transfer of possession of those articles; and

(B) in the case of defense services, the provision of those services; and

(4) the term "value" means—

(A) in the case of defense articles, the greater of—

(i) the original acquisition cost to the United States Government, plus the cost of improvements or other modifications made by or on behalf of the Government; or

(ii) the replacement cost; and

(B) in the case of defense services, the full cost to the Government of providing the services.

(July 26, 1947, ch. 343, title V, §505, formerly §503, as added Pub. L. 99–569, title VI, §602(a), Oct. 27, 1986, 100 Stat. 3203; renumbered §505 and amended Pub. L. 102–88, title VI, §§602(a)(1), (c)(2), 604, Aug. 14, 1991, 105 Stat. 441, 444, 445; Pub. L. 103–160, div. A, title VIII, §828(d)(1), Nov. 30, 1993, 107 Stat. 1715.)

REFERENCES IN TEXT

The Foreign Assistance Act of 1961, referred to in subsec. (a)(2)(B)(i), is Pub. L. 87–195, Sept. 4, 1961, 75 Stat. 424, as amended. Part II of the Act is classified generally to subchapter II (§2301 et seq.) of chapter 32 of Title 22, Foreign Relations and Intercourse. For provisions deeming references to subchapter II to exclude parts IV (§2346 et seq.), VI (§2348 et seq.), and VIII (§2349aa et seq.) of subchapter II, see section 202(b) of Pub. L. 92–228, set out as a note under section 2346 of Title 22, and sections 2348c and 2349aa–5 of Title 22. For complete classification of this Act to the Code, see Short Title note set out under section 2151 of Title 22 and Tables.

The Arms Export Control Act, referred to in subsec. (a)(2)(B)(i), is Pub. L. 90–269, Oct. 22, 1968, 82 Stat. 1320, as amended, which is classified principally to chapter 39 (§2751 et seq.) of Title 22. For complete classification of this Act to the Code, see Short Title note set out under section 2751 of Title 22 and Tables.

The Federal Property and Administrative Services Act of 1949, referred to in subsec. (a)(2)(B)(i), is act June 30, 1949, ch. 288, 63 Stat. 377, as amended. Provisions of that Act relating to management and disposal of government property are classified to chapter 10 (§471 et seq.) of Title 40, Public Buildings, Property, and Works. For complete classification of this Act to the Code, see Short Title note set out under section 471 of Title 40 and Tables.

AMENDMENTS

1993—Subsec. (a)(2)(B)(i). Pub. L. 103–160 substituted "section 7307(a)" for "section 7307(b)(1)".

1991—Subsec. (a)(1). Pub. L. 102–88 inserted ", or the anticipated transfer in any fiscal year of any aggregation of defense articles or defense services," after "service" and substituted "this subchapter" for "section 413 of this title".

SECTION REFERRED TO IN OTHER SECTIONS

This section is referred to in title 22 section 7304.

SUBCHAPTER IV—PROTECTION OF CERTAIN NATIONAL SECURITY INFORMATION

SUBCHAPTER REFERRED TO IN OTHER SECTIONS

This subchapter is referred to in section 411 of this title.

§421. Protection of identities of certain United States undercover intelligence officers, agents, informants, and sources

(a) Disclosure of information by persons having or having had access to classified information that identifies covert agent

Whoever, having or having had authorized access to classified information that identifies a covert agent, intentionally discloses any information identifying such covert agent to any individual not authorized to receive classified information, knowing that the information disclosed so identifies such covert agent and that the United States is taking affirmative measures to conceal such covert agent's intelligence relationship to the United States, shall be fined under title 18 or imprisoned not more than ten years, or both.

(b) Disclosure of information by persons who learn identity of covert agents as result of having access to classified information

Whoever, as a result of having authorized access to classified information, learns the identify of a covert agent and intentionally discloses any information identifying such covert agent to any individual not authorized to receive classified information, knowing that the information disclosed so identifies such covert agent and that the United States is taking affirmative measures to conceal such covert agent's intelligence relationship to the United States, shall be fined under title 18 or imprisoned not more than five years, or both.

(c) Disclosure of information by persons in course of pattern of activities intended to identify and expose covert agents

Whoever, in the course of a pattern of activities intended to identify and expose covert agents and with reason to believe that such activities would impair or impede the foreign intelligence activities of the United States, discloses any information that identifies an individual as a covert agent to any individual not authorized to receive classified information, knowing that the information disclosed so identifies such individual and that the United States is taking affirmative measures to conceal such individual's classified intelligence relationship to the United States, shall be fined under title 18 or imprisoned not more than three years, or both.

(d) Imposition of consecutive sentences

A term of imprisonment imposed under this section shall be consecutive to any other sentence of imprisonment.

(July 26, 1947, ch. 343, title VI, §601, as added Pub. L. 97–200, §2(a), June 23, 1982, 96 Stat. 122; amended Pub. L. 106–120, title III, §304(b), Dec. 3, 1999, 113 Stat. 1611.)

AMENDMENTS

1999—Subsec. (a). Pub. L. 106–120, §304(b)(2)(A), substituted "shall be fined under title 18" for "shall be fined not more than $50,000".

Subsec. (b). Pub. L. 106–120, §304(b)(2)(B), substituted "shall be fined under title 18" for "shall be fined not more than $25,000".

Subsec. (c). Pub. L. 106–120, §304(b)(2)(C), substituted "shall be fined under title 18" for "shall be fined not more than $15,000".

Subsec. (d). Pub. L. 106–120, §304(b)(1), added subsec. (d).

SHORT TITLE

For short title of this subchapter as the "Intelligence Identities Protection Act of 1982", see section 1 of Pub. L. 97–200, set out as a Short Title of 1982 Amendment note under section 401 of this title.

SECTION REFERRED TO IN OTHER SECTIONS

This section is referred to in sections 422, 424 of this title; title 5 section 8312; title 8 section 1101; title 18 section 3239; title 22 section 2778.

§422. Defenses and exceptions

(a) Disclosure by United States of identity of covert agent

It is a defense to a prosecution under section 421 of this title that before the commission of the offense with which the defendant is charged, the United States had publicly acknowledged or revealed the intelligence relationship to the United States of the individual the disclosure of whose intelligence relationship to the United States is the basis for the prosecution.

(b) Conspiracy, misprision of felony, aiding and abetting, etc.

(1) Subject to paragraph (2), no person other than a person committing an offense under section 421 of this title shall be subject to prosecution under such section by virtue of section 2 or 4 of title 18 or shall be subject to prosecution for conspiracy to commit an offense under such section.

(2) Paragraph (1) shall not apply (A) in the case of a person who acted in the course of a pattern of activities intended to identify and expose covert agents and with reason to believe that such activities would impair or impede the foreign intelligence activities of the United States, or (B) in the case of a person who has authorized access to classified information.

(c) Disclosure to select Congressional committees on intelligence

It shall not be an offense under section 421 of this title to transmit information described in such section directly to the Select Committee on Intelligence of the Senate or to the Permanent Select Committee on Intelligence of the House of Representatives.

(d) Disclosure by agent of own identity

It shall not be an offense under section 421 of this title for an individual to disclose information that solely identifies himself as a covert agent.

(July 26, 1947, ch. 343, title VI, §602, as added Pub. L. 97–200, §2(a), June 23, 1982, 96 Stat. 122.)

§ 423. Report

(a) Annual report by President to Congress on measures to protect identities of covert agents

The President, after receiving information from the Director of Central Intelligence, shall submit to the Select Committee on Intelligence of the Senate and the Permanent Select Committee on Intelligence of the House of Representatives an annual report on measures to protect the identities of covert agents, and on any other matter relevant to the protection of the identities of covert agents.

(b) Exemption from disclosure; date of initial submission

The report described in subsection (a) of this section shall be exempt from any requirement for publication or disclosure. The first such report shall be submitted no later than February 1, 1983.

(July 26, 1947, ch. 343, title VI, § 603, as added Pub. L. 97–200, § 2(a), June 23, 1982, 96 Stat. 123.)

TERMINATION OF REPORTING REQUIREMENTS

For termination, effective May 15, 2000, of provisions in subsec. (a) of this section relating to the requirement that the President submit an annual report to certain committees of Congress, see section 3003 of Pub. L. 104–66, as amended, set out as a note under section 1113 of Title 31, Money and Finance, and the 8th item on page 156 of House Document No. 103–7.

§ 424. Extraterritorial jurisdiction

There is jurisdiction over an offense under section 421 of this title committed outside the United States if the individual committing the offense is a citizen of the United States or an alien lawfully admitted to the United States for permanent residence (as defined in section 1101(a)(20) of title 8).

(July 26, 1947, ch. 343, title VI, § 604, as added Pub. L. 97–200, § 2(a), June 23, 1982, 96 Stat. 123.)

§ 425. Providing information to Congress

Nothing in this subchapter may be construed as authority to withhold information from the Congress or from a committee of either House of Congress.

(July 26, 1947, ch. 343, title VI, § 605, as added Pub. L. 97–200, § 2(a), June 23, 1982, 96 Stat. 123.)

§ 426. Definitions

For the purposes of this subchapter:

(1) The term "classified information" means information or material designated and clearly marked or clearly represented, pursuant to the provisions of a statute or Executive order (or a regulation or order issued pursuant to a statute or Executive order), as requiring a specific degree of protection against unauthorized disclosure for reasons of national security.

(2) The term "authorized", when used with respect to access to classified information, means having authority, right, or permission pursuant to the provisions of a statute, Executive order, directive of the head of any department or agency engaged in foreign intelligence or counterintelligence activities, order of any United States court, or provisions of any Rule of the House of Representatives or resolution of the Senate which assigns responsibility within the respective House of Congress for the oversight of intelligence activities.

(3) The term "disclose" means to communicate, provide, impart, transmit, transfer, convey, publish, or otherwise make available.

(4) The term "covert agent" means—

(A) a present or retired officer or employee of an intelligence agency or a present or retired member of the Armed Forces assigned to duty with an intelligence agency—

(i) whose identity as such an officer, employee, or member is classified information, and

(ii) who is serving outside the United States or has within the last five years served outside the United States; or

(B) a United States citizen whose intelligence relationship to the United States is classified information, and—

(i) who resides and acts outside the United States as an agent of, or informant or source of operational assistance to, an intelligence agency, or

(ii) who is at the time of the disclosure acting as an agent of, or informant to, the foreign counterintelligence or foreign counterterrorism components of the Federal Bureau of Investigation; or

(C) an individual, other than a United States citizen, whose past or present intelligence relationship to the United States is classified information and who is a present or former agent of, or a present or former informant or source of operational assistance to, an intelligence agency.

(5) The term "intelligence agency" means the Central Intelligence Agency, a foreign intelligence component of the Department of Defense, or the foreign counterintelligence or foreign counterterrorism components of the Federal Bureau of Investigation.

(6) The term "informant" means any individual who furnishes information to an intelligence agency in the course of a confidential relationship protecting the identity of such individual from public disclosure.

(7) The terms "officer" and "employee" have the meanings given such terms by section 2104 and 2105, respectively, of title 5.

(8) The term "Armed Forces" means the Army, Navy, Air Force, Marine Corps, and Coast Guard.

(9) The term "United States", when used in a geographic sense, means all areas under the territorial sovereignty of the United States and the Trust Territory of the Pacific Islands.

(10) The term "pattern of activities" requires a series of acts with a common purpose or objective.

(July 26, 1947, ch. 343, title VI, § 606, as added Pub. L. 97–200, § 2(a), June 23, 1982, 96 Stat. 123; amended Pub. L. 106–120, title III, § 304(a), Dec. 3, 1999, 113 Stat. 1611.)

AMENDMENTS

1999—Par. (4)(A). Pub. L. 106–120 substituted "a present or retired officer or employee" for "an officer or employee'' and ''a present or retired member'' for ''a member''.

TERMINATION OF TRUST TERRITORY OF THE PACIFIC ISLANDS

For termination of Trust Territory of the Pacific Islands, see note set out preceding section 1681 of Title 48, Territories and Insular Possessions.

SUBCHAPTER V—PROTECTION OF OPERATIONAL FILES OF THE CENTRAL INTELLIGENCE AGENCY

SUBCHAPTER REFERRED TO IN OTHER SECTIONS

This subchapter is referred to in section 411 of this title; title 44 section 3511.

§431. Exemption of certain operational files from search, review, publication, or disclosure

(a) Exemption by Director of Central Intelligence

Operational files of the Central Intelligence Agency may be exempted by the Director of Central Intelligence from the provisions of section 552 of title 5 (Freedom of Information Act) which require publication or disclosure, or search or review in connection therewith.

(b) "Operational files" defined

For the purposes of this title the term ''operational files'' means—

(1) files of the Directorate of Operations which document the conduct of foreign intelligence or counterintelligence operations or intelligence or security liaison arrangements or information exchanges with foreign governments or their intelligence or security services;

(2) files of the Directorate for Science and Technology which document the means by which foreign intelligence or counterintelligence is collected through scientific and technical systems; and

(3) files of the Office of Personnel Security which document investigations conducted to determine the suitability of potential foreign intelligence or counterintelligence sources;

except that files which are the sole repository of disseminated intelligence are not operational files.

(c) Search and review for information

Notwithstanding subsection (a) of this section, exempted operational files shall continue to be subject to search and review for information concerning—

(1) United States citizens or aliens lawfully admitted for permanent residence who have requested information on themselves pursuant to the provisions of section 552 of title 5 (Freedom of Information Act) or section 552a of title 5 (Privacy Act of 1974);

(2) any special activity the existence of which is not exempt from disclosure under the provisions of section 552 of title 5 (Freedom of Information Act); or

(3) the specific subject matter of an investigation by the intelligence committees of the Congress, the Intelligence Oversight Board, the Department of Justice, the Office of General Counsel of the Central Intelligence Agency, the Office of Inspector General of the Central Intelligence Agency, or the Office of the Director of Central Intelligence for any impropriety, or violation of law, Executive order, or Presidential directive, in the conduct of an intelligence activity.

(d) Information derived or disseminated from exempted operational files

(1) Files that are not exempted under subsection (a) of this section which contain information derived or disseminated from exempted operational files shall be subject to search and review.

(2) The inclusion of information from exempted operational files in files that are not exempted under subsection (a) of this section shall not affect the exemption under subsection (a) of this section of the originating operational files from search, review, publication, or disclosure.

(3) Records from exempted operational files which have been disseminated to and referenced in files that are not exempted under subsection (a) of this section and which have been returned to exempted operational files for sole retention shall be subject to search and review.

(e) Supersedure of prior law

The provisions of subsection (a) of this section shall not be superseded except by a provision of law which is enacted after October 15, 1984, and which specifically cites and repeals or modifies its provisions.

(f) Allegation; improper withholding of records; judicial review

Whenever any person who has requested agency records under section 552 of title 5 (Freedom of Information Act), alleges that the Central Intelligence Agency has improperly withheld records because of failure to comply with any provision of this section, judicial review shall be available under the terms set forth in section 552(a)(4)(B) of title 5, except that—

(1) in any case in which information specifically authorized under criteria established by an Executive order to be kept secret in the interest of national defense or foreign relations which is filed with, or produced for, the court by the Central Intelligence Agency, such information shall be examined ex parte, in camera by the court;

(2) the court shall, to the fullest extent practicable, determine issues of fact based on sworn written submissions of the parties;

(3) when a complaint alleges that requested records were improperly withheld because of improper placement solely in exempted operational files, the complainant shall support such allegation with a sworn written submission, based upon personal knowledge or otherwise admissible evidence;

(4)(A) when a complainant alleges that requested records were improperly withheld because of improper exemption of operational files, the Central Intelligence Agency shall meet its burden under section 552(a)(4)(B) of title 5 by demonstrating to the court by sworn written submission that exempted operational files likely to contain responsive records currently perform the functions set forth in subsection (b) of this section; and

(B) the court may not order the Central Intelligence Agency to review the content of any exempted operational file or files in order to make the demonstration required under subparagraph (A) of this paragraph, unless the complainant disputes the Central Intelligence Agency's showing with a sworn written submission based on personal knowledge or otherwise admissible evidence;

(5) in proceedings under paragraphs (3) and (4) of this subsection, the parties shall not obtain discovery pursuant to rules 26 through 36 of the Federal Rules of Civil Procedure, except that requests for admission may be made pursuant to rules 26 and 36;

(6) if the court finds under this subsection that the Central Intelligence Agency has improperly withheld requested records because of failure to comply with any provision of this section, the court shall order the Central Intelligence Agency to search and review the appropriate exempted operational file or files for the requested records and make such records, or portions thereof, available in accordance with the provisions of section 552 of title 5 (Freedom of Information Act), and such order shall be the exclusive remedy for failure to comply with this section; and

(7) if at any time following the filing of a complaint pursuant to this subsection the Central Intelligence Agency agrees to search the appropriate exempted operational file or files for the requested records, the court shall dismiss the claim based upon such complaint.

(July 26, 1947, ch. 343, title VII, § 701, as added Pub. L. 98–477, § 2(a), Oct. 15, 1984, 98 Stat. 2209; amended Pub. L. 104–93, title VII, § 702, Jan. 6, 1996, 109 Stat. 978.)

REFERENCES IN TEXT

The Federal Rules of Civil Procedure, referred to in subsec. (f)(5), are set out in the Appendix to Title 28, Judiciary and Judicial Procedure.

AMENDMENTS

1996—Subsec. (b)(3). Pub. L. 104–93 substituted "Office of Personnel Security" for "Office of Security".

EFFECTIVE DATE

Section 4 of Pub. L. 98–477 provided that: "The amendments made by subsections (a) and (b) of section 2 [enacting this subchapter and amending section 552a of Title 5, Government Organization and Employees] shall be effective upon enactment of this Act [Oct. 15, 1984] and shall apply with respect to any requests for records, whether or not such request was made prior to such enactment, and shall apply to all civil actions not commenced prior to February 7, 1984."

SECTION REFERRED TO IN OTHER SECTIONS

This section is referred to in section 432 of this title; title 10 section 457.

§ 432. Decennial review of exempted operational files

(a) Review by Director of Central Intelligence

Not less than once every ten years, the Director of Central Intelligence shall review the exemptions in force under subsection (a) of section 431 of this title to determine whether such exemptions may be removed from any category of exempted files or any portion thereof.

(b) Consideration; historical value; public interest

The review required by subsection (a) of this section shall include consideration of the historical value or other public interest in the subject matter of the particular category of files or portions thereof and the potential for declassifying a significant part of the information contained therein.

(c) Judicial review

A complainant who alleges that the Central Intelligence Agency has improperly withheld records because of failure to comply with this section may seek judicial review in the district court of the United States of the district in which any of the parties reside, or in the District of Columbia. In such a proceeding, the court's review shall be limited to determining (1) whether the Central Intelligence Agency has conducted the review required by subsection (a) of this section within ten years of enactment of this title or within ten years after the last review, and (2) whether the Central Intelligence Agency, in fact, considered the criteria set forth in subsection (b) of this section in conducting the required review.

(July 26, 1947, ch. 343, title VII, § 702, as added Pub. L. 98–477, § 2(a), Oct. 15, 1984, 98 Stat. 2211.)

EFFECTIVE DATE

Section effective Oct. 15, 1984, and applicable with respect to any request for records, whether or not such request was made prior to Oct. 15, 1984, and applicable to all civil actions not commenced prior to Feb. 7, 1984, see section 4 of Pub. L. 98–477, set out as a note under section 431 of this title.

DECLASSIFICATION AND RELEASE OF CIA INFORMATION OF HISTORICAL VALUE

Section 3 of Pub. L. 98–477 directed Director of Central Intelligence, in consultation with Archivist of the United States, Librarian of Congress, and appropriate representatives of historical discipline selected by Archivist, to prepare and submit report to Congress by June 1, 1985, on feasibility of conducting systematic review for declassification and release of Central Intelligence Agency information of historical value. Director was also required to prepare and submit four unclassified reports, one each six months beginning by Apr. 15, 1985, which were to include a description of the specific measures established by Director to improve processing of requests under section 552 of title 5, United States Code, current budgetary and personnel allocations for such processing, the number of such requests (i) received and processed during the preceding six months, and (ii) pending at time of submission of such report, and an estimate of current average response time for completing the processing of such requests.

SUBCHAPTER VI—ACCESS TO CLASSIFIED INFORMATION

§ 435. Procedures

(a) Not later than 180 days after October 14, 1994, the President shall, by Executive order or regulation, establish procedures to govern access to classified information which shall be binding upon all departments, agencies, and offices of the executive branch of Government. Such procedures shall, at a minimum—

(1) provide that, except as may be permitted by the President, no employee in the executive

branch of Government may be given access to classified information by any department, agency, or office of the executive branch of Government unless, based upon an appropriate background investigation, such access is determined to be clearly consistent with the national security interests of the United States;

(2) establish uniform minimum requirements governing the scope and frequency of background investigations and reinvestigations for all employees in the executive branch of Government who require access to classified information as part of their official responsibilities;

(3) provide that all employees in the executive branch of Government who require access to classified information shall be required as a condition of such access to provide to the employing department or agency written consent which permits access by an authorized investigative agency to relevant financial records, other financial information, consumer reports, travel records, and computers used in the performance of Government duties, as determined by the President, in accordance with section 436 of this title, during the period of access to classified information and for a period of three years thereafter;

(4) provide that all employees in the executive branch of Government who require access to particularly sensitive classified information, as determined by the President, shall be required, as a condition of maintaining access to such information, to submit to the employing department or agency, during the period of such access, relevant information concerning their financial condition and foreign travel, as determined by the President, as may be necessary to ensure appropriate security; and

(5) establish uniform minimum standards to ensure that employees in the executive branch of Government whose access to classified information is being denied or terminated under this subchapter are appropriately advised of the reasons for such denial or termination and are provided an adequate opportunity to respond to all adverse information which forms the basis for such denial or termination before final action by the department or agency concerned.

(b)(1) Subsection (a) of this section shall not be deemed to limit or affect the responsibility and power of an agency head pursuant to other law or Executive order to deny or terminate access to classified information if the national security so requires. Such responsibility and power may be exercised only when the agency head determines that the procedures prescribed by subsection (a) of this section cannot be invoked in a manner that is consistent with the national security.

(2) Upon the exercise of such responsibility, the agency head shall submit a report to the Permanent Select Committee on Intelligence of the House of Representatives and the Select Committee on Intelligence of the Senate.

(July 26, 1947, ch. 343, title VIII, §801, as added Pub. L. 103–359, title VIII, §802(a), Oct. 14, 1994, 108 Stat. 3435; amended Pub. L. 106–120, title III, §305(a), Dec. 3, 1999, 113 Stat. 1611.)

AMENDMENTS

1999—Subsec. (a)(3). Pub. L. 106–120 substituted "travel records, and computers used in the performance of Government duties" for "and travel records".

EFFECTIVE DATE OF 1999 AMENDMENT

Pub. L. 106–120, title III, §305(c), Dec. 3, 1999, 113 Stat. 1612, provided that: "The President shall modify the procedures required by section 801(a)(3) of the National Security Act of 1947 [50 U.S.C. 435(a)(3)] to take into account the amendment to that section made by subsection (a) of this section not later than 90 days after the date of the enactment of this Act [Dec. 3, 1999]."

EFFECTIVE DATE

Section 802(c) of Pub. L. 103–359 provided that: "The amendments made by subsections (a) and (b) [enacting this subchapter] shall take effect 180 days after the date of enactment of this Act [Oct. 14, 1994]."

DECLASSIFICATION OF INFORMATION

Pub. L. 106–567, title VII, Dec. 27, 2000, 114 Stat. 2856, provided that:

"SEC. 701. SHORT TITLE.

"This title may be cited as the 'Public Interest Declassification Act of 2000'.

"SEC. 702. FINDINGS.

"Congress makes the following findings:

"(1) It is in the national interest to establish an effective, coordinated, and cost-effective means by which records on specific subjects of extraordinary public interest that do not undermine the national security interests of the United States may be collected, retained, reviewed, and disseminated to Congress, policymakers in the executive branch, and the public.

"(2) Ensuring, through such measures, public access to information that does not require continued protection to maintain the national security interests of the United States is a key to striking the balance between secrecy essential to national security and the openness that is central to the proper functioning of the political institutions of the United States.

"SEC. 703. PUBLIC INTEREST DECLASSIFICATION BOARD.

"(a) ESTABLISHMENT.—There is established within the executive branch of the United States a board to be known as the 'Public Interest Declassification Board' (in this title referred to as the 'Board').

"(b) PURPOSES.—The purposes of the Board are as follows:

"(1) To advise the President, the Assistant to the President for National Security Affairs, the Director of the Office of Management and Budget, and such other executive branch officials as the Board considers appropriate on the systematic, thorough, coordinated, and comprehensive identification, collection, review for declassification, and release to Congress, interested agencies, and the public of declassified records and materials (including donated historical materials) that are of archival value, including records and materials of extraordinary public interest.

"(2) To promote the fullest possible public access to a thorough, accurate, and reliable documentary record of significant United States national security decisions and significant United States national security activities in order to—

"(A) support the oversight and legislative functions of Congress;

"(B) support the policymaking role of the executive branch;

"(C) respond to the interest of the public in national security matters; and

"(D) promote reliable historical analysis and new avenues of historical study in national security matters.

"(3) To provide recommendations to the President for the identification, collection, and review for declassification of information of extraordinary public interest that does not undermine the national security of the United States, to be undertaken in accordance with a declassification program that has been established or may be established by the President by Executive order.

"(4) To advise the President, the Assistant to the President for National Security Affairs, the Director of the Office of Management and Budget, and such other executive branch officials as the Board considers appropriate on policies deriving from the issuance by the President of Executive orders regarding the classification and declassification of national security information.

"(c) MEMBERSHIP.—(1) The Board shall be composed of nine individuals appointed from among citizens of the United States who are preeminent in the fields of history, national security, foreign policy, intelligence policy, social science, law, or archives, including individuals who have served in Congress or otherwise in the Federal Government or have otherwise engaged in research, scholarship, or publication in such fields on matters relating to the national security of the United States, of whom—

"(A) five shall be appointed by the President;

"(B) one shall be appointed by the Speaker of the House of Representatives;

"(C) one shall be appointed by the majority leader of the Senate;

"(D) one shall be appointed by the minority leader of the Senate; and

"(E) one shall be appointed by the minority leader of the House of Representatives.

"(2)(A) Of the members initially appointed to the Board by the President—

"(i) three shall be appointed for a term of 4 years;

"(ii) one shall be appointed for a term of 3 years; and

"(iii) one shall be appointed for a term of 2 years.

"(B) The members initially appointed to the Board by the Speaker of the House of Representatives or by the majority leader of the Senate shall be appointed for a term of 3 years.

"(C) The members initially appointed to the Board by the minority leader of the House of Representatives or the Senate shall be appointed for a term of 2 years.

"(D) Any subsequent appointment to the Board shall be for a term of 3 years.

"(3) A vacancy in the Board shall be filled in the same manner as the original appointment. A member of the Board appointed to fill a vacancy before the expiration of a term shall serve for the remainder of the term.

"(4) A member of the Board may be appointed to a new term on the Board upon the expiration of the member's term on the Board, except that no member may serve more than three full terms on the Board.

"(d) CHAIRPERSON; EXECUTIVE SECRETARY.—(1)(A) The President shall designate one of the members of the Board as the Chairperson of the Board.

"(B) The term of service as Chairperson of the Board shall be 2 years.

"(C) A member serving as Chairperson of the Board may be redesignated as Chairperson of the Board upon the expiration of the member's term as Chairperson of the Board, except that no member shall serve as Chairperson of the Board for more than 6 years.

"(2) The Director of the Information Security Oversight Office shall serve as the Executive Secretary of the Board.

"(e) MEETINGS.—The Board shall meet as needed to accomplish its mission, consistent with the availability of funds. A majority of the members of the Board shall constitute a quorum.

"(f) STAFF.—Any employee of the Federal Government may be detailed to the Board, with the agreement of and without reimbursement to the detailing agency, and such detail shall be without interruption or loss of civil, military, or foreign service status or privilege.

"(g) SECURITY.—(1) The members and staff of the Board shall, as a condition of appointment to or employment with the Board, hold appropriate security clearances for access to the classified records and materials to be reviewed by the Board or its staff, and shall follow the guidance and practices on security under applicable Executive orders and Presidential or agency directives.

"(2) The head of an agency shall, as a condition of granting access to a member of the Board, the Executive Secretary of the Board, or a member of the staff of the Board to classified records or materials of the agency under this title, require the member, the Executive Secretary, or the member of the staff, as the case may be, to—

"(A) execute an agreement regarding the security of such records or materials that is approved by the head of the agency; and

"(B) hold an appropriate security clearance granted or recognized under the standard procedures and eligibility criteria of the agency, including any special access approval required for access to such records or materials.

"(3) The members of the Board, the Executive Secretary of the Board, and the members of the staff of the Board may not use any information acquired in the course of their official activities on the Board for nonofficial purposes.

"(4) For purposes of any law or regulation governing access to classified information that pertains to the national security of the United States, and subject to any limitations on access arising under section 706(b), and to facilitate the advisory functions of the Board under this title, a member of the Board seeking access to a record or material under this title shall be deemed for purposes of this subsection to have a need to know the contents of the record or material.

"(h) COMPENSATION.—(1) Each member of the Board shall receive compensation at a rate not to exceed the daily equivalent of the annual rate of basic pay payable for positions at ES–1 of the Senior Executive Service under section 5382 of title 5, United States Code, for each day such member is engaged in the actual performance of duties of the Board.

"(2) Members of the Board shall be allowed travel expenses, including per diem in lieu of subsistence at rates authorized for employees of agencies under subchapter I of chapter 57 of title 5, United States Code, while away from their homes or regular places of business in the performance of the duties of the Board.

"(i) GUIDANCE; ANNUAL BUDGET.—(1) On behalf of the President, the Assistant to the President for National Security Affairs shall provide guidance on policy to the Board.

"(2) The Executive Secretary of the Board, under the direction of the Chairperson of the Board and the Board, and acting in consultation with the Archivist of the United States, the Assistant to the President for National Security Affairs, and the Director of the Office of Management and Budget, shall prepare the annual budget of the Board.

"(j) SUPPORT.—The Information Security Oversight Office may support the activities of the Board under this title. Such support shall be provided on a reimbursable basis.

"(k) PUBLIC AVAILABILITY OF RECORDS AND REPORTS.—(1) The Board shall make available for public inspection records of its proceedings and reports prepared in the course of its activities under this title to the extent such records and reports are not classified and would not be exempt from release under the provisions of section 552 of title 5, United States Code.

"(2) In making records and reports available under paragraph (1), the Board shall coordinate the release of such records and reports with appropriate officials from agencies with expertise in classified information in order to ensure that such records and reports do not inadvertently contain classified information.

"(*l*) APPLICABILITY OF CERTAIN ADMINISTRATIVE LAWS.—The provisions of the Federal Advisory Committee Act (5 U.S.C. App.) shall not apply to the activities of the Board under this title. However, the records of the Board shall be governed by the provisions of the Federal Records Act of 1950 [June 30, 1949, ch. 288, title V, as added Sept. 5, 1950, ch. 849, §6(d), 64 Stat. 583, see Tables for classification].

"SEC. 704. IDENTIFICATION, COLLECTION, AND REVIEW FOR DECLASSIFICATION OF INFORMATION OF ARCHIVAL VALUE OR EXTRAORDINARY PUBLIC INTEREST.

"(a) BRIEFINGS ON AGENCY DECLASSIFICATION PROGRAMS.—(1) As requested by the Board, or by the Select Committee on Intelligence of the Senate or the Permanent Select Committee on Intelligence of the House of Representatives, the head of any agency with the authority under an Executive order to classify information shall provide to the Board, the Select Committee on Intelligence of the Senate, or the Permanent Select Committee on Intelligence of the House of Representatives, on an annual basis, a summary briefing and report on such agency's progress and plans in the declassification of national security information. Such briefing shall cover the declassification goals set by statute, regulation, or policy, the agency's progress with respect to such goals, and the agency's planned goals and priorities for its declassification activities over the next 2 fiscal years. Agency briefings and reports shall give particular attention to progress on the declassification of records and materials that are of archival value or extraordinary public interest to the people of the United States.

"(2)(A) The annual briefing and report under paragraph (1) for agencies within the Department of Defense, including the military departments and the elements of the intelligence community, shall be provided on a consolidated basis.

"(B) In this paragraph, the term 'elements of the intelligence community' means the elements of the intelligence community specified or designated under section 3(4) of the National Security Act of 1947 (50 U.S.C. 401a(4)).

"(b) RECOMMENDATIONS ON AGENCY DECLASSIFICATION PROGRAMS.—(1) Upon reviewing and discussing declassification plans and progress with an agency, the Board shall provide to the head of the agency the written recommendations of the Board as to how the agency's declassification program could be improved. A copy of each recommendation shall also be submitted to the Assistant to the President for National Security Affairs and the Director of the Office of Management and Budget.

"(2) Consistent with the provisions of section 703(k), the Board's recommendations to the head of an agency under paragraph (1) shall become public 60 days after such recommendations are sent to the head of the agency under that paragraph.

"(c) RECOMMENDATIONS ON SPECIAL SEARCHES FOR RECORDS OF EXTRAORDINARY PUBLIC INTEREST.—(1) The Board shall also make recommendations to the President regarding proposed initiatives to identify, collect, and review for declassification classified records and materials of extraordinary public interest.

"(2) In making recommendations under paragraph (1), the Board shall consider the following:

"(A) The opinions and requests of Members of Congress, including opinions and requests expressed or embodied in letters or legislative proposals.

"(B) The opinions and requests of the National Security Council, the Director of Central Intelligence, and the heads of other agencies.

"(C) The opinions of United States citizens.

"(D) The opinions of members of the Board.

"(E) The impact of special searches on systematic and all other on-going declassification programs.

"(F) The costs (including budgetary costs) and the impact that complying with the recommendations would have on agency budgets, programs, and operations.

"(G) The benefits of the recommendations.

"(H) The impact of compliance with the recommendations on the national security of the United States.

"(d) PRESIDENT'S DECLASSIFICATION PRIORITIES.—(1) Concurrent with the submission to Congress of the budget of the President each fiscal year under section 1105 of title 31, United States Code, the Director of the Office of Management and Budget shall publish a description of the President's declassification program and priorities, together with a listing of the funds requested to implement that program.

"(2) Nothing in this title shall be construed to substitute or supersede, or establish a funding process for, any declassification program that has been established or may be established by the President by Executive order.

"SEC. 705. PROTECTION OF NATIONAL SECURITY INFORMATION AND OTHER INFORMATION.

"(a) IN GENERAL.—Nothing in this title shall be construed to limit the authority of the head of an agency to classify information or to continue the classification of information previously classified by that agency.

"(b) SPECIAL ACCESS PROGRAMS.—Nothing in this title shall be construed to limit the authority of the head of an agency to grant or deny access to a special access program.

"(c) AUTHORITIES OF DIRECTOR OF CENTRAL INTELLIGENCE.—Nothing in this title shall be construed to limit the authorities of the Director of Central Intelligence as the head of the intelligence community, including the Director's responsibility to protect intelligence sources and methods from unauthorized disclosure as required by section 103(c)(6) of the National Security Act of 1947 (50 U.S.C. 403–3(c)(6)).

"(d) EXEMPTIONS TO RELEASE OF INFORMATION.—Nothing in this title shall be construed to limit any exemption or exception to the release to the public under this title of information that is protected under subsection (b) of section 552 of title 5, United States Code (commonly referred to as the 'Freedom of Information Act'), or section 552a of title 5, United States Code (commonly referred to as the 'Privacy Act').

"(e) WITHHOLDING INFORMATION FROM CONGRESS.—Nothing in this title shall be construed to authorize the withholding of information from Congress.

"SEC. 706. STANDARDS AND PROCEDURES.

"(a) LIAISON.—(1) The head of each agency with the authority under an Executive order to classify information and the head of each Federal Presidential library shall designate an employee of such agency or library to act as liaison to the Board for purposes of this title.

"(2) The Board may establish liaison and otherwise consult with such other historical and advisory committees as the Board considers appropriate for purposes of this title.

"(b) LIMITATIONS ON ACCESS.—(1)(A) Except as provided in paragraph (2), if the head of an agency or the head of a Federal Presidential library determines it necessary to deny or restrict access of the Board, or of the agency or library liaison to the Board, to information contained in a record or material, in whole or in part, the head of the agency or the head of the library shall promptly notify the Board in writing of such determination.

"(B) Each notice to the Board under subparagraph (A) shall include a description of the nature of the records or materials, and a justification for the determination, covered by such notice.

"(2) In the case of a determination referred to in paragraph (1) with respect to a special access program created by the Secretary of Defense, the Director of Central Intelligence, or the head of any other agency, the notification of denial of access under paragraph (1), including a description of the nature of the Board's request for access, shall be submitted to the Assistant to the President for National Security Affairs rather than to the Board.

"(c) DISCRETION TO DISCLOSE.—At the conclusion of a declassification review, the head of an agency may, in the discretion of the head of the agency, determine that the public's interest in the disclosure of records or materials of the agency covered by such review, and still properly classified, outweighs the Government's need to protect such records or materials, and may release such records or materials in accordance with the provisions of Executive Order No. 12958 [set out below] or any successor order to such Executive order.

"(d) DISCRETION TO PROTECT.—At the conclusion of a declassification review, the head of an agency may, in the discretion of the head of the agency, determine that the interest of the agency in the protection of records or materials of the agency covered by such review, and still properly classified, outweighs the public's need for access to such records or materials, and may deny release of such records or materials in accordance with the provisions of Executive Order No. 12958 or any successor order to such Executive order.

"(e) REPORTS.—(1)(A) Except as provided in paragraph (2), the Board shall annually submit to the appropriate congressional committees a report on the activities of the Board under this title, including summary information regarding any denials to the Board by the head of an agency or the head of a Federal Presidential library of access to records or materials under this title.

"(B) In this paragraph, the term 'appropriate congressional committees' means the Select Committee on Intelligence and the Committee on Governmental Affairs of the Senate and the Permanent Select Committee on Intelligence and the Committee on Government Reform of the House of Representatives.

"(2) Notwithstanding paragraph (1), notice that the Board has been denied access to records and materials, and a justification for the determination in support of the denial, shall be submitted by the agency denying the access as follows:

"(A) In the case of the denial of access to a special access program created by the Secretary of Defense, to the Committees on Armed Services and Appropriations of the Senate and to the Committees on Armed Services and Appropriations of the House of Representatives.

"(B) In the case of the denial of access to a special access program created by the Director of Central Intelligence, or by the head of any other agency (including the Department of Defense) if the special access program pertains to intelligence activities, or of access to any information and materials relating to intelligence sources and methods, to the Select Committee on Intelligence of the Senate and the Permanent Select Committee on Intelligence of the House of Representatives.

"(C) In the case of the denial of access to a special access program created by the Secretary of Energy or the Administrator for Nuclear Security, to the Committees on Armed Services and Appropriations and the Select Committee on Intelligence of the Senate and to the Committees on Armed Services and Appropriations and the Permanent Select Committee on Intelligence of the House of Representatives.

"SEC. 707. JUDICIAL REVIEW.

"Nothing in this title limits the protection afforded to any information under any other provision of law. This title is not intended and may not be construed to create any right or benefit, substantive or procedural, enforceable against the United States, its agencies, its officers, or its employees. This title does not modify in any way the substantive criteria or procedures for the classification of information, nor does this title create any right or benefit subject to judicial review.

"SEC. 708. FUNDING.

"(a) AUTHORIZATION OF APPROPRIATIONS.—There is hereby authorized to be appropriated to carry out the provisions of this title amounts as follows:

"(1) For fiscal year 2001, $650,000.

"(2) For each fiscal year after fiscal year 2001, such sums as may be necessary for such fiscal year.

"(b) FUNDING REQUESTS.—The President shall include in the budget submitted to Congress for each fiscal year under section 1105 of title 31, United States Code, a request for amounts for the activities of the Board under this title during such fiscal year.

"SEC. 709. DEFINITIONS.

"In this title:

"(1) AGENCY.—(A) Except as provided in subparagraph (B), the term 'agency' means the following:

"(i) An Executive agency, as that term is defined in section 105 of title 5, United States Code.

"(ii) A military department, as that term is defined in section 102 of such title.

"(iii) Any other entity in the executive branch that comes into the possession of classified information.

"(B) The term does not include the Board.

"(2) CLASSIFIED MATERIAL OR RECORD.—The terms 'classified material' and 'classified record' include any correspondence, memorandum, book, plan, map, drawing, diagram, pictorial or graphic work, photograph, film, microfilm, sound recording, videotape, machine readable records, and other documentary material, regardless of physical form or characteristics, that has been determined pursuant to Executive order to require protection against unauthorized disclosure in the interests of the national security of the United States.

"(3) DECLASSIFICATION.—The term 'declassification' means the process by which records or materials that have been classified are determined no longer to require protection from unauthorized disclosure to protect the national security of the United States.

"(4) DONATED HISTORICAL MATERIAL.—The term 'donated historical material' means collections of personal papers donated or given to a Federal Presidential library or other archival repository under a deed of gift or otherwise.

"(5) FEDERAL PRESIDENTIAL LIBRARY.—The term 'Federal Presidential library' means a library operated and maintained by the United States Government through the National Archives and Records Administration under the applicable provisions of the Federal Records Act of 1950 [June 30, 1949, ch. 288, title V, as added Sept. 5, 1950, ch. 849, § 6(d), 64 Stat. 583, see Tables for classification].

"(6) NATIONAL SECURITY.—The term 'national security' means the national defense or foreign relations of the United States.

"(7) RECORDS OR MATERIALS OF EXTRAORDINARY PUBLIC INTEREST.—The term 'records or materials of extraordinary public interest' means records or materials that—

"(A) demonstrate and record the national security policies, actions, and decisions of the United States, including—

"(i) policies, events, actions, and decisions which led to significant national security outcomes; and

"(ii) the development and evolution of significant United States national security policies, actions, and decisions;

"(B) will provide a significantly different perspective in general from records and materials publicly available in other historical sources; and

"(C) would need to be addressed through ad hoc record searches outside any systematic declassification program established under Executive order.

"(8) RECORDS OF ARCHIVAL VALUE.—The term 'records of archival value' means records that have been determined by the Archivist of the United States to have sufficient historical or other value to warrant their continued preservation by the Federal Government.

"SEC. 710. EFFECTIVE DATE; SUNSET.

"(a) EFFECTIVE DATE.—This title shall take effect on the date that is 120 days after the date of the enactment of this Act [Dec. 27, 2000].

"(b) SUNSET.—The provisions of this title shall expire 4 years after the date of the enactment of this Act, unless reauthorized by statute."

COMPILATION AND ORGANIZATION OF PREVIOUSLY DECLASSIFIED RECORDS

Pub. L. 106–398, §1 [[div. A], title X, §1075(c), (d)], Oct. 30, 2000, 114 Stat. 1654, 1654A–280, provided that:

"(c) COMPILATION AND ORGANIZATION OF RECORDS.—The Department of Defense may not be required, when conducting a special search, to compile or organize records that have already been declassified and placed into the public domain.

"(d) SPECIAL SEARCHES.—For the purpose of this section, the term 'special search' means the response of the Department of Defense to any of the following:

"(1) A statutory requirement to conduct a declassification review on a specified set of agency records.

"(2) An Executive order to conduct a declassification review on a specified set of agency records.

"(3) An order from the President or an official with delegated authority from the President to conduct a declassification review on a specified set of agency records."

CERTIFICATION AND REPORT RELATED TO AUTOMATIC DECLASSIFICATION OF DEPARTMENT OF DEFENSE RECORDS

Pub. L. 106–65, div. A, title X, §1041(c), (d), Oct. 5, 1999, 113 Stat. 758, provided that:

"(c) CERTIFICATION REQUIRED WITH RESPECT TO AUTOMATIC DECLASSIFICATION OF RECORDS.—No records of the Department of Defense that have not been reviewed for declassification shall be subject to automatic declassification unless the Secretary of Defense certifies to Congress that such declassification would not harm the national security.

"(d) REPORT ON AUTOMATIC DECLASSIFICATION OF DEPARTMENT OF DEFENSE RECORDS.—Not later than February 1, 2001, the Secretary of Defense shall submit to the Committee on Armed Services of the House of Representatives and the Committee on Armed Services of the Senate a report on the efforts of the Department of Defense relating to the declassification of classified records under the control of the Department of Defense. Such report shall include the following:

"(1) An assessment of whether the Department will be able to review all relevant records for declassification before any date established for automatic declassification.

"(2) An estimate of the cost of reviewing records to meet any requirement to review all relevant records for declassification by a date established for automatic declassification.

"(3) An estimate of the number of records, if any, that the Department will be unable to review for declassification before any such date and the affect [sic] on national security of the automatic declassification of those records.

"(4) An estimate of the length of time by which any such date would need to be extended to avoid the automatic declassification of records that have not yet been reviewed as of such date."

SUPPLEMENT TO PLAN FOR DECLASSIFICATION OF RESTRICTED DATA AND FORMERLY RESTRICTED DATA

Pub. L. 106–65, div. C, title XXXI, §3149, Oct. 5, 1999, 113 Stat. 938, provided that:

"(a) SUPPLEMENT TO PLAN.—The Secretary of Energy and the Archivist of the United States shall, after consultation with the members of the National Security Council and in consultation with the Secretary of Defense and the heads of other appropriate Federal agencies, develop a supplement to the plan required under subsection (a) of section 3161 of the Strom Thurmond National Defense Authorization Act for Fiscal Year 1999 (Public Law 105–261; 112 Stat. 2260 [2259]; 50 U.S.C. 435 note).

"(b) CONTENTS OF SUPPLEMENT.—The supplement shall provide for the application of that plan (including in particular the element of the plan required by section 3161(b)(1) of that Act) to all records subject to Executive Order No. 12958 [set out below] that were determined before the date of the enactment of that Act [Oct. 17, 1998] to be suitable for declassification.

"(c) LIMITATION ON DECLASSIFICATION OF RECORDS.—All records referred to in subsection (b) shall be treated, for purposes of section 3161(c) of that Act, in the same manner as records referred to in section 3161(a) of that Act.

"(d) SUBMISSION OF SUPPLEMENT.—The Secretary of Energy shall submit the supplement required under subsection (a) to the recipients of the plan referred to in section 3161(d) of that Act."

IDENTIFICATION IN BUDGET MATERIALS OF AMOUNTS FOR DECLASSIFICATION ACTIVITIES AND LIMITATION ON EXPENDITURES FOR SUCH ACTIVITIES

Pub. L. 106–65, div. C, title XXXI, §3173, Oct. 5, 1999, 113 Stat. 949, provided that:

"(a) AMOUNTS FOR DECLASSIFICATION OF RECORDS.—The Secretary of Energy shall include in the budget justification materials submitted to Congress in support of the Department of Energy budget for any fiscal year (as submitted with the budget of the President under section 1105(a) of title 31, United States Code) specific identification, as a budgetary line item, of the amounts required to carry out programmed activities during that fiscal year to declassify records pursuant to Executive Order No. 12958 (50 U.S.C. 435 note), or any successor Executive order, or to comply with any statutory requirement to declassify Government records.

"(b) CERTIFICATION REQUIRED WITH RESPECT TO AUTOMATIC DECLASSIFICATION OF RECORDS.—No records of the Department of Energy that have not as of the date of the enactment of this Act [Oct. 5, 1999] been reviewed for declassification shall be subject to automatic declassification unless the Secretary of Energy certifies to Congress that such declassification would not harm the national security.

"(c) REPORT ON AUTOMATIC DECLASSIFICATION OF DEPARTMENT OF ENERGY RECORDS.—Not later than February 1, 2001, the Secretary of Energy shall submit to the Committee on Armed Services of the House of Representatives and the Committee on Armed Services of the Senate a report on the efforts of the Department of Energy relating to the declassification of classified records under the control of the Department of Energy. Such report shall include the following:

"(1) An assessment of whether the Department will be able to review all relevant records for declassification before any date established for automatic declassification.

"(2) An estimate of the number of records, if any, that the Department will be unable to review for declassification before any such date and the effect on national security of the automatic declassification of those records.

"(3) An estimate of the length of time by which any such date would need to be extended to avoid the automatic declassification of records that have not yet been reviewed as of such date."

PROTECTION AGAINST INADVERTENT RELEASE OF RESTRICTED DATA AND FORMERLY RESTRICTED DATA

Pub. L. 105–261, div. C, title XXXI, §3161, Oct. 17, 1998, 112 Stat. 2259, as amended by Pub. L. 106–65, div. A, title X, §1067(3), Oct. 5, 1999, 113 Stat. 774; Pub. L. 106–398, §1 [div. C, title XXXI, §3193(a)], Oct. 30, 2000, 114 Stat. 1654, 1654A–480, provided that:

"(a) PLAN FOR PROTECTION AGAINST RELEASE.—The Secretary of Energy and the Archivist of the United States shall, after consultation with the members of the National Security Council and in consultation with the Secretary of Defense and the heads of other appropriate Federal agencies, develop a plan to prevent the inadvertent release of records containing Restricted Data or Formerly Restricted Data during the automatic declassification of records under Executive Order No. 12958 (50 U.S.C. 435 note).

"(b) PLAN ELEMENTS.—The plan under subsection (a) shall include the following:

"(1) The actions to be taken in order to ensure that records subject to Executive Order No. 12958 are reviewed on a page-by-page basis for Restricted Data and Formerly Restricted Data unless they have been determined to be highly unlikely to contain Restricted Data or Formerly Restricted Data.

"(2) The criteria and process by which documents are determined to be highly unlikely to contain Restricted Data or Formerly Restricted Data.

"(3) The actions to be taken in order to ensure proper training, supervision, and evaluation of personnel engaged in declassification under that Executive order so that such personnel recognize Restricted Data and Formerly Restricted Data.

"(4) The extent to which automated declassification technologies will be used under that Executive order to protect Restricted Data and Formerly Restricted Data from inadvertent release.

"(5) Procedures for periodic review and evaluation by the Secretary of Energy, in consultation with the Director of the Information Security Oversight Office of the National Archives and Records Administration, of compliance by Federal agencies with the plan.

"(6) Procedures for resolving disagreements among Federal agencies regarding declassification procedures and decisions under the plan.

"(7) The funding, personnel, and other resources required to carry out the plan.

"(8) A timetable for implementation of the plan.

"(c) LIMITATION ON DECLASSIFICATION OF CERTAIN RECORDS.—(1) Effective on the date of the enactment of this Act [Oct. 17, 1998] and except as provided in paragraph (3), a record referred to in subsection (a) may not be declassified unless the agency having custody of the record reviews the record on a page-by-page basis to ensure that the record does not contain Restricted Data or Formerly Restricted Data.

"(2) Any record determined as a result of a review under paragraph (1) to contain Restricted Data or Formerly Restricted Data may not be declassified until the Secretary of Energy, in conjunction with the head of the agency having custody of the record, determines that the document is suitable for declassification.

"(3) After the date occurring 60 days after the submission of the plan required by subsection (a) to the committees referred to in paragraphs (1) and (2) of subsection (d), the requirement under paragraph (1) to review a record on a page-by-page basis shall not apply in the case of a record determined, under the actions specified in the plan pursuant to subsection (b)(1), to be a record that is highly unlikely to contain Restricted Data or Formerly Restricted Data.

"(d) SUBMISSION OF PLAN.—The Secretary of Energy shall submit the plan required under subsection (a) to the following:

"(1) The Committee on Armed Services of the Senate.

"(2) The Committee on Armed Services of the House of Representatives.

"(3) The Assistant to the President for National Security Affairs.

"(e) SUBMISSION OF REVIEWS.—The Secretary of Energy shall, on a periodic basis, submit a summary of the results of the periodic reviews and evaluations specified in the plan pursuant to subsection (b)(4) to the committees and Assistant to the President specified in subsection (d).

"(f) REPORT AND NOTIFICATION REGARDING INADVERTENT RELEASES.—(1) The Secretary of Energy shall submit to the committees and Assistant to the President specified in subsection (d) a report on inadvertent releases of Restricted Data or Formerly Restricted Data under Executive Order No. 12958 that occurred before the date of the enactment of this Act.

"(2) The Secretary of Energy shall, on a quarterly basis, submit a report to the committees and Assistant to the President specified in subsection (d). The report shall state whether any inadvertent releases described in paragraph (1) occurred during the immediately preceding quarter and, if so, shall identify each such release.

"(g) DEFINITION.—In this section, the term 'Restricted Data' has the meaning given that term in section 11 y. of the Atomic Energy Act of 1954 (42 U.S.C. 2014(y))."

[Pub. L. 106–398, §1 [div. C, title XXXI, §3193(b)], Oct. 30, 2000, 114 Stat. 1654, 1654A–481, provided that: "The amendment made by subsection (a) [amending section 3161 of Pub. L. 105–261, set out above] apply [sic] with respect to inadvertent releases of Restricted Data and Formerly Restricted Data that are discovered on or after the date of the enactment of this Act [Oct. 30, 2000]."]

SECRECY AGREEMENTS USED IN INTELLIGENCE ACTIVITIES

Pub. L. 104–93, title III, §306, Jan. 6, 1996, 109 Stat. 966, provided that: "Notwithstanding any other provision of law not specifically referencing this section, a nondisclosure policy form or agreement that is to be executed by a person connected with the conduct of an intelligence or intelligence-related activity, other than an employee or officer of the United States Government, may contain provisions appropriate to the particular activity for which such document is to be used. Such form or agreement shall, at a minimum—

"(1) require that the person will not disclose any classified information received in the course of such activity unless specifically authorized to do so by the United States Government; and

"(2) provide that the form or agreement does not bar—

"(A) disclosures to Congress; or

"(B) disclosures to an authorized official of an executive agency that are deemed essential to reporting a violation of United States law."

VOLUNTARY SERVICE PROGRAM

Pub. L. 104–93, title IV, §402, Jan. 6, 1996, 109 Stat. 969, provided that:

"(a) GENERAL AUTHORITY.—The Director of Central Intelligence is authorized to establish and maintain a program from fiscal years 1996 through 2001 to utilize the services contributed by not more than 50 annuitants who serve without compensation as volunteers in aid of the review for declassification or downgrading of classified information by the Central Intelligence Agency under applicable Executive orders governing the classification and declassification of national security information and Public Law 102–526 [44 U.S.C. 2107 note].

"(b) COSTS INCIDENTAL TO SERVICES.—The Director is authorized to use sums made available to the Central Intelligence Agency by appropriations or otherwise for paying the costs incidental to the utilization of services contributed by individuals under subsection (a). Such costs may include (but need not be limited to) training, transportation, lodging, subsistence, equipment, and supplies. The Director may authorize either direct procurement of equipment, supplies, and services, or reimbursement for expenses, incidental to the effective use of volunteers. Such expenses or services shall be in accordance with volunteer agreements made with such individuals. Sums made available for such costs may not exceed $100,000.

"(c) APPLICATION OF CERTAIN PROVISIONS OF LAW.—A volunteer under this section shall be considered to be a Federal employee for the purposes of subchapter I of title [chapter] 81 [of title 5] (relating to compensation of Federal employees for work injuries) and section 1346(b) and chapter 171 of title 28 (relating to tort claims). A volunteer under this section shall be covered by and subject to the provisions of chapter 11 of title 18 of the United States Code as if they were employees or special Government employees depending upon the days of expected service at the time they begin volunteering."

COMMISSION ON PROTECTING AND REDUCING GOVERNMENT SECRECY

Pub. L. 103–236, title IX, Apr. 30, 1994, 108 Stat. 525, provided that:

"SEC. 901. SHORT TITLE.

"This title may be cited as the 'Protection and Reduction of Government Secrecy Act'.

"SEC. 902. FINDINGS.

"The Congress makes the following findings:

"(1) During the Cold War an extensive secrecy system developed which limited public access to information and reduced the ability of the public to participate with full knowledge in the process of governmental decisionmaking.

"(2) In 1992 alone 6,349,532 documents were classified and approximately three million persons held some form of security clearance.

"(3) The burden of managing more than 6 million newly classified documents every year has led to tremendous administrative expense, reduced communication within the government and within the scientific community, reduced communication between the government and the people of the United States, and the selective and unauthorized public disclosure of classified information.

"(4) It has been estimated that private businesses spend more than $14 billion each year implementing government mandated regulations for protecting classified information.

"(5) If a smaller amount of truly sensitive information were classified the information could be held more securely.

"(6) In 1970 a Task Force organized by the Defense Science Board and headed by Dr. Frederick Seitz concluded that 'more might be gained than lost if our Nation were to adopt—unilaterally, if necessary—a policy of complete openness in all areas of information'.

"(7) The procedures for granting security clearances have themselves become an expensive and inefficient part of the secrecy system and should be closely examined.

"(8) A bipartisan study commission specially constituted for the purpose of examining the consequences of the secrecy system will be able to offer comprehensive proposals for reform.

"SEC. 903. PURPOSE.

"It is the purpose of this title to establish for a two-year period a Commission on Protecting and Reducing Government Secrecy—

"(1) to examine the implications of the extensive classification of information and to make recommendations to reduce the volume of information classified and thereby to strengthen the protection of legitimately classified information; and

"(2) to examine and make recommendations concerning current procedures relating to the granting of security clearances.

"SEC. 904. COMPOSITION OF THE COMMISSION.

"(a) ESTABLISHMENT.—To carry out the purpose of this title, there is established a Commission on Protecting and Reducing Government Secrecy (in this title referred to as the 'Commission').

"(b) COMPOSITION.—The Commission shall be composed of twelve members, as follows:

"(1) Four members appointed by the President, of whom two shall be appointed from the executive branch of the Government and two shall be appointed from private life.

"(2) Two members appointed by the Majority Leader of the Senate, of whom one shall be a Member of the Senate and one shall be appointed from private life.

"(3) Two members appointed by the Minority Leader of the Senate, of whom one shall be a Member of the Senate and one shall be appointed from private life.

"(4) Two members appointed by the Speaker of the House of Representatives, of whom one shall be a Member of the House and one shall be appointed from private life.

"(5) Two members appointed by the Minority Leader of the House of Representatives, of whom one shall be a Member of the House and one shall be appointed from private life.

"(c) CHAIRMAN.—The Commission shall elect a Chairman from among its members.

"(d) QUORUM; VACANCIES.—After its initial meeting, the Commission shall meet upon the call of the Chairman or a majority of its members. Seven members of the Commission shall constitute a quorum. Any vacancy in the Commission shall not affect its powers but shall be filled in the same manner in which the original appointment was made.

"(e) APPOINTMENT OF MEMBERS; INITIAL MEETING.—(1) It is the sense of the Congress that members of the Commission should be appointed not later than 60 days after the date of enactment of this title [Apr. 30, 1994].

"(2) If after 60 days from the date of enactment of this Act seven or more members of the Commission have been appointed, those members who have been appointed may meet and select a Chairman who thereafter shall have authority to begin the operations of the Commission, including the hiring of staff.

"SEC. 905. FUNCTIONS OF THE COMMISSION.

"The functions of the Commission shall be—

"(1) to conduct, for a period of 2 years from the date of its first meeting, an investigation into all matters in any way related to any legislation, executive order, regulation, practice, or procedure relating to classified information or granting security clearances; and

"(2) to submit to the Congress a final report containing such recommendations concerning the classification of national security information and the granting of security clearances as the Commission shall determine, including proposing new procedures, rules, regulations, or legislation.

"SEC. 906. POWERS OF THE COMMISSION.

"(a) IN GENERAL.—(1) The Commission or, on the authorization of the Commission, any subcommittee or member thereof, may, for the purpose of carrying out the provisions of this title—

"(A) hold such hearings and sit and act at such times and places, take such testimony, receive such evidence, administer such oaths, and

"(B) require, by subpoena or otherwise, the attendance and testimony of such witnesses and the production of such books, records, correspondence, memoranda, papers, and documents,

as the Commission or such designated subcommittee or designated member may deem advisable.

"(2) Subpoenas issued under paragraph (1)(B) may be issued under the signature of the Chairman of the Commission, the chairman of any designated subcommittee, or any designated member, and may be served by any person designated by such Chairman, subcommittee chairman, or member. The provisions of sections 102 through 104 of the Revised Statutes of the United States (2 U.S.C. 192–194) shall apply in the case of any failure of any witness to comply with any subpoena or to testify when summoned under authority of this section.

"(b) CONTRACTING.—The Commission may, to such extent and in such amounts as are provided in appropriation Acts, enter into contracts to enable the Commission to discharge its duties under this title.

"(c) INFORMATION FROM FEDERAL AGENCIES.—The Commission is authorized to secure directly from any executive department, bureau, agency, board, commission, office, independent establishment, or instrumentality of the Government information, suggestions, estimates, and statistics for the purposes of this title. Each such department, bureau, agency, board, commission, office, establishment, or instrumentality shall, to the extent authorized by law, furnish such information, suggestions, estimates, and statistics directly to the Commission, upon request made by the Chairman.

"(d) ASSISTANCE FROM FEDERAL AGENCIES.—(1) The Secretary of State is authorized on a reimbursable or non-reimbursable basis to provide the Commission with administrative services, funds, facilities, staff, and other support services for the performance of the Commission's functions.

"(2) The Administrator of General Services shall provide to the Commission on a reimbursable basis such administrative support services as the Commission may request.

"(3) In addition to the assistance set forth in paragraphs (1) and (2), departments and agencies of the United States are authorized to provide to the Commission such services, funds, facilities, staff, and other support services as they may deem advisable and as may be authorized by law.

"(e) GIFTS.—The Commission may accept, use, and dispose of gifts or donations of services or property.

"(f) POSTAL SERVICES.—The Commission may use the United States mails in the same manner and under the same conditions as departments and agencies of the United States.

"SEC. 907. STAFF OF THE COMMISSION.

"(a) IN GENERAL.—The Chairman, in accordance with rules agreed upon by the Commission, may appoint and fix the compensation of a staff director and such other personnel as may be necessary to enable the Commission to carry out its functions, without regard to the provisions of title 5, United States Code, governing appointments in the competitive service, and without regard to the provisions of chapter 51 and subchapter III of chapter 53 of such title relating to classification and General Schedule pay rates, except that no rate of pay fixed under this subsection may exceed the equivalent of that payable to a person occupying a position at level V of the Executive Schedule under section 5316 of title 5, United States Code. Any Federal Government employee may be detailed to the Commission without reimbursement from the Commission, and such detailee shall retain the rights, status, and privileges of his or her regular employment without interruption.

"(b) CONSULTANT SERVICES.—The Commission is authorized to procure the services of experts and consultants in accordance with section 3109 of title 5, United States Code, but at rates not to exceed the daily rate paid a person occupying a position at level IV of the Executive Schedule under section 5315 of title 5, United States Code.

"SEC. 908. COMPENSATION AND TRAVEL EXPENSES.

"(a) COMPENSATION.—(1) Except as provided in paragraph (2), each member of the Commission may be compensated at not to exceed the daily equivalent of the annual rate of basic pay in effect for a position at level IV of the Executive Schedule under section 5315 of title 5, United States Code, for each day during which that member is engaged in the actual performance of the duties of the Commission.

"(2) Members of the Commission who are officers or employees of the United States or Members of Congress shall receive no additional pay on account of their service on the Commission.

"(b) TRAVEL EXPENSES.—While away from their homes or regular places of business in the performance of services for the Commission, members of the Commission shall be allowed travel expenses, including per diem in lieu of subsistence, in the same manner as persons employed intermittently in the Government service are allowed expenses under section 5703(b) of title 5, United States Code.

"SEC. 909. SECURITY CLEARANCES FOR COMMISSION MEMBERS AND STAFF.

"The appropriate executive departments and agencies shall cooperate with the Commission in expeditiously providing to the Commission members and staff appropriate security clearances in a manner consistent with existing procedures and requirements, except that no person shall be provided with access to classified information pursuant to this section who would not otherwise qualify for such security clearance.

"SEC. 910. FINAL REPORT OF COMMISSION; TERMINATION.

"(a) FINAL REPORT.—Not later than two years after the date of the first meeting of the Commission, the Commission shall submit to the Congress its final report, as described in section 905(2).

"(b) TERMINATION.—(1) The Commission, and all the authorities of this title, shall terminate on the date which is 60 days after the date on which a final report is required to be transmitted under subsection (a).

"(2) The Commission may use the 60-day period referred to in paragraph (1) for the purpose of concluding its activities, including providing testimony to committees of Congress concerning its final report and disseminating that report."

REPORTS RELATING TO CERTAIN SPECIAL ACCESS PROGRAMS AND SIMILAR PROGRAMS

Pub. L. 103–160, div. A, title XI, §1152, Nov. 30, 1993, 107 Stat. 1758, as amended by Pub. L. 106–65, div. C, title XXXII, §3294(e)(2), Oct. 5, 1999, 113 Stat. 970, provided that:

"(a) IN GENERAL.—(1) Not later than February 1 of each year, the head of each covered department or agency shall submit to Congress a report on each special access program carried out in the department or agency.

"(2) Each such report shall set forth—

"(A) the total amount requested by the department or agency for special access programs within the budget submitted under section 1105 of title 31, United States Code, for the fiscal year following the fiscal year in which the report is submitted; and

"(B) for each program in such budget that is a special access program—

"(i) a brief description of the program;

"(ii) in the case of a procurement program, a brief discussion of the major milestones established for the program;

"(iii) the actual cost of the program for each fiscal year during which the program has been conducted before the fiscal year during which that budget is submitted; and

"(iv) the estimated total cost of the program and the estimated cost of the program for (I) the current fiscal year, (II) the fiscal year for which the budget is submitted, and (III) each of the four succeeding fiscal years during which the program is expected to be conducted.

"(b) NEWLY DESIGNATED PROGRAMS.—(1) Not later than February 1 of each year, the head of each covered department or agency shall submit to Congress a report that, with respect to each new special access program of that department or agency, provides—

"(A) notice of the designation of the program as a special access program; and

"(B) justification for such designation.

"(2) A report under paragraph (1) with respect to a program shall include—

"(A) the current estimate of the total program cost for the program; and

"(B) an identification, as applicable, of existing programs or technologies that are similar to the technology, or that have a mission similar to the technology, or that have a mission similar to the mission, of the program that is the subject of the notice.

"(3) In this subsection, the term 'new special access program' means a special access program that has not previously been covered in a notice and justification under this subsection.

"(c) REVISION IN CLASSIFICATION OF PROGRAMS.—(1) Whenever a change in the classification of a special access program of a covered department or agency is planned to be made or whenever classified information concerning a special access program of a covered department or agency is to be declassified and made public, the head of the department or agency shall submit to Congress a report containing a description of the proposed change or the information to be declassified, the reasons for the proposed change or declassification, and notice of any public announcement planned to be made with respect to the proposed change or declassification.

"(2) Except as provided in paragraph (3), a report referred to in paragraph (1) shall be submitted not less than 14 days before the date on which the proposed change, declassification, or public announcement is to occur.

"(3) If the head of the department or agency determines that because of exceptional circumstances the requirement of paragraph (2) cannot be met with respect to a proposed change, declassification, or public announcement concerning a special access program of the department or agency, the head of the department or agency may submit the report required by paragraph (1) regarding the proposed change, declassification, or public announcement at any time before the proposed change, declassification, or public announcement is made and shall include in the report an explanation of the exceptional circumstances.

"(d) REVISION OF CRITERIA FOR DESIGNATING PROGRAMS.—Whenever there is a modification or termination of the policy and criteria used for designating a program of a covered department or agency as a special access program, the head of the department or agency shall promptly notify Congress of such modification or termination. Any such notification shall contain the reasons for the modification or termination and, in the case of a modification, the provisions of the policy as modified.

"(e) WAIVER OF REPORTING REQUIREMENT.—(1) The head of a covered department or agency may waive any requirement under subsection (a), (b), or (c) that certain information be included in a report under that subsection if the head of the department or agency determines that inclusion of that information in the report would adversely affect the national security. Any such waiver shall be made on a case-by-case basis.

"(2) If the head of a department or agency exercises the authority provided under paragraph (1), the head of the department or agency shall provide the information described in that subsection with respect to the special access program concerned, and the justification for the waiver, to Congress.

"(f) INITIATION OF PROGRAMS.—A special access program may not be initiated by a covered department or agency until—

"(1) the appropriate oversight committees are notified of the program; and

"(2) a period of 30 days elapses after such notification is received.

"(g) DEFINITIONS.—For purposes of this section:

"(1) COVERED DEPARTMENT OR AGENCY.—(A) Except as provided in subparagraph (B), the term 'covered department or agency' means any department or agency of the Federal Government that carries out a special access program.

"(B) Such term does not include—

"(i) the Department of Defense (which is required to submit reports on special access programs under section 119 of title 10, United States Code);

"(ii) the National Nuclear Security Administration (which is required to submit reports on special access programs under section 3236 of the National Nuclear Security Administration Act [50 U.S.C. 2426]); or

"(iii) an agency in the Intelligence Community (as defined in section 3(4) of the National Security Act of 1947 (50 U.S.C. 401a)).

"(2) SPECIAL ACCESS PROGRAM.—The term 'special access program' means any program that, under the authority of Executive Order 12356 [formerly set out below] (or any successor Executive order), is established by the head of a department or agency whom the President has designated in the Federal Register as an original 'secret' or 'top secret' classification authority that imposes 'need-to-know' controls or access controls beyond those controls normally required (by regulations applicable to such department or agency) for access to information classified as 'confidential', 'secret', or 'top secret'."

DISCLOSURE OF INFORMATION CONCERNING UNACCOUNTED FOR UNITED STATES PERSONNEL OF COLD WAR, KOREAN CONFLICT, AND VIETNAM ERA

Pub. L. 102–190, div. A, title X, §1082, Dec. 5, 1991, 105 Stat. 1480, as amended by Pub. L. 103–337, div. A, title X, §1036, Oct. 5, 1994, 108 Stat. 2841; Pub. L. 104–106, div. A, title X, §1085, Feb. 10, 1996, 110 Stat. 457, provided that:

"(a) PUBLIC AVAILABILITY OF INFORMATION.—(1) Except as provided in subsection (b), the Secretary of Defense shall, with respect to any information referred to in paragraph (2), place the information in a suitable library-like location within a facility within the National Capital region for public review and photocopying.

"(2) Paragraph (1) applies to any record, live-sighting report, or other information in the custody of the official custodian referred to in subsection (d)(3) that may pertain to the location, treatment, or condition of (A) United States personnel who remain not accounted for as a result of service in the Armed Forces or other Federal Government service during the Korean conflict, the Vietnam era, or the Cold War, or (B) their remains.

"(b) EXCEPTIONS.—(1) The Secretary of Defense may not make a record or other information available to the public pursuant to subsection (a) if—

"(A) the record or other information is exempt from the disclosure requirements of section 552 of title 5, United States Code, by reason of subsection (b) of that section; or

"(B) the record or other information is in a system of records exempt from the requirements of subsection (d) of section 552a of such title pursuant to subsection (j) or (k) of that section.

"(2) The Secretary of Defense may not make a record or other information available to the public pursuant to subsection (a) if the record or other information specifically mentions a person by name unless—

"(A) in the case of a person who is alive (and not incapacitated) and whose whereabouts are known, that person expressly consents in writing to the disclosure of the record or other information; or

"(B) in the case of a person who is dead or incapacitated or whose whereabouts are unknown, a family member or family members of that person determined by the Secretary of Defense to be appropriate for such purpose expressly consent in writing to the disclosure of the record or other information.

"(3)(A) The limitation on disclosure in paragraph (2) does not apply in the case of a person who is dead or incapacitated or whose whereabouts are unknown if the family member or members of that person determined pursuant to subparagraph (B) of that paragraph cannot be located by the Secretary of Defense—

"(i) in the case of a person missing from the Vietnam era, after a reasonable effort; and

"(ii) in the case of a person missing from the Korean Conflict or Cold War, after a period of 90 days from the date on which any record or other information referred to in paragraph (2) is received by the Department of Defense for disclosure review from the Archivist of the United States, the Library of Congress, or the Joint United States-Russian Commission on POW/MIAs.

"(B) Paragraph (2) does not apply to the access of an adult member of the family of a person to any record or information to the extent that the record or other information relates to that person.

"(C) The authority of a person to consent to disclosure of a record or other information for the purposes of paragraph (2) may be delegated to another person or an organization only by means of an express legal power of attorney granted by the person authorized by that paragraph to consent to the disclosure.

"(c) DEADLINES.—(1) In the case of records or other information originated by the Department of Defense, the official custodian shall make such records and other information available to the public pursuant to this section not later than January 2, 1996. Such records or other information shall be made available as soon as a review carried out for the purposes of subsection (b) is completed.

"(2) Whenever a department or agency of the Federal Government receives any record or other information referred to in subsection (a) that is required by this section to be made available to the public, the head of that department or agency shall ensure that such record or other information is provided to the Secretary of Defense, and the Secretary shall make such record or other information available in accordance with subsection (a) as soon as possible and, in any event, not later than one year after the date on which the record or information is received by the department or agency of the Federal Government.

"(3) If the Secretary of Defense determines that the disclosure of any record or other information referred to in subsection (a) by the date required by paragraph (1) or (2) may compromise the safety of any United States personnel referred to in subsection (a)(2) who remain not accounted for but who may still be alive in captivity, then the Secretary may withhold that record or other information from the disclosure otherwise required by this section. Whenever the Secretary makes a determination under the preceding sentence, the Secretary shall immediately notify the President and the Congress of that determination.

"(d) DEFINITIONS.—For purposes of this section:

"(1) The terms 'Korean conflict' and 'Vietnam era' have the meanings given those terms in section 101 of title 38, United States Code.

"(2) The term 'Cold War' means the period from the end of World War II to the beginning of the Korean conflict and the period from the end of the Korean conflict to the beginning of the Vietnam era.

"(3) The term 'official custodian' means—

"(A) in the case of records, reports, and information relating to the Korean conflict or the Cold War, the Archivist of the United States; and

"(B) in the case of records, reports, and information relating to the Vietnam era, the Secretary of Defense."

DISCLOSURE OF INFORMATION CONCERNING AMERICAN PERSONNEL LISTED AS PRISONER, MISSING, OR UNACCOUNTED FOR IN SOUTHEAST ASIA

Pub. L. 100–453, title IV, § 404, Sept. 29, 1988, 102 Stat. 1908, provided that:

"(a) This section is enacted to ensure that current disclosure policy is incorporated into law.

"(b) Except as provided in subsection (c), the head of each department or agency—

"(1) with respect to which funds are authorized under this Act [see Tables for classification], and

"(2) which holds or receives live sighting reports of any United States citizen reported missing in action, prisoner of war, or unaccounted for from the Vietnam Conflict,

shall make available to the next-of-kin of that United States citizen all reports, or portions thereof, held by that department or agency which have been correlated or possibly correlated to that citizen.

"(c) Subsection (b) does not apply with respect to—

"(1) information that would reveal or compromise sources and methods of intelligence collection; or

"(2) specific information that previously has been made available to the next-of-kin.

"(d) The head of each department or agency covered by subsection (a) shall make information available under this section in a timely manner."

EXECUTIVE ORDER NO. 10501

Ex. Ord. No. 10501, Nov. 5, 1953, 18 F.R. 7049, as amended by Ex. Ord. No. 10816, May 7, 1959, 24 F.R. 3777; Ex. Ord. No. 10901, Jan. 9, 1961, 26 F.R. 217; Ex. Ord. No. 10964, Sept. 20, 1961, 26 F.R. 8932; Ex. Ord. No. 10985, Jan. 12, 1962, 27 F.R. 439; Ex. Ord. No. 11097, Feb. 28, 1963, 28 F.R. 2225; Ex. Ord. No. 11382, Nov. 28, 1967, 32 F.R. 16247, which related to safeguarding official information, was superseded by Ex. Ord. No. 11652, Mar. 8, 1972, 37 F.R. 5209, formerly set out below.

EX. ORD. NO. 10865. SAFEGUARDING CLASSIFIED INFORMATION WITHIN INDUSTRY

Ex. Ord. No. 10865, Feb. 20, 1960, 25 F.R. 1583, as amended by Ex. Ord. No. 10909, Jan. 17, 1961, 26 F.R. 508; Ex. Ord. No. 11382, Nov. 28, 1967, 32 F.R. 16247; Ex. Ord. No. 12829, § 203(g), Jan. 6, 1993, 58 F.R. 3479, provided:

WHEREAS it is mandatory that the United States protect itself against hostile or destructive activities by preventing unauthorized disclosures of classified information relating to the national defense; and

WHEREAS it is a fundamental principle of our Government to protect the interests of individuals against unreasonable or unwarranted encroachment; and

WHEREAS I find that the provisions and procedures prescribed by this order are necessary to assure the preservation of the integrity of classified defense information and to protect the national interest; and

WHEREAS I find that those provisions and procedures recognize the interest of individuals affected thereby and provide maximum possible safeguards to protect such interests:

NOW, THEREFORE, under and by virtue of the authority vested in me by the Constitution and statutes of the United States, and as President of the United States and as Commander in Chief of the armed forces of the United States, it is hereby ordered as follows:

SECTION 1. When used in this order, the term "head of a department" means the Secretary of State, the Secretary of Defense, the Secretary of Transportation, the Secretary of Energy, the Nuclear Regulatory Commission, the Administrator of the National Aeronautics and Space Administration, and, in section 4, the Attorney General. The term "head of a department" also means the head of any department or agency, including but not limited to those referenced above with whom the Department of Defense makes an agreement to extend regulations prescribed by the Secretary of Defense concerning authorizations for access to classified information pursuant to Executive Order No. 12829 [set out below].

SEC. 2. An authorization for access to classified information pursuant to Executive Order No. 12829 [set out below] may be granted by the head of a department or his designee, including but not limited to, those officials named in section 8 of this order, to an individual, hereinafter termed an "applicant", for a specific classification category only upon a finding that it is clearly consistent with the national interest to do so.

SEC. 3. Except as provided in section 9 of this order, an authorization for access to a specific classification category may not be finally denied or revoked pursuant to Executive Order No. 12829 [set out below] by the head of a department or his designee, including, but not limited to, those officials named in section 8 of this order, unless the applicant has been given the following:

(1) A written statement of the reasons why his access authorization may be denied or revoked, which shall be as comprehensive and detailed as the national security permits.

(2) A reasonable opportunity to reply in writing under oath or affirmation to the statement of reasons.

(3) After he has filed under oath or affirmation a written reply to the statement of reasons, the form and sufficiency of which may be prescribed by regulations issued by the head of the department concerned, an opportunity to appear personally before the head of the department concerned or his designee including, but not limited to, those officials named in section 8 of this order for the purpose of supporting his eligibility for access authorization and to present evidence on his behalf.

(4) A reasonable time to prepare for that appearance.

(5) An opportunity to be represented by counsel.

(6) An opportunity to cross-examine persons either orally or through written interrogatories in accordance with section 4 on matters not relating to the characterization in the statement of reasons of any organization or individual other than the applicant.

(7) A written notice of the final decision in his case which, if adverse, shall specify whether the head of the department or his designee, including, but not limited to, those officials named in section 8 of this order, found for or against him with respect to each allegation in the statement of reasons.

SEC. 4. (a) An applicant shall be afforded an opportunity to cross-examine persons who have made oral or written statements adverse to the applicant relating to a controverted issue except that any such statement may be received and considered without affording such opportunity in the circumstances described in either of the following paragraphs:

(1) The head of the department supplying the statement certifies that the person who furnished the information is a confidential informant who has been engaged in obtaining intelligence information for the Government and that disclosure of his identity would be substantially harmful to the national interest.

(2) The head of the department concerned or his special designee for that particular purpose has preliminarily determined, after considering information furnished by the investigative agency involved as to the reliability of the person and the accuracy of the statement concerned, that the statement concerned appears to be reliable and material, and the head of the department or such special designee has determined that failure to receive and consider such statement would, in view of the level of access sought, be substantially harmful to the national security and that the person who furnished the information cannot appear to testify (A) due to death, severe illness, or similar cause, in which case the identity of the person and the information to be considered shall be made available to the applicant, or (B) due to some other cause determined by the head of the department to be good and sufficient.

(b) Whenever procedures under paragraphs (1) or (2) of subsection (a) of this section are used (1) the applicant shall be given a summary of the information which shall be as comprehensive and detailed as the national security permits, (2) appropriate consideration shall be accorded to the fact that the applicant did not have an opportunity to cross-examine such person or persons, and (3) a final determination adverse to the applicant shall be made only by the head of the department based upon his personal review of the case.

SEC. 5. (a) Records compiled in the regular course of business, or other physical evidence other than investigative reports, may be received and considered subject to rebuttal without authenticating witnesses, provided that such information has been furnished to the department concerned by an investigative agency pursuant to its responsibilities in connection with assisting the head of the department concerned to safeguard classified information within industry pursuant to this order.

(b) Records compiled in the regular course of business, or other physical evidence other than investigative reports, relating to a controverted issue which, because they are classified, may not be inspected by the applicant, may be received and considered provided that: (1) the head of the department concerned or his special designee for that purpose has made a preliminary determination that such physical evidence appears to be material, (2) the head of the department concerned or such designee has made a determination that failure to receive and consider such physical evidence would, in view of the level of access sought, be substantially harmful to the national security, and (3) to the extent that the national security permits, a summary or description of such physical evidence is made available to the applicant. In every such case, information as to the authenticity and accuracy of such physical evidence furnished by the investigative agency involved shall be considered. In such instances a final determination adverse to the applicant shall be made only by the head of the department based upon his personal review of the case.

SEC. 6. The head of a department of the United States or his representative, may issue, in appropriate cases, invitations and requests to appear and testify in order that the applicant may have the opportunity to cross-examine as provided by this order. Whenever a witness is so invited or requested to appear and testify at a proceeding and the witness is an officer or employee of the executive branch of the Government or a member of the armed forces of the United States, and the proceeding involves the activity in connection with which the witness is employed, travel expenses and per diem are authorized as provided by the Standardized Government Travel Regulations or the Joint Travel Regulations, as appropriate. In all other cases (including non-Government employees as well as officers or employees of the executive branch of the Government or members of the armed forces of the United States not covered by the foregoing sentence), transportation in kind and reimbursement for actual expenses are authorized in an amount not to exceed the amount payable under Standardized Government Travel Regulations. An officer or employee of the executive branch of the Government or a member of the armed forces of the United States who is invited or requested to appear pursuant to this paragraph shall be deemed to be in the performance of his official duties. So far as the national security permits, the head of the investigative agency involved shall cooperate with the Secretary, the Administrator, or the head of the other department or agency, as the case may be, in identifying persons who have made statements adverse to the applicant and in assisting him in making them available for cross-examination. If a person so invited is an officer or employee of the executive branch of the government or a member of the armed forces of the United States, the head of the department or agency concerned shall cooperate in making that person available for cross-examination.

SEC. 7. Any determination under this order adverse to an applicant shall be a determination in terms of the national interest and shall in no sense be a determination as to the loyalty of the applicant concerned.

SEC. 8. Except as otherwise specified in the preceding provisions of this order, any authority vested in the head of a department by this order may be delegated to the the [sic] deputy of that department, or the principal assistant to the head of that department, as the case may be.

SEC. 9. Nothing contained in this order shall be deemed to limit or affect the responsibility and powers of the head of a department to deny or revoke access to a specific classification category if the security of the nation so requires. Such authority may not be delegated and may be exercised only when the head of a department determines that the procedures prescribed in sections 3, 4, and 5 cannot be invoked consistently with the national security and such determination shall be conclusive.

MODIFICATION OF EXECUTIVE ORDER NO. 10865

Ex. Ord. No. 10865, Feb. 20, 1960, 25 F.R. 1583, as amended, set out above, when referring to functions of the Atomic Energy Commission is modified to provide that all such functions shall be exercised by the Secretary of Energy and the Nuclear Regulatory Commission, see section 4(a)(1) of Ex. Ord. No. 12038, Feb. 3, 1978, 43 F.R. 4957, set out under section 7151 of Title 42, The Public Health and Welfare.

EXECUTIVE ORDER NO. 10985

Ex. Ord. No. 10985, Jan. 12, 1962, 27 F.R. 439, which amended Executive Order No. 10501, which related to safeguarding official information, was superseded by Ex. Ord. No. 11652, Mar. 8, 1972, 37 F.R. 5209, formerly set out below.

EXECUTIVE ORDER NO. 11097

Ex. Ord. No. 11097, Feb. 28, 1963, 28 F.R. 2225, which amended Executive Order No. 10501, which related to safeguarding official information, was superseded by Ex. Ord. No. 11652, Mar. 8, 1972, 37 F.R. 5209, formerly set out below.

EXECUTIVE ORDER NO. 11652

Ex. Ord. No. 11652, Mar. 8, 1972, 37 F.R. 5209, as amended by Ex. Ord. No. 11714, Apr. 24, 1973, 38 F.R. 10245; Ex. Ord. No. 11862, June 11, 1975, 40 F.R. 25197; Ex. Ord. No. 12038, Feb. 3, 1978, 43 F.R. 4957, which related to the classification and declassification of national security information and material, was revoked by Ex. Ord. No. 12065, June 28, 1978, 43 F.R. 28949, formerly set out below.

EX. ORD. NO. 11932. CLASSIFICATION OF CERTAIN INFORMATION AND MATERIAL OBTAINED FROM ADVISORY BODIES CREATED TO IMPLEMENT THE INTERNATIONAL ENERGY PROGRAM

Ex. Ord. No. 11932, Aug. 4, 1976, 41 F.R. 32691, provided:

The United States has entered into the Agreement on an International Energy Program of November 18, 1974, which created the International Energy Agency. This program is a substantial factor in the conduct of our foreign relations and an important element of our national security. The effectiveness of the Agreement depends significantly upon the provision and exchange of information and material by participants in advisory bodies created by the International Energy Agency. Confidentiality is essential to assure the free and open discussion necessary to accomplish the tasks assigned to those bodies. I have consulted with the Secretary of State, the Attorney General and the Administrator of the Federal Energy Administration concerning the handling and safeguarding of information and material in the possession of the United States which has been obtained pursuant to the program, and I find that some of such information and material requires protection as provided in Executive Order No. 11652 of March 8, 1972, as amended [formerly set out above].

NOW, THEREFORE, by virtue of the authority vested in me by the Constitution and statutes of the United States, and as President of the United States, it is hereby ordered as follows:

SECTION 1. Information and material obtained pursuant to the International Energy Program and which requires protection against unauthorized disclosure in the interest of the national defense or foreign relations of the United States shall be classified pursuant to Executive Order No. 11652 of March 8, 1972, as amended [formerly set out above]. The Secretary of State shall have the responsibility for the classification, declassification and safeguarding of information and material in the possession of the United States Government which has been obtained pursuant to:

(a) Section 252(c)(3), (d)(2), or (e)(3) of the Energy Policy and Conservation Act (89 Stat. 871; 42 U.S.C. 6272(c)(3), (d)(2), (e)(3)), or

(b) The Voluntary Agreement and Program relating to the International Energy Program (40 F.R. 16041, April 8, 1975), or

(c) Any similar Voluntary Agreement and Program entered into under the Energy Policy and Conservation Act [42 U.S.C. 6201 et seq.] after the date of this Order.

SEC. 2. Information or material classified pursuant to Section 1 of this Order may be exempted from the General Declassification Schedule established by Section 5 of Executive Order No. 11652 [formerly set out above] if it was obtained by the United States on the understanding that it be kept in confidence, or if it might otherwise be exempted under Section 5(B) of such Order.

SEC. 3. (a) Within 60 days of the date of this Order, the Secretary of State shall promulgate regulations which implement his responsibilities under this Order.

(b) The directives issued under Section 6 of Executive Order No. 11652 [formerly set out above] shall not apply to information and material classified under this Order. However, the regulations promulgated by the Secretary of State shall:

(1) conform, to the extent practicable, to the policies set forth in Section 6 of Executive Order No. 11652 [formerly set out above], and

(2) provide that he may take such measures as he deems necessary and appropriate to ensure the confidentiality of any information and material classified under this Order that may remain in the custody or control of any person outside the United States Government.

GERALD R. FORD.

EXECUTIVE ORDER NO. 12065

Ex. Ord. No. 12065, June 28, 1978, 43 F.R. 28949, as amended by Ex. Ord. No. 12148, July 20, 1979, 44 F.R. 43239; Ex. Ord. No. 12163, Sept. 29, 1979, 44 F.R. 56673, which related to classification and declassification of national security information and material, was revoked by Ex. Ord. No. 12356, Apr. 2, 1982, 47 F.R. 14874, 15557, formerly set out below.

EXECUTIVE ORDER NO. 12356

Ex. Ord. No. 12356, Apr. 2, 1982, 47 F.R. 14874, 15557, which prescribed a uniform system for classifying, declassifying, and safeguarding national security information, was revoked by Ex. Ord. No. 12958, § 6.1(d), Apr. 17, 1995, 60 F.R. 19843, set out below.

EX. ORD. NO. 12812. DECLASSIFICATION AND RELEASE OF MATERIALS PERTAINING TO PRISONERS OF WAR AND MISSING IN ACTION

Ex. Ord. No. 12812, July 22, 1992, 57 F.R. 32879, provided:

WHEREAS, the Senate, by S. Res. 324 of July 2, 1992, has asked that I "expeditiously issue an Executive order requiring all executive branch departments and agencies to declassify and publicly release without compromising United States national security all documents, files, and other materials pertaining to POWs and MIAs;" and

WHEREAS, indiscriminate release of classified material could jeopardize continuing United States Government efforts to achieve the fullest possible accounting of Vietnam-era POWs and MIAs; and

WHEREAS, I have concluded that the public interest would be served by the declassification and public release of materials pertaining to Vietnam-era POWs and MIAs as provided below;

NOW, THEREFORE, by the authority vested in me as President by the Constitution and the laws of the United States of America, I hereby order as follows:

SECTION 1. All executive departments and agencies shall expeditiously review all documents, files, and other materials pertaining to American POWs and MIAs lost in Southeast Asia for the purposes of declassification in accordance with the standards and procedures of Executive Order No. 12356 [formerly set out above].

SEC. 2. All executive departments and agencies shall make publicly available documents, files, and other materials declassified pursuant to section 1, except for those the disclosure of which would constitute a clearly unwarranted invasion of personal privacy of returnees, family members of POWs and MIAs, or other persons, or would impair the deliberative processes of the executive branch.

SEC. 3. This order is not intended to create any right or benefit, substantive or procedural, enforceable by a party against the United States, its agencies or instrumentalities, its officers or employees, or any other person.

GEORGE BUSH.

EX. ORD. NO. 12829. NATIONAL INDUSTRIAL SECURITY PROGRAM

Ex. Ord. No. 12829, Jan. 6, 1993, 58 F.R. 3479, as amended by Ex. Ord. No. 12885, Dec. 14, 1993, 58 F.R. 65863, provided:

This order establishes a National Industrial Security Program to safeguard Federal Government classified information that is released to contractors, licensees, and grantees of the United States Government. To promote our national interests, the United States Government issues contracts, licenses, and grants to nongovernment organizations. When these arrangements require access to classified information, the national security requires that this information be safeguarded in a manner equivalent to its protection within the executive branch of Government. The national security also requires that our industrial security program promote the economic and technological interests of the United States. Redundant, overlapping, or unnecessary requirements impede those interests. Therefore, the National Industrial Security Program shall serve as a single, integrated, cohesive industrial security program to protect classified information and to preserve our Nation's economic and technological interests.

Therefore, by the authority vested in me as President by the Constitution and the laws of the United States of America, including the Atomic Energy Act of 1954, as amended (42 U.S.C. 2011–2286) [42 U.S.C. 2011 *et seq.*], the National Security Act of 1947, as amended (codified as amended in scattered sections of the United States Code) [see Short Title note set out under section 401 of this title], and the Federal Advisory Committee Act, as amended (5 U.S.C. App. 2) [5 App. U.S.C.], it is hereby ordered as follows:

PART 1. ESTABLISHMENT AND POLICY

SECTION 101. *Establishment.* (a) There is established a National Industrial Security Program. The purpose of this program is to safeguard classified information that may be released or has been released to current, prospective, or former contractors, licensees, or grantees of United States agencies. For the purposes of this order, the terms "contractor, licensee, or grantee" means current, prospective, or former contractors, licensees, or grantees of United States agencies. The National Industrial Security Program shall be applicable to all executive branch departments and agencies.

(b) The National Industrial Security Program shall provide for the protection of information classified pursuant to Executive Order No. 12356 of April 2, 1982 [formerly set out above], or its successor, and the Atomic Energy Act of 1954, as amended [42 U.S.C. 2011 *et seq.*].

(c) For the purposes of this order, the term "contractor" does not include individuals engaged under personal services contracts.

SEC. 102. *Policy Direction.* (a) The National Security Council shall provide overall policy direction for the National Industrial Security Program.

(b) The Director of the Information Security Oversight Office, established under Executive Order No. 12356 of April 2, 1982 [formerly set out above], shall be responsible for implementing and monitoring the National Industrial Security Program and shall:

(1) develop, in consultation with the agencies, and promulgate subject to the approval of the National Security Council, directives for the implementation of this order, which shall be binding on the agencies;

(2) oversee agency, contractor, licensee, and grantee actions to ensure compliance with this order and implementing directives;

(3) review all agency implementing regulations, internal rules, or guidelines. The Director shall require any regulation, rule, or guideline to be changed if it is not consistent with this order or implementing directives. Any such decision by the Director may be appealed to the National Security Council. The agency regulation, rule, or guideline shall remain in effect pending a prompt decision on the appeal;

(4) have the authority, pursuant to terms of applicable contracts, licenses, grants, or regulations, to conduct on-site reviews of the implementation of the National Industrial Security Program by each agency, contractor, licensee, and grantee that has access to or stores classified information and to require of each agency, contractor, licensee, and grantee those reports, information, and other cooperation that may be necessary to fulfill the Director's responsibilities. If these reports, inspections, or access to specific classified information, or other forms of cooperation, would pose an exceptional national security risk, the affected agency head or the senior official designated under section 203(a) of this order may request the National Security Council to deny access to the Director. The Director shall not have access pending a prompt decision by the National Security Council;

(5) report any violations of this order or its implementing directives to the head of the agency or to the senior official designated under section 203(a) of this order so that corrective action, if appropriate, may be taken. Any such report pertaining to the implementation of the National Industrial Security Program by a contractor, licensee, or grantee shall be directed to the agency that is exercising operational oversight over the contractor, licensee, or grantee under section 202 of this order;

(6) consider and take action on complaints and suggestions from persons within or outside the Government with respect to the administration of the National Industrial Security Program;

(7) consider, in consultation with the advisory committee established by this order, affected agencies, contractors, licensees, and grantees, and recommend to the President through the National Security Council changes to this order; and

(8) report at least annually to the President through the National Security Council on the implementation of the National Industrial Security Program.

(c) Nothing in this order shall be construed to supersede the authority of the Secretary of Energy or the Nuclear Regulatory Commission under the Atomic Energy Act of 1954, as amended [42 U.S.C. 2011 *et seq.*], or the authority of the Director of Central Intelligence under the National Security Act of 1947, as amended [see Short Title note set out under section 401 of this title], or Executive Order No. 12333 of December 8, 1981 [50 U.S.C. 401 note].

SEC. 103. *National Industrial Security Program Policy Advisory Committee.* (a) *Establishment.* There is established the National Industrial Security Program Policy Advisory Committee ("Committee"). The Director of the Information Security Oversight Office shall serve as Chairman of the Committee and appoint the members of the Committee. The members of the Committee shall be the representatives of those departments and agencies most affected by the National Industrial Security Program and nongovernment representatives of contractors, licensees, or grantees involved with classified contracts, licenses, or grants, as determined by the Chairman.

(b) *Functions.* (1) The Committee members shall advise the Chairman of the Committee on all matters concerning the policies of the National Industrial Security Program, including recommended changes to those policies as reflected in this order, its implementing directives, or the operating manual established under this order, and serve as a forum to discuss policy issues in dispute.

(2) The Committee shall meet at the request of the Chairman, but at least twice during the calendar year.

(c) *Administration.* (1) Members of the Committee shall serve without compensation for their work on the Committee. However, nongovernment members may be allowed travel expenses, including per diem in lieu of subsistence, as authorized by law for persons serving intermittently in the Government service (5 U.S.C. 5701–5707).

(2) To the extent permitted by law and subject to the availability of funds, the Administrator of General Services shall provide the Committee with administrative services, facilities, staff, and other support services necessary for the performance of its functions.

(d) *General.* Notwithstanding any other Executive order, the functions of the President under the Federal Advisory Committee Act, as amended [5 App. U.S.C.], except that of reporting to the Congress, which are applicable to the Committee, shall be performed by the Administrator of General Services in accordance with the guidelines and procedures established by the General Services Administration.

PART 2. OPERATIONS

SEC. 201. *National Industrial Security Program Operating Manual.* (a) The Secretary of Defense, in consultation with all affected agencies and with the concurrence of the Secretary of Energy, the Nuclear Regulatory Commission, and the Director of Central Intelligence, shall issue and maintain a National Industrial Security Program Operating Manual (''Manual''). The Secretary of Energy and the Nuclear Regulatory Commission shall prescribe and issue that portion of the Manual that pertains to information classified under the Atomic Energy Act of 1954, as amended [42 U.S.C. 2011 *et seq.*]. The Director of Central Intelligence shall prescribe and issue that portion of the Manual that pertains to intelligence sources and methods, including Sensitive Compartmented Information.

(b) The Manual shall prescribe specific requirements, restrictions, and other safeguards that are necessary to preclude unauthorized disclosure and control authorized disclosure of classified information to contractors, licensees, or grantees. The Manual shall apply to the release of classified information during all phases of the contracting process including bidding, negotiation, award, performance, and termination of contracts, the licensing process, or the grant process, with or under the control of departments or agencies.

(c) The Manual shall also prescribe requirements, restrictions, and other safeguards that are necessary to protect special classes of classified information, including Restricted Data, Formerly Restricted Data, intelligence sources and methods information, Sensitive Compartmented Information, and Special Access Program information.

(d) In establishing particular requirements, restrictions, and other safeguards within the Manual, the Secretary of Defense, the Secretary of Energy, the Nuclear Regulatory Commission, and the Director of Central Intelligence shall take into account these factors: (i) the damage to the national security that reasonably could be expected to result from an unauthorized disclosure; (ii) the existing or anticipated threat to the disclosure of information; and (iii) the short- and long-term costs of the requirements, restrictions, and other safeguards.

(e) To the extent that is practicable and reasonable, the requirements, restrictions, and safeguards that the Manual establishes for the protection of classified information by contractors, licensees, and grantees shall be consistent with the requirements, restrictions, and safeguards that directives implementing Executive Order No. 12356 of April 2, 1982 [formerly set out above], or the Atomic Energy Act of 1954, as amended, establish for the protection of classified information by agencies. Upon request by the Chairman of the Committee, the Secretary of Defense shall provide an explanation and justification for any requirement, restriction, or safeguard that results in a standard for the protection of classified information by contractors, licensees, and grantees that differs from the standard that applies to agencies.

(f) The Manual shall be issued to correspond as closely as possible to pertinent decisions of the Secretary of Defense and the Director of Central Intelligence made pursuant to the recommendations of the Joint Security Review Commission and to revisions to the security classification system that result from Presidential Review Directive 29, but in any event no later than June 30, 1994.

SEC. 202. *Operational Oversight.* (a) The Secretary of Defense shall serve as Executive Agent for inspecting and monitoring the contractors, licensees, and grantees who require or will require access to, or who store or will store classified information; and for determining the eligibility for access to classified information of contractors, licensees, and grantees and their respective employees. The heads of agencies shall enter into agreements with the Secretary of Defense that establish the terms of the Secretary's responsibilities on behalf of these agency heads.

(b) The Director of Central Intelligence retains authority over access to intelligence sources and methods, including Sensitive Compartmented Information. The Director of Central Intelligence may inspect and monitcr [sic] contractor, licensee, and grantee programs and facilities that involve access to such information or may enter into written agreements with the Secretary of Defense, as Executive Agent, to inspect and monitor these programs or facilities, in whole or in part, on the Director's behalf.

(c) The Secretary of Energy and the Nuclear Regulatory Commission retain authority over access to information under their respective programs classified under the Atomic Energy Act of 1954, as amended [42 U.S.C. 2011 *et seq.*]. The Secretary or the Commission may inspect and monitor contractor, licensee, and grantee programs and facilities that involve access to such information or may enter into written agreements with the Secretary of Defense, as Executive Agent, to inspect and monitor these programs or facilities, in whole or in part, on behalf of the Secretary or the Commission, respectively.

(d) The Executive Agent shall have the authority to issue, after consultation with affected agencies, standard forms or other standardization that will promote the implementation of the National Industrial Security Program.

SEC. 203. *Implementation.* (a) The head of each agency that enters into classified contracts, licenses, or grants shall designate a senior agency official to direct and administer the agency's implementation and compliance with the National Industrial Security Program.

(b) Agency implementing regulations, internal rules, or guidelines shall be consistent with this order, its implementing directives, and the Manual. Agencies shall issue these regulations, rules, or guidelines no later than 180 days from the issuance of the Manual. They may incorporate all or portions of the Manual by reference.

(c) Each agency head or the senior official designated under paragraph (a) above shall take appropriate and prompt corrective action whenever a violation of this order, its implementing directives, or the Manual occurs.

(d) The senior agency official designated under paragraph (a) above shall account each year for the costs within the agency associated with the implementation of the National Industrial Security Program. These costs shall be reported to the Director of the Information Security Oversight Office, who shall include them in the reports to the President prescribed by this order.

(e) The Secretary of Defense, with the concurrence of the Administrator of General Services, the Administrator of the National Aeronautics and Space Administration, and such other agency heads or officials who may be responsible, shall amend the Federal Acquisition Regulation to be consistent with the implementation of the National Industrial Security Program.

(f) All contracts, licenses, or grants that involve access to classified information and that are advertised or proposed following the issuance of agency regulations, rules, or guidelines described in paragraph (b) above shall comply with the National Industrial Security Program. To the extent that is feasible, economical, and permitted by law, agencies shall amend, modify, or convert preexisting contracts, licenses, or grants, or previously advertised or proposed contracts, licenses, or grants, that involve access to classified information for operation under the National Industrial Security Program. Any direct inspection or monitoring of contractors, licensees, or grantees specified by this order shall be carried out pursuant to the terms of a contract, license, grant, or regulation.

(g) Executive Order No. 10865 of February 20, 1960 [set out above], as amended by Executive Order No. 10909 of January 17, 1961, and Executive Order No. 11382 of November 27, 1967, is hereby amended as follows:

(1) Section 1(a) and (b) are revoked as of the effective date of this order.

(2) Section 1(c) is renumbered as Section 1 and is amended to read as follows:

"SECTION 1. When used in this order, the term 'head of a department' means the Secretary of State, the Secretary of Defense, the Secretary of Transportation, the Secretary of Energy, the Nuclear Regulatory Commission, the Administrator of the National Aeronautics and Space Administration, and, in section 4, the Attorney General. The term 'head of a department' also means the head of any department or agency, including but not limited to those referenced above with whom the Department of Defense makes an agreement to extend regulations prescribed by the Secretary of Defense concerning authorizations for access to classified information pursuant to Executive Order No. 12829."

(3) Section 2 is amended by inserting the words "pursuant to Executive Order No. 12829" after the word "information."

(4) Section 3 is amended by inserting the words "pursuant to Executive Order No. 12829" between the words "revoked" and "by" in the second clause of that section.

(5) Section 6 is amended by striking out the words "The Secretary of State, the Secretary of Defense, the Administrator of the National Aeronautics and Space Administration, the Secretary of Transportation, or his representative, or the head of any other department or agency of the United States with which the Department of Defense makes an agreement under section (1)(b)," at the beginning of the first sentence, and inserting in their place "The head of a department of the United States . . . ."

(6) Section 8 is amended by striking out paragraphs (1) through (7) and inserting in their place ". . . the deputy of that department, or the principal assistant to the head of that department, as the case may be."

(h) All delegations, rules, regulations, orders, directives, agreements, contracts, licenses, and grants issued under preexisting authorities, including section 1(a) and (b) of Executive Order No. 10865 of February 20, 1960, as amended, by Executive Order No. 10909 of January 17, 1961, and Executive Order No. 11382 of November 27, 1967, shall remain in full force and effect until amended, modified, or terminated pursuant to authority of this order.

(i) This order shall be effective immediately.

EX. ORD. NO. 12937. DECLASSIFICATION OF SELECTED RECORDS WITHIN NATIONAL ARCHIVES OF UNITED STATES

Ex. Ord. No. 12937, Nov. 10, 1994, 59 F.R. 59097, provided:

By the authority vested in me as President by the Constitution and the laws of the United States of America, it is hereby ordered:

SECTION 1. The records in the National Archives of the United States referenced in the list accompanying this order are hereby declassified.

SEC. 2. The Archivist of the United States shall take such actions as are necessary to make such records available for public research no later than 30 days from the date of this Order, except to the extent that the head of an affected agency and the Archivist have determined that specific information within such records must be protected from disclosure pursuant to an authorized exemption to the Freedom of Information Act, 5 U.S.C. 552, other than the exemption that pertains to national security information.

SEC. 3. Nothing contained in this order shall create any right or benefit, substantive or procedural, enforceable by any party against the United States, its agencies or instrumentalities, its officers or employees, or any other person.

WILLIAM J. CLINTON.

Records in the following record groups ("RG") in the National Archives of the United States shall be declassified. Page numbers are approximate. A complete list of the selected records is available from the Archivist of the United States.

I. All unreviewed World War II and earlier records, including:		
A.	RG 18, Army Air Forces	1,722,400 pp.
B.	RG 65, Federal Bureau of Investigation	362,500 pp.
C.	RG 127, United States Marine Corps	195,000 pp.
D.	RG 216, Office of Censorship	112,500 pp.
E.	RG 226, Office of Strategic Services	415,000 pp.
F.	RG 60, United States Occupation Headquarters	4,422,500 pp.
G.	RG 331, Allied Operational and Occupation Headquarters, World War II (including 350 reels of Allied Force Headquarters)	3,097,500 pp.
H.	RG 332, United States Theaters of War, World War II	1,182,500 pp.
I.	RG 338, Mediterranean Theater of Operations and European Command	9,500,000 pp.
	Subtotal for World War II and earlier	21.0 million pp.
II. Post-1945 Collections (Military and Civil)		
A.	RG 19, Bureau of Ships, Pre-1950 General Correspondence (selected records)	1,732,500 pp.
B.	RG 51, Bureau of the Budget, 52.12 Budget Preparation Branch, 1952–69	142,500 pp.
C.	RG 72, Bureau of Aeronautics (Navy) (selected records)	5,655,000 pp.
D.	RG 166, Foreign Agricultural Service, Narrative Reports, 1955–61	1,272,500 pp.
E.	RG 313, Naval Operating Forces (selected records)	407,500 pp.
F.	RG 319, Office of the Chief of Military History Manuscripts and Background Papers (selected records)	933,000 pp.
G.	RG 337, Headquarters, Army Ground Forces (selected records)	1,269,700 pp.
H.	RG 341, Headquarters, United States Air Force (selected records)	4,870,000 pp.
I.	RG 389, Office of the Provost Marshal General (selected records)	448,000 pp.
J.	RG 391, United States Army Regular Army Mobil Units	240,000 pp.
K.	RG 428, General Records of the Department of the Navy (selected records)	31,250 pp.
L.	RG 472, Army Vietnam Collection (selected records)	5,864,000 pp.
	Subtotal for Other	22.9 million pp.
	TOTAL	43.9 million pp.

EX. ORD. NO. 12951. RELEASE OF IMAGERY ACQUIRED BY SPACE-BASED NATIONAL INTELLIGENCE RECONNAISSANCE SYSTEMS

Ex. Ord. No. 12951, Feb. 22, 1995, 60 F.R. 10789, provided:

By the authority vested in me as President by the Constitution and the laws of the United States of America and in order to release certain scientifically or environmentally useful imagery acquired by space-based national intelligence reconnaissance systems, consistent with the national security, it is hereby ordered as follows:

SECTION 1. *Public Release of Historical Intelligence Imagery*. Imagery acquired by the space-based national intelligence reconnaissance systems known as the Corona, Argon, and Lanyard missions shall, within 18 months of the date of this order, be declassified and transferred to the National Archives and Records Administration with a copy sent to the United States Geological Survey of the Department of the Interior consistent with procedures approved by the Director of Central Intelligence and the Archivist of the United States. Upon transfer, such imagery shall be deemed declassified and shall be made available to the public.

SEC. 2. *Review for Future Public Release of Intelligence Imagery*. (a) All information that meets the criteria in section 2(b) of this order shall be kept secret in the interests of national defense and foreign policy until deemed otherwise by the Director of Central Intelligence. In consultation with the Secretaries of State and Defense, the Director of Central Intelligence shall establish a comprehensive program for the periodic review of imagery from systems other than the Corona, Argon, and Lanyard missions, with the objective of making available to the public as much imagery as possible consistent with the interests of national defense and foreign policy. For imagery from obsolete broad-area film-return systems other than Corona, Argon, and Lanyard missions, this review shall be completed within 5 years of the date of this order. Review of imagery from any other system that the Director of Central Intelligence deems to be obsolete shall be accomplished according to a timetable established by the Director of Central Intelligence. The Director of Central Intelligence shall report annually to the President on the implementation of this order.

(b) The criteria referred to in section 2(a) of this order consist of the following: imagery acquired by a space-based national intelligence reconnaissance system other than the Corona, Argon, and Lanyard missions.

SEC. 3. *General Provisions*. (a) This order prescribes a comprehensive and exclusive system for the public release of imagery acquired by space-based national intelligence reconnaissance systems. This order is the exclusive Executive order governing the public release of imagery for purposes of section 552(b)(1) of the Freedom of Information Act [5 U.S.C. 552(b)(1)].

(b) Nothing contained in this order shall create any right or benefit, substantive or procedural, enforceable by any party against the United States, its agencies or instrumentalities, its officers or employees, or any other person.

SEC. 4. *Definition*. As used herein, "imagery" means the product acquired by space-based national intelligence reconnaissance systems that provides a likeness or representation of any natural or man-made feature or related objective or activities and satellite positional data acquired at the same time the likeness or representation was acquired.

WILLIAM J. CLINTON.

EX. ORD. NO. 12958. CLASSIFIED NATIONAL SECURITY INFORMATION

Ex. Ord. No. 12958, Apr. 17, 1995, 60 F.R. 19825, as amended by Ex. Ord. No. 12972, Sept. 18, 1995, 60 F.R. 48863; Ex. Ord. No. 13142, Nov. 19, 1999, 64 F.R. 66089, provided:

This order prescribes a uniform system for classifying, safeguarding, and declassifying national security information. Our democratic principles require that the American people be informed of the activities of their Government. Also, our Nation's progress depends on the free flow of information. Nevertheless, throughout our history, the national interest has required that certain information be maintained in confidence in order to protect our citizens, our democratic institutions, and our participation within the community of nations. Protecting information critical to our Nation's security remains a priority. In recent years, however, dramatic changes have altered, although not eliminated, the national security threats that we confront. These changes provide a greater opportunity to emphasize our commitment to open Government.

NOW, THEREFORE, by the authority vested in me as President by the Constitution and the laws of the United States of America, it is hereby ordered as follows:

PART 1—ORIGINAL CLASSIFICATION

SECTION 1.1. *Definitions*. For purposes of this order:

(a) "National security" means the national defense or foreign relations of the United States.

(b) "Information" means any knowledge that can be communicated or documentary material, regardless of its physical form or characteristics, that is owned by, produced by or for, or is under the control of the United States Government. "Control" means the authority of the agency that originates information, or its successor in function, to regulate access to the information.

(c) "Classified national security information" (hereafter "classified information") means information that has been determined pursuant to this order or any predecessor order to require protection against unauthorized disclosure and is marked to indicate its classified status when in documentary form.

(d) "Foreign Government Information" means:

(1) information provided to the United States Government by a foreign government or governments, an international organization of governments, or any element thereof, with the expectation that the information, the source of the information, or both, are to be held in confidence;

(2) information produced by the United States pursuant to or as a result of a joint arrangement with a foreign government or governments, or an international organization of governments, or any element thereof, requiring that the information, the arrangement, or both, are to be held in confidence; or

(3) information received and treated as "Foreign Government Information" under the terms of a predecessor order.

(e) "Classification" means the act or process by which information is determined to be classified information.

(f) "Original classification" means an initial determination that information requires, in the interest of national security, protection against unauthorized disclosure.

(g) "Original classification authority" means an individual authorized in writing, either by the President, or by agency heads or other officials designated by the President, to classify information in the first instance.

(h) "Unauthorized disclosure" means a communication or physical transfer of classified information to an unauthorized recipient.

(i) "Agency" means any "Executive agency," as defined in 5 U.S.C. 105; any "Military department" as defined in 5 U.S.C. 102; and any other entity within the executive branch that comes into the possession of classified information.

(j) "Senior agency official" means the official designated by the agency head under section 5.6(c) of this order to direct and administer the agency's program under which information is classified, safeguarded, and declassified.

(k) "Confidential source" means any individual or organization that has provided, or that may reasonably be expected to provide, information to the United States on matters pertaining to the national security with the expectation that the information or relationship, or both, are to be held in confidence.

(*l*) "Damage to the national security" means harm to the national defense or foreign relations of the United States from the unauthorized disclosure of information, to include the sensitivity, value, and utility of that information.

SEC. 1.2. *Classification Standards*. (a) Information may be originally classified under the terms of this order only if all of the following conditions are met:

(1) an original classification authority is classifying the information;

(2) the information is owned by, produced by or for, or is under the control of the United States Government;

(3) the information falls within one or more of the categories of information listed in section 1.5 of this order; and

(4) the original classification authority determines that the unauthorized disclosure of the information reasonably could be expected to result in damage to the national security and the original classification authority is able to identify or describe the damage.

(b) If there is significant doubt about the need to classify information, it shall not be classified. This provision does not:

(1) amplify or modify the substantive criteria or procedures for classification; or

(2) create any substantive or procedural rights subject to judicial review.

(c) Classified information shall not be declassified automatically as a result of any unauthorized disclosure of identical or similar information.

SEC. 1.3. *Classification Levels.* (a) Information may be classified at one of the following three levels:

(1) "Top Secret" shall be applied to information, the unauthorized disclosure of which reasonably could be expected to cause exceptionally grave damage to the national security that the original classification authority is able to identify or describe.

(2) "Secret" shall be applied to information, the unauthorized disclosure of which reasonably could be expected to cause serious damage to the national security that the original classification authority is able to identify or describe.

(3) "Confidential" shall be applied to information, the unauthorized disclosure of which reasonably could be expected to cause damage to the national security that the original classification authority is able to identify or describe.

(b) Except as otherwise provided by statute, no other terms shall be used to identify United States classified information.

(c) If there is significant doubt about the appropriate level of classification, it shall be classified at the lower level.

SEC. 1.4. *Classification Authority.* (a) The authority to classify information originally may be exercised only by:

(1) the President;

(2) agency heads and officials designated by the President in the Federal Register; or

(3) United States Government officials delegated this authority pursuant to paragraph (c), below.

(b) Officials authorized to classify information at a specified level are also authorized to classify information at a lower level.

(c) Delegation of original classification authority.

(1) Delegations of original classification authority shall be limited to the minimum required to administer this order. Agency heads are responsible for ensuring that designated subordinate officials have a demonstrable and continuing need to exercise this authority.

(2) "Top Secret" original classification authority may be delegated only by the President or by an agency head or official designated pursuant to paragraph (a)(2), above.

(3) "Secret" or "Confidential" original classification authority may be delegated only by the President; an agency head or official designated pursuant to paragraph (a)(2), above; or the senior agency official, provided that official has been delegated "Top Secret" original classification authority by the agency head.

(4) Each delegation of original classification authority shall be in writing and the authority shall not be redelegated except as provided in this order. Each delegation shall identify the official by name or position title.

(d) Original classification authorities must receive training in original classification as provided in this order and its implementing directives.

(e) Exceptional cases. When an employee, contractor, licensee, certificate holder, or grantee of an agency that does not have original classification authority originates information believed by that person to require classification, the information shall be protected in a manner consistent with this order and its implementing directives. The information shall be transmitted promptly as provided under this order or its implementing directives to the agency that has appropriate subject matter interest and classification authority with respect to this information. That agency shall decide within 30 days whether to classify this information. If it is not clear which agency has classification responsibility for this information, it shall be sent to the Director of the Information Security Oversight Office. The Director shall determine the agency having primary subject matter interest and forward the information, with appropriate recommendations, to that agency for a classification determination.

SEC. 1.5. *Classification Categories.*

Information may not be considered for classification unless it concerns:

(a) military plans, weapons systems, or operations;

(b) foreign government information;

(c) intelligence activities (including special activities), intelligence sources or methods, or cryptology;

(d) foreign relations or foreign activities of the United States, including confidential sources;

(e) scientific, technological, or economic matters relating to the national security;

(f) United States Government programs for safeguarding nuclear materials or facilities; or

(g) vulnerabilities or capabilities of systems, installations, projects or plans relating to the national security.

SEC. 1.6. *Duration of Classification.* (a) At the time of original classification, the original classification authority shall attempt to establish a specific date or event for declassification based upon the duration of the national security sensitivity of the information. The date or event shall not exceed the time frame in paragraph (b), below.

(b) If the original classification authority cannot determine an earlier specific date or event for declassification, information shall be marked for declassification 10 years from the date of the original decision, except as provided in paragraph (d), below.

(c) An original classification authority may extend the duration of classification or reclassify specific information for successive periods not to exceed 10 years at a time if such action is consistent with the standards and procedures established under this order. This provision does not apply to information contained in records that are more than 25 years old and have been determined to have permanent historical value under title 44, United States Code.

(d) At the time of original classification, the original classification authority may exempt from declassification within 10 years specific information, the unauthorized disclosure of which could reasonably be expected to cause damage to the national security for a period greater than that provided in paragraph (b), above, and the release of which could reasonably be expected to:

(1) reveal an intelligence source, method, or activity, or a cryptologic system or activity;

(2) reveal information that would assist in the development or use of weapons of mass destruction;

(3) reveal information that would impair the development or use of technology within a United States weapons system;

(4) reveal United States military plans, or national security emergency preparedness plans;

(5) reveal foreign government information;

(6) damage relations between the United States and a foreign government, reveal a confidential source, or seriously undermine diplomatic activities that are reasonably expected to be ongoing for a period greater than that provided in paragraph (b), above;

(7) impair the ability of responsible United States Government officials to protect the President, the

Vice President, and other individuals for whom protection services, in the interest of national security, are authorized; or

(8) violate a statute, treaty, or international agreement.

(e) Information marked for an indefinite duration of classification under predecessor orders, for example, "Originating Agency's Determination Required," or information classified under predecessor orders that contains no declassification instructions shall be declassified in accordance with part 3 of this order.

SEC. 1.7. *Identification and Markings.* (a) At the time of original classification, the following shall appear on the face of each classified document, or shall be applied to other classified media in an appropriate manner:

(1) one of the three classification levels defined in section 1.3 of this order;

(2) the identity, by name or personal identifier and position, of the original classification authority;

(3) the agency and office of origin, if not otherwise evident;

(4) declassification instructions, which shall indicate one of the following:

(A) the date or event for declassification, as prescribed in section 1.6(a) or section 1.6(c); or

(B) the date that is 10 years from the date of original classification, as prescribed in section 1.6(b); or

(C) the exemption category from declassification, as prescribed in section 1.6(d); and

(5) a concise reason for classification which, at a minimum, cites the applicable classification categories in section 1.5 of this order.

(b) Specific information contained in paragraph (a), above, may be excluded if it would reveal additional classified information.

(c) Each classified document shall, by marking or other means, indicate which portions are classified, with the applicable classification level, which portions are exempt from declassification under section 1.6(d) of this order, and which portions are unclassified. In accordance with standards prescribed in directives issued under this order, the Director of the Information Security Oversight Office may grant waivers of this requirement for specified classes of documents or information. The Director shall revoke any waiver upon a finding of abuse.

(d) Markings implementing the provisions of this order, including abbreviations and requirements to safeguard classified working papers, shall conform to the standards prescribed in implementing directives issued pursuant to this order.

(e) Foreign government information shall retain its original classification markings or shall be assigned a U.S. classification that provides a degree of protection at least equivalent to that required by the entity that furnished the information.

(f) Information assigned a level of classification under this or predecessor orders shall be considered as classified at that level of classification despite the omission of other required markings. Whenever such information is used in the derivative classification process or is reviewed for possible declassification, holders of such information shall coordinate with an appropriate classification authority for the application of omitted markings.

(g) The classification authority shall, whenever practicable, use a classified addendum whenever classified information constitutes a small portion of an otherwise unclassified document.

SEC. 1.8. *Classification Prohibitions and Limitations.* (a) In no case shall information be classified in order to:

(1) conceal violations of law, inefficiency, or administrative error;

(2) prevent embarrassment to a person, organization, or agency;

(3) restrain competition; or

(4) prevent or delay the release of information that does not require protection in the interest of national security.

(b) Basic scientific research information not clearly related to the national security may not be classified.

(c) Information may not be reclassified after it has been declassified and released to the public under proper authority.

(d) Information that has not previously been disclosed to the public under proper authority may be classified or reclassified after an agency has received a request for it under the Freedom of Information Act (5 U.S.C. 552) or the Privacy Act of 1974 (5 U.S.C. 552a), or the mandatory review provisions of section 3.6 of this order only if such classification meets the requirements of this order and is accomplished on a document-by-document basis with the personal participation or under the direction of the agency head, the deputy agency head, or the senior agency official designated under section 5.6 of this order. This provision does not apply to classified information contained in records that are more than 25 years old and have been determined to have permanent historical value under title 44, United States Code.

(e) Compilations of items of information which are individually unclassified may be classified if the compiled information reveals an additional association or relationship that:

(1) meets the standards for classification under this order; and

(2) is not otherwise revealed in the individual items of information.

As used in this order, "compilation" means an aggregation of pre-existing unclassified items of information.

SEC. 1.9. *Classification Challenges.* (a) Authorized holders of information who, in good faith, believe that its classification status is improper are encouraged and expected to challenge the classification status of the information in accordance with agency procedures established under paragraph (b), below.

(b) In accordance with implementing directives issued pursuant to this order, an agency head or senior agency official shall establish procedures under which authorized holders of information are encouraged and expected to challenge the classification of information that they believe is improperly classified or unclassified. These procedures shall assure that:

(1) individuals are not subject to retribution for bringing such actions;

(2) an opportunity is provided for review by an impartial official or panel; and

(3) individuals are advised of their right to appeal agency decisions to the Interagency Security Classification Appeals Panel established by section 5.4 of this order.

PART 2—DERIVATIVE CLASSIFICATION

SEC. 2.1. *Definitions.* For purposes of this order:

(a) "Derivative classification" means the incorporating, paraphrasing, restating or generating in new form information that is already classified, and marking the newly developed material consistent with the classification markings that apply to the source information. Derivative classification includes the classification of information based on classification guidance. The duplication or reproduction of existing classified information is not derivative classification.

(b) "Classification guidance" means any instruction or source that prescribes the classification of specific information.

(c) "Classification guide" means a documentary form of classification guidance issued by an original classification authority that identifies the elements of information regarding a specific subject that must be classified and establishes the level and duration of classification for each such element.

(d) "Source document" means an existing document that contains classified information that is incorporated, paraphrased, restated, or generated in new form into a new document.

(e) "Multiple sources" means two or more source documents, classification guides, or a combination of both.

SEC. 2.2. *Use of Derivative Classification.* (a) Persons who only reproduce, extract, or summarize classified information, or who only apply classification markings derived from source material or as directed by a classification guide, need not possess original classification authority.

(b) Persons who apply derivative classification markings shall:

(1) observe and respect original classification decisions; and

(2) carry forward to any newly created documents the pertinent classification markings. For information derivatively classified based on multiple sources, the derivative classifier shall carry forward:

(A) the date or event for declassification that corresponds to the longest period of classification among the sources; and

(B) a listing of these sources on or attached to the official file or record copy.

SEC. 2.3. *Classification Guides.* (a) Agencies with original classification authority shall prepare classification guides to facilitate the proper and uniform derivative classification of information. These guides shall conform to standards contained in directives issued under this order.

(b) Each guide shall be approved personally and in writing by an official who:

(1) has program or supervisory responsibility over the information or is the senior agency official; and

(2) is authorized to classify information originally at the highest level of classification prescribed in the guide.

(c) Agencies shall establish procedures to assure that classification guides are reviewed and updated as provided in directives issued under this order.

PART 3—DECLASSIFICATION AND DOWNGRADING

SEC. 3.1. *Definitions.* For purposes of this order:

(a) "Declassification" means the authorized change in the status of information from classified information to unclassified information.

(b) "Automatic declassification" means the declassification of information based solely upon:

(1) the occurrence of a specific date or event as determined by the original classification authority; or

(2) the expiration of a maximum time frame for duration of classification established under this order.

(c) "Declassification authority" means:

(1) the official who authorized the original classification, if that official is still serving in the same position;

(2) the originator's current successor in function;

(3) a supervisory official of either; or

(4) officials delegated declassification authority in writing by the agency head or the senior agency official.

(d) "Mandatory declassification review" means the review for declassification of classified information in response to a request for declassification that meets the requirements under section 3.6 of this order.

(e) "Systematic declassification review" means the review for declassification of classified information contained in records that have been determined by the Archivist of the United States ("Archivist") to have permanent historical value in accordance with chapter 33 of title 44, United States Code.

(f) "Declassification guide" means written instructions issued by a declassification authority that describes the elements of information regarding a specific subject that may be declassified and the elements that must remain classified.

(g) "Downgrading" means a determination by a declassification authority that information classified and safeguarded at a specified level shall be classified and safeguarded at a lower level.

(h) "File series" means documentary material, regardless of its physical form or characteristics, that is arranged in accordance with a filing system or maintained as a unit because it pertains to the same function or activity.

SEC. 3.2. *Authority for Declassification.* (a) Information shall be declassified as soon as it no longer meets the standards for classification under this order.

(b) It is presumed that information that continues to meet the classification requirements under this order requires continued protection. In some exceptional cases, however, the need to protect such information may be outweighed by the public interest in disclosure of the information, and in these cases the information should be declassified. When such questions arise, they shall be referred to the agency head or the senior agency official. That official will determine, as an exercise of discretion, whether the public interest in disclosure outweighs the damage to national security that might reasonably be expected from disclosure. This provision does not:

(1) amplify or modify the substantive criteria or procedures for classification; or

(2) create any substantive or procedural rights subject to judicial review.

(c) If the Director of the Information Security Oversight Office determines that information is classified in violation of this order, the Director may require the information to be declassified by the agency that originated the classification. Any such decision by the Director may be appealed to the President through the Assistant to the President for National Security Affairs. The information shall remain classified pending a prompt decision on the appeal.

(d) The provisions of this section shall also apply to agencies that, under the terms of this order, do not have original classification authority, but had such authority under predecessor orders.

SEC. 3.3. *Transferred Information.* (a) In the case of classified information transferred in conjunction with a transfer of functions, and not merely for storage purposes, the receiving agency shall be deemed to be the originating agency for purposes of this order.

(b) In the case of classified information that is not officially transferred as described in paragraph (a), above, but that originated in an agency that has ceased to exist and for which there is no successor agency, each agency in possession of such information shall be deemed to be the originating agency for purposes of this order. Such information may be declassified or downgraded by the agency in possession after consultation with any other agency that has an interest in the subject matter of the information.

(c) Classified information accessioned into the National Archives and Records Administration ("National Archives") as of the effective date of this order shall be declassified or downgraded by the Archivist in accordance with this order, the directives issued pursuant to this order, agency declassification guides, and any existing procedural agreement between the Archivist and the relevant agency head.

(d) The originating agency shall take all reasonable steps to declassify classified information contained in records determined to have permanent historical value before they are accessioned into the National Archives. However, the Archivist may require that records containing classified information be accessioned into the National Archives when necessary to comply with the provisions of the Federal Records Act [probably means chapters 21 to 31 of Title 44, Public Printing and Documents]. This provision does not apply to information being transferred to the Archivist pursuant to section 2203 of title 44, United States Code, or information for which the National Archives and Records Administration serves as the custodian of the records of an agency or organization that goes out of existence.

(e) To the extent practicable, agencies shall adopt a system of records management that will facilitate the public release of documents at the time such documents are declassified pursuant to the provisions for automatic declassification in sections 1.6 and 3.4 of this order.

SEC. 3.4. *Automatic Declassification.* (a) Subject to paragraph (b), below, within six and one half years from the date of this order, all classified information contained in records that (1) are more than 25 years old, and (2) have been determined to have permanent historical value under title 44, United States Code, shall be automatically declassified whether or not the records have been reviewed. Subsequently, all classified information in such records shall be automatically declassified no longer than 25 years from the date of its original classification, except as provided in paragraph (b), below. For records otherwise subject to this paragraph for which a review or assessment conducted by the agency and confirmed by the Information Security Oversight Office has determined that they: (1) contain information that was created by or is under the control of more than one agency, or (2) are within file series containing information that almost invariably pertains to intelligence sources or methods, all classified information in such records shall be automatically declassified, whether or not the records have been reviewed, within 8 years from the date of this order, except as provided in paragraph (b), below. For records that contain information that becomes subject to automatic declassification after the dates otherwise established in this paragraph, all classified information in such records shall be automatically declassified, whether or not the records have been reviewed on December 31 of the year that is 25 years from the origin of the information, except as provided in paragraph (b), below.

(b) An agency head may exempt from automatic declassification under paragraph (a), above, specific information, the release of which should be expected to:

(1) reveal the identity of a confidential human source, or reveal information about the application of an intelligence source or method, or reveal the identity of a human intelligence source when the unauthorized disclosure of that source would clearly and demonstrably damage the national security interests of the United States;

(2) reveal information that would assist in the development or use of weapons of mass destruction;

(3) reveal information that would impair U.S. cryptologic systems or activities;

(4) reveal information that would impair the application of state of the art technology within a U.S. weapon system;

(5) reveal actual U.S. military war plans that remain in effect;

(6) reveal information that would seriously and demonstrably impair relations between the United States and a foreign government, or seriously and demonstrably undermine ongoing diplomatic activities of the United States;

(7) reveal information that would clearly and demonstrably impair the current ability of United States Government officials to protect the President, Vice President, and other officials for whom protection services, in the interest of national security, are authorized;

(8) reveal information that would seriously and demonstrably impair current national security emergency preparedness plans; or

(9) violate a statute, treaty, or international agreement.

(c) No later than the effective date of this order, an agency head shall notify the President through the Assistant to the President for National Security Affairs of any specific file series of records for which a review or assessment has determined that the information within those file series almost invariably falls within one or more of the exemption categories listed in paragraph (b), above, and which the agency proposes to exempt from automatic declassification. The notification shall include:

(1) a description of the file series;

(2) an explanation of why the information within the file series is almost invariably exempt from automatic declassification and why the information must remain classified for a longer period of time; and

(3) except for the identity of a confidential human source or a human intelligence source, as provided in paragraph (b), above, a specific date or event for declassification of the information.

The President may direct the agency head not to exempt the file series or to declassify the information within that series at an earlier date than recommended.

(d) At least 180 days before information is automatically declassified under this section, an agency head or senior agency official shall notify the Director of the Information Security Oversight Office, serving as Executive Secretary of the Interagency Security Classification Appeals Panel, of any specific information beyond that included in a notification to the President under paragraph (c), above, that the agency proposes to exempt from automatic declassification. The notification shall include:

(1) a description of the information;

(2) an explanation of why the information is exempt from automatic declassification and must remain classified for a longer period of time; and

(3) except for the identity of a confidential human source or a human intelligence source, as provided in paragraph (b), above, a specific date or event for declassification of the information. The Panel may direct the agency not to exempt the information or to declassify it at an earlier date than recommended. The agency head may appeal such a decision to the President through the Assistant to the President for National Security Affairs. The information will remain classified while such an appeal is pending.

(e) No later than the effective date of this order, the agency head or senior agency official shall provide the Director of the Information Security Oversight Office with a plan for compliance with the requirements of this section, including the establishment of interim target dates. Each such plan shall include the requirement that the agency declassify at least 15 percent of the records affected by this section no later than 1 year from the effective date of this order, and similar commitments for subsequent years until the effective date for automatic declassification.

(f) Information exempted from automatic declassification under this section shall remain subject to the mandatory and systematic declassification review provisions of this order.

(g) The Secretary of State shall determine when the United States should commence negotiations with the appropriate officials of a foreign government or international organization of governments to modify any treaty or international agreement that requires the classification of information contained in records affected by this section for a period longer than 25 years from the date of its creation, unless the treaty or international agreement pertains to information that may otherwise remain classified beyond 25 years under this section.

SEC. 3.5. *Systematic Declassification Review.* (a) Each agency that has originated classified information under this order or its predecessors shall establish and conduct a program for systematic declassification review. This program shall apply to historically valuable records exempted from automatic declassification under section 3.4 of this order. Agencies shall prioritize the systematic review of records based upon:

(1) recommendations of the Information Security Policy Advisory Council, established in section 5.5 of this order, on specific subject areas for systematic review concentration; or

(2) the degree of researcher interest and the likelihood of declassification upon review.

(b) The Archivist shall conduct a systematic declassification review program for classified information: (1) accessioned into the National Archives as of the effective date of this order; (2) information transferred to the Archivist pursuant to section 2203 of title 44, United States Code; and (3) information for which the National Archives and Records Administration serves as the custodian of the records of an agency or organization that has gone out of existence. This program shall apply to pertinent records no later than 25 years from the date of their creation. The Archivist shall establish priorities for the systematic review of these records based upon the recommendations of the Information Security Policy Advisory Council; or the degree of researcher interest and the likelihood of declassification upon review. These records shall be reviewed in accordance with the standards of this order, its implementing directives, and declassification guides provided to the Archivist by each agency that originated the records. The Director of the Information Security Oversight Office shall assure that agencies provide the Archivist with adequate and current declassification guides.

(c) After consultation with affected agencies, the Secretary of Defense may establish special procedures for systematic review for declassification of classified cryptologic information, and the Director of Central Intelligence may establish special procedures for systematic review for declassification of classified information pertaining to intelligence activities (including special activities), or intelligence sources or methods.

SEC. 3.6. *Mandatory Declassification Review.* (a) Except as provided in paragraph (b), below, all information classified under this order or predecessor orders shall be subject to a review for declassification by the originating agency if:

(1) the request for a review describes the document or material containing the information with sufficient specificity to enable the agency to locate it with a reasonable amount of effort;

(2) the information is not exempted from search and review under the Central Intelligence Agency Information Act [see Short Title of 1984 Amendment note, set out under section 401 of this title]; and

(3) the information has not been reviewed for declassification within the past 2 years. If the agency has reviewed the information within the past 2 years, or the information is the subject of pending litigation, the agency shall inform the requester of this fact and of the requester's appeal rights.

(b) Information originated by:

(1) the incumbent President;

(2) the incumbent President's White House Staff;

(3) committees, commissions, or boards appointed by the incumbent President; or

(4) other entities within the Executive Office of the President that solely advise and assist the incumbent President is exempted from the provisions of paragraph (a), above. However, the Archivist shall have the authority to review, downgrade, and declassify information of former Presidents under the control of the Archivist pursuant to sections 2107, 2111, 2111 note, or 2203 of title 44, United States Code. Review procedures developed by the Archivist shall provide for consultation with agencies having primary subject matter interest and shall be consistent with the provisions of applicable laws or lawful agreements that pertain to the respective Presidential papers or records. Agencies with primary subject matter interest shall be notified promptly of the Archivist's decision. Any final decision by the Archivist may be appealed by the requester or an agency to the Interagency Security Classification Appeals Panel. The information shall remain classified pending a prompt decision on the appeal.

(c) Agencies conducting a mandatory review for declassification shall declassify information that no longer meets the standards for classification under this order. They shall release this information unless withholding is otherwise authorized and warranted under applicable law.

(d) In accordance with directives issued pursuant to this order, agency heads shall develop procedures to process requests for the mandatory review of classified information. These procedures shall apply to information classified under this or predecessor orders. They also shall provide a means for administratively appealing a denial of a mandatory review request, and for notifying the requester of the right to appeal a final agency decision to the Interagency Security Classification Appeals Panel.

(e) After consultation with affected agencies, the Secretary of Defense shall develop special procedures for the review of cryptologic information, the Director of Central Intelligence shall develop special procedures for the review of information pertaining to intelligence activities (including special activities), or intelligence sources or methods, and the Archivist shall develop special procedures for the review of information accessioned into the National Archives.

SEC. 3.7. *Processing Requests and Reviews.* In response to a request for information under the Freedom of Information Act [5 U.S.C. 552], the Privacy Act of 1974 [5 U.S.C. 552a], or the mandatory review provisions of this order, or pursuant to the automatic declassification or systematic review provisions of this order:

(a) An agency may refuse to confirm or deny the existence or nonexistence of requested information whenever the fact of its existence or nonexistence is itself classified under this order.

(b) When an agency receives any request for documents in its custody that contain information that was originally classified by another agency, or comes across such documents in the process of the automatic declassification or systematic review provisions of this order, it shall refer copies of any request and the pertinent documents to the originating agency for processing, and may, after consultation with the originating agency, inform any requester of the referral unless such association is itself classified under this order. In cases in which the originating agency determines in writing that a response under paragraph (a), above, is required, the referring agency shall respond to the requester in accordance with that paragraph.

SEC. 3.8. *Declassification Database.* (a) The Archivist in conjunction with the Director of the Information Security Oversight Office and those agencies that originate classified information, shall establish a Governmentwide database of information that has been declassified. The Archivist shall also explore other possible uses of technology to facilitate the declassification process.

(b) Agency heads shall fully cooperate with the Archivist in these efforts.

(c) Except as otherwise authorized and warranted by law, all declassified information contained within the database established under paragraph (a), above, shall be available to the public.

PART 4—SAFEGUARDING

SEC. 4.1. *Definitions.* For purposes of this order: (a) "Safeguarding" means measures and controls that are prescribed to protect classified information.

(b) "Access" means the ability or opportunity to gain knowledge of classified information.

(c) "Need-to-know" means a determination made by an authorized holder of classified information that a prospective recipient requires access to specific classified information in order to perform or assist in a lawful and authorized governmental function.

(d) "Automated information system" means an assembly of computer hardware, software, or firmware configured to collect, create, communicate, compute, disseminate, process, store, or control data or information.

(e) "Integrity" means the state that exists when information is unchanged from its source and has not been accidentally or intentionally modified, altered, or destroyed.

(f) "Network" means a system of two or more computers that can exchange data or information.

(g) "Telecommunications" means the preparation, transmission, or communication of information by electronic means.

(h) "Special access program" means a program established for a specific class of classified information that imposes safeguarding and access requirements that exceed those normally required for information at the same classification level.

SEC. 4.2. *General Restrictions on Access.* (a) A person may have access to classified information provided that:

(1) a favorable determination of eligibility for access has been made by an agency head or the agency head's designee;

(2) the person has signed an approved nondisclosure agreement; and

(3) the person has a need-to-know the information.

(b) Classified information shall remain under the control of the originating agency or its successor in function. An agency shall not disclose information originally classified by another agency without its authorization. An official or employee leaving agency service may not remove classified information from the agency's control.

(c) Classified information may not be removed from official premises without proper authorization.

(d) Persons authorized to disseminate classified information outside the executive branch shall assure the protection of the information in a manner equivalent to that provided within the executive branch.

(e) Consistent with law, directives, and regulation, an agency head or senior agency official shall establish uniform procedures to ensure that automated information systems, including networks and telecommunications systems, that collect, create, communicate, compute, disseminate, process, or store classified information have controls that:

(1) prevent access by unauthorized persons; and

(2) ensure the integrity of the information.

(f) Consistent with law, directives, and regulation, each agency head or senior agency official shall establish controls to ensure that classified information is used, processed, stored, reproduced, transmitted, and destroyed under conditions that provide adequate protection and prevent access by unauthorized persons.

(g) Consistent with directives issued pursuant to this order, an agency shall safeguard foreign government information under standards that provide a degree of protection at least equivalent to that required by the government or international organization of governments that furnished the information. When adequate to achieve equivalency, these standards may be less restrictive than the safeguarding standards that ordinarily apply to United States "Confidential" information, including allowing access to individuals with a need-to-know who have not otherwise been cleared for access to classified information or executed an approved nondisclosure agreement.

(h) Except as provided by statute or directives issued pursuant to this order, classified information originating in one agency may not be disseminated outside any other agency to which it has been made available without the consent of the originating agency. An agency head or senior agency official may waive this requirement for specific information originated within that agency. For purposes of this section, the Department of Defense shall be considered one agency.

SEC. 4.3. *Distribution Controls.* (a) Each agency shall establish controls over the distribution of classified information to assure that it is distributed only to organizations or individuals eligible for access who also have a need-to-know the information.

(b) Each agency shall update, at least annually, the automatic, routine, or recurring distribution of classified information that they distribute. Recipients shall cooperate fully with distributors who are updating distribution lists and shall notify distributors whenever a relevant change in status occurs.

SEC. 4.4. *Special Access Programs.* (a) Establishment of special access programs. Unless otherwise authorized by the President, only the Secretaries of State, Defense and Energy, and the Director of Central Intelligence, or the principal deputy of each, may create a special access program. For special access programs pertaining to intelligence activities (including special activities, but not including military operational, strategic and tactical programs), or intelligence sources or methods, this function will be exercised by the Director of Central Intelligence. These officials shall keep the number of these programs at an absolute minimum, and shall establish them only upon a specific finding that:

(1) the vulnerability of, or threat to, specific information is exceptional; and

(2) the normal criteria for determining eligibility for access applicable to information classified at the same level are not deemed sufficient to protect the information from unauthorized disclosure; or

(3) the program is required by statute.

(b) *Requirements and Limitations.* (1) Special access programs shall be limited to programs in which the number of persons who will have access ordinarily will be reasonably small and commensurate with the objective of providing enhanced protection for the information involved.

(2) Each agency head shall establish and maintain a system of accounting for special access programs consistent with directives issued pursuant to this order.

(3) Special access programs shall be subject to the oversight program established under section 5.6(c) of this order. In addition, the Director of the Information Security Oversight Office shall be afforded access to these programs, in accordance with the security requirements of each program, in order to perform the functions assigned to the Information Security Oversight Office under this order. An agency head may limit access to a special access program to the Director and no more than one other employee of the Information Security Oversight Office; or, for special access programs that are extraordinarily sensitive and vulnerable, to the Director only.

(4) The agency head or principal deputy shall review annually each special access program to determine whether it continues to meet the requirements of this order.

(5) Upon request, an agency shall brief the Assistant to the President for National Security Affairs, or his or her designee, on any or all of the agency's special access programs.

(c) Within 180 days after the effective date of this order, each agency head or principal deputy shall review all existing special access programs under the agency's jurisdiction. These officials shall terminate any special access programs that do not clearly meet the provisions of this order. Each existing special access program that an agency head or principal deputy validates shall be treated as if it were established on the effective date of this order.

(d) Nothing in this order shall supersede any requirement made by or under 10 U.S.C. 119.

SEC. 4.5. *Access by Historical Researchers and Former Presidential Appointees.* (a) The requirement in section 4.2(a)(3) of this order that access to classified information may be granted only to individuals who have a need-to-know the information may be waived for persons who:

(1) are engaged in historical research projects; or

(2) previously have occupied policy-making positions to which they were appointed by the President.

(b) Waivers under this section may be granted only if the agency head or senior agency official of the originating agency:

(1) determines in writing that access is consistent with the interest of national security;

(2) takes appropriate steps to protect classified information from unauthorized disclosure or compromise, and ensures that the information is safeguarded in a manner consistent with this order; and

(3) limits the access granted to former Presidential appointees to items that the person originated, reviewed, signed, or received while serving as a Presidential appointee.

PART 5—IMPLEMENTATION AND REVIEW

SEC. 5.1. *Definitions.* For purposes of this order: (a) "Self-inspection" means the internal review and evaluation of individual agency activities and the agency as a whole with respect to the implementation of the program established under this order and its implementing directives.

(b) "Violation" means:

(1) any knowing, willful, or negligent action that could reasonably be expected to result in an unauthorized disclosure of classified information;

(2) any knowing, willful, or negligent action to classify or continue the classification of information con-

trary to the requirements of this order or its implementing directives; or

(3) any knowing, willful, or negligent action to create or continue a special access program contrary to the requirements of this order.

(c) "Infraction" means any knowing, willful, or negligent action contrary to the requirements of this order or its implementing directives that does not comprise a "violation," as defined above.

SEC. 5.2. *Program Direction.* (a) The Director of the Information Security Oversight Office, under the direction of the Archivist of the United States and in consultation with the Assistant to the President for National Security Affairs and the co-chairs of the Security Policy Board, shall issue such directives as are necessary to implement this order. These directives shall be binding upon the agencies. Directives issued by the Director of the Information Security Oversight Office shall establish standards for:

(1) classification and marking principles;

(2) agency security education and training programs;

(3) agency self-inspection programs; and

(4) classification and declassification guides.

(b) The Archivist of the United States shall delegate the implementation and monitorship functions of this program to the Director of the Information Security Oversight Office.

(c) The Security Policy Board, established by a Presidential Decision Directive, shall make a recommendation to the President through the Assistant to the President for National Security Affairs with respect to the issuance of a Presidential directive on safeguarding classified information. The Presidential directive shall pertain to the handling, storage, distribution, transmittal, and destruction of and accounting for classified information.

SEC. 5.3. *Information Security Oversight Office.* (a) There is established within the National Archives and Records Administration an Information Security Oversight Office. The Archivist of the United States shall appoint the Director of the Information Security Oversight Office, subject to the approval of the President.

(b) Under the direction of the Archivist of the United States, acting in consultation with the Assistant to the President for National Security Affairs, the Director of the Information Security Oversight Office shall:

(1) develop directives for the implementation of this order;

(2) oversee agency actions to ensure compliance with this order and its implementing directives;

(3) review and approve agency implementing regulations and agency guides for systematic declassification review prior to their issuance by the agency;

(4) have the authority to conduct on-site reviews of each agency's program established under this order, and to require of each agency those reports, information, and other cooperation that may be necessary to fulfill its responsibilities. If granting access to specific categories of classified information would pose an exceptional national security risk, the affected agency head or the senior agency official shall submit a written justification recommending the denial of access to the President through the Assistant to the President for National Security Affairs within 60 days of the request for access. Access shall be denied pending the response,[;]

(5) review requests for original classification authority from agencies or officials not granted original classification authority and, if deemed appropriate, recommend Presidential approval through the Director of the Office of Management and Budget;

(6) consider and take action on complaints and suggestions from persons within or outside the Government with respect to the administration of the program established under this order;

(7) have the authority to prescribe, after consultation with affected agencies, standardization of forms or procedures that will promote the implementation of the program established under this order;

(8) report at least annually to the President on the implementation of this order; and

(9) convene and chair interagency meetings to discuss matters pertaining to the program established by this order.

SEC. 5.4. *Interagency Security Classification Appeals Panel.*

(a) Establishment and Administration.

(1) There is established an Interagency Security Classification Appeals Panel ("Panel"). The Secretaries of State and Defense, the Attorney General, the Director of Central Intelligence, the Archivist of the United States, and the Assistant to the President for National Security Affairs shall each appoint a senior level representative to serve as a member of the Panel. The President shall select the Chair of the Panel from among the Panel members.

(2) A vacancy on the Panel shall be filled as quickly as possible as provided in paragraph (1), above.

(3) The Director of the Information Security Oversight Office shall serve as the Executive Secretary. The staff of the Information Security Oversight Office shall provide program and administrative support for the Panel.

(4) The members and staff of the Panel shall be required to meet eligibility for access standards in order to fulfill the Panel's functions.

(5) The Panel shall meet at the call of the Chair. The Chair shall schedule meetings as may be necessary for the Panel to fulfill its functions in a timely manner.

(6) The Information Security Oversight Office shall include in its reports to the President a summary of the Panel's activities.

(b) *Functions.* The Panel shall:

(1) decide on appeals by persons who have filed classification challenges under section 1.9 of this order;

(2) approve, deny, or amend agency exemptions from automatic declassification as provided in section 3.4 of this order; and

(3) decide on appeals by persons or entities who have filed requests for mandatory declassification review under section 3.6 of this order.

(c) *Rules and Procedures.* The Panel shall issue bylaws, which shall be published in the Federal Register no later than 120 days from the effective date of this order. The bylaws shall establish the rules and procedures that the Panel will follow in accepting, considering, and issuing decisions on appeals. The rules and procedures of the Panel shall provide that the Panel will consider appeals only on actions in which: (1) the appellant has exhausted his or her administrative remedies within the responsible agency; (2) there is no current action pending on the issue within the federal courts; and (3) the information has not been the subject of review by the federal courts or the Panel within the past 2 years.

(d) Agency heads will cooperate fully with the Panel so that it can fulfill its functions in a timely and fully informed manner. An agency head may appeal a decision of the Panel to the President through the Assistant to the President for National Security Affairs. The Panel will report to the President through the Assistant to the President for National Security Affairs any instance in which it believes that an agency head is not cooperating fully with the Panel.

(e) The Appeals Panel is established for the sole purpose of advising and assisting the President in the discharge of his constitutional and discretionary authority to protect the national security of the United States. Panel decisions are committed to the discretion of the Panel, unless reversed by the President.

SEC. 5.5. *Information Security Policy Advisory Council.*

(a) *Establishment.* There is established an Information Security Policy Advisory Council ("Council"). The Council shall be composed of seven members appointed by the President for staggered terms not to exceed 4 years, from among persons who have demonstrated interest and expertise in an area related to the subject matter of this order and are not otherwise employees of the Federal Government. The President shall appoint the Council Chair from among the members. The Council shall comply with the Federal Advisory Committee Act, as amended, 5 U.S.C. App. 2.

(b) *Functions.* The Council shall:

(1) advise the President, the Assistant to the President for National Security Affairs, the Director of the Office of Management and Budget, or such other executive branch officials as it deems appropriate, on policies established under this order or its implementing directives, including recommended changes to those policies;

(2) provide recommendations to agency heads for specific subject areas for systematic declassification review; and

(3) serve as a forum to discuss policy issues in dispute.

(c) *Meetings.* The Council shall meet at least twice each calendar year, and as determined by the Assistant to the President for National Security Affairs or the Director of the Office of Management and Budget.

(d) *Administration.*

(1) Each Council member may be compensated at a rate of pay not to exceed the daily equivalent of the annual rate of basic pay in effect for grade GS–18 of the general schedule under section 5376 of title 5, United States Code, for each day during which that member is engaged in the actual performance of the duties of the Council.

(2) While away from their homes or regular place of business in the actual performance of the duties of the Council, members may be allowed travel expenses, including per diem in lieu of subsistence, as authorized by law for persons serving intermittently in the Government service (5 U.S.C. 5703(b)).

(3) To the extent permitted by law and subject to the availability of funds, the Information Security Oversight Office shall provide the Council with administrative services, facilities, staff, and other support services necessary for the performance of its functions.

(4) Notwithstanding any other Executive order, the functions of the President under the Federal Advisory Committee Act, as amended [5 App. U.S.C.], that are applicable to the Council, except that of reporting to the Congress, shall be performed by the Director of the Information Security Oversight Office in accordance with the guidelines and procedures established by the General Services Administration.

SEC. 5.6. *General Responsibilities.* Heads of agencies that originate or handle classified information shall:

(a) demonstrate personal commitment and commit senior management to the successful implementation of the program established under this order;

(b) commit necessary resources to the effective implementation of the program established under this order; and

(c) designate a senior agency official to direct and administer the program, whose responsibilities shall include:

(1) overseeing the agency's program established under this order, provided, an agency head may designate a separate official to oversee special access programs authorized under this order. This official shall provide a full accounting of the agency's special access programs at least annually;

(2) promulgating implementing regulations, which shall be published in the Federal Register to the extent that they affect members of the public;

(3) establishing and maintaining security education and training programs;

(4) establishing and maintaining an ongoing self-inspection program, which shall include the periodic review and assessment of the agency's classified product;

(5) establishing procedures to prevent unnecessary access to classified information, including procedures that: (i) require that a need for access to classified information is established before initiating administrative clearance procedures; and (ii) ensure that the number of persons granted access to classified information is limited to the minimum consistent with operational and security requirements and needs;

(6) developing special contingency plans for the safeguarding of classified information used in or near hostile or potentially hostile areas;

(7) assuring that the performance contract or other system used to rate civilian or military personnel performance includes the management of classified information as a critical element or item to be evaluated in the rating of: (i) original classification authorities; (ii) security managers or security specialists; and (iii) all other personnel whose duties significantly involve the creation or handling of classified information;

(8) accounting for the costs associated with the implementation of this order, which shall be reported to the Director of the Information Security Oversight Office for publication; and

(9) assigning in a prompt manner agency personnel to respond to any request, appeal, challenge, complaint, or suggestion arising out of this order that pertains to classified information that originated in a component of the agency that no longer exists and for which there is no clear successor in function.

SEC. 5.7. *Sanctions.* (a) If the Director of the Information Security Oversight Office finds that a violation of this order or its implementing directives may have occurred, the Director shall make a report to the head of the agency or to the senior agency official so that corrective steps, if appropriate, may be taken.

(b) Officers and employees of the United States Government, and its contractors, licensees, certificate holders, and grantees shall be subject to appropriate sanctions if they knowingly, willfully, or negligently:

(1) disclose to unauthorized persons information properly classified under this order or predecessor orders;

(2) classify or continue the classification of information in violation of this order or any implementing directive;

(3) create or continue a special access program contrary to the requirements of this order; or

(4) contravene any other provision of this order or its implementing directives.

(c) Sanctions may include reprimand, suspension without pay, removal, termination of classification authority, loss or denial of access to classified information, or other sanctions in accordance with applicable law and agency regulation.

(d) The agency head, senior agency official, or other supervisory official shall, at a minimum, promptly remove the classification authority of any individual who demonstrates reckless disregard or a pattern of error in applying the classification standards of this order.

(e) The agency head or senior agency official shall:

(1) take appropriate and prompt corrective action when a violation or infraction under paragraph (b), above, occurs; and

(2) notify the Director of the Information Security Oversight Office when a violation under paragraph (b)(1), (2) or (3), above, occurs.

PART 6—GENERAL PROVISIONS

SEC. 6.1. *General Provisions.* (a) Nothing in this order shall supersede any requirement made by or under the Atomic Energy Act of 1954, as amended [42 U.S.C. 2011 *et seq.*], or the National Security Act of 1947, as amended [act July 26, 1947, see Short Title note set out under section 401 of this title]. "Restricted Data" and "Formerly Restricted Data" shall be handled, protected, classified, downgraded, and declassified in conformity with the provisions of the Atomic Energy Act of 1954, as amended, and regulations issued under that Act.

(b) The Attorney General, upon request by the head of an agency or the Director of the Information Security Oversight Office, shall render an interpretation of this order with respect to any question arising in the course of its administration.

(c) Nothing in this order limits the protection afforded any information by other provisions of law, including the exemptions to the Freedom of Information Act [5 U.S.C. 552], the Privacy Act [5 U.S.C. 552a], and the National Security Act of 1947, as amended. This order is not intended, and should not be construed, to create any right or benefit, substantive or procedural, enforceable at law by a party against the United States, its agencies, its officers, or its employees. The foregoing is in addition to the specific provisos set forth in sections 1.2(b), 3.2(b) and 5.4(e) of this order.

(d) Executive Order No. 12356 of April 6, 1982, is revoked as of the effective date of this order.

SEC. 6.2. *Effective Date.* This order shall become effective 180 days from the date of this order.

WILLIAM J. CLINTON.

OFFICIALS DESIGNATED TO CLASSIFY NATIONAL SECURITY INFORMATION

Executive Secretary of National Security Council designated to exercise authority of President to classify certain information originally as "Top Secret" by section 7(b) of Ex. Ord. No. 13010, July 15, 1996, 61 F.R. 37347, as amended, set out as a note under section 5195 of Title 42, The Public Health and Welfare.

Order of President of the United States, dated Oct. 13, 1995, 60 F.R. 53845, provided:

Pursuant to the provisions of Section 1.4 of Executive Order No. 12958 of April 17, 1995, entitled "Classified National Security Information," [set out above] I hereby designate the following officials to classify information originally as "Top Secret", "Secret", or "Confidential":

TOP SECRET

EXECUTIVE OFFICE OF THE PRESIDENT:

The Vice President
The Chief of Staff to the President
The Director, Office of Management and Budget
The Assistant to the President for National Security Affairs
The Director, Office of National Drug Control Policy
The Chairman, President's Foreign Intelligence Advisory Board

DEPARTMENTS AND AGENCIES:

The Secretary of State
The Secretary of the Treasury
The Secretary of Defense
The Secretary of the Army
The Secretary of the Navy
The Secretary of the Air Force
The Attorney General
The Secretary of Energy
The Chairman, Nuclear Regulatory Commission
The Director, United States Arms Control and Disarmament Agency
The Director of Central Intelligence
The Administrator, National Aeronautics and Space Administration
The Director, Federal Emergency Management Agency

SECRET

EXECUTIVE OFFICE OF THE PRESIDENT:

The United States Trade Representative
The Chairman, Council of Economic Advisers
The Director, Office of Science and Technology Policy

DEPARTMENTS AND AGENCIES:

The Secretary of Commerce
The Secretary of Transportation
The Administrator, Agency for International Development
The Director, United States Information Agency

CONFIDENTIAL

The President, Export-Import Bank of the United States
The President, Overseas Private Investment Corporation

Any delegation of this authority shall be in accordance with Section 1.4(c) of Executive Order No. 12958.

This Order shall be published in the Federal Register.

WILLIAM J. CLINTON.

[For abolition of United States Arms Control and Disarmament Agency and United States Information Agency (other than Broadcasting Board of Governors and International Broadcasting Bureau), transfer of functions, and treatment of references, see sections 6511–6521, 6531, 6532, and 6551 of Title 22, Foreign Relations and Intercourse.]

Order of President of the United States, dated Feb. 27, 1996, 61 F.R. 7977, provided:

Pursuant to the provisions of section 1.4 of Executive Order No. 12958 of April 17, 1995, entitled "Classified National Security Information," [set out above] I hereby designate the following additional officials to classify information originally as "Top Secret":

The Chair, Commission on the Roles and Capabilities of the United States Intelligence Community
The Director, National Counterintelligence Center

The Chair of the Commission on the Roles and Capabilities of the United States Intelligence Community, shall exercise the authority to classify information originally as "Top Secret" during the existence of the Commission and for such time afterwards as may be necessary to complete the Commission's administrative affairs.

The authority of the Director of the National Counterintelligence Center to classify information originally as "Top Secret" is limited to those circumstances in which the original classification of information is necessary in order for the Center to fulfill its mission and functions.

Any delegation of this authority shall be in accordance with section 1.4(c) of Executive Order No. 12958.

This order shall be published in the Federal Register.

WILLIAM J. CLINTON.

Order of President of the United States, dated Feb. 26, 1997, 62 F.R. 9349, provided:

Pursuant to the provisions of section 1.4 of Executive Order 12958 of April 17, 1995, entitled "Classified National Security Information," [set out above] I hereby designate the following additional official to classify information originally as "Top Secret":

The Chair, President's Commission on Critical Infrastructure Protection.

The Chair of the President's Commission on Critical Infrastructure Protection, established under Executive Order 13010 of July 15, 1996 [42 U.S.C. 5195 note], shall exercise the authority to classify information originally as "Top Secret" during the existence of the Commission.

Any delegation of this authority shall be in accordance with section 1.4(c) of Executive Order 12958.

This order shall be published in the Federal Register.

WILLIAM J. CLINTON.

EX. ORD. NO. 12968. ACCESS TO CLASSIFIED INFORMATION

Ex. Ord. No. 12968, Aug. 2, 1995, 60 F.R. 40245, provided:

The national interest requires that certain information be maintained in confidence through a system of classification in order to protect our citizens, our democratic institutions, and our participation within the community of nations. The unauthorized disclosure of information classified in the national interest can cause irreparable damage to the national security and loss of human life.

Security policies designed to protect classified information must ensure consistent, cost effective, and efficient protection of our Nation's classified information, while providing fair and equitable treatment to those Americans upon whom we rely to guard our national security.

This order establishes a uniform Federal personnel security program for employees who will be considered for initial or continued access to classified information.

NOW, THEREFORE, by the authority vested in me as President by the Constitution and the laws of the United States of America, it is hereby ordered as follows:

PART 1—DEFINITIONS, ACCESS TO CLASSIFIED INFORMATION, FINANCIAL DISCLOSURE, AND OTHER ITEMS

SECTION 1.1. *Definitions.* For the purposes of this order: (a) "Agency" means any "Executive agency," as defined in 5 U.S.C. 105, the "military departments," as defined in 5 U.S.C. 102, and any other entity within the executive branch that comes into the possession of classified information, including the Defense Intelligence Agency, National Security Agency, and the National Reconnaissance Office.

(b) "Applicant" means a person other than an employee who has received an authorized conditional offer of employment for a position that requires access to classified information.

(c) "Authorized investigative agency" means an agency authorized by law or regulation to conduct a counterintelligence investigation or investigation of persons who are proposed for access to classified information to ascertain whether such persons satisfy the criteria for obtaining and retaining access to such information.

(d) "Classified information" means information that has been determined pursuant to Executive Order No. 12958 [set out above], or any successor order, Executive Order No. 12951 [set out above], or any successor order, or the Atomic Energy Act of 1954 (42 U.S.C. 2011 [*et seq.*]), to require protection against unauthorized disclosure.

(e) "Employee" means a person, other than the President and Vice President, employed by, detailed or assigned to, an agency, including members of the Armed Forces; an expert or consultant to an agency; an industrial or commercial contractor, licensee, certificate holder, or grantee of an agency, including all subcontractors; a personal services contractor; or any other category of person who acts for or on behalf of an agency as determined by the appropriate agency head.

(f) "Foreign power" and "agent of a foreign power" have the meaning provided in 50 U.S.C. 1801.

(g) "Need for access" means a determination that an employee requires access to a particular level of classified information in order to perform or assist in a lawful and authorized governmental function.

(h) "Need-to-know" means a determination made by an authorized holder of classified information that a prospective recipient requires access to specific classified information in order to perform or assist in a lawful and authorized governmental function.

(i) "Overseas Security Policy Board" means the Board established by the President to consider, develop, coordinate and promote policies, standards and agreements on overseas security operations, programs and projects that affect all United States Government agencies under the authority of a Chief of Mission.

(j) "Security Policy Board" means the Board established by the President to consider, coordinate, and recommend policy directives for U.S. security policies, procedures, and practices.

(k) "Special access program" has the meaning provided in section 4.1 of Executive Order No. 12958 [set out above], or any successor order.

SEC. 1.2. *Access to Classified Information.* (a) No employee shall be granted access to classified information unless that employee has been determined to be eligible in accordance with this order and to possess a need-to-know.

(b) Agency heads shall be responsible for establishing and maintaining an effective program to ensure that access to classified information by each employee is clearly consistent with the interests of the national security.

(c) Employees shall not be granted access to classified information unless they:

(1) have been determined to be eligible for access under section 3.1 of this order by agency heads or designated officials based upon a favorable adjudication of an appropriate investigation of the employee's background;

(2) have a demonstrated need-to-know; and

(3) have signed an approved nondisclosure agreement.

(d) All employees shall be subject to investigation by an appropriate government authority prior to being granted access to classified information and at any time during the period of access to ascertain whether they continue to meet the requirements for access.

(e)(1) All employees granted access to classified information shall be required as a condition of such access to provide to the employing agency written consent permitting access by an authorized investigative agency, for such time as access to classified information is maintained and for a period of 3 years thereafter, to:

(A) relevant financial records that are maintained by a financial institution as defined in 31 U.S.C. 5312(a) or by a holding company as defined in section 1101(6) of the Right to Financial Privacy Act of 1978 (12 U.S.C. 3401[(6)]);

(B) consumer reports pertaining to the employee under the Fair Credit Reporting Act (15 U.S.C. 1681a [1681 *et seq.*]); and

(C) records maintained by commercial entities within the United States pertaining to any travel by the employee outside the United States.

(2) Information may be requested pursuant to employee consent under this section where:

(A) there are reasonable grounds to believe, based on credible information, that the employee or former employee is, or may be, disclosing classified information in an unauthorized manner to a foreign power or agent of a foreign power;

(B) information the employing agency deems credible indicates the employee or former employee has incurred excessive indebtedness or has acquired a level of affluence that cannot be explained by other information; or

(C) circumstances indicate the employee or former employee had the capability and opportunity to disclose classified information that is known to have been lost or compromised to a foreign power or an agent of a foreign power.

(3) Nothing in this section shall be construed to affect the authority of an investigating agency to obtain information pursuant to the Right to Financial Privacy Act [of 1978, 12 U.S.C. 3401 *et seq.*], the Fair Credit Reporting Act [15 U.S.C. 1681 *et seq.*] or any other applicable law.

SEC. 1.3. *Financial Disclosure.* (a) Not later than 180 days after the effective date of this order, the head of each agency that originates, handles, transmits, or possesses classified information shall designate each employee, by position or category where possible, who has a regular need for access to classified information that, in the discretion of the agency head, would reveal:

(1) the identity of covert agents as defined in the Intelligence Identities Protection Act of 1982 (50 U.S.C. 421 [*et seq.*]);

(2) technical or specialized national intelligence collection and processing systems that, if disclosed in an unauthorized manner, would substantially negate or impair the effectiveness of the system;

(3) the details of:

(A) the nature, contents, algorithm, preparation, or use of any code, cipher, or cryptographic system or;

(B) the design, construction, functioning, maintenance, or repair of any cryptographic equipment; but not including information concerning the use of cryptographic equipment and services;

(4) particularly sensitive special access programs, the disclosure of which would substantially negate or impair the effectiveness of the information or activity involved; or

(5) especially sensitive nuclear weapons design information (but only for those positions that have been certified as being of a high degree of importance or sen-

sitivity, as described in section 145(f) of the Atomic Energy Act of 1954, as amended [42 U.S.C. 2165(f)]).

(b) An employee may not be granted access, or hold a position designated as requiring access, to information described in subsection (a) unless, as a condition of access to such information, the employee:

(1) files with the head of the agency a financial disclosure report, including information with respect to the spouse and dependent children of the employee, as part of all background investigations or reinvestigations;

(2) is subject to annual financial disclosure requirements, if selected by the agency head; and

(3) files relevant information concerning foreign travel, as determined by the Security Policy Board.

(c) Not later than 180 days after the effective date of this order, the Security Policy Board shall develop procedures for the implementation of this section, including a standard financial disclosure form for use by employees under subsection (b) of this section, and agency heads shall identify certain employees, by position or category, who are subject to annual financial disclosure.

SEC. 1.4. *Use of Automated Financial Record Data Bases.* As part of all investigations and reinvestigations described in section 1.2(d) of this order, agencies may request the Department of the Treasury, under terms and conditions prescribed by the Secretary of the Treasury, to search automated data bases consisting of reports of currency transactions by financial institutions, international transportation of currency or monetary instruments, foreign bank and financial accounts, transactions under $10,000 that are reported as possible money laundering violations, and records of foreign travel.

SEC. 1.5. *Employee Education and Assistance.* The head of each agency that grants access to classified information shall establish a program for employees with access to classified information to: (a) educate employees about individual responsibilities under this order; and

(b) inform employees about guidance and assistance available concerning issues that may affect their eligibility for access to classified information, including sources of assistance for employees who have questions or concerns about financial matters, mental health, or substance abuse.

PART 2—ACCESS ELIGIBILITY POLICY AND PROCEDURE

SEC. 2.1. *Eligibility Determinations.* (a) Determinations of eligibility for access to classified information shall be based on criteria established under this order. Such determinations are separate from suitability determinations with respect to the hiring or retention of persons for employment by the government or any other personnel actions.

(b) The number of employees that each agency determines are eligible for access to classified information shall be kept to the minimum required for the conduct of agency functions.

(1) Eligibility for access to classified information shall not be requested or granted solely to permit entry to, or ease of movement within, controlled areas when the employee has no need for access and access to classified information may reasonably be prevented. Where circumstances indicate employees may be inadvertently exposed to classified information in the course of their duties, agencies are authorized to grant or deny, in their discretion, facility access approvals to such employees based on an appropriate level of investigation as determined by each agency.

(2) Except in agencies where eligibility for access is a mandatory condition of employment, eligibility for access to classified information shall only be requested or granted based on a demonstrated, foreseeable need for access. Requesting or approving eligibility in excess of actual requirements is prohibited.

(3) Eligibility for access to classified information may be granted where there is a temporary need for access, such as one-time participation in a classified project, provided the investigative standards established under this order have been satisfied. In such cases, a fixed date or event for expiration shall be identified and access to classified information shall be limited to information related to the particular project or assignment.

(4) Access to classified information shall be terminated when an employee no longer has a need for access.

SEC. 2.2. *Level of Access Approval.* (a) The level at which an access approval is granted for an employee shall be limited, and relate directly, to the level of classified information for which there is a need for access. Eligibility for access to a higher level of classified information includes eligibility for access to information classified at a lower level.

(b) Access to classified information relating to a special access program shall be granted in accordance with procedures established by the head of the agency that created the program or, for programs pertaining to intelligence activities (including special activities but not including military operational, strategic, and tactical programs) or intelligence sources and methods, by the Director of Central Intelligence. To the extent possible and consistent with the national security interests of the United States, such procedures shall be consistent with the standards and procedures established by and under this order.

SEC. 2.3. *Temporary Access to Higher Levels.* (a) An employee who has been determined to be eligible for access to classified information based on favorable adjudication of a completed investigation may be granted temporary access to a higher level where security personnel authorized by the agency head to make access eligibility determinations find that such access:

(1) is necessary to meet operational or contractual exigencies not expected to be of a recurring nature;

(2) will not exceed 180 days; and

(3) is limited to specific, identifiable information that is made the subject of a written access record.

(b) Where the access granted under subsection (a) of this section involves another agency's classified information, that agency must concur before access to its information is granted.

SEC. 2.4. *Reciprocal Acceptance of Access Eligibility Determinations.* (a) Except when an agency has substantial information indicating that an employee may not satisfy the standards in section 3.1 of this order, background investigations and eligibility determinations conducted under this order shall be mutually and reciprocally accepted by all agencies.

(b) Except where there is substantial information indicating that the employee may not satisfy the standards in section 3.1 of this order, an employee with existing access to a special access program shall not be denied eligibility for access to another special access program at the same sensitivity level as determined personally by the agency head or deputy agency head, or have an existing access eligibility readjudicated, so long as the employee has a need for access to the information involved.

(c) This section shall not preclude agency heads from establishing additional, but not duplicative, investigative or adjudicative procedures for a special access program or for candidates for detail or assignment to their agencies, where such procedures are required in exceptional circumstances to protect the national security.

(d) Where temporary eligibility for access is granted under sections 2.3 or 3.3 of this order or where the determination of eligibility for access is conditional, the fact of such temporary or conditional access shall be conveyed to any other agency that considers affording the employee access to its information.

SEC. 2.5. *Specific Access Requirement.* (a) Employees who have been determined to be eligible for access to classified information shall be given access to classified information only where there is a need-to-know that information.

(b) It is the responsibility of employees who are authorized holders of classified information to verify that a prospective recipient's eligibility for access has been granted by an authorized agency official and to ensure that a need-to-know exists prior to allowing such access, and to challenge requests for access that do not appear well-founded.

SEC. 2.6. *Access by Non-United States Citizens.* (a) Where there are compelling reasons in furtherance of an agency mission, immigrant alien and foreign national employees who possess a special expertise may, in the discretion of the agency, be granted limited access to classified information only for specific programs, projects, contracts, licenses, certificates, or grants for which there is a need for access. Such individuals shall not be eligible for access to any greater level of classified information than the United States Government has determined may be releasable to the country of which the subject is currently a citizen, and such limited access may be approved only if the prior 10 years of the subject's life can be appropriately investigated. If there are any doubts concerning granting access, additional lawful investigative procedures shall be fully pursued.

(b) Exceptions to these requirements may be permitted only by the agency head or the senior agency official designated under section 6.1 of this order to further substantial national security interests.

PART 3—ACCESS ELIGIBILITY STANDARDS

SEC. 3.1. *Standards.* (a) No employee shall be deemed to be eligible for access to classified information merely by reason of Federal service or contracting, licensee, certificate holder, or grantee status, or as a matter of right or privilege, or as a result of any particular title, rank, position, or affiliation.

(b) Except as provided in sections 2.6 and 3.3 of this order, eligibility for access to classified information shall be granted only to employees who are United States citizens for whom an appropriate investigation has been completed and whose personal and professional history affirmatively indicates loyalty to the United States, strength of character, trustworthiness, honesty, reliability, discretion, and sound judgment, as well as freedom from conflicting allegiances and potential for coercion, and willingness and ability to abide by regulations governing the use, handling, and protection of classified information. A determination of eligibility for access to such information is a discretionary security decision based on judgments by appropriately trained adjudicative personnel. Eligibility shall be granted only where facts and circumstances indicate access to classified information is clearly consistent with the national security interests of the United States, and any doubt shall be resolved in favor of the national security.

(c) The United States Government does not discriminate on the basis of race, color, religion, sex, national origin, disability, or sexual orientation in granting access to classified information.

(d) In determining eligibility for access under this order, agencies may investigate and consider any matter that relates to the determination of whether access is clearly consistent with the interests of national security. No inference concerning the standards in this section may be raised solely on the basis of the sexual orientation of the employee.

(e) No negative inference concerning the standards in this section may be raised solely on the basis of mental health counseling. Such counseling can be a positive factor in eligibility determinations. However, mental health counseling, where relevant to the adjudication of access to classified information, may justify further inquiry to determine whether the standards of subsection (b) of this section are satisfied, and mental health may be considered where it directly relates to those standards.

(f) Not later than 180 days after the effective date of this order, the Security Policy Board shall develop a common set of adjudicative guidelines for determining eligibility for access to classified information, including access to special access programs.

SEC. 3.2. *Basis for Eligibility Approval.* (a) Eligibility determinations for access to classified information shall be based on information concerning the applicant or employee that is acquired through the investigation conducted pursuant to this order or otherwise available to security officials and shall be made part of the applicant's or employee's security record. Applicants or employees shall be required to provide relevant information pertaining to their background and character for use in investigating and adjudicating their eligibility for access.

(b) Not later than 180 days after the effective date of this order, the Security Policy Board shall develop a common set of investigative standards for background investigations for access to classified information. These standards may vary for the various levels of access.

(c) Nothing in this order shall prohibit an agency from utilizing any lawful investigative procedure in addition to the investigative requirements set forth in this order and its implementing regulations to resolve issues that may arise during the course of a background investigation or reinvestigation.

SEC. 3.3. *Special Circumstances.* (a) In exceptional circumstances where official functions must be performed prior to the completion of the investigative and adjudication process, temporary eligibility for access to classified information may be granted to an employee while the initial investigation is underway. When such eligibility is granted, the initial investigation shall be expedited.

(1) Temporary eligibility for access under this section shall include a justification, and the employee must be notified in writing that further access is expressly conditioned on the favorable completion of the investigation and issuance of an access eligibility approval. Access will be immediately terminated, along with any assignment requiring an access eligibility approval, if such approval is not granted.

(2) Temporary eligibility for access may be granted only by security personnel authorized by the agency head to make access eligibility determinations and shall be based on minimum investigative standards developed by the Security Policy Board not later than 180 days after the effective date of this order.

(3) Temporary eligibility for access may be granted only to particular, identified categories of classified information necessary to perform the lawful and authorized functions that are the basis for the granting of temporary access.

(b) Nothing in subsection (a) shall be construed as altering the authority of an agency head to waive requirements for granting access to classified information pursuant to statutory authority.

(c) Where access has been terminated under section 2.1(b)(4) of this order and a new need for access arises, access eligibility up to the same level shall be reapproved without further investigation as to employees who were determined to be eligible based on a favorable adjudication of an investigation completed within the prior 5 years, provided they have remained employed by the same employer during the period in question, the employee certifies in writing that there has been no change in the relevant information provided by the employee for the last background investigation, and there is no information that would tend to indicate the employee may no longer satisfy the standards established by this order for access to classified information.

(d) Access eligibility shall be reapproved for individuals who were determined to be eligible based on a favorable adjudication of an investigation completed within the prior 5 years and who have been retired or otherwise separated from United States Government employment for not more than 2 years; provided there is no indication the individual may no longer satisfy the standards of this order, the individual certifies in writing that there has been no change in the relevant information provided by the individual for the last background investigation, and an appropriate record check reveals no unfavorable information.

SEC. 3.4. *Reinvestigation Requirements.* (a) Because circumstances and characteristics may change dramatically over time and thereby alter the eligibility of employees for continued access to classified information, reinvestigations shall be conducted with the same priority and care as initial investigations.

(b) Employees who are eligible for access to classified information shall be the subject of periodic reinvestigations and may also be reinvestigated if, at any time, there is reason to believe that they may no longer meet the standards for access established in this order.

(c) Not later than 180 days after the effective date of this order, the Security Policy Board shall develop a common set of reinvestigative standards, including the frequency of reinvestigations.

PART 4—INVESTIGATIONS FOR FOREIGN GOVERNMENTS

SEC. 4. *Authority.* Agencies that conduct background investigations, including the Federal Bureau of Investigation and the Department of State, are authorized to conduct personnel security investigations in the United States when requested by a foreign government as part of its own personnel security program and with the consent of the individual.

PART 5—REVIEW OF ACCESS DETERMINATIONS

SEC. 5.1. *Determinations of Need for Access.* A determination under section 2.1(b)(4) of this order that an employee does not have, or no longer has, a need for access is a discretionary determination and shall be conclusive.

SEC. 5.2. *Review Proceedings for Denials or Revocations of Eligibility for Access.* (a) Applicants and employees who are determined to not meet the standards for access to classified information established in section 3.1 of this order shall be:

(1) provided as comprehensive and detailed a written explanation of the basis for that conclusion as the national security interests of the United States and other applicable law permit;

(2) provided within 30 days, upon request and to the extent the documents would be provided if requested under the Freedom of Information Act (5 U.S.C. 552) or the Privacy Act (3 U.S.C. 552a), as applicable, any documents, records, and reports upon which a denial or revocation is based;

(3) informed of their right to be represented by counsel or other representative at their own expense; to request any documents, records, and reports as described in section 5.2(a)(2) upon which a denial or revocation is based; and to request the entire investigative file, as permitted by the national security and other applicable law, which, if requested, shall be promptly provided prior to the time set for a written reply;

(4) provided a reasonable opportunity to reply in writing to, and to request a review of, the determination;

(5) provided written notice of and reasons for the results of the review, the identity of the deciding authority, and written notice of the right to appeal;

(6) provided an opportunity to appeal in writing to a high level panel, appointed by the agency head, which shall be comprised of at least three members, two of whom shall be selected from outside the security field. Decisions of the panel shall be in writing, and final except as provided in subsection (b) of this section; and

(7) provided an opportunity to appear personally and to present relevant documents, materials, and information at some point in the process before an adjudicative or other authority, other than the investigating entity, as determined by the agency head. A written summary or recording of such appearance shall be made part of the applicant's or employee's security record, unless such appearance occurs in the presence of the appeals panel described in subsection (a)(6) of this section.

(b) Nothing in this section shall prohibit an agency head from personally exercising the appeal authority in subsection (a)(6) of this section based upon recommendations from an appeals panel. In such case, the decision of the agency head shall be final.

(c) Agency heads shall promulgate regulations to implement this section and, at their sole discretion and as resources and national security considerations permit, may provide additional review proceedings beyond those required by subsection (a) of this section. This section does not require additional proceedings, however, and creates no procedural or substantive rights.

(d) When the head of an agency or principal deputy personally certifies that a procedure set forth in this section cannot be made available in a particular case without damaging the national security interests of the United States by revealing classified information, the particular procedure shall not be made available. This certification shall be conclusive.

(e) This section shall not be deemed to limit or affect the responsibility and power of an agency head pursuant to any law or other Executive order to deny or terminate access to classified information in the interests of national security. The power and responsibility to deny or terminate access to classified information pursuant to any law or other Executive order may be exercised only where the agency head determines that the procedures prescribed in subsection (a) of this section cannot be invoked in a manner that is consistent with national security. This determination shall be conclusive.

(f)(1) This section shall not be deemed to limit or affect the responsibility and power of an agency head to make determinations of suitability for employment.

(2) Nothing in this section shall require that an agency provide the procedures prescribed in subsection (a) of this section to an applicant where a conditional offer of employment is withdrawn for reasons of suitability or any other reason other than denial of eligibility for access to classified information.

(3) A suitability determination shall not be used for the purpose of denying an applicant or employee the review proceedings of this section where there has been a denial or revocation of eligibility for access to classified information.

PART 6—IMPLEMENTATION

SEC. 6.1. *Agency Implementing Responsibilities.* Heads of agencies that grant employees access to classified information shall: (a) designate a senior agency official to direct and administer the agency's personnel security program established by this order. All such programs shall include active oversight and continuing security education and awareness programs to ensure effective implementation of this order;

(b) cooperate, under the guidance of the Security Policy Board, with other agencies to achieve practical, consistent, and effective adjudicative training and guidelines; and

(c) conduct periodic evaluations of the agency's implementation and administration of this order, including the implementation of section 1.3(a) of this order. Copies of each report shall be provided to the Security Policy Board.

SEC. 6.2. *Employee Responsibilities.* (a) Employees who are granted eligibility for access to classified information shall:

(1) protect classified information in their custody from unauthorized disclosure;

(2) report all contacts with persons, including foreign nationals, who seek in any way to obtain unauthorized access to classified information;

(3) report all violations of security regulations to the appropriate security officials; and

(4) comply with all other security requirements set forth in this order and its implementing regulations.

(b) Employees are encouraged and expected to report any information that raises doubts as to whether another employee's continued eligibility for access to classified information is clearly consistent with the national security.

SEC. 6.3. *Security Policy Board Responsibilities and Implementation.* (a) With respect to actions taken by the

Security Policy Board pursuant to sections 1.3(c), 3.1(f), 3.2(b), 3.3(a)(2), and 3.4(c) of this order, the Security Policy Board shall make recommendations to the President through the Assistant to the President for National Security Affairs for implementation.

(b) Any guidelines, standards, or procedures developed by the Security Policy Board pursuant to this order shall be consistent with those guidelines issued by the Federal Bureau of Investigation in March 1994 on Background Investigations Policy/Guidelines Regarding Sexual Orientation.

(c) In carrying out its responsibilities under this order, the Security Policy Board shall consult where appropriate with the Overseas Security Policy Board. In carrying out its responsibilities under section 1.3(c) of this order, the Security Policy Board shall obtain the concurrence of the Director of the Office of Management and Budget.

SEC. 6.4. *Sanctions*. Employees shall be subject to appropriate sanctions if they knowingly and willfully grant eligibility for, or allow access to, classified information in violation of this order or its implementing regulations. Sanctions may include reprimand, suspension without pay, removal, and other actions in accordance with applicable law and agency regulations.

PART 7—GENERAL PROVISIONS

SEC. 7.1. *Classified Information Procedures Act*. Nothing in this order is intended to alter the procedures established under the Classified Information Procedures Act (18 U.S.C. App.).

SEC. 7.2. *General*. (a) Information obtained by an agency under sections 1.2(e) or 1.3 of this order may not be disseminated outside the agency, except to:

(1) the agency employing the employee who is the subject of the records or information;

(2) the Department of Justice for law enforcement or counterintelligence purposes; or

(3) any agency if such information is clearly relevant to the authorized responsibilities of such agency.

(b) The Attorney General, at the request of the head of an agency, shall render an interpretation of this order with respect to any question arising in the course of its administration.

(c) No prior Executive orders are repealed by this order. To the extent that this order is inconsistent with any provision of any prior Executive order, this order shall control, except that this order shall not diminish or otherwise affect the requirements of Executive Order No. 10450 [5 U.S.C. 7311 note], the denial and revocation procedures provided to individuals covered by Executive Order No. 10865, as amended [set out above], or access by historical researchers and former presidential appointees under Executive Order No. 12958 [set out above] or any successor order.

(d) If any provision of this order or the application of such provision is held to be invalid, the remainder of this order shall not be affected.

(e) This Executive order is intended only to improve the internal management of the executive branch and is not intended to, and does not, create any right to administrative or judicial review, or any other right or benefit or trust responsibility, substantive or procedural, enforceable by a party against the United States, its agencies or instrumentalities, its officers or employees, or any other person.

(f) This order is effective immediately.

WILLIAM J. CLINTON.

§ 435a. Limitation on handling, retention, and storage of certain classified materials by the Department of State

(a) Certification regarding full compliance with requirements

The Director of Central Intelligence shall certify to the appropriate committees of Congress whether or not each covered element of the Department of State is in full compliance with all applicable directives of the Director of Central Intelligence relating to the handling, retention, or storage of covered classified material.

(b) Limitation on certification

The Director of Central Intelligence may not certify a covered element of the Department of State as being in full compliance with the directives referred to in subsection (a) of this section if the covered element is currently subject to a waiver of compliance with respect to any such directive.

(c) Report on noncompliance

Whenever the Director of Central Intelligence determines that a covered element of the Department of State is not in full compliance with any directive referred to in subsection (a) of this section, the Director shall promptly notify the appropriate committees of Congress of such determination.

(d) Effects of certification of non-full compliance

(1) Subject to subsection (e) of this section, effective as of January 1, 2001, a covered element of the Department of State may not retain or store covered classified material unless the Director has certified under subsection (a) of this section as of such date that the covered element is in full compliance with the directives referred to in subsection (a) of this section.

(2) If the prohibition in paragraph (1) takes effect in accordance with that paragraph, the prohibition shall remain in effect until the date on which the Director certifies under subsection (a) of this section that the covered element involved is in full compliance with the directives referred to in that subsection.

(e) Waiver by Director of Central Intelligence

(1) The Director of Central Intelligence may waive the applicability of the prohibition in subsection (d) of this section to an element of the Department of State otherwise covered by such prohibition if the Director determines that the waiver is in the national security interests of the United States.

(2) The Director shall submit to appropriate committees of Congress a report on each exercise of the waiver authority in paragraph (1).

(3) Each report under paragraph (2) with respect to the exercise of authority under paragraph (1) shall set forth the following:

(A) The covered element of the Department of State addressed by the waiver.

(B) The reasons for the waiver.

(C) The actions that will be taken to bring such element into full compliance with the directives referred to in subsection (a) of this section, including a schedule for completion of such actions.

(D) The actions taken by the Director to protect any covered classified material to be handled, retained, or stored by such element pending achievement of full compliance of such element with such directives.

(f) Definitions

In this section:

(1) The term "appropriate committees of Congress" means the following:

(A) The Select Committee on Intelligence and the Committee on Foreign Relations of the Senate.

(B) The Permanent Select Committee on Intelligence and the Committee on International Relations of the House of Representatives.

(2) The term ''covered classified material'' means any material classified at the Sensitive Compartmented Information (SCI) level.

(3) The term ''covered element of the Department of State'' means each element of the Department of State that handles, retains, or stores covered classified material.

(4) The term ''material'' means any data, regardless of physical form or characteristic, including written or printed matter, automated information systems storage media, maps, charts, paintings, drawings, films, photographs, engravings, sketches, working notes, papers, reproductions of any such things by any means or process, and sound, voice, magnetic, or electronic recordings.

(5) The term ''Sensitive Compartmented Information (SCI) level'', in the case of classified material, means a level of classification for information in such material concerning or derived from intelligence sources, methods, or analytical processes that requires such information to be handled within formal access control systems established by the Director of Central Intelligence.

(Pub. L. 106–567, title III, §309, Dec. 27, 2000, 114 Stat. 2840.)

CODIFICATION

Section was enacted as part of the Intelligence Authorization Act for Fiscal Year 2001, and not as part of the National Security Act of 1947 which comprises this chapter.

§436. Requests by authorized investigative agencies

(a) Generally

(1) Any authorized investigative agency may request from any financial agency, financial institution, or holding company, or from any consumer reporting agency, such financial records, other financial information, and consumer reports as may be necessary in order to conduct any authorized law enforcement investigation, counterintelligence inquiry, or security determination. Any authorized investigative agency may also request records maintained by any commercial entity within the United States pertaining to travel by an employee in the executive branch of Government outside the United States.

(2) Requests may be made under this section where—

(A) the records sought pertain to a person who is or was an employee in the executive branch of Government required by the President in an Executive order or regulation, as a condition of access to classified information, to provide consent, during a background investigation and for such time as access to the information is maintained, and for a period of not more than three years thereafter, permitting access to financial records, other financial information, consumer reports, and travel records; and

(B)(i) there are reasonable grounds to believe, based on credible information, that the person is, or may be, disclosing classified information in an unauthorized manner to a foreign power or agent of a foreign power;

(ii) information the employing agency deems credible indicates the person has incurred excessive indebtedness or has acquired a level of affluence which cannot be explained by other information known to the agency; or

(iii) circumstances indicate the person had the capability and opportunity to disclose classified information which is known to have been lost or compromised to a foreign power or an agent of a foreign power.

(3) Each such request—

(A) shall be accompanied by a written certification signed by the department or agency head or deputy department or agency head concerned, or by a senior official designated for this purpose by the department or agency head concerned (whose rank shall be no lower than Assistant Secretary or Assistant Director), and shall certify that—

(i) the person concerned is or was an employee within the meaning of paragraph (2)(A);

(ii) the request is being made pursuant to an authorized inquiry or investigation and is authorized under this section; and

(iii) the records or information to be reviewed are records or information which the employee has previously agreed to make available to the authorized investigative agency for review;

(B) shall contain a copy of the agreement referred to in subparagraph (A)(iii);

(C) shall identify specifically or by category the records or information to be reviewed; and

(D) shall inform the recipient of the request of the prohibition described in subsection (b) of this section.

(b) Disclosure of requests

Notwithstanding any other provision of law, no governmental or private entity, or officer, employee, or agent of such entity, may disclose to any person, other than those officers, employees, or agents of such entity necessary to satisfy a request made under this section, that such entity has received or satisfied a request made by an authorized investigative agency under this section.

(c) Records or information; inspection or copying

(1) Notwithstanding any other provision of law (other than section 6103 of title 26), an entity receiving a request for records or information under subsection (a) of this section shall, if the request satisfies the requirements of this section, make available such records or information within 30 days for inspection or copying, as may be appropriate, by the agency requesting such records or information.

(2) Any entity (including any officer, employee, or agent thereof) that discloses records or information for inspection or copying pursuant to this section in good faith reliance upon the certifications made by an agency pursuant to this section shall not be liable for any such disclosure to any person under this subchapter, the constitution of any State, or any law or reg-

ulation of any State or any political subdivision of any State.

(d) Reimbursement of costs

Any agency requesting records or information under this section may, subject to the availability of appropriations, reimburse a private entity for any cost reasonably incurred by such entity in responding to such request, including the cost of identifying, reproducing, or transporting records or other data.

(e) Dissemination of records or information received

An agency receiving records or information pursuant to a request under this section may disseminate the records or information obtained pursuant to such request outside the agency only—

(1) to the agency employing the employee who is the subject of the records or information;

(2) to the Department of Justice for law enforcement or counterintelligence purposes; or

(3) with respect to dissemination to an agency of the United States, if such information is clearly relevant to the authorized responsibilities of such agency.

(f) Construction of section

Nothing in this section may be construed to affect the authority of an investigative agency to obtain information pursuant to the Right to Financial Privacy Act (12 U.S.C. 3401 et seq.) or the Fair Credit Reporting Act (15 U.S.C. 1681 et seq.).

(July 26, 1947, ch. 343, title VIII, § 802, as added Pub. L. 103–359, title VIII, § 802(a), Oct. 14, 1994, 108 Stat. 3436.)

REFERENCES IN TEXT

The Right to Financial Privacy Act, referred to in subsec. (f), probably means the Right to Financial Privacy Act of 1978, which is title XI of Pub. L. 95–630, Nov. 10, 1978, 92 Stat. 3697, as amended, and is classified generally to chapter 35 (§ 3401 et seq.) of Title 12, Banks and Banking. For complete classification of this Act to the Code, see Short Title note set out under section 3401 of Title 12 and Tables.

The Fair Credit Reporting Act, referred to in subsec. (f), is title VI of Pub. L. 90–321, as added by Pub. L. 91–508, title VI, § 601, Oct. 26, 1970, 84 Stat. 1127, as amended, which is classified generally to subchapter III (§ 1681 et seq.) of chapter 41 of Title 15, Commerce and Trade. For complete classification of this Act to the Code, see Short Title of 1970 Amendment note set out under section 1601 of Title 15 and Tables.

SECTION REFERRED TO IN OTHER SECTIONS

This section is referred to in section 435 of this title.

§ 437. Exceptions

Except as otherwise specifically provided, the provisions of this subchapter shall not apply to the President and Vice President, Members of the Congress, Justices of the Supreme Court, and Federal judges appointed by the President.

(July 26, 1947, ch. 343, title VIII, § 803, as added Pub. L. 103–359, title VIII, § 802(a), Oct. 14, 1994, 108 Stat. 3437.)

§ 438. Definitions

For purposes of this subchapter—

(1) the term "authorized investigative agency" means an agency authorized by law or regulation to conduct a counterintelligence investigation or investigations of persons who are proposed for access to classified information to ascertain whether such persons satisfy the criteria for obtaining and retaining access to such information;

(2) the term "classified information" means any information that has been determined pursuant to Executive Order No. 12356 of April 2, 1982, or successor orders, or the Atomic Energy Act of 1954 [42 U.S.C. 2011 et seq.], to require protection against unauthorized disclosure and that is so designated;

(3) the term "consumer reporting agency" has the meaning given such term in section 1681a of title 15;

(4) the term "employee" includes any person who receives a salary or compensation of any kind from the United States Government, is a contractor of the United States Government or an employee thereof, is an unpaid consultant of the United States Government, or otherwise acts for or on behalf of the United States Government, except as otherwise determined by the President;

(5) the terms "financial agency" and "financial institution" have the meanings given to such terms in section 5312(a) of title 31 and the term "holding company" has the meaning given to such term in section 3401(6) of title 12;

(6) the terms "foreign power" and "agent of a foreign power" have the same meanings as set forth in sections[1] 1801(a) and (b), respectively, of this title;

(7) the term "State" means each of the several States of the United States, the District of Columbia, the Commonwealth of Puerto Rico, the Commonwealth of the Northern Mariana Islands, the United States Virgin Islands, Guam, American Samoa, the Republic of the Marshall Islands, the Federated States of Micronesia, and the Republic of Palau, and any other possession of the United States; and

(8) the term "computer" means any electronic, magnetic, optical, electrochemical, or other high speed data processing device performing logical, arithmetic, or storage functions, and includes any data storage facility or communications facility directly related to or operating in conjunction with such device and any data or other information stored or contained in such device.

(July 26, 1947, ch. 343, title VIII, § 804, as added Pub. L. 103–359, title VIII, § 802(a), Oct. 14, 1994, 108 Stat. 3438; amended Pub. L. 106–120, title III, § 305(b), Dec. 3, 1999, 113 Stat. 1611.)

REFERENCES IN TEXT

Executive Order No. 12356, referred to in par. (2), is set out as a note under section 435 of this title.

The Atomic Energy Act of 1954, referred to in par. (2), is act Aug. 1, 1946, ch. 724, as added by act Aug. 30, 1954, ch. 1073, § 1, 68 Stat. 921, and amended, which is classified generally to chapter 23 (§ 2011 et seq.) of Title 42, The Public Health and Welfare. For complete classi-

[1] So in original. Probably should be "section".

fication of this Act to the Code, see Short Title note set out under section 2011 of Title 42 and Tables.

AMENDMENTS

1999—Par. (8). Pub. L. 106–120 added par. (8).

SUBCHAPTER VII—APPLICATION OF SANCTIONS LAWS TO INTELLIGENCE ACTIVITIES

§§441 to 441d. Omitted

CODIFICATION

Sections 441 to 441d were omitted pursuant to section 441d which provided that this subchapter ceased to be effective on Jan. 6, 2000.

Section 441, act July 26, 1947, ch. 343, title IX, §901, as added Pub. L. 104–93, title III, §303(a), Jan. 6, 1996, 109 Stat. 964, authorized the President to stay the imposition of an economic, cultural, diplomatic, or other sanction or related action by the United States Government concerning a foreign country, organization, or person when to proceed without delay would seriously risk the compromise of an ongoing criminal investigation directly related to the activities giving rise to the sanction or an intelligence source or method directly related to the activities giving rise to the sanction.

Section 441a, act July 26, 1947, ch. 343, title IX, §902, as added Pub. L. 104–93, title III, §303(a), Jan. 6, 1996, 109 Stat. 964, authorized the President to extend the period of a stay obtained pursuant to section 441 of this title.

Section 441b, act July 26, 1947, ch. 343, title IX, §903, as added Pub. L. 104–93, title III, §303(a), Jan. 6, 1996, 109 Stat. 964, related to reports to Congress.

Section 441c, act July 26, 1947, ch. 343, title IX, §904, as added Pub. L. 104–93, title III, §303(a), Jan. 6, 1996, 109 Stat. 965, authorized the President to stay the imposition of a sanction related to the proliferation of weapons of mass destruction, their delivery systems, or advanced conventional weapons otherwise required to be imposed by certain other laws.

Section 441d, act July 26, 1947, ch. 343, title IX, §905, as added Pub. L. 104–93, title III, §303(a), Jan. 6, 1996, 109 Stat. 965; amended Pub. L. 104–293, title III, §304, Oct. 11, 1996, 110 Stat. 3464; Pub. L. 105–107, title III, §304, Nov. 20, 1997, 111 Stat. 2252; Pub. L. 105–272, title III, §303, Oct. 20, 1998, 112 Stat. 2400, provided that this subchapter would cease to be effective on Jan. 6, 2000.

SUBCHAPTER VIII—ADDITIONAL MISCELLANEOUS PROVISIONS

§442. Applicability to United States intelligence activities of Federal laws implementing international treaties and agreements

(a) In general

No Federal law enacted on or after December 27, 2000, that implements a treaty or other international agreement shall be construed as making unlawful an otherwise lawful and authorized intelligence activity of the United States Government or its employees, or any other person to the extent such other person is carrying out such activity on behalf of, and at the direction of, the United States, unless such Federal law specifically addresses such intelligence activity.

(b) Authorized intelligence activities

An intelligence activity shall be treated as authorized for purposes of subsection (a) of this section if the intelligence activity is authorized by an appropriate official of the United States Government, acting within the scope of the official duties of that official and in compliance with Federal law and any applicable Presidential directive.

(July 26, 1947, ch. 343, title X, §1001, as added Pub. L. 106–567, title III, §308(a), Dec. 27, 2000, 114 Stat. 2839.)

CHAPTER 16—DEFENSE INDUSTRIAL RESERVES

CHAPTER REFERRED TO IN OTHER SECTIONS

This chapter is referred to in title 40 sections 474, 490.

§§451 to 453. Transferred

CODIFICATION

Sections 451, 452, and 453 of this title were transferred to section 2535 of Title 10, Armed Forces, and redesignated as subsecs. (a), (c), and (b), respectively, of section 2535 by Pub. L. 102–484, div. D, title XLII, §4235(a)(2), (3), (b), Oct. 23, 1992, 106 Stat. 2690, 2691.

Section 451, acts July 2, 1948, ch. 811, §2, 62 Stat. 1225; Nov. 16, 1973, Pub. L. 93–155, title VIII, §809, 87 Stat. 617, related to Congressional declaration of purpose and policy in enacting this chapter.

Section 452, acts July 2, 1948, ch. 811, §3, 62 Stat. 1225; Nov. 16, 1973, Pub. L. 93–155, title VIII, §809, 87 Stat. 617, defined "Secretary", "Defense Industrial Reserve", and "plant equipment package" for purposes of this chapter.

Section 453, acts July 2, 1948, ch. 811, §4, 62 Stat. 1226; Nov. 16, 1973, Pub. L. 93–155, title VIII, §809, 87 Stat. 617; Nov. 14, 1986, Pub. L. 99–661, div. A, title XIII, §1359(a), 100 Stat. 3999, related to powers and duties of Secretary of Defense, reimbursement for transferred Defense Industrial Reserve equipment, and regulations.

SHORT TITLE

Section 1 of act July 2, 1948, as amended by Pub. L. 93–155, §809, provided: "That this Act [enacting this chapter] may be cited as the 'Defense Industrial Reserve Act'."

§454. Repealed. Pub. L. 101–510, div. A, title XIII, §1303(a), Nov. 5, 1990, 104 Stat. 1669

Section, acts July 2, 1948, ch. 811, §5, 62 Stat. 1226; Nov. 16, 1973, Pub. L. 93–155, title VIII, §809, 87 Stat. 618, related to reports concerning status of defense industrial reserve.

§455. Authorization of appropriations

There are authorized to be appropriated such sums as the Congress may from time to time determine to be necessary to enable the Secretary to carry out the provisions of this chapter.

(July 2, 1948, ch. 811, §6, 62 Stat. 1226; Pub. L. 93–155, title VIII, §809, Nov. 16, 1973, 87 Stat. 618.)

PRIOR PROVISIONS

Provisions similar to those in this section were contained in section 14 of act July 2, 1948, ch. 811, 62 Stat. 1228 (classified to section 462 of this title) prior to the general amendment of act July 2, 1948, by Pub. L. 93–155.

AMENDMENTS

1973—Pub. L. 93–155 substituted provisions respecting authorization of appropriations, for prior provisions respecting acceptance of plants by Administrator of General Services, disposition of plants, and conditions of lease, now covered in section 453 of this title.

SECTION REFERRED TO IN OTHER SECTIONS

This section is referred to in section 1941f of Appendix to this title.

§§ 456 to 462. Omitted

CODIFICATION

Sections 456 to 462 were omitted in the general amendment of act July 2, 1948, ch. 811 by Pub. L. 93–155, title VIII, § 809, Nov. 16, 1973, 87 Stat. 617. See sections 453 to 455 of this title.

Section 456, act July 2, 1948, ch. 811, § 7, 62 Stat. 1227, related to powers of Secretary of Defense respecting property in national industrial reserve. See section 453 of this title.

Section 457, act July 2, 1948, ch. 811, § 8, 62 Stat. 1227, related to transportation, maintenance, disposition, etc., of transferred property. See section 453 of this title.

Section 458, act July 2, 1948, ch. 811, § 9, 62 Stat. 1227, related to limitation on acquisition of property.

Section 459, act July 2, 1948, ch. 811, § 10, 62 Stat. 1227, provided for an Industrial Reserve Review Committee, its composition, appointment, tenure, and compensation and related to inapplicability of certain laws to Committee solely by reason of appointment to and membership on such Committee.

Section 460, act July 2, 1948, ch. 811, § 11, 62 Stat. 1228, related to duties of Industrial Reserve Review Committee, including making of recommendations to Secretary of Defense.

Section 461, act July 2, 1948, ch. 811, § 12, 62 Stat. 1228, provided for reports to Congress. See section 454 of this title.

Section 462, acts July 2, 1948, ch. 811, § 14, 62 Stat. 1228; June 30, 1949, ch. 288, title I, § 103, 63 Stat. 380, authorized appropriations. See section 455 of this title.

CHAPTER 17—ARMING AMERICAN VESSELS

§ 481. Repealed. Aug. 10, 1956, ch. 1041, § 53, 70A Stat. 641

Section, act June 29, 1948, ch. 715, § 1, 62 Stat. 1095, provided for arming of American vessels during a war or national emergency. See section 351 of Title 10, Armed Forces.

CHAPTER 18—AIR-WARNING SCREEN

§ 491. Establishment and development of land-based air warning and control installations and facilities; extent of appropriation; procurement of communication services

The Secretary of the Air Force is authorized to establish and develop within and without the continental limits of the United States in fulfilling the air defense responsibilities of the Department of the Air Force such land-based air warning and control installations and facilities, by the construction, installation, or equipment of temporary or permanent public works, including buildings, facilities, appurtenances, utilities, and access roads, and to provide for necessary administration and planning therefor, without regard to section 3324(a) and (b) of title 31, as he may deem necessary in the interest of national security: *Provided*, That not to exceed $85,500,000 shall be appropriated for the construction of public works authorized by this section.

The Secretary of the Air Force is authorized to procure communication services required for the semiautomatic ground environment system. No contract for such services may be for a period of more than ten years from the date communication services are first furnished under such contract. The aggregate contingent liability of the Government under the termination provisions of all contracts authorized hereunder may not exceed a total of $222,000,000 and the General Accounting Office shall have access to such carrier records and accounts as it may deem necessary for the purpose of audit. In procuring such services, the Secretary of the Air Force shall utilize to the fullest extent practicable the facilities and capabilities of communication common carriers, including rural telephone cooperatives, within their respective service areas and for power supply, shall utilize to the fullest extent practicable, the facilities and capabilities of public utilities and rural electric cooperatives within their respective service areas. Negotiations with communication common carriers, including cooperatives, and representation in proceedings involving such carriers before Federal and State regulatory bodies where such negotiations or proceedings involve contracts authorized by this paragraph shall be in accordance with the provisions of section 481 of title 40.

(Mar. 30, 1949, ch. 41, § 1, 63 Stat. 17; Aug. 3, 1956, ch. 939, title III, § 303, 70 Stat. 1012; Pub. L. 97–214, § 10(b)(4), July 12, 1982, 96 Stat. 175; Pub. L. 104–316, title I, § 128(a), Oct. 19, 1996, 110 Stat. 3841.)

CODIFICATION

"Section 3324(a) and (b) of title 31" substituted in text for "section 3648 of the Revised Statutes (31 U.S.C. 529)" on authority of Pub. L. 97–258, § 4(b), Sept. 13, 1982, 96 Stat. 1067, the first section of which enacted Title 31, Money and Finance.

AMENDMENTS

1996—Pub. L. 104–316, in third sentence of second par., struck out "no termination payment shall be final until audited and approved by" after "$222,000,000 and", struck out "which" after "Office", and inserted "of audit" after "for the purpose".

1982—Pub. L. 97–214 struck out reference to sections 1136 [10 U.S.C. 4774, 9774] and 3734 [40 U.S.C. 259, 267] of the Revised Statutes.

1956—Act Aug. 3, 1956, authorized procurement of communication services required for the semiautomatic ground environment system.

EFFECTIVE DATE OF 1982 AMENDMENT

Amendment by Pub. L. 97–214 effective Oct. 1, 1982, and applicable to military construction projects, and to construction and acquisition of military family housing, authorized before, on, or after such date, see section 12(a) of Pub. L. 97–214, set out as an Effective Date note under section 2801 of Title 10, Armed Forces.

SECTION REFERRED TO IN OTHER SECTIONS

This section is referred to in section 492 of this title.

§ 492. Acquisition of land

In furtherance of section 491 of this title, the Secretary of the Air Force is authorized to make surveys and to acquire lands and rights pertaining thereto or other interests therein, including the temporary use thereof, by donation, purchase, exchange of Government-owned lands, or otherwise, and to place permanent and temporary improvements thereon whether such lands are held in fee or under lease, or under other temporary tenure.

(Mar. 30, 1949, ch. 41, § 2, 63 Stat. 17.)

§493. Authorization of appropriations

There is authorized to be appropriated, out of any moneys in the Treasury of the United States not otherwise appropriated, such sums as may be necessary to carry out the purposes of this chapter, and when so specified in an appropriation Act such amounts shall remain available until expended.

(Mar. 30, 1949, ch. 41, §3, 63 Stat. 18.)

§494. Supervision and control of project

The provisions of this chapter shall be subject to the duties and authority of the Secretary of Defense and the departments and agencies of the Department of Defense as provided in the National Security Act of 1947.

(Mar. 30, 1949, ch. 41, §4, 63 Stat. 18; Aug. 10, 1949, ch. 412, §12(a), 63 Stat. 591.)

REFERENCES IN TEXT

The National Security Act of 1947, referred to in text, is act July 26, 1947, ch. 343, 61 Stat. 495, as amended. For complete classification of this Act to the Code, see Short Title note set out under section 401 of this title and Tables.

CHANGE OF NAME

"Department of Defense" substituted in text for "National Military Establishment" on authority of act Aug. 10, 1949, ch. 412, §12(a), 63 Stat. 591.

CHAPTER 19—GUIDED MISSILES

§501. Establishment of long-range proving ground for guided missiles and other weapons; jurisdiction of Secretary of the Air Force; use by all Services

The Secretary of the Air Force is authorized to establish a joint long-range proving ground for guided missiles and other weapons by the construction, installation, or equipment of temporary or permanent public works, including buildings, facilities, appurtenances, and utilities, within or without the continental limits of the United States, for scientific study, testing, and training purposes by the Departments of the Army, Navy, and Air Force.

(May 11, 1949, ch. 98, §1, 63 Stat. 66.)

SECTION REFERRED TO IN OTHER SECTIONS

This section is referred to in sections 502, 503, 504 of this title.

§502. Acquisition of land

The Secretary of the Air Force is authorized in discharging the authority given in section 501 of this title to make surveys, to acquire lands and rights or other interests pertaining thereto, including the temporary use thereof, by donation, purchase, exchange of Government-owned lands, or otherwise, without regard to section 3324(a) and (b) of title 31. Prior to the acquisition under the authority of this section of any lands or rights or other interests pertaining thereto, the Secretary of the Air Force shall come into agreement with the Armed Services Committees of the Senate and the House of Representatives with respect to the acquisition of such lands, rights, or other interests.

(May 11, 1949, ch. 98, §2, 63 Stat. 66.)

CODIFICATION

"Section 3324(a) and (b) of title 31" substituted in text for "section 3648, Revised Statutes, as amended [31 U.S.C. 529]" on authority of Pub. L. 97–258, §4(b), Sept. 13, 1982, 96 Stat. 1067, the first section of which enacted Title 31, Money and Finance.

SECTION REFERRED TO IN OTHER SECTIONS

This section is referred to in sections 503, 504 of this title.

§503. Authorization of appropriations

There is authorized to be appropriated, out of any money in the Treasury not otherwise appropriated, not to exceed $75,000,000 to carry out the purposes of sections 501 and 502 of this title.

(May 11, 1949, ch. 98, §3, 63 Stat. 66.)

§504. Delegation of authority by Secretary of Defense; contributions for support

The Secretary of Defense is authorized, in his discretion, to transfer to the Secretary of the Army or the Secretary of the Navy, and to retransfer from either of such Secretaries to the other or to the Secretary of the Air Force, all, or any part of, the authority granted by sections 501 and 502 of this title; and, in connection with any such transfer or retransfer, to transfer all or any part of the funds available for the establishment and support of the joint long-range proving ground for guided missiles and other weapons. The Secretary of Defense is further authorized to permit, to the extent that he may deem appropriate, the Secretaries of the Army, the Navy, and the Air Force to contribute, with or without reimbursement, to the establishment and support of the joint long-range proving ground for guided missiles authorized by this chapter, by the loan, assignment, or transfer of personnel, supplies, equipment, and services.

(May 11, 1949, ch. 98, §4, 63 Stat. 66.)

CHAPTER 20—WIND TUNNELS

SUBCHAPTER I—CONSTRUCTION OF WIND-TUNNEL FACILITIES

SUBCHAPTER REFERRED TO IN OTHER SECTIONS

This subchapter is referred to in section 521 of this title.

§ 511. Joint development of unitary plan for construction of facilities; construction at educational institutions

The Administrator of the National Aeronautics and Space Administration (hereinafter referred to as the "Administrator") and the Secretary of Defense are authorized and directed jointly to develop a unitary plan for the construction of transsonic, supersonic, and hypersonic wind-tunnel facilities for the solution of research, development, and evaluation problems in aeronautics, including the construction of facilities at educational institutions within the continental limits of the United States for training and research in aeronautics, and to revise the uncompleted portions of the unitary plan from time to time to accord with changes in national defense requirements and scientific and technical advances. The Administrator and the Secretaries of the Army, the Navy, and the Air Force are authorized to proceed with the construction and equipment of facilities in implementation of the unitary plan to the extent permitted by appropriations pursuant to existing authority and the authority contained in this chapter. Any further implementation of the unitary plan shall be subject to such additional authorizations as may be approved by Congress.

(Oct. 27, 1949, ch. 766, title I, § 101, 63 Stat. 936; Pub. L. 85–568, title III, § 301(d)(1), (2), July 29, 1958, 72 Stat. 433; Pub. L. 106–391, title III, § 312(1), Oct. 30, 2000, 114 Stat. 1594.)

AMENDMENTS

2000—Pub. L. 106–391 substituted "transsonic, supersonic, and hypersonic" for "transsonic and supersonic".

1958—Pub. L. 85–568 substituted "The Administrator of the National Aeronautics and Space Administration (hereinafter referred to as the 'Administrator')" for "The National Advisory Committee for Aeronautics (hereinafter referred to as the 'Committee')", and "Administrator" for "Committee" in second sentence.

EFFECTIVE DATE OF 1958 AMENDMENT

Amendment by Pub. L. 85–568 effective 90 days after July 29, 1958, or on any earlier date on which the Administrator of the National Aeronautics and Space Administration determines, and announces by proclamation, that the Administration has been organized and is prepared to discharge the duties and exercise the powers conferred upon it, see section 301(e) of Pub. L. 85–568, set out as a note under section 2302 of Title 10, Armed Forces.

SHORT TITLE

Section 106 of title I of act Oct. 27, 1949, provided that: "This title [enacting this subchapter] may be cited as the 'Unitary Wind Tunnel Plan Act of 1949'."

Section 205 of title II of act Oct. 27, 1949, provided that: "This title [enacting subchapter II of this chapter] may be cited as the 'Air Engineering Development Center Act of 1949'."

§ 512. Limitation on cost of construction and equipment; vesting of title to facilities

The Administrator is authorized, in implementation of the unitary plan, to construct and equip transsonic or supersonic wind tunnels of a size, design and character adequate for the efficient conduct of experimental work in support of long-range fundamental research at educational institutions within the continental United States, to be selected by the Administrator, or to enter into contracts with such institutions to provide for such construction and equipment, at a total cost not to exceed $10,000,000: *Provided*, That the Administrator may, in his discretion, after consultation with the Committees on Armed Services of both Houses of the Congress, vest title to the facilities completed pursuant to this section in such educational institutions under such terms and conditions as may be deemed in the best interests of the United States.

(Oct. 27, 1949, ch. 766, title I, § 102, 63 Stat. 936; Pub. L. 85–568, title III, § 301(d)(2), (3), July 29, 1958, 72 Stat. 433.)

AMENDMENTS

1958—Pub. L. 85–568 substituted "Administrator" for "Committee" in three places, and "his" for "its".

EFFECTIVE DATE OF 1958 AMENDMENT

Amendment by Pub. L. 85–568 effective 90 days after July 29, 1958, or on any earlier date on which the Administrator of the National Aeronautics and Space Administration determines, and announces by proclamation, that the Administration has been organized and is prepared to discharge the duties and exercise the powers conferred upon it, see section 301(e) of Pub. L. 85–568, set out as a note under section 2302 of Title 10, Armed Forces.

SECTION REFERRED TO IN OTHER SECTIONS

This section is referred to in section 515 of this title.

§ 513. Expansion of existing facilities; appropriations; testing of models

(a) The Administrator is authorized to expand the facilities at his existing laboratories and centers by the construction of additional transsonic, supersonic, and hypersonic wind tunnels, including buildings, equipment, and accessory construction, and by the acquisition of land and installation of utilities.

(b) There is authorized to be appropriated such sums as may be necessary to carry out the purposes of this section, but not to exceed $136,000,000.

(c) The facilities authorized by this section shall be operated and staffed by the Administrator but shall be available primarily to industry for testing experimental models in connection with the development of aircraft and missiles. Such tests shall be scheduled and conducted in accordance with industry's requirements and allocation of facility time shall be made in accordance with the public interest, with proper emphasis upon the requirements of each military service and due consideration of civilian needs.

(Oct. 27, 1949, ch. 766, title I, § 103, 63 Stat. 937; Pub. L. 85–568, title III, § 301(d)(2), (3), July 29, 1958, 72 Stat. 433; Pub. L. 106–391, title III, § 312(2), Oct. 30, 2000, 114 Stat. 1594.)

AMENDMENTS

2000—Subsec. (a). Pub. L. 106–391, §312(2)(A), (B), substituted "laboratories and centers" for "laboratories" and "transsonic, supersonic, and hypersonic" for "supersonic".

Subsec. (c). Pub. L. 106–391, §312(2)(C), substituted "facility" for "laboratory".

1958—Subsecs. (a), (c). Pub. L. 85–568 substituted "Administrator" for "Committee" in subsecs. (a) and (c), and "his" for "its" in subsec. (a).

EFFECTIVE DATE OF 1958 AMENDMENT

Amendment by Pub. L. 85–568 effective 90 days after July 29, 1958, or on any earlier date on which the Administrator of the National Aeronautics and Space Administration determines, and announces by proclamation, that the Administration has been organized and is prepared to discharge the duties and exercise the powers conferred upon it, see section 301(e) of Pub. L. 85–568, set out as a note under section 2302 of Title 10, Armed Forces.

ADDITIONAL APPROPRIATIONS

Act June 29, 1950, ch. 405, §801, 64 Stat. 286, provided in part for an additional appropriation of $75,000,000, to remain available until expended; for the construction and completion and equipment of facilities at the Langley Aeronautical Laboratory, Langley Air Force Base, Virginia.

§514. Expansion of facilities at Carderock, Maryland

The Secretary of the Navy is authorized, in implementation of the unitary plan, to expand the naval facilities at the David W. Taylor Model Basin, Carderock, Maryland, by the construction of a wind tunnel, including buildings, equipment, utilities, and accessory construction, at a cost not to exceed $6,600,000.

(Oct. 27, 1949, ch. 766, title I, §104, 63 Stat. 937.)

§515. Reports to Congress

The Administrator shall submit semi-annual written reports to the Congress covering the selection of institutions and contracts entered into pursuant to section 512 of this title together with other pertinent information relative to the Administrator's activities and accomplishments thereunder.

(Oct. 27, 1949, ch. 766, title I, §105, 63 Stat. 937; Pub. L. 85–568, title III, §301(d)(2), July 29, 1958, 72 Stat. 433.)

AMENDMENTS

1958—Pub. L. 85–568 substituted "Administrator" for "Committee" and "Administrator's" for "Committee's".

EFFECTIVE DATE OF 1958 AMENDMENT

Amendment by Pub. L. 85–568 effective 90 days after July 29, 1958, or on any earlier date on which the Administrator of the National Aeronautics and Space Administration determines, and announces by proclamation, that the Administration has been organized and is prepared to discharge the duties and exercise the powers conferred upon it, see section 301(e) of Pub. L. 85–568, set out as a note under section 2302 of Title 10, Armed Forces.

SUBCHAPTER II—AIR ENGINEERING DEVELOPMENT CENTER

§521. Establishment; construction, maintenance, and operation of public works and wind tunnels

The Secretary of the Air Force is authorized to establish an Air Engineering Development Center, and to construct, install, and equip (1) temporary and permanent public works, including housing accommodations and community facilities for military and civilian personnel, buildings, facilities, appurtenances, and utilities; and (2) wind tunnels in implementation of the unitary plan referred to in subchapter I of this chapter; and to maintain and operate the public works and wind tunnels authorized by this subchapter.

(Oct. 27, 1949, ch. 766, title II, §201, 63 Stat. 937.)

§522. Acquisition of lands; advance payments for construction

To accomplish the purposes of this subchapter, the Secretary of the Air Force is authorized to acquire lands and rights pertaining thereto, or other interest therein, including the temporary use thereof, by donation, purchase, exchange of Government-owned lands, or otherwise, and construction under this subchapter may be prosecuted without regard to section 3324(a) and (b) of title 31.

(Oct. 27, 1949, ch. 766, title II, §202, 63 Stat. 937.)

CODIFICATION

"Section 3324(a) and (b) of title 31" substituted in text for "section 3648, Revised Statutes, as amended [31 U.S.C. 529]" on authority of Pub. L. 97–258, §4(b), Sept. 13, 1982, 96 Stat. 1067, the first section of which enacted Title 31, Money and Finance.

§523. Employment of civilian personnel

The Secretary of the Air Force is authorized to employ such civilian personnel as may be necessary to carry out the purposes of this subchapter without regard to the limitation on maximum number of employees imposed by section 14(a)[1] of the Federal Employees Pay Act of 1946 (5 U.S.C. 947(g)).

(Oct. 27, 1949, ch. 766, title II, §203, 63 Stat. 937.)

REFERENCES IN TEXT

Section 14(a) of the Federal Employees Pay Act of 1946 (5 U.S.C. 947(g)), referred to in text, was repealed by act Sept. 12, 1950, ch. 946, title III, §301(85), 64 Stat. 843.

§524. Authorization of appropriations

There is authorized to be appropriated, out of any moneys in the Treasury not otherwise appropriated, to remain available until expended when so specified in the appropriation act concerned, (a) not to exceed $157,500,000 for the establishment and for initial construction, installation, and equipment of the Air Engineering Development Center authorized in this subchapter, including expenses for necessary surveys and acquisition of land, and (b) such sums

[1] See References in Text note below.

as may be necessary to carry out the other purposes of this subchapter.

(Oct. 27, 1949, ch. 766, title II, §204, 63 Stat. 937; Sept. 21, 1950, ch. 969, 64 Stat. 895.)

AMENDMENTS

1950—Act Sept. 21, 1950, substituted "$157,500,000" for "$100,000,000".

CHAPTER 21—ABACÁ PRODUCTION

§§541 to 546. Omitted

CODIFICATION

Sections 541 to 546, act Aug. 10, 1950, ch. 673, §§2–7, 64 Stat. 435–437, terminated not later than ten years after Apr. 1, 1950. See Effective and Termination Date note below.

Section 541 related to Congressional declaration of policy.

Section 542 related to production program of abacá.

Section 543 related to administration.

Section 544 related to financing.

Section 545 related to disposal of property.

Section 546 related to reports to Congress.

EFFECTIVE AND TERMINATION DATE

Act Aug. 10, 1950, ch. 673, §8, 64 Stat. 437, provided that this chapter become effective Apr. 1, 1950, and remain effective for ten years thereafter, unless Congress or President direct earlier termination of operations, and for such further period as necessary to earliest practicable liquidation of operations under this chapter.

CHAPTER 22—UNIFORM CODE OF MILITARY JUSTICE

SUBCHAPTER I—GENERAL PROVISIONS

§§551 to 556. Repealed. Aug. 10, 1956, ch. 1041, §53, 70A Stat. 641

Section 551, act May 5, 1950, ch. 169, §1, 64 Stat. 108, defined terms used in this chapter. See sections 101 and 801 of Title 10, Armed Forces.

Section 552, acts May 5, 1950, ch. 169, §1, 64 Stat. 109; Aug. 1, 1956, ch. 852, §23, 70 Stat. 911, related to persons subject to Articles of War. See section 802 of Title 10. Act Aug. 1, 1956, ch. 852, §23, 70 Stat. 911 was repealed by Pub. L. 87–651, title III, §307A, Sept. 7, 1962, 76 Stat. 526.

Section 553, act May 5, 1950, ch. 169, §1, 64 Stat. 109, related to jurisdiction to try certain personnel. See section 803 of Title 10.

Section 554, act May 5, 1950, ch. 169, §1, 64 Stat. 110, provided for dismissed officer's right to trial by court-martial. See section 804 of Title 10.

Section 555, act May 5, 1950, ch. 169, §1, 64 Stat. 110, provided that this chapter should be applicable in all places. See section 805 of Title 10.

Section 556, act May 5, 1950, ch. 169, §1, 64 Stat. 110, related to judge advocates and legal officers. See section 806 of Title 10.

EFFECTIVE DATE OF REPEAL

Repeal effective Jan. 1, 1957, see act Aug. 10, 1956, ch. 1041, §53 footnote, 70A Stat. 680.

SUBCHAPTER II—APPREHENSION AND RESTRAINT

§§561 to 568. Repealed. Aug. 10, 1956, ch. 1041, §53, 70A Stat. 641

Section 561, act May 5, 1950, ch. 169, §1, 64 Stat. 111, related to apprehension. See section 807 of Title 10, Armed Forces.

Section 562, act May 5, 1950, ch. 169, §1, 64 Stat. 111, provided for apprehension of deserters. See section 808 of Title 10.

Section 563, act May 5, 1950, ch. 169, §1, 64 Stat. 111, related to imposition of restraint. See section 809 of Title 10.

Section 564, act May 5, 1950, ch. 169, §1, 64 Stat. 111, related to restraint of persons charged with offenses. See section 810 of Title 10.

Section 565, act May 5, 1950, ch. 169, §1, 64 Stat. 112, provided for reports and receiving of prisoners. See section 811 of Title 10.

Section 566, act May 5, 1950, ch. 169, §1, 64 Stat. 112, prohibited confinement of members of armed forces with enemy prisoners. See section 812 of Title 10.

Section 567, act May 5, 1950, ch. 169, §1, 64 Stat. 112, prohibited punishment before trial. See section 813 of Title 10.

Section 568, act May 5, 1950, ch. 169, §1, 64 Stat. 112, related to delivery of offenders to civil authorities. See section 814 of Title 10.

EFFECTIVE DATE OF REPEAL

Repeal effective Jan. 1, 1957, see act Aug. 10, 1956, ch. 1041, §53 footnote, 70A Stat. 680.

SUBCHAPTER III—NON-JUDICIAL PUNISHMENT

§571. Repealed. Aug. 10, 1956, ch. 1041, §53, 70A Stat. 641

Section, act May 5, 1950, ch. 169, §1, 64 Stat. 112, related to commanding officer's non-judicial punishment. See section 815 of Title 10, Armed Forces.

EFFECTIVE DATE OF REPEAL

Repeal effective Jan. 1, 1957, see act Aug. 10, 1956, ch. 1041, §53 footnote, 70A Stat. 680.

SUBCHAPTER IV—COURTS-MARTIAL JURISDICTION

§§576 to 581. Repealed. Aug. 10, 1956, ch. 1041, §53, 70A Stat. 641

Section 576, act May 5, 1950, ch. 169, §1, 64 Stat. 113, classified types of courts-martial. See section 816 of Title 10, Armed Forces.

Section 577, act May 5, 1950, ch. 169, §1, 64 Stat. 114, related to jurisdiction of courts-martial in general. See section 817 of Title 10.

Section 578, act May 5, 1950, ch. 169, §1, 64 Stat. 114, related to jurisdiction of general courts-martial. See section 818 of Title 10.

Section 579, act May 5, 1950, ch. 169, §1, 64 Stat. 114, related to jurisdiction of special courts-martial. See section 819 of Title 10.

Section 580, act May 5, 1950, ch. 169, §1, 64 Stat. 114, related to jurisdiction of summary courts-martial. See section 820 of Title 10.

Section 581, act May 5, 1950, ch. 169, §1, 64 Stat. 115, provided that jurisdiction of courts-martial was not exclusive. See section 821 of Title 10.

EFFECTIVE DATE OF REPEAL

Repeal effective Jan. 1, 1957, see act Aug. 10, 1956, ch. 1041, §53 footnote, 70A Stat. 680.

SUBCHAPTER V—APPOINTMENT AND COMPOSITION OF COURTS-MARTIAL

§§586 to 593. Repealed. Aug. 10, 1956, ch. 1041, §53, 70A Stat. 641

Section 586, act May 5, 1950, ch. 169, §1, 64 Stat. 115, prescribed persons who may convene general courts-martial. See section 822 of Title 10, Armed Forces.

Section 587, act May 5, 1950, ch. 169, §1, 64 Stat. 115, prescribed persons who may convene special courts-martial. See section 823 of Title 10.

Section 588, act May 5, 1950, ch. 169, §1, 64 Stat. 116, prescribed persons who may convene summary courts-martial. See section 824 of Title 10.

Section 589, act May 5, 1950, ch. 169, §1, 64 Stat. 116, related to persons who may serve on courts-martial. See section 825 of Title 10.

Section 590, act May 5, 1950, ch. 169, §1, 64 Stat. 117, provided for law officer of a general court-martial. See section 826 of Title 10.

Section 591, act May 5, 1950, ch. 169, §1, 64 Stat. 117, related to appointment of trial counsel and defense counsel. See section 827 of Title 10.

Section 592, act May 5, 1950, ch. 169, §1, 64 Stat. 117, provided for appointment of reporters and interpreters. See section 828 of Title 10.

Section 593, act May 5, 1950, ch. 169, §1, 64 Stat. 117, related to absent and additional members of courts-martial. See section 829 of Title 10.

EFFECTIVE DATE OF REPEAL

Repeal effective Jan. 1, 1957, see act Aug. 10, 1956, ch. 1041, §53 footnote, 70A Stat. 680.

SUBCHAPTER VI—PRETRIAL PROCEDURE

§§601 to 606. Repealed. Aug. 10, 1956, ch. 1041, §53, 70A Stat. 641

Section 601, act May 5, 1950, ch. 169, §1, 64 Stat. 118, related to charges and specifications. See section 830 of Title 10, Armed Forces.

Section 602, act May 5, 1950, ch. 169, §1, 64 Stat. 118, prohibited compulsory self-incrimination. See section 831 of Title 10.

Section 603, act May 5, 1950, ch. 169, §1, 64 Stat. 118, related to investigations. See section 832 of Title 10.

Section 604, act May 5, 1950, ch. 169, §1, 64 Stat. 119, provided for forwarding of charges. See section 833 of Title 10.

Section 605, act May 5, 1950, ch. 169, §1, 64 Stat. 119, related to advice of staff judge advocate and reference for trial. See section 834 of Title 10.

Section 606, act May 5, 1950, ch. 169, §1, 64 Stat. 119, provided for service of charges. See section 835 of Title 10.

EFFECTIVE DATE OF REPEAL

Repeal effective Jan. 1, 1957, see act Aug. 10, 1956, ch. 1041, §53 footnote, 70A Stat. 680.

SUBCHAPTER VII—TRIAL PROCEDURE

§§611 to 629. Repealed. Aug. 10, 1956, ch. 1041, §53, 70A Stat. 641

Section 611, act May 5, 1950, ch. 169, §1, 64 Stat. 120, authorized President to prescribe rules. See section 836 of Title 10, Armed Forces.

Section 612, act May 5, 1950, ch. 169, §1, 64 Stat. 120, related to unlawfully influencing action of court. See section 837 of Title 10.

Section 613, act May 5, 1950, ch. 169, §1, 64 Stat. 120, provided for duties of trial counsel and defense counsel. See section 838 of Title 10.

Section 614, act May 5, 1950, ch. 169, §1, 64 Stat. 121, related to sessions of the courts-martial. See section 839 of Title 10.

Section 615, act May 5, 1950, ch. 169, §1, 64 Stat. 121, provided for continuances. See section 840 of Title 10.

Section 616, act May 5, 1950, ch. 169, §1, 64 Stat. 121, provided for challenges. See section 841 of Title 10.

Section 617, act May 5, 1950, ch. 169, §1, 64 Stat. 121, related to oaths. See section 842 of Title 10.

Section 618, act May 5, 1950, ch. 169, §1, 64 Stat. 121, related to statutes of limitation. See section 843 of Title 10.

Section 619, act May 5, 1950, ch. 169, §1, 64 Stat. 122, related to former jeopardy. See section 844 of Title 10.

Section 620, act May 5, 1950, ch. 169, §1, 64 Stat. 122, related to pleas of the accused. See section 845 of Title 10.

Section 621, act May 5, 1950, ch. 169, §1, 64 Stat. 122, related to opportunity to obtain witnesses and other evidence. See section 846 of Title 10.

Section 622, act May 5, 1950, ch. 169, §1, 64 Stat. 123, provided for refusal to appear or testify. See section 847 of Title 10.

Section 623, act May 5, 1950, ch. 169, §1, 64 Stat. 123, related to contempts. See section 848 of Title 10.

Section 624, act May 5, 1950, ch. 169, §1, 64 Stat. 123, related to depositions. See section 849 of Title 10.

Section 625, act May 5, 1950, ch. 169, §1, 64 Stat. 124, provided for admissibility of records of courts of inquiry. See section 850 of Title 10.

Section 626, act May 5, 1950, ch. 169, §1, 64 Stat. 124, provided for methods of voting and rulings. See section 851 of Title 10.

Section 627, act May 5, 1950, ch. 169, §1, 64 Stat. 125, prescribed number of votes required. See section 852 of Title 10.

Section 628, act May 5, 1950, ch. 169, 64 Stat. 125, required every court-martial to announce its findings and sentence. See section 853 of Title 10.

Section 629, act May 5, 1950, ch. 169, §1, 64 Stat. 125, related to record of trial. See section 858 of Title 10.

EFFECTIVE DATE OF REPEAL

Repeal effective Jan. 1, 1957, see act Aug. 10, 1956, ch. 1041, §53 footnote, 70A Stat. 680.

SUBCHAPTER VIII—SENTENCES

§§636 to 639. Repealed. Aug. 10, 1956, ch. 1041, §53, 70A Stat. 641

Section 636, act May 5, 1950, ch. 169, §1, 64 Stat. 126, prohibited cruel and unusual punishments. See section 855 of Title 10, Armed Forces.

Section 637, act May 5, 1950, ch. 169, §1, 64 Stat. 126, related to maximum limits of punishment. See section 856 of Title 10.

Section 638, act May 5, 1950, ch. 169, §1, 64 Stat. 126, provided for effective date of sentences. See section 857 of Title 10.

Section 639, act May 5, 1950, ch. 169, §1, 64 Stat. 126, related to execution of confinement. See section 854 of Title 10.

EFFECTIVE DATE OF REPEAL

Repeal effective Jan. 1, 1957, see act Aug. 10, 1956, ch. 1041, §53 footnote, 70A Stat. 680.

SUBCHAPTER IX—REVIEW OF COURTS-MARTIAL

§§646 to 663. Repealed. Aug. 10, 1956, ch. 1041, §53, 70A Stat. 641

Section 646, act May 5, 1950, ch. 169, §1, 64 Stat. 127, related to errors of law and to lesser included offense. See section 859 of Title 10, Armed Forces.

Section 647, act May 5, 1950, ch. 169, §1, 64 Stat. 127, provided for initial action on record. See section 860 of Title 10.

Section 648, act May 5, 1950, ch. 169, §1, 64 Stat. 127, provided for initial action on general court-martial records. See section 861 of Title 10.

Section 649, act May 5, 1950, ch. 169, §1, 64 Stat. 127, provided for reconsideration and revision. See section 862 of Title 10.

Section 650, act May 5, 1950, ch. 169, §1, 64 Stat. 127, related to rehearings. See section 863 of Title 10.

Section 651, act May 5, 1950, ch. 169, §1, 64 Stat. 128, related to approval by convening authority. See section 864 of Title 10.

Section 652, act May 5, 1950, ch. 169, §1, 64 Stat. 128, provided for disposition of records after review by convening authority. See section 865 of Title 10.

Section 653, act May 5, 1950, ch. 169, §1, 64 Stat. 128, provided for review by board of review. See section 866 of Title 10.

Section 654, acts May 5, 1950, ch. 169, §1, 64 Stat. 130; Mar. 2, 1955, ch. 9, §1(i), 69 Stat. 10, provided for review by the Court of Military Appeals. See section 867 of Title 10.

Section 655, act May 5, 1950, ch. 169, §1, 64 Stat. 130, authorized establishment of branch offices of The Judge Advocate General. See section 868 of Title 10.

Section 656, act May 30, 1950, ch. 169, §1, 64 Stat. 130, provided for review in office of The Judge Advocate General. See section 869 of Title 10.

Section 657, act May 5, 1950, ch. 169, §1, 64 Stat. 130, provided for appellate counsel. See section 870 of Title 10.

Section 658, act May 5, 1950, ch. 169, §1, 64 Stat. 131, provided for execution of sentence and suspension of sentence. See section 871 of Title 10.

Section 659, act May 5, 1950, ch. 169, §1, 64 Stat. 131, related to vacation of suspension of a court-martial sentence. See section 872 of Title 10.

Section 660, act May 5, 1950, ch. 169, §1, 64 Stat. 132, provided for a petition for a new trial. See section 873 of Title 10.

Section 661, act May 5, 1950, ch. 169, §1, 64 Stat. 132, authorized remission and suspension of sentences. See section 874 of Title 10.

Section 662, act May 5, 1950, ch. 169, §1, 64 Stat. 132, related to restoration of rights, privileges, and property. See section 875 of Title 10.

Section 663, act May 5, 1950, ch. 169, §1, 64 Stat. 132, related to finality of court-martial judgments. See section 876 of Title 10.

Effective Date of Repeal

Repeal effective Jan. 1, 1957, see act Aug. 10, 1956, ch. 1041, §53 footnote, 70A Stat. 680.

SUBCHAPTER X—PUNITIVE ARTICLES

§§671 to 728. Repealed. Aug. 10, 1956, ch. 1041, §53, 70A Stat. 641

Section 671, act May 5, 1950, ch. 169, §1, 64 Stat. 134, defined "principal". See section 877 of Title 10, Armed Forces.

Section 672, act May 5, 1950, ch. 169, §1, 64 Stat. 134, related to accessories after the fact. See section 878 of Title 10.

Section 673, act May 5, 1950, ch. 169, §1, 64 Stat. 134, authorized conviction of lesser included offense. See section 879 of Title 10.

Section 674, act May 5, 1950, ch. 169, §1, 64 Stat. 138, related to attempts. See section 880 of Title 10.

Section 675, act May 5, 1950, ch. 169, §1, 64 Stat. 138, related to conspiracy. See section 881 of Title 10.

Section 676, act May 5, 1950, ch. 169, §1, 64 Stat. 134, related to solicitation. See section 882 of Title 10.

Section 677, act May 5, 1950, ch. 169, §1, 64 Stat. 134, related to fraudulent enlistment, appointment, or separation. See section 883 of Title 10.

Section 678, act May 5, 1950, ch. 169, §1, 64 Stat. 135, related to unlawful enlistment, appointment, or separation. See section 884 of Title 10.

Section 679, act May 5, 1950, ch. 169, §1, 64 Stat. 135, provided for desertion. See section 885 of Title 10.

Section 680, act May 5, 1950, ch. 169, §1, 64 Stat. 135, related to absence without leave. See section 886 of Title 10.

Section 681, act May 5, 1950, ch. 169, §1, 64 Stat. 135, related to missing movement of a ship, aircraft, or unit. See section 887 of Title 10.

Section 682, act May 5, 1950, ch. 169, §1, 64 Stat. 135, related to contempt towards officials. See section 888 of Title 10.

Section 683, act May 5, 1950, ch. 169, §1, 64 Stat. 135, related to disrespect towards superior officer. See section 889 of Title 10.

Section 684, act May 5, 1950, ch. 169, §1, 64 Stat. 135, related to assaulting or willfully disobeying officer. See section 890 of Title 10.

Section 685, act May 5, 1950, ch. 169, §1, 64 Stat. 136, related to insubordinate conduct towards noncommissioned officer. See section 891 of Title 10.

Section 686, act May 5, 1950, ch. 169, §1, 64 Stat. 136, related to failure to obey order or regulation. See section 892 of Title 10.

Section 687, act May 5, 1950, ch. 169, §1, 64 Stat. 136, related to cruelty and maltreatment. See section 893 of Title 10.

Section 688, act May 5, 1950, ch. 169, §1, 64 Stat. 136, related to mutiny or sedition. See section 894 of Title 10.

Section 689, act May 5, 1950, ch. 169, §1, 64 Stat. 136, related to arrest and confinement. See section 895 of Title 10.

Section 690, act May 5, 1950, ch. 169, §1, 64 Stat. 136, related to releasing prisoner without proper authority. See section 896 of Title 10.

Section 691, act May 5, 1950, ch. 169, §1, 64 Stat. 137, related to unlawful detention of another. See section 897 of Title 10.

Section 692, act May 5, 1950, ch. 169, §1, 64 Stat. 137, related to noncompliance with procedural rules. See section 898 of Title 10.

Section 693, act May 5, 1950, ch. 169, §1, 64 Stat. 137, related to misbehavior before the enemy. See section 899 of Title 10.

Section 694, act May 5, 1950, ch. 169, §1, 64 Stat. 137, related to subordinate compelling surrender. See section 900 of Title 10.

Section 695, act May 5, 1950, ch. 169, §1, 64 Stat. 137, related to improper use of countersign. See section 901 of Title 10.

Section 696, act May 5, 1950, ch. 169, §1, 64 Stat. 137, related to forcing a safeguard. See section 902 of Title 10.

Section 697, act May 5, 1950, ch. 169, §1, 64 Stat. 138, related to captured or abandoned property. See section 903 of Title 10.

Section 698, act May 5, 1950, ch. 169, §1, 64 Stat. 138, related to aiding the enemy. See section 904 of Title 10.

Section 699, act May 5, 1950, ch. 169, §1, 64 Stat. 138, related to misconduct as a prisoner. See section 905 of Title 10.

Section 700, act May 5, 1950, ch. 169, §1, 64 Stat. 138, related to spies. See section 906 of Title 10.

Section 701, act May 5, 1950, ch. 169, §1, 64 Stat. 138, related to false official statements. See section 907 of Title 10.

Section 702, act May 5, 1950, ch. 169, §1, 64 Stat. 138, related to loss, damage, destruction, or wrongful disposition of military property. See section 908 of Title 10.

Section 703, act May 5, 1950, ch. 169, §1, 64 Stat. 139, related to waste, spoil or destruction of property other than military property. See section 909 of Title 10.

Section 704, act May 5, 1950, ch. 169, §1, 64 Stat. 139, related to improper hazarding of vessel. See section 910 of Title 10.

Section 705, act May 5, 1950, ch. 169, §1, 64 Stat. 139, related to drunken or reckless driving. See section 911 of Title 10.

Section 706, act May 5, 1950, ch. 169, §1, 64 Stat. 139, related to drunk on duty. See section 912 of Title 10.

Section 707, act May 5, 1950, ch. 169, §1, 64 Stat. 139, related to misbehavior of sentinel. See section 913 of Title 10.

Section 708, act May 5, 1950, ch. 169, §1, 64 Stat. 139, related to dueling. See section 914 of Title 10.

Section 709, act May 5, 1950, ch. 169, §1, 64 Stat. 139, related to malingering. See section 915 of Title 10.

Section 710, act May 5, 1950, ch. 169, §1, 64 Stat. 139, related to riot or breach of peace. See section 916 of Title 10.

Section 711, act May 5, 1950, ch. 169, §1, 64 Stat. 139, related to provoking speeches or gestures. See section 917 of Title 10.

Section 712, act May 5, 1950, ch. 169, §1, 64 Stat. 140, related to murder. See section 918 of Title 10.

Section 713, act May 5, 1950, ch. 169, §1, 64 Stat. 140, related to manslaughter. See section 919 of Title 10.

Section 714, act May 5, 1950, ch. 169, §1, 64 Stat. 140, related to rape and carnal knowledge. See section 920 of Title 10.

Section 715, act May 5, 1950, ch. 169, §1, 64 Stat. 140, related to larceny and wrongful appropriation. See section 921 of Title 10.

Section 716, act May 5, 1950, ch. 169, §1, 64 Stat. 140, related to robbery. See section 922 of Title 10.

Section 717, act May 5, 1950, ch. 169, §1, 64 Stat. 141, related to forgery. See section 923 of Title 10.

Section 718, act May 5, 1950, ch. 169, §1, 64 Stat. 141, related to maiming. See section 924 of Title 10.

Section 719, act May 5, 1950, ch. 169, §1, 64 Stat. 141, related to sodomy. See section 925 of Title 10.

Section 720, act May 5, 1950, ch. 169, §1, 64 Stat. 141, related to arson. See section 926 of Title 10.

Section 721, act May 5, 1950, ch. 169, §1, 64 Stat. 141, related to extortion. See section 927 of Title 10.

Section 722, act May 5, 1950, ch. 169, §1, 64 Stat. 141, related to assault. See section 928 of Title 10.

Section 723, act May 5, 1950, ch. 169, §1, 64 Stat. 142, related to burglary. See section 929 of Title 10.

Section 724, act May 5, 1950, ch. 169, §1, 64 Stat. 142, related to housebreaking. See section 930 of Title 10.

Section 725, act May 5, 1950, ch. 169, §1, 64 Stat. 142, related to perjury. See section 931 of Title 10.

Section 726, act May 5, 1950, ch. 169, §1, 64 Stat. 142, related to frauds against Government. See section 932 of Title 10.

Section 727, act May 5, 1950, ch. 169, §1, 64 Stat. 142, related to conduct unbecoming an officer and gentleman. See section 933 of Title 10.

Section 728, act May 5, 1950, ch. 169, §1, 64 Stat. 142, was a general article covering offenses not specifically defined. See section 934 of Title 10.

EFFECTIVE DATE OF REPEAL

Repeal effective Jan. 1, 1957, see act Aug. 10, 1956, ch. 1041, §53 footnote, 70A Stat. 680.

SUBCHAPTER XI—MISCELLANEOUS PROVISIONS

§§731 to 739. Repealed. Aug. 10, 1956, ch. 1041, §53, 70A Stat. 641

Section 731, act May 5, 1950, ch. 169, §1, 64 Stat. 143, related to courts of inquiry. See section 935 of Title 10, Armed Forces.

Section 732, act May 5, 1950, ch. 169, §1, 64 Stat. 143, related to authority to administer oaths and to act as notary. See section 936 of Title 10.

Section 733, act May 5, 1950, ch. 169, §1, 64 Stat. 144, required reading and explanation of certain sections of this chapter. See section 937 of Title 10.

Section 734, act May 5, 1950, ch. 169, §1, 64 Stat. 144, related to complaints of wrongs. See section 938 of Title 10.

Section 735, act May 5, 1950, ch. 169, §1, 64 Stat. 144, related to redress of injuries to property. See section 939 of Title 10.

Section 736, act May 5, 1950, ch. 169, §1, 64 Stat. 145, authorized President to delegate his authority. See section 940 of Title 10.

Section 737, act May 5, 1950, ch. 169, §8, 64 Stat. 146, provided for oath of enlistment. See section 502 of Title 10.

Section 738, act May 5, 1950, ch. 169, §9, 64 Stat. 146, provided for removal of suits. See section 1442a of Title 28, Judiciary and Judicial Procedure.

Section 739, act May 5, 1950, ch. 169, §10, 64 Stat. 146, related to dismissal of officers. See sections 1161 and 6408 of Title 10.

EFFECTIVE DATE OF REPEAL

Repeal effective Jan. 1, 1957, see act Aug. 10, 1956, ch. 1041, §53 footnote, 70A Stat. 680.

§740. Omitted

CODIFICATION

Section, act May 5, 1950, ch. 169, §12, 64 Stat. 147, which authorized the Judge Advocate General of any of the armed forces to grant a new trial, vacate a sentence, restore rights and property, and substitute an administrative discharge for a dismissal or for a dishonorable or bad-conduct discharge in any court-martial case for offenses committed during World War II upon application made within one year after termination of the war or after final disposition upon initial appellate review, whichever was the later, limited new trial applications to one as to any one case, and provided that World War II was deemed to have ended as of May 31, 1951.

EXECUTIVE ORDER NO. 10190

Ex. Ord. No. 10190, Dec. 6, 1950, 15 F.R. 8711, provided for the petition to the Judge Advocate General of the Navy or to the General Counsel of the Treasury Department, in respect to violations of Navy or Coast Guard disciplinary laws committed between Dec. 7, 1941 and May 30, 1951, for a new trial, the vacatur of sentence and restoration of rights and property, or the substitution of an administrative discharge for a dismissal, dishonorable discharge, or bad-conduct discharge; limited such petition to within one year after final disposition of the case upon initial appellate review or to any time before May 31, 1952 (whichever was the later date); prohibited submission of more than one such petition in any one case and submission after death of an accused; specified the ground for relief and the form and contents of the petition; permitted oral agreement; prescribed the rules for a hearing; authorized additional investigation; required the action granting or denying a remedy to be in writing and published; provided the procedure for a new trial; and specified the effect of a new trial upon the prior trial and sentence.

§741. Repealed. Aug. 10, 1956, ch. 1041, §53, 70A Stat. 641, eff. Jan. 1, 1957

Section, act May 5, 1950, ch. 169, §13, 64 Stat. 147, prescribed qualifications of Judge Advocate Generals of armed forces. See sections 3037, 5148, and 8072 of Title 10, Armed Forces.

EFFECTIVE DATE OF REPEAL

Repeal effective Jan. 1, 1957, see act Aug. 10, 1956, ch. 1041, §53 footnote, 70A Stat. 680.

CHAPTER 22A—REPRESENTATION OF ARMED FORCES PERSONNEL BEFORE FOREIGN JUDICIAL TRIBUNALS

§§751 to 755. Repealed. Pub. L. 85–861, §36A, Sept. 2, 1958, 72 Stat. 1570

Section 751, act July 24, 1956, ch. 689, §1, 70 Stat. 630, related to representation of members of the Armed Forces before foreign judicial tribunals and employment of counsel.

Section 752, act July 24, 1956, ch. 689, §2, 70 Stat. 630, provided for enactment of regulations.

Section 753, act July 24, 1956, ch. 689, §3, 70 Stat. 630, provided that sections 189 and 365 of the Revised Statutes not apply to action taken under this act.

Section 754, act July 24, 1956, ch. 689, §4, 70 Stat. 630, related to claims for reimbursement.

Section 755, act July 24, 1956, ch. 689, §5, 70 Stat. 630, related to appropriations.

CHAPTER 23—INTERNAL SECURITY

SUBCHAPTER I—CONTROL OF SUBVERSIVE ACTIVITIES

APPLICATION TO COMMUNIST PARTY MEMBERS

Application of subchapters I and II of this chapter and other provisions of the Internal Security Act of 1950, as amended, to members of the Communist Party and other subversive organizations, see section 843 of this title, and References in Text note set out under that section.

CHAPTER REFERRED TO IN OTHER SECTIONS

This chapter is referred to in sections 842, 843 of this title; title 26 section 3121; title 42 section 410.

SUBCHAPTER I—CONTROL OF SUBVERSIVE ACTIVITIES

APPLICATION TO COMMUNIST PARTY MEMBERS

Application of this subchapter to members of the Communist Party and other subversive organizations, see section 843 of this title, and References in Text note set out under that section.

SUBCHAPTER REFERRED TO IN OTHER SECTIONS

This subchapter is referred to in title 42 section 2000e–2.

§ 781. Repealed. Pub. L. 103–199, title VIII, § 803(1), Dec. 17, 1993, 107 Stat. 2329

Section, acts Sept. 23, 1950, ch. 1024, title I, § 2, 64 Stat. 987; Jan. 2, 1968, Pub. L. 90–237, § 1, 81 Stat. 765, related to Congressional finding of necessity to control subversive activities.

SHORT TITLE OF 1954 AMENDMENT

Act Aug. 24, 1954, ch. 886, § 1, 68 Stat. 775, provided: "That this Act [enacting sections 792a and 841 to 844 of this title, amending sections 782, 784, 785, 789 to 792, and 793 of this title, and enacting a provision set out as a note under section 841 of this title] may be cited as the 'Communist Control Act of 1954'."

SHORT TITLE

Act Sept. 23, 1950, provided that: "This Act [enacting subchapters I to III of this chapter and section 1507 of Title 18, Crimes and Criminal Procedure, amending sections 137 to 137–8, 156, 456, 457, 704, 705, 725, 729, 733, 734, and 735 of Title 8, Aliens and Nationality, section 793 of Title 18, and sections 611 and 618 of Title 22, Foreign Relations and Intercourse, enacting provisions set out as notes under sections 781 and 811 of this title and section 792 of Title 18, and amending a provision set out as a note under section 402 of this title] may be cited as the 'Internal Security Act of 1950'."

Section 1(a) of act Sept. 23, 1950, which provided that title I of act Sept. 23, 1950, which enacted this subchapter and section 1507 of Title 18, Crimes and Criminal Procedure, amended sections 137 to 137–8, 156, 456, 457, 704, 705, 725, 729, 733, 734, and 735 of Title 8, Aliens and Nationality, section 793 of Title 18, and sections 611 and 618 of Title 22, Foreign Relations and Intercourse, and enacted provisions set out as notes under section 781 of this title and section 792 of Title 18, be cited as the "Subversive Activities Control Act of 1950", was repealed by Pub. L. 103–199, title VIII, § 803(1), Dec. 17, 1993, 107 Stat. 2329.

SEPARABILITY

Section 32 of title I of act Sept. 23, 1950, provided: "If any provision of this title [see Short Title note above] or the application thereof to any person or circumstances, is held invalid, the remaining provisions of this title, or the application of such provision to other persons or circumstances, shall not be affected thereby."

§ 782. Repealed. Pub. L. 103–199, title VIII, § 803(1), Dec. 17, 1993, 107 Stat. 2329

Section, acts Sept. 23, 1950, ch. 1024, title I, § 3, 64 Stat. 989; Aug. 24, 1954, ch. 886, § 7(a), (b), 68 Stat. 777; May 31, 1962, Pub. L. 87–474, § 1(a), 76 Stat. 91; Jan. 2, 1968, Pub. L. 90–237, § 2, 81 Stat. 765, defined terms for purposes of this subchapter.

§ 783. Offenses

(a) Communication of classified information by Government officer or employee

It shall be unlawful for any officer or employee of the United States or of any department or agency thereof, or of any corporation the stock of which is owned in whole or in major part by the United States or any department or agency thereof, to communicate in any manner or by any means, to any other person whom such officer or employee knows or has reason to believe to be an agent or representative of any foreign government, any information of a kind which shall have been classified by the President (or by the head of any such department, agency, or corporation with the approval of the President) as affecting the security of the United States, knowing or having reason to know that such information has been so classified, unless such officer or employee shall have been specifically authorized by the President, or by the head of the department, agency, or corporation by which this officer or employee is employed, to make such disclosure of such information.

(b) Receipt of, or attempt to receive, by foreign agent or member of Communist organization, classified information

It shall be unlawful for any agent or representative of any foreign government knowingly to obtain or receive, or attempt to obtain or receive, directly or indirectly, from any officer or employee of the United States or of any department or agency thereof or of any corporation the stock of which is owned in whole or in major part by the United States or any department or agency thereof, any information of a kind which shall have been classified by the President (or by the head of any such department, agency, or corporation with the approval of the President) as affecting the security of the United States, unless special authorization for such communication shall first have been obtained from the head of the department, agency, or corporation having custody of or control over such information.

(c) Penalties for violation

Any person who violates any provision of this section shall, upon conviction thereof, be punished by a fine of not more than $10,000, or imprisonment for not more than ten years, or by both such fine and such imprisonment, and shall, moreover, be thereafter ineligible to hold any office, or place of honor, profit, or trust created by the Constitution or laws of the United States.

(d) Limitation period

Any person may be prosecuted, tried, and punished for any violation of this section at any time within ten years after the commission of such offense, notwithstanding the provisions of any other statute of limitations: *Provided*, That if at the time of the commission of the offense such person is an officer or employee of the United States or of any department or agency thereof, or of any corporation the stock of which is owned in whole or in major part by the United States or any department or agency thereof, such person may be prosecuted, tried, and punished for any violation of this section at any time within ten years after such person has ceased to be employed as such officer or employee.

(e) Forfeiture of property

(1) Any person convicted of a violation of this section shall forfeit to the United States irrespective of any provision of State law—

(A) any property constituting, or derived from, any proceeds the person obtained, directly or indirectly, as the result of such violation; and

(B) any of the person's property used, or intended to be used, in any manner or part, to commit, or to facilitate the commission of, such violation.

(2) The court, in imposing sentence on a defendant for a conviction of a violation of this section, shall order that the defendant forfeit to the United States all property described in paragraph (1).

(3) Except as provided in paragraph (4), the provisions of subsections (b), (c), and (e) through (p) of section 853 of title 21 shall apply to—

(A) property subject to forfeiture under this subsection;

(B) any seizure or disposition of such property; and

(C) any administrative or judicial proceeding in relation to such property,

if not inconsistent with this subsection.

(4) Notwithstanding section 524(c) of title 28, there shall be deposited in the Crime Victims Fund established under section 10601 of title 42 all amounts from the forfeiture of property under this subsection remaining after the payment of expenses for forfeiture and sale authorized by law.

(5) As used in this subsection, the term "State" means any State of the United States, the District of Columbia, the Commonwealth of Puerto Rico, the Trust Territory of the Pacific Islands, and any territory or possession of the United States.

(Sept. 23, 1950, ch. 1024, title I, §4, 64 Stat. 991; Pub. L. 90–237, §3, Jan. 2, 1968, 81 Stat. 765; Pub. L. 103–199, title VIII, §803(2), Dec. 17, 1993, 107 Stat. 2329; Pub. L. 103–359, title VIII, §804(c), Oct. 14, 1994, 108 Stat. 3440.)

AMENDMENTS

1994—Subsec. (e). Pub. L. 103–359 added subsec. (e).

1993—Subsec. (a). Pub. L. 103–199, §803(2)(A)–(C), redesignated subsec. (b) as (a), struck out "or an officer or member of any Communist organization as defined in paragraph (5) of section 782 of this title" after "foreign government", and struck out former subsec. (a) which read as follows: "It shall be unlawful for any person knowingly to combine, conspire, or agree with any other person to perform any act which would substantially contribute to the establishment within the United States of a totalitarian dictatorship, as defined in paragraph (15) of section 782 of this title, the direction and control of which is to be vested in, or exercised by or under the domination or control of, any foreign government, foreign organization, or foreign individual: *Provided, however*, That this subsection shall not apply to the proposal of a constitutional amendment."

Subsec. (b). Pub. L. 103–199, §803(2)(B), (D), redesignated subsec. (c) as (b) and struck out ", or any officer or member of any Communist organization as defined in paragraph (5) of section 782 of this title," after "foreign government". Former subsec. (b) redesignated (a).

Subsecs. (c) to (e). Pub. L. 103–199, §803(2)(B), redesignated subsecs. (d) and (e) as (c) and (d), respectively. Former subsec. (c) redesignated (b).

Subsec. (f). Pub. L. 103–199, §803(2)(A), struck out subsec. (f) which read as follows: "Neither the holding of office nor membership in any Communist organization by any person shall constitute per se a violation of subsection (a) or subsection (c) of this section or of any other criminal statute."

1968—Subsec. (f). Pub. L. 90–237 struck out prohibition against receiving the fact of the registration of any person under section 787 or 788 of this title as an officer or member of any Communist organization in evidence against such person in any prosecution for any alleged violation of subsection (a) or (c) of this section or for any alleged violation of any other criminal statute.

TERMINATION OF TRUST TERRITORY OF THE PACIFIC ISLANDS

For termination of Trust Territory of the Pacific Islands, see note set out preceding section 1681 of Title 48, Territories and Insular Possessions.

SECTION REFERRED TO IN OTHER SECTIONS

This section is referred to in section 2410 of Appendix to this title; title 5 section 8312; title 18 sections 3077, 3239; title 22 section 2778; title 38 section 6105; title 42 sections 402, 2000aa.

§§ 784, 785. Repealed. Pub. L. 103–199, title VIII, § 803(1), Dec. 17, 1993, 107 Stat. 2329

Section 784, acts Sept. 23, 1950, ch. 1024, title I, § 5, 64 Stat. 992; Aug. 24, 1954, ch. 886, §§ 6, 7(c), 68 Stat. 777, 778; May 31, 1962, Pub. L. 87–474, § 1(b), 76 Stat. 91; Jan. 2, 1968, Pub. L. 90–237, § 4, 81 Stat. 765, related to employment of members of Communist organizations.

Section 785, acts Sept. 23, 1950, ch. 1024, title I, § 6, 64 Stat. 993; Aug. 24, 1954, ch. 886, § 7(c), 68 Stat. 778, related to denial of United States passports to members of Communist organizations.

§§ 786, 787. Repealed. Pub. L. 90–237, § 5, Jan. 2, 1968, 81 Stat. 766

Section 786, acts Sept. 23, 1950, ch. 1024, title I, § 7, 64 Stat. 993; July 29, 1954, ch. 646, 68 Stat. 586, related to registration of Communist-action and Communist-front organizations with the Attorney General, the preparation and filing of a registration statement and subsequent annual reports by such organizations, duty of such organizations to keep certain specified records and accounts, duty of Attorney General to notify individuals listed in any registration statement as an officer or member of such organization that such individual is so listed, investigation and determination of denials of membership and petition for relief in cases where Attorney General declines or fails to strike name of any individual from an annual report or registration statement.

Section 787, act Sept. 23, 1950, ch. 1024, title I, § 8, 64 Stat. 995, related to registration of members of Communist-action organizations with Attorney General and preparation and filing of a registration statement by such individuals.

§§ 788 to 795. Repealed. Pub. L. 103–199, title VIII, § 803(1), Dec. 17, 1993, 107 Stat. 2329

Section 788, acts Sept. 23, 1950, ch. 1024, title I, § 9, 64 Stat. 995; Jan. 2, 1968, Pub. L. 90–237, § 6, 81 Stat. 766, related to records of final orders of Subversive Activities Control Board and to public inspection of those records.

Section 789, acts Sept. 23, 1950, ch. 1024, title I, § 10, 64 Stat. 996; Aug. 24, 1954, ch. 886, § 8(a), 68 Stat. 778; Jan. 2, 1968, Pub. L. 90–237, § 7, 81 Stat. 766, related to use of mails and instrumentalities of interstate or foreign commerce by Communist organizations.

Section 790, acts Sept. 23, 1950, ch. 1024, title I, § 11, 64 Stat. 996; Aug. 24, 1954, ch. 886, § 8(b), 68 Stat. 778; Jan. 2, 1968, Pub. L. 90–237, § 8, 81 Stat. 767; Oct. 22, 1986, Pub. L. 99–514, § 2, 100 Stat. 2095, related to denial of tax deductions and exemptions for contributions to Communist organizations.

Section 791, acts Sept. 23, 1950, ch. 1024, title I, § 12, 64 Stat. 977; July 12, 1952, ch. 697, 66 Stat. 590; Aug. 24, 1954, ch. 886, § 9(a), 68 Stat. 778; Aug. 5, 1955, ch. 580, § 1, 69 Stat. 539; Jan. 2, 1968, Pub. L. 90–237, § 9, 81 Stat. 767, established the Subversive Activities Control Board and provided for its Chairman, membership, filling of vacancies, duties, appointment and compensation of personnel, reports to Congress and President, appropriations, and termination of the Board on June 30, 1969, unless in the period beginning Jan. 2, 1968 and ending Dec. 31, 1968, a proceeding was instituted.

Section 792, acts Sept. 23, 1950, ch. 1024, title I, § 13, 64 Stat. 998; Aug. 24, 1954, ch. 886, § 9(b), 68 Stat. 778; Jan. 2, 1968, Pub. L. 90–237, § 10, 81 Stat. 768; Oct. 15, 1970, Pub. L. 91–452, title II, § 247, 84 Stat. 931, related to Board proceedings with respect to Communist action and Communist front organizations and provided for petition by Attorney General to Board for determination of Communist action or Communist front organizations, petition for review, not more than once every calendar year, for redetermination by Board, public hearings, criteria to be considered in making determinations, written report of findings to be served on Attorney General, and publication of final orders in the Federal Register.

Section 792a, acts Sept. 23, 1950, ch. 1024, title I, § 13A, as added Aug. 24, 1954, ch. 886, § 10, 68 Stat. 778; amended July 26, 1955, ch. 381, 69 Stat. 375; Jan. 2, 1968, Pub. L. 90–237, § 11, 81 Stat. 771; Nov. 8, 1984, Pub. L. 98–620, title IV, § 402(53), 98 Stat. 3361, related to labor organizations determined by Board to be Communist.

Section 793, acts Sept. 23, 1950, ch. 1024, title I, § 14, 64 Stat. 1001; Aug. 24, 1954, ch. 886, § 11, 68 Stat. 780; Aug. 28, 1958, Pub. L. 85–791, § 29, 72 Stat. 950; Jan. 2, 1968, Pub. L. 90–237, § 12, 81 Stat. 771, provided for judicial review of orders of Board to United States Court of Appeals for the District of Columbia if petition was filed within sixty days from date of service of such order and specified time of finality of the Board's orders.

Section 794, acts Sept. 23, 1950, ch. 1024, title I, § 15, 64 Stat. 1002; Jan. 2, 1968, Pub. L. 90–237, § 13, 81 Stat. 771, provided for penalties for violation of former sections 784 and 789 of this title.

Section 795, act Sept. 23, 1950, ch. 1024, title I, § 16, 64 Stat. 1003, related to applicability of administrative procedure provisions to Board.

§ 796. Effect of subchapter on other criminal laws

The foregoing provisions of this subchapter shall be construed as being in addition to and not in modification of existing criminal statutes.

(Sept. 23, 1950, ch. 1024, title I, § 17, 64 Stat. 1003.)

REFERENCES IN TEXT

This subchapter, referred to in text, was in the original "this title", meaning title I of act Sept. 23, 1950, ch. 1024, 64 Stat. 987, as amended, known as the Subversive Activities Control Act of 1950, which is classified principally to this subchapter. For complete classification of title I of such act to the Code, see Short Title note set out under section 781 of this title and Tables.

§ 797. Security regulations and orders; penalty for violation

(a) Whoever willfully shall violate any such regulation or order as, pursuant to lawful authority, shall be or has been promulgated or approved by the Secretary of Defense, or by any military commander designated by the Secretary of Defense, or by the Director of the National Advisory Committee for Aeronautics, for the protection or security of military or naval aircraft, airports, airport facilities, vessels, harbors, ports, piers, water-front facilities, bases, forts, posts, laboratories, stations, vehicles, equipment, explosives, or other property or places subject to the jurisdiction, administration, or in the custody of the Department of Defense, any Department or agency of which said Department consists, or any officer or employee of said Department or agency, or of the National

Advisory Committee for Aeronautics or any officer or employee thereof, relating to fire hazards, fire protection, lighting, machinery, guard service, disrepair, disuse or other unsatisfactory conditions thereon, or the ingress thereto or egress or removal of persons therefrom, or otherwise providing for safeguarding the same against destruction, loss, or injury by accident or by enemy action, sabotage or other subversive actions, shall be guilty of a misdemeanor and upon conviction thereof shall be liable to a fine of not to exceed $5,000 or to imprisonment for not more than one year, or both.

(b) Every such regulation or order shall be posted in conspicuous and appropriate places.

(Sept. 23, 1950, ch. 1024, title I, §21, 64 Stat. 1005.)

TERMINATION OF NATIONAL ADVISORY COMMITTEE FOR AERONAUTICS

The National Advisory Committee for Aeronautics, as established by act Mar. 3, 1915, ch. 83, 38 Stat. 930, was terminated pursuant to section 301(a) of Pub. L. 85–568, title III, July 29, 1958, 72 Stat. 432, set out as a note under section 2472 of Title 42, The Public Health and Welfare, which transferred all its functions, powers, duties, and obligations to the National Aeronautics and Space Administration. See section 2451 et seq. of Title 42.

§ 798. Repealed. Pub. L. 103–199, title VIII, § 803(1), Dec. 17, 1993, 107 Stat. 2329

Section, act Sept. 23, 1950, ch. 1024, title I, §1(b), 64 Stat. 987, provided that the Internal Security Act of 1950 not be construed to authorize, require, or establish military or civilian censorship or in any way to limit or infringe upon freedom of press or of speech as guaranteed by Constitution.

SUBCHAPTER II—EMERGENCY DETENTION OF SUSPECTED SECURITY RISKS

§§ 811 to 826. Repealed. Pub. L. 92–128, § 2(a), Sept. 25, 1971, 85 Stat. 348

Section 811, act Sept. 23, 1950, ch. 1024, title II, §101, 64 Stat. 1019, related to Congressional finding of necessity.

Section 812, act Sept. 23, 1950, ch. 1024, title II, §102, 64 Stat. 1021, related to declaration of "internal security emergency" by the President, events warranting the declaration, and period of existence.

Section 813, act Sept. 23, 1950, ch. 1024, title II, §103, 64 Stat. 1021, related to detention during emergency and to release.

Section 814, act Sept. 23, 1950, ch. 1024, title II, §104, 64 Stat. 1022, related to procedure for apprehension and detention, providing in subsecs. (a) to (h), respectively, for warrants and applications; service of warrants and apprehension, and copies for persons apprehended; places of confinement, provision for transportation, food, shelter, etc., and supervision; preliminary hearing, rights of detainee, evidence, orders and reports of hearing officer, and appointment of preliminary hearing officers; receipt of additional information upon request of detainee, and revocation or modification of detention order; presentation of evidence in case of Board or court review and right to withhold certain information; regulations by Attorney General and exclusion of forced labor and confinement with criminals; and bimonthly reports to President and Congress during emergency.

Section 815, act Sept. 23, 1950, ch. 1024, title II, §105, 64 Stat. 1023, related to the Detention Review Board, providing in subsecs. (a) to (d), respectively, for creation of Board, membership, terms, designation of Chairman, and removal; Board divisions, vacancies, powers of remaining members, quorums, official seal, and judicial notice thereof; reports to Congress and its contents; and dissolution upon termination of emergency, release of detainees, conclusion of proceedings, and subsequent establishment.

Section 816, act Sept. 23, 1950, ch. 1024, title II, §106, 64 Stat. 1024, related to salaries of Board members, other personnel, use of agencies and services, expenses, and appropriations.

Section 817, act Sept. 23, 1950, ch. 1024, title II, §107, 64 Stat. 1024, specified the District of Columbia as Board headquarters and related to meetings and hearings outside the District.

Section 818, act Sept. 23, 1950, ch. 1024, title II, §108, 64 Stat. 1024, related to rules and regulations by the Board and applicability of the Administrative Procedure Act.

Section 819, act Sept. 23, 1950, ch. 1024, title II, §109, 64 Stat. 1025, related to powers and duties of Board, providing in subsecs. (a) to (j), respectively, for review of, and action on, orders and claims, and determination of security risks; time for hearing on petition for review, the notice and place; information which may be given to detainee in review cases; subpenas, oaths, affirmations, witnesses, evidence, aid of courts, and contempt; service of papers, fees and mileage, and information from other Government agencies; rights of detainee at hearing; consideration of confidential evidence, reduction of evidence to writing, and additional testimony, and argument; evidentiary matters considered in deciding questions as to security risks; necessity for reasonable ground for belief, and claims for indemnity and receipt of evidence having probative value.

Section 820, acts Sept. 23, 1950, ch. 1024, title II, §110, 64 Stat. 1027; Aug. 28, 1958, Pub. L. 85–791, §30(a), 72 Stat. 950, related to orders of Board, providing in subsecs. (a) to (e), respectively, for revocation of detention order; orders sustaining or denying indemnity claims; dismissal of petition and confirmation of detention order; report and recommended order of hearing examiner, and effectiveness after expiration of time period; and modification or setting aside by Board of its own findings or orders prior to court review.

Section 821, acts Sept. 23, 1950, ch. 1024, title II, §111, 64 Stat. 1028; Aug. 28, 1958, Pub. L. 85–791, §30(b), (c), 72 Stat. 950, 951, related to judicial review, providing in subsecs. (a) to (g), respectively, for rights of petitioner; orders granting indemnity and right of Attorney General; courts of appeals, place, petition, time, service, record, statement, powers of court, and conclusiveness of Board's finding; additional evidence, modification of, or new, findings by Board, recommendations, exclusiveness of court jurisdiction, finality of judgment, and review by Supreme Court; commencement of review proceeding as stay of Board's order; time of finality of Board's order; and applicability of Administrative Procedure Act.

Section 822, act Sept. 23, 1950, ch. 1024, title II, §112, 64 Stat. 1029, related to resisting, disregarding, or evading apprehension, escape or attempts at escape, conspiracy, and to penalties.

Section 823, act Sept. 23, 1950, ch. 1024, title II, §113, 64 Stat. 1030, related to aiding evasion of apprehension or escape, concealment, conspiracy, and to penalties.

Section 824, act Sept. 23, 1950, ch. 1024, title II, §114, 64 Stat. 1030, related to resistance of, or interference with, Board members or agents and to penalties.

Section 825, act Sept. 23, 1950, ch. 1024, title II, §115, 64 Stat. 1030, related to definitions.

Section 826, act Sept. 23, 1950, ch. 1024, title II, §116, 64 Stat. 1030, related to preservation of privilege of habeas corpus.

SUBCHAPTER III—PERSONNEL SECURITY PROCEDURES IN NATIONAL SECURITY AGENCY

SUBCHAPTER REFERRED TO IN OTHER SECTIONS

This subchapter is referred to in title 5 section 2305.

§ 831. Regulations for employment security

Subject to the provisions of this subchapter, the Secretary of Defense (hereafter in this subchapter referred to as the "Secretary") shall prescribe such regulations relating to continuing security procedures as he considers necessary to assure—

(1) that no person shall be employed in, or detailed or assigned to, the National Security Agency (hereafter in this subchapter referred to as the "Agency"), or continue to be so employed, detailed, or assigned; and

(2) that no person so employed, detailed, or assigned shall have access to any classified information;

unless such employment, detail, assignment, or access to classified information is clearly consistent with the national security.

(Sept. 23, 1950, ch. 1024, title III, § 301, as added Pub. L. 88–290, Mar. 26, 1964, 78 Stat. 168.)

§ 832. Full field investigation and appraisal

(a) Conditional employment; other current security clearance; circumstances authorizing employment on temporary basis

No person shall be employed in, or detailed or assigned to, the Agency unless he has been the subject of a full field investigation in connection with such employment, detail, or assignment, and is cleared for access to classified information in accordance with the provisions of this subchapter; excepting that conditional employment without access to sensitive cryptologic information or material may be tendered any applicant, under such regulations as the Secretary may prescribe, pending the completion of such full field investigation: *And provided further*, That such full field investigation at the discretion of the Secretary need not be required in the case of persons assigned or detailed to the Agency who have a current security clearance for access to sensitive cryptologic information under equivalent standards of investigation and clearance. During any period of war declared by the Congress, or during any period when the Secretary determines that a national disaster exists, or in exceptional cases in which the Secretary (or his designee for such purpose) makes a determination in writing that his action is necessary or advisable in the national interest, he may authorize the employment of any person in, or the detail or assignment of any person to, the Agency, and may grant to any such person access to classified information, on a temporary basis, pending the completion of the full field investigation and the clearance for access to classified information required by this subsection, if the Secretary determines that such action is clearly consistent with the national security.

(b) Boards of appraisal; establishment; membership; appointment; appraisal in doubtful cases; report and recommendation; qualifications of members; Secretary's clearance contrary to board's recommendation

To assist the Secretary and the Director of the Agency in carrying out their personnel security responsibilities, one or more boards of appraisal of three members each, to be appointed by the Director of the Agency, shall be established in the Agency. Such a board shall appraise the loyalty and suitability of persons for access to classified information, in those cases in which the Director of the Agency determines that there is a doubt whether their access to that information would be clearly consistent with the national security, and shall submit a report and recommendation on each such a case. However, appraisal by such a board is not required before action may be taken under sections 7512 and 7532 of title 5, or any other similar provision of law. Each member of such a board shall be specially qualified and trained for his duties as such a member, shall have been the subject of a full field investigation in connection with his appointment as such a member, and shall have been cleared by the Director for access to classified information at the time of his appointment as such a member. No person shall be cleared for access to classified information, contrary to the recommendations of any such board, unless the Secretary (or his designee for such purpose) shall make a determination in writing that such employment, detail, assignment, or access to classified information is in the national interest.

(Sept. 23, 1950, ch. 1024, title III, § 302, as added Pub. L. 88–290, Mar. 26, 1964, 78 Stat. 168.)

CODIFICATION

In subsec. (b), "sections 7512 and 7532 of title 5" substituted for "section 14 of the Act of June 27, 1944, chapter 287, as amended (5 U.S.C. 863), section 1 of the Act of August 26, 1950, chapter 803, as amended (5 U.S.C. 22–1)" on authority of Pub. L. 89–554, § 7(b), Sept. 6, 1966, 80 Stat. 631, the first section of which enacted Title 5, Government Organization and Employees. Sections 7511 and 7512 (which related to adverse actions against preference eligible employees and comprised subchapter II of chapter 75) were repealed by Pub. L. 95–454 and replaced by a new subchapter II (§§ 7511–7514) of chapter 75 (relating to removal, suspension for more than 14 days, reduction in grade or pay, or furlough for 30 days or less).

§ 833. Repealed. Pub. L. 104–201, div. A, title XVI, § 1633(b)(2), Sept. 23, 1996, 110 Stat. 2751

Section, act Sept. 23, 1950, ch. 1024, title III, § 303, as added Mar. 26, 1964, Pub. L. 88–290, 78 Stat. 169; amended Oct. 27, 1972, Pub. L. 92–596, § 7, 86 Stat. 1318; Oct. 21, 1977, Pub. L. 95–140, § 3(c), 91 Stat. 1173; 1978 Reorg. Plan No. 2, § 102, eff. Jan. 1, 1979, 43 F.R. 36037, 92 Stat. 3783; Oct. 1, 1986, Pub. L. 99–433, title I, § 110(h)(3), 100 Stat. 1004, related to termination of employment.

EFFECTIVE DATE OF REPEAL

Repeal effective Oct. 1, 1996, see section 1635 of Pub. L. 104–201, set out as an Effective Date of 1996 Amendment note under section 1593 of Title 10, Armed Forces.

§ 834. "Classified information" defined

For the purposes of this section, the term "classified information" means information which, for reasons of national security, is specifically designated by a United States Government agency for limited or restricted dissemination or distribution.

(Sept. 23, 1950, ch. 1024, title III, § 304, as added Pub. L. 88–290, Mar. 26, 1964, 78 Stat. 170.)

§835. Nonapplicability of administrative procedure provisions

Subchapter II of chapter 5, and chapter 7, of title 5, shall not apply to the use or exercise of any authority granted by this subchapter.

(Sept. 23, 1950, ch. 1024, title III, §305, as added Pub. L. 88–290, Mar. 26, 1964, 78 Stat. 170.)

CODIFICATION

"Subchapter II of chapter 5, and chapter 7, of title 5" substituted in text for "the Administrative Procedure Act, as amended" on authority of Pub. L. 89–554, §7(b), Sept. 6, 1966, 80 Stat. 631, the first section of which enacted Title 5, Government Organization and Employees.

SUBCHAPTER IV—COMMUNIST CONTROL

§841. Findings and declarations of fact

The Congress finds and declares that the Communist Party of the United States, although purportedly a political party, is in fact an instrumentality of a conspiracy to overthrow the Government of the United States. It constitutes an authoritarian dictatorship within a republic, demanding for itself the rights and privileges accorded to political parties, but denying to all others the liberties guaranteed by the Constitution. Unlike political parties, which evolve their policies and programs through public means, by the reconciliation of a wide variety of individual views, and submit those policies and programs to the electorate at large for approval or disapproval, the policies and programs of the Communist Party are secretly prescribed for it by the foreign leaders of the world Communist movement. Its members have no part in determining its goals, and are not permitted to voice dissent to party objectives. Unlike members of political parties, members of the Communist Party are recruited for indoctrination with respect to its objectives and methods, and are organized, instructed, and disciplined to carry into action slavishly the assignments given them by their hierarchical chieftains. Unlike political parties, the Communist Party acknowledges no constitutional or statutory limitations upon its conduct or upon that of its members. The Communist Party is relatively small numerically, and gives scant indication of capacity ever to attain its ends by lawful political means. The peril inherent in its operation arises not from its numbers, but from its failure to acknowledge any limitation as to the nature of its activities, and its dedication to the proposition that the present constitutional Government of the United States ultimately must be brought to ruin by any available means, including resort to force and violence. Holding that doctrine, its role as the agency of a hostile foreign power renders its existence a clear present and continuing danger to the security of the United States. It is the means whereby individuals are seduced into the service of the world Communist movement, trained to do its bidding, and directed and controlled in the conspiratorial performance of their revolutionary services. Therefore, the Communist Party should be outlawed.

(Aug. 24, 1954, ch. 886, §2, 68 Stat. 775.)

CODIFICATION

Section was enacted as part of the Communist Control Act of 1954, and not as part of the Internal Security Act of 1950 which comprises subchapters I to III of this chapter.

SHORT TITLE

Section 1 of act Aug. 24, 1954, provided: "That this Act [enacting this subchapter and section 792a of this title, amending sections 782, 784, 785, 789 to 792, and 793 of this title, and enacting provisions set out below] may be cited as the 'Communist Control Act of 1954'."

SEPARABILITY

Section 12 of act Aug. 24, 1954, provided: "If any provision of this title [see Short Title note above] or the application thereof to any person or circumstances is held invalid, the remainder of the title and the application of such provisions to other persons or circumstances, shall not be affected thereby."

The use of the word "Act", in place of the word "title" as used in section 12 of act of Aug. 24, 1954, quoted above, was probably intended, since that act is not divided into titles.

§842. Proscription of Communist Party, its successors, and subsidiary organizations

The Communist Party of the United States, or any successors of such party regardless of the assumed name, whose object or purpose is to overthrow the Government of the United States, or the government of any State, Territory, District, or possession thereof, or the government of any political subdivision therein by force and violence, are not entitled to any of the rights, privileges, and immunities attendant upon legal bodies created under the jurisdiction of the laws of the United States or any political subdivision thereof; and whatever rights, privileges, and immunities which have heretofore been granted to said party or any subsidiary organization by reason of the laws of the United States or any political subdivision thereof, are terminated: *Provided, however*, That nothing in this section shall be construed as amending the Internal Security Act of 1950, as amended [50 U.S.C. 781 et seq.]

(Aug. 24, 1954, ch. 886, §3, 68 Stat. 776.)

REFERENCES IN TEXT

The Internal Security Act of 1950, as amended, referred to in text, is act Sept. 23, 1950, ch. 1024, 64 Stat. 987, as amended, which is classified principally to subchapters I to III of this chapter. For complete classification of this Act to the Code, see Short Title note set out under section 781 of this title and Tables.

CODIFICATION

Section was enacted as part of the Communist Control Act of 1954, and not as part of the Internal Security Act of 1950 which comprises subchapters I to III of this chapter.

§843. Application of Internal Security Act of 1950 to members of Communist Party and other subversive organizations; "Communist Party" defined

(a) Whoever knowingly and willfully becomes or remains a member of (1) the Communist Party, or (2) any other organization having for one of its purposes or objectives the establishment, control, conduct, seizure, or overthrow of the Government of the United States, or the government of any State or political subdivision thereof, by the use of force or violence, with knowledge of the purpose or objective of such organization shall be subject to all the provisions and penalties of the Internal Security Act of 1950, as amended [50 U.S.C. 781 et seq.], as a member of a "Communist-action" organization.

(b) For the purposes of this section, the term "Communist Party" means the organization now known as the Communist Party of the United States of America, the Communist Party of any State or subdivision thereof, and any unit or subdivision of any such organization, whether or not any change is hereafter made in the name thereof.

(Aug. 24, 1954, ch. 886, § 4, 68 Stat. 776.)

REFERENCES IN TEXT

The Internal Security Act of 1950, as amended, referred to in subsec. (a), is act Sept. 23, 1950, ch. 1024, 64 Stat. 987, as amended, which is classified principally to subchapters I to III of this chapter. For complete classification of this Act to the Code, see Short Title note set out under section 781 of this title and Tables.

CODIFICATION

Section was enacted as part of the Communist Control Act of 1954, and not as part of the Internal Security Act of 1950 which comprises subchapters I to III of this chapter.

§ 844. Determination by jury of membership in Communist Party, participation, or knowledge of purpose

In determining membership or participation in the Communist Party or any other organization defined in this Act, or knowledge of the purpose or objective of such party or organization, the jury, under instructions from the court, shall consider evidence, if presented, as to whether the accused person:

(1) Has been listed to his knowledge as a member in any book or any of the lists, records, correspondence, or any other document of the organization;

(2) Has made financial contribution to the organization in dues, assessments, loans, or in any other form;

(3) Has made himself subject to the discipline of the organization in any form whatsoever;

(4) Has executed orders, plans, or directives of any kind of the organization;

(5) Has acted as an agent, courier, messenger, correspondent, organizer, or in any other capacity in behalf of the organization;

(6) Has conferred with officers or other members of the organization in behalf of any plan or enterprise of the organization;

(7) Has been accepted to his knowledge as an officer or member of the organization or as one to be called upon for services by other officers or members of the organization;

(8) Has written, spoken or in any other way communicated by signal, semaphore, sign, or in any other form of communication orders, directives, or plans of the organization;

(9) Has prepared documents, pamphlets, leaflets, books, or any other type of publication in behalf of the objectives and purposes of the organization;

(10) Has mailed, shipped, circulated, distributed, delivered, or in any other way sent or delivered to others material or propaganda of any kind in behalf of the organization;

(11) Has advised, counseled or in any other way imparted information, suggestions, recommendations to officers or members of the organization or to anyone else in behalf of the objectives of the organization;

(12) Has indicated by word, action, conduct, writing or in any other way a willingness to carry out in any manner and to any degree the plans, designs, objectives, or purposes of the organization;

(13) Has in any other way participated in the activities, planning, actions, objectives, or purposes of the organization;

(14) The enumeration of the above subjects of evidence on membership or participation in the Communist Party or any other organization as above defined, shall not limit the inquiry into and consideration of any other subject of evidence on membership and participation as herein stated.

(Aug. 24, 1954, ch. 886, § 5, 68 Stat. 776.)

REFERENCES IN TEXT

This Act, referred to in the provision preceding par. (1), is act Aug. 24, 1954, ch. 886, 68 Stat. 775, known as the Communist Control Act of 1954, which is classified principally to this subchapter. For complete classification of this Act to the Code, see Short Title note set out under section 841 of this title and Tables.

CODIFICATION

Section was enacted as part of the Communist Control Act of 1954, and not as part of the Internal Security Act of 1950 which comprises subchapters I to III of this chapter.

SUBCHAPTER V—REGISTRATION OF CERTAIN PERSONS TRAINED IN FOREIGN ESPIONAGE SYSTEMS

§ 851. Registration of certain persons; filing statement; regulations

Except as provided in section 852 of this title, every person who has knowledge of, or has received instruction or assignment in, the espionage, counter-espionage, or sabotage service or tactics of a government of a foreign country or of a foreign political party, shall register with the Attorney General by filing with the Attorney General a registration statement in duplicate, under oath, prepared and filed in such manner and form, and containing such statements, information, or documents pertinent to the purposes and objectives of this subchapter as the Attorney General, having due regard for the national security and the public interest, by regulations prescribes.

(Aug. 1, 1956, ch. 849, § 2, 70 Stat. 899.)

CODIFICATION

Section was not enacted as part of the Internal Security Act of 1950 which comprises subchapters I to III of this chapter.

SEPARABILITY

Section 9 of act Aug. 1, 1956, provided: "If any provision of this Act [enacting this subchapter] or the application thereof to any person or circumstances is held invalid, the remainder of the Act, and the application of such provisions to other persons or circumstances, is not affected thereby."

SECTION REFERRED TO IN OTHER SECTIONS

This section is referred to in section 852 of this title.

§852. Exemption from registration

The registration requirements of section 851 of this title do not apply to any person—

(a) who has obtained knowledge of or received instruction or assignment in the espionage, counter-espionage, or sabotage service or tactics of a foreign government or foreign political party by reason of civilian, military, or police service or employment with the United States Government, the governments of the several States, their political subdivisions, the District of Columbia, the Territories, or the Canal Zone;

(b) who has obtained such knowledge solely by reason of academic or personal interest not under the supervision of or in preparation for service with the government of a foreign country or a foreign political party;

(c) who has made full disclosure of such knowledge, instruction, or assignment to officials within an agency of the United States Government having responsibilities in the field of intelligence, which disclosure has been made a matter of record in the files of such agency, and concerning whom a written determination has been made by the Attorney General or the Director of Central Intelligence that registration would not be in the interest of national security;

(d) whose knowledge of, or receipt of instruction or assignment in, the espionage, counter-espionage, or sabotage service or tactics of a government of a foreign country or of a foreign political party, is a matter of record in the files of an agency of the United States Government having responsibilities in the field of intelligence and concerning whom a written determination is made by the Attorney General or the Director of Central Intelligence, based on all information available, that registration would not be in the interest of national security;

(e) who is a duly accredited diplomatic or consular officer of a foreign government, who is so recognized by the Department of State, while he is engaged exclusively in activities which are recognized by the Department of State as being within the scope of the functions of such officer, and any member of his immediate family who resides with him;

(f) who is an official of a foreign government recognized by the United States, whose name and status and the character of whose duties as such official are of record in the Department of State, and while he is engaged exclusively in activities which are recognized by the Department of State as being within the scope of the functions of such official, and any member of his immediate family who resides with him;

(g) who is a member of the staff of or employed by a duly accredited diplomatic or consular officer of a foreign government who is so recognized by the Department of State, and whose name and status and the character of whose duties as such member or employee are a matter of record in the Department of State, while he is engaged exclusively in the performance of activities recognized by the Department of State as being within the scope of the functions of such member or employee;

(h) Who[1] is an officially acknowledged and sponsored representative of a foreign government and is in the United States on an official mission for the purpose of conferring or otherwise cooperating with United States intelligence or security personnel;

(i) who is a civilian or one of the military personnel of a foreign armed service coming to the United States pursuant to arrangements made under a mutual defense treaty or agreement, or who has been invited to the United States at the request of an agency of the United States Government; or

(j) who is a person designated by a foreign government to serve as its representative in or to an international organization in which the United States participates or is an officer or employee of such an organization or who is a member of the immediate family of, and resides with, such a representative, officer, or employee.

(Aug. 1, 1956, ch. 849, §3, 70 Stat. 899.)

CODIFICATION

Section was not enacted as part of the Internal Security Act of 1950 which comprises subchapters I to III of this chapter.

SECTION REFERRED TO IN OTHER SECTIONS

This section is referred to in section 851 of this title.

§853. Retention of registration statements; public examination; withdrawal

The Attorney General shall retain in permanent form one copy of all registration statements filed under this subchapter. They shall be public records and open to public examination at such reasonable hours and under such regulations as the Attorney General prescribes, except that the Attorney General, having due regard for the national security and public interest, may withdraw any registration statement from public examination.

(Aug. 1, 1956, ch. 849, §4, 70 Stat. 900.)

CODIFICATION

Section was not enacted as part of the Internal Security Act of 1950 which comprises subchapters I to III of this chapter.

§854. Rules, regulations, and forms

The Attorney General may at any time, make, prescribe, amend, and rescind such rules, regulations and forms as he deems necessary to carry out the provisions of this subchapter.

(Aug. 1, 1956, ch. 849, §5, 70 Stat. 900.)

CODIFICATION

Section was not enacted as part of the Internal Security Act of 1950 which comprises subchapters I to III of this chapter.

[1] So in original. Probably should not be capitalized.

§855. Violations; penalties; deportation

(a) Whoever willfully violates any provision of this subchapter or any regulation thereunder, or in any registration statement willfully make[1] a false statement of a material fact or willfully omits any material fact, shall be fined not more than $10,000 or imprisoned for not more than five years, or both.

(b) Any alien convicted of a violation of this subchapter or any regulation thereunder is subject to deportation in the manner provided by chapter 4 of title II of the Immigration and Nationality Act [8 U.S.C. 1221 et seq.].

(Aug. 1, 1956, ch. 849, §6, 70 Stat. 900; Pub. L. 104–208, div. C, title III, §308(g)(9)(B), Sept. 30, 1996, 110 Stat. 3009–624.)

REFERENCES IN TEXT

The Immigration and Nationality Act, referred to in subsec. (b), is act June 27, 1952, ch. 477, 66 Stat. 163, as amended. Chapter 4 of title II of the Act is classified generally to part IV (§1221 et seq.) of subchapter II of chapter 12 of Title 8, Aliens and Nationality. For complete classification of this Act to the Code, see Short Title note set out under section 1101 of Title 8 and Tables.

CODIFICATION

Section was not enacted as part of the Internal Security Act of 1950 which comprises subchapters I to III of this chapter.

AMENDMENTS

1996—Subsec. (b). Pub. L. 104–208 substituted "chapter 4 of title II of the Immigration and Nationality Act" for "chapter 5, title II, of the Immigration and Nationality Act (66 Stat. 163)".

EFFECTIVE DATE OF 1996 AMENDMENT

Amendment by Pub. L. 104–208 effective, with certain transitional provisions, on the first day of the first month beginning more than 180 days after Sept. 30, 1996, see section 309 of Pub. L. 104–208, set out as a note under section 1101 of Title 8, Aliens and Nationality.

§856. Continuing offense

Failure to file a registration statement as required by this subchapter is a continuing offense for as long as such failure exists, notwithstanding any statute of limitation or other statute to the contrary.

(Aug. 1, 1956, ch. 849, §7, 70 Stat. 900.)

CODIFICATION

Section was not enacted as part of the Internal Security Act of 1950 which comprises subchapters I to III of this chapter.

§857. Compliance with other registration statutes

Compliance with the registration provisions of this subchapter does not relieve any person from compliance with any other applicable registration statute.

(Aug. 1, 1956, ch. 849, §8, 70 Stat. 900.)

CODIFICATION

Section was not enacted as part of the Internal Security Act of 1950 which comprises subchapters I to III of this chapter.

[1] So in original. Probably should be "makes".

§858. Applicability to Canal Zone

This subchapter applies to and within the Canal Zone.

(Aug. 1, 1956, ch. 849, §10, as added Pub. L. 87–845, §13, Oct. 18, 1962, 76A Stat. 700.)

REFERENCES IN TEXT

For definition of Canal Zone, referred to in text, see section 3602(b) of Title 22, Foreign Relations and Intercourse.

CODIFICATION

Section was not enacted as part of the Internal Security Act of 1950 which comprises subchapters I to III of this chapter.

EFFECTIVE DATE

Section effective Jan. 2, 1963, see section 25 of Pub. L. 87–845, set out as an Effective Date of 1962 Amendment note under section 14 of Title 18, Crimes and Criminal Procedure.

CHAPTER 24—NATIONAL DEFENSE FACILITIES

§§881 to 887. Repealed. Aug. 10, 1956, ch. 1041, §53, 70A Stat. 641

Section 881, act Sept. 11, 1950, ch. 945, §2, 64 Stat. 829, stated purpose of this chapter, which provided for national defense facilities. See section 18231 of Title 10, Armed Forces.

Section 882, acts Sept. 11, 1950, ch. 945, §3, 64 Stat. 830; Aug. 9, 1955, ch. 662, §1(a), (b), 69 Stat. 593; Aug. 3, 1956, ch. 939, title IV, §414, 70 Stat. 1018; Aug. 29, 1957, Pub. L. 85–215, §2, 71 Stat. 490; Pub. L. 85–685, title VI, §602, Aug. 20, 1958, 72 Stat. 665, related to acquisition and construction of defense facilities. See section 18233 of Title 10 and Codification note thereunder. Acts Aug. 9, 1955, ch. 662, §1(a), (b), 69 Stat. 593; Aug. 3, 1956, ch. 939, title IV, §414, 70 Stat. 1018; Aug. 29, 1957, Pub. L. 85–215, §2, 71 Stat. 490, were repealed by Pub. L. 85–861, §36A, Sept. 2, 1958, 72 Stat. 1569, 1570.

Section 883, acts Sept. 11, 1950, ch. 945, §4, 64 Stat. 830; Aug. 9, 1955, ch. 662, §1(c)–(e), 69 Stat. 593, related to location of facilities, change of location of units, title and maintenance of facilities, and to use of Federal and State facilities. See sections 18233, 18236, and 18238 of Title 10. Act Aug. 9, 1955, ch. 662, §1(c)–(e), 69 Stat. 593, was repealed by Pub. L. 85–861, §36A, Sept. 2, 1958, 72 Stat. 1569.

Section 884, act Sept. 11, 1950, ch. 945, §5, 64 Stat. 831, authorized Secretary of Defense to delegate his authority under this chapter. See section 18233 of Title 10.

Section 885, acts Sept. 11, 1950, ch. 945, §6, 64 Stat. 831; Aug. 9, 1955, ch. 662, §1(f), 69 Stat. 594, related to supervision of construction, expansion, rehabilitation or conversion of facilities. See section 18237 of Title 10. Act Aug. 9, 1955, ch. 662, §1(f), 69 Stat. 594, was repealed by Pub. L. 85–861, §36A, Sept. 2, 1958, 72 Stat. 1569.

Section 886, acts Sept. 11, 1950, ch. 945, §7, 64 Stat. 831; Aug. 9, 1955, ch. 662, §1(g), (h), 69 Stat. 594, defined terms used in sections 881 to 887 of this title. See section 18232 of Title 10. Act Aug. 9, 1955, ch. 662, §1(g), (h), 69 Stat. 594, was repealed by Pub. L. 85–861, §36A, Sept. 2, 1958, 72 Stat. 1569.

Section 887, act Sept. 11, 1950, ch. 945, §8, 64 Stat. 832, authorized appropriations to carry out purposes of this chapter.

CHAPTER 25—ARMED FORCES RESERVE

§§901 to 905. Repealed. Aug. 10, 1956, ch. 1041, §53, 70A Stat. 641

Section 901, act July 9, 1952, ch. 608, pt. I, §101, 66 Stat. 481, defined terms used in this chapter. See sections 101 and 10207 of Title 10, Armed Forces.

Section 902, act July 9, 1952, ch. 608, pt. VIII, §809, 66 Stat. 509, related to savings provisions for laws relating to appointment in reserve components.

Section 903, act July 9, 1952, ch. 608, pt. VIII, §810, 66 Stat. 509, related to accrued rights.

Section 904, act July 9, 1952, ch. 608, pt. VIII, §811, 66 Stat. 509, related to authority to order reservists to active duty and the responsibilities and functions of Chief of National Guard Bureau.

Section 905, act July 9, 1952, ch. 608, pt. VIII, §812, 66 Stat. 509, related to retroactive pay.

§§921 to 935. Repealed. Aug. 10, 1956, ch. 1041, §53, 70A Stat. 641

Section 921, act July 9, 1952, ch. 608, pt. II, §201, 66 Stat. 482, stated purpose of reserve components, and provided for maintenance of National Guard and Air National Guard. See sections 10102 and 10103 of Title 10, Armed Forces, and section 102 of Title 32, National Guard.

Section 922, act July 9, 1952, ch. 608, pt. II, §202, 66 Stat. 482, enumerated reserve components. See section 10101 of Title 10, Armed Forces.

Section 923, act July 9, 1952, ch. 608, pt. II, §203, 66 Stat. 483, provided for maximum numerical strength of reserve components. See section 12001 of Title 10, Armed Forces, and section 702 of Title 14, Coast Guard.

Section 924, act July 9, 1952, ch. 608, pt. II, §204, 66 Stat. 483, provided for composition of reserve components. See section 10141 of Title 10, Armed Forces.

Section 925, acts July 9, 1952, ch. 608, pt. II, §205, 66 Stat. 483; Aug. 9, 1955, ch. 665, §2(a), 69 Stat. 598, prescribed composition and maximum strength of Ready Reserve. See section 10142 of Title 10. Act Aug. 9, 1955, ch. 665, §2(a), 69 Stat. 598 was repealed by Pub. L. 85–861, §36A, Sept. 2, 1958, 72 Stat. 1569.

Section 926, act July 9, 1952, ch. 608, pt. II, §206, 66 Stat. 483, related to Standby Reserve, its composition, and for ordering units to active duty. See sections 10151 and 12306 of Title 10.

Section 927, act July 9, 1952, ch. 608, pt. II, §207, 66 Stat. 483, related to Retired Reserve, its composition, establishment of reserve retired lists, ordering members into active duty. See sections 1376, 10154, and 12307 of Title 10.

Section 928, acts July 9, 1952, ch. 608, pt. II, §208, 66 Stat. 484; Aug. 9, 1955, ch. 665, §2(b) to (d), 69 Stat. 598, 599, related to term of service in Ready Reserve, placement, requests for assignment, training duty, extension of membership, transfer to Standby Reserve, applications for transfer and screening of units and members. See sections 10145 to 10150 of Title 10. Act Aug. 9, 1955, ch. 665, §2(b)–(d), 69 Stat. 598, was repealed by Pub. L. 85–861, §36A, Sept. 2, 1958, 72 Stat. 1569.

Section 929, act July 9, 1952, ch. 608, pt. II, §209, 66 Stat. 484, related to transferees, enlistment or appointment in Armed Forces. See sections 12104 and 12208 of Title 10.

Section 930, act July 9, 1952, ch. 608, pt. II, §210, 66 Stat. 485, related to composition of Standby Reserve. See section 10141 of Title 10.

Section 931, act July 9, 1952, ch. 608, pt. II, §211, 66 Stat. 485, provided for inactive status list in Standby Reserve, regulations governing transfer, limitation on benefits. See sections 10152, 10153, and 12734 of Title 10.

Section 932, act July 9, 1952, ch. 608, pt. II, §212, 66 Stat. 485, prescribed status of members of reserve components. See section 10141 of Title 10.

Section 933, act July 9, 1952, ch. 608, pt. II, §213, 66 Stat. 485, related to retention of status of members of reserve components, and to honorary status.

Section 934, act July 9, 1952, ch. 608, pt. II, §214, 66 Stat. 485, related to training categories for each reserve component. See section 10141(c) of Title 10.

Section 935, act July 9, 1952, ch. 608, pt. II, §215, 66 Stat. 486, provided for officer candidates and for distribution of personnel in various ranks and grades. See sections 12001 and 12209 of Title 10, Armed Forces, and section 702 of Title 14, Coast Guard.

§936. Repealed. Sept. 3, 1954, ch. 1257, title VII, §702(d), 68 Stat. 1189

Section, act July 9, 1952, ch. 608, pt. II, §216, 66 Stat. 486, related to promotion and precedence.

ADDITIONAL REPEAL

Section was also repealed by act Aug. 10, 1956, ch. 1041, §53, 70A Stat. 641.

§§941 to 956. Repealed. Aug. 10, 1956, ch. 1041, §53, 70A Stat. 641

Section 941, acts July 9, 1952, ch. 608, pt. II, §217, 66 Stat. 486; July 30, 1956, ch. 789, §4(a), 70 Stat. 729, related to qualifications for appointments and enlistments in the Reserves. See sections 12102, 12201, and 12204 of Title 10, Armed Forces. Act July 30, 1956, ch. 789, §4(a), 70 Stat. 729, was repealed by Pub. L. 85–861, §36A, Sept. 2, 1958, 72 Stat. 1570.

Section 942, act July 9, 1952, ch. 608, pt. II, §218, 66 Stat. 487, authorized the President, by and with the advice and consent of the Senate, to make appointments to general or flag officer grade. See section 12203 of Title 10.

Section 943, act July 9, 1952, ch. 608, pt. II, §219, 66 Stat. 487, authorized the President to make appointments in commissioned grades below general or flag officer grades. See section 12203 of Title 10.

Section 944, act July 9, 1952, ch. 608, pt. II, §220, 66 Stat. 487, related to appointments in warrant officer grades. See section 12241 of Title 10.

Section 945, act July 9, 1952, ch. 608, pt. II, §221, 66 Stat. 487, related to tenure of appointments of commissioned officers. See section 12203 of Title 10.

Section 946, act July 9, 1952, ch. 608, pt. II, §222, 66 Stat. 487, provided for a common Federal appointment for officers. See section 12201(a) of Title 10.

Section 947, act July 9, 1952, ch. 608, pt. II, §223, 66 Stat. 487, prescribed tenure of appointments of warrant officers. See section 12241 of Title 10.

Section 948, act July 9, 1952, ch. 608, pt. II, §224, 66 Stat. 487, provided for indefinite term of appointment, conversion of appointments and enlistments. See sections 12203 and 12241 of Title 10 and note set out under section 12203 of Title 10.

Section 949, act July 9, 1952, ch. 608, pt. II, §225, 66 Stat. 488, provided for physical examinations. See section 12644 of Title 10.

Section 950, act July 9, 1952, ch. 608, pt. II, §226, 66 Stat. 488, provided for discharge or transfer of physically disqualified personnel. See section 12644 of Title 10.

Section 951, act July 9, 1952, ch. 608, pt. II, §227, 66 Stat. 488, related to term of enlistment. See section 12103 of Title 10.

Section 952, act July 9, 1952, ch. 608, pt. II, §228, 66 Stat. 488, related to common Federal enlistments. See sections 12102 and 12107 of Title 10.

Section 953, act July 9, 1952, ch. 608, pt. II, §229, 66 Stat. 488, prohibited dual membership in reserve components. See section 10213 of Title 10.

Section 954, act July 9, 1952, ch. 608, pt. II, §230, 66 Stat. 489, related to enlisted personnel as officer candidates. See section 12209 of Title 10.

Section 955, act July 9, 1952, ch. 608, pt. II, §231, 66 Stat. 489, related to age limitation for officers.

Section 956, act July 9, 1952, ch. 608, pt. II, §232, 66 Stat. 489, authorized appointment or enlistment of limited-service personnel. See sections 12102 and 12201 of Title 10.

§§961 to 967. Repealed. Aug. 10, 1956, ch. 1041, §53, 70A Stat. 641

Section 961, acts July 9, 1952, ch. 608, pt. II, §233, 66 Stat. 489; Aug. 9, 1955, ch. 665, §2(e)–(g), 69 Stat. 599, related to liability of members for active duty, limitation on recall, annual training, voluntary active duty, notification prior to active-duty orders, utilization of officers, protection of members of organized units, and to ministers of religion. See sections 12102, 12201, 12204, 12301, 12302, 12317, and 12682 of Title 10, Armed Forces. Act Aug. 9, 1955, ch. 665, §2(e)–(g), 69 Stat. 599, was repealed by Pub. L. 85–861, §36A, Sept. 2, 1958, 72 Stat. 1569.

Section 962, act July 9, 1952, ch. 608, pt. II, §234, 66 Stat. 490, related to active duty in connection with Reserve training and administration. See sections 12301 and 12310 of Title 10.

Section 963, act July 9, 1952, ch. 608, pt. II, §235, 66 Stat. 491, provided for active duty agreements, involuntary release, obligation to serve full term, prior obligated or involuntary service, uniformity of agreements. See sections 12311 and 12312 of Title 10.

Section 964, act July 9, 1952, ch. 608, pt. II, §236, 66 Stat. 491, provided for continuation of active duty. See section 12311 of Title 10.

Section 965, act July 9, 1952, ch. 608, pt. II, §237, 66 Stat. 492, authorized detail or assignment to duties authorized for regulars. See section 12314 of Title 10.

Section 966, act July 9, 1952, ch. 608, pt. II, §238, 66 Stat. 492, related to maintenance of Reserve forces in time of partial mobilization. See section 10207 of Title 10.

Section 967, act July 9, 1952, ch. 608, pt. II, §239, 66 Stat. 492, provided for release from active duty. See section 12313 of Title 10.

§§971 to 975. Repealed. Aug. 10, 1956, ch. 1041, §53, 70A Stat. 641

Section 971, act July 9, 1952, ch. 608, pt. II, §240, 66 Stat. 492, provided for active duty with or without pay. See section 12315 of Title 10, Armed Forces.

Section 972, act July 9, 1952, ch. 608, pt. II, §241, 66 Stat. 492, related to pay and allowances of persons retained beyond the term of service. See section 12315 of Title 10.

Section 973, act July 9, 1952, ch. 608, pt. II, §242, 66 Stat. 492, related to pay for officer candidates. See section 12209 of Title 10.

Section 974, act July 9, 1952, ch. 608, pt. II, §243, 66 Stat. 492, related to uniform allowances. See sections 415 to 419 of Title 37, Pay and Allowances of the Uniformed Services.

Section 975, act July 9, 1952, ch. 608, pt. II, §245, 66 Stat. 494, provided for continuation of existing benefits.

§§981, 982. Repealed. Aug. 10, 1956, ch. 1041, §53, 70A Stat. 641

Section 981, act July 9, 1952, ch. 608, pt. II, §246, 66 Stat. 495, related to civil status of reservists. See section 502 of Title 5, Government Organization and Employees.

Section 982, act July 9, 1952, ch. 608, pt. II, §247, 66 Stat. 495, authorized members of reserve components to accept employment with and compensation from any foreign government or any concern which is controlled in whole or in part by a foreign government. See section 1032 of Title 10, Armed Forces.

§§991, 992. Repealed. Aug. 10, 1956, ch. 1041, §53, 70A Stat. 641

Section 991, act July 9, 1952, ch. 608, pt. II, §248, 66 Stat. 495, provided for discharge of commissioned officers and other members of reserve components. See sections 12681 and 12682 of Title 10, Armed Forces.

Section 992, act July 9, 1952, ch. 608, pt. II, §249, 66 Stat. 495, related to limitation on discharges, dropping from rolls, and character of discharge. See sections 12683 to 12686 of Title 10.

§§1001 to 1010. Repealed. Aug. 10, 1956, ch. 1041, §53, 70A Stat. 641

Section 1001, act July 9, 1952, ch. 608, pt. II, §250, 66 Stat. 495, prohibited discrimination between Regulars and reserve components. See section 10209 of Title 10, Armed Forces.

Section 1002, act July 9, 1952, ch. 608, pt. II, §251, 66 Stat. 495, authorized Secretaries of the Army, Navy, Air Force, and the Treasury, to make and publish regulations. See section 10202 of Title 10 and section 417(a) of Title 37, Pay and Allowances of the Uniformed Services.

Section 1003, act July 9, 1952, ch. 608, pt. II, §252, 66 Stat. 496, provided for reserve participation in administration of policy and regulations. See section 10211 of Title 10, Armed Forces.

Section 1004, act July 9, 1952, ch. 608, pt. II, §253, 66 Stat. 496, related to support of reserve components. See section 12501 of Title 10.

Section 1005, act July 9, 1952, ch. 608, pt. II, §254, 66 Stat. 496, related to boards, membership of boards, seniority. See section 12643 of Title 10.

Section 1006, act July 9, 1952, ch. 608, pt. II, §255, 66 Stat. 496, related to availability of supplies, equipment, and facilities. See section 18502 of Title 10.

Section 1007, act July 9, 1952, ch. 608, pt. II, §256, 66 Stat. 496, provided for responsibility for Reserve affairs. See sections 10203 and 18501 of Title 10.

Section 1008, act July 9, 1952, ch. 608, pt. II, §257(a)–(d), 66 Stat. 497, related to creation, composition and representation on the Reserve Forces Policy Board, provided that the Board should be the principal policy adviser to the Secretary of Defense. See section 10301 of Title 10. Subsec. (e) of section 257 of act July 9, 1952, as amended Sept. 3, 1954, ch. 1257, title VII, §702(c), 68 Stat. 1189, was restated in section 133 [now 113] of Title 10.

Section 1009, act July 9, 1952, ch. 608, pt. II, §258, 66 Stat. 498, related to personnel records. See section 10204 of Title 10.

Section 1010, act July 9, 1952, ch. 608, pt. II, §259, 66 Stat. 498, related to dissemination of information. See section 10210 of Title 10.

§§1011, 1012. Repealed. Pub. L. 85–861, §36A, Sept. 2, 1958, 72 Stat. 1569

Section 1011, act July 9, 1952, ch. 608, pt. II, §260, as added Aug. 9, 1955, ch. 665, §2(h), 69 Stat. 599, related to records of persons participating in active and inactive duty training. See section 10204 of Title 10, Armed Forces.

Section 1012, act July 9, 1952, ch. 608, pt. II, §261, as added Aug. 9, 1955, ch. 665, §2(i), 69 Stat. 600, related to period of enlistment in Reserve components. See section 12103 of Title 10.

§1013. Repealed. Pub. L. 88–110, §1, Sept. 3, 1963, 77 Stat. 134

Section, act July 9, 1952, ch. 608, pt. II, §262, as added Aug. 9, 1955, ch. 665, §2(i), 69 Stat. 600; amended Apr. 23, 1956, ch. 209, §1, 70 Stat. 115; July 17, 1959, Pub. L. 86–96, 73 Stat. 221; July 12, 1960, Pub. L. 86–632, §2, 74 Stat. 468, authorized President to accept enlistments in the Ready Reserve, to maintain them at a level necessary for national defense, of persons not having attained age 18, and six months and who had not been ordered to report for induction, or who possessed critical skills and were engaged in defense industry, fixed period of enlistment at eight years with active duty therein for three to six months, deferred such persons from universal military training, and required National Security Training Commission to advise President and Secretary of Defense and to report annually to Congress regarding welfare of trainees.

§1014. Omitted

CODIFICATION

Section, act July 9, 1952, ch. 608, pt. II, §263, as added Aug. 9, 1955, ch. 665, §2(i), 69 Stat. 602, which provided for release from active duty in Armed Forces prior to serving periods for which inducted or enlisted, expired by its own terms on July 1, 1957.

§1015. Repealed. Pub. L. 85–861, §36A, Sept. 2, 1958, 72 Stat. 1569

Section, act July 9, 1952, ch. 608, pt. II, §264, as added Apr. 23, 1956, ch. 209, §2, 70 Stat. 115, related to training period and to eligibility for benefits. See sections 3687, 3721, 6148, 8687, and 8721 of Title 10, Armed Forces.

§1016. Repealed. Pub. L. 87–651, title III, §307A, Sept. 7, 1962, 76 Stat. 526

Section, act July 9, 1952, ch. 608, pt. II, §265, as added July 9, 1956, ch. 534, 70 Stat. 517; amended Sept. 2, 1958, Pub. L. 85–857, §13(r), 72 Stat. 1266; Sept. 21, 1959, Pub. L. 86–324, §1, 73 Stat. 596; June 28, 1962, Pub. L. 87–509, §1, 76 Stat. 120, provided for a lump-sum readjustment payment for involuntary release from active duty. See section 12686 of Title 10, Armed Forces.

Pub. L. 87–509, §1, June 28, 1962, 76 Stat. 120, was repealed by Pub. L. 89–718, §75(4), Nov. 2, 1966, 80 Stat. 1124.

§§1021 to 1024. Repealed. Aug. 10, 1956, ch. 1041, §53, 70A Stat. 641

Section 1021, act July 9, 1952, ch. 608, pt. III, §301, 66 Stat. 498, established National Guard and Army Reserve as reserve components of the Army. See section 3062 of Title 10, Armed Forces.

Section 1022, act July 9, 1952, ch. 608, pt. III, §302, 66 Stat. 498, redesignated Organized Reserve Corps as Army Reserve.

Section 1023, act July 9, 1952, ch. 608, pt. III, §303, 66 Stat. 498, related to composition of Army Reserve. See section 10104 of Title 10.

Section 1024, act July 9, 1952, ch. 608, pt. III, §304, 66 Stat. 498, related to women in Army Reserve.

§§1041 to 1053. Repealed. Aug. 10, 1956, ch. 1041, §53, 70A Stat. 641

Section 1041, act July 9, 1952, ch. 608, pt. IV, §401, 66 Stat. 498, established Naval Reserve as Reserve component of Navy. See section 10108 of Title 10, Armed Forces.

Section 1042, act July 9, 1952, ch. 608, pt. IV, §402, 66 Stat. 498, established Marine Corps Reserve as reserve component of Marine Corps. See section 10109 of Title 10.

Section 1043, act July 9, 1952, ch. 608, pt. IV, §403, 66 Stat. 498, provided that Coast Guard Reserve is reserve component of Coast Guard. See section 701 of Title 14, Coast Guard.

Section 1044, act July 9, 1952, ch. 608, pt. IV, §404, 66 Stat. 498, provided for integration of Naval Reserve. See section 10108 of Title 10, Armed Forces.

Section 1045, act July 9, 1952, ch. 608, pt. IV, §405, 66 Stat. 498, provided for integration of Marine Corps Reserve. See section 10109 of Title 10.

Section 1046, act July 9, 1952, ch. 608, pt. IV, §406, 66 Stat. 499, provided for integration of Coast Guard Reserve. See section 701 of Title 14, Coast Guard.

Section 1047, act July 9, 1952, ch. 608, pt. IV, §407, 66 Stat. 499, provided for a Naval Reserve Policy Board, a Marine Corps Reserve Policy Board, a Coast Guard Policy Board, and for membership on such boards. See sections 10303 and 10304 of Title 10, Armed Forces, and section 703 of Title 14, Coast Guard.

Section 1048, act July 9, 1952, ch. 608, pt. IV, §409, 66 Stat. 499, authorized Secretary of Navy to prescribe a suitable flag to be known as Naval Reserve flag, and provided class of vessels which may fly such flag. See section 7225 of Title 10, Armed Forces.

Section 1049, act July 9, 1952, ch. 608, pt. IV, §410, 66 Stat. 499, authorized Secretary of Navy to prescribe a Naval Reserve yacht pennant and enumerated class of vessels which may fly such pennant. See section 7226 of Title 10.

Section 1050, act July 9, 1952, ch. 608, pt. IV, §411, 66 Stat. 499, related to appointment and duty of temporary officers in Naval Reserve and Marine Corps Reserve. See section 603 of Title 10.

Section 1051, act July 9, 1952, ch. 608, pt. IV, §412, 66 Stat. 499, related to temporary members of Coast Guard Reserve.

Section 1052, act July 9, 1952, ch. 608, pt. IV, §413, 66 Stat. 499, provided for a Retired Reserve, membership, pay, recall to active duty. See sections 6327 and 6483 of Title 10.

Section 1053, act July 9, 1952, ch. 608, pt. IV, §414, 66 Stat. 500, related to applicability of laws to women in Naval Reserve, Marine Corps Reserve, and Coast Guard Reserve. See section 762 of Title 14, Coast Guard.

§§1071 to 1074. Repealed. Aug. 10, 1956, ch. 1041, §53, 70A Stat. 641

Section 1071, act July 9, 1952, ch. 608, pt. V, §501, 66 Stat. 500, prescribed composition of Naval Militia. See section 7851 of Title 10, Armed Forces.

Section 1072, act July 9, 1952, ch. 608, pt. V, §502, 66 Stat. 500, provided for appointment and enlistment of militia members in Naval Reserve or Marine Corps Reserve. See section 7852 of Title 10.

Section 1073, act July 9, 1952, ch. 608, pt. V, §503, 66 Stat. 500, provided for release from militia duty upon order to active duty in service of United States. See section 7853 of Title 10.

Section 1074, act July 9, 1952, ch. 608, pt. V, §504, 66 Stat. 500, related to availability of supplies and equipment. See section 7854 of Title 10.

§§1091 to 1093. Repealed. Aug. 10, 1956, ch. 1041, §53, 70A Stat. 641

Section 1091, act July 9, 1952, ch. 608, pt. VI, §601, 66 Stat. 501, provided that Air National Guard and Air Force Reserve are reserve components of Air Force. See section 8062 of Title 10, Armed Forces.

Section 1092, act July 9, 1952, ch. 608, pt. VI, §602, 66 Stat. 501, provided for composition of Air Force Reserve. See section 10110 of Title 10.

Section 1093, act July 9, 1952, ch. 608, pt. VI, §603, 66 Stat. 501, related to women in Air Force Reserve.

§§1111 to 1124. Repealed. Aug. 10, 1956, ch. 1041, §53, 70A Stat. 641

Section 1111, act July 9, 1952, ch. 608, pt. VII, §701, 66 Stat. 501, provided that National Guard and Air National Guard are reserve components of Army and Air Force. See sections 10105 and 10111 of Title 10, Armed Forces.

Section 1112, act July 9, 1952, ch. 608, pt. VII, §702, 66 Stat. 501, related to composition of National Guard and Air National Guard. See sections 101, 10105, and 10111 of Title 10, Armed Forces, and section 101 of Title 32, National Guard.

Section 1113, act July 9, 1952, ch. 608, pt. VII, §703, 66 Stat. 502, related to Federal recognition and appointments. See sections 12211 and 12212 of Title 10, Armed Forces, and sections 301, 307 of Title 32, National Guard.

Section 1114, act July 9, 1952, ch. 608, pt. VII, §704, 66 Stat. 502, related to temporary extension of Federal recognition to any officer of National Guard or Air National Guard. See sections 12211 and 12212 of Title 10, Armed Forces, and section 308 of Title 32, National Guard.

Section 1115, act July 9, 1952, ch. 608, pt. VII, §705, 66 Stat. 502, related to transfers from Army Reserve or Air Force Reserve to National Guard or Air National Guard. See sections 12107, 12211, and 12212 of Title 10, Armed Forces, and section 307 of Title 32, National Guard.

Section 1116, act July 9, 1952, ch. 608, pt. VII, §706, 66 Stat. 503, related to transfers from National Guard or Air National Guard to Army Reserve or Air Force Reserve. See sections 12105, 12213, and 12214 of Title 10, Armed Forces, and section 323 of Title 32, National Guard.

Section 1117, act July 9, 1952, ch. 608, pt. VII, §707, 66 Stat. 503, provided for automatic transfers. See sections 12106, 12213, and 12214 of Title 10, Armed Forces.

Section 1118, acts July 9, 1952, ch. 608, pt. VII, §708, 66 Stat. 503; Sept. 3, 1954, ch. 1257, title VII, §702(e), 68 Stat. 1189, permitted warrant officers and enlisted members of National Guard and of Air National Guard of United States to hold appointments as Reserve commissioned officers of Army or of Air Force, provided for determination of their status.

Section 1119, act July 9, 1952, ch. 608, pt. VII, §709, 66 Stat. 503, provided for training in State status. See sections 10107, 10113, and 12401 of Title 10.

Section 1120, act July 9, 1952, ch. 608, pt. VII, §710, 66 Stat. 503, provided for relief from National Guard duty when ordered to active duty. See section 325 of Title 32, National Guard.

Section 1121, act July 9, 1952, ch. 608, pt. VII, §711, 66 Stat. 504, related to relief from liability for issued United States property. See section 704 of Title 32.

Section 1122, act July 9, 1952, ch. 608, pt. VII, §712, 66 Stat. 504, related to maintenance of integrity of units, and to return to State status. See section 12404 of Title 10, Armed Forces, and sections 325 and 706 of Title 32, National Guard.

Section 1123, act July 9, 1952, ch. 608, pt. VII, §713, 66 Stat. 504, related to Federal status of personnel ordered to active duty. See sections 12211, 12212, and 12403 of Title 10, Armed Forces.

Section 1124, act July 9, 1952, ch. 608, pt. VII, §714, 66 Stat. 504, related to benefits for members of National Guard of United States. See section 12602 of Title 10, Armed Forces, and section 501(c) of Title 37, Pay and Allowances of the Uniformed Services.

§1125. Repealed. Pub. L. 85–861, §36A, Sept. 2, 1958, 72 Stat. 1569

Section, act July 9, 1952, ch. 608, pt. VII, §715, as added July 30, 1956, ch. 789, §4(b), 70 Stat. 729, related to applicability of laws to female officers, their dependents and beneficiaries and to determination of dependency.

CHAPTER 26—GIFTS FOR DEFENSE PURPOSES

§§1151 to 1156. Repealed. Pub. L. 101–403, title II, §202(b), Oct. 1, 1990, 104 Stat. 874

Section 1151, act July 27, 1954, ch. 582, §1, 68 Stat. 566, authorized Secretary of the Treasury and Administrator of General Services to accept gifts of money or property on behalf of the United States made on condition that such gifts be used for particular defense purposes. See section 2608 of Title 10, Armed Forces.

Section 1152, act July 27, 1954, ch. 582, §2, 68 Stat. 566, authorized Secretary of the Treasury and Administrator of General Services to convert into money any gifts of property.

Section 1153, act July 27, 1954, ch. 582, §3, 68 Stat. 566, established a special account in the Treasury for depositing gifts.

Section 1154, act July 27, 1954, ch. 582, §4, 68 Stat. 566, directed Secretary of the Treasury to pay to various appropriation accounts any moneys in the special account which in his judgment would best effectuate the purpose of the gifts.

Section 1155, act July 27, 1954, ch. 582, §5, 68 Stat. 566, directed Secretary of the Treasury and Administrator of General Services to consult with interested Federal agencies in carrying out this chapter.

Section 1156, act July 27, 1954, ch. 582, §6, 68 Stat. 566, provided that nothing in this chapter was to be construed to modify or repeal the authority to accept conditional gifts under any other provision of law.

TRANSFER OF FUNDS

Section 202(c) of Pub. L. 101–403 provided that: "Any money in the special account provided for in section 3 of the Act [former 50 U.S.C. 1153] referred to in subsection (b) [repealing this chapter] on the date of the enactment of this Act [Oct. 1, 1990] shall be credited to the Defense Cooperation Account provided for in section 2608(b) of title 10, United States Code, as added by subsection (a)."

CHAPTER 27—RESERVE OFFICER PERSONNEL PROGRAM

§§1181, 1182. Repealed. Pub. L. 85–861, §36A, Sept. 2, 1958, 72 Stat. 1569

Section 1181, act Sept. 3, 1954, ch. 1257, title I, §102, 68 Stat. 1149, defined terms used in the Reserve Officer Personnel Act of 1954. See sections 101(d)(4), 12003 to 12005, 12202, 12642, 12646, 12647, and 12772 of Title 10, Armed Forces, and section 720 of Title 14, Coast Guard.

Section 1182, act Sept. 3, 1954, ch. 1257, title VII, §703, 68 Stat. 1189, contained savings provisions. See section 723 of Title 14.

§§1191 to 1202. Repealed. Pub. L. 85–861, §36A, Sept. 2, 1958, 72 Stat. 1569

Section 1191, acts Sept. 3, 1954, ch. 1257, title II, §201, 68 Stat. 1150; June 30, 1955, ch. 247, §1(a), 69 Stat. 218, related to constructive service credit on initial appointment. See section 12207 of Title 10, Armed Forces, and section 727 of Title 14, Coast Guard.

Section 1192, act Sept. 3, 1954, ch. 1257, title II, §202, 68 Stat. 1150, related to eligibility for promotion and to standards and qualifications for active status. See sections 12642 and 14301 et seq. of Title 10, Armed Forces, and section 732 of Title 14, Coast Guard.

Section 1193, act Sept. 3, 1954, ch. 1257, title II, §203, 68 Stat. 1150, related to appointment, composition, duration of service, quorum, and oath of service of selection boards, and to communications by officers eligible for promotion. See section 14101 et seq. of Title 10, Armed Forces, and section 730 of Title 14, Coast Guard.

Section 1194, act Sept. 3, 1954, ch. 1257, title II, §204, 68 Stat. 1151, authorized retention of officers with incomplete reserve service. See section 12645 of Title 10, Armed Forces.

Section 1195, acts Sept. 3, 1954, ch. 1257, title II, §205, 68 Stat. 1151; June 30, 1955, ch. 247, §1(b), 69 Stat. 218, related to retention of officers with eighteen or more years of service. See section 12646 of Title 10.

Section 1196, act Sept. 3, 1954, ch. 1257, title II, §206, 68 Stat. 1152, provided for advancement in grade on retirement or transfer to Retired Reserve. See sections 12771 to 12773 of Title 10.

Section 1197, act Sept. 3, 1954, ch. 1257, title II, §207, 68 Stat. 1152, related to grade on entry upon active duty. See section 12320 of Title 10, Armed Forces, and section 745 of Title 14, Coast Guard.

Section 1198, act Sept. 3, 1954, ch. 1257, title II, §208, 68 Stat. 1152, provided for recommendation for promotion of officer previously removed from active status. See section 14317 of Title 10, Armed Forces, and section 733 of Title 14, Coast Guard.

Section 1199, act Sept. 3, 1954, ch. 1257, title II, §209, 68 Stat. 1152, authorized the President to suspend provisions of Reserve Officer Personnel Act of 1954 in time of war or national emergency. See section 123 of Title 10, Armed Forces, section 722 of Title 14, Coast Guard, and section 111 of Title 32, National Guard.

Section 1200, act Sept. 3, 1954, ch. 1257, title II, §210, 68 Stat. 1152, provided that there shall be no requirement for sea or foreign service for promotion of Reserve officers. See section 779 of Title 14, Coast Guard.

Section 1201, act Sept. 3, 1954, ch. 1257, title II, §211, 68 Stat. 1153, related to grades of Reserve officers. See section 12202 of Title 10, Armed Forces.

Section 1202, act Sept. 3, 1954, ch. 1257, title II, §212, 68 Stat. 1153, related to active status of officers assigned to Selective Service System. See section 12647 of Title 10, Armed Forces, and section 740 of Title 14, Coast Guard.

§§1221 to 1227. Repealed. Pub. L. 85–861, §36A, Sept. 2, 1958, 72 Stat. 1569

Section 1221, act Sept. 3, 1954, ch. 1257, title III, §301, 68 Stat. 1153, provided that sections 1221 to 1281 should apply only to Reserve officers of the Army.

Section 1222, acts Sept. 3, 1954, ch. 1257, title III, §302, 68 Stat. 1153; June 30, 1955, ch. 247, §6, 69 Stat. 221, defined terms used in sections 1221 to 1281 of this title. See section 12007 of Title 10, Armed Forces.

Section 1223, acts Sept. 3, 1954, ch. 1257, title III, §303, 68 Stat. 1154; June 30, 1955, ch. 247, §7, 69 Stat. 221, provided for promotion procedures. See sections 14101 et seq. and 14301 et seq. of Title 10.

Section 1224, act Sept. 3, 1954, ch. 1257, title III, §304, 68 Stat. 1154, related to maximum grades for female officers.

Section 1225, act Sept. 3, 1954, ch. 1257, title III, §305, 68 Stat. 1154, related to constructive service credit. See section 12201 et seq. of Title 10, Armed Forces.

Section 1226, act Sept. 3, 1954, ch. 1257, title III, §306, 68 Stat. 1155, related to minimum service in grade. See section 14303 of Title 10.

Section 1227, act Sept. 3, 1954, ch. 1257, title III, §307, 68 Stat. 1155, prescribed the authorized number of officers and for distribution in grade. See sections 12003 to 12005, 12007, and 12646 of Title 10.

§§1231 to 1238. Repealed. Pub. L. 85–861, §36A, Sept. 2, 1958, 72 Stat. 1569

Section 1231, act Sept. 3, 1954, ch. 1257, title III, §308, 68 Stat. 1155, provided for promotion to first lieutenant. See section 14301 et seq. of Title 10, Armed Forces.

Section 1232, act Sept. 3, 1954, ch. 1257, title III, §309, 68 Stat. 1156, provided for promotion to captain, major, and lieutenant colonel to fill vacancies. See section 14301 et seq. of Title 10.

Section 1233, act Sept. 3, 1954, ch. 1257, title III, §310, 68 Stat. 1156, related to promotion to captain, major, and lieutenant colonel regardless of vacancies. See sections 12009 and 14301 et seq. of Title 10.

Section 1234, act Sept. 3, 1954, ch. 1257, title III, §311, 68 Stat. 1157, related to second consideration for promotion. See section 14301 et seq. of Title 10.

Section 1235, act Sept. 3, 1954, ch. 1257, title III, §312, 68 Stat. 1157, related to promotion to colonel and female field grades to fill vacancies. See section 14301 et seq. of Title 10.

Section 1236, act Sept. 3, 1954, ch. 1257, title III, §313, 68 Stat. 1157, provided for promotion to brigadier general and major general to fill vacancies. See section 14301 et seq. of Title 10.

Section 1237, acts Sept. 3, 1954, ch. 1257, title III, §314, 68 Stat. 1158; June 30, 1955, ch. 247, §8, 69 Stat. 222, related to method of selection and order of promotion. See section 14301 et seq. of Title 10.

Section 1238, act Sept. 3, 1954, ch. 1257, title III, §315, 68 Stat. 1158, related to total years of service for first nonunit promotion.

§§1241 to 1243. Repealed. Pub. L. 85–861, §36A, Sept. 2, 1958, 72 Stat. 1569

Section 1241, act Sept. 3, 1954, ch. 1257, title III, §316, 68 Stat. 1159, provided for promotion to first lieutenant. See section 14301 et seq. of Title 10, Armed Forces.

Section 1242, act Sept. 3, 1954, ch. 1257, title III, §317, 68 Stat. 1159, provided for promotion to captain, major, lieutenant colonel, and colonel to fill unit vacancies. See section 14301 et seq. of Title 10.

Section 1243, act Sept. 3, 1954, ch. 1257, title III, §318, 68 Stat. 1159, provided for promotion to brigadier general and major general to fill vacancies. See section 14315 of Title 10.

§§1251 to 1255. Repealed. Pub. L. 85–861, §36A, Sept. 2, 1958, 72 Stat. 1569

Section 1251, act Sept. 3, 1954, ch. 1257, title III, §319, 68 Stat. 1160, related to examination for Federal recognition upon unit vacancy promotion. See section 309 of Title 32, National Guard.

Section 1252, act Sept. 3, 1954, ch. 1257, title III, §320, 68 Stat. 1160, related to extension of automatic Federal recognition to higher grade. See section 310 of Title 32.

Section 1253, act Sept. 3, 1954, ch. 1257, title III, §321, 68 Stat. 1160, provided for promotion to higher grade upon recognition. See section 14308(f) of Title 10, Armed Forces.

Section 1254, act Sept. 3, 1954, ch. 1257, title III, §322, 68 Stat. 1161, provided for promotion upon transfer to Army Reserve. See section 12213 of Title 10.

Section 1255, act Sept. 3, 1954, ch. 1257, title III, §323, 68 Stat. 1161, provided for appointment of adjutants general and assistant adjutants general as Reserve officers. See section 12215(a) of Title 10.

§§1261 to 1264. Repealed. Pub. L. 85–861, §36A, Sept. 2, 1958, 72 Stat. 1569

Section 1261, act Sept. 3, 1954, ch. 1257, title III, §324, 68 Stat. 1161, related to discharge of second lieutenants. See sections 14503 and 14907 of Title 10, Armed Forces, and section 323 of Title 32, National Guard.

Section 1262, acts Sept. 3, 1954, ch. 1257, title III, §325, 68 Stat. 1161; June 30, 1955, ch. 247, §9, 69 Stat. 222, provided for discharge or transfer to Retired Reserve of first lieutenants, captains, and majors. See section 14501 et seq. of Title 10, Armed Forces.

Section 1263, act Sept. 3, 1954, ch. 1257, title III, §326, 68 Stat. 1161, prescribed maximum age for discharge or transfer to Retired Reserve. See sections 14508 to 14512 of Title 10.

Section 1264, act Sept. 3, 1954, ch. 1257, title III, §327, 68 Stat. 1162, provided for discharge or transfer to Retired Reserve for length of service. See section 14501 et seq. of Title 10.

§1265. Omitted

Codification

Section, act Sept. 3, 1954, ch. 1257, title III, §328, 68 Stat. 1163, which provided for retention of officers to complete 20 years of service.

§§1266, 1267. Repealed. Pub. L. 85–861, §36A, Sept. 2, 1958, 72 Stat. 1569

Section 1266, act Sept. 3, 1954, ch. 1257, title III, §329, 68 Stat. 1163, related to disposition of general officers ceasing to occupy position. See section 14314(a) of Title 10, Armed Forces.

Section 1267, act Sept. 3, 1954, ch. 1257, title III, §330, 68 Stat. 1163, related to excess numbers in grade. See sections 14514 and 14704 of Title 10.

§§1271 to 1279. Repealed. Pub. L. 85–861, §36A, Sept. 2, 1958, 72 Stat. 1569

Section 1271, act Sept. 3, 1954, ch. 1257, title III, §331, 68 Stat. 1164, related to applicability of sections 1221 to 1227, 1231 to 1238, and 1261 to 1267 of this title. See section 14301 et seq. of Title 10, Armed Forces.

Section 1272, act Sept. 3, 1954, ch. 1257, title III, §332, 68 Stat. 1164, related to officers eligible for vacancy promotion entering on active duty. See section 14301 et seq. of Title 10.

Section 1273, acts Sept. 3, 1954, ch. 1257, title III, §333, 68 Stat. 1164; June 30, 1955, ch. 247, §§2, 10, 69 Stat. 218, 222, provided for promotion to higher grade while on active duty. See section 14311 of Title 10.

Section 1274, act Sept. 3, 1954, ch. 1257, title III, §334, 68 Stat. 1164, provided for promotion under mandatory consideration of officers with higher temporary grade. See section 14301 et seq. of Title 10.

Section 1275, act Sept. 3, 1954, ch. 1257, title III, §335, 68 Stat. 1165, related to appointment in appropriate higher grade after temporary appointment. See section 14301 et seq. of Title 10.

Section 1276, act Sept. 3, 1954, ch. 1257, title III, §336, 68 Stat. 1165, related to officers of the National Guard of the United States. See section 14301 et seq. of Title 10.

Section 1277, act Sept. 3, 1954, ch. 1257, title III, §337, 68 Stat. 1165, which related to withholding promotion on release from active duty, was also repealed by act June 30, 1955, ch. 247, §11, 69 Stat. 222.

Section 1278, act Sept. 3, 1954, ch. 1257, title III, §338, 68 Stat. 1165, related to promotion upon release from active duty. See section 14301 et seq. of Title 10.

Section 1279, acts Sept. 3, 1954, ch. 1257, title III, §339, 68 Stat. 1165; June 30, 1955, ch. 247, §1(c), 69 Stat. 218, related to retention for additional service.

§1281. Repealed. Pub. L. 85–861, §36A, Sept. 2, 1958, 72 Stat. 1569

Section, act Sept. 3, 1954, ch. 1257, title III, §340, 68 Stat. 1166, related to assimilation of regulations relating to promotion.

§§1301 to 1314. Repealed. Pub. L. 85–861, §36A, Sept. 2, 1958, 72 Stat. 1569

Section 1301, act Sept. 3, 1954, ch. 1257, title IV, §401, 68 Stat. 1166, related to applicability of sections 1301 to 1314 of this title, and defined terms.

Section 1302, acts Sept. 3, 1954, ch. 1257, title IV, §402, 68 Stat. 1166; June 30, 1955, ch. 247, §3(a), 69 Stat. 218, provided for authorized numbers and distribution of officers in the Naval Reserve. See sections 12003 to 12005 and 14001 et seq. of Title 10, Armed Forces.

Section 1303, acts Sept. 3, 1954, ch. 1257, title IV, §403, 68 Stat. 1167; June 30, 1955, ch. 247, §3(b), 69 Stat. 218, related to applicability of laws relating to selection for promotion of Regular officers. See sections 14001 et seq., 14101 et seq., 14307, and 14501 et seq. of Title 10.

Section 1304, act Sept. 3, 1954, ch. 1257, title IV, §404, 68 Stat. 1167, provided for running mates. See section 14306 of Title 10.

Section 1305, acts Sept. 3, 1954, ch. 1257, title IV, §405, 68 Stat. 1168; June 30, 1955, ch. 247, §3(c), (d), 69 Stat. 218, related to eligibility for promotion. See sections 14001 et seq., 14306, and 14501 et seq. of Title 10.

Section 1306, act Sept. 3, 1954, ch. 1257, title IV, §406, 68 Stat. 1168, related to applicability of laws relating to eligibility for promotion of Regular officers. See sections 14001 et seq. and 14308 of Title 10, Armed Forces and section 209 of Title 37, Pay and Allowances of the Uniformed Services.

Section 1307, act Sept. 3, 1954, ch. 1257, title IV, §407, 68 Stat. 1169, related to restriction on applicability of subchapter to officers on active status. See section 14301 et seq. of Title 10, Armed Forces.

Section 1308, act Sept. 3, 1954, ch. 1257, title IV, §408, 68 Stat. 1169, provided for qualifications for promotion.

Section 1309, act Sept. 3, 1954, ch. 1257, title IV, §409, 68 Stat. 1169, provided for removal from promotion list by the President. See section 14310 of Title 10.

Section 1310, act Sept. 3, 1954, ch. 1257, title IV, §410, 68 Stat. 1169, provided for precedence.

Section 1311, act Sept. 3, 1954, ch. 1257, title IV, §411, 68 Stat. 1169, provided for elimination from active status. See sections 6389 and 14512(b) of Title 10.

Section 1312, act Sept. 3, 1954, ch. 1257, title IV, §412, 68 Stat. 1171, provided for transfer to Retired Reserve for age, and exempted certain flag and general officers. See section 14512(b) of Title 10.

Section 1313, act Sept. 3, 1954, ch. 1257, title IV, §413, 68 Stat. 1171, provided for promotions under Secretary's regulations. See section 14301 et seq. of Title 10.

Section 1314, act Sept. 3, 1954, ch. 1257, title IV, §414, as added June 30, 1955, ch. 247, §3(e), 69 Stat. 219, related to promotion of Naval and Marine officers selected for promotion prior to July 1, 1955.

§§1331 to 1357. Repealed. Pub. L. 85–861, §36A, Sept. 2, 1958, 72 Stat. 1569

Section 1331, acts Sept. 3, 1954, ch. 1257, title V, §501, 68 Stat. 1171; June 30, 1955, ch. 247, §4(a), 69 Stat. 219, related to applicability of sections 1331 to 1357 of this title, and defined terms.

Section 1332, acts Sept. 3, 1954, ch. 1257, title V, §502, 68 Stat. 1172; June 30, 1955, ch. 247, §4(b), 69 Stat. 219, related to promotion and promotion service. See sections 14001 et seq. and 14301 et seq. of Title 10, Armed Forces.

Section 1333, act Sept. 3, 1954, ch. 1257, title V, §503, 68 Stat. 1172, related to authorized numbers and distribution of Reserve officers of the Air Force. See sections 12003 to 12005, 12009, and 12646 of Title 10.

Section 1334, acts Sept. 3, 1954, ch. 1257, title V, §504, 68 Stat. 1173; June 30, 1955, ch. 247, §4(c), 69 Stat. 219, related to seniority for promotion purposes. See section 14301 et seq. of Title 10.

Section 1335, act Sept. 3, 1954, ch. 1257, title V, §505, 68 Stat. 1173, provided for constructive service credit on appointment. See section 12201 et seq. of Title 10.

Section 1336, acts Sept. 3, 1954, ch. 1257, title V, §506, 68 Stat. 1173; June 30, 1955, ch. 247, §4(d), 69 Stat. 219, related to minimum service in grade. See section 14301 et seq. of Title 10.

Section 1337, act Sept. 3, 1954, ch. 1257, title V, §507, 68 Stat. 1174, related to time limit for consideration. See section 14301 et seq. of Title 10.

Section 1338, acts Sept. 3, 1954, ch. 1257, title V, §508, 68 Stat. 1174; June 30, 1955, ch. 247, §4(e), 69 Stat. 219, related to selection boards. See sections 14101 et seq. and 14301 et seq. of Title 10.

Section 1339, acts Sept. 3, 1954, ch. 1257, title V, §509, 68 Stat. 1174; June 30, 1955, ch. 247, §4(f), 69 Stat. 219, provided for promotion to first lieutenant, and to discharge for failure to qualify for permanent grade. See sections 14301 et seq. and 14503 of Title 10.

Section 1340, acts Sept. 3, 1954, ch. 1257, title V, §510, 68 Stat. 1174; June 30, 1955, ch. 247, §4(g), 69 Stat. 220, related to consideration for promotion to captain, major, and lieutenant colonel. See section 14301 et seq. of Title 10.

Section 1341, acts Sept. 3, 1954, ch. 1257, title V, §511, 68 Stat. 1175; June 30, 1955, ch. 247, §4(h), 69 Stat. 220, provided for promotion to captain, major or lieutenant colonel. See section 14301 et seq. of Title 10.

Section 1342, act Sept. 3, 1954, ch. 1257, title V, §512, 68 Stat. 1175, related to method of selection for promotion to captain, major, or lieutenant colonel. See section 14001 et seq. of Title 10.

Section 1343, act Sept. 3, 1954, ch. 1257, title V, §513, 68 Stat. 1176, authorized special promotions. See section 14301 et seq. of Title 10.

Section 1344, act Sept. 3, 1954, ch. 1257, title V, §514, 68 Stat. 1176, related to promotion of officers serving in temporary grade higher than permanent grade. See section 14301 et seq. of Title 10.

Section 1345, act Sept. 3, 1954, ch. 1257, title V, §515, 68 Stat. 1177, related to female Reserve officers.

Section 1346, act Sept. 3, 1954, ch. 1257, title V, §516, 68 Stat. 1177, related to promotion to colonel. See section 14301 et seq. of Title 10.

Section 1347, act Sept. 3, 1954, ch. 1257, title V, §517, 68 Stat. 1177, provided for promotion to brigadier general and major general. See sections 14314 and 14315 of Title 10.

Section 1348, act Sept. 3, 1954, ch. 1257, title V, §518, 68 Stat. 1178, provided for removal from the promotion list by the President. See section 14301 et seq. of Title 10.

Section 1349, act Sept. 3, 1954, ch. 1257, title V, §519, 68 Stat. 1179, related to Air National Guard. See section 14301 et seq. of Title 10, Armed Forces, and section 307 of Title 32, National Guard.

Section 1350, act Sept. 3, 1954, ch. 1257, title V, §520, 68 Stat. 1179, provided for promotion to first lieutenant in Air National Guard of the United States. See sections 14301 et seq. and 14503 of Title 10, Armed Forces.

Section 1351, act Sept. 3, 1954, ch. 1257, title V, §521, 68 Stat. 1179, provided for promotion to captain, major, and lieutenant colonel in the Air National Guard. See section 14301 et seq. of Title 10.

Section 1352, act Sept. 3, 1954, ch. 1257, title V, §522, 68 Stat. 1180, related to deferred officers. See section

14301 et seq. of Title 10, Armed Forces, and section 323 of Title 32, National Guard.

Section 1353, acts Sept. 3, 1954, ch. 1257, title V, §523, 68 Stat. 1181; June 30, 1955, ch. 247, §4(i), 69 Stat. 220, related to maximum ages for retention in active status. See sections 14510 to 14512 of Title 10, Armed Forces.

Section 1354, acts Sept. 3, 1954, ch. 1257, title V, §524, 68 Stat. 1182; June 30, 1955, ch. 247, §4(j), 69 Stat. 220, related to elimination of officers for length of service. See section 14501 et seq. of Title 10.

Section 1355, act Sept. 3, 1954, ch. 1257, title V, §525, 68 Stat. 1183, provided for elimination of excess officers. See sections 14514 and 14704 of Title 10.

Section 1356, act Sept. 3, 1954, ch. 1257, title V, §526, 68 Stat. 1183, provided for elimination or transfer of adjutants general or assistant adjutants general. See section 14314(a), (c) of Title 10.

Section 1357, act Sept. 3, 1954, ch. 1257, title V, §527, as added June 30, 1955, ch. 247, §4(k), 69 Stat. 220, related to civilian employees of the Air National Guard.

§§1381 to 1398. Repealed. Pub. L. 85–861, §36A, Sept. 2, 1958, 72 Stat. 1569

Section 1381, act Sept. 3, 1954, ch. 1257, title VI, §601, 68 Stat. 1183, defined terms used in sections 1381 to 1399 of this title. See section 720 of Title 14, Coast Guard.

Section 1382, act Sept. 3, 1954, ch. 1257, title VI, §602, 68 Stat. 1183, related to applicability of sections 1381 to 1399 of this title. See section 721 of Title 14.

Section 1383, act Sept. 3, 1954, ch. 1257, title VI, §603, 68 Stat. 1184, related to authorized numbers and distribution of officers in the Coast Guard Reserve. See section 724 of Title 14.

Section 1384, act Sept. 3, 1954, ch. 1257, title VI, §604, 68 Stat. 1184, related to promotions and selection boards. See section 729 of Title 14.

Section 1385, act Sept. 3, 1954, ch. 1257, title VI, §605, 68 Stat. 1185, provided for precedence. See section 725 of Title 14.

Section 1386, acts Sept. 3, 1954, ch. 1257, title VI, §606, 68 Stat. 1185; June 30, 1955, ch. 247, §5(a), 69 Stat. 221, related to running mates. See section 726 of Title 14.

Section 1387, act Sept. 3, 1954, ch. 1257, title VI, §607, 68 Stat. 1186, related to promotion zones. See section 731 of Title 14.

Section 1388, acts Sept. 3, 1954, ch. 1257, title VI, §608, 68 Stat. 1186; June 30, 1955, ch. 247, §5(b), 69 Stat. 221, related to date of rank upon promotion. See section 736 of Title 14.

Section 1389, act Sept. 3, 1954, ch. 1257, title VI, §609, 68 Stat. 1186, related to minimum points for consideration for promotion. See section 785 of Title 14.

Section 1390, act Sept. 3, 1954, ch. 1257, title VI, §610, 68 Stat. 1186, related to qualifications for promotion. See section 734 of Title 14.

Section 1391, act Sept. 3, 1954, ch. 1257, title VI, §611, 68 Stat. 1186, related to failure of selection and elimination. See section 740 of Title 14.

Section 1392, act Sept. 3, 1954, ch. 1257, title VI, §612, 68 Stat. 1187, provided for removal from promotion list by the President. See section 738 of Title 14.

Section 1393, act Sept. 3, 1954, ch. 1257, title VI, §613, 68 Stat. 1187, related to maximum ages for active status. See section 742 of Title 14.

Section 1394, act Sept. 3, 1954, ch. 1257, title VI, §614, 68 Stat. 1187, related to type of promotion. See section 737 of Title 14.

Section 1395, act Sept. 3, 1954, ch. 1257, title VI, §615, 68 Stat. 1188, related to promotion of officers serving on active duty. See section 728 of Title 14.

Section 1396, act Sept. 3, 1954, ch. 1257, title VI, §616, 68 Stat. 1188, provided for appointment of former Navy and Coast Guard officers. See section 744 of Title 14.

Section 1397, act Sept. 3, 1954, ch. 1257, title VI, §617, 68 Stat. 1188, provided for recall of retired officers. See section 746 of Title 14.

Section 1398, act Sept. 3, 1954, ch. 1257, title VI, §618, 68 Stat. 1188, authorized the Secretary to promulgate regulations. See section 794 of Title 14.

§1399. Omitted

CODIFICATION

Section, act Sept. 3, 1954, ch. 1257, title VI, §619, as added June 30, 1955, ch. 247, §5(c), 69 Stat. 221, which authorized promotion of officers who were selected for promotion prior to July 1, 1955.

CHAPTER 28—STATUS OF ARMED FORCES PERSONNEL APPOINTED TO SERVICE ACADEMIES

§§1411 to 1414. Repealed. Pub. L. 85–861, §36A, Sept. 2, 1958, 72 Stat. 1570

Section 1411, act June 25, 1956, ch. 439, §1, 70 Stat. 333, related to continuance of enlisted contract or period of obligated service and to pay allowance and benefits. See section 516 of Title 10, Armed Forces.

Section 1412, act June 25, 1956, ch. 439, §2, 70 Stat. 333, related to reversion to enlisted status upon separation from the service academies. See section 516 of Title 10.

Section 1413, act June 25, 1956, ch. 439, §3, 70 Stat. 333, related to charge against allowed number of personnel in Armed Forces.

Section 1414, act June 25, 1956, ch. 439, §4, 70 Stat. 333, related to restriction on counting Academy service towards length of service as an officer.

CHAPTER 29—NATIONAL DEFENSE CONTRACTS

CHAPTER REFERRED TO IN OTHER SECTIONS

This chapter is referred to in section 1651 of this title; title 10 section 2410; title 42 section 2210.

§1431. Authorization; official approval; Congressional action: notification of committees of certain proposed obligations, resolution of disapproval, continuity of session, computation of period

The President may authorize any department or agency of the Government which exercises functions in connection with the national defense, acting in accordance with regulations prescribed by the President for the protection of the Government, to enter into contracts or into amendments or modifications of contracts heretofore or hereafter made and to make advance payments thereon, without regard to other provisions of law relating to the making, performance, amendment, or modification of contracts, whenever he deems that such action would facilitate the national defense. The authority conferred by this section shall not be utilized to obligate the United States in an amount in excess of $50,000 without approval by an official at or above the level of an Assistant Secretary or his Deputy, or an assistant head or his deputy, of such department or agency, or by a Contract Adjustment Board established therein. The authority conferred by this section may not be utilized to obligate the United States in any amount in excess of $25,000,000 unless the Committees on Armed Services of the Senate and the House of Representatives have been notified in writing of such proposed obligation and 60 days of continuous session of Congress have expired following the date on which such notice was transmitted to such Committees. For purposes of this section, the continuity of a session of Congress is broken only by an adjournment of the Congress sine die at the end of a Congress, and the days on which either House is not in session because of an adjournment of more than 3 days to a day certain, or because of an adjournment sine die other than at the end of a Congress, are excluded in the computation of such 60-day period.

(Pub. L. 85–804, §1, Aug. 28, 1958, 72 Stat. 972; Pub. L. 93–155, title VIII, §807(a), Nov. 16, 1973, 87 Stat. 615; Pub. L. 101–510, div. A, title XIII, §1313, Nov. 5, 1990, 104 Stat. 1670; Pub. L. 102–25, title VII, §705(f), Apr. 6, 1991, 105 Stat. 120.)

AMENDMENTS

1991—Pub. L. 102–25, §705(f)(1), inserted before period at end of third sentence "and 60 days of continuous session of Congress have expired following the date on which such notice was transmitted to such Committees".

Pub. L. 102–25, §705(f)(2), in fourth sentence, inserted "at the end of a Congress" after "sine die" and ", or because of an adjournment sine die other than at the end of a Congress," after "to a day certain".

1990—Pub. L. 101–510 struck out before period at end of third sentence "and 60 days of continuous session of Congress have expired following the date on which such notice was transmitted to such Committees and neither House of Congress has adopted, within such 60-day period, a resolution disapproving such obligation".

1973—Pub. L. 93–155 provided for notification of Congressional Committees with respect to certain proposed obligations, Congressional resolution of disapproval, continuity of Congressional session, and computation of period.

EFFECTIVE DATE OF 1991 AMENDMENT

Section 705(f)(1) of Pub. L. 102–25 provided that the amendment made by that section is effective as of Nov. 6, 1990.

NONAPPLICABILITY OF NATIONAL EMERGENCIES ACT

The provisions of the National Emergencies Act [see Short Title note set out under section 1601 of this title] shall not apply to the powers and authorities conferred by this section and actions taken hereunder, see section 1651(a)(6) of this title.

OBLIGATIONS ENTERED INTO BEFORE NOVEMBER 16, 1973

Amendment by Pub. L. 93–155 not affecting the carrying out of any contract, loan, guarantee, commitment, or other obligation entered into prior to Nov. 16, 1973, see section 807(e) of Pub. L. 93–155, set out as a note under section 2307 of Title 10, Armed Forces.

EX. ORD. NO. 10789. CONTRACTING AUTHORITY OF GOVERNMENT AGENCIES IN CONNECTION WITH NATIONAL DEFENSE FUNCTIONS

Ex. Ord. No. 10789, Nov. 14, 1958, 23 F.R. 8897, as amended by Ex. Ord. No. 11051, Sept. 27, 1962, 27 F.R. 9683; Ex. Ord. No. 11382, Nov. 28, 1967, 32 F.R. 16247; Ex. Ord. No. 11610, July 22, 1971, 36 F.R. 13755; Ex. Ord. No. 12148, July 20, 1979, 44 F.R. 43239; Ex. Ord. No. 12919, §904(b), June 3, 1994, 59 F.R. 29534, provided:

By virtue of the authority vested in me by the act of August 28, 1958, 72 Stat. 972, hereinafter called the act [this chapter], and as President of the United States, and deeming that such action will facilitate the national defense, it is hereby ordered as follows:

PART I—DEPARTMENT OF DEFENSE

Under such regulations, which shall be uniform to the extent practicable, as may be prescribed or approved by the Secretary of Defense:

1. The Department of Defense is authorized, within the limits of the amounts appropriated and the contract authorization provided therefor, to enter into contracts and into amendments or modifications of contracts heretofore or hereafter made, and to make advance payments thereon, without regard to the provisions of law relating to the making, performance, amendment, or modification of contracts, whenever, in the judgment of the Secretary of Defense, the Secretary of the Army, the Secretary of the Navy, or the Secretary of the Air Force, or the duly authorized representative of any such Secretary, the national defense will be facilitated thereby.

1A. (a) The limitation in paragraph 1 to amounts appropriated and the contract authorization provided therefor shall not apply to contractual provisions which provide that the United States will hold harmless and indemnify the contractor against any of the claims or losses set forth in subparagraph (b), whether resulting from the negligence or wrongful act or omission of the contractor or otherwise (except as provided in subparagraph (b)(2)). This exception from the limitations of paragraph 1 shall apply only to claims or losses arising out of or resulting from risks that the contract defines as unusually hazardous or nuclear in nature. Such a contractual provision shall be approved in advance by an official at a level not below that of the Secretary of a military department and may require each contractor so indemnified to provide and maintain financial protection of such type and in such amounts as is determined by the approving official to be appropriate under the circumstances. In deciding whether to approve the use of an indemnification provision and in determining the amount of financial protection to be provided and maintained by the indemnified contractor, the appropriate official shall take into account such factors as the availability, cost and terms of private insurance, self-insurance, other proof of financial responsibility and workmen's compensation insurance. Such approval and determination, as required by the preceding two sentences, shall be final.

(b)(1) Subparagraph (a) shall apply to claims (including reasonable expenses of litigation and settlement) or losses, not compensated by insurance or otherwise, of the following types:

(A) Claims by third persons, including employees of the contractor, for death, personal injury, or loss of, damage to, or loss of use of property;

(B) Loss of, damage to, or loss of use of property of the contractor;

(C) Loss of, damage to, or loss of use of property of the Government;

(D) Claims arising (i) from indemnification agreements between the contractor and a subcontractor or subcontractors, or (ii) from such arrangements and further indemnification arrangements between subcontractors at any tier; provided that all such arrangements were entered into pursuant to regulations prescribed or approved by the Secretaries of Defense, the Army, the Navy, or the Air Force.

(2) Indemnification and hold harmless agreements entered into pursuant to this subsection, whether between the United States and a contractor, or between a contractor and a subcontractor, or between two subcontractors, shall not cover claims or losses caused by the willful misconduct or lack of good faith on the part of any of the contractor's or subcontractor's directors or officers or principal officials which are (i) claims by the United States (other than those arising through subrogation) against the contractor or subcontractor, or (ii) losses affecting the property of such contractor or subcontractor. Regulations to be prescribed or approved by the Secretaries of Defense, the Army, the

Navy or the Air Force shall define the scope of the term principal officials.

(3) The United States may discharge its obligation under a provision authorized by subparagraph (a) by making payments directly to subcontractors or to third persons to whom a contractor or subcontractor may be liable.

(c) A contractual provision made under subparagraph (a) that provides for indemnification must also provide for—

(1) notice to the United States of any claim or action against, or of any loss by, the contractor or subcontractor which is covered by such contractual provision; and

(2) control or assistance by the United States, at its election, in the settlement or defense of any such claim or action.

2. The Secretaries of Defense, the Army, the Navy, and the Air Force, respectively, may exercise the authority herein conferred and, in their discretion and by their direction, may delegate such authority to any other military or civilian officers or officials of their respective departments, and may confer upon any such military or civilian officers or officials the power to make further delegations of such authority within their respective commands or organizations: *Provided*, That the authority herein conferred shall not be utilized to obligate the United States in an amount in excess of $50,000 without approval by an official at or above the level of an Assistant Secretary or his Deputy, or by a departmental Contract Adjustment Board.

3. The contracts hereby authorized to be made shall include agreements of all kinds (whether in the form of letters of intent, purchase orders, or otherwise) for all types and kinds of property or services necessary, appropriate, or convenient for the national defense, or for the invention, development, or production of, or research concerning, any such property or services, including, but not limited to, aircraft, missiles, buildings, vessels, arms, armament, equipment or supplies of any kind, or any portion thereof, including plans, spare parts and equipment therefor, materials, supplies, facilities, utilities, machinery, machine tools, and any other equipment without any restriction of any kind as to type, character, location, or form.

4. The Department of Defense may by agreement modify or amend or settle claims under contracts heretofore or hereafter made, may make advance payments upon such contracts of any portion of the contract price, and may enter into agreements with contractors or obligors modifying or releasing accrued obligations of any sort, including accrued liquidated damages or liability under surety or other bonds. Amendments or modifications of contracts may be with or without consideration and may be utilized to accomplish the same things as any original contract could have accomplished hereunder, irrespective of the time or circumstances of the making, or the form, of the contract amended or modified, or of the amending or modifying contract, and irrespective of rights which may have accrued under the contract or the amendments or modifications thereof.

5. Proper records of all actions taken under the authority of the act shall be maintained within the Department of Defense. The Secretaries of Defense, the Army, the Navy, and the Air Force shall make such records available for public inspection except to the extent that they, or their duly authorized representatives, may respectively deem the disclosure of information therein to be detrimental to the national security.

6. The Department of Defense shall, by March 15 of each year, report to the Congress all actions taken within that department under the authority of the act during the preceding calendar year. With respect to actions which involve actual or potential cost to the United States in excess of $50,000, the report shall (except as the disclosure of such information may be deemed to be detrimental to the national security)—

(a) name the contractor;

(b) state the actual cost or estimated potential cost involved;

(c) describe the property or services involved; and

(d) state further the circumstances justifying the action taken.

7. There shall be no discrimination in any act performed hereunder against any person on the ground of race, religion, color, or national origin, and all contracts entered into, amended, or modified hereunder shall contain such nondiscrimination provision as otherwise may be required by statute or Executive order.

8. No claim against the United States arising under any purchase or contract made under the authority of the act and this order shall be assigned except in accordance with the Assignment of Claims Act of 1940 (54 Stat. 1029), as amended [section 3727 of Title 31, Money and Finance, and section 15 of Title 41, Public Contracts].

9. Advance payments shall be made hereunder only upon obtaining adequate security.

10. Every contract entered into, amended, or modified pursuant to this order shall contain a warranty by the contractor in substantially the following terms:

"The Contractor warrants that no person or selling agency has been employed or retained to solicit or secure this contract upon an agreement or understanding for a commission, percentage, brokerage, or contingent fee, except bonafide employees or bonafide established commercial or selling agencies maintained by the Contractor for the purpose of securing business. For breach or violation of this warranty the Government shall have the right to annul this contract without liability or, in its discretion, to deduct from the contract price or consideration, or otherwise recover, the full amount of such commission, percentage, brokerage, or contingent fee."

11. Except as provided in the Act of September 27, 1966, 80 Stat. 850 [which amended section 1433 of this title, sections 2310 and 2313 of Title 10, Armed Forces, and section 254 of Title 41, Public Contracts] contracts entered into, amended, or modified pursuant to authority of this order shall include a clause to the effect that the Comptroller General of the United States or any of his duly authorized representatives shall, until the expiration of three years after final payment, have access to and the right to examine any directly pertinent books, documents, papers, and records of the contractor or any of his subcontractors engaged in the performance of, and involving transactions related to, such contracts or subcontracts. Before exercising the authority provided in the Act of September 27, 1966, 80 Stat. 850 the Secretaries of Defense, the Army, the Navy, or the Air Force, or their designees, shall first determine that all reasonable efforts have been made to include the clause prescribed above and that alternate sources of supply are not reasonably available.

12. Nothing herein contained shall be construed to constitute authorization hereunder for—

(a) the use of the cost-plus-a-percentage-of-cost system of contracting;

(b) any contract in violation of existing law relating to limitation of profits or fees;

(c) the negotiation of purchases of or contracts for property or services required by law to be procured by formal advertising and competitive bidding;

(d) the waiver of any bid, payment, performance, or other bond required by law;

(e) the amendment of a contract negotiated under section 2304(a)(15) of Title 10 of the United States Code to increase the contract price to an amount higher than the lowest rejected bid of any responsible bidder; or

(f) the formalization of an informal commitment, unless the Secretary of Defense, the Secretary of the Army, the Secretary of the Navy, or the Secretary of the Air Force, or the duly authorized representative of any such Secretary, finds that at the time the commitment was made it was impracticable to use normal procurement procedures.

13. The provisions of the Walsh-Healey Act (49 Stat. 2036), as amended [sections 35 to 45 of Title 41, Public

Contracts], the Davis-Bacon Act (49 Stat. 1011), as amended [sections 276a to 276a–5 of Title 40, Public Buildings, Property, and Works], the Copeland Act (48 Stat. 948), as amended, and the Eight-Hour Law (37 Stat. 137), as amended [sections 321 to 323 of Title 40], if otherwise applicable, shall apply to contracts made and performed under the authority of this order.

14. Nothing herein contained shall prejudice anything heretofore done under Executive Order No. 9001 of December 27, 1941, or Executive Order No. 10210 of February 2, 1951, or any amendments or extensions thereof, or the continuance in force of an action heretofore taken under those orders or any amendments or extensions thereof.

15. Nothing herein contained shall prejudice any other authority which the Department of Defense may have to enter into, amend, or modify contracts, and to make advance payments.

PART II—EXTENSION OF PROVISIONS OF PARAGRAPHS 1 TO 14

21. Subject to the limitations and regulations contained in paragraphs 1 to 14, inclusive, hereof, and under any regulations prescribed by him in pursuance of the provisions of paragraph 22 hereof, the head of each of the following-named agencies is authorized to perform or exercise as to his agency, independently of any Secretary referred to in the said paragraphs 1 to 14, all the functions and authority vested by those paragraphs in the Secretaries mentioned therein:

Department of the Treasury.
Department of the Interior.
Department of Agriculture.
Department of Commerce.
Department of Transportation.
Atomic Energy Commission.
General Services Administration.
National Aeronautics and Space Administration.
Tennessee Valley Authority.
Government Printing Office.
The Federal Emergency Management Agency.

22. The head of each agency named in paragraph 21 hereof is authorized to prescribe regulations governing the carrying out of the functions and authority vested with respect to his agency by the provisions of paragraph 21 hereof. Such regulations shall, to the extent practicable, be uniform with the regulations prescribed or approved by the Secretary of Defense under the provisions of Part I of this order.

23. Nothing contained herein shall prejudice any other authority which any agency named in paragraph 21 hereof may have to enter into, amend, or modify contracts and to make advance payments.

24. Nothing contained in this Part shall constitute authorization thereunder for the amendment of a contract negotiated under section 322(c)(14) of the Federal Property and Administrative Services Act of 1949 (63 Stat. 394), as amended by section 2(b) of the act of August 28, 1958, 72 Stat. 966 [section 252(c)(14) of Title 41, Public Contracts], to increase the contract price to an amount higher than the lowest rejected bid of any responsible bidder.

§ 1432. Restrictions

Nothing in this chapter shall be construed to constitute authorization hereunder for—

(a) the use of the cost-plus-a-percentage-of-cost system of contracting;

(b) any contract in violation of existing law relating to limitation of profits;

(c) the negotiation of purchases of or contracts for property or services required by law to be procured by formal advertising and competitive bidding;

(d) the waiver of any bid, payment, performance, or other bond required by law;

(e) the amendment of a contract negotiated under section 2304(a)(15)[1] of title 10 or under section 252(c)(13)[1] of title 41, to increase the contract price to an amount higher than the lowest rejected bid of any responsible bidder; or

(f) the formalization of an informal commitment, unless it is found that at the time the commitment was made it was impracticable to use normal procurement procedures.

(Pub. L. 85–804, § 2, Aug. 28, 1958, 72 Stat. 972.)

REFERENCES IN TEXT

Section 2304 of title 10, referred to in subd. (e), was amended generally by Pub. L. 98–369 and, as so amended, does not contain a subsec. (a)(15).

Section 252(c)(13) of title 41, referred to in subd. (e), was renumbered section 252(c)(14) of Title 41, Public Contracts, by Pub. L. 85–800, § 2(b), Aug. 28, 1958, 72 Stat. 966. Subsequently, Pub. L. 98–369 amended section 252 of Title 41 by striking out subsec. (c), redesignating subsec. (e) as (c)(1), and adding subsec. (c)(2).

NONAPPLICABILITY OF NATIONAL EMERGENCIES ACT

The provisions of the National Emergencies Act [see Short Title note set out under section 1601 of this title] shall not apply to the powers and authorities conferred by this section and actions taken hereunder, see section 1651(a)(6) of this title.

§ 1433. Public record; examination of records by Comptroller General; exemptions: exceptional conditions; reports to Congress

(a) All actions under the authority of this chapter shall be made a matter of public record under regulations prescribed by the President and when deemed by him not to be detrimental to the national security.

(b) All contracts entered into, amended, or modified pursuant to authority contained in this chapter shall include a clause to the effect that the Comptroller General of the United States or any of his duly authorized representatives shall, until the expiration of three years after final payment, have access to and the right to examine any directly pertinent books, documents, papers, and records of the contractor or any of his subcontractors engaged in the performance of and involving transactions related to such contracts or subcontracts. Under regulations to be prescribed by the President, however, such clause may be omitted from contracts with foreign contractors or foreign subcontractors if the agency head determines, with the concurrence of the Comptroller General of the United States or his designee, that the omission will serve the best interests of the United States. However, the concurrence of the Comptroller General of the United States or his designee is not required for the omission of such clause—

(1) where the contractor or subcontractor is a foreign government or agency thereof or is precluded by the laws of the country involved from making its books, documents, papers, or records available for examination; and

(2) where the agency head determines, after taking into account the price and availability of the property or services from United States sources, that the public interest would be best served by the omission of the clause.

If the clause is omitted based on a determination under clause (2), a written report shall be furnished to the Congress.

[1] See References in Text note below.

(Pub. L. 85–804, §3, Aug. 28, 1958, 72 Stat. 972; Pub. L. 89–607, §3, Sept. 27, 1966, 80 Stat. 851.)

AMENDMENTS

1966—Subsec. (b). Pub. L. 89–607 provided for exemption of certain contracts with foreign contractors from the requirement for an examination-of-records clause, such determination to be reported to Congress.

EXEMPTION OF FUNCTIONS

Functions with respect to purchases authorized to be made outside the limits of the United States or the District of Columbia under the Foreign Assistance Act of 1961, as amended [see Short Title note set out under section 2151 of Title 22, Foreign Relations and Intercourse], as exempt, see Ex. Ord. No. 11223, eff. May 12, 1965, 30 F.R. 6635, set out under section 2393 of Title 22.

FOREIGN CONTRACTORS

Secretaries of Defense, Army, Navy, or Air Force, or their designees, to determine, prior to exercising the authority provided in the amendment by Pub. L. 89–607 to exempt certain contracts with foreign contractors from the requirement of an examination-of-records clause, that all reasonable efforts have been made to include such examination-of-records clause, as required by par. 11 of Part I of Ex. Ord. No. 10789, and that alternate sources of supply are not reasonably available, see par. 11 of Part I of Ex. Ord. No. 10789, eff. Nov. 14, 1958, 23 F.R. 8897, as amended, set out under section 1431 of this title.

NONAPPLICABILITY OF THE NATIONAL EMERGENCIES ACT

The provisions of the National Emergencies Act [see Short Title note set out under section 1601 of this title] shall not apply to the powers and authorities conferred by this section and actions taken hereunder, see section 1651(a)(6) of this title.

§1434. Repealed. Pub. L. 105–362, title IX, §901(r)(1)(A), Nov. 10, 1998, 112 Stat. 3291

Section, Pub. L. 85–804, §4, Aug. 28, 1958, 72 Stat. 972; Pub. L. 104–66, title III, §3001(g), Dec. 21, 1995, 109 Stat. 734, related to reports to Congress by departments and agencies acting under authority of this chapter and requirement that such reports be published in the Congressional Record.

§1435. Effective period

This chapter shall be effective only during a national emergency declared by Congress or the President and for six months after the termination thereof or until such earlier time as Congress, by concurrent resolution, may designate.

(Pub. L. 85–804, §4, formerly §5, Aug. 28, 1958, 72 Stat. 973; renumbered §4, Pub. L. 105–362, title IX, §901(r)(1)(B), Nov. 10, 1998, 112 Stat. 3291.)

PRIOR PROVISIONS

A prior section 4 of Pub. L. 85–804 was classified to section 1434 of this title prior to repeal by Pub. L. 105–362.

NONAPPLICABILITY OF NATIONAL EMERGENCIES ACT

The provisions of the National Emergencies Act [see Short Title note under section 1601 of this title] shall not apply to the powers and authorities conferred by this section and actions taken hereunder, see section 1651(a)(6) of this title.

§1436. Repealed. Pub. L. 97–295, §6(b), Oct. 12, 1982, 96 Stat. 1314

Section, Pub. L. 91–121, title IV, §410, Nov. 19, 1969, 83 Stat. 210; Pub. L. 94–273, §§4(4), 5(6), 14, Apr. 21, 1976, 90 Stat. 377, 378, related to reporting requirements for former military and civilian officials employed by defense contractors and by Department of Defense employees previously employed by defense contractors.

CHAPTER 30—FEDERAL ABSENTEE VOTING ASSISTANCE

§§1451 to 1454. Transferred

CODIFICATION

Section 1451, acts Aug. 9, 1955, ch. 656, title I, §101, 69 Stat. 584; June 18, 1968, Pub. L. 90–343, §1, 82 Stat. 180, which related to State enactment of absentee voting legislation, was transferred to section 1973cc of Title 42, The Public Health and Welfare.

Section 1452, acts Aug. 9, 1955, ch. 656, title I, §102, 69 Stat. 584; June 18, 1968, Pub. L. 90–344, §1(1), 82 Stat. 181, which related to balloting procedures, was transferred to section 1973cc–1 of Title 42.

Section 1453, act Aug. 9, 1955, ch. 656, title I, §103, 69 Stat. 584, which related to statistical data, was transferred to section 1973cc–2 of Title 42.

Section 1454, act Aug. 9, 1955, ch. 656, title I, §104, as added June 18, 1968, Pub. L. 90–344, §1(2), 82 Stat. 181, which related to personnel residing on military installations and acquisition of legal residence for voting purposes, was transferred to section 1973cc–3 of Title 42.

Sections 1451 to 1453 were formerly classified to sections 2171 to 2173 of Title 5 prior to the general revision and enactment of Title 5, Government Organization and Employees, by Pub. L. 89–554, §1, Sept. 6, 1966, 80 Stat. 378.

§§1461 to 1465. Transferred

CODIFICATION

Section 1461, act Aug. 9, 1955, ch. 656, title II, §201, 69 Stat. 585, which provided for a Presidential designee to coordinate and facilitate actions to discharge Federal responsibilities and to reports submitted by the designee, was transferred to section 1973cc–11 of Title 42, The Public Health and Welfare.

Section 1462, act Aug. 9, 1955, ch. 656, title II, §202, 69 Stat. 586, which related to current absentee voting information, was transferred to section 1973cc–12 of Title 42.

Section 1463, acts Aug. 9, 1955, ch. 656, title II, §203, 69 Stat. 586; June 18, 1968, Pub. L. 90–344, §1(3), 82 Stat. 181, which related to cooperation of Government officials, drafts of state legislation, and printing and transmitting post cards, was transferred to section 1973cc–13 of Title 42.

Section 1464, acts Aug. 9, 1955, ch. 656, title II, §204, 69 Stat. 586; June 18, 1968, Pub. L. 90–343, §2, 82 Stat. 181; June 18, 1968, Pub. L. 90–344, §1(4), (5), (6), 82 Stat. 182, which related to form and content of post card application, was transferred to section 1973cc–14 of Title 42.

Section 1465, act Aug. 9, 1955, ch. 656, title II, §205, 69 Stat. 588, which provided for use of post card for election of Members of Congress, was transferred to section 1973cc–15 of Title 42.

Sections 1461 to 1465 were formerly classified to sections 2181 to 2185 of Title 5 prior to the general revision and enactment of Title 5, Government Organization and Employees, by Pub. L. 89–554, §1, Sept. 6, 1966, 80 Stat. 378.

§§1471 to 1476. Transferred

CODIFICATION

Section 1471, act Aug. 9, 1955, ch. 656, title III, §301, 69 Stat. 588, which related to definitions, was transferred to section 1973cc–21 of Title 42, The Public Health and Welfare.

Section 1472, act Aug. 9, 1955, ch. 656, title III, §302, 69 Stat. 588, which related to free postage, was transferred to section 1973cc–22 of Title 42.

Section 1473, act Aug. 9, 1955, ch. 656, title III, §303, 69 Stat. 588, which related to prevention of fraud and coercion, was transferred to section 1973cc–23 of Title 42.

Section 1474, act Aug. 9, 1955, ch. 656, title III, §304, 69 Stat. 589, which related to acts done in good faith, was transferred to section 1973cc–24 of Title 42.

Section 1475, act Aug. 9, 1955, ch. 656, title III, §305, 69 Stat. 589, which related to undue influence and free discussion, was transferred to section 1973cc–25 of Title 42.

Section 1476, act Aug. 9, 1955, ch. 656, title III, §308, 69 Stat. 589, which authorized appropriations, was transferred to section 1973cc–26 of Title 42.

Sections 1471 to 1476 were formerly classified to sections 2191 to 2196 of Title 5 prior to the general revision and enactment of Title 5, Government Organization and Employees, by Pub. L. 89–554, §1, Sept. 6, 1966, 80 Stat. 378.

CHAPTER 31—ADVISORY COMMISSION ON INTERGOVERNMENTAL RELATIONS

§§1501 to 1509. Transferred

CODIFICATION

Section 1501, Pub. L. 86–380, §1, Sept. 24, 1959, 73 Stat. 703, which related to establishment of the Advisory Commission on Intergovernmental Relations, was transferred to section 4271 of Title 42, The Public Health and Welfare.

Section 1502, Pub. L. 86–380, §2, Sept. 24, 1959, 73 Stat. 703, which related to declaration of purpose, was transferred to section 4272 of Title 42.

Section 1503, Pub. L. 86–380, §3, Sept. 24, 1959, 73 Stat. 704; Pub. L. 89–733, §§1, 2, Nov. 2, 1966, 80 Stat. 1162, which related to membership of Commission, was transferred to section 4273 of Title 42.

Section 1504, Pub. L. 86–380, §4, Sept. 24, 1959, 73 Stat. 705, which related to organization of Commission, was transferred to section 4274 of Title 42.

Section 1505, Pub. L. 86–380, §5, Sept. 24, 1959, 73 Stat. 705, which related to duties of Commission, was transferred to section 4275 of Title 42.

Section 1506, Pub. L. 86–380, §6, Sept. 24, 1959, 73 Stat. 705; Pub. L. 88–426, title III, §306(e), Aug. 14, 1964, 78 Stat. 429; Pub. L. 89–733, §§3, 4, Nov. 2, 1966, 80 Stat. 1162, which related to powers of Commission and administrative provisions, was transferred to section 4276 of Title 42.

Section 1507, Pub. L. 86–380, §7, Sept. 24, 1959, 73 Stat. 706; Pub. L. 89–733, §5, Nov. 2, 1966, 80 Stat. 1162, which related to compensation of members of Commission, was transferred to section 4277 of Title 42.

Section 1508, Pub. L. 86–380, §8, Sept. 24, 1959, 73 Stat. 706, which authorized appropriations, was transferred to section 4278 of Title 42.

Section 1509, Pub. L. 86–380, §9, as added Pub. L. 89–733, §6, Nov. 2, 1966, 80 Stat. 1162, which related to receipt of funds and to consideration of these funds by Congress in making appropriations for Commission, was transferred to section 4279 of Title 42.

CHAPTER 32—CHEMICAL AND BIOLOGICAL WARFARE PROGRAM

§1511. Repealed. Pub. L. 104–106, div. A, title X, §1061(k), Feb. 10, 1996, 110 Stat. 443

Section, Pub. L. 91–121, title IV, §409(a), Nov. 19, 1969, 83 Stat. 209; Pub. L. 93–608, §2(4), Jan. 2, 1975, 88 Stat. 1971; Pub. L. 97–375, title II, §203(a)(2), Dec. 21, 1982, 96 Stat. 1822, directed Secretary of Defense to submit an annual report to Congress on expenditures for research, development, test, and evaluation of all lethal and nonlethal chemical and biological agents.

§1512. Transportation, open air testing, and disposal; Presidential determination; report to Congress; notice to Congress and State Governors

None of the funds authorized to be appropriated by this Act or any other Act may be used for the transportation of any lethal chemical or any biological warfare agent to or from any military installation in the United States, or the open air testing of any such agent within the United States, or the disposal of any such agent within the United States until the following procedures have been implemented:

(1) the Secretary of Defense (hereafter referred to in this chapter as the "Secretary") has determined that the transportation or testing proposed to be made is necessary in the interests of national security;

(2) the Secretary has brought the particulars of the proposed transportation, testing, or disposal to the attention of the Secretary of Health and Human Services, who in turn may direct the Surgeon General of the Public Health Service and other qualified persons to review such particulars with respect to any hazards to public health and safety which such transportation, testing, or disposal may pose and to recommend what precautionary measures are necessary to protect the public health and safety;

(3) the Secretary has implemented any precautionary measures recommended in accordance with paragraph (2) above (including, where practicable, the detoxification of any such agent, if such agent is to be transported to or from a military installation for disposal): *Provided, however*, That in the event the Secretary finds the recommendation submitted by the Surgeon General would have the effect of preventing the proposed transportation, testing, or disposal, the President may determine that overriding considerations of national security require such transportation, testing, or disposal be conducted. Any transportation, testing, or disposal conducted pursuant to such a Presidential determination shall be carried out in the safest practicable manner, and the President shall report his determination and an explanation thereof to the President of the Senate and the Speaker of the House of Representatives as far in advance as practicable; and

(4) the Secretary has provided notification that the transportation, testing, or disposal will take place, except where a Presidential determination has been made: (A) to the President of the Senate and the Speaker of the House of Representatives at least 10 days before any such transportation will be commenced and at least 30 days before any such testing or disposal will be commenced; (B) to the Governor of any State through which such agents will be transported, such notification to be provided appropriately in advance of any such transportation.

(Pub. L. 91–121, title IV, §409(b), Nov. 19, 1969, 83 Stat. 209; Pub. L. 91–441, title V, §506(b)(1), Oct. 7, 1970, 84 Stat. 912; Pub. L. 96–88, title V, §509(b), Oct. 17, 1979, 93 Stat. 695.)

REFERENCES IN TEXT

This Act, referred to in provision preceding par. (1), means Pub. L. 91–121, Nov. 19, 1969, 83 Stat. 204, as amended. Provisions authorizing the appropriation of funds are not classified to the Code. For complete classification of this Act to the Code, see Tables.

AMENDMENTS

1970—Pub. L. 91–441 inserted reference to the disposal of lethal chemical or biological warfare agents in the United States.

CHANGE OF NAME

"Secretary of Health and Human Services" substituted for "Secretary of Health, Education, and Welfare" in par. (2), pursuant to section 509(b) of Pub. L. 96–88 which is classified to section 3508(b) of Title 20, Education.

CHEMICAL MUNITIONS TRANSPORTATION FROM OKINAWA TO THE UNITED STATES

Pub. L. 91–672, §13, Jan. 12, 1971, 84 Stat. 2055, provided that: "No funds authorized or appropriated pursuant to this or any other law may be used to transport chemical munitions from the Island of Okinawa to the United States. Such funds as are necessary for the detoxification or destruction of the above described chemical munitions are hereby authorized and shall be used for the detoxification or destruction of chemical munitions only outside the United States. For purposes of this section, the term 'United States' means the several States and the District of Columbia."

EX ORD. NO. 11850. RENUNCIATION OF CERTAIN USES IN WAR OF CHEMICAL HERBICIDES AND RIOT CONTROL AGENTS

Ex. Ord. No. 11850, Apr. 8, 1975, 40 F.R. 16187, provided:

The United States renounces, as a matter of national policy, first use of herbicides in war except use, under regulations applicable to their domestic use, for control of vegetation within U.S. bases and installations or around their immediate defensive perimeters, and first use of riot control agents in war except in defensive military modes to save lives such as:

(a) Use of riot control agents in riot control situations in areas under direct and distinct U.S. military control, to include controlling rioting prisoners of war.

(b) Use of riot control agents in situations in which civilians are used to mask or screen attacks and civilian casualties can be reduced or avoided.

(c) Use of riot control agents in rescue missions in remotely isolated areas, of downed aircrews and passengers, and escaping prisoners.

(d) Use of riot control agents in rear echelon areas outside the zone of immediate combat to protect convoys from civil disturbances, terrorists and paramilitary organizations.

I have determined that the provisions and procedures prescribed by this Order are necessary to ensure proper implementation and observance of such national policy.

NOW, THEREFORE, by virtue of the authority vested in me as President of the United States of America by the Constitution and laws of the United States and as Commander-in-Chief of the Armed Forces of the United States, it is hereby ordered as follows:

SECTION 1. The Secretary of Defense shall take all necessary measures to ensure that the use by the Armed Forces of the United States of any riot control agents and chemical herbicides in war is prohibited unless such use has Presidential approval, in advance.

SEC. 2. The Secretary of Defense shall prescribe the rules and regulations he deems necessary to ensure that the national policy herein announced shall be observed by the Armed Forces of the United States.

GERALD R. FORD.

§1512a. Transportation of chemical munitions

(a) Prohibition of transportation across State lines

The Secretary of Defense may not transport any chemical munition that constitutes part of the chemical weapons stockpile out of the State in which that munition is located on October 5, 1994, and, in the case of any such chemical munition not located in a State on October 5, 1994, may not transport any such munition into a State.

(b) Transportation of chemical munitions not in chemical weapons stockpile

In the case of any chemical munitions that are discovered or otherwise come within the control of the Department of Defense and that do not constitute part of the chemical weapons stockpile, the Secretary of Defense may transport such munitions to the nearest chemical munitions stockpile storage facility that has necessary permits for receiving and storing such items if the transportation of such munitions to that facility—

(1) is considered by the Secretary of Defense to be necessary; and

(2) can be accomplished while protecting public health and safety.

(Pub. L. 103–337, div. A, title I, §143, Oct. 5, 1994, 108 Stat. 2689.)

CODIFICATION

Section was enacted as part of the National Defense Authorization Act for Fiscal Year 1995, and not as part of Pub. L. 91–121, title IV, §409, Nov. 19, 1969, 83 Stat. 209, which comprises this chapter.

§1513. Deployment, storage, and disposal; notification to host country and Congress; international law violations; reports to Congress and international organizations

(1) None of the funds authorized to be appropriated by this Act or any other Act may be used for the future deployment, storage, or disposal, at any place outside the United States of—

(A) any lethal chemical or any biological warfare agent, or

(B) any delivery system specifically designed to disseminate any such agent,

unless prior notice of such deployment, storage, or disposal has been given to the country exercising jurisdiction over such place. In the case of any place outside the United States which is under the jurisdiction or control of the United States Government, no such action may be taken unless the Secretary gives prior notice of such action to the President of the Senate and the Speaker of the House of Representatives. As used in this paragraph, the term "United States" means the several States and the District of Columbia.

(2) None of the funds authorized by this Act or any other Act shall be used for the future testing, development, transportation, storage, or disposal of any lethal chemical or any biological warfare agent outside the United States, or for the disposal of any munitions in international waters, if the Secretary of State, after appropriate notice by the Secretary whenever any such action is contemplated, determines that such testing, development, transportation, storage, or disposal will violate international law. The Secretary of State shall report all determinations made by him under this paragraph to the President of the Senate and the Speaker of the House of Representatives, and to all appropriate international organizations, or organs thereof, in the event such report is required by treaty or other international agreement.

(Pub. L. 91–121, title IV, §409(c), Nov. 19, 1969, 83 Stat. 210; Pub. L. 91–441, title V, §506(b)(2), (3), Oct. 7, 1970, 84 Stat. 912.)

REFERENCES IN TEXT

This Act, referred to in pars. (1) and (2), means Pub. L. 91–121, Nov. 19, 1969, 83 Stat. 204, as amended. Provisions authorizing the appropriation of funds are not classified to the Code. For complete classification of this Act to the Code, see Tables.

AMENDMENTS

1970—Par. (1). Pub. L. 91–441, §506(b)(2), inserted reference to disposal of lethal chemical or biological warfare agents or delivery systems for such agents.

Par. (2). Pub. L. 91–441, §506(b)(3), inserted reference to disposal of munitions in international waters.

WITHDRAWAL OF EUROPEAN CHEMICAL STOCKPILE

Pub. L. 100–180, div. A, title I, §126, Dec. 4, 1987, 101 Stat. 1044, provided that: "Chemical munitions of the United States stored in Europe on the date of the enactment of this Act [Dec. 4, 1987] should not be removed from Europe unless such munitions are replaced contemporaneously with binary chemical munitions stationed on the soil of at least one European member nation of the North Atlantic Treaty Organization."

§1514. "United States" defined

Unless otherwise indicated, as used in this chapter the term "United States" means the several States the District of Columbia, and the territories and possessions of the United States.

(Pub. L. 91–121, title IV, §409(d), Nov. 19, 1969, 83 Stat. 210.)

§1515. Suspension; Presidential authorization

After November 19, 1969, the operation of this chapter, or any portion thereof, may be suspended by the President during the period of any war declared by Congress and during the period of any national emergency declared by Congress or by the President.

(Pub. L. 91–121, title IV, §409(e), Nov. 19, 1969, 83 Stat. 210.)

§1516. Delivery systems

None of the funds authorized to be appropriated by this Act shall be used for the procurement of delivery systems specifically designed to disseminate lethal chemical or any biological warfare agents, or for the procurement of delivery system parts or components specifically designed for such purpose, unless the President shall certify to the Congress that such procurement is essential to the safety and security of the United States.

(Pub. L. 91–441, title V, §506(a), Oct. 7, 1970, 84 Stat. 912.)

REFERENCES IN TEXT

This Act, referred to in text, means Pub. L. 91–441, Oct. 7, 1970, 84 Stat. 912. Provisions authorizing the appropriation of funds are not classified to the Code. For complete classification of this Act to the Code, see Tables.

CODIFICATION

Section was not enacted as part of Pub. L. 91–121, title IV, §409, Nov. 19, 1969, 83 Stat. 209, which comprises this chapter.

Section is from the Armed Forces-Military Procurement, 1971 act, Pub. L. 91–441. Provisions similar to those in this section were contained in Pub. L. 91–121, title IV, §409(f), Nov. 19, 1969, 83 Stat. 210.

§1517. Immediate disposal when health or safety are endangered

Nothing contained in this chapter shall be deemed to restrict the transportation or disposal of research quantities of any lethal chemical or any biological warfare agent, or to delay or prevent, in emergency situations either within or outside the United States, the immediate disposal together with any necessary associated transportation, of any lethal chemical or any biological warfare agent when compliance with the procedures and requirements of this chapter would clearly endanger the health or safety of any person.

(Pub. L. 91–121, title IV, §409(g), as added Pub. L. 91–441, title V, §506(b)(4), Oct. 7, 1970, 84 Stat. 912.)

§1518. Disposal; detoxification; report to Congress; emergencies

On and after October 7, 1970, no chemical or biological warfare agent shall be disposed of within or outside the United States unless such agent has been detoxified or made harmless to man and his environment unless immediate disposal is clearly necessary, in an emergency, to safeguard human life. An immediate report should be made to Congress in the event of such disposal.

(Pub. L. 91–441, title V, §506(d), Oct. 7, 1970, 84 Stat. 913.)

CODIFICATION

Section was not enacted as part of Pub. L. 91–121, title IV, §409, Nov. 19, 1969, 83 Stat. 209, which comprises this chapter.

§1519. Lethal binary chemical munitions

(a) Notwithstanding any other provision of law, none of the funds authorized to be appropriated by this or any other Act shall be used for the purpose of production of lethal binary chemical munitions unless the President certifies to Congress that the production of such munitions is essential to the national interest and submits a full report thereon to the President of the Senate and the Speaker of the House of Representatives as far in advance of the production of such munitions as is practicable.

(b) For purposes of this section the term "lethal binary chemical munitions" means (1) any toxic chemical (solid, liquid, or gas) which, through its chemical properties, is intended to be used to produce injury or death to human beings, and (2) any unique device, instrument, apparatus, or contrivance, including any components or accessories thereof, intended to be used to disperse or otherwise disseminate any such toxic chemical.

(Pub. L. 94–106, title VIII, §818, Oct. 7, 1975, 89 Stat. 544.)

REFERENCES IN TEXT

This Act, referred to in text, is Pub. L. 94–106, Oct. 7, 1975, 89 Stat. 531, as amended, known as the Department of Defense Appropriation Authorization Act, 1976. Provisions authorizing the appropriation of funds are not classified to the Code. For complete classification of this Act to the Code, see Tables.

CODIFICATION

Section was not enacted as part of Pub. L. 91–121, title IV, §409, Nov. 19, 1969, 83 Stat. 209, which comprises this chapter.

§1519a. Limitation on procurement of binary chemical weapons

(a) Notwithstanding any other provision of law, no funds may be obligated or expended after September 24, 1983, for the production of binary chemical weapons unless the President certifies to the Congress that for each 155-millimeter binary artillery shell or aircraft-delivered binary aerial bomb produced a serviceable unitary artillery shell from the existing arsenal shall be rendered permanently useless for military purposes.

(b)(1) Funds appropriated pursuant to the authorization of appropriations for the Army in section 101 of this Act may be used for the establishment of a production base for binary chemical munitions and for the procurement of components for 155-millimeter binary chemical artillery projectiles, but such funds may not be used for the actual production of binary chemical munitions before October 1, 1985.

(2) Notwithstanding the provisions of paragraph (1), before the production of binary chemical munitions may begin after September 30, 1985, the President must certify to Congress in writing that, in light of circumstances prevailing at the time the certification is made, the production of such munitions is essential to the national interest.

(3) For purposes of this subsection, "production of binary chemical munitions" means the final assembly of weapon components and the filling or loading of components with binary chemicals.

(Pub. L. 98–94, title XII, §1233, Sept. 24, 1983, 97 Stat. 695.)

REFERENCES IN TEXT

Section 101 of this Act, referred to in subsec. (b)(1), is section 101 of Pub. L. 98–94, title I, Sept. 24, 1983, 97 Stat. 618, which was not classified to the Code.

CODIFICATION

Section was enacted as part of the Department of Defense Authorization Act, 1984, and not as part of Pub. L. 91–121, title IV, §409, Nov. 19, 1969, 83 Stat. 209, which comprises this chapter.

§1520. Repealed. Pub. L. 105–85, div. A, title X, §1078(g), Nov. 18, 1997, 111 Stat. 1916, and Pub. L. 105–277, div. I, title VI, §601, Oct. 21, 1998, 112 Stat. 2681–886

Section, Pub. L. 95–79, title VIII, §808, July 30, 1977, 91 Stat. 334; Pub. L. 97–375, title II, §203(a)(1), Dec. 21, 1982, 96 Stat. 1822, related to use by the Department of Defense of human subjects for testing of chemical or biological agents, accounting to congressional committees with respect to experiments and studies, and notification of local civilian officials.

§1520a. Restrictions on use of human subjects for testing of chemical or biological agents

(a) Prohibited activities

The Secretary of Defense may not conduct (directly or by contract)—

(1) any test or experiment involving the use of a chemical agent or biological agent on a civilian population; or

(2) any other testing of a chemical agent or biological agent on human subjects.

(b) Exceptions

Subject to subsections (c), (d), and (e) of this section, the prohibition in subsection (a) of this section does not apply to a test or experiment carried out for any of the following purposes:

(1) Any peaceful purpose that is related to a medical, therapeutic, pharmaceutical, agricultural, industrial, or research activity.

(2) Any purpose that is directly related to protection against toxic chemicals or biological weapons and agents.

(3) Any law enforcement purpose, including any purpose related to riot control.

(c) Informed consent required

The Secretary of Defense may conduct a test or experiment described in subsection (b) of this section only if informed consent to the testing was obtained from each human subject in advance of the testing on that subject.

(d) Prior notice to Congress

Not later than 30 days after the date of final approval within the Department of Defense of plans for any experiment or study to be conducted by the Department of Defense (whether directly or under contract) involving the use of human subjects for the testing of a chemical agent or a biological agent, the Secretary of Defense shall submit to the Committee on Armed Services of the Senate and the Committee on Armed Services of the House of Representatives a report setting forth a full accounting of those plans, and the experiment or study may then be conducted only after the end of the 30-day period beginning on the date such report is received by those committees.

(e) "Biological agent" defined

In this section, the term ''biological agent'' means any micro-organism (including bacteria, viruses, fungi, rickettsiac, or protozoa), pathogen, or infectious substance, and any naturally occurring, bioengineered, or synthesized component of any such micro-organism, pathogen, or infectious substance, whatever its origin or method of production, that is capable of causing—

(1) death, disease, or other biological malfunction in a human, an animal, a plant, or another living organism;

(2) deterioration of food, water, equipment, supplies, or materials of any kind; or

(3) deleterious alteration of the environment.

(Pub. L. 105–85, div. A, title X, § 1078, Nov. 18, 1997, 111 Stat. 1915; Pub. L. 106–65, div. A, title X, § 1067(4), Oct. 5, 1999, 113 Stat. 774.)

CODIFICATION

Section is comprised of section 1078 of Pub. L. 105–85. Subsec. (f) of section 1078 of Pub. L. 105–85 amended section 1523(b) of this title. Subsec. (g) of section 1078 of Pub. L. 105–85 repealed section 1520 of this title.

Section was enacted as part of the National Defense Authorization Act for Fiscal Year 1998, and not as part of Pub. L. 91–121, title IV, § 409, Nov. 19, 1969, 83 Stat. 209, which comprises this chapter.

AMENDMENTS

1999—Subsec. (d). Pub. L. 106–65 substituted ''and the Committee on Armed Services'' for ''and the Committee on National Security''.

§ 1521. Destruction of existing stockpile of lethal chemical agents and munitions

(a) In general

Notwithstanding any other provision of law, the Secretary of Defense (hereinafter in this section referred to as the ''Secretary'') shall, in accordance with the provisions of this section, carry out the destruction of the United States' stockpile of lethal chemical agents and munitions that exists on November 8, 1985.

(b) Date for completion

(1) Except as provided by paragraphs (2) and (3), the destruction of such stockpile shall be completed by the stockpile elimination deadline.

(2) If a treaty banning the possession of chemical agents and munitions is ratified by the United States, the date for completing the destruction of the United States' stockpile of such agents and munitions shall be the date established by such treaty.

(3)(A) In the event of a declaration of war by the Congress or of a national emergency by the President or the Congress or if the Secretary of Defense determines that there has been a significant delay in the acquisition of an adequate number of binary chemical weapons to meet the requirements of the Armed Forces (as defined by the Joint Chiefs of Staff as of September 30, 1985), the Secretary may defer, beyond the stockpile elimination deadline, the destruction of not more than 10 percent of the stockpile described in subsection (a)(1) of this section.

(B) The Secretary shall transmit written notice to the Congress of any deferral made under subparagraph (A) not later than the earlier of (A) 30 days after the date on which the decision to defer is made, or (B) 30 days before the stockpile elimination deadline.

(4) If the Secretary determines at any time that there will be a delay in meeting the requirement in paragraph (1) for the completion of the destruction of chemical weapons by the stockpile elimination deadline, the Secretary shall immediately notify the Committee on Armed Services of the Senate and the Committee on Armed Services of the House of Representatives of that projected delay.

(5) For purposes of this section, the term ''stockpile elimination deadline'' means December 31, 2004.

(c) Environmental protection and use of facilities

(1) In carrying out the requirement of subsection (a) of this section, the Secretary shall provide for—

(A) maximum protection for the environment, the general public, and the personnel who are involved in the destruction of the lethal chemical agents and munitions referred to in subsection (a) of this section; and

(B) adequate and safe facilities designed solely for the destruction of lethal chemical agents and munitions.

(2) Facilities constructed to carry out this section shall, when no longer needed for the purposes for which they were constructed, be disposed of in accordance with applicable laws and regulations and mutual agreements between the

Secretary of the Army and the Governor of the State in which the facility is located.

(3)(A) Facilities constructed to carry out this section may not be used for a purpose other than the destruction of the stockpile of lethal chemical agents and munitions that exists on November 8, 1985.

(B) The prohibition in subparagraph (A) shall not apply with respect to items designated by the Secretary of Defense as lethal chemical agents, munitions, or related materials after November 8, 1985, if the State in which a destruction facility is located issues the appropriate permit or permits for the destruction of such items at the facility.

(4) In order to carry out subparagraph (A) of paragraph (1), the Secretary may make grants to State and local governments (either directly or through the Federal Emergency Management Agency) to assist those governments in carrying out functions relating to emergency preparedness and response in connection with the disposal of the lethal chemical agents and munitions referred to in subsection (a) of this section. Funds available to the Department of Defense for the purpose of carrying out this section may be used for such grants. Additionally, the Secretary may provide funds through cooperative agreements with State and local governments for the purpose of assisting them in processing, approving, and overseeing permits and licenses necessary for the construction and operation of facilities to carry out this section. The Secretary shall ensure that funds provided through such a cooperative agreement are used only for the purpose set forth in the preceding sentence.

(5)(A) In coordination with the Secretary of the Army and in accordance with agreements between the Secretary of the Army and the Director of the Federal Emergency Management Agency, the Director shall carry out a program to provide assistance to State and local governments in developing capabilities to respond to emergencies involving risks to the public health or safety within their jurisdictions that are identified by the Secretary as being risks resulting from—

(i) the storage of lethal chemical agents and munitions referred to in subsection (a) of this section at military installations in the continental United States; or

(ii) the destruction of such agents and munitions at facilities referred to in paragraph (1)(B).

(B) No assistance may be provided under this paragraph after the completion of the destruction of the United States' stockpile of lethal chemical agents and munitions.

(C) Not later than December 15 of each year, the Director shall transmit a report to Congress on the activities carried out under this paragraph during the fiscal year preceding the fiscal year in which the report is submitted.

(d) Plan

(1) The Secretary shall develop a comprehensive plan to carry out this section.

(2) In developing such plan, the Secretary shall consult with the Secretary of Health and Human Services and the Administrator of the Environmental Protection Agency.

(3) The Secretary shall transmit a copy of such plan to the Congress not later than March 15, 1986.

(4) Such plan shall provide—

(A) an evaluation of the comparison of on-site destruction, regional destruction centers, and a national destruction site both inside and outside of the United States;

(B) for technological advances in techniques used to destroy chemical munitions;

(C) for the maintenance of a permanent, written record of the destruction of lethal chemical agents and munitions carried out under this section; and

(D) a description of—

(i) the methods and facilities to be used in the destruction of agents and munitions under this section;

(ii) the schedule for carrying out this section; and

(iii) the management organization established under subsection (e) of this section.

(e) Management organization

(1) In carrying out this section, the Secretary shall provide for the establishment, not later than May 1, 1986, of a management organization within the Department of the Army.

(2) Such organization shall be responsible for management of the destruction of agents and munitions under this section.

(3) The Secretary shall designate a general officer or civilian equivalent as the director of the management organization established under paragraph (1). Such officer shall have—

(A) experience in the acquisition, storage, and destruction of chemical agents and munitions;

(B) training in chemical warfare defense operations; and

(C) outstanding qualifications regarding safety in handling chemical agents and munitions.

(f) Identification of funds

(1) Funds for carrying out this section, including funds for military construction projects necessary to carry out this section, shall be set forth in the budget of the Department of Defense for any fiscal year as a separate account. Such funds shall not be included in the budget accounts for any military department.

(2) Amounts appropriated to the Secretary for the purpose of carrying out subsection (c)(5) of this section shall be promptly made available to the Director of the Federal Emergency Management Agency.

(g) Periodic reports

(1) Except as provided by paragraph (3), the Secretary shall transmit, by December 15 of each year, a report to the Congress on the activities carried out under this section during the fiscal year ending on September 30 of the calendar year in which the report is to be made.

(2) Each annual report shall include the following:

(A) A site-by-site description of the construction, equipment, operation, and dismantling of facilities (during the fiscal year for which the report is made) used to carry out the destruction of agents and munitions under this section, including any accidents or other unplanned occurrences associated with such construction and operation.

(B) A site-by-site description of actions taken to assist State and local governments (either directly or through the Federal Emergency Management Agency) in carrying out functions relating to emergency preparedness and response in accordance with subsection (c)(4) of this section.

(C) An accounting of all funds expended (during such fiscal year) for activities carried out under this section, with a separate accounting for amounts expended for—

(i) the construction of and equipment for facilities used for the destruction of agents and munitions;

(ii) the operation of such facilities;

(iii) the dismantling or other closure of such facilities;

(iv) research and development;

(v) program management;

(vi) travel and associated travel costs for Citizens' Advisory Commissioners under section 172(g) of Public Law 102–484 (50 U.S.C. 1521 note); and

(vii) grants to State and local governments to assist those governments in carrying out functions relating to emergency preparedness and response in accordance with subsection (c)(3)[1] of this section.

(D) An assessment of the safety status and the integrity of the stockpile of lethal chemical agents and munitions subject to this section, including—

(i) an estimate on how much longer that stockpile can continue to be stored safely;

(ii) a site-by-site assessment of the safety of those agents and munitions; and

(iii) a description of the steps taken (to the date of the report) to monitor the safety status of the stockpile and to mitigate any further deterioration of that status.

(3) The Secretary shall transmit the final report under paragraph (1) not later than 120 days following the completion of activities under this section.

(h) Prohibition on acquiring certain lethal chemical agents and munitions

(1) Except as provided in paragraph (2), no agency of the Federal Government may, after November 8, 1985, develop or acquire lethal chemical agents or munitions other than binary chemical weapons.

(2)(A) The Secretary of Defense may acquire any chemical agent or munition at any time for purposes of intelligence analysis.

(B) Chemical agents and munitions may be acquired for research, development, test, and evaluation purposes at any time, but only in quantities needed for such purposes and not in production quantities.

(i) Reaffirmation of United States position on first use of chemical agents and munitions

It is the sense of Congress that the President should publicly reaffirm the position of the United States as set out in the Geneva Protocol of 1925, which the United States ratified with reservations in 1975.

(j) Definitions

For purposes of this section:

(1) The term "chemical agent and munition" means an agent or munition that, through its chemical properties, produces lethal or other damaging effects on human beings, except that such term does not include riot control agents, chemical herbicides, smoke and other obscuration materials.

(2) The term "lethal chemical agent and munition" means a chemical agent or munition that is designed to cause death, through its chemical properties, to human beings in field concentrations.

(3) The term "destruction" means, with respect to chemical munitions or agents—

(A) the demolishment of such munitions or agents by incineration or by any other means; or

(B) the dismantling or other disposal of such munitions or agents so as to make them useless for military purposes and harmless to human beings under normal circumstances.

(k) Operational verification

(1) Until the Secretary of the Army successfully completes (through the prove-out work to be conducted at Johnston Atoll) operational verification of the technology to be used for the destruction of live chemical agents and munitions under this section, the Secretary may not conduct any activity for equipment prove out and systems test before live chemical agents are introduced at a facility (other than the Johnston Atoll facility) at which the destruction of chemical agent[2] and munitions weapons is to take place under this section. The limitation in the preceding sentence shall not apply with respect to the Chemical Agent Munition Disposal System in Tooele, Utah.

(2) Upon the successful completion of the prove out of the equipment and facility at Johnston Atoll, the Secretary of Defense shall submit to the Committee on Armed Services of the Senate and the Committee on Armed Services of the House of Representatives a report certifying that the prove out is completed.

(3) If the Secretary determines at any time that there will be a delay in meeting the deadline of December 31, 1990, scheduled by the Department of Defense for completion of the operational verification at Johnston Atoll referred to in paragraph (1), the Secretary shall immediately notify the Committees of that projected delay.

(Pub. L. 99–145, title XIV, §1412, Nov. 8, 1985, 99 Stat. 747; Pub. L. 100–456, div. A, title I, §118, Sept. 29, 1988, 102 Stat. 1934; Pub. L. 101–510, div. A, title I, §§171, 172, Nov. 5, 1990, 104 Stat. 1507; Pub. L. 102–190, div. A, title I, §151, Dec. 5, 1991, 105 Stat. 1313; Pub. L. 102–484, div. A, title I, §§171, 179, Oct. 23, 1992, 106 Stat. 2341, 2347; Pub. L. 103–160, div. A, title I, §107(c), Nov. 30, 1993, 107 Stat. 1564; Pub. L. 103–337, div. A, title I, §142, Oct. 5, 1994, 108 Stat. 2689; Pub. L. 104–106, div. A,

[1] See References in Text note below.

[2] So in original. Probably should be "agents".

title I, §153(b), (c), title XV, §1502(c)(6), Feb. 10, 1996, 110 Stat. 216, 508; Pub. L. 104–201, div. A, title X, §1074(d)(2), Sept. 23, 1996, 110 Stat. 2661; Pub. L. 105–85, div. A, title X, §1041(d), Nov. 18, 1997, 111 Stat. 1885; Pub. L. 105–261, div. A, title I, §141, Oct. 17, 1998, 112 Stat. 1942; Pub. L. 106–65, div. A, title I, §141(b), title X, §1067(11), Oct. 5, 1999, 113 Stat. 537, 775.)

REFERENCES IN TEXT

Subsection (c)(3) of this section, referred to in subsec. (g)(2)(C)(vii), was redesignated subsec. (c)(4) of this section by Pub. L. 106–65, div. A, title I, §141(b)(1)(B), Oct. 5, 1999, 113 Stat. 538.

CODIFICATION

Section was enacted as part of the Department of Defense Authorization Act, 1986, and not as part of Pub. L. 91–121, title IV, §409, Nov. 19, 1969, 83 Stat. 209, which comprises this chapter.

AMENDMENTS

1999—Subsec. (b)(4). Pub. L. 106–65, §1067(11), substituted "and the Committee on Armed Services" for "and the Committee on National Security".

Subsec. (c)(2). Pub. L. 106–65, §141(b)(1)(A), added par. (2) and struck out former par. (2) which read as follows: "Facilities constructed to carry out this section may not be used for any purpose other than the destruction of lethal chemical weapons and munitions, and when no longer needed to carry out this section, such facilities shall be cleaned, dismantled, and disposed of in accordance with applicable laws and regulations."

Subsec. (c)(3) to (5). Pub. L. 106–65, §141(b)(1)(B), (C), added par. (3) and redesignated former pars. (3) and (4) as (4) and (5), respectively.

Subsec. (f)(2). Pub. L. 106–65, §141(b)(2), substituted "(c)(5)" for "(c)(4)".

Subsec. (g)(2)(B). Pub. L. 106–65, §141(b)(3), substituted "(c)(4)" for "(c)(3)".

Subsec. (k)(2). Pub. L. 106–65, §1067(11), substituted "and the Committee on Armed Services" for "and the Committee on National Security".

1998—Subsec. (c)(4). Pub. L. 105–261, §141(a), added par. (4).

Subsec. (f). Pub. L. 105–261, §141(b), designated existing provisions as par. (1) and added par. (2).

Subsec. (g)(2)(B). Pub. L. 105–261, §141(c)(3), added subpar. (B). Former subpar. (B) redesignated (C).

Subsec. (g)(2)(B)(vii). Pub. L. 105–261, §141(c)(1), added cl. (vii).

Subsec. (g)(2)(C), (D). Pub. L. 105–261, §141(c)(2), redesignated subpars. (B) and (C) as (C) and (D), respectively.

1997—Subsec. (g)(3), (4). Pub. L. 105–85 struck out "No quarterly report is required under paragraph (3) after the transmittal of the final report under paragraph (1)." at end of par. (4), redesignated par. (4) as (3), and struck out former par. (3) which read as follows: "The Secretary shall transmit to the Committee on Armed Services and the Committee on Appropriations of the Senate and the Committee on National Security and the Committee on Appropriations of the House of Representatives a quarterly report containing an accounting of all funds expended (during the quarter covered by the report) for travel and associated travel costs for Citizens' Advisory Commissioners under section 172(g) of Public Law 102–484 (50 U.S.C. 1521 note). The quarterly report for the final quarter of the period covered by a report under paragraph (1) may be included in that report."

1996—Subsec. (b)(4). Pub. L. 104–106, §1502(c)(6), substituted "Committee on Armed Services of the Senate and the Committee on National Security of the House of Representatives" for "Committees on Armed Services of the Senate and House of Representatives".

Subsec. (e)(3). Pub. L. 104–106, §153(c), inserted "or civilian equivalent" after "general officer" in introductory provisions.

Subsec. (g). Pub. L. 104–106, §153(b)(1), substituted "Periodic reports" for "Annual report" in heading.

Subsec. (g)(2). Pub. L. 104–201, §1074(d)(2)(A), substituted "shall include the following:" for "shall contain—" in introductory provisions.

Pub. L. 104–106, §153(b)(2)(A), substituted "Each annual report shall contain—" for "Each such report shall contain—" in introductory provisions.

Subsec. (g)(2)(A). Pub. L. 104–201, §1074(d)(2)(B), substituted "A site-by-site" for "a site-by-site" and "and operation." for "and operation;".

Subsec. (g)(2)(B). Pub. L. 104–201, §1074(d)(2)(C), substituted "An accounting" for "an accounting" in introductory provisions.

Subsec. (g)(2)(B)(iv). Pub. L. 104–106, §153(b)(2)(B)(i), struck out "and" after "development;".

Subsec. (g)(2)(B)(v). Pub. L. 104–106, §153(b)(2)(B)(ii), which directed substitution of "; and" for period at end of cl. (v), could not be executed because cl. (v) ended with "; and" and not with a period.

Subsec. (g)(2)(B)(vi). Pub. L. 104–106, §153(b)(2)(B)(iii), added cl. (vi).

Subsec. (g)(2)(C). Pub. L. 104–201, §1074(d)(2)(C), substituted "An assessment" for "an assessment" in introductory provisions.

Subsec. (g)(3). Pub. L. 104–106, §153(b)(4), added par. (3). Former par. (3) redesignated (4).

Subsec. (g)(4). Pub. L. 104–106, §153(b)(5), substituted "paragraph (1) not later" for "this subsection not later" and inserted at end "No quarterly report is required under paragraph (3) after the transmittal of the final report under paragraph (1)."

Pub. L. 104–106, §153(b)(3), redesignated par. (3) as (4).

Subsec. (k)(2). Pub. L. 104–106, §1502(c)(6), substituted "Committee on Armed Services of the Senate and the Committee on National Security of the House of Representatives" for "Committees on Armed Services of the Senate and House of Representatives".

1994—Subsec. (f). Pub. L. 103–337 inserted ", including funds for military construction projects necessary to carry out this section," after "carrying out this section" and struck out at end "Funds for military construction projects necessary to carry out this section may be set out in the annual military construction budget separately from other funds for such project."

1993—Subsec. (c)(3). Pub. L. 103–160 substituted "processing, approving, and overseeing" for "processing and approving".

1992—Subsec. (a). Pub. L. 102–484, §179(1), struck out par. (1) designation before "Notwithstanding" and struck out par. (2) which read as follows: "Such destruction shall be carried out in conjunction with the acquisition of binary chemical weapons for use by the Armed Forces."

Subsec. (b)(5). Pub. L. 102–484, §171, substituted "December 31, 2004" for "July 31, 1999".

Subsec. (c)(1). Pub. L. 102–484, §179(2), substituted "subsection (a)" for "subsection (a)(1)" in introductory provisions.

Subsec. (g)(1). Pub. L. 102–484, §179(3)(A), substituted "paragraph (3)" for "paragraph (4)".

Subsec. (g)(2). Pub. L. 102–484, §179(3)(B), (C), redesignated par. (3) as (2), substituted "such report" for "report other than the first one" in introductory provisions, and struck out former par. (2) which read as follows: "The first such report shall be transmitted by December 15, 1985, and shall contain—

"(A) an accounting of the United States' stockpile of lethal chemical agents and munitions on November 8, 1985; and

"(B) a schedule of the activities planned to be carried out under this section during fiscal year 1986."

Subsec. (g)(3), (4). Pub. L. 102–484, §179(3)(D), redesignated par. (4) as (3). Former par. (3) redesignated (2).

1991—Subsec. (b)(5). Pub. L. 102–190, §151(a), substituted "July 31, 1999" for "April 30, 1997".

Subsec. (c)(3). Pub. L. 102–190, §151(b), inserted at end "Additionally, the Secretary may provide funds through cooperative agreements with State and local governments for the purpose of assisting them in processing and approving permits and licenses necessary for the construction and operation of facilities to carry out this section. The Secretary shall ensure that funds provided through such a cooperative agreement are used only for the purpose set forth in the preceding sentence.''

1990—Subsec. (a)(1). Pub. L. 101–510, §171(b), substituted ''November 8, 1985'' for ''the date of the enactment of this Act''.

Subsec. (c)(3). Pub. L. 101–510, §172, added par. (3).

Subsec. (g)(3)(C). Pub. L. 101–510, §171(a), added subpar. (C).

Subsec. (h)(1). Pub. L. 101–510, §171(b), substituted ''November 8, 1985'' for ''the date of the enactment of this Act''.

1988—Subsec. (b)(1), (3)(A). Pub. L. 100–456, §118(a)(1), substituted ''the stockpile elimination deadline'' for ''September 30, 1994''.

Subsec. (b)(3)(B). Pub. L. 100–456, §118(a)(2), substituted ''not later than the earlier of (A) 30 days after the date on which the decision to defer is made, or (B) 30 days before the stockpile elimination deadline'' for ''within 30 days after the date on which the determination to defer is made or by August 31, 1994, whichever is earlier''.

Subsec. (b)(4), (5). Pub. L. 100–456, §118(a)(3), added pars. (4) and (5).

Subsec. (k). Pub. L. 100–456, §118(b), amended subsec. (k) generally. Prior to amendment, subsec. (k) read as follows: ''The provisions of this section shall take effect on October 1, 1985.''

ALTERNATIVE TECHNOLOGIES FOR DESTRUCTION OF ASSEMBLED CHEMICAL WEAPONS

Pub. L. 105–261, div. A, title I, §142, Oct. 17, 1998, 112 Stat. 1943, as amended by Pub. L. 106–65, div. A, title IX, §911(a)(1), Oct. 5, 1999, 113 Stat. 717; Pub. L. 106–398, §1 [[div. A], title X, §1087(d)(1)], Oct. 30, 2000, 114 Stat. 1654, 1654A–292, provided that:

''(a) PROGRAM MANAGEMENT.—The program manager for the Assembled Chemical Weapons Assessment shall continue to manage the development and testing (including demonstration and pilot-scale testing) of technologies for the destruction of lethal chemical munitions that are potential or demonstrated alternatives to the baseline incineration program. In performing such management, the program manager shall act independently of the program manager for Chemical Demilitarization and shall report to the Under Secretary of Defense for Acquisition, Technology, and Logistics.

''(b) POST-DEMONSTRATION ACTIVITIES.—(1) The program manager for the Assembled Chemical Weapons Assessment may carry out those activities necessary to ensure that an alternative technology for the destruction of lethal chemical munitions can be implemented immediately after—

''(A) the technology has been demonstrated to be successful; and

''(B) the Under Secretary of Defense for Acquisition, Technology, and Logistics has submitted a report on the demonstration to Congress that includes a decision to proceed with the pilot-scale facility phase for an alternative technology.

''(2) To prepare for the immediate implementation of any such technology, the program manager may, during fiscal years 1998 and 1999, take the following actions:

''(A) Establish program requirements.

''(B) Prepare procurement documentation.

''(C) Develop environmental documentation.

''(D) Identify and prepare to meet public outreach and public participation requirements.

''(E) Prepare to award a contract for the design, construction, and operation of a pilot facility for the technology to the provider team for the technology not later than December 30, 1999.

''(c) INDEPENDENT EVALUATION.—The Under Secretary of Defense for Acquisition, Technology, and Logistics shall provide for an independent evaluation of the cost and schedule of the Assembled Chemical Weapons Assessment, which shall be performed and submitted to the Under Secretary not later than September 30, 1999. The evaluation shall be performed by a nongovernmental organization qualified to make such an evaluation.

''(d) PILOT FACILITIES CONTRACTS.—(1) The Under Secretary of Defense for Acquisition, Technology, and Logistics shall determine whether to proceed with pilot-scale testing of a technology referred to in paragraph (2) in time to award a contract for the design, construction, and operation of a pilot facility for the technology to the provider team for the technology not later than December 30, 1999. If the Under Secretary determines to proceed with such testing, the Under Secretary shall (exercising the acquisition authority of the Secretary of Defense) so award a contract not later than such date.

''(2) Paragraph (1) applies to an alternative technology for the destruction of lethal chemical munitions, other than incineration, that the Under Secretary—

''(A) certifies in writing to Congress is—

''(i) as safe and cost effective for disposing of assembled chemical munitions as is incineration of such munitions; and

''(ii) is capable of completing the destruction of such munitions on or before the later of the date by which the destruction of the munitions would be completed if incineration were used or the deadline date for completing the destruction of the munitions under the Chemical Weapons Convention; and

''(B) determines as satisfying the Federal and State environmental and safety laws that are applicable to the use of the technology and to the design, construction, and operation of a pilot facility for use of the technology.

''(3) The Under Secretary shall consult with the National Research Council in making determinations and certifications for the purpose of paragraph (2).

''(4) In this subsection, the term 'Chemical Weapons Convention' means the Convention on the Prohibition of Development, Production, Stockpiling and Use of Chemical Weapons and on their Destruction, opened for signature on January 13, 1993, together with related annexes and associated documents.

''(e) PLAN FOR PILOT PROGRAM.—If the Secretary of Defense proceeds with a pilot program under section 152(f) of the National Defense Authorization Act for Fiscal Year 1996 (Public Law 104–106; 110 Stat. 214; 50 U.S.C. 1521 note), the Secretary shall prepare a plan for the pilot program and shall submit to Congress a report on such plan (including information on the cost of, and schedule for, implementing the pilot program).

''(f) FUNDING.—(1) Of the amount authorized to be appropriated under section 107 [112 Stat. 1937], funds shall be available for the program manager for the Assembled Chemical Weapons Assessment for the following:

''(A) Demonstrations of alternative technologies under the Assembled Chemical Weapons Assessment.

''(B) Planning and preparation to proceed from demonstration of an alternative technology immediately into the development of a pilot-scale facility for the technology, including planning and preparation for—

''(i) continued development of the technology leading to deployment of the technology for use;

''(ii) satisfaction of requirements for environmental permits;

''(iii) demonstration, testing, and evaluation;

''(iv) initiation of actions to design a pilot plant;

''(v) provision of support at the field office or depot level for deployment of the technology for use; and

''(vi) educational outreach to the public to engender support for the deployment.

''(C) The independent evaluation of cost and schedule required under subsection (c).

''(2) Funds authorized to be appropriated under section 107(1) are authorized to be used for awarding contracts in accordance with subsection (d) and for taking any other action authorized in this section.

"(g) ASSEMBLED CHEMICAL WEAPONS ASSESSMENT DEFINED.—In this section, the term 'Assembled Chemical Weapons Assessment' means the pilot program carried out under section 8065 of the Department of Defense Appropriations Act, 1997 (section 101(b) of Public Law 104–208; 110 Stat. 3009–101; 50 U.S.C. 1521 note)."

PILOT PROGRAM FOR DEMILITARIZATION OF ASSEMBLED CHEMICAL MUNITIONS

Pub. L. 104–208, div. A, title I, § 101(b) [title VIII, § 8065], Sept. 30, 1996, 110 Stat. 3009–71, 3009–101, as amended by Pub. L. 106–65, div. A, title IX, § 911(a)(1), Oct. 5, 1999, 113 Stat. 717, provided that: "Notwithstanding section 142 of H.R. 3230, the National Defense Authorization Act for Fiscal Year 1997, as passed by the Senate on September 10, 1996 [section 142 of Pub. L. 104–201, which amended section 152 of Pub. L. 104–106, set out below], of the funds provided in title VI of this Act [Pub. L. 104–208, div. A, title I, § 101(b) [title VI], Sept. 30, 1996, 110 Stat. 3009–71, 3009–85], under the heading 'Chemical Agents and Munitions Destruction, Defense', $40,000,000 shall only be available for the conduct of a pilot program to identify and demonstrate not less than two alternatives to the baseline incineration process for the demilitarization of assembled chemical munitions: *Provided*, That the Under Secretary of Defense for Acquisition, Technology, and Logistics shall, not later than December 1, 1996, designate a program manager who is not, nor has been, in direct or immediate control of the baseline reverse assembly incineration demilitarization program to carry out the pilot program: *Provided further*, That the Under Secretary of Defense for Acquisition, Technology, and Logistics shall evaluate the effectiveness of each alternative chemical munitions demilitarization technology identified and demonstrated under the pilot program to demilitarize munitions and assembled chemical munitions while meeting all applicable Federal and State environmental and safety requirements: *Provided further*, That the Under Secretary of Defense for Acquisition, Technology, and Logistics shall transmit, by December 15 of each year, a report to the congressional defense committees on the activities carried out under the pilot program during the preceding fiscal year in which the report is to be made: *Provided further*, That section 142(f)(3) of H.R. 3230, the National Defense Authorization Act for Fiscal Year 1997, as passed by the Senate on September 10, 1996 [probably means section 152(f)(3) of Pub. L. 104–106, set out below], is repealed: *Provided further*, That no funds may be obligated for the construction of a baseline incineration facility at the Lexington Blue Grass Army Depot or the Pueblo Depot activity until 180 days after the Secretary of Defense has submitted to the congressional defense committees a report detailing the effectiveness of each alternative chemical munitions demilitarization technology identified and demonstrated under the pilot program and its ability to meet the applicable safety and environmental requirements: *Provided further*, That none of the funds in this or any other Act may be obligated for the preparation of studies, assessments, or planning of the removal and transportation of stockpile assembled unitary chemical weapons or neutralized chemical agent to any of the eight chemical weapons storage sites within the continental United States."

DESTRUCTION OF EXISTING STOCKPILE OF LETHAL CHEMICAL AGENTS AND MUNITIONS

Pub. L. 106–65, div. A, title I, § 141, Oct. 5, 1999, 113 Stat. 537, provided that:

"(a) PROGRAM ASSESSMENT.—(1) The Secretary of Defense shall conduct an assessment of the current program for destruction of the United States' stockpile of chemical agents and munitions, including the Assembled Chemical Weapons Assessment, for the purpose of reducing significantly the cost of such program and ensuring completion of such program in accordance with the obligations of the United States under the Chemical Weapons Convention while maintaining maximum protection of the general public, the personnel involved in the demilitarization program, and the environment.

"(2) Based on the results of the assessment conducted under paragraph (1), the Secretary may take those actions identified in the assessment that may be accomplished under existing law to achieve the purposes of such assessment and the chemical agents and munitions stockpile destruction program.

"(3) Not later than March 1, 2000, the Secretary shall submit to Congress a report on—

"(A) those actions taken, or planned to be taken, under paragraph (2); and

"(B) any recommendations for additional legislation that may be required to achieve the purposes of the assessment conducted under paragraph (1) and of the chemical agents and munitions stockpile destruction program.

"(b) CHANGES AND CLARIFICATIONS REGARDING PROGRAM.—[Amended this section.]

"(c) COMPTROLLER GENERAL ASSESSMENT AND REPORT.—(1) Not later than March 1, 2000, the Comptroller General of the United States shall review and assess the program for destruction of the United States stockpile of chemical agents and munitions and report the results of the assessment to the congressional defense committees.

"(2) The assessment conducted under paragraph (1) shall include a review of the program execution and financial management of each of the elements of the program, including—

"(A) the chemical stockpile disposal project;

"(B) the nonstockpile chemical materiel project;

"(C) the alternative technologies and approaches project;

"(D) the chemical stockpile emergency preparedness program; and

"(E) the assembled chemical weapons assessment program.

"(d) DEFINITIONS.—As used in this section:

"(1) The term 'Assembled Chemical Weapons Assessment' means the pilot program carried out under section 8065 of the Department of Defense Appropriations Act, 1997 (section 101(b) of Public Law 104–208; 110 Stat. 3009–101; 50 U.S.C. 1521 note).

"(2) The term 'Chemical Weapons Convention' means the Convention on the Prohibition of the Development, Production, Stockpiling and Use of Chemical Weapons and on Their Destruction, ratified by the United States on April 25, 1997, and entered into force on April 29, 1997."

Section 152 of Pub. L. 104–106, as amended by Pub. L. 104–201, div. A, title I, § 142, Sept. 23, 1996, 110 Stat. 2448; Pub. L. 104–208, div. A, title I, § 101(b) [title VIII, § 8065], Sept. 30, 1996, 110 Stat. 3009–71, 3009–102, provided that:

"(a) IN GENERAL.—The Secretary of Defense shall proceed with the program for destruction of the chemical munitions stockpile of the Department of Defense while maintaining the maximum protection of the environment, the general public, and the personnel involved in the actual destruction of the munitions. In carrying out such program, the Secretary shall use technologies and procedures that will minimize the risk to the public at each site.

"(b) INITIATION OF DEMILITARIZATION OPERATIONS.—The Secretary of Defense may not initiate destruction of the chemical munitions stockpile stored at a site until the following support measures are in place:

"(1) Support measures that are required by Department of Defense and Army chemical surety and security program regulations.

"(2) Support measures that are required by the general and site chemical munitions demilitarization plans specific to that installation.

"(3) Support measures that are required by the permits required by the Solid Waste Disposal Act (42 U.S.C. 6901 et seq.) and the Clean Air Act (42 U.S.C. 7401 et seq.) for chemical munitions demilitarization operations at that installation, as approved by the appropriate State regulatory agencies.

"(c) ASSESSMENT OF ALTERNATIVES.—(1) The Secretary of Defense shall conduct an assessment of the current chemical demilitarization program and of measures that could be taken to reduce significantly the total cost of the program, while ensuring maximum protection of the general public, the personnel involved in the demilitarization program, and the environment. The measures considered shall be limited to those that would minimize the risk to the public. The assessment shall be conducted without regard to any limitation that would otherwise apply to the conduct of such an assessment under any provision of law.

"(2) The assessment shall be conducted in coordination with the National Research Council.

"(3) Based on the results of the assessment, the Secretary shall develop appropriate recommendations for revision of the chemical demilitarization program.

"(4) Not later than March 1, 1996, the Secretary of Defense shall submit to the congressional defense committees [Committees on Armed Services and on Appropriations of the Senate and House of Representatives] an interim report assessing the current status of the chemical stockpile demilitarization program, including the results of the Army's analysis of the physical and chemical integrity of the stockpile and implications for the chemical demilitarization program, and providing recommendations for revisions to that program that have been included in the budget request of the Department of Defense for fiscal year 1997. The Secretary shall submit to the congressional defense committees with the submission of the budget request of the Department of Defense for fiscal year 1998 a final report on the assessment conducted in accordance with paragraph (1) and recommendations for revision to the program, including an assessment of alternative demilitarization technologies and processes to the baseline incineration process and potential reconfiguration of the stockpile that should be incorporated in the program.

"(d) ASSISTANCE FOR CHEMICAL WEAPONS STOCKPILE COMMUNITIES AFFECTED BY BASE CLOSURE.—(1) The Secretary of Defense shall review and evaluate issues associated with closure and reutilization of Department of Defense facilities co-located with continuing chemical stockpile and chemical demilitarization operations.

"(2) The review shall include the following:

"(A) An analysis of the economic impacts on these communities and the unique reuse problems facing local communities associated with ongoing chemical weapons programs.

"(B) Recommendations of the Secretary on methods for expeditious and cost-effective transfer or lease of these facilities to local communities for reuse by those communities.

"(3) The Secretary shall submit to the congressional defense committees a report on the review and evaluation under this subsection. The report shall be submitted not later than 90 days after the date of the enactment of this Act [Feb. 10, 1996].

"(e) ASSESSMENT OF ALTERNATIVE TECHNOLOGIES FOR DEMILITARIZATION OF ASSEMBLED CHEMICAL MUNITIONS.—(1) In addition to the assessment required by subsection (c), the Secretary of Defense shall conduct an assessment of the chemical demilitarization program for destruction of assembled chemical munitions and of the alternative demilitarization technologies and processes (other than incineration) that could be used for the destruction of the lethal chemical agents that are associated with these munitions, while ensuring maximum protection for the general public, the personnel involved in the demilitarization program, and the environment. The measures considered shall be limited to those that would minimize the risk to the public and reduce the total cost of the chemical agents and munitions destruction program. The assessment shall be conducted without regard to any limitation that would otherwise apply to the conduct of such assessment under any provision of law.

"(2) The assessment shall be conducted in coordination with the National Research Council.

"(3) Among the alternatives, the assessment shall include a determination of the cost of incineration of the current chemical munitions stockpile by building incinerators at each existing facility compared to the proposed cost of dismantling those same munitions, neutralizing them at each storage site (other than Tooele Army Depot or Johnston Atoll), and transporting the neutralized remains and all munitions parts to a treatment, storage, and disposal facility within the United States that has the necessary environmental permits to undertake incineration of the material.

"(4) Based on the results of the assessment, the Secretary shall develop appropriate recommendations for revision of the chemical demilitarization program.

"(5) Not later than December 31, 1997, the Secretary of Defense shall submit to Congress a report on the assessment conducted in accordance with paragraph (1) and any recommendations for revision of the chemical demilitarization program, including the continued development of alternative demilitarization technologies and processes other than incineration that could be used for the destruction of the lethal chemical agents that are associated with these assembled chemical munitions and the chemical munitions demilitarization sites for which the selected technologies should be developed.

"(f) PILOT PROGRAM FOR DEMILITARIZATION OF CHEMICAL AGENTS FOR ASSEMBLED MUNITIONS.—(1) If the Secretary of Defense makes a decision to continue the development of an alternative demilitarization technology or process (other than incineration) that could be used for the destruction of the lethal chemical agents that are associated with assembled chemical munitions, $25,000,000 shall be available from the funds authorized to be appropriated in section 107 of the National Defense Authorization Act for Fiscal Year 1997 [Pub. L. 104–201, 110 Stat. 2440] for the chemical agents and munitions destruction program, in order to initiate a pilot program using the selected alternative technology or process for the destruction of chemical agents that are stored at these sites.

"(2) Not less than 30 days before using funds to initiate the pilot program under paragraph (1), the Secretary shall submit notice in writing to Congress of the Secretary's intent to do so.

"[(3) Repealed. Pub. L. 104–208, div. A, title I, §101(b) [title VIII, §8065], Sept. 30, 1996, 110 Stat. 3009–71, 3009–102.]"

CHEMICAL DEMILITARIZATION CITIZENS ADVISORY COMMISSIONS

Section 172 of Pub. L. 102–484, as amended by Pub. L. 104–106, div. A, title I, §153(a), Feb. 10, 1996, 110 Stat. 215; Pub. L. 104–201, div. A, title X, §1073(d), Sept. 23, 1996, 110 Stat. 2658, provided that:

"(a) ESTABLISHMENT.—(1) The Secretary of the Army shall establish a citizens' commission for each State in which there is a low-volume site (as defined in section 180 [set out below]). Each such commission shall be known as the 'Chemical Demilitarization Citizens' Advisory Commission' for that State.

"(2) The Secretary shall also establish a Chemical Demilitarization Citizens' Advisory Commission for any State in which there is located a chemical weapons storage site other than a low-volume site, if the establishment of such a commission for such State is requested by the Governor of that State.

"(b) FUNCTIONS.—The Secretary of the Army shall provide for a representative from the Office of the Assistant Secretary of the Army (Research, Development and Acquisition) to meet with each commission under this section to receive citizen and State concerns regarding the ongoing program of the Army for the disposal of the lethal chemical agents and munitions in the stockpile referred to in section 1412(a)(1) of the Department of Defense Authorization Act, 1986 (50 U.S.C. 1521(a)(1)) at each of the sites with respect to which a commission is established pursuant to subsection (a).

"(c) MEMBERSHIP.—(1) Each commission established for a State pursuant to subsection (a) shall be composed of nine members appointed by the Governor of the State. Seven of such members shall be citizens from the local affected areas in the State; the other two shall be representatives of State government who have direct responsibilities related to the chemical demilitarization program.

"(2) For purposes of paragraph (1), affected areas are those areas located within a 50-mile radius of a chemical weapons storage site.

"(d) CONFLICTS OF INTEREST.—For a period of five years after the termination of any commission, no corporation, partnership, or other organization in which a member of that commission, a spouse of a member of that commission, or a natural or adopted child of a member of that commission has an ownership interest may be awarded—

"(1) a contract related to the disposal of lethal chemical agents or munitions in the stockpile referred to in section 1412(a)(1) of the Department of Defense Authorization Act, 1986 (50 U.S.C. 1521(a)(1)); or

"(2) a subcontract under such a contract.

"(e) CHAIRMAN.—The members of each commission shall designate the chairman of the commission from among the members of the commission.

"(f) MEETINGS.—Each commission shall meet with a representative from the Office of the Assistant Secretary of the Army (Research, Development and Acquisition) upon joint agreement between the chairman of the commission and that representative. The two parties shall meet not less often than twice a year and may meet more often at their discretion.

"(g) PAY AND EXPENSES.—Members of each commission shall receive no pay for their involvement in the activities of their commissions. Funds appropriated for the Chemical Stockpile Demilitarization Program may be used for travel and associated travel costs for Citizens' Advisory Commissioners, when such travel is conducted at the invitation of the Assistant Secretary of the Army (Research, Development, and Acquisition).

"(h) TERMINATION OF COMMISSIONS.—Each commission shall be terminated after the stockpile located in that commission's State has been destroyed."

ALTERNATIVE DISPOSAL PROCESS FOR LOW-VOLUME SITES; REVISED DISPOSAL CONCEPT PLAN

Sections 174 and 175 of Pub. L. 102–484, as amended by Pub. L. 103–160, div. A, title I, §155(b), Nov. 30, 1993, 107 Stat. 1579, provided that:

"SEC. 174. ALTERNATIVE DISPOSAL PROCESS FOR LOW-VOLUME SITES.

"(a) REQUIREMENT FOR ALTERNATIVE PROCESS.—If the date by which chemical weapons destruction and demilitarization operations can be completed at a low-volume site using an alternative technology process evaluated by the Secretary of the Army falls within the deadline established by the amendment made by section 171 [amending this section] and the Secretary determines that the use of that alternative technology process for the destruction of chemical weapons at that site is significantly safer and equally or more cost-effective than the use of the baseline disassembly and incineration process, then the Secretary of the Army, as part of the requirement of section 1412(a) of Public Law 99–145 [subsec. (a) of this section], shall carry out the disposal of chemical weapons at that site using such alternative technology process. In addition, the Secretary may carry out the disposal of chemical weapons at sites other than low-volume sites using an alternative technology process (rather than the baseline process) after notifying Congress of the Secretary's intent to do so.

"(b) APPLICABILITY OF CERTAIN PROVISIONS OF SECTION 1412.—Subsections (c), (e), (f), and (g) of section 1412 of Public Law 99–145 (50 U.S.C. 1521) shall apply to this section and to activities under this section in the same manner as if this section were part of that section 1412.

"SEC. 175. REVISED CHEMICAL WEAPONS DISPOSAL CONCEPT PLAN.

"(a) REVISED PLAN.—If, pursuant to section 174, the Secretary of the Army is required to implement an alternative technology process for destruction of chemical weapons at any low-volume site, the Secretary shall submit to Congress a revised chemical weapons disposal concept plan incorporating the alternative technology process and reflecting the revised stockpile disposal schedule developed under section 1412(b) of Public Law 99–145 (50 U.S.C. 1521(b)), as amended by section 171. In developing the revised concept plan, the Secretary should consider, to the maximum extent practicable, revisions to the program and program schedule that capitalize on the changes to the chemical demilitarization schedule resulting from the revised stockpile elimination deadline by reducing cost and decreasing program risk.

"(b) MATTERS TO BE INCLUDED.—The revised concept plan should include—

"(1) life-cycle cost estimates and schedules; and

"(2) a description of the facilities and operating procedures to be employed using the alternative technology process.

"(c) APPLICABILITY OF CERTAIN PROVISIONS OF SECTION 1412.—Subsection (c) of section 1412 of Public Law 99–145 (50 U.S.C. 1521) shall apply to the revised concept plan in the same manner as if this section were part of that section 1412.

"(d) SUBMISSION OF REVISED PLAN.—If the Secretary is required to submit a revised concept plan under this section, the Secretary shall submit the revised concept plan during the 120-day period beginning at the end of the 60-day period following the submission of the report of the Secretary required under section 173 [106 Stat. 2342].

"(e) LIMITATION.—If the Secretary is required to submit a revised concept plan under this section, no funds may be obligated for procurement of equipment or for facilities planning and design activities (other than for those preliminary planning and design activities required to comply with subsection(b)(2)) for a chemical weapons disposal facility at any low-volume site at which the Secretary intends to implement an alternative technology process until the Secretary submits the revised concept plan."

SENSE OF CONGRESS CONCERNING INTERNATIONAL CONSULTATION AND EXCHANGE PROGRAM

Section 178 of Pub. L. 102–484 provided that: "It is the sense of Congress that the Secretary of Defense, in consultation with the Secretary of State, should establish, with other nations that are anticipated to be signatories to an international agreement or treaty banning chemical weapons, a program under which consultation and exchange concerning chemical weapons disposal technology could be enhanced. Such a program shall be used to facilitate the exchange of technical information and advice concerning the disposal of chemical weapons among signatory nations and to further the development of safer, more cost-effective methods for the disposal of chemical weapons."

"LOW-VOLUME SITE" DEFINED

Section 180 of Pub. L. 102–484 provided that: "For purposes of this subtitle [subtitle G (§§ 171–180) of title I of div. A of Pub. L. 102–484, amending this section and enacting provisions set out as notes above], the term 'low-volume site' means one of the three chemical weapons storage sites in the United States at which there is stored 5 percent or less of the total United States stockpile of unitary chemical weapons."

REVISION OF CHEMICAL DEMILITARIZATION PROGRAM

Pub. L. 100–180, div. A, title I, §125, Dec. 4, 1987, 101 Stat. 1043, provided that:

"(a) DEFINITION.—For purposes of this section, the term 'chemical stockpile demilitarization program' means the program established by section 1412 of the Department of Defense Authorization Act, 1986 (50 U.S.C. 1521), to provide for the destruction of the United States' stockpile of lethal chemical agents and munitions.

"(b) ENVIRONMENTAL IMPACT STATEMENT.—The Secretary of Defense shall issue the final Programmatic Environmental Impact Statement on the chemical stockpile demilitarization program by January 1, 1988. The Environmental Impact Statement shall be prepared in accordance with all applicable laws.

"(c) DISPOSAL TECHNOLOGIES.—(1) Funds appropriated pursuant to this Act [see Tables for classification] or otherwise made available for fiscal year 1988 for the chemical stockpile demilitarization program may not be obligated for procurement or for an Army military construction project at a military installation or facility inside the continental United States until the Secretary of Defense certifies to Congress in writing that the concept plan under the program includes the following:

"(A) Evaluation of alternate technologies for disposal of the existing stockpile and selection of the technology or technologies to be used for such purpose.

"(B) Full-scale operational verification of the technology or technologies selected for such disposal.

"(C) Maximum protection for public health and the environment.

"(2) The limitation in paragraph (1) shall not apply with respect to the obligation of funds for the technology evaluation or development program.

"(d) ALTERNATIVE CONCEPT PLAN.—The Secretary of Defense shall submit to the Committees on Armed Services of the Senate and House of Representatives an alternative concept plan for the chemical stockpile demilitarization program. The alternative concept plan shall—

"(1) incorporate the requirements of subsections (b) and (c); and

"(2) specify any revised schedule or revised funding requirement necessary to enable the Secretary to meet the requirements of subsections (b) and (c).

The alternative concept plan shall be submitted by March 15, 1988.

"(e) SURVEILLANCE AND ASSESSMENT PROGRAM.—The Secretary of Defense shall conduct an ongoing comprehensive program of—

"(1) surveillance of the existing United States stockpile of chemical weapons; and

"(2) assessment of the condition of the stockpile."

§ 1522. Conduct of chemical and biological defense program

(a) General

The Secretary of Defense shall carry out the chemical and biological defense program of the United States in accordance with the provisions of this section.

(b) Management and oversight

In carrying out his responsibilities under this section, the Secretary of Defense shall do the following:

(1) Assign responsibility for overall coordination and integration of the chemical and biological warfare defense program and the chemical and biological medical defense program to a single office within the Office of the Secretary of Defense.

(2) Take those actions necessary to ensure close and continuous coordination between (A) the chemical and biological warfare defense program, and (B) the chemical and biological medical defense program.

(3) Exercise oversight over the chemical and biological defense program through the Defense Acquisition Board process.

(c) Coordination of program

(1) The Secretary of Defense shall designate the Army as executive agent for the Department of Defense to coordinate and integrate research, development, test, and evaluation, and acquisition, requirements of the military departments for chemical and biological warfare defense programs of the Department of Defense.

(2) The Director of the Defense Advanced Research Projects Agency may conduct a program of basic and applied research and advanced technology development on chemical and biological warfare defense technologies and systems. In conducting such program, the Director shall seek to avoid unnecessary duplication of the activities under the program with chemical and biological warfare defense activities of the military departments and defense agencies and shall coordinate the activities under the program with those of the military departments and defense agencies.

(d) Funding

(1) The budget for the Department of Defense for each fiscal year after fiscal year 1994 shall reflect a coordinated and integrated chemical and biological defense program for the Department of Defense.

(2) Funding requests for the program (other than for activities under the program conducted by the Defense Advanced Research Projects Agency under subsection (c)(2) of this section) shall be set forth in the budget of the Department of Defense for each fiscal year as a separate account, with a single program element for each of the categories of research, development, test, and evaluation, acquisition, and military construction. Amounts for military construction projects may be set forth in the annual military construction budget. Funds for military construction for the program in the military construction budget shall be set forth separately from other funds for military construction projects. Funding requests for the program may not be included in the budget accounts of the military departments.

(3) The program conducted by the Defense Advanced Research Projects Agency under subsection (c)(2) of this section shall be set forth as a separate program element in the budget of that agency.

(4) All funding requirements for the chemical and biological defense program shall be reviewed by the Secretary of the Army as executive agent pursuant to subsection (c) of this section.

(e) Management review and report

(1) The Secretary of Defense shall conduct a review of the management structure of the Department of Defense chemical and biological warfare defense program, including—

(A) research, development, test, and evaluation;

(B) procurement;

(C) doctrine development;

(D) policy;

(E) training;

(F) development of requirements;

(G) readiness; and

(H) risk assessment.

(2) Not later than May 1, 1994, the Secretary shall submit to Congress a report that describes the details of measures being taken to improve joint coordination and oversight of the program

and ensure a coherent and effective approach to its management.

(Pub. L. 103–160, div. A, title XVII, §1701, Nov. 30, 1993, 107 Stat. 1853; Pub. L. 104–201, div. A, title II, §228, Sept. 23, 1996, 110 Stat. 2460.)

CODIFICATION

Section was enacted as part of the National Defense Authorization Act for Fiscal Year 1994, and not as part of Pub. L. 91–121, title IV, §409, Nov. 19, 1969, 83 Stat. 209, which comprises this chapter.

AMENDMENTS

1996—Subsec. (c). Pub. L. 104–201, §228(a), designated existing provisions as par. (1) and added par. (2).

Subsec. (d)(1). Pub. L. 104–201, §228(b)(1), substituted "program for the Department of Defense" for "program for the military departments".

Subsec. (d)(2). Pub. L. 104–201, §228(b)(2), in first sentence, inserted "(other than for activities under the program conducted by the Defense Advanced Research Projects Agency under subsection (c)(2) of this section)" after "requests for the program".

Subsec. (d)(3), (4). Pub. L. 104–201, §228(b)(3), (4), added par. (3) and redesignated former par. (3) as (4).

CHEMICAL WARFARE DEFENSE

Pub. L. 105–261, div. A, title II, §247, Oct. 17, 1998, 112 Stat. 1956, provided that:

"(a) REVIEW AND MODIFICATION OF POLICIES AND DOCTRINES.—The Secretary of Defense shall review the policies and doctrines of the Department of Defense on chemical warfare defense and modify the policies and doctrine as appropriate to achieve the objectives set forth in subsection (b).

"(b) OBJECTIVES.—The objectives for the modification of policies and doctrines of the Department of Defense on chemical warfare defense are as follows:

"(1) To provide for adequate protection of personnel from any exposure to a chemical warfare agent (including chronic and low-level exposure to a chemical warfare agent) that would endanger the health of exposed personnel because of the deleterious effects of—

"(A) a single exposure to the agent;

"(B) exposure to the agent concurrently with other dangerous exposures, such as exposures to—

"(i) other potentially toxic substances in the environment, including pesticides, other insect and vermin control agents, and environmental pollutants;

"(ii) low-grade nuclear and electromagnetic radiation present in the environment;

"(iii) preventive medications (that are dangerous when taken concurrently with other dangerous exposures referred to in this paragraph);

"(iv) diesel fuel, jet fuel, and other hydrocarbon-based fuels; and

"(v) occupational hazards, including battlefield hazards; and

"(C) repeated exposures to the agent, or some combination of one or more exposures to the agent and other dangerous exposures referred to in subparagraph (B), over time.

"(2) To provide for—

"(A) the prevention of and protection against, and the detection (including confirmation) of, exposures to a chemical warfare agent (whether intentional or inadvertent) at levels that, even if not sufficient to endanger health immediately, are greater than the level that is recognized under Department of Defense policies as being the maximum safe level of exposure to that agent for the general population; and

"(B) the recording, reporting, coordinating, and retaining of information on possible exposures described in subparagraph (A), including the monitoring of the health effects of exposures on humans and animals, environmental effects, and ecological effects, and the documenting and reporting of those effects specifically by location.

"(3) To provide solutions for the concerns and mission requirements that are specifically applicable for one or more of the Armed Forces in a protracted conflict when exposures to chemical agents could be complex, dynamic, and occurring over an extended period.

"(c) RESEARCH PROGRAM.—The Secretary of Defense shall develop and carry out a plan to establish a research program for determining the effects of exposures to chemical warfare agents of the type described in subsection (b). The research shall be designed to yield results that can guide the Secretary in the evolution of policy and doctrine on exposures to chemical warfare agents and to develop new risk assessment methods and instruments with respect to such exposures. The plan shall state the objectives and scope of the program and include a 5-year funding plan.

"(d) REPORT.—Not later than May 1, 1999, the Secretary of Defense shall submit to the Committee on Armed Services of the Senate and the Committee on National Security of the House of Representatives [now Committee on Armed Services of the House of Representatives] a report on the results of the review under subsection (a) and on the research program developed under subsection (c). The report shall include the following:

"(1) Each modification of chemical warfare defense policy and doctrine resulting from the review.

"(2) Any recommended legislation regarding chemical warfare defense.

"(3) The plan for the research program."

STUDY OF FACILITY FOR TRAINING AND EVALUATION OF CHEMICAL OR BIOLOGICAL WEAPONS RESPONSE PERSONNEL

Pub. L. 104–132, title V, §521(b), Apr. 24, 1996, 110 Stat. 1286, provided that:

"(1) FINDINGS.—The Congress finds that—

"(A) the threat of the use of chemical and biological weapons by Third World countries and by terrorist organizations has increased in recent years and is now a problem of worldwide significance;

"(B) the military and law enforcement agencies in the United States that are responsible for responding to the use of such weapons require additional testing, training, and evaluation facilities to ensure that the personnel of such agencies discharge their responsibilities effectively; and

"(C) a facility that recreates urban and suburban locations would provide an especially effective environment in which to test, train, and evaluate such personnel for that purpose.

"(2) STUDY OF FACILITY.—

"(A) IN GENERAL.—The President shall establish an interagency task force to determine the feasibility and advisability of establishing a facility that recreates both an urban environment and a suburban environment in such a way as to permit the effective testing, training, and evaluation in such environments of government personnel who are responsible for responding to the use of chemical and biological weapons in the United States.

"(B) DESCRIPTION OF FACILITY.—The facility considered under subparagraph (A) shall include—

"(i) facilities common to urban environments (including a multistory building and an underground rail transit system) and to suburban environments;

"(ii) the capacity to produce controllable releases of chemical and biological agents from a variety of urban and suburban structures, including laboratories, small buildings, and dwellings;

"(iii) the capacity to produce controllable releases of chemical and biological agents into sewage, water, and air management systems common to urban areas and suburban areas;

"(iv) chemical and biocontaminant facilities at the P3 and P4 levels;

"(v) the capacity to test and evaluate the effectiveness of a variety of protective clothing and facilities and survival techniques in urban areas and suburban areas; and

"(vi) the capacity to test and evaluate the effectiveness of variable sensor arrays (including video, audio, meteorological, chemical, and biosensor arrays) in urban areas and suburban areas.

"(C) SENSE OF CONGRESS.—It is the sense of Congress that the facility considered under subparagraph (A) shall, if established—

"(i) be under the jurisdiction of the Secretary of Defense; and

"(ii) be located at a principal facility of the Department of Defense for the testing and evaluation of the use of chemical and biological weapons during any period of armed conflict."

CONSOLIDATION OF CHEMICAL AND BIOLOGICAL DEFENSE TRAINING ACTIVITIES

Section 1702 of Pub. L. 103–160 provided that: "The Secretary of Defense shall consolidate all chemical and biological warfare defense training activities of the Department of Defense at the United States Army Chemical School."

SENSE OF CONGRESS CONCERNING FEDERAL EMERGENCY PLANNING FOR RESPONSE TO TERRORIST THREATS

Section 1704 of Pub. L. 103–160 provided that: "It is the sense of Congress that the President should strengthen Federal interagency emergency planning by the Federal Emergency Management Agency and other appropriate Federal, State, and local agencies for development of a capability for early detection and warning of and response to—

"(1) potential terrorist use of chemical or biological agents or weapons; and

"(2) emergencies or natural disasters involving industrial chemicals or the widespread outbreak of disease."

§1523. Annual report on chemical and biological warfare defense

(a) Report required

The Secretary of Defense shall include in the annual report of the Secretary under section 113(c) of title 10 a report on chemical and biological warfare defense. The report shall assess—

(1) the overall readiness of the Armed Forces to fight in a chemical-biological warfare environment and shall describe steps taken and planned to be taken to improve such readiness; and

(2) requirements for the chemical and biological warfare defense program, including requirements for training, detection, and protective equipment, for medical prophylaxis, and for treatment of casualties resulting from use of chemical or biological weapons.

(b) Matters to be included

The report shall include information on the following:

(1) The quantities, characteristics, and capabilities of fielded chemical and biological defense equipment to meet wartime and peacetime requirements for support of the Armed Forces, including individual protective items.

(2) The status of research and development programs, and acquisition programs, for required improvements in chemical and biological defense equipment and medical treatment, including an assessment of the ability of the Department of Defense and the industrial base to meet those requirements.

(3) Measures taken to ensure the integration of requirements for chemical and biological defense equipment and material among the Armed Forces.

(4) The status of nuclear, biological, and chemical (NBC) warfare defense training and readiness among the Armed Forces and measures being taken to include realistic nuclear, biological, and chemical warfare simulations in war games, battle simulations, and training exercises.

(5) Measures taken to improve overall management and coordination of the chemical and biological defense program.

(6) Problems encountered in the chemical and biological warfare defense program during the past year and recommended solutions to those problems for which additional resources or actions by the Congress are required.

(7) A description of the chemical warfare defense preparations that have been and are being undertaken by the Department of Defense to address needs which may arise under article X of the Chemical Weapons Convention.

(8) A summary of other preparations undertaken by the Department of Defense and the On-Site Inspection Agency to prepare for and to assist in the implementation of the convention, including activities such as training for inspectors, preparation of defense installations for inspections under the convention using the Defense Treaty Inspection Readiness Program, provision of chemical weapons detection equipment, and assistance in the safe transportation, storage, and destruction of chemical weapons in other signatory nations to the convention.

(9) A description of any program involving the testing of biological or chemical agents on human subjects that was carried out by the Department of Defense during the period covered by the report, together with—

(A) a detailed justification for the testing;

(B) a detailed explanation of the purposes of the testing;

(C) a description of each chemical or biological agent tested; and

(D) the Secretary's certification that informed consent to the testing was obtained from each human subject in advance of the testing on that subject.

(Pub. L. 103–160, div. A, title XVII, §1703, Nov. 30, 1993, 107 Stat. 1854; Pub. L. 105–85, div. A, title X, §1078(f), Nov. 18, 1997, 111 Stat. 1915.)

CODIFICATION

Section was enacted as part of the National Defense Authorization Act for Fiscal Year 1994, and not as part of Pub. L. 91–121, title IV, §409, Nov. 19, 1969, 83 Stat. 209, which comprises this chapter.

AMENDMENTS

1997—Subsec. (b)(9). Pub. L. 105–85 added par. (9).

§1524. Agreements to provide support to vaccination programs of Department of Health and Human Services

(a) Agreements authorized

The Secretary of Defense may enter into agreements with the Secretary of Health and Human Services to provide support for vaccination programs of the Secretary of Health and Human Services in the United States through use of the excess peacetime biological weapons defense capability of the Department of Defense.

(b) Report

Not later than February 1, 1994, the Secretary of Defense shall submit to the congressional defense committees a report on the feasibility of providing Department of Defense support for vaccination programs under subsection (a) of this section and shall identify resource requirements that are not within the Department's capability.

(Pub. L. 103–160, div. A, title XVII, § 1705, Nov. 30, 1993, 107 Stat. 1856.)

CODIFICATION

Section was enacted as part of the National Defense Authorization Act for Fiscal Year 1994, and not as part of Pub. L. 91–121, title IV, § 409, Nov. 19, 1969, 83 Stat. 209, which comprises this chapter.

"CONGRESSIONAL DEFENSE COMMITTEES" DEFINED

Congressional defense committees means the Committees on Armed Services and the Committees on Appropriations of the Senate and House of Representatives, see section 3 of Pub. L. 103–160, 107 Stat. 1562.

§ 1525. Assistance for facilities subject to inspection under Chemical Weapons Convention

(a) Assistance authorized

Upon the request of the owner or operator of a facility that is subject to a routine inspection or a challenge inspection under the Chemical Weapons Convention, the Secretary of Defense may provide technical assistance to that owner or operator related to compliance of that facility with the Convention. Any such assistance shall be provided through the On-Site Inspection Agency of the Department of Defense.

(b) Reimbursement requirement

The Secretary may provide assistance under subsection (a) of this section only to the extent that the Secretary determines that the Department of Defense will be reimbursed for costs incurred in providing the assistance. The United States National Authority may provide such reimbursement from amounts available to it. Any such reimbursement shall be credited to amounts available for the On-Site Inspection Agency.

(c) Definitions

In this section:

(1) The terms "Chemical Weapons Convention" and "Convention" mean the Convention on the Prohibition of the Development, Production, Stockpiling and Use of Chemical Weapons and on Their Destruction, ratified by the United States on April 25, 1997, and entered into force on April 29, 1997.

(2) The term "facility that is subject to a routine inspection" means a declared facility, as defined in paragraph 15 of part X of the Annex on Implementation and Verification of the Convention.

(3) The term "challenge inspection" means an inspection conducted under Article IX of the Convention.

(4) The term "United States National Authority" means the United States National Authority established or designated pursuant to Article VII, paragraph 4, of the Convention.

(Pub. L. 105–85, div. A, title XIII, § 1303, Nov. 18, 1997, 111 Stat. 1951.)

CODIFICATION

Section was enacted as part of the National Defense Authorization Act for Fiscal Year 1998, and not as part of Pub. L. 91–121, title IV, § 409, Nov. 19, 1969, 83 Stat. 209, which comprises this chapter.

§ 1526. Effective use of resources for nonproliferation programs

(a) Prohibition

Except as provided in subsection (b) of this section, no assistance may be provided by the United States Government to any person who is involved in the research, development, design, testing, or evaluation of chemical or biological weapons for offensive purposes.

(b) Exception

The prohibition contained in subsection (a) of this section shall not apply to any activity conducted pursuant to title V of the National Security Act of 1947 (50 U.S.C. 413 et seq.).

(Pub. L. 106–113, div. B, § 1000(a)(7) [div. B, title XI, § 1132], Nov. 29, 1999, 113 Stat. 1536, 1501A–493).

REFERENCES IN TEXT

The National Security Act of 1947, referred to in subsec. (b), is act July 26, 1947, ch. 343, 61 Stat. 495, as amended. Title V of the Act is classified generally to subchapter III (§ 413 et seq.) of chapter 15 of this title. For complete classification of this Act to the Code, see Short Title note set out under section 401 of this title and Tables.

CODIFICATION

Section was enacted as part of the Arms Control and Nonproliferation Act of 1999, and also as part of the Arms Control, Nonproliferation, and Security Assistance Act of 1999, and the Admiral James W. Nance and Meg Donovan Foreign Relations Authorization Act, Fiscal Years, 2000 and 2001, and not as part of Pub. L. 91–121, title IV, § 409, Nov. 19, 1969, 83 Stat. 209, which comprises this chapter.

CHAPTER 33—WAR POWERS RESOLUTION

CHAPTER REFERRED TO IN OTHER SECTIONS

This chapter is referred to in title 10 sections 127a, 12304; title 22 section 3426.

§1541. Purpose and policy

(a) Congressional declaration

It is the purpose of this chapter to fulfill the intent of the framers of the Constitution of the United States and insure that the collective judgment of both the Congress and the President will apply to the introduction of United States Armed Forces into hostilities, or into situations where imminent involvement in hostilities is clearly indicated by the circumstances, and to the continued use of such forces in hostilities or in such situations.

(b) Congressional legislative power under necessary and proper clause

Under article I, section 8, of the Constitution, it is specifically provided that the Congress shall have the power to make all laws necessary and proper for carrying into execution, not only its own powers but also all other powers vested by the Constitution in the Government of the United States, or in any department or officer hereof.

(c) Presidential executive power as Commander-in-Chief; limitation

The constitutional powers of the President as Commander-in-Chief to introduce United States Armed Forces into hostilities, or into situations where imminent involvement in hostilities is clearly indicated by the circumstances, are exercised only pursuant to (1) a declaration of war, (2) specific statutory authorization, or (3) a national emergency created by attack upon the United States, its territories or possessions, or its armed forces.

(Pub. L. 93–148, §2, Nov. 7, 1973, 87 Stat. 555.)

EFFECTIVE DATE

Section 10 of Pub. L. 93–148 provided that: "This joint resolution [enacting this chapter] shall take effect on the date of its enactment [Nov. 7, 1973]."

SHORT TITLE

Section 1 of Pub. L. 93–148 provided that: "This joint resolution [enacting this chapter] may be cited as the 'War Powers Resolution'."

LIMITATION ON DEPLOYMENT OF ARMED FORCES IN HAITI DURING FISCAL YEAR 2000 AND CONGRESSIONAL NOTICE OF DEPLOYMENTS TO HAITI

Pub. L. 106–65, div. A, title XII, §1232, Oct. 5, 1999, 113 Stat. 788, provided that:

"(a) LIMITATION ON DEPLOYMENT.—No funds available to the Department of Defense during fiscal year 2000 may be expended after May 31, 2000, for the continuous deployment of United States Armed Forces in Haiti pursuant to the Department of Defense operation designated as Operation Uphold Democracy.

"(b) REPORT.—Whenever there is a deployment of United States Armed Forces to Haiti after May 31, 2000, the President shall, not later than 96 hours after such deployment begins, transmit to Congress a written report regarding the deployment. In any such report, the President shall specify (1) the purpose of the deployment, and (2) the date on which the deployment is expected to end."

INVOLVEMENT OF ARMED FORCES IN HAITI

Pub. L. 103–423, Oct. 25, 1994, 108 Stat. 4358, provided that:

"SECTION 1. SENSE OF CONGRESS REGARDING UNITED STATES ARMED FORCES OPERATIONS IN HAITI.

"It is the sense of Congress that—

"(a) the men and women of the United States Armed Forces in Haiti who are performing with professional excellence and dedicated patriotism are to be commended;

"(b) the President should have sought and welcomed Congressional approval before deploying United States Armed Forces to Haiti;

"(c) the departure from power of the de facto authorities in Haiti, and Haitian efforts to achieve national reconciliation, democracy and the rule of law are in the best interests of the Haitian people;

"(d) the President's lifting of the unilateral economic sanctions on Haiti, and his efforts to bring about the lifting of economic sanctions imposed by the United Nations are appropriate; and

"(e) Congress supports a prompt and orderly withdrawal of all United States Armed Forces from Haiti as soon as possible.

"SEC. 2. PRESIDENTIAL STATEMENT OF NATIONAL SECURITY OBJECTIVES.

"The President shall prepare and submit to the President pro tempore of the Senate and the Speaker of the House of Representatives (hereafter, 'Congress') not later than seven days after enactment of this resolution [Oct. 25, 1994] a statement of the national security objectives to be achieved by Operation Uphold Democracy, and a detailed description of United States policy, the military mission and the general rules of engagement under which operations of United States Armed Forces are conducted in and around Haiti, including the role of United States Armed Forces regarding Haitian on Haitian violence, and efforts to disarm Haitian military or police forces, or civilians. Changes or modifications to such objectives, policy, military mission, or general rules of engagement shall be submitted to Congress within forty-eight hours of approval.

"SEC. 3. REPORT ON THE SITUATION IN HAITI.

"Not later than November 1, 1994, and monthly thereafter until the cessation of Operation Uphold Democracy, the President shall submit a report to Congress on the situation in Haiti, including—

"(a) a listing of the units of the United States Armed Forces and of the police and military units of other nations participating in operations in and around Haiti;

"(b) the estimated duration of Operation Uphold Democracy and progress toward the withdrawal of all United States Armed Forces from Haiti consistent with the goal of section 1(e) of this resolution;

"(c) armed incidents or the use of force in or around Haiti involving United States Armed Forces or Coast Guard personnel in the time period covered by the report;

"(d) the estimated cumulative incremental cost of all United States activities subsequent to September 30, 1993, in and around Haiti, including but not limited to—

"(1) the cost of all deployments of United States Armed Forces and Coast Guard personnel, training, exercises, mobilization, and preparation activities, including the preparation of police and military units of the other nations of the multinational force involved in enforcement of sanctions, limits on migration, establishment and maintenance of migrant facilities at Guantanamo Bay and elsewhere, and all other activities relating to operations in and around Haiti; and

"(2) the costs of all other activities relating to United States policy toward Haiti, including humanitarian assistance, reconstruction, aid and other financial assistance, and all other costs to the United States Government;

"(e) a detailed accounting of the source of funds obligated or expended to meet the costs described in subparagraph (d), including—

"(1) in the case of funds expended from the Department of Defense budget, a breakdown by military service or defense agency, line item and program, and

"(2) in the case of funds expended from the budgets of departments and agencies other than the Department of Defense, by department or agency and program;

"(f) the Administration plan for financing the costs of the operations and the impact on readiness without supplemental funding;

"(g) a description of the situation in Haiti, including—

"(1) the security situation;

"(2) the progress made in transferring the functions of government to the democratically elected government of Haiti; and

"(3) progress toward holding free and fair parliamentary elections;

"(h) a description of issues relating to the United Nations Mission in Haiti (UNMIH), including—

"(1) the preparedness of the United Nations Mission in Haiti (UNMIH) to deploy to Haiti to assume its functions;

"(2) troop commitments by other nations to UNMIH;

"(3) the anticipated cost to the United States of participation in UNMIH, including payments to the United Nations and financial, material and other assistance to UNMIH;

"(4) proposed or actual participation of United States Armed Forces in UNMIH;

"(5) proposed command arrangements for UNMIH, including proposed or actual placement of United States Armed Forces under foreign command; and

"(6) the anticipated duration of UNMIH.

"SEC. 4. REPORT ON HUMAN RIGHTS.

"Not later than January 1, 1995, the Secretary of State shall report to Congress on the participation or involvement of any member of the de jure or de facto Haitian government in violations of internationally-recognized human rights from December 15, 1990, to December 15, 1994.

"SEC. 5. REPORT ON UNITED STATES AGREEMENTS.

"Not later than November 15, 1994, the Secretary of State shall provide a comprehensive report to Congress on all agreements the United States has entered into with other nations, including any assistance pledged or provided, in connection with United States efforts in Haiti. Such report shall also include information on any agreements or commitments relating to United Nations Security Council actions concerning Haiti since 1992.

"SEC. 6. TRANSITION TO UNITED NATIONS MISSION IN HAITI.

"Nothing in this resolution should be construed or interpreted to constitute Congressional approval or disapproval of the participation of United States Armed Forces in the United Nations Mission in Haiti."

INVOLVEMENT OF ARMED FORCES IN SOMALIA

Pub. L. 103–160, div. A, title XV, §1512, Nov. 30, 1993, 107 Stat. 1840, provided that:

"(a) SENSE OF CONGRESS REGARDING UNITED STATES POLICY TOWARD SOMALIA.—

"(1) Since United States Armed Forces made significant contributions under Operation Restore Hope towards the establishment of a secure environment for humanitarian relief operations and restoration of peace in the region to end the humanitarian disaster that had claimed more than 300,000 lives.

"(2) Since the mission of United States forces in support of the United Nations appears to be evolving from the establishment of 'a secure environment for humanitarian relief operations,' as set out in United Nations Security Council Resolution 794 of December 3, 1992, to one of internal security and nation building.

"(b) STATEMENT OF CONGRESSIONAL POLICY.—

"(1) CONSULTATION WITH THE CONGRESS.—The President should consult closely with the Congress regarding United States policy with respect to Somalia, including in particular the deployment of United States Armed Forces in that country, whether under United Nations or United States command.

"(2) PLANNING.—The United States shall facilitate the assumption of the functions of United States forces by the United Nations.

"(3) REPORTING REQUIREMENT.—

"(A) The President shall ensure that the goals and objectives supporting deployment of United States forces to Somalia and a description of the mission, command arrangements, size, functions, location, and anticipated duration in Somalia of those forces are clearly articulated and provided in a detailed report to the Congress by October 15, 1993.

"(B) Such report shall include the status of planning to transfer the function contained in paragraph (2).

"(4) CONGRESSIONAL APPROVAL.—Upon reporting under the requirements of paragraph (3) Congress believes the President should by November 15, 1993, seek and receive congressional authorization in order for the deployment of United States forces to Somalia to continue."

DURATION OF AUTHORIZATION FOR UNITED STATES PARTICIPATION IN MULTINATIONAL FORCE IN SOMALIA

Pub. L. 103–139, title VIII, §8151, Nov. 11, 1993, 107 Stat. 1475, provided that:

"(a) The Congress finds that—

"(1) the United States entered into Operation Restore Hope in December of 1992 for the purpose of relieving mass starvation in Somalia;

"(2) the original mission in Somalia, to secure the environment for humanitarian relief, had the unanimous support of the Senate, expressed in Senate Joint Resolution 45, passed on February 4, 1993, and was endorsed by the House when it amended S.J. Res. 45 on May 25, 1993;

"(3) Operation Restore Hope was being successfully accomplished by United States forces, working with forces of other nations, when it was replaced by the UNOSOM II mission, assumed by the United Nations on May 4, 1993, pursuant to United Nations Resolution 814 of March 26, 1993;

"(4) neither the expanded United Nations mission of national reconciliation, nor the broad mission of disarming the clans, nor any other mission not essential to the performance of the humanitarian mission has been endorsed or approved by the Senate;

"(5) the expanded mission of the United Nations was, subsequent to an attack upon United Nations forces, diverted into a mission aimed primarily at capturing certain persons, pursuant to United Nations Security Council Resolution 837, of June 6, 1993;

"(6) the actions of hostile elements in Mogadishu, and the United Nations mission to subdue those elements, have resulted in open conflict in the city of Mogadishu and the deaths of 29 Americans, at least 159 wounded, and the capture of American personnel; and

"(7) during fiscal years 1992 and 1993, the United States incurred expenses in excess of $1,100,000,000 to support operations in Somalia.

"(b) The Congress approves the use of United States Armed Forces in Somalia for the following purposes:

"(1) The protection of United States personnel and bases; and

"(2) The provision of assistance in securing open lines of communication for the free flow of supplies and relief operations through the provision of—

"(A) United States military logistical support services to United Nations forces; and

"(B) United States combat forces in a security role and as an interim force protection supplement to United Nations units: *Provided*, That funds appropriated, or otherwise made available, in this or any other Act to the Department of Defense may be obligated for expenses incurred only through March 31, 1994, for the operations of United States Armed Forces in Somalia: *Provided further*, That such date may be extended if so requested by the President and authorized by the Congress: *Provided further*, That funds may be obligated beyond March 31, 1994 to support a limited number of United States military personnel sufficient only to protect American diplomatic facilities and American citizens, and noncombat personnel to advise the United Nations commander in Somalia: *Provided further*, That United States combat forces in Somalia shall be under the command and control of United States commanders under the ultimate direction of the President of the United States: *Provided further*, That the President should intensify efforts to have United Nations member countries immediately deploy additional troops to Somalia to fulfill previous force commitments made to the United Nations and to deploy additional forces to assume the security missions of United States Armed Forces: *Provided further*, That—

"(i) captured United States personnel in Somalia should be treated humanely and fairly; and

"(ii) the United States and the United Nations should make all appropriate efforts to ensure the immediate and safe return of any future captured United States personnel: *Provided further*, That the President should ensure that, at all times, United States military personnel in Somalia have the capacity to defend themselves, and American citizens: *Provided further*, That the United States Armed Forces should remain deployed in or around Somalia until such time as all American service personnel missing in action in Somalia are accounted for, and all American service personnel held prisoner in Somalia are released: *Provided further*, That nothing herein shall be deemed to restrict in any way the authority of the President under the Constitution to protect the lives of Americans."

AUTHORIZATION FOR USE OF MILITARY FORCE AGAINST IRAQ RESOLUTION

Pub. L. 102–1, Jan. 14, 1991, 105 Stat. 3, as amended by Pub. L. 106–113, div. B, §1000(a)(7) [div. A, title II, §207], Nov. 29, 1999, 113 Stat. 1536, 1501A–422, provided that:

"Whereas the Government of Iraq without provocation invaded and occupied the territory of Kuwait on August 2, 1990;

"Whereas both the House of Representatives (in H.J. Res. 658 of the 101st Congress) and the Senate (in S. Con. Res. 147 of the 101st Congress) have condemned Iraq's invasion of Kuwait and declared their support for international action to reverse Iraq's aggression;

"Whereas, Iraq's conventional, chemical, biological, and nuclear weapons and ballistic missile programs and its demonstrated willingness to use weapons of mass destruction pose a grave threat to world peace;

"Whereas the international community has demanded that Iraq withdraw unconditionally and immediately from Kuwait and that Kuwait's independence and legitimate government be restored;

"Whereas the United Nations Security Council repeatedly affirmed the inherent right of individual or collective self-defense in response to the armed attack by Iraq against Kuwait in accordance with Article 51 of the United Nations Charter;

"Whereas, in the absence of full compliance by Iraq with its resolutions, the United Nations Security Council in Resolution 678 has authorized member states of the United Nations to use all necessary means, after January 15, 1991, to uphold and implement all relevant Security Council resolutions and to restore international peace and security in the area; and

"Whereas Iraq has persisted in its illegal occupation of, and brutal aggression against Kuwait: Now, therefore, be it

"Resolved by the Senate and House of Representatives of the United States of America in Congress assembled,

"SECTION 1. SHORT TITLE.

"This joint resolution may be cited as the 'Authorization for Use of Military Force Against Iraq Resolution'.

"SEC. 2. AUTHORIZATION FOR USE OF UNITED STATES ARMED FORCES.

"(a) AUTHORIZATION.—The President is authorized, subject to subsection (b), to use United States Armed Forces pursuant to United Nations Security Council Resolution 678 (1990) in order to achieve implementation of Security Council Resolutions 660, 661, 662, 664, 665, 666, 667, 669, 670, 674, and 677.

"(b) REQUIREMENT FOR DETERMINATION THAT USE OF MILITARY FORCE IS NECESSARY.—Before exercising the authority granted in subsection (a), the President shall make available to the Speaker of the House of Representatives and the President pro tempore of the Senate his determination that—

"(1) the United States has used all appropriate diplomatic and other peaceful means to obtain compliance by Iraq with the United Nations Security Council resolutions cited in subsection (a); and

"(2) that those efforts have not been and would not be successful in obtaining such compliance.

"(c) WAR POWERS RESOLUTION REQUIREMENTS.—

"(1) SPECIFIC STATUTORY AUTHORIZATION.—Consistent with section 8(a)(1) of the War Powers Resolution [50 U.S.C. 1547(a)(1)], the Congress declares that this section is intended to constitute specific statutory authorization within the meaning of section 5(b) of the War Powers Resolution [50 U.S.C. 1544(b)].

"(2) APPLICABILITY OF OTHER REQUIREMENTS.—Nothing in this resolution supersedes any requirement of the War Powers Resolution [50 U.S.C. 1541 et seq.].

"SEC. 3. REPORTS TO CONGRESS.

"At least once every 90 days, the President shall submit to the Congress a summary on the status of efforts to obtain compliance by Iraq with the resolutions adopted by the United Nations Security Council in response to Iraq's aggression."

INTRODUCTION OF UNITED STATES ARMED FORCES INTO CENTRAL AMERICA FOR COMBAT

Pub. L. 98–525, title III, §310, Oct. 19, 1984, 98 Stat. 2516, provided that:

"(a) The Congress makes the following findings:

"(1) The President has stated that there is no need to introduce United States Armed Forces into Central America for combat and that he has no intention of doing so.

"(2) The President of El Salvador has stated that there is no need for United States Armed Forces to conduct combat operations in El Salvador and that he has no intention of asking that they do so.

"(3) The possibility of the introduction of United States Armed Forces into Central America for combat raises very grave concern in the Congress and the American people.

"(b) It is the sense of Congress that—

"(1) United States Armed Forces should not be introduced into or over the countries of Central America for combat; and

"(2) if circumstances change from those present on the date of the enactment of this Act and the President believes that those changed circumstances require the introduction of United States Armed Forces into or over a country of Central America for combat, the President should consult with Congress before any decision to so introduce United States Armed Forces and any such introduction of United States Armed Forces must comply with the War Powers Resolution [this chapter]."

Pub. L. 98–473, title I, §101(h) [title VIII, §8101], Oct. 12, 1984, 98 Stat. 1904, 1942, provided that:

"(a) The Congress makes the following findings:

"(1) The President has stated that there is no need to introduce United States Armed Forces into Central America for combat and that he has no intention of doing so.

"(2) The President of El Salvador has stated that there is no need for United States Armed Forces to conduct combat operations in El Salvador and that he has no intention of asking that they do so.

"(3) The possibility of the introduction of United States Armed Forces into Central America for combat raises very grave concern in the Congress and the American people.

"(b) It is the sense of Congress that—

"(1) United States Armed Forces should not be introduced into or over the countries of Central America for combat; and

"(2) if circumstances change from those present on the date of the enactment of this Act [Oct. 12, 1984] and the President believes that those changed circumstances require the introduction of United States Armed Forces into or over a country of Central America for combat, the President should consult with Congress before any decision to so introduce United States Armed Forces and any such introduction of United States Armed Forces must comply with the War Powers Resolution [this chapter]."

MULTINATIONAL FORCE IN LEBANON RESOLUTION

Pub. L. 98–119, Oct. 12, 1983, 97 Stat. 805, provided that:

"SHORT TITLE

"SECTION 1. This joint resolution may be cited as the 'Multinational Force in Lebanon Resolution'.

"FINDINGS AND PURPOSE

"SEC. 2. (a) The Congress finds that—

"(1) the removal of all foreign forces from Lebanon is an essential United States foreign policy objective in the Middle East;

"(2) in order to restore full control by the Government of Lebanon over its own territory, the United States is currently participating in the multinational peacekeeping force (hereafter in this resolution referred to as the 'Multinational Force in Lebanon') which was established in accordance with the exchange of letters between the Governments of the United States and Lebanon dated September 25, 1982;

"(3) the Multinational Force in Lebanon better enables the Government of Lebanon to establish its unity, independence, and territorial integrity;

"(4) progress toward national political reconciliation in Lebanon is necessary; and

"(5) United States Armed Forces participating in the Multinational Force in Lebanon are now in hostilities requiring authorization of their continued presence under the War Powers Resolution [50 U.S.C. 1541 et seq.].

"(b) The Congress determines that the requirements of section 4(a)(1) of the War Powers Resolution [50 U.S.C. 1543(a)(1)] became operative on August 29, 1983. Consistent with section 5(b) of the War Powers Resolution [50 U.S.C. 1544(b)], the purpose of this joint resolution is to authorize the continued participation of United States Armed Forces in the Multinational Force in Lebanon.

"(c) The Congress intends this joint resolution to constitute the necessary specific statutory authorization under the War Powers Resolution for continued participation by United States Armed Forces in the Multinational Force in Lebanon.

"AUTHORIZATION FOR CONTINUED PARTICIPATION OF UNITED STATES ARMED FORCES IN THE MULTINATIONAL FORCE IN LEBANON

"SEC. 3. The President is authorized, for purposes of section 5(b) of the War Powers Resolution [50 U.S.C. 1544(b)], to continue participation by United States Armed Forces in the Multinational Force in Lebanon, subject to the provisions of section 6 of this joint resolution. Such participation shall be limited to performance of the functions, and shall be subject to the limitations, specified in the agreement establishing the Multinational Force in Lebanon as set forth in the exchange of letters between the Governments of the United States and Lebanon dated September 25, 1982, except that this shall not preclude such protective measures as may be necessary to ensure the safety of the Multinational Force in Lebanon.

"REPORTS TO THE CONGRESS

"SEC. 4. As required by section 4(c) of the War Powers Resolution [50 U.S.C. 1543(c)], the President shall report periodically to the Congress with respect to the situation in Lebanon, but in no event shall he report less often than once every three months. In addition to providing the information required by that section on the status, scope, and duration of hostilities involving United States Armed Forces, such reports shall describe in detail—

"(1) the activities being performed by the Multinational Force in Lebanon;

"(2) the present composition of the Multinational Force in Lebanon, including a description of the responsibilities and deployment of the armed forces of each participating country;

"(3) the results of efforts to reduce and eventually eliminate the Multinational Force in Lebanon;

"(4) how continued United States participation in the Multinational Force in Lebanon is advancing United States foreign policy interests in the Middle East; and

"(5) what progress has occurred toward national political reconciliation among all Lebanese groups.

"STATEMENTS OF POLICY

"SEC. 5. (a) The Congress declares that the participation of the armed forces of other countries in the Multinational Force in Lebanon is essential to maintain the international character of the peacekeeping function in Lebanon.

"(b) The Congress believes that it should continue to be the policy of the United States to promote continuing discussions with Israel, Syria, and Lebanon with the objective of bringing about the withdrawal of all foreign troops from Lebanon and establishing an environment which will permit the Lebanese Armed Forces to carry out their responsibilities in the Beirut area.

"(c) It is the sense of the Congress that, not later than one year after the date of enactment of this joint resolution [Oct. 12, 1983] and at least once a year thereafter, the United States should discuss with the other members of the Security Council of the United Nations the establishment of a United Nations peacekeeping force to assume the responsibilities of the Multinational Force in Lebanon. An analysis of the implications of the response to such discussions for the continuation of the Multinational Force in Lebanon shall be included in the reports required under paragraph (3) of section 4 of this resolution.

"DURATION OF AUTHORIZATION FOR UNITED STATES PARTICIPATION IN THE MULTINATIONAL FORCE IN LEBANON

"SEC. 6. The participation of United States Armed Forces in the Multinational Force in Lebanon shall be authorized for purposes of the War Powers Resolution [50 U.S.C. 1541 et seq.] until the end of the eighteen-month period beginning on the date of enactment of this resolution [Oct. 12, 1983] unless the Congress extends such authorization, except that such authorization shall terminate sooner upon the occurrence of any one of the following:

"(1) the withdrawal of all foreign forces from Lebanon, unless the President determines and certifies to the Congress that continued United States Armed Forces participation in the Multinational Force in Lebanon is required after such withdrawal in order to accomplish the purposes specified in the September 25, 1982, exchange of letters providing for the establishment of the Multinational Force in Lebanon; or

"(2) the assumption by the United Nations or the Government of Lebanon of the responsibilities of the Multinational Force in Lebanon; or

"(3) the implementation of other effective security arrangements in the area; or

"(4) the withdrawal of all other countries from participation in the Multinational Force in Lebanon.

"INTERPRETATION OF THIS RESOLUTION

"SEC. 7. (a) Nothing in this joint resolution shall preclude the President from withdrawing United States Armed Forces participation in the Multinational Force in Lebanon if circumstances warrant, and nothing in this joint resolution shall preclude the Congress by joint resolution from directing such a withdrawal.

"(b) Nothing in this joint resolution modifies, limits, or supersedes any provision of the War Powers Resolution [50 U.S.C. 1541 et seq.] or the requirement of section 4(a) of the Lebanon Emergency Assistance Act of 1983, relating to congressional authorization for any substantial expansion in the number or role of United States Armed Forces in Lebanon.

"CONGRESSIONAL PRIORITY PROCEDURES FOR AMENDMENTS

"SEC. 8. (a) Any joint resolution or bill introduced to amend or repeal this Act shall be referred to the Committee on Foreign Affairs [now Committee on International Relations] of the House of Representatives or the Committee on Foreign Relations of the Senate, as the case may be. Such joint resolution or bill shall be considered by such committee within fifteen calendar days and may be reported out, together with its recommendations, unless such House shall otherwise determine pursuant to its rules.

"(b) Any joint resolution or bill so reported shall become the pending business of the House in question (in the case of the Senate the time for debate shall be equally divided between the proponents and the opponents) and shall be voted on within three calendar days thereafter, unless such House shall otherwise determine by the yeas and nays.

"(c) Such a joint resolution or bill passed by one House shall be referred to the committee of the other House named in subsection (a) and shall be reported out by such committee together with its recommendations within fifteen calendar days and shall thereupon become the pending business of such House and shall be voted upon within three calendar days, unless such House shall otherwise determine by the yeas and nays.

"(d) In the case of any disagreement between the two Houses of Congress with respect to a joint resolution or bill passed by both Houses, conferees shall be promptly appointed and the committee of conference shall make and file a report with respect to such joint resolution within six calendar days after the legislation is referred to the committee of conference. Notwithstanding any rule in either House concerning the printing of conference reports in the Record or concerning any delay in the consideration of such reports, such report shall be acted on by both Houses not later than six calendar days after the conference report is filed. In the event the conferees are unable to agree within forty-eight hours, they shall report back to their respective Houses in disagreement."

ADHERENCE TO WAR POWERS RESOLUTION

Pub. L. 96–342, title X, § 1008, Sept. 8, 1980, 94 Stat. 1122, provided that: "Whereas, the National Command Authority must have the capacity to carry out any military mission which is essential to the national security of the United States having in its hands in the Rapid Deployment Force an increased capability to extend the reach of our military power in an expedited manner; and whereas, without the significant safeguard of the War Powers Resolution (Public Law 93–148) [this chapter], United States foreign and defense policies could be subject to misinterpretation; it is therefore the sense of the Congress that the provisions of the War Powers Resolution be strictly adhered to and that the congressional consultation process specified by such Resolution be utilized strictly according to the terms of the War Powers Resolution."

§ 1542. Consultation; initial and regular consultations

The President in every possible instance shall consult with Congress before introducing United States Armed Forces into hostilities or into situations where imminent involvement in hostilities is clearly indicated by the circumstances, and after every such introduction shall consult regularly with the Congress until United States Armed Forces are no longer engaged in hostilities or have been removed from such situations.

(Pub. L. 93–148, § 3, Nov. 7, 1973, 87 Stat. 555.)

§ 1543. Reporting requirement

(a) Written report; time of submission; circumstances necessitating submission; information reported

In the absence of a declaration of war, in any case in which United States Armed Forces are introduced—

(1) into hostilities or into situations where imminent involvement in hostilities is clearly indicated by the circumstances;

(2) into the territory, airspace or waters of a foreign nation, while equipped for combat, except for deployments which relate solely to supply, replacement, repair, or training of such forces; or

(3) in numbers which substantially enlarge United States Armed Forces equipped for combat already located in a foreign nation;

the President shall submit within 48 hours to the Speaker of the House of Representatives and to the President pro tempore of the Senate a report, in writing, setting forth—

(A) the circumstances necessitating the introduction of United States Armed Forces;

(B) the constitutional and legislative authority under which such introduction took place; and

(C) the estimated scope and duration of the hostilities or involvement.

(b) Other information reported

The President shall provide such other information as the Congress may request in the fulfillment of its constitutional responsibilities with respect to committing the Nation to war and to the use of United States Armed Forces abroad.

(c) Periodic reports; semiannual requirement

Whenever United States Armed Forces are introduced into hostilities or into any situation described in subsection (a) of this section, the President shall, so long as such armed forces continue to be engaged in such hostilities or situation, report to the Congress periodically on the status of such hostilities or situation as well as on the scope and duration of such hostilities or situation, but in no event shall he report to the Congress less often than once every six months.

(Pub. L. 93–148, §4, Nov. 7, 1973, 87 Stat. 555.)

SECTION REFERRED TO IN OTHER SECTIONS

This section is referred to in section 1544 of this title.

§1544. Congressional action

(a) Transmittal of report and referral to Congressional committees; joint request for convening Congress

Each report submitted pursuant to section 1543(a)(1) of this title shall be transmitted to the Speaker of the House of Representatives and to the President pro tempore of the Senate on the same calendar day. Each report so transmitted shall be referred to the Committee on Foreign Affairs of the House of Representatives and to the Committee on Foreign Relations of the Senate for appropriate action. If, when the report is transmitted, the Congress has adjourned sine die or has adjourned for any period in excess of three calendar days, the Speaker of the House of Representatives and the President pro tempore of the Senate, if they deem it advisable (or if petitioned by at least 30 percent of the membership of their respective Houses) shall jointly request the President to convene Congress in order that it may consider the report and take appropriate action pursuant to this section.

(b) Termination of use of United States Armed Forces; exceptions; extension period

Within sixty calendar days after a report is submitted or is required to be submitted pursuant to section 1543(a)(1) of this title, whichever is earlier, the President shall terminate any use of United States Armed Forces with respect to which such report was submitted (or required to be submitted), unless the Congress (1) has declared war or has enacted a specific authorization for such use of United States Armed Forces, (2) has extended by law such sixty-day period, or (3) is physically unable to meet as a result of an armed attack upon the United States. Such sixty-day period shall be extended for not more than an additional thirty days if the President determines and certifies to the Congress in writing that unavoidable military necessity respecting the safety of United States Armed Forces requires the continued use of such armed forces in the course of bringing about a prompt removal of such forces.

(c) Concurrent resolution for removal by President of United States Armed Forces

Notwithstanding subsection (b) of this section, at any time that United States Armed Forces are engaged in hostilities outside the territory of the United States, its possessions and territories without a declaration of war or specific statutory authorization, such forces shall be removed by the President if the Congress so directs by concurrent resolution.

(Pub. L. 93–148, §5, Nov. 7, 1973, 87 Stat. 556.)

CHANGE OF NAME

Committee on Foreign Affairs of House of Representatives treated as referring to Committee on International Relations of House of Representatives by section 1(a) of Pub. L. 104–14, set out as a note preceding section 21 of Title 2, The Congress.

SECTION REFERRED TO IN OTHER SECTIONS

This section is referred to in sections 1545, 1546 of this title.

§1545. Congressional priority procedures for joint resolution or bill

(a) Time requirement; referral to Congressional committee; single report

Any joint resolution or bill introduced pursuant to section 1544(b) of this title at least thirty calendar days before the expiration of the sixty-day period specified in such section shall be referred to the Committee on Foreign Affairs of the House of Representatives or the Committee on Foreign Relations of the Senate, as the case may be, and such committee shall report one such joint resolution or bill, together with its recommendations, not later than twenty-four calendar days before the expiration of the sixty-day period specified in such section, unless such House shall otherwise determine by the yeas and nays.

(b) Pending business; vote

Any joint resolution or bill so reported shall become the pending business of the House in question (in the case of the Senate the time for debate shall be equally divided between the proponents and the opponents), and shall be voted on within three calendar days thereafter, unless such House shall otherwise determine by yeas and nays.

(c) Referral to other House committee

Such a joint resolution or bill passed by one House shall be referred to the committee of the other House named in subsection (a) of this section and shall be reported out not later than fourteen calendar days before the expiration of the sixty-day period specified in section 1544(b) of this title. The joint resolution or bill so reported shall become the pending business of the House in question and shall be voted on within three calendar days after it has been reported, unless such House shall otherwise determine by yeas and nays.

(d) Disagreement between Houses

In the case of any disagreement between the two Houses of Congress with respect to a joint resolution or bill passed by both Houses, conferees shall be promptly appointed and the committee of conference shall make and file a report with respect to such resolution or bill not later than four calendar days before the expiration of the sixty-day period specified in section 1544(b) of this title. In the event the conferees are unable to agree within 48 hours, they shall report back to their respective Houses in disagreement. Notwithstanding any rule in either House concerning the printing of conference reports in the Record or concerning any delay in the consideration of such reports, such report shall be acted on by both Houses not later than the expiration of such sixty-day period.

(Pub. L. 93–148, §6, Nov. 7, 1973, 87 Stat. 557.)

CHANGE OF NAME

Committee on Foreign Affairs of House of Representatives treated as referring to Committee on International Relations of House of Representatives by section 1(a) of Pub. L. 104–14, set out as a note preceding section 21 of Title 2, The Congress.

§1546. Congressional priority procedures for concurrent resolution

(a) Referral to Congressional committee; single report

Any concurrent resolution introduced pursuant to section 1544(c) of this title shall be referred to the Committee on Foreign Affairs of the House of Representatives or the Committee on Foreign Relations of the Senate, as the case may be, and one such concurrent resolution shall be reported out by such committee together with its recommendations within fifteen calendar days, unless such House shall otherwise determine by the yeas and nays.

(b) Pending business; vote

Any concurrent resolution so reported shall become the pending business of the House in question (in the case of the Senate the time for debate shall be equally divided between the proponents and the opponents) and shall be voted on within three calendar days thereafter, unless such House shall otherwise determine by yeas and nays.

(c) Referral to other House committee

Such a concurrent resolution passed by one House shall be referred to the committee of the other House named in subsection (a) of this section and shall be reported out by such committee together with its recommendations within fifteen calendar days and shall thereupon become the pending business of such House and shall be voted upon within three calendar days, unless such House shall otherwise determine by yeas and nays.

(d) Disagreement between Houses

In the case of any disagreement between the two Houses of Congress with respect to a concurrent resolution passed by both Houses, conferees shall be promptly appointed and the committee of conference shall make and file a report with respect to such concurrent resolution within six calendar days after the legislation is referred to the committee of conference. Notwithstanding any rule in either House concerning the printing of conference reports in the Record or concerning any delay in the consideration of such reports, such report shall be acted on by both Houses not later than six calendar days after the conference report is filed. In the event the conferees are unable to agree within 48 hours, they shall report back to their respective Houses in disagreement.

(Pub. L. 93–148, §7, Nov. 7, 1973, 87 Stat. 557.)

CHANGE OF NAME

Committee on Foreign Affairs of House of Representatives treated as referring to Committee on International Relations of House of Representatives by section 1(a) of Pub. L. 104–14, set out as a note preceding section 21 of Title 2, The Congress.

§1546a. Expedited procedures for certain joint resolutions and bills

Any joint resolution or bill introduced in either House which requires the removal of United States Armed Forces engaged in hostilities outside the territory of the United States, its possessions and territories, without a declaration of war or specific statutory authorization shall be considered in accordance with the procedures of section 601(b) of the International Security Assistance and Arms Export Control Act of 1976, except that any such resolution or bill shall be amendable. If such a joint resolution or bill should be vetoed by the President, the time for debate in consideration of the veto message on such measure shall be limited to twenty hours in the Senate and in the House shall be determined in accordance with the Rules of the House.

(Pub. L. 98–164, title X, §1013, Nov. 22, 1983, 97 Stat. 1062.)

REFERENCES IN TEXT

Section 601(b) of the International Security Assistance and Arms Export Control Act of 1976, referred to in text, is section 601(b) of Pub. L. 94–329, title VI, June 30, 1976, 90 Stat. 765, which was not classified to the Code.

CODIFICATION

Section was enacted as part of the Department of State Authorization Act, Fiscal Years 1984 and 1985, and not as part of the War Powers Resolution which comprises this chapter.

§1547. Interpretation of joint resolution

(a) Inferences from any law or treaty

Authority to introduce United States Armed Forces into hostilities or into situations wherein involvement in hostilities is clearly indicated by the circumstances shall not be inferred—

(1) from any provision of law (whether or not in effect before November 7, 1973), including any provision contained in any appropriation Act, unless such provision specifically authorizes the introduction of United States Armed Forces into hostilities or into such situations and states that it is intended to constitute specific statutory authorization within the meaning of this chapter; or

(2) from any treaty heretofore or hereafter ratified unless such treaty is implemented by

legislation specifically authorizing the introduction of United States Armed Forces into hostilities or into such situations and stating that it is intended to constitute specific statutory authorization within the meaning of this chapter.

(b) Joint headquarters operations of high-level military commands

Nothing in this chapter shall be construed to require any further specific statutory authorization to permit members of United States Armed Forces to participate jointly with members of the armed forces of one or more foreign countries in the headquarters operations of high-level military commands which were established prior to November 7, 1973, and pursuant to the United Nations Charter or any treaty ratified by the United States prior to such date.

(c) Introduction of United States Armed Forces

For purposes of this chapter, the term "introduction of United States Armed Forces" includes the assignment of members of such armed forces to command, coordinate, participate in the movement of, or accompany the regular or irregular military forces of any foreign country or government when such military forces are engaged, or there exists an imminent threat that such forces will become engaged, in hostilities.

(d) Constitutional authorities or existing treaties unaffected; construction against grant of Presidential authority respecting use of United States Armed Forces

Nothing in this chapter—

(1) is intended to alter the constitutional authority of the Congress or of the President, or the provisions of existing treaties; or

(2) shall be construed as granting any authority to the President with respect to the introduction of United States Armed Forces into hostilities or into situations wherein involvement in hostilities is clearly indicated by the circumstances which authority he would not have had in the absence of this chapter.

(Pub. L. 93–148, §8, Nov. 7, 1973, 87 Stat. 558.)

§1548. Separability

If any provision of this chapter or the application thereof to any person or circumstance is held invalid, the remainder of the chapter and the application of such provision to any other person or circumstance shall not be affected thereby.

(Pub. L. 93–148, §9, Nov. 7, 1973, 87 Stat. 559.)

CHAPTER 34—NATIONAL EMERGENCIES

CHAPTER REFERRED TO IN OTHER SECTIONS

This chapter is referred to in section 1706 of this title; title 10 sections 2350j, 2662, 2808; title 30 section 185; title 33 section 2293.

SUBCHAPTER I—TERMINATING EXISTING DECLARED EMERGENCIES

§1601. Termination of existing declared emergencies

(a) All powers and authorities possessed by the President, any other officer or employee of the Federal Government, or any executive agency, as defined in section 105 of title 5, as a result of the existence of any declaration of national emergency in effect on September 14, 1976, are terminated two years from September 14, 1976. Such termination shall not affect—

(1) any action taken or proceeding pending not finally concluded or determined on such date;

(2) any action or proceeding based on any act committed prior to such date; or

(3) any rights or duties that matured or penalties that were incurred prior to such date.

(b) For the purpose of this section, the words "any national emergency in effect" means a general declaration of emergency made by the President.

(Pub. L. 94–412, title I, §101, Sept. 14, 1976, 90 Stat. 1255.)

SHORT TITLE

Section 1 of Pub. L. 94–412 provided: "That this Act [enacting this chapter, amending section 1481 of Title 8,

Aliens and Nationality, and section 2667 of Title 10, Armed Forces, repealing section 249 of Title 12, Banks and Banking, section 831d of Title 16, Conservation, section 1383 of Title 18, Crimes and Criminal Procedure, section 211b of Title 42, The Public Health and Welfare, and section 1742 of the Appendix to this title, and enacting provisions set out below] may be cited as the 'National Emergencies Act'."

SAVINGS PROVISION

Section 501(h) of Pub. L. 94–412 provided that: "This section [amending section 1481 of Title 8, Aliens and Nationality and section 2667 of Title 10, Armed Forces, and repealing section 249 of Title 12, Banks and Banking, section 831d of Title 16, Conservation, section 1383 of Title 18, Crimes and Criminal Procedure, and section 211b of Title 42, The Public Health and Welfare] shall not affect—

"(1) any action taken or proceeding pending not finally concluded or determined at the time of repeal;

"(2) any action or proceeding based on any act committee prior to repeal; or

"(3) any rights or duties that matured or penalties that were incurred prior to repeal."

SECTION REFERRED TO IN OTHER SECTIONS

This section is referred to in section 1706 of this title.

SUBCHAPTER II—DECLARATIONS OF FUTURE NATIONAL EMERGENCIES

SUBCHAPTER REFERRED TO IN OTHER SECTIONS

This subchapter is referred to in section 1706 of this title; title 10 sections 123, 527, 12006; title 42 section 8374.

§ 1621. Declaration of national emergency by President; publication in Federal Register; effect on other laws; superseding legislation

(a) With respect to Acts of Congress authorizing the exercise, during the period of a national emergency, of any special or extraordinary power, the President is authorized to declare such national emergency. Such proclamation shall immediately be transmitted to the Congress and published in the Federal Register.

(b) Any provisions of law conferring powers and authorities to be exercised during a national emergency shall be effective and remain in effect (1) only when the President (in accordance with subsection (a) of this section), specifically declares a national emergency, and (2) only in accordance with this chapter. No law enacted after September 14, 1976, shall supersede this subchapter unless it does so in specific terms, referring to this subchapter, and declaring that the new law supersedes the provisions of this subchapter.

(Pub. L. 94–412, title II, § 201, Sept. 14, 1976, 90 Stat. 1255.)

§ 1622. National emergencies

(a) Termination methods

Any national emergency declared by the President in accordance with this subchapter shall terminate if—

(1) there is enacted into law a joint resolution terminating the emergency; or

(2) the President issues a proclamation terminating the emergency.

Any national emergency declared by the President shall be terminated on the date specified in any joint resolution referred to in clause (1) or on the date specified in a proclamation by the President terminating the emergency as provided in clause (2) of this subsection, whichever date is earlier, and any powers or authorities exercised by reason of said emergency shall cease to be exercised after such specified date, except that such termination shall not affect—

(A) any action taken or proceeding pending not finally concluded or determined on such date;

(B) any action or proceeding based on any act committed prior to such date; or

(C) any rights or duties that matured or penalties that were incurred prior to such date.

(b) Termination review of national emergencies by Congress

Not later than six months after a national emergency is declared, and not later than the end of each six-month period thereafter that such emergency continues, each House of Congress shall meet to consider a vote on a joint resolution to determine whether that emergency shall be terminated.

(c) Joint resolution; referral to Congressional committees; conference committee in event of disagreement; filing of report; termination procedure deemed part of rules of House and Senate

(1) A joint resolution to terminate a national emergency declared by the President shall be referred to the appropriate committee of the House of Representatives or the Senate, as the case may be. One such joint resolution shall be reported out by such committee together with its recommendations within fifteen calendar days after the day on which such resolution is referred to such committee, unless such House shall otherwise determine by the yeas and nays.

(2) Any joint resolution so reported shall become the pending business of the House in question (in the case of the Senate the time for debate shall be equally divided between the proponents and the opponents) and shall be voted on within three calendar days after the day on which such resolution is reported, unless such House shall otherwise determine by yeas and nays.

(3) Such a joint resolution passed by one House shall be referred to the appropriate committee of the other House and shall be reported out by such committee together with its recommendations within fifteen calendar days after the day on which such resolution is referred to such committee and shall thereupon become the pending business of such House and shall be voted upon within three calendar days after the day on which such resolution is reported, unless such House shall otherwise determine by yeas and nays.

(4) In the case of any disagreement between the two Houses of Congress with respect to a joint resolution passed by both Houses, conferees shall be promptly appointed and the committee of conference shall make and file a report with respect to such joint resolution within six calendar days after the day on which managers on the part of the Senate and the House have been appointed. Notwithstanding any rule in either House concerning the printing of con-

ference reports or concerning any delay in the consideration of such reports, such report shall be acted on by both Houses not later than six calendar days after the conference report is filed in the House in which such report is filed first. In the event the conferees are unable to agree within forty-eight hours, they shall report back to their respective Houses in disagreement.

(5) Paragraphs (1)–(4) of this subsection, subsection (b) of this section, and section 1651(b) of this title are enacted by Congress—

(A) as an exercise of the rulemaking power of the Senate and the House of Representatives, respectively, and as such they are deemed a part of the rules of each House, respectively, but applicable only with respect to the procedure to be followed in the House in the case of resolutions described by this subsection; and they supersede other rules only to the extent that they are inconsistent therewith; and

(B) with full recognition of the constitutional right of either House to change the rules (so far as relating to the procedure of that House) at any time, in the same manner, and to the same extent as in the case of any other rule of that House.

(d) Automatic termination of national emergency; continuation notice from President to Congress; publication in Federal Register

Any national emergency declared by the President in accordance with this subchapter, and not otherwise previously terminated, shall terminate on the anniversary of the declaration of that emergency if, within the ninety-day period prior to each anniversary date, the President does not publish in the Federal Register and transmit to the Congress a notice stating that such emergency is to continue in effect after such anniversary.

(Pub. L. 94–412, title II, §202, Sept. 14, 1976, 90 Stat. 1255; Pub. L. 99–93, title VIII, §801, Aug. 16, 1985, 99 Stat. 448.)

AMENDMENTS

1985—Subsecs. (a) to (c). Pub. L. 99–93 substituted "there is enacted into law a joint resolution terminating the emergency" for "Congress terminates the emergency by concurrent resolution" in par. (1) of subsec. (a), and substituted "joint resolution" for "concurrent resolution" wherever appearing in second sentence of subsec. (a), subsec. (b), and pars. (1) to (4) of subsec. (c).

SECTION REFERRED TO IN OTHER SECTIONS

This section is referred to in section 1706 of this title.

SUBCHAPTER III—EXERCISE OF EMERGENCY POWERS AND AUTHORITIES

§1631. Declaration of national emergency by Executive order; authority; publication in Federal Register; transmittal to Congress

When the President declares a national emergency, no powers or authorities made available by statute for use in the event of an emergency shall be exercised unless and until the President specifies the provisions of law under which he proposes that he, or other officers will act. Such specification may be made either in the declaration of a national emergency, or by one or more contemporaneous or subsequent Executive orders published in the Federal Register and transmitted to the Congress.

(Pub. L. 94–412, title III, §301, Sept. 14, 1976, 90 Stat. 1257.)

RELEASE OF AMERICAN HOSTAGES IN IRAN

For provisions relating to the release of the American hostages in Iran, see Ex. Ord. Nos. 12276 to 12285, Jan. 19, 1981, 46 F.R. 7913 to 7932, set out under section 1701 of this title.

SUBCHAPTER IV—ACCOUNTABILITY AND REPORTING REQUIREMENTS OF PRESIDENT

SUBCHAPTER REFERRED TO IN OTHER SECTIONS

This subchapter is referred to in section 1703 of this title.

§1641. Accountability and reporting requirements of President

(a) Maintenance of file and index of Presidential orders, rules and regulations during national emergency

When the President declares a national emergency, or Congress declares war, the President shall be responsible for maintaining a file and index of all significant orders of the President, including Executive orders and proclamations, and each Executive agency shall maintain a file and index of all rules and regulations, issued during such emergency or war issued pursuant to such declarations.

(b) Presidential orders, rules and regulations; transmittal to Congress

All such significant orders of the President, including Executive orders, and such rules and regulations shall be transmitted to the Congress promptly under means to assure confidentiality where appropriate.

(c) Expenditures during national emergency; Presidential reports to Congress

When the President declares a national emergency or Congress declares war, the President shall transmit to Congress, within ninety days after the end of each six-month period after such declaration, a report on the total expenditures incurred by the United States Government during such six-month period which are directly attributable to the exercise of powers and authorities conferred by such declaration. Not later than ninety days after the termination of each such emergency or war, the President shall transmit a final report on all such expenditures.

(Pub. L. 94–412, title IV, §401, Sept. 14, 1976, 90 Stat. 1257.)

SUBCHAPTER V—APPLICATION TO POWERS AND AUTHORITIES OF OTHER PROVISIONS OF LAW AND ACTIONS TAKEN THEREUNDER

§1651. Other laws, powers and authorities conferred thereby, and actions taken thereunder; Congressional studies

(a) The provisions of this chapter shall not apply to the following provisions of law, the powers and authorities conferred thereby, and actions taken thereunder:

(1) Repealed. Pub. L. 95–223, title I, § 101(d), Dec. 28, 1977, 91 Stat. 1625.

(2) Act of April 28, 1942 (40 U.S.C. 278b); [1]

(3) Act of June 30, 1949 (41 U.S.C. 252);

(4) Section 3727(a)–(e)(1) of title 31;

(5) Section 3737 of the Revised Statutes, as amended (41 U.S.C. 15);

(6) Public Law 85–804 (Act of Aug. 28, 1958, 72 Stat. 972; 50 U.S.C. 1431 et seq.);

(7) Section 2304(a)(1) [1] of title 10; [2]

(b) Each committee of the House of Representatives and the Senate having jurisdiction with respect to any provision of law referred to in subsection (a) of this section shall make a complete study and investigation concerning that provision of law and make a report, including any recommendations and proposed revisions such committee may have, to its respective House of Congress within two hundred and seventy days after September 14, 1976.

(Pub. L. 94–412, title V, § 502, Sept. 14, 1976, 90 Stat. 1258; Pub. L. 95–223, title I, § 101(d), Dec. 28, 1977, 91 Stat. 1625; Pub. L. 96–513, title V, § 507(b), Dec. 12, 1980, 94 Stat. 2919; Pub. L. 105–362, title IX, § 901(r)(2), Nov. 10, 1998, 112 Stat. 3291.)

References in Text

Act of April 28, 1942, referred to in subsec. (a)(2), is act Apr. 28, 1942, ch. 249, 56 Stat. 247, which was classified to section 278b of Title 40, Public Buildings, Property, and Works, and was omitted from the Code.

Act of June 30, 1949 (41 U.S.C. 252), referred to in subsec. (a)(3), is act June 30, 1949, ch. 288, 63 Stat. 377, as amended, known as the Federal Property and Administrative Services Act of 1949. For complete classification of this Act to the Code, see Short Title note set out under section 471 of Title 40 and Tables.

Section 2304(a)(1) of title 10, referred to in subsec. (a)(7), originally authorized purchases or contracts without formal advertising when necessary in the public interest during a national emergency declared by Congress or the President, and as amended generally by Pub. L. 98–369 now sets forth the competition requirements for procurement of property or services.

Codification

In subsec. (a)(4), "Section 3727(a)–(e)(1) of title 31" substituted for "Section 3477 of the Revised Statutes, as amended (31 U.S.C. 203)" on authority of Pub. L. 97–258, § 4(b), Sept. 13, 1982, 96 Stat. 1067, the first section of which enacted Title 31, Money and Finance.

Amendments

1998—Subsec. (a)(6). Pub. L. 105–362 substituted "1431 et seq." for "1431–1435".

1980—Subsec. (a)(8). Pub. L. 96–513 struck out par. (8) which made reference to sections 3313, 6386(c), and 8313 of title 10.

1977—Subsec. (a)(1). Pub. L. 95–223 struck out par. (1) which read as follows: "Section 5(b) of the Act of October 6, 1917, as amended (12 U.S.C. 95a; 50 U.S.C. App. 5(b));".

Effective Date of 1980 Amendment

Amendment by Pub. L. 96–513 effective Sept. 15, 1981, see section 701 of Pub. L. 96–513, set out as a note under section 101 of Title 10, Armed Forces.

Section Referred to in Other Sections

This section is referred to in section 1622 of this title.

[1] See References in Text note below.

[2] So in original. The semicolon probably should be a period.

CHAPTER 35—INTERNATIONAL EMERGENCY ECONOMIC POWERS

Chapter Referred to in Other Sections

This chapter is referred to in section 2332 of this title; sections 2170, 2405, 2410 of the Appendix to this title; title 12 sections 3409, 3413, 4407; title 19 sections 1675, 2581; title 21 section 1901; title 22 section 6004; title 26 section 911; title 30 section 185.

§ 1701. Unusual and extraordinary threat; declaration of national emergency; exercise of Presidential authorities

(a) Any authority granted to the President by section 1702 of this title may be exercised to deal with any unusual and extraordinary threat, which has its source in whole or substantial part outside the United States, to the national security, foreign policy, or economy of the United States, if the President declares a national emergency with respect to such threat.

(b) The authorities granted to the President by section 1702 of this title may only be exercised to deal with an unusual and extraordinary threat with respect to which a national emergency has been declared for purposes of this chapter and may not be exercised for any other purpose. Any exercise of such authorities to deal with any new threat shall be based on a new declaration of national emergency which must be with respect to such threat.

(Pub. L. 95–223, title II, § 202, Dec. 28, 1977, 91 Stat. 1626.)

Short Title

Section 201 of title II of Pub. L. 95–223 provided that: "This title [enacting this chapter] may be cited as the 'International Emergency Economic Powers Act'."

Separability

Section 208 of Pub. L. 95–223 provided that: "If any provision of this Act [enacting this chapter] is held invalid, the remainder of the Act shall not be affected thereby."

ASSISTANCE EFFORTS IN SUDAN

Pub. L. 106–570, title V, §501, Dec. 27, 2000, 114 Stat. 3050, provided that:

"(a) ADDITIONAL AUTHORITIES.—Notwithstanding any other provision of law, the President is authorized to undertake appropriate programs using Federal agencies, contractual arrangements, or direct support of indigenous groups, agencies, or organizations in areas outside of control of the Government of Sudan in an effort to provide emergency relief, promote economic self-sufficiency, build civil authority, provide education, enhance rule of law and the development of judicial and legal frameworks, support people-to-people reconciliation efforts, or implement any program in support of any viable peace agreement at the local, regional, or national level in Sudan.

"(b) EXCEPTION TO EXPORT PROHIBITIONS.—Notwithstanding any other provision of law, the prohibitions set forth with respect to Sudan in Executive Order No. 13067 of November 3, 1997 (62 Fed. Register 59989) [set out below] shall not apply to any export from an area in Sudan outside of control of the Government of Sudan, or to any necessary transaction directly related to that export, if the President determines that the export or related transaction, as the case may be, would directly benefit the economic development of that area and its people."

IRAN NONPROLIFERATION

Pub. L. 106–178, Mar. 14, 2000, 114 Stat. 38, provided that:

"SECTION 1. SHORT TITLE.

"This Act may be cited as the 'Iran Nonproliferation Act of 2000'.

"SEC. 2. REPORTS ON PROLIFERATION TO IRAN.

"(a) REPORTS.—The President shall, at the times specified in subsection (b), submit to the Committee on International Relations of the House of Representatives and the Committee on Foreign Relations of the Senate a report identifying every foreign person with respect to whom there is credible information indicating that that person, on or after January 1, 1999, transferred to Iran—

"(1) goods, services, or technology listed on—

"(A) the Nuclear Suppliers Group Guidelines for the Export of Nuclear Material, Equipment and Technology (published by the International Atomic Energy Agency as Information Circular INFCIRC/254/ Rev.3/ Part 1, and subsequent revisions) and Guidelines for Transfers of Nuclear-Related Dual-Use Equipment, Material, and Related Technology (published by the International Atomic Energy Agency as Information Circular INFCIRC/254/ Rev.3/ Part 2, and subsequent revisions);

"(B) the Missile Technology Control Regime Equipment and Technology Annex of June 11, 1996, and subsequent revisions;

"(C) the lists of items and substances relating to biological and chemical weapons the export of which is controlled by the Australia Group;

"(D) the Schedule One or Schedule Two list of toxic chemicals and precursors the export of which is controlled pursuant to the Convention on the Prohibition of the Development, Production, Stockpiling and Use of Chemical Weapons and on Their Destruction; or

"(E) the Wassenaar Arrangement list of Dual Use Goods and Technologies and Munitions list of July 12, 1996, and subsequent revisions; or

"(2) goods, services, or technology not listed on any list identified in paragraph (1) but which nevertheless would be, if they were United States goods, services, or technology, prohibited for export to Iran because of their potential to make a material contribution to the development of nuclear, biological, or chemical weapons, or of ballistic or cruise missile systems.

"(b) TIMING OF REPORTS.—The reports under subsection (a) shall be submitted not later than 90 days after the date of the enactment of this Act [Mar. 14, 2000], not later than 6 months after such date of enactment, and not later than the end of each 6-month period thereafter.

"(c) EXCEPTIONS.—Any foreign person who—

"(1) was identified in a previous report submitted under subsection (a) on account of a particular transfer; or

"(2) has engaged in a transfer on behalf of, or in concert with, the Government of the United States,

is not required to be identified on account of that same transfer in any report submitted thereafter under this section, except to the degree that new information has emerged indicating that the particular transfer may have continued, or been larger, more significant, or different in nature than previously reported under this section.

"(d) SUBMISSION IN CLASSIFIED FORM.—When the President considers it appropriate, reports submitted under subsection (a), or appropriate parts thereof, may be submitted in classified form.

"SEC. 3. APPLICATION OF MEASURES TO CERTAIN FOREIGN PERSONS.

"(a) APPLICATION OF MEASURES.—Subject to sections 4 and 5, the President is authorized to apply with respect to each foreign person identified in a report submitted pursuant to section 2(a), for such period of time as he may determine, any or all of the measures described in subsection (b).

"(b) DESCRIPTION OF MEASURES.—The measures referred to in subsection (a) are the following:

"(1) EXECUTIVE ORDER NO. 12938 PROHIBITIONS.—The measures set forth in subsections (b) and (c) of section 4 of Executive Order No. 12938.

"(2) ARMS EXPORT PROHIBITION.—Prohibition on United States Government sales to that foreign person of any item on the United States Munitions List as in effect on August 8, 1995, and termination of sales to that person of any defense articles, defense services, or design and construction services under the Arms Export Control Act [22 U.S.C. 2751 et seq.].

"(3) DUAL USE EXPORT PROHIBITION.—Denial of licenses and suspension of existing licenses for the transfer to that person of items the export of which is controlled under the Export Administration Act of 1979 [50 App. U.S.C. 2401 et seq.] or the Export Administration Regulations.

"(c) EFFECTIVE DATE OF MEASURES.—Measures applied pursuant to subsection (a) shall be effective with respect to a foreign person no later than—

"(1) 90 days after the report identifying the foreign person is submitted, if the report is submitted on or before the date required by section 2(b);

"(2) 90 days after the date required by section 2(b) for submitting the report, if the report identifying the foreign person is submitted within 60 days after that date; or

"(3) on the date that the report identifying the foreign person is submitted, if that report is submitted more than 60 days after the date required by section 2(b).

"(d) PUBLICATION IN FEDERAL REGISTER.—The application of measures to a foreign person pursuant to subsection (a) shall be announced by notice published in the Federal Register.

"SEC. 4. PROCEDURES IF MEASURES ARE NOT APPLIED.

"(a) REQUIREMENT TO NOTIFY CONGRESS.—Should the President not exercise the authority of section 3(a) to apply any or all of the measures described in section 3(b) with respect to a foreign person identified in a report submitted pursuant to section 2(a), he shall so notify the Committee on International Relations of the House of Representatives and the Committee on Foreign Relations of the Senate no later than the effective date under section 3(c) for measures with respect to that person.

"(b) WRITTEN JUSTIFICATION.—Any notification submitted by the President under subsection (a) shall include a written justification describing in detail the facts and circumstances relating specifically to the foreign person identified in a report submitted pursuant to section 2(a) that support the President's decision not to exercise the authority of section 3(a) with respect to that person.

"(c) SUBMISSION IN CLASSIFIED FORM.—When the President considers it appropriate, the notification of the President under subsection (a), and the written justification under subsection (b), or appropriate parts thereof, may be submitted in classified form.

"SEC. 5. DETERMINATION EXEMPTING FOREIGN PERSON FROM SECTIONS 3 AND 4.

"(a) IN GENERAL.—Sections 3 and 4 shall not apply to a foreign person 15 days after the President reports to the Committee on International Relations of the House of Representatives and the Committee on Foreign Relations of the Senate that the President has determined, on the basis of information provided by that person, or otherwise obtained by the President, that—

"(1) the person did not, on or after January 1, 1999, knowingly transfer to Iran the goods, services, or technology the apparent transfer of which caused that person to be identified in a report submitted pursuant to section 2(a);

"(2) the goods, services, or technology the transfer of which caused that person to be identified in a report submitted pursuant to section 2(a) did not materially contribute to Iran's efforts to develop nuclear, biological, or chemical weapons, or ballistic or cruise missile systems;

"(3) the person is subject to the primary jurisdiction of a government that is an adherent to one or more relevant nonproliferation regimes, the person was identified in a report submitted pursuant to section 2(a) with respect to a transfer of goods, services, or technology described in section 2(a)(1), and such transfer was made consistent with the guidelines and parameters of all such relevant regimes of which such government is an adherent; or

"(4) the government with primary jurisdiction over the person has imposed meaningful penalties on that person on account of the transfer of the goods, services, or technology which caused that person to be identified in a report submitted pursuant to section 2(a).

"(b) OPPORTUNITY TO PROVIDE INFORMATION.—Congress urges the President—

"(1) in every appropriate case, to contact in a timely fashion each foreign person identified in each report submitted pursuant to section 2(a), or the government with primary jurisdiction over such person, in order to afford such person, or governments, the opportunity to provide explanatory, exculpatory, or other additional information with respect to the transfer that caused such person to be identified in a report submitted pursuant to section 2(a); and

"(2) to exercise the authority in subsection (a) in all cases where information obtained from a foreign person identified in a report submitted pursuant to section 2(a), or from the government with primary jurisdiction over such person, establishes that the exercise of such authority is warranted.

"(c) SUBMISSION IN CLASSIFIED FORM.—When the President considers it appropriate, the determination and report of the President under subsection (a), or appropriate parts thereof, may be submitted in classified form.

"SEC. 6. RESTRICTION ON EXTRAORDINARY PAYMENTS IN CONNECTION WITH THE INTERNATIONAL SPACE STATION.

"(a) RESTRICTION ON EXTRAORDINARY PAYMENTS IN CONNECTION WITH THE INTERNATIONAL SPACE STATION.—Notwithstanding any other provision of law, no agency of the United States Government may make extraordinary payments in connection with the International Space Station to the Russian Aviation and Space Agency, any organization or entity under the jurisdiction or control of the Russian Aviation and Space Agency, or any other organization, entity, or element of the Government of the Russian Federation, unless, during the fiscal year in which the extraordinary payments in connection with the International Space Station are to be made, the President has made the determination described in subsection (b), and reported such determination to the Committee on International Relations and the Committee on Science of the House of Representatives and the Committee on Foreign Relations and the Committee on Commerce, Science, and Transportation of the Senate.

"(b) DETERMINATION REGARDING RUSSIAN COOPERATION IN PREVENTING PROLIFERATION TO IRAN.—The determination referred to in subsection (a) is a determination by the President that—

"(1) it is the policy of the Government of the Russian Federation to oppose the proliferation to Iran of weapons of mass destruction and missile systems capable of delivering such weapons;

"(2) the Government of the Russian Federation (including the law enforcement, export promotion, export control, and intelligence agencies of such government) has demonstrated and continues to demonstrate a sustained commitment to seek out and prevent the transfer to Iran of goods, services, and technology that could make a material contribution to the development of nuclear, biological, or chemical weapons, or of ballistic or cruise missile systems; and

"(3) neither the Russian Aviation and Space Agency, nor any organization or entity under the jurisdiction or control of the Russian Aviation and Space Agency, has, during the 1-year period prior to the date of the determination pursuant to this subsection, made transfers to Iran reportable under section 2(a) of this Act (other than transfers with respect to which a determination pursuant to section 5 has been or will be made).

"(c) PRIOR NOTIFICATION.—Not less than 5 days before making a determination under subsection (b), the President shall notify the Committee on International Relations and the Committee on Science of the House of Representatives and the Committee on Foreign Relations and the Committee on Commerce, Science, and Transportation of the Senate of his intention to make such determination.

"(d) WRITTEN JUSTIFICATION.—A determination of the President under subsection (b) shall include a written justification describing in detail the facts and circumstances supporting the President's conclusion.

"(e) SUBMISSION IN CLASSIFIED FORM.—When the President considers it appropriate, a determination of the President under subsection (b), a prior notification under subsection (c), and a written justification under subsection (d), or appropriate parts thereof, may be submitted in classified form.

"(f) EXCEPTION FOR CREW SAFETY.—

"(1) EXCEPTION.—The National Aeronautics and Space Administration may make extraordinary payments that would otherwise be prohibited under this section to the Russian Aviation and Space Agency or any organization or entity under the jurisdiction or control of the Russian Aviation and Space Agency if the President has notified the Congress in writing that such payments are necessary to prevent the imminent loss of life by or grievous injury to individuals aboard the International Space Station.

"(2) REPORT.—Not later than 30 days after notifying Congress that the National Aeronautics and Space Administration will make extraordinary payments under paragraph (1), the President shall submit to Congress a report describing—

"(A) the extent to which the provisions of subsection (b) had been met as of the date of notification; and

"(B) the measures that the National Aeronautics and Space Administration is taking to ensure that—

"(i) the conditions posing a threat of imminent loss of life by or grievous injury to individuals aboard the International Space Station necessitating the extraordinary payments are not repeated; and

"(ii) it is no longer necessary to make extraordinary payments in order to prevent imminent loss of life by or grievous injury to individuals aboard the International Space Station.

"(g) SERVICE MODULE EXCEPTION.—

"(1) The National Aeronautics and Space Administration may make extraordinary payments that would otherwise be prohibited under this section to the Russian Aviation and Space Agency, any organization or entity under the jurisdiction or control of the Russian Aviation and Space Agency, or any subcontractor thereof for the construction, testing, preparation, delivery, launch, or maintenance of the Service Module, and for the purchase (at a total cost not to exceed $14,000,000) of the pressure dome for the Interim Control Module and the Androgynous Peripheral Docking Adapter and related hardware for the United States propulsion module, if—

"(A) the President has notified Congress at least 5 days before making such payments;

"(B) no report has been made under section 2 with respect to an activity of the entity to receive such payment, and the President has no credible information of any activity that would require such a report; and

"(C) the United States will receive goods or services of value to the United States commensurate with the value of the extraordinary payments made.

"(2) For purposes of this subsection, the term 'maintenance' means activities which cannot be performed by the National Aeronautics and Space Administration and which must be performed in order for the Service Module to provide environmental control, life support, and orbital maintenance functions which cannot be performed by an alternative means at the time of payment.

"(3) This subsection shall cease to be effective 60 days after a United States propulsion module is in place at the International Space Station.

"(h) EXCEPTION.—Notwithstanding subsections (a) and (b), no agency of the United States Government may make extraordinary payments in connection with the International Space Station to any foreign person subject to measures applied pursuant to—

"(1) section 3 of this Act; or

"(2) section 4 of Executive Order No. 12938 (November 14, 1994), as amended by Executive Order No. 13094 (July 28, 1998).

Such payments shall also not be made to any other entity if the agency of the United States Government anticipates that such payments will be passed on to such a foreign person.

"SEC. 7. DEFINITIONS.

"For purposes of this Act, the following terms have the following meanings:

"(1) EXTRAORDINARY PAYMENTS IN CONNECTION WITH THE INTERNATIONAL SPACE STATION.—The term 'extraordinary payments in connection with the International Space Station' means payments in cash or in kind made or to be made by the United States Government—

"(A) for work on the International Space Station which the Russian Government pledged at any time to provide at its expense; or

"(B) for work on the International Space Station, or for the purchase of goods or services relating to human space flight, that are not required to be made under the terms of a contract or other agreement that was in effect on January 1, 1999, as those terms were in effect on such date.

"(2) FOREIGN PERSON; PERSON.—The terms 'foreign person' and 'person' mean—

"(A) a natural person that is an alien;

"(B) a corporation, business association, partnership, society, trust, or any other nongovernmental entity, organization, or group, that is organized under the laws of a foreign country or has its principal place of business in a foreign country;

"(C) any foreign governmental entity operating as a business enterprise; and

"(D) any successor, subunit, or subsidiary of any entity described in subparagraph (B) or (C).

"(3) EXECUTIVE ORDER NO. 12938.—The term 'Executive Order No. 12938' means Executive Order No. 12938 [set out below] as in effect on January 1, 1999.

"(4) ADHERENT TO RELEVANT NONPROLIFERATION REGIME.—A government is an 'adherent' to a 'relevant nonproliferation regime' if that government—

"(A) is a member of the Nuclear Suppliers Group with respect to a transfer of goods, services, or technology described in section 2(a)(1)(A);

"(B) is a member of the Missile Technology Control Regime with respect to a transfer of goods, services, or technology described in section 2(a)(1)(B), or is a party to a binding international agreement with the United States that was in effect on January 1, 1999, to control the transfer of such goods, services, or technology in accordance with the criteria and standards set forth in the Missile Technology Control Regime;

"(C) is a member of the Australia Group with respect to a transfer of goods, services, or technology described in section 2(a)(1)(C);

"(D) is a party to the Convention on the Prohibition of the Development, Production, Stockpiling and Use of Chemical Weapons and on Their Destruction with respect to a transfer of goods, services, or technology described in section 2(a)(1)(D); or

"(E) is a member of the Wassenaar Arrangement with respect to a transfer of goods, services, or technology described in section 2(a)(1)(E).

"(5) ORGANIZATION OR ENTITY UNDER THE JURISDICTION OR CONTROL OF THE RUSSIAN AVIATION AND SPACE AGENCY.—

"(A) The term 'organization or entity under the jurisdiction or control of the Russian Aviation and Space Agency' means an organization or entity that—

"(i) was made part of the Russian Space Agency upon its establishment on February 25, 1992;

"(ii) was transferred to the Russian Space Agency by decree of the Russian Government on July 25, 1994, or May 12, 1998;

"(iii) was or is transferred to the Russian Aviation and Space Agency or Russian Space Agency by decree of the Russian Government at any other time before, on, or after the date of the enactment of this Act [Mar. 14, 2000]; or

"(iv) is a joint stock company in which the Russian Aviation and Space Agency or Russian Space Agency has at any time held controlling interest.

"(B) Any organization or entity described in subparagraph (A) shall be deemed to be under the jurisdiction or control of the Russian Aviation and Space Agency regardless of whether—

"(i) such organization or entity, after being part of or transferred to the Russian Aviation and Space Agency or Russian Space Agency, is removed from or transferred out of the Russian Aviation and Space Agency or Russian Space Agency; or

"(ii) the Russian Aviation and Space Agency or Russian Space Agency, after holding a controlling interest in such organization or entity, divests its controlling interest."

[Memorandum of President of the United States, Sept. 11, 2000, 65 F.R. 56209, delegated to the Secretary of State functions and authorities conferred on the President under Pub. L. 106–178, set out above, with the exception of section 6(f) and (g), from which were delegated to the Secretary of State only section 6(f)(2)(A) and (g)(1)(B), with the remaining functions and authorities under section 6(f) and (g) delegated to the Administrator of the National Aeronautics and Space Administration, and provided that authorities and functions delegated by the memorandum could be redelegated.]

APPLICATION OF AUTHORITIES UNDER THE INTERNATIONAL EMERGENCY ECONOMIC POWERS ACT TO COMMUNIST CHINESE MILITARY COMPANIES

Pub. L. 105–261, div. A, title XII, §1237, Oct. 17, 1998, 112 Stat. 2160, as amended by Pub. L. 106–398, §1 [[div. A], title XII, §1233], Oct. 30, 2000, 114 Stat. 1654, 1654A–330, provided that:

"(a) PRESIDENTIAL AUTHORITY.—

"(1) IN GENERAL.—The President may exercise IEEPA authorities (other than authorities relating to importation) without regard to section 202 of the International Emergency Economic Powers Act (50 U.S.C. 1701) in the case of any commercial activity in the United States by a person that is on the list published under subsection (b).

"(2) PENALTIES.—The penalties set forth in section 206 of the International Emergency Economic Powers Act (50 U.S.C. 1705) apply to violations of any license, order, or regulation issued under paragraph (1).

"(3) IEEPA AUTHORITIES.—For purposes of paragraph (1), the term 'IEEPA authorities' means the authorities set forth in section 203(a) of the International Emergency Economic Powers Act (50 U.S.C. 1702(a)).

"(b) DETERMINATION AND REPORTING OF COMMUNIST CHINESE MILITARY COMPANIES OPERATING IN UNITED STATES.—

"(1) INITIAL DETERMINATION AND REPORTING.—Not later than March 1, 2001, the Secretary of Defense shall make a determination of those persons operating directly or indirectly in the United States or any of its territories and possessions that are Communist Chinese military companies and shall submit a list of those persons in classified and unclassified form to the following:

"(A) The Committee on Armed Services of the House of Representatives.

"(B) The Committee on Armed Services of the Senate.

"(C) The Secretary of State.

"(D) The Secretary of the Treasury.

"(E) The Attorney General.

"(F) The Secretary of Commerce.

"(G) The Secretary of Energy.

"(H) The Director of Central Intelligence.

"(2) ANNUAL REVISIONS TO THE LIST.—The Secretary of Defense shall make additions or deletions to the list submitted under paragraph (1) on an annual basis based on the latest information available and shall submit the updated list not later than February 1, each year to the committees and officers specified in paragraph (1).

"(3) CONSULTATION.—The Secretary of Defense shall consult with the following officers in carrying out paragraphs (1) and (2):

"(A) The Attorney General.

"(B) The Director of Central Intelligence.

"(C) The Director of the Federal Bureau of Investigation.

"(4) COMMUNIST CHINESE MILITARY COMPANY.—For purposes of making the determination required by paragraph (1) and of carrying out paragraph (2), the term 'Communist Chinese military company' means—

"(A) any person identified in the Defense Intelligence Agency publication numbered VP–1920–271–90, dated September 1990, or PC–1921–57–95, dated October 1995, and any update of those publications for the purposes of this section; and

"(B) any other person that—

"(i) is owned or controlled by the People's Liberation Army; and

"(ii) is engaged in providing commercial services, manufacturing, producing, or exporting.

"(c) PEOPLE'S LIBERATION ARMY.—For purposes of this section, the term 'People's Liberation Army' means the land, naval, and air military services, the police, and the intelligence services of the Communist Government of the People's Republic of China, and any member of any such service or of such police."

IRAN AND LIBYA SANCTIONS

Pub. L. 104–172, Aug. 5, 1996, 110 Stat. 1541, provided that:

"SECTION 1. SHORT TITLE.

"This Act may be cited as the 'Iran and Libya Sanctions Act of 1996'.

"SEC. 2. FINDINGS.

"The Congress makes the following findings:

"(1) The efforts of the Government of Iran to acquire weapons of mass destruction and the means to deliver them and its support of acts of international terrorism endanger the national security and foreign policy interests of the United States and those countries with which the United States shares common strategic and foreign policy objectives.

"(2) The objective of preventing the proliferation of weapons of mass destruction and acts of international terrorism through existing multilateral and bilateral initiatives requires additional efforts to deny Iran the financial means to sustain its nuclear, chemical, biological, and missile weapons programs.

"(3) The Government of Iran uses its diplomatic facilities and quasi-governmental institutions outside of Iran to promote acts of international terrorism and assist its nuclear, chemical, biological, and missile weapons programs.

"(4) The failure of the Government of Libya to comply with Resolutions 731, 748, and 883 of the Security Council of the United Nations, its support of international terrorism, and its efforts to acquire weapons of mass destruction constitute a threat to international peace and security that endangers the national security and foreign policy interests of the United States and those countries with which it shares common strategic and foreign policy objectives.

"SEC. 3. DECLARATION OF POLICY.

"(a) POLICY WITH RESPECT TO IRAN.—The Congress declares that it is the policy of the United States to deny Iran the ability to support acts of international terrorism and to fund the development and acquisition of weapons of mass destruction and the means to deliver them by limiting the development of Iran's ability to explore for, extract, refine, or transport by pipeline petroleum resources of Iran.

"(b) POLICY WITH RESPECT TO LIBYA.—The Congress further declares that it is the policy of the United States to seek full compliance by Libya with its obligations under Resolutions 731, 748, and 883 of the Security Council of the United Nations, including ending all support for acts of international terrorism and efforts to develop or acquire weapons of mass destruction.

"SEC. 4. MULTILATERAL REGIME.

"(a) MULTILATERAL NEGOTIATIONS.—In order to further the objectives of section 3, the Congress urges the President to commence immediately diplomatic efforts, both in appropriate international fora such as the United Nations, and bilaterally with allies of the United States, to establish a multilateral sanctions regime against Iran, including provisions limiting the development of petroleum resources, that will inhibit Iran's efforts to carry out activities described in section 2.

"(b) REPORTS TO CONGRESS.—The President shall report to the appropriate congressional committees, not later than 1 year after the date of the enactment of this Act [Aug. 5, 1996], and periodically thereafter, on the extent that diplomatic efforts described in subsection (a) have been successful. Each report shall include—

"(1) the countries that have agreed to undertake measures to further the objectives of section 3 with respect to Iran, and a description of those measures; and

"(2) the countries that have not agreed to measures described in paragraph (1), and, with respect to those countries, other measures (in addition to that provided in subsection (d)) the President recommends that the United States take to further the objectives of section 3 with respect to Iran.

"(c) WAIVER.—The President may waive the application of section 5(a) with respect to nationals of a country if—

"(1) that country has agreed to undertake substantial measures, including economic sanctions, that will inhibit Iran's efforts to carry out activities described in section 2 and information required by subsection (b)(1) has been included in a report submitted under subsection (b); and

"(2) the President, at least 30 days before the waiver takes effect, notifies the appropriate congressional committees of his intention to exercise the waiver.

"(d) ENHANCED SANCTION.—

"(1) SANCTION.—With respect to nationals of countries except those with respect to which the President has exercised the waiver authority of subsection (c), at any time after the first report is required to be submitted under subsection (b), section 5(a) shall be applied by substituting '$20,000,000' for '$40,000,000' each place it appears, and by substituting '$5,000,000' for '$10,000,000'.

"(2) REPORT TO CONGRESS.—The President shall report to the appropriate congressional committees any country with respect to which paragraph (1) applies.

"(e) INTERIM REPORT ON MULTILATERAL SANCTIONS; MONITORING.—The President, not later than 90 days after the date of the enactment of this Act, shall report to the appropriate congressional committees on—

"(1) whether the member states of the European Union, the Republic of Korea, Australia, Israel, or Japan have legislative or administrative standards providing for the imposition of trade sanctions on persons or their affiliates doing business or having investments in Iran or Libya;

"(2) the extent and duration of each instance of the application of such sanctions; and

"(3) the disposition of any decision with respect to such sanctions by the World Trade Organization or its predecessor organization.

"SEC. 5. IMPOSITION OF SANCTIONS.

"(a) SANCTIONS WITH RESPECT TO IRAN.—Except as provided in subsection (f), the President shall impose 2 or more of the sanctions described in paragraphs (1) through (6) of section 6 if the President determines that a person has, with actual knowledge, on or after the date of the enactment of this Act [Aug. 5, 1996], made an investment of $40,000,000 or more (or any combination of investments of at least $10,000,000 each, which in the aggregate equals or exceeds $40,000,000 in any 12-month period), that directly and significantly contributed to the enhancement of Iran's ability to develop petroleum resources of Iran.

"(b) MANDATORY SANCTIONS WITH RESPECT TO LIBYA.—

"(1) VIOLATIONS OF PROHIBITED TRANSACTIONS.—Except as provided in subsection (f), the President shall impose 2 or more of the sanctions described in paragraphs (1) through (6) of section 6 if the President determines that a person has, with actual knowledge, on or after the date of the enactment of this Act, exported, transferred, or otherwise provided to Libya any goods, services, technology, or other items the provision of which is prohibited under paragraph 4(b) or 5 of Resolution 748 of the Security Council of the United Nations, adopted March 31, 1992, or under paragraph 5 or 6 of Resolution 883 of the Security Council of the United Nations, adopted November 11, 1993, if the provision of such items significantly and materially—

"(A) contributed to Libya's ability to acquire chemical, biological, or nuclear weapons or destabilizing numbers and types of advanced conventional weapons or enhanced Libya's military or paramilitary capabilities;

"(B) contributed to Libya's ability to develop its petroleum resources; or

"(C) contributed to Libya's ability to maintain its aviation capabilities.

"(2) INVESTMENTS THAT CONTRIBUTE TO THE DEVELOPMENT OF PETROLEUM RESOURCES.—Except as provided in subsection (f), the President shall impose 2 or more of the sanctions described in paragraphs (1) through (6) of section 6 if the President determines that a person has, with actual knowledge, on or after the date of the enactment of this Act [Aug. 5, 1996], made an investment of $40,000,000 or more (or any combination of investments of at least $10,000,000 each, which in the aggregate equals or exceeds $40,000,000 in any 12-month period), that directly and significantly contributed to the enhancement of Libya's ability to develop its petroleum resources.

"(c) PERSONS AGAINST WHICH THE SANCTIONS ARE TO BE IMPOSED.—The sanctions described in subsections (a) and (b) shall be imposed on—

"(1) any person the President determines has carried out the activities described in subsection (a) or (b); and

"(2) any person the President determines—

"(A) is a successor entity to the person referred to in paragraph (1);

"(B) is a parent or subsidiary of the person referred to in paragraph (1) if that parent or subsidiary, with actual knowledge, engaged in the activities referred to in paragraph (1); or

"(C) is an affiliate of the person referred to in paragraph (1) if that affiliate, with actual knowledge, engaged in the activities referred to in paragraph (1) and if that affiliate is controlled in fact by the person referred to in paragraph (1).

For purposes of this Act, any person or entity described in this subsection shall be referred to as a 'sanctioned person'.

"(d) PUBLICATION IN FEDERAL REGISTER.—The President shall cause to be published in the Federal Register a current list of persons and entities on whom sanctions have been imposed under this Act. The removal of persons or entities from, and the addition of persons and entities to, the list, shall also be so published.

"(e) PUBLICATION OF PROJECTS.—The President shall cause to be published in the Federal Register a list of all significant projects which have been publicly tendered in the oil and gas sector in Iran.

"(f) EXCEPTIONS.—The President shall not be required to apply or maintain the sanctions under subsection (a) or (b)—

"(1) in the case of procurement of defense articles or defense services—

"(A) under existing contracts or subcontracts, including the exercise of options for production quantities to satisfy requirements essential to the national security of the United States;

"(B) if the President determines in writing that the person to which the sanctions would otherwise be applied is a sole source supplier of the defense articles or services, that the defense articles or services are essential, and that alternative sources are not readily or reasonably available; or

"(C) if the President determines in writing that such articles or services are essential to the national security under defense coproduction agreements;

"(2) in the case of procurement, to eligible products, as defined in section 308(4) of the Trade Agreements Act of 1979 (19 U.S.C. 2518(4)), of any foreign country or instrumentality designated under section 301(b)(1) of that Act (19 U.S.C. 2511(b)(1));

"(3) to products, technology, or services provided under contracts entered into before the date on which the President publishes in the Federal Register the name of the person on whom the sanctions are to be imposed;

"(4) to—

"(A) spare parts which are essential to United States products or production;

"(B) component parts, but not finished products, essential to United States products or production; or

"(C) routine servicing and maintenance of products, to the extent that alternative sources are not readily or reasonably available;

"(6) to information and technology essential to United States products or production; or

"(7) to medicines, medical supplies, or other humanitarian items.

"SEC. 6. DESCRIPTION OF SANCTIONS.

"The sanctions to be imposed on a sanctioned person under section 5 are as follows:

"(1) EXPORT-IMPORT BANK ASSISTANCE FOR EXPORTS TO SANCTIONED PERSONS.—The President may direct the Export-Import Bank of the United States not to give approval to the issuance of any guarantee, insurance, extension of credit, or participation in the extension of credit in connection with the export of any goods or services to any sanctioned person.

"(2) EXPORT SANCTION.—The President may order the United States Government not to issue any specific license and not to grant any other specific permission or authority to export any goods or technology to a sanctioned person under—

"(i) the Export Administration Act of 1979 [50 App. 2401 et seq.];

"(ii) the Arms Export Control Act [22 U.S.C. 2751 et seq.];

"(iii) the Atomic Energy Act of 1954 [42 U.S.C. 2011 et seq.]; or

"(iv) any other statute that requires the prior review and approval of the United States Government as a condition for the export or reexport of goods or services.

"(3) LOANS FROM UNITED STATES FINANCIAL INSTITUTIONS.—The United States Government may prohibit any United States financial institution from making loans or providing credits to any sanctioned person totaling more than $10,000,000 in any 12-month period unless such person is engaged in activities to relieve human suffering and the loans or credits are provided for such activities.

"(4) PROHIBITIONS ON FINANCIAL INSTITUTIONS.—The following prohibitions may be imposed against a sanctioned person that is a financial institution:

"(A) PROHIBITION ON DESIGNATION AS PRIMARY DEALER.—Neither the Board of Governors of the Federal Reserve System nor the Federal Reserve Bank of New York may designate, or permit the continuation of any prior designation of, such financial institution as a primary dealer in United States Government debt instruments.

"(B) PROHIBITION ON SERVICE AS A REPOSITORY OF GOVERNMENT FUNDS.—Such financial institution may not serve as agent of the United States Government or serve as repository for United States Government funds.

The imposition of either sanction under subparagraph (A) or (B) shall be treated as 1 sanction for purposes of section 5, and the imposition of both such sanctions shall be treated as 2 sanctions for purposes of section 5.

"(5) PROCUREMENT SANCTION.—The United States Government may not procure, or enter into any contract for the procurement of, any goods or services from a sanctioned person.

"(6) ADDITIONAL SANCTIONS.—The President may impose sanctions, as appropriate, to restrict imports with respect to a sanctioned person, in accordance with the International Emergency Economic Powers Act (50 U.S.C. 1701 and following).

"SEC. 7. ADVISORY OPINIONS.

"The Secretary of State may, upon the request of any person, issue an advisory opinion to that person as to whether a proposed activity by that person would subject that person to sanctions under this Act. Any person who relies in good faith on such an advisory opinion which states that the proposed activity would not subject a person to such sanctions, and any person who thereafter engages in such activity, will not be made subject to such sanctions on account of such activity.

"SEC. 8. TERMINATION OF SANCTIONS.

"(a) IRAN.—The requirement under section 5(a) to impose sanctions shall no longer have force or effect with respect to Iran if the President determines and certifies to the appropriate congressional committees that Iran—

"(1) has ceased its efforts to design, develop, manufacture, or acquire—

"(A) a nuclear explosive device or related materials and technology;

"(B) chemical and biological weapons; and

"(C) ballistic missiles and ballistic missile launch technology; and

"(2) has been removed from the list of countries the governments of which have been determined, for purposes of section 6(j) of the Export Administration Act of 1979 [50 App. 2405(j)], to have repeatedly provided support for acts of international terrorism.

"(b) LIBYA.—The requirement under section 5(b) to impose sanctions shall no longer have force or effect with respect to Libya if the President determines and certifies to the appropriate congressional committees that Libya has fulfilled the requirements of United Nations Security Council Resolution 731, adopted January 21, 1992, United Nations Security Council Resolution 748, adopted March 31, 1992, and United Nations Security Council Resolution 883, adopted November 11, 1993.

"SEC. 9. DURATION OF SANCTIONS; PRESIDENTIAL WAIVER.

"(a) DELAY OF SANCTIONS.—

"(1) CONSULTATIONS.—If the President makes a determination described in section 5(a) or 5(b) with respect to a foreign person, the Congress urges the President to initiate consultations immediately with the government with primary jurisdiction over that foreign person with respect to the imposition of sanctions under this Act.

"(2) ACTIONS BY GOVERNMENT OF JURISDICTION.—In order to pursue consultations under paragraph (1) with the government concerned, the President may delay imposition of sanctions under this Act for up to 90 days. Following such consultations, the President shall immediately impose sanctions unless the President determines and certifies to the Congress that the government has taken specific and effective actions, including, as appropriate, the imposition of appropriate penalties, to terminate the involvement of the foreign person in the activities that resulted in the determination by the President under section 5(a) or 5(b) concerning such person.

"(3) ADDITIONAL DELAY IN IMPOSITION OF SANCTIONS.—The President may delay the imposition of sanctions for up to an additional 90 days if the President determines and certifies to the Congress that the government with primary jurisdiction over the person concerned is in the process of taking the actions described in paragraph (2).

"(4) REPORT TO CONGRESS.—Not later than 90 days after making a determination under section 5(a) or 5(b), the President shall submit to the appropriate congressional committees a report on the status of consultations with the appropriate foreign government under this subsection, and the basis for any determination under paragraph (3).

"(b) DURATION OF SANCTIONS.—A sanction imposed under section 5 shall remain in effect—

"(1) for a period of not less than 2 years from the date on which it is imposed; or

"(2) until such time as the President determines and certifies to the Congress that the person whose activities were the basis for imposing the sanction is no longer engaging in such activities and that the President has received reliable assurances that such person will not knowingly engage in such activities in the future, except that such sanction shall remain in effect for a period of at least 1 year.

"(c) PRESIDENTIAL WAIVER.—

"(1) AUTHORITY.—The President may waive the requirement in section 5 to impose a sanction or sanctions on a person described in section 5(c), and may waive the continued imposition of a sanction or sanctions under subsection (b) of this section, 30 days or more after the President determines and so reports to the appropriate congressional committees that it is important to the national interest of the United States to exercise such waiver authority.

"(2) CONTENTS OF REPORT.—Any report under paragraph (1) shall provide a specific and detailed rationale for the determination under paragraph (1), including—

"(A) a description of the conduct that resulted in the determination under section 5(a) or (b), as the case may be;

"(B) in the case of a foreign person, an explanation of the efforts to secure the cooperation of the government with primary jurisdiction over the sanctioned person to terminate or, as appropriate, penalize the activities that resulted in the determination under section 5(a) or (b), as the case may be;

"(C) an estimate as to the significance—

"(i) of the provision of the items described in section 5(a) to Iran's ability to develop its petroleum resources, or

"(ii) of the provision of the items described in section 5(b)(1) to the abilities of Libya described in subparagraph (A), (B), or (C) of section 5(b)(1), or of the investment described in section 5(b)(2) on Libya's ability to develop its petroleum resources,

as the case may be; and

"(D) a statement as to the response of the United States in the event that the person concerned engages in other activities that would be subject to section 5(a) or (b).

"(3) EFFECT OF REPORT ON WAIVER.—If the President makes a report under paragraph (1) with respect to a waiver of sanctions on a person described in section 5(c), sanctions need not be imposed under section 5(a) or (b) on that person during the 30-day period referred to in paragraph (1).

"SEC. 10. REPORTS REQUIRED.

"(a) REPORT ON CERTAIN INTERNATIONAL INITIATIVES.—Not later than 6 months after the date of the enactment of this Act [Aug. 5, 1996], and every 6 months thereafter, the President shall transmit a report to the appropriate congressional committees describing—

"(1) the efforts of the President to mount a multilateral campaign to persuade all countries to pressure Iran to cease its nuclear, chemical, biological, and missile weapons programs and its support of acts of international terrorism;

"(2) the efforts of the President to persuade other governments to ask Iran to reduce the presence of Iranian diplomats and representatives of other government and military or quasi-governmental institutions of Iran and to withdraw any such diplomats or representatives who participated in the takeover of the United States embassy in Tehran on November 4, 1979, or the subsequent holding of United States hostages for 444 days;

"(3) the extent to which the International Atomic Energy Agency has established regular inspections of all nuclear facilities in Iran, including those presently under construction; and

"(4) Iran's use of Iranian diplomats and representatives of other government and military or quasi-governmental institutions of Iran to promote acts of international terrorism or to develop or sustain Iran's nuclear, chemical, biological, and missile weapons programs.

"(b) OTHER REPORTS.—The President shall ensure the continued transmittal to the Congress of reports describing—

"(1) the nuclear and other military capabilities of Iran, as required by section 601(a) of the Nuclear Non-Proliferation Act of 1978 [22 U.S.C. 3281(a)] and section 1607 of the National Defense Authorization Act for Fiscal Year 1993 [Pub. L. 102–484 set out below]; and

"(2) the support provided by Iran for acts of international terrorism, as part of the Department of State's annual report on international terrorism.

"SEC. 11. DETERMINATIONS NOT REVIEWABLE.

"A determination to impose sanctions under this Act shall not be reviewable in any court.

"SEC. 12. EXCLUSION OF CERTAIN ACTIVITIES.

"Nothing in this Act shall apply to any activities subject to the reporting requirements of title V of the National Security Act of 1947 [50 U.S.C. 413 et seq.].

"SEC. 13. EFFECTIVE DATE; SUNSET.

"(a) EFFECTIVE DATE.—This Act shall take effect on the date of the enactment of this Act [Aug. 5, 1996].

"(b) SUNSET.—This Act shall cease to be effective on the date that is 5 years after the date of the enactment of this Act.

"SEC. 14. DEFINITIONS.

"As used in this Act:

"(1) ACT OF INTERNATIONAL TERRORISM.—The term 'act of international terrorism' means an act—

"(A) which is violent or dangerous to human life and that is a violation of the criminal laws of the United States or of any State or that would be a criminal violation if committed within the jurisdiction of the United States or any State; and

"(B) which appears to be intended—

"(i) to intimidate or coerce a civilian population;

"(ii) to influence the policy of a government by intimidation or coercion; or

"(iii) to affect the conduct of a government by assassination or kidnapping.

"(2) APPROPRIATE CONGRESSIONAL COMMITTEES.—The term 'appropriate congressional committees' means the Committee on Finance, the Committee on Banking, Housing, and Urban Affairs, and the Committee on Foreign Relations of the Senate and the Committee on Ways and Means, the Committee on Banking and Financial Services [now Committee on Financial Services], and the Committee on International Relations of the House of Representatives.

"(3) COMPONENT PART.—The term 'component part' has the meaning given that term in section 11A(e)(1) of the Export Administration Act of 1979 (50 U.S.C. App. 2410a(e)(1)).

"(4) DEVELOP AND DEVELOPMENT.—To 'develop', or the 'development' of, petroleum resources means the exploration for, or the extraction, refining, or transportation by pipeline of, petroleum resources.

"(5) FINANCIAL INSTITUTION.—The term 'financial institution' includes—

"(A) a depository institution (as defined in section 3(c)(1) of the Federal Deposit Insurance Act [12 U.S.C. 1813(c)(1)]), including a branch or agency of a foreign bank (as defined in section 1(b)(7) of the International Banking Act of 1978 [12 U.S.C. 3101(b)(7)]);

"(B) a credit union;

"(C) a securities firm, including a broker or dealer;

"(D) an insurance company, including an agency or underwriter; and

"(E) any other company that provides financial services.

"(6) FINISHED PRODUCT.—The term 'finished product' has the meaning given that term in section 11A(e)(2) of the Export Administration Act of 1979 (50 U.S.C. App. 2410a(e)(2)).

"(7) FOREIGN PERSON.—The term 'foreign person' means—

"(A) an individual who is not a United States person or an alien lawfully admitted for permanent residence into the United States; or

"(B) a corporation, partnership, or other nongovernmental entity which is not a United States person.

"(8) GOODS AND TECHNOLOGY.—The terms 'goods' and 'technology' have the meanings given those terms in section 16 of the Export Administration Act of 1979 (50 U.S.C. App. 2415).

"(9) INVESTMENT.—The term 'investment' means any of the following activities if such activity is undertaken pursuant to an agreement, or pursuant to the exercise of rights under such an agreement, that is entered into with the Government of Iran or a nongovenmental [sic] entity in Iran, or with the Government of Libya or a nongovernmental entity in Libya, on or after the date of the enactment of this Act [Aug. 5, 1996]:

"(A) The entry into a contract that includes responsibility for the development of petroleum resources located in Iran or Libya (as the case may be), or the entry into a contract providing for the general supervision and guarantee of another person's performance of such a contract.

"(B) The purchase of a share of ownership, including an equity interest, in that development.

"(C) The entry into a contract providing for the participation in royalties, earnings, or profits in that development, without regard to the form of the participation.

The term 'investment' does not include the entry into, performance, or financing of a contract to sell or purchase goods, services, or technology.

"(10) IRAN.—The term 'Iran' includes any agency or instrumentality of Iran.

"(11) IRANIAN DIPLOMATS AND REPRESENTATIVES OF OTHER GOVERNMENT AND MILITARY OR QUASI-GOVERNMENTAL INSTITUTIONS OF IRAN.—The term 'Iranian diplomats and representatives of other government and military or quasi-governmental institutions of Iran' includes employees, representatives, or affiliates of Iran's—

"(A) Foreign Ministry;

"(B) Ministry of Intelligence and Security;

"(C) Revolutionary Guard Corps;

"(D) Crusade for Reconstruction;

"(E) Qods (Jerusalem) Forces;

"(F) Interior Ministry;

"(G) Foundation for the Oppressed and Disabled;

"(H) Prophet's Foundation;

"(I) June 5th Foundation;

"(J) Martyr's Foundation;

"(K) Islamic Propagation Organization; and

"(L) Ministry of Islamic Guidance.

"(12) LIBYA.—The term 'Libya' includes any agency or instrumentality of Libya.

"(13) NUCLEAR EXPLOSIVE DEVICE.—The term 'nuclear explosive device' means any device, whether assembled or disassembled, that is designed to produce an instantaneous release of an amount of nuclear energy from special nuclear material (as defined in section 11(aa) of the Atomic Energy Act of 1954 [42 U.S.C. 2014(aa)]) that is greater than the amount of energy that would be released from the detonation of one pound of trinitrotoluene (TNT).

"(14) PERSON.—The term 'person' means—

"(A) a natural person;

"(B) a corporation, business association, partnership, society, trust, any other nongovernmental entity, organization, or group, and any governmental entity operating as a business enterprise; and

"(C) any successor to any entity described in subparagraph (B).

"(15) PETROLEUM RESOURCES.—The term 'petroleum resources' includes petroleum and natural gas resources.

"(16) UNITED STATES OR STATE.—The term 'United States' or 'State' means the several States, the District of Columbia, the Commonwealth of Puerto Rico, the Commonwealth of the Northern Mariana Islands, American Samoa, Guam, the United States Virgin Islands, and any other territory or possession of the United States.

"(17) UNITED STATES PERSON.—The term 'United States person' means—

"(A) a natural person who is a citizen of the United States or who owes permanent allegiance to the United States; and

"(B) a corporation or other legal entity which is organized under the laws of the United States, any State or territory thereof, or the District of Columbia, if natural persons described in subparagraph (A) own, directly or indirectly, more than 50 percent of the outstanding capital stock or other beneficial interest in such legal entity."

[Memorandum of President of the United States, Nov. 21, 1996, 61 F.R. 64249, delegated to the Secretary of State, in consultation with the Departments of the Treasury and Commerce and the United States Trade Representative, and with the Export-Import Bank and Federal Reserve Board and other interested agencies as appropriate functions vested in the President by sections 4(c), 5(a), (b), (c), (f), 6(1), (2), and 9(c) of Pub. L. 104–172, set out above, delegated to the Secretary of State functions vested in the President by sections 4(a), (b), (d), (e), 5(d), (e), 9(a), (b), and 10 of Pub. L. 104–172, provided that any reference to provisions of any Act related to the subject of the memorandum be deemed to include references to any subsequent provision of law that is the same or substantially the same as such provisions, and provided that only the functions vested in the President by sections 4(a), (b), (d), (e), 5(d), (e), and 10 of Pub. L. 104–172 and delegated by the memorandum could be redelegated.]

SANCTIONS AGAINST SERBIA AND MONTENEGRO

Pub. L. 106–113, div. B, §1000(a)(2) [title V, §599], Nov. 29, 1999, 113 Stat. 1535, 1501A–127, provided that:

"(a) CONTINUATION OF EXECUTIVE BRANCH SANCTIONS.—The sanctions listed in subsection (b) shall remain in effect for fiscal year 2000, unless the President submits to the Committees on Appropriations and Foreign Relations in the Senate and the Committees on Appropriations and International Relations of the House of Representatives a certification described in subsection (c).

"(b) APPLICABLE SANCTIONS.—

"(1) The Secretary of the Treasury shall instruct the United States executive directors of the international financial institutions to work in opposition to, and vote against, any extension by such institutions of any financial or technical assistance or grants of any kind to the government of Serbia.

"(2) The Secretary of State should instruct the United States Ambassador to the Organization for Security and Cooperation in Europe (OSCE) to block any consensus to allow the participation of Serbia in the OSCE or any organization affiliated with the OSCE.

"(3) The Secretary of State should instruct the United States Representative to the United Nations to vote against any resolution in the United Nations Security Council to admit Serbia to the United Nations or any organization affiliated with the United Nations, to veto any resolution to allow Serbia to assume the United Nations' membership of the former Socialist Federal Republic of Yugoslavia, and to take action to prevent Serbia from assuming the seat formerly occupied by the Socialist Federal Republic of Yugoslavia.

"(4) The Secretary of State should instruct the United States Permanent Representative on the Council of the North Atlantic Treaty Organization to oppose the extension of the Partnership for Peace program or any other organization affiliated with NATO to Serbia.

"(5) The Secretary of State should instruct the United States Representatives to the Southeast European Cooperative Initiative (SECI) to oppose and to work to prevent the extension of SECI membership to Serbia.

"(c) CERTIFICATION.—A certification described in this subsection is a certification that—

"(1) the representatives of the successor states to the Socialist Federal Republic of Yugoslavia have successfully negotiated the division of assets and liabilities and all other succession issues following the dissolution of the Socialist Federal Republic of Yugoslavia;

"(2) the Government of Serbia is fully complying with its obligations as a signatory to the General

Framework Agreement for Peace in Bosnia and Herzegovina;

"(3) the Government of Serbia is fully cooperating with and providing unrestricted access to the International Criminal Tribunal for the former Yugoslavia, including surrendering persons indicted for war crimes who are within the jurisdiction of the territory of Serbia, and with the investigations concerning the commission of war crimes and crimes against humanity in Kosova;

"(4) the Government of Serbia is implementing internal democratic reforms; and

"(5) Serbian federal governmental officials, and representatives of the ethnic Albanian community in Kosova have agreed on, signed, and begun implementation of a negotiated settlement on the future status of Kosova.

"(d) STATEMENT OF POLICY.—It is the sense of the Congress that the United States should not restore full diplomatic relations with Serbia until the President submits to the Committees on Appropriations and Foreign Relations in the Senate and the Committees on Appropriations and International Relations in the House of Representatives the certification described in subsection (c).

"(e) EXEMPTION OF MONTENEGRO AND KOSOVA.—The sanctions described in subsection (b) shall not apply to Montenegro or Kosova.

"(f) DEFINITION.—The term 'international financial institution' includes the International Monetary Fund, the International Bank for Reconstruction and Development, the International Development Association, the International Finance Corporation, the Multilateral Investment Guaranty Agency, and the European Bank for Reconstruction and Development.

"(g) WAIVER AUTHORITY.—The President may waive the application in whole or in part, of any sanction described in subsection (b) if the President certifies to the Congress that the President has determined that the waiver is necessary to meet emergency humanitarian needs."

Pub. L. 105–277, div. A, §101(d) [title V, §539], Oct. 21, 1998, 112 Stat. 2681–150, 2681–182, provided that:

"(a) RESTRICTIONS.—None of the funds in this or any other Act may be made available to modify or remove any sanction, prohibition or requirement with respect to Serbia-Montenegro unless the President first submits to the Congress a certification described in subsection (c).

"(b) INTERNATIONAL FINANCIAL INSTITUTIONS.—The Secretary of the Treasury shall instruct the United States executive directors of the international financial institutions to work in opposition to, and vote against, any extension by such institutions of any financial or technical assistance or grants of any kind to the government of Serbia-Montenegro, unless the President first submits to the Congress a certification described in subsection (c).

"(c) CERTIFICATION.—A certification described in this subsection is a certification that—

"(1) there is substantial improvement in the human rights situation in Kosova;

"(2) international human rights observers are allowed to return to Kosova;

"(3) Serbian, Serbian-Montenegrin federal government officials, and representatives of the ethnic Albanian community in Kosova have agreed on and begun implementation of a negotiated settlement on the future status of Kosova; and

"(4) the government of Serbia-Montenegro is fully complying with its obligations as a signatory to the General Framework Agreement for Peace in Bosnia-Herzegovina including fully cooperating with the International Criminal Tribunal for the Former Yugoslavia.

"(d) WAIVER AUTHORITY.—The President may waive the application, in whole or in part, of subsections (a) and (b) if he certifies in writing to the Congress that the waiver is necessary to meet emergency humanitarian needs or to advance negotiations toward a peaceful settlement of the conflict in Kosova that is acceptable to the parties.

"(e) EXEMPTION FOR MONTENEGRO.—This section shall not apply to Montenegro."

[For delegation of functions of President under section 101(d) [title V, §539] of div. A of Pub. L. 105–277, set out above, see Ex. Ord. No. 12163, Sept. 29, 1979, 44 F.R. 56673, as amended, set out as a note under section 2381 of Title 22, Foreign Relations and Intercourse.]

Similar provisions were contained in the following prior appropriation acts:

Pub. L. 104–208, div. A, title I, §101(c) [title V, §540], Sept. 30, 1996, 110 Stat. 3009–121, 3009–155.

Pub. L. 104–107, title V, §540A(a)–(c), Feb. 12, 1996, 110 Stat. 737.

Pub. L. 103–160, div. A, title XV, §1511, Nov. 30, 1993, 107 Stat. 1839, provided that:

"(a) CODIFICATION OF EXECUTIVE BRANCH SANCTIONS.—The sanctions imposed on Serbia and Montenegro, as in effect on the date of the enactment of this Act [Nov. 30, 1993], that were imposed by or pursuant to the following directives of the executive branch shall (except as provided under subsections (d) and (e)) remain in effect until changed by law:

"(1) Executive Order 12808 of May 30, 1992 [set out below], as continued in effect on May 25, 1993.

"(2) Executive Order 12810 of June 5, 1992 [set out below].

"(3) Executive Order 12831 of January 15, 1993 [set out below].

"(4) Executive Order 12846 of April 25, 1993 [set out below].

"(5) Department of State Public Notice 1427, effective July 11, 1991.

"(6) Proclamation 6389 of December 5, 1991 (56 Fed. Register 64467).

"(7) Department of Transportation Order 92–5–38 of May 20, 1992.

"(8) Federal Aviation Administration action of June 19, 1992 (14 C.F.R. Part 91).

"(b) PROHIBITION ON ASSISTANCE.—No funds appropriated or otherwise made available by law may be obligated or expended on behalf of the government of Serbia or the government of Montenegro.

"(c) INTERNATIONAL FINANCIAL INSTITUTIONS.—The Secretary of the Treasury shall instruct the United States executive director of each international financial institution to use the voice and vote of the United States to oppose any assistance from that institution to the government of Serbia or the government of Montenegro, except for basic human needs.

"(d) EXCEPTION.—Notwithstanding any other provision of law, the President is authorized and encouraged to exempt from sanctions imposed against Serbia and Montenegro that are described in subsection (a) those United States-supported programs, projects, or activities that involve reform of the electoral process, the development of democratic institutions or democratic political parties, or humanitarian assistance (including refugee care and human rights observation).

"(e) WAIVER AUTHORITY.—(1) The President may waive or modify the application, in whole or in part, of any sanction described in subsection (a), the prohibition in subsection (b), or the requirement in subsection (c).

"(2) Such a waiver or modification may only be effective upon certification by the President to Congress that the President has determined that the waiver or modification is necessary (A) to meet emergency humanitarian needs, or (B) to achieve a negotiated settlement of the conflict in Bosnia-Herzegovina that is acceptable to the parties."

PRESIDENTIAL CERTIFICATION TO SUSPEND SANCTIONS IMPOSED ON THE GOVERNMENT OF SERBIA AND THE GOVERNMENT OF MONTENEGRO

Determination of President of the United States, No. 01–7, Dec. 19, 2000, 66 F.R. 1013, provided:

Memorandum for the Secretary of Defense [and] the Secretary of the Treasury

Pursuant to the authority vested in me by the laws of the United States, including section 1511 of the National Defense Authorization Act for Fiscal Year 1994 (Public Law 103–160) [set out as a note above], I hereby certify to the Congress that I have determined that the waiver of the application of subsections 1511(b) and (c) of Public Law 103–160 is necessary to achieve a negotiated settlement of the conflict in Bosnia-Herzegovina that is acceptable to the parties, to the extent that such provisions apply to the furnishing of assistance to the Government of Serbia and to the support of assistance from international financial institutions to the Government of Serbia and the Government of Montenegro.

Therefore, I hereby waive the application of these provisions with respect to such assistance and support.

The Secretary of Defense is authorized and directed to transmit a copy of this determination to the Congress and arrange for its publication in the Federal Register.

WILLIAM J. CLINTON.

Determination of President of the United States, No. 99–14, Feb. 16, 1999, 64 F.R. 9263, provided:

Memorandum for the Secretary of Defense

Pursuant to the authority vested in me by the laws of the United States, including section 1511 of the National Defense Authorization Act for Fiscal Year 1994 (Public Law 103–160) [set out as a note above], I hereby certify to the Congress that I have determined that the waiver of the application of the prohibition in section 1511(b) of Public Law 103–160 is necessary to achieve a negotiated settlement of the conflict in Bosnia-Herzegovina that is acceptable to the parties, to the extent that such provision applies to the furnishing of assistance to the Republic of Montenegro.

Therefore, I hereby waive the application of this provision with respect to such assistance.

You are authorized and directed to transmit a copy of this determination to the Congress and arrange for its publication in the Federal Register.

WILLIAM J. CLINTON.

Determination of President of the United States, No. 97–26, May 30, 1997, 62 F.R. 32015, provided:

Memorandum for the Secretary of State

Pursuant to the authority vested in me by the laws of the United States, including section 1511 of the National Defense Authorization Act for Fiscal Year 1994 (Public Law 103–160) [set out as a note above] and section 540 of the Foreign Operations, Export Financing, and Related Programs Appropriations Act, 1997 (contained in Public Law 104–208 (the "Act")) [set out as a note above], I hereby certify to the Congress that I have determined that the waiver of the application of the prohibition in section 1511(b) of Public Law 103–160 and of the application of section 540(a) of the Act is necessary to achieve a negotiated settlement of the conflict in Bosnia and Herzegovina that is acceptable to the parties, to the extent that such provisions apply to the furnishing of assistance to facilitate destruction of military equipment.

Therefore, I hereby waive the application of these provisions with respect to such assistance.

You are authorized and directed to transmit a copy of this determination to the Congress and arrange for its publication in the Federal Register.

WILLIAM J. CLINTON.

Determination of the President of the United States, No. 96–7, Dec. 27, 1995, 61 F.R. 2887, provided:

Memorandum for the Secretary of State, the Secretary of the Treasury [and] the Secretary of Transportation

Pursuant to the authority vested in me by section 1511(e)(2) of the National Defense Authorization Act for Fiscal Year 1994 (Public Law 103–160) [set out above] (the "Act"), I hereby determine that the waiver or modification of the sanctions on Serbia and Montenegro that were imposed by or pursuant to the directives described in section 1511(a)(1–5) and (7–8) of the Act, in conformity with the provisions of United Nations Security Council Resolutions 1021 and 1022 of November 22, 1995, is necessary to achieve a negotiated settlement of the conflict in Bosnia-Herzegovina that is acceptable to the parties.

Therefore, I hereby direct the Secretary of the Treasury to take appropriate action to suspend the application of the sanctions imposed on Serbia and Montenegro pursuant to Executive Order No. 12808 of May 30, 1992 [set out below], Executive Order No. 12810 of June 5, 1992 [set out below], Executive Order No. 12831 of January 15, 1993 [set out below], and Executive Order No. 12846 of April 25, 1993 [set out below], effective upon the transmittal of this determination to the Congress. The property and interests in property previously blocked remain blocked until provision is made to address claims or encumbrances, including the claims of the other successor states of the former Yugoslavia.

I hereby direct the Secretary of Transportation to take appropriate action to suspend the application of the sanctions imposed pursuant to Department of Transportation Order 92–5–38 of May 20, 1992, Department of Transportation Order 92–6–27 of June 12, 1992, and Special Federal Aviation Regulation No. 66–2 of May 31, 1995 (14 C.F.R. Part 91, 60 Federal Register 28477), effective upon the transmittal of this determination to the Congress.

I hereby authorize the Secretary of State to take appropriate action to suspend the application of the sanctions imposed pursuant to Department of State Public Notice 1427 of July 11, 1991, at the appropriate time in conformity with the provisions of United Nations Security Council Resolution 1021 of November 22, 1995.

The national emergency declared in Executive Order No. 12808 [set out below] and expanded in Executive Order No. 12934 [set out below] shall continue in effect.

The Secretary of State is authorized and directed to publish this determination in the Federal Register.

WILLIAM J. CLINTON.

IRAN-IRAQ ARMS NON-PROLIFERATION

Pub. L. 102–484, div. A, title XVI, Oct. 23, 1992, 106 Stat. 2571, as amended by Pub. L. 104–106, div. A, title XIV, §1408(a)–(c), Feb. 10, 1996, 110 Stat. 494, provided that:

"SEC. 1601. SHORT TITLE.

"This title may be cited as the 'Iran-Iraq Arms Non-Proliferation Act of 1992'.

"SEC. 1602. UNITED STATES POLICY.

"(a) IN GENERAL.—It shall be the policy of the United States to oppose, and urgently to seek the agreement of other nations also to oppose, any transfer to Iran or Iraq of any goods or technology, including dual-use goods or technology, wherever that transfer could materially contribute to either country's acquiring chemical, biological, nuclear, or destabilizing numbers and types of advanced conventional weapons.

"(b) SANCTIONS.—(1) In the furtherance of this policy, the President shall apply sanctions and controls with respect to Iran, Iraq, and those nations and persons who assist them in acquiring weapons of mass destruction in accordance with the Foreign Assistance Act of 1961 [22 U.S.C. 2151 et seq.], the Nuclear Non-Proliferation Act of 1978 [22 U.S.C. 3201 et seq.], the Chemical and Biological Weapons Control and Warfare Elimination Act of 1991 [22 U.S.C. 5601 et seq.], chapter 7 of the Arms Export Control Act [22 U.S.C. 2797 et seq.], and other relevant statutes, regarding the non-proliferation of weapons of mass destruction and the means of their delivery.

"(2) The President should also urgently seek the agreement of other nations to adopt and institute, at the earliest practicable date, sanctions and controls comparable to those the United States is obligated to apply under this subsection.

"(c) PUBLIC IDENTIFICATION.—The Congress calls on the President to identify publicly (in the report required by section 1607) any country or person that transfers goods or technology to Iran or Iraq contrary to the policy set forth in subsection (a).

"SEC. 1603. APPLICATION TO IRAN OF CERTAIN IRAQ SANCTIONS.

"The sanctions against Iraq specified in paragraphs (1) through (4) of section 586G(a) of the Iraq Sanctions Act of 1990 (as contained in Public Law 101–513) [set out below], including denial of export licenses for United States persons and prohibitions on United States Government sales, shall be applied to the same extent and in the same manner with respect to Iran.

"SEC. 1604. SANCTIONS AGAINST CERTAIN PERSONS.

"(a) PROHIBITION.—If any person transfers or retransfers goods or technology so as to contribute knowingly and materially to the efforts by Iran or Iraq (or any agency or instrumentality of either such country) to acquire chemical, biological, or nuclear weapons or to acquire destabilizing numbers and types of advanced conventional weapons, then the sanctions described in subsection (b) shall be imposed.

"(b) MANDATORY SANCTIONS.—The sanctions to be imposed pursuant to subsection (a) are as follows:

"(1) PROCUREMENT SANCTION.—For a period of two years, the United States Government shall not procure, or enter into any contract for the procurement of, any goods or services from the sanctioned person.

"(2) EXPORT SANCTION.—For a period of two years, the United States Government shall not issue any license for any export by or to the sanctioned person.

"SEC. 1605. SANCTIONS AGAINST CERTAIN FOREIGN COUNTRIES.

"(a) PROHIBITION.—If the President determines that the government of any foreign country transfers or retransfers goods or technology so as to contribute knowingly and materially to the efforts by Iran or Iraq (or any agency or instrumentality of either such country) to acquire chemical, biological, or nuclear weapons or to acquire destabilizing numbers and types of advanced conventional weapons, then—

"(1) the sanctions described in subsection (b) shall be imposed on such country; and

"(2) in addition, the President may apply, in the discretion of the President, the sanction described in subsection (c).

"(b) MANDATORY SANCTIONS.—Except as provided in paragraph (2), the sanctions to be imposed pursuant to subsection (a)(1) are as follows:

"(1) SUSPENSION OF UNITED STATES ASSISTANCE.—The United States Government shall suspend, for a period of one year, United States assistance to the sanctioned country.

"(2) MULTILATERAL DEVELOPMENT BANK ASSISTANCE.—The Secretary of the Treasury shall instruct the United States Executive Director to each appropriate international financial institution to oppose, and vote against, for a period of one year, the extension by such institution of any loan or financial or technical assistance to the sanctioned country.

"(3) SUSPENSION OF CODEVELOPMENT OR COPRODUCTION AGREEMENTS.—The United States shall suspend, for a period of one year, compliance with its obligations under any memorandum of understanding with the sanctioned country for the codevelopment or coproduction of any item on the United States Munitions List (established under section 38 of the Arms Export Control Act [22 U.S.C. 2778]), including any obligation for implementation of the memorandum of understanding through the sale to the sanctioned country of technical data or assistance or the licensing for export to the sanctioned country of any component part.

"(4) SUSPENSION OF MILITARY AND DUAL-USE TECHNICAL EXCHANGE AGREEMENTS.—The United States shall suspend, for a period of one year, compliance with its obligations under any technical exchange agreement involving military and dual-use technology between the United States and the sanctioned country that does not directly contribute to the security of the United States, and no military or dual-use technology may be exported from the United States to the sanctioned country pursuant to that agreement during that period.

"(5) UNITED STATES MUNITIONS LIST.—No item on the United States Munitions List (established pursuant to section 38 of the Arms Export Control Act) may be exported to the sanctioned country for a period of one year.

"(c) DISCRETIONARY SANCTION.—The sanction referred to in subsection (a)(2) is as follows:

"(1) USE OF AUTHORITIES OF INTERNATIONAL EMERGENCY ECONOMIC POWERS ACT.—Except as provided in paragraph (2), the President may exercise, in accordance with the provisions of that Act [50 U.S.C. 1701 et seq.], the authorities of the International Emergency Economic Powers Act with respect to the sanctioned country.

"(2) EXCEPTION.—Paragraph (1) does not apply with respect to urgent humanitarian assistance.

"SEC. 1606. WAIVER.

"The President may waive the requirement to impose a sanction described in section 1603, in the case of Iran, or a sanction described in section 1604(b) or 1605(b), in the case of Iraq and Iran, 15 days after the President determines and so reports to the Committees on Armed Services and Foreign Relations of the Senate and the Committees on Armed Services and Foreign Affairs [now Committee on International Relations] of the House of Representatives that it is essential to the national interest of the United States to exercise such waiver authority. Any such report shall provide a specific and detailed rationale for such determination.

"SEC. 1607. REPORTING REQUIREMENT.

"(a) ANNUAL REPORT.—Beginning one year after the date of the enactment of this Act [Oct. 23, 1992], and every 12 months thereafter, the President shall submit to the Committees on Armed Services and Foreign Relations of the Senate and the Committees on Armed Services and Foreign Affairs [now Committee on International Relations] of the House of Representatives a report detailing—

"(1) all transfers or retransfers made by any person or foreign government during the preceding 12-month period which are subject to any sanction under this title; and

"(2) the actions the President intends to undertake or has undertaken pursuant to this title with respect to each such transfer.

"(b) REPORT ON INDIVIDUAL TRANSFERS.—Whenever the President determines that a person or foreign government has made a transfer which is subject to any sanction under this title, the President shall, within 30 days after such transfer, submit to the Committees on Armed Services and Foreign Relations of the Senate and the Committees on Armed Services and Foreign Affairs [now Committee on International Relations] of the House of Representatives a report—

"(1) identifying the person or government and providing the details of the transfer; and

"(2) describing the actions the President intends to undertake or has undertaken under the provisions of this title with respect to each such transfer.

"(c) FORM OF TRANSMITTAL.—Reports required by this section may be submitted in classified as well as in unclassified form.

"SEC. 1608. DEFINITIONS.

"For purposes of this title:

"(1) The term 'advanced conventional weapons' includes—

"(A) such long-range precision-guided munitions, fuel air explosives, cruise missiles, low observability aircraft, other radar evading aircraft, advanced military aircraft, military satellites, electromagnetic weapons, and laser weapons as the President determines destabilize the military balance or enhance offensive capabilities in destabilizing ways;

"(B) such advanced command, control, and communications systems, electronic warfare systems, or intelligence collection systems as the President determines destabilize the military balance or enhance offensive capabilities in destabilizing ways; and

"(C) such other items or systems as the President may, by regulation, determine necessary for purposes of this title.

"(2) The term 'cruise missile' means guided missiles that use aerodynamic lift to offset gravity and propulsion to counteract drag.

"(3) The term 'goods or technology' means—

"(A) any article, natural or manmade substance, material, supply, or manufactured product, including inspection and test equipment; and

"(B) any information and know-how (whether in tangible form, such as models, prototypes, drawings, sketches, diagrams, blueprints, or manuals, or in intangible form, such as training or technical services) that can be used to design, produce, manufacture, utilize, or reconstruct goods, including computer software and technical data.

"(4) The term 'person' means any United States or foreign individual, partnership, corporation, or other form of association, or any of their successor entities, parents, or subsidiaries.

"(5) The term 'sanctioned country' means a country against which sanctions are required to be imposed pursuant to section 1605.

"(6) The term 'sanctioned person' means a person that makes a transfer described in section 1604(a).

"(7) The term 'United States assistance' means—

"(A) any assistance under the Foreign Assistance Act of 1961 (22 U.S.C. 2151 et seq.), other than urgent humanitarian assistance or medicine;

"(B) sales and assistance under the Arms Export Control Act [22 U.S.C. 2751 et seq.];

"(C) financing by the Commodity Credit Corporation for export sales of agricultural commodities; and

"(D) financing under the Export-Import Bank Act [of 1945] [22 U.S.C. 635 et seq.]."

[Memorandum of President of the United States, Sept. 27, 1994, 59 F.R. 50685, delegated to Secretary of State, in consultation with heads of other departments and agencies, all functions vested in President under title XVI of Pub. L. 102–484, set out above, without limitation of authority of other officials to exercise powers heretofore or hereafter delegated to them to implement sanctions imposed or actions directed by the Secretary pursuant to this delegation of authority.]

PAYMENT OF CLAIMS BY UNITED STATES NATIONALS AGAINST IRAQ

Pub. L. 101–519, §131, Nov. 5, 1990, 104 Stat. 2249, which authorized President to vest title in a portion of property in which transactions were blocked pursuant to Executive Order 12722 in order to satisfy obligations owed to United States Government and United States nationals for which Iraq had suspended repayment, was repealed by Pub. L. 102–27, title IV, §402(a), Apr. 10, 1991, 105 Stat. 155, as amended by Pub. L. 102–136, §126, Oct. 25, 1991, 105 Stat. 643, effective Nov. 5, 1990.

IRAQ SANCTIONS

Pub. L. 101–513, title V, §§586–586J, Nov. 5, 1990, 104 Stat. 2047–2054, provided that:

"SEC. 586. SHORT TITLE.

"Sections 586 through 586J of this Act may be cited as the 'Iraq Sanctions Act of 1990'.

"SEC. 586A. DECLARATIONS REGARDING IRAQ'S INVASION OF KUWAIT.

"The Congress—

"(1) condemns Iraq's invasion of Kuwait on August 2, 1990;

"(2) supports the actions that have been taken by the President in response to that invasion;

"(3) calls for the immediate and unconditional withdrawal of Iraqi forces from Kuwait;

"(4) supports the efforts of the United Nations Security Council to end this violation of international law and threat to international peace;

"(5) supports the imposition and enforcement of multilateral sanctions against Iraq;

"(6) calls on United States allies and other countries to support fully the efforts of the United Nations Security Council, and to take other appropriate actions, to bring about an end to Iraq's occupation of Kuwait; and

"(7) condemns the brutal occupation of Kuwait by Iraq and its gross violations of internationally recognized human rights in Kuwait, including widespread arrests, torture, summary executions, and mass extrajudicial killings.

"SEC. 586B. CONSULTATIONS WITH CONGRESS.

"The President shall keep the Congress fully informed, and shall consult with the Congress, with respect to current and anticipated events regarding the international crisis caused by Iraq's invasion of Kuwait, including with respect to United States actions.

"SEC. 586C. TRADE EMBARGO AGAINST IRAQ.

"(a) CONTINUATION OF EMBARGO.—Except as otherwise provided in this section, the President shall continue to impose the trade embargo and other economic sanctions with respect to Iraq and Kuwait that the United States is imposing, in response to Iraq's invasion of Kuwait, pursuant to Executive Orders Numbered 12724 and 12725 [set out below] (August 9, 1990) and, to the extent they are still in effect, Executive Orders Numbered 12722 and 12723 [set out below] (August 2, 1990). Notwithstanding any other provision of law, no funds, credits, guarantees, or insurance appropriated or otherwise made available by this or any other Act for fiscal year 1991 or any fiscal year thereafter shall be used to support or administer any financial or commercial operation of any United States Government department, agency, or other entity, or of any person subject to the jurisdiction of the United States, for the benefit of the Government of Iraq, its agencies or instrumentalities, or any person working on behalf of the Government of Iraq, contrary to the trade embargo and other economic sanctions imposed in accordance with this section.

"(b) HUMANITARIAN ASSISTANCE.—To the extent that transactions involving foodstuffs or payments for foodstuffs are exempted 'in humanitarian circumstances' from the prohibitions established by the United States pursuant to United Nations Security Council Resolution 661 (1990), those exemptions shall be limited to foodstuffs that are to be provided consistent with United Nations Security Council Resolution 666 (1990) and other relevant Security Council resolutions.

"(c) NOTICE TO CONGRESS OF EXCEPTIONS TO AND TERMINATION OF SANCTIONS.—

"(1) NOTICE OF REGULATIONS.—Any regulations issued after the date of enactment of this Act [Nov. 5, 1990] with respect to the economic sanctions imposed with respect to Iraq and Kuwait by the United States under Executive Orders Numbered 12722 and 12723 (August 2, 1990) and Executive Orders Numbered 12724 and 12725 (August 9, 1990) shall be submitted to the Congress before those regulations take effect.

"(2) NOTICE OF TERMINATION OF SANCTIONS.—The President shall notify the Congress at least 15 days before the termination, in whole or in part, of any sanction imposed with respect to Iraq or Kuwait pursuant to those Executive orders.

"(d) RELATION TO OTHER LAWS.—

"(1) SANCTIONS LEGISLATION.—The sanctions that are described in subsection (a) are in addition to, and not in lieu of the sanctions provided for in section 586G of this Act or any other provision of law.

"(2) NATIONAL EMERGENCIES AND UNITED NATIONS LEGISLATION.—Nothing in this section supersedes any provision of the National Emergencies Act [50 U.S.C. 1601 et seq.] or any authority of the President under the International Emergency Economic Powers Act [50 U.S.C. 1701 et seq.] or section 5(a) of the United Nations Participation Act of 1945 [22 U.S.C. 287c(a)].

"SEC. 586D. COMPLIANCE WITH UNITED NATIONS SANCTIONS AGAINST IRAQ.

"(a) DENIAL OF ASSISTANCE.—None of the funds appropriated or otherwise made available pursuant to this Act [see Tables for classification] to carry out the Foreign Assistance Act of 1961 [22 U.S.C. 2151 et seq.] (including title IV of chapter 2 of part I [22 U.S.C. 2191 et seq.], relating to the Overseas Private Investment Corporation) or the Arms Export Control Act [22 U.S.C. 2751 et seq.] may be used to provide assistance to any country that is not in compliance with the United Nations Security Council sanctions against Iraq unless the President determines and so certifies to the Congress that—

"(1) such assistance is in the national interest of the United States;

"(2) such assistance will directly benefit the needy people in that country; or

"(3) the assistance to be provided will be humanitarian assistance for foreign nationals who have fled Iraq and Kuwait.

"(b) IMPORT SANCTIONS.—If the President considers that the taking of such action would promote the effectiveness of the economic sanctions of the United Nations and the United States imposed with respect to Iraq, and is consistent with the national interest, the President may prohibit, for such a period of time as he considers appropriate, the importation into the United States of any or all products of any foreign country that has not prohibited—

"(1) the importation of products of Iraq into its customs territory, and

"(2) the export of its products to Iraq.

"SEC. 586E. PENALTIES FOR VIOLATIONS OF EMBARGO.

"Notwithstanding section 206 of the International Emergency Economic Powers Act (50 U.S.C. 1705) and section 5(b) of the United Nations Participation Act of 1945 (22 U.S.C. 287c(b))—

"(1) a civil penalty of not to exceed $250,000 may be imposed on any person who, after the date of enactment of this Act [Nov. 5, 1990], violates or evades or attempts to violate or evade Executive Order Numbered 12722, 12723, 12724, or 12725 [set out below] or any license, order, or regulation issued under any such Executive order; and

"(2) whoever, after the date of enactment of this Act, willfully violates or evades or attempts to violate or evade Executive Order Numbered 12722, 12723, 12724, or 12725 or any license, order, or regulation issued under any such Executive order—

"(A) shall, upon conviction, be fined not more than $1,000,000, if a person other than a natural person; or

"(B) if a natural person, shall, upon conviction, be fined not more than $1,000,000, be imprisoned for not more than 12 years, or both.

Any officer, director, or agent of any corporation who knowingly participates in a violation, evasion, or attempt described in paragraph (2) may be punished by imposition of the fine or imprisonment (or both) specified in subparagraph (B) of that paragraph.

"SEC. 586F. DECLARATIONS REGARDING IRAQ'S LONG-STANDING VIOLATIONS OF INTERNATIONAL LAW.

"(a) IRAQ'S VIOLATIONS OF INTERNATIONAL LAW.—The Congress determines that—

"(1) the Government of Iraq has demonstrated repeated and blatant disregard for its obligations under international law by violating the Charter of the United Nations, the Protocol for the Prohibition of the Use in War of Asphyxiating, Poisonous or Other Gases, and of Bacteriological Methods of Warfare (done at Geneva, June 17, 1925), as well as other international treaties;

"(2) the Government of Iraq is a party to the International Covenant on Civil and Political Rights and the International Covenant on Economic, Social, and Cultural Rights and is obligated under the Covenants, as well as the Universal Declaration of Human Rights, to respect internationally recognized human rights;

"(3) the State Department's Country Reports on Human Rights Practices for 1989 again characterizes Iraq's human rights record as 'abysmal';

"(4) Amnesty International, Middle East Watch, and other independent human rights organizations have documented extensive, systematic, and continuing human rights abuses by the Government of Iraq, including summary executions, mass political killings, disappearances, widespread use of torture, arbitrary arrests and prolonged detention without trial of thousands of political opponents, forced relocation and deportation, denial of nearly all civil and political rights such as freedom of association, assembly, speech, and the press, and the imprisonment, torture, and execution of children;

"(5) since 1987, the Government of Iraq has intensified its severe repression of the Kurdish minority of Iraq, deliberately destroyed more than 3,000 villages and towns in the Kurdish regions, and forcibly expelled more than 500,000 people, thus effectively depopulating the rural areas of Iraqi Kurdistan;

"(6) Iraq has blatantly violated international law by initiating use of chemical weapons in the Iran-Iraq war;

"(7) Iraq has also violated international law by using chemical weapons against its own Kurdish citizens, resulting in tens of thousands of deaths and more than 65,000 refugees;

"(8) Iraq continues to expand its chemical weapons capability, and President Saddam Hussein has threatened to use chemical weapons against other nations;

"(9) persuasive evidence exists that Iraq is developing biological weapons in violation of international law;

"(10) there are strong indications that Iraq has taken steps to produce nuclear weapons and has attempted to smuggle from the United States, in violation of United States law, components for triggering devices used in nuclear warheads whose manufacture would contravene the Treaty on the Non-Proliferation of Nuclear Weapons, to which Iraq is a party; and

"(11) Iraqi President Saddam Hussein has threatened to use terrorism against other nations in violation of international law and has increased Iraq's support for the Palestine Liberation Organization and other Palestinian groups that have conducted terrorist acts.

"(b) HUMAN RIGHTS VIOLATIONS.—The Congress determines that the Government of Iraq is engaged in a consistent pattern of gross violations of internationally recognized human rights. All provisions of law that impose sanctions against a country whose government is engaged in a consistent pattern of gross violations of internationally recognized human rights shall be fully enforced against Iraq.

"(c) SUPPORT FOR INTERNATIONAL TERRORISM.—(1) The Congress determines that Iraq is a country which has repeatedly provided support for acts of international terrorism, a country which grants sanctuary from prosecution to individuals or groups which have committed an act of international terrorism, and a country which otherwise supports international terrorism. The provisions of law specified in paragraph (2) and all other provisions of law that impose sanctions against a country which has repeatedly provided support for acts of international terrorism, which grants sanctuary from prosecution to an individual or group which has committed an act of international terrorism, or which otherwise supports international terrorism shall be fully enforced against Iraq.

"(2) The provisions of law referred to in paragraph (1) are—

"(A) section 40 of the Arms Export Control Act [22 U.S.C. 2780];

"(B) section 620A of the Foreign Assistance Act of 1961 [22 U.S.C. 2371];

"(C) sections 555 and 556 of this Act [104 Stat. 2021, 2022] (and the corresponding sections of predecessor foreign operations appropriations Acts); and

"(D) section 555 of the International Security and Development Cooperation Act of 1985 [99 Stat. 227].

"(d) MULTILATERAL COOPERATION.—The Congress calls on the President to seek multilateral cooperation—

"(1) to deny dangerous technologies to Iraq;

"(2) to induce Iraq to respect internationally recognized human rights; and

"(3) to induce Iraq to allow appropriate international humanitarian and human rights organizations to have access to Iraq and Kuwait, including the areas in northern Iraq traditionally inhabited by Kurds.

"SEC. 586G. SANCTIONS AGAINST IRAQ.

"(a) IMPOSITION.—Except as provided in section 586H, the following sanctions shall apply with respect to Iraq:

"(1) FMS SALES.—The United States Government shall not enter into any sale with Iraq under the Arms Export Control Act [22 U.S.C. 2751 et seq.].

"(2) COMMERCIAL ARMS SALES.—Licenses shall not be issued for the export to Iraq of any item on the United States Munitions List.

"(3) EXPORTS OF CERTAIN GOODS AND TECHNOLOGY.—The authorities of section 6 of the Export Administration Act of 1979 (50 U.S.C. App. 2405) shall be used to prohibit the export to Iraq of any goods or technology listed pursuant to that section or section 5(c)(1) of that Act (50 U.S.C. App. 2404(c)(1)) on the control list provided for in section 4(b) of that Act (50 U.S.C. App. 2403(b)).

"(4) NUCLEAR EQUIPMENT, MATERIALS, AND TECHNOLOGY.—

"(A) NRC LICENSES.—The Nuclear Regulatory Commission shall not issue any license or other authorization under the Atomic Energy Act of 1954 (42 U.S.C. 2011 and following) for the export to Iraq of any source or special nuclear material, any production or utilization facility, any sensitive nuclear technology, any component, item, or substance determined to have significance for nuclear explosive purposes pursuant to section 109b. of the Atomic Energy Act of 1954 (42 U.S.C. 2139(b)), or any other material or technology requiring such a license or authorization.

"(B) DISTRIBUTION OF NUCLEAR MATERIALS.—The authority of the Atomic Energy Act of 1954 shall not be used to distribute any special nuclear material, source material, or byproduct material to Iraq.

"(C) DOE AUTHORIZATIONS.—The Secretary of Energy shall not provide a specific authorization under section 57b.(2) of the Atomic Energy Act of 1954 (42 U.S.C. 2077(b)(2)) for any activity that would constitute directly or indirectly engaging in Iraq in activities that require a specific authorization under that section.

"(5) ASSISTANCE FROM INTERNATIONAL FINANCIAL INSTITUTIONS.—The United States shall oppose any loan or financial or technical assistance to Iraq by international financial institutions in accordance with section 701 of the International Financial Institutions Act (22 U.S.C. 262d).

"(6) ASSISTANCE THROUGH THE EXPORT-IMPORT BANK.—Credits and credit guarantees through the Export-Import Bank of the United States shall be denied to Iraq.

"(7) ASSISTANCE THROUGH THE COMMODITY CREDIT CORPORATION.—Credit, credit guarantees, and other assistance through the Commodity Credit Corporation shall be denied to Iraq.

"(8) FOREIGN ASSISTANCE.—All forms of assistance under the Foreign Assistance Act of 1961 (22 U.S.C. 2151 and following) other than emergency assistance for medical supplies and other forms of emergency humanitarian assistance, and under the Arms Export Control Act (22 U.S.C. 2751 and following) shall be denied to Iraq.

"(b) CONTRACT SANCTITY.—For purposes of the export controls imposed pursuant to subsection (a)(3), the date described in subsection (m)(1) of section 6 of the Export Administration Act of 1979 (50 U.S.C. App. 2405) shall be deemed to be August 1, 1990.

"SEC. 586H. WAIVER AUTHORITY.

"(a) IN GENERAL.—The President may waive the requirements of any paragraph of section 586G(a) if the President makes a certification under subsection (b) or subsection (c).

"(b) CERTIFICATION OF FUNDAMENTAL CHANGES IN IRAQI POLICIES AND ACTIONS.—The authority of subsection (a) may be exercised 60 days after the President certifies to the Congress that—

"(1) the Government of Iraq—

"(A) has demonstrated, through a pattern of conduct, substantial improvement in its respect for internationally recognized human rights;

"(B) is not acquiring, developing, or manufacturing (i) ballistic missiles, (ii) chemical, biological, or nuclear weapons, or (iii) components for such weapons; has forsworn the first use of such weapons; and is taking substantial and verifiable steps to destroy or otherwise dispose of any such missiles and weapons it possesses; and

"(C) does not provide support for international terrorism;

"(2) the Government of Iraq is in substantial compliance with its obligations under international law, including—

"(A) the Charter of the United Nations;

"(B) the International Covenant on Civil and Political Rights (done at New York, December 16, 1966) and the International Covenant on Economic, Social, and Cultural Rights (done at New York, December 16, 1966);

"(C) the Convention on the Prevention and Punishment of the Crime of Genocide (done at Paris, December 9, 1948);

"(D) the Protocol for the Prohibition of the Use in War of Asphyxiating, Poisonous or Other Gases, and of Bacteriological Methods of Warfare (done at Geneva, June 17, 1925);

"(E) the Treaty on the Non-Proliferation of Nuclear Weapons (done at Washington, London, and Moscow, July 1, 1968); and

"(F) the Convention on the Prohibition of the Development, Production and Stockpiling of Bacteriological (Biological) and Toxin Weapons and on Their Destruction (done at Washington, London, and Moscow, April 10, 1972); and

"(3) the President has determined that it is essential to the national interests of the United States to exercise the authority of subsection (a).

"(c) CERTIFICATION OF FUNDAMENTAL CHANGES IN IRAQI LEADERSHIP AND POLICIES.—The authority of subsection (a) may be exercised 30 days after the President certifies to the Congress that—

"(1) there has been a fundamental change in the leadership of the Government of Iraq; and

"(2) the new Government of Iraq has provided reliable and credible assurance that—

"(A) it respects internationally recognized human rights and it will demonstrate such respect through its conduct;

"(B) it is not acquiring, developing, or manufacturing and it will not acquire, develop, or manufacture (i) ballistic missiles, (ii) chemical, biological, or nuclear weapons, or (iii) components for such weapons; has forsworn the first use of such weapons; and is taking substantial and verifiable steps to destroy or otherwise dispose of any such missiles and weapons it possesses;

"(C) it is not and will not provide support for international terrorism; and

"(D) it is and will continue to be in substantial compliance with its obligations under international law, including all the treaties specified in subparagraphs (A) through (F) of subsection (b)(2).

"(d) INFORMATION TO BE INCLUDED IN CERTIFICATIONS.—Any certification under subsection (b) or (c) shall include the justification for each determination required by that subsection. The certification shall also specify which paragraphs of section 586G(a) the President will waive pursuant to that certification.

"SEC. 586I. DENIAL OF LICENSES FOR CERTAIN EXPORTS TO COUNTRIES ASSISTING IRAQ'S ROCKET OR CHEMICAL, BIOLOGICAL, OR NUCLEAR WEAPONS CAPABILITY.

"(a) RESTRICTION ON EXPORT LICENSES.—None of the funds appropriated by this or any other Act may be used to approve the licensing for export of any supercomputer to any country whose government the President determines is assisting, or whose government officials the President determines are assisting, Iraq to improve its rocket technology or chemical, biological, or nuclear weapons capability.

"(b) NEGOTIATIONS.—The President is directed to begin immediate negotiations with those governments with which the United States has bilateral supercomputer agreements, including the Government of the United Kingdom and the Government of Japan, on conditions restricting the transfer to Iraq of supercomputer or associated technology.

"SEC. 586J. REPORTS TO CONGRESS.

"(a) STUDY AND REPORT ON THE INTERNATIONAL EXPORT TO IRAQ OF NUCLEAR, BIOLOGICAL, CHEMICAL, AND BALLISTIC MISSILE TECHNOLOGY. (1) The President shall conduct a study on the sale, export, and third party transfer or development of nuclear, biological, chemical, and ballistic missile technology to or with Iraq including—

"(A) an identification of specific countries, as well as companies and individuals, both foreign and domestic, engaged in such sale or export of, nuclear, biological, chemical, and ballistic missile technology;

"(B) a detailed description and analysis of the international supply, information, support, and coproduction network, individual, corporate, and state, responsible for Iraq's current capability in the area of nuclear, biological, chemical, and ballistic missile technology; and

"(C) a recommendation of standards and procedures against which to measure and verify a decision of the Government of Iraq to terminate the development, production, coproduction, and deployment of nuclear, biological, chemical, and offensive ballistic missile technology as well as the destruction of all existing facilities associated with such technologies.

"(2) The President shall include in the study required by paragraph (1) specific recommendations on new mechanisms, to include, but not be limited to, legal, political, economic and regulatory, whereby the United States might contribute, in conjunction with its friends, allies, and the international community, to the management, control, or elimination of the threat of nuclear, biological, chemical, and ballistic missile proliferation.

"(3) Not later than March 30, 1991, the President shall submit to the Committee on Appropriations and the Committee on Foreign Relations of the Senate and the Committee on Appropriations and the Committee on Foreign Affairs [now Committee on International Relations] of the House of Representatives, a report, in both classified and unclassified form, setting forth the findings of the study required by paragraph (1) of this subsection.

"(b) STUDY AND REPORT ON IRAQ'S OFFENSIVE MILITARY CAPABILITY.—(1) The President shall conduct a study on Iraq's offensive military capability and its effect on the Middle East balance of power including an assessment of Iraq's power projection capability, the prospects for another sustained conflict with Iran, joint Iraqi-Jordanian military cooperation, the threat Iraq's arms transfer activities pose to United States allies in the Middle East, and the extension of Iraq's political-military influence into Africa and Latin America.

"(2) Not later than March 30, 1991, the President shall submit to the Committee on Appropriations and the Committee on Foreign Relations of the Senate and the Committee on Appropriations and the Committee on Foreign Affairs [now Committee on International Relations] of the House of Representatives, a report, in both classified and unclassified form, setting forth the findings of the study required by paragraph (1).

"(c) REPORT ON SANCTIONS TAKEN BY OTHER NATIONS AGAINST IRAQ.—(1) The President shall prepare a report on the steps taken by other nations, both before and after the August 2, 1990, invasion of Kuwait, to curtail the export of goods, services, and technologies to Iraq which might contribute to, or enhance, Iraq's nuclear, biological, chemical, and ballistic missile capability.

"(2) The President shall provide a complete accounting of international compliance with each of the sanctions resolutions adopted by the United Nations Security Council against Iraq since August 2, 1990, and shall list, by name, each country which to his knowledge, has provided any assistance to Iraq and the amount and type of that assistance in violation of each United Nations resolution.

"(3) The President shall make every effort to encourage other nations, in whatever forum or context, to adopt sanctions toward Iraq similar to those contained in this section.

"(4) Not later than every 6 months after the date of enactment of this Act [Nov. 5, 1990], the President shall submit to the Committee on Appropriations and the Committee on Foreign Relations of the Senate and the Committee on Appropriations and the Committee on Foreign Affairs [now Committee on International Relations] of the House of Representatives, a report in both classified and unclassified form, setting forth the findings of the study required by paragraph (1) of this subsection."

[Provisions similar to section 586D of Pub. L. 101–513, set out above, relating to compliance with sanctions against Iraq were contained in the following appropriations acts:

[Pub. L. 106–429, §101(a) [title V, §534], Nov. 6, 2000, 114 Stat. 1900, 1900A–34.

[Pub. L. 106–113, div. B, §1000(a)(2) [title V, §534], Nov. 29, 1999, 113 Stat. 1535, 1501A–93.

[Pub. L. 105–277, div. A, §101(d) [title V, §535], Oct. 21, 1998, 112 Stat. 2681–150, 2681–181.

[Pub. L. 105–118, title V, §534, Nov. 26, 1997, 111 Stat. 2416.

[Pub. L. 104–208, div. A, title I, §101(c) [title V, §533], Sept. 30, 1996, 110 Stat. 3009–121, 3009–152.

[Pub. L. 104–107, title V, §534, Feb. 12, 1996, 110 Stat. 734.

[Pub. L. 103–306, title V, §538, Aug. 23, 1994, 108 Stat. 1639.

[Pub. L. 103–87, title V, §539, Sept. 30, 1993, 107 Stat. 957.

[Pub. L. 102–391, title V, §573, Oct. 6, 1992, 106 Stat. 1683.]

Pub. L. 101–510, div. A, title XIV, §1458, Nov. 5, 1990, 104 Stat. 1697, provided that: "If the President considers that the taking of such action would promote the effectiveness of the economic sanctions of the United Nations and the United States imposed with respect to Iraq, and is consistent with the national interest, the President may prohibit, for such a period of time as he considers appropriate, the importation into the United States of any or all products of any foreign country that has not—

"(1) prohibited—

"(A) the importation of products of Iraq into its customs territory, and

"(B) the export of its products to Iraq; or

"(2) given assurances satisfactory to the President that such import and export sanctions will be promptly implemented."

IRAN CLAIMS SETTLEMENT

Pub. L. 99–93, title V, Aug. 16, 1985, 99 Stat. 437, provided that:

"SEC. 501. RECEIPT AND DETERMINATION OF CERTAIN CLAIMS.

"(a) AUTHORITY OF FOREIGN CLAIMS SETTLEMENT COMMISSION.—The Foreign Claims Settlement Commission of the United States is authorized to receive and determine the validity and amounts of claims by nationals of the United States against Iran which are settled en bloc by the United States. In deciding such claims, the Commission shall apply, in the following order—

"(1) the terms of any settlement agreement;

"(2) the relevant provisions of the Declarations of the Government of the Democratic and Popular Republic of Algeria of January 19, 1981, giving consideration to interpretations thereof by the Iran-United States Claims Tribunal; and

"(3) applicable principles of international law, justice, and equity.

Except as otherwise provided in this title, the provisions of title I of the International Claims Settlement Act of 1949 (22 U.S.C. 1621 et seq.) shall apply with respect to claims under this section. Any reference in such provisions to 'this title' [translated therein as 'this subchapter'] shall be deemed to refer to those provisions and to this section.

"(b) CERTIFICATION AND PAYMENT.—The Commission shall certify to the Secretary of the Treasury any awards determined pursuant to subsection (a) in accordance with section 5 of title I of the International Claims Settlement Act of 1949 (22 U.S.C. 1624). Such awards shall be paid in accordance with sections 7 and 8 of such title (22 U.S.C. 1626 and 1627), except that—

"(1) the Secretary of the Treasury is authorized to make payments pursuant to paragraphs (1) and (2) of section 8(c) of such title in the amount of $10,000 or the principal amount of the award, whichever is less; and

"(2) the Secretary of the Treasury may deduct, pursuant to section 7(b) of such title, an amount calculated in accordance with section 502(a) of this Act, instead of 5 percent of payments made pursuant to section 8(c) of such title.

"SEC. 502. DEDUCTIONS FROM ARBITRAL AWARDS.

"(a) DEDUCTION FOR EXPENSES OF THE UNITED STATES.—Except as provided in section 503, the Federal Reserve Bank of New York shall deduct from the aggregate amount awarded under each enumerated claim before the Iran-United States Claims Tribunal in favor of a United States claimant, an amount equal to 1½ percent of the first $5,000,000 and 1 percent of any amount over $5,000,000, as reimbursement to the United States Government for expenses incurred in connection with the arbitration of claims of United States claimants against Iran before that Tribunal and the maintenance of the Security Account established pursuant to the Declarations of the Democratic and Popular Republic of Algeria of January 19, 1981. The Federal Reserve Bank of New York shall make the deduction required by the preceding sentence whenever the Bank receives an amount from the Security Account in satisfaction of an award rendered by the Iran-United States Claim Tribunal on the enumerated claim involved.

"(b) DEDUCTION TREATED AS MISCELLANEOUS RECEIPT.—Amounts deducted by the Federal Reserve Bank of New York pursuant to subsection (a) shall be deposited into the Treasury of the United States to the credit of miscellaneous receipts.

"(c) PAYMENT TO UNITED STATES CLAIMANTS.—Nothing in this section shall be construed to affect the payment to United States claimants of amounts received by the Federal Reserve Bank of New York in respect of awards by the Iran-United States Claims Tribunal, after deduction of the amounts calculated in accordance with subsection (a).

"(d) EFFECTIVE DATE.—This section shall be effective as of June 7, 1982.

"SEC. 503. EN BLOC SETTLEMENT.

"The deduction by the Federal Reserve Bank of New York provided for in section 502(a) of this Act shall not apply in the case of a sum received by the Bank pursuant to an en bloc settlement of any category of claims of United States nationals against Iran when such sum is to be used for payments in satisfaction of awards certified by the Foreign Claims Settlement Commission pursuant to section 501(b) of this Act.

"SEC. 504. REIMBURSEMENT TO THE FEDERAL RESERVE BANK OF NEW YORK.

"The Secretary of the Treasury may reimburse the Federal Reserve Bank of New York for expenses incurred by the Bank in the performance of fiscal agency agreements relating to the settlement or arbitration of claims pursuant to the Declarations of the Democratic and Popular Republic of Algeria of January 19, 1981.

"SEC. 505. CONFIDENTIALITY OF RECORDS.

"Notwithstanding section 552 of title 5, United States Code (commonly referred to as the Freedom of Information Act), records pertaining to the arbitration of claims before the Iran-United States Claims Tribunal may not be disclosed to the general public, except that—

"(1) rules, awards, and other decisions of the Tribunal and claims and responsive pleadings filed at the Tribunal by the United States on its own behalf shall be made available to the public, unless the Secretary of State determines that public disclosure would be prejudicial to the interests of the United States or United States claimants in proceedings before the Tribunal, or that public disclosure would be contrary to the rules of the Tribunal; and

"(2) the Secretary of State may determine on a case-by-case basis to make such information available when in the judgment of the Secretary the interests of justice so require."

EX. ORD. NO. 12170. BLOCKING IRANIAN GOVERNMENT PROPERTY

Ex. Ord. No. 12170, Nov. 14, 1979, 44 F.R. 65729, provided:

Pursuant to the authority vested in me as President by the Constitution and laws of the United States including the International Emergency Economic Powers Act, 50 U.S.C.A. sec. 1701 et seq., the National Emergencies Act, 50 U.S.C. sec. 1601 et seq., and 3 U.S.C. sec. 301,

I, JIMMY CARTER, President of the United States, find that the situation in Iran constitutes an unusual and extraordinary threat to the national security, foreign policy and economy of the United States and hereby declare a national emergency to deal with that threat.

I hereby order blocked all property and interests in property of the Government of Iran, its instrumentalities and controlled entities and the Central Bank of Iran which are or become subject to the jurisdiction of the United States or which are in or come within the possession or control of persons subject to the jurisdiction of the United States.

The Secretary of the Treasury is authorized to employ all powers granted to me by the International Emergency Economic Powers Act [this chapter] to carry out the provisions of this order.

This order is effective immediately and shall be transmitted to the Congress and published in the Federal Register.

JIMMY CARTER.

CONTINUATION OF NATIONAL EMERGENCY DECLARED BY EX. ORD. NO. 12170

Notice of President of the United States, dated Nov. 9, 2000, 65 F.R. 68061, provided:

On November 14, 1979, by Executive Order 12170 [set out above], the President declared a national emergency to deal with the threat to the national security, foreign policy, and economy of the United States constituted by the situation in Iran. Since that time, notices of the continuation of this national emergency have been transmitted annually by the President to the

Congress and published in the Federal Register. The most recent notice appeared in the Federal Register on November 5, 1999. Because our relations with Iran have not yet returned to normal, and the process of implementing the January 19, 1981, agreements with Iran is still underway, the national emergency declared on November 14, 1979, must continue in effect beyond November 14, 2000. Therefore, in accordance with section 202(d) of the National Emergencies Act (50 U.S.C. 1622(d)), I am continuing the national emergency with respect to Iran for 1 year. This notice shall be published in the Federal Register and transmitted to the Congress.

WILLIAM J. CLINTON.

Prior continuations of national emergency declared by Ex. Ord. No. 12170 were contained in the following:

Notice of President of the United States, dated Nov. 5, 1999, 64 F.R. 61471.

Notice of President of the United States, dated Nov. 9, 1998, 63 F.R. 63125.

Notice of President of the United States, dated Sept. 30, 1997, 62 F.R. 51591.

Notice of President of the United States, dated Oct. 29, 1996, 61 F.R. 56107.

Notice of President of the United States, dated Oct. 31, 1995, 60 F.R. 55651.

Notice of President of the United States, dated Oct. 31, 1994, 59 F.R. 54785.

Notice of President of the United States, dated Nov. 1, 1993, 58 F.R. 58639.

Notice of President of the United States, dated Oct. 25, 1992, 57 F.R. 48719.

Notice of President of the United States, dated Nov. 12, 1991, 56 F.R. 57791.

Notice of the President of the United States, dated Nov. 9, 1990, 55 F.R. 47453.

Notice of the President of the United States, dated Oct. 30, 1989, 54 F.R. 46043.

Notice of the President of the United States, dated Nov. 8, 1988, 53 F.R. 45750.

Notice of the President of the United States, dated Nov. 10, 1987, 52 F.R. 43549.

Notice of the President of the United States, dated Nov. 10, 1986, 51 F.R. 41067.

Notice of the President of the United States, dated Nov. 1, 1985, 50 F.R. 45901.

Notice of the President of the United States, dated Nov. 7, 1984, 49 F.R. 44741.

Notice of the President of the United States, dated Nov. 8, 1982, 47 F.R. 50841.

EX. ORD. NO. 12205. PROHIBITING CERTAIN TRANSACTIONS WITH IRAN

Ex. Ord. No. 12205, Apr. 7, 1980, 45 F.R. 24099, as amended by Ex. Ord. No. 12211, Apr. 17, 1980, 45 F.R. 26685, provided:

By the authority vested in me as President by the Constitution and statutes of the United States, including Section 203 of the International Emergency Economic Powers Act (50 U.S.C. 1702), Section 301 of Title 3 of the United States Code, and Section 301 of the National Emergencies Act (50 U.S.C. 1631), in order to take steps additional to those set forth in Executive Order No. 12170 of November 14, 1979 [set out as a note above], to deal with the threat to the national security, foreign policy and economy of the United States referred to in that Order, and in furtherance of the objectives of United Nations Security Council Resolution 461 (1979) adopted on December 31, 1979, it is hereby ordered as follows:

1–101. The following are prohibited effective immediately, notwithstanding any contracts entered into or licenses granted before the date of this Order [Apr. 7, 1980]:

(a) The sale, supply or other transfer, by any person subject to the jurisdiction of the United States, of any items, commodities or products, except food, medicine and supplies intended strictly for medical purposes, and donations of clothing intended to be used to relieve human suffering, from the United States, or from any foreign country, whether or not originating in the United States, either to or destined for Iran, an Iranian governmental entity in Iran, any other person or body in Iran or any other person or body for the purposes of any enterprise carried on in Iran.

(b) The shipment by vessel, aircraft, railway or other land transport of United States registration or owned by or under charter to any person subject to the jurisdiction of the United States or the carriage (whether or not in bond) by land transport facilities across the United States of any of the items, commodities and products covered by paragraph (a) of this section which are consigned to or destined for Iran, an Iranian governmental entity or any person or body in Iran, or to any enterprise carried on in Iran.

(c) The shipment from the United States of any of the items, products and commodities covered by paragraph (a) of this section on vessels or aircraft registered in Iran.

(d) The following acts, when committed by any person subject to the jurisdiction of the United States in connection with any transaction involving Iran, an Iranian governmental entity, an enterprise controlled by Iran or an Iranian governmental entity, or any person in Iran:

(i) Making available any new credits or loans;

(ii) Making available any new deposit facilities or allowing substantial increases in non-dollar deposits which exist as of the date of this Order [Apr. 7, 1980];

(iii) Allowing more favorable terms of payment than are customarily used in international commercial transactions; or

(iv) Failing to act in a businesslike manner in exercising any rights when payments due on existing credits or loans are not made in a timely manner.

(v) Make any payment, transfer of credit, or other transfer of funds or other property or interests therein, except for purposes of family remittances.

(e) The engaging by any person subject to the jurisdiction of the United States in any service contract in support of an industrial project in Iran, except any such contract entered into prior to the date of this Order [Apr. 7, 1980] or concerned with medical care.

(f) The engaging by any person subject to the jurisdiction of the United States in any transaction which evades or avoids, or has the purpose or effect of evading or avoiding, any of the prohibitions set forth in this section.

1–102. The prohibitions in section 1–101 above shall not apply to transactions by any person subject to the jurisdiction of the United States which is a nonbanking association, corporation, or other organization organized and doing business under the laws of any foreign country.

1–103. The Secretary of the Treasury is delegated, and authorized to exercise, all functions vested in the President by the International Emergency Economic Powers Act (50 U.S.C. 1701 et seq.) to carry out the purposes of this Order. The Secretary may redelegate any of these functions to other officers and agencies of the Federal government.

1–104. The Secretary of the Treasury shall ensure that actions taken pursuant to this Order and Executive Order No. 12170 [set out above] are accounted for as required by Section 401 of the National Emergencies Act (50 U.S.C. 1641).

1–105. This Order is effective immediately. In accord with Section 401 of the National Emergencies Act (50 U.S.C. 1641) and Section 204 of the International Emergency Economic Powers Act (50 U.S.C. 1703), it shall be immediately transmitted to the Congress and published in the Federal Register.

JIMMY CARTER.

REVOCATION OF PROHIBITIONS CONTAINED IN EXECUTIVE ORDER NO. 12205

For provisions relating to the revocation of prohibitions contained in Ex. Ord. No. 12205, Apr. 7, 1980, 45 F.R. 24099, as amended, which prohibited certain transactions with Iran, see Ex. Ord. No. 12282, Jan. 19, 1981, 46 F.R. 7925, set out below.

EX. ORD. NO. 12211. PROHIBITING CERTAIN TRANSACTIONS WITH IRAN

Ex. Ord. No. 12211, Apr. 17, 1980, 45 F.R. 26685, provided:

By the authority vested in me as President by the Constitution and statutes of the United States, including Section 203 of the International Emergency Economic Powers Act (50 U.S.C. 1702), Section 301 of Title 3 of the United States Code, Sections 1732 and 2656 of Title 22 of the United States Code, and Section 301 of the National Emergencies Act (50 U.S.C. 1631), in order to take steps additional to those set forth in Executive Order No. 12170 of November 14, 1979 [set out above], and Executive Order No. 12205 of April 7, 1980 [set out above], to deal with the threat to the national security, foreign policy and economy of the United States referred to in those Orders, and the added unusual and extraordinary threat to the national security, foreign policy and economy of the United States created by subsequent events in Iran and neighboring countries, including the Soviet invasion of Afghanistan, with respect to which I hereby declare a national emergency, and to carry out the policy of the United States to deny the use of its resources to aid, encourage or give sanctuary to those persons involved in directing, supporting or participating in acts of international terrorism, it is hereby ordered as follows:

1–101. Paragraph 1–101(d) of Executive Order No. 12205 [set out above] is hereby amended by the addition of a new subparagraph (v) as follows:

(v) Make any payment, transfer of credit, or other transfer of funds or other property or interests therein, except for purposes of family remittances.

1–102. The following transactions are prohibited, notwithstanding any contracts entered into or licenses granted before the date of this Order [Apr. 17, 1980]:

(a) Effective immediately, the direct or indirect import from Iran into the United States of Iranian goods or services, other than materials imported for news publication or news broadcast dissemination.

(b) Effective immediately, any transactions with a foreign person or foreign entity by any citizen or permanent resident of the United States relating to that person's travel to Iran after the date of this Order [Apr. 17, 1980].

(c) Effective seven days from the date of this Order [Apr. 17, 1980], the payment by or on behalf of any citizen or permanent resident of the United States who is within Iran of any expenses for transactions within Iran.

The prohibitions in paragraphs (b) and (c) of this section shall not apply to a person who is also a citizen of Iran and those prohibitions and the prohibitions in section 1–101 shall not apply to a journalist or other person who is regularly employed by a news gathering or transmitting organization and who travels to Iran or is within Iran for the purpose of gathering or transmitting news, making news or documentary films, or similar activities.

1–103. The Secretary of the Treasury is hereby directed, effective fourteen days from the date of this Order [Apr. 17, 1980], to revoke existing licenses for transactions by persons subject to the jurisdiction of the United States with Iran Air, the National Iranian Oil Company, and the National Iranian Gas Company previously issued pursuant to regulations under Executive Order No. 12170 [set out above], or Executive Order No. 12205 [set out above].

1–104. The Secretary of the Treasury is delegated, and authorized to exercise, all functions vested in the President by the International Emergency Economic Powers Act (50 U.S.C. 1701 et seq.) to carry out the purposes of this Order. The Secretary may redelegate any of these functions to other officers and agencies of the Federal government.

1–105. The Secretary of the Treasury shall ensure that actions taken by him pursuant to the above provisions of this Order, Executive Order No. 12170 [set out above] and Executive Order No. 12205 [set out above] are accounted for as required by Section 401 of the National Emergencies Act (50 U.S.C. 1641).

1–106. The Secretary of State is delegated, and authorized to exercise in furtherance of the purposes of this Order, the powers vested in the President by Section 2001 of the Revised Statutes (22 U.S.C. 1732), Section 1 of the Act of July 3, 1926 (22 U.S.C. 211a), and Section 215 of the Immigration and Nationality Act (8 U.S.C. 1185), with respect to:

(a) the restriction of the use of United States passports for travel to, in or through Iran; and

(b) the regulation of departures from and entry into the United States in connection with travel to Iran by citizens and permanent residents of the United States.

1–107. Except as otherwise indicated herein, this Order is effective immediately. In accord with Section 401 of the National Emergencies Act (50 U.S.C. 1641) and Section 204 of the International Emergency Economic Powers Act (50 U.S.C. 1703), it shall be immediately transmitted to the Congress and published in the Federal Register.

JIMMY CARTER.

REVOCATION OF PROHIBITIONS CONTAINED IN EXECUTIVE ORDER NO. 12211

For provisions relating to the revocation of prohibitions contained in Ex. Ord. No. 12211, Apr. 17, 1980, 45 F.R. 26685, which prohibited certain transactions with Iran, see Ex. Ord. No. 12282, Jan. 19, 1981, 46 F.R. 7925, set out below.

EX. ORD. NO. 12276. RELEASE OF AMERICAN HOSTAGES IN IRAN—DIRECTION RELATING TO ESTABLISHMENT OF ESCROW ACCOUNTS

Ex. Ord. No. 12276, Jan. 19, 1981, 46 F.R. 7913, provided:

By the authority vested in me as President by the Constitution and statutes of the United States, including Section 203 of the International Emergency Economic Powers Act (50 U.S.C. 1702), Section 301 of Title 3 of the United States Code, Section 1732 of Title 22 of the United States Code, and Section 301 of the National Emergencies Act (50 U.S.C. 1631), in view of the continuing unusual and extraordinary threat to the national security, foreign policy and economy of the United States upon which I based my declarations of national emergency in Executive Order 12170 [set out above], issued November 14, 1979, and in Executive Order 12211 [set out above], issued April 17, 1980, in order to implement agreements with the Government of Iran, as reflected in Declarations of the Government of the Democratic and Popular Republic of Algeria dated January 19, 1981, relating to the release of U.S. diplomats and nationals being held as hostages and to the resolution of claims of United States nationals against Iran, and to begin the process of normalization of relations between the United States and Iran, it is hereby ordered that as of the effective date of this Order:

1–101. The Secretary of the Treasury is authorized to enter into, and to license, authorize, direct, and compel any appropriate official and/or the Federal Reserve Bank of New York, as fiscal agent of the United States, to enter into escrow or related agreements with a foreign central bank and with the Central Bank of Algeria under which certain money and other assets, as and when directed by the Secretary of the Treasury, shall be credited by the foreign central bank to an escrow account on its books in the name of the Central Bank of Algeria for transfer to the Government of Iran if and when the Central Bank of Algeria receives from the Government of Algeria a certification that the 52 U.S. diplomats and nationals being held hostage in Iran have safely departed from Iran. Such agreements shall include other parties and terms as determined by the Secretary of the Treasury to be appropriate to carry out the purposes of this Order.

1–102. The Secretary of the Treasury is authorized to license, authorize, direct, and compel the Federal Reserve Bank of New York, as fiscal agent of the United States, to receive certain money and other assets in which Iran or its agencies, instrumentalities, or controlled entities have an interest and to hold or transfer such money and other assets, and any interest earned thereon, in such a manner as he deems necessary to fulfill the rights and obligations of the United States under the Declaration of the Government of the Democratic and Popular Republic of Algeria dated January 19, 1981, and the escrow and related agreements described in paragraph 1–101 of this Order. Such money and other assets may be held in interest-bearing form and where possible shall be invested with or through the entity holding the money or asset on the effective date of this Order.

1–103. Compliance with this Executive Order, any other Executive Order licensing, authorizing, directing or compelling the transfer of the assets referred to in paragraphs 1–101 and 1–102 of this Order, or any regulations, instructions, or directions issued thereunder shall to the extent thereof be a full acquittance and discharge for all purposes of the obligation of the person making the same. No person shall be held liable in any court for or with respect to anything done or omitted in good faith in connection with the administration of, or pursuant to and in reliance on, such orders, regulations, instructions, or directions.

1–104. The Attorney General shall seek to intervene in any litigation within the United States which arises out of this Order and shall, among other things, defend the legality of, and all actions taken pursuant to, each of its provisions.

1–105. The Secretary of the Treasury is delegated and authorized to exercise all functions vested in the President by the International Emergency Economic Powers Act (50 U.S.C. 1701 et seq.) to carry out the purposes of this Order.

1–106. This Order shall be effective immediately.

JIMMY CARTER.

EX. ORD. NO. 12277. RELEASE OF AMERICAN HOSTAGES IN IRAN—DIRECTION TO TRANSFER IRANIAN GOVERNMENT ASSETS

Ex. Ord. No. 12277, Jan. 19, 1981, 46 F.R. 7915, provided:

By the authority vested in me as President by the Constitution and statutes of the United States, including Section 203 of the International Emergency Economic Powers Act (50 U.S.C. 1702), Section 301 of Title 3 of the United States Code, Section 1732 of Title 22 of the United States Code, and Section 301 of the National Emergencies Act (50 U.S.C. 1631), in view of the continuing unusual and extraordinary threat to the national security, foreign policy and economy of the United States upon which I based my declarations of national emergency in Executive Order 12170 [set out above], issued November 14, 1979, and in Executive Order 12211 [set out above], issued April 17, 1980, in order to implement agreements with the Government of Iran, as reflected in Declarations of the Government of the Democratic and Popular Republic of Algeria dated January 19, 1981, relating to the release of U.S. diplomats and nationals being held as hostages and to the resolution of claims of United States nationals against Iran, and to begin the process of normalization of relations between the United States and Iran and in which Iran and the United States instruct and require that the assets described in this order shall be transferred as set forth below by the holders of such assets, it is hereby ordered that as of the effective date of this Order:

1–101. The Federal Reserve Bank of New York is licensed, authorized, directed, and compelled to transfer to accounts at the Bank of England, and subsequently to transfer to accounts at the Bank of England established pursuant to an escrow agreement approved by the Secretary of the Treasury, all gold bullion, and other assets (or the equivalent thereof) in its custody, of the Government of Iran, or its agencies, instrumentalities or controlled entities. Such transfers shall be executed when and in the manner directed by the Secretary of the Treasury. The Secretary of the Treasury is also authorized to license, authorize, direct, and compel the Federal Reserve Bank of New York to engage in whatever further transactions he deems appropriate and consistent with the purposes of this Order, including any transactions related to the return of such bullion and other assets pursuant to the escrow agreement.

1–102. (a) All licenses and authorizations for acquiring or exercising any right, power, or privilege, by court order, attachment, or otherwise, including the license contained in Section 535.504 of the Iranian Assets Control Regulations, with respect to the properties described in Section 1–101 of this Order are revoked and withdrawn.

(b) All rights, powers, and privileges relating to the properties described in section 1–101 of this Order and which derive from any attachment, injunction, other like proceedings or process, or other action in any litigation after November 14, 1979, at 8:10 a.m. EST, including those derived from Section 535.504 of the Iranian Assets Control Regulations, other than rights, powers, and privileges of the Government of Iran and its agencies, instrumentalities, and controlled entities, whether acquired by court order or otherwise, are nullified, and all persons claiming any such right, power, or privilege are hereafter barred from exercising the same.

(c) All persons subject to the jurisdiction of the United States are prohibited from acquiring or exercising any right, power, or privilege, whether by court order or otherwise, with respect to the properties (and any income earned thereon) referred to in Section 1–101 of this Order.

1–103. Compliance with this Order, any other Executive Order licensing, authorizing, directing, or compelling the transfer of the assets described in section 1–101 of this Order, or any regulations, instructions, or directions issued thereunder shall to the extent thereof be a full acquittance and discharge for all purposes of the obligation of the person making the same. No person shall be held liable in any court for or with respect to anything done or omitted in good faith in connection with the administration of, or pursuant to and in reliance on, such orders, regulations, instructions, or directions.

1–104. The Attorney General shall seek to intervene in any litigation within the United States which arises out of this Order and shall, among other things, defend the legality of, and all actions taken pursuant to, each of its provisions.

1–105. The Secretary of the Treasury is delegated and authorized to exercise all functions vested in the President by the International Emergency Economic Powers Act (50 U.S.C. 1701 et seq.) to carry out the purposes of this Order.

1–106. This Order shall be effective immediately.

JIMMY CARTER.

EX. ORD. NO. 12278. RELEASE OF AMERICAN HOSTAGES IN IRAN—DIRECTION TO TRANSFER IRANIAN GOVERNMENT ASSETS OVERSEAS

Ex. Ord. No. 12278, Jan. 19, 1981, 46 F.R. 7917, provided:

By the authority vested in me as President by the Constitution and statutes of the United States, including Section 203 of the International Emergency Economic Powers Act (50 U.S.C. 1702), Section 301 of Title 3 of the United States Code, Section 1732 of Title 22 of the United States Code, and Section 301 of the National Emergencies Act (50 U.S.C. 1631), in view of the continuing unusual and extraordinary threat to the national security, foreign policy and economy of the United States upon which I based my declarations of national emergency in Executive Order 12170 [set out above], issued November 14, 1979, and in Executive Order 12211 [set out above], issued April 17, 1980, in order to implement agreements with the Government of Iran, as reflected in Declarations of the Government of the Democratic and Popular Republic of Algeria dated January 19, 1981, relating to the release of U.S. diplomats and nationals being held as hostages and to the resolution of claims of United States nationals against Iran, and to begin the process of normalization of relations between the United States and Iran and in which Iran and the United States instruct and require that the assets described in this Order shall be transferred as set forth below by the holders of such assets, it is hereby ordered that as of the effective date of this Order:

1–101. Any branch or office of a United States bank or subsidiary thereof, which branch or office is located outside the territory of the United States and which on or after 8:10 a.m. E.S.T. on November 14, 1979 (a) has been or is in possession of funds or securities legally or beneficially owned by the Government of Iran or its agencies, instrumentalities, or controlled entities, or (b) has carried or is carrying on its books deposits standing to the credit of or beneficially owned by such Government, agencies, instrumentalities, or controlled entities, is licensed, authorized, directed, and compelled to transfer such funds, securities, and deposits, including interest from November 14, 1979, at commercially reasonable rates, to the account of the Federal Reserve Bank of New York at the Bank of England, to be held or transferred as directed by the Secretary of the Treasury. The Secretary of the Treasury shall determine when the transfers required by this section shall take place. The funds, securities and deposits described in this section shall be further transferred as provided for in the Declaration of the Government of the Democratic and Popular Republic of Algeria and its Annex.

1–102. Any banking institution subject to the jurisdiction of the United States that has executed a set-off on or after November 14, 1979, at 8:10 a.m. E.S.T. against Iranian funds, securities, or deposits referred to in section 1–101 is hereby licensed, authorized, directed, and compelled to cancel such set-off and to transfer all funds, securities, and deposits which have been subject to such set-off, including interest from November 14, 1979, at commercially reasonable rates, pursuant to the provisions of section 1–101 of this Order.

1–103. If the funds, securities, and deposits described in section 1–101 are not promptly transferred to the control of the Government of Iran, such funds, securities, and deposits shall be returned to the banking institutions holding them on the effective date of this Order and the set-offs described in section 1–102 shall be in force as if this Order had not been issued and the status of all such funds, securities, deposits and set-offs shall be status quo ante.

1–104. (a) All licenses and authorizations for acquiring or exercising any right, power, or privilege, by court order, attachment, or otherwise, including the license contained in Section 535.504 of the Iranian Assets Control Regulations, with respect to the properties described in Sections 1–101 and 1–102 of this Order are revoked and withdrawn.

(b) All rights, powers, and privileges relating to the properties described in Sections 1–101 and 1–102 of this Order and which derive from any attachment, injunction, other like proceedings or process, or other action in any litigation after November 14, 1979, at 8:10 a.m. E.S.T., including those derived from Section 535.504 of the Iranian Assets Control Regulations, other than rights, powers, and privileges of the Government of Iran and its agencies, instrumentalities, and controlled entities, whether acquired by court order or otherwise, are nullified, and all persons claiming any such right, power, or privilege are hereafter barred from exercising the same.

(c) All persons subject to the jurisdiction of the United States are prohibited from acquiring or exercising any right, power, or privilege, whether by court order or otherwise, with respect to the properties (and any income earned thereon) referred to in Sections 1–101 and 1–102 of this Order.

1–105. Compliance with this Order, any other Executive Order licensing, authorizing, directing, or compelling the transfer of the assets described in Sections 1–101 and 1–102 of this Order, or any regulations, instructions, or directions issued thereunder shall to the extent thereof be a full acquittance and discharge for all purposes of the obligation of the person making the same. No person shall be held liable in any court for or with respect to anything done or omitted in good faith in connection with the administration of, or pursuant to and in reliance on, such orders, regulations, instructions, or directions.

1–106. The Attorney General shall seek to intervene in any litigation within the United States which arises out of this Order and shall, among other things, defend the legality of, and all actions taken pursuant to, each of its provisions.

1–107. The Secretary of the Treasury is delegated and authorized to exercise all functions vested in the President by the International Emergency Economic Powers Act (50 U.S.C. 1701 et seq.) to carry out the purposes of this Order.

1–108. This Order shall be effective immediately.

JIMMY CARTER.

EX. ORD. NO. 12279. RELEASE OF AMERICAN HOSTAGES IN IRAN—DIRECTION TO TRANSFER IRANIAN GOVERNMENT ASSETS HELD BY DOMESTIC BANKS

Ex. Ord. No. 12279, Jan. 19, 1981, 46 F.R. 7919, provided:

By the authority vested in me as President by the Constitution and statutes of the United States, including Section 203 of the International Emergency Economic Powers Act (50 U.S.C. 1702), Section 301 of Title 3 of the United States Code, Section 1732 of Title 22 of the United States Code, and Section 301 of the National Emergencies Act (50 U.S.C. 1631), in view of the continuing unusual and extraordinary threat to the national security, foreign policy and economy of the United States upon which I based my declarations of national emergency in Executive Order 12170 [set out above], issued November 14, 1979, and in Executive Order 12211 [set out above], issued April 17, 1980, in order to implement agreements with the Government of Iran, as reflected in Declarations of the Government of the Democratic and Popular Republic of Algeria dated January 19, 1981, relating to the release of U.S. diplomats and nationals being held as hostages and to the resolution of claims of United States nationals against Iran, and to begin the process of normalization of relations between the United States and Iran and in which Iran and the United States instruct and require that the assets described in this Order shall be transferred as set forth below by the holders of such assets, it is hereby ordered that as of the effective date of this Order:

1–101. Any branch or office of a banking institution subject to the jurisdiction of the United States, which branch or office is located within the United States and is, on the effective date, either (a) in possession of funds or securities legally or beneficially owned by the Government of Iran or its agencies, instrumentalities, or controlled entities, or (b) carrying on its books deposits standing to the credit of or beneficially owned by such Government, agencies, instrumentalities, or controlled entities is licensed, authorized, directed and compelled to transfer such funds, securities, and deposits, including interest from November 14, 1979, at commercially reasonable rates, to the Federal Reserve Bank of New York, to be held or transferred as directed by the Secretary of the Treasury.

1–102. (a) All licenses and authorizations for acquiring or exercising any right, power, or privilege, by court order, attachment, or otherwise, including the license contained in Section 535.504 of the Iranian Assets Control Regulations, with respect to the properties described in Section 1–101 of this Order are revoked and withdrawn.

(b) All rights, powers, and privileges relating to the properties described in section 1–101 of this Order and which derive from any attachment, injunction, other like proceedings or process, or other action in any litigation after November 14, 1979, at 8:10 a.m. EST, including those derived from Section 535.504 of the Iranian Assets Control Regulations, other than rights, powers, and privileges of the Government of Iran and its agencies, instrumentalities, and controlled entities, whether acquired by court order or otherwise, are nullified, and all persons claiming any such right, power, or privilege are hereafter barred from exercising the same.

(c) All persons subject to the jurisdiction of the United States are prohibited from acquiring or exercising any right, power, or privilege whether by court order or otherwise, with respect to the properties (and any income earned thereon) referred to in Section 1–101 of this Order.

1–103. Compliance with this Order, any other Executive Order licensing, authorizing, directing or compelling the transfer of the assets described in section 1–101 of this Order, or any regulations, instructions, or directions issued thereunder shall to the extent thereof be a full acquittance and discharge for all purposes of the obligation of the person making the same. No person shall be held liable in any court for or with respect to anything done or omitted in good faith in connection with the administration of, or pursuant to and in reliance on, such orders, regulations, instructions, or directions.

1–104. The Attorney General shall seek to intervene in any litigation within the United States which arises out of this Order and shall, among other things, defend the legality of, and all actions taken pursuant to, each of its provisions.

1–105. The Secretary of the Treasury is delegated and authorized to exercise all functions vested in the President by the International Emergency Economic Powers Act (50 U.S.C. 1701 et seq.) to carry out the purposes of this Order.

1–106. This Order shall be effective immediately.

JIMMY CARTER.

EX. ORD. NO. 12280. RELEASE OF AMERICAN HOSTAGES IN IRAN—DIRECTION TO TRANSFER IRANIAN GOVERNMENT FINANCIAL ASSETS HELD BY NON-BANKING INSTITUTIONS

Ex. Ord. No. 12280, Jan. 19, 1981, 46 F.R. 7921, provided:

By the authority vested in me as President by the Constitution and statutes of the United States, including Section 203 of the International Emergency Economic Powers Act (50 U.S.C. 1702), Section 301 of Title 3 of the United States Code, Section 1732 of Title 22 of the United States Code, and Section 301 of the National Emergencies Act (50 U.S.C. 1631), in view of the continuing unusual and extraordinary threat to the national security, foreign policy and economy of the United States upon which I based my declarations of national emergency in Executive Order 12170 [set out above], issued November 14, 1979, and in Executive Order 12211 [set out above], issued April 17, 1980, in order to implement agreements with the Government of Iran, as reflected in Declarations of the Government of the Democratic and Popular Republic of Algeria dated January 19, 1981, relating to the release of U.S. diplomats and nationals being held as hostages and to the resolution of claims of United States nationals against Iran, and to begin the process of normalization of relations between the United States and Iran and in which Iran and the United States instruct and require that the assets described in this Order shall be transferred as set forth below by the holders of such assets, it is hereby ordered that as of the effective date of this Order:

1–101. Any person subject to the jurisdiction of the United States which is not a banking institution and is on the effective date in possession or control of funds or securities of Iran or its agencies, instrumentalities, or controlled entities is licensed, authorized, directed and compelled to transfer such funds or securities to the Federal Reserve Bank of New York to be held or transferred as directed by the Secretary of the Treasury.

1–102. (a) All licenses and authorizations for acquiring or exercising any right, power, or privilege, by court order, attachment, or otherwise, including the license contained in Section 535.504 of the Iranian Assets Control Regulations, with respect to the properties described in Section 1–101 of this Order are revoked and withdrawn.

(b) All rights, powers, and privileges relating to the properties described in section 1–101 of this Order and which derive from any attachment, injunction, other like proceedings or process, or other action in any litigation after November 14, 1979, at 8:10 a.m. EST, including those derived from Section 535.504 of the Iranian Assets Control Regulations, other than rights, powers, and privileges of the Government of Iran and its agencies, instrumentalities, and controlled entities, whether acquired by court order or otherwise, are nullified, and all persons claiming any such right, power, or privilege are hereafter barred from exercising the same.

(c) All persons subject to the jurisdiction of the United States are prohibited from acquiring or exercising any right, power, or privilege, whether by court order or otherwise, with respect to the properties (and any income earned thereon) referred to in Section 1–101 of this Order.

1–103. Compliance with this Executive Order, any other Executive Order licensing, authorizing, directing or compelling the transfer of the assets described in paragraph 1–101 of this Order, or any regulations, instructions, or directions issued thereunder shall to the extent thereof be a full acquittance and discharge for all purposes of the obligation of the person making the same. No person shall be held liable in any court for or with respect to anything done or omitted in good faith in connection with the administration of, or pursuant to and in reliance on, such orders, regulations, instructions, or directions.

1–104. The Attorney General shall seek to intervene in any litigation within the United States which arises out of this Order and shall, among other things, defend the legality of and all actions taken pursuant to, each of its provisions.

1–105. The Secretary of the Treasury is delegated and authorized to exercise all functions vested in the President by the International Emergency Economic Powers Act (50 U.S.C. 1701 et seq.) to carry out the purposes of this Order.

1–106. This Order shall be effective immediately.

JIMMY CARTER.

EX. ORD. NO. 12281. RELEASE OF AMERICAN HOSTAGES IN IRAN—DIRECTION TO TRANSFER CERTAIN IRANIAN GOVERNMENT ASSETS

Ex. Ord. No. 12281, Jan. 19, 1981, 46 F.R. 7923, provided:

By the authority vested in me as President by the Constitution and statutes of the United States, including Section 203 of the International Emergency Economic Powers Act (50 U.S.C. 1702), Section 301 of Title 3 of the United States Code, Section 1732 of Title 22 of the United States Code, and Section 301 of the National Emergencies Act (50 U.S.C. 1631), in view of the continuing unusual and extraordinary threat to the national security, foreign policy and economy of the United States upon which I based my declarations of national emergency in Executive Order 12170 [set out above], issued November 14, 1979, and in Executive Order 12211 [set out above], issued April 17, 1980, in order to implement agreements with the Government of Iran, as reflected in Declarations of the Government of the Democratic and Popular Republic of Algeria dated January 19, 1981, relating to the release of U.S. diplomats and nationals being held as hostages and to the resolution of claims of United States nationals against Iran, and to begin the process of normalization of relations between the United States and Iran and in which Iran and the United States instruct and require that the assets described in this Order shall be transferred as set forth below by the holders of such assets, it is hereby ordered that as of the effective date of this Order:

1–101. All persons subject to the jurisdiction of the United States in possession or control of properties, not including funds and securities, owned by Iran or its agencies, instrumentalities, or controlled entities are licensed, authorized, directed and compelled to transfer such properties, as directed after the effective date of this Order by the Government of Iran, acting through its authorized agent. Except where specifically stated, this license, authorization, and direction does not relieve persons subject to the jurisdiction of the United States from existing legal requirements other than those based upon the International Emergency Economic Powers Act [this chapter].

1–102. (a) All licenses and authorizations for acquiring or exercising any right, power, or privilege, by court order, attachment, or otherwise, including the license contained in Section 535.504 of the Iranian Assets Control Regulations, with respect to the properties described in Section 1–101 of this Order are revoked and withdrawn.

(b) All rights, powers, and privileges relating to the properties described in section 1–101 of this Order and which derive from any attachment, injunction, other like proceedings or process, or other action in any litigation after November 14, 1979, at 8:10 a.m. EST, including those derived from Section 535.504 of the Iranian Assets Control Regulations, other than rights, powers, and privileges of the Government of Iran and its agencies, instrumentalities, and controlled entities, whether acquired by court order or otherwise, are nullified, and all persons claiming any such right, power, or privilege are hereafter barred from exercising the same.

(c) All persons subject to the jurisdiction of the United States are prohibited from acquiring or exercising any right, power, or privilege, whether by court order or otherwise, with respect to the properties (and any income earned thereon) referred to in Section 1–101 of this Order.

1–103. Compliance with this Executive Order, any other Executive Order licensing, authorizing, directing or compelling the transfer of the assets described in paragraph 1–101 of this Order, or any regulations, instructions, or directions issued thereunder shall to the extent thereof be a full acquittance and discharge for all purposes of the obligation of the person making the same. No person shall be held liable in any court for or with respect to anything done or omitted in good faith in connection with the administration of, or pursuant to and in reliance on, such orders, regulations, instructions, or directions.

1–104. The Attorney General shall seek to intervene in any litigation within the United States which arises out of this Order and shall, among other things, defend the legality of, and all actions taken pursuant to, each of its provisions.

1–105. The Secretary of the Treasury is delegated and authorized to exercise all functions vested in the President by the International Emergency Economic Powers Act (50 U.S.C. 1701 et seq.) to carry out the purposes of this Order.

1–106. This Order shall be effective immediately.

JIMMY CARTER.

EX. ORD. NO. 12282. RELEASE OF AMERICAN HOSTAGES IN IRAN—REVOCATION OF PROHIBITIONS AGAINST TRANSACTIONS INVOLVING IRAN

Ex. Ord. No. 12282, Jan. 19, 1981, 46 F.R. 7925, provided:

By the authority vested in me as President by the Constitution and statutes of the United States, including Section 203 of the International Emergency Economic Powers Act (50 U.S.C. 1702), Section 301 of Title 3 of the United States Code, Section 1732 of Title 22 of the United States Code, and Section 301 of the National Emergencies Act (50 U.S.C. 1631), in view of the continuing unusual and extraordinary threat to the national security, foreign policy and economy of the United States upon which I based my declarations of national emergency in Executive Order 12170 [set out above], issued November 14, 1979, and in Executive Order 12211 [set out above], issued April 17, 1980, in order to implement agreements with the Government of Iran, as reflected in Declarations of the Government of the Democratic and Popular Republic of Algeria dated January 19, 1981, relating to the release of U.S. diplomats and nationals being held as hostage and to the resolution of claims of United States nationals against Iran, and to begin the process of normalization of relations between the United States and Iran, it is hereby ordered that as of the effective date of this Order:

1–101. The prohibitions contained in Executive Order 12205 of April 7, 1980 [set out above], and Executive Order 12211 of April 17, 1980 [set out above], and Proclamation 4702 of November 12, 1979 [amending Proc. No. 3279, set out under section 1862 of Title 19, Customs Duties], are hereby revoked.

1–102. The Secretary of the Treasury is delegated and authorized to exercise all functions vested in the President by the International Emergency Economic Powers Act (50 U.S.C. 1701 et seq.) to carry out the purpose of this Order.

1–103. This Order shall be effective immediately.

JIMMY CARTER.

EX. ORD. NO. 12283. RELEASE OF AMERICAN HOSTAGES IN IRAN—NON-PROSECUTION OF CLAIMS OF HOSTAGES AND FOR ACTIONS AT THE UNITED STATES EMBASSY AND ELSEWHERE

Ex. Ord. No. 12283, Jan. 19, 1981, 46 F.R. 7927, provided:

By the authority vested in me as President by the Constitution and statutes of the United States, including Section 203 of the International Emergency Economic Powers Act (50 U.S.C. 1702), Section 301 of Title 3 of the United States Code, Section 1732 of Title 22 of the United States Code, and Section 301 of the National Emergencies Act (50 U.S.C. 1631), in view of the continuing unusual and extraordinary threat to the national security, foreign policy and economy of the United States upon which I based my declarations of national emergency in Executive Order 12170 [set out above], issued November 14, 1979, and in Executive Order 12211 [set out above], issued April 17, 1980, in order to implement agreements with the Government of Iran, as reflected in Declarations of the Government of the Democratic and Popular Republic of Algeria dated January 19, 1981, relating to the release of U.S. diplomats and nationals being held as hostages and to the resolution of claims of United States nationals against Iran, and to begin the process of normalization of relations between the United States and Iran, it is hereby ordered that as of the effective date of this Order:

1–101. The Secretary of the Treasury shall promulgate regulations: (a) prohibiting any person subject to U.S. jurisdiction from prosecuting in any court within the United States or elsewhere any claim against the Government of Iran arising out of events occurring before the date of this Order relating to (1) the seizure of the hostages on November 4, 1979, (2) their subsequent detention, (3) injury to United States property or property of United States nationals within the United States Embassy compound in Tehran after November 3, 1979, or (4) injury to United States nationals or their property as a result of popular movements in the course of the Islamic Revolution in Iran which were not an act of the Government of Iran; (b) prohibiting any person not a U.S. national from prosecuting any such claim in any court within the United States; (c) ordering the termination of any previously instituted judicial proceedings based upon such claims; and (d) prohibiting the enforcement of any judicial order issued in the course of such proceedings.

1–102. The Attorney General of the United States is authorized and directed, immediately upon the issuance of regulations in accordance with Section 1–101, to take all appropriate measures to notify all appropriate courts of the existence of this Order and implementing regulations and the resulting termination of litigation.

1–103. The Secretary of the Treasury is delegated and authorized to exercise all functions vested in the President by the International Emergency Economic Powers Act (50 U.S.C. 1701 et seq.) to carry out the purpose of this Order.

1–104. This Order shall be effective immediately.

JIMMY CARTER.

EX. ORD. NO. 12284. RELEASE OF AMERICAN HOSTAGES IN IRAN—RESTRICTIONS ON TRANSFER OF PROPERTY OF FORMER SHAH OF IRAN

Ex. Ord. No. 12284, Jan. 19, 1981, 46 F.R. 7929, provided:

By the authority vested in me as President by the Constitution and statutes of the United States, including Section 203 of the International Emergency Economic Powers Act (50 U.S.C. 1702), Section 301 of Title 3 of the United States Code, Section 1732 of Title 22 of the United States Code, and Section 301 of the National Emergencies Act (50 U.S.C. 1631), in view of the continuing unusual and extraordinary threat to the national security, foreign policy and economy of the United States upon which I based my declarations of national emergency in Executive Order 12170 [set out above], issued November 14, 1979, and in Executive Order 12211 [set out above], issued April 17, 1980, in order to implement agreements with the Government of Iran, as reflected in Declarations of the Government of the Democratic and Popular Republic of Algeria dated January 19, 1981, relating to the release of U.S. diplomats and nationals being held as hostages and to the resolution of claims of United States nationals against Iran, and to begin the process of normalization of relations between the United States and Iran, it is hereby ordered that as of the effective date of this Order:

1–101. For the purpose of protecting the rights of litigants in courts within the United States, all property and assets located in the United States within the control of the estate of Mohammad Reza Pahlavi, the former Shah of Iran, or any close relative of the former Shah served as a defendant in litigation in such courts brought by Iran seeking the return of property alleged to belong to Iran, is hereby blocked as to each such estate or person until all such litigation against such estate or person is finally terminated.

1–102. The Secretary of the Treasury is authorized and directed (a) to promulgate regulations requiring all persons who are subject to the jurisdiction of the United States and who, as of November 3, 1979, or as of this date, have actual or constructive possession of property of the kind described in Section 1–101, or knowledge of such possession by others, to report such possession or knowledge thereof, to the Secretary of the Treasury in accordance with such regulations and (b) to make available to the Government of Iran or its designated agents all identifying information derived from such reports to the fullest extent permitted by law. Such reports shall be required as to all individuals described in 1–101 and shall be required to be filed within 30 days after publication of a notice in the Federal Register.

1–103. The Secretary of the Treasury is authorized and directed (a) to require all agencies within the Executive Branch of the United States Government to deliver to the Secretary all official financial books and records which serve to identify any property of the kind described in Section 1–101 of this Order, and (b) to make available to the Government of Iran or its designated agents all identifying information derived from such books and records to the fullest extent permitted by law.

1–104. The Attorney General of the United States having advised the President of his opinion that no claim on behalf of the Government of Iran for recovery of property of the kind described in Section 1–101 of this Order should be considered legally barred either by sovereign immunity principles or by the act of state doctrine, the Attorney General is authorized and directed to prepare, and upon the request of counsel representing the Government of Iran to present to the appropriate court or courts within the United States, suggestions of interest reflecting that such is the position of the United States, and that it is also the position of the United States that Iranian decrees and judgments relating to the assets of the former Shah and the persons described in Section 1–101 should be enforced by such courts in accordance with United States law.

1–105. The Secretary of the Treasury is delegated and authorized to exercise all functions vested in the President by the International Emergency Economic Powers Act (50 U.S.C. 1701 et seq.) to carry out the purposes of this Order.

1–106. This Order shall be effective immediately.

JIMMY CARTER.

EXECUTIVE ORDER NO. 12285

Ex. Ord. No. 12285, Jan. 19, 1981, 46 F.R. 7931, as amended by Ex. Ord. No. 12307, June 4, 1981, 46 F.R. 30483; Ex. Ord. No. 12317, Aug. 14, 1981, 46 F.R. 42241, which established the President's Commission on Hostage Compensation and provided for its membership, functions, etc., was revoked by Ex. Ord. No. 12379, §21, Aug. 17, 1982, 47 F.R. 36100, set out as a note under section 14 of the Federal Advisory Committee Act in the Appendix to Title 5, Government Organization and Employees.

EX. ORD. NO. 12294. SUSPENSION OF LITIGATION AGAINST IRAN

Ex. Ord. No. 12294, Feb. 24, 1981, 46 F.R. 14111, provided:

By the authority vested in me as President by the Constitution and statutes of the United States, including Section 203 of the International Emergency Economic Powers Act (50 U.S.C. 1702), Section 301 of Title 3 of the United States Code, Section 1732 of Title 22 of the United States Code, and Section 301 of the National Emergencies Act (50 U.S.C. 1631), in view of the continuing unusual and extraordinary threat to the national security, foreign policy and economy of the United States upon which were based the declarations of national emergency in Executive Order No. 12170, issued November 14, 1979 [set out above], and in Executive Order No. 12211, issued April 17, 1980 [set out above], in light of the agreement with the Government of Iran, as reflected in the Declarations of the Government of the Democratic and Popular Republic of Algeria dated January 19, 1981, relating to the release of United States diplomats and nationals being held as hostages and to the resolution of claims of United States nationals against Iran, in order to implement Article II of the Declaration of Algeria concerning the settlement of claims and to begin the process of normalization of relations between the United States and Iran, it is hereby ordered that as of the effective date of this Order:

SECTION 1. All claims which may be presented to the Iran-United States Claims Tribunal under the terms of Article II of the Declaration of the Government of the Democratic and Popular Republic of Algeria Concerning the Settlement of Claims by the Government of the United States of America and the Government of the Islamic Republic of Iran, and all claims for equitable or other judicial relief in connection with such claims, are hereby suspended, except as they may be presented to the Tribunal. During the period of this suspension, all such claims shall have no legal effect in any action now pending in any court of the United States, including the courts of any state or any locality thereof, the District of Columbia and Puerto Rico, or in any action commenced in any such court after the effective date of this Order. Nothing in this action precludes the commencement of an action after the effective date of this Order for the purpose of tolling the period of limitations for commencement of such action.

SEC. 2. Nothing in this Order shall require dismissal of any action for want of prosecution.

SEC. 3. Suspension under this Order of a claim or a portion thereof submitted to the Iran-United States Claims Tribunal for adjudication shall terminate upon a determination by the Tribunal that it does not have jurisdiction over such claim or such portion thereof.

SEC. 4. A determination by the Iran-United States Claims Tribunal on the merits that a claimant is not entitled to recover on a claim shall operate as a final resolution and discharge of the claim for all purposes. A determination by the Tribunal that a claimant shall have recovery on a claim in a specified amount shall operate as a final resolution and discharge of the claim for all purposes upon payment to the claimant of the full amount of the award, including any interest awarded by the Tribunal.

SEC. 5. Nothing in this Order shall apply to any claim concerning the validity or payment of a standby letter of credit, performance or payment bond or other similar instrument.

SEC. 6. Nothing in this Order shall prohibit the assertion of a counterclaim or set-off by a United States national in any judicial proceeding pending or hereafter commenced by the Government of Iran, any political subdivision of Iran, or any agency, instrumentality, or entity controlled by the Government of Iran or any political subdivision thereof.

SEC. 7. The Secretary of the Treasury is authorized to employ all powers granted to me by the International Emergency Economic Powers Act [this chapter] and by 22 U.S.C. §1732 to carry out the purposes of this Order.

SEC. 8. Executive Order Nos. 12276 through 12285 of January 19, 1981 [set out above], are ratified.

This Order shall be effective immediately and copies shall be transmitted to the Congress.

RONALD REAGAN.

EXECUTIVE ORDER NO. 12444

Ex. Ord. No. 12444, Oct. 14, 1983, 48 F.R. 48215, which continued effectiveness of the Export Administration Act of 1979, 50 App. U.S.C. 2401 et seq., and of orders, rules and regulations promulgated thereunder, was revoked by Ex. Ord. No. 12451, Dec. 20, 1983, 48 F.R. 56563, set out below.

EX. ORD. NO. 12451. CONTINUATION OF EXPORT CONTROL REGULATIONS

Ex. Ord. No. 12451, Dec. 20, 1983, 48 F.R. 56563, provided:

By the authority vested in me as President by the Constitution and laws of the United States of America, including section 203 of the International Emergency Economic Powers Act (50 U.S.C. 1702) (hereinafter referred to as "IEEPA"), 22 U.S.C. 287c, and the Export Administration Act of 1979, as amended (50 U.S.C. App. 2401 *et seq.*) (hereinafter referred to as "the Act), it is hereby ordered as follows:

SECTION 1. In view of the extension by Public Law 98–207 (December 5, 1983) [amending 50 App. U.S.C. 2419], of the authorities contained in the Act, Executive Order No. 12444 of October 14, 1983, which continued in effect export control regulations under IEEPA, is revoked, and the declaration of economic emergency is rescinded.

SEC. 2. The revocation of Executive Order No. 12444 shall not affect any violation of any rules, regulations, orders, licenses and other forms of administrative action under that Order which occurred during the period that Order was in effect. All rules and regulations issued or continued in effect under the authority of the IEEPA and that Order, including those published in Title 15, Chapter III, Subchapter C, of the Code of Federal Regulations, Parts 368 to 399 inclusive, and all orders, regulations, licenses and other forms of administrative action issued, taken or continued in effect pursuant thereto, shall remain in full force and effect, as if issued, taken or continued in effect pursuant to the Act until amended or revoked by the proper authority. Nothing in this Order shall affect the continued applicability of the provision for the administration of the Act and delegations of authority set forth in Executive Order No. 12002 of July 7, 1977 and Executive Order No. 12214 of May 2, 1980 [50 App. U.S.C. 2403 note].

SEC. 3. All orders, licenses, and other forms of administrative action issued, taken or continued in effect pursuant to the authority of the IEEPA and Executive Order No. 12444 relating to the administration of section 38(e) of the Arms Export Control Act (22 U.S.C. 2778(e)) shall remain in full force and effect until amended or revoked under proper authority.

SEC. 4. This Order shall take effect immediately.

RONALD REAGAN.

EXECUTIVE ORDER NO. 12470

Ex. Ord. No. 12470, Mar. 30, 1984, 49 F.R. 13099, which continued effectiveness of the Export Administration Act of 1979, 50 App. U.S.C. 2401 et seq., and of the orders, rules and regulations promulgated thereunder, was revoked by Ex. Ord. No. 12525, July 12, 1985, 50 F.R. 28757, set out below.

Continuation of emergency declared by Ex. Ord. No. 12470 was contained in Notice of the President of the United States, dated Mar. 28, 1985, 50 F.R. 12513.

EXECUTIVE ORDER NO. 12513

Ex. Ord. No. 12513, May 1, 1985, 50 F.R. 18629, which prohibited trade and certain other transactions involving Nicaragua, was revoked by Ex. Ord. No. 12707, Mar. 13, 1990, 55 F.R. 9707, set out below.

Continuations of national emergency declared by Ex. Ord. No. 12513 were contained in the following:

Notice of the President of the United States, dated Apr. 21, 1989, 54 F.R. 17701.

Notice of the President of the United States, dated Apr. 25, 1988, 53 F.R. 15011.

Notice of the President of the United States, dated Apr. 21, 1987, 52 F.R. 13425.

Notice of the President of the United States, dated Apr. 22, 1986, 51 F.R. 15461.

EX. ORD. NO. 12525. TERMINATION OF EMERGENCY AUTHORITY FOR EXPORT CONTROLS

Ex. Ord. No. 12525, July 12, 1985, 50 F.R. 28757, provided:

By the authority vested in me as President by the Constitution and laws of the United States of America, including section 203 of the International Emergency Economic Powers Act (50 U.S.C. 1702) (hereinafter referred to as "IEEPA"), 22 U.S.C. 287c, and the Export Administration Act of 1979, as amended (50 U.S.C. App. 2401 *et seq.*) (hereinafter referred to as "the Act"), it is hereby ordered as follows:

SECTION 1. In view of the extension by Public Law 99–64 (July 12, 1985) [amending 50 App. U.S.C. 2419] of the authorities contained in the Act, Executive Order No. 12470 of March 30, 1984, which continued in effect export control regulations under IEEPA, is revoked, and the declaration of economic emergency is rescinded.

SEC. 2. The revocation of Executive Order No. 12470 shall not affect any violation of any rules, regulations, orders, licenses, and other forms of administrative action under that Order that occurred during the period that Order was in effect. All rules and regulations issued or continued in effect under the authority of the IEEPA and that Order, including those published in Title 15, Chapter III, Subchapter C, of the Code of Federal Regulations, Parts 368 to 399 inclusive, and all orders, regulations, licenses, and other forms of administrative action issued, taken or continued in effect pursuant thereto, shall remain in full force and effect, as if issued, taken or continued in effect pursuant to and as authorized by the Act or by other appropriate authority until amended or revoked by the proper authority. Nothing in this Order shall affect the continued applicability of the provision for the administration of the Act and delegations of authority set forth in Executive Order No. 12002 of July 7, 1977, and Executive Order No. 12214 of May 2, 1980 [set out under 50 App. U.S.C. 2403].

SEC. 3. All rules, regulations, orders, licenses, and other forms of administrative action issued, taken or continued in effect pursuant to the authority of the IEEPA and Executive Order No. 12470 relating to the administration of Section 38(e) of the Arms Export Control Act (22 U.S.C. 2778(e)) shall remain in full force and effect until amended or revoked under proper authority.

SEC. 4. This Order shall take effect immediately.

RONALD REAGAN.

EXECUTIVE ORDER NO. 12532

Ex. Ord. No. 12532, Sept. 9, 1985, 50 F.R. 36861, which prohibited trade and certain other transactions involving South Africa, was revoked by Ex. Ord. No. 12769, §4, July 10, 1991, 56 F.R. 31855, set out as a note under section 5061 of Title 22, Foreign Relations and Intercourse.

Continuation of national emergency declared by Ex. Ord. No. 12532 was contained in Notice of the President of the United States, dated Sept. 4, 1986, 51 F.R. 31925.

EXECUTIVE ORDER NO. 12535

Ex. Ord. No. 12535, Oct. 1, 1985, 50 F.R. 40325, which prohibited importation into United States of South African Krugerrands, was revoked by Ex. Ord. No. 12769, §4, July 10, 1991, 56 F.R. 31855, set out as a note under section 5061 of Title 22, Foreign Relations and Intercourse.

EX. ORD. NO. 12543. PROHIBITING TRADE AND CERTAIN TRANSACTIONS INVOLVING LIBYA

Ex. Ord. No. 12543, Jan. 7, 1986, 51 F.R. 875, provided:

By the authority vested in me as President by the Constitution and laws of the United States of America, including the International Emergency Economic Powers Act (50 U.S.C. 1701 *et seq.*), the National Emergencies Act (50 U.S.C. 1601 *et seq.*), sections 504 and 505 of the International Security and Development Cooperation Act of 1985 (Public Law 99–83) [22 U.S.C. 2349aa–8, 2349aa–9], section 1114 of the Federal Aviation Act of 1958, as amended (49 U.S.C. 1514) [now 49 U.S.C. 40106(b)], and section 301 of title 3 of the United States Code.

I, RONALD REAGAN, President of the United States of America, find that the policies and actions of the Government of Libya constitute an unusual and extraordinary threat to the national security and foreign policy of the United States and hereby declare a national emergency to deal with that threat.

I hereby order:

SECTION 1. The following are prohibited, except to the extent provided in regulations which may hereafter be issued pursuant to this Order:

(a) The import into the United States of any goods or services of Libyan origin, other than publications and materials imported for news publications or news broadcast dissemination;

(b) The export to Libya of any goods, technology (including technical data or other information) or services from the United States, except publications and donations of articles intended to relieve human suffering, such as food, clothing, medicine and medical supplies intended strictly for medical purposes;

(c) Any transaction by a United States person relating to transportation to or from Libya; the provision of transportation to or from the United States by any Libyan person or any vessel or aircraft of Libyan registration; or the sale in the United States by any person holding authority under the Federal Aviation Act [of 1958, now 49 U.S.C. 40101 et seq.] of any transportation by air which includes any stop in Libya;

(d) The purchase by any United States person of goods for export from Libya to any country;

(e) The performance by any United States person of any contract in support of an industrial or other commercial or governmental project in Libya;

(f) The grant or extension of credits or loans by any United States person to the Government of Libya, its instrumentalities and controlled entities;

(g) Any transaction by a United States person relating to travel by any United States citizen or permanent resident alien to Libya, or to activities by any such person within Libya, after the date of this Order, other than transactions necessary to effect such person's departure from Libya, to perform acts permitted until February 1, 1986, by Section 3 of this Order, or travel for journalistic activity by persons regularly employed in such capacity by a newsgathering organization; and

(h) Any transaction by any United States person which evades or avoids, or has the purpose of evading or avoiding, any of the prohibitions set forth in this Order.

For purposes of this Order, the term "United States person" means any United States citizen, permanent resident alien, juridical person organized under the laws of the United States or any person in the United States.

SEC. 2. In light of the prohibition in Section 1(a) of this Order, section 251 of the Trade Expansion Act of 1962, as amended (19 U.S.C. 1881), and section 126 of the Trade Act of 1974, as amended (19 U.S.C. 2136) will have no effect with respect to Libya.

SEC. 3. This Order is effective immediately, except that the prohibitions set forth in Section 1(a), (b), (c), (d) and (e) shall apply as of 12:01 a.m. Eastern Standard Time, February 1, 1986.

SEC. 4. The Secretary of the Treasury, in consultation with the Secretary of State, is hereby authorized to take such actions, including the promulgation of rules and regulations, as may be necessary to carry out the purposes of this Order. Such actions may include prohibiting or regulating payments or transfers of any property or any transactions involving the transfer of anything of economic value by any United States person to the Government of Libya, its instrumentalities and controlled entities, or to any Libyan national or entity owned or controlled, directly or indirectly, by Libya or Libyan nationals. The Secretary may redelegate any of these functions to other officers and agencies of the Federal government. All agencies of the United States government are directed to take all appropriate measures within their authority to carry out the provisions of this Order, including the suspension or termination of licenses or other authorizations in effect as of the date of this Order.

This Order shall be transmitted to the Congress and published in the Federal Register.

RONALD REAGAN.

CONTINUATION OF NATIONAL EMERGENCY DECLARED BY EX. ORD. NO. 12543

Notice of President of the United States, dated Jan. 4, 2001, 66 F.R. 1251, provided:

On January 7, 1986, by Executive Order 12543 [set out above], President Reagan declared a national emergency to deal with the unusual and extraordinary threat to the national security and foreign policy of the United States constituted by the actions and policies of the Government of Libya. On January 8, 1986, by Executive Order 12544 [set out below], the President took additional measures to block Libyan assets in the United States. The President has transmitted a notice continuing this emergency to the Congress and the Federal Register every year since 1986.

The crisis between the United States and Libya that led to the declaration of a national emergency on January 7, 1986, has not been resolved. Despite the United Nations Security Council's suspension of U.N. sanctions against Libya upon the Libyan government's hand over of the Pan Am 103 bombing suspects, there are still concerns about the Libyan government's support for terrorist activities and its noncompliance with United Nations Security Council Resolutions 731 (1992), 748 (1992), and 883 (1993).

Therefore, in accordance with section 202(d) of the National Emergencies Act (50 U.S.C. 1622(d)), I am continuing the national emergency with respect to Libya. This notice shall be published in the Federal Register and transmitted to the Congress.

WILLIAM J. CLINTON.

Prior continuations of national emergency declared by Ex. Ord. No. 12543 were contained in the following:

Notice of President of the United States, dated Dec. 29, 1999, 65 F.R. 1999.

Notice of President of the United States, dated Dec. 30, 1998, 64 F.R. 383.

Notice of President of the United States, dated Jan. 2, 1998, 63 F.R. 653.

Notice of President of the United States, dated Jan. 2, 1997, 62 F.R. 587.

Notice of President of the United States, dated Jan. 3, 1996, 61 F.R. 383.

Notice of President of the United States, dated Dec. 22, 1994, 59 F.R. 67119.

Notice of President of the United States, dated Dec. 2, 1993, 58 F.R. 64361.

Notice of President of the United States, dated Dec. 14, 1992, 57 F.R. 59895.

Notice of President of the United States, dated Dec. 26, 1991, 56 F.R. 67465.

Notice of the President of the United States, dated Jan. 2, 1991, 56 F.R. 477.

Notice of the President of the United States, dated Jan. 4, 1990, 55 F.R. 589.

Notice of the President of the United States, dated Dec. 28, 1988, 53 F.R. 52971.

Notice of the President of the United States, dated Dec. 15, 1987, 52 F.R. 47891.

Notice of the President of the United States, dated Dec. 23, 1986, 51 F.R. 46849.

EX. ORD. NO. 12544. BLOCKING LIBYAN GOVERNMENT PROPERTY IN THE UNITED STATES OR HELD BY U.S. PERSONS

Ex. Ord. No. 12544, Jan. 8, 1986, 51 F.R. 1235, provided:

By the authority vested in me as President by the Constitution and laws of the United States, including the International Emergency Economic Powers Act (50 U.S.C. 1701 *et seq.*), the National Emergencies Act (50 U.S.C. 1601 *et seq.*) and section 301 of title 3 of the United States Code, in order to take steps with respect to Libya additional to those set forth in Executive Order No. 12543 of January 7, 1986 [set out above], to deal with the threat to the national security and foreign policy of the United States referred to in that Order,

I, RONALD REAGAN, President of the United States, hereby order blocked all property and interests in property of the Government of Libya, its agencies, instrumentalities and controlled entities and the Central Bank of Libya that are in the United States, that hereafter come within the United States or that are or hereafter come within the possession or control of U.S. persons, including overseas branches of U.S. persons.

The Secretary of the Treasury, in consultation with the Secretary of State, is authorized to employ all powers granted to me by the International Emergency Economics [sic] Power[s] Act, 50 U.S.C. 1701 *et seq.*, to carry out the provisions of this Order.

This Order is effective immediately and shall be transmitted to the Congress and published in the Federal Register.

RONALD REAGAN.

EXECUTIVE ORDER NO. 12613

Ex. Ord. No. 12613, Oct. 29, 1987, 52 F.R. 41940, which prohibited imports from Iran, was revoked by Ex. Ord. No. 13059, §7, Aug. 19, 1997, 62 F.R. 44533, set out below.

EXECUTIVE ORDER NO. 12635

Ex. Ord. No. 12635, Apr. 8, 1988, 53 F.R. 12134, which blocked property and interests in property of the Government of Panama that were in the United States, was revoked by Ex. Ord. No. 12710, Apr. 5, 1990, 55 F.R. 13099, set out below.

Continuation of national emergency declared by Ex. Ord. No. 12635 was contained in Notice of the President of the United States, dated Apr. 6, 1989, 54 F.R. 14197.

EX. ORD. NO. 12707. TERMINATION OF EMERGENCY WITH RESPECT TO NICARAGUA

Ex. Ord. No. 12707, Mar. 13, 1990, 55 F.R. 9707, provided:

By the authority vested in me as President by the Constitution and laws of the United States of America, including the International Emergency Economic Powers Act (50 U.S.C. 1701 *et seq.*), the National Emergencies Act (50 U.S.C. 1601 *et seq.*), chapter 12 of title 50 of the United States Code (50 U.S.C. 191 *et seq.*), and section 301 of title 3 of the United States Code.

I, GEORGE BUSH, President of the United States of America, find that the February 25, 1990, democratic election in Nicaragua has ended the unusual and extraordinary threat to the national security and foreign policy of the United States previously posed by the policies and actions of the Sandinista government in that country, and the need to continue the national emergency declared in Executive Order No. 12513 of May 1, 1985, to deal with that threat.

I hereby revoke Executive Order No. 12513 and terminate the national emergency declared in that order with respect to Nicaragua.

Pursuant to section 202 of the National Emergencies Act (50 U.S.C. 1622), termination of the national emergency with respect to Nicaragua shall not affect any action taken or proceeding pending and not finally concluded or determined at the effective date of this order, or any action or proceeding based on any act committed prior to the effective date of this order, or any rights or duties that matured or penalties that were incurred prior to the effective date of this order.

This order shall take effect immediately.

GEORGE BUSH.

EX. ORD. NO. 12710. TERMINATION OF EMERGENCY WITH RESPECT TO PANAMA

Ex. Ord. No. 12710, Apr. 5, 1990, 55 F.R. 13099, provided:

By the authority vested in me as President by the Constitution and laws of the United States of America, including the International Emergency Economic Powers Act (50 U.S.C. 1701 *et seq.*) (hereinafter referred to as "IEEPA"), the National Emergencies Act (50 U.S.C. 1601 *et seq.*) (hereinafter referred to as "the NEA"), chapter 12 of title 50 of the United States Code (50 U.S.C. 191 *et seq.*), and section 301 of title 3 of the United States Code.

I, GEORGE BUSH, President of the United States of America, find that the restoration of a democratically elected government in Panama has ended the unusual and extraordinary threat to the national security, foreign policy, and economy of the United States previously posed by the policies and actions of Manuel Antonio Noriega in that country, and the need to continue the national emergency declared in Executive Order No. 12635 of April 8, 1988, to deal with that threat.

I hereby revoke Executive Order No. 12635 and terminate the national emergency declared in that order with respect to Panama.

Pursuant to section 202 of the NEA (50 U.S.C. 1622), termination of the national emergency with respect to Panama shall not affect any action taken or proceeding pending not finally concluded or determined as of the effective date of this order, or any action or proceeding based on any act committed prior to the effective date of this order, or any rights or duties that matured or penalties that were incurred prior to the effective date of this order. Pursuant to section 207 (50 U.S.C. 1706) of IEEPA, I hereby determine that the continuation of prohibitions with regard to transactions involving property in which the Government of Panama has an interest is necessary on account of claims involving Panama.

This order shall take effect immediately.

GEORGE BUSH.

EX. ORD. NO. 12722. BLOCKING IRAQI GOVERNMENT PROPERTY AND PROHIBITING TRANSACTIONS WITH IRAQ

Ex. Ord. No. 12722, Aug. 2, 1990, 55 F.R. 31803, provided:

By the authority vested in me as President by the constitution and laws of the United States of America, including the International Emergency Economic Powers Act (50 U.S.C. 1701 *et seq.*), the National Emergencies Act (50 U.S.C. 1601 *et seq.*), and section 301 of title 3 of the United States Code.

I, GEORGE BUSH, President of the United States of America, find that the policies and actions of the Government of Iraq constitute an unusual and extraordinary threat to the national security and foreign policy of the United States and hereby declare a national emergency to deal with that threat.

I hereby order:

SECTION 1. All property and interests in property of the Government of Iraq, its agencies, instrumentalities and controlled entities and the Central Bank of Iraq that are in the United States, that hereafter come within the United States or that are or hereafter come within the possession or control of United States persons, including their overseas branches, are hereby blocked.

SECTION 2. The following are prohibited, except to the extent provided in regulations which may hereafter be issued pursuant to this Order:

(a) The import into the United States of any goods or services of Iraqi origin, other than publications and other informational materials;

(b) The export to Iraq of any goods, technology (including technical data or other information controlled for export pursuant to Section 5 of the Export Administration Act (50 U.S.C. App. 2404)) or services from the United States, except publications and other informational materials, and donations of articles intended to relieve human suffering, such as food, clothing, medicine and medical supplies intended strictly for medical purposes;

(c) Any transaction by a United States person relating to transportation to or from Iraq; the provision of transportation to or from the United States by any Iraqi person or any vessel or aircraft of Iraqi registration; or the sale in the United States by any person holding authority under the Federal Aviation Act of 1958, as amended [now 49 U.S.C. 40101 et seq.] (49 U.S.C. 1514), of any transportation by air which includes any stop in Iraq;

(d) The purchase by any United States person of goods for export from Iraq to any country;

(e) The performance by any United States person of any contract in support of an industrial or other commercial or governmental project in Iraq;

(f) The grant or extension of credits or loans by any United States person to the Government of Iraq, its instrumentalities and controlled entities;

(g) Any transaction by a United States person relating to travel by any United States citizen or permanent resident alien to Iraq, or to activities by any such person within Iraq, after the date of this Order, other than transactions necessary to effect such person's departure from Iraq, or travel for journalistic activity by persons regularly employed in such capacity by a newsgathering organization; and

(h) Any transaction by any United States person which evades or avoids, or has the purpose of evading or avoiding, any of the prohibitions set forth in this Order.

For purposes of this Order, the term "United States person" means any United States citizen, permanent resident alien, juridical person organized under the laws of the United States, or any person in the United States.

SECTION 3. This Order is effective immediately.

SECTION 4. The Secretary of the Treasury, in consultation with the Secretary of State, is hereby authorized to take such actions, including the promulgation of rules and regulations, as may be necessary to carry out the purposes of this Order. Such actions may include prohibiting or regulating payments or transfers of any property or any transactions involving the transfer of anything of economic value by any United States person to the Government of Iraq, its instrumentalities and controlled entities, or to any Iraqi national or entity owned or controlled, directly or indirectly, by Iraq or Iraqi nationals. The Secretary may redelegate any of these functions to other officers and agencies of the Federal government. All agencies of the United States government are directed to take all appropriate measures within their authority to carry out the provisions of this Order, including the suspension or termination of licenses or other authorizations in effect as of the date of this Order.

This Order shall be transmitted to the Congress and published in the Federal Register.

GEORGE BUSH.

[Ex. Ord. No. 12722 was revoked by Ex. Ord. No. 12724, §6, Aug. 9, 1990, 55 F.R. 33090, set out below, to the extent inconsistent with Ex. Ord. No. 12724.]

CONTINUATION OF NATIONAL EMERGENCY DECLARED BY EX. ORD. NO. 12722

Notice of President of the United States, dated July 28, 2000, 65 F.R. 47241, provided:

On August 2, 1990, by Executive Order 12722 [set out above], President Bush declared a national emergency to deal with the unusual and extraordinary threat to the national security and foreign policy of the United States constituted by the actions and policies of the Government of Iraq. By Executive Orders 12722 of August 2, 1990, and 12724 of August 9, 1990 [set out below], the President imposed trade sanctions on Iraq and blocked Iraqi government assets. Because the Government of Iraq has continued its activities hostile to United States interests in the Middle East, the national emergency declared on August 2, 1990, and the measures adopted on August 2 and August 9, 1990, to deal with that emergency must continue in effect beyond August 2, 2000. Therefore, in accordance with section 202(d) of the National Emergencies Act (50 U.S.C. 1622(d)), I am continuing the national emergency with respect to Iraq.

This notice shall be published in the Federal Register and transmitted to the Congress.

WILLIAM J. CLINTON.

Prior continuations of national emergency declared by Ex. Ord. No. 12722 were contained in the following:

Notice of President of the United States, dated July 20, 1999, 64 F.R. 39897.

Notice of President of the United States, dated July 28, 1998, 63 F.R. 41175.

Notice of President of the United States, dated July 31, 1997, 62 F.R. 41803.

Notice of President of the United States, dated July 22, 1996, 61 F.R. 38561.

Notice of President of the United States, dated July 28, 1995, 60 F.R. 39099.

Notice of President of the United States, dated July 19, 1994, 59 F.R. 37151.

Notice of President of the United States, dated July 20, 1993, 58 F.R. 39111.

Notice of President of the United States, dated July 21, 1992, 57 F.R. 32875.

Notice of President of the United States, dated July 26, 1991, 56 F.R. 35995.

EXECUTIVE ORDER NO. 12723

Ex. Ord. No. 12723, Aug. 2, 1990, 55 F.R. 31805, which directed Secretary of the Treasury to block all property and interests in Kuwaiti Government property that are in the United States or within possession or control of United States persons, was revoked by Ex. Ord. No. 12771, July 25, 1991, 56 F.R. 35993, set out below.

EX. ORD. NO. 12724. BLOCKING IRAQI GOVERNMENT PROPERTY AND PROHIBITING TRANSACTIONS WITH IRAQ

Ex. Ord. No. 12724, Aug. 9, 1990, 55 F.R. 33089, provided:

By the authority vested in me as President by the Constitution and laws of the United States of America, including the International Emergency Economic Powers Act (50 U.S.C. 1701 *et seq.*), the National Emergencies Act (50 U.S.C. 1601 *et seq.*), section 301 of title 3 of the United States Code, and the United Nations Participation Act [22 U.S.C. 287 et seq.] (22 U.S.C. 287c), in view of United Nations Security Council Resolution No. 661 of August 6, 1990, and in order to take additional steps with respect to Iraq's invasion of Kuwait and the national emergency declared in Executive Order No. 12722 [set out above],

I, GEORGE BUSH, President of the United States of America, hereby order:

SECTION 1. Except to the extent provided in regulations that may hereafter be issued pursuant to this order, all property and interests in property of the Government of Iraq that are in the United States, that hereafter come within the United States, or that are or hereafter come within the possession or control of United States persons, including their overseas branches, are hereby blocked.

SEC. 2. The following are prohibited, except to the extent provided in regulations that may hereafter be issued pursuant to this order:

(a) The importation into the United States of any goods or services of Iraqi origin, or any activity that promotes or is intended to promote such importation;

(b) The exportation to Iraq, or to any entity operated from Iraq, or owned or controlled by the Government of Iraq, directly or indirectly, of any goods, technology (including technical data or other information), or services either (i) from the United States, or (ii) requiring the issuance of a license by a Federal agency, or any activity that promotes or is intended to promote such exportation, except donations of articles intended to relieve human suffering, such as food and supplies intended strictly for medical purposes;

(c) Any dealing by a United States person related to property of Iraqi origin exported from Iraq after August 6, 1990, or property intended for exportation from Iraq to any country, or exportation to Iraq from any country, or any activity of any kind that promotes or is intended to promote such dealing;

(d) Any transaction by a United States person relating to travel by any United States citizen or permanent resident alien to Iraq, or to activities by any such person within Iraq, after the date of this order, other than transactions necessary to effect (i) such person's departure from Iraq, (ii) travel and activities for the conduct of the official business of the Federal Government or the United Nations, or (iii) travel for journalistic activity by persons regularly employed in such capacity by a news-gathering organization;

(e) Any transaction by a United States person relating to transportation to or from Iraq; the provision of transportation to or from the United States by any Iraqi person or any vessel or aircraft of Iraqi registration; or the sale in the United States by any person holding authority under the Federal Aviation Act of 1958, as amended (49 U.S.C. 1301 *et seq.*) [now 49 U.S.C. 40101 et seq.], of any transportation by air that includes any stop in Iraq;

(f) The performance by any United States person of any contract, including a financing contract, in support of an industrial, commercial, public utility, or governmental project in Iraq;

(g) Except as otherwise authorized herein, any commitment or transfer, direct or indirect, of funds, or other financial or economic resources by any United States person to the Government of Iraq or any other person in Iraq;

(h) Any transaction by any United States person that evades or avoids, or has the purpose of evading or avoiding, any of the prohibitions set forth in this order.

SEC. 3. For purposes of this order:

(a) the term "United States person" means any United States citizen, permanent resident alien, juridical person organized under the laws of the United States (including foreign branches), or any person in the United States, and vessels of U.S. registration.

(b) the term "Government of Iraq" includes the Government of Iraq, its agencies, instrumentalities and controlled entities, and the Central Bank of Iraq.

SEC. 4. This order is effective immediately.

SEC. 5. The Secretary of the Treasury, in consultation with the Secretary of State, is hereby authorized to take such actions, including the promulgation of rules and regulations, as may be necessary to carry out the purposes of this order. Such actions may include prohibiting or regulating payments or transfers of any property or any transactions involving the transfer of anything of economic value by any United States person to the Government of Iraq, or to any Iraqi national or entity owned or controlled, directly or indirectly, by the Government of Iraq or Iraqi nationals. The Secretary of the Treasury may redelegate any of these functions to other officers and agencies of the Federal Government. All agencies of the Federal Government are directed to take all appropriate measures within their authority to carry out the provisions of this order, including the suspension or termination of licenses or other authorizations in effect as of the date of this order.

SEC. 6. Executive Order No. 12722 of August 2, 1990 [set out above], is hereby revoked to the extent inconsistent with this order. All delegations, rules, regulations, orders, licenses, and other forms of administrative action made, issued, or otherwise taken under Executive Order No. 12722 and not revoked administratively shall remain in full force and effect under this order until amended, modified, or terminated by proper authority. The revocation of any provision of Executive Order No. 12722 pursuant to this section shall not affect any violation of any rules, regulations, orders, licenses, or other forms of administrative action under that order during the period that such provision of that order was in effect.

This order shall be transmitted to the Congress and published in the Federal Register.

GEORGE BUSH.

EXECUTIVE ORDER NO. 12725

Ex. Ord. No. 12725, Aug. 9, 1990, 55 F.R. 33091, which directed Secretary of the Treasury to block all property and interests in Kuwaiti Government property that are in the United States or within possession or control of United States persons and which prohibited transactions with Kuwait, was revoked by Ex. Ord. No. 12771, July 25, 1991, 56 F.R. 35993, set out below.

EXECUTIVE ORDER NO. 12730

Ex. Ord. No. 12730, Sept. 30, 1990, 55 F.R. 40373, which continued effectiveness of the Export Administration Act of 1979, 50 App. U.S.C. 2401 et seq., and of the orders, rules and regulations promulgated thereunder, was revoked by Ex. Ord. No. 12867, §1, Sept. 30, 1993, 58 F.R. 51747, set out below.

Continuations of national emergency declared by Ex. Ord. No. 12730 were contained in the following:

Notice of President of the United States, dated Sept. 25, 1992, 57 F.R. 44649.

Notice of President of the United States, dated Sept. 26, 1991, 56 F.R. 49385.

EXECUTIVE ORDER NO. 12735

Ex. Ord. No. 12735, Nov. 16, 1990, 55 F.R. 48587, which declared a national emergency to deal with threat of proliferation of chemical and biological weapons and imposed controls on exports that would assist a country in developing, stockpiling, delivering, or using chemical or biological weapons and associated sanctions, was revoked by Ex. Ord. No. 12938, §10, Nov. 14, 1994, 59 F.R. 59099, set out below.

Continuations of national emergency declared by Ex. Ord. No. 12735 were contained in the following:

Notice of President of the United States, dated Nov. 12, 1993, 58 F.R. 60361.

Notice of President of the United States, dated Nov. 11, 1992, 57 F.R. 53979.

Notice of President of the United States, dated Nov. 14, 1991, 56 F.R. 58171.

EX. ORD. NO. 12771. REVOKING EARLIER ORDERS WITH RESPECT TO KUWAIT

Ex. Ord. No. 12771, July 25, 1991, 56 F.R. 35993, provided:

By the authority vested in me as President by the Constitution and the laws of the United States of America, including the International Emergency Economic Powers Act (50 U.S.C.1701 *et seq.*), the National Emergencies Act (50 U.S.C. 1601 *et seq.*), section 301 of title 3 of the United States Code, and United Nations Participation Act [22 U.S.C. 287 et seq.] (22 U.S.C. 287c),

I, GEORGE BUSH, President of the United States of America, find that the expulsion from Kuwait of Iraq's occupation forces, the restoration of Kuwait to its citizens, and the reinstatement of the lawful Government of Kuwait eliminate the need for Executive Order No. 12723 of August 2, 1990, entitled "Blocking Kuwaiti Government Property," and Executive Order No. 12725 of August 9, 1990, entitled "Blocking Kuwaiti Government Property and Prohibiting Transactions With Kuwait." Those orders were issued to protect the assets of the Government of Kuwait which were subject to United States jurisdiction, and to prevent the transfer of benefits by United States persons to Iraq based upon its invasion of Kuwait. Those orders also implemented the foreign policy and protected the national security of the United States, in conformity with applicable resolutions of the United Nations Security Council. Finding continuation of these orders unnecessary, I hereby order:

SECTION 1. Executive Order No. 12723 and Executive Order No. 12725 are hereby revoked. This revocation shall not affect the national emergency declared in Executive Order No. 12722 [set out above] to deal with the unusual and extraordinary threat to the national security and foreign policy of the United States posed by the policies and action of the Government of Iraq.

SEC. 2. This revocation shall not affect:

(a) any action taken or proceeding pending and not finally concluded or determined on the effective date of this order;

(b) any action or proceeding based on any act committed prior to the effective date of this order; or

(c) any rights or duties that matured or penalties that were incurred prior to the effective date of this order.

SEC. 3. This order shall take effect immediately.

GEORGE BUSH.

EXECUTIVE ORDER NO. 12775

Ex. Ord. No. 12775, Oct. 4, 1991, 56 F.R. 50641, which declared a national emergency to deal with Republic of Haiti, directed Secretary of Treasury to block all property and interests in property of Government of Haiti that were in United States or within possession or control of United States persons, and prohibited transactions with Haiti, was revoked, and such national emergency terminated, by Ex. Ord. No. 12932, Oct. 14, 1994, 59 F.R. 52403, set out below.

Continuations of national emergency declared by Ex. Ord. No. 12775 were contained in the following:

Notice of President of the United States, dated Sept. 30, 1994, 59 F.R. 50479.

Notice of President of the United States, dated Sept. 30, 1993, 58 F.R. 51563.

Notice of President of the United States, dated Sept. 30, 1992, 57 F.R. 45557.

EXECUTIVE ORDER NO. 12779

Ex. Ord. No. 12779, Oct. 28, 1991, 56 F.R. 55975, which directed Secretary of the Treasury to block all property and interests in property of Government of Haiti that were in United States or within possession or control of United States persons and which prohibited transactions with Haiti and most imports from and exports to Haiti, was revoked by Ex. Ord. No. 12932, Oct. 14, 1994, 59 F.R. 52403, set out below.

EX. ORD. NO. 12801. BARRING OVERFLIGHT, TAKEOFF, AND LANDING OF AIRCRAFT FLYING TO OR FROM LIBYA

Ex. Ord. No. 12801, Apr. 15, 1992, 57 F.R. 14319, provided:

By the authority vested in me as President by the Constitution and the laws of the United States of America, including the International Emergency Economic Powers Act (50 U.S.C. 1701, *et seq.*), the National Emergencies Act (50 U.S.C. 1601, *et seq.*), section 1114 of the Federal Aviation Act of 1958, as amended (49 U.S.C. App. 1514) [now 49 U.S.C. 40106(b)], section 5 of the United Nations Participation Act of 1945, as amended (22 U.S.C. 287c), and section 301 of title 3 of the United States Code, in view of United Nations Security Council Resolutions Nos. 731 of January 21, 1992, and 748 of March 31, 1992, and in order to take additional steps with respect to Libya's continued support for international terrorism and the national emergency declared in Executive Order No. 12543 of January 7, 1986 [set out above], it is hereby ordered that:

SECTION 1. Except to the extent provided in regulations, orders, directives, authorizations, or licenses that may hereafter be issued pursuant to this order, and notwithstanding the existence of any rights or obligations conferred or imposed by any international agreement or any contract entered into or any license or permit granted before the effective date of this order, the granting of permission to any aircraft to take off from, land in, or overfly the United States, if the aircraft, as part of the same flight or as a continuation of that flight, is destined to land in or has taken off from the territory of Libya, is hereby prohibited.

SEC. 2. The Secretary of the Treasury, in consultation with the Secretary of Transportation, is hereby authorized to take such actions, including the promulgation of rules and regulations, as may be necessary to carry out the provisions of section 1 of this order. The Secretary of the Treasury may redelegate the authority set forth in this order to other officers in the Department of the Treasury and may confer or impose such authority upon any other officer of the United States, with the consent of the head of the department or agency within which such officer is serving. All executive branch agencies of the Federal Government hereby affected are directed to consult as appropriate on the implementation of this order and to take all necessary measures within their authority to carry out the provisions of this order, including the suspension or termination of licenses or other authorizations in effect as of the date of this order.

SEC. 3. Nothing contained in this order shall confer any substantive or procedural right or privilege on any person or organization, enforceable against the United States, its agencies or instrumentalities, its officers, or its employees.

SEC. 4. This order is effective 11:59 p.m. eastern daylight time, April 15, 1992.

SEC. 5. This order shall be transmitted to the Congress and published in the Federal Register.

GEORGE BUSH.

EX. ORD. NO. 12808. BLOCKING "YUGOSLAV GOVERNMENT" PROPERTY AND PROPERTY OF GOVERNMENTS OF SERBIA AND MONTENEGRO

Ex. Ord. No. 12808, May 30, 1992, 57 F.R. 23299, provided:

By the authority vested in me as President by the Constitution and the laws of the United States of America, including the International Emergency Economic Powers Act (50 U.S.C. 1701, *et seq.*), the National Emergencies Act (50 U.S.C. 1601, *et seq.*), and section 301 of title 3 of the United States Code,

I, GEORGE BUSH, President of the United States of America, find that the actions and policies of the Governments of Serbia and Montenegro, acting under the name of the Socialist Federal Republic of Yugoslavia or the Federal Republic of Yugoslavia, in their involvement in and support for groups attempting to seize territory in Croatia and Bosnia-Hercegovina by force and violence utilizing, in part, the forces of the so-called Yugoslav National Army, constitute an unusual and extraordinary threat to the national security, foreign policy, and economy of the United States, and hereby declare a national emergency to deal with that threat.

I hereby order:

SECTION 1. Except to the extent provided in regulations, orders, directives, or licenses which may hereafter be issued pursuant to this order, all property and interests in property of the Government of Serbia and the Government of Montenegro that are in the United States, that hereafter come within the United States, or that are or hereafter come within the possession or control of United States persons, including their overseas branches, are hereby blocked.

SEC. 2. Except to the extent provided in regulations, orders, directives, or licenses which may hereafter be issued pursuant to this order, all property and interests in property in the name of the Government of the Socialist Federal Republic of Yugoslavia or the Government of the Federal Republic of Yugoslavia that are in the United States, that hereafter come within the United States, or that are or hereafter come within the possession or control of United States persons, including their overseas branches, are hereby blocked.

SEC. 3. Any transaction by any United States person that evades or avoids, or has the purpose of evading or avoiding, or attempts to violate, any of the prohibitions set forth in this order is prohibited.

SEC. 4. For the purposes of this order:

(a) The term "United States person" means any United States citizen, permanent resident alien, juridical person organized under the laws of the United States (including foreign branches), or person in the United States;

(b) The terms "Government of Serbia" and "Government of Montenegro" include the governments of Serbia and Montenegro, including any subdivisions thereof or local government therein, their respective agencies, instrumentalities and controlled entities, and any persons acting or purporting to act for or on behalf of any of the foregoing, including the National Bank of Serbia, the Serbian Chamber of Economy, the National Bank of Montenegro, and the Montenegrin Chamber of Economy;

(c) The terms "Government of the Socialist Federal Republic of Yugoslavia" and "Government of the Federal Republic of Yugoslavia" include the government of the former Socialist Federal Republic of Yugoslavia, the government of the newly constituted Federal Republic of Yugoslavia, their respective agencies, instrumentalities and controlled entities, and any persons acting or purporting to act for or on behalf of any of the foregoing, including the National Bank of Yugoslavia, the Yugoslav National Army, and the Yugoslav Chamber of Economy.

SEC. 5. The Secretary of the Treasury, in consultation with the Secretary of State, is hereby authorized to take such actions, including the promulgation of rules and regulations, and to employ all powers granted to the President by the International Emergency Economic Powers Act [50 U.S.C. 1701 et seq.], as may be necessary to carry out the purposes of this order. Such actions may include prohibiting or regulating payments or transfers of any property, or any transactions involving the transfer of anything of economic value by any United States person to the Government of the Socialist Federal Republic of Yugoslavia, the Government of the Federal Republic of Yugoslavia, the Government of Serbia, the Government of Montenegro, any person in Serbia or Montenegro, or any person or entity acting for or on behalf of, or owned or controlled, directly or indirectly, by any of the foregoing. The Secretary of the Treasury may redelegate any of these functions to other officers and agencies of the United States Government, all agencies of which are hereby directed to take all appropriate measures within their authority to carry out the provisions of this order, including suspension or termination of licenses or other authorizations in effect as of the date of this order.

SEC. 6. Nothing contained in this order shall create any right or benefit, substantive or procedural, enforceable by any party against the United States, its agencies or instrumentalities, its officers or employees, or any other person.

SEC. 7. (a) This order shall take effect at 11:59 p.m. Eastern Daylight Time, May 30, 1992.

(b) This order shall be transmitted to the Congress and published in the Federal Register.

GEORGE BUSH.

CONTINUATION OF NATIONAL EMERGENCY DECLARED BY EX. ORD. NOS. 12808 AND 13088

Notice of President of the United States, dated May 25, 2000, 65 F.R. 34379, provided:

In accordance with section 202(d) of the National Emergencies Act (50 U.S.C. 1622(d)), I am continuing for 1 year the national emergency declared on May 30, 1992 [see Ex. Ord. No. 12808, set out above], with respect to the Federal Republic of Yugoslavia (Serbia and Montenegro), as expanded on October 25, 1994 [see Ex. Ord. No. 12934, set out below], in response to the actions and policies of the Bosnian Serbs. In addition, I am continuing for 1 year the national emergency declared on June 9, 1998 [see Ex. Ord. No. 13088, set out below], with respect to the Federal Republic of Yugoslavia's policies and actions in Kosovo. This notice shall be published in the Federal Register and transmitted to the Congress.

On May 30, 1992, by Executive Order 12808, President Bush declared a national emergency to deal with the unusual and extraordinary threat to the national security, foreign policy, and economy of the United States constituted by the actions and policies of the Governments of Serbia and Montenegro, blocking all property and interests in property of those Governments. President Bush took additional measures to prohibit trade and other transactions with the Federal Republic of Yugoslavia (Serbia and Montenegro) by Executive Orders 12810 and 12831 [set out below], issued on June 5, 1992, and January 15, 1993, respectively, and on April 25, 1993, I issued Executive Order 12846 [set out below] imposing additional measures.

On October 25, 1994, I expanded the scope of the national emergency by issuing Executive Order 12934 to address the unusual and extraordinary threat to the national security, foreign policy, and economy of the United States posed by the actions and policies of the Bosnian Serb forces and the authorities in the territory that they controlled within Bosnia and Herzegovina.

On December 27, 1995, I issued Presidential Determination 96–7 [set out above], directing the Secretary of the Treasury, *inter alia*, to suspend the application of sanctions imposed on the Federal Republic of Yugoslavia (Serbia and Montenegro) pursuant to the above-referenced Executive orders and to continue to block property previously blocked until provision is made to address claims or encumbrances, including the claims of the other successor states of the former Yugoslavia. This sanctions relief, in conformity with United Nations Security Council Resolution 1022 of November 22, 1995 (hereinafter the "Resolution"), was an essential factor motivating Serbia and Montenegro's acceptance of the General Framework Agreement for Peace in Bosnia and Herzegovina initialed by the parties in Dayton on November 21, 1995, and signed in Paris on December 14, 1995 (hereinafter the "Peace Agreement"). The sanctions imposed on the Federal Republic of Yugoslavia (Serbia and Montenegro) were accordingly suspended prospectively, effective January 16, 1996. Sanctions imposed on the Bosnian Serb forces and authorities and on the territory that they control within Bosnia and Herzegovina were subsequently suspended prospectively, effective May 10, 1996, also in conformity with the Peace Agreement and the Resolution. Sanctions against both the Federal Republic of Yugoslavia (Serbia and Montenegro) and the Bosnian Serbs were subsequently terminated by United Nations Security Council Resolution 1074 of October 1, 1996. This termination, however, did not end the requirement of the Resolution that those blocked funds and assets that are subject to claims and encumbrances remain blocked, until unblocked in accordance with applicable law.

Until the status of all remaining blocked property is resolved, the Peace Agreement implemented, and the terms of the Resolution met, the national emergency declared on May 30, 1992, as expanded in scope on October 25, 1994, must continue beyond May 30, 2000.

On June 9, 1998, by Executive Order 13088, I found that the actions and policies of the Federal Republic of Yugoslavia (Serbia and Montenegro) and the Republic of Serbia with respect to Kosovo, by promoting ethnic conflict and human suffering, threatened to destabilize countries in the region and to disrupt progress in Bosnia and Herzegovina in implementing the Dayton peace agreement, constituted an unusual and extraordinary threat to the national security and foreign policy of the United States. I therefore declared a national emergency to deal with that threat. On April 30, 1999, I issued Executive Order 13121 [set out below] to take additional steps with respect to the continuing human rights and humanitarian crisis in Kosovo and the national emergency declared with respect to Kosovo. Because the crisis with respect to the situation in Kosovo has not been resolved, I have determined that it is necessary to maintain in force these emergency authorities beyond June 9, 2000.

WILLIAM J. CLINTON.

Prior continuations of national emergency declared by Ex. Ord. No. 12808 were contained in the following:

Notice of President of the United States, dated May 27, 1999, 64 F.R. 29205.

Notice of President of the United States, dated May 28, 1998, 63 F.R. 29527.

Notice of President of the United States, dated May 28, 1997, 62 F.R. 29283.

Notice of President of the United States, dated May 24, 1996, 61 F.R. 26773.

Determination of President, No. 96–7, Dec. 27, 1995, 61 F.R. 2887.

Notice of President of the United States, dated May 10, 1995, 60 F.R. 25599.

Notice of President of the United States, dated May 25, 1994, 59 F.R. 27429.

Notice of President of the United States, dated May 25, 1993, 58 F.R. 30693.

EX. ORD. NO. 12810. BLOCKING PROPERTY OF AND PROHIBITING TRANSACTIONS WITH FEDERAL REPUBLIC OF YUGOSLAVIA (SERBIA AND MONTENEGRO)

Ex. Ord. No. 12810, June 5, 1992, 57 F.R. 24347, as amended by Ex. Ord. No. 12831, § 4, Jan. 15, 1993, 58 F.R. 5253, provided:

By the authority vested in me as President by the Constitution and the laws of the United States of America, including the International Emergency Economic Powers Act (50 U.S.C. 1701, *et seq.*), the National Emergencies Act (50 U.S.C. 1601, *et seq.*), section 1114 of the Federal Aviation Act of 1958, as amended (49 U.S.C. App. 1514), section 5 of the United Nations Participation Act of 1945, as amended (22 U.S.C. 287c), and section 301 of title 3 of the United States Code, in view of United Nations Security Council Resolution No. 757 of May 30, 1992, and in order to take additional steps with respect to the actions and policies of the Federal Republic of Yugoslavia (Serbia and Montenegro) and the national emergency described and declared in Executive Order No. 12808 [set out above],

I, GEORGE BUSH, President of the United States of America, hereby order:

SECTION 1. Except to the extent provided in regulations, orders, directives, or licenses which may hereafter be issued pursuant to this order, and notwithstanding the existence of any rights or obligations conferred or imposed by any international agreement or any contract entered into or any license or permit granted before the effective date of this order, all property and interests in property of the Government of the Federal Republic of Yugoslavia (Serbia and Montenegro), and property and interests in property held in the name of the Government of the Federal Republic of Yugoslavia or of the former Government of the Socialist Federal Republic of Yugoslavia, that are in the United States, that hereafter come within the United States, or that are or hereafter come within the possession or control of United States persons, including their overseas branches, are blocked.

SEC. 2. The following are prohibited, notwithstanding the existence of any rights or obligations conferred or imposed by any international agreement or any contract entered into or any license or permit granted before the effective date of this order, except to the extent provided in regulations, orders, directives, or licenses which may hereafter be issued pursuant to this order:

(a) The importation into the United States of any goods originating in, or services performed in, the Federal Republic of Yugoslavia (Serbia and Montenegro), exported from the Federal Republic of Yugoslavia (Serbia and Montenegro) after May 30, 1992, or any activity that promotes or is intended to promote such importation;

(b) The exportation to the Federal Republic of Yugoslavia (Serbia and Montenegro), or to any entity operated from the Federal Republic of Yugoslavia (Serbia and Montenegro), or owned or controlled by the Government of the Federal Republic of Yugoslavia (Serbia and Montenegro), directly or indirectly, of any goods, technology (including technical data or other information controlled for export pursuant to the Export Administration Regulations, 15 C.F.R. Parts 768, *et seq.*), or services, either (i) from the United States, (ii) requiring the issuance of a license by a Federal agency, or (iii) involving the use of U.S.-registered vessels or aircraft, or any activity that promotes or is intended to promote such exportation;

(c) Any dealing by a United States person related to property originating in the Federal Republic of Yugoslavia (Serbia and Montenegro) exported from the Federal Republic of Yugoslavia (Serbia and Montenegro) after May 30, 1992, or property intended for exportation from the Federal Republic of Yugoslavia (Serbia and Montenegro) to any country, or exportation to the Federal Republic of Yugoslavia (Serbia and Montenegro) from any country, or any activity of any kind that promotes or is intended to promote such dealing;

(d) Any transaction by a United States person, or involving the use of U.S.-registered vessels and aircraft, relating to transportation to or from the Federal Republic of Yugoslavia (Serbia and Montenegro), the provision of transportation to or from the United States by any person in the Federal Republic of Yugoslavia (Serbia and Montenegro) or any vessel or aircraft registered in the Federal Republic of Yugoslavia (Serbia and Montenegro), or the sale in the United States by any person holding authority under the Federal Aviation Act of 1958, as amended (49 U.S.C. 1301, *et seq.*) [now 49 U.S.C. 40101 et seq.], of any transportation by air that includes any stop in the Federal Republic of Yugoslavia (Serbia and Montenegro);

(e) The granting of permission to any aircraft to take off from, land in, or overfly the United States, if the aircraft, as part of the same flight or as a continuation of that flight, is destined to land in or has taken off from the territory of the Federal Republic of Yugoslavia (Serbia and Montenegro);

(f) The performance by any United States person of any contract, including a financing contract, in support of an industrial, commercial, public utility, or governmental project in the Federal Republic of Yugoslavia (Serbia and Montenegro);

(g) Any commitment or transfer, direct or indirect, of funds, or other financial or economic resources by any United States person to or for the benefit of the Government of the Federal Republic of Yugoslavia (Serbia and Montenegro) or any other person in the Federal Republic of Yugoslavia (Serbia and Montenegro);

(h) Any transaction in the United States or by a United States person related to participation in sporting events in the United States by persons or groups representing the Federal Republic of Yugoslavia (Serbia and Montenegro);

(i) [Revoked by Ex. Ord. No. 12831, §4, Jan. 15, 1993, 58 F.R. 5253.]

SEC. 3. Nothing in this order shall apply to (i) the transshipment through the Federal Republic of Yugoslavia (Serbia and Montenegro) of commodities and products originating outside the Federal Republic of Yugoslavia (Serbia and Montenegro) and temporarily present in the territory of the Federal Republic of Yugoslavia (Serbia and Montenegro) only for the purpose of such transshipment, and (ii) activities related to the United Nations Protection Force (UNPROFOR), the Conference on Yugoslavia, or the European Community Monitor Mission.

SEC. 4. Any transaction by any United States person that evades or avoids, or has the purpose of evading or avoiding, or attempts to violate, any of the prohibitions set forth in this order is prohibited.

SEC. 5. For the purposes of this order:

(a) The term "United States person" means any United States citizen, permanent resident alien, juridical person organized under the laws of the United States (including foreign branches), or any person in the United States, and vessels and aircraft of U.S. registration;

(b) The term "the Federal Republic of Yugoslavia (Serbia and Montenegro)" means the territory of Serbia and Montenegro;

(c) The term "the Government of the Federal Republic of Yugoslavia (Serbia and Montenegro)" includes the government of the newly constituted Federal Republic of Yugoslavia, the Government of Serbia, and the Government of Montenegro, including any subdivisions thereof or local governments therein, their respective agencies, instrumentalities and controlled entities, and any persons acting or purporting to act for or on behalf of any of the foregoing, including the National Bank of Yugoslavia, the Yugoslav National Army, and the Yugoslav Chamber of Economy, the National Bank of Serbia, the Serbian Chamber of Economy, the National Bank of Montenegro, and the Montenegrin Chamber of Economy.

SEC. 6. The Secretary of the Treasury, in consultation with the Secretary of State, is hereby authorized to take such actions, including the promulgation of rules and regulations, and to employ all powers granted to the President by the International Emergency Economic Powers Act [50 U.S.C. 1701 et seq.] and the United Nations Participation Act [22 U.S.C. 287 et seq.], as may be necessary to carry out the purposes of this order. Such actions may include prohibiting or regulating payments or transfers of any property, or any transactions involving the transfer of anything of economic value by the [sic] any United States person to the Government of the Federal Republic of Yugoslavia (Serbia and Montenegro), any person in the Federal Republic of Yugoslavia (Serbia and Montenegro), or any person or entity acting for or on behalf of, or owned or controlled, directly or indirectly, by any of the foregoing. The Secretary of the Treasury may redelegate any of these functions to other officers and agencies of the United States Government, all agencies of which are hereby directed to take all appropriate measures within their authority to carry out the provisions of this order, including suspension or termination of licenses or other authorizations in effect as of the date of this order.

SEC. 7. All delegations, rules, regulations, orders, licenses, and other forms of administrative action made, issued, or otherwise taken under Executive Order No. 12808 [set out above] and not revoked administratively shall remain in full force and effect under this order until amended, modified, or terminated by proper authority.

SEC. 8. Nothing contained in this order shall create any right or benefit, substantive or procedural, enforceable by any party against the United States, its agencies or instrumentalities, its officers or employees, or any other person.

SEC. 9. (a) This order is effective immediately.

(b) This order shall be transmitted to the Congress and published in the Federal Register.

GEORGE BUSH.

EX. ORD. NO. 12817. TRANSFER OF CERTAIN IRAQI GOVERNMENT ASSETS HELD BY DOMESTIC BANKS

Ex. Ord. No. 12817, Oct. 21, 1992, 57 F.R. 48433, provided:

By the authority vested in me as President by the Constitution and the laws of the United States of America, including the International Emergency Economic Powers Act (50 U.S.C. 1701 *et seq.*), the National Emergencies Act (50 U.S.C. 1601 *et seq.*), section 5 of the United Nations Participation Act of 1945, as amended (22 U.S.C. 287c), and section 301 of title 3 of the United States Code, in order to apply in the United States measures adopted in United Nations Security Council Resolution No. 778 of October 2, 1992, and in order to take additional steps with respect to the actions and policies of the Government of Iraq and the national emergency described and declared in Executive Order No. 12722 [set out above],

I, GEORGE BUSH, President of the United States of America, hereby order:

SECTION 1. The Secretary of the Treasury is authorized and directed to take all actions necessary to carry out the provisions of United Nations Security Council Resolution No. 778 with respect to blocked funds and other assets described in section 2 of this order, or funds and other assets received from the United Nations in repayment of funds and assets transferred pursuant to section 2 of this order. For this purpose, the Secretary of the Treasury is delegated and authorized to exercise all authorities vested in the President by sections 203 and 205 of the International Emergency Economic Powers Act (50 U.S.C. 1702 and 1704) and section 5 of the United Nations Participation Act (22 U.S.C. 287c).

SEC. 2. Upon a determination by the Secretary of the Treasury that funds or other assets in which the Government of Iraq or its agencies, instrumentalities, or controlled entities have an interest represent the proceeds of the sale of Iraqi petroleum or petroleum products, paid for by or on behalf of the purchaser on or after August 6, 1990, each and every United States financial institution is directed and compelled to transfer such funds or assets held by it or carried on its books to the Federal Reserve Bank of New York, when, to the extent, and in the manner required by the Secretary of the Treasury.

SEC. 3. The Federal Reserve Bank of New York, as fiscal agent of the United States, is authorized, directed, and compelled to receive funds and other assets in which the Government of Iraq or its agencies, instrumentalities, or controlled entities have an interest, and to hold, invest, or transfer such funds and assets, and any earnings thereon, when, to the extent, and in the manner required by the Secretary of the Treasury in order to fulfill the rights and obligations of the United States under United Nations Security Council Resolution No. 778.

SEC. 4. Compliance with this order, or any regulation, instruction, or direction issued under this order, licensing, authorizing, directing, or compelling the transfer of the blocked funds and other assets described in section 2 of this order, or funds and other assets received from the United Nations in repayment of funds and assets transferred pursuant to section 2 of this order, shall, to the extent thereof, be a full acquittance and discharge for all purposes of the obligation of the person making the transfer. No person shall be held liable in any court for or with respect to anything done or omitted in good faith in connection with the administration of, or pursuant to and in reliance on, this order or any regulation, instruction, or direction issued hereunder. The operation of this order shall have no effect on rights, debts, and claims existing with respect to funds or other assets prior to their transfer to the Federal Reserve Bank of New York.

SEC. 5. For the purposes of this order, the term "United States financial institution" means any United States citizen, permanent resident alien, juridical person organized under the laws of the United States, or any person located in the United States, which is engaged in the business of accepting deposits, making, granting, transferring, holding, or brokering loans or credits, or purchasing or selling foreign exchange or securities, including, but not limited to, depository institutions, banks, saving banks, trust companies, securities brokers and dealers, clearing corporations, investment companies, and U.S. holding companies, U.S. affiliates, or U.S. subsidiaries of the foregoing. This term includes branches, offices, and agencies of foreign financial institutions which are located in the United States.

SEC. 6. The Secretary of the Treasury, in consultation with the Secretary of State, is authorized to take such actions, including the issuance of directive licenses, rules, and regulations, as may be necessary to carry out the purposes of this order. The Secretary of the Treasury may redelegate any of these functions to other officers and agencies of the Federal Government. All agencies of the Federal Government are directed to take all appropriate measures within their authority to carry out the provisions of this order.

SEC. 7. Nothing contained in this order shall create any right or benefit, substantive or procedural, enforceable by any party (other than the United States) against the United States, its agencies or instrumentalities, its officers or employees, or any other person.

SEC. 8.

(a) This order is effective immediately.

(b) This order shall be transmitted to the Congress and published in the Federal Register.

GEORGE BUSH.

EX. ORD. NO. 12831. ADDITIONAL MEASURES WITH RESPECT TO FEDERAL REPUBLIC OF YUGOSLAVIA (SERBIA AND MONTENEGRO)

Ex. Ord. No. 12831, Jan. 15, 1993, 58 F.R. 5253, provided:

By the authority vested in me as President by the Constitution and the laws of the United States of America, including the International Emergency Economic Powers Act (50 U.S.C. 1701 *et seq.*), the National Emergencies Act (50 U.S.C. 1601 *et seq.*), section 5 of the United Nations Participation Act of 1945, as amended (22 U.S.C. 287c), and section 301 of title 3 of the United States Code, in view of United Nations Security Council Resolutions No. 757 of May 30, 1992, and No. 787 of November 16, 1992, and in order to take additional steps with respect to the actions and policies of the Federal Republic of Yugoslavia (Serbia and Montenegro) and the national emergency described and declared in Executive Order No. 12808 [set out above] and expanded in Executive Order No. 12810 [set out above],

I, GEORGE BUSH, President of the United States of America, hereby order:

SECTION 1. The following are prohibited, except to the extent provided in regulations, orders, directives, or licenses which may hereafter be issued pursuant to this order, and notwithstanding the existence of any rights or obligations conferred or imposed by any international agreement or any contract entered into or any license or permit granted before the effective date of this order:

(a) Any transaction within the United States or by a United States person related to the transshipment of commodities or products through the Federal Republic of Yugoslavia (Serbia and Montenegro); and

(b) Any transaction within the United States or by a United States person relating to any vessel in which a majority or controlling interest is held by a person or entity in, or operating from, the Federal Republic of Yugoslavia (Serbia and Montenegro) regardless of the flag under which the vessel sails.

SEC. 2. Any vessel in which a majority or controlling interest is held by a person or entity in, or operating from, the Federal Republic of Yugoslavia (Serbia and Montenegro) shall be considered as a vessel of the Federal Republic of Yugoslavia (Serbia and Montenegro) regardless of the flag under which the vessel sails.

SEC. 3. The Secretary of the Treasury, in consultation with the Secretary of State, is hereby authorized to take such actions, including the promulgation of rules and regulations, and to employ all powers granted to the President by the International Emergency Economic Powers Act [50 U.S.C. 1701 et seq.] and the United Nations Participation Act [22 U.S.C. 287 et seq.], as may be necessary to carry out the purpose of this order. Such actions may include prohibiting or regulating trade and financial transactions involving any areas of the territory of the former Socialist Federal Republic of Yugoslavia as to which there is inadequate assurance that such transactions will not be diverted to the benefit of the Federal Republic of Yugoslavia (Serbia and Montenegro). The Secretary of the Treasury may redelegate the authority set forth in this order to other officers and agencies of the United States Government, all agencies of which are hereby directed to take all appropriate measures within their authority to carry out the provisions of this order, including suspension or termination of licenses or other authorizations in effect as of the date of this order.

SEC. 4. Section 3[2](i) of Executive Order No. 12810 [set out above] is hereby revoked.

SEC. 5. The definitions contained in Section 5 of Executive Order No. 12810 [set out above] apply to the terms used in this order.

SEC. 6. Nothing contained in this order shall create any right or benefit, substantive or procedural, enforceable by any party against the United States, its agencies or instrumentalities, its officers or employees, or any other person.

SEC. 7. (a) This order is effective immediately.

(b) This order shall be transmitted to the Congress and published in the Federal Register.

GEORGE BUSH.

EX. ORD. NO. 12846. ADDITIONAL MEASURES WITH RESPECT TO FEDERAL REPUBLIC OF YUGOSLAVIA (SERBIA AND MONTENEGRO)

Ex. Ord. No. 12846, Apr. 25, 1993, 58 F.R. 25771, provided:

By the authority vested in me as President by the Constitution and the laws of the United States of America, including the International Emergency Economic Powers Act (50 U.S.C. 1701 *et seq.*), the National Emergencies Act (50 U.S.C. 1601 *et seq.*), section 5 of the United Nations Participation Act of 1945, as amended (22 U.S.C. 287c), and section 301 of title 3, United States Code, in view of United Nations Security Council Resolution No. 757 of May 30, 1992, No. 787 of November 16, 1992, and No. 820 of April 17, 1993, and in order to take additional steps with respect to the actions and policies of the Federal Republic of Yugoslavia (Serbia and Montenegro) and the national emergency described and declared in Executive Order No. 12808 [set out above] and expanded in Executive Order No. 12810 [set out above] and No. 12831 [set out above],

I, WILLIAM J. CLINTON, President of the United States of America, hereby order:

SECTION 1. Notwithstanding the existence of any rights or obligations conferred or imposed by any international agreement or any contract entered into or any license or permit granted before the effective date of this order, except to the extent provided in regulations, orders, directives, or licenses which may hereafter be issued pursuant to this order:

(a) All property and interests in property of all commercial, industrial, or public utility undertakings or entities organized or located in the Federal Republic of Yugoslavia (Serbia and Montenegro), including, without limitation, the property and interests in property of entities (wherever organized or located) owned or controlled by such undertakings or entities, that are in the United States, that hereafter come within the United States, or that are or hereafter come within the possession or control of United States persons, including their overseas branches, are hereby blocked;

(b) All expenses incident to the blocking and maintenance of property blocked under Executive Order Nos. 12808, 12810, 12831 [set out above] or this order shall be charged to the owners or operators of such property, which expenses shall not be met from blocked funds. Such property may also be sold or liquidated and the proceeds placed in a blocked interest-bearing account in the name of the owner;

(c) All vessels, freight vehicles, rolling stock, aircraft and cargo that are within or hereafter come within the United States and are not subject to blocking under Executive Order Nos. 12808, 12810, 12831 or this order, but which are suspected of a violation of United Nations Security Council Resolution Nos. 713, 757, 787 or 820, shall be detained pending investigation and, upon a determination by the Secretary of the Treasury that they have been in violation of any of these resolutions, shall be blocked. Such blocked conveyances and cargo may also be sold or liquidated and the proceeds placed in a blocked interest-bearing account in the name of the owner;

(d) No vessel registered in the United States or owned or controlled by United States persons, other than a United States naval vessel, may enter the territorial waters of the Federal Republic of Yugoslavia (Serbia and Montenegro); and

(e) Any dealing by a United States person relating to the importation from, exportation to, or transshipment through the United Nations Protected Areas in the Republic of Croatia and those areas of the Republic of Bosnia-Hercegovina under the control of Bosnian Serb forces, or activity of any kind that promotes or is intended to promote such dealing, is prohibited.

SEC. 2. The Secretary of the Treasury, in consultation with the Secretary of State, is hereby authorized to take such actions, including the promulgation of rules and regulations, and to employ all powers granted to the President by the International Emergency Economic Powers Act [50 U.S.C. 1701 et seq.] and the United Nations Participation Act [22 U.S.C. 287 et seq.] as may be necessary to carry out the purposes of this order. The Secretary of the Treasury may redelegate the authority set forth in this order to other officers and agencies of the Federal Government, all agencies of which are hereby directed to take all appropriate measures within their authority to carry out the provisions of this order, including suspension or termination of licenses or other authorizations in effect as of the date of this order.

SEC. 3. Nothing in this order shall apply to activities related to the United Nations Protection Force, the International Conference on the Former Yugoslavia, and the European Community Monitor Mission.

SEC. 4. The definitions contained in section 5 of Executive Order No. 12810 [set out above] apply to the terms used in this order.

SEC. 5. Nothing contained in this order shall create any right or benefit, substantive or procedural, enforceable by any party against the United States, its agencies or instrumentalities, its officers or employees, or any other person.

SEC. 6. This order shall not affect the provisions of licenses and authorizations issued pursuant to Executive Order Nos. 12808, 12810, 12831 [set out above] and in force on the effective date of this order, except as such licenses or authorization may hereafter be terminated, modified or suspended by the issuing federal agency.

SEC. 7. (a) This order shall take effect at 12:01 a.m. Eastern Daylight Time, April 26, 1993.

(b) This order shall be transmitted to the Congress and published in the Federal Register.

WILLIAM J. CLINTON.

EXECUTIVE ORDER NO. 12853

Ex. Ord. No. 12853, June 30, 1993, 58 F.R. 35843, which directed Secretary of the Treasury to block all property and interests in property of Government of Haiti and the de facto regime in Haiti or controlled directly or indirectly by either that were in United States or within possession or control of United States persons and which prohibited sale or supply to Haiti of petroleum or arms and related materiel by United States persons or from United States or using U.S.-registered vessels or aircraft, was revoked by Ex. Ord. No. 12932, Oct. 14, 1994, 59 F.R. 52403, set out below.

EX. ORD. NO. 12865. PROHIBITING CERTAIN TRANSACTIONS WITH RESPECT TO UNITA

Ex. Ord. No. 12865, Sept. 26, 1993, 58 F.R. 51005, provided:

By the authority vested in me as President by the Constitution and the laws of the United States of America, including the International Emergency Economic Powers Act (50 U.S.C. 1701 *et seq.*), the National Emergencies Act (50 U.S.C. 1601 *et seq.*), section 5 of the United Nations Participation Act of 1945, as amended (22 U.S.C. 287c), and section 301 of title 3, United States Code, and in view of United Nations Security Council Resolution No. 864 of September 15, 1993,

I, WILLIAM J. CLINTON, President of the United States of America, take note of the United Nations Security Council's determination that, as a result of UNITA's military actions, the situation in Angola constitutes a threat to international peace and security, and find that the actions and policies of UNITA, in continuing military actions, repeated attempts to seize additional territory and failure to withdraw its troops from locations that it has occupied since the resumption of hostilities, in repeatedly attacking United Nations personnel working to provide humanitarian assistance, in holding foreign nationals against their will, in refusing to accept the results of the democratic elections held in Angola in 1992, and in failing to abide by the "Acordos de Paz," constitute an unusual and extraordinary threat to the foreign policy of the United States, and hereby declare a national emergency to deal with that threat.

I hereby order:

SECTION 1. The following are prohibited, notwithstanding the existence of any rights or obligations conferred or imposed by any international agreement or contract entered into or any license or permit granted before the effective date of this order, except to the extent provided in regulations, orders, directives, or licenses which may hereafter be issued pursuant to this order:

(a) The sale or supply by United States persons or from the United States, or using U.S.-registered vessels or aircraft, of arms and related materiel of all types, including weapons and ammunition, military vehicles and equipment and spare parts for the aforementioned, as well as petroleum and petroleum products, regardless of origin:

(1) to UNITA;

(2) to the territory of Angola, other than through points of entry to be designated by the Secretary of the Treasury, or any activity by United States persons or in the United States which promotes or is calculated to promote such sale or supply.

(b) Any transaction by any United States person that evades or avoids, or has the purpose of evading or avoiding, or attempts to violate, any of the prohibitions set forth in this order.

SEC. 2. For purposes of this order:

(a) The term "United States person" means any United States citizen, permanent resident alien, juridical person organized under the laws of the United States (including foreign branches), or person in the United States;

(b) The term "UNITA" includes:

(1) the Uniao Nacional para a Independencia Total de Angola (UNITA), known in English as the "National Union for the Total Independence of Angola;"

(2) the Forcas Armadas para a Liberacao de Angola (FALA), known in English as the "Armed Forces for the Liberation of Angola;" and

(3) any person acting or purporting to act for or on behalf of any of the foregoing, including the Free Angola Information Service, Inc.

SEC. 3. The Secretary of the Treasury, in consultation with the Secretary of State, is hereby authorized to take such actions, including the promulgation of rules and regulations, and to employ all powers granted to the President by the International Emergency Economic Powers Act [50 U.S.C. 1701 et seq.] and the United Nations Participation Act [22 U.S.C. 287 et seq.] as may be necessary to carry out the purpose of this order. The Secretary of the Treasury may redelegate any of these functions to other officers and agencies of the United States Government.

SEC. 4. Nothing contained in the order shall be construed to supersede the requirements established under the Arms Export Control Act (22 U.S.C. 2751 *et seq.*) and the Export Administration Act (50 U.S.C. App. 2401 *et seq.*) to obtain licenses for the exportation from the United States or from a third country of any goods, data, or services subject to the export jurisdiction of the Department of State or the Department of Commerce.

SEC. 5. All Federal agencies are hereby directed to take all appropriate measures within their authority to carry out the provisions of this order, including suspension or termination of licenses or other authorizations in effect as of the date of this order.

SEC. 6. Nothing contained in this order shall create any right or benefit, substantive or procedural, enforceable by any party against the United States, its agencies or instrumentalities, its officers or employees, or any other person.

SEC. 7. (a) This order shall take effect immediately.

(b) This order shall be transmitted to the Congress and published in the Federal Register.

WILLIAM J. CLINTON.

CONTINUATION OF NATIONAL EMERGENCY DECLARED BY EX. ORD. NO. 12865

Notice of President of the United States, dated Sept. 22, 2000, 65 F.R. 57721, provided:

On September 26, 1993, by Executive Order 12865 [set out above], I declared a national emergency to deal with the unusual and extraordinary threat to the foreign policy of the United States constituted by the actions and policies of the National Union for the Total Independence of Angola (UNITA), prohibiting the sale or supply by United States persons or from the United States, or using U.S. registered vessels or aircraft, of arms, related materiel of all types, petroleum, and petroleum products to the territory of Angola, other than through designated points of entry. The order also prohibits the sale or supply of such commodities to UNITA. On December 12, 1997, in order to take additional steps with respect to the national emergency declared in Executive Order 12865, I issued Executive Order 13069 [set out below], closing all UNITA offices in the United States and imposing additional sanctions with regard to the sale or supply of aircraft or aircraft parts, the granting of take-off, landing and overflight permission, and the provision of certain aircraft-related services. On August 18, 1998, in order to take further steps with respect to the national emergency declared in Executive Order 12865, I issued Executive Order 13098 [set out below], blocking all property and interests in property of UNITA and designated UNITA officials and adult members of their immediate families, prohibiting the importation of certain diamonds exported from Angola, and imposing additional sanctions with regard to the sale or supply of equipment used in mining, motorized vehicles, watercraft, spare parts for motorized vehicles or watercraft, mining services, and ground or waterborne transportation services.

Because of our continuing international obligations and because of the prejudicial effect that discontinuation of the sanctions would have on prospects for peace in Angola, the national emergency declared on September 26, 1993, and the measures adopted pursuant thereto to deal with that emergency, must continue in effect beyond September 26, 2000. Therefore, in accordance with section 202(d) of the National Emergencies Act (50 U.S.C. 1622(d)), I am continuing the national emergency with respect to UNITA.

This notice shall be published in the Federal Register and transmitted to the Congress.

WILLIAM J. CLINTON.

Prior continuations of national emergency declared by Ex. Ord. No. 12865 were contained in the following:

Notice of President of the United States, dated Sept. 21, 1999, 64 F.R. 51419.

Notice of President of the United States, dated Sept. 23, 1998, 63 F.R. 51509.

Notice of President of the United States, dated Sept. 24, 1997, 62 F.R. 50477.

Notice of President of the United States, dated Sept. 16, 1996, 61 F.R. 49047.

Notice of President of the United States, dated Sept. 18, 1995, 60 F.R. 48621.

Notice of President of the United States, dated Aug. 17, 1994, 59 F.R. 42749.

EX. ORD. NO. 12867. TERMINATION OF EMERGENCY AUTHORITY FOR CERTAIN EXPORT CONTROLS

Ex. Ord. No. 12867, Sept. 30, 1993, 58 F.R. 51747, provided:

By the authority vested in me as President by the Constitution and the laws of the United States of America, including section 203 of the International Emergency Economic Powers Act (50 U.S.C. 1702) (“the IEEPA”), the National Emergencies Act (50 U.S.C. 1601 *et seq.*), the Export Administration Act of 1979, as amended (50 U.S.C. App. 2401 *et seq.*) (“the Act”), and section 301 of title 3 of the United States Code, it is hereby ordered as follows:

SECTION 1. In view of the extension of the Act by Public Law 103–10 (March 27, 1993) [amending 50 App. U.S.C. 2419], Executive Order No. 12730 of September 30, 1990, which continued the effect of export control regulations under the IEEPA, is revoked, and the declaration of economic emergency is rescinded, as provided in this order.

SEC. 2. The revocation of Executive Order No. 12730 shall not affect any violation of any rules, regulations, orders, licenses, and other forms of administrative action under that Order that occurred during the period the order was in effect. All rules and regulations issued or continued in effect under the authority of the IEEPA and Executive Order No. 12735, including those codified at 15 CFR Sections 768–799 (1993), and all orders, regulations, licenses, and other forms of administrative action issued, taken, or continued in effect pursuant thereto, shall remain in full force and effect, as if issued, taken, or continued in effect pursuant to and as authorized by the Act or by other appropriate authority until amended or revoked by the proper authority. Nothing in this order shall affect the continued applicability of the provision for the administration of the Act and delegations of authority set forth in Executive Order No. 12002 of July 7, 1977, Executive Order No. 12214 of May 2, 1980 [50 App. U.S.C. 2403 notes], and Executive Order No. 12735 of November 16, 1990.

SEC. 3. All rules, regulations, orders, licenses, and other forms of administrative action issued, taken, or continued in effect pursuant to the authority of the IEEPA and Executive Order No. 12730 relating to the administration of Section 38(e) of the Arms Export Control Act (22 U.S.C. 2778(e)) shall remain in full force and effect until amended or revoked under proper authority.

SEC. 4. This order shall take effect immediately.

WILLIAM J. CLINTON.

EXECUTIVE ORDER NO. 12868

Ex. Ord. No. 12868, Sept. 30, 1993, 58 F.R. 51749, which directed Secretary of Commerce to regulate activities of United States persons to prevent participation in weapons proliferation activities, was revoked, with savings provision, by Ex. Ord. No. 12930, §3, Sept. 29, 1994, 59 F.R. 50475, formerly set out below.

EXECUTIVE ORDER NO. 12872

Ex. Ord. No. 12872, Oct. 18, 1993, 58 F.R. 54029, which directed Secretary of the Treasury to block property of persons obstructing democratization in Haiti, was revoked by Ex. Ord. No. 12932, Oct. 14, 1994, 59 F.R. 52403, set out below.

EXECUTIVE ORDER NO. 12914

Ex. Ord. No. 12914, May 7, 1994, 59 F.R. 24339, which directed Secretary of the Treasury to block all funds and financial resources of officers and employees of Haitian military, including police, and of all major participants in coup d'état in Haiti of 1991 and in illegal governments that followed, and which prohibited air travel between United States territory and Haiti except regularly scheduled commercial passenger flights, was revoked by Ex. Ord. No. 12932, Oct. 14, 1994, 59 F.R. 52403, set out below.

EXECUTIVE ORDER NO. 12917

Ex. Ord. No. 12917, May 21, 1994, 59 F.R. 26925, which prohibited imports into United States from Haiti and activity by United States persons or in United States promoting or dealing in Haitian exports, with certain exceptions, was revoked by Ex. Ord. No. 12932, Oct. 14, 1994, 59 F.R. 52403, set out below.

EXECUTIVE ORDER NO. 12920

Ex. Ord. No. 12920, June 10, 1994, 59 F.R. 30501, which prohibited payment or transfer of funds or other financial or investment assets or credits to Haiti from or through United States or from Haiti to or through United States and the sale, supply, or exportation of goods, technology, or services to Haiti or promotion of such activity, with certain exceptions, was revoked by Ex. Ord. No. 12932, Oct. 14, 1994, 59 F.R. 52403, set out below.

EXECUTIVE ORDER NO. 12922

Ex. Ord. No. 12922, June 21, 1994, 59 F.R. 32645, which directed Secretary of the Treasury to block property and interests in property of Haitian national residents in Haiti and to continue blocking property of certain other persons that were in United States or within possession and control of United States persons, was revoked by Ex. Ord. No. 12932, Oct. 14, 1994, 59 F.R. 52403, set out below.

EXECUTIVE ORDER NO. 12923

Ex. Ord. No. 12923, June 30, 1994, 59 F.R. 34551, which continued effectiveness of the Export Administration Act of 1979, 50 App. U.S.C. 2401 et seq., and of the orders, rules and regulations promulgated thereunder, was revoked by Ex. Ord. No. 12924, §4, Aug. 19, 1994, 59 F.R. 43438, set out below.

EX. ORD. NO. 12924. CONTINUATION OF EXPORT CONTROL REGULATIONS

Ex. Ord. No. 12924, Aug. 19, 1994, 59 F.R. 43437, provided:

By the authority vested in me as President by the Constitution and the laws of the United States of America, including but not limited to section 203 of the International Emergency Economic Powers Act ("Act") (50 U.S.C. 1702), I, WILLIAM J. CLINTON, President of the United States of America, find that the unrestricted access of foreign parties to U.S. goods, technology, and technical data and the existence of certain boycott practices of foreign nations, in light of the expiration of the Export Administration Act of 1979, as amended (50 U.S.C. App. 2401 *et seq.*), constitute an unusual and extraordinary threat to the national security, foreign policy, and economy of the United States and hereby declare a national emergency with respect to that threat.

Accordingly, in order (a) to exercise the necessary vigilance over exports and activities affecting the national security of the United States; (b) to further significantly the foreign policy of the United States, including its policy with respect to cooperation by U.S. persons with certain foreign boycott activities, and to fulfill its international responsibilities; and (c) to protect the domestic economy from the excessive drain of scarce materials and reduce the serious economic impact of foreign demand, it is hereby ordered as follows:

SECTION 1. To the extent permitted by law, the provisions of the Export Administration Act of 1979, as amended, and the provisions for administration of the Export Administration Act of 1979, as amended, shall be carried out under this order so as to continue in full force and effect and amend, as necessary, the export control system heretofore maintained by the Export Administration regulations issued under the Export Administration Act of 1979, as amended. The delegations of authority set forth in Executive Order No. 12002 of July 7, 1977 [50 App. U.S.C. 2403 note], as amended by Executive Order No. 12755 of March 12, 1991; Executive Order No. 12214 of May 2, 1980 [50 App. U.S.C. 2403 note]; Executive Order No. 12735 of November 16, 1990; and Executive Order No. 12851 of June 11, 1993 [22 U.S.C. 2797 note], shall be incorporated in this order and shall apply to the exercise of authorities under this order.

SEC. 2. All rules and regulations issued or continued in effect by the Secretary of Commerce under the authority of the Export Administration Act of 1979, as amended [50 App. U.S.C. 2401 et seq.], including those published in Title 15, Subtitle B, Chapter VII, Subchapter C, of the Code of Federal Regulations, Parts 768 through 799, and all orders, regulations, licenses, and other forms of administrative action issued, taken, or continued in effect pursuant thereto, shall, until amended or revoked by the Secretary of Commerce, remain in full force and effect as if issued or taken pursuant to this order, except that the provisions of sections 203(b)(2) and 206 of the Act (50 U.S.C. 1702(b)(2) and 1705) shall control over any inconsistent provisions in the regulations. Nothing in this section shall affect the continued applicability of administrative sanctions provided for by the regulations described above.

SEC. 3. Provisions for administration of section 38(e) of the Arms Export Control Act (22 U.S.C. 2778(e)) may be made and shall continue in full force and effect until amended or revoked under the authority of section 203 of the Act (50 U.S.C. 1702). To the extent permitted by law, this order also shall constitute authority for the issuance and continuation in full force and effect of all rules and regulations by the President or his delegate, and all orders, licenses, and other forms of administrative actions issued, taken, or continued in effect pursuant thereto, relating to the administration of section 38(e).

SEC. 4. Executive Order No. 12923 of June 30, 1994, is revoked, and that declaration of emergency is rescinded. The revocation of Executive Order No. 12923 shall not affect any violation of any rules, regulations, orders, licenses, and other forms of administrative action under that order that occurred during the period the order was in effect.

SEC. 5. This order shall be effective as of midnight between August 20, 1994, and August 21, 1994, and shall remain in effect until terminated.

WILLIAM J. CLINTON.

CONTINUATION OF NATIONAL EMERGENCY DECLARED BY EX. ORD. NO. 12924

Notice of President of the United States, dated Aug. 3, 2000, 65 F.R. 48347, provided:

On August 19, 1994, consistent with the authority provided me under the International Emergency Economic Powers Act (50 U.S.C. 1701 *et seq.*), I issued Executive Order 12924 [set out above]. In that order, I declared a national emergency with respect to the unusual and extraordinary threat to the national security, foreign policy, and economy of the United States in light of the expiration of the Export Administration Act of 1979, as amended (50 U.S.C. App. 2401 *et seq.*). Because the Export Administration Act has not been renewed by the

Congress, the national emergency declared on August 19, 1994, must continue in effect beyond August 19, 2000. Therefore, in accordance with section 202(d) of the National Emergencies Act (50 U.S.C. 1622(d)), I am continuing the national emergency declared in Executive Order 12924.

This notice shall be published in the Federal Register and transmitted to the Congress.

WILLIAM J. CLINTON.

Prior continuations of national emergency declared by Ex. Ord. No. 12924 were contained in the following:

Notice of President of the United States, dated Aug. 10, 1999, 64 F.R. 44101.

Notice of President of the United States, dated Aug. 13, 1998, 63 F.R. 44121.

Notice of President of the United States, dated Aug. 13, 1997, 62 F.R. 43629.

Notice of President of the United States, dated Aug. 14, 1996, 61 F.R. 42527.

Notice of President of the United States, dated Aug. 15, 1995, 60 F.R. 42767.

EXECUTIVE ORDER NO. 12930

Ex. Ord. No. 12930, Sept. 29, 1994, 59 F.R. 50475, which directed Secretary of Commerce to take measures to restrict participation by United States persons in weapons proliferation activities, was revoked by Ex. Ord. No. 12938, §10, Nov. 14, 1994, 59 F.R. 59099, set out below.

EX. ORD. NO. 12932. TERMINATION OF EMERGENCY WITH RESPECT TO HAITI

Ex. Ord. No. 12932, Oct. 14, 1994, 59 F.R. 52403, provided:

By the authority vested in me as President by the Constitution and laws of the United States of America, including the International Emergency Economic Powers Act (50 U.S.C. 1701 *et seq.*), the National Emergencies Act ("NEA") (50 U.S.C. 1601 *et seq.*), section 5 of the United Nations Participation Act of 1945, as amended (22 U.S.C. 287c), and section 301 of title 3, United States Code, and taking into consideration United Nations Security Council Resolution 944 of September 29, 1994,

I, WILLIAM J. CLINTON, President of the United States of America, find that the restoration of a democratically elected government in Haiti has ended the unusual and extraordinary threat to the national security, foreign policy, and economy of the United States previously posed by the policies and actions of the *de facto* regime in Haiti and the need to continue the national emergency declared in Executive Order No. 12775 of October 4, 1991, to deal with that threat.

I hereby revoke Executive Order Nos. 12775, 12779, 12853, 12872, 12914, 12917, 12920, and 12922 and terminate the national emergency declared in Executive Order No. 12775 with respect to Haiti.

Pursuant to section 202 of the NEA (50 U.S.C. 1622), termination of the national emergency with respect to Haiti shall not affect any action taken or proceeding pending not finally concluded or determined as of the effective date of this order, or any action or proceeding based on any act committed prior to the effective date of this order, or any rights or duties that matured or penalties that were incurred prior to the effective date of this order.

This order shall take effect at 12:01 a.m. eastern daylight time on October 16, 1994.

WILLIAM J. CLINTON.

EX. ORD. NO. 12934. BLOCKING PROPERTY AND ADDITIONAL MEASURES WITH RESPECT TO BOSNIAN SERB-CONTROLLED AREAS OF REPUBLIC OF BOSNIA AND HERZEGOVINA

Ex. Ord. No. 12934, Oct. 25, 1994, 59 F.R. 54117, provided:

By the authority vested in me as President by the Constitution and the laws of the United States of America, including the International Emergency Economic Powers Act (50 U.S.C. 1701 *et seq.*), the National Emergencies Act (50 U.S.C. 1601 *et seq.*), section 5 of the United Nations Participation Act of 1945, as amended (22 U.S.C. 287c), and section 301 of title 3, United States Code, in view of United Nations Security Council Resolution 942 of September 23, 1994, and in order to take additional steps with respect to the crisis in the former Yugoslavia, I hereby expand the scope of the national emergency declared in Executive Order No. 12808 [set out above] to address the unusual and extraordinary threat to the national security, foreign policy, and economy of the United States posed by the actions and policies of the Bosnian Serb forces and the authorities in the territory that they control, including their refusal to accept the proposed territorial settlement of the conflict in the Republic of Bosnia and Herzegovina.

I, WILLIAM J. CLINTON, President of the United States of America, hereby order:

SECTION 1. Notwithstanding the existence of any rights or obligations conferred or imposed by any international agreement or any contract entered into or any license or permit granted before the effective date of this order, except to the extent provided in regulations, orders, directives, or licenses, which may hereafter be issued pursuant to this order, all property and interests in property of: (a) the Bosnian Serb military and paramilitary forces and the authorities in those areas of the Republic of Bosnia and Herzegovina under the control of those forces;

(b) any entity, including any commercial, industrial, or public utility undertaking, organized or located in those areas of the Republic of Bosnia and Herzegovina under the control of Bosnian Serb forces;

(c) any entity, wherever organized or located, which is owned or controlled directly or indirectly by any person in, or resident in, those areas of the Republic of Bosnia and Herzegovina under the control of Bosnian Serb forces;

(d) any person acting for or on behalf of any person included within the scope of paragraph (a), (b), or (c) of this section; that are in the United States, that hereafter come within the United States, or that are or hereafter come within the possession or control of United States persons, including their overseas branches, are blocked.

SEC. 2. Notwithstanding the existence of any rights or obligations conferred or imposed by any international agreement or any contract entered into or any license or permit granted before the effective date of this order, except to the extent provided in regulations, orders, directives, or licenses, which may hereafter be issued pursuant to this order: (a) the provision or exportation of services to those areas of the Republic of Bosnia and Herzegovina under the control of Bosnian Serb forces, or to any person for the purpose of any business carried on in those areas, either from the United States or by a United States person, is prohibited; and

(b) no vessel registered in the United States or owned or controlled by a United States person, other than a United States naval vessel, may enter the riverine ports of those areas of the Republic of Bosnia and Herzegovina under the control of Bosnian Serb forces.

SEC. 3. Any transaction by any United States person that evades or avoids, or has the purpose of evading or avoiding, or attempts to violate, any of the prohibitions set forth in this order is prohibited.

SEC. 4. The Secretary of the Treasury, in consultation with the Secretary of State, is hereby authorized to take such actions, including the promulgation of rules and regulations, and to employ all powers granted to me by the International Emergency Economic Powers Act [50 U.S.C. 1701 et seq.] and the United Nations Participation Act of 1945 [22 U.S.C. 287 et seq.], as amended, as may be necessary to carry out the purposes of this order. The Secretary of the Treasury may redelegate the authority set forth in this order to other officers and agencies of the United States Government, all agencies of which are hereby directed to take all appropriate measures within their authority to carry out the provisions of this order, including suspension or termination of licenses or other authorizations in effect as of the date of this order.

SEC. 5. Nothing in this order shall apply to activities related to the United Nations Protection Force, the International Conference on the Former Yugoslavia, or the European Community Monitoring Missions.

SEC. 6. For the purposes of this order:

(a) The term "person" means an individual or entity;

(b) The term "entity" means a corporation, partnership, association, or other organization;

(c) The term "United States person" is as defined in section 5 of Executive Order No. 12810 [set out above].

SEC. 7. Nothing contained in this order shall create any right or benefit, substantive or procedural, enforceable by any party against the United States, its agencies or instrumentalities, its officers or employees, or any other person.

SEC. 8 (a) This order shall take effect at 11:59 p.m. eastern daylight time on October 25, 1994.

(b) This order shall be transmitted to the Congress and published in the Federal Register.

WILLIAM J. CLINTON.

EX. ORD. NO. 12938. PROLIFERATION OF WEAPONS OF MASS DESTRUCTION

Ex. Ord. No. 12938, Nov. 14, 1994, 59 F.R. 59099, as amended by Ex. Ord. No. 13094, §1, July 28, 1998, 63 F.R. 40803; Ex. Ord. No. 13128, June 25, 1999, 64 F.R. 34704, provided:

By the authority vested in me as President by the Constitution and the laws of the United States of America, including the International Emergency Economic Powers Act (50 U.S.C. 1701 *et seq.*), the National Emergencies Act (50 U.S.C. 1601 *et seq.*), the Arms Export Control Act, as amended (22 U.S.C. 2751 *et seq.*), Executive Orders Nos. 12851 [22 U.S.C. 2797 note] and 12924 [set out above], and section 301 of title 3, United States Code,

I, WILLIAM J. CLINTON, President of the United States of America, find that the proliferation of nuclear, biological, and chemical weapons ("weapons of mass destruction") and of the means of delivering such weapons, constitutes an unusual and extraordinary threat to the national security, foreign policy, and economy of the United States, and hereby declare a national emergency to deal with that threat.

Accordingly, I hereby order:

SECTION 1. *International Negotiations.* It is the policy of the United States to lead and seek multilaterally coordinated efforts with other countries to control the proliferation of weapons of mass destruction and the means of delivering such weapons. Accordingly, the Secretary of State shall cooperate in and lead multilateral efforts to stop the proliferation of weapons of mass destruction and their means of delivery.

SEC. 2. *Imposition of Controls.* As provided herein, the Secretary of State and the Secretary of Commerce shall use their respective authorities, including the Arms Export Control Act [22 U.S.C. 2751 et seq.] and the International Emergency Economic Powers Act [50 U.S.C. 1701 et seq.], to control any exports, to the extent they are not already controlled by the Department of Energy and the Nuclear Regulatory Commission, that either Secretary determines would assist a country in acquiring the capability to develop, produce, stockpile, deliver, or use weapons of mass destruction or their means of delivery. The Secretary of State shall pursue early negotiations with foreign governments to adopt effective measures comparable to those imposed under this order.

SEC. 3. *Department of Commerce Controls.* (a) The Secretary of Commerce shall prohibit the export of any goods, technology, or services subject to the Secretary's export jurisdiction that the Secretary of Commerce determines, in consultation with the Secretary of State, the Secretary of Defense, and other appropriate officials, would assist a foreign country in acquiring the capability to develop, produce, stockpile, deliver, or use weapons of mass destruction or their means of delivery. The Secretary of State shall pursue early negotiations with foreign governments to adopt effective measures comparable to those imposed under this section.

(b) Subsection (a) of this section will not apply to exports relating to a particular category of weapons of mass destruction (i.e., nuclear, chemical, or biological weapons) if their destination is a country with whose government the United States has entered into a bilateral or multilateral arrangement for the control of that category of weapons of mass destruction-related goods (including delivery systems) and technology, or maintains domestic export controls comparable to controls that are imposed by the United States with respect to that category of goods and technology, or that are otherwise deemed adequate by the Secretary of State.

(c) The Secretary of Commerce shall require validated licenses to implement this order and shall coordinate any license applications with the Secretary of State and the Secretary of Defense.

(d) The Secretary of Commerce, in consultation with the Secretary of State, shall take such actions, including the promulgation of rules, regulations, and amendments thereto, as may be necessary to continue to regulate the activities of United States persons in order to prevent their participation in activities that could contribute to the proliferation of weapons of mass destruction or their means of delivery, as provided in the Export Administration Regulations, set forth in Title 15, Chapter VII, Subchapter C, of the Code of Federal Regulations, Parts 768 to 799 inclusive.

(e) the Secretary of Commerce shall impose and enforce such restrictions on the importation of chemicals into the United States as may be necessary to carry out the requirements of the Convention on the Prohibition of the Development, Production, Stockpiling and Use of Chemical Weapons and on Their Destruction.

SEC. 4. *Measures Against Foreign Persons.*

(a) *Determination by Secretary of State; Imposition of Measures.* Except to the extent provided in section 203(b) of the International Emergency Economic Powers Act (50 U.S.C. 1702(b)), where applicable, if the Secretary of State determines that a foreign person, on or after November 16, 1990, the effective date of Executive Order 12735, the predecessor order to Executive Order 12938, has materially contributed or attempted to contribute materially to the efforts of any foreign country, project, or entity of proliferation concern to use, acquire, design, develop, produce, or stockpile weapons of mass destruction or missiles capable of delivering such weapons, the measures set forth in subsections (b), (c), and (d) of this section shall be imposed on that foreign person to the extent determined by the Secretary of State in consultation with the implementing agency and other relevant agencies. Nothing in this section is intended to preclude the imposition on that foreign person of other measures or sanctions available under this order or under other authorities.

(b) *Procurement Ban.* No department or agency of the United States Government may procure, or enter into any contract for the procurement of, any goods, technology, or services from any foreign person described in subsection (a) of this section.

(c) *Assistance Ban.* No department or agency of the United States Government may provide any assistance to any foreign person described in subsection (a) of this section, and no such foreign person shall be eligible to participate in any assistance program of the United States Government.

(d) *Import Ban.* The Secretary of the Treasury shall prohibit the importation into the United States of goods, technology, or services produced or provided by any foreign person described in subsection (a) of this section, other than information or informational materials within the meaning of section 203(b)(3) of the International Emergency Economic Powers Act (50 U.S.C. 1702(b)(3)).

(e) *Termination.* Measures pursuant to this section may be terminated against a foreign person if the Secretary of State determines that there is reliable evidence that such foreign person has ceased all activities referred to in subsection (a) of this section.

(f) *Exceptions.* Departments and agencies of the United States Government, acting in consultation with the Secretary of State, may, by license, regulation, order, directive, exception, or otherwise, provide for:

(i) Procurement contracts necessary to meet U.S. operational military requirements or requirements under defense production agreements; intelligence requirements; sole source suppliers, spare parts, components, routine servicing and maintenance of products for the United States Government; and medical and humanitarian items; and

(ii) Performance pursuant to contracts in force on the effective date of this order under appropriate circumstances.

SEC. 5. *Sanctions Against Foreign Countries.* (a) In addition to the sanctions imposed on foreign countries as provided in the Chemical and Biological Weapons Control and Warfare Elimination Act of 1991 [22 U.S.C. 5601 et seq.], sanctions also shall be imposed on a foreign country as specified in subsection (b) of this section, if the Secretary of State determines that the foreign country has, on or after the effective date of this order or its predecessor, Executive Order No. 12735 of November 16, 1990, (1) used chemical or biological weapons in violation of international law; (2) made substantial preparations to use chemical or biological weapons in violation of international law; or (3) developed, produced, stockpiled, or otherwise acquired chemical or biological weapons in violation of international law.

(b) The following sanctions shall be imposed on any foreign country identified in subsection (a)(1) of this section unless the Secretary of State determines, on grounds of significant foreign policy or national security, that any individual sanction should not be applied. The sanctions specified in this section may be made applicable to the countries identified in subsections (a)(2) or (a)(3) when the Secretary of State determines that such action will further the objectives of this order pertaining to proliferation. The sanctions specified in subsection (b)(2) below shall be imposed with the concurrence of the Secretary of the Treasury.

(1) *Foreign Assistance.* No assistance shall be provided to that country under the Foreign Assistance Act of 1961 [22 U.S.C. 2151 et seq.], or any successor act, or the Arms Export Control Act [22 U.S.C. 2751 et seq.], other than assistance that is intended to benefit the people of that country directly and that is not channeled through governmental agencies or entities of that country.

(2) *Multilateral Development Bank Assistance.* The United States shall oppose any loan or financial or technical assistance to that country by international financial institutions in accordance with section 701 of the International Financial Institutions Act (22 U.S.C. 262d).

(3) *Denial of Credit or Other Financial Assistance.* The United States shall deny to that country any credit or financial assistance by any department, agency, or instrumentality of the United States Government.

(4) *Prohibition of Arms Sales.* The United States Government shall not, under the Arms Export Control Act, sell to that country any defense articles or defense services or issue any license for the export of items on the United States Munitions List.

(5) *Exports of National Security-Sensitive Goods and Technology.* No exports shall be permitted of any goods or technologies controlled for national security reasons under the Export Administration Regulations.

(6) *Further Export Restrictions.* The Secretary of Commerce shall prohibit or otherwise substantially restrict exports to that country of goods, technology, and services (excluding agricultural commodities and products otherwise subject to control).

(7) *Import Restrictions.* Restrictions shall be imposed on the importation into the United States of articles (that may include petroleum or any petroleum product) that are the growth, product, or manufacture of that country.

(8) *Landing Rights.* At the earliest practicable date, the Secretary of State shall terminate, in a manner consistent with international law, the authority of any air carrier that is controlled in fact by the government of that country to engage in air transportation (as defined in section 101(10) of the Federal Aviation Act of 1958 (49 U.S.C. App. 1301(10) [see 49 U.S.C. 40102(5)]).

SEC. 6. *Duration.* Any sanctions imposed pursuant to sections 4 or 5 of this order shall remain in force until the Secretary of State determines that lifting any sanction is in the foreign policy or national security interests of the United States or, as to sanctions under section 4 of this order, until the Secretary has made the determination under section 4(e).

SEC. 7. *Implementation.* The Secretary of State, the Secretary of the Treasury, and the Secretary of Commerce are hereby authorized and directed to take such actions, including the promulgation of rules and regulations, as may be necessary to carry out the purposes of this order. These actions, and in particular those in sections 4 and 5 of this order, shall be made in consultation with the Secretary of Defense and, as appropriate, other agency heads and shall be implemented in accordance with procedures established pursuant to Executive Order No. 12851 [22 U.S.C. 2797 note]. The Secretary concerned may redelegate any of these functions to other officers in agencies of the Federal Government. All heads of departments and agencies of the United States Government are directed to take all appropriate measures within their authority to carry out the provisions of this order, including the suspension or termination of licenses or other authorizations.

SEC. 8. *Preservation of Authorities.* Nothing in this order is intended to affect the continued effectiveness of any rules, regulations, orders, licenses, or other forms of administrative action issued, taken, or continued in effect heretofore or hereafter under the authority of the International Economic Emergency Powers Act [International Emergency Economic Powers Act, 50 U.S.C. 1701 et seq.], the Export Administration Act [50 App. U.S.C. 2401 et seq.], the Arms Export Control Act [22 U.S.C. 2751 et seq.], the Nuclear Non-proliferation Act [22 U.S.C. 3201 et seq.], Executive Order No. 12730 of September 30, 1990 [50 U.S.C. 1701 note], Executive Order No. 12735 of November 16, 1990, Executive Order No. 12924 of August 18, 1994 [50 U.S.C. 1701 note], and Executive Order No. 12930 of September 29, 1994.

SEC. 9. *Judicial Review.* This order is not intended to create, nor does it create, any right or benefit, substantive or procedural, enforceable at law by a party against the United States, its agencies, officers, or any other person.

SEC. 10. *Revocation of Executive Orders Nos. 12735 and 12930.* Executive Order No. 12735 of November 16, 1990, and Executive Order No. 12930 of September 29, 1994, are hereby revoked.

SEC. 11. *Effective Date.* This order is effective immediately.

This order shall be transmitted to the Congress and published in the Federal Register.

WILLIAM J. CLINTON.

CONTINUATION OF NATIONAL EMERGENCY DECLARED BY EX. ORD. NO. 12938

Notice of President of the United States, dated Nov. 9, 2000, 65 F.R. 68063, provided:

On November 14, 1994, by Executive Order 12938 [set out above], I declared a national emergency with respect to the unusual and extraordinary threat to the national security, foreign policy, and economy of the United States posed by the proliferation of nuclear, biological, and chemical weapons (weapons of mass destruction) and the means of delivering such weapons. Because the proliferation of weapons of mass destruction and the means of delivering them continues to pose an unusual and extraordinary threat to the national security, foreign policy, and economy of the United States, the national emergency first declared on November 14, 1994, and extended on November 14, 1995,

November 12, 1996, November 13, 1997, November 12, 1998, and November 10, 1999, must continue in effect beyond November 14, 2000. Therefore, in accordance with section 202(d) of the National Emergencies Act (50 U.S.C. 1622(d)), I am continuing the national emergency declared in Executive Order 12938.

This notice shall be published in the Federal Register and transmitted to the Congress.

WILLIAM J. CLINTON.

Prior continuations of national emergency declared by Ex. Ord. No. 12938 were contained in the following:

Notice of President of the United States, dated Nov. 10, 1999, 64 F.R. 61767.

Notice of President of the United States, dated Nov. 12, 1998, 63 F.R. 63589.

Notice of President of the United States, dated Nov. 12, 1997, 62 F.R. 60993.

Notice of President of the United States, dated Nov. 12, 1996, 61 F.R. 58309.

Notice of President of the United States, dated Nov. 8, 1995, 60 F.R. 57137.

EX. ORD. NO. 12947. PROHIBITING TRANSACTIONS WITH TERRORISTS WHO THREATEN TO DISRUPT MIDDLE EAST PEACE PROCESS

Ex. Ord. No. 12947, Jan. 23, 1995, 60 F.R. 5079, as amended by Ex. Ord. No. 13099, §§1, 2, Aug. 20, 1998, 63 F.R. 45167, provided:

By the authority vested in me as President by the Constitution and the laws of the United States of America, including the International Emergency Economic Powers Act (50 U.S.C. 1701 *et seq.*) (IEEPA), the National Emergencies Act (50 U.S.C. 1601 *et seq.*), and section 301 of title 3, United States Code,

I, WILLIAM J. CLINTON, President of the United States of America, find that grave acts of violence committed by foreign terrorists that disrupt the Middle East peace process constitute an unusual and extraordinary threat to the national security, foreign policy, and economy of the United States, and hereby declare a national emergency to deal with that threat.

I hereby order:

SECTION 1. Except to the extent provided in section 203(b)(3) and (4) of IEEPA (50 U.S.C. 1702(b)(3) and (4)) and in regulations, orders, directives, or licenses that may be issued pursuant to this order, and notwithstanding any contract entered into or any license or permit granted prior to the effective date: (a) all property and interests in property of:

(i) the persons listed in the Annex to this order;

(ii) foreign persons designated by the Secretary of State, in coordination with the Secretary of the Treasury and the Attorney General, because they are found:

(A) to have committed, or to pose a significant risk of committing, acts of violence that have the purpose or effect of disrupting the Middle East peace process, or

(B) to assist in, sponsor, or provide financial, material, or technological support for, or services in support of, such acts of violence; and

(iii) persons determined by the Secretary of the Treasury, in coordination with the Secretary of State and the Attorney General, to be owned or controlled by, or to act for or on behalf of, any of the foregoing persons, that are in the United States, that hereafter come within the United States, or that hereafter come within the possession or control of United States persons, are blocked;

(b) any transaction or dealing by United States persons or within the United States in property or interests in property of the persons designated in or pursuant to this order is prohibited, including the making or receiving of any contribution of funds, goods, or services to or for the benefit of such persons;

(c) any transaction by any United States person or within the United States that evades or avoids, or has the purpose of evading or avoiding, or attempts to violate, any of the prohibitions set forth in this order, is prohibited.

SEC. 2. For the purposes of this order: (a) the term "person" means an individual or entity;

(b) the term "entity" means a partnership, association, corporation, or other organization, group, or subgroup;

(c) the term "United States person" means any United States citizen, permanent resident alien, entity organized under the laws of the United States (including foreign branches), or any person in the United States; and

(d) the term "foreign person" means any citizen or national of a foreign state (including any such individual who is also a citizen or national of the United States) or any entity not organized solely under the laws of the United States or existing solely in the United States, but does not include a foreign state.

SEC. 3. I hereby determine that the making of donations of the type specified in section 203(b)(2)(A) of IEEPA (50 U.S.C. 1702(b)(2)(A)) by United States persons to persons designated in or pursuant to this order would seriously impair my ability to deal with the national emergency declared in this order, and hereby prohibit such donations as provided by section 1 of this order.

SEC. 4. (a) The Secretary of the Treasury, in consultation with the Secretary of State and, as appropriate, the Attorney General, is hereby authorized to take such actions, including the promulgation of rules and regulations, and to employ all powers granted to me by IEEPA as may be necessary to carry out the purposes of this order. The Secretary of the Treasury may redelegate any of these functions to other officers and agencies of the United States Government. All agencies of the United States Government are hereby directed to take all appropriate measures within their authority to carry out the provisions of this order.

(b) Any investigation emanating from a possible violation of this order, or of any license, order, or regulation issued pursuant to this order, shall first be coordinated with the Federal Bureau of Investigation (FBI), and any matter involving evidence of a criminal violation shall be referred to the FBI for further investigation. The FBI shall timely notify the Department of the Treasury of any action it takes on such referrals.

SEC. 5. Nothing contained in this order shall create any right or benefit, substantive or procedural, enforceable by any party against the United States, its agencies or instrumentalities, its officers or employees, or any other person.

SEC. 6. (a) This order is effective at 12:01 a.m., eastern standard time on January 24, 1995.

(b) This order shall be transmitted to the Congress and published in the Federal Register.

WILLIAM J. CLINTON.

ANNEX

TERRORISTS WHO THREATEN TO DISRUPT THE MIDDLE EAST PEACE PROCESS

Abu Hafs al-Masri

Abu Nidal Organization (ANO)

Democratic Front for the Liberation of Palestine (DFLP)

Hizballah

Islamic Army (a.k.a. Al-Qaida, Islamic Salvation Foundation, The Islamic Army for the Liberation of the Holy Places, The World Islamic Front for Jihad Against Jews and Crusaders, and The Group for the Preservation of the Holy Sites)

Islamic Gama'at (IG)

Islamic Resistance Movement (HAMAS)

Jihad

Kach

Kahane Chai

Palestinian Islamic Jihad-Shiqaqi faction (PIJ)

Palestine Liberation Front-Abu Abbas faction (PLF-Abu Abbas)

Popular Front for the Liberation of Palestine (PFLP)

Popular Front for the Liberation of Palestine-General Command (PFLP–GC)

Rifa'i Ahmad Taha Musa

Usama bin Muhammad bin Awad bin Ladin (a.k.a. Usama bin Ladin)

CONTINUATION OF NATIONAL EMERGENCY DECLARED BY EX. ORD. NO. 12947

Notice of President of the United States, dated Jan. 19, 2001, 66 F.R. 7371, provided:

On January 23, 1995, by Executive Order 12947 [set out above], I declared a national emergency to deal with the unusual and extraordinary threat to the national security, foreign policy, and economy of the United States constituted by grave acts of violence committed by foreign terrorists that disrupt the Middle East peace process. The order, issued pursuant to the International Emergency Economic Powers Act [50 U.S.C. 1701 et seq.], among other authorities, blocks the assets in the United States, or in the control of United States persons, of foreign terrorists who threaten to disrupt the Middle East peace process. I also prohibited transactions or dealings by United States persons in such property. On August 20, 1998, by Executive Order 13099 [set out below], I identified four additional persons, including Usama bin Ladin, who threaten to disrupt the Middle East peace process. I have annually transmitted notices of the continuation of this national emergency to the Congress and the Federal Register. Last year's notice of continuation was published in the Federal Register on January 21, 2000. Because terrorist activities continue to threaten the Middle East peace process and vital interests of the United States in the Middle East, the national emergency declared on January 23, 1995, and the measures made effective on January 24, 1995, to deal with that emergency must continue in effect beyond January 23, 2001. Therefore, in accordance with section 202(d)2 of the National Emergencies Act (50 U.S.C. 1622(d) of the National Emergencies Act (50 U.S.C. 1622(d)) [sic], I am continuing the national emergency with respect to foreign terrorists who threaten to disrupt the Middle East peace process.

This notice shall be published in the Federal Register and transmitted to the Congress.

WILLIAM J. CLINTON.

Prior continuations of national emergency declared by Ex. Ord. No. 12947 were contained in the following:

Notice of President of the United States, dated Jan. 19, 2000, 65 F.R. 3581.

Notice of President of the United States, dated Jan. 20, 1999, 64 F.R. 3393.

Notice of President of the United States, dated Jan. 21, 1998, 63 F.R. 3445.

Notice of President of the United States, dated Jan. 21, 1997, 62 F.R. 3439.

Notice of President of the United States, dated Jan. 18, 1996, 61 F.R. 1695.

EX. ORD. NO. 12957. PROHIBITING CERTAIN TRANSACTIONS WITH RESPECT TO DEVELOPMENT OF IRANIAN PETROLEUM RESOURCES

Ex. Ord. No. 12957, Mar. 15, 1995, 60 F.R. 14615, provided:

By the authority vested in me as President by the Constitution and the laws of the United States of America, including the International Emergency Economic Powers Act (50 U.S.C. 1701 *et seq.*), the National Emergencies Act (50 U.S.C. 1601 *et seq.*), and section 301 of title 3, United States Code,

I, WILLIAM J. CLINTON, President of the United States of America, find that the actions and policies of the Government of Iran constitute an unusual and extraordinary threat to the national security, foreign policy, and economy of the United States, and hereby declare a national emergency to deal with that threat.

I hereby order:

SECTION 1. The following are prohibited, except to the extent provided in regulations, orders, directives, or licenses that may be issued pursuant to this order, and notwithstanding any contract entered into or any license or permit granted prior to the effective date of this order: (a) the entry into or performance by a United States person, or the approval by a United States person of the entry into or performance by an entity owned or controlled by a United States person, of (i) a contract that includes overall supervision and management responsibility for the development of petroleum resources located in Iran, or (ii) a guaranty of another person's performance under such a contract;

(b) the entry into or performance by a United States person, or the approval by a United States person of the entry into or performance by an entity owned or controlled by a United States person, of (i) a contract for the financing of the development of petroleum resources located in Iran, or (ii) a guaranty of another person's performance under such a contract; and

(c) any transaction by any United States person or within the United States that evades or avoids, or has the purpose of evading or avoiding, or attempts to violate, any of the prohibitions set forth in this order.

SEC. 2. For the purposes of this order: (a) The term "person" means an individual or entity;

(b) The term "entity" means a partnership, association, trust, joint venture, corporation, or other organization;

(c) The term "United States person" means any United States citizen, permanent resident alien, entity organized under the laws of the United States (including foreign branches), or any person in the United States; and

(d) The term "Iran" means the land territory claimed by Iran and any other area over which Iran claims sovereignty, sovereign rights or jurisdiction, including the territorial sea, exclusive economic zone, and continental shelf claimed by Iran.

SEC. 3. The Secretary of the Treasury, in consultation with the Secretary of State, is hereby authorized to take such actions, including the promulgation of rules and regulations, and to employ all powers granted to me by the International Emergency Economic Powers Act as may be necessary to carry out the purposes of this order. The Secretary of the Treasury may redelegate any of these functions to other officers and agencies of the United States Government. All agencies of the United States Government are hereby directed to take all appropriate measures within their authority to carry out the provisions of this order.

SEC. 4. Nothing contained in this order shall create any right or benefit, substantive or procedural, enforceable by any party against the United States, its agencies or instrumentalities, its officers or employees, or any other person.

SEC. 5. (a) This order is effective at 12:01 a.m., eastern standard time, on March 16, 1995.

(b) This order shall be transmitted to the Congress and published in the Federal Register.

WILLIAM J. CLINTON.

[Sections 1 and 2 of Ex. Ord. No. 12957 were revoked by Ex. Ord. No. 12959, §5, May 6, 1995, 60 F.R. 24758, set out below, to the extent inconsistent with Ex. Ord. No. 12959.]

CONTINUATION OF NATIONAL EMERGENCY DECLARED BY EX. ORD. NO. 12957

Notice of President of the United States, dated Mar. 13, 2000, 65 F.R. 13863, provided:

On March 15, 1995, by Executive Order 12957 [set out above], I declared a national emergency with respect to Iran pursuant to the International Emergency Economic Powers Act (50 U.S.C. 1701–1706) to deal with the threat to the national security, foreign policy, and economy of the United States constituted by the actions and policies of the Government of Iran, including its support for international terrorism, efforts to undermine the Middle East peace process, and acquisition of weapons of mass destruction and the means to deliver them. On May 6, 1995, I issued Executive Order 12959 [set out below] imposing more comprehensive sanctions to further respond to this threat, and on August 19, 1997, I issued Executive Order 13059 [set out below] consolidating and clarifying these previous orders. The last notice of continuation was published in the Federal Register on March 12, 1999.

Because the actions and policies of the Government of Iran continue to threaten the national security, foreign policy, and economy of the United States, the national emergency declared on March 15, 1995, must continue in effect beyond March 15, 2000. Therefore, in accordance with section 202(d) of the National Emergencies Act (50 U.S.C. 1622(d)), I am continuing the national emergency with respect to Iran. Because the emergency declared by Executive Order 12957 constitutes an emergency separate from that declared on November 14, 1979, by Executive Order 12170 [set out above], this renewal is distinct from the emergency renewal of November 1999. This notice shall be published in the Federal Register and transmitted to the Congress.

WILLIAM J. CLINTON.

Prior continuations of national emergency declared by Ex. Ord. No. 12957 were contained in the following:

Notice of President of the United States, dated Mar. 10, 1999, 64 F.R. 12239.

Notice of President of the United States, dated Mar. 4, 1998, 63 F.R. 11099.

Notice of President of the United States, dated Mar. 5, 1997, 62 F.R. 10409.

Notice of President of the United States, dated Mar. 8, 1996, 61 F.R. 9897.

EX. ORD. NO. 12959. PROHIBITING CERTAIN TRANSACTIONS WITH RESPECT TO IRAN

Ex. Ord. No. 12959, May 6, 1995, 60 F.R. 24757, as amended by Ex. Ord. No. 13059, §7, Aug. 19, 1997, 62 F.R. 44533, provided:

By the authority vested in me as President by the Constitution and the laws of the United States of America, including the International Emergency Economic Powers Act (50 U.S.C. 1701 *et seq.*) (IEEPA), the National Emergencies Act (50 U.S.C. 1601 *et seq.*), section 505 of the International Security and Development Cooperation Act of 1985 (22 U.S.C. 2349aa-9) (ISDCA), and section 301 of title 3, United States Code,

I, WILLIAM J. CLINTON, President of the United States of America, in order to take steps with respect to Iran in addition to those set forth in Executive Order No. 12957 of March 15, 1995 [set out above], to deal with the unusual and extraordinary threat to the national security, foreign policy, and economy of the United States referred to in that order, hereby order:

SECTION 1. The following are prohibited, except to the extent provided in regulations, orders, directives, or licenses that may be issued pursuant to this order, and notwithstanding any contract entered into or any license or permit granted prior to the effective date of this order:

[(a) to (d) Revoked by Ex. Ord. No. 13059, §7, Aug. 19, 1997, 62 F.R. 44533, set out below.]

(e) any new investment by a United States person in Iran or in property (including entities) owned or controlled by the Government of Iran;

[(f) Revoked by Ex. Ord. No. 13059, §7, Aug. 19, 1997, 62 F.R. 44533, set out below.]

(g) any transaction by any United States person or within the United States that evades or avoids, or has the purpose of evading or avoiding, or attempts to violate, any of the prohibitions set forth in this order.

SEC. 2. For the purposes of this order:

(a) the term "person" means an individual or entity;

(b) the term "entity" means a partnership, association, trust, joint venture, corporation, or other organization;

(c) the term "United States person" means any United States citizen, permanent resident alien, entity organized under the laws of the United States (including foreign branches), or any person in the United States;

(d) the term "Iran" means the territory of Iran and any other territory or marine area, including the exclusive economic zone and continental shelf, over which the Government of Iran claims sovereignty, sovereign rights or jurisdiction, provided that the Government of Iran exercises partial or total de facto control over the area or derives a benefit from economic activity in the area pursuant to international arrangements; and

(e) the term "new investment" means (i) a commitment or contribution of funds or other assets, or (ii) a loan or other extension of credit.

SEC. 3. The Secretary of the Treasury, in consultation with the Secretary of State, is hereby authorized to take such actions, including the promulgation of rules and regulations, the requirement of reports, including reports by United States persons on oil transactions engaged in by their foreign affiliates with Iran or the Government of Iran, and to employ all powers granted to the President by IEEPA and ISDCA [Pub. L. 99–83, see Short Title of 1985 Amendments note set out under section 2151 of Title 22, Foreign Relations and Intercourse] as may be necessary to carry out the purposes of this order. The Secretary of the Treasury may redelegate any of these functions to other officers and agencies of the United States Government. All agencies of the United States Government are hereby directed to take all appropriate measures within their authority to carry out the provisions of this order.

SEC. 4. The Secretary of the Treasury may not authorize the exportation or reexportation to Iran, the Government of Iran, or an entity owned or controlled by the Government of Iran of any goods, technology, or services subject to export license application requirements of another agency of the United States Government, if authorization of the exportation or reexportation by that agency would be prohibited by law.

SEC. 5. Sections 1 and 2 of Executive Order No. 12613 of October 29, 1987 [formerly set out above], and sections 1 and 2 of Executive Order No. 12957 of March 15, 1995 [set out above], are hereby revoked to the extent inconsistent with this order. Otherwise, the provisions of this order supplement the provisions of Executive Orders No. 12613 and 12957.

SEC. 6. Nothing contained in this order shall create any right or benefit, substantive or procedural, enforceable by any party against the United States, its agencies or instrumentalities, its officers or employees, or any other person.

SEC. 7. The measures taken pursuant to this order are in response to actions of the Government of Iran occurring after the conclusion of the 1981 Algiers Accords, and are intended solely as a response to those later actions.

SEC. 8. (a) This order is effective at 12:01 a.m., eastern daylight time, on May 7, 1995, except that (i) section 1(b), (c), and (d) of this order shall not apply until 12:01 a.m., eastern daylight time, on June 6, 1995, to trade transactions under contracts in force as of the date of this order if such transactions are authorized pursuant to Federal regulations in force immediately prior to the date of this order ("existing trade contracts"), and (ii) letters of credit and other financing agreements with respect to existing trade contracts may be performed pursuant to their terms with respect to underlying trade transactions occurring prior to 12:01 a.m., eastern daylight time, on June 6, 1995.

(b) This order shall be transmitted to the Congress and published in the Federal Register.

WILLIAM J. CLINTON.

EX. ORD. NO. 12978. BLOCKING ASSETS AND PROHIBITING TRANSACTIONS WITH SIGNIFICANT NARCOTICS TRAFFICKERS

Ex. Ord. No. 12978, Oct. 21, 1995, 60 F.R. 54579, provided:

By the authority vested in me as President by the Constitution and the laws of the United States of America, including the International Emergency Economic Powers Act (50 U.S.C. 1701 *et seq.*) (IEEPA), the National Emergencies Act (50 U.S.C. 1601 *et seq.*), and section 301 of title 3, United States Code,

I, WILLIAM J. CLINTON, President of the United States of America, find that the actions of significant foreign narcotics traffickers centered in Colombia, and the unparalleled violence, corruption, and harm that they cause in the United States and abroad, constitute an unusual and extraordinary threat to the national security, foreign policy, and economy of the United States, and hereby declare a national emergency to deal with that threat.

SECTION 1. Except to the extent provided in section 203(b) of IEEPA (50 U.S.C. 1702(b)) and in regulations, orders, directives, or licenses that may be issued pursuant to this order, and notwithstanding any contract entered into or any license or permit granted prior to the effective date, I hereby order blocked all property and interests in property that are or hereafter come within the United States, or that are or hereafter come within the possession or control of United States persons, of:

(a) the foreign persons listed in the Annex to this order;

(b) foreign persons determined by the Secretary of the Treasury, in consultation with the Attorney General and the Secretary of State:

(i) to play a significant role in international narcotics trafficking centered in Colombia; or

(ii) materially to assist in, or provide financial or technological support for or goods or services in support of, the narcotics trafficking activities of persons designated in or pursuant to this order; and

(c) persons determined by the Secretary of the Treasury, in consultation with the Attorney General and the Secretary of State, to be owned or controlled by, or to act for or on behalf of, persons designated in or pursuant to this order.

SEC. 2. Further, except to the extent provided in section 203(b) of IEEPA and in regulations, orders, directives, or licenses that may be issued pursuant to this order, and notwithstanding any contract entered into or any license or permit granted prior to the effective date, I hereby prohibit the following:

(a) any transaction or dealing by United States persons or within the United States in property or interests in property of the persons designated in or pursuant to this order;

(b) any transaction by any United States person or within the United States that evades or avoids, or has the purpose of evading or avoiding, or attempts to violate, any of the prohibitions set forth in this order.

SEC. 3. For the purposes of this order:

(a) the term "person" means an individual or entity;

(b) the term "entity" means a partnership, association, corporation, or other organization, group or subgroup;

(c) the term "United States person" means any United States citizen or national, permanent resident alien, entity organized under the laws of the United States (including foreign branches), or any person in the United States;

(d) the term "foreign person" means any citizen or national of a foreign state (including any such individual who is also a citizen or national of the United States) or any entity not organized solely under the laws of the United States or existing solely in the United States, but does not include a foreign state; and

(e) the term "narcotics trafficking" means any activity undertaken illicitly to cultivate, produce, manufacture, distribute, sell, finance or transport, or otherwise assist, abet, conspire, or collude with others in illicit activities relating to, narcotic drugs, including, but not limited to, cocaine.

SEC. 4. The Secretary of the Treasury, in consultation with the Attorney General and the Secretary of State, is hereby authorized to take such actions, including the promulgation of rules and regulations, and to employ all powers granted to the President by IEEPA as may be necessary to carry out this order. The Secretary of the Treasury may redelegate any of these functions to other officers and agencies of the United States Government. All agencies of the United States Government are hereby directed to take all appropriate measures within their authority to carry out this order.

SEC. 5. Nothing contained in this order shall create any right or benefit, substantive or procedural, enforceable by any party against the United States, its agencies or instrumentalities, its officers or employees, or any other person.

SEC. 6. (a) This order is effective at 12:01 a.m. Eastern Daylight Time on October 22, 1995.

(b) This order shall be transmitted to the Congress and published in the Federal Register.

WILLIAM J. CLINTON.

ANNEX

Gilberto Rodriguez Orejuela
Miguel Angel Rodriguez Orejuela
José Santacruz Londoño
Helmer Herrera Buitrago

CONTINUATION OF NATIONAL EMERGENCY DECLARED BY EX. ORD. NO. 12978

Notice of President of the United States, dated Oct. 19, 2000, 65 F.R. 63193, provided:

On October 21, 1995, by Executive Order 12978 [set out above], I declared a national emergency to deal with the unusual and extraordinary threat to the national security, foreign policy, and economy of the United States constituted by the actions of significant narcotics traffickers centered in Colombia, and the unparalleled violence, corruption, and harm they cause in the United States and abroad. The order blocks all property and interests in property of foreign persons listed in an Annex to the order [see note above], as well as persons determined to play a significant role in international narcotics trafficking centered in Colombia, to materially assist in, or provide financial or technological support for or goods or services in support of, narcotics trafficking activities of persons designated in or pursuant to the order, or to be owned or controlled by, or to act for or on behalf of, persons designated in or pursuant to the order. The order also prohibits any transaction or dealing by United States persons or within the United States in such property or interests in property. Because the activities of significant narcotics traffickers centered in Colombia continue to threaten the national security, foreign policy, and economy of the United States and to cause unparalleled violence, corruption, and harm in the United States and abroad, the national emergency declared on October 21, 1995, and the measures adopted pursuant thereto to deal with that emergency, must continue in effect beyond October 21, 2000. Therefore, in accordance with section 202(d) of the National Emergencies Act (50 U.S.C. 1622(d)), I am continuing the national emergency for 1 year with respect to significant narcotics traffickers centered in Colombia. This notice shall be published in the Federal Register and transmitted to the Congress.

WILLIAM J. CLINTON.

Prior continuations of national emergency declared by Ex. Ord. No. 12978 were contained in the following:

Notice of President of the United States, dated Oct. 19, 1999, 64 F.R. 56667.

Notice of President of the United States, dated Oct. 19, 1998, 63 F.R. 56079.

Notice of President of the United States, dated Oct. 17, 1997, 62 F.R. 54561.

Notice of President of the United States, dated Oct. 16, 1996, 61 F.R. 54531.

EX. ORD. NO. 13047. PROHIBITING NEW INVESTMENT IN BURMA

Ex. Ord. No. 13047, May 20, 1997, 62 F.R. 28301, provided:

By the authority vested in me as President by the Constitution and the laws of the United States of America, including section 570 of the Foreign Operations, Export Financing, and Related Programs Appropriations Act, 1997 (Public Law 104–208) (the "Act") [110 Stat. 3009–166], the International Emergency Economic Powers Act (50 U.S.C. 1701 *et seq.*) (IEEPA), the National Emergencies Act (50 U.S.C. 1601 *et seq.*), and section 301 of title 3 of the United States Code;

I, WILLIAM J. CLINTON, President of the United States of America, hereby determine and certify that, for purposes of section 570(b) of the Act, the Government of Burma has committed large-scale repression of the democratic opposition in Burma after September 30, 1996, and further determine that the actions and policies of the Government of Burma constitute an unusual and extraordinary threat to the national security and foreign policy of the United States and declare a national emergency to deal with that threat.

SECTION 1. Except to the extent provided in regulations, orders, directives, or licenses that may be issued in conformity with section 570 of the Act and pursuant to this order, I hereby prohibit new investment in Burma by United States persons.

SEC. 2. The following are also prohibited, except to the extent provided in section 203(b) of IEEPA (50 U.S.C. 1702(b)) or in regulations, orders, directives, or licenses that may be issued pursuant to this order:

(a) any approval or other facilitation by a United States person, wherever located, of a transaction by a foreign person where the transaction would constitute new investment in Burma prohibited by this order if engaged in by a United States person or within the United States; and

(b) any transaction by a United States person or within the United States that evades or avoids, or has the purpose of evading or avoiding, or attempts to violate, any of the prohibitions set forth in this order.

SEC. 3. Nothing in this order shall be construed to prohibit the entry into, performance of, or financing of a contract to sell or purchase goods, services, or technology, except:

(a) where the entry into such contract on or after the effective date of this order is for the general supervision and guarantee of another person's performance of a contract for the economic development of resources located in Burma; or

(b) where such contract provides for payment, in whole or in part, in:

(i) shares of ownership, including an equity interest, in the economic development of resources located in Burma; or

(ii) participation in royalties, earnings, or profits in the economic development of resources located in Burma.

SEC. 4. For the purposes of this order:

(a) the term "person" means an individual or entity;

(b) the term "entity" means a partnership, association, trust, joint venture, corporation, or other organization;

(c) the term "United States person" means any United States citizen, permanent resident alien, juridical person organized under the laws of the United States (including foreign branches), or any person in the United States;

(d) the term "new investment" means any of the following activities, if such an activity is undertaken pursuant to an agreement, or pursuant to the exercise of rights under such an agreement, that is entered into with the Government of Burma or a nongovernmental entity in Burma on or after the effective date of this order:

(i) the entry into a contract that includes the economic development of resources located in Burma;

(ii) the entry into a contract providing for the general supervision and guarantee of another person's performance of a contract that includes the economic development of resources located in Burma;

(iii) the purchase of a share of ownership, including an equity interest, in the economic development of resources located in Burma; or

(iv) the entry into a contract providing for the participation in royalties, earnings, or profits in the economic development of resources located in Burma, without regard to the form of the participation;

(e) the term "resources located in Burma" means any resources, including natural, agricultural, commercial, financial, industrial, and human resources, located within the territory of Burma, including the territorial sea, or located within the exclusive economic zone or continental shelf of Burma;

(f) the term "economic development of resources located in Burma" shall not be construed to include not-for-profit educational, health, or other humanitarian programs or activities.

SEC. 5. I hereby delegate to the Secretary of State the functions vested in me under section 570(c) and (d) of the Act, to be exercised in consultation with the heads of other agencies of the United States Government as appropriate.

SEC. 6. The Secretary of the Treasury, in consultation with the Secretary of State, is hereby authorized to take such actions, including the promulgation of rules and regulations, and to employ all powers granted to me by section 570(b) of the Act and by IEEPA, as may be necessary to carry out the purposes of this order. The Secretary of the Treasury may redelegate the authority set forth in this order to other officers and agencies of the United States Government. All agencies of the United States Government are hereby directed to take all appropriate measures within their authority to carry out the provisions of this order.

SEC. 7. Nothing contained in this order shall create any right or benefit, substantive or procedural, enforceable by any party against the United States, its agencies or instrumentalities, its officers or employees, or any other person.

SEC. 8. (a) This order shall take effect at 12:01 a.m., eastern daylight time, May 21, 1997.

(b) This order shall be transmitted to the Congress and published in the Federal Register.

WILLIAM J. CLINTON.

CONTINUATION OF NATIONAL EMERGENCY DECLARED BY EX. ORD. NO. 13047

Notice of President of the United States, dated May 18, 2000, 65 F.R. 32005, provided:

On May 20, 1997, I issued Executive Order 13047 [set out above], effective at 12:01 a.m. eastern daylight time on May 21, 1997, certifying to the Congress under section 570(b) of the Foreign Operations, Export Financing, and Related Programs Appropriations Act, 1997 (Public Law 104–208 [110 Stat. 3009–166]), that the Government of Burma has committed large-scale repression of the democratic opposition in Burma after September 30, 1996, thereby invoking the prohibition on new investment in Burma by United States persons, contained in that section. I also declared a national emergency to deal with the threat posed to the national security and foreign policy of the United States by the actions and policies of the Government of Burma, invoking the authority, *inter alia*, of the International Emergency Economic Powers Act (50 U.S.C. 1701–1706).

The National Emergency declared on May 20, 1997, must continue beyond May 20, 2000, because the Government of Burma continues its policies of committing large-scale repression of the democratic opposition in Burma. Therefore, in accordance with section 202(d) of the National Emergencies Act (50 U.S.C. 1622(d)), I am continuing the national emergency with respect to Burma. This notice shall be published in the Federal Register and transmitted to the Congress.

WILLIAM J. CLINTON.

Prior continuations of national emergency declared by Ex. Ord. No. 13047 were contained in the following:

Notice of President of the United States, dated May 18, 1999, 64 F.R. 27443.

Notice of President of the United States, dated May 18, 1998, 63 F.R. 27661.

EX. ORD. NO. 13059. PROHIBITING CERTAIN TRANSACTIONS WITH RESPECT TO IRAN

Ex. Ord. No. 13059, Aug. 19, 1997, 62 F.R. 44531, provided:

By the authority vested in me as President by the Constitution and the laws of the United States of America, including the International Emergency Economic Powers Act (50 U.S.C. 1701 *et seq.*) ("IEEPA"), the National Emergencies Act (50 U.S.C. 1601 *et seq.*), section 505 of the International Security and Development Cooperation Act of 1985 (22 U.S.C. 2349aa-9) ("ISDCA"), and section 301 of title 3, United States Code,

I, WILLIAM J. CLINTON, President of the United States of America, in order to clarify the steps taken in Executive Orders 12957 of March 15, 1995, and 12959 of May 6, 1995 [set out above], to deal with the unusual and extraordinary threat to the national security, foreign policy, and economy of the United States declared in Executive Order 12957 in response to the actions and policies of the Government of Iran, hereby order:

SECTION 1. Except to the extent provided in section 3 of this order or in regulations, orders, directives, or licenses issued pursuant to this order, and notwithstanding any contract entered into or any license or permit granted prior to the effective date of this order, the importation into the United States of any goods or services of Iranian origin or owned or controlled by the Government of Iran, other than information or informational materials within the meaning of section 203(b)(3) of IEEPA (50 U.S.C. 1702(b)(3)), is hereby prohibited.

SEC. 2. Except to the extent provided in section 3 of this order, in section 203(b) of IEEPA (50 U.S.C. 1702(b)), or in regulations, orders, directives, or licenses issued pursuant to this order, and notwithstanding any contract entered into or any license or permit granted prior to the effective date of this order, the following are prohibited:

(a) the exportation, reexportation, sale, or supply, directly or indirectly, from the United States, or by a United States person, wherever located, of any goods, technology, or services to Iran or the Government of Iran, including the exportation, reexportation, sale, or supply of any goods, technology, or services to a person in a third country undertaken with knowledge or reason to know that:

(i) such goods, technology, or services are intended specifically for supply, transshipment, or reexportation, directly or indirectly, to Iran or the Government of Iran; or

(ii) such goods, technology, or services are intended specifically for use in the production of, for commingling with, or for incorporation into goods, technology, or services to be directly or indirectly supplied, transshipped, or reexported exclusively or predominantly to Iran or the Government of Iran;

(b) the reexportation from a third country, directly or indirectly, by a person other than a United States person of any goods, technology, or services that have been exported from the United States, if:

(i) undertaken with knowledge or reason to know that the reexportation is intended specifically for Iran or the Government of Iran, and

(ii) the exportation of such goods, technology, or services to Iran from the United States was subject to export license application requirements under any United States regulations in effect on May 6, 1995, or thereafter is made subject to such requirements imposed independently of the actions taken pursuant to the national emergency declared in Executive Order 12957; provided, however, that this prohibition shall not apply to those goods or that technology subject to export license application requirements if such goods or technology have been:

(A) substantially transformed into a foreign-made product outside the United States; or

(B) incorporated into a foreign-made product outside the United States if the aggregate value of such controlled United States goods and technology constitutes less than 10 percent of the total value of the foreign-made product to be exported from a third country;

(c) any new investment by a United States person in Iran or in property, including entities, owned or controlled by the Government of Iran;

(d) any transaction or dealing by a United States person, wherever located, including purchasing, selling, transporting, swapping, brokering, approving, financing, facilitating, or guaranteeing, in or related to:

(i) goods or services of Iranian origin or owned or controlled by the Government of Iran; or

(ii) goods, technology, or services for exportation, reexportation, sale, or supply, directly or indirectly, to Iran or the Government of Iran;

(e) any approval, financing, facilitation, or guarantee by a United States person, wherever located, of a transaction by a foreign person where the transaction by that foreign person would be prohibited by this order if performed by a United States person or within the United States; and

(f) any transaction by a United States person or within the United States that evades or avoids, or has the purpose of evading or avoiding, or attempts to violate, any of the prohibitions set forth in this order.

SEC. 3. Specific licenses issued pursuant to Executive Orders 12613 (of October 29, 1987) [formerly set out above], 12957, or 12959 continue in effect in accordance with their terms except to the extent revoked, amended, or modified by the Secretary of the Treasury. General licenses, regulations, orders, and directives issued pursuant to those orders continue in effect in accordance with their terms except to the extent inconsistent with this order or to the extent revoked, amended, or modified by the Secretary of the Treasury.

SEC. 4. For the purposes of this order:

(a) the term "person" means an individual or entity;

(b) the term "entity" means a partnership, association, trust, joint venture, corporation, or other organization;

(c) the term "United States person" means any United States citizen, permanent resident alien, entity organized under the laws of the United States (including foreign branches), or any person in the United States;

(d) the term "Iran" means the territory of Iran and any other territory or marine area, including the exclusive economic zone and continental shelf, over which the Government of Iran claims sovereignty, sovereign rights, or jurisdiction, provided that the Government of Iran exercises partial or total de facto control over the area or derives a benefit from economic activity in the area pursuant to international arrangements;

(e) the term "Government of Iran" includes the Government of Iran, any political subdivision, agency, or instrumentality thereof, and any person owned or controlled by, or acting for or on behalf of, the Government of Iran;

(f) the term "new investment" means:

(i) a commitment or contribution of funds or other assets; or

(ii) a loan or other extension of credit, made after the effective date of Executive Order 12957 [Mar. 16, 1995] as to transactions prohibited by that order, or otherwise made after the effective date of Executive Order 12959 [see Ex. Ord. No. 12959, §8(a), set out above].

SEC. 5. The Secretary of the Treasury, in consultation with the Secretary of State and, as appropriate, other agencies, is hereby authorized to take such actions, including the promulgation of rules and regulations, the requirement of reports, including reports by United States persons on oil and related transactions engaged in by their foreign affiliates with Iran or the Government of Iran, and to employ all powers granted to me by IEEPA and the ISDCA as may be necessary to carry out the purposes of this order. The Secretary of the Treasury may redelegate any of these functions to other officers and agencies of the United States Government. All agencies of the United States Government are hereby directed to take all appropriate measures within their authority to carry out the provisions of this order.

SEC. 6. (a) The Secretary of the Treasury may authorize the exportation or reexportation to Iran or the Government of Iran of any goods, technology, or services also subject to export license application requirements of another agency of the United States Government only if authorization by that agency of the exportation or reexportation to Iran would be permitted by law.

(b) Nothing contained in this order shall be construed to supersede the requirements established under any other provision of law or to relieve a person from any requirement to obtain a license or other authorization from another department or agency of the United States Government in compliance with applicable laws and regulations subject to the jurisdiction of that department or agency.

SEC. 7. The provisions of this order consolidate the provisions of Executive Orders 12613, 12957, and 12959. Executive Order 12613 and subsections (a), (b), (c), (d), and (f) of section 1 of Executive Order 12959 are hereby revoked with respect to transactions occurring after the effective date of this order. The revocation of those provisions shall not alter their applicability to any transaction or violation occurring before the effective date of this order, nor shall it affect the applicability of any rule, regulation, order, license, or other form of administrative action previously taken pursuant to Executive Orders 12613 or 12959.

SEC. 8. Nothing contained in this order shall create any right or benefit, substantive or procedural, enforceable by any party against the United States, its agencies or instrumentalities, its officers or employees, or any other person.

SEC. 9. The measures taken pursuant to this order are in response to actions of the Government of Iran occurring after the conclusion of the 1981 Algiers Accords, and are intended solely as a response to those later actions.

SEC. 10. (a) This order is effective at 12:01 a.m. eastern daylight time on August 20, 1997.

(b) This order shall be transmitted to the Congress and published in the Federal Register.

WILLIAM J. CLINTON.

EX. ORD. NO. 13067. BLOCKING SUDANESE GOVERNMENT PROPERTY AND PROHIBITING TRANSACTIONS WITH SUDAN

Ex. Ord. No. 13067, Nov. 3, 1997, 62 F.R. 59989, provided:

By the authority vested in me as President by the Constitution and the laws of the United States of America, including the International Emergency Economic Powers Act (50 U.S.C. 1701 *et seq.*) (IEEPA), the National Emergencies Act (50 U.S.C. 1601 *et seq.*), and section 301 of title 3, United States Code;

I, WILLIAM J. CLINTON, President of the United States of America, find that the policies and actions of the Government of Sudan, including continued support for international terrorism; ongoing efforts to destabilize neighboring governments; and the prevalence of human rights violations, including slavery and the denial of religious freedom, constitute an unusual and extraordinary threat to the national security and foreign policy of the United States, and hereby declare a national emergency to deal with that threat. I hereby order:

SECTION 1. Except to the extent provided in section 203(b) of IEEPA (50 U.S.C. 1702(b)) and in regulations, orders, directives, or licenses that may be issued pursuant to this order, all property and interests in property of the Government of Sudan that are in the United States, that hereafter come within the United States, or that hereafter come within the possession or control of United States persons, including their overseas branches, are blocked.

SEC. 2. The following are prohibited, except to the extent provided in section 203(b) of IEEPA (50 U.S.C. 1702(b)) and in regulations, orders, directives, or licenses that may be issued pursuant to this order:

(a) the importation into the United States of any goods or services of Sudanese origin, other than information or informational materials;

(b) the exportation or reexportation, directly or indirectly, to Sudan of any goods, technology (including technical data, software, or other information), or services from the United States or by a United States person, wherever located, or requiring the issuance of a license by a Federal agency, except for donations of articles intended to relieve human suffering, such as food, clothing, and medicine;

(c) the facilitation by a United States person, including but not limited to brokering activities, of the exportation or reexportation of goods, technology, or services from Sudan to any destination, or to Sudan from any location;

(d) the performance by any United States person of any contract, including a financing contract, in support of an industrial, commercial, public utility, or governmental project in Sudan;

(e) the grant or extension of credits or loans by any United States person to the Government of Sudan;

(f) any transaction by a United States person relating to transportation of cargo to or from Sudan; the provision of transportation of cargo to or from the United States by any Sudanese person or any vessel or aircraft of Sudanese registration; or the sale in the United States by any person holding authority under subtitle 7 of title 49, United States Code, of any transportation of cargo by air that includes any stop in Sudan; and

(g) any transaction by any United States person or within the United States that evades or avoids, or has the purpose of evading or avoiding, or attempts to violate, any of the prohibitions set forth in this order.

SEC. 3. Nothing in this order shall prohibit:

(a) transactions for the conduct of the official business of the Federal Government or the United Nations by employees thereof; or

(b) transactions in Sudan for journalistic activity by persons regularly employed in such capacity by a newsgathering organization.

SEC. 4. For the purposes of this order:

(a) the term "person" means an individual or entity;

(b) the term "entity" means a partnership, association, trust, joint venture, corporation, or other organization;

(c) the term "United States person" means any United States citizen, permanent resident alien, entity organized under the laws of the United States (including foreign branches), or any person in the United States; and

(d) the term "Government of Sudan" includes the Government of Sudan, its agencies, instrumentalities and controlled entities, and the Central Bank of Sudan.

SEC. 5. The Secretary of the Treasury, in consultation with the Secretary of State and, as appropriate, other agencies, is hereby authorized to take such actions, including the promulgation of rules and regulations, and to employ all powers granted to me by IEEPA, as may be necessary to carry out the purposes of this order. The Secretary of the Treasury may redelegate any of these functions to other officers and agencies of the United States Government. All agencies of the United States Government are hereby directed to take all appropriate measures within their authority to carry out the provisions of this order.

SEC. 6. Nothing contained in this order shall create any right or benefit, substantive or procedural, enforceable by any party against the United States, its agencies or instrumentalities, its officers or employees, or any other person.

SEC. 7. (a) This order shall take effect at 12:01 a.m. eastern standard time on November 4, 1997, except that trade transactions under contracts in force as of the effective date of this order may be performed pursuant to their terms through 12:01 a.m. eastern standard time on December 4, 1997, and letters of credit and other financing agreements for such underlying trade transactions may be performed pursuant to their terms.

(b) This order shall be transmitted to the Congress and published in the Federal Register.

WILLIAM J. CLINTON.

CONTINUATION OF NATIONAL EMERGENCY DECLARED BY EX. ORD. NO. 13067

Notice of President of the United States, dated Oct. 31, 2000, 65 F.R. 66163, provided:

On November 3, 1997, by Executive Order 13067 [set out above], I declared a national emergency to deal with the unusual and extraordinary threat to the national security and foreign policy of the United States constituted by the actions and policies of the Government of Sudan. By Executive Order 13067, I imposed trade sanctions on Sudan and blocked Sudanese government assets. Because the Government of Sudan has continued its activities hostile to United States interests, the national emergency declared on November 3, 1997, and the measures adopted on that date to deal with that emergency must continue in effect beyond November 3, 2000. Therefore, in accordance with section 202(d) of the National Emergencies Act (50 U.S.C. 1622(d)), I am continuing the national emergency for 1 year with respect to Sudan.

This notice shall be published in the Federal Register and transmitted to the Congress.

WILLIAM J. CLINTON.

Prior continuations of national emergency declared by Ex. Ord. No. 13067 were contained in the following:

Notice of President of the United States, dated Oct. 29, 1999, 64 F.R. 59105.

Notice of President of the United States, dated Oct. 27, 1998, 63 F.R. 58617.

EX. ORD. NO. 13069. PROHIBITING CERTAIN TRANSACTIONS WITH RESPECT TO UNITA

Ex. Ord. No. 13069, Dec. 12, 1997, 62 F.R. 65989, provided:

By the authority vested in me as President by the Constitution and the laws of the United States of America, including the International Emergency Economic Powers Act (50 U.S.C. 1701 *et seq.*) (IEEPA), the National Emergencies Act (50 U.S.C. 1601 *et seq.*), section 5 of the United Nations Participation Act of 1945, as amended (22 U.S.C. 287c)(UNPA), and section 301 of title 3, United States Code, in view of United Nations Security Council Resolution 1127 of August 28, 1997, and 1130 of September 29, 1997, and in order to take additional steps with respect to the actions and policies of the National Union for the Total Independence of Angola (UNITA) and the national emergency declared in Executive Order 12865 [set out above], I, WILLIAM J. CLINTON, President of the United States of America, hereby order:

SECTION 1. Except to the extent provided in regulations, orders, directives, or licenses issued pursuant to this order, and notwithstanding the existence of any rights or obligations conferred or imposed by any international agreement or any contract entered into or any license or permit granted prior to the effective date of this order, all UNITA offices located in the United States shall be immediately and completely closed.

SEC. 2. Except to the extent provided in regulations, orders, directives, or licenses issued pursuant to this order, and notwithstanding the existence of any rights or obligations conferred or imposed by any international agreement or any contract entered into or any license or permit granted prior to the effective date of this order, the following are prohibited:

(a) the sale, supply, or making available in any form, by United States persons or from the United States or using U.S.-registered vessels or aircraft, of any aircraft or aircraft components, regardless of origin:

(i) to UNITA; or

(ii) to the territory of Angola other than through a point of entry specified pursuant to section 4 of this order;

(b) the insurance, engineering, or servicing by United States persons or from the United States of any aircraft owned or controlled by UNITA;

(c) the granting of permission to any aircraft to take off from, land in, or overfly the United States if the aircraft, as part of the same flight or as a continuation of that flight, is destined to land in or has taken off from a place in the territory of Angola other than one specified pursuant to section 4 of this order;

(d) the provision or making available by United States persons or from the United States of engineering and maintenance servicing, the certification of airworthiness, the payment of new claims against existing insurance contracts, or the provision, renewal, or making available of direct insurance with respect to:

(i) any aircraft registered in Angola other than those specified pursuant to section 4 of this order; or

(ii) any aircraft that entered the territory of Angola other than through a point of entry specified pursuant to section 4 of this order;

(e) any transaction by any United States person or within the United States that evades or avoids, or has the purpose of evading or avoiding, or attempts to violate, any of the prohibitions set forth in this order.

SEC. 3. For the purposes of this order:

(a) the term "person" means an individual or entity;

(b) the term "entity" means a partnership, association, trust, joint venture, corporation, or other organization;

(c) the term "United States person" means any United States citizen, permanent resident alien, entity organized under the laws of the United States (including foreign branches), or any person in the United States;

(d) the term "UNITA" includes:

(i) the Uniao Nacional para a Independencia Total de Angola (UNITA), known in English as the "National Union for the Total Independence of Angola;"

(ii) the Forcas Armadas para a Liberacao de Angola (FALA), known in English as the "Armed Forces for the Liberation of Angola;" and

(iii) any person acting or purporting to act for or on behalf of any of the foregoing, including the Center for Democracy in Angola (CEDA).

SEC. 4. The Secretary of the Treasury, in consultation with the Secretary of State and, as appropriate, other agencies, is hereby authorized to take such actions, including the specification of places, points of entry, and aircraft registered in Angola for purposes of section 2(a), (c), and (d) of this order, the authorization in appropriate cases of medical emergency flights or flights of aircraft carrying food, medicine, or supplies for essential humanitarian needs, and the promulgation of rules and regulations, and to employ all powers granted to the President by IEEPA and UNPA [22 U.S.C. 287 et seq.] as may be necessary to carry out the purposes of this order. The Secretary of the Treasury may redelegate any of these functions to other officers and agencies of the United States Government. All agencies of the United States Government are hereby directed to take all appropriate measures within their authority to carry out the provisions of this order, including suspension or termination of licenses or other authorizations in effect as of the effective date of this order.

SEC. 5. Nothing contained in this order shall create any right or benefit, substantive or procedural, enforceable by any party against the United States, its agencies or instrumentalities, its officers or employees, or any other person.

SEC. 6. (a) This order is effective at 12:01 a.m. eastern standard time on December 15, 1997.

(b) This order shall be transmitted to the Congress and published in the Federal Register.

WILLIAM J. CLINTON.

EX. ORD. NO. 13088. BLOCKING PROPERTY OF THE GOVERNMENTS OF THE FEDERAL REPUBLIC OF YUGOSLAVIA (SERBIA AND MONTENEGRO), THE REPUBLIC OF SERBIA, AND THE REPUBLIC OF MONTENEGRO, AND PROHIBITING NEW INVESTMENT IN THE REPUBLIC OF SERBIA IN RESPONSE TO THE SITUATION IN KOSOVO

Ex. Ord. No. 13088, June 9, 1998, 63 F.R. 32109, as amended by Ex. Ord. No. 13121, Apr. 30, 1999, 64 F.R. 24021, eff. May 1, 1999; Ex. Ord. No. 13192, Jan. 17, 2001, 66 F.R. 7379, eff. Jan. 19, 2001, provided:

By the authority vested in me as President by the Constitution and the laws of the United States of America, including the International Emergency Economic Powers Act (IEEPA) (50 U.S.C. 1701 *et seq.*), the National Emergencies Act (50 U.S.C. 1601 *et seq.*), and section 301 of title 3, United States Code,

I, WILLIAM J. CLINTON, President of the United States of America, find that the actions and policies of the Governments of the Federal Republic of Yugoslavia (Serbia and Montenegro) and the Republic of Serbia with respect to Kosovo, by promoting ethnic conflict and human suffering, threaten to destabilize countries of the region and to disrupt progress in Bosnia and Herzegovina in implementing the Dayton peace agreement, and therefore constitute an unusual and extraordinary threat to the national security and foreign policy of the United States, and hereby declare a national emergency to deal with that threat.

I hereby order:

SECTION 1. (a) Except to the extent provided in section 203(b) of IEEPA (50 U.5.C. 1702(b)), and in regulations, orders, directives, or licenses that may hereafter be issued pursuant to this order, and notwithstanding any contract entered into or any license or permit granted prior to the effective date, I hereby order blocked all property and interests in property that are or hereafter come within the United States or that are or hereafter come within the possession or control of United States persons, of:

(i) any person listed in the Annex to this order [Ex. Ord. No. 13088 does not contain an Annex, however, Ex. Ord. No. 13192 does contain an Annex which is not set out under this section. See 66 F.R. 7382.]; and

(ii) any person determined by the Secretary of the Treasury, in consultation with the Secretary of State:

(A) to be under open indictment by the International Criminal Tribunal for the former Yugoslavia, subject to applicable laws and procedures;

(B) to have sought, or to be seeking, through repressive measures or otherwise, to maintain or reestablish illegitimate control over the political processes or institutions or the economic resources or enterprises of the Federal Republic of Yugoslavia, the Republic of Serbia, the Republic of Montenegro, or the territory of Kosovo;

(C) to have provided material support or resources to any person designated in or pursuant to section 1(a) of this order; or

(D) to be owned or controlled by or acting or purporting to act directly or indirectly for or on behalf of any person designated in or pursuant to section 1(a) of this order.

(b) All property and interests in property blocked pursuant to this order prior to 12:01 a.m., eastern standard time, on January 19, 2001, shall remain blocked except as otherwise authorized by the Secretary of the Treasury.

SEC. 2. Further, except to the extent provided in section 203(b) of IEEPA (50 U.S.C. 1702(b)), and in regulations, orders, directives, or licenses that may hereafter be issued pursuant to this order, and notwithstanding any contract entered into or any license or permit granted prior to the effective date, I hereby prohibit any transaction or dealing by a United States person or within the United States in property or interests in property of any person designated in or pursuant to section 1(a) of this order.

SEC. 3. Any transaction by a United States person that evades or avoids, or has the purpose of evading or avoiding, or attempts to violate, any of the prohibitions set forth in this order is prohibited. Any conspiracy formed to violate the prohibitions of this order is prohibited.

SEC. 4. For the purposes of this order:

(a) The term ''person'' means an individual or entity;

(b) The term ''entity'' means a partnership, association, trust, joint venture, corporation or other organization; and

(c) The term ''United States person'' means any United States citizen, permanent resident alien, entity organized under the laws of the United States or any jurisdiction within the United States (including foreign branches), or any person in the United States.

SEC. 5. The Secretary of the Treasury, in consultation with the Secretary of State, is hereby authorized to take such actions, including the promulgation of rules and regulations, and to employ all powers granted to me by IEEPA and UNPA [United Nations Participation Act of 1945, 22 U.S.C. 287 et seq.], as may be necessary to carry out the purposes of this order. The Secretary of the Treasury may redelegate any of these functions to other officers and agencies of the United States Government. All agencies of the United States Government are hereby directed to take all appropriate measures within their statutory authority to carry out the provisions of this order.

SEC. 6. The Secretary of the Treasury, in consultation with the Secretary of State, is hereby authorized to remove any person from the Annex to this order [Ex. Ord. No. 13088 does not contain an Annex, however, Ex. Ord. No. 13192 does contain an Annex which is not set out under this section. See 66 F.R. 7382.] as circumstances warrant.

SEC. 7. [Revoked by Ex. Ord. No. 13192, §1(h), Jan. 17, 2001, 66 F.R. 7381, eff. Jan. 19, 2001.]

SEC. 8. Nothing contained in this order shall confer any substantive or procedural right or privilege on any person or organization, enforceable against the United States, its agencies or its officers.

SEC. 9. (a) This order is effective at 12:01 a.m. eastern daylight time on June 10, 1998.

(b) This order shall be transmitted to the Congress and published in the Federal Register.

WILLIAM J. CLINTON.

CONTINUATIONS OF NATIONAL EMERGENCY DECLARED BY EX. ORD. NO. 13088

Continuations of national emergency declared by Ex. Ord. No. 13088 were contained in the following Presidential documents, set out above:

Notice of President of the United States, dated May 25, 2000, 65 F.R. 34379.

Notice of President of the United States, dated May 27, 1999, 64 F.R. 29205.

EX. ORD. NO. 13098. BLOCKING PROPERTY OF UNITA AND PROHIBITING CERTAIN TRANSACTIONS WITH RESPECT TO UNITA

Ex. Ord. No. 13098, Aug. 18, 1998, 63 F.R. 44771, provided:

By the authority vested in me as President by the Constitution and the laws of the United States of America, including the International Emergency Economic Powers Act (50 U.S.C. 1701 *et seq.*) (IEEPA), the National Emergencies Act (50 U.S.C. 1601 *et seq.*), section 5 of the United Nations Participation Act of 1945, as amended (22 U.S.C. 287c) (UNPA), and section 301 of title 3, United States Code, in view of United Nations Security Council Resolutions 1173 of June 12, 1998, and 1176 of June 24, 1998, and in order to take additional steps with respect to the actions and policies of the National Union for the Total Independence of Angola (UNITA) and the national emergency declared in Executive Order 12865 [set out above], I, WILLIAM J. CLINTON, President of the United States of America, hereby order:

SECTION 1. Except to the extent provided in regulations, orders, directives, or licenses issued pursuant to this order, and notwithstanding the existence of any rights or obligations conferred or imposed by any international agreement or any contract entered into or any license or permit granted prior to the effective date of this order, all property and interests in property that are in the United States, that hereafter come within the United States, or that are or hereafter come within the possession or control of United States persons, of UNITA, or of those senior officials of UNITA, or adult members of their immediate families, who are designated pursuant to section 5 of this order, are hereby blocked.

SEC. 2. Except to the extent provided in regulations, orders, directives, or licenses issued pursuant to this order, and notwithstanding the existence of any rights or obligations conferred or imposed by any international agreement or any contract entered into or any license or permit granted prior to the effective date of this order, the following are prohibited:

(a) the direct or indirect importation into the United States of all diamonds exported from Angola on or after the effective date of this order that are not controlled through the Certificate of Origin regime of the Angolan Government of Unity and National Reconciliation;

(b) the sale or supply by United States persons or from the United States or using U.S.-registered vessels or aircraft, of equipment used in mining, regardless of origin, to the territory of Angola other than through a point of entry designated pursuant to section 5 of this order;

(c) the sale or supply by United States persons or from the United States or using U.S.-registered vessels or aircraft, of motorized vehicles, watercraft, or spare parts for the foregoing, regardless of origin, to the territory of Angola other than through a point of entry designated pursuant to section 5 of this order; and

(d) the sale or supply by United States persons or from the United States or using U.S.-registered vessels or aircraft, of mining services or ground or waterborne transportation services, regardless of origin, to persons in areas of Angola to which State administration has not been extended, as designated pursuant to section 5 of this order.

SEC. 3. Any transaction by a United States person or within the United States that evades or avoids, or has the purpose of evading or avoiding, or attempts to violate, any of the prohibitions set forth in this order is prohibited.

SEC. 4. For the purposes of this order:

(a) the term "person" means an individual or entity;

(b) the term "entity" means a partnership, association, trust, joint venture, corporation, or other organization;

(c) the term "United States person" means any United States citizen, permanent resident alien, entity organized under the laws of the United States (including foreign branches), or any person in the United States;

(d) the term "UNITA" includes:

(i) the Uniao Nacional para a Independencia Total de Angola (UNITA), known in English as the "National Union for the Total Independence of Angola;"

(ii) the Forcas Armadas para a Liberacao de Angola (FALA), known in English as the "Armed Forces for the Liberation of Angola;" and

(iii) any person acting or purporting to act for or on behalf of any of the foregoing, including the Center for Democracy in Angola (CEDA);

(e) the term "controlled through the Certificate of Origin regime of the Angolan Government of Unity and National Reconciliation" means accompanied by any documentation that demonstrates to the satisfaction of the United States Customs Service that the diamonds were legally exported from Angola with the approval of the Angolan Government of Unity and National Reconciliation.

SEC. 5. The Secretary of the Treasury, in consultation with the Secretary of State, is hereby authorized to take such actions, including designating senior officials of UNITA and adult members of their immediate families for purposes of section 1 of this order, designating points of entry in Angola and areas of Angola to which State administration has not been extended for purposes of section 2 of this order, establishing exemptions from the prohibitions set forth in this order for medical and humanitarian purposes, and promulgating rules and regulations, and to employ all powers granted to the President by IEEPA and UNPA, as may be necessary to carry out the purposes of this order. The Secretary of the Treasury may redelegate any of these functions to other officers and agencies of the United States Government. All agencies of the United States Government are hereby directed to take all appropriate measures within their authority to carry out the provisions of this order, including suspension or termination of licenses or other authorizations in effect as of the effective date of this order.

SEC. 6. Nothing contained in this order shall create any right or benefit, substantive or procedural, enforceable by any party against the United States, its agencies or instrumentalities, its officers or employees, or any other person.

SEC. 7. (a) This order is effective at 12:01 a.m., eastern daylight time on August 19, 1998.

(b) This order shall be transmitted to the Congress and published in the Federal Register.

WILLIAM J. CLINTON.

EX. ORD. NO. 13129. BLOCKING PROPERTY AND PROHIBITING TRANSACTIONS WITH TALIBAN

Ex. Ord. No. 13129, July 4, 1999, 64 F.R. 36759, provided:

By the authority vested in me as President by the Constitution and the laws of the United States of America, including the International Emergency Economic Powers Act (50 U.S.C. 1701 *et seq.*)("IEEPA"), the National Emergencies Act (50 U.S.C. 1601 *et seq.*), and section 301 of title 3, United States Code,

I, WILLIAM J. CLINTON, President of the United States of America, find that the actions and policies of the Taliban in Afghanistan, in allowing territory under its control in Afghanistan to be used as a safe haven and base of operations for Usama bin Ladin and the Al-Qaida organization who have committed and threaten to continue to commit acts of violence against the United States and its nationals, constitute an unusual and extraordinary threat to the national security and foreign policy of the United States, and hereby declare a national emergency to deal with that threat.

I hereby order:

SECTION 1. Except to the extent provided in section 203(b) of IEEPA (50 U.S.C. 1702(b)) and in regulations, orders, directives, or licenses that may be issued pursuant to this order, and notwithstanding any contract entered into or any license or permit granted prior to the effective date:

(a) all property and interests in property of the Taliban; and

(b) all property and interests in property of persons determined by the Secretary of the Treasury, in consultation with the Secretary of State and the Attorney General:

(i) to be owned or controlled by, or to act for or on behalf of, the Taliban; or

(ii) to provide financial, material, or technological support for, or services in support of, any of the foregoing, that are in the United States, that hereafter come within the United States, or that are or hereafter come within the possession or control of United States persons, are blocked.

SEC. 2. Except to the extent provided in section 203(b) of IEEPA (50 U.S.C. 1702(b)) and in regulations, orders, directives, or licenses that may be issued pursuant to this order, and notwithstanding any contract entered into or any license or permit granted prior to the effective date:

(a) any transaction or dealing by United States persons or within the United States in property or interests in property blocked pursuant to this order is prohibited, including the making or receiving of any contribution of funds, goods, or services to or for the benefit of the Taliban or persons designated pursuant to this order;

(b) the exportation, reexportation, sale, or supply, directly or indirectly, from the United States, or by a United States person, wherever located, of any goods, software, technology (including technical data), or services to the territory of Afghanistan controlled by the Taliban or to the Taliban or persons designated pursuant to this order is prohibited;

(c) the importation into the United States of any goods, software, technology, or services owned or controlled by the Taliban or persons designated pursuant to this order or from the territory of Afghanistan controlled by the Taliban is prohibited;

(d) any transaction by any United States person or within the United States that evades or avoids, or has the purpose of evading or avoiding, or attempts to violate, any of the prohibitions set forth in this order is prohibited; and

(e) any conspiracy formed to violate any of the prohibitions set forth in this order is prohibited.

SEC. 3. The Secretary of the Treasury, in consultation with the Secretary of State, is hereby directed to authorize commercial sales of agricultural commodities and products, medicine, and medical equipment for civilian end use in the territory of Afghanistan controlled by the Taliban under appropriate safeguards to prevent diversion to military, paramilitary, or terrorist end users or end use or to political end use.

SEC. 4. For the purposes of this order:

(a) the term "person" means an individual or entity;

(b) the term "entity" means a partnership, association, corporation, or other organization, group, or subgroup;

(c) the term "the Taliban" means the political/military entity headquartered in Kandahar, Afghanistan that as of the date of this order exercises de facto control over the territory of Afghanistan described in paragraph (d) of this section, its agencies and instrumentalities, and the Taliban leaders listed in the Annex to this order or designated by the Secretary of State in consultation with the Secretary of the Treasury and the Attorney General. The Taliban is also known as the "Taleban," "Islamic Movement of Taliban," "the Taliban Islamic Movement," "Talibano Islami Tahrik," and "Tahrike Islami'a Taliban"[;]

(d) the term "territory of Afghanistan controlled by the Taliban" means the territory referred to as the "Islamic Emirate of Afghanistan," known in Pashtun as "de Afghanistan Islami Emarat" or in Dari as "Emarat Islami-e Afghanistan," including the following provinces of the country of Afghanistan: Kandahar, Farah, Helmund, Nimruz, Herat, Badghis, Ghowr, Oruzghon, Zabol, Paktiha, Ghazni, Nangarhar, Lowgar, Vardan, Faryab, Jowlan, Balkh, and Paktika. The Secretary of State, in consultation with the Secretary of the Treasury, is hereby authorized to modify the description of the term "territory of Afghanistan controlled by the Taliban"[;]

(e) the term "United States person" means any United States citizen, permanent resident alien, entity organized under the laws of the United States (including foreign branches), or any person in the United States.

SEC. 5. The Secretary of the Treasury, in consultation with the Secretary of State and the Attorney General, is hereby authorized to take such actions, including the promulgation of rules and regulations, and to employ all powers granted to me by IEEPA as may be necessary to carry out the purposes of this order. The Secretary of the Treasury may redelegate any of these functions to other officers and agencies of the United States Government. All agencies of the United States Government are hereby directed to take all appropriate measures within their authority to carry out the provisions of this order.

SEC. 6. Nothing contained in this order shall create any right or benefit, substantive or procedural, enforceable by any party against the United States, its agencies or instrumentalities, its officers or employees, or any other person.

SEC. 7. (a) This order is effective at 12:01 a.m. Eastern Daylight Time on July 6, 1999.

(b) This order shall be transmitted to the Congress and published in the Federal Register.

WILLIAM J. CLINTON.

ANNEX

Mohammed Omar (Amir al-Mumineen [Commander of the Faithful]);[.]

CONTINUATION OF NATIONAL EMERGENCY DECLARED BY EX. ORD. NO. 13129

Notice of President of the United States, dated June 30, 2000, 65 F.R. 41549, provided:

On July 4, 1999, I issued Executive Order 13129, "Blocking Property and Prohibiting Transactions with the Taliban," [set out above] to deal with the unusual and extraordinary threat to the national security and foreign policy of the United States posed by the actions and policies of the Taliban in Afghanistan. The order blocks all property and interests in property of the Taliban and prohibits trade-related transactions by United States persons involving the territory of Afghanistan controlled by the Taliban.

The Taliban continues to allow territory under its control in Afghanistan to be used as a safe haven and base of operations for Usama bin Laden and the Al-Qaida organization who have committed and threaten to continue to commit acts of violence against the United States and its nationals. For these reasons, I have determined that it is necessary to maintain in force these emergency authorities beyond July 5, 2000. Therefore, in accordance with section 202(d) of the National Emergencies Act (50 U.S.C. 1622(d)), I am continuing the national emergency declared on July 4, 1999, with respect to the Taliban. This notice shall be published in the Federal Register and transmitted to the Congress.

WILLIAM J. CLINTON.

EX. ORD. NO. 13159. BLOCKING PROPERTY OF THE GOVERNMENT OF THE RUSSIAN FEDERATION RELATING TO THE DISPOSITION OF HIGHLY ENRICHED URANIUM EXTRACTED FROM NUCLEAR WEAPONS

Ex. Ord. No. 13159, June 21, 2000, 65 F.R. 39279, provided:

By the authority vested in me as President by the Constitution and the laws of the United States of America, including the International Emergency Economic Powers Act (IEEPA) (50 U.S.C. 1701 *et seq.*), the National Emergencies Act (50 U.S.C. 1601 *et seq.*), and section 301 of title 3, United States Code.

I, WILLIAM J. CLINTON, President of the United States of America, in view of the policies underlying Executive Order 12938 of November 14, 1994 [set out above], and Executive Order 13085 of May 26, 1998 [42 U.S.C. 2297h note], find that the risk of nuclear proliferation created by the accumulation of a large volume of weapons-usable fissile material in the territory of the Russian Federation constitutes an unusual and extraordinary threat to the national security and foreign policy of the United States, and hereby declare a national emergency to deal with that threat.

I hereby order:

SECTION 1. A major national security goal of the United States is to ensure that fissile material removed from Russian nuclear weapons pursuant to various arms control and disarmament agreements is dedicated to peaceful uses, subject to transparency measures, and protected from diversion to activities of proliferation concern. As reflected in Executive Order 13085, the full implementation of the Agreement Between the Government of the United States of America and the Government of the Russian Federation Concerning the Disposition of Highly Enriched Uranium Extracted from Nuclear Weapons, dated February 18, 1993, and related contracts and agreements (collectively, the "HEU Agreements") is essential to the attainment of this goal. The HEU Agreements provide for the conversion of approximately 500 metric tons of highly enriched uranium contained in Russian nuclear weapons into low-enriched uranium for use as fuel in commercial nuclear reactors. In furtherance of our national security goals, all heads of departments and agencies of the United States Government shall continue to take all appropriate measures within their authority to further the full implementation of the HEU Agreements.

SEC. 2. Government of the Russian Federation assets directly related to the implementation of the HEU Agreements currently may be subject to attachment, judgment, decree, lien, execution, garnishment, or other judicial process, thereby jeopardizing the full implementation of the HEU Agreements to the detriment of U.S. foreign policy. In order to ensure the preservation and proper and complete transfer to the Government of the Russian Federation of all payments due to it under the HEU Agreements, and except to the extent provided in regulations, orders, directives, or licenses that may hereafter be issued pursuant to this order, all property and interests in property of the Government of the Russian Federation directly related to the implementation of the HEU Agreements that are in the United States, that hereafter come within the United States, or that are or hereafter come within the possession or control of United States persons, including their overseas branches, are hereby blocked and may not be transferred, paid, exported, withdrawn, or otherwise dealt in. Unless licensed or authorized pursuant to this order, any attachment, judgment, decree, lien, execution, garnishment, or other judicial process is null and void with respect to any property or interest in property blocked pursuant to this order.

SEC. 3. For the purposes of this order: (a) The term "person" means an individual or entity;

(b) The term "entity" means a partnership, association, trust, joint venture, corporation, or other organization;

(c) The term "United States person" means any United States citizen; permanent resident alien; juridical person organized under the laws of the United States or any jurisdiction within the United States, including foreign branches; or any person in the United States; and

(d) The term "Government of the Russian Federation" means the Government of the Russian Federation, any political subdivision, agency, or instrumentality thereof, and any person owned or controlled by, or acting for or on behalf of, the Government of the Russian Federation.

SEC. 4. (a) The Secretary of the Treasury, in consultation with the Secretary of State, the Secretary of Energy, and, as appropriate, other agencies, is hereby authorized to take such actions, including the promulgation of rules and regulations, and to employ all powers granted to me by IEEPA, as may be necessary to carry out the purposes of this order. The Secretary of the Treasury may redelegate any of these functions to other officers and agencies of the United States Government. All agencies of the United States Government are hereby directed to take all appropriate measures within their statutory authority to carry out the provisions of this order.

(b) Nothing contained in this order shall relieve a person from any requirement to obtain a license or other authorization from any department or agency of the United States Government in compliance with applicable laws and regulations subject to the jurisdiction of the department or agency.

SEC. 5. This order is not intended to create, nor does it create, any right, benefit, or privilege, substantive or procedural, enforceable at law by a party against the United States, its agencies, officers, or any other person.

SEC. 6. (a) This order is effective at 12:01 a.m. eastern daylight time on June 22, 2000.

(b) This order shall be transmitted to the Congress and published in the Federal Register.

WILLIAM J. CLINTON.

EX. ORD. NO. 13194. PROHIBITING THE IMPORTATION OF ROUGH DIAMONDS FROM SIERRA LEONE

Ex. Ord. No. 13194, Jan. 18, 2001, 66 F.R. 7389, provided:

By the authority vested in me as President by the Constitution and the laws of the United States of America, including the International Emergency Economic Powers Act (50 U.S.C. 1701 *et seq.*) (IEEPA), the National Emergencies Act (50 U.S.C. 1601 *et seq.*), section 5 of the United Nations Participation Act of 1945, as amended (22 U.S.C. 287c) (UNPA), and section 301 of title 3, United States Code, and in view of United Nations Security Council Resolution 1306 of July 5, 2000,

I, WILLIAM J. CLINTON, President of the United States of America, take note that the people of Sierra Leone have suffered the ravages of a brutal civil war for nearly 10 years, and that the United Nations Security Council has determined that the situation in Sierra Leone constitutes a threat to international peace and security in the region and also has expressed concerns regarding the role played by the illicit trade in diamonds in fueling the conflict in Sierra Leone. Sierra Leone's insurgent Revolutionary United Front's (RUF's) illicit trade in diamonds from Sierra Leone to fund its operations and procurement of weapons, the RUF's flagrant violation of the Lome Peace Agreement of July 7, 1999, and its attacks on personnel of the United Nations Mission in Sierra Leone are direct challenges to the United States foreign policy objectives in the region as well as a direct challenge to the rule-based international order which is crucial to the peace and prosperity of the United States. Therefore, I find these actions constitute an unusual and extraordinary threat to the foreign policy of the United States and hereby declare a national emergency to deal with that threat. In order to implement United Nations Security Council Resolution 1306 and to ensure that the direct or indirect importation into the United States of rough diamonds from Sierra Leone will not contribute financial support to aggressive actions by the RUF or to the RUF's procurement of weapons, while at the same time seeking to avoid undermining the legitimate diamond trade or diminishing confidence in the integrity of the legitimate diamond industry, I hereby order:

SECTION 1. Except to the extent provided in section 2 of this order and to the extent provided in regulations, orders, directives, or licenses issued pursuant to this order, and notwithstanding the existence of any rights or obligations conferred or imposed by any international agreement or any contract entered into or any license or permit granted prior to the effective date of this order, the direct or indirect importation into the United States of all rough diamonds from Sierra Leone on or after the effective date of this order is prohibited.

SEC. 2. The prohibition in section 1 of this order shall not apply to the importation of rough diamonds controlled through the Certificate of Origin regime of the Government of Sierra Leone.

SEC. 3. Any transaction by a United States person or within the United States that evades or avoids, or has the purpose of evading or avoiding, or attempts to violate, any of the prohibitions set forth in this order is prohibited.

SEC. 4. For the purposes of this order:

(a) the term "person" means an individual or entity;

(b) the term "entity" means a partnership, association, trust, joint venture, corporation, or other organization;

(c) the term "United States person" means any United States citizen, permanent resident alien, entity organized under the laws of the United States or any jurisdiction within the United States (including foreign branches), or any person in the United States;

(d) the term "rough diamond" means all unworked diamonds classifiable in heading 7102 of the Harmonized Tariff Schedule of the United States [see Publication of Harmonized Tariff Schedule note set out under 19 U.S.C. 1202]; and

(e) the term "controlled through the Certificate of Origin regime of the Government of Sierra Leone" means accompanied by a Certificate of Origin or other documentation that demonstrates to the satisfaction of the United States Customs Service (or analogous officials of a United States territory or possession with its own customs administration) that the rough diamonds were legally exported from Sierra Leone with the approval of the Government of Sierra Leone.

SEC. 5. The Secretary of the Treasury, in consultation with the Secretary of State, is hereby authorized to take such actions, including the promulgation of rules and regulations, and to employ all powers granted to the President by IEEPA and UNPA, as may be necessary to carry out the purposes of this order. The Secretary of the Treasury may redelegate any of these functions to other officers and agencies of the United States Government. All agencies of the United States Government are hereby directed to take all appropriate measures within their authority to carry out the provisions of this order.

SEC. 6. This order is not intended to create, nor does it create, any right, benefit, or privilege, substantive or procedural, enforceable at law by a party against the United States, its agencies, officers, or any other person.

SEC. 7. This order is effective at 12:01 a.m. eastern standard time on January 19, 2001.

WILLIAM J. CLINTON.

SECTION REFERRED TO IN OTHER SECTIONS

This section is referred to in section 1702 of this title; title 22 section 7108; title 28 section 1610.

§ 1702. Presidential authorities

(a)(1) At the times and to the extent specified in section 1701 of this title, the President may, under such regulations as he may prescribe, by means of instructions, licenses, or otherwise—

(A) investigate, regulate, or prohibit—

(i) any transactions in foreign exchange,

(ii) transfers of credit or payments between, by, through, or to any banking institution, to the extent that such transfers or payments involve any interest of any foreign country or a national thereof,

(iii) the importing or exporting of currency or securities; and

(B) investigate, regulate, direct and compel, nullify, void, prevent or prohibit, any acquisition, holding, withholding, use, transfer, withdrawal, transportation, importation or exportation of, or dealing in, or exercising any right, power, or privilege with respect to, or transactions involving, any property in which any foreign country or a national thereof has any interest;

by any person, or with respect to any property, subject to the jurisdiction of the United States.

(2) In exercising the authorities granted by paragraph (1), the President may require any person to keep a full record of, and to furnish under oath, in the form of reports or otherwise, complete information relative to any act or transaction referred to in paragraph (1) either before, during, or after the completion thereof, or relative to any interest in foreign property, or relative to any property in which any foreign country or any national thereof has or has had any interest, or as may be otherwise necessary to enforce the provisions of such paragraph. In any case in which a report by a person could be required under this paragraph, the President may require the production of any books of account, records, contracts, letters, memoranda, or other papers, in the custody or control of such person.

(3) Compliance with any regulation, instruction, or direction issued under this chapter shall to the extent thereof be a full acquittance and discharge for all purposes of the obligation of the person making the same. No person shall be held liable in any court for or with respect to anything done or omitted in good faith in connection with the administration of, or pursuant to and in reliance on, this chapter, or any regulation, instruction, or direction issued under this chapter.

(b) The authority granted to the President by this section does not include the authority to regulate or prohibit, directly or indirectly—

(1) any postal, telegraphic, telephonic, or other personal communication, which does not involve a transfer of anything of value;

(2) donations, by persons subject to the jurisdiction of the United States, of articles, such as food, clothing, and medicine, intended to be used to relieve human suffering, except to the extent that the President determines that such donations (A) would seriously impair his ability to deal with any national emergency declared under section 1701 of this title, (B) are in response to coercion against the proposed recipient or donor, or (C) would endanger Armed Forces of the United States which are engaged in hostilities or are in a situation where imminent involvement in hostilities is clearly indicated by the circumstances; or[1]

(3) the importation from any country, or the exportation to any country, whether commercial or otherwise, regardless of format or medium of transmission, of any information or informational materials, including but not limited to, publications, films, posters, phonograph records, photographs, microfilms, microfiche, tapes, compact disks, CD ROMs, artworks, and news wire feeds. The exports exempted from regulation or prohibition by this paragraph do not include those which are otherwise controlled for export under section 2404 of the Appendix to this title, or under section 2405 of the Appendix to this title to the extent that such controls promote the nonproliferation or antiterrorism policies of the United States, or with respect to which acts are prohibited by chapter 37 of title 18; or

(4) any transactions ordinarily incident to travel to or from any country, including importation of accompanied baggage for personal use, maintenance within any country including payment of living expenses and acquisition of goods or services for personal use, and arrangement or facilitation of such travel including nonscheduled air, sea, or land voyages.

(Pub. L. 95–223, title II, § 203, Dec. 28, 1977, 91 Stat. 1626; Pub. L. 100–418, title II, § 2502(b)(1), Aug. 23, 1988, 102 Stat. 1371; Pub. L. 103–236, title V, § 525(c)(1), Apr. 30, 1994, 108 Stat. 474.)

AMENDMENTS

1994—Subsec. (b)(3), (4). Pub. L. 103–236 added pars. (3) and (4) and struck out former par. (3) which read as follows: "the importation from any country, or the exportation to any country, whether commercial or otherwise, of publications, films, posters, phonograph records, photographs, microfilms, microfiche, tapes, or other informational materials, which are not otherwise controlled for export under section 2404 of the Appendix to this title or with respect to which no acts are prohibited by chapter 37 of title 18."

1988—Subsec. (b)(3). Pub. L. 100–418 added par. (3).

EFFECTIVE DATE OF 1994 AMENDMENT

Section 525(c)(2) and (3) of Pub. L. 103–236 provided that:

"(2) The amendments made by paragraph (1) to section 203(b)(3) of the International Emergency Economic

[1] So in original. The word "or" probably should not appear.

Powers Act [50 U.S.C. 1702(b)(3)] apply to actions taken by the President under section 203 of such Act before the date of enactment of this Act [Apr. 30, 1994] which are in effect on such date and to actions taken under such section on or after such date.

"(3) Section 203(b)(4) of the International Emergency Economic Powers Act (as added by paragraph (1)) shall not apply to restrictions on the transactions and activities described in section 203(b)(4) in force on the date of enactment of this Act, with respect to countries embargoed under the International Emergency Economic Powers Act [50 U.S.C. 1701 et seq.] on the date of enactment of this Act."

EFFECTIVE DATE OF 1988 AMENDMENT

Section 2502(b)(2) of Pub. L. 100–418 provided that: "The amendments made by paragraph (1) [amending this section] apply to actions taken by the President under section 203 of the International Emergency Economic Powers Act [this section] before the date of the enactment of this Act [Aug. 23, 1988] which are in effect on such date of enactment, and to actions taken under such section on or after such date of enactment."

SECTION REFERRED TO IN OTHER SECTIONS

This section is referred to in section 1701 of this title; title 22 sections 6004, 7108; title 28 section 1610.

§1703. Consultation and reports

(a) Consultation with Congress

The President, in every possible instance, shall consult with the Congress before exercising any of the authorities granted by this chapter and shall consult regularly with the Congress so long as such authorities are exercised.

(b) Report to Congress upon exercise of Presidential authorities

Whenever the President exercises any of the authorities granted by this chapter, he shall immediately transmit to the Congress a report specifying—

(1) the circumstances which necessitate such exercise of authority;

(2) why the President believes those circumstances constitute an unusual and extraordinary threat, which has its source in whole or substantial part outside the United States, to the national security, foreign policy, or economy of the United States;

(3) the authorities to be exercised and the actions to be taken in the exercise of those authorities to deal with those circumstances;

(4) why the President believes such actions are necessary to deal with those circumstances; and

(5) any foreign countries with respect to which such actions are to be taken and why such actions are to be taken with respect to those countries.

(c) Periodic follow-up reports

At least once during each succeeding six-month period after transmitting a report pursuant to subsection (b) of this section with respect to an exercise of authorities under this chapter, the President shall report to the Congress with respect to the actions taken, since the last such report, in the exercise of such authorities, and with respect to any changes which have occurred concerning any information previously furnished pursuant to paragraphs (1) through (5) of subsection (b) of this section.

(d) Supplemental requirements

The requirements of this section are supplemental to those contained in title IV of the National Emergencies Act [50 U.S.C. 1641].

(Pub. L. 95–223, title II, §204, Dec. 28, 1977, 91 Stat. 1627.)

REFERENCES IN TEXT

The National Emergencies Act, referred to in subsec. (d), is Pub. L. 94–412, Sept. 14, 1976, 90 Stat. 1255, as amended. Title IV of the National Emergencies Act enacted subchapter IV (§1641) of chapter 34 of this title. For complete classification of this Act to the Code, see Short Title note set out under section 1601 of this title and Tables.

§1704. Authority to issue regulations

The President may issue such regulations, including regulations prescribing definitions, as may be necessary for the exercise of the authorities granted by this chapter.

(Pub. L. 95–223, title II, §205, Dec. 28, 1977, 91 Stat. 1628.)

§1705. Penalties

(a) A civil penalty of not to exceed $10,000 may be imposed on any person who violates, or attempts to violate, any license, order, or regulation issued under this chapter.

(b) Whoever willfully violates, or willfully attempts to violate, any license, order, or regulation issued under this chapter shall, upon conviction, be fined not more than $50,000, or, if a natural person, may be imprisoned for not more than ten years, or both; and any officer, director, or agent of any corporation who knowingly participates in such violation may be punished by a like fine, imprisonment, or both.

(Pub. L. 95–223, title II, §206, Dec. 28, 1977, 91 Stat. 1628; Pub. L. 102–393, title VI, §629, Oct. 6, 1992, 106 Stat. 1773; Pub. L. 102–396, title IX, §9155, Oct. 6, 1992, 106 Stat. 1943; Pub. L. 104–201, div. A, title XIV, §1422, Sept. 23, 1996, 110 Stat. 2725.)

AMENDMENTS

1996—Subsec. (a). Pub. L. 104–201, §1422(1), inserted ", or attempts to violate," after "violates".

Subsec. (b). Pub. L. 104–201, §1422(2), inserted ", or willfully attempts to violate," after "violates".

1992—Subsec. (a). Pub. L. 102–396 substituted "$10,000" for "$50,000".

Pub. L. 102–393 substituted "$50,000" for "$10,000".

SECTION REFERRED TO IN OTHER SECTIONS

This section is referred to in title 18 section 1956; title 22 sections 2778, 7108.

§1706. Savings provisions

(a) Termination of national emergencies pursuant to National Emergencies Act

(1) Except as provided in subsection (b) of this section, notwithstanding the termination pursuant to the National Emergencies Act [50 U.S.C. 1601 et seq.] of a national emergency declared for purposes of this chapter, any authorities granted by this chapter, which are exercised on the date of such termination on the basis of such national emergency to prohibit transactions involving property in which a foreign country or

national thereof has any interest, may continue to be so exercised to prohibit transactions involving that property if the President determines that the continuation of such prohibition with respect to that property is necessary on account of claims involving such country or its nationals.

(2) Notwithstanding the termination of the authorities described in section 101(b) of this Act, any such authorities, which are exercised with respect to a country on the date of such termination to prohibit transactions involving any property in which such country or any national thereof has any interest, may continue to be exercised to prohibit transactions involving that property if the President determines that the continuation of such prohibition with respect to that property is necessary on account of claims involving such country or its nationals.

(b) Congressional termination of national emergencies by concurrent resolution

The authorities described in subsection (a)(1) of this section may not continue to be exercised under this section if the national emergency is terminated by the Congress by concurrent resolution pursuant to section 202 of the National Emergencies Act [50 U.S.C. 1622] and if the Congress specifies in such concurrent resolution that such authorities may not continue to be exercised under this section.

(c) Supplemental savings provisions; supersedure of inconsistent provisions

(1) The provisions of this section are supplemental to the savings provisions of paragraphs (1), (2), and (3) of section 101(a) [50 U.S.C. 1601(a)(1), (2), (3)] and of paragraphs (A), (B), and (C) of section 202(a) [50 U.S.C. 1622(a)(A), (B), and (C)] of the National Emergencies Act.

(2) The provisions of this section supersede the termination provisions of section 101(a) [50 U.S.C. 1601(a)] and of title II [50 U.S.C. 1621 et seq.] of the National Emergencies Act to the extent that the provisions of this section are inconsistent with these provisions.

(d) Periodic reports to Congress

If the President uses the authority of this section to continue prohibitions on transactions involving foreign property interests, he shall report to the Congress every six months on the use of such authority.

(Pub. L. 95–223, title II, §207, Dec. 28, 1977, 91 Stat. 1628.)

REFERENCES IN TEXT

The National Emergencies Act, referred to in subsecs. (a)(1) and (c)(2), is Pub. L. 94–412, Sept. 14, 1976, 90 Stat. 1255, as amended, which is classified principally to chapter 34 (§1601 et seq.) of this title. Title II of the National Emergencies Act is classified generally to subchapter II (§1621 et seq.) of chapter 34 of this title. For complete classification of this Act to the Code, see Short Title note set out under section 1601 of this title and Tables.

Section 101(b) of this Act, referred to in subsec. (a)(2), is section 101(b) of Pub. L. 95–223, which is set out as a note under section 5 of the Appendix to this title.

TERMINATION OF REPORTING REQUIREMENTS

For termination, effective May 15, 2000, of provisions of law requiring submittal to Congress of any annual, semiannual, or other regular periodic report listed in House Document No. 103–7 (in which a report required under subsec. (d) of this section is listed as the 11th item on page 27), see section 3003 of Pub. L. 104–66, as amended, set out as a note under section 1113 of Title 31, Money and Finance.

§1707. Multinational economic embargoes against governments in armed conflict with the United States

(a) Policy on the establishment of embargoes

It is the policy of the United States, that upon the use of the Armed Forces of the United States to engage in hostilities against any foreign country, the President shall, as appropriate—

(1) seek the establishment of a multinational economic embargo against such country; and

(2) seek the seizure of its foreign financial assets.

(b) Reports to Congress

Not later than 20 days after the first day of the engagement of the United States in hostilities described in subsection (a) of this section, the President shall, if the armed conflict has continued for 14 days, submit to Congress a report setting forth—

(1) the specific steps the United States has taken and will continue to take to establish a multinational economic embargo and to initiate financial asset seizure pursuant to subsection (a) of this section; and

(2) any foreign sources of trade or revenue that directly or indirectly support the ability of the adversarial government to sustain a military conflict against the United States.

(Pub. L. 106–65, div. A, title XII, §1231, Oct. 5, 1999, 113 Stat. 788.)

CODIFICATION

This section enacted as part of the National Defense Authorization Act for Fiscal Year 2000, and not as part of the International Emergency Economic Powers Act which comprises this chapter.

CHAPTER 36—FOREIGN INTELLIGENCE SURVEILLANCE

SUBCHAPTER I—ELECTRONIC SURVEILLANCE

CHAPTER REFERRED TO IN OTHER SECTIONS

This chapter is referred to in title 8 sections 1532, 1534; title 18 sections 2232, 2511, 2522, 3121; title 47 section 1008.

SUBCHAPTER I—ELECTRONIC SURVEILLANCE

SUBCHAPTER REFERRED TO IN OTHER SECTIONS

This subchapter is referred to in section 1842 of this title.

§ 1801. Definitions

As used in this subchapter:

(a) ''Foreign power'' means—

(1) a foreign government or any component thereof, whether or not recognized by the United States;

(2) a faction of a foreign nation or nations, not substantially composed of United States persons;

(3) an entity that is openly acknowledged by a foreign government or governments to be directed and controlled by such foreign government or governments;

(4) a group engaged in international terrorism or activities in preparation therefor;

(5) a foreign-based political organization, not substantially composed of United States persons; or

(6) an entity that is directed and controlled by a foreign government or governments.

(b) ''Agent of a foreign power'' means—

(1) any person other than a United States person, who—

(A) acts in the United States as an officer or employee of a foreign power, or as a member of a foreign power as defined in subsection (a)(4) of this section;

(B) acts for or on behalf of a foreign power which engages in clandestine intelligence activities in the United States contrary to the interests of the United States, when the circumstances of such person's presence in the United States indicate that such person may engage in such activities in the United States, or when such person knowingly aids or abets any person in the conduct of such activities or knowingly conspires with any person to engage in such activities; or

(2) any person who—

(A) knowingly engages in clandestine intelligence gathering activities for or on behalf of a foreign power, which activities involve or may involve a violation of the criminal statutes of the United States;

(B) pursuant to the direction of an intelligence service or network of a foreign power, knowingly engages in any other clandestine intelligence activities for or on behalf of such foreign power, which activities involve or are about to involve a violation of the criminal statutes of the United States;

(C) knowingly engages in sabotage or international terrorism, or activities that are in preparation therefor, for or on behalf of a foreign power;

(D) knowingly enters the United States under a false or fraudulent identity for or on behalf of a foreign power or, while in the United States, knowingly assumes a false or fraudulent identity for or on behalf of a foreign power; or

(E) knowingly aids or abets any person in the conduct of activities described in subparagraph (A), (B), or (C) or knowingly conspires with any person to engage in activities described in subparagraph (A), (B), or (C).

(c) ''International terrorism'' means activities that—

(1) involve violent acts or acts dangerous to human life that are a violation of the criminal laws of the United States or of any State, or that would be a criminal violation if committed within the jurisdiction of the United States or any State;

(2) appear to be intended—

(A) to intimidate or coerce a civilian population;

(B) to influence the policy of a government by intimidation or coercion; or

(C) to affect the conduct of a government by assassination or kidnapping; and

(3) occur totally outside the United States, or transcend national boundaries in terms of the means by which they are accomplished, the persons they appear intended to coerce or intimidate, or the locale in which their perpetrators operate or seek asylum.

(d) ''Sabotage'' means activities that involve a violation of chapter 105 of title 18, or that would involve such a violation if committed against the United States.

(e) ''Foreign intelligence information'' means—

(1) information that relates to, and if concerning a United States person is necessary to, the ability of the United States to protect against—

(A) actual or potential attack or other grave hostile acts of a foreign power or an agent of a foreign power;

(B) sabotage or international terrorism by a foreign power or an agent of a foreign power; or

(C) clandestine intelligence activities by an intelligence service or network of a foreign power or by an agent of a foreign power; or

(2) information with respect to a foreign power or foreign territory that relates to, and if concerning a United States person is necessary to—

(A) the national defense or the security of the United States; or

(B) the conduct of the foreign affairs of the United States.

(f) "Electronic surveillance" means—

(1) the acquisition by an electronic, mechanical, or other surveillance device of the contents of any wire or radio communication sent by or intended to be received by a particular, known United States person who is in the United States, if the contents are acquired by intentionally targeting that United States person, under circumstances in which a person has a reasonable expectation of privacy and a warrant would be required for law enforcement purposes;

(2) the acquisition by an electronic, mechanical, or other surveillance device of the contents of any wire communication to or from a person in the United States, without the consent of any party thereto, if such acquisition occurs in the United States;

(3) the intentional acquisition by an electronic, mechanical, or other surveillance device of the contents of any radio communication, under circumstances in which a person has a reasonable expectation of privacy and a warrant would be required for law enforcement purposes, and if both the sender and all intended recipients are located within the United States; or

(4) the installation or use of an electronic, mechanical, or other surveillance device in the United States for monitoring to acquire information, other than from a wire or radio communication, under circumstances in which a person has a reasonable expectation of privacy and a warrant would be required for law enforcement purposes.

(g) "Attorney General" means the Attorney General of the United States (or Acting Attorney General) or the Deputy Attorney General.

(h) "Minimization procedures", with respect to electronic surveillance, means—

(1) specific procedures, which shall be adopted by the Attorney General, that are reasonably designed in light of the purpose and technique of the particular surveillance, to minimize the acquisition and retention, and prohibit the dissemination, of nonpublicly available information concerning unconsenting United States persons consistent with the need of the United States to obtain, produce, and disseminate foreign intelligence information;

(2) procedures that require that nonpublicly available information, which is not foreign intelligence information, as defined in subsection (e)(1) of this section, shall not be disseminated in a manner that identifies any United States person, without such person's consent, unless such person's identity is necessary to understand foreign intelligence information or assess its importance;

(3) notwithstanding paragraphs (1) and (2), procedures that allow for the retention and dissemination of information that is evidence of a crime which has been, is being, or is about to be committed and that is to be retained or disseminated for law enforcement purposes; and

(4) notwithstanding paragraphs (1), (2), and (3), with respect to any electronic surveillance approved pursuant to section 1802(a) of this title, procedures that require that no contents of any communication to which a United States person is a party shall be disclosed, disseminated, or used for any purpose or retained for longer than twenty-four hours unless a court order under section 1805 of this title is obtained or unless the Attorney General determines that the information indicates a threat of death or serious bodily harm to any person.

(i) "United States person" means a citizen of the United States, an alien lawfully admitted for permanent residence (as defined in section 1101(a)(20) of title 8), an unincorporated association a substantial number of members of which are citizens of the United States or aliens lawfully admitted for permanent residence, or a corporation which is incorporated in the United States, but does not include a corporation or an association which is a foreign power, as defined in subsection (a)(1), (2), or (3) of this section.

(j) "United States", when used in a geographic sense, means all areas under the territorial sovereignty of the United States and the Trust Territory of the Pacific Islands.

(k) "Aggrieved person" means a person who is the target of an electronic surveillance or any other person whose communications or activities were subject to electronic surveillance.

(*l*) "Wire communication" means any communication while it is being carried by a wire, cable, or other like connection furnished or operated by any person engaged as a common carrier in providing or operating such facilities for the transmission of interstate or foreign communications.

(m) "Person" means any individual, including any officer or employee of the Federal Government, or any group, entity, association, corporation, or foreign power.

(n) "Contents", when used with respect to a communication, includes any information concerning the identity of the parties to such communication or the existence, substance, purport, or meaning of that communication.

(*o*) "State" means any State of the United States, the District of Columbia, the Commonwealth of Puerto Rico, the Trust Territory of the Pacific Islands, and any territory or possession of the United States.

(Pub. L. 95–511, title I, §101, Oct. 25, 1978, 92 Stat. 1783; Pub. L. 106–120, title VI, §601, Dec. 3, 1999, 113 Stat. 1619.)

AMENDMENTS

1999—Subsec. (b)(2)(D), (E). Pub. L. 106–120 added subpar. (D) and redesignated former subpar. (D) as (E).

EFFECTIVE DATE; EXCEPTION

Pub. L. 95–511, title VI, §601, formerly title III, §301, Oct. 25, 1978, 92 Stat. 1798, as renumbered title IV, §401, and amended by Pub. L. 103–359, title VIII, §807(a)(1), (2), Oct. 14, 1994, 108 Stat. 3443; renumbered title VI, §601, and amended Pub. L. 105–272, title VI, §§601(1), 603(a), Oct. 20, 1998, 112 Stat. 2404, 2412, provided that: "The provisions of this Act [enacting this chapter, amending sections 2511, 2518, and 2519 of Title 18, Crimes and Criminal Procedure, and enacting provision set out as a note below] (other than titles III, IV, and V [enacting subchapters II, III, and IV, respectively, of this chapter]) and the amendments made hereby shall become effective upon the date of enactment of this Act [Oct. 25, 1978], except that any electronic surveillance approved by the Attorney General to gather foreign intelligence information shall not be deemed unlawful for failure to follow the procedures of this Act, if that surveillance is terminated or an order approving that surveillance is obtained under title I of this Act [enacting this subchapter] within ninety days following the designation of the first judge pursuant to section 103 of this Act [section 1803 of this title].''

SHORT TITLE OF 2000 AMENDMENT

Pub. L. 106–567, title VI, § 601, Dec. 27, 2000, 114 Stat. 2850, provided that: ''This title [enacting section 9A of the Classified Information Procedures Act, set out in the Appendix to Title 18, Crimes and Criminal Procedure, amending sections 402a, 1804, 1805, 1808, 1823, and 1824 of this title, and enacting provisions set out as notes under this section and section 1806 of this title] may be cited as the 'Counterintelligence Reform Act of 2000'.''

SHORT TITLE

Section 1 of Pub. L. 95–511 provided in part: ''That this Act [enacting this chapter, amending sections 2511, 2518, and 2519 of Title 18, Crimes and Criminal Procedure, and enacting provisions set out as a note above] may be cited as the 'Foreign Intelligence Surveillance Act of 1978'.''

SEVERABILITY

Pub. L. 106–567, title VI, § 608, Dec. 27, 2000, 114 Stat. 2856, provided that: ''If any provision of this title [see Short Title of 2000 Amendment note above] (including an amendment made by this title), or the application thereof, to any person or circumstance, is held invalid, the remainder of this title (including the amendments made by this title), and the application thereof, to other persons or circumstances shall not be affected thereby.''

TERMINATION OF TRUST TERRITORY OF THE PACIFIC ISLANDS

For termination of Trust Territory of the Pacific Islands, see note set out preceding section 1681 of Title 48, Territories and Insular Possessions.

SECTION REFERRED TO IN OTHER SECTIONS

This section is referred to in sections 402a, 438, 1802, 1804, 1805, 1810, 1821, 1822, 1823, 1824, 1828, 1841, 1861 of this title; title 12 section 3414; title 15 section 1681u; title 18 sections 794, 2511, 2709; title 22 section 1442a; title 42 section 10603b.

§ 1802. Electronic surveillance authorization without court order; certification by Attorney General; reports to Congressional committees; transmittal under seal; duties and compensation of communication common carrier; applications; jurisdiction of court

(a)(1) Notwithstanding any other law, the President, through the Attorney General, may authorize electronic surveillance without a court order under this subchapter to acquire foreign intelligence information for periods of up to one year if the Attorney General certifies in writing under oath that—

(A) the electronic surveillance is solely directed at—

(i) the acquisition of the contents of communications transmitted by means of communications used exclusively between or among foreign powers, as defined in section 1801(a)(1), (2), or (3) of this title; or

(ii) the acquisition of technical intelligence, other than the spoken communications of individuals, from property or premises under the open and exclusive control of a foreign power, as defined in section 1801(a)(1), (2), or (3) of this title;

(B) there is no substantial likelihood that the surveillance will acquire the contents of any communication to which a United States person is a party; and

(C) the proposed minimization procedures with respect to such surveillance meet the definition of minimization procedures under section 1801(h) of this title; and

if the Attorney General reports such minimization procedures and any changes thereto to the House Permanent Select Committee on Intelligence and the Senate Select Committee on Intelligence at least thirty days prior to their effective date, unless the Attorney General determines immediate action is required and notifies the committees immediately of such minimization procedures and the reason for their becoming effective immediately.

(2) An electronic surveillance authorized by this subsection may be conducted only in accordance with the Attorney General's certification and the minimization procedures adopted by him. The Attorney General shall assess compliance with such procedures and shall report such assessments to the House Permanent Select Committee on Intelligence and the Senate Select Committee on Intelligence under the provisions of section 1808(a) of this title.

(3) The Attorney General shall immediately transmit under seal to the court established under section 1803(a) of this title a copy of his certification. Such certification shall be maintained under security measures established by the Chief Justice with the concurrence of the Attorney General, in consultation with the Director of Central Intelligence, and shall remain sealed unless—

(A) an application for a court order with respect to the surveillance is made under sections 1801(h)(4) and 1804 of this title; or

(B) the certification is necessary to determine the legality of the surveillance under section 1806(f) of this title.

(4) With respect to electronic surveillance authorized by this subsection, the Attorney General may direct a specified communication common carrier to—

(A) furnish all information, facilities, or technical assistance necessary to accomplish the electronic surveillance in such a manner as will protect its secrecy and produce a minimum of interference with the services that such carrier is providing its customers; and

(B) maintain under security procedures approved by the Attorney General and the Director of Central Intelligence any records concerning the surveillance or the aid furnished which such carrier wishes to retain.

The Government shall compensate, at the prevailing rate, such carrier for furnishing such aid.

(b) Applications for a court order under this subchapter are authorized if the President has, by written authorization, empowered the Attorney General to approve applications to the court having jurisdiction under section 1803 of this title, and a judge to whom an application is made may, notwithstanding any other law, grant an order, in conformity with section 1805 of this title, approving electronic surveillance of a foreign power or an agent of a foreign power for the purpose of obtaining foreign intelligence information, except that the court shall not have jurisdiction to grant any order approving electronic surveillance directed solely as described in paragraph (1)(A) of subsection (a) of this section unless such surveillance may involve the acquisition of communications of any United States person.

(Pub. L. 95–511, title I, §102, Oct. 25, 1978, 92 Stat. 1786.)

EX. ORD. NO. 12139. EXERCISE OF CERTAIN AUTHORITY RESPECTING ELECTRONIC SURVEILLANCE

Ex. Ord. No. 12139, May 23, 1979, 44 F.R. 30311, provided:

By the authority vested in me as President by Sections 102 and 104 of the Foreign Intelligence Surveillance Act of 1978 (50 U.S.C. 1802 and 1804), in order to provide as set forth in that Act [this chapter] for the authorization of electronic surveillance for foreign intelligence purposes, it is hereby ordered as follows:

1–101. Pursuant to Section 102(a)(1) of the Foreign Intelligence Surveillance Act of 1978 (50 U.S.C. 1802(a)), the Attorney General is authorized to approve electronic surveillance to acquire foreign intelligence information without a court order, but only if the Attorney General makes the certifications required by that Section.

1–102. Pursuant to Section 102(b) of the Foreign Intelligence Act of 1978 (50 U.S.C. 1802(b)), the Attorney General is authorized to approve applications to the court having jurisdiction under Section 103 of that Act [50 U.S.C. 1803] to obtain orders for electronic surveillance for the purpose of obtaining foreign intelligence information.

1–103. Pursuant to Section 104(a)(7) of the Foreign Intelligence Surveillance Act of 1978 (50 U.S.C. 1804(a)(7)), the following officials, each of whom is employed in the area of national security or defense, is designated to make the certifications required by Section 104(a)(7) of the Act in support of applications to conduct electronic surveillance:

(a) Secretary of State.
(b) Secretary of Defense.
(c) Director of Central Intelligence.
(d) Director of the Federal Bureau of Investigation.
(e) Deputy Secretary of State.
(f) Deputy Secretary of Defense.
(g) Deputy Director of Central Intelligence.

None of the above officials, nor anyone officially acting in that capacity, may exercise the authority to make the above certifications, unless that official has been appointed by the President with the advice and consent of the Senate.

1–104. Section 2–202 of Executive Order No. 12036 [set out under section 401 of this title] is amended by inserting the following at the end of that section: "Any electronic surveillance, as defined in the Foreign Intelligence Surveillance Act of 1978, shall be conducted in accordance with that Act as well as this Order.".

1–105. Section 2–203 of Executive Order No. 12036 [set out under section 401 of this title] is amended by inserting the following at the end of that section: "Any monitoring which constitutes electronic surveillance as defined in the Foreign Intelligence Surveillance Act of 1978 shall be conducted in accordance with that Act as well as this Order.".

JIMMY CARTER.

SECTION REFERRED TO IN OTHER SECTIONS

This section is referred to in sections 1801, 1805 of this title.

§1803. Designation of judges

(a) Court to hear applications and grant orders; record of denial; transmittal to court of review

The Chief Justice of the United States shall publicly designate seven district court judges from seven of the United States judicial circuits who shall constitute a court which shall have jurisdiction to hear applications for and grant orders approving electronic surveillance anywhere within the United States under the procedures set forth in this chapter, except that no judge designated under this subsection shall hear the same application for electronic surveillance under this chapter which has been denied previously by another judge designated under this subsection. If any judge so designated denies an application for an order authorizing electronic surveillance under this chapter, such judge shall provide immediately for the record a written statement of each reason of his decision and, on motion of the United States, the record shall be transmitted, under seal, to the court of review established in subsection (b) of this section.

(b) Court of review; record, transmittal to Supreme Court

The Chief Justice shall publicly designate three judges, one of whom shall be publicly designated as the presiding judge, from the United States district courts or courts of appeals who together shall comprise a court of review which shall have jurisdiction to review the denial of any application made under this chapter. If such court determines that the application was properly denied, the court shall immediately provide for the record a written statement of each reason for its decision and, on petition of the United States for a writ of certiorari, the record shall be transmitted under seal to the Supreme Court, which shall have jurisdiction to review such decision.

(c) Expeditious conduct of proceedings; security measures for maintenance of records

Proceedings under this chapter shall be conducted as expeditiously as possible. The record of proceedings under this chapter, including applications made and orders granted, shall be maintained under security measures established by the Chief Justice in consultation with the Attorney General and the Director of Central Intelligence.

(d) Tenure

Each judge designated under this section shall so serve for a maximum of seven years and shall not be eligible for redesignation, except that the judges first designated under subsection (a) of this section shall be designated for terms of from one to seven years so that one term expires each year, and that judges first designated under subsection (b) of this section shall be designated for terms of three, five, and seven years.

(Pub. L. 95–511, title I, §103, Oct. 25, 1978, 92 Stat. 1788.)

REFERENCES IN TEXT

This chapter, referred to in subsecs. (a), (b), and (c), was in the original "this Act", meaning Pub. L. 95–511, Oct. 25, 1978, 92 Stat. 1783, as amended, which is classified principally to this chapter. For complete classification of this Act to the Code, see Short Title note set out under section 1801 of this title and Tables.

SECTION REFERRED TO IN OTHER SECTIONS

This section is referred to in sections 1802, 1804, 1805, 1821, 1822, 1824, 1842, 1862 of this title; title 8 section 1532.

§ 1804. Applications for court orders

(a) Submission by Federal officer; approval of Attorney General; contents

Each application for an order approving electronic surveillance under this subchapter shall be made by a Federal officer in writing upon oath or affirmation to a judge having jurisdiction under section 1803 of this title. Each application shall require the approval of the Attorney General based upon his finding that it satisfies the criteria and requirements of such application as set forth in this subchapter. It shall include—

(1) the identity of the Federal officer making the application;

(2) the authority conferred on the Attorney General by the President of the United States and the approval of the Attorney General to make the application;

(3) the identity, if known, or a description of the target of the electronic surveillance;

(4) a statement of the facts and circumstances relied upon by the applicant to justify his belief that—

(A) the target of the electronic surveillance is a foreign power or an agent of a foreign power; and

(B) each of the facilities or places at which the electronic surveillance is directed is being used, or is about to be used, by a foreign power or an agent of a foreign power;

(5) a statement of the proposed minimization procedures;

(6) a detailed description of the nature of the information sought and the type of communications or activities to be subjected to the surveillance;

(7) a certification or certifications by the Assistant to the President for National Security Affairs or an executive branch official or officials designated by the President from among those executive officers employed in the area of national security or defense and appointed by the President with the advice and consent of the Senate—

(A) that the certifying official deems the information sought to be foreign intelligence information;

(B) that the purpose of the surveillance is to obtain foreign intelligence information;

(C) that such information cannot reasonably be obtained by normal investigative techniques;

(D) that designates the type of foreign intelligence information being sought according to the categories described in section 1801(e) of this title; and

(E) including a statement of the basis for the certification that—

(i) the information sought is the type of foreign intelligence information designated; and

(ii) such information cannot reasonably be obtained by normal investigative techniques;

(8) a statement of the means by which the surveillance will be effected and a statement whether physical entry is required to effect the surveillance;

(9) a statement of the facts concerning all previous applications that have been made to any judge under this subchapter involving any of the persons, facilities, or places specified in the application, and the action taken on each previous application;

(10) a statement of the period of time for which the electronic surveillance is required to be maintained, and if the nature of the intelligence gathering is such that the approval of the use of electronic surveillance under this subchapter should not automatically terminate when the described type of information has first been obtained, a description of facts supporting the belief that additional information of the same type will be obtained thereafter; and

(11) whenever more than one electronic, mechanical or other surveillance device is to be used with respect to a particular proposed electronic surveillance, the coverage of the devices involved and what minimization procedures apply to information acquired by each device.

(b) Exclusion of certain information respecting foreign power targets

Whenever the target of the electronic surveillance is a foreign power, as defined in section 1801(a)(1), (2), or (3) of this title, and each of the facilities or places at which the surveillance is directed is owned, leased, or exclusively used by that foreign power, the application need not contain the information required by paragraphs (6), (7)(E), (8), and (11) of subsection (a) of this section, but shall state whether physical entry is required to effect the surveillance and shall contain such information about the surveillance techniques and communications or other information concerning United States persons likely to be obtained as may be necessary to assess the proposed minimization procedures.

(c) Additional affidavits or certifications

The Attorney General may require any other affidavit or certification from any other officer in connection with the application.

(d) Additional information

The judge may require the applicant to furnish such other information as may be necessary to make the determinations required by section 1805 of this title.

(e) Personal review by Attorney General

(1)(A) Upon written request of the Director of the Federal Bureau of Investigation, the Secretary of Defense, the Secretary of State, or the Director of Central Intelligence, the Attorney General shall personally review under subsection (a) of this section an application under that subsection for a target described in section 1801(b)(2) of this title.

(B) Except when disabled or otherwise unavailable to make a request referred to in subparagraph (A), an official referred to in that subparagraph may not delegate the authority to make a request referred to in that subparagraph.

(C) Each official referred to in subparagraph (A) with authority to make a request under that subparagraph shall take appropriate actions in advance to ensure that delegation of such authority is clearly established in the event such official is disabled or otherwise unavailable to make such request.

(2)(A) If as a result of a request under paragraph (1) the Attorney General determines not to approve an application under the second sentence of subsection (a) of this section for purposes of making the application under this section, the Attorney General shall provide written notice of the determination to the official making the request for the review of the application under that paragraph. Except when disabled or otherwise unavailable to make a determination under the preceding sentence, the Attorney General may not delegate the responsibility to make a determination under that sentence. The Attorney General shall take appropriate actions in advance to ensure that delegation of such responsibility is clearly established in the event the Attorney General is disabled or otherwise unavailable to make such determination.

(B) Notice with respect to an application under subparagraph (A) shall set forth the modifications, if any, of the application that are necessary in order for the Attorney General to approve the application under the second sentence of subsection (a) of this section for purposes of making the application under this section.

(C) Upon review of any modifications of an application set forth under subparagraph (B), the official notified of the modifications under this paragraph shall modify the application if such official determines that such modification is warranted. Such official shall supervise the making of any modification under this subparagraph. Except when disabled or otherwise unavailable to supervise the making of any modification under the preceding sentence, such official may not delegate the responsibility to supervise the making of any modification under that preceding sentence. Each such official shall take appropriate actions in advance to ensure that delegation of such responsibility is clearly established in the event such official is disabled or otherwise unavailable to supervise the making of such modification.

(Pub. L. 95–511, title I, §104, Oct. 25, 1978, 92 Stat. 1788; Pub. L. 106–567, title VI, §602(a), Dec. 27, 2000, 114 Stat. 2851.)

AMENDMENTS

2000—Subsec. (e). Pub. L. 106–567 added subsec. (e).

DESIGNATION OF CERTAIN OFFICIALS TO MAKE CERTIFICATIONS

For designation of certain officials to make certifications required by subsec. (a)(7) of this section, see Ex. Ord. No. 12139, May 23, 1979, 44 F.R. 30311, set out under section 1802 of this title.

SECTION REFERRED TO IN OTHER SECTIONS

This section is referred to in sections 1802, 1805 of this title.

§ 1805. Issuance of order

(a) Necessary findings

Upon an application made pursuant to section 1804 of this title, the judge shall enter an ex parte order as requested or as modified approving the electronic surveillance if he finds that—

(1) the President has authorized the Attorney General to approve applications for electronic surveillance for foreign intelligence information;

(2) the application has been made by a Federal officer and approved by the Attorney General;

(3) on the basis of the facts submitted by the applicant there is probable cause to believe that—

(A) the target of the electronic surveillance is a foreign power or an agent of a foreign power: *Provided*, That no United States person may be considered a foreign power or an agent of a foreign power solely upon the basis of activities protected by the first amendment to the Constitution of the United States; and

(B) each of the facilities or places at which the electronic surveillance is directed is being used, or is about to be used, by a foreign power or an agent of a foreign power;

(4) the proposed minimization procedures meet the definition of minimization procedures under section 1804(h) of this title; and

(5) the application which has been filed contains all statements and certifications required by section 1804 of this title and, if the target is a United States person, the certification or certifications are not clearly erroneous on the basis of the statement made under section 1804(a)(7)(E) of this title and any other information furnished under section 1804(d) of this title.

(b) Determination of probable cause

In determining whether or not probable cause exists for purposes of an order under subsection (a)(3) of this section, a judge may consider past activities of the target, as well as facts and circumstances relating to current or future activities of the target.

(c) Specifications and directions of orders

An order approving an electronic surveillance under this section shall—

(1) specify—

(A) the identity, if known, or a description of the target of the electronic surveillance;

(B) the nature and location of each of the facilities or places at which the electronic surveillance will be directed;

(C) the type of information sought to be acquired and the type of communications or activities to be subjected to the surveillance;

(D) the means by which the electronic surveillance will be effected and whether physical entry will be used to effect the surveillance;

(E) the period of time during which the electronic surveillance is approved; and

(F) whenever more than one electronic, mechanical, or other surveillance device is to be used under the order, the authorized coverage of the devices involved and what minimization procedures shall apply to information subject to acquisition by each device; and

(2) direct—

(A) that the minimization procedures be followed;

(B) that, upon the request of the applicant, a specified communication or other common carrier, landlord, custodian, or other specified person furnish the applicant forthwith all information, facilities, or technical assistance necessary to accomplish the electronic surveillance in such a manner as will protect its secrecy and produce a minimum of interference with the services that such carrier, landlord, custodian, or other person is providing that target of electronic surveillance;

(C) that such carrier, landlord, custodian, or other person maintain under security procedures approved by the Attorney General and the Director of Central Intelligence any records concerning the surveillance or the aid furnished that such person wishes to retain; and

(D) that the applicant compensate, at the prevailing rate, such carrier, landlord, custodian, or other person for furnishing such aid.

(d) Exclusion of certain information respecting foreign power targets

Whenever the target of the electronic surveillance is a foreign power, as defined in section 1801(a)(1), (2), or (3) of this title, and each of the facilities or places at which the surveillance is directed is owned, leased, or exclusively used by that foreign power, the order need not contain the information required by subparagraphs (C), (D), and (F) of subsection (c)(1) of this section, but shall generally describe the information sought, the communications or activities to be subjected to the surveillance, and the type of electronic surveillance involved, including whether physical entry is required.

(e) Duration of order; extensions; review of circumstances under which information was acquired, retained or disseminated

(1) An order issued under this section may approve an electronic surveillance for the period necessary to achieve its purpose, or for ninety days, whichever is less, except that an order under this section shall approve an electronic surveillance targeted against a foreign power, as defined in section 1801(a)(1), (2), or (3) of this title, for the period specified in the application or for one year, whichever is less.

(2) Extensions of an order issued under this subchapter may be granted on the same basis as an original order upon an application for an extension and new findings made in the same manner as required for an original order, except that an extension of an order under this chapter for a surveillance targeted against a foreign power, as defined in section 1801(a)(5) or (6) of this title, or against a foreign power as defined in section 1801(a)(4) of this title that is not a United States person, may be for a period not to exceed one year if the judge finds probable cause to believe that no communication of any individual United States person will be acquired during the period.

(3) At or before the end of the period of time for which electronic surveillance is approved by an order or an extension, the judge may assess compliance with the minimization procedures by reviewing the circumstances under which information concerning United States persons was acquired, retained, or disseminated.

(f) Emergency orders

Notwithstanding any other provision of this subchapter, when the Attorney General reasonably determines that—

(1) an emergency situation exists with respect to the employment of electronic surveillance to obtain foreign intelligence information before an order authorizing such surveillance can with due diligence be obtained; and

(2) the factual basis for issuance of an order under this subchapter to approve such surveillance exists;

he may authorize the emergency employment of electronic surveillance if a judge having jurisdiction under section 1803 of this title is informed by the Attorney General or his designee at the time of such authorization that the decision has been made to employ emergency electronic surveillance and if an application in accordance with this subchapter is made to that judge as soon as practicable, but not more than twenty-four hours after the Attorney General authorizes such surveillance. If the Attorney General authorizes such emergency employment of electronic surveillance, he shall require that the minimization procedures required by this subchapter for the issuance of a judicial order be followed. In the absence of a judicial order approving such electronic surveillance, the surveillance shall terminate when the information sought is obtained, when the application for the order is denied, or after the expiration of twenty-four hours from the time of authorization by the Attorney General, whichever is earliest. In the event that such application for approval is denied, or in any other case where the electronic surveillance is terminated and no order is issued approving the surveillance, no information obtained or evidence derived from such surveillance shall be received in evidence or otherwise disclosed in any trial, hearing, or other proceeding in or before any court, grand jury, department, office, agency, regulatory body, legislative committee, or other authority of the United States, a State, or political subdivision thereof, and no information concerning any United States person acquired from such surveillance shall subsequently be used or disclosed in any other manner by Federal officers or employees without the consent of such person, except with the approval of the Attorney General if the information indicates a threat of death or serious bodily harm to any person. A denial of the application made under this subsection may be reviewed as provided in section 1803 of this title.

(g) Testing of electronic equipment; discovering unauthorized electronic surveillance; training of intelligence personnel

Notwithstanding any other provision of this subchapter, officers, employees, or agents of the

United States are authorized in the normal course of their official duties to conduct electronic surveillance not targeted against the communications of any particular person or persons, under procedures approved by the Attorney General, solely to—

(1) test the capability of electronic equipment, if—

(A) it is not reasonable to obtain the consent of the persons incidentally subjected to the surveillance;

(B) the test is limited in extent and duration to that necessary to determine the capability of the equipment;

(C) the contents of any communication acquired are retained and used only for the purpose of determining the capability of the equipment, are disclosed only to test personnel, and are destroyed before or immediately upon completion of the test; and:

(D) *Provided*, That the test may exceed ninety days only with the prior approval of the Attorney General;

(2) determine the existence and capability of electronic surveillance equipment being used by persons not authorized to conduct electronic surveillance, if—

(A) it is not reasonable to obtain the consent of persons incidentally subjected to the surveillance;

(B) such electronic surveillance is limited in extent and duration to that necessary to determine the existence and capability of such equipment; and

(C) any information acquired by such surveillance is used only to enforce chapter 119 of title 18, or section 605 of title 47, or to protect information from unauthorized surveillance; or

(3) train intelligence personnel in the use of electronic surveillance equipment, if—

(A) it is not reasonable to—

(i) obtain the consent of the persons incidentally subjected to the surveillance;

(ii) train persons in the course of surveillances otherwise authorized by this subchapter; or

(iii) train persons in the use of such equipment without engaging in electronic surveillance;

(B) such electronic surveillance is limited in extent and duration to that necessary to train the personnel in the use of the equipment; and

(C) no contents of any communication acquired are retained or disseminated for any purpose, but are destroyed as soon as reasonably possible.

(h) Retention of certifications, applications and orders

Certifications made by the Attorney General pursuant to section 1802(a) of this title and applications made and orders granted under this subchapter shall be retained for a period of at least ten years from the date of the certification or application.

(Pub. L. 95–511, title I, §105, Oct. 25, 1978, 92 Stat. 1790; Pub. L. 98–549, §6(b)(3), Oct. 30, 1984, 98 Stat. 2804; Pub. L. 106–567, title VI, §602(b), Dec. 27, 2000, 114 Stat. 2851.)

AMENDMENTS

2000—Subsecs. (b), (c). Pub. L. 106–567, §602(b)(1), (2), added subsec. (b) and redesignated former subsec. (b) as (c). Former subsec. (c) redesignated (d).

Subsec. (d). Pub. L. 106–567, §602(b)(1), (3), redesignated subsec. (c) as (d) and substituted "subsection (c)(1)" for "subsection (b)(1)". Former subsec. (d) redesignated (e).

Subsecs. (e) to (h). Pub. L. 106–567, §602(b)(1), redesignated subsecs. (d) to (g) as (e) to (h), respectively.

1984—Subsec. (f)(2)(C). Pub. L. 98–549 substituted "section 705" for "section 605" in the original to accommodate renumbering of sections in subchapter VI (section 601 et seq.) of chapter 5 of Title 47, Telegraphs, Telephones, and Radiotelegraphs, by section 6(a) of Pub. L. 98–549. Because both sections translate as "section 605 of Title 47", the amendment by Pub. L. 98–549 resulted in no change in text.

EFFECTIVE DATE OF 1984 AMENDMENT

Amendment by Pub. L. 98–549 effective 60 days after Oct. 30, 1984, except where otherwise expressly provided, see section 9(a) of Pub. L. 98–549, set out as a note under section 521 of Title 47, Telegraphs, Telephones, and Radiotelegraphs.

SECTION REFERRED TO IN OTHER SECTIONS

This section is referred to in sections 1801, 1802, 1804, 1806, 1842 of this title; title 47 section 1002.

§1806. Use of information

(a) Compliance with minimization procedures; privileged communications; lawful purposes

Information acquired from an electronic surveillance conducted pursuant to this subchapter concerning any United States person may be used and disclosed by Federal officers and employees without the consent of the United States person only in accordance with the minimization procedures required by this subchapter. No otherwise privileged communication obtained in accordance with, or in violation of, the provisions of this subchapter shall lose its privileged character. No information acquired from an electronic surveillance pursuant to this subchapter may be used or disclosed by Federal officers or employees except for lawful purposes.

(b) Statement for disclosure

No information acquired pursuant to this subchapter shall be disclosed for law enforcement purposes unless such disclosure is accompanied by a statement that such information, or any information derived therefrom, may only be used in a criminal proceeding with the advance authorization of the Attorney General.

(c) Notification by United States

Whenever the Government intends to enter into evidence or otherwise use or disclose in any trial, hearing, or other proceeding in or before any court, department, officer, agency, regulatory body, or other authority of the United States, against an aggrieved person, any information obtained or derived from an electronic surveillance of that aggrieved person pursuant to the authority of this subchapter, the Government shall, prior to the trial, hearing, or other proceeding or at a reasonable time prior to an effort to so disclose or so use that information or submit it in evidence, notify the aggrieved person and the court or other authority in which the information is to be disclosed or used that the Government intends to so disclose or so use such information.

(d) Notification by States or political subdivisions

Whenever any State or political subdivision thereof intends to enter into evidence or otherwise use or disclose in any trial, hearing, or other proceeding in or before any court, department, officer, agency, regulatory body, or other authority of a State or a political subdivision thereof, against an aggrieved person any information obtained or derived from an electronic surveillance of that aggrieved person pursuant to the authority of this subchapter, the State or political subdivision thereof shall notify the aggrieved person, the court or other authority in which the information is to be disclosed or used, and the Attorney General that the State or political subdivision thereof intends to so disclose or so use such information.

(e) Motion to suppress

Any person against whom evidence obtained or derived from an electronic surveillance to which he is an aggrieved person is to be, or has been, introduced or otherwise used or disclosed in any trial, hearing, or other proceeding in or before any court, department, officer, agency, regulatory body, or other authority of the United States, a State, or a political subdivision thereof, may move to suppress the evidence obtained or derived from such electronic surveillance on the grounds that—

(1) the information was unlawfully acquired; or

(2) the surveillance was not made in conformity with an order of authorization or approval.

Such a motion shall be made before the trial, hearing, or other proceeding unless there was no opportunity to make such a motion or the person was not aware of the grounds of the motion.

(f) In camera and ex parte review by district court

Whenever a court or other authority is notified pursuant to subsection (c) or (d) of this section, or whenever a motion is made pursuant to subsection (e) of this section, or whenever any motion or request is made by an aggrieved person pursuant to any other statute or rule of the United States or any State before any court or other authority of the United States or any State to discover or obtain applications or orders or other materials relating to electronic surveillance or to discover, obtain, or suppress evidence or information obtained or derived from electronic surveillance under this chapter, the United States district court or, where the motion is made before another authority, the United States district court in the same district as the authority, shall, notwithstanding any other law, if the Attorney General files an affidavit under oath that disclosure or an adversary hearing would harm the national security of the United States, review in camera and ex parte the application, order, and such other materials relating to the surveillance as may be necessary to determine whether the surveillance of the aggrieved person was lawfully authorized and conducted. In making this determination, the court may disclose to the aggrieved person, under appropriate security procedures and protective orders, portions of the application, order, or other materials relating to the surveillance only where such disclosure is necessary to make an accurate determination of the legality of the surveillance.

(g) Suppression of evidence; denial of motion

If the United States district court pursuant to subsection (f) of this section determines that the surveillance was not lawfully authorized or conducted, it shall, in accordance with the requirements of law, suppress the evidence which was unlawfully obtained or derived from electronic surveillance of the aggrieved person or otherwise grant the motion of the aggrieved person. If the court determines that the surveillance was lawfully authorized and conducted, it shall deny the motion of the aggrieved person except to the extent that due process requires discovery or disclosure.

(h) Finality of orders

Orders granting motions or requests under subsection (g) of this section, decisions under this section that electronic surveillance was not lawfully authorized or conducted, and orders of the United States district court requiring review or granting disclosure of applications, orders, or other materials relating to a surveillance shall be final orders and binding upon all courts of the United States and the several States except a United States court of appeals and the Supreme Court.

(i) Destruction of unintentionally acquired information

In circumstances involving the unintentional acquisition by an electronic, mechanical, or other surveillance device of the contents of any radio communication, under circumstances in which a person has a reasonable expectation of privacy and a warrant would be required for law enforcement purposes, and if both the sender and all intended recipients are located within the United States, such contents shall be destroyed upon recognition, unless the Attorney General determines that the contents indicate a threat of death or serious bodily harm to any person.

(j) Notification of emergency employment of electronic surveillance; contents; postponement, suspension or elimination

If an emergency employment of electronic surveillance is authorized under section 1805(e)[1] of this title and a subsequent order approving the surveillance is not obtained, the judge shall cause to be served on any United States person named in the application and on such other United States persons subject to electronic surveillance as the judge may determine in his discretion it is in the interest of justice to serve, notice of—

(1) the fact of the application;

(2) the period of the surveillance; and

(3) the fact that during the period information was or was not obtained.

On an ex parte showing of good cause to the judge the serving of the notice required by this

[1] See References in Text note below.

subsection may be postponed or suspended for a period not to exceed ninety days. Thereafter, on a further ex parte showing of good cause, the court shall forego ordering the serving of the notice required under this subsection.

(Pub. L. 95–511, title I, §106, Oct. 25, 1978, 92 Stat. 1793.)

REFERENCES IN TEXT

Section 1805(e) of this title, referred to in subsec. (j), was redesignated section 1805(f) of this title by Pub. L. 106–567, title VI, §602(b)(1), Dec. 27, 2000, 114 Stat. 2851.

REPORT ON MECHANISMS FOR DETERMINATIONS OF DISCLOSURE OF INFORMATION FOR LAW ENFORCEMENT PURPOSES

Pub. L. 106–567, title VI, §604(b), Dec. 27, 2000, 114 Stat. 2853, provided that:

"(1) The Attorney General shall submit to the appropriate committees of Congress a report on the authorities and procedures utilized by the Department of Justice for determining whether or not to disclose information acquired under the Foreign Intelligence Surveillance Act of 1978 (50 U.S.C. 1801 et seq.) for law enforcement purposes.

"(2) In this subsection, the term 'appropriate committees of Congress' means the following:

"(A) The Select Committee on Intelligence and the Committee on the Judiciary of the Senate.

"(B) The Permanent Select Committee on Intelligence and the Committee on the Judiciary of the House of Representatives."

SECTION REFERRED TO IN OTHER SECTIONS

This section is referred to in section 1802 of this title; title 8 section 1534.

§1807. Report to Administrative Office of the United States Court and to Congress

In April of each year, the Attorney General shall transmit to the Administrative Office of the United States Court and to Congress a report setting forth with respect to the preceding calendar year—

(a) the total number of applications made for orders and extensions of orders approving electronic surveillance under this subchapter; and

(b) the total number of such orders and extensions either granted, modified, or denied.

(Pub. L. 95–511, title I, §107, Oct. 25, 1978, 92 Stat. 1795.)

§1808. Report of Attorney General to Congressional committees; limitation on authority or responsibility of information gathering activities of Congressional committees; report of Congressional committees to Congress

(a)(1) On a semiannual basis the Attorney General shall fully inform the House Permanent Select Committee on Intelligence and the Senate Select Committee on Intelligence concerning all electronic surveillance under this subchapter. Nothing in this subchapter shall be deemed to limit the authority and responsibility of the appropriate committees of each House of Congress to obtain such information as they may need to carry out their respective functions and duties.

(2) Each report under the first sentence of paragraph (1) shall include a description of—

(A) each criminal case in which information acquired under this chapter has been passed for law enforcement purposes during the period covered by such report; and

(B) each criminal case in which information acquired under this chapter has been authorized for use at trial during such reporting period.

(b) On or before one year after October 25, 1978, and on the same day each year for four years thereafter, the Permanent Select Committee on Intelligence and the Senate Select Committee on Intelligence shall report respectively to the House of Representatives and the Senate, concerning the implementation of this chapter. Said reports shall include but not be limited to an analysis and recommendations concerning whether this chapter should be (1) amended, (2) repealed, or (3) permitted to continue in effect without amendment.

(Pub. L. 95–511, title I, §108, Oct. 25, 1978, 92 Stat. 1795; Pub. L. 106–567, title VI, §604(a), Dec. 27, 2000, 114 Stat. 2853.)

AMENDMENTS

2000—Subsec. (a). Pub. L. 106–567 designated existing provisions as par. (1) and added par. (2).

SECTION REFERRED TO IN OTHER SECTIONS

This section is referred to in sections 1802, 1842 of this title.

§1809. Criminal sanctions

(a) Prohibited activities

A person is guilty of an offense if he intentionally—

(1) engages in electronic surveillance under color of law except as authorized by statute; or

(2) discloses or uses information obtained under color of law by electronic surveillance, knowing or having reason to know that the information was obtained through electronic surveillance not authorized by statute.

(b) Defense

It is a defense to a prosecution under subsection (a) of this section that the defendant was a law enforcement or investigative officer engaged in the course of his official duties and the electronic surveillance was authorized by and conducted pursuant to a search warrant or court order of a court of competent jurisdiction.

(c) Penalties

An offense described in this section is punishable by a fine of not more than $10,000 or imprisonment for not more than five years, or both.

(d) Federal jurisdiction

There is Federal jurisdiction over an offense under this section if the person committing the offense was an officer or employee of the United States at the time the offense was committed.

(Pub. L. 95–511, title I, §109, Oct. 25, 1978, 92 Stat. 1796.)

SECTION REFERRED TO IN OTHER SECTIONS

This section is referred to in section 1810 of this title.

§1810. Civil liability

An aggrieved person, other than a foreign power or an agent of a foreign power, as defined in section 1801(a) or (b)(1)(A) of this title, respectively, who has been subjected to an electronic surveillance or about whom information obtained by electronic surveillance of such person has been disclosed or used in violation of section 1809 of this title shall have a cause of action against any person who committed such violation and shall be entitled to recover—

(a) actual damages, but not less than liquidated damages of $1,000 or $100 per day for each day of violation, whichever is greater;

(b) punitive damages; and

(c) reasonable attorney's fees and other investigation and litigation costs reasonably incurred.

(Pub. L. 95–511, title I, § 110, Oct. 25, 1978, 92 Stat. 1796.)

§ 1811. Authorization during time of war

Notwithstanding any other law, the President, through the Attorney General, may authorize electronic surveillance without a court order under this subchapter to acquire foreign intelligence information for a period not to exceed fifteen calendar days following a declaration of war by the Congress.

(Pub. L. 95–511, title I, § 111, Oct. 25, 1978, 92 Stat. 1796.)

SUBCHAPTER II—PHYSICAL SEARCHES

§ 1821. Definitions

As used in this subchapter:

(1) The terms "foreign power", "agent of a foreign power", "international terrorism", "sabotage", "foreign intelligence information", "Attorney General", "United States person", "United States", "person", and "State" shall have the same meanings as in section 1801 of this title, except as specifically provided by this subchapter.

(2) "Aggrieved person" means a person whose premises, property, information, or material is the target of physical search or any other person whose premises, property, information, or material was subject to physical search.

(3) "Foreign Intelligence Surveillance Court" means the court established by section 1803(a) of this title.

(4) "Minimization procedures" with respect to physical search, means—

(A) specific procedures, which shall be adopted by the Attorney General, that are reasonably designed in light of the purposes and technique of the particular physical search, to minimize the acquisition and retention, and prohibit the dissemination, of nonpublicly available information concerning unconsenting United States persons consistent with the need of the United States to obtain, produce, and disseminate foreign intelligence information;

(B) procedures that require that nonpublicly available information, which is not foreign intelligence information, as defined in section 1801(e)(1) of this title, shall not be disseminated in a manner that identifies any United States person, without such person's consent, unless such person's identity is necessary to understand such foreign intelligence information or assess its importance;

(C) notwithstanding subparagraphs (A) and (B), procedures that allow for the retention and dissemination of information that is evidence of a crime which has been, is being, or is about to be committed and that is to be retained or disseminated for law enforcement purposes; and

(D) notwithstanding subparagraphs (A), (B), and (C), with respect to any physical search approved pursuant to section 1822(a) of this title, procedures that require that no information, material, or property of a United States person shall be disclosed, disseminated, or used for any purpose or retained for longer than 24 hours unless a court order under section 1824 of this title is obtained or unless the Attorney General determines that the information indicates a threat of death or serious bodily harm to any person.

(5) "Physical search" means any physical intrusion within the United States into premises or property (including examination of the interior of property by technical means) that is intended to result in a seizure, reproduction, inspection, or alteration of information, material, or property, under circumstances in which a person has a reasonable expectation of privacy and a warrant would be required for law enforcement purposes, but does not include (A) "electronic surveillance", as defined in section 1801(f) of this title, or (B) the acquisition by the United States Government of foreign intelligence information from international or foreign communications, or foreign intelligence activities conducted in accordance with otherwise applicable Federal law involving a foreign electronic communications system, utilizing a means other than electronic surveillance as defined in section 1801(f) of this title.

(Pub. L. 95–511, title III, § 301, as added Pub. L. 103–359, title VIII, § 807(a)(3), Oct. 14, 1994, 108 Stat. 3443.)

PRIOR PROVISIONS

A prior section 301 of Pub. L. 95–511 was renumbered section 601 and is set out as a note under section 1801 of this title.

EFFECTIVE DATE

Section 807(c) of Pub. L. 103–359 provided that: "The amendments made by subsections (a) and (b) [enacting this subchapter and amending provisions set out as a note under section 1801 of this title] shall take effect 90 days after the date of enactment of this Act [Oct. 14, 1994], except that any physical search approved by the Attorney General of the United States to gather foreign intelligence information shall not be deemed unlawful for failure to follow the procedures of title III of the Foreign Intelligence Surveillance Act of 1978 [this subchapter] (as added by this Act), if that search is conducted within 180 days after the date of enactment of this Act pursuant to regulations issued by the Attorney General, which were in the possession of the Select Committee on Intelligence of the Senate and the Permanent Select Committee on Intelligence of the House of Representatives before the date of enactment of this Act."

SECTION REFERRED TO IN OTHER SECTIONS

This section is referred to in section 1822 of this title.

§1822. Authorization of physical searches for foreign intelligence purposes

(a) Presidential authorization

(1) Notwithstanding any other provision of law, the President, acting through the Attorney General, may authorize physical searches without a court order under this subchapter to acquire foreign intelligence information for periods of up to one year if—

(A) the Attorney General certifies in writing under oath that—

(i) the physical search is solely directed at premises, information, material, or property used exclusively by, or under the open and exclusive control of, a foreign power or powers (as defined in section 1801(a)(1), (2), or (3) of this title);

(ii) there is no substantial likelihood that the physical search will involve the premises, information, material, or property of a United States person; and

(iii) the proposed minimization procedures with respect to such physical search meet the definition of minimization procedures under paragraphs (1) through (4)[1] of section 1821(4) of this title; and

(B) the Attorney General reports such minimization procedures and any changes thereto to the Permanent Select Committee on Intelligence of the House of Representatives and the Select Committee on Intelligence of the Senate at least 30 days before their effective date, unless the Attorney General determines that immediate action is required and notifies the committees immediately of such minimization procedures and the reason for their becoming effective immediately.

(2) A physical search authorized by this subsection may be conducted only in accordance with the certification and minimization procedures adopted by the Attorney General. The Attorney General shall assess compliance with such procedures and shall report such assessments to the Permanent Select Committee on Intelligence of the House of Representatives and the Select Committee on Intelligence of the Senate under the provisions of section 1826 of this title.

(3) The Attorney General shall immediately transmit under seal to the Foreign Intelligence Surveillance Court a copy of the certification. Such certification shall be maintained under security measures established by the Chief Justice of the United States with the concurrence of the Attorney General, in consultation with the Director of Central Intelligence, and shall remain sealed unless—

(A) an application for a court order with respect to the physical search is made under section 1821(4) of this title and section 1823 of this title; or

(B) the certification is necessary to determine the legality of the physical search under section 1825(g) of this title.

(4)(A) With respect to physical searches authorized by this subsection, the Attorney General may direct a specified landlord, custodian, or other specified person to—

(i) furnish all information, facilities, or assistance necessary to accomplish the physical search in such a manner as will protect its secrecy and produce a minimum of interference with the services that such landlord, custodian, or other person is providing the target of the physical search; and

(ii) maintain under security procedures approved by the Attorney General and the Director of Central Intelligence any records concerning the search or the aid furnished that such person wishes to retain.

(B) The Government shall compensate, at the prevailing rate, such landlord, custodian, or other person for furnishing such aid.

(b) Application for order; authorization

Applications for a court order under this subchapter are authorized if the President has, by written authorization, empowered the Attorney General to approve applications to the Foreign Intelligence Surveillance Court. Notwithstanding any other provision of law, a judge of the court to whom application is made may grant an order in accordance with section 1824 of this title approving a physical search in the United States of the premises, property, information, or material of a foreign power or an agent of a foreign power for the purpose of collecting foreign intelligence information.

(c) Jurisdiction of Foreign Intelligence Surveillance Court

The Foreign Intelligence Surveillance Court shall have jurisdiction to hear applications for and grant orders approving a physical search for the purpose of obtaining foreign intelligence information anywhere within the United States under the procedures set forth in this subchapter, except that no judge shall hear the same application which has been denied previously by another judge designated under section 1803(a) of this title. If any judge so designated denies an application for an order authorizing a physical search under this subchapter, such judge shall provide immediately for the record a written statement of each reason for such decision and, on motion of the United States, the record shall be transmitted, under seal, to the court of review established under section 1803(b) of this title.

(d) Court of review; record; transmittal to Supreme Court

The court of review established under section 1803(b) of this title shall have jurisdiction to review the denial of any application made under this subchapter. If such court determines that the application was properly denied, the court shall immediately provide for the record a written statement of each reason for its decision and, on petition of the United States for a writ of certiorari, the record shall be transmitted under seal to the Supreme Court, which shall have jurisdiction to review such decision.

(e) Expeditious conduct of proceedings; security measures for maintenance of records

Judicial proceedings under this subchapter shall be concluded as expeditiously as possible.

[1] So in original. Probably should be "subparagraphs (A) through (D)".

The record of proceedings under this subchapter, including applications made and orders granted, shall be maintained under security measures established by the Chief Justice of the United States in consultation with the Attorney General and the Director of Central Intelligence.

(Pub. L. 95–511, title III, § 302, as added Pub. L. 103–359, title VIII, § 807(a)(3), Oct. 14, 1994, 108 Stat. 3444.)

EX. ORD. NO. 12949. FOREIGN INTELLIGENCE PHYSICAL SEARCHES

Ex. Ord. No. 12949, Feb. 9, 1995, 60 F.R. 8169, provided:

By the authority vested in me as President by the Constitution and the laws of the United States, including sections 302 and 303 of the Foreign Intelligence Surveillance Act of 1978 ("Act") (50 U.S.C. 1801, *et seq.*), as amended by Public Law 103–359 [50 U.S.C. 1822, 1823], and in order to provide for the authorization of physical searches for foreign intelligence purposes as set forth in the Act, it is hereby ordered as follows:

SECTION 1. Pursuant to section 302(a)(1) of the Act, the Attorney General is authorized to approve physical searches, without a court order, to acquire foreign intelligence information for periods of up to one year, if the Attorney General makes the certifications required by that section.

SEC. 2. Pursuant to section 302(b) of the Act, the Attorney General is authorized to approve applications to the Foreign Intelligence Surveillance Court under section 303 of the Act to obtain orders for physical searches for the purpose of collecting foreign intelligence information.

SEC. 3. Pursuant to section 303(a)(7) of the Act, the following officials, each of whom is employed in the area of national security or defense, is designated to make the certifications required by section 303(a)(7) of the Act in support of applications to conduct physical searches:

(a) Secretary of State;
(b) Secretary of Defense;
(c) Director of Central Intelligence;
(d) Director of the Federal Bureau of Investigation,
(e) Deputy Secretary of State;
(f) Deputy Secretary of Defense; and
(g) Deputy Director of Central Intelligence.

None of the above officials, nor anyone officially acting in that capacity, may exercise the authority to make the above certifications, unless that official has been appointed by the President, by and with the advice and consent of the Senate.

WILLIAM J. CLINTON.

SECTION REFERRED TO IN OTHER SECTIONS

This section is referred to in sections 1821, 1824 of this title.

§ 1823. Application for order

(a) Submission by Federal officer; approval of Attorney General; contents

Each application for an order approving a physical search under this subchapter shall be made by a Federal officer in writing upon oath or affirmation to a judge of the Foreign Intelligence Surveillance Court. Each application shall require the approval of the Attorney General based upon the Attorney General's finding that it satisfies the criteria and requirements for such application as set forth in this subchapter. Each application shall include—

(1) the identity of the Federal officer making the application;

(2) the authority conferred on the Attorney General by the President and the approval of the Attorney General to make the application;

(3) the identity, if known, or a description of the target of the search, and a detailed description of the premises or property to be searched and of the information, material, or property to be seized, reproduced, or altered;

(4) a statement of the facts and circumstances relied upon by the applicant to justify the applicant's belief that—

(A) the target of the physical search is a foreign power or an agent of a foreign power;

(B) the premises or property to be searched contains foreign intelligence information; and

(C) the premises or property to be searched is owned, used, possessed by, or is in transit to or from a foreign power or an agent of a foreign power;

(5) a statement of the proposed minimization procedures;

(6) a statement of the nature of the foreign intelligence sought and the manner in which the physical search is to be conducted;

(7) a certification or certifications by the Assistant to the President for National Security Affairs or an executive branch official or officials designated by the President from among those executive branch officers employed in the area of national security or defense and appointed by the President, by and with the advice and consent of the Senate—

(A) that the certifying official deems the information sought to be foreign intelligence information;

(B) that the purpose of the search is to obtain foreign intelligence information;

(C) that such information cannot reasonably be obtained by normal investigative techniques;

(D) that designates the type of foreign intelligence information being sought according to the categories described in section 1801(e) of this title; and

(E) includes a statement explaining the basis for the certifications required by subparagraphs (C) and (D);

(8) where the physical search involves a search of the residence of a United States person, the Attorney General shall state what investigative techniques have previously been utilized to obtain the foreign intelligence information concerned and the degree to which these techniques resulted in acquiring such information; and

(9) a statement of the facts concerning all previous applications that have been made to any judge under this subchapter involving any of the persons, premises, or property specified in the application, and the action taken on each previous application.

(b) Additional affidavits or certifications

The Attorney General may require any other affidavit or certification from any other officer in connection with the application.

(c) Additional information

The judge may require the applicant to furnish such other information as may be necessary to make the determinations required by section 1824 of this title.

(d) Personal review by Attorney General

(1)(A) Upon written request of the Director of the Federal Bureau of Investigation, the Secretary of Defense, the Secretary of State, or the Director of Central Intelligence, the Attorney General shall personally review under subsection (a) of this section an application under that subsection for a target described in section 1801(b)(2) of this title.

(B) Except when disabled or otherwise unavailable to make a request referred to in subparagraph (A), an official referred to in that subparagraph may not delegate the authority to make a request referred to in that subparagraph.

(C) Each official referred to in subparagraph (A) with authority to make a request under that subparagraph shall take appropriate actions in advance to ensure that delegation of such authority is clearly established in the event such official is disabled or otherwise unavailable to make such request.

(2)(A) If as a result of a request under paragraph (1) the Attorney General determines not to approve an application under the second sentence of subsection (a) of this section for purposes of making the application under this section, the Attorney General shall provide written notice of the determination to the official making the request for the review of the application under that paragraph. Except when disabled or otherwise unavailable to make a determination under the preceding sentence, the Attorney General may not delegate the responsibility to make a determination under that sentence. The Attorney General shall take appropriate actions in advance to ensure that delegation of such responsibility is clearly established in the event the Attorney General is disabled or otherwise unavailable to make such determination.

(B) Notice with respect to an application under subparagraph (A) shall set forth the modifications, if any, of the application that are necessary in order for the Attorney General to approve the application under the second sentence of subsection (a) of this section for purposes of making the application under this section.

(C) Upon review of any modifications of an application set forth under subparagraph (B), the official notified of the modifications under this paragraph shall modify the application if such official determines that such modification is warranted. Such official shall supervise the making of any modification under this subparagraph. Except when disabled or otherwise unavailable to supervise the making of any modification under the preceding sentence, such official may not delegate the responsibility to supervise the making of any modification under that preceding sentence. Each such official shall take appropriate actions in advance to ensure that delegation of such responsibility is clearly established in the event such official is disabled or otherwise unavailable to supervise the making of such modification.

(Pub. L. 95–511, title III, §303, as added Pub. L. 103–359, title VIII, §807(a)(3), Oct. 14, 1994, 108 Stat. 3446; amended Pub. L. 106–567, title VI, §603(a), Dec. 27, 2000, 114 Stat. 2852.)

AMENDMENTS

2000—Subsec. (d). Pub. L. 106–567 added subsec. (d).

OFFICIALS DESIGNATED TO MAKE CERTIFICATIONS

For provisions listing officials designated by President to make certifications required by subsec. (a)(7) of this section, see Ex. Ord. No. 12949, §3, Feb. 9, 1995, 60 F.R. 8169, set out as a note under section 1822 of this title.

SECTION REFERRED TO IN OTHER SECTIONS

This section is referred to in sections 1822, 1824 of this title.

§1824. Issuance of order

(a) Necessary findings

Upon an application made pursuant to section 1823 of this title, the judge shall enter an ex parte order as requested or as modified approving the physical search if the judge finds that—

(1) the President has authorized the Attorney General to approve applications for physical searches for foreign intelligence purposes;

(2) the application has been made by a Federal officer and approved by the Attorney General;

(3) on the basis of the facts submitted by the applicant there is probable cause to believe that—

(A) the target of the physical search is a foreign power or an agent of a foreign power, except that no United States person may be considered an agent of a foreign power solely upon the basis of activities protected by the first amendment to the Constitution of the United States; and

(B) the premises or property to be searched is owned, used, possessed by, or is in transit to or from an agent of a foreign power or a foreign power;

(4) the proposed minimization procedures meet the definition of minimization contained in this subchapter; and

(5) the application which has been filed contains all statements and certifications required by section 1823 of this title, and, if the target is a United States person, the certification or certifications are not clearly erroneous on the basis of the statement made under section 1823(a)(7)(E) of this title and any other information furnished under section 1823(c) of this title.

(b) Determination of probable cause

In determining whether or not probable cause exists for purposes of an order under subsection (a)(3) of this section, a judge may consider past activities of the target, as well as facts and circumstances relating to current or future activities of the target.

(c) Specifications and directions of orders

An order approving a physical search under this section shall—

(1) specify—

(A) the identity, if known, or a description of the target of the physical search;

(B) the nature and location of each of the premises or property to be searched;

(C) the type of information, material, or property to be seized, altered, or reproduced;

(D) a statement of the manner in which the physical search is to be conducted and, whenever more than one physical search is authorized under the order, the authorized scope of each search and what minimization procedures shall apply to the information acquired by each search; and

(E) the period of time during which physical searches are approved; and

(2) direct—

(A) that the minimization procedures be followed;

(B) that, upon the request of the applicant, a specified landlord, custodian, or other specified person furnish the applicant forthwith all information, facilities, or assistance necessary to accomplish the physical search in such a manner as will protect its secrecy and produce a minimum of interference with the services that such landlord, custodian, or other person is providing the target of the physical search;

(C) that such landlord, custodian, or other person maintain under security procedures approved by the Attorney General and the Director of Central Intelligence any records concerning the search or the aid furnished that such person wishes to retain;

(D) that the applicant compensate, at the prevailing rate, such landlord, custodian, or other person for furnishing such aid; and

(E) that the Federal officer conducting the physical search promptly report to the court the circumstances and results of the physical search.

(d) Duration of order; extensions; assessment of compliance

(1) An order issued under this section may approve a physical search for the period necessary to achieve its purpose, or for forty-five days, whichever is less, except that an order under this section shall approve a physical search targeted against a foreign power, as defined in paragraph (1), (2), or (3) of section 1801(a) of this title, for the period specified in the application or for one year, whichever is less.

(2) Extensions of an order issued under this subchapter may be granted on the same basis as the original order upon an application for an extension and new findings made in the same manner as required for the original order, except that an extension of an order under this chapter for a physical search targeted against a foreign power, as defined in section 1801(a)(5) or (6) of this title, or against a foreign power, as defined in section 1801(a)(4) of this title, that is not a United States person, may be for a period not to exceed one year if the judge finds probable cause to believe that no property of any individual United States person will be acquired during the period.

(3) At or before the end of the period of time for which a physical search is approved by an order or an extension, or at any time after a physical search is carried out, the judge may assess compliance with the minimization procedures by reviewing the circumstances under which information concerning United States persons was acquired, retained, or disseminated.

(e) Emergency orders

(1)(A) Notwithstanding any other provision of this subchapter, whenever the Attorney General reasonably makes the determination specified in subparagraph (B), the Attorney General may authorize the execution of an emergency physical search if—

(i) a judge having jurisdiction under section 1803 of this title is informed by the Attorney General or the Attorney General's designee at the time of such authorization that the decision has been made to execute an emergency search, and

(ii) an application in accordance with this subchapter is made to that judge as soon as practicable but not more than 24 hours after the Attorney General authorizes such search.

(B) The determination referred to in subparagraph (A) is a determination that—

(i) an emergency situation exists with respect to the execution of a physical search to obtain foreign intelligence information before an order authorizing such search can with due diligence be obtained, and

(ii) the factual basis for issuance of an order under this subchapter to approve such a search exists.

(2) If the Attorney General authorizes an emergency search under paragraph (1), the Attorney General shall require that the minimization procedures required by this subchapter for the issuance of a judicial order be followed.

(3) In the absence of a judicial order approving such a physical search, the search shall terminate the earlier of—

(A) the date on which the information sought is obtained;

(B) the date on which the application for the order is denied; or

(C) the expiration of 24 hours from the time of authorization by the Attorney General.

(4) In the event that such application for approval is denied, or in any other case where the physical search is terminated and no order is issued approving the search, no information obtained or evidence derived from such search shall be received in evidence or otherwise disclosed in any trial, hearing, or other proceeding in or before any court, grand jury, department, office, agency, regulatory body, legislative committee, or other authority of the United States, a State, or political subdivision thereof, and no information concerning any United States person acquired from such search shall subsequently be used or disclosed in any other manner by Federal officers or employees without the consent of such person, except with the approval of the Attorney General, if the information indicates a threat of death or serious bodily harm to any person. A denial of the application made under this subsection may be reviewed as provided in section 1822 of this title.

(f) Retention of applications and orders

Applications made and orders granted under this subchapter shall be retained for a period of at least 10 years from the date of the application.

(Pub. L. 95–511, title III, §304, as added Pub. L. 103–359, title VIII, §807(a)(3), Oct. 14, 1994, 108 Stat. 3447; amended Pub. L. 106–567, title VI, §603(b), Dec. 27, 2000, 114 Stat. 2853.)

REFERENCES IN TEXT

This chapter, referred to in subsec. (d)(2), was in the original "this Act", meaning Pub. L. 95–511, Oct. 25, 1978, 92 Stat. 1783, as amended, which is classified principally to this chapter. For complete classification of this Act to the Code, see Short Title note set out under section 1801 of this title and Tables.

AMENDMENTS

2000—Subsecs. (b) to (f). Pub. L. 106–567 added subsec. (b) and redesignated former subsecs. (b) to (e) as (c) to (f), respectively.

SECTION REFERRED TO IN OTHER SECTIONS

This section is referred to in sections 1821, 1822, 1823, 1825 of this title.

§ 1825. Use of information

(a) Compliance with minimization procedures; lawful purposes

Information acquired from a physical search conducted pursuant to this subchapter concerning any United States person may be used and disclosed by Federal officers and employees without the consent of the United States person only in accordance with the minimization procedures required by this subchapter. No information acquired from a physical search pursuant to this subchapter may be used or disclosed by Federal officers or employees except for lawful purposes.

(b) Notice of search and identification of property seized, altered, or reproduced

Where a physical search authorized and conducted pursuant to section 1824 of this title involves the residence of a United States person, and, at any time after the search the Attorney General determines there is no national security interest in continuing to maintain the secrecy of the search, the Attorney General shall provide notice to the United States person whose residence was searched of the fact of the search conducted pursuant to this chapter and shall identify any property of such person seized, altered, or reproduced during such search.

(c) Statement for disclosure

No information acquired pursuant to this subchapter shall be disclosed for law enforcement purposes unless such disclosure is accompanied by a statement that such information, or any information derived therefrom, may only be used in a criminal proceeding with the advance authorization of the Attorney General.

(d) Notification by United States

Whenever the United States intends to enter into evidence or otherwise use or disclose in any trial, hearing, or other proceeding in or before any court, department, officer, agency, regulatory body, or other authority of the United States, against an aggrieved person, any information obtained or derived from a physical search pursuant to the authority of this subchapter, the United States shall, prior to the trial, hearing, or the other proceeding or at a reasonable time prior to an effort to so disclose or so use that information or submit it in evidence, notify the aggrieved person and the court or other authority in which the information is to be disclosed or used that the United States intends to so disclose or so use such information.

(e) Notification by States or political subdivisions

Whenever any State or political subdivision thereof intends to enter into evidence or otherwise use or disclose in any trial, hearing, or other proceeding in or before any court, department, officer, agency, regulatory body, or other authority of a State or a political subdivision thereof against an aggrieved person any information obtained or derived from a physical search pursuant to the authority of this subchapter, the State or political subdivision thereof shall notify the aggrieved person, the court or other authority in which the information is to be disclosed or used, and the Attorney General that the State or political subdivision thereof intends to so disclose or so use such information.

(f) Motion to suppress

(1) Any person against whom evidence obtained or derived from a physical search to which he is an aggrieved person is to be, or has been, introduced or otherwise used or disclosed in any trial, hearing, or other proceeding in or before any court, department, officer, agency, regulatory body, or other authority of the United States, a State, or a political subdivision thereof, may move to suppress the evidence obtained or derived from such search on the grounds that—

(A) the information was unlawfully acquired; or

(B) the physical search was not made in conformity with an order of authorization or approval.

(2) Such a motion shall be made before the trial, hearing, or other proceeding unless there was no opportunity to make such a motion or the person was not aware of the grounds of the motion.

(g) In camera and ex parte review by district court

Whenever a court or other authority is notified pursuant to subsection (d) or (e) of this section, or whenever a motion is made pursuant to subsection (f) of this section, or whenever any motion or request is made by an aggrieved person pursuant to any other statute or rule of the United States or any State before any court or other authority of the United States or any State to discover or obtain applications or orders or other materials relating to a physical search authorized by this subchapter or to discover, obtain, or suppress evidence or information obtained or derived from a physical search authorized by this subchapter, the United States district court or, where the motion is made before another authority, the United States district court in the same district as the authority shall, notwithstanding any other provision of law, if the Attorney General files an affidavit under oath that disclosure or any adversary hearing would harm the national security of the United States, review in camera and ex parte the application, order, and such other materials relating to the physical search as may be necessary to determine whether the physical search of the aggrieved person was lawfully authorized and conducted. In making this determination, the court may disclose to the aggrieved person, under appropriate security procedures and protective orders, portions of the application, order, or other materials relating to the physical search, or may require the Attorney General to provide to the aggrieved person a summary of such materials, only where such disclosure is necessary to make an accurate determination of the legality of the physical search.

(h) Suppression of evidence; denial of motion

If the United States district court pursuant to subsection (g) of this section determines that the physical search was not lawfully authorized or conducted, it shall, in accordance with the requirements of law, suppress the evidence which was unlawfully obtained or derived from the physical search of the aggrieved person or otherwise grant the motion of the aggrieved person. If the court determines that the physical search was lawfully authorized or conducted, it shall deny the motion of the aggrieved person except to the extent that due process requires discovery or disclosure.

(i) Finality of orders

Orders granting motions or requests under subsection (h) of this section, decisions under this section that a physical search was not lawfully authorized or conducted, and orders of the United States district court requiring review or granting disclosure of applications, orders, or other materials relating to the physical search shall be final orders and binding upon all courts of the United States and the several States except a United States Court of Appeals or the Supreme Court.

(j) Notification of emergency execution of physical search; contents; postponement, suspension, or elimination

(1) If an emergency execution of a physical search is authorized under section 1824(d)[1] of this title and a subsequent order approving the search is not obtained, the judge shall cause to be served on any United States person named in the application and on such other United States persons subject to the search as the judge may determine in his discretion it is in the interests of justice to serve, notice of—

(A) the fact of the application;

(B) the period of the search; and

(C) the fact that during the period information was or was not obtained.

(2) On an ex parte showing of good cause to the judge, the serving of the notice required by this subsection may be postponed or suspended for a period not to exceed 90 days. Thereafter, on a further ex parte showing of good cause, the court shall forego ordering the serving of the notice required under this subsection.

(Pub. L. 95–511, title III, §305, as added Pub. L. 103–359, title VIII, §807(a)(3), Oct. 14, 1994, 108 Stat. 3449.)

REFERENCES IN TEXT

Section 1824(d) of this title, referred to in subsec. (j)(1), was redesignated section 1824(e) of this title by Pub. L. 106–567, title VI, §603(b)(1), Dec. 27, 2000, 114 Stat. 2853.

SECTION REFERRED TO IN OTHER SECTIONS

This section is referred to in sections 1822, 1826 of this title.

[1] See References in Text note below.

§1826. Congressional oversight

On a semiannual basis the Attorney General shall fully inform the Permanent Select Committee on Intelligence of the House of Representatives and the Select Committee on Intelligence of the Senate concerning all physical searches conducted pursuant to this subchapter. On a semiannual basis the Attorney General shall also provide to those committees and the Committees on the Judiciary of the House of Representatives and the Senate a report setting forth with respect to the preceding six-month period—

(1) the total number of applications made for orders approving physical searches under this subchapter;

(2) the total number of such orders either granted, modified, or denied; and

(3) the number of physical searches which involved searches of the residences, offices, or personal property of United States persons, and the number of occasions, if any, where the Attorney General provided notice pursuant to section 1825(b) of this title.

(Pub. L. 95–511, title III, §306, as added Pub. L. 103–359, title VIII, §807(a)(3), Oct. 14, 1994, 108 Stat. 3451.)

SECTION REFERRED TO IN OTHER SECTIONS

This section is referred to in section 1822 of this title.

§1827. Penalties

(a) Prohibited activities

A person is guilty of an offense if he intentionally—

(1) under color of law for the purpose of obtaining foreign intelligence information, executes a physical search within the United States except as authorized by statute; or

(2) discloses or uses information obtained under color of law by physical search within the United States, knowing or having reason to know that the information was obtained through physical search not authorized by statute, for the purpose of obtaining intelligence information.

(b) Defense

It is a defense to a prosecution under subsection (a) of this section that the defendant was a law enforcement or investigative officer engaged in the course of his official duties and the physical search was authorized by and conducted pursuant to a search warrant or court order of a court of competent jurisdiction.

(c) Fine or imprisonment

An offense described in this section is punishable by a fine of not more than $10,000 or imprisonment for not more than five years, or both.

(d) Federal jurisdiction

There is Federal jurisdiction over an offense under this section if the person committing the offense was an officer or employee of the United States at the time the offense was committed.

(Pub. L. 95–511, title III, § 307, as added Pub. L. 103–359, title VIII, § 807(a)(3), Oct. 14, 1994, 108 Stat. 3452.)

SECTION REFERRED TO IN OTHER SECTIONS

This section is referred to in section 1828 of this title.

§ 1828. Civil liability

An aggrieved person, other than a foreign power or an agent of a foreign power, as defined in section 1801(a) or (b)(1)(A), respectively, of this title, whose premises, property, information, or material has been subjected to a physical search within the United States or about whom information obtained by such a physical search has been disclosed or used in violation of section 1827 of this title shall have a cause of action against any person who committed such violation and shall be entitled to recover—

(1) actual damages, but not less than liquidated damages of $1,000 or $100 per day for each day of violation, whichever is greater;

(2) punitive damages; and

(3) reasonable attorney's fees and other investigative and litigation costs reasonably incurred.

(Pub. L. 95–511, title III, § 308, as added Pub. L. 103–359, title VIII, § 807(a)(3), Oct. 14, 1994, 108 Stat. 3452.)

§ 1829. Authorization during time of war

Notwithstanding any other provision of law, the President, through the Attorney General, may authorize physical searches without a court order under this subchapter to acquire foreign intelligence information for a period not to exceed 15 calendar days following a declaration of war by the Congress.

(Pub. L. 95–511, title III, § 309, as added Pub. L. 103–359, title VIII, § 807(a)(3), Oct. 14, 1994, 108 Stat. 3452.)

SUBCHAPTER III—PEN REGISTERS AND TRAP AND TRACE DEVICES FOR FOREIGN INTELLIGENCE PURPOSES

§ 1841. Definitions

As used in this subchapter:

(1) The terms "foreign power", "agent of a foreign power", "international terrorism", "foreign intelligence information", "Attorney General", "United States person", "United States", "person", and "State" shall have the same meanings as in section 1801 of this title.

(2) The terms "pen register" and "trap and trace device" have the meanings given such terms in section 3127 of title 18.

(3) The term "aggrieved person" means any person—

(A) whose telephone line was subject to the installation or use of a pen register or trap and trace device authorized by this subchapter; or

(B) whose communication instrument or device was subject to the use of a pen register or trap and trace device authorized by this subchapter to capture incoming electronic or other communications impulses.

(Pub. L. 95–511, title IV, § 401, as added Pub. L. 105–272, title VI, § 601(2), Oct. 20, 1998, 112 Stat. 2404.)

PRIOR PROVISIONS

A prior section 401 of Pub. L. 95–511 was renumbered section 601 and is set out as a note under section 1801 of this title.

§ 1842. Pen registers and trap and trace devices for foreign intelligence and international terrorism investigations

(a) Application for authorization or approval

(1) Notwithstanding any other provision of law, the Attorney General or a designated attorney for the Government may make an application for an order or an extension of an order authorizing or approving the installation and use of a pen register or trap and trace device for any investigation to gather foreign intelligence information or information concerning international terrorism which is being conducted by the Federal Bureau of Investigation under such guidelines as the Attorney General approves pursuant to Executive Order No. 12333, or a successor order.

(2) The authority under paragraph (1) is in addition to the authority under subchapter I of this chapter to conduct the electronic surveillance referred to in that paragraph.

(b) Form of application; recipient

Each application under this section shall be in writing under oath or affirmation to—

(1) a judge of the court established by section 1803(a) of this title; or

(2) a United States Magistrate Judge under chapter 43 of title 28 who is publicly designated by the Chief Justice of the United States to have the power to hear applications for and grant orders approving the installation and use of a pen register or trap and trace device on behalf of a judge of that court.

(c) Executive approval; contents of application

Each application under this section shall require the approval of the Attorney General, or a designated attorney for the Government, and shall include—

(1) the identity of the Federal officer seeking to use the pen register or trap and trace device covered by the application;

(2) a certification by the applicant that the information likely to be obtained is relevant to an ongoing foreign intelligence or international terrorism investigation being conducted by the Federal Bureau of Investigation under guidelines approved by the Attorney General; and

(3) information which demonstrates that there is reason to believe that the telephone line to which the pen register or trap and trace device is to be attached, or the communication instrument or device to be covered by the pen register or trap and trace device, has been or is about to be used in communication with—

(A) an individual who is engaging or has engaged in international terrorism or clandestine intelligence activities that involve or may involve a violation of the criminal laws of the United States; or

(B) a foreign power or agent of a foreign power under circumstances giving reason to believe that the communication concerns or concerned international terrorism or clandestine intelligence activities that involve or may involve a violation of the criminal laws of the United States.

(d) Ex parte judicial order of approval

(1) Upon an application made pursuant to this section, the judge shall enter an ex parte order as requested, or as modified, approving the installation and use of a pen register or trap and trace device if the judge finds that the application satisfies the requirements of this section.

(2) An order issued under this section—

(A) shall specify—

(i) the identity, if known, of the person who is the subject of the foreign intelligence or international terrorism investigation;

(ii) in the case of an application for the installation and use of a pen register or trap and trace device with respect to a telephone line—

(I) the identity, if known, of the person to whom is leased or in whose name the telephone line is listed; and

(II) the number and, if known, physical location of the telephone line; and

(iii) in the case of an application for the use of a pen register or trap and trace device with respect to a communication instrument or device not covered by clause (ii)—

(I) the identity, if known, of the person who owns or leases the instrument or device or in whose name the instrument or device is listed; and

(II) the number of the instrument or device; and

(B) shall direct that—

(i) upon request of the applicant, the provider of a wire or electronic communication service, landlord, custodian, or other person shall furnish any information, facilities, or technical assistance necessary to accomplish the installation and operation of the pen register or trap and trace device in such a manner as will protect its secrecy and produce a minimum amount of interference with the services that such provider, landlord, custodian, or other person is providing the person concerned;

(ii) such provider, landlord, custodian, or other person—

(I) shall not disclose the existence of the investigation or of the pen register or trap and trace device to any person unless or until ordered by the court; and

(II) shall maintain, under security procedures approved by the Attorney General and the Director of Central Intelligence pursuant to section 1805(b)(2)(C)[1] of this title, any records concerning the pen register or trap and trace device or the aid furnished; and

(iii) the applicant shall compensate such provider, landlord, custodian, or other person for reasonable expenses incurred by such provider, landlord, custodian, or other person in providing such information, facilities, or technical assistance.

(e) Time limitation

An order issued under this section shall authorize the installation and use of a pen register or trap and trace device for a period not to exceed 90 days. Extensions of such an order may be granted, but only upon an application for an order under this section and upon the judicial finding required by subsection (d) of this section. The period of extension shall be for a period not to exceed 90 days.

(f) Cause of action barred

No cause of action shall lie in any court against any provider of a wire or electronic communication service, landlord, custodian, or other person (including any officer, employee, agent, or other specified person thereof) that furnishes any information, facilities, or technical assistance under subsection (d) of this section in accordance with the terms of a court under this section.

(g) Furnishing of results

Unless otherwise ordered by the judge, the results of a pen register or trap and trace device shall be furnished at reasonable intervals during regular business hours for the duration of the order to the authorized Government official or officials.

(Pub. L. 95–511, title IV, § 402, as added Pub. L. 105–272, title VI, § 601(2), Oct. 20, 1998, 112 Stat. 2405.)

REFERENCES IN TEXT

Executive Order No. 12333, referred to in subsec. (a)(1), is set out as a note under section 401 of this title.

Section 1805(b)(2)(C) of this title, referred to in subsec. (d)(2)(B)(ii)(II), was redesignated section 1805(c)(2)(C) of this title by Pub. L. 106–567, title VI, § 602(b)(1), Dec. 27, 2000, 114 Stat. 2851.

The criminal laws of the United States, referred to in subsec. (c)(3), are classified generally to Title 18, Crimes and Criminal Procedure.

SECTION REFERRED TO IN OTHER SECTIONS

This section is referred to in section 1843 of this title.

§ 1843. Authorization during emergencies

(a) Requirements for authorization

Notwithstanding any other provision of this subchapter, when the Attorney General makes a determination described in subsection (b) of this section, the Attorney General may authorize the installation and use of a pen register or trap and trace device on an emergency basis to gather foreign intelligence information or information concerning international terrorism if—

(1) a judge referred to in section 1842(b) of this title is informed by the Attorney General or his designee at the time of such authorization that the decision has been made to install and use the pen register or trap and trace device, as the case may be, on an emergency basis; and

(2) an application in accordance with section 1842 of this title is made to such judge as soon as practicable, but not more than 48 hours, after the Attorney General authorizes the in-

[1] See References in Text note below.

stallation and use of the pen register or trap and trace device, as the case may be, under this section.

(b) Determination of emergency and factual basis

A determination under this subsection is a reasonable determination by the Attorney General that—

(1) an emergency requires the installation and use of a pen register or trap and trace device to obtain foreign intelligence information or information concerning international terrorism before an order authorizing the installation and use of the pen register or trap and trace device, as the case may be, can with due diligence be obtained under section 1842 of this title; and

(2) the factual basis for issuance of an order under such section 1842 of this title to approve the installation and use of the pen register or trap and trace device, as the case may be, exists.

(c) Effect of absence of order

(1) In the absence of an order applied for under subsection (a)(2) of this section approving the installation and use of a pen register or trap and trace device authorized under this section, the installation and use of the pen register or trap and trace device, as the case may be, shall terminate at the earlier of—

(A) when the information sought is obtained;

(B) when the application for the order is denied under section 1842 of this title; or

(C) 48 hours after the time of the authorization by the Attorney General.

(2) In the event that an application for an order applied for under subsection (a)(2) of this section is denied, or in any other case where the installation and use of a pen register or trap and trace device under this section is terminated and no order under section 1842 of this title is issued approving the installation and use of the pen register or trap and trace device, as the case may be, no information obtained or evidence derived from the use of the pen register or trap and trace device, as the case may be, shall be received in evidence or otherwise disclosed in any trial, hearing, or other proceeding in or before any court, grand jury, department, office, agency, regulatory body, legislative committee, or other authority of the United States, a State, or political subdivision thereof, and no information concerning any United States person acquired from the use of the pen register or trap and trace device, as the case may be, shall subsequently be used or disclosed in any other manner by Federal officers or employees without the consent of such person, except with the approval of the Attorney General if the information indicates a threat of death or serious bodily harm to any person.

(Pub. L. 95–511, title IV, § 403, as added Pub. L. 105–272, title VI, § 601(2), Oct. 20, 1998, 112 Stat. 2407.)

§ 1844. Authorization during time of war

Notwithstanding any other provision of law, the President, through the Attorney General, may authorize the use of a pen register or trap and trace device without a court order under this subchapter to acquire foreign intelligence information for a period not to exceed 15 calendar days following a declaration of war by Congress.

(Pub. L. 95–511, title IV, § 404, as added Pub. L. 105–272, title VI, § 601(2), Oct. 20, 1998, 112 Stat. 2408.)

§ 1845. Use of information

(a) In general

(1) Information acquired from the use of a pen register or trap and trace device installed pursuant to this subchapter concerning any United States person may be used and disclosed by Federal officers and employees without the consent of the United States person only in accordance with the provisions of this section.

(2) No information acquired from a pen register or trap and trace device installed and used pursuant to this subchapter may be used or disclosed by Federal officers or employees except for lawful purposes.

(b) Disclosure for law enforcement purposes

No information acquired pursuant to this subchapter shall be disclosed for law enforcement purposes unless such disclosure is accompanied by a statement that such information, or any information derived therefrom, may only be used in a criminal proceeding with the advance authorization of the Attorney General.

(c) Notification of intended disclosure by United States

Whenever the United States intends to enter into evidence or otherwise use or disclose in any trial, hearing, or other proceeding in or before any court, department, officer, agency, regulatory body, or other authority of the United States against an aggrieved person any information obtained or derived from the use of a pen register or trap and trace device pursuant to this subchapter, the United States shall, before the trial, hearing, or the other proceeding or at a reasonable time before an effort to so disclose or so use that information or submit it in evidence, notify the aggrieved person and the court or other authority in which the information is to be disclosed or used that the United States intends to so disclose or so use such information.

(d) Notification of intended disclosure by State or political subdivision

Whenever any State or political subdivision thereof intends to enter into evidence or otherwise use or disclose in any trial, hearing, or other proceeding in or before any court, department, officer, agency, regulatory body, or other authority of the State or political subdivision thereof against an aggrieved person any information obtained or derived from the use of a pen register or trap and trace device pursuant to this subchapter, the State or political subdivision thereof shall notify the aggrieved person, the court or other authority in which the information is to be disclosed or used, and the Attorney General that the State or political subdivision thereof intends to so disclose or so use such information.

(e) Motion to suppress

(1) Any aggrieved person against whom evidence obtained or derived from the use of a pen register or trap and trace device is to be, or has been, introduced or otherwise used or disclosed in any trial, hearing, or other proceeding in or before any court, department, officer, agency, regulatory body, or other authority of the United States, or a State or political subdivision thereof, may move to suppress the evidence obtained or derived from the use of the pen register or trap and trace device, as the case may be, on the grounds that—

(A) the information was unlawfully acquired; or

(B) the use of the pen register or trap and trace device, as the case may be, was not made in conformity with an order of authorization or approval under this subchapter.

(2) A motion under paragraph (1) shall be made before the trial, hearing, or other proceeding unless there was no opportunity to make such a motion or the aggrieved person concerned was not aware of the grounds of the motion.

(f) In camera and ex parte review

(1) Whenever a court or other authority is notified pursuant to subsection (c) or (d) of this section, whenever a motion is made pursuant to subsection (e) of this section, or whenever any motion or request is made by an aggrieved person pursuant to any other statute or rule of the United States or any State before any court or other authority of the United States or any State to discover or obtain applications or orders or other materials relating to the use of a pen register or trap and trace device authorized by this subchapter or to discover, obtain, or suppress evidence or information obtained or derived from the use of a pen register or trap and trace device authorized by this subchapter, the United States district court or, where the motion is made before another authority, the United States district court in the same district as the authority shall, notwithstanding any other provision of law and if the Attorney General files an affidavit under oath that disclosure or any adversary hearing would harm the national security of the United States, review in camera and ex parte the application, order, and such other materials relating to the use of the pen register or trap and trace device, as the case may be, as may be necessary to determine whether the use of the pen register or trap and trace device, as the case may be, was lawfully authorized and conducted.

(2) In making a determination under paragraph (1), the court may disclose to the aggrieved person, under appropriate security procedures and protective orders, portions of the application, order, or other materials relating to the use of the pen register or trap and trace device, as the case may be, or may require the Attorney General to provide to the aggrieved person a summary of such materials, only where such disclosure is necessary to make an accurate determination of the legality of the use of the pen register or trap and trace device, as the case may be.

(g) Effect of determination of lawfulness

(1) If the United States district court determines pursuant to subsection (f) of this section that the use of a pen register or trap and trace device was not lawfully authorized or conducted, the court may, in accordance with the requirements of law, suppress the evidence which was unlawfully obtained or derived from the use of the pen register or trap and trace device, as the case may be, or otherwise grant the motion of the aggrieved person.

(2) If the court determines that the use of the pen register or trap and trace device, as the case may be, was lawfully authorized or conducted, it may deny the motion of the aggrieved person except to the extent that due process requires discovery or disclosure.

(h) Binding final orders

Orders granting motions or requests under subsection (g) of this section, decisions under this section that the use of a pen register or trap and trace device was not lawfully authorized or conducted, and orders of the United States district court requiring review or granting disclosure of applications, orders, or other materials relating to the installation and use of a pen register or trap and trace device shall be final orders and binding upon all courts of the United States and the several States except a United States Court of Appeals or the Supreme Court.

(Pub. L. 95–511, title IV, §405, as added Pub. L. 105–272, title VI, §601(2), Oct. 20, 1998, 112 Stat. 2408.)

§1846. Congressional oversight

(a) On a semiannual basis, the Attorney General shall fully inform the Permanent Select Committee on Intelligence of the House of Representatives and the Select Committee on Intelligence of the Senate concerning all uses of pen registers and trap and trace devices pursuant to this subchapter.

(b) On a semiannual basis, the Attorney General shall also provide to the committees referred to in subsection (a) of this section and to the Committees on the Judiciary of the House of Representatives and the Senate a report setting forth with respect to the preceding 6-month period—

(1) the total number of applications made for orders approving the use of pen registers or trap and trace devices under this subchapter; and

(2) the total number of such orders either granted, modified, or denied.

(Pub. L. 95–511, title IV, §406, as added Pub. L. 105–272, title VI, §601(2), Oct. 20, 1998, 112 Stat. 2410.)

SUBCHAPTER IV—ACCESS TO CERTAIN BUSINESS RECORDS FOR FOREIGN INTELLIGENCE PURPOSES

§1861. Definitions

As used in this subchapter:

(1) The terms "foreign power", "agent of a foreign power", "foreign intelligence information", "international terrorism", and "Attorney General" shall have the same meanings as in section 1801 of this title.

(2) The term "common carrier" means any person or entity transporting people or property by land, rail, water, or air for compensation.

(3) The term "physical storage facility" means any business or entity that provides space for the storage of goods or materials, or services related to the storage of goods or materials, to the public or any segment thereof.

(4) The term "public accommodation facility" means any inn, hotel, motel, or other establishment that provides lodging to transient guests.

(5) The term "vehicle rental facility" means any person or entity that provides vehicles for rent, lease, loan, or other similar use to the public or any segment thereof.

(Pub. L. 95–511, title V, §501, as added Pub. L. 105–272, title VI, §602, Oct. 20, 1998, 112 Stat. 2410.)

§1862. Access to certain business records for foreign intelligence and international terrorism investigations

(a) Application for authorization

The Director of the Federal Bureau of Investigation or a designee of the Director (whose rank shall be no lower than Assistant Special Agent in Charge) may make an application for an order authorizing a common carrier, public accommodation facility, physical storage facility, or vehicle rental facility to release records in its possession for an investigation to gather foreign intelligence information or an investigation concerning international terrorism which investigation is being conducted by the Federal Bureau of Investigation under such guidelines as the Attorney General approves pursuant to Executive Order No. 12333, or a successor order.

(b) Recipient and contents of application

Each application under this section—

(1) shall be made to—

(A) a judge of the court established by section 1803(a) of this title; or

(B) a United States Magistrate Judge under chapter 43 of title 28 who is publicly designated by the Chief Justice of the United States to have the power to hear applications and grant orders for the release of records under this section on behalf of a judge of that court; and

(2) shall specify that—

(A) the records concerned are sought for an investigation described in subsection (a) of this section; and

(B) there are specific and articulable facts giving reason to believe that the person to whom the records pertain is a foreign power or an agent of a foreign power.

(c) Ex parte judicial order of approval

(1) Upon application made pursuant to this section, the judge shall enter an ex parte order as requested, or as modified, approving the release of records if the judge finds that the application satisfies the requirements of this section.

(2) An order under this subsection shall not disclose that it is issued for purposes of an investigation described in subsection (a) of this section.

(d) Compliance; nondisclosure

(1) Any common carrier, public accommodation facility, physical storage facility, or vehicle rental facility shall comply with an order under subsection (c) of this section.

(2) No common carrier, public accommodation facility, physical storage facility, or vehicle rental facility, or officer, employee, or agent thereof, shall disclose to any person (other than those officers, agents, or employees of such common carrier, public accommodation facility, physical storage facility, or vehicle rental facility necessary to fulfill the requirement to disclose information to the Federal Bureau of Investigation under this section) that the Federal Bureau of Investigation has sought or obtained records pursuant to an order under this section.

(Pub. L. 95–511, title V, §502, as added Pub. L. 105–272, title VI, §602, Oct. 20, 1998, 112 Stat. 2411.)

REFERENCES IN TEXT

Executive Order No. 12333, referred to in subsec. (a), is set out as a note under section 401 of this title.

§1863. Congressional oversight

(a) On a semiannual basis, the Attorney General shall fully inform the Permanent Select Committee on Intelligence of the House of Representatives and the Select Committee on Intelligence of the Senate concerning all requests for records under this subchapter.

(b) On a semiannual basis, the Attorney General shall provide to the Committees on the Judiciary of the House of Representatives and the Senate a report setting forth with respect to the preceding 6-month period—

(1) the total number of applications made for orders approving requests for records under this subchapter; and

(2) the total number of such orders either granted, modified, or denied.

(Pub. L. 95–511, title V, §503, as added Pub. L. 105–272, title VI, §602, Oct. 20, 1998, 112 Stat. 2412.)

CHAPTER 37—NATIONAL SECURITY SCHOLARSHIPS, FELLOWSHIPS, AND GRANTS

§ 1901. Short title, findings, and purposes

(a) Short title

This chapter may be cited as the "David L. Boren National Security Education Act of 1991".

(b) Findings

The Congress makes the following findings:

(1) The security of the United States is and will continue to depend on the ability of the United States to exercise international leadership.

(2) The ability of the United States to exercise international leadership is, and will increasingly continue to be, based on the political and economic strength of the United States, as well as on United States military strength around the world.

(3) Recent changes in the world pose threats of a new kind to international stability as Cold War tensions continue to decline while economic competition, regional conflicts, terrorist activities, and weapon proliferations have dramatically increased.

(4) The future national security and economic well-being of the United States will depend substantially on the ability of its citizens to communicate and compete by knowing the languages and cultures of other countries.

(5) The Federal Government has an interest in ensuring that the employees of its departments and agencies with national security responsibilities are prepared to meet the challenges of this changing international environment.

(6) The Federal Government also has an interest in taking actions to alleviate the problem of American undergraduate and graduate students being inadequately prepared to meet the challenges posed by increasing global interaction among nations.

(7) American colleges and universities must place a new emphasis on improving the teaching of foreign languages, area studies, counterproliferation studies, and other international fields to help meet those challenges.

(c) Purposes

The purposes of this chapter are as follows:

(1) To provide the necessary resources, accountability, and flexibility to meet the national security education needs of the United States, especially as such needs change over time.

(2) To increase the quantity, diversity, and quality of the teaching and learning of subjects in the fields of foreign languages, area studies, counterproliferation studies, and other international fields that are critical to the Nation's interest.

(3) To produce an increased pool of applicants for work in the departments and agencies of the United States Government with national security responsibilities.

(4) To expand, in conjunction with other Federal programs, the international experience, knowledge base, and perspectives on which the United States citizenry, Government employees, and leaders rely.

(5) To permit the Federal Government to advocate the cause of international education.

(Pub. L. 102–183, title VIII, § 801, Dec. 4, 1991, 105 Stat. 1271; Pub. L. 102–496, title IV, § 404(a), Oct. 24, 1992, 106 Stat. 3185; Pub. L. 105–272, title III, § 305(a)(1), Oct. 20, 1998, 112 Stat. 2400.)

AMENDMENTS

1998—Subsecs. (b)(7), (c)(2). Pub. L. 105–272 inserted "counterproliferation studies," after "area studies,".

1992—Subsec. (a). Pub. L. 102–496 amended subsec. (a) generally, inserting "David L. Boren".

§ 1902. Scholarship, fellowship, and grant program

(a) Program required

(1) In general

The Secretary of Defense shall carry out a program for—

(A) awarding scholarships to undergraduate students who—

(i) are United States citizens in order to enable such students to study, for at least one academic semester or equivalent term, in foreign countries that are critical countries (as determined under section 1903(d)(4)(A) of this title) in those languages and study areas where deficiencies exist (as identified in the assessments undertaken pursuant to section 1906(d) of this title); and

(ii) pursuant to subsection (b)(2)(A) of this section, enter into an agreement to work in a national security position or work in the field of higher education in the area of study for which the scholarship was awarded;

(B) awarding fellowships to graduate students who—

(i) are United States citizens to enable such students to pursue education as part of a graduate degree program of a United States institution of higher education in the disciplines of foreign languages, area studies, counterproliferation studies, and other international fields relating to the national security interests of the United

States that are critical areas of those disciplines (as determined under section 1903(d)(4)(B) of this title) and in which deficiencies exist (as identified in the assessments undertaken pursuant to section 1906(d) of this title); and

(ii) pursuant to subsection (b)(2)(B) of this section, enter into an agreement to work in a national security position or work in the field of education in the area of study for which the fellowship was awarded; and

(C) awarding grants to institutions of higher education to enable such institutions to establish, operate, or improve programs in foreign languages, area studies, counterproliferation studies, and other international fields that are critical areas of those disciplines (as determined under section 1903(d)(4)(C) of this title).

(2) Funding allocations

Of the amount available for obligation out of the National Security Education Trust Fund for any fiscal year for the purposes stated in paragraph (1), the Secretary shall have a goal of allocating—

(A) ⅓ of such amount for the awarding of scholarships pursuant to paragraph (1)(A);

(B) ⅓ of such amount for the awarding of fellowships pursuant to paragraph (1)(B); and

(C) ⅓ of such amount for the awarding of grants pursuant to paragraph (1)(C).

(3) Consultation with National Security Education Board

The program required under this chapter shall be carried out in consultation with the National Security Education Board established under section 1903 of this title.

(4) Contract authority

The Secretary may enter into one or more contracts, with private national organizations having an expertise in foreign languages, area studies, counterproliferation studies, and other international fields, for the awarding of the scholarships, fellowships, and grants described in paragraph (1) in accordance with the provisions of this chapter. The Secretary may enter into such contracts without regard to section 5 of title 41 or any other provision of law that requires the use of competitive procedures. In addition, the Secretary may enter into personal service contracts for periods up to one year for program administration, except that not more than 10 such contracts may be in effect at any one time.

(b) Service agreement

In awarding a scholarship or fellowship under the program, the Secretary or contract organization referred to in subsection (a)(4) of this section, as the case may be, shall require a recipient of any fellowship or any scholarship to enter into an agreement that, in return for such assistance, the recipient—

(1) will maintain satisfactory academic progress, as determined in accordance with regulations issued by the Secretary, and agrees that failure to maintain such progress shall constitute grounds upon which the Secretary or contract organization referred to in subsection (a)(4) of this section may terminate such assistance;

(2) will—

(A) not later than eight years after such recipient's completion of the study for which scholarship assistance was provided under the program, and in accordance with regulations issued by the Secretary—

(i) work in a national security position for a period specified by the Secretary, which period shall be no longer than the period for which scholarship assistance was provided; or

(ii) if the recipient demonstrates to the Secretary (in accordance with such regulations) that no national security position is available, work in the field of higher education in a discipline relating to the foreign country, foreign language, area study, counterproliferation study, or international field of study for which the scholarship was awarded, for a period specified by the Secretary, which period shall be determined in accordance with clause (i); or

(B) upon completion of such recipient's education under the program, and in accordance with such regulations—

(i) work in a national security position for a period specified by the Secretary, which period shall be not less than one and not more than three times the period for which the fellowship assistance was provided; or

(ii) if the recipient demonstrates to the Secretary (in accordance with such regulations) that no national security position is available upon the completion of the degree, work in the field of higher education in a discipline relating to the foreign country, foreign language, area study, counterproliferation study, or international field of study for which the fellowship was awarded, for a period specified by the Secretary, which period shall be established in accordance with clause (i); and

(3) if the recipient fails to meet either of the obligations set forth in paragraph (1) or (2), will reimburse the United States Government for the amount of the assistance provided the recipient under the program, together with interest at a rate determined in accordance with regulations issued by the Secretary.

(c) Evaluation of progress in language skills

The Secretary shall, through the National Security Education Program office, administer a test of the foreign language skills of each recipient of a scholarship or fellowship under this chapter before the commencement of the study or education for which the scholarship or fellowship is awarded and after the completion of such study or education. The purpose of these tests is to evaluate the progress made by recipients of scholarships and fellowships in developing foreign language skills as a result of assistance under this chapter.

(d) Distribution of assistance

In selecting the recipients for awards of scholarships, fellowships, or grants pursuant to this chapter, the Secretary or a contract organization referred to in subsection (a)(4) of this section, as the case may be, shall take into consideration (1) the extent to which the selections will result in there being an equitable geographic distribution of such scholarships, fellowships, or grants (as the case may be) among the various regions of the United States, and (2) the extent to which the distribution of scholarships and fellowships to individuals reflects the cultural, racial, and ethnic diversity of the population of the United States.

(e) Merit review

The Secretary shall award scholarships, fellowships, and grants under the program based upon a merit review process.

(f) Limitation on use of program participants

No person who receives a grant, scholarship, or fellowship or any other type of assistance under this chapter shall, as a condition of receiving such assistance or under any other circumstances, be used by any department, agency, or entity of the United States Government engaged in intelligence activities to undertake any activity on its behalf during the period such person is pursuing a program of education for which funds are provided under the program carried out under this chapter.

(g) Determination of agencies and offices of Federal Government having national security responsibilities

(1) The Secretary, in consultation with the Board, shall annually determine and develop a list identifying each agency or office of the Federal Government having national security responsibilities at which a recipient of a fellowship or scholarship under this chapter will be able to make the recipient's foreign area and language skills available to such agency or office. The Secretary shall submit the first such list to the Congress and include each subsequent list in the annual report to the Congress, as required by section 1906(b)(6) of this title.

(2) Notwithstanding section 1904 of this title, funds may not be made available from the Fund to carry out this chapter for fiscal year 1997 until 30 days after the date on which the Secretary of Defense submits to the Congress the first such list required by paragraph (1).

(Pub. L. 102–183, title VIII, § 802, Dec. 4, 1991, 105 Stat. 1271; Pub. L. 102–496, title IV, § 404(b), (c), Oct. 24, 1992, 106 Stat. 3185; Pub. L. 103–178, title III, § 311(b)(2), (d), Dec. 3, 1993, 107 Stat. 2037; Pub. L. 104–201, div. A, title X, § 1078(b)–(d), (f)(2), Sept. 23, 1996, 110 Stat. 2664–2666; Pub. L. 105–272, title III, § 305(a)(2), Oct. 20, 1998, 112 Stat. 2400.)

AMENDMENTS

1998—Subsec. (a)(1)(B)(i), (C), (4). Pub. L. 105–272, § 305(a)(2)(A), inserted "counterproliferation studies," after "area studies,".

Subsec. (b)(2)(A)(ii), (B)(ii). Pub. L. 105–272, § 305(a)(2)(B), inserted "counterproliferation study," after "area study,".

1996—Subsec. (a)(1)(A). Pub. L. 104–201, § 1078(b)(1), amended subpar. (A) generally. Prior to amendment, subpar. (A) read as follows: "awarding scholarships to undergraduate students who are United States citizens in order to enable such students to study, for at least one academic semester or equivalent term, in foreign countries that are critical countries (as determined under section 1903(d)(4)(A) of this title) in those language and study areas where deficiencies exist (as identified in the assessments undertaken pursuant to section 1906(d) of this title);".

Subsec. (a)(1)(B)(i). Pub. L. 104–201, § 1078(b)(2)(A), inserted "relating to the national security interests of the United States" after "international fields".

Subsec. (a)(1)(B)(ii). Pub. L. 104–201, § 1078(b)(2)(B), substituted "subsection (b)(2)(B)" for "subsection (b)(2)" and "work in a national security position or work in" for "work for an agency or office of the Federal Government or in".

Subsec. (b). Pub. L. 104–201, § 1078(c)(1), in introductory provisions, substituted "or any scholarship" for ", or of scholarships that provide assistance for periods that aggregate 12 months or more,".

Subsec. (b)(2). Pub. L. 104–201, § 1078(c)(2), amended par. (2) generally. Prior to amendment, par. (2) read as follows: "will, upon completion of such recipient's baccalaureate degree or education under the program, as the case may be, and in accordance with regulations issued by the Secretary, work for the Federal Government or in the field of education in the area of study for which the scholarship or fellowship was awarded for a period specified by the Secretary, which period for the recipients of scholarships shall be no more than the same period for which scholarship assistance was provided and for the recipients of fellowships shall be not less than one and not more than three times the period for which the fellowship assistance was provided; and".

Subsecs. (c) to (f). Pub. L. 104–201, § 1078(d), added subsec. (c) and redesignated former subsecs. (c) to (e) as (d) to (f), respectively.

Subsec. (g). Pub. L. 104–201, § 1078(f)(2), added subsec. (g).

1993—Subsec. (a)(1)(A). Pub. L. 103–178, § 311(b)(2)(A), (d), struck out comma after "term," and inserted before semicolon at end "in those language and study areas where deficiencies exist (as identified in the assessments undertaken pursuant to section 1906(d) of this title)".

Subsec. (a)(1)(B)(i). Pub. L. 103–178, § 311(b)(2)(B), inserted before semicolon at end "and in which deficiencies exist (as identified in the assessments undertaken pursuant to section 1906(d) of this title)".

1992—Subsec. (a)(1)(A). Pub. L. 102–496, § 404(b)(1), inserted "or equivalent term," after "semester".

Subsec. (a)(1)(B)(i). Pub. L. 102–496, § 404(b)(2), substituted "as part of a graduate degree program of a United States institution of higher education" for "in the United States".

Subsec. (a)(4). Pub. L. 102–496, § 404(b)(3), inserted at end "In addition, the Secretary may enter into personal service contracts for periods up to one year for program administration, except that not more than 10 such contracts may be in effect at any one time."

Subsecs. (e), (f). Pub. L. 102–496, § 404(c), redesignated subsec. (f) as (e) and struck out former subsec. (e) which read as follows: "The Secretary shall administer the program through the Defense Intelligence College."

SECTION REFERRED TO IN OTHER SECTIONS

This section is referred to in sections 1903, 1904, 1906, 1908 of this title.

§ 1903. National Security Education Board

(a) Establishment

The Secretary of Defense shall establish a National Security Education Board.

(b) Composition

The Board shall be composed of the following individuals or the representatives of such individuals:

(1) The Secretary of Defense, who shall serve as the chairman of the Board.

(2) The Secretary of Education.

(3) The Secretary of State.

(4) The Secretary of Commerce.

(5) The Director of Central Intelligence.

(6) The Chairperson of the National Endowment for the Humanities.

(7) Six individuals appointed by the President, by and with the advice and consent of the Senate, who shall be experts in the fields of international, language, area, and counterproliferation studies education and who may not be officers or employees of the Federal Government.

(c) Term of appointees

Each individual appointed to the Board pursuant to subsection (b)(6) of this section shall be appointed for a period specified by the President at the time of the appointment, but not to exceed four years. Such individuals shall receive no compensation for service on the Board but may receive reimbursement for travel and other necessary expenses.

(d) Functions

The Board shall perform the following functions:

(1) Develop criteria for awarding scholarships, fellowships, and grants under this chapter, including an order of priority in such awards that favors individuals expressing an interest in national security issues or pursuing a career in a national security position.

(2) Provide for wide dissemination of information regarding the activities assisted under this chapter.

(3) Establish qualifications for students desiring scholarships or fellowships, and institutions of higher education desiring grants, under this chapter, including, in the case of students desiring a scholarship or fellowship, a requirement that the student have a demonstrated commitment to the study of the discipline for which the scholarship or fellowship is to be awarded.

(4) After taking into account the annual analyses of trends in language, international, area, and counterproliferation studies under section 1906(b)(1) of this title, make recommendations to the Secretary regarding—

(A) which countries are not emphasized in other United States study abroad programs, such as countries in which few United States students are studying and countries which are of importance to the national security interests of the United States, and are, therefore, critical countries for the purposes of section 1902(a)(1)(A) of this title;

(B) which areas within the disciplines described in section 1902(a)(1)(B) of this title relating to the national security interests of the United States are areas of study in which United States students are deficient in learning and are, therefore, critical areas within those disciplines for the purposes of that section;

(C) which areas within the disciplines described in section 1902(a)(1)(C) of this title are areas in which United States students, educators, and Government employees are deficient in learning and in which insubstantial numbers of United States institutions of higher education provide training and are, therefore, critical areas within those disciplines for the purposes of that section; and

(D) how students desiring scholarships or fellowships can be encouraged to work for an agency or office of the Federal Government involved in national security affairs or national security policy upon completion of their education.

(5) Encourage applications for fellowships under this chapter from graduate students having an educational background in any academic discipline, particularly in the areas of science or technology.

(6) Provide the Secretary biennially with a list of scholarship recipients and fellowship recipients, including an assessment of their foreign area and language skills, who are available to work in a national security position.

(7) Not later than 30 days after a scholarship or fellowship recipient completes the study or education for which assistance was provided under the program, provide the Secretary with a report fully describing the foreign area and language skills obtained by the recipient as a result of the assistance.

(8) Review the administration of the program required under this chapter.

(Pub. L. 102–183, title VIII, §803, Dec. 4, 1991, 105 Stat. 1273; Pub. L. 102–496, title IV, §404(d), Oct. 24, 1992, 106 Stat. 3186; Pub. L. 104–201, div. A, title X, §1078(e), Sept. 23, 1996, 110 Stat. 2666; Pub. L. 105–272, title III, §305(a)(3), (b), Oct. 20, 1998, 112 Stat. 2401; Pub. L. 105–277, div. G, title XIII, §1335(g), Oct. 21, 1998, 112 Stat. 2681–788.)

AMENDMENTS

1998—Subsec. (b)(6). Pub. L. 105–277, §1335(g)(1), redesignated par. (7) as (6) and struck out former par. (6) which read as follows: "The Secretary of Energy."

Pub. L. 105–272, §305(b), amended par. (6) generally. Prior to amendment, par. (6) read as follows: "The Director of the United States Information Agency."

Subsec. (b)(7). Pub. L. 105–277, §1335(g)(1)(B), redesignated par. (8) as (7). Former par. (7) redesignated (6).

Subsec. (b)(8). Pub. L. 105–277, §1335(g)(1)(B), redesignated par. (8) as (7).

Pub. L. 105–272, §305(a)(3), substituted "area, and counterproliferation" for "and area".

Subsec. (c). Pub. L. 105–277, §1335(g)(2), substituted "subsection (b)(6)" for "subsection (b)(7)".

Subsec. (d)(4). Pub. L. 105–272, §305(a)(3), substituted "area, and counterproliferation" for "and area" in introductory provisions.

1996—Subsec. (d)(1). Pub. L. 104–201, §1078(e)(1), inserted before period at end ", including an order of priority in such awards that favors individuals expressing an interest in national security issues or pursuing a career in a national security position".

Subsec. (d)(4). Pub. L. 104–201, §1078(e)(2)(A), in introductory provisions, substituted "After taking into account the annual analyses of trends in language, international, and area studies under section 1906(b)(1) of this title, make recommendations" for "Make recommendations".

Subsec. (d)(4)(A). Pub. L. 104–201, §1078(e)(2)(B), substituted "and countries which are of importance to the national security interests of the United States" after "are studying".

Subsec. (d)(4)(B). Pub. L. 104–201, §1078(e)(2)(C), substituted "relating to the national security interests of the United States" after "section 1902(a)(1)(B) of this title".

Subsec. (d)(5) to (8). Pub. L. 104–201, §1078(e)(3), (4), added pars. (5) to (7) and redesignated former par. (5) as (8).

1992—Subsec. (b)(7). Pub. L. 102–496, §404(d)(2), added par. (7). Former par. (7) redesignated (8).

Subsec. (b)(8). Pub. L. 102–496, §404(d)(1), (3), redesignated par. (7) as (8), substituted "Six individuals" for "Four individuals", and inserted before period at end "and who may not be officers or employees of the Federal Government".

EFFECTIVE DATE OF 1998 AMENDMENT

Amendment by Pub. L. 105–277 effective on earlier of Oct. 1, 1999, or date of abolition of the United States Information Agency pursuant to reorganization plan described in section 6601 of Title 22, Foreign Relations and Intercourse, see section 1301 of Pub. L. 105–277, set out as an Effective Date note under section 6531 of Title 22.

SECTION REFERRED TO IN OTHER SECTIONS

This section is referred to in sections 1902, 1906, 1908 of this title.

§1904. National Security Education Trust Fund

(a) Establishment of Fund

There is established in the Treasury of the United States a trust fund to be known as the "National Security Education Trust Fund". The assets of the Fund consist of amounts appropriated to the Fund and amounts credited to the Fund under subsection (e) of this section.

(b) Availability of sums in Fund

Sums in the Fund shall, to the extent provided in appropriations Acts, be available—

(1) for awarding scholarships, fellowships, and grants in accordance with the provisions of this chapter; and

(2) for properly allocable costs of the Federal Government for the administration of the program under this chapter.

(c) Investment of Fund assets

The Secretary of the Treasury shall invest in full the amount in the Fund that is not immediately necessary for expenditure. Such investments may be made only in interest-bearing obligations of the United States or in obligations guaranteed as to both principal and interest by the United States. For such purpose, such obligations may be acquired on original issue at the issue price or by purchase of outstanding obligations at the market price. The purposes for which obligations of the United States may be issued under chapter 31 of title 31 are hereby extended to authorize the issuance at par of special obligations exclusively to the Fund. Such special obligations shall bear interest at a rate equal to the average rate of interest, computed as to the end of the calendar month next preceding the date of such issue, borne by all marketable interest-bearing obligations of the United States then forming a part of the public debt, except that where such average rate is not a multiple of ⅛ of 1 percent, the rate of interest of such special obligations shall be the multiple of ⅛ of 1 percent next lower than such average rate. Such special obligations shall be issued only if the Secretary of the Treasury determines that the purchases of other interest-bearing obligations of the United States, or of obligations guaranteed as to both principal and interest by the United States or original issue or at the market price, is not in the public interest.

(d) Authority to sell obligations

Any obligation acquired by the Fund (except special obligations issued exclusively to the Fund) may be sold by the Secretary of the Treasury at the market price, and such special obligations may be redeemed at par plus accrued interest.

(e) Amounts credited to Fund

(1) The interest on, and the proceeds from the sale or redemption of, any obligations held in the Fund shall be credited to and form a part of the Fund.

(2) Any amount paid to the United States under section 1902(b)(3) of this title shall be credited to and form a part of the Fund.

(3) Any gifts of money shall be credited to and form a part of the Fund.

(Pub. L. 102–183, title VIII, §804, Dec. 4, 1991, 105 Stat. 1274; Pub. L. 102–496, title IV, §404(e), Oct. 24, 1992, 106 Stat. 3186; Pub. L. 103–160, div. A, title III, §375, Nov. 30, 1993, 107 Stat. 1637.)

AMENDMENTS

1993—Subsec. (b). Pub. L. 103–160, §375(b), struck out "(1)" before "Sums in the Fund", redesignated former subpars. (A) and (B) as pars. (1) and (2), respectively, and struck out former par. (2) which read as follows: "No amount may be appropriated to the Fund, or obligated from the Fund, unless authorized by law."

Subsec. (e)(3). Pub. L. 103–160, §375(a), added par. (3).

1992—Subsec. (c). Pub. L. 102–496 substituted "expenditure" for "obligation" in first sentence.

SECTION REFERRED TO IN OTHER SECTIONS

This section is referred to in sections 1902, 1905, 1908, 1910 of this title.

§1905. Regulations and administrative provisions

(a) Regulations

The Secretary may prescribe regulations to carry out the program required by this chapter. Before prescribing any such regulations, the Secretary shall submit a copy of the proposed regulations to the Select Committee on Intelligence of the Senate and the Permanent Select Committee on Intelligence of the House of Representatives. Such proposed regulations may not take effect until 30 days after the date on which they are submitted to those committees.

(b) Acceptance and use of gifts

In order to conduct the program required by this chapter, the Secretary may—

(1) receive money and other property donated, bequeathed, or devised, without condition or restriction other than that it be used for the purpose of conducting the program required by this chapter; and

(2) may use, sell, or otherwise dispose of such property for that purpose.

(c) Voluntary services

In order to conduct the program required by this chapter, the Secretary may accept and use the services of voluntary and noncompensated personnel.

(d) Necessary expenditures

Expenditures necessary to conduct the program required by this chapter shall be paid from the Fund, subject to section 1904(b) of this title.

(Pub. L. 102–183, title VIII, § 805, Dec. 4, 1991, 105 Stat. 1275.)

§ 1906. Annual report

(a) Annual report

The Secretary shall submit to the President and to the Congress an annual report of the conduct of the program required by this chapter. The report shall be submitted each year at the time that the President's budget for the next fiscal year is submitted to Congress pursuant to section 1105 of title 31.

(b) Contents of report

Each such report shall contain—

(1) an analysis of the trends within language, international, area, and counterproliferation studies, along with a survey of such areas as the Secretary determines are receiving inadequate attention;

(2) the effect on those trends of activities under the program required by this chapter;

(3) an analysis of the assistance provided under the program for the previous fiscal year, to include the subject areas being addressed and the nature of the assistance provided;

(4) an analysis of the performance of the individuals who received assistance under the program during the previous fiscal year, to include the degree to which assistance was terminated under the program and the extent to which individual recipients failed to meet their obligations under the program;

(5) an analysis of the results of the program for the previous fiscal year, and cumulatively, to include, at a minimum—

(A) the percentage of individuals who have received assistance under the program who subsequently became employees of the United States Government;

(B) in the case of individuals who did not subsequently become employees of the United States Government, an analysis of the reasons why they did not become employees and an explanation as to what use, if any, was made of the assistance by those recipients; and

(C) the uses made of grants to educational institutions;

(6) the current list of agencies and offices of the Federal Government required to be developed by section 1902(g) of this title; and

(7) any legislative changes recommended by the Secretary to facilitate the administration of the program or otherwise to enhance its objectives.

(c) Submission of initial report

The first report under this section shall be submitted at the time the budget for fiscal year 1994 is submitted to Congress.

(d) Consultation

During the preparation of each report required by subsection (a) of this section, the Secretary shall consult with the members of the Board specified in paragraphs (1) through (7) of section 1903(b) of this title. Each such member shall submit to the Secretary an assessment of their hiring needs in the areas of language and area studies and a projection of the deficiencies in such areas. The Secretary shall include all assessments in the report required by subsection (a) of this section.

(Pub. L. 102–183, title VIII, § 806, Dec. 4, 1991, 105 Stat. 1276; Pub. L. 103–178, title III, § 311(b)(1), Dec. 3, 1993, 107 Stat. 2037; Pub. L. 104–201, div. A, title X, § 1078(f)(3), Sept. 23, 1996, 110 Stat. 2667; Pub. L. 105–272, title III, § 305(a)(4), Oct. 20, 1998, 112 Stat. 2401.)

AMENDMENTS

1998—Subsec. (b)(1). Pub. L. 105–272 substituted "area, and counterproliferation" for "and area".

1996—Subsec. (b)(5) to (7). Pub. L. 104–201 struck out "and" at end of par. (5), added par. (6), and redesignated former par. (6) as (7).

1993—Subsec. (d). Pub. L. 103–178 added subsec. (d).

SECTION REFERRED TO IN OTHER SECTIONS

This section is referred to in sections 1902, 1903 of this title.

§ 1907. General Accounting Office audits

The conduct of the program required by this chapter may be audited by the General Accounting Office under such rules and regulations as may be prescribed by the Comptroller General of the United States. Representatives of the General Accounting Office shall have access to all books, accounts, records, reports, and files and all other papers, things, or property of the Department of Defense pertaining to such activities and necessary to facilitate the audit.

(Pub. L. 102–183, title VIII, § 807, Dec. 4, 1991, 105 Stat. 1276.)

§ 1908. Definitions

For the purpose of this chapter:

(1) The term "Board" means the National Security Education Board established pursuant to section 1903 of this title.

(2) The term "Fund" means the National Security Education Trust Fund established pursuant to section 1904 of this title.

(3) The term "institution of higher education" has the meaning given that term by section 1001 of title 20.

(4) The term "national security position" means a position—

(A) having national security responsibilities in a[1] agency or office of the Federal Government that has national security responsibilities, as determined under section 1902(g) of this title; and

(B) in which the individual in such position makes their foreign language skills available to such agency or office.

(Pub. L. 102–183, title VIII, § 808, Dec. 4, 1991, 105 Stat. 1276; Pub. L. 104–201, div. A, title X, § 1078(f)(1), Sept. 23, 1996, 110 Stat. 2666; Pub. L. 105–244, title I, § 102(a)(15), Oct. 7, 1998, 112 Stat. 1622.)

AMENDMENTS

1998—Par. (3). Pub. L. 105–244 substituted "section 1001" for "section 1141(a)".

1996—Par. (4). Pub. L. 104–201 added par. (4).

EFFECTIVE DATE OF 1998 AMENDMENT

Amendment by Pub. L. 105–244 effective Oct. 1, 1998, except as otherwise provided in Pub. L. 105–244, see sec-

[1] So in original. Probably should be "an".

tion 3 of Pub. L. 105–244, set out as a note under section 1001 of Title 20, Education.

§ 1909. Fiscal year 1992 funding

(a) Authorization of appropriations to Fund

There is hereby authorized to be appropriated to the Fund for fiscal year 1992 the sum of $150,000,000.

(b) Authorization of obligations from Fund

During fiscal year 1992, there may be obligated from the Fund such amounts as may be provided in appropriations Acts, not to exceed $35,000,000. Amounts made available for obligation from the Fund for fiscal year 1992 shall remain available until expended.

(Pub. L. 102–183, title VIII, § 809, Dec. 4, 1991, 105 Stat. 1277.)

§ 1910. Funding

(a) Fiscal years 1993 and 1994

Amounts appropriated to carry out this chapter for fiscal years 1993 and 1994 shall remain available until expended.

(b) Fiscal years 1995 and 1996

There is authorized to be appropriated from, and may be obligated from, the Fund for each of the fiscal years 1995 and 1996 not more than the amount credited to the Fund in interest only for the preceding fiscal year under section 1904(e) of this title.

(Pub. L. 102–183, title VIII, § 810, as added Pub. L. 103–178, title III, § 311(c), Dec. 3, 1993, 107 Stat. 2037.)

CHAPTER 38—CENTRAL INTELLIGENCE AGENCY RETIREMENT AND DISABILITY

SUBCHAPTER I—DEFINITIONS

SUBCHAPTER II—CENTRAL INTELLIGENCE AGENCY RETIREMENT AND DISABILITY SYSTEM

PART A—ESTABLISHMENT OF SYSTEM

PART B—CONTRIBUTIONS

PART C—COMPUTATION OF ANNUITIES

PART D—BENEFITS ACCRUING TO CERTAIN PARTICIPANTS

CODIFICATION

The Central Intelligence Agency Retirement Act, comprising this chapter, was originally enacted as the Central Intelligence Agency Retirement Act of 1964 for Certain Employees by Pub. L. 88–643, Oct. 13, 1964, 78 Stat. 1043, as amended by Pub. L. 90–539, Sept. 30, 1968, 82 Stat. 902; Pub. L. 91–185, Dec. 30, 1969, 83 Stat. 847; Pub. L. 91–626, §§ 1–6, Dec. 31, 1970, 84 Stat. 1872–1874; Pub. L. 93–31, May 8, 1973, 87 Stat. 65; Pub. L. 93–210, § 1(a), Dec. 28, 1973, 87 Stat. 908; Pub. L. 94–361, title VIII, § 801(b), July 14, 1976, 90 Stat. 929; Pub. L. 94–522, title I, §§ 101, 102, title II, §§ 201–213, Oct. 17, 1976, 90 Stat. 2467–2471; Ex. Ord. No. 12273, Jan. 16, 1981, 46 F.R. 5854; Ex. Ord. No. 12326, Sept. 30, 1981, 46 F.R. 48889; Pub. L. 97–269, title VI, §§ 602–611, Sept. 27, 1982, 96 Stat. 1145–1148, 1152–1153; Ex. Ord. No. 12443, Sept. 27, 1983, 48 F.R. 44751; Ex. Ord. No. 12485, July 13, 1984, 49 F.R. 28827; Pub. L. 98–618, title III, § 302, Nov. 8, 1984, 98 Stat. 3300; Pub. L. 99–169, title VII, § 702, Dec. 4, 1985, 99 Stat. 1008; Pub. L. 99–335, title V, §§ 501–506, June 6, 1986, 100 Stat. 622–624; Pub. L. 99–514, § 2, Oct. 22, 1986, 100 Stat. 2095; Pub. L. 99–569, title III, § 302(a), Oct. 27, 1986, 100 Stat. 3192; Pub. L. 100–178, title IV, §§ 401(a), 402(a), (b)(1), (2), Dec. 2, 1987, 101 Stat. 1012–1014; Pub. L. 100–453, title III, § 302(a), (b)(1), (c)(1), (d)(1), (2), title V, § 502, Sept. 29, 1988, 102 Stat. 1906, 1907, 1909; Pub. L. 101–193, title III, §§ 302–304(a), 307(b), Nov. 30, 1989, 103 Stat. 1703, 1707; Pub. L. 102–83, § 5(c)(2), Aug. 6, 1991, 105 Stat. 406; Pub. L. 102–88, title III, §§ 302–305(a), 306–307(b), Aug. 14, 1991, 105 Stat. 431–433; Pub. L. 102–183, title III, §§ 302(a)–(c), 303(a), 304–306(b), 307, 309(a), 310(a), Dec. 4, 1991, 105 Stat. 1262–1266; Pub. L. 102–496, title III, § 304(b), Oct. 24, 1992, 106 Stat. 3183, and was set out as a note under section 403 of this title. The Act is shown herein, however, as having been added by Pub. L. 102–496, title VIII, § 802, Oct. 24, 1992, 106 Stat. 3196, without reference to such intervening amendments because of the extensive revision and restatement of the Act's provisions by Pub. L. 102–496.

SUBCHAPTER I—DEFINITIONS

§ 2001. Definitions relating to the system

When used in this chapter:

(1) Agency

The term "Agency" means the Central Intelligence Agency.

(2) Director

The term "Director" means the Director of Central Intelligence.

(3) Qualifying service

The term "qualifying service" means service determined by the Director to have been performed in carrying out duties described in section 2013 of this title.

(4) Fund balance

The term "fund balance" means the sum of—

(A) the investments of the fund calculated at par value; and

(B) the cash balance of the fund on the books of the Treasury.

(5) Unfunded liability

The term "unfunded liability" means the estimated amount by which—

(A) the present value of all benefits payable from the fund exceeds

(B) the sum of—

(i) the present value of deductions to be withheld from the future basic pay of participants subject to subchapter II of this chapter and of future Agency contributions to be made on the behalf of such participants;

(ii) the present value of Government payments to the fund under sections 2091(c) and 2091(d) of this title; and

(iii) the fund balance as of the date on which the unfunded liability is determined.

(6) Normal cost

The term "normal cost" means the level percentage of payroll required to be deposited in the fund to meet the cost of benefits payable under the system (computed in accordance with generally accepted actuarial practice on an entry-age basis) less the value of retirement benefits earned under another retirement system for government employees and less the cost of credit allowed for military service.

(7) Lump-sum credit

The term "lump-sum credit" means the unrefunded amount consisting of retirement deductions made from a participant's basic pay and amounts deposited by a participant covering earlier service, including any amounts deposited under section 2082(h) of this title.

(8) Congressional intelligence committees

The term "congressional intelligence committees" means the Permanent Select Committee on Intelligence of the House of Representatives and the Select Committee on Intelligence of the Senate.

(9) Employee

The term "employee" includes an officer of the Agency.

(Pub. L. 88–643, title I, § 101, as added Pub. L. 102–496, title VIII, § 802, Oct. 24, 1992, 106 Stat. 3197; amended Pub. L. 103–178, title II, § 202(a)(1), Dec. 3, 1993, 107 Stat. 2025.)

PRIOR PROVISIONS

A prior section 101 of Pub. L. 88–643, title I, Oct. 13, 1964, 78 Stat. 1043, provided a short title for Pub. L. 88–643 as the "Central Intelligence Agency Retirement Act of 1964 for Certain Employees" and was set out as a note under section 403 of this title prior to the general amendment of Pub. L. 88–643 by section 802 of Pub. L. 102–496.

AMENDMENTS

1993—Par. (7). Pub. L. 103–178 substituted "basic pay and amounts deposited" for "basic pay, amounts deposited" and struck out ", and interest determined under section 2121 of this title" after "section 2082(h) of this title".

EFFECTIVE DATE OF 1993 AMENDMENT

Section 202(b) of Pub. L. 103–178 provided that: "The amendments made by subsection (a) [amending this section and sections 2011, 2021, 2031, 2032, 2034, 2035, 2051, 2052, 2054, 2071, 2094, 2095, 2131, and 2154 of this title] shall take effect as of February 1, 1993."

EFFECTIVE DATE

Section 805 of Pub. L. 102–496 provided that: "The amendments made by sections 802 and 803 [enacting this chapter and amending sections 403n, 403r, and 403s of this title, sections 8347 and 8423 of Title 5, Government Organization and Employees, section 1605 of Title 10, Armed Forces, and provisions set out as a note under section 402 of this title] shall take effect on the first day of the fourth month beginning after the date of the enactment of this Act [Oct. 24, 1992]."

EFFECTIVE DATE OF AMENDMENTS TO PUB. L. 88–643 PRIOR TO ENACTMENT OF PUB. L. 102–496

Pub. L. 102–183, title III, §302(d), Dec. 4, 1991, 105 Stat. 1263, provided that: "The amendments made by this section [amending sections 204(b)(3), 221(c)–(e), and 232(c)–(e) of Pub. L. 88–643] shall take effect on the first day of the fourth month beginning after the date of the enactment of this Act [Dec. 4, 1991] and shall apply with respect to annuities payable to children by reason of the death of a participant or annuitant on or after that date."

Pub. L. 102–183, title III, §303(b), Dec. 4, 1991, 105 Stat. 1264, provided that: "(1) The amendments made by subsection (a) [amending section 221(p)–(r) of Pub. L. 88–643] shall take effect on the first day of the fourth month beginning after the date of the enactment of this Act [Dec. 4, 1991].

"(2)(A) The amendment made by subsection (a)(2) [enacting section 221(q) of Pub. L. 88–643] shall apply with respect to participants and former participants regardless of whether they retire before, on, or after the effective date specified in paragraph (1), except that paragraph (1)(A) of section 221(q) of the Central Intelligence Agency Retirement Act of 1964 for Certain Employees (as added by subsection (a)(2)) shall apply only with respect to participants who retire on or after that effective date.

"(B) In applying the provisions of paragraph (1)(B) of section 221(q) of the Central Intelligence Agency Retirement Act of 1964 for Certain Employees (as added by subsection (a)(2)) to a participant or former participant who retires before the effective date specified in paragraph (1)—

"(i) the 18-month period referred to in that paragraph shall be considered to begin on the effective date specified in paragraph (1); and

"(ii) the amount referred to in paragraph (2) of that section (as added by subsection (a)(2)) shall be computed without regard to the provisions of subparagraph (B)(ii) of such paragraph (relating to interest)."

Pub. L. 102–183, title III, §306(c), Dec. 4, 1991, 105 Stat. 1265, provided that:

"(1) The amendment made by subsection (a)(1) [amending section 226(a) of Pub. L. 88–643] shall be deemed to have become effective as of September 30, 1990, and shall apply in the case of annuitants whose divorce occurs on or after that date.

"(2) The amendments made by subsections (a)(2) and (a)(3) [amending section 226(a) of Pub. L. 88–643] shall be deemed to have become effective as of September 29, 1988."

Pub. L. 102–183, title III, §309(b), Dec. 4, 1991, 105 Stat. 1266, provided that: "Subsection (h) of section 304 of the Central Intelligence Agency Retirement Act of 1964 for Certain Employees [Pub. L. 88–643], as added by subsection (a), shall be deemed to have become effective as of December 2, 1987."

Pub. L. 102–183, title III, §310(b), Dec. 4, 1991, 105 Stat. 1267, provided that: "The amendment made by subsection (a) [amending section 204(b)(4) of Pub. L. 88–643] shall apply only to a former husband or wife of a participant or former participant whose divorce from the participant or former participant becomes final after the date of the enactment of this Act [Dec. 4, 1991]."

Pub. L. 102–88, title III, §305(b), Aug. 14, 1991, 105 Stat. 432, provided that:

"(1) The amendments made by subsection (a) [amending sections 221, 222, and 232 of Pub. L. 88–643] relating to widows or widowers shall apply in the case of a surviving spouse's remarriage occurring on or after July 27, 1989, and with respect to periods beginning after such date.

"(2) The amendments made by subsection (a) relating to former spouses shall apply with respect to any former spouse whose remarriage occurs after the date of enactment of this Act [Aug. 14, 1991]."

Amendment by section 307 of Pub. L. 102–88 (amending sections 224 and 225 of Pub. L. 88–643) effective as of Oct. 1, 1990, and no benefits provided pursuant to such amendment to be payable with respect to any period before such date, see section 307(d) of Pub. L. 102–88, set out as an Effective Date of 1991 Amendment note under section 403p of this title.

Pub. L. 101–193, title III, §304(b), Nov. 30, 1989, 103 Stat. 1703, provided that: "The amendment made by this section [amending section 224(a)(2) of Pub. L. 88–643] shall be effective as of October 1, 1986."

Pub. L. 100–453, title III, §302(b)(2), Sept. 29, 1988, 102 Stat. 1907, provided that: "The amendments made by paragraph (1) [amending section 224 of Pub. L. 88–643] shall take effect as of October 1, 1986."

Pub. L. 100–453, title III, §302(c)(2), Sept. 29, 1988, 102 Stat. 1907, provided that: "The amendment made by paragraph (1) [amending section 225(a) of Pub. L. 88–643] shall take effect as of December 2, 1987."

Pub. L. 100–453, title III, §302(d)(3), Sept. 29, 1988, 102 Stat. 1907, provided that: "The amendment made by this subsection [amending section 221(n), (p) of Pub. L. 88–643] shall apply to marriages which occur on or after May 7, 1985."

Pub. L. 100–178, title IV, §402(c)–(e), Dec. 2, 1987, 101 Stat. 1014, provided that:

"(c)(1) Except as provided in paragraph (2), the amendments made by this section [amending section 403n of this title and sections 221(*o*)(2), 232(b), and 304 of Pub. L. 88–643] shall take effect on November 15, 1982, the effective date of the Central Intelligence Agency Spouses' Retirement Equity Act of 1982.

"(2) The amendment made by subsection (b)(2) [amending section 304 of Pub. L. 88–643] shall take effect on January 1, 1987, the effective date of the Federal Employees' Retirement System Act of 1986.

"(d) Nothing in this section or any amendment made by this section shall be construed to require the forfeiture by any individual of benefits received before the date of the enactment of this Act [Dec. 2, 1987].

"(e) Nothing in this section or any amendment made by this section shall be construed to require a reduction in the level of benefits received by any individual who was receiving benefits under section 232 of the Central Intelligence Agency Retirement Act of 1964 for Certain Employees [Pub. L. 88–643] before the date of enactment of this Act [Dec. 2, 1987]".

Amendment by section 302(a) of Pub. L. 99–569 (enacting section 224 of Pub. L. 88–643) effective Oct. 1, 1986, see section 302(d) of Pub. L. 99–569, set out as an Effective Date of 1986 Amendment note under section 403n of this title.

Pub. L. 97–269, title VI, §613, Sept. 27, 1982, 96 Stat. 1154, provided that:

"(a) Except as provided in subsections (b) and (c) of this section, this title [enacting section 403n of this title and sections 222 and 223 of Pub. L. 88–643 and amending sections 204, 211, 221, 234, and 263 of Pub. L. 88–643] shall take effect on November 15, 1982.

"(b) The provisions of section 222(a) of the Central Intelligence Agency Retirement Act of 1964 for Certain Employees [Pub. L. 88–643], as added by this title, regarding the rights of former spouses to an annuity shall apply in the case of any individual who after the effective date of this title [Nov. 15, 1982] becomes a former spouse of an individual who separates from service with the Agency after such date.

"(c) Except to the extent provided in section 223 of the Central Intelligence Agency Retirement Act of 1964 for Certain Employees [Pub. L. 88–643], the provisions of section 221(b) (as amended by this title) and the provisions of subsections (b) and (c) of section 222 of such

Act, as added by this title, regarding the rights of former spouses to receive survivor annuities shall apply in the case of any individual who after the effective date of this title [Nov. 15, 1982] becomes a former spouse of a participant or former participant in the Central Intelligence Agency Retirement and Disability System.''

Pub. L. 94–522, title II, § 215, Oct. 17, 1976, 90 Stat. 2472, provided that:

''(a) This Act [amending Pub. L. 88–643] shall become effective October 1, 1976.

''(b) The amendments made by sections 201(a), (b), (c), and (d), 202, and 208 [amending sections 204(a), (b)(2), (3)(i), 221(b) and 232(b) of Pub. L. 88–643] shall not apply in the case of participants who died before January 8, 1971. The amendments made by section 201(e) [amending section 204 of Pub. L. 88–643] shall not apply in the case of participants who died before April 9, 1974. The rights of such persons and their survivors shall continue in the same manner and to the same extent as if such amendments had not been enacted.

''(c) The amendment made by section 203 [enacting section 221(f)(2) of Pub. L. 88–643] shall apply to a participant who married prior to enactment [Oct. 17, 1976] but only if the election is made within one year after enactment [Oct. 17, 1976].

''(d) The amendment made by section 210 [amending section 251 of Pub. L. 88–643] is effective only with respect to annuity accruing for full months beginning after January 8, 1971; but any part of a period of separation referred to in such amendment in which the participant or former participant was receiving benefits under chapter 81 of title 5, United States Code or any earlier statute on which such chapter is based shall be counted whether the person returns to duty before, on, or after January 8, 1971. With respect to any person retired before such date of enactment, any such part of a period of separation shall be counted only upon application of the retired person.

''(e) The amendment in section 211 [amending section 252(a)(2) of Pub. L. 88–643] to credit certain service in the Public Health Service is effective as of April 8, 1960, and the amendment to credit certain service in the National Oceanic and Atmospheric Administration is effective as of September 14, 1961.

''(f) The amendment in section 212 [enacting section 264 of Pub. L. 88–643] is effective as of June 30, 1974.

''(g) The amendment to recompute a reduced annuity during periods when not married in section 202 [amending section 221(b) of Pub. L. 88–643] shall apply to annuities which commence before, on, or after the date of enactment of this Act [Oct. 17, 1976], but no increase in annuity shall be paid for any period prior to November 1, 1974.

''(h) Annuity increases under sections 204 [enacting section 221(*l*) of Pub. L. 88–643] and 214 [set out below] shall apply to annuities which commence before, on, or after the date of enactment of this Act [Oct. 17, 1976], but no increase in annuity shall be paid for any period prior to August 1, 1974, or the date on which the annuity commences, whichever is later.''

Pub. L. 93–210, § 1(b), Dec. 28, 1973, 87 Stat. 908, provided that: ''The amendments made by subsection (a) [amending section 291(b) of Pub. L. 88–643] shall apply only with respect to annuities which commence on or after July 2, 1973.''

Pub. L. 91–185, § 6, Dec. 30, 1969, 83 Stat. 849, provided that:

''(a) The amendments made by section 1 [amending section 211(a) of Pub. L. 88–643, set out above] shall become effective at the beginning of the first applicable pay period beginning after December 31, 1969.

''(b) The amendments made by sections 3, 4 [amending sections 231(a) and 232(h) of Pub. L. 88–643], and 2 [amending section 221 of Pub. L. 88–643], with the exception of 2(c) [amending subsec. (c) thereof], shall become effective October 20, 1969.

''(c) The amendments made by sections 2(c) and 5 [amending sections 221(c) and 291 of Pub. L. 88–643] shall become effective November 1, 1969.

''(d) The amendments made by sections 2(a), 2(e), 3, and 4(a)(1)–(2) [amending section 221(a), adding section 221(h), and amending sections 231(a) and 232(b) of Pub. L. 88–643] shall not apply in the cases of persons retired or otherwise separated prior to October 20, 1969, and the rights of such persons and their survivors shall continue in the same manner and to the same extent as if such sections had not been enacted.''

SHORT TITLE OF 1993 AMENDMENT

Pub. L. 103–36, § 1, June 8, 1993, 107 Stat. 104, provided that: ''This Act [amending section 2053 of this title and enacting provisions set out as a note under section 403–4 of this title] may be cited as the 'Central Intelligence Agency Voluntary Separation Pay Act'.''

SHORT TITLE OF 1992 AMENDMENT

Section 801 of title VIII of Pub. L. 102–496 provided that: ''This title [enacting this chapter, amending sections 403n, 403r, 403r–1, and 403s of this title, sections 8347 and 8423 of Title 5, Government Organization and Employees, section 1605 of Title 10, Armed Forces and sections 4071b to 4071d of Title 22, Foreign Relations and Intercourse, enacting provisions set out as notes under this section, and amending provisions set out as a note under section 402 of this title] may be cited as the 'CIARDS Technical Corrections Act of 1992'.''

SHORT TITLE OF 1982 AMENDMENT

Pub. L. 97–269, title VI, § 601, Sept. 27, 1982, 96 Stat. 1145, provided that: ''This title [enacting section 403n of this title and amending Pub. L. 88–643] may be cited as the 'Central Intelligence Agency Spouses' Retirement Equity Act of 1982'.''

SHORT TITLE

Section 1(a) of Pub. L. 88–643, as added by Pub. L. 102–496, title VIII, § 802, Oct. 24, 1992, 106 Stat. 3196, provided that: ''This Act [enacting this chapter] may be cited as the 'Central Intelligence Agency Retirement Act'.''

SAVINGS PROVISION

Section 804 of Pub. L. 102–496 provided that:

''(a) PRIOR ELECTIONS.—Any election made under the Central Intelligence Agency Retirement Act of 1964 for Certain Employees [Pub. L. 88–643 prior to enactment of Pub. L. 102–496, formerly set out as a note under section 403 of this title] before the effective date specified in section 805 [set out as an Effective Date note above] shall not be affected by the amendment made by section 802 [enacting this chapter] and shall be deemed to have been made under the corresponding provision of that Act as restated by section 802 as the Central Intelligence Agency Retirement Act.

''(b) REFERENCES.—Any reference in any other Act, or in any Executive order, rule, or regulation, to the Central Intelligence Agency Retirement Act of 1964 for Certain Employees, or to a provision of that Act, shall be deemed to refer to that Act and to the corresponding provision of that Act, as restated by section 802 as the Central Intelligence Agency Retirement Act.''

FUNDING REQUIREMENTS FOR AMENDMENTS TO PUB. L. 88–643 PRIOR TO ENACTMENT OF PUB. L. 102–496

Pub. L. 100–453, title III, § 302(e), Sept. 29, 1988, 102 Stat. 1907, provided that: ''Any new spending authority (within the meaning of section 401(c) of the Congressional Budget Act of 1974 [2 U.S.C. 651(c)]) provided pursuant to the amendments made by this section [enacting section 226 and amending sections 221, 224, and 225 of Pub. L. 88–643] shall be effective for any fiscal year only to such extent or in such amounts as are provided in appropriations Acts.''

For provision that any new spending authority (within the meaning of section 401(c) of the Congressional Budget Act of 1974) provided pursuant to the amendments made to sections 224 and 225 of Pub. L. 88–643 by section 307 of Pub. L. 102–88 be effective for any fiscal year only to such extent or in such amounts as are provided in advance in appropriation Acts, see section 307(c) of Pub. L. 102–88, set out as a Compliance With Budget Act note under section 403p of this title.

CENTRAL INTELLIGENCE AGENCY RETIREMENT AND DISABILITY FUND; ANNUITY INCREASE PAYMENT; MONTHLY RATE

Pub. L. 94–522, title II, § 214, Oct. 17, 1976, 90 Stat. 2472, provided that:

"(a) An annuity payable from the Central Intelligence Agency Retirement and Disability Fund to an annuitant which is based on a separation occurring prior to October 20, 1969, is increased by $240 per annum.

"(b) In lieu of any increase based on an increase under subsection (a) of this section, an annuity payable from the Central Intelligence Agency Retirement and Disability Fund to the surviving spouse of an annuitant, which is based on a separation occurring prior to October 20, 1969, shall be increased by $132 per annum.

"(c) The monthly rate of an annuity resulting from an increase under this section shall be considered as the monthly rate of annuity payable under section 221(a) of the Central Intelligence Agency Retirement Act of 1964 for Certain Employees, as amended (78 Stat. 1043; 50 U.S.C. 403 note) [section 221 of Pub. L. 88–643 prior to enactment of Pub. L. 102–496; see 50 U.S.C. 2031(a)] for purposes of computing the minimum annuity under new section 221(*l*) of the Act, as added by section 204 of this Act."

TEMPORARY RETIREMENT CONTRIBUTIONS AND PROCEDURES FOR CERTAIN PARTICIPANTS

For temporary provisions providing modified contributions and procedures for officers and employees participating in the Central Intelligence Agency Retirement and Disability System who are also required to pay employment taxes relating to benefits under title II of the Social Security Act, 42 U.S.C. 401 et seq., until they are covered by a new Government retirement system or Jan. 1, 1986, whichever is earlier, see title II of Pub. L. 98–168, set out as a note under section 8331 of Title 5, Government Organization and Employees.

CONTINGENT ONCE-A-YEAR ADJUSTMENT IN ANNUITIES

For provisions which directed the President, subject to certain conditions, to provide for a single cost-of-living adjustment in the annuities paid under the Central Intelligence Agency Retirement Act of 1964 for Certain Employees [Pub. L. 88–643] during the period Sept. 1, 1980, to Aug. 31, 1981, and which further directed that, subject to the enactment of specified legislation providing for the adjustment of annuities paid under section 8331 et seq. of Title 5, Government Organization and Employees, the President exercise the authority vested in him under section 292 of the Central Intelligence Agency Retirement Act of 1964 for Certain Employees [Pub. L. 88–643] to provide for cost-of-living adjustments in the annuities paid under that Act on an identical basis, see Pub. L. 96–342, title VIII, § 812(a)(3), (4), (b)(3), (4), (c), Sept. 8, 1980, 94 Stat. 1098, set out as a note under section 1401a of Title 10, Armed Forces.

EXECUTIVE ORDER NO. 11950

Ex. Ord. No. 11950, Jan. 6, 1977, 42 F.R. 1451, conformed Central Intelligence Agency and Civil Service Retirement and Disability Systems with respect to cost of living increases in annuities when there were increases in the price index.

EXECUTIVE ORDER NO. 12023

Ex. Ord. No. 12023, Dec. 1, 1977, 42 F.R. 61443, conformed Central Intelligence Agency and Civil Service Retirement and Disability Systems with regard to allotments or assignments of moneys by annuitants.

EXECUTIVE ORDER NO. 12197

Ex. Ord. No. 12197, Mar. 5, 1980, 45 F.R. 14833, conformed Central Intelligence Agency Retirement and Disability System to amendments to Civil Service Retirement and Disability System with regard to restoration of previously reduced annuities.

EXECUTIVE ORDER NO. 12253

Ex. Ord. No. 12253, Nov. 25, 1980, 45 F.R. 78995, conformed Central Intelligence Agency and Civil Service Retirement and Disability Systems with regard to definition of "dependent".

EXECUTIVE ORDER NO. 12273

Ex. Ord. No. 12273, Jan. 16, 1981, 46 F.R. 5854, conformed Central Intelligence Agency and Civil Service Retirement and Disability Systems with regard to cost-of-living increases to annuities.

EXECUTIVE ORDER NO. 12326

Ex. Ord. No. 12326, Sept. 30, 1981, 46 F.R. 48889, as amended by Ex. Ord. No. 12443, Sept. 27, 1983, 48 F.R. 44751, conformed Central Intelligence Agency and Civil Service Retirement and Disability Systems with regard to notification of loss or reduction of survivor benefits, computation of annuities, cost-of-living increases, accuracy of information, and withholding of State income tax.

EXECUTIVE ORDER NO. 12443

Ex. Ord. No. 12443, Sept. 27, 1983, 48 F.R. 44751, conformed Central Intelligence Agency and Civil Service Retirement and Disability Systems with regard to restoration of disability retirement annuities, entitlement to and computation and payment of annuities, accuracy of information, and adjustments in amounts.

EXECUTIVE ORDER NO. 12485

Ex. Ord. No. 12485, July 13, 1984, 49 F.R. 28827, conformed Central Intelligence Agency Retirement and Disability System and Civil Service Retirement and Disability System with regard to prior service credit.

EXECUTIVE ORDER NO. 12684

Ex. Ord. No. 12684, July 27, 1989, 54 F.R. 31643, conformed Central Intelligence Agency and Civil Service Retirement and Disability Systems with regard to considering part-time service in computing annuities and remarriage of surviving spouses.

§ 2002. Definitions relating to participants and annuitants

(a) General definitions

When used in subchapter II of this chapter:

(1) Former participant

The term "former participant" means a person who—

(A) while an employee of the Agency was a participant in the system; and

(B) separates from the Agency without entitlement to immediate receipt of an annuity from the fund.

(2) Retired participant

The term "retired participant" means a person who—

(A) while an employee of the Agency was a participant in the system; and

(B) is entitled to receive an annuity from the fund based upon such person's service as a participant.

(3) Surviving spouse

(A) In general

The term "surviving spouse" means the surviving wife or husband of a participant or retired participant who (i) was married to the participant or retired participant for at least 9 months immediately preceding the participant's or retired participant's death, or (ii) who is the parent of a child born of the marriage.

(B) Treatment when participant dies less than 9 months after marriage

In a case in which the participant or retired participant dies within the 9-month period beginning on the date of the marriage, the requirement under subparagraph (A)(i) that a marriage have a duration of at least 9 months immediately preceding the death of the participant or retired participant shall be treated as having been met if—

(i) the death of the participant or retired participant was accidental; or

(ii) the surviving wife or husband had been previously married to the participant or retired participant (and subsequently divorced) and the aggregate time married is at least 9 months.

(4) Former spouse

The term "former spouse" means a former wife or husband of a participant, former participant, or retired participant as follows:

(A) Divorces on or before December 4, 1991

In the case of a divorce that became final on or before December 4, 1991, such term means a former wife or husband of a participant, former participant, or retired participant who was married to such participant for not less than 10 years during periods of the participant's creditable service, at least 5 years of which were spent outside the United States by both such participant and former wife or husband during the participant's service as an employee of the Agency.

(B) Divorces after December 4, 1991

In the case of a divorce that becomes final after December 4, 1991, such term means a former wife or husband of a participant, former participant, or retired participant who was married to such participant for not less than 10 years during periods of the participant's creditable service, at least 5 years of which were spent by the participant during the participant's service as an employee of the Agency (i) outside the United States, or (ii) otherwise in a position the duties of which qualified the participant for designation by the Director as a participant under section 2013 of this title.

(C) Creditable service

For purposes of subparagraphs (A) and (B), the term "creditable service" means all periods of a participant's service that are creditable under sections 2081, 2082, and 2083 of this title.

(5) Previous spouse

The term "previous spouse" means an individual who was married for at least 9 months to a participant, former participant, or retired participant who had at least 18 months of service which are creditable under sections 2081, 2082, and 2083 of this title.

(6) Spousal agreement

The term "spousal agreement" means an agreement between a participant, former participant, or retired participant and the participant, former participant, or retired participant's spouse or former spouse that—

(A) is in writing, is signed by the parties, and is notarized;

(B) has not been modified by court order; and

(C) has been authenticated by the Director.

(7) Court order

The term "court order" means—

(A) a court decree of divorce, annulment, or legal separation; or

(B) a court order or court-approved property settlement agreement incident to such court decree of divorce, annulment, or legal separation.

(8) Court

The term "court" means a court of a State, the District of Columbia, the Commonwealth of Puerto Rico, Guam, the Northern Mariana Islands, or the Virgin Islands, and any Indian court.

(b) "Child" defined

For purposes of sections 2031 and 2052 of this title:

(1) In general

The term "child" means any of the following:

(A) Minor children

An unmarried dependent child under 18 years of age, including—

(i) an adopted child;

(ii) a stepchild, but only if the stepchild lived with the participant or retired participant in a regular parent-child relationship;

(iii) a recognized natural child; and

(iv) a child who lived with the participant, for whom a petition of adoption was filed by the participant or retired participant, and who is adopted by the surviving spouse after the death of the participant or retired participant.

(B) Disabled adult children

An unmarried dependent child, regardless of age, who is incapable of self-support because of a physical or mental disability incurred before age 18.

(C) Students

An unmarried dependent child between 18 and 22 years of age who is a student regularly pursuing a full-time course of study or training in residence in a high school, trade school, technical or vocational institute, junior college, college, university, or comparable recognized educational institution.

(2) Special rules for students

(A) Extension of age termination of status as "child"

For purposes of this subsection, a child whose 22nd birthday occurs before July 1 or after August 31 of a calendar year, and while regularly pursuing such a course of study or training, shall be treated as having attained the age of 22 on the first day of July following that birthday.

(B) Treatment of interim period between school years

A child who is a student is deemed not to have ceased to be a student during an interim between school years if the interim does not exceed 5 months and if the child shows to the satisfaction of the Director that the child has a bona fide intention of continuing to pursue a course of study or training in the same or different school during the school semester (or other period into which the school year is divided) immediately following the interim.

(3) "Dependent" defined

For purposes of this subsection, the term "dependent", with respect to the child of a participant or retired participant, means that the participant or retired participant was, at the time of the death of the participant or retired participant, either living with or contributing to the support of the child, as determined in accordance with regulations prescribed under subchapter II of this chapter.

(4) Exclusion of stepchildren from lump-sum payment

For purposes of section 2071(c) of this title, the term "child" includes an adopted child and a natural child, but does not include a stepchild.

(Pub. L. 88–643, title I, §102, as added Pub. L. 102–496, title VIII, §802, Oct. 24, 1992, 106 Stat. 3198.)

PRIOR PROVISIONS

A prior section 111 of Pub. L. 88–643, title I, Oct. 13, 1964, 78 Stat. 1043; Pub. L. 94–522, title I, §101, Oct. 17, 1976, 90 Stat. 2467, provided definitions for Pub. L. 88–643 and was set out as a note under section 403 of this title prior to the general amendment of Pub. L. 88–643 by section 802 of Pub. L. 102–496.

SECTION REFERRED TO IN OTHER SECTIONS

This section is referred to in sections 403n, 403s, 2031, 2154 of this title.

SUBCHAPTER II—CENTRAL INTELLIGENCE AGENCY RETIREMENT AND DISABILITY SYSTEM

SUBCHAPTER REFERRED TO IN OTHER SECTIONS

This subchapter is referred to in sections 2001, 2002, 2151, 2154 of this title; title 22 sections 4071b, 4071c, 4071d.

PART A—ESTABLISHMENT OF SYSTEM

§2011. CIARDS system

(a) In general

(1) Establishment of system

There is a retirement and disability system for certain employees of the Central Intelligence Agency known as the Central Intelligence Agency Retirement and Disability System (hereinafter in this chapter referred to as the "system"), originally established pursuant to title II of the Central Intelligence Agency Retirement Act of 1964 for Certain Employees.

(2) DCI regulations

The Director shall prescribe regulations for the system. The Director shall submit any proposed regulations for the system to the congressional intelligence committees not less than 14 days before they take effect.

(b) Administration of system

The Director shall administer the system in accordance with regulations prescribed under this subchapter and with the principles established by this subchapter.

(c) Finality of decisions of DCI

In the interests of the security of the foreign intelligence activities of the United States and in order further to implement paragraph (6) of section 403–3(c) of this title that the Director of Central Intelligence shall be responsible for protecting intelligence sources and methods from unauthorized disclosure, and notwithstanding the provisions of chapter 7 of title 5 or any other provision of law (except section 2155(b) of this title), any determination by the Director authorized by this chapter shall be final and conclusive and shall not be subject to review by any court.

(Pub. L. 88–643, title II, §201, as added Pub. L. 102–496, title VIII, §802, Oct. 24, 1992, 106 Stat. 3201; amended Pub. L. 103–178, title II, §202(a)(2), Dec. 3, 1993, 107 Stat. 2026; Pub. L. 105–272, title IV, §403(b), Oct. 20, 1998, 112 Stat. 2404.)

REFERENCES IN TEXT

The Central Intelligence Agency Retirement Act of 1964 for Certain Employees, referred to in subsec. (a)(1), is Pub. L. 88–643, Oct. 13, 1964, 78 Stat. 1043, as amended, which was formerly set out as a note under section 403 of this title. Pub. L. 88–643 was revised generally by Pub. L. 102–496, title VIII, §802, Oct. 24, 1992, 106 Stat. 3196, and is now known as the Central Intelligence Agency Retirement Act. As so revised, title II of Pub. L. 88–643 is classified generally to this subchapter.

PRIOR PROVISIONS

A prior section 201 of Pub. L. 88–643, title II, Oct. 13, 1964, 78 Stat. 1043; Pub. L. 98–618, title III, §302, Nov. 8, 1984, 98 Stat. 3300; Pub. L. 99–335, title V, §501(1), June 6, 1986, 100 Stat. 622, related to rules and regulations and was set out as a note under section 403 of this title prior to the general amendment of Pub. L. 88–643 by section 802 of Pub. L. 102–496.

AMENDMENTS

1998—Subsec. (c). Pub. L. 105–272 substituted "paragraph (6) of section 403–3(c) of this title" for "section 403–3(c)(5) of this title".

1993—Subsec. (c). Pub. L. 103–178 substituted "section 403–3(c)(5) of this title" for "the proviso of section 403(d)(3) of this title".

EFFECTIVE DATE OF 1993 AMENDMENT

Amendment by Pub. L. 103–178 effective Feb. 1, 1993, see section 202(b) of Pub. L. 103–178, set out as a note under section 2001 of this title.

SECTION REFERRED TO IN OTHER SECTIONS

This section is referred to in section 2155 of this title.

§ 2012. Central Intelligence Agency Retirement and Disability Fund

The Director shall maintain the fund in the Treasury known as the "Central Intelligence Agency Retirement and Disability Fund" (hereinafter in this chapter referred to as the "fund"), originally created pursuant to title II of the Central Intelligence Agency Retirement Act of 1964 for Certain Employees.

(Pub. L. 88–643, title II, § 202, as added Pub. L. 102–496, title VIII, § 802, Oct. 24, 1992, 106 Stat. 3201.)

REFERENCES IN TEXT

The Central Intelligence Agency Retirement Act of 1964 for Certain Employees, referred to in text, is Pub. L. 88–643, Oct. 13, 1964, 78 Stat. 1043, as amended, which was formerly set out as a note under section 403 of this title. Pub. L. 88–643 was revised generally by Pub. L. 102–496, title VIII, § 802, Oct. 24, 1992, 106 Stat. 3196, and is now known as the Central Intelligence Agency Retirement Act. As so revised, title II of Pub. L. 88–643 is classified generally to this subchapter.

PRIOR PROVISIONS

A prior section 202 of Pub. L. 88–643, title II, Oct. 13, 1964, 78 Stat. 1043, related to establishment and maintenance of the Central Intelligence Agency Retirement and Disability Fund and was set out as a note under section 403 of this title prior to the general amendment of Pub. L. 88–643 by section 802 of Pub. L. 102–496.

SECTION REFERRED TO IN OTHER SECTIONS

This section is referred to in section 403j of this title.

§ 2013. Participants in CIARDS system

(a) Designation of participants

The Director may from time to time designate employees of the Agency who shall be entitled to participate in the system. Employees so designated who elect to participate in the system are referred to in this chapter as "participants".

(b) Qualifying service

Designation of employees under this section may be made only from among employees of the Agency who have completed at least 5 years of qualifying service. For purposes of this chapter, qualifying service is service in the Agency performed in carrying out duties that are determined by the Director—

(1) to be in support of Agency activities abroad hazardous to life or health; or

(2) to be so specialized because of security requirements as to be clearly distinguishable from normal government employment.

(c) Election of employee to be participant

(1) Permanence of election

An employee of the Agency who elects to accept designation as a participant in the system shall remain a participant of the system for the duration of that individual's employment with the Agency.

(2) Irrevocability of election

Such an election shall be irrevocable except as and to the extent provided in section 2151(d) of this title.

(3) Election not subject to approval

An election under this section is not subject to review or approval by the Director.

(Pub. L. 88–643, title II, § 203, as added Pub. L. 102–496, title VIII, § 802, Oct. 24, 1992, 106 Stat. 3202.)

PRIOR PROVISIONS

A prior section 203 of Pub. L. 88–643, title II, Oct. 13, 1964, 78 Stat. 1044; Pub. L. 102–88, title III, § 303, Aug. 14, 1991, 105 Stat. 431, related to participants in the system and was set out as a note under section 403 of this title prior to the general amendment of Pub. L. 88–643 by section 802 of Pub. L. 102–496.

SECTION REFERRED TO IN OTHER SECTIONS

This section is referred to in sections 403p, 403r, 403s, 2001, 2002, 2151, 2152, 2154 of this title.

§ 2014. Annuitants

Persons who are annuitants under the system are—

(1) those persons who, on the basis of their service in the Agency, have met all requirements for an annuity under this subchapter or any other Act and are receiving an annuity from the fund; and

(2) those persons who, on the basis of someone else's service, meet all the requirements under this subchapter or any other Act for an annuity payable from the fund.

(Pub. L. 88–643, title II, § 204, as added Pub. L. 102–496, title VIII, § 802, Oct. 24, 1992, 106 Stat. 3202.)

PRIOR PROVISIONS

A prior section 204 of Pub. L. 88–643, title II, Oct. 13, 1964, 78 Stat. 1044; Pub. L. 91–626, § 1, Dec. 31, 1970, 84 Stat. 1872; Pub. L. 94–552, title II, § 201, Oct. 17, 1976, 90 Stat. 2468; Pub. L. 97–269, title VI, § 602, Sept. 27, 1982, 96 Stat. 1145; Pub. L. 99–335, title V, § 501(2), June 6, 1986, 100 Stat. 622; Pub. L. 102–88, title III, § 302, Aug. 14, 1991, 105 Stat. 431; Pub. L. 102–183, title III, §§ 302(c), 310(a), Dec. 4, 1991, 105 Stat. 1263, 1266, related to annuitants under the system and was set out as a note under section 403 of this title prior to the general amendment of Pub. L. 88–643 by section 802 of Pub. L. 102–496.

PART B—CONTRIBUTIONS

§ 2021. Contributions to fund

(a) In general

(1) Participant's contributions

Except as provided in subsection (d) of this section, 7 percent of the basic pay received by a participant for any pay period shall be deducted and withheld from the pay of that participant and contributed to the fund.

(2) Agency contributions

An equal amount shall be contributed to the fund for that pay period from the appropriation or fund which is used for payment of the participant's basic pay.

(3) Deposits to the fund

The amounts deducted and withheld from basic pay, together with the amounts so contributed from the appropriation or fund, shall be deposited by the Director to the credit of the fund.

(b) Consent of participant to deductions from pay

Each participant shall be deemed to consent and agree to such deductions from basic pay, and payment less such deductions shall be a full and complete discharge and acquittance of all claims and demands whatsoever for all regular services during the period covered by such payment, except the right to the benefits to which the participant is entitled under this subchapter, notwithstanding any law, rule, or regulation affecting the individual's pay.

(c) Treatment of contributions after 35 years of service

(1) Accrual of interest

Amounts deducted and withheld from the basic pay of a participant under this section for pay periods after the first day of the first pay period beginning after the day on which the participant completes 35 years of creditable service computed under sections 2081 and 2082 of this title (excluding service credit for unused sick leave under section 2031(a)(2) of this title) shall accrue interest. Such interest shall accrue at the rate of 3 percent a year through December 31, 1984, and thereafter at the rate computed under section 8334(e) of title 5, and shall be compounded annually from the date on which the amount is so deducted and withheld until the date of the participant's retirement or death.

(2) Use of amounts withheld after 35 years of service

(A) Use for deposits due under section 2082(b)

Amounts described in paragraph (1), including interest accrued on such amounts, shall be applied upon the participant's retirement or death toward any deposit due under section 2082(b) of this title.

(B) Lump-sum payment

Any balance of such amounts not so required for such a deposit shall be refunded to the participant in a lump sum after the participant's separation (or, in the event of a death in service, to a beneficiary in order of precedence specified in subsection[1] 2071(c) of this title), subject to prior notification of a current spouse, if any, unless the participant establishes to the satisfaction of the Director, in accordance with regulations which the Director may prescribe, that the participant does not know, and has taken all reasonable steps to determine, the whereabouts of the current spouse.

(C) Purchases of additional elective benefits

In lieu of such a lump-sum payment, the participant may use such amounts—

(i) to purchase an additional annuity in accordance with section 2121 of this title; or

(ii) provide any additional survivor benefit for a current or former spouse or spouses.

(d) Offset for social security taxes

(1) Persons covered

In the case of a participant who was a participant subject to this subchapter before January 1, 1984, and whose service—

(A) is employment for the purposes of title II of the Social Security Act [42 U.S.C. 401 et seq.] and chapter 21 of title 26, and

(B) is not creditable service for any purpose under subchapter III of this chapter or chapter 84 of title 5,

there shall be deducted and withheld from the basic pay of the participant under this section during any pay period only the amount computed under paragraph (2).

(2) Reduction in contribution

The amount deducted and withheld from the basic pay of a participant during any pay period pursuant to paragraph (1) shall be the excess of—

(A) the amount determined by multiplying the percent applicable to the participant under subsection (a) of this section by the basic pay payable to the participant for that pay period, over

(B) the amount of the taxes deducted and withheld from such basic pay under section 3101(a) of title 26 (relating to old-age, survivors, and disability insurance) for that pay period.

(Pub. L. 88–643, title II, § 211, as added Pub. L. 102–496, title VIII, § 802, Oct. 24, 1992, 106 Stat. 3202; amended Pub. L. 103–178, title II, § 202(a)(3), Dec. 3, 1993, 107 Stat. 2026.)

REFERENCES IN TEXT

The Social Security Act, referred to in subsec. (d)(1)(A), is act Aug. 14, 1935, ch. 531, 49 Stat. 620, as amended. Title II of the Act is classified generally to subchapter II (§ 401 et seq.) of chapter 7 of Title 42, The Public Health and Welfare. For complete classification of this Act to the Code, see section 1305 of Title 42 and Tables.

PRIOR PROVISIONS

A prior section 211 of Pub. L. 88–643, title II, Oct. 13, 1964, 78 Stat. 1045; Pub. L. 91–185, § 1, Dec. 30, 1969, 83 Stat. 847; Pub. L. 97–269, title VI, § 611, Sept. 27, 1982, 96 Stat. 1153; Pub. L. 99–335, title V, §§ 501(2), 502, June 6, 1986, 100 Stat. 622, 623; Pub. L. 99–514, § 2, Oct. 22, 1986, 100 Stat. 2095, related to compulsory contributions to the fund and was set out as a note under section 403 of this title prior to the general amendment of Pub. L. 88–643 by section 802 of Pub. L. 102–496.

AMENDMENTS

1993—Subsec. (c)(2)(B). Pub. L. 103–178 substituted "prior notification of a current spouse, if any, unless the participant establishes to the satisfaction of the Director, in accordance with regulations which the Director may prescribe, that the participant does not know, and has taken all reasonable steps to determine, the whereabouts of the current spouse" for "the requirement under section 2071(b)(4) of this title".

EFFECTIVE DATE OF 1993 AMENDMENT

Amendment by Pub. L. 103–178 effective Feb. 1, 1993, see section 202(b) of Pub. L. 103–178, set out as a note under section 2001 of this title.

TEMPORARY ADJUSTMENT OF CONTRIBUTION LEVELS

Pub. L. 106–346, § 101(a) [title V, § 505(g)], Oct. 23, 2000, 114 Stat. 1356, 1356A–54, provided that: "Notwithstanding section 211(a)(2) of the Central Intelligence Agency Retirement Act (50 U.S.C. 2021(a)(2)), during the period beginning on October 1, 2002, through December 31, 2002, the Central Intelligence Agency shall contribute 7.5 percent of the basic pay of an employee participating

[1] So in original. Probably should be "section".

in the Central Intelligence Agency Retirement and Disability System in lieu of the agency contribution otherwise required under section 211(a)(2) of such Act."

Pub. L. 105–33, title VII, § 7001(c)(1), (2), Aug. 5, 1997, 111 Stat. 658, as amended by Pub. L. 106–346, § 101(a) [title V, § 505(c)(1)], Oct. 23, 2000, 114 Stat. 1356, 1356A–53, provided that:

"(1) AGENCY CONTRIBUTIONS.—Notwithstanding section 211(a)(2) of the Central Intelligence Agency Retirement Act (50 U.S.C. 2021(a)(2)), during the period beginning on October 1, 1997, through September 30, 2002, the Central Intelligence Agency shall contribute 8.51 percent of the basic pay of an employee participating in the Central Intelligence Agency Retirement and Disability System in lieu of the agency contribution otherwise required under section 211(a)(2) of such Act.

"(2) INDIVIDUAL DEDUCTIONS, WITHHOLDINGS, AND DEPOSITS.—Notwithstanding section 211(a)(1) of the Central Intelligence Agency Retirement Act (50 U.S.C. 2021(a)(1)) beginning on January 1, 1999, through December 31, 2000, the percentage deducted and withheld from the basic pay of an employee participating in the Central Intelligence Agency Retirement and Disability System shall be as follows:

7.25	January 1, 1999, to December 31, 1999.
7.4	January 1, 2000, to December 31, 2000."

SECTION REFERRED TO IN OTHER SECTIONS

This section is referred to in sections 2031, 2091, 2111 of this title.

PART C—COMPUTATION OF ANNUITIES

§ 2031. Computation of annuities

(a) Annuity of participant

(1) Computation of annuity

The annuity of a participant is the product of—

(A) the participant's high-3 average pay (as defined in paragraph (4)); and

(B) the number of years, not exceeding 35, of service credit (determined in accordance with sections 2081 and 2082 of this title) multiplied by 2 percent.

(2) Credit for unused sick leave

The total service of a participant who retires on an immediate annuity (except under section 2051 of this title) or who dies leaving a survivor or survivors entitled to an annuity shall include (without regard to the 35-year limitation prescribed in paragraph (1)) the days of unused sick leave to the credit of the participant. Days of unused sick leave may not be counted in determining average basic pay or eligibility for an annuity under this subchapter. A deposit shall not be required for days of unused sick leave credited under this paragraph.

(3) Crediting of part-time service

(A) In general

In the case of a participant whose service includes service on a part-time basis performed after April 6, 1986, the participant's annuity shall be the sum of the amounts determined under subparagraphs (B) and (C).

(B) Computation of pre-April 7, 1986, annuity

The portion of an annuity referred to in subparagraph (A) with respect to service before April 7, 1986, shall be the amount computed under paragraph (1) using the participant's length of service before that date (increased by the unused sick leave to the credit of the participant at the time of retirement) and the participant's high-3 average pay.

(C) Computation of post-April 6, 1986, annuity

The portion of an annuity referred to in subparagraph (A) with respect to service after April 6, 1986, shall be the product of—

(i) the amount computed under paragraph (1), using the participant's length of service after that date and the participant's high-3 average pay, as determined by using the annual rate of basic pay that would be payable for full-time service; and

(ii) the ratio which the participant's actual service after April 6, 1986 (as determined by prorating the participant's total service after that date to reflect the service that was performed on a part-time basis) bears to the total service after that date that would be creditable for the participant if all the service had been performed on a full-time basis.

(D) Treatment of employment on temporary or intermittent basis

Employment on a temporary or intermittent basis shall not be considered to be service on a part-time basis for purposes of this paragraph.

(4) High-3 average pay defined

For purposes of this subsection, a participant's high-3 average pay is the amount of the participant's average basic pay for the highest 3 consecutive years of the participant's service for which full contributions have been made to the fund.

(5) Computation of service

In determining the aggregate period of service upon which an annuity is to be based, any fractional part of a month shall not be counted.

(b) Spouse or former spouse survivor annuity

(1) Reduction in participant's annuity to provide spouse or former spouse survivor annuity

(A) General rule

Except to the extent provided otherwise under a written election under subparagraph (B) or (C), if at the time of retirement a participant or former participant is married (or has a former spouse who has not remarried before attaining age 55), the participant shall receive a reduced annuity and provide a survivor annuity for the participant's spouse under this subsection or former spouse under section 2032(b) of this title, or a combination of such annuities, as the case may be.

(B) Joint election for waiver or reduction of spouse survivor annuity

A married participant or former participant and the participant's spouse may jointly elect in writing at the time of retirement to waive a survivor annuity for that spouse under this section or to reduce such survivor annuity under this section by designating a portion of the annuity of the participant as the base for the survivor annuity. If the marriage is dissolved following an election for such a reduced annuity and the spouse qualifies as a former spouse, the base used in calculating any annuity of the former spouse under section 2032(b) of this title may not exceed the portion of the participant's annuity designated under this subparagraph.

(C) Joint election of participant and former spouse

If a participant or former participant has a former spouse, such participant and the participant's former spouse may jointly elect by spousal agreement under section 2094(b) of this title to waive, reduce, or increase a survivor annuity under section 2032(b) of this title for that former spouse. Any such election must be made (i) before the end of the 12-month period beginning on the date on which the divorce or annulment involving that former spouse becomes final, or (ii) at the time of retirement of the participant, whichever is later.

(D) Unilateral elections in absence of spouse or former spouse

The Director may prescribe regulations under which a participant or former participant may make an election under subparagraph (B) or (C) without the participant's spouse or former spouse if the participant establishes to the satisfaction of the Director that the participant does not know, and has taken all reasonable steps to determine, the whereabouts of the spouse or former spouse.

(2) Amount of reduction in participant's annuity

The annuity of a participant or former participant providing a survivor annuity under this section (or section 2032(b) of this title), excluding any portion of the annuity not designated or committed as a base for any survivor annuity, shall be reduced by 2½ percent of the first $3,600 plus 10 percent of any amount over $3,600. The reduction under this paragraph shall be calculated before any reduction under section 2032(a)(5) of this title.

(3) Amount of surviving spouse annuity

(A) In general

If a retired participant receiving a reduced annuity under this subsection dies and is survived by a spouse, a survivor annuity shall be paid to the surviving spouse. The amount of the annuity shall be equal to 55 percent of (i) the full amount of the participant's annuity computed under subsection (a) of this section, or (ii) any lesser amount elected as the base for the survivor annuity under paragraph (1)(B).

(B) Limitation

Notwithstanding subparagraph (A), the amount of the annuity calculated under subparagraph (A) for a surviving spouse in any case in which there is also a surviving former spouse of the retired participant who qualifies for an annuity under section 2032(b) of this title may not exceed 55 percent of the portion (if any) of the base for survivor annuities which remains available under section 2032(b)(4)(B) of this title.

(C) Effective date and termination of annuity

An annuity payable from the fund to a surviving spouse under this paragraph shall commence on the day after the retired participant dies and shall terminate on the last day of the month before the surviving spouse's death or remarriage before attaining age 55. If such survivor annuity is terminated because of remarriage, it shall be restored at the same rate commencing on the date such remarriage is dissolved by death, annulment, or divorce if any lump sum paid upon termination of the annuity is returned to the fund.

(c) 18-month open period after retirement to provide spouse coverage

(1) Survivor annuity elections

(A) Election when spouse coverage waived at time of retirement

A participant or former participant who retires after March 31, 1992 and who—

(i) is married at the time of retirement; and

(ii) elects at that time (in accordance with subsection (b) of this section) to waive a survivor annuity for the spouse,

may, during the 18-month period beginning on the date of the retirement of the participant, elect to have a reduction under subsection (b) of this section made in the annuity of the participant (or in such portion thereof as the participant may designate) in order to provide a survivor annuity for the participant's spouse.

(B) Election when reduced spouse annuity elected

A participant or former participant who retires after March 31, 1992, and—

(i) who, at the time of retirement, is married, and

(ii) who, at that time designates (in accordance with subsection (b) of this section) that a portion of the annuity of such participant is to be used as the base for a survivor annuity,

may, during the 18-month period beginning on the date of the retirement of such participant, elect to have a greater portion of the annuity of such participant so used.

(2) Deposit required

(A) Requirement

An election under paragraph (1) shall not be effective unless the amount specified in subparagraph (B) is deposited into the fund before the end of that 18-month period.

(B) Amount of deposit

The amount to be deposited with respect to an election under this subsection is the amount equal to the sum of the following:

(i) Additional cost to system

The additional cost to the system that is associated with providing a survivor annuity under subsection (b) of this section and that results from such election, taking into account—

(I) the difference (for the period between the date on which the annuity of the participant or former participant commences and the date of the election) between the amount paid to such participant or former participant under this subchapter and the amount which would have been paid if such election had been made at the time the participant or former participant applied for the annuity; and

(II) the costs associated with providing for the later election.

(ii) Interest

Interest on the additional cost determined under clause (i), computed using the interest rate specified or determined under section 8334(e) of title 5 for the calendar year in which the amount to be deposited is determined.

(3) Voiding of previous elections

An election by a participant or former participant under this subsection voids prospectively any election previously made in the case of such participant under subsection (b) of this section.

(4) Reductions in annuity

An annuity that is reduced in connection with an election under this subsection shall be reduced by the same percentage reductions as were in effect at the time of the retirement of the participant or former participant whose annuity is so reduced.

(5) Rights and obligations resulting from reduced annuity election

Rights and obligations resulting from the election of a reduced annuity under this subsection shall be the same as the rights and obligations that would have resulted had the participant involved elected such annuity at the time of retirement.

(d) Annuities for surviving children

(1) Participants dying before April 1, 1992

In the case of a retired participant who died before April 1, 1992, and who is survived by a child or children—

(A) if the retired participant was survived by a spouse, there shall be paid from the fund to or on behalf of each such surviving child an annuity determined under paragraph (3)(A); and

(B) if the retired participant was not survived by a spouse, there shall be paid from the fund to or on behalf of each such surviving child an annuity determined under paragraph (3)(B).

(2) Participants dying on or after April 1, 1992

In the case of a retired participant who dies on or after April 1, 1992, and who is survived by a child or children—

(A) if the retired participant is survived by a spouse or former spouse who is the natural or adoptive parent of a surviving child of the participant, there shall be paid from the fund to or on behalf of each such surviving child an annuity determined under paragraph (3)(A); and

(B) if the retired participant is not survived by a spouse or former spouse who is the natural or adoptive parent of a surviving child of the participant, there shall be paid to or on behalf of each such surviving child an annuity determined under paragraph (3)(B).

(3) Amount of annuity

(A) The annual amount of an annuity for the surviving child of a participant covered by paragraph (1)(A) or (2)(A) of this subsection (or covered by paragraph (1)(A) or (2)(A) of section 2052(c) of this title) is the smallest of the following:

(i) 60 percent of the participant's high-3 average pay, as determined under subsection (a)(4) of this section, divided by the number of children.

(ii) $900, as adjusted under section 2131 of this title.

(iii) $2,700, as adjusted under section 2131 of this title, divided by the number of children.

(B) The amount of an annuity for the surviving child of a participant covered by paragraph (1)(B) or (2)(B) of this subsection (or covered by paragraph (1)(B) or (2)(B) of section 2052(c) of this title) is the smallest of the following:

(i) 75 percent of the participant's high-3 average pay, as determined under subsection (a)(4) of this section, divided by the number of children.

(ii) $1,080, as adjusted under section 2131 of this title.

(iii) $3,240, as adjusted under section 2131 of this title, divided by the number of children.

(4) Recomputation of child annuities

(A) In the case of a child annuity payable under paragraph (1), upon the death of a surviving spouse or the termination of the annuity of a child, the annuities of any remaining children shall be recomputed and paid as though the spouse or child had not survived the retired participant.

(B) In the case of a child annuity payable under paragraph (2), upon the death of a surviving spouse or former spouse or termination of the annuity of a child, the annuities of any remaining children shall be recomputed and paid as though the spouse, former spouse, or child had not survived the retired participant. If the annuity of a surviving child who has not been receiving an annuity is initiated or resumed, the annuities of any other children shall be recomputed and paid from that date as though the annuities of all currently eligible children were then being initiated.

(5) "Former spouse" defined

For purposes of this subsection, the term "former spouse" includes any former wife or husband of the retired participant, regardless of the length of marriage or the amount of creditable service completed by the participant.

(e) Commencement and termination of child annuities

(1) Commencement

An annuity payable to a child under subsection (d) of this section, or under section 2052(c) of this title, shall begin on the day after the date on which the participant or retired participant dies or, in the case of an individual over the age of 18 who is not a child within the meaning of section 2002(b) of this title, shall begin or resume on the first day of the month in which the individual later becomes or again becomes a student as described in section 2002(b) of this title. Such annuity may not commence until any lump-sum that has been paid is returned to the fund.

(2) Termination

Such an annuity shall terminate on the last day of the month before the month in which the recipient of the annuity dies or no longer qualifies as a child (as defined in section 2002(b) of this title).

(f) Participants not married at time of retirement

(1) Designation of persons with insurable interest

(A) Authority to make designation

Subject to the rights of former spouses under subsection (b) of this section and section 2032 of this title, at the time of retirement an unmarried participant found by the Director to be in good health may elect to receive an annuity reduced in accordance with subparagraph (B) and designate in writing an individual having an insurable interest in the participant to receive an annuity under the system after the participant's death. The amount of such an annuity shall be equal to 55 percent of the participant's reduced annuity.

(B) Reduction in participant's annuity

The annuity payable to the participant making such election shall be reduced by 10 percent of an annuity computed under subsection (a) of this section and by an additional 5 percent for each full 5 years the designated individual is younger than the participant. The total reduction under this subparagraph may not exceed 40 percent.

(C) Commencement of survivor annuity

The annuity payable to the designated individual shall begin on the day after the retired participant dies and terminate on the last day of the month before the designated individual dies.

(D) Recomputation of participant's annuity on death of designated individual

An annuity which is reduced under this paragraph shall, effective the first day of the month following the death of the designated individual, be recomputed and paid as if the annuity had not been so reduced.

(2) Election of survivor annuity upon subsequent marriage

A participant who is unmarried at the time of retirement and who later marries may irrevocably elect, in a signed writing received by the Director within one year after the marriage, to receive a reduced annuity as provided in subsection (b) of this section. Such election and reduction shall be effective on the first day of the month beginning 9 months after the date of marriage. The election voids prospectively any election previously made under paragraph (1).

(g) Effect of divorce after retirement

(1) Recomputation of retired participant's annuity upon divorce

An annuity which is reduced under this section (or any similar prior provision of law) to provide a survivor annuity for a spouse shall, if the marriage of the retired participant to such spouse is dissolved, be recomputed and paid for each full month during which a retired participant is not married (or is remarried, if there is no election in effect under paragraph (2)) as if the annuity had not been so reduced, subject to any reduction required to provide a survivor annuity under subsection (b) or (c) of section 2032 of this title or under section 2036 of this title.

(2) Election of survivor annuity upon subsequent remarriage

(A) In general

Upon remarriage, the retired participant may irrevocably elect, by means of a signed writing received by the Director within one year after such remarriage, to receive a reduced annuity for the purpose of providing an annuity for the new spouse of the retired participant in the event such spouse survives the retired participant. Such reduction shall be equal to the reduction in effect immediately before the dissolution of the previous marriage (unless such reduction is adjusted under section 2032(b)(5) of this title or elected under subparagraph (B)).

(B) When annuity previously not (or not fully) reduced

(i) Election

If the retired participant's annuity was not reduced (or was not fully reduced) to provide a survivor annuity for the participant's spouse or former spouse as of the time of retirement, the retired participant may make an election under the first sentence of subparagraph (A) upon remarriage to a spouse other than the spouse at the time of retirement. For any remarriage that occurred before August 14, 1991, the retired participant may make such an election within 2 years after such date.

(ii) Deposit required

(I) The retired participant shall, within one year after the date of the remarriage (or by August 14, 1993 for any remarriage that occurred before August 14, 1991), deposit in the fund an amount determined by the Director, as nearly as may be administratively feasible, to reflect the amount by which the retired participant's annuity would have been reduced if the election had been in effect since the date the annuity commenced, plus interest.

(II) The annual rate of interest for each year during which the retired participant's annuity would have been reduced if the election had been in effect since the date the annuity commenced shall be 6 percent.

(III) If the retired participant does not make the deposit, the Director shall collect such amount by offset against the participant's annuity, up to a maximum of 25 percent of the net annuity otherwise payable to the retired participant, and the retired participant is deemed to consent to such offset.

(IV) The deposit required by this subparagraph may be made by the surviving spouse of the retired participant.

(C) Effects of election

An election under this paragraph and the reduction in the participant's annuity shall be effective on the first day of the month beginning 9 months after the date of remarriage. A survivor annuity elected under this paragraph shall be treated in all respects as a survivor annuity under subsection (b) of this section.

(h) Coordination of annuities

(1) Surviving spouse

A surviving spouse whose survivor annuity was terminated because of remarriage before attaining age 55 shall not be entitled under subsection (b)(3)(C) of this section to the restoration of that survivor annuity payable from the fund unless the surviving spouse elects to receive it instead of any other survivor annuity to which the surviving spouse may be entitled under the system or any other retirement system for Government employees by reason of the remarriage.

(2) Former spouse

A surviving former spouse of a participant or retired participant shall not become entitled under section 2032(b) or 2034 of this title to a survivor annuity or to the restoration of a survivor annuity payable from the fund unless the surviving former spouse elects to receive it instead of any other survivor annuity to which the surviving former spouse may be entitled under this or any other retirement system for Government employees on the basis of a marriage to someone other than the participant.

(3) Surviving spouse of post-retirement marriage

A surviving spouse who married a participant after the participant's retirement shall be entitled to a survivor annuity payable from the fund only upon electing that annuity instead of any other survivor annuity to which the surviving spouse may be entitled under this or any other retirement system for Government employees on the basis of a marriage to someone other than the retired participant.

(i) Supplemental survivor annuities

(1) Spouse of recalled annuitant

A married recalled annuitant who reverts to retired status with entitlement to a supplemental annuity under section 2111(b) of this title shall, unless the annuitant and the annuitant's spouse jointly elect in writing to the contrary at the time of reversion to retired status, have the supplemental annuity reduced by 10 percent to provide a supplemental survivor annuity for the annuitant's spouse. Such supplemental survivor annuity shall be equal to 55 percent of the supplemental annuity of the annuitant.

(2) Regulations

The Director shall prescribe regulations to provide for the application of paragraph (1) of this subsection and of subsection (b) of section 2111 of this title in any case in which an annuitant has a former spouse who was married to the recalled annuitant at any time during the period of recall service and who qualifies for an annuity under section 2032(b) of this title.

(j) Offset of annuities by amount of social security benefit

Notwithstanding any other provision of this subchapter, an annuity (including a disability annuity) payable under this subchapter to an individual described in sections 2021(d)(1) and 2151(c)(1) of this title and any survivor annuity payable under this subchapter on the basis of the service of such individual shall be reduced in a manner consistent with section 8349 of title 5, under conditions consistent with the conditions prescribed in that section.

(k) Information from other agencies

(1) Other agencies

For the purpose of ensuring the accuracy of the information used in the determination of eligibility for and the computation of annuities payable from the fund under this subchapter, at the request of the Director—

(A) the Secretary of Defense shall provide information on retired or retainer pay paid under title 10;

(B) the Secretary of Veterans Affairs shall provide information on pensions or compensation paid under title 38;

(C) the Secretary of Health and Human Services shall provide information contained in the records of the Social Security Administration; and

(D) the Secretary of Labor shall provide information on benefits paid under subchapter I of chapter 81 of title 5.

(2) Limitation on information requested

The Director shall request only such information as the Director determines is necessary.

(3) Limitation on uses of information

The Director, in consultation with the officials from whom information is requested, shall ensure that information made available under this subsection is used only for the purposes authorized.

(*l*) Information on rights under system

The Director shall, on an annual basis—

(1) inform each retired participant of the participant's right of election under subsections (c), (f)(2), and (g) of this section; and

(2) to the maximum extent practicable, inform spouses and former spouses of partici-

pants, former participants, and retired participants of their rights under this chapter.

(Pub. L. 88–643, title II, § 221, as added Pub. L. 102–496, title VIII, § 802, Oct. 24, 1992, 106 Stat. 3204; amended Pub. L. 103–178, title II, § 202(a)(4), Dec. 3, 1993, 107 Stat. 2026.)

PRIOR PROVISIONS

A prior section 221 of Pub. L. 88–643, title II, Oct. 13, 1964, 78 Stat. 1045; Pub. L. 91–185, § 2, Dec. 30, 1969, 83 Stat. 847; Pub. L. 91–626, §§ 2, 3, Dec. 31, 1970, 84 Stat. 1872; Pub. L. 94–522, title II, §§ 202–204, Oct. 17, 1976, 90 Stat. 2468, 2469; Ex. Ord. No. 12326, §§ 1, 3, 6, Sept. 30, 1981, 46 F.R. 48889, 48890; Pub. L. 97–269, title VI, §§ 603–605, 610, Sept. 27, 1982, 96 Stat. 1146, 1147, 1153; Ex. Ord. No. 12443, §§ 4, 7, 8, Sept. 27, 1983, 48 F.R. 44752; Pub. L. 99–335, title V, §§ 501(2), (3), 503, June 6, 1986, 100 Stat. 622, 623; Pub. L. 100–178, title IV, § 402(b)(1), Dec. 2, 1987, 101 Stat. 1014; Pub. L. 100–453, title III, § 302(d)(1), (2), Sept. 29, 1988, 102 Stat. 1907; Pub. L. 102–88, title III, §§ 304(a), 305(a)(1), 306, Aug. 14, 1991, 105 Stat. 431, 432; Pub. L. 102–183, title III, §§ 302(a), 303(a), Dec. 4, 1991, 105 Stat. 1262, 1263, related to computation of annuities for other than former spouses and was set out as a note under section 403 of this title prior to the general amendment of Pub. L. 88–643 by section 802 of Pub. L. 102–496.

AMENDMENTS

1993—Subsec. (a)(4). Pub. L. 103–178, § 202(a)(4)(A), struck out "(or, in the case of an annuity computed under section 2052 of this title and based on less than 3 years, over the total service)" after "years of the participant's service".

Subsec. (f)(1)(A). Pub. L. 103–178, § 202(a)(4)(B), inserted "after the participant's death" after "under the system" and struck out "after the participant's death" after "participant's reduced annuity".

Subsec. (g)(1). Pub. L. 103–178, § 202(a)(4)(C), substituted "(or is remarried, if" for "(or is remarried if".

Subsec. (j). Pub. L. 103–178, § 202(a)(4)(D), struck out "(except as provided in paragraph (2))" after "individual shall be reduced".

EFFECTIVE DATE OF 1993 AMENDMENT

Amendment by Pub. L. 103–178 effective Feb. 1, 1993, see section 202(b) of Pub. L. 103–178, set out as a note under section 2001 of this title.

SECTION REFERRED TO IN OTHER SECTIONS

This section is referred to in sections 403n, 2002, 2021, 2032, 2033, 2034, 2051, 2052, 2053, 2054, 2055, 2071, 2082, 2111, 2131 of this title.

§ 2032. Annuities for former spouses

(a) Former spouse share of participant's annuity

(1) Pro rata share

Unless otherwise expressly provided by a spousal agreement or court order under section 2094(b) of this title, a former spouse of a participant, former participant, or retired participant is entitled to an annuity—

(A) if married to the participant, former participant, or retired participant throughout the creditable service of the participant, equal to 50 percent of the annuity of the participant; or

(B) if not married to the participant throughout such creditable service, equal to that proportion of 50 percent of such annuity that is the proportion that the number of days of the marriage of the former spouse to the participant during periods of creditable service of such participant under this subchapter bears to the total number of days of such creditable service.

(2) Disqualification upon remarriage before age 55

A former spouse is not qualified for an annuity under this subsection if before the commencement of that annuity the former spouse remarries before becoming 55 years of age.

(3) Commencement of annuity

The annuity of a former spouse under this subsection commences on the day the participant upon whose service the annuity is based becomes entitled to an annuity under this subchapter or on the first day of the month after the divorce or annulment involved becomes final, whichever is later.

(4) Termination of annuity

The annuity of such former spouse and the right thereto terminate on—

(A) the last day of the month before the month in which the former spouse dies or remarries before 55 years of age; or

(B) the date on which the annuity of the participant terminates (except in the case of an annuity subject to paragraph (5)(B)).

(5) Treatment of participant's annuity

(A) Reduction in participant's annuity

The annuity payable to any participant shall be reduced by the amount of an annuity under this subsection paid to any former spouse based upon the service of that participant. Such reduction shall be disregarded in calculating—

(i) the survivor annuity for any spouse, former spouse, or other survivor under this subchapter; and

(ii) any reduction in the annuity of the participant to provide survivor benefits under subsection (b) of this section or under section 2031(b) of this title.

(B) Treatment when annuitant returns to service

If an annuitant whose annuity is reduced under subparagraph (A) is recalled to service under section 2111 of this title, or reinstated or reappointed, in the case of a recovered disability annuitant, or if any annuitant is reemployed as provided for under sections 2112 and 2113 of this title, the pay of that annuitant shall be reduced by the same amount as the annuity would have been reduced if it had continued. Amounts equal to the reductions under this subparagraph shall be deposited in the Treasury of the United States to the credit of the fund.

(6) Disability annuitant

Notwithstanding paragraph (3), in the case of a former spouse of a disability annuitant—

(A) the annuity of that former spouse shall commence on the date on which the participant would qualify on the basis of the participant's creditable service for an annuity under this subchapter (other than a disability annuity) or the date on which the disability annuity begins, whichever is later, and

(B) the amount of the annuity of the former spouse shall be calculated on the basis of the annuity for which the participant would otherwise so qualify.

(7) Election of benefits

A former spouse of a participant, former participant, or retired participant shall not become entitled under this subsection to an annuity payable from the fund unless the former spouse elects to receive it instead of any survivor annuity to which the former spouse may be entitled under this or any other retirement system for Government employees on the basis of a marriage to someone other than the participant.

(8) Limitation in case of multiple former spouse annuities

No spousal agreement or court order under section 2094(b) of this title involving a participant may provide for an annuity or a combination of annuities under this subsection that exceeds the annuity of the participant.

(b) Former spouse survivor annuity

(1) Pro rata share

Subject to any election under section 2031(b)(1)(B) and (C) of this title and unless otherwise expressly provided by a spousal agreement or court order under section 2094(b) of this title, if an annuitant is survived by a former spouse, the former spouse shall be entitled—

(A) if married to the annuitant throughout the creditable service of the annuitant, to a survivor annuity equal to 55 percent of the unreduced amount of the annuitant's annuity, as computed under section 2031(a) of this title; and

(B) if not married to the annuitant throughout such creditable service, to a survivor annuity equal to that proportion of 55 percent of the unreduced amount of such annuity that is the proportion that the number of days of the marriage of the former spouse to the participant during periods of creditable service of such participant under this subchapter bears to the total number of days of such creditable service.

(2) Disqualification upon remarriage before age 55

A former spouse shall not be qualified for an annuity under this subsection if before the commencement of that annuity the former spouse remarries before becoming 55 years of age.

(3) Commencement, termination, and restoration of annuity

An annuity payable from the fund under this subchapter to a surviving former spouse under this subsection shall commence on the day after the annuitant dies and shall terminate on the last day of the month before the former spouse's death or remarriage before attaining age 55. If such a survivor annuity is terminated because of remarriage, it shall be restored at the same rate commencing on the date such remarriage is dissolved by death, annulment, or divorce if any lump sum paid upon termination of the annuity is returned to the fund.

(4) Survivor annuity amount

(A) Maximum amount

The maximum survivor annuity or combination of survivor annuities under this subsection (and section 2031(b)(3) of this title) with respect to any participant may not exceed 55 percent of the full amount of the participant's annuity, as calculated under section 2031(a) of this title.

(B) Limitation on other survivor annuities based on service of same participant

Once a survivor annuity has been provided under this subsection for any former spouse, a survivor annuity for another individual may thereafter be provided under this subsection (or section 2031(b)(3) of this title) with respect to the participant only for that portion (if any) of the maximum available which is not committed for survivor benefits for any former spouse whose prospective right to such annuity has not terminated by reason of death or remarriage.

(C) Finality of court order upon death of participant

After the death of a participant or retired participant, a court order under section 2094(b) of this title may not adjust the amount of the annuity of a former spouse of that participant or retired participant under this section.

(5) Effect of termination of former spouse entitlement

(A) Recomputation of participant's annuity

If a former spouse of a retired participant dies or remarries before attaining age 55, the annuity of the retired participant, if reduced to provide a survivor annuity for that former spouse, shall be recomputed and paid, effective on the first day of the month beginning after such death or remarriage, as if the annuity had not been so reduced, unless an election is in effect under subparagraph (B).

(B) Election of spouse annuity

Subject to paragraph (4)(B), the participant may elect in writing within one year after receipt of notice of the death or remarriage of the former spouse to continue the reduction in order to provide a higher survivor annuity under section 2031(b)(3) of this title for any spouse of the participant.

(c) Optional additional survivor annuities for other former spouse or surviving spouse

(1) In general

In the case of any participant providing a survivor annuity under subsection (b) of this section for a former spouse—

(A) such participant may elect, or

(B) a spousal agreement or court order under section 2094(b) of this title may provide for,

an additional survivor annuity under this subsection for any other former spouse or spouse surviving the participant, if the participant satisfactorily passes a physical examination as prescribed by the Director.

(2) Limitation

Neither the total amount of survivor annuity or annuities under this subsection with respect to any participant, nor the survivor annuity or annuities for any one surviving spouse or former spouse of such participant under this section or section 2031 of this title, may exceed 55 percent of the unreduced amount of the participant's annuity, as computed under section 2031(a) of this title.

(3) Contribution for additional annuities

(A) Provision of additional survivor annuity

In accordance with regulations which the Director shall prescribe, the participant involved may provide for any annuity under this subsection—

(i) by a reduction in the annuity or an allotment from the basic pay of the participant;

(ii) by a lump-sum payment or installment payments to the fund; or

(iii) by any combination thereof.

(B) Actuarial equivalence to benefit

The present value of the total amount to accrue to the fund under subparagraph (A) to provide any annuity under this subsection shall be actuarially equivalent in value to such annuity, as calculated upon such tables of mortality as may from time to time be prescribed for this purpose by the Director.

(C) Effect of former spouse's death or disqualification

If a former spouse predeceases the participant or remarries before attaining age 55 (or, in the case of a spouse, the spouse predeceases the participant or does not qualify as a former spouse upon dissolution of the marriage)—

(i) if an annuity reduction or pay allotment under subparagraph (A) is in effect for that spouse or former spouse, the annuity shall be recomputed and paid as if it had not been reduced or the pay allotment terminated, as the case may be; and

(ii) any amount accruing to the fund under subparagraph (A) shall be refunded, but only to the extent that such amount may have exceeded the actuarial cost of providing benefits under this subsection for the period such benefits were provided, as determined under regulations prescribed by the Director.

(D) Recomputation upon death or remarriage of former spouse

Under regulations prescribed by the Director, an annuity shall be recomputed (or a pay allotment terminated or adjusted), and a refund provided (if appropriate), in a manner comparable to that provided under subparagraph (C), in order to reflect a termination or reduction of future benefits under this subsection for a spouse in the event a former spouse of the participant dies or remarries before attaining age 55 and an increased annuity is provided for that spouse in accordance with this section.

(4) Commencement and termination of additional survivor annuity

An annuity payable under this subsection to a spouse or former spouse shall commence on the day after the participant dies and shall terminate on the last day of the month before the spouse's or the former spouse's death or remarriage before attaining age 55.

(5) Nonapplicability of COLA provision

Section 2131 of this title does not apply to an annuity under this subsection, unless authorized under regulations prescribed by the Director.

(Pub. L. 88–643, title II, §222, as added Pub. L. 102–496, title VIII, §802, Oct. 24, 1992, 106 Stat. 3212; amended Pub. L. 103–178, title II, §202(a)(5), Dec. 3, 1993, 107 Stat. 2026.)

PRIOR PROVISIONS

A prior section 222 of Pub. L. 88–643, as added Pub. L. 97–269, title VI, §606, Sept. 27, 1982, 96 Stat. 1148; amended Pub. L. 99–335, title V, §501(2), (3), June 6, 1986, 100 Stat. 622; Pub. L. 102–88, title III, §305(a)(2), Aug. 14, 1991, 105 Stat. 432, related to computation of annuities for former spouses and was set out as a note under section 403 of this title prior to the general amendment of Pub. L. 88–643 by section 802 of Pub. L. 102–496.

AMENDMENTS

1993—Subsec. (a)(7). Pub. L. 103–178, §202(a)(5)(A), substituted "any survivor annuity" for "any other annuity".

Subsec. (c)(3)(C). Pub. L. 103–178, §202(a)(5)(B), inserted "the participant" before "or does not qualify".

Subsec. (c)(4). Pub. L. 103–178, §202(a)(5)(C), substituted "before the spouse's or the former spouse's death" for "before the former spouse's death".

EFFECTIVE DATE OF 1993 AMENDMENT

Amendment by Pub. L. 103–178 effective Feb. 1, 1993, see section 202(b) of Pub. L. 103–178, set out as a note under section 2001 of this title.

SURVIVOR ANNUITY, RETIREMENT ANNUITY, AND HEALTH BENEFITS FOR CERTAIN EX-SPOUSES OF CENTRAL INTELLIGENCE AGENCY EMPLOYEES; EFFECTIVE DATE

Section 203 of Pub. L. 103–178 provided that:

"(a) SURVIVOR ANNUITY.—

"(1) IN GENERAL.—

"(A) ENTITLEMENT OF FORMER WIFE OR HUSBAND.—Any person who was divorced on or before December 4, 1991, from a participant or retired participant in the Central Intelligence Agency Retirement and Disability System and who was married to such participant for not less than 10 years during such participant's creditable service, at least five years of which were spent by the participant during the participant's service as an employee of the Central Intelligence Agency outside the United States, or otherwise in a position the duties of which qualified the participant for designation by the Director of Central Intelligence as a participant under section 203 of the Central Intelligence Agency Retirement Act (50 U.S.C. 2013), shall be entitled, except to the extent such person is disqualified under paragraph (2), to a survivor annuity equal to 55 percent of the greater of—

"(i) the unreduced amount of the participant's annuity, as computed under section 221(a) of such Act [50 U.S.C. 2031(a)]; or

"(ii) the unreduced amount of what such annuity as so computed would be if the participant had not elected payment of the lump-sum credit under section 294 of such Act [50 U.S.C. 2143].

"(B) REDUCTION IN SURVIVOR ANNUITY.—A survivor annuity payable under this subsection shall be reduced by an amount equal to any survivor annuity payments made to the former wife or husband under section 226 of such Act [50 U.S.C. 2036].

"(2) LIMITATIONS.—A former wife or husband is not entitled to a survivor annuity under this subsection if—

"(A) the former wife or husband remarries before age 55, except that the entitlement of the former wife or husband to such a survivor annuity shall be restored on the date such remarriage is dissolved by death, annulment, or divorce;

"(B) the former wife or husband is less than 50 years of age; or

"(C) the former wife or husband meets the definition of 'former spouse' that was in effect under section 204(b)(4) of the Central Intelligence Agency Retirement Act of 1964 for Certain Employees before December 4, 1991 [section 204(b)(4) of Pub. L. 88–643 prior to enactment of Pub. L. 102–496, formerly set out as a note under section 403 of this title].

"(3) COMMENCEMENT AND TERMINATION OF ANNUITY.—

"(A) COMMENCEMENT OF ANNUITY.—The entitlement of a former wife or husband to a survivor annuity under this subsection shall commence—

"(i) in the case of a former wife or husband of a participant or retired participant who is deceased as of October 1, 1994, beginning on the later of—

"(I) the 60th day after such date; or

"(II) the date on which the former wife or husband reaches age 50; and

"(ii) in the case of any other former wife or husband, beginning on the latest of—

"(I) the date on which the participant or retired participant to whom the former wife or husband was married dies;

"(II) the 60th day after October 1, 1994; or

"(III) the date on which the former wife or husband attains age 50.

"(B) TERMINATION OF ANNUITY.—The entitlement of a former wife or husband to a survivor annuity under this subsection terminates on the last day of the month before the former wife's or husband's death or remarriage before attaining age 55. The entitlement of a former wife or husband to such a survivor annuity shall be restored on the date such remarriage is dissolved by death, annulment, or divorce.

"(4) ELECTION OF BENEFITS.—A former wife or husband of a participant or retired participant shall not become entitled under this subsection to a survivor annuity or to the restoration of the survivor annuity unless the former wife or husband elects to receive it instead of any other survivor annuity to which the former wife or husband may be entitled under the Central Intelligence Agency Retirement and Disability System or any other retirement system for Government employees on the basis of a marriage to someone other than the participant.

"(5) APPLICATION—

"(A) TIME LIMIT; WAIVER.—A survivor annuity under this subsection shall not be payable unless appropriate written application is provided to the Director, complete with any supporting documentation which the Director may by regulation require. Any such application shall be submitted not later than October 1, 1995. The Director may waive the application deadline under the preceding sentence in any case in which the Director determines that the circumstances warrant such a waiver.

"(B) RETROACTIVE BENEFITS.—Upon approval of an application provided under subparagraph (A), the appropriate survivor annuity shall be payable to the former wife or husband with respect to all periods before such approval during which the former wife or husband was entitled to such annuity under this subsection, but in no event shall a survivor annuity be payable under this subsection with respect to any period before October 1, 1994.

"(6) RESTORATION OF ANNUITY.—Notwithstanding paragraph (5)(A), the deadline by which an application for a survivor annuity must be submitted shall not apply in cases in which a former spouse's entitlement to such a survivor annuity is restored after October 1, 1994, under paragraph (2)(A) or (3)(B).

"(7) APPLICABILITY IN CASES OF PARTICIPANTS TRANSFERRED TO FERS.—

"(A) ENTITLEMENT.—Except as provided in paragraph (2), this subsection shall apply to a former wife or husband of a participant under the Central Intelligence Agency Retirement and Disability System who has elected to become subject to chapter 84 of title 5, United States Code.

"(B) AMOUNT OF ANNUITY.—The survivor annuity of a person covered by subparagraph (A) shall be equal to 50 percent of the unreduced amount of the participant's annuity computed in accordance with section 302(a) of the Federal Employees' Retirement System Act of 1986 [Pub. L. 99–335, 5 U.S.C. 8331 note] and shall be reduced by an amount equal to any survivor annuity payments made to the former wife or husband under section 8445 of title 5, United States Code.

"(b) RETIREMENT ANNUITY.—

"(1) IN GENERAL.—

"(A) ENTITLEMENT OF FORMER WIFE OR HUSBAND.—A person described in subsection (a)(1)(A) shall be entitled, except to the extent such former spouse is disqualified under paragraph (2), to an annuity—

"(i) if married to the participant throughout the creditable service of the participant, equal to 50 percent of the annuity of the participant; or

"(ii) if not married to the participant throughout such creditable service, equal to that former wife's or husband's pro rata share of 50 percent of such annuity (determined in accordance with section 222(a)(1)(B) of the Central Intelligence Agency Retirement Act (50 U.S.C. 2032 (a)(1)(B)).

"(B) REDUCTION IN RETIREMENT ANNUITIES.—

"(i) AMOUNT OF REDUCTION.—An annuity payable under this subsection shall be reduced by an amount equal to any apportionment payments payable to the former wife or husband pursuant to the terms of a court order incident to the dissolution of the marriage of such former spouse and the participant, former participant, or retired participant.

"(ii) DEFINITION OF TERMS.—For purposes of clause (i):

"(I) APPORTIONMENT.—The term 'apportionment' means a portion of a retired participant's annuity payable to a former wife or husband either by the retired participant or the Government in accordance with the terms of a court order.

"(II) COURT ORDER.—The term 'court order' means any decree of divorce or annulment or any court order or court-approved property settlement agreement incident to such decree.

"(2) LIMITATIONS.—A former wife or husband is not entitled to an annuity under this subsection if—

"(A) the former wife or husband remarries before age 55, except that the entitlement of the former wife or husband to an annuity under this subsection shall be restored on the date such remarriage is dissolved by death, annulment, or divorce;

"(B) the former wife or husband is less than 50 years of age; or

"(C) the former wife or husband meets the definition of 'former spouse' that was in effect under section 204(b)(4) of the Central Intelligence Agency Retirement Act of 1964 for Certain Employees before December 4, 1991 [section 204(b)(4) of Pub. L. 88–643 prior to enactment of Pub. L. 102–496, formerly set out as a note under section 403 of this title].

"(3) COMMENCEMENT AND TERMINATION.—

"(A) RETIREMENT ANNUITIES.—The entitlement of a former wife or husband to an annuity under this subsection—

"(i) shall commence on the later of—

"(I) October 1, 1994;

"(II) the day the participant upon whose service the right to the annuity is based becomes entitled to an annuity under such Act [probably means Central Intelligence Agency Retirement Act, 50 U.S.C. 2001 et seq.]; or

"(III) such former wife's or husband's 50th birthday; and

"(ii) shall terminate on the earlier of—

"(I) the last day of the month before the former wife or husband dies or remarries before 55 years of age, except that the entitlement of the former wife or husband to an annuity under this subsection shall be restored on the date such remarriage is dissolved by death, annulment, or divorce; or

"(II) the date on which the annuity of the participant terminates.

"(B) DISABILITY ANNUITIES.—Notwithstanding subparagraph (A)(i)(II), in the case of a former wife or husband of a disability annuitant—

"(i) the annuity of the former wife or husband shall commence on the date on which the participant would qualify on the basis of the participant's creditable service for an annuity under the Central Intelligence Agency Retirement Act [50 U.S.C. 2001 et seq.] (other than a disability annuity) or the date the disability annuity begins, whichever is later; and

"(ii) the amount of the annuity of the former wife or husband shall be calculated on the basis of the annuity for which the participant would otherwise so qualify.

"(C) ELECTION OF BENEFITS.—A former wife or husband of a participant or retired participant shall not become entitled under this subsection to an annuity or to the restoration of an annuity unless the former wife or husband elects to receive it instead of any survivor annuity to which the former wife or husband may be entitled under the Central Intelligence Agency Retirement and Disability System or any other retirement system for Government employees on the basis of a marriage to someone other than the participant.

"(D) APPLICATION.—

"(i) TIME LIMIT; WAIVER.—An annuity under this subsection shall not be payable unless appropriate written application is provided to the Director of Central Intelligence, complete with any supporting documentation which the Director may by regulation require, not later than October 1, 1995. The Director may waive the application deadline under the preceding sentence in any case in which the Director determines that the circumstances warrant such a waiver.

"(ii) RETROACTIVE BENEFITS.—Upon approval of an application under clause (i), the appropriate annuity shall be payable to the former wife or husband with respect to all periods before such approval during which the former wife or husband was entitled to an annuity under this subsection, but in no event shall an annuity be payable under this subsection with respect to any period before October 1, 1994.

"(4) RESTORATION OF ANNUITIES.—Notwithstanding paragraph (3)(D)(i), the deadline by which an application for a retirement annuity must be submitted shall not apply in cases in which a former spouse's entitlement to such annuity is restored after October 1, 1994, under paragraph (2)(A) or (3)(A)(ii).

"(5) APPLICABILITY IN CASES OF PARTICIPANTS TRANSFERRED TO FERS.—The provisions of this subsection shall apply to a former wife or husband of a participant under the Central Intelligence Agency Retirement and Disability System who has elected to become subject to chapter 84 of title 5, United States Code. For purposes of this paragraph, any reference in this section to a participant's annuity under the Central Intelligence Agency Retirement and Disability System shall be deemed to refer to the transferred participant's annuity computed in accordance with section 302(a) of the Federal Employee's Retirement System Act of 1986 [Pub. L. 99–335, 5 U.S.C. 8331 note].

"(6) SAVINGS PROVISION.—Nothing in this subsection shall be construed to impair, reduce, or otherwise affect the annuity or the entitlement to an annuity of a participant or former participant under title II or III of the Central Intelligence Agency Retirement Act [50 U.S.C. 2011 et seq., 2151 et seq.].

"(c) HEALTH BENEFITS.—[Amended section 403p of this title.]

"(d) SOURCE OF PAYMENT FOR ANNUITIES.—Annuities provided under subsections (a) and (b) shall be payable from the Central Intelligence Agency Retirement and Disability Fund maintained under section 202 of the Central Intelligence Agency Retirement Act (50 U.S.C. 2012).

"(e) EFFECTIVE DATE.—

"(1) IN GENERAL.—Except as provided in paragraph (2), subsections (a) and (b) shall take effect as of October 1, 1994, the amendments made by subsection (c) [amending section 403p of this title] shall apply to individuals on and after October 1, 1994, and no benefits provided pursuant to those subsections shall be payable with respect to any period before October 1, 1994.

"(2) Section 16(d) of the Central Intelligence Agency Act of 1949 (as added by subsection (c) of this section) [50 U.S.C. 403p(d)] shall apply to individuals beginning on the date of enactment of this Act [Dec. 3, 1993]."

SECTION REFERRED TO IN OTHER SECTIONS

This section is referred to in sections 403n, 2031, 2033, 2052, 2094 of this title.

§2033. Election of survivor benefits for certain former spouses divorced as of November 15, 1982

(a) Former spouses as of November 15, 1982

A participant, former participant, or retired participant in the system who on November 15, 1982, had a former spouse may, by a spousal agreement, elect to receive a reduced annuity and provide a survivor annuity for such former spouse under section 2032(b) of this title.

(b) Time for making election

(1) If the participant or former participant has not retired under such system on or before November 15, 1982, an election under this section may be made at any time before retirement.

(2) If the participant or former participant has retired under such system on or before November 15, 1982, an election under this section may be made within such period after November 15, 1982, as the Director may prescribe.

(3) For the purposes of applying this subchapter, any such election shall be treated in the same manner as if it were a spousal agreement under section 2094(b) of this title.

(c) Base for annuity

An election under this section may provide for a survivor annuity based on all or any portion of that part of the annuity of the participant which is not designated or committed as a base for a survivor annuity for a spouse or any other former spouse of the participant. The participant and the participant's spouse may make an election under section 2031(b)(1)(B) of this title before the time of retirement for the purpose of allowing an election to be made under this section.

(d) Reduction in participant's annuity

(1) Computation

The amount of the reduction in the participant's annuity shall be determined in accordance with section 2031(b)(2) of this title.

(2) Effective date of reduction

Such reduction shall be effective as of—

(A) the commencing date of the participant's annuity, in the case of an election under subsection (b)(1) of this section; or

(B) November 15, 1982, in the case of an election under subsection (b)(2) of this section.

(Pub. L. 88–643, title II, § 223, as added Pub. L. 102–496, title VIII, § 802, Oct. 24, 1992, 106 Stat. 3216.)

PRIOR PROVISIONS

A prior section 223 of Pub. L. 88–643, as added Pub. L. 97–269, title VI, § 607, Sept. 27, 1982, 96 Stat. 1151; amended Pub. L. 99–335, title V, § 501(2), June 6, 1986, 100 Stat. 622, related to election of survivor benefits for certain former spouses and was set out as a note under section 403 of this title prior to the general amendment of Pub. L. 88–643 by section 802 of Pub. L. 102–496.

SECTION REFERRED TO IN OTHER SECTIONS

This section is referred to in sections 403n, 2034 of this title.

§ 2034. Survivor annuity for certain other former spouses

(a) Survivor annuity

(1) In general

An individual who was a former spouse of a participant or retired participant on November 15, 1982, shall be entitled, except to the extent such former spouse is disqualified under subsection (b) of this section, to a survivor annuity equal to 55 percent of the greater of—

(A) the unreduced amount of the participant's or retired participant's annuity, as computed under section 2031(a) of this title; or

(B) the unreduced amount of what such annuity as so computed would be if the participant, former participant, or retired participant had not elected payment of the lump-sum credit under section 2143 of this title.

(2) Reduction in survivor annuity

A survivor annuity payable under this section shall be reduced by an amount equal to any survivor annuity payments made to the former spouse under section 2033 of this title.

(b) Limitations

A former spouse is not entitled to a survivor annuity under this section if—

(1) the former spouse remarries before age 55, except that the entitlement of the former spouse to such a survivor annuity shall be restored on the date such remarriage is dissolved by death, annulment, or divorce; or

(2) the former spouse is less than 50 years of age.

(c) Commencement and termination of annuity

(1) Commencement of annuity

The entitlement of a former spouse to a survivor annuity under this section shall commence—

(A) in the case of a former spouse of a participant or retired participant who is deceased as of October 1, 1986, beginning on the later of—

(i) the 60th day after such date; or

(ii) the date on which the former spouse reaches age 50; and

(B) in the case of any other former spouse, beginning on the latest of—

(i) the date on which the participant or retired participant to whom the former spouse was married dies;

(ii) the 60th day after October 1, 1986; or

(iii) the date on which the former spouse attains age 50.

(2) Termination of annuity

The entitlement of a former spouse to a survivor annuity under this section terminates on the last day of the month before the former spouse's death or remarriage before attaining age 55. The entitlement of a former spouse to such a survivor annuity shall be restored on the date such remarriage is dissolved by death, annulment, or divorce.

(d) Application

(1) Time limit; waiver

A survivor annuity under this section shall not be payable unless appropriate written application is provided to the Director, complete with any supporting documentation which the Director may by regulation require. Any such application shall be submitted not later than April 1, 1989. The Director may waive the application deadline under the preceding sentence in any case in which the Director determines that the circumstances warrant such a waiver.

(2) Retroactive benefits

Upon approval of an application provided under paragraph (1), the appropriate survivor annuity shall be payable to the former spouse with respect to all periods before such approval during which the former spouse was entitled to such annuity under this section, but in no event shall a survivor annuity be payable under this section with respect to any period before October 1, 1986.

(e) Restoration of annuity

Notwithstanding subsection (d)(1) of this section, the deadline by which an application for a survivor annuity must be submitted shall not apply in cases in which a former spouse's entitlement to such a survivor annuity is restored under subsection (b)(1) or (c)(2) of this section.

(Pub. L. 88–643, title II, § 224, as added Pub. L. 102–496, title VIII, § 802, Oct. 24, 1992, 106 Stat. 3217; amended Pub. L. 103–178, title II, § 202(a)(6), Dec. 3, 1993, 107 Stat. 2026.)

PRIOR PROVISIONS

A prior section 224 of Pub. L. 88–643, as added Pub. L. 99–569, title III, § 302(a), Oct. 27, 1986, 100 Stat. 3192; amended Pub. L. 100–453, title III, § 302(b)(1), Sept. 29, 1988, 102 Stat. 1907; Pub. L. 101–193, title III, § 304(a), Nov. 30, 1989, 103 Stat. 1703; Pub. L. 102–88, title III, § 307(a), Aug. 14, 1991, 105 Stat. 432; Pub. L. 102–183, title III, § 304, Dec. 4, 1991, 105 Stat. 1264, related to survivor annuities for certain other former spouses and was set out as a note under section 403 of this title prior to the general amendment of Pub. L. 88–643 by section 802 of Pub. L. 102–496.

AMENDMENTS

1993—Subsec. (c)(1)(B)(i). Pub. L. 103–178 substituted "retired participant" for "former participant".

EFFECTIVE DATE OF 1993 AMENDMENT

Amendment by Pub. L. 103–178 effective Feb. 1, 1993, see section 202(b) of Pub. L. 103–178, set out as a note under section 2001 of this title.

SECTION REFERRED TO IN OTHER SECTIONS

This section is referred to in sections 403n, 2031, 2052, 2154 of this title.

§2035. Retirement annuity for certain former spouses

(a) Retirement annuity

An individual who was a former spouse of a participant, former participant, or retired participant on November 15, 1982, and any former spouse divorced after November 15, 1982, from a participant or former participant who retired before November 15, 1982, shall be entitled, except to the extent such former spouse is disqualified under subsection (b) of this section, to an annuity—

(1) if married to the participant throughout the creditable service of the participant, equal to 50 percent of the annuity of the participant; or

(2) if not married to the participant throughout such creditable service, equal to that former spouse's pro rata share of 50 percent of such annuity.

(b) Limitations

A former spouse is not entitled to an annuity under this section if—

(1) the former spouse remarries before age 55, except that the entitlement of the former spouse to an annuity under this section shall be restored on the date such remarriage is dissolved by death, annulment, or divorce; or

(2) the former spouse is less than 50 years of age.

(c) Commencement and termination

(1) Retirement annuities

The entitlement of a former spouse to an annuity under this section—

(A) shall commence on the later of—

(i) the day the participant upon whose service the right to the annuity is based becomes entitled to an annuity under this subchapter;

(ii) the first day of the month in which the divorce or annulment involved becomes final; or

(iii) such former spouse's 50th birthday; and

(B) shall terminate on the earlier of—

(i) the last day of the month before the former spouse dies or remarries before 55 years of age, except that the entitlement of the former spouse to an annuity under this section shall be restored on the date such remarriage is dissolved by death, annulment, or divorce; or

(ii) the date on which the annuity of the participant terminates.

(2) Disability annuities

Notwithstanding paragraph (1)(A)(i), in the case of a former spouse of a disability annuitant—

(A) the annuity of the former spouse shall commence on the date on which the participant would qualify on the basis of the participant's creditable service for an annuity under this subchapter (other than disability annuity) or the date the disability annuity begins, whichever is later; and

(B) the amount of the annuity of the former spouse shall be calculated on the basis of the annuity for which the participant would otherwise so qualify.

(3) Election of benefits

A former spouse of a participant or retired participant shall not become entitled under this section to an annuity or to the restoration of an annuity payable from the fund unless the former spouse elects to receive it instead of any survivor annuity to which the former spouse may be entitled under this or any other retirement system for Government employees on the basis of a marriage to someone other than the participant.

(4) Application

(A) Time limit; waiver

An annuity under this section shall not be payable unless appropriate written application is provided to the Director, complete with any supporting documentation which the Director may by regulation require, not later than June 2, 1990. The Director may waive the application deadline under the preceding sentence in any case in which the Director determines that the circumstances warrant such a waiver.

(B) Retroactive benefits

Upon approval of an application under subparagraph (A), the appropriate annuity shall be payable to the former spouse with respect to all periods before such approval during which the former spouse was entitled to an annuity under this section, but in no event shall an annuity be payable under this section with respect to any period before December 2, 1987.

(d) Restoration of annuities

Notwithstanding subsection (c)(4)(A) of this section, the deadline by which an application for a retirement annuity must be submitted shall not apply in cases in which a former spouse's entitlement to such annuity is restored under subsection (b)(1) or (c)(1)(B) of this section.

(e) Savings provision

Nothing in this section shall be construed to impair, reduce, or otherwise affect the annuity or the entitlement to an annuity of a participant or former participant under this subchapter.

(Pub. L. 88–643, title II, §225, as added Pub. L. 102–496, title VIII, §802, Oct. 24, 1992, 106 Stat. 3218; amended Pub. L. 103–178, title II, §202(a)(7), Dec. 3, 1993, 107 Stat. 2026.)

PRIOR PROVISIONS

A prior section 225 of Pub. L. 88–643, as added Pub. L. 100–178, title IV, §401(a), Dec. 2, 1987, 101 Stat. 1012; amended Pub. L. 100–453, title III, §302(c)(1), Sept. 29, 1988, 102 Stat. 1907; Pub. L. 102–88, title III, §307(b), Aug. 14, 1991, 105 Stat. 433, related to retirement benefits for certain other former spouses and was set out as a note under section 403 of this title prior to the general amendment of Pub. L. 88–643 by section 802 of Pub. L. 102–496.

AMENDMENTS

1993—Subsec. (c)(3). Pub. L. 103–178, § 202(a)(7)(A), substituted "any survivor annuity" for "any other annuity".

Subsec. (c)(4)(A). Pub. L. 103–178, § 202(a)(7)(B), substituted "June 2, 1990" for "June 2, 1991".

EFFECTIVE DATE OF 1993 AMENDMENT

Amendment by Pub. L. 103–178 effective Feb. 1, 1993, see section 202(b) of Pub. L. 103–178, set out as a note under section 2001 of this title.

SECTION REFERRED TO IN OTHER SECTIONS

This section is referred to in sections 403n, 2154 of this title.

§ 2036. Survivor annuities for previous spouses

The Director shall prescribe regulations under which a previous spouse who is divorced after September 29, 1988, from a participant, former participant, or retired participant shall be eligible for a survivor annuity to the same extent and, to the greatest extent practicable, under the same conditions (including reductions to be made in the annuity of the participant) applicable to former spouses (as defined in section 8331(23) of title 5) of participants in the Civil Service Retirement and Disability System (CSRS) as prescribed by the Civil Service Retirement Spouse Equity Act of 1984.

(Pub. L. 88–643, title II, § 226, as added Pub. L. 102–496, title VIII, § 802, Oct. 24, 1992, 106 Stat. 3220.)

REFERENCES IN TEXT

The Civil Service Retirement Spouse Equity Act of 1984, referred to in text, is Pub. L. 98–615, Nov. 8, 1984, 98 Stat. 3195, as amended. For complete classification of this Act to the Code, see Short Title of 1984 Amendment note set out under section 8331 of Title 5, Government Organization and Employees, and Tables.

PRIOR PROVISIONS

A prior section 226 of Pub. L. 88–643, as added Pub. L. 100–453, title III, § 302(a), Sept. 29, 1988, 102 Stat. 1906; amended Pub. L. 102–88, title III, § 304(b), (c), Aug. 14, 1991, 105 Stat. 431, 432; Pub. L. 102–183, title III, § 306(a), (b), Dec. 4, 1991, 105 Stat. 1265, related to survivor annuities for previous spouses and second chance to elect survivor annuity for certain spouses and was set out as a note under section 403 of this title prior to the general amendment of Pub. L. 88–643 by section 802 of Pub. L. 102–496.

SECTION REFERRED TO IN OTHER SECTIONS

This section is referred to in sections 2031, 2071 of this title.

PART D—BENEFITS ACCRUING TO CERTAIN PARTICIPANTS

§ 2051. Retirement for disability or incapacity; medical examination; recovery

(a) Disability retirement

(1) Eligibility

A participant who has become disabled shall, upon the participant's own application or upon order of the Director, be retired on an annuity computed under subsection (b) of this section.

(2) Standard for disability determination

A participant shall be considered to be disabled only if the participant—

(A) is found by the Director to be unable, because of disease or injury, to render useful and efficient service in the participant's position; and

(B) is not qualified for reassignment, under procedures prescribed by the Director, to a vacant position in the Agency at the same grade or level and in which the participant would be able to render useful and efficient service.

(3) Time limit for application

(A) One year requirement

A claim may be allowed under this section only if the application is submitted before the participant is separated from the Agency or within one year thereafter.

(B) Waiver for mentally incompetent participant

The time limitation may be waived by the Director for a participant who, at the date of separation from the Agency or within one year thereafter, is mentally incompetent, if the application is filed with the Agency within one year from the date of restoration of the participant to competency or the appointment of a fiduciary, whichever is earlier.

(b) Computation of disability annuity

(1) In general

Except as provided in paragraph (2), an annuity payable under subsection (a) of this section shall be computed under section 2031(a) of this title. However, if the disabled or incapacitated participant has less than 20 years of service credit toward retirement under the system at the time of retirement, the annuity shall be computed on the assumption that the participant has had 20 years of service, but the additional service credit that may accrue to a participant under this paragraph may not exceed the difference between the participant's age at the time of retirement and age 60.

(2) Coordination with military retired pay and veterans' compensation and pension

If a participant retiring under this section is receiving retired pay or retainer pay for military service (except that specified in section 2082(e)(3) of this title) or Department of Veterans Affairs compensation or pension in lieu of such retired or retainer pay, the annuity of that participant shall be computed under section 2031(a) of this title, excluding credit for such military service from that computation. If the amount of the annuity so computed, plus the retired or retainer pay which is received, or which would be received but for the application of the limitation in section 5532[1] of title 5, or the Department of Veterans Affairs compensation or pension in lieu of such retired or retainer pay, is less than the annuity that would be payable under this section in the absence of the previous sentence, an amount equal to the difference shall be added to the annuity payable under section 2031(a) of this title.

[1] See References in Text note below.

(c) Medical examinations

(1) Medical examination required for determination of disability

In each case, the participant shall be given a medical examination by one or more duly qualified physicians or surgeons designated by the Director to conduct examinations, and disability shall be determined by the Director on the basis of the advice of such physicians or surgeons.

(2) Annual reexaminations until age 60

Unless the disability is permanent, like examinations shall be made annually until the annuitant becomes age 60. If the Director determines on the basis of the advice of one or more duly qualified physicians or surgeons conducting such examinations that an annuitant has recovered to the extent that the annuitant can return to duty, the annuitant may apply for reinstatement or reappointment in the Agency within one year from the date the annuitant's recovery is determined.

(3) Reinstatement

Upon application, the Director may reinstate any such recovered disability annuitant in the grade held at time of retirement, or the Director may, taking into consideration the age, qualifications, and experience of such annuitant, and the present grade of the annuitant's contemporaries in the Agency, appoint the annuitant to a grade higher than the one held before retirement.

(4) Termination of disability annuity

Payment of the annuity shall continue until a date one year after the date of examination showing recovery or until the date of reinstatement or reappointment in the Agency, whichever is earlier.

(5) Payment of fees

Fees for examinations under this subsection, together with reasonable traveling and other expenses incurred in order to submit to examination, may be paid out of the fund.

(6) Suspension of annuity pending required examination

If the annuitant fails to submit to examination as required under this section, payment of the annuity shall be suspended until continuance of the disability is satisfactorily established.

(7) Termination of annuity upon restoration of earning capacity

If the annuitant receiving a disability retirement annuity is restored to earning capacity before becoming age 60, payment of the annuity terminates on reemployment by the Government or 180 days after the end of the calendar year in which earning capacity is restored, whichever is earlier. Earning capacity shall be considered to be restored if in any calendar year the income of the annuitant from wages or self-employment, or both, equals at least 80 percent of the current rate of pay for the grade and step the annuitant held at the time of retirement.

(d) Treatment of recovered disability annuitant who is not reinstated

(1) Separation

If a recovered or restored disability annuitant whose annuity is discontinued is for any reason not reinstated or reappointed in the Agency, the annuitant shall be considered, except for service credit, to have been separated within the meaning of section 2054 of this title as of the date of termination of the disability annuity.

(2) Retirement

After such termination, the recovered or restored annuitant shall be entitled to the benefits of section 2054 or 2071(a) of this title, except that the annuitant may elect voluntary retirement under section 2053 of this title, if qualified thereunder, or may be placed by the Director in an involuntary retirement status under section 2055(a) of this title, if qualified thereunder. Retirement rights under this paragraph shall be based on the provisions of this subchapter in effect as of the date on which the disability annuity is discontinued.

(3) Further disability before age 62

If, based on a current medical examination, the Director determines that a recovered annuitant has, before reaching age 62, again become totally disabled due to recurrence of the disability for which the annuitant was originally retired, the annuitant's terminated disability annuity (same type and rate) shall be reinstated from the date of such medical examination. If a restored-to-earning-capacity annuitant has not medically recovered from the disability for which retired and establishes to the Director's satisfaction that the annuitant's income from wages and self-employment in any calendar year before reaching age 62 was less than 80 percent of the rate of pay for the grade and step the annuitant held at the time of retirement, the annuitant's terminated disability annuity (same type and rate) shall be reinstated from the first of the next following year. If the annuitant has been allowed an involuntary or voluntary retirement annuity in the meantime, the annuitant's reinstated disability annuity shall be substituted for it unless the annuitant elects to retain the former benefit.

(e) Coordination of benefits

(1) Workers' compensation

A participant is not entitled to receive for the same period of time—

(A) an annuity under this subchapter, and

(B) compensation for injury to, or disability of, such participant under subchapter I of chapter 81 of title 5, other than compensation payable under section 8107 of such title.

(2) Survivor annuities

An individual is not entitled to receive an annuity under this subchapter and a concurrent benefit under subchapter I of chapter 81 of title 5 on account of the death of the same person.

(3) Greater benefit

Paragraphs (1) and (2) do not bar the right of a claimant to the greater benefit conferred by either this subchapter or subchapter I of chapter 81 of title 5.

(f) Offset from survivor annuity for workers' compensation payment

(1) Refund to Department of Labor

If an individual is entitled to an annuity under this subchapter and the individual receives a lump-sum payment for compensation under section 8135 of title 5 based on the disability or death of the same person, so much of the compensation as has been paid for a period extended beyond the date payment of the annuity commences, as determined by the Secretary of Labor, shall be refunded to the Department for credit to the Employees' Compensation Fund. Before the individual may receive the annuity, the individual shall—

(A) refund to the Secretary of Labor the amount representing the commuted compensation payments for the extended period; or

(B) authorize the deduction of the amount from the annuity.

(2) Source of deduction

Deductions from the annuity may be made from accrued or accruing payments. The amounts deducted and withheld from the annuity shall be transmitted to the Secretary for reimbursement to the Employees' Compensation Fund.

(3) Prorating deduction

If the Secretary finds that the financial circumstances of an individual entitled to an annuity under this subchapter warrant deferred refunding, deductions from the annuity may be prorated against and paid from accruing payments in such manner as the Secretary determines appropriate.

(Pub. L. 88–643, title II, § 231, as added Pub. L. 102–496, title VIII, § 802, Oct. 24, 1992, 106 Stat. 3220; amended Pub. L. 103–178, title II, § 202(a)(8), Dec. 3, 1993, 107 Stat. 2026.)

REFERENCES IN TEXT

Section 5532 of title 5, referred to in subsec. (b)(2), was repealed by Pub. L. 106–65, div. A, title VI, § 651(a)(1), Oct. 5, 1999, 113 Stat. 664.

PRIOR PROVISIONS

A prior section 231 of Pub. L. 88–643, title II, Oct. 13, 1964, 78 Stat. 1046; Ex. Ord. No. 12326, § 2, Sept. 30, 1981, 46 F.R. 48889; Pub. L. 94–522, title II, §§ 205–207, Oct. 17, 1976, 90 Stat. 2470; Ex. Ord. No. 12443, § 1, Sept. 27, 1983, 48 F.R. 44751; Pub. L. 99–335, title V, § 501(2), June 6, 1986, 100 Stat. 622; Pub. L. 102–183, title III, § 305, Dec. 4, 1991, 105 Stat. 1265, related to retirement for disability or incapacity, medical examination, and recovery and was set out as a note under section 403 of this title prior to the general amendment of Pub. L. 88–643 by section 802 of Pub. L. 102–496.

AMENDMENTS

1993—Subsec. (d)(2). Pub. L. 103–178 substituted "2071(a) of this title" for "2071(b) of this title".

EFFECTIVE DATE OF 1993 AMENDMENT

Amendment by Pub. L. 103–178 effective Feb. 1, 1993, see section 202(b) of Pub. L. 103–178, set out as a note under section 2001 of this title.

SECTION REFERRED TO IN OTHER SECTIONS

This section is referred to in sections 403s, 2031, 2093, 2111, 2143 of this title.

§ 2052. Death in service

(a) Return of contributions when no annuity payable

If a participant dies and no claim for an annuity is payable under this subchapter, the participant's lump-sum credit and any voluntary contributions made under section 2121 of this title, with interest, shall be paid in the order of precedence shown in section 2071(c) of this title.

(b) Survivor annuity for surviving spouse or former spouse

(1) In general

If a participant dies before separation or retirement from the Agency and is survived by a spouse or by a former spouse qualifying for a survivor annuity under section 2032(b) of this title, such surviving spouse shall be entitled to an annuity equal to 55 percent of the annuity computed in accordance with paragraphs (2) and (3) of this subsection and section 2031(a) of this title, and any such surviving former spouse shall be entitled to an annuity computed in accordance with section 2032(b) of this title and paragraph (2) of this subsection as if the participant died after being entitled to an annuity under this subchapter. The annuity of such surviving spouse or former spouse shall commence on the day after the participant dies and shall terminate on the last day of the month before the death or remarriage before attaining age 55 of the surviving spouse or former spouse (subject to the payment and restoration provisions of sections 2031(b)(3)(C), 2031(h), and 2032(b)(3) of this title).

(2) Computation

The annuity payable under paragraph (1) shall be computed in accordance with section 2031(a) of this title, except that the computation of the annuity of the participant under such section shall be at least the smaller of (A) 40 percent of the participant's high-3 average pay, or (B) the sum obtained under such section after increasing the participant's length of service by the difference between the participant's age at the time of death and age 60.

(3) Limitation

Notwithstanding paragraph (1), if the participant had a former spouse qualifying for an annuity under section 2032(b) of this title, the annuity of a surviving spouse under this section shall be subject to the limitation of section 2031(b)(3)(B) of this title, and the annuity of a former spouse under this section shall be subject to the limitation of section 2032(b)(4)(B) of this title.

(4) Precedence of section 2034 survivor annuity over death-in-service annuity

If a former spouse who is eligible for a death-in-service annuity under this section is or becomes eligible for an annuity under section 2034 of this title, the annuity provided under this section shall not be payable and shall be superseded by the annuity under section 2034 of this title.

(c) Annuities for surviving children

(1) Participants dying before April 1, 1992

In the case of a participant who before April 1, 1992, died before separation or retirement from the Agency and who was survived by a child or children—

(A) if the participant was survived by a spouse, there shall be paid from the fund to or on behalf of each such surviving child an annuity determined under section 2031(d)(3)(A) of this title; and

(B) if the participant was not survived by a spouse, there shall be paid from the fund to or on behalf of each such surviving child an annuity determined under section 2031(d)(3)(B) of this title.

(2) Participants dying on or after April 1, 1992

In the case of a participant who on or after April 1, 1992, dies before separation or retirement from the Agency and who is survived by a child or children—

(A) if the participant is survived by a spouse or former spouse who is the natural or adoptive parent of a surviving child of the participant, there shall be paid from the fund to or on behalf of each such surviving child an annuity determined under section 2031(d)(3)(A) of this title; and

(B) if the participant is not survived by a spouse or former spouse who is the natural or adoptive parent of a surviving child of the participant, there shall be paid to or on behalf of each such surviving child an annuity determined under section 2031(d)(3)(B) of this title.

(3) "Former spouse" defined

For purposes of this subsection, the term "former spouse" includes any former wife or husband of a participant, regardless of the length of marriage or the amount of creditable service completed by the participant.

(Pub. L. 88–643, title II, § 232, as added Pub. L. 102–496, title VIII, § 802, Oct. 24, 1992, 106 Stat. 3223; amended Pub. L. 103–178, title II, § 202(a)(9), Dec. 3, 1993, 107 Stat. 2026.)

PRIOR PROVISIONS

A prior section 232 of Pub. L. 88–643, title II, Oct. 13, 1964, 78 Stat. 1048; Pub. L. 91–185, § 4, Dec. 30, 1969, 83 Stat. 848; Pub. L. 94–522, title II, § 208, Oct. 17, 1976, 90 Stat. 2471; Pub. L. 99–335, title V, § 501(2), June 6, 1986, 100 Stat. 622; Pub. L. 100–178, title IV, § 402(a), Dec. 2, 1987, 101 Stat. 1013; Pub. L. 101–193, title III, § 303, Nov. 30, 1989, 103 Stat. 1703; Pub. L. 102–88, title III, § 305(a)(3), Aug. 14, 1991, 105 Stat. 432; Pub. L. 102–183, title III, § 302(b), (c), Dec. 4, 1991, 105 Stat. 1262, 1263; Pub. L. 102–496, title III, § 304(b), Oct. 24, 1992, 106 Stat. 3183, related to death in service and was set out as a note under section 403 of this title prior to the general amendment of Pub. L. 88–643 by section 802 of Pub. L. 102–496.

AMENDMENTS

1993—Subsec. (b)(4). Pub. L. 103–178 substituted "eligible for an annuity under section 2034" for "eligible for an annuity under section 2032".

EFFECTIVE DATE OF 1993 AMENDMENT

Amendment by Pub. L. 103–178 effective Feb. 1, 1993, see section 202(b) of Pub. L. 103–178, set out as a note under section 2001 of this title.

SECTION REFERRED TO IN OTHER SECTIONS

This section is referred to in sections 403n, 403s, 2002, 2031 of this title.

§ 2053. Voluntary retirement

(a) A participant who is at least 50 years of age and has completed 20 years of service may, on the participant's application and with the consent of the Director, be retired from the Agency and receive benefits in accordance with the provisions of section 2031 of this title if the participant has not less than 10 years of service with the Agency.

(b) A participant who has at least 25 years of service, ten years of which are with the Agency, may retire, with the consent of the Director, at any age and receive benefits in accordance with the provisions of section 2031 of this title if the Office of Personnel Management has authorized separation from service voluntarily for Agency employees under section 8336(d)(2) of title 5 with respect to the Civil Service Retirement System or section 8414(b)(1)(B) of such title with respect to the Federal Employees' Retirement System.

(Pub. L. 88–643, title II, § 233, as added Pub. L. 102–496, title VIII, § 802, Oct. 24, 1992, 106 Stat. 3225; amended Pub. L. 103–36, § 3, June 8, 1993, 107 Stat. 106.)

PRIOR PROVISIONS

A prior section 233 of Pub. L. 88–643, title II, Oct. 13, 1964, 78 Stat. 1048, related to voluntary retirement and was set out as a note under section 403 of this title prior to the general amendment of Pub. L. 88–643 by section 802 of Pub. L. 102–496.

AMENDMENTS

1993—Pub. L. 103–36 designated existing provisions as subsec. (a) and added subsec. (b).

SECTION REFERRED TO IN OTHER SECTIONS

This section is referred to in sections 2051, 2152 of this title.

§ 2054. Discontinued service benefits

(a) Deferred annuity

A participant who separates from the Agency may, upon separation or at any time before the commencement of an annuity under this subchapter, elect—

(1) to have the participant's contributions to the fund returned to the participant in accordance with section 2071(a) of this title; or

(2) except in a case in which the Director determines that separation was based in whole or in part on the ground of disloyalty to the United States, to leave the contributions in the fund and receive an annuity, computed as prescribed in section 2031 of this title, commencing at age 62.

(b) Refund of contributions if former participant dies before age 62

If a participant who qualifies under subsection (a) of this section to receive a deferred annuity commencing at age 62 dies before reaching age 62, the participant's contributions to the fund, with interest, shall be paid in accordance with the provisions of section 2071 of this title.

(Pub. L. 88–643, title II, § 234, as added Pub. L. 102–496, title VIII, § 802, Oct. 24, 1992, 106 Stat.

3225; amended Pub. L. 103–178, title II, § 202(a)(10), Dec. 3, 1993, 107 Stat. 2026.)

PRIOR PROVISIONS

A prior section 234 of Pub. L. 88–643, title II, Oct. 13, 1964, 78 Stat. 1048; Pub. L. 97–269, title VI, § 608, Sept. 27, 1982, 96 Stat. 1152; Pub. L. 99–335, title V, § 501(2), June 6, 1986, 100 Stat. 622, related to discontinued service benefits and was set out as a note under section 403 of this title prior to the general amendment of Pub. L. 88–643 by section 802 of Pub. L. 102–496.

AMENDMENTS

1993—Subsec. (b). Pub. L. 103–178 substituted "section 2071" for "sections 2071 and 2121".

EFFECTIVE DATE OF 1993 AMENDMENT

Amendment by Pub. L. 103–178 effective Feb. 1, 1993, see section 202(b) of Pub. L. 103–178, set out as a note under section 2001 of this title.

SECTION REFERRED TO IN OTHER SECTIONS

This section is referred to in sections 2051, 2071 of this title.

§ 2055. Mandatory retirement

(a) Involuntary retirement

(1) AUTHORITY OF DIRECTOR.—The Director may, in the Director's discretion, place in a retired status any participant in the system described in paragraph (2).

(2) Paragraph (1) applies with respect to any participant who has not less than 10 years of service with the Agency and who—

(A) has completed at least 25 years of service; or

(B) is at least 50 years of age and has completed at least 20 years of service.

(b) Mandatory retirement for age

(1) In general

A participant in the system shall be automatically retired from the Agency—

(A) upon reaching age 65, in the case of a participant in the system receiving compensation under the Senior Intelligence Service pay schedule at the rate of level 4 or above; and

(B) upon reaching age 60, in the case of any other participant in the system.

(2) Effective date of retirement

Retirement under paragraph (1) shall be effective on the last day of the month in which the participant reaches the age applicable to that participant under that paragraph.

(3) Authority for extension

In any case in which the Director determines it to be in the public interest, the Director may extend the mandatory retirement date for a participant under this subsection by a period of not to exceed 5 years.

(c) Retirement benefits

A participant retired under this section shall receive retirement benefits in accordance with section 2031 of this title.

(Pub. L. 88–643, title II, § 235, as added Pub. L. 102–496, title VIII, § 802, Oct. 24, 1992, 106 Stat. 3225.)

PRIOR PROVISIONS

A prior section 235 of Pub. L. 88–643, title II, Oct. 13, 1964, 78 Stat. 1049; Ex. Ord. No. 12443, § 13, Sept. 27, 1983, 48 F.R. 44754; Pub. L. 99–335, title V, § 501(2), June 6, 1986, 100 Stat. 622; Pub. L. 102–183, title III, § 307, Dec. 4, 1991, 105 Stat. 1265, related to mandatory retirement and was set out as a note under section 403 of this title prior to the general amendment of Pub. L. 88–643 by section 802 of Pub. L. 102–496.

SECTION REFERRED TO IN OTHER SECTIONS

This section is referred to in sections 2051, 2152 of this title.

§ 2056. Eligibility for annuity

(a) One-out-of-two requirement

A participant must complete, within the last two years before any separation from service (except a separation because of death or disability) at least one year of creditable civilian service during which the participant is subject to this subchapter and in a pay status before the participant or the participant's survivors are eligible for an annuity under this subchapter based on that separation.

(b) Refund of contributions for time not allowed for credit

If a participant (other than a participant separated from the service because of death or disability) fails to meet the service and pay status requirement of subsection (a) of this section, any amounts deducted from the participant's pay during the period for which no eligibility is established based on the separation shall be returned to the participant on the separation.

(c) Exception

Failure to meet the service and pay status requirement of subsection (a) of this section shall not deprive the participant or the participant's survivors of any annuity to which they may be entitled under this subchapter based on a previous separation.

(Pub. L. 88–643, title II, § 236, as added Pub. L. 102–496, title VIII, § 802, Oct. 24, 1992, 106 Stat. 3226.)

PRIOR PROVISIONS

A prior section 236 of Pub. L. 88–643, as added Pub. L. 101–193, title III, § 302(2), Nov. 30, 1989, 103 Stat. 1703, related to eligibility for annuity and was set out as a note under section 403 of this title prior to the general amendment of Pub. L. 88–643 by section 802 of Pub. L. 102–496.

A prior section 237 of Pub. L. 88–643, title II, formerly § 236, Oct. 13, 1964, 78 Stat. 1049; Pub. L. 91–626, § 4, Dec. 31, 1970, 84 Stat. 1873; Pub. L. 93–31, May 8, 1973, 87 Stat. 65; Pub. L. 99–335, title V, § 501(2), June 6, 1986, 100 Stat. 622, renumbered § 237, Pub. L. 101–193, title III, § 302(1), Nov. 30, 1989, 103 Stat. 1703, related to limitation on number of retirements and was set out as a note under section 403 of this title prior to the general amendment of Pub. L. 88–643 by section 802 of Pub. L. 102–496.

PART E—LUMP-SUM PAYMENTS

§ 2071. Lump-sum payments

(a) Entitlement to lump-sum credit

Subject to section 2082(d) of this title and subsection (b) of this section, a participant who—

(1) is separated from the Agency for at least 31 consecutive days and is not transferred to employment covered by another retirement system for Government employees;

(2) files an application with the Director for payment of the lump-sum credit;

(3) is not reemployed in a position in which the participant is subject to this subchapter at the time the participant files the application; and

(4) will not become eligible to receive an annuity under this subchapter within 31 days after filing the application,

is entitled to be paid the lump-sum credit. Receipt of the payment of the lump-sum credit by the former participant voids all annuity rights under this subchapter based on the service on which the lump-sum credit is based, until the former participant is reemployed in service subject to this subchapter.

(b) Conditions for payment of lump-sum credit

(1) In general

Whenever a former participant becomes entitled to receive payment of the lump-sum credit under subsection (a) of this section, such lump-sum credit shall be paid to the former participant and to any former spouse or former wife or husband of the former participant in accordance with paragraphs (2) through (4). The former participant's lump-sum credit shall be reduced by the amount of the lump-sum credit payable to any former spouse or former wife or husband.

(2) Pro rata share for former spouse

Unless otherwise expressly provided by any spousal agreement or court order under section 2094(b) of this title, a former spouse of the former participant shall be entitled to receive a share of such participant's lump-sum credit—

(A) if married to the participant throughout the period of creditable service of the participant, equal to 50 percent of such lump-sum credit; or

(B) if not married to the participant throughout such creditable service, equal to a proportion of 50 percent of such lump-sum credit which is the proportion that the number of days of the marriage of the former spouse to the participant during periods of creditable service of such participant bears to the total number of days of such creditable service.

(3) Share for former wife or husband

Payment of the former participant's lump-sum credit shall be subject to the terms of a court order under section 2094(c) of this title concerning any former wife or husband of the former participant if—

(A) the court order expressly relates to any portion of such lump-sum credit; and

(B) payment of the lump-sum credit would extinguish entitlement of such former wife or husband to a survivor annuity under section 2036 of this title or to any portion of the participant's annuity under section 2094(c) of this title.

(4) Notification

A lump-sum credit may be paid to or for the benefit of a former participant—

(A) only upon written notification to (i) the current spouse, if any, (ii) any former spouse, and (iii) any former wife or husband who has a court order covered by paragraph (3); and

(B) only if the express written concurrence of the current spouse has been received by the Director.

This paragraph may be waived under circumstances described in section 2031(b)(1)(D) of this title.

(c) Order of precedence of payment

A lump-sum payment authorized by subsection (d) or (e) of this section 2121(d)[1] of this title and a payment of any accrued and unpaid annuity authorized by subsection (f) of this section shall be paid in the following order of precedence to individuals surviving the participant and alive on the date entitlement to the payment arises, upon establishment of a valid claim therefor, and such payment bars recovery by any other individual:

(1) To the beneficiary or beneficiaries designated by such participant in a signed and witnessed writing received by the Director before the participant's death. For this purpose, a designation, change, or cancellation of beneficiary in a will or other document not so executed and filed with the Director shall have no force or effect.

(2) If there is no designated beneficiary, to the surviving wife or husband of such participant.

(3) If none of the above, to the child or children of such participant and descendent of deceased children by representation.

(4) If none of the above, to the parents of such participant or the survivor of them.

(5) If none of the above, to the duly appointed executor or administrator of the estate of such participant.

(6) If none of the above, to such other next of kin of such participant as the Director determines to be legally entitled to such payment.

(d) Death of former participant before retirement

(1) In general

Except as provided in paragraph (2), if a former participant eligible for a deferred annuity under section 2054 of this title dies before reaching age 62, such former participant's lump-sum credit shall be paid in accordance with subsection (c) of this section.

(2) Limitation

In any case where there is a surviving former spouse or surviving former wife or husband of such participant who is entitled to a share of such participant's lump-sum credit under paragraphs (2) and (3) of subsection (b) of this section, the lump-sum credit payable under paragraph (1) shall be reduced by the lump-sum credit payable to such former spouse or former wife or husband.

(e) Termination of all annuity rights

If all annuity rights under this subchapter based on the service of a deceased participant or annuitant terminate before the total annuity paid equals the lump-sum credit, the difference shall be paid in accordance with subsection (c) of this section.

[1] So in original. The words "of this section 2121(d)" probably should be "of this section or by section 2121(d)".

(f) Payment of accrued and unpaid annuity when retired participant dies

If a retired participant dies, any annuity accrued and unpaid shall be paid in accordance with subsection (c) of this section.

(g) Termination of survivor annuity

An annuity accrued and unpaid on the termination, except by death, of the annuity of a survivor annuitant shall be paid to that individual. An annuity accrued and unpaid on the death of a survivor annuitant shall be paid in the following order of precedence, and the payment bars recovery by any other individual:

(1) To the duly appointed executor or administrator of the estate of the survivor annuitant.

(2) If there is no executor or administrator, to such next of kin of the survivor annuitant as the Director determines to be legally entitled to such payment, except that no payment shall be made under this paragraph until after the expiration of 30 days from the date of death of the survivor annuitant.

(Pub. L. 88–643, title II, § 241, as added Pub. L. 102–496, title VIII, § 802, Oct. 24, 1992, 106 Stat. 3226; amended Pub. L. 103–178, title II, § 202(a)(11), Dec. 3, 1993, 107 Stat. 2026.)

PRIOR PROVISIONS

A prior section 241 of Pub. L. 88–643, title II, Oct. 13, 1964, 78 Stat. 1049; Pub. L. 94–522, title II, § 209, Oct. 17, 1976, 90 Stat. 2471; Ex. Ord. No. 12443, § 5, Sept. 27, 1983, 48 F.R. 44752; Pub. L. 99–335, title V, § 501(2), June 6, 1986, 100 Stat. 622, related to disposition of contributions and interest in excess of benefits received and was set out as a note under section 403 of this title prior to the general amendment of Pub. L. 88–643 by section 802 of Pub. L. 102–496.

AMENDMENTS

1993—Subsec. (c). Pub. L. 103–178, § 202(a)(11)(A), substituted "A lump-sum payment authorized by subsection (d) or (e) of this section 2121(d) of this title and a payment of any accrued and unpaid annuity authorized by subsection (f) of this section" for "A lump-sum benefit that would have been payable to a participant, former participant, or annuitant, or to a survivor annuitant, authorized by subsection (d) or (e) of this section or by section 2054(b) or 2121(d) of this title".

Subsecs. (f), (g). Pub. L. 103–178, § 202(a)(11)(B), added subsec. (f) and redesignated former subsec. (f) as (g).

EFFECTIVE DATE OF 1993 AMENDMENT

Amendment by Pub. L. 103–178 effective Feb. 1, 1993, see section 202(b) of Pub. L. 103–178, set out as a note under section 2001 of this title.

SECTION REFERRED TO IN OTHER SECTIONS

This section is referred to in sections 403n, 2002, 2021, 2051, 2052, 2054, 2094, 2121 of this title.

PART F—PERIOD OF SERVICE FOR ANNUITIES

§ 2081. Computation of length of service

(a) In general

(1) Crediting service as participant

For the purposes of this subchapter, the period of service of a participant shall be computed from the date on which the participant becomes a participant under this subchapter.

(2) Exclusion of certain periods

In computing the period of service of a participant, all periods of separation from the Agency and so much of any leave of absence without pay as may exceed six months in the aggregate in any calendar year shall be excluded, except leaves of absence while receiving benefits under chapter 81 of title 5 and leaves of absence granted participants while performing active and honorable service in the Armed Forces.

(3) Crediting certain periods of separation

A participant or former participant who returns to Government duty after a period of separation shall have included in the participant or former participant's period of service that part of the period of separation in which the participant or former participant was receiving benefits under chapter 81 of title 5.

(b) Extra credit for periods served at unhealthful posts overseas

(1) Classification of certain posts as unhealthful

The Director may from time to time establish a list of places outside the United States that, by reason of climatic or other extreme conditions, are to be classed as unhealthful posts. Such list shall be established in consultation with the Secretary of State.

(2) Extra credit

Each year of duty at a post on the list established under paragraph (1), inclusive of regular leaves of absence, shall be counted as one and a half years in computing the length of service of a participant under this subchapter for the purpose of retirement. In computing such service, any fractional month shall be treated as a full month.

(3) Coordination with benefits under title 5

Extra credit for service at an unhealthful post may not be credited to a participant who is paid a differential under section 5925 or 5928 of title 5 for the same service.

(Pub. L. 88–643, title II, § 251, as added Pub. L. 102–496, title VIII, § 802, Oct. 24, 1992, 106 Stat. 3228.)

PRIOR PROVISIONS

A prior section 251 of Pub. L. 88–643, title II, Oct. 13, 1964, 78 Stat. 1050; Pub. L. 94–522, title II, § 210, Oct. 17, 1976, 90 Stat. 2471; Pub. L. 99–169, title VII, § 702, Dec. 4, 1985, 99 Stat. 1008; Pub. L. 99–335, title V, § 501(2), June 6, 1986, 100 Stat. 622, related to computation of length of service and was set out as a note under section 403 of this title prior to the general amendment of Pub. L. 88–643 by section 802 of Pub. L. 102–496.

SECTION REFERRED TO IN OTHER SECTIONS

This section is referred to in sections 2002, 2021, 2031 of this title.

§ 2082. Prior service credit

(a) In general

A participant may, subject to the provisions of this section, include in the participant's period of service—

(1) civilian service in the Government before becoming a participant that would be creditable toward retirement under subchapter III of chapter 83 of title 5 (as determined under section 8332(b) of such title); and

(2) honorable active service in the Armed Forces before the date of the separation upon which eligibility for an annuity is based, or honorable active service in the Regular or Reserve Corps of the Public Health Service after June 30, 1960, or as a commissioned officer of the National Oceanic and Atmospheric Administration after June 30, 1961.

(b) Limitations

(1) In general

Except as provided in paragraphs (2) and (3), the total service of any participant shall exclude—

(A) any period of civilian service on or after October 1, 1982, for which retirement deductions or deposits have not been made,

(B) any period of service for which a refund of contributions has been made, or

(C) any period of service for which contributions were not transferred pursuant to subsection (c)(1) of this section;

unless the participant makes a deposit to the fund in an amount equal to the percentages of basic pay received for such service as specified in the table contained in section 8334(c) of title 5, together with interest computed in accordance with section 8334(e) of such title. The deposit may be made in one or more installments (including by allotment from pay), as determined by the Director.

(2) Effect of retirement deductions not made

If a participant has not paid a deposit for civilian service performed before October 1, 1982, for which retirement deductions were not made, such participant's annuity shall be reduced by 10 percent of the deposit described in paragraph (1) remaining unpaid, unless the participant elects to eliminate the service involved for the purpose of the annuity computation.

(3) Effect of refund of retirement contributions

A participant who received a refund of retirement contributions under this or any other retirement system for Government employees covering service for which the participant may be allowed credit under this subchapter may deposit the amount received, with interest computed under paragraph (1). Credit may not be allowed for the service covered by the refund until the deposit is made, except that a participant who—

(A) separated from Government service before October 1, 1990, and received a refund of the participant's retirement contributions covering a period of service ending before October 1, 1990;

(B) is entitled to an annuity under this subchapter (other than a disability annuity) which commences after December 1, 1992; and

(C) does not make the deposit required to receive credit for the service covered by the refund;

shall be entitled to an annuity actuarially reduced in accordance with section 8334(d)(2)(B) of title 5.

(4) Entitlement under another system

Credit toward retirement under the system shall not be allowed for any period of civilian service on the basis of which the participant is receiving (or will in the future be entitled to receive) an annuity under another retirement system for Government employees, unless the right to such annuity is waived and a deposit is made under paragraph (1) covering that period of service, or a transfer is made pursuant to subsection (c) of this section.

(c) Transfer from other Government retirement systems

(1) In general

If an employee who is under another retirement system for Government employees becomes a participant in the system by direct transfer, the Government's contributions (including interest accrued thereon computed in accordance with section 8334(e) of title 5) under such retirement system on behalf of the employee as well as such employee's total contributions and deposits (including interest accrued thereon), except voluntary contributions, shall be transferred to the employee's credit in the fund effective as of the date such employee becomes a participant in the system.

(2) Consent of employee

Each such employee shall be deemed to consent to the transfer of such funds, and such transfer shall be a complete discharge and acquittance of all claims and demands against the other Government retirement fund on account of service rendered before becoming a participant in the system.

(3) Additional contributions; refunds

A participant whose contributions are transferred pursuant to paragraph (1) shall not be required to make additional contributions for periods of service for which full contributions were made to the other Government retirement fund, nor shall any refund be made to any such participant on account of contributions made during any period to the other Government retirement fund at a higher rate than that fixed for employees by section 8334(c) of title 5 for contributions to the fund.

(d) Transfer to other Government retirement systems

(1) In general

If a participant in the system becomes an employee under another Government retirement system by direct transfer to employment covered by such system, the Government's contributions (including interest accrued thereon computed in accordance with section 8334(e) of title 5) to the fund on the participant's behalf as well as the participant's total contributions and deposits (including interest accrued thereon), except voluntary contributions, shall be transferred to the participant's credit in the fund of such other retirement system effective as of the date on which the participant becomes eligible to participate in such other retirement system.

(2) Consent of employee

Each such employee shall be deemed to consent to the transfer of such funds, and such transfer shall be a complete discharge and acquittance of all claims and demands against the fund on account of service rendered before the participant's becoming eligible for participation in that other system.

(e) Prior military service credit

(1) Application to obtain credit

If a deposit required to obtain credit for prior military service described in subsection (a)(2) of this section was not made to another Government retirement fund and transferred under subsection (c)(1) of this section, the participant may obtain credit for such military service, subject to the provisions of this subsection and subsections (f) through (h) of this section, by applying for it to the Director before retirement or separation from the Agency.

(2) Employment starting before, on, or after October 1, 1982

Except as provided in paragraph (3)—

(A) the service of a participant who first became a Federal employee before October 1, 1982, shall include credit for each period of military service performed before the date of separation on which entitlement to an annuity under this subchapter is based, subject to subsection (f) of this section; and

(B) the service of a participant who first becomes a Federal employee on or after October 1, 1982, shall include credit for—

(i) each period of military service performed before January 1, 1957, and

(ii) each period of military service performed after December 31, 1956, and before the separation on which entitlement to an annuity under this subchapter is based, only if a deposit (with interest, if any) is made with respect to that period, as provided in subsection (h) of this section.

(3) Effect of receipt of military retired pay

In the case of a participant who is entitled to retired pay based on a period of military service, the participant's service may not include credit for such period of military service unless the retired pay is paid—

(A) on account of a service-connected disability—

(i) incurred in combat with an enemy of the United States; or

(ii) caused by an instrumentality of war and incurred in the line of duty during a period of war (as defined in section 1101 of title 38); or

(B) under chapter 67 [1] of title 10.

(4) Survivor annuity

Notwithstanding paragraph (3), the survivor annuity of a survivor of a participant—

(A) who was awarded retired pay based on any period of military service, and

(B) whose death occurs before separation from the Agency,

shall be computed in accordance with section 8332(c)(3) of title 5.

(f) Effect of entitlement to social security benefits

(1) In general

Notwithstanding any other provision of this section (except paragraph (3) of this subsection) or section 2083 of this title, any military service (other than military service covered by military leave with pay from a civilian position) performed by a participant after December 1956 shall be excluded in determining the aggregate period of service on which an annuity payable under this subchapter to such participant or to the participant's spouse, former spouse, previous spouse, or child is based, if such participant, spouse, former spouse, previous spouse, or child is entitled (or would upon proper application be entitled), at the time of such determination, to monthly old-age or survivors' insurance benefits under section 402 of title 42, based on such participant's wages and self-employment income. If the military service is not excluded under the preceding sentence, but upon attaining age 62, the participant or spouse, former spouse, or previous spouse becomes entitled (or would upon proper application be entitled) to such benefits, the aggregate period of service on which the annuity is based shall be redetermined, effective as of the first day of the month in which the participant or spouse, former spouse, or previous spouse attains age 62, so as to exclude such service.

(2) Limitation

The provisions of paragraph (1) relating to credit for military service do not apply to—

(A) any period of military service of a participant with respect to which the participant has made a deposit with interest, if any, under subsection (h) of this section; or

(B) the military service of any participant described in subsection (e)(2)(B) of this section.

(3) Effect of entitlement before September 8, 1982

(A) The annuity recomputation required by paragraph (1) shall not apply to any participant who was entitled to an annuity under this subchapter on or before September 8, 1982, or who is entitled to a deferred annuity based on separation from the Agency occurring on or before such date. Instead of an annuity recomputation, the annuity of such participant shall be reduced at age 62 by an amount equal to a fraction of the participant's old-age or survivors' insurance benefits under section 402 of title 42. The reduction shall be determined by multiplying the participant's monthly Social Security benefit by a fraction, the numerator of which is the participant's total military wages and deemed additional wages (within the meaning of section 429 of title 42) that were subject to Social Security deductions and the denominator of which is the total of all the participant's wages, including military wages, and all self-employment income that were subject to Social Security deductions before the calendar year in which the determination month occurs.

(B) The reduction determined in accordance with subparagraph (A) shall not be greater than the reduction that would be required under paragraph (1) if such paragraph applied to the participant. The new formula shall be applicable to any annuity payment payable after October 1, 1982, including annuity pay-

[1] See References in Text note below.

ments to participants who had previously reached age 62 and whose annuities had already been recomputed.

(C) For purposes of this paragraph, the term "determination month" means—

(i) the first month for which the participant is entitled to old-age or survivors' insurance benefits (or would be entitled to such benefits upon application therefor); or

(ii) October 1982, in the case of any participant entitled to such benefits for that month.

(g) Deposits paid by survivors

For the purpose of survivor annuities, deposits authorized by subsections (b) and (h) of this section may also be made by the survivor of a participant.

(h) Deposits for periods of military service

(1)(A) Each participant who has performed military service before the date of separation on which entitlement to an annuity under this subchapter is based may pay to the Agency an amount equal to 7 percent of the amount of basic pay paid under section 204 of title 37 to the participant for each period of military service after December 1956; except, the amount to be paid for military service performed beginning on January 1, 1999, through December 31, 2000, shall be as follows:

7.25 percent of basic pay.	January 1, 1999, to December 31, 1999.
7.4 percent of basic pay.	January 1, 2000, to December 31, 2000.

(B) The amount of such payments shall be based on such evidence of basic pay for military service as the participant may provide or, if the Director determines sufficient evidence has not been provided to adequately determine basic pay for military service, such payment shall be based upon estimates of such basic pay provided to the Director under paragraph (4).

(2) Any deposit made under paragraph (1) more than two years after the later of—

(A) October 1, 1983, or

(B) the date on which the participant making the deposit first becomes an employee of the Federal Government,

shall include interest on such amount computed and compounded annually beginning on the date of expiration of the two-year period. The interest rate that is applicable in computing interest in any year under this paragraph shall be equal to the interest rate that is applicable for such year under section 8334(e) of title 5.

(3) Any payment received by the Director under this subsection shall be deposited in the Treasury of the United States to the credit of the fund.

(4) The provisions of section 2031(k) of this title shall apply with respect to such information as the Director determines to be necessary for the administration of this subsection in the same manner that such section applies concerning information described in that section.

(Pub. L. 88–643, title II, §252, as added Pub. L. 102–496, title VIII, §802, Oct. 24, 1992, 106 Stat. 3229; amended Pub. L. 105–33, title VII, §7001(c)(3), Aug. 5, 1997, 111 Stat. 659; Pub. L. 106–346, §101(a) [title V, §505(c)(2)], Oct. 23, 2000, 114 Stat. 1356, 1356A–53.)

REFERENCES IN TEXT

Chapter 67 of title 10, referred to in subsec. (e)(3)(B), was transferred to part II of subtitle E of Title 10, Armed Forces, renumbered as chapter 1223, and amended generally by Pub. L. 103–337, div. A, title XVI, §1662(j)(1), Oct. 5, 1994, 108 Stat. 2998. A new chapter 67 (§1331) of Title 10 was added by section 1662(j)(7) of Pub. L. 103–337.

PRIOR PROVISIONS

A prior section 252 of Pub. L. 88–643, title II, Oct. 13, 1964, 78 Stat. 1050; Pub. L. 91–626, §§5, 6, Dec. 31, 1970, 84 Stat. 1872; Pub. L. 94–522, title II, §211, Oct. 17, 1976, 90 Stat. 2471; Ex. Ord. No. 12443, §§9–11, 15, Sept. 27, 1983, 48 F.R. 44753, 44755; Ex. Ord. No. 12485, July 13, 1984, 49 F.R. 28827; Pub. L. 99–335, title V, §501(2), June 6, 1986, 100 Stat. 622; Pub. L. 102–83, §5(c)(2), Aug. 6, 1991, 105 Stat. 406, related to prior service credit and was set out as a note under section 403 of this title prior to the general amendment of Pub. L. 88–643 by section 802 of Pub. L. 102–496.

AMENDMENTS

2000—Subsec. (h)(1)(A). Pub. L. 106–346, in introductory provisions, substituted "December 31, 2000" for "December 31, 2002" and in table struck out item at end relating to payment of 7.5 percent of basic pay for service period January 1, 2001, to December 31, 2002.

1997—Subsec. (h)(1). Pub. L. 105–33 amended par. (1) generally. Prior to amendment, par. (1) read as follows: "Each participant who has performed military service before the date of separation on which entitlement to an annuity under this subchapter is based may pay to the Agency an amount equal to 7 percent of the amount of basic pay paid under section 204 of title 37 to the participant for each period of military service after December 1956. The amount of such payments shall be based on such evidence of basic pay for military service as the participant may provide or, if the Director determines sufficient evidence has not been provided to adequately determine basic pay for military service, such payment shall be based upon estimates of such basic pay provided to the Director under paragraph (4)."

EFFECTIVE DATE OF 2000 AMENDMENT

Amendment by Pub. L. 106–346 effective upon the close of calendar year 2000 and applicable thereafter, see section 101(a) [title V, §505(i)] of Pub. L. 106–346, set out as a note under section 8334 of Title 5, Government Organization and Employees.

EFFECTIVE DATE OF 1997 AMENDMENT

Amendment by Pub. L. 105–33 effective Oct. 1, 1997, see section 7001(f) of Pub. L. 105–33, set out as a note under section 8334 of Title 5, Government Organization and Employees.

SECTION REFERRED TO IN OTHER SECTIONS

This section is referred to in sections 2001, 2002, 2021, 2031, 2051, 2071, 2083, 2091 of this title.

§2083. Credit for service while on military leave

(a) General rule

A participant who, during the period of any war or of any national emergency as proclaimed by the President or declared by the Congress, leaves the participant's position in the Agency to enter military service shall not be considered, for purposes of this subchapter, as separated from the participant's position in the Agency by reason of such military service, unless the participant applies for and receives a refund of contributions under this subchapter. Such a participant may not be considered as retaining such position in the Agency after December 31, 1956, or upon the expiration of five years of such military service, whichever is later.

(b) Waiver of contributions

Except to the extent provided under section 2082(e) or 2082(h) of this title, contributions shall not be required covering periods of leave of absence from the Agency granted a participant while performing active service in the Armed Forces.

(Pub. L. 88–643, title II, § 253, as added Pub. L. 102–496, title VIII, § 802, Oct. 24, 1992, 106 Stat. 3234.)

PRIOR PROVISIONS

A prior section 253 of Pub. L. 88–643, title II, Oct. 13, 1964, 78 Stat. 1052; Pub. L. 99–335, title V, § 501(2), June 6, 1986, 100 Stat. 622, related to credit for service while on military leave and was set out as a note under section 403 of this title prior to the general amendment of Pub. L. 88–643 by section 802 of Pub. L. 102–496.

SECTION REFERRED TO IN OTHER SECTIONS

This section is referred to in sections 2002, 2082 of this title.

PART G—MONEYS

§ 2091. Estimate of appropriations needed

(a) Estimates of annual appropriations

The Director shall prepare the estimates of the annual appropriations required to be made to the fund.

(b) Actuarial valuations

The Director shall cause to be made actuarial valuations of the fund at such intervals as the Director determines to be necessary, but not less often than every five years.

(c) Changes in law affecting actuarial status of fund

Any statute which authorizes—

(1) new or increased benefits payable from the fund under this subchapter, including annuity increases other than under section 2131 of this title;

(2) extension of the coverage of this subchapter to new groups of employees; or

(3) increases in pay on which benefits are computed;

is deemed to authorize appropriations to the fund in order to provide funding for the unfunded liability created by that statute, in 30 equal annual installments with interest computed at the rate used in the then most recent valuation of the system and with the first payment thereof due as of the end of the fiscal year in which such new or liberalized benefit, extension of coverage, or increase in pay is effective.

(d) Authorization

There is hereby authorized to be appropriated to the fund for each fiscal year such amounts as may be necessary to meet the amount of normal cost for each year that is not met by contributions under section 2021(a) of this title.

(e) Unfunded liability; credit allowed for military service

There is hereby authorized to be appropriated to the fund for each fiscal year such sums as may be necessary to provide the amount equivalent to—

(1) interest on the unfunded liability computed for that year at the interest rate used in the then most recent valuation of the system; and

(2) that portion of disbursement for annuities for that year that the Director estimates is attributable to credit allowed for military service,

less an amount determined by the Director to be appropriate to reflect the value of the deposits made to the credit of the fund under section 2082(h) of this title.

(Pub. L. 88–643, title II, § 261, as added Pub. L. 102–496, title VIII, § 802, Oct. 24, 1992, 106 Stat. 3234.)

PRIOR PROVISIONS

A prior section 261 of Pub. L. 88–643, title II, Oct. 13, 1964, 78 Stat. 1052; Pub. L. 94–522, title I, § 102, Oct. 17, 1976, 90 Stat. 2467; Ex. Ord. No. 12443, § 12, Sept. 27, 1983, 48 F.R. 44754; Pub. L. 99–335, title V, § 501(2), (3), June 6, 1986, 100 Stat. 622, related to estimate of appropriations needed and was set out as a note under section 403 of this title prior to the general amendment of Pub. L. 88–643 by section 802 of Pub. L. 102–496.

SECTION REFERRED TO IN OTHER SECTIONS

This section is referred to in section 2001 of this title.

§ 2092. Investment of moneys in fund

The Director may, with the approval of the Secretary of the Treasury, invest from time to time in interest-bearing securities of the United States such portions of the fund as in the Director's judgment may not be immediately required for the payment of annuities, cash benefits, refunds, and allowances from the fund. The income derived from such investments shall be credited to and constitute a part of the fund.

(Pub. L. 88–643, title II, § 262, as added Pub. L. 102–496, title VIII, § 802, Oct. 24, 1992, 106 Stat. 3235.)

PRIOR PROVISIONS

A prior section 262 of Pub. L. 88–643, title II, Oct. 13, 1964, 78 Stat. 1052, related to investment of moneys in the fund and was set out as a note under section 403 of this title prior to the general amendment of Pub. L. 88–643 by section 802 of Pub. L. 102–496.

§ 2093. Payment of benefits

(a) Annuities stated as annual amounts

Each annuity is stated as an annual amount, $1/12$ of which, rounded to the next lowest dollar, constitutes the monthly rate payable on the first business day of the month after the month or other period for which it has accrued.

(b) Commencement of annuity

(1) Commencement of annuity for participants generally

Except as otherwise provided in paragraph (2), the annuity of a participant who has met the eligibility requirements for an annuity shall commence on the first day of the month after separation from the Agency or after pay ceases and the service and age requirements for title to an annuity are met.

(2) Exceptions

The annuity of—

(A) a participant involuntarily separated from the Agency;

(B) a participant retiring under section 2051 of this title due to a disability; and

(C) a participant who serves 3 days or less in the month of retirement;

shall commence on the day after separation from the Agency or the day after pay ceases and the service and age or disability requirements for title to annuity are met.

(3) Other annuities

Any other annuity payable from the fund commences on the first day of the month after the occurrence of the event on which payment thereof is based.

(c) Termination of annuity

An annuity payable from the fund shall terminate—

(1) in the case of a retired participant, on the day death or any other terminating event provided by this subchapter occurs; or

(2) in the case of a former spouse or a survivor, on the last day of the month before death or any other terminating event occurs.

(d) Application for survivor annuities

The annuity to a survivor shall become effective as otherwise specified but shall not be paid until the survivor submits an application for such annuity, supported by such proof of eligibility as the Director may require. If such application or proof of eligibility is not submitted during the lifetime of an otherwise eligible individual, no annuity shall be due or payable to the individual's estate.

(e) Waiver of annuity

An individual entitled to an annuity from the fund may decline to accept all or any part of the annuity by submitting a signed waiver to the Director. The waiver may be revoked in writing at any time. Payment of the annuity waived may not be made for the period during which the waiver is in effect.

(f) Limitations

(1) Application before 115th anniversary

No payment shall be made from the fund unless an application for benefits based on the service of the participant is received by the Director before the 115th anniversary of the participant's birth.

(2) Application within 30 years

Notwithstanding paragraph (1), after the death of a participant or retired participant, no benefit based on that participant's service may be paid from the fund unless an application for the benefit is received by the Director within 30 years after the death or other event which gives rise to eligibility for the benefit.

(g) Withholding of State income tax from annuities

(1) Agreements with States

The Director shall, in accordance with this subsection, enter into an agreement with any State within 120 days of a request for agreement from the proper State official. The agreement shall provide that the Director shall withhold State income tax in the case of the monthly annuity of any annuitant who voluntarily requests, in writing, such withholding. The amounts withheld during any calendar quarter shall be held in the Fund[1] and disbursed to the States during the month following that calendar quarter.

(2) Limitation on multiple requests

An annuitant may have in effect at any time only one request for withholding under this subsection, and an annuitant may not have more than two such requests during any one calendar year.

(3) Change in State designation

Subject to paragraph (2), an annuitant may change the State designated by that annuitant for purposes of having withholdings made, and may request that the withholdings be remitted in accordance with such change. An annuitant also may revoke any request of that annuitant for withholding. Any change in the State designated or revocation is effective on the first day of the month after the month in which the request or the revocation is processed by the Director, but in no event later than on the first day of the second month beginning after the day on which such request or revocation is received by the Director.

(4) General provisions

This subsection does not give the consent of the United States to the application of a statute which imposes more burdensome requirements of the United States than on employers generally, or which subjects the United States or any annuitant to a penalty or liability because of this subsection. The Director may not accept pay from a State for services performed in withholding State income taxes from annuities. Any amount erroneously withheld from an annuity and paid to a State by the Director shall be repaid by the State in accordance with regulations prescribed by the Director.

(5) "State" defined

For the purpose of this subsection, the term "State" includes the District of Columbia and any territory or possession of the United States.

(Pub. L. 88–643, title II, §263, as added Pub. L. 102–496, title VIII, §802, Oct. 24, 1992, 106 Stat. 3235.)

PRIOR PROVISIONS

A prior section 263 of Pub. L. 88–643, title II, Oct. 13, 1964, 78 Stat. 1052; Pub. L. 97–269, title VI, §609, Sept. 27, 1982, 96 Stat. 1153; Pub. L. 99–335, title V, §501(2), June 6, 1986, 100 Stat. 622, related to attachment of moneys and was set out as a note under section 403 of this title prior to the general amendment of Pub. L. 88–643 by section 802 of Pub. L. 102–496.

§ 2094. Attachment of moneys

(a) Exemption from legal process

Except as provided in subsections (b), (c), and (e) of this section, none of the moneys men-

[1] So in original. Probably should not be capitalized.

tioned in this subchapter shall be assignable either in law or equity, or be subject to execution, levy, attachment, garnishment, or other legal process, except as otherwise may be provided by Federal laws.

(b) Payment to former spouses under court order or spousal agreement

In the case of any participant, former participant, or retired participant who has a former spouse who is covered by a court order or who is a party to a spousal agreement—

(1) any right of the former spouse to any annuity under section 2032(a) of this title in connection with any retirement or disability annuity of the participant, and the amount of any such annuity;

(2) any right of the former spouse of a participant or retired participant to a survivor annuity under section 2032(b) or 2032(c) of this title, and the amount of any such annuity; and

(3) any right of the former spouse of a former participant to any payment of a lump-sum credit under section 2071(b) of this title, and the amount of any such payment;

shall be determined in accordance with that spousal agreement or court order, if and to the extent expressly provided for in the terms of the spousal agreement or court order that are not inconsistent with the requirements of this subchapter.

(c) Other payments under court orders

Payments under this subchapter that would otherwise be made to a participant, former participant, or retired participant based upon that participant's service shall be paid, in whole or in part, by the Director to another individual if and to the extent expressly provided for in the terms of any court decree of divorce, annulment, or legal separation, or the terms of any court order or court-approved property settlement agreement incident to any court decree of divorce, annulment, or legal separation.

(d) Prospective payments; bar to recovery

(1) Subsections (b) and (c) of this section apply only to payments made under this subchapter for periods beginning after the date of receipt by the Director of written notice of such decree, order, or agreement and such additional information and documentation as the Director may require.

(2) Any payment under subsection (b) or (c) of this section to an individual bars recovery by any other individual.

(e) Allotments

An individual entitled to an annuity from the fund may make allotments or assignments of amounts from such annuity for such purposes as the Director considers appropriate.

(Pub. L. 88–643, title II, § 264, as added Pub. L. 102–496, title VIII, § 802, Oct. 24, 1992, 106 Stat. 3237; amended Pub. L. 103–178, title II, § 202(a)(12), Dec. 3, 1993, 107 Stat. 2027.)

PRIOR PROVISIONS

A prior section 264 of Pub. L. 88–643, as added Pub. L. 94–522, title II, § 212, Oct. 17, 1976, 90 Stat. 2471, related to recovery of payments and was set out as a note under section 403 of this title prior to the general amendment of Pub. L. 88–643 by section 802 of Pub. L. 102–496. See section 2095 of this title.

AMENDMENTS

1993—Subsec. (b)(2). Pub. L. 103–178, § 202(a)(12)(A), inserted "and" at end.

Subsec. (b)(3). Pub. L. 103–178, § 202(a)(12)(B), substituted ", and the amount of any such payment;" for "and to any payment of a return of contributions under section 2054(a) of this title; and".

Subsec. (b)(4). Pub. L. 103–178, § 202(a)(12)(C), struck out par. (4) which read as follows: "any right of the former spouse of a participant or former participant to a lump-sum payment or additional annuity payable from a voluntary contribution account under section 2121 of this title;".

EFFECTIVE DATE OF 1993 AMENDMENT

Amendment by Pub. L. 103–178 effective Feb. 1, 1993, see section 202(b) of Pub. L. 103–178, set out as a note under section 2001 of this title.

SECTION REFERRED TO IN OTHER SECTIONS

This section is referred to in sections 403n, 2031, 2032, 2033, 2071 of this title.

§ 2095. Recovery of payments

Recovery of payments under this subchapter may not be made from an individual when, in the judgment of the Director, the individual is without fault and recovery would be against equity and good conscience. Withholding or recovery of money payable pursuant to this subchapter on account of a certification or payment made by a former employee of the Agency in the discharge of the former employee's official duties may be made if the Director certifies that the certification or payment involved fraud on the part of the former employee.

(Pub. L. 88–643, title II, § 265, as added Pub. L. 102–496, title VIII, § 802, Oct. 24, 1992, 106 Stat. 3237; amended Pub. L. 103–178, title II, § 202(a)(13), Dec. 3, 1993, 107 Stat. 2027.)

AMENDMENTS

1993—Pub. L. 103–178 substituted "subchapter" for "chapter" in two places.

EFFECTIVE DATE OF 1993 AMENDMENT

Amendment by Pub. L. 103–178 effective Feb. 1, 1993, see section 202(b) of Pub. L. 103–178, set out as a note under section 2001 of this title.

PART H—RETIRED PARTICIPANTS RECALLED, REINSTATED, OR REAPPOINTED IN AGENCY OR REEMPLOYED IN GOVERNMENT

§ 2111. Recall

(a) Authority to recall

The Director may, with the consent of a retired participant, recall that participant to service in the Agency whenever the Director determines that such recall is in the public interest.

(b) Pay of retired participant while serving

A retired participant recalled to duty in the Agency under subsection (a) of this section or reinstated or reappointed in accordance with section 2051(b)[1] of this title shall, while so serving, be entitled, in lieu of the retired participant's annuity, to the full basic pay of the grade

[1] So in original. Probably should be section "2051(c)".

in which the retired participant is serving. During such service, the retired participant shall make contributions to the fund in accordance with section 2021 of this title.

(c) Recomputation of annuity

When the retired participant reverts to retired status, the annuity of the retired participant shall be redetermined in accordance with section 2031 of this title.

(Pub. L. 88–643, title II, § 271, as added Pub. L. 102–496, title VIII, § 802, Oct. 24, 1992, 106 Stat. 3238.)

PRIOR PROVISIONS

A prior section 271 of Pub. L. 88–643, title II, Oct. 13, 1964, 78 Stat. 1052, related to recalled participants and was set out as a note under section 403 of this title prior to the general amendment of Pub. L. 88–643 by section 802 of Pub. L. 102–496.

SECTION REFERRED TO IN OTHER SECTIONS

This section is referred to in sections 2031, 2032, 2152 of this title.

§ 2112. Reemployment

A participant retired under this subchapter shall not, by reason of that retired status, be barred from employment in Federal Government service in any appointive position for which the participant is qualified.

(Pub. L. 88–643, title II, § 272, as added Pub. L. 102–496, title VIII, § 802, Oct. 24, 1992, 106 Stat. 3238.)

PRIOR PROVISIONS

A prior section 272 of Pub. L. 88–643, title II, Oct. 13, 1964, 78 Stat. 1053; Pub. L. 99–335, title V, § 501(2), June 6, 1986, 100 Stat. 622, related to reemployed participants and was set out as a note under section 403 of this title prior to the general amendment of Pub. L. 88–643 by section 802 of Pub. L. 102–496.

SECTION REFERRED TO IN OTHER SECTIONS

This section is referred to in section 2032 of this title.

§ 2113. Reemployment compensation

(a) Deduction from basic pay

An annuitant who has retired under this subchapter and who is reemployed in the Federal Government service in any appointive position (either on a part-time or full-time basis) shall be entitled to receive the annuity payable under this subchapter, but there shall be deducted from the annuitant's basic pay a sum equal to the annuity allocable to the period of actual employment.

(b) Recovery of overpayments

In the event of an overpayment under this section, the amount of the overpayment shall be recovered by withholding the amount involved from the basic pay payable to such reemployed annuitant or from any other moneys, including the annuitant's annuity, payable in accordance with this subchapter.

(c) Deposit in fund

Sums deducted from the basic pay of a reemployed annuitant under this section shall be deposited in the Treasury of the United States to the credit of the fund.

(Pub. L. 88–643, title II, § 273, as added Pub. L. 102–496, title VIII, § 802, Oct. 24, 1992, 106 Stat. 3238.)

PRIOR PROVISIONS

A prior section 273 of Pub. L. 88–643, title II, Oct. 13, 1964, 78 Stat. 1053; Pub. L. 99–335, title V, § 501(2), June 6, 1986, 100 Stat. 622, related to reemployment compensation and was set out as a note under section 403 of this title prior to the general amendment of Pub. L. 88–643 by section 802 of Pub. L. 102–496.

SECTION REFERRED TO IN OTHER SECTIONS

This section is referred to in section 2032 of this title.

PART I—VOLUNTARY CONTRIBUTIONS

§ 2121. Voluntary contributions

(a) Authority for voluntary contributions

(1) In general

Under such regulations as may be prescribed by the Director, a participant may voluntarily contribute additional sums in multiples of one percent of the participant's basic pay, but not in excess of 10 percent of such basic pay.

(2) Interest

The voluntary contribution account in each case is the sum of unrefunded contributions, plus interest—

(A) for periods before January 1, 1985, at 3 percent a year; and

(B) for periods on or after January 1, 1985, at the rate computed under section 8334(e) of title 5,

compounded annually to the date of election under subsection (b) of this section or the date of payment under subsection (d) of this section.

(b) Treatment of voluntary contributions

Effective on the date of retirement and at the election of the participant, the participant's account shall be—

(1) returned in a lump sum;

(2) used to purchase an additional life annuity;

(3) used to purchase an additional life annuity for the participant and to provide for a cash payment on the participant's death to a beneficiary; or

(4) used to purchase an additional life annuity for the participant and a life annuity commencing on the participant's death payable to a beneficiary, with a guaranteed return to the beneficiary or the beneficiary's legal representative of an amount equal to the cash payment referred to in paragraph (3).

In the case of a benefit provided under paragraph (3) or (4), the participant shall notify the Director in writing of the name of the beneficiary of the cash payment or life annuity to be paid upon the participant's death.

(c) Value of benefits

The benefits provided by subsection (b)(2), (3), or (4) of this section shall be actuarially equivalent in value to the payment provided for in subsection (b)(1) of this section and shall be calculated upon such tables of mortality as may be from time to time prescribed for this purpose by the Director.

(d) Lump-sum payment

A voluntary contribution account shall be paid in a lump sum at such time as the participant dies or separates from the Agency without entitlement to an annuity. In the case of death, the account shall be paid in the order of precedence specified in section 2071(c) of this title.

(e) Benefits in addition to other benefits

Any benefit payable to a participant or to the participant's beneficiary with respect to the additional contributions provided under this section shall be in addition to benefits otherwise provided under this subchapter.

(Pub. L. 88–643, title II, § 281, as added Pub. L. 102–496, title VIII, § 802, Oct. 24, 1992, 106 Stat. 3239.)

PRIOR PROVISIONS

A prior section 281 of Pub. L. 88–643, title II, Oct. 13, 1964, 78 Stat. 1053; Ex. Ord. No. 12443, § 3, Sept. 27, 1983, 48 F.R. 44751; Pub. L. 99–335, title V, § 501(2), June 6, 1986, 100 Stat. 622, related to voluntary contributions and was set out as a note under section 403 of this title prior to the general amendment of Pub. L. 88–643 by section 802 of Pub. L. 102–496.

SECTION REFERRED TO IN OTHER SECTIONS

This section is referred to in sections 2021, 2052, 2071 of this title.

PART J—COST-OF-LIVING ADJUSTMENT OF ANNUITIES

§ 2131. Cost-of-living adjustment of annuities

(a) In general

Each annuity payable from the fund shall be adjusted as follows:

(1) Each cost-of-living annuity increase under this section shall be identical to the corresponding percentage increase under section 8340(b) of title 5.

(2) A cost-of-living increase made under paragraph (1) shall become effective under this section on the effective date of each such increase under section 8340(b) of title 5. Except as provided in subsection (b) of this section, each such increase shall be applied to each annuity payable from the fund which has a commencing date not later than the effective date of the increase.

(b) Eligibility

Eligibility for an annuity increase under this section shall be governed by the commencing date of each annuity payable from the fund as of the effective date of an increase, except as follows:

(1) The first cost-of-living increase (if any) made under subsection (a) of this section to an annuity which is payable from the fund to a participant who retires, to the surviving spouse, former spouse, or previous spouse of a participant who dies in service, or to the surviving spouse, former spouse, previous spouse, or insurable interest designee of a deceased annuitant whose annuity has not been increased under this subsection or subsection (a) of this section, shall be equal to the product (adjusted to the nearest $\frac{1}{10}$ of one percent) of—

(A) $\frac{1}{12}$ of the applicable percent change computed under subsection (a) of this section, multiplied by

(B) the number of months (not to exceed 12 months, counting any portion of a month as a month)—

(i) for which the annuity was payable from the fund before the effective date of the increase, or

(ii) in the case of a surviving spouse, former spouse, previous spouse, or insurable interest designee of a deceased annuitant whose annuity has not been so increased, since the annuity was first payable to the deceased annuitant.

(2) Effective from its commencing date, an annuity payable from the fund to an annuitant's survivor (other than a child entitled to an annuity under section 2031(d) of this title) shall be increased by the total percentage increase the annuitant was receiving under this section at death.

(3) For purposes of computing the annuity of a child under section 2031(d) of this title that commences after October 31, 1969, the dollar amounts specified in section 2031(d)(3) of this title shall each be increased by the total percentage increases allowed and in force under this section on or after such day and, in the case of a deceased annuitant, the percentages specified in that section shall be increased by the total percent allowed and in force to the annuitant under this section on or after such day.

(c) Limitation

An annuity increase provided by this section may not be computed on any additional annuity purchased at retirement by voluntary contributions.

(d) Rounding to next lower dollar

The monthly annuity installment, after adjustment under this section, shall be rounded to the next lowest dollar, except that such installment shall, after adjustment, reflect an increase of at least $1.

(e) Limitation on maximum amount of annuity

(1) In general

An annuity shall not be increased by reason of an adjustment under this section to an amount which exceeds the greater of—

(A) the maximum pay payable for GS–15 30 days before the effective date of the adjustment under this section; or

(B) the final pay (or average pay, if higher) of the participant with respect to whom the annuity is paid, increased by the overall annual average percentage adjustments (compounded) in the rates of pay of the General Schedule under subchapter I of chapter 53 of title 5 during the period—

(i) beginning on the date on which the annuity commenced (or, in the case of a survivor of the retired participant, the date on which the participant's annuity commenced), and

(ii) ending on the effective date of the adjustment under this section.

(2) "Pay" defined

For purposes of paragraph (1), the term ''pay'' means the rate of salary or basic pay as payable under any provision of law, including any provision of law limiting the expenditure of appropriated funds.

(Pub. L. 88–643, title II, §291, as added Pub. L. 102–496, title VIII, §802, Oct. 24, 1992, 106 Stat. 3240; amended Pub. L. 103–178, title II, §202(a)(14), Dec. 3, 1993, 107 Stat. 2027.)

REFERENCES IN TEXT

GS–15, referred to in subsec. (e)(1)(A), probably means GS–15 of the General Schedule which is set out under section 5332 of Title 5, Government Organization and Employees.

PRIOR PROVISIONS

A prior section 291 of Pub. L. 88–643, title II, Oct. 13, 1964, 78 Stat. 1054; Pub. L. 90–539, Sept. 30, 1968, 82 Stat. 902; Pub. L. 91–185, §5, Dec. 30, 1969, 83 Stat. 849; Pub. L. 93–210, §1(a), Dec. 28, 1973, 87 Stat. 908; Pub. L. 94–361, title VIII, §801(b), July 14, 1976, 90 Stat. 929; Ex. Ord. No. 12326, §4, Sept. 30, 1981, 46 F.R. 48889; Ex. Ord. No. 12443, §§6, 14, Sept. 27, 1983, 48 F.R. 44752, 44754; Pub. L. 99–335, title V, §501(3), June 6, 1986, 100 Stat. 622, related to cost-of-living adjustment of annuities and was set out as a note under section 403 of this title prior to the general amendment of Pub. L. 88–643 by section 802 of Pub. L. 102–496.

AMENDMENTS

1993—Subsec. (b)(2). Pub. L. 103–178 struck out "or section 2052(c) of this title" after "section 2031(d) of this title".

EFFECTIVE DATE OF 1993 AMENDMENT

Amendment by Pub. L. 103–178 effective Feb. 1, 1993, see section 202(b) of Pub. L. 103–178, set out as a note under section 2001 of this title.

DELAY IN COST-OF-LIVING ADJUSTMENTS DURING FISCAL YEARS 1994, 1995, AND 1996

Any cost-of-living increase scheduled to take effect during fiscal year 1994, 1995, or 1996 under this section delayed until first day of third calendar month after date such increase would otherwise take effect, see section 11001 of Pub. L. 103–66, set out as a note under section 8340 of Title 5, Government Organization and Employees.

SECTION REFERRED TO IN OTHER SECTIONS

This section is referred to in sections 2031, 2032, 2091 of this title.

PART K—CONFORMITY WITH CIVIL SERVICE RETIREMENT SYSTEM

§2141. Authority to maintain existing areas of conformity between Civil Service and Central Intelligence Agency Retirement and Disability Systems

(a) Presidential authority

(1) Conformity to CSRS by Executive order

Whenever the President determines that it would be appropriate for the purpose of maintaining existing conformity between the Civil Service Retirement and Disability System and the Central Intelligence Agency Retirement and Disability System with respect to substantially identical provisions, the President may, by Executive order, extend to current or former participants in the Central Intelligence Agency Retirement and Disability System, or to their survivors, a provision of law enacted after January 1, 1975, which—

(A) amends subchapter III of chapter 83 of title 5 and is applicable to civil service employees generally; or

(B) otherwise affects current or former participants in the Civil Service Retirement and Disability System, or their survivors.

(2) Extension to CIARDS

Any such order shall extend such provision of law so that it applies in like manner with respect to such Central Intelligence Agency Retirement and Disability System participants, former participants, or survivors.

(3) Legal status

Any such order shall have the force and effect of law.

(4) Effective date

Any such order may be given retroactive effect to a date not earlier than the effective date of the corresponding provision of law applicable to employees under the Civil Service Retirement System.

(b) Effect of Executive order

Provisions of an Executive order issued pursuant to this section shall modify, supersede, or render inapplicable, as the case may be, to the extent inconsistent therewith—

(1) provisions of law enacted before the effective date of the Executive order; and

(2) any prior provision of an Executive order issued under this section.

(Pub. L. 88–643, title II, §292, as added Pub. L. 102–496, title VIII, §802, Oct. 24, 1992, 106 Stat. 3241.)

PRIOR PROVISIONS

A prior section 292 of Pub. L. 88–643, as added Pub. L. 94–522, title II, §213, Oct. 17, 1976, 90 Stat. 2471, 2472, related to authority to maintain existing areas of conformity between Civil Service and Central Intelligence Agency Retirement and Disability Systems and was set out as a note under section 403 of this title prior to the general amendment of Pub. L. 88–643 by section 802 of Pub. L. 102–496.

OPEN ENROLLMENT SEASON FOR PARTICIPANTS IN THE CENTRAL INTELLIGENCE AGENCY RETIREMENT AND DISABILITY SYSTEM

The Director to provide an open enrollment period for employee participants in the Central Intelligence Agency Retirement and Disability System to elect the Federal Employees' Retirement System, see Ex. Ord. No. 13105, §2, Nov. 2, 1998, 63 F.R. 60201, set out as a note under section 4067 of Title 22, Foreign Relations and Intercourse.

§2142. Thrift Savings Plan participation

(a) Eligibility for Thrift Savings Plan

Participants in the system shall be deemed to be employees for the purposes of section 8351 of title 5.

(b) Management of Thrift Savings Plan accounts by Director

Subsections (k) and (m) of section 8461 of title 5 shall apply with respect to contributions made by participants to the Thrift Savings Fund under section 8351 of such title and to earnings attributable to the investment of such contributions.

(Pub. L. 88–643, title II, §293, as added Pub. L. 102–496, title VIII, §802, Oct. 24, 1992, 106 Stat. 3242.)

PRIOR PROVISIONS

A prior section 293 of Pub. L. 88–643, as added Pub. L. 99–335, title V, § 504, June 6, 1986, 100 Stat. 623, related to Thrift Savings Fund participation by participants in the Central Intelligence Agency Retirement and Disability System and was set out as a note under section 403 of this title prior to the general amendment of Pub. L. 88–643 by section 802 of Pub. L. 102–496.

§ 2143. Alternative forms of annuities

(a) Authority for alternative form of annuity

The Director shall prescribe regulations under which any participant who has a life-threatening affliction or other critical medical condition may, at the time of retiring under this subchapter (other than under section 2051 of this title), elect annuity benefits under this section instead of any other benefits under this subchapter (including any survivor benefits under this subchapter) based on the service of the participant creditable under this subchapter.

(b) Basis for alternative forms of annuity

The regulations and alternative forms of annuity shall, to the maximum extent practicable, meet the requirements prescribed in section 8343a of title 5.

(c) Lump-sum credit

Any lump-sum credit provided pursuant to an election under subsection (a) of this section shall not preclude an individual from receiving other benefits provided under that subsection.

(d) Submission of regulations to congressional intelligence committees

The Director shall submit the regulations prescribed under subsection (a) of this section to the congressional intelligence committees before the regulations take effect.

(Pub. L. 88–643, title II, § 294, as added Pub. L. 102–496, title VIII, § 802, Oct. 24, 1992, 106 Stat. 3242; amended Pub. L. 103–66, title XI, § 11002(c), Aug. 10, 1993, 107 Stat. 409.)

PRIOR PROVISIONS

A prior section 294 of Pub. L. 88–643, as added Pub. L. 99–335, title V, § 505, June 6, 1986, 100 Stat. 624, related to alternative forms of annuities and was set out as a note under section 403 of this title prior to the general amendment of Pub. L. 88–643 by section 802 of Pub. L. 102–496.

AMENDMENTS

1993—Subsec. (a). Pub. L. 103–66 substituted "any participant who has a life-threatening affliction or other critical medical condition" for "a participant".

EFFECTIVE DATE OF 1993 AMENDMENT

Amendment by Pub. L. 103–66 effective Oct. 1, 1994, and applicable with respect to any annuity commencing on or after that date, see section 11002(d) of Pub. L. 103–66, set out as a note under section 8343a of Title 5, Government Organization and Employees.

SECTION REFERRED TO IN OTHER SECTIONS

This section is referred to in section 2034 of this title.

§ 2144. Payments from CIARDS fund for portions of certain Civil Service Retirement System annuities

The amount of the increase in any annuity that results from the application of section 403r of this title, if and when such increase is based on an individual's overseas service as an employee of the Central Intelligence Agency, shall be paid from the fund.

(Pub. L. 88–643, title II, § 295, as added Pub. L. 102–496, title VIII, § 802, Oct. 24, 1992, 106 Stat. 3242.)

PRIOR PROVISIONS

A prior section 295 of Pub. L. 88–643, as added Pub. L. 101–193, title III, § 307(b), Nov. 30, 1989, 103 Stat. 1707, related to payments from CIARDS fund for portions of certain Civil Service Retirement System annuities and was set out as a note under section 403 of this title prior to the general amendment of Pub. L. 88–643 by section 802 of Pub. L. 102–496.

SUBCHAPTER III—PARTICIPATION IN FEDERAL EMPLOYEES' RETIREMENT SYSTEM

SUBCHAPTER REFERRED TO IN OTHER SECTIONS

This subchapter is referred to in section 2021 of this title; title 22 section 4071c.

§ 2151. Application of Federal Employees' Retirement System to Agency employees

(a) General rule

Except as provided in subsections (b) and (c) of this section, all employees of the Agency, any of whose service after December 31, 1983, is employment for the purpose of title II of the Social Security Act [42 U.S.C. 401 et seq.] and chapter 21 of title 26, shall be subject to chapter 84 of title 5.

(b) Exception for pre-1984 employees

Participants in the Central Intelligence Agency Retirement and Disability System who were participants in such system on or before December 31, 1983, and who have not had a break in service in excess of one year since that date, are not subject to chapter 84 of title 5 without regard to whether they are subject to title II of the Social Security Act [42 U.S.C. 401 et seq.].

(c) Nonapplicability of FERS to certain employees

(1) The provisions of chapter 84 of title 5 shall not apply with respect to—

(A) any individual who separates, or who has separated, from Federal Government service after having been an employee of the Agency subject to subchapter II of this chapter; and

(B) any employee of the Agency having at least 5 years of civilian service which was performed before January 1, 1987, and is creditable under subchapter II of this chapter (determined without regard to any deposit or redeposit requirement under subchapter III of chapter 83 of title 5, or under subchapter II of this chapter, or any requirement that the individual become subject to such subchapter or to subchapter II of this chapter after performing the service involved).

(2) Paragraph (1) shall not apply with respect to an individual who has elected under regulations prescribed under section 2157 of this title to become subject to chapter 84 of title 5 to the extent provided in such regulations.

(3) An individual described in paragraph (1) shall be deemed to be an individual excluded under section 8402(b)(2) of title 5.

(d) Election to become subject to FERS

An employee who is designated as a participant in the Central Intelligence Agency Retirement and Disability System after December 31, 1987, pursuant to section 2013 of this title may elect to become subject to chapter 84 of title 5. Such election—

(1) shall not be effective unless it is made during the six-month period beginning on the date on which the employee is so designated;

(2) shall take effect beginning with the first pay period beginning after the date of the election; and

(3) shall be irrevocable.

(e) Special rules

The application of the provisions of chapter 84 of title 5 to an employee referred to in subsection (a) of this section shall be subject to the exceptions and special rules provided in this subchapter. Any provision of that chapter which is inconsistent with a special rule provided in this subchapter shall not apply to such employees.

(Pub. L. 88–643, title III, §301, as added Pub. L. 102–496, title VIII, §802, Oct. 24, 1992, 106 Stat. 3243.)

REFERENCES IN TEXT

The Social Security Act, referred to in subsecs. (a) and (b), is act Aug. 14, 1935, ch. 531, 49 Stat. 620, as amended. Title II of the Act is classified generally to subchapter II (§401 et seq.) of chapter 7 of Title 42, The Public Health and Welfare. For complete classification of this Act to the Code, see section 1305 of Title 42 and Tables.

PRIOR PROVISIONS

A prior section 301 of Pub. L. 88–643, as added Pub. L. 99–335, title V, §506, June 6, 1986, 100 Stat. 624; amended Pub. L. 99–514, §2, Oct. 22, 1986, 100 Stat. 2095; Pub. L. 100–453, title V, §502, Sept. 29, 1988, 102 Stat. 1909, related to application of Federal Employees' Retirement System to Agency employees and was set out as a note under section 403 of this title prior to the general amendment of Pub. L. 88–643 by section 802 of Pub. L. 102–496.

SECTION REFERRED TO IN OTHER SECTIONS

This section is referred to in sections 2013, 2031 of this title.

§2152. Special rules relating to section 2013 criteria employees

(a) In general

Except as otherwise provided in this section, in the application of chapter 84 of title 5 to an employee of the Agency who is subject to such chapter and is designated by the Director under the criteria prescribed in section 2013 of this title, such employee shall be treated for purposes of determining such employee's retirement benefits and obligations under such chapter as if the employee were a law enforcement officer (as defined in section 8401(17) of title 5).

(b) Voluntary and mandatory retirement

The provisions of sections 2053 and 2055 of this title shall apply to employees referred to in subsection (a) of this section, except that the retirement benefits shall be determined under chapter 84 of title 5.

(c) Recall

(1) Except as provided in paragraph (2), section 2111 of this title shall apply to an employee referred to in subsection (a) of this section.

(2) Contributions during recall service shall be made as provided in section 8422 of title 5.

(3) When an employee recalled under this subsection reverts to a retired status, the annuity of such employee shall be redetermined under the provisions of chapter 84 of title 5.

(Pub. L. 88–643, title III, §302, as added Pub. L. 102–496, title VIII, §802, Oct. 24, 1992, 106 Stat. 3244.)

PRIOR PROVISIONS

A prior section 302 of Pub. L. 88–643, as added Pub. L. 99–335, title V, §506, June 6, 1986, 100 Stat. 625, related to special rules relating to employees designated under criteria of former section 203 of Pub. L. 88–643 and was set out as a note under section 403 of this title prior to the general amendment of Pub. L. 88–643 by section 802 of Pub. L. 102–496.

SECTION REFERRED TO IN OTHER SECTIONS

This section is referred to in sections 2153, 2154, 2155 of this title; title 22 section 4071d.

§2153. Special rules for other employees for service abroad

(a) Special computation rule

Notwithstanding any provision of chapter 84 of title 5, the annuity under subchapter II of such chapter of a retired employee of the Agency who is not designated under section 2152(a) of this title and who has served abroad as an employee of the Agency after December 31, 1986, shall be computed as provided in subsection (b) of this section.

(b) Computation

(1) Service abroad

The portion of the annuity relating to such service abroad shall be computed as provided in section 8415(d) of title 5.

(2) Other service

The portions of the annuity relating to other creditable service shall be computed as provided in section 8415 of such title that is applicable to such service under the conditions prescribed in chapter 84 of such title.

(Pub. L. 88–643, title III, §303, as added Pub. L. 102–496, title VIII, §802, Oct. 24, 1992, 106 Stat. 3244.)

PRIOR PROVISIONS

A prior section 303 of Pub. L. 88–643, as added Pub. L. 99–335, title V, §506, June 6, 1986, 100 Stat. 626, related to special rules for other employees for service abroad and was set out as a note under section 403 of this title prior to the general amendment of Pub. L. 88–643 by section 802 of Pub. L. 102–496.

SECTION REFERRED TO IN OTHER SECTIONS

This section is referred to in section 403r–1 of this title; title 10 section 1605; title 22 section 4071d.

§2154. Special rules for former spouses

(a) General rule

Except as otherwise specifically provided in this section, the provisions of chapter 84 of title

5 shall apply in the case of an employee of the Agency who is subject to chapter 84 of title 5 and who has a former spouse (as defined in section 8401(12) of title 5) or a qualified former spouse.

(b) Definitions

For purposes of this section:

(1) Employee

The term "employee" means an employee of the Agency who is subject to chapter 84 of title 5, including an employee referred to in section 2152(a) of this title.

(2) Qualified former spouse

The term "qualified former spouse" means a former spouse of an employee or retired employee who—

(A) in the case of a former spouse whose divorce from such employee became final on or before December 4, 1991, was married to such employee for not less than 10 years during periods of the employee's service which are creditable under section 8411 of title 5, at least 5 years of which were spent outside the United States by both the employee and the former spouse during the employee's service with the Agency; and

(B) in the case of a former spouse whose divorce from such employee becomes final after December 4, 1991, was married to such employee for not less than 10 years during periods of the employee's service which are creditable under section 8411 of title 5, at least 5 years of which were spent by the employee outside the United States during the employee's service with the Agency or otherwise in a position the duties of which qualified the employee for designation by the Director under the criteria prescribed in section 2013 of this title.

(3) Pro rata share

The term "pro rata share" means the percentage that is equal to (A) the number of days of the marriage of the qualified former spouse to the employee during the employee's periods of creditable service under chapter 84 of title 5, divided by (B) the total number of days of the employee's creditable service.

(4) Spousal agreement

The term "spousal agreement" means an agreement between an employee, former employee, or retired employee and such employee's spouse or qualified former spouse that—

(A) is in writing, is signed by the parties, and is notarized;

(B) has not been modified by court order; and

(C) has been authenticated by the Director.

(5) Court order

The term "court order" means any court decree of divorce, annulment or legal separation, or any court order or court-approved property settlement agreement incident to such court decree of divorce, annulment, or legal separation.

(c) Entitlement of qualified former spouse to retirement benefits

(1) Entitlement

(A) In general

Unless otherwise expressly provided by a spousal agreement or court order governing disposition of benefits payable under subchapter II or V of chapter 84 of title 5, a qualified former spouse of an employee is entitled to a share (determined under subparagraph (B)) of all benefits otherwise payable to such employee under subchapter II or V of chapter 84 of title 5.

(B) Amount of share

The share referred to in subparagraph (A) equals—

(i) 50 percent, if the qualified former spouse was married to the employee throughout the entire period of the employee's service which is creditable under chapter 84 of title 50;[1] or

(ii) a pro rata share of 50 percent, if the qualified former spouse was not married to the employee throughout such creditable service.

(2) Annuity supplement

The benefits payable to an employee under subchapter II of chapter 84 of title 5 shall include, for purposes of this subsection, any annuity supplement payable to such employee under sections 8421 and 8421a of such title.

(3) Disqualification upon remarriage before age 55

A qualified former spouse shall not be entitled to any benefit under this subsection if, before the commencement of any benefit, the qualified former spouse remarries before becoming 55 years of age.

(4) Commencement and termination

(A) Commencement

The benefits of a qualified former spouse under this subsection commence on the later of—

(i) the day on which the employee upon whose service the benefits are based becomes entitled to the benefits; or

(ii) the first day of the second month beginning after the date on which the Director receives written notice of the court order or spousal agreement, together with such additional information or documentation as the Director may prescribe.

(B) Termination

The benefits of the qualified former spouse and the right thereto terminate on—

(i) the last day of the month before the qualified former spouse remarries before 55 years of age or dies; or

(ii) the date on which the retired employee's benefits terminate (except in the case of benefits subject to paragraph (5)(B)).

(5) Payments to retired employees

(A) Calculation of survivor annuity

Any reduction in payments to a retired employee as a result of payments to a quali-

[1] So in original. Probably should be title "5".

fied former spouse under this subsection shall be disregarded in calculating—

(i) the survivor annuity for any spouse, former spouse (qualified or otherwise), or other survivor under chapter 84 of title 5, and

(ii) any reduction in the annuity of the retired employee to provide survivor benefits under subsection (d) of this section or under sections[2] 8442 or 8445 of title 5.

(B) Reduction in basic pay upon recall to service

If a retired employee whose annuity is reduced under paragraph (1) is recalled to service under section 2152(c) of this title, the basic pay of that annuitant shall be reduced by the same amount as the annuity would have been reduced if it had continued. Amounts equal to the reductions under this subparagraph shall be deposited in the Treasury of the United States to the credit of the Civil Service Retirement and Disability Fund.

(6) Special rules for disability annuitants

Notwithstanding paragraphs (1) and (4), in the case of any qualified former spouse of a disability annuitant—

(A) the annuity of such former spouse shall commence on the date on which the employee would qualify, on the basis of the employee's creditable service, for benefits under subchapter II of chapter 84 of title 5 or on the date on which the disability annuity begins, whichever is later; and

(B) the amount of the annuity of the qualified former spouse shall be calculated on the basis of the benefits for which the employee would otherwise qualify under subchapter II of chapter 84 of such title.

(7) Pro rata share in case of employees transferred to FERS

Notwithstanding paragraph (1)(B), in the case of an employee who has elected to become subject to chapter 84 of title 5, the share of such employee's qualified former spouse shall equal the sum of—

(A) 50 percent of the employee's annuity under subchapter III of chapter 83 of title 5 or under subchapter II of this chapter (computed in accordance with section 302(a) of the Federal Employees' Retirement System Act of 1986 or section 2157 of this title), multiplied by the proportion that the number of days of marriage during the period of the employee's creditable service before the effective date of the election to transfer bears to the employee's total creditable service before such effective date; and

(B) if applicable, 50 percent of the employee's benefits under chapter 84 of title 5 or section 2152(a) of this title (computed in accordance with section 302(a) of the Federal Employees' Retirement System Act of 1986 or section 2157 of this title), multiplied by the proportion that the number of days of marriage during the period of the employee's creditable service on and after the effective date of the election to transfer bears to the employee's total creditable service after such effective date.

(8) Treatment of pro rata share under title 26

For purposes of title 26, payments to a qualified former spouse under this subsection shall be treated as income to the qualified former spouse and not to the employee.

(d) Qualified former spouse survivor benefits

(1) Entitlement

(A) In general

Subject to an election under section 8416(a) of title 5, and unless otherwise expressly provided by any spousal agreement or court order governing survivor benefits payable under this subsection to a qualified former spouse, such former spouse is entitled to a share, determined under subparagraph (B), of all survivor benefits that would otherwise be payable under subchapter IV of chapter 84 of title 5 to an eligible surviving spouse of the employee.

(B) Amount of share

The share referred to in subparagraph (A) equals—

(i) 100 percent, if the qualified former spouse was married to the employee throughout the entire period of the employee's service which is creditable under chapter 84 of title 5; or

(ii) a pro rata share of 100 percent, if the qualified former spouse was not married to the employee throughout such creditable service.

(2) Survivor benefits

(A) The survivor benefits payable under this subsection to a qualified former spouse shall include the amount payable under section 8442(b)(1)(A) of title 5 and any supplementary annuity under section 8442(f) of such title that would be payable if such former spouse were a widow or widower entitled to an annuity under such section.

(B) Any calculation under section 8442(f) of title 5 of the supplementary annuity payable to a widow or widower of an employee referred to in section 2152(a) of this title shall be based on an "assumed CIARDS annuity" rather than an "assumed CSRS annuity" as stated in section 8442(f) of such title. For the purpose of this subparagraph, the term "assumed CIARDS annuity" means the amount of the survivor annuity to which the widow or widower would be entitled under subchapter II of this chapter based on the service of the deceased annuitant determined under section 8442(f)(5) of such title.

(3) Disqualification upon remarriage before age 55

A qualified former spouse shall not be entitled to any benefit under this subsection if, before commencement of any benefit, the qualified former spouse remarries before becoming 55 years of age.

(4) Restoration

If the survivor annuity payable under this subsection to a surviving qualified former

[2] So in original. Probably should be "section".

spouse is terminated because of remarriage before becoming age 55, the annuity shall be restored at the same rate commencing on the date such remarriage is dissolved by death, divorce, or annulment, if—

(A) such former spouse elects to receive this survivor annuity instead of any other survivor benefit to which such former spouse may be entitled under subchapter IV of chapter 84 of title 5, or under another retirement system for Government employees by reason of the remarriage; and

(B) any lump sum paid on termination of the annuity is returned to the Civil Service Retirement and Disability Fund.

(5) Modification of court order or spousal agreement

A modification in a court order or spousal agreement to adjust a qualified former spouse's share of the survivor benefits shall not be effective if issued after the retirement or death of the employee, former employee, or annuitant, whichever occurs first.

(6) Effect of termination of qualified former spouse's entitlement

After a qualified former spouse of a retired employee remarries before becoming age 55 or dies, the reduction in the retired employee's annuity for the purpose of providing a survivor annuity for such former spouse shall be terminated. The annuitant may elect, in a signed writing received by the Director within 2 years after the qualified former spouse's remarriage or death, to continue the reduction in order to provide or increase the survivor annuity for such annuitant's spouse. The annuitant making such election shall pay a deposit in accordance with the provisions of section 8418 of title 5.

(7) Pro rata share in case of employees transferred to FERS

Notwithstanding paragraph (1)(B), in the case of an employee who has elected to become subject to chapter 84 of title 5, the share of such employee's qualified former spouse to survivor benefits shall equal the sum of—

(A) 50 percent of the employee's annuity under subchapter III of chapter 83 of title 5 or under subchapter II of this chapter (computed in accordance with section 302(a) of the Federal Employees' Retirement System Act of 1986 or section 2157 of this title), multiplied by the proportion that the number of days of marriage during the period of the employee's creditable service before the effective date of the election to transfer bears to the employee's total creditable service before such effective date; and

(B) if applicable—

(i) 50 percent of the employee's annuity under chapter 84 of title 5 or section 2152(a) of this title (computed in accordance with section 302(a) of the Federal Employees' Retirement System Act of 1986 or section 2157 of this title), plus

(ii) the survivor benefits referred to in subsection (d)(2)(A) of this section,

multiplied by the proportion that the number of days of marriage during the period of the employee's creditable service on and after the effective date of the election to transfer bears to the employee's total creditable service after such effective date.

(e) Qualified former spouse Thrift Savings Plan benefit

(1) Entitlement

(A) In general

Unless otherwise expressly provided by a spousal agreement or court order governing disposition of the balance of an account in the Thrift Savings Fund under subchapter III of chapter 84 of title 5, a qualified former spouse of an employee is entitled to a share (determined under subparagraph (B)) of the balance in the employee's account in the Thrift Savings Fund on the date the divorce of the qualified former spouse and employee becomes final.

(B) Amount of share

The share referred to in subparagraph (A) equals 50 percent of the employee's account balance in the Thrift Savings Fund that accrued during the period of marriage. For purposes of this subsection, the employee's account balance shall not include the amount of any outstanding loan.

(2) Payment of benefit

(A) Time of payment

The entitlement of a qualified former spouse under paragraph (1) shall be effective on the date the divorce of the qualified former spouse and employee becomes final. The qualified former spouse's benefit shall be payable after the date on which the Director receives the divorce decree or any applicable court order or spousal agreement, together with such additional information or documentation as the Director may require.

(B) Method of payment

The qualified former spouse's benefit under this subsection shall be paid in a lump sum.

(C) Limitation

A spousal agreement or court order may not provide for payment to a qualified former spouse under this subsection of an amount that exceeds the employee's account balance in the Thrift Savings Fund.

(D) Death of qualified former spouse

If the qualified former spouse dies before payment of the benefit provided under this subsection, such payment shall be made to the estate of the qualified former spouse.

(E) Bar to recovery

Any payment under this subsection to an individual bars recovery by any other individual.

(3) Closed account

No payment under this subsection may be made by the Director if the date on which the divorce becomes final is after the date on which the total amount of the employee's account balance has been withdrawn or transferred, or the date on which an annuity contract has been purchased, in accordance with section 8433 of title 5.

(f) Preservation of rights of qualified former spouses

An employee may not make an election or modification of election under section 8417 or 8418 of title 5, or other section relating to the employee's annuity under subchapter II of chapter 84 of title 5, that would diminish the entitlement of a qualified former spouse to any benefit granted to such former spouse by this section or by court order or spousal agreement.

(g) Payment of share of lump-sum credit

Whenever an employee or former employee becomes entitled to receive the lump-sum credit under section 8424(a) of title 5, a share (determined under subsection (c)(1)(B) of this section) of that lump-sum credit shall be paid to any qualified former spouse of such employee, unless otherwise expressly provided by any spousal agreement or court order governing disposition of the lump-sum credit involved.

(h) Payment to qualified former spouses under court order or spousal agreement

In the case of any employee or retired employee who has a qualified former spouse who is covered by a court order or who is a party to a spousal agreement—

(1) any right of the qualified former spouse to any retirement benefits under subsection (c) of this section and to any survivor benefits under subsection (d) of this section, and the amount of any such benefits;

(2) any right of the qualified former spouse to any Thrift Savings Plan benefit under subsection (e) of this section, and the amount of any such benefit; and

(3) any right of the qualified former spouse to any payment of a lump-sum credit under subsection (g) of this section, and the amount of any such payment;

shall be determined in accordance with that spousal agreement or court order, if and to the extent expressly provided for in the terms of the spousal agreement or court order that are not inconsistent with the requirements of this section.

(i) Applicability of CIARDS former spouse benefits

(1) Except as provided in paragraph (2), in the case of an employee who has elected to become subject to chapter 84 of title 5, the provisions of sections 2034 and 2035 of this title shall apply to such employee's former spouse (as defined in section 2002(a)(4) of this title) who would otherwise be eligible for benefits under sections 2034 and 2035 of this title but for the employee having elected to become subject to such chapter.

(2) For the purposes of computing such former spouse's benefits under sections 2034 and 2035 of this title—

(A) the retirement benefits shall be equal to the amount determined under subsection (c)(7)(A) of this section; and

(B) the survivor benefits shall be equal to 55 percent of the full amount of the employee's annuity computed in accordance with section 302(a) of the Federal Employees' Retirement System Act of 1986 or regulations prescribed under section 2157 of this title.

(3) Benefits provided pursuant to this subsection shall be payable from the Central Intelligence Agency Retirement and Disability Fund.

(Pub. L. 88–643, title III, §304, as added Pub. L. 102–496, title VIII, §802, Oct. 24, 1992, 106 Stat. 3244; amended Pub. L. 103–178, title II, §202(a)(15), Dec. 3, 1993, 107 Stat. 2027.)

REFERENCES IN TEXT

Section 302(a) of the Federal Employees' Retirement System Act of 1986, referred to in subsecs. (c)(7)(A), (B), (d)(7)(A), (B)(i), and (i)(2)(B), is section 302(a) of Pub. L. 99–335, which is set out as a note under section 8331 of Title 5, Government Organization and Employees.

PRIOR PROVISIONS

A prior section 304 of Pub. L. 88–643, as added Pub. L. 99–335, title V, §506, June 6, 1986, 100 Stat. 626; amended Pub. L. 100–178, title IV, §402(b)(2), Dec. 2, 1987, 101 Stat. 1014; Pub. L. 102–183, title III, §309(a), Dec. 4, 1991, 105 Stat. 1266, related to special rules for former spouses and was set out as a note under section 403 of this title prior to the general amendment of Pub. L. 88–643 by section 802 of Pub. L. 102–496.

AMENDMENTS

1993—Subsec. (i)(1). Pub. L. 103–178 substituted "section 2002(a)(4)" for "section 2002(a)(3)".

EFFECTIVE DATE OF 1993 AMENDMENT

Amendment by Pub. L. 103–178 effective Feb. 1, 1993, see section 202(b) of Pub. L. 103–178, set out as a note under section 2001 of this title.

§2155. Administrative provisions

(a) Finality of decisions of Director

Section 2011(c) of this title shall apply in the administration of chapter 84 of title 5 with respect to employees of the Agency.

(b) Exception

Notwithstanding subsection (a) of this section, section 8461(e) of title 5 shall apply with respect to employees of the Agency who are not participants in the Central Intelligence Agency Retirement and Disability System and are not designated under section 2152(a) of this title.

(Pub. L. 88–643, title III, §305, as added Pub. L. 102–496, title VIII, §802, Oct. 24, 1992, 106 Stat. 3251.)

PRIOR PROVISIONS

A prior section 305 of Pub. L. 88–643, as added Pub. L. 99–335, title V, §506, June 6, 1986, 100 Stat. 627, related to administrative provisions and was set out as a note under section 403 of this title prior to the general amendment of Pub. L. 88–643 by section 802 of Pub. L. 102–496.

SECTION REFERRED TO IN OTHER SECTIONS

This section is referred to in section 2011 of this title.

§2156. Regulations

(a) Requirement

The Director shall prescribe in regulations appropriate procedures to carry out this subchapter. Such regulations shall be prescribed in consultation with the Director of the Office of

Personnel Management and the Executive Director of the Federal Retirement Thrift Investment Board.

(b) Congressional review

The Director shall submit regulations prescribed under subsection (a) of this section to the congressional intelligence committees before they take effect.

(Pub. L. 88–643, title III, §306, as added Pub. L. 102–496, title VIII, §802, Oct. 24, 1992, 106 Stat. 3251.)

PRIOR PROVISIONS

A prior section 306 of Pub. L. 88–643, as added Pub. L. 99–335, title V, §506, June 6, 1986, 100 Stat. 628, related to regulations and was set out as a note under section 403 of this title prior to the general amendment of Pub. L. 88–643 by section 802 of Pub. L. 102–496.

§2157. Transition regulations

(a) Regulations

The Director shall prescribe regulations providing for the transition from the Central Intelligence Agency Retirement and Disability System to the Federal Employees' Retirement System provided in chapter 84 of title 5 in a manner consistent with sections 301 through 304 of the Federal Employees' Retirement System Act of 1986.

(b) Congressional review

The Director shall submit regulations prescribed under subsection (a) of this section to the congressional intelligence committees before they take effect.

(Pub. L. 88–643, title III, §307, as added Pub. L. 102–496, title VIII, §802, Oct. 24, 1992, 106 Stat. 3251.)

REFERENCES IN TEXT

Sections 301 through 304 of the Federal Employees' Retirement System Act of 1986, referred to in subsec. (a), are sections 301 to 304 of Pub. L. 99–335, which amended section 3121 of Title 26, Internal Revenue Code, and section 410 of Title 42, The Public Health and Welfare, and enacted provisions set out as a note under section 8331 of Title 5, Government Organization and Employees.

PRIOR PROVISIONS

A prior section 307 of Pub. L. 88–643, as added Pub. L. 99–335, title V, §506, June 6, 1986, 100 Stat. 628, related to transition provisions and regulations and was set out as a note under section 403 of this title prior to the general amendment of Pub. L. 88–643 by section 802 of Pub. L. 102–496.

SECTION REFERRED TO IN OTHER SECTIONS

This section is referred to in sections 2151, 2154 of this title; title 26 section 3121; title 42 section 410.

CHAPTER 39—SPOILS OF WAR

§2201. Transfers of spoils of war

(a) Eligibility for transfer

Spoils of war in the possession, custody, or control of the United States may be transferred to any other party, including any government, group, or person, by sale, grant, loan or in any other manner, only to the extent and in the same manner that property of the same type, if otherwise owned by the United States, may be so transferred.

(b) Terms and conditions

Any transfer pursuant to subsection (a) of this section shall be subject to all of the terms, conditions, and requirements applicable to the transfer of property of the same type otherwise owned by the United States.

(Pub. L. 103–236, title V, §552, Apr. 30, 1994, 108 Stat. 482.)

SHORT TITLE

Section 551 of Pub. L. 103–236 provided that: "This part [part B (§§551–556) of title V of Pub. L. 103–236, enacting this chapter] may be cited as the 'Spoils of War Act of 1994'."

§2202. Prohibition on transfers to countries which support terrorism

Spoils of war in the possession, custody, or control of the United States may not be transferred to any country determined by the Secretary of State, for purposes of section 2780 of title 22, to be a nation whose government has repeatedly provided support for acts of international terrorism.

(Pub. L. 103–236, title V, §553, Apr. 30, 1994, 108 Stat. 482.)

§2203. Report on previous transfers

Not later than 90 days after April 30, 1994, the President shall submit to the appropriate congressional committees a report describing any spoils of war obtained subsequent to August 2, 1990 that were transferred to any party, including any government, group, or person, before April 30, 1994. Such report shall be submitted in unclassified form to the extent possible.

(Pub. L. 103–236, title V, §554, Apr. 30, 1994, 108 Stat. 482.)

§2204. Definitions

As used in this chapter—

(1) the term "appropriate congressional committees" means the Committee on Foreign Relations of the Senate and the Committee on Foreign Affairs of the House of Representatives, or, where required by law for certain reporting purposes, the Select Committee on Intelligence of the Senate and the Select[1] Committee on Intelligence of the House of Representatives;

(2) the term "enemy" means any country, government, group, or person that has been engaged in hostilities, whether or not lawfully authorized, with the United States;

(3) the term "person" means—

[1] So in original. Probably should be preceded by "Permanent".

(A) any natural person;

(B) any corporation, partnership, or other legal entity; and

(C) any organization, association, or group; and

(4) the term "spoils of war" means enemy movable property lawfully captured, seized, confiscated, or found which has become United States property in accordance with the laws of war.

(Pub. L. 103–236, title V, § 555, Apr. 30, 1994, 108 Stat. 482.)

CHANGE OF NAME

Committee on Foreign Affairs of House of Representatives treated as referring to Committee on International Relations of House of Representatives by section 1(a) of Pub. L. 104–14, set out as a note preceding section 21 of Title 2, The Congress.

§ 2205. Construction

Nothing in this chapter shall apply to—

(1) the abandonment or failure to take possession of spoils of war by troops in the field for valid military reasons related to the conduct of the immediate conflict, including the burden of transporting such property or a decision to allow allied forces to take immediate possession of certain property solely for use during an ongoing conflict;

(2) the abandonment or return of any property obtained, borrowed, or requisitioned for temporary use during military operations without intent to retain possession of such property;

(3) the destruction of spoils of war by troops in the field;

(4) the return of spoils of war to previous owners from whom such property had been seized by enemy forces; or

(5) minor articles of personal property which have lawfully become the property of individual members of the armed forces as war trophies pursuant to public written authorization from the Department of Defense.

(Pub. L. 103–236, title V, § 556, Apr. 30, 1994, 108 Stat. 483.)

CHAPTER 40—DEFENSE AGAINST WEAPONS OF MASS DESTRUCTION

§ 2301. Findings

Congress makes the following findings:

(1) Weapons of mass destruction and related materials and technologies are increasingly available from worldwide sources. Technical information relating to such weapons is readily available on the Internet, and raw materials for chemical, biological, and radiological weapons are widely available for legitimate commercial purposes.

(2) The former Soviet Union produced and maintained a vast array of nuclear, biological, and chemical weapons of mass destruction.

(3) Many of the states of the former Soviet Union retain the facilities, materials, and technologies capable of producing additional quantities of weapons of mass destruction.

(4) The disintegration of the former Soviet Union was accompanied by disruptions of command and control systems, deficiencies in accountability for weapons, weapons-related materials and technologies, economic hardships, and significant gaps in border control among the states of the former Soviet Union. The problems of organized crime and corruption in the states of the former Soviet Union increase the potential for proliferation of nuclear, radiological, biological, and chemical weapons and related materials.

(5) The conditions described in paragraph (4) have substantially increased the ability of potentially hostile nations, terrorist groups, and individuals to acquire weapons of mass destruction and related materials and technologies from within the states of the former Soviet Union and from unemployed scientists who worked on those programs.

(6) As a result of such conditions, the capability of potentially hostile nations and terrorist groups to acquire nuclear, radiological, biological, and chemical weapons is greater than at any time in history.

(7) The President has identified North Korea, Iraq, Iran, and Libya as hostile states which already possess some weapons of mass destruction and are developing others.

(8) The acquisition or the development and use of weapons of mass destruction is well within the capability of many extremist and terrorist movements, acting independently or as proxies for foreign states.

(9) Foreign states can transfer weapons to or otherwise aid extremist and terrorist movements indirectly and with plausible deniability.

(10) Terrorist groups have already conducted chemical attacks against civilian targets in the United States and Japan, and a radiological attack in Russia.

(11) The potential for the national security of the United States to be threatened by nuclear, radiological, chemical, or biological terrorism must be taken seriously.

(12) There is a significant and growing threat of attack by weapons of mass destruction on targets that are not military targets in the usual sense of the term.

(13) Concomitantly, the threat posed to the citizens of the United States by nuclear, radiological, biological, and chemical weapons delivered by unconventional means is significant and growing.

(14) Mass terror may result from terrorist incidents involving nuclear, radiological, biological, or chemical materials.

(15) Facilities required for production of radiological, biological, and chemical weapons are much smaller and harder to detect than nuclear weapons facilities, and biological and chemical weapons can be deployed by alternative delivery means other than long-range ballistic missiles.

(16) Covert or unconventional means of delivery of nuclear, radiological, biological, and chemical weapons include cargo ships, passenger aircraft, commercial and private vehicles and vessels, and commercial cargo shipments routed through multiple destinations.

(17) Traditional arms control efforts assume large state efforts with detectable manufacturing programs and weapons production programs, but are ineffective in monitoring and controlling smaller, though potentially more dangerous, unconventional proliferation efforts.

(18) Conventional counterproliferation efforts would do little to detect or prevent the rapid development of a capability to suddenly manufacture several hundred chemical or biological weapons with nothing but commercial supplies and equipment.

(19) The United States lacks adequate planning and countermeasures to address the threat of nuclear, radiological, biological, and chemical terrorism.

(20) The Department of Energy has established a Nuclear Emergency Response Team which is available in case of nuclear or radiological emergencies, but no comparable units exist to deal with emergencies involving biological or chemical weapons or related materials.

(21) State and local emergency response personnel are not adequately prepared or trained for incidents involving nuclear, radiological, biological, or chemical materials.

(22) Exercises of the Federal, State, and local response to nuclear, radiological, biological, or chemical terrorism have revealed serious deficiencies in preparedness and severe problems of coordination.

(23) The development of, and allocation of responsibilities for, effective countermeasures

to nuclear, radiological, biological, or chemical terrorism in the United States requires well-coordinated participation of many Federal agencies, and careful planning by the Federal Government and State and local governments.

(24) Training and exercises can significantly improve the preparedness of State and local emergency response personnel for emergencies involving nuclear, radiological, biological, or chemical weapons or related materials.

(25) Sharing of the expertise and capabilities of the Department of Defense, which traditionally has provided assistance to Federal, State, and local officials in neutralizing, dismantling, and disposing of explosive ordnance, as well as radiological, biological, and chemical materials, can be a vital contribution to the development and deployment of countermeasures against nuclear, biological, and chemical weapons of mass destruction.

(26) The United States lacks effective policy coordination regarding the threat posed by the proliferation of weapons of mass destruction.

(Pub. L. 104–201, div. A, title XIV, §1402, Sept. 23, 1996, 110 Stat. 2715.)

SHORT TITLE OF 1996 AMENDMENT

Pub. L. 104–293, title VII, §701, Oct. 11, 1996, 110 Stat. 3470, provided that: "This title [enacting section 2366 of this title and provisions set out as a note under section 2351 of this title] may be cited as the 'Combatting Proliferation of Weapons of Mass Destruction Act of 1996'."

SHORT TITLE

Section 1401 of title XIV of div. A of Pub. L. 104–201 provided that: "This title [enacting this chapter, section 382 of Title 10, Armed Forces, and sections 175a and 2332d of Title 18, Crimes and Criminal Procedure, amending section 1705 of this title, section 372 of Title 10, and provisions set out as a note under section 5955 of Title 22, Foreign Relations and Intercourse] may be cited as the 'Defense Against Weapons of Mass Destruction Act of 1996'."

COMMISSION TO ASSESS THE THREAT TO THE UNITED STATES FROM ELECTROMAGNETIC PULSE (EMP) ATTACK

Pub. L. 106–398, §1 [[div. A], title XIV], Oct. 30, 2000, 114 Stat. 1654, 1654A–345, provided that:

"SEC. 1401. ESTABLISHMENT OF COMMISSION.

"(a) ESTABLISHMENT.—There is hereby established a commission to be known as the 'Commission to Assess the Threat to the United States from Electromagnetic Pulse Attack' (hereafter in this title referred to as the 'Commission').

"(b) COMPOSITION.—The Commission shall be composed of nine members. Seven of the members shall be appointed by the Secretary of Defense and two of the members shall be appointed by the Director of the Federal Emergency Management Agency. In selecting individuals for appointment to the Commission, the Secretary of Defense shall consult with the chairmen and ranking minority members of the Committees on Armed Services of the Senate and House of Representatives.

"(c) QUALIFICATIONS.—Members of the Commission shall be appointed from among private United States citizens with knowledge and expertise in the scientific, technical, and military aspects of electromagnetic pulse (hereafter in this title referred to as 'EMP') effects resulting from the detonation of a nuclear weapon or weapons at high altitude, sometimes referred to as high-altitude electromagnetic pulse effects (HEMP).

"(d) CHAIRMAN OF COMMISSION.—The Secretary of Defense shall designate one of the members of the Commission to serve as chairman of the Commission.

"(e) PERIOD OF APPOINTMENT; VACANCIES.—Members shall be appointed for the life of the Commission. Any vacancy in the Commission shall be filled in the same manner as the original appointment.

"(f) SECURITY CLEARANCES.—All members of the Commission shall hold appropriate security clearances.

"(g) INITIAL ORGANIZATION REQUIREMENTS.—All appointments to the Commission shall be made not later than 90 days after the date of the enactment of this Act [Oct. 30, 2000]. The Commission shall convene its first meeting not later than 60 days after the date as of which all members of the Commission have been appointed.

"SEC. 1402. DUTIES OF COMMISSION.

"(a) REVIEW OF EMP THREAT.—The Commission shall assess—

"(1) the nature and magnitude of potential high-altitude EMP threats to the United States from all potentially hostile states or non-state actors that have or could acquire nuclear weapons and ballistic missiles enabling them to perform a high-altitude EMP attack against the United States within the next 15 years;

"(2) the vulnerability of United States military and especially civilian systems to an EMP attack, giving special attention to vulnerability of the civilian infrastructure as a matter of emergency preparedness;

"(3) the capability of the United States to repair and recover from damage inflicted on United States military and civilian systems by an EMP attack, and

"(4) the feasibility and cost of hardening select military and civilian systems against EMP attack.

"(b) RECOMMENDATION.—The Commission shall recommend any steps it believes should be taken by the United States to better protect its military and civilian systems from EMP attack.

"(c) COOPERATION FROM GOVERNMENT OFFICIALS.—In carrying out its duties, the Commission should receive the full and timely cooperation of the Secretary of Defense, the Director of the Federal Emergency Management Agency, and any other United States Government official serving in the Department of Defense or Armed Forces in providing the Commission with analyses, briefings, and other information necessary for the fulfillment of its responsibilities.

"SEC. 1403. REPORTS.

"(a) COMMISSION REPORT.—The Commission shall, not later than one year after the date of its first meeting, submit to Congress, the Secretary of Defense, and the Director of the Federal Emergency Management Agency a report on the Commission's findings and conclusions.

"(b) SECRETARY OF DEFENSE REPORT.—Not later than one year after the date of the Commission's report under subsection (a), the Secretary of Defense shall submit to Congress a report—

"(1) commenting on the Commission's findings and conclusions;

"(2) describing political-military scenarios that could possibly lead to an EMP attack against the United States;

"(3) evaluating the relative likelihood of an EMP attack against the United States compared to other threats involving nuclear weapons; and

"(4) explaining what actions, if any, the Secretary intends to take to implement the recommendations of the Commission and the Secretary's reasons for doing so.

"SEC. 1404. POWERS.

"(a) HEARINGS.—The Commission or, at its direction, any panel or member of the Commission, may, for the purpose of carrying out the provisions of this title, hold hearings, take testimony, receive evidence, and administer oaths to the extent that the Commission or any panel or member considers advisable.

"(b) INFORMATION.—The Commission may secure directly from the Department of Defense, the Central Intelligence Agency, and any other Federal department or agency information that the Commission considers necessary to enable the Commission to carry out its responsibilities under this title.

"SEC. 1405. COMMISSION PROCEDURES.

"(a) MEETINGS.—The Commission shall meet at the call of the Chairman.

"(b) QUORUM.—(1) Five members of the Commission shall constitute a quorum other than for the purpose of holding hearings.

"(2) The Commission shall act by resolution agreed to by a majority of the members of the Commission.

"(c) COMMISSION.—The Commission may establish panels composed of less than full membership of the Commission for the purpose of carrying out the Commission's duties. The actions of each such panel shall be subject to the review and control of the Commission. Any findings and determinations made by such a panel shall not be considered the findings and determinations of the Commission unless approved by the Commission.

"(d) AUTHORITY OF INDIVIDUALS TO ACT FOR COMMISSION.—Any agent or member of the Commission may, if authorized by the Commission, take any action which the Commission is authorized to take under this title.

"SEC. 1406. PERSONNEL MATTERS.

"(a) PAY OF MEMBERS.—Members of the Commission shall serve without pay by reason of their work on the Commission.

"(b) TRAVEL EXPENSES.—The members of the Commission shall be allowed travel expenses, including per diem in lieu of subsistence, at rates authorized for employees of agencies under subchapter I of chapter 57 of title 5, United States Code, while away from their homes or regular places of business in the performance of services for the Commission.

"(c) STAFF.—(1) The chairman of the Commission may, without regard to the provisions of title 5, United States Code, governing appointments in the competitive service, appoint a staff director and such additional personnel as may be necessary to enable the Commission to perform its duties. The appointment of a staff director shall be subject to the approval of the Commission.

"(2) The chairman of the Commission may fix the pay of the staff director and other personnel without regard to the provisions of chapter 51 and subchapter III of chapter 53 of title 5, United States Code, relating to classification of positions and General Schedule pay rates, except that the rate of pay fixed under this paragraph for the staff director may not exceed the rate payable for level V of the Executive Schedule under section 5316 of such title and the rate of pay for other personnel may not exceed the maximum rate payable for grade GS–15 of the General Schedule.

"(d) DETAIL OF GOVERNMENT EMPLOYEES.—Upon request of the chairman of the Commission, the head of any Federal department or agency may detail, on a nonreimbursable basis, any personnel of that department or agency to the Commission to assist it in carrying out its duties.

"(e) PROCUREMENT OF TEMPORARY AND INTERMITTENT SERVICES.—The chairman of the Commission may procure temporary and intermittent services under section 3109(b) of title 5, United States Code, at rates for individuals which do not exceed the daily equivalent of the annual rate of basic pay payable for level V of the Executive Schedule under section 5316 of such title.

"SEC. 1407. MISCELLANEOUS ADMINISTRATIVE PROVISIONS.

"(a) POSTAL AND PRINTING SERVICES.—The Commission may use the United States mails and obtain printing and binding services in the same manner and under the same conditions as other departments and agencies of the Federal Government.

"(b) MISCELLANEOUS ADMINISTRATIVE AND SUPPORT SERVICES.—The Secretary of Defense shall furnish the Commission, on a reimbursable basis, any administrative and support services requested by the Commission.

"SEC. 1408. FUNDING.

"Funds for activities of the Commission shall be provided from amounts appropriated for the Department of Defense for operation and maintenance for Defense-wide activities for fiscal year 2001. Upon receipt of a written certification from the Chairman of the Commission specifying the funds required for the activities of the Commission, the Secretary of Defense shall promptly disburse to the Commission, from such amounts, the funds required by the Commission as stated in such certification.

"SEC. 1409. TERMINATION OF THE COMMISSION.

"The Commission shall terminate 60 days after the date of the submission of its report under section 1403(a)."

DOMESTIC PREPAREDNESS FOR DEFENSE AGAINST WEAPONS OF MASS DESTRUCTION

Pub. L. 105–261, div. A, title XIV, Oct. 17, 1998, 112 Stat. 2167, as amended by Pub. L. 106–65, div. A, title X, § 1064, Oct. 5, 1999, 113 Stat. 769, Pub. L. 106–398, § 1 [[div. A], title X, § 1087(d)(7)], Oct. 30, 2000, 114 Stat. 1654, 1654A–293, provided that:

"SEC. 1401. SHORT TITLE.

"This title may be cited as the 'Defense Against Weapons of Mass Destruction Act of 1998'.

"SEC. 1402. DOMESTIC PREPAREDNESS FOR RESPONSE TO THREATS OF TERRORIST USE OF WEAPONS OF MASS DESTRUCTION.

"(a) ENHANCED RESPONSE CAPABILITY.—In light of the continuing potential for terrorist use of weapons of mass destruction against the United States and the need to develop a more fully coordinated response to that threat on the part of Federal, State, and local agencies, the President shall act to increase the effectiveness at the Federal, State, and local level of the domestic emergency preparedness program for response to terrorist incidents involving weapons of mass destruction by utilizing the President's existing authorities to develop an integrated program that builds upon the program established under the Defense Against Weapons of Mass Destruction Act of 1996 (title XIV of Public Law 104–201; 110 Stat. 2714; 50 U.S.C. 2301 et seq.).

"(b) REPORT.—Not later than January 31, 1999, the President shall submit to Congress a report containing information on the actions taken at the Federal, State, and local level to develop an integrated program to prevent and respond to terrorist incidents involving weapons of mass destruction.

"SEC. 1403. REPORT ON DOMESTIC EMERGENCY PREPAREDNESS.

"[Amended section 1051 of Pub. L. 105–85, set out as a note under section 1113 of Title 31, Money and Finance.]

"SEC. 1404. THREAT AND RISK ASSESSMENTS.

"(a) THREAT AND RISK ASSESSMENTS.—Assistance to Federal, State, and local agencies provided under the program under section 1402 shall include the performance of assessments of the threat and risk of terrorist employment of weapons of mass destruction against cities and other local areas. Such assessments shall be used by Federal, State, and local agencies to determine the training and equipment requirements under this program and shall be performed as a collaborative effort with State and local agencies.

"(b) CONDUCT OF ASSESSMENTS.—The Department of Justice, as lead Federal agency for domestic crisis management in response to terrorism involving weapons of mass destruction, shall—

"(1) conduct any threat and risk assessment performed under subsection (a) in coordination with appropriate Federal, State, and local agencies; and

"(2) develop procedures and guidance for conduct of the threat and risk assessment in consultation with officials from the intelligence community.

"SEC. 1405. ADVISORY PANEL TO ASSESS DOMESTIC RESPONSE CAPABILITIES FOR TERRORISM INVOLVING WEAPONS OF MASS DESTRUCTION.

"(a) REQUIREMENT FOR PANEL.—The Secretary of Defense, in consultation with the Attorney General, the

Secretary of Energy, the Secretary of Health and Human Services, and the Director of the Federal Emergency Management Agency, shall enter into a contract with a federally funded research and development center to establish a panel to assess the capabilities for domestic response to terrorism involving weapons of mass destruction.

"(b) COMPOSITION OF PANEL; SELECTION.—(1) The panel shall be composed of members who shall be private citizens of the United States with knowledge and expertise in emergency response matters.

"(2) Members of the panel shall be selected by the federally funded research and development center in accordance with the terms of the contract established pursuant to subsection (a).

"(c) PROCEDURES FOR PANEL.—The federally funded research and development center shall be responsible for establishing appropriate procedures for the panel, including procedures for selection of a panel chairman.

"(d) DUTIES OF PANEL.—The panel shall—

"(1) assess Federal agency efforts to enhance domestic preparedness for incidents involving weapons of mass destruction;

"(2) assess the progress of Federal training programs for local emergency responses to incidents involving weapons of mass destruction;

"(3) assess deficiencies in programs for response to incidents involving weapons of mass destruction, including a review of unfunded communications, equipment, and planning requirements, and the needs of maritime regions;

"(4) recommend strategies for ensuring effective coordination with respect to Federal agency weapons of mass destruction response efforts, and for ensuring fully effective local response capabilities for weapons of mass destruction incidents; and

"(5) assess the appropriate roles of State and local government in funding effective local response capabilities.

"(e) DEADLINE TO ENTER INTO CONTRACT.—The Secretary of Defense shall enter into the contract required under subsection (a) not later than 60 days after the date of the enactment of this Act [Oct. 17, 1998].

"(f) DEADLINE FOR SELECTION OF PANEL MEMBERS.—Selection of panel members shall be made not later than 30 days after the date on which the Secretary enters into the contract required by subsection (a).

"(g) INITIAL MEETING OF THE PANEL.—The panel shall conduct its first meeting not later than 30 days after the date that all the selections to the panel have been made.

"(h) REPORTS.—(1) Not later than 6 months after the date of the first meeting of the panel, the panel shall submit to the President and to Congress an initial report setting forth its findings, conclusions, and recommendations for improving Federal, State, and local domestic emergency preparedness to respond to incidents involving weapons of mass destruction.

"(2) Not later than December 15 of each year, beginning in 1999 and ending in 2001, the panel shall submit to the President and to the Congress a report setting forth its findings, conclusions, and recommendations for improving Federal, State, and local domestic emergency preparedness to respond to incidents involving weapons of mass destruction.

"(i) COOPERATION OF OTHER AGENCIES.—(1) The panel may secure directly from the Department of Defense, the Department of Energy, the Department of Health and Human Services, the Department of Justice, and the Federal Emergency Management Agency, or any other Federal department or agency information that the panel considers necessary for the panel to carry out its duties.

"(2) The Attorney General, the Secretary of Defense, the Secretary of Energy, the Secretary of Health and Human Services, the Director of the Federal Emergency Management Agency, and any other official of the United States shall provide the panel with full and timely cooperation in carrying out its duties under this section.

"(j) FUNDING.—The Secretary of Defense shall provide the funds necessary for the panel to carry out its duties from the funds available to the Department of Defense for weapons of mass destruction preparedness initiatives.

"(k) COMPENSATION OF PANEL MEMBERS.—(1) Members of the panel shall serve without pay by reason of their work on the panel.

"(2) Members of the panel shall be allowed travel expenses, including per diem in lieu of subsistence, at rates authorized for employees of agencies under chapter 57 of title 5, United States Code, while away from their homes or regular place of business in performance of services for the panel.

"(*l*) TERMINATION OF THE PANEL.—The panel shall terminate three years after the date of the appointment of the member selected as chairman of the panel.

"(m) DEFINITION.—In this section, the term 'weapon of mass destruction' has the meaning given that term in section 1403(1) of the Defense Against Weapons of Mass Destruction Act of 1996 (50 U.S.C. 2302(1))."

§2302. Definitions

In this chapter:

(1) The term "weapon of mass destruction" means any weapon or device that is intended, or has the capability, to cause death or serious bodily injury to a significant number of people through the release, dissemination, or impact of—

(A) toxic or poisonous chemicals or their precursors;

(B) a disease organism; or

(C) radiation or radioactivity.

(2) The term "independent states of the former Soviet Union" has the meaning given that term in section 5801 of title 22.

(3) The term "highly enriched uranium" means uranium enriched to 20 percent or more in the isotope U–235.

(Pub. L. 104–201, div. A, title XIV, §1403, Sept. 23, 1996, 110 Stat. 2717.)

REFERENCES IN TEXT

This chapter, referred to in text, was in the original "this title", meaning title XIV of div. A of Pub. L. 104–201, Sept. 23, 1996, 110 Stat. 2714, which is classified principally to this chapter. For complete classification of title XIV to the Code, see Short Title note set out under section 2301 of this title and Tables.

SECTION REFERRED TO IN OTHER SECTIONS

This section is referred to in title 10 sections 12304, 12310.

SUBCHAPTER I—DOMESTIC PREPAREDNESS

§2311. Response to threats of terrorist use of weapons of mass destruction

(a) Enhanced response capability

In light of the potential for terrorist use of weapons of mass destruction against the United States, the President shall take immediate action—

(1) to enhance the capability of the Federal Government to prevent and respond to terrorist incidents involving weapons of mass destruction; and

(2) to provide enhanced support to improve the capabilities of State and local emergency response agencies to prevent and respond to such incidents at both the national and the local level.

(b) Report required

Not later than January 31, 1997, the President shall transmit to Congress a report containing—

(1) an assessment of the capabilities of the Federal Government to prevent and respond to terrorist incidents involving weapons of mass destruction and to support State and local prevention and response efforts;

(2) requirements for improvements in those capabilities; and

(3) the measures that should be taken to achieve such improvements, including additional resources and legislative authorities that would be required.

(Pub. L. 104–201, div. A, title XIV, § 1411, Sept. 23, 1996, 110 Stat. 2717.)

§ 2312. Emergency response assistance program

(a) Program required

(1) The Secretary of Defense shall carry out a program to provide civilian personnel of Federal, State, and local agencies with training and expert advice regarding emergency responses to a use or threatened use of a weapon of mass destruction or related materials.

(2) The President may designate the head of an agency other than the Department of Defense to assume the responsibility for carrying out the program on or after October 1, 1999, and relieve the Secretary of Defense of that responsibility upon the assumption of the responsibility by the designated official.

(3) In this section, the official responsible for carrying out the program is referred to as the ''lead official''.

(b) Coordination

In carrying out the program, the lead official shall coordinate with each of the following officials who is not serving as the lead official:

(1) The Director of the Federal Emergency Management Agency.

(2) The Secretary of Energy.

(3) The Secretary of Defense.

(4) The heads of any other Federal, State, and local government agencies that have an expertise or responsibilities relevant to emergency responses described in subsection (a)(1) of this section.

(c) Eligible participants

The civilian personnel eligible to receive assistance under the program are civilian personnel of Federal, State, and local agencies who have emergency preparedness responsibilities.

(d) Involvement of other Federal agencies

(1) The lead official may use personnel and capabilities of Federal agencies outside the agency of the lead official to provide training and expert advice under the program.

(2)(A) Personnel used under paragraph (1) shall be personnel who have special skills relevant to the particular assistance that the personnel are to provide.

(B) Capabilities used under paragraph (1) shall be capabilities that are especially relevant to the particular assistance for which the capabilities are used.

(3) If the lead official is not the Secretary of Defense, and requests assistance from the Department of Defense that, in the judgment of the Secretary of Defense would affect military readiness or adversely affect national security, the Secretary of Defense may appeal the request for Department of Defense assistance by the lead official to the President.

(e) Available assistance

Assistance available under this program shall include the following:

(1) Training in the use, operation, and maintenance of equipment for—

(A) detecting a chemical or biological agent or nuclear radiation;

(B) monitoring the presence of such an agent or radiation;

(C) protecting emergency personnel and the public; and

(D) decontamination.

(2) Establishment of a designated telephonic link (commonly referred to as a ''hot line'') to a designated source of relevant data and expert advice for the use of State or local officials responding to emergencies involving a weapon of mass destruction or related materials.

(3) Use of the National Guard and other reserve components for purposes authorized under this section that are specified by the lead official (with the concurrence of the Secretary of Defense if the Secretary is not the lead official).

(4) Loan of appropriate equipment.

(f) Limitations on Department of Defense assistance to law enforcement agencies

Assistance provided by the Department of Defense to law enforcement agencies under this section shall be provided under the authority of, and subject to the restrictions provided in, chapter 18 of title 10.

(g) Administration of Department of Defense assistance

The Secretary of Defense shall designate an official within the Department of Defense to serve as the executive agent of the Secretary for the coordination of the provision of Department of Defense assistance under this section.

(h) Funding

(1) Of the total amount authorized to be appropriated under section 301,[1] $35,000,000 is available for the program required under this section.

(2) Of the amount available for the program pursuant to paragraph (1), $10,500,000 is available for use by the Secretary of Defense to assist the Secretary of Health and Human Services in the establishment of metropolitan emergency medical response teams (commonly referred to as ''Metropolitan Medical Strike Force Teams'') to provide medical services that are necessary or potentially necessary by reason of a use or threatened use of a weapon of mass destruction.

(3) The amount available for the program under paragraph (1) is in addition to any other amounts authorized to be appropriated for the program under section 301.[1]

(Pub. L. 104–201, div. A, title XIV, § 1412, Sept. 23, 1996, 110 Stat. 2718.)

[1] See References in Text note below.

REFERENCES IN TEXT

Section 301, referred to in subsec. (h)(1), (3), is section 301 of Pub. L. 104–201, div. A, title III, Sept. 23, 1996, 110 Stat. 2475, which is not classified to the Code.

§2313. Nuclear, chemical, and biological emergency response

(a) Department of Defense

The Secretary of Defense shall designate an official within the Department of Defense as the executive agent for—

(1) the coordination of Department of Defense assistance to Federal, State, and local officials in responding to threats involving biological or chemical weapons or related materials or technologies, including assistance in identifying, neutralizing, dismantling, and disposing of biological and chemical weapons and related materials and technologies; and

(2) the coordination of Department of Defense assistance to the Department of Energy in carrying out that department's responsibilities under subsection (b) of this section.

(b) Department of Energy

The Secretary of Energy shall designate an official within the Department of Energy as the executive agent for—

(1) the coordination of Department of Energy assistance to Federal, State, and local officials in responding to threats involving nuclear, chemical, and biological weapons or related materials or technologies, including assistance in identifying, neutralizing, dismantling, and disposing of nuclear weapons and related materials and technologies; and

(2) the coordination of Department of Energy assistance to the Department of Defense in carrying out that department's responsibilities under subsection (a) of this section.

(c) Funding

Of the total amount authorized to be appropriated under section 301,[1] $15,000,000 is available for providing assistance described in subsection (a) of this section.

(Pub. L. 104–201, div. A, title XIV, §1413, Sept. 23, 1996, 110 Stat. 2719.)

REFERENCES IN TEXT

Section 301, referred to in subsec. (c), is section 301 of Pub. L. 104–201, div. A, title III, Sept. 23, 1996, 110 Stat. 2475, which is not classified to the Code.

§2314. Chemical-biological emergency response team

(a) Department of Defense rapid response team

The Secretary of Defense shall develop and maintain at least one domestic terrorism rapid response team composed of members of the Armed Forces and employees of the Department of Defense who are capable of aiding Federal, State, and local officials in the detection, neutralization, containment, dismantlement, and disposal of weapons of mass destruction containing chemical, biological, or related materials.

(b) Addition to Federal response plan

Not later than December 31, 1997, the Director of the Federal Emergency Management Agency shall develop and incorporate into existing Federal emergency response plans and programs prepared under section 5196(b) of title 42 guidance on the use and deployment of the rapid response teams established under this section to respond to emergencies involving weapons of mass destruction. The Director shall carry out this subsection in consultation with the Secretary of Defense and the heads of other Federal agencies involved with the emergency response plans.

(Pub. L. 104–201, div. A, title XIV, §1414, Sept. 23, 1996, 110 Stat. 2720.)

§2315. Testing of preparedness for emergencies involving nuclear, radiological, chemical, and biological weapons

(a) Emergencies involving chemical or biological weapons

(1) The Secretary of Defense shall develop and carry out a program for testing and improving the responses of Federal, State, and local agencies to emergencies involving biological weapons and related materials and emergencies involving chemical weapons and related materials.

(2) The program shall include exercises to be carried out during each of five successive fiscal years beginning with fiscal year 1997.

(3) In developing and carrying out the program, the Secretary shall coordinate with the Director of the Federal Bureau of Investigation, the Director of the Federal Emergency Management Agency, the Secretary of Energy, and the heads of any other Federal, State, and local government agencies that have an expertise or responsibilities relevant to emergencies described in paragraph (1).

(b) Emergencies involving nuclear and radiological weapons

(1) The Secretary of Energy shall develop and carry out a program for testing and improving the responses of Federal, State, and local agencies to emergencies involving nuclear and radiological weapons and related materials.

(2) The program shall include exercises to be carried out during each of five successive fiscal years beginning with fiscal year 1997.

(3) In developing and carrying out the program, the Secretary shall coordinate with the Director of the Federal Bureau of Investigation, the Director of the Federal Emergency Management Agency, the Secretary of Defense, and the heads of any other Federal, State, and local government agencies that have an expertise or responsibilities relevant to emergencies described in paragraph (1).

(c) Annual revisions of programs

The official responsible for carrying out a program developed under subsection (a) or (b) of this section shall revise the program not later than June 1 in each fiscal year covered by the program. The revisions shall include adjustments that the official determines necessary or appropriate on the basis of the lessons learned from the exercise or exercises carried out under the program in the fiscal year, including lessons learned regarding coordination problems and equipment deficiencies.

[1] See References in Text note below.

(d) Option to transfer responsibility

(1) The President may designate the head of an agency outside the Department of Defense to assume the responsibility for carrying out the program developed under subsection (a) of this section beginning on or after October 1, 1999, and relieve the Secretary of Defense of that responsibility upon the assumption of the responsibility by the designated official.

(2) The President may designate the head of an agency outside the Department of Energy to assume the responsibility for carrying out the program developed under subsection (b) of this section beginning on or after October 1, 1999, and relieve the Secretary of Energy of that responsibility upon the assumption of the responsibility by the designated official.

(e) Funding

Of the total amount authorized to be appropriated under section 301,[1] $15,000,000 is available for the development and execution of the programs required by this section, including the participation of State and local agencies in exercises carried out under the programs.

(Pub. L. 104–201, div. A, title XIV, § 1415, Sept. 23, 1996, 110 Stat. 2720.)

REFERENCES IN TEXT

Section 301, referred to in subsec. (e), is section 301 of Pub. L. 104–201, div. A, title III, Sept. 23, 1996, 110 Stat. 2475, which is not classified to the Code.

§ 2316. Actions to increase civilian expertise

(a) to (c) Omitted

(d) Civilian expertise

The President shall take reasonable measures to reduce the reliance of civilian law enforcement officials on Department of Defense resources to counter the threat posed by the use or potential use of biological and chemical weapons of mass destruction within the United States. The measures shall include—

(1) actions to increase civilian law enforcement expertise to counter such a threat; and

(2) actions to improve coordination between civilian law enforcement officials and other civilian sources of expertise, within and outside the Federal Government, to counter such a threat.

(e) Reports

The President shall submit to Congress the following reports:

(1) Not later than 90 days after September 23, 1996, a report describing the respective policy functions and operational roles of Federal agencies in countering the threat posed by the use or potential use of biological and chemical weapons of mass destruction within the United States.

(2) Not later than one year after September 23, 1996, a report describing—

(A) the actions planned to be taken to carry out subsection (d) of this section; and

(B) the costs of such actions.

(3) Not later than three years after September 23, 1996, a report updating the information provided in the reports submitted pursuant to paragraphs (1) and (2), including the measures taken pursuant to subsection (d) of this section.

(Pub. L. 104–201, div. A, title XIV, § 1416, Sept. 23, 1996, 110 Stat. 2721.)

CODIFICATION

Section is comprised of subsecs. (d) and (e) of section 1416 of Pub. L. 104–201. Subsecs. (a) to (c) of section 1416 enacted section 382 of Title 10, Armed Forces, and sections 175a and 2332d of Title 18, Crimes and Criminal Procedure, and amended section 372 of Title 10.

§ 2317. Rapid response information system

(a) Inventory of rapid response assets

(1) The head of each Federal Response Plan agency shall develop and maintain an inventory of physical equipment and assets under the jurisdiction of that agency that could be made available to aid State and local officials in search and rescue and other disaster management and mitigation efforts associated with an emergency involving weapons of mass destruction. The agency head shall submit a copy of the inventory, and any updates of the inventory, to the Director of the Federal Emergency Management Agency for inclusion in the master inventory required under subsection (b) of this section.

(2) Each inventory shall include a separate listing of any equipment that is excess to the needs of that agency and could be considered for disposal as excess or surplus property for use for response and training with regard to emergencies involving weapons of mass destruction.

(b) Master inventory

The Director of the Federal Emergency Management Agency shall compile and maintain a comprehensive listing of all inventories prepared under subsection (a) of this section. The first such master list shall be completed not later than December 31, 1997, and shall be updated annually thereafter.

(c) Addition to Federal response plan

Not later than December 31, 1997, the Director of the Federal Emergency Management Agency shall develop and incorporate into existing Federal emergency response plans and programs prepared under section 5196(b) of title 42 guidance on accessing and using the physical equipment and assets included in the master list developed under subsection[1] to respond to emergencies involving weapons of mass destruction.

(d) Database on chemical and biological materials

The Director of the Federal Emergency Management Agency, in consultation with the Secretary of Defense, shall prepare a database on chemical and biological agents and munitions characteristics and safety precautions for civilian use. The initial design and compilation of the database shall be completed not later than December 31, 1997.

(e) Access to inventory and database

The Director of the Federal Emergency Management Agency shall design and maintain a

[1] See References in Text note below.

[1] So in original. Probably should be "subsection (b) of this section".

system to give Federal, State, and local officials access to the inventory listing and database maintained under this section in the event of an emergency involving weapons of mass destruction or to prepare and train to respond to such an emergency. The system shall include a secure but accessible emergency response hotline to access information and request assistance.

(Pub. L. 104–201, div. A, title XIV, §1417, Sept. 23, 1996, 110 Stat. 2724.)

SUBCHAPTER II—INTERDICTION OF WEAPONS OF MASS DESTRUCTION AND RELATED MATERIALS

§2331. Procurement of detection equipment for United States border security

Of the amount authorized to be appropriated by section 301,[1] $15,000,000 is available for the procurement of—

(1) equipment capable of detecting the movement of weapons of mass destruction and related materials into the United States;

(2) equipment capable of interdicting the movement of weapons of mass destruction and related materials into the United States; and

(3) materials and technologies related to use of equipment described in paragraph (1) or (2).

(Pub. L. 104–201, div. A, title XIV, §1421, Sept. 23, 1996, 110 Stat. 2725.)

REFERENCES IN TEXT

Section 301, referred to in text, is section 301 of Pub. L. 104–201, div. A, title III, Sept. 23, 1996, 110 Stat. 2475, which is not classified to the Code.

§2332. Sense of Congress concerning criminal penalties

(a) Sense of Congress concerning inadequacy of sentencing guidelines

It is the sense of Congress that the sentencing guidelines prescribed by the United States Sentencing Commission for the offenses of importation, attempted importation, exportation, and attempted exportation of nuclear, biological, and chemical weapons materials constitute inadequate punishment for such offenses.

(b) Urging of revision to guidelines

Congress urges the United States Sentencing Commission to revise the relevant sentencing guidelines to provide for increased penalties for offenses relating to importation, attempted importation, exportation, and attempted exportation of nuclear, biological, or chemical weapons or related materials or technologies under the following provisions of law:

(1) Section 2410 of the Appendix to this title.

(2) Sections 2778 and 2780 of title 22.

(3) The International Emergency Economic Powers Act (50 U.S.C. 1701 et seq.).

(4) Section 2139a(c) of title 42.

(Pub. L. 104–201, div. A, title XIV, §1423, Sept. 23, 1996, 110 Stat. 2725; Pub. L. 105–261, div. A, title X, §1069(c)(1), Oct. 17, 1998, 112 Stat. 2136.)

REFERENCES IN TEXT

The International Emergency Economic Powers Act, referred to in subsec. (b)(3), is title II of Pub. L. 95–223, Dec. 28, 1977, 91 Stat. 1626, which is classified generally to chapter 35 (§1701 et seq.) of this title. For complete classification of this Act to the Code, see Short Title note set out under section 1701 of this title and Tables.

CODIFICATION

Section is comprised of section 1423 of Pub. L. 104–201 which also enacted provisions listed in a table of provisions for review, promulgation, or amendment of Federal sentencing guidelines relating to specific offenses set out under section 994 of Title 28, Judiciary and Judicial Procedure.

AMENDMENTS

1998—Subsec. (b)(4). Pub. L. 105–261 made technical amendment to reference in original act which appears in text as reference to section 2139a(c) of title 42.

§2333. International border security

(a) Secretary of Defense responsibility

The Secretary of Defense, in consultation and cooperation with the Commissioner of Customs, shall carry out programs for assisting customs officials and border guard officials in the independent states of the former Soviet Union, the Baltic states, and other countries of Eastern Europe in preventing unauthorized transfer and transportation of nuclear, biological, and chemical weapons and related materials. Training, expert advice, maintenance of equipment, loan of equipment, and audits may be provided under or in connection with the programs.

(b) Funding

Of the total amount authorized to be appropriated by section 301,[1] $15,000,000 is available for carrying out the programs referred to in subsection (a) of this section.

(c) Assistance to states of former Soviet Union

Assistance under programs referred to in subsection (a) of this section may (notwithstanding any provision of law prohibiting the extension of foreign assistance to any of the newly independent states of the former Soviet Union) be extended to include an independent state of the former Soviet Union if the President certifies to Congress that it is in the national interest of the United States to extend assistance under this section to that state.

(Pub. L. 104–201, div. A, title XIV, §1424, Sept. 23, 1996, 110 Stat. 2726.)

REFERENCES IN TEXT

Section 301, referred to in subsec. (b), is section 301 of Pub. L. 104–201, div. A, title III, Sept. 23, 1996, 110 Stat. 2475, which is not classified to the Code.

DELEGATION OF AUTHORITY

Memorandum of President of the United States, July 24, 1997, 62 F.R. 40727, provided:

Memorandum for the Secretary of Defense

By the authority vested in me by the Constitution and the laws of the United States of America, including section 301 of title 3 of the United States Code, I hereby delegate to you, in consultation with the Secretary of State, the authority vested in the President under section 1424(c) of the National Defense Authorization Act for Fiscal Year 1997 (Public Law 104–201) [50 U.S.C. 2333(c)].

You are authorized and directed to publish this memorandum in the Federal Register.

WILLIAM J. CLINTON.

[1] See References in Text note below.

[1] See References in Text note below.

SUBCHAPTER III—CONTROL AND DISPOSITION OF WEAPONS OF MASS DESTRUCTION AND RELATED MATERIALS THREATENING THE UNITED STATES

SUBCHAPTER REFERRED TO IN OTHER SECTIONS

This subchapter is referred to in section 2361 of this title.

§2341. Elimination of plutonium production

(a) Replacement program

The Secretary of Energy, in consultation with the Secretary of Defense, shall develop a cooperative program with the Government of Russia to eliminate the production of weapons grade plutonium by modifying or replacing the reactor cores at Tomsk–7 and Krasnoyarsk–26 with reactor cores that are less suitable for the production of weapons-grade plutonium.

(b) Program requirements

(1) The program shall be designed to achieve completion of the modifications or replacements of the reactor cores within three years after the modification or replacement activities under the program are begun.

(2) The plan for the program shall—

(A) specify—

(i) successive steps for the modification or replacement of the reactor cores; and

(ii) clearly defined milestones to be achieved; and

(B) include estimates of the costs of the program.

(c) Submission of program plan to Congress

Not later than 180 days after September 23, 1996, the Secretary of Defense shall submit to Congress—

(1) a plan for the program under subsection (a) of this section;

(2) an estimate of the United States funding that is necessary for carrying out the activities under the program for each fiscal year covered by the program; and

(3) a comparison of the benefits of the program with the benefits of other nonproliferation programs.

(Pub. L. 104–201, div. A, title XIV, §1432, Sept. 23, 1996, 110 Stat. 2726.)

SUBCHAPTER IV—COORDINATION OF POLICY AND COUNTERMEASURES AGAINST PROLIFERATION OF WEAPONS OF MASS DESTRUCTION

§2351. National coordinator on nonproliferation

(a) Designation of position

The President shall designate an individual to serve in the Executive Office of the President as the National Coordinator for Nonproliferation Matters.

(b) Duties

The Coordinator, under the direction of the National Security Council, shall advise and assist the President by—

(1) advising the President on nonproliferation of weapons of mass destruction, including issues related to terrorism, arms control, and international organized crime;

(2) chairing the Committee on Nonproliferation of the National Security Council; and

(3) taking such actions as are necessary to ensure that there is appropriate emphasis in, cooperation on, and coordination of, nonproliferation research efforts of the United States, including activities of Federal agencies as well as activities of contractors funded by the Federal Government.

(c) Allocation of funds

Of the total amount authorized to be appropriated under section 301,[1] $2,000,000 is available to the Department of Defense for carrying out research referred to in subsection (b)(3) of this section.

(Pub. L. 104–201, div. A, title XIV, §1441, Sept. 23, 1996, 110 Stat. 2727; Pub. L. 105–261, div. A, title X, §1069(c)(2), Oct. 17, 1998, 112 Stat. 2136.)

REFERENCES IN TEXT

Section 301, referred to in subsec. (c), is section 301 of Pub. L. 104–201, div. A, title III, Sept. 23, 1996, 110 Stat. 2475, which is not classified to the Code.

AMENDMENTS

1998—Subsec. (b)(2). Pub. L. 105–261 substituted "of the National Security Council" for "established under section 1342".

COMMISSION TO ASSESS ORGANIZATION OF FEDERAL GOVERNMENT TO COMBAT PROLIFERATION OF WEAPONS OF MASS DESTRUCTION

Pub. L. 104–293, title VII, subtitle A, Oct. 11, 1996, 110 Stat. 3470, as amended by Pub. L. 105–277, div. A, §101(f) [title VII, §708], Oct. 21, 1998, 112 Stat. 2681–337, 2681–390, provided that:

"SEC. 711. ESTABLISHMENT OF COMMISSION.

"(a) ESTABLISHMENT.—There is established a commission to be known as the Commission to Assess the Organization of the Federal Government to Combat the Proliferation of Weapons of Mass Destruction (in this subtitle [subtitle A (§§711–717) of title VII of Pub. L. 104–293] referred to as the 'Commission').

"(b) MEMBERSHIP.—The Commission shall be composed of twelve members, none of whom may, during the period of their service on the Commission, be an officer or employee of any department, agency, or other establishment of the Executive Branch (other than the Commission), and of whom—

"(1) four shall be appointed by the President;

"(2) three shall be appointed by the Majority Leader of the Senate;

"(3) one shall be appointed by the Minority Leader of the Senate;

"(4) three shall be appointed by the Speaker of the House of Representatives; and

"(5) one shall be appointed by the Minority Leader of the House of Representatives.

"(c) QUALIFICATIONS OF MEMBERS.—(1) To the maximum extent practicable, the individuals appointed as members of the Commission shall be individuals who are nationally recognized for expertise regarding—

"(A) the nonproliferation of weapons of mass destruction;

"(B) the efficient and effective implementation of United States nonproliferation policy; or

"(C) the implementation, funding, or oversight of the national security policies of the United States.

"(2) An official who appoints members of the Commission may not appoint an individual as a member if, in the judgment of the official, the individual possesses any personal or financial interest in the discharge of any of the duties of the Commission.

[1] See References in Text note below.

"(d) PERIOD OF APPOINTMENT; VACANCIES.—Members shall be appointed for the life of the Commission. Any vacancy in the Commission shall not affect its powers, but shall be filled in the same manner as the original appointment.

"(e) INITIAL MEETING.—Not later than 30 days after the date of enactment of an Act making appropriations for the Departments of Labor, Health and Human Services, and Education, and related agencies, for the fiscal year ending September 30, 1999 [Oct. 21, 1998], regardless of whether all the members of the Commission have been appointed as of that date,,[sic] the Commission shall hold its first meeting.

"(f) QUORUM.—A majority of the members of the Commission shall constitute a quorum, but a lesser number of members may hold hearings.

"(g) CHAIRMAN AND VICE CHAIRMAN.—The Commission shall select a Chairman and Vice Chairman from among its members.

"(h) MEETINGS.—The Commission shall meet at the call of the Chairman.

"SEC. 712. DUTIES OF COMMISSION.

"(a) STUDY.—

"(1) IN GENERAL.—The Commission shall carry out a thorough study of the organization of the Federal Government, including the elements of the intelligence community, with respect to combatting the proliferation of weapons of mass destruction.

"(2) SPECIFIC REQUIREMENTS.—In carrying out the study, the Commission shall—

"(A) assess the current structure and organization of the departments and agencies of the Federal Government having responsibilities for combatting the proliferation of weapons of mass destruction; and

"(B) assess the effectiveness of United States cooperation with foreign governments with respect to nonproliferation activities, including cooperation—

"(i) between elements of the intelligence community and elements of the intelligence-gathering services of foreign governments;

"(ii) between other departments and agencies of the Federal Government and the counterparts to such departments and agencies in foreign governments; and

"(iii) between the Federal Government and international organizations.

"(3) ASSESSMENTS.—In making the assessments under paragraph (2), the Commission should address—

"(A) the organization of the export control activities (including licensing and enforcement activities) of the Federal Government relating to the proliferation of weapons of mass destruction;

"(B) arrangements for coordinating the funding of United States nonproliferation activities;

"(C) existing arrangements governing the flow of information among departments and agencies of the Federal Government responsible for nonproliferation activities;

"(D) the effectiveness of the organization and function of interagency groups in ensuring implementation of United States treaty obligations, laws, and policies with respect to nonproliferation;

"(E) the administration of sanctions for purposes of nonproliferation, including the measures taken by departments and agencies of the Federal Government to implement, assess, and enhance the effectiveness of such sanctions;

"(F) the organization, management, and oversight of United States counterproliferation activities;

"(G) the recruitment, training, morale, expertise, retention, and advancement of Federal Government personnel responsible for the nonproliferation functions of the Federal Government, including any problems in such activities;

"(H) the role in United States nonproliferation activities of the National Security Council, the Office of Management and Budget, the Office of Science and Technology Policy, and other offices in the Executive Office of the President having responsibilities for such activities;

"(I) the organization of the activities of the Federal Government to verify government-to-government assurances and commitments with respect to nonproliferation, including assurances regarding the future use of commodities exported from the United States; and

"(J) the costs and benefits to the United States of increased centralization and of decreased centralization in the administration of the nonproliferation activities of the Federal Government.

"(4) RESTRICTIONS.—In carrying out the study under paragraph (1), making the assessments under paragraph (2), and addressing the matters identified in paragraph (3), the Commission shall not review, evaluate, or report on—

"(A) United States domestic response capabilities with respect to weapons of mass destruction; or

"(B) the adequacy or usefulness of United States laws that provide for the imposition of sanctions on countries or entities that engage in the proliferation of weapons of mass destruction.

"(b) RECOMMENDATIONS.—In conducting the study, the Commission shall develop recommendations on means of improving the effectiveness of the organization of the departments and agencies of the Federal Government in meeting the national security interests of the United States with respect to the proliferation of weapons of mass destruction. Such recommendations shall include specific recommendations to eliminate duplications of effort, and other inefficiencies, in and among such departments and agencies.

"(c) REPORT.—(1) Not later than 18 months after January 18, 1998, the Commission shall submit to Congress a report containing a detailed statement of the findings and conclusions of the Commission, together with its recommendations for such legislation and administrative actions as it considers appropriate.

"(2) The report shall be submitted in unclassified form, but may include a classified annex.

"SEC. 713. POWERS OF COMMISSION.

"(a) HEARINGS.—The Commission may hold such hearings, sit and act at such times and places, take such testimony, and receive such evidence as the Commission considers advisable to carry out the purposes of this subtitle.

"(b) INFORMATION FROM FEDERAL AGENCIES.—

"(1) IN GENERAL.—The Commission may secure directly from any Federal department or agency such information as the Commission considers necessary to carry out the provisions of this subtitle. Upon request of the Chairman of the Commission, the head of such department or agency shall furnish such information to the Commission.

"(2) CLASSIFIED INFORMATION.—A department or agency may furnish the Commission classified information under this subsection. The Commission shall take appropriate actions to safeguard classified information furnished to the Commission under this paragraph.

"(c) POSTAL SERVICES.—The Commission may use the United States mails in the same manner and under the same conditions as other departments and agencies of the Federal Government.

"(d) GIFTS.—The Commission may accept, use, and dispose of gifts or donations of services or property.

"SEC. 714. COMMISSION PERSONNEL MATTERS.

"(a) COMPENSATION OF MEMBERS.—Each member of the Commission who is not an officer or employee of the Federal Government shall be compensated at a rate equal to the daily equivalent of the annual rate of basic pay prescribed for level IV of the Executive Schedule under section 5315 of title 5, United States Code, for each day (including travel time) during which such member is engaged in the performance of the duties of the Commission. All members of the Commission who are officers or employees of the United States shall serve without compensation in addition to that received for their services as officers or employees of the United States.

"(b) TRAVEL EXPENSES.—The members of the Commission shall be allowed travel expenses, including per diem in lieu of subsistence, at rates authorized for employees of agencies under subchapter I of chapter 57 of title 5, United States Code, while away from their homes or regular places of business in the performance of services for the Commission.

"(c) STAFF.—

"(1) IN GENERAL.—The Chairman of the Commission may, without regard to the civil service laws and regulations, appoint and terminate an executive director and such other additional personnel as may be necessary to enable the Commission to perform its duties. The employment of an executive director shall be subject to confirmation by the Commission.

"(2) COMPENSATION.—The Chairman of the Commission may fix the compensation of the executive director and other personnel without regard to the provisions of chapter 51 and subchapter III of chapter 53 of title 5, United States Code, relating to classification of positions and General Schedule pay rates, except that the rate of pay for the executive director and other personnel may not exceed the rate payable for level V of the Executive Schedule under section 5316 of such title.

"(d) DETAIL OF GOVERNMENT EMPLOYEES.—Any Federal Government employee may be detailed to the Commission without reimbursement, and such detail shall be without interruption or loss of civil service status or privilege.

"(e) PROCUREMENT OF TEMPORARY AND INTERMITTENT SERVICES.—The Chairman of the Commission may procure temporary and intermittent services under section 3109(b) of title 5, United States Code, at rates for individuals which do not exceed the daily equivalent of the annual rate of basic pay prescribed for level V of the Executive Schedule under section 5316 of such title.

"SEC. 715. TERMINATION OF COMMISSION.

"The Commission shall terminate 60 days after the date on which the Commission submits its report under section 712(c).

"SEC. 716. DEFINITION.

"For purposes of this subtitle, the term 'intelligence community' shall have the meaning given such term in section 3(4) of the National Security Act of 1947 (50 U.S.C. 401a(4)).

"SEC. 717. PAYMENT OF COMMISSION EXPENSES.

"The compensation, travel expenses, per diem allowances of members and employees of the Commission, and other expenses of the Commission shall not exceed $1,000,000, and shall be paid out of funds available to the Director of Central Intelligence for the payment of compensation, travel allowances, and per diem allowances, respectively, of employees of the Central Intelligence Agency."

SECTION REFERRED TO IN OTHER SECTIONS

This section is referred to in section 2354 of this title.

§2352. National Security Council Committee on Nonproliferation

(a) Establishment

The Committee on Nonproliferation (in this section referred to as the "Committee") is established as a committee of the National Security Council.

(b) Membership

(1) The Committee shall be composed of representatives of the following:

(A) The Secretary of State.

(B) The Secretary of Defense.

(C) The Director of Central Intelligence.

(D) The Attorney General.

(E) The Secretary of Energy.

(F) The Administrator of the Federal Emergency Management Agency.

(G) The Secretary of the Treasury.

(H) The Secretary of Commerce.

(I) Such other members as the President may designate.

(2) The National Coordinator for Nonproliferation Matters shall chair the Committee on Nonproliferation.

(c) Responsibilities

The Committee has the following responsibilities:

(1) To review and coordinate Federal programs, policies, and directives relating to the proliferation of weapons of mass destruction and related materials and technologies, including matters relating to terrorism and international organized crime.

(2) To make recommendations through the National Security Council to the President regarding the following:

(A) Integrated national policies for countering the threats posed by weapons of mass destruction.

(B) Options for integrating Federal agency budgets for countering such threats.

(C) Means to ensure that Federal, State, and local governments have adequate capabilities to manage crises involving nuclear, radiological, biological, or chemical weapons or related materials or technologies, and to manage the consequences of a use of such weapon or related materials or technologies, and that use of those capabilities is coordinated.

(D) Means to ensure appropriate cooperation on, and coordination of, the following:

(i) Preventing the smuggling of weapons of mass destruction and related materials and technologies.

(ii) Promoting domestic and international law enforcement efforts against proliferation-related efforts.

(iii) Countering the involvement of organized crime groups in proliferation-related activities.

(iv) Safeguarding weapons of mass destruction materials and related technologies.

(v) Improving coordination and cooperation among intelligence activities, law enforcement, and the Departments of Defense, State, Commerce, and Energy in support of nonproliferation and counterproliferation efforts.

(vi) Improving export controls over materials and technologies that can contribute to the acquisition of weapons of mass destruction.

(vii) Reducing proliferation of weapons of mass destruction and related materials and technologies.

(Pub. L. 104–201, div. A, title XIV, §1442, Sept. 23, 1996, 110 Stat. 2727.)

SECTION REFERRED TO IN OTHER SECTIONS

This section is referred to in sections 2353, 2354 of this title.

§ 2353. Comprehensive preparedness program

(a) Program required

The President, acting through the Committee on Nonproliferation established under section 2352 of this title, shall develop a comprehensive program for carrying out this chapter.

(b) Content of program

The program set forth in the report shall include specific plans as follows:

(1) Plans for countering proliferation of weapons of mass destruction and related materials and technologies.

(2) Plans for training and equipping Federal, State, and local officials for managing a crisis involving a use or threatened use of a weapon of mass destruction, including the consequences of the use of such a weapon.

(3) Plans for providing for regular sharing of information among intelligence, law enforcement, and customs agencies.

(4) Plans for training and equipping law enforcement units, customs services, and border security personnel to counter the smuggling of weapons of mass destruction and related materials and technologies.

(5) Plans for establishing appropriate centers for analyzing seized nuclear, radiological, biological, and chemical weapons, and related materials and technologies.

(6) Plans for establishing in the United States appropriate legal controls and authorities relating to the exporting of nuclear, radiological, biological, and chemical weapons, and related materials and technologies.

(7) Plans for encouraging and assisting governments of foreign countries to implement and enforce laws that set forth appropriate penalties for offenses regarding the smuggling of weapons of mass destruction and related materials and technologies.

(8) Plans for building the confidence of the United States and Russia in each other's controls over United States and Russian nuclear weapons and fissile materials, including plans for verifying the dismantlement of nuclear weapons.

(9) Plans for reducing United States and Russian stockpiles of excess plutonium, reflecting—

(A) consideration of the desirability and feasibility of a United States-Russian agreement governing fissile material disposition and the specific technologies and approaches to be used for disposition of excess plutonium; and

(B) an assessment of the options for United States cooperation with Russia in the disposition of Russian plutonium.

(10) Plans for studying the merits and costs of establishing a global network of means for detecting and responding to terroristic or other criminal use of biological agents against people or other forms of life in the United States or any foreign country.

(c) Report

(1) At the same time that the President submits the budget for fiscal year 1998 to Congress pursuant to section 1105(a) of title 31, the President shall submit to Congress a report that sets forth the comprehensive program developed under subsection (a) of this section.

(2) The report shall include the following:

(A) The specific plans for the program that are required under subsection (b) of this section.

(B) Estimates of the funds necessary, by agency or department, for carrying out such plans in fiscal year 1998 and the following five fiscal years.

(3) The report shall be in an unclassified form. If there is a classified version of the report, the President shall submit the classified version at the same time.

(Pub. L. 104–201, div. A, title XIV, § 1443, Sept. 23, 1996, 110 Stat. 2728.)

REFERENCES IN TEXT

This chapter, referred to in subsec. (a), was in the original "this title", meaning title XIV of div. A of Pub. L. 104–201, Sept. 23, 1996, 110 Stat. 2714, which is classified principally to this chapter. For complete classification of title XIV to the Code, see Short Title note set out under section 2301 of this title and Tables.

§ 2354. Termination

After September 30, 1999, the President—

(1) is not required to maintain a National Coordinator for Nonproliferation Matters under section 2351 of this title; and

(2) may terminate the Committee on Nonproliferation established under section 2352 of this title.

(Pub. L. 104–201, div. A, title XIV, § 1444, Sept. 23, 1996, 110 Stat. 2730; Pub. L. 105–261, div. A, title X, § 1069(c)(3), Oct. 17, 1998, 112 Stat. 2136.)

AMENDMENTS

1998—Pub. L. 105–261 made technical amendments to references in original act which appear in par. (1) as reference to section 2351 of this title and in par. (2) as reference to section 2352 of this title.

SUBCHAPTER V—MISCELLANEOUS

§ 2361. Sense of Congress concerning contracting policy

It is the sense of Congress that the Secretary of Defense, the Secretary of Energy, the Secretary of the Treasury, and the Secretary of State, to the extent authorized by law, should—

(1) contract directly with suppliers in independent states of the former Soviet Union when such action would—

(A) result in significant savings of the programs referred to in subchapter III of this chapter; and

(B) substantially expedite completion of the programs referred to in subchapter III of this chapter; and

(2) seek means to use innovative contracting approaches to avoid delay and increase the effectiveness of such programs and of the exercise of such authorities.

(Pub. L. 104–201, div. A, title XIV, § 1451, Sept. 23, 1996, 110 Stat. 2730.)

§2362. Transfers of allocations among cooperative threat reduction programs

Congress finds that—

(1) the various Cooperative Threat Reduction programs are being carried out at different rates in the various countries covered by such programs; and

(2) it is necessary to authorize transfers of funding allocations among the various programs in order to maximize the effectiveness of United States efforts under such programs.

(Pub. L. 104–201, div. A, title XIV, §1452, Sept. 23, 1996, 110 Stat. 2730.)

SPECIFICATION OF COOPERATIVE THREAT REDUCTION PROGRAMS

Section 1501 of Pub. L. 104–201, as amended by Pub. L. 105–261, div. A, title XIII, §1301(a)(2), Oct. 17, 1998, 112 Stat. 2161, provided that:

"(a) IN GENERAL.—For purposes of section 301 [110 Stat. 2475] and other provisions of this Act [see Tables for classification], Cooperative Threat Reduction programs are the programs specified in subsection (b).

"(b) SPECIFIED PROGRAMS.—The programs referred to in subsection (a) are the following programs with respect to states of the former Soviet Union:

"(1) Programs to facilitate the elimination, and the safe and secure transportation and storage, of nuclear, chemical, and other weapons and their delivery vehicles.

"(2) Programs to facilitate the safe and secure storage of fissile materials derived from the elimination of nuclear weapons.

"(3) Programs to prevent the proliferation of weapons, weapons components, materials, and weapons-related technology and expertise.

"(4) Programs to expand military-to-military and defense contacts."

§2363. Sense of Congress concerning assistance to states of former Soviet Union

It is the sense of Congress that—

(1) the Cooperative Threat Reduction programs and other United States programs authorized in title XIV of the National Defense Authorization Act for Fiscal Year 1993 (Public Law 102–484; 22 U.S.C. 5901 et seq.) should be expanded by offering assistance under those programs to other independent states of the former Soviet Union in addition to Russia, Ukraine, Kazakstan, and Belarus; and

(2) the President should offer assistance to additional independent states of the former Soviet Union in each case in which the participation of such states would benefit national security interests of the United States by improving border controls and safeguards over materials and technology associated with weapons of mass destruction.

(Pub. L. 104–201, div. A, title XIV, §1453, Sept. 23, 1996, 110 Stat. 2730; Pub. L. 105–261, div. A, title X, §1069(c)(4), Oct. 17, 1998, 112 Stat. 2136.)

REFERENCES IN TEXT

Title XIV of the National Defense Authorization Act for Fiscal Year 1993, referred to in par. (1), is title XIV of div. A of Pub. L. 102–484, Oct. 23, 1992, 106 Stat. 2563, known as the Former Soviet Union Demilitarization Act of 1992, which is classified generally to chapter 68 (§5901 et seq.) of Title 22, Foreign Relations and Intercourse.

AMENDMENTS

1998—Par. (1). Pub. L. 105–261 substituted "title XIV of the National Defense Authorization Act for Fiscal Year 1993 (Public Law 102–484; 22 U.S.C. 5901 et seq.)" for "the National Defense Authorization Act for Fiscal Years 1993 and 1994".

SPECIFICATION OF COOPERATIVE THREAT REDUCTION PROGRAM

For specification of Cooperative Threat Reduction programs, see section 1501(b) of Pub. L. 104–201, set out as a note under section 2362 of this title.

§2364. Purchase of low-enriched uranium derived from Russian highly enriched uranium

(a) Sense of Congress

It is the sense of Congress that the allies of the United States and other nations should participate in efforts to ensure that stockpiles of weapons-grade nuclear material are reduced.

(b) Actions by Secretary of State

Congress urges the Secretary of State to encourage, in consultation with the Secretary of Energy, other countries to purchase low-enriched uranium that is derived from highly enriched uranium extracted from Russian nuclear weapons.

(Pub. L. 104–201, div. A, title XIV, §1454, Sept. 23, 1996, 110 Stat. 2730.)

§2365. Sense of Congress concerning purchase, packaging, and transportation of fissile materials at risk of theft

It is the sense of Congress that—

(1) the Secretary of Defense, the Secretary of Energy, the Secretary of the Treasury, and the Secretary of State should purchase, package, and transport to secure locations weapons-grade nuclear materials from a stockpile of such materials if such officials determine that—

(A) there is a significant risk of theft of such materials; and

(B) there is no reasonable and economically feasible alternative for securing such materials; and

(2) if it is necessary to do so in order to secure the materials, the materials should be imported into the United States, subject to the laws and regulations that are applicable to the importation of such materials into the United States.

(Pub. L. 104–201, div. A, title XIV, §1455, Sept. 23, 1996, 110 Stat. 2731.)

§2366. Reports on acquisition of technology relating to weapons of mass destruction and advanced conventional munitions

(a) Reports

Not later than 6 months after October 11, 1996, and every 6 months thereafter, the Director of Central Intelligence shall submit to Congress a report on—

(1) the acquisition by foreign countries during the preceding 6 months of dual-use and other technology useful for the development or production of weapons of mass destruction (including nuclear weapons, chemical weap-

ons, and biological weapons) and advanced conventional munitions; and

(2) trends in the acquisition of such technology by such countries.

(b) Form of reports

The reports submitted under subsection (a) of this section shall be submitted in unclassified form, but may include a classified annex.

(Pub. L. 104–293, title VII, § 721, Oct. 11, 1996, 110 Stat. 3474.)

CODIFICATION

Section was enacted as part of the Intelligence Authorization Act for Fiscal Year 1997, and not as part of the Defense Against Weapons of Mass Destruction Act of 1996 which comprises this chapter.

§ 2367. Annual report on threat posed to United States by weapons of mass destruction, ballistic missiles, and cruise missiles

(a) Annual report

The Secretary of Defense shall submit to Congress by January 30 of each year a report on the threats posed to the United States and allies of the United States—

(1) by weapons of mass destruction, ballistic missiles, and cruise missiles; and

(2) by the proliferation of weapons of mass destruction, ballistic missiles, and cruise missiles.

(b) Consultation

Each report submitted under subsection (a) of this section shall be prepared in consultation with the Director of Central Intelligence.

(c) Matters to be included

Each report submitted under subsection (a) of this section shall include the following:

(1) Identification of each foreign country and non-State organization that possesses weapons of mass destruction, ballistic missiles, or cruise missiles, and a description of such weapons and missiles with respect to each such foreign country and non-State organization.

(2) A description of the means by which any foreign country and non-State organization that has achieved capability with respect to weapons of mass destruction, ballistic missiles, or cruise missiles has achieved that capability, including a description of the international network of foreign countries and private entities that provide assistance to foreign countries and non-State organizations in achieving that capability.

(3) An examination of the doctrines that guide the use of weapons of mass destruction in each foreign country that possesses such weapons.

(4) An examination of the existence and implementation of the control mechanisms that exist with respect to nuclear weapons in each foreign country that possesses such weapons.

(5) Identification of each foreign country and non-State organization that seeks to acquire or develop (indigenously or with foreign assistance) weapons of mass destruction, ballistic missiles, or cruise missiles, and a description of such weapons and missiles with respect to each such foreign country and non-State organization.

(6) An assessment of various possible timelines for the achievement by foreign countries and non-State organizations of capability with respect to weapons of mass destruction, ballistic missiles, and cruise missiles, taking into account the probability of whether the Russian Federation and the People's Republic of China will comply with the Missile Technology Control Regime, the potential availability of assistance from foreign technical specialists, and the potential for independent sales by foreign private entities without authorization from their national governments.

(7) For each foreign country or non-State organization that has not achieved the capability to target the United States or its territories with weapons of mass destruction, ballistic missiles, or cruise missiles as of November 18, 1997, an estimate of how far in advance the United States is likely to be warned before such foreign country or non-State organization achieves that capability.

(8) For each foreign country or non-State organization that has not achieved the capability to target members of the United States Armed Forces deployed abroad with weapons of mass destruction, ballistic missiles, or cruise missiles as of November 18, 1997, an estimate of how far in advance the United States is likely to be warned before such foreign country or non-State organization achieves that capability.

(d) Classification

Each report under subsection (a) of this section shall be submitted in classified and unclassified form.

(Pub. L. 105–85, div. A, title II, § 234, Nov. 18, 1997, 111 Stat. 1664.)

CODIFICATION

Section was enacted as part of the National Defense Authorization Act for Fiscal Year 1998, and not as part of the Defense Against Weapons of Mass Destruction Act of 1996 which comprises this chapter.

CHAPTER 41—NATIONAL NUCLEAR SECURITY ADMINISTRATION

SUBCHAPTER I—ESTABLISHMENT AND ORGANIZATION

SUBCHAPTER I—ESTABLISHMENT AND ORGANIZATION

§ 2401. Establishment and mission

(a) Establishment

There is established within the Department of Energy a separately organized agency to be known as the National Nuclear Security Administration (in this chapter referred to as the "Administration").

(b) Mission

The mission of the Administration shall be the following:

(1) To enhance United States national security through the military application of nuclear energy.

(2) To maintain and enhance the safety, reliability, and performance of the United States nuclear weapons stockpile, including the ability to design, produce, and test, in order to meet national security requirements.

(3) To provide the United States Navy with safe, militarily effective nuclear propulsion plants and to ensure the safe and reliable operation of those plants.

(4) To promote international nuclear safety and nonproliferation.

(5) To reduce global danger from weapons of mass destruction.

(6) To support United States leadership in science and technology.

(c) Operations and activities to be carried out consistent with certain principles

In carrying out the mission of the Administration, the Administrator shall ensure that all operations and activities of the Administration are consistent with the principles of protecting the environment and safeguarding the safety and health of the public and of the workforce of the Administration.

(Pub. L. 106–65, div. C, title XXXII, §3211, Oct. 5, 1999, 113 Stat. 957.)

REFERENCES IN TEXT

This chapter, referred to in subsec. (a), was in the original "this title", meaning title XXXII of div. C of Pub. L. 106–65, Oct. 5, 1999, 113 Stat. 953, as amended, which is classified principally to this chapter. For complete classification of title XXXII to the Code, see Short Title note set out below and Tables.

EFFECTIVE DATE

Pub. L. 106–65, div. C, title XXXII, §3299, Oct. 5, 1999, 113 Stat. 971, provided that:

"(a) IN GENERAL.—Except as provided in subsection (b), the provisions of this title [see Short Title note below] shall take effect on March 1, 2000.

"(b) EXCEPTIONS.—(1) Sections 3202, 3204, 3251, 3295, and 3297 [enacting sections 2451 and 2483 of this title and sections 7144a to 7144c of Title 42, amending section 7132 of Title 42, and enacting provisions set out as a note below] shall take effect on the date of the enactment of this Act [Oct. 5, 1999].

"(2) Sections 3234 and 3235 [enacting sections 2424 and 2425 of this title] shall take effect on the date of the enactment of this Act. During the period beginning on the date of the enactment of this Act and ending on the effective date of this title, the Secretary of Energy shall carry out those sections and any reference in those sections to the Administrator and the Administration shall be treated as references to the Secretary and the Department of Energy, respectively."

SHORT TITLE

Pub. L. 106–65, div. C, title XXXII, §3201, Oct. 5, 1999, 113 Stat. 953, provided that: "This title [enacting this chapter and sections 7144 to 7144c of Title 42, The Public Health and Welfare, amending sections 5314, 5315, 5595, and 8905a of Title 5, Government Organization and Employees, and sections 7132, 7133, and 7158 of Title 42, repealing sections 2122a, 7143, and 7271b of Title 42, enacting provisions set out as notes under this section, and amending provisions set out as a note under section 435 of this title] may be cited as the 'National Nuclear Security Administration Act'."

STUDY AND REPORT RELATED TO IMPROVING MISSION EFFECTIVENESS, PARTNERSHIPS, AND TECHNOLOGY TRANSFER AT NATIONAL SECURITY LABORATORIES AND NUCLEAR WEAPONS PRODUCTION FACILITIES

Pub. L. 106–398, §1 [div. C, title XXXI, §3163], Oct. 30, 2000, 114 Stat. 1654, 1654A–473, provided that:

"(a) STUDY AND REPORT REQUIRED.—The Secretary of Energy shall direct the Secretary of Energy Advisory Board to study and to submit to the Secretary not later than one year after the date of the enactment of this Act [Oct. 30, 2000] a report regarding the following topics:

"(1) The advantages and disadvantages of providing the Administrator for Nuclear Security with authority, notwithstanding the limitations otherwise imposed by the Federal Acquisition Regulation, to enter into transactions with public agencies, private organizations, or individuals on terms the Administrator considers appropriate to the furtherance of basic, applied, and advanced research functions. The Advisory Board shall consider, in its assessment of this authority, the management history of the Department of Energy and the effect of this authority on the National Nuclear Security Administration's use of contractors to operate the national security laboratories.

"(2) The advantages and disadvantages of establishing and implementing policies and procedures to facilitate the transfer of scientific, technical, and professional personnel among national security laboratories and nuclear weapons production facilities.

"(3) The advantages and disadvantages of making changes in—

"(A) the indemnification requirements for patents or other intellectual property licensed from a national security laboratory or nuclear weapons production facility;

"(B) the royalty and fee schedules and types of compensation that may be used for patents or other intellectual property licensed to a small business concern from a national security laboratory or nuclear weapons production facility;

"(C) the licensing procedures and requirements for patents and other intellectual property;

"(D) the rights given to a small business concern that has licensed a patent or other intellectual property from a national security laboratory or nuclear weapons production facility to bring suit against third parties infringing such intellectual property;

"(E) the advance funding requirements for a small business concern funding a project at a national security laboratory or nuclear weapons production facility through a funds-in agreement;

"(F) the intellectual property rights allocated to a business when it is funding a project at a national security laboratory or nuclear weapons production facility through a funds-in agreement; and

"(G) policies on royalty payments to inventors employed by a contractor operating a national security laboratory or nuclear weapons production facility, including those for inventions made under a funds-in agreement.

"(b) DEFINITION OF FUNDS-IN AGREEMENT.—For the purposes of this section, the term 'funds-in agreement' means a contract between the Department and a non-Federal organization under which that organization pays the Department to provide a service or material not otherwise available in the domestic private sector.

"(c) SUBMISSION TO CONGRESS.—Not later than one month after receiving the report under subsection (a), the Secretary shall submit to Congress that report, along with the Secretary's recommendations for action and proposals for legislation to implement the recommendations."

DEFINITIONS FOR PURPOSES OF PUB. L. 106–398

Pub. L. 106–398, §1 [div. C, title XXXI, §3165], Oct. 30, 2000, 114 Stat. 1654, 1654A–475, provided that: "For purposes of this subtitle [subtitle E (§§3161–3165) of title XXXI of div. C of H.R. 5408, as enacted by section 1 of Pub. L. 106–398, enacting provisions set out as notes under this section and section 2402 of this title], the terms 'national security laboratory' and 'nuclear weapons production facility' have the meanings given such terms in section 3281 of the National Nuclear Security Administration Act (title XXXII of Public Law 106–65; 113 Stat. 968; 50 U.S.C. 2471)."

REPORT CONTAINING IMPLEMENTATION PLAN OF SECRETARY OF ENERGY

Pub. L. 106–65, div. C, title XXXII, § 3297, Oct. 5, 1999, 113 Stat. 971, provided that: "Not later than January 1, 2000, the Secretary of Energy shall submit to the Committee on Armed Services of the Senate and the Committee on Armed Services of the House of Representatives a report containing the Secretary's plan for the implementation of the provisions of this title [see Short Title note set out above]."

CLASSIFICATION IN UNITED STATES CODE

Pub. L. 106–65, div. C, title XXXII, § 3298, Oct. 5, 1999, 113 Stat. 971, provided that: "Subtitles A through F of this title [§§ 3211–3281, enacting this chapter and amending sections 5595 and 8905a of Title 5, Government Organization and Employees] (other than provisions of those subtitles amending existing provisions of law) shall be classified to the United States Code as a new chapter of title 50, United States Code."

SECTION REFERRED TO IN OTHER SECTIONS

This section is referred to in section 2464 of this title.

§ 2402. Administrator for Nuclear Security

(a) In general

(1) There is at the head of the Administration an Administrator for Nuclear Security (in this chapter referred to as the "Administrator").

(2) Pursuant to subsection (c) of section 7132 of title 42, the Under Secretary for Nuclear Security of the Department of Energy serves as the Administrator.

(b) Functions

The Administrator has authority over, and is responsible for, all programs and activities of the Administration (except for the functions of the Deputy Administrator for Naval Reactors specified in the Executive order referred to in section 2406(b) of this title), including the following:

(1) Strategic management.

(2) Policy development and guidance.

(3) Budget formulation, guidance, and execution, and other financial matters.

(4) Resource requirements determination and allocation.

(5) Program management and direction.

(6) Safeguards and security.

(7) Emergency management.

(8) Integrated safety management.

(9) Environment, safety, and health operations.

(10) Administration of contracts, including the management and operations of the nuclear weapons production facilities and the national security laboratories.

(11) Intelligence.

(12) Counterintelligence.

(13) Personnel, including the selection, appointment, distribution, supervision, establishing of compensation, and separation of personnel in accordance with subchapter III of this chapter.

(14) Procurement of services of experts and consultants in accordance with section 3109 of title 5.

(15) Legal matters.

(16) Legislative affairs.

(17) Public affairs.

(18) Liaison with other elements of the Department of Energy and with other Federal agencies, State, tribal, and local governments, and the public.

(c) Procurement authority

The Administrator is the senior procurement executive for the Administration for the purposes of section 414(3) of title 41.

(d) Policy authority

The Administrator may establish Administration-specific policies, unless disapproved by the Secretary of Energy.

(e)[1] Membership on Joint Nuclear Weapons Council

The Administrator serves as a member of the Joint Nuclear Weapons Council under section 179 of title 10.

(e)[1] Reorganization authority

Except as provided by subsections (b) and (c) of section 2481 of this title:

(1) The Administrator may establish, abolish, alter, consolidate, or discontinue any organizational unit or component of the Administration, or transfer any function of the Administration.

(2) Such authority does not apply to the abolition of organizational units or components established by law or the transfer of functions vested by law in any organizational unit or component.

(Pub. L. 106–65, div. C, title XXXII, § 3212, Oct. 5, 1999, 113 Stat. 957; Pub. L. 106–398, § 1 [div. C, title XXXI, §§ 3152(b), 3159(a)], Oct. 30, 2000, 114 Stat. 1654, 1654A–464, 1654A–469.)

AMENDMENTS

2000—Subsec. (e). Pub. L. 106–398, § 1 [div. C, title XXXI, § 3159(a)], added subsec. (e) relating to reorganization authority.

Pub. L. 106–398, § 1 [div. C, title XXXI, § 3152(b)], added subsec. (e) relating to membership on Joint Nuclear Weapons Council.

TECHNOLOGY INFRASTRUCTURE PILOT PROGRAM

Pub. L. 106–398, § 1 [div. C, title XXXI, § 3161], Oct. 30, 2000, 114 Stat. 1654, 1654A–470, provided that:

"(a) ESTABLISHMENT.—The Administrator for Nuclear Security shall establish a Technology Infrastructure Pilot Program in accordance with this section.

"(b) PURPOSE.—The purpose of the program shall be to explore new methods of collaboration and improvements in the management and effectiveness of collaborative programs carried out by the national security laboratories and nuclear weapons production facilities in partnership with private industry and institutions of higher education and to improve the ability of those laboratories and facilities to support missions of the Administration.

"(c) FUNDING.—(1) Except as provided in paragraph (2), funding shall be available for the pilot program only to the extent of specific authorizations and appropriations enacted after the date of the enactment of this Act [Oct. 30, 2000].

"(2) From amounts available in fiscal years 2001 and 2002 for technology partnership programs of the Administration, the Administrator may allocate to carry out the pilot program not more than $5,000,000.

"(d) PROJECT REQUIREMENTS.—A project may not be approved for the pilot program unless the project meets the following requirements:

"(1) The participants in the project include—

[1] So in original. Two subsecs. (e) have been enacted.

"(A) a national security laboratory or nuclear weapons production facility; and

"(B) one or more of the following:

"(i) A business.

"(ii) An institution of higher education.

"(iii) A nonprofit institution.

"(iv) An agency of a State, local, or tribal government.

"(2)(A) Not less than 50 percent of the costs of the project are to be provided by non-Federal sources.

"(B)(i) The calculation of the amount of the costs of the project provided by non-Federal sources shall include cash, personnel, services, equipment, and other resources expended on the project.

"(ii) No funds or other resources expended before the start of the project or outside the project's scope of work may be credited toward the costs provided by non-Federal sources to the project.

"(3) The project (other than in the case of a project under which the participating laboratory or facility receives funding under this section) shall be competitively selected by that laboratory or facility using procedures determined to be appropriate by the Administrator.

"(4) No Federal funds shall be made available under this section for—

"(A) construction; or

"(B) any project for more than five years.

"(e) SELECTION CRITERIA.—(1) The projects selected for the pilot program shall—

"(A) stimulate the development of technology expertise and capabilities in private industry and institutions of higher education that can support the nuclear weapons and nuclear nonproliferation missions of the national security laboratories and nuclear weapons production facilities on a continuing basis;

"(B) improve the ability of those laboratories and facilities [to] benefit from commercial research, technology, products, processes, and services that can support the nuclear weapons and nuclear nonproliferation missions of those laboratories and facilities on a continuing basis; and

"(C) encourage the exchange of scientific and technological expertise between those laboratories and facilities and—

"(i) institutions of higher education;

"(ii) technology-related business concerns;

"(iii) nonprofit institutions; and

"(iv) agencies of State, tribal, or local governments;

that can support the missions of those laboratories and facilities.

"(2) The Administrator may authorize the provision of Federal funds for a project under this section only if the director of the laboratory or facility managing the project determines that the project is likely to improve the ability of that laboratory or facility to achieve technical success in meeting nuclear weapons and nuclear nonproliferation missions of the Administration.

"(3) The Administrator shall require the director of the laboratory or facility to consider the following criteria in selecting a project to receive Federal funds:

"(A) The potential of the project to succeed, based on its technical merit, team members, management approach, resources, and project plan.

"(B) The potential of the project to promote the development of a commercially sustainable technology, determined by considering whether the project will derive sufficient demand for its products or services from the private sector to support the nuclear weapons and nuclear nonproliferation missions of the participating laboratory or facility on a continuing basis.

"(C) The potential of the project to promote the use of commercial research, technology, products, processes, and services by the participating laboratory or facility to achieve its nuclear weapons and nuclear nonproliferation missions.

"(D) The commitment shown by non-Federal organizations to the project, based primarily on the nature and amount of the financial and other resources they will risk on the project.

"(E) The extent to which the project involves a wide variety and number of institutions of higher education, nonprofit institutions, and technology-related business concerns that can support the nuclear weapons and nuclear nonproliferation missions of the participating laboratory or facility on a continuing basis and that will make substantive contributions to achieving the goals of the project.

"(F) The extent of participation in the project by agencies of State, tribal, or local governments that will make substantive contributions to achieving the goals of the project.

"(G) The extent to which the project focuses on promoting the development of technology-related business concerns that are small business concerns or involves small business concerns substantively in the project.

"(f) IMPLEMENTATION PLAN.—No funds may be allocated for the pilot program until 30 days after the date on which the Administrator submits to the congressional defense committees [Committees on Armed Services and Appropriations of the Senate and the House of Representatives] a plan for the implementation of the pilot program. The plan shall, at a minimum—

"(1) identify the national security laboratories and nuclear weapons production facilities that have been designated by the Administrator to participate in the pilot program; and

"(2) with respect to each laboratory or facility identified under paragraph (1)—

"(A) identify the businesses, institutions of higher education, nonprofit institutions, and agencies of State, local, or tribal government that are expected to participate in the pilot program at that laboratory or facility;

"(B) identify the technology areas to be addressed by the pilot program at that laboratory or facility and the manner in which the pilot program will support high-priority missions of that laboratory or facility on a continuing basis; and

"(C) describe the management controls that have been put into place to ensure that the pilot program as conducted at that laboratory or facility is conducted in a cost-effective manner consistent with the objectives of the pilot program.

"(g) REPORT ON IMPLEMENTATION.—(1) Not later than February 1, 2002, the Administrator shall submit to the congressional defense committees a report on the implementation and management of the pilot program. The report shall take into consideration the results of the pilot program to date and the views of the directors of the participating laboratories and facilities. The report shall include any recommendations the Administrator may have concerning the future of the pilot program.

"(2) Not later than 30 days after the date on which the Administrator submits the report required by paragraph (1), the Comptroller General shall submit to the congressional defense committees a report containing the Comptroller General's assessment of that report."

[For definitions of "national security laboratory" and "nuclear weapons production facility" as used in section 1 [div. C, title XXXI, §3161] of Pub. L. 106–398, set out above, see section 1 [div. C, title XXXI, §3165] of Pub. L. 106–398, set out as a note under section 2401 of this title.]

SECTION REFERRED TO IN OTHER SECTIONS

This section is referred to in section 2403 of this title; title 42 sections 7132, 7253.

§2403. Status of Administration and contractor personnel within Department of Energy

(a) Status of Administration personnel

Each officer or employee of the Administration—

(1) shall be responsible to and subject to the authority, direction, and control of—

(A) the Secretary acting through the Administrator and consistent with section 7132(c)(3) of title 42;

(B) the Administrator; or

(C) the Administrator's designee within the Administration; and

(2) shall not be responsible to, or subject to the authority, direction, or control of, any other officer, employee, or agent of the Department of Energy.

(b) Status of contractor personnel

Each officer or employee of a contractor of the Administration shall not be responsible to, or subject to the authority, direction, or control of, any officer, employee, or agent of the Department of Energy who is not an employee of the Administration, except for the Secretary of Energy consistent with section 7132(c)(3) of title 42.

(c) Construction of section

Subsections (a) and (b) of this section may not be interpreted to in any way preclude or interfere with the communication of technical findings derived from, and in accord with, duly authorized activities between (1) the head, or any contractor employee, of a national security laboratory or of a nuclear weapons production facility, and (2) the Department of Energy, the President, or Congress.

(d) Prohibition on dual office holding

Except in accordance with sections 2402(a)(2) and 2406(a)(1) of this title:

(1) An individual may not concurrently hold or carry out the responsibilities of—

(A) a position within the Administration; and

(B) a position within the Department of Energy not within the Administration.

(2) No funds appropriated or otherwise made available for any fiscal year may be used to pay, to an individual who concurrently holds or carries out the responsibilities of a position specified in paragraph (1)(A) and a position specified in paragraph (1)(B), the basic pay, salary, or other compensation relating to any such position.

(Pub. L. 106–65, div. C, title XXXII, § 3213, Oct. 5, 1999, 113 Stat. 958; Pub. L. 106–398, § 1 [div. C, title XXXI, § 3157], Oct. 30, 2000, 114 Stat. 1654, 1654A–468.)

AMENDMENTS

2000—Subsec. (a). Pub. L. 106–398, § 1 [div. C, title XXXI, § 3157(1)], struck out "Administration, in carrying out any function of the" after "employee of the" in introductory provisions.

Subsec. (b). Pub. L. 106–398, § 1 [div. C, title XXXI, § 3157(2)], struck out ", in carrying out any function of the Administration," after "contractor of the Administration".

Subsec. (d). Pub. L. 106–398, § 1 [div. C, title XXXI, § 3157(3)], added subsec. (d).

§ 2404. Deputy Administrator for Defense Programs

(a) In general

There is in the Administration a Deputy Administrator for Defense Programs, who is appointed by the President, by and with the advice and consent of the Senate.

(b) Duties

Subject to the authority, direction, and control of the Administrator, the Deputy Administrator for Defense Programs shall perform such duties and exercise such powers as the Administrator may prescribe, including the following:

(1) Maintaining and enhancing the safety, reliability, and performance of the United States nuclear weapons stockpile, including the ability to design, produce, and test, in order to meet national security requirements.

(2) Directing, managing, and overseeing the nuclear weapons production facilities and the national security laboratories.

(3) Directing, managing, and overseeing assets to respond to incidents involving nuclear weapons and materials.

(c) Relationship to laboratories and facilities

The head of each national security laboratory and nuclear weapons production facility shall, consistent with applicable contractual obligations, report to the Deputy Administrator for Defense Programs.

(Pub. L. 106–65, div. C, title XXXII, § 3214, Oct. 5, 1999, 113 Stat. 959.)

§ 2405. Deputy Administrator for Defense Nuclear Nonproliferation

(a) In general

There is in the Administration a Deputy Administrator for Defense Nuclear Nonproliferation, who is appointed by the President, by and with the advice and consent of the Senate.

(b) Duties

Subject to the authority, direction, and control of the Administrator, the Deputy Administrator for Defense Nuclear Nonproliferation shall perform such duties and exercise such powers as the Administrator may prescribe, including the following:

(1) Preventing the spread of materials, technology, and expertise relating to weapons of mass destruction.

(2) Detecting the proliferation of weapons of mass destruction worldwide.

(3) Eliminating inventories of surplus fissile materials usable for nuclear weapons.

(4) Providing for international nuclear safety.

(Pub. L. 106–65, div. C, title XXXII, § 3215, Oct. 5, 1999, 113 Stat. 959.)

§ 2406. Deputy Administrator for Naval Reactors

(a) In general

(1) There is in the Administration a Deputy Administrator for Naval Reactors. The director of the Naval Nuclear Propulsion Program provided for under the Naval Nuclear Propulsion Executive Order shall serve as the Deputy Administrator for Naval Reactors.

(2) Within the Department of Energy, the Deputy Administrator shall report to the Secretary of Energy through the Administrator and shall have direct access to the Secretary and other senior officials in the Department.

(b) Duties

The Deputy Administrator shall be assigned the responsibilities, authorities, and accountability for all functions of the Office of Naval Reactors under the Naval Nuclear Propulsion Executive Order.

(c) Effect on Executive Order

Except as otherwise specified in this section and notwithstanding any other provision of this chapter, the provisions of the Naval Nuclear Propulsion Executive Order remain in full force and effect until changed by law.

(d) Naval Nuclear Propulsion Executive Order

As used in this section, the Naval Nuclear Propulsion Executive Order is Executive Order No. 12344, dated February 1, 1982 (42 U.S.C. 7158 note) (as in force pursuant to section 1634 of the Department of Defense Authorization Act, 1985 (Public Law 98–525; 42 U.S.C. 7158 note)).

(Pub. L. 106–65, div. C, title XXXII, § 3216, Oct. 5, 1999, 113 Stat. 959.)

SECTION REFERRED TO IN OTHER SECTIONS

This section is referred to in sections 2402, 2403 of this title.

§ 2407. General Counsel

There is a General Counsel of the Administration. The General Counsel is the chief legal officer of the Administration.

(Pub. L. 106–65, div. C, title XXXII, § 3217, Oct. 5, 1999, 113 Stat. 960.)

§ 2408. Staff of Administration

(a) In general

The Administrator shall maintain within the Administration sufficient staff to assist the Administrator in carrying out the duties and responsibilities of the Administrator.

(b) Responsibilities

The staff of the Administration shall perform, in accordance with applicable law, such of the functions of the Administrator as the Administrator shall prescribe. The Administrator shall assign to the staff responsibility for the following functions:

(1) Personnel.

(2) Legislative affairs.

(3) Public affairs.

(4) Liaison with other elements of the Department of Energy and with other Federal agencies, State, tribal, and local governments, and the public.

(Pub. L. 106–65, div. C, title XXXII, § 3218, Oct. 5, 1999, 113 Stat. 960.)

§ 2409. Scope of authority of Secretary of Energy to modify organization of Administration

Notwithstanding the authority granted by section 7253 of title 42 or any other provision of law, the Secretary of Energy may not establish, abolish, alter, consolidate, or discontinue any organizational unit or component, or transfer any function, of the Administration, except as authorized by subsection (b) or (c) of section 2481 of this title.

(Pub. L. 106–65, div. C, title XXXII, § 3219, as added Pub. L. 106–377, § 1(a)(2) [title III, § 314(a)], Oct. 27, 2000, 114 Stat. 1441, 1441A–81.)

SECTION REFERRED TO IN OTHER SECTIONS

This section is referred to in title 42 section 7253.

SUBCHAPTER II—MATTERS RELATING TO SECURITY

§ 2421. Protection of national security information

(a) Policies and procedures required

The Administrator shall establish procedures to ensure the maximum protection of classified information in the possession of the Administration.

(b) Prompt reporting

The Administrator shall establish procedures to ensure prompt reporting to the Administrator of any significant problem, abuse, violation of law or Executive order, or deficiency relating to the management of classified information by personnel of the Administration.

(Pub. L. 106–65, div. C, title XXXII, § 3231, Oct. 5, 1999, 113 Stat. 960.)

§ 2422. Office of Defense Nuclear Counterintelligence and Office of Defense Nuclear Security

(a) Establishment

(1) There are within the Administration—

(A) an Office of Defense Nuclear Counterintelligence; and

(B) an Office of Defense Nuclear Security.

(2) Each office established under paragraph (1) shall be headed by a Chief appointed by the Secretary of Energy. The Administrator shall recommend to the Secretary suitable candidates for each such position.

(b) Chief of Defense Nuclear Counterintelligence

(1) The head of the Office of Defense Nuclear Counterintelligence is the Chief of Defense Nuclear Counterintelligence, who shall report to the Administrator and shall implement the counterintelligence policies directed by the Secretary and Administrator.

(2) The Secretary shall appoint the Chief, in consultation with the Director of the Federal Bureau of Investigation, from among individuals who have special expertise in counterintelligence. If an individual to serve as the Chief of Defense Nuclear Counterintelligence is a Federal employee of an entity other than the Administration, the service of that employee as Chief shall not result in any loss of employment status, right, or privilege by that employee.

(3) The Chief shall have direct access to the Secretary and all other officials of the Department and the contractors of the Department concerning counterintelligence matters.

(4) The Chief shall be responsible for—

(A) the development and implementation of the counterintelligence programs of the Administration to prevent the disclosure or loss of classified or other sensitive information; and

(B) the development and administration of personnel assurance programs within the Administration.

(c) Chief of Defense Nuclear Security

(1) The head of the Office of Defense Nuclear Security is the Chief of Defense Nuclear Security, who shall report to the Administrator and shall implement the security policies directed by the Secretary and Administrator.

(2) The Chief shall have direct access to the Secretary and all other officials of the Department and the contractors of the Department concerning security matters.

(3) The Chief shall be responsible for the development and implementation of security programs for the Administration, including the protection, control and accounting of materials, and for the physical and cyber security for all facilities of the Administration.

(Pub. L. 106–65, div. C, title XXXII, § 3232, Oct. 5, 1999, 113 Stat. 960.)

§ 2423. Counterintelligence programs

(a) National security laboratories and nuclear weapons production facilities

The Administrator shall, at each national security laboratory and nuclear weapons production facility, establish and maintain a counterintelligence program adequate to protect national security information at that laboratory or production facility.

(b) Other facilities

The Administrator shall, at each Administration facility not described in subsection (a) of this section at which Restricted Data is located, assign an employee of the Office of Defense Nuclear Counterintelligence who shall be responsible for and assess counterintelligence matters at that facility.

(Pub. L. 106–65, div. C, title XXXII, § 3233, Oct. 5, 1999, 113 Stat. 961.)

§ 2424. Procedures relating to access by individuals to classified areas and information of Administration

The Administrator shall establish appropriate procedures to ensure that any individual is not permitted unescorted access to any classified area, or access to classified information, of the Administration until that individual has been verified to hold the appropriate security clearances.

(Pub. L. 106–65, div. C, title XXXII, § 3234, Oct. 5, 1999, 113 Stat. 961.)

§ 2425. Government access to information on Administration computers

(a) Procedures required

The Administrator shall establish procedures to govern access to information on Administration computers. Those procedures shall, at a minimum, provide that any individual who has access to information on an Administration computer shall be required as a condition of such access to provide to the Administrator written consent which permits access by an authorized investigative agency to any Administration computer used in the performance of the duties of such employee during the period of that individual's access to information on an Administration computer and for a period of three years thereafter.

(b) Expectation of privacy in Administration computers

Notwithstanding any other provision of law (including any provision of law enacted by the Electronic Communications Privacy Act of 1986), no user of an Administration computer shall have any expectation of privacy in the use of that computer.

(c) Definition

For purposes of this section, the term "authorized investigative agency" means an agency authorized by law or regulation to conduct a counterintelligence investigation or investigations of persons who are proposed for access to classified information to ascertain whether such persons satisfy the criteria for obtaining and retaining access to such information.

(Pub. L. 106–65, div. C, title XXXII, § 3235, Oct. 5, 1999, 113 Stat. 961.)

REFERENCES IN TEXT

The Electronic Communications Privacy Act of 1986, referred to in subsec. (b), is Pub. L. 99–508, Oct. 21, 1986, 100 Stat. 1848, as amended. For complete classification of this Act to the Code, see Short Title of 1986 Amendment note set out under section 2510 of Title 18, Crimes and Criminal Procedure, and Tables.

SECTION REFERRED TO IN OTHER SECTIONS

This section is referred to in section 2483 of this title.

§ 2426. Congressional oversight of special access programs

(a) Annual report on special access programs

(1) Not later than February 1 of each year, the Administrator shall submit to the congressional defense committees a report on special access programs of the Administration.

(2) Each such report shall set forth—

(A) the total amount requested for such programs in the President's budget for the next fiscal year submitted under section 1105 of title 31; and

(B) for each such program in that budget, the following:

(i) A brief description of the program.

(ii) A brief discussion of the major milestones established for the program.

(iii) The actual cost of the program for each fiscal year during which the program has been conducted before the fiscal year during which that budget is submitted.

(iv) The estimated total cost of the program and the estimated cost of the program for (I) the current fiscal year, (II) the fiscal year for which the budget is submitted, and (III) each of the four succeeding fiscal years during which the program is expected to be conducted.

(b) Annual report on new special access programs

(1) Not later than February 1 of each year, the Administrator shall submit to the congressional defense committees a report that, with respect to each new special access program, provides—

(A) notice of the designation of the program as a special access program; and

(B) justification for such designation.

(2) A report under paragraph (1) with respect to a program shall include—

(A) the current estimate of the total program cost for the program; and

(B) an identification of existing programs or technologies that are similar to the technology, or that have a mission similar to the mission, of the program that is the subject of the notice.

(3) In this subsection, the term "new special access program" means a special access program that has not previously been covered in a notice and justification under this subsection.

(c) Reports on changes in classification of special access programs

(1) Whenever a change in the classification of a special access program of the Administration is planned to be made or whenever classified information concerning a special access program of the Administration is to be declassified and made public, the Administrator shall submit to the congressional defense committees a report containing a description of the proposed change, the reasons for the proposed change, and notice of any public announcement planned to be made with respect to the proposed change.

(2) Except as provided in paragraph (3), any report referred to in paragraph (1) shall be submitted not less than 14 days before the date on which the proposed change or public announcement is to occur.

(3) If the Administrator determines that because of exceptional circumstances the requirement of paragraph (2) cannot be met with respect to a proposed change or public announcement concerning a special access program of the Administration, the Administrator may submit the report required by paragraph (1) regarding the proposed change or public announcement at any time before the proposed change or public announcement is made and shall include in the report an explanation of the exceptional circumstances.

(d) Notice of change in SAP designation criteria

Whenever there is a modification or termination of the policy and criteria used for designating a program of the Administration as a special access program, the Administrator shall promptly notify the congressional defense committees of such modification or termination. Any such notification shall contain the reasons for the modification or termination and, in the case of a modification, the provisions of the policy as modified.

(e) Waiver authority

(1) The Administrator may waive any requirement under subsection (a), (b), or (c) of this section that certain information be included in a report under that subsection if the Administrator determines that inclusion of that information in the report would adversely affect the national security. The Administrator may waive the report-and-wait requirement in subsection (f) of this section if the Administrator determines that compliance with such requirement would adversely affect the national security. Any waiver under this paragraph shall be made on a case-by-case basis.

(2) If the Administrator exercises the authority provided under paragraph (1), the Administrator shall provide the information described in that subsection with respect to the special access program concerned, and the justification for the waiver, jointly to the chairman and ranking minority member of each of the congressional defense committees.

(f) Report and wait for initiating new programs

A special access program may not be initiated until—

(1) the congressional defense committees are notified of the program; and

(2) a period of 30 days elapses after such notification is received.

(Pub. L. 106–65, div. C, title XXXII, §3236, Oct. 5, 1999, 113 Stat. 962.)

PRIOR PROVISIONS

Provisions similar to those in this section were contained in section 2122a of Title 42, The Public Health and Welfare, prior to repeal by Pub. L. 106–65, §3294(e)(1)(A).

SUBCHAPTER III—MATTERS RELATING TO PERSONNEL

SUBCHAPTER REFERRED TO IN OTHER SECTIONS

This subchapter is referred to in section 2402 of this title.

§2441. Authority to establish certain scientific, engineering, and technical positions

The Administrator may, for the purposes of carrying out the responsibilities of the Administrator under this chapter, establish not more than 300 scientific, engineering, and technical positions in the Administration, appoint individuals to such positions, and fix the compensation of such individuals. Subject to the limitations in the preceding sentence, the authority of the Administrator to make appointments and fix compensation with respect to positions in the Administration under this section shall be equivalent to, and subject to the limitations of, the authority under section 2201(d) of title 42 to make appointments and fix compensation with respect to officers and employees described in such section.

(Pub. L. 106–65, div. C, title XXXII, §3241, Oct. 5, 1999, 113 Stat. 964.)

REFERENCES IN TEXT

This chapter, referred to in text, was in the original "this title", meaning title XXXII of div. C of Pub. L. 106–65, Oct. 5, 1999, 113 Stat. 953, as amended, which is classified principally to this chapter. For complete classification of title XXXII to the Code, see Short Title note set out under section 2401 of this title and Tables.

§2442. Voluntary early retirement authority

(a) Authority

An employee of the Department of Energy who is separated from the service under conditions described in subsection (b) of this section after completing 25 years of service or after becoming 50 years of age and completing 20 years of service is entitled to an annuity in accordance with the provisions in chapter 83 or 84 of title 5, as applicable.

(b) Conditions of separation

Subsection (a) of this section applies to an employee who—

(1) has been employed continuously by the Department of Energy for more than 30 days before the date on which the Secretary of Energy makes the determination required under paragraph (4)(A);

(2) is serving under an appointment that is not limited by time;

(3) has not received a decision notice of involuntary separation for misconduct or unacceptable performance that is pending decision; and

(4) is separated from the service voluntarily during a period with respect to which—

(A) the Secretary of Energy determines that the Department of Energy is undergoing a major reorganization as a result of the establishment of the National Nuclear Security Administration; and

(B) the employee is within the scope of an offer of voluntary early retirement (as defined by organizational unit, occupational series or level, geographical location, any other similar factor that the Office of Personnel Management determines appropriate, or any combination of such definitions of scope), as determined by the Secretary under regulations prescribed by the Office.

(c) Treatment of employees

For purposes of chapters 83 and 84 of title 5 (including for purposes of computation of an annuity under such chapters), an employee entitled to an annuity under this section shall be treated as an employee entitled to an annuity under section 8336(d) or 8414(b) of such title, as applicable.

(d) Definitions

As used in this section, the terms "employee" and "annuity"—

(1) with respect to individuals covered by the Civil Service Retirement System established in subchapter III of chapter 83 of title 5 have the meaning of such terms as used in such chapter; and

(2) with respect to individuals covered by the Federal Employees Retirement System established in chapter 84 of such title, have the meaning of such terms as used in such chapter.

(e) Limitation and termination of authority

The authority provided in subsection (a) of this section—

(1) may be applied with respect to a total of not more than 600 employees of the Department of Energy; and

(2) shall expire on September 30, 2003.

(Pub. L. 106–65, div. C, title XXXII, § 3242, Oct. 5, 1999, 113 Stat. 964.)

§ 2443. Prohibition on pay of personnel engaged in concurrent service or duties inside and outside Administration

(a) Except as otherwise expressly provided by statute, no funds authorized to be appropriated or otherwise made available for the Department of Energy may be obligated or utilized to pay the basic pay of an officer or employee of the Department of Energy who—

(1) serves concurrently in a position in the Administration and a position outside the Administration; or

(2) performs concurrently the duties of a position in the Administration and the duties of a position outside the Administration.

(b) The provision of this section shall take effect 60 days after October 27, 2000.

(Pub. L. 106–65, div. C, title XXXII, § 3245, as added Pub. L. 106–377, § 1(a)(2) [title III, § 315], Oct. 27, 2000, 114 Stat. 1441, 1441A–81.)

SUBCHAPTER IV—BUDGET AND FINANCIAL MANAGEMENT

§ 2451. Separate treatment in budget

(a) President's budget

In each budget submitted by the President to the Congress under section 1105 of title 31, amounts requested for the Administration shall be set forth separately within the other amounts requested for the Department of Energy.

(b) Budget justification materials

In the budget justification materials submitted to Congress in support of each such budget, the amounts requested for the Administration shall be specified in individual, dedicated program elements.

(Pub. L. 106–65, div. C, title XXXII, § 3251, Oct. 5, 1999, 113 Stat. 966.)

§ 2452. Planning, programming, and budgeting process

(a) Procedures required

The Administrator shall establish procedures to ensure that the planning, programming, budgeting, and financial activities of the Administration comport with sound financial and fiscal management principles. Those procedures shall, at a minimum, provide for the planning, programming, and budgeting of activities of the Administration using funds that are available for obligation for a limited number of years.

(b) Annual plan for obligation of funds

(1) Each year, the Administrator shall prepare a plan for the obligation of the amounts that, in the President's budget submitted to Congress that year under section 1105(a) of title 31, are proposed to be appropriated for the Administration for the fiscal year that begins in that year (in this section referred to as the "budget year") and the two succeeding fiscal years.

(2) For each program element and construction line item of the Administration, the plan shall provide the goal of the Administration for the obligation of those amounts for that element or item for each fiscal year of the plan, expressed as a percentage of the total amount proposed to be appropriated in that budget for that element or item.

(c) Submission of plan and report

The Administrator shall submit to Congress each year, at or about the time that the President's budget is submitted to Congress under section 1105(a) of title 31, each of the following:

(1) The plan required by subsection (b) of this section prepared with respect to that budget.

(2) A report on the plans prepared with respect to the preceding years' budgets, which

shall include, for each goal provided in those plans—

(A) the assessment of the Administrator as to whether or not that goal was met; and

(B) if that assessment is that the goal was not met—

(i) the reasons why that goal was not met; and

(ii) the plan of the Administrator for meeting or, if necessary, adjusting that goal.

(Pub. L. 106–65, div. C, title XXXII, §3252, Oct. 5, 1999, 113 Stat. 966; Pub. L. 106–398, §1 [div. C, title XXXI, §3158(a)], Oct. 30, 2000, 114 Stat. 1654, 1654A–469.)

AMENDMENTS

2000—Pub. L. 106–398 designated existing provisions as subsec. (a), inserted heading, and added subsecs. (b) and (c).

FIRST REPORT ON ASSESSMENT OF PRIOR PLANS; GAO REPORT

Pub. L. 106–398, §1 [div. C, title XXXI, §3158(b), (c)], Oct. 30, 2000, 114 Stat. 1654, 1654A–469, provided that:

"(b) EFFECTIVE DATE OF REQUIREMENT TO ASSESS PRIOR PLAN.—The first report submitted under paragraph (2) of subsection (c) of such section [subsec. (c)(2) of this section] (as added by subsection (a)) shall be the report on the plan prepared with respect to the budget submitted in calendar year 2001.

"(c) GAO REPORT.—Not later than March 15, 2001, the Comptroller General shall submit to the congressional defense committees [Committees on Armed Services and Appropriations of the Senate and the House of Representatives] an assessment of the adequacy of the planning, programming, and budgeting processes of the National Nuclear Security Administration."

SECTION REFERRED TO IN OTHER SECTIONS

This section is referred to in section 2483 of this title.

§2453. Future-years nuclear security program

(a) Submission to Congress

The Administrator shall submit to Congress each year, at or about the time that the President's budget is submitted to Congress that year under section 1105(a) of title 31, a future-years nuclear security program (including associated annexes) reflecting the estimated expenditures and proposed appropriations included in that budget. Any such future-years nuclear security program shall cover the fiscal year with respect to which the budget is submitted and at least the four succeeding fiscal years.

(b) Elements

Each future-years nuclear security program shall contain the following:

(1) A detailed description of the program elements (and the projects, activities, and construction projects associated with each such program element) during the applicable five-fiscal year period for at least each of the following:

(A) For defense programs—

(i) directed stockpile work;

(ii) campaigns;

(iii) readiness in technical base and facilities; and

(iv) secure transportation asset.

(B) For defense nuclear nonproliferation—

(i) nonproliferation and verification, research, and development;

(ii) arms control; and

(iii) fissile materials disposition.

(C) For naval reactors, naval reactors operations and maintenance.

(2) A statement of proposed budget authority, estimated expenditures, and proposed appropriations necessary to support each program element specified pursuant to paragraph (1).

(3) A detailed description of how the funds identified for each program element specified pursuant to paragraph (1) in the budget for the Administration for each fiscal year during that five-fiscal year period will help ensure that the nuclear weapons stockpile is safe and reliable, as determined in accordance with the criteria established under section 3158 of the Strom Thurmond National Defense Authorization Act for Fiscal Year 1999 (42 U.S.C. 2121 note).

(4) A description of the anticipated workload requirements for each Administration site during that five-fiscal year period.

(c) Consistency in budgeting

(1) The Administrator shall ensure that amounts described in subparagraph (A) of paragraph (2) for any fiscal year are consistent with amounts described in subparagraph (B) of paragraph (2) for that fiscal year.

(2) Amounts referred to in paragraph (1) are the following:

(A) The amounts specified in program and budget information submitted to Congress by the Administrator in support of expenditure estimates and proposed appropriations in the budget submitted to Congress by the President under section 1105(a) of title 31 for any fiscal year, as shown in the future-years nuclear security program submitted pursuant to subsection (a) of this section.

(B) The total amounts of estimated expenditures and proposed appropriations necessary to support the programs, projects, and activities of the Administration included pursuant to paragraph (5) of section 1105(a) of such title in the budget submitted to Congress under that section for any fiscal year.

(d) Treatment of management contingencies

Nothing in this section shall be construed to prohibit the inclusion in the future-years nuclear security program of amounts for management contingencies, subject to the requirements of subsection (c) of this section.

(Pub. L. 106–65, div. C, title XXXII, §3253, Oct. 5, 1999, 113 Stat. 966; Pub. L. 106–398, §1 [div. C, title XXXI, §3154], Oct. 30, 2000, 114 Stat. 1654, 1654A–465.)

REFERENCES IN TEXT

Section 3158 of the Strom Thurmond National Defense Authorization Act for Fiscal Year 1999, referred to in subsec. (b)(3), is section 3158 of Pub. L. 105–261, as amended, which is set out as a note under section 2121 of Title 42, The Public Health and Welfare.

AMENDMENTS

2000—Subsec. (b). Pub. L. 106–398, §1 [div. C, title XXXI, §3154(a)], added pars. (1) to (3), redesignated former par. (2) as (4), and struck out former par. (1) which read as follows: "The estimated expenditures and proposed appropriations necessary to support the programs, projects, and activities of the Administration during the five-fiscal year period covered by the program, expressed in a level of detail comparable to that contained in the budget submitted by the President to Congress under section 1105 of title 31."

Subsec. (c). Pub. L. 106–398, §1 [div. C, title XXXI, §3154(b)(1), (2)], redesignated subsec. (d) as (c) and struck out heading and text of former subsec. (c). Text read as follows: "The Administrator shall include in the materials the Administrator submits to Congress in support of the budget for any fiscal year that is submitted by the President pursuant to section 1105 of title 31 a description of how the funds identified for each program element in the weapons activities budget of the Administration for such fiscal year will help ensure that the nuclear weapons stockpile is safe and reliable as determined in accordance with the criteria established under section 3158 of the Strom Thurmond National Defense Authorization Act for Fiscal Year 1999 (Public Law 105–261; 112 Stat. 2257; 42 U.S.C. 2121 note)."

Subsec. (d). Pub. L. 106–398, §1 [div. C, title XXXI, §3154(b)(2), (3)], redesignated subsec. (e) as (d) and substituted "subsection (c)" for "subsection (d)". Former subsec. (d) redesignated (c).

Subsec. (e). Pub. L. 106–398, §1 [div. C, title XXXI, §3154(b)(2)], redesignated subsec. (e) as (d).

SECTION REFERRED TO IN OTHER SECTIONS

This section is referred to in section 2483 of this title.

SUBCHAPTER V—MISCELLANEOUS PROVISIONS

§ 2461. Environmental protection, safety, and health requirements

(a) Compliance required

The Administrator shall ensure that the Administration complies with all applicable environmental, safety, and health statutes and substantive requirements.

(b) Procedures required

The Administrator shall develop procedures for meeting such requirements.

(c) Rule of construction

Nothing in this chapter shall diminish the authority of the Secretary of Energy to ascertain and ensure that such compliance occurs.

(Pub. L. 106–65, div. C, title XXXII, §3261, Oct. 5, 1999, 113 Stat. 967.)

REFERENCES IN TEXT

This chapter, referred to in subsec. (c), was in the original "this title", meaning title XXXII of div. C of Pub. L. 106–65, Oct. 5, 1999, 113 Stat. 953, as amended, which is classified principally to this chapter. For complete classification of title XXXII to the Code, see Short Title note set out under section 2401 of this title and Tables.

§ 2462. Compliance with Federal Acquisition Regulation

The Administrator shall establish procedures to ensure that the mission and programs of the Administration are executed in full compliance with all applicable provisions of the Federal Acquisition Regulation issued pursuant to the Office of Federal Procurement Policy Act (41 U.S.C. 401 et seq.).

(Pub. L. 106–65, div. C, title XXXII, §3262, Oct. 5, 1999, 113 Stat. 967.)

REFERENCES IN TEXT

The Office of Federal Procurement Policy Act, referred to in text, is Pub. L. 93–400, Aug. 30, 1974, 88 Stat. 796, as amended, which is classified principally to chapter 7 (§401 et seq.) of Title 41, Public Contracts. For complete classification of this Act to the Code, see Short Title note set out under section 401 of Title 41 and Tables.

SECTION REFERRED TO IN OTHER SECTIONS

This section is referred to in section 2483 of this title.

§ 2463. Sharing of technology with Department of Defense

The Administrator shall, in cooperation with the Secretary of Defense, establish procedures and programs to provide for the sharing of technology, technical capability, and expertise between the Administration and the Department of Defense to further national security objectives.

(Pub. L. 106–65, div. C, title XXXII, §3263, Oct. 5, 1999, 113 Stat. 967.)

§ 2464. Use of capabilities of national security laboratories by entities outside the Administration

The Secretary, in consultation with the Administrator, shall establish appropriate procedures to provide for the use, in a manner consistent with the national security mission of the Administration under section 2401(b) of this title, of the capabilities of the national security laboratories by elements of the Department of Energy not within the Administration, other Federal agencies, and other appropriate entities, including the use of those capabilities to support efforts to defend against weapons of mass destruction.

(Pub. L. 106–65, div. C, title XXXII, §3264, Oct. 5, 1999, 113 Stat. 967.)

SUBCHAPTER VI—DEFINITIONS

§ 2471. Definitions

For purposes of this chapter:

(1) The term "national security laboratory" means any of the following:

(A) Los Alamos National Laboratory, Los Alamos, New Mexico.

(B) Sandia National Laboratories, Albuquerque, New Mexico, and Livermore, California.

(C) Lawrence Livermore National Laboratory, Livermore, California.

(2) The term "nuclear weapons production facility" means any of the following:

(A) The Kansas City Plant, Kansas City, Missouri.

(B) The Pantex Plant, Amarillo, Texas.

(C) The Y–12 Plant, Oak Ridge, Tennessee.

(D) The tritium operations facilities at the Savannah River Site, Aiken, South Carolina.

(E) The Nevada Test Site, Nevada.

(F) Any facility of the Department of Energy that the Secretary of Energy, in consultation with the Administrator and the Congress, determines to be consistent with the mission of the Administration.

(3) The term "classified information" means any information that has been determined pursuant to Executive Order No. 12333 of December 4, 1981 (50 U.S.C. 401 note), Executive Order No. 12958 of April 17, 1995 (50 U.S.C. 435 note), or successor orders, to require protection against unauthorized disclosure and that is so designated.

(4) The term "Restricted Data" has the meaning given such term in section 2014(y) of title 42.

(5) The term "congressional defense committees" means—

(A) the Committee on Armed Services and the Committee on Appropriations of the Senate; and

(B) the Committee on Armed Services and the Committee on Appropriations of the House of Representatives.

(Pub. L. 106–65, div. C, title XXXII, §3281, Oct. 5, 1999, 113 Stat. 968.)

REFERENCES IN TEXT

This chapter, referred to in text, was in the original "this title", meaning title XXXII of div. C of Pub. L. 106–65, Oct. 5, 1999, 113 Stat. 953, as amended, which is classified principally to this chapter. For complete classification of title XXXII to the Code, see Short Title note set out under section 2401 of this title and Tables.

SUBCHAPTER VII—TRANSITION PROVISIONS

§2481. Functions transferred

(a) Transfers

There are hereby transferred to the Administrator all national security functions and activities performed immediately before October 5, 1999, by the following elements of the Department of Energy:

(1) The Office of Defense Programs.

(2) The Office of Nonproliferation and National Security.

(3) The Office of Fissile Materials Disposition.

(4) The nuclear weapons production facilities.

(5) The national security laboratories.

(6) The Office of Naval Reactors.

(b) Authority to transfer additional functions

The Secretary of Energy may transfer to the Administrator any other facility, mission, or function that the Secretary, in consultation with the Administrator and Congress, determines to be consistent with the mission of the Administration.

(c) Environmental remediation and waste management activities

In the case of any environmental remediation and waste management activity of any element specified in subsection (a) of this section, the Secretary of Energy may determine to transfer responsibility for that activity to another element of the Department.

(Pub. L. 106–65, div. C, title XXXII, §3291, Oct. 5, 1999, 113 Stat. 968.)

SECTION REFERRED TO IN OTHER SECTIONS

This section is referred to in sections 2402, 2409, 2484 of this title.

§2482. Transfer of funds and employees

(a) Transfer of funds

(1) Any balance of appropriations that the Secretary of Energy determines is available and needed to finance or discharge a function, power, or duty or an activity that is transferred to the Administration shall be transferred to the Administration and used for any purpose for which those appropriations were originally available. Balances of appropriations so transferred shall—

(A) be credited to any applicable appropriation account of the Administration; or

(B) be credited to a new account that may be established on the books of the Department of the Treasury;

and shall be merged with the funds already credited to that account and accounted for as one fund.

(2) Balances of appropriations credited to an account under paragraph (1)(A) are subject only to such limitations as are specifically applicable to that account. Balances of appropriations credited to an account under paragraph (1)(B) are subject only to such limitations as are applicable to the appropriations from which they are transferred.

(b) Personnel

(1) With respect to any function, power, or duty or activity of the Department of Energy that is transferred to the Administration, those employees of the element of the Department of Energy from which the transfer is made that the Secretary of Energy determines are needed to perform that function, power, or duty, or for that activity, as the case may be, shall be transferred to the Administration.

(2) The authorized strength in civilian employees of any element of the Department of Energy from which employees are transferred under this section is reduced by the number of employees so transferred.

(Pub. L. 106–65, div. C, title XXXII, §3292, Oct. 5, 1999, 113 Stat. 969.)

§2483. Transition provisions

(a) Compliance with financial principles

(1) The Under Secretary of Energy for Nuclear Security shall ensure that the compliance with sound financial and fiscal management principles specified in section 2452 of this title is achieved not later than October 1, 2000.

(2) In carrying out paragraph (1), the Under Secretary of Energy for Nuclear Security shall conduct a review and develop a plan to bring applicable activities of the Administration into full compliance with those principles not later than such date.

(3) Not later than January 1, 2000, the Under Secretary of Energy for Nuclear Security shall submit to the Committees on Armed Services of the Senate and the House of Representatives a report containing the results of that review and a description of that plan.

(b) Initial report for future-years nuclear security program

The first report under section 2453 of this title shall be submitted in conjunction with the budget submitted for fiscal year 2001.

(c) Procedures for computer access

The regulations to implement the procedures under section 2425 of this title shall be prescribed not later than 90 days after the effective date of this chapter.

(d) Compliance with FAR

(1) The Under Secretary of Energy for Nuclear Security shall ensure that the compliance with the Federal Acquisition Regulation specified in section 2462 of this title is achieved not later than October 1, 2000.

(2) In carrying out paragraph (1), the Under Secretary of Energy for Nuclear Security shall conduct a review and develop a plan to bring applicable activities of the Administration into full compliance with the Federal Acquisition Regulation not later than such date.

(3) Not later than January 1, 2000, the Under Secretary of Energy for Nuclear Security shall submit to the Committees on Armed Services of the Senate and the House of Representatives a report containing the results of that review and a description of that plan.

(Pub. L. 106–65, div. C, title XXXII, § 3295, Oct. 5, 1999, 113 Stat. 970.)

REFERENCES IN TEXT

For effective date of this chapter, referred to in subsec. (c), see section 3299 of Pub. L. 106–65, set out as an Effective Date note under section 2401 of this title.

§ 2484. Applicability of preexisting laws and regulations

Unless otherwise provided in this chapter, all provisions of law and regulations in effect immediately before the effective date of this chapter that are applicable to functions of the Department of Energy specified in section 2481 of this title shall continue to apply to the corresponding functions of the Administration.

(Pub. L. 106–65, div. C, title XXXII, § 3296, Oct. 5, 1999, 113 Stat. 971.)

REFERENCES IN TEXT

This chapter, referred to in text, was in the original "this title", meaning title XXXII of div. C of Pub. L. 106–65, Oct. 5, 1999, 113 Stat. 953, as amended, which is classified principally to this chapter. For effective date of this chapter, see section 3299 of Pub. L. 106–65, set out as an Effective Date note under section 2401 of this title. For complete classification of title XXXII to the Code, see Short Title note set out under section 2401 of this title and Tables.

TITLE 50, APPENDIX—WAR AND NATIONAL DEFENSE

PROCLAMATIONS, EXECUTIVE ORDERS, JOINT RESOLUTIONS AND TREATIES RESPECTING WAR, NEUTRALITY AND PEACE

I. PROCLAMATIONS OF STATE OF WAR

War between Germany and France; Poland; and the United Kingdom, India, Australia, Canada, New Zealand and the Union of South Africa	Proc. No. 2374
War between Germany and Norway	Proc. No. 2398
War between Germany and Belgium, Luxemburg, and the Netherlands	Proc. No. 2404
War between Italy and France and United Kingdom	Proc. No. 2407
War between Italy and Greece	Proc. No. 2443
War between Germany-Italy and Yugoslavia	Proc. No. 2473
War between Hungary and Yugoslavia	Proc. No. 2477
War between Bulgaria and Yugoslavia and Greece	Proc. No. 2479

II. PROCLAMATIONS OF UNITED STATES NEUTRALITY

War between Germany and France; Poland; United Kingdom, India, Australia and New Zealand	Proc. No. 2348
War between Germany and Union of South Africa, Canada	Proc. Nos. 2353, 2359
War between Germany and Norway	Proc. No. 2399
War between Germany and Belgium, Luxemburg, and the Netherlands	Proc. No. 2405
War between Italy and France and United Kingdom	Proc. No. 2408
War between Italy and Greece	Proc. No. 2444

III. MISCELLANEOUS PROCLAMATIONS AND EXECUTIVE ORDERS

Neutrality of the United States	Ex. Ord. No. 8233
Vessels through Panama Canal in any War in which the United States is Neutral	Ex. Ord. No. 8234
Neutrality in the Canal Zone	Proc. No. 2350
National Emergency, 1950	Proc. No. 2914
National Emergency of 1939	Proc. No. 2352
National Emergency of 1941	Proc. No. 2487
Removal of Alien Enemies	Proc. No. 2685
Termination of President's War Relief Control Board	Ex. Ord. No. 9723
Termination of Wartime Emergencies	Proc. No. 2974

IV. DECLARATIONS OF WAR BY UNITED STATES

War between United States and Germany	Joint Res. April 6, 1917, 40 Stat. 1
War between United States and Austria-Hungary	Joint Res. Dec. 7, 1917, 40 Stat. 429
War between United States and Japan	Res. Dec. 8, 1941, ch. 561
War between United States and Germany	Res. Dec. 11, 1941, ch. 564
War between United States and Italy	Res. Dec. 11, 1941, ch. 565
War between United States and Bulgaria	Res. June 5, 1942, ch. 323
War between United States and Hungary	Res. June 5, 1942, ch. 324
War between United States and Rumania	Res. June 5, 1942, ch. 325
War between United States and Hungary, Bulgaria, and Rumania	Proc. No. 2563

V. TERMINATION OF STATE OF WAR

Cessation of Hostilities of World War II	Proc. No. 2714
Treaties of Peace with Italy, Bulgaria, Hungary, Rumania and Finland	Feb. 10, 1947
Treaty of Peace with Japan	Sept. 8, 1951
Termination of War with Germany	Jt. Res. Oct. 19, 1951, Proc. No. 2950
Ratification of Japanese Peace Treaty	Mar. 20, 1952

VI. AUTHORIZATION TO EMPLOY ARMED FORCES

Termination of Hostilities in Indochina	Pub. L. 92–129, Sept. 28, 1971, 85 Stat. 360
Maintenance of International Peace and Security in Southeast Asia	Pub. L. 88–408, Aug. 10, 1964, 78 Stat. 384
Interdiction of the Delivery of Offensive Weapons to Cuba	Proc. No. 3504, Oct. 23, 1962
Termination of Authority Granted and Orders Issued in Proc. No. 3504	Proc. 3507, Nov. 21, 1962

Middle East Stabilization	Pub. L. 85–7, Mar. 9, 1957, 71 Stat. 5
Protection of Security of Formosa	Res. Jan. 29, 1955

See, also, notes under the Neutrality Act of 1939, sections 441, 444, 445, 447 to 451, 453 to 457 of Title 22, Foreign Relations and Intercourse.

I. PROCLAMATIONS OF STATE OF WAR

Proc. No. 2374, Nov. 4, 1939, 12:04 p.m., 4 F.R. 4493, 54 Stat. 2671, proclaimed a state of war between Germany and France; Poland; and the United Kingdom, India, Australia, Canada, New Zealand and the Union of South Africa.

Proc. No. 2398, Apr. 25, 1940, 5 F.R. 1569, 54 Stat. 2698, proclaimed a state of war between Germany and Norway.

Proc. No. 2404, May 11, 1940, 5 F.R. 1689, 54 Stat. 2703, proclaimed a state of war between Germany and Belgium, Luxemburg, and the Netherlands.

Proc. No. 2407, June 10, 1940, 10:20 p.m., E.S.T., 5 F.R. 2191, 54 Stat. 2706, proclaimed a state of war between Italy and France and United Kingdom.

Proc. No. 2443, Nov. 15, 1940, 5 F.R. 4523, 54 Stat. 2763, proclaimed a state of war between Italy and Greece.

Proc. No. 2473, Apr. 10, 1941, 6 F.R. 1905, 55 Stat. 1627, proclaimed a state of war between Germany-Italy and Yugoslavia.

Proc. No. 2477, Apr. 15, 1941, 6 F.R. 1995, 55 Stat. 1631, proclaimed a state of war between Hungary and Yugoslavia.

Proc. No. 2479, Apr. 24, 1941, 6 F.R. 2133, 55 Stat. 1636, proclaimed a state of war between Bulgaria and Yugoslavia and Greece.

II. PROCLAMATIONS OF UNITED STATES NEUTRALITY

Proc. No. 2348, Sept. 5, 1939, 4 F.R. 3809, 54 Stat. 2629, proclaimed neutrality of United States in war between Germany and France; Poland; United Kingdom, India, Australia, and New Zealand.

Proc. No. 2353, Sept. 8, 1939, 4 F.R. 3851, 54 Stat. 2643, proclaimed neutrality of United States in war between Germany and Union of South Africa.

Proc. No. 2359, Sept. 10, 1939, 4 F.R. 3857, 54 Stat. 2652, proclaimed neutrality of United States in war between Germany and Canada.

Proc. No. 2399, Apr. 25, 1940, 5 F.R. 1569, 54 Stat. 2699, proclaimed neutrality of United States in war between Germany and Norway.

Proc. No. 2405, May 11, 1940, 5 F.R. 1689, 54 Stat. 2704, proclaimed neutrality of United States in war between Germany and Belgium, Luxemburg, and the Netherlands.

Proc. No. 2408, June 10, 1940, 10:20 p.m. E.S.T., 5 F.R. 2191, 54 Stat. 2707, proclaimed neutrality of United States in war between Italy and France and United Kingdom.

Proc. No. 2444, Nov. 15, 1940, 5 F.R. 4523, 54 Stat. 2764, proclaimed neutrality of United States in war between Italy and Greece.

III. MISCELLANEOUS PROCLAMATIONS AND EXECUTIVE ORDERS

National Emergency of 1939

Proc. No. 2352, Sept. 8, 1939, 4 F.R. 3851, 54 Stat. 2643, proclaimed national emergency in connection with enforcement of neutrality which was terminated by Proc. No. 2974, set out below.

National Emergency of 1941

Proc. No. 2487, May 27, 1941, 6 F.R. 2617, 55 Stat. 1647, proclaimed an unlimited national emergency which was terminated by Proc. No. 2974, set out below.

Proc. No. 2685. Removal of Alien Enemies

Proc. No. 2685, Apr. 11, 1946, 11 F.R. 4079, 60 Stat. Pt. 2, p. 1342, provided:

1. All alien enemies within the continental limits of the United States brought here from other American republics after December 7, 1941, who are within the territory of the United States without admission under the immigration laws, shall, if their continued residence in the Western Hemisphere is deemed by the Secretary of State to be prejudicial to the future security or welfare of the Americas, be subject upon the order of the Secretary of State to removal from the United States and may be required to depart therefrom in accordance with such regulations as the Secretary of State may prescribe.

2. In all cases in which the Secretary of State shall have ordered the removal of an alien enemy under the authority of this proclamation or in which the Attorney General shall have ordered the removal of an alien enemy under the authority of Proclamation No. 2655 of July 14, 1945, thirty days shall be considered, and is hereby declared to be, a reasonable time for such alien enemy to effect the recovery, disposal, and removal of his goods and effects, and for his departure.

3. This proclamation supersedes Proclamation No. 2662 of September 8, 1945, entitled "Removal of Alien Enemies."

Harry S Truman.

Proc. No. 2914. National Emergency, 1950

Proc. No. 2914, Dec. 16, 1950, 15 F.R. 9029, 64 Stat. a454 provided:

WHEREAS recent events in Korea and elsewhere constitute a grave threat to the peace of the world and imperil the efforts of this country and those of the United Nations to prevent aggression and armed conflict; and

WHEREAS world conquest by communist imperialism is the goal of the forces of aggression that have been loosed upon the world; and

WHEREAS, if the goal of communist imperialism were to be achieved, the people of this country would no longer enjoy the full and rich life they have with God's help built for themselves and their children; they would no longer enjoy the blessings of the freedom of worshipping as they severally choose, the freedom of reading and listening to what they choose, the right of free speech including the right to criticize their Government, the right to choose those who conduct their Government, the right to engage freely in collective bargaining, the right to engage freely in their own business enterprises, and the many other freedoms and rights which are a part of our way of life; and

Whereas the increasing menace of the forces of communist aggression requires that the national defense of the United States be strengthened as speedily as possible:

NOW, THEREFORE, I, HARRY S. TRUMAN, President of the United States of America, do proclaim the existence of a national emergency, which requires that the military, naval, air, and civilian defenses of this country be strengthened as speedily as possible to the end that we may be able to repeal any and all threats against our national security and to fulfill our responsibilities in the efforts being made through the United Nations and otherwise to bring about lasting peace.

I summon all citizens to make a united effort for the security and well-being of our beloved country and to place its needs foremost in thought and action that the full moral and material strength of the Nation may be readied for the dangers which threaten us.

I summon our farmers, our workers in industry, and our businessmen to make a mighty production effort to meet the defense requirements of the Nation and to this end to eliminate all waste and inefficiency and to subordinate all lesser interests to the common good.

I summon every person and every community to make, with a spirit of neighborliness, whatever sacrifices are necessary for the welfare of the Nation.

I summon all State and local leaders and officials to cooperate fully with the military and civilian defense agencies of the United States in the national defense program.

I summon all citizens to be loyal to the principles upon which our Nation is founded, to keep faith with our friends and allies, and to be firm in our devotion to the peaceful purposes for which the United Nations was founded.

I am confident that we will meet the dangers that confront us with courage and determination, strong in the faith that we can thereby "secure the Blessings of Liberty to ourselves and our Posterity."

HARRY S. TRUMAN.

PROC. NO. 2974. TERMINATION OF WARTIME EMERGENCIES

Proc. No. 2974, Apr. 28, 1952, 17 F.R. 3813, 66 Stat. c31, provided in part:

NOW, THEREFORE, I, HARRY S. TRUMAN, President of the United States of America, do proclaim that the national emergencies declared to exist by the proclamations of September 8, 1939 [set out above], and May 27, 1941 [set out above], terminated this day upon the entry into force of the Treaty of Peace with Japan.

Nothing in this proclamation shall be construed to affect Proclamation No. 2914 [set out above], issued by the President on December 16, 1950, declaring that world conquest by communist imperialism is the goal of the forces of aggression that have been loosed upon the world, and proclaiming the existence of a national emergency requiring that the military, naval, air, and civilian defenses of this country be strengthened as speedily as possible to the end that we may be able to repel any and all threats against our national security and to fulfill our responsibilities in the efforts being made through the United Nations and otherwise to bring about lasting peace; and nothing herein shall be construed to affect the continuation of the said emergency of September 8, 1939, as specified in the Emergency Powers Interim Continuation Act, approved April 14, 1952 (Public Law 313—82d Congress), for the purpose of continuing the use of property held under the Act of October 14, 1940, ch. 862, 54 Stat. 1125, as amended [sections 1521 to 1524, 1531 to 1536, 1541 to 1553, 1561 to 1564, 1571 to 1576, 1581 to 1590 of Title 42, The Public Health and Welfare].

HARRY S TRUMAN.

EXECUTIVE ORDER NO. 8233

Ex. Ord. No. 8233, Sept. 5, 1939, 4 F.R. 3822, referred to regulations governing enforcement of neutrality of the United States.

EX. ORD. NO. 8234. REGULATIONS GOVERNING PASSAGE AND CONTROL OF VESSELS THROUGH PANAMA CANAL IN ANY WAR IN WHICH THE UNITED STATES IS NEUTRAL

Ex. Ord. No. 8234, Sept. 5, 1939, 4 F.R. 3823, as amended by Ex. Ord. No. 8382, Mar. 25, 1940, 5 F.R. 1185, provided:

WHEREAS the treaties of the United States, in any war in which the United States is a neutral, impose on the United States certain obligations to both neutral and belligerent nations;

AND WHEREAS the treaties of the United States, in any war in which the United States is a neutral, require that the United States exert all the vigilance within their power to carry out their obligations as a neutral;

AND WHEREAS treaties of the United States require that the Panama Canal shall be free and open, on terms of entire equality, to the vessels of commerce and of war of all nations observing the rules laid down in Article 3 of the so-called Hay-Pauncefote treaty concluded between the United States and Great Britain, November 18, 1901:

NOW, THEREFORE, by virtue of the authority vested in me by section 5 of the Panama Canal Act, approved August 24, 1912 (ch. 390, sec. 5, 37 Stat. 562), as amended by the act of July 5, 1932 (ch. 425, 47 Stat. 578), I hereby prescribe the following regulations governing the passage and control of vessels through the Panama Canal or any part thereof, including the locks and approaches thereto, in any war in which the United States is a neutral;

1. Whenever considered necessary, in the opinion of the Governor of the Panama Canal, to prevent damage or injury to vessels or to prevent damage or injury to the Canal or its appurtenances, or to secure the observance of the rules, regulations, rights, or obligations of the United States, the Canal authorities may at any time, as a condition precedent to transit of the Canal, inspect any vessel, belligerent or neutral, other than a public vessel, including its crew and cargo, and, for and during the passage through the Canal, place armed guards thereon, and take full possession and control of such vessel and remove therefrom the officers and crew thereof and all other persons not specially authorized by the Canal authorities to go or remain on board thereof during such passage.

2. A public vessel of a belligerent or neutral nation shall be permitted to pass through the Canal only after her commanding officer has given written assurance to the authorities of the Panama Canal that the rules, regulations, and treaties of the United States will be faithfully observed.

3. *Possession of cameras on board vessels; photographing from vessels.* While on board any vessel in transit through the Panama Canal, no person shall (a) have or remain in possession of any camera, or (b) make any photograph, sketch, picture, drawing, map, or graphical representation of any of the locks of the Panama Canal, or of any portion of any such lock, or of any area within or adjacent to any such lock, or of any object or structure within or upon any such area, without first obtaining the permission of the Governor of The Panama Canal, and promptly submitting the product obtained to the Governor for such action as he may deem necessary. The master of every vessel that transmits the Panama Canal (a) shall prior to the beginning of each transit cause all cameras on board such vessel, or which are brought on board by embarking passengers, or otherwise, to be collected and delivered to him, and shall retain the said cameras in his possession, in a secure and inaccessible place, until the disembarkation of the original possessors thereof or until the transit through the Canal is completed, and (b) shall during such transit take such further action, in cooperation with the Canal authorities, as may be necessary to prevent the making, by any person on board such vessel in the waters of the Canal Zone, of any photograph, sketch, picture, drawing, map, or graphical representation which is forbidden by this paragraph; but these provisions shall not apply with respect to any person who has obtained permission as provided in this paragraph. Any person who shall violate any provision of this paragraph shall be punishable as provided in section 9 of title 2 of the [former] Canal Zone Code.

The foregoing regulations are in addition to the "Rules and Regulations for the Operation and Navigation of the Panama Canal and Approaches Thereto, including all Waters under its Jurisdiction" prescribed by Executive Order No. 4314 of September 25, 1925, as amended, and the provisions of proclamations and executive orders pertaining to the Canal Zone issued in conformity with the laws and treaties of the United States.

Proc. No. 2350, eff. Sept. 5, 1939, 4 F.R. 3821, 54 Stat. 2368, referred to regulations concerning neutrality in the Canal Zone.

FRANKLIN D. ROOSEVELT.

EX. ORD. NO. 9723. TERMINATION OF PRESIDENT'S WAR RELIEF CONTROL BOARD

Ex. Ord. No. 9723, May 14, 1946, 11 F.R. 5345, provided:

Executive Order No. 9205 of July 25, 1942, is revoked, and the President's War Relief Control Board established by that order is hereby terminated. The Secretary of State is authorized and directed to liquidate all of the activities and obligations and wind up all of the affairs of the Board as rapidly as practicable, and to utilize therefore such of the personnel property, records, and unexpended appropriations of the Board as may be necessary.

HARRY S TRUMAN.

IV. DECLARATIONS OF WAR BY UNITED STATES

WAR BETWEEN UNITED STATES AND GERMANY

Declared by Joint Res. April 6, 1917, 40 Stat. 1.

WAR BETWEEN UNITED STATES AND AUSTRIA-HUNGARY

Declared by Joint Res. Dec. 7, 1917, 40 Stat. 429.

WAR BETWEEN UNITED STATES AND JAPAN

Declared by Joint Res. Dec. 8, 1941, 4:10 p.m., E.S.T., ch. 561, 55 Stat. 795.

WAR BETWEEN UNITED STATES AND GERMANY

Declared by Joint Res. Dec. 11, 1941, 3:05 p.m. E.S.T., ch. 564, 55 Stat. 796.

WAR BETWEEN UNITED STATES AND ITALY

Declared by Joint Res. Dec. 11, 1941, 3:06 p.m., E.S.T., ch. 565, 55 Stat. 797.

WAR BETWEEN THE UNITED STATES AND BULGARIA

Declared by Joint Res. June 5, 1942, ch. 323, 56 Stat. 307.

WAR BETWEEN UNITED STATES AND HUNGARY

Declared by Joint Res. June 5, 1942, ch. 324, 56 Stat. 307.

WAR BETWEEN UNITED STATES AND RUMANIA

Declared by Joint Res. June 5, 1942, ch. 325, 56 Stat. 307.

PROC. NO. 2563. PROCLAMATION OF STATE OF WAR BETWEEN UNITED STATES AND HUNGARY, BULGARIA, AND RUMANIA

Proc. No. 2563, July 17, 1942, 7 F.R. 5535, 56 Stat. 1970, proclaimed that a state of war existed between the United States and Hungary, Rumania, and Bulgaria.

V. TERMINATION OF STATE OF WAR

CESSATION OF HOSTILITIES

The cessation of hostilities of World War II was officially proclaimed by the President of the United States, Proclamation No. 2714, Dec. 31, 1946, 12 F.R. 1, 61 Stat. 1048, in the following language:

> NOW, THEREFORE, I, HARRY S. TRUMAN, President of the United States of America, do hereby proclaim the cessation of hostilities of World War II, effective twelve o'clock noon, December 31, 1946.

TREATIES OF PEACE WITH ITALY, BULGARIA, HUNGARY, RUMANIA, AND FINLAND

On the 10th day of February 1947, separate Treaties of Peace were concluded by designated Allied and Associated Powers, including the United States of America, with Italy, Bulgaria, Hungary and Rumania.

Each of these Treaties contained a recital in the Preamble that the Allied and Associated Powers named therein

> Have therefore agreed to declare the cessation of the state of war and for this purpose to conclude the present Treaty of Peace, and have accordingly appointed the undersigned Plenipotentiaries who, after presentation of their full powers, found in good and due form, have agreed on the following provisions: * * *.

The full text of the Treaties of Peace with Italy, Bulgaria, Hungary, Rumania and Finland are set out in 61 Stat. 1245, 1915, 2065, 1757.

On the same date a Treaty of Peace was concluded with Finland. The United States is not a signatory thereto.

TREATY OF PEACE WITH JAPAN

The Treaty of Peace with Japan signed at the city of San Francisco on the 8th day of September 1951, Chapter I, Article 1, provides:

> (a) The state of war between Japan and each of the Allied Powers is terminated as from the date on which the present Treaty comes into force between Japan and the Allied Power concerned as provided for in Article 23.

Article 23 of Chapter VII, above referred to, provides:

> (a) The present Treaty shall be ratified by the States which sign it, including Japan, and will come into force for all the States which have then ratified it, when instruments of ratification have been deposited by Japan and by a majority, including the United States of America as the principal occupying Power, of the following States [here would appear the names of such of the following States as are signatories to the present Treaty], namely Australia, Burma, Canada, Ceylon, France, India, Indonesia, the Netherlands, New Zealand, Pakistan, the Philippines, the United Kingdom of Great Britain and Northern Ireland, the Union of Soviet Socialist Republics, and the United States of America. The present Treaty shall come into force for each State which subsequently ratifies it, on the date of the deposit of its instrument of ratification.
>
> (b) If the Treaty has not come into force within nine months after the date of the deposit of Japan's ratification, any State which has ratified it may bring the Treaty into force between itself and Japan by a notification to that effect given to the Government of Japan and of the United States of America not later than three years after the date of deposit of Japan's ratification.

RATIFICATION OF JAPANESE PEACE TREATY

The Treaty of Peace with Japan, signed at San Francisco on September 8, 1951, was ratified by the United States Senate on March 20, 1952. For Resolution of ratification, see Congressional Record, Vol. 98, No. 46, Thursday, March 20, 1952, p. 2634.

GERMANY

JOINT RESOLUTION OF CONGRESS

Joint Res. Oct. 19, 1951, ch. 519, 65 Stat. 451, provided: "That the state of war declared to exist between the United States and the Government of Germany by the joint resolution of Congress approved December 11, 1941, is hereby terminated and such termination shall take effect on the date of enactment of this resolution [Oct. 19, 1951]: *Provided, however*, That notwithstanding this resolution and any proclamation issued by the President pursuant thereto, any property or interest which prior to January 1, 1947, was subject to vesting or seizure under the provisions of the Trading With the Enemy Act of October 6, 1917 (40 Stat. 411), as amended [sections 1 to 6, 7 to 39, 41 to 44 of this Appendix] or which has heretofore been vested or seized under that Act, including accruals to or proceeds of any such property or interest, shall continue to be subject to the provisions of that Act in the same manner and to the same extent as if this resolution had not been adopted and such proclamation had not been issued. Nothing herein and nothing in such proclamation shall alter the status, as it existed immediately prior hereto, under that Act, of Germany or of any person with respect to any such property or interest."

PROCLAMATION NO. 2950

Proc. No. 2950, Oct. 25, 1951, 16 F.R. 10915, 66 Stat. c3, proclaimed that the state of war between the United States and the Government of Germany declared on Dec. 11, 1941 was terminated on Oct. 19, 1951.

VI. AUTHORIZATION TO EMPLOY ARMED FORCES

MAINTENANCE OF INTERNATIONAL PEACE AND SECURITY IN SOUTHEAST ASIA

Pub. L. 88–408, Aug. 10, 1964, 78 Stat. 384, which authorized the President to take all necessary measures to repeal armed attack against the forces of the United States in the interest of the maintenance of peace and security in Southeast Asia, was terminated by Pub. L. 91–672, §12, Jan. 12, 1971, 84 Stat. 2055, effective upon the day that the second session of the Ninety-first Congress was last adjourned. The second session of the Ninety-first Congress adjourned sine die on January 2, 1971.

TERMINATION OF HOSTILITIES IN INDOCHINA

Pub. L. 92–129, title IV, §401, Sept. 28, 1971, 85 Stat. 360, provided that: "It is hereby declared to be the sense of Congress that the United States terminate at the earliest practicable date all military operations of the United States in Indochina, and provide for the prompt and orderly withdrawal of all United States military forces at a date certain subject to the release of all American prisoners of war held by the Government of North Vietnam and forces allied with such Government, and an accounting for all Americans missing in action who have been held by or known to such Government or such forces. The Congress hereby urges and requests the President to implement the above expressed policy by initiating immediately the following actions:

"(1) Negotiate with the Government of North Vietnam for an immediate cease-fire by all parties to the hostilities in Indochina.

"(2) Negotiate with the Government of North Vietnam for the establishing of a final date for the withdrawal from Indochina of all military forces of the United States contingent upon the release at a date certain of all American prisoners of war held by the Government of North Vietnam and forces allied with such Government.

"(3) Negotiate with the Government of North Vietnam for an agreement which would provide for a series of phased and rapid withdrawals of United States military forces from Indochina subject to a corresponding series of phased releases of American prisoners of war, and for the release of any remaining American prisoners of war concurrently with the withdrawal of all remaining military forces of the United States by not later than the date established pursuant to paragraph (2) hereof."

PROC. NO. 3504. INTERDICTION OF THE DELIVERY OF OFFENSIVE WEAPONS TO CUBA

Proc. No. 3504, Oct. 23, 1962, 27 F.R. 10401, 77 Stat. 958, provided:

WHEREAS the peace of the world and the security of the United States and of all American States are endangered by reason of the establishment by the Sino-Soviet powers of an offensive military capability in Cuba, including bases for ballistic missiles with a potential range covering most of North and South America;

WHEREAS by a Joint Resolution passed by the Congress of the United States and approved on October 3, 1962, it was declared that the United States is determined to prevent by whatever means may be necessary, including the use of arms, the Marxist-Leninist regime in Cuba from extending, by force or the threat of force, its aggressive or subversive activities to any part of this hemisphere, and to prevent in Cuba the creation or use of an externally supported military capability endangering the security of the United States; and

WHEREAS the Organ of Consultation of the American Republics meeting in Washington on October 23, 1962, recommended that the Member States, in accordance with Articles 6 and 8 of the Inter-American Treaty of Reciprocal Assistance, take all measures, individually and collectively, including the use of armed force, which they may deem necessary to ensure that the Government of Cuba cannot continue to receive from the Sino-Soviet powers military material and related supplies which may threaten the peace and security of the Continent and to prevent the missiles in Cuba with offensive capability from ever becoming an active threat to the peace and security of the Continent:

NOW, THEREFORE, I, JOHN F. KENNEDY, President of the United States of America, acting under and by virtue of the authority conferred upon me by the Constitution and statutes of the United States, in accordance with the aforementioned resolutions of the United States Congress and of the Organ of Consultation of the American Republics, and to defend the security of the United States, do hereby proclaim that the forces under my command are ordered, beginning at 2:00 P.M. Greenwich time October 24, 1962, to interdict, subject to the instructions herein contained, the delivery of offensive weapons and associated material to Cuba.

For the purposes of this Proclamation, the following are declared to be prohibited materiel:

Surface-to-surface missiles; bomber aircraft; bombs, air-to-surface rockets and guided missiles; warheads for any of the above weapons; mechanical or electronic equipment to support or operate the above items; and any other classes of materiel hereafter designated by the Secretary of Defense for the purpose of effectuating this Proclamation.

To enforce this order, the Secretary of Defense shall take appropriate measures to prevent the delivery of prohibited materiel to Cuba, employing the land, sea and air forces of the United States in cooperation with any forces that may be made available by other American States.

The Secretary of Defense may make such regulations and issue such directives as he deems necessary to ensure the effectiveness of this order, including the designation, within a reasonable distance of Cuba, of prohibited or restricted zones and of prescribed routes.

Any vessel or craft which may be proceeding toward Cuba may be intercepted and may be directed to identify itself, its cargo, equipment and stores and its ports of call, to stop, to lie to, to submit to visit and search, or to proceed as directed. Any vessel or craft which fails or refuses to respond to or comply with directions shall be subject to being taken into custody. Any vessel or craft which it is believed is en route to Cuba and may be carrying prohibited materiel or may itself constitute such materiel shall, wherever possible, be directed to proceed to another destination of its own choice and shall be taken into custody if it fails or refuses to obey such directions. All vessels or craft taken into custody shall be sent into a port of the United States for appropriate disposition.

In carrying out this order, force shall not be used except in case of failure or refusal to comply with directions, or with regulations or directives of the Secretary of Defense issued hereunder, after reasonable efforts have been made to communicate them to the vessel or craft, or in case of self-defense. In any case, force shall be used only to the extent necessary.

IN WITNESS WHEREOF, I have hereunto set my hand and caused the seal of the United States of America to be affixed.

Done in the City of Washington this twenty-third day of October in the year of our Lord nineteen hundred and sixty-two, and of the Independence of the United States of America the one hundred and eighty-seventh.

[SEAL]

JOHN FITZGERALD KENNEDY.

PROC. NO. 3507. TERMINATING AUTHORITY GRANTED AND ORDERS ISSUED IN PROC. NO. 3504

Proc. No. 3507, Nov. 21, 1962, 27 F.R. 11525, 77 Stat. 961, provided:

I, JOHN F. KENNEDY, President of the United States of America, acting under and by virtue of the authority vested in me by the Constitution and statutes of the United States, do hereby proclaim that at 11 p.m., Greenwich Time, November 20, 1962, I terminated the authority conferred upon the Secretary of Defense by Proclamation No. 3504, dated October 23, 1962 [set out above], and revoked the orders contained therein to forces under my command.

IN WITNESS WHEREOF, I have hereunto set my hand and caused the Seal of the United States of America to be affixed.

DONE at the City of Washington this 21st day of November, in the year of our Lord nineteen hundred and sixty-two and of the Independence of the United States of America the one hundred and eighty-seventh.

[SEAL]

JOHN F. KENNEDY.

MIDDLE EAST STABILIZATION

Pub. L. 85–7, §§1–6, Mar. 9, 1957, 71 Stat. 5, set out as chapter 24A (§1961 et seq.) of Title 22, Foreign Relations and Intercourse, authorizes the President to provide economic and military assistance, and, if he determines it necessary, to use armed forces under certain circumstances to maintenance of national independence in the Middle East.

PROTECTION OF SECURITY OF FORMOSA

Joint Res. Jan. 29, 1955, ch. 4, 8:42 A.M., 69 Stat. 7, which authorized the President of the United States to employ the Armed Forces of the United States for the purpose of securing and protecting Formosa and Pescadores against armed attack, was repealed by Pub. L. 93–475, §3, Oct. 26, 1974, 88 Stat. 1439.

TRADING WITH THE ENEMY ACT OF 1917

ACT OCT. 6, 1917, CH. 106, 40 STAT. 411

TERMINATION OF WORLD WAR AND EMERGENCY

The Trading with the enemy Act was expressly excepted from the operation and effect of Joint Res. Mar. 3, 1921, ch. 136, 41 Stat. 1359, declaring that certain Acts of Congress, joint resolutions, and proclamations should be construed as though the World War had ended and the then present or existing emergency expired.

ACT REFERRED TO IN OTHER SECTIONS

The Trading with the enemy Act is referred to in section 1982 of this Appendix; title 8 section 1227; title 12 section 4407; title 18 section 983; title 19 section 2581; title 22 sections 1382, 1384, 1631a, 1631*o*, 6009, 7207; title 26 section 911; title 28 section 2680.

§1. Designation of Act

This Act [sections 1 to 6, 7 to 39, and 41 to 44 of this Appendix] shall be known as the "Trading with the enemy[1] Act."

(Oct. 6, 1917, ch. 106, §1, 40 Stat. 411.)

SECTION REFERRED TO IN OTHER SECTIONS

This section is referred to in title 28 section 2680.

§2. Definitions

The word "enemy," as used herein, shall be deemed to mean, for the purposes of such trading and of this Act [sections 1 to 6, 7 to 39, and 41 to 44 of this Appendix]—

(a) Any individual, partnership, or other body of individuals, of any nationality, resident within the territory (including that occupied by the military and naval forces) of any nation with which the United States is at war, or resident outside the United States and doing business within such territory, and any corporation incorporated within such territory of any nation with which the United States is at war or incorporated within any country other than the United States and doing business within such territory.

(b) The government of any nation with which the United States is at war, or any political or municipal subdivision thereof, or any officer, official, agent, or agency thereof.

(c) Such other individuals, or body or class of individuals, as may be natives, citizens, or subjects of any nation with which the United States is at war, other than citizens of the United States, wherever resident or wherever doing business, as the President, if he shall find the safety of the United States or the successful prosecution of the war shall so require, may, by proclamation, include within the term "enemy."

The words "ally of enemy," as used herein, shall be deemed to mean—

(a) Any individual, partnership, or other body of individuals, of any nationality, resident within the territory (including that occupied by the military and naval forces) of any nation which is an ally of a nation with which the United States is at war, or resident outside the United States and doing business within such territory, and any corporation incorporated within such territory of such ally nation, or incorporated within any country other than the United States and doing business within such territory.

(b) The government of any nation which is an ally of a nation with which the United States is at war, or any political or municipal subdivision of such ally nation, or any officer, official, agent, or agency thereof.

(c) Such other individuals, or body or class of individuals, as may be natives, citizens, or subjects of any nation which is an ally of a nation with which the United States is at war, other than citizens of the United States, wherever resident or wherever doing business, as the President, if he shall find the safety of the United States or the successful prosecution of the war shall so require, may, by proclamation, include within the term "ally of enemy."

The word "person," as used herein, shall be deemed to mean an individual, partnership, association, company, or other unincorporated body of individuals, or corporation or body politic.

The words "United States," as used herein, shall be deemed to mean all land and water, continental or insular, in any way within the jurisdiction of the United States or occupied by the military or naval forces thereof.

The words "the beginning of the war," as used herein, shall be deemed to mean midnight ending the day on which Congress has declared or shall declare war or the existence of a state of war.

The words "end of the war," as used herein, shall be deemed to mean the date of proclamation of exchange of ratifications of the treaty of peace, unless the President shall, by proclamation, declare a prior date, in which case the date so proclaimed shall be deemed to be the "end of the war" within the meaning of this Act [sections 1 to 6, 7 to 39, and 41 to 44 of this Appendix].

[1] So in original. Probably should be capitalized.

The words "bank or banks," as used herein, shall be deemed to mean and include national banks, State banks, trust companies, or other banks or banking associations doing business under the laws of the United States, or of any State of the United States.

The words "to trade," as used herein, shall be deemed to mean—

(a) Pay, satisfy, compromise, or give security for the payment or satisfaction of any debt or obligation.

(b) Draw, accept, pay, present for acceptance or payment, or indorse any negotiable instrument or chose in action.

(c) Enter into, carry on, complete, or perform any contract, agreement, or obligation.

(d) Buy or sell, loan or extend credit, trade in, deal with, exchange, transmit, transfer, assign, or otherwise dispose of, or receive any form of property.

(e) To have any form of business or commercial communication or intercourse with.

(Oct. 6, 1917, ch. 106, §2, 40 Stat. 411.)

WORLD WAR I PROCLAMATIONS ENUMERATING ENEMIES

The following Presidential Proclamations issued during World War I declared the partnerships and persons enumerated therein to be "enemies":

Proc. Feb. 5, 1918, 40 Stat. 1745.
Proc. May 31, 1918, 40 Stat. 1786.
Proc. Aug. 10, 1918, 40 Stat. 1833.
Proc. Aug. 14, 1918, 40 Stat. 1837.
Proc. Nov. 29, 1918, 40 Stat. 1899.

SECTION REFERRED TO IN OTHER SECTIONS

This section is referred to in title 28 section 2680.

§3. Acts prohibited

It shall be unlawful—

(a) For any person in the United States, except with the license of the President, granted to such person, or to the enemy, or ally of enemy, as provided in this Act [sections 1 to 6, 7 to 39, and 41 to 44 of this Appendix] to trade, or attempt to trade, either directly or indirectly, with, to, or from, or for, or on account of, or on behalf of, or for the benefit of, any other person, with knowledge or reasonable cause to believe that such other person is an enemy or ally of enemy, or is conducting or taking part in such trade, directly or indirectly, for, or on account of, or on behalf of, or for the benefit of, an enemy or ally of enemy.

(b) For any person, except with the license of the President, to transport or attempt to transport into or from the United States, or for any owner, master, or other person in charge of a vessel of American registry to transport or attempt to transport from any place to any other place, any subject or citizen of an enemy or ally of enemy nation, with knowledge or reasonable cause to believe that the person transported or attempted to be transported is such subject or citizen.

(c) For any person (other than a person in the service of the United States Government or of the Government of any nation, except that of an enemy or ally of enemy nation, and other than such persons or classes of persons as may be exempted hereunder by the President or by such person as he may direct), to send, or take out of, or bring into, or attempt to send, or take out of, or bring into the United States, any letter or other writing or tangible form of communication, except in the regular course of the mail; and it shall be unlawful for any person to send, take, or transmit, or attempt to send, take, or transmit out of the United States, any letter or other writing, book, map, plan, or other paper, picture, or any telegram, cablegram, or wireless message, or other form of communication intended for or to be delivered, directly or indirectly, to an enemy or ally of enemy: *Provided, however*, That any person may send, take, or transmit out of the United States anything herein forbidden if he shall first submit the same to the President, or to such officer as the President may direct, and shall obtain the license or consent of the President, under such rules and regulations, and with such exemptions, as shall be prescribed by the President.

(d) Whenever, during the present war, the President shall deem that the public safety demands it, he may cause to be censored under such rules and regulations as he may from time to time establish, communications by mail, cable, radio, or other means of transmission passing between the United States and any foreign country he may from time to time specify, or which may be carried by any vessel or other means of transportation touching at any port, place, or territory of the United States and bound to or from any foreign country. Any person who willfully evades or attempts to evade the submission of any such communication to such censorship or willfully uses or attempts to use any code or other device for the purpose of concealing from such censorship the intended meaning of such communication shall be punished as provided in section sixteen of this Act [section 16 of this Appendix].

(Oct. 6, 1917, ch. 106, §3, 40 Stat. 412.)

DELEGATION OF FUNCTIONS

Delegation of President's powers under subsec. (a) of this section to Secretary of the Treasury and Alien Property Custodian; and transfer of Alien Property Custodian's powers to Attorney General, see Ex. Ord. Nos. 9095 and 9788, set out under section 6 of this Appendix.

Powers conferred upon President by subsec. (a) of this section delegated to Secretary of the Treasury by Memorandum of the President dated Feb. 12, 1942, 7 F.R. 1409.

WORLD WAR II ALIEN PROPERTY CUSTODIAN

Reestablishment and termination of Office of Alien Property Custodian during World War II, see notes set out under section 6 of this Appendix.

SECTION REFERRED TO IN OTHER SECTIONS

This section is referred to in sections 4, 5, 7 of this Appendix; title 28 section 2680.

§4. Licenses to enemy or ally of enemy insurance or reinsurance companies; change of name; doing business in United States

(a) Every enemy or ally of enemy insurance or reinsurance company, and every enemy or ally of enemy, doing business within the United States through an agency or branch office, or otherwise, may within thirty days after the passage of this Act [Oct. 6, 1917], apply to the President for a license to continue to do business; and, within thirty days after such application, the President may enter an order either granting or refusing to grant such license. The license, if granted, may be temporary or otherwise, and for such period of time, and may contain such provisions and conditions regulating the business, agencies, managers and trustees and the control and disposition of the funds of the company, or of such enemy or ally of enemy, as the President shall deem necessary for the safety of the United States; and any license granted hereunder may be revoked or regranted or renewed in such manner and at such times as the President shall determine: *Provided, however*, That reasonable notice of his intent to refuse to grant a license or to revoke a license granted to any reinsurance company shall be given by him to all insurance companies incorporated within the United States and known to the President to be doing business with such reinsurance company: *Provided further*, That no insurance company, organized within the United States, shall be obligated to continue any existing contract, entered into prior to the beginning of the war, with any enemy or ally of enemy insurance or reinsurance company, but any such company may abrogate and cancel any such contract by serving thirty days' notice in writing upon the President of its election to abrogate such contract.

For a period of thirty days after the passage of this Act [Oct. 6, 1917], and further pending the entry of such order by the President, after application made by any enemy or ally of enemy insurance or reinsurance company, within such thirty days as above provided, the provisions of the President's proclamation of April sixth, nineteen hundred and seventeen, relative to agencies in the United States of certain insurance companies, as modified by the provisions of the President's proclamation of July thirteenth, nineteen hundred and seventeen, relative to marine and war-risk insurance, shall remain in full force and effect so far as it applies to such German insurance companies, and the conditions of said proclamation of April sixth, nineteen hundred and seventeen, as modified by said proclamation of July thirteenth, nineteen hundred and seventeen, shall also during said period of thirty days after the passage of this Act [Oct. 6, 1917], and pending the order of the President as herein provided, apply to any enemy or ally of enemy insurance or reinsurance company, anything in this Act [sections 1 to 6, 7 to 39, and 41 to 44 of this Appendix] to the contrary notwithstanding. It shall be unlawful for any enemy or ally of enemy insurance or reinsurance company, to whom license is granted, to transmit out of the United States any funds belonging to or held for the benefit of such company or to use any such funds as the basis for the establishment directly or indirectly of any credit within or outside of the United States to, or for the benefit of, or on behalf of, or on account of, an enemy or ally of enemy.

For a period of thirty days after the passage of this Act [Oct. 6, 1917], and further pending the entry of such order by the President, after application made within such thirty days by any enemy or ally of enemy, other than an insurance or reinsurance company as above provided, it shall be lawful for such enemy or ally of enemy to continue to do business in this country and for any person to trade with, to, from, for, on account of, on behalf of or for the benefit of such enemy or ally of enemy, anything in this Act [said sections] to the contrary notwithstanding: *Provided, however*, That the provisions of sections three and sixteen hereof [sections 3 and 16 of this Appendix] shall apply to any act or attempted act of transmission or transfer of money or other property out of the United States and to the use or attempted use of such money or property as the basis for the establishment of any credit within or outside of the United States to, or for the benefit of, or on behalf of, or on account of, an enemy or ally of enemy.

If no license is applied for within thirty days after the passage of this Act [Oct. 6, 1917], or if a license shall be refused to any enemy or ally of enemy, whether insurance or reinsurance company, or other person, making application, or if any license granted shall be revoked by the President, the provisions of sections three and sixteen hereof [sections 3 and 16 of this Appendix] shall forthwith apply to all trade or to any attempt to trade with, to, from, for, buy, on account of, or on behalf of, or for the benefit of such company or other person: *Provided, however*, That after such refusal or revocation, anything in this Act [said sections] to the contrary notwithstanding, it shall be lawful for a policyholder or for an insurance company, not an enemy or ally of enemy, holding insurance or having effected reinsurance in or with such enemy or ally of enemy insurance or reinsurance company, to receive payment of, and for such enemy or ally of enemy insurance or reinsurance company to pay any premium, return premium, claim, money, security, or other property due or which may become due on or in respect to such insurance or reinsurance in force at the date of such refusal or revocation of license; and nothing in this Act [said sections] shall vitiate or nullify then existing policies or contracts of insurance or reinsurance, or the conditions thereof; and any such policyholder or insurance company, not an enemy or ally of enemy, having any claim to or upon money or other property of the enemy or ally of enemy insurance or reinsurance company in the custody or control of the alien property custodian, hereinafter provided for, or of the Treasurer of the United States, may make application for the payment thereof and may institute suit as provided in section nine hereof [section 9 of this Appendix].

(b) During the present war, no enemy, or ally of enemy, and no partnership of which he is a member or was a member at the beginning of the war, shall for any purpose assume or use any name other than that by which such enemy or partnership was ordinarily known at the beginning of the war, except under license from the President.

Whenever, during the present war, in the opinion of the President the public safety or public interest requires, the President may prohibit any or all foreign insurance companies from doing business in the United States, or the

President may license such company or companies to do business upon such terms as he may deem proper.

(Oct. 6, 1917, ch. 106, §4, 40 Stat. 413.)

REFERENCES IN TEXT

Proclamation of April 6, 1917, 40 Stat. 1654, and Proclamation of July 13, 1917, 40 Stat. 1684, referred to in subsec. (a), are set out below.

TRANSFER OF FUNCTIONS

Functions of Alien Property Custodian and Office of Alien Property Custodian, except those relating to property or interest in Philippines, vested in Attorney General. See notes set out under section 6 of this Appendix.

PROCLAMATION OF APRIL 6, 1917

40 STAT. 1654

WHEREAS, certain insurance companies, incorporated under the laws of the German Empire, have been admitted to transact the business of insurance in various States of the United States, by means of separate United States branches established pursuant to the laws of such States, and are now engaged in business under the supervision of the Insurance Departments thereof, with assets in the United States deposited with Insurance Departments or in the hands of resident trustees, citizens of the United States, for the protection of all policyholders in the United States;

AND WHEREAS, the interests of the citizens of the United States in the protection afforded by such insurance are of great magnitude, so that it is deemed to be important that the agencies of such companies in the United States be permitted to continue in business;

NOW, THEREFORE, I, WOODROW WILSON, President of the United States of America, by virtue of the powers vested in me as such, hereby declare and proclaim that such branch establishments of German insurance companies now engaged in the transaction of business in the United States pursuant to the laws of the several States are hereby authorized and permitted to continue the transaction of their business in accordance with the laws of such States in the same manner and to the same extent as though a state of war did not now exist; provided, however, that all funds of such establishments now in the possession of their managers or agents, or which shall hereafter come into their possession, shall be subject to such rules and regulations concerning the payment and disposition thereof as shall be prescribed by the insurance supervising officials of the State in which the principal office of such establishment in the United States is located, but in no event shall any funds belonging to or held for the benefit of such companies be transmitted outside of the United States nor be used as the basis for the establishment directly or indirectly of any credit within or outside of the United States to or for the benefit or use of the enemy or any of his allies without the permission of this Government.

PROCLAMATION OF JULY 13, 1917

40 STAT. 1684

WHEREAS, certain insurance companies, incorporated under the laws of the German Empire, have been admitted to transact the business of marine and war risk insurance in various States of the United States, by means of separate United States branches established pursuant to the laws of such States, and are now engaged in such business under the supervision of the Insurance Departments thereof, with assets in the United States deposited with Insurance Departments or in the hands of resident trustees, citizens of the United States, for the protection of all policyholders in the United States;

AND WHEREAS, the nature of marine and war risk insurance is such that those conducting it must of necessity be in touch with the movements of ships and cargoes, and it has been considered by the Government of great importance that this information should not be obtained by alien enemies;

NOW, THEREFORE, I, WOODROW WILSON, President of the United States of America, by virtue of the powers vested in me as such, hereby declare and proclaim that such branch establishments of German insurance companies now engaged in the transaction of business in the United States pursuant to the laws of the several States are hereby prohibited from continuing the transaction of the business of marine and war risk insurance either as direct insurers or re-insurers; and all individuals, firms, and insurance companies incorporated under the laws of any of the States or Territories of the United States, or of any foreign country, and established pursuant to the laws of such States and now engaged in the United States in the business of marine and war risk insurance either as direct insurers or re-insurers are hereby prohibited from reinsuring with companies incorporated under the laws of the German Empire, no matter where located; and all persons in the United States are prohibited from insuring against marine or war risks with insurance companies incorporated under the laws of the German Empire or with individuals, firms, and insurance companies incorporated under the laws of any of the States or Territories of the United States or of any foreign country and now engaged in the business of marine or war risk insurance in the United States, which re-insure business originating in the United States with companies incorporated under the laws of the German Empire, no matter where located.

The foregoing prohibitions shall extend and operate as to all existing contracts for insurance and re-insurance which are hereby suspended for the period of the war, except that they shall not operate to vitiate or prevent the insurance or re-insurance of, and the payment or receipt of, premiums on insurance or re-insurance under existing contracts on vessels or interest at risk on the date of this proclamation, and such insurance or re-insurance, if for a voyage, shall continue in force until arrival at destination, and if for time, until thirty days from the date of this proclamation.

SECTION REFERRED TO IN OTHER SECTIONS

This section is referred to in section 5 of this Appendix; title 28 section 2680.

§5. Suspension of provisions relating to ally of enemy; regulation of transactions in foreign exchange of gold or silver, property transfers, vested interests, enforcement and penalties

(a) The President, if he shall find it compatible with the safety of the United States and with the successful prosecution of the war, may, by proclamation, suspend the provisions of this Act [sections 1 to 6, 7 to 39, and 41 to 44 of this Appendix] so far as they apply to an ally of enemy, and he may revoke or renew such suspension from time to time; and the President may grant licenses, special or general, temporary or otherwise, and for such period of time and containing such provisions and conditions as he shall prescribe, to any person or class of persons to do business as provided in subsection (a) of section four hereof [section 4(a) of this Appendix], and to perform any act made unlawful without such license in section three hereof [section 3 of this Appendix], and to file and prosecute applications under subsection (b) of section ten hereof [section 10(b) of this Appendix]; and he may revoke or renew such licenses from time to time, if he shall be of opinion that such grant or revocation or renewal shall be compatible with the safety of the United States and with the successful prosecution of the war; and he may make such rules and regulations, not inconsistent with law, as may be necessary and proper to carry out the provisions of this Act [said sections]; and the President may exercise any power or authority conferred by this Act [said sections] through such officer or officers as he shall direct.

If the President shall have reasonable cause to believe that any act is about to be performed in violation of section three hereof [section 3 of this Appendix] he shall have authority to order the postponement of the performance of such act for a period not exceeding ninety days, pending investigation of the facts by him.

(b)(1) During the time of war, the President may, through any agency that he may designate, and under such rules and regulations as he may prescribe, by means of instructions, licenses, or otherwise—

(A) investigate, regulate, or prohibit, any transactions in foreign exchange, transfers of credit or payments between, by, through, or to any banking institution, and the importing, exporting, hoarding, melting, or earmarking of gold or silver coin or bullion, currency or securities, and

(B) investigate, regulate, direct and compel, nullify, void, prevent or prohibit, any acquisition holding, withholding, use, transfer, withdrawal, transportation, importation or exportation of, or dealing in, or exercising any right, power, or privilege with respect to, or transactions involving, any property in which any foreign country or a national thereof has any interest,

by any person, or with respect to any property, subject to the jurisdiction of the United States; and any property or interest of any foreign country or national thereof shall vest, when, as, and upon the terms, directed by the President, in such agency or person as may be designated from time to time by the President, and upon such terms and conditions as the President may prescribe such interest or property shall be held, used, administered, liquidated, sold, or otherwise dealt with in the interest of and for the benefit of the United States, and such designated agency or person may perform any and all acts incident to the accomplishment or furtherance of these purposes; and the President shall, in the manner hereinabove provided, require any person to keep a full record of, and to furnish under oath, in the form of reports or otherwise, complete information relative to any act or transaction referred to in this subdivision either before, during, or after the completion thereof, or relative to any interest in foreign property, or relative to any property in which any foreign country or any national thereof has or has had any interest, or as may be otherwise necessary to enforce the provisions of this subdivision, and in any case in which a report could be required, the President may, in the manner hereinabove provided, require the production, or if necessary to the national security or defense, the seizure, of any books of account, records, contracts, letters, memoranda, or other papers, in the custody or control of such person.

(2) Any payment, conveyance, transfer, assignment, or delivery of property or interest therein, made to or for the account of the United States, or as otherwise directed, pursuant to this subdivision or any rule, regulation, instruction, or direction issued hereunder shall to the extent thereof be a full acquittance and discharge for all purposes of the obligation of the person making the same; and no person shall be held liable in any court for or in respect to anything done or omitted in good faith in connection with the administration of, or in pursuance of and in reliance on, this subdivision, or any rule, regulation, instruction, or direction issued hereunder.

(3) As used in this subdivision the term "United States" means the United States and any place subject to the jurisdiction thereof: *Provided, however*, That the foregoing shall not be construed as a limitation upon the power of the President, which is hereby conferred, to prescribe from time to time, definitions, not inconsistent with the purposes of this subdivision, for any or all of the terms used in this subdivision. As used in this subdivision the term "person" means an individual, partnership, association, or corporation.

(4) The authority granted to the President by this section does not include the authority to regulate or prohibit, directly or indirectly, the importation from any country, or the exportation to any country, whether commercial or otherwise, regardless of format or medium of transmission, of any information or informational materials, including but not limited to, publications, films, posters, phonograph records, photographs, microfilms, microfiche, tapes, compact disks, CD ROMs, artworks, and news wire feeds. The exports exempted from regulation or prohibition by this paragraph do not include those which are otherwise controlled for export under section 5 of the Export Administration Act of 1979 [section 2404 of this Appendix], or under section 6 of that Act [section 2405 of this Appendix] to the extent that such controls promote the nonproliferation or antiterrorism policies of the United States, or with respect to which acts are prohibited by chapter 37 of title 18, United States Code.

(Oct. 6, 1917, ch. 106, §5, 40 Stat. 415; Sept. 24, 1918, ch. 176, §5, 40 Stat. 966; Mar. 9, 1933, ch. 1, §2, 48 Stat. 1; May 7, 1940, ch. 185, §1, 54 Stat. 179; Dec. 18, 1941, ch. 593, title III, §301, 55 Stat. 839; Proc. No. 2695, eff. July 4, 1946, 11 F.R. 7517, 60 Stat. 1352; Pub. L. 95–223, title I, §§101(a), 102, 103(b), Dec. 28, 1977, 91 Stat. 1625, 1626; Pub. L. 100–418, title II, §2502(a)(1), Aug. 23, 1988, 102 Stat. 1371; Pub. L. 103–236, title V, §525(b)(1), Apr. 30, 1994, 108 Stat. 474.)

CODIFICATION

Words ", including the Philippine Islands, and the several courts of first instance of the Commonwealth of the Philippine Islands shall have jurisdiction in all cases, civil or criminal, arising under this subdivision in the Philippine Islands and concurrent jurisdiction with the district courts of the United States of all cases, civil or criminal, arising upon the high seas" following "to the jurisdiction thereof:" in subsec. (b)(3) were omitted upon the authority of 1946 Proc. No. 2695, which granted the Philippine Islands independence, and which was issued pursuant to section 1394 of Title 22, Foreign Relations and Intercourse. Proc. No. 2695 is set out as a note under section 1394 of Title 22.

Subsec. (b) is also classified to section 95a of Title 12, Banks and Banking.

AMENDMENTS

1994—Subsec. (b)(4). Pub. L. 103–236 amended par. (4) generally. Prior to amendment, par. (4) read as follows: "The authority granted to the President in this subsection does not include the authority to regulate or prohibit, directly or indirectly, the importation from any country, or the exportation to any country, whether commercial or otherwise, of publications, films, posters, phonograph records, photographs, microfilms, microfiche, tapes, or other informational materials, which are not otherwise controlled for export under section 5 of the Export Administration Act of 1979 or with respect to which no acts are prohibited by chapter 37 of title 18, United States Code."

1988—Subsec. (b)(4). Pub. L. 100–418 added par. (4).

1977—Subsec. (b)(1). Pub. L. 95–223, §§101(a), 102, substituted "During the time of war, the President may, through any agency that he may designate, and under such rules and regulations" for "During the time of war or during any other period of national emergency declared by the President, the President may, through any agency, that he may designate, or otherwise, and under such rules and regulations" in provisions preceding subpar. (A), and, in provisions following subpar. (B), struck out "; and the President may, in the manner hereinabove provided, take other and further measures not inconsistent herewith for the enforcement of this subdivision" after "control of such person".

Subsec. (b)(3). Pub. L. 95–22, §103(b), struck out provisions that whoever willfully violated any of the provisions of this subdivision or of any license, order, rule, or regulation issued thereunder, could be fined not more than $10,000, or, if a natural person, could be imprisoned for not more than ten years, or both; and that any officer, director, or agent of any corporation who knowingly participated in that violation could be punished by a like fine, imprisonment, or both.

1941—Subsec. (b). Act Dec. 18, 1941, considerably broadened the powers of the President to take, administer, control, use and liquidate foreign-owned property and added a flexibility of control which enabled the President and the agencies designated by him to cope with the problems surrounding alien property, its ownership or control, on the basis of the particular facts in each case.

1940—Subsec. (b). Act May 7, 1940, included dealings in evidences of indebtedness or ownership of property in which foreign states, nationals or political subdivisions thereof have an interest.

1933—Subsec. (b). Act Mar. 9, 1933, among other things, extended President's power to any time of war national emergency, permitted regulations to be issued by any agency designated by President, provided for furnishing under oath of complete information relative to transactions under the subsection, and placed sanctions on violations to the extent of a $10,000 fine or ten years imprisonment.

1918—Subsec. (b). Act Sept. 24, 1918, inserted provisions relating to hoarding or melting of gold or silver coin or bullion or currency and to regulation of transactions in bonds or certificates of indebtedness.

DELEGATION OF FUNCTIONS

Delegation of President's powers under subsec. (b) of this section to Secretary of the Treasury and Alien Property Custodian; and transfer of Alien Property Custodian's powers to Attorney General, see Ex. Ord. Nos. 9095 and 9788, set out under section 6 of this Appendix.

Powers conferred upon President by subsec. (b) of this section delegated to Secretary of the Treasury by Memorandum of President dated Feb. 12, 1942, 7 F.R. 1409.

LIMITATION ON EXERCISE OF EMERGENCY AUTHORITIES

Section 525(b)(2) of Pub. L. 103–236 provided that: "The authorities conferred upon the President by section 5(b) of the Trading With the Enemy Act [subsec. (b) of this section], which were being exercised with respect to a country on July 1, 1977, as a result of a national emergency declared by the President before such date, and are being exercised on the date of the enactment of this Act [Apr. 30, 1994], do not include the authority to regulate or prohibit, directly or indirectly, any activity which, under section 5(b)(4) of the Trading With the Enemy Act, as amended by paragraph (1) of this subsection, may not be regulated or prohibited."

Section 2502(a)(2) of Pub. L. 100–418 provided that: "The authorities conferred upon the President by section 5(b) of the Trading With the Enemy Act [subsec. (b) of this section], which were being exercised with respect to a country on July 1, 1977, as a result of a national emergency declared by the President before such date, and are being exercised on the date of the enactment of this Act [Aug. 23, 1988], do not include the authority to regulate or prohibit, directly or indirectly, any activity which, under section 5(b)(4) of the Trading With the Enemy Act, as added by paragraph (1) of this subsection, may not be regulated or prohibited."

EXTENSION AND TERMINATION OF NATIONAL EMERGENCY POWERS UNDER THE TRADING WITH THE ENEMY ACT

Section 101(b), (c) of Pub. L. 95–223 provided that:

"(b) Notwithstanding the amendment made by subsection (a) [amending subsec. (b)(1) of this section], the authorities conferred upon the President by section 5(b) of the Trading With the Enemy Act [subsec. (b) of this section], which were being exercised with respect to a country on July 1, 1977, as a result of a national emergency declared by the President before such date, may continue to be exercised with respect to such country, except that, unless extended, the exercise of such authorities shall terminate (subject to the savings provisions of the second sentence of section 101(a) of the National Emergencies Act [section 1601(a) of this title]) at the end of the two-year period beginning on the date of enactment of the National Emergencies Act [Sept. 14, 1976]. The President may extend the exercise of such authorities for one-year periods upon a determination for each such extension that the exercise of such authorities with respect to such country for another year is in the national interest of the United States.

"(c) The termination and extension provisions of subsection (b) of this section supersede the provisions of section 101(a) [section 1601(a) of this title] and of title II [section 1621 et seq. of this title] of the National Emergencies Act to the extent that the provisions of subsection (b) of this section are inconsistent with those provisions."

EXTENSION OF THE EXERCISE OF CERTAIN AUTHORITIES UNDER THE TRADING WITH THE ENEMY ACT

Determination of President of the United States, No. 2000–29, Sept. 12, 2000, 65 F.R. 55883, provided:

Memorandum for the Secretary of State [and] the Secretary of the Treasury

Under section 101(b) of Public Law 95–223 (91 Stat. 1625; 50 U.S.C. App. 5(b) note), and a previous determination made by me on September 10, 1999 (64 Fed. Reg. 51885), the exercise of certain authorities under the Trading With the Enemy Act [sections 1 to 6, 7 to 39, and 41 to 44 of this Appendix] is scheduled to terminate on September 14, 2000.

I hereby determine that the continuation for 1 year of the exercise of those authorities with respect to the applicable countries is in the national interest of the United States.

Therefore, pursuant to the authority vested in me by section 101(b) of Public Law 95–223, I continue for 1 year, until September 14, 2001, the exercise of those authorities with respect to countries affected by:

(1) the Foreign Assets Control Regulations, 31 CFR part 500;

(2) the Transaction Control Regulations, 31 CFR part 505; and

(3) the Cuban Assets Control Regulations, 31 CFR part 515.

The Secretary of the Treasury is authorized and directed to publish this determination in the Federal Register.

WILLIAM J. CLINTON.

Prior extensions were contained in the following:

Determination of President of the United States, No. 99–36, Sept. 10, 1999, 64 F.R. 51885.

Determination of President of the United States, No. 98–35, Sept. 11, 1998, 63 F.R. 50455.

Determination of President of the United States, No. 97–32, Sept. 12, 1997, 62 F.R. 48729.

Determination of President of the United States, No. 96–43, Aug. 27, 1996, 61 F.R. 46529.

Determination of President of the United States, No. 95–41, Sept. 8, 1995, 60 F.R. 47659.

Determination of President of the United States, No. 94–46, Sept. 8, 1994, 59 F.R. 47229.

Determination of President of the United States, No. 93–38, Sept. 13, 1993, 58 F.R. 51209.

Determination of President of the United States, No. 92–45, Aug. 28, 1992, 57 F.R. 43125.

Determination of President of the United States, No. 91–52, Sept. 13, 1991, 56 F.R. 48415.

Determination of President of the United States, No. 90–38, Sept. 5, 1990, 55 F.R. 37309.

Determination of President of the United States, No. 89–25, Aug. 28, 1989, 54 F.R. 37089.

Determination of President of the United States, No. 88–22, Sept. 8, 1988, 53 F.R. 35289.

Memorandum of President of the United States, Aug. 27, 1987, 51 F.R. 33397.

Memorandum of President of the United States, Aug. 20, 1986, 51 F.R. 30201.

Memorandum of President of the United States, Sept. 5, 1985, 50 F.R. 36563.

Memorandum of President of the United States, Sept. 11, 1984, 49 F.R. 35927.

Memorandum of President of the United States, Sept. 7, 1983, 48 F.R. 40695.

Memorandum of President of the United States, Sept. 8, 1982, 47 F.R. 39797.

Memorandum of President of the United States, Sept. 10, 1981, 46 F.R. 45321.

Memorandum of President of the United States, Sept. 8, 1980, 45 F.R. 59549.

Memorandum of President of the United States, Sept. 12, 1979, 44 F.R. 53153.

Memorandum of President of the United States, Sept. 8, 1978, 43 F.R. 40449.

NON-APPLICABILITY OF NATIONAL EMERGENCIES ACT

The provisions of the National Emergencies Act [see Short Title note set out under section 1601 of Title 50, War and National Defense] shall not apply to the powers and authorities conferred by this section and actions taken hereunder, see section 1651(a)(1) of Title 50.

WORLD WAR II ALIEN PROPERTY CUSTODIAN

Reestablishment and termination of Office of Alien Property Custodian during World War II, see notes set out under section 6 of this Appendix.

APPROVAL OF REGULATIONS

Act Mar. 9, 1933, ch. 1, title I, §1, 48 Stat. 1, provided that: "The actions, regulations, rules, licenses, orders and proclamations heretofore or hereafter taken, promulgated, made, or issued by the President of the United States or the Secretary of the Treasury since March 4, 1933, pursuant to the authority conferred by subdivision (b) of section 5 of the act of October 6, 1917, as amended [section 5(b) of this Appendix], are hereby approved and confirmed."

EXECUTIVE ORDERS

Ex. Ord. No. 6260, as amended, respecting hoarding, export, and earmarking of gold coin, bullion, or currency and transactions in foreign exchange; Ex. Ord. No. 6560, as amended, respecting transactions in foreign exchange, transfers of credit, and export of coin and currency; Ex. Ord. No. 8389, as amended, regulating transactions in foreign exchange and foreign-owned property and providing for the reporting of all foreign-owned property; Ex. Ord. No. 9747, respecting continuance of functions of Alien Property Custodian and Treasury Department in Philippines; Ex. Ord. No. 9760, respecting diplomatic property of Germany and Japan; and Ex. Ord. No. 10348, continuing in force orders and regulations relating to blocked property, see notes set out under section 95a of Title 12, Banks and Banking, and section 6 of this Appendix.

SECTION REFERRED TO IN OTHER SECTIONS

This section is referred to in title 12 sections 212, 3409, 3413; title 22 sections 6004, 6005, 6023, 6082; title 28 sections 1610, 2680; title 31 section 5315.

§ 6. Alien Property Custodian; general powers and duties

The President is authorized to appoint, prescribe the duties of, and fix the salary of an official to be known as the alien property custodian, who shall be empowered to receive all money and property in the United States due or belonging to an enemy, or ally of enemy, which may be paid, conveyed, transferred, assigned, or delivered to said custodian under the provisions of this Act [sections 1 to 6, 7 to 39, and 41 to 44 of this Appendix]; and to hold, administer, and account for the same under the general direction of the President and as provided in this Act [said sections]. The President may further employ in the District of Columbia and elsewhere and fix the compensation of such clerks, attorneys, investigators, accountants, and other employees as he may find necessary for the due administration of the provisions of this Act [said sections]; *Provided*, That such clerks, investigators, accountants, and other employees shall be appointed from lists of eligibles to be supplied by the Civil Service Commission[1] and in accordance with the civil-service law.

(Oct. 6, 1917, ch. 106, §6, 40 Stat. 415; Pub. L. 92–310, title II, §235, June 6, 1972, 86 Stat. 214; Pub. L. 94–273, §11(5), Apr. 21, 1976, 90 Stat. 378; Pub. L. 100–418, title II, §2501(b), Aug. 23, 1988, 102 Stat. 1371.)

REFERENCES IN TEXT

The civil-service law, referred to in text, is set forth in Title 5, Government Organization and Employees. See, particularly, section 3301 et seq. of Title 5.

CODIFICATION

Provisions that limited the salary of the alien property custodian to not more than $5,000 per annum have been omitted as obsolete and superseded. Sections 1202 and 1204 of the Classification Act of 1949, 63 Stat. 972, 973, repealed the Classification Act of 1923 and all other laws or parts of laws inconsistent with the 1949 Act. The Classification Act of 1949 was repealed by Pub. L. 89–554, Sept. 6, 1966, §8(a), 80 Stat. 632, and reenacted as chapter 51 and subchapter III of chapter 53 of Title 5, Government Organization and Employees. Section 5102 of Title 5 contains the applicability provisions of the 1949 Act, and section 5103 of Title 5 authorizes the Office of Personnel Management to determine the applicability to specific positions and employees.

AMENDMENTS

1988—Pub. L. 100–418 struck out before period at end ": *Provided further*, That the President shall cause a de-

[1] See Transfer of Functions note below.

tailed report to be made to Congress on the first day of April of each year of all proceedings had under this Act during the year preceding. Such report shall contain a list of all persons appointed or employed, with the salary or compensation paid to each, and a statement of the different kinds of property taken into custody and the disposition made thereof".

1976—Pub. L. 94–273 substituted "April" for "January".

1972—Pub. L. 92–310 struck out provisions which required the Alien Property Custodian to give a bond.

TRANSFER OF FUNCTIONS

Functions vested by statute in United States Civil Service Commission transferred to Director of Office of Personnel Management (except as otherwise specified) by Reorg. Plan No. 2 of 1978, §102, 43 F.R. 36037, 92 Stat. 3783, set out under section 1101 of Title 5, Government Organization and Employees, effective Jan. 1, 1979, as provided by section 1–102 of Ex. Ord. No. 12107, Dec. 28, 1978, 44 F.R. 1055, set out under section 1101 of Title 5.

Reorg. Plan No. 1 of 1947, §101, eff. July 1, 1947, 12 F.R. 4534, 61 Stat. 951, transferred functions vested by law in Alien Property Custodian or Office of Alien Property Custodian to Attorney General, except that those relating to property or interests in Philippines transferred to President. For text of this plan and provisions relating to transfer of records, property, personnel, and funds, see the text of the plan, set out in the Appendix to Title 5.

Previous office of Alien Property Custodian abolished and functions and personnel transferred to Department of Justice by Ex. Ord. No. 6694, eff. July 1, 1934.

EXPENSES AND COMPENSATION OF ALIEN PROPERTY CUSTODIAN

Act May 16, 1928, ch. 580, §1, 45 Stat. 574, contained the following provision: "All expenses of the office of the Alien Property Custodian authorized by * * * [the Trading With the Enemy Act], including compensation of the Alien Property Custodian at not to exceed $10,000 per annum; shall be paid from interest and collections on trust funds and other properties under the control of such Custodian."

REPORT TO CONGRESS; INCLUSION OF CLAIMS FILED UNDER SECTION 32(a)(2)(D) OF THIS APPENDIX

Act Sept. 29, 1950, ch. 1108, §2, 64 Stat. 1081, provided that: "There shall be included in the report made to Congress pursuant to section 6 of the Trading With the Enemy Act, as amended [this section], a statement of (1) the names and nationalities of persons who have filed notice of claim for the return of any property or interest under section 1 of this Act [section 32(a)(2)(D) of this Appendix], the date of the filing of such notice of claim, and the estimated value of the property or interest, and (2) the names and nationalities of persons to whom returns have been made of any property or interest under section 1 of this Act [section 32(a)(2)(D) of this Appendix] and the value of such property or interest."

EXECUTIVE ORDER NO. 9095

Ex. Ord. No. 9095, Mar. 11, 1942, 7 F.R. 1971, as amended by Ex. Ord. No. 9193, July 6, 1942, 7 F.R. 5205; Ex. Ord. No. 9567, June 8, 1945, 10 F.R. 6917, which established the Office of the World War II Alien Property Custodian and provided for the compensation, functions, etc., of the Alien Property Custodian, was revoked by Ex. Ord. No. 12553, Feb. 25, 1986, 51 F.R. 7237.

EX. ORD. NO. 9142. TRANSFER OF CERTAIN FUNCTIONS, PROPERTY AND PERSONNEL FROM DEPARTMENT OF JUSTICE TO ALIEN PROPERTY CUSTODIAN

Ex. Ord. No. 9142, Apr. 21, 1942, 7 F.R. 2985, provided:

1. All authority, rights, privileges, powers, duties, and functions transferred or delegated to the Department of Justice, to be administered under the supervision of the Attorney General, by Executive Order No. 6694 of May 1, 1934, or vested in, transferred or delegated to, the Attorney General or the Assistant Attorney General in charge of the Claims Division of the Department of Justice, by Executive Order No. 8136 of May 15, 1939, are hereby transferred to the Alien Property Custodian provided for by Executive Order No. 9095, dated March 11, 1942.

2. Subject to the provisions of paragraph 5 hereof, all property of the Alien Property Division of the Department of Justice, including records, files, supplies, furniture, and equipment, and all funds, securities, choses in action, real estate, patents, trade-marks, copyrights, and all other property of whatsoever kind, held or administered by the Attorney General under and pursuant to the Trading With the Enemy Act, as amended [sections 1 to 6, 7 to 39, and 41 to 44 of this Appendix], are hereby transferred to the Alien Property Custodian, to be administered and disposed of under his supervision and direction.

3. All administrative or general or other expenses of the Office of the Alien Property Custodian in the administration of the Trading With the Enemy Act, as amended [sections 1 to 6, 7 to 39, and 41 to 44 of this Appendix], including the administration of Executive Order No. 9095, may be paid out of any funds or other property transferred to the Alien Property Custodian hereunder, whether or not such expenses relate to the property transferred hereunder, or were incurred before or after March 11, 1942.

4. The personnel of the Alien Property Division of the Department of Justice is hereby transferred to the Office of the Alien Property Custodian without loss of such civil service status or eligibility therefor as they may have.

5. All litigation in which the Alien Property Custodian or the Office of the Alien Property Custodian is interested shall be conducted under the supervision of the Attorney General. The Department of Justice and the Attorney General shall from time to time render such advice on legal matters to the Alien Property Custodian and the Office of the Alien Property Custodian as the Attorney General and the Alien Property Custodian may from time to time agree upon. For the purpose of defraying such expenses as may be incurred by the Department of Justice or the Attorney General in the rendering of advice as aforesaid or in the conduct of litigation in which the Alien Property Custodian or the Office of Alien Property Custodian is interested, including expenses for salaries of personnel and all other charges, the Alien Property Custodian may from time to time make available out of the funds or other property in his possession or control such funds as the Attorney General and the Alien Property Custodian may from time to time agree to be necessary therefor. Nothing in this order shall be construed to require the Department of Justice to surrender possession of any files and records relating to any litigation heretofore or hereafter conducted by it.

6. This order shall not be construed as modifying or limiting in any way the authority heretofore granted to the Federal Bureau of Investigation.

7. This order shall remain in force during the continuance of the present war and for six months after the termination thereof.

8. All prior Executive orders insofar as they are in conflict herewith are hereby superseded.

FRANKLIN D. ROOSEVELT.

EX. ORD. NO. 9325. PAYMENT OF EXPENSES OF THE OFFICE OF ALIEN PROPERTY CUSTODIAN

Ex. Ord. No. 9325, Apr. 7, 1943, 8 F.R. 1682, provided:

1. Until it is otherwise provided, the Alien Property Custodian is authorized and empowered to pay out of any funds lawfully in his custody or under his control all necessary expenses incurred by the Office of Alien Property Custodian in carrying out the powers and duties vested in him pursuant to Title III of the First War Powers Act, 1941 [sections 616 to 618 of this Appendix], and the applicable orders issued thereunder. Such ex-

penses shall be allocated and recovered as provided in section 2 hereof.

2. The Alien Property Custodian is authorized to retain, allocate and recover, as a charge against any specific property or any other property of which the former owner of the specific property was divested, expenses attributable to such specific property with respect to which he has exercised or may hereafter exercise any power heretofore or hereafter conferred upon him. In addition to such expenses, the Alien Property Custodian is authorized to retain, allocate and recover at such time or times as he may deem practicable, as a charge against money or property in his custody or under his control, such amounts as may be necessary in connection with the general administrative expenses of the Office of Alien Property Custodian which have been or may be paid and which are not practicably allocable to a specific property.

3. The power and authority herein granted shall not be limited by the filing of a claim or the institution of a suit relating to any property subject to the authority of the Alien Property Custodian.

4. This order shall not be construed as a limitation upon or in derogation of any powers heretofore granted.

5. The Office of Alien Property Custodian shall submit to the Bureau of the Budget [now the Office of Management and Budget] (a) prior to April 30, 1943, an estimate of general administrative expenses for the remainder of the current fiscal year, (b) prior to the end of the current and of each subsequent fiscal year, at such time as may be specified by the Director of the Bureau of the Budget, an estimate of such expenses for the succeeding fiscal year, and (c) any supplemental estimates of such expenses if and as the need arises. After April 30, 1943, no general administrative expenses authorized to be paid pursuant to this order shall be incurred or paid by the Office of Alien Property Custodian beyond the amounts approved by the Director of the Bureau of the Budget upon submissions as above set forth.

FRANKLIN D. ROOSEVELT.

EX. ORD. NO. 9747. FUNCTIONS OF ALIEN PROPERTY CUSTODIAN AND TREASURY DEPARTMENT CONTINUED IN PHILIPPINES

Ex. Ord. No. 9747, July 3, 1946, 11 F.R. 7518, provided that the powers of the Alien Property Custodian under Ex. Ord. No. 9095, formerly set out above, should continue to be exercised in the Philippines after July 4, 1946. It also provided that the Secretary of the Treasury should continue to exercise his powers in the Philippines under Ex. Ord. No. 8389, eff. Apr. 10, 1940, set out as a note under section 95a of Title 12, Banks and Banking.

EX. ORD. NO. 9760. AUTHORITY OF SECRETARY OF STATE REGARDING DIPLOMATIC PROPERTY OF GERMANY AND JAPAN

Ex. Ord. No. 9760, July 23, 1946, 11 F.R. 7999, provided:

1. The Secretary of State is authorized and empowered as he deems necessary in the national interest to direct, manage, supervise, or control diplomatic and consular property within the United States owned or controlled by Germany or Japan, including all assets on the premises of such property.

2. The Alien Property Custodian shall not exercise any power and authority conferred upon him by any other Executive order with respect to diplomatic and consular property within the United States owned or controlled by Germany or Japan except so far as the Secretary of State releases his authority over such diplomatic and consular property under this order and so notifies the Alien Property Custodian in writing.

3. When the Secretary of State determines to exercise any power and authority conferred upon him by this order with respect to any property over which the Secretary of the Treasury is exercising any control and so notifies the Secretary of the Treasury in writing, the Secretary of the Treasury shall release all control of such property, except as authorized or directed by the Secretary of State.

4. This order supersedes all conflicting provisions of prior Executive orders, including Executive Orders Nos. 8389, as amended [set out under section 95a of Title 12, Banks and Banking] and 9095, as amended [set out above].

5. The Secretary of State is authorized to prescribe from time to time regulations, rulings, and instructions to carry out the purposes of this order.

HARRY S TRUMAN.

EX. ORD. NO. 9788. TERMINATION OF OFFICE OF WORLD WAR II ALIEN PROPERTY CUSTODIAN AND TRANSFERENCE OF ITS FUNCTIONS TO THE ATTORNEY GENERAL

Ex. Ord. No. 9788, Oct. 14, 1946, 11 F.R. 11981, provided:

1. The Office of Alien Property Custodian in the Office for Emergency Management of the Executive Office of the President, established by Executive Order No. 9095 of March 11, 1942 [formerly set out above], is hereby terminated; and all authority, rights, privileges, powers, duties, and functions vested in such Office or in the Alien Property Custodian or transferred or delegated thereto are hereby vested in or transferred or delegated to the Attorney General, as the case may be, and shall be administered by him or under his direction and control by such officers and agencies of the Department of Justice as he may designate.

2. All property or interests vested in or transferred to the Alien Property Custodian or seized by him, and all proceeds thereof, which are held or administered by him on the effective date of this order are hereby transferred to the Attorney General.

3. All personnel, property, records, and funds of the Office of Alien Property Custodian are hereby transferred to the Department of Justice.

4. This order supersedes all prior Executive orders to the extent that they are in conflict with this order.

5. This order shall become effective on October 15, 1946.

HARRY S TRUMAN.

EXECUTIVE ORDER NO. 9818

Ex. Ord. No. 9818, Jan. 7, 1947, 12 F.R. 133, formerly set out under section 1382 of Title 22, Foreign Relations and Intercourse, established the Philippine Alien Property Administration.

EXECUTIVE ORDER NO. 9989

Ex. Ord. No. 9989, Aug. 20, 1948, 13 F.R. 4891, which transferred jurisdiction over blocked assets to the Attorney General, was superseded by Ex. Ord. No. 11281, May 13, 1966, 31 F.R. 7215, set out below.

EXECUTIVE ORDER NO. 10348

Ex. Ord. No. 10348, Apr. 26, 1952, 17 F.R. 3769, which continued in force Ex. Ord. No. 9989, was superseded by Ex. Ord. No. 11281, May 13, 1966, 31 F.R. 7215, set out below.

EX. ORD. NO. 11281. TRANSFERRING JURISDICTION OVER BLOCKED ASSETS FROM ATTORNEY GENERAL TO SECRETARY OF THE TREASURY

Ex. Ord. No. 11281, May 13, 1966, 31 F.R. 7215, provided:

WHEREAS before October 1, 1948, the Secretary of the Treasury administered the blocking controls and other restrictions over property and interests of certain foreign countries or their nationals that had been imposed, under the authority of section 5(b) of the Trading with the Enemy Act, as amended (50 U.S.C. App. 5(b)), by means of and under Executive Order No. 8389 of April 10, 1940, as amended [set out under section 95a of Title 12, Banks and Banking]; and

WHEREAS by Executive Order No. 9989 of August 20, 1948, jurisdiction over the property and interests which remained blocked or restricted under Executive Order No. 8389 on September 30, 1948, was transferred, effective October 1, 1948, to the Attorney General to aid him in carrying out his functions as successor to the Alien Property Custodian, including, among others, the function of vesting property pursuant to the provisions of the Trading with the Enemy Act, as amended [sections 1 to 6, 7 to 39,and 41 to 44 of this Appendix]; and

WHEREAS by Executive Order No. 10644 of November 7, 1955 [formerly set out under section 1631a of Title 22, Foreign Relations and Intercourse], the Attorney General was designated to carry out the functions of the President under Title II of the International Claims Settlement Act of 1949 (as added by the Act of August 9, 1955, Public Law 285, 84th Congress, 69 Stat. 562) [sections 1631 to 1631*o* of Title 22], including certain vesting and blocking functions required by section 202 of that Act (22 U.S.C. 1631a), and the Attorney General, as designee of the President, exercises controls under Executive Order No. 8389 with respect to the net proceeds of certain property that are carried, pursuant to section 202, in blocked accounts with the Treasury; and

WHEREAS the functions of vesting property under the Trading with the Enemy Act and under section 202 of the International Claims Settlement Act of 1949 have been terminated; and

WHEREAS the blocking controls not exercised by the Attorney General under Executive Order No. 8389 are limited in application to property of Hungary or its nationals acquired on or before January 1, 1945; property of Czechoslovakia, Estonia, Latvia, Lithuania or nationals of those countries acquired on or before December 7, 1945; property of East Germany or its nationals acquired on or before December 31, 1946, and certain securities scheduled in General Rulings No. 5 and No. 5B, as amended (8 CFR 511.205 and 511.205b); and

WHEREAS the Office of Alien Property, through which the Attorney General carries out or has carried out the various responsibilities described above, will be abolished on or before June 30, 1966, and the Attorney General thereafter will not be in a position to administer blocking controls under Executive Order No. 8389 efficiently; and

WHEREAS in the interest of efficiency it is desirable to return to the Secretary of the Treasury jurisdiction over the property and interests remaining subject to such blocking controls:

NOW, THEREFORE, by virtue of the authority vested in me by the Constitution and the laws of the United States, including the Trading with the Enemy Act, as amended [sections 1 to 6, 7 to 39, and 41 to 44 of this Appendix], Title II of the International Claims Settlement Act of 1949 and section 301 of Title 3 of the United States Code, and as President of the United States, it is hereby ordered as follows:

SECTION 1. The authority granted to the Attorney General by Executive Order No. 9989 with respect to property and interests blocked or otherwise subject to restriction under Executive Order No. 8389 [set out under section 95a of Title 12, Banks and Banking] is hereby terminated and Executive Order No. 9989 [formerly set out above] is hereby superseded.

SEC. 2. The Secretary of the Treasury shall hereafter be responsible for the administration of the controls exercisable under Executive Order No. 8389 [set out under section 95a of Title 12, Banks and Banking] and he is authorized and directed to take such action as he may deem necessary with respect to any property or interest that remains blocked or restricted under Executive Order No. 8389 on the effective date of this order. In the performance of the functions and duties hereby reassigned to him, the Secretary of the Treasury may act personally or through any officer, person, agency or instrumentality designated by him.

SEC. 3. All orders, regulations, rulings, instructions or licenses issued prior to the effective date of this order by the Attorney General or the Secretary of the Treasury with respect to any of the property or interests referred to in Section 2 shall continue in full force and effect except as hereafter amended, modified or revoked by the Secretary of the Treasury.

SEC. 4. No person affected by any order, regulation, ruling, instruction, license or other action issued or taken by either the Attorney General or the Secretary of the Treasury in the administration of Executive Order No. 8389 may challenge the validity thereof or otherwise excuse any action, or failure to act, on the ground that it was within the jurisdiction of the Secretary of the Treasury rather than the Attorney General or *vice versa*.

SEC. 5. Section 1 of Executive Order No. 10644 of November 7, 1955 [formerly set out under section 1631a of Title 22, Foreign Relations and Intercourse], is hereby amended to read as follows:

"SECTION 1. (a) With the exception of the functions referred to in subsection (b) of this section, the Attorney General, and, as designated by the Attorney General for this purpose, any Assistant Attorney General are hereby designated and empowered to perform the functions conferred by Title II of the International Claims Settlement Act of 1949 upon the President, and the functions conferred by that title upon any designee of the President.

"(b) The Secretary of the Treasury, and any officer, person, agency or instrumentality designated by the Secretary of the Treasury for this purpose, as hereby designated and empowered to perform the functions conferred upon the President by section 202 of Title II with respect to the release of blocked property and of the net proceeds of property that are carried in blocked accounts with the Treasury."

SEC. 6. Executive Order No. 8389, this order and all delegations, designations, regulations, rulings, instructions and licenses issued or to be issued under Executive Order No. 8389 or this order are hereby continued in force according to their terms for the duration of the period of the national emergency proclaimed by Proclamation No. 2914 of December 16, 1950 [set out preceding section 1 of this Appendix]. Executive Order No. 10348 of April 26, 1952 [formerly set out above] is hereby superseded.

SEC. 7. Nothing in this order shall be deemed to revoke or limit any powers heretofore conferred on the Secretary of the Treasury by or under any statute or Executive order, or to revoke or limit any powers heretofore conferred upon the Attorney General by or under any statute or Executive order other than Executive Order No. 9989 [formerly set out above] or No. 10644.

SEC. 8. This order shall become effective at midnight, May 15, 1966.

LYNDON B. JOHNSON.

SECTION REFERRED TO IN OTHER SECTIONS

This section is referred to in sections 1 to 5, 7 to 39, 41 to 44 of this Appendix; title 28 section 2680.

§ 6a. Incurment of expenses by Office of Alien Property Custodian

After June 30, 1945, the Office of Alien Property Custodian shall not incur any obligations for the expenses of said Office except pursuant to a further annual authorization by the Congress specifically therefor.

(Dec. 22, 1944, ch. 660, title I, 58 Stat. 855.)

CODIFICATION

Section was not enacted as part of the Trading with the enemy Act which comprises sections 1 to 6, 7 to 39, and 41 to 44 of this Appendix.

TRANSFER OF FUNCTIONS

Functions of Alien Property Custodian and Office of Alien Property Custodian, except those relating to property or interest in Philippines, vested in Attorney General. See notes set out under section 6 of this Appendix.

WORLD WAR II ALIEN PROPERTY CUSTODIAN

Reestablishment and termination of Office of Alien Property Custodian during World War II, see notes set out under section 6 of this Appendix.

REPORT TO CONGRESS ON EXPENSES

Act Dec. 22, 1944, ch. 660, title I, 58 Stat. 855, provided in part that on or before Apr. 1, 1945, the Alien Property Custodian make a report to the Appropriations Committees of the House and Senate giving detailed information on all administrative and nonadministrative expenses incurred in connection with the activities of the Office of Alien Property Custodian.

§ 6b. Omitted

CODIFICATION

Section, Pub. L. 90–470, title II, Aug. 9, 1968, 82 Stat. 673, which authorized Attorney General to pay, out of certain funds or other property or interest, expenses incurred in carrying out Trading With the Enemy Act and International Claims Settlement Act, was from the Department of Justice Appropriation Act, 1969, and was not repeated in subsequent appropriation acts. Similar provisions were carried in the following prior appropriation acts:

Nov. 8, 1967, Pub. L. 90–133, title II, 81 Stat. 416.
Nov. 8, 1966, Pub. L. 89–797, title II, 80 Stat. 1484.
Sept. 2, 1965, Pub. L. 89–164, title II, 79 Stat. 625.
Aug. 31, 1964, Pub. L. 88–527, title II, 78 Stat. 716.
Dec. 30, 1963, Pub. L. 88–245, title II, 77 Stat. 781.
Oct. 18, 1962, Pub. L. 87–843, title II, 76 Stat. 1085.
Sept. 21, 1961, Pub. L. 87–264, title II, 75 Stat. 550.
Aug. 31, 1960, Pub. L. 86–678, title II, 74 Stat. 564.
July 13, 1959, Pub. L. 86–84, title II, 73 Stat. 189.
June 30, 1958, Pub. L. 85–474, title II, 72 Stat. 252.
June 11, 1957, Pub. L. 85–49, title II, 71 Stat. 63.
June 20, 1956, ch. 414, title II, 70 Stat. 308.
July 7, 1955, ch. 279, title II, 69 Stat. 273.
July 2, 1954, ch. 456, title II, 68 Stat. 421.
Aug. 5, 1953, ch. 328, title II, 67 Stat. 375.
July 10, 1952, ch. 651, title II, 66 Stat. 559.
Oct. 22, 1951, ch. 533, title II, 65 Stat. 585.
Sept. 6, 1950, ch. 896, Ch. III, title II, 64 Stat. 619.
July 20, 1949, ch. 354, title II, 63 Stat. 461.

§ 7. Lists of enemy or ally of enemy officers, directors or stockholders of corporations in United States; acts constituting trade with enemy prior to passage of Act; conveyance of property to custodian; voluntary payment to custodian by holder; acts under order, rule, or regulation

(a) Every corporation incorporated within the United States, and every unincorporated association, or company, or trustee, or trustees within the United States, issuing shares or certificates representing beneficial interests, shall, under such rules and regulations as the President may prescribe and, within sixty days after the passage of this Act [Oct. 6, 1917] and at such other times thereafter as the President may require, transmit to the alien property custodian a full list, duly sworn to, of every officer, director, or stockholder known to be, or whom the representative of such corporation, association, company, or trustee has reasonable cause to believe to be an enemy or ally of enemy resident within the territory, or a subject or citizen residing outside of the United States, of any nation with which the United States is at war, or resident within the territory, or a subject or citizen residing outside of the United States, of any ally of any nation with which the United States is at war, together with the amount of stock or shares owned by each such officer, director, or stockholder, or in which he has any interest.

The President may also require a similar list to be transmitted of all stock or shares owned on February third, nineteen hundred and seventeen, by any person now defined as an enemy or ally of enemy, or in which any such person had any interest; and he may also require a list to be transmitted of all cases in which said corporation, association, company, or trustee has reasonable cause to believe that the stock or shares on February third, nineteen hundred and seventeen, were owned or are owned by such enemy or ally of enemy, though standing on the books in the name of another: *Provided, however*, That the name of any such officer, director, or stockholder, shall be stricken permanently or temporarily from such list by the alien property custodian when he shall be satisfied that he is not such enemy or ally of enemy.

Any person in the United States who holds or has or shall hold or have custody or control of any property beneficial or otherwise, alone or jointly with others, of, for, or on behalf of an enemy or ally of enemy, or of any person whom he may have reasonable cause to believe to be an enemy or ally of enemy and any person in the United States who is or shall be indebted in any way to an enemy or ally of enemy, or to any person whom he may have reasonable cause to believe to be an enemy or ally of enemy, shall, with such exceptions and under such rules and regulations as the President shall prescribe, and within thirty days after the passage of this Act [Oct. 6, 1917], or within thirty days after such property shall come within his custody or control, or after such debt shall become due, report the fact to the alien-property custodian by written statement under oath containing such particulars as said custodian shall require. The President may also require a similar report of all property so held, of, for, or on behalf of, and of all debts so owed to, any person now defined as an enemy or ally of enemy, on February third, nineteen hundred and seventeen: *Provided*, That the name of any person shall be stricken from the said report by the alien property custodian, either temporarily or permanently, when he shall be satisfied that such person is not an enemy or ally of enemy. The President may extend the time for filing the lists or reports required by this section for an additional period not exceeding ninety days.

(b) Nothing in this Act [sections 1 to 6, 7 to 39, and 41 to 44 of this Appendix] contained shall render valid or legal, or be construed to recognize as valid or legal, any act or transaction constituting trade with, to, from, for or on account of, or on behalf or for the benefit of an enemy performed or engaged in since the beginning of the war and prior to the passage of this Act [said sections] or any such act or transaction hereafter performed or engaged in except as authorized hereunder, which would otherwise have been or be void, illegal, or invalid at law. No conveyance, transfer, delivery, payment, or loan of money or other property, in violation of section three hereof [section 3 of this Appendix], made after the passage of this Act [Oct. 6, 1917] and not under license as herein provided shall confer or create any right or remedy in respect thereof; and no person shall by virtue of any assignment, indorsement, or delivery to him of any debt, bill, note, or other obligation or chose in action by, from, or on behalf of, or on account of, or for the benefit of an enemy or ally of enemy have any right or remedy against the debtor, obligor, or other person liable to pay, fulfill, or perform the same unless said assignment, indorsement, or delivery was made prior to the beginning of the war or shall be made under license as herein provided, or unless, if made after the beginning of the war and prior to the date of passage of this Act [Oct. 6, 1917], the person to whom the same was made shall prove lack of knowledge and of reasonable cause to believe on his part that the same was made by, from or on behalf of, or on account of, or for the benefit of an enemy or ally of enemy; and any person who knowingly pays, discharges, or satisfies any such debt, note, bill, or other obligation or chose in action shall, on conviction thereof, be deemed to violate section three hereof [section 3 of this Appendix]: *Provided*, That nothing in this Act [said sections] contained shall prevent the carrying out, completion, or performance of any contract, agreement, or obligation originally made with or entered into by an enemy or ally of enemy where, prior to the beginning of the war and not in contemplation thereof, the interest of such enemy or ally of enemy devolved by assignment or otherwise upon a person not an enemy or ally of enemy, and no enemy or ally of enemy will be benefited by such carrying out, completion, or performance otherwise than by release from obligation thereunder.

Nothing in this Act [said sections] shall be deemed to prevent payment of money belonging or owing to an enemy or ally of enemy to a person within the United States not an enemy or ally of enemy, for the benefit of such person or of any other person within the United States, not an enemy or ally of enemy, if the funds so paid shall have been received prior to the beginning of the war and such payments arise out of transactions entered into prior to the beginning of the war, and not in contemplation thereof: *Provided*, That such payment shall not be made without the license of the President, general or special, as provided in this Act [said sections].

Nothing in this Act [said sections] shall be deemed to authorize the prosecution of any suit or action at law or in equity in any court within the United States by an enemy or ally of enemy prior to the end of the war, except as provided in section ten hereof [section 10 of this Appendix]: *Provided, however*, That an enemy or ally of enemy licensed to do business under this Act [said sections] may prosecute and maintain any such suit or action so far as the same arises solely out of the business transacted within the United States under such license and so long as such license remains in full force and effect: *And provided further*, That an enemy or ally of enemy may defend by counsel any suit in equity or action at law which may be brought against him.

Receipt of notice from the President to the effect that he has reasonable ground to believe that any person is an enemy or ally of enemy shall be prima facie defense to any one receiving the same, in any suit or action at law or in equity brought or maintained, or to any right or set-off or recoupment asserted by, such person and based on failure to complete or perform since the beginning of the war any contract or other obligation. In any prosecution under section sixteen hereof [section 16 of this Appendix] proof of receipt of notice from the President to the effect that he has reasonable cause to believe that any person is an enemy or ally of enemy shall be prima facie evidence that the person receiving such notice has reasonable cause to believe such other person to be an enemy or ally of enemy within the meaning of section three hereof [section 3 of this Appendix].

(c) If the President shall so require any money or other property including (but not thereby limiting the generality of the above) patents, copyrights, applications therefor, and rights to apply for the same, trade marks, choses in action, and rights and claims of every character and description owing or belonging to or held for, by, on account of, or on behalf of, or for the benefit of, an enemy or ally of enemy not holding a license granted by the President hereunder, which the President after investigation shall determine is so owning or so belongs or is so held, shall be conveyed, transferred, assigned, delivered, or paid over to the Alien Property Custodian, or the same may be seized by the Alien Property Custodian; and all property thus acquired shall be held, administered and disposed of as elsewhere provided in this Act [sections 1 to 6, 7 to 39, and 41 to 44 of this Appendix].

Any requirement made pursuant to this Act [said sections], or a duly certified copy thereof, may be filed, registered, or recorded in any office for the filing, registering, or recording of conveyances, transfers, or assignments of any such property or rights as may be covered by such requirement (including the proper office for filing, registering, or recording conveyances, transfers, or assignments of patents, copyrights, trade-marks, or any rights therein or any other rights); and if so filed, registered, or recorded shall impart the same notice and have the same force and effect as a duly executed conveyance, transfer, or assignment to the Alien Property Custodian so filed, registered, or recorded.

Whenever any such property shall consist of shares of stock or other beneficial interest in any corporation, association, or company or trust, it shall be the duty of the corporation, association, or company or trustee or trustees issuing such shares or any certificates or other instruments representing the same or any other beneficial interest to cancel upon its, his, or their books all shares of stock or other beneficial interest standing upon its, his, or their books in the name of any person or persons, or held for, on account of, or on behalf of, or for the benefit of any person or persons who shall have been determined by the President, after investigation, to be an enemy or ally of enemy, and which shall have been required to be conveyed, transferred, assigned, or delivered to the Alien Property Custodian or seized by him, and in lieu thereof to issue certificates or other instruments for such shares or other beneficial interest to the Alien Property Custodian or otherwise, as the Alien Property Custodian shall require.

The sole relief and remedy of any person having any claim to any money or other property heretofore or hereafter conveyed, transferred, assigned, delivered, or paid over to the Alien Property Custodian, or required so to be, or seized by him shall be that provided by the terms of this Act [said sections], and in the event of sale or other disposition of such property by the Alien Property Custodian, shall be limited to and enforced against the net proceeds received therefrom and held by the Alien Property Custodian or by the Treasurer of the United States.

(d) If not required to pay, convey, transfer, assign, or deliver under the provisions of subsection (c) of this section, any person not an enemy or ally of enemy who owes to, or holds for, or on account of, or on behalf of, or for the benefit of an enemy or of an ally of enemy not holding a license granted by the President hereunder, any money or other property, or to whom any obligation or form of liability to such enemy or ally of enemy is presented for payment, may, at his option, with the consent of the President, pay, convey, transfer, assign, or deliver to the alien property custodian said money or other property under such rules and regulations as the President shall prescribe.

(e) No person shall be held liable in any court for or in respect to anything done or omitted in pursuance of any order, rule, or regulation made by the President under the authority of this Act [sections 1 to 6, 7 to 39, and 41 to 44 of this Appendix].

Any payment, conveyance, transfer, assignment, or delivery of money or property made to the alien property custodian hereunder shall be a full acquittance and discharge for all purposes of the obligation of the person making the same to the extent of same. The alien property custodian and such other persons as the President may appoint shall have power to execute, acknowledge, and deliver any such instrument or instruments as may be necessary or proper to evidence upon the record or otherwise such acquittance and discharge, and shall, in case of payment to the alien property custodian of any debt or obligation owed to an enemy or ally of enemy, deliver up any notes, bonds, or other evidences of indebtedness or obligation, or any security therefor in which such enemy or ally of enemy had any right or interest that may have come into the possession of the alien property custodian, with like effect as if he or they, respectively, were duly appointed by the enemy or ally of enemy, creditor, or obligee. The President shall issue to every person so appointed a certificate of the appointment and authority of such person, and such certificate shall be received in evidence in all courts within the United States. Whenever any such certificate of authority shall be offered to any registrar, clerk, or other recording officer, Federal or otherwise, within the United States, such officer shall record the same in like manner as a power of attorney, and such record or a duly certified copy thereof shall be received in evidence in all courts of the United States or other courts within the United States.

(Oct. 6, 1917, ch. 106, §7, 40 Stat. 416; Nov. 4, 1918, ch. 201, §1, 40 Stat. 1020.)

AMENDMENTS

1918—Subsec. (c). Act Nov. 4, 1918, amended subsec. (c) generally, inserting provisions on recording of property transfers, cancellation of enemy owned stock by corporations, and restriction of claims to relief provided by terms of the Act.

TRANSFER OF FUNCTIONS

Functions of Alien Property Custodian and Office of Alien Property Custodian, except those relating to property or interest in Philippines, vested in Attorney General. See notes set out under section 6 of this Appendix.

WORLD WAR II ALIEN PROPERTY CUSTODIAN

Reestablishment and termination of Office of Alien Property Custodian during World War II, see notes set out under section 6 of this Appendix.

SECTION REFERRED TO IN OTHER SECTIONS

This section is referred to in title 28 section 2680.

§8. Contracts, mortgages, or pledges against or with enemy or ally of enemy; abrogation of contracts; suspension of limitations

(a) Any person not an enemy or ally of enemy holding a lawful mortgage, pledge, or lien, or other right in the nature of security in property of an enemy or ally of enemy which, by law or by the terms of the instrument creating such mortgage, pledge, or lien, or right, may be disposed of on notice or presentation or demand, and any person not an enemy or ally of enemy who is a party to any lawful contract with an enemy or ally of enemy, the terms of which provide for a termination thereof upon notice or for acceleration of maturity on presentation or demand, may continue to hold said property, and, after default, may dispose of the property in accordance with law or may terminate or mature such contract by notice or presentation or demand served or made on the alien property custodian in accordance with the law and the terms of such instrument or contract and under such rules and regulations as the President shall prescribe; and such notice and such presentation and demand shall have, in all respects, the same force and effect as if duly served or made upon the enemy or ally of enemy personally: *Provided*, That no such rule or regulation shall require that notice or presentation or demand shall be served or made in any case in which, by law or by the terms of said instrument or contract, no notice, presentation, or demand was, prior to the passage of this Act [Oct. 6, 1917], required; and that in case were, by law or by the terms of such instrument or contract, notice is required, no longer period of notice shall be required: *Provided further*, That if, on any such disposition of property, a surplus shall remain after the satisfaction of the mortgage, pledge, lien, or other right in the nature of security, notice of that fact shall be given to the President pursuant to such rules and regulations as he may prescribe, and such surplus shall be held subject to his further order.

(b) Any contract entered into prior to the beginning of the war between any citizen of the United States or any corporation organized within the United States, and an enemy or ally of an enemy, the terms of which provide for the delivery, during or after any war in which a present enemy or ally of enemy nation has been or is now engaged, of anything produced, mined, or manufactured in the United States, may be abrogated by such citizen or corporation by serving thirty days' notice in writing upon the alien property custodian of his or its election to abrogate such contract.

(c) The running of any statute of limitations shall be suspended with reference to the rights or remedies on any contract or obligation entered into prior to the beginning of the war between parties neither of whom is an enemy or ally of enemy, and containing any promise to pay or liability for payment which is evidenced by drafts or other commercial paper drawn against or secured by funds or other property situated in an enemy or ally of enemy country, and no suit shall be maintained on any such contract or obligation in any court within the United States until after the end of the war, or until the said funds or property shall be released for the payment or satisfaction of such contract or obligation: *Provided, however*, That nothing herein contained shall be construed to prevent the suspension of the running of the statute of limitations in all other cases where such suspension would occur under existing law.

(Oct. 6, 1917, ch. 106, §8, 40 Stat. 418.)

TRANSFER OF FUNCTIONS

Functions of Alien Property Custodian and Office of Alien Property Custodian, except those relating to property or interest in Philippines, vested in Attorney General. See notes set out under section 6 of this Appendix.

WORLD WAR II ALIEN PROPERTY CUSTODIAN

Reestablishment and termination of Office of Alien Property Custodian during World War II, see notes set out under section 6 of this Appendix.

SECTION REFERRED TO IN OTHER SECTIONS

This section is referred to in title 28 section 2680.

§9. Claims to property transferred to custodian; notice of claim; filing; return of property; suits to recover; sale of claimed property in time of war or during national emergency

(a) Any person not an enemy or ally of enemy claiming any interest, right, or title in any money or other property which may have been conveyed, transferred, assigned, delivered, or paid to the Alien Property Custodian or seized by him hereunder and held by him or by the Treasurer of the United States, or to whom any debt may be owing from an enemy or ally of enemy whose property or any part thereof shall have been conveyed, transferred, assigned, delivered, or paid to the Alien Property Custodian or seized by him hereunder and held by him or by the Treasurer of the United States may file with the said custodian a notice of his claim under oath and in such form and containing such particulars as the said custodian shall require; and the President, if application is made therefor by the claimant, may order the payment, conveyance, transfer, assignment, or delivery to said claimant of the money or other property so held by the Alien Property Custodian or by the Treasurer of the United States, or of the interest therein to which the President shall determine said claimant is entitled: *Provided*, That no such order by the President shall bar any person from the prosecution of any suit at law or in equity against the claimant to establish any right, title, or interest which he may have in such money or other property. If the President shall not so order within sixty days after the filing of such application or if the claimant shall have filed the notice as above required and shall have made no application to the President, said claimant may institute a suit in equity in the United States District Court for the District of Columbia or in the district court of the United States for the district in which such claimant resides, or, if a corporation, where it has its principal place of business (to which suit the Alien Property Custodian or the Treasurer of the United States, as the case may be, shall be made a party defendant), to establish the interest, right, title, or debt so claimed, and if so established the court shall order the payment, conveyance, transfer, assignment, or delivery to said claimant of the money or other property so held by the Alien Property Custodian or by the Treasurer of the United States or the interest therein to which the court shall determine said claimant is entitled. If suit shall be so instituted, then such money or property shall be retained in the custody of the Alien Property Custodian, or in the Treasury of the United States, as provided in this Act [sections 1 to 6, 7 to 39, and 41 to 44 of this Appendix], and until any final judgment or decree which shall be entered in favor of the claimant shall be fully satisfied by payment or conveyance, transfer, assignment, or delivery by the defendant, or by the Alien Property Custodian, or Treasurer of the United States on order of the court, or until final judgment or decree shall be entered against the claimant or suit otherwise terminated: *Provided further*, That upon a determination made by the President, in time of war or during any national emergency declared by the President, that the interest and welfare of the United States require the sale of any property or interest or any part thereof claimed in any suit filed under this subsection and pending on or after the date of enactment [Oct. 22, 1962] of this proviso the Alien Property Custodian or any successor officer, or agency may sell such property or interest or part thereof, in conformity with law applicable to sales of property by him, at any time prior to the entry of final judgment in such suit. No such sale shall be made until thirty days have passed after the publication of notice in the Federal Register of the intention to sell. The net proceeds of any such sale shall be deposited in a special account established in the Treasury, and shall be held in trust by the Secretary of the Treasury pending the entry of final judgment in such suit. Any recovery of any claimant in any such suit in respect of the property or interest or part thereof so sold shall be satisfied from the net proceeds of such sale unless such claimant, within sixty days after receipt of notice of the amount of net proceeds of sale serves upon the Alien Property Custodian, or any successor officer or agency, and files with the court an election to waive all claims to the net proceeds, or any part thereof, and to claim just compensation instead. If the court finds that the claimant has established an interest, right, or title in any property in respect of which such an election has been served and filed, it shall proceed to determine the amount which will constitute just compensation for such interest, right, or title, and shall order payment to the claimant of the amount so determined. An order for the payment of just compensation hereunder shall be a judgment against the United States and shall be payable first from the net proceeds of the sale in an amount not to exceed the amount the claimant would have received had he elected to accept his proportionate part of the net proceeds of the sale, and the balance, if any, shall be payable in the same manner as are judgments in cases arising under section 1346 of title 28, United States Code. The Alien Property Custodian or any successor officer or agency shall, immediately upon the entry of final judgment, notify the Secretary of the Treasury of the determination by final judgment of the claimant's interest and right to the proportionate part of the net proceeds from the sale, and the final determination by judgment of the amount of just compensation in the event the claimant has elected to recover just compensation for the interest in the property he claimed.

(b) In respect of all money or other property conveyed, transferred, assigned, delivered, or paid to the Alien Property Custodian or seized by him hereunder and held by him or by the Treasurer of the United States, if the President shall determine that the owner thereof at the time such money or other property was required to be so conveyed, transferred, assigned, delivered, or paid to the Alien Property Custodian or at the time when it was voluntarily delivered to him or was seized by him was—

(1) A citizen or subject of any nation or State or free city other than Germany or Austria or Hungary or Austria-Hungary, and is at the time of the return of such money or other property hereunder a citizen or subject of any such nation or State or free city; or

(2) A woman who, at the time of her marriage, was a subject or citizen of a nation which has remained neutral in the war, or of a nation which was associated with the United States in the prosecution of said war, and who, prior to April 6, 1917, intermarried with a subject or citizen of Germany or Austria-Hungary and that the money or other property concerned was not acquired by such woman, either directly or indirectly from any subject or citizen of Germany or Austria-Hungary subsequent to January 1, 1917; or

(3) A woman who at the time of her marriage was a citizen of the United States, and who prior to April 6, 1917, intermarried with a subject or citizen of Germany or Austria-Hungary, and that the money or other property concerned, was not acquired by such woman, either directly or indirectly, from any subject or citizen of Germany or Austria-Hungary subsequent to January 1, 1917; or who was a daughter of a resident citizen of the United States and herself a resident or former resident thereof, or the minor daughter or daughters of such woman, she being deceased; or

(3A) An individual who was at such time a citizen or subject of Germany, Austria, Hungary, or Austria-Hungary, or not a citizen or subject of any nation, state or free city, and that the money or other property concerned was acquired by such individual while a bona fide resident of the United States, and that such individual, on January 1, 1926, and at the time of the return of the money or other property, shall be a bona fide resident of the United States; or

(3B) Any individual who at such time was not a subject or citizen of Germany, Austria, Hungary, or Austria-Hungary, and who is now a citizen or subject of a neutral or allied country: *Provided, however*, That nothing contained herein shall be construed as limiting or abrogating any existing rights of an individual under the provisions of this Act [sections 1 to 6, 7 to 39, and 41 to 44 of this Appendix]; or

(4) A citizen or subject of Germany or Austria or Hungary or Austria-Hungary and was at the time of the severance of diplomatic relations between the United States and such nations, respectively, accredited to the United States as a diplomatic or consular officer of any such nation, or the wife or minor child of such officer, and that the money or other property concerned was within the territory of the United States by reason of the service of such officer in such capacity; or

(5) A citizen or subject of Germany or Austria-Hungary, who by virtue of the provisions of sections 4067, 4068, 4069, and 4070 of the Revised Statutes [sections 21 to 24 of title 50] and of the proclamations and regulations thereunder, was transferred, after arrest, into the custody of the War Department of the United States for detention during the war and is at the time of the return of his money or other property hereunder living within the United States; or

(6) A partnership, association, or other unincorporated body of individuals outside the United States, or a corporation incorporated within any country other than the United States, and was entirely owned at such time by subjects or citizens of nations, States, or free cities other than Germany or Austria or Hungary or Austria-Hungary and is so owned at the time of the return of its money or other property hereunder; or

(7) The Government of Bulgaria or Turkey, or any political or municipal subdivision thereof; or

(8) The Government of Germany or Austria or Hungary or Austria-Hungary, and that the money or other property concerned was the diplomatic or consular property of such Government; or

(9) An individual who was at such time a citizen or subject of Germany, Austria, Hungary, or Austria-Hungary, or who is not a citizen or subject of any nation, State or free city, and that such money or other property, or the proceeds thereof, if the same has been converted, does not exceed in value the sum of $10,000, or although exceeding in value the sum of $10,000 is nevertheless susceptible of division, and the part thereof to be returned hereunder does not exceed in value the sum of $10,000: *Provided*, That an individual shall not be entitled, under this paragraph, to the return of any money or other property owned by a partnership, association, unincorporated body of individuals, or corporation at the time it was conveyed, transferred, assigned, delivered, or paid to the Alien Property Custodian, or seized by him hereunder; or

(10) A partnership, association, other unincorporated body of individuals, or corporation, and that it is not otherwise entitled to the return of its money or other property, or any part thereof, under this section, and that such money or other property, or the proceeds thereof, if the same has been converted, does not exceed in value the sum of $10,000, or although exceeding in value the sum of $10,000, is nevertheless susceptible of division, and the part thereof to be returned hereunder does not exceed in value the sum of $10,000; or

(11) A partnership, association, or other unincorporated body of individuals, having its principal place of business within any country other than Germany, Austria, Hungary, or Austria-Hungary, or a corporation, organized or incorporated within any country other than Germany, Austria, Hungary, or Austria-Hungary, and that the control of, or more than 50 per centum of the interests or voting power in, any such partnership, association, other unincorporated body of individuals, or corporation, was at such time, and is at the time of the return of any money or other property, vested in citizens or subjects of nations, States, or free cities other than Germany, Austria, Hungary, or Austria-Hungary: *Provided, however*, That this subsection shall not affect any rights which any citizen or subject may have under paragraph (1) of this subsection; or

(12) A partnership, association, or other unincorporated body of individuals, or a corporation, and was entirely owned at such time by subjects or citizens of nations, States, or free cities other than Austria or Hungary, or Austria-Hungary and is so owned at the time of the return of its money or other property, and has filed the written consent provided for in subsection (m) of this section; or

(13) A partnership, association or other unincorporated body of individuals, having its principal place of business at such time within any country other than Austria, Hungary, or Austria-Hungary, or a corporation organized or incorporated within any country other than Austria, Hungary, or Austria-Hungary, and that the written consent provided for in subsection (m) has been filed; or

(14) An individual who at such time was a citizen or subject of Germany or who, at the time of the return of any money or other property, is a citizen or subject of Germany or is not a citizen or subject of any nation, State, or free city, and that the written consent provided for in subsection (m) of this section has been filed; or

(15) Repealed. Aug. 6, 1956, ch. 1016, §3, 70 Stat. 1073.

(16) An individual, partnership, association, or other unincorporated body of individuals, or a corporation, and that the written consent provided for in subsection (m) has been filed, and that no suit or proceeding against the United States or any agency thereof is pending in respect of such return, and that such individual has filed a written waiver renouncing on behalf of himself, his heirs, successors, and assigns any claim based upon the fact that at the time of such return he was in fact entitled to such return under any other provision of this Act [sections 1 to 6, 7 to 39, and 41 to 44 of this Appendix]; or

(17) A partnership, association, or other unincorporated body of individuals, or a corporation, and was entirely owned at such time by citizens of Austria and is so owned at the time of the return of its money or other property; or

(18) A partnership, association, or other unincorporated body of individuals, having its principal place of business at such time within Austria, or a corporation organized or incorporated within Austria; or

(19) An individual who at such time was a citizen of Austria or who, at the time of the return of any money or other property, is a citizen of Austria; or

(20) A partnership, association, or other unincorporated body of individuals, or a corporation, and was entirely owned at such time by citizens of Hungary and is so owned at the time of the return of its money or other property; or

(21) A partnership, association, or other unincorporated body of individuals, having its principal place of business at such time within Hungary, or a corporation organized or incorporated within Hungary; or

(22) An individual who at such time was a citizen of Hungary or who, at the time of the return of any money or other property, is a citizen of Hungary;

Then the President, without any application being made therefor, may order the payment, conveyance, transfer, assignment, or delivery of such money or other property held by the Alien Property Custodian or by the Treasurer of the United States, or of the interest therein to which the President shall determine such person entitled, either to the said owner or to the person by whom said property was conveyed, transferred, assigned, delivered, or paid over to the Alien Property Custodian: *Provided*, That no person shall be deemed or held to be a citizen or subject of Germany or Austria or Hungary or Austria-Hungary for the purposes of this section, even though he was such citizen or subject at the time first specified in this subsection, if he has become or shall become, ipso facto or through exercise of option, a citizen or subject of any nation or State or free city other than Germany, Austria, or Hungary, (first) under the terms of such treaties of peace as have been or may be concluded subsequent to November 11, 1918, between Germany or Austria or Hungary (of the one part) and the United States and/or three or more of the following-named powers: The British Empire, France, Italy, and Japan (of the other part), or (second) under the terms of such treaties as have been or may be concluded in pursuance of the treaties of peace aforesaid between any nation, State, or free city (of the one part) whose territories, in whole or in part, on August 4, 1914, formed a portion of the territory of Germany or Austria-Hungary and the United States and/or three or more of the following-named powers: The British Empire, France, Italy, and Japan (of the other part). For the purposes of this section any citizen or subject of a State or free city which at the time of the proposed return of money or other property of such citizen or subject hereunder forms a part of the territory of any one of the following nations: Germany, Austria, or Hungary, shall be deemed to be a citizen or subject of such nation.

And the receipt of the said owner or of the person by whom said money or other property was conveyed, transferred, assigned, delivered, or paid over to the Alien Property Custodian shall be a full acquittance and discharge of the Alien Property Custodian or the Treasurer of the United States, as the case may be, and of the United States in respect to all claims of all persons heretofore or hereafter claiming any right, title, or interest in said money or other property, or compensation or damages arising from the capture of such money or other property by the President or the Alien Property Custodian: *Provided further, however*, That except as herein provided no such action by the President shall bar any person from the prosecution of any suit at law or in equity to establish any right, title, or interest which he may have therein.

(c) Any person whose money or other property the President is authorized to return under the provisions of subsection (b) hereof may file notice of claim for the return of such money or other property, as provided in subsection (a) hereof, and thereafter may make application to the President for allowance of such claim and/or may institute suit in equity to recover such money or other property, as provided in said subsection, and with like effect. The President or the court, as the case may be, may make the same determinations with respect to citizenship and other relevant facts that the President is authorized to make under the provisions of subsection (b) hereof.

(d) Whenever an individual, deceased, would have been entitled, if living, to the return of any money or other property without filing the written consent provided for in subsection (m), then his legal representative may proceed for the return of such money or other property in the same manner as such individual might proceed if living, and such money or other property may be returned to such legal representative without requiring the appointment of an administrator, or an ancillary administrator, by a court in the United States, or to any such ancillary administrator, for distribution directly to the persons entitled thereto. Return in accordance with the provisions of this subsection may be made in any case where an application or court proceeding by any legal representative, under the provisions of this subsection before its amendment by the Settlement of War Claims Act of 1928 [Act Mar. 10, 1928, ch. 167, §12(a), 45 Stat. 271] is pending and undetermined at the time of the enactment of such Act. All bonds or other security given under the provisions of this subsection before such amendment shall be canceled or released and all sureties thereon discharged.

(e) No money or other property shall be returned nor any debt allowed under this section to any person who is a citizen or subject of any nation which was associated with the United States in the prosecution of the war, unless such nation in like case extends reciprocal rights to citizens of the United States: *Provided*, That any arrangement made by a foreign nation for the release of money and other property of American citizens and certified by the Secretary of State to the Attorney General as fair and the most advantageous arrangement obtainable shall be regarded as meeting this requirement; nor in any event shall a debt be allowed under this section unless it was owing to and owned by the claimant prior to October 6, 1917, and as to claimants other than citizens of the United States unless it arose with reference to the money or other property held by the Alien Property Custodian or Treasurer of the United States hereunder; nor shall a debt be allowed under this section unless notice of the claim has been filed, or application therefor has been made, prior to the date of the enactment of the Settlement of War Claims Act of 1928 [Act Mar. 10, 1928, ch. 167, 45 Stat. 254].

(f) Except as herein provided, the money or other property conveyed, transferred, assigned, delivered, or paid to the Alien Property Custodian, shall not be liable to lien, attachment, garnishment, trustee process, or execution, or subject to any order or decree of any court.

(g) Whenever an individual, deceased, would have been entitled, if living, to the return of any money or other property upon filing the written consent provided for in subsection (m), then his legal representative may proceed for the return of such money or other property in the same manner as such individual might proceed if living, and such money or other property may be returned, upon filing the written consent provided for in subsection (m), to such legal representative without requiring the appointment of an administrator, or an ancillary administrator, by a court in the United States, or to any such ancillary administrator, for distribution to the persons entitled thereto. This subsection shall not be construed as extinguishing or diminishing any right which any citizen of the United States may have had under this subsection prior to its amendment by the Settlement of War Claims Act of 1928 [Act Mar. 10, 1928, ch. 167, §12(c), 45 Stat. 271] to receive in full his interest in the property of any individual dying before such amendment.

(h) The aggregate value of the money or other property returned under paragraphs (9) and (10) of subsection (b) to any one person, irrespective of the number of trusts involved, shall in no case exceed $10,000.

(i) For the purposes of paragraphs (9) and (10) of subsection (b) of this section accumulated net income, dividends, interest, annuities, and other earnings, shall be considered as part of the principal.

(j) The Alien Property Custodian is authorized and directed to return to the person entitled thereto, whether or not an enemy or ally of enemy and regardless of the value, any patent, trademark, print, label, copyright, or right therein or claim thereto, which was conveyed, transferred, assigned, or delivered to the Alien Property Custodian, or seized by him, and which has not been sold, licensed, or otherwise disposed of under the provisions of this Act [sections 1 to 6, 7 to 39, and 41 to 44 of this Appendix], and to return any such patent, trademark, print, label, copyright, or right therein or claim thereto, which has been licensed, except that any patent, trade-mark, print, label, copyright, or right therein or claim thereto, which is returned by the Alien Property Custodian and which has been licensed, or in respect of which any contract has been entered into, or which is subject to any lien or encumbrance, shall be returned subject to the license, contract, lien, or encumbrance.

(k) Except as provided in section 27 [section 27 of this Appendix], paragraphs (12) to (22), both inclusive, of subsection (b) of this section shall apply to the proceeds received from the sale, license, or other disposition of any patent, trademark, print, label, copyright, or right therein or claim thereto, conveyed, transferred, assigned, or delivered to the Alien Property Custodian, or seized by him.

(*l*) This section shall apply to royalties paid to the Alien Property Custodian, in accordance with a judgment or decree in a suit brought under subsection (f) of section 10 [section 10(f) of this Appendix]; but shall not apply to any other money paid to the Alien Property Custodian under section 10 [section 10 of this Appendix].

(m) No money or other property shall be returned under paragraph (12), (13), (14), or (16) of subsection (b) or under subsection (g) or (n) or (to the extent therein provided) under subsection (p), unless the person entitled thereto files a written consent to a postponement of the return of an amount equal to 20 per centum of the aggregate value of such money or other property (at the time, as nearly as may be, of the return), as determined by the Alien Property Custodian, and the investment of such amount in accordance with the provisions of section 25 [section 25 of this Appendix]. Such amount shall be deducted from the money to be returned to such person, so far as possible, and the balance shall be deducted from the proceeds of the sale of so much of the property as may be necessary, unless such person pays the balance to the Alien Property Custodian, except that no property shall be sold prior to the expiration of six years from the date of the enactment of the Settlement of War Claims Act of 1928 [Act Mar. 10, 1928, ch. 167, 45 Stat. 254] without the consent of the person entitled thereto. The amounts so deducted shall be returned to the persons entitled thereto as provided in subsection (f) of section 25 [section 25(f) of this Appendix]. The sale of any such property shall be made in accordance with the provisions of section 12 [section 12 of this Appendix], except that the provisions of such section relating to sales or resales to, or for the benefit of, citizens of the United States shall not be applicable. If such aggregate value of the money or other property to be returned under paragraph (12), (13), (14), or (16) of subsection (b) or under subsection (g) is less than $2,000, then the written consent shall not be required and the money or other property shall be returned in full without the temporary retention and investment of 20 per centum thereof.

(n) In the case of property consisting of stock or other interest in any corporation, association, company, or trust, or of bonded or other indebtedness thereof, evidenced by certificates of stock or by bonds or by other certificates of interest therein or indebtedness thereof, or consisting of dividends or interest or other accruals thereon, where the right, title, and interest in the property (but not the actual certificate or bond or other certificate of interest or indebtedness) was conveyed, transferred, assigned, delivered, or paid to the Alien Property Custodian, or seized by him, if the President determines that the owner thereof or of any interest therein has acquired such ownership by assignment, transfer, or sale of such certificate or bond or other certificate of interest or indebtedness, (it being the intent of this subsection that such assignment, transfer, or sale shall not be deemed invalid hereunder by reason of such conveyance, transfer, assignment, delivery, or payment to the Alien Property Custodian or seizure by him) and that the written consent provided for in subsection (m) of this section has been filed, then the President may make in respect of such property an order of the same character, upon the same conditions, and with the same effect, as in cases provided for in subsection (b), including the benefits of subsection (c).

(*o*) The provisions of paragraph (12), (13), (14), (17), (18), (19), (20), (21), or (22) of subsection (b), or of subsection (m) or (n) of this section, and (except to the extent therein provided) the provisions of paragraph (16) of subsection (b), shall not be construed as diminishing or extinguishing any right under any other provision of this Act [sections 1 to 6, 7 to 39, and 41 to 44 of this Appendix] in force immediately prior to the enactment of the Settlement of War Claims Act of 1928 [Act Mar. 10, 1928, ch. 167, 45 Stat. 254].

(p) The Alien Property Custodian shall transfer the money or other property in the trust of any partnership, association, or other unincorporated body of individuals, or corporation, the existence of which has terminated, to trusts in the names of the persons (including the German Government and members of the former ruling family) who have succeeded to its claim or interest; and the provisions of subsection (a) of this section relating to the collection of a debt (by order of the President or of a court) out of money or other property held by the Alien Property Custodian or the Treasurer of the United States shall be applicable to the debts of such successor and any such debt may be collected out of the money or other property in any of such trusts if not returnable under subsection (a) of this section. Subject to the above provisions as to the collection of debts, each such successor (except the German Government and members of the former ruling family) may proceed for the return of the amount so transferred to his trust, in the same manner as such partnership, association, or other unincorporated body of individuals, or corporation might proceed if still in existence. If such partnership, association, or other unincorporated body of individuals, or corporation, would have been entitled to the return of its money or other property only upon filing the written consent provided for in subsection (m), then the successor shall be entitled to the return under this subsection only upon filing such written consent.

(q) The return of money or other property under paragraph (15), (17), (18), (19), (20), (21), or (22) of subsection (b) (relating to the return of Austrian and Hungarian nationals) shall be subject to the limitations imposed by subsections (d) and (e) of section 7 of the Settlement of War Claims Act of 1928 [Act Mar. 10, 1928, ch. 167, §7(d), (e), 45 Stat. 265, 266].

(Oct. 6, 1917, ch. 106, §9, 40 Stat. 419; July 11, 1919, ch. 6, §1, 41 Stat. 35; June 5, 1920, ch. 241, 41 Stat.

977; Feb. 27, 1921, ch. 76, 41 Stat. 1147; Dec. 21, 1921, ch. 13, 42 Stat. 351; Dec. 27, 1922, ch. 13, 42 Stat. 1065; Mar. 4, 1923, ch. 285, §1, 42 Stat. 1511; May 7, 1926, ch. 252, 44 Stat. 406; Mar. 10, 1928, ch. 167, §§11–14, 20, 45 Stat. 270–273, 277; June 25, 1936, ch. 804, 49 Stat. 1921; Aug. 24, 1937, ch. 745, 50 Stat. 748; June 25, 1948, ch. 646, §32(a), 62 Stat. 991; May 24, 1949, ch. 139, §127, 63 Stat. 107; Aug. 6, 1956, ch. 1016, §3, 70 Stat. 1073; Pub. L. 87–846, title II, §203, Oct. 22, 1962, 76 Stat. 1113.)

AMENDMENTS

1962—Subsec. (a). Pub. L. 87–846 inserted provisions for sale of claimed property in time of war or during national emergency, publication of notice in Federal Register of intention to sell, deposit of net proceeds of sale in a special account in the Treasury, satisfaction of the claim from such net proceeds, election to waive claims to net proceeds and to claim just compensation, judicial determination of amount of compensation, order for payment, judgment against United States and notification of Secretary of the Treasury respecting the determination of election made.

1956—Subsec. (b)(15). Act Aug. 6, 1956, repealed par. (15) which related to property of the Austro-Hungarian Bank.

1937—Subsec. (e). Act Aug. 24, 1937, inserted proviso that arrangements by foreign nations certified by Secretary of State would be regarded as meeting reciprocity requirement for return of property.

1928—Subsec. (b)(12) to (22). Act Mar. 10, 1928, §11, added pars. (12) to (22).

Subsec. (d). Act Mar. 10, 1928, §12(a), amended subsec. (d) generally.

Subsec. (e). Act Mar. 10, 1928, §12(b), inserted "; nor shall a debt be allowed under this section unless notice of the claim has been filed, or application therefor has been made, prior to the date of the enactment of the Settlement of War Claims Act of 1928" before period at end.

Subsec. (g). Act Mar. 10, 1928, §12(c), amended subsec. (g) generally.

Subsecs. (*l*) to (q). Act Mar. 10, 1928, §§13, 14, added subsecs. (*l*) to (q).

1926—Subsec. (b)(3A), (3B). Act May 7, 1926, added pars. (3A) and (3B).

1923—Act Mar. 4, 1923, added pars. (9) to (11) of subsec. (b), and subsecs. (g) to (j) and redesignated former subsec. (g) as (k).

1922—Subsec. (a). Act Dec. 27, 1922, increased time limit for instituting a suit from eighteen to thirty months.

1921—Subsec. (a). Act Dec. 21, 1921, increased time limit for instituting a suit from six to eighteen months.

Subsec. (b). Act Feb. 27, 1921, added to pars. (2) and (3) requirement that money or property be acquired subsequent to Jan. 1, 1917, and struck out in par. (3) requirement that citizenship be by birth in the United States.

1920—Act June 5, 1920, added pars. (1) to (8) of subsec. (b) and added subsecs. (c) to (g), latter two subsecs. having formerly been last two paragraphs, respectively, of subsec. (b).

1919—Act July 11, 1919, struck out requirement of owner's assent to the transfer of property to the Custodian, gave the Supreme Court of the District of Columbia co-extensive jurisdiction with the District Courts over suits, and inserted proviso permitting the Custodian to acquit his responsibility by transferring the property of persons, who were enemies by reason of residence in enemy occupied countries, to those persons or their designated representatives.

CHANGE OF NAME

In subsec. (a), act June 25, 1936, substituted "the district court of the United States for the District of Columbia" for "the Supreme Court of the District of Columbia", and act June 25, 1948, as amended by act May 24, 1949, substituted "United States District Court for the District of Columbia" for "district court of the United States for the District of Columbia".

TRANSFER OF FUNCTIONS

Functions of Alien Property Custodian and Office of Alien Property Custodian, except those relating to property or interest in Philippines, vested in Attorney General. See notes set out under section 6 of this Appendix.

SETTLEMENT OF WAR CLAIMS ACT OF 1928

Act Mar. 10, 1928, ch. 167, 45 Stat. 254, known as the Settlement of War Claims Act of 1928, provided for the settlement of certain claims of American nationals against Germany, Austria, and Hungary, and the nationals of Germany, Austria, and Hungary against the United States, and for the ultimate return of all property held by the Alien Property Custodian.

Sections 9(c) to 19 of the act were classified to sections 9, 10, 20, and 22 to 31 of this Appendix. Sections 1 to 9(b) of the act are not classified to the Code.

The act has been amended to extend the time of presenting claims under it several times as follows: Acts Mar. 10, 1930, ch. 175, 46 Stat. 84; June 14, 1932, ch. 259, 47 Stat. 318; Mar. 3, 1933, ch. 210, 47 Stat. 1488; June 12, 1933, ch. 60, 48 Stat. 125; June 18, 1934, ch. 608, 48 Stat. 1019; June 27, 1934, ch. 851, 48 Stat. 1267; June 26, 1936, ch. 852, 49 Stat. 1984; May 23, 1938, ch. 263, 52 Stat. 437. The act of May 23, 1938, was the final extension and it allowed the presentation of claims up to 12 years after Mar. 10, 1938.

Act Aug. 6, 1947, ch. 506, 61 Stat. 789, amended section 4(b), (c) of act Mar. 10, 1928, to change the order of priority for payment of claims out of the German special deposit account.

EFFECT OF TERMINATION OF STATE OF WAR BETWEEN UNITED STATES AND GERMANY

Termination of war by Joint Res. Oct. 19, 1951, ch. 519, 65 Stat. 451, as not affecting property already vested, see said Joint Res. Oct. 19, 1951, set out as a note preceding section 1 of this Appendix.

WORLD WAR II ALIEN PROPERTY CUSTODIAN

Reestablishment and termination of Office of Alien Property Custodian during World War II, see notes set out under section 6 of this Appendix.

SECTION REFERRED TO IN OTHER SECTIONS

This section is referred to in sections 4, 12, 25, 26, 29, 30, 32, 33, 35, 36, 44 of this Appendix; title 28 section 2680.

§10. Acts permitted; applications for patents, or registration of trade-marks or copyrights; payment of tax in relation thereto; licenses under enemy owned patent or copyright; statements by licensees; term and cancellation; suits against licensees; restraining infringements; powers of attorney; keeping secret inventions

Nothing contained in this Act [sections 1 to 6, 7 to 39, and 41 to 44 of this Appendix] shall be held to make unlawful any of the following acts:

(a) Repealed. Aug. 8, 1946, ch. 910, §13, 60 Stat. 944.

(b) Any citizen of the United States, or any corporation organized within the United States, may, when duly authorized by the President, pay to an enemy or ally of enemy any tax, annuity, or fee which may be required by the laws of such enemy or ally of enemy nation in relation to patents and trade-marks, prints, labels, and copyrights; and any such citizen or corporation may file and prosecute an application for letters patent or for registration of trade-mark, print, label, or copyright in the country of an enemy, or of an ally of enemy after first submitting such application to the President and receiving license so to file and prosecute, and to pay the fees required by law and customary agents' fees, the maximum amount of which in each case shall be subject to the control of the President.

(c) Any citizen of the United States or any corporation organized within the United States desiring to manufacture, or cause to be manufactured, a machine, manufacture, composition of matter, or design, or to carry on, or to use any trade-mark, print, label or cause to be carried on, a process under any patent or copyrighted matter owned or controlled by an enemy or ally of enemy at any time during the existence of a state of war may apply to the President for a license; and the President is authorized to grant such a license, nonexclusive or exclusive as he shall deem best, provided he shall be of the opinion that such grant is for the public welfare, and that the applicant is able and intends in good faith to manufacture, or cause to be manufactured, the machine, manufacture, composition of matter, or design, or to carry on, or cause to be carried on, the process or to use the trade-mark, print, label or copyrighted matter. The President may prescribe the conditions of this license, including the fixing of prices of articles and products necessary to the health of the military and naval forces of the United States or the successful prosecution of the war, and the rules and regulations under which such license may be granted and the fee which shall be charged therefor, not exceeding $100, and not exceeding one per centum of the fund deposited as hereinafter provided. Such license shall be a complete defense to any suit at law or in equity instituted by the enemy or ally of enemy owners of the letters patent, trade-mark, print, label or copyright, or otherwise, against the licensee for infringement or for damages, royalty, or other money award on account of anything done by the licensee under such license, except as provided in subsection (f) hereof.

(d) The licensee shall file with the President a full statement of the extent of the use and enjoyment of the license, and of the prices received in such form and at such stated periods (at least annually) as the President may prescribe; and the licensee shall pay at such times as may be required to the alien property custodian not to exceed five per centum of the gross sums received by the licensee from the sale of said inventions or use of the trade-mark, print, label or copyrighted matter, or, if the President shall so order, five per centum of the value of the use of such inventions, trade-marks, prints, labels or copyrighted matter to the licensee as established by the President; and sums so paid shall be deposited by said alien property custodian forthwith in the Treasury of the United States as a trust fund for the said licensee and for the owner of the said patent, trade-mark, print, label or copyright registration as hereinafter provided, to be paid from the Treasury upon order of the court, as provided in subsection (f) of this section, or upon the direction of the alien property custodian.

(e) Unless surrendered or terminated as provided in this Act [sections 1 to 6, 7 to 39, and 41 to 44 of this Appendix], any license granted hereunder shall continue during the term fixed in the license or in the absence of any such limitation during the term of the patent, trade-mark, print, label, or copyright registration under which is it granted. Upon violation by the licensee of any of the provisions of this Act [said sections], or of the conditions of the license, the President may, after due notice and hearing, cancel any license granted by him.

(f) The owner of any patent, trade-mark, print, label, or copyright under which a license is granted hereunder may, after the end of the war and until the expiration of one year thereafter, file a bill in equity against the licensee in the district court of the United States for the district in which the said licensee resides, or, if a corporation, in which it has its principal place of business (to which suit the Treasurer of the United States shall be made a party), for recovery from the said licensee for all use and enjoyment of the said patented invention, trade-mark, print, label, or copyrighted matter: *Provided, however*, That whenever suit is brought, as above, notice shall be filed with the alien property custodian within thirty days after date of entry of suit: *Provided further*, That the licensee may make any and all defenses which would be available were no license granted. The court on due proceedings had may adjudge and decree to the said owner payment of a reasonable royalty. The amount of said judgment and decree, when final, shall be paid on order of the court to the owner of the patent from the fund deposited by the licensee, so far as such deposit will satisfy said judgment and decree; and the said payment shall be in full or partial satisfaction of said judgment and decree, as the facts may appear; and if, after payment of all such judgments and decrees, there shall remain any balance of said deposit, such balance shall be repaid to the licensee on order of the alien property custodian. If no suit is brought within one year after the end of the war, or no notice is filed as above required, then the licensee shall not be liable to make any further deposits, and all funds deposited by him shall be repaid to him on order of the alien property custodian. Upon entry of suit and notice filed as above required, or upon repayment of funds as above provided, the liability of the licensee to make further reports to the President shall cease.

If suit is brought as above provided, the court may, at any time, terminate the license, and may, in such event, issue an injunction to restrain the licensee from infringement thereafter, or the court, in case the licensee, prior to suit, shall have made investment of capital based on possession of the license, may continue the license for such period and upon such terms and with such royalties as it shall find to be just and reasonable.

In the case of any such patent, trade-mark, print, label, or copyright, conveyed, assigned, transferred, or delivered to the Alien Property Custodian or seized by him, any suit brought under this subsection, within the time limited therein, shall be considered as having been brought by the owner within the meaning of this subsection, in so far as such suit relates to royalties for the period prior to the sale by the

Alien Property Custodian of such patent, trade-mark, print, label, or copyright, if brought either by the Alien Property Custodian or by the person who was the owner thereof immediately prior to the date such patent, trade-mark, print, label, or copyright was seized or otherwise acquired by the Alien Property Custodian.

(g) Any enemy, or ally of enemy, may institute and prosecute suits in equity against any person other than a licensee under this Act [sections 1 to 6, 7 to 39, and 41 to 44 of this Appendix] to enjoin infringement of letters patent, trade-mark, print, label, and copyrights in the United States owned or controlled by said enemy or ally of enemy, in the same manner and to the extent that he would be entitled so to do if the United States was not at war: *Provided*, That no final judgment or decree shall be entered in favor of such enemy or ally of enemy by any court except after thirty days' notice to the alien property custodian. Such notice shall be in writing and shall be served in the same manner as civil process of Federal courts.

(h) All powers of attorney heretofore or hereafter granted by an enemy or ally of enemy to any person within the United States, in so far as they may be requisite to the performance of acts authorized in subsections (a) and (g) of this section, shall be valid.

(i) Whenever the publication of an invention by the granting of a patent may, in the opinion of the President, be detrimental to the public safety or defense, or may assist the enemy or endanger the successful prosecution of the war, he may order that the invention be kept secret and withhold the grant of a patent until the end of the war: *Provided*, That the invention disclosed in the application for said patent may be held abandoned upon it being established before or by the Under Secretary of Commerce for Intellectual Property and Director of the United States Patent and Trademark Office that, in violation of said order, said invention has been published or that an application for a patent therefor has been filed in any other country, by the inventor or his assigns or legal representatives, without the consent or approval of the commissioner or under a license of the President.

When an applicant whose patent is withheld as herein provided and who faithfully obeys the order of the President above referred to shall tender his invention to the Government of the United States for its use, he shall, if he ultimately receives a patent, have the right to sue for compensation in the United States Court of Federal Claims, such right to compensation to begin from the date of the use of the invention by the Government.

(Oct. 6, 1917, ch. 106, §10, 40 Stat. 420; Mar. 10, 1928, ch. 167, §19, 45 Stat. 277; Aug. 8, 1946, ch. 910, §13, 60 Stat. 944; Pub. L. 97–164, title I, §160(a)(17), Apr. 2, 1982, 96 Stat. 48; Pub. L. 102–572, title IX, §902(b)(1), Oct. 29, 1992, 106 Stat. 4516; Pub. L. 106–113, div. B, §1000(a)(9) [title IV, §4732(b)(26)], Nov. 29, 1999, 113 Stat. 1536, 1501A–585.)

PRIOR PROVISIONS

The provisions of subsection (i) of this section are similar to the provisions of act Oct. 6, 1917, ch. 95, 40 Stat. 394 (formerly classified to section 42 of Title 35, Patents), which was repealed and superseded by act Feb. 1, 1952, ch. 4, 66 Stat. 3. Act Feb. 1, 1952 was also repealed by act July 19, 1952, ch. 950, §5, 66 Stat. 815. See section 181 et seq. of Title 35.

AMENDMENTS

1999—Subsec. (i). Pub. L. 106–113 substituted "Under Secretary of Commerce for Intellectual Property and Director of the United States Patent and Trademark Office" for "Commissioner of Patents".

1992—Subsec. (i). Pub. L. 102–572 substituted "United States Court of Federal Claims" for "United States Claims Court".

1982—Subsec. (i). Pub. L. 97–164 substituted "United States Claims Court" for "Court of Claims".

1946—Subsec. (a). Act Aug. 8, 1946, repealed subsec. (a).

1928—Subsec. (f). Act Mar. 10, 1928, added par. at end.

EFFECTIVE DATE OF 1999 AMENDMENT

Amendment by Pub. L. 106–113 effective 4 months after Nov. 29, 1999, see section 1000(a)(9) [title IV, §4731] of Pub. L. 106–113, set out as a note under section 1 of Title 35, Patents.

EFFECTIVE DATE OF 1992 AMENDMENT

Amendment by Pub. L. 102–572 effective Oct. 29, 1992, see section 911 of Pub. L. 102–572, set out as a note under section 171 of Title 28, Judiciary and Judicial Procedure.

EFFECTIVE DATE OF 1982 AMENDMENT

Amendment by Pub. L. 97–164 effective Oct. 1, 1982, see section 402 of Pub. L. 97–164, set out as a note under section 171 of Title 28, Judiciary and Judicial Procedure.

TRANSFER OF FUNCTIONS

Functions of Alien Property Custodian and Office of Alien Property Custodian, except those relating to property or interest in Philippines, vested in Attorney General. See notes set out under section 6 of this Appendix.

WORLD WAR II ALIEN PROPERTY CUSTODIAN

Reestablishment and termination of Office of Alien Property Custodian during World War II, see notes set out under section 6 of this Appendix.

PRESIDENT'S PROCLAMATION

Proclamation of May 24, 1917, 40 Stat. 1669, authorized citizens owning letters patent issued by the German Empire to pay any tax, annuity or fee required by the laws of the German Empire for preservation of their rights in the letters patent.

SECTION REFERRED TO IN OTHER SECTIONS

This section is referred to in sections 5, 7, 9, 12 of this Appendix; title 28 section 2680.

§11. Importations prohibited

Whenever during the present war the President shall find that the public safety so requires and shall make proclamation thereof it shall be unlawful to import into the United States from any country named in such proclamation any article or articles mentioned in such proclamation except at such time or times, and under such regulations or orders, and subject to such limitations and exceptions as the President shall prescribe, until otherwise ordered by the President or by Congress: *Provided, however*, That no preference shall be given to the ports of one State over those of another.

(Oct. 6, 1917, ch. 106, §11, 40 Stat. 422.)

EXTENSION OF IMPORT LIMITATIONS

Joint Res. Nov. 19, 1919, ch. 121, 41 Stat. 361, continued provisions of section 1 et seq. of this Appendix and proclamations limiting imports to Jan. 15, 1920.

PRESIDENT'S PROCLAMATIONS

Proclamation of Nov. 28, 1917, 40 Stat. 1722, forbade importation of various articles except under license granted by War Trade Board.

Proclamation of Feb. 14, 1918, 40 Stat. 1748, added other articles to list of articles upon which import limitations were placed.

SECTION REFERRED TO IN OTHER SECTIONS

This section is referred to in title 28 section 2680.

§12. Property transferred to Alien Property Custodian

All moneys (including checks and drafts payable on demand) paid to or received by the alien property custodian pursuant to this Act [sections 1 to 6, 7 to 39, and 41 to 44 of this Appendix] shall be deposited forthwith in the Treasury of the United States, and may be invested and reinvested by the Secretary of the Treasury in United States bonds or United States certificates of indebtedness, under such rules and regulations as the President shall prescribe for such deposit, investment, and sale of securities; and as soon after the end of the war as the President shall deem practicable, such securities shall be sold and the proceeds deposited in the Treasury.

All other property of an enemy, or ally of enemy, conveyed, transferred, assigned, delivered, or paid to the alien property custodian hereunder shall be safely held and administered by him except as hereinafter provided; and the President is authorized to designate as a depositary, or depositaries, of property of an enemy or ally of enemy, any bank, or banks, or trust company, or trust companies, or other suitable depositary or depositaries, located and doing business in the United States. The alien property custodian may deposit with such designated depositary or depositaries, or with the Secretary of the Treasury, any stocks, bonds, notes, time drafts, time bills of exchange, or other securities, or property (except money or checks or drafts payable on demand which are required to be deposited with the Secretary of the Treasury) and such depositary or depositaries shall be authorized and empowered to collect any dividends or interest or income that may become due and any maturing obligations held for the account of such custodian. Any moneys collected on said account shall be paid and deposited forthwith by said depositary or by the alien property custodian into the Treasury of the United States as hereinbefore provided.

The President shall require all such designated depositaries to execute and file bonds sufficient in his judgment to protect property on deposit, such bonds to be conditioned as he may direct.

The alien property custodian shall be vested with all of the powers of a common-law trustee in respect of all property, other than money, which has been or shall be, or which has been or shall be required to be, conveyed, transferred, assigned, delivered, or paid over to him in pursuance of the provisions of this Act [said sections], and, in addition thereto, acting under the supervision and direction of the President, and under such rules and regulations as the President shall prescribe, shall have power to manage such property and do any act or things in respect thereof or make any disposition thereof or of any part thereof, by sale or otherwise, and exercise any rights or powers which may be or become appurtenant thereto or to the ownership thereof in like manner as though he were the absolute owner thereof: *Provided*, That any property sold under this Act [said sections] except when sold to the United States, shall be sold only to American citizens, at public sale to the highest bidder, after public advertisement of time and place of sale which shall be where the property or a major portion thereof is situated, unless the President stating the reasons therefor, in the public interest shall otherwise determine: *Provided further*, That when sold at public sale, the alien property custodian upon the order of the President stating the reasons therefor, shall have the right to reject all bids and resell such property at public sale or otherwise as the President may direct. Any person purchasing property from the alien property custodian for an undisclosed principal, or for re-sale to a person not a citizen of the United States, or for the benefit of a person not a citizen of the United States, shall be guilty of a misdemeanor, and, upon conviction, shall be subject to a fine of not more than $10,000, or imprisonment for not more than ten years, or both, and the property shall be forfeited to the United States. It shall be the duty of every corporation incorporated within the United States and every unincorporated association, or company, or trustee, or trustees within the United States issuing shares or certificates representing beneficial interests to transfer such shares or certificates upon its, his, or their books into the name of the alien property custodian upon demand, accompanied by the presentation of the certificates which represent such shares or beneficial interests. The alien property custodian shall forthwith deposit in the Treasury of the United States, as hereinbefore provided, the proceeds of any such property or rights so sold by him.

Any money or property required or authorized by the provisions of this Act [said sections] to be paid, conveyed, transferred, assigned, or delivered to the alien property custodian shall, if said custodian shall so direct by written order, be paid, conveyed, transferred, assigned, or delivered to the Treasurer of the United States with the same effect as if to the alien property custodian.

After the end of the war any claim of any enemy or of an ally of enemy to any money or other property received and held by the alien property custodian or deposited in the United States Treasury, shall be settled as Congress shall direct: *Provided, however*, That on order of the President as set forth in section nine hereof [section 9 of this Appendix], or of the court, as set forth in sections nine and ten hereof [sections 9 and 10 of this Appendix], the alien property custodian or the Treasurer of the United States, as the case may be, shall forthwith convey, transfer, assign, and pay to the person to whom the President shall so order, or in whose behalf the court shall enter final judgment or decree, any property of an enemy or ally of enemy held by said custodian or by said Treasurer, so far as may be necessary to comply with said order of the President or said final judgment or decree of the court: *And provided further*, That the Treasurer of the United States, on order of the alien property custodian shall, as provided in section ten hereof [section 10 of this Appendix], repay to the licensee any funds deposited by said licensee.

(Oct. 6, 1917, ch. 106, §12, 40 Stat. 423; Mar. 28, 1918, ch. 28, §1, 40 Stat. 460.)

AMENDMENTS

1918—Act Mar. 28, 1918, required that property sold be sold at public sale to American citizens, gave Custodian right to reject bids, and made violations of sale regulations subject to fine or imprisonment as misdemeanors.

TRANSFER OF FUNCTIONS

Functions of Alien Property Custodian and Office of Alien Property Custodian, except those relating to property or interest in Philippines, vested in Attorney General. See notes set out under section 6 of this Appendix.

DELEGATION OF POWER

Ex. Ord. No. 6237–A, eff. July 30, 1933, provided:

"I hereby vest in the Alien Property Custodian, and in the event of his death, resignation, absence, or disability, in the General Counsel, and in the event of his death, resignation, absence, or disability during his period of authority, then in the Director of Finance and Accounts of the Office of the Alien Property Custodian, all power and authority conferred upon me by the provisions of the act approved October 6, 1917, known as the "Trading With the Enemy Act," as amended [sections 1 to 6, 7 to 39, and 41 to 44 of this Appendix] pertaining to the deposit, transfer, and payment of moneys, and interest which may have accrued thereon, which may be or have been deposited with the Treasurer of the United States, and to release and deliver property held under and by virtue of said acts: *Provided, however*, That all claims which are required to be submitted to the Attorney General and to the President, as provided in Executive Order No. 4862 of April 23, 1928, shall continue to be submitted to the Attorney General and to the President. Any order of payment of money, and interest, which may be executed by said officials shall constitute a ratification of all previous orders or acts, by virtue of which the funds in the possession of the Treasurer of the United States have been placed to the credit of the particular trusts on which such orders are drawn. I hereby revoke all former orders in conflict herewith."

Ex. Ord. No. 7894, eff. May 23, 1938, 3 F.R. 998 authorized and directed "the Attorney General of the United States to exercise all power and authority conferred upon the President by section 12 of the said [Trading with the Enemy] act, as amended [section 12 of this Appendix]."

WORLD WAR II ALIEN PROPERTY CUSTODIAN

Reestablishment and termination of Office of Alien Property Custodian during World War II, see notes set out under section 6 of this Appendix.

SECTION REFERRED TO IN OTHER SECTIONS

This section is referred to in sections 9, 26, 28 of this Appendix; title 28 section 2680.

§13. Statements by masters of vessels and owners of cargoes before granting clearances

During the present war, in addition to the facts required by sections forty-one hundred and ninety-seven [46 App. U.S.C. 91], forty-one hundred and ninety-eight,[1] and forty-two hundred[1] of the Revised Statutes, as amended by the Act of June fifteenth, nineteen hundred and seventeen, to be set out in the master's and shipper's manifests before clearance will be issued to vessels bound to foreign ports, the master or person in charge of any vessel, before departure of such vessel from port, shall deliver to the collector of customs of the district wherein such vessel is located a statement duly verified by oath that the cargo is not shipped or to be delivered in violation of this Act [sections 1 to 6, 7 to 39, and 41 to 44 of this Appendix], and the owners, shippers, or consignors of the cargo of such vessels shall in like manner deliver to the collector like statement under oath as to the cargo or the parts thereof laden or shipped by them, respectively, which statement shall contain also the names and addresses of the actual consignees of the cargo, or if the shipment is made to a bank or other broker, factor, or agent, the names and addresses of the persons who are the actual consignees on whose account the shipment is made. The master or person in control of the vessel shall, on reaching port of destination of any of the cargo, deliver a copy of the manifest and of the said master's, owner's shipper's, or consignor's statement to the American consular officer of the district in which the cargo is unladen.

(Oct. 6, 1917, ch. 106, §13, 40 Stat. 424.)

REFERENCES IN TEXT

The amendment by act June 15, 1917, referred to in text, probably means the amendment made by section 4 of title V of act June 15, 1917, ch. 30, 40 Stat. 222.

Section 4198 of the Revised Statutes, referred to in text, which was classified to section 94 of former Title 46, Shipping, was repealed by Pub. L. 103–182, title VI, §690(a)(8), Dec. 8, 1993, 107 Stat. 2223.

Section 4200 of the Revised Statutes, referred to in text, which was classified to section 92 of former Title 46, was repealed by Pub. L. 87–826, §3, Oct. 15, 1962, 76 Stat. 953.

TRANSFER OF FUNCTIONS

All offices of collector of customs, comptroller of customs, surveyor of customs, and appraiser of merchandise in Bureau of Customs of Department of the Treasury to which appointments were required to be made by President with advice and consent of Senate ordered abolished with such offices to be terminated not later than Dec. 31, 1966, by Reorg. Plan No. 1 of 1965, eff. May 25, 1965, 30 F.R. 7035, 79 Stat. 1317, set out in the Appendix to Title 5, Government Organization and Employees. All functions of offices eliminated were already vested in Secretary of the Treasury by Reorg. Plan No. 26 of 1950, eff. July 31, 1950, 15 F.R. 4935, 64 Stat. 1280, set out in the Appendix to Title 5.

SECTION REFERRED TO IN OTHER SECTIONS

This section is referred to in section 14 of this Appendix; title 28 section 2680.

§14. False manifest; refusal of clearance; reports of gold or silver coin in cargoes for export

During the present war, whenever there is reasonable cause to believe that the manifest or the additional statements under oath required by the preceding section [section 13 of this Appendix] are false or that any vessel, domestic or for-

[1] See References in Text note below.

eign, is about to carry out of the United States any property to or for the account or benefit of an enemy, or ally of enemy, or any property or person whose export, taking out, or transport will be in violation of law, the collector of customs for the district in which such vessel is located is authorized and empowered subject to review by the President to refuse clearance to any such vessel, domestic or foreign, for which clearance is required by law, and by formal notice served upon the owners, master, or person or persons in command or charge of any domestic vessel for which clearance is not required by law, to forbid the departure of such vessel from the port, and it shall thereupon be unlawful for such vessel to depart.

The collector of customs shall, during the present war, in each case report to the President the amount of gold or silver coin or bullion or other moneys of the United States contained in any cargo intended for export. Such report shall include the names and addresses of the consignors and consignees, together with any facts known to the collector with reference to such shipment and particularly those which may indicate that such gold or silver coin or bullion or moneys of the United States may be intended for delivery or may be delivered, directly or indirectly, to an enemy or an ally of enemy.

(Oct. 6, 1917, ch. 106, §14, 40 Stat. 424.)

TRANSFER OF FUNCTIONS

All offices of collector of customs, comptroller of customs, surveyor of customs, and appraiser of merchandise in Bureau of Customs of Department of the Treasury to which appointments were required to be made by President with advice and consent of Senate ordered abolished with such offices to be terminated not later than Dec. 31, 1966, by Reorg. Plan No. 1 of 1965, eff. May 25, 1965, 30 F.R. 7035, 79 Stat. 1317, set out in the Appendix to Title 5, Government Organization and Employees. All functions of offices eliminated were already vested in Secretary of the Treasury by Reorg. Plan No. 26 of 1950, eff. July 31, 1950, 15 F.R. 4935, 64 Stat. 1280, set out in the Appendix to Title 5.

SECTION REFERRED TO IN OTHER SECTIONS

This section is referred to in title 28 section 2680.

§15. Omitted

CODIFICATION

Section, act Oct. 6, 1917, ch. 106, §15, 40 Stat. 425, made an appropriation of $450,000 for purpose of carrying out the Act during fiscal year ending June 30, 1918.

§16. Offenses; punishment; forfeitures of property

(a) Whoever shall willfully violate any of the provisions of this Act [sections 1 to 6, 7 to 39, and 41 to 44 of this Appendix] or of any license, rule, or regulation issued thereunder, and whoever shall willfully violate, neglect, or refuse to comply with any order of the President issued in compliance with the provisions of the Act [said sections] shall, upon conviction, be fined not more than $1,000,000, or if a natural person, be fined not more than $100,000, or imprisoned for not more than ten years or both; and the officer, director, or agent of any corporation who knowingly participates in such violation shall, upon conviction, be fined not more than $100,000 or imprisoned for not more than ten years or both.

(b)(1) A civil penalty of not to exceed $50,000 may be imposed by the Secretary of the Treasury on any person who violates any license, order, rule, or regulation issued in compliance with the provisions of this Act [sections 1 to 6, 7 to 39, and 41 to 44 of this Appendix].

(2) Any property, funds, securities, papers, or other articles or documents, or any vessel, together with its tackle, apparel, furniture, and equipment, that is the subject of a violation under paragraph (1) shall, at the direction of the Secretary of the Treasury, be forfeited to the United States Government.

(3) The penalties provided under this subsection may be imposed only on the record after opportunity for an agency hearing in accordance with sections 554 through 557 of title 5, United States Code, with the right to prehearing discovery.

(4) Judicial review of any penalty imposed under this subsection may be had to the extent provided in section 702 of title 5, United States Code.

(c) Upon conviction, any property, funds, securities, papers, or other articles or documents, or any vessel, together with tackle, apparel, furniture, and equipment, concerned in any violation of subsection (a) may be forfeited to the United States.

(Oct. 6, 1917, ch. 106, §16, 40 Stat. 425; Pub. L. 95–223, title I, §103(a), Dec. 28, 1977, 91 Stat. 1626; Pub. L. 102–393, title VI, §628, Oct. 6, 1992, 106 Stat. 1772; Pub. L. 102–484, div. A, title XVII, §1710(c), Oct. 23, 1992, 106 Stat. 2580; Pub. L. 104–114, title I, §102(d), Mar. 12, 1996, 110 Stat. 792.)

AMENDMENTS

1996—Pub. L. 104–114, §102(d)(3)(A), made technical amendment inserting section designation in original.

Subsec. (a). Pub. L. 104–114, §102(d)(3)(B), substituted "participates" for "participants".

Subsec. (b). Pub. L. 104–114, §102(d)(1), amended subsec. (b), as added by Pub. L. 102–484, generally. Prior to amendment, subsec. (b) read as follows:

"(b)(1) The Secretary of the Treasury may impose a civil penalty of not more than $50,000 on any person who violates any license, order, rule, or regulation issued under this Act.

"(2) Any property, funds, securities, papers, or other articles or documents, or any vessel, together with its tackle, apparel, furniture, and equipment, that is the subject of a violation under paragraph (1) shall, at the discretion of the Secretary of the Treasury, be forfeited to the United States Government.

"(3) The penalties provided under this subsection may not be imposed for—

"(A) news gathering, research, or the export or import of, or transmission of, information or informational materials; or

"(B) clearly defined educational or religious activities, or activities of recognized human rights organizations, that are reasonably limited in frequency, duration, and number of participants.

"(4) The penalties provided under this subsection may be imposed only on the record after opportunity for an agency hearing in accordance with sections 554 through 557 of title 5, United States Code, with the right to prehearing discovery.

"(5) Judicial review of any penalty imposed under this subsection may be had to the extent provided in section 702 of title 5, United States Code."

Pub. L. 104–114, §102(d)(2), struck out subsec. (b), as added by Pub. L. 102–393, which read as follows:

"(b)(1) A civil penalty of not to exceed $50,000 may be imposed by the Secretary of the Treasury on any person who violates any license, order, rule, or regulation issued in compliance with the provisions of this Act.

"(2) The penalties provided under this subsection may not be imposed for—

"(A) news gathering, research, or the export or import of, or transmission of, information or informational materials; or

"(B) clearly defined educational or religious activities, or activities of recognized human rights organizations, that are reasonably limited in frequency, duration, and number of participants."

1992—Pub. L. 102–484, which directed substitution of "(a) Whoever" for "That whoever" and addition of subsec. (b) at end, was executed to reflect the probable intent of Congress in light of the intervening general amendment by Pub. L. 102–393 (see below), by adding subsec. (b) after subsec. (a).

Pub. L. 102–393 amended section generally, substituting subsecs. (a) to (c) for former undesignated provisions which read as follows: "Whoever shall willfully violate any of the provisions of this Act or of any license, rule, or regulation issued thereunder, and whoever shall willfully violate, neglect, or refuse to comply with any order of the President issued in compliance with the provisions of this Act shall, upon conviction, be fined not more than $50,000, or, if a natural person, imprisoned for not more than ten years, or both; and the officer, director, or agent of any corporation who knowingly participates in such violation shall be punished by a like fine, imprisonment, or both, and any property, funds, securities, papers, or other articles or documents, or any vessel, together with her tackle, apparel, furniture, and equipment, concerned in such violation shall be forfeited to the United States."

1977—Pub. L. 95–223 substituted "$50,000" for "$10,000".

SECTION REFERRED TO IN OTHER SECTIONS

This section is referred to in sections 3, 4, 7 of this Appendix; title 18 section 1956; title 22 sections 2778, 6009; title 28 section 2680.

§17. Rules by district courts; appeals

The district courts of the United States are given jurisdiction to make and enter all such rules as to notice and otherwise, and all such orders and decrees, and to issue such process as may be necessary and proper in the premises to enforce the provisions of this Act [sections 1 to 6, 7 to 39, and 41 to 44 of this Appendix], with a right of appeal from the final order or decree of such court as provided in sections one hundred and twenty-eight and two hundred and thirty-eight of the Act of March third, nineteen hundred and eleven, entitled "An Act to codify, revise, and amend the laws relating to the judiciary."

(Oct. 6, 1917, ch. 106, §17, 40 Stat. 425.)

REFERENCES IN TEXT

Sections one hundred and twenty-eight and two hundred and thirty-eight of the Act of March third, nineteen hundred and eleven, entitled "An Act to codify, revise, and amend the laws relating to the judiciary", referred to in text, enacted sections 225 and 345 of former Title 28, Judicial Code and Judiciary, respectively. Section 225 of former Title 28 was repealed by act June 25, 1948, ch. 646, §39, 62 Stat. 992, and reenacted as sections 1291, 1292, 1293, and 1294 of Title 28, Judiciary and Judicial Procedure. Section 345 of former Title 28 was repealed by act June 25, 1948, ch. 646, §39, 62 Stat. 992.

SECTION REFERRED TO IN OTHER SECTIONS

This section is referred to in title 28 section 2680.

§18. Jurisdiction of courts of Philippines and Canal Zone of offenses

The several courts of first instance in the Philippine Islands and the district court of the Canal Zone shall have jurisdiction of offenses under this Act [sections 1 to 6, 7 to 39, and 41 to 44 of this Appendix] committed within their respective districts, and concurrent jurisdiction with the district courts of the United States of offenses under this Act [said sections] committed upon the high seas and of conspiracies to commit such offenses as defined by section thirty-seven of the Act entitled "An Act to codify, revise, and amend the penal laws of the United States," approved March fourth, nineteen hundred and nine, and the provisions of such section for the purpose of this Act [said sections] are extended to the Philippine Islands and to the Canal Zone.

(Oct. 6, 1917, ch. 106, §18, 40 Stat. 425.)

REFERENCES IN TEXT

Section thirty-seven of the Act entitled "An Act to codify, revise, and amend the penal laws of the United States," approved March fourth, nineteen hundred and nine, referred to in text, enacted section 88 of former Title 18, Criminal Code and Criminal Procedure, and was repealed by act June 25, 1948, ch. 645, §21, 62 Stat. 862, and reenacted as section 371 of Title 18, Crimes and Criminal Procedure.

TERMINATION OF UNITED STATES DISTRICT COURT FOR THE DISTRICT OF THE CANAL ZONE

For termination of the United States District Court for the District of the Canal Zone at end of the "transition period", being the 30-month period beginning Oct. 1, 1979, and ending midnight Mar. 31, 1982, see Paragraph 5 of Article XI of the Panama Canal Treaty of 1977 and sections 2101 and 2201 to 2203 of Pub. L. 96–70, title II, Sept. 27, 1979, 93 Stat. 493, formerly classified to sections 3831 and 3841 to 3843, respectively, of Title 22, Foreign Relations and Intercourse.

PHILIPPINE INDEPENDENCE

Proc. No. 2695, eff. July 4, 1946, 11 F.R. 7517, 60 Stat. 1352, issued pursuant to section 1394 of Title 22, Foreign Relations and Intercourse, recognized the independence of the Philippine Islands as of July 4, 1946, and is set out under that section.

SECTION REFERRED TO IN OTHER SECTIONS

This section is referred to in title 28 section 2680.

§19. Print, newspaper or publication in foreign languages

Ten days after the approval of this act [Oct. 6, 1917] and until the end of the war, it shall be unlawful for any person, firm, corporation, or association, to print, publish, or circulate, or cause to be printed, published, or circulated in any foreign language, any news item, editorial or other printed matter, respecting the Government of the United States, or of any nation engaged in the present war, its policies, international relations, the state or conduct of the war, or any matter relating thereto: *Provided*, That this section shall not apply to any print, newspaper, or publication where the publisher or distributor thereof, on or before offering the same for mailing, or in any manner distributing it to the public, has filed with the postmaster at the place of publication, in the form of an affidavit, a true and complete translation of the entire article containing such matter proposed to be published in such print, newspaper, or publication, and has caused to be printed, in plain type in the English language, at the head of each such item, editorial, or other matter, on each copy of such print, newspaper, or publication, the words "True translation filed with the postmaster at _______ on _______ (naming the post office where the translation was filed, and the date of filing thereof), as required by the Act of _______ (here giving the date of this Act [Oct. 6, 1917])."

Any print, newspaper, or publication in any foreign language which does not conform to the provisions of this section is declared to be nonmailable, and it shall be unlawful for any person, firm, corporation, or association, to transport, carry, or otherwise publish or distribute the same, or to transport, carry or otherwise publish or distribute any matter which is made nonmailable by the provisions of the Act relating to espionage, approved June fifteenth, nineteen hundred and seventeen: *Provided, further*, That upon evidence satisfactory to him that any print, newspaper, or publication, printed in a foreign language may be printed, published, and distributed free from the foregoing restrictions and conditions without detriment to the United States in the conduct of the present war, the President may cause to be issued to the printers or publishers of such print, newspaper, or publication, a permit to print, publish, and circulate the issue or issues of their print, newspaper, or publication, free from such restrictions and requirements, such permits to be subject to revocation at his discretion. And the Postmaster General[1] shall cause copies of all such permits and revocations of permits to be furnished to the postmaster of the post office serving the place from which the print, newspaper, or publication, granted the permit is to emanate. All matter printed, published and distributed under permits shall bear at the head thereof in plain type in the English language, the words, "Published and distributed under permit authorized by the Act of _______ (here giving date of this Act [Oct. 6, 1917]), on file at the post office of _______ (giving name of office)."

Any person who shall make an affidavit containing any false statement in connection with the translation provided for in this section shall be guilty of the crime of perjury and subject to the punishment provided therefor by section one hundred and twenty-five of the Act of March fourth, nineteen hundred and nine, entitled "An Act to codify, revise, and amend the penal laws of the United States," and any person, firm, corporation, or association, violating any other requirement of this section shall, on conviction thereof, be punished by a fine of not more than $500, or by imprisonment of not more than one year, or, in the discretion of the court, may be both fined and imprisoned.

(Oct. 6, 1917, ch. 106, §19, 40 Stat. 425.)

REFERENCES IN TEXT

Provision of the Act relating to espionage approved June fifteenth, nineteen hundred and seventeen, referred to in text, means act June 15, 1917, ch. 30, title I, §§1–8, 40 Stat. 217, as amended, which enacted sections 31 to 38 of Title 50, War and National Defense, and which was repealed by act June 25, 1948, ch. 645, §21, 62 Stat. 862, and reenacted as sections 792 to 794 and 2388 of Title 18, Crimes and Criminal Procedure.

Section one hundred and twenty-five of the Act of March fourth, nineteen hundred and nine, entitled "An Act to codify, revise, and amend the penal laws of the United States", referred to in text, enacted section 231 of former Title 18, Criminal Code and Criminal Procedure, was repealed by act June 25, 1948, ch. 645, §21, 62 Stat. 862, and reenacted as section 1621 of Title 18, Crimes and Criminal Procedure.

TRANSFER OF FUNCTIONS

Office of Postmaster General of Post Office Department abolished and functions, powers, and duties of Postmaster General transferred to United States Postal Service by Pub. L. 91–375, §4(a), Aug. 12, 1970, 84 Stat. 773, set out as a note under section 201 of Title 39, Postal Service.

SECTION REFERRED TO IN OTHER SECTIONS

This section is referred to in title 28 section 2680.

§20. Fees of agents, attorneys, or representatives

No property or interest or proceeds shall be returned under this Act [sections 1 to 6, 7 to 39, and 41 to 44 of this Appendix], nor shall any payment be made or judgment awarded in respect of any property or interest vested in or transferred to any officer or agency of the United States under this Act [said sections] unless satisfactory evidence is furnished to the President or such officer or agency as he may designate, or the court, as the case may be, that the aggregate of the fees to be paid to all agents, attorneys at law or in fact, or representatives, for services rendered in connection with such return or payment or judgment does not exceed 10 per centum of the value of such property or interest or proceeds or of such payment. Any agent, attorney at law or in fact, or representative, believing that the aggregate of the fees should be in excess of such 10 per centum may in the case of any return of, or the making of any payment in respect of, such property or interest or proceeds by the President or such officer or agency as he may designate, petition the district court of the United States for the district in which he resides for an order authorizing fees in excess of 10 per centum and shall name such officer or agency as respondent. The court hearing such petition, or a court awarding any judgment in respect of any such property or interest or proceeds, as the case may be, shall approve an aggregate of fees in excess of 10 per centum of the value of such property or interest or proceeds only upon a finding that there exist special circumstances of unusual hardship which require the payment of such excess. Any person accepting any fee in excess of an amount approved hereunder, or retaining for more than thirty days any portion of a fee, accepted prior to approval hereunder, in excess of the fee as approved, shall be guilty of a violation of this Act [said sections].

(Oct. 6, 1917, ch. 106, §20, as added Mar. 4, 1923, ch. 285, §2, 42 Stat. 1515; amended Mar. 10, 1928, ch. 167, §9(c), 45 Stat. 267; Mar. 8, 1946, ch. 83, §2, 60 Stat. 54; June 25, 1956, ch. 436, 70 Stat. 331.)

[1] See Transfer of Functions note below.

AMENDMENTS

1956—Act June 25, 1956, struck out provisions which required a schedule of fees to be furnished to, and approved by, the President or such officer or agency as he designated, and which permitted approval of such schedule of fees only upon a determination that the individual fees did not exceed fair compensation for services rendered.

1946—Act Mar. 8, 1946, raised limitation of fees from 3 per centum of amount involved to 10 per centum.

1928—Act Mar. 10, 1928, inserted "at law or in fact" after "attorney" wherever appearing.

TRANSFER OF FUNCTIONS

Functions of Alien Property Custodian and Office of Alien Property Custodian, except those relating to property or interest in Philippines, vested in Attorney General. See notes set out under section 6 of this Appendix.

EX. ORD. NO. 9725. ADMINISTRATION OF POWERS AND AUTHORITY OF PRESIDENT BY ALIEN PROPERTY CUSTODIAN

Ex. Ord. No. 9725, May 16, 1946, 11 F.R. 5381, provided:

The Alien Property Custodian is designated as the officer to administer the powers and authority conferred upon the President by section 20 of the Trading with the Enemy Act, as amended by Public Law 322, 79th Congress, approved March 8, 1946 [this section], and by section 32 of the said act, as added by the said Public Law 322 [section 32 of this Appendix].

The Alien Property Custodian may delegate to officers and employees of the Office of Alien Property Custodian such functions as he may deem necessary to carry out the provisions of this order.

This order shall not be construed as revoking or limiting any power or authority heretofore delegated to the Alien Property Custodian.

HARRY S. TRUMAN.

SECTION REFERRED TO IN OTHER SECTIONS

This section is referred to in title 28 section 2680.

§21. Claims of naturalized citizens as affected by expatriation

The claim of any naturalized American citizen under the provisions of this Act [sections 1 to 6, 7 to 39, and 41 to 44 of this Appendix] shall not be denied on the ground of any presumption of expatriation which has arisen against him, under the second sentence of section 2 of the Act entitled "An Act in reference to the expatriation of citizens and their protection abroad," approved March 2, 1907, if he shall give satisfactory evidence to the President, or the court, as the case may be, of his uninterrupted loyalty to the United States during his absence, and that he has returned to the United States, or that he, although desiring to return, has been prevented from so returning by circumstances beyond his control.

(Oct. 6, 1917, ch. 106, §21, as added Mar. 4, 1923, ch. 285, §2, 42 Stat. 1516.)

REFERENCES IN TEXT

The second sentence of section 2 of the Act entitled "An Act in reference to the expatriation of citizens and their protection abroad," approved March 2, 1907, referred to in text, is the second sentence of section 2 of act Mar. 2, 1907, ch. 2534, 34 Stat. 1228, which was classified to section 17 of Title 8, Aliens and Nationality, and which was repealed by act Oct. 14, 1940, ch. 876, title I, subch. V, §504, 54 Stat. 1172.

SECTION REFERRED TO IN OTHER SECTIONS

This section is referred to in title 28 section 2680.

§22. Fugitives from justice barred from recovery

No person shall be entitled to the return of any property or money under any provision of this Act [sections 1 to 6, 7 to 39, and 41 to 44 of this Appendix], or any amendment of this Act [said sections], who is a fugitive from justice of the United States or any State or Territory thereof, or the District of Columbia.

(Oct. 6, 1917, ch. 106, §22, as added Mar. 4, 1923, ch. 285, §2, 42 Stat. 1516; amended Mar. 10, 1928, ch. 167, §16, 45 Stat. 275.)

AMENDMENTS

1928—Act Mar. 10, 1928, inserted "or any amendment of this Act" after "any provision of this Act".

SECTION REFERRED TO IN OTHER SECTIONS

This section is referred to in title 28 section 2680.

§23. Payment of income, etc., by Alien Property Custodian

The Alien Property Custodian is directed to pay to the person entitled thereto, from and after March 4, 1923, the net income (including dividends, interest, annuities, and other earnings), accruing and collected thereafter, in respect of any money or property held in trust for such person by the Alien Property Custodian or by the Treasurer of the United States for the account of the Alien Property Custodian, under such rules and regulations as the President may prescribe.

(Oct. 6, 1917, ch. 106, §23, as added Mar. 4, 1923, ch. 285, §2, 42 Stat. 1516; amended Mar. 10, 1928, ch. 167, §17, 45 Stat. 275.)

AMENDMENTS

1928—Act Mar. 10, 1928, struck out restriction that no person be paid any amount over $10,000 per annum.

TRANSFER OF FUNCTIONS

Functions of Alien Property Custodian and Office of Alien Property Custodian, except those relating to property or interest in Philippines, vested in Attorney General. See notes set out under section 6 of this Appendix.

WORLD WAR II ALIEN PROPERTY CUSTODIAN

Reestablishment and termination of Office of Alien Property Custodian during World War II, see notes set out under section 6 of this Appendix.

SECTION REFERRED TO IN OTHER SECTIONS

This section is referred to in title 28 section 2680.

§24. Payment of taxes and expenses by Alien Property Custodian

(a) The Alien Property Custodian is authorized to pay all taxes (including special assessments), heretofore or hereafter lawfully assessed by any body politic against any money or other property held by him or by the Treasurer of the United States under this Act [sections 1 to 6, 7 to 39, and 41 to 44 of this Appendix], and to pay the necessary expenses incurred by him or by any depositary for him in securing the possession, collection, or control of any such money or other property, or in protecting or administering the same. Such taxes and expenses shall be paid out of the money or other property against which such taxes are assessed or in respect of which such expenses are incurred, or (if such money or other property is insufficient) out of any other money or property held for the same person, notwithstanding the fact that a claim may have been filed or suit instituted under this Act [said sections]. No claim shall be filed with the Alien Property Custodian or allowed by him or by the President of the United States, nor shall any suit be instituted or maintained against the Alien Property Custodian or the Treasurer of the United States, or the United States, under any provisions of law, by any person who was an enemy or ally of enemy as defined in the Trading with the Enemy Act, as amended [said sections], and no allowance of any such claim now pending shall be made, nor judgment entered in any such suit heretofore or hereafter instituted, for the recovery of any deduction or deductions, heretofore or hereafter made by the Alien Property Custodian from money or properties, or income therefrom, held by him or by the Treasurer of the United States hereunder, for the general or administrative expenses of the office of the Alien Property Custodian, which deduction or deductions on the collection of any income do not exceed the sum of two per centum of such income or which on the return of any moneys or properties or income therefrom, do not exceed the sum of two per centum of the aggregate value thereof at the time or times as nearly as may be, of such deduction or deductions, or, for the recovery of any deduction or deductions heretofore or hereafter made by the Alien Property Custodian from money or properties or income therefrom held by him or by the Treasurer of the United States hereunder, for any and all necessary expenses incurred and actually disbursed by the Alien Property Custodian or by any depositary for him in securing the possession, collection or control of any such money or properties or income therefrom, or in protecting or administering the same, as said general or administrative and other expenses and said aggregate value of returned money or properties or income therefrom have been heretofore or shall be hereafter determined by said Alien Property Custodian.

(b) In the case of income, war-profits, excess-profits, or estate taxes imposed by any Act of Congress, the amount thereof shall, under regulations prescribed by the Commissioner of Internal Revenue with the approval of the Secretary of the Treasury, be computed in the same manner (except as hereinafter in this section provided) as though the money or other property had not been seized by or paid to the Alien Property Custodian, and shall be paid as far as practicable, in accordance with subsection (a) of this section. Pending final determination of the tax liability the Alien Property Custodian is authorized to return, in accordance with the provisions of this Act [sections 1 to 6, 7 to 39, and 41 to 44 of this Appendix], money or other property in any trust in such amounts as may be determined, under regulations prescribed by the Commissioner of Internal Revenue with the approval of the Secretary of the Treasury, to be consistent with the prompt payment of the full amount of the internal-revenue taxes. Notwithstanding the expiration of any period of limitation provided by law, credit or refund of any income, war-profits, or excess-profits tax erroneously or illegally assessed or collected may be made or allowed if claim therefor was filed with the Commissioner of Internal Revenue by the Alien Property Custodian on or before February 15, 1933.

(c) So much of the net income of a taxpayer for the taxable year 1917, or any succeeding taxable year, as represents the gain derived from the sale or exchange by the Alien Property Custodian of any property conveyed, transferred, assigned, delivered, or paid to him, or seized by him, may at the option of the taxpayer be segregated from the net income and separately taxed at the rate of 30 per centum. This subsection shall be applied and the amount of net income to be so segregated shall be determined, under regulations prescribed by the Commissioner of Internal Revenue with the approval of the Secretary of the Treasury, as nearly as may be in the same manner as provided in section 208 of the Revenue Act of 1926 (relating to capital net gains), but without regard to the period for which the property was held by the Alien Property Custodian before its sale or exchange, and whether or not the taxpayer is an individual.

(d) Any property sold or exchanged by the Alien Property Custodian (whether before or after the date of the enactment of the Settlement of War Claims Act of 1928 [Mar. 10, 1928]) shall be considered as having been compulsorily or involuntarily converted, within the meaning of the income, excess-profits, and war-profits tax laws and regulations; and the provisions of such laws and regulations relating to such a conversion shall (under regulations prescribed by the Commissioner of Internal Revenue with the approval of the Secretary of the Treasury) apply in the case of the proceeds of such sale or exchange. For the purpose of determining whether the proceeds of such conversion have been expended within such time as will entitle the taxpayer to the benefits of such laws and regulations relating to such a conversion, the date of the return of the proceeds to the person entitled thereto shall be considered as the date of the conversion.

(e) In case of any internal-revenue tax imposed in respect of property conveyed, transferred, assigned, delivered, or paid to the Alien Property Custodian, or seized by him, and imposed in respect of any period (in the taxable year 1917 or any succeeding taxable year) during which such property was held by him or by the Treasurer of the United States, no interest or civil penalty shall be assessed upon, collected from, or paid by or on behalf of, the taxpayer; nor shall any interest be credited or paid to the taxpayer in respect of any credit or refund allowed or made in respect of such tax.

(f) The benefits of subsections (c), (d), and (e) shall be extended to the taxpayer if claim therefor is filed before the expiration of the period of limitations properly applicable thereto, or before the expiration of six months after the date of the enactment of the Settlement of War Claims Act of 1928 [Mar. 10, 1928], whichever date is the later. The benefits of subsection (d) shall also be extended to the taxpayer if claim therefor is filed before the expiration of six months after the return of the proceeds.

(Oct. 6, 1917, ch. 106, § 24, as added Mar. 4, 1923, ch. 285, § 2, 42 Stat. 1516; amended Mar. 10, 1928, ch. 167, § 18, 45 Stat. 276, 277; Mar. 28, 1934, ch. 102, title I, § 1, 48 Stat. 510; June 18, 1934, ch. 567, 48 Stat. 978.)

REFERENCES IN TEXT

Section 208 of the Revenue Act of 1926 (relating to capital net gains), referred to in subsec. (c), is act Feb. 26, 1926, ch. 27, § 208, 44 Stat. 19, which enacted section 939 of former Title 26, Internal Revenue, prior to its repeal by act May 29, 1928, ch. 852, § 63, 45 Stat. 810. See section 1201 et seq. of Title 26, Internal Revenue Code.

PRIOR PROVISIONS

Provisions similar to subdivision (a) of this section was contained in the sundry civil appropriation act for the fiscal year 1919, act July 1, 1918, ch. 113, 40 Stat. 646.

AMENDMENTS

1934—Subsec. (a). Act Mar. 28, 1934, inserted provisions relating to recovery by enemies of deductions made by Alien Property Custodian for administrative expenses.

Subsec. (b). Act June 18, 1934, provided that credit or refund of income or war profits erroneously collected might be allowed if claim was filed on or before Feb. 15, 1933.

1928—Subsecs. (b) to (f). Act Mar. 10, 1928, designated existing provisions as subsec. (a) and added subsecs. (b) to (f).

TRANSFER OF FUNCTIONS

Functions of Alien Property Custodian and Office of Alien Property Custodian, except those relating to property or interest in Philippines, vested in Attorney General. See notes set out under section 6 of this Appendix.

WORLD WAR II ALIEN PROPERTY CUSTODIAN

Reestablishment of Office of Alien Property Custodian during World War II, see notes set out under section 6 of this Appendix.

SECTION REFERRED TO IN OTHER SECTIONS

This section is referred to in title 28 section 2680.

§ 25. Investments by Custodian in participating certificates issued by Secretary of the Treasury; transfers to and payments from German, Austrian or Hungarian special deposit accounts; allocation of payments

(a)(1) The Alien Property Custodian is authorized and directed to invest, from time to time upon the request of the Secretary of the Treasury, out of the funds held by the Alien Property Custodian or by the Treasurer of the United States for the Alien Property Custodian, an amount not to exceed $40,000,000 in the aggregate, in one or more participating certificates issued by the Secretary of the Treasury in accordance with the provisions of this section.

(2) When in the case of any trust written consent under subsection (m) of section 9 [section 9(m) of this Appendix] has been filed, an amount equal to the portion of such trust the return of which is temporarily postponed under such subsection shall be credited against the investment made under paragraph (1) of this subsection. If the total amount so credited is in excess of the amount invested under paragraph (1) of this subsection, the excess shall be invested by the Alien Property Custodian in accordance with the provisions of this subsection, without regard to the $40,000,000 limitation in paragraph (1). If the amount invested under paragraph (1) of this subsection is in excess of the total amount so credited, such excess shall, from time to time on request of the Alien Property Custodian, be paid to him out of the funds in the German special deposit account created by section 4 of the Settlement of War Claims Act of 1928, and such payments shall have priority over any payments therefrom other than the payments under paragraph (1) of subsection (c) of such section (relating to expenses of administration).

(b) The Alien Property Custodian is authorized and directed to invest, in one or more participating certificates issued by the Secretary of the Treasury, out of the unallocated interest fund, as defined in section 28 [section 28 of this Appendix]—

(1) The sum of $25,000,000. If, after the allocation under section 26 [section 26 of this Appendix] has been made, the amount of the unallocated interest fund allocated to the trust described in subsection (c) of such section is found to be in excess of $25,000,000, such excess shall be invested by the Alien Property Custodian in accordance with the provisions of this subsection. If the amount so allocated is found to be less than $25,000,000 any participating certificate or certificates that have been issued shall be corrected accordingly; and

(2) The balance of such unallocated interest fund remaining after the investment provided for in paragraph (1) and the payment of allocated earnings in accordance with the provisions of subsection (b) of section 26 [section 26(b) of this Appendix] have been made.

(c) If the amount of such unallocated interest fund, remaining after the investment required by paragraph (1) of subsection (b) of this section has been made, is insufficient to pay the allocated earnings in accordance with subsection (b) of section 26 [section 26(b) of this Appendix], then the amount necessary to make up the deficiency shall be paid out of the funds in the German special deposit account created by section 4 of the Settlement of War Claims Act of 1928, and such payment shall have priority over any payments therefrom other than the payments under paragraph (1) of subsection (c) of such section (relating to expenses of administration) and the payments under paragraph (2) of subsection (a) of this section.

(d) The Alien Property Custodian is authorized and directed (after the payment of debts under section 9 [section 9 of this Appendix]) to transfer to the Secretary of the Treasury, for deposit in such special deposit account, all money and the proceeds of all property, including all income, dividends, interest, annuities, and earnings accumulated in respect thereof, owned by the German Government or any member of the former ruling family. All money and other property shall be held to be owned by the German Government (1) if no claim thereto has been filed with the Alien Property Custodian prior to the expiration of three years from the date of the enactment of the Settlement of War Claims Act of 1928 [Mar. 10, 1928], or (2) if any claim has been filed before the expiration of such period (whether before or after the enactment of such Act), then if the ownership thereof under any such claim is not established by a decision of the Alien Property Custodian or by suit in court instituted, under section 9 [section 9 of this Appendix], within one year after the decision of the Alien Property Custodian, or after the date of the enactment of the Settlement of War Claims Act of 1928, whichever date is later. The amounts so transferred under this subsection shall be credited upon the final payment due the United States from the German Government on account of the awards of the Mixed Claims Commission.

(e) The Secretary of the Treasury is authorized and directed to issue to the Alien Property Custodian, upon such terms and conditions and under such regulations as the Secretary of the Treasury may prescribe, one or more participating certificates, bearing interest payable annually (as nearly as may be) at the rate of 5 per centum per annum, as evidence of the investment by the Alien Property Custodian under subsection (a), and one or more non-interest bearing participating certificates, as evidence of the investment by the Alien Property Custodian under subsection (b). All such certificates shall evidence a participating interest, in accordance with, and subject to the priorities of, the provisions of section 4 of the Settlement of War Claims Act of 1928, in the funds in the German special deposit account created by such section, except that—

(1) The United States shall assume no liability, directly or indirectly, for the payment of any such certificates, or of the interest thereon, except out of funds in such special deposit account available therefor, and all such certificates shall so state on their face; and

(2) Such certificates shall not be transferable, except that the Alien Property Custodian may transfer any such participating certificate evidencing the interest of a substantial number of the owners of the money invested, to a trustee duly appointed by such owners.

(f) Any amount of principal or interest paid to the Alien Property Custodian in accordance with the provisions of subsection (c) of section 4 of the Settlement of War Claims Act of 1928 shall be allocated pro rata among the persons filing written consents under subsection (m) of section 9 of this Act [section 9(m) of this Appendix], and the amounts so allocated shall be paid to such persons. If any person to whom any amount is payable under this subsection has died (or if, in the case of a partnership, association, or other unincorporated body of individuals, or a corporation, its existence has terminated), payment shall be made to the persons determined by the Alien Property Custodian to be entitled thereto.

(g) The Alien Property Custodian is authorized and directed (after the payment of debts under section 9 [section 9 of this Appendix]) to transfer to the Secretary of the Treasury, for deposit in the special deposit account (Austrian or Hungarian, as the case may be), created by section 7 of the Settlement of War Claims Act of 1928, all money and the proceeds of all property, including all income, dividends, interest, annuities, and earnings accumulated in respect thereof, owned by the Austrian Government or any corporation all the stock of which was owned by or on behalf of the Austrian Government (including the property of the Imperial Royal Tobacco Monopoly, also known under the name of K. K. Oesterreichische Tabak Regie), or owned by the Hungarian Government or by any corporation all the stock of which was owned by or on behalf of the Hungarian Government.

(Oct. 6, 1917, ch. 106, §25, as added Mar. 10, 1928, ch. 167, §10, 45 Stat. 268; amended Feb. 21, 1929, ch. 291, 45 Stat. 1255; Mar. 10, 1930, ch. 75, §2, 46 Stat. 84.)

REFERENCES IN TEXT

Section 4 of the Settlement of War Claims Act of 1928, referred to in subsecs. (a)(2), (c), (e), and (f), is section 4 of act Mar. 10, 1928, ch. 167, 45 Stat. 254, which is not classified to the Code.

Section 7 of the Settlement of War Claims Act of 1928, referred to in subsec. (g), is section 7 of act Mar. 10, 1928, ch. 167, 45 Stat. 254, which is not classified to the Code.

AMENDMENTS

1930—Subsec. (d)(1). Act Mar. 10, 1930, substituted "three years" for "two years".

1929—Subsec. (d)(1). Act Feb. 21, 1929, substituted "two years" for "one year".

TRANSFER OF FUNCTIONS

Functions of Alien Property Custodian and Office of Alien Property Custodian, except those relating to property or interest in Philippines, vested in Attorney General. See notes set out under section 6 of this Appendix.

WORLD WAR II ALIEN PROPERTY CUSTODIAN

Reestablishment of Office of Alien Property Custodian during World War II, see notes set out under section 6 of this Appendix.

SECTION REFERRED TO IN OTHER SECTIONS

This section is referred to in sections 26, 29 of this Appendix; title 28 section 2680.

§26. Allocation of "unallocated interest fund"

(a) The Alien Property Custodian shall allocate among the various trusts the funds in the "unallocated interest fund" (as defined in section 28 [section 28 of this Appendix]). Such allocation shall be based upon the earnings (determined by the Secretary of the Treasury) on the total amounts deposited under section 12 [section 12 of this Appendix].

(b) The Alien Property Custodian, when the allocation has been made, is authorized and directed to pay to each person entitled, in accordance with a final decision of a court of the United States or of the District of Columbia, or of an opinion of the Attorney General, to the distribution of any portion of such unallocated interest fund, the amount allocated to his trust, except as provided in subsection (c) of this section.

(c) In the case of persons entitled, under paragraph (12), (13), (14), or (16) of subsection (b) of section 9 [section 9(b)(12), (13), (14), or (16) of this Appendix], to such return, and in the case of persons who would be entitled to such return thereunder if all such money or property had not been returned under paragraph (9) or (10) of such subsection [section 9(b)(9) or (10) of this Appendix], and in the case of persons entitled to such return under subsection (n) of section 9 [section

9(n) of this Appendix], an amount equal to the aggregate amount allocated to their trusts shall be credited against the sum of $25,000,000 invested in participating certificates under paragraph (1) of subsection (b) of section 25 [section 25(b)(1) of this Appendix]. If the aggregate amount so allocated is in excess of $25,000,000, an amount equal to the excess shall be invested in the same manner. Upon the repayment of any of the amounts so invested, under the provisions of section 4 of the Settlement of War Claims Act of 1928, the amount so repaid shall be distributed pro rata among such persons, notwithstanding any receipts or releases given by them.

(d) The unallocated interest fund shall be available for carrying out the provisions of this section, including the expenses of making the allocation.

(Oct. 6, 1917, ch. 106, § 26, as added Mar. 10, 1928, ch. 167, § 15, 45 Stat. 273; amended June 11, 1929, ch. 14, 46 Stat. 6.)

REFERENCES IN TEXT

Section 4 of the Settlement of War Claims Act of 1928, referred to in subsec. (c), is section 4 of act Mar. 10, 1928, ch. 167, 45 Stat. 254, which is not classified to the Code.

AMENDMENTS

1929—Subsec. (a). Act June 11, 1929, struck out "average rate of" before "earnings" in second sentence.

TRANSFER OF FUNCTIONS

Functions of Alien Property Custodian and Office of Alien Property Custodian, except those relating to property or interest in Philippines, vested in Attorney General. See notes set out under section 6 of this Appendix.

WORLD WAR II ALIEN PROPERTY CUSTODIAN

Reestablishment and termination of Office of Alien Property Custodian during World War II, see notes set out under section 6 of this Appendix.

SECTION REFERRED TO IN OTHER SECTIONS

This section is referred to in section 25 of this Appendix; title 28 section 2680.

§ 27. Return by Custodian, to United States, of payments under licenses, assignments or sales of patents

The Alien Property Custodian is authorized and directed to return to the United States any consideration paid to him by the United States under any license, assignment, or sale by the Alien Property Custodian to the United States of any patent (or any right therein or claim thereto, and including an application therefor and any patent issued pursuant to any such application).

(Oct. 6, 1917, ch. 106, § 27, as added Mar. 10, 1928, ch. 167, § 15, 45 Stat. 274.)

TRANSFER OF FUNCTIONS

Functions of Alien Property Custodian and Office of Alien Property Custodian, except those relating to property or interest in Philippines, vested in Attorney General. See notes set out under section 6 of this Appendix.

WORLD WAR II ALIEN PROPERTY CUSTODIAN

Reestablishment and termination of Office of Alien Property Custodian during World War II, see notes set out under section 6 of this Appendix.

SECTION REFERRED TO IN OTHER SECTIONS

This section is referred to in title 28 section 2680.

§ 28. "Unallocated interest fund" defined

As used in this Act [sections 1 to 6, 7 to 39, and 41 to 44 of this Appendix], the term "unallocated interest fund" means the sum of (1) the earnings and profits accumulated prior to March 4, 1923, and attributable to investments and reinvestments under section 12 [section 12 of this Appendix] by the Secretary of the Treasury, plus (2) the earnings and profits accumulated on or after March 4, 1923, in respect of the earnings and profits referred to in clause (1) of this section.

(Oct. 6, 1917, ch. 106, § 28, as added Mar. 10, 1928, ch. 167, § 15, 45 Stat. 274.)

SECTION REFERRED TO IN OTHER SECTIONS

This section is referred to in sections 25, 26 of this Appendix; title 28 section 2680.

§ 29. Waiver by Custodian of demand for property; acceptance of less amount; approval of Attorney General

(a) Where the Alien Property Custodian has made demand or requirement for the conveyance, transfer, assignment, delivery, or payment to him of any money or other property of any enemy or ally of enemy (whether or not suit or proceeding for the enforcement thereof has been begun and whether or not any judgment or decree in respect thereof has been made or entered) and where the whole or any part of such money or other property would, if conveyed, transferred, assigned, delivered, or paid to him, be returnable under any provision of this Act [sections 1 to 6, 7 to 39, and 41 to 44 of this Appendix], the Alien Property Custodian may, in his discretion, and on such terms and conditions as he may prescribe, waive such demand or requirement, or accept in full satisfaction of such demand, requirement, judgment, or decree, a less amount than that demanded or required by him.

(b) The Alien Property Custodian shall not make any such waiver or compromise except with the approval of the Attorney General; nor (if any part of such money or property would be returnable only upon the filing of the written consent required by subsection (m) of section 9 [section 9(m) of this Appendix]) unless, after compliance with the terms and conditions of such waiver or compromise, the Alien Property Custodian or the Treasurer of the United States will hold (in respect of such enemy or ally of enemy) for investment as provided in section 25 [section 25 of this Appendix], an amount equal to 20 per centum of the sum of (1) the value of the money or other property held by the Alien Property Custodian or the Treasurer of the United States at the time of such waiver or compromise, plus (2) the value of the money or other property to which the Alien Property Custodian would be entitled under such demand or requirement if the waiver or compromise had not been made.

(c) Where the Alien Property Custodian has made demand or requirement for the conveyance, transfer, assignment, delivery, or payment to him of any money or other property of any enemy or ally of enemy (whether or not suit or proceeding for the enforcement thereof has been begun and whether or not any judgment or decree in respect thereof has been made or entered) and where the interest or right of such enemy or ally of enemy in such money or property has not, prior to the enactment of the Settlement of War Claims Act of 1928 [Mar. 10, 1928], vested in enjoyment, the Alien Property Custodian may, in his discretion, and on such terms and conditions as he may prescribe, waive such demand and requirement, without compliance with the requirements of subsection (b) of this section, but only with the approval of the Attorney General.

(d) Nothing in this section shall be construed as requiring the Alien Property Custodian to make any waiver or compromise authorized by this section, and the Alien Property Custodian may proceed in respect of any demand or requirement referred to in subsection (a) or (c) as if this section had not been enacted.

(e) All money or other property received by the Alien Property Custodian as a result of any action or proceeding (whether begun before or after the enactment of the Settlement of War Claims Act of 1928 [Mar. 10, 1928], and whether or not for the enforcement of a demand or requirement as above specified) shall for the purposes of this Act [sections 1 to 6, 7 to 39, and 41 to 44 of this Appendix] be considered as forming a part of the trust in respect of which such action or proceeding was brought, and shall be subject to return in the same manner and upon the same conditions as any other money or property in such trust, except as otherwise provided in subsection (b) of this section.

(Oct. 6, 1917, ch. 106, §29, as added Mar. 10, 1928, ch. 167, §15, 45 Stat. 274.)

TRANSFER OF FUNCTIONS

Functions of Alien Property Custodian and Office of Alien Property Custodian, except those relating to property or interest in Philippines, vested in Attorney General. See notes set out under section 6 of this Appendix.

WORLD WAR II ALIEN PROPERTY CUSTODIAN

Reestablishment and termination of Office of Alien Property Custodian during World War II, see notes set out under section 6 of this Appendix.

SECTION REFERRED TO IN OTHER SECTIONS

This section is referred to in title 28 section 2680.

§30. Attachment or garnishment of funds or property held by Custodian

Any money or other property returnable under subsection (b) or (n) of section 9 [section 9(b) or (n) of this Appendix] shall, at any time prior to such return, be subject to attachment in accordance with the provisions of the code of law for the District of Columbia, as amended, relating to attachments in suits at law and to attachments for the enforcement of judgments at law and decrees in equity, but any writ of attachment or garnishment issuing in any such suit, or for the enforcement of any judgment or decree, shall be served only upon the Alien Property Custodian, who shall for the purposes of this section be considered as holding credits in favor of the person entitled to such return to the extent of the value of the money or other property so returnable. Nothing in this section shall be construed as authorizing the taking of actual possession, by any officer of any court, of any money or other property held by the Alien Property Custodian or by the Treasurer of the United States.

(Oct. 6, 1917, ch. 106, §30, as added Mar. 10, 1928, ch. 167, §15, 45 Stat. 275.)

TRANSFER OF FUNCTIONS

Functions of Alien Property Custodian and Office of Alien Property Custodian, except those relating to property or interest in Philippines, vested in Attorney General. See notes set out under section 6 of this Appendix.

WORLD WAR II ALIEN PROPERTY CUSTODIAN

Reestablishment and termination of Office of Alien Property Custodian during World War II, see notes set out under section 6 of this Appendix.

SECTION REFERRED TO IN OTHER SECTIONS

This section is referred to in title 28 section 2680.

§31. "Member of the former ruling family" defined

As used in this Act [sections 1 to 6, 7 to 39, and 41 to 44 of this Appendix], the term "member of the former ruling family" means (1) any person who was at any time between April 6, 1917, and July 2, 1921, the German Emperor or the ruler of any constituent kingdom of the German Empire, or (2) the wife or any child of such person.

(Oct. 6, 1917, ch. 106, §31, as added Mar. 10, 1928, ch. 167, §15, 45 Stat. 275.)

SECTION REFERRED TO IN OTHER SECTIONS

This section is referred to in title 28 section 2680.

§32. Return of property

(a) Conditions precedent

The President, or such officer or agency as he may designate, may return any property or interest vested in or transferred to the Alien Property Custodian (other than any property or interest acquired by the United States prior to December 18, 1941), or the net proceeds thereof, whenever the President or such officer or agency shall determine—

(1) that the person who has filed a notice of claim for return, in such form as the President or such officer or agency may prescribe, was the owner of such property or interest immediately prior to its vesting in or transfer to the Alien Property Custodian, or is the legal representative (whether or not appointed by a court in the United States), or successor in interest by inheritance, devise, bequest, or operation of law, of such owner; and

(2) that such owner, and legal representative or successor in interest, if any, are not—

(A) the Government of Germany, Japan, Bulgaria, Hungary, or Rumania; or

(B) a corporation or association organized under the laws of such nation: *Provided*, That any property or interest or proceeds which, but for the provisions of this subdivision (B), might be returned under this section to any such corporation or association, may be returned to the owner or owners of all the stock of such corporation or of all the proprietary and beneficial interest in such association, if their ownership of such stock or proprietary and beneficial interest existed immediately prior to vesting in or transfer to the Alien Property Custodian and continuously thereafter to the date of such return (without regard to purported divestments or limitations of such ownership by any government referred to in subdivision (A) hereof) and if such ownership was by one or more citizens of the United States or by one or more corporations organized under the laws of the United States or any State, Territory, or possession thereof, or the District of Columbia: *Provided further*, That such owner or owners shall succeed to those obligations limited in aggregate amount to the value of such property or interest or proceeds, which are lawfully assertible against the corporation or association by persons not ineligible to receive a return under this section; or

(C) an individual voluntarily resident at any time since December 7, 1941, within the territory of such nation, other than a citizen of the United States or a diplomatic or consular officer of Italy or of any nation with which the United States has not at any time since December 7, 1941, been at war: *Provided*, That an individual who, while in the territory of a nation with which the United States has at any time since December 7, 1941, been at war, was deprived of life or substantially deprived of liberty pursuant to any law, decree, or regulation of such nation discriminating against political, racial, or religious groups, shall not be deemed to have voluntarily resided in such territory; or

(D) an individual who was at any time after December 7, 1941, a citizen or subject of Germany, Japan, Bulgaria, Hungary, or Rumania, and who on or after December 7, 1941, and prior to the date of the enactment of this section [Mar. 8, 1946], was present (other than in the service of the United States) in the territory of such nation or in any territory occupied by the military or naval forces thereof or engaged in any business in any such territory: *Provided*, That notwithstanding the provisions of this subdivision (D) return may be made to an individual who, as a consequence of any law, decree, or regulation of the nation of which he was then a citizen or subject, discriminating against political, racial, or religious groups, has at no time between December 7, 1941, and the time when such law, decree, or regulation was abrogated, enjoyed full rights of citizenship under the law of such nation: *And provided further*, That, notwithstanding the provisions of subdivision (C) hereof and of this subdivision (D), return may be made to an individual who at all times since December 7, 1941, was a citizen of the United States, or to an individual who, having lost United States citizenship solely by reason of marriage to a citizen or subject of a foreign country, reacquired such citizenship prior to September 29, 1950, if such individual would have been a citizen of the United States at all times since December 7, 1941, but for such marriage: *And provided further*, That the aggregate book value of returns made pursuant to the foregoing proviso shall not exceed $9,000,000; and any return under such proviso may be made if the book value of any such return, taken together with the aggregate book value of returns already made under such proviso does not exceed $9,000,000; and for the purposes of this proviso the term "book value" means the value, as of the time of vesting, entered on the books of the Alien Property Custodian for the purpose of accounting for the property or interest involved; or

(E) a foreign corporation or association which at any time after December 7, 1941, was controlled or 50 per centum or more of the stock of which was owned by any person or persons ineligible to receive a return under subdivisions (A), (B), (C), or (D) hereof: *Provided*, That notwithstanding the provisions of this subdivision (E) return may be made to a corporation or association so controlled or owned, if such corporation or association was organized under the laws of a nation any of whose territory was occupied by the military or naval forces of any nation with which the United Stats has at any time since December 7, 1941, been at war, and if such control or ownership arose after March 1, 1938, as an incident to such occupation and was terminated prior to the enactment of this section [Mar. 8, 1946];

and

(3) that the property or interest claimed, or the net proceeds of which are claimed, was not at any time after September 1, 1939, held or used, by or with the assent of the person who was the owner thereof immediately prior to vesting in or transfer to the Alien Property Custodian, pursuant to any arrangement to conceal any property or interest within the United States of any person ineligible to receive a return under subsection (a)(2) hereof;

(4) that the Alien Property Custodian has no actual or potential liability under the Renegotiation Act [section 1191 of this Appendix] or the Act of October 31, 1942 (56 Stat. 1013; 35 U.S.C. §§89 to 96), in respect of the property or interest or proceeds to be returned and that the claimant and his predecessor in interest, if any, have no actual or potential liability of any kind under the Renegotiation Act or the said Act of October 31, 1942; or in the alternative that the claimant has provided security or undertakings adequate to assure satisfaction of all such liabilities or that property or interest or proceeds to be retained by the Alien Property Custodian are adequate therefor; and

(5) that such return is in the interest of the United States.

(b) Extension of filing time limitation for redetermination of excessive profits

Notwithstanding the limitation prescribed in the Renegotiation Act [section 1191 of this Appendix] upon the time within which petitions may be filed in The Tax Court of the United States,[1] any person to whom any property or interest or proceeds are returned hereunder shall, for a period of ninety days (not counting Sunday or a legal holiday in the District of Columbia as the last day) following return, have the right to file such a petition for a redetermination in respect of any final order of the Renegotiation Board[2] determining excessive profits, made against the Alien Property Custodian, or of any determination, not embodied in an agreement, of excessive profits, so made by or on behalf of a Secretary.

(c) Inventions

Any person to whom any invention, whether patented or unpatented, or any right or interest therein is returned hereunder shall be bound by any notice or order issued or agreement made pursuant to the Act of October 31, 1942 (56 Stat. 1013; 35 U.S.C. §§89 to 96), in respect of such invention or right or interest, and such person to whom a licensor's interest is returned shall have all rights assertible by a licensor pursuant to section 2 of the said Act.

(d) Rights and duties

Except as otherwise provided herein, and except to the extent that the President or such officer or agency as he may designate may otherwise determine, any person to whom return is made hereunder shall have all rights, privileges, and obligations in respect to the property or interest returned or the proceeds of which are returned which would have existed if the property or interest had not vested in the Alien Property Custodian, but no cause of action shall accrue to such person in respect of any deduction or retention of any part of the property or interest or proceeds by the Alien Property Custodian for the purpose of paying taxes, costs, or expenses in connection with such property or interest or proceeds: *Provided*, That except as provided in subsections (b) and (c) hereof, no person to whom a return is made pursuant to this section, nor the successor in interest of such person, shall acquire or have any claim or right of action against the United States or any department, establishment or agency thereof, or corporation owned thereby, or against any person authorized or licensed by the United States, founded upon the retention, sale, or other disposition, or use, during the period it was vested in the Alien Property Custodian, of the returned property, interest, or proceeds. Any notice to the Alien Property Custodian in respect of any property or interest or proceeds shall constitute notice to the person to whom such property or interest or proceeds is returned and such person shall succeed to all burdens and obligations in respect of such property or interest or proceeds which accrued during the time of retention by the Alien Property Custodian, but the period during which the property or interest or proceeds returned were vested in the Alien Property Custodian shall not be included for the purpose of determining the application of any statute of limitations to the assertion of any rights by such person in respect of such property or interest or proceeds.

[1] See Change of Name note below.

[2] See Transfer of Functions note below.

(e) Legal proceeding unaffected

No return hereunder shall bar the prosecution of any suit at law or in equity against a person to whom return has been made, to establish any right, title, or interest, which may exist or which may have existed at the time of vesting, in or to the property or interest returned, but no such suit may be prosecuted by any person ineligible to receive a return under subsection (a)(2) hereof. With respect to any such suit, the period during which the property or interest or proceeds returned were vested in the Alien Property Custodian shall not be included for the purpose of determining the application of any statute of limitations.

(f) Notice of intention

At least thirty days before making any return to any person other than a resident of the United States or a corporation organized under the laws of the United States, or any State, Territory, or possession thereof, or the District of Columbia, the President or such officer or agency as he may designate shall publish in the Federal Register a notice of intention to make such return, specifying therein the person to whom return is to be made and the place where the property or interest or proceeds to be returned are located. Publication of a notice of intention to return shall confer no right of action upon any person to compel the return of any such property or interest or proceeds, and such notice of intention to return may be revoked by appropriate notice in the Federal Register. After publication of such notice of intention and prior to revocation thereof, the property or interest or proceeds specified shall be subject to attachment at the suit of any citizen or resident of the United States or any corporation organized under the laws of the United States, or any State, Territory, or possession thereof, or the District of Columbia, in the same manner as property of the person to whom return is to be made: *Provided*, That notice of any writ of attachment which may issue prior to return shall be served upon the Alien Property Custodian. Any such attachment proceeding shall be subject to the provisions of law relating to limitation of actions applicable to actions at law in the jurisdiction in which such proceeding is brought, but the period during which the property or interest or proceeds were vested in the Alien Property Custodian shall not be included for the purpose of determining the period of limitation. No officer of any court shall take actual possession, without the consent of the Alien Property Custodian, of any property or interest or proceeds so attached, and publication of a notice of revocation of intention to return shall invalidate any attachment with respect to the specified property or interest or proceeds, but if there is no such revocation, the President or such officer or agency as he may designate shall accord full effect to any such attachment in returning any such property or interest or proceeds.

(g) Payment of expenses of Custodian

Without limitation by or upon any other existing provision of law with respect to the payment of expenses by the Alien Property Custodian, the

Custodian may retain or recover from any property or interest or proceeds returned pursuant to this section or section 9(a) of this Act [section 9(a) of this Appendix] an amount not exceeding that expended or incurred by him for the conservation, preservation, or maintenance of such property or interest or proceeds, or other property or interest or proceeds returned to the same person.

(h) Designation of successor organizations to receive heirless property; time for application; payment of funds: time, allocation, claims barred by acceptance and conditions

The President may designate one or more organizations as successors in interest to deceased persons who, if alive, would be eligible to receive returns under the provisos of subdivision (C) or (D) of subsection (a)(2) thereof.[3] In the case of any organization not so designated before the date of enactment of this amendment, such organization may be so designated only if it applies for such designation within three months after such date of enactment.

The President, or such officer as he may designate, shall, before the expiration of the one-year period which begins on the date of enactment of this amendment, pay out of the War Claims Fund to organizations designated before or after the date of enactment of this amendment pursuant to this subsection the sum of $500,000. If there is more than one such designated organization, such sum shall be allocated among such organizations in the proportions in which the proceeds of heirless property were distributed, pursuant to agreements to which the United States was a party, by the Intergovernmental Committee for Refugees and successor organizations thereto. Acceptance of payment pursuant to this subsection by any such organization shall constitute a full and complete discharge of all claims filed by such organization pursuant to this section, as it existed before the date of enactment of this amendment.

No payment may be made to any organization designated under this section unless it has given firm and responsible assurances approved by the President that (1) the payment will be used on the basis of need in the rehabilitation and settlement of persons in the United States who suffered substantial deprivation of liberty or failed to enjoy the full rights of citizenship within the meaning of subdivisions (C) and (D) of subsection (a)(2) of this section; (2) it will make to the President, with a copy to be furnished to the Congress, such reports (including a detailed annual report on the use of the payment made to it) and permit such examination of its books as the President, or such officer or agency as he may designate, may from time to time require; and (3) it will not use any part of such payment for legal fees, salaries, or other administrative expenses connected with the filing of claims for such payment or for the recovery of any property or interest under this section.

As used in this subsection, "organization" means only a nonprofit charitable corporation incorporated on or before January 1, 1950, under the laws of any State of the United States or of the District of Columbia with the power to sue and be sued.

(Oct. 6, 1917, ch. 106, §32 as added Dec. 18, 1941, ch. 593, title III, §304, as added Mar. 8, 1946, ch. 83, §1, 60 Stat. 50; amended Aug. 8, 1946, ch. 878, §2, 60 Stat. 930; Aug. 5, 1947, ch. 499, §2, 61 Stat. 784; Sept. 29, 1950, ch. 1108, §1, 64 Stat. 1080; Mar. 23, 1951, ch. 15, title II, §201(a), (b), 65 Stat. 23; June 6, 1952, ch. 372, 66 Stat. 129; Aug. 23, 1954, ch. 830, §1, 68 Stat. 767; Pub. L. 87–846, title II, §204(a), Oct. 22, 1962, 76 Stat. 1114.)

REFERENCES IN TEXT

The Renegotiation Act, referred to in subsecs. (a)(4) and (b), is act Apr. 28, 1942, ch. 247, title IV, §403, 56 Stat. 245, as amended, which enacted section 1191 of this Appendix, and which was omitted from the Code.

Act of October 31, 1942 (56 Stat. 1013; 35 U.S.C. §§89 to 96), referred to in subsecs. (a)(4) and (c), is act Oct. 31, 1942, ch. 634, 56 Stat. 1013, which enacted sections 89 to 96 of former Title 35, Patents, and which was omitted from the Code.

Section 2 of said Act, referred to in subsec. (c), means section 2 of act Oct. 31, 1942, ch. 634, 56 Stat. 1013, which enacted section 90 of former Title 35, Patents, and which was omitted from the Code.

Date of enactment of this amendment, referred to in subsec. (h), probably means date of enactment of Pub. L. 87–846, which was approved Oct. 22, 1962.

CODIFICATION

Section was formerly classified to section 619 of this Appendix.

AMENDMENTS

1962—Subsec. (h). Pub. L. 87–846 permitted application for designation as successor organization to be made within three months after Oct. 22, 1962, required payments in sum of $500,000 to be made from the War Claims Fund before expiration of one year from Oct. 22, 1962, provided for allocation of funds to multiple successor organizations and acceptance of payments as discharge of all claims, and eliminated provisions deeming a successor organization as successor in interest by operation of law, respecting time for making return to such organizations, limiting the return to $3,000,000, requiring filing of notice of claim before expiration of one year from Aug. 23, 1954, for transfer of property to eligible persons, and declaring that filing of notice of claim would not bar payment of debt claims under section 34 of this Appendix.

1954—Subsec. (h). Act Aug. 23, 1954, added subsec. (h).

1952—Subsec. (a)(2)(D). Act June 6, 1952, increased from $5,000,000 to $9,000,000 the limitation on amount of property which may be returned to nationals.

1950—Subsec. (a)(2)(D). Act Sept. 29, 1950, clarified authority of Alien Property Custodian to return vested property to a person who possessed American citizenship at all times since Dec. 7, 1941, despite concurrent enemy citizenship and residence in enemy territory, and authorized return of vested property to American women who lost their citizenship solely because of marriage, and who have reacquired their citizenship prior to Sept. 29, 1950.

1947—Subsec. (a)(2). Act Aug. 5, 1947, provided that returns shall not be made to any owner, legal representative, or successor in interest, of the Governments of Germany, Japan, Rumania, Bulgaria, or Hungary; or to corporations or associations organized under the laws of such countries; or to an individual voluntarily resident in such countries at any time since Dec. 7, 1941; or to an individual who was at any time after Dec. 7, 1941, a citizen or subject of such country and present in the territory of such nation.

1946—Subsec. (a)(2)(C), (D). Act Aug. 8, 1946, inserted provisos in subdivs. (C) and (D).

[3] So in original. Probably should be "hereof."

CHANGE OF NAME

Tax Court of the United States redesignated United States Tax Court pursuant to Pub. L. 91–172, title IX, §951, Dec. 30, 1969, 83 Stat. 730. See section 7441 of Title 26, Internal Revenue Code.

TRANSFER OF FUNCTIONS

War Contracts Price Adjustment Board abolished and powers, functions, and duties conferred upon Board by the Renegotiation Act, section 1191 of this Appendix, except those transferred to Administrator of General Services, transferred to Renegotiation Board by section 201(a), (b) of act Mar. 23, 1951, which was classified to section 1231(a), (b) of this Appendix. Renegotiation Board terminated and all property, including records, of Board transferred to Administrator of General Services on Mar. 31, 1979, pursuant to Pub. L. 95–431, title V, §501, Oct. 10, 1978, 92 Stat. 1043, and sections 1191 and 1231 of this Appendix were omitted from the Code.

Functions of Alien Property Custodian and Office of Alien Property Custodian, except those relating to property or interest in Philippines, vested in Attorney General. See notes set out under section 6 of this Appendix.

PURPOSE OF ACT AUGUST 5, 1947

Congress in enacting act Aug. 5, 1947, outlined the purpose of the act as follows:

"Whereas article 79 of the Treaty of Peace with Italy, signed at Paris on February 10, 1947, grants to the Allied and Associated Powers the right to seize and retain 'all property rights and interests which on the coming into force of the present treaty are within its territory and belong to Italy or to Italian nationals, and to apply such property or the proceeds thereof to such purposes as it may desire, within the limits of its claims and those of its nationals against Italy or Italian nationals, including debts, other than claims fully satisfied under other articles of the present treaty' and further provides that 'All Italian property, or the proceeds thereof, in excess of the amount of such claims, shall be returned'; and

"Whereas, pursuant to article 79 of the treaty of peace, negotiations have been entered into between the Governments of the United States and of Italy looking toward an agreement under which, upon the return of property, formerly Italian, in the United States, Italy will place at the disposal of the United States funds to be used in meeting certain claims of nationals of the United States; and

"Whereas, for the purpose of carrying out such agreement, it is desirable to authorize, in accordance with the procedures provided for in section 32 of the Trading With the Enemy Act of October 6, 1917 (40 Stat. 411), as amended [this section], return to Italy or citizens or subjects of Italy, or corporations or associations organized under the laws of Italy, of property vested in or transferred to the United States or its agencies; and

"Whereas, for the purpose of aiding the revival of the Italian economy and establishing it on a self-sustaining basis, it is desirable that there be returned or transferred to Italy those Italian vessels acquired by the United States after December 7, 1941, for use in the war effort and now owned by the United States and vessels of a total tonnage approximately equal to the tonnage of those Italian vessels seized by the United States after September 1, 1939, and lost while being employed in the United States war effort."

RETURN OF ITALIAN PROPERTY

Section 1 of act Aug. 5, 1947, provided: "That the President, or such officer or agency as he may designate, is hereby authorized to return, in accordance with the procedures provided for in section 32 of the Trading With the Enemy Act, as amended [this section], any property or interest, or the net proceeds thereof, which has been, since December 18, 1941, vested in or transferred to any officer or agency of the United States pursuant to the Trading With the Enemy Act, as amended [sections 1 to 6, 7 to 39, and 41 to 44 of this Appendix], and which immediately prior to such vesting or transfer was the property or interest of Italy or a citizen or subject of Italy, or a corporation or association organized under the laws of Italy."

TRANSFER OF VESSELS TO ITALIAN GOVERNMENT

Section 4 of act Aug. 5, 1947, provided: "The President is authorized upon such terms as he deems necessary (a) to transfer to the Government of Italy all vessels which were under Italian registry and flag on September 1, 1939, and were thereafter acquired by the United States and are now owned by the United States; and (b) with respect to any vessel under Italian registry and flag on September 1, 1939, and subsequently seized in United States ports and thereafter lost while being employed in the United States war effort, to transfer to the Government of Italy surplus merchant vessels of the United States of a total tonnage approximately equal to the total tonnage of the Italian vessels lost: *Provided*, That no monetary compensation shall be paid either for the use by the United States or its agencies of former Italian vessels so acquired or seized or for the return or transfer of such vessels or substitute vessels."

EXECUTIVE ORDER NO. 10587

Ex. Ord. No. 10587, Jan. 13, 1955, 20 F.R. 361, as amended by Ex. Ord. No. 11086, Feb. 26, 1963, 28 F.R. 1833, which designated the Jewish Restitution Successor Organization as successor in interest to deceased persons under subsec. (h) of this section and delegated to the Foreign Claims Settlement Commission the functions provided for in subsec. (h) of this section, was revoked by Ex. Ord. No. 12553, Feb. 25, 1986, 51 F.R. 7237.

SECTION REFERRED TO IN OTHER SECTIONS

This section is referred to in sections 33, 35, 36, 44 of this Appendix.

§33. Notice of claim; institution of suits; computation of time

No return may be made pursuant to section 9 or 32 [section 9 or 32 of this Appendix] unless notice of claim has been filed: (a) in the case of any property or interest acquired by the United States prior to December 18, 1941, by August 9, 1948; or (b) in the case of any property or interest acquired by the United States on or after December 18, 1941, not later than one year from February 9, 1954, or two years from the vesting of the property or interest in respect of which the claim is made, whichever is later. No suit pursuant to section 9 [section 9 of this Appendix] may be instituted after April 30, 1949, or after the expiration of two years from the date of the seizure by or vesting in the Alien Property Custodian, as the case may be, of the property or interest in respect of which relief is sought, whichever is later, but in computing such two years there shall be excluded any period during which there was pending a suit or claim for return pursuant to section 9 or 32(a) hereof [section 9 or 32(a) of this Appendix].

(Oct. 6, 1917, ch. 106, §33, as added Dec. 18, 1941, ch. 593, title III, §305, as added Aug. 8, 1946, ch. 878, §1, 60 Stat. 925; amended Aug. 5, 1947, ch. 499, §3, 61 Stat. 786; July 1, 1948, ch. 794, 62 Stat. 1218; Feb. 9, 1954, ch. 4, 68 Stat. 7; Aug. 23, 1954, ch. 830, §2, 68 Stat. 768; Pub. L. 87–846, title II, §204(b), Oct. 22, 1962, 76 Stat. 1115.)

CODIFICATION

Section was formerly classified to section 620 of this Appendix.

AMENDMENTS

1962—Pub. L. 87–846 struck out provision for return of property to successor organizations pursuant to section 32(h) of this Appendix if notice of claim was filed before expiration of one year from Aug. 23, 1954.

1954—Act Aug. 23, 1954, inserted before period at end of first sentence "except that return may be made to successor organizations designated pursuant to section 32(h) hereof if notice of claim is filed before the expiration of one year from the effective date of this Act".

Act Feb. 9, 1954, substituted "not later than one year from February 9, 1954" for "by April 30, 1949" in first sentence.

1948—Act July 1, 1948, amended section generally, extending time for filing claims under section 9 or 32 of this Appendix.

1947—Act Aug. 5, 1947, provided that notice of certain claims could be filed by Aug. 8, 1948, or that Italian notice of claim could be filed by July 31, 1949.

TRANSFER OF FUNCTIONS

Functions of Alien Property Custodian and Office of Alien Property Custodian, except those relating to property or interest in Philippines, vested in Attorney General. See notes set out under section 6 of this Appendix.

§34. Payment of debts

(a) Claims allowable; defenses

Any property or interest vested in or transferred to the Alien Property Custodian (other than any property or interest acquired by the United States prior to December 18, 1941), or the net proceeds thereof, shall be equitably applied by the Custodian in accordance with the provisions of this section to the payment of debts owed by the person who owned such property or interest immediately prior to its vesting in or transfer to the Alien Property Custodian. No debt claim shall be allowed under this section if it was not due and owing at the time of such vesting or transfer, or if it arose from any action or transactions prohibited by or pursuant to this Act [sections 1 to 6, 7 to 39, and 41 to 44 of this Appendix] and not licensed or otherwise authorized pursuant thereto, or (except in the case of debt claims acquired by the Custodian) if it was at the time of such vesting or transfer due and owing to any person who has since the beginning of the war been convicted of violation of this Act, as amended [said sections], sections 1 to 6 of the Criminal Code, title I of the Act of June 15, 1917 (ch. 30, 40 Stat. 217), as amended; the Act of April 20, 1918 (ch. 59, 40 Stat. 534), as amended; the Act of June 8, 1934[1] (ch. 327, 52 Stat. 631), as amended; the Act of January 12, 1938 (ch. 2, 52 Stat. 3); title I, Alien Registration Act, 1940 (ch. 439, 54 Stat. 670); the Act of October 17, 1940 (ch. 897, 54 Stat. 1201); or the Act of June 25, 1942 (ch. 447, 56 Stat. 390). Any defense to the payment of such claims which would have been available to the debtor shall be available to the Custodian, except that the period from and after the beginning of the war shall not be included for the purpose of determining the application of any statute of limitations. Debt claims allowable hereunder shall include only those of citizens of the United States or of the Philippine Islands; those of corporations organized under the laws of the United States or any State, Territory, or possession thereof, or the District of Columbia or the Philippine Islands; those of other natural persons who are and have been since the beginning of the war residents of the United States and who have not during the war been interned or paroled pursuant to the Alien Enemy Act; and those acquired by the Custodian. Legal representatives (whether or not appointed by a court in the United States) or successors in interest by inheritance, devise, bequest, or operation of law or debt claimants, other than persons who would themselves be disqualified hereunder from allowance of a debt claim, shall be eligible for payment to the same extent as their principals or predecessors would have been.

(b) Time limit for filing claims; extension; notice

The Custodian shall fix a date or dates after which the filing of debt claims in respect of any or all debtors shall be barred, and may extend the time so fixed, and shall give at least sixty days' notice thereof by publication in the Federal Register. In no event shall the time extend beyond the expiration of two years from the date of the last vesting in or transfer to the Custodian of any property or interest of a debtor in respect of whose debts the date is fixed, or from the date of enactment of this section [Aug. 8, 1946], whichever is later. No debt shall be paid prior to the expiration of one hundred and twenty days after publication of the first such notice in respect of the debtor, nor in any event shall any payment of a debt claim be made out of any property or interest or proceeds in respect of which a suit or proceeding pursuant to this Act [sections 1 to 6, 7 to 39, and 41 to 44 of this Appendix] for return is pending and was instituted prior to the expiration of such one hundred and twenty days.

(c) Examination of claims

The Custodian shall examine the claims, and such evidence in respect thereof as may be presented to him or as he may introduce into the record, and shall make a determination, with respect to each claim, of allowance or disallowance, in whole or in part.

(d) Funds for debt payments

Payment of debt claims shall be made only out of such money included in, or received as net proceeds from the sale, use, or other disposition of, any property or interest owned by the debtor immediately prior to its vesting in or transfer to the Alien Property Custodian, as shall remain after deduction of (1) the amount of the expenses of the Office of Alien Property Custodian (including both expenses in connection with such property or interest or proceeds thereof, and such portion as the Custodian shall fix of the other expenses of the Office of Alien Property Custodian), and of taxes, as defined in section 36 hereof [section 36 of this Appendix], paid by the Custodian in respect of such property or interest or proceeds, and (2) such amount, if any, as the Custodian may establish as a cash reserve for the future payment of such expenses and taxes. If the money available hereunder for the payment of debt claims against the debtor is insufficient for the satisfaction of all claims allowed by the Custodian, ratable payments shall

[1] So in original. Probably should be "1938".

be made in accordance with subsection (g) hereof to the extent permitted by the money available and additional payments shall be made whenever the Custodian shall determine that substantial further money has become available, through liquidation of any such property or interest or otherwise. The Custodian shall not be required through any judgment of any court, levy of execution, or otherwise to sell or liquidate any property or interest vested in or transferred to him, for the purpose of paying or satisfying any debt claim.

(e) Amount payable; disallowance; notice; review; additional evidence; judgment

If the aggregate of debt claims filed as prescribed does not exceed the money from which, in accordance with subsection (d) of this section, payment may be made, the Custodian shall pay each claim to the extent allowed, and shall serve by registered mail, on each claimant whose claim is disallowed in whole or in part, a notice of such disallowance. Within sixty days after the date of mailing of the Custodian's determination, any debt claimant whose claim has been disallowed in whole or in part may file in the United States District Court for the District of Columbia a complaint for review of such disallowance naming the Custodian as defendant. Such complaint shall be served on the Custodian. The Custodian, within forty-five days after service on him, shall certify and file in said court a transcript of the record of proceedings in the Office of Alien Property Custodian with respect to the claim in question. Upon good cause shown such time may be extended by the court. Such record shall include the claim as filed, such evidence with respect thereto as may have been presented to the Custodian or introduced into the record by him, and the determination of the Custodian with respect thereto, including any findings made by him. The court may, in its discretion, take additional evidence, upon a showing that such evidence was offered to and excluded by the Custodian, or could not reasonably have been adduced before him or was not available to him. The court shall enter judgment affirming, modifying, or reversing the Custodian's determination, and directing payment in the amount, if any, which it finds due.

(f) Pro rata payments; notice; review; additional evidence; intervention; judgment

If the aggregate of debt claims filed as prescribed exceeds the money from which, in accordance with subsection (d) hereof, payment may be made, the Custodian shall prepare and serve by registered mail on all claimants a schedule of all debt claims allowed and the proposed payment to each claimant. In preparing such schedule, the Custodian shall assign priorities in accordance with the provisions of subsection (g) hereof. Within sixty days after the date of mailing of such schedule, any claimant considering himself aggrieved may file in the United States District Court for the District of Columbia a complaint for review of such schedule, naming the Custodian as defendant. A copy of such complaint shall be served upon the Custodian and on each claimant named in the schedule. The Custodian, within forty-five days after service on him, shall certify and file in said court a transcript of the record of proceedings in the Office of Alien Property Custodian with respect to such schedule. Upon good cause shown such time may be extended by the court. Such record shall include the claims in question as filed, such evidence with respect thereto as may have been presented to the Custodian or introduced into the record by him, any findings or other determinations made by the Custodian with respect thereto, and the schedule prepared by the Custodian. The court may, in its discretion, take additional evidence, upon a showing that such evidence was offered to and excluded by the Custodian or could not reasonably have been adduced before him or was not available to him. Any interested debt claimant who has filed a claim with the Custodian pursuant to this section, upon timely application to the court, shall be permitted to intervene in such review proceedings. The court shall enter judgment affirming or modifying the schedule as prepared by the Custodian and directing payment, if any be found due, pursuant to the schedule as affirmed or modified and to the extent of the money from which, in accordance with subsection (d) hereof, payment may be made. Pending the decision of the court on such complaint for review, and pending final determination of any appeal from such decision, payment may be made only to an extent, if any, consistent with the contentions of all claimants for review.

(g) Priority of claims

Debt claims shall be paid in the following order of priority: (1) Wage and salary claims, not to exceed $600; (2) claims entitled to priority under sections 191 and 193 of title 31[2] of the United States Code [31 U.S.C. 3713(a) and 9309], except as provided in subsection (h) hereof, (3) all other claims for services rendered, for expenses incurred in connection with such services, for rent, for goods and materials delivered to the debtor, and for payments made to the debtor for goods or services not received by the claimant; (4) all other debt claims. No payment shall be made to claimants within a subordinate class unless the money from which, in accordance with subsection (d) hereof, payment may be made permits payment in full of all allowed claims in every prior class.

(h) Priority as debt due United States

No debt of any kind shall be entitled to priority under any law of the United States or any State, Territory, or possession thereof, or the District of Columbia, solely by reason of becoming a debt due or owing to the United States as a result of its acquisition by the Alien Property Custodian.

(i) Exclusiveness of relief

The sole relief and remedy available to any person seeking satisfaction of a debt claim out of any property or interest which shall have been vested in or transferred to the Alien Property Custodian (other than any property or interest acquired by the United States prior to December 18, 1941), or the proceeds thereof, shall be the relief and remedy provided in this section, and suits for the satisfaction of debt claims

[2] See References in Text note below.

shall not be instituted, prosecuted, or further maintained except in conformity with this section: *Provided*, That no person asserting any interest, right, or title in any property or interest or proceeds acquired by the Alien Property Custodian, shall be barred from proceeding pursuant to this Act [sections 1 to 6, and 7 to 39, and 41 to 44 of this Appendix] for the return thereof, by reason of any proceeding which he may have brought pursuant to this section; nor shall any security interest asserted by the creditor in any such property or interest or proceeds be deemed to have been waived solely by reason of such proceeding. The Alien Property Custodian shall treat all debt claims now filed with him as claims filed pursuant to this section. Nothing contained in this section shall bar any person from the prosecution of any suit at law or in equity against the original debtor or against any other person who may be liable for the payment of any debt for which a claim might have been filed hereunder. No purchaser, lessee, licensee, or other transferee of any property or interest from the Alien Property Custodian shall, solely by reason of such purchase, lease, license, or transfer, become liable for the payment of any debt owed by the person who owned such property or interest prior to its vesting in or transfer to the Alien Property Custodian. Payment by the Alien Property Custodian to any debt claimant shall constitute, to the extent of payment, a discharge of the indebtedness represented by the claim.

(Oct. 6, 1917, ch. 106, §34, as added Dec. 18, 1941, ch. 593, title III, §305, as added Aug. 8, 1946, ch. 878, §1, 60 Stat. 925; amended June 25, 1948, ch. 646, §32(a), 62 Stat. 991; May 24, 1949, ch. 139, §127, 63 Stat. 107.)

REFERENCES IN TEXT

Sections 1 to 6 of the Criminal Code, referred to in subsec. (a), are sections 1 to 6 of act Mar. 4, 1909, ch. 321, 35 Stat. 1088, which enacted sections 1 to 6 of former Title 18, Criminal Code and Criminal Procedure. Sections 1 to 6 of former Title 18 were repealed by act June 25, 1948, ch. 645, §21, 62 Stat. 862, and reenacted as sections 953 and 2381 to 2384 of Title 18, Crimes and Criminal Procedure.

Title I of act of June 15, 1917 (ch. 30, 40 Stat. 217), as amended, referred to in subsec. (a), is act June 15, 1917, ch. 30, title I, 40 Stat. 217, as amended, which enacted sections 31 to 38 of Title 50, War and National Defense, and which was repealed by act June 25, 1948, ch. 645, §21, 62 Stat. 862, and reenacted as sections 792 to 794 and 2388 of Title 18, Crimes and Criminal Procedure.

Act of April 20, 1918 (ch. 59, 40 Stat. 534), as amended, referred to in subsec. (a), is act Apr. 20, 1918, ch. 59, 40 Stat. 534, as amended, which enacted sections 101 to 106 of Title 50, and which was repealed by act June 25, 1948, ch. 645, §21, 62 Stat. 862, and reenacted as sections 2151 and 2153 to 2156 of Title 18.

Act of June 8, 1934 (ch. 327, 52 Stat. 631), as amended, referred to in subsec. (a), probably means act June 8, 1938, ch. 327, 52 Stat. 631, as amended, known as the Foreign Agents Registration Act of 1938, which is classified generally to subchapter II (§611 et seq.) of chapter 11 of Title 22, Foreign Relations and Intercourse. For complete classification of this Act to the Code, see Short Title note set out under section 611 of Title 22 and Tables.

Act January 12, 1938 (ch. 2, 52 Stat. 3), referred to in subsec. (a), is act Jan. 12, 1938, ch. 2, 52 Stat. 3, which enacted sections 45 to 45d of Title 50, War and National Defense, and which was repealed by act June 25, 1948, ch. 645, §21, 62 Stat. 862, and reenacted as sections 791 and 795 to 797 of Title 18, Crimes and Criminal Procedure.

Title I, Alien Registration Act, 1940 (ch. 439, 54 Stat. 670), referred to in subsec. (a), is act June 28, 1940, ch. 439, title I, 54 Stat. 670, which enacted sections 9 to 13 of former Title 18, Criminal Code and Criminal Procedure, and which was repealed by act June 25, 1948, ch. 645, §21, 62 Stat. 862, and reenacted as sections 2385 and 2387 of Title 18, Crimes and Criminal Procedure.

Act October 17, 1940 (ch. 897, 54 Stat. 1201), referred to in subsec. (a), is act Oct. 17, 1940, ch. 897, 54 Stat. 1201, which enacted sections 14 to 17 of former Title 18, Criminal Code and Criminal Procedure, and which was repealed by act June 25, 1948, ch. 645, §21, 62 Stat. 862, and reenacted as section 2386 of Title 18, Crimes and Criminal Procedure.

Act of June 25, 1942 (ch. 447, 56 Stat. 390), referred to in subsec. (a), is act June 25, 1942, ch. 447, 56 Stat. 390, as amended, which was classified to sections 781 to 785 of this Appendix and was omitted from the Code as terminated.

The Alien Enemy Act, referred to in subsec. (a), probably means sections 4067 to 4070 of the Revised Statutes, which are classified to sections 21 to 24 of Title 50, War and National Defense.

Sections 191 and 193 of title 31 of the United States Code, referred to in subsec. (g), were repealed by Pub. L. 97–258, §5(b), Sept. 13, 1982, 96 Stat. 1068, and reenacted by the first section thereof as sections 3713(a) and 9309 of Title 31, Money and Finance.

CODIFICATION

Section was formerly classified to section 620 of this Appendix.

CHANGE OF NAME

In subsecs. (e) and (f), "United States District Court for the District of Columbia" substituted for "the district court of the United States for the District of Columbia" on authority of act June 25, 1948, as amended by act May 24, 1949.

TRANSFER OF FUNCTIONS

Functions of Alien Property Custodian and Office of Alien Property Custodian, except those relating to property or interest in Philippines, vested in Attorney General. See notes set out under section 6 of this Appendix.

SECTION REFERRED TO IN OTHER SECTIONS

This section is referred to in section 35 of this Appendix.

§35. Hearings on claims; rules and regulations; delegation of powers

The officer or agency empowered to entertain claims under sections 9(a), 32, and 34 hereof [sections 9(a), 32, and 34 of this Appendix] shall have power to hold such hearings as may be deemed necessary; to prescribe rules and regulations governing the form and contents of claims, the proof thereof, and all other matters related to proceedings on such claims; and in connection with such proceedings to issue subpenas, administer oaths, and examine witnesses. Such powers, and any other powers conferred upon such officer or agency by sections 9(a), 32, and 34 hereof [said sections] may be exercised through subordinate officers designated by such officer or agency.

(Oct. 6, 1917, ch. 106, §35, as added Dec. 18, 1941, ch. 593, title III, §305, as added Aug. 8, 1946, ch. 878, §1, 60 Stat. 928.)

CODIFICATION

Section was formerly classified to section 620 of this Appendix.

§36. Taxes

(a) Liability; exemptions

The vesting in or transfer to the Alien Property Custodian of any property or interest (other than any property or interest acquired by the United States prior to December 18, 1941), or the receipt by him of any earnings, increment, or proceeds thereof shall not render inapplicable any Federal, State, Territorial, or local tax for any period prior or subsequent to the date of such vesting or transfer, nor render applicable the exemptions provided in title II of the Social Security Act [42 U.S.C. 401 et seq.] with respect to service performed in the employ of the United States Government or of any instrumentality of the United States.

(b) Payment by Custodian; liability of former owner; enforcement of tax liability; transfer of property

The Alien Property Custodian shall, notwithstanding the filing of any claim or the institution of any suit under this Act [sections 1 to 6, 7 to 39, and 41 to 44 of this Appendix], pay any tax incident to any such property or interest, or the earnings, increment, or proceeds thereof, at the earliest time appearing to him to be not contrary to the interest of the United States. The former owner shall not be liable for any such tax accruing while such property, interest, earnings, increment, or proceeds are held by the Alien Property Custodian, unless they are returned pursuant to this Act [said sections] without payment of such tax by the Alien Property Custodian. Every such tax shall be paid by the Alien Property Custodian to the same extent, as nearly as may be deemed practicable, as though the property or interest had not been vested in or transferred to the Alien Property Custodian, and shall be paid only out of the property or interest, or earnings, increment, or proceeds thereof, to which they are incident or out of other property or interests acquired from the same former owner, or earnings, increment, or proceeds thereof. No tax liability may be enforced from any property or interest or the earnings, increment or proceeds thereof while held by the Alien Property Custodian except with his consent. Where any property or interest is transferred, otherwise than pursuant to section 9(a) or 32 hereof [section 9(a) or 32(a) of this Appendix], the Alien Property Custodian may transfer the property or interest free and clear of any tax, except to the extent of any lien for a tax existing and perfected at the date of vesting, and the proceeds of such transfer shall, for tax purposes, replace the property or interest in the hands of the Alien Property Custodian.

(c) Computation; suspension of limitations, etc.

Subject to the provisions of subsection (b) of this section, the manner of computing any Federal taxes, including without limitation by reason of this enumeration, the applicability in such computation of credits, deductions, and exemptions to which the former owner is or would be entitled, and the time and manner of any payment of such taxes and the extent of any compliance by the Custodian with provisions of Federal law and regulations applicable with respect to Federal taxes, shall be in accordance with regulations prescribed by the Commissioner of Internal Revenue with the approval of the Secretary of the Treasury to effectuate this section. Statutes of limitations on assessment, collection, refund, or credit of Federal taxes shall be suspended, with respect to any vested property or interest, or the earnings, increment or proceeds thereof, while vested and for six months thereafter; but no interest shall be paid upon any refund with respect to any period during which the statute of limitations is so suspended.

(d) "Tax" defined

The word "tax" as used in this section shall include, without limitation by reason of this enumeration, any property, income, excess-profits, war-profits, excise, estate and employment tax, import duty, and special assessment; and also any interest, penalty, additional amount, or addition thereto not arising from any act, omission, neglect, failure, or delay on the part of the Custodian.

(e) Exemptions

Any tax exemption accorded to the Alien Property Custodian by specific provision of existing law shall not be affected by this section.

(Oct. 6, 1917, ch. 106, §36, as added Dec. 18, 1941, ch. 593, title III, §305, as added Aug. 8, 1946, ch. 878, §1, 60 Stat. 929.)

References in Text

The Social Security Act, referred to in subsec. (a), is act Aug. 14, 1935, ch. 531, 49 Stat. 620, as amended. Title II of the Social Security Act is classified generally to subchapter II (§401 et seq.) of chapter 7 of Title 42, The Public Health and Welfare. For complete classification of this Act to the Code, see section 1305 of Title 42 and Tables.

Codification

Section was formerly classified to section 620 of this Appendix.

Transfer of Functions

Functions of Alien Property Custodian and Office of Alien Property Custodian, except those relating to property or interest in Philippines, vested in Attorney General. See notes set out under section 6 of this Appendix.

Section Referred to in Other Sections

This section is referred to in section 34 of this Appendix.

§37. Insurance of property

The Alien Property Custodian may procure insurance in such amounts, and from such insurers, as he believes will adequately protect him against loss in connection with property or interest or proceeds held by him.

(Oct. 6, 1917, ch. 106, §37, as added Dec. 18, 1941, ch. 593, title III, §305, as added Aug. 8, 1946, ch. 878, §1, 60 Stat. 930.)

Codification

Section was formerly classified to section 620 of this Appendix.

Transfer of Functions

Functions of the Alien Property Custodian and the Office of Alien Property Custodian, except those relating to property or interest in the Philippines, vested in the Attorney General. See notes set out under section 6 of this Appendix.

§ 38. Shipment of relief supplies; definitions

(a) Notwithstanding any other provision of this Act [sections 1 to 6, 7 to 39, and 41 to 44 of this Appendix], it shall be lawful, at any time after the date of cessation of hostilities with any country with which the United States is at war, for any person in the United States to donate, or otherwise dispose of to, and to transport or deliver to, any person in such country any article or articles (including food, clothing, and medicine) intended to be used solely to relieve human suffering.

(b) As used in this section—

(1) the term "person" means any individual, partnership, association, company, or other unincorporated body of individuals, or corporation or body politic;

(2) with respect to any country with which the United States was at war on January 1, 1946, the term "date of cessation of hostilities" shall mean the date of enactment of this Act [May 16, 1946];

(3) with respect to any other war the term "date of cessation of hostilities" shall mean the date specified by proclamation of the President or by a concurrent resolution of the two Houses of Congress whichever is the earlier.

(Oct. 6, 1917, ch. 106, § 38, formerly § —, as added May 16, 1946, ch. 260, 60 Stat. 182, numbered Aug. 8, 1946, ch. 878, § 3, 60 Stat. 930.)

REFERENCES IN TEXT

The date of enactment of this Act, referred to in subsec. (b)(2), probably means May 16, 1946, the date of approval of act May 16, 1946, which added this section.

§ 39. Retention of properties or interests of Germany and Japan and their nationals; proceeds covered into Treasury; ex gratia payment to Switzerland

(a) No property or interest therein of Germany, Japan, or any national of either such country vested in or transferred to any officer or agency of the Government at any time after December 17, 1941, pursuant to the provisions of this Act [sections 1 to 6, 7 to 39, and 41 to 44 of this Appendix], shall be returned to former owners thereof or their successors in interest, and the United States shall not pay compensation for any such property or interest therein. The net proceeds remaining upon the completion of administration, liquidation, and disposition pursuant to the provisions of this Act [said sections] of any such property or interest therein shall be covered into the Treasury at the earliest practicable date. Nothing in this section shall be construed to repeal or otherwise affect the operation of the provisions of section 32, 40, 41, 42 or 43 of this Act [section 32, 40, 41, 42 or 43 of this Appendix] or of the Philippine Property Act of 1946 [22 U.S.C. 1381 et seq.].

(b) The Attorney General shall cover into the Treasury, to the credit of miscellaneous receipts, all sums from property vested in or transferred to the Attorney General under this Act [sections 1 to 6, 7 to 39, and 41 to 44 of this Appendix]—

(1) which the Attorney General receives after the date of the enactment of the Export Enhancement Act of 1988 [August 23, 1988], or

(2) which the Attorney General received before that date and which, as of that date, the Attorney General had not covered into the Treasury for deposit in the War Claims Fund, other than any such sums which the Attorney General determines in his or her discretion are the subject matter of any judicial action or proceeding.

(c) Notwithstanding any of the provisions of subsections (a) and (b) of this section, the Attorney General is authorized to pay from property vested in or transferred to the Attorney General under this Act [sections 1 to 6, 7 to 39, and 41 to 44 of this Appendix], the sum of $20,000 as an ex gratia payment to the Government of Switzerland in accordance with the terms of the agreement entered into by that Government and the Government of the United States on March 12, 1980.

(Oct. 6, 1917, ch. 106, § 39, as added July 3, 1948, ch. 826, § 12, 62 Stat. 1246; amended Aug. 7, 1953, ch. 344, 67 Stat. 461; Pub. L. 85–884, Sept. 2, 1958, 72 Stat. 1708; Pub. L. 87–846, title II, §§ 202, 204(c), Oct. 22, 1962, 76 Stat. 1113, 1115; Pub. L. 87–861, § 1, Oct. 23, 1962, 76 Stat. 1139; Pub. L. 89–619, Oct. 4, 1966, 80 Stat. 871; Pub. L. 99–93, title VIII, § 803, Aug. 16, 1985, 99 Stat. 449; Pub. L. 100–418, title II, § 2501(a), Aug. 23, 1988, 102 Stat. 1370.)

REFERENCES IN TEXT

The Philippine Property Act of 1946, referred to in subsec. (a), is act July 3, 1946, ch. 536, 60 Stat. 418, as amended, which is classified generally to subchapter V (§ 1381 et seq.) of chapter 15 of Title 22, Foreign Relations and Intercourse. For complete classification of this Act to the Code, see Short Title note set out under section 1381 of Title 22 and Tables.

AMENDMENTS

1988—Subsecs. (b) to (f). Pub. L. 100–418 substituted subsec. (b) for former subsecs. (b) to (e), redesignated subsec. (f) as (c), and substituted "and (b)" for "through (d)".

1985—Subsec. (f). Pub. L. 99–93 added subsec. (f).

1966—Subsec. (e). Pub. L. 89–619 added subsec. (e).

1962—Subsec. (a). Pub. L. 87–861 provided that nothing in this section shall be construed to repeal or otherwise affect the operation of section 40, 41, 42, or 43 of this Appendix.

Subsec. (b). Pub. L. 87–846, § 204(c), required Attorney General to cover $500,000 into Treasury for deposit into War Claims Fund for payments to successor organizations receiving heirless property.

Subsec. (d). Pub. L. 87–846, § 202, added subsec. (d).

1958—Subsec. (c). Pub. L. 85–884 added subsec. (c).

1953—Act Aug. 7, 1953, designated existing provisions as subsec. (a) and added subsec. (b).

SECTION REFERRED TO IN OTHER SECTION

This section is referred to in sections 2012, 2017p of this Appendix.

§ 40. Intercustodial conflicts involving enemy property; authority of President to conclude; delegation of authority

The President, or such officer or agency as he may designate, is authorized to conclude and give effect to agreements to further the amicable and expeditious settlement of intercustodial conflicts involving enemy property, subject to the following:

(1) The authority granted in this section shall extend only to agreements with governments with which the United States was not at war in World War II.

(2) Such agreements shall be in accordance with the policy of protecting and making available for utilization the American and nonenemy interests in such property and further the elimination of enemy interests in such property and the efficient administration and liquidation of enemy property in the United States.

(3) For the purposes of this section, the United States as to any intergovernmental agreements hereafter negotiated shall seek treatment equal to that accorded United States nationals for persons who, although citizens or residents of any enemy country before or during World War II, were deprived of full rights of citizenship or substantially deprived of liberty by laws, decrees, or regulations of such enemy country discriminating against racial, religious, or political groups: *Provided*, That on September 28, 1950, such persons were (1) permanent residents of the United States and (2) had declared their intention to become citizens of the United States in conformity with the provisions of the Nationality Act of 1940, as amended; and that such persons shall have acquired citizenship of the United States prior to the effective date of any intergovernmental agreement hereafter negotiated.

(4) Reimbursement to the United States by other governments pursuant to such agreements shall be administered as vested property: *Provided*, That nothing contained in this section shall hinder, restrict or limit the payment of claims from the War Claims Fund established by section 13 of the War Claims Act of 1948 (Public Law 896, 80th Congress, July 3, 1948; 62 Stat. 1240; 50 U.S.C. app. 2001–2013), as amended [section 2012 of this Appendix].

(Sept. 28, 1950, ch. 1094, 64 Stat. 1079.)

REFERENCES IN TEXT

The Nationality Act of 1940, as amended, referred to in par. (3), is act Oct. 14, 1940, ch. 876, 54 Stat. 1137, as amended, which was classified principally to chapter 11 (§501 et seq.) of Title 8, Aliens and Nationality, prior to its repeal by act June 27, 1952, ch. 477, title IV, §403(a)(42), 66 Stat. 280. See section 1101 et seq. of Title 8.

CODIFICATION

Section was not enacted as part of the Trading with the Enemy Act which comprises sections 1 to 6, 7 to 39, and 41 to 44 of this Appendix.

EX. ORD. NO. 10244. AUTHORIZATION OF SECRETARY OF STATE AND ATTORNEY GENERAL TO PERFORM CERTAIN FUNCTIONS

Ex. Ord. No. 10244, May 17, 1951, 16 F.R. 4639, provided:

1. The Secretary of State and the Attorney General are hereby jointly designated as the officers authorized to conclude and give effect to agreements relating to the settlement of intercustodial conflicts involving enemy property made pursuant to the said act of September 28, 1950 [this section], and to exercise all powers incident thereto which are conferred by such act, including, without limitation, the powers to receive, transfer, release or return property, interests therein, or proceeds thereof.

2. It is the policy of this order that the Secretary of State, with the concurrence of the Attorney General, shall perform all functions necessary or appropriate to give effect to any agreement made pursuant to the said act of September 28, 1950 [this section], with relation to the protection of American interests in property outside the United States, and that the Attorney General, with the concurrence of the Secretary of State, shall perform all functions necessary or appropriate to give effect to any such agreement with relation to property subject to the jurisdiction of the United States, and that all other functions relating to the effectuation of any such agreement shall be performed as may be agreed by the Secretary of State and the Attorney General. However, no action taken hereunder by either the Secretary of State or the Attorney General shall be considered to be invalid on the ground that under the provisions of this order such action was within the jurisdiction of the Secretary of State rather than the Attorney General, or vice versa, or that concurrence was not obtained, or that such action was not joint.

3. The Secretary of State and the Attorney General may each delegate to the other or to any other officer, person, or agency within his respective department such of his functions under this order as he may deem necessary.

4. Any money, property, or interest received as reimbursement by the United States by virtue of any agreement made pursuant to the said act of September 28, 1950 [this section], shall be administered and disposed of by the Attorney General as vested property pursuant to the said Trading With the Enemy Act, as amended [sections 1 to 6, 7 to 39, and 41 to 44 of this Appendix]. Any other money, property, or interest received by the Secretary of State or the Attorney General pursuant to any such agreement shall be administered and disposed of pursuant to the provisions of such agreement.

HARRY S. TRUMAN.

SECTION REFERRED TO IN OTHER SECTIONS

This section is referred to in section 39 of this Appendix.

§41. Divestment of estates, trusts, insurance policies, annuities, remainders, pensions, workmen's compensation and veterans' benefits; exceptions; notice of divestment

(a) Subject to the provisions of subsection (b) hereof [of this section], all rights and interests of individuals in estates, trusts, insurance policies, annuities, remainders, pensions, workmen's compensation and veterans' benefits vested under this Act [sections 1 to 6, 7 to 39, and 41 to 44 of this Appendix] after December 17, 1941, which have not become payable or deliverable to or have not vested in possession in the Attorney General prior to December 31, 1961, are divested: *Provided*, That the provisions of this section shall not affect the right of the Attorney General to retain all such property rights and interests and to collect all income which is payable to or vested in possession in him prior to December 31, 1961.

(b) Nothing contained in this section shall divest or require the divestment of any portion of any such interest the beneficial owner of which is a natural person who has been convicted personally and by name by a court of competent jurisdiction of murder, ill treatment, or deportation for slave labor of prisoners of war, political opponents, hostages, or civilian population in occupied territories, or of murder or ill treatment of military or naval persons, or of plunder or wanton destruction without justified military necessity.

(c) At the earliest practicable time after the effective date of this Act, the Attorney General shall transmit to the lawful owner or custodian of any interest divested by this section written notice of such divestment.

(Oct. 6, 1917, ch. 106, §40, as added Pub. L. 87–846, title II, §205, Oct. 22, 1962, 76 Stat. 1115.)

REFERENCES IN TEXT

Effective date of this Act, referred to in subsec. (c), probably means the effective date of Pub. L. 87–846, which was approved Oct. 22, 1962, which added this section.

SECTION REFERRED TO IN OTHER SECTIONS

This section is referred to in section 39 of this Appendix.

§42. Claims for proceeds from sale of certain certificates: jurisdiction, limitations; divestment of copyrights: "copyrights" defined, rights of licensees and assignees, reproduction rights of United States, transfer of interests, payment of royalties to Attorney General, suits for infringement

(a) Notwithstanding any statute of limitation, lapse of time, any prior decision by any court of the United States, or any compromise, release or assignment to the Alien Property Custodian, jurisdiction is hereby conferred upon the United States Court of Federal Claims to hear, determine, and render judgment upon the claims against the United States for the proceeds received by the United States from the sale of the property vested under the provisions of the Trading With the Enemy Act [sections 1 to 6, 7 to 39, and 41 to 44 of this Appendix] by vesting order numbered 33 relating to certificate numbers 104 to 121, inclusive, 125, 126, 128 to 134, inclusive, and 137 to 139, inclusive. Proceedings with respect to such claims may be instituted hereunder not later than two years after the date of the enactment of this section [Oct. 22, 1962].

(b) As used in this section the word "copyrights" includes copyrights, claims of copyrights, rights to copyrights, and rights to copyright renewals.

(c) All copyrights vested in the Alien Property Custodian or the Attorney General under the provisions of this Act [sections 1 to 6, 7 to 39, and 41 to 44 of this Appendix] subsequent to December 17, 1941, which have not been returned or otherwise disposed of under this Act [said sections], except copyrights vested by vesting orders 128 (7 F.R. 7578), 13111 (14 F.R. 1730), 14349 (15 F.R. 1575), 17366 (16 F.R. 2483), and 17952 (16 F.R. 6162) and copyrights vested with respect to the motion picture listed last in exhibit A of vesting order 11803, as amended (13 F.R. 5167, 15 F.R. 1626), are hereby divested as a matter of grace, effective the ninety-first day after the date of enactment of this section [Oct. 22, 1962], and the persons entitled thereto shall on that day succeed to the rights, privileges, and obligations arising out of such copyrights, subject, however, to—

(1) the rights of licensees under licenses issued by the Alien Property Custodian or the Attorney General in respect of such copyrights;

(2) the rights of assignees under assignments by the Alien Property Custodian or the Attorney General of interests in such licenses; and

(3) the right retained by the United States to reproduce, for its own use, or exhibit any divested copyrighted motion picture films.

The rights and interests remaining in the Attorney General under licenses issued by him or by the Alien Property Custodian in respect to copyrights divested hereunder are hereby transferred, effective the day of divestment, to the persons entitled to such copyrights: *Provided*, That all unpaid royalties or other income accrued in favor of the Attorney General under such licenses prior to the day of divestment shall be paid by the licensees to the Attorney General.

(d) All rights or interests vested in the Alien Property Custodian or the Attorney General under the provisions of this Act [sections 1 to 6, 7 to 39, and 41 to 44 of this Appendix] subsequent to December 17, 1941, arising out of prevesting contracts entered into with respect to copyrights, except—

(1) royalties or other income received by or accrued in favor of the Alien Property Custodian or the Attorney General under such contracts;

(2) rights or interests which have been returned or otherwise disposed of under this Act [sections 1 to 6, 7 to 39, and 41 to 44 of this Appendix]; and

(3) rights or interests vested by vesting orders 128 (7 F.R. 7578), 13111 (14 F.R. 1730), 14349 (15 F.R. 1575), and 17366 (16 F.R. 2483),

are hereby divested as a matter of grace, effective the ninety-first day after the date of enactment of this section [Oct. 22, 1962], and the persons entitled to such rights or interests shall succeed thereto, subject to the right of the Attorney General to collect and receive all unpaid royalties or other income accrued in his favor under such prevesting contracts prior to the day of divestment.

(e) Nothing in this section shall be construed to transfer to a person entitled to a copyright divested hereunder the right of the Attorney General to sue for the infringement of such copyright during the period between (1) the vesting thereof or the vesting of rights and interests in a contract entered into with respect thereto, and (2) the day of divestment. The right to sue for infringement shall remain in the Attorney General.

(Oct. 6, 1917, ch. 106, §41, as added Pub. L. 87–846, title II, §206, Oct. 22, 1962, 76 Stat. 1115; amended Pub. L. 88–490, Aug. 26, 1964, 78 Stat. 607; Pub. L. 97–164, title I, §161(9), Apr. 2, 1982, 96 Stat. 49; Pub. L. 102–572, title IX, §902(b)(1), Oct. 29, 1992, 106 Stat. 4516.)

AMENDMENTS

1992—Subsec. (a). Pub. L. 102–572 substituted "United States Court of Federal Claims" for "United States Claims Court".

1982—Subsec. (a). Pub. L. 97–164 substituted "Claims Court" for "Court of Claims".

1964—Subsec. (a). Pub. L. 88–490 substituted "render judgment upon" for "report to the Congress concerning" and "two years after the date of enactment of this section [October 22, 1962]" for "one year after the date of the enactment of this Act".

EFFECTIVE DATE OF 1992 AMENDMENT

Amendment by Pub. L. 102–572 effective Oct. 29, 1992, see section 911 of Pub. L. 102–572, set out as a note under section 171 of Title 28, Judiciary and Judicial Procedure.

EFFECTIVE DATE OF 1982 AMENDMENT

Amendment by Pub. L. 97–164 effective Oct. 1, 1982, see section 402 of Pub. L. 97–164, set out as a note under section 171 of Title 28, Judiciary and Judicial Procedure.

TRANSFER OF FUNCTIONS

Functions of Alien Property Custodian and Office of Alien Property Custodian, except those relating to property or interest in Philippines, are vested in Attorney General. See notes set out under section 6 of this Appendix.

SECTION REFERRED TO IN OTHER SECTIONS

This section is referred to in section 39 of this Appendix.

§43. Divestment of trademarks

(a) "Trademarks" defined

As used in this section, the word "trademarks" includes trademarks, trade names, and the goodwill of the business to which a trademark or trade name is appurtenant.

(b) Effective date of divestment; rights of licensees; transfer of interests; payment of royalties to Attorney General

Trademarks vested in the Alien Property Custodian or the Attorney General under the provisions of this Act [sections 1 to 6, 7 to 39, and 41 to 44 of this Appendix] subsequent to December 17, 1941, which have not been returned or otherwise disposed of under this Act [said sections], except trademarks vested by vesting orders 284, as amended (7 Fed. Reg. 9754, 9 Fed. Reg. 1038), 2354 (8 Fed. Reg. 14635), 5592 (11 Fed. Reg. 1675), and 18805 (17 Fed. Reg. 4364), are hereby divested as a matter of grace, effective the ninety-first day after the day of enactment of this section [Oct. 23, 1962], and the persons entitled to such trademarks shall on that day succeed to the rights, privileges, and obligations arising therefrom, subject, however, to the rights of licensees under licenses issued by the Alien Property Custodian or the Attorney General in respect to such trademarks. The rights and interests remaining in the Attorney General under licenses issued by him or by the Alien Property Custodian in respect to trademarks divested hereunder are transferred, effective the day of divestment, to the persons entitled to such trademarks: *Provided*, That all unpaid royalties or other income accrued in favor of the Attorney General under such licenses prior to the day of divestment shall be paid by the licensees to the Attorney General.

(c) Prevesting contracts; exceptions; payment of royalties to Attorney General

All rights or interests vested in the Alien Property Custodian or the Attorney General under the provisions of this Act [sections 1 to 6, 7 to 39, and 41 to 44 of this Appendix] subsequent to December 17, 1941, arising out of prevesting contracts entered into with respect to trademarks, except—

(1) royalties or other income received by or accrued in favor of the Alien Property Custodian or the Attorney General under such contracts;

(2) rights or interests which have been returned or otherwise disposed of under this Act [said sections];

(3) rights or interests vested by vesting orders 284, as amended (7 Fed. Reg. 9754; 9 Fed. Reg. 1038), 2354 (8 Fed. Reg. 14635), 5592 (11 Fed. Reg. 1675), and 18805 (17 Fed. Reg. 4364),

are hereby divested as a matter of grace, effective the ninety-first day after the date of enactment of this section [Oct. 23, 1962], and the persons entitled to such rights or interests shall succeed thereto, subject to the right of the Attorney General to collect and receive all unpaid royalties or other income accrued in his favor under such prevesting contracts prior to the day of divestment.

(d) Publication of ownership list in Federal Register; effective date of divestment; succession to ownership of equivalent trademarks

The Attorney General shall within forty-five days after the date of enactment of this section [Oct. 23, 1962] publish in the Federal Register a list of trademarks which at the date of vesting in the Alien Property Custodian or Attorney General were owned by persons who were resident in or had their sole or primary seat in the area of Germany now in the Soviet Zone of Occupation or in the Soviet sector of Berlin or in German territory under provisional Soviet or Polish administration. Notwithstanding the provisions of subsection (b) of this section, the effective date of divestment of the trademarks so listed and published in the Federal Register shall be the date of publication in the Federal Register by the Secretary of State of a certification identifying the cases in which an equivalent trademark has been registered in the Federal Republic of Germany for a person residing or having its sole or primary seat in the Federal Republic of Germany or in the western sectors of Berlin. In those cases of an equivalent trademark certified by the Secretary of State, the person registered by the Federal Republic of Germany as owner of such equivalent trademark shall succeed to the ownership of the divested trademark in the United States.

(Oct. 6, 1917, ch. 106, §42, as added Pub. L. 87–861, §2, Oct. 23, 1962, 76 Stat. 1139.)

TRANSFER OF FUNCTIONS

Functions of Alien Property Custodian and Office of Alien Property Custodian, except those relating to property or interest in Philippines, are vested in Attorney General. See notes set out under section 6 of this Appendix.

§44. Motion picture prints, transfer of title

(a) Prints in custody of Library of Congress; exception

The Attorney General is authorized and directed to transfer to the Library of Congress the title to all prints of motion pictures now in the custody of the Library, which prints were vested in or transferred to the Alien Property Custodian or the Attorney General pursuant to this Act [sections 1 to 6, 7 to 39, and 41 to 44 of this Appendix] after December 17, 1941, except prints of motion pictures which are the subject of suits or claims under section 9(a) or section 32 of this Act [section 9(a) or section 32 of this Appendix].

(b) Prints in custody of Attorney General; exception; right of selection by Library of Congress; disposal of unselected prints by Attorney General

Subject to the right of selection by the Library of Congress, the authorization, direction, and exception contained in subsection (a) hereof shall apply with respect to such prints now in the custody of the Attorney General. Prints not selected by the Library of Congress may be disposed of by the Attorney General in any manner he deems appropriate.

(c) Retention, reproduction, and disposal of prints by Library of Congress

With respect to all prints concerning which title is transferred to the Library of Congress pursuant to subsections (a) and (b) hereof, the Library shall have complete discretion to retain such prints and to reproduce copies thereof, or to dispose of them in any manner it deems appropriate.

(Oct. 6, 1917, ch. 106, § 43, as added Pub. L. 87–861, § 2, Oct. 23, 1962, 76 Stat. 1140.)

TRANSFER OF FUNCTIONS

Functions of Alien Property Custodian and Office of Alien Property Custodian, except those relating to property or interest in Philippines, are vested in Attorney General. See notes set out under section 6 of this Appendix.

SECTION REFERRED TO IN OTHER SECTIONS

This section is referred to in section 39 of this Appendix.

SOLDIERS' AND SAILORS' CIVIL RELIEF ACT OF 1918

ACT MAR. 8, 1918, CH. 20, 40 STAT. 440

§§ 101 to 104. Omitted

CODIFICATION

Sections 101 to 104 were omitted as expired. See Termination note set out under sections 161 to 165 of this Appendix.

Section 101, act Mar. 8, 1918, ch. 20, § 100, 40 Stat. 440, related to declaration of purpose of this act.

Section 102, act Mar. 8, 1918, ch. 20, § 101, 40 Stat. 440, related to definitions.

Section 103, act Mar. 8, 1918, ch. 20, § 102, 40 Stat. 441, related to territorial application of this act, jurisdiction of courts, and form of procedure.

Section 104, act Mar. 8, 1918, ch. 20, § 103, 40 Stat. 441, related to protection of persons secondarily liable.

§§ 111 to 116. Omitted

CODIFICATION

Sections 111 to 116 were omitted as expired. See Termination note set out under sections 161 to 165 of this Appendix.

Section 111, act Mar. 8, 1918, ch. 20, § 200, 40 Stat. 441, related to default judgments, affidavits and bonds, and attorneys for persons in service. See Default Judgment note set out under sections 161 to 165 of this Appendix.

Section 112, act Mar. 8, 1918, ch. 20, § 201, 40 Stat. 442, related to stay of proceedings where military service affected conduct.

Section 113, act Mar. 8, 1918, ch. 20, § 202, 40 Stat. 442, related to relief against fines and penalties on contracts, etc., while in service.

Section 114, act Mar. 8, 1918, ch. 20, § 203, 40 Stat. 442, related to stay of execution of judgments, attachments, etc., against persons in service.

Section 115, act Mar. 8, 1918, ch. 20, § 204, 40 Stat. 442, related to duration and terms of stay and to codefendants not in service.

Section 116, act Mar. 8, 1918, ch. 20, § 205, 40 Stat. 443, related to exclusion of period of military service from time of statutes of limitation.

§§ 121 to 124. Omitted

CODIFICATION

Sections 121 to 124 were omitted as expired. See Termination note set out under sections 161 to 165 of this Appendix.

Section 121, act Mar. 8, 1918, ch. 20, § 300, 40 Stat. 443, related to rents, evictions, stay of proceedings, and allotment of pay to discharge.

Section 122, act Mar. 8, 1918, ch. 20, § 301, 40 Stat. 443, related to contracts for the purchase of real or personal property and to actions on such contracts.

Section 123, act Mar. 8, 1918, ch. 20, § 302, 40 Stat. 444, related to mortgages or trust deeds, actions thereon, stays, and sales under powers. See Limitation of Actions note set out under sections 161 to 165 of this Appendix.

Section 124, act Mar. 8, 1918, ch. 20, § 303, as added Sept. 16, 1940, ch. 720, § 13(c), 54 Stat. 896, related to installments contracts and agreements to terminate, repossess, or retain property transferred.

§§ 131 to 146. Omitted

CODIFICATION

Sections 131 to 146 were omitted as expired. See Termination note set out under sections 161 to 165 of this Appendix.

Section 131, act Mar. 8, 1918, ch. 20, § 400, 40 Stat. 444, related to definitions concerning insurance.

Section 132, act Mar. 8, 1918, ch. 20, § 401, 40 Stat. 444, related to application for insurance benefits and forms.

Section 133, act Mar. 8, 1918, ch. 20, § 402, 40 Stat. 444, related to persons entitled to insurance benefits.

Section 134, act Mar. 8, 1918, ch. 20, § 403, 40 Stat. 445, related to lists of persons entitled to insurance benefits.

Section 135, act Mar. 8, 1918, ch. 20, § 404, 40 Stat. 445, related to applications on policies totaling more than $5,000.

Section 136, act Mar. 8, 1918, ch. 20, § 405, 40 Stat. 445, related to lapse of policies for nonpayment of premiums.

Section 137, act Mar. 8, 1918, ch. 20, § 406, 40 Stat. 445, related to reports to the Bureau of War Risk Insurance.

Section 138, act Mar. 8, 1918, ch. 20, § 407, 40 Stat. 446, related to verification of differences between premiums defaulted and paid.

Section 139, act Mar. 8, 1918, ch. 20, § 408, 40 Stat. 446, related to bonds of the United States for the difference between premiums defaulted and paid.

Section 140, act Mar. 8, 1918, ch. 20, § 409, 40 Stat. 446, related to holding of United States bonds as security for payment of premiums.

Section 141, act Mar. 8, 1918, ch. 20, § 410, 40 Stat. 446, related to deduction of unpaid premiums from proceeds of policies.

Section 142, act Mar. 8, 1918, ch. 20, § 411, 40 Stat. 446, related to payment of past due premiums on termination of service.

Section 143, act Mar. 8, 1918, ch. 20, § 412, 40 Stat. 446, related to accounts stated between insurers and the United States.

Section 144, act Mar. 8, 1918, ch. 20, § 413, 40 Stat. 447, related to payments of balances due insurers.

Section 145, act Mar. 8, 1918, ch. 20, § 414, 40 Stat. 447, related to policies to which these provisions did not apply.

Section 146, act Mar. 8, 1918, ch. 20, § 415, 40 Stat. 447, related to companies or associations to which these provisions applied.

§§151, 152. Omitted

CODIFICATION

Sections 151 and 152 were omitted as expired. See Termination note set out under sections 161 to 165 of this Appendix.

Section 151, act Mar. 8, 1918, ch. 20, §500, 40 Stat. 447, related to application of this section to taxes or assessments and to sale of property for failure to pay taxes or assessments.

Section 152, act Mar. 8, 1918, ch. 20, §501, 40 Stat. 448, related to rights to public lands as not forfeited.

§§161 to 165. Omitted

CODIFICATION

Sections 161 to 165 were omitted as expired. See Termination note set out below.

Section 161, act Mar. 8, 1918, ch. 20, §600, 40 Stat. 448, related to transfers to take advantage of this act.

Section 162, act Mar. 8, 1918, ch. 20, §601, 40 Stat. 448, related to certificates of military service, persons reported missing, and presumptions.

Section 163, act Mar. 8, 1918, ch. 20, §602, 40 Stat. 449, related to revocation of interlocutory orders.

Section 164, act Mar. 8, 1918, ch. 20, §603, 40 Stat. 449, provided that the act of Mar. 8, 1918, remain in force until the termination of the war and for six months thereafter and that the provisions of the Act remain in effect as long as necessary for the exercise or enjoyment of any proceeding, remedy, privilege, stay, limitation, accounting, or other transaction authorized by the Act.

Section 165, act Mar. 8, 1918, ch. 20, §604, 40 Stat. 449, provided that this Act be cited as the Soldiers' and Sailors' Civil Relief Act.

TERMINATION AFTER OCTOBER 17, 1940

Sections 101 to 104, 111 to 116, 121 to 124, 131 to 146, 151, 152, and 161 to 165 of this Appendix were rendered inapplicable to military service performed after Oct. 17, 1940, under Selective Training and Service Act of 1940 and Army Reserve and Retired Personnel Law of 1940 by section 585 of this Appendix. Some of the sections had previously been made applicable to those 1940 acts by sections 313 and 404 of this Appendix. Present provisions on soldier's and sailor's civil relief are contained in section 501 et seq. of this Appendix.

DEFAULT JUDGMENTS

Act Sept. 3, 1919, ch. 55, 41 Stat. 282, provided that where default judgments were entered and no affidavits required by section 111 of this Appendix had been filed, the plaintiff, on notice, could file an affidavit stating that persons in default were not in military service at time of entry of default judgment and authorized court to enter an order making the judgment effective as of date of entry.

LIMITATION OF ACTIONS ON CLAIMS UNDER SECTION 123(3)

Act Mar. 4, 1923, ch. 284, 42 Stat. 1510, provided that claims under section 123(3) of this Appendix must have been asserted prior to Mar. 4, 1923 or within one year thereafter.

SELECTIVE DRAFT ACT OF 1917

ACT MAY 18, 1917, CH. 15, 40 STAT. 76

§§201 to 211. Omitted

CODIFICATION

Sections 201 to 211 were omitted pursuant to section 4 of act June 15, 1917, set out as an Effect of Termination of World War I note under sections 213, 214 of this Appendix.

Section 201, act May 18, 1917, ch. 15, §1, 40 Stat. 76, related to emergency increase in the Army, draft of National Guard and additional forces, volunteer divisions, and to the organization of the Army.

Section 202, acts May 18, 1917, ch. 15, §2, 40 Stat. 77; July 9, 1918, ch. 143, subch. XII, 40 Stat. 885; Aug. 31, 1918, ch. 166, §1, 40 Stat. 955; Oct. 14, 1940, ch. 876, §504, 54 Stat. 1172, related to manner of attaining increased forces, eligibility for the draft, quotas, period of service, and the government of the forces raised.

Section 203, act May 18, 1917, ch. 15, §3, 40 Stat. 78, related to bounties to induce enlistments, substitutes, and payments to escape service.

Section 204, acts May 18, 1917, ch. 15, §4, 40 Stat. 78; Aug. 31, 1918, ch. 166, §2, 40 Stat. 955, related to exemptions from the draft and to draft and appeal boards, and was repealed by Pub. L. 89–554, §8(a), Sept. 6, 1966, 80 Stat. 643.

Section 205, acts May 18, 1917, ch. 15, §5, 40 Stat. 80; Aug. 31, 1918, ch. 166, §3, 40 Stat. 955, related to registration, the persons required to register, and to penalties for failure to register.

Section 206, act May 18, 1917, ch. 15, §6, 40 Stat. 80, related to utilization of departments and officers, etc., use of franks, and offenses and punishments, and was repealed by Pub. L. 89–554, §8(a), Sept. 6, 1966, 80 Stat. 643.

Section 207, acts May 18, 1917, ch. 15, §7, 40 Stat. 81; July 9, 1918, ch. 143, subch. XIII, 40 Stat. 885, related to voluntary enlistments and to geographical groupings of enlisted or drafted men.

Section 208, acts May 18, 1917, ch. 15, §8, 40 Stat. 81; Apr. 20, 1918, ch. 61, 40 Stat. 534, related to temporary appointment of general officers and to vacancies in the Regular Army.

Section 209, act May 18, 1917, ch. 15, §9, 40 Stat. 82, related to periods of appointments and discharges for cause.

Section 210, act May 18, 1917, ch. 15, §10, 40 Stat. 82, related to pay, allowances, and pensions.

Section 211, act May 18, 1917, ch. 15, §11, 40 Stat. 82, related to suspension of restrictions on detail, detachment and employment of personnel.

§212. Repealed. Aug. 27, 1935, ch. 740, title II, §203, 49 Stat. 878

Section, act May 18, 1917, ch. 15, §12, 40 Stat. 82, related to regulation and prohibition of alcoholic liquors by the President.

§§213, 214. Omitted

CODIFICATION

Sections 213 and 214 were omitted pursuant to section 4 of act June 15, 1917, set out as an Effect of Termination of World War I note below.

Section 213, acts May 18, 1917, ch. 15, §13, 40 Stat. 83; July 9, 1918, ch. 143, subch. XIV, 40 Stat. 885, related to prohibition of prostitution. See section 1384 of Title 18, Crimes and Criminal Procedure.

Section 214, act May 18, 1917, ch. 15, §14, 40 Stat. 83, related to suspension of conflicting laws.

EFFECT OF TERMINATION OF WORLD WAR I

Act June 15, 1917, ch. 29, §4, 40 Stat. 217, provided in part that compulsory military service under sections 201 to 214 of this Appendix should cease four months after proclamation of peace by the President.

DURATION OF SERVICE

Act June 15, 1917, ch. 29, §4, 40 Stat. 217, provided in part that draftees and enlistees should serve for the duration of the war.

SUPPLEMENTAL PROVISIONS RELATING TO GENERAL OFFICERS

Act Oct. 6, 1917, ch. 105, §3, 40 Stat. 410, provided that section 208 of this Appendix should be construed to authorize the President to appoint the Chief of Staff and the commander of United States forces in France as generals, the commander of an army corps as lieutenant general, and their rate of pay and allowances.

EXTENSION OF SECTIONS 212 AND 213 OF THIS APPENDIX TO THE NAVY

Act Oct. 6, 1917, ch. 92, 40 Stat. 393, extended the provisions of sections 212 and 213 of this Appendix to include the Navy.

CALLING OF CERTAIN DEFERRED CLASSES FOR SERVICE

Act May 16, 1918, ch. 76, 40 Stat. 554, authorized the President to call for immediate military service persons who were placed in deferred classes.

REGISTRATION OF PERSONS ATTAINING AGE OF 21 SINCE JUNE 5, 1917

Act May 20, 1918, ch. 79, 40 Stat. 557, authorized the President to proclaim a registration date for persons who attained the age of 21 since June 5, 1917, and authorized further proclamations from time to time as necessary.

POWER OF PRESIDENT TO INCREASE DRAFTED ARMY

Act July 9, 1918, ch. 143, subch. XXI, 40 Stat. 894, authorized the President to draft the maximum number of men necessary for prosecution of the war.

SERVICES FOR WHICH DRAFTEE LIABLE

Act Aug. 31, 1918, ch. 166, §4, 40 Stat. 955, provided for allotment of draftees to Army, Navy, and Marine Corps.

REPEAL OF RESTRICTIONS ON ENLISTMENTS; PERIOD OF ENLISTMENTS; SERVICE WITH RESERVES; PAY OF ENLISTED MEN

Act Feb. 28, 1919, ch. 79, 40 Stat. 1211, provided for repeal of so much of sections 207 and 214 of this Appendix as imposed restrictions on enlistments in Regular Army, the period of such enlistments, did not require service with the reserves, rate of pay, and discharge after one year's service to those who enlisted for three years, in discretion of Secretary of the Army.

STATUS OF DESERTERS; PROSECUTION OF DRAFT VIOLATORS

Act Mar. 8, 1922, ch. 101, 42 Stat. 421, provided for extension of time within which deserters and draft violators could be prosecuted.

PROC. NO. 2068. PARDON OF PERSONS CONVICTED OF VIOLATING SECTION 205

Proc. No. 2068, Dec. 23, 1933, 48 Stat. 1725, granted full pardon to all persons who had theretofore been convicted of a violation of or of a conspiracy to violate section 205 of this Appendix, and who had complied with their sentences.

SELECTIVE TRAINING AND SERVICE ACT OF 1940

ACT SEPT. 16, 1940, CH. 720, 54 STAT. 885

§§301 to 309a. Omitted

CODIFICATION

Section 301, acts Sept. 16, 1940, ch. 720, §1, 54 Stat. 885; June 29, 1946, ch. 522, §1, 60 Stat. 341, which related to declaration of emergency and policy, expired on Mar. 31, 1947, pursuant to section 316 of this Appendix. See section 451 of this Appendix.

Section 302, acts Sept. 16, 1940, ch. 720, §2, 54 Stat. 885; Dec. 20, 1941, ch. 602, §1, 55 Stat. 844; June 29, 1946, ch. 522, §1, 60 Stat. 341, which related to registration and age limits, expired on Mar. 31, 1947, pursuant to section 316 of this Appendix. See section 453 of this Appendix.

Section 303, acts Sept. 16, 1940, ch. 720, §3, 54 Stat. 885; Aug. 18, 1941, ch. 362, §5, 55 Stat. 627; Dec. 20, 1941, ch. 602, §§2, 9, 55 Stat. 845, 846; Nov. 13, 1942, ch. 638, §§1, 5, 56 Stat. 1018, 1019; May 9, 1945, ch. 112, §2, 59 Stat. 166; May 14, 1946, ch. 253, §3, 60 Stat. 181; June 29, 1946, ch. 522, §§2–4, 60 Stat. 341, which related to liability for service, number of armed forces and term of service, expired in part on Mar. 31, 1947 and after July 1, 1947, pursuant to section 316 of this Appendix. See section 454 of this Appendix.

Section 303a, acts June 28, 1944, ch. 301, title I, 58 Stat. 544; July 17, 1945, ch. 319, 59 Stat. 485; July 23, 1946, ch. 591, title I, 60 Stat. 613, related to medical and burial expenses of registrants. See section 461 of this Appendix.

Section 303a was enacted as part of act July 23, 1946, known as the Third Deficiency Appropriation Act, 1946, and not as part of act Sept. 16, 1940, ch. 720, 54 Stat. 885, known as the Selective Training and Service Act of 1940.

Section 304, acts Sept. 16, 1940, ch. 720, §4, 54 Stat. 887; Dec. 20, 1941, ch. 602, §3, 55 Stat. 815; June 29, 1946, ch. 522, §1, 60 Stat. 341, which related to manner of selecting men, expired on Mar. 31, 1947, pursuant to section 316 of this Appendix. See section 455 of this Appendix.

Section 304a, act Dec. 5, 1943, ch. 342, §5, 57 Stat. 599, related to pre-induction physical examinations.

Section 304a was not enacted as part of act Sept. 16, 1940, ch. 720, 54 Stat. 885, known as the Selective Training and Service Act of 1940.

Section 305, acts Sept. 16, 1940, ch. 720, §5, 54 Stat. 887; May 29, 1941, ch. 155, 55 Stat. 211; Aug. 16, 1941, ch. 355, §§1, 2, 55 Stat. 621; Dec. 20, 1941, ch. 602, §§4–6, 55 Stat. 845; June 23, 1942, ch. 443, title II, §201(a), 56 Stat. 386; Nov. 13, 1942, ch. 638, §§2, 4, 56 Stat. 1019; July 9, 1943, ch. 211, 57 Stat. 391; Dec. 5, 1943, ch. 342, §1, 57 Stat. 596; May 14, 1946, ch. 253, §2, 60 Stat. 181; June 29, 1946, ch. 522, §§5, 6, 60 Stat. 342; Oct. 12, 1949, ch. 681, title V, §531(d), 63 Stat. 841, which related to exceptions, exemptions and deferments, expired on Mar. 31, 1947, pursuant to section 316 of this Appendix. See section 456 of this Appendix.

Section 305a, act Apr. 8, 1943, ch. 33, 57 Stat. 57, related to deferments of Federal Government employees.

Section 305a was not enacted as part of act Sept. 16, 1940, ch. 720, 54 Stat. 885, known as the Selective Training and Service Act of 1940.

Section 305b, act Dec. 5, 1943, ch. 342, §6, 57 Stat. 599, related to monthly reports by Director of Selective Service.

Section 305b was not enacted as part of act Sept. 16, 1940, ch. 720, 54 Stat. 885, known as the Selective Training and Service Act of 1940.

Section 306, acts Sept. 16, 1940, ch. 720, §6, 54 Stat. 889; June 29, 1946, ch. 522, §1, 60 Stat. 341, which related to number inducted as limited by appropriations, expired on Mar. 31, 1947, pursuant to section 316 of this Appendix.

Section 307, acts Sept. 16, 1940, ch. 720, §7, 54 Stat. 890; June 29, 1946, ch. 522, §1, 60 Stat. 341, which related to bounties for enlistment and substitutes, expired on Mar. 31, 1947, pursuant to section 316 of this Appendix. See section 458 of this Appendix.

Section 308, acts Sept. 16, 1940, ch. 720, §8, 54 Stat. 890; July 28, 1942, ch. 529, §2, 56 Stat. 724; Dec. 8, 1944, ch. 548, §1, 58 Stat. 798; June 29, 1946, ch. 522, §1, 60 Stat. 341, which related to service certificates and reemployment rights, expired on Mar. 31, 1947, pursuant to section 316 of this Appendix. See section 459 of this Appendix.

Section 309, acts Sept. 16, 1940, ch. 720, §9, 54 Stat. 892; June 25, 1943, ch. 144, §3, 57 Stat. 164; June 29, 1946, ch. 522, §1, 60 Stat. 341, which related to conscription of industry, expired on Mar. 31, 1947, pursuant to section 316 of this Appendix. See section 468 of this Appendix.

Section 309a, acts July 12, 1943, ch. 221, title VII, 57 Stat. 518; June 28, 1944, ch. 301, title I, 58 Stat. 544; July 17, 1945, ch. 319, 59 Stat. 485; July 23, 1946, ch. 591, title I, 60 Stat. 614, related to a work program for conscientious objectors. See section 456 of this Appendix.

Section 309a was enacted as part of act July 23, 1946, known as the Third Deficiency Appropriation Act, 1946, and not as part of act Sept. 16, 1940, ch. 720, 54 Stat. 885, known as the Selective Training and Service Act of 1940.

§310. Repealed. Pub. L. 89–554, §8(a), Sept. 16, 1966, 80 Stat. 651, 652

Section, acts Sept. 16, 1940, ch. 720, §10, 54 Stat. 893; Dec. 5, 1943, ch. 342, §§2–4, 57 Stat. 597, 598; June 29, 1946, ch. 522, §1, 60 Stat. 341; 1950 Reorg. Plan No. 26, §§1, 2, eff. July 31, 1950, 15 F.R. 4935, 64 Stat. 1280, 1281, related to administrative provisions. See section 460 of this Appendix.

§§310a to 318. Omitted

Section 310a, acts Oct. 8, 1940, ch. 756, title I, 54 Stat. 971; Apr. 5, 1941, ch. 40, 55 Stat. 117; Apr. 28, 1942, ch. 247, title III, 56 Stat. 237; July 12, 1943, ch. 221, title VII, 57 Stat. 519; June 28, 1944, ch. 301, title I, 58 Stat. 544; July 17, 1945, ch. 319, 59 Stat. 485; July 23, 1946, ch. 591, title I, 60 Stat. 614, related to travel expenses. See section 460(f) of this Appendix.

Section 310a was enacted as part of act July 23, 1946, known as the Third Deficiency Appropriation Act, 1946, and not as part of act Sept. 16, 1940, ch. 720, 54 Stat. 885, known as the Selective Training and Service Act of 1940.

Section 310b, act July 2, 1945, ch. 219, §§1–4, 59 Stat. 312, related to Selective Service Medal.

Section 310b was not enacted as part of act Sept. 16, 1940, ch. 720, 54 Stat. 885, known as the Selective Training and Service Act of 1940.

Section 311, acts Sept. 16, 1940, ch. 720, §11, 54 Stat. 894; June 29, 1946, ch. 522, §1, 60 Stat. 341, related to offenses and punishment, expired on Mar. 31, 1947, pursuant to section 316 of this Appendix. See section 462 of this Appendix.

Section 312, acts Sept. 16, 1940, ch. 720, §12, 54 Stat. 895; Mar. 28, 1942, ch. 206, 56 Stat. 190; June 16, 1942, ch. 413, §19, 56 Stat. 369, eff. June 1, 1942; June 29, 1946, ch. 522, §1, 60 Stat. 341, related to pay and allowances. Subsections (a) to (c) were repealed on June 1, 1942, and the other subsections expired on Mar. 31, 1947, pursuant to section 316 of this Appendix.

Section 313, acts Sept. 16, 1940, ch. 720, §13, 54 Stat. 895; June 29, 1946, ch. 522, §1, 60 Stat. 341, which related to applicability of Soldiers' and Sailors' Civil Relief Act, section 501 et seq. of this Appendix, expired on Mar. 31, 1947, pursuant to section 316 of this Appendix. See section 464 of this Appendix.

Section 314, acts Sept. 16, 1940, ch. 720, §14, 54 Stat. 896; June 29, 1946, ch. 522, §1, 60 Stat. 341, which related to notice of requirements of the act, expired on Mar. 31, 1947, pursuant to section 316 of this Appendix. See section 465 of this Appendix.

Section 315, acts Sept. 16, 1940, ch. 720, §15, 54 Stat. 896; Dec. 20, 1941, ch. 602, §7, 55 Stat. 845; June 23, 1942, ch. 443, title II, §201(b), 56 Stat. 387; Nov. 13, 1942, ch. 638, §3, 56 Stat. 1019; July 1, 1944, ch. 376, 58 Stat. 720; June 29, 1946, ch. 522, §1, 60 Stat. 341, which related to definitions, expired on Mar. 31, 1947, pursuant to section 316 of this Appendix. See section 466 of this Appendix.

Section 316, act Sept. 16, 1940, ch. 720, §16, 54 Stat. 897; May 9, 1945, ch. 112, §1, 59 Stat. 166; May 14, 1946, ch. 253, §1, 60 Stat. 181; June 29, 1946, ch. 522, §7, 60 Stat. 342, related to suspension of conflicting laws and expiration of the act. See section 467 of this Appendix.

Section 317, acts Sept. 16, 1940, ch. 720, §17, 54 Stat. 897; June 29, 1946, ch. 522, §1, 60 Stat. 341, related to the effective date of the act.

Section 318, acts Sept. 16, 1940, ch. 720, §18, 54 Stat. 897; June 29, 1946, ch. 522, §1, 60 Stat. 341, which related to short title of act, expired on Mar. 31, 1947, pursuant to section 316 of this Appendix.

STATUS AND TERM OF SERVICE OF PERSONS INDUCTED INTO NAVY, MARINE CORPS OR COAST GUARD

Act Dec. 20, 1941, ch. 602, §8, 55 Stat. 846, related to the status and term of service of persons inducted into Navy, Marine Corps, or Coast Guard under Selective Training and Service Act of 1940.

RECOGNITION OF UNCOMPENSATED SERVICE OF MEMBERS OF LOCAL BOARDS, ETC.

Act June 30, 1947, ch. 167, 61 Stat. 210, directed the Director of Selective Service to issue to uncompensated personnel of the Selective Service System, upon the expiration of the Selective Training and Service Act of 1940, as amended, suitable certificates of separation.

OFFICE OF SELECTIVE SERVICE RECORDS

ACT MAR. 31, 1947, CH. 26, 61 STAT. 31

TERMINATION AND REESTABLISHMENT OF OFFICE OF SELECTIVE SERVICE RECORDS; TRANSFER OF FUNCTIONS, PERSONNEL, PROPERTY, ETC.

Act June 24, 1948, ch. 625, title I, §10(a)(4), 62 Stat. 618, provided that: "The functions of the Office of Selective Service Records (established by the Act of March 31, 1947) [sections 321 to 329 of this Appendix] and of the Director of the Office of Selective Service Records are hereby transferred to the Selective Service System and the Director of Selective Service, respectively. The personnel, property, records, and unexpended balances (available or to be made available) of appropriations, allocations, and other funds of the Office of Selective Service Records are hereby transferred to the Selective Service System. The Office of Selective Service Records shall cease to exist upon the taking of effect of the provisions of this title [sections 451, 453, 454 and 455 to 471 of this Appendix]: *Provided*, That, effective upon the termination of this title [said sections] and notwithstanding such termination in other respects, (A) the said Office of Selective Service Records is hereby reestablished on the same basis and with the same functions as obtained prior to the effective date of this title [June 24, 1948], (B) said reestablished Office shall be responsible for liquidating any other outstanding affairs of the Selective Service System, and (C) the personnel, property, records, and unexpended balances (available or to be made available) of appropriations, allocations, and other funds of the Selective Service System shall be transferred to such reestablished Office of Selective Service Records."

ACT REFERRED TO IN OTHER SECTIONS

This Act is referred to in section 460 of this Appendix.

§321. Establishment of Office of Selective Service Records; appointment of Director

There is hereby established an Office of Selective Service Records, to be headed by a Director who shall be appointed by the President, by and with the advice and consent of the Senate.

(Mar. 31, 1947, ch. 26, § 1, 61 Stat. 31.)

CODIFICATION

Provisions that fixed the compensation of the Director at $10,000 per year were omitted as obsolete and superseded. Sections 1202 and 1204 of the Classification Act of 1949, 63 Stat. 972, 973, repealed the Classification Act of 1923 and all other laws or parts of laws inconsistent with the 1949 Act. The Classification Act of 1949 was repealed by Pub. L. 89–554, Sept. 6, 1966, § 8(a), 80 Stat. 632, and reenacted as chapter 51 and subchapter III of chapter 53 of Title 5, Government Organization and Employees. Section 5102 of Title 5 contains the applicability provisions of the 1949 Act, and section 5103 of Title 5 authorizes the Office of Personnel Management to determine the applicability to specific positions and employees.

§ 322. Functions, duties, and responsibilities of Office

The functions, duties, and responsibilties[1] of the Office of Selective Service Records shall be (a) to liquidate the Selective Service System, which liquidation shall be completed as rapidly as possible after March 31, 1947, but in any event not later than March 31, 1948, except as herein provided; (b) to preserve and service the records of Selective Service; and (c) to perform such other duties relating to the preservation of records, knowledge, and methods of Selective Service, not inconsistent with law.

(Mar. 31, 1947, ch. 26, § 2, 61 Stat. 31.)

REESTABLISHMENT OF OFFICE

For termination and reestablishment dates, see note set out preceding section 321 of this Appendix.

§ 323. Transfer of funds; appropriations

The unexpended balances of funds available to the Selective Service System are made available to the Office of Selective Service Records for the purposes of this Act [sections 321 to 329 of this Appendix] and such additional appropriations as are necessary therefor are authorized.

(Mar. 31, 1947, ch. 26, § 3, 61 Stat. 31.)

REESTABLISHMENT OF OFFICE

For termination and reestablishment dates, see note set out preceding section 321 of this Appendix.

§ 324. Transfer of property, records, and personnel to Office; transfer of surplus property to National Guard

All property, records, and personnel of the Selective Service System are hereby transferred to the Office of Selective Service Records and authority is hereby granted to the Director of the Office of Selective Service Records to transfer, without reimbursement, and with the approval of the War Assets Administration,[2] to the National Guard in the several States, the District of Columbia, and Territories and possessions of the United States, or to the Organized Reserves of the armed forces, surplus property of the Selective Service System.

(Mar. 31, 1947, ch. 26, § 4, 61 Stat. 31; June 30, 1949, ch. 288, title I, § 105, 63 Stat. 381.)

[1] So in original. Should be "responsibilities".

[2] See Transfer of Functions note below.

TRANSFER OF FUNCTIONS

War Assets Administration abolished and functions, records, etc., transferred to General Services Administration by act June 30, 1949, ch. 288, title I, § 105, 63 Stat. 381, effective July 1, 1949, see section 605 of act June 30, 1949, set out as an Effective Date note under section 471 of Title 40, Public Buildings, Property, and Works.

REESTABLISHMENT OF OFFICE

For termination and reestablishment dates, see note set out preceding section 321 of this Appendix.

§ 325. Transfer of functions and responsibilities of Personnel Division, National Headquarters, Selective Service System to Office; effective date

Pursuant to the third sentence of section 7 of Public Law 473, approved June 29, 1946 [section 316(b) of this Appendix], all functions and responsibilities of the Personnel Division, National Headquarters, Selective Service System, established under authority of section 8(g) of the Selective Training and Service Act of 1940, as amended [section 308(g) of this Appendix], together with so much of the records of the Selective Service System, and so much of the unexpended balances of appropriations of the Selective Service System, as the Director of the Bureau of the Budget[1] may determine to relate primarily to such functions, are transferred, effective March 29, 1947, from the Selective Service System to the Secretary of Labor.

(Mar. 31, 1947, ch. 26, § 5(a), 61 Stat. 32.)

TRANSFER OF FUNCTIONS

Functions vested by law (including reorganization plan) in Bureau of the Budget or Director of Bureau of the Budget transferred to President by section 101 of Reorg. Plan No. 2, of 1970, eff. July 1, 1970, 35 F.R. 7959, 84 Stat. 2085, set out in the Appendix to Title 5, Government Organization and Employees. Section 102 of Reorg. Plan No. 2 of 1970, redesignated Bureau of the Budget as Office of Management and Budget.

§ 326. Powers and duties of Director; acceptance of voluntary services; fiscal, disbursing, and accounting agent; status of officers of military and naval Services and Reserves and departments or agencies detailed to Office

(a) The Director is authorized—

(1) to prescribe the necessary rules and regulations to carry out the provisions of this Act [sections 321 to 329 of this Appendix];

(2) to create and establish, on the date hereinafter specified, Federal record depots in the several States, the District of Columbia, Territories, and possessions of the United States, and to maintain such other offices as may be necessary for the purposes of this Act [said sections];

(3) to utilize the agencies of the Federal Government with the consent of the heads thereof, and to accept the services of all officers and agents of the several States, the District of Columbia, Territories, and possessions of the United States, and subdivisions thereof, in the execution of this Act [said sections];

(4) to appoint and fix the compensation of such officers and employees (not to exceed

[1] See Transfer of Functions note below.

1,200 in number by November 1, 1947), as may be necessary for the purposes of this Act [said sections];

(5) to delegate and provide for the delegation of any authority vested in him under this Act [said sections] to such officers, agents, or persons as he may designate or appoint for such purpose or as may be designated or appointed for such purpose pursuant to such rules and regulations as he may prescribe.

(b) In the administration of this Act [sections 321 to 329 of this Appendix] voluntary services may be accepted.

(c) The Chief of Finance, United States Army,[1] is designated, empowered, and directed to act as the fiscal, disbursing, and accounting agent of the Director of the Office of Selective Service Records in carrying out the provisions of this Act [sections 321 to 329 of this Appendix].

(d) Any officer of the Armed Forces or any officer or employee of any department or agency of the United States who may be assigned or detailed to any office or position to carry out the provisions of this Act [sections 321 to 329 of this Appendix] may serve in and perform the functions of such office or position without loss of or prejudice to his status as such officer of the Armed Forces or as such officer or employee in any department or agency of the United States.

(Mar. 31, 1947, ch. 26, §6, 61 Stat. 32; Pub. L. 96–513, title V, §507(c), Dec. 12, 1980, 94 Stat. 2919.)

CODIFICATION

Provisions of subsec. (a)(4) that authorized the Director to fix the compensation of officers and employees "with or without regard to the Classification Act of 1923, as amended: *Provided*, That the compensation of such persons shall not be in excess of that provided in said Act" were omitted as obsolete and superseded. Sections 1202 and 1204 of the Classification Act of 1949, 63 Stat. 972, 973, repealed the Classification Act of 1923 and all other laws or parts of laws inconsistent with the 1949 Act. The Classification Act of 1949 was repealed by Pub. L. 89–554, Sept. 6, 1966, §8(a), 80 Stat. 632, and reenacted as chapter 51 and subchapter III of chapter 53 of Title 5, Government Organization and Employees. Section 5102 of Title 5 contains the applicability provisions of the 1949 Act, and section 5103 of Title 5 authorizes the Office of Personnel Management to determine the applicability to specific positions and employees.

AMENDMENTS

1980—Subsec. (d). Pub. L. 96–513 substituted "Any officer of the Armed Forces" for "Any officer on the active or retired list of the Army, Navy, Marine Corps, or Coast Guard, or of any Reserve component thereof," and "as such officer of the Armed Forces" for "as such officer in the Army, Navy, Marine Corps, or Coast Guard or Reserve component thereof,".

EFFECTIVE DATE OF 1980 AMENDMENT

Amendment by Pub. L. 96–513 effective Sept. 15, 1981, see section 701 of Pub. L. 96–513, set out as a note under section 101 of Title 10, Armed Forces.

TRANSFER OF FUNCTIONS

Pursuant to Department of Defense Reorganization Order, Jan. 10, 1962, set out as a note under section 3036 of Title 10, Armed Forces, Office of Chief of Finance, United States Army, abolished and functions transferred to Secretary of the Army, with power in Secretary to delegate.

REESTABLISHMENT OF OFFICES

For termination and reestablishment dates, see note set out preceding section 321 of this Appendix.

§327. Rules and regulations; penalties

The Director is authorized to prescribe such rules and regulations as may be necessary to preserve the confidential nature of the individual confidential records previously obtained under the Selective Training and Service Act of 1940, as amended [sections 301 to 318 of this Appendix]. Any person charged with the duty of carrying out any of the provisions of this Act [sections 321 to 329 of this Appendix], and who fails to carry out such provisions or who shall knowingly violate the regulations promulgated under this section, or any person or persons who shall unlawfully obtain, gain access to, or use such records, shall, upon conviction in the district court of the United States having jurisdiction thereof, be punished by imprisonment for not more than five years, or a fine of not more than $10,000, or by both such fine and imprisonment, or if subject to military or naval law, may be tried by court martial, and, on conviction, shall suffer such punishment as the court martial may direct.

(Mar. 31, 1947, ch. 26, §7, 61 Stat. 32.)

REESTABLISHMENT OF OFFICE

For termination and reestablishment dates, see note set out preceding section 321 of this Appendix.

§328. Suspension of conflicting laws

Except as provided in this Act [sections 321 to 329 of this Appendix], all laws and parts of laws in conflict with the provisions of this Act [said sections] are suspended to the extent of such conflict for the period in which this Act [said sections] shall be in force.

(Mar. 31, 1947, ch. 26, §8, 61 Stat. 33.)

REESTABLISHMENT OF OFFICE

For termination and reestablishment dates, see note set out preceding section 321 of this Appendix.

§329. Effective date

Except as otherwise provided by the terms of this Act [sections 321 to 329 of this Appendix], the provisions hereof shall take effect at 12 o'clock post meridian, March 31, 1947.

(Mar. 31, 1947, ch. 26, §9, 61 Stat. 33.)

§330. Destruction of records; use of appropriations; procedures; transfers to other agencies

Appropriations for the Selective Service System may on and after August 28, 1958, be used for the destruction of records accumulated under the Selective Training and Service Act of 1940, as amended [sections 301 to 318 of this Appendix], by the Director of Selective Service after compliance with the procedures for the destruction of records prescribed pursuant to the Records Disposal Act of 1943, as amended (44 U.S.C. 366–380): *Provided*, That no records may be transferred to any other agency without the approval of the Director of Selective Service.

[1] See Transfer of Functions note below.

(Pub. L. 85–844, title I, Aug. 28, 1958, 72 Stat. 1073.)

REFERENCES IN TEXT

The Records Disposal Act of 1943, as amended (44 U.S.C. 366–380), is act July 7, 1943, ch. 192, 57 Stat. 380, which enacted sections 366 to 380 of former Title 44, Public Printing and Documents. Sections 366 to 376, and 378 to 380 of former Title 44 were repealed by Pub. L. 90–620, §3, Oct. 22, 1968, 82 Stat. 1306, and reenacted as sections 3301 to 3303 and 3304 to 3314, respectively, of Title 44, Public Printing and Documents. Sections 3304 to 3307 of Title 44 were repealed by Pub. L. 91–287, §2(c), June 23, 1970, 84 Stat. 321. Section 377 of former Title 44 was also repealed by Pub. L. 90–620, §3, Oct. 22, 1968, 82 Stat. 1306.

CODIFICATION

Section was enacted as part of Pub. L. 85–844, known as the Independent Offices Appropriation Act, 1959, and not as part of act Mar. 31, 1947, ch. 26, 61 Stat. 31, which comprises sections 321 to 329 of this Appendix.

PRIOR PROVISIONS

Similar provisions were contained in the following prior appropriation acts:
Pub. L. 85–69, title I, June 29, 1957, 71 Stat. 235.
June 27, 1956, ch. 452, title I, 70 Stat. 348.
June 30, 1955, ch. 244, title I, 69 Stat. 209.
June 24, 1954, ch. 359, title I, 68 Stat. 287.
July 27, 1953, ch. 241, title I, 67 Stat. 189.
July 5, 1952, ch. 578, title I, 66 Stat. 406.

SERVICE EXTENSION ACT OF 1941

ACT AUG. 18, 1941, CH. 362, 55 STAT. 626–628

§§351 to 357. Repealed. Aug. 10, 1956, ch. 1041, §53, 70A Stat. 641

Section 351, act Aug. 18, 1941, ch. 362, §1, 55 Stat. 626, related to the declaration of national peril for purposes of extending service under section 303(b) of this Appendix.

Section 352, act Aug. 18, 1941, ch. 362, §2, 55 Stat. 626, authorized an eighteen-month extension of periods of service for persons inducted under the Selective Training and Service Act of 1940, sections 301 to 318 of this Appendix.

Section 353, act Aug. 18, 1941, ch. 362, §3, 55 Stat. 626, extended time for application for National Service Life Insurance.

Section 354, act Aug. 18, 1941, ch. 362, §4, 55 Stat. 627, related to release from service in hardship cases.

Section 355, act Aug. 18, 1941, ch. 362, amended section 303(c) of this Appendix.

Section 356, act Aug. 18, 1941, ch. 362, §6, 55 Stat. 627, authorized President to order Regular Army retired personnel to active duty. See section 471 of this Appendix.

Section 357, acts Aug. 18, 1941, ch. 362, §7, 55 Stat. 627; Dec. 8, 1944, ch. 548, §3, 58 Stat. 799; Aug. 9, 1946, ch. 936, 60 Stat. 971, related to reemployment rights. See section 459 of this Appendix.

§358. Repealed. June 16, 1942, ch. 413, §19, 56 Stat. 369, eff. June 1, 1942

Section, act Aug. 18, 1941, ch. 362, §8, 55 Stat. 627, related to additional compensation for active service in excess of twelve months.

ADDITIONAL REPEAL

Section was also repealed by act Aug. 10, 1956, ch. 1041, §53, 70A Stat. 641.

§§359 to 362. Repealed. Aug. 10, 1956, ch. 1041, §53, 70A Stat. 641

Section 359, acts Aug. 18, 1941, ch. 362, §9, 55 Stat. 628; Aug. 7, 1946, ch. 770, §1(58), 60 Stat. 871, suspended limitations on number of inductees.

Section 360, act Aug. 18, 1941, ch. 362, §10, 55 Stat. 628, related to enlistments in Army without regard to component. See section 3252 of Title 10, Armed Forces.

Section 361, act Aug. 18, 1941, ch. 362, §11, 55 Stat. 628, amended section 401 of this Appendix.

Section 362, act Aug. 18, 1941, ch. 362, §12, 55 Stat. 628, gave short title of act.

ARMY RESERVE AND RETIRED PERSONNEL SERVICE LAW OF 1940

ACT AUG. 27, 1940, CH. 689, 54 STAT. 858

§§401 to 405. Omitted

CODIFICATION

Section 401, acts Aug. 27, 1940, ch. 689, §1, 54 Stat. 858; Aug. 18, 1941, ch. 362, §11, 55 Stat. 628, authorized for the period ending the later of June 30, 1942, or 6 months after the termination of the authority under section 352 of this Appendix the President to order reserve and retired personnel to active service. See section 471 of this Appendix.

Section 402, act Aug. 27, 1940, ch. 689, §2, 54 Stat. 859, related to laws and regulations governing personnel called to active service.

Section 403, acts Aug. 27, 1940, ch. 689, §3, 54 Stat. 859; Sept. 16, 1940, ch. 720, §8(d), (f), 54 Stat. 891; July 28, 1942, ch. 529, §1, 56 Stat. 723; Dec. 8, 1944, ch. 548, §2, 58 Stat. 799, related to service and health certificates and reemployment rights. See section 459 of this Appendix.

Section 404, act Aug. 27, 1940, ch. 689, §4, 54 Stat. 860, made applicable the Soldiers' and Sailors' Civil Relief Act and section 101 et seq. of this Appendix. See sections 464 and 501 et seq. of this Appendix.

Section 405, act Aug. 27, 1940, ch. 689, §5, 54 Stat. 860, suspended all laws in conflict with sections 401 to 405 of this Appendix.

PAY OF PERSONS INDUCTED IN ERRONEOUS RANK OR GRADE

Act Feb. 6, 1942, ch. 42, 56 Stat. 50, related to pay of persons inducted in erroneous rank or grade under sections 401 to 405 of this Appendix.

MILITARY SELECTIVE SERVICE ACT

ACT JUNE 24, 1948, CH. 625, 62 STAT. 604

ACT REFERRED TO IN OTHER SECTIONS

This Act is referred to in section 516 of this Appendix; title 8 sections 1227, 1255a; title 10 sections 513, 1475, 12103, 12104, 12208; title 22 section 2520; title 26 section 3121; title 29 sections 2886, 2939; title 42 sections 410, 2996f.

§451. Short title; Congressional declaration of policy

(a) This Act may be cited as the "Military Selective Service Act".

(b) The Congress declares that an adequate armed strength must be achieved and maintained to insure the security of this Nation.

(c) The Congress further declares that in a free society the obligations and privileges of serving in the armed forces and the reserve components thereof should be shared generally, in accordance with a system of selection which is fair and just, and which is consistent with the maintenance of an effective national economy.

(d) The Congress further declares, in accordance with our traditional military policy as expressed in the National Defense Act of 1916, as amended, that it is essential that the strength and organization of the National Guard, both Ground and Air, as an integral part of the first line defenses of this Nation, be at all times maintained and assured.

To this end, it is the intent of the Congress that whenever Congress shall determine that units and organizations are needed for the national security in excess of those of the Regular components of the Ground Forces and the Air Forces, and those in active service under this title [sections 451 to 471a of this Appendix], the National Guard of the United States, both Ground and Air, or such part thereof as may be necessary, together with such units of the Reserve components as are necessary for a balanced force, shall be ordered to active Federal service and continued therein so long as such necessity exists.

(e) The Congress further declares that adequate provision for national security requires maximum effort in the fields of scientific research and development, and the fullest possible utilization of the Nation's technological, scientific, and other critical manpower resources.

(f) The Congress further declares that the Selective Service System should remain administratively independent of any other agency, including the Department of Defense.

(June 24, 1948, ch. 625, title I, §1, 62 Stat. 604; June 19, 1951, ch. 144, title I, §1(a), 65 Stat. 75; Pub. L. 90–40, §1(1), June 30, 1967, 81 Stat. 100; Pub. L. 92–129, title I, §101(a)(1), Sept. 28, 1971, 85 Stat. 348; Pub. L. 96–107, title VIII, §812, Nov. 9, 1979, 93 Stat. 816.)

REFERENCES IN TEXT

The Military Selective Service Act, referred to in subsec. (a), is act June 24, 1948, ch. 625, 62 Stat. 604, as amended, originally called the "Selective Service Act of 1948", renamed the "Universal Military Training and Service Act" by act June 19, 1951, ch. 144, title I, §1(a), 65 Stat. 75, then renamed the "Military Selective Service Act of 1967" by Pub. L. 90–40, §1(1), June 30, 1967, 81 Stat. 100, and now designated the Military Selective Service Act by Pub. L. 92–129, title I, §101(a)(1), Sept. 28, 1971, 85 Stat. 348. Act June 24, 1948 consisted of titles I and II. Title I of such act enacted sections 451 to 454 and 455 to 471a of this Appendix. Title II of such act was classified to the Articles of War set out in former Title 10, Army and Air Force, to sections 61, 61a, 62a, 65, and 652a of former Title 10, and to section 180 of former Title 14, Coast Guard. Title II of act June 24, 1948 was repealed by act Aug. 10, 1956, ch. 1041, §53, 70A Stat. 641.

The National Defense Act of 1916, as amended, referred to in subsec. (d), is act June 3, 1916, ch. 134, 39 Stat. 166, as amended, which was classified generally throughout former Title 10, Army and Air Force. The Act was repealed by act Aug. 10, 1956, ch. 1041, §53, 70A Stat. 641, and the provisions thereof were reenacted as parts of Title 10, Armed Forces, and Title 32, National Guard.

AMENDMENTS

1979—Subsec. (f). Pub. L. 96–107 added subsec. (f).

1971—Subsec. (a). Pub. L. 92–129 substituted "Military Selective Service Act" for "Military Selective Service Act of 1967".

1967—Subsec. (a). Pub. L. 90–40 substituted "Military Selective Service Act of 1967" for "Universal Military Training and Service Act".

1951—Subsec. (a). Act June 19, 1951, substituted "Universal Military Training and Service Act" for "Selective Service Act of 1948".

SHORT TITLE OF 1969 AMENDMENT

Pub. L. 91–124, § 1, Nov. 26, 1969, 83 Stat. 220, provided: "That this Act [amending section 455 of this Appendix] may be cited as the 'Selective Service Amendment Act of 1969'."

SHORT TITLE OF 1955 AMENDMENT

Act June 30, 1955, ch. 250, § 1, 69 Stat. 223, provided: "That this Act [amending sections 454, 454a, 456, 467, and 2216 of this Appendix, and section 234 of former Title 37, Pay and Allowances] may be cited as the '1955 Amendments to the Universal Military Training and Service Act'."

SHORT TITLE OF 1951 AMENDMENT

Section 7 of title I of act June 19, 1951, provided that: "This title [enacting sections 472 and 473 of this Appendix, amending this section and sections 452 to 454, 455, 456, 459, 460, 463, 466, 467, and 471 of this Appendix, repealing section 457 of this Appendix, enacting provisions set out as notes under this section, and amending provisions set out as notes under section 454 of this Appendix and section 351 of Title 14, Coast Guard] may be cited as the '1951 Amendments to the Universal Military Training and Service Act'."

SHORT TITLE OF 1950 AMENDMENTS

Act Sept. 9, 1950, ch. 939, 64 Stat. 826, which amended section 454 of this Appendix, is popularly known as the "Doctors Draft Act".

Act June 30, 1950, ch. 445, § 4, 64 Stat. 319, provided that: "This Act [enacting section 471 and amending sections 460 and 467 of this Appendix] may be cited as the 'Selective Service Extension Act of 1950'."

SEPARABILITY

Section 5 of act June 19, 1951, provided that: "If any provisions of this Act [enacting sections 472 and 473 of this Appendix, amending this section, sections 452 to 454, 455, 456, 459, 460, 463, 466, 467, and 471 of this Appendix, and section 621c of former Title 10, Army and Air Force, repealing section 457 of this Appendix, enacting provisions set out as notes under this section, and amending provisions set out as notes under section 454 of this Appendix and section 351 of Title 14, Coast Guard] or the application thereof to any person or circumstances is held invalid, the validity of the remainder of the Act and of the application of such provision to other persons and circumstances shall not be affected thereby."

SELECTIVE SERVICE REFORM; PRESIDENTIAL PLAN, LEGISLATIVE PROPOSALS, ETC.

Section 811 of Pub. L. 96–107 directed President to prepare and transmit to Congress a plan for reform of law providing for registration and induction of persons in the Armed Forces, along with proposals for implementing legislation, on the later of Jan. 15, 1980, or the end of the three-month period beginning on Nov. 9, 1979.

§ 452. Repealed. Aug. 10, 1956, ch. 1041, § 53, 70A Stat. 641

Section, acts June 24, 1948, ch. 625, title I, § 2, 62 Stat. 605; June 19, 1951, ch. 144, title I, § 1(b), 65 Stat. 75, related to authorized personnel strength of various services.

§ 453. Registration

(a) Except as otherwise provided in this title [sections 451 to 471a of this Appendix] it shall be the duty of every male citizen of the United States, and every other male person residing in the United States, who, on the day or days fixed for the first or any subsequent registration, is between the ages of eighteen and twenty-six, to present himself for and submit to registration at such time or times and place or places, and in such manner, as shall be determined by proclamation of the President and by rules and regulations prescribed hereunder. The provisions of this section shall not be applicable to any alien lawfully admitted to the United States as a nonimmigrant under section 101(a)(15) of the Immigration and Nationality Act, as amended (66 Stat. 163; 8 U.S.C. 1101), for so long as he continues to maintain a lawful nonimmigrant status in the United States.

(b) Regulations prescribed pursuant to subsection (a) may require that persons presenting themselves for and submitting to registration under this section provide, as part of such registration, such identifying information (including date of birth, address, and social security account number) as such regulations may prescribe.

(June 24, 1948, ch. 625, title I, § 3, 62 Stat. 605; June 19, 1951, ch. 144, title I, § 1(c), 65 Stat. 76; Pub. L. 92–129, title I, § 101(a)(2), Sept. 28, 1971, 85 Stat. 348; Pub. L. 97–86, title IX, § 916(a), Dec. 1, 1981, 95 Stat. 1129.)

AMENDMENTS

1981—Pub. L. 97–86 designated existing provisions as subsec. (a) and added subsec. (b).

1971—Pub. L. 92–129 substituted "male person residing in the United States" for "male person now or hereafter in the United States" and inserted provision making section inapplicable to aliens lawfully admitted to the United States as nonimmigrants under section 1101(a)(15) of Title 8 for so long as they maintain lawful nonimmigrant status in the United States.

1951—Act June 19, 1951, made all male persons now or hereafter in the United States subject to registration.

PROCLAMATION NO. 2799

Proc. No. 2799, July 20, 1948, 13 F.R. 4173, 62 Stat. 1531, which related to registration, was revoked by Proc. No. 4360, Mar. 29, 1975, 40 F.R. 14567, 89 Stat. 1255, set out below.

PROCLAMATION NO. 2937

Proc. No. 2937, Aug. 16, 1951, 16 F.R. 8263, 65 Stat. c.27, which related to registration in the Canal Zone, was revoked by Proc. No. 4360, Mar. 29, 1975, 40 F.R. 14567, 89 Stat. 1255, set out below.

PROCLAMATION NO. 2938

Proc. No. 2938, Aug. 16, 1951, 16 F.R. 8265, 65 Stat. c.30, which related to registration in Guam, was revoked by Proc. No. 4360, Mar. 29, 1975, 40 F.R. 14567, 89 Stat. 1255, set out below.

PROCLAMATION NO. 2942

Proc. No. 2942, Aug. 30, 1951, 16 F.R. 8969, 65 Stat. c.35, which concerned the supplementing of prior Proclamations relating to registration, was revoked by Proc. No. 4360, Mar. 29, 1975, 40 F.R. 14567, 89 Stat. 1255, set out below.

PROCLAMATION NO. 2972

Proc. No. 2972, Apr. 17, 1952, 17 F.R. 3473, 66 Stat. c.28, which related to extra registration, was revoked by Proc. No. 4360, Mar. 29, 1975, 40 F.R. 14567, 89 Stat. 1255, set out below.

PROCLAMATION NO. 3314

Proc. No. 3314, Sept. 14, 1959, 24 F.R. 7517, 73 Stat. c.78, which concerned the supplementing of prior Proclamations relating to registration, was revoked by Proc. No. 4360, Mar. 29, 1975, 40 F.R. 14567, 89 Stat. 1255, set out below.

PROCLAMATION NO. 4101

Proc. No. 4101, Jan. 13, 1972, 37 F.R. 659, which concerned the supplementing of prior Proclamations relating to registration, was revoked by Proc. No. 4360, Mar. 29, 1975, 40 F.R. 14567, 89 Stat. 1255, set out below.

PROC. NO. 4360. TERMINATION OF REGISTRATION PROCEDURES

Proc. No. 4360, Mar. 29, 1975, 40 F.R. 14567, 89 Stat. 1255, provided:

Under authority vested in the President by the Military Selective Service Act (62 Stat. 604), as amended [see References In Text note set out under section 451 of this Appendix], procedures have been established for the registration of male citizens of the United States and of other male persons who are subject to registration under section 3 of said act, as amended (85 Stat. 348) [this section].

In order to evaluate an annual registration system, existing procedures are being terminated and will be replaced by new procedures which will provide for periodic registration.

NOW, THEREFORE, I, GERALD R. FORD, President of the United States of America, by virtue of the authority vested in me by the Constitution and the statutes of the United States, including the Military Selective Service Act, as amended, do hereby revoke Proclamations No. 2799 of July 20, 1948, No. 2937 of August 16, 1951, No. 2938 of August 16, 1951, No. 2942 of August 30, 1951, No. 2972 of April 17, 1952, No. 3314 of September 14, 1959, and No. 4101 of January 13, 1972; thereby terminating the present procedures for registration under the Military Selective Service Act, as amended.

IN WITNESS WHEREOF, I have hereunto set my hand this twenty-ninth day of March in the year of our Lord nineteen hundred seventy-five, and of the Independence of the United States of America the one hundred ninety-ninth.

GERALD R. FORD.

PROC. NO. 4771. REGISTRATION UNDER THE SELECTIVE SERVICE ACT

Proc. No. 4771, July 2, 1980, 45 F.R. 45247, 94 Stat. 3775, as amended by Proc. No. 7275, Feb. 22, 2000, 65 F.R. 9199, provided:

Section 3 of the Military Selective Service Act, as amended (50 U.S.C. App. 453), provides that male citizens of the United States and other male persons residing in the United States who are between the ages of 18 and 26, except those exempted by Sections 3 and 6(a) of the Military Selective Service Act [50 U.S.C. App. 453 and 456(a)], must present themselves for registration at such time or times and place or places, and in such manner as determined by the President. Section 6(k) [50 U.S.C. App. 456(k)] provides that such exceptions shall not continue after the cause for the exemption ceases to exist.

The Congress of the United States has made available the funds (H.J. Res. 521, approved by me on June 27, 1980 [Pub. L. 96–282, June 27, 1980, 93 Stat. 552]), which are needed to initiate this registration, beginning with those born on or after January 1, 1960.

NOW, THEREFORE, I, JIMMY CARTER, President of the United States of America, by the authority vested in me by the Military Selective Service Act, as amended (50 U.S.C. App. 451 et seq.), do hereby proclaim as follows:

1–1. PERSONS TO BE REGISTERED AND DAYS OF REGISTRATION

1–101. Male citizens of the United States and other males residing in the United States, unless exempted by the Military Selective Service Act, as amended, who were born on or after January 1, 1960, and who have attained their eighteenth birthday, shall present themselves for registration in the manner and at the time and places as hereinafter provided.

1–102. Persons born in calendar year 1960 shall present themselves for registration on any of the six days beginning Monday, July 21, 1980.

1–103. Persons born in calendar year 1961 shall present themselves for registration on any of the six days beginning Monday, July 28, 1980.

1–104. Persons born in calendar year 1962 shall present themselves for registration on any of the six days beginning Monday, January 5, 1981.

1–105. Persons born on or after January 1, 1963, shall present themselves for registration on the day they attain the 18th anniversary of their birth or on any day within the period of 60 days beginning 30 days before such date; however, in no event shall such persons present themselves for registration prior to January 5, 1981.

1–106. Aliens who would be required to present themselves for registration pursuant to Sections 1–101 to 1–105, but who are in processing centers on the dates fixed for registration, shall present themselves for registration within 30 days after their release from such centers.

1–107. Aliens and noncitizen nationals of the United States who reside in the United States, but who are absent from the United States on the days fixed for their registration, shall present themselves for registration within 30 days after their return to the United States.

1–108. Aliens and noncitizen nationals of the United States who, on or after July 1, 1980, come into and reside in the United States shall present themselves for registration in accordance with Sections 1–101 to 1–105 or within 30 days after coming into the United States, whichever is later.

1–109. Persons who would have been required to present themselves for registration pursuant to Sections 1–101 to 1–108 but for an exemption pursuant to Section 3 or 6(a) of the Military Selective Service Act, as amended [50 U.S.C. App. 453 or 456(a)], or but for some condition beyond their control such as hospitalization or incarceration, shall present themselves for registration within 30 days after the cause for their exempt status ceases to exist or within 30 days after the termination of the condition which was beyond their control.

1–2. PLACES AND TIMES FOR REGISTRATION

1–201. Persons who are required to be registered and who are in the United States shall register at the places and by the means designated by the Director of Selective Service. These places and means may include but are not limited to any classified United States Post Office, the Selective Service Internet web site, telephonic registration, registration on approved Government forms, registration through high school and college registrars, and the Selective Service reminder mailback card.

1–202. Citizens of the United States who are required to be registered and who are not in the United States, shall register via any of the places and methods authorized by the Director of Selective Service pursuant to paragraph 1–201 or present themselves at a United States Embassy or Consulate for registration before a diplomatic or consular officer of the United States or before a registrar duly appointed by a diplomatic or consular officer of the United States.

1–203. The hours for registration in United States Post Offices shall be the business hours during the days of operation of the particular United States Post Office. The hours for registration in United States Embassies and Consulates shall be those prescribed by the United States Embassies and Consulates.

1–3. MANNER OF REGISTRATION

1–301. Persons who are required to be registered shall comply with the registration procedures and other rules and regulations prescribed by the Director of Selective Service.

1–302. When reporting for registration each person shall present for inspection reasonable evidence of his identity. After registration, each person shall keep the Selective Service System informed of his current address.

Having proclaimed these requirements for registration, I urge everyone, including employers in the private and public sectors, to cooperate with and assist those persons who are required to be registered in order to ensure a timely and complete registration. Also, I direct the heads of Executive agencies, when requested by the Director of Selective Service and to the extent permitted by law, to cooperate and assist in carrying out the purposes of this Proclamation.

IN WITNESS WHEREOF, I have hereunto set my hand this second day of July, in the year of our Lord nineteen hundred and eighty, and of the Independence of the United States of America the two hundred and fourth.

JIMMY CARTER.

SECTION REFERRED TO IN OTHER SECTIONS

This section is referred to in sections 454, 456, 462, 465 of this Appendix; title 5 section 3328; title 29 section 2939; title 42 sections 292d, 292r.

§ 454. Persons liable for training and service

(a) Age limits; training in National Security Training Corps; physical and mental fitness; adequate training facilities; assignment to stations and units; training period; medical specialist categories

Except as otherwise provided in this title [sections 451 to 471a of this Appendix], every person required to register pursuant to section 3 of this title [section 453 of this Appendix] who is between the ages of eighteen years and six months and twenty-six years, at the time fixed for his registration, or who attains the age of eighteen years and six months after having been required to register pursuant to section 3 of this title [section 453 of this Appendix], or who is otherwise liable as provided in section 6(h) of this title [section 456(h) of this Appendix], shall be liable for training and service in the Armed Forces of the United States: *Provided*, That each registrant shall be immediately liable for classification and examination, and shall, as soon as practicable following his registration, be so classified and examined, both physically and mentally, in order to determine his availability for induction for training and service in the Armed Forces: *Provided further*, That, notwithstanding any other provision of law, any registrant who has failed or refused to report for induction shall continue to remain liable for induction and when available shall be immediately inducted. The President is authorized, from time to time, whether or not a state of war exists, to select and induct into the Armed Forces of the United States for training and service in the manner provided in this title [said sections] (including but not limited to selection and induction by age group or age groups) such number of persons as may be required to provide and maintain the strength of the Armed Forces.

At such time as the period of active service in the Armed Forces required under this title [said sections] of persons who have not attained the nineteenth anniversary of the day of their birth has been reduced or eliminated pursuant to the provisions of section 4(k) of this title [subsection (k) of this section], and except as otherwise provided in this title [said sections], every person who is required to register under this title [said sections] and who has not attained the nineteenth anniversary of the day of his birth on the date such period of active service is reduced or eliminated or who is otherwise liable as provided in section 6(h) of this title [section 456(h) of this Appendix], shall be liable for training in the National Security Training Corps: *Provided*, That persons deferred under the provisions of section 6 of this title [section 456 of this Appendix] shall not be relieved from liability for induction into the National Security Training Corps solely by reason of having exceeded the age of nineteen years during the period of such deferment. The President is authorized, from time to time, whether or not a state of war exists, to select and induct for training in the National Security Training Corps as hereinafter provided such number of persons as may be required to further the purposes of this title [said sections].

No person shall be inducted into the Armed Forces for training and service or shall be inducted for training in the National Security Training Corps under this title [said sections] until his acceptability in all respects, including his physical and mental fitness, has been satisfactorily determined under standards prescribed by the Secretary of Defense: *Provided*, That the minimum standards for physical acceptability established pursuant to this subsection shall not be higher than those applied to persons inducted between the ages of 18 and 26 in January 1945: *Provided further*, That the passing requirement for the Armed Forces Qualification Test shall be fixed at a percentile score of 10 points: *And provided further*, That except in time of war or national emergency declared by the Congress the standards and requirements fixed by the preceding two provisos may be modified by the President under such rules and regulations as he may prescribe.

No persons shall be inducted for such training and service until adequate provision shall have been made for such shelter, sanitary facilities, water supplies, heating and lighting arrangements, medical care, and hospital accommodations for such persons as may be determined by the Secretary of Defense or the Secretary of Transportation to be essential to the public and personal health.

The persons inducted into the Armed Forces for training and service under this title [said sections] shall be assigned to stations or units of such forces. Persons inducted into the land forces of the United States pursuant to this title [said sections] shall be deemed to be members of the Army of the United States; persons inducted into the naval forces of the United States pursuant to this title [said sections] shall be deemed to be members of the United States Navy or the United States Marine Corps or the United States Coast Guard, as appropriate; and persons inducted into the air forces of the United States pursuant to this title [said sections] shall be deemed to be members of the Air Force of the United States.

Every person inducted into the Armed Forces pursuant to the authority of this subsection after the date of enactment of the 1951 Amendments to the Universal Military Training and Service Act [June 19, 1951] shall, following his induction, be given full and adequate military training for service in the armed force into which he is inducted for a period of not less than twelve weeks, and no such person shall, during this twelve weeks period, be assigned for duty at any installation located on land outside the United States, its Territories and possessions (including the Canal Zone): *Provided*, That no funds appropriated by the Congress shall be used for the purpose of transporting or maintaining in violation of the provisions of this paragraph any person inducted into, or enlisted, appointed, or ordered to active duty in, the Armed Forces under the provisions of this title [said sections].

No person, without his consent, shall be inducted for training and service in the Armed Forces or for training in the National Security Training Corps under this title [said sections], except as otherwise provided herein, after he has attained the twenty-sixth anniversary of the day of his birth.

(b) Length of service; release of individuals accepted into Army National Guard, Air National Guard, and other Reserve components

Each person inducted into the Armed Forces under the provisions of subsection (a) of this section shall serve on active training and service for a period of twenty-four consecutive months, unless sooner released, transferred, or discharged in accordance with procedures prescribed by the Secretary of Defense (or the Secretary of Transportation with respect to the United States Coast Guard) or as otherwise prescribed by subsection (d) of section 4 of this title [subsection (d) of this section]. The Secretaries of the Army, Navy, and Air Force, with the approval of the Secretary of Defense (and the Secretary of Transportation with respect to the United States Coast Guard), may provide, by regulations which shall be as nearly uniform as practicable, for the release from training and service in the armed forces prior to serving the periods required by this subsection of individuals who volunteered for and are accepted into organized units of the Army National Guard and Air National Guard and other reserve components.

(c) Opportunity to enlist in Regular Army; voluntary induction; volunteers under 18 years old

(1) Under the provisions of applicable laws and regulations any person between the ages of eighteen years and six months and twenty-six years shall be offered an opportunity to enlist in the regular army for a period of service equal to that prescribed in subsection (b) of this section: *Provided*, That, notwithstanding the provisions of this or any other Act, any person so enlisting shall not have his enlistment extended without his consent until after a declaration of war or national emergency by the Congress after the date of enactment of the 1951 Amendments to the Universal Military Training and Service Act [June 19, 1951].

(2) Any enlisted member of any reserve component of the Armed Forces may, during the effective period of this Act, apply for a period of service equal to that prescribed in subsection (b) of this section and his application shall be accepted: *Provided*, That his services can be effectively utilized and that his physical and mental fitness for such service meet the standards prescribed by the head of the department concerned: *Provided further*, That active service performed pursuant to this section shall not prejudice his status as such member of such reserve component: *And provided further*, That any person who was a member of a reserve component on June 25, 1950, and who thereafter continued to serve satisfactorily in such reserve component, shall, if his application for active duty made pursuant to this paragraph is denied, be deferred from induction under this title [sections 451 to 471a of this Appendix] until such time as he is ordered to active duty or ceases to serve satisfactorily in such reserve component.

(3) Within the limits of the quota determined under sections 5(b) [section 455(b) of this Appendix] for the subdivision in which he resides, any person, between the ages of eighteen and twenty-six, shall be afforded an opportunity to volunteer for induction into the Armed Forces of the United States for the training and service prescribed in subsection (b), but no person who so volunteers shall be inducted for such training and service so long as he is deferred after classification.

(4) Within the limits of the quota determined under section 5(b) [section 455(b) of this Appendix] for the subdivision in which he resides, any person after attaining the age of seventeen shall with the written consent of his parents or guardian be afforded an opportunity to volunteer for induction into the Armed Forces of the United States for the training and service prescribed in subsection (b).

(5) Within the limits of the quota determined under section 5(b) [section 455(b) of this Appendix] for the subdivision in which he resides, at such time as induction into the National Security Training Corps is authorized pursuant to the provisions of this title [sections 451 to 471a of this Appendix], any person after attaining the age of seventeen shall with the written consent of his parents or guardian be afforded an opportunity to volunteer for induction into the National Security Training Corps for the training prescribed in subsection (k) of section 4 of this title [subsection (k) of this section].

(d) Transfer to Reserve component; period of service

(1) Each person who hereafter and prior to the enactment of the 1951 Amendments to the Universal Military Training and Service Act [June 19, 1951] is inducted, enlisted, or appointed and serves for a period of less than three years in one of the armed forces and meets the qualifica-

tions for enlistment or appointment in a reserve component of the armed force in which he serves, shall be transferred to a reserve component of such armed force, and until the expiration of a period of five years after such transfer, or until he is discharged from such reserve component, whichever occurs first, shall be deemed to be a member of such reserve component and shall be subject to such additional training and service as may now or hereafter be prescribed by law for such reserve component: *Provided*, That any such person who completes at least twenty-one months of service in the armed forces and who thereafter serves satisfactorily (1) on active duty in the armed forces under a voluntary extension for a period of at least one year, which extension is authorized, or (2) in an organized unit of any reserve component of any of the armed forces for a period of at least thirty-six consecutive months, shall, except in time of war or national emergency declared by the Congress, be relieved from any further liability under this subsection to serve in any reserve component of the armed forces of the United States, but nothing in this subsection shall be construed to prevent any such person, while in a reserve component of such forces, from being ordered or called to active duty in such forces.

(2) Each person who hereafter and prior to the enactment of the 1951 Amendments to the Universal Military Training and Service Act [June 19, 1951] is enlisted under the provisions of subsection (g) of this section and who meets the qualifications for enlistment or appointment in a reserve component of the armed forces shall, upon discharge from such enlistment under honorable conditions, be transferred to a reserve component of the armed forces of the United States and shall serve therein for a period of six years or until sooner discharged. Each such person shall, so long as he is a member of such reserve component, be liable to be ordered to active duty, but except in time of war or national emergency declared by the Congress no such person shall be ordered to active duty, without his consent and except as hereinafter provided, for more than one month in any year. In case the Secretary of the Army, the Secretary of the Navy, or the Secretary of the Air Force determines that enlistment, enrollment, or appointment in, or assignment to, an organized unit of a reserve component or an officers' training program of the armed force in which he served is available to, and can without undue hardship be filled by, any such person, it shall be the duty of such person to enlist, enroll, or accept appointment in, or accept assignment to, such organized unit or officers' training program and to serve satisfactorily therein for a period of four years. Any such person who fails or refuses to perform such duty may be ordered to active duty, without his consent, for an additional period of not more than twelve consecutive months. Any such person who enlists or accepts appointment in any such organized unit and serves satisfactorily therein for a period of four years shall, except in time of war or national emergency declared by the Congress, be relieved from any further liability under this subsection to serve in any reserve component of the armed forces of the United States, but nothing in this subsection shall be construed to prevent any such person, while in a reserve component of such forces, from being ordered or called to active duty in such forces. The Secretary of Defense is authorized to prescribe regulations governing the transfer of such persons within and between reserve components of the armed forces and determining, for the purpose of the requirements of the foregoing provisions of this paragraph, the credit to be allowed any person so transferring for his previous service in one or more reserve components.

(3) Each person who, subsequent to June 19, 1951, and on or before August 9, 1955, is inducted, enlisted, or appointed, under any provision of law, in the Armed Forces, including the reserve components thereof, or in the National Security Training Corps prior to attaining the twenty-sixth anniversary of his birth, shall be required to serve on active training and service in the Armed Forces or in training in the National Security Training Corps, and in a reserve component, for a total period of eight years, unless sooner discharged on grounds of personal hardship, in accordance with regulations and standards prescribed by the Secretary of Defense (or the Secretary of Transportation with respect to the United States Coast Guard). Each such person, on release from active training and service in the Armed Forces or from training in the National Security Training Corps, shall, if physically and mentally qualified, be transferred to a reserve component of the Armed Forces, and shall serve therein for the remainder of the period which he is required to serve under this paragraph and shall be deemed to be a member of the reserve component during that period. If the Secretary of the Army, the Secretary of the Navy, or the Secretary of the Air Force, or the Secretary of Transportation with respect to the United States Coast Guard, determines that enlistment, enrollment, or appointment in, or assignment to, an organized unit of a reserve component or an officers' training program of the armed force in which he served is available to, and can, without undue personal hardship, be filled by such a person, that person shall enlist, enroll, or accept appointment in, or accept assignment to, the organized unit or officers' training program, and serve satisfactorily therein.

(e) Pay and allowances

With respect to the persons inducted for training and service under this title [sections 451 to 471a of this Appendix] there shall be paid, allowed, and extended the same pay, allowances, pensions, disability and death compensation, and other benefits as are provided by law in the case of other enlisted men of like grades and length of service of that component of the armed forces to which they are assigned. Section 3 of the Act of July 25, 1947 (Public Law 239, Eightieth Congress), is amended by deleting therefrom the following: "Act of March 7, 1942 (56 Stat. 143 to 148, ch. 166), as amended". The Act of March 7, 1942 (56 Stat. 143 to 148), as amended, is made applicable to persons inducted into the armed forces pursuant to this title [said sections].

(f) Additional compensation from civilian sources

Notwithstanding any other provision of law, any person who is inducted into the armed forces under this Act and who, before being inducted, was receiving compensation from any person may, while serving under that induction, receive compensation from that person.

(g) Occupational deferment recommendations by National Security Council

The National Security Council shall periodically advise the Director of the Selective Service System and coordinate with him the work of such State and local volunteer advisory committees which the Director of Selective Service may establish, with respect to the identification, selection, and deferment of needed professional and scientific personnel and those engaged in, and preparing for, critical skills and other essential occupations. In the performance of its duties under this subsection the National Security Council shall consider the needs of both the Armed Forces and the civilian segment of the population.

(h) Repealed. June 19, 1951, ch. 144, title I, § 1(h), 65 Stat. 80

(i), (j) Omitted

(k) Reduction of periods of service; establishment of National Security Training Corps; composition; service; pay

(1) Upon a finding by him that such action is justified by the strength of the Armed Forces in the light of international conditions, the President, upon recommendation of the Secretary of Defense, is authorized, by Executive order, which shall be uniform in its application to all persons inducted under this title [sections 451 to 471a of this Appendix] but which may vary as to age groups, to provide for (A) decreasing periods of service under this title [said sections] but in no case to a lesser period of time than can be economically utilized, or (B) eliminating periods of service required under this title [said sections].

(2) Whenever the Congress shall by concurrent resolution declare—

(A) that the period of active service required of any age group or groups of persons inducted under this title [said sections] should be decreased to any period less than twenty-four months which may be designated in such resolution; or

(B) that the period of active service required of any age group or groups of persons inducted under this title [said sections] should be eliminated,

the period of active service in the Armed Forces of the age group or groups designated in any such resolution shall be so decreased or eliminated, as the case may be. Whenever the period of active service required under this title [said sections] of persons who have not attained the nineteenth anniversary of the day of their birth has been reduced or eliminated by the President or as a result of the adoption of a concurrent resolution of the Congress in accordance with the foregoing provisions of this section, all individuals then or thereafter liable for registration under this title [said sections] who on that date have not attained the nineteenth anniversary of the day of their birth and have not been inducted into the Armed Forces shall be liable, effective on such date, for induction into the National Security Training Corps as hereinafter established for initial military training for a period of six months.

(3), (4) Repealed. Pub. L. 89–554, §8(a), Sept. 6, 1966, 80 Stat. 656.

(5) The Commission shall, subject to the direction of the President, exercise general supervision over the training of the National Security Training Corps, which training shall be basic military training. The Commission shall establish such policies and standards with respect to the conduct of the training of members of the National Security Training Corps as are necessary to carry out the purposes of this Act. The Commission shall make adequate provisions for the moral and spiritual welfare of members of the National Security Training Corps. The Secretary of Defense shall designate the military departments to carry out such training. Each military department so designated shall carry out such military training in accordance with the policies and standards of the Commission. The military department or departments so designated to carry out such military training shall, subject to the approval of the Secretary of Defense, and subject to the policies and standards established by the Commission, determine the type or types of basic military training to be given to members of the National Security Training Corps.

(6) Repealed. Pub. L. 89–554, §8(a), Sept. 6, 1966, 80 Stat. 656.

(7) Not later than four months following confirmation of the members of the Commission, the Commission shall submit to the Congress legislative recommendations which shall include, but not be limited to—

(A) a broad outline for a program deemed by the Commission and approved by the Secretary of Defense to be appropriate to assure that the training carried out under the provisions of this Act shall be of a military nature, but nothing contained in this paragraph shall be construed to grant to the Commission the authority to prescribe the basic type or types of military training to be given members of the National Security Training Corps;

(B) measures for the personal safety, health, welfare and morals of members of the National Security Training Corps;

(C) a code of conduct, together with penalties for violation thereof;

(D) measures deemed necessary to implement the policies and standards established under the provisions of paragraph (5) of this subsection; and

(E) disability and death benefits and other benefits, and the obligations, duties, liabilities and responsibilities, to be granted to or imposed upon members of the National Security Training Corps.

All legislative recommendations submitted under this paragraph shall be referred to the Committees on Armed Services of the two Houses, and each of such committees shall, not later than the expiration of the first period of 45 calendar days of continuous sessions of the Congress, following the date on which the recommendations provided for in this paragraph are transmitted to the Congress, report thereon to its House: *Provided*, That any bill or resolution reported with respect to such recommendations shall be privileged and may be called up by any member of either House but shall be subject to amendment as if it were not so privileged.

(8) No person shall be inducted into the National Security Training Corps until after—

(A) a code of conduct, together with penalties for violation thereof, and measures providing for disability and death benefits have been enacted into law; and

(B) such other legislative recommendations as are provided for in paragraph (7) shall have been considered and such recommendations or any portion thereof shall have been enacted with or without amendments into law; and

(C) the period of service required under this title [sections 451 to 471a of this Appendix] of persons who have not attained the nineteenth anniversary of the day of their birth has been reduced or eliminated by the President or as a result of the adoption of a concurrent resolution of the Congress in accordance with paragraph (2) of this subsection.

(9) Six months following the commencement of induction of persons into the National Security Training Corps, and semiannually thereafter, the Commission shall submit to the Congress a comprehensive report describing in detail the operation of the National Security Training Corps, including the number of persons inducted therein, a list of camps and stations at which training is being conducted, a report on the number of deaths and injuries occurring during such training and the causes thereof, an estimate of the performance of the persons inducted therein, including an analysis of the disciplinary problems encountered during the preceding six months, the number of civilian employees of the Commission and the administrative costs of the Commission. Simultaneously, there shall be submitted to the Congress by the Secretary of Defense a report setting forth an estimate of the value of the training conducted during the preceding six months, the cost of the training program chargeable to the appropriations made to the Department of Defense, and the number of personnel of the Armed Forces directly engaged in the conduct of such training.

(10) Each person inducted into the National Security Training Corps shall be compensated at the monthly rate of $30: *Provided, however*, That each such person, having a dependent or dependents shall be entitled to receive a dependency allowance equal to the basic allowance for housing provided for persons in pay grade E–1 under section 403 of title 37 plus $40 so long as such person has in effect an allotment equal to the amount of such dependency allowance for the support of the dependent or dependents on whose account the allowance is claimed.

(11) No person inducted into the National Security Training Corps shall be assigned for training at an installation located on land outside the continental United States, except that residents of Territories and possessions of the United States may be trained in the Territory or possession from which they were inducted.

(*l*) Terminated

(June 24, 1948, ch. 625, title I, §4, 62 Stat. 605; Sept. 9, 1950, ch. 939, §1, 64 Stat. 826; Sept. 27, 1950, ch. 1059, §§1(1)–(5), 3(a), 64 Stat. 1073; June 19, 1951, ch. 144, title I, §1(d)–(j), 65 Stat. 76; July 9, 1952, ch. 608, pt. VIII, §813, 66 Stat. 509; June 29, 1953, ch. 158, §§1, 2, 6, 67 Stat. 86, 89; June 30, 1955, ch. 250, title II, §202, 69 Stat. 224; Aug. 9, 1955, ch. 665, §3(a), 69 Stat. 602; Aug. 10, 1956, ch. 1041, §§22(a)–(c), 53, 70A Stat. 630, 641; Pub. L. 85–62, §§1–3, June 27, 1957, 71 Stat. 206, 207; Pub. L. 85–564, July 28, 1958, 72 Stat. 424; Pub. L. 85–861, §§9, 36A, Sept. 2, 1958, 72 Stat. 1556, 1569; Pub. L. 87–651, title III, §301, Sept. 7, 1962, 76 Stat. 524; Pub. L. 89–554, §8(a), Sept. 6, 1966, 80 Stat. 656; Pub. L. 90–40, §1(2), June 30, 1967, 81 Stat. 100; Pub. L. 92–129, title I, §101(a)(3)–(7), Sept. 28, 1971, 85 Stat. 348, 349; Pub. L. 94–106, title VIII, §802(c), Oct. 7, 1975, 89 Stat. 537; Pub. L. 105–85, div. A, title VI, §603(d)(5), Nov. 18, 1997, 111 Stat. 1783.)

REFERENCES IN TEXT

This Act, referred to in subsecs. (c)(1), (2), (f), and (k)(5), (7)(A), is act June 24, 1948, ch. 625, 62 Stat. 604, as amended, known as the Military Selective Service Act. For complete classification of this Act to the Code, see References in Text note set out under section 451 of this Appendix and Tables.

The effective period of this Act, referred to in subsec. (c)(2), is set out in section 467 of this Appendix.

Section 3 of the Act of July 25, 1947 (Public Law 239, Eightieth Congress), referred to in subsec. (e), is section of act July 25, 1947, ch. 327, 61 Stat. 451, which is not classified to the Code.

Act of March 7, 1942 (56 Stat. 143 to 148), as amended, referred to in subsec. (e), popularly known as the Missing Persons Act, was classified to sections 1001 to 1018 of this Appendix. The Act was repealed by Pub. L. 89–554, Sept. 6, 1966, §8(a), 80 Stat. 632, and reenacted as subchapter VII of chapter 55 of Title 5, Government Organization and Employees, and chapter 10 of Title 37, Pay and Allowances of the Uniformed Services.

Subsection (g) of this section, referred to in subsec. (d)(2), refers to the subsection (g) that was repealed by act June 19, 1951, §1(h).

The Commission, referred to in subsec. (k)(5), means the National Security Training Commission, which expired June 30, 1957, pursuant to letter of the President on Mar. 25, 1957, following the Commission's own recommendation for its termination.

AMENDMENTS

1997—Subsec. (k)(10). Pub. L. 105–85 substituted "shall be entitled to receive a dependency allowance equal to the basic allowance for housing provided for persons in pay grade E–1 under section 403 of title 37" for "as such terms are defined in the Career Compensation Act of 1949, shall be entitled to receive a dependency allowance equal to the sum of the basic allowance for quarters provided for persons in pay grade E–1 by section 302(f) of the Career Compensation Act of 1949 as amended by section 3 of the Dependents' Assistance Act of 1950 as may be extended or amended".

1975—Subsec. (a). Pub. L. 94–106 in paragraph relating to military training for persons inducted after June 19, 1951, for service in the armed force into which they were inducted, substituted twelve weeks for four months in two places.

1971—Subsec. (a). Pub. L. 92–129, §101(a)(3), (4), struck out provisions which had given special coverage for male aliens and substituted "Secretary of Transportation" for "Secretary of the Treasury".

Subsec. (b). Pub. L. 92–129, §101(a)(5), substituted "Secretary of Transportation" for "Secretary of the Treasury".

Subsec. (d)(1). Pub. L. 92–129, §101(a)(6), struck out "(except a person enlisted under subsection (g) of this section)" after "inducted, enlisted, or appointed".

Subsec. (d)(3). Pub. L. 92–129, §101(a)(7), substituted "Secretary of Transportation" for "Secretary of the Treasury".

1967—Subsec. (a). Pub. L. 90–40, §1(2)(a), inserted proviso that registrants failing or refusing to report for induction continue to remain liable for induction and to be immediately inducted when available.

Subsec. (g). Pub. L. 90–40, §1(2)(b), added subsec. (g). A former subsec. (g), authorizing one year enlistments in the armed services by male persons between 18 and 19, was repealed by act June 19, 1951, ch. 144, §1(h), 65 Stat. 80.

1966—Subsec. (k)(3), (4), (6). Pub. L. 89–554 repealed pars. (3), (4) and (6) which established the National Security Training Commission, provided for its composition, tenure, pay and duties, and authorized appointment and pay of employees.

1962—Subsec. (d)(3). Pub. L. 87–651 amended par. (3) generally, striking out provisions which required each person inducted into the National Security Training Corps to serve in the Armed Forces or the National Security Training Corps for a total of eight years, unless sooner discharged because of personal hardship, and requiring each person covered by this subsection who is not a reserve, and who is qualified, upon his release from training, to be transferred to a reserve component to complete the service required by this subsection.

1958—Subsec. (a). Pub. L. 85–564 inserted, at end of third par., proviso authorizing President to modify standards fixed by preceding two provisos, except in war or national emergency.

Subsec. (d)(3). Pub. L. 85–861 repealed provisions that required persons inducted, enlisted, or appointed, in the Armed Forces to serve on active training and service in the Armed Forces and in a reserve component for a total of six years, and inserted provisions requiring transfer to reserve components of persons released from active training and service in the Armed Forces or from training in the National Security Training Corps and authorizing enlistment, enrollment, or appointment in, or assignment to, an organized unit of a reserve component or an officers' training program of the armed force in which a person served. See section 651 of Title 10, Armed Forces.

1957—Subsec. (a). Pub. L. 85–62, §§1, 9, temporarily inserted next to last paragraph providing that no medical, dental, or allied specialist shall be inducted if he applies or applied for appointment as a Reserve officer in one of such categories and is rejected on the sole ground of physical disqualification. See Effective and Termination Dates of 1957 Amendment note below.

Subsec. (j). Pub. L. 85–62, §§3, 9, temporarily struck out "as referred to in subsection (i)" after "categories of persons" at end of first sentence, and substituted "thirty-fifth" for "fifty-first" in last sentence of second par. See Effective and Termination Dates of 1957 Amendment note below.

Subsec. (*l*). Pub. L. 85–62, §§2, 9, temporarily added subsec. (*l*). See Effective and Termination Dates of 1957 Amendment note below.

1956—Subsec. (a). Act Aug. 10, 1956, §53, repealed provisions prohibiting assignment to duty outside the United States until the member of the Armed Forces has had the equivalent of four months of basic training, and relating to communications with Members of Congress. See sections 671 and 1034 of Title 10, Armed Forces.

Subsec. (b). Act Aug. 10, 1956, §22(a), authorized Secretaries of the Army, Navy, Air Force, and Treasury, to provide by regulations for release from training and service in the Armed Forces of those individuals who are accepted into organized units of the Army National Guard and Air National Guard and other reserve components.

Subsec. (d)(3). Act Aug. 10, 1956, §22(b), purportedly repealed par. (3) and amended it to provide that "Each person who is inducted into the National Security Training Corps shall serve in the armed forces or the National Security Training Corps for a total of eight years, unless he is sooner discharged because of personal hardship under regulations prescribed by the Secretary of Defense. Each person covered by this subsection who is not a Reserve, and who is qualified, shall, upon his release from training, be transferred to a reserve component of an armed force to complete the service required by this subsection." See 1958 and 1962 Amendment notes above.

Subsec. (f). Act Aug. 10, 1956, §53, purportedly repealed subsec. (f). However, section 22(c) of the act amended subsection to clarify authority to receive compensation. See also section 103 of Title 10, Armed Forces.

1955—Subsec. (d)(3). Act Aug. 9, 1955, provided for a six-year term of duty for persons who are inducted, enlisted, or appointed after Aug. 9, 1955.

Subsec. (i)(1). Act June 30, 1955, exempted from service persons who attained their thirty-fifth anniversary of their date of birth and who were rejected for service on the ground of physical disqualification, and to reduce maximum age of liability of induction from 51 to 46 years of age.

1953—Subsec. (i)(2). Act June 29, 1953, §6, in cl. "First" struck out "subsequent to the completion of or release from the program or course of instruction" after "Public Health Service"; and, in cl. "Second", substituted "seventeen months" for "twenty-one months", and struck out "subsequent to the completion of or release from the program or course of instruction" after "Public Health Service".

Subsec. (i)(4) to (7). Act June 29, 1953, §1, added pars. (4) to (7).

Subsec. (j). Act June 29, 1953, §2, added third par.

1952—Subsec. (d)(3). Act July 9, 1952, substituted "appointed under any provision of law, in the Armed Forces, including the reserve components thereof," for "appointed in the Armed Forces".

1951—Subsec. (a). Act June 19, 1951, §1(d), lowered age limit from 19 years to 18½, provided for training in National Security Training Corps, lowered physical and mental standards, provided for a basic training period, and allowed communication with Members of Congress.

Subsec. (b). Act June 19, 1951, §1(e), increased length of service from 21 to 24 months.

Subsec. (c). Act June 19, 1951, §1(f), struck out short-term Army enlistment period and the General Classification Test, and established age for voluntary induction.

Subsec. (d). Act June 19, 1951, §1(g), inserted "and prior to the enactment of the 1951 Amendments to the Universal Military Training and Service Act" after "hereafter" in pars. (1) and (2), and added par. (3).

Subsec. (e). Act June 19, 1951, §1(i), inserted "6g" after "sections" in par. (1), and extended period of service from 21 to 24 months.

Subsec. (g). Act June 19, 1951, §1(h), repealed subsec. (g) which related to enlistments in armed service for one year by male persons between 18 and 19 years.

Subsec. (h). Act June 19, 1951, §1(h), repealed subsec. (h) which related to permanent assignment outside continental United States.

Subsec. (k). Act June 19, 1951, §1(j), added subsec. (k).

1950—Subsec. (a). Act Sept. 27, 1950, §1(1)–(4), inserted before period in third sentence of first par. "and such number of persons as in his judgment may be required for the United States Coast Guard", inserted before period in second par. "or the Secretary of the Treasury", inserted after "the Secretary of Defense" in third par. "or the Secretary of the Treasury", inserted after "United States Marine Corps" in fourth par. "or the United States Coast Guard".

Subsec. (b). Act Sept. 27, 1950, §1(5), inserted before period "or the Secretary of the Treasury".

Subsec. (c). Act Sept. 27, 1950, §3(a), added par. (4).

Subsecs. (i), (j). Act Sept. 9, 1950, §§1, 9, temporarily added subsecs. (i) and (j). See Termination Date of Subsection (i) and Former Subsection (j) note below.

EFFECTIVE DATE OF 1997 AMENDMENT

Amendment by Pub. L. 105–85 effective Jan. 1, 1998, see section 603(e) of Pub. L. 105–85, set out as a note under section 5561 of Title 5, Government Organization and Employees.

EFFECTIVE AND TERMINATION DATES OF 1957 AMENDMENT

Pub. L. 85–62, §9, June 27, 1957, 71 Stat. 208, as amended by Pub. L. 86–4, §4, Mar. 23, 1959, 73 Stat. 13; Pub. L. 88–2, §4, Mar. 28, 1963, 77 Stat. 4; Pub. L. 90–40, §4, June 30, 1967, 81 Stat. 105; Pub. L. 92–129, title I, §103, Sept. 28, 1971, 85 Stat. 355, provided that: "This Act [amending this section, sections 454a to 456 of this Appendix, and provisions set out as a note under this section] takes effect July 1, 1957, and shall terminate July 1, 1973."

EFFECTIVE DATE OF 1952 AMENDMENT

Section 813 of act July 9, 1952, provided that the amendment made by that section is effective as of June 19, 1951.

REPEAL OF PRIOR ACTS CONTINUING SECTION

Section 6 of act July 3, 1952, repealed act Apr. 14, 1952, ch. 204, 66 Stat. 54 as amended by acts May 28, 1952, ch. 339, 66 Stat. 96; June 14, 1952, ch. 437, 66 Stat. 137; June 30, 1952, ch. 526, 66 Stat. 296, which continued provisions until July 3, 1952. This repeal shall take effect as of June 16, 1952, by section 7 of act July 3, 1952.

TERMINATION DATE OF SUBSECTION (i) AND FORMER SUBSECTION (j)

Section 7 of act Sept. 9, 1950, as amended by acts June 19, 1951, §2(b); June 29, 1953, §9; and June 30, 1955, §201, and by Pub. L. 85–62, §8, provided that subsecs. (i) and (j) of this section, which were added by act Sept. 9, 1950, shall terminate as of June 30, 1957. See Effective and Termination Dates of 1957 Amendment note set out above with respect to subsec. (j) as reenacted and amended by Pub. L. 85–62.

EXECUTIVE ORDER NO. 10164

Ex. Ord. No. 10164, Sept. 27, 1950, 15 F.R. 6570, provided for extension for a period of twelve months of all enlistments in the United States Coast Guard, including the Coast Guard Reserve, which would have expired at any time after Sept. 27, 1950, and prior to July 9, 1951.

EXECUTIVE ORDER NO. 10166

Ex. Ord. No. 10166, Oct. 4, 1950, 15 F.R. 6777, as amended by Ex. Ord. No. 10185, Dec. 1, 1950, 15 F.R. 8557, which established the National Advisory Committee on the Selection of Physicians, Dentists, and Allied Specialists, was revoked by Ex. Ord. No. 11415, June 24, 1968, 33 F.R. 9329, formerly set out below.

EX. ORD. NO. 10762. DELEGATION OF AUTHORITY TO SECRETARY OF DEFENSE

Ex. Ord. No. 10762, Mar. 28, 1958, 23 F.R. 2119, provided:

1. There is hereby delegated to the Secretary of Defense:

(a) The authority vested in the President by section 4(*l*)(1) of the Universal Military Training and Service Act, as added by section 2 of the Act of June 27, 1957 (P.L. 85–62; 71 Stat. 206) [subsection (*l*)(1) of this section], to order to active duty (other than for training) for a period of not more than 24 consecutive months, with or without his consent, any member of a reserve component of the armed forces of the United States who is in a medical, dental, or allied specialist category, who has not attained the thirty-fifth anniversary of the date of his birth, and who has not performed at least one year of active duty (other than for training).

(b) The authority vested in the President by section 5(c) of the Universal Military Training and Service Act, as added by section 5 of the Act of June 27, 1957 (P.L. 85–62; 71 Stat. 207) [section 455(c) of this Appendix], to prescribe regulations with respect to the appointment, reappointment, or promotion of any qualified person who (1) is liable for induction or (2) as a member of a reserve component is ordered to active duty as a physician or dentist or in an allied specialist category in the armed forces of the United States.

2. Executive Order No. 10478 of August 5, 1953, as amended by Executive Order No. 10658 of February 15, 1956, is hereby revoked.

DWIGHT D. EISENHOWER.

EX. ORD. NO. 10776. DELEGATION OF PRESIDENT'S AUTHORITY

Ex. Ord. No. 10776, July 28, 1958, 23 F.R. 5683, provided:

By virtue of the authority vested in me by title 3 of the United States Code, and as President of the United States and Commander in Chief of the Armed Forces, there is hereby delegated to the Secretary of Defense the authority (relating to the prescribing of rules and regulations modifying the standards and requirements with respect to induction of persons into the armed forces) vested in the President by the last proviso of section 4(a) of the Universal Military Training and Service Act [subsec. (a) of this section], added by the act of July 28, 1958 [Pub. L. 85–564]. The Secretary of Defense is hereby authorized to re-delegate that authority to any official of the Department of Defense who is required to be appointed by and with the advice and consent of the Senate. No person shall be inducted into the armed forces for training and service who does not meet the standards and requirements specified in the rules and regulations prescribed by the Secretary or his designee pursuant to this order.

DWIGHT D. EISENHOWER.

EXECUTIVE ORDER NO. 11415

Ex. Ord. No. 11415, June 24, 1968, 33 F.R. 9329, which established the National Advisory Committee on the Selection of Physicians, Dentists, and Allied Specialists and the National Health Resources Advisory Committee, was revoked by section 5–110 of Ex. Ord. No. 12148, July 20, 1979, 44 F.R. 43243, set out as a note under section 5195 of Title 42, The Public Health and Welfare.

PROC. NO. 2906. REGISTRATION OF DOCTORS, DENTISTS AND ALLIED SPECIALISTS

Proc. No. 2906, Oct. 6, 1950, 15 F.R. 6845, 64 Stat. Pt. 2, p. A437, as amended Proc. No. 2915, Dec. 28, 1950, 15 F.R. 9419, 64 Stat. Pt. 2, p. A455, provided:

1. Every male person who participated as a student in the Army specialized training program or any similar program administered by the Navy, or was deferred from service during World War II for the purpose of pursuing a course of instruction leading to education in a medical, dental, or allied specialist category, and has had less than twenty-one months of active duty in the Army, the Air Force, the Navy, the Marine Corps, the Coast Guard, or the Public Health Service subsequent to the completion of, or release from, such program or course of instruction (exclusive of time spent in postgraduate training), and who, on the day or any of the days hereinafter fixed for his registration (a) shall have received from any school, college, university, or similar institution of learning, one or more of the degrees of bachelor of medicine, doctor of medicine, doctor of dental surgery, doctor of dental medicine, doctor of veterinary surgery, and doctor of veterinary medicine, (b) is within any of the several States of the United States, the District of Columbia, the Territory of Alaska, the Territory of Hawaii, Puerto Rico, or the Virgin Islands, (c) is not a member of any reserve component of the armed forces of the United States, and (d) shall not have attained the fiftieth anniversary of the day of his birth is required to and shall on that day or any of those days present himself for and submit to registration before a duly designated registration official or selective service local board having jurisdiction in the area in which he has his permanent home or in which he may happen to be on that day or any of those days.

2. The special registration of the male persons required to submit to registration by paragraph numbered 1 hereof shall take place in the several States of the United States, the District of Columbia, the Territories of Alaska and Hawaii, Puerto Rico, and the Virgin Islands between the hours of 8:00 a.m. and 5:00 p.m. on the day or days hereinafter designated for their registration, as follows:

(a) Persons who shall have received any of the degrees above referred to on or before October 16, 1950, shall be registered on Monday, the 16th day of October, 1950.

(b) Persons who receive any of the degrees above referred to after October 16, 1950, shall be registered on the day they receive any such degree, or within five days thereafter.

(c) Persons who shall have received any of the degrees above referred to and who enter any of the several States of the United States, the District of Columbia, the Territory of Alaska, the Territory of Hawaii, Puerto Rico, or the Virgin Islands after October 16, 1950, shall be registered on the day of such entrance, or within five days thereafter.

3. Every male person who has not had active service in the Army, the Air Force, the Navy, the Marine Corps, the Coast Guard, or the Public Health Service subsequent to September 16, 1940, and every male person not included in the first or the second of the priorities defined in section 4(i)(2) of the Selective Service Act of 1948, as amended [now the Military Selective Service Act, formerly subsec. (i)(2) of this section], who has had active service in the Army, the Air Force, the Navy, the Marine Corps, the Coast Guard, or the Public Health Service subsequent to September 16, 1940, who on the day or any of the days hereafter fixed by the Director of Selective Service for his registration (a) shall have received from a school, college, university, or similar institution of learning one or more of the degrees of bachelor of medicine, doctor of medicine, doctor of dental surgery, doctor of dental medicine, doctor of veterinary surgery, and doctor of veterinary medicine, (b) is within any of the several States of the United States, the District of Columbia, the Territory of Alaska, the Territory of Hawaii, Puerto Rico, or the Virgin Islands, (c) is not a member of any reserve component of the armed forces of the United States, and (d) shall not have attained the fiftieth anniversary of the day of his birth is required to and shall on that day or any of those days present himself for and submit to registration before a duly designated registration official or selective service local board having jurisdiction in the area in which he has his permanent home or in which he may happen to be on that day or any of those days.

4. The Director of Selective Service is hereby authorized and directed to fix the date or dates for the special registration required under paragraph numbered 3 hereof: *Provided*, that the date or dates so fixed shall be not later than January 16, 1951.

5. The Director of Selective Service is hereby authorized to require special registration of, and fix the date or dates of registration for, all other persons who are subject to registration under section 4(i) of the Selective Service Act of 1948, as amended [subsection (i) of this section], and who are not required to register under or pursuant to this proclamation.

6. All orders and directives of the Director of Selective Service issued pursuant to paragraph numbered 4 or paragraph numbered 5 hereof shall be published in the Federal Register.

7. (a) A person subject to registration under or pursuant to this proclamation who, because of circumstances beyond his control, is unable to present himself for and submit to registration during the hours of the day or any of the days fixed for registration shall do so as soon as possible after the cause for such inability ceases to exist.

(b) Every person subject to registration under or pursuant to this proclamation who has registered in accordance with Proclamation No. 2799 of July 20, 1948 [formerly set out under section 453 of this Appendix], issued under the Selective Service Act of 1948, as amended, [now the Military Selective Service Act] and the regulations prescribed thereunder, shall, notwithstanding such registration, present himself for and submit to registration as required by or pursuant to this proclamation.

(c) The duty of any person to present himself for and submit to registration in accordance with Proclamation No. 2799 of July 20, 1948, issued under the Selective Service Act of 1948, as amended [now the Military Selective Service Act] and the regulations prescribed thereunder, shall not be affected by this proclamation.

8. Every person subject to registration under or pursuant to this proclamation is required to familiarize himself with the rules and regulations governing such registration and to comply therewith.

9. I call upon the Governors of each of the several States, the Territories of Alaska and Hawaii, Puerto Rico, and the Virgin Islands and the Board of Commissioners of the District of Columbia, and all officers and agents of the United States and all officers and agents of the several States, the Territories of Alaska and Hawaii, Puerto Rico, the Virgin Islands, and the District of Columbia, and political subdivisions thereof, and all local boards and agents thereof appointed under the provisions of title I of the Selective Service Act of 1948, as amended [now the Military Selective Service Act, sections 451 to 471a of this Appendix], or the regulations prescribed thereunder, to do and perform all acts and services necessary to accomplish effective and complete registration.

10. In order that there may be full cooperation in carrying into effect the purposes of section 4(i) of title I of the Selective Service Act of 1948, as amended [now the Military Selective Service Act, formerly subsec. (i) of this section], I urge all employers and Government agencies of all kinds—Federal, State, territorial, and local—to give those under their charge sufficient time in which to fulfill the obligations of registration incumbent upon them under the said Act and under or pursuant to this proclamation.

PROC. NO. 2915. EXEMPTIONS FROM REGISTRATION

Proc. No. 2915, Dec. 28, 1950, 15 F.R. 9419, 64 Stat. 494, provided:

Proclamation No. 2906 of October 6, 1950 [set out above], be, and it is hereby, amended, effective as of October 6, 1950, so as to exempt from the force and effect thereof, until otherwise directed by the President by proclamation, (1) commissioned officers, warrant officers, pay clerks, enlisted men, and aviation cadets of the Regular Army, the Navy, the Air Force, the Marine Corps, the Coast Guard, the Coast and Geodetic Survey, and the Public Health Service, and (2) aliens who are residing in the United States and have not declared their intention of becoming citizens of the United States and who are also in one of the following categories: (a) alien students admitted under subdivision (e) of section 4 of the Immigration Act approved May 26, 1924, as amended [former section 204 of Title 8 Aliens and Nationality], (b) aliens recognized as diplomatic, consular, military or civilian officials or employees of a foreign government and members of their families, (c) aliens who are officials or employees of a public international organization recognized under the International Organizations Immunities Act, approved December 29, 1945 (59 Stat. 669) [22 U.S.C. 288 et seq.], and members of their families, (d) aliens who have entered the United States and remain therein pursuant to the provisions of section 11 of the Agreement between the United Nations and the United States of America regarding the Headquarters of the United Nations, as approved in Public Law 357, 80th Congress (61 Stat. 756) [set out as a note under section 287 of Title 22, Foreign Relations and Intercourse], (e) aliens who are nationals of a country with which there is in effect a treaty or international agreement exempting its nationals from military service while they are within the United States, or (f) other aliens whose admission to the

United States is for a temporary stay only: *Provided*, That such exemption shall not continue after the cause thereof shall cease to exist.

SECTION REFERRED TO IN OTHER SECTIONS

This section is referred to in sections 455, 456, 458, 459, 465 of this Appendix; title 8 section 1101; title 10 section 671.

§§ 454a, 454b. Omitted

CODIFICATION

Section 454a, acts Sept. 9, 1950, ch. 939, § 4, 64 Stat. 828; June 29, 1953, ch. 158, § 3, 67 Stat. 88; June 18, 1954, ch. 307, 68 Stat. 254; June 30, 1955, ch. 250, title II, § 201, 69 Stat. 224, which provided for promotion of physicians, dentists, and allied specialist categories, period of service, and discharge and resignation of such personnel, expired on June 30, 1957. See sections 451 and 455 of this Appendix.

Section 454b, act Sept. 9, 1950, ch. 939, § 6, 64 Stat. 828, which defined "allied specialist categories" as used in sections 454(i) and 454a of this Appendix, expired on June 30, 1957.

TERMINATION DATE

Section 7 of act Sept. 9, 1950, as amended by acts June 19, 1951, ch. 144, title I, § 2(b), 65 Stat. 88; June 29, 1953, § 9; June 30, 1955, § 201 and by Pub. L. 85–62, § 8, June 27, 1957, 71 Stat. 208, provided that sections 454a and 454b of this Appendix shall terminate as of June 30, 1957.

§§ 454c, 454d. Omitted

Section 454c, act June 29, 1953, ch. 158, § 4, 67 Stat. 88, provided for release, discharge, or resignation of special registrants who made application therefor on or before 90th day after June 29, 1953.

Section 454d, act June 29, 1953, ch. 158, § 5, 67 Stat. 89, provided for extension of reserve commissions of certain doctors, dentists, and other special registrants.

§ 454e. Volunteer service of physicians and dentists; minimum period

Any physician or dentist who meets the qualifications for a reserve commission in the respective military departments shall, so long as there is a need for the services of such a physician or dentist, be afforded an opportunity to volunteer for a period of active duty of not less than twenty-four months. Any physician or dentist who so volunteers his service, and meets the qualifications for a reserve commission shall be ordered to active duty for not less than twenty-four months, notwithstanding the grade or rank to which such physician or dentist is entitled under the provisions of the Act of September 9, 1950, as amended.

(June 29, 1953, ch. 158, § 7, 67 Stat. 89.)

REFERENCES IN TEXT

Act of September 9, 1950, as amended, referred to in text, is act Sept. 9, 1950, ch. 939, 64 Stat. 826, as amended. Section 7 of the Act, as amended (71 Stat. 208), provided that the Act, except for sections 3 and 5, shall terminate as of June 30, 1957. Section 3 of the Act amended section 202 of the National Security Act of 1947, by adding subsections (g) to (i) which were classified to section 171a(g) to (i) of former Title 5 and which were later omitted from the Code following the codification of section 202(a) to (f) and (j) of the National Security Act of 1947 in Title 10, Armed Forces, by Pub. L. 87–651, Sept. 7, 1972, 76 Stat. 506. Section 5 of the Act was classified to section 234b of former Title 37, and was later omitted from the Code following the enactment of Title 37, Pay and Allowances of the Uniformed Services, by Pub. L. 87–649, Sept. 7, 1962, 76 Stat. 451.

CODIFICATION

Section was not enacted as part of the Military Selective Service Act, title I of which comprises sections 451 to 471a of this Appendix.

§ 455. Manner of selection of men for training and service; quotas

(a)(1) The selection of persons for training and service under section 4 [section 454 of this Appendix] shall be made in an impartial manner, under such rules and regulations as the President may prescribe, from the persons who are liable for such training and service and who at the time of selection are registered and classified, but not deferred or exempted: *Provided*, That in the selection of persons for training and service under this title [sections 451 to 471a of this Appendix], and in the interpretation and execution of the provisions of this title [said sections], there shall be no discrimination against any person on account of race or color: *Provided further*, That in the classification of registrants within the jurisdiction of any local board, the registrants of any particular registration may be classified, in the manner prescribed by and in accordance with rules and regulations prescribed by the President, before, together with, or after the registrants of any prior registration or registrations; and in the selection for induction of persons within the jurisdiction of any local board and within any particular classification, persons who were registered at any particular registration may be selected, in the manner prescribed by and in accordance with rules and regulations prescribed by the President, before, together with, or after persons who were registered at any prior registration or registrations: *And provided further*, That nothing herein shall be construed to prohibit the selection or induction of persons by age group or groups under rules and regulations prescribed by the President: *And provided further*, That—

(1) no local board shall order for induction for training and service in the Armed Forces of the United States any person who has not attained the age of nineteen unless there is not within the jurisdiction of such local board a sufficient number of persons who are deemed by such local board to be available for induction and who have attained the age of nineteen to enable such local board to meet a call for men which it has been ordered to furnish for induction;

(2) no local board shall order for induction for training and service in the Armed Forces of the United States any person who has not attained the age of nineteen, if there is any person within the jurisdiction of such local board who (i) is as much as ninety days older, (ii) has not attained the age of nineteen, and (iii) is deemed by the local board to be available for induction; and

(3) no local board shall order for induction for training and service in the Armed Forces of the United States an alien unless such alien shall have resided in the United States for one year.

(2) Repealed. Pub. L. 91–124, § 2, Nov. 26, 1969, 83 Stat. 220.

(b) Quotas of men to be inducted for training and service under this title [sections 451 to 471a of this Appendix] shall be determined for each State, Territory, possession, and the District of Columbia, and for subdivisions thereof, on the basis of the actual number of men in the several States, Territories, possessions, and the District of Columbia, and the subdivisions thereof, who are liable for such training and service but who are not deferred after classification, except that credits shall be given in fixing such quotas for residents of such subdivisions who are in the armed forces of the United States on the date fixed for determining such quotas. After such quotas are fixed, credits shall be given in filling such quotas for residents of such subdivisions who subsequently become members of such forces. Until the actual numbers necessary for determining the quotas are known, the quotas may be based on estimates, and subsequent adjustments therein shall be made when such actual numbers are known. All computations under this subsection shall be made in accordance with such rules and regulations as the President may prescribe.

(c) Terminated

(d) Whenever the President has provided for the selection of persons for training and service in accordance with random selection under subsection (a) of this section, calls for induction may be placed under such rules and regulations as he may prescribe, notwithstanding the provisions of subsection (b) of this section.

(e) Notwithstanding any other provision of this Act, not more than 130,000 persons may be inducted into the Armed Forces under this Act in the fiscal year ending June 30, 1972, and not more than 140,000 in the fiscal year ending June 30, 1973, unless a number greater than that authorized in this subsection for such fiscal year or years is authorized by a law enacted after the date of enactment of this subsection [Sept. 28, 1971].

(June 24, 1948, ch. 625, title I, §5, 62 Stat. 608; June 19, 1951, ch. 144, title I, §1(k), 65 Stat. 83; Pub. L. 85–62, §§4, 5, June 27, 1957, 71 Stat. 207; Pub. L. 90–40, §1(3), June 30, 1967, 81 Stat. 100; Pub. L. 91–124, §2, Nov. 26, 1969, 83 Stat. 220; Pub. L. 92–129, title I, §101(a)(8), (9), Sept. 28, 1971, 85 Stat. 349.)

REFERENCES IN TEXT

This Act, referred to in subsec. (e), is act June 24, 1948, ch. 625, 62 Stat. 604, as amended, known as the Military Selective Service Act. For complete classification of this Act to the Code, see References in Text note set out under section 451 of this Appendix and Tables.

AMENDMENTS

1971—Subsec. (a)(1). Pub. L. 92–129, §101(a)(8), added cl. (3) covering induction orders for aliens residing in the United States for one year, to last proviso.

Subsecs. (d), (e). Pub. L. 92–129, §101(a)(9), added subsecs. (d) and (e).

1969—Subsec. (a). Pub. L. 91–124 repealed cl. (2) which prohibited President from effecting any change in method of determining relative order of induction.

1967—Subsec. (a). Pub. L. 90–40 designated existing provisions as par. (1) and added par. (2).

1957—Subsec. (a). Pub. L. 85–62, §§4, 9, temporarily, substituted third and fourth provisos for former third proviso "that nothing herein shall be construed to prohibit the selection or induction of persons by age group or groups under rules and regulations prescribed by the President:". See Effective and Termination Dates of 1957 Amendment note below.

Subsec. (c). Pub. L. 85–62, §§5, 9, temporarily added subsec. (c). See Effective and Termination Dates of 1957 Amendment note below.

1951—Subsec. (a). Act June 19, 1951, inserted last two provisos.

EFFECTIVE AND TERMINATION DATES OF 1957 AMENDMENT

Amendment by Pub. L. 85–62 to take effect on July 1, 1957, and terminate on July 1, 1973, see section 9 of Pub. L. 85–62, set out as a note under section 454 of this Appendix.

PROC. NO. 3945. RANDOM SELECTION FOR MILITARY SERVICE

Proc. No. 3945, Nov. 26, 1969, 34 F.R. 19017, 83 Stat. 972, provided:

WHEREAS section 5(a)(1) of the Military Selective Service Act of 1967, as amended (50 U.S.C. App. 455(a)(1)) [now the Military Selective Service Act], provides that selection of persons for training and service under that Act shall be made in an impartial manner without discrimination on account of race or color, under such rules and regulations as the President may prescribe; and

WHEREAS section 5(a)(2) of that Act (50 U.S.C. App. 455(a)(2)) limited the President's authority to prescribe rules and regulations by requiring, in effect, the selection of registrants through a method known as "oldest first"; and

WHEREAS such section 5(a)(2) has been repealed by Public Law 91–124 of November 26, 1969:

NOW, THEREFORE, I, RICHARD NIXON, President of the United States of America, acting under and by virtue of the authority vested in me by section 5(a) of the Military Selective Service Act of 1967, as amended, and having determined that a method of random selection will provide the most equitable basis for selection of registrants for military training and service, do hereby proclaim the following:

That a random selection sequence will be established by a drawing to be conducted in Washington, D.C., on December 1, 1969, and will be applied nationwide. The random selection method will use 366 days to represent the birthdays (month and day only) of all registrants who, prior to January 1, 1970, shall have attained their nineteenth year of age but not their twenty-sixth. The drawing, commencing with the first day selected and continuing until all 366 days are drawn, shall be accomplished impartially.

On the day designated above, a supplemental drawing or drawings will be conducted to determine alphabetically the random selection sequence by name among registrants who have the same birthday.

The random selection sequence obtained as described above shall determine the order of selection of registrants who prior to January 1, 1970, shall have attained their nineteenth year of age but not their twenty-sixth and who are not volunteers and not delinquents. New random selection sequences shall be established, in a similar manner, for registrants who attain their nineteenth year of age on or after January 1, 1970.

The random sequence number determined for any registrant shall apply to him so long as he remains subject to induction for military training and service by random selection.

IN WITNESS WHEREOF, I have hereunto set my hand this twenty-sixth day of November, in the year of our Lord nineteen hundred and sixty-nine, and of the Independence of the United States of America the one hundred and ninety-fourth.

RICHARD NIXON.

SECTION REFERRED TO IN OTHER SECTIONS

This section is referred to in sections 454, 456 of this Appendix.

§ 456. Deferments and exemptions from training and service

(a)(1) Commissioned officers, warrant officers, pay clerks, enlisted men, and aviation cadets of the Regular Army, the Navy, the Air Force, the Marine Corps, the Coast Guard, and the Environmental Science Services Administration;[1] cadets, United States Military Academy; midshipmen, United States Naval Academy; cadets, United States Air Force Academy; cadets, United States Coast Guard Academy; midshipmen, Merchant Marine Reserve, United States Naval Reserves; students enrolled in an officer procurement program at military colleges the curriculum of which is approved by the Secretary of Defense; members of the reserve components of the Armed Forces and the Coast Guard, while on active duty; and foreign diplomatic representatives, technical attachés of foreign embassies and legations, consuls general, consuls, vice consuls and other consular agents of foreign countries who are not citizens of the United States, and members of their families, and persons in other categories to be specified by the President who are not citizens of the United States, shall not be required to be registered under section 3 [section 453 of this Appendix] and shall be relieved from liability for training and service under section 4 [section 454 of this Appendix], except that aliens admitted for permanent residence in the United States shall not be so exempted: *Provided*, That any alien lawfully admitted for permanent residence as defined in paragraph (20) of section 101(a) of the Immigration and Nationality Act, as amended (66 Stat. 163, 8 U.S.C. 1101), and who by reason of occupational status is subject to adjustment to nonimmigrant status under paragraph (15)(A), (15)(E), or (15)(G) of such section 101(a) [8 U.S.C. 1101(a)(15)(A), (E), or (G)] but who executes a waiver in accordance with section 247(b) of that Act [8 U.S.C. 1257(b)] of all rights, privileges, exemptions, and immunities which would otherwise accrue to him as a result of that occupational status, shall be subject to registration under section 3 of this Act [section 453 of this Appendix], but shall be deferred from induction for training and service for so long as such occupational status continues. Any person who subsequent to June 24, 1948, serves on active duty for a period of not less than twelve months in the armed forces of a nation with which the United States is associated in mutual defense activities as defined by the President, may be exempted from training and service, but not from registration, in accordance with regulations prescribed by the President, except that no such exemption shall be granted to any person who is a national of a country which does not grant reciprocal privileges to citizens of the United States: *Provided*, That any active duty performed prior to June 24, 1948, by a person in the armed forces of a country allied with the United States during World War II and with which the United States is associated in such mutual defense activities, shall be credited in the computation of such twelve-month period: *Provided further*, That any person who is in a medical, dental, or allied specialist category not otherwise deferred or exempted under this subsection shall be liable for registration and training and service until the thirty-fifth anniversary of the date of his birth.

(2) Commissioned officers of the Public Health Service and members of the Reserve of the Public Health Service while on active duty and assigned to staff the various offices and bureaus of the Public Health Service, including the National Institutes of Health, or assigned to the Coast Guard, the Bureau of Prisons, Department of Justice, the Environmental Protection Agency, or the Environmental Science Services Administration[1] or who are assigned to assist Indian tribes, groups, bands, or communities pursuant to the Act of August 5, 1954 (68 Stat. 674), as amended [42 U.S.C. 2001 et seq.], shall not be required to be registered under section 3 [section 453 of this Appendix] and shall be relieved from liability for training and service under section 4 [section 454 of this Appendix]. Notwithstanding the preceding sentence, commissioned officers of the Public Health Service and members of the Reserve of the Public Health Service who, prior to the enactment of this paragraph [June 30, 1967], had been detailed or assigned to duty other than that specified in the preceding sentence shall not be required to be registered under section 3 [section 453 of this Appendix] and shall be relieved from liability for training and service under section 4 [section 454 of this Appendix].

(b)(1) No person who served honorably on active duty between September 16, 1940, and the date of enactment of this title [June 24, 1948] for a period of twelve months or more, or between December 7, 1941, and September 2, 1945, for a period in excess of ninety days, in the Army, the Air Force, the Navy, the Marine Corps, the Coast Guard, the Public Health Service, or the armed forces of any country allied with the United States in World War II prior to September 2, 1945, shall be liable for induction for training and service under this title [sections 451 to 471a of this Appendix], except after a declaration of war or national emergency made by the Congress subsequent to the date of enactment of this title [June 24, 1948].

(2) No person who served honorably on active duty between September 16, 1940, and the date of enactment of this title [June 24, 1948] for a period of ninety days or more but less than twelve months in the Army, the Air Force, the Navy, the Marine Corps, the Coast Guard, the Public Health Service, or the armed forces of any country allied with the United States in World War II prior to September 2, 1945, shall be liable for induction for training and service under this title [sections 451 to 471a of this Appendix], except after a declaration of war or national emergency made by the Congress subsequent to the date of enactment of this title [June 24, 1948], if—

(A) the local board determines that he is regularly enlisted or commissioned in any organized unit of a reserve component of the armed force in which he served, provided such unit is reasonably accessible to such person without unduly interrupting his normal pursuits and activities (including attendance at a

[1] See Transfer of Functions note below.

college or university in which he is regularly enrolled), or in a reserve component (other than in an organized unit) of such armed force in any case in which enlistment or commission in an organized unit of a reserve component of such armed force is not available to him; or

(B) the local board determines that enlistment or commission in a reserve component of such armed force is not available to him or that he has voluntarily enlisted or accepted appointment in an organized unit of a reserve component of an armed force other than the armed force in which he served.

Nothing in this paragraph shall be deemed to be applicable to any person to whom paragraph (1) of this subsection is applicable.

(3) Except as provided in section 5(a) of this Act [section 455(a) of this Appendix], and notwithstanding any other provision of this Act, no person who (A) has served honorably on active duty after September 16, 1940, for a period of not less than one year in the Army, the Air Force, the Navy, the Marine Corps, or the Coast Guard, or (B) subsequent to September 16, 1940, was discharged for the convenience of the Government after having served honorably on active duty for a period of not less than six months in the Army, the Air Force, the Navy, the Marine Corps, or the Coast Guard, or (C) has served for a period of not less than twenty-four months (i) as a commissioned officer in the Public Health Service or (ii) as a commissioned officer in the Coast and Geodetic Survey,[2] shall be liable for induction for training and service under this Act, except after a declaration of war or national emergency made by the Congress subsequent to the date of enactment of this title [June 24, 1948].

(4) No person who is honorably discharged upon the completion of an enlistment pursuant to section 4(c) [section 454(c) of this Appendix] shall be liable for induction for training and service under this title [sections 451 to 471a of this Appendix], except after a declaration of war or national emergency made by the Congress subsequent to the date of enactment of this title [June 24, 1948].

(5) For the purposes of computation of the periods of active duty referred to in paragraphs (1), (2), or (3) of this subsection, no credit shall be allowed for—

(A) periods of active duty training performed as a member of a reserve component pursuant to an order or call to active duty solely for training purposes;

(B) periods of active duty in which the service consisted solely of training under the Army specialized training program, the Army Air Force college training program, or any similar program under the jurisdiction of the Navy, Marine Corps, or Coast Guard;

(C) periods of active duty as a cadet at the United States Military Academy or United States Coast Guard Academy, or as a midshipman at the United States Naval Academy, or in a preparatory school after nomination as a principal, alternate, or candidate for admission to any of such academies; or

(D) periods of active duty in any of the armed forces while being processed for entry into or separation from any educational program or institution referred to in paragraphs (B) or (C);

(c)(1) Persons who, on February 1, 1951, were members of organized units of the federally recognized National Guard, the federally recognized Air National Guard, the Officers' Reserve Corps, the Regular Army Reserve, the Air Force Reserve, the Enlisted Reserve Corps, the Naval Reserve, the Marine Corps Reserve, the Coast Guard Reserve, or the Public Health Service Reserve, shall, so long as they continue to be such members and satisfactorily participate in scheduled drills and training periods as prescribed by the Secretary of Defense, be exempt from training and service by induction under the provisions of this title [sections 451 to 471a of this Appendix], but shall not be exempt from registration unless on active duty.

(2)(A) Any person, other than a person referred to in subsection (d) of this section, who—

(i) prior to the issuance of orders for him to report for induction; or

(ii) prior to the date scheduled for his induction and pursuant to a proclamation by the Governor of a State to the effect that the authorized strength of any organized unit of the National Guard of that State cannot be maintained by the enlistment or appointment of persons who have not been issued orders to report for induction under this title [sections 451 to 471a of this Appendix]; or

(iii) prior to the date scheduled for his induction and pursuant to a determination by the President that the strength of the Ready Reserve of the Army Reserve, Naval Reserve, Marine Corps Reserve, Air Force Reserve, or Coast Guard Reserve cannot be maintained by the enlistment or appointment of persons who have not been issued orders to report for induction under this title [sections 451 to 471a of this Appendix];

enlists or accepts appointment, before attaining the age of 26 years, in the Ready Reserve of any Reserve component of the Armed Forces, the Army National Guard, or the Air National Guard, shall be deferred from training and service under this title [sections 451 to 471a of this Appendix] so long as he serves satisfactorily as a member of an organized unit of such Reserve or National Guard in accordance with section 10147 of title 10 or section 502 of title 32, United States Code, as the case may be, or satisfactorily performs such other Ready Reserve service as may be prescribed by the Secretary of Defense. Enlistments or appointments under subparagraphs (ii) and (iii) of this clause may be accepted notwithstanding the provisions of section 15(d) of this title [section 465(d) of this Appendix]. Notwithstanding the provisions of subsection (h) of this section, no person deferred under this clause who has completed six years of such satisfactory service as a member of the Ready Reserve or National Guard, and who during such service has performed active duty for training with an armed force for not less than twelve consecutive weeks, shall be liable for induction for training and service under this Act,

[2] See Transfer of Functions note below.

except after a declaration of war or national emergency made by the Congress after August 9, 1955. In no event shall the number of enlistments or appointments made under authority of this paragraph in any fiscal year in any Reserve component of the Armed Forces or in the Army National Guard or the Air National Guard cause the personnel strength of such Reserve component or the Army National Guard or the Air National Guard, as the case may be, to exceed the personnel strength for which funds have been made available by the Congress for such fiscal year.

(B) A person who, under any provision of law, is exempt or deferred from training and service under this Act by reason of membership in a reserve component, the Army National Guard, or the Air National Guard, as the case may be, shall, if he becomes a member of another reserve component, the Army National Guard, or the Air National Guard, as the case may be, continue to be exempt or deferred to the same extent as if he had not become a member of another reserve component, the Army National Guard, or the Air National Guard, as the case may be, so long as he continues to serve satisfactorily.

(C) Except as provided in subsection (b) and the provisions of this subsection, no person who becomes a member of a reserve component after February 1, 1951, shall thereby be exempt from registration or training and service by induction under the provisions of this Act.

(D) Notwithstanding any other provision of this Act, the President, under such rules and regulations as he may prescribe, may provide that any person enlisted or appointed after October 4, 1961, in the Ready Reserve of any reserve component of the Armed Forces (other than under section 12103 of title 10, United States Code), the Army National Guard, or the Air National Guard, prior to attaining age of twenty-six years, or any person enlisted or appointed in the Army National Guard or the Air National Guard or enlisted in the Ready Reserve of any reserve component prior to attaining the age of eighteen years and six months and deferred under the prior provisions of this paragraph as amended by the Act of October 4, 1961, Public Law 87–378 (75 Stat. 807), or under section 262 of the Armed Forces Reserve Act of 1952, as amended [50 U.S.C. 1013], who fails to serve satisfactorily during his obligated period of service as a member of such Ready Reserve or National Guard or the Ready Reserve of another reserve component or the National Guard of which he becomes a member, may be selected for training and service and inducted into the armed force of which such reserve component is a part, prior to the selection and induction of other persons liable therefor.

(d)(1) Within such numbers as may be prescribed by the Secretary of Defense, any person who (A) has been or may hereafter be selected for enrollment or continuance in the senior division, Reserve Officers' Training Corps, or the Air Reserve Officers' Training Corps, or the Naval Reserve Officers' Training Corps, or the naval and Marine Corps officer candidate training program established by the Act of August 13, 1946 (60 Stat. 1057), as amended, or the Reserve officers' candidate program of the Navy, or the platoon leaders' class of the Marine Corps, or the officer procurement programs of the Coast Guard and the Coast Guard Reserve, or appointed an ensign, United States Naval Reserve, while undergoing professional training; (B) agrees, in writing, to accept a commission, if tendered, and to serve, subject to order of the Secretary of the military department having jurisdiction over him (or the Secretary of Transportation with respect to the United States Coast Guard), not less than two years on active duty after receipt of a commission; and (C) agrees to remain a member of a regular or reserve component until the eighth anniversary of the receipt of a commission in accordance with his obligation under the first sentence of section 651 of title 10, United States Code, or until the sixth anniversary of the receipt of a commission in accordance with his obligation under the second sentence of section 651 of title 10, United States Code, shall be deferred from induction under this title [sections 451 to 471a of this Appendix] until after completion or termination of the course of instruction and so long as he continues in a regular or reserve status upon being commissioned, but shall not be exempt from registration. Such persons, except those persons who have previously completed an initial period of military training or an equivalent period of active military training and service, shall be required while enrolled in such programs to complete a period of training equal (as determined under regulations approved by the Secretary of Defense or the Secretary of Transportation with respect to the United States Coast Guard) in duration and type of training to an initial period of military training. There shall be added to the obligated active commissioned service of any person who has agreed to perform such obligatory service in return for financial assistance while attending a civilian college under any such training program a period of not to exceed one year. Except as provided in paragraph (5), upon the successful completion by any person of the required course of instruction under any program listed in clause (A) of the first sentence of this paragraph, such person shall be tendered a commission in the appropriate reserve component of the Armed Forces if he is otherwise qualified for such appointment. If, at the time of, or subsequent to, such appointment, the armed force in which such person is commissioned does not require his service on active duty in fulfillment of the obligation undertaken by him in compliance with clause (B) of the first sentence of this paragraph, such person shall be ordered to active duty for training with such armed force in the grade in which he was commissioned for a period of active duty for training of not more than six months (not including duty performed under section 10147 of title 10, United States Code), as determined by the Secretary of the military department concerned to be necessary to qualify such person for a mobilization assignment. Upon being commissioned and assigned to a reserve component, such person shall be required to serve therein, or in a reserve component of any other armed force in which he is later appointed, until the eighth anniversary of the receipt of such commission pursuant to the provisions of this section. So long as such person performs satisfactory service, as determined under regulations prescribed by the Secretary of Defense, he shall be deferred from training and service under the provisions of this Act. If such person fails to perform satisfactory service, and such failure is not excused under regulations prescribed by the Secretary of Defense, his commission may be revoked by the Secretary of the military department concerned.

(2) In addition to the training programs enumerated in paragraph (1) of this subsection, and under such regulations as the Secretary of Defense (or the Secretary of the Treasury[3] with respect to the United States Coast Guard) may approve, the Secretaries of the military departments and the Secretary of the Treasury[3] are authorized to establish officer candidate programs leading to the commissioning of persons on active duty. Any person heretofore or hereafter enlisted in the Army Reserve, the Naval Reserve, the Marine Corps Reserve, the Air Force Reserve, or the Coast Guard Reserve who thereafter has been or may be commissioned therein upon graduation from an Officers' Candidate School of such Armed Force shall, if not ordered to active duty as a commissioned officer, be deferred from training and service under the provisions of this Act so long as he performs satisfactory service as a commissioned officer in an appropriate unit of the Ready Reserve, as determined under regulations prescribed by the Secretary of the department concerned. If such person fails to perform satisfactory service in such unit, and such failure is not excused under such regulations, his commission may be revoked by such Secretary.

(3) Nothing in this subsection shall be deemed to preclude the President from providing, by regulations prescribed under subsection (h) of this section, for the deferment from training and service of any category or categories of students for such periods of time as he may deem appropriate.

(4) Omitted.

(5) Notwithstanding paragraph (1), upon the successful completion by any person of the required course of instruction under any Reserve Officers' Training Corps program listed in clause (A) of the first sentence of paragraph (1) and subject to the approval of the Secretary of the military department having jurisdiction over him, such person may, without being relieved of his obligation under that sentence, be tendered, and accept, a commission in the National Oceanic and Atmospheric Administration instead of a commission in the appropriate reserve component of the Armed Forces. If he does not serve on active duty as a commissioned officer of the National Oceanic and Atmospheric Administration for at least six years, he shall, upon discharge therefrom, be tendered a commission in the appropriate reserve component of the Armed Forces, if he is otherwise qualified for such appointment, and, in fulfillment of his obligation under the first sentence of paragraph (1), remain a member of a reserve component until the sixth anniversary of the receipt of his commission in the National Oceanic and Atmospheric Administration. While a member of a reserve component he may, in addition to as otherwise provided by law, be ordered to active duty for such period that, when added to the period he served on active duty as a commissioned officer of the National Oceanic and Atmospheric Administration, equals two years.

(e) Fully qualified and accepted aviation cadet applicants of the Army, Navy, or Air Force who have signed an agreement of service shall, in such numbers as may be designated by the Secretary of Defense, be deferred, during the period covered by the agreement but not to exceed four months, from induction for training and service under this title [sections 451 to 471a of this Appendix] but shall not be exempt from registration.

(f) The Vice President of the United States; the governors of the several States, Territories, and possessions, and all other officials chosen by the voters of the entire State, Territory, or possession; members of the legislative bodies of the United States and of the several States, Territories, and possessions; judges of the courts of record of the United States and of the several States, Territories, possessions, and the District of Columbia shall, while holding such offices, be deferred from training and service under this title [sections 451 to 471a of this Appendix] in the armed forces of the United States.

(g)(1) Regular or duly ordained ministers of religion, as defined in this title [sections 451 to 471a of this Appendix], shall be exempt from training and service, but not from registration, under this title [said sections].

(2) Students preparing for the ministry under the direction of recognized churches or religious organizations, who are satisfactorily pursuing full-time courses of instruction in recognized theological or divinity schools, or who are satisfactorily pursuing full-time courses of instruction leading to their entrance into recognized theological or divinity schools in which they have been preenrolled, shall be deferred from training and service, but not from registration, under this title [sections 451 to 471a of this Appendix]. Persons who are or may be deferred under the provisions of this subsection shall remain liable for training and service in the Armed Forces under the provisions of section 4(a) of this Act [section 454(a) of this Appendix] until the thirty-fifth anniversary of the date of their birth. The foregoing sentence shall not be construed to prevent the exemption or continued deferment of such persons if otherwise exempted or deferrable under any other provision of this Act.

(h) Except as otherwise provided in this subsection the President is authorized, under such rules and regulations as he may prescribe, to provide for the deferment from training and service in the Armed Forces of any or all categories of persons whose employment in industry, agriculture, or other occupations or employment, or whose continued service in an Office (other than an Office described in subsection (f)) under the United States or any State, territory, or possession, or the District of Columbia, or whose activity in study, research, or medical, dental, veterinary, optometric, osteopathic, scientific, pharmaceutical, chiropractic, chiro-

[3] See Transfer of Functions note below.

podial, or other endeavors is found to be necessary to the maintenance of the national health, safety, or interest: *Provided*, That no person within any such category shall be deferred except upon the basis of his individual status: *Provided further*, That persons who are or may be deferred under the provisions of this section shall remain liable for training and service in the Armed Forces under the provisions of section 4(a) of this Act [section 454(a) of this Appendix] until the thirty-fifth anniversary of the date of their birth. This proviso shall not be construed to prevent the continued deferment of such persons if otherwise deferrable under any other provisions of this Act. The President is also authorized, under such rules and regulations as he may prescribe, to provide for the deferment from training and service in the Armed Forces (1) of any or all categories of persons in a status with respect to persons (other than wives alone, except in cases of extreme hardship) dependent upon them for support which renders their deferment advisable, and (2) of any or all categories of those persons found to be physically, mentally, or morally deficient or defective. For the purpose of determining whether or not the deferment of any person is advisable, because of his status with respect to persons dependent upon him for support, any payments of allowances which are payable by the United States to the dependents of persons serving in the Armed Forces of the United States shall be taken into consideration, but the fact that such payments of allowances are payable shall not be deemed conclusively to remove the grounds for deferment when the dependency is based upon financial considerations and shall not be deemed to remove the ground for deferment when the dependency is based upon other than financial considerations and cannot be eliminated by financial assistance to the dependents. Except as otherwise provided in this subsection, the President is also authorized, under such rules and regulations as he may prescribe, to provide for the deferment from training and service in the Armed Forces of any or all categories of persons who have children, or wives and children, with whom they maintain a bona fide family relationship in their homes. No deferment from such training and service in the Armed Forces shall be made in the case of any individual except upon the basis of the status of such individual. There shall be posted in a conspicuous place at the office of each local board a list setting forth the names and classifications of those persons who have been classified by such local board. The President may, in carrying out the provisions of this title [sections 451 to 471a of this Appendix], recommend criteria for the classification of persons subject to induction under this title [said sections], and to the extent that such action is determined by the President to be consistent with the national interest, recommend that such criteria be administered uniformly throughout the United States whenever practicable; except that no local board, appeal board, or other agency of appeal of the Selective Service System shall be required to postpone or defer any person by reason of his activity in study, research, or medical, dental, veterinary, optometric, osteopathic, scientific, pharmaceutical, chiropractic, chiropodial, or other endeavors found to be necessary to the maintenance of the national health, safety, or interest solely on the basis of any test, examination, selection system, class standing, or any other means conducted, sponsored, administered, or prepared by any agency or department of the Federal Government, or any private institution, corporation, association, partnership, or individual employed by an agency or department of the Federal Government.

(i)(1) Any person who is satisfactorily pursuing a full-time course of instruction at a high school or similar institution of learning and is issued an order for induction shall, upon the facts being presented to the local board, have his induction postponed (A) until the time of his graduation therefrom, or (B) until he attains the twentieth anniversary of his birth, or (C) until he ceases satisfactorily to pursue such course of instruction, whichever is the earliest. Notwithstanding the preceding sentence, any person who attains the twentieth anniversary of his birth after beginning his last academic year of high school shall have his induction postponed until the end of that academic year if and so long as he continues to pursue satisfactorily a full-time course of instruction.

(2) Any person who while satisfactorily pursuing a full-time course of instruction at a college, university, or similar institution is ordered to report for induction under this title [sections 451 to 471a of this Appendix], shall, upon the appropriate facts being presented to the local board, have his induction postponed (A) until the end of the semester or term, or academic year in the case of his last academic year, or (B) until he ceases satisfactorily to pursue such course of instruction, whichever is the earlier.

(j) Nothing contained in this title [sections 451 to 471a of this Appendix] shall be construed to require any person to be subject to combatant training and service in the armed forces of the United States who, by reason of religious training and belief, is conscientiously opposed to participation in war in any form. As used in this subsection, the term "religious training and belief" does not include essentially political, sociological, or philosophical views, or a merely personal moral code. Any person claiming exemption from combatant training and service because of such conscientious objections whose claim is sustained by the local board shall, if he is inducted into the armed forces under this title [said sections], be assigned to noncombatant service as defined by the President, or shall, if he is found to be conscientiously opposed to participation in such noncombatant service, in lieu of such induction, be ordered by his local board, subject to such regulations as the President may prescribe, to perform for a period equal to the period prescribed in section 4(b) [section 454(b) of this Appendix] such civilian work contributing to the maintenance of the national health, safety, or interest as the Director may deem appropriate and any such person who knowingly fails or neglects to obey any such order from his local board shall be deemed, for the purposes of section 12 of this title [section 462 of this Appendix], to have knowingly failed or neglected to perform a duty required of him under this title [said sections].The Director shall be responsible for finding civilian work for persons exempted from training and service under this subsection and for the placement of such persons in appropriate civilian work contributing to the maintenance of the national health, safety, or interest.

(k) No exception from registration, or exemption or deferment from training and service, under this title [sections 451 to 471a of this Appendix], shall continue after the cause therefor ceases to exist.

(*l*) Notwithstanding any other provisions of law, no person between the ages of eighteen and twenty-one shall be discharged from service in the armed forces of the United States while this title [sections 451 to 471a of this Appendix] is in effect because such person entered such service without the consent of his parent or guardian.

(m) No person shall be relieved from training and service under this title [sections 451 to 471a of this Appendix] by reason of conviction of a criminal offense, except where the offense of which he has been convicted may be punished by death, or by imprisonment for a term exceeding one year.

(n) In the case of any registrant whose principal place of employment is located outside the appeal board area in which the local board having jurisdiction over the registrant is located, any occupational deferment made under subsection (h) of this section may, within five days after such deferment is made, be submitted for review and decision to the appeal board having jurisdiction over the area in which is located the principal place of employment of the registrant. Such decision of the appeal board shall be final unless modified or changed by the President, and such decision shall be made public.

(*o*) Except during the period of a war or a national emergency declared by Congress, no person may be inducted for training and service under this title [sections 451 to 471a of this Appendix] unless he volunteers for such induction—

(1) if the father or the mother or a brother or a sister of such person was killed in action or died in line of duty while serving in the Armed Forces after December 31, 1959, or died subsequent to such date as a result of injuries received or disease incurred in line of duty during such service, or

(2) during any period of time in which the father or the mother or a brother or a sister of such person is in a captured or missing status as a result of such service.

As used in this subsection, the term "brother" or "sister" means a brother of the whole blood or a sister of the whole blood, as the case may be.

(June 24, 1948, ch. 625, title I, §6, 62 Stat. 609; Sept. 27, 1950, ch. 1059, §1(6), 64 Stat. 1074; June 19, 1951, ch. 144, title I, §1(*l*)–(q), 65 Stat. 83; June 30, 1955, ch. 250, title I, §101, 69 Stat. 223; Aug. 9, 1955, ch. 665, §3(b)–(d), 69 Stat. 603, 604; Pub. L. 85–62, §§6, 7, June 27, 1957, 71 Stat. 208; Pub. L. 85–722, Aug. 21, 1958, 72 Stat. 711; Pub. L. 87–378, §1, Oct. 4, 1961, 75 Stat. 807; Pub. L. 87–536, July 18, 1962, 76 Stat. 167; Pub. L. 88–110, §2, Sept. 3, 1963, 77 Stat. 134; Pub. L. 88–360, July 7, 1964, 78 Stat. 296; Pub. L. 90–40, §1(4)–(7), June 30, 1967, 81 Stat. 100–102, 104; Pub. L. 91–604, §15(b)(8)(B), Dec. 31, 1970, 84 Stat. 1712; Pub. L. 92–129, title I, §101(a)(10)–(22), Sept. 28, 1971, 85 Stat. 349–351; Pub. L. 93–638, title I, §104(c), formerly §105(c), Jan. 4, 1975, 88 Stat. 2208, renumbered §104(c), Pub. L. 100–472, title II, §203(a), Oct. 5, 1988, 102 Stat. 2290; Pub. L. 94–106, title VIII, §802(d), Oct. 7, 1975, 89 Stat. 537; Pub. L. 96–584, §3(a), Dec. 23, 1980, 94 Stat. 3377; Pub. L. 98–525, title XV, §1531, Oct. 19, 1984, 98 Stat. 2631; Pub. L. 103–337, div. A, title XVI, §1677(f), Oct. 5, 1994, 108 Stat. 3020.)

References in Text

Act of August 5, 1954 (68 Stat. 674), as amended, referred to in subsec. (a)(2), is act Aug. 5, 1954, ch. 658, 68 Stat. 674, as amended, which is classified generally to subchapter I (§2001 et seq.) of chapter 22 of Title 42, The Public Health and Welfare. For complete classification of this Act to the Code, see Tables.

This Act, referred to in subsecs. (a)(3), (b)(3), (c)(2)(A) to (D), (d)(1), (2), (g)(2), and (h), is act June 24, 1948, ch. 625, 62 Stat. 604, as amended, known as the Military Selective Service Act. For complete classification of this Act to the Code, see References in Text note set out under section 451 of this Appendix and Tables.

Section 262 of the Armed Forces Reserve Act of 1952, as amended [50 U.S.C. 1013], referred to in subsec. (c)(2)(D), was repealed by Pub. L. 88–110, §1, Sept. 3, 1963, 77 Stat. 134.

Act of August 13, 1946 (60 Stat. 1057), as amended, referred to in subsec. (d)(1), is act Aug. 13, 1946, ch. 962, 60 Stat. 1057, as amended. The Act was repealed by section 53 of act Aug. 10, 1956, ch. 1041, 70A Stat. 641, section 1 of which enacted Title 10, Armed Forces. Provisions of the 1946 Act relating to the naval and Marine Corps officer candidate training program were reenacted in sections 6903 to 6908 of Title 10. Sections 6903 to 6908 of Title 10 were repealed by Pub. L. 88–647, §301(17), Oct. 13, 1964, 78 Stat. 1072, and replaced by chapters 102 and 103 of Title 10.

Amendments

1994—Subsec. (c)(2)(A). Pub. L. 103–337, §1677(f)(1), substituted "section 10147 of title 10" for "section 270 of title 10" in concluding provisions.

Subsec. (c)(2)(D). Pub. L. 103–337, §1677(f)(2), substituted "section 12103 of title 10" for "section 511(b) of title 10".

Subsec. (d)(1). Pub. L. 103–337, §1677(f)(3), substituted "section 10147 of title 10" for "section 270(a) of title 10".

1984—Subsec. (*o*). Pub. L. 98–525 inserted reference to mother in cls. (1) and (2), exempting from induction any person whose mother was killed in line of duty.

1980—Subsec. (d)(1). Pub. L. 96–584 struck out minimum active duty requirement of not less than three months.

1975—Subsec. (a)(2). Pub. L. 93–638 inserted provision relating to assignment of personnel to assist Indian tribes, groups, bands or communities.

Subsec. (c)(2)(A). Pub. L. 94–106, in provisions relating to deferment of certain persons from induction who completed six years of active service as members of the Ready Reserve or National Guard, substituted requirement of performance of active duty for training with an armed force for not less than twelve consecutive weeks during such service for requirement of performance of such active duty for not less than four consecutive months.

1971—Subsec. (a)(1). Pub. L. 92–129, §101(a)(10), (11), inserted proviso making subject to registration an alien lawfully admitted for permanent residence who by reason of occupational status is subject to adjustment to non-immigrant status but who executes a waiver of all rights, privileges, exemptions, and immunities which would otherwise accrue to him as a result of that occupational status, and granting a deferment from induction to such alien for so long as such occupational status continues, and substituted "twelve months" for "eighteen months" as the period of requisite service in the armed forces of a nation with which the United States is associated in mutual defense activities in order to gain an exemption from training and service.

Subsec. (b)(3). Pub. L. 92–129, § 101(a)(12), substituted reference to "section 5(a) of this Act [section 455(a) of this Appendix] for reference to "section 4(i) of this Act [section 454(i) of this Appendix]".

Subsec. (b)(4). Pub. L. 92–129, § 101(a)(13), struck out reference to section 4(g) [section 454(g) of this Appendix].

Subsec. (d)(1). Pub. L. 92–129, § 101(a)(14), substituted "Secretary of Transportation" for "Secretary of the Treasury" and "section 651 of Title 10" for "section 4(d)(3) of this Act", respectively.

Subsec. (d)(5). Pub. L. 92–129, § 101(a)(15), reflected creation of National Oceanic and Atmospheric Administration and transfer to such newly created Administration of former Coast and Geodetic Survey.

Subsec. (g). Pub. L. 92–129, § 101(a)(16), changed from an exemption to a deferment the status to be accorded divinity students, with such students to remain liable for training and service until their 35th birthday.

Subsec. (h). Pub. L. 92–129, § 101(a)(17), (18), struck out provisions formerly designated as par. (1) which had covered college student deferments, struck the designation "(2)" preceding the remaining provisions which had theretofore been designated par. (2), and, in such provisions, struck out reference to deferments for persons engaged in graduate study.

Subsec. (i)(1). Pub. L. 92–129, § 101(a)(19), substituted provisions allowing a postponement of induction for high school students for provisions creating a deferment for such students and inserted provisions allowing an additional postponement of induction until the end of the academic year for high school students who turn 20 during their last year of high school provided that they continue to pursue satisfactorily a full-time course of instruction.

Subsec. (i)(2). Pub. L. 91–129, § 101(a)(20), substituted provisions allowing a postponement of induction for college students for provisions creating a deferment for such students and struck out references to previous deferments and postponements and to the President's former authority to allow for student deferments.

Subsec. (j). Pub. L. 92–129, § 101(a)(21), substituted "Director" for "local board pursuant to Presidential regulations" and inserted sentence charging the Director with the responsibility for finding civilian work for persons exempted from training and service and for their placement in appropriate civilian work.

Subsec. (*o*). Pub. L. 92–129, § 101(a)(22), inserted provisions for an exemption from training and service during a period of time in which the father or a brother or sister of a person is in a captured or missing status and struck out provisions limiting the exemption from service provided under this subsection to the sole surviving son of the family.

1970—Subsec. (b)(2). Pub. L. 91–604 inserted "the Environmental Protection Agency," after "Department of Justice,".

1967—Subsec. (a). Pub. L. 90–40, § 1(5), designated existing provisions as par. (1), substituted "Environmental Science Services Administration" for "Coast and Geodetic Survey", removed commissioned officers, warrant officers, pay clerks, enlisted men, aviation cadets, and, while on active duty, members of the reserve component, of the Public Health Service from the list of enumerated personnel relieved from the registration requirement of section 453 and the training and service requirement of section 454, added cadets, United States Air Force Academy, to such lists, and inserted proviso that a person in a medical, dental, or allied specialist category not otherwise deferred or exempted under subsec. (a) be liable for registration, training, and service until the thirty-fifth anniversary of the date of his birth, and added par. (2).

Subsec. (c)(2)(A). Pub. L. 90–40, § 1(4), gave standby authority to both the Governors of the individual States, in the case of the National Guard, and to the President, in the case of the other reserve components, to permit the voluntary enlistment of registrants into these components during the period following their receipt of an induction notice and the date required for their actual induction, provided that there had previously issued a proclamation that the Governor or the President is not otherwise able to maintain the personnel strengths of the respective components.

Subsec. (h). Pub. L. 90–40, § 1(6), established uniform criteria for all undergraduate deferments to continue only until a registrant receives a baccalaureate degree, fails to pursue a full-time course of instruction satisfactorily, or reaches the age of 24, whichever occurs first, at which point students are required to be exposed to the hazards of induction in the prime age group in the same manner as their contemporaries who had not been provided student deferments, continued the President's wide latitude in providing deferments for graduate students in medicine, dentistry, or other subjects deemed essential to the national health, safety, or interest, continued the President's authority to prescribe areas of deferment based upon occupations or professions essential to the national interest, and called for greater uniformity in the administration of classification criteria for persons subject to induction.

Subsec. (j). Pub. L. 90–40, § 1(7), struck out provision that religious training and belief stem from the individual's belief in a relation to a Supreme Being involving duties superior to those arising from any human relationship, and struck out requirement for a hearing by the Department of Justice when there is an appeal from a local board decision denying conscientious objector status.

1964—Subsec. (*o*). Pub. L. 88–360 exempted sole surviving sons from induction in cases where the father was killed in action or in line of duty, permitted the sole surviving son to volunteer for induction, and terminated the exemption during time of war or national emergency thereafter declared by Congress.

1963—Subsec. (c)(2). Pub. L. 88–110, among other changes, authorized deferment of persons who prior to attaining age 26 and to the issuance of induction orders enlisted or accepted appointment in the Ready Reserve of any reserve component, Army National Guard, or Air National Guard, and served satisfactorily, exempted such persons from induction after completing 6 years service and who during such service performed active duty for training for not less than 4 consecutive months, and struck out provisions which deferred persons who prior to attaining 18 years and 6 months of age, and prior to issuance of induction orders, enlisted or accepted appointment in any organized unit of the National Guard, exempted such persons from training and service by reason of subsec. (h) of this section after they attained age 28, or who completed 8 years of service in such unit and performed active duty for training for not less than 3 consecutive months, authorized the President to accept enlistments in the Ready Reserve, whenever he determined its strength could not be maintained at a necessary level for defense, of persons who had not attained age 18 years and 6 months, and who had not been ordered to report for induction, and exempted such persons from liability under subsec. (h) of this section after attaining age 28 years, permitted volunteers to perform a period of active duty pursuant to section 1013 of Title 50, and exempted such persons from induction after serving 8 years in the Ready Reserve.

1962—Subsec. (d). Pub. L. 87–536 inserted "Except as provided in paragraph (5)," before "upon the successful completion by any person" and added par. (5).

1961—Subsec. (c)(2). Pub. L. 87–378, § 1(1), included members of the National Guard deferred by clause (A) of this paragraph, or any person enlisted or appointed in the Ready Reserve of any reserve component other than under section 511(b) of this title, the Army National Guard or the Air National Guard after Oct. 4, 1961, but prior to attaining age 26, who fail to serve satisfactorily as a member of their components within clause (E) of this paragraph, and struck out "or appointed" after "may provide that any person enlisted".

Subsec. (d)(1). Pub. L. 87–378, §1(2), substituted "If, at the time of, or subsequent to, such appointment" for "If, at the time of such appointment", changed the period of active duty for training in grade, where the armed force in which such person is commissioned does not require his service on active duty, from 6 months to a period of not less than 3 months or more than 6 months, not including duty performed under section 270(a) of Title 10, Armed Forces, as is determined to qualify such person for a mobilization assignment, and substituted the requirement that upon being commissioned and assigned to a reserve component, such person must serve therein, or in a reserve component of any other armed force in which he is later appointed, for provisions which required such person to be returned to inactive duty and assigned to an appropriate reserve unit upon completion of the required period of active duty for training.

1958—Subsec. (c)(2)(F). Pub. L. 85–722 added subpar. (F).

1957—Subsec. (b)(5)(E). Pub. L. 85–62, §§6, 9, temporarily, added subpar. (E). See Effective and Termination Dates of 1957 Amendment note below.

Subsec. (d)(4). Pub. L. 85–62, §§7, 9, added par. (4). See Effective and Termination Dates of 1957 Amendment note below.

1955—Subsec. (a). Act June 30, 1955, §101(a), exempted from training and service, but not from registration, those persons who served on active duty for not less than 18 months since June 24, 1948 in the armed forces of a nation with which the United States is associated in mutual defense activities.

Subsec. (b)(3). Act June 30, 1955, §101(b), exempted individuals who have served not less than one year after September 16, 1940, or who were discharged after such date for the convenience of the Government and had served not less than six months, or who served not less than twenty-four months in the Public Health Service or in the Coast and Geodetic Survey.

Subsec. (c)(2). Act Aug. 9, 1955, §3(b), exempted from induction persons who have completed eight years of satisfactory service as members of an organized unit of the National Guard, with a minimum of not less than three consecutive months of active duty for training, and added cls. (C), (D), and (E).

Subsec. (c)(2)(A). Act June 30, 1955, §101(c), inserted provisions to exempt persons from liability for induction after attaining age 28.

Subsec. (d)(1). Act Aug. 9, 1955, §3(c), deferred from induction any person who agrees to remain a member of a regular or reserve component until the sixth anniversary of the receipt of a commission, provided that all qualified graduates must be tendered a commission in the appropriate reserve component, and permitted active duty for training for a period of six months upon completion of which he must serve in the component in which appointed until the eighth anniversary of the receipt of the commission.

Subsec. (d)(2). Act Aug. 9, 1955, §3(d), permitted deferment of commissioned officers who perform satisfactory service in an appropriate unit of the Ready Reserve.

Subsec. (h). Act June 30, 1955, §101(d), provided that determination of deferment shall not be based on existence of a shortage or a surplus of any agricultural commodity.

1951—Subsec. (a). Act June 19, 1951, §1(*l*), exempted Naval reserve midshipmen attending merchant marine schools and students enrolled in military colleges which have approved ROTC courses from registration and induction.

Subsec. (c). Act June 19, 1951, §1(m), substituted "February 1, 1941" for "the effective date of this title" in par. (1), inserted "prior to the determination by the Secretary of Defense that adequate trained personnel are available to the National Guard to enable it to maintain its strength authorized by current appropriations, and prior to the issuance of orders for him to report for induction" after "six months" in par. (2)(A), and inserted ", paragraph (1) of this subsection" after "subsection (b)" in par. (2)(B).

Subsec. (d). Act June 19, 1951, §1(n), continued deferments to ROTC members but increased their period of service from 2 years to 6 years after receiving their commission (including 2 years active duty or 3 years active duty if financial assistance is received), authorized establishment of other training programs, and provided for the President's deferment power.

Subsec. (h). Act June 19, 1951, §1(*o*), removed the President's authority to defer married men who have no dependents other than a wife solely on a basis of such marriage unless extreme hardship is involved, permitted the induction of persons now deferred until the thirty-fifth anniversary of their birth should the basis for deferment terminate after their 26th birthday, and inserted "dental, optometric, osteopathic, and chiropractic" to list of endeavors which may be considered for deferment purposes.

Subsec. (i). Act June 19, 1951, §1(p), authorized deferment of high school and college students in lieu of postponement of induction in order to give them an opportunity to enlist in the branch of service of their choice during such deferment period.

Subsec. (j). Act June 19, 1951, §1(q), substituted "in lieu of such induction, be ordered by his local board, subject to such regulations as the President may prescribe, to perform for a period equal to the period prescribed in section 4(b) such civilian work contributing to the maintenance of the national health, safety, or interest as the local board may deem appropriate and any such person who knowingly fails or neglects to obey any such order from his local board shall be deemed, for the purposes of section 12 of this title, to have knowingly failed or neglected to perform a duty required of him under this title" for "be deferred" in third sentence, and "he shall in lieu of such induction be ordered by his local board, subject to such regulations as the President may prescribe, to perform for a period equal to the period prescribed in section 4(b) such civilian work contributing to the maintenance of the national health, safety, or interest as the local board may deem appropriate and any such person who knowingly fails or neglects to obey any such order from his local board shall be deemed, for the purposes of section 12 of this title, to have knowingly failed or neglected to perform a duty required of him under this title" for "he shall be deferred" in seventh sentence.

1950—Subsec. (b)(2). Act Sept. 27, 1950, struck out of subpars. (A) and (B) "or the Coast Guard", "(or the Coast Guard)", and "or in the Coast Guard" wherever appearing.

Effective Date of 1994 Amendment

Amendment by Pub. L. 103–337 effective Dec. 1, 1994, except as otherwise provided, see section 1691 of Pub. L. 103–337, set out as an Effective Date note under section 10001 of Title 10, Armed Forces.

Effective Date of 1980 Amendment

Section 3(b) of Pub. L. 96–584 provided that: "The amendment made by subsection (a) [amending this section] shall apply only to persons ordered to active duty for training after the effective date of this Act [Dec. 23, 1980]."

Effective and Termination Dates of 1957 Amendment

Amendment by Pub. L. 85–62 to take effect on July 1, 1957, and terminate on July 1, 1973, see section 9 of Pub. L. 85–62, set out as a note under section 454 of this Appendix.

Savings Provision; Repeal of College Student Deferment

Section 101(b) of Pub. L. 92–129 provided that: "Notwithstanding the repeal of section 6(h)(1) of the Military Selective Service Act of 1967 [subsec. (h)(1) of this section] made by subsection (a)(17) of this section, any person (1) who is satisfactorily pursuing a full-time course of instruction at a college, university, or similar institution of higher learning, (2) who met the academic requirements of a student deferment prescribed in such section 6(h)(1), and (3) who was satisfactorily pursuing such a full-time course prior to the date of enactment of this Act [Sept. 28, 1971] and during the 1970–1971 regular academic school year shall be deferred from induction for training and service in the Armed Forces under the same terms and conditions such person would have been deferred under the provisions of such section 6(h)(1) had such provision not been repealed."

TRANSFER OF FUNCTIONS

Coast Guard transferred to Department of Transportation, and functions, powers, and duties relating to Coast Guard of Secretary of the Treasury and of all other officers and offices of Department of the Treasury transferred to Secretary of Transportation by Pub. L. 89–670, §6(b)(1), Oct. 15, 1966, 80 Stat. 938. Section 6(b)(2) of Pub. L. 89–670, however, provided that notwithstanding such transfer of functions, Coast Guard shall operate as part of Navy in time of war or when President directs as provided in section 3 of Title 14, Coast Guard. See section 108 of Title 49, Transportation.

For transfer of functions of other officers, employees, and agencies of Department of the Treasury, with certain exceptions, to Secretary of the Treasury with power to delegate, see Reorg. Plan No. 26 of 1950, §§1, 2, eff. July 31, 1950, 15 F.R. 4935, 64 Stat. 1280, 1281, set out in the Appendix to Title 5, Government Organization and Employees. Functions of Coast Guard, and Commandant of Coast Guard, excepted from transfer when Coast Guard is operating as part of Navy under sections 1 and 3 of Title 14, Coast Guard.

Environmental Science Services Administration in Department of Commerce, including offices of Administrator and Deputy Administrator thereof, abolished by Reorg. Plan No. 4 of 1970, eff. Oct. 3, 1970, 35 F.R. 15627, 84 Stat. 2090, set out in the Appendix to Title 5, Government Organization and Employees, which created National Oceanic and Atmospheric Administration in Department of Commerce and transferred personnel, property, records, and unexpended balances of funds of Environmental Science Services Administration to such newly created National Oceanic and Atmospheric Administration. Components of Environmental Science Services Administration thus transferred included Weather Bureau [now National Weather Service], Coast and Geodetic Survey [now National Ocean Survey], Environmental Data Service, National Environmental Satellite Center, and ESSA Research Laboratories.

In order to implement the provisions of Reorganization Plan No. 4 of 1970, eff. Oct. 3, 1970, 35 F.R. 15627, 84 Stat. 2090, the following organizational names appearing in chapter IX of subtitle B of Title 15, Code of Federal Regulations, which covers administration of National Oceanic and Atmospheric Administration, were changed by order of Acting Associate Administrator, 35 F.R. 19249, Dec. 19, 1970, as follows: Environmental Science Services Administration to National Oceanic and Atmospheric Administration (ESSA to NOAA); Coast and Geodetic Survey to National Ocean Survey; and Weather Bureau to National Weather Service.

Coast and Geodetic Survey consolidated with National Weather Bureau in 1965 to form Environmental Science Services Administration by Reorg. Plan No. 2 of 1965, eff. July 13, 1965, 30 F.R. 8819, 79 Stat. 1318. Environmental Science Services Administration abolished in 1970 and its personnel, property, records, etc., transferred to National Oceanic and Atmospheric Administration by Reorg. Plan No. 4 of 1970, eff. Oct. 3, 1970, 35 F.R. 15627, 84 Stat. 2090. By order of Acting Associate Administrator of National Oceanic and Atmospheric Administration, 35 F.R. 19249, Dec. 19, 1970, Coast and Geodetic Survey redesignated National Ocean Survey. See notes set out under section 311 of Title 15, Commerce and Trade.

Functions of Public Health Service, Surgeon General of Public Health Service, and all other officers and employees of Public Health Service, and functions of all agencies of or in Public Health Service transferred to Secretary of Health, Education, and Welfare by Reorg. Plan No. 3 of 1966, eff. June 25, 1966, 31 F.R. 8855, 80 Stat. 1610, set out in the Appendix to Title 5, Government Organization and Employees. Secretary of Health, Education, and Welfare redesignated Secretary of Health and Human Services by section 3508(b) of Title 20, Education.

DELEGATION OF FUNCTIONS

Functions of President delegated to Director of Selective Service concerning establishment, implementation, and administration of program for return of Vietnam era draft evaders and military deserters, see Ex. Ord. No. 11804, Sept. 16, 1974, 39 F.R. 33299, set out under section 462 of this Appendix.

DISCHARGE OF SURVIVING SONS

Section 101(d) of Pub. L. 92–129 provided that:

"(1) Subject to the provisions of paragraph (2) of this subsection any surviving son or sons of a family who (A) were inducted into the Armed Forces under the Military Selective Service Act of 1967 [see References in Text note set out under section 451 of this Appendix], (B) have not reenlisted or otherwise voluntarily extended their period of active duty in the Armed Forces, and (C) are serving on active duty with the Armed Forces on or after the date of enactment of this subsection [Sept. 28, 1971], and such son or sons could not, if they were not in the Armed Forces, be involuntarily inducted into military service under the Military Selective Service Act as a result of the amendment made by paragraph (22) of subsection (a) of this section [amending subsec. (*o*) of this section], such surviving son or sons shall, upon application, be promptly discharged from the Armed Forces.

"(2) The provisions of paragraph (1) of this subsection shall not apply in the case of any member of the Armed Forces against whom court-martial charges are pending, or in the case of any member who has been tried and convicted by a court-martial for an offense and whose case is being reviewed or appealed, or in the case of any member who has been tried and convicted by a court-martial for an offense and who is serving a sentence (or otherwise satisfying punishment) imposed by such court-martial, until final action (including completion of any punishment imposed pursuant to such court-martial) has been completed with respect to such charges, review, or appeal, or until the sentence has been served (or until any other punishment imposed has been satisfied), as the case may be. The President shall have authority to implement the provisions of this subsection by regulations.

"(3) Notwithstanding the amendment made by paragraph (22) of subsection (a) of this section [amending subsec. (*o*) of this section], except during the period of a war or a national emergency declared by Congress, the sole surviving son of any family in which the father or one or more sons or daughters thereof were killed in action before January 1, 1960, or died in line of duty before January 1, 1960, while serving in the Armed Forces of the United States, or died subsequent to such date as a result of injuries received or disease incurred before such date during such service shall not be inducted under the Military Selective Service Act [see References in Text note set out under section 451 of this Appendix] unless he volunteers for induction."

PRIOR OBLIGATED SERVICE

Section 5 of Pub. L. 88–110 provided that: "This Act [amending subsec. (c)(2) of this section, section 463(a) of this Appendix and sections 270(b) and 511 [now 12103] of Title 10, Armed Forces, and repealing section 1013 of Title 50, War and National Defense] shall not affect any term of obligated service incurred before the effective date of this Act [Sept. 3, 1963]. In addition, the enactment of this Act [Sept. 3, 1963] shall not increase the minimum period of active duty or active duty for training that is required on the day before the effective date of this Act to earn an exemption from training and service under the Universal Military Training and Service Act, as amended (50 U.S.C. App. 451 et seq.), in the case of persons who entered the Armed Forces before the effective date of this Act."

PROGRAM FOR RETURN OF VIETNAM ERA DRAFT EVADERS AND MILITARY DESERTERS

Proc. No. 4313, Sept. 16, 1974, 39 F.R. 33293, 88 Stat. 2504, set out under section 462 of this Appendix, provided for a program for return of Vietnam era draft evaders and military deserters.

EXECUTIVE ORDER NO. 11803

Ex. Ord. No. 11803, Sept. 16, 1974, 39 F.R. 33297, set out under section 462 of this Appendix, provided for review by Clemency Board of convictions of violations under subsec. (j) of this section.

EX. ORD. NO. 10028. DEFINITION OF NONCOMBATANT SERVICE AND NONCOMBATANT TRAINING

Ex. Ord. No. 10028, Jan. 13, 1949, 14 F.R. 211, provided:

1. The term "noncombatant service" shall mean (a) service in any unit of the armed forces which is unarmed at all times; (b) service in the medical department of any of the armed forces, wherever performed; or (c) any other assignment the primary function of which does not require the use of arms in combat; provided that such other assignment is acceptable to the individual concerned and does not require him to bear arms or to be trained in their use.

2. The term "noncombatant training" shall mean any training which is not concerned with the study, use, or handling of arms or weapons.

HARRY S TRUMAN.

SECTION REFERRED TO IN OTHER SECTIONS

This section is referred to in sections 454, 467 of this Appendix; title 10 sections 513, 651, 12103, 12104; title 37 sections 209, 308e.

§457. Repealed. June 19, 1951, ch. 144, §1(r), 65 Stat. 86

Section, act June 24, 1948, ch. 625, title I, §7, 62 Stat. 614, related to active duty for certain members of reserve components.

§458. Bounties for induction; substitutes; purchase of release

No bounty may be paid to induce any person to be inducted into an armed force. A clothing allowance authorized by law is not a bounty for the purposes of this section. No person liable for training and service under this Act may furnish a substitute for that training or service. No person may be enlisted, inducted, or appointed in an armed force as a substitute for another. No person liable for training and service under section 4 [section 454 of this Appendix] may escape that training and service or be discharged before the end of his period of training and service by paying money or any other valuable thing as consideration for his release from that training and service or liability therefor.

(June 24, 1948, ch. 625, title I, §8, 62 Stat. 614; Aug. 10, 1956, ch. 1041, §22(d), 70A Stat. 630.)

REFERENCES IN TEXT

This Act, referred to in text, is act June 24, 1948, ch. 625, 62 Stat. 604, as amended, known as the Military Selective Service Act. For complete classification of this Act to the Code, see References in Text note set out under section 451 of this Appendix and Tables.

CODIFICATION

Section 8 of act June 24, 1948, 62 Stat. 614, cited as a credit to this section, was repealed by act Aug. 10, 1956, ch. 1041, §53, 70A Stat. 641, 678, and provisions thereof (as applicable to induction) were restated in this section by section 22(d) of act Aug. 10, 1956. Provisions of such section 8 (less applicability to induction) were restated by first section of act Aug. 10, 1956, as section 514 of Title 10, Armed Forces.

AMENDMENTS

1956—Act Aug. 10, 1956, struck out provisions which prohibited payment of any bounty to induce any person to enlist into Armed Forces. See section 514 of Title 10, Armed Forces.

§459. Separation from service

(a) Certificate recording proficiency and merit; physical examination

Any person inducted into the armed forces under this title [sections 451 to 471a of this Appendix] for training and service, who, in the judgment of those in authority over him, satisfactorily completes his period of training and service under section 4(b) [section 454(b) of this Appendix] shall be entitled to a certificate to that effect upon the completion of such period of training and service, which shall include a record of any special proficiency or merit attained. In addition, each such person who is inducted into the armed forces under this title [said sections] for training and service shall be given a physical examination at the beginning of such training and service, and upon the completion of his period of training and service under this title [said sections], each such person shall be given another physical examination and, upon his written request, shall be given a statement of physical condition by the Secretary concerned: *Provided*, That such statement shall not contain any reference to mental or other conditions which in the judgment of the Secretary concerned would prove injurious to the physical or mental health of the person to whom it pertains: *Provided further*, That, if upon completion of training and service under this title [said sections], such person continues on active duty without an interruption of more than seventy-two hours as a member of the Armed Forces of the United States, a physical examination upon completion of such training and service shall not be required unless it is requested by such person, or the medical authorities of the Armed Force concerned determine that the physical examination is warranted.

(b) Right to vote; manner; poll tax

Any person inducted into the armed forces for training and service under this title [sections 451 to 471a of this Appendix] shall, during the period of such service, be permitted to vote in person or by absentee ballot in any general, special, or primary election occurring in the State of which he is a resident, whether he is within or outside such State at the time of such election, if under the laws of such State he is otherwise entitled so to vote in such election; but nothing in this subsection shall be construed to require granting to any such person a leave of absence or furlough for longer than one day in order to permit him to vote in person in any such election. No person inducted into, or enlisted in, the armed forces for training and service under this title [said sections] shall, during the period of such service, as a condition of voting in any election for President, Vice President, electors for President or Vice President, or for Senator or Member of the House of Representatives, be required to pay any poll tax or other tax or make any other payment to any State or political subdivision thereof.

(c) Reports on separated personnel

The Secretaries of Army, Navy, Air Force, or Transportation shall furnish to the Selective Service System hereafter established a report of separation for each person separated from active duty.

(June 24, 1948, ch. 625, title I, § 9, 62 Stat. 614; Sept. 27, 1950, ch. 1059, § 1(7)–(10), 64 Stat. 1074; June 19, 1951, ch. 144, title I, § 1(s), 65 Stat. 86; July 12, 1955, ch. 327, 69 Stat. 295; July 9, 1956, ch. 523, § 1, 70 Stat. 509; Pub. L. 86–632, § 1, July 12, 1960, 74 Stat. 467; Pub. L. 87–391, Oct. 4, 1961, 75 Stat. 821; Pub. L. 90–491, § 1, Aug. 17, 1968, 82 Stat. 790; Pub. L. 92–129, title I, § 101(a)(23), Sept. 28, 1971, 85 Stat. 351; Pub. L. 93–508, title IV, § 405, Dec. 3, 1974, 88 Stat. 1600.)

AMENDMENTS

1974—Subsecs. (b), (c). Pub. L. 93–508, § 405(1), (2), redesignated subsecs. (i) and (j) as (b) and (c), respectively. Former subsecs. (b) and (c), relating to reemployment rights and consideration of training and service in the armed forces as furlough or leave of absence, were struck out. See section 2021 et seq. of Title 38, Veterans' Benefits.

Subsecs. (d) to (h). Pub. L. 93–508, § 405(1), repealed subsecs. (d) to (h) relating to jurisdiction of district courts to enforce compliance with the reemployment provisions, legal assistance by United States attorneys to claimants of reemployment benefits, reemployment by Federal Government, priority of rights to reemployment, and reemployment benefits to persons enlisting or called to active duty. See section 2021 et seq. of Title 38, Veterans' Benefits.

Subsecs. (i), (j). Pub. L. 93–508, § 405(2), redesignated subsecs. (i) and (j) as (b) and (c), respectively.

1971—Subsec. (j). Pub. L. 92–129 substituted "or Transportation" for "or Treasury".

1968—Subsec. (c)(3). Pub. L. 90–491, § 1(1), added par. (3).

Subsec. (d). Pub. L. 90–491, § 1(2), included cases where any private employer fails or refuses to comply with provisions of subsec. (c)(3) of this section.

Subsec. (g)(1). Pub. L. 90–491, § 1(3), substituted "does not exceed five years, provided that the service in excess of four years after August 1, 1961, is at the request and for the convenience of the Federal Government" for "does not exceed four years".

Subsec. (g)(2). Pub. L. 90–491, § 1(4), designated existing provisions as par. (A) and added par. (B).

1961—Subsec. (g)(1). Pub. L. 87–391 permitted four years service after Aug. 1, 1961, in addition to four years service between June 24, 1948, and Aug. 1, 1961, without loss of reemployment rights.

Subsec. (g)(2). Pub. L. 87–391 permitted four years service after Aug. 1, 1961, in addition to four years service between June 24, 1948, and Aug. 1, 1961, without loss of reemployment rights.

Subsec. (g)(4). Pub. L. 87–391 struck out requirement that persons who are rejected for military service must have requested a leave of absence from their employers for purpose of determining their physical fitness to enter Armed Forces in order to insure reemployment rights.

Subsec. (g)(5), (6). Pub. L. 87–391 added par. (5) and redesignated former par. (5) as (6).

1960—Subsec. (g)(2). Pub. L. 86–632, § 1(1), inserted "and other than for training" after "physical fitness" in parenthetical phrase.

Subsec. (g)(3). Pub. L. 86–632, § 1(2), substituted the existing reemployment provisions for provisions granting a leave of absence to perform training duty or to be examined to determine fitness to enter the armed forces and requiring application for reinstatement to be made within thirty days following release from training duty or rejection for service.

Subsec. (g)(4), (5). Pub. L. 86–632, § 1(3), added pars. (4) and (5).

1956—Subsec. (d). Act July 9, 1956, inserted reference to subsection (g) of this section.

1955—Subsec. (a). Act July 12, 1955, inserted proviso removing requirement for a final physical examination for inductees who continue on active duty in another status in the Armed Forces.

1951—Subsec. (g). Act June 19, 1951, clarified reemployment rights with respect to restoration to a position of like seniority, status, and pay.

1950—Subsec. (g)(1). Act Sept. 27, 1950, § 1(7), struck out "or the Coast Guard (other than a reserve component)" and "or the Coast Guard" after "(other than in a reserve component)".

Subsec. (g)(2). Act Sept. 27, 1950, § 1(8), struck out ", the Coast Guard" after "United States".

Subsec. (h). Act Sept. 27, 1950, § 1(9), struck out ", the Coast Guard" after "United States".

Subsec. (j). Act Sept. 27, 1950, § 1(10), struck out "or" after "Navy" and inserted ", or Treasury" after "Air Force".

EFFECTIVE DATE OF 1974 AMENDMENT

Amendment by Pub. L. 93–508 effective Dec. 3, 1974, see section 503 of Pub. L. 93–508, set out as a note under section 3452 of Title 38, Veterans' Benefits.

EFFECTIVE DATE OF 1960 AMENDMENT

Section 3 of Pub. L. 86–632 provided that: "This Act [amending this section and section 1013 of Title 50, War and National Defense] shall take effect upon the expiration of sixty days from the date of its enactment [July 12, 1960]."

EFFECTIVE DATE OF 1956 AMENDMENT

Section 2 of act July 9, 1956, provided that: "The amendment made by the first section of this Act [amending this section] shall take effect as of June 19, 1951."

§ 460. Selective Service System

(a) Establishment; construction; appointment of Director; termination and reestablishment of Office of Selective Service Records

(1) There is established in the executive branch of the Government an agency to be known as the Selective Service System, and a Director of Selective Service who shall be the head thereof.

(2) The Selective Service System shall include a national headquarters, at least one State headquarters in each State, Territory, and possession of the United States, and in the District of Columbia, and the local boards, appeal boards, and other agencies provided for in subsection (b)(3) of this section.

(3) The Director shall be appointed by the President, by and with the advice and consent of the Senate.

(4) The functions of the Office of Selective Service Records (established by the Act of March 31, 1947 [sections 321 to 329 of this Appen-

dix]) and of the Director of the Office of Selective Service Records are transferred to the Selective Service System and the Director of Selective Service, respectively. The personnel, property, records, and unexpended balances (available or to be made available) of appropriations, allocations, and other funds of the Office of Selective Service Records are transferred to the Selective Service System. The Office of Selective Service Records shall cease to exist upon the taking effect of the provisions of this title [sections 451 to 471a of this Appendix]: *Provided*, That, effective upon the termination of this title [said sections] and notwithstanding such termination in other respects, (A) the said Office of Selective Service Records is reestablished on the same basis and with the same functions as obtained prior to the effective date of this title [June 24, 1948], (B) said reestablished Office shall be responsible for liquidating any other outstanding affairs of the Selective Service System, and (C) the personnel, property, records, and unexpended balances (available or to be made available) of appropriations, allocations, and other funds of the Selective Service System shall be transferred to such reestablished Office of Selective Service Records.

(b) Administrative provisions

The President is authorized to undertake the following:

(1) To prescribe the necessary rules and regulations to carry out the provisions of this title [sections 451 to 471a of this Appendix].

(2) To appoint, upon recommendation of the respective governor or comparable executive official, a State director of the Selective Service System for each headquarters in each State, Territory, and possession of the United States and for the District of Columbia, who shall represent the governor and be in immediate charge of the state headquarters of the Selective Service System: *Provided*, That no State director shall serve concurrently in an elected or appointed position of a State or local government; to employ such number of civilians, and, subject to subsection (e), to order to active duty with their consent and to assign to the Selective Service System such officers of the selective-service section of the State headquarters and headquarters detachments and such other officers of the federally recognized National Guard of the United States or other armed forces personnel (including personnel of the reserve components thereof), as may be necessary for the administration of the national and of the several State headquarters of the Selective Service System.

(3) To create and establish within the Selective Service System civilian local boards, civilian appeal boards, and such other civilian agencies, including agencies of appeal, as may be necessary to carry out its functions with respect to the registration, examination, classification, selection, assignment, delivery for induction, and maintenance of records of persons registered under this title [sections 451 to 471a of this Appendix], together with such other duties as may be assigned under this title [said sections]: *Provided*, That no person shall be disqualified from serving as a counselor to registrants, including service as Government appeal agent, because of his membership in a Reserve component of the Armed Forces. He shall create and establish one or more local boards in each county or political subdivision corresponding thereto of each State, territory, and possession of the United States, and in the District of Columbia. The local board and/or its staff shall perform their official duties only within the county or political subdivision corresponding thereto for which the local board is established, or in the case of an intercounty board, within the area for which such board is established, except that the staffs of local boards in more than one county of a State or comparable jurisdiction may be collocated or one staff may serve local boards in more than one county of a State or comparable jurisdiction when such action is approved by the Governor or comparable executive official or officials. Each local board shall consist of three or more members to be appointed by the President from recommendations made by the respective Governors or comparable executive officials. In making such appointments after the date of the enactment of the Act enacting this sentence [Sept. 28, 1971], the President is requested to appoint the membership of each local board so that to the maximum extent practicable it is proportionately representative of the race and national origin of those registrants within its jurisdiction, but no action by any local board shall be declared invalid on the ground that any board failed to conform to any particular quota as to race or national origin. No citizen shall be denied membership on any local board or appeal board on account of sex. After December 31, 1971, no person shall serve on any local board or appeal board who has served on any local board or appeal board for a period of more than 20 years. Notwithstanding any other provision of this paragraph, an intercounty local board consisting of at least one member from each component county or corresponding subdivision may, with the approval of the Governor or comparable executive official or officials, be established for an area not exceeding five counties or political subdivisions corresponding thereto within a State or comparable jurisdiction when the President determines, after considering the public interest involved, that the establishment of such local board area will result in a more efficient and economical operation. Any such intercounty local board shall have within its area the same power and jurisdiction as a local board has in its area. A local board may include among its members any citizen otherwise qualified under Presidential regulations, provided he is at least eighteen years of age. No member of any local board shall be a member of the Armed Forces of the United States, but each member of any local board shall be a civilian who is a citizen of the United States residing in the county or political subdivision corresponding thereto in which such local board has jurisdiction, and each intercounty local board shall have at least one member from each county or

political subdivision corresponding thereto included within the intercounty local board area. Such local boards, or separate panels thereof each consisting of three or more members, shall, under rules and regulations prescribed by the President, have the power within the respective jurisdictions of such local boards to hear and determine, subject to the right of appeal to the appeal boards herein authorized, all questions or claims with respect to inclusion for, or exemption or deferment from, training and service under this title [said sections], of all individuals within the jurisdiction of such local boards. The decisions of such local board shall be final, except where an appeal is authorized and is taken in accordance with such rules and regulations as the President may prescribe. There shall be not less than one appeal board located within the area of each Federal judicial district in the United States and within each Territory and possession of the United States, and such additional separate panels thereof, as may be prescribed by the President. Appeal boards within the Selective Service System shall be composed of civilians who are citizens of the United States and who are not members of the armed forces. The decision of such appeal boards shall be final in cases before them on appeal unless modified or changed by the President. The President, upon appeal or upon his own motion, shall have power to determine all claims or questions with respect to inclusion for, or exemption or deferment from training and service under this title [said sections], and the determination of the President shall be final. No judicial review shall be made of the classification or processing of any registrant by local boards, appeal boards, or the President, except as a defense to a criminal prosecution instituted under section 12 of this title [section 462 of this Appendix], after the registrant has responded either affirmatively or negatively to an order to report for induction or for civilian work in the case of a registrant determined to be opposed to participation in war in any form: *Provided*, That such review shall go to the question of the jurisdiction herein reserved to local boards, appeal boards, and the President only when there is no basis in fact for the classification assigned to such registrant. No person who is a civilian officer, member, agent, or employee of the Office of Selective Service Records or the Selective Service System, or of any local board or appeal board or other agency of such Officer or system, shall be excepted from registration or deferred or exempted from training and service, as provided for in this title [said sections], by reason of his status as such civilian officer, member, agent, or employee.

(4) To appoint, and to fix, in accordance with the provisions of chapter 51 and subchapter III of chapter 53 of title 5, United States Code, relating to classification and General Schedule pay rates, the basic pay of such officers, agents, and employees as he may deem necessary to carry out the provisions of this title [sections 451 to 471a of this Appendix], however, any officer of the armed forces or any officer or employee of any department or agency of the United States who may be assigned or detailed to any office or position to carry out the provisions of this title [said sections] (except to offices or positions on local boards or appeal boards established or created pursuant to section 10(b)(3) [subsection (b)(3) of this section]) may serve in and perform the functions of such office or position without loss of or prejudice to his status as such officer in the armed forces or as such officer or employee in any department or agency of the United States.

(5) To utilize the services of any or all departments and any and all officers or agents of the United States, and to accept the services of all officers and agents of the several States, Territories, and possessions, and subdivisions thereof, and the District of Columbia, and of private welfare organizations, in the execution of this title [sections 451 to 471a of this Appendix].

(6) To purchase such printing, binding, and blank-book work from public, commercial, or private printing establishments or binderies upon orders placed by the Public Printer or upon waivers issued in accordance with section 12 of the Printing Act approved January 12, 1895, as amended [44 U.S.C. 504], and to obtain by purchase, loan, or gift such equipment and supplies for the Selective Service System, as he may deem necessary to carry out the provisions of this title [sections 451 to 471a of this Appendix], with or without advertising or formal contract.

(7) To prescribe eligibility, rules, and regulations governing the release for service in the armed forces, or for any other special service established pursuant to this title [sections 451 to 471a of this Appendix], of any person convicted of a violation of any of the provisions of this title [said sections].

(8) Subject to the availability of funds appropriated for such purpose, to procure such space as he may deem necessary to carry out the provisions of this title [sections 451 to 471a of this Appendix] and Public Law 26, Eightieth Congress, approved March 31, 1947 [sections 321 to 329 of this Appendix], by lease pursuant to existing statutes, except that the provisions of the Act of June 30, 1932 (47 Stat. 412), as amended by section 15 of the Act of March 3, 1933 (47 Stat. 1517) [40 U.S.C. 278a],[1] shall not apply to any lease entered into under the authority of this title [said sections].

(9) Subject to the availability of funds appropriated for such purposes, to determine the location of such additional temporary installations as he may deem essential; to utilize and enlarge such existing installations; to construct, install, and equip, and to complete the construction, installation, and equipment of such buildings, structures, utilities, and appurtenances (including the necessary grading and removal, repair or remodeling of existing structures and installations), as may be necessary to carry out the provisions of this title [sections 451 to 471a of this Appendix]; and, in order to accomplish the purpose of this title [said sections], to acquire lands, and rights

[1] See References in Text note below.

pertaining thereto, or other interests therein, for temporary use thereof, by donation or lease, and to prosecute construction thereon prior to the approval of the title [said sections] by the Attorney General as required by section 355, Revised Statutes, as amended [40 U.S.C. 255].

(10) Subject to the availability of funds appropriated for such purposes, to utilize, in order to provide and furnish such services as may be deemed necessary or expedient to accomplish the purposes of this title [sections 451 to 471a of this Appendix], such personnel of the armed forces and of Reserve components thereof with their consent, and such civilian personnel, as may be necessary. For the purposes of this title [said sections], the provisions of section 14 of the Federal Employees' Pay Act of 1946 (Public Law 390, Seventy-ninth Congress) with respect to the maximum limitations as to the number of civilian employees shall not be applicable to the Department of the Army, the Department of the Navy, or the Department of the Air Force.

(c) Delegation of President's authority

The President is authorized to delegate any authority vested in him under this title [sections 451 to 471a of this Appendix], and to provide for the subdelegation of any such authority.

(d) Acceptance of gifts and voluntary services

In the administration of this title [sections 451 to 471a of this Appendix], gifts of supplies, equipment, and voluntary services may be accepted.

(e) Assignment of armed forces personnel

The total number of armed forces personnel assigned to the Selective Service System under subsection (b)(2) at any time may not be less than the number of such personnel determined by the Director of Selective Service to be necessary, but not to exceed 745 persons, except that the President may assign additional armed forces personnel to the Selective Service System during a time of war or a national emergency declared by Congress or the President.

(f) Settlement of travel claims, etc.

The Director is authorized to make final settlement of individual claims, for amounts not exceeding $500, for travel and other expenses of uncompensated personnel of the Office of Selective Service Records, or the Selective Service System, incurred while in the performance of official duties, without regard to other provisions of law governing the travel of civilian employees of the Federal Government.

(g) Reports to Congress

The Director of Selective Service shall submit to the Congress annually a written report covering the operation of the Selective Service System and such report shall include, by States, information as to the number of persons registered under this Act; the number of persons inducted in to the military service under this Act; and the number of deferments granted under this Act and the basis for such deferments; and such other specific kinds of information as the Congress may from time to time request.

(h) Maintenance of System after institution of all volunteer program for meeting manpower needs

The Selective Service system[2] shall be maintained as an active standby organization, with (1) a complete registration and classification structure capable of immediate operation in the event of a national emergency (including a structure for registration and classification of persons qualified for practice or employment in a health care occupation essential to the maintenance of the Armed Forces), and (2) personnel adequate to reinstitute immediately the full operation of the System, including military reservists who are trained to operate such System and who can be ordered to active duty for such purpose in the event of a national emergency.

(June 24, 1948, ch. 625, title I, §10, 62 Stat. 618; Oct. 28, 1949, ch. 782, title XI, §1106(a), 63 Stat. 972; June 30, 1950, ch. 445, §3, 64 Stat. 319; Sept. 27, 1950, ch. 1059, §3(b), 64 Stat. 1074; June 19, 1951, ch. 144, title I, §1(u), 65 Stat. 87; Pub. L. 90–40, §1(8)–(10), June 30, 1967, 81 Stat. 104, 105; Pub. L. 92–129, title I, §101(a)(24)–(29), Sept. 28, 1971, 85 Stat. 351, 352; Pub. L. 93–176, §3, Dec. 5, 1973, 87 Stat. 693; Pub. L. 96–513, title V, §507(d), Dec. 12, 1980, 94 Stat. 2919; Pub. L. 97–60, title II, §208, Oct. 14, 1981, 95 Stat. 1008; Pub. L. 98–473, title II, §234, Oct. 12, 1984, 98 Stat. 2031; Pub. L. 100–180, div. A, title VII, §715, Dec. 4, 1987, 101 Stat. 1113; Pub. L. 102–190, div. A, title X, §1091, Dec. 5, 1991, 105 Stat. 1486; Pub. L. 104–201, div. A, title IV, §414, Sept. 23, 1996, 110 Stat. 2508.)

REFERENCES IN TEXT

Act of June 30, 1932 (47 Stat. 412), as amended by section 15 of the Act of March 3, 1933 (47 Stat. 1517) [40 U.S.C. 278a], referred to in subsec. (b)(8), was repealed by Pub. L. 100–678, §7, Nov. 17, 1988, 102 Stat. 4052.

Section 14 of the Federal Employees' Pay Act of 1946 (Public Law 390, Seventy-ninth Congress), referred to in subsec. (b)(10), means section 14 of act May 24, 1946, ch. 270, 60 Stat. 219, which amended section 947 of former Title 5, Executive Departments and Government Officers and Employees, and which was repealed by act Sept. 12, 1950, ch. 946, title III, §301(85), 64 Stat. 843.

This Act, referred to in subsec. (g), is act June 24, 1948, ch. 625, 62 Stat. 604, as amended, known as the Military Selective Service Act. For complete classification of this Act to the Code, see References in Text note set out under section 451 of this Appendix and Tables.

AMENDMENTS

1996—Subsec. (b). Pub. L. 104–201, §414(b)(1), substituted "authorized to undertake the following:" for "authorized—" in introductory provisions.

Subsec. (b)(1). Pub. L. 104–201, §414(b)(2), (4), substituted "To" for "to" at beginning and a period for a semicolon at end.

Subsec. (b)(2). Pub. L. 104–201, §414(a)(1), (b)(2), (4), substituted "To" for "to" at beginning, inserted ", subject to subsection (e)," after "to employ such number of civilians, and", and substituted a period for a semicolon at end.

Subsec. (b)(3) to (7). Pub. L. 104–201, §414(b)(2), (4), substituted "To" for "to" at beginning and a period for a semicolon at end.

Subsec. (b)(8), (9). Pub. L. 104–201, §414(b)(3), (4), substituted "Subject" for "subject" at beginning and a period for a semicolon at end.

Subsec. (b)(10). Pub. L. 104–201, §414(b)(3), substituted "Subject" for "subject" at beginning.

[2] So in original. Probably should be capitalized.

Subsec. (e). Pub. L. 104–201, §414(a)(2), added subsec. (e).

1991—Subsec. (b)(2). Pub. L. 102–190, §1091(1), struck out "without the approval of the Director" after "local government".

Subsec. (g). Pub. L. 102–190, §1091(2), substituted "annually" for "semiannually".

1987—Subsec. (h). Pub. L. 100–180 substituted "The Selective Service system shall" for "If at any time calls under this section for the induction of persons for training and service in the Armed Forces are discontinued because the Armed Forces are placed on an all volunteer basis for meeting their active duty manpower needs, the Selective Service System, as it is constituted on the date of the enactment of this subsection [Sept. 28, 1971], shall, nevertheless," and directed the insertion of "(including a structure for registration and classification of persons qualified for practice or employment in a health care occupation essential to the maintenance of the Armed Forces)" after "national emergency", which was inserted in cl. (1) as the probable intent of Congress.

1984—Subsec. (b)(7). Pub. L. 98–473 substituted "release" for "parole".

1981—Subsec. (b)(3). Pub. L. 97–60 struck out provision that had prohibited service on local boards or appeal boards by persons who had attained the age of 65.

1980—Subsec. (b)(4). Pub. L. 96–513 substituted "however, any officer of the armed forces" for "however, any officer on the active or retired list of the armed forces, or any reserve component thereof with his consent," and struck out "or reserve component thereof," after "without loss of or prejudice to his status as such officer in the armed forces".

1973—Subsec. (b)(4). Pub. L. 93–176 substituted "the provisions of chapter 51 and subchapter III of chapter 53 of title 5, United States Code, relating to classification and General Schedule pay rates, the basic pay" for "the Classification Act of 1949, the compensation" and struck out provisos that compensation of employees of local boards and appeal boards may be fixed without regard to Classification Act of 1949, that employees of local boards having supervisory duties with respect to other employees of one or more local boards be designated as the executive secretary of the local board or boards, and that the term of employment of executive secretaries not exceed ten years except when reappointed.

1971—Subsec. (a)(3). Pub. L. 92–129, §101(a)(24), struck out provisions setting compensation of Director.

Subsec. (b)(2). Pub. L. 92–129, §101(a)(25), inserted proviso that no State director shall serve concurrently in an elected or appointed position of a State or local government without the approval of the Director.

Subsec. (b)(3). Pub. L. 92–129, §101(a)(26), inserted provisions requiring that local boards and their staffs perform their duties only within the counties or political subdivisions for which they are established with special provisions for intercounty boards and the collocation or multiple use of staffs with executive approval, provided for board membership proportionately representative of the area served, reduced the maximums applicable to board members from 75 years of age or 25 years of service on the board to 65 years of age or 20 years of service respectively, and authorized local boards to include among their members any citizens otherwise qualified under Presidential regulations provided they are at least 18 years of age.

Subsec. (e). Pub. L. 92–129, §101(a)(27), struck out subsec. (e) which authorized Chief of Finance of the United States Army to act as the fiscal, disbursing, and accounting agent of Director.

Subsec. (f). Pub. L. 92–129, §101(a)(28), substituted "$500" for "$50".

Subsec. (h). Pub. L. 92–129, §101(a)(29), added subsec. (h).

1967—Subsec. (b)(3). Pub. L. 90–40, §1(8), prohibited disqualification of members of armed forces reserve components from serving as counselors to registrants, including services as government appeal agents, merely because of such membership in the reserve, set 25 years as maximum length of service on local and appeal boards and 75 years as age after attainment of which members may not serve, prohibited discrimination as to service on boards because of sex, with new limitations on age and sex to be implemented not later than January 1, 1968, and prohibited judicial review of classification or processing of registrants except as a defense to a criminal prosecution instituted under section 462 of this Appendix, and then only after registrant has responded either affirmatively or negatively to an order to report for induction or for civilian work and to question of jurisdiction reserved to local boards, appeal boards, and President only when there is no basis in fact for classification.

Subsec. (b)(4). Pub. L. 90–40, §1(9), provided for designation of a local board employee having supervisory duties with respect to other employees of one or more local boards as "executive secretary", with such employee to serve in that position for a maximum of ten years except when reappointed.

Subsec. (g). Pub. L. 90–40, §1(10), substituted "semiannually" for "on or before the 3rd day of January of each year," as time for submission of Director's written report to Congress, and inserted "such other specific kinds of information as the Congress may from time to time request" to enumeration of subjects to be covered by the report.

1951—Subsec. (b)(3). Act June 19, 1951, §1(u)(1), provided for one appeal board in each Federal judicial district in the United States, its territories and possessions, and such necessary panels as the President deems necessary.

Subsec. (g). Act June 19, 1951, §1(u)(2), added subsec. (g).

1950—Subsec. (b)(3). Act Sept. 27, 1950, inserted ", or separate panels thereof each consisting of three or more members" after "Such local boards" in sixth sentence.

Subsec. (b)(4). Act June 30, 1950, struck out comma between "the compensation of" and "such officers".

1949—Subsec. (b)(4). Act Oct. 28, 1949, substituted "Classification Act of 1949" for "Classification Act of 1923".

Effective Date of 1984 Amendment

Amendment by Pub. L. 98–473 effective Nov. 1, 1987, and applicable only to offenses committed after the taking effect of such amendment, see section 235(a)(1) of Pub. L. 98–473, set out as an Effective Date note under section 3551 of Title 18, Crimes and Criminal Procedure.

Effective Date of 1980 Amendment

Amendment by Pub. L. 96–513 effective Sept. 15, 1981, see section 701 of Pub. L. 96–513, set out as a note under section 101 of Title 10, Armed Forces.

Effective Date of 1973 Amendment

Section 4 of Pub. L. 93–176 provided that: "This Act [amending this section and section 5102 of Title 5, Government Organization and Employees, and enacting provisions set out as notes under this section] shall take effect not later than the beginning of the first pay period which begins on or after the ninetieth day following the date of the enactment of this Act [Dec. 5, 1973]."

Repeals

Act Oct. 28, 1949, ch. 782, cited as a credit to this section, was repealed (subject to a savings clause) by Pub. L. 89–554, Sept. 6, 1966, §8, 80 Stat. 632, 655.

Emergency Preparedness Functions

For assignment of certain emergency preparedness functions to the Director of Selective Service, see Parts 1, 2, and 23 of Ex. Ord. No. 12656, Nov. 18, 1988, 53 F.R. 47491, set out as a note under section 5195 of Title 42, The Public Health and Welfare.

COMPENSATION INCREASES FOR EMPLOYEES OF LOCAL OR APPEAL BOARDS

Section 2 of Pub. L. 93–176 provided that: "The rate of basic pay of each employee in a position under a local board or appeal board of the Selective Service System on and immediately prior to the effective date of this Act [designated as a date not later than the beginning of the first pay period which begins on or after the 90th day following Dec. 5, 1973] shall be adjusted, as of such effective date, under the provisions of section 5334(d) of title 5, United States Code."

Act June 5, 1952, ch. 369, Ch. VII, §701, 66 Stat. 109, authorized increases in the rate of compensation of any employees of local or appeal boards effective as of the first day of the first pay period which began after June 30, 1951 and within ninety days from June 5, 1952, pursuant to the authority contained in section 460 of this Appendix.

COMPENSATION OF DIRECTOR OF SELECTIVE SERVICE

Compensation of Director, see section 5315 of Title 5, Government Organization and Employees.

EX. ORD. NO. 10271. DELEGATION OF PRESIDENT'S AUTHORITY

Ex. Ord. No. 10271, July 7, 1951, 16 F.R. 6659, set out as a note under section 471 of this Appendix, delegates to the Secretary of Defense the President's authority to order members and units of Reserve components into active Federal service.

EX. ORD. NO. 11623. DELEGATION OF AUTHORITY TO ISSUE RULES AND REGULATIONS TO DIRECTOR OF SELECTIVE SERVICE

Ex. Ord. No. 11623, Oct. 12, 1971, 36 F.R. 19963, as amended by Ex. Ord. No. 12608, Sept. 9, 1987, 52 F.R. 34617, provided:

By virtue of the authority vested in me by the Constitution and statutes of the United States, including the Military Selective Service Act, as amended (50 U.S. Code App., sections 451 *et seq.*, hereinafter referred to as the Act), and section 301 of title 3 of the United States Code, it is hereby ordered as follows:

SECTION 1. The Director of Selective Service (hereinafter referred to as the Director) is authorized to prescribe the necessary rules and regulations to carry out the provisions of the Act. Regulations heretofore issued by the President to carry out such provisions shall continue in effect until amended or revoked by the Director pursuant to the authority conferred by this Order.

SEC. 2. (a) In carrying out the provisions of this Order, the Director shall cause any rule or regulation which he proposes to issue hereunder to be published in the FEDERAL REGISTER as required by section 13(b) of the Act [section 463(b) of this Appendix]. Prior to such publication, the Director shall request the views of the Secretary of Defense, the Attorney General, the Secretary of Labor, the Secretary of Health and Human Services, the Secretary of Transportation (when the Coast Guard is serving under the Department of Transportation), the Director of the Office of Emergency Preparedness, and the Chairman of the National Selective Service Appeal Board with regard to such proposed rule or regulation, and shall allow not less than 10 days for the submission of such views before publication of the proposed rule or regulation.

(b) Any proposed rule or regulation as published by the Director shall be furnished to the officials required to be consulted pursuant to subsection (a). The Director may (not less than 30 days after publication in the FEDERAL REGISTER) issue such rule or regulation as published unless, within 10 days after being furnished with the proposed rule or regulation as published, any such official shall notify the Director that he disagrees therewith and requests that the matter be referred to the President for decision.

(c) Any rule or regulation issued by the Director pursuant to this Order shall be published in the FEDERAL REGISTER with (1) a statement reciting compliance with the prepublication requirement of section 13(b) of the Act [section 463(b) of this Appendix], and (2) either (i) approval of such rule or regulation by the President, or (ii) a certification of the Director that he has requested the views of the officials required to be consulted pursuant to subsection (a) and that none of them has timely requested that the matter be referred to the President for decision. Such rule or regulation shall be effective upon such publication in the FEDERAL REGISTER or on such later date as may be specified therein.

SEC. 3. Nothing in this Order shall be deemed to (i) authorize the exercise by the Director of the President's authority to waive the requirements of section 13(b) of the Act [section 463(b) of this Appendix], or (ii) derogate from the authority of the President himself to waive the requirements of such section 13(b), or (iii) derogate from the authority of the President himself to issue such rules or regulations as he may deem necessary to carry out the provisions of the Act.

SECTION REFERRED TO IN OTHER SECTIONS

This section is referred to in title 10 sections 101, 523, 641.

§461. Emergency medical care

Under such rules and regulations as may be prescribed by the President, funds available to carry out the provisions of this title [sections 451 to 471a of this Appendix] shall also be available for the payment of actual and reasonable expenses of emergency medical care, including hospitalization, of registrants who suffer illness or injury, and the transportation and burial of the remains of registrants who suffer death, while acting under orders issued under the provisions of this title [said sections], but such burial expenses shall not exceed the maximum that the Secretary of Veterans Affairs may pay under the provisions of section 2302(a) of title 38, United States Code, in any one case.

(June 24, 1948, ch. 625, title I, §11, 62 Stat. 621; Pub. L. 92–129, title I, §101(a)(30), Sept. 28, 1971, 85 Stat. 352; Pub. L. 102–54, §13(t), June 13, 1991, 105 Stat. 282; Pub. L. 102–83, §5(c)(2), Aug. 6, 1991, 105 Stat. 406.)

AMENDMENTS

1991—Pub. L. 102–83 substituted "section 2302(a) of title 38" for "section 902(a) of title 38".

Pub. L. 102–54 substituted "Secretary of Veterans Affairs" for "Administrator of Veterans' Affairs".

1971—Pub. L. 92–129 substituted "the maximum that the Administrator of Veterans' Affairs may pay under the provisions of section 902(a) of title 38, United States Code" for "$150".

§462. Offenses and penalties

(a) Any member of the Selective Service System or any other person charged as herein provided with the duty of carrying out any of the provisions of this title [sections 451 to 471a of this Appendix], or the rules or regulations made or directions given thereunder, who shall knowingly fail or neglect to perform such duty, and any person charged with such duty, or having and exercising any authority under said title [said sections], rules, regulations, or directions who shall knowingly make, or be a party to the making, of any false, improper, or incorrect registration, classification, physical or mental examination, deferment, induction, enrollment, or muster, and any person who shall knowingly make, or be a party to the making, of any false statement or certificate regarding or bearing upon a classification or in support of any request for a particular classification, for service under the provisions of this title [said sections], or rules, regulations, or directions made pursuant thereto, or who otherwise evades or refuses registration or service in the armed forces or any of the requirements of this title [said sections], or who knowingly counsels, aids, or abets another to refuse or evade registration or service in the armed forces or any of the requirements of this title [said sections], or of said rules, regulations, or directions, or who in any manner shall knowingly fail or neglect or refuse to perform any duty required of him under or in the execution of this title [said sections], or rules, regulations, or directions made pursuant to this title [said sections], or any person or persons who shall knowingly hinder or interfere or attempt to do so in any way, by force or violence or otherwise, with the administration of this title [said sections] or the rules or regulations made pursuant thereto, or who conspires to commit any one or more of such offenses, shall, upon conviction in any district court of the United States of competent jurisdiction, be punished by imprisonment for not more than five years or a fine of not more than $10,000, or by both such fine and imprisonment, or if subject to military or naval law may be tried by court martial, and, on conviction, shall suffer such punishment as a court martial may direct. No person shall be tried by court martial in any case arising under this title [said sections] unless such person has been actually inducted for the training and service prescribed under this title [said sections] or unless he is subject to trial by court martial under laws in force prior to the enactment of this title [June 24, 1948].

(b) Any person (1) who knowingly transfers or delivers to another, for the purpose of aiding or abetting the making of any false identification or representation, any registration certificate, alien's certificate of nonresidence, or any other certificate issued pursuant to or prescribed by the provisions of this title [sections 451 to 471a of this Appendix], or rules or regulations promulgated hereunder; or (2) who, with intent that it be used for any purpose of false identification or representation, has in his possession any such certificate not duly issued to him; or (3) who forges, alters, knowingly destroys, knowingly mutilates, or in any manner changes any such certificate or any notation duly and validly inscribed thereon; or (4) who, with intent that it be used for any purpose of false identification or representation, photographs, prints, or in any manner makes or executes any engraving, photograph, print, or impression in the likeness of any such certificate, or any colorable imitation thereof; or (5) who has in his possession any certificate purporting to be a certificate issued pursuant to this title [said sections], or rules and regulations promulgated hereunder, which he knows to be falsely made, reproduced, forged, counterfeited, or altered; or (6) who knowingly violates or evades any of the provisions of this title [said sections] or rules and regulations promulgated pursuant thereto relating to the issuance, transfer, or possession of such certificate, shall, upon conviction, be fined not to exceed $10,000 or be imprisoned for not more than five years, or both. Whenever on trial for a violation of this subsection the defendant is shown to have or to have had possession of any certificate not duly issued to him, such possession shall be deemed sufficient evidence to establish an intent to use such certificate for purposes of false identification or representation, unless the defendant explains such possession to the satisfaction of the jury.

(c) The Department of Justice shall proceed as expeditiously as possible with a prosecution under this section, or with an appeal, upon the request of the Director of Selective Service System or shall advise the House of Representatives and the Senate in writing the reasons for its failure to do so.

(d) No person shall be prosecuted, tried, or punished for evading, neglecting, or refusing to perform the duty of registering imposed by section 3 of this title [section 453 of this Appendix] unless the indictment is found within five years next after the last day before such person attains the age of twenty-six, or within five years next after the last day before such person does perform his duty to register, whichever shall first occur.

(e) The President may require the Secretary of Health and Human Services to furnish to the Director, from records available to the Secretary, the following information with respect to individuals who are members of any group of individuals required by a proclamation of the President under section 3 [section 453 of this Appendix] to present themselves for and submit to registration under such section: name, date of birth, social security account number, and address. Information furnished to the Director by the Secretary under this subsection shall be used only for the purpose of the enforcement of this Act.

(f)(1) Except as provided in subsection (g), any person who is required under section 3 [section 453 of this Appendix] to present himself for and submit to registration under such section and fails to do so in accordance with any proclamation issued under such section, or in accordance with any rule or regulation issued under such section, shall be ineligible for any form of assistance or benefit provided under title IV of the Higher Education Act of 1965 [20 U.S.C. 1070 et seq.; 42 U.S.C. 2751 et seq.].

(2) In order to receive any grant, loan, or work assistance under title IV of the Higher Education Act of 1965 (20 U.S.C. 1070 et seq. [and 42 U.S.C. 2751 et seq.]), a person who is required under section 3 [section 453 of this Appendix] to present himself for and submit to registration under such section shall file with the institution of higher education which the person intends to attend, or is attending, a statement of compliance with section 3 and regulations issued thereunder.

(3) The Secretary of Education, in agreement with the Director, shall prescribe methods for verifying such statements of compliance filed pursuant to paragraph (2). Such methods may include requiring institutions of higher education to provide a list to the Secretary of Education or to the Director of persons who have submitted such statements of compliance.

(4) The Secretary of Education, in consultation with the Director, shall issue regulations to implement the requirements of this subsection. Such regulations shall provide that any person to whom the Secretary of Education proposes to deny assistance or benefits under title IV [20 U.S.C. 1070 et seq.; 42 U.S.C. 2751 et seq.] for failure to meet the registration requirements of section 3 [section 453 of this Appendix] and regulations issued thereunder shall be given notice of the proposed denial and shall have a suitable period (of not less than thirty days) after such notice to provide the Secretary with information and materials establishing that he has complied with the registration requirement under section 3. Such regulations shall also provide that the Secretary may afford such person an opportunity for a hearing to establish his compliance or for any other purpose.

(g) A person may not be denied a right, privilege, or benefit under Federal law by reason of failure to present himself for and submit to registration under section 3 [section 453 of this Appendix] if—

(1) the requirement for the person to so register has terminated or become inapplicable to the person; and

(2) the person shows by a preponderance of the evidence that the failure of the person to register was not a knowing and willful failure to register.

(June 24, 1948, ch. 625, title I, §12, 62 Stat. 622; Pub. L. 89–152, Aug. 30, 1965, 79 Stat. 586; Pub. L. 90–40, §1(11), June 30, 1967, 81 Stat. 105; Pub. L. 92–129, title I, §101(a)(31), Sept. 28, 1971, 85 Stat. 352; Pub. L. 97–86, title IX, §916(b), Dec. 1, 1981, 95 Stat. 1129; Pub. L. 97–252, title XI, §1113(a), Sept. 8, 1982, 96 Stat. 748; Pub. L. 98–620, title IV, §402(54), Nov. 8, 1984, 98 Stat. 3361; Pub. L. 99–661, div. A, title XIII, §1366, Nov. 14, 1986, 100 Stat. 4002.)

References in Text

This Act, referred to in subsec. (e), is act June 24, 1948, ch. 625, 62 Stat. 604, as amended, known as the Military Selective Service Act. For complete classification of this Act to the Code, see References in Text note set out under section 451 of this Appendix and Tables.

The Higher Education Act of 1965, referred to in subsec. (f), is Pub. L. 89–329, Nov. 8, 1965, 79 Stat. 1219, as amended. Title IV of the Higher Education Act of 1965 is classified generally to subchapter IV (§1070 et seq.) of chapter 28 of Title 20, Education, and part C (§2751 et seq.) of subchapter I of chapter 34 of Title 42, The Public Health and Welfare. For complete classification of this Act to the Code, see Short Title note set out under section 1001 of Title 20 and Tables.

Amendments

1986—Subsec. (f)(1). Pub. L. 99–661, §1366(1), substituted "Except as provided in subsection (g), any person" for "Any person".

Subsec. (g). Pub. L. 99–661, §1366(2), added subsec. (g).

1984—Subsec. (a). Pub. L. 98–620 struck out sentence at end requiring that precedence be given by courts to the trial of cases arising under sections 451 to 471a of this Appendix, and that such cases had to be advanced on the docket for immediate hearing, and that an appeal from the decision or decree of any United States district court or United States court of appeals would take precedence over all other cases pending before the court to which the case had been referred.

1982—Subsec. (f). Pub. L. 97–252 added subsec. (f).

1981—Subsec. (e). Pub. L. 97–86 added subsec. (e).

1971—Subsec. (d). Pub. L. 92–129 added subsec. (d).

1967—Subsec. (a). Pub. L. 90–40, §1(11)(a), struck out requirement that a request of the Attorney General precede the granting of precedence to the trial of cases arising under this title and inserted provision that appeals from a decision or decree of any United States District Court or United States Court of Appeals take precedence over all other cases pending before the court to which the case has been referred.

Subsec. (c). Pub. L. 90–40, §1(11)(b), added subsec. (c).

1965—Subsec. (b)(3). Pub. L. 89–152 prohibited a person from knowingly destroying or knowingly mutilating any registration certificate or other prescribed certificate.

Effective Date of 1984 Amendment

Amendment by Pub. L. 98–620 not applicable to cases pending on Nov. 8, 1984, see section 403 of Pub. L. 98–620, set out as a note under section 1657 of Title 28, Judiciary and Judicial Procedure.

Effective Date of 1982 Amendment

Section 1113(b) of Pub. L. 97–252 provided that: "The amendment made by subsection (a) [amending this section] shall apply to loans, grants, or work assistance under title IV of the Higher Education Act [20 U.S.C. 1070 et seq.; 42 U.S.C. 2751 et seq.] for periods of instruction beginning after June 30, 1983."

Study on Compliance of Health Professions Schools With Military Selective Service Act

Pub. L. 99–129, title II, §222, Oct. 22, 1985, 99 Stat. 544, directed Secretary of Health and Human Services, in cooperation with Director of Selective Service, to conduct a study to determine if health professions schools are engaged in a pattern or practice of failure to comply with section 12(f) of the Military Selective Service Act (50 U.S.C. App. 462(f)) (or regulations issued under such section) or are engaged in a pattern or practice of providing loans or work assistance to persons who are required to register under section 3 of such Act [50 App. U.S.C. 453] (and any proclamation of the President and regulations prescribed under that section) and have not so registered with Secretary and to complete the study and report its results to Congress not later than one year after Oct. 22, 1985.

Advertising Prohibition on Special Discharge Review Program

Pub. L. 95–79, title VIII, §810, July 30, 1977, 91 Stat. 335, prohibited the use of funds authorized or appropriated under this or any other Act to purchase advertising of the special discharge review program.

Proc. No. 4313. Program for Return of Vietnam Era Draft Evaders and Military Deserters

Proc. No. 4313, Sept. 16, 1974, 39 F.R. 33293, 88 Stat. 2504, as amended by Proc. No. 4345, Jan. 30, 1975, 40 F.R. 4893, 89 Stat. 1236; Proc. No. 4353, Feb. 28, 1975, 40 F.R. 8931, 10433, 89 Stat. 1246, provided:

The United States withdrew the last of its forces from the Republic of Vietnam on March 28, 1973.

In the period of its involvement in armed hostilities in Southeast Asia, the United States suffered great losses. Millions served their country, thousands died in combat, thousands more were wounded, others are still listed as missing in action.

Over a year after the last American combatant had left Vietnam, the status of thousands of our countrymen—convicted, charged, investigated or still sought for violations of the Military Selective Service Act [see References in Text note set out under section 451 of this Appendix] or of the Uniform Code of Military Justice [10 U.S.C. 801 et seq.]—remains unresolved.

In furtherance of our national commitment to justice and mercy these young Americans should have the chance to contribute a share to the rebuilding of peace among ourselves and with all nations. They should be allowed the opportunity to earn return to their country, their communities, and their families, upon their agreement to a period of alternate service in the national interest, together with an acknowledgment of their allegiance to the country and its Constitution.

Desertion in time of war is a major, serious offense; failure to respond to the country's call for duty is also a serious offense. Reconciliation among our people does not require that these acts be condoned. Yet, reconciliation calls for an act of mercy to bind the Nation's wounds and to heal the scars of divisiveness.

NOW, THEREFORE, I, GERALD R. FORD, President of the United States, pursuant to my powers under Article II, Sections 1, 2 and 3 of the Constitution, do hereby proclaim a program to commence immediately to afford reconciliation to Vietnam era draft evaders and military deserters upon the following terms and conditions:

1. *Draft Evaders*—An individual who allegedly unlawfully failed under the Military Selective Service Act [see References in Text note set out under section 451 of this Appendix] or any rule or regulation promulgated thereunder, to register or register on time, to keep the local board informed of his current address, to report for or submit to preinduction or induction examination, to report for or submit to induction itself, or to report for or submit to, or complete service under section 6(j) of such Act [section 456(j) of this Appendix] during the period from August 4, 1964 to March 28, 1973, inclusive, and who has not been adjudged guilty in a trial for such offense, will be relieved of prosecution and punishment for such offense if he:

(i) presents himself to a United States Attorney before March 31, 1975,

(ii) executes an agreement acknowledging his allegiance to the United States and pledging to fulfill a period of alternate service under the auspices of the Director of Selective Service, and

(iii) satisfactorily completes such service.

The alternate service shall promote the national health, safety, or interest. No draft evader will be given the privilege of completing a period of alternate service by service in the Armed Forces.

However, this program will not apply to an individual who is precluded from re-entering the United States under 8 U.S.C. 1182(a)(22) or other law. Additionally, if individuals eligible for this program have other criminal charges outstanding, their participation in the program may be conditioned upon, or postponed until after, final disposition of the other charges has been reached in accordance with law.

The period of service shall be twenty-four months, which may be reduced by the Attorney General because of mitigating circumstances.

2. *Military Deserters*—A member of the armed forces who has been administratively classified as a deserter by reason of unauthorized absence and whose absence commenced during the period from August 4, 1964 to March 28, 1973, inclusive, will be relieved of prosecution and punishment under Articles 85, 86 and 87 of the Uniform Code of Military Justice [10 U.S.C. 885, 886, 887] for such absence and for offenses directly related thereto if before March 31, 1975 he takes an oath of allegiance to the United States and executes an agreement with the Secretary of the Military Department from which he absented himself or for members of the Coast Guard, with the Secretary of Transportation, pledging to fulfill a period of alternate service under the auspices of the Director of Selective Service. The alternate service shall promote the national health, safety, or interest.

The period of service shall be twenty-four months, which may be reduced by the Secretary of the appropriate Military Department, or Secretary of Transportation for members of the Coast Guard, because of mitigating circumstances.

However, if a member of the armed forces has additional outstanding charges pending against him under the Uniform Code of Military Justice [10 U.S.C. 801 et seq.], his eligibility to participate in this program may be conditioned upon, or postponed until after, final disposition of the additional charges has been reached in accordance with law.

Each member of the armed forces who elects to seek relief through this program will receive an undesirable discharge. Thereafter, upon satisfactory completion of a period of alternate service prescribed by the Military Department or Department of Transportation, such individual will be entitled to receive, in lieu of his undesirable discharge, a clemency discharge in recognition of his fulfillment of the requirements of the program. Such clemency discharge shall not bestow entitlement to benefits administered by the Veterans Administration.

Procedures of the Military Departments implementing this Proclamation will be in accordance with guidelines established by the Secretary of Defense, present Military Department regulations notwithstanding.

3. *Presidential Clemency Board*—By Executive Order I have this date established a Presidential Clemency Board which will review the records of individuals within the following categories: (*i*) those who have been convicted of draft evasion offenses as described above, (*ii*) those who have received a punitive or undesirable discharge from service in the armed forces for having violated Article 85, 86, or 87 of the Uniform Code of Military Justice [10 U.S.C. 885, 886, 887] between August 4, 1964 and March 28, 1973, or are serving sentences of confinement for such violations. Where appropriate, the Board may recommend that clemency be conditioned upon completion of a period of alternate service. However, if any clemency discharge is recommended, such discharge shall not bestow entitlement to benefits administered by the Veterans Administration.

4. *Alternate Service*—In prescribing the length of alternate service in individual cases, the Attorney General, the Secretary of the appropriate Department, or the Clemency Board shall take into account such honorable service as an individual may have rendered prior to his absence, penalties already paid under law, and such other mitigating factors as may be appropriate to seek equity among those who participate in this program.

IN WITNESS WHEREOF, I have hereunto set my hand this sixteenth day of September in the year of our Lord nineteen hundred seventy-four, and of the Independence of the United States of America the one hundred and ninety-nineth.

GERALD R. FORD.

PROC. NO. 4483. PARDON FOR VIOLATIONS OF ACT, AUGUST 4, 1964 TO MARCH 28, 1973

Proc. No. 4483, Jan. 21, 1977, 42 F.R. 4391, 91 Stat. 1719, provided:

Acting pursuant to the grant of authority in Article II, Section 2, of the Constitution of the United States, I, Jimmy Carter, President of the United States, do hereby grant a full, complete and unconditional pardon to: (1) all persons who may have committed any offense between August 4, 1964 and March 28, 1973 in violation of the Military Selective Service Act [see References in Text note set out under section 451 of this Appendix] or any rule or regulation promulgated thereunder; and (2) all persons heretofore convicted, irrespective of the date of conviction, of any offense committed between August 4, 1964 and March 28, 1973 in violation of the Military Selective Service Act, or any rule or regulation promulgated thereunder, restoring to them full political, civil and other rights.

This pardon does not apply to the following who are specifically excluded therefrom:

(1) All persons convicted of or who may have committed any offense in violation of the Military Selective Service Act, or any rule or regulation promulgated thereunder, involving force or violence; and

(2) All persons convicted of or who may have committed any offense in violation of the Military Selective Service Act, or any rule or regulation promulgated thereunder, in connection with duties or responsibilities arising out of employment as agents, officers or employees of the Military Selective Service system.

IN WITNESS WHEREOF, I have hereunto set my hand this 21st day of January, in the year of our Lord nineteen hundred and seventy-seven, and of the Independence of the United States of America the two hundred and first.

JIMMY CARTER.

EX. ORD. NO. 11803. CLEMENCY BOARD TO REVIEW CERTAIN CONVICTIONS AND DISCHARGES

Ex. Ord. No. 11803, Sept. 16, 1974, 39 F.R. 33297, as amended by Ex. Ord. No. 11837, Jan. 30, 1975, 40 F.R. 4895; Ex. Ord. No. 11842, Feb. 28, 1975, 40 F.R. 8935; Ex. Ord. No. 11857, May 7, 1975, 40 F.R. 20261; Ex. Ord. No. 11878, Sept. 10, 1975, 40 F.R. 42731, provided:

By virtue of the authority vested in me as President of the United States by Section 2 of Article II of the Constitution of the United States, and in the interest of the internal management of the Government, it is ordered as follows:

SECTION 1. There is hereby established in the Executive Office of the President a board of 9 members, which shall be known as the Presidential Clemency Board. The members of the Board shall be appointed by the President, who shall also designate its Chairman. The President may appoint such additional members to the board as he shall from time to time determine to be necessary to carry out its functions.

SEC. 2. The Board, under such regulations as it may prescribe, shall examine the cases of persons who apply for Executive clemency prior to March 31, 1975, and who (i) have been convicted of violating Section 12 or 6(j) of the Military Selective Service Act (50 App. U.S.C. §462) [this section and section 456(j) of this Appendix], or of any rule or regulation promulgated pursuant to that section, for acts committed between August 4, 1964 and March 28, 1973, inclusive, or (ii) have received punitive or undesirable discharges as a consequence of violations of Articles 85, 86 or 87 of the Uniform Code of Military Justice (10 U.S.C. §§885, 886, 887) that occurred between August 4, 1964 and March 28, 1973, inclusive, or are serving sentences of confinement for such violations. The Board will only consider the cases of Military Selective Service Act violators who were convicted of unlawfully failing (i) to register or register on time, (ii) to keep the local board informed of their current address, (iii) to report for or submit to preinduction or induction examination, (iv) to report for or submit to induction itself, or (v) to report for or submit to, or complete service under Section 6(j) of such Act [section 456(j) of this Appendix]. However, the Board will not consider the cases of individuals who are precluded from reentering the United States under [former] 8 U.S.C. 182(a)(22) or other law.

SEC. 3. The Board shall report to the President its findings and recommendations as to whether Executive clemency should be granted or denied in any case. If clemency is recommended, the Board shall also recommend the form that such clemency should take, including clemency conditioned upon a period of alternate service in the national interest. In the case of an individual discharged from the armed forces with a punitive or undesirable discharge, the Board may recommend to the President that a clemency discharge be substituted for a punitive or undesirable discharge. Determination of any period of alternate service shall be in accord with the Proclamation [Proc. No. 4313, set out above] announcing a program for the return of Vietnam era draft evaders and military deserters.

SEC. 4. The Board shall give priority consideration to those applicants who are presently confined and have been convicted only of an offense set forth in section 2 of this order, and who have no outstanding criminal charges.

SEC. 5. Each member of the Board, except any member who then receives other compensation from the United States, may receive compensation for each day he or she is engaged upon the work of the Board at not to exceed the daily rate now or hereafter prescribed by law for persons and positions in GS–18, as authorized by law (5 U.S.C. 3109), and may also receive travel expenses, including per diem in lieu of subsistence, as authorized by law (5 U.S.C. 5703) for persons in the government service employed intermittently.

SEC. 6. Necessary expenses of the Board may be paid from the Unanticipated Personnel Needs Fund of the President or from such other funds as may be available.

SEC. 7. Necessary administrative services and support may be provided the Board by the General Services Administration on a reimbursable basis.

SEC. 8. All department and agencies in the Executive branch are authorized and directed to cooperate with the Board in its work, and to furnish the Board all appropriate information and assistance, to the extent permitted by law.

SEC. 9. The Board shall submit its final recommendations to the President not later than September 15, 1975, at which time it shall cease to exist.

GERALD R. FORD.

EX. ORD. NO. 11804. DELEGATION OF CERTAIN FUNCTIONS OF PRESIDENT TO DIRECTOR OF SELECTIVE SERVICE

Ex. Ord. No. 11804, Sept. 16, 1974, 39 F.R. 33299, provided:

By virtue of the authority vested in me as President of the United States, pursuant to my powers under Article II, Sections 1, 2 and 3 of the Constitution, and under Section 301 of Title 3 of the United States Code, it is hereby ordered as follows:

SECTION 1. The Director of Selective Service is designated and empowered, without the approval, ratification or other action of the President, under such regulations as he may prescribe, to establish, implement, and administer the program of alternate service authorized in the Proclamation [set out above] announcing a program for the return of Vietnam era draft evaders and military deserters.

SEC. 2. Departments and agencies in the Executive branch shall, upon the request of the Director of Selective Service, cooperate and assist in the implementation or administration of the Director's duties under this Order, to the extent permitted by law.

GERALD R. FORD.

EX. ORD. NO. 11878. ASSIGNING RESPONSIBILITIES RELATING TO ACTIVITIES OF PRESIDENTIAL CLEMENCY BOARD

Ex. Ord. No. 11878, Sept. 10, 1975, 40 F.R. 42731, provided:

By virtue of the authority vested in me by the Constitution of the United States of America, and as President of the United States of America, it is hereby ordered as follows:

SECTION 1. Section 9 of Executive Order No. 11803 of September 16, 1974, as amended [set out above] is amended to read:

"The Board shall submit its final recommendations to the President not later than September 15, 1975, at which time it shall cease to exist."

SEC. 2. Any applications for Executive clemency, as to which the Presidential Clemency Board (established by Executive Order No. 11803) [set out above] has not taken final action shall be transferred, together with the files related thereto, to the Attorney General.

SEC. 3. The Attorney General, with respect to the applications and related files transferred to him by Section 2 of this Order, shall take all actions appropriate or necessary to complete the clemency process and shall expeditiously report to the President his findings and recommendations as to whether Executive clemency should be granted or denied in any case. In performing his responsibilities under this Order, the Attorney General shall apply the relevant criteria and comply with the appropriate and applicable instructions and procedures established by Executive Order No. 11803 of September 16, 1974, as amended [set out above], Proclamation No. 4313 of September 16, 1974, as amended [set out above], Executive Order No. 11804 of September 16, 1974 [set out above], and, to the extent that he deems appropriate, the regulations of the Presidential Clemency Board and the Selective Service System issued pursuant to the foregoing Executive orders.

SEC. 4. The Director of the Office of Management and Budget is hereby designated and empowered to take such action as he deems necessary to ensure the orderly and prompt termination of the activities of the Presidential Clemency Board and the assignment of responsibilities directed by this Order.

SEC. 5. Departments and agencies in the Executive branch shall, to the extent permitted by law, cooperate with and assist the Attorney General, the Director of the Selective Service and the Director of the Office of Management and Budget in the performance of their responsibilities under this Order.

SEC. 6. The responsibilities assigned under this Order are to be completed no later than March 31, 1976, at which time the Attorney General shall submit his final recommendations to the President.

GERALD R. FORD.

EX. ORD. NO. 11967. IMPLEMENTATION OF PARDON FOR VIOLATIONS OF ACT, AUGUST 4, 1964 TO MARCH 28, 1973

Ex. Ord. No. 11967, Jan. 21, 1977, 42 F.R. 4393, provided:

The following actions shall be taken to facilitate Presidential Proclamation of Pardon of January 21, 1977 [set out above]:

1. The Attorney General shall cause to be dismissed with prejudice to the Government all pending indictments for violations of the Military Selective Service Act [see References in Text note set out under section 451 of this Appendix] alleged to have occurred between August 4, 1964 and March 28, 1973 with the exception of the following:

(a) Those cases alleging acts of force or violence deemed to be so serious by the Attorney General as to warrant continued prosecution; and

(b) Those cases alleging acts in violation of the Military Selective Service Act by agents, employees or officers of the Selective Service System arising out of such employment.

2. The Attorney General shall terminate all investigations now pending and shall not initiate further investigations alleging violations of the Military Selective Service Act [see References in Text note set out under section 451 of this Appendix] between August 4, 1964 and March 28, 1973, with the exception of the following:

(a) Those cases involving allegations of force or violence deemed to be so serious by the Attorney General as to warrant continued investigation, or possible prosecution; and

(b) Those cases alleging acts in violation of the Military Selective Service Act by agents, employees or officers of the Selective Service System arising out of such employment.

3. Any person who is or may be precluded from reentering the United States under [former] 8 U.S.C. 1182(a)(22) or under any other law, by reason of having committed or apparently committed any violation of the Military Selective Service Act [see References in Text note set out under section 451 of this Appendix] shall be permitted as any other alien to reenter the United States.

The Attorney General is directed to exercise his discretion under 8 U.S.C. 1182(d)(5) or other applicable law to permit the reentry of such persons under the same terms and conditions as any other alien.

This shall not include anyone who falls into the exceptions of paragraphs 1(a) and (b) and 2(a) and (b) above.

4. Any individual offered conditional clemency or granted a pardon or other clemency under Executive Order 11803 [set out above] or Presidential Proclamation 4313, dated September 16, 1974 [set out above], shall receive the full measure of relief afforded by this program if they are otherwise qualified under the terms of this Executive Order.

JIMMY CARTER.

SECTION REFERRED TO IN OTHER SECTIONS

This section is referred to in sections 456, 460 of this Appendix.

§ 463. Nonapplicability of certain laws

(a) Nothing in sections 203, 205, or 207 of title 18 of the United States Code, or in the second sentence of subsection (a) of section 9 of the Act of August 2, 1939 (53 Stat. 1148), entitled "An Act to prevent pernicious political activities", as amended, shall be deemed to apply to any person because of his appointment under authority of this title [sections 451 to 471a of this Appendix] or the regulations made pursuant thereto as an uncompensated official of the Selective Service System, or as an individual to conduct hearings on appeals of persons claiming exemption from combatant or noncombatant training because of conscientious objections, or as a member of the National Selective Service Appeal Board.

(b) All functions performed under this title [sections 451 to 471a of this Appendix] shall be excluded from the operation of the Administrative Procedure Act (60 Stat. 237) [5 U.S.C. 551 et seq. and 701 et seq.] except as to the requirements of section 3 of such Act [5 U.S.C. 552]. Notwithstanding the foregoing sentence, no regulation issued under this Act shall become effective until the expiration of thirty days following the date on which such regulation has been published in the Federal Register. After the publication of any regulation and prior to the date on which such regulation becomes effective, any person shall be given an opportunity to submit his views to the Director on such regulation, but no formal hearing shall be required on any such regulation. The requirements of this subsection may be waived by the President in the case of any regulation if he (1) determines that compliance with such requirements would materially impair the national defense, and (2) gives public notice to that effect at the time such regulation is issued.

(c) In computing the lump-sum payments made to Air Force reserve officers under the provisions of section 2 of the Act of June 16, 1936, as amended and to reserve officers of the Navy or to their beneficiaries under section 12 of the Act of August 4, 1942, as amended, no credit shall be allowed for any period of active service performed from the effective date of this title [June 24, 1948] to the date on which this title [sections 451 to 471a of this Appendix] shall cease to be effective. Each such lumpsum payment shall be prorated for a fractional part of a year of active service in the case of any reserve officer subject to the provisions of either such section, if such reserve officer performs continuous active service for one or more years (inclusive of such service performed during the period in which this title [said sections] is effective) and such active service includes a fractional part of a year immediately prior to the effective date of this title [June 24, 1948], or immediately following the date on which this title [said sections] shall cease to be effective, or both.

(June 24, 1948, ch. 625, title I, § 13, 62 Stat. 623; June 19, 1951, ch. 144, title I, § 1(t), 65 Stat. 87; Pub. L. 88–110, § 6, Sept. 3, 1963, 77 Stat. 136; Pub. L. 92–129, title I, § 101(a)(32), Sept. 28, 1971, 85 Stat. 353.)

REFERENCES IN TEXT

The second sentence of subsection (a) of section 9 of the Act of August 2, 1939, referred to in subsec. (a), was classified to section 118i(a) of former Title 5 and was repealed by Pub. L. 89–554, Sept. 6, 1966, 80 Stat. 378, and reenacted as section 7324(a)(2) of Title 5, Government Organization and Employees. Section 7324 of Title 5 was omitted and a new section 7324 enacted in the general amendment of subchapter III of chapter 73 of Title 5 by Pub. L. 103–94, §2(a), Oct. 6, 1993, 107 Stat. 1001. See section 7323(b)(2)(A) of Title 5.

The Administrative Procedure Act, referred to in subsec. (b), is act June 11, 1946, ch. 324, 60 Stat. 237, as amended, which was classified to sections 1001 to 1011 of former Title 5 and which was repealed by Pub. L. 89–554, Sept. 6, 1966, 80 Stat. 378, and reenacted as subchapter II (§551 et seq.) of chapter 5, and chapter 7 (§701 et seq.), of Title 5, Government Organization and Employees.

This Act, referred to in subsec. (b), is act June 24, 1948, ch. 625, 62 Stat. 604, as amended, known as the Military Selective Service Act. For complete classification of this Act to the Code, see References in Text note set out under section 451 of this Appendix and Tables.

Section 2 of the Act of June 16, 1936, as amended, referred to in subsec. (c), is section 2 of act June 16, 1936, ch. 587, 49 Stat. 1524, as amended Apr. 3, 1939, ch. 35, §11, 53 Stat. 559; June 3, 1941, ch. 165, §6, 55 Stat. 240; July 25, 1947, ch. 323, 61 Stat. 424; July 26, 1947, ch. 343, title II, §205(a), 61 Stat. 501, which is not classified to the Code.

Section 12 of the Act of August 4, 1942, as amended, referred to in subsec. (c), is section 12 of act Aug. 4, 1942, ch. 547, 56 Stat. 738, as amended Oct. 25, 1943, ch. 275, §1, 57 Stat. 574; July 25, 1947, ch. 323, 61 Stat. 421, which is not classified to the Code.

Date on which this title shall cease to be effective, referred to in subsec. (c), is defined in section 467 of this Appendix.

AMENDMENTS

1971—Subsec. (b). Pub. L. 92–129 inserted provisions covering the publication of regulations in the Federal Register.

1963—Subsec. (a). Pub. L. 88–110 substituted "sections 203, 205, or 207 of title 18 of the United States Code" for "sections 281, 283, or 284 of title 18 of the United States Code, in section 190 of the Revised Statutes (U.S.C., title 5, sec. 99)".

1951—Subsec. (a). Act June 19, 1951, brought within its provisions members of the National Selective Service Appeal Board.

§464. Soldiers' and Sailors' Civil Relief Act as applicable

Notwithstanding the provisions of section 604 of the Act of October 17, 1940 (54 Stat. 1191) [section 584 of this Appendix], and the provisions of section 4 of the Act of July 25, 1947 (Public Law 239, Eightieth Congress) [section 584 note of this Appendix], all of the provisions of the Soldiers' and Sailors' Civil Relief Act of 1940, as amended [sections 501 to 593 of this Appendix], including specifically article IV thereof [sections 540 to 548 of this Appendix], shall be applicable to all persons in the armed forces of the United States, including all persons inducted into the armed forces pursuant to this title [sections 451 to 471a of this Appendix] or the Public Health Service, until such time as the Soldiers' and Sailors' Civil Relief Act of 1940, as amended [sections 501 to 593 of this Appendix] is repealed or otherwise terminated by subsequent Act of the Congress: *Provided*, That, with respect to persons inducted into the armed forces while this title [said sections] is in effect, wherever under any section or provision of the Soldiers' and Sailors' Civil Relief Act of 1940, as amended [sections 501 to 593 of this Appendix] a proceeding, remedy, privilege, stay, limitation, accounting, or other transaction has been authorized or provided with respect to military service performed while such Act is in force, such section or provision shall be deemed to continue in full force and effect so long as may be necessary to the exercise or enjoyment of such proceeding, remedy, privilege, stay, limitation, accounting, or other transaction.

(June 24, 1948, ch. 625, title I, §14, 62 Stat. 623; Sept. 27, 1950, ch. 1059, §1(11), 64 Stat. 1074.)

REFERENCES IN TEXT

The Soldiers' and Sailors' Civil Relief Act of 1940, as amended, referred to in text, is act Oct. 17, 1940, ch. 888, 54 Stat. 1178, as amended, which is classified to section 501 et seq. of this Appendix. For complete classification of this Act to the Code, see section 501 of this Appendix.

AMENDMENTS

1950—Act Sept. 27, 1950, struck out ", the Coast Guard" after "to this title".

TRANSFER OF FUNCTIONS

Functions of Public Health Service, Surgeon General of Public Health Service, and all other officers and employees of Public Health Service, and functions of all agencies of or in Public Health Service transferred to Secretary of Health, Education, and Welfare by Reorg. Plan No. 3 of 1966, eff. June 25, 1966, 31 F.R. 8855, 80 Stat. 1610, set out in the Appendix to Title 5, Government Organization and Employees. Secretary of Health, Education, and Welfare redesignated Secretary of Health and Human Services by section 3508(b) of Title 20, Education.

TERMINATION OF WAR

Termination of war with respect to article IV of Soldiers' and Sailors' Civil Relief Act, referred to in text, see note set out under section 584 of this Appendix.

§465. Notice of requirements of Act; voluntary enlistments unaffected

(a) Every person shall be deemed to have notice of the requirements of this title [sections 451 to 471a of this Appendix] upon publication by the President of a proclamation or other public notice fixing a time for any registration under section 3 [section 453 of this Appendix].

(b) It shall be the duty of every registrant to keep his local board informed as to his current address and changes in status as required by such rules and regulations as may be prescribed by the President.

(c) If any provision of this title [sections 451 to 471a of this Appendix], or the application thereof to any person or circumstance, is held invalid, the remainder of the title [said sections], and the application of such provision to other persons or circumstances, shall not be affected thereby.

(d) Except as provided in section 4(c) [section 454(c) of this Appendix], nothing contained in this title [sections 451 to 471a of this Appendix] shall be construed to repeal, amend, or suspend the laws now in force authorizing voluntary enlistment or reenlistment in the Armed Forces of the United States, including the reserve components thereof, except that no person shall be accepted for enlistment after he has been issued an order to report for induction unless authorized by the Director and the Secretary of Defense and except that, whenever the Congress or the

President has declared that the national interest is imperiled, voluntary enlistment or reenlistment in such forces, and their reserve components, may be suspended by the President to such extent as he may deem necessary in the interest of national defense.

(e) In order to assist the Armed Forces in recruiting individuals for voluntary service in the Armed Forces, the Director shall, upon the request of the Secretary of Defense or the Secretary of Transportation, furnish to the Secretary the names and addresses of individuals registered under this Act. Names and addresses furnished pursuant to the preceding sentence may be used by the Secretary of Defense or Secretary of Transportation only for recruiting purposes.

(June 24, 1948, ch. 625, title I, § 15, 62 Stat. 624; Pub. L. 92–129, title I, § 101(a)(33), Sept. 28, 1971, 85 Stat. 353; Pub. L. 97–86, title IX, § 916(c), Dec. 1, 1981, 95 Stat. 1129.)

REFERENCES IN TEXT

This Act, referred to in subsec. (e), is act June 24, 1948, ch. 625, 62 Stat. 604, as amended, known as the Military Selective Service Act. For complete classification of this Act to the Code, see References in Text note set out under section 451 of this Appendix and Tables.

AMENDMENTS

1981—Subsec. (e). Pub. L. 97–86 added subsec. (e).

1971—Subsec. (d). Pub. L. 92–129 inserted provision empowering the Director and the Secretary of Defense to authorize voluntary enlistments and reenlistments in the Armed Forces after a person has been issued an order to report for induction and struck out reference to section 454(g) of this Appendix.

SECTION REFERRED TO IN OTHER SECTIONS

This section is referred to in section 456 of this Appendix.

§ 466. Definitions

When used in this title [sections 451 to 471a of this Appendix]—

(a) The term "between the ages of eighteen and twenty-six" shall refer to men who have attained the eighteenth anniversary of the day of their birth and who have not attained the twenty-sixth anniversary of the day of their birth; and other terms designating different age groups shall be construed in a similar manner.

(b) The term "United States", when used in a geographical sense, shall be deemed to mean the several States, the District of Columbia, Puerto Rico, the Virgin Islands, and Guam.

(c) The term "armed forces" shall be deemed to include the Army, the Navy, the Marine Corps, the Air Force, and the Coast Guard.

(d) The term "district court of the United States" shall be deemed to include the courts of the United States for the Territories and possessions of the United States.

(e) The term "local board" shall be deemed to include an intercounty local board in the case of any registrant who is subject to the jurisdiction of an intercounty local board.

(f) The term "Director" shall be deemed to mean the Director of the Selective Service System.

(g)(1) The term "duly ordained minister of religion" means a person who has been ordained, in accordance with the ceremonial, ritual, or discipline of a church, religious sect, or organization established on the basis of a community of faith and belief, doctrines and practices of a religious character, to preach and to teach the doctrines of such church, sect, or organization and to administer the rites and ceremonies thereof in public worship, and who as his regular and customary vocation preaches and teaches the principles of religion and administers the ordinances of public worship as embodied in the creed or principles of such church, sect, or organization.

(2) The term "regular minister of religion" means one who as his customary vocation preaches and teaches the principles of religion of a church, a religious sect, or organization of which he is a member, without having been formally ordained as a minister of religion, and who is recognized by such church, sect, or organization as a regular minister.

(3) The term "regular or duly ordained minister of religion" does not include a person who irregularly or incidentally preaches and teaches the principles of religion of a church, religious sect, or organization and does not include any person who may have been duly ordained a minister in accordance with the ceremonial, rite, or discipline of a church, religious sect or organization, but who does not regularly, as a bona fide vocation, teach and preach the principles of religion and administer the ordinances of public worship as embodied in the creed or principles of his church, sect, or organization.

(h) The term "organized unit", when used with respect to a reserve component, shall be deemed to mean a unit in which the members thereof are required satisfactorily to participate in scheduled drills and training periods as prescribed by the Secretary of Defense.

(i) The term "reserve components of the armed forces" shall, unless the context otherwise requires, be deemed to include the federally recognized National Guard of the United States, the federally recognized Air National Guard of the United States, the Officers' Reserve Corps, the Regular Army Reserve, the Air Force Reserve, the Enlisted Reserve Corps, the Naval Reserve, the Marine Corps Reserve, and the Coast Guard Reserve, and shall include, in addition to the foregoing, the Public Health Service Reserve when serving with the armed forces.

(June 24, 1948, ch. 625, title I, § 16, 62 Stat. 624; Sept. 27, 1950, ch. 1059, § 1(12), (13), 64 Stat. 1074; June 19, 1951, ch. 144, title I, § 1(v), 65 Stat. 87; Pub. L. 86–70, § 36, June 25, 1959, 73 Stat. 150; Pub. L. 86–624, § 39, July 12, 1960, 74 Stat. 422; Pub. L. 92–129, title I, § 101(a)(34), Sept. 28, 1971, 85 Stat. 353.)

AMENDMENTS

1971—Subsec. (g)(3). Pub. L. 92–129 inserted "bona fide" before "vocation".

1960—Subsec. (b). Pub. L. 86–624 struck out "Hawaii," before "Puerto Rico".

1959—Subsec. (b). Pub. L. 86–70 struck out "Alaska," after "District of Columbia,".

1951—Subsec. (b). Act June 19, 1951, brought "Guam" within definition of "United States".

1950—Subsec. (c). Act Sept. 27, 1950, § 1(12), struck out "and" after "Corps" and inserted ", and the Coast Guard" before the period.

Subsec. (i). Act Sept. 27, 1950, § 1(13), struck out "and" after "Naval Reserve" and ", the Coast Guard Reserve" after "foregoing" and inserted "and the Coast Guard Reserve" after "Marine Corps Reserve".

TRANSFER OF FUNCTIONS

Coast Guard transferred to Department of Transportation, and functions, powers, and duties relating to Coast Guard of Secretary of the Treasury and of all other officers and offices of Department of the Treasury transferred to Secretary of Transportation by Pub. L. 89–670, § 6(b)(1), Oct. 15, 1966, 80 Stat. 938. Section 6(b)(2) of Pub. L. 89–670, however, provided that notwithstanding such transfer of functions, Coast Guard shall operate as part of Navy in time of war or when President directs as provided in section 3 of Title 14, Coast Guard. See section 108 of Title 49, Transportation.

For transfer of functions of other officers, employees, and agencies of Department of the Treasury, with certain exceptions, to Secretary of the Treasury with power to delegate, see Reorg. Plan No. 26 of 1950, §§ 1, 2, eff. July 31, 1950, 15 F.R. 4935, 64 Stat. 1280, 1281, set out in the Appendix to Title 5, Government Organization and Employees. Functions of Coast Guard, and Commandant of Coast Guard, excepted from transfer when Coast Guard is operating as part of Navy under sections 1 and 3 of Title 14, Coast Guard.

Functions of Public Health Service, Surgeon General of Public Health Service, and all other officers and employees of Public Health Service, and functions of all agencies of or in Public Health Service transferred to Secretary of Health, Education, and Welfare by Reorg. Plan No. 3 of 1966, eff. June 25, 1966, 31 F.R. 8855, 80 Stat. 1610, set out in the Appendix to Title 5, Government Organization and Employees. Secretary of Health, Education, and Welfare redesignated Secretary of Health and Human Services by section 3508(b) of Title 20, Education.

§ 467. Repeals; appropriations; termination date

(a) Except as provided in this title [sections 451 to 471a of this Appendix] all laws or any parts of laws in conflict with the provisions of the title [said sections] are repealed to the extent of such conflict.

(b) There are authorized to be appropriated, out of any money in the Treasury not otherwise appropriated, such sums as may be necessary to carry out the provisions of this title [sections 451 to 471a of this Appendix]. All funds appropriated for the administrative expenses of the National Security Training Commission shall be appropriated directly to the Commission and all funds appropriated to pay the expenses of training carried out by the military departments designated by the Commission shall be appropriated directly to the Department of Defense.

(c) Notwithstanding any other provisions of this title [sections 451 to 471a of this Appendix], no person shall be inducted for training and service in the Armed Forces after July 1, 1973, except persons now or hereafter deferred under section 6 of this title [section 456 of this Appendix] after the basis for such deferment ceases to exist.

(June 24, 1948, ch. 625, title I, § 17, 62 Stat. 625; June 23, 1950, ch. 351, 64 Stat. 254; June 30, 1950, ch. 445, § 1, 64 Stat. 318; June 19, 1951, ch. 144, title I, § 1(w), 65 Stat. 87; June 30, 1955, ch. 250, title I, § 102, 69 Stat. 224; Pub. L. 86–4, § 1, Mar. 23, 1959, 73 Stat. 13; Pub. L. 88–2, § 1, Mar. 28, 1963, 77 Stat. 4; Pub. L. 90–40, § 1(12), June 30, 1967, 81 Stat. 105; Pub. L. 92–129, title I, § 101(a)(35), Sept. 28, 1971, 85 Stat. 353.)

AMENDMENTS

1971—Subsec. (c). Pub. L. 92–129 extended termination date from July 1, 1971, to July 1, 1973.

1967—Subsec. (c). Pub. L. 90–40 extended termination date from July 1, 1967, to July 1, 1971.

1963—Subsec. (c). Pub. L. 88–2 extended termination date from July 1, 1963, to July 1, 1967.

1959—Subsec. (c). Pub. L. 86–4 extended termination date from July 1, 1959, to July 1, 1963.

1955—Subsec. (c). Act June 30, 1955, extended termination date from July 1, 1955, to July 1, 1959.

1951—Act June 19, 1951, amended section generally to provide for repeal of all conflicting laws, to appropriate certain funds directly to the Commission, and to provide for the termination date of July 1, 1955.

1950—Subsec. (b). Acts June 23, 1950 and June 30, 1950, extended period of effectiveness for fifteen days until July 9, 1950, and again from July 9, 1950, to July 9, 1951.

EFFECTIVE DATE OF 1971 AMENDMENT

Section 101(a)(35) of Pub. L. 92–129 provided in part that: "The amendment made by the preceding sentence [amending this section] shall take effect July 2, 1971."

TERMINATION OF NATIONAL SECURITY TRAINING COMMISSION

National Security Training Commission expired June 30, 1957, pursuant to a Presidential letter on Mar. 25, 1957, following its own recommendation for its termination.

§ 468. Utilization of industry

(a) Placement of orders; Congressional action: notification of committees of certain proposed payment orders, resolution of disapproval, continuity of session, computation of period; "small business" defined

Whenever the President after consultation with and receiving advice from the National Security Resources Board[1] determines that it is in the interest of the national security for the Government to obtain prompt delivery of any articles or materials the procurement of which has been authorized by the Congress exclusively for the use of the armed forces of the United States, or for the use of the Atomic Energy Commission,[1] he is authorized, through the head of any Government agency, to place with any person operating a plant, mine, or other facility capable of producing such articles or materials an order for such quantity of such articles or materials as the President deems appropriate, except that no order which requires payments thereunder in excess of $25,000,000 shall be placed with any person unless the Committees on Armed Services of the Senate and the House of Representatives have been notified in writing of such proposed order and 60 days of continuous session of Congress have expired following the date on which such notice was transmitted to such Committees and neither House of Congress has adopted, within such 60-day period, a resolution disapproving such order. For purposes of the preceding sentence, the continuity of a session of Congress is broken only by an adjournment of the Congress sine die, and the days on which either House is not in session because of an adjournment of more than 3 days to a day certain are excluded in the computation of such 60-day period. Any person with whom an order is placed pursuant to the provisions of this section

[1] See Transfer of Functions note below.

shall be advised that such order is placed pursuant to the provisions of this section. Under any such program of national procurement, the President shall recognize the valid claim of American small business to participate in such contracts, in such manufactures, and in such distribution of materials, and small business shall be granted a fair share of the orders placed, exclusively for the use of the armed forces or for other Federal agencies now or hereafter designated in this section. For the purposes of this section, a business enterprise shall be determined to be "small business" if (1) its position in the trade or industry of which it is a part is not dominant, (2) the number of its employees does not exceed 500, and (3) it is independently owned and operated.

(b) Precedence of Government placed orders

It shall be the duty of any person with whom an order is placed pursuant to the provisions of subsection (a), (1) to give such order such precedence with respect to all other orders (Government or private) theretofore or thereafter placed with such person as the President may prescribe, and (2) to fill such order within the period of time prescribed by the President or as soon thereafter as possible.

(c) Failure to give precedence; Government possession

In case any person with whom an order is placed pursuant to the provisions of subsection (a) of this section refuses or fails—

(1) to give such order such precedence with respect to all other orders (Government or private) theretofore or thereafter placed with such person as the President may have prescribed;

(2) to fill such order within the period of time prescribed by the President or as soon thereafter as possible as determined by the President;

(3) to produce the kind or quality of articles or materials ordered; or

(4) to furnish the quantity, kind, and quality of articles or materials ordered at such price as shall be negotiated between such person and the Government agency concerned; or in the event of failure to negotiate a price, to furnish the quantity, kind, and quality of articles or materials ordered at such price as he may subsequently be determined to be entitled to receive under subsection (d);

the President is authorized to take immediate possession of any plant, mine, or other facility of such person and to operate it, through any Government agency, for the production of such articles or materials as may be required by the Government.

(d) Payment of compensation by United States

Fair and just compensation shall be paid by the United States (1) for any articles or materials furnished pursuant to an order placed under subsection (a) of this section, or (2) as rental for any plant, mine, or other facility of which possession is taken under subsection (c).

(e) Application of Federal and State laws governing employees

Nothing contained in this section shall be deemed to render inapplicable to any plant, mine, or facility of which possession is taken pursuant to subsection (c) any State or Federal laws concerning the health, safety, security, or employment standards of employees.

(f) Penalties

Any person, or any officer of any person as defined in this section, who willfully fails or refuses to carry out any duty imposed upon him by subsection (b) of this section shall be guilty of a felony and, upon conviction thereof, shall be punished by imprisonment for not more than three years, or by a fine of not more than $50,000, or by both such imprisonment and fine.

(g) "Person" and "Government agency" defined

(1) As used in this section—

(A) The term "person" means any individual, firm, company, association, corporation, or other form of business organization.

(B) The term "Government agency" means any department, agency, independent establishment, or corporation in the Executive branch of the United States Government.

(2) For the purposes of this section, a plant, mine, or other facility shall be deemed capable of producing any articles or materials if it is then producing or furnishing such articles or materials or if the President after consultation with and receiving advice from the National Security Resources Board determines that it can be readily converted to the production or furnishing of such articles or materials.

(h) Rules and regulations governing steel industry; mandatory

The President is empowered, through the Secretary of Defense, to require all producers of steel in the United States to make available, to individuals, firms, associations, companies, corporations, or organized manufacturing industries having orders for steel products or steel materials required by the armed forces, such percentages of the steel production of such producers, in equal proportion deemed necessary for the expeditious execution of orders for such products or materials. Compliance with such requirement shall be obligatory on all such producers of steel and such requirement shall take precedence over all orders and contracts theretofore placed with such producers. If any such producer of steel or the responsible head or heads thereof refuses to comply with such requirement, the President, through the Secretary of Defense, is authorized to take immediate possession of the plant or plants of such producer and, through the appropriate branch, bureau, or department of the armed forces, to insure compliance with such requirement. Any such producer of steel or the responsible head or heads thereof refusing to comply with such requirement shall be deemed guilty of a felony and upon conviction thereof shall be punished by imprisonment for not more than three years and a fine not exceeding $50,000.

(June 24, 1948, ch. 625, title I, § 18, 62 Stat. 625; Pub. L. 93–155, title VIII, § 807(d), Nov. 16, 1973, 87 Stat. 616; Pub. L. 101–510, div. A, title XIII, § 1303(c), Nov. 5, 1990, 104 Stat. 1669.)

AMENDMENTS

1990—Subsec. (h). Pub. L. 101–510 struck out "(1)" before "The President is empowered" and struck out par.

(2) which read as follows: "The President shall report to the Congress on the final day of each six-month period following the date of enactment of this Act the percentage figure, or if such information is not available, the approximate percentage figure, of the total steel production in the United States required to be made available during such period for the execution of orders for steel products and steel materials required by the armed forces, if such percentage figure is in excess of 10 per centum."

1973—Subsec. (a). Pub. L. 93–155 provided for notification of Congressional Committees with respect to certain proposed payment orders, Congressional resolution of disapproval, continuity of Congressional session, and computation of period.

TRANSFER OF FUNCTIONS

Functions of Chairman of National Security Resources Board under this section, with respect to being consulted by and furnishing advice to President as required by this section, abolished by Reorg. Plan No. 3 of 1953, §5(a), eff. June 12, 1953, 18 F.R. 3375, 67 Stat. 634, set out in the Appendix to Title 5, Government Organization and Employees.

National Security Resources Board, together with its functions, records, property, personnel, and unexpended balances of appropriations, allocations, and other funds (available or to be made available) transferred to Executive Office of President by Reorg. Plan No. 4 of 1949, eff. Aug. 19, 1949, 14 F.R. 5227, 63 Stat. 1067, set out in the Appendix to Title 5, Government Organization and Employees. For subsequent transfers to Office of Defense Mobilization, Office of Emergency Planning, Office of Emergency Preparedness, and President, see notes set out under section 404 of this title.

Atomic Energy Commission abolished and functions transferred by sections 5814 and 5841 of Title 42, The Public Health and Welfare. See also Transfer of Functions notes set out under those sections.

DELEGATION OF AUTHORITY

For delegation of President's authority under this section with respect to placing of orders for prompt delivery of articles or materials, see section 102 of Ex. Ord. No. 12742, Jan. 8, 1991, 56 F.R. 1079, set out as a note under section 82 of Title 50, War and National Defense.

OBLIGATIONS ENTERED INTO BEFORE NOVEMBER 16, 1973

Amendment by Pub. L. 93–155 not affecting the carrying out of any contract, loan, guarantee, commitment, or other obligation entered into prior to Nov. 16, 1973, see section 807(e) of Pub. L. 93–155, set out as a note under section 2307 of Title 10, Armed Forces.

§469. Savings provision

Nothing in this title [sections 451 to 471a of this Appendix] shall be deemed to amend any provision of the National Security Act of 1947 (61 Stat. 495).

(June 24, 1948, ch. 625, title I, §19, 62 Stat. 627.)

REFERENCES IN TEXT

The National Security Act of 1947 (61 Stat. 495), referred to in text, is act July 26, 1947, ch. 343, 61 Stat. 495, as amended. For complete classification of this Act to the Code, see Short Title note set out under section 401 of Title 50, War and National Defense, and Tables.

§470. Effective date

This title [sections 451 to 471a of this Appendix] shall become effective immediately; except that unless the President, or the Congress by concurrent resolution, declares a national emergency after the date of enactment of this Act [June 24, 1948], no person shall be inducted or ordered into active service without his consent under this title [said sections] within ninety days after the date of its enactment.

(June 24, 1948, ch. 625, title I, §20, 62 Stat. 627; Sept. 27, 1950, ch. 1059, §1(14), 64 Stat. 1074; Aug. 10, 1956, ch. 1041, §53, 70A Stat. 641.)

AMENDMENTS

1956—Act Aug. 10, 1956, repealed provisions requiring the Secretaries of the Army, Navy, and the Treasury to initiate and carry forward intensified voluntary enlistment campaigns for the Army, Air Force, Navy, Marine Corps, and the Coast Guard, which provisions are now covered by sections 3255 and 5531 of Title 10, Armed Forces, and section 350 of Title 14, Coast Guard.

1950—Act Sept. 27, 1950, struck out "and" after "Air Force" and inserted "and the Secretary of the Treasury, for the Coast Guard" after "Marine Corps".

§471. Authority of President to order Reserve components to active service; release from active duty; retention of unit organizations and equipment

Until July 1, 1953, and subject to the limitations imposed by section 2 of the Selective Service Act of 1948, as amended [section 452 of this Appendix], the President shall be authorized to order into the active military or naval service of the United States for a period of not to exceed twenty-four consecutive months, with or without their consent, any or all members and units of any or all Reserve components of the Armed Forces of the United States and retired personnel of the Regular Armed Forces. Unless he is sooner released under regulations prescribed by the Secretary of the military department concerned, any member of the inactive or volunteer reserve who served on active duty for a period of 12 months or more in any branch of the Armed Forces between the period December 7, 1941, and September 2, 1945, inclusive, who is now or may hereafter be ordered to active duty pursuant to this section, shall upon completion of 17 or more months of active duty since June 25, 1950, if he makes application therefor to the Secretary of the branch of service in which he is serving, be released from active duty and shall not thereafter be ordered to active duty for periods in excess of 30 days without his consent except in time of war or national emergency hereafter declared by the Congress: *Provided*, That the foregoing shall not apply to any member of the inactive or volunteer reserve ordered to active duty whose rating or specialty is found by the Secretary of the military department concerned to be critical and whose release to inactive duty prior to the period for which he was ordered to active duty would impair the efficiency of the military department concerned.

The President may retain the unit organizations and the equipment thereof, exclusive of the individual members thereof, in the active Federal service for a total period of five consecutive years, and upon being relieved by the appropriate Secretary from active Federal service, National Guard, or Air National Guard units, shall, insofar as practicable, be returned to their National Guard or Air National Guard status in their respective States, Territories, the District of Columbia, and Puerto Rico, with pertinent records, colors, histories, trophies, and other historical impedimenta.

(June 24, 1948, ch. 625, title I, §21, as added June 30, 1950, ch. 445, §2, 64 Stat. 318; amended June 19, 1951, ch. 144, title I, §1(x), 65 Stat. 87; July 7, 1952, ch. 584, §1, 66 Stat. 440.)

AMENDMENTS

1952—Act July 7, 1952, authorized the President to retain unit organizations and their equipment, exclusive of individual members, for a period of five years.

1951—Act June 19, 1951, substituted "July 1, 1953" for "July 9, 1951", "twenty-four months" for "twenty-one months", and inserted last sentence.

EX. ORD. NO. 10271. DELEGATION OF PRESIDENT'S AUTHORITY

Ex. Ord. No. 10271, July 7, 1951, 16 F.R. 6661, provided:

There is hereby delegated to the Secretary of Defense the authority vested in the President by section 21 of the Universal Military Training and Service Act (64 Stat. 318), as amended by the 1951 Amendments to the Universal Military Training and Service Act (65 Stat. 87; Public Law 51, 82d Congress) [this section], to order into the active military or naval service of the United States for a period not to exceed twenty-four months, with or without their consent, any or all members and units of any or all Reserve components of the Armed Forces of the United States and retired personnel of the Regular Armed Forces: *Provided*, that so much of the authority of the President under the said section 21, as amended [this section], as relates to any Reserve component of the United States Coast Guard or to retired personnel of the Regular Coast Guard is hereby delegated to the Secretary of the Treasury.

The Secretary of Defense is hereby authorized to redelegate, subject to such conditions as the Secretary may deem appropriate, to the Secretaries of the Army, Navy, and Air Force such functions under this order as affect their respective services.

HARRY S TRUMAN.

§471a. Procedural rights

(a) It is hereby declared to be the purpose of this section to guarantee to each registrant asserting a claim before a local or appeal board, a fair hearing consistent with the informal and expeditious processing which is required by selective service cases.

(b) Pursuant to such rules and regulations as the President may prescribe—

(1) Each registrant shall be afforded the opportunity to appear in person before the local or any appeal board of the Selective Service System to testify and present evidence regarding his status.

(2) Subject to reasonable limitations on the number of witnesses and the total time allotted to each registrant, each registrant shall have the right to present witnesses on his behalf before the local board.

(3) A quorum of any local board or appeal board shall be present during the registrant's personal appearance.

(4) In the event of a decision adverse to the claim of a registrant, the local or appeal board making such decision shall, upon request, furnish to such registrant a brief written statement of the reasons for its decision.

(June 24, 1948, ch. 625, title I, §22, as added Pub. L. 92–129, title I, §101(a)(36), Sept. 28, 1971, 85 Stat. 353.)

§472. Period of increased service applicable to all personnel

Wherever in this amendatory Act the period of active service for any category of persons is increased, such increased period of service shall be applicable to all persons in such category serving on active duty in the Armed Forces on the date of the enactment of this amendatory Act [June 19, 1951].

(June 19, 1951, ch. 144, title I, §4, 65 Stat. 88.)

CODIFICATION

Section was enacted as part of the 1951 Amendments to the Universal Military Training and Service Act, and not as part of the Military Selective Service Act, title I of which comprises sections 451 to 471a of this Appendix.

§473. Regulations governing liquor sales; penalties

Subject to section 2683(c) of title 10, United States Code, the Secretary of Defense is authorized to make such regulations as he may deem to be appropriate governing the sale, consumption, possession of or traffic in beer, wine, or any other intoxicating liquors to or by members of the Armed Forces or the National Security Training Corps at or near any camp, station, post, or other place primarily occupied by members of the Armed Forces or the National Security Training Corps. Any person, corporation, partnership, or association who knowingly violates the regulations which may be made hereunder shall, unless otherwise punishable under the Uniform Code of Military Justice, be deemed guilty of a misdemeanor and be punished by a fine of not more than $1,000 or imprisonment for not more than twelve months, or both.

(June 19, 1951, ch. 144, title I, §6, 65 Stat. 88; Pub. L. 99–145, title XII, §1224(b)(2), Nov. 8, 1985, 99 Stat. 729.)

REFERENCES IN TEXT

The Uniform Code of Military Justice, referred to in text, is classified generally to chapter 47 (§801 et seq.) of Title 10, Armed Forces.

CODIFICATION

Section was enacted as a part of the 1951 Amendments to the Universal Military Training and Service Act, and not as a part of the Military Selective Service Act, title I of which comprises sections 451 to 471a of this Appendix.

AMENDMENTS

1985—Pub. L. 99–145 substituted "Subject to section 2683(c) of title 10, United States Code, the" for "The".

EFFECTIVE DATE OF 1985 AMENDMENT

Amendment by Pub. L. 99–145 effective 90 days after Nov. 8, 1985, see section 1224(d) of Pub. L. 99–145, set out as a note under section 2683 of Title 10, Armed Forces.

SOLDIERS' AND SAILORS' CIVIL RELIEF ACT OF 1940

ACT OCT. 17, 1940, CH. 888, 54 STAT. 1178

EXTENSION OF BENEFITS TO INDUCTEES UNDER UNIVERSAL MILITARY TRAINING AND SERVICE ACT

The benefits of the Soldiers' and Sailors' Civil Relief Act of 1940 (see section 501 of this Appendix) are extended to inductees under the Universal Military Training and Service Act by section 464 of this Appendix.

SOLDIERS' AND SAILORS' CIVIL RELIEF ACT OF 1918

Former provisions on this subject were contained in act Mar. 8, 1918, ch. 20, 40 Stat. 440, known as the Soldiers' and Sailors' Civil Relief Act of 1918, section 101 et seq. of this Appendix.

ACT REFERRED TO IN OTHER SECTIONS

This Act is referred to in section 464 of this Appendix; title 5 sections 5520a, 5569; title 10 section 1408; title 26 section 7654; title 33 section 857–3; title 42 section 213.

§501. Short title

This Act [sections 501 to 593 of this Appendix] may be cited as the Soldiers' and Sailors' Civil Relief Act of 1940.

(Oct. 17, 1940, ch. 888, §1, 54 Stat. 1178.)

SHORT TITLE OF 1991 AMENDMENT

Pub. L. 102–12, §1, Mar. 18, 1991, 105 Stat. 34, provided that: "This Act [enacting sections 518, 592, and 593 of this Appendix, amending sections 511 to 513, 515, 516, 525, 526, 530 to 532, 534, 535, 540 to 545, 547, 564 to 567, 570, 574, 580, 581, 584, and 591 of this Appendix and sections 2021 and 2024 of Title 38, Veterans' Benefits, repealing section 548 of this Appendix, and enacting provisions set out as notes under sections 521 and 530 of this Appendix and sections 2021 and 2024 of Title 38] may be cited as the 'Soldiers' and Sailors' Civil Relief Act Amendments of 1991'."

SHORT TITLE OF 1942 AMENDMENT

Act Oct. 6, 1942, ch. 581, §1, 56 Stat. 769, provided: "That this Act [enacting sections 514 to 517, 526, 533 to 536, 574, and 590 of this Appendix and amending sections 513, 525, 530 to 532, 540 to 548, 560, 569, and 572 of this Appendix] may be cited as the 'Soldiers' and Sailors' Civil Relief Act Amendments of 1942'."

ARTICLE I—GENERAL PROVISIONS

ARTICLE REFERRED TO IN OTHER SECTIONS

This article is referred to in section 516 of this Appendix.

§510. Purpose; suspension of enforcement of civil liabilities

In order to provide for, strengthen, and expedite the national defense under the emergent conditions which are threatening the peace and security of the United States and to enable the United States the more successfully to fulfill the requirements of the national defense, provision is made to suspend enforcement of civil liabilities, in certain cases, of persons in the military service of the United States in order to enable such persons to devote their entire energy to the defense needs of the Nation, and to this end the following provisions are made for the temporary suspension of legal proceedings and transactions which may prejudice the civil rights of persons in such service during the period herein specified over which this Act [sections 501 to 593 of this Appendix] remains in force.

(Oct. 17, 1940, ch. 888, art. I, §100, 54 Stat. 1179.)

§511. Definitions

(1) The term "person in the military service", the term "persons in military service", and the term "persons in the military service of the United States", as used in this Act [sections 501 to 593 of this Appendix], shall include the following persons and not other: All members of the Army of the United States, the United States Navy, the Marine Corps, the Air Force, the Coast Guard, and all officers of the Public Health Service detailed by proper authority for duty either with the Army or the Navy. The term "military service", as used in this Act [said sections], shall signify Federal service on active duty with any branch of service heretofore referred to or mentioned as well as training or education under the supervision of the United States preliminary to induction into the military service. The terms "active service" or "active duty" shall include the period during which a person in military service is absent from duty on account of sickness, wounds, leave, or other lawful cause.

(2) The term "period of military service", as used in this Act [said sections], means, in the case of any person, the period beginning on the date on which the person enters active service and ending on the date of the person's release from active service or death while in active service, but in no case later than the date when this Act [said sections] ceases to be in force.

(3) The term "person", when used in this Act [said sections], with reference to the holder of any right alleged to exist against a person in military service or against a person secondarily liable under such right, shall include individuals, partnerships, corporations, and any other forms of business association.

(4) The term "court", as used in this Act [said sections], shall include any court of competent jurisdiction of the United States or of any State, whether or not a court of record.

(Oct. 17, 1940, ch. 888, art. I, §101, 54 Stat. 1179; Pub. L. 92–540, title V, §504(1), Oct. 24, 1972, 86 Stat. 1098; Pub. L. 102–12, §9(1), Mar. 18, 1991, 105 Stat. 38.)

AMENDMENTS

1991—Par. (1). Pub. L. 102–12, §9(1)(A), inserted "the Air Force," after "the Marine Corps,".

Par. (2). Pub. L. 102–12, §9(1)(B), substituted "means, in the case of any person, the period beginning on the date on which the person enters active service and ending on the date of the person's release" for "shall include the time between the following dates: For persons in active service at the date of approval of this Act it shall begin with the date of approval of this Act; for persons entering active service after the date of this Act, with the date of entering active service. It shall terminate with the date of discharge".

1972—Par. (1). Pub. L. 92–540 inserted provision relating to "person in the military service".

EFFECTIVE DATE OF 1972 AMENDMENT

Amendment by Pub. L. 92–540 effective 90 days after Oct. 24, 1972, see section 601(b) of Pub. L. 92–540, set out as a note under section 4101 of Title 38, Veterans' Benefits.

TRANSFER OF FUNCTIONS

Coast Guard transferred to Department of Transportation, and functions, powers, and duties relating to Coast Guard of Secretary of the Treasury and of all other officers and offices of Department of the Treasury transferred to Secretary of Transportation, by Pub. L. 89–670, §6(b)(1), Oct. 15, 1966, 80 Stat. 938. Section 6(b)(2) of Pub. L. 89–670, however, provided that notwithstanding such transfer of functions, Coast Guard shall operate as part of Navy in time of war or when President directs as provided in section 3 of Title 14, Coast Guard. See section 108 of Title 49, Transportation.

For transfer of functions of other officers, employees, and agencies of Department of the Treasury, with certain exceptions, to Secretary of the Treasury with power to delegate, see Reorg. Plan No. 26 of 1950, §§1, 2, eff. July 31, 1950, 15 F.R. 4935, 64 Stat. 1280, 1281, set out in the Appendix to Title 5, Government Organization and Employees. Functions of Coast Guard, and Commandant of Coast Guard, excepted from transfer when Coast Guard is operating as part of Navy under sections 1 and 3 of Title 14, Coast Guard.

Functions of Public Health Service, Surgeon General of Public Health Service, and all other officers and employees of Public Health Service, and functions of all agencies of or in Public Health Service transferred to Secretary of Health, Education, and Welfare by Reorg. Plan No. 3 of 1966, eff. June 25, 1966, 31 F.R. 8855, 80 Stat. 1610, set out in the Appendix to Title 5, Government Organization and Employees. Secretary of Health, Education, and Welfare redesignated Secretary of Health and Human Services by section 3508(b) of Title 20, Education.

SECTION REFERRED TO IN OTHER SECTIONS

This section is referred to in section 540 of this Appendix.

§512. Territorial application; jurisdiction of courts; form of procedure

(1) The provisions of this Act [sections 501 to 593 of this Appendix] shall apply to the United States, the several States and Territories, the District of Columbia, and all territory subject to the jurisdiction of the United States and to proceedings commenced in any court therein, and shall be enforced through the usual forms of procedure obtaining in such courts or under such regulations as may be by them prescribed.

(2) When under this Act [sections 501 to 593 of this Appendix], any application is required to be made to a court in which no proceeding has already been commenced with respect to the matter, such application may be made to any court.

(Oct. 17, 1940, ch. 888, art. I, §102, 54 Stat. 1179; Pub. L. 102–12, §9(2), Mar. 18, 1991, 105 Stat. 39.)

AMENDMENTS

1991—Par. (1). Pub. L. 102–12 struck out provision including the Philippine Islands while under sovereignty of the United States within territories to which this Act applies.

§513. Protection of persons secondarily liable

(1) Whenever pursuant to any of the provisions of this Act [sections 501 to 593 of this Appendix] the enforcement of any obligation or liability, the prosecution of any suit or proceeding, the entry or enforcement of any order, writ, judgment, or decree, or the performance of any other act, may be stayed, postponed, or suspended, such stay, postponement, or suspension may, in the discretion of the court, likewise be granted to sureties, guarantors, endorsers, accommodation makers, and others, whether primarily or secondarily subject to the obligation or liability, the performance or enforcement of which is stayed, postponed, or suspended.

(2) When a judgment or decree is vacated or set aside in whole or in part, as provided in this Act [sections 501 to 593 of this Appendix], the same may, in the discretion of the court, likewise be set aside and vacated as to any surety, guarantor, endorser, accommodation maker, or other person whether primarily or secondarily liable upon the contract or liability for the enforcement of which the judgment or decree was entered.

(3) Whenever, by reason of the military service of a principal upon a criminal bail bond the sureties upon such bond are prevented from enforcing the attendance of their principal and performing their obligation the court shall not enforce the provisions of such bond during the military service of the principal thereon and may in accordance with principles of equity and justice either during or after such service discharge such sureties and exonerate the bail.

(4) Nothing contained in this Act [sections 501 to 593 of this Appendix] shall prevent a waiver in writing of the benefits afforded by subsections (1) and (2) of this section by any surety, guarantor, endorser, accommodation maker, or other person whether primarily or secondarily liable upon the obligation or liability, except that no such waiver shall be valid unless it is executed as an instrument separate from the obligation or liability in respect of which it applies, and no such waiver shall be valid after the beginning of the period of military service if executed by an individual who subsequent to the execution of such waiver becomes a person in military service, or if executed by a dependent of such individual, unless executed by such individual or dependent during the period specified in section 106 [section 516 of this Appendix].

(Oct. 17, 1940, ch. 888, art. I, §103, 54 Stat. 1179; Oct. 6, 1942, ch. 581, §§2, 3, 56 Stat. 769; Pub. L. 102–12, §9(3), Mar. 18, 1991, 105 Stat. 39.)

AMENDMENTS

1991—Par. (4). Pub. L. 102–12, which directed that "after the date of the enactment of the Soldiers' and Sailors' Civil Relief Act Amendments of 1942" be struck out, was executed by striking out "after the date of enactment of the Soldiers' and Sailors' Civil Relief Act Amendments of 1942" before "no such waiver" to reflect the probable intent of Congress.

1942—Subsec. (1). Act Oct. 6, 1942, §2(a), substituted "accommodation makers, and others, whether primarily or secondarily" for "and others".

Subsec. (2). Act Oct. 6, 1942, §2(b), substituted "accommodation maker, or other person whether primarily or secondarily" for "or other person".

Subsecs. (3), (4). Act Oct. 6, 1942, §3, added subsecs. (3) and (4).

§514. Extension of benefits to citizens serving with forces of war allies

Persons who serve with the forces of any nation with which the United States may be allied in the prosecution of any war in which the United States engages while this Act [sections 501 to 593 of this Appendix] remains in force and who immediately prior to such service were citizens of the United States shall, except in those cases provided for in section 512 [section 572 of this Appendix], be entitled to the relief and benefits afforded by this Act [said sections] if such service is similar to military service as defined in this Act [said sections], unless they are dishonorably discharged therefrom, or it appears that they do not intend to resume United States citizenship.

(Oct. 17, 1940, ch. 888, art. I, §104, as added Oct. 6, 1942, ch. 581, §4, 56 Stat. 770.)

SECTION REFERRED TO IN OTHER SECTIONS

This section is referred to in title 5 section 5569.

§515. Notice of benefits to persons in and persons entering military service

The Secretary of Defense and the Secretary of Transportation, with respect to the Coast Guard when it is not operating as a service in the Navy, shall ensure the giving of notice of the benefits accorded by this Act [sections 501 to 593 of this Appendix] to persons in and to persons entering military service. The Director of Selective Service shall cooperate with the Secretary of Defense and the Secretary of Transportation in carrying out the provisions of this section.

(Oct. 17, 1940, ch. 888, art. I, §105, as added Oct. 6, 1942, ch. 581, §4, 56 Stat. 770; amended Pub. L. 102–12, §9(4), Mar. 18, 1991, 105 Stat. 39.)

AMENDMENTS

1991—Pub. L. 102–12 substituted "The Secretary of Defense and the Secretary of Transportation, with respect to the Coast Guard when it is not operating as a service in the Navy, shall ensure" for "The Secretary of War and the Secretary of the Navy shall make provision, in such manner as each may deem appropriate for his respective Department, to insure" in first sentence and "the Secretary of Defense and the Secretary of Transportation" for "the Secretary of War and the Secretary of the Navy" in second sentence.

SECTION REFERRED TO IN OTHER SECTIONS

This section is referred to in title 5 section 5569.

§516. Extension of benefits to persons ordered to report for induction or military service

Any person who has been ordered to report for induction under the Military Selective Service Act (50 U.S.C. App. 451 et seq.) shall be entitled to the relief and benefits accorded persons in military service under articles I, II, and III of this Act [sections 510 to 518, 520 to 527, and 530 to 536 of this Appendix] during the period beginning on the date of receipt of such order and ending on the date upon which such person reports for induction; and any member of a reserve component of the Armed Forces who is ordered to report for military service shall be entitled to such relief and benefits during the period beginning on the date of receipt of such order and ending on the date upon which such member reports for military service or the date on which the order is revoked, whichever is earlier.

(Oct. 17, 1940, ch. 888, art. I, §106, as added Oct. 6, 1942, ch. 581, §4, 56 Stat. 770; amended Pub. L. 102–12, §9(5), Mar. 18, 1991, 105 Stat. 39.)

REFERENCES IN TEXT

The Military Selective Service Act, referred to in text, is act June 24, 1948, ch. 625, 62 Stat. 604, as amended, which is classified principally to section 451 et seq. of this Appendix. For complete classification of this Act to the Code, see note set out under section 451 of this Appendix and Tables.

AMENDMENTS

1991—Pub. L. 102–12 substituted "Military Selective Service Act (50 U.S.C. App. 451 et seq.)" for "Selective Training and Service Act of 1940, as amended,", "a reserve component of the Armed Forces" for "the Enlisted Reserve Corps", and "such member reports for military service or the date on which the order is revoked, whichever is earlier" for "he reports for such service".

SECTION REFERRED TO IN OTHER SECTIONS

This section is referred to in sections 513, 517 of this Appendix; title 5 section 5569.

§517. Effect on rights, remedies, etc., pursuant to written agreements entered after commencement of military service

Nothing contained in this Act [sections 501 to 593 of this Appendix] shall prevent—

(a) the modification, termination, or cancellation of any contract, lease, or bailment or any obligation secured by mortgage, trust deed, lien, or other security in the nature of a mortgage, or

(b) the repossession, retention, foreclosure, sale, forfeiture, or taking possession of property which is security for any obligation or which has been purchased or received under a contract, lease, or bailment,

pursuant to a written agreement of the parties thereto (including the person in military service concerned, or the person to whom section 106 [section 516 of this Appendix] is applicable, whether or not such person is a party to the obligation), or their assignees, executed during or after the period of military service of the person concerned or during the period specified in section 106 [section 516 of this Appendix].

(Oct. 17, 1940, ch. 888, art. I, §107, as added Oct. 6, 1942, ch. 581, §4, 56 Stat. 770.)

SECTIONS REFERRED TO IN OTHER SECTIONS

This section is referred to in sections 531, 532 of this Appendix.

§518. Exercise of rights under Act not to affect certain future financial transactions

Application by a person in military service for, or receipt by a person in military service of, a stay, postponement, or suspension pursuant to the provisions of this Act [sections 501 to 593 of this Appendix] in the payment of any tax, fine, penalty, insurance premium, or other civil obligation or liability of that person shall not itself (without regard to other considerations) provide the basis for any of the following:

(1) A determination by any lender or other person that such person in military service is unable to pay such civil obligation or liability in accordance with its terms.

(2) With respect to a credit transaction between a creditor and such person in military service—

(A) a denial or revocation of credit by the creditor;

(B) a change by the creditor in the terms of an existing credit arrangement; or

(C) a refusal by the creditor to grant credit to such person in substantially the amount or on substantially the terms requested.

(3) An adverse report relating to the creditworthiness of such person in military service by or to any person or entity engaged in the practice of assembling or evaluating consumer credit information.

(4) A refusal by an insurer to insure such person.

(Oct. 17, 1940, ch. 888, art. I, §108, as added Pub. L. 102–12, §7, Mar. 18, 1991, 105 Stat. 38.)

ARTICLE II—GENERAL RELIEF

ARTICLE REFERRED TO IN OTHER SECTIONS

This article is referred to in section 516 of this Appendix.

§520. Default judgments; affidavits; bonds; attorneys for persons in service

(1) In any action or proceeding commenced in any court, if there shall be a default of any ap-

pearance by the defendant, the plaintiff, before entering judgment shall file in the court an affidavit setting forth facts showing that the defendant is not in military service. If unable to file such affidavit plaintiff shall in lieu thereof file an affidavit setting forth either that the defendant is in the military service or that plaintiff is not able to determine whether or not defendant is in such service. If an affidavit is not filed showing that the defendant is not in the military service, no judgment shall be entered without first securing an order of court directing such entry, and no such order shall be made if the defendant is in such service until after the court shall have appointed an attorney to represent defendant and protect his interest, and the court shall on application make such appointment. Unless it appears that the defendant is not in such service the court may require, as a condition before judgment is entered, that the plaintiff file a bond approved by the court conditioned to indemnify the defendant, if in military service, against any loss or damage that he may suffer by reason of any judgment should the judgment be thereafter set aside in whole or in part. And the court may make such other and further order or enter such judgment as in its opinion may be necessary to protect the rights of the defendant under this Act [sections 501 to 593 of this Appendix]. Whenever, under the laws applicable with respect to any court, facts may be evidenced, established, or proved by an unsworn statement, declaration, verification, or certificate, in writing, subscribed and certified or declared to be true under penalty of perjury, the filing of such an unsworn statement, declaration, verification, or certificate shall satisfy the requirement of this subsection that facts be established by affidavit.

(2) Any person who shall make or use an affidavit required under this section, or a statement, declaration, verification, or certificate certified or declared to be true under penalty of perjury permitted under subsection (1), knowing it to be false, shall be guilty of a misdemeanor and shall be punishable by imprisonment not to exceed one year or by fine not to exceed $1,000, or both.

(3) In any action or proceeding in which a person in military service is a party if such party does not personally appear therein or is not represented by an authorized attorney, the court may appoint an attorney to represent him; and in such case a like bond may be required and an order made to protect the rights of such person. But no attorney appointed under this Act [sections 501 to 593 of this Appendix], to protect a person in military service shall have power to waive any right of the person for whom he is appointed or bind him by his acts.

(4) If any judgment shall be rendered in any action or proceeding governed by this section against any person in military service during the period of such service or within thirty days thereafter, and it appears that such person was prejudiced by reason of his military service in making his defense thereto, such judgment may, upon application, made by such person or his legal representative, not later than ninety days after the termination of such service, be opened by the court rendering the same and such defendant or his legal representative let in to defend; provided it is made to appear that the defendant has a meritorious or legal defense to the action or some part thereof. Vacating, setting aside, or reversing any judgment because of any of the provisions of this Act [said sections], shall not impair any right or title acquired by any bona fide purchaser for value under such judgment.

(Oct. 17, 1940, ch. 888, art. II, §200, 54 Stat. 1180; Pub. L. 86–721, §§1, 2, Sept. 8, 1960, 74 Stat. 820.)

AMENDMENTS

1960—Subsec. (1). Pub. L. 86–721, §1, permitted establishment of certain facts by a declaration under penalty of perjury in lieu of an affidavit.

Subsec. (2). Pub. L. 86–721, §2, inserted "or a statement, declaration, verification, or certificate certified or declared to be true under penalty of perjury permitted under subsection (1)," after "affidavit required under this section,".

§521. Stay of proceedings where military service affects conduct thereof

At any stage thereof any action or proceeding in any court in which a person in military service is involved, either as plaintiff or defendant, during the period of such service or within sixty days thereafter may, in the discretion of the court in which it is pending, on its own motion, and shall, on application to it by such person or some person on his behalf, be stayed as provided in this Act [sections 501 to 593 of this Appendix] unless, in the opinion of the court, the ability of plaintiff to prosecute the action or the defendant to conduct his defense is not materially affected by reason of his military service.

(Oct. 17, 1940, ch. 888, art. II, §201, 54 Stat. 1181.)

STAY OF JUDICIAL PROCEEDINGS

Pub. L. 102–12, §6, Mar. 18, 1991, 105 Stat. 37, provided that:

"(a) STAY OF ACTION OR PROCEEDING.—In any judicial action or proceeding (other than a criminal proceeding) in which a member of the Armed Forces described in subsection (b) is involved (either as plaintiff or defendant), the court shall, upon application by such member (or some other person on the member's behalf) at any stage before final judgment is entered, stay the action or proceeding until a date after June 30, 1991.

"(b) MEMBERS COVERED.—A member of the Armed Forces is covered by subsection (a) if at the time of application for the stay of a judicial action or proceeding the member—

"(1) is on active duty; and

"(2) is serving outside the State in which the court having jurisdiction over the action or proceeding is located.

"(c) DEFINITION.—For purposes of this section, the term 'State' includes the District of Columbia, the Commonwealth of Puerto Rico, the Virgin Islands, and Guam."

§522. Fines and penalties on contracts, etc.

When an action for compliance with the terms of any contract is stayed pursuant to this Act [sections 501 to 593 of this Appendix] no fine or penalty shall accrue by reason of failure to comply with the terms of such contract during the period of such stay, and in any case where a person fails to perform any obligation and a fine or penalty for such nonperformance is incurred a court may, on such terms as may be just, relieve against the enforcement of such fine or penalty if it shall appear that the person who would suffer by such fine or penalty was in the military service when the penalty was incurred and that by reason of such service the ability of such person to pay or perform was thereby materially impaired.

(Oct. 17, 1940, ch. 888, art. II, § 202, 54 Stat. 1181.)

§ 523. Stay or vacation of execution of judgments, attachments, etc.

In any action or proceeding commenced in any court against a person in military service, before or during the period of such service, or within sixty days thereafter, the court may, in its discretion, on its own motion, or on application to it by such person or some person on his behalf shall, unless in the opinion of the court the ability of the defendant to comply with the judgment or order entered or sought is not materially affected by reason of his military service—

(a) Stay the execution of any judgment or order entered against such person, as provided in this Act [sections 501 to 593 of this Appendix]; and

(b) Vacate or stay any attachment or garnishment of property, money, or debts in the hands of another, whether before or after judgment as provided in this Act [said sections].

(Oct. 17, 1940, ch. 888, art. II, § 203, 54 Stat. 1181.)

§ 524. Duration and term of stays; codefendants not in service

Any stay of any action, proceeding, attachment, or execution, ordered by any court under the provisions of this Act [sections 501 to 593 of this Appendix] may, except as otherwise provided, be ordered for the period of military service and three months thereafter or any part of such period, and subject to such terms as may be just, whether as to payment in installments of such amounts and at such times as the court may fix or otherwise. Where the person in military service is a codefendant with others the plaintiff may nevertheless by leave of court proceed against the others.

(Oct. 17, 1940, ch. 888, art. II, § 204, 54 Stat. 1181.)

§ 525. Statutes of limitations as affected by period of service

The period of military service shall not be included in computing any period now or hereafter to be limited by any law, regulation, or order for the bringing of any action or proceeding in any court, board, bureau, commission, department, or other agency of government by or against any person in military service or by or against his heirs, executors, administrators, or assigns, whether such cause of action or the right or privilege to institute such action or proceeding shall have accrued prior to or during the period of such service, nor shall any part of such period which occurs after October 6, 1942 be included in computing any period now or hereafter provided by any law for the redemption of real property sold or forfeited to enforce any obligation, tax, or assessment.

(Oct. 17, 1940, ch. 888, art. II, § 205, 54 Stat. 1181; Oct. 6, 1942, ch. 581, § 5, 56 Stat. 770; Pub. L. 102–12, § 9(6), Mar. 18, 1991, 105 Stat. 39.)

AMENDMENTS

1991—Pub. L. 102–12 substituted "October 6, 1942" for "the date of enactment of the Soldiers' and Sailors' Civil Relief Act Amendments of 1942".

1942—Act Oct. 6, 1942, included proceedings before boards, bureaus, commissions, departments, or other agencies of government, and inserted provision for omission of service period in computing period for redemption of real property.

SECTION REFERRED TO IN OTHER SECTIONS

This section is referred to in section 527 of this Appendix.

§ 526. Maximum rate of interest

No obligation or liability bearing interest at a rate in excess of 6 percent per year incurred by a person in military service before that person's entry into that service shall, during any part of the period of military service, bear interest at a rate in excess of 6 percent per year unless, in the opinion of the court, upon application thereto by the obligee, the ability of such person in military service to pay interest upon such obligation or liability at a rate in excess of 6 percent per year is not materially affected by reason of such service, in which case the court may make such order as in its opinion may be just. As used in this section the term "interest" includes service charges, renewal charges, fees, or any other charges (except bona fide insurance) in respect of such obligation or liability.

(Oct. 17, 1940, ch. 888, art. II, § 206, as added Oct. 6, 1942, ch. 581, § 6, 56 Stat. 771; amended Pub. L. 102–12, § 9(7), Mar. 18, 1991, 105 Stat. 39.)

AMENDMENTS

1991—Pub. L. 102–12 substituted "percent per year" for "per centum per annum" wherever appearing and "before that person's entry into that service shall, during any part of the period of military service, bear interest" for "prior to his entry into such service shall, during any part of the period of military service which occurs after the date of enactment of the Soldiers' and Sailors' Civil Relief Act Amendments of 1942, bear interest".

§ 527. Limitations prescribed by internal revenue laws as affected by period of service

Section 205 of this Act [section 525 of this Appendix] shall not apply with respect to any period of limitation prescribed by or under the internal revenue laws of the United States.

(Oct. 17, 1940, ch. 888, art. II, § 207, as added Oct. 21, 1942, ch. 619, title V, § 507(b)(2)(B), 56 Stat. 964.)

REFERENCES IN TEXT

The internal revenue laws of the United States, referred to in text, are classified generally to Title 26, Internal Revenue Code.

ARTICLE III—RENT, INSTALLMENT CONTRACTS, MORTGAGES, LIENS, ASSIGNMENTS, LEASES

AMENDMENTS

1942—Article heading was amended by act Oct. 6, 1942, ch. 581, § 7, 56 Stat. 771. Article was formerly entitled "Rent, Installment Contracts, Mortgages".

ARTICLE REFERRED TO IN OTHER SECTIONS

This article is referred to in sections 516, 536 of this Appendix.

§530. Eviction or distress during military service; stay; penalty for noncompliance; allotment of pay for payment

(a) No eviction or distress shall be made during the period of military service in respect of any premises for which the agreed rent does not exceed $1,200 per month, occupied chiefly for dwelling purposes by the wife, children, or other dependents of a person in military service, except upon leave of court granted upon application therefor or granted in an action or proceeding affecting the right of possession.

(b) On any such application or in any such action the court may, in its discretion, on its own motion, and shall, on application, unless in the opinion of the court the ability of the tenant to pay the agreed rent is not materially affected by reason of such military service, stay the proceedings for not longer than three months, as provided in this Act [sections 501 to 593 of this Appendix], or it may make such other order as may be just. Where such stay is granted or other order is made by the court, the owner of the premises shall be entitled, upon application therefor, to relief in respect of such premises similar to that granted persons in military service in sections 301, 302, and 500 of this Act [sections 531, 532, and 560 of this Appendix] to such extent and for such period as may appear to the court to be just.

(c) Any person who shall knowingly take part in any eviction or distress otherwise than as provided in subsection (a), or attempts so to do, shall be fined as provided in title 18, United States Code, or imprisoned for not to exceed one year, or both.

(d) The Secretary of Defense or Secretary of Transportation, with respect to the Coast Guard when it is not operating as a service in the Navy, is empowered, subject to such regulations as he may prescribe, to order an allotment of the pay of a person in military service in reasonable proportion to discharge the rent of premises occupied for dwelling purposes by the wife, children, or other dependents of such person.

(Oct. 17, 1940, ch. 888, art. III, §300, 54 Stat. 1181; Oct. 6, 1942, ch. 581, §8, 56 Stat. 771; Pub. L. 89–358, §10, Mar. 3, 1966, 80 Stat. 28; Pub. L. 102–12, §§2(a), (b), 9(8), Mar. 18, 1991, 105 Stat. 34, 39.)

AMENDMENTS

1991—Subsec. (a). Pub. L. 102–12, §2(a), (b)(1), redesignated par. (1) as subsec. (a) and substituted "$1,200" for "$150".

Subsec. (b). Pub. L. 102–12, §2(b)(1), redesignated par. (2) as subsec. (b).

Subsec. (c). Pub. L. 102–12, §§2, 9(8)(A), redesignated par. (3) as subsec. (c) and substituted "subsection (a)" for "subsection (1) hereof" and "shall be fined as provided in title 18, United States Code, or imprisoned for not to exceed one year," for "shall be guilty of a misdemeanor, and shall be punishable by imprisonment not to exceed one year or by fine not to exceed $1,000,".

Subsec. (d). Pub. L. 102–12, §§2(b)(1), 9(8)(B), redesignated par. (4) as subsec. (d) and substituted "Secretary of Defense or Secretary of Transportation, with respect to the Coast Guard when it is not operating as a service in the Navy," for "Secretary of War, the Secretary of the Navy, or the Secretary of the Treasury with respect to the Coast Guard, as the case may be,".

1966—Subsec. (1). Pub. L. 89–358 increased the limitation of rents from $80 to $150 per month.

1942—Subsec. (2). Act Oct. 6, 1942, §8(a), inserted last sentence.

Subsec. (3). Act Oct. 6, 1942, §8(b), inserted "or attempts so to do,".

EFFECTIVE DATE OF 1991 AMENDMENT

Section 2(c) of Pub. L. 102–12 provided that: "The amendment made by subsection (a) [amending this section] applies to actions for eviction or distress that are commenced after July 31, 1990."

§531. Installment contracts for purchase of property

(1) No person who has received, or whose assignor has received, under a contract for the purchase of real or personal property, or of lease or bailment with a view to purchase of such property, a deposit or installment of the purchase price, or a deposit or installment under the contract, lease, or bailment, from a person or from the assignor of a person who, after the date of payment of such deposit or installment, has entered military service, shall exercise any right or option under such contract to rescind or terminate the contract or resume possession of the property for nonpayment of any installment thereunder due or for any other breach of the terms thereof occurring prior to or during the period of such military service, except by action in a court of competent jurisdiction.

(2) Any person who shall knowingly resume possession of property which is the subject of this section otherwise than as provided in subsection (1) of this section or in section 107 [section 517 of this Appendix], or attempts so to do, shall be fined as provided in title 18, United States Code, or imprisoned for not to exceed one year, or both.

(3) Upon the hearing of such action the court may order the repayment of prior installments or deposits or any part thereof, as a condition of terminating the contract and resuming possession of the property, or may, in its discretion, on its own motion, and shall, on application to it by such person in military service or some person on his behalf, order a stay of proceedings as provided in this Act [sections 501 to 593 of this Appendix] unless, in the opinion of the court, the ability of the defendant to comply with the terms of the contract is not materially affected by reason of such service; or it may make such other disposition of the case as may be equitable to conserve the interests of all parties.

(Oct. 17, 1940, ch. 888, art. III, §301, 54 Stat. 1182; Oct. 6, 1942, ch. 581, §9(a), (c), (d), 56 Stat. 771; Pub. L. 102–12, §9(9), Mar. 18, 1991, 105 Stat. 40.)

AMENDMENTS

1991—Par. (2). Pub. L. 102–12 substituted "shall be fined as provided in title 18, United States Code, or imprisoned for not to exceed one year," for "shall be guilty of a misdemeanor and shall be punished by imprisonment not to exceed one year or by fine not to exceed $1,000,".

1942—Subsec. (1). Act Oct. 6, 1942, §9(a), in amending subsec. (1) generally, omitted provision limiting applicability to transactions prior to Oct. 10, 1940, and proviso relating to modification, termination, or cancellation of contracts and repossession or retention of property by mutual written agreement of the parties, inserted provision relating to deposit or installment under contract, lease, or bailment, and included other breaches of terms in addition to nonpayment of installments.

Subsec. (2). Act Oct. 6, 1942, §9(d), substituted "of this section or in section 107, or attempts so to do," for "hereof".

Subsec. (3). Act Oct. 6, 1942, §9(c), struck out "except as provided in section 303," before "on application".

SECTION REFERRED TO IN OTHER SECTIONS

This section is referred to in section 530 of this Appendix.

§532. Mortgages, trust deeds, etc.

(1) The provisions of this section shall apply only to obligations secured by mortgage, trust deed, or other security in the nature of a mortgage upon real or personal property owned by a person in military service at the commencement of the period of the military service and still so owned by him which obligations originated prior to such person's period of military service.

(2) In any proceeding commenced in any court during the period of military service to enforce such obligation arising out of nonpayment of any sum thereunder due or out of any other breach of the terms thereof occurring prior to or during the period of such service the court may, after hearing, in its discretion, on its own motion, and shall, on application to it by such person in military service or some person on his behalf, unless in the opinion of the court the ability of the defendant to comply with the terms of the obligation is not materially affected by reason of his military service—

(a) stay the proceedings as provided in this Act [sections 501 to 593 of this Appendix]; or

(b) make such other disposition of the case as may be equitable to conserve the interests of all parties.

(3) No sale, foreclosure, or seizure of property for nonpayment of any sum due under any such obligation, or for any other breach of the terms thereof, whether under a power of sale, under a judgment entered upon warrant of attorney to confess judgment contained therein, or otherwise, shall be valid if made during the period of military service or within three months thereafter, except pursuant to an agreement as provided in section 107 [section 517 of this Appendix], unless upon an order previously granted by the court and a return thereto made and approved by the court.

(4) Any person who shall knowingly make or cause to be made any sale, foreclosure, or seizure of property, defined as invalid by subsection (3) hereof, or attempts so to do, shall be fined as provided in title 18, United States Code, or imprisoned for not to exceed one year, or both.

(Oct. 17, 1940, ch. 888, art. III, §302, 54 Stat. 1182; Oct. 6, 1942, ch. 581, §§9(b), (c), 10, 56 Stat. 771, 772; June 23, 1952, ch. 450, 66 Stat. 151; Pub. L. 102–12, §9(9), (10), Mar. 18, 1991, 105 Stat. 40.)

AMENDMENTS

1991—Par. (3). Pub. L. 102–12, §9(10), struck out "after the date of enactment of the Soldiers' and Sailors' Civil Relief Act Amendments of 1942 and" after "shall be valid if made".

Par. (4). Pub. L. 102–12, §9(9), substituted "shall be fined as provided in title 18, United States Code, or imprisoned for not to exceed one year," for "shall be guilty of a misdemeanor and shall be punished by imprisonment not to exceed one year or by fine not to exceed $1,000,".

1952—Subsec. (4). Act June 23, 1952, prohibited the making of sales, foreclosures, or seizures defined as invalid by subsec. (3) of this section.

1942—Subsec. (1). Act Oct. 6, 1942, §9(b), struck out "originating prior to the date of approval of this Act and" after "obligations" and inserted matter at end of subsection following "him".

Subsec. (2). Act Oct. 6, 1942, §9(c), struck out "except as provided in section 303," before "on application".

Subsecs. (3), (4). Act Oct. 6, 1942, §10, amended subsec. (3) generally and added subsec. (4).

SECTION REFERRED TO IN OTHER SECTIONS

This section is referred to in sections 530, 535 of this Appendix; title 12 sections 1739, 1750c.

§533. Settlement of cases involving stayed proceedings to foreclose mortgage on, resume possession of, or terminate contract for purchase of, personal property

Where a proceeding to foreclose a mortgage upon or to resume possession of personal property, or to rescind or terminate a contract for the purchase thereof, has been stayed as provided in this Act [sections 501 to 593 of this Appendix], the court may, unless in its opinion an undue hardship would result to the dependents of the person in military service, appoint three disinterested parties to appraise the property and, based upon the report of the appraisers, order such sum, if any, as may be just, paid to the person in military service or his dependent, as the case may be, as a condition of foreclosing the mortgage, resuming possession of the property, or rescinding or terminating the contract.

(Oct. 17, 1940, ch. 888, art. III, §303, as added Oct. 6, 1942, ch. 581, §12, 56 Stat. 772.)

PRIOR PROVISIONS

A prior section 533, act Oct. 17, 1940, ch. 888, art. III, §303, 54 Stat. 1183, related to stay of action to resume possession of motor vehicle, tractor, or their accessories, encumbered by purchase money mortgage, conditional sales contract, etc., prior to repeal by act Oct. 6, 1942, ch. 581, §11, 56 Stat. 772.

§534. Termination of leases by lessees

(1) The provisions of this section shall apply to any lease covering premises occupied for dwelling, professional, business, agricultural, or similar purposes in any case in which (a) such lease was executed by or on the behalf of a person who, after the execution of such lease, entered military service, and (b) the premises so leased have been occupied for such purposes, or for a combination of such purposes, by such person or by him and his dependents.

(2) Any such lease may be terminated by notice in writing delivered to the lessor (or his grantee) or to the lessor's (or his grantee's) agent by the lessee at any time following the date of the beginning of his period of military service. Delivery of such notice may be accomplished by placing it in an envelope properly stamped and duly addressed to the lessor (or his

grantee) or to the lessor's (or his grantee's) agent and depositing the notice in the United States mails. Termination of any such lease providing for monthly payment of rent shall not be effective until thirty days after the first date on which the next rental payment is due and payable subsequent to the date when such notice is delivered or mailed. In the case of all other leases, termination shall be effected on the last day of the month following the month in which such notice is delivered or mailed and in such case any unpaid rental for a period preceding termination shall be proratably computed and any rental paid in advance for a period succeeding termination shall be refunded by the lessor (or his assignee). Upon application by the lessor to the appropriate court prior to the termination period provided for in the notice, any relief granted in this subsection shall be subject to such modifications or restrictions as in the opinion of the court justice and equity may in the circumstances require.

(3) Any person who shall knowingly seize, hold, or detain the personal effects, clothing, furniture, or other property of any person who has lawfully terminated a lease covered by this section, or in any manner interfere with the removal of such property from the premises covered by such lease, for the purpose of subjecting or attempting to subject any of such property to a claim for rent accruing subsequent to the date of termination of such lease, or attempts so to do, shall be fined as provided in title 18, United States Code, or imprisoned for not to exceed one year, or both.

(Oct. 17, 1940, ch. 888, art. III, §304, as added Oct. 6, 1942, ch. 581, §12, 56 Stat. 772; amended Pub. L. 102–12, §9(9), Mar. 18, 1991, 105 Stat. 40.)

AMENDMENTS

1991—Par. (3). Pub. L. 102–12 substituted "shall be fined as provided in title 18, United States Code, or imprisoned for not to exceed one year," for "shall be guilty of a misdemeanor and shall be punished by imprisonment not to exceed one year or by fine not to exceed $1,000,".

§535. Protection of assignor of life insurance policy; enforcement of storage liens; penalties

(1) Where any life insurance policy on the life of a person in military service has been assigned prior to such person's period of military service to secure the payment of any obligation of such person, no assignee of such policy (except the insurer in connection with a policy loan) shall, during the period of military service of the insured or within one year thereafter, except upon the consent in writing of the insured made during such period or when the premiums thereon are due and unpaid or upon the death of the insured, exercise any right or option by virtue of such assignment unless upon leave of court granted upon an application made therefor by such assignee. The court may thereupon refuse to grant such leave unless in the opinion of the court the ability of the obligor to comply with the terms of the obligation is not materially affected by reason of his military service. For the purpose of this subsection premiums which are guaranteed under the provisions of article IV of this Act [sections 540 to 548 of this Appendix] shall not be deemed to be due and unpaid.

(2) No person shall exercise any right to foreclose or enforce any lien for storage of household goods, furniture, or personal effects of a person in military service during such person's period of military service and for three months thereafter except upon an order previously granted by a court upon application therefor and a return thereto made and approved by the court. In such proceeding the court may, after hearing, in its discretion, on its own motion, and shall, on application to it by such person in military service or some person on his behalf, unless in the opinion of the court the ability of the defendant to pay the storage charges due is not materially affected by reason of his military service—

(a) stay the proceedings as provided in this Act [sections 501 to 593 of this Appendix]; or

(b) make such other disposition of the case as may be equitable to conserve the interest of all parties.

The enactment of the provisions of this subsection shall not be construed in any way as affecting or as limiting the scope of section 302 of this Act [section 532 of this Appendix].

(3) Any person who shall knowingly take any action contrary to the provisions of this section, or attempts so to do, shall be fined as provided in title 18, United States Code, or imprisoned for not to exceed one year, or both.

(Oct. 17, 1940, ch. 888, art. III, §305, as added Oct. 6, 1942, ch. 581, §12, 56 Stat. 773; amended Pub. L. 102–12, §9(9), Mar. 18, 1991, 105 Stat. 40.)

AMENDMENTS

1991—Par. (3). Pub. L. 102–12 substituted "shall be fined as provided in title 18, United States Code, or imprisoned for not to exceed one year," for "shall be guilty of a misdemeanor and shall be punished by imprisonment not to exceed one year or by fine not to exceed $1,000,".

§536. Extension of benefits to dependents

Dependents of a person in military service shall be entitled to the benefits accorded to persons in military service under the provisions of this article [sections 530 to 536 of this Appendix] upon application to a court therefor, unless in the opinion of the court the ability of such dependents to comply with the terms of the obligation, contract, lease, or bailment has not been materially impaired by reason of the military service of the person upon whom the applicants are dependent.

(Oct. 17, 1940, ch. 888, art. III, §306, as added Oct. 6, 1942, ch. 581, §12, 56 Stat. 773.)

SECTION REFERRED TO IN OTHER SECTIONS

This section is referred to in title 12 sections 1739, 1750c.

ARTICLE IV—INSURANCE

ARTICLE REFERRED TO IN OTHER SECTIONS

This article is referred to in section 535 of this Appendix.

§540. Definitions

As used in this article [sections 540 to 548 of this Appendix]—

(a) The term "policy" shall include any contract of life insurance or policy on a life, endowment, or term plan, including any benefit in the nature of life insurance arising out of membership in any fraternal or beneficial association, which does not provide for the payment of any sum less than the face value thereof or for the payment of an additional amount as premiums if the insured engages in the military service of the United States as defined in section 101 of article I of this Act [section 511 of this Appendix] or which does not contain any limitation or restriction upon coverage relating to engagement in or pursuit of certain types of activities which a person might be required to engage in by virtue of his being in such military service, and (1) which is in force on a premium-paying basis at the time of application for benefits hereunder, and (2) which was made and a premium paid thereon not less than 180 days before the date the insured entered into the military service. The provisions of this Act [sections 501 to 593 of this Appendix] shall not be applicable to policies or contracts of life insurance issued under the War Risk Insurance Act, as amended, the World War Veterans Act, as amended, or the National Service Life Insurance Act of 1940, as amended.

(b) The term "premium" shall include the amount specified in the policy as the stipend to be paid by the insured at regular intervals during the period therein stated.

(c) The term "insured" shall include any person in the military service of the United States as defined in section 101, article I, of this Act [section 511 of this Appendix], whose life is insured under and who is the owner and holder of and has an interest in a policy as above defined.

(d) The term "insurer" shall include any firm, corporation, partnership, or association chartered or authorized to engage in the insurance business and to issue a policy as above defined by the laws of a State of the United States or the United States.

(Oct. 17, 1940, ch. 888, art. IV, §400, 54 Stat. 1183; Oct. 6, 1942, ch. 581, §13, 56 Stat. 773; July 11, 1956, ch. 570, §1, 70 Stat. 528; Pub. L. 102–12, §9(11), Mar. 18, 1991, 105 Stat. 40.)

REFERENCES IN TEXT

The War Risk Insurance Act, as amended, referred to in subsec. (a), is act Oct. 6, 1917, ch. 105, 40 Stat. 398, as amended, which enacted sections 502 and 575 of former Title 38, Pensions, Bonuses, and Veterans' Relief, amended section 241 of former Title 34, Navy, and sections 287 and 357 of former Title 38, and enacted provisions set out as notes under section 211 of this Appendix, and which was repealed by acts June 7, 1924, ch. 320, title VI, §§600(5), 601(1), 43 Stat. 629, and June 17, 1957, Pub. L. 85–56, title XXII, §2202(96), 71 Stat. 166. For complete classification of this Act to the Code prior to its repeal, see Tables.

The World War Veterans' Act, as amended, referred to in subsec. (a), probably means act June 7, 1924, ch. 320, 43 Stat. 607, known as the World War Veterans' Act, 1924, which was classified principally to chapter 10 (§§421 to 574) of former Title 38, Pensions, Bonuses, and Veterans' Relief, and which was repealed by Pub. L. 85–857, §14(51), Sept. 2, 1958, 72 Stat. 1271. For distribution of sections 421 to 574 of former Title 38 in Title 38, Veterans' Benefits, see Table preceding section 101 of Title 38.

The National Service Life Insurance Act of 1940, as amended, referred to in subsec. (a), is act Oct. 8, 1940, ch. 757, title VI, pt. I, §§601 to 623, 54 Stat. 1008, as amended, which was classified generally to subchapter I (§§801 to 824) of chapter 13 of former Title 38, Pensions, Bonuses, and Veterans' Relief, and which was repealed by Pub. L. 85–857, §14(75), Sept. 2, 1958, 72 Stat. 1272, and the provisions thereof reenacted generally as subchapter I (§701 [now 1901] et seq.) of chapter 19 of Title 38, Veterans' Benefits, by the first section of Pub. L. 85–857 which enacted Title 38. Section 5(a) of Pub. L. 85–857 provides that references in other laws to any provision of law replaced by Title 38 shall, where applicable, be deemed to refer also to the corresponding provision of Title 38. For distribution of sections 801 and 824 of former Title 38, see Tables preceding section 101 of Title 38.

AMENDMENTS

1991—Subsec. (a). Pub. L. 102–12 substituted "not less than 180 days before" for "before the date of enactment of the Soldiers' and Sailors' Civil Relief Act Amendments of 1942 or not less than one hundred and eighty days before".

1956—Subsec. (a). Act July 11, 1956, substituted "one hundred and eighty" for "thirty" before "days before the date the insured entered into the military service".

1942—Act Oct. 6, 1942, amended section generally, substituting provisions defining "policy", "premium", "insured", and "insurer" for provisions defining the same terms.

EFFECTIVE DATE OF 1956 AMENDMENT

Section 2 of act July 11, 1956, provided that: "The amendment made by this Act [amending this section] shall take effect with respect to applications for benefits made after the date of enactment of this Act [July 11, 1956]".

VETERANS' LIFE INSURANCE REFUNDS

Pub. L. 85–586, Aug. 1, 1958, 72 Stat. 487, authorized Administrator of Veterans' Affairs to make refunds, without interest, which were due on account of amounts collected by United States Government by offset or otherwise from persons who made valid application for and were legally entitled to protection of article IV of the Soldiers' and Sailors' Civil Relief Act of 1940 (sections 540 to 554 of this Appendix), as it existed prior to amendments of Oct. 6, 1942, application to be made to Veterans' Administration, within two years after Aug. 1, 1958, and authorized appropriation of additional sums for such purposes.

SECTION REFERRED TO IN OTHER SECTIONS

This section is referred to in title 5 section 5569.

§541. Persons entitled to benefits of article; applications; amount of insurance protected

The benefits and privileges of this article [sections 540 to 548 of this Appendix] shall apply to any insured, when such insured, or a person designated by him, or, in case the insured is outside the continental United States (excluding Alaska and the Panama Canal Zone), a beneficiary, shall make written application for protection under this article [said sections], unless the Secretary of Veterans Affairs in passing upon such application as provided in this article [said sections] shall find that the policy is not entitled to protection hereunder. The Secretary shall give notice to the military and naval authorities of the provisions of this article [said sections], and shall include in such notice an explanation of such provisions for the information of those desiring to make application for the benefits thereof. The original of such application shall be sent by the insured to the insurer, and a copy thereof to the Secretary. The total amount of insurance on the life of one insured under policies protected by the provisions of this article [said sections] shall not exceed $10,000. If an insured makes application for protection of policies on his life totaling insurance in excess of $10,000, the Secretary is authorized to have the amount of insurance divided into two or more policies so that the protection of this article [said sections] may be extended to include policies for a total amount of insurance not to exceed $10,000, and a policy which affords the best security to the Government shall be given preference.

(Oct. 17, 1940, ch. 888, art. IV, §401, 54 Stat. 1183; Oct. 6, 1942, ch. 581, §13, 56 Stat. 774; Pub. L. 102–12, §9(12), Mar. 18, 1991, 105 Stat. 40.)

AMENDMENTS

1991—Pub. L. 102–12 substituted "Secretary of Veterans Affairs" for "Administrator of Veterans' Affairs", "Secretary" for "Veterans' Administration" in two places, and "Secretary" for "Administrator" in last sentence.

1942—Act Oct. 6, 1942, amended section generally, substituting provisions relating to persons entitled to benefits, applications, and amount of insurance protected for provisions relating to applications for benefits and forms.

SECTION REFERRED TO IN OTHER SECTIONS

This section is referred to in title 5 section 5569.

§542. Form of application; reports to Secretary of Veterans Affairs by insurer; policy deemed modified upon application for protection

Any writing signed by the insured and identifying the policy and the insurer, and agreeing that his rights under the policy are subject to and modified by the provisions of this article [sections 540 to 548 of this Appendix], shall be sufficient as an application for the benefits of this article [said sections], but the Secretary of Veterans Affairs may require the insured and insurer to execute such other forms as may be deemed advisable. Upon receipt of the application of the insured the insurer shall furnish such report to the Secretary concerning the policy as shall be prescribed by regulations. The insured who has made application for protection under this article [said sections] and the insurer shall be deemed to have agreed to such modification of the policy as may be required to give this article [said sections] full force and effect with respect to such policy.

(Oct. 17, 1940, ch. 888, art. IV, §402, 54 Stat. 1183; Oct. 6, 1942, ch. 581, §13, 56 Stat. 774; Pub. L. 102–12, §9(13), Mar. 18, 1991, 105 Stat. 40.)

AMENDMENTS

1991—Pub. L. 102–12 substituted "Secretary of Veterans Affairs" for "Veterans' Administration" in first sentence and "Secretary" for "Veterans' Administration" in second sentence.

1942—Act Oct. 6, 1942, amended section generally, substituting provisions relating to form of application, reports to Veterans' Administration by insurer, and policy being deemed modified upon application for protection for provisions relating to persons entitled to benefits.

SECTION REFERRED TO IN OTHER SECTIONS

This section is referred to in title 5 section 5569.

§543. Determination of policies entitled to protection; notice to parties; lapse of policies for nonpayment of premiums, etc.

The Secretary of Veterans Affairs shall find whether the policy is entitled to protection under this article [sections 540 to 548 of this Appendix] and shall notify the insured and the insurer of such finding. Any policy found by the Secretary to be entitled to protection under this article [said sections] shall not, subsequent to date of application, and during the period of military service of the insured or during two years after the expiration of such service, lapse or otherwise terminate or be forfeited for the nonpayment of a premium becoming due and payable, or the nonpayment of any indebtedness or interest.

(Oct. 17, 1940, ch. 888, art. IV, §403, 54 Stat. 1184; Oct. 6, 1942, ch. 581, §13, 56 Stat. 775; Pub. L. 102–12, §9(14), Mar. 18, 1991, 105 Stat. 40.)

AMENDMENTS

1991—Pub. L. 102–12 substituted "Secretary of Veterans Affairs" for "Administrator of Veterans' Affairs" in first sentence and "Secretary" for "Administrator of Veterans' Affairs" in second sentence.

1942—Act Oct. 6, 1942, amended section generally, substituting provisions relating to determining entitlement to protection, notice, and lapse of policies for nonpayment of premiums for provisions relating to list of applicants for benefits and rejection of improper applications.

SECTION REFERRED TO IN OTHER SECTIONS

This section is referred to in title 5 section 5569.

§544. Rights and privileges of insured during period of protection

No dividend or other monetary benefit under a policy shall be paid to an insured or used to purchase dividend additions while a policy is protected by the provisions of this article [sections 540 to 548 of this Appendix] except with the consent and approval of the Secretary of Veterans Affairs. If such consent is not procured, such dividends or benefits shall be added to the value of the policy to be used as a credit when final settlement is made with the insurer. No cash value, loan value, or withdrawal of dividend accumulation, or unearned premium, or other value of similar character shall be available to the insured while the policy is protected under this article [said sections] except upon approval by the Secretary of Veterans Affairs. The insured's right to change a beneficiary designation or select an optional settlement for a beneficiary shall not be affected by the provisions of this article [said sections].

(Oct. 17, 1940, ch. 888, art. IV, §404, 54 Stat. 1184; Oct. 6, 1942, ch. 581, §13, 56 Stat. 775; Pub. L. 102–12, §9(15), Mar. 18, 1991, 105 Stat. 40.)

AMENDMENTS

1991—Pub. L. 102–12 substituted "Secretary of Veterans Affairs" for "Veterans' Administration" in two places.

1942—Act Oct. 6, 1942, amended section generally, substituting provisions relating to rights and privileges of insured during period of protection for provisions relating to applications on policies exceeding $5,000.

SECTION REFERRED TO IN OTHER SECTIONS

This section is referred to in title 5 section 5569.

§ 545. Deduction of unpaid premiums upon settlement of policies maturing during protection

In the event of maturity of a policy as a death claim or otherwise before the expiration of the period of protection under the provisions of this article [sections 540 to 548 of this Appendix], the insurer in making settlement will deduct from the amount of insurance the premiums guaranteed under this article [said sections], together with interest thereon at the rate fixed in the policy for policy loans. If no rate of interest is specifically fixed in the policy, the rate shall be the rate fixed for policy loans in other policies issued by the insurer at the time the policy brought under the Act [sections 501 to 593 of this Appendix] was issued. The amount deducted by reason of the protection afforded by this article [sections 540 to 548 of this Appendix] shall be reported by the insurer to the Secretary of Veterans Affairs.

(Oct. 17, 1940, ch. 888, art. IV, § 405, 54 Stat. 1184; Oct. 6, 1942, ch. 581, § 13, 56 Stat. 775; Pub. L. 102–12, § 9(16), Mar. 18, 1991, 105 Stat. 40.)

AMENDMENTS

1991—Pub. L. 102–12 substituted "Secretary of Veterans Affairs" for "Administrator of Veterans' Affairs".

1942—Act Oct. 6, 1942, amended section generally, substituting provisions relating to deduction of unpaid premiums upon settlement of policies maturing during protection for provisions relating to lapse of policies for nonpayment of premiums.

SECTION REFERRED TO IN OTHER SECTIONS

This section is referred to in section 546 of this Appendix; title 5 section 5569.

§ 546. Guaranty of premiums and interest by United States; settlement of amounts due upon expiration of protection; subrogation of United States; crediting debt repayments

Payment of premiums and interest thereon at the rate specified in section 405 hereof [section 545 of this Appendix] becoming due on a policy while protected under the provisions of this article [sections 540 to 548 of this Appendix] is guaranteed by the United States, and if the amount so guaranteed is not paid to the insurer prior to the expiration of the period of insurance protection under this article [said sections], the amount then due shall be treated by the insurer as a policy loan on such policy, but if at the expiration of said period the cash surrender value is less than the amount then due, the policy shall then cease and terminate and the United States shall pay the insurer the difference between such amount and the cash surrender value. The amount paid by the United States to an insurer on account of applications approved under the provisions of this article, as amended [said sections], shall become a debt due to the United States by the insured on whose account payment was made and, notwithstanding any other Act, such amount may be collected either by deduction from any amount due said insured by the United States or as otherwise authorized by law. Any moneys received as repayment of debts incurred under this article, as originally enacted and as amended [said sections], shall be credited to the appropriation for the payment of claims under this article [said sections].

(Oct. 17, 1940, ch. 888, art. IV, § 406, 54 Stat. 1184; Oct. 6, 1942, ch. 581, § 13, 56 Stat. 775; Apr. 3, 1948, ch. 170, § 6, 62 Stat. 160.)

AMENDMENTS

1948—Act Apr. 3, 1948, inserted last sentence.

1942—Act Oct. 6, 1942, amended section generally, substituting provisions relating to guaranty of premiums and interest by United States, settlement of amounts due upon expiration of protection, subrogation of United States, and crediting debt repayments for provisions relating to reports by insurers to Veterans' Administration.

SECTION REFERRED TO IN OTHER SECTIONS

This section is referred to in title 5 section 5569.

§ 547. Regulations; finality of determinations

The Secretary of Veterans Affairs shall provide by regulations for such rules of procedure and forms as he may deem advisable in carrying out the provisions of this article [sections 540 to 548 of this Appendix]. The findings of fact and conclusions of law made by the Secretary in administering the provisions of this article [said sections] shall be final, and shall not be subject to review by any other official or agency of the Government.

(Oct. 17, 1940, ch. 888, art. IV, § 407, 54 Stat. 1185; Oct. 6, 1942, ch. 581, § 13, 56 Stat. 775; Pub. L. 85–857, § 14(76), Sept. 2, 1958, 72 Stat. 1272; Pub. L. 102–12, § 9(17), Mar. 18, 1991, 105 Stat. 40.)

PRIOR PROVISIONS

Section 407 of act Oct. 17, 1940, as originally enacted, which, by the provisions of section 408 of act Oct. 17, 1940, as amended (section 548 of this Appendix), is continued in force as to applications for protection executed prior to Oct. 6, 1942, read as follows: "The Administrator of Veterans' Affairs shall verify the computation of monthly difference reported by each insurer and shall, within ten days thereafter, deliver each month to the proper officer of such insurer, a certificate in the amount of the monthly difference certified in respect of each insurer. Such certificate shall be signed by said Administrator in the name of the United States, shall be in such form as the Administrator shall determine, shall be payable to the insurer within sixty days after the approval of the statement of account, as provided in section 411 hereof [section 551 of this Appendix], and shall bear interest at a rate to be prescribed by the Secretary of the Treasury, payable with the principal. Such certificate shall not be transferred except with the approval of said Administrator and shall remain with the insurer until settlement is made in accordance with this article."

AMENDMENTS

1991—Pub. L. 102–12 substituted "The Secretary of Veterans Affairs shall" for "The Administrator of Veterans' Affairs is hereby authorized and directed to" in first sentence and "Secretary" for "Administrator of Veterans' Affairs" in second sentence.

1958—Pub. L. 85–857 struck out provisions which required the Administrator of Veterans' Affairs to report annually to the Congress on the administration of sections 540 to 548 of this Appendix. See section 529 of Title 38, Veterans' Benefits.

1942—Act Oct. 6, 1942, amended section generally, substituting provisions relating to regulations and finality of determinations for provisions relating to certificate of difference between premiums defaulted and paid and interest.

EFFECTIVE DATE OF 1958 AMENDMENT

Amendment by Pub. L. 85–857 effective Jan. 1, 1959, see section 2 of Pub. L. 85–857, set out as an Effective

Date note preceding part I of Title 38, Veterans' Benefits.

SECTION REFERRED TO IN OTHER SECTIONS

This section is referred to in title 5 section 5569.

§548. Repealed. Pub. L. 102–12, §9(18), Mar. 18, 1991, 105 Stat. 40

Section, acts Oct. 17, 1940, ch. 888, art. IV, §408, 54 Stat. 1185; Oct. 6, 1942, ch. 581, §13, 56 Stat. 776, related to law governing applications for protection prior to Oct. 6, 1942.

§§549 to 554. Omitted

CODIFICATION

Sections 549 to 554 of this Appendix were omitted in the general amendment of article IV by act Oct. 6, 1942, ch. 581, §13, 56 Stat. 773.

Section 549, act Oct. 17, 1940, ch. 888, art. IV, §409, 54 Stat. 1185, related to deduction of unpaid premiums from proceeds of policies.

Section 550, act Oct. 17, 1940, ch. 888, art. IV, §410, 54 Stat. 1185, related to lapsing of policy for failure to pay past due premiums upon termination of service.

Section 551, act Oct. 17, 1940, ch. 888, art. IV, §411, 54 Stat. 1185, related to accounts stated between insurers and United States.

Section 552, act Oct. 17, 1940, ch. 888, art. IV, §412, 54 Stat. 1185, related to payment of balances due insurers by Secretary of the Treasury.

Section 553, act Oct. 17, 1940, ch. 888, art. IV, §413, 54 Stat. 1186, related to policies excepted from application of article.

Section 554, act Oct. 17, 1940, ch. 888, art. IV, §414, 54 Stat. 1186, related to insurers within application of article.

ARTICLE V—TAXES AND PUBLIC LANDS

§560. Taxes respecting personalty, money, credits, or realty; sale of property to enforce collection; redemption of property sold; penalty for nonpayment; notice of rights to beneficiaries of section

(1) The provisions of this section shall apply when any taxes or assessments, whether general or special (other than taxes on income), whether falling due prior to or during the period of military service, in respect of personal property, money, or credits, or real property owned and occupied for dwelling, professional, business, or agricultural purposes by a person in military service or his dependents at the commencement of his period of military service and still so occupied by his dependents or employees are not paid.

(2) No sale of such property shall be made to enforce the collection of such tax or assessment, or any proceeding or action for such purpose commenced, except upon leave of court granted upon application made therefor by the collector of taxes or other officer whose duty it is to enforce the collection of taxes or assessments. The court thereupon, unless in its opinion the ability of the person in military service to pay such taxes or assessments is not materially affected by reason of such service, may stay such proceedings or such sale, as provided in this Act [sections 501 to 593 of this Appendix], for a period extending not more than six months after the termination of the period of military service of such person.

(3) When by law such property may be sold or forfeited to enforce the collection of such tax or assessment, such person in military service shall have the right to redeem or commence an action to redeem such property, at any time not later than six months after the termination of such service, but in no case later than six months after the date when this Act [said sections] ceases to be in force; but this shall not be taken to shorten any period, now or hereafter provided by the laws of any State or Territory for such redemption.

(4) Whenever any tax or assessment shall not be paid when due, such tax or assessment due and unpaid shall bear interest until paid at the rate of 6 per centum per annum, and no other penalty or interest shall be incurred by reason of such nonpayment. Any lien for such unpaid taxes or assessment shall also include such interest thereon.

(Oct. 17, 1940, ch. 888, art. V, §500, 54 Stat. 1186; Oct. 6, 1942, ch. 581, §14, 56 Stat. 776.)

AMENDMENTS

1942—Subsec. (1). Act Oct. 6, 1942, inserted parenthetical clause excepting income taxes, included taxes and assessments falling due prior to period of military service, and extended benefits to cover personal property, money, or credits, and real property owned and occupied for professional purposes.

Subsec. (2). Act Oct. 6, 1942, §14(a), amended subsec. (2) generally.

Subsec. (5). Act Oct. 6, 1942, §14(b), repealed subsec. (5) which required the Secretaries of War, Navy, and Treasury to give notice of the benefits of this section to persons in the military service.

SECTION REFERRED TO IN OTHER SECTIONS

This section is referred to in section 530 of this Appendix.

§561. Rights to public lands not forfeited; grazing lands

(1) No right to any lands owned or controlled by the United States initiated or acquired under any laws of the United States, including the mining and mineral leasing laws, by any person prior to entering military service shall during the period of such service be forfeited or prejudiced by reason of his absence from the land or his failure to perform any work or make any improvements thereon or his failure to do any other act required by or under such laws.

(2) If a permittee or licensee under the Act of June 28, 1934 (48 Stat. 1269) [43 U.S.C. 315 et seq.] enters military service, he may elect to suspend his permit or license for the period of his military service and six months thereafter, and the Secretary of the Interior by regulations shall provide for such suspension of permits and licenses and for the remission, reduction, or refund of grazing fees during such suspension.

(3) This section shall not be construed to control specific requirements contained in this article [sections 560 to 574 of this Appendix].

(Oct. 17, 1940, ch. 888, art. V, §501, 54 Stat. 1187.)

REFERENCES IN TEXT

The mining laws of the United States and the mineral leasing laws, referred to in subsec. (1), are classified generally to Title 30, Mineral Lands and Mining.

Act of June 28, 1934 (48 Stat. 1269), referred to in subsec. (2), is act June 28, 1934, ch. 865, 48 Stat. 1269, as amended, popularly known as the Taylor Grazing Act, which is classified principally to subchapter I (§ 315 et seq.) of chapter 8A of Title 43, Public Lands. For complete classification of this Act to the Code, see Short Title note set out under section 315 of Title 43 and Tables.

SECTION REFERRED TO IN OTHER SECTIONS

This section is referred to in sections 567, 572 of this Appendix; title 5 section 5569.

§ 562. Homestead entries and settlement claims; service as equivalent to residence and cultivation

If any person whose application for a homestead entry has been allowed or who has made application for homestead entry which may thereafter be allowed, after such entry or application enters military service, or if any person who has a valid settlement claim enters military service, the Department of the Interior shall construe his military service to be equivalent to residence and cultivation upon the tract entered or settled upon for the period of such service. From the effective date of this Act [Oct. 17, 1940] no contest shall be initiated on the ground of abandonment and no allegation of abandonment shall be sustained against any such person, unless it shall be alleged in the preliminary affidavit or affidavits of contest and proved at the hearing in cases initiated subsequent to the effective date of this Act [Oct. 17, 1940] that the alleged absence from the land was not due to such military service. If such person is discharged on account of wounds received or disability incurred in the line of duty, the term of his enlistment and any period of hospitalization due to such wounds or disability shall be deducted from the required length of residence, without reference to the time of actual service. No patent shall issue to any such person who has not resided upon, improved, and cultivated his homestead for a period of at least one year.

(Oct. 17, 1940, ch. 888, art. V, § 502, 54 Stat. 1187.)

SECTION REFERRED TO IN OTHER SECTIONS

This section is referred to in sections 563, 567, 572 of this Appendix; title 5 section 5569.

§ 563. Death or incapacity during or resulting from service as affecting rights; perfection of rights

(1) If any person whose application for a homestead entry has been allowed or who has made application for homestead entry which may thereafter be allowed or who has a valid settlement claim dies while in military service or as a result of such service, his widow, if unmarried, or in the case of her death or marriage, his minor children, or his or their legal representatives, may proceed forthwith to make final proof upon such entry or upon an application which is allowed after the applicant's death, or upon a homestead application thereafter allowed based on a valid settlement claim, and shall be entitled to receive a patent for such land. The death of such person while in military service or as a result of such service shall be construed to be equivalent to a performance of all requirements as to residence and cultivation upon such homestead or claim, notwithstanding the provisions of section 502 of this Act [section 562 of this Appendix].

(2) If such person is honorably discharged and because of physical incapacities due to such service is unable to return to the land, he may make final proof without further residence, improvement, or cultivation, at such time and place as the Secretary of the Interior may authorize, and receive a patent to the land entered.

(3) The Act of July 28, 1917 (40 Stat. 248) [43 U.S.C. 241, 242], is repealed.

(Oct. 17, 1940, ch. 888, art. V, § 503, 54 Stat. 1187.)

SECTION REFERRED TO IN OTHER SECTIONS

This section is referred to in sections 567, 572 of this Appendix; title 5 section 5569.

§ 564. Desert-land entries; suspension of requirements

(1) No desert-land entry made or held under the desert-land laws prior to the entrance of the entryman or his successor in interest into military service shall be subject to contest or cancelation for failure to make or expend the sum of $1 per acre per year in improvements upon the claim or to effect the reclamation of the claim during the period the entryman or his successor in interest is engaged in military service or during a period of six months thereafter or during any period of hospitalization because of wounds or disability incurred in the line of duty. The time within which such entryman or claimant is required to make such expenditures and effect reclamation of the land shall be exclusive of his period of service and the six-months' period and any such period of hospitalization.

(2) If such entryman or claimant is honorably discharged and because of physical incapacities due to such service is unable to accomplish reclamation of, and payment for, the land, he may make proof without further reclamation or payments under such rules as the Secretary of the Interior may prescribe and receive patent for the land entered or claimed.

(3) In order to obtain the benefits of this section, such entryman or claimant shall, within six months after his entrance into military service, file or cause to be filed in the land office of the district in which his claim is situated a notice that he has entered military service and that he desires to hold the desert claim under this section.

(Oct. 17, 1940, ch. 888, art. V, § 504, 54 Stat. 1187; Pub. L. 102–12, § 9(19), Mar. 18, 1991, 105 Stat. 40.)

REFERENCES IN TEXT

The desert-land laws, referred to in par. (1), are classified generally to chapter 9 (§ 321 et seq.) of Title 43, Public Lands.

AMENDMENTS

1991—Par. (3). Pub. L. 102–12 struck out "within six months after the effective date of this Act or" after "claimant shall,".

SECTION REFERRED TO IN OTHER SECTIONS

This section is referred to in sections 567, 572 of this Appendix; title 5 section 5569.

§ 565. Mining claims; requirements suspended

(1) The provisions of section 2324 of the Revised Statutes of the United States (30 U.S.C.

28), which require that on each mining claim located after May 10, 1872, and until patent has been issued therefor not less than $100 worth of labor shall be performed or improvements made during each year, shall not apply during the period of his service, or until six months after the termination of such service, or during any period of hospitalization because of wounds or disability incurred in line of duty, to claims or interests in claims which are owned by a person in military service and which have been regularly located and recorded. No mining claim or any interest in a claim which is owned by such a person and which has been regularly located and recorded shall be subject to forfeiture by nonperformance of the annual assessments during the period of such military service, or until six months after the termination of such service or of such hospitalization.

(2) In order to obtain the benefits of this section, the claimant of any mining location shall, before the expiration of the assessment year during which he enters military service, file or cause to be filed in the office where the location notice or certificate is recorded a notice that he has entered such service and that he desires to hold his mining claim under this section.

(Oct. 17, 1940, ch. 888, art. V, §505, 54 Stat. 1188; Pub. L. 102–12, §9(20), Mar. 18, 1991, 105 Stat. 41.)

AMENDMENTS

1991—Par. (1). Pub. L. 102–12 inserted "(30 U.S.C. 28)" after "section 2324 of the Revised Statutes of the United States".

SECTION REFERRED TO IN OTHER SECTIONS

This section is referred to in sections 567, 572 of this Appendix; title 5 section 5569.

§566. Mineral permits and leases; suspension of operations and term of permits and leases

(1) Any person holding a permit or lease on the public domain under the Federal mineral leasing laws who enters military service may, at his election, suspend all operations under his permit or lease for a period of time equivalent to the period of his military service and six months thereafter. The term of the permit or lease shall not run during such period of suspension nor shall any rentals or royalties be charged against the permit or lease during the period of suspension.

(2) In order to obtain the benefit of this section, such permittee or lessee shall, within six months after his entrance into military service, notify the Bureau of Land Management by registered mail of his entrance into such service and of his desire to avail himself of the benefits of this section.

(3) This section shall not be construed to supersede the terms of any contract for operation of a permit or lease.

(Oct. 17, 1940, ch. 888, art. V, §506, 54 Stat. 1188; Pub. L. 102–12, §9(21), Mar. 18, 1991, 105 Stat. 41.)

REFERENCES IN TEXT

The Federal mineral leasing laws, referred to in par. (1), are classified generally to Title 30, Mineral Lands and Mining.

AMENDMENTS

1991—Par. (2). Pub. L. 102–12 struck out "six months after the effective date of this Act or" after "lessee shall, within" and substituted "Bureau of Land Management" for "General Land Office".

SECTION REFERRED TO IN OTHER SECTIONS

This section is referred to in sections 560 to 565, 567 to 590 of this Appendix; title 5 section 5569.

§567. Right to take action for perfection, defense, etc., of rights as unaffected; affidavits and proofs

Nothing in this article [sections 560 to 574 of this Appendix] shall be construed to limit or affect the right of a person in military service to take any action during his period of service which may be authorized by law or the regulations of the Department of the Interior for the perfection, defense, or further assertion of rights initiated or acquired prior to the date of entering military service. It shall be lawful for any person while in such service to make any affidavit or submit any proof which may be required by law or the practice or regulations of the Bureau of Land Management in connection with the entry, perfection, defense, or further assertion of any rights initiated or acquired prior to entering such service, before the officer in immediate command and holding a commission in the branch of the service in which the person is engaged. Such affidavits shall be as binding in law and with like penalties as if taken before an officer designated by the Secretary of the Interior. The Secretary of the Interior may issue rules and regulations to effectuate the purposes of sections 501 to 512 [sections 561 to 572 of this Appendix].

(Oct. 17, 1940, ch. 888, art. V, §507, 54 Stat. 1188; Pub. L. 102–12, §9(22), Mar. 18, 1991, 105 Stat. 41.)

AMENDMENTS

1991—Pub. L. 102–12 substituted "Bureau of Land Management" for "General Land Office", substituted "an officer designated by the Secretary of the Interior" for "a register of a United States land office", and struck out ", inclusive" after "sections 501 to 512".

SECTION REFERRED TO IN OTHER SECTIONS

This section is referred to in section 572 of this Appendix; title 5 section 5569.

§568. Irrigation rights; residence requirements suspended

The Secretary of the Interior is authorized, in his discretion, to suspend as to persons in military service during the period while this Act [sections 501 to 593 of this Appendix] remains in force and for a period of six months thereafter or during any period of hospitalization because of wounds or disability incurred in line of duty that provision of the act known as the "Reclamation Act" requiring residence upon lands in private ownership or within the neighborhood for securing water for the irrigation of the same [43 U.S.C. 431], and he is authorized to permit the use of available water thereon upon such terms and conditions as he may deem proper.

(Oct. 17, 1940, ch. 888, art. V, §508, 54 Stat. 1189.)

SECTION REFERRED TO IN OTHER SECTIONS

This section is referred to in sections 567, 572 of this Appendix; title 5 section 5569.

§ 569. Distribution of information concerning benefits of article; forms

The Secretary of the Interior shall issue through appropriate military and naval channels a notice for distribution by appropriate military and naval authorities to persons in the military service explaining the provisions of this article [sections 560 to 574 of this Appendix] except as to sections 500, 513, and 514 hereof [sections 560, 573, and 574 of this Appendix] and shall furnish forms to be distributed in like manner to those desiring to make application for its benefits, except as to said sections.

(Oct. 17, 1940, ch. 888, art. V, § 509, 54 Stat. 1189; Oct. 6, 1942, ch. 581, § 15, 56 Stat. 776.)

AMENDMENTS

1942—Act Oct. 6, 1942, substituted "sections 500, 513, and 514" for "section 500" and "sections" for "section" before period at end.

SECTION REFERRED TO IN OTHER SECTIONS

This section is referred to in sections 567, 572 of this Appendix; title 5 section 5569.

§ 570. Homestead entrymen permitted to leave entries to perform farm labor

(1) During the pendency of any war in which the United States may be engaged while this Act [sections 501 to 593 of this Appendix] remains in force any homestead entryman shall be entitled to a leave of absence from his entry for the purpose of performing farm labor. The time actually spent in farm labor shall be counted as constructive residence, if within fifteen days after leaving his entry to engage in such labor the entryman files a notice of absence in the land office of the district in which his entry is situated, and if at the expiration of the calendar year the entryman files in that office a written statement under oath and corroborated by two witnesses giving the date or dates when he left his entry, the date or dates of his return, and the place where and person for whom he was engaged in farm labor during such period or periods of absence.

(2) Nothing in this section shall excuse any homestead entryman from making improvements or performing the cultivation upon his entry required by law. The provisions of this section shall apply only to persons whose applications have been allowed or filed before October 17, 1940.

(Oct. 17, 1940, ch. 888, art. V, § 510, 54 Stat. 1189; Pub. L. 102–12, § 9(23), Mar. 18, 1991, 105 Stat. 41.)

AMENDMENTS

1991—Par. (2). Pub. L. 102–12 substituted "before October 17, 1940" for "prior to the effective date of this Act".

SECTION REFERRED TO IN OTHER SECTIONS

This section is referred to in sections 567, 572 of this Appendix; title 5 section 5569.

§ 571. Land rights of persons under 21

Any person under the age of twenty-one who serves in the military service while this Act [sections 501 to 593 of this Appendix] remains in force shall be entitled to the same rights under the laws relating to lands owned or controlled by the United States, including the mining and mineral leasing laws, as those over twenty-one now possess under such laws. Any requirements as to establishment of residence within a limited time shall be suspended as to entry by such person until six months after his discharge from military service. Applications for entry may be verified before any officer in the United States or any foreign country authorized to administer oaths by the laws of the State or Territory in which the land may be situated.

(Oct. 17, 1940, ch. 888, art. V, § 511, 54 Stat. 1189.)

REFERENCES IN TEXT

The mining laws and the mineral leasing laws, referred to in text, are classified generally to Title 30, Mineral Lands and Mining.

SECTION REFERRED TO IN OTHER SECTIONS

This section is referred to in sections 567, 572 of this Appendix; title 5 section 5569.

§ 572. Extension of benefits to persons serving with war allies of United States

Citizens of the United States who serve with the forces of any nation with which the United States may be allied in the prosecution of any war in which the United States engages while this Act [sections 501 to 593 of this Appendix] remains in force shall be entitled to the relief and benefits afforded by sections 501 to 511, inclusive [sections 561 to 571 of this Appendix], if such service is similar to military service as defined in this Act [sections 501 to 593 of this Appendix], and if they are honorably discharged and resume United States citizenship or die in the service of the allied forces or as a result of such service.

(Oct. 17, 1940, ch. 888, art. V, § 512, 54 Stat. 1190; Oct. 6, 1942, ch. 581, § 16, 56 Stat. 776.)

AMENDMENTS

1942—Act Oct. 6, 1942, substituted "sections 501 to 511, inclusive" for "this article".

REPEAL OF PRIOR ACTS CONTINUING SECTION

Section 6 of act July 3, 1952, ch. 570, 66 Stat. 334, repealed act Apr. 14, 1952, ch. 204, 66 Stat. 54, as amended by acts May 28, 1952, ch. 339, 66 Stat. 96; June 14, 1952, ch. 437, 66 Stat. 137; June 30, 1952, ch. 526, 66 Stat. 296, which continued provisions until July 3, 1952. This repeal took effect as of June 16, 1952, by section 7 of act July 3, 1952.

SECTION REFERRED TO IN OTHER SECTIONS

This section is referred to in sections 514, 567 of this Appendix; title 5 section 5569.

§ 573. Income taxes; collection deferred; interest; statute of limitations

The collection from any person in the military service of any tax on the income of such person, whether falling due prior to or during his period of military service, shall be deferred for a period extending not more than six months after the termination of his period of military service if such person's ability to pay such tax is materially impaired by reason of such service. No interest on any amount of tax, collection of which is deferred for any period under this section, and no penalty for nonpayment of such amount during such period, shall accrue for such period of deferment by reason of such nonpayment. The running of any statute of limitations against the collection of such tax by distraint or otherwise shall be suspended for the period of military service of any individual the collection of whose tax is deferred under this section, and for an additional period of nine months beginning with the day following the period of military service. The provisions of this section shall not apply to the income tax on employees imposed by section 1400 of the Federal Insurance Contributions Act.

(Oct. 17, 1940, ch. 888, art. V, §513, 54 Stat. 1190.)

REFERENCES IN TEXT

Section 1400 of the Federal Insurance Contributions Act, referred to in text, is section 1400 of act Feb. 10, 1939, ch. 2, 53 Stat. 175, which enacted section 1400 of former Title 26, Internal Revenue Code of 1939. Section 1400 was repealed by section 7851(a)(3) of Title 26, Internal Revenue Code. For table of comparisons of the 1939 Code to the 1986 Code, see Table I preceding section 1 of Title 26, Internal Revenue Code. See also section 7851(e) of Title 26, Internal Revenue Code, for provision that references in the 1986 Code to a provision of the 1939 Code, not then applicable, shall be deemed a reference to the corresponding provision of the 1986 Code, which is then applicable.

FORMER PROVISIONS FOR ABATEMENT OF TAX

Internal Revenue Code, §421, as added by act June 9, 1943, ch. 120, §8, 57 Stat. 149, and amended by acts Aug. 5, 1947, ch. 496, §1, 61 Stat. 778; Aug. 8, 1947, ch. 515, §9, 61 Stat. 918 (section 421 of former Title 26, Internal Revenue Code of 1939), provided for abatement of income tax for members of armed forces dying on or after December 7, 1941, while in active service and prior to January 1, 1948. These provisions were omitted in the general amendment of that section by act Sept. 23, 1950, ch. 994, title III, part I, §301, 64 Stat. 947.

EXTENSION OF DUE DATE UNDER OTHER LAWS

Section 507(b)(2)(A) of the Revenue Act of 1942, act Oct. 21, 1942, ch. 619, title V, 56 Stat. 964, provided: "The amendments made by this section [adding sections 3804 and 3805 of former Title 26, Internal Revenue Code of 1939, and adding section 527 of this Appendix] shall not be construed to shorten any period fixed under the provisions of section 513 of the Soldiers' and Sailors' Civil Relief Act of 1940 [this section] within which any act may be done, except that any action or proceeding authorized under section 3804(d)(1) of the Internal Revenue Code [section 3804(d)(1) of former Title 26, Internal Revenue Code of 1939], as well as any other action or proceeding authorized by law in connection therewith, may be taken, begun, or prosecuted without regard to the period so fixed."

§574. Residence for tax purposes

(1) For the purposes of taxation in respect of any person, or of his personal property, income, or gross income, by any State, Territory, possession, or political subdivision of any of the foregoing, or by the District of Columbia, such person shall not be deemed to have lost a residence or domicile in any State, Territory, possession, or political subdivision of any of the foregoing, or in the District of Columbia, solely by reason of being absent therefrom in compliance with military or naval orders, or to have acquired a residence or domicile in, or to have become resident in or a resident of, any other State, Territory, possession, or political subdivision of any of the foregoing, or the District of Columbia, while, and solely by reason of being, so absent. For the purposes of taxation in respect of the personal property, income, or gross income of any such person by any State, Territory, possession, or political subdivision of any of the foregoing, or the District of Columbia, of which such person is not a resident or in which he is not domiciled, compensation for military or naval service shall not be deemed income for services performed within, or from sources within, such State, Territory, possession, political subdivision, or District, and personal property shall not be deemed to be located or present in or to have a situs for taxation in such State, Territory, possession, or political subdivision, or district. Where the owner of personal property is absent from his residence or domicile solely by reason of compliance with military or naval orders, this section applies with respect to personal property, or the use thereof, within any tax jurisdiction other than such place of residence or domicile, regardless of where the owner may be serving in compliance with such orders. Nothing contained in this section shall prevent taxation by any State, Territory, possession, or political subdivision of any of the foregoing, or the District of Columbia in respect of personal property used in or arising from a trade or business, if it otherwise has jurisdiction. This section shall be effective as of September 8, 1939, except that it shall not require the crediting or refunding of any tax paid prior to October 6, 1942.

(2) When used in this section, (a) the term "personal property" shall include tangible and intangible property (including motor vehicles), and (b) the term "taxation" shall include but not be limited to licenses, fees, or excises imposed in respect to motor vehicles or the use thereof, but only if a license, fee, or excise required by the State or territory, possession, or District of Columbia of which the person is a resident or in which the person is domiciled has been paid.

(Oct. 17, 1940, ch. 888, art. V, §514, as added Oct. 6, 1942, ch. 581, §17, 56 Stat. 777; amended July 3, 1944, ch. 397, §1, 58 Stat. 722; Pub. L. 87–771, Oct. 9, 1962, 76 Stat. 768; Pub. L. 102–12, §9(24), Mar. 18, 1991, 105 Stat. 41.)

AMENDMENTS

1991—Par. (1). Pub. L. 102–12, §9(24)(A), substituted "orders. Nothing" for "orders: *Provided*, That nothing".

Par. (2). Pub. L. 102–12, §9(24)(B), substituted "the use thereof, but only if a license, fee, or excise required by the State or territory, possession, or District of Columbia of which the person is a resident or in which the person is domiciled has been paid" for "the use thereof: *Provided*, That the license, fee, or excise required by the State, Territory, possession, or District of Columbia of which the person is a resident or in which he is domiciled has been paid".

1962—Pub. L. 87–771 inserted sentence in par. (1) making this section applicable with respect to personal property, or the use thereof, within any tax jurisdiction other than the place of residence or domicile, regardless of where the owner may be serving in compliance with military or naval orders where the owner of personal property is absent from his residence or domicile solely by reason of compliance with such orders.

1944—Act July 3, 1944, inserted "personal" before "property" in first sentence, "personal property", before "income or gross income", "and personal property shall not be deemed to be located or present in or to have a situs for taxation in such State, Territory, possession, or political subdivision, or district: *Provided*, That nothing contained in this section shall prevent taxation by any State, Territory, possession, or political subdivision of any of the foregoing, or the District of Columbia in respect of personal property used in or arising from a trade or business, if it otherwise has jurisdiction'' after ''or District'' in second sentence, and substituted ''October 6, 1942'' for ''the date of the enactment of the Soldiers' and Sailors' Civil Relief Act amendments of 1942'' in third sentence.

CREDITING OR REFUNDING TANGIBLE PERSONAL PROPERTY TAX

Section 2 of act July 3, 1944, provided: ''Nothing contained in this Act [amending this section] shall be construed to require the crediting or refunding of any tax in respect of tangible personal property (including licenses, fees, or excise imposed in respect of motor vehicles or the use thereof) paid prior to the date of its enactment [July 3, 1944].''

SECTION REFERRED TO IN OTHER SECTIONS

This section is referred to in title 5 section 5569; title 20 section 7701.

ARTICLE VI—ADMINISTRATIVE REMEDIES

§ 580. Transfers to take advantage of act

Where in any proceeding to enforce a civil right in any court it is made to appear to the satisfaction of the court that any interest, property, or contract has since October 17, 1940, been transferred or acquired with intent to delay the just enforcement of such right by taking advantage of this Act [sections 501 to 593 of this Appendix], the court shall enter such judgment or make such order as might lawfully be entered or made, the provisions of this Act [said sections] to the contrary notwithstanding.

(Oct. 17, 1940, ch. 888, art. VI, § 600, 54 Stat. 1190; Pub. L. 102–12, § 9(25), Mar. 18, 1991, 105 Stat. 41.)

AMENDMENTS

1991—Pub. L. 102–12 substituted ''October 17, 1940,'' for ''the date of the approval of this Act''.

§ 581. Certificates of service; persons reported missing

(1) In any proceeding under this Act [sections 501 to 593 of this Appendix] a certificate signed by The Adjutant General of the Army as to persons in the Army or in any branch of the United States service while serving pursuant to law with the Army of the United States, signed by the Chief of Naval Personnel as to persons in the United States Navy or in any other branch of the United States service while serving pursuant to law with the United States Navy, and signed by the Commandant, United States Marine Corps, as to persons in the Marine Corps, or in any other branch of the United States service while serving pursuant to law with the Marine Corps, or signed by an officer designated by any of them, respectively, for the purpose, shall when produced be prima facie evidence as to any of the following facts stated in such certificate:

That a person named has not been, or is, or has been in military service; the time when and the place where such person entered military service, his residence at that time, and the rank, branch, and unit of such service that he entered, the dates within which he was in military service, the monthly pay received by such person at the date of issuing the certificate, the time when and the place where such person died in or was discharged from such service.

(2) It shall be the duty of the foregoing officers to furnish such certificate on application, and any such certificate when purporting to be signed by any one of such officers or by any person purporting upon the face of the certificates to have been so authorized shall be prima facie evidence of its contents and of the authority of the signer to issue the same.

(3) Where a person in military service has been reported missing he shall be presumed to continue in the service until accounted for, and no period herein limited which begins or ends with the death of such person shall begin or end until the death of such person is in fact reported to or found by the Department of Defense, or any court or board thereof, or until such death is found by a court of competent jurisdiction. No period herein limited which begins or ends with the death of such person shall be extended beyond a period of six months after the time when this Act [said sections] ceases to be in force.

(Oct. 17, 1940, ch. 888, art. VI, § 601, 54 Stat. 1190; Jan. 20, 1942, ch. 10, §§ 1, 2, 56 Stat. 10; Pub. L. 102–12, § 9(26), Mar. 18, 1991, 105 Stat. 41.)

REFERENCES IN TEXT

The time when this Act ceases to be in force, referred to in subsec. (3), is defined in section 584 of this Appendix.

AMENDMENTS

1991—Par. (1). Pub. L. 102–12, § 9(26)(A), substituted ''Chief of Naval Personnel'' for ''Chief of the Bureau of Navigation of the Navy Department''.

Par. (3). Pub. L. 102–12, § 9(26)(B)(i), which directed the substitution of ''Department of Defense'' for ''Department of War or the Navy'', was executed by making the substitution for ''Department of War or Navy'' to reflect the probable intent of Congress.

Pub. L. 102–12, § 9(26)(B)(ii), substituted ''jurisdiction. No'' for ''jurisdiction: *Provided*, That no''.

1942—Act Jan. 20, 1942, changed ''Major General Commandant of the Marine Corps'' to ''Commandant of the Marine Corps''.

§ 582. Revocation, etc., of interlocutory orders

Any interlocutory order made by any court under the provisions of this Act [sections 501 to 593 of this Appendix] may, upon the court's own motion or otherwise, be revoked, modified, or extended by it upon such notice to the parties affected as it may require.

(Oct. 17, 1940, ch. 888, art. VI, § 602, 54 Stat. 1191.)

§ 583. Separability

If any provision of this Act [sections 501 to 593 of this Appendix], or the application thereof to any person or circumstances, is held invalid, the remainder of the Act [said sections], and the application of such provision to other persons or circumstances, shall not be affected thereby.

(Oct. 17, 1940, ch. 888, art. VI, § 603, 54 Stat. 1191.)

§ 584. Termination date

This Act [sections 501 to 593 of this Appendix] shall remain in force until May 15, 1945, except that should the United States be then engaged in a war, this Act [said sections] shall remain in force until such war is terminated by a treaty of peace proclaimed by the President and for six months thereafter. Whenever under any section or provision of this Act [said sections] a proceeding, remedy, privilege, stay, limitation, accounting, or other transaction has been authorized or provided with respect to military service performed prior to the date herein fixed for the termination of this Act [said sections], such section or provision shall be deemed to continue in full force and effect so long as may be necessary to the exercise or enjoyment of such proceeding, remedy, privilege, stay, limitation, accounting, or other transaction.

(Oct. 17, 1940, ch. 888, art. VI, §604, 54 Stat. 1191; Pub. L. 102–12, §9(27), Mar. 18, 1991, 105 Stat. 41.)

AMENDMENTS

1991—Pub. L. 102–12, §9(27)(A), substituted "1945, except that" for "1945: *Provided*, That".

Pub. L. 102–12, §9(27)(B), which directed the substitution of "thereafter. Whenever" for "thereafter: *Provided further*, That whenever", was executed by making the substitution for "thereafter: *Provided further*, That wherever" to reflect the probable intent of Congress.

EXTENSION OF ACT

Notwithstanding the provisions of act July 25, 1947, ch. 327, 61 Stat. 449, set out below, this entire act, sections 501 to 593 of this Appendix, are in force and effect and shall so remain until a subsequent Act of Congress terminates them, under the provisions of section 464 of this Appendix.

TERMINATION OF WAR

Joint Res. July 25, 1947, ch. 327, §4, 61 Stat. 454, provided: "For the purposes of article IV of the Act of October 17, 1940 (54 Stat. 1183–1186), as amended [sections 540 to 548 of this Appendix], the present war shall be deemed to have terminated within the meaning of section 604 (54 Stat. 1191) of the said Act [this section], as of the effective date of this joint resolution [July 25, 1947]."

SECTION REFERRED TO IN OTHER SECTIONS

This section is referred to in section 464 of this Appendix.

§585. Omitted

CODIFICATION

Section, act Oct. 17, 1940, ch. 888, art. VI, §605, 54 Stat. 1191, related to the inapplicability of the Soldiers' and Sailors' Relief Act of 1918 [section 101 et seq. of this Appendix], to military service performed after Oct. 17, 1940.

ARTICLE VII—FURTHER RELIEF

§590. Stay of enforcement of obligations, liabilities, taxes, etc.

(1) A person may, at any time during his period of military service or within six months thereafter, apply to a court for relief in respect of any obligation or liability incurred by such person prior to his period of military service or in respect of any tax or assessment whether falling due prior to or during his period of military service. The court, after appropriate notice and hearing, unless in its opinion the ability of the applicant to comply with the terms of such obligation or liability or to pay such tax or assessment has not been materially affected by reason of his military service, may grant the following relief:

(a) In the case of an obligation payable under its terms in installments under a contract for the purchase of real estate, or secured by a mortgage or other instrument in the nature of a mortgage upon real estate, a stay of the enforcement of such obligation during the applicant's period of military service and, from the date of termination of such period of military service or from the date of application if made after such service, for a period equal to the period of the remaining life of the installment contract or other instrument plus a period of time equal to the period of military service of the applicant or any part of such combined period, subject to payment of the balance of principal and accumulated interest due and unpaid at the date of termination of the period of military service or from the date of application, as the case may be, in equal installments during such combined period at such rate of interest on the unpaid balance as is prescribed in such contract, or other instrument evidencing the obligation, for installments paid when due, and subject to such other terms as may be just.

(b) In the case of any other obligation, liability, tax, or assessment, a stay of the enforcement thereof during the applicant's period of military service and, from the date of termination of such period of military service or from the date of application if made after such service, for a period of time equal to the period of military service of the applicant or any part of such period, subject to payment of the balance of principal and accumulated interest due and unpaid at the date of termination of such period of military service or the date of application, as the case may be, in equal periodic installments during such extended period at such rate of interest as may be prescribed for such obligation, liability, tax, or assessment, if paid when due, and subject to such other terms as may be just.

(2) When any court has granted a stay as provided in this section no fine or penalty shall accrue during the period the terms and conditions of such stay are complied with by reason of failure to comply with the terms or conditions of the obligation, liability, tax, or assessment in respect of which such stay was granted.

(Oct. 17, 1940, ch. 888, art. VII, §700, as added Oct. 6, 1942, ch. 581, §18, 56 Stat. 777.)

§591. Power of attorney

(a) Extension for period person in missing status

Notwithstanding any other provision of law, a power of attorney which—

(1) was duly executed by a person in the military service who is in a missing status (as defined in section 551(2) of title 37, United States Code);

(2) designates that person's spouse, parent, or other named relative as his attorney in fact for certain specified, or all, purposes; and

(3) expires by its terms after that person entered a missing status, and before or after the effective date of this section;

shall be automatically extended for the period that the person is in a missing status.

(b) Limitation on extension

No power of attorney executed after the effective date of this section by a person in the military service may be extended under subsection (a) of this section if the document by its terms clearly indicates that the power granted expires on the date specified even though that person, after the date of execution of the document, enters a missing status.

(c) Persons subject to coverage

This section applies to the following powers of attorney executed by a person in military service or under a call or order to report for military service (or who has been advised by an official of the Department of Defense that such person may receive such a call or order):

(1) A power of attorney that is executed during the Vietnam era (as defined in section 101(29) of title 38, United States Code).

(2) A power of attorney that expires by its terms after July 31, 1990.

(Oct. 17, 1940, ch. 888, art. VII, § 701, as added Pub. L. 92–540, title V, § 504(2), Oct. 24, 1972, 86 Stat. 1098; amended Pub. L. 102–12, § 3, Mar. 18, 1991, 105 Stat. 34.)

AMENDMENTS

1991—Subsec. (c). Pub. L. 102–12 amended subsec. (c) generally. Prior to amendment, subsec. (c) read as follows: "This section applies only to persons in military service who executed powers of attorney during the Vietnam era (as defined in section 101(29) of title 38, United States Code)."

EFFECTIVE DATE

Section effective 90 days after Oct. 24, 1972, see section 601(b) of Pub. L. 92–540, set out as an Effective Date of 1972 Amendment note under section 4101 of Title 38, Veterans' Benefits.

SECTION REFERRED TO IN OTHER SECTIONS

This section is referred to in title 5 section 5569.

§ 592. Professional liability protection for certain persons ordered to active duty in armed forces

(a) Applicability

This section applies to a person who—

(1) after July 31, 1990, is ordered to active duty (other than for training) pursuant to section 688, 12301(a), 12301(g), 12302, 12304, 12306, or 12307 of title 10, United States Code, or who is ordered to active duty under section 12301(d) of such title during a period when members are on active duty pursuant to any of the preceding sections; and

(2) immediately before receiving the order to active duty—

(A) was engaged in the furnishing of health-care services or other services determined by the Secretary of Defense to be professional services; and

(B) had in effect a professional liability insurance policy that does not continue to cover claims filed with respect to such person during the period of the person's active duty unless the premiums are paid for such coverage for such period.

(b) Suspension of coverage

(1) Coverage of a person referred to in subsection (a) by a professional liability insurance policy shall be suspended in accordance with this subsection upon receipt of the written request of such person by the insurance carrier.

(2) A professional liability insurance carrier—

(A) may not require that premiums be paid by or on behalf of a person for any professional liability insurance coverage suspended pursuant to paragraph (1); and

(B) shall refund any amount paid for coverage for the period of such suspension or, upon the election of such person, apply such amount for the payment of any premium becoming due upon the reinstatement of such coverage.

(3) A professional liability insurance carrier shall not be liable with respect to any claim that is based on professional conduct (including any failure to take any action in a professional capacity) of a person that occurs during a period of suspension of that person's professional liability insurance under this subsection. For the purposes of the preceding sentence, a claim based upon the failure of a professional to make adequate provision for patients to be cared for during the period of the professional's active duty service shall be considered to be based on an action or failure to take action before the beginning of the period of suspension of professional liability insurance under this subsection, except in a case in which professional services were provided after the date of the beginning of such period.

(c) Reinstatement of coverage

(1) Professional liability insurance coverage suspended in the case of any person pursuant to subsection (b) shall be reinstated by the insurance carrier on the date on which that person transmits to the insurance carrier a written request for reinstatement.

(2) The request of a person for reinstatement shall be effective only if the person transmits the request to the insurance carrier within 30 days after the date on which the person is released from active duty. The insurance carrier shall notify the person of the due date for payment of the premium of such insurance. Such premium shall be paid by the person within 30 days after the receipt of that notice.

(3) The period for which professional liability insurance coverage shall be reinstated for a person under this subsection may not be less than the balance of the period for which coverage would have continued under the insurance policy if the coverage had not been suspended.

(d) Increase in premium

An insurance carrier may not increase the amount of the premium charged for professional liability insurance coverage of any person for the minimum period of the reinstatement of such coverage required under subsection (c)(3) to an amount greater than the amount chargeable for such coverage for such period before the suspension, except to the extent of any general increase in the premium amounts charged by that carrier for the same professional liability coverage for persons similarly covered by such insurance during the period of the suspension.

(e) Continuation of coverage of unaffected persons

This section does not—

(1) require a suspension of professional liability insurance coverage for any person who is not a person referred to in subsection (a) and who is covered by the same professional liability insurance as a person referred to in such subsection; or

(2) relieve any person of the obligation to pay premiums for the coverage not required to be suspended.

(f) Stay of civil or administrative actions

(1) A civil or administrative action for damages on the basis of the alleged professional negligence or other professional liability of a person whose professional liability insurance coverage has been suspended under subsection (b) shall be stayed until the end of the period of the suspension if—

(A) the action was commenced during that period;

(B) the action is based on an act or omission that occurred before the date on which the suspension became effective; and

(C) the suspended professional liability insurance would, except for the suspension, on its face cover the alleged professional negligence or other professional liability negligence or other professional liability of the person.

(2) Whenever a civil or administrative action for damages is stayed under paragraph (1) in the case of any person, the action shall be deemed to have been filed on the date on which the professional liability insurance coverage of such person is reinstated under subsection (c).

(g) Effect of suspension upon limitations period

In the case of a civil or administrative action for which a stay could have been granted under subsection (f) by reason of the suspension of professional liability insurance coverage of the defendant under this section, the period of the suspension of the coverage shall be excluded from the computation of any statutory period of limitation on the commencement of such action.

(h) Death during period of suspension

If a person whose professional liability insurance coverage is suspended under subsection (b) dies during the period of the suspension—

(1) the requirement for the grant or continuance of a stay in any civil or administrative action against such person under subsection (f)(1) shall terminate on the date of the death of such person; and

(2) the carrier of the professional liability insurance so suspended shall be liable for any claim for damages for professional negligence or other professional liability of the deceased person in the same manner and to the same extent as such carrier would be liable if the person had died while covered by such insurance but before the claim was filed.

(i) Definitions

In this section:

(1) The term "active duty" has the meaning given that term in section 101 of title 10, United States Code.

(2) The term "profession" includes occupation.

(3) The term "professional" includes occupational.

(Oct. 17, 1940, ch. 888, art. VII, §702, as added Pub. L. 102–12, §4, Mar. 18, 1991, 105 Stat. 34; amended Pub. L. 104–106, div. A, title XV, §1501(e)(3), Feb. 10, 1996, 110 Stat. 501.)

AMENDMENTS

1996—Subsec. (a)(1). Pub. L. 104–106 substituted "section 688, 12301(a), 12301(g), 12302, 12304, 12306, or 12307 of title 10" for "section 672(a) or (g), 673, 673b, 674, 675, or 688 of title 10" and "section 12301(d) of such title" for "section 672(d) of such title".

EFFECTIVE DATE OF 1996 AMENDMENT

Amendment by Pub. L. 104–106 effective as if included in the Reserve Officer Personnel Management Act, title XVI of Pub. L. 103–337, as enacted on Oct. 5, 1994, see section 1501(f)(3) of Pub. L. 104–106, set out as a note under section 113 of Title 10, Armed Forces.

SECTION REFERRED TO IN OTHER SECTIONS

This section is referred to in section 593 of this Appendix.

§593. Reinstatement of health insurance coverage upon release from service

(a) Right to reinstatement of coverage

A person who, by reason of military service described in section 702(a)(1) [section 592(a)(1) of this Appendix], is entitled to the rights and benefits of this Act [sections 501 to 593 of this Appendix] shall also be entitled upon release from such military service to reinstatement of any health insurance which (1) was in effect on the day before such service commenced, and (2) was terminated effective on a date during the period of such service.

(b) Exclusion or waiting period

An exclusion or a waiting period may not be imposed in connection with reinstatement of health insurance coverage of a health or physical condition of a person under subsection (a), or a health or physical condition of any other person who is covered by the insurance by reason of the coverage of such person, if—

(1) the condition arose before or during that person's period of training or service in the Armed Forces;

(2) an exclusion or waiting period would not have been imposed for the condition during a period of coverage resulting from participation by such person in the insurance; and

(3) the condition of such person has not been determined by the Secretary of Veterans Affairs to be a disability incurred or aggravated in the line of duty (within the meaning of section 105 of title 38, United States Code).

(c) Employer-offered insurance benefits

Subsection (a) does not apply in the case of employer-offered insurance benefits in which a person referred to in such subsection is entitled to participate pursuant to the provisions of chapter 43 of title 38, United States Code.

(Oct. 17, 1940, ch. 888, art. VII, §703, as added Pub. L. 102–12, §5(b), Mar. 18, 1991, 105 Stat. 37.)

EFFECTIVE DATE

Section 5(c) of Pub. L. 102–12 provided that: "The amendments made by this section [enacting this section and amending section 4301 of Title 38, Veterans' Benefits] shall take effect as of August 1, 1990.''

FIRST WAR POWERS ACT, 1941

ACT DEC. 18, 1941, CH. 593, 55 STAT. 838

TITLE I—COORDINATION OF EXECUTIVE BUREAUS IN THE INTEREST OF THE MORE EFFICIENT CONCENTRATION OF THE GOVERNMENT

§§ 601 to 605. Repealed. Pub. L. 89–554, § 8(a), Sept. 6, 1966, 80 Stat. 651

Section 601, act Dec. 18, 1941, ch. 593, title I, § 1, 55 Stat. 838, related to coordination of executive bureaus and offices by the President for national defense.

Section 602, act Dec. 18, 1941, ch. 593, title I, § 2, 55 Stat. 838, related to consolidation of offices.

Section 603, act Dec. 18, 1941, ch. 593, title I, § 3, 55 Stat. 838, related to expenditure of appropriations.

Section 604, act Dec. 18, 1941, ch. 593, title I, § 4, 55 Stat. 839, related to elimination of certain bureaus.

Section 605, act Dec. 18, 1941, ch. 593, title I, § 5, 55 Stat. 839, related to suspension of conflicting laws.

TITLE II—CONTRACTS

§ 611. Repealed. Pub. L. 89–554, § 8(a), Sept. 6, 1966, 80 Stat. 651

Section, acts Dec. 18, 1941, ch. 593, title II, § 201, 55 Stat. 839; Jan. 12, 1951, ch. 1230, § 1, 64 Stat. 1257, related to exemption of war contracts from certain restrictions.

TITLE III—TRADING WITH THE ENEMY

§ 616. Omitted

CODIFICATION

Section, act Dec. 18, 1941, ch. 593, title III, § 301, 55 Stat. 839, amended section 5 of the Trading with the Enemy Act, which is classified to section 5 of this Appendix and section 95a of Title 12, Banks and Banking.

§ 617. Repealed. Pub. L. 89–554, 8(a), Sept. 6, 1966, 80 Stat. 651

Section, act Dec. 18, 1941, ch. 593, title III, § 302, 55 Stat. 840, confirmed certain acts, etc., made under the Trading with the Enemy Act.

§ 618. Repealed. July 5, 1947, ch. 327, § 1, 61 Stat. 449

Section, act Dec. 18, 1941, ch. 593, title III, § 303, 55 Stat. 840, related to censorship of communications during World War II and penalties and forfeitures for violations thereof.

§§ 619, 620. Transferred

CODIFICATION

Section 619, act Dec. 18, 1941, ch. 593, title III, § 304, as added Mar. 8, 1946, ch. 83, § 1, 60 Stat. 50, amended the Trading with the Enemy Act by adding a section 32, and was transferred to section 32 of this Appendix.

Section 620, act Dec. 18, 1941, ch. 593, title III, § 305, as added Aug. 8, 1946, ch. 878, § 1, 60 Stat. 925, amended the Trading with the Enemy Act by adding sections 33 to 37, and was transferred to sections 33 to 37 of this Appendix.

TITLE IV—TIME LIMIT AND SHORT TITLE

§§ 621, 622. Repealed. Pub. L. 89–554, § 8(a), Sept. 6, 1966, 80 Stat. 651

Section 621, act Dec. 18, 1941, ch. 593, title IV, § 401, 55 Stat. 841, provided that sections 601 to 605 and 611 of this Appendix would terminate six months after the termination of the war or such earlier time as the Congress or President may designate.

Section 622, act Dec. 18, 1941, ch. 593, title IV, § 402, 55 Stat. 841, provided that act Dec. 18, 1941, may be cited as the ''First Powers Act, 1941''.

SECOND WAR POWERS ACT, 1942

ACT MAR. 27, 1942, CH. 199, 56 STAT. 176

TITLE I—EMERGENCY POWERS OF THE INTERSTATE COMMERCE COMMISSION OVER MOTOR AND WATER CARRIERS

§§ 631 to 631b. Repealed. Pub. L. 95–473, § 4(b), Oct. 17, 1978, 92 Stat. 1468

Section 631, act Mar. 27, 1942, ch. 199, title I, § 101, 56 Stat. 177, amended section 304 of former Title 49, Transportation.

Section 631a, act Mar. 27, 1942, ch. 199, title I, § 102, 56 Stat. 177, amended section 310a of former Title 49.

Section 631b, act Mar. 27, 1942, ch. 199, title I, § 103, 56 Stat. 177, amended section 911 of former Title 49.

TITLE II—ACQUISITION AND DISPOSITION OF PROPERTY

§§ 632, 632a. Omitted

CODIFICATION

Sections 632 and 632a were omitted as terminated pursuant to section 645 of this Appendix.

Section 632, act Mar. 27, 1942, ch. 199, title II, § 201, 56 Stat. 177, added section 2 to act July 2, 1917, ch. 35, section 171a of Title 50, War and National Defense, authorizing the acquisition and disposition of property for military, naval, or other war purposes.

Section 632a, act Mar. 27, 1942, ch. 199, title II, § 202, as added Dec. 28, 1945, ch. 590, § 1(a), 59 Stat. 658, provided that the authority granted by section 2 of act July 2, 1917, should not be exercised after Dec. 28, 1945.

The following Executive Orders related to the exercise of authority under section 632: No. 9129, eff. Apr. 13, 1942, 7 F.R. 2810; No. 9150, eff. Apr. 28, 1942, 7 F.R. 3217; No. 9186, eff. June 5, 1942, 7 F.R. 4317; No. 9194, eff. July 7, 1942, 7 F.R. 5257; No. 9211, eff. Aug. 1, 1942, 7 F.R. 6030; No. 9217, eff. Aug. 7, 1942, 7 F.R. 6177; No. 9218, eff. Aug. 11, 1942, 7 F.R. 6381; No. 9249, eff. Oct. 1, 1942, 7 F.R. 7874; No. 9280, eff. Dec. 5, 1942, 7 F.R. 10179; No. 9321, eff. Mar. 25, 1943, 8 F.R. 3749; and President's letter of July 31, 1943, 8 F.R. 10702.

TITLE III—PRIORITIES POWERS

§ 633. Omitted

CODIFICATION

Section, acts Mar. 27, 1942, ch. 199, title III, § 301, 56 Stat. 177; Dec. 20, 1944, ch. 614, 58 Stat. 827; Aug. 7, 1946, ch. 770, § 1(26), (31), 60 Stat. 868, which amended section 1152 of this Appendix, was omitted as terminated pursuant to the provisions of section 645 of this Appendix.

TITLE IV—PURCHASE BY FEDERAL RESERVE BANKS OF GOVERNMENT OBLIGATIONS

§ 634. Omitted

CODIFICATION

Section, act Mar. 27, 1942, ch. 199, title IV, § 401, 56 Stat. 180, which amended section 355(b) of Title 12, Banks and Banking, was omitted as terminated pursuant to the provisions of section 645 of this Appendix.

TITLE V—WAIVER OF NAVIGATION AND INSPECTION LAWS

§635. Omitted

CODIFICATION

Section, act Mar. 27, 1942, ch. 199, title V, §501, 56 Stat. 180, which authorized waiver of navigation and inspection laws, was omitted as terminated pursuant to the provisions of section 645 of this Appendix.

VESSELS OF WAR SHIPPING ADMINISTRATION AND THOSE TRAVELLING BETWEEN PUERTO RICO AND UNITED STATES

Treasury Decisions No. 50756, Oct. 30, 1942, 7 F.R. 9005 and No. 50811, Feb. 5, 1943, 8 F.R. 1757, related respectively to those vessels.

TITLE VI—POWER TO REQUISITION

§§636, 636a. Omitted

CODIFICATION

Section 636, act Mar. 27, 1942, ch. 199, title VI, §601, 56 Stat. 181, amended section 721 of this Appendix, which was omitted from the Code.

Section 636a, act Mar. 27, 1942, ch. 199, title VI, §602, 56 Stat. 181, amended section 721 of this Appendix, which was omitted from the Code.

TITLE VII—POLITICAL ACTIVITY

§637. Repealed. Pub. L. 89–554, §8(a), Sept. 6, 1966, 80 Stat. 651

Section, act Mar. 27, 1942, ch. 199, title VII, §701, 56 Stat. 181, amended section 118i of former Title 5, Executive Departments and Government Officers and Employees.

TITLE VIII—PROTECTION OF WAR INDUSTRIES AND PROTECTION OF RESOURCES SUBJECT TO HAZARDS OF FOREST FIRES

§638. Repealed. Pub. L. 89–554, §8(a), Sept. 6, 1966, 80 Stat. 651

Section, act Mar. 27, 1942, ch. 199, title VIII, §801, 56 Stat. 181, related to utilization of Civilian Conservation Corps.

TITLE IX—FREE POSTAGE FOR SOLDIERS, SAILORS, AND MARINES

§639. Repealed. Dec. 28, 1945, ch. 590, §1(b), 59 Stat. 658

Section, act Mar. 27, 1942, ch. 199, title IX, §901, 56 Stat. 181, related to free postage for members of the armed forces.

§639a. Repealed. Aug. 10, 1956, ch. 1041, §53, 70A Stat. 641

Section, act Oct. 6, 1945, ch. 393, §10, 59 Stat. 542, related to first class mail matter for members of the armed forces and termination date.

TITLE X—NATURALIZATION OF PERSONS SERVING IN THE ARMED FORCES OF THE UNITED STATES DURING THE PRESENT WAR

§640. Repealed. June 27, 1952, ch. 477, title IV, §403(a)(42), 66 Stat. 280

Section, acts Mar. 27, 1942, ch. 199, title X, §1001, 56 Stat. 182; Dec. 28, 1945, ch. 590, §1(c), 59 Stat. 658, were amendments to the Nationality Act of 1940 which were formerly classified to sections 1001 to 1006 of Title 8, Aliens and Nationality (relating to naturalization of persons serving in the armed forces of the United States during World War II). See section 1440 of Title 8.

TITLE XI—ACCEPTANCE OF CONDITIONAL GIFTS TO FURTHER THE WAR PROGRAM

§§641 to 641f. Repealed. June 29, 1946, ch. 526, §1, 60 Stat. 345

Section 641, act Mar. 27, 1942, ch. 199, title XI, §1101, 56 Stat. 183, related to acceptance by Secretary of the Treasury of gifts for war purposes.

Section 641a, act Mar. 27, 1942, ch. 199, title XI, §1102, 56 Stat. 183, related to conversion of gift property into money.

Section 641b, act Mar. 27, 1942, ch. 199, title XI, §1103, 56 Stat. 183, related to deposit of moneys in War Contributions Fund.

Section 641c, act Mar. 27, 1942, ch. 199, title XI, §1104, 56 Stat. 183, related to allocation of deposits to pertinent appropriations.

Section 641d, act Mar. 27, 1942, ch. 199, title XI, §1105, 56 Stat. 184, related to reports to Congress.

Section 641e, act Mar. 27, 1942, ch. 199, title XI, §1106, 56 Stat. 184, related to penalties for wrongful solicitation or use of gifts. Section was also repealed by act June 25, 1948, ch. 645, §21, 62 Stat. 862. See section 663 of Title 18, Crimes and Criminal Procedure.

Section 641f, act Mar. 27, 1942, ch. 199, title XI, §1107, as added by act Dec. 28, 1945, ch. 590, §1(d), 59 Stat. 658, limited scope of authority granted by these sections to the personnel of the armed forces stationed abroad.

TITLE XII—COINAGE OF 5-CENT PIECES

§§642 to 642e. Omitted

CODIFICATION

Section 642, acts Mar. 27, 1942, ch. 199, title XII, §1201, 56 Stat. 184; Dec. 28, 1945, ch. 590, §1(e), 59 Stat. 658, which related to temporary coinage of silver and copper 5-cent pieces, expired Dec. 31, 1945, by its own terms.

Section 642a, act Mar. 27, 1942, ch. 199, title XII, §1202, 56 Stat. 184, related to allocation of silver bullion to Director of Mint for coinage of 5 cent pieces pursuant to section 642 of this Appendix.

Section 642b, act Mar. 27, 1942, ch. 199, title XII, §1203, 56 Stat. 184, set standard for silver-copper ingots used for coinage pursuant to section 642 of this Appendix and set the weight deviation of such coinage.

Section 642c, act Mar. 27, 1942, ch. 199, title XII, §1204, 56 Stat. 184, provided that for purposes of section 341 of former Title 31, Money and Finance, the coinage authorized by section 642 of this Appendix was to be deemed to be copper.

Section 642d, acts Mar. 27, 1942, ch. 199, title XII, §1205, 56 Stat. 184; Dec. 28, 1945, ch. 590, §1(e), 59 Stat. 658, related to redemption, melting, and use of 5-cent pieces for subsidiary silver coinage.

Section 642e, act Mar. 27, 1942, ch. 199, title XII, §1206, 56 Stat. 185, related to effective date of sections 642 to 642e of this Appendix.

TITLE XIII—INSPECTION AND AUDIT OF WAR CONTRACTORS

§§643 to 643c. Omitted

CODIFICATION

Sections 643 to 643c of this Appendix were omitted as terminated six months after the termination of the national emergency proclaimed by the President on Dec. 16, 1950, which emergency terminated two years from Sept. 14, 1976, pursuant to section 1601 of Title 50, War and National Defense.

Section 643, act Mar. 27, 1942, ch. 199, title XIII, §1301, 56 Stat. 185, related to inspection of plants and audits of books and records of defense contractors, definition of defense contract, and designation of the governmental agency or officer to administer these functions.

Section 643a, acts Mar. 27, 1942, ch. 199, title XIII, § 1302, 56 Stat. 185; Oct. 15, 1970, Pub. L. 91–452, title II, § 248, 84 Stat. 931, related to oaths and affirmations, attendance and testimony of witnesses, production of records and other evidence, and unlawful disclosure of information obtained.

Section 643b, act Mar. 27, 1942, ch. 199, title XIII, § 1303, 56 Stat. 186, related to refusal to give evidence, etc., assistance of courts to obtain such evidence, and penalties for such refusal.

Section 643c, act Mar. 27, 1942, ch. 199, title XIII, § 1304, 56 Stat. 186, defined "person" for purposes of sections 643 to 643c of this Appendix.

CONTINUATION OF PROVISIONS UNTIL TERMINATION OF NATIONAL EMERGENCY

Act June 30, 1953, ch. 169, 67 Stat. 120, provided that sections 643 to 643c of this Appendix as extended by subsection 1(a)(2) of the Emergency Powers Continuation Act (Public Law 450, Eighty-second Congress), as amended, remain in full force and effect until six months after the termination of the national emergency proclaimed by the President on Dec. 16, 1950 (Proc. 2914, 3 C.F.R. 71, set out as a note preceding section 1 of this Appendix), notwithstanding any limitation by reference to war of the time during which the powers and authorizations therein granted may be exercised, or until such earlier date as may be provided by the Congress by concurrent resolution or by the President.

Provisions of this section were previously extended to July 1, 1953 by act July 3, 1952, ch. 570, § 1(a)(2), 66 Stat. 331, as amended by act Mar. 31, 1953, ch. 13, § 1, 67 Stat. 18.

Act Apr. 4, 1953, ch. 21, § 2, 67 Stat. 23, repealed act July 3, 1952, ch. 570, § 1(a)(18), 66 Stat. 331, which continued the effectiveness of this section until Apr. 1, 1953. Section 6 of act July 3, 1952, repealed act Apr. 14, 1952, ch. 204, 66 Stat. 54, as amended by act May 28, 1952, ch. 339, 66 Stat. 96; act June 14, 1952, ch. 437, 66 Stat. 137; act June 30, 1952, ch. 526, 66 Stat. 296, which continued provisions until July 3, 1952. This repeal took effect as of June 16, 1952, by section 7 of act July 3, 1952.

EXECUTIVE ORDER NO. 9127

Ex. Ord. No. 9127, eff. Apr. 10, 1942, 7 F.R. 2753, provided for the inspection of plants and audit of books of defense contractors.

TITLE XIV—UTILIZATION OF VITAL WAR INFORMATION

§§ 644 to 644b. Omitted

CODIFICATION

Sections 644 to 644b were omitted as terminated pursuant to section 645 of this Appendix.

Section 644, act Mar. 27, 1942, ch. 199, title XIV, § 1401, 56 Stat. 186, related to special investigations and reports and to penalties for refusal to answer questions or for supplying false information.

Section 644a, act Mar. 27, 1942, ch. 199, title XIV, § 1402, 56 Stat. 186, related to availability of reports to other government agencies.

Section 644b, act Mar. 27, 1942, ch. 199, title XIV, § 1403, 56 Stat. 186, defined person as used in this title.

TITLE XV—TIME LIMIT AND SHORT TITLE

§§ 645 to 645b. Omitted

CODIFICATION

Sections 645 to 645b of this Appendix, which were part of the Second War Powers Act, 1942, were omitted in view of the repeal or omission of the remaining provisions of the Second War Powers Act, 1942.

Section 645, acts Mar. 27, 1942, ch. 199, title XV, § 1501, 56 Stat. 187; Dec. 20, 1944, ch. 614, 58 Stat. 827; Dec. 28, 1945, ch. 590, § 1(f), 59 Stat. 658; June 29, 1946, ch. 526, § 1, 60 Stat. 345; Mar. 31, 1947, ch. 29, § 3, 61 Stat. 34; June 30, 1947, ch. 184, § 1, 61 Stat. 214; July 15, 1947, ch. 248, § 3, 61 Stat. 322; Feb. 28, 1948, ch. 85, 62 Stat. 58; June 4, 1948, ch. 419, § 1, 62 Stat. 342; June 30, 1949, ch. 289, 63 Stat. 404, provided for termination of portions of the Second War Powers Act, 1942, former sections 631 to 642e, 643 to 643c, 644 to 644b, and 645 to 645b of this Appendix, on certain specified dates.

Section 645a, act Mar. 27, 1942, ch. 199, title XV, § 1502, 56 Stat. 187, provided that act Mar. 27, 1942, ch. 199, 56 Stat. 176, be cited as the "Second War Powers Act, 1942".

Section 645b, act Mar. 27, 1942, ch. 199, title XV, § 1503, as added June 29, 1946, ch. 526, § 2, 60 Stat. 346, provided that nothing in the Second War Powers Act, 1942, or any other Federal Act, except the Emergency Price Control Act of 1942, sections 901 to 946 of this Appendix, the Stabilization Act of 1942, sections 961 to 971 of this Appendix, or the District of Columbia Emergency Rent Act be construed to authorize the establishment of price and rent controls.

FIRST DECONTROL ACT OF 1947

Act Mar. 31, 1947, ch. 29, 61 Stat. 34, known as the "First Decontrol Act of 1947", provided that it was vital to a free economy and full production in the United States that all emergency controls and war powers under the Second War Powers Act, sections 631 to 642e, 643 to 643c, 644 to 644b, and 645 to 645b of this Appendix, be removed except in certain limited instances, and amended section 645 of this Appendix for the purpose of liquidating existing emergency controls and war powers and for the purpose of affording Congressional committees an opportunity to consider specific legislation granting restricted authority in limited instances.

SECOND DECONTROL ACT OF 1947

Act July 15, 1947, ch. 248, 61 Stat. 321, as amended Feb. 28, 1948, ch. 85, 62 Stat. 58; June 4, 1948, ch. 419, § 1, 62 Stat. 342, known as the "Second Decontrol Act of 1947", provided that it was the general policy of the United States to eliminate emergency wartime controls of materials except to the minimum extent necessary, and amended sections 645 and 701 of this Appendix to effectuate this policy.

APPROPRIATIONS

Act June 30, 1947, ch. 184, § 2, 61 Stat. 214, authorized appropriations, out of any money in the Treasury not otherwise appropriated, as may be necessary to carry out the provisions of act June 30, 1947, amending sections 645 and 701 of this Appendix.

EXPORTATION RESTRICTIONS ON CERTAIN ARTICLES

ACT JULY 2, 1940, CH. 508, 54 STAT. 714

§ 701. Repealed. Aug. 10, 1956, ch. 1041, § 53, 70A Stat. 641

Section, acts July 2, 1940, ch. 508, § 6, 54 Stat. 714; June 30, 1942, ch. 461, 56 Stat. 463; July 1, 1944, ch. 360, 58 Stat. 671; June 30, 1945, ch. 205, 59 Stat. 270; May 23, 1946, ch. 269, 60 Stat. 215; June 30, 1947, ch. 184, § 1, 61 Stat. 214; July 15, 1947, ch. 248, § 4, 61 Stat. 323; Dec. 30, 1947, ch. 526, § 3(a), 61 Stat. 946, authorized President, until Feb. 28, 1949, to prohibit or curtail exportation of any articles, technical data, materials, or supplies, except under those rules and regulations as he should prescribe. See section 2401 et seq. of this Appendix.

§ 702. Omitted

CODIFICATION

Section, act May 28, 1941, ch. 134, 55 Stat. 206, extended application of section 701 of this Appendix to territories and possessions of the United States.

REQUISITION OF MILITARY EQUIPMENT, MATERIALS AND SUPPLIES

ACT OCT. 10, 1940, CH. 836, 54 STAT. 1090

§§711 to 713. Omitted

CODIFICATION

Sections 711 to 713 were omitted as terminated pursuant to section 713 of this Appendix.

Section 711, acts Oct. 10, 1940, ch. 836, §1, 54 Stat. 1090; July 2, 1942, ch. 471, §1, 56 Stat. 467, authorized President to requisition certain military and naval materials, the exportation of which had been prohibited or curtailed by law. Authority to requisition under Defense Production Act of 1950 was contained in section 2081 of this Appendix.

Section 712, act Oct. 10, 1940, ch. 836, §2, 54 Stat. 1091, provided for compensation for materials requisitioned under sections 711 to 713 of this Appendix. Compensation for property requisitioned under Defense Production Act of 1950 was provided for in section 2081 of this Appendix.

Section 713, acts Oct. 10, 1940, ch. 836, §3, 54 Stat. 1091; July 2, 1942, ch. 471, §2, 56 Stat. 468; June 28, 1944, ch. 308, 58 Stat. 625; June 30, 1945, ch. 207, 59 Stat. 270, provided that authority granted in sections 711 to 713 of this Appendix should remain in force only until June 30, 1946.

EXECUTIVE ORDER NO. 8567

Ex. Ord. No. 8567, Oct. 15, 1940, 5 F.R. 4121, provided for administration of sections 711 to 713 of this Appendix.

ACT OCT. 16, 1941, CH. 445, 55 STAT. 742

§§721 to 724. Omitted

CODIFICATION

Section 721, acts Oct. 16, 1941, ch. 445, §1, 55 Stat. 742; Mar. 27, 1942, ch. 199, title VI, §§601, 602, 56 Stat. 181; June 30, 1943, ch. 181, §1, 57 Stat. 271; June 28, 1944, ch. 307, §1, 58 Stat. 624; June 30, 1945, ch. 208, §1, 59 Stat. 271, authorized President, not later than June 30, 1946, to requisition certain military materials needed for defense and provided for payment of just compensation which might be recovered by suits against United States. Authority to requisition under Defense Production Act of 1950 was contained in section 2081 of this Appendix.

Section 722, acts Oct. 16, 1941, ch. 445, §2, 55 Stat. 742; June 30, 1943, ch. 181, §2, 57 Stat. 271; June 28, 1944, ch. 307, §2, 58 Stat. 624; June 30, 1945, ch. 208, §2, 59 Stat. 271, provided for return of property acquired under sections 721 to 724 to the owner not later than Dec. 31, 1946, if owner desired it and paid fair value thereof.

Section 723, act Oct. 16, 1941, ch. 445, §3, 55 Stat. 743, related to reports to Congress.

Section 724, act Oct. 16, 1941, ch. 445, §4, 55 Stat. 743, related to administration of sections 721 to 724 of this Appendix.

TERRITORIAL USE OF ARMY AND EXTENSION OF SERVICE PERIOD

ACT DEC. 13, 1941, CH. 571, 55 STAT. 799

§731. Omitted

CODIFICATION

Section, act Dec. 13, 1941, ch. 571, §1, 55 Stat. 799, suspended restrictions on territorial use of Army in sections 301 to 318 and 401 to 405 of this Appendix.

§732. Transferred

CODIFICATION

Section, act Dec. 13, 1941, ch. 571, §2, 55 Stat. 800, which extended service periods during any war, was transferred to section 16a of former Title 10, Army and Air Force. Section 16a of former Title 10 was repealed by act Aug. 10, 1956, ch. 1041, §53, 70A Stat. 641, and reenacted as sections 3492 and 8492 of Title 10, Armed Forces. Said sections 3492 and 8492 of Title 10 were repealed by Pub. L. 90–235, §1(a)(2), Jan. 2, 1968, 81 Stat. 753. See section 671a of Title 10.

§733. Repealed. June 28, 1950, ch. 383, title IV, §401(a), 64 Stat. 271

Section, act Dec. 13, 1941, ch. 571, §3, 55 Stat. 800, amended section 2 of former Title 10, Army and Air Force.

CIVILIAN PROTECTION FROM WAR HAZARDS

ACT JAN. 27, 1942, CH. 20, 56 STAT. 19

§§741, 742. Omitted

CODIFICATION

Sections 741 and 742 were omitted pursuant to Ex. Ord. No. 9562, June 5, 1945, 10 F.R. 6639, which terminated the Office of Civilian Defense and abolished the functions of the Office and its Director. See section 5195 et seq. of Title 42, The Public Health and Welfare.

Section 741, act Jan. 27, 1942, ch. 20, §1, 56 Stat. 19, related to provision by the Director of Civilian Defense of protection from bombing attacks and other war hazards.

Section 742, act Jan. 27, 1942, ch. 20, §2, 56 Stat. 19, related to unlawful use of insignia prescribed by the Director of Civilian Defense and interference by the Director of Civilian Defense or his agents with local districts or officials.

DECORATIONS, ETC., FOR MERCHANT MARINE

JOINT RES. APR. 11, 1942, CH. 241, 56 STAT. 217

§§751, 752. Repealed. July 25, 1947, ch. 327, §1, 61 Stat. 449

Section 751, act Apr. 11, 1942, ch. 241, 56 Stat. 217, related to medals for outstanding conduct or service by persons serving in the merchant marines on or after Sept. 3, 1939.

Section 752, act Apr. 11, 1942, ch. 241, 56 Stat. 217, related to use of rosettes or other devices, number of medals to be issued, awards for repeated distinguished service, and posthumous award of medals.

ACT MAY 10, 1943, CH. 96, 57 STAT. 81

§§753 to 753f. Repealed. July 24, 1956, ch. 671, §5(a)(1), 70 Stat. 606, eff. July 1, 1954

Section 753, act May 10, 1943, ch. 96, §1, 57 Stat. 81, related to seamen's service and war zone insignias and the persons eligible therefor.

Section 753a, act May 10, 1943, ch. 96, §2, 57 Stat. 81, related to seamen's honor bar and to persons eligible therefor.

Section 753b, act May 10, 1943, ch. 96, §3, 57 Stat. 82, related to a medal for seamen wounded, physically injured, or suffering from dangerous exposure from acts of enemy.

Section 753c, act May 10, 1943, ch. 96, §4, 57 Stat. 82, related to conditions for eligibility of awards, limitation and termination of awards, and posthumous awards.

Section 753d, act May 10, 1943, ch. 96, §5, 57 Stat. 82, related to seamen's service flag and lapel button and persons entitled to display it.

Section 753e, act May 10, 1943, ch. 96, §6, 57 Stat. 82, related to rules and regulations and expenditures of funds.

Section 753f, act May 10, 1943, ch. 96, § 7, as added July 31, 1945, ch. 337, 59 Stat. 511; amended Aug. 7, 1946, ch. 786, 60 Stat. 884, prescribed regulations governing manufacture, sale, possession, or display of awards and decorations, and penalties for violations.

See sections 249 to 249c of Title 46, Appendix, Shipping.

REPLACEMENT OF AWARDS, MEDALS, AND DECORATIONS

Section 5(b) of act July 24, 1956, which authorized the Secretary of Commerce, notwithstanding the repeal of sections 753 to 753f, 754 to 754b, and 1471 to 1475 of this Appendix, under such rules and regulations as he may from time to time prescribe, to make replacements at cost or permit replacements at reasonable prices by persons authorized by him of the awards, medals, decorations, or other articles issued under such sections, if lost, destroyed, or rendered unfit for use, without fault or neglect on the part of the owner, was repealed by Pub. L. 100–324, § 9, May 30, 1988, 102 Stat. 577. See section 2004(c) of Title 46, Appendix, Shipping.

ACT AUG. 8, 1946, CH. 918, 60 STAT. 960

§§ 754 to 754b. Repealed. July 24, 1956, ch. 671, § 5(a)(2), 70 Stat. 606, eff. July 1, 1954

Section 754, act Aug. 8, 1946, ch. 918, § 1, 60 Stat. 960, provided for award of service medals and honorable discharge buttons (including posthumous award) to officers and crew in merchant marine who served honorably in a war zone for thirty days between Dec. 7, 1941, and Sept. 3, 1945, and who were entitled to a certificate of substantially continuous service between May 1, 1940 and July 25, 1947, pursuant to regulations prescribed by Maritime Commission.

Section 754a, act Aug. 8, 1946, ch. 918, § 2, 60 Stat. 960, authorized funds required to make awards of service medals and honorable discharge buttons pursuant to sections 754 to 754b of this Appendix.

Section 754b, act Aug. 8, 1946, ch. 918, § 3, 60 Stat. 960, related to regulations governing manufacture, sale, or use of decorations, and the penalties for violation.

REPLACEMENT OF AWARDS, MEDALS, AND DECORATIONS

For replacement of awards, medals, and decorations, see section 2004(c) of Title 46, Appendix, Shipping.

USE OF PUBLIC LANDS FOR WAR PURPOSES

ACT JUNE 5, 1942, CH. 346, 56 STAT. 323

§§ 756 to 759. Repealed. July 25, 1947, ch. 327, § 1, 61 Stat. 449

Section 756, act June 5, 1942, ch. 346, § 1, 56 Stat. 323, provided for lease or sale of vacant public lands withdrawn or reserved under certain Executive Orders or within a grazing district for use in connection with manufacture of arms, etc.

Section 757, act June 5, 1942, ch. 346, § 2, 56 Stat. 323, provided that lessee's interest in public lands leased under sections 756 to 759 should be taxable by States and political subdivisions thereof.

Section 758, act June 5, 1942, ch. 346, § 3, 56 Stat. 323, provided for rules and regulations.

Section 759, act June 5, 1942, ch. 346, § 4, 56 Stat. 323, provided a termination date for sections 756 to 759 of this Appendix.

MISCELLANEOUS PROVISIONS AFFECTING MILITARY ESTABLISHMENT

ACT JUNE 5, 1942, CH. 340, 56 STAT. 314

§§ 761, 762. Omitted

CODIFICATION

Sections 761 and 762 were omitted as terminated pursuant to section 776 of this Appendix.

Section 761, act June 5, 1942, ch. 340, § 1, 56 Stat. 314, authorized Secretary of War to provide for entertainment and instruction of enlisted personnel and employment of interns in the Medical Department at not to exceed $720 per annum. See Continuation of Section 761 note set out below.

Section 762, act June 5, 1942, ch. 340, § 2, 56 Stat. 314, suspended all provisions of law existing on June 5, 1942, limiting the strength of any branch of the Army, the number of aviation cadets in the Army Air Corps, the number of assistant superintendents of the Army Nurse Corps, the number and grade of reserve officers who might be ordered to extended active duty, and the number of officers of the Army who might be required to participate in aerial flights. Such strength limitations were superseded by section 452 of this Appendix and sections 3201, 3205, 3213, 3222, 3223, 3225 [see 522, 12002, and 12008] of Title 10, Armed Forces. Appointments as assistant superintendents of the Army Nurse Corps have ceased to exist under section 166*l* of former Title 10, Army and Air Force, and limitations as to number of reserve officers on active duty and number of officers participating in aerial flights, sections 369a and 292 of former Title 10, were repealed by act Aug. 10, 1956, ch. 1041, § 53, 70A Stat. 641.

CONTINUATION OF SECTION 761 UNTIL AUGUST 1, 1953

Act June 30, 1953, ch. 172, 67 Stat. 132, and act Mar. 31, 1953, ch. 13, § 1, 67 Stat. 18, amended act July 3, 1952, ch. 570, 66 Stat. 332, which provided that section 761 of this Appendix should continue in force in no event beyond Aug. 1, 1953.

REPEAL OF PRIOR ACTS CONTINUING SECTION 761

Act Apr. 4, 1953, ch. 21, § 2, 67 Stat. 23, repealed act July 3, 1952, ch. 570, § 1(a)(18), which continued the effectiveness of section 761 of this Appendix until Apr. 1, 1953. Section 6 of act July 3, 1952, repealed act Apr. 14, 1952, ch. 204, 66 Stat. 54; amended May 28, 1952, ch. 339, 66 Stat. 96; June 14, 1952, ch. 437, 66 Stat. 137; June 30, 1952, ch. 526, 66 Stat. 296, which continued provisions until July 3, 1952. This repeal took effect as of June 16, 1952, by section 7 of act July 3, 1952.

§ 763. Repealed. Sept. 23, 1950, ch. 1010, § 3(a), 64 Stat. 986

Section, act June 5, 1942, ch. 340, § 3, 56 Stat. 314, related to appointment and transfer of civilian employers for foreign service and transportation of employees, dependents, and effects.

§ 764. Omitted

CODIFICATION

Section 764, act June 5, 1942, ch. 340, § 4(a)–(d), 56 Stat. 315, relating to travel allowances for dependents and effects of military personnel, were repealed by act Oct. 12, 1949, ch. 681, title V, § 531(c)(11), 63 Stat. 840, eff. Jan. 1, 1950. See section 404 et seq. of Title 37, Pay and Allowances of the Uniformed Services.

Section 764, act June 5, 1942, ch. 340, § 4(e), as added Feb. 12, 1946, ch. 6, § 4, 60 Stat. 5; amended Oct. 12, 1949, ch. 681, title V, § 525(a), 63 Stat. 836, provided for monetary payments in lieu of transportation authorized by section 763(b), (c) of this Appendix.

§ 765. Repealed. Sept. 23, 1950, ch. 1010, § 3(a), 64 Stat. 986

Section, acts June 5, 1942, ch. 340, § 5, 56 Stat. 316; Oct. 12, 1949, ch. 681, title V, § 525(b), 63 Stat. 836, related to availability of funds for transportation of baggage, etc. See section 5701 et seq. of Title 5, Government Organization and Employees.

§§ 766 to 776. Omitted

CODIFICATION

Sections 766 to 776 were omitted as terminated pursuant to section 776 of this Appendix.

Section 766, act June 5, 1942, ch. 340, §6, 56 Stat. 316, made available for lease of vessels Army transportation funds.

Section 767, act June 5, 1942, ch. 340, §7, 56 Stat. 316, made funds available for acquisition of land, rights pertaining thereto, leasehold and other interests, temporary uses, and approval of title. Such provisions continued until Aug. 1, 1953, as provided in Continuation of Section 767 note set out below.

Section 768, act June 5, 1942, ch. 340, §8, 56 Stat. 316, limited fixed fee to 6 per centum on cost-plus contracts for military posts.

Section 769, act June 5, 1942, ch. 340, §9, 56 Stat. 316, extended act Mar. 5, 1940, ch. 44, 54 Stat. 45, relating to aircraft procurement, which was repealed by act July 25, 1947, ch. 327, §1, 61 Stat. 449.

Section 770, act June 5, 1942, ch. 340, §10, 56 Stat. 316, made available the funds of Engineer Service, Army, for expenses of operation of railroad.

Section 771, act June 5, 1942, ch. 340, §11, 56 Stat. 316, made funds available for acquisition of leasehold and other interests in land, temporary uses, and approval of title. Such provisions continued until Aug. 1, 1953, as provided in Continuation of Section 771 note set out below.

Section 772, act June 5, 1942, ch. 340, §12, 56 Stat. 316, related to employment of necessary personnel for production of plans for Army projects and their compensation.

Section 773, act June 5, 1942, ch. 340, §13, 56 Stat. 317, extended provisions of section 1171(a), (b) of this Appendix to moneys appropriated for Department of the Army for national defenses during World War II and was repealed by act Aug. 10, 1956, ch. 1041, §53, 70A Stat. 672.

Section 774, act June 5, 1942, ch. 340, §14, 56 Stat. 317, related to suspension of limitations on number of aircraft.

Section 775, act June 5, 1942, ch. 340, §15, 56 Stat. 317, provided that sections 761 to 776 of this Appendix were not to limit or effect any power or authority granted or conferred by the First War Powers Act, 1941 [sections 601 to 605, 611, and 616 to 622 of this Appendix] or the Second War Powers Act, 1942 [sections 631 to 642e, 643 to 643c, 644 to 644b, and 645 to 645b of this Appendix].

Section 776, act June 5, 1942, ch. 340, §16, 56 Stat. 317, provided that provisions of sections 761 to 776 of this Appendix should remain in force during the continuance of World War II and for six months after its termination. For termination of state of war, see notes set out preceding section 1 of this Appendix.

CONTINUATION OF SECTIONS 767, 771 UNTIL AUGUST 1, 1953

Section 1(a)(5) of act July 3, 1952, ch. 570, 66 Stat. 331, as amended Mar. 31, 1953, ch. 13, §1, 67 Stat. 18; June 30, 1953, ch. 172, 67 Stat. 132, provided that sections 767 and 771 of this Appendix should continue in force until six months after the termination of the national emergency proclaimed by the President on Dec. 16, 1950 by Proc. No. 2914, 15 F.R. 9029, set out as a note preceding section 1 of this Appendix, or such earlier date or dates as may be provided for by Congress, but in no event beyond Aug. 1, 1953, as extended from Apr. 1, 1953.

REPEAL OF PRIOR ACTS CONTINUING SECTIONS 767, 771

Act Apr. 4, 1953, ch. 21, §2, 67 Stat. 23, repealed act July 3, 1952, ch. 570, §1(a)(18), 66 Stat. 331, which continued the effectiveness of this section until Apr. 1, 1953. Section 6 of act July 3, 1952, repealed act Apr. 14, 1952, ch. 204, 66 Stat. 54; amended May 28, 1952, ch. 339, 66 Stat. 96; June 14, 1952, ch. 437, 66 Stat. 137; June 30, 1952, ch. 526, 66 Stat. 296, which continued provisions until July 3, 1952. This repeal took effect as of June 16, 1952, by section 7 of Joint Res. July 3, 1952.

ACT JUNE 28, 1944, CH. 306, 58 STAT. 624

§777. Transferred

CODIFICATION

Section, act June 28, 1944, ch. 306, 58 Stat. 624, which related to naval plantations outside the continental United States and to availability of appropriations for management and operation, was originally a temporary war measure and was made permanent legislation and transferred to section 1213 of former Title 10, Army and Air Force, and to section 555a of former Title 34, Navy. Section 1213 of former Title 10 and section 555a of former Title 34 were repealed by act Aug. 10, 1956, ch. 1041, §53, 70A Stat. 641 and reenacted as section 2421 of Title 10, Armed Forces.

ACT FEB. 21, 1946, CH. 34, §3, 60 STAT. 27

§778. Repealed. Aug. 10, 1956, ch. 1041, §53, 70A Stat. 641

Section, act Feb. 21, 1946, ch. 34, §3, 60 Stat. 27, authorized Secretary of the Navy to convene boards of officers to recommend retirement of Regular Navy and Marine Corps Officers in certain ranks and by section 12 of that act provided that those provisions terminate on June 30 of fiscal year following that in which World War II is declared ended.

PHOTOGRAPHING, MAPPING OR OTHER REPRESENTATION OF MILITARY OR DEFENSE PROPERTIES

ACT JUNE 25, 1942, CH. 447, 56 STAT. 390

§§781 to 785. Omitted

CODIFICATION

Sections 781 to 785 of this Appendix were omitted as terminated six months after the termination of the national emergency proclaimed by the President on Dec. 16, 1950, which emergency terminated two years from Sept. 14, 1976, pursuant to section 1601 of Title 50, War and National Defense.

Section 781, act June 25, 1942, ch. 447, §1, 56 Stat. 390, provided that photographing, sketching, mapping, etc., of military or naval reservations, properties, equipment, etc., is unlawful.

Section 782, act June 25, 1942, ch. 447, §2, 56 Stat. 391, provided authority to grant permission to photograph, sketch, map, etc., if national defense interests were not adversely affected.

Section 783, act June 25, 1942, ch. 447, §3, 56 Stat. 391, provided penalties for violations of sections 781 to 785 of this Appendix.

Section 784, act June 25, 1942, ch. 447, §4, 56 Stat. 391; Proc. No. 2695, eff. July 4, 1946, 11 F.R. 7817, 60 Stat. 1352, provided that sections 781 to 785 of this Appendix apply in all places within territory or jurisdiction of United States.

Section 785, acts June 25, 1942, ch. 447, §5, 56 Stat. 391; June 4, 1953, ch. 97, 67 Stat. 41, provided that sections 781 to 785 of this Appendix be effective only until six months after termination of national emergency proclaimed by President on Dec. 16, 1950.

EXEMPTION OF CERTAIN ARTICLES FROM IMPORT DUTIES AND TAXES

JOINT RES. JUNE 27, 1942, CH. 455, 56 STAT. 461

§§791 to 795. Omitted

CODIFICATION

Sections 791 to 795 were omitted as terminated pursuant to section 795 of this Appendix.

Section 791, Joint Res. June 27, 1942, ch. 455, §1, 56 Stat. 461, provided for importation of articles for members of armed forces of United Nations, other than those of the United States, free of duties, internal-revenue taxes, and customs charges.

Section 792, Joint Res. June 27, 1942, ch. 455, §2, 56 Stat. 462, contained similar exemptions for articles for enemy prisoners of war and enemy civilian internees and detainees.

Section 793, Joint Res. June 27, 1942, ch. 455, §3, 56 Stat. 462, contained similar exemptions for articles made by members of United Nations armed forces detained as prisoners of war or made by nationals of United States interned or detained by enemy.

Section 794, Joint Res. June 27, 1942, ch. 455, §4, 56 Stat. 462, authorized regulations by Secretary of the Treasury governing exemptions under sections 791 to 795 of this Appendix.

Section 795, Joint Res. June 27, 1942, ch. 455, §5, 56 Stat. 462; Aug. 8, 1947, ch. 515, §2, 61 Stat. 917, provided that sections 791 to 795 of this Appendix should be effective as to articles entered for consumption or withdrawn from warehouse for consumption on or after June 27, 1942, and before July 1, 1948.

ACT JUNE 27, 1942, CH. 453, 56 STAT. 461

§801. Omitted

CODIFICATION

Section, acts June 27, 1942, ch. 453, §1, 56 Stat. 461; June 30, 1955, ch. 258, §1(a), 69 Stat. 242, provided for free importation of personal and household effects brought into United States under Government orders. Provisions were superseded and incorporated in Tariff Schedules of the United States, as item 915.20 of the temporary legislation in the Appendix to the Tariff Schedules, and upon repeal of such item 915.00 as item 817.00 of the permanent legislation in Schedule 8, Special Classification Provisions. See Publication of Harmonized Tariff Schedule note set out under section 1202 of Title 19, Customs Duties.

§802. Repealed. June 30, 1955, ch. 258, §1(a), 69 Stat. 242

Section, acts June 27, 1942, ch. 453, §2, 56 Stat. 461; Apr. 4, 1953, ch. 21, §1, 67 Stat. 22, prescribed effective date of section 801 of this Appendix.

TEMPORARY APPOINTMENTS, PROMOTIONS, ETC., OF NAVY, MARINE CORPS, AND COAST GUARD OFFICERS

ACT JUNE 30, 1942, CH. 462, 56 STAT. 463

§§806 to 810. Omitted

CODIFICATION

Sections 806 to 810 were omitted as terminated pursuant to section 814 of this Appendix.

Section 806, act June 30, 1942, ch. 462, §1, 56 Stat. 463, suspended the provisions of existing law relating to periodic computations for the purpose of determining the authorized number of commissioned officers in the various grades of the line of the Regular Navy and of the Marine Corps, the permanent promotion or advancement of all officers of the Navy and Marine Corps, and the involuntary retirement or honorable discharge of such officers by reason of failure of selection or upon completion of designated periods of service. Under section 813 of this Appendix, this section also applied to officer personnel of the Coast Guard. This section was repealed insofar as it related to the Navy and Marine Corps by act Aug. 7, 1947, ch. 512, title IV, §426(a), 61 Stat. 880. It was superseded with respect to the Coast Guard by section 42 of Title 14, Coast Guard.

Section 807, act June 30, 1942, ch. 462, §2, 56 Stat. 464, related to the number of rear admirals entitled to pay and allowances of rear admirals of the upper half. It was repealed insofar as it related to the Navy and Marine Corps by act Aug. 7, 1947, ch. 512, title IV, §426(a), 61 Stat. 880, and superseded with respect to the Coast Guard by section 462 of former Title 14, Coast Guard, which is covered by section 202 of Title 37, Pay and Allowances of the Uniformed Services.

Section 808, act June 30, 1942, ch. 462, §3, 56 Stat. 464, provided for modification of age limits for original appointments to commissioned rank in staff corps.

Section 809, act June 30, 1942, ch. 462, §4, 56 Stat. 464, which was an amendment of provisions concerning appointment of certain reserve officers to regular Navy or Marine Corps, was a permanent provision under section 814 of this Appendix, and was set out as sections 737a and 853c–2a of former Title 34, Navy, which were repealed by act Aug. 10, 1956, ch. 1041, §53, 70A Stat. 641. See sections 2104, 2106, and 6914 of Title 10, Armed Forces.

Section 810, act June 30, 1942, ch. 462, §5, 56 Stat. 465, related to temporarily promoted officers, pay and allowances, and date of acceptance of appointment. It was repealed insofar as it related to the Navy and Marine Corps by act Aug. 7, 1947, ch. 512, title IV, §426(a), 61 Stat. 880, and reenacted as section 350k of former Title 34, Navy, by act May 22, 1950, ch. 193, §3, 64 Stat. 187. Although section 810 applied to the Coast Guard under section 813 of this Appendix, it was superseded in this respect by section 350k of Title 34, which applied to the Coast Guard under section 350j of former Title 34. Sections 350j and 350k of former Title 34 were repealed by act Aug. 10, 1956, ch. 1041, §53, 70A Stat. 641, and replaced by sections 5597 and 5787 of Title 10, Armed Forces, section 351 of Title 14, Coast Guard, and section 212(f) of Title 42, The Public Health and Welfare.

§811. Repealed. Feb. 21, 1946, ch. 34, §11(b), 60 Stat. 29

Section, act June 30, 1942, ch. 462, §6, 56 Stat. 465, related to retired grade and pay of officers retired for age while serving under temporary promotion. See section 6151 of Title 10, Armed Forces.

§§812 to 814. Omitted

CODIFICATION

Sections 812 to 814 were omitted as terminated pursuant to section 814 of this Appendix.

Section 812, act June 30, 1942, ch. 462, §7, 56 Stat. 465, amended sections 350 and 350i of former Title 34, Navy. It was repealed insofar as it related to the Navy and Marine Corps by act Aug. 7, 1947, ch. 512, title IV, §426(a), 61 Stat. 880. It was superseded with respect to the Coast Guard by act June 3, 1948, ch. 395, 62 Stat. 302.

Section 813, act June 30, 1942, ch. 462, §8, 56 Stat. 465, provided: "The provisions of this Act [sections 806 to 814 of this Appendix] except as may be necessary to adapt the said provisions to the Coast Guard, shall apply to officer personnel of the Coast Guard in like manner and to the same extent and with the same relative conditions in all respects as are provided for the officer personnel of the Navy and Marine Corps." It appears that section 808 of this Appendix does not apply to the Coast Guard since it has no staff officers and that section 809 does not apply because it amends provisions relating only to the Navy and Marine Corps. As pointed out in notes under sections 806, 807, 810, and 812, they have been superseded with respect to the Coast Guard.

Section 814, act June 30, 1942, ch. 462, §9, 56 Stat. 465, prohibited any reduction of pay by virtue of sections 806 to 814 of this Appendix, and provided for termination of sections 806 to 814 of this Appendix on June 30 of fiscal year following that in which World War II ended. See Termination of State of War notes preceding section 1, of this Appendix. See note for former section 809 of this Appendix for its disposition, such section having been excepted from the termination provisions.

JURISDICTION OF PRIZES AND PRIZE PROCEEDINGS

ACT AUG. 18, 1942, CH. 553, 56 STAT. 746

§§821 to 828. Transferred

CODIFICATION

Section 821, act Aug. 18, 1942, ch. 553, §1, 56 Stat. 746, which related to jurisdiction of prizes and proceedings for their condemnation, was transferred to section 1159 of former Title 34, Navy. Section 1159 of former Title 34 was repealed by act Aug. 10, 1956, ch. 1041, §53, 70A Stat. 641, and reenacted as sections 7651 and 7652(a) and (b) of Title 10, Armed Forces.

Section 822, act Aug. 18, 1942, ch. 553, §2, 56 Stat. 746, which related to venue of proceedings, was transferred to section 1160 of former Title 34, Navy. Section 1160 of former Title 34 was repealed by act Aug. 10, 1956, ch. 1041, §53, 70A Stat. 641, and reenacted as section 7653 of Title 10, Armed Forces.

Section 823, act Aug. 18, 1942, ch. 553, §3, 56 Stat. 746, which related to consent of cobelligerent to exercise of jurisdiction or taking of prize involving territorial waters of cobelligerent, was transferred to section 1161 of former Title 34, Navy. Section 1161 of former Title 34 was repealed by act Aug. 10, 1956, ch. 1041, §53, 70A Stat. 641, and reenacted as section 7652(c) of Title 10, Armed Forces.

Section 824, act Aug. 18, 1942, ch. 553, §4, 56 Stat. 746, which related to the power of the War Shipping Administration to appropriate property, was transferred to section 1162 of former Title 34, Navy. Section 1162 of former Title 34 was repealed by act Aug. 10, 1956, ch. 1041, §53, 70A Stat. 641, and reenacted as section 7663(a) of Title 10, Armed Forces.

Section 825, act Aug. 18, 1942, ch. 553, §5, 56 Stat. 746, which related to appointment, qualifications, and powers and duties of special prize commissioners, was transferred to section 1163 of former Title 34, Navy. Section 1163 of former Title 34 was repealed by act Aug. 10, 1956, ch. 1041, §53, 70A Stat. 641, and reenacted as sections 7655 and 7676 of Title 10, Armed Forces.

Section 826, act Aug. 18, 1942, ch. 553, §6, 56 Stat. 746, which related to rules governing jurisdiction and construction with other laws relating to prizes, was transferred to section 1164 of former Title 34, Navy. Section 1164 of former Title 34 was repealed by act Aug. 10, 1956, ch. 1041, §53, 70A Stat. 641.

Section 827, act Aug. 18, 1942, ch. 553, §7, 56 Stat. 746, which related to reciprocal privileges and jurisdiction of cobelligerents, was transferred to section 1165 of former Title 34, Navy. Section 1165 of former Title 34 was repealed by act Aug. 10, 1956, ch. 1041, §53, 70A Stat. 641, and reenacted as section 7681 of Title 10, Armed Forces.

Section 828, act Aug. 18, 1942, ch. 553, §8, 56 Stat. 746, which related to effect on jurisdiction under other laws, was transferred to section 1166 of former Title 34, Navy. Section 1166 of former Title 34 was repealed by act Aug. 10, 1956, ch. 1041, §53, 70A Stat. 641.

CERTAIN ALLOWANCE ASSISTANCE FOR CIVILIAN AND MILITARY PERSONNEL

ACTS OCT. 14, 1942, CH. 603, 56 STAT. 786; NOV. 28, 1943, CH. 330, 57 STAT. 593

§§831 to 833f. Repealed. Oct. 12, 1949, ch. 681, title V, §531(c)(13), (16), 63 Stat. 840, eff. Jan. 1, 1950

Section 831, acts Oct. 14, 1942, ch. 603, §1, 56 Stat. 786; Feb. 21, 1946, ch. 6, §2(a), 60 Stat. 5; July 1, 1947, ch. 190, §1, 61 Stat. 236, related to transportation of dependents and household effects of Navy, Marine Corps, and Coast Guard personnel incident to secret orders. See section 404 et seq. of Title 37, Pay and Allowances of the Uniformed Services.

Section 832, act Oct. 14, 1942, ch. 603, §3, 56 Stat. 786, made sections 831 to 833 applicable to personnel of the Coast and Geodetic Survey.

Section 833, act Oct. 14, 1942, ch. 603, §2, 56 Stat. 786, provided for effective date and termination of sections 831 to 833 of this Appendix.

Section 833a, acts Nov. 28, 1943, ch. 330, §1, 57 Stat. 593; July 1, 1947, ch. 190, §2(a), (b), 61 Stat. 236 related to transportation of dependents and household effects of Navy, Marine Corps, and Coast Guard personnel in case of evacuation of dependents or transfer of personnel to sea duty or places where dependents could not join them. See section 404 et seq. of Title 37, Pay and Allowances of the Uniformed Services.

Section 833b, acts Nov. 28, 1943, ch. 330, §2, 57 Stat. 593; July 1, 1947, ch. 190, §2(c), 61 Stat. 237, related to certificates in connection with transportation under sections 833a to 833f of this Appendix.

Section 833c, act Nov. 28, 1943, ch. 330, §3, 57 Stat. 594, provided for allowance of credit in disbursing officers' accounts for prior payments which would have been authorized under section 833a of this Appendix.

Section 833d, act Nov. 28, 1943, ch. 330, §4, 57 Stat. 594, related to mode of transportation of household effects of naval and civilian personnel of the Naval Establishment without regard to comparative costs. With respect to naval personnel, see section 404 et seq. of Title 37, Pay and Allowances of the Uniformed Services.

Section 833e, act Nov. 28, 1943, ch. 330, §5, as added Feb. 12, 1946, ch. 6, §3(a), 60 Stat. 5, provided for monetary payments in lieu of transportation authorized by sections 833a to 833f of this Appendix.

Section 833f, act Nov. 28, 1943, ch. 330, §6, 57 Stat. 594, renumbered Feb. 12, 1946, ch. 6, §3(a), 60 Stat. 5, provided for effective date and termination of sections 833a to 833f of this Appendix.

ACT OCT. 26, 1942, CH. 624, 56 STAT. 987

§836. Omitted

CODIFICATION

Section, act Oct. 26, 1942, ch. 624, 56 Stat. 987, which related to certificates in connection with pay and allowance accounts of civilian and military personnel of the Departments of the Army and Navy, was omitted as terminated. See Continuation of Provisions note below.

CONTINUATION OF PROVISIONS UNTIL AUGUST 1, 1953

Section 1(a)(9) of act July 3, 1952, ch. 570, 66 Stat. 331, as amended Mar. 31, 1953, ch. 13, §1, 67 Stat. 18; act June 30, 1953, ch. 172, 67 Stat. 132, provided that this section continue in force until six months after the termination of the national emergency proclaimed by the President on Dec. 16, 1950 by 1950 Proc. No. 2914, 15 F.R. 9029, set out as a note preceding section 1 of this Appendix, or such earlier date or dates as may be provided for by Congress, but in no event beyond Aug. 1, 1953, as extended from Apr. 1, 1953.

REPEAL OF PRIOR ACTS CONTINUING SECTION

Act Apr. 4, 1953, ch. 21, §2, 67 Stat. 23, repealed act July 3, 1952, ch. 570, §1(a)(18), 66 Stat. 331, which continued the effectiveness of this section until Apr. 1, 1953. Section 6 of act July 3, 1952, repealed act Apr. 14, 1952, ch. 204, 66 Stat. 54, as amended by act May 28, 1952, ch. 339, 66 Stat. 96; act June 14, 1952, ch. 437, 66 Stat. 137; act June 30, 1952, ch. 526, 66 Stat. 296, which continued provisions until July 3, 1952. This repeal took effect as of June 16, 1952, by section 7 of act July 3, 1952.

ACT JULY 16, 1953, CH. 197, §1, 67 STAT. 172

§837. Omitted

CODIFICATION

Section, act July 16, 1953, ch. 197, §1, 67 Stat. 172, which related to certificates in connection with pay and allowance accounts of civilian and military personnel of the Armed Forces, expired on Apr. 1, 1954, pursuant to section 2 of that act.

ACT DEC. 1, 1942, CH. 651, 56 STAT. 1024

§§ 841, 842. Repealed. May 28, 1948, ch. 352, § 3, 62 Stat. 277

Section 841, acts Dec. 1, 1942, ch. 651, §1, 56 Stat. 1024; Apr. 9, 1946, ch. 121, §1(a), 60 Stat. 86, related to transportation for personnel of the War and Navy Departments, Maritime Commission, and private plants engaged at war production. See section 2632 of Title 10, Armed Forces.

Section 842, acts Dec. 1, 1942, ch. 651, §2, 56 Stat. 1025; Apr. 9, 1946, ch. 121, §1(b), 60 Stat. 86, related to reports to be filed with Congress.

FREE ENTRY OF GIFTS FROM MEMBERS OF ARMED FORCES

ACT DEC. 5, 1942, CH. 680, 56 STAT. 1041

§§ 846, 847. Omitted

CODIFICATION

Section 846, acts Dec. 5, 1942, ch. 680, §1, 56 Stat. 1041; Aug. 8, 1947, ch. 515, §3(a), 61 Stat. 917; May 14, 1957, Pub. L. 85–30, §1 71 Stat. 29, which authorized free entry for gifts from members of the armed forces on duty abroad, expired on July 1, 1961, pursuant to section 847 of this Appendix.

Section 847, acts Dec. 5, 1942, ch. 680, §2, 56 Stat. 1041; Aug. 8, 1947, ch. 515, §33(c), 61 Stat. 917; Aug. 17, 1949, ch. 454, 63 Stat. 612; Feb. 21, 1951, ch. 1, 65 Stat. 3; Apr. 4, 1954, ch. 20, 67 Stat. 22; July 28, 1955, ch. 425, 69 Stat. 394; May 14, 1957, Pub. L. 85–30, §2, 71 Stat. 29; July 17, 1959, Pub. L. 86–99, 73 Stat. 223, provided that section 846 of this title shall be effective with respect to articles entered for consumption or withdrawn from warehouse for consumption on or after Dec. 5, 1942, and before July 1, 1961.

FREE POSTAGE FOR ARMED FORCES PERSONNEL

ACT JULY 12, 1950, CH. 460, 64 STAT. 336

§§ 891, 892. Omitted

CODIFICATION

Section 891, acts July 12, 1950, ch. 460, §1, 64 Stat. 336; Mar. 23, 1953, ch. 9, §1, 67 Stat. 7, which authorized free postage to Armed Forces personnel in specified areas, expired on June 30, 1955, pursuant to section 892 of this Appendix.

Section 892, acts July 12, 1950, ch. 460, §2, 64 Stat. 336; June 26, 1951, ch. 152, 65 Stat. 90; Mar. 23, 1953, ch. 9, §2, 67 Stat. 7, provided that the free mailing privileges authorized by section 891 of this Appendix shall be effective from July 12, 1950 to June 30, 1955.

EMERGENCY PRICE CONTROL ACT OF 1942

ACT JAN. 30, 1942, CH. 26, 56 STAT. 23

TERMINATION DATE

Sections 901 to 906, 921, 922, 923 to 926, and 941 to 946 of this Appendix terminated June 30, 1947 under the provisions of act July 25, 1946, ch. 671, §1, 60 Stat. 664.

TITLE I—GENERAL PROVISIONS AND AUTHORITY

§§ 901 to 906. Omitted

CODIFICATION

Sections 901 to 906 were omitted as terminated.

Section 901, acts Jan. 30, 1942, ch. 26, title I, §1, 56 Stat. 23; Oct. 2, 1942, ch. 578, §7(a), 56 Stat. 767; June 30, 1944, ch. 325, title I, §101, 58 Stat. 632; June 30, 1945, ch. 214, §1, 59 Stat. 306; July 25, 1946, ch. 671, §1, 60 Stat. 664, related to purposes, time limit, and applicability of section 901 et seq. of this Appendix.

Section 901a, act Jan. 30, 1942, ch. 26, title I, §1a, as added July 25, 1946, ch. 671, §3, 60 Stat. 664, related to purposes and policies of decontrol during transition period. Subsec. (h) of section 1a of act Jan. 30, 1942, ch. 26, title I, as added July 25, 1946, ch. 671, §3, 60 Stat. 669, formerly classified to subsec. (h) of section 901a of this Appendix, was repealed by Pub. L. 89–554, §8(a), Sept. 6, 1966, 80 Stat. 653.

Section 902, acts Jan. 30, 1942, ch. 26, title I, §2, 56 Stat. 24; July 16, 1943, ch. 241, §5(a), 57 Stat. 566; June 30, 1944, ch. 325, title I, §102, 58 Stat. 632; June 30, 1945, ch. 214, §§3, 4, 59 Stat. 306; July 25, 1946, ch. 671, §§4, 5, 7–10, 60 Stat. 670, 671, 673, related to regulation of prices, rents, and market and renting practices. Act Jan. 30, 1942, ch. 26, title I, §2, 56 Stat. 24, was repealed by Pub. L. 89–554, §8(a), Sept. 6, 1966, 80 Stat. 651.

Section 903, acts Jan. 30, 1942, ch. 26, title I, §3, 56 Stat. 27; June 30, 1944, ch. 325, title I, §103, 58 Stat. 636; June 30, 1945, ch. 214, §5(a), 59 Stat. 307, related to maximum prices of agricultural commodities.

Section 904, act Jan. 30, 1942, ch. 26, title I, §4, 56 Stat. 28, prohibited violation of rules and regulations relating to prices, rents, and market and renting practices and disclosure or use of information otherwise than in course of official duty. Act Jan. 30, 1942, ch. 26, title I, §4(c), 56 Stat. 28, was repealed by Pub. L. 89–554, §8(a), Sept. 6, 1966, 80 Stat. 651.

Section 905, act Jan. 30, 1942, ch. 26, title I, §5, 56 Stat. 28, authorized Administrator to confer with groups having to do with commodities and to enter into voluntary agreements relating to purposes of section 901 et seq. of this Appendix.

Section 906, act Jan. 30, 1942, ch. 26, title I, §6, as added July 5, 1946, ch. 671, §11, 60 Stat. 675, provided for the establishment and adjustment of maximum prices.

TITLE II—ADMINISTRATION AND ENFORCEMENT

§§ 921 to 926. Omitted

CODIFICATION

Section 921, acts Jan. 30, 1942, ch. 26, title II, §201, 56 Stat. 29; June 30, 1944, ch. 325, title I, §104, 58 Stat. 637, which related to the administration of section 901 et seq. of this Appendix, with provisions for Office of Price Administration under Price Administrator, regional offices, issuance of regulations and orders and transfer of functions, was omitted as terminated. Act Jan. 30, 1942, ch. 26, title II, §201, 56 Stat. 29, was repealed by Pub. L. 89–554, §8(a), Sept. 6, 1966, 80 Stat. 651.

Section 922, acts Jan. 30, 1942, ch. 26, title II, §202, 56 Stat. 30; June 30, 1944, ch. 325, title I, §105, 58 Stat. 637, which authorized Administrator to conduct investigations, require records and reports, and initiate contempt proceedings for violation of subpenas, and established right to specifically claim privilege against self-incrimination, was omitted as terminated. Act Jan. 30, 1942, ch. 26, title II, §202, 56 Stat. 30, was repealed by Pub. L. 89–554, §8(a), Sept. 6, 1966, 80 Stat. 651.

Section 922a, was from appropriation acts June 28, 1944, ch. 304, title I, §101, 58 Stat. 601; July 5, 1945, ch. 271, title I, §101, 59 Stat. 415; July 23, 1946, ch. 591, title I, §101, 60 Stat. 610, which authorized Office of Price Administration employees, when designated, to administer oaths, etc., in connection with Office functions, and was not repeated in subsequent appropriation acts.

Section 922a was enacted as part of the Second Deficiency Appropriation Act, 1944, and not as part of act Jan. 30, 1942, ch. 26, 56 Stat. 23, known as the Emergency Price Control Act of 1942, which enacted sections 901 to 906, 921, 922, 923 to 926, and 941 to 946 of this Appendix.

Section 923, acts Jan. 30, 1942, ch. 26, title II, §203, 56 Stat. 31; June 30, 1944, ch. 325, title I, §106, 58 Stat. 638;

July 30, 1947, ch. 361, title I, §101, 61 Stat. 619, which related to protest proceedings, was omitted as terminated. Section 101 of act July 30, 1947 provided in part for the dismissal of protest under section 923 of this Appendix on the ground of laches.

Section 924, acts Jan. 30, 1942, ch. 26, title II, §204, 56 Stat. 31; June 30, 1944, ch. 325, title I, §107, 58 Stat. 639; June 30, 1945, ch. 214, §6, 59 Stat. 308; July 30, 1947, ch. 361, title I, §101, 61 Stat. 619; June 25, 1948, ch. 646, §32(a), 62 Stat. 991; May 24, 1949, ch. 139, §127, 63 Stat. 107, authorized review of orders of the Office of Price Administrator under the Emergency Price Control Act of 1942, and created the Emergency Court of Appeals for this purpose. The Emergency Price Control Act of 1942 terminated on June 30, 1947, under the provisions of act July 25, 1946, ch. 671, §1, 60 Stat. 664. The Housing and Rent Act of 1948, act Mar. 30, 1948, ch. 161, 62 Stat. 93, classified to section 1881 of this Appendix, continued the Court for the purpose of reviewing recommendations of local advisory boards for the decontrol or adjustment of maximum rents. Later, the Defense Production Act of 1950, act Sept. 8, 1950, ch. 932, 64 Stat. 798, classified to sections 2061 to 2166 of this Appendix, continued the Court to review regulations and orders relating to price control. The Housing and Rent Act of 1948 and the Defense Production Act of 1950 both terminated, however, the Court remained in existence "to complete the adjudication of rights and liabilities incurred prior to their termination dates." (Transcript of Proceedings of the Final Session of the Court, 299 F.2d 1.) The final decision of the Court, Rosenzweig v. General Services Administration, 1961, 299 F.2d 22, was decided on Dec. 6, 1961. A petition for rehearing was denied on Jan. 2, 1962, and a petition for writ of certiorari to the Supreme Court of the United States was denied on Mar. 19, 1962, 82 S. Ct. 830.

The order of Chief Judge Albert B. Maris, set forth in 299 F.2d 20, provided:

"The business of this Court having been completed, it is ordered that at the expiration of 30 days from this date, if a petition for certiorari has not been filed in the Supreme Court in Case No. 676 [Rosenzweig v. General Services Administration], just decided, the acting clerk shall deliver the records and papers of the Court in his office to the General Services Administration for permanent custody as records of the Government, and shall thereupon inform the Chief Justice of the United States that the work of the Court has been completed and that the designations of the judges of the Court may therefore appropriately be terminated.

"If a petition for certiorari is filed in Case No. 676 this order shall take effect and be carried out at the expiration of 30 days after the final disposition of Case No. 676."

In accordance with the terms of this order, the petition for certiorari having been filed, and denied Mar. 19, 1962, the Court terminated on Apr. 18, 1962.

Section 925, acts Jan. 30, 1942, ch. 26, title II, §205, 56 Stat. 33; June 30, 1944, ch. 325, title I, §108, 58 Stat. 640; July 25, 1946, ch. 671, §§12, 13, 60 Stat. 676, 677; July 30, 1947, ch. 361, title I, §101, 61 Stat. 619, which related to enforcement and recovery of damages and penalties, was omitted as terminated.

Section 926, act Jan. 30, 1942, ch. 26, title II, §206, 56 Stat. 35, which provided for standards, limitations, publication in Federal Register, protest and review of price schedules issued prior to the Administrator's taking of office, was omitted as terminated.

TITLE III—MISCELLANEOUS

§§941 to 946. Omitted

CODIFICATION

Sections 941 to 946 were omitted as terminated.

Section 941, act Jan. 30, 1942, ch. 26, title III, §301, 56 Stat. 36, related to transmission of quarterly reports to Congress.

Section 942, acts Jan. 30, 1942, ch. 26, title III, §302, 56 Stat. 36; June 30, 1945, ch. 214, §5(b), 59 Stat. 308, contained definitions of terms used in the Emergency Price Control Act of 1942, section 901 et seq. of this Appendix.

Section 943, act Jan. 30, 1942, ch. 26, title III, §303, 56 Stat. 37, contained separability provisions.

Section 944, act Jan. 30, 1942, ch. 26, title III, §304, 56 Stat. 37, authorized appropriations.

Section 945, act Jan. 30, 1942, ch. 26, title III, §305, 56 Stat. 37, related to application of existing law.

Section 946, act Jan. 30, 1942, ch. 26, title III, §306, 56 Stat. 37, provided as short title for section 901 et seq. of this Appendix, "Emergency Price Control Act of 1942".

STABILIZATION ACT OF 1942

ACT OCT. 2, 1942, CH. 578, 56 STAT. 765

§§961 to 971. Omitted

CODIFICATION

Sections 961 to 971 were omitted as terminated pursuant to section 966 of this Appendix.

Section 961, act Oct. 2, 1942, ch. 578, §1, 56 Stat. 765, related to stabilization by President of prices, wages and salaries affecting cost of living and to public utility rate increases.

Section 962, act Oct. 2, 1942, ch. 578, §2, 56 Stat. 765, provided for promulgation of regulations, delegation of authority and suspension of certain provisions of Emergency Price Control Act of 1942, section 901 et seq. of this Appendix.

Section 963, acts Oct. 2, 1942, ch. 578, §3, 56 Stat. 766; June 30, 1944, ch. 325, title II, §201, 58 Stat. 642; June 30, 1945, ch. 214, §7, 59 Stat. 309; June 25, 1946, ch. 671, §14, 60 Stat. 677, related to maximum prices for agricultural commodities and products.

Section 963a, act Oct. 2, 1942, ch. 578, §3A, as added June 30, 1945, ch. 214, §8, 59 Stat. 309, related to slaughter of animals, certification of plants, conditions, partial plant certification, inspection, status of meat for transportation purposes and revocation and termination of certification.

Section 964, acts Oct. 2, 1942, ch. 578, §4, 56 Stat. 766; Apr. 11, 1943, ch. 52, §4(a), 57 Stat. 63; June 30, 1944, ch. 325, title II, §202, 58 Stat. 642, related to wages and salaries and limitations on control.

Section 964a, act Apr. 11, 1943, ch. 52, §4(b), 57 Stat. 63, which related to rescission of stabilization of wages order, was not enacted as part of act Oct. 2, 1942, ch. 578, 56 Stat. 765, known as the Stabilization Act of 1942, which enacted sections 961 to 964 and 965 to 971 of this Appendix. Act Apr. 11, 1943, ch. 52, was repealed by Pub. L. 97–258, §5(b), Sept. 13, 1982, 96 Stat. 1068, 1076.

Section 965, act Oct. 2, 1942, ch. 578, §5, 56 Stat. 767, related to wages and salaries, prohibition of violation of regulations, employer's reduction of salaries over $5,000 and regulation of payment of double time.

Section 966, acts Oct. 2, 1942, ch. 578, §6, 56 Stat. 767; June 30, 1944, ch. 325, title II, §203, 58 Stat. 643; June 30, 1945, ch. 214, §2, 59 Stat. 306; June 25, 1946, ch. 671, §2, 60 Stat. 664, provided for the expiration of sections 961 to 964, 965 to 967, 970, and 971 of this Appendix on June 30, 1947, or on such earlier date as the Congress by concurrent resolution or the President by proclamation might prescribe.

Section 967, act Oct. 2, 1942, ch. 578, §7, 56 Stat. 767, amended Emergency Price Control Act of 1942, §1(b), section 901(b) of this Appendix, and made that act, section 901 et seq. of this Appendix, applicable to, and provided for its construction with, section 961 et seq. of this Appendix.

Section 968, acts Oct. 2, 1942, ch. 578, §8, 56 Stat. 767; June 30, 1944, ch. 325, title II, §204, 58 Stat. 643; Oct. 3, 1944, ch. 479, §37(a), 58 Stat. 784, which related to crop loans, expired by its own terms on Dec. 31, 1948.

Section 969, act Oct. 2, 1942, ch. 578, §9, 56 Stat. 768, which amended provision in section 713a–8 of Title 15, Commerce and Trade, relating to encouragement of production of non-basic agricultural commodities, expired by its own terms on Dec. 31, 1948.

Section 970, act Oct. 2, 1942, ch. 578, §10, 56 Stat. 768, defined wages and salaries.

Section 971, act Oct. 2, 1942, ch. 578, §11, 56 Stat. 768, provided penalties for violations.

EXTENSION OF SUGAR CONTROLS

ACT MAR. 31, 1947, CH. 30, 61 STAT. 35

§§981 to 985. Omitted

CODIFICATION

Sections 981 to 985 were omitted as expired pursuant to section 981 of this Appendix.

Section 981, act Mar. 31, 1947, ch. 30, §1, 61 Stat. 35, extended certain laws with respect to sugar until Oct. 31, 1947, and the authority to continue inventory controls over other than household users until Mar. 31, 1948, and provided for certain powers and duties of the Secretary of Agriculture and specified limitations in connection with the control of said commodity.

Section 982, act Mar. 31, 1947, ch. 30, §2, 61 Stat. 36, authorized the Secretary of Agriculture to remove controls prior to the termination of sections 981 to 985 of this Appendix when sugar supplies were sufficient to warrant such action.

Section 983, act Mar. 31, 1947, ch. 30, §3, 61 Stat. 36, provided for the transfer of functions, powers and duties relating to sugar, which were vested in the President, any executive department and the Price Administrator by certain acts, to the Secretary of Agriculture, the continuance of rules and regulations promulgated by said persons and the transfer of appropriations.

Section 984, act Mar. 31, 1947, ch. 30, §4, 61 Stat. 37, related to unlawful actions and penalties therefor. Act Mar. 31, 1947, ch. 30, §4, 61 Stat. 37, was repealed by Pub. L. 89–544, §8(a), Sept. 6, 1966, 80 Stat. 654.

Section 985, act Mar. 31, 1947, ch. 30, §5, 61 Stat. 37, defined the terms person and sugar.

MISSING PERSONS ACT

ACT MAR. 7, 1942, CH. 166, 56 STAT. 143

§§1001 to 1012. Repealed. Pub. L. 89–554, §8(a), Sept. 6, 1966, 80 Stat. 651–654, 656, 657, 659, 662

Section 1001, acts Mar. 7, 1942, ch. 166, §1, 56 Stat. 143; July 1, 1944, ch. 371, §1, 58 Stat. 679; May 16, 1947, ch. 70, §1, 61 Stat. 96; Aug. 29, 1957, Pub. L. 85–217, §1(a), 71 Stat. 491; Aug. 14, 1964, Pub. L. 88–428, §1(1), (2), 78 Stat. 437, defined terms used in sections 1001 to 1018 of this Appendix. For that portion of this section applicable to civilian officers and employees and their dependents, see section 5561 of Title 5, Government Organization and Employees, and for that portion applicable to members of the uniformed services and their dependents, see section 551 of Title 37, Pay and Allowances of the Uniformed Services.

Section 1002, acts Mar. 7, 1942, ch. 166, §2, 56 Stat. 144; July 1, 1944, ch. 371, §2, 58 Stat. 679; Apr. 4, 1953, ch. 17, §1(a), 67 Stat. 21; Aug. 29, 1957, Pub. L. 85–217, §1(b), 71 Stat. 491; Aug. 14, 1964, Pub. L. 88–428, §1(3), 78 Stat. 437, related to continuance of pay and allowances for missing interned or captive persons, and limited fees of agents or attorneys. For that portion of this section applicable to civilian officers and employees and their dependents, see sections 5561 and 5562 of Title 5, Government Organization and Employees, and for that portion applicable to members of the uniformed services and their dependents, see sections 551 and 552 of Title 37, Pay and Allowances of the Uniformed Services.

Act June 23, 1942, ch. 444, §1, 56 Stat. 389, which authorized use of funds for payments to persons subject to section 1002 of this Appendix, was repealed by Pub. L. 89–554, §8(a), Sept. 6, 1966, 80 Stat. 651.

Section 1003, acts Mar. 7, 1942, ch. 166, §3, 56 Stat. 144; Dec. 24, 1942, ch. 828, §1, 56 Stat. 1092; July 1, 1944, ch. 371, §3, 58 Stat. 680, provided for continuance or establishment by department head of allotments for dependents and insurance. For that portion of this section applicable to civilian officers and employees and their dependents, see section 5563 of Title 5, Government Organization and Employees, and for that portion applicable to members of the uniformed services and their dependents, see section 553 of Title 37, Pay and Allowances of the Uniformed Services.

Section 1004, acts Mar. 7, 1942, ch. 166, §4, 56 Stat. 144; Dec. 24, 1942, ch. 828, §1, 56 Stat. 1093; July 1, 1944, ch. 371, §4, 58 Stat. 680, provided for continuance, suspension, or resumption of pay and allowances by department head, and limited duration of allotments. For that portion of this section applicable to civilian officers and employees and their dependents, see section 5563 of Title 5, Government Organization and Employees, and for that portion applicable to members of the uniformed services and their dependents, see section 553 of Title 37, Pay and Allowances of the Uniformed Services.

Section 1005, acts Mar. 7, 1942, ch. 166, §5, 56 Stat. 145; Dec. 24, 1942, ch. 828, §1, 56 Stat. 1093; Aug. 14, 1964, Pub. L. 88–428, §1(4), 78 Stat. 437, related to departmental review, continuance of missing status or finding of death after year's absence, and date of termination of pay and allowances. For that portion of this section applicable to civilian officers and employees and their dependents, see section 5565 of Title 5, Government Organization and Employees, and for that portion applicable to members of the uniformed services and their dependents, see section 555 of Title 37, Pay and Allowances of the Uniformed Services.

Section 1006, acts Mar. 7, 1942, ch. 166, §6, 56 Stat. 145; Dec. 24, 1942, ch. 828, §1, 56 Stat. 1093; Apr. 4, 1953, ch. 17, §1(b), 67 Stat. 21; Aug. 14, 1964, Pub. L. 88–428, §1(5), 78 Stat. 437, related to payment of allotments in case of captured or interned persons until death or return to jurisdiction. For that portion of this section applicable to civilian officers and employees and their dependents, see sections 5562 and 5563 of Title 5, Government Organization and Employees, and for that portion applicable to members of the uniformed services, see sections 552 and 553 of Title 37, Pay and Allowances of the Uniformed Services.

Section 1007, acts Mar. 7, 1942, ch. 166, §7, 56 Stat. 145; Aug. 14, 1964, Pub. L. 88–428, §1(6), 78 Stat. 437, related to authority of department head to create new allotments and to continue or change amounts of old allotments. For that portion of this section applicable to civilian officers and employees and their dependents, see section 5563 of Title 5, Government Organization and Employees, and for that portion applicable to members of the uniformed services and their dependents, see section 553 of Title 37, Pay and Allowances of the Uniformed Services.

Section 1008, act Mar. 7, 1942, ch. 166, §8, 56 Stat. 145, provided penalty for fraudulent receipt of payments.

Section 1009, acts Mar. 7, 1942, ch. 166, §9, 56 Stat. 145; July 1, 1944, ch. 371, §5, 58 Stat. 680; Apr. 4, 1953, ch. 17, §1(c), 67 Stat. 21; Aug. 29, 1957, Pub. L. 85–217, §1(c), 71 Stat. 492, related to determinations by department heads or designees, and to conclusiveness relative to status of personnel, payments, or death. For that portion of this section applicable to civilian officers and employees and their dependents, see sections 5565 to 5567 of Title 5, Government Organization and Employees, and for that portion applicable to members of the uniformed services and their dependents, see sections 555 to 557 of Title 37, Pay and Allowances of the Uniformed Services.

Section 1010, acts Mar. 7, 1942, ch. 166, §10, 56 Stat. 145; July 1, 1944, ch. 371, §6, 58 Stat. 681; Aug. 14, 1964, Pub. L. 88–428, §1(7), 78 Stat. 437, provided for fact of dependency, and authority to determine. For that portion of this section applicable to civilian officers and employees and their dependents, see section 5566 of Title 5, Government Organization and Employees, and for that portion applicable to members of the uniformed services and their dependents, see section 556 of Title 37, Pay and Allowances of the Uniformed Services.

Section 1011, act Mar. 7, 1942, ch. 166, §11, 56 Stat. 146, related to settlement of accounts. For that portion of this section applicable to civilian officers and employees and their dependents, see section 5567 of Title 5, Government Organization and Employees, and for that portion applicable to members of the uniformed services and their dependents, see section 557 of Title 37, Pay and Allowances of the Uniformed Services.

Section 1012, acts Mar. 7, 1942, ch. 166, §12, 56 Stat. 146; Feb. 12, 1946, ch. 6, §1(a), 60 Stat. 5; Aug. 29, 1951, ch. 356, §1, 65 Stat. 207; Apr. 4, 1953, ch. 17, §1(a), 67 Stat. 21; Aug. 29, 1957, Pub. L. 85–217, §1(d), 71 Stat. 492; Aug. 14, 1964, Pub. L. 88–428, §1(8), 78 Stat. 437; Oct. 19, 1965, Pub. L. 89–271, 79 Stat. 992, provided for moving dependents and effects of persons dead, injured, missing, or captured, for sale of motor vehicles and other bulky items, and claims for proceeds. For portions of this section applicable to civilian officers and employees and their dependents, see section 5564 of Title 5, Government Organization and Employees, and for that portion applicable to members of the uniformed services and their dependents, see section 554 of Title 37, Pay and Allowances of the Uniformed Services.

§1012a. Repealed. Pub. L. 89–554, §8(a), Sept. 6, 1966, 80 Stat. 656

Section, act Aug. 29, 1951, ch. 356, §2, 65 Stat. 208, allowed presentation, for consideration, reconsideration, or reimbursement during a period of 3 years following Aug. 29, 1951, of previously unpresented, rejected or disallowed claims for travel by dependents and for transportation of household and personal effects arising between Sept. 8, 1939, and Aug. 29, 1951, under section 1012 of this Appendix, ratified payments for travel by dependents and transportation of household and personal effects made by disbursing officers pursuant to section 1012 of this Appendix, on or after Mar. 7, 1942, and prior to Aug. 29, 1951, previously not allowed by virtue of inability to establish death or injury as a result of military or naval operations, and ratified payments made on and after June 25, 1950, and prior to Aug. 29, 1951, for transportation, packing, and unpacking of privately owned motor vehicles transported under the conditions set forth in section 1012 of this Appendix.

Section was not enacted as part of act Mar. 7, 1942, ch. 166, 56 Stat. 143, known as the Missing Persons Act, which enacted sections 1001 to 1012 and 1013 to 1017 of this Appendix.

§§1013 to 1017. Repealed. Pub. L. 89–554, §8(a), Sept. 6, 1966, 80 Stat. 651, 654, 657, 658, 659, 662

Section 1013, acts Mar. 7, 1942, ch. 166, §13, 56 Stat. 146; Aug. 8, 1947, ch. 515, §6, 61 Stat. 918; Aug. 14, 1964, Pub. L. 88–428, §1(9), 78 Stat. 437, provided for income tax deferment for certain persons in Government service not in position to pay taxes because of service. For that portion of this section applicable to civilian officers and employees and their dependents, see section 5568 of Title 5, Government Organization and Employees, and for that portion applicable to members of the uniformed services and their dependents, see section 558 of Title 37, Pay and Allowances of the Uniformed Services.

Section 1014, acts Mar. 7, 1942, ch. 166, §14, 56 Stat. 147; Apr. 4, 1953, ch. 17, §1(e), 67 Stat. 21, related to application of the Missing Persons Act to persons besieged by a hostile force. For that portion of this section applicable to civilian officers and employees and their dependents, see sections 5561 to 5564 and 5566 of Title 5, Government Organization and Employees, and for that portion applicable to members of the uniformed services and their dependents, see sections 551 to 554 and 556 of Title 37, Pay and Allowances of the Uniformed Services.

Section 1015, acts Mar. 7, 1942, ch. 166, §15, 56 Stat. 147; Dec. 24, 1942, ch. 828, §1, 56 Stat. 1092; Apr. 4, 1953, ch. 17, §1(f), 67 Stat. 21; Jan. 30, 1954, ch. 3, 68 Stat. 7; June 30, 1955, ch. 254, 69 Stat. 238; July 20, 1956, ch. 658, 70 Stat. 595; Aug. 7, 1957, Pub. L. 85–121, 71 Stat. 341; Aug. 29, 1957, Pub. L. 85–217, §1(e), 71 Stat. 493, prescribed the effective date.

Section 1016, act Mar. 7, 1942, ch. 166, §16, 56 Stat. 147, amended the Civil Service Retirement Act.

Section 1017, act Mar. 7, 1942, ch. 166, §17, 56 Stat. 148, authorized a lock for Saint Marys Falls Canal, Mich.

§1018. Repealed. June 16, 1942, ch. 413, §19, 56 Stat. 369, eff. June 1, 1942

Section, act Mar. 7, 1942, ch. 166, §18, 56 Stat. 148, related to base pay increases for military and naval personnel serving at sea or outside United States. See section 305 of Title 37, Pay and Allowances of the Uniformed Services.

SMALL BUSINESS MOBILIZATION ACT

ACT JUNE 11, 1942, CH. 404, 56 STAT. 351

§§1101 to 1109. Omitted

CODIFICATION

Section 1101, act June 11, 1942, ch. 404, §1, 56 Stat. 351, which related to mobilization of productive capacity by Chairman of War Production Board, was omitted in view of the termination of the Board on Nov. 3, 1945. Act June 11, 1942, ch. 404, §1, 56 Stat. 351, was repealed by Pub. L. 89–554, §8(a), Sept. 6, 1966, 80 Stat. 651.

Section 1102, act June 11, 1942, ch. 404, §2, 56 Stat. 352, which related to powers of Chairman of War Production Board, was omitted in view of the termination of the Board on Nov. 3, 1945.

Section 1103, act June 11, 1942, ch. 404, §3, 56 Stat. 352, which related to certification of contractors by Chairman, was omitted in view of the termination of the Board on Nov. 3, 1945.

Section 1104, acts June 11, 1942, ch. 404, §4, 56 Stat. 353; Dec. 8, 1944, ch. 549, 58 Stat. 799; Apr. 27, 1945, ch. 98, §§1, 2(a), 59 Stat. 95, which created the Smaller War Plants Corporation and enumerated its powers and duties, expired on Dec. 31, 1946, by its own terms. Act June 11, 1942, ch. 404, §4, 56 Stat. 353, was repealed by Pub. L. 89–554, §8(a), Sept. 6, 1966, 80 Stat. 651.

Section 1105, act June 11, 1942, ch. 404, §5, 56 Stat. 355, which related to reports of Chairman of War Production Board, was omitted in view of the termination of the Board on Nov. 3, 1945.

Section 1106, act June 11, 1942, ch. 404, §6, 56 Stat. 355, which related to Defense Plant Corporation, expired upon dissolution of Corporation by Joint Res. June 30, 1945, ch. 215, §1, 59 Stat. 310, eff. July 1, 1945.

Section 1107, acts June 11, 1942, ch. 404, §7, 56 Stat. 355; July 26, 1947, ch. 343, title II, §205(a), 61 Stat. 501, which related to participation, by the Army and Navy Departments and the United States Maritime Commission, in loans, guaranties, and commitments in accordance with Ex. Ord. No. 9112, eff. Mar. 26, 1942, 7 F.R. 2367, and to participation in or guarantee of, by those Departments and Commission, any loans made pursuant to act June 11, 1942, ch. 404, 56 Stat. 351, formerly classified to sections 1101 to 1111 of this Appendix, with a view to increasing the production of war materials, etc., was omitted as obsolete. Ex. Ord. No. 9112 was superseded by Ex. Ord. No. 10161, eff. Sept. 9, 1950, 15 F.R. 6105, and set out under section 2071 of this Appendix, and all of act June 11, 1942, to which section 1107 could have related, has expired.

Section 1108, act June 11, 1942, ch. 404, §8, 56 Stat. 355, amended R.S. §5200, which is classified to section 84 of Title 12, Banks and Banking.

Section 1109, act June 11, 1942, ch. 404, §9, 56 Stat. 355, amended section 5d of the Reconstruction Finance Corporation Act, which was classified to section 606b of Title 15, Commerce and Trade, and was omitted from the Code.

§1110. Transferred

CODIFICATION

Section, act June 11, 1942, ch. 404, §10, 56 Stat. 356, which related to insured banks as depositaries of public money, duties and security of these banks, prohibition of discrimination between banks, and to repeal of inconsistent laws, was transferred to section 265 of Title 12, Banks and Banking.

§1111. Omitted

CODIFICATION

Section, act June 11, 1942, ch. 404, §11, 56 Stat. 357, which related to construction with other laws and Executive Orders of the authority of the Chairman of the War Production Board and of the Reconstruction Finance Corporation, was omitted in view of the termination of the War Production Board and the abolition of the Reconstruction Finance Corporation.

§1112. Repealed. July 25, 1947, ch. 327, §1, 61 Stat. 449

Section, act June 11, 1942, ch. 404, §12, 56 Stat. 357, related to suspension of the anti-trust laws.

OUTSTANDING CERTIFICATES

Act July 25, 1947, ch. 327, §1, 61 Stat. 449, which repealed this section, provided that outstanding certificates issued under this section should continue in effect for a period of six months from July 25, 1947, unless sooner revoked.

WAR AND DEFENSE CONTRACT ACTS

ACT JUNE 28, 1940

ACT JUNE 28, 1940, CH. 440, 54 STAT. 676

§§1151, 1152. Omitted

CODIFICATION

Section 1151, act June 28, 1940, ch. 440, title I, §1, 54 Stat. 676, which related to advance and partial payments on defense contracts and liens on payments, terminated on June 30, 1942 pursuant to the provisions of section 1162 of this Appendix. A provision of this section concerning reports to Congress was repealed by act Aug. 7, 1946, ch. 770, §1(25), 60 Stat. 868. Advance payments on government contracts are covered by section 255 of Title 41, Public Contracts and sections 1431 to 1435 of Title 50, War and National Defense.

Section 1152, acts June 28, 1940, ch. 440, title I, §2, 54 Stat. 676; Sept. 9, 1940, ch. 717, title II, §201, 54 Stat. 875; May 31, 1941, ch. 157, 55 Stat. 236; Mar. 27, 1942, ch. 199, title III, §301, 56 Stat. 177; Dec. 20, 1944, ch. 614, 58 Stat. 827; Proc. No. 2695, eff. July 4, 1946, 11 F.R. 7817, 60 Stat. 1352; Aug. 7, 1946, ch. 770, §1(26), (31), 60 Stat. 868, was omitted as terminated. Subsec. (a) of this section, which related to the powers, duties, and discretion of the President to contract for the acquisition, construction, and repair of naval vessels, aircraft, and equipment, was omitted pursuant to the provisions of section 645 of this Appendix. See Continuation of Import Controls note set out below. Subsec. (b) of this section, which required contracts for naval vessels under section 496 of former Title 34, Navy, to contain limitations on excess profits, terminated on June 30, 1942, pursuant to the provisions of section 1162 of this Appendix.

Pub. L. 91–452, title II, §249, Oct. 15, 1970, 84 Stat. 931, purported to amend subsec. (a)(4) of section 1152, by striking out provisions which related to immunity from prosecution of any individual compelled to testify or produce evidence, documentary or otherwise, after claiming his privilege against self-incrimination, subsequent to termination of subsec. (a)(4).

CONTINUATION OF IMPORT CONTROLS OVER FATS AND OILS AND RICE AND RICE PRODUCTS UNTIL AUGUST 1, 1951

Act June 30, 1950, ch. 426, 64 Stat. 308, as amended June 30, 1951, ch. 198, §3, 65 Stat. 111, continued Title III of the Second War Powers Act, 1942, as amended [this section] until Aug. 1, 1951, for the purpose of authorizing and exercising, administering, and enforcing of import controls with respect to fats and oils (including oil-bearing materials, fatty acids, butter, soap and soap powder, but excluding petroleum and petroleum products and coconuts and coconut products) and rice and rice products, upon a determination by the President that such controls are (a) essential to the acquisition or distribution of products in world short supply or (b) essential to the orderly liquidation of temporary surpluses of stocks owned or controlled by the Government.

Similar provisions continuing the controls until July 1, 1950, were contained in act July 1, 1949, ch. 292, 63 Stat. 405.

EXECUTIVE ORDER NO. 9729

Ex. Ord. No. 9729, May 23, 1946, 11 F.R. 5641, related to the functions and duties of the Office of Defense Transportation, which was terminated by Ex. Ord. No. 10065, July 6, 1949, eff. July 1, 1949, 14 F.R. 3719.

§§1153 to 1162. Omitted

CODIFICATION

Sections 1153, 1154, and 1156 to 1162 terminated June 30, 1942, and section 1155 terminated Apr. 30, 1943, pursuant to the provisions of section 1162 of this Appendix.

Section 1153, act June 28, 1940, ch. 440, title I, §3, 54 Stat. 677, limited the provisions of section 496 of former Title 34, Navy, to contracts exceeding $25,000.

Section 1154, act June 28, 1940, ch. 440, title I, §4, 54 Stat. 677, provided for certification as to necessity and cost of special additional equipment and facilities acquired to facilitate construction of aircraft or naval vessels under section 496 of former Title 34. A provision of this section concerning reports to Congress was repealed by act Aug. 7, 1946, ch. 770, §1(27), 60 Stat. 868.

Section 1155, act June 28, 1940, ch. 440, title I, §5, 54 Stat. 678, related to working hours and overtime compensation of Navy, Coast Guard, and Army employees. Act July 3, 1942, ch. 482, 56 Stat. 645, as amended Oct. 2, 1942, ch. 577, 56 Stat. 765; Dec. 22, 1942, ch. 798, 56 Stat. 1068, extended from June 30, 1942, to and including Apr. 30, 1943, the provisions for the payment of overtime rates of compensation contained in sections 1151 to 1162.

Section 1156, act June 28, 1940, ch. 440, title I, §6, 54 Stat. 679; Aug. 21, 1941, ch. 385, 55 Stat. 654, related to reemployment of retired employees and to summary removal of civil service employees of the War and Navy Departments and the Coast Guard for national security reasons. Act Aug. 21, 1941, ch. 385, 55 Stat. 654, was repealed by Pub. L. 89–554, §8(a), Sept. 6, 1966, 80 Stat. 651.

Section 1157, act June 28, 1940, ch. 440, title I, §7, 54 Stat. 679, added a temporary section 8 to act Mar. 14, 1936, ch. 140, 49 Stat. 611, providing for vacation pay in lieu of vacation for Navy and Coast Guard employees. The act of Mar. 14, 1936, was repealed by act Oct. 30, 1951, ch. 631, title II, §207(a)(1), 65 Stat. 682. For accumulation of annual leave, see section 6301 et seq. of Title 5, Government Organization and Employees.

Section 1158, acts June 28, 1940, ch. 440, title I, §8, 54 Stat. 680; Sept. 16, 1940, ch. 720, §9, 54 Stat. 892, increased the limit of cost of vessels under section 498c–1 of former Title 34, Navy, and other statutes, suspended limitations on payments to certain Navy Department employees, and authorized the Secretary of the Navy to employ additional personnel and to provide and operate the necessary buildings, facilities, utilities, and appurtenances thereto for the purposes of sections 1151 to 1162 of this Appendix. The latter provision is covered by section 1201 of this Appendix. Act Aug. 21, 1941, ch. 395,

55 Stat. 664, made the provisions of section 1158 applicable to naval public-works projects authorized by that act and all prior acts. A provision of this section concerning reports to Congress was repealed by act Aug. 7, 1946, ch. 770, §1(28), 60 Stat. 868.

Section 1159, act June 28, 1940, ch. 440, title I, §9, 54 Stat. 680, authorized modification of existing Navy and Coast Guard contracts to expedite defense.

Section 1160, act June 28, 1940, ch. 440, title I, §10, 54 Stat. 680, related to approval of certain Naval public-works contracts under act April 25, 1939, ch. 87, §4, 53 Stat. 590.

Section 1161, act June 28, 1940, ch. 440, title I, §11, 54 Stat. 680, related to employment of aliens in performance of secret, confidential, or restricted Government contracts.

Section 1162, act June 28, 1940, ch. 440, title I, §12, 54 Stat. 681, provided that sections 1151 to 1161 of this Appendix terminate June 30, 1942, unless Congress otherwise provided, was omitted from the Code as terminated.

ACT JULY 2, 1940, CH. 508, 54 STAT. 712

§§1171, 1172. Repealed. Aug. 10, 1956, ch. 1041, §53, 70A Stat. 641

Section 1171, acts July 2, 1940, ch. 508, §1, 54 Stat. 712; Sept. 9, 1940, ch. 717, title I, §103, 54 Stat. 875; June 5, 1942, ch. 340, §13, 56 Stat. 317, related to contracts for Army defense facilities, construction of facilities, acquisition of military equipment munitions, and supplies, suspension of limitations on costs, operation and maintenance of facilities, and disposal of land and facilities.

Section 1172, act July 2, 1940, ch. 508, §5, 54 Stat. 714, related to contracts for emergencies affecting national defense; limitation of amount; report of expenditures; compliance with statutory conditions for contracts.

ACT JULY 17, 1953, CH. 221, 67 STAT. 177

§§1173 to 1175. Omitted

Codification

Sections 1173 to 1175 were omitted pursuant to act June 21, 1956, ch. 420, 70 Stat. 325, which provided that sections 1173 to 1175 of this Appendix remain in effect until six months after the national emergency proclaimed by the President on Dec. 16, 1950, or until such date as specified by a concurrent resolution of the Congress or until July 1, 1957, whichever was earliest.

Section 1173, acts July 17, 1953, ch. 221, §1, 67 Stat. 177; July 26, 1954, ch. 570, §2, 68 Stat. 531, related to construction authority for the Armed Forces.

Section 1174, act July 17, 1953, ch. 221, §2, 67 Stat. 178, related to activity reports by the Secretary of Defense.

Section 1175, act July 17, 1953, ch. 221, §3, 67 Stat. 178, prohibited construction of section 1173 to 1175 of this Appendix as a repeal or modification of section 555 of Title 40, Public Buildings, Property, and Works.

ACT JULY 11, 1941, CH. 290, §3, 55 STAT. 585

§1181. Repealed. July 25, 1947, ch. 327, §1, 61 Stat. 449

Section, act July 11, 1941, ch. 290, §3, 55 Stat. 585, authorized the Secretary of the Treasury to negotiate contracts for Coast Guard vessels, aircraft and equipment on the basis provided by section 1152(a) of this Appendix.

ACT APR. 28, 1942, CH. 247, TITLE IV, §403, 56 STAT. 245

§1191. Omitted

Codification

Section, acts Apr. 28, 1942, ch. 247, title IV, §403, 56 Stat. 245; Oct. 21, 1942, ch. 619, title VIII, §801(a)–(c), 56 Stat. 982; July 1, 1943, ch. 185, §1, 57 Stat. 347, 348; July 14, 1943, ch. 239, §§1–4, 57 Stat. 564; Feb. 25, 1944, ch. 63, title VII, §701(b), 58 Stat. 78; June 30, 1945, ch. 210, §1, 59 Stat. 294; June 14, 1947, ch. 105, 61 Stat. 133; June 28, 1949, ch. 268, §2(a), 63 Stat. 280; Mar. 23, 1951, ch. 15, title II, §201(a)–(d), 65 Stat. 23; Oct. 20, 1951, ch. 521, title VI, §617, 65 Stat. 569; July 17, 1952, ch. 924, §2, 66 Stat. 753, which provided that this section be cited as the Renegotiation Act and which related to the renegotiation of contracts and determination and recovery of excess profits, was omitted in view of the application of the provisions of this section to profits derived from contracts determined under regulations prescribed by the Board (meaning the War Contracts Price Adjustment Board, prior to its abolition sixty days after Mar. 23, 1951, by section 201(a) and (k) of act Mar. 23, 1951, and thereafter the Renegotiation Board) to be reasonably allocable to performance prior to the close of Dec. 31, 1945, and the termination of the Renegotiation Board and transfer of all property, including records, of the Renegotiation Board to the Administrator, General Services Administration, on Mar. 31, 1979, pursuant to Pub. L. 95–431, title V, §501, Oct. 10, 1978, 92 Stat. 1043.

Terms Used

Act Feb. 25, 1944, ch. 63, title VII, §701(a), 58 Stat. 78, which provided that terms used in section 701 of act Feb. 25, 1944, have same meaning as when used in this section.

ACT FEB. 25, 1944, CH. 63, TITLE VIII, §801, 58 STAT. 92

§1192. Omitted

Codification

Section, act Feb. 25, 1944, ch. 63, title VIII, §801, 58 Stat. 92, which related to repricing of war contracts, terminated on Dec. 31, 1945 under the provisions of section 802(b) of act Feb. 25, 1944.

ACT MAY 21, 1948, CH. 333, §3, 62 STAT. 259

§1193. Omitted

Codification

Section, acts May 21, 1948, ch. 333, §3, 62 Stat. 259; Aug. 10, 1949, ch. 412, §12(a), 63 Stat. 591, provided that this section be cited as the Renegotiation Act of 1948 and related to renegotiation of airplane contracts, authorizing the Secretary of Defense, by utilizing provisions of the Renegotiation Act, section 1191 of this title, to renegotiate contracts for the purpose of eliminating excess profits.

Department of Defense Procurement Contracts for Fiscal Year 1950 Subject to This Section

Act Oct. 29, 1949, ch. 787, §622(a), 63 Stat. 1021, which provided that all negotiated contracts for procurement in excess of $1,000 entered into during the fiscal year 1950 by or on behalf of the Department of Defense, including the Department of the Army, Department of the Navy, and Department of the Air Force, and all subcontracts thereunder in excess of $1,000, are made subject to this section in the same manner and to the same extent as if such contracts and subcontracts were required by this section to contain the renegotiation article prescribed in subsec. (a) of this section.

ACT DEC. 17, 1942, CH. 739, 56 STAT. 1053

§1201. Omitted

Codification

Section, acts Dec. 17, 1942, ch. 739, §1, 56 Stat. 1053; Aug. 7, 1946, ch. 770, §1(32), 60 Stat. 868; July 3, 1952, ch. 570, §1(a)(1), 66 Stat. 330, which related to acquisition and operation of buildings and facilities by the Secretary of the Navy, terminated Aug. 1, 1953.

CONTINUATION OF PROVISIONS UNTIL AUGUST 1, 1953

Act July 3, 1952, ch. 570, §6, 66 Stat. 334, repealed act Apr. 14, 1952, ch. 204, 66 Stat. 54 as amended by acts May 28, 1952, ch. 339, 66 Stat. 96; June 14, 1952, ch. 437, 66 Stat. 137; June 30, 1952, ch. 526, 66 Stat. 296, which had continued the effectiveness of the provisions of this section until July 3, 1952. Section 1(a) of act July 3, 1952, as amended by acts Mar. 31, 1953, ch. 13, §1, 67 Stat. 18 and June 30, 1953, ch. 172, 67 Stat. 132, extended the time limitation on the effectiveness of the provisions of this section from Apr. 1, 1953 to Aug. 1, 1953.

ACT MAR. 23, 1951, CH. 15, 65 STAT. 7

TITLE I—RENEGOTIATION OF CONTRACTS

§§1211 to 1217. Omitted

CODIFICATION

Sections were omitted pursuant to section 1212(c)(1) of this Appendix, which provided that sections 1211 to 1217, and 1218 to 1224 of this Appendix not be applicable to receipts and accruals under contracts attributable to performance after Sept. 30, 1976, and in view of the termination of the Renegotiation Board and transfer of all property, including records, of the Renegotiation Board to the Administrator, General Services Administration, on Mar. 31, 1979, pursuant to Pub. L. 95–431, title V, §501, Oct. 10, 1978, 92 Stat. 1043.

Section 1211, act Mar. 23, 1951, ch. 15, title I, §101, 65 Stat. 7, set forth the Congressional declaration of policy concerning renegotiation of contracts.

Section 1212, acts Mar. 23, 1951, ch. 15, title I, §102, 65 Stat. 8; Sept. 1, 1954, ch. 1209, §1, 68 Stat. 1116; Aug. 3, 1955, ch. 499, §§1, 2(a), 69 Stat. 447; Aug. 1, 1956, ch. 821, §§2, 9(b), 70 Stat. 786, 791; Sept. 6, 1958, Pub. L. 85–930, §1, 72 Stat. 1789; July 13, 1959, Pub. L. 86–89, §1, 73 Stat. 210; July 3, 1962, Pub. L. 87–520, §1, 76 Stat. 134; June 30, 1964, Pub. L. 88–339, §1, 78 Stat. 233; June 30, 1966, Pub. L. 89–480, 80 Stat. 232; Oct. 24, 1968, Pub. L. 90–634, title I, §102, 82 Stat. 1345; July 1, 1971, Pub. L. 92–41, §1, 85 Stat. 97; July 9, 1973, Pub. L. 93–66, §1, 87 Stat. 152; June 30, 1974, Pub. L. 93–329, §1, 88 Stat. 288; Dec. 31, 1975, Pub. L. 94–185, 89 Stat. 1061, which related to contracts subject to renegotiation and provided that sections 1211 to 1214 of this Appendix not be applicable to receipts and accruals under contracts attributable to performance after Sept. 30, 1976.

Section 1213, acts Mar. 23, 1951, ch. 15, title I, §103, 65 Stat. 8; Aug. 1, 1956, ch. 821, §§3(a), 4, 70 Stat. 786; Sept. 6, 1958, Pub. L. 85–930, §2(a), 72 Stat. 1789; July 13, 1959, Pub. L. 86–89, §2, 73 Stat. 210; June 30, 1964, Pub. L. 88–339, §2(a), 78 Stat. 233; July 1, 1971, Pub. L. 92–41, §3(d), 85 Stat. 98; Apr. 2, 1982, Pub. L. 97–164, title I, §160(a)(18), 96 Stat. 48, related to definitions for the purposes of sections 1211 to 1224 of this Appendix.

Section 1214, act Mar. 23, 1951, ch. 15, title I, §104, 65 Stat. 11, related to renegotiation clauses in contracts.

Section 1215, acts Mar. 23, 1951, ch. 15, title I, §105, 65 Stat. 12; Sept. 1, 1954, ch. 1209, §§2, 7(a), 68 Stat. 1116, 1118; Aug. 1, 1956, ch. 821, §§5(a)–(c), 6, 7(a), 70 Stat. 787; June 11, 1960, Pub. L. 86–507, §1(39), 74 Stat. 202; July 3, 1962, Pub. L. 87–520, §2(c), 76 Stat. 134; Oct. 24, 1968, Pub. L. 90–634, title I, §103, 82 Stat. 1345; July 1, 1971, Pub. L. 92–41, §§2(a), 3(d), 85 Stat. 97, 98; Apr. 2, 1982, Pub. L. 97–164, title I, §160(a)(18), 96 Stat. 48, related to renegotiation proceedings.

Section 1216, acts Mar. 23, 1951, ch. 15, title I, §106, 65 Stat. 17; Sept. 1, 1954, ch. 1209, §§3(a), 4(a)–(c), 5(a), 6(a), 68 Stat. 1116, 1118; Aug. 3, 1955, ch. 499, §§3(a), 4(a), 5(a), 69 Stat. 447, 448; Aug. 1, 1956, ch. 821, §§8(a), 9(a), 70 Stat. 789; Oct. 24, 1968, Pub. L. 90–634, title I, §104, 82 Stat. 1345; July 1, 1971, Pub. L. 92–41, §3(d), 85 Stat. 98; Apr. 2, 1982, Pub. L. 97–164, title I, §160(a)(18), 96 Stat. 48, related to exemptions.

Section 1217, acts Mar. 23, 1951, ch. 15, title I, §107, 65 Stat. 19; Aug. 1, 1956, ch. 821, §10, 70 Stat. 791; July 13, 1959, Pub. L. 86–89, §3, 73 Stat. 211; June 11, 1960, Pub. L. 86–507, §1(40), 74 Stat. 202; Aug. 14, 1964, Pub. L. 88–426, title III, §305(31), 78 Stat. 426, established the Renegotiation Board and provided for its operation. The Renegotiation Board was terminated and all property, including records, of the Board was transferred to the Administrator, General Services Administration, on Mar. 31, 1979, pursuant to Pub. L. 95–431, title V, §501, Oct. 10, 1978, 92 Stat. 1043.

§1217a. Repealed. June 28, 1955, ch. 189, §12(c)(5), 69 Stat. 181

Section, act Nov. 1, 1951, ch. 665, Ch. V, 65 Stat. 763, authorized the Board to place not more than five positions in grades 16, 17, or 18 of the General Schedule established by the Classification Act of 1949.

§§1218 to 1224. Omitted

CODIFICATION

Sections were omitted pursuant to section 1212(c)(1) of this Appendix, which provided that sections 1211 to 1217, and 1218 to 1224 of this Appendix not be applicable to receipts and accruals under contracts attributable to performance after Sept. 30, 1976, and in view of the termination of the Renegotiation Board and transfer of all property, including records, of the Renegotiation Board to the Administrator, General Services Administration, on Mar. 31, 1979, pursuant to Pub. L. 95–431, title V, §501, Oct. 10, 1978, 92 Stat. 1043.

Section 1218, acts Mar. 23, 1951, ch. 15, title I, §108, 65 Stat. 21; Aug. 1, 1956, ch. 821, §11(a), 70 Stat. 791; July 3, 1962, Pub. L. 87–520, §2(b), 76 Stat. 134; July 1, 1971, Pub. L. 92–41, §§2(b), 3(a), 85 Stat. 97, 98; Apr. 2, 1982, Pub. L. 97–164, title I, §160(a)(18), 96 Stat. 48, provided for review by the United States Claims Court [now United States Court of Federal Claims] of Renegotiation Board determinations.

Section 1218a, acts Mar. 23, 1951, ch. 15, title I, §108A, as added Aug. 1, 1956, ch. 821, §12, 70 Stat. 791; amended July 3, 1962, Pub. L. 87–520, §2(a), 76 Stat. 134; July 1, 1971, Pub. L. 92–41, §3(b), 85 Stat. 98; Apr. 2, 1982, Pub. L. 97–164, title I, §160(a)(18), (c), 96 Stat. 48, provided for review of United States Claims Court [now United States Court of Federal Claims] decisions.

Section 1219, act Mar. 23, 1951, ch. 15, title I, §109, 65 Stat. 22, authorized the Renegotiation Board to make rules and regulations as deemed necessary.

Section 1220, act Mar. 23, 1951, ch. 15, title I, §110, 65 Stat. 22, provided that no person be held liable for damages or penalties for compliance with any rule, regulation, or order.

Section 1221, act Mar. 23, 1951, ch. 15, title I, §111, 65 Stat. 22, related to application of the Administrative Procedure Act.

Section 1222, act Mar. 23, 1951, ch. 15, title I, §112, 65 Stat. 22, related to authorization of appropriations.

Section 1223, acts Mar. 23, 1951, ch. 15, title I, §113, 65 Stat. 22; Aug. 1, 1956, ch. 821, §13, 70 Stat. 792, related to prosecution of claims against United States by former personnel.

Section 1224, acts Mar. 23, 1951, ch. 15, title I, §114, as added Aug. 1, 1956, ch. 821, §14, 70 Stat. 792; amended July 1, 1971, Pub. L. 92–41, §3(c), 85 Stat. 98; Apr. 2, 1982, Pub. L. 97–164, title I, §160(a)(18), 96 Stat. 48, required the Renegotiation Board to report to Congress on or before Jan. 1, 1957, and on or before Jan. 1, of each year thereafter on its activities for the preceding year ending on June 30.

TITLE II—GENERAL PROVISIONS

§§1231 to 1233. Omitted

CODIFICATION

Section 1231, acts Mar. 23, 1951, ch. 15, title II, §201, 65 Stat. 23; July 17, 1952, ch. 924, §3, 66 Stat. 753; Sept. 1, 1954, ch. 1209, §8, 68 Stat. 1118, which abolished the War Contracts Price Adjustment Board and transferred its functions under section 1191 of this Appendix to the Renegotiation Board, with the exception of the functions under section 1191(a)(4)(D) of this Appendix, which were transferred to the Administrator of General Services, was omitted in view of the termination of the Renegotiation Board and transfer of all property, including records, of the Board to the Administrator, General Services Administration, on Mar. 31, 1979, pursuant to Pub. L. 95–431, title V, §501, Oct. 10, 1978, 92 Stat. 1043, and the omission of section 1191 of this Appendix.

Section 1232, act Mar. 23, 1951, ch. 15, title II, §202, 65 Stat. 24, which prescribed a period of limitations for actions under the Renegotiation Act of 1948, section 1193 of this Appendix, was omitted in view of the omission of section 1193 of this Appendix.

Section 1233, act Mar. 23, 1951, ch. 15, title II, §203, 65 Stat. 25, amended section 3806(a)(1) of the Internal Revenue Code of 1939. Provisions of section 3806 of the I.R.C. of 1939 are covered by section 1481 of Title 26, Internal Revenue Code.

NATIONAL EMERGENCY AND WAR SHIPPING ACTS

ACT JUNE 11, 1940

ACT JUNE 11, 1940, CH. 327, 54 STAT. 306

§1251. Repealed. July 25, 1947, ch. 327, §1, 61 Stat. 449

Section, acts June 11, 1940, ch. 327, 54 Stat. 306; May 2, 1941, ch. 84, §1, 55 Stat. 148; June 16, 1942, ch. 416, 56 Stat. 370, related to determination of foreign construction costs of vessels.

ACT MAY 2, 1941, CH. 84, 55 STAT. 148

§§1261, 1262. Repealed. July 25, 1947, ch. 327, §1, 61 Stat. 449

Section 1261, acts May 2, 1941, ch. 84, §2, 55 Stat. 148; June 16, 1942, ch. 416, 56 Stat. 370, authorized United States Maritime Commission to negotiate contracts without advertisement or bids.

Section 1262, acts May 2, 1941, ch. 84, §3, 55 Stat. 149; June 16, 1942, ch. 416, 56 Stat. 370, authorized charter of Commission vessels to private operators for foreign trade until six months after the end of World War II.

§1263. Repealed. May 7, 1943, ch. 93, §5, 57 Stat. 77

Section, acts May 2, 1941, ch. 84, §4, 55 Stat. 150; June 16, 1942, ch. 416, 56 Stat. 370, related to working hours and overtime pay of United States Maritime Commission ship construction and other employees.

ACT JUNE 6, 1941, CH. 174, 55 STAT. 242

§§1271 to 1275. Omitted

CODIFICATION

Section 1271, acts June 6, 1941, ch. 174, §1, 55 Stat. 242; June 16, 1942, ch. 416, 56 Stat. 370; Mar. 24, 1943, ch. 26, §3(a), 57 Stat. 48, which related to purchase, requisition, etc., of foreign vessels authorized during national emergency and compensation, expired on July 1, 1953. See section 196 of Title 50.

Section 1272, acts June 6, 1941, ch. 174, §2, 55 Stat. 243; June 16, 1942, ch. 416, 56 Stat. 370, which related to availability of appropriations for carrying out provisions of section 1271 to 1275 of this Appendix, expired on July 1, 1953.

Section 1273, acts June 6, 1941, ch. 174, §3, 55 Stat. 243; June 16, 1942, ch. 416, 56 Stat. 370; Mar. 24, 1943, ch. 26, §3(j), 57 Stat. 51, which related to charter of domestic and foreign vessels, expired on July 1, 1953. See sections 197 and 198 of Title 50.

Section 1274, acts June 6, 1942, ch. 174, §4, 55 Stat. 244; June 16, 1942, ch. 416, 56 Stat. 370; Mar. 24, 1943, ch. 26, §3(k), 57 Stat. 51, which related to purchase of domestic or foreign vessels, expired on July 1, 1953. See sections 197 and 198 of Title 50.

Section 1275, acts June 6, 1941, ch. 174, §5, 55 Stat. 244; June 16, 1942, ch. 416, 56 Stat. 370, which related to documentation of vessels requisitioned, purchased, etc., expired on July 1, 1953. See section 198 of Title 50.

Ex. Ord. No. 9848, eff. May 8, 1947, 12 F.R. 3059, and Ex. Ord. No. 8869, eff. Aug. 23, 1941, 6 F.R. 4351, related to administration of sections 1271 to 1275 of this Appendix.

ACT JULY 14, 1941, CH. 297, 55 STAT. 591

§§1281 to 1286. Repealed. July 25, 1947, ch. 327, §1, 61 Stat. 449

Section 1281, acts July 14, 1941, ch. 297, §1, 55 Stat. 591; June 16, 1942, ch. 416, 56 Stat. 370, related to transportation priorities for merchant vessels during World War II.

Section 1282, acts July 14, 1941, ch. 297, §2, 55 Stat. 591; June 16, 1942, ch. 416, 56 Stat. 370, related to form and content of warrants.

Section 1283, acts July 14, 1941, ch. 297, §3, 55 Stat. 592; June 16, 1942, ch. 416, 56 Stat. 370, related to priorities for vessels holding warrants.

Section 1284, acts July 14, 1941, ch. 297, §4, 55 Stat. 592; June 16, 1942, ch. 416, 56 Stat. 370, related to Commission policy regarding priorities.

Section 1285, acts July 14, 1941, ch. 297, §5, 55 Stat. 592; June 16, 1942, ch. 416, 56 Stat. 370, defined citizens of the United States for purposes of sections 1281 to 1286 of this Appendix.

Section 1286, acts July 14, 1941, ch. 297, §6, 55 Stat. 592; June 16, 1942, ch. 416, 56 Stat. 370, related to penalties for violations of sections 1281 to 1286 of this Appendix and jurisdiction of offenses committed in the Canal Zone and the Philippine Islands.

EXTENSION OF TERMINATION DATE

Prior to repeal, sections 1281 to 1286 had been extended until six months after termination of World War II by act June 16, 1942, ch. 416, 56 Stat. 370.

ACT MAR. 24, 1943, CH. 26, 57 STAT. 45

§1291. Rights of American seamen on privately owned and operated American vessels extended to seamen employed through the War Shipping Administration; exceptions; definitions

(a) Officers and members of crews (hereinafter referred to as "seamen") employed on United States or foreign flag vessels as employees of the United States through the War Shipping Administration[1] shall, with respect to (1) laws administered by the Public Health Service and the Social Security Act [42 U.S.C. 301 et seq.], as amended by subsection (b)(2) and (3) of this section; (2) death, injuries, illness, maintenance and cure, loss of effects, detention, or repatriation, or claims arising therefrom not covered by the foregoing clause (1); and (3) collection of wages and bonuses and making of allotments, have all of the rights, benefits, exemptions, privileges, and liabilities, under law applicable to citizens of the United States employed as seamen on privately owned and operated American vessels. Such seamen, because of the temporary wartime character of their employment by the War Shipping Administration, shall not be considered as officers or employees of the United States for the purposes of the United States Employees Compensation Act, as amended [5 U.S.C. 8101 et seq.]; the Civil Service Retirement Act, as amended [5 U.S.C. 8331 et seq.]; the Act of Congress approved March 7, 1942 (Pub. Law 490, Seventy-seventh Congress) or the Act entitled "An Act to provide benefits for the injury, disability, death, or detention of employees of contractors with the United States and certain other persons or reimbursement therefor", approved December 2, 1942 (Public Law 784, Seventy-seventh Congress) [42 U.S.C. 1701 et seq.]. Claims arising under clause (1) hereof shall be enforced in the same manner as such claims would be enforced if the seaman were employed on a privately owned and operated American vessel. Any claim referred to in clause (2) or (3) hereof shall, if administratively disallowed in whole or in part, be enforced pursuant to the provisions of the Suits in Admiralty Act [46 App. U.S.C. 741 et seq.], notwithstanding the vessel on which the seaman is employed is not a merchant vessel within the meaning of such Act [said sections]. Any claim, right, or cause of action of or in respect of any such seaman accruing on or after October 1, 1941, and prior to the date of enactment of this section [Mar. 24, 1943] may be enforced, and upon the election of the seaman or his surviving dependent or beneficiary, or his legal representative to do so shall be governed, as if this section had been in effect when such claim, right, or cause of action accrued, such election to be made in accordance with rules and regulations prescribed by the Administrator, War Shipping Administration. Rights of any seaman under the Social Security Act [42 U.S.C. 301 et seq.], as amended by subsection (b)(2) and (3), and claims therefor shall be governed solely by the provisions of such Act, so amended. When used in this subsection the term "administratively disallowed" means a denial of a written claim in accordance with rules or regulations prescribed by the Administrator, War Shipping Administration. When used in this subsection the terms "War Shipping Administration" and "Administrator, War Shipping Administration" shall be deemed to include the United States Maritime Commission with respect to the period beginning October 1, 1941, and ending February 11, 1942, and the term "seaman" shall be deemed to include any seaman employed as an employee of the United States through the War Shipping Administration on vessels made available to or subchartered to other agencies or departments of the United States.

(b)(1) Omitted [Amendment of section 1426 of the Internal Revenue Code of 1939].

(2) Omitted [Amendment of section 209 of the Social Security Act, as amended (42 U.S.C. 409)].

(3) Omitted [Amendment of section 907 of the Social Security Act Amendments of 1939 (53 Stat. 1402)].

(c) The War Shipping Administration and its agents or persons acting on its behalf or for its account may, for convenience of administration, with the approval of the Administrator, make payments of any taxes, fees, charges, or exactions to the United States or its agencies.

(Mar. 24, 1943, ch. 26, §1, 57 Stat. 45; Apr. 4, 1944, ch. 161, §§1, 2, 58 Stat. 188; Mar. 24, 1945, ch. 36, §1(a), 59 Stat. 38.)

REFERENCES IN TEXT

The Social Security Act, referred to in subsec. (a), is act Aug. 14, 1935, ch. 531, 49 Stat. 620, as amended, which is classified generally to chapter 7 (§301 et seq.) of Title 42, The Public Health and Welfare. For complete classification of this Act to the Code, see section 1305 of Title 42 and Tables.

The United States Employees Compensation Act, as amended, referred to in subsec. (a), is act Sept. 7, 1916, ch. 458, 39 Stat. 742, as amended, which was repealed by Pub. L. 89–554, §8(a), Sept. 6, 1966, 80 Stat. 632, and the provisions thereof were reenacted by the first section thereof as subchapter I (§8101 et seq.) of chapter 81 of Title 5, Government Organization and Employees.

The Civil Service Retirement Act, as amended, referred to in subsec. (a), is act May 29, 1930, ch. 349, 46 Stat. 468, as amended generally by act July 31, 1956, ch. 804, §401, 70 Stat. 743, which was repealed by Pub. L. 89–554, §8(a), Sept. 6, 1966, 80 Stat. 632, and reenacted by the first section thereof as subchapter III (§8331 et seq.) of chapter 83 of Title 5.

The Act of Congress approved March 7, 1942 (Public Law 784, Seventy-seventh Congress), referred to in subsec. (a), is act Mar. 7, 1942, ch. 166, 56 Stat. 143, as amended, popularly known as the Missing Persons Act, and was classified to sections 1001 to 1018 of this Appendix. The Act was repealed by Pub. L. 89–554, Sept. 6, 1966, §8(a), 80 Stat. 632, and reenacted by the first section thereof as subchapter VII of chapter 55 of Title 5, Government Organization and Employees, and chapter 10 of Title 37, Pay and Allowances of the Uniformed Services.

The Act entitled "An Act to provide benefits for the injury, disability, death, or detention of employees of contractors with the United States and certain other persons or reimbursement therefor", approved December 2, 1942 (Public Law 784, Seventy-seventh Congress), referred to in subsec. (a), is act Dec. 2, 1942, ch. 668, 56 Stat. 1028, as amended, titles I and II of which are popularly known as the War Hazards Compensation Act, and is classified principally to chapter 12 (§1701 et seq.) of Title 42, The Public Health and Welfare. For complete classification of this Act to the Code, see Short Title note set out under section 1701 of Title 42 and Tables.

[1] See Transfer of Functions note below.

The Suits in Admiralty Act, referred to in subsec. (a), is act Mar. 9, 1920, ch. 95, 41 Stat. 525, as amended, which is classified generally to chapter 20 (§741 et seq.) of Title 46, Appendix, Shipping. For complete classification of this Act to the Code, see Short Title note set out under section 741 of Title 46, Appendix, and Tables.

AMENDMENTS

1945—Subsec. (b)(1). Act Mar. 24, 1945, inserted last sentence.

1944—Subsec. (b)(1), (2). Act Apr. 4, 1944, inserted provisions excluding from term employment service performed under contract entered into without the United States and during the performance of which the vessel does not touch a port in the United States, or a vessel documented under the laws of a foreign country and bareboat chartered to the War Shipping Administration.

EFFECTIVE DATE

Section 1(b) of act Mar. 24, 1945, provided that the amendment made by that act shall be effective as if made by section 1 of act Mar. 24, 1943.

TRANSFER OF FUNCTIONS

War Shipping Administration terminated as of Sept. 1, 1946, and functions, powers, duties, etc., transferred to United States Maritime Commission for period Sept. 1, 1946, to Dec. 31, 1946, for purpose of liquidating Administration, by act July 8, 1946, ch. 543, title II, §202, 60 Stat. 501.

United States Maritime Commission abolished by Reorg. Plan No. 21 of 1950, eff. May 24, 1950, 15 F.R. 3178, 64 Stat. 1273, set out in the Appendix to Title 5, Government Organization and Employees, which transferred part of its functions and part of functions of its Chairman to Federal Maritime Board and Chairman thereof, that Board having been created by that Plan as an agency within Department of Commerce with an independent status in some respects, and transferred remainder of Commission's functions and functions of its Chairman to Secretary of Commerce, with power vested in Secretary to authorize their performance by Maritime Administrator, the head of Maritime Administration, which likewise was established by the Plan in Department of Commerce with provision that Chairman of Federal Maritime Board should, ex officio, be that Administrator.

Federal Maritime Board, including offices of members of Board, abolished by section 304 of Reorg. Plan No. 7 of 1961, eff. Aug. 12, 1961, 26 F.R. 7315, 75 Stat. 843, set out in the Appendix to Title 5, Government Organization and Employees. Functions of Board transferred either to Federal Maritime Commission or to Secretary of Commerce by sections 103 and 202 of Reorg. Plan No. 7 of 1961.

Maritime Administration transferred from Department of Commerce to Department of Transportation by Pub. L. 97–31, Aug. 6, 1981, 95 Stat. 151 (46 App. U.S.C. 1601 et seq.).

Functions of Public Health Service, Surgeon General of Public Health Service, and all other officers and employees of Public Health Service, and functions of all agencies of or in Public Health Service transferred to Secretary of Health, Education, and Welfare by Reorg. Plan No. 3 of 1966, 31 F.R. 8855, 80 Stat. 1610, effective June 25, 1966, set out in the Appendix to Title 5, Government Organization and Employees. Secretary of Health, Education, and Welfare redesignated Secretary of Health and Human Services by section 3508(b) of Title 20, Education.

VESSEL OPERATIONS UNDER REVOLVING FUND

Vessel operations conducted under Vessel Operations Revolving Fund, applicability of subsecs. (a) and (c) of this section to, see section 1241a of Title 46, Appendix, Shipping.

SECTION REFERRED TO IN OTHER SECTIONS

This section is referred to in title 5 section 5541; title 46 App. section 1241a.

§1292. Insurance awards by War Shipping Administrators; findings and actions as conclusive

(a) Repealed. July 25, 1947, ch. 327, §1, 61 Stat. 449.

(b) Whenever the Administrator, War Shipping Administration,[1] finds that, on or after October 1, 1941, and before thirty days after the date of enactment of this subsection [Mar. 24, 1943], a master, officer, or member of the crew of, or any persons transported on, a vessel owned by or chartered to the Maritime Commission, the War Shipping Administration, or the War Department[2] or operated by, or for the account of, or at the direction or under the control of the Commission, the Administration, or the War Department, has suffered death, injury, detention, or other casualty, for which the War Shipping Administration would be authorized to provide insurance under Subtitle—Insurance of title II of the Merchant Marine Act, 1936, as amended by this Act, the Administrator may declare that such death, injury, detention, or other casualty, shall be deemed and considered to be covered by such insurance at the time of the disaster or accident, if the Administrator finds that such action is required to make equitable provision for loss or injury related to the war effort and not otherwise adequately provided for: *Provided*, That in making provision for insurance under this subsection the Administrator shall not provide for payments in excess of those generally provided for in comparable cases under insurance hereafter furnished under the said Subtitle—Insurance of title II, as amended: *Provided further*, That any money paid to any person by reason of insurance provided for under this subsection shall apply in pro tanto satisfaction of the claim of such person against the United States arising from the same loss or injury. There shall be no recovery of any money paid on account of insurance provided for the master, officers, or members of the crew of, or individuals transported on, any vessel under this subsection or under Subtitle—Insurance of title II of the Merchant Marine Act, 1936, as amended, from any person who in the judgment of the Administrator, War Shipping Administration, is without fault, and when in the judgment of the Administrator such recovery would defeat the purposes of benefits otherwise authorized or would be against equity and good conscience. The declarations, findings, and actions of or by the Administrator under this subsection shall be final and conclusive.

(c) The Administrator, War Shipping Administration, is also authorized to make payments, in accordance with rate schedules provided by the United States Employees' Compensation Act [5 U.S.C. 8101 et seq.], to a master, officer, or member of the crew of, or any persons transported on, a vessel owned by or chartered to the Maritime Commission or the War Shipping Administration or operated by, or for the account of, or

[1] See Transfer of Functions note below.

[2] See Change of Name note below.

at the direction or under the control of the Commission or the Administration, for permanent total or partial disability as long as such disability resulting from causes related to the war effort whether heretofore or hereafter arising exists; such payments to commence if and when insurance benefits provided by the War Shipping Administration for such person shall have been exhausted.

(d) The War Shipping Administration shall have the right of intervention and a lien and right of recovery in the cases and to the extent of any payments paid and payable under this section or under Subtitle—Insurance of Title II of the Merchant Marine Act, 1936, as amended, in the manner provided in the last paragraph of subsection (c) of section 105 of the Act approved December 2, 1942 (Public Law 784, 77th Congress; 42 U.S.C., sec. 1701), as amended by Public Law 216, 78th Congress, approved December 23, 1943. Any amounts recovered under this provision shall be covered into the Marine and War-risk insurance fund, War Shipping Administration.

(Mar. 24, 1943, ch. 26, § 2, 57 Stat. 47; Sept. 30, 1944, ch. 451, 58 Stat. 758; Aug. 8, 1946, ch. 905, 60 Stat. 937; July 25, 1947, ch. 327, § 1, 61 Stat. 449.)

REFERENCES IN TEXT

Title II of the Merchant Marine Act, 1936, as amended, referred to in subsecs. (b) and (d), is title II of act June 29, 1936, ch. 858, 49 Stat. 1985, as amended, which was classified to sections 1128 to 1128h of former Title 46, Shipping, and which was repealed by act July 25, 1947, ch. 327, § 1, 61 Stat. 449.

The United States Employees' Compensation Act, as amended, referred to in subsec. (c), is act Sept. 7, 1916, ch. 458, 39 Stat. 742, as amended, which was repealed by Pub. L. 89–554, § 8(a), Sept. 6, 1966, 80 Stat. 632, and the provisions thereof were reenacted by the first section thereof as subchapter I (§ 8101 et seq.) of chapter 81 of Title 5, Government Organization and Employees.

AMENDMENTS

1947—Subsec. (a). Act July 25, 1947, repealed subsec. (a) which amended section 1128a of former Title 46, Shipping.

1946—Subsec. (b). Act Aug. 8, 1946, amended subsec. (b) generally, making section applicable to employees of the War Department.

1944—Subsec. (b). Act Sept. 30, 1944, inserted sentence beginning "There shall be no".

Subsecs. (c), (d). Act Sept. 30, 1944, added subsecs. (c) and (d).

CHANGE OF NAME

Department of War designated Department of the Army and title of Secretary of War changed to Secretary of the Army by section 205(a) of act July 26, 1947, ch. 343, title II, 61 Stat. 501. Section 207(a), (f) of act July 26, 1947, established Department of the Air Force, headed by a Secretary, and transferred functions (relating to Army Air Forces) of Secretary of the Army and Department of the Army to Secretary of the Air Force and Department of the Air Force. Sections 205(a) and 207(a), (f) of act July 26, 1947, were repealed by section 53 of act Aug. 10, 1956, ch. 1041, 70A Stat. 641. Section 1 of act Aug. 10, 1956, enacted "Title 10, Armed Forces", which in sections 3010 to 3013 and 8010 to 8013 continued Departments of the Army and Air Force under administrative supervision of Secretary of the Army and Secretary of the Air Force, respectively.

EFFECTIVE DATE OF 1946 AMENDMENT

Act Aug. 8, 1946, provided that the amendment made by that Act is effective as of Mar. 24, 1943.

TRANSFER OF FUNCTIONS

War Shipping Administration terminated as of Sept. 1, 1946, and functions, powers, duties, etc., transferred to United States Maritime Commission for period Sept. 1, 1946, to Dec. 31, 1946, for purpose of liquidating Administration, by act July 8, 1946, ch. 543, title II, § 202, 60 Stat. 501.

Maritime Commission, meaning United States Maritime Commission, abolished by Reorg. Plan No. 21 of 1950, eff. May 24, 1950, 15 F.R. 3178, 64 Stat. 1273, set out in the Appendix to Title 5, Government Organization and Employees, which transferred part of its functions and part of functions of its Chairman to Federal Maritime Board and Chairman thereof, that Board having been created by that Plan as an agency within Department of Commerce with an independent status in some respects, and transferred remainder of that Commission's functions and functions of its Chairman to Secretary of Commerce, with power vested in Secretary to authorize their performance by Maritime Administrator, the head of Maritime Administration, which likewise was established by the Plan in Department of Commerce with provision that Chairman of Federal Maritime Board should, ex officio, be that Administrator.

Federal Maritime Board, including offices of members of Board, abolished by section 304 of Reorg. Plan No. 7 of 1961, eff. Aug. 12, 1961, 26 F.R. 7315, 75 Stat. 843, set out in the Appendix to Title 5, Government Organization and Employees. Functions of Board transferred either to Federal Maritime Commission or to Secretary of Commerce by sections 103 and 202 of Reorg. Plan No. 7 of 1961.

Maritime Administration transferred from Department of Commerce to Department of Transportation by Pub. L. 97–31, Aug. 6, 1981, 95 Stat. 151 (46 App. U.S.C. 1601 et seq.).

§ 1293. Payment of compensation; insurance

(a) Omitted [Amendment of section 1271 of this Appendix].

(b) Omitted.

(c) In the event that a vessel the title or use and possession of which is requisitioned or taken pursuant to section 902 of the Merchant Marine Act, 1936, as amended [46 App. U.S.C. 1242], or the Act of June 6, 1941 (Public Law 101, Seventy-seventh Congress) [sections 1271 to 1275 of this Appendix], is in the custody of any court, State or Federal, it shall be the duty of all agents and officers of the court having possession, custody, or control of said vessel, forthwith upon the filing with the clerk of said court of a certified copy of the order of requisitioning or taking, and without further order of the court, to comply with said requisitioning or taking and to permit the representatives of the United States Maritime Commission or the War Shipping Administration,[1] as the case may be, to take possession, custody, and control of said vessel.

(d) Omitted [Amendment of section 902 of the Merchant Marine Act, 1936 (46 App. U.S.C. 1242)].

(e) to (i) Repealed. July 25, 1947, ch. 327, § 1, 61 Stat. 449.

(j) Omitted [Amendment of section 1273 of this Appendix].

(k) Omitted [Amendment of section 1274 of this Appendix].

(Mar. 24, 1943, ch. 26, § 3, 57 Stat. 48; July 25, 1947, ch. 327, § 1, 61 Stat. 449.)

[1] See Transfer of Functions note below.

CODIFICATION

Subsec. (b). Act Mar. 24, 1943, dealing with power of War Shipping Administrator to determine whether a vessel was required by United States, expired with the termination on Sept. 1, 1946, of War Shipping Administration, as set forth in note below.

Subsecs. (e) to (i). Act Mar. 24, 1943, amended sections 1128b to 1128e and 1128h of former Title 46, Shipping, by providing compensation for servicing insurance, placing 5 percent limitation on commissions, for action in nature of bill of interpleader against interested persons, defining risks of war, and reinsurance of insurance companies.

TRANSFER OF FUNCTIONS

War Shipping Administration terminated as of Sept. 1, 1946, and functions, powers, duties, etc., transferred to United States Maritime Commission for period Sept. 1, 1946, to Dec. 31, 1946, for purpose of liquidating Administration, by act July 8, 1946, ch. 543, title II, § 202, 60 Stat. 501.

United States Maritime Commission abolished by Reorg. Plan No. 21, 1950, eff. May 24, 1950, 15 F.R. 3178, 64 Stat. 1273, set out in the Appendix to Title 5, Government Organization and Employees, which transferred part of its functions and part of functions of its Chairman to Federal Maritime Board and Chairman thereof, that Board having been created by that Plan as an agency within Department of Commerce with an independent status in some respects, and transferred remainder of Commission's functions and functions of its Chairman to Secretary of Commerce, with power vested in Secretary to authorize their performance by Maritime Administrator, the head of Maritime Administration, which likewise was established by the Plan in Department of Commerce with provision that Chairman of Federal Maritime Board should, ex officio, be that Administrator.

Federal Maritime Board, including offices of members of Board, abolished by section 304 of Reorg. Plan No. 7 of 1961, eff. Aug. 12, 1961, 26 F.R. 7315, 75 Stat. 843, set out in the Appendix to Title 5, Government Organization and Employees. Functions of Board transferred either to Federal Maritime Commission or to Secretary of Commerce by sections 103 and 202 of Reorg. Plan No. 7 of 1961.

Maritime Administration transferred from Department of Commerce to Department of Transportation by Pub. L. 97–31, Aug. 6, 1981, 95 Stat. 151 (46 App. U.S.C. 1601 et seq.).

VESSEL OPERATIONS UNDER REVOLVING FUND

Vessel operations conducted under Vessel Operations Revolving Fund, applicability of subsec. (c) of this section to, see section 1241a of Title 46, Appendix, Shipping.

SECTION REFERRED TO IN OTHER SECTIONS

This section is referred to in title 46 App. section 1241a.

§ 1294. United States as entitled to all benefits of exemption and limitation of liability accorded to owners of vessels

The United States shall, with respect to vessels owned by or chartered to the War Shipping Administrator[1] under bareboat charter or time charter or operated directly by such Administrator or for his account, be entitled to the benefits of all exemptions and of all limitations of liability accorded by law to the owners of vessels. With respect to any such vessel, the term "the United States" shall include agents or other persons acting for or on behalf of the Administrator in connection with the operation thereof.

(Mar. 24, 1943, ch. 26, § 4, 57 Stat. 51.)

[1] See Transfer of Functions note below.

TRANSFER OF FUNCTIONS

War Shipping Administration terminated as of Sept. 1, 1946, and functions, powers, duties, etc., transferred to United States Maritime Commission for period Sept. 1, 1946, to Dec. 31, 1946, for purpose of liquidating Administration, by act July 8, 1946, ch. 543, title II, § 202, 60 Stat. 501.

VESSEL OPERATIONS UNDER REVOLVING FUND

Vessel operations conducted under Vessel Operations Revolving Fund, applicability of this section to, see section 1241a of Title 46, Appendix, Shipping.

SECTION REFERRED TO IN OTHER SECTIONS

This section is referred to in title 46 App. section 1241a.

§ 1295. Omitted

CODIFICATION

Section, act Mar. 24, 1943, ch. 26, § 5, 57 Stat. 51, which provided that section 1291(a) of this Appendix should remain in force until termination of sections 601 to 605 of this Appendix by section 621 of this Appendix, was omitted in view of termination on Sept. 1, 1946, of War Shipping Administration.

ACT APR. 29, 1943, CH. 81, 57 STAT. 69

§§ 1301 to 1305. Repealed. Aug. 13, 1954, ch. 725, § 1(a), 68 Stat. 701

Section 1301, acts Apr. 29, 1943, ch. 81, § 1, 57 Stat. 69; May 18, 1944, ch. 199, § 1, 58 Stat. 223, related to return of fishing vessels, vessels of 100 tons or less and Great Lakes vessels to private owners.

Section 1302, acts Apr. 29, 1943, ch. 81, § 2, 57 Stat. 69; May 18, 1944, ch. 199, § 2, 58 Stat. 223, related to determination of availability of vessels mentioned in section 1301 of this Appendix, repayment of compensation to United States.

Section 1303, acts Apr. 29, 1943, ch. 81, § 3, 57 Stat. 69; May 18, 1944, ch. 199, § 3, 58 Stat. 244; Aug. 10, 1946, ch. 948, 60 Stat. 976, related to failure or waiver of return rights, sale of vessels.

Section 1304, acts Apr. 29, 1943, ch. 81, § 4, 57 Stat. 70; May 18, 1944, ch. 199, § 4, 58 Stat. 224, related to payment of expenses incurred by War Shipping Administration in return or sale of vessels.

Section 1305, act Apr. 29, 1943, ch. 81, § 5, as added Aug. 10, 1946, ch. 948, 60 Stat. 976, related to vessels for exclusive disposal to veterans.

SAVINGS PROVISION

See section 1(b) of act Aug. 13, 1954, set out as a note under sections 1306 to 1308 of this Appendix.

ACT AUG. 10, 1946, CH. 949, 60 STAT. 977

§§ 1306 to 1308. Repealed. Aug. 13, 1954, ch. 725, § 1(b), 68 Stat. 701

Section 1306, act Aug. 10, 1946, ch. 949, § 1, 60 Stat. 977, related to sale of surplus vessels for fishing.

Section 1307, act Aug. 10, 1946, ch. 949, § 2, 60 Stat. 977, related to definitions of terms used in sections 1306 to 1308 of this Appendix and rights of former owners.

Section 1308, act Aug. 10, 1946, ch. 949, § 3, 60 Stat. 977, related to terms of sale of vessels and other methods of disposal.

SAVINGS PROVISION

Section 1(b) of act Aug. 13, 1954, provided in part that: "Notwithstanding the enactment of this joint resolution, the aforesaid statutory provisions shall apply to any vessels which prior to such enactment [Aug. 13, 1954] have been declared available for return to former owners by notice to the Department of Commerce under the Act of April 29, 1943, as amended [sections 1301 to 1305 of this Appendix], or determined to be surplus for sale to former owners of fishing vessels in accordance with the Act of August 10, 1946 (Public Law 717, Seventy-ninth Congress) [sections 1306 to 1308 of this Appendix]. Any other vessels which, but for the enactment of this joint resolution, would be disposed of in accordance with any of the aforesaid statutory provisions, shall be disposed of in accordance with the provisions of other existing laws.''

ACT JULY 9, 1943, CH. 212, 57 STAT. 391

§§1311, 1312. Omitted

CODIFICATION

Section 1311, act July 9, 1943, ch. 212, §1, 57 Stat. 391, which created penalty for violation of regulations or orders relating to protection of vessels, harbors, ports, or waterways, terminated pursuant to section 1312 of this Appendix.

Section 1312, act July 9, 1943, ch. 212, §2, 57 Stat. 391, provided for the termination of sections 1311 and 1312 of this Appendix six months after the cessation of hostilities, which was proclaimed by Proc. No. 2714, eff. Dec. 31, 1946, 12 F.R. 1.

FARM LABOR SUPPLY APPROPRIATION ACT, 1944

ACT FEB. 14, 1944, CH. 16, 58 STAT. 11

§§1351 to 1355. Omitted

CODIFICATION

Sections 1351 to 1355 were omitted as terminating Jan. 30, 1948, pursuant to act May 26, 1947, ch. 82, title I, §101, 61 Stat. 109, set out as an Extension and Liquidation of Program note below.

Section 1351, act Feb. 14, 1944, ch. 16, title I, §1, 58 Stat. 11, appropriated money to provide adequate supply of agricultural workers during World War II.

Section 1352, act Feb. 14, 1944, ch. 16, title I, §2, 58 Stat. 12, related to payments to the various States to assist in supplying an adequate number of agricultural workers during World War II.

Section 1353, act Feb. 14, 1944, ch. 16, title I, §3, 58 Stat. 12, related to expenditures by the Administrator of Food Production and Distribution.

Section 1354, act Feb. 14, 1944, ch. 16, title I, §4, 58 Stat. 14, related to limitations on use of funds.

Section 1355, acts Feb. 14, 1944, ch. 16, title I, §5, 58 Stat. 14; Apr. 1, 1944, ch. 152, title I, 58 Stat. 157; Apr. 25, 1945, ch. 95, title I, 59 Stat. 80; June 30, 1947, ch. 165, 61 Stat. 202, related to miscellaneous provisions for implementing sections 1351 to 1355 of this Appendix.

PRIOR PROVISIONS

Sections 1351 to 1355 are from act Feb. 14, 1944, ch. 16, title I, §§1–5, 58 Stat. 11–14, known as the Farm Labor Supply Appropriation Act, 1944. Similar provisions were contained in act Apr. 29, 1943, ch. 82, §§1–5, 57 Stat. 70, as amended June 9, 1943, ch. 119, 57 Stat. 125; Dec. 23, 1943, ch. 381, §1, 57 Stat. 643. Section 3 of act Apr. 29, 1943, was repealed by Pub. L. 89–554, §8(a), Sept. 6, 1966, 80 Stat. 651.

ANNUAL APPROPRIATIONS

Additional funds were authorized to be merged with available funds as follows:

$3,000,000—Act May 26, 1947, ch. 82, title I, 61 Stat. 109.

$12,000,000—Act July 23, 1946, ch. 591, title I, 60 Stat. 617.

$25,000,000—Act Dec. 28, 1945, ch. 589, title I, 59 Stat. 645.

$20,000,000—Act Dec. 22, 1944, ch. 660, title I, 58 Stat. 862.

EXTENSION AND LIQUIDATION OF PROGRAM

Acts May 26, 1947, ch. 82, title I, 61 Stat. 109; Apr. 28, 1947, ch. 43, 61 Stat. 55; Aug. 9, 1946, ch. 934, 60 Stat. 617, provided in part that the funds as provided and supplemented for carrying out the purposes of sections 1351 to 1355 of this Appendix were continued available until Jan. 30, 1948, which allowed for a six months extension and final liquidation of the program.

WAR OVERTIME PAY ACT OF 1943

ACT MAY 7, 1943, CH. 93, 57 STAT. 75

§§1401 to 1415. Repealed. Pub. L. 89–554, §8(a), Sept. 6, 1966, 80 Stat. 651, 652

Section 1401, act May 7, 1943, ch. 93, §1, 57 Stat. 75, related to officers and employees subject to sections 1401 to 1415 of this Appendix.

Section 1402, act May 7, 1943, ch. 93, §2, 57 Stat. 76, related to computation of overtime compensation.

Section 1403, acts May 7, 1943, ch. 93, §3, 57 Stat. 76; Sept. 30, 1944, ch. 450, 58 Stat. 758, related to additional officers and employees subject to sections 1401 to 1415 of this Appendix.

Section 1404, act May 7, 1943, ch. 93, §4, 57 Stat. 77, related to Senate official reporters and employees subject to sections 1401 to 1415 of this Appendix.

Section 1405, act May 7, 1943, ch. 93, §5, 57 Stat. 77, related to repeal of certain wage overtime provisions.

Section 1406, act May 7, 1943, ch. 93, §6, 57 Stat. 77, related to suspension of the Saturday half-holiday rule.

Section 1407, act May 7, 1943, ch. 93, §7, 57 Stat. 77, related to construction of other laws with sections 1401 to 1415 of this Appendix.

Section 1408, act May 7, 1943, ch. 93, §8, 57 Stat. 77, related to adjustment of gross inequities in pay differentials.

Section 1409, act May 7, 1943, ch. 93, §9, 57 Stat. 77, related to administrative rules and regulations.

Section 1410, act May 7, 1943, ch. 93, §10, 57 Stat. 77, related to change of salaries and number of legislative employees.

Section 1411, act May 7, 1943, ch. 93, §11, 57 Stat. 78, related to report on the number of employees required in executive branch departments.

Section 1412, act May 7, 1943, ch. 93, §12, 57 Stat. 78, related to overtime or additional compensation as part of annual income.

Section 1413, act May 7, 1943, ch. 93, §13, 57 Stat. 78, related to certain employees of the Army Engineering Corps and the Coast and Geodetic Survey as subject to sections 1401 to 1415 of this Appendix.

Section 1414, act May 7, 1943, ch. 93, §14, 57 Stat. 78, related to effective and termination dates of sections 1401 to 1415 of this Appendix.

Section 1415, act May 7, 1943, ch. 93, §15, 57 Stat. 78, provided that sections 1401 to 1415 of this Appendix were to be cited as the War Overtime Pay Act of 1943.

WAIVER OF RESTRICTIONS

Act Apr. 1, 1944, ch. 152, title II, §202, 58 Stat. 176, related to waiver of restrictions in appropriations limiting amounts payable for personal services to meet cost of overtime and additional compensation authorized by sections 1401 to 1415 of this Appendix.

BASIC RATE FOR OVERTIME COMPENSATION

Act Apr. 1, 1944, ch. 152, title II, §203, 58 Stat. 176, provided that the basic rate for overtime compensation should be one and one-half times basic rate for work performed in excess of forty hours per week.

TRAINING OF NURSES THROUGH GRANTS TO INSTITUTIONS

ACT JUNE 15, 1943, CH. 126, 57 STAT. 153

§§1451 to 1462. Omitted

CODIFICATION

Sections 1451 to 1462 were omitted as terminating Dec. 31, 1946, pursuant to section 1460 of this Appendix.

Section 1451, act June 15, 1943, ch. 126, §1, 57 Stat. 153, authorized appropriations to assure supply of nurses for armed forces and other needs during World War II.

Section 1452, act June 15, 1943, ch. 126, §2, 57 Stat. 153, related to approval of submitted plans for training nurses.

Section 1453, act June 15, 1943, ch. 126, §3, 57 Stat. 154, related to payments to institutions with approved training plans.

Section 1454, act June 15, 1943, ch. 126, §4, 57 Stat. 154, related to recruitment of nurses.

Section 1455, act June 15, 1943, ch. 126, §5, 57 Stat. 155, related to conclusiveness of determinations under sections 1453 and 1454 of this Appendix.

Section 1456, act June 15, 1943, ch. 126, §6, 57 Stat. 155, related to computation of payments under sections 1453 and 1454 of this Appendix.

Section 1457, acts June 15, 1943, ch. 126, §7, 57 Stat. 155; Mar. 4, 1944, ch. 83, 58 Stat. 112, related to insignia for student nurses.

Section 1458, act June 15, 1943, ch. 126, §8, 57 Stat. 155, related to prohibitions of discrimination against particular institutions.

Section 1459, act June 15, 1943, ch. 126, §9, 57 Stat. 155, authorized issuance of rules and regulations and established an advisory committee to aid in such issuance. Section was repealed by Pub. L. 89–554, §8(a), Sept. 6, 1966, 80 Stat. 651.

Section 1460, act June 15, 1943, ch. 126, §10, 57 Stat. 155, related to effective and termination dates of sections 1451 to 1462 of this Appendix and provided that said sections were to terminate upon the proclamation of the cessation of hostilities of World War II, which was proclaimed Dec. 31, 1946, by Proc. No. 2714, eff. Dec. 31, 1946, 12 F.R. 1, set out preceding section 1 of this Appendix.

Section 1461, act June 15, 1943, ch. 126, §11, as added Mar. 4, 1944, ch. 83, 58 Stat. 112, related to transfer of student nurses.

Section 1462, act June 15, 1943, ch. 126, §12, as added Mar. 4, 1944, ch. 83, 58 Stat. 112, related to the designation of nurse insignia and uniforms.

TERMINATION OF APPROPRIATIONS

Section 803 of the Labor-Federal Security Appropriation Act of 1946, act July 3, 1945, ch. 263, 59 Stat. 383, provided that no part of any appropriation for training of defense workers contained in said act should be available for obligation longer than 60 days after cessation of hostilities of World War II, which was proclaimed at 12 o'clock noon of December 31, 1946, by Proc. No. 2714, eff. Dec. 31, 1946, 12 F.R. 1, set out preceding section 1 of this Appendix.

MERGER OF APPROPRIATIONS

The Federal Security Agency Appropriation Act, 1948, act July 8, 1947, ch. 210, title II, 61 Stat. 270, provided in part that the appropriation contained therein for the training of nurses under sections 1451 to 1462 of this Appendix was available for transfer and consolidation with the appropriations of St. Elizabeths and Freedmen's Hospitals to cover cost of items furnished to student nurses in training.

Similar provisions were contained in the following acts:

July 26, 1946, ch. 672, title II, 60 Stat. 692.
July 3, 1945, ch. 263, title II, 59 Stat. 370.
June 28, 1944, ch. 302, title II, 58 Stat. 557.
Apr. 1, 1944, ch. 152, title I, 58 Stat. 152.

CIVILIAN REEMPLOYMENT OF MEMBERS OF MERCHANT MARINE

ACT JUNE 23, 1943, CH. 142, 57 STAT. 162

§§1471 to 1475. Repealed. July 24, 1956, ch. 671, §5(a)(3), 70 Stat. 606

Section 1471, acts June 23, 1943, ch. 142, §1, 57 Stat. 162; Aug. 8, 1946, ch. 867, 60 Stat. 905; Aug. 8, 1946, ch. 912, 60 Stat. 945, authorized a certificate of service for service in merchant marine after May 1, 1940, and before the termination of the national emergency (July 25, 1947).

Section 1472, acts June 23, 1943, ch. 142, §2, 57 Stat. 162; Aug. 8, 1946, ch. 867, 60 Stat. 906, related to restoration of members of merchant marine to civilian employment.

Section 1473, acts June 23, 1943, ch. 142, §3, 57 Stat. 162; Aug. 8, 1946, ch. 867, 60 Stat. 907, related to proceedings to compel employer compliance with section 1472 of this Appendix.

Section 1474, acts June 23, 1943, ch. 142, §4, 57 Stat. 163; Aug. 8, 1946, ch. 867, 60 Stat. 907, related to additional compensation to certain members of merchant marine.

Section 1475, acts June 23, 1943, ch. 142, §5, 57 Stat. 163; Aug. 8, 1946, ch. 867, 60 Stat. 907, related to issuance of rules and regulations.

EFFECTIVE DATE OF REPEAL

Repeal effective July 1, 1954, see section 5(a) of act July 24, 1956.

REPLACEMENT OF AWARDS, MEDALS, AND DECORATIONS

For replacement of awards, medals, and decorations, see section 2004(c) of Title 46, Appendix, Shipping.

WAR LABOR DISPUTES ACT

ACT JUNE 25, 1943, CH. 144, 57 STAT. 163

§§1501 to 1511. Omitted

CODIFICATION

Sections 1501 to 1511 were omitted as terminating six months after Dec. 31, 1946, under the terms of section 510 of this Appendix, pursuant to the proclamation of the cessation of hostilities of World War II by Proc. No. 2714, eff. Dec. 31, 1946, 12. F.R. 1, set out preceding section 1 of this Appendix.

Section 1501, act June 25, 1943, ch. 144, §1, 57 Stat. 163, provided that sections 1501 to 1511 of this Appendix were to be known as the War Labor Disputes Act.

Section 1502, act June 25, 1943, ch. 144, §2, 57 Stat. 164, defined terms for purposes of sections 1501 to 1511 of this Appendix.

Section 1503, act June 25, 1943, ch. 144, §3, 57 Stat. 164, amended section 309 of this Appendix and related to power of President to take possession of certain manufacturing facilities.

Section 1504, act June 25, 1943, ch. 144, §4, 57 Stat. 165, related to terms of employment at government operated plants.

Section 1505, act June 25, 1943, ch. 144, §5, 57 Stat. 165, related to applications to War Labor Board for changes in terms of employment at government operated plants.

Section 1506, act June 25, 1943, ch. 144, §6, 57 Stat. 165, related to interference with government operation of plants.

Section 1507, act June 25, 1943, ch. 144, §7, 57 Stat. 166, related to functions and duties of National War Labor Board.

Section 1508, act June 25, 1943, ch. 144, §8, 57 Stat. 167, related to notice of threatened interruptions in war production.

Section 1509, act June 25, 1943, ch. 144, §9, 57 Stat. 167, related to political contributions by labor organizations. Section 1509 was also repealed by act June 25, 1948, ch. 645, §21, 62 Stat. 862.

Section 1510, act June 25, 1943, ch. 144, §10, 57 Stat. 168, provided that sections 1501 to 1511 of this Appendix were to cease to be effective, six months after Dec. 31, 1946, the date on which the cessation of hostilities of World War II was proclaimed by Proc. No. 2714, eff. Dec. 31, 1946, 12 F.R. 1, set out preceding section 1 of this Appendix.

Section 1511, act June 25, 1943, ch. 144, §11, 57 Stat. 168, contained separability provisions.

EFFECTIVE DATE OF REPEAL

Repeal of section 1509 effective Sept. 1, 1948, see section 38 of act June 25, 1948, set out as an Effective Date note preceding section 1 of Title 28, Judiciary and Judicial Procedure.

VOLUNTARY ENLISTMENTS IN REGULAR MILITARY ESTABLISHMENT

ACT JUNE 1, 1945, CH. 168, 59 STAT. 230

§§1531 to 1534. Repealed. Aug. 10, 1956, ch. 1041, §53, 70A Stat. 641

Section 1531, acts June 1, 1945, ch. 168, §1, 59 Stat. 230; Oct. 6, 1945, ch. 393, §3(a), 59 Stat. 538, related to enlistments and reenlistments in the Regular Army.

Section 1532, act June 1, 1945, ch. 168, §2, as added Oct. 6, 1945, ch. 393, §3(a), 59 Stat. 539, related to regulations.

Section 1533, act June 1, 1945, ch. 168, §3, as added Oct. 6, 1945, ch. 393, §3(a), 59 Stat. 539, relating to termination of authority to accept enlistments, terminated on June 30, 1947, by its own terms.

Section 1534, act June 1, 1945, ch. 168, §4, as added Oct. 6, 1945, ch. 393, §3(a), 59 Stat. 539, related to promotion after six months service in seventh grade.

WOMEN'S ARMY CORPS

ACT JULY 1, 1943, CH. 187, 57 STAT. 371

§§1551 to 1555. Repealed. July 25, 1947, ch. 327, §2a, 61 Stat. 451

Section 1551, act July 1, 1943, ch. 187, §1, 57 Stat. 371, related to establishment and duration of Women's Army Corps.

Section 1552, act July 1, 1943, ch. 187, §2, 57 Stat. 371, related to qualifications for membership.

Section 1553, act July 1, 1943, ch. 187, §3, 57 Stat. 371, related to officers in the Corps.

Section 1554, act July 1, 1943, ch. 187, §4, 57 Stat. 371, related to Corps' uniforms, insignia, accessories and equipment.

Section 1555, act July 1, 1943, ch. 187, §5, 57 Stat. 371, repealed certain prior provisions.

EFFECTIVE DATE OF REPEAL

Repeal was to be effective July 1, 1948, but section 110 of act June 12, 1948, ch. 449, title I, 62 Stat. 363, provided in part that the effective date of repeal be postponed until June 12, 1949.

UNITED NATIONS RELIEF AND REHABILITATION ADMINISTRATION

ACT MAR. 28, 1944, CH. 135, 58 STAT. 122

§§1571 to 1578. Omitted

CODIFICATION

Sections 1571 to 1578 were omitted as terminating on June 30, 1947, pursuant to section 9 of Act Mar. 28, 1944, set out as a Termination Date note below.

Section 1571, acts Mar. 28, 1944, ch. 135, §1, 58 Stat. 122; Dec. 18, 1945, ch. 580, 59 Stat. 612, authorized appropriations for purposes of sections 1571 to 1578 of this Appendix.

Section 1572, act Mar. 28, 1944, ch. 135, §2, 58 Stat. 127, related to disbursements under Presidential direction.

Section 1573, act Mar. 28, 1944, ch. 135, §3, 58 Stat. 127, related to extent of rehabilitation.

Section 1574, act Mar. 28, 1944, ch. 135, §4, 58 Stat. 127, related to area included for relief.

Section 1575, act Mar. 28, 1944, ch. 135, §5, 58 Stat. 128, related to need for Congressional approval for new applications.

Section 1576, act Mar. 28, 1944, ch. 135, §6, 58 Stat. 128, related to approval of contributions by Congress.

Section 1577, act Mar. 28, 1944, ch. 135, §7, 58 Stat. 128, related to extent of rehabilitation.

Section 1578, acts Mar. 28, 1944, ch. 135, §8, 58 Stat. 128; Dec. 18, 1945, ch. 580, 59 Stat. 612, related to limitation on contracts and obligations.

TERMINATION DATE

Section 9 of act Mar. 28, 1944, as amended by act Dec. 18, 1945, provided that the authorizations contained in sections 1571 to 1578 were to expire on June 30, 1947.

OFFICERS AND EMPLOYEES

Act June 30, 1944, ch. 324, title II, §201, 58 Stat. 629, provided in part for retention of all rights and privileges by officers and employees detailed to the Administration.

ADDITIONAL APPROPRIATIONS

Act Dec. 14, 1945, ch. 577, 59 Stat. 609, appropriated $550,000,000 to the Administration to be available during fiscal year 1946.

LIQUIDATION EXPENDITURES

Act July 8, 1947, ch. 209, 61 Stat. 260, appropriated not to exceed $2,370,000 for the liquidation expenses of the Administration.

TEMPORARY APPOINTMENTS OF ARMY NURSE CORPS MEMBERS, ETC., AS OFFICERS OF ARMY OF UNITED STATES

ACT JUNE 22, 1944, CH. 272, 58 STAT. 324

§§1591 to 1598. Repealed. Pub. L. 99–145, title XIII, §1301(e)(1), Nov. 8, 1985, 99 Stat. 737

Section 1591, act June 22, 1944, ch. 272, §1, 58 Stat. 324, related to temporary appointments as officers in the Army of the United States under the provisions of act Sept. 22, 1941, ch. 414, 55 Stat. 728, of members of the Army Nurse Corps, females qualified for appointment in such Corps, female dietetic and physical-therapy personnel of the Army Medical Department, and females qualified for appointment in such Department as female dietetic or physical-therapy personnel.

Section 1592, act June 22, 1944, ch. 272, §2, 58 Stat. 325, provided that persons appointed as officers in the United States Army under section 1591 of this Appendix, and their dependents and beneficiaries, have all rights, privileges, and benefits accorded in like cases to persons appointed under act Sept. 22, 1941.

Section 1593, act June 22, 1944, ch. 272, §3, 58 Stat. 325, related to retirement of persons appointed under section 1591 of this Appendix, and retirement for disability of Army Nurse Corps members between Dec. 7, 1941, and June 22, 1944, or of any female dietitian or physical-therapy aide between Jan. 12, 1943, and June 22, 1944.

Section 1594, act June 22, 1944, ch. 272, §4, 58 Stat. 325, related to computation of years of service of Army Nurse Corps members appointed under section 1591 of this Appendix.

Section 1595, act June 22, 1944, ch. 272, §5, 58 Stat. 325, related to computation of years of service of female dietetic and physical-therapy personnel appointed under section 1591 of this Appendix, and included service rendered under Act December 22, 1942, ch. 805, 56 Stat. 1072.

Section 1596, act June 22, 1944, ch. 272, §6, 58 Stat. 325, related to uniform allowances and issues for women appointed as officers in the Army of the United States under section 1591 of this Appendix.

Section 1597, act June 22, 1944, ch. 272, §7, 58 Stat. 326, related to blanket order appointments by the President of persons described in section 1591 of this Appendix, acceptance or declination of such appointments, and oaths of office.

Section 1598, act June 22, 1944, ch. 272, §8, 58 Stat. 326, related to award of mileage allowances to women appointed in the Army Nurse Corps, female dietitians and physical-therapy aides appointed in the Army Medical Department, and women appointed from civilian life under section 1591 of this Appendix in the same amount as for persons appointed under act Sept. 22, 1941, ch. 414, 55 Stat. 728.

PERSON APPOINTED AND ASSIGNED UNDER FORMER SECTION 1591

Section 1301(e)(2) of Pub. L. 99–145 provided that: "The repeal made by paragraph (1) [repealing sections 1591 to 1598 of this Appendix] shall not apply in the case of any person appointed and assigned under the first section of the Act [section 1591 of this Appendix] repealed by such paragraph, as such Act was in effect on the day before the date of the enactment of this Act [Nov. 8, 1985]."

DISPOSAL OF MATERIALS ON PUBLIC LANDS

ACT SEPT. 27, 1944, CH. 416, 58 STAT. 745

§§1601 to 1603. Omitted

CODIFICATION

Sections 1601 to 1603 were omitted as terminated pursuant to section 1603 of this Appendix.

Section 1601, act Sept. 27, 1944, ch. 416, §1, 58 Stat. 745, related to rules and regulations governing disposal of materials on public lands.

Section 1602, act Sept. 27, 1944, ch. 416, §2, 58 Stat. 745, related to disposition of moneys received from sale of materials.

Section 1603, act Sept. 27, 1944, ch. 416, §3, 58 Stat. 745, provided for termination of sections 1601 to 1603 of this Appendix on the cessation of hostilities of World War II as determined by Presidential proclamation or congressional resolution. Proc. No. 2714, eff. Dec. 31, 1946, 12 F.R. 1, provided for the cessation of hostilities of World War II and is set out preceding section 1 of this Appendix.

For similar provisions, see sections 601 to 604 of Title 30, Mineral Lands and Mining.

SURPLUS PROPERTY ACT OF 1944

ACT OCT. 3, 1944, CH. 479, 58 STAT. 765

ACT REFERRED TO IN OTHER SECTIONS

The Surplus Property Act of 1944 is referred to in title 7 section 439; title 16 section 666g; title 22 section 2681; title 30 section 352; title 40 sections 166c, 473, 484, 485, 490, 511; title 45 section 1212.

§§1611 to 1614. Repealed. June 30, 1949, ch. 288, title VI, §602(a)(1), formerly title V, §502(a)(1), 63 Stat. 399; renumbered title VI, §602(a)(1), Sept. 5, 1950, ch. 849, §6(a), (b), 64 Stat. 583

Section 1611, act Oct. 3, 1944, ch. 479, §2, 58 Stat. 766, related to declaration of general objectives.

Section 1612, acts Oct. 3, 1944, ch. 479, §3, 58 Stat. 768; Sept. 18, 1945, ch. 368, §2, 59 Stat. 533, related to definitions.

Section 1613, act Oct. 3, 1944, ch. 479, §4, 58 Stat. 768, related to a general rule regarding disposition of surplus property.

Section 1614, act Oct. 3, 1944, ch. 479, §5, 58 Stat. 768, related to establishment of Surplus Property Board.

See section 471 et seq. of Title 40, Public Buildings, Property, and Works.

EFFECTIVE DATE OF REPEAL

Repeal effective July 1, 1949, with priorities and preferences for surplus real estate continued until Dec. 31, 1949, see sections 602(a)(1) and 605, formerly sections 502(a)(1) and 505, of act June 30, 1949.

§§1614a, 1614b. Repealed. Pub. L. 89–554, §8(a), Sept. 6, 1966, 80 Stat. 653

Section 1614a, act Sept. 18, 1945, ch. 368, §1, 59 Stat. 533, related to establishment of Surplus Property Administration.

Section 1614b, act Sept. 18, 1945, ch. 368, §2, 59 Stat. 533, related to abolishment of Surplus Property Board.

§§1615 to 1621. Repealed. June 30, 1949, ch. 288, title VI, §602(a)(1), formerly title V, §502(a)(1), 63 Stat. 399; renumbered title VI, §602(a)(1), Sept. 5, 1950, ch. 849, §6(a), (b), 64 Stat. 583

Section 1615, acts Oct. 3, 1944, ch. 479, §6, 58 Stat. 768; Sept. 18, 1945, ch. 368, §2, 59 Stat. 533, related to duties and authority of Surplus Property Administrator.

Section 1616, acts Oct. 3, 1944, ch. 479, §7, 58 Stat. 768; Sept. 18, 1945, ch. 368, §2, 59 Stat. 533, related to Surplus Property Administrator's cooperation with other government agencies.

Section 1617, acts Oct. 3, 1944, ch. 479, §8, 58 Stat. 768; Sept. 18, 1945, ch. 368, §2, 59 Stat. 533, related to delegation of authority by other government agencies.

Section 1618, acts Oct. 3, 1944, ch. 479, §9, 58 Stat. 769; Sept. 18, 1945, ch. 368, §2, 59 Stat. 533, related to issuance of regulations by Surplus Property Administrator.

Section 1619, acts Oct. 3, 1944, ch. 479, §10, 58 Stat. 769; Sept. 18, 1945, ch. 368, §2, 59 Stat. 533; Aug. 1, 1946, ch. 723, §1, 60 Stat. 754, related to designation of disposal agencies.

Section 1620, acts Oct. 3, 1944, ch. 479, §11, 58 Stat. 769; Sept. 18, 1945, ch. 368, §2, 59 Stat. 533, related to declaration and disposition of surplus property.

Section 1621, acts Oct. 3, 1944, ch. 479, §12, 58 Stat. 770; Sept. 18, 1945, ch. 368, §2, 59 Stat. 533; May 3, 1946, ch. 248, §§2–4, 60 Stat. 168, related to utilization of surplus property by Federal agencies.

See section 471 et seq. of Title 40, Public Buildings, Property, and Works.

EFFECTIVE DATE OF REPEAL

Repeal effective July 1, 1949, with priorities and preferences for surplus real estate continued until Dec. 31, 1949, see sections 602(a)(1) and 605, formerly sections 502(a)(1) and 505, of act June 30, 1949.

§1621a. Transferred

CODIFICATION

Section, act June 29, 1948, ch. 719, §4, 62 Stat. 1100, relating to the utilization of surplus property by Federal Prisons Industries, Incorporated, is set out as a note under section 4122 of Title 18, Crimes and Criminal Procedure.

§1622. Disposal to local governments and nonprofit institutions

(a) to (c) Repealed. June 30, 1949, ch. 288, title VI, §602(a)(1), formerly title V, §502(a)(1), 63 Stat. 399, renumbered Sept. 5, 1950, ch. 849, §6(a), (b), 64 Stat. 583

(d) Power transmission lines

Whenever any State or political subdivision thereof, or any State or Government agency or instrumentality certifies to the Administrator of General Services that any power transmission line determined to be surplus property under the provisions of this Act [sections 1611 to 1646 of this Appendix] is needful for or adaptable to the requirements of any public or cooperative power project, such line and the right-of-way acquired for its construction shall not be sold, leased for more than one year, or otherwise disposed of, except as provided in section 12[1] [section 1621 of this Appendix] or this section, unless specifically authorized by Act of Congress.

(e), (f) Repealed. June 30, 1949, ch. 288, title VI, §602(a)(1), formerly title V, §502(a)(1), 63 Stat. 399, renumbered Sept. 5, 1950, ch. 849, §6(a), (b), 64 Stat. 583

(g) Repealed. Pub. L. 103–272, §7(b), July 5, 1994, 108 Stat. 1379

(Oct. 3, 1944, ch. 479, §13, 58 Stat. 770; Sept. 18, 1945, ch. 368, §2, 59 Stat. 533; May 3, 1946, ch. 248, §5, 60 Stat. 169; 1947 Reorg. Plan No. 1, §501, eff. July 1, 1947, 12 F.R. 4535, 61 Stat. 952; July 30, 1947, ch. 404, 61 Stat. 678; June 10, 1948, ch. 433, §§1, 2, 62 Stat. 350; June 29, 1948, ch. 727, 62 Stat. 1103; June 30, 1949, ch. 288, title I, §105, title VI, §602(a)(1), formerly title V, §502(a)(1), 63 Stat. 381, 399, renumbered Sept. 5, 1950, ch. 849, §6(a), (b), 64 Stat. 583; amended Oct. 1, 1949, ch. 589, §§1, 5, 63 Stat. 701; Pub. L. 85–726, title XIV, §1402(c), Aug. 23, 1958, 72 Stat. 807; Pub. L. 87–90, July 20, 1961, 75 Stat. 211; Pub. L. 91–258, title I, §52(b)(6), May 21, 1970, 84 Stat. 235; Pub. L. 91–485, §5, Oct. 22, 1970, 84 Stat. 1085; Pub. L. 92–362, §2, Aug. 4, 1972, 86 Stat. 504; Pub. L. 97–248, title V, §524(c), Sept. 3, 1982, 96 Stat. 696; Pub. L. 103–272, §7(b), July 5, 1994, 108 Stat. 1379.)

References in Text

Section 12, referred to in subsec. (d), is section 12 of act Oct. 3, 1944, ch. 479, which was classified to section 1621 of this Appendix prior to repeal by act June 30, 1949, ch. 288, title VI, §602(a)(1), formerly title V, §502(a)(1), 63 Stat. 399, renumbered Sept. 5, 1950, ch. 849, §6(a), (b), 64 Stat. 583.

Amendments

1994—Subsec. (g). Pub. L. 103–272 struck out subsec. (g) which provided for conveyance or disposal of surplus real or personal property to States, political subdivisions, municipalities, or tax-supported institutions for development, improvement, operation, or maintenance of public airports. See sections 47151 to 47153 of Title 49, Transportation.

1982—Subsec. (g)(1). Pub. L. 97–248 substituted "Airport and Airway Improvement Act of 1982" for "Airport and Airway Development Act of 1970".

1972—Subsec. (h). Pub. L. 92–362 repealed subsec. (h) which related to conveyance of surplus lands to local government agencies, determined to be historic monuments, without monetary consideration and for reversion to United States when purposes of conveyance were unfulfilled.

1970—Subsec. (g)(1). Pub. L. 91–258 substituted "Airport and Airway Development Act of 1970" for "Federal Airport Act (60 Stat. 170)".

Subsec. (h)(1). Pub. L. 91–485, §5(1), limited the conveyance of surplus land for use as a historic monument by striking out public park and public recreational area.

Subsec. (h)(2). Pub. L. 91–485, §5(2), struck out provisions relating to the price adjustment of conveyances for park or recreational purposes.

1961—Subsec. (h)(2). Pub. L. 87–90 substituted "its historical significance relates to a period of time within the fifty years immediately preceding the determination of suitability and desirability for such use" for "it was acquired by the United States at any time subsequent to January 1, 1900".

1958—Subsec. (g). Pub. L. 85–726 substituted "Administrator of the Federal Aviation Agency" for "Administrator of Civil Aeronautics" in six places.

1949—Subsecs. (a) to (c), (e), (f). Act June 30, 1949, eff. July 1, 1949, repealed subsecs. (a) to (c), (e), and (f).

Subsec. (g)(2)(A). Act Oct. 1, 1949, §1, struck out "*Provided*, That no structures disposed of hereunder shall be used as an industrial plant, factory or similar facility within the meaning of section 23 of this Act, unless the public agency receiving title to such structures shall pay to the United States such sum as the Administrator shall determine to be fair consideration for the removal of the restrictions imposed by this proviso."

Subsec. (g)(4). Act Oct. 1, 1949, §5, repealed par. (4) which related to sole responsibility of Administrator for determining and enforcing compliance with the terms, conditions, reservations, and restrictions upon or subject to which surplus property is disposed of pursuant to this subsection.

1948—Subsec. (a)(3). Act June 29, 1948, made available without charge, except for reimbursement of disposal expenses, to local governments who maintain a civilian unit, certain surplus property.

Subsec. (f). Act June 10, 1948, §2, gave State and local governments a higher priority than the Reconstruction Finance Corporation with regard to certain properties.

Subsec. (h). Act June 10, 1948, §1, added subsec. (h).

1947—Subsec. (c). Act July 30, 1947, §1, struck out reference to airport.

Subsec. (g). Act July 30, 1947, §2, added subsec. (g).

1946—Subsec. (f). Act May 3, 1946, substituted provisions relating to priorities for disposal of surplus property to the United States for provisions relating to property donated by the American Red Cross.

Effective Date of 1982 Amendment

Amendment by Pub. L. 97–248 effective Sept. 3, 1982, see section 523(b) of Pub. L. 97–248.

Effective Date of 1958 Amendment

Amendment by Pub. L. 85–726 effective on 60th day following date on which Administrator of Federal Aviation Agency first appointed under Pub. L. 85–726 qualifies and takes office, see section 1505(2) of Pub. L. 85–726. Administrator appointed, qualified, and took office on Oct. 31, 1958.

Effective Date of 1949 Amendment

Amendment by act June 30, 1949, effective July 1, 1949, with priorities and preferences for surplus real estate continued until Dec. 31, 1949, see sections 602(a)(1) and 605, formerly sections 502(a)(1) and 505, of act June 30, 1949.

Transfer of Functions

Reference to Administrator of General Services substituted in subsec. (d) for reference to War Assets Administrator on authority of section 105 of act June 30, 1949, in view of transfer of functions, records, property, etc., of War Assets Administration to General Services

[1] See References in Text note below.

Administration and abolition of War Assets Administration. Previously, reference to War Assets Administrator was substituted in subsec. (d) for reference to Surplus Property Administrator on authority of Reorg. Plan No. 1, 1947, §501, eff. July 1, 1947, 12 F.R. 4535, 61 Stat. 952, which was later repealed by act June 30, 1949, ch. 288, title VI, §602(a)(1), formerly title V, §502(a)(1), 63 Stat. 399, renumbered Sept. 5, 1950, ch. 849, §6(a), (b), 64 Stat. 583. Previously, reference to Surplus Property Administrator was substituted in subsec. (d) for reference to Surplus Property Board on authority of section 2 of act Sept. 18, 1945, in view of transfer of functions of Surplus Property Board to Surplus Property Administrator and abolition of Surplus Property Board.

SURPLUS ATHLETIC EQUIPMENT

Act June 16, 1948, ch. 478, 62 Stat. 458, provided for disposal of surplus athletic equipment to State, public and government institutions, and private charitable and nonprofit organizations for use in sports by the youth of the country, prior to repeal by act Oct. 31, 1951, ch. 654, §1(128), 65 Stat. 706.

SECTION REFERRED TO IN OTHER SECTIONS

This section is referred to in title 25 section 450j; title 40 section 485.

§§1622a to 1622c. Repealed. Pub. L. 103–272, §7(b), July 5, 1994, 108 Stat. 1379

Section 1622a, acts Oct. 1, 1949, ch. 589, §2, 63 Stat. 700; Aug. 23, 1958, Pub. L. 85–726, title XIV, §1402(c), 72 Stat. 807, provided for extinguishment of restrictions on use of structures in disposal of surplus airport property.

Section 1622b, acts Oct. 1, 1949, ch. 589, §3, 63 Stat. 700; Aug. 23, 1958, Pub. L. 85–726, title XIV, §1402(c), 72 Stat. 807, related to terms and conditions of disposal instruments. See section 47151 of Title 49, Transportation.

Section 1622c, acts Oct. 1, 1949, ch. 589, §4, 63 Stat. 700; Aug. 23, 1958, Pub. L. 85–726, title XIV, §1402(c), 72 Stat. 807, related to granting of releases from terms and conditions of disposal instruments and terms and conditions of releases. See section 47153 of Title 49, Transportation.

§§1623 to 1630. Repealed. June 30, 1949, ch. 288, title VI, §602(a)(1), formerly title V, §502(a)(1), 63 Stat. 399; renumbered title VI, §602(a)(1), Sept. 5, 1950, ch. 849, §6(a), (b), 64 Stat. 583

Section 1623, acts Oct. 3, 1944, ch. 479, §14, 58 Stat. 772; Sept. 18, 1945, ch. 368, §2, 59 Stat. 533; July 23, 1946, ch. 590, 60 Stat. 599, related to disposition of property by any owning agency.

Section 1624, acts Oct. 3, 1944, ch. 479, §15, 58 Stat. 772; Sept. 18, 1945, ch. 368, §2, 59 Stat. 533, related to methods of disposition of property by government agencies.

Section 1625, acts Oct. 3, 1944, ch. 479, §16, 58 Stat. 773; Sept. 18, 1945, ch. 368, §2, 59 Stat. 533; May 3, 1946, ch. 248, §1, 60 Stat. 168, related to disposition of surplus property to veterans.

Section 1626, acts Oct. 3, 1944, ch. 479, §17, 58 Stat. 773; Ex. Ord. No. 9577, eff. June 30, 1945, 10 F.R. 8087; Sept. 18, 1945, ch. 368, §2, 59 Stat. 533; Reorg. Plan No. 3 of 1946, §501, eff. July 16, 1946, 11 F.R. 7877, 60 Stat. 1100, related to disposition of surplus property in rural areas.

Section 1627, acts Oct. 3, 1944, ch. 479, §18, 58 Stat. 773; Sept. 18, 1945, ch. 368, §2, 59 Stat. 533; May 3, 1946, ch. 248, §6, 60 Stat. 169; June 10, 1948, ch. 433, §3, 62 Stat. 351, related to disposition of surplus property to small businesses.

Section 1628, acts Oct. 3, 1944, ch. 479, §19, 58 Stat. 774; Oct. 22, 1945, ch. 432, 59 Stat. 546, related to disposition of surplus plants.

Section 1629, acts Oct. 3, 1944, ch. 479, §20, 59 Stat. 775; Sept. 18, 1945, ch. 368, §2, 59 Stat. 533, related to applicability of antitrust laws to disposition of surplus property.

Section 1630, acts Oct. 3, 1944, ch. 479, §21, 58 Stat. 775; Sept. 18, 1945, ch. 368, §2, 59 Stat. 533, related to formulation of policies for disposal of surplus agricultural commodities.

See section 471 et seq. of Title 40, Public Buildings, Property, and Works.

EFFECTIVE DATE OF REPEAL

Repeal effective July 1, 1949, with priorities and preferences for surplus real estate continued until Dec. 31, 1949, see sections 602(a)(1) and 605, formerly sections 502(a)(1) and 505, of act June 30, 1949.

§1631. Repealed. June 7, 1939, ch. 190, §6(e), as added July 23, 1946, ch. 590, 60 Stat. 599

Section, act Oct. 3, 1944, ch. 479, §22, 58 Stat. 776, related to stock piling of surplus materials. See section 98 et seq. of Title 50, War and National Defense.

§1632. Repealed. June 30, 1949, ch. 288, title VI, §602(a)(1), formerly title V, §502(a)(1), 63 Stat. 399; renumbered title VI, §602(a)(1), Sept. 5, 1950, ch. 849, §6(a), (b), 64 Stat. 583

Section, acts Oct. 3, 1944, ch. 479, §23, 58 Stat. 777; Sept. 18, 1945, ch. 368, §2, 59 Stat. 533; Aug. 7, 1946, ch. 790, §§1, 2, 60 Stat. 886, related to disposal of surplus real property. See section 471 et seq. of Title 40, Public Buildings, Property, and Works.

EFFECTIVE DATE OF REPEAL

Repeal effective July 1, 1949, with priorities and preferences for surplus real estate continued until Dec. 31, 1949, see sections 602(a)(1) and 605, formerly sections 502(a)(1) and 505, of act June 30, 1949.

§§1632a, 1632b. Omitted

CODIFICATION

Section 1632a, act Apr. 24, 1948, ch. 230, §1, 62 Stat. 199, authorizing transfer of surplus real property to Department of the Interior, expired July 1, 1952, under the provisions of section 1632b of this Appendix.

Section 1632b, act Apr. 24, 1948, ch. 230, §2, 62 Stat. 199, subjecting any surplus real property transferred to Department of the Interior to all laws and regulations applicable to area with which it is consolidated, was omitted, the authorization to make such transfers having expired by its own terms on July 1, 1952.

§§1633 to 1636. Repealed. June 30, 1949, ch. 288, title VI, §602(a)(1), formerly title V, §502(a)(1), 63 Stat. 399; renumbered title VI, §602(a)(1), Sept. 5, 1950, ch. 849, §6(a), (b), 64 Stat. 583

Section 1633, acts Oct. 3, 1944, ch. 479, §24, 58 Stat. 780; Sept. 18, 1945, ch. 368, §2, 59 Stat. 533, related to a report concerning disposition of surplus property.

Section 1634, act Oct. 3, 1944, ch. 479, §25, 58 Stat. 780, related to conclusiveness of purchaser's title to property received from government agencies.

Section 1635, act Oct. 3, 1944, ch. 479, §26, 58 Stat. 780, related to civil remedies for fraudulent acts with respect to disposition of surplus property.

Section 1636, act Oct. 3, 1944, ch. 479, §27, 58 Stat. 781, related to the limitation on the practice of law, etc., by former employees in matters involving the disposition of surplus property.

See section 471 et seq. of Title 40, Public Buildings, Property, and Works.

EFFECTIVE DATE OF REPEAL

Repeal effective July 1, 1949, with priorities and preferences for surplus real estate continued until Dec. 31, 1949, see sections 602(a)(1) and 605, formerly sections 502(a)(1) and 505, of act June 30, 1949.

§ 1637. Repealed. June 25, 1948, ch. 645, § 21, 62 Stat. 862

Section, act Oct. 3, 1944, ch. 479, § 28, 58 Stat. 781, related to an amendment of section 590a of former Title 18, Criminal Code and Criminal Procedure. See section 3287 of Title 18, Crimes and Criminal Procedure.

EFFECTIVE DATE OF REPEAL

Repeal effective Sept. 1, 1948, see section 20 of act June 25, 1948.

§§ 1638 to 1640. Repealed. June 30, 1949, ch. 288, title VI, § 602(a)(1), formerly title V, § 502(a)(1), 63 Stat. 399; renumbered title VI, § 602(a)(1), Sept. 5, 1950, ch. 849, § 6(a), (b), 64 Stat. 583

Section 1638, acts Oct. 3, 1944, ch. 479, § 29, 58 Stat. 781; Sept. 18, 1945, ch. 368, § 2, 59 Stat. 533, related to competitive bidding with regard to surplus property disposals.

Section 1639, acts Oct. 3, 1944, ch. 479, § 30, 58 Stat. 781; Sept. 18, 1945, ch. 368, § 2, 59 Stat. 533, related to disposition of proceeds from transfer or or disposition of surplus property.

Section 1640, act Oct. 3, 1944, ch. 479, § 31, 58 Stat. 782, related to use of appropriated funds for the care and handling of surplus property pending its disposition.

See section 471 et seq. of Title 40, Public Buildings, Property, and works.

EFFECTIVE DATE OF REPEAL

Repeal effective July 1, 1949, with priorities and preferences for surplus real estate continued until Dec. 31, 1949, see sections 602(a)(1) and 605, formerly sections 502(a)(1) and 505, of act June 30, 1949.

§ 1641. Repealed. Pub. L. 87–256, § 111(a)(1), Sept. 21, 1961, 75 Stat. 538

Section, acts Oct. 3, 1944, ch. 479, § 32, 58 Stat. 782; Sept. 18, 1945, ch. 368, § 2, 59 Stat. 533; Aug. 1, 1946, ch. 723, § 2, 60 Stat. 754; June 30, 1949, ch. 288, title VI, § 602(a)(1), formerly title V, § 502(a)(1), 63 Stat. 399, renumbered Sept. 5, 1950, ch. 849, § 6(a), (b), 64 Stat. 583; June 20, 1952, ch. 449, § 11, 66 Stat. 151; Aug. 26, 1954, ch. 937, title V, § 544(d), as added July 18, 1956, ch. 627, § 11(a), 70 Stat. 563, and amended Aug. 14, 1957, Pub. L. 85–141, § 11(b)(1), 71 Stat. 365; Aug. 17, 1961, Pub. L. 87–153, 75 Stat. 390, related to use of foreign currencies, foreign scholarships, and establishment of Board of Foreign Scholarships. See section 2451 et seq. of Title 22, Foreign Relations and Intercourse.

CONTINUATION OF CERTAIN EXECUTIVE ORDERS, AGREEMENTS, DETERMINATIONS, REGULATIONS, CONTRACTS, APPOINTMENTS, AND OTHER ACTIONS

Continuation in full force and effect, and applicability to the appropriate provisions of the Mutual Educational and Cultural Exchange Act of 1961, section 2451 et seq. of Title 22, Foreign Relations and Intercourse, until modified or superseded by appropriate authority, of all Executive orders, agreements, determinations, regulations, contracts, appointments, and other actions issued, concluded, or taken under authority of this section, see section 111(b) of Pub. L. 87–256, set out as a note under section 2451 of Title 22.

§§ 1642 to 1646. Repealed. June 30, 1949, ch. 288, title VI, § 602(a)(1), formerly title V, § 502(a)(1), 63 Stat. 399; renumbered title VI, § 602(a)(1), Sept. 5, 1950, ch. 849, § 6(a), (b), 64 Stat. 583

Section 1642, act Oct. 3, 1944, ch. 479, § 33, 58 Stat. 782; Sept. 18, 1945, ch. 368, § 2, 59 Stat. 533, related to restrictions on importation of surplus property into the United States.

Section 1643, acts Oct. 3, 1944, ch. 479, § 34, 58 Stat. 783; Sept. 18, 1945, ch. 368, § 2, 59 Stat. 533, related to savings provisions.

Section 1644, acts Oct. 3, 1944, ch. 479, § 35, 58 Stat. 783; Sept. 18, 1945, ch. 368, § 2, 59 Stat. 533, related to temporary applicability of existing procedures with regard to surplus property.

Section 1645, acts Oct. 3, 1944, ch. 479, § 36, 58 Stat. 783; Sept. 18, 1945, ch. 368, § 2, 59 Stat. 533, related to disposition and removal of termination inventories from plants of war contractors.

Section 1646, act Oct. 3, 1944, ch. 479, § 37, 58 Stat. 784, related to an amendment and effective date with regard to section 968 of this Appendix.

See section 471 et seq. of Title 40, Public Buildings, Property, and Works.

EFFECTIVE DATE OF REPEAL

Repeal effective July 1, 1949, with priorities and preferences for surplus real estate continued until Dec. 31, 1949, see sections 602(a)(1) and 605, formerly sections 502(a)(1) and 505, of act June 30, 1949.

WAR MOBILIZATION AND RECONVERSION ACT OF 1944

ACT OCT. 3, 1944, CH. 480, 58 STAT. 785

§§ 1651, 1652. Omitted

CODIFICATION

Sections 1651 and 1652 were omitted as terminated on June 30, 1947, pursuant to section 603 of act Oct. 3, 1944, set out as a Termination Date note below, and were subsequently repealed by Pub. L. 89–554, § 8(a), Sept. 6, 1966, 80 Stat. 652.

Section 1651, act Oct. 3, 1944, ch. 480, title I, § 101, 58 Stat. 785, related to establishment of Office of War Mobilization and Reconversion.

Section 1652, act Oct. 3, 1944, ch. 480, title I, § 102, 58 Stat. 786, related to creation of an advisory board.

SHORT TITLE

Act Oct. 3, 1944, ch. 480, title VI, § 607, 58 Stat. 792, provided that sections 1651, 1652, 1656 to 1663, 1666, 1667, 1671, and 1676 to 1678 of this Appendix be cited as the "War Mobilization and Reconversion Act of 1944".

TERMINATION DATE

Act Oct. 3, 1944, ch. 480, title VI, § 603, 58 Stat. 792, provided that the provisions of sections 1651, 1652, 1656 to 1663, 1671, and 1676 to 1678 of this Appendix terminate on June 30, 1947.

SEPARABILITY CLAUSE

Act Oct. 4, 1944, ch. 480, title VI, § 604, 58 Stat. 792, provided that if any provision of sections 1651, 1652, 1656 to 1663, 1666, 1667, 1671, and 1676 to 1678 of this Appendix, or the application of such provision to any person or circumstance, is held invalid, the remainder of such sections or the application of such provision to persons or circumstances, other than those as to which it is held invalid, shall not be affected thereby.

APPROPRIATION

Act Oct. 3, 1944, ch. 480, title VI, § 602, 58 Stat. 792, authorized to be appropriated such sums as might be necessary or appropriate to carry out the purposes and provisions of act Oct. 3, 1944.

§§ 1656 to 1663. Omitted

CODIFICATION

Sections 1656 to 1663 were omitted as terminated on June 30, 1947, pursuant to section 603 of act Oct. 3, 1944, set out as a Termination Date note under former section 1652 of this Appendix.

Section 1656, act Oct. 3, 1944, ch. 480, title II, § 201, 58 Stat. 787, related to a prohibition of indefinite military service.

Section 1657, act Oct. 3, 1944, ch. 480, title II, §202, 58 Stat. 787, related to termination of prime war contracts.

Section 1658, act Oct. 3, 1944, ch. 480, title II, §203, 58 Stat. 787, related to integration of termination of war contracts with resumption of civilian production.

Section 1659, act Oct. 3, 1944, ch. 480, title II, §204, 58 Stat. 788, related to small plant participation in civilian production.

Section 1660, act Oct. 3, 1944, ch. 480, title II, §205, 58 Stat. 788, related to surveys by Attorney General.

Section 1661, act Oct. 3, 1944, ch. 480, title III, §301, 58 Stat. 788, related to establishment of a Retraining and Reemployment Administration, and was subsequently repealed by Pub. L. 89–554, §8(a), Sept. 6, 1966, 80 Stat. 652.

Section 1662, act Oct. 3, 1944, ch. 480, title III, §302, 58 Stat. 789, related to functions of Retraining and Reemployment Administration.

Section 1663, act Oct. 3, 1944, ch. 480, title III, §303, 58 Stat. 789, related to employment of Assistant Administrators, officers and employees, and was subsequently repealed by Pub. L. 89–554, §8(a), Sept. 6, 1966, 80 Stat. 652.

§§1666, 1667. Omitted

CODIFICATION

Section 1666, act Oct. 3, 1944, ch. 480, title IV, §401, 58 Stat. 789; Reorg. Plan. No. 2 of 1946, §4, eff. July 16, 1946, 11 F.R. 7873, 60 Stat. 1095, consisted of provisions amending section 1104 of Title 42, The Public Health and Welfare.

Section 1667, act Oct. 3, 1944, ch. 480, title IV, §402, 58 Stat. 790; Reorg. Plan No. 2 of 1946, §4, eff. July 16, 1946, 11 F.R. 7873, 60 Stat. 1095, consisted of provisions enacting section 1321 of Title 42, The Public Health and Welfare.

§1671. Omitted

CODIFICATION

Section, act Oct. 3, 1944, ch. 480, title V, §501, 58 Stat. 791, which related to advance provision by States and other agencies for construction of public works, terminated on June 30, 1947, pursuant to section 603 of act Oct. 4, 1944, set out as a Termination Date note under section 1652 of this Appendix.

REVOLVING FUND

Establishment of revolving fund under which to account for assets and liabilities in connection with loans or advances made pursuant to section 1671 of this Appendix, see section 1701g–5 of Title 12, Banks and Banking, and References in Text note thereunder.

§§1676 to 1678. Omitted

CODIFICATION

Sections 1676 to 1678 were omitted as terminated on June 30, 1947, pursuant to section 603 of act Oct. 3, 1944, set out as a Termination Date note under former section 1652 of this Appendix.

Section 1676, act Oct. 3, 1944, ch. 480, title VI, §601, 58 Stat. 791, defined "executive agency" and "contracting agency".

Section 1677, act Oct. 3, 1944, ch. 480, title VI, §605, 58 Stat. 792, related to disbandment and transfer of functions of certain offices, boards, etc.

Section 1678, act Oct. 3, 1944, ch. 480, title VI, §606, 58 Stat. 792, provided for a saving clause.

FLEET ADMIRAL OF NAVY AND GENERAL OF ARMY

ACT DEC. 14, 1944, CH. 580, 58 STAT. 802

§§1691 to 1697. Repealed. Aug. 10, 1956, ch. 1041, §53, 70A Stat. 641, 674

Section 1691, act Dec. 14, 1944, ch. 580, §1, 58 Stat. 802, established Fleet Admiral of United States Navy as highest grade in Navy with provision for appointment of four on active list at any one time.

Section 1692, act Dec. 14, 1944, ch. 580, §2, 58 Stat. 802, established General of the Army as highest grade in Army with provision for appointment of four on active list at any one time.

Section 1693, act Dec. 14, 1944, ch. 580, §3, 58 Stat. 802, related to appointment without examination, tenure, effect on permanent or temporary status, appointment and reversion of retired officers.

Section 1694, act Dec. 14, 1944, ch. 580, §4, 58 Stat. 803, related to pay and allowances of appointees under sections 1691 to 1697 of this Appendix.

Section 1695, act Dec. 14, 1944, ch. 580, §5, 58 Stat. 803, related to rank and pay on retirement of appointees under sections 1691 to 1697 of this Appendix.

Section 1696, act Dec. 14, 1944, ch. 580, §6, 58 Stat. 803, related to rank and precedence of appointees under sections 1691 to 1697 of this Appendix according to date of appointment.

Section 1697, act Dec. 14, 1944, ch. 580, §7, 58 Stat. 803, left unaffected by sections 1691 to 1697 of this Appendix, any other law relating to office of General of the Armies of the United States.

DISPOSAL OF CENSORED MAIL

ACT DEC. 22, 1944, CH. 673, 58 STAT. 913

§1701. Omitted

CODIFICATION

Section, act Dec. 22, 1944, ch. 673, §1, 58 Stat. 913, relating to disposal of censored mail, expired six months after termination of hostilities in World War II, which was proclaimed at 12 o'clock noon on Dec. 31, 1946 by Proc. No. 2714, Dec. 31, 1946, 12 F.R. 1, set out preceding section 1 of this Appendix, pursuant to section 2 of act Dec. 22, 1944.

DISBURSING OFFICERS' ADDITIONAL FUNCTIONS

ACT DEC. 23, 1944, CH. 716, 58 STAT. 921

§§1705 to 1707. Transferred

CODIFICATION

Sections 1705 to 1707, acts Dec. 23, 1944, ch. 716, §§1, 2, 58 Stat. 921; June 16, 1953, ch. 115, 67 Stat. 62, were transferred to sections 492a to 492c, respectively, of former Title 31, Money and Finance, and subsequently repealed by section 5(b) of Pub. L. 97–258, Sept. 13, 1982, 96 Stat. 1076, the first section of which enacted Title 31. See section 3342 of Title 31.

Section 1705 related to check cashing and exchange transactions authorized for official and accommodation purposes.

Section 1706 related to coverage into Treasury of any gains realized from the operations conducted pursuant to sections 1705 to 1707 of this Appendix.

Section 1707 related to the issuance of regulation by Secretary of the Treasury to carry out purposes of sections 1705 to 1707 of this Appendix.

GENERAL OF MARINE CORPS

ACT MAR. 21, 1945, CH. 29, 59 STAT. 36

§§1711 to 1715. Omitted

CODIFICATION

Sections 1711 to 1715 were omitted as terminated pursuant to section 1715 of this Appendix.

Section 1711, act Mar. 21, 1945, ch. 29, §1, 59 Stat. 36, established grade and rank of General of Marine Corps and provided for appointment of Commandant of Marine Corps thereto.

Section 1712, act Mar. 21, 1945, ch. 29, §2, 59 Stat. 36, related to appointment without examination, tenure and effect on permanent or temporary status.

Section 1713, act Mar. 21, 1945, ch. 29, §3, 59 Stat. 36, related to pay and allowances of appointees under sections 1711 to 1715 of this Appendix.

Section 1714, act Mar. 21, 1945, ch. 29, §4, 59 Stat. 36, related to rank and pay on retirement of appointees under sections 1711 to 1715 of this Appendix.

Section 1715, act Mar. 21, 1945, ch. 29, §5, 59 Stat. 37, provided for the termination of sections 1711 to 1715 of this Appendix six months after the termination of the wars in which the United States was engaged as proclaimed by the President or such earlier date as Congress, by concurrent resolution, might fix. Cessation of hostilities of World War II, eff. twelve o'clock noon, Dec. 31, 1946, was proclaimed by the President in Proc. No. 2714, Dec. 31, 1946, 12 F.R. 1. The Treaty of Peace with Japan, signed at San Francisco on Sept. 8, 1951, was ratified by the United States Senate on Mar. 20, 1952 and came into force on Apr. 28, 1952. See Termination of State of War notes set out preceding section 1 of this Appendix.

PERMANENT APPOINTMENT

Section 2 of act Mar. 23, 1946, ch. 112, 60 Stat. 60, provided for permanent appointment in grade of General in Regular Marine Corps of General Alexander A. Vandegrift. Section also provided for full pay upon retirement.

ADMIRAL IN COAST GUARD

ACT MAR. 21, 1945, CH. 30, 59 STAT. 37

§§1721 to 1725. Repealed. Pub. L. 101–225, title III, §307(15), Dec. 12, 1989, 103 Stat. 1925

Section 1721, act Mar. 21, 1945, ch. 30, §1, 59 Stat. 37, established grade and rank of Admiral in Coast Guard and provided for appointment of Commandant of Coast Guard thereto.

Section 1722, act Mar. 21, 1945, ch. 30, §2, 59 Stat. 37, related to appointment without examination, tenure and effect on permanent or temporary status.

Section 1723, act Mar. 21, 1945, ch. 30, §3, 59 Stat. 37, related to pay and allowances of appointees under sections 1721 to 1725 of this Appendix.

Section 1724, act Mar. 21, 1945, ch. 30, §4, 59 Stat. 37, related to rank and pay on retirement of appointees under sections 1721 to 1725 of this Appendix.

Section 1725, act Mar. 21, 1945, ch. 30, §5, 59 Stat. 37, provided for termination of sections 1721 to 1725 of this Appendix six months after termination of wars in which United States was engaged as proclaimed by President or such earlier date as Congress, by concurrent resolution, might fix. Cessation of hostilities of World War II, eff. twelve o'clock noon, Dec. 31, 1946, proclaimed by President in Proc. No. 2714, Dec. 31, 1946, 12 F.R. 1. Treaty of Peace with Japan, signed at San Francisco on Sept. 8, 1951, ratified by United States Senate on Mar. 20, 1952, and came into force on Apr. 28, 1952. See Termination of State of War notes set out preceding section 1 of this Appendix.

PERMANENT APPOINTMENT

Section 3 of act Mar. 3, 1946, ch. 112, 60 Stat. 60, provided for permanent appointment in grade of Admiral in Coast Guard of Admiral Russell R. Waesche. Section also provided for full pay upon retirement.

EXCEPTION OF NAVY OR COAST GUARD VESSELS FROM CERTAIN NAVIGATION RULES

ACT DEC. 3, 1945, CH. 511, 59 STAT. 590

§§1731, 1732. Transferred

CODIFICATION

Section 1731, act Dec. 3, 1945, ch. 511, §1, 59 Stat. 590, which related to an exemption from requirements as to number, position, etc., of lights for vessels of special construction, was transferred to section 360 of Title 33, Navigation and Navigable Waters, and was subsequently repealed by Pub. L. 96–591, §8(a), Dec. 24, 1980, 94 Stat. 3435.

Section 1732, act Dec. 3, 1945, ch. 511, §2, 59 Stat. 591, which related to publication of notice of findings or certification and character and number of lights, was transferred to section 360a of Title 33, Navigation and Navigable Waters, and was subsequently repealed by Pub. L. 96–591, §8(a), Dec. 24, 1980, 94 Stat. 3435.

SALE OF SURPLUS WAR-BUILT VESSELS

ACT MAR. 8, 1946, CH. 82, 60 STAT. 41

ACT REFERRED TO IN OTHER SECTIONS

This Act is referred to in title 40 section 270f.

§1735. Declaration of policy

(a) It is necessary for the national security and development and maintenance of the domestic and the export and import foreign commerce of the United States that the United States have an efficient and adequate American-owned merchant marine (1) sufficient to carry its domestic water-borne commerce and a substantial portion of its water-borne export and import foreign commerce and to provide shipping service on all routes essential for maintaining the flow of such domestic and foreign water-borne commerce at all times; (2) capable of serving as a naval and military auxiliary in time of war or national emergency; (3) owned and operated under the United States flag by citizens of the United States; (4) composed of the best-equipped, safest, and most suitable types of vessels, constructed in the United States and manned with a trained and efficient citizen personnel; and (5) supplemented by efficient American-owned facilities for shipbuilding and ship repair, marine insurance, and other auxiliary services.

(b) It is hereby declared to be the policy of this Act [sections 1735 to 1746 of this Appendix] to foster the development and encourage the maintenance of such a merchant marine.

(Mar. 8, 1946, ch. 82, §2, 60 Stat. 41.)

SHORT TITLE

Section 1 of act Mar. 8, 1946, provided that: "This Act [enacting this section and sections 1736 to 1746 of this Appendix] may be cited as the 'Merchant Ship Sales Act of 1946'."

TERMINATION DATE

Section 14 of act Mar. 8, 1946, as amended June 28, 1947, ch. 161, §1, 61 Stat. 190; Feb. 27, 1948, ch. 78, §1(a), 62 Stat. 38; Feb. 28, 1949, ch. 12, 63 Stat. 9; June 29, 1949, ch. 281, §1, 63 Stat. 349; June 30, 1950, ch. 427, §1, 64 Stat. 308; Aug. 17, 1950, ch. 725, 64 Stat. 452, provided that: "No contract of sale shall be made under this Act [sections 1735 to 1746 of this Appendix] after January 15, 1951, and no contract of charter shall be made under this Act [sections 1735 to 1746 of this Appendix] after June 30, 1950, except as provided for charter under subsections (e) and (f) of section 5 hereof, as amended [section 1738(e), (f) of this Appendix]."

DETERMINATION OF SELLING PRICE

Elements to be considered in determination of the selling price of vessels, see section 864b of Title 46, Appendix, Shipping.

GREAT LAKES VESSELS

Section 3 of act Sept. 28, 1950, ch. 1093, 64 Stat. 1078, provided: "Contracts for the sale of vessels for exclusive use on the Great Lakes, including the Saint Lawrence River and Gulf and their connecting waterways, may be made until December 31, 1950. Such contracts shall require that transfer to the Great Lakes of such vessels by the buyers shall be completed by December 31, 1951."

§1736. Definitions

As used in this Act [sections 1735 to 1746 of this Appendix] the term—

(a) "Secretary" means the Secretary of Transportation.

(b) to (f) Repealed. Pub. L. 101–225, title III, §307(12), Dec. 12, 1989, 103 Stat. 1925.

(g) "Citizen of the United States" includes a corporation, partnership, or association only if it is a citizen of the United States within the meaning of section 2 of the Shipping Act of 1916, as amended [46 App. U.S.C. 802, 803]. The term "affiliated interest" as used in sections 9 and 10 of this Act [sections 1742 and 1743 of this Appendix] includes any person affiliated or associated with a citizen applicant for benefits under this Act [sections 1735 to 1746 of this Appendix] who the Secretary, pursuant to rules and regulations prescribed hereunder, determines should be so included in order to carry out the policy and purposes of this Act [said sections].

(Mar. 8, 1946, ch. 82, §3, 60 Stat. 41; Pub. L. 97–31, §12(153), Aug. 6, 1981, 95 Stat. 167; Pub. L. 101–225, title III, §307(12), Dec. 12, 1989, 103 Stat. 1925.)

AMENDMENTS

1989—Subsecs. (b) to (f). Pub. L. 101–225 struck out subsecs. (b) to (f) which defined "war-built vessel", "prewar domestic cost", "statutory sales price", "domestic war cost", and "cessation of hostilities", respectively.

1981—Subsec. (a). Pub. L. 97–31, §12(153)(A), (B), substituted "Secretary" for "Commission" and "Secretary of Transportation" for "United States Maritime Commission".

Subsecs. (c) to (e), (g). Pub. L. 97–31, §12(153)(C), substituted "Secretary" for "Commission" wherever appearing.

SECTION REFERRED TO IN OTHER SECTIONS

This section is referred to in sections 1738, 1739 of this Appendix; title 46 App. section 864a.

§1737. Repealed. Pub. L. 101–225, title III, §307(12), Dec. 12, 1989, 103 Stat. 1925

Section, acts Mar. 8, 1946, ch. 82, §4, 60 Stat. 43; June 12, 1960, Pub. L. 86–518, §1, 74 Stat. 216; Aug. 6, 1981, Pub. L. 97–31, §12(154), 95 Stat. 167, provided for sales of vessels to citizens, sales price, down payment and installment payments, and restrictions on vessel operations.

§1738. Charter of vessels

(a), (b) Repealed. Pub. L. 101–225, title III, §307(12), Dec. 12, 1989, 103 Stat. 1925

(c) Laws applicable to charter hire

The provisions of sections 708, 709, 710, 712, and 713 of the Merchant Marine Act, 1936, as amended [46 App. U.S.C. 1198 to 1200, 1202, 1203], shall be applicable to charters made under this section.

(d) Repealed. Pub. L. 101–225, title III, §307(12), Dec. 12, 1989, 103 Stat. 1925

(e) Proceedings and findings; extension of charters

(1) Notwithstanding the provisions of sections 11 and 14 of this Act, as amended [sections 1744 and 1735 note of this Appendix], war-built dry-cargo vessels owned by the United States on or after June 30, 1950, may be chartered pursuant to this Act [sections 1735 to 1746 of this Appendix] for bareboat use in any service which, in the opinion of the Maritime Administration, is required in the public interest and is not adequately served, and for which privately owned American flag vessels are not available for charter by private operators on reasonable conditions and at reasonable rates for use in such service. No charters shall be made by the Secretary of Transportation under authority of this subsection until the Maritime Administration shall have given due notice to all interested parties and shall have afforded such parties an opportunity for a public hearing on such charters and shall have certified its findings to the Secretary of Transportation. The Secretary of Transportation is authorized to include in such charters such restrictions and conditions as the Maritime Administration determines to be necessary or appropriate to protect the public interest in respect of such charters and to protect privately owned vessels against competition from vessels chartered under this section: *Provided, however*, That all such charters shall contain a provision that they will be reviewed annually by the Maritime Administration, with recommendations to the Secretary of Transportation, for the purpose of determining whether conditions exist justifying continuance of the charters under the provisions of this subsection.

(2) A charter existing on June 30, 1950, with respect to a war-built dry-cargo vessel may be extended to October 31, 1950, if application is made within ten days after the enactment hereof [June 30, 1950] for the charter of such vessel under this subsection and if the Secretary of Transportation deems such extension is justified in accordance with the provisions of subdivision (1) of this subsection: *Provided, however*, That a new voyage under such extended charter shall not be begun after October 31, 1950, unless it has been determined prior to such date, in accordance with the procedure set forth in this sub-

section, that the continued use of the vessel in the service is required. The Maritime Administration shall conduct all hearings on applications made under this paragraph immediately upon receipt thereof and shall promptly certify its findings to the Secretary of Transportation, provided that all such certifications shall be made not later than October 31, 1950.

(f) Charter of passenger vessels

(1) Notwithstanding the provisions of sections 11 and 14 of this Act, as amended [sections 1744 and 1735 note of this Appendix], the Secretary of Transportation may charter any passenger vessel, whether or not war-built, owned by the United States on or after June 30, 1950, pursuant to title VII of the Merchant Marine Act, 1936, as amended [46 App. U.S.C. 1191 et seq.] and may charter any war-built passenger vessel owned by the United States for use in the domestic trade of the United States, under the conditions prescribed for the charter of war-built cargo vessels in subsection (e) of this section.

(2) Charters existing on June 30, 1950, with respect to passenger vessels may be continued until December 31, 1951, or until expiration thereof by the terms of their provisions.

(Mar. 8, 1946, ch. 82, § 5, 60 Stat. 43; June 28, 1947, ch. 161, § 2, 61 Stat. 191; June 30, 1950, ch. 427, § 3, 64 Stat. 308; Aug. 31, 1954, ch. 1175, 68 Stat. 1050; Pub. L. 97–31, § 12(155), Aug. 6, 1981, 95 Stat. 167; Pub. L. 101–225, title III, § 307(12), Dec. 12, 1989, 103 Stat. 1925.)

References in Text

The Merchant Marine Act, 1936, as amended, referred to in subsec. (f)(1), is act June 29, 1936, ch. 858, 49 Stat. 1985, as amended. Title VII of the Merchant Marine Act, 1936, is classified generally to subchapter VII (§ 1191 et seq.) of chapter 27 of Title 46, Appendix, Shipping. For complete classification of this Act to the Code, see section 1245 of Title 46, Appendix, and Tables.

Amendments

1989—Subsecs. (a), (b), (d). Pub. L. 101–225 struck out subsec. (a) which related to charter of vessels to citizens and publication of domestic prewar cost as a prerequisite, subsec. (b) which related to rate of charter hire, and subsec. (d) which related to computation of charter hire where an operator is engaged in both foreign and domestic trade.

1981—Subsec. (a). Pub. L. 97–31, § 12(155)(A), (B), substituted "Secretary" for "Commission" and "his" for "its" wherever appearing.

Subsec. (b). Pub. L. 97–31, § 12(155)(A), substituted "Secretary" for "Commission" wherever appearing.

Subsec. (d). Pub. L. 97–31, § 12(155)(C), substituted "Secretary of Transportation" for "Maritime Commission".

Subsec. (e). Pub. L. 97–31, § 12(155)(D), (E), substituted "Maritime Administration" for "Federal Maritime Board" and "Secretary of Transportation" for "Secretary of Commerce" wherever appearing.

Subsec. (f)(1). Pub. L. 97–31, § 12(155)(E), substituted "Secretary of Transportation" for "Secretary of Commerce".

1954—Subsec. (f)(1). Act Aug. 31, 1954, allowed the chartering of war-built passenger vessels.

1950—Subsecs. (e), (f). Act June 30, 1950, added subsecs. (e) and (f).

1947—Subsec. (d). Act June 28, 1947, added subsec. (d).

Authorization for Payments by Secretary of Commerce to Persons to Whom He Chartered Vessels

Pub. L. 85–721, Aug. 21, 1958, 72 Stat. 710, provided: "That the Secretary of Commerce [now Secretary of Transportation] is authorized to pay to any person to whom he has chartered any vessel under authority of section 5 of the Merchant Ship Sales Act of 1946, as amended (50 U.S.C. App., sec. 1738), out of the Vessel Operations Revolving Fund established in chapter VIII of the Third Supplemental Appropriations Act, 1951 [46 App. U.S.C., sec. 1241a], an amount equal to the fair and reasonable expenses incurred by such person, as determined by the Maritime Administrator, during the calendar year beginning January 1, 1957, to activate such vessel. Such amount shall be reduced by the amount of the difference, as determined by the Maritime Administrator, between the charter hire which such person paid for such vessel, and the charter hire which was paid for similar vessels which the United States activated at its own expense during such calendar year."

§ 1738a. Repealed. Pub. L. 101–225, title III, § 307(13), Dec. 12, 1989, 103 Stat. 1925

Section, acts June 29, 1949, ch. 281, § 2, 63 Stat. 349; Aug. 6, 1981, Pub. L. 97–31, § 12(156), 95 Stat. 167, provided for termination of charters, except passenger vessel charters.

§ 1738b. Omitted

Codification

Section, Pub. L. 94–121, title III, Oct. 21, 1975, 89 Stat. 628, which related to conditions for chartering vessels, was from the Department of Commerce Appropriation Act, 1976, and was not repeated in subsequent appropriation acts. Similar provisions were contained in the following prior appropriation acts:

Oct. 5, 1974, Pub. L. 93–433, title III, 88 Stat. 1199.
Nov. 27, 1973, Pub. L. 93–162, title III, 87 Stat. 649.
Oct. 25, 1972, Pub. L. 92–544, title III, 86 Stat. 1124.
Aug. 10, 1971, Pub. L. 92–77, title III, 85 Stat. 260.
Oct. 21, 1970, Pub. L. 91–472, title III, 84 Stat. 1054.
Dec. 24, 1969, Pub. L. 91–153, title III, 83 Stat. 417.
Aug. 9, 1968, Pub. L. 90–470, title III, 82 Stat. 682.
Nov. 8, 1967, Pub. L. 90–133, title III, 81 Stat. 425.
Nov. 8, 1966, Pub. L. 89–797, title III, 80 Stat. 1494.
Sept. 2, 1965, Pub. L. 89–164, title III, 79 Stat. 634.
Aug. 31, 1964, Pub. L. 88–527, title III, 78 Stat. 726.
Dec. 30, 1963, Pub. L. 88–245, title III, 77 Stat. 791.
Oct. 18, 1962, Pub. L. 87–843, title III, 76 Stat. 1093.
Aug. 3, 1961, Pub. L. 87–125, title II, 75 Stat. 274.
May 13, 1960, Pub. L. 86–451, title I, 74 Stat. 97.
July 13, 1959, Pub. L. 86–88, title I, 73 Stat. 204.
June 25, 1958, Pub. L. 85–469, title I, 72 Stat. 231.
June 13, 1957, Pub. L. 85–52, title I, 71 Stat. 74.
June 20, 1956, ch. 415, title I, 70 Stat. 318.
June 30, 1955, ch. 253, title I, 69 Stat. 231.
July 2, 1954, ch. 456, title III, 68 Stat. 426.
Aug. 5, 1953, ch. 328, title III, 67 Stat. 381.
July 5, 1952, ch. 578, title II, 66 Stat. 414.
Aug. 31, 1951, ch. 376, title II, 65 Stat. 286.
Sept. 6, 1950, ch. 896, Ch. VIII, title I, 64 Stat. 717.
Oct. 10, 1949, ch. 662, title I, 63 Stat. 743.

§§ 1739, 1740. Repealed. Pub. L. 101–225, title III, § 307(12), Dec. 12, 1989, 103 Stat. 1925

Section 1739, acts Mar. 8, 1946, ch. 82, § 6, 60 Stat. 43; Aug. 6, 1981, Pub. L. 97–31, § 12(154), 95 Stat. 167, provided for sale of vessels to non-citizens, sales conditions and priority of mortgage on unpaid balance.

Section 1740, acts Mar. 8, 1946, ch. 82, § 7, 60 Stat. 44; Sept. 26, 1950, ch. 1049, § 2(a)(2), 64 Stat. 1038; Sept. 27, 1979, Pub. L. 96–70, § 3(b)(5), 93 Stat. 455; Aug. 6, 1981, Pub. L. 97–31, § 12(154), 95 Stat. 167, provided for order of preference in sales and charters, determining relevant factors, and operation of commercial vessels by Government.

§ 1741. Exchange of vessels

(a) to (c) Repealed. Pub. L. 101–225, title III, § 307(12), Dec. 12, 1989, 103 Stat. 1925

(d) Transfer of substitute vessels

In the case of any vessel constructed in the United States after January 1, 1937, which has been taken by the United States for use in any manner, the Secretary, if in his opinion the transfer would aid in carrying out the policies of this Act [sections 1735 to 1746 of this Appendix], is authorized to transfer to the owner of such vessel another vessel which is deemed by the Secretary to be of comparable type with adjustments for depreciation and difference in design or speed, and to the extent applicable, adjustments with respect to the retained vessel as provided for in section 9 [section 1742 of this Appendix], and such other adjustments and terms and conditions, including transfer of mortgage obligations in favor of the United States binding upon the old vessel, as the Secretary may prescribe.

(Mar. 8, 1946, ch. 82, §8, 60 Stat. 45; Pub. L. 97–31, §12(154), Aug. 6, 1981, 95 Stat. 167; Pub. L. 101–225, title III, §307(12), Dec. 12, 1989, 103 Stat. 1925.)

AMENDMENTS

1989—Subsecs. (a) to (c). Pub. L. 101–225 struck out subsecs. (a) to (c) which related to allowance as credit on purchase price and vessels acceptable, amount of allowance, and transfers in settlement of claims, respectively.

1981—Pub. L. 97–31 substituted "Secretary" for "Commission" wherever appearing.

SECTION REFERRED TO IN OTHER SECTIONS

This section is referred to in title 26 section 1061.

§1742. Repealed. Pub. L. 94–412, title V, §501(g), Sept. 14, 1976, 90 Stat. 1258

Section, acts Mar. 8, 1946, ch. 82, §9, 60 Stat. 46; Aug. 6, 1956, ch. 1013, 70 Stat. 1068, made provision for price adjustments on prior sales of surplus war-built vessels to citizens.

SAVINGS PROVISION

Repeal not to affect any action taken or proceeding pending at the time of repeal, see section 501(h) of Pub. L. 94–412, set out as a note under section 1601 of Title 50, War and National Defense.

§1743. Repealed. Pub. L. 101–225, title III, §307(12), Dec. 12, 1989, 103 Stat. 1925

Section, acts Mar. 8, 1946, ch. 82, §10, 60 Stat. 49; Aug. 6, 1981, Pub. L. 97–31, §12(154), 95 Stat. 167, limited eligibility for benefits under Merchant Ship Sales Act of 1946.

§1744. National Defense Reserve Fleet

(a) Fleet components

The Secretary of Transportation shall maintain a National Defense Reserve Fleet, including any vessel assigned by the Secretary to the Ready Reserve Force component of the fleet, consisting of those vessels owned or acquired by the United States Government that the Secretary of Transportation, after consultation with the Secretary of the Navy, determines are of value for national defense purposes and that the Secretary of Transportation decides to place and maintain in the fleet.

(b) Permitted uses

Except as otherwise provided by law, a vessel in the fleet may be used—

(1) for an account of an agency of the United States Government in a period during which vessels may be requisitioned under section 902 of the Merchant Marine Act, 1936 (46 App. U.S.C. 1242); or

(2) on the request of the Secretary of Defense, and in accordance with memoranda of agreement between the Secretary of Transportation and the Secretary of Defense, for—

(A) testing for readiness and suitability for mission performance;

(B) defense sealift functions for which other sealift assets are not reasonably available; and

(C) support of the deployment of the United States armed forces in a military contingency, for military contingency operations, or for civil contingency operations upon orders from the National Command Authority;

(3) for otherwise lawfully permitted storage or transportation of non-defense-related cargo as directed by the Secretary of Transportation with the concurrence of the Secretary of Defense; or

(4) for training purposes to the extent authorized by the Secretary of Transportation with the concurrence of the Secretary of Defense.

(c) Ready Reserve Force management

(1) Minimum requirements

To ensure the readiness of vessels in the Ready Reserve Force component of the National Defense Reserve Fleet, the Secretary of Transportation shall, at a minimum—

(A) maintain all of the vessels in a manner that will enable each vessel to be activated within a period specified in plans for mobilization of the vessels;

(B) activate and conduct sea trials on each vessel at least once every twenty-four months;

(C) maintain in an enhanced activation status those vessels that are scheduled to be activated within 5 days;

(D) locate those vessels that are scheduled to be activated within 5 days near embarkation ports specified for those vessels; and

(E) notwithstanding section 2109 of title 46, United States Code, have each vessel inspected by the Secretary of the department in which the Coast Guard is operating to determine if the vessel meets the safety standards that would apply under part B of subtitle II of that title if the vessel were not a public vessel.

(2) Vessel managers

(A) Eligibility for contract

A person, including a shipyard, is eligible for a contract for the management of a vessel in the Ready Reserve Force if the Secretary determines, at a minimum, that the person has—

(i) experience in the operation of commercial-type vessels or public vessels owned by the United States Government; and

(ii) the management capability necessary to operate, maintain, and activate the vessel at a reasonable price.

(B) Contract requirement

The Secretary of Transportation shall include in each contract for the management of a vessel in the Ready Reserve Force a requirement that each seaman who performs services on any vessel covered by the contract hold the license or merchant mariner's document that would be required under chapter 71 or chapter 73 of title 46, United States Code, for a seaman performing that service while operating the vessel if the vessel were not a public vessel.

(e)[1] Exemption from tank vessel construction standards

Vessels in the National Defense Reserve Fleet are exempt from the provisions of section 3703a of title 46, United States Code.

(Mar. 8, 1946, ch. 82, §11, 60 Stat. 49; June 28, 1947, ch. 161, §1, 61 Stat. 190; Feb. 27, 1948, ch. 78, §1(a), 62 Stat. 38; Feb. 28, 1949, ch. 12, 63 Stat. 9; June 29, 1949, ch. 281, §1, 63 Stat. 349; June 30, 1950, ch. 427, §2, 64 Stat. 308; Pub. L. 97–31, §12(157), Aug. 6, 1981, 95 Stat. 167; Pub. L. 101–115, §6, Oct. 13, 1989, 103 Stat. 693; Pub. L. 101–225, title III, §307(12), Dec. 12, 1989, 103 Stat. 1925; Pub. L. 102–241, §57, Dec. 19, 1991, 105 Stat. 2234; Pub. L. 102–587, title VI, §6205(a), Nov. 4, 1992, 106 Stat. 5094; Pub. L. 104–106, div. A, title X, §1014(b), Feb. 10, 1996, 110 Stat. 424; Pub. L. 104–239, §9, Oct. 8, 1996, 110 Stat. 3133.)

AMENDMENTS

1996—Subsec. (b)(2). Pub. L. 104–239, §9(1), substituted "of the Secretary of Defense" for "of the Secretary of the Navy".

Subsecs. (c), (d). Pub. L. 104–239, §9(2), redesignated subsec. (d) as (c) and struck out former subsec. (c) which read as follows: "The Secretary of Transportation shall not require bid, payment, performance, payment and performance, or completion bonds from contractors for repair, alteration, or maintenance of vessels of the National Defense Reserve Fleet unless—

"(1) required by law; or

"(2) the Secretary determines, after investigation, that the imposition of such bonding requirements would not preclude any responsible potential bidder or offeror from competing for award of the contract."

Subsec. (e). Pub. L. 104–106 added subsec. (e).

1992—Subsec. (b). Pub. L. 102–587 amended subsec. (b) to read as if it had not been repealed by Pub. L. 101–225. See 1989 Amendment note below.

1991—Subsec. (d). Pub. L. 102–241 added subsec. (d).

1989—Pub. L. 101–225 struck out subsec. (b) as it appeared after a general amendment by Pub. L. 101–115, see below. See also 1992 Amendment note above.

Pub. L. 101–115 amended section generally. Prior to amendment, section read as follows:

"(a) The Secretary of Transportation shall place in a national defense reserve (1) such vessels owned by the Department of Transportation as, after consultation with the Secretary of the Army and the Secretary of the Navy, he deems should be retained for the national defense, and (2) all vessels owned by the Department of Transportation on June 30, 1950, for the sale of which a contract has not been made by that time, except those determined by the Secretary of Transportation to be of insufficient value for commercial and national defense purposes to warrant their maintenance and preservation, and except those vessels, the contracts for the construction of which are made after September 2, 1945, under the provisions of the Merchant Marine Act, 1936, as amended. A vessel under charter on March 1, 1948, shall not be placed in the reserve until the termination of such charter. Unless otherwise provided for by law, all vessels placed in such reserve shall be preserved and maintained by the Secretary of Transportation for the purpose of national defense. A vessel placed in such reserve shall in no case be used for any purpose whatsoever except that any such vessel may be used for account of any agency or department of the United States during any period in which vessels may be requisitioned under section 902 of the Merchant Marine Act, 1936, as amended, and that any such vessel may be used under a bare-boat charter entered into pursuant to authority vested in the Secretary of Transportation on July 1, 1950, or granted to the Secretary of Transportation after such date.

"(b) Any war-built vessel may be made available by the Secretary of Transportation to any State maintaining a marine school or nautical branch in accordance with the Act of July 29, 1941 (Public Law 191, Seventy-seventh Congress; 55 Stat. 607)."

1981—Subsec. (a). Pub. L. 97–31 substituted "Secretary of Transportation" first three times it appears for "Commission" and last two times it appears for "Secretary of Commerce"; "Department of Transportation" for "it"; and "he" for "it".

Subsec. (b). Pub. L. 97–31 substituted "Secretary of Transportation" for "Commission".

1950—Subsec. (a). Act June 30, 1950, amended subsec. (a) to provide that a vessel placed in reserve may not be used for any purpose whatsoever except (1) for the account of any Federal agency or department during the period in which vessels may be requisitioned under section 1242 of Title 46 and (2) and any such vessel may be used under a bare-boat charter entered into pursuant to the authority vested in the Secretary of Commerce.

1949—Subsec. (a). Joint Res. June 29, 1949, extended provisions of section from June 30, 1949, to June 30, 1950. Joint Res. Feb. 28, 1949, extended provisions of section from Mar. 1, 1949, to June 30, 1949.

1948—Subsec. (a). Act Feb. 27, 1948, extended provisions of section from Mar. 1, 1948, to Mar. 1, 1949.

1947—Subsec. (a). Act June 28, 1947, extended provisions of section from Dec. 31, 1947, to Mar. 1, 1948.

EFFECTIVE DATE OF 1992 AMENDMENT

Section 6205(a) of Pub. L. 102–587 provided in part that: "The effective date of this subsection [amending this section] is December 12, 1989."

VESSEL REPAIR AND MAINTENANCE PILOT PROGRAM

Section 16 of Pub. L. 104–239 provided that:

"(a) IN GENERAL.—The Secretary of Transportation shall conduct a pilot program to evaluate the feasibility of using renewable contracts for the maintenance and repair of outported vessels in the Ready Reserve Force to enhance the readiness of those vessels. Under the pilot program, the Secretary, subject to the availability of appropriations and within 6 months after the date of the enactment of this Act [Oct. 8, 1996], shall award 9 contracts for this purpose.

"(b) USE OF VARIOUS CONTRACTING ARRANGEMENTS.—In conducting a pilot program under this section, the Secretary of Transportation shall use contracting arrangements similar to those used by the Department of Defense for procuring maintenance and repair of its vessels.

"(c) CONTRACT REQUIREMENTS.—Each contract with a shipyard under this section shall—

"(1) subject to subsection (d), provide for the procurement from the shipyard of all repair and maintenance (including activation, deactivation, and drydocking) for 1 vessel in the Ready Reserve Force that is outported in the geographical vicinity of the shipyard;

"(2) be effective for 1 fiscal year; and

"(3) be renewable, subject to the availability of appropriations, for each subsequent fiscal year through fiscal year 1998.

"(d) LIMITATION OF WORK UNDER CONTRACTS.—A contract under this section may not provide for the procurement of operation or manning for a vessel that may be procured under another contract for the vessel

[1] So in original. Probably should be "(d)".

to which section 11(d)(2) of the Merchant Ship Sales Act of 1946 (50 U.S.C. App. 1774(d)(2)) applies.

"(e) GEOGRAPHIC DISTRIBUTION.—The Secretary shall seek to distribute contract awards under this section to shipyards located throughout the United States.

"(f) REPORTS.—The Secretary shall submit to the Congress—

"(1) an interim report on the effectiveness of each contract under this section in providing for economic and efficient repair and maintenance of the vessel included in the contract, no later than 20 months after the date of the enactment of this Act [Oct. 8, 1996]; and

"(2) a final report on that effectiveness no later than 6 months after the termination of all contracts awarded pursuant to this section."

SECTION REFERRED TO IN OTHER SECTIONS

This section is referred to in section 1738 of this Appendix; title 10 section 2218; title 46 section 3703a; title 46 App. sections 1132, 1152, 1160.

§1745. Reconversion of vessels for normal commercial operation; applicability of other laws to construction contracts; coastwise trade; disposition of moneys; Great Lakes trade

(a) The Secretary is authorized to reconvert or restore for normal operation in commercial services and to convert for operation on the Great Lakes, including the Saint Lawrence River and Gulf, and their connecting waterways, including removal of national defense or war-service features, any vessel authorized to be sold or chartered under this Act [sections 1735 to 1746 of this Appendix]. The Secretary is authorized to make such replacements, alterations, or modifications with respect to any vessel authorized to be sold or chartered under this Act [said sections], and to install therein such special features, as may be necessary or advisable to make such vessel suitable for commercial operation on trade routes or services or comparable as to commercial utility to other such vessels of the same general type.

(b) to (e) Repealed. Pub. L. 101–225, title III, §307(12), Dec. 12, 1989, 103 Stat. 1925.

(Mar. 8, 1946, ch. 82, §12, 60 Stat. 49; Sept. 28, 1950, ch. 1093, §§1, 2, 64 Stat. 1078; Pub. L. 97–31, §12(158), Aug. 6, 1981, 95 Stat. 168; Pub. L. 101–225, title III, §307(12), Dec. 12, 1989, 103 Stat. 1925.)

AMENDMENTS

1989—Subsecs. (b) to (e). Pub. L. 101–225, which directed repeal of subsecs. (b) to (f), was executed by striking out subsecs. (b) to (e) as the probable intent of Congress because there was no subsec. (f). Subsecs. (b) to (e) provided in subsec. (b) that section 202 of the War Mobilization and Reconversion Act was inapplicable to contracts of the Commission for or relating to construction of ships, in subsec. (c) that no vessel sold or chartered to a citizen of the United States be prohibited from engaging in the coastwise trade of the United States merely because it was under foreign registry on or after May 27, 1941, in subsec. (d) that all moneys received be deposited in the Treasury to the credit of miscellaneous receipts, and in subsec. (e) that the Secretary make allowances to purchasers of not more than ten vessels sold for exclusive use on the Great Lakes.

1981—Subsecs. (a), (c), (d). Pub. L. 97–31, §12(158)(A), substituted "Secretary" for "Commission" wherever appearing.

Subsec. (e). Pub. L. 97–31, §12(158)(B), substituted "Secretary of Transportation" for "Secretary of Commerce".

1950—Subsec. (a). Act Sept. 28, 1950, §1, provided for conversion for operation on the Great Lakes, including the Saint Lawrence River and Gulf, and their connecting waterways.

Subsec. (e). Act Sept. 28, 1950, §2, added subsec. (e).

§1745a. Repealed. Pub. L. 101–225, title III, §307(14), Dec. 12, 1989, 103 Stat. 1925

Section, Pub. L. 86–315, Sept. 21, 1959, 73 Stat. 588, accorded Great Lakes vessels operation status of documented vessels.

§1746. Repealed. Pub. L. 99–386, title I, §107, Aug. 22, 1986, 100 Stat. 822; Pub. L. 101–225, title III, §307(12), Dec. 12, 1989, 103 Stat. 1925

Section, acts Mar. 8, 1946, ch. 82, §13, 60 Stat. 50; Aug. 6, 1981, Pub. L. 97–31, §12(154), 95 Stat. 167, required submission of quarterly reports by Secretary to Congress with respect to all activities or transactions under sections 1735 to 1746 of this Appendix not covered by any previous such report.

Pub. L. 89–348, §2(1), Nov. 8, 1965, 79 Stat. 1312, modified this section to require annual instead of quarterly reports.

REHABILITATION OF PHILIPPINES

ACT APR. 30, 1946, CH. 243, 60 STAT. 128

§§1751 to 1763. Omitted

PAYMENT OF BALANCE OF AWARDS TO PHILIPPINES

Pub. L. 87–616, Aug. 30, 1962, 76 Stat. 411, as amended by Pub. L. 88–94, §3, Aug. 12, 1963, 77 Stat. 122, provided:

"[SEC. 1. *Conditions; limitations on amount*]. That the Foreign Claims Settlement Commission (hereafter in this Act referred to as the "Commission") shall provide, out of funds appropriated pursuant to this Act, for the payment of the unpaid balance of awards heretofore made by the Philippine War Damage Commission under title I of the Philippine Rehabilitation Act of 1946 [sections 1751 to 1763 of this Appendix]. No payment shall be made under this Act to any person, or to his successors in interest, on account of any award unless payment was made on such award under the Philippine Rehabilitation Act of 1946 [sections 1751 to 1806 of this Appendix], and the maximum amount paid under this Act, when added to amounts paid under the Philippine Rehabilitation Act of 1946 [sections 1751 to 1806 of this Appendix] and section 7 of the War Claims Act of 1948 [section 2006 of this Appendix] on account of any claim shall not exceed the aggregate amount of claims approved in favor of such claimant after reduction under the last proviso of section 102(a) of the Philippine Rehabilitation Act of 1946 [section 1752(a) of this Appendix], or $25,000, whichever is the lesser. All payments under this Act in amounts over 25,000 pesos or equivalent value in dollars shall be subject to the provisions of section 104(c) of the Philippine Rehabilitation Act of 1946 [section 1754(c) of this Appendix].

"SEC. 2. [*Applications; commencement and duration of period; determination of Commission*]. Within sixty days after the enactment of this Act [Aug. 30, 1962], or of legislation appropriating for administration expenses incurred in carrying out this Act, whichever is later, the Commission shall prescribe and publish in the Federal Register and give appropriate publicity in the Republic of the Philippines concerning the period, not in excess of twelve additional months, within which application must be filed under this Act. The Commission shall complete its determination and take final action with respect to applications filed under this Act not later than one year after the last date on which applications may be filed.

"SEC. 3. [*Publicity to payments provisions; notice to claimants*]. The Commission shall give maximum publicity in the Republic of the Philippines to the provisions of this Act, and through utilization of the records of the former Philippine War Damage Commission shall attempt to notify individual claimants of their right to file applications for payment under this Act, by mailing notice thereof to the last known address of such claimants as shown by such records.

"SEC. 4. [*Notice of approval or denial of applications; hearings; finality of determinations*]. The Commission shall notify all applicants of the approval or denial of their applications and, if approved, shall notify such applicants of the amount for which such applications are approved. Any applicant whose application is denied, or is approved for less than the amount of such application, shall be entitled, under such regulations as the Commission may prescribe, to a hearing before the Commission or its representative with respect to such application. Upon such hearing, the Commission may affirm, modify, or reverse its former action with respect to such application, including a denial or reduction in the amount of award theretofore approved. All findings of the Commission concerning the persons to whom compensation pursuant to this Act is payable, and the amounts thereof, shall be conclusive and not be reviewable by any court.

"SEC. 5. [*Payments; exchange rate; medium; extraterritorial claimants; purchasers of claims; Educational Programs Fund; reversion of funds to United States Treasury*]. (a) Each award made under this Act shall be certified to the Secretary of the Treasury in terms of United States currency on the basis of the rate of exchange (that is, P/2 equals $1) which was applied in the Philippine Rehabilitation Act of 1946 [sections 1751 to 1806 of this Appendix], for payment out of sums appropriated pursuant to section 8 of this Act. Such payments shall be made in accordance with such regulations as the Secretary of the Treasury may prescribe. Payments authorized under this Act shall be made in United States dollars or in Philippine pesos at the option of the Secretary of the Treasury; however, notwithstanding the last sentence of the first section of this Act, payment shall not be made outside of the Republic of the Philippines to any claimant residing outside the Republic of the Philippines unless he establishes to the satisfaction of the Commission that since the date of the loss or damage on account of which the original award was made he has heretofore invested in such manner as furthered the rehabilitation or economic development of the Philippines an amount not less than the claims approved in his favor after reduction under the last proviso of section 102(a) of the Philippine Rehabilitation Act of 1946 [section 1752(a) of this Appendix]. Any balance of the appropriation made pursuant to section 8 remaining after the payments authorized by the first section of this Act have been made and after any administrative expenses incurred by the Commission in connection with such payments have been paid shall be paid into a special fund in the United States Treasury to be used for the purpose of furthering educational exchange and other educational programs to the mutual advantage of the Republic of the Philippines and the United States in such manner as the Presidents of those two Republics shall from time to time determine. There shall be withheld from the payment authorized by the preceding sentence a sum equal to the difference between $73,000,000 (less administrative expenses) and the total amount which would have been paid to the claimants under the provisions of Public Law 87–616, which sum shall revert to the general funds in the United States Treasury. The acceptance by any claimant of a payment under this Act shall be considered to be in full satisfaction and final settlement of all claims of such claimant arising out of awards for war damage compensation made by the Philippine War Damage Commission. Payment shall not be made under this Act on any claim filed under the Philippine Rehabilitation Act of 1946 [sections 1751 to 1806 of this Appendix] or under this Act which was acquired from a predecessor in interest by purchase, except where such purchase was in the ordinary course of business in connection with the acquisition of all assets of a business firm.

"(b) Such of the records of the Philippine War Damage Commission as the Foreign Claims Settlement Commission may deem necessary for carrying out its functions under this Act shall be transferred to the Foreign Claims Settlement Commission.

"SEC. 6. [*Remuneration for services to applicants; prohibition against certain payments; penalties; forfeitures; recovery of payments*]. (a) The total remuneration on account of services rendered or to be rendered to or on behalf of any applicant in connection with any application filed under this Act shall not exceed 5 per centum of the amount paid by the Commission on account of such application. Any agreement to the contrary shall be unlawful and void. Whoever, subject to the jurisdiction of the United States, violates this subsection shall be fined not more than $5,000 or imprisoned for not more than one year, or both. Where any payment is made in violation of this subsection, the Commission shall take such action as may be appropriate to recover the same.

"(b) Notwithstanding the provisions of subsection (a), no sum shall be paid by any claimant directly or indirectly to, or received or accepted by, any former commissioner or employee of the Philippine War Damage Commission or their assigns, or any person employed by or associated with any such former commissioner or employee in connection with the preparation, filing, allowance, or collection of any claim under this Act, as compensation on account of services rendered or as reimbursement on account of expenses incurred in connection with any application filed under this Act. Whoever, subject to the jurisdiction of the United States, makes a payment in violation of the provisions of this subsection shall be fined not more than $5,000 or imprisoned for not more than one year or both. Whoever, subject to the jurisdiction of the United States, receives or accepts a payment in violation of this subsection, shall be fined not more than $5,000 or imprisoned for not more than five years or both. Whoever, subject to the jurisdiction of the United States, receives or accepts a payment in violation of this subsection, shall forfeit to the Government of the United States a sum equal to three times the amount of such payment, and the Commission shall take action to recover such sum from the person receiving the payment.

"SEC. 7. [*Application of International Claims Settlement Act of 1949*]. For the purposes of carrying out this Act, the following provisions of the International Claims Settlement Act of 1949 [section 1621 et seq. of Title 22, Foreign Relations and Intercourse] shall, to the extent not inconsistent with this Act, be applicable in the administration of this Act: Subsections (c), (d), (e), and (i) of section 4 [section 1623 of Title 22]; subsections (d) and (e) of section 7 [section 1626 of Title 22]; and subsection (c) of section 7 [section 1626 of Title 22] except that with respect to applicants not subject to the jurisdiction of the United States, references in such subsection (c) to the Comptroller General of the United States shall be deemed to refer to the Secretary of the Treasury.

"SEC. 8. [*Appropriations for payment of awards and administrative expenses*]. There is authorized to be appropriated not more than $73,000,000 to make payments on awards certified pursuant to this Act, plus such additional sums as may be necessary for the administrative expenses of the Commission and of the Secretary of the Treasury in carrying out this Act."

CODIFICATION

Sections 1751 to 1763 terminated Apr. 30, 1951, pursuant to section 1751 of this Appendix.

Section 1751, acts Apr. 30, 1946, ch. 243, title I, §101, 60 Stat. 128; Jan. 26, 1948, ch. 16, §§1, 2, 62 Stat. 4; Oct. 15, 1949, ch. 695, §6(a), 63 Stat. 881, established the Philippine War Damage Commission and provided for the winding up of its affairs not later than two years after expiration of time for filing claims under sections 1751 to 1763 of this Appendix if possible but in no event later than Apr. 30, 1951. Acts Apr. 30, 1946, ch. 243, title I, §101, 60 Stat. 128; Oct. 15, 1949, ch. 695, §6(a), 63 Stat. 881, were repealed by Pub. L. 89–554, §8(a), Sept. 6, 1966, 80 Stat. 653, 655.

Section 1752, act Apr. 30, 1946, ch. 243, title I, §102, 60 Stat. 129, related to payment for destruction and damage to property, perils and persons covered, claim limitations and definitions.

Section 1753, act Apr. 30, 1946, ch. 243, title I, §103, 60 Stat. 130, excluded from payment certain enumerated claims.

Section 1754, acts Apr. 30, 1946, ch. 243, title I, §104, 60 Stat. 130; Aug. 2, 1946, ch. 741, §1, 60 Stat. 805, related to claim payments.

Section 1755, acts Apr. 30, 1946, ch. 243, title I, §105, 60 Stat. 131; Aug. 2, 1946, ch. 741, §2, 60 Stat. 805, required Philippine War Damage Commission to make reports to Congress at intervals of six months.

Section 1756, acts Apr. 30, 1946, ch. 243, title I, §106, 60 Stat. 131; Jan. 26, 1948, ch. 16, §3, 62 Stat. 5, authorized to be appropriated the amount of $400,000,000 for compensation payments under sections 1751 to 1763 of this Appendix, including the sum of $12,000,000 for expenses of Philippine War Damage Commission, all appropriations under the sections remaining available until Apr. 30, 1951, and provided for disposition of Japanese reparations, including individual reparations.

Section 1757, act Apr. 30, 1946, ch. 243, title I, §107, 60 Stat. 132, provided penalties for false and fraudulent claims.

Section 1758, act Apr. 30, 1946, ch. 243, title I, §108, 60 Stat. 132, set limitation on fees for claim services and provided penalties for violations thereof.

Section 1759, act Apr. 30, 1946, ch. 243, title I, §109, 60 Stat. 132, related to the authority of the Philippine War Damage Commission and the prohibition on War Damage Corporation payments.

Section 1760, act Apr. 30, 1946, ch. 243, title I, §110, 60 Stat. 133, excluded from coverage certain enumerated classes of property.

Section 1761, act Apr. 30, 1946, ch. 243, title I, §111, 60 Stat. 133, related to transfer of surplus property, valuation of property and payment.

Section 1762, act Apr. 30, 1946, ch. 243, title I, §112, 60 Stat. 133, provided for cooperation between the Philippine War Damage Commission and the War Damage Corporation.

Section 1763, act Apr. 30, 1946, ch. 243, title I, §113, 60 Stat. 134, provided for notification of disposal and amount of claim, hearings and conclusiveness of findings.

§§1771 to 1776. Omitted

CODIFICATION

Section 1771, acts Apr. 30, 1946, ch. 243, title II, §201, 60 Stat. 134; Aug. 2, 1946, ch. 741, §3, 60 Stat. 805, related to transfer and disposal of surplus property, by Department of State acting through a Foreign Liquidation Commissioner, and terms and conditions thereof.

Section 1772, act Apr. 30, 1946, ch. 243, title II, §202, 60 Stat. 134, required recordation of number, condition and value of transferred items and quarterly reports thereof to the President and Congress.

Section 1773, act Apr. 30, 1946, ch. 243, title II, §203, 60 Stat. 134, related to law governing disposal.

Section 1774, act Apr. 30, 1946, ch. 243, title II, §204, 60 Stat. 134, prohibited transfer of military equipment and toxic gas.

Section 1775, act Apr. 30, 1946, ch. 243, title II, §205, 60 Stat. 134, limited gross amount transferable to Commonwealth of Philippines, provincial governments, and chartered cities or municipalities to $100,000,000.

Section 1776, act Apr. 30, 1946, ch. 243, title II, §206, 60 Stat. 135, authorized Foreign Liquidation Commissioner to prescribe rules and regulations necessary for performance of his functions under sections 1771 to 1776 of this Appendix and to delegate any authority conferred upon him by the sections.

§§1781 to 1791. Omitted

CODIFICATION

Section 1781, act Apr. 30, 1946, ch. 243, title III, §301, 60 Stat. 135, authorized to be appropriated the sum of $120,000,000 for allocation, but not later than the fiscal year 1950, among the programs set forth in sections 1782 to 1785 of this Appendix and such additional sums as might be necessary for the purposes of sections 1786 to 1791 of this Appendix. Appropriations remained available for the purposes of sections 1782(a) and 1783(a) of this Appendix until June 30, 1951 under the provisions of section 1791(e) of this Appendix.

Section 1782, acts Apr. 30, 1946, ch. 243, title III, §302, 60 Stat. 135; July 2, 1948, ch. 810, §1, 62 Stat. 1224, related to restoration and construction of roads and bridges and training of Filipino engineers. Section 1782(a) authority continued in effect until June 30, 1951, under the provisions of section 1791(e) of this Appendix.

Section 1783, act Apr. 30, 1946, ch. 243, title III, §303, 60 Stat. 135, related to rehabilitation and construction of port and harbor facilities and training of Filipino engineers. Section 1783(a) authority continued in effect until June 30, 1951, under the provisions of section 1791(e) of this Appendix.

Section 1784, act Apr. 30, 1946, ch. 243, title III, §304, 60 Stat. 136, related to compensation for damage and destruction of public property, repairs and replacement and powers of the Philippine War Damage Commission.

Section 1785, acts Apr. 30, 1946, ch. 243, title III, §305, 60 Stat. 136; July 2, 1948, ch. 810, §2, 62 Stat. 1224, related to rehabilitation and improvement of public health services, training of Filipinos and replacement of equipment.

Section 1786, act Apr. 30, 1946, ch. 243, title III, §306, 60 Stat. 137, related to restoration and improvement of inter-island commerce and training of Filipino merchant marine personnel.

Section 1787, act Apr. 30, 1946, ch. 243, title III, §307, 60 Stat. 137, related to establishment and operation of inter-island air facilities and training of Filipino personnel.

Section 1788, act Apr. 30, 1946, ch. 243, title III, §308, 60 Stat. 138, related to establishment of metrological facilities and training of Filipino personnel.

Section 1789, act Apr. 30, 1946, ch. 243, title III, §309, 60 Stat. 138, related to rehabilitation and development of fisheries, training of Filipino personnel, operation of research and experimental stations and vessels and transfer of vessels.

Section 1790, act Apr. 30, 1946, ch. 243, title III, §310, 60 Stat. 139, provided for continuation of Coast and Geodetic surveys and training of Filipino personnel.

Section 1791, acts Apr. 30, 1946, ch. 243, title III, §311, 60 Stat. 139; July 2, 1948, ch. 810, §3, 62 Stat. 1225; Sept. 7, 1949, ch. 545, 63 Stat. 692, related to acquisition of lands and easements, cooperation between Governments, rules and regulations governing training courses, admission to United States, and conditions for carrying out training and termination date. Section 1791(e) provided for the expiration of sections 1781, 1782(b), 1783(b), 1784 to 1791 on June 30, 1950 with the following exceptions. Appropriations under section 1781 for the purposes of sections 1782(a) and 1783(a) of this Appendix and the authority contained in sections 1782(a) and 1783(a) continued available and in effect, respectively, until June 30, 1951. Section 1791(d) last proviso, relating to the deportation of Filipinos designated for training or instruction in the United States for failure to depart within reasonable time fixed by regulation.

EXTENSION OF CHARTERS; TERMINATION DATE

Joint Res. July 1, 1954, ch. 454, 68 Stat. 396, provided that: "Notwithstanding any other provisions of existing law, the Secretary of Commerce is authorized to extend and continue the present charters of vessels to citizens of the Republic of the Philippines, which charters were made and entered into under the terms of section 306(a) of the Act of April 30, 1946 (Public Law 370, Seventy-ninth Congress) [section 1786(a) of this Appendix], and which charters were extended by the Secretary of Commerce under the terms of a joint resolution, approved June 30, 1953 (ch. 163, 67 Stat. 110). Such charters may be further extended for such periods of time and under such terms and conditions as the Secretary may, from time to time, determine to be required in the interest of the economy of the Philippines, but any such charter shall contain a provision requiring that the vessel shall be operated only in the inter-island commerce in the Philippines. No such vessel shall be continued under charter, as authorized herein, beyond the completion of the first voyage terminating after June 30, 1955."

Similar provisions were contained in the following acts:

Joint Res. June 30, 1953, ch. 163, 67 Stat. 110.

Joint Res. Apr. 30, 1952, ch. 242, 66 Stat. 65.

LIMITATION ON EXPENDITURES

Act July 23, 1946, ch. 591, title I, § 101, 60 Stat. 622, provided in part that the total expenditure under subsec. (a) of section 1787 of this Appendix should not exceed $8,000,000.

§§ 1796, 1797. Omitted

CODIFICATION

Section 1796, act Apr. 30, 1946, ch. 243, title IV, § 401, 60 Stat. 140, providing for the supervision of functions, powers and duties of Federal agencies and employees in carrying out the provisions of act Apr. 30, 1946, as amended, by the United States High Commissioner to the Philippines, until the Philippines attained their independence, was omitted, independence having been granted to the Philippine Islands by 1946 Proc. No. 2695, eff. July 4, 1946, 11 F.R. 7517, 60 Stat. 1352, which was issued under the authority of section 1394 of Title 22, Foreign Relations and Intercourse, and is set out as a note under section 1394 of Title 22.

Section 1797, act Apr. 30, 1946, ch. 243, title IV, § 402, 60 Stat. 140, provided for the transfer of functions under act Apr. 30, 1946, as amended, from the High Commissioner to the Philippines to such United States representative or representatives as the President might appoint on and after the date the Philippines attained their independence.

§ 1801. Omitted

CODIFICATION

Section, act Apr. 30, 1946, ch. 243, title V, § 501, 60 Stat. 140, authorized $5,000,000 to be appropriated for the restoration, repair of damage to and improvement of lands and buildings referred to in section 1394(c)(3) of Title 22, Foreign Relations and Intercourse, and for the acquisition or construction of additional buildings to house the civil agencies, including the diplomatic and consular establishments of the United States operating in the Philippine Islands.

§ 1806. Omitted

CODIFICATION

Section, act Apr. 30, 1946, ch. 243, title VI, § 601, 60 Stat. 140, required an executive agreement to be entered into between the Presidents of the United States and the Philippines as a condition precedent for certain private-aid payments under sections 1751 to 1763 of this Appendix which have been omitted from the Code.

RETURN AND INTERMENT OF PERSONS BURIED OUTSIDE UNITED STATES

ACT MAY 16, 1946, CH. 261, 60 STAT. 182

§§ 1811 to 1820. Repealed. Pub. L. 89–554, § 8(a), Sept. 6, 1966, 80 Stat. 653, 654

Sections 1811 to 1820 of this Appendix terminated Dec. 31, 1951, pursuant to section 1818 of this Appendix. The sections remained in force as to any application under sections 1813 and 1814 of this Appendix filed prior to Dec. 31, 1951.

Section 1811, acts May 16, 1946, ch. 261, § 1, 60 Stat. 182; Aug. 5, 1947, ch. 497, 61 Stat. 779, contained the Congressional declaration of purpose for sections 1811 to 1820 of this Appendix.

Section 1812, acts May 16, 1946, ch. 261, § 2, 60 Stat. 183; Aug. 5, 1947, ch. 497, 61 Stat. 779; May 16, 1946, ch. 261, § 11, as added June 3, 1948, ch. 402, 62 Stat. 334, provided for administration by Secretary of the Army of sections 1811 to 1820 of this Appendix with exception of activities reserved for American Battle Monuments Commission by section 1819 of this Appendix.

Section 1813, acts May 16, 1946, ch. 261, § 3, 60 Stat. 183; Aug. 5, 1947, ch. 497, 61 Stat. 779; May 16, 1946, ch. 261, § 11, as added June 3, 1948, ch. 402, 62 Stat. 334, related to remains returnable and place of interment.

Section 1814, acts May 16, 1946, ch. 261, § 4, 60 Stat. 183; Aug. 5, 1947, ch. 497, 61 Stat. 779; May 16, 1946, ch. 261, § 11, as added June 3, 1948, ch. 402, 62 Stat. 334, related to interment in military cemeteries outside United States.

Section 1815, acts May 16, 1946, ch. 261, § 5, 60 Stat. 183; Aug. 5, 1947, ch. 497, 61 Stat. 779; May 16, 1946, ch. 261, § 11, as added June 3, 1948, ch. 402, 62 Stat. 334, provided for acquisition of land in foreign countries for establishment of cemeteries.

Section 1816, acts May 16, 1946, ch. 261, § 6, 60 Stat. 183; Aug. 5, 1947, ch. 497, 61 Stat. 779; May 16, 1946, ch. 261, § 11, as added June 3, 1948, ch. 402, 62 Stat. 334, authorized Secretary of the Army to prescribe rules and regulations to carry out sections 1811 to 1820 of this Appendix.

Section 1817, acts May 16, 1946, ch. 261, § 7, as added Aug. 5, 1947, ch. 497, 61 Stat. 779, and amended May 16, 1946, ch. 261, § 11, as added June 3, 1948, ch. 402, 62 Stat. 334, related to appropriations.

Section 1818, act May 16, 1946, ch. 261, § 8, as added Aug. 5, 1947, ch. 497, 61 Stat. 779, provided for termination of sections 1811 to 1820 of this Appendix on Dec. 31, 1951. The sections remained in force as to any applications under sections 1813 and 1814 of this Appendix filed prior to Dec. 31, 1951.

Section 1819, act May 16, 1946, ch. 261, § 9, as added Aug. 5, 1947, ch. 497, 61 Stat. 779, and amended May 16, 1946, ch. 261, § 11, as added June 3, 1948, ch. 402, 62 Stat. 334, related to duties and responsibilities of American Battle Monuments Commission and transfer to Commission of temporary administrative functions of Secretary of the Army.

Section 1820, act May 16, 1946, ch. 261, § 10, as added June 3, 1948, ch. 402, 62 Stat. 334, related to allowances for escort personnel.

VETERANS' EMERGENCY HOUSING PROGRAM

ACT MAY 22, 1946, CH. 268, 60 STAT. 207

§ 1821. Repealed. June 30, 1947, ch. 163, title I, § 1(a), 61 Stat. 193

Section, act May 22, 1946, ch. 268, § 1, 60 Stat. 207, related to purpose, termination date, and applicability of the Veterans' Emergency Housing Act of 1946.

Effect of repeal on existing allocations and priorities, see section 1881 of this Appendix.

§ 1822. Repealed. Pub. L. 89–554, § 8(a), Sept. 6, 1966, 80 Stat. 653

Section, acts May 22, 1946, ch. 268, § 2, 60 Stat. 208; June 30, 1947, ch. 163, title I, § 1(a), 61 Stat. 193; Oct. 15, 1949, ch. 695, § 6(a), 63 Stat. 881, related to appointment, compensation, and functions of Housing Expediter.

ACT JUNE 30, 1948, CH. 775, 62 STAT. 1197

§ 1822a. Repealed. Pub. L. 89–554, § 8(a), Sept. 6, 1966, 80 Stat. 654

Section, act June 30, 1948, ch. 775, § 101, 62 Stat. 1197, related to administration of oaths by employees of Office of Housing Expediter.

ACT MAY 22, 1946, CH. 268, 60 STAT. 207

§§1823 to 1829. Repealed. June 30, 1947, ch. 163, title I, §1(a), 61 Stat. 193

Section 1823, act May 22, 1946, ch. 268, §3, 60 Stat. 209, related to establishment of maximum sales prices for housing accommodations.

Section 1824, act May 22, 1946, ch. 268, §4, 60 Stat. 210, related to establishment of material priorities.

Section 1825, act May 22, 1946, ch. 268, §5, 60 Stat. 210, related to prohibited practices.

Section 1826, act May 22, 1946, ch. 268, §6, 60 Stat. 211, related to review of action taken pursuant to any regulation or order issued under act May 22, 1946.

Section 1827, act May 22, 1946, ch. 268, §7, 60 Stat. 211, related to penalties for violation of section 1825 of this Appendix.

Section 1828, act May 22, 1946, ch. 268, §8, 60 Stat. 211, related to definitions.

Section 1829, act May 22, 1946, ch. 268, §9, 60 Stat. 212, related to authorization of appropriations.

§1830. Omitted

CODIFICATION

Section, act May 22, 1946, ch. 268, §10, 60 Stat. 212, amended sections 603(a), 603(b)(2), 603(b)(5), 603(c), 604(b), 608(b)(2), (3)(C) and 608(c) of the National Housing Act, as amended, sections 1738(a), 1738(b)(2), 1738(b)(5), 1738(c), 1739(b), 1743(b)(2), (3)(C) and 1743(c) of Title 12, Banks and Banking, respectively. The amendments are incorporated in the latter sections.

§§1831, 1832. Repealed. June 30, 1947, ch. 163, title I, §1(a), 61 Stat. 193

Section 1831, act May 22, 1946, ch. 268, §11, 60 Stat. 214, related to subsidies for prefabricated houses.

Section 1832, act May 22, 1946, ch. 268, §12, 60 Stat. 215, related to guaranty of markets for prefabricated houses.

Effect of repeal on existing allocations and priorities, see section 1881 of this Appendix.

§1833. Omitted

CODIFICATION

Section, act May 22, 1946, ch. 268, §13, 60 Stat. 215, contained a saving clause.

NAVAL VESSELS AS ATOMIC TARGETS

ACT JUNE 25, 1946, CH. 487, 60 STAT. 308

§§1841 to 1845. Omitted

CODIFICATION

Sections 1841 to 1845 terminated June 25, 1948, pursuant to section 5 of act June 25, 1946.

Section 1841, act June 25, 1946, ch. 487, §1, 60 Stat. 308, related to use of vessels as targets for atomic weapons.

Section 1842, act June 25, 1946, ch. 487, §2, 60 Stat. 308, related to disposal of vessels after experiments.

Section 1843, act June 25, 1946, ch. 487, §3, 60 Stat. 308, related to number of combatant vessels to be employed.

Section 1844, act June 25, 1946, ch. 487, §4, 60 Stat. 309, related to safeguarding of information on results of tests.

Section 1845, act June 25, 1946, ch. 487, §4A, 60 Stat. 309, related to appointment and compensation of an advisory board.

ADMISSION OF ALIEN FIANCEES INTO UNITED STATES

ACT JUNE 29, 1946, CH. 520, 60 STAT. 339

§§1851 to 1855. Omitted

CODIFICATION

Sections 1851 to 1855 were omitted as terminated pursuant to section 1851 of this Appendix.

Section 1851, acts June 29, 1946, ch. 520, §1, 60 Stat. 339; June 28, 1947, ch. 160, 61 Stat. 190; Mar. 24, 1948, ch. 141, §§1, 2, 62 Stat. 84, related to the admission of alien fiancees or fiances of members of the armed forces, on or before Dec. 31, 1948.

Section 1852, act June 29, 1946, ch. 520, §2, 60 Stat. 340, related to deportation upon nonoccurrence of marriage.

Section 1853, act June 29, 1946, ch. 520, §3, 60 Stat. 340, related to regulations governing functions of diplomatic or consular officers.

Section 1854, act June 29, 1946, ch. 520, §4, 60 Stat. 340, related to regulations governing functions of the Immigration and Naturalization Service.

Section 1855, act June 29, 1946, ch. 520, §5, 60 Stat. 340, defined the period of World War II.

COMPLETION OF PROCESSING OF VISA CASES

Act Apr. 21, 1949, ch. 85, 63 Stat. 56, provided for the completion of processing of cases of the alien fiances or fiancees of citizens of the United States pending on Dec. 31, 1948 under sections 1851 to 1855 of this Appendix.

MILITARY ASSISTANCE TO PHILIPPINE REPUBLIC

ACT JUNE 26, 1946, CH. 500, 60 STAT. 315

§§1861 to 1866. Omitted

CODIFICATION

Sections 1861 to 1866 of this Appendix terminated July 4, 1951, under the provisions of act June 26, 1946, ch. 500, §8, 60 Stat. 316.

Section 1861, act June 26, 1946, ch. 500, §2, 60 Stat. 315, authorized the President to provide military assistance upon application by the Philippines.

Section 1862, act June 26, 1946, ch. 500, §3, 60 Stat. 315, related to terms and conditions for military assistance to the Philippines.

Section 1863, act June 26, 1946, ch. 500, §4, 60 Stat. 315, set forth condition precedent to receipt of assistance.

Section 1864, act June 26, 1946, ch. 500, §5, 60 Stat. 315, related to detail of personnel of United States armed forces to Philippine Government and their compensation and emoluments.

Section 1865, act June 26, 1946, ch. 500, §6, 60 Stat. 316, related to appropriations and limitation on amount of assistance.

Section 1866, act June 26, 1946, ch. 500, §7, 60 Stat. 316, related to authority to promulgate rules and regulations, delegation of authority by President and transfer of property.

NAVAL AID TO CHINA

ACT JULY 16, 1946, CH. 580, 60 STAT. 539

§§1871, 1872. Omitted

CODIFICATION

Sections 1871 and 1872 terminated July 16, 1951, pursuant to section 3 of act July 16, 1946.

Section 1871, act July 16, 1946, ch. 580, §1, 60 Stat. 539, related to furnishing of naval services, training and vessels to Republic of China and to restrictions on vessel disposals.

Section 1872, act July 16, 1946, ch. 580, §2, 60 Stat. 539, related to detail of Naval and Marine Corps personnel and restrictions on service.

NAVAL AID TO FOREIGN NATIONS

ACT JULY 8, 1952, CH. 591, 66 STAT. 443

§1876. Omitted

CODIFICATION

Section, act July 8, 1952, ch. 591, 66 Stat. 443, authorized loan to Japanese Government of eighteen patrol frigates and fifty landing craft suitable for patrol purposes for an initial five year period and for an additional requested five year period and provided for return of the vessels in substantially the original condition.

ACT AUG. 5, 1953, CH. 321, 67 STAT. 363

§§ 1878 to 1878d. Omitted

CODIFICATION

Section 1878, act Aug. 5, 1953, ch. 321, §1, 67 Stat. 363, authorized loan of two submarines to Italian Government for five year period to provide training for Italian units in antisubmarine warfare.

Section 1878a, acts Aug. 5, 1953, ch. 321, §2, 67 Stat. 363; July 26, 1955, ch. 376, 69 Stat. 373, authorized loan of a small aircraft carrier to French Government until June 30, 1958.

Section 1878b, act Aug. 5, 1953, ch. 321, §3, 67 Stat. 363, conditioned loan of submarines and aircraft carrier to return of the vessels in substantially the original condition unless damaged or lost through enemy action.

Section 1878c, acts Aug. 5, 1953, ch. 321, §4, 67 Stat. 363; Aug. 3, 1956, ch. 914, §1(a), (b), 70 Stat. 967, made available to friendly foreign nations in the Far Eastern or European area naval vessels not larger than destroyers, twenty-five in number, and assorted minor miscellaneous craft, naval services, training, technical advice, facilities and equipment, with or without reimbursement and subject to appropriate terms and conditions; required the Secretary of Defense to determine the transfers to be in the best interests of the United States and to report the transfers to Congress; authorized promulgation of rules and regulations; prohibited communication of secret or top secret classifications; and prescribed Dec. 31, 1957, as termination date for executive exercise of naval vessel transfer authority under this section.

Section 1878d, acts Aug. 5, 1953, ch. 321, §5, 67 Stat. 363; Aug. 3, 1956, ch. 914, §1(c), 70 Stat. 967, provided for the charging of activation expenses (submarines, air carrier, and other vessels) to funds programed for recipient Governments under Mutual Security Act of 1954, or to funds provided by recipient Governments under reimbursable provisions of such Act.

PUB. L. 85–532, JULY 18, 1958, 72 STAT. 376

§§ 1878e to 1878i. Omitted

CODIFICATION

Section 1878e, Pub. L. 85–532, §1, July 18, 1958, 72 Stat. 376, authorized extension of loan of aircraft carrier to French Government until June 30, 1960 [originally until June 30, 1958, under section 1878a of this Appendix], and made available to friendly foreign nations destroyers, destroyer escorts, and submarines from the reserve fleet, as follows: North Atlantic Treaty Organization and European area, nineteen ships; Latin American area, eighteen ships; Far Eastern area, four ships; emergency loans, two ships, and authorized promulgation of rules and regulations.

Section 1878f, Pub. L. 85–532, §2, July 18, 1958, 72 Stat. 376, limited the loans to five year periods terminable earlier because of defense requirements of United States.

Section 1878g, Pub. L. 85–532, §3, July 18, 1958, 72 Stat. 376, provided for the charging of activation, rehabilitation, and outfitting expenses to funds programed for recipient government under Mutual Security Act of 1954, or to funds provided by recipient government under reimbursable provisions of such Act and for reimbursement of recipient government by Secretary of Defense on a pro rata basis for funds provided by it under the reimbursable provisions where loan was terminated prior to the expiration date.

Section 1878h, Pub. L. 85–532, §4, July 18, 1958, 72 Stat. 376, required Secretary of Defense to determine transfers to be in best interests of United States and to report transfers to Congress.

Section 1878i, Pub. L. 85–532, §5, July 18, 1958, 72 Stat. 376, prescribed Dec. 31, 1960, as termination date for executive exercise of naval vessel transfer authority under sections 1878e to 1878i of this Appendix.

PUB. L. 86–57, JUNE 23, 1959, 73 STAT. 90

§§ 1878j to 1878*l*. Omitted

CODIFICATION

Section 1878j, Pub. L. 86–57, §§1, 2, June 23, 1959, 73 Stat. 90, authorized extension of loans of: two submarines to Italian Government (originally authorized by sections 1878 to 1878d of this Appendix), two submarines to Turkish Government (originally authorized by section 1879 of this Appendix), and two destroyers to Government of Republic of China (originally authorized by sections 1878 to 1878d of this Appendix), subject to appropriate terms and conditions, and authorized promulgation of rules and regulations.

Section 1878k, Pub. L. 86–57, §3, June 23, 1959, 73 Stat. 90, limited extension of loans to a five year period terminable earlier because of defense requirements of United States.

Section 1878*l*, Pub. L. 86–57, §4, June 23, 1959, 73 Stat. 90, required Secretary of Defense to determine extension of loans to be in best interest of United States and to report extensions to Congress.

PUB. L. 86–482, JUNE 1, 1960, 74 STAT. 153

§§ 1878m to 1878p. Omitted

CODIFICATION

Section 1878m, Pub. L. 86–482, §§1, 2, June 1, 1960, 74 Stat. 153, authorized extension of loan of one destroyer to Government of Republic of China (originally authorized by sections 1878 to 1878d of this Appendix), subject to appropriate terms and conditions, and authorized promulgation of rules and regulations.

Section 1878n, Pub. L. 86–482, §3, June 1, 1960, 74 Stat. 153, limited extension of loans to a five year period terminable earlier because of defense requirements of United States.

Section 1878*o*, Pub. L. 86–482, §4, June 1, 1960, 74 Stat. 153, required Secretary of Defense to determine extension of loans to be in best interest of United States and to report extensions to Congress.

Section 1878p, Pub. L. 86–482, §5, June 1, 1960, 74 Stat. 153, authorized loan of one submarine to Canadian Government for a five year period and extension of the loan for a similar period, required the Canadian Government to pay for activation expenses, and prescribed Dec. 31, 1961, as termination date for executive exercise of submarine transfer authority under this section.

PUB. L. 87–387, OCT. 4, 1961, 75 STAT. 815

§§ 1878q to 1878x. Omitted

CODIFICATION

Sections 1878q to 1878x terminated pursuant to section 1878x of this Appendix.

Section 1878q, Pub. L. 87–387, §§1, 2, Oct. 4, 1961, 75 Stat. 815, authorized extension of loans of two destroyer escorts to Portuguese Government and two destroyers to Spanish Government (originally authorized by sections 1878 to 1878d of this Appendix), subject to appropriate terms and conditions.

Section 1878r, Pub. L. 87–387, §3, Oct. 4, 1961, 75 Stat. 815, limited extension of existing loans to a five year period terminable earlier because of defense requirements of United States.

Section 1878s, Pub. L. 87–387, §4, Oct. 4, 1961, 75 Stat. 815, made available to friendly foreign nations destroyers, destroyer escorts, and submarines from the Reserve Fleet, as follows: North Atlantic Treaty Organization and European area, six ships; Southern Asia, two ships; Far Eastern area, six ships; emergency loans, two ships, for replacement of loaned vessels lost by enemy action or by an act of God.

Section 1878t, Pub. L. 87–387, § 5, Oct. 4, 1961, 75 Stat. 815, limited new loans to five year periods terminable earlier because of defense requirements of United States.

Section 1878u, Pub. L. 87–387, § 6, Oct. 4, 1961, 75 Stat. 815, provided for the charging of activation, rehabilitation, and outfitting expenses to funds programed for recipient government under Mutual Security Act of 1954, or successor legislation, or to funds provided by recipient government.

Section 1878v, Pub. L. 87–387, § 7, Oct. 4, 1961, 75 Stat. 815, required Secretary of Defense to determine loans or extension of loans to be in best interest of United States and to report loans or extensions to Congress.

Section 1878w, Pub. L. 87–387, § 8, Oct. 4, 1961, 75 Stat. 815, authorized promulgation of rules and regulations.

Section 1878x, Pub. L. 87–387, § 9, Oct. 4, 1961, 75 Stat. 815, prescribed Dec. 31, 1963, as termination date for executive exercise of naval vessel transfer authority under sections 1878q to 1878x of this Appendix.

PUB. L. 88–437, AUG. 14, 1964, 78 STAT. 444

§§ 1878y to 1878bb. Omitted

CODIFICATION

Section 1878y, Pub. L. 88–437, § 1, Aug. 14, 1964, 78 Stat. 444, authorized extension of loan of ships, subject to appropriate terms and conditions, as follows: Argentina, two submarines, and Brazil, two destroyers (authorized by sections 1878e to 1878i of this Appendix); China, four destroyers (authorized by sections 1878 to 1878d of this Appendix); Germany, five destroyers, and Greece, four destroyers (authorized by sections 1878e to 1878i of this Appendix); Italy, three submarines, and Japan, one submarine, four destroyers, two destroyer escorts (authorized by sections 1878 to 1878i of this Appendix); Netherlands, two submarines (authorized by Act July 11, 1952, 66 Stat. 587, as amended); Peru, one destroyer, Spain, one submarine, three destroyers, and Thailand, one destroyer escort (authorized by sections 1878e to 1878i of this Appendix); and Turkey, five submarines (authorized by sections 1878e to 1878i and 1879 of this Appendix).

Section 1878z, Pub. L. 88–437, § 2, Aug. 14, 1964, 78 Stat. 444, limited extension of loans to a five year period and to an additional five year period, terminable earlier because of defense requirements of United States.

Section 1878aa, Pub. L. 88–437, § 3, Aug. 14, 1964, 78 Stat. 444, required Secretary of Defense to determine extension of loans to be in best interest of United States and to report extensions to Congress.

Section 1878bb, Pub. L. 88–437, § 4, Aug. 14, 1964, 78 Stat. 444, authorized promulgation of rules and regulations.

PUB. L. 89–324, NOV. 5, 1965, 79 STAT. 1214

§§ 1878cc to 1878mm. Omitted

CODIFICATION

Sections 1878cc to 1878mm terminated pursuant to section 1878mm of this Appendix.

Section 1878cc, Pub. L. 89–324, title I, § 101, Nov, 5, 1965, 79 Stat. 1214, authorized loan of two submarines to Italy and one helicopter carrier to Spain from reserve fleet, subject to appropriate terms and conditions.

Section 1878dd, Pub. L. 89–324, title I, § 102, Nov. 5, 1965, 79 Stat. 1214, provided for charging of activation, rehabilitation, and outfitting expenses to funds provided by recipient government under reimbursable provisions of the Foreign Assistance Act of 1961, or successor legislation, for vessels transferred under section 1878cc of this Appendix.

Section 1878ee, Pub. L. 89–324, title II, § 201, Nov. 5, 1965, 79 Stat. 1214, authorized sale or loan of two and three destroyers to Argentina and Brazil from reserve fleet, subject to appropriate terms and conditions.

Section 1878ff, Pub. L. 89–324, title II, § 202, Nov. 5, 1965, 79 Stat. 1214, provided for charging of activation, rehabilitation, and outfitting expenses to funds provided by recipient government under reimbursable provisions of Foreign Assistance Act of 1961, or successor legislation for vessels transferred under section 1878ee of this Appendix.

Section 1878gg, Pub. L. 89–324, title II, § 203, Nov. 5, 1965, 79 Stat. 1214, required stricken from the Naval Vessel Register vessels up for sale and sold for not less than $1,000,000 each plus cost of activation, overhaul, or modification under Foreign Assistance Act of 1961, or successor legislation.

Section 1878hh, Pub. L. 89–324, title III, § 301, Nov. 5, 1965, 79 Stat. 1214, authorized loan of two destroyers to Turkey and one destroyer escort to Philippines from reserve fleet, subject to appropriate terms and conditions.

Section 1878ii, Pub. L. 89–324, title III, § 302, Nov. 5, 1965m, 79 Stat. 1214, provided for charging of activation, rehabilitation, and outfitting expenses to funds programed for recipient government as grant military assistance, or as reimbursable, under provisions of Foreign Assistance Act of 1961, or successor legislation for vessels transferred under section 1878hh of this Appendix.

Section 1878jj, Pub. L. 89–324, title IV, § 401, Nov. 5, 1965, 79 Stat. 1215, limited loans to five year periods and an additional five year extension, terminable earlier because of defense requirements of United States.

Section 1878kk, Pub. L. 89–324, title IV, § 402, Nov. 5, 1965, 79 Stat. 1215, required Secretary of Defense to determine sales or loans to be in best interest of United States and to report sales or loans to Congress.

Section 1878*ll*, Pub. L. 89–324, title IV, § 403, Nov. 5, 1965, 79 Stat. 1215, authorized promulgation of rules and regulations.

Section 1878mm, Pub. L. 89–324, title IV, § 404, Nov. 5, 1965, 79 Stat. 1215, prescribed Dec. 31, 1967, as termination for executive exercise of naval vessel sale or loan authority under sections 1878cc to 1878mm of this Appendix.

PUB. L. 89–398, APR. 16, 1966, 80 STAT. 121

§§ 1878nn to 1878ss. Omitted

CODIFICATION

Sections 1878nn to 1878ss terminated Dec. 31, 1967, pursuant to section 1878ss of this Appendix.

Section 1878nn, Pub. L. 89–398, § 1, Apr. 16, 1966, 80 Stat. 121, authorized loan to Republic of China of one destroyer and one destroyer escort from reserve fleet subject to appropriate terms and conditions.

Section 1878*oo*, Pub. L. 89–398, § 2, Apr. 16, 1966, 80 Stat. 121, which provided for charging of activation, rehabilitation, and outfitting expense to funds programed for recipient government as grant military assistance, or as reimbursable, under provisions of Foreign Assistance Act of 1961, or successor legislation.

Section 1878pp, Pub. L. 89–398, § 3, Apr. 16, 1966, 80 Stat. 121, limited loans to five year periods with provision for a five year extension, terminable earlier because of defense requirements of United States.

Section 1878qq, Pub. L. 89–398, § 4, Apr. 16, 1966, 80 Stat. 121, required Secretary of Defense to determine loans to be in best interest of United States and to report extensions or loans to Congress.

Section 1878rr, Pub. L. 89–398, § 5, Apr. 16, 1966, 80 Stat. 121, authorized promulgation of rules and regulations.

Section 1878ss, Pub. L. 89–398, § 6, Apr. 16, 1966, 80 Stat. 121, prescribed Dec. 31, 1967, as termination date for executive exercise of naval vessel loan authority under sections 1878nn to 1878ss of this Appendix.

PUB. L. 90–224, DEC. 26, 1967, 81 STAT. 729

§§ 1878tt to 1878xx. Omitted

CODIFICATION

Section 1878tt, Pub. L. 90–224, §1, Dec. 26, 1967, 81 Stat. 729, authorized extension of loan of ships subject to appropriate terms and conditions, as follows: Argentina, three destroyers, Brazil, two destroyers and two submarines, Chile, two submarines and two destroyers, and Columbia, one destroyer (authorized by sections 1878e to 1878i of this Appendix); Federal Republic of Germany, one destroyer (authorized by sections 1878 to 1878d of this Appendix): Greece, one submarine, and two destroyers (authorized by sections 1878 to 1878d and 1878q to 1878x of this Appendix); Korea, two destroyer escorts and one destroyer and one destroyer escort (authorized by sections 1878 to 1878d and 1878q to 1878x of this Appendix); Portugal, two destroyer escorts, and Spain, two destroyers (authorized by sections 1878 to 1878d of this Appendix); and Peru, one destroyer (authorized by sections 1878e to 1878i of this Appendix).

Section 1878uu, Pub. L. 90–224, §2, Dec. 26, 1967, 81 Stat. 729, authorized additional loan of two destroyers to Korean Government and one destroyer to Republic of China, with or without reimbursement, subject to appropriate terms and conditions; provided for charging activation, rehabilitation, and outfitting expenses to funds programed for recipient government as grant military assistance, or as reimbursable, under provision of Foreign Assistance Act of 1961, or successor legislation; and prescribed Dec. 31, 1969, as termination date for executive exercise of naval vessel loan authority under this section.

Section 1878vv, Pub. L. 90–224, §3, Dec. 26, 1967, 81 Stat. 729, authorized new loans and loan extensions for five year periods, and an additional five year extension, terminable: for acts of warfare by armed forces of borrowing country against a country party to a mutual defense treaty ratified by the United States; upon an executive finding of seizure of United States fishing vessels on account of fishing activities in international waters by country party to the agreement, except in cases governed by international agreement to which United States is a party; and earlier because of defense requirements of the United States.

Section 1878ww, Pub. L. 90–224, §4, Dec. 26, 1967, 81 Stat. 730, required Secretary of Defense to determine loans or extension of loans to be in best interest of United States and to report loans or extensions to Congress.

Section 1878xx, Pub. L. 90–224, §5, Dec. 26, 1967, 81 Stat. 730, authorized promulgation of rules and regulations.

PUB. L. 91–682, JAN. 12, 1971, 84 STAT. 2066

§§ 1878yy to 1878zz–3. Omitted

CODIFICATION

Section 1878yy, Pub. L. 91–682, §1, Jan. 12, 1971, 84 Stat. 2066, authorized extension of loans, subject to appropriate terms and conditions, of one submarine to Greece and Pakistan (authorized under sections 1878q to 1878x of this Appendix).

Section 1878zz, Pub. L. 91–682, §2, Jan. 12, 1971, 84 Stat. 2066, authorized additional loans of two destroyer escorts to Republic of Vietnam and two destroyers and two submarines to Turkish Government, with or without reimbursement, subject to appropriate terms and conditions, provided for the charging of activation, rehabilitation, and outfitting expenses to funds programed for recipient government as grant military assistance under provisions of Foreign Assistance Act of 1961, or successor legislation, or to funds provided by the recipient government, and prescribed Dec. 31, 1971, as termination date for executive exercise of naval vessel loan authority under this section.

Section 1878zz–1, Pub. L. 91–682, §3, Jan. 12, 1971, 84 Stat. 2066, authorized new loans and loan extensions for five year periods, and additional five year extensions, terminable for acts of warfare by armed forces of borrowing country against a country party to a mutual defense treaty ratified by the United States and earlier because of defense requirements of the United States.

Section 1878zz–2, Pub. L. 91–682, §4, Jan. 12, 1971, 84 Stat. 2067, required Secretary of Defense to determine loans or extension of loans to be in best interest of United States and to report loans or extensions to Congress.

Section 1878zz–3, Pub. L. 91–682, §5, Jan. 12, 1971, 84 Stat. 2067, authorized promulgation of rules and regulations.

PUB. L. 92–270, APR. 6, 1972, 86 STAT. 118

§§ 1878zz–4 to 1878zz–8. Omitted

CODIFICATION

Section 1878zz–4, Pub. L. 92–270, §1, Apr. 6, 1972, 86 Stat. 118, authorized loan of additional naval vessels, with or without reimbursement, and subject to appropriate terms and conditions, as follows: five destroyers and two submarines, Spanish Government; one destroyer and two submarines, Turkish Government; two destroyers, Greek Government; two destroyers, Republic of Korea; and two submarines, Italian Government; provided for the charging of activation, rehabilitation, and outfitting expenses to funds programed for recipient government as grant military assistance under provisions of Foreign Assistance Act of 1961, or successor legislation, or to funds provided by recipient government; and prescribed Dec. 31, 1974, as termination date for executive exercise of naval vessel loan authority under this section.

Section 1878zz–5, Pub. L. 92–270, §2, Apr. 6, 1972, 86 Stat. 118, limited loan of ships to five-year period, required designation by Secretary of Defense of place of return, and made loans terminable for acts of warfare by armed forces of borrowing country against a country party to a mutual defense treaty ratified by United States and earlier where no longer contributory to defense requirements of United States.

Section 1878zz–6, Pub. L. 92–270, §3, Apr. 6, 1972, 86 Stat. 118, required Secretary of Defense to determine loans to be in best interest of United States and to report loans and loan extensions to Congress.

Section 1878zz–7, Pub. L. 92–270, §4, Apr. 6, 1972, 86 Stat. 118, authorized promulgation of rules and regulations.

Section 1878zz–8, Pub. L. 92–270, §5, Apr. 6, 1972, 86 Stat. 118, prohibited construction of a loan as a commitment to defense of borrowing country.

ACT AUG. 7, 1953, CH. 347, 67 STAT. 471

§ 1879. Omitted

CODIFICATION

Section, act Aug. 7, 1953, ch. 347, 67 Stat. 471, provided for loan of two submarines to Turkish Government for a five year period, subject to agreement for their return in substantially the original condition, and for charging activation expenses to funds programed for Turkish Government under Mutual Security Act.

HOUSING AND RENT ACTS

ACTS JUNE 30, 1947, CH. 163, 61 STAT. 193; MAR. 30, 1948, CH. 161, 62 STAT. 93; MAR. 30, 1949, CH. 42, 63 STAT. 18; JUNE 23, 1950, CH. 354, 64 STAT. 255

TITLE I—AMENDMENTS TO EXISTING LAW

Sec.
1881 to 1884. Omitted.

TITLE II—MAXIMUM RENTS

1891 to 1894. Omitted.

TITLE I—AMENDMENTS TO EXISTING LAW

§§ 1881 to 1884. Omitted

CODIFICATION

Section 1881, acts June 30, 1947, ch. 163, title I, §1, 61 Stat. 193; Mar. 30, 1948, ch. 161, title I, §2, 62 Stat. 93, repealed in part Veterans' Emergency Housing Act of 1946, sections 1821, 1822(b)–(d), 1823 to 1829, 1831, and 1832 of this Appendix, and provided continuing allocations made or priorities granted for delivery of housing materials or facilities under regulation issued under the Act and before June 30, 1947.

Section 1882, act June 30, 1947, ch. 163, title I, §2, 61 Stat. 193, extended the limitation date of the mortgage insurance provisions of section 1738(a) of Title 12, Banks and Banking, from June 30, 1947 to Mar. 31, 1948.

Section 1883, act June 30, 1947, ch. 163, title I, §3, 61 Stat. 193, amended title VI of the National Housing Act, as amended, sections 1736 to 1743 of Title 12, Banks and Banking, by adding section 609, relating to insurance of loans for manufacture of houses, the provisions of which are classified to section 1744 of Title 12.

Section 1884, acts June 30, 1947, ch. 163, title I, §4, 61 Stat. 195; Feb. 27, 1948, ch. 77, §1, 62 Stat. 37; Mar. 30, 1948, ch. 161, title I, §3, 62 Stat. 93; Mar. 30, 1949, ch. 42, title I, §2, 63 Stat. 18; June 23, 1950, ch. 354, §2, 64 Stat. 255; June 30, 1951, ch. 198, §2(a), 65 Stat. 110; July 31, 1951, ch. 275, title II, §§202(a), 211, 65 Stat. 145; June 30, 1952, ch. 530, title II, §201(a), 66 Stat. 306; Apr. 30, 1953, ch. 31, §2, 67 Stat. 24, which provided for a priority in sale or rental of housing accommodations for veterans of World War II and the Korean conflict, terminated by its own terms.

SHORT TITLE OF 1953 AMENDMENT

Act Apr. 30, 1953, ch. 31, §1, 67 Stat. 23, provided that act Apr. 30, 1953, be cited as the Housing and Rent Act of 1953.

SHORT TITLE OF 1950 AMENDMENT

Act June 23, 1950, ch. 354, §1, 64 Stat. 255, provided that act June 23, 1950, be cited as the Housing and Rent Act of 1950.

SHORT TITLE OF 1949 AMENDMENT

Act Mar. 30, 1949, ch. 42, title I, §1, 63 Stat. 18, provided that act Mar. 30, 1949, be cited as the Housing and Rent Act of 1949.

SHORT TITLE OF 1948 AMENDMENT

Act Mar. 30, 1948, ch. 161, title I, §1, 62 Stat. 93, provided that act Mar. 30, 1948 be cited as the Housing and Rent Act of 1948.

SHORT TITLE

Act June 30, 1947, ch. 163, title II, §213, 61 Stat. 201, provided that act June 30, 1947, be cited as the Housing and Rent Act of 1947.

SEPARABILITY

Act Mar. 30, 1948, ch. 161, title III, §305, 62 Stat. 100, provided that if provisions of act Mar. 30, 1948, or the application of such provisions to any person or circumstances be held invalid, the validity of the remainder of the Act, and the applicability of such provision to other persons or circumstances, shall not be affected thereby.

Act June 30, 1947, ch. 163, title III, §301, 61 Stat. 201, provided that if any provision of act June 30, 1947, or the application of such provisions to any person or circumstances be held invalid, the validity of the remainder of the Act, and the applicability of such provision to other persons or circumstances, shall not be affected thereby.

TITLE II—MAXIMUM RENTS

§§ 1891 to 1894. Omitted

CODIFICATION

Sections 1891 to 1894 terminated Sept. 30, 1952, with certain exceptions, pursuant to section 1894 of this Appendix.

Section 1891, act June 30, 1947, ch. 163, title II, §201, 61 Stat. 196, stated the congressional declaration of policy for controls for rental housing accommodations in defense-rental areas.

Section 1892, acts June 30, 1947, ch. 163, title II, §202, 61 Stat. 196; Mar. 10, 1948, ch. 161, title II, §201, 62 Stat. 93; Mar. 30, 1949, ch. 42, title II, §201, 63 Stat. 19; July 31, 1951, ch. 275, title II, §§202(a), 206, 207(a), (b), 208, 65 Stat. 145, 148, defined terms used in sections 1891 to 1894 and 1895 to 1902 of this Appendix.

Section 1893, acts June 30, 1947, ch. 163, title II, §203, 61 Stat. 197; Mar. 30, 1949, ch. 42, title II, §202, 63 Stat. 21; July 31, 1951, ch. 275, title II, §202(a), 65 Stat. 145, terminated rent control under the Emergency Price Control Act of 1942 after July 1, 1947.

Section 1894, acts June 30, 1947, ch. 163, title II, §204, 61 Stat. 197; Feb. 27, 1948, ch. 77, §2, 62 Stat. 37; Mar. 30, 1948, ch. 161, title II, §202, 62 Stat. 94; Mar. 30, 1949, ch. 42, title II, §203, 63 Stat. 21; June 23, 1950, ch. 354, §§3–5, 64 Stat. 255; Dec. 20, 1950, ch. 1139, §§1, 2, 64 Stat. 1113; Mar. 23, 1951, ch. 14, 65 Stat. 7; June 30, 1951, ch. 198, §2(b), (c), 65 Stat. 111; July 31, 1951, ch. 275, title II, §§201, 203(a), (b), 205, 207(c), 209, 65 Stat. 144, 145, 148, 149; June 30, 1952, ch. 530, title II, §§201(b), 202, 66 Stat. 306; July 15, 1952, ch. 758, ch. XII, §1201, 66 Stat. 657; Apr. 30, 1953, ch. 31, §§3–7, 67 Stat. 24, provided for rent control under sections 1891 to 1894 and 1895 to 1902 of this Appendix, prescribed procedures, empowered the President to remove controls, to promulgate rules and regulations and to create local advisory boards, and declared that the provisions of such sections shall cease to be in effect at the close of Sept. 30, 1952, except for certain areas where they ceased to be in effect at the close of Apr. 30, 1953.

§ 1894a. Defense Areas Advisory Committee; creation; composition; duties

The Director of Defense Mobilization[1] is authorized to appoint a Defense Areas Advisory Committee to advise him in connection with the exercise of any function or authority vested in him by section 204(*l*) of the Housing and Rent Act of 1947, as amended [section 1894(*l*) of this Appendix], or section 101 of the Defense Housing and Community Facilities and Services Act of 1951, as amended [42 U.S.C. 1591], or by delegation thereunder, with respect to determining any area to be a critical defense housing area. Any committee so appointed shall consist, in addition to a chairman, of representatives of the Department of Defense and the Housing and Home Finance Agency.[1] Any Federal agency shall, to the fullest practicable extent, furnish such information in its possession to the Defense Areas Advisory Committee as such Committee may request from time to time relevant to its operations.

(June 30, 1952, ch. 530, title II, §203, 66 Stat. 307; Apr. 30, 1953, ch. 31, §10, 67 Stat. 25.)

REFERENCES IN TEXT

Section 204(*l*) of the Housing and Rent Act of 1947, as amended [section 1894(*l*) of this Appendix], referred to in text, was omitted from the Code.

[1] See Transfer of Functions note below.

AMENDMENTS

1953—Act Apr. 30, 1953, amended last sentence generally, eliminating reference to Office of Rent Stabilization.

TRANSFER OF FUNCTIONS

Functions vested by any statute in Director of Defense Mobilization or Office of Defense Mobilization provided for in Executive Order No. 10193, eff. Dec. 16, 1950, 15 F.R. 9031, transferred to Director of Office of Defense Mobilization by Reorg. Plan No. 3 of 1953, §2(d), eff. June 12, 1953, 18 F.R. 3375, 67 Stat. 634, set out in the Appendix to Title 5, Government Organization and Employees.

Functions vested in Office of Defense Mobilization or Director of Office of Defense Mobilization transferred to Office of Emergency Planning by section 2 of Reorg. Plan No. 1 of 1958, eff. July 1, 1958, 23 F.R. 4991, 72 Stat. 1799, set out under section 5195 of Title 42, The Public Health and Welfare.

Office of Emergency Planning changed to Office of Emergency Preparedness pursuant to section 402 of Pub. L. 90–608, Oct. 21, 1968, 82 Stat. 1194, which provided that references in laws to Office of Emergency Planning after Oct. 21, 1968, should be deemed references to Office of Emergency Preparedness.

Office of Emergency Preparedness, including offices of Director, Deputy Director, Assistant Directors, and Regional Directors, abolished and functions vested by law in Office of Emergency Preparedness transferred to President by sections 1 and 3(a)(1) of Reorg. Plan No. 1 of 1973, eff. July 1, 1973, 38 F.R. 9579, 87 Stat. 1089, set out under section 5195 of Title 42, The Public Health and Welfare.

Functions vested in Director of Office of Emergency Preparedness as of June 30, 1973, by Executive Order, proclamation, or other directive issued by or on behalf of President or otherwise, with certain exceptions, transferred to Administrator of General Services, effective July 1, 1973, by Ex. Ord. No. 11725, §3, eff. June 29, 1973, 38 F.R. 17175, formerly set out under section 2271 of this Appendix.

Housing and Home Finance Agency lapsed and functions, powers, and duties transferred to Secretary of Housing and Urban Development who was authorized to delegate such functions, powers, and duties to such officers and employees of Department of Housing and Urban Development as Secretary may delegate, see sections 3531 note, 3534, and 3535 of Title 42, The Public Health and Welfare.

TERMINATION OF ADVISORY COMMITTEES

Advisory committees in existence on Jan. 5, 1973, to terminate not later than the expiration of the 2-year period following Jan. 5, 1973, unless, in the case of a committee established by the President or an officer of the Federal Government, such committee is renewed by appropriate action prior to the expiration of such 2-year period, or in the case of a committee established by the Congress, its duration is otherwise provided by law. Advisory committees established after Jan. 5, 1973, to terminate not later than the expiration of the 2-year period beginning on the date of their establishment, unless, in the case of a committee established by the President or an officer of the Federal Government, such committee is renewed by appropriate action prior to the expiration of such 2-year period, or in the case of a committee established by the Congress, its duration is otherwise provided by law. See section 14 of Pub. L. 92–463, Oct. 6, 1972, 86 Stat. 776, set out in the Appendix to Title 5, Government Organization and Employees.

§§1895 to 1903. Omitted

CODIFICATION

Sections 1895 to 1903 terminated Sept. 30, 1952, with certain exceptions, pursuant to section 1894 of this Appendix.

Section 1895, acts June 30, 1947, ch. 163, title II, §205, 61 Stat. 199; Mar. 30, 1949, ch. 42, title II, §204, 63 Stat. 27; July 31, 1951, ch. 275, title II, §204, 65 Stat. 147, authorized suits for damages for violations of sections 1891 to 1894 and 1895 to 1902 of this Appendix.

Section 1896, acts June 30, 1947, ch. 163, title II, §206, 61 Stat. 199; Mar. 30, 1948, ch. 161, title II, §203, 62 Stat. 98; Mar. 30, 1949, ch. 42, title II, §205, 63 Stat. 27; July 31, 1951, ch. 275, title II, §§202(a), (c), 205, 65 Stat. 144, 148, related to prohibitions and enforcement.

Section 1897, act June 30, 1947, ch. 163, title II, §207, 61 Stat. 200, prohibited maintenance of actions for certain past violations.

Section 1898, acts June 30, 1947, ch. 163, title II, §208, 61 Stat. 200; July 31, 1951, ch. 275, title II, §202(2), (d), 65 Stat. 145; Apr. 30, 1953, ch. 31, §8, 67 Stat. 25, related to property, personnel, and appropriations.

Section 1899, acts June 30, 1947, ch. 163, title II, §209, 61 Stat. 200; Mar. 30, 1948, ch. 161, title II, §204, 62 Stat. 98; Mar. 30, 1949, ch. 42, title II, §206, 63 Stat. 29; July 13, 1951, ch. 275, title II, §202(a), 65 Stat. 145, empowered the President to regulate speculative or manipulative renting or leasing practices.

Section 1900, acts June 30, 1947, ch. 163, title II, §210, 61 Stat. 201; Mar. 30, 1948, ch. 161, title II, §301, 62 Stat. 99, amended section 2(a) of the Administrative Procedure Act.

Section 1901, act June 30, 1947, ch. 163, title II, §211, 61 Stat. 201, stated the territorial applicability of sections 1891 to 1894 and 1895 to 1902 of this Appendix.

Section 1902, act June 30, 1947, ch. 163, title II, §212, 61 Stat. 201, prescribed the effective date of sections 1891 to 1894 and 1895 to 1902 of this Appendix.

Section 1903, act Mar. 30, 1948, ch. 161, title III, §302, 62 Stat. 99, provided that nothing in act Mar. 30, 1948, shall be construed to require any person to offer any housing accommodations for rent.

§1904. Repealed. Mar. 30, 1949, ch. 42, title III, §302, 63 Stat. 29

Section, act Mar. 30, 1948, ch. 161, title III, §303, 62 Stat. 100, related to reimposition of rent ceilings after decontrol.

EFFECTIVE DATE OF REPEAL

Repeal effective Apr. 1, 1949, see section 305 of act Mar. 30, 1949.

§§1905 to 1910. Omitted

CODIFICATION

Section 1905, act Mar. 30, 1948, ch. 161, title III, §304, 62 Stat. 100, amended section 1413a of Title 42, The Public Health and Welfare, relating to recovery of possession of housing accommodations.

Section 1906, act Mar. 30, 1948, ch. 161, title III, §306, 62 Stat. 100, prescribed effective date of Housing and Rent Act of 1948.

Section 1907, act Mar. 30, 1949, ch. 42, title III, §301, 63 Stat. 29, related to non-offer of housing accommodations.

Section 1908, act Mar. 30, 1949, ch. 42, title III, §303, 63 Stat. 29, related to separability of provisions.

Section 1909, act Mar. 30, 1949, ch. 42, title III, §304, 63 Stat. 29, amended section 1738(a) of Title 12, Banks and Banking.

Section 1910, act Mar. 30, 1949, ch. 42, title III, §305, 63 Stat. 29, prescribed effective date of Housing and Rent Act of 1949.

STABILIZATION OF ECONOMY AND COMMODITY PRICES

ACT DEC. 30, 1947, CH. 526, 61 STAT. 945

§1911. Declaration of purpose

The purposes of this joint resolution [sections 1911 to 1919 of this Appendix] are to aid in stabilizing the economy of the United States, to aid in curbing inflationary tendencies, to promote the orderly and equitable distribution of goods and facilities, and to aid in preventing maldistribution of goods and facilities which basically affect the cost of living or industrial production.

(Dec. 30, 1947, ch. 526, §1, 61 Stat. 945.)

EX. ORD. NO. 9919. DELEGATION OF AUTHORITY AND ESTABLISHMENT OF PROCEDURES UNDER SECTIONS 1911 TO 1919 OF THIS APPENDIX

Ex. Ord. No. 9919, Jan. 3, 1948, 13 F.R. 59, provided:

By virtue of the authority vested in me by the joint resolution approved December 30, 1947 (Public Law 395, 80th Congress) [sections 1911 to 1919 of this Appendix], and as President of the United States, it is hereby ordered as follows:

1. The authority to consult with representatives of industry, business, and agriculture with a view to encouraging the making of voluntary agreements or plans provided for in section 2 of the said joint resolution of December 30, 1947 [former section 1912 of this Appendix] (hereinafter referred to as the joint resolution), and the authority to approve any such agreements or plans and to make written requests for compliance with any such agreements or plans is delegated severally to the Secretary of the Interior, the Secretary of Agriculture, the Secretary of Commerce, and the Director of the Office of Defense Transportation as provided in paragraphs 2, 3, 4, and 5 hereof: *Provided, however*, that no such agreement or plan shall be approved by any of such officers unless it is first submitted to and approved by the Attorney General. The consultation above referred to may be through advisory committees approved by the appropriate governmental officer or agency as representative of the various segments of the industry involved. Prior to submitting any such proposed agreement or plan to the Attorney General the appropriate governmental officer or agency shall give industry, labor, and the public generally an opportunity to present their views with respect to the agreement or plan. The submission of the proposed agreement or plan to the Attorney General shall be accompanied by the favorable recommendation of the head of the appropriate department or agency and by a statement of (a) the circumstances which require the proposed agreement or plan, (b) the means by which the agreement or plan will be carried out, (c) the effect of the agreement or plan on persons and industries affected, including where appropriate the proposed degree of curtailment in amount and prospective use of any material, commodity, or product by any processor or user thereof, and the formulae for such curtailment, (d) the criteria used in the establishment of such formulae, and (e) the factual evidence on which the recommendation for approval is made, showing which information, if any, is subject to restrictions for reasons of military security.

2 (a). The authority delegated to the Secretary of the Interior by paragraph 1 hereof shall be exercised by him with respect to priority, allocation, and inventory control of fuels.

(b). For the purposes of this order the term "fuels" means coal, coke, petroleum and petroleum products, and natural and manufactured gas.

3 (a). The authority delegated to the Secretary of Agriculture by paragraph 1 hereof shall be exercised by him with respect to priority, allocation, and inventory control of agricultural commodities and with respect to speculative trading on commodity exchanges.

(b). For the purposes of this order, the term "agricultural commodities" means all commodities and products, simple, mixed, or compound, or complements to such commodities or products that are or may be eaten or drunk by human beings or animals, irrespective of other uses to which such commodities or products may be put, and at all stages of processing from the raw commodity to the product thereof in a vendible form for immediate human or animal consumption, but exclusive of such commodities and products as the Secretary of Agriculture shall determine. For the purposes of this order, the term "agricultural commodities" shall also include all starches, sugars, fats and oils of animal, vegetable, or marine origin (including oil seeds and other oil bearing materials, fatty acids, soap and soap powder), cotton, tobacco, wool, hemp, flax, fiber, and alcohol, and also such other commodities and products as the President may designate.

4 (a). The authority delegated to the Director of the Office of Defense Transportation by paragraph 1 hereof shall be exercised by him with respect to allocation of transportation facilities and equipment.

(b). The powers, authority, and discretion conferred on the President by section 4(a) of the joint resolution [section 1914(a) of this Appendix] with respect to the use of transportation equipment and facilities by rail carriers are hereby included within the powers, authority, and discretion delegated to the Director of the Office of Defense Transportation under Executive Order No. 8989 of December 18, 1941 (6 F.R. 6725), as amended by Executive Order No. 9389 of October 18, 1943 (8 F.R. 14183), Executive Order No. 9156 of May 2, 1942 (7 F.R. 3349), Executive Order No. 9214 of August 5, 1942 (7 F.R. 6097), and Executive Order No. 9729 of May 23, 1946 (11 F.R. 5641). The said Executive orders are amended accordingly.

5. The authority delegated to the Secretary of Commerce by paragraph 1 hereof shall be exercised by him with respect to priority, allocation, and inventory control of scarce commodities which basically affect the cost of living or industrial production, other than fuels as provided in paragraph 2, agricultural commodities as provided in paragraph 3, and transportation facilities and equipment as provided in paragraph 4.

6. The Secretary of Agriculture is hereby authorized to carry out a program for the conservation of food and feed and for that purpose to exercise the authority conferred upon the President by section 8 of the joint resolution [section 1918 of this Appendix].

7. The Secretary of Commerce is hereby authorized to continue exercising the powers, authority, and discretion conferred upon the President by section 6 of the act of July 2, 1940, 54 Stat. 714, as amended [section 701 of this Appendix]. Such powers, authority, and discretion, and the powers, authority, and discretion vested in the President by section 3 of the joint resolution [section 1913 of this Appendix] are hereby included within the delegation made to the Secretary of Commerce by Executive Order No. 9630 of September 27, 1945 (10 F.R. 12245), and the said Executive order is modified accordingly.

8. Each governmental officer or agency exercising authority delegated under this order shall, in exercising such authority, consult with other agencies or committees having special information or sources of such information about the supply of or demand for the materials, commodities, or facilities involved and with other agencies or committees having responsibilities related to such authority. Each agency shall establish such committees and other working groups as may be appropriate to consult with and obtain the advice of other agencies.

9. Nothing in this order shall be deemed to affect the powers, authority, or discretion delegated to the Secretary of Agriculture by Executive Order No. 9915 of December 30, 1947.

HARRY S TRUMAN.

§§1912 to 1915. Omitted

CODIFICATION

Section 1912, acts Dec. 30, 1947, ch. 526, §2, 61 Stat. 945; Feb. 9, 1949, ch. 6, 63 Stat. 5, relating to voluntary agreements, expired by its own terms on Sept. 30, 1949.

Section 1913, act Dec. 30, 1947, ch. 526, §3, 61 Stat. 946, amending section 701 of this Appendix, expired on Feb. 28, 1949, when section 701 expired.

Section 1914, act Dec. 30, 1947, ch. 526, §4, 61 Stat. 946, relating to allocation of transportation facilities and grain, expired on Feb. 28, 1949, as to transportation facilities and on Jan. 31, 1948, as to grain.

Section 1915, act Dec. 30, 1947, ch. 526, §5, 61 Stat. 946, relating to delegation of President's authority under sections 701 and 1912 of this Appendix, expired with the expiration of those sections.

§1916. Critical shortages; recommendations by President; public hearings

(a) Whenever the President shall determine that there is or threatens to be a critical shortage of any raw material, commodity, or product which jeopardizes the health or safety of the people of the United States or its national security or welfare and that there is no prospect that such critical shortage may soon be remedied by an increase in the available supply without additional governmental action and that the situation cannot be solved by voluntary agreement under the provisions of this Act [sections 1911 to 1919 of this Appendix], he may prepare proposed measures for conserving such raw material, commodity, or product which he shall submit to the Congress in the following form:

(1) A statement of the circumstances which, in the President's judgment, require the proposed conservation measures.

(2) A detailed procedure for the administration of the proposed measures including the additional budget and additional personnel required for their enforcement.

(3) The proposed degree of curtailment in current and prospective use of each such raw material, commodity, or product by each processor and/or user thereof, including the specific formulae proposed for such curtailment with respect to each class or classes of processors or users and the criteria used in the establishment of such formulae.

(4) A complete record of the factual evidence upon which his recommendations are based, including all information provided by any agency of the Federal Government which may have been made available to him in the course of his consideration of the matter.

(b) Within fifteen days after the submission of such proposed conservation measures, the Joint Economic Committee shall conduct public hearings thereon and shall make such recommendations to the Congress for legislative action as in its judgment the recommendations of the President and any additional information disclosed at the public hearings may require.

(Dec. 30, 1947, ch. 526, §6, 61 Stat. 947; June 18, 1956, ch. 399, §2, 70 Stat. 290.)

AMENDMENTS

1956—Subsec. (b). Act June 18, 1956, changed "Joint Committee on the Economic Report" to "Joint Economic Committee".

§1917. Repealed. Pub. L. 104–127, title II, §229, Apr. 4, 1996, 110 Stat. 963

Section, act Dec. 30, 1947, ch. 526, §7, 61 Stat. 947, authorized Commodity Credit Corporation to carry out projects to stimulate and increase production of foods, agricultural commodities, and products thereof, in non-European foreign countries.

§1918. Food and conservation program; appropriations; administrative expenses

(a) In order to alleviate shortages in foods and feeds, and to assist in stabilizing prices, the President shall carry out a program for the conservation of food and feed. In carrying out such program, the President is authorized, through the dissemination of information, educational and other campaigns, the furnishing of assistance, and such other voluntary and cooperative measures as he deems necessary or appropriate, to encourage and promote the efficient utilization, care, and preservation of food and feed, the elimination of practices which waste food and feed, the control and eradication of insects and rodents, the consumption of less of these foods and feeds which are in short supply and more of those foods and feeds which are in abundant supply, and other conservation practices. The authority herein conferred may be exercised by the President through such departments, agencies, independent establishments, and officials of the Federal Government and such State, local, and private agencies as he may determine.

(b) There is hereby authorized to be appropriated to the President such sums as may be necessary to carry out this section. To enable the President to carry out this section for the remainder of the fiscal year ending June 30, 1948, there is made available not to exceed $1,000,000 from any funds made available by the Congress for carrying out Public Law 84, Eightieth Congress, or from any funds made available by the Congress for interim foreign aid. Funds made available for the purpose of this section may be used for necessary administrative expenses, including personal services in the District of Columbia and elsewhere, purchase or hire of motor vehicles, temporary or intermittent services of experts or consultants or organizations thereof, including stenographic reporting services, by contract, without regard to the civil service and classification laws (the compensation of any such individual not to exceed $50 per day). Funds made available for the purposes of this section may be allotted for any of the purposes of this section to any department, agency, or independent establishment of the Government, or transferred to any other agency requested to assist in carrying out this section. Funds allotted to any department, agency, or independent establishment of the Government shall be available for obligation and expenditure in accordance with the laws governing obligations and expenditures of the department, agency, or independent establishment, or organizational unit thereof concerned, and without regard to sections 3709 and 3648 of the Revised Statutes, as amended [41 U.S.C. 5; 31 U.S.C. 3324(a), (b)].

(Dec. 30, 1947, ch. 526, §8, 61 Stat. 947.)

REFERENCES IN TEXT

Public Law 84, Eightieth Congress, referred to in subsec. (b), is act May 31, 1947, ch. 90, 61 Stat. 125, which was classified generally to chapter 17 (§1411 et seq.) of Title 22, Foreign Relations and Intercourse, and which was repealed by act Aug. 26, 1954, ch. 937, title V, §542(a)(2), 68 Stat. 861. For complete classification of this Act to the Code, see Tables.

The civil service laws, referred to in subsec. (b), are set forth in Title 5, Government Organization and Employees. See, particularly, section 3301 et seq. of Title 5.

The classification laws, referred to in subsec. (b), are classified generally to chapter 51 (§5101 et seq.) and to subchapter III (§5331 et seq.) of chapter 53 of Title 5.

Section 3648 of the Revised Statutes, as amended, referred to in subsec. (b), which was classified to section 529 of former Title 31, was repealed by Pub. L. 97–258, §5(b), Sept. 13, 1982, 96 Stat. 1068, and reenacted by the first section thereof as section 3324(a) and (b) of Title 31, Money and Finance.

§1919. Authorizations for appropriations

There is authorized to be appropriated such amounts as may be necessary for purposes of carrying out the provisions of this joint resolution [sections 1911 to 1919 of this Appendix].

(Dec. 30, 1947, ch. 526, §9, 61 Stat. 948.)

DOMESTIC RUBBER-PRODUCING INDUSTRY

ACT MAR. 31, 1948, CH. 166, 62 STAT. 101

§§1921 to 1938. Omitted

CODIFICATION

Sections 1921 to 1938 terminated May 1, 1955, pursuant to section 1938 of this Appendix.

Section 1921, act Mar. 31, 1948, ch. 166, §2, 62 Stat. 102, related to Congressional declaration of policy.

Section 1922, act Mar. 31, 1948, ch. 166, §3, 62 Stat. 102, authorized certain controls over natural and synthetic rubber and rubber products.

Section 1923, act Mar. 31, 1948, ch. 166, §4, 62 Stat. 102, related to importation and exportation of rubber products.

Section 1924, act Mar. 31, 1948, ch. 166, §5, 62 Stat. 103, related to maintenance of domestic rubber-producing capacity.

Section 1925, act Mar. 31, 1948, ch. 166, §6, 62 Stat. 103, related to rubber research and development.

Section 1926, act Mar. 31, 1948, ch. 166, §7, 62 Stat. 103, related to operation of rubber-producing facilities by the Government.

Section 1927, act Mar. 31, 1948, ch. 166, §8, 62 Stat. 104, related to placing in adequate stand-by condition rubber-producing facilities and their maintenance.

Section 1928, acts Mar. 31, 1948, ch. 166, §9, 62 Stat. 105; June 24, 1950, ch. 357, §1(a), 64 Stat. 256; June 23, 1952, ch. 453, §1(a), 66 Stat. 154, related to disposal of Government-owned rubber-producing facilities.

Section 1929, act Mar. 31, 1948, ch. 166, §10, 62 Stat. 1929, provided administrative provisions respecting rules and regulations; delegation of powers and duties by President; consolidation of powers and functions, creation of corporation, powers, subscription to capital stock; transfer of facilities, personnel, funds, etc.; and annual report.

Section 1930, act Mar. 31, 1948, ch. 166, §11, 62 Stat. 106, related to patent pooling and use of technical information.

Section 1931, act Mar. 31, 1948, ch. 166, §12, 62 Stat. 106, related to information, records, etc., for enforcement or administrative purposes; oaths, affidavits, subpenas, etc.; witnesses; testimony; publication of information; and penalties.

Section 1932, act Mar. 31, 1948, ch. 166, §13, 62 Stat. 107, related to penalties.

Section 1933, act Mar. 31, 1948, ch. 166, §14, 62 Stat. 107, related to jurisdiction of courts, venue, process and costs.

Section 1934, act Mar. 31, 1948, ch. 166, §15, 62 Stat. 107, was an exculpatory clause.

Section 1935, act Mar. 31, 1948, ch. 166, §16, 62 Stat. 108, related to exemption from Administrative Procedure Act. Act Mar. 31, 1948, ch. 166, §16, 62 Stat. 108, formerly classified to section 1935 of this Appendix, was repealed by Pub. L. 89–554, §8(a), Sept. 6, 1966, 80 Stat. 654.

Section 1936, act Mar. 31, 1948, ch. 166, §18, 62 Stat. 1936, defined the terms "natural rubber", "synthetic rubber", "general-purpose synthetic rubber", "special-purpose synthetic rubber", "rubber-producing facilities", "rated production capacity", "component materials", "stand-by condition", "person" and "United States".

Section 1937, act Mar. 31, 1948, ch. 166, §19, 62 Stat. 109, related to appropriations.

Section 1938, acts Mar. 31, 1948, ch. 166, §20, 62 Stat. 109; June 24, 1950, ch. 357, §1(b), 64 Stat. 256; June 23, 1952, ch. 453, §1(b), 66 Stat. 154; Aug. 7, 1953, ch. 338, §22, 67 Stat. 415, provided that sections 1921 to 1938 of this Appendix should become effective on Apr. 1, 1948, and should remain in effect until May 1, 1955.

TRANSFER OF FUNCTIONS

Ex. Ord. No. 9942, Apr. 1, 1948, 13 F.R. 1823, as amended by Ex. Ord. No. 10539, June 22, 1954, 19 F.R. 3827, which provided for the performance of certain functions under sections 1921 to 1938 of this Appendix by the Secretary of Commerce and by the Federal Facilities Corporation as successor of the Reconstruction Finance Corporation, was revoked by Ex. Ord. No. 12553, Feb. 25, 1986, 51 F.R. 7237.

Act July 30, 1953, ch. 282, title I, §107(a)(1), (b), 67 Stat. 231, provided for Presidential transfer of all functions, powers, duties, and authority of the Reconstruction Finance Corporation under sections 1921 to 1938 of this Appendix not later than June 30, 1954, and for the transfer of all assets, funds, contracts, loans, liabilities, commitments, authorizations, allocations, personnel, and records of the Reconstruction Finance Corporation which the Director of the Bureau of the Budget shall determine to be primarily related to, and necessary for, the exercise of such functions, powers, duties, and authority, to the officer or agency of the Government to which such functions, powers, duties, and authority are transferred.

EXTENSION WITH RESPECT TO DISPOSAL OF COPOLYMER PLANT AT INSTITUTE, WEST VIRGINIA

Act Aug. 9, 1955, ch. 696, §3, 69 Stat. 629, provided that: "Notwithstanding the provisions of sections 14 and 22 of the Rubber Producing Facilities Disposal Act of 1953 [sections 1941*l* and 1941t of this Appendix], the Rubber Act of 1948, as amended [sections 1921 to 1938 of this Appendix], is hereby extended with respect to the rubber-producing facilities covered by this Act [section 1941x of this Appendix], to the close of the day of transfer of possession of Plancor Numbered 980 to a purchaser in accordance with the provisions of section 26 of the Rubber Producing Facilities Disposal Act [section 1941x of this Appendix]."

EXTENSION WITH RESPECT TO DISPOSAL OF COPOLYMER PLANT AT BAYTOWN, TEXAS

Act Mar. 31, 1955, ch. 19, §3, 69 Stat. 16, provided that: "Notwithstanding the provisions of sections 14 and 22 of the Rubber Producing Facilities Disposal Act of 1953 [sections 1941*l* and 1941t of this Appendix], the Rubber Act of 1948, as amended [sections 1921 to 1938 of this Appendix], is hereby extended with respect to the rubber-producing facilities covered by this Act [section 1941w of this Appendix], to the close of the day of transfer of possession of Plancor Numbered 877 to a purchaser in accordance with the provisions of section 25 of the Rubber Producing Facilities Disposal Act [section 1941w of this Appendix]: *Provided*, That if no such transfer is made, the Rubber Act of 1948, as amended [sections 1921 to 1938 of this Appendix], is hereby extended to the close of the day upon which Plancor Numbered 877 is placed in standby condition pursuant to the provisions of this Act."

DISSOLUTION OF FEDERAL FACILITIES CORPORATION

Pub. L. 87–190, Aug. 30, 1961, 75 Stat. 418, provided:

"[SEC. 1. *Administration of sales of rubber producing facilities by Administrator of General Services; exercise of authority of Rubber Producing Facilities Disposal Commission by Administrator; transfer of contracts from Federal Facilities Corporation to Administrator*]. That, subject to the provisions of section 2 of this Act, the Administrator of General Services is hereby designated to administer the contracts of sale of the Government-owned rubber producing facilities made pursuant to the Rubber Producing Facilities Disposal Act of 1953 (67 Stat. 414) [section 1941 et seq. of this Appendix], as amended, and to administer other matters involving the Rubber Producing Facilities Disposal Commission, including the exercise of all powers and authority conferred upon the said Commission by section 6 of the Act of March 21, 1956 (70 Stat. 51, 53) [set out as a note under section 1941f of this Appendix], and also including the winding up of the affairs of the Commission. The said contracts are hereby transferred from Federal Facilities Corporation to the Administrator of General Services.

"SEC. 2. [*National defense as guide for execution of national security clause in rubber producing facilities' contracts of sale*]. The administration of the national security clause contained in the contracts of sale referred to in section 1 of this Act shall be carried out in accordance with the needs and requirements of the national defense as determined by the Secretary of Defense.

"SEC. 3. [*Transfer of records, assets and liabilities of Rubber Producing Facilities Disposal Commission*]. The records and the remaining assets and liabilities of the Rubber Producing Facilities Disposal Commission are hereby transferred from the Federal Facilities Corporation to the Administrator of General Services for use of the Administrator in connection with the administration or performance of his functions and duties under sections 1 and 2 of this Act, or for other disposition as may be determined, consonant with law, by the Administrator.

"SEC. 4. [*Transfer of property, assets and liabilities of Federal Facilities Corporation to Administrator for liquidation; transfer of functions; assumption of liabilities; deposits into Treasury; cancellation of obligations*].

"(a) Notwithstanding any other provision of law, the books of account, records, documents, property, assets and liabilities of every kind and nature, including, but not limited to, all funds, notes (and accrued interest thereon), mortgages, deeds of trust, contracts, commitments, claims, and causes of action, of Federal Facilities Corporation are transferred to the Administrator of General Services for liquidation and, in connection therewith, there are also transferred to the Administrator, notwithstanding the provisions of section 6 of this Act, all functions, powers, duties, authority, rights, and immunities now vested in, or available or applicable to, the Corporation which shall be performed, exercised, and administered by the Administrator in the same manner and to the same extent as if the same were performed, exercised, and administered by the Corporation. The Administrator shall assume and be subject, in his official capacity, to all liabilities and commitments, whether arising out of contract or otherwise, of the corporation but he shall pay into the Treasury, as miscellaneous receipts, all future receipts and all remaining funds of the Corporation transferred to, or received by, him pursuant to this Act.

"(b) Any obligation of General Services Administration to Federal Facilities Corporation existing by virtue of the provisions of section 5(b) of the joint resolution, 'To authorize the disposal of the Government-owned tin smelter at Texas City, Texas, and for other purposes', approved June 22, 1956 (Public Law 608, Eighty-fourth Congress, chapter 426, second session (70 Stat. 329)) [set out as a note under section 98 of Title 50], is canceled.

"SEC. 5. [*Delegation of powers*]. The Administrator of General Services is authorized to delegate, from time to time as he may deem to be appropriate, to any officer, employee, or administrative unit under his jurisdiction the performance of any function and the exercise of the related authority transferred to the Administrator by this Act.

"SEC. 6. [*Termination of succession and dissolution of Corporation; repeal of charter*]. The succession of Federal Facilities Corporation is terminated and the Corporation is dissolved. The charter of the Corporation, as amended, is repealed.

"SEC. 7. [*Suits against corporation before dissolution; United States as party*]. No suit, action, or other proceeding lawfully commenced by or against Federal Facilities Corporation before the dissolution of the Corporation shall abate by reason of such dissolution; but the court may, on motion or supplemental petition filed at any time within twelve months after such dissolution and showing a necessity for the survival of such suit, action, or other proceeding to obtain a settlement of the questions involved, allow the same to be maintained by or against the United States in such court. After the dissolution of the Corporation, any suit, action, or other proceeding which, but for such dissolution, would be commenced by or against the Corporation, shall be commenced by or against the United States in a Federal court of competent jurisdiction.

"SEC. 8. [*Special assessments and taxes*]. In the event that title to any real property which was sold by the Rubber Producing Facilities Disposal Commission or by the Federal Facilities Corporation to private industry on credit, under mortgage, deed of trust, or similar arrangement, is acquired by the United States by reason of default by, or failure of performance of, the purchaser, or its successor in interest, of any of its obligations, such real property shall continue to be subject to special assessments for local improvements and to State, county, municipal, or local taxation to the same extent according to its value as other real property is taxed and the Administrator of General Services is authorized and directed to pay such special assessments and taxes.

"SEC. 9. [*Effective date*]. This Act shall take effect at the close of September 30, 1961."

DISPOSAL OF GOVERNMENT-OWNED RUBBER-PRODUCING FACILITIES

ACT AUG. 7, 1953, CH. 338, 67 STAT. 408

§ 1941. Congressional declaration of policy

It is declared that disposal of the Government-owned rubber-producing facilities pursuant to the provisions of this Act [sections 1941 to 1941y of this Appendix] is consistent with the national security and will further effectuate the policy set forth in section 2 of the Rubber Act of 1948, as amended (62 Stat. 101, 50 U.S.C. App. 1921), with respect to the development within the United States of a free, competitive, synthetic rubber industry.

(Aug. 7, 1953, ch. 338, § 2, 67 Stat. 408.)

SHORT TITLE

Section 1 of act Aug. 7, 1953, provided that: "This Act [enacting sections 1941 to 1941y of this Appendix] shall be known as the 'Rubber Producing Facilities Disposal Act of 1953'."

SECTION REFERRED TO IN OTHER SECTIONS

This section is referred to in section 1941*o* of this Appendix.

§ 1941a. Rubber Producing Facilities Disposal Commission [1]

(a) Repealed. Pub. L. 89–554 § 8(a), Sept. 6, 1966, 80 Stat. 657

(b) Duties; sales contracts, instruments of conveyance, leases and additional powers

With respect to the Government-owned rubber-producing facilities it shall be the duty of the Commission, and it is authorized in accordance with the provisions of this Act [sections 1941 to 1941y of this Appendix] (1) to invite and receive proposals for the purchase of the facilities; to negotiate for their sale and make recommendations therefor to the Congress; to enter into appropriate contracts for their sale, which contracts shall be binding upon the Government and the prospective purchasers upon their execution subject only to the further provisions of this Act [said sections]; and in the performance of such contracts to execute and deliver such deeds or other instruments appropriate to effectively transfer to the purchaser thereof title to the facilities, no matter by what officer, agent, department, Government corporation, or instrumentality of the United States the same is held; (2) to lease and thereunder deliver possession of the alcohol butadiene facilities, if practicable; and (3) to take such action and exercise such powers as may be necessary or appropriate to effectuate the purposes of this Act [said sections].

(c) Consultation with Attorney General

From the time of its appointment and throughout the course of the performance of its

[1] See Transfer of Functions note below.

duties, the Commission shall consult and advise with the Attorney General in order (1) to secure guidance as to the type of disposal program which would best foster the development of a free competitive synthetic rubber industry, and (2) to supply the Attorney General with such information as he may deem requisite to enable him to provide the advice contemplated by this section and sections 9(a)(4) and 9 (f) of this Act [section 1941g(a)(4), (f) of this Appendix].

(d) Submission of disposal report to Attorney General

Before submission of its proposed disposal report to the Congress, as provided for in section 9 of this Act [section 1941g of this Appendix], the Commission shall submit it to the Attorney General, who shall within a reasonable time, in no event to exceed ninety days, after receiving such report, advise the Commission whether, in his opinion, the proposed disposition will violate the antitrust laws.

(e) Antitrust laws as unaffected

Nothing in this Act [sections 1941 to 1941y of this Appendix] shall impair, amend, or modify the antitrust laws or limit and prevent their application to persons who acquire property under the provisions of this Act [said sections]. As used in this section, the term "antitrust laws" includes the Act of July 2, 1890 (ch. 647, 26 Stat. 209), as amended [15 U.S.C. 1 to 7]; the Act of October 15, 1914 (ch. 323, 38 Stat. 730), as amended; the Federal Trade Commission Act [15 U.S.C. 41 et seq.]; and the Act of August 27, 1894 (ch. 349, secs. 73, 74, 28 Stat. 570), as amended [15 U.S.C. 8, 9].

(Aug. 7, 1953, ch. 338, § 3, 67 Stat. 408; Pub. L. 89–554, § 8(a), Sept. 6, 1966, 80 Stat. 657.)

REFERENCES IN TEXT

Act of July 2, 1890, referred to in subsec. (e), is act July 2, 1890, ch. 647, 26 Stat. 209, as amended, known as the Sherman Act, which is classified to sections 1 to 7 of Title 15, Commerce and Trade. For complete classification of this Act to the Code, see Short Title note set out under section 1 of Title 15 and Tables.

Act of October 15, 1914, as amended, referred to in subsec. (e), is act Oct. 15, 1914, ch. 323, 38 Stat. 730, as amended, known as the Clayton Act, which is classified generally to sections 12, 13, 14 to 19, 20, 21, and 22 to 27 of Title 15 and sections 52 and 53 of Title 29, Labor. For further details and complete classification of this Act to the Code, see References in Text note set out under section 12 of Title 15 and Tables.

The Federal Trade Commission Act, referred to in subsec. (e), is act Sept. 26, 1914, ch. 311, 38 Stat. 717, as amended, which is classified generally to subchapter I (§ 41 et seq.) of chapter 2 of Title 15. For complete classification of this Act to the Code, see section 58 of Title 15 and Tables.

AMENDMENTS

1966—Subsec. (a). Pub. L. 89–554 repealed subsec. (a) which established the Rubber Producing Facilities Disposal Commission and provided for appointment, qualifications, and pay of the Commissioners.

TRANSFER OF FUNCTIONS

Functions, property, records, etc., of Rubber Producing Facilities Disposal Commission transferred to Federal Facilities Corporation by Ex. Ord. No. 10678, Sept. 20, 1956, 21 F.R. 7199, set out under section 1941r of this Appendix.

Federal Facilities Corporation dissolved and functions, property, records, etc., transferred to Administrator of General Services by Pub. L. 87–190, Aug. 30, 1961, 75 Stat. 418, set out as a note under section 1938 of this Appendix.

SECTION REFERRED TO IN OTHER SECTIONS

This section is referred to in section 1941g of this Appendix.

§ 1941b. Furnishing of information concerning facilities to Commission on request

The Commission shall be furnished upon its request all available information concerning the Government-owned rubber-producing facilities in the possession of any department, agency, officer, Government corporation, or instrumentality of the United States concerned with Government-owned rubber-producing facilities.

(Aug. 7, 1953, ch. 338, § 4, 67 Stat. 409.)

TRANSFER OF FUNCTIONS

Functions, property, records, etc., of Rubber Producing Facilities Disposal Commission transferred to Federal Facilities Corporation by Ex. Ord. No. 10678, Sept. 20, 1956, 21 F.R. 7199, set out under section 1941r of this Appendix.

Federal Facilities Corporation dissolved and functions, property, records, etc., transferred to the Administrator of General Services by Pub. L. 87–190, Aug. 30, 1961, 75 Stat. 418, set out as a note under section 1938 of this Appendix.

§ 1941c. Prompt disposal of facilities by Commission; hearings

The Commission shall proceed as promptly as practicable, conducting such hearings as may be necessary, with the disposal of the rubber-producing facilities in compliance with the provisions of this Act [sections 1941 to 1941y of this Appendix].

(Aug. 7, 1953, ch. 338, § 5, 67 Stat. 409.)

TRANSFER OF FUNCTIONS

Functions, property, records, etc., of Rubber Producing Facilities Disposal Commission transferred to Federal Facilities Corporation by Ex. Ord. No. 10678, Sept. 20, 1956, 21 F.R. 7199, set out under section 1941r of this Appendix.

Federal Facilities Corporation dissolved and functions, property, records, etc., transferred to Administrator of General Services by Pub. L. 87–190, Aug. 30, 1961, 75 Stat. 418, set out as a note under section 1938 of this Appendix.

§ 1941d. Restriction on activities of members and employees after leaving Commission; penalty

(a) Repealed. Pub. L. 89–554, § 8(a), Sept. 6, 1966, 80 Stat. 657.

(b) No member of the Commission and no person employed by the Commission as an attorney, agent, or employee in activities involving discretion with respect to negotiations or contracts of sale of the Government-owned rubber-producing facilities, shall, during the period of such employment, or for a period of two years thereafter, be employed in any capacity by any purchaser, or affiliate thereof. No purchaser or affiliate thereof shall employ in any capacity any person, who has served as a member of the Commission or who was employed by the Commission and served the Commission as an attorney, agent, or employee in activities involving discretion with respect to negotiations or contracts of sale of the Government-owned rubber-producing facilities, while any such person is serving as a member or employee of the Commission or for a period of two years thereafter. Any person violating the provisions of this subsection shall be fined not more than $10,000 or imprisoned not more than one year, or both.

(Aug. 7, 1953, ch. 338, §6, 67 Stat. 409; Pub. L. 89–554, §8(a), Sept. 6, 1966, 80 Stat. 657.)

AMENDMENTS

1966—Subsec. (a). Pub. L. 89–554 repealed subsec. (a) which authorized the Commission to employ persons and fix their compensation.

TRANSFER OF FUNCTIONS

Functions, property, records, etc., of Rubber Producing Facilities Disposal Commission transferred to Federal Facilities Corporation by Ex. Ord. No. 10678, Sept. 20, 1956, 21 F.R. 7199, set out under section 1941r of this Appendix.

Federal Facilities Corporation dissolved and functions, property, records, etc., transferred to Administrator of General Services by Pub. L. 87–190, Aug. 30, 1961, 75 Stat. 418, set out as a note under section 1938 of this Appendix.

§1941e. Disposal procedure

(a) Invitation of purchase proposals; notice and advertisement; period for receipt of proposals; data to accompany proposals

The Commission shall invite, upon adequate notice and advertisement, proposals for the purchase of the Government-owned rubber-producing facilities, hereafter referred to as the "facilities". The period for the receipt of proposals shall be determined and publicly announced by the Commission, and in no event shall be less than six months after the first day on which proposals may be received pursuant to the advertisement. The advertisement shall be in such form, contain such specifications and reservations, and be published in such manner as the Commission in its discretion determines will best effectuate the purposes of this Act [sections 1941 to 1941y of this Appendix]. All data concerning such facilities which in the judgment of the Commission may be reasonably required for the submission of a bona fide proposal shall be furnished by the Commission upon request by any prospective purchaser unless the Commission has reason to believe that such prospective purchaser has not identified his principal, or is not financially responsible, or is a poor security risk.

(b) Form and contents of proposals

Proposals shall be in writing, and shall contain, among other things—

(1) identification of the person in whose behalf the proposal is submitted, including the business affiliation of such person;

(2) the facility or facilities which are proposed to be purchased, and the order of preference if more than one facility is proposed to be purchased; or the order of preference if proposals are submitted on more than one facility, if only one facility is proposed to be purchased;

(3) the arrangements or plans, if any, formal or informal, for the supply of feedstock to, and the disposition of the end products of, the respective facilities proposed to be purchased;

(4) the amount proposed to be paid for each of the facilities, and, if such amount is not to be paid in cash, then the principal terms of the financing arrangement proposed;

(5) the general terms and conditions which the prospective purchaser of a copolymer facility would be willing to accept in order to make the end product of such facility available for sale to small business enterprises, and the general terms and conditions which the prospective purchaser of a butadiene or styrene facility would be willing to accept in order to make the end product of such facility available for sale to purchasers of copolymer facilities; and

(6) such other information as the Commission in its notice and advertisement for proposals shall require be set forth in proposals including the prospective purchaser's acceptance of the terms, conditions, restrictions and reservations contained in subsection (h) of this section, and the interest rate to be charged on the purchase-money mortgage referred to in subsection (e) of this section.

(c) Disclosure of contents of proposals

Should it become necessary to the effective prosecution of the disposal program, the Commission may, after the termination of the period for the submission of proposals provided for in subsection (a) of this section, disclose the contents of the proposals at such time, in such manner, and to such extent as it deems appropriate.

(d) Deposit of cash or Government bonds to accompany proposals

Proposals shall be accompanied by a deposit of cash or United States Government bonds of face amount equal to 2½ per centum of the gross amount proposed to be paid but not exceeding $250,000 for each facility: *Provided, however*, That the deposit required in the case of a proposal for one of a number of facilities on an alternative basis shall be the same as would be required if such proposal were for only the facility for which the particular prospective purchaser proposed to pay the highest amount. Except in the case of purchasers, deposits made hereunder shall be refunded without interest and not later than upon the termination of the period for congressional review as provided in section 9 of this Act [section 1941g of this Appendix]. In the case of purchasers, deposits made hereunder shall be applied without interest to the purchase price: *Provided, however*, That upon the closing of the contract of sale the purchaser shall be required to substitute cash equal to the face amount of the Government bonds then held in connection with such purchaser's proposal.

(e) Payment of purchase price; amount and terms of mortgages

Payment of the purchase price may be made in part by a first lien purchase-money mortgage, in an amount not to exceed 75 per centum of the purchase price. The terms of any such mortgage obligation, to be determined by negotiation, shall provide among other things for a maturity of not more than ten years, periodic amortization, and a uniform interest rate of not less than 3 per centum per annum.

(f) Negotiation with those submitting proposals

Promptly after the termination of the period for the receipt of proposals, pursuant to subsection (a) of this section, and for such period thereafter not less than seven months as may be determined and publicly announced by the Commission, it shall negotiate with those submitting proposals for the purpose of entering into definitive contracts of sale.

(g) Securing of additional information from those submitting proposals

Nothing contained in this Act [sections 1941 to 1941y of this Appendix] shall be construed to prevent the Commission from securing such additional information from those submitting proposals at any time as the Commission may deem necessary or appropriate to fulfill its responsibilities under this Act [said sections].

(h) National security clause in contracts of sale

All contracts of sale and instruments in execution thereof shall contain a national security clause having terms, conditions, restrictions and reservations which will assure the prompt availability of the rubber-producing facilities, or facilities of equivalent capacity, for the production of synthetic rubber and the component materials thereof for a period of ten years from the date of the contract.

(i) Effective date of contracts of sale; time for transfer of possession of facilities; failure to complete transfer prior to termination date

Subject to the conditions prescribed in section 24 of this Act [section 1941v of this Appendix], any contract of sale shall become fully effective upon the expiration of the period for congressional review provided for in section 9 of this Act [section 1941g of this Appendix] unless the Congress within such period has disapproved such sale. The transfer of possession of all of the rubber-producing facilities to be sold shall be made as promptly as is practicable after the effective date, in accordance with the terms of the contracts, but in any event within a period terminating sixty days after the expiration of the period for congressional review as provided in section 9(b) of this Act [section 1941g(b) of this Appendix]. The failure to complete transfer of possession prior to said termination date shall not give rise to or be the basis of rescission of the contract of sale.

(j) Limitation on Government rubber sales

Upon termination of the transfer period, as provided in subsection (i) of this section, the operating agency last designated by the President shall make no further sales of synthetic rubber and its component materials except as otherwise provided in this Act [sections 1941 to 1941y of this Appendix].

(k) Offer of Government rubber for sale to purchasers of facilities after termination of transfer period

During the period of one year following the termination of the transfer period, the operating agency last designated by the President shall offer for sale to the purchasers of the facilities the synthetic rubber and its component materials held by it at a price determined in accordance with its pricing policy prevailing at the close of the transfer period, in amounts prorated in accordance with the ratio of the capacity of each such facility purchased to the total capacity of all facilities of the same type sold. Any synthetic rubber or component materials not purchased by an eligible purchaser during periodic intervals, as determined by the operating agency, shall be made available to other eligible purchasers on a like equitable basis. Any synthetic rubber or component materials not sold during such one-year period shall thereafter be disposed of in such manner as said agency deems advisable.

(Aug. 7, 1953, ch. 338, § 7, 67 Stat. 409.)

TRANSFER OF FUNCTIONS

Functions, property, records, etc., of Rubber Producing Facilities Disposal Commission transferred to Federal Facilities Corporation by Ex. Ord. No. 10678, Sept. 20, 1956, 21 F.R. 7199, set out under section 1941r of this Appendix.

Federal Facilities Corporation dissolved and functions, property, records, etc., transferred to Administrator of General Services by Pub. L. 87–190, Aug. 30, 1961, 75 Stat. 418, set out as a note under section 1938 of this Appendix.

SECTION REFERRED TO IN OTHER SECTIONS

This section is referred to in sections 1941g, 1941*l*, 1941m, 1941r, 1941w, 1941x, 1941y of this Appendix.

§ 1941f. Disposition of unsold facilities; transfer to General Services Administration; lease of alcohol-butadiene facilities; advice of Attorney General; standby funds

(a) Upon the termination of the transfer period, the operating agency last designated by the President, shall, as promptly as possible consistent with sound operating procedures, take out of production and place in adequate standby condition the rubber-producing facilities which shall not have been sold. At any time after the termination of production, such facilities may be transferred without reimbursement or transfer of funds to the General Services Administration and administered in accordance with the provisions of sections 6, 7, and 8 of the National Industrial Reserve Act of 1948, as amended (62 Stat. 1227, 50 U.S.C. 456–458) [50 U.S.C. 455 to 457], or to such other agency as the President may designate for administration in such manner as he may direct. In such event (1) no such facility shall thereafter be operated as a rubber-producing facility for the account of, or by, the Government except pursuant to further Act of Congress; (2) no such facility, other than alcohol-butadiene facilities, shall be leased for operation as a rubber-producing facility at any time: *Provided*, That nothing contained in this Act [sections 1941 to 1941y of this Appendix] shall preclude the leasing of alcohol-butadiene facilities for purposes other than the manufacture of alcohol butadiene so long as such leases are in accordance with the provisions of section 8(a) or section 9(f) of this Act [subsection (a) of this section or section 1941g (f) of this Appendix]; and (3) no such facility shall be disposed of by sale within a period of three years from the termination of the transfer period, and in any subsequent lease or sale, the Government agency acting under authority of this section shall within a reasonable time and in no event less than sixty days prior to the lease or sale, request the advice of the Attorney General as to whether the proposed lease or sale would tend to create or maintain a situation inconsistent with the antitrust laws. The Attorney General shall give his advice within forty-five days of the receipt of such request. Upon the request of the Attorney General, the Government agency shall furnish, or cause to be furnished, such information as it may possess which the Attorney General determines to be appropriate or necessary to enable him to give the advice called for by this section.

(b) Whenever any transfer to any Government agency is made pursuant to this section, all unexpended funds budgeted as provided in section 9(e) [section 1941g(e) of this Appendix] for standby and maintenance in such condition shall also be transferred.

(Aug. 7, 1953, ch. 338, § 8, 67 Stat. 411.)

REFERENCES IN TEXT

Sections 7 and 8 of the National Industrial Reserve Act of 1948, referred to in subsec. (a), were classified to sections 456 and 457 of Title 50, War and National Defense, and were omitted from the Code.

The antitrust laws, referred to in subsec. (a), are classified generally to chapter 1 (§1 et seq.) of Title 15, Commerce and Trade. See section 1941a(e) of this Appendix and References in Text notes thereunder.

SALE OF LEASE OF CATALYST EQUIPMENT; TERMS AND CONDITIONS; SECURITY CLAUSE; PRICE; STANDBY CONDITION; AUTHORITY

Administration by Administrator of General Services of matters involving the Rubber Producing Facilities Disposal Commission, including the exercise of authority conferred upon the Commission by section 6 of Act Mar. 21, 1956, set out below, see Dissolution of Federal Facilities Corporation note set out under section 1938 of this Appendix.

Section 6 of act Mar. 21, 1956, ch. 89, 70 Stat. 53, provided that:

"(a) Notwithstanding any provision of the Rubber Producing Facilities Disposal Act of 1953, as amended [sections 1941 to 1941x of this Appendix], or of this Act [enacting section 1941y and provisions set out as notes under sections 1941r and 1941y of this Appendix], the Rubber Producing Facilities Disposal Commission may enter into contracts of sale and may from time to time enter into leases for all or any part of the catalyst manufacturing equipment now situated in Baltimore, Maryland, and generally described in the Commission's brochure M–2 dated March 1954.

"(b) Except as provided in this paragraph, each such lease or contract may be made on such terms and conditions, including type of use and duration (up to fifteen years) of any lease, as the Commission deems advisable in the public interest. Before making such sale or lease, the Commission shall secure the advice of the Attorney General as to whether the proposed sale or lease would tend to create or maintain a situation inconsistent with the antitrust laws. Each such lease or contract of sale shall contain a national security clause, containing such terms and for such duration (ten years or less) as the Commission deems desirable in the public interest, and any such lease shall provide for the recapture of the equipment thereby leased and the termination of the lease, if the President determines that the national interest so requires.

"The price for any part or all of such equipment shall be an amount which the Commission determines to be the maximum amount obtainable in the public interest, but not less than fair value as determined by the Commission.

"(c) Any of such equipment not sold or leased under subsection (a) shall be placed and maintained in adequate standby condition pursuant to, and be otherwise subject to, the provisions of section 8 of the Rubber Producing Facilities Disposal Act of 1953 [this section] (other than the provision prohibiting leases).

"(d) All the powers and authority conferred by this section upon the Commission may, after the termination of the existence of the Commission, be exercised by such agency of the Government as the President may designate for the purpose, and for this purpose such successor agency may exercise all the authority conferred in the Rubber Producing Facilities Disposal Act of 1953 [sections 1941 to 1941y of this Appendix] upon the Commission."

SECTION REFERRED TO IN OTHER SECTIONS

This section is referred to in sections 1941w, 1941x of this Appendix.

§ 1941g. Report of recommended disposal by Commission to Congress

(a) Contents and requirements

Not later than thirty days after the termination of the negotiating period provided in section 7 of this Act [section 1941e of this Appendix], and in no event later than January 31, 1955, the Commission shall prepare and submit to the Congress a report setting forth—

(1) the steps taken to elicit proposals and the proposals which have been received;

(2) the principal terms of all sales contracted for and the Commission's recommendations in respect thereto;

(3) in the event that there may have been a financially more advantageous proposal for any rubber-producing facility than the sale recommended, a statement of the reasons why such sale is nevertheless proposed;

(4) the statement from the Attorney General setting forth findings approving the proposed disposals in accordance with the standards set forth in section 3(c) of this Act [section 1941a(c) of this Appendix];

(5) the program to be followed to place in standby condition the rubber-producing facilities not sold;

(6) an inventory report concerning the Government's current stocks of synthetic rubber and its component materials;

(7) a program for the continuance, to the extent it deems necessary, during the fiscal year following the fiscal year in which the transfer period terminates, of the research program on synthetic rubber and its component materials then being carried on by the operating agency; and

(8) the names of persons who have represented the Government or the purchasers in conducting negotiations or in making contracts for disposal of the rubber-producing facilities.

(b) Time of submission of report; period for action by Congress

The report shall be submitted to both Houses of Congress on the same day. Upon the expiration of sixty days of continuous session of the Congress following the date upon which the report is submitted to it, the Commission shall proceed to carry out the contracts and proposals, as outlined in its report, to the extent that such contracts and proposals are not disapproved by either House of Congress by a resolution within the sixty-day period.

(c) Computation of period for Congressional action

For the purposes of subsection (b) of this section—

(1) continuity of session shall be considered as broken only by an adjournment of the Congress sine die; but

(2) in the computation of the sixty-day period there shall be excluded the days on which either House is not in session because of an adjournment of more than three days to a day certain.

(d) Restriction on sale or lease of rubber-producing facilities

No rubber-producing facility shall be sold or leased except in accordance with this Act [sections 1941 to 1941y of this Appendix] or in accordance with section 7(d)(4) of the Rubber Act of 1948, as amended [section 1926(d)(4) of this Appendix].

(e) Funds for expenses; annual budget

Such sums as may be required for the foregoing purposes may be provided out of the proceeds of disposal, and annual budgets for the expenses necessary for such purposes shall be submitted in accordance with the Government Corporation Control Act of 1945, as amended (59 Stat. 597, 31 U.S.C. 841) [31 U.S.C. 9101 et seq.].

(f) Leases of alcohol-butadiene facilities; requirements; advice of Attorney General

Notwithstanding any other provisions of this Act [sections 1941 to 1941y of this Appendix], the Commission may, after securing the advice of the Attorney General as to whether the proposed lease would tend to create or maintain a situation inconsistent with the antitrust laws, enter into leases for the alcohol-butadiene facilities for a period of not less than one year, nor more than three years: *Provided*, That any such lease shall contain among other things (1) a national security clause, and (2) provisions for the recapture of such facilities by the Government and the termination of the lease, if the President determines that the national interest so requires. Not less than sixty days prior to said lease the Commission shall request such advice from the Attorney General who shall give the same within forty-five days of the receipt of such request.

(Aug. 7, 1953, ch. 338, § 9, 67 Stat. 412.)

REFERENCES IN TEXT

The Government Corporation Control Act of 1945, as amended, referred to in subsec. (e), is act Dec. 6, 1945, ch. 557, 59 Stat. 597, as amended, which was classified to chapter 14 (§ 841 et seq.) of former Title 31, and which was repealed by Pub. L. 97–258, § 5(b), Sept. 13, 1982, 96 Stat. 1068, and reenacted by the first section thereof as chapter 91 (§ 9101 et seq.) of Title 31, Money and Finance.

The antitrust laws, referred to in subsec. (f), are classified generally to chapter 1 (§ 1 et seq.) of Title 15, Commerce and Trade. See section 1941a(e) of this Appendix and References in Text notes thereunder.

TRANSFER OF FUNCTIONS

Functions, property, records, etc., of Rubber Producing Facilities Disposal Commission transferred to Federal Facilities Corporation by Ex. Ord. No. 10678, Sept. 20, 1956, 21 F.R. 7199, set out under section 1941r of this Appendix.

Federal Facilities Corporation dissolved and functions, property, records, etc., transferred to Administrator of General Services by Pub. L. 87–190, Aug. 30, 1961, 75 Stat. 418, set out as a note under section 1938 of this Appendix.

SECTION REFERRED TO IN OTHER SECTIONS

This section is referred to in sections 1941a, 1941e, 1941f, 1941*l*, 1941w, 1941x, 1941y of this Appendix.

§ 1941h. President's report to Congress on Nation's rubber requirements and resources

At the expiration of one year after the transfer period or as soon thereafter as the Congress is in session, the President shall report to the Congress concerning the Nation's rubber requirements and resources, and the need, if any, for further research by the Government relative to the production or use of synthetic rubber and its component materials.

(Aug. 7, 1953, ch. 338, § 10, 67 Stat. 413.)

§ 1941i. Exclusion from term "rubber-producing facilities"

The term "rubber-producing facilities" as used in this Act [sections 1941 to 1941y of this Appendix] shall not include the Government-owned evaluation laboratory at Akron, Ohio.

(Aug. 7, 1953, ch. 338, § 11, 67 Stat. 413.)

DISPOSAL OF RESEARCH LABORATORIES AT AKRON, OHIO

Act July 26, 1956, ch. 738, 70 Stat. 657, provided: "That the Government laboratories at Akron, Ohio, now under control of the National Science Foundation are hereby transferred to the General Services Administration for disposal in accordance with the Federal Property and Administrative Services Act of 1949 [see Short Title note set out under section 471 of Title 40, Public Buildings, Property, and Works], except that the Administrator of General Services shall first offer the laboratories for public sale before seeking to dispose of them by transfer or assignment to any Federal agency. The Administrator of General Services, before he offers the laboratories to the public for sale, shall ascertain what the value of the laboratories would be to Government agencies which would make substantial use thereof, and the Administrator shall not sell the laboratories to the public unless he finds, after consultation with the Director of the Budget Bureau, that such sale to the public would be in the best interests of the United States, taking into consideration among other relevant factors the value of the laboratories to any interested agency and the amounts offered by public bidders. The National Science Foundation is authorized to reimburse the General Services Administration in advance for expenses necessary for the protection and maintenance of the laboratories up to June 30, 1957."

§ 1941j. Disposition of proceeds from disposal of facilities

All final net proceeds from disposal of the rubber-producing facilities shall be covered into the Treasury as miscellaneous receipts except as otherwise provided by this Act [sections 1941 to 1941y of this Appendix].

(Aug. 7, 1953, ch. 338, § 12, 67 Stat. 413.)

§ 1941k. Prior disposal of facilities as unaffected

The sales, leases, or other dispositions made prior to the enactment of this Act [Aug. 7, 1953], pursuant to section 9(b) of the Rubber Act of 1948, as amended [section 1928(b) of this Appendix], shall not be affected by this Act [sections 1941 to 1941y of this Appendix].

(Aug. 7, 1953, ch. 338, § 13, 67 Stat. 413.)

§ 1941*l*. Conditional termination dates for Rubber Act of 1948

Notwithstanding the provisions of section 20 of the Rubber Act of 1948, as amended [section 1938 of this Appendix], (1) if no report is submitted by the Commission, or if the report submitted by the Commission pursuant to section 9 of this Act [section 1941g of this Appendix] is disapproved in its entirety, then the Rubber Act of 1948, as amended [sections 1921 to 1938 of this Appendix] shall be extended until March 31, 1956; and (2) if the Commission submits a report and it is not disapproved in its entirety, the Rubber Act of 1948, as amended [said sections], shall terminate at the termination of the transfer period as provided in section 7(i) of this Act [section 1941e(i) of this Appendix].

(Aug. 7, 1953, ch. 338, § 14, 67 Stat. 413.)

TRANSFER OF FUNCTIONS

Functions, property, records, etc., of Rubber Producing Facilities Disposal Commission transferred to Federal Facilities Corporation by Ex. Ord. No. 10678, Sept. 20, 1956, 21 F.R. 7199, set out under section 1941r of this Appendix.

Federal Facilities Corporation dissolved and functions, property, records, etc., transferred to Administrator of General Services by Pub. L. 87–190, Aug. 30, 1961, 75 Stat. 418, set out as a note under section 1938 of this Appendix.

§ 1941m. Monthly reports by Commission to Congress of expenditures and obligations

Thirty days following the receipt of proposals, as provided in section 7 of this Act [section 1941e of this Appendix] the Commission shall submit to the Congress a report stating the amount of funds expended by or obligated by the operating agency for the repair, replacement, additions, improvements, or maintenance of each synthetic rubber-producing facility for which proposals have been submitted. Thereafter reports shall be made monthly until such time as the Congress shall have permitted or disapproved in whole or in part the disposal recommended by the Commission.

(Aug. 7, 1953, ch. 338, § 15, 67 Stat. 413.)

TRANSFER OF FUNCTIONS

Functions, property, records, etc., of Rubber Producing Facilities Disposal Commission transferred to Federal Facilities Corporation by Ex. Ord. No. 10678, Sept. 20, 1956, 21 F.R. 7199, set out under section 1941r of this Appendix.

Federal Facilities Corporation dissolved and functions, property, records, etc., transferred to Administrator of General Services by Pub. L. 87–190, Aug. 30, 1961, 75 Stat. 418, set out as a note under section 1938 of this Appendix.

§ 1941n. Basis for negotiating sale of a facility

In arriving at its recommendations for the disposal of the facilities, the Commission shall use, as the basis for negotiating the sale of each facility the highest amount proposed to be paid for each facility, if, in the opinion of the Commission, the highest amount proposed to be paid was a bona fide proposal and was submitted by a person competent to operate a rubber-producing facility: *Provided*, That the words "competent to operate a rubber-producing facility" shall not be interpreted so as to require prior experience in the operation of a rubber-producing facility: *Provided further*, That in using such highest proposed amount as a basis for negotiations the Commission may negotiate with respect to any facility with any person who submitted a proposal on that or any similar facility and may recommend sale of any facility to any person who submitted a proposal on that or any similar facility at a price which is equal to, higher than, or lower than the highest amount proposed to be paid for each facility as the Commission determines will best effectuate the purposes of this Act [sections 1941 to 1941y of this Appendix].

(Aug. 7, 1953, ch. 338, § 16, 67 Stat. 413.)

TRANSFER OF FUNCTIONS

Functions, property, records, etc., of Rubber Producing Facilities Disposal Commission transferred to Federal Facilities Corporation by Ex. Ord. No. 10678, Sept. 20, 1956, 21 F.R. 7199, set out under section 1941r of this Appendix.

Federal Facilities Corporation dissolved and functions, property, records, etc., transferred to Administrator of General Services by Pub. L. 87–190, Aug. 30, 1961, 75 Stat. 418, set out as a note under section 1938 of this Appendix.

§ 1941*o*. Criteria for disposal recommendations

The following criteria, together with such other criteria as the Commission deems necessary or desirable to best effectuate the purposes of this Act [sections 1941 to 1941y of this Appendix], shall be used by the Commission in arriving at its recommendations for disposal:

(1) That the disposal program be designed best to afford small-business enterprises and users, other than the purchser[1] of a facility, the opportunity to obtain a fair share of the end products of the facilities sold and at fair prices;

(2) That the prospective purchaser has the technical competence necessary to operate a rubber-producing facility, except that prior experience in operating a rubber-producing facility shall not be required as a basis for determining whether a prospective purchaser has the technical competence necessary to operate a rubber-producing facility;

(3) That the recommended sales shall provide for the development within the United States of a free, competitive, synthetic rubber industry, and do not permit any person to possess unreasonable control over the manufacture of synthetic rubber or its component materials;

(4) That the prospective purchaser is acting in good faith, and actually intends to operate the facility or facilities for the purpose of manufacturing synthetic rubber or its component materials;

(5) That full fair value for the facility or facilities will be received by the Government,

[1] So in original. Probably should be "purchaser".

taking into consideration the policy set forth in section 2 of this Act [section 1941 of this Appendix];

(6) That disposal of the facility or facilities to the purchasers is consistent with national security; and

(7) That the facilities recommended for sale will in the aggregate be capable of annually producing not less than five hundred thousand long tons of general-purpose synthetic rubber, and not less than forty-three thousand long tons annually of butyl rubber.

(Aug. 7, 1953, ch. 338, §17, 67 Stat. 414.)

TRANSFER OF FUNCTIONS

Functions, property, records, etc., of Rubber Producing Facilities Disposal Commission transferred to Federal Facilities Corporation by Ex. Ord. No. 10678, Sept. 20, 1956, 21 F.R. 7199, set out under section 1941r of this Appendix.

Federal Facilities Corporation dissolved and functions, property, records, etc., transferred to Administrator of General Services by Pub. L. 87–190, Aug. 30, 1961, 75 Stat. 418, set out as a note under section 1938 of this Appendix.

§1941p. Authorization of disposal of facilities notwithstanding Rubber Act of 1948

Unless otherwise provided in this Act [sections 1941 to 1941y of this Appendix], the disposal of the Government-owned rubber-producing facilities shall be authorized notwithstanding the provisions of the Rubber Act of 1948, as amended [sections 1921 to 1938 of this Appendix].

(Aug. 7, 1953, ch. 338, §18, 67 Stat. 414.)

§1941q. Payment of costs of disposal from operating income

Unless otherwise provided in this Act [sections 1941 to 1941y of this Appendix], all costs incurred by the Commission or any other department, agency, officer, Government corporation, or instrumentality of the United States pursuant to the provisions of this Act [said sections] shall, so long as synthetic rubber is produced for the account of the Government in the Government-owned rubber-producing facilities, be paid from and charged against the operating income of the Government-owned synthetic rubber program, administered by the operating agency.

(Aug. 7, 1953, ch. 338, §19, 67 Stat. 414.)

TRANSFER OF FUNCTIONS

Functions, property, records, etc., of Rubber Producing Facilities Disposal Commission transferred to Federal Facilities Corporation by Ex. Ord. No. 10678, Sept. 20, 1956, 21 F.R. 7199, set out under section 1941r of this Appendix.

Federal Facilities Corporation dissolved and functions, property, records, etc., transferred to Administrator of General Services by Pub. L. 87–190, Aug. 30, 1961, 75 Stat. 418, set out as a note under section 1938 of this Appendix.

§1941r. Termination of Commission; administration after termination

The Commission shall cease to exist thirty days after the termination of the transfer period as provided by section 7(i) of this Act [section 1941e(i) of this Appendix], but nothing contained in this section shall be construed in any way so as to abrogate, modify, or adversely affect any contract of sale or lease of the Government-owned rubber-producing facilities pursuant to this Act [sections 1941 to 1941y of this Appendix]. After the Commission ceases to exist, such contracts and leases and other matters involving the Commission shall be administered by such agency of the Government as the President may designate.

(Aug. 7, 1953, ch. 338, §20, 67 Stat. 414.)

TRANSFER OF FUNCTIONS

Functions, property, records, etc., of Rubber Producing Facilities Disposal Commission transferred to Federal Facilities Corporation by Ex. Ord. No. 10678, Sept. 20, 1956, 21 F.R. 7199, set out under this section.

Federal Facilities Corporation dissolved and functions, property, records, etc., transferred to Administrator of General Services by Pub. L. 87–190, Aug. 30, 1961, 75 Stat. 418, set out as a note under section 1938 of this Appendix.

TERMINATION OF COMMISSION

Section 3 of act Mar. 21, 1956, ch. 89, 70 Stat. 52, provided that: "Notwithstanding the provisions of section 4 of Public Law 336, Eighty-fourth Congress, approved August 9, 1955 [set out as a note below], of section 4 of Public Law 19, Eighty-fourth Congress, approved March 31, 1955 [set out as a note below], and section 20 of the Rubber Producing Facilities Disposal Act of 1953 [this section], the Commission established by the last-mentioned Act shall cease to exist at the close of the ninetieth day following the termination of the review period provided for in section 27(c) of that Act [section 1941y(c) of this Appendix], unless no sale of the Louisville plant is recommended by the Commission pursuant to section 27(c) of that Act [section 1941y(c) of this Appendix], in which event the Commission shall cease to exist at the close of the ninetieth day following the termination of the maximum period allowed for negotiation in section 27(b) [section 1941y(b) of this Appendix]."

Act Aug. 9, 1955, ch. 696, §4, 69 Stat. 629, provided that: "Notwithstanding the provisions of section 4 of Public Law 19 [set out as a note below], approved March 31, 1955, and notwithstanding the provisions of section 20 of the Rubber Producing Facilities Disposal Act of 1953 [this section], the Commission established by the latter Act [sections 1941 to 1941y of this Appendix] shall cease to exist at the close of the thirtieth day following the termination of the transfer period provided for in section 26(c) of that Act [section 1941x(c) of this Appendix], unless no sale of Plancor Numbered 980 is recommended by the Commission pursuant to section 26(c) of that Act [section 1941x(c) of this Appendix], in which event the Commission shall cease to exist at the close of the one hundred and thirtieth day following the date of the enactment of this Act [Aug. 9, 1955]."

Act Mar. 31, 1955, ch. 19, §4, 69 Stat. 16, provided that: "Notwithstanding the provisions of section 20 of the Rubber Producing Facilities Disposal Act of 1953 [this section], the Commission established by that Act [sections 1941 to 1941y of this Appendix] shall cease to exist at the close of the thirtieth day following the termination of the transfer period provided for in section 25(c) of that Act [section 1941w(c) of this Appendix], unless no sale of Plancor Numbered 877 is recommended by the Commission pursuant to section 25(c) of that Act [section 1941w(c) of this Appendix], in which event the Commission shall cease to exist at the close of the one hundred and thirtieth day following the date of enactment of this Act [March 31, 1955]."

EX. ORD. NO. 10678. ADMINISTRATION OF FUNCTIONS OF COMMISSION

Ex. Ord. No. 10678, Sept. 20, 1956, 21 F.R. 7199, as amended by Ex. Ord. No. 10720, July 11, 1957, 22 F.R. 5521, provided:

By virtue of the authority vested in me by section 20 of the Rubber Producing Facilities Disposal Act of 1953 67 Stat. 414, as amended or modified (50 U.S.C. App. 1941r), and by section 6(d) of the act of March 21, 1956, 70 Stat. 53 [set out as a note under section 1941f of this Appendix], and as President of the United States, it is ordered as follows:

SECTION 1. Subject to the provisions of section 2 of this order, the Federal Facilities Corporation (hereinafter referred to as the Corporation) is hereby designated as the agency to administer the contracts of sale or lease of the Government-owned rubber producing facilities made pursuant to the Rubber Producing Facilities Disposal Act of 1953, as amended [sections 1941 to 1941y of this Appendix], and to administer other matters involving the Rubber Producing Facilities Disposal Commission, including all powers and authority conferred upon the said Commission by sections 4, 5, and 6 of the said act of March 21, 1956 [set out as notes under sections 1941f and 1941y of this Appendix], and also including the winding up of the affairs of the Commission. The said contracts are hereby transferred to the Corporation.

SEC. 2. The administration of the national-security clause contained in such contracts of sale, including any contract of sale made under the act of March 31, 1955 69 Stat. 15 [enacting section 1941w and provisions set out under section 1938 and sections 1941w and 1941r of this Appendix], or under the said act of March 21, 1956 [set out as notes under sections 1941f and 1941y of this Appendix], and the administration of the national-security clause (including the recapture clause) contained in any lease of the unsold facilities made under any of the aforesaid acts shall be carried out in accordance with the needs and requirements of the national defense as determined by the Secretary of Defense.

SEC. 3. The records, property, liabilities, employees and unexpended balances of appropriations, allocations, and other funds, available or to be made available, of the Rubber Producing Facilities Disposal Commission are hereby transferred to the Corporation, for use or employment by the Corporation in connection with the administration or performance of its functions and duties under section 1 of this order, or for other disposition as determined, consonant with law, by the Corporation.

SEC. 4. All matters placed under the administration or jurisdiction of the Corporation by sections 1 and 3 of this order shall be subject to direction and control by the Administrator of General Services.

SEC. 5. This order shall become effective on September 24, 1956.

DWIGHT D. EISENHOWER.

ADMINISTRATION AFTER TERMINATION

Administration by Administrator of General Services of matters involving the Rubber Producing Facilities Disposal Commission, including the winding up of the affairs of the Commission, see Dissolution of Federal Facilities Corporation note set out under section 1938 of this Appendix.

§ 1941s. Definitions

(a) The term "synthetic rubber" means any product of chemical synthesis similar in general properties and applications to natural rubber, and specifically capable of vulcanization, produced in the United States, not including reclaimed synthetic rubber.

(b) The term "general-purpose synthetic rubber" means a synthetic rubber of the butadiene-styrene type generally suitable for use in the manufacture of transportation items such as tires or camelback, as well as any other type of synthetic rubber equally or better suited for use in the manufacture of transportation items such as tires or camelback as determined from time to time by the President.

(c) The term "rubber-producing facilities" means facilities, in whole or in part, for the manufacture of synthetic rubber, and the component materials thereof, including, but not limited to, buildings and land in which or on which such facilities may be located and all machinery and utilities associated therewith.

(d) The term "component materials" means the material, raw, semifinished, and finished, necessary for the manufacture of synthetic rubber.

(e) The term "standby condition" means the condition in which rubber-producing facilities, in whole or in part, are placed if not sold or leased in accordance with this Act [sections 1941 to 1941y of this Appendix], but are maintained so as to be readily available for the production of synthetic rubber or component materials.

(f) The term "person" means any individual, firm, copartnership, business trust, corporation, or any organized group of persons whether incorporated or not.

(g) The term "operating agency" means the Department, agency, officer, Government corporation, or instrumentality of the United States designated from time to time by the President pursuant to section 7(a) of the Rubber Act of 1948, as amended [section 1926(a) of this Appendix].

(h) The term "small business enterprise" means an enterprise independently owned and operated which is not dominant in its field of operation, due regard being given to the number of its employees and dollar volume of business.

(Aug. 7, 1953, ch. 338, § 21, 67 Stat. 415.)

§ 1941t. Omitted

CODIFICATION

Section, act Aug. 7, 1953, ch. 338, § 22, 67 Stat. 415, amended section 20 of the Rubber Act of 1949, as amended (50 App. U.S.C. 1938), which was omitted from the Code.

§ 1941u. Congressional resolutions respecting facilities

(a) Resolutions as rules of Congress; changes

The provisions of this section are enacted by the Congress:

(1) As an exercise of the rule-making power of the Senate and the house of Representatives, respectively, and as such they shall be considered as part of the rules of each House, respectively, but applicable only with respect to the procedure to be followed in such House in the case of resolutions (as defined in subsection (b)); and such rules shall supersede other rules only to the extent that they are inconsistent therewith; and

(2) With full recognition of the constitutional right of either House to change such rules (so far as relating to the procedure in such House) at any time, in the same manner and to the same extent as in the case of any other rule of such House.

(b) Form of resolution

As used in this section, the term "resolution" means only a resolution of either of the two Houses of Congress, the matter after the resolving clause of which is as follows: (1) "That the

______________ does not favor sale of the facilities as recommended in the report of the Rubber Producing Facilities Disposal Commission.", the blank therein being filled with the name of the resolving House; or (2) "That the ______________ does not favor the sale of the ______________ as recommended in the report of the Rubber Producing Facilities Disposal Commission.", the first blank therein being filled with the name of the resolving House and the other blank being filled with a description of the facility or facilities proposed to be sold.

(c) Reference to committee

A resolution with respect to a facility or facilities shall be referred to a committee (and all such resolutions shall be referred to the same committee) by the President of the Senate or the Speaker of the House of Representatives, as the case may be.

(d) Report by committee; motion to discharge

(1) If the committee to which has been referred a resolution with respect to a facility or facilities has not reported it before the expiration of ten calendar days after its introduction, it shall then (but not before) be in order to move either to discharge the committee from further consideration of such resolution, or to discharge the committee from further consideration of any other resolution with respect to such facility or facilities which has been referred to the committee.

(2) Such motion may be made only by a person favoring the resolution, shall be highly privileged (except that it may not be made after the committee has reported a resolution with respect to the same facility or facilities), and debate thereon shall be limited to not to exceed one hour, to be equally divided between those favoring and those opposing the resolution. No amendment to such motion shall be in order, and it shall not be in order to move to reconsider the vote by which such motion is agreed to or disagreed to.

(3) If the motion to discharge is agreed to or disagreed to, such motion may not be renewed, nor may another motion to discharge the committee be made with respect to any other resolution with respect to the same facility or facilities.

(e) Motion to consider resolution; amendment

(1) Where the committee has reported, or has been discharged from further consideration of, a resolution with respect to a facility or facilities, it shall at any time thereafter be in order (even though a previous motion to the same effect has been disagreed to) to move to proceed to the consideration of such resolution. Such motion shall be highly privileged and shall not be debatable. No amendment to such motion shall be in order and it shall not be in order to move to reconsider the vote by which such motion is agreed to or disagreed to.

(2) Debate on the resolution shall be limited to not to exceed ten hours, which shall be equally divided between those favoring and those opposing the resolution. A motion further to limit debate shall not be debatable. No amendment to, or motion to recommit, the resolution shall be in order, and it shall not be in order to move to reconsider the vote by which the resolution is agreed to or disagreed to.

(f) Motions and appeals from decisions on rules to be decided without debate

(1) All motions to postpone, made with respect to the discharge from committee, or the consideration of, a resolution with respect to a facility or facilities, and all motions to proceed to the consideration of other business, shall be decided without debate.

(2) All appeals from the decisions of the Chair relating to the application of the rules of the Senate or the House of Representatives, as the case may be, to the procedure relating to a resolution with respect to a facility or facilities, shall be decided without debate.

(Aug. 7, 1953, ch. 338, §23, 67 Stat. 415.)

TRANSFER OF FUNCTIONS

Functions, property, records, etc., of Rubber Producing Facilities Disposal Commission transferred to Federal Facilities Corporation by Ex. Ord. No. 10678, Sept. 20, 1956, 21 F.R. 7199, set out under section 1941r of this Appendix.

Federal Facilities Corporation dissolved and functions, property, records, etc., transferred to Administrator of General Services by Pub. L. 87–190, Aug. 30, 1961, 75 Stat. 418, set out as a note under section 1938 of this Appendix.

§1941v. Rejection of recommended sales contract; right to review of purchaser of other facilities; minimum annual production necessary to sustain disposal report

Notwithstanding any provisions of this Act [sections 1941 to 1941y of this Appendix], in the event that the recommended sale of any facility is disapproved by either House of the Congress, any prospective purchaser of any other facility shall have a period of thirty days after the termination of the period for review by the Congress in which to reject the recommended sales contract with regard to the facility or facilities which he has agreed to purchase: *Provided*, That if as a result of the disapproval by either House of the Congress of the sale of any facility or facilities, or as a result of the rejection of one or more sales contracts by any prospective purchaser as provided in this section, the remaining facilities to be sold will in the aggregate not be capable of annually producing at least 500,000 long tons of general purpose synthetic rubber and at least 43,000 long tons of butyl rubber, then no facility shall be sold under this Act [said sections], and for the purposes of this Act [said sections] the report of the Commission shall be deemed to have been disapproved in its entirety.

(Aug. 7, 1953, ch. 338, §24, 67 Stat. 416.)

TRANSFER OF FUNCTIONS

Functions, property, records, etc., of Rubber Producing Facilities Disposal Commission transferred to Federal Facilities Corporation by Ex. Ord. No. 10678, Sept. 20, 1956, 21 F.R. 7199, set out under section 1941r of this Appendix.

Federal Facilities Corporation dissolved and functions, property, records, etc., transferred to Administrator of General Services by Pub. L. 87–190, Aug. 30, 1961, 75 Stat. 418, set out as a note under section 1938 of this Appendix.

§ 1941w. Disposal of rubber-producing facility at Baytown, Texas

(a) Receipt of proposal

Notwithstanding the second sentence of section 7(a) [section 1941e(a) of this Appendix], the period for receipt of proposals for the purchase of the Government-owned rubber-producing facility at Baytown, Texas, known as Plancor Numbered 877, shall not expire until the end of the thirty-day period which begins on the date of the enactment of this section [Mar. 31, 1955].

(b) Negotiation period

If one or more proposals are received for the purchase of Plancor Numbered 877 within the time period specified in subsection (a), the Commission, notwithstanding the expiration of the period for negotiation specified in section 7 (f) [section 1941e(f) of this Appendix], shall negotiate with those submitting the proposals for a period of not to exceed sixty days for the purpose of entering into a definite contract of sale.

(c) Report to Congress; transfer period

Within ten days after the termination of the actual negotiation period referred to in subsection (b), the Commission shall prepare and submit to the Congress a report containing, with respect to the disposal under this section of Plancor Numbered 877, the information described in paragraphs (1) to (5), inclusive, and paragraph (8) of section 9(a) [section 1941g(a) of this Appendix]. Unless the contract is disapproved by either House of the Congress by a resolution prior to the expiration of thirty days of continuous session (as defined in section 9(c) [section 1941g(c) of this Appendix]) of the Congress following the date upon which the report is submitted to it, upon the expiration of such thirty-day period the contract shall become fully effective and the Commission shall proceed to carry it out, and transfer of possession of the facility sold shall be made as soon as practicable but in any event within thirty days after the expiration of such thirty-day period. The failure to complete transfer of possession within thirty days after the expiration of the period for congressional review shall not give rise to or be the basis of rescission of the contract of sale.

(d) Standby condition

If, upon termination of the transfer period provided for in subsection (c), no contract for the sale of Plancor Numbered 877 has become effective, the operating agency last designated by the President shall, as promptly as possible consistent with sound operating procedures, take said Plancor out of production and place it in adequate standby condition under the provisions of section 8 of the Rubber Producing Facilities Disposal Act of 1953 [section 1941f of this Appendix]: *Provided*, That the provisions in said section relating to the time for placing facilities in standby condition shall not apply to Plancor Numbered 877.

(Aug. 7, 1953, ch. 338, § 25, as added Mar. 31, 1955, ch. 19, § 1, 69 Stat. 15.)

Transfer of Functions

Functions, property, records, etc., of Rubber Producing Facilities Disposal Commission transferred to Federal Facilities Corporation by Ex. Ord. No. 10678, Sept. 20, 1956, 21 F.R. 7199, set out under section 1941r of this Appendix.

Federal Facilities Corporation dissolved and functions, property, records, etc., transferred to Administrator of General Services by Pub. L. 87–190, Aug. 30, 1961, 75 Stat. 418, set out as a note under section 1938 of this Appendix.

Submission of Disposal Report to Attorney General

Section 2 of act Mar. 31, 1955, provided that: "Notwithstanding the provisions of section 3(d) of the Rubber Producing Facilities Disposal Act of 1953 [section 1941a(d) of this Appendix], the Rubber Producing Facilities Disposal Commission (hereinafter referred to as the 'Commission') before submission to the Congress of its report relative to Plancor Numbered 877, shall submit it to the Attorney General, who shall, within seven days after receiving the report, advise the Commission whether, in his opinion, the proposed disposition, if carried out, will violate the antitrust laws."

Disposal Criteria

Section 5 of act Mar. 31, 1955, provided that: "Except as otherwise provided in this Act [enacting this section and provisions set out as notes under sections 1938, 1941r, and 1941w of this Appendix], disposal of Plancor Numbered 877 shall be fully subject to all the provisions of the Rubber Producing Facilities Disposal Act of 1953 [sections 1941 to 1941y of this Appendix] and such criteria as have been established by the Commission in handling disposal of other Government-owned rubber producing facilities under that Act: *Provided*, That the provisions of sections 7(j), 7 (k), 9(d), 9(f), 10, 11, 15, and 24 of that Act [sections 1941e(j), 1941e(k), 1941g(d), 1941g(f), 1941h, 1941i, 1941m, and 1941v of this Appendix] shall not apply to the disposal of Plancor Numbered 877. As promptly as practicable following the date of transfer of possession of Plancor Numbered 877 to a purchaser under this Act, the operating agency last designated by the President shall offer for sale to such purchaser the end products produced at such plant and held in inventory for Government account on the day of such transfer of possession, together with the feedstocks then located at such plant or purchased by the operating agency for use at such plant. Sale of such end products shall be made at the Government sales price prevailing on the business day next preceding the date of transfer of possession of such plant. Sale of such feedstocks shall be made at not less than their cost to the Government. In the event the purchaser declines to purchase such end products or feedstocks when first offered to it by the operating agency, they may be thereafter disposed of in such manner as the operating agency deems advisable. In the event Plancor Numbered 877 is not sold under the provisions of this Act, any end products produced at such plant and held in inventory for Government account on the day such plant is placed in standby condition pursuant to section 25(d) of the Rubber Producing Facilities Disposal Act of 1953, as added by this Act [subsec. (d) of this section], and any feedstocks then located at such plant or purchased by the operating agency for use at such plant shall be disposed of in such manner as the operating agency deems advisable, at the prevailing market price for such end products and feedstocks."

Lease or Sale of Tank Cars

Section 6 of act Mar. 31, 1955, provided that: "Notwithstanding any provision of the Rubber Producing Facilities Disposal Act of 1953 [sections 1941 to 1941y of this Appendix] and notwithstanding any other provision of this Act [enacting this section and provisions set out as notes under sections 1938, 1941r, and 1941w of this Appendix], the Commission or, after it ceases to exist, such agency of the Government as the President may designate, may, after securing the advice of the Attorney General as to whether the proposed lease or sale would tend to create or maintain a situation inconsistent with the antitrust laws, enter into leases or contracts of sale for all or any number of 448 pressure tank cars (ICC Classification ICC–104AW) for which the Commission invited proposals to purchase pursuant to that Act. Each such lease may be for such duration and each such lease or contract of sale may be made on such terms (including type of use) as the Commission or such other agency deems advisable in the public interest: *Provided*, That each such lease or contract of sale shall contain, among other provisions, a national security clause, and each such lease shall contain provisions for the recapture of the tank cars leased by the Government and the termination of the lease, if the President determines that the national interest so requires. The rental or price for any such tank car or cars shall be an amount which the Commission or such agency determines to be the maximum amount obtainable in the public interest, but not less than fair value as determined by the Commission. Any of such tank cars not under lease or contract of sale to non-Federal lessees or purchasers may be transferred without charge by the Commission or such agency to any Government department or agency upon request, for such use as the Commission or such agency deems advisable and subject to national security and recapture provisions of the type hereinabove provided for in this section running in favor of the Commission or other agency transferring the tank car or cars. Any of such tank cars not sold or under lease or transferred as hereinabove provided shall be placed and maintained in adequate standby condition pursuant to the provisions of section 8 of the Rubber Producing Facilities Disposal Act of 1953 [section 1941f of this Appendix]."

LIMITATION

Section 7 of act Mar. 31, 1955, provided that: "The provisions of this Act [enacting this section and provisions set out as notes under sections 1938, 1941r, and 1941w of this Appendix] shall not be applicable to the disposal of any Government-owned rubber-producing facilities other than Plancor Numbered 877 and 448 pressure tank cars (ICC Classification–ICC 104AW); and all action taken pursuant to the provisions of the Rubber Producing Facilities Disposal Act of 1953 [sections 1941 to 1941y of this Appendix] prior to the enactment of this Act [Mar. 31, 1955] shall be governed by the provisions of that Act [sections 1941 to 1941y of this Appendix] as it existed prior to the enactment of this Act and shall have the same force and effect as if this Act had not been enacted."

§ 1941x. Disposal of rubber-producing facility at Institute, West Virginia

(a) Receipt of proposal

Notwithstanding the second sentence of section 7(a) [section 1941e(a) of this Appendix], the period for receipt of proposals for the purchase of the Government-owned rubber-producing facility at Institute, West Virginia, known as Plancor Numbered 980, shall not expire until the end of the sixty-day period which begins on the date of the enactment of this section [Aug. 9, 1955].

(b) Negotiation period

If one or more proposals are received for the purchase of Plancor Numbered 980 within the time period specified in subsection (a), the Commission, notwithstanding the expiration of the period for negotiation specified in section 7 (f) [section 1941e(f) of this Appendix], shall negotiate with those submitting the proposals for a period of not to exceed seventy-five days for the purpose of entering into a definite contract of sale.

(c) Report to Congress; transfer period

Within ten days after the termination of the actual negotiation period referred to in subsection (b), or, if Congress is not then in session, within ten days after Congress next convenes, the Commission shall prepare and submit to the Congress a report containing with respect to the disposal under this section of Plancor Numbered 980, the information described in paragraphs (1) to (5), inclusive, and paragraph (8) of section 9(a) [section 1941g(a) of this Appendix]. Unless the contract is disapproved by either House of the Congress by a resolution prior to the expiration of thirty days of continuous session (as defined in section 9(c) [section 1941g(c) of this Appendix]) of the Congress following the date upon which the report is submitted to it, upon the expiration of such thirty-day period the contract shall become fully effective and the Commission shall proceed to carry it out, and transfer of possession of the facility sold shall be made as soon as practicable but in any event within thirty days after the expiration of such thirty-day period. The failure to complete transfer of possession within thirty days after the expiration of the period for congressional review shall not give rise to or be the basis of rescission of the contract of sale.

(d) Standby condition

If, upon termination of the transfer period provided for in subsection (c), no contract for the sale of Plancor Numbered 980 has become effective, the operating agency last designated by the President shall continue to maintain said Plancor in adequate standby condition under the provisions of section 8 of the Rubber Producing Facilities Disposal Act of 1953 [section 1941f of this Appendix].

(Aug. 7, 1953, ch. 338, § 26, as added Aug. 9, 1955, ch. 696, § 1, 69 Stat. 628.)

TRANSFER OF FUNCTIONS

Functions, property, records, etc., of Rubber Producing Facilities Disposal Commission transferred to Federal Facilities Corporation by Ex. Ord. No. 10678, Sept. 20, 1956, 21 F.R. 7199, set out under section 1941r of this Appendix.

Federal Facilities Corporation dissolved and functions, property, records, etc., transferred to Administrator of General Services by Pub. L. 87–190, Aug. 30, 1961, 75 Stat. 418, set out as a note under section 1938 of this Appendix.

SUBMISSION OF DISPOSAL REPORT TO ATTORNEY GENERAL

Section 2 of act Aug. 9, 1955, provided that: "Notwithstanding the provisions of section 3(d) of the Rubber Producing Facilities Disposal Act of 1953 [section 1941a(d) of this Appendix], the Rubber Producing Facilities Disposal Commission (hereinafter referred to as the 'Commission') before submission to the Congress of its report relative to Plancor Numbered 980, shall submit it to the Attorney General, who shall, within seven days after receiving the report, advise the Commission whether, in his opinion, the proposed disposition, if carried out, will violate the antitrust laws."

DISPOSAL CRITERIA

Section 5 of act Aug. 9, 1955, provided that: "Except as otherwise provided in this Act [enacting this section and provisions set out as notes under sections 1938, 1941r, and 1941x of this Appendix], disposal of Plancor

Numbered 980 shall be fully subject to all the provisions of the Rubber Producing Facilities Disposal Act of 1953 [sections 1941 to 1941y of this Appendix] and such criteria as have been established by the Commission in handling disposal of other Government-owned rubber producing facilities under that Act: *Provided*, That the provisions of sections 7(j), 7(k), 9(d), 9(f), 10, 11, 15, and 24 of that Act [sections 1941e(j), 1941e(k), 1941g(d), 1941g(f), 1941h, 1941i, 1941m, and 1941v of this Appendix] shall not apply to the disposal of Plancor Numbered 980. As promptly as practicable following the date of transfer of possession of Plancor Numbered 980 to a purchaser under this Act, the operating agency last designated by the President shall offer for sale to such purchaser the end products at such plant and held in inventory for Government account on the day of such transfer of possession, together with the feedstocks then located at such plant or purchased by the operating agency for use at such plant. Sale of such end products shall be made at the Government sales price prevailing on the business day next preceding the date of transfer of possession of such plant. Sale of such feedstocks shall be made at not less than their cost to the Government. In the event the purchaser declines to purchase such end products or feedstocks when first offered to it by the operating agency, they may be thereafter disposed of in such manner as the operating agency deems advisable. In the event Plancor Numbered 980 is not sold under the provisions of this Act, any end products at such plant and held in inventory for Government account and any feedstocks located at such plant or purchased by the operating agency for use at such plant shall be disposed of in such manner as the operating agency deems advisable, at the prevailing market price for such end products and feedstocks.''

LIMITATION

Section 6 of act Aug. 9, 1955, provided that: ''The provisions of this Act [enacting this section and provisions set out as notes under sections 1938, 1941r, and 1941x of this Appendix] shall not be applicable to the disposal of any Government-owned rubber-producing facilities other than Plancor Numbered 980; and all action taken pursuant to the provisions of the Rubber Producing Facilities Disposal Act of 1953 [sections 1941 to 1941y of this Appendix], or the amendment thereto known as Public Law 19 [section 1941w of this Appendix], enacted March 31, 1955, prior to the enactment of this Act [Aug. 9, 1955] shall be governed by the provisions of that Act as it existed prior to the enactment of this Act and shall have the same force and effect as if this Act had not been enacted.''

§ 1941y. Disposal of rubber-producing facility at Louisville, Kentucky

(a) Receipt of proposal

Notwithstanding the second sentence of section 7(a) [section 1941e(a) of this Appendix], the period for receipt of proposals for the purchase of the Government-owned rubber-producing facility at Louisville, Kentucky, known as Plancor Numbered 1207 and hereinafter referred to as the ''Louisville plant'', shall not expire until the end of the thirty-day period which begins on the date of the enactment of this section [Mar. 21, 1956].

(b) Negotiation period

If one or more proposals are received for the purchase of the Louisville plant within the time period specified in subsection (a), the Commission, notwithstanding the expiration of the period for negotiation specified in section 7(f) [section 1941e(f) of this Appendix], shall negotiate with those submitting the proposals for a period of not to exceed thirty days for the purpose of entering into a contract of sale.

(c) Report to Congress; transfer period

Within ten days after the termination of the actual negotiation period referred to in subsection (b), or, if Congress is not then in session, within ten days after Congress next convenes, the Commission shall prepare and submit to the Congress a report containing, with respect to the disposal under this section of the Louisville plant, the information described in paragraphs 1, 2, 3, 4, and 8 of section 9(a) [section 1941g(a) of this Appendix]. Unless the contract is disapproved by either House of the Congress by a resolution prior to the expiration of thirty days of continuous session (as defined in section 9(c) [section 1941g(c) of this Appendix]) of the Congress following the date upon which the report is submitted to it, upon the expiration of such thirty-day period the contract shall become fully effective and the Commission shall proceed to carry it out, and transfer of possession of the facility sold shall be made as soon as practicable but in any event within thirty days after the expiration or termination of the existing lease on the Louisville plant. The failure to complete transfer of possession within thirty days after expiration or termination of the existing lease shall not give rise to or be the basis of rescission of the contract of sale.

(Aug. 7, 1953, ch. 338, § 27, as added Mar. 21, 1956, ch. 89, § 1, 70 Stat. 51.)

TRANSFER OF FUNCTIONS

Functions, property, records, etc., of Rubber Producing Facilities Disposal Commission transferred to Federal Facilities Corporation by Ex. Ord. No. 10678, Sept. 20, 1956, 21 F.R. 7199, set out under section 1941r of this Appendix.

Federal Facilities Corporation dissolved and functions, property, records, etc., transferred to Administrator of General Services by Pub. L. 87–190, Aug. 30, 1961, 75 Stat. 418, set out as a note under section 1938 of this Appendix.

SUBMISSION OF DISPOSAL REPORT TO ATTORNEY GENERAL

Section 2 of act Mar. 21, 1956, provided that: ''Notwithstanding the provisions of section 3(d) of the Rubber Producing Facilities Disposal Act of 1953 [section 1941a(d) of this Appendix], the Rubber Producing Facilities Disposal Commission (hereinafter referred to as the 'Commission'), before submission to the Congress of its report relative to the Louisville plant shall submit it to the Attorney General, who shall, within seven days after receiving the report, advise the Commission whether, in his opinion, the proposed disposition, if carried out, will violate the antitrust laws.''

LEASE; TRANSMITTAL TO ATTORNEY GENERAL; CONGRESSIONAL REVIEW

Section 4 of act Mar. 21, 1956, provided that:

''(a) Notwithstanding the provisions of section 9(d) [section 1941g(d) of this Appendix] and notwithstanding the period of lease limitation in section 9(f) [section 1941g(f) of this Appendix] of the Rubber Producing Facilities Disposal Act of 1953, the Commission or its successor may, provided the period for receipt of proposals for the purchase of the Louisville plant has expired as provided in section 27(a) of that Act [subsection (a) of this section] and no proposal or contract for the purchase of the Louisville plant is then pending or in effect, extend the existing lease or enter into a new lease on the Louisville plant for a term of not less than five years nor more than fifteen years from the date of termination of said existing lease.

"(b) Notwithstanding the provisions of sections 8(a)(3) and 9(f) of the Rubber Producing Facilities Disposal Act of 1953 [sections 1941f(a)(3) and 1941g(f) of this Appendix] relating to the period for review by the Attorney General, the Commission, before submission to the Congress of a lease or lease extension relative to the Louisville plant, shall submit it to the Attorney General, who shall, within seven days after receiving the lease or lease extension, advise the Commission whether the proposed lease or lease extension would tend to create or maintain a situation inconsistent with the antitrust laws.

"(c) Within ten days after the termination of the lease negotiations authorized in subsection (a) of this section, or, if Congress is not then in session, within ten days after Congress next convenes, the Commission shall report to the Congress the lease or lease extension negotiated pursuant to this section. The Commission shall submit at the same time the statement of the Attorney General approving the proposed lease or lease extension in accordance with the standard set forth in subsection (b) of this section, and the names of the persons who have represented the Government or lessee in conducting negotiations for the lease or lease extension on the Louisville plant. Unless the lease or lease extension is disapproved by either House of the Congress by resolution prior to the expiration of thirty days of continuous session (as defined in section 9(c) of the Rubber Producing Facilities Disposal Act of 1953 [section 1941g(c) of this Appendix]) of the Congress following the date upon which the lease or lease extension is submitted to it, upon the expiration of such thirty-day period the lease or lease extension shall become fully effective and the Commission shall proceed to carry it out in accordance with its terms."

DISPOSAL CRITERIA

Section 5 of act Mar. 21, 1956, provided that: "Except as otherwise provided in this Act [enacting this section and provisions set out as notes under sections 1941f, 1941r, and 1941y of this Appendix], the disposal or lease of the Louisville plant shall be fully subject to all the provisions of the Rubber Producing Facilities Disposal Act of 1953 [sections 1941 to 1941y of this Appendix] and such criteria as have been established by the Commission in handling disposal of other Government-owned rubber producing facilities under this Act: *Provided*, That the provisions of sections 7(j), 7(k), 10, 15 and 24 of that Act [sections 1941e(j), 1941e(k), 1941h, 1941m and 1941v of this Appendix] shall not apply to the disposal or lease of the Louisville plants."

DISPLACED PERSONS, REFUGEES AND ORPHANS

ADMISSION OF DISPLACED PERSONS

ACT JUNE 25, 1948, CH. 647, 62 STAT. 1009

§§ 1951 to 1965. Omitted

CODIFICATION

Sections 1951 to 1965 authorized admission of displaced persons and permitted the issuance of immigration visas without regard to quota limitations prior to June 30, 1952.

Section 1951, acts June 25, 1948, ch. 647, §2, 62 Stat. 1009; June 16, 1950, ch. 262, §§1 to 3, 64 Stat. 219; June 28, 1951, ch. 167, §2, 65 Stat. 96, defined terms used in sections 1951 to 1965 of this Appendix.

Section 1952, acts June 25, 1948, ch. 647, §3, 62 Stat. 1010; June 16, 1950, ch. 262, §4, 64 Stat. 221; June 28, 1951, ch. 167, §1, 65 Stat. 96; June 27, 1952, ch. 477, title IV, §402(h)(1), (2), 66 Stat. 277, authorized issuance of visas prior to June 30, 1952, and provided for use of quota numbers.

Section 1953, acts June 25, 1948, ch. 647, §4, 62 Stat. 1011; June 16, 1950, ch. 262, §5, 64 Stat. 224; June 27, 1952, ch. 477, title IV, §402(h)(3), 66 Stat. 277, provided for adjustment of immigration status of aliens who entered prior to Apr. 30, 1949, if application for adjustment was made within two years after June 25, 1948.

Section 1954, acts June 25, 1948, ch. 647, §5, 62 Stat. 1011; June 28, 1951, ch. 167, §3, 65 Stat. 96; June 27, 1952, ch. 477, title IV, §402(h)(4), 66 Stat. 277, related to determination of quota nationality.

Section 1955, acts June 25, 1948, ch. 647, §6, 62 Stat. 1012; June 16, 1950, ch. 262, §6, 64 Stat. 224; June 27, 1952, ch. 477, title IV, §402(h)(5), 66 Stat. 277, related to preferences and priorities and authorized a "good faith" oath.

Section 1956, acts June 25, 1948, ch. 647, §7, 62 Stat. 1012; June 12, 1950, ch. 262, §7, 64 Stat. 225, required priority to be given to persons who bore arms against enemies of the United States or who served in labor service or guard units of the U.S. Army.

Section 1957, acts June 25, 1948, ch. 647, §8, 62 Stat. 1012; Oct. 15, 1949, ch. 695, §6(a), 63 Stat. 881; June 16, 1950, ch. 262, §8, 64 Stat. 225, created a Displaced Persons Commission of three members appointed for a term ending August 31, 1952 and provided for appropriations, employment of personnel, issuance of rules and regulations and reports to the President and the Congress, including a final report at the end of the Commission's term. Acts June 25, 1948, ch. 647, §8, 62 Stat. 1012; Oct. 15, 1949, ch. 695, §6(a), 63 Stat. 881, were subsequently repealed by Pub. L. 89–554, §8(a), Sept. 6, 1966, 80 Stat. 654, 655.

Section 1958, act June 25, 1948, ch. 647, §9, 62 Stat. 1013, related to reporting to Displaced Persons Commission by admitted persons.

Section 1959, acts June 25, 1948, ch. 647, §10, 62 Stat. 1013; June 16, 1950, ch. 262, §9, 64 Stat. 225, provided for investigation and report on all persons prior to admittance.

Section 1960, act June 25, 1948, ch. 647, §11, 62 Stat. 1013, prohibited preference or priority for visas under other laws after June 30, 1948.

Section 1961, acts June 25, 1948, ch. 647, §12, 62 Stat. 1013; June 16, 1950, ch. 262, §10, 64 Stat. 226; June 27, 1952, ch. 477, title IV, §402(h)(6), 66 Stat. 278, related to admission of persons of German ethnic origin.

Section 1962, acts June 25, 1948, ch. 647, §13, 62 Stat. 1014; June 16, 1950, ch. 262, §11, 64 Stat. 227, enumerated persons excluded from provisions authorizing visas.

Section 1962a, act June 25, 1948, ch. 647, §14, as added June 16, 1950, ch. 262, §12, 64 Stat. 227, authorized the Reconstruction Finance Corporation to make advances to the Displaced Persons Commission.

Section 1963, act June 25, 1948, ch. 647, §15, formerly §14, 62 Stat. 1014, renumbered June 16, 1950, ch. 262, §12, 64 Stat. 227, prescribed penalties for violations of sections 1951 to 1965 of this Appendix.

Section 1964, act June 25, 1948, ch. 647, §16, as added June 16, 1950, ch. 262, §13, 64 Stat. 228, related to conferences respecting problems of persons of German ethnic origin.

Section 1965, act June 25, 1948, ch. 647, §17, as added June 16, 1950, ch. 262, §14, 64 Stat. 228, required transportation by American flagships or planes.

ADMISSION OF REFUGEES AND ORPHANS

ACT AUG. 7, 1953, CH. 336, 67 STAT. 400

§§ 1971 to 1971q. Omitted

CODIFICATION

Sections 1971 to 1971q were omitted as terminated Dec. 31, 1956, pursuant to section 1971q of this Appendix.

Section 1971, act Aug. 7, 1953, ch. 336, §2, 67 Stat. 400, defined terms used in sections 1971 to 1971q of this Appendix.

Section 1971a, act Aug. 7, 1953, ch. 336, §3, 67 Stat. 401, authorized issuance of 205,000 special nonquota immigrant visas to aliens and their spouses, unmarried children under 21 years of age, stepchildren, and children adopted prior to July 1, 1953.

Section 1971b, acts Aug. 7, 1953, ch. 336, §4, 67 Stat. 401; Aug. 31, 1954, ch. 1169, §1, 68 Stat. 1044, provided for allocation among classes of visas issued under section 1971a of this Appendix.

Section 1971c, acts Aug. 7, 1953, ch. 336, §5, 67 Stat. 402; Aug. 31, 1954, ch. 1169, §2, 68 Stat. 1044, authorized not more than 4,000 special nonquota immigrants visas to eligible orphans.

Section 1971d, acts Aug. 7, 1953, ch. 336, §6, 67 Stat. 403; Aug. 31, 1954, ch. 1169, §3, 68 Stat. 1044, permitted applications not later than June 30, 1955, to adjust immigrant status of temporary residents.

Section 1971e, acts Aug. 7, 1953, ch. 336, §7, 67 Stat. 403; Aug. 31, 1954, ch. 1169, §4, 68 Stat. 1045, related to assurances of citizen sponsors, and deportation for inadmissibility.

Section 1971f, act Aug. 7, 1953, ch. 336, §8, 67 Stat. 404, related to intergovernmental arrangements for assistance to immigrants and use of American ships and airplanes.

Section 1971g, act Aug. 7, 1953, ch. 336, §9, 67 Stat. 405, related to determination of eligibility on a nondiscriminatory basis.

Section 1971h, act Aug. 7, 1953, ch. 336, §10, 67 Stat. 405, related to an exemption from visa fees.

Section 1971i, act Aug. 7, 1953, ch. 336, §11, 67 Stat. 405, related to safeguards in regards to security-screening.

Section 1971j, act Aug. 7, 1953, ch. 336, §12, 67 Stat. 405, related to priorities in consideration of visa applications.

Section 1971k, act Aug. 7, 1953, ch. 336, §13, 67 Stat. 406, related to priorities of persons eligible under the Displaced Persons Act of 1948.

Section 1971*l*, act Aug. 7, 1953, ch. 336, §14, 67 Stat. 406, related to ineligibility of certain persons.

Section 1971m, act Aug. 7, 1953, ch. 336, §15, 67 Stat. 406, related to applicability of Immigration and Nationality Act.

Section 1971n, act Aug. 7, 1953, ch. 336, §16, 67 Stat. 406, related to loans to pay transportation.

Section 1971*o*, act Aug. 7, 1953, ch. 336, §17, 67 Stat. 407, related to eligible aliens as nonquota immigrants.

Section 1971p, act Aug. 7, 1953, ch. 336, §19, 67 Stat. 407, related to semi-annual reports to President and Congress.

Section 1971q, act Aug. 7, 1953, ch. 336, §20, 67 Stat. 407, provided that no immigrant visa would issue under sections 1971 to 1971q of this Appendix after Dec. 31, 1956.

ADMISSION OF ORPHANS ADOPTED BY CITIZENS SERVING ABROAD

ACT JULY 29, 1953, CH. 268, 67 STAT. 229

§§1975 to 1975c. Omitted

CODIFICATION

Sections 1975 to 1975c were omitted as terminated pursuant to section 1975 of this Appendix.

Section 1975, act July 29, 1953, ch. 268, §1, 67 Stat. 229, authorized 500 special quota nonimmigrant visas for certain orphans and provided that the issuance of such visas under sections 1975 to 1975c of this Appendix would terminate no later than Dec. 31, 1954.

Section 1975a, act July 29, 1953, ch. 268, §2, 67 Stat. 229, defined "eligible orphan".

Section 1975b, act July 29, 1953, ch. 268, §3, 67 Stat. 230, related to rights of natural parents under Immigration and Nationality Act.

Section 1975c, act July 29, 1953, ch. 268, §4, 67 Stat. 230, related to eligible orphans as nonquota immigrants.

AMERICAN-JAPANESE EVACUATION CLAIMS

ACT JULY 2, 1948, CH. 814, 62 STAT. 1231

§1981. Attorney General's jurisdiction; uncompensated claims; condition precedent; definitions

(a) The Attorney General shall have jurisdiction to compromise and settle and make an award in an amount not to exceed $100,000 as hereinafter provided on any claim by a person of Japanese ancestry against the United States arising on or after December 7, 1941, when such claim is not compensated for by insurance or otherwise, for damage to or loss of real or personal property (including without limitation as to amount damage to or loss of personal property bailed to or in the custody of the Government or any agent thereof), that is (except as is otherwise provided by subsections 1(b)(2) and (1)(b)(3)) [subsections (b)(2) and (b)(3) of this section] a reasonable and natural consequence of the evacuation or exclusion of such person by the appropriate military commander from a military area in Arizona, California, Oregon, or Washington; or from the Territory of Alaska, or the Territory of Hawaii, under authority of Executive Order Numbered 9066, dated February 19, 1942 (3 C.F.R. Cum. Supp. 1092), section 67 of the Act of April 30, 1900 (48 U.S.C. 532), or Executive Order Numbered 9489, dated October 18, 1944 (3 C.F.R. 1944 Supp. 45).

(b) As used herein—

(1) "Evacuation" shall include voluntary departure from a military area prior to but in anticipation of an order of exclusion therefrom.

(2) "Claims by a person of Japanese ancestry" shall include claims that were filed by any profit or nonprofit organization, corporate or otherwise, the majority of whose stock was owned by, or the majority of whose stockholders or members were, on December 7, 1941, and on the date of the filing of the claim, persons of Japanese ancestry actually residing within the continental limits of the United States or its Territories: *Provided, however*, That the losses sustained by the particular organization were the result (1) of the evacuation and exclusion of its stockholders or members, or (2) of the evacuation and exclusion of persons of Japanese ancestry upon whom the organization depended for its business or support. Such claims shall not be barred by awards or disallowances heretofore made.

(3) "Claim by a person of Japanese ancestry" shall also include claims which have been timely filed for such damage or loss as heretofore defined incurred by persons of Japanese ancestry detained, interned, or paroled, and subsequently released, pursuant to Revised Statutes, sections 4067–70, as amended (relating to alien enemies) [50 U.S.C. 21 to 24]. Such claims shall also include losses due to the exclusion of the families and relatives of such persons during their deten-

tion or internment. Any such person shall be deemed to have been excluded from such military areas and territories as of the date he would have been evacuated had he not been detained or interned. The claim of or on behalf of such person shall not be barred by any award or disallowance heretofore made.

(July 2, 1948, ch. 814, §1, 62 Stat. 1231; July 9, 1956, ch. 531, 70 Stat. 513.)

REFERENCES IN TEXT

Section 67 of the Act of April 30, 1900 (48 U.S.C. 532), referred to in subsec. (a), was omitted from the Code.

AMENDMENTS

1956—Subsec. (a). The former first sentence of section was designated subsec. (a) by act July 9, 1956, which permitted the Attorney General to compromise and settle and make an award in an amount not to exceed $100,000.

Subsec. (b). The former second sentence of section was designated subsec. (b) by act July 9, 1956, which defined ''claims by a person of Japanese ancestry'' and ''claim by a person of Japanese ancestry''.

SHORT TITLE OF 2000 AMENDMENT

Pub. L. 106–451, §1, Nov. 7, 2000, 114 Stat. 1947, provided that: ''This Act [enacting provisions set out as a note under this section] may be cited as the 'Wartime Violation of Italian American Civil Liberties Act'.''

VIOLATION OF CIVIL LIBERTIES OF ITALIAN AMERICANS DURING WORLD WAR II

Pub. L. 106–451, §3, Nov. 7, 2000, 114 Stat. 1947, provided that: ''The Attorney General shall conduct a comprehensive review of the treatment by the United States Government of Italian Americans during World War II, and not later than 1 year after the date of the enactment of this Act [Nov. 7, 2000] shall submit to the Congress a report that documents the findings of such review. The report shall cover the period between September 1, 1939, and December 31, 1945, and shall include the following:

''(1) The names of all Italian Americans who were taken into custody in the initial roundup following the attack on Pearl Harbor, and prior to the United States declaration of war against Italy.

''(2) The names of all Italian Americans who were taken into custody.

''(3) The names of all Italian Americans who were interned and the location where they were interned.

''(4) The names of all Italian Americans who were ordered to move out of designated areas under the United States Army's 'Individual Exclusion Program'.

''(5) The names of all Italian Americans who were arrested for curfew, contraband, or other violations under the authority of Executive Order No. 9066 [not classified to the Code].

''(6) Documentation of Federal Bureau of Investigation raids on the homes of Italian Americans.

''(7) A list of ports from which Italian American fishermen were restricted.

''(8) The names of Italian American fishermen who were prevented from fishing in prohibited zones and therefore unable to pursue their livelihoods.

''(9) The names of Italian Americans whose boats were confiscated.

''(10) The names of Italian American railroad workers who were prevented from working in prohibited zones.

''(11) A list of all civil liberties infringements suffered by Italian Americans during World War II, as a result of Executive Order No. 9066, including internment, hearings without benefit of counsel, illegal searches and seizures, travel restrictions, enemy alien registration requirements, employment restrictions, confiscation of property, and forced evacuation from homes.

''(12) An explanation of whether Italian Americans were subjected to civil liberties infringements, as a result of Executive Order No. 9066, and if so, why other Italian Americans were not.

''(13) A review of the wartime restrictions on Italian Americans to determine how civil liberties can be better protected during national emergencies.''

COMMISSION ON WARTIME RELOCATION AND INTERNMENT OF CIVILIANS

Pub. L. 96–317, July 31, 1980, 94 Stat. 964, as amended by Pub. L. 97–3, Feb. 10, 1981, 95 Stat. 5; Pub. L. 97–152, Mar. 16, 1982, 96 Stat. 11; Pub. L. 97–377, title I, §111A, Dec. 21, 1982, 96 Stat. 1911, provided for establishment of Commission on Wartime Relocation and Internment of Civilians which was to, not later than June 30, 1983, submit to Congress a final report and study concerning facts and circumstances surrounding Ex. Ord. No. 9066, issued Feb. 19, 1942, pursuant to which thousands of American citizens and permanent resident aliens were relocated and detained in internment camps, and which was to further review U.S. military directives requiring relocation and detention of American citizens, including Aleut civilians, and permanent resident aliens of Aleutian and Pribilof Islands, as well as recommend appropriate remedies for such actions, and further provided for establishment of Commission as well as powers, administrative procedures, appropriations, and termination of Commission 90 days after submission of final report to Congress.

§1982. Time limitation on presentation of claims; claims excluded

(a) The Attorney General shall receive claims for a period of eighteen months from the date of the original enactment of this Act [July 2, 1948]. All claims not presented within that time shall be forever barred: *Provided, however*, That any claim received by the Attorney General bearing a postmark prior to midnight, January 3, 1950, shall be considered to be timely filed within the said eighteen months. Any claim, timely filed, may be amended at any time prior to its final determination in order to include then compensable items of claim which, by the provisions of this Act [sections 1981 to 1987 of this Appendix] as they existed when the claim was filed, the Attorney General was not authorized to determine or consider.

(b) The Attorney General shall not consider any claim—

(1) by or on behalf of any person who after December 7, 1941, was voluntarily or involuntarily deported from the United States to Japan or by and on behalf of any alien who on December 7, 1941, was not actually residing in the United States;

(2) Except[1] as provided in section 1(b)(3) [section 1981(b)(3) of this Appendix], for damage or loss arising out of action taken by any Federal agency pursuant to sections 4067, 4068, 4069, and 4070 (relating to alien enemies) of the Revised Statutes, as amended (50 U.S.C. 21 to 24), or pursuant to the Trading With the Enemy Act, as amended (50 U.S.C. App., and Supp., 1–31, 616);

(3) for damage or loss to any property, or interest therein, vested in the United States pursuant to said Trading With the Enemy Act, as amended [sections 1 to 6, 7 to 39, and 41 to 44 of this Appendix];

[1] So in original. Probably should not be capitalized.

(4) for damage or loss on account of death or personal injury, personal inconvenience, physical hardship, or mental suffering; and

(5) for loss of anticipated profits or loss of anticipated earnings.

(July 2, 1948, ch. 814, § 2, 62 Stat. 1231; July 9, 1956, ch. 531, 70 Stat. 514.)

AMENDMENTS

1956—Subsec. (a). Act July 9, 1956, validated claims received by the Attorney General bearing a postmark prior to midnight, Jan. 3, 1950, and permitted amendment of claims timely filed.

Subsec. (b)(2). Act July 9, 1956, amended par. (2) generally, inserting at beginning "Except as provided in section 1(b)(3),".

§ 1983. Notice; evidence; records

(a) The Attorney General shall give reasonable notice to the interested parties and an opportunity for them to present evidence before making a final determination upon any claim.

(b) For the purpose of any investigation authorized under this Act [sections 1981 to 1987 of this Appendix], the provisions of sections 9 and 10 (relating to examination of documentary evidence, attendance of witnesses, and production of books, papers, and documents) of the Federal Trade Commission Act of September 26, 1914, as amended (15 U.S.C. 49, 50), are made applicable to the jurisdiction, powers, and duties of the Attorney General. Subpenas may be served personally, by registered mail, by telegraph, or by leaving a copy thereof at the residence or principal place of business of the person required to be served. A verified return by the individual so serving the same, setting forth the manner of service, shall be proof of service. The United States marshals or their deputies shall serve such process in their respective districts.

(c) A record shall be kept of all proceedings under this Act [sections 1981 to 1987 of this Appendix] and shall be open to public inspection.

(July 2, 1948, ch. 814, § 3, 62 Stat. 1231; July 9, 1956, ch. 531, 70 Stat. 515.)

AMENDMENTS

1956—Subsec. (a). Act July 9, 1956, struck out provisions permitting interested parties to be heard.

Subsec. (b). Act July 9, 1956, struck out provisions relating to hearings.

Subsec. (c). Act July 9, 1956, struck out provisions relating to hearings and substituted "records" for "written record".

§ 1984. Compromise of claims by Attorney General; jurisdiction of United States Court of Federal Claims to determine claims timely filed; report to Congress; payment of awards; finality of decisions

(a) The Attorney General is authorized to compromise and settle and make an award in an amount not to exceed $100,000 on any claim timely filed under this Act, as amended [sections 1981 to 1987 of this Appendix], on the basis of affidavits, available Government records, and other information satisfactory to him.

(b) The United States Court of Federal Claims shall have jurisdiction to determine any claim timely filed under this Act [sections 1981 to 1987 of this Appendix]. A petition for the determination of a claim by the United States Court of Federal Claims shall be filed with the clerk of the said court and a copy of the petition shall be served upon the Attorney General by registered mail. Such a petition may be filed at any time after enactment of this subsection except that it must be filed within ninety days after the date of a notice by the Attorney General served on the claimant by registered mail that no further consideration will be given to the compromise of the claim. Upon the timely filing and serving of such petition, the United States Court of Federal Claims shall have jurisdiction to hear and determine said claim in the same manner and under the same rules as any other cause properly before it and applying rules of equity and justice. Upon being served with a copy of such petition, the Attorney General shall forthwith certify and transmit to the clerk of the United States Court of Federal Claims the original statement of the claim and any requested amendments thereto for filing with the said clerk as a preliminary record in the case.

(c) On the first day of each regular session of Congress the Attorney General shall transmit to Congress a full and complete statement of all compromise settlements effected by the Attorney General under this Act, as amended [sections 1981 to 1987 of this Appendix], during the previous year, stating the name and address of each claimant, the amount claimed, and the amount awarded. All awards shall be paid in like manner as are final judgments of the United States Court of Federal Claims.

(d) Except as herein provided, the payment of an award shall be final and conclusive for all purposes, notwithstanding any other provision of law to the contrary, and shall be a full discharge of the United States and all of its officers, agents, servants, and employees with respect to all claims arising out of the same subject matter.

(July 2, 1948, ch. 814, § 4, 62 Stat. 1232; Aug. 17, 1951, ch. 327, § 1, 65 Stat. 192; July 9, 1956, ch. 531, 70 Stat. 514; Pub. L. 97–164, title I, § 160(a)(19), Apr. 2, 1982, 96 Stat. 48; Pub. L. 98–620, title IV, § 402(55), Nov. 8, 1984, 98 Stat. 3361; Pub. L. 102–572, title IX, § 902(b)(1), Oct. 29, 1992, 106 Stat. 4516.)

REFERENCES IN TEXT

Any time after enactment of this subsection, referred to in subsec. (b), probably means any time after July 9, 1956, which was the date of enactment of the 1956 amendment of subsec. (b).

AMENDMENTS

1992—Subsecs. (b), (c). Pub. L. 102–572 substituted "United States Court of Federal Claims" for "United States Claims Court" wherever appearing.

1984—Subsec. (b). Pub. L. 98–620 struck out provisions that required that such petitions be treated for docketing, hearing and determination, to the fullest practicable extent, as if the petition had been filed with the United States Claims Court on the date the original claim was received by the Attorney General, but that no such petition would have precedence over petitions involving interest-bearing obligations of the United States.

1982—Subsecs. (b), (c). Pub. L. 97–164 substituted "United States Claims Court" for "Court of Claims" wherever appearing.

1956—Subsec. (a). Act July 9, 1956, substituted provisions permitting the Attorney General to compromise and settle and make an award in an amount not to exceed $100,000 for provisions which required him to adjudicate, except as to compromised claims, all claims filed, by award or order of dismissal, upon written findings of fact and reasons for the decision.

Subsec. (b). Act July 9, 1956, substituted provisions granting jurisdiction to the Court of Claims to determine timely claims for provisions which authorized the Attorney General to make payment of any award not exceeding $2,500 in amount.

Subsec. (c). Act July 9, 1956, required the Attorney General to report on all compromise settlements effected during the previous year.

Subsec. (d). Act July 9, 1956, inserted "Except as herein provided", and struck out provisions which barred any further claim against the United States where there is an order of dismissal against a claimant, unless set aside by the Attorney General.

1951—Subsec. (a). Act Aug. 17, 1951, inserted exception as to claims compromised.

EFFECTIVE DATE OF 1992 AMENDMENT

Amendment by Pub. L. 102–572 effective Oct. 29, 1992, see section 911 of Pub. L. 102–572, set out as a note under section 171 of Title 28, Judiciary and Judicial Procedure.

EFFECTIVE DATE OF 1984 AMENDMENT

Amendment by Pub. L. 98–620 not applicable to cases pending on Nov. 8, 1984, see section 403 of Pub. L. 98–620, set out as a note under section 1657 of Title 28, Judiciary and Judicial Procedure.

EFFECTIVE DATE OF 1982 AMENDMENT

Amendment by Pub. L. 97–164 effective Oct. 1, 1982, see section 402 of Pub. L. 97–164 set out as a note under section 171 of Title 28, Judiciary and Judicial Procedure.

EXCLUSION FROM GROSS INCOME OF CERTAIN AWARDS MADE PURSUANT TO EVACUATION CLAIMS OF JAPANESE-AMERICAN PERSONS

Pub. L. 87–834, §27, Oct. 16, 1962, 76 Stat. 1067, as amended by Pub. L. 99–514, §2, Oct. 22, 1986, 100 Stat. 2095, provided that:

"(a) IN GENERAL.—No amount received as an award under the Act entitled 'An Act to authorize the Attorney General to adjudicate certain claims resulting from evacuation of certain persons of Japanese ancestry under military orders', approved July 2, 1948, as amended by Public Law 116, Eighty-second Congress, and Public Law 673, Eighty-fourth Congress (50 U.S.C. App., secs. 1981–1987), shall be included in gross income for purposes of chapter 1 of the Internal Revenue Code of 1939 or chapter 1 of the Internal Revenue Code of 1986 [formerly I.R.C. 1954].

"(b) EFFECTIVE DATE, ETC.—Subsection (a) shall apply with respect to taxable years ending after July 2, 1948. If refund or credit of any overpayment of Federal income tax resulting from the application of subsection (a) (including interest, additions to the tax, additional amounts, and penalties) is prevented on the date of the enactment of this Act [Oct. 16, 1962], or within one year from such date, by the operation of any law or rule of law, the refund or credit of such overpayment may nevertheless be made or allowed if claim therefor is filed within one year after the date of enactment of this Act [Oct. 16, 1962]. In the case of a claim to which the preceding sentence applies, the amount to be refunded or credited as an overpayment shall not be diminished by any credit or setoff based upon any item other than the amount of the award referred to in subsection (a). No interest shall be allowed or paid on any overpayment resulting from the application of this section."

§ 1985. Attorney's fees; penalty for overcharging

The Attorney General, in rendering an award in favor of any claimant, may as a part of the award determine and allow reasonable attorneys' fees, which shall not exceed 10 per centum of the amount allowed, to be paid out of, but not in addition to, the amount of such award.

Any attorney who charges, demands, receives, or collects for services rendered in connection with such claim any amount in excess of that allowed under this section, if recovery be had, shall be guilty of a misdemeanor, and shall upon conviction thereof be subject to a fine of not more than $2,000, or imprisonment for not more than one year, or both.

(July 2, 1948, ch. 814, §5, 62 Stat. 1232.)

§ 1986. Administration

For the purposes of this Act [sections 1981 to 1987 of this Appendix] the Attorney General may—

(a) appoint a clerk and such attorneys, examiners, interpreters, appraisers, and other employees as may be necessary;

(b) call upon any Federal department or agency for any information or records necessary;

(c) secure the cooperation of State and local agencies, governmental or otherwise, and reimburse such agencies for services rendered;

(d) utilize such voluntary and uncompensated services as may from time to time be needed and available;

(e) assist needy claimants in the preparation and filing of claims;

(f) make such investigations as may be necessary;

(g) make expenditures for witness fees and mileage and for other administrative expenses;

(h) prescribe such rules and regulations, perform such acts not inconsistent with law, and delegate such authority as he may deem proper in carrying out the provisions of this Act [sections 1981 to 1987 of this Appendix].

(July 2, 1948, ch. 814, §6, 62 Stat. 1232.)

§ 1987. Authorization of appropriations

There are hereby authorized to be appropriated for the purposes of this Act [sections 1981 to 1987 of this Appendix] such sums as Congress may from time to time determine to be necessary.

(July 2, 1948, ch. 814, §7, 62 Stat. 1233; Aug. 17, 1951, ch. 327, §2, 65 Stat. 192; July 9, 1956, ch. 531, 70 Stat. 515.)

AMENDMENTS

1956—Act July 9, 1956, struck out provisions which made funds available for payment of settlement awards.

1951—Act Aug. 17, 1951, inserted provisions giving the Attorney General authority to effect compromise settlement of certain claims, not to exceed $2,500 in amount with respect to each such claim.

RESTITUTION FOR WORLD WAR II INTERNMENT OF JAPANESE-AMERICANS AND ALEUTS

PUB. L. 100–383, AUG. 10, 1988, 102 STAT. 903

§ 1989. Purposes

The purposes of this Act [sections 1989 to 1989d of this Appendix] are to—

(1) acknowledge the fundamental injustice of the evacuation, relocation, and internment of United States citizens and permanent resident aliens of Japanese ancestry during World War II;

(2) apologize on behalf of the people of the United States for the evacuation, relocation, and internment of such citizens and permanent resident aliens;

(3) provide for a public education fund to finance efforts to inform the public about the internment of such individuals so as to prevent the recurrence of any similar event;

(4) make restitution to those individuals of Japanese ancestry who were interned;

(5) make restitution to Aleut residents of the Pribilof Islands and the Aleutian Islands west of Unimak Island, in settlement of United States obligations in equity and at law, for—

(A) injustices suffered and unreasonable hardships endured while those Aleut residents were under United States control during World War II;

(B) personal property taken or destroyed by United States forces during World War II;

(C) community property, including community church property, taken or destroyed by United States forces during World War II; and

(D) traditional village lands on Attu Island not rehabilitated after World War II for Aleut occupation or other productive use;

(6) discourage the occurrence of similar injustices and violations of civil liberties in the future; and

(7) make more credible and sincere any declaration of concern by the United States over violations of human rights committed by other nations.

(Pub. L. 100–383, § 1, Aug. 10, 1988, 102 Stat. 903.)

§ 1989a. Statement of the Congress

(a) With regard to individuals of Japanese ancestry

The Congress recognizes that, as described by the Commission on Wartime Relocation and Internment of Civilians, a grave injustice was done to both citizens and permanent resident aliens of Japanese ancestry by the evacuation, relocation, and internment of civilians during World War II. As the Commission documents, these actions were carried out without adequate security reasons and without any acts of espionage or sabotage documented by the Commission, and were motivated largely by racial prejudice, wartime hysteria, and a failure of political leadership. The excluded individuals of Japanese ancestry suffered enormous damages, both material and intangible, and there were incalculable losses in education and job training, all of which resulted in significant human suffering for which appropriate compensation has not been made. For these fundamental violations of the basic civil liberties and constitutional rights of these individuals of Japanese ancestry, the Congress apologizes on behalf of the Nation.

(b) With respect to the Aleuts

The Congress recognizes that, as described by the Commission on Wartime Relocation and Internment of Civilians, the Aleut civilian residents of the Pribilof Islands and the Aleutian Islands west of Unimak Island were relocated during World War II to temporary camps in isolated regions of southeast Alaska where they remained, under United States control and in the care of the United States, until long after any potential danger to their home villages had passed. The United States failed to provide reasonable care for the Aleuts, and this resulted in widespread illness, disease, and death among the residents of the camps; and the United States further failed to protect Aleut personal and community property while such property was in its possession or under its control. The United States has not compensated the Aleuts adequately for the conversion or destruction of personal property, and the conversion or destruction of community property caused by the United States military occupation of Aleut villages during World War II. There is no remedy for injustices suffered by the Aleuts during World War II except an Act of Congress providing appropriate compensation for those losses which are attributable to the conduct of United States forces and other officials and employees of the United States.

(Pub. L. 100–383, § 2, Aug. 10, 1988, 102 Stat. 903.)

SECTION REFERRED TO IN OTHER SECTIONS

This section is referred to in sections 1989b–1, 1989b–2 of this Appendix.

TITLE I—UNITED STATES CITIZENS OF JAPANESE ANCESTRY AND RESIDENT JAPANESE ALIENS

§ 1989b. Short title

This title [sections 1989b to 1989b–9 of this Appendix] may be cited as the "Civil Liberties Act of 1988".

(Pub. L. 100–383, title I, § 101, Aug. 10, 1988, 102 Stat. 904.)

SHORT TITLE OF 1992 AMENDMENT

Pub. L. 102–371, § 1, Sept. 27, 1992, 106 Stat. 1167, provided that: "This Act [amending sections 1989b–3, 1989b–4, 1989b–7, and 1989b–9 of this Appendix and enacting provisions set out as a note under section 1989b–4 of this Appendix] may be cited as the 'Civil Liberties Act Amendments of 1992'."

§ 1989b–1. Remedies with respect to criminal convictions

(a) Review of convictions

The Attorney General is requested to review any case in which an individual living on the date of the enactment of this Act [Aug. 10, 1988] was, while a United States citizen or permanent resident alien of Japanese ancestry, convicted of a violation of—

(1) Executive Order Numbered 9066, dated February 19, 1942;

(2) the Act entitled "An Act to provide a penalty for violation of restrictions or orders with respect to persons entering, remaining in, leaving, or committing any act in military areas or zones", approved March 21, 1942 (56 Stat. 173); or

(3) any other Executive order, Presidential proclamation, law of the United States, directive of the Armed Forces of the United States, or other action taken by or on behalf of the United States or its agents, representatives, officers, or employees, respecting the evacuation, relocation, or internment of individuals solely on the basis of Japanese ancestry;

on account of the refusal by such individual, during the evacuation, relocation, and internment period, to accept treatment which discriminated against the individual on the basis of the individual's Japanese ancestry.

(b) Recommendations for pardons

Based upon any review under subsection (a), the Attorney General is requested to recommend to the President for pardon consideration those convictions which the Attorney General considers appropriate.

(c) Action by the President

In consideration of the statement of the Congress set forth in section 2(a) [section 1989a(a) of this Appendix], the President is requested to offer pardons to any individuals recommended by the Attorney General under subsection (b).

(Pub. L. 100–383, title I, § 102, Aug. 10, 1988, 102 Stat. 904.)

REFERENCES IN TEXT

Executive Order Numbered 9066, dated February 19, 1942, referred to in subsec. (a)(1), is not classified to the Code.

The Act entitled "An Act to provide a penalty for violation of restrictions or orders with respect to persons entering, remaining in, leaving, or committing any act in military areas or zones", approved March 21, 1942 (56 Stat. 173), referred to in subsec. (a)(2), is act Mar. 21, 1942, ch. 191, 56 Stat. 173, which was classified to section 97a of former Title 18, Criminal Code and Criminal Procedure, and was repealed by act of June 25, 1948, ch. 645, § 21, 62 Stat. 868 and reenacted as section 1383 of Title 18, Crimes and Criminal Procedure. Section 1383 of Title 18 was repealed by Pub. L. 94–412, title V, § 501(e), Sept. 14, 1976, 90 Stat. 1258.

§ 1989b–2. Consideration of Commission findings by departments and agencies

(a) Review of applications by eligible individuals

Each department and agency of the United States Government shall review with liberality, giving full consideration to the findings of the Commission and the statement of the Congress set forth in section 2(a) [section 1989a(a) of this Appendix], any application by an eligible individual for the restitution of any position, status, or entitlement lost in whole or in part because of any discriminatory act of the United States Government against such individual which was based upon the individual's Japanese ancestry and which occurred during the evacuation, relocation, and internment period.

(b) No new authority created

Subsection (a) does not create any authority to grant restitution described in that subsection, or establish any eligibility to apply for such restitution.

(Pub. L. 100–383, title I, § 103, Aug. 10, 1988, 102 Stat. 905.)

§ 1989b–3. Trust Fund

(a) Establishment

There is established in the Treasury of the United States the Civil Liberties Public Education Fund, which shall be administered by the Secretary of the Treasury.

(b) Investment of amounts in the Fund

Amounts in the Fund shall be invested in accordance with section 9702 of title 31, United States Code.

(c) Uses of the Fund

Amounts in the Fund shall be available only for disbursement by the Attorney General under section 105 [section 1989b–4 of this Appendix] and by the Board under section 106 [section 1989b–5 of this Appendix].

(d) Termination

The Fund shall terminate not later than the earlier of the date on which an amount has been expended from the Fund which is equal to the amount authorized to be appropriated to the Fund by subsection (e), and any income earned on such amount, or 10 years after the date of the enactment of this Act [Aug. 10, 1988]. If all of the amounts in the Fund have not been expended by the end of that 10-year period, investments of amounts in the Fund shall be liquidated and receipts thereof deposited in the Fund and all funds remaining in the Fund shall be deposited in the miscellaneous receipts account in the Treasury.

(e) Authorization of appropriations

There are authorized to be appropriated to the Fund $1,650,000,000, of which not more than $500,000,000 may be appropriated for any fiscal year. Any amounts appropriated pursuant to this section are authorized to remain available until expended.

(Pub. L. 100–383, title I, § 104, Aug. 10, 1988, 102 Stat. 905; Pub. L. 102–371, § 2, Sept. 27, 1992, 106 Stat. 1167.)

AMENDMENTS

1992—Subsec. (e). Pub. L. 102–371 substituted "$1,650,000,000" for "$1,250,000,000".

MAXIMUM AMOUNT AUTHORIZED FOR FUND

Pub. L. 101–162, title II, Nov. 21, 1989, 103 Stat. 996, provided that: "Subject to the provisions of section 104(e) of the Civil Liberties Act of 1988 (Public Law 100–383; 50 U.S.C. App. 1989(b-3(e)) [subsec. (e) of this section], the maximum amount authorized under such section for any fiscal year is appropriated, from money in the Treasury not otherwise appropriated, for each fiscal year beginning on or after October 1, 1990, to the Civil Liberties Public Education Fund established by section 104(a) of the Civil Liberties Act of 1988, for payments to eligible individuals under section 105 of that Act [50 App. U.S.C. 1989b–4]."

SECTION REFERRED TO IN OTHER SECTIONS

This section is referred to in sections 1989b–7, 1989b–9 of this Appendix.

§ 1989b–4. Restitution

(a) Location and payment of eligible individuals

(1) In general

Subject to paragraph (7), the Attorney General shall, subject to the availability of funds appropriated to the Fund for such purpose, pay out of the Fund to each eligible individual the sum of $20,000, unless such individual refuses, in the manner described in paragraph (5), to accept the payment.

(2) Location of eligible individuals

The Attorney General shall identify and locate, without requiring any application for payment and using records already in the possession of the United States Government, each eligible individual. The Attorney General should use funds and resources available to the Attorney General, including those described in subsection (c), to attempt to complete such identification and location within 12 months after the date of the enactment of this Act [Aug. 10, 1988]. Any eligible individual may notify the Attorney General that such individual is an eligible individual, and may provide documentation therefor. The Attorney General shall designate an officer or employee to whom such notification and documentation may be sent, shall maintain a list of all individuals who submit such notification and documentation, and shall, subject to the availability of funds appropriated for such purpose, encourage, through a public awareness campaign, each eligible individual to submit his or her current address to such officer or employee. To the extent that resources referred to in the second sentence of this paragraph are not sufficient to complete the identification and location of all eligible individuals, there are authorized to be appropriated such sums as may be necessary for such purpose. In any case, the identification and location of all eligible individuals shall be completed within 12 months after the appropriation of funds under the preceding sentence. Failure to be identified and located by the end of the 12-month period specified in the preceding sentence shall not preclude an eligible individual from receiving payment under this section.

(3) Benefit of the doubt

When, after consideration of all evidence and relevant material for determining whether an individual is an eligible individual, there is an approximate balance of positive and negative evidence regarding the merits of an issue material to the determination of eligibility, the benefit of the doubt in resolving each such issue shall be given to such individual.

(4) Notice from the Attorney General

The Attorney General shall, when funds are appropriated to the Fund for payments to an eligible individual under this section, notify that eligible individual in writing of his or her eligibility for payment under this section. Such notice shall inform the eligible individual that—

(A) acceptance of payment under this section shall be in full satisfaction of all claims against the United States arising out of acts described in section 108(2)(B) [section 1989b–7(2)(B) of this Appendix], and

(B) each eligible individual who does not refuse, in the manner described in paragraph (5), to accept payment under this section within 18 months after receiving such written notice shall be deemed to have accepted payment for purposes of paragraph (6).

(5) Effect of refusal to accept payment

If an eligible individual refuses, in a written document filed with the Attorney General, to accept any payment under this section, the amount of such payment shall remain in the Fund and no payment may be made under this section to such individual at any time after such refusal.

(6) Payment in full settlement of claims against the United States

The acceptance of payment by an eligible individual under this section shall be in full satisfaction of all claims against the United States arising out of acts described in section 108(2)(B) [section 1989b–7(2)(B) of this Appendix]. This paragraph shall apply to any eligible individual who does not refuse, in the manner described in paragraph (5), to accept payment under this section within 18 months after receiving the notification from the Attorney General referred to in paragraph (4).

(7) Exclusion of certain individuals

No payment may be made under this section to any individual who, after September 1, 1987, accepts payment pursuant to an award of a final judgment or a settlement on a claim against the United States for acts described in section 108(2)(B) [section 1989b–7(2)(B) of this Appendix], or to any surviving spouse, child, or parent of such individual to whom paragraph (8) applies.

(8) Payments in the case of deceased persons

(A) In the case of an eligible individual who is deceased at the time of payment under this section, such payment shall be made only as follows:

(i) If the eligible individual is survived by a spouse who is living at the time of payment, such payment shall be made to such surviving spouse.

(ii) If there is no surviving spouse described in clause (i), such payment shall be made in equal shares to all children of the eligible individual who are living at the time of payment.

(iii) If there is no surviving spouse described in clause (i) and if there are no children described in clause (ii), such payment shall be made in equal shares to the parents of the eligible individual who are living at the time of payment.

If there is no surviving spouse, children, or parents described in clauses (i), (ii), and (iii), the amount of such payment shall remain in the Fund, and may be used only for the purposes set forth in section 106(b) [section 1989b–5(b) of this Appendix].

(B) After the death of an eligible individual, this subsection and subsections (c) and (f) shall apply to the individual or individuals specified in subparagraph (A) to whom payment under this section will be made, to the same extent as such subsections apply to the eligible individual.

(C) For purposes of this paragraph—

(i) the "spouse" of an eligible individual means a wife or husband of an eligible individual who was married to that eligible individual for at least 1 year immediately before the death of the eligible individual;

(ii) a "child" of an eligible individual includes a recognized natural child, a stepchild who lived with the eligible individual in a regular parent-child relationship, and an adopted child; and

(iii) a "parent" of an eligible individual includes fathers and mothers through adoption.

(b) Order of payments

The Attorney General shall endeavor to make payments under this section to eligible individuals in the order of date of birth (with the oldest individual on the date of the enactment of this Act [Aug. 10, 1988] (or, if applicable, that individual's survivors under paragraph (8)) receiving full payment first), until all eligible individuals have received payment in full.

(c) Resources for locating eligible individuals

In attempting to locate any eligible individual, the Attorney General may use any facility or resource of any public or nonprofit organization or any other record, document, or information that may be made available to the Attorney General.

(d) Administrative costs not paid from the Fund

No costs incurred by the Attorney General in carrying out this section shall be paid from the Fund or set off against, or otherwise deducted from, any payment under this section to any eligible individual.

(e) Termination of duties of Attorney General

The duties of the Attorney General under this section shall cease 180 days after the Fund terminates.

(f) Clarification of treatment of payments under other laws

Amounts paid to an eligible individual under this section—

(1) shall be treated for purposes of the internal revenue laws of the United States as damages for human suffering; and

(2) shall not be included as income or resources for purposes of determining eligibility to receive benefits described in section

3803(c)(2)(C) of title 31, United States Code[1] or available under any other law administered by the Secretary of Veterans Affairs, or for purposes of determining the amount of such benefits.

(g) Liability of United States limited to amount in Fund

(1) General rule

An eligible individual may be paid under this section only from amounts in the Fund.

(2) Coordination with other provisions

Nothing in this title [sections 1989b to 1989b–9 of this Appendix] shall authorize the payment to an eligible individual by the United States Government of any amount authorized by this section from any source other than the Fund.

(3) Order in which unpaid claims to be paid

If at any time the Fund has insufficient funds to pay all eligible individuals at such time, such eligible individuals shall, to the extent permitted under paragraph (1), be paid in full in the order specified in subsection (b).

(h) Judicial review

(1) Review by the Court of Federal Claims

A claimant may seek judicial review of a denial of compensation under this section solely in the United States Court of Federal Claims, which shall review the denial upon the administrative record and shall hold unlawful and set aside the denial if it is found to be arbitrary, capricious, an abuse of discretion, or otherwise not in accordance with law.

(2) Applicability

This subsection shall apply only to any claim filed in court on or after the date of the enactment of this subsection [Sept. 27, 1992].

(Pub. L. 100–383, title I, § 105, Aug. 10, 1988, 102 Stat. 905; Pub. L. 101–162, title II, § 209(b), Nov. 21, 1989, 103 Stat. 1005; Pub. L. 102–371, §§ 4–6(a), Sept. 27, 1992, 106 Stat. 1167, 1168; Pub. L. 102–572, title IX, § 902(b)(1), Oct. 29, 1992, 106 Stat. 4516.)

AMENDMENTS

1992—Subsec. (a)(1). Pub. L. 102–371, § 4(c)(1)(A), substituted "(7)" for "(6)" and "(5)" for "(4)".

Subsec. (a)(3). Pub. L. 102–371, § 4(a)(2), added par. (3). Former par. (3) redesignated (4).

Subsec. (a)(4). Pub. L. 102–371, § 4(a)(1), (c)(1)(B), redesignated par. (3) as (4) and in subpar. (B) substituted "(5)" for "(4)" and "(6)" for "(5)". Former par. (4) redesignated (5).

Subsec. (a)(5). Pub. L. 102–371, § 4(a)(1), redesignated par. (4) as (5). Former par. (5) redesignated (6).

Subsec. (a)(6). Pub. L. 102–371, § 4(a)(1), (c)(1)(C), redesignated par. (5) as (6) and substituted "(5)" for "(4)" and "(4)" for "(3)". Former par. (6) redesignated (7).

Subsec. (a)(7). Pub. L. 102–371, § 4(a)(1), (c)(1)(D), redesignated par. (6) as (7) and substituted "(8)" for "(6)". Former par. (7) redesignated (8).

Subsec. (a)(8). Pub. L. 102–371, § 4(a)(1), redesignated par. (7) as (8).

Subsec. (b). Pub. L. 102–371, § 4(c)(2), substituted "(8)" for "(6)".

Subsec. (e). Pub. L. 102–371, § 5, substituted "180 days after the Fund terminates" for "when the Fund terminates".

[1] So in original. Probably should be followed by a comma.

Subsec. (f)(2). Pub. L. 102–371, § 6(a), substituted "or available under any other law administered by the Secretary of Veterans Affairs, or for purposes of determining the" for ", or the".

Subsec. (h). Pub. L. 102–572 substituted "United States Court of Federal Claims" for "United States Claims Court" in par. (1).

Pub. L. 102–371, § 4(b), added subsec. (h).

1989—Subsec. (g). Pub. L. 101–162 added subsec. (g).

EFFECTIVE DATE OF 1992 AMENDMENTS

Amendment by Pub. L. 102–572 effective Oct. 29, 1992, see section 911 of Pub. L. 102–572, set out as a note under section 171 of Title 28, Judiciary and Judicial Procedure.

Section 6(b) of Pub. L. 102–371 provided that: "The amendment made by subsection (a) [amending this section] shall be effective as of August 10, 1988."

SECTION REFERRED TO IN OTHER SECTIONS

This section is referred to in sections 1989b–3, 1989b–9 of this Appendix.

§ 1989b–5. Board of Directors of the Fund

(a) Establishment

There is established the Civil Liberties Public Education Fund Board of Directors, which shall be responsible for making disbursements from the Fund in the manner provided in this section.

(b) Uses of the Fund

The Board may make disbursements from the Fund only—

(1) to sponsor research and public educational activities, and to publish and distribute the hearings, findings, and recommendations of the Commission, so that the events surrounding the evacuation, relocation, and internment of United States citizens and permanent resident aliens of Japanese ancestry will be remembered, and so that the causes and circumstances of this and similar events may be illuminated and understood; and

(2) for reasonable administrative expenses of the Board, including expenses incurred under subsections (c)(3), (d), and (e).

(c) Membership

(1) Appointment

The Board shall be composed of 9 members appointed by the President, by and with the advice and consent of the Senate, from individuals who are not officers or employees of the United States Government.

(2) Terms

(A) Except as provided in subparagraphs (B) and (C), members shall be appointed for terms of 3 years.

(B) Of the members first appointed—

(i) 5 shall be appointed for terms of 3 years, and

(ii) 4 shall be appointed for terms of 2 years,

as designated by the President at the time of appointment.

(C) Any member appointed to fill a vacancy occurring before the expiration of the term for which such member's predecessor was appointed shall be appointed only for the remainder of such term. A member may serve after the expiration of such member's term until such member's successor has taken office. No individual may be appointed as a member for more than 2 consecutive terms.

(3) Compensation

Members of the Board shall serve without pay, except that members of the Board shall be entitled to reimbursement for travel, subsistence, and other necessary expenses incurred by them in carrying out the functions of the Board, in the same manner as persons employed intermittently in the United States Government are allowed expenses under section 5703 of title 5, United States Code.

(4) Quorum

5 members of the Board shall constitute a quorum but a lesser number may hold hearings.

(5) Chair

The Chair of the Board shall be elected by the members of the Board.

(d) Director and staff

(1) Director

The Board shall have a Director who shall be appointed by the Board.

(2) Additional staff

The Board may appoint and fix the pay of such additional staff as it may require.

(3) Applicability of civil service laws

The Director and the additional staff of the Board may be appointed without regard to section 5311(b)[1] of title 5, United States Code, and without regard to the provisions of such title governing appointments in the competitive service, and may be paid without regard to the provisions of chapter 51 and subchapter III of chapter 53 of such title relating to classification and General Schedule pay rates, except that the compensation of any employee of the Board may not exceed a rate equivalent to the minimum rate of basic pay payable for GS–18 of the General Schedule under section 5332(a) of such title.

(e) Administrative support services

The Administrator of General Services shall provide to the Board on a reimbursable basis such administrative support services as the Board may request.

(f) Gifts and donations

The Board may accept, use, and dispose of gifts or donations of services or property for purposes authorized under subsection (b).

(g) Annual reports

Not later than 12 months after the first meeting of the Board and every 12 months thereafter, the Board shall transmit to the President and to each House of the Congress a report describing the activities of the Board.

(h) Termination

90 days after the termination of the Fund, the Board shall terminate and all obligations of the Board under this section shall cease.

(Pub. L. 100–383, title I, §106, Aug. 10, 1988, 102 Stat. 908.)

[1] See References in Text note below.

REFERENCES IN TEXT

Section 5311(b) of title 5, referred to in subsec. (d)(3), was repealed by Pub. L. 101–509, title V, §529 [title I, §104(c)(1)], Nov. 5, 1990, 104 Stat. 1427, 1447.

The provisions of title 5 governing appointments in the competitive service, referred to in subsec. (d)(3), are classified to section 3301 et seq. of Title 5, Government Organization and Employees.

REFERENCES IN OTHER LAWS TO GS–16, 17, OR 18 PAY RATES

References in laws to the rates of pay for GS–16, 17, or 18, or to maximum rates of pay under the General Schedule, to be considered references to rates payable under specified sections of Title 5, Government Organization and Employees, see section 529 [title I, §101(c)(1)] of Pub. L. 101–509, set out in a note under section 5376 of Title 5.

SECTION REFERRED TO IN OTHER SECTIONS

This section is referred to in sections 1989b–3, 1989b–4, 1989b–7 of this Appendix.

§ 1989b–6. Documents relating to the internment

(a) Preservation of documents in National Archives

All documents, personal testimony, and other records created or received by the Commission during its inquiry shall be kept and maintained by the Archivist of the United States who shall preserve such documents, testimony, and records in the National Archives of the United States. The Archivist shall make such documents, testimony, and records available to the public for research purposes.

(b) Public availability of certain records of the House of Representatives

(1) The Clerk of the House of Representatives is authorized to permit the Archivist of the United States to make available for use records of the House not classified for national security purposes, which have been in existence for not less than thirty years, relating to the evacuation, relocation, and internment of individuals during the evacuation, relocation, and internment period.

(2) This subsection is enacted as an exercise of the rulemaking power of the House of Representatives, but is applicable only with respect to the availability of records to which it applies, and supersedes other rules only to the extent that the time limitation established by this section with respect to such records is specifically inconsistent with such rules, and is enacted with full recognition of the constitutional right of the House to change its rules at any time, in the same manner and to the same extent as in the case of any other rule of the House.

(Pub. L. 100–383, title I, §107, Aug. 10, 1988, 102 Stat. 909.)

§ 1989b–7. Definitions

For the purposes of this title [sections 1989b to 1989b–9 of this Appendix]—

(1) the term "evacuation, relocation, and internment period" means that period beginning on December 7, 1941, and ending on June 30, 1946;

(2) the term "eligible individual" means any individual of Japanese ancestry, or the spouse

or a parent of an individual of Japanese ancestry, who is living on the date of the enactment of this Act [Aug. 10, 1988] and who, during the evacuation, relocation, and internment period—

(A) was a United States citizen or a permanent resident alien; and

(B)(i) was confined, held in custody, relocated, or otherwise deprived of liberty or property as a result of—

(I) Executive Order Numbered 9066, dated February 19, 1942;

(II) the Act entitled "An Act to provide a penalty for violation of restrictions or orders with respect to persons entering, remaining in, leaving, or committing any act in military areas or zones", approved March 21, 1942 (56 Stat. 173); or

(III) any other Executive order, Presidential proclamation, law of the United States, directive of the Armed Forces of the United States, or other action taken by or on behalf of the United States or its agents, representatives, officers, or employees, respecting the evacuation, relocation, or internment of individuals solely on the basis of Japanese ancestry; or

(ii) was enrolled on the records of the United States Government during the period beginning on December 7, 1941, and ending on June 30, 1946, as being in a prohibited military zone;

except that the term "eligible individual" does not include any individual who, during the period beginning on December 7, 1941, and ending on September 2, 1945, relocated to a country while the United States was at war with that country;

(3) the term "permanent resident alien" means an alien lawfully admitted into the United States for permanent residence;

(4) the term "Fund" means the Civil Liberties Public Education Fund established in section 104 [section 1989b–3 of this Appendix];

(5) the term "Board" means the Civil Liberties Public Education Fund Board of Directors established in section 106 [section 1989b–5 of this Appendix]; and

(6) the term "Commission" means the Commission on Wartime Relocation and Internment of Civilians, established by the Commission on Wartime Relocation and Internment of Civilians Act (Public Law 96–317; 50 U.S.C. App. 1981 note).

(Pub. L. 100–383, title I, §108, Aug. 10, 1988, 102 Stat. 910; Pub. L. 102–371, §3, Sept. 27, 1992, 106 Stat. 1167.)

REFERENCES IN TEXT

Executive Order Numbered 9066, dated February 19, 1942, referred to in par. (2)(B)(i)(I), is not classified to the Code.

The Act entitled "An Act to provide a penalty for violation of restrictions or orders with respect to persons entering, remaining in, leaving, or committing any act in military areas or zones", approved March 21, 1942 (56 Stat. 173), referred to in par. (2)(B)(i)(II), is act Mar. 21, 1942, ch. 191, 56 Stat. 173, which was classified to section 97a of former Title 18, Criminal Code and Criminal Procedure, and was repealed by act of June 25, 1948, ch. 645, §21, 62 Stat. 868 and reenacted as section 1383 of Title 18, Crimes and Criminal Procedure. Section 1383 of Title 18 was repealed by Pub. L. 94–412, title V, §501(e), Sept. 14, 1976, 90 Stat. 1258.

AMENDMENTS

1992—Par. (2). Pub. L. 102–371 inserted ", or the spouse or a parent of an individual of Japanese ancestry," after "Japanese ancestry" in introductory provisions.

SECTION REFERRED TO IN OTHER SECTIONS

This section is referred to in section 1989b–4 of this Appendix.

§ 1989b–8. Compliance with Budget Act

No authority under this title [sections 1989b to 1989b–9 of this Appendix] to enter into contracts or to make payments shall be effective in any fiscal year except to such extent and in such amounts as are provided in advance in appropriations Acts. In any fiscal year, total benefits conferred by this title shall be limited to an amount not in excess of the appropriations for such fiscal year. Any provision of this title which, directly or indirectly, authorizes the enactment of new budget authority shall be effective only for fiscal year 1989 and thereafter.

(Pub. L. 100–383, title I, §109, Aug. 10, 1988, 102 Stat. 910.)

REFERENCES IN TEXT

The Budget Act, referred to in section catchline, probably means the Congressional Budget Act of 1974, titles I through IX of Pub. L. 93–344, July 12, 1974, 88 Stat. 297, as amended. For complete classification of this Act to the Code, see Short Title note set out under section 621 of Title 2, The Congress, and Tables.

§ 1989b–9. Entitlements to eligible individuals

(a) In general

Subject to sections 104(e) and 105(g) of this title [sections 1989b–3(e) and 1989b–4(g) of this Appendix] and except as provided in subsection (b), beginning on October 1, 1990, the payments to be made to any eligible individual under the provisions of this title [sections 1989b to 1989b–9 of this Appendix] shall be an entitlement.

(b) Payments from discretionary appropriations

(1) Payments

Any such payment made to an individual who is not of Japanese ancestry and who is an eligible individual on the basis of the amendment made by section 3 of the Civil Liberties Act Amendments of 1992 shall not be an entitlement and shall be made from discretionary appropriations.

(2) Authorization of appropriations

There are authorized to be appropriated for fiscal year 1993 and each subsequent fiscal year such sums as may be necessary for the payments from discretionary appropriations described in paragraph (1).

(c) Definitions

As used in this section—

(1) the term "discretionary appropriations" has the meaning given that term in section 250(c)(7) of the Balanced Budget and Emergency Deficit Control Act of 1985 (2 U.S.C. 900(c)(7)); and

(2) the term "entitlement" means "spending authority" as defined in section 401(c)(2)(C) of the Congressional Budget Act of 1974 (2 U.S.C. 651(c)(2)(C)).

(Pub. L. 100–383, title I, § 110, as added Pub. L. 101–162, title II, § 209(a), Nov. 21, 1989, 103 Stat. 1005; amended Pub. L. 102–371, § 7, Sept. 27, 1992, 106 Stat. 1168.)

REFERENCES IN TEXT

Section 3 of the Civil Liberties Act Amendments of 1992, referred to in subsec. (b)(1), is section 3 of Pub. L. 102–371, which amended paragraph (2) of section 1989b–7 of this Appendix.

AMENDMENTS

1992—Pub. L. 102–371 designated existing provisions as subsec. (a), inserted heading, inserted "and except as provided in subsection (b)" after "105(g) of this title", struck out "As used in this section, the term 'entitlement' means 'spending authority' as defined in section 401(c)(2)(C) of the Congressional Budget Act of 1974." after "shall be an entitlement.", and added subsecs. (b) and (c).

TITLE II—ALEUTIAN AND PRIBILOF ISLANDS RESTITUTION

§ 1989c. Short title

This title [sections 1989c to 1989c–8 of this Appendix] may be cited as the "Aleutian and Pribilof Islands Restitution Act".

(Pub. L. 100–383, title II, § 201, Aug. 10, 1988, 102 Stat. 911.)

§ 1989c–1. Definitions

As used in this title [sections 1989c to 1989c–8 of this Appendix]—

(1) the term "Administrator" means the person appointed by the Secretary under section 204 [section 1989c–3 of this Appendix];

(2) the term "affected Aleut villages" means the surviving Aleut villages of Akutan, Atka, Nikolski, Saint George, Saint Paul, and Unalaska, and the Aleut village of Attu, Alaska;

(3) the term "Association" means the Aleutian/Pribilof Islands Association, Inc., a nonprofit regional corporation established for the benefit of the Aleut people and organized under the laws of the State of Alaska;

(4) the term "Corporation" means the Aleut Corporation, a for-profit regional corporation for the Aleut region organized under the laws of the State of Alaska and established under section 7 of the Alaska Native Claims Settlement Act (Public Law 92–203; 43 U.S.C. 1606);

(5) the term "eligible Aleut" means any Aleut living on the date of the enactment of this Act [Aug. 10, 1988]—

(A) who, as a civilian, was relocated by authority of the United States from his or her home village on the Pribilof Islands or the Aleutian Islands west of Unimak Island to an internment camp, or other temporary facility or location, during World War II; or

(B) who was born while his or her natural mother was subject to such relocation;

(6) the term "Secretary" means the Secretary of the Interior;

(7) the term "Fund" means the Aleutian and Pribilof Islands Restitution Fund established in section 203 [section 1989c–2 of this Appendix]; and

(8) the term "World War II" means the period beginning on December 7, 1941, and ending on September 2, 1945.

(Pub. L. 100–383, title II, § 202, Aug. 10, 1988, 102 Stat. 911.)

SECTION REFERRED TO IN OTHER SECTIONS

This section is referred to in section 1989c–5 of this Appendix.

§ 1989c–2. Aleutian and Pribilof Islands Restitution Fund

(a) Establishment

There is established in the Treasury of the United States the Aleutian and Pribilof Islands Restitution Fund, which shall be administered by the Secretary. The Fund shall consist of amounts appropriated to it pursuant to this title [sections 1989c to 1989c–8 of this Appendix].

(b) Report

The Secretary shall report to the Congress, not later than 60 days after the end of each fiscal year, on the financial condition of the Fund, and the results of operations of the Fund, during the preceding fiscal year and on the expected financial condition and operations of the Fund during the current fiscal year.

(c) Investment

Amounts in the Fund shall be invested in accordance with section 9702 of title 31, United States Code.

(d) Termination

The Secretary shall terminate the Fund 3 years after the date of the enactment of this Act [Aug. 10, 1988], or 1 year following disbursement of all payments from the Fund, as authorized by this title [sections 1989c to 1989c–8 of this Appendix], whichever occurs later. On the date the Fund is terminated, all investments of amounts in the Fund shall be liquidated by the Secretary and receipts thereof deposited in the Fund and all funds remaining in the Fund shall be deposited in the miscellaneous receipts account in the Treasury.

(Pub. L. 100–383, title II, § 203, Aug. 10, 1988, 102 Stat. 911.)

REESTABLISHMENT OF FUND; USE OF FUNDS

For provisions that the Fund, if terminated pursuant to subsec. (d) of this section, is to be reestablished upon appropriation of additional funds, and restricting use of appropriated funds, see section 1(b), (c), of Pub. L. 103–402, set out as a note under section 1989c–4 of this Appendix.

SECTION REFERRED TO IN OTHER SECTIONS

This section is referred to in sections 1989c–1, 1989c–7 of this Appendix.

§ 1989c–3. Appointment of Administrator

As soon as practicable after the date of the enactment of this Act [Aug. 10, 1986], the Secretary shall offer to undertake negotiations with the Association, leading to the execution of an agreement with the Association to serve as Administrator under this title [sections 1989c to

1989c–8 of this Appendix]. The Secretary may appoint the Association as Administrator if such agreement is reached within 90 days after the date of the enactment of this title. If no such agreement is reached within such period, the Secretary shall appoint another person as Administrator under this title, after consultation with leaders of affected Aleut villages and the Corporation.

(Pub. L. 100–383, title II, § 204, Aug. 10, 1988, 102 Stat. 912.)

SECTION REFERRED TO IN OTHER SECTIONS

This section is referred to in section 1989c–1 of this Appendix.

§ 1989c–4. Compensation for community losses

(a) In general

Subject to the availability of funds appropriated to the Fund, the Secretary shall make payments from the Fund, in accordance with this section, as restitution for certain Aleut losses sustained in World War II.

(b) Trust

(1) Establishment

The Secretary shall, subject to the availability of funds appropriated for this purpose, establish a trust for the purposes set forth in this section. Such trust shall be established pursuant to the laws of the State of Alaska, and shall be maintained and operated by not more than seven trustees, as designated by the Secretary. Each affected Aleut village may submit to the Administrator a list of three prospective trustees. The Secretary, after consultation with the Administrator, affected Aleut villages, and the Corporation, shall designate not more than seven trustees from such lists as submitted.

(2) Administration of trust

The trust established under this subsection shall be administered in a manner that is consistent with the laws of the State of Alaska, and as prescribed by the Secretary, after consultation with representatives of eligible Aleuts, the residents of affected Aleut villages, and the Administrator.

(c) [1] Accounts for benefit of Aleuts

(1) In general

The Secretary shall deposit in the trust such sums as may be appropriated for the purposes set forth in this subsection. The trustees shall maintain and operate 8 independent and separate accounts in the trust for purposes of this subsection, as follows:

(A) One account for the independent benefit of the wartime Aleut residents of Attu and their descendants.

(B) Six accounts for the benefit of the 6 surviving affected Aleut villages, one each for the independent benefit of Akutan, Atka, Nikolski, Saint George, Saint Paul, and Unalaska, respectively.

(C) One account for the independent benefit of those Aleuts who, as determined by the Secretary, upon the advice of the trustees, are deserving but will not benefit directly from the accounts established under subparagraphs (A) and (B).

The trustees shall credit to the account described in subparagraph (C) an amount equal to 5 percent of the principal amount deposited by the Secretary in the trust under this subsection. Of the remaining principal amount, an amount shall be credited to each account described in subparagraphs (A) and (B) which bears the same proportion to such remaining principal amount as the Aleut civilian population, as of June 1, 1942, of the village with respect to which such account is established bears to the total civilian Aleut population on such date of all affected Aleut villages.

(2) Uses of accounts

The trustees may use the principal, accrued interest, and other earnings of the accounts maintained under paragraph (1) for—

(A) the benefit of elderly, disabled, or seriously ill persons on the basis of special need;

(B) the benefit of students in need of scholarship assistance;

(C) the preservation of Aleut cultural heritage and historical records;

(D) the improvement of community centers in affected Aleut villages; and

(E) other purposes to improve the condition of Aleut life, as determined by the trustees.

(3) Authorization of appropriations

There are authorized to be appropriated $5,000,000 to the Fund to carry out this subsection.

(d) Compensation for damaged or destroyed church property

(1) Inventory and assessment of property

The Administrator shall make an inventory and assessment of real and personal church property of affected Aleut villages which was damaged or destroyed during World War II. In making such inventory and assessment, the Administrator shall consult with the trustees of the trust established under subsection (b), residents of affected Aleut villages, affected church members and leaders, and the clergy of the churches involved. Within 1 year after the date of the enactment of this Act [Aug. 10, 1988], the Administrator shall submit such inventory and assessment, together with an estimate of the present replacement value of lost or destroyed furnishings and artifacts, to the Secretary.

(2) Review by the Secretary; deposit in the trust

The Secretary shall review the inventory and assessment provided under paragraph (1), and shall deposit in the trust established under subsection (b) an amount reasonably calculated by the Secretary to compensate affected Aleut villages for church property lost, damaged, or destroyed during World War II.

(3) Distribution of compensation

The trustees shall distribute the amount deposited in the trust under paragraph (2) for the

[1] So in original. Two subsecs. (c) have been enacted.

benefit of the churches referred to in this subsection.

(4) Authorization of appropriations

There are authorized to be appropriated to the Fund $4,700,000 to carry out this subsection.

(c)[2] Administrative and legal expenses

(1) Reimbursement for expenses

The Secretary shall reimburse the Administrator, not less often than annually, for reasonable and necessary administrative and legal expenses in carrying out the Administrator's responsibilities under this title [sections 1989c to 1989c–8 of this Appendix].

(2) Authorization of appropriations

There are authorized to be appropriated to the Fund such sums as are necessary to carry out this subsection.

(Pub. L. 100–383, title II, § 205, Aug. 10, 1988, 102 Stat. 912; Pub. L. 103–402, § 1(a), Oct. 22, 1994, 108 Stat. 4174.)

AMENDMENTS

1994—Subsec. (d)(4). Pub. L. 103–402 substituted "$4,700,000" for "$1,400,000".

REESTABLISHMENT OF FUND; USE OF FUNDS

Section 1(b), (c), of Pub. L. 103–402 provided that:

"(b) FUND.—If the Fund referred to in section 205(a) of the Aleutian and Pribilof Islands Restitution Act (50 U.S.C. App. 1989c–4(a)) has been terminated pursuant to section 203(d) of such Act (50 U.S.C. App. 1989c–2(d)), upon the appropriation of additional funds pursuant to this Act, the Fund shall be reestablished.

"(c) USE OF FUNDS.—The funds appropriated pursuant to this Act shall be used solely for the renovation, replacement, and restoration of church property lost, damaged, or destroyed during World War II."

SECTION REFERRED TO IN OTHER SECTIONS

This section is referred to in sections 1989c–5, 1989c–7 of this Appendix.

§ 1989c–5. Individual compensation of eligible Aleuts

(a) Payments to eligible Aleuts

In addition to payments made under section 205 [section 1989c–4 of this Appendix], the Secretary shall, in accordance with this section, make per capita payments out of the Fund to eligible Aleuts. The Secretary shall pay, subject to the availability of funds appropriated to the Fund for such payments, to each eligible Aleut the sum of $12,000.

(b) Assistance of Attorney General

The Secretary may request the Attorney General to provide reasonable assistance in locating eligible Aleuts residing outside the affected Aleut villages, and upon such request, the Attorney General shall provide such assistance. In so doing, the Attorney General may use available facilities and resources of the International Committee of the Red Cross and other organizations.

(c) Assistance of Administrator

The Secretary may request the assistance of the Administrator in identifying and locating eligible Aleuts for purposes of this section.

[2] So in original. Two subsecs. (c) have been enacted.

(d) Clarification of treatment of payments under other laws

Amounts paid to an eligible Aleut under this section—

(1) shall be treated for purposes of the internal revenue laws of the United States as damages for human suffering, and

(2) shall not be included as income or resources for purposes of determining eligibility to receive benefits described in section 3803(c)(2)(C) of title 31, United States Code, or the amount of such benefits.

(e) Payment in full settlement of claims against United States

The payment to an eligible Aleut under this section shall be in full satisfaction of all claims against the United States arising out of the relocation described in section 202(5) [section 1989c–1(5) of this Appendix].

(f) Authorization of appropriations

There are authorized to be appropriated to the Fund such sums as are necessary to carry out this section.

(Pub. L. 100–383, title II, § 206, Aug. 10, 1988, 102 Stat. 914.)

SECTION REFERRED TO IN OTHER SECTIONS

This section is referred to in section 1989c–7 of this Appendix.

§ 1989c–6. Attu Island restitution program

(a) Purpose of section

In accordance with section (3)(c)[1] of the Wilderness Act (78 Stat. 892; 16 U.S.C. 1132(c)), the public lands on Attu Island, Alaska, within the National Wildlife Refuge System have been designated as wilderness by section 702(1) of the Alaska National Interest Lands Conservation Act (94 Stat. 2417; 16 U.S.C. 1132 note). In order to make restitution for the loss of traditional Aleut lands and village properties on Attu Island, while preserving the present designation of Attu Island lands as part of the National Wilderness Preservation System, compensation to the Aleut people, in lieu of the conveyance of Attu Island, shall be provided in accordance with this section.

(b) Acreage determination

Not later than 90 days after the date of the enactment of this Act [Aug. 10, 1988], the Secretary shall, in accordance with this subsection, determine the total acreage of land on Attu Island, Alaska, that, at the beginning of World War II, was subject to traditional use by the Aleut villagers of that island for subsistence and other purposes. In making such acreage determination, the Secretary shall establish a base acreage of not less than 35,000 acres within that part of eastern Attu Island traditionally used by the Aleut people, and shall, from the best available information, including information that may be submitted by representatives of the Aleut people, identify any such additional acreage on Attu Island that was subject to such use. The combination of such base acreage and such additional acreage shall constitute the acreage de-

[1] So in original. Probably should be section "3(c)".

termination upon which payment to the Corporation under this section is based. The Secretary shall promptly notify the Corporation of the results of the acreage determination made under this subsection.

(c) Valuation

(1) Determination of value

Not later than 120 days after the date of the enactment of this Act [Aug. 10, 1988], the Secretary shall determine the value of the Attu Island acreage determined under subsection (b), except that—

(A) such acreage may not be valued at less than $350 per acre nor more than $500 per acre; and

(B) the total valuation of all such acreage may not exceed $15,000,000.

(2) Factors in making determination

In determining the value of the acreage under paragraph (1), the Secretary shall take into consideration such factors as the Secretary considers appropriate, including—

(A) fair market value;

(B) environmental and public interest value; and

(C) established precedents for valuation of comparable wilderness lands in the State of Alaska.

(3) Notification of determination; appeal

The Secretary shall promptly notify the Corporation of the determination of value made under this subsection, and such determination shall constitute the final determination of value unless the Corporation, within 30 days after the determination is made, appeals the determination to the Secretary. If such appeal is made, the Secretary shall, within 30 days after the appeal is made, review the determination in light of the appeal, and issue a final determination of the value of that acreage determined to be subject to traditional use under subsection (b).

(d) In lieu compensation payment

(1) Payment

The Secretary shall pay, subject to the availability of funds appropriated for such purpose, to the Corporation, as compensation for the Aleuts' loss of lands on Attu Island, the full amount of the value of the acreage determined under subsection (c), less the value (as determined under subsection (c)) of any land conveyed under subsection (e).

(2) Payment in full settlement of claims against the United States

The payment made under paragraph (1) shall be in full satisfaction of any claim against the United States for the loss of traditional Aleut lands and village properties on Attu Island.

(e) Village site conveyance

The Secretary may convey to the Corporation all right, title, and interest of the United States to the surface estate of the traditional Aleut village site on Attu Island, Alaska (consisting of approximately 10 acres) and to the surface estate of a parcel of land consisting of all land outside such village that is within 660 feet of any point on the boundary of such village. The conveyance may be made under the authority contained in section 14(h)(1) of the Alaska Native Claims Settlement Act (Public Law 92–203; 43 U.S.C. 1613(h)(1)), except that after the enactment of this Act [Aug. 10, 1988], no site on Attu Island, Alaska, other than such traditional Aleut village site and such parcel of land, may be conveyed to the Corporation under such section 14(h)(1).

(f) Authorization of appropriations

There are authorized to be appropriated $15,000,000 to the Secretary to carry out this section.

(Pub. L. 100–383, title II, § 207, Aug. 10, 1988, 102 Stat. 914.)

REFERENCES IN TEXT

Section 702(1) of the Alaska National Interest Lands Conservation Act, referred to in subsec. (a), is section 702(1) of Pub. L. 96–487, title VII, Dec. 2, 1980, 94 Stat. 2417, which is included in the listing of wilderness areas set out as a note under section 1132 of Title 16, Conservation.

SECTION REFERRED TO IN OTHER SECTIONS

This section is referred to in section 1989c–7 of this Appendix.

§ 1989c–7. Compliance with Budget Act

No authority under this title [sections 1989c to 1989c–8 of this Appendix] to enter into contracts or to make payments shall be effective in any fiscal year except to such extent and in such amounts as are provided in advance in appropriations Acts. In any fiscal year, the Secretary, with respect to—

(1) the Fund established under section 203 [section 1989c–2 of this Appendix],

(2) the trust established under section 205(b) [section 1989c–4(b) of this Appendix], and

(3) the provisions of sections 206 and 207 [sections 1989c–5 and 1989c–6 of this Appendix],

shall limit the total benefits conferred to an amount not in excess of the appropriations for such fiscal year. Any provision of this title which, directly or indirectly, authorizes the enactment of new budget authority shall be effective only for fiscal year 1989 and thereafter.

(Pub. L. 100–383, title II, § 208, Aug. 10, 1988, 102 Stat. 916.)

REFERENCES IN TEXT

The Budget Act, referred to in section catchline, probably means the Congressional Budget Act of 1974, titles I through IX of Pub. L. 93–344, July 12, 1974, 88 Stat. 297, as amended. For complete classification of this Act to the Code, see Short Title note set out under section 621 of Title 2, The Congress, and Tables.

§ 1989c–8. Severability

If any provision of this title [sections 1989c to 1989c–8 of this Appendix], or the application of such provision to any person or circumstance, is held invalid, the remainder of this title and the application of such provision to other persons not similarly situated or to other circumstances shall not be affected by such invalidation.

(Pub. L. 100–383, title II, § 209, Aug. 10, 1988, 102 Stat. 916.)

TITLE III—TERRITORY OR PROPERTY CLAIMS AGAINST UNITED STATES

§ 1989d. Exclusion of claims

Notwithstanding any other provision of law or of this Act [sections 1989 to 1989d of this Appendix], nothing in this Act shall be construed as recognition of any claim of Mexico or any other country or any Indian tribe (except as expressly provided in this Act with respect to the Aleut tribe of Alaska) to any territory or other property of the United States, nor shall this Act be construed as providing any basis for compensation in connection with any such claim.

(Pub. L. 100–383, title III, § 301, Aug. 10, 1988, 102 Stat. 916.)

MEDICAL CARE FOR PHILIPPINE VETERANS

ACT JULY 1, 1948, CH. 785, 62 STAT. 1210

§§ 1991 to 1996. Repealed. Pub. L. 85–461, § 5, June 18, 1958, 72 Stat. 203

Section 1991, act July 1, 1948, ch. 785, § 1, 62 Stat. 1210, related to grants-in-aid for construction of hospitals and expenses for medical care for treatment of Philippine veterans.

Section 1992, act July 1, 1948, ch. 785, § 2, 62 Stat. 1210, defined "veteran".

Section 1993, act July 1, 1948, ch. 785, § 3, 62 Stat. 1210, related to time and amount of hospital construction grants.

Section 1994, acts July 1, 1948, ch. 785, § 4, 62 Stat. 1210; June 18, 1954, ch. 329, 68 Stat. 268, related to time and amount of medical care grants.

Section 1995, act July 1, 1948, ch. 785, § 5, 62 Stat. 1210, related to issuance of rules and regulations.

Section 1996, act July 1, 1948, ch. 785, § 6, 62 Stat. 1210, related to authorization of appropriations.

WAR CLAIMS

ACT JULY 3, 1948, CH. 826, 62 STAT. 1240

TITLE I

ACT REFERRED TO IN OTHER SECTIONS

This Act is referred to in title 22 sections 1622b, 1622g.

TITLE I

TITLE I OF ACT

Section 101 of Pub. L. 87–846, Oct. 22, 1962, 76 Stat. 1107, designated sections 2 to 17 of act July 3, 1948, as amended [sections 2001 to 2016 of this Appendix], as title I.

TITLE REFERRED TO IN OTHER SECTIONS

This title is referred to in section 2017n of this Appendix.

§2001. Foreign Claims Settlement Commission of the United States

(a) Employment of personnel; use of other facilities and services

The Foreign Claims Settlement Commission of the United States (hereinafter referred to as the "Commission") may, in accordance with the provisions of the civil-service laws and the Classification Act of 1949, as amended [5 U.S.C. 5101 et seq., 5331 et seq.], appoint and fix the compensation of such officers, attorneys, and employees, and may make such expenditures, as may be necessary to carry out its functions. Officers and employees of any other department or agency of the Government may, with the consent of the head of such department or agency, be assigned to assist the Commission in carrying out its functions. The Commission may, with the consent of the head of any other department or agency of the Government, utilize the facilities and services of such department or agency in carrying out the functions of the Commission.

(b) Rules and regulations; delegation of functions; time limit on filing of claims

The Commission may prescribe such rules and regulations as may be necessary to enable it to carry out its functions, and may delegate functions to any member, officer, or employee of the Commission. The Commission shall give public notice of the time when, and the limit of time within which, claims may be filed, which notice shall be published in the Federal Register. The limit of time within which claims may be filed with the Commission shall in no event be later than March 31, 1952. The Commission shall take immediate action to advise all persons entitled to file claims under the provisions of this title [sections 2001 to 2016 of this Appendix] administered by the Commission of their rights under such provisions, and to assist them in the preparation and filing of their claims.

(c) Subpenas; issuance; contempt; witness fees; administration of oaths

(1) For the purpose of any hearing, examination, or investigation under this title [sections 2001 to 2016 of this Appendix], the Commission and those employees designated by the Commission shall have the power to issue subpenas requiring persons to appear and testify or to appear and produce documents, or both, at any designated place where such hearing, examination, or investigation is being held. The Commission or any employee so designated shall, upon application of a claimant, issue to such claimant subpenas requiring the attendance and testimony of witnesses or the production of documents, or both, required by such claimant in hearings upon his claim: *Provided*, That the claimant making such application pay the witness fees and mileage of any witness or witnesses subpenaed upon his request. The production of a person's documents at any place other than his place of business shall not be required, however, in any case in which, prior to the return date specified in the subpena with respect thereto, such person either has furnished the issuer of the subpena with a copy of such documents (certified by such person under oath to be a true and correct copy) or has entered into a stipulation with the issuer of the subpena as to the information contained in such documents.

(2) The Commission may, in case of a failure or refusal on the part of any person to comply with any such subpena, invoke the aid of any United States district court within the jurisdiction of which the hearing, examination, or investigation is being conducted, or such person resides or transacts business. Such court may issue an order requiring such person to appear at the designated place of hearing, examination, or investigation, there to give or produce testimony or documentary evidence concerning the matter in question. Any failure to obey such order of the court shall be punishable by such court as a contempt thereof. All process in any such case may be served in the judicial district wherein such person resides or transacts business or wherever such person may be found.

(3) Witnesses subpenaed under this subsection shall be paid the same fees and mileage that are allowed and paid witnesses in United States district courts.

(4) Any member of the Commission, and any employee of the Commission authorized by the Commission to do so, may administer to, or take from, any person an oath, affirmation, or

affidavit when such action is necessary or appropriate in the performance of the functions or activities of the Commission.

(July 3, 1948, ch. 826, title I, § 2, 62 Stat. 1240; May 27, 1949, ch. 145, § 1(1), 63 Stat. 112; Oct. 28, 1949, ch. 782, title XI, § 1106(a), 63 Stat. 972; Aug. 16, 1950, ch. 718, 64 Stat. 449; Apr. 5, 1951, ch. 27, 65 Stat. 28; 1954 Reorg. Plan No. 1 §§ 2, 4, eff. July 1, 1954, 19 F.R. 3985, 68 Stat. 1279; Aug. 21, 1954, ch. 784, § 3, 68 Stat. 762; Pub. L. 87–846, title I, §§ 102, 104(a), Oct. 22, 1962, 76 Stat. 1107, 1113; Pub. L. 96–209, title I, § 108, Mar. 14, 1980, 94 Stat. 97.)

REFERENCES IN TEXT

The civil-service laws, referred to in subsec. (a), are set out in Title 5, Government Organization and Employees. See, particularly, section 3301 et seq. of Title 5.

The Classification Act of 1949, as amended, referred to in subsec. (a), is act Oct. 28, 1949, ch. 782, 63 Stat. 954, as amended. The Classification Act of 1949 was repealed by Pub. L. 89–554, § 8(a), Sept. 6, 1966, 80 Stat. 632, and reenacted by the first section thereof as chapter 51 (§ 5101 et seq.) and subchapter III (§ 5331 et seq.) of chapter 53 of Title 5.

AMENDMENTS

1980—Subsec. (d). Pub. L. 96–209 struck out subsec. (d) which provided for terms of office of Chairman and members of Foreign Claims Settlement Commission of United States. See section 1622c(c) of Title 22, Foreign Relations and Intercourse.

1962—Subsecs. (b), (c)(1). Pub. L. 87–846, § 102, substituted "title" for "Act".

Subsec. (d). Pub. L. 87–846, § 104(a), added subsec. (d).

1954—Subsec. (a). Act Aug. 21, 1954, struck out subsec. (a) which related to establishment and composition of the former War Claims Commission, and which had been affected by Reorg. Plan No. 1 of 1954 (see Transfer of Functions note below), redesignated subsec. (b) as (a) and substituted "The Foreign Claims Settlement Commission of the United States (hereinafter referred to as the 'Commission')" for "The Commission", meaning the former War Claims Commission.

Subsecs. (b) to (d). Act Aug. 21, 1954, § 3(a), designated subsecs. (b) to (d) as (a) to (c), respectively.

Former subsec. (e). Act Aug. 21, 1954, § 3(a), repealed subsec. (e) which related to termination of former War Claims Commission.

1951—Subsec. (c). Act Apr. 5, 1951, extended time limit on filing of claims from Mar. 1, 1951 to Mar. 31, 1952, and authorized Commission to advise claimants of their rights.

1950—Subsecs. (d), (e). Act Aug. 16, 1950, added subsec. (d) and redesignated former subsec. (d) as (e).

1949—Subsec. (b). Act Oct. 28, 1949, substituted "Classification Act of 1949" for "Classification Act of 1923".

Subsec. (c). Act May 27, 1949, extended time within which persons may file claims until Mar. 1, 1951.

EFFECTIVE DATE OF 1980 AMENDMENT

Amendment by Pub. L. 96–209 effective Mar. 14, 1980, see title VI of Pub. L. 96–209, set out as an Effective Date note under section 1622a of Title 22, Foreign Relations and Intercourse.

EFFECTIVE DATE OF 1951 AMENDMENT

Act Apr. 5, 1951, provided that the amendment made by that Act is effective as of Mar. 1, 1951.

EFFECTIVE DATE OF 1949 AMENDMENT

The increased compensation provided for by act Oct. 15, 1949, took effect on first day of first pay period which began after Oct. 15, 1949, see section 9 of act Oct. 15, 1949.

SHORT TITLE OF 1954 AMENDMENT

Act Aug. 31, 1954, ch. 1162, title I, § 1, 68 Stat. 1033, provided: "That this Act [enacting sections 2014 to 2016 of this Appendix, amending sections 2004, 2005, and 2012 of this Appendix and section 801 of former Title 5, Executive Departments and Government Officers and Employees, and enacting provisions set out as notes under this section and section 2008 of this Appendix] may be cited as the 'War Claims Act Amendments of 1954'."

SHORT TITLE

Section 1 of act July 3, 1948, provided that: "This Act [enacting this section and sections 2002 to 2017p of this Appendix] may be cited as the 'War Claims Act of 1948'."

REPEALS

Act Oct. 28, 1949, ch. 782, cited as a credit to this section, was repealed (subject to a savings clause) by Pub. L. 89–554, Sept. 6, 1966, § 8, 80 Stat. 632, 655.

TRANSFER OF FUNCTIONS

For provisions transferring Foreign Claims Settlement Commission of the United States to Department of Justice, as a separate agency, see section 1622a et seq. of Title 22, Foreign Relations and Intercourse.

"Foreign Claims Settlement Commission" substituted in text for "War Claims Commission" pursuant to Reorg. Plan No. 1 of 1954, §§ 2, 4, eff. July 1, 1954, 19 F.R. 3985, 68 Stat. 1279, set out in the Appendix to Title 5, Government Organization and Employees, which abolished War Claims Commission, including offices of its members, and transferred functions of Commission and members, officers, and employees thereof to Foreign Claims Settlement Commission of the United States.

TIME LIMIT FOR SETTLEMENT OF CLAIMS UNDER WAR CLAIMS ACT AMENDMENTS OF 1954

Act Aug. 31, 1954, ch. 1162, title I, § 105, 68 Stat. 1037, required the Foreign Claims Settlement Commission to wind up its affairs in settling claims for benefits authorized by act Aug. 31, 1954 within two years after Aug. 31, 1954.

REAPPOINTMENT OF MEMBERS OF FOREIGN CLAIMS SETTLEMENT COMMISSION

Section 104(b) of Pub. L. 87–846 provided that: "Nothing in this section shall be construed to preclude the reappointment as a member of the Foreign Claims Settlement Commission of any person holding office as a member of such Commission on the date of enactment of this Act [Oct. 22, 1962]."

TENURE OF WAR CLAIMS COMMISSION

Act Apr. 9, 1952, ch. 167, § 4, 66 Stat. 49, provided that nothing in that act or the amendments made by it, amending sections 2005 and 2006 of this Appendix, should extend the life of the War Claims Commission for any period of time.

SECTION REFERRED TO IN OTHER SECTIONS

This section is referred to in sections 2007, 2017n of this Appendix.

§ 2002. Jurisdiction of Commission

The Commission shall have jurisdiction to receive and adjudicate according to law claims as hereinafter provided.

(July 3, 1948, ch. 826, title I, § 3, 62 Stat. 1241.)

TRANSFER OF FUNCTIONS

For provisions transferring Foreign Claims Settlement Commission of the United States to Department of Justice, as a separate agency, see section 1622a et seq. of Title 22, Foreign Relations and Intercourse.

War Claims Commission, including offices of its members, abolished and functions transferred to Foreign Claims Settlement Commission of the United

States by Reorg. Plan No. 1 of 1954, §§2, 4, eff. July 1, 1954, 19 F.R. 3985, 68 Stat. 1279, set out in the Appendix to Title 5, Government Organization and Employees. See, also, section 2001 of this Appendix and notes thereunder.

SECTION REFERRED TO IN OTHER SECTIONS

This section is referred to in section 2007 of this Appendix.

§ 2003. Claims of employees of contractors

(a) Payment by Secretary of Labor of certain claims; execution of releases

The Secretary of Labor is authorized to receive, adjudicate according to law, and provide for the payment of any claim filed by any person specified in section 101(a) of the Act entitled "An Act to provide benefits for the injury, disability, death, or enemy detention of employees of contractors with the United States, and for other purposes", approved December 2, 1942, as amended [42 U.S.C. 1701(a)], or by the legal representative of any such person who may have died, for the amount by which (1) the total sum which would have been payable to such person by his employer (not including any payments for overtime), if such person's contract of employment had been in effect and he had been paid under it for the entire period during which he was entitled to receive benefits under section 101(b) of such Act [42 U.S.C. 1701(b)], exceeds (2) the entire amount creditable to such person's account for such period under the provisions of such section plus any amounts paid to such person by such employer for such period or recovered by such person in any legal action against such employer based upon such person's right against such employer for such period under the contract of employment, including payments in settlement of the liability of the employer arising under or out of such contract. No claim shall be allowed to any person under the provisions of this section unless such person executes a full release to the employer and to the United States in respect to the liability of the employer arising under or out of the contract of employment, except liability for workmen's compensation benefits under the Act of August 16, 1941, as amended (42 U.S.C. 1651 and the following) or detention or other benefits paid under the Act of December 2, 1942, as amended (42 U.S.C. 1751 and the following) [42 U.S.C. 1701 et seq.]. Any claim allowed under the provisions of this section shall be certified by the Secretary of Labor to the Secretary of the Treasury for payment out of the War Claims Fund established by section 13 of this title [section 2012 of this Appendix].

(b) Cancellation of employees' obligations; repayment to employees

(1) The Secretary of State is authorized and directed to cancel any obligation to the United States of any person specified in section 101(a) of such Act of December 2, 1942 [42 U.S.C. 1701(a)], to pay any sum which may have been advanced to or on behalf of any such person by the Department of State for the purpose of paying the costs of food and medical services furnished to such person during his period of internment by the Imperial Japanese Government or for the purpose of paying transportation or other expenses of repatriation.

(2) The Secretary of Labor is authorized to receive, adjudicate according to law, and provide for the payment of any claim filed by any person specified in section 101(a) of such Act of December 2, 1942 [42 U.S.C. 1701(a)], for the repayment of any sum which may have been paid by such person to the Department of State in settlement of any obligation of the type referred to in paragraph (1) of this subsection. Any claim allowed under the provisions of this paragraph shall be certified by the Secretary of Labor to the Secretary of the Treasury for payment out of the War Claims Fund established by section 13 of this title [section 2012 of this Appendix].

(c) Omitted [Amendment of section 1702(a) of Title 42]

(July 3, 1948, ch. 826, title I, §4, 62 Stat. 1241; 1950 Reorg. Plan No. 19, §1, eff. May 24, 1950, 15 F.R. 3178, 64 Stat. 1271; Pub. L. 87–846, title I, §102, Oct. 22, 1962, 76 Stat. 1107.)

REFERENCES IN TEXT

Act of August 16, 1941, as amended, referred to in subsec. (a), is act Aug. 16, 1941, ch. 357, 55 Stat. 622, as amended, known as the Defense Base Act, which is classified generally to chapter 11 (§1651 et seq.) of Title 42, The Public Health and Welfare. For complete classification of this Act to the Code, see Short Title note set out under section 1651 of Title 42 and Tables.

Act of December 2, 1942, as amended, referred to in subsec. (a), is act Dec. 2, 1942, ch. 668, 56 Stat. 1028, as amended, titles I and II of which are popularly known as the War Hazards Compensation Act, and is classified principally to chapter 12 (§1701 et seq.) of Title 42. For complete classification of this Act to the Code, see Tables.

AMENDMENTS

1962—Pub. L. 87–846 substituted "title" for "Act".

TRANSFER OF FUNCTIONS

"Secretary of Labor" substituted in subsecs. (a) and (b) for "Federal Security Administrator" and "Administrator" pursuant to Reorg. Plan No. 19 of 1950, §1, eff. May 24, 1950, 15 F.R. 3178, 64 Stat. 1271, set out in the Appendix to Title 5, Government Organization and Employees, which transferred functions of Federal Security Administrator and Federal Security Agency under this section to Secretary of Labor, with power to delegate.

For provisions transferring Foreign Claims Settlement Commission of the United States to Department of Justice, as a separate agency, see section 1622a et seq. of Title 22, Foreign Relations and Intercourse.

War Claims Commission, including offices of its members, abolished and functions and funds transferred to Foreign Claims Settlement Commission of the United States by Reorg. Plan No. 1 of 1954, §§2, 4, 6(c), eff. July 1, 1954, 19 F.R. 3985, 68 Stat. 1279, set out in the Appendix to Title 5, Government Organization and Employees. See, also, section 2001 of this Appendix and notes thereunder.

SECTION REFERRED TO IN OTHER SECTIONS

This section is referred to in sections 2007, 2012 of this Appendix.

§ 2004. Internees

(a) "Civilian American citizen" defined

As used in subsections (b) and (f) of this section, the term "civilian American citizen" means any person who, being then a citizen of the United States, was captured by the Imperial Japanese Government on or after December 7,

1941, at Midway. Guam, Wake Island, the Philippine Islands, or any Territory or possession of the United States attacked or invaded by such government, or while in transit to or from any such place, or who went into hiding at any such place in order to avoid capture or internment by such government; except (1) a person who at any time voluntarily gave aid to, collaborated with, or in any manner served such government, or (2) a person who at the time of his capture or entrance into hiding was a regularly appointed, enrolled, enlisted, or inducted member of any military or naval force.

(b) Payment of detention benefits

The Commission is authorized to receive, adjudicate according to law, and provide for the payment of any claim filed by, or on behalf of, any civilian American citizen for detention benefits for any period of time subsequent to December 6, 1941, during which he was held by the Imperial Japanese Government as a prisoner, internee, hostage, or in any other capacity, or remained in hiding to avoid being captured or interned by such Imperial Japanese Government.

(c) Amount of detention benefits

The detention benefit allowed to any person under the provisions of subsection (b) shall be at the rate of $60 for each calendar month during which such person was at least eighteen years of age and at the rate of $25 per month for each calendar month during which such person was less than eighteen years of age.

(d) Persons entitled to detention benefits

The detention benefits allowed under subsection (b) of this section shall be allowed to the person entitled thereto, or, in the event of his death, only to the following persons:

(1) Widow or husband if there is no child or children of the deceased;

(2) Widow or husband and child or children of the deceased, one-half to the widow or husband and the other half to the child or children in equal shares;

(3) Child or children of the deceased (in equal shares) if there is no widow or husband; and

(4) Parents (in equal shares) if there is no husband, or child.

(e) Certification of claims

Any claim allowed by the Commission under this section (except under subsections (g) and (i)) shall be certified to the Secretary of the Treasury for payment out of the war claims funds established by section 13 of this title [section 2012 of this Appendix], and shall be payable by the Secretary of the Treasury to the person entitled thereto; except that where the person entitled to payment is under any legal disability, any part of the amount payable may, in the discretion of the Commission, be paid, for the use of the claimant, to the natural or legal guardian, committee, conservator, or curator of the claimant, or, if there is no such guardian, committee, conservator, or curator, then the Commission may, in its discretion, make payment to any other person, including the spouse of such claimant, whom the Commission may determine is vested with the care of the claimant or his estate for the use and benefit of such claimant or estate; and if such person is a minor, any part of the amount payable may, in the discretion of the Commission, be paid to such minor.

(f) Application of sections 1701 to 1706 and 1711 to 1717 of Title 42; factors for determining benefits; effective date

(1) Except as otherwise provided in this subsection, the provisions of titles I [42 U.S.C. 1701 to 1706] and II [42 U.S.C. 1711 to 1717] of the Act entitled "An Act to provide benefits for the injury, disability, death, or enemy detention of employees of contractors with the United States, and for other purposes", approved December 2, 1942, as amended, are extended and shall apply with respect to the injury, disability, or death resulting from injury of a civilian American citizen occurring while he was held by or in hiding from the Imperial Japanese Government, to the same extent as if such civilian American citizen were an employee within the purview of such Act of December 2, 1942, as amended [42 U.S.C. 1701 to 1717].

(2) For the purpose of determining the benefits extended and made applicable by paragraph (1)—

(A) the average weekly wage of any such civilian American citizen, whether employed, self-employed, or not employed, shall be deemed to have been $37.50;

(B) the provisions of such Act [42 U.S.C. 1701 to 1717], shall be applicable whether or not any such civilian American citizen was employed;

(C) notice of injury or death shall not be required; and limitation provisions with respect to the filing of claims for injury, disability, or death shall not begin to run until the date of enactment of this section [July 3, 1948]; and

(D) the monthly compensation in cases involving partial disability shall be determined by the percentage the degree of partial disability bears to total disability and shall not be determined with respect to the extent of loss of wage earning capacity.

(3) The following provisions of such Act of December 2, 1942, as amended [42 U.S.C. 1701 to 1717], shall not apply in the case of such civilian American citizens: The last sentence of section 101(a), section 101(b), section 101(d) [42 U.S.C. 1701(a), (b), (d)], section 104 [42 U.S.C. 1704], and section 105 [42 U.S.C. 1705].

(4) Rights or benefits which, under this subsection, are to be determined with reference to other provisions of law shall be determined with reference to such provisions of law as in force on January 3, 1948.

(5) The money benefit for disability or death shall be paid only to the person entitled thereto, or to his legal or natural guardian if he has one, and shall not upon death of the person so entitled survive for the benefit of his estate or any other person.

(6) The benefit of a minor or of an incompetent person who has no natural or legal guardian may, in the discretion of the Secretary of Labor, be paid, in whole or in such part as he may determine for and on behalf of such minor or incompetent directly to the person or institution caring for, supporting, or having custody of such minor or incompetent.

(7) No person, except a widow or a child, shall be entitled to benefits for disability with respect

to himself, and to death benefits on account of the death of another.

(8) If a civilian American citizen or his dependent receives or has received from the United States any payments on account of the same injury or death, or from his employer, in the form of wages, or payments in lieu of wages, or in any form of support or compensation (including workmen's compensation) in respect to the same objects, the benefits under this section shall be diminished by the amount of such payments in the following manner: (A) Benefits on account of injury or disability shall be reduced by the amount of payments to the injured person on account of the same injury or disability; and (B) benefits on account of death shall be reduced by the amount of payments to the dependents of the deceased civilian American citizen on account of the same death.

(9) This subsection shall take effect as of December 7, 1941, and the right of individuals to benefits shall be held to have begun to accrue as though this subsection had been in effect as of such date.

(10) No benefits provided by this subsection for injury, disability, or death shall accrue to any person who, without regard to this subsection, is entitled to or has received benefits for the same injury, disability, or death under such Act of December 2, 1942, as amended [42 U.S.C. 1701 to 1717].

(11) No benefits provided by this subsection shall accrue to any person to whom benefits have been paid, or are payable, under the Federal Employees' Compensation Act [5 U.S.C. 8101 et seq.], or any extension thereof, by reason of disability or death of an employee of the United States suffered after capture, detention, or other restraint by an enemy of the United States, when such disability or death is deemed, in the administration of the Federal Employees' Compensation Act to have resulted from injury occurring while in the performance of duty, under subsection (b) of section 5 of the Act entitled "An Act to amend the Act entitled 'An Act to provide compensation for employees of the United States suffering injuries while in the performance of their duties, and for other purposes', as amended", approved July 28, 1945, as amended.

(g) Benefits for civilian internees in Korea, and dependents; time

(1) As used in this subsection, the term "civilian American citizens" means any person who, being then a citizen of the United States, was captured in Korea on or after June 25, 1950, by any hostile force with which the Armed Forces of the United States were actually engaged in armed conflict subsequent to such date and prior to August 21, 1954, or who went into hiding in Korea in order to avoid capture or internment by any such hostile force; except (A) a person who at any time voluntarily, knowingly, and without duress, gave aid to or collaborated with or in any manner served any such hostile force, or (B) a regularly appointed, enrolled, enlisted, or inducted member of the Armed Forces of the United States.

(2) The Commission is authorized to receive and to determine, according to law, the amount and validity, and provide for the payment of any claim filed by, or on behalf of, any civilian American citizen for detention benefits for any period of time subsequent to June 25, 1950, during which he was held by any such hostile force as a prisoner, internee, hostage, or in any other capacity, or remained in hiding to avoid being captured or interned by any such hostile force.

(3) The detention benefit allowed to any person under the provisions of paragraph (2) of this subsection shall be at the rate of $60 for each calendar month during which such person was at least eighteen years of age and at the rate of $25 per month for each calendar month during which such person was less than eighteen years of age.

(4) The detention benefits allowed under paragraph (2) of this subsection shall be allowed to the person entitled thereto, or, in the event of his death, only to the following persons:

(A) widow or husband if there is no child or children of the deceased;

(B) widow or dependent husband and child or children of the deceased, one-half to the widow or dependent husband and the other half to the child or children in equal shares;

(C) child or children of the deceased (in equal shares) if there is no widow or dependent husband.

(5) Any claim allowed by the Commission under this subsection shall be certified to the Secretary of the Treasury for payment out of funds appropriated pursuant to this subsection, and shall be paid by the Secretary of the Treasury to the person entitled thereto, except that where any person entitled to payment under this subsection is under any legal disability, payment may be made in accordance with the provisions of subsection (e) of this section.

(6) Each claim filed under this subsection must be filed not later than one year from whichever of the following dates last occurs:

(A) The date of enactment of this subsection [Aug. 21, 1954];

(B) The date the civilian American citizen by whom the claim is filed returned to the jurisdiction of the United States; or

(C) The date upon which the Commission, at the request of a potentially eligible survivor, makes a determination that the civilian American citizen has actually died or may be presumed to be dead, in the case of any civilian American citizen who has not returned to the jurisdiction of the United States.

The Commission shall complete its determinations with respect to each claim filed under this subsection at the earliest practicable date, but in no event later than one year after the date on which such claim was filed.

(7)(A) There are authorized to be appropriated such amounts as may be necessary to carry out the purposes of this subsection, including necessary administrative expenses.

(B) The Commission shall determine, from time to time, the share of its administrative expenses attributable to the performance of its functions under this subsection and make the appropriate adjustments in its accounts, and determinations and adjustments made pursuant to this subparagraph shall be final and conclusive.

(h) Benefits for Guamanians killed or captured at Wake Island on or after December 7, 1941

In the case of any Guamanian killed or captured by the Imperial Japanese Government on or after December 7, 1941, at Wake Island, benefits shall be granted under subsections (a) through (f) of this section in the same manner and to the same extent as apply in the case of civilian American citizens so killed or captured. Claims for benefits under subsections (a) through (e) of this section must be filed within six months after the date of enactment of this subsection [Aug. 31, 1962], and the time limitation applicable to any individual by subsection (f) shall not begin to run until the date of enactment of this subsection [Aug. 31, 1962], with respect to any individual who is entitled to such benefits solely by reason of this subsection. The preceding sentence shall not be construed to affect the right of any individual to receive such benefits with respect to any period prior to the date of enactment of this subsection [Aug. 31, 1962].

(i) Detention benefits for civilian internees in Southeast Asia; definitions; authority of Commission; claim for benefits; rate of compensation; persons entitled to payments; certification for payment; filing date; determination of claims; appropriations

(1) As used in this subsection—

(A) the term "Vietnam conflict" relates to the period beginning on February 28, 1961, and ending on such date as shall thereafter be determined by Presidential proclamation or concurrent resolution of the Congress; and

(B) the term "civilian American citizen" means any person who, being then a citizen of the United States, was captured in Southeast Asia during the Vietnam conflict by any force hostile to the United States, or who went into hiding in Southeast Asia, in order to avoid capture or internment by any such hostile force, except (i) a person who voluntarily, knowingly, and without duress, gave aid to or collaborated with or in any manner served any such hostile force, or (ii) a regularly appointed, enrolled, enlisted, or inducted member of the Armed Forces of the United States.

(2) The Commission is authorized to receive and to determine, according to law, the amount and validity, and provide for the payment of any claim filed by, or on behalf of, any civilian American citizen for detention benefits for any period of time subsequent to February 27, 1961, during which he was held by any such hostile force as a prisoner, internee, hostage, or in any other capacity, or remained in hiding to avoid capture or internment by any such hostile force.

(3) The detention benefits allowed under paragraph (2) of this subsection shall be at the rate of $150 for each calendar month.

(4) The detention benefits allowed under paragraph (2) of this subsection shall be allowed to the civilian American citizen entitled thereto, or, in the event of his death, only to the following persons:

(A) the widow or husband if there is no child or children of the deceased;

(B) the widow or dependent husband and child or children of the deceased, one-half to the widow or dependent husband and the other half to the child or children in equal shares;

(C) the child or children of the deceased in equal shares if there is no widow or dependent husband.

(5) Any claim allowed by the Commission under this subsection shall be certified to the Secretary of the Treasury for payment out of funds appropriated pursuant to this subsection, and shall be paid to the person entitled thereto, except that if a person entitled to payment under this section is under any legal disability, payment shall be made in accordance with the provisions of subsection (e) of this section.

(6) Each claim filed under this section must be filed not later than three years from whichever of the following dates last occurs:

(A) the date of enactment of this subsection [June 24, 1970];

(B) the date the civilian American citizen by whom the claim is filed returned to the jurisdiction of the United States; or

(C) the date upon which the Commission, at the request of a potentially eligible survivor, makes a determination that the civilian American citizen has actually died or may be presumed to be dead, in the case of any civilian American citizen who has not returned to the jurisdiction of the United States.

The Commission shall complete its determinations for each claim filed under this subsection at the earliest practicable date, but not later than one year after the date on which such claim was filed.

(7) There are authorized to be appropriated such amounts as may be necessary to carry out the purposes of this subsection, including necessary administrative expenses.

(July 3, 1948, ch. 826, title I, §5, 62 Stat. 1242; 1950 Reorg. Plan No. 19, §1, eff. May 24, 1950, 15 F.R. 3178, 64 Stat. 1271; Apr. 9, 1952, ch. 168, §1, 66 Stat. 49; Aug. 21, 1954, ch. 784, §1, 68 Stat. 759; Aug. 31, 1954, ch. 1162, title I, §§101 (a)–(c), 102(a), 68 Stat. 1034; Pub. L. 87–617, Aug. 31, 1962, 76 Stat. 413; Pub. L. 87–846, title I, §102, Oct. 22, 1962, 76 Stat. 1107; Pub. L. 91–289, §3, June 24, 1970, 84 Stat. 324; Pub. L. 94–383, Aug. 12, 1976, 90 Stat. 1122.)

REFERENCES IN TEXT

The Act entitled "An Act to provide benefits for the injury, disability, death, or enemy detention of employees of contractors with the United States, and for other purposes", approved December 2, 1942, as amended, referred to in subsec. (f)(1), means act Dec. 2, 1942, ch. 668, 56 Stat. 1028, as amended, titles I and II of which are popularly known as the War Hazards Compensation Act, and is classified principally to chapter 12 (§1701 et seq.) of Title 42, The Public Health and Welfare. For complete classification of this Act to the Code, see Tables.

The Federal Employees' Compensation Act, referred to in subsec. (f)(11), is act Sept. 7, 1916, ch. 458, 39 Stat. 742, as amended, which was repealed and the provisions thereof were reenacted as subchapter 1 (§8101 et seq.) of chapter 81 of Title 5, Government Organization and Employees, by Pub. L. 89–554, Sept. 6, 1966, 80 Stat. 378.

Subsection (b) of section 5 of the Act entitled "An Act to amend the Act entitled 'An Act to provide compensation for employees of the United States suffering injuries while in the performance of their duties, and for other purposes', as amended", approved July 28,

1945, as amended, referred to in subsec. (f)(11), means section 5 of act July 28, 1945, ch. 328, 59 Stat. 504, as amended, which enacted section 801 of former Title 5, Executive Departments and Government Officers and Employees, amended sections 760, 761, 770, and 793 of former Title 5, and enacted provisions set out as notes under section 770 of former Title 5, and which was repealed by Pub. L. 85–608, §303, Aug. 8, 1958, 72 Stat. 539. See section 8102(b) of Title 5, Government Organization and Employees.

AMENDMENTS

1976—Subsec. (i)(3). Pub. L. 94–383 substituted "$150" for "$60".

1970—Subsec. (e). Pub. L. 91–289, §3(1), included reference to subsec. (i) in parenthetical phrase.

Subsec. (i). Pub. L. 91–289, §3(2), added subsec. (i).

1962—Subsec. (e). Pub. L. 87–846 substituted "title" for "Act".

Subsec. (h). Pub. L. 87–617 added subsec. (h).

1954—Subsec. (a). Act Aug. 31, 1954, §101(a), included as eligible for detention benefits, civilian American citizens who were captured at certain Pacific islands by the Japanese, but who were formerly expressly excluded from these benefits by reason of being Federal employees or employees of contractors with the United States, and to make them eligible for disability compensation. Act Aug. 21, 1954, §1(b), limited the application of such section's definition of "civilian American citizen" to subsecs. (b) and (f) of this section.

Subsec. (d). Act Aug. 31, 1954, §102(a), (b), struck out "dependent" wherever appearing, and added cl. (4).

Subsec. (e). Act Aug. 21, 1954, §1(c), inserted "(except under subsection (g))" after "under this section".

Subsec. (f)(3). Act Aug. 31, 1954, §101(b), provided that last sentence of section 101(a) [1701(a) of this Appendix] and section 101(d) [1701(d) of this Appendix] should not operate to exclude civilian American citizens from entitlement to medical care or disability compensation.

Subsec. (f)(10), (11). Act Aug. 31, 1954, §101(c), added pars. (10) and (11).

Subsec. (g). Act Aug. 21, 1954, §1(a), added subsec. (g).

1952—Subsec. (e). Act Apr. 9, 1952, allowed the award for the benefit of claimant to be paid to the claimant's natural or legal guardian, committee, conservator, or curator, or to such other person as is charged with the care of the claimant, and permitted the payment of an award payable to a minor, directly to such minor.

TRANSFER OF FUNCTIONS

"Secretary of Labor" substituted for "Federal Security Administrator" in subsec. (f)(6) pursuant to Reorg. Plan No. 19 of 1950, §1, eff. May 24, 1950, 15 F.R. 3178, 64 Stat. 1271, set out in the Appendix to Title 5, Government Organization and Employees, which transferred functions of Federal Security Administrator and Federal Security Agency under this section to Secretary of Labor, with power to delegate.

For provisions transferring Foreign Claims Settlement Commission of the United States to Department of Justice, as a separate agency, see section 1622a et seq. of Title 22, Foreign Relations and Intercourse.

War Claims Commission, including offices of its members, abolished and functions transferred to Foreign Claims Settlement Commission of the United States by Reorg. Plan No. 1 of 1954, §§2, 4, eff. July 1, 1954, 19 F.R. 3985, 68 Stat. 1279, set out in the Appendix to Title 5, Government Organization and Employees. See, also, section 2001 of this Appendix and notes thereunder.

FILING DATES FOR CLAIMS OF NEW CLASSES OF BENEFICIARIES; TOLLING OF LIMITATIONS

Section 101(e) of act Aug. 31, 1954, required persons entitled to benefits under subsec. (b), (c), or (d) of this section solely by reason of the amendments made to this section by act Aug. 31, 1954, to file claims therefor within one year from Aug. 31, 1954, and provided that the time limitations applicable to claims under subsec. (f) of this section were not to begin to run until Aug. 31, 1954, with regard to any person entitled to such benefits solely by reason of the amendments to this section by act Aug. 31, 1954.

Section 102(c) of act Aug. 31, 1954, required persons entitled to benefits solely by reason of amendments made to this section by section 102 of act Aug. 31, 1954 to file claims within one year from Aug. 31, 1954.

PRIOR BENEFITS AS AFFECTING RIGHTS

Section 102(b) of act Aug. 31, 1954, provided that the amendments to sections 2004(d) and 2005(c), (d)(4) of this Appendix by section 102 of act Aug. 31, 1954, should not apply with respect to benefits paid prior to Aug. 31, 1954.

SECTION REFERRED TO IN OTHER SECTIONS

This section is referred to in sections 2005, 2006, 2007, 2012, 2015, 2016 of this Appendix.

§2005. Prisoners of war

(a) "Prisoner of war" defined

As used in subsection (b) of this section, the term "prisoner of war" means any regularly appointed, enrolled, enlisted, or inducted member of the military or naval forces of the United States who was held as a prisoner of war for any period of time subsequent to December 7, 1941, by any government of any nation with which the United States has been at war subsequent to such date.

(b) Payment of claims; rate allowed; certification of claims

The Commission is authorized to receive, adjudicate according to law, and provide for the payment of any claim filed by any prisoner of war for compensation for the violation by the enemy government by which he was held as a prisoner of war, or its agents, of its obligation to furnish him the quantity or quality of food to which he was entitled as a prisoner of war under the terms of the Geneva Convention of July 27, 1929. The compensation allowed to any prisoner of war under the provisions of this subsection shall be at the rate of $1 for each day he was held as a prisoner of war on which the enemy government or its agents failed to furnish him such quantity or quality of food. Any claim allowed under the provisions of this subsection shall be certified to the Secretary of the Treasury for payment out of the War Claims Fund established by section 13 of this title [section 2012 of this Appendix].

(c) Persons entitled to payments

Claims pursuant to subsection (b) shall be paid to the person entitled thereto, and shall in case of death of the persons who are entitled be payable only to or for the benefit of the following persons:

(1) Widow or husband if there is no child or children of the deceased;

(2) Widow or husband and child or children of the deceased, one-half to the widow or husband and the other half to the child or children of the deceased in equal shares;

(3) Child or children of the deceased (in equal shares) if there is no widow or husband; and

(4) Parents (in equal shares) if there is no widow, husband, or child.

(d) Additional definition of "prisoner of war"; payment of claims; rate allowed; persons entitled to payments

(1) As used in this subsection the term "prisoner of war" means any regularly appointed, enrolled, enlisted, or inducted member of the military or naval forces of the United States, who was held a prisoner of war for any period of time subsequent to December 7, 1941, by any government of any nation with which the United States has been at war subsequent to such date.

(2) The Commission is authorized to receive, adjudicate according to law, and to provide for the payment of any claim filed by any prisoner of war for compensation—

(A) for the violations by the enemy government by which he was held as a prisoner of war, or its agents, of such government's obligations under title III, section III, of the Geneva Convention of July 27, 1929, relating to labor of prisoners of war; or

(B) for inhumane treatment by the enemy government by which he was held, or its agents. The term "inhumane treatment" as used herein shall include, but not be limited to, violation by such enemy government, or its agents, of one or more of the provisions of articles 2, 3, 7, 10, 12, 13, 21, 22, 54, 56, or 57, of the Geneva Convention of July 27, 1929.

(3) Compensation shall be allowed to any prisoner of war under this subsection at the rate of $1.50 per day for each day he was held as a prisoner of war on which he alleges and proves in a manner acceptable to the Commission—

(A) the violation by such enemy government or its agents of the provisions of title III, section III, of the Geneva Convention of July 27, 1929; or

(B) any inhumane treatment as defined herein.

Any claim allowed under the provisions of this subsection shall be certified to the Secretary of the Treasury for payment out of the War Claims Fund established by section 13 of this title [section 2012 of this Appendix]. In no event shall the compensation allowed to any prisoner of war under this subsection exceed the sum of $1.50 with respect to any one day.

(4) Claims pursuant to subsection (d)(2) shall be paid to the person entitled thereto, or to his legal or natural guardian if he has one, and shall, in case of death of the persons who are entitled be payable only to or for the benefit of the following persons:

(A) widow or husband if there is no child or children of the deceased;

(B) widow or husband and child or children of the deceased, one-half to the widow or husband and the other half to the child or children of the deceased in equal shares;

(C) child or children of the deceased (in equal shares) if there is no widow or husband; and

(D) parents (in equal shares) if there is no widow, husband, or child.

(e) Extension to Korean War prisoners

(1) As used in this subsection the term "prisoner of war" means any regularly appointed, enrolled, enlisted, or inducted member of the Armed Forces of the United States who was held as a prisoner of war for any period of time subsequent to June 25, 1950, by any hostile force with which the Armed Forces of the United States were actually engaged in armed conflict subsequent to such date and prior to the date of enactment of this subsection [Aug. 21, 1954], or any person (military or civilian) assigned to duty in the U.S.S. Pueblo who was captured by the military forces of North Korea on January 23, 1968, and thereafter held prisoner by the Government of North Korea for any period of time ending on or before December 23, 1968, except any person who, at any time, voluntarily, knowingly, and without duress, gave aid to or collaborated with or in any manner served any such hostile force.

(2) The Commission is authorized to receive and to determine, according to law, the amount and validity, and provide for the payment of any claim filed by any prisoner of war for compensation for the failure of the hostile force by which he was held as a prisoner of war, or its agents, to furnish him the quantity or quality of food prescribed for prisoners of war under the terms of the Geneva Convention of July 27, 1929. The compensation allowed to any prisoner of war under the provisions of this paragraph shall be at the rate of $1 for each day on which he was held as a prisoner of war and on which such hostile force, or its agents, failed to furnish him such quantity or quality of food.

(3) The Commission is authorized to receive and to determine, according to law, the amount and validity and provide for the payment of any claim filed by any prisoner of war for compensation—

(A) for the failure of the hostile force by which he was held as a prisoner of war, or its agents, to meet the conditions and requirements prescribed under title III, section III, of the Geneva Convention of July 27, 1929, relating to labor of prisoners of war; or

(B) for inhumane treatment by the hostile force by which he was held, or its agents. The term "inhumane treatment" as used herein shall include, but not be limited to, failure of such hostile force, or its agents, to meet the conditions and requirements of one or more of the provisions of articles 2, 3, 7, 10, 12, 13, 21, 22, 54, 56, or 57 of the Geneva Convention of July 27, 1929.

Compensation shall be allowed to any prisoner of war under this paragraph at the rate of $1.50 per day for each day on which he was held as a prisoner of war and with respect to which he alleges and proves in a manner acceptable to the Commission the failure to meet the conditions and requirements described in subparagraph (A) or the inhumane treatment described in subparagraph (B). In no event shall the compensation allowed to any prisoner of war under this paragraph exceed the sum of $1.50 with respect to any one day.

(4) Any claim allowed by the Commission under this subsection shall be certified to the Secretary of the Treasury for payment out of funds appropriated pursuant to this subsection and shall be paid by the Secretary of the Treasury to the person entitled thereto, and shall, in case of death or determination of death of the persons who are entitled, be paid only to or for

the benefit of the persons specified, and in the order established, by paragraph (4) of subsection (d) of this section.

(5) Each claim filed under this subsection must be filed not later than one year from whichever of the following dates last occurs:

(A) The date of enactment of this subsection [Aug. 21, 1954];

(B) The date the prisoner of war by whom the claim is filed returned to the jurisdiction of the Armed Forces of the United States; or

(C) The date upon which the Department of Defense makes a determination that the prisoner of war has actually died or is presumed to be dead, in the case of any prisoner of war who has not returned to the jurisdiction of the Armed Forces of the United States;

(D) In the case of any person assigned to duty in the U.S.S. Pueblo referred to in paragraph (1) of this subsection, one year after the date of enactment of this subparagraph [June 24, 1970].

The Commission shall complete its determinations with respect to each claim filed under this subsection at the earliest practicable date, but in no event later than one year after the date on which such claim was filed.

(6) Any claim allowed under the provisions of this subsection shall be paid from funds appropriated pursuant to paragraph (7) of this subsection.

(7)(A) There are authorized to be appropriated such amounts as may be necessary to carry out the purposes of this subsection, including necessary administrative expenses.

(B) The Commission shall determine, from time to time, the share of its administrative expenses attributable to the performance of its functions under this subsection and make the appropriate adjustments in its accounts, and determinations and adjustments made pursuant to this subparagraph shall be final and conclusive.

(f) Vietnam conflict; definitions; authority of Commission; classes of claims; rate of compensation; certification for payment; persons entitled to payments; filing date; determination of claims; fund for payment; appropriations

(1) As used in this subsection—

(A) the term "Vietnam conflict" relates to the period beginning February 28, 1961, and ending on such date as shall thereafter be determined by Presidential proclamation or concurrent resolution of the Congress; and

(B) the term "prisoner of war" means any regularly appointed, enrolled, enlisted, or inducted member of the Armed Forces of the United States who was held as a prisoner of war for any period of time during the Vietnam conflict by any force hostile to the United States, except any such member who, at any time, voluntarily, knowingly, and without duress, gave aid to collaborated with, or in any manner served, such hostile force.

(2) The Commission is authorized to receive and to determine, according to law, the amount and validity, and provide for the payment of any claim filed by any prisoner of war for compensation for the failure of the hostile force by which he was held as a prisoner of war, or its agents, to furnish him the quantity or quality of food prescribed for prisoners of war under the terms of the Geneva Convention of August 12, 1949. The compensation allowed to any prisoner of war under the provisions of this paragraph shall be at the rate of $2 for each day on which he was held as a prisoner of war and on which such hostile force, or its agents, failed to furnish him such quantity or quality of food.

(3) The Commission is authorized to receive and to determine, according to law, the amount and validity and provide for the payment of any claim filed by any prisoner of war for compensation—

(A) for the failure of the hostile force by which he was held as a prisoner of war, or its agents, to meet the conditions and requirements prescribed under chapter VIII, section III, of the Geneva Convention of August 12, 1949, relating to labor of prisoners of war; or

(B) for inhumane treatment by the hostile force by which he was held, or its agents. The term "inhumane treatment" as used in this subparagraph shall include, but not be limited to, failure of such hostile force, or its agents, to meet the conditions and requirements of one or more of the provisions of articles 3, 12, 13, 14, 17, 19, 22, 23, 24, 25, 27, 29, 43, 44, 45, 46, 47, 48, 84, 85, 86, 87, 88, 89, 90, 97, or 98 of the Geneva Convention of August 12, 1949.

Compensation shall be allowed to any prisoner of war under this paragraph at the rate of $3 per day for each day on which he was held as a prisoner of war and with respect to which he alleges and proves in a manner acceptable to the Commission the failure to meet the conditions and requirements described in subparagraph (A) of this paragraph or the inhumane treatment described in subparagraph (B) of this paragraph. In no event shall the compensation allowed to any prisoner of war under this paragraph exceed the sum of $3 with respect to any one day.

(4) Any claim allowed by the Commission under this subsection shall be certified to the Secretary of the Treasury for payment out of funds appropriated pursuant to this subsection and shall be paid by the Secretary of the Treasury to the person entitled thereto, and shall, in the case of death or determination of death of the persons who are entitled, be paid only to or for the benefit of the persons specified, and in the order established, by subsection (d)(4) of this section.

(5) Each claim filed under this subsection must be filed not later than three years from whichever of the following dates last occurs:

(A) the date of enactment of this subsection [June 24, 1970];

(B) the date the prisoner of war by whom the claim is filed returned to the jurisdiction of the Armed Forces of the United States; or

(C) the date upon which the Department of Defense makes a determination that the prisoner of war has actually died or is presumed to be dead, in the case of any prisoner of war who has not returned to the jurisdiction of the Armed Forces of the United States.

The Commission shall complete its determinations with respect to each claim filed under this subsection at the earliest practicable date, but in no event later than one year after the date on which such claim was filed.

(6) Any claim allowed under the provisions of this subsection shall be paid from funds appropriated pursuant to paragraph (7) of this subsection.

(7) There are authorized to be appropriated such amounts as may be necessary to carry out the purposes of this subsection, including necessary administrative expenses.

(g) Manner of payment

Where any person entitled to payment under this section is under any legal disability, payment may be made in accordance with the provisions of subsection (e) of section 5 [section 2004(e) of this Appendix].

(July 3, 1948, ch. 826, title I, § 6, 62 Stat. 1244; Sept. 30, 1950, ch. 1116, 64 Stat. 1090; Apr. 9, 1952, ch. 167, § 1, 66 Stat. 47; Apr. 9, 1952, ch. 168, § 2, 66 Stat. 49; Aug. 21, 1954, ch. 784, § 2, 68 Stat. 761; Aug. 31, 1954, ch. 1162, title I, § 102(a)(1), 68 Stat. 1034; Pub. L. 87–846, title I, § 102, Oct. 22, 1962, 76 Stat. 1107; Pub. L. 91–289, §§ 1, 2, June 24, 1970, 84 Stat. 323.)

AMENDMENTS

1970—Subsec. (e)(1). Pub. L. 91–289, § 2(1), defined "prisoner of war" to include any person (military or civilian) assigned to duty in the U.S.S. Pueblo who was captured by the military forces of North Korea on January 23, 1968, and thereafter held prisoner by Government of North Korea for any period of time ending on or before December 23, 1968, and substituted "except any person" for "except any such member".

Subsec. (e)(5)(D). Pub. L. 91–289, § 2(2), added subpar. (D).

Subsecs. (f), (g). Pub. L. 91–289, § 1, added subsec. (f) and redesignated former subsec. (f) as (g).

1962—Pub. L. 87–846 substituted "title" for "Act".

1954—Subsecs. (c), (d)(4). Act Aug. 31, 1954, § 102(a), struck out "dependent" wherever appearing.

Subsec. (e). Act Aug. 21, 1954, § 2(b), added subsec. (e).

Subsec. (f). Act Apr. 9, 1952, ch. 168, added subsec. as a second subsec. (d) which was redesignated "(f)" by act Aug. 21, 1954, § 2(a).

1952—Subsec. (a). Act Apr. 9, 1952, ch. 167, inserted "subsection (b) of" after "As used in".

Subsec. (c). Act Apr. 9, 1952, ch. 168, struck out "or to his legal or natural guardian if he has one" after "person entitled thereto".

Subsec. (d). Act Apr. 9, 1952, ch. 167, added subsec. (d). Another subsec. (d), which was added by act Apr. 9, 1952, ch. 168, was redesignated "(f)". See 1954 Amendment note above.

1950—Subsec. (c)(4). Act Sept. 30, 1950, removed requirement of dependency upon which parents were entitled to benefits.

TRANSFER OF FUNCTIONS

For provisions transferring Foreign Claims Settlement Commission of the United States to Department of Justice, as a separate agency, see section 1622a et seq. of Title 22, Foreign Relations and Intercourse.

War Claims Commission, including offices of its members, abolished and functions transferred to Foreign Claims Settlement Commission of the United States by Reorg. Plan No. 1 of 1954, §§ 2, 4, eff. July 1, 1954, 19 F.R. 3985, 68 Stat. 1279, set out in the Appendix to Title 5, Government Organization and Employees. See, also, section 2001 of this Appendix and notes thereunder.

COMPENSATION FOR PERSONS AWARDED PRISONER OF WAR MEDAL WHO DID NOT PREVIOUSLY RECEIVE COMPENSATION AS PRISONER OF WAR

Pub. L. 104–201, div. A, title VI, § 656, Sept. 23, 1996, 110 Stat. 2584, provided that:

"(a) AUTHORITY TO MAKE PAYMENTS.—The Secretary of the military department concerned shall make payments in the manner provided in section 6 of the War Claims Act of 1948 (50 U.S.C. App. 2005) to (or on behalf of) any person described in subsection (b) who submits an application for such payment in accordance with subsection (d).

"(b) ELIGIBLE PERSONS.—This section applies with respect to a member or former member of the Armed Forces who—

"(1) has received the prisoner of war medal under section 1128 of title 10, United States Code; and

"(2) has not previously received a payment under section 6 of the War Claims Act of 1948 (50 U.S.C. App. 2005) with respect to the period of internment for which the person received the prisoner of war medal.

"(c) AMOUNT OF PAYMENT.—The amount of the payment to any person under this section shall be determined based upon the provisions of section 6 of the War Claims Act of 1948 that are applicable with respect to the period of time during which the internment occurred for which the person received the prisoner of war medal.

"(d) ONE-YEAR PERIOD FOR SUBMISSION OF APPLICATIONS.—A payment may be made by reason of this section only in the case of a person who submits an application to the Secretary concerned for such payment during the one-year period beginning on the date of the enactment of this Act [Sept. 23, 1996]. Any such application shall be submitted in such form and manner as the Secretary may require."

FILING DATE FOR CLAIMS OF NEW CLASS OF BENEFICIARIES

Persons entitled to benefits solely by reason of amendments made to this section by section 102(a) of act Aug. 31, 1954, were required to file claims within one year of Aug. 31, 1954, see section 102(c) of act Aug. 31, 1954.

PRIOR BENEFITS AS AFFECTING RIGHTS

Section 102(b) of act Aug. 31, 1954, provided that the amendments to sections 2004(d) and 2005(c), (d)(4) of this Appendix by section 102 of act Aug. 31, 1954, should not apply with respect to benefits paid prior to Aug. 31, 1954.

TIME FOR FILING CLAIMS

Section 3 of act Apr. 9, 1952, ch. 167, as amended by act May 13, 1954, ch. 202, § 1, 68 Stat. 97, provided that claims for compensation under subsec. (d) of this section were to be filed on or before Aug. 1, 1954.

Sections 2 and 3 of act May 13, 1954, provided:

"SEC. 2. The amendment made by this Act [amending section 3 of act Apr. 9, 1952, ch. 167, by extending the time for filing claims from one year after April 9, 1952 to August 1, 1954] shall not be construed to extend the life of the War Claims Commission for any period of time.

"SEC. 3. The amendment made by this Act shall take effect as of April 9, 1953."

SECTION REFERRED TO IN OTHER SECTIONS

This section is referred to in sections 2006, 2007, 2014, 2016 of this Appendix.

§ 2006. Religious organizations

(a) Reimbursement for services furnished members of armed services and American civilians; certification of claims

The Commission is authorized to receive, adjudicate according to law, and provide for the payment of any claim filed by any religious organization functioning in the Philippine Islands and affiliated with a religious organization in the United States, or by the personnel of any such Philippine organization, for reimbursement of expenditures incurred, or for payment of the fair value of supplies used, by such organization or such personnel for the purpose of furnishing shelter, food, clothing, hospitalization, medicines and medical services, and other relief in the Philippines to members of the armed forces of the United States or to civilian American citizens (as defined in section 5 [section 2004 of this Appendix]) at any time subsequent to December 6, 1941, and before August 15, 1945. Any claim allowed under the provisions of this section shall be certified to the Secretary of the Treasury for payment out of the War Claims Fund established by section 13 of this title [section 2012 of this Appendix].

(b) Compensation for loss or damage to real property used in educational, medical, or welfare work

Any such religious organization or its personnel functioning in the Philippines and affiliated with a religious organization in the United States, which furnished relief in the Philippines to members of the Armed Forces of the United States or to civilian American citizens in accordance with the provisions of subsection (a) shall be compensated from the War Claims Fund, as hereinafter provided, for the loss and damage sustained as a consequence of the war to its schools, colleges, universities, scientific observatories, hospitals, dispensaries, orphanages, and other property or facilities connected with its educational, medical, or welfare work.

(c) Compensation to replace facilities

Any such affiliated organization furnishing relief which possessed any interest in, and whose personnel of American citizens substantially composed the administrative staff of, any hospital whose prewar facilities and capacity have not been restored shall be compensated in an amount sufficient to enable such organization to replace the hospital's facilities and capacity equal to that which existed at the time of the outbreak of the war, irrespective of what disposition was made subsequently of the land, buildings, and contents.

(d) Determination of claims

Claims filed pursuant to subsection (b) shall be determined and paid upon the basis of postwar cost of replacement which shall be ascertained by the War Claims Commission. In making such determinations the Commission shall utilize but not be limited to the factual information and evidence contained in the records of the Philippine War Damage Commission; the technical advice of experts in the field; the substantiating evidence submitted by the claimants; and any other technical and legal means by which fair and equitable postwar replacement costs shall be determined.

(e) Investigation; determination of replacement costs; basis used

The Commission is authorized and directed to proceed at once with the necessary investigation, study, and establishment of procedures in order to determine the replacement costs of the claims to be filed under subsections (b) and (c), using as a basis for beginning such investigation and study the evidence contained in the claims of those religious organizations or their personnel which have already filed and are eligible to be paid under the terms of subsection (a) of this section.

(f) Filing of claims; adjudication; place and use of payments

All claims under subsections (b) and (c) must be filed on or before October 1, 1952; and not later than March 31, 1953, the Commission shall adjudicate according to law and provide for the payment of any claim filed pursuant to this section. In any case in which any money is payable as a result of subsections (b) and (c) to a religious organization or its personnel functioning in the Philippines, such money shall be paid upon request of such organization to its affiliate in the United States: *Provided*, That all money thus paid to such affiliated religious organization in the United States shall be used by such affiliate for the purpose of restoring the educational, medical, and welfare facilities described in subsections (b) and (c) and located in the Philippines.

(g) Claims of internees and prisoners of war unaffected

The Commission shall expedite the payments under this section without reducing payment of claims of American civilian internees and prisoners of war filed before March 31, 1953, pursuant to the provisions of sections 5 and 6 of this title [sections 2004 and 2005 of this Appendix].

(h) Denominational organizations

(1) Any religious organization functioning in the Philippines and of the same denomination as a religious organization functioning in the United States which furnished relief (as described, and during the period designated, in subsection (a) of this section) in the Philippines to members of the Armed Forces of the United States or to civilian American citizens shall be compensated from the War Claims Fund (A) for expenditures incurred, or for payment of the fair value of supplies used by such organization, for the purpose of furnishing such relief and (B) for loss and damage sustained as a consequence of the war to its schools, colleges, universities, scientific observatories, hospitals, dispensaries, orphanages, and other property or facilities connected with its educational, medical, or welfare work. No payments shall be made to any organization under this subsection if such organization has received an award under subsection (a) or (b) of this section, and no payments shall be made to any organization pursuant to clause (B) of this paragraph unless such organization has received an award for war damages from the Philippine War Damage Commission under the provisions of the Philippine Rehabilitation Act of 1946, as amended [sections 1751 to 1806 of this Appendix].

(2) The Commission is authorized to receive, determine according to law, and provide for the payment of claims filed under this subsection. Each claim allowed by the Commission under this subsection shall be certified to the Secretary of the Treasury for payment out of the War Claims Fund. All payments under this subsection shall be made to an organization or individual in the United States designated by the

claimant, and, in the case of claims under clause (B) of paragraph (1) of this subsection such payments shall be used for the purpose of restoring the educational, medical, and welfare facilities described in such clause.

(3) Claims for benefits under this subsection must be filed within six months after the date of enactment of this subsection [Aug. 6, 1956]. The Commission shall complete its determination with respect to each claim filed under this subsection at the earliest practicable date, but in no event later than one year after the date on which such claim was filed.

(4) Claims filed pursuant to clause (B) of paragraph (1) of this subsection shall be determined and paid upon the basis of postwar cost of replacement for the twelve-month period ending October 1, 1952, as ascertained by the Commission.

(July 3, 1948, ch. 826, title I, § 7, 62 Stat. 1245; Apr. 9, 1952, ch. 167, § 2, 66 Stat. 48; Aug. 6, 1956, ch. 985, 70 Stat. 1063; Pub. L. 87–846, title I, § 102, Oct. 22, 1962, 76 Stat. 1107.)

AMENDMENTS

1962—Pub. L. 87–846 substituted "title" for "Act".

1956—Subsec. (h). Act Aug. 6, 1956, added subsec. (h).

1952—Subsec. (a). Subsec. constituted entire section prior to amendment by act Apr. 9, 1952.

Subsecs. (b) to (g). Act Apr. 9, 1952, added subsecs. (b) to (g).

TRANSFER OF FUNCTIONS

For provisions transferring Foreign Claims Settlement Commission of the United States to Department of Justice, as a separate agency, see section 1622a et seq. of Title 22, Foreign Relations and Intercourse.

War Claims Commission, including offices of its members, abolished and functions transferred to Foreign Claims Settlement Commission of the United States by Reorg. Plan No. 1 of 1954, §§ 2, 4, eff. July 1, 1954, 19 F.R. 3985, 68 Stat. 1279, set out in the Appendix to Title 5, Government Organization and Employees. See, also, section 2001 of this Appendix and notes thereunder.

TERMINATION OF PHILIPPINE WAR DAMAGE COMMISSION

The Philippine War Damage Commission established by section 1751 of this Appendix terminated under the provisions of subsec. (d) of section 1751 which provided for the winding up of the Commission's affairs not later than two years after expiration of time for filing claims under former sections 1751 to 1763 of this Appendix if possible but in no event later than Apr. 30, 1951.

SECTION REFERRED TO IN OTHER SECTIONS

This section is referred to in section 2007 of this Appendix.

§ 2007. Commission's report on personal injury and property claims to President; findings; recommendations; public property; legislative effect

(a) The Commission shall inquire into and report to the President, for submission of such report to the Congress on or before March 31, 1950, with respect to war claims arising out of World War II, other than claims which may be received and adjudicated under the preceding sections of this Act [sections 2001 to 2006 of this Appendix], and shall present in such report its findings on—

(1) the estimated number and amount of such claims, classified by types and categories; and

(2) the extent to which such claims have been or may be satisfied under international agreements or domestic or foreign laws.

(b) The report of the Commission shall contain recommendations with respect to—

(1) categories and types of claims, if any, which should be received and considered and the legal and equitable bases therefor;

(2) the administrative method by which such claims should be considered, and any priorities or limitations which should be applicable; and

(3) any limitations which should be applied to the allowance and payment of fees in connection with such claims.

(c) The Commission shall include in such report—

(1) such other recommendations as it deems appropriate; and

(2) such proposals for legislation as it deems appropriate for carrying out the recommendations made in such report.

(d) Such report, with accompanying evidence, shall be printed as a public document when received by the Congress.

(e) Nothing in this section shall be deemed to imply that the Congress will enact legislation—

(1) adopting any recommendations made under this section with respect to the consideration or payment of any type of claim; or

(2) making any moneys, including moneys remaining in the war claims fund after the making of payments from such fund provided for by this title [sections 2001 to 2016 of this Appendix], available for the payment of such claims.

(July 3, 1948, ch. 826, title I, § 8, 62 Stat. 1245; May 27, 1949, ch. 145, § 1(2), 63 Stat. 112; Pub. L. 87–846, title I, § 102, Oct. 22, 1962, 76 Stat. 1107.)

AMENDMENTS

1962—Pub. L. 87–846 substituted "title" for "Act".

1949—Subsec. (a). Act May 27, 1949, extended until March 31, 1950, time within which Commission is required to file its reports and recommendations.

TRANSFER OF FUNCTIONS

For provisions transferring Foreign Claims Settlement Commission of the United States to Department of Justice, as a separate agency, see section 1622a et seq. of Title 22, Foreign Relations and Intercourse.

War Claims Commission, including offices of its members, abolished and functions transferred to Foreign Claims Settlement Commission of the United States by Reorg. Plan No. 1 of 1954, §§ 2, 4, eff. July 1, 1954, 19 F.R. 3985, 68 Stat. 1279, set out in the Appendix to Title 5, Government Organization and Employees. See, also, section 2001 of this Appendix and notes thereunder.

§ 2008. Reports to Congress

Not later than six months after its organization, and every six months thereafter, the Commission shall make a report to the Congress concerning its operations under this title [sections 2001 to 2016 of this Appendix].

(July 3, 1948, ch. 826, title I, § 9, 62 Stat. 1246; Pub. L. 87–846, title I, § 102, Oct. 22, 1962, 76 Stat. 1107.)

ANNUAL SUBMISSION OF REPORTS

Pub. L. 89–348, § 2(6), Nov. 8, 1965, 79 Stat. 1312, modified the provisions of this section, be-

ginning Jan. 1, 1967, to require annual instead of semiannual submission to Congress by Foreign Claims Settlement Commission of report concerning its operations under War Claims Act of 1948.

AMENDMENTS

1962—Pub. L. 87–846 substituted "title" for "Act".

TRANSFER OF FUNCTIONS

For provisions transferring Foreign Claims Settlement Commission of the United States to Department of Justice, as a separate agency, see section 1622a et seq. of Title 22, Foreign Relations and Intercourse.

War Claims Commission, including offices of its members, abolished and functions transferred to Foreign Claims Settlement Commission of the United States by Reorg. Plan No. 1 of 1954, §§ 2, 4, eff. July 1, 1954, 19 F.R. 3985, 68 Stat. 1279, set out in the Appendix to Title 5, Government Organization and Employees. See, also, section 2001 of this Appendix and notes thereunder.

MALNUTRITION STUDY; DEFINITIONS; REPORT TO CONGRESS

Act Aug. 31, 1954, ch. 1162, title II, §§ 201–203, 68 Stat. 1037, defined terms "prisoner of war" and "civilian American citizen" and directed Secretary of Health, Education, and Welfare to conduct malnutrition study and report results thereof, not later than Aug. 31, 1955, to President for transmittal to Congress.

§ 2009. Fee limitation for representing claimants; penalties

No remuneration on account of services rendered or to be rendered to or on behalf of any claimant in connection with any claim filed with the administering agency under this title [sections 2001 to 2016 of this Appendix] shall exceed 10 per centum (or such lesser per centum as may be fixed by the administering agency with respect to any class of claims) of the amount allowed by the administering agency on account of such claim. Any agreement to the contrary shall be unlawful and void. Whoever, in the United States or elsewhere, pays or offers to pay, or promises, to pay, or receives, on account of services rendered or to be rendered in connection with any such claim, any remuneration in excess of the maximum permitted by this section, shall be deemed guilty of a misdemeanor, and, upon conviction thereof, shall be fined not more than $5,000 or imprisoned not more than twelve months, or both, and, if any such payment shall have been made or granted, the administering agency shall take such action as may be necessary to recover the same, and, in addition thereto any such claimant shall forfeit all rights under this title [said sections].

(July 3, 1948, ch. 826, title I, § 10, 62 Stat. 1246; Pub. L. 87–846, title I, § 102, Oct. 22, 1962, 76 Stat. 1107.)

AMENDMENTS

1962—Pub. L. 87–846 substituted "title" for "Act".

TRANSFER OF FUNCTIONS

For provisions transferring Foreign Claims Settlement Commission of the United States to Department of Justice, as a separate agency, see section 1622a et seq. of Title 22, Foreign Relations and Intercourse.

War Claims Commission, including offices of its members, abolished and functions transferred to Foreign Claims Settlement Commission of the United States by Reorg. Plan No. 1 of 1954, §§ 2, 4, eff. July 1, 1954, 19 F.R. 3985, 68 Stat. 1279, set out in the Appendix to Title 5, Government Organization and Employees. See, also, section 2001 of this Appendix and notes thereunder.

§ 2010. Hearings on claims; finality of decision

The Commission shall notify all claimants of the approval or denial of their claims, and, if approved, shall notify such claimants of the amount for which such claims are approved. Any claimant whose claim is denied, or is approved for less than the full allowable amount of such claim, shall be entitled, under such regulations as the Commission may prescribe, to a hearing before the Commission or its representatives with respect to such claim. Upon such hearing, the Commission may affirm, modify, or revise its former action with respect to such claim, including a denial or reduction in the amount theretofore allowed with respect to such claim. The action of the Commission in allowing or denying any claim under this title [sections 2001 to 2016 of this Appendix] shall be final and conclusive on all questions of law and fact and not subject to review by any other official of the United States or by any court by mandamus or otherwise, and the Comptroller General is authorized and directed to allow credit in the accounts of any certifying or disbursing officer for payments in accordance with such action.

(July 3, 1948, ch. 826, title I, § 11, 62 Stat. 1246; Pub. L. 87–846, title I, § 102, Oct. 22, 1962, 76 Stat. 1107.)

AMENDMENTS

1962—Pub. L. 87–846 substituted "title" for "Act".

TRANSFER OF FUNCTIONS

For provisions transferring Foreign Claims Settlement Commission of the United States to Department of Justice, as a separate agency, see section 1622a et seq. of Title 22, Foreign Relations and Intercourse.

War Claims Commission, including offices of its members, abolished and functions transferred to Foreign Claims Settlement Commission of the United States by 68 Reorg. Plan No. 1 of 1954, §§ 2, 4, eff. July 1, 1954, 19 F.R. 3985, 68 Stat. 1279, set out in the Appendix to Title 5, Government Organization and Employees. See, also, section 2001 of this Appendix and notes thereunder.

SECTION REFERRED TO IN OTHER SECTIONS

This section is referred to in section 2017n of this Appendix.

§ 2011. Omitted

CODIFICATION

Section, act July 3, 1948, ch. 826, title I, § 12, 62 Stat. 1246, enacted section 39 of this Appendix.

§ 2012. War Claims Fund

(a) Composition; expenditure

There is hereby created on the books of the Treasury of the United States a trust fund to be known as the War Claims Fund. The War Claims Fund shall consist of all sums covered into the Treasury pursuant to the provisions of section 39 of the Trading With the Enemy Act of October 6, 1917, as amended [section 39 of this Appendix]. The moneys in such fund shall be available for expenditure only as provided in this Act [sections 2001 to 2017p of this Appendix] or as may be provided hereafter by the Congress.

(b) Estimation and certification to Treasury of total amount necessary under section 2004(f)

Before August 1, 1956, the Secretary of Labor shall estimate and report to the President the total amount which will be required to pay all benefits payable by reason of section 5(f) of this title [section 2004(f) of this Appendix]. If the President approves the amount so estimated as reasonably accurate, the total amount so estimated and approved shall be certified to the Secretary of the Treasury; if the President does not so approve he shall determine such amount, and the amount so determined shall be certified to the Secretary of the Treasury. Such certification shall be made on or before September 1, 1956. The Secretary of the Treasury shall then transfer from the War Claims Fund to the general fund of the Treasury a sum equal to the total amount certified to him under this subsection.

(c) Estimation and certification to Treasury of total amount necessary under section 2003(c)

Before August 1, 1956, the Secretary of Labor shall estimate and report to the President the total amount which will be required to pay all additional benefits payable as a result of the enactment of section 4(c) of this title [section 2003(c) of this Appendix]. If the President approves the amount so estimated as reasonably accurate, the total amount so estimated and approved shall be certified to the Secretary of the Treasury; if the President does not so approve, he shall determine such amount, and the amount so determined shall be certified to the Secretary of the Treasury. Such certification shall be made on or before September 1, 1956. The Secretary of the Treasury shall then transfer from the War Claims Fund to the general fund of the Treasury a sum equal to the total amount certified to him under this subsection.

(d) Certification to Treasury of total canceled obligations under section 2003(b)(1)

On or before August 1, 1956, the Secretary of State is authorized and directed to certify to the Secretary of the Treasury the total amount of all obligations canceled pursuant to the provisions of section 4(b)(1) of this title [section 2003(b)(1) of this Appendix]. The Secretary of the Treasury shall transfer from the war claims fund to the general fund of the Treasury an amount equal to the total amount so certified.

(e) Authorization of appropriations for Commission's work

There are hereby authorized to be appropriated, out of any money in the war claims fund, such sums as may be necessary to enable the Commission to carry out its functions under this title [sections 2001 to 2016 of this Appendix].

(July 3, 1948, ch. 826, title I, § 13, 62 Stat. 1247; 1950 Reorg. Plan No. 19, § 1, eff. May 24, 1950, 15 F.R. 3178, 64 Stat. 1271; Aug. 31, 1954, ch. 1162, title I, § 104, 68 Stat. 1036; Pub. L. 87–846, title I, § 102, Oct. 22, 1962, 76 Stat. 1107.)

REFERENCES IN TEXT

Section 4(c) of this title, referred to in subsec. (c), which amended section 1702 of Title 42, The Public Health and Welfare, was classified to section 2003(c) of this Appendix, and was omitted from the Code.

AMENDMENTS

1962—Subsecs. (b) to (e). Pub. L. 87–846 substituted "title" for "Act".

1954—Subsec. (b). Act Aug. 31, 1954, § 104(a), provided that President may approve or disapprove of Secretary of Labor's estimate, and if he disapproves he shall estimate total amount of claims under section 2004(f) of this Appendix, and provided that all transfers which are to be made from the War Claims Fund to the Treasury general fund shall be made before Aug. 1, 1956.

Subsec. (c). Act Aug. 31, 1954, § 104(a), provided that President may approve or disapprove Secretary of Labor's estimate, and if he disapproves he shall estimate total amount of claims under section 2003 (c) of this Appendix, and provided that all transfers which are to be made from War Claims Fund to Treasury general fund shall be made before Aug. 1, 1956.

Subsec. (d). Act Aug. 31, 1954, § 104(b), inserted "on or before August 1, 1956" before "Secretary of State".

TRANSFER OF FUNCTIONS

"Secretary of Labor" substituted for "Federal Security Administrator" in subsecs. (b) and (c) pursuant to Reorg. Plan No. 19 of 1950, § 1, eff. May 24, 1950, 15 F.R. 3178, 64 Stat. 1271, set out in the Appendix to Title 5, Government Organization and Employees, which transferred functions of Federal Security Administrator and Federal Security Agency under this section to Secretary of Labor with power to delegate.

For provisions transferring Foreign Claims Settlement Commission of the United States to Department of Justice, as a separate agency, see section 1622a et seq. of Title 22, Foreign Relations and Intercourse.

War Claims Commission, including offices of its members, abolished and functions transferred to Foreign Claims Settlement Commission of the United States by Reorg. Plan No. 1 of 1954, §§ 2, 4, eff. July 1, 1954, 19 F.R. 3985, 68 Stat. 1279, set out in the Appendix to Title 5, Government Organization and Employees. See, also, section 2001 of this Appendix and notes thereunder.

SECTION REFERRED TO IN OTHER SECTIONS

This section is referred to in sections 40, 2003, 2004, 2005, 2006, 2014, 2015, 2016 of this Appendix; title 22 section 1641c.

§ 2012a. Omitted

CODIFICATION

Section, act June 29, 1955, ch. 226, title I, 69 Stat. 195, which placed a limitation on funds used for payment of claims, was from the General Government Matters Appropriation Act, 1956, and was not repeated in subsequent appropriation acts. Similar provisions were contained in the following prior appropriation acts:

1954—June 24, 1954, ch. 359, title I, 68 Stat. 293.

1953—July 31, 1953, ch. 302, title I, 67 Stat. 312.

1952—July 5, 1952, ch. 578, title I, 66 Stat. 410.

1951—Aug. 31, 1951, ch. 376, title I, 65 Stat. 282.

1950—Sept. 6, 1950, ch. 896, Ch. VIII, title I, 64 Stat. 720.

§ 2013. Payments to certain members of religious orders

In any case in which any money is payable as a result of the enactment of this title [sections 2001 to 2016 of this Appendix] to any person who is prevented from accepting such money by the rules, regulations, or customs of the church or the religious order or organization of which he is a member, such money shall be paid, upon the request of such person, to such church or to such religious order or organization.

(July 3, 1948, ch. 826, title I, §14, 62 Stat. 1247; Pub. L. 87–846, title I, §102, Oct. 22, 1962, 76 Stat. 1107.)

AMENDMENTS

1962—Pub. L. 87–846 substituted "title" for "Act".

TRANSFER OF FUNCTIONS

For provisions transferring Foreign Claims Settlement Commission of the United States to Department of Justice, as a separate agency, see section 1622a et seq. of Title 22, Foreign Relations and Intercourse.

War Claims Commission, including offices of its members, abolished and functions of Commission and of members, officers, and employees thereof transferred to Foreign Claims Settlement Commission of the United States by Reorg. Plan No. 1 of 1954, §§2, 4, eff. July 1, 1954, 19 F.R. 3985, 68 Stat. 1279, set out in the Appendix to Title 5, Government Organization and Employees. See, also, section 2001 of this Appendix and notes thereunder.

§2014. United States citizens serving in allied forces

(a) Right to compensation

The Commission is authorized to receive and to determine, according to law, the amount and validity, and provide for the payment of any claim for compensation filed by or on behalf of any individual who, being then an American citizen, served in the military or naval forces of any government allied with the United States during World War II who was held as a prisoner of war for any period of time subsequent to December 7, 1941, by any government of any nation with which such allied government has been at war subsequent to such date. Compensation shall be payable under this section in accordance with the standards established by, and at the rates prescribed in, subsection (b) of section 6 of this title [section 2005(b) of this Appendix], and paragraphs (2) and (3) of subsection (d) of such section 6 [section 2005(d) (2), (3) of this Appendix].

(b) Deductions

The amount payable under this section shall be reduced by such sum as the individual entitled to compensation under this section has received or is entitled to receive from any government by reason of the same detention.

(c) Payments on death

In the event of death of the individual entitled to compensation under this section, payment may be made to the persons specified in paragraph (4) of subsection (d) of section 6 of this title [section 2005(d)(4) of this Appendix].

(d) Filing date for claims

Claims for benefits under this section must be filed within one year after the date of enactment of this section [Aug. 31, 1954].

(e) Certification of claim for payment

Any claim allowed under the provisions of this section shall be certified to the Secretary of the Treasury for payment out of the War Claims Fund established by section 13 of this title [section 2012 of this Appendix].

(July 3, 1948, ch. 826, title I, §15, as added Aug. 31, 1954, ch. 1162, title I, §103, 68 Stat. 1034; amended Pub. L. 87–846, title I, §102, Oct. 22, 1962, 76 Stat. 1107.)

AMENDMENTS

1962—Pub. L. 87–846 substituted "title" for "Act".

TRANSFER OF FUNCTIONS

For provisions transferring Foreign Claims Settlement Commission of the United States to Department of Justice, as a separate agency, see section 1622a et seq. of Title 22, Foreign Relations and Intercourse.

§2015. Detention benefits to merchant seamen

(a) "Merchant seaman" defined

As used in this section, the term "merchant seaman" means any individual who was employed as a seaman or crew member on any vessel registered under the laws of the United States, or under the laws of any government friendly to the United States during World War II, and who was a citizen of the United States on and after December 7, 1941, to the date of his death or the date of filing claim under this section; except any such individual who is entitled to, or who has received, benefits under section 5 of this title [section 2004 of this Appendix] as a "civilian American citizen".

(b) Determination of claim; rate of payment

The Commission is authorized to receive and determine, according to law, the amount and validity, and provide for the payment of any claim for detention benefits filed by or on behalf of any merchant seaman who, being then a merchant seaman, was captured or interned or held by the Government of Germany or the Imperial Japanese Government, its agent or instrumentalities in World War II for any period of time subsequent to December 7, 1941, during which he was held by either such government as a prisoner, internee, hostage, or in any other capacity. Detention benefits shall be paid under this section at the rates prescribed and in the manner provided in subsections (c) and (d) of section 5 of this title [section 2004(c), (d) of this Appendix].

(c) Collaborationists excluded

Payment of any claim filed under this section shall not be made to any merchant seaman, or to any survivor or survivors thereof, who, voluntarily, knowingly, and without duress, gave aid to or collaborated with or in any manner served any government hostile to the United States during World War II.

(d) Time of filing claim

Claims for benefits under this section must be filed within one year after the date of enactment of this section [Aug. 31, 1954].

(e) Certification of claim for payment

Any claim allowed under the provisions of this section shall be certified to the Secretary of the Treasury for payment out of the War Claims Fund established by section 13 of this title [section 2012 of this Appendix].

(July 3, 1948, ch. 826, title I, §16, as added Aug. 31, 1954, ch. 1162, title I, §103, 68 Stat. 1034; amended Pub. L. 87–846, title I, §102, Oct. 22, 1962, 76 Stat. 1107.)

AMENDMENTS

1962—Pub. L. 87–846 substituted "title" for "Act".

TRANSFER OF FUNCTIONS

For provisions transferring Foreign Claims Settlement Commission of the United States to Department of Justice, as a separate agency, see section 1622a et seq. of Title 22, Foreign Relations and Intercourse.

§ 2016. Philippines

(a) Losses by individual from sequestered credits; loss by banks or other financial institutions

(1) The Commission is authorized to receive and to determine, according to law, the amount and validity, and provide for the payment of any claim filed by—

(A) any individual who—

(i) on or after December 7, 1941, was a member of the military or naval forces of the United States;

(ii) is the survivor of any deceased individual described in subparagraph (i);

(iii) was a national of the United States on December 7, 1941, and is a national of the United States on the date of enactment of this section [Aug. 31, 1954]; or

(iv) is the survivor of any deceased individual who was a national of the United States on December 7, 1941, and would be a national of the United States on the date of enactment of this section [Aug. 31, 1954] if living; or

(B) any partnership, firm, corporation, or other legal entity, in which more than 50 per centum of the ownership was vested, directly or indirectly, both on December 7, 1941, and on the date of enactment of this section [Aug. 31, 1954], in individuals referred to in subparagraph (A) of this paragraph;

for losses arising as a result of the sequestration of accounts, deposits, or other credits of such individual or legal entity in the Philippines by the Imperial Japanese Government.

(2) The Commission is authorized to receive and to determine, according to law, the amount and validity, and provide for the payment of any claim filed by any bank or other financial institution doing business in the Philippines which reestablished sequestered accounts, deposits, or other credits of—

(A) any individual referred to in subparagraph (A) of paragraph (1) of this subsection; or

(B) any partnership, firm, corporation, or other legal entity, in which more than 50 per centum of the ownership was vested, directly or indirectly, both on December 7, 1941, and on the date of reestablishment of such sequestered credits, in individuals referred to in such subparagraph (A);

for reimbursement of the amounts of such sequestered credits paid by such bank or financial institution.

(b) Filing date for claims

Claims must be filed under this section within one year after the date of enactment of this section [Aug. 31, 1954].

(c) Death or legal disability as affecting payments

Where any individual entitled to payment under this section is under any legal disability, payment may be made in accordance with the provisions of subsection (e) of section 5 of this title [section 2004(e) of this Appendix]. In the case of the death of any individual entitled to payment of any claim under this section, payment of such claim shall be made to the individuals specified, and in the order provided, in subsection (d) of section 6 of this title [section 2005(d) of this Appendix]; except that no payment shall be made under this section to any individual who voluntarily, knowingly, and without duress, gave aid to or collaborated with or in any manner served any government hostile to the United States during World War II.

(d) Certification of claims for payment

Each claim allowed under this section shall be certified to the Secretary of the Treasury for payment out of the War Claims Fund established under section 13 of this title [section 2012 of this Appendix]. The Secretary of the Treasury shall pay such claims as follows:

(1) In the case of each claim allowed in an amount equal to or less than $500, such claim shall be paid in full; and

(2) In the case of each claim allowed in an amount greater than $500, such claim shall be paid in two installments. The first installment shall be paid in an amount equal to $500 plus 66⅔ per centum of the amount of such claim allowed in excess of $500. The last installment shall be computed as of September 1, 1956, under the next sentence of this paragraph, and, as so computed, shall be paid from the sums remaining in the War Claims Fund on that date. If the sums remaining in the War Claims Fund on September 1, 1956, are sufficient to satisfy all claims allowed under this section and not paid in full, the unpaid portion of each such claim shall be paid in full; if the sums remaining in the War Claims Fund on September 1, 1956, are not sufficient to satisfy all claims allowed under this section and not paid in full, the last installment payable on each such claim shall be reduced ratably, and, as so reduced, shall be paid from the War Claims Fund.

(July 3, 1948, ch. 826, title I, § 17, as added Aug. 31, 1954, ch. 1162, title I, § 103, 68 Stat. 1035; amended Pub. L. 87–846, title I, § 102, Oct. 22, 1962, 76 Stat. 1107.)

AMENDMENTS

1962—Pub. L. 87–846 substituted "title" for "Act".

TRANSFER OF FUNCTIONS

For provisions transferring Foreign Claims Settlement Commission of the United States to Department of Justice, as a separate agency, see section 1622a et seq. of Title 22, Foreign Relations and Intercourse.

TITLE II

TITLE II OF ACT

Section 103 of Pub. L. 87–846, Oct. 22, 1962, 76 Stat. 1107, added sections 201 to 217 of act July 3, 1948, as amended [sections 2017 to 2017p of this Appendix], as title II.

§ 2017. Definitions

As used in this title [sections 2017 to 2017p of this Appendix] the term or terms—

(a) ''Albania'', ''Austria'', ''Czechoslovakia'', ''the Free Territory of Danzig'', ''Estonia'', ''Germany'', ''Greece'', ''Latvia'', ''Lithuania'', ''Poland'', and ''Yugoslavia'', when used in their respective geographical senses, mean the territorial limits of each such country or free territory, as the case may be, in continental Europe as such limits existed on December 1, 1937.

(b) ''Commission'' means the Foreign Claims Settlement Commission of the United States established pursuant to Reorganization Plan Numbered 1 of 1954 (68 Stat. 1279).

(c) ''National of the United States'' means (1) a natural person who is a citizen of the United States, (2) a natural person who, though not a citizen of the United States, owes permanent allegiance to the United States, and (3) a corporation, partnership, unincorporated body, or other entity, organized under the laws of the United States, or of any State, the Commonwealth of Puerto Rico, the District of Columbia, or any possession of the United States and in which more than 50 per centum of the outstanding capital stock or other proprietary or similar interest is owned, directly or indirectly, by persons referred to in clauses (1) and (2) of this subsection. It does not include aliens.

(d) ''Property'' means real property and such items of tangible personalty as can be identified and evaluated.

(July 3, 1948, ch. 826, title II, § 201, as added Pub. L. 87–846, title I, § 103, Oct. 22, 1962, 76 Stat. 1107.)

REFERENCES IN TEXT

Reorganization Plan Numbered 1 of 1954 (68 Stat. 1279), referred to in subsec. (b), is set out in the Appendix to Title 5, Government Organization and Employees.

SEPARABILITY

Section 301 of Pub. L. 87–846 provided that: ''If any provision of this Act [enacting sections 41, 42, and 2017 to 2017p of this Appendix, amending sections 9, 32, 33, 39, 2001, 2003 to 2010, 2012, and 2013 to 2016 of this Appendix, and exacting provisions set out as notes under this section and section 2001 of this Appendix], or the application thereof to any person or circumstances, shall be held invalid, the remainder of this Act, or the application of such provisions to other persons or circumstances, shall not be affected.''

TRANSFER OF FUNCTIONS

For provisions transferring Foreign Claims Settlement Commission of the United States to Department of Justice, as a separate agency, see section 1622a et seq. of Title 22, Foreign Relations and Intercourse.

§ 2017a. Claims authorized

The Commission is directed to receive and to determine according to the provisions of this title [sections 2017 to 2017p of this Appendix] the validity and amount of claims of nationals of the United States for—

(a) loss or destruction of, or physical damage to, property located in Albania, Austria, Czechoslovakia, the Free Territory of Danzig, Estonia, Germany, Greece, Latvia, Lithuania, Poland, or Yugoslavia, or in territory which was part of Hungary or Rumania on December 1, 1937, but which was not included in such countries on September 15, 1947, which loss, destruction, or physical damage occurred during the period beginning September 1, 1939, and ending May 8, 1945, or which occurred in the period beginning July 1, 1937, and ending September 2, 1945, to property in territory occupied or attacked by the Imperial Japanese military forces (including territory to which Japan has renounced all right, title, and claim under article 2 of the Treaty of Peace Between the Allied Powers and Japan) except the island of Guam: *Provided*, That claims for loss, destruction, or damage occurring in the Commonwealth of the Philippines shall not be allowed except on behalf of nationals of the United States who have received no payment, and certify under oath or affirmation that they have received no payment, on account of the same loss, destruction, or damage under the Philippine Rehabilitation Act of 1946 [sections 1751 to 1806 of this Appendix], whether or not claim was filed thereunder: *Provided further*, That such loss, destruction, or damage must have occurred, as a direct consequence of (1) military operations of war or (2) special measures directed against property in such countries or territories during the respective periods specified, because of the enemy or alleged enemy character of the owner, which property was owned, directly or indirectly, by a national of the United States at the time of such loss, damage or destruction;

(b) damage to, or loss or destruction of, ships or ship cargoes directly or indirectly owned by a national of the United States at the time such damage, loss, or destruction occurred, which was a direct consequence of military action by Germany or Japan during the period beginning September 1, 1939, and ending September 2, 1945; no award shall be made under this subsection in favor of any insurer or reinsurer as assignee or otherwise as successor in interest to the right of the insured;

(c) net losses under war-risk insurance or reinsurance policies or contracts, incurred in the settlement of claims for insured losses of ships directly or indirectly owned by a national of the United States at the time of the loss, damage, or destruction of such ships and at the time of the settlement of such claims, which insured losses were a direct consequence of military action by Germany or Japan during the period beginning September 1, 1939, and ending September 2, 1945; such net losses shall be determined by deducting from the aggregate of all payments made in the settlement of such insured losses the aggregate of the net amounts received by any such insurance companies on all policies of contracts of war-risk insurance or reinsurance on ships under which the insured was a national of the United States, after deducting expenses; and

(d) loss or damage on account of—

(1) the death of any person who, being then a civilian national of the United States and a passenger on any vessel engaged in commerce on the high seas, died or was killed as a result of military action by Germany or Japan which occurred during the period beginning September 1, 1939, and ending De-

cember 11, 1941; awards under this paragraph shall be made only to or for the benefit of the following persons in the order of priority named:

(A) widow or husband if there is no child or children of the deceased;

(B) widow or husband and child or children of the deceased, one-half to the widow or husband and the other half to the child or children of the deceased in equal shares;

(C) child or children of the deceased (in equal shares) if there is no widow or husband; and

(D) parents of the deceased (in equal shares) if there is no widow, husband, or child;

(2) injury or permanent disability sustained by any person, who being then a civilian national of the United States and a passenger on any vessel engaged in commerce on the high seas, was injured or permanently disabled as a result of military action by Germany or Japan which occurred during the period beginning September 1, 1939, and ending December 11, 1941; awards under this paragraph shall be payable solely to the person so injured or disabled;

(3) the loss or destruction, as a result of such action, of property on such vessel, as determined by the Commission to be reasonable, useful, necessary, or proper under the circumstances, which property was owned by any civilian national of the United States who was then a passenger on such vessel; and in the case of the death of any person suffering such loss, awards under this paragraph shall be made only to or for the benefit of the persons designated in paragraph (1) of this subsection and in the order of priority named therein.

(July 3, 1948, ch. 826, title II, § 202, as added Pub. L. 87–846, title I, § 103, Oct. 22, 1962, 76 Stat. 1107.)

SECTION REFERRED TO IN OTHER SECTIONS

This section is referred to in sections 2017b, 2017c, 2017d, 2017h, 2017k, 2017*l* of this Appendix; title 22 section 1641c.

§ 2017b. Transfers and assignments

The transfer or assignment for value of any property forming the subject matter of a claim under subsection (a) or (b) of section 202 [section 2017a of this Appendix] subsequent to its damage, loss, or destruction shall not operate to extinguish any claim of the transferor otherwise compensable under either of such subsections. If a claim which could otherwise be allowed under subsection (a) or (b) of section 202 [section 2017a of this Appendix] has been assigned for value prior to the enactment of this title [Oct. 22, 1962], the assignee shall be the party entitled to claim thereunder.

(July 3, 1948, ch. 826, title II, § 203, as added Pub. L. 87–846, title I, § 103, Oct. 22, 1962, 76 Stat. 1109.)

§ 2017c. Nationality of claimants

No claim shall be allowed under subsection (a), (b), or (c) of section 202 of this title [section 2017a of this Appendix] unless the property upon which it is based was owned by a national or nationals of the United States on the date of loss, damage, or destruction and unless the claim was owned by a national or nationals of the United States continuously thereafter until the date of filing with the Commission pursuant to this title [sections 2017 to 2017p of this Appendix]. Where any person who lost United States citizenship solely by reason of marriage to a citizen or subject of a foreign country reacquired such citizenship before the date of enactment of this title [Oct. 22, 1962], then if such individual, but for such marriage would have been a national of the United States at all times on and after the date of such loss, damage, or destruction until the filing of the claim, such individual shall be treated for all purposes of this title [sections 2017 to 2017p of this Appendix] as having been a national of the United States at all such times.

(July 3, 1948, ch. 826, title II, § 204, as added Pub. L. 87–846, title I, § 103, Oct. 22, 1962, 76 Stat. 1109.)

§ 2017d. Claims of stockholders

(a) A claim under section 202 of this title [section 2017a of this Appendix] based upon an ownership interest in any corporation, association, or other entity which is a national of the United States shall be denied.

(b) A claim under section 202 of this title [section 2017a of this Appendix], based upon a direct ownership interest in a corporation, association, or other entity which suffered a loss within the meaning of said section, shall be allowed, subject to other provisions of this title [sections 2017 to 2017p of this Appendix], if such corporation, association, or other entity on the date of the loss was not a national of the United States, without regard to the per centum of ownership vested in the claimant in any such claim.

(c) A claim under section 202 of this title [section 2017a of this Appendix], based upon an indirect ownership interest in a corporation, association, or other entity which suffered a loss within the meaning of said section, shall be allowed, subject to other provisions of this title [sections 2017 to 2017p of this Appendix], only if at least 25 per centum of the entire ownership interest thereof at the time of such loss was vested in nationals of the United States.

(d) Any award on a claim under subsection (b) or (c) of this section shall be calculated on the basis of the total loss suffered by such corporation, association, or other entity, and shall bear the same proportion to such loss as the ownership interest of the claimant bears to the entire ownership interest thereof.

(July 3, 1948, ch. 826, title II, § 205, as added Pub. L. 87–846, title I, § 103, Oct. 22, 1962, 76 Stat. 1109.)

§ 2017e. Deductions in making awards

(a) In determining the amount of any award there shall be deducted all amounts the claimant has received on account of the same loss or losses with respect to which an award is made under this title [sections 2017 to 2017p of this Appendix].

(b) Each claim in excess of $10,000 filed under this title [sections 2017 to 2017p of this Appendix] by a corporation shall include a statement under oath disclosing the aggregate amount of Federal tax benefits derived by such corporation in any prior taxable year or years resulting from any deduction or deductions claimed for the loss or losses with respect to which such claim is filed. In determining the amount of any award where the allowable loss exceeds $10,000 there shall be deducted an amount equal to the aggregate amount of Federal tax benefits so derived by the claimant. For the purposes of this subsection, such Federal tax benefits shall be the aggregate of the amounts by which the claimant's taxes for such year or years under chapters 1, 2A, 2B, 2D, and 2E of the Internal Revenue Code of 1939, or subtitle A of the Internal Revenue Code of 1986 [26 U.S.C. 1 et seq.] were decreased with respect to such loss or losses. Any payments made on an award reduced by reason of this subsection shall be exempt from Federal income taxes.

(July 3, 1948, ch. 826, title II, §206, as added Pub. L. 87–846, title I, §103, Oct. 22, 1962, 76 Stat. 1110; amended Pub. L. 99–514, §2, Oct. 22, 1986, 100 Stat. 2095.)

REFERENCES IN TEXT

The Internal Revenue Code of 1939, referred to in text, was generally repealed by section 7851 of the Internal Revenue Code of 1986, Title 26. For table of comparisons of the 1939 Code to the 1986 Code, see Table I preceding section 1 of Title 26, Internal Revenue Code. See, also, section 7852(b) of Title 26 for provision that references in any other law to a provision of the 1939 Code, unless expressly incompatible with the intent thereof, shall be deemed a reference to the corresponding provision of the 1986 Code.

Chapter 1 of the Internal Revenue Code of 1939, referred to in subsec. (b), was comprised of sections 1 to 482 of former Title 26, Internal Revenue Code. Section 14 of former Title 26 was repealed by act Oct. 20, 1951, ch. 521, title I, pt. II, §121(g), 65 Stat. 469. Sections 34 and 185 of former Title 26 were repealed by act Feb. 25, 1944, ch. 63, title I, §§106(c)(2), 107(a), 58 Stat. 31. Sections 264 and 363 of former Title 26 were repealed by act Oct. 21, 1942, ch. 619, title I, §§159(e), 170(a), 56 Stat. 860, 878. Sections 430 to 474 of former Title 26 were omitted from the Code, and subsequently, along with the remaining sections of former Title 26 comprising chapter 1, except sections 143 and 144, were repealed by sections 7851(a)(1)(A) of Title 26, Internal Revenue Code. Sections 143 and 144 of former Title 26 were repealed by section 7851(a)(1)(B) of Title 26.

Chapter 2A of the Internal Revenue Code of 1939, referred to in subsec. (b), was comprised of sections 500 to 511 of former Title 26, Internal Revenue Code. Sections 500 to 511 were repealed by section 7851(a)(1)(A) of Title 26, Internal Revenue Code.

Chapter 2B of the Internal Revenue Code of 1939, referred to in subsec. (b), was comprised of sections 600 to 605 of former Title 26, Internal Revenue Code. Sections 600 to 605 were repealed by act Nov. 8, 1945, ch. 453, title II, §202, 59 Stat. 574, eff. with respect to taxable years ending June 30, 1946.

Chapter 2D of the Internal Revenue Code of 1939, referred to in subsec. (b), was comprised of sections 700 to 706 of former Title 26, Internal Revenue Code. Sections 700 to 716 were repealed by section 7851(a)(1)(A) of Title 26, Internal Revenue Code.

Chapter 2E of the Internal Revenue Code of 1939, referred to in subsec. (b), was comprised of sections 710 to 784 of former Title 26, Internal Revenue Code. Sections 710 to 736, 740, 742 to 744, 750, 751, 760, 761 and 780 to 784 were repealed by act Nov. 8, 1945, ch. 453, title I, §122(a), 59 Stat. 568. Section 741 was repealed by act Oct. 21, 1942, ch. 619, title II, §§224(b), 228(b), 56 Stat. 920, 925. Section 752 was repealed by act Oct. 21, 1942, ch. 619, title II, §229(a)(1), 56 Stat. 931, eff. as of Oct. 8, 1940.

Subtitle A of the Internal Revenue Code of 1986, referred to in subsec. (b), is subtitle A of act Aug. 16, 1954, ch. 736, 68A Stat. 4, as amended, which comprises subtitle A (§1 et seq.) of Title 26, Internal Revenue Code.

AMENDMENTS

1986—Subsec. (b). Pub. L. 99–514 substituted "Internal Revenue Code of 1986" for "Internal Revenue Code of 1954".

§2017f. Consolidated awards

With respect to any claim which, at the time of the award, is vested in persons other than the person by whom the loss was sustained, the Commission may issue a consolidated award in favor of all claimants then entitled thereto, which award shall indicate the respective interests of such claimant therein; and all such claimants shall participate, in proportion to their indicated interests, in the payments authorized by this title [sections 2017 to 2017p of this Appendix] in all respects as if the award had been in favor of a single person.

(July 3, 1948, ch. 826, title II, §207, as added Pub. L. 87–846, title I, §103, Oct. 22, 1962, 76 Stat. 1110.)

§2017g. Certain awards prohibited

No award shall be made under this title [sections 2017 to 2017p of this Appendix] to or for the benefit of (1) any person who has been convicted of a violation of any provision of chapter 115, title 18, United States Code, or of any other crime involving disloyalty to the United States, or (2) any claimant whose claim under this title [said sections] is within the scope of title III of the International Claims Settlement Act of 1949, as amended (69 Stat. 570) [22 U.S.C. 1641 et seq.], except any claimant whose award under section 303(1) of title III of the International Claims Settlement Act of 1949, as amended [22 U.S.C. 1641b(1)], is recertified pursuant to subsection (b) of section 209 of this title [section 2017h of this Appendix].

(July 3, 1948, ch. 826, title II, §208, as added Pub. L. 87–846, title I, §103, Oct. 22, 1962, 76 Stat. 1110.)

REFERENCES IN TEXT

The International Claims Settlement Act of 1949, as amended, referred to in text, is act Mar. 10, 1950, ch. 54, 64 Stat. 12, as amended. Title III of the International Claims Settlement Act of 1949, as amended (69 Stat. 570) is classified generally to subchapter III (§1641 et seq.) of chapter 21 of Title 22, Foreign Relations and Intercourse. For complete classification of this Act to the Code, see Short Title note set out under section 1621 of Title 22 and Tables.

§2017h. Certification of awards

(a) The Commission shall certify to the Secretary of the Treasury, in terms of United States currency, for payment out of the War Claims Fund each award made pursuant to section 202 [section 2017a of this Appendix].

(b) The Commission shall recertify to the Secretary of the Treasury, in terms of United States currency, for payment out of the War Claims Fund, awards heretofore made with respect to claims against the Government of Hungary under section 303(1) of title III of the International Claims Settlement Act of 1949, as amended [22 U.S.C. 1641b(1)]. Nothing contained in this subsection shall be construed as authorizing the filing of new claims against Hungary.

(July 3, 1948, ch. 826, title II, § 209, as added Pub. L. 87–846, title I, § 103, Oct. 22, 1962, 76 Stat. 1111.)

SECTION REFERRED TO IN OTHER SECTIONS

This section is referred to in sections 2017g, 2017*l* of this Appendix.

§ 2017i. Claim filing period

Within sixty days after the enactment of this title [Oct. 22, 1962] or of legislation making appropriations to the Commission for payment of administrative expenses incurred in carrying out its functions under this title [sections 2017 to 2017p of this Appendix], whichever date is later, the Commission shall give public notice by publication in the Federal Register of the time when, and the limit of time within which claims may be filed, which limit shall not be more than eighteen months after such publication.

(July 3, 1948, ch. 826, title II, § 210, as added Pub. L. 87–846, title I, § 103, Oct. 22, 1962, 76 Stat. 1111.)

PROTESTS RELATING TO AWARDS BY COMMISSION; NOTICE BY PUBLICATION IN FEDERAL REGISTER

Notwithstanding the provisions of this section and section 2017j of this Appendix, receipt and consideration of filed and published protests relating to awards made by the Foreign Claims Settlement Commission which result in modification of such awards shall be certified and paid by the Secretary of the Treasury out of the War Claims Fund in accordance with section 2017*l* of this Appendix. See section 615 of act Mar. 10, 1950, ch. 54, as added by Pub. L. 94–542, Oct. 18, 1976, 90 Stat. 2512, set out as a note under section 1623 of Title 22, Foreign Relations and Intercourse.

§ 2017j. Claims settlement period

The Commission shall complete its affairs in connection with the settlement of claims pursuant to this title [sections 2017 to 2017p of this Appendix] not later than four years following the enactment of legislation making appropriations to the Commission for payment of administrative expenses incurred in carrying out its functions under this title [said sections].

(July 3, 1948, ch. 826, title II, § 211, as added Pub. L. 87–846, title I, § 103, Oct. 22, 1962, 76 Stat. 1111.)

PROTESTS RELATING TO AWARDS BY COMMISSION; NOTICE BY PUBLICATION IN FEDERAL REGISTER

Notwithstanding the provisions of this section and section 2017i of this Appendix, receipt and consideration of filed and published protests relating to awards made by the Foreign Claims Settlement Commission which result in modification of such awards shall be certified and paid by the Secretary of the Treasury out of the War Claims Fund in accordance with section 2017*l* of this Appendix. See section 615 of act Mar. 10, 1950, ch. 54, as added by Pub. L. 94–542, Oct. 18, 1976; 90 Stat. 2512, set out as a note under section 1623 of Title 22, Foreign Relations and Intercourse.

§ 2017k. Notification to claimants

Each award or denial of a claim by the Commission whether rendered before or after a hearing, shall include a specific statement of the facts and of the reasoning of the Commission in support of its conclusion.

(July 3, 1948, ch. 826, title II, § 212, as added Pub. L. 87–846, title I, § 103, Oct. 22, 1962, 76 Stat. 1111.)

§ 2017*l*. Payment of awards; priorities; limitations

(a) The Secretary of the Treasury shall pay out of the War Claims Fund on account of award certified by the Commission pursuant to this title [sections 2017 to 2017p of this Appendix] as follows and in the following order of priority:

(1) Payment in full of awards made pursuant to section 202(d)(1) and (2) [section 2017a(d)(1) and (2) of this Appendix], and thereafter of any award made pursuant to section 202(a) [section 2017a(a) of this Appendix] to any claimant (A) certified to the Commission by the Small Business Administration as having been, on the date of loss, damage, or destruction, a small business concern within the meaning now set forth in the Small Business Act, as amended [15 U.S.C. 631 et seq.], or (B) determined by the Commission to have been, on the date of loss, damage, or destruction, a nonprofit organization operated exclusively for the promotion of social welfare, religious, charitable, or educational purposes.

(2) Thereafter, payments from time to time on account of the other awards made pursuant to section 202 [section 2017a of this Appendix] in an amount which shall be the same for each award or in the amount of the award, whichever is less. The total payment made pursuant to this paragraph on account of any award shall not exceed $10,000.

(3) Thereafter, payments from time to time on account of the other awards made to individuals and corporations pursuant to section 202 [section 2017a of this Appendix] and not compensated in full under paragraph (1) or (2) of this subsection in an amount which shall be the same for each award or in the amount of the award, whichever is less. The total payment pursuant to this paragraph on account of any award shall not exceed $35,000.

(4) Thereafter, payments from time to time on account of the unpaid balance of each remaining award made pursuant to section 202 [section 2017a of this Appendix] or recertified pursuant to subsection (b) of section 209 [section 2017h of this Appendix] which shall bear to such unpaid balance the same proportion as the total amount in the War Claims Fund and available for distribution at the time such payments are made bears to the aggregate unpaid balances of all such awards. No payment made pursuant to this paragraph on account of any award shall exceed the unpaid balance of such award. Payments heretofore made under section 310 of title III of the International Claims Settlement Act of 1949, as amended [22 U.S.C. 1641i], on awards made against the Government of Hungary under section 303(1) of title III of the International Claims Settlement Act of 1949, as amended [22 U.S.C. 1641b(1)], and recertified under subsection (b) of section 209 [section 2017h(b) of this Appendix], shall be considered as payments under this paragraph and no payment shall be made on any recertified award until the percentage of distribution on awards made under section 202 [section 2017a of this Appendix] exceeds the corresponding percentage of distribution on such recertified award: *Provided*, That no payment made on awards recertified under subsection (b) of section 209 [section 2017h(b) of this Appendix] shall exceed 40 per centum of the amount of the award recertified.

(b) Such payments, and applications for such payments, shall be made in accordance with such regulations as the Secretary of the Treasury shall prescribe.

(c) For the purpose of making any such payments, other than under section 213(a)(1) [subsec. (a)(1) of this section], an "award" shall be deemed to mean the aggregate of all awards certified for payment in favor of the same claimant.

(d) If any person to whom any payment is to be made pursuant to this title [sections 2017 to 2017p of this Appendix] is deceased or is under a legal disability, payment shall be made to his legal representative, except that if any payment to be made is not over $1,000 and there is no qualified executor or administrator, payment may be made to the person or persons found by the Secretary of the Treasury to be entitled thereto, without the necessity of compliance with the requirements of law with respect to the administration of estates.

(e) Payment on account of any award pursuant to this title [sections 2017 to 2017p of this Appendix] shall not, unless such payment is for the full amount of the award, extinguish any rights against any foreign government for the unpaid balance of the award.

(f) Payments made under this section on account of any award for loss, damage, or destruction occurring in the Commonwealth of the Philippines shall not exceed the amount paid on account of awards in the same amount under the Philippine Rehabilitation Act of 1946 [sections 1751 to 1806 of this Appendix].

(July 3, 1948, ch. 826, title II, § 213, as added Pub. L. 87–846, title I, § 103, Oct. 22, 1962, 76 Stat. 1111; amended Pub. L. 91–571, § 1(a), Dec. 24, 1970, 84 Stat. 1503; Pub. L. 104–316, title I, § 128(b), Oct. 19, 1996, 110 Stat. 3841.)

REFERENCES IN TEXT

The Small Business Act, as amended, referred to in subsec. (a)(1), is Pub. L. 85–536, July 18, 1958, 72 Stat. 384, as amended, which is classified generally to chapter 14A (§ 631 et seq.) of Title 15, Commerce and Trade. For complete classification of this Act to the Code, see Short Title note set out under section 631 of Title 15 and Tables.

AMENDMENTS

1996—Subsec. (d). Pub. L. 104–316 substituted "Secretary of the Treasury" for "Comptroller General".

1970—Subsec. (a)(1). Pub. L. 91–571, § 1(a)(1), included payment to any claimant determined by Commission to have been, on date of loss, damage, or destruction, a nonprofit organization operated exclusively for promotion of social welfare, religious, charitable, or educational purposes.

Subsec. (a)(3), (4). Pub. L. 91–571, § 1(a)(2), added par. (3) and redesignated former par. (3) as (4).

PROTEST RELATING TO AWARDS BY COMMISSION; NOTICE BY PUBLICATION IN FEDERAL REGISTER

Notwithstanding the provisions of sections 2017i and 2017j of this Appendix receipt and consideration of filed and published protests relating to awards made by the Foreign Claims Settlement Commission which result in modification of such awards shall be certified and paid by the Secretary of the Treasury out of the War Claims Fund in accordance with this section. See section 615 of Act Mar. 10, 1950, ch. 54, as added by Pub. L. 94–542, Oct. 18, 1976, 90 Stat. 2512, set out as a note under section 1623 of Title 22, Foreign Relations and Intercourse.

RECERTIFICATION OF CERTAIN AWARDS

Section 1(b) of Pub. L. 91–571 provided that: "The Foreign Claims Settlement Commission is authorized to recertify to the Secretary of the Treasury each award which has been certified before the date of enactment of this Act [Dec. 24, 1970] pursuant to title II of the War Claims Act of 1948, as added by the Act of October 22, 1962 (76 Stat. 1107) [sections 2017 to 2017p of this Appendix], but which as of the date of enactment of this Act has not been paid in full, in such manner as it may determine to be required to give effect to the amendments made by this Act [amending this section] to the same extent and with the same effect as if such amendments had taken effect on October 22, 1962."

§ 2017m. Fees of attorneys and agents

No remuneration on account of services rendered on behalf of any claimant in connection with any claim filed with the Commission under this title [sections 2017 to 2017p of this Appendix] shall exceed 10 per centum (or such lesser per centum as may be fixed by the Commission with respect to any class of claims) of the total amount paid pursuant to any award certified under the provisions of this title [said sections] on account of such claim. Any agreement to the contrary shall be unlawful and void. Whoever, in the United States or elsewhere, demands or receives, on account of services so rendered, any remuneration in excess of the maximum permitted by this section shall be guilty of a misdemeanor and, upon conviction thereof, shall be fined not more than $5,000 or imprisoned not more than twelve months, or both.

(July 3, 1948, ch. 826, title II, § 214, as added Pub. L. 87–846, title I, § 103, Oct. 22, 1962, 76 Stat. 1112.)

§ 2017n. Application of other laws

To the extent they are not inconsistent with the provisions of this title [sections 2017 to 2017p of this Appendix], the following provisions of title I of this Act [sections 2001 to 2016 of this Appendix] and title I of the International Claims Settlement Act of 1949, as amended [22 U.S.C. 1621 et seq.], shall apply to this title [sections 2017 to 2017p of this Appendix]: The first sentence of subsection (b) of section 2 [section 2001 of this Appendix], all of subsection (c) of section 2 [section 2001 of this Appendix] and section 11 [section 2010 of this Appendix] of title I of this Act, and subsections (c), (d), (e), and (f) of section 7 of the International Claims Settlement Act of 1949, as amended [22 U.S.C. 1626].

(July 3, 1948, ch. 826, title II, § 215, as added Pub. L. 87–846, title I, § 103, Oct. 22, 1962, 76 Stat. 1112.)

REFERENCES IN TEXT

The International Claims Settlement Act of 1949, as amended, referred to in text, is act Mar. 10, 1950, ch. 54, 64 Stat. 12, as amended. Title I of that Act is classified generally to subchapter I (§ 1621 et seq.) of chapter 21 of Title 22, Foreign Relations and Intercourse. For complete classification of this Act to the Code, see Short Title note set out under section 1621 of Title 22 and Tables.

§ 2017*o*. Transfer of records

The Secretary of State is authorized and directed to transfer or otherwise make available to the Commission such records and documents relating to claims authorized by this title [sections 2017 to 2017p of this Appendix] as may be required by the Commission in carrying out its functions under this title [said sections].

(July 3, 1948, ch. 826, title II, § 216, as added Pub. L. 87–846, title I, § 103, Oct. 22, 1962, 76 Stat. 1113.)

§ 2017p. Administrative expenses

There are authorized to be appropriated out of any moneys in the Treasury not otherwise appropriated such sums as may be necessary (but not to exceed the total covered into the Treasury to the credit of miscellaneous receipts under section 39 subsection (d)[1] of the Trading With the Enemy Act [section 39(d) of this Appendix]) to enable the Commission and the Treasury Department to pay their administrative expenses in carrying out their respective functions under this title [sections 2017 to 2017p of this Appendix].

(July 3, 1948, ch. 826, title II, § 217, as added Pub. L. 87–846, title I, § 103, Oct. 22, 1962, 76 Stat. 1113.)

References in Text

Section 39 subsection (d) of the Trading With the Enemy Act, referred to in text, was repealed by Pub. L. 100–418, title II, § 2501(a)(1), Aug. 23, 1988, 102 Stat. 1371.

MICRONESIAN WAR AND POSTWAR CLAIMS

PUB. L. 92–39, JULY 1, 1971, 85 STAT. 92

§§ 2018 to 2020b. Omitted

Codification

Sections 2018 to 2020b terminated Aug. 3, 1976, pursuant to section 2019b of this Appendix.

Section 2018, Pub. L. 92–39, § 1, July 1, 1971, 85 Stat. 92, provided that sections 2018 to 2020b of this Appendix were to be cited as the Micronesian Claims Act of 1971.

Section 2019, Pub. L. 92–39, title I, § 101, July 1, 1971, 85 Stat. 92; Pub. L. 93–131, § 1, Oct. 19, 1973, 87 Stat. 460, related to purpose of sections 2019 to 2019e of this Appendix to implement an ex gratia contribution by the United States to meritorious Micronesian war claimants inhabiting the Trust Territory of Pacific Islands.

Section 2019a, Pub. L. 92–39, title I, § 102, July 1, 1971, 85 Stat. 93, authorized appropriations for purposes of sections 2018 to 2020b of this Appendix and authorized the establishment and management of a Micronesian Claims Fund.

Section 2019b, Pub. L. 92–39, title I, § 103, July 1, 1971, 85 Stat. 93, established Micronesian Claims Commission, provided for compensation and allowances of its members, authorized prescription of rules and regulations by Commission, and provided that Commission was to wind up its affairs no later than three years after expiration of time for filing claims under sections 2018 to 2020b of this Appendix. The Commission terminated on Aug. 3, 1976.

Section 2019c, Pub. L. 92–39, title I, § 104, July 1, 1971, 85 Stat. 94; Pub. L. 93–131, § 2, Oct. 19, 1973, 87 Stat. 461, related to powers of Commission.

Section 2019d, Pub. L. 92–39, title I, § 105, July 1, 1971, 85 Stat. 95, authorized appropriations necessary for operational and administrative expenses of Foreign Claims Settlement Commission and Micronesian Claims Commission in carrying out the purposes of sections 2018 to 2020b of this Appendix.

Section 2019e, Pub. L. 92–39, title I, § 106, July 1, 1971, 85 Stat. 95, related to remuneration limitation for filing services and prescribed penalties for violations of sections 2018 to 2020b of this Appendix.

Section 2020, Pub. L. 92–39, title II, § 201, July 1, 1971, 85 Stat. 96, authorized Commission to determine personal or property loss claims against United States by Micronesian inhabitants and provided that administrative settlements by Commission were to be final and conclusive.

Section 2020a, Pub. L. 92–39, title II, § 202, July 1, 1971, 85 Stat. 96, authorized appropriations for making payments to extent authorized by sections 2020 to 2020b of this Appendix.

Section 2020b, Pub. L. 92–39, title II, § 203, July 1, 1971, 85 Stat. 96, authorized transfer of any funds remaining after settlement of claims under sections 2020 to 2020b of this Appendix to Treasury of United States.

EXPORT CONTROLS

ACT FEB. 26, 1949, CH. 11, 63 STAT. 7

§§ 2021 to 2032. Omitted

Codification

Sections 2021 to 2032 terminated pursuant to section 2032 of this Appendix. See section 2401 et seq. of this Appendix.

Section 1, in part, of act Feb. 26, 1949, ch. 11, 63 Stat. 7, as amended, provided that act Feb. 26, 1949, may be cited as the Export Control Act of 1949.

Section 2021, acts Feb. 26, 1949, ch. 11, § 1(a), (b), 63 Stat. 7; July 1, 1962, Pub. L. 87–515, § 2, 76 Stat. 127, set out Congressional findings.

Section 2022, acts Feb. 26, 1949, ch. 11, § 2, 63 Stat. 7; July 1, 1962, Pub. L. 87–515, § 3, 76 Stat. 127; June 30, 1965, Pub. L. 89–63, § 3(a), 79 Stat. 209, set out Congressional declaration of policy.

Section 2023, acts Feb. 26, 1949, ch. 11, § 3, 63 Stat. 7; July 1, 1962, Pub. L. 87–515, § 4, 76 Stat. 127; June 30, 1965, Pub. L. 89–63, §§ 3(b), 4(a), (d), 79 Stat. 210, set out authority to effectuate export control policy and delegated authority to prescribe rules and regulations.

Section 2024, acts Feb. 26, 1949, ch. 11, § 4, 63 Stat. 8; June 30, 1965, Pub. L. 89–63, § 4(b), 79 Stat. 210, laid down criteria for establishment of standards for carrying out policies and for consultation among departments and agencies.

Section 2025, acts Feb. 26, 1949, ch. 11, § 5, 63 Stat. 8; July 1, 1962, Pub. L. 87–515, § 5, 76 Stat. 128; June 30, 1965, Pub. L. 89–63, §§ 2, 4(c), 79 Stat. 209, 210, provided for penalties for violations of export control policy.

Section 2026, act Feb. 26, 1949, ch. 11, § 6, 63 Stat. 8, provided for enforcement and for keeping certain information confidential.

Subsec. (b) of section 2026, which provided that no person would be excused from complying with any requirements under this section because of his privilege against self-incrimination, but that immunity provisions of section 46 of Title 49, Transportation, would apply with respect to any individual specifically claiming such privilege, was repealed by Pub. L. 91–452, title II, § 250, Oct. 15, 1970, 84 Stat. 931. See section 6001 et seq. of Title 18, Crimes and Criminal Procedure.

Section 2027, act Feb. 26, 1949, ch. 11, § 7, 63 Stat. 9, exempted functions under Act from Administrative Procedure Act.

Section 2028, act Feb. 26, 1949, ch. 11, § 8, 63 Stat. 9, required quarterly reports to be submitted to President and Congress.

Section 2029, act Feb. 26, 1949, ch. 11, § 9, 63 Stat. 9, defined "person".

Section 2030, act Feb. 26, 1949, ch. 11, § 10, 63 Stat. 9, provided for effect of Act on other legislation.

Section 2031, act Feb. 26, 1949, ch. 11, § 11, 63 Stat. 9, set out effective date of sections 2021 to 2032 of this Appendix.

Section 2032, acts Feb. 26, 1949, ch. 11, § 12, 63 Stat. 9; May 16, 1951, ch. 83, 65 Stat. 43; June 16, 1953, ch. 116, 67 Stat. 62; June 29, 1956, ch. 473, § 1, 70 Stat. 407; June 25, 1958, Pub. L. 85–466, 72 Stat. 220; May 13, 1960, Pub. L. 86–464, 74 Stat. 130; July 1, 1962, Pub. L. 87–515, § 1, 76 Stat. 127; June 30, 1965, Pub. L. 89–63, § 1, 79 Stat. 209; June 30, 1969, Pub. L. 91–35, 83 Stat. 42; Aug. 18, 1969, Pub. L. 91–59, 83 Stat. 101; Oct. 31, 1969, Pub. L. 91–105,

[1] See References in Text note below.

§1, 83 Stat. 169, provided for termination date of sections 2021 to 2032 of this Appendix, on Dec. 31, 1969.

ALIEN PROPERTY DAMAGE CLAIMS

ACT MAR. 15, 1949, CH. 19, 63 STAT. 12

§§2041 to 2045. Omitted

CODIFICATION

Sections 2041 to 2045 were omitted pursuant to section 2042 of this Appendix.

Section 2041, act Mar. 15, 1949, ch. 19, §1, 63 Stat. 12, related to adjustment and settlement of claims.

Section 2042, act Mar. 15, 1949, ch. 19, §2, 63 Stat. 13, related to time limitation for presentment of claims under sections 2041 to 2045 of this Appendix and required presentment within one year of Mar. 15, 1949.

Section 2043, act Mar. 15, 1949, ch. 19, §3, 63 Stat. 13, related to finality and conclusiveness of Attorney General's decisions.

Section 2044, act Mar. 15, 1949, ch. 19, §4, 63 Stat. 13, related to claims in excess of one thousand dollars.

Section 2045, act Mar. 15, 1949, ch. 19, §5, 63 Stat. 13, related to authorization of appropriations for use under sections 2041 to 2045 of this Appendix.

DEFENSE PRODUCTION ACT OF 1950

ACT SEPT. 8, 1950, CH. 932, 64 STAT. 798

AMENDMENTS

1952—Act June 30, 1952, ch. 530, title I, §116(a), 66 Stat. 305, struck out "CONSUMER AND" in title VI heading.

1951—Act July 31, 1951, ch. 275, title I, §107, 65 Stat. 138, amended heading of title II by inserting "AND CONDEMN".

TERMINATION DATE

For termination of certain provisions of act Sept. 8, 1950, see section 2166 of this Appendix.

ACT REFERRED TO IN OTHER SECTIONS

This Act is referred to in sections 2182, 2183 of this Appendix; title 30 section 1604; title 42 sections 1591a, 1593o, 5105a.

§2061. Short title

This Act [sections 2061 to 2171 of this Appendix], divided into titles, may be cited as "the Defense Production Act of 1950".

(Sept. 8, 1950, ch. 932, §1, 64 Stat. 798.)

SHORT TITLE OF 1995 AMENDMENT

Pub. L. 104–64, §1, Dec. 18, 1995, 109 Stat. 689, provided that: "This Act [amending sections 2161 and 2166 of this Appendix and enacting provisions set out as a note under section 2062 of this Appendix] may be cited as the 'Defense Production Act Amendments of 1995'."

SHORT TITLE OF 1992 AMENDMENT

Pub. L. 102–558, §1(a), Oct. 28, 1992, 106 Stat. 4198, provided that: "This Act [enacting sections 2074, 2077, 2078, 2099a, and 2171 of this Appendix, amending sections 2062, 2091 to 2094, 2097, 2099, 2151 to 2155, 2159 to 2161, 2166, and 2170 of this Appendix, sections 1815, 1817, 1818, 1820, 1834, 1834a, and 3104 of Title 12, Banks and Banking, and section 1143 of Title 30, Mineral Lands and Mining, repealing sections 2162, 2165, 2167, and 2169 of this Appendix, enacting provisions set out as notes under sections 2062, 2099, and 2159 of this Appendix and sections 1815, 1817, 1834, 1834a, and 3104 of Title 12, and repealing provisions set out as notes under sections 1817, 1834, and 1834a of Title 12] may be cited as the 'Defense Production Act Amendments of 1992'."

SHORT TITLE OF 1991 AMENDMENT

Pub. L. 102–99, §1, Aug. 17, 1991, 105 Stat. 487, provided that: "This Act [amending sections 2071, 2158, 2161, and 2166 of this Appendix, repealing section 2158a of this Appendix, and enacting provisions set out as a note under section 2071 of this Appendix] may be cited as the 'Defense Production Act Extension and Amendments of 1991'."

SHORT TITLE OF 1986 AMENDMENT

Pub. L. 99–441, §1, Oct. 3, 1986, 100 Stat. 1117, provided that: "This Act [amending sections 2099, 2161, and 2166 of this Appendix and provisions set out as a note under section 5314 of Title 5, Government Organization and Employees] may be cited as the 'Defense Production Act Amendments of 1986'."

SHORT TITLE OF 1984 AMENDMENT

Pub. L. 98–265, §1, Apr. 17, 1984, 98 Stat. 149, provided that: "This Act [enacting section 2099 of this Appendix and amending sections 2091, 2092, 2093, 2161, and 2166 of this Appendix] may be cited as the 'Defense Production Act Amendments of 1984'."

SHORT TITLE OF 1980 AMENDMENT

Pub. L. 96–294, title I, part A (§§101–107), §101, June 30, 1980, 94 Stat. 617, provided that: "This part [enacting sections 2075, 2076, and 2095 to 2098 of this Appendix, amending sections 2062, 2091 to 2093, 2151, 2161, and 2166 of this Appendix, and enacting a provision set out as a note under section 2062 of this Appendix] may be cited as the 'Defense Production Act Amendments of 1980'."

SHORT TITLE OF 1977 AMENDMENT

Pub. L. 95–37, §1, June 1, 1977, 91 Stat. 178, provided: "That this Act [amending section 2166 of this Appendix] may be cited as the 'Defense Production Act Extension Amendments of 1977'."

SHORT TITLE OF 1975 AMENDMENT

Pub. L. 94–152, §1, Dec. 16, 1975, 89 Stat. 810, provided: "That this Act [enacting section 2158a of this Appendix, amending sections 2158, 2160, 2162, 2166, 2168, and 2169 of this Appendix, and enacting provisions set out as notes under section 2158 of this Appendix] may be cited as the 'Defense Production Act Amendments of 1975'."

SHORT TITLE OF 1974 AMENDMENT

Pub. L. 93–426, §1, Sept. 30, 1974, 88 Stat. 1166, provided: "That this Act [enacting section 2169 of this Appendix and amending sections 2094, 2161, and 2166 of this Appendix] may be cited as the 'Defense Production Act Amendments of 1974'."

SHORT TITLE OF 1955 AMENDMENT

Act Aug. 9, 1955, ch. 655, §1, 69 Stat. 580, provided: "That this Act [amending sections 2062, 2093, 2151, 2158, 2160, 2162, and 2166 of this Appendix and enacting provisions set out as notes under section 2062 of this Appendix] may be cited as the 'Defense Production Act Amendments of 1955'."

SHORT TITLE OF 1953 AMENDMENT

Act June 30, 1953, ch. 171, §1, 67 Stat. 129, provided: "That this Act [amending sections 2062, 2071, 2091, 2093, 2151, 2152, 2155, 2163a, and 2166 of this Appendix] may be cited as the 'Defense Production Act Amendments of 1953'."

SHORT TITLE OF 1952 AMENDMENT

Act June 30, 1952, ch. 530, §1, 66 Stat. 296, provided: "That this Act [enacting sections 1894a, 2111, 2112, and 2137 of this Appendix and section 43a of Title 41, Public Contracts, and amending sections 1884, 1894, 1894a, 2071, 2074, 2092, 2102, 2103, 2107, 2108, 2123, 2155, 2157, 2158, 2162, 2163a, and 2166 of this Appendix and sections 44 and 45 of Title 41] may be cited as the 'Defense Production Act Amendments of 1952'."

SHORT TITLE OF 1951 AMENDMENT

Act July 31, 1951, ch. 275, §1, 65 Stat. 131, provided: "That this Act [amending sections 1884, 1892 to 1896, 1898, 1899, 2071, 2072, 2074, 2081, 2093, 2094, 2102, 2103, 2105, 2109, 2122, 2123, 2131, 2133, 2135, 2151, 2153 to 2156, 2160, and 2163a to 2166 of this Appendix, repealing section 694f of former Title 38, Pensions, Bonuses, and Veterans' Relief, and enacting provisions set out as a note under section 1907 of this Appendix] may be cited as the 'Defense Production Act Amendments of 1951'."

DELEGATION OF FUNCTIONS

Functions of President under act Sept. 8, 1950 [section 2061 et seq. of this Appendix], relating to production, conservation, use, control, distribution, and allocation of energy, delegated to Secretary of Energy, see section 4 of Ex. Ord. No. 11790, eff. June 25, 1974, 39 F.R. 23185, set out as a note under section 761 of Title 15, Commerce and Trade.

For delegation of certain authority of President under act Sept. 8, 1950 [section 2061 et seq. of this Appendix] relating to national defense industrial resource preparedness and statement of related policy, see Ex. Ord. No. 12919, June 3, 1994, 59 F.R. 29525, set out as a note under section 2153 of this Appendix.

§ 2062. Declaration of policy

(a) Findings

The Congress finds that—

(1) the vitality of the industrial and technology base of the United States is a foundation of national security that provides the industrial and technological capabilities employed to meet national defense requirements, in peacetime and in time of national emergency;

(2) in peacetime, the health of the industrial and technological base contributes to the technological superiority of United States defense equipment, which is a cornerstone of the national security strategy, and the efficiency with which defense equipment is developed and produced;

(3) in times of crisis, a healthy industrial base will be able to effectively provide the graduated response needed to effectively meet the demands of the emergency;

(4) in view of continuing international problems, the Nation's demonstrated reliance on imports of materials and components, and the need for measures to reduce defense production lead times and bottlenecks, and in order to provide for the national defense and national security, the United States defense mobilization preparedness effort continues to require the development of—

(A) preparedness programs;

(B) domestic defense industrial base improvement measures;

(C) provisions for a graduated response to any threatening international or military situation;

(D) the expansion of domestic productive capacity beyond the levels needed to meet the civilian demand; and

(E) some diversion of certain materials and facilities from civilian use to military and related purposes.[1]

(5) to meet the requirements referred to in this subsection, this Act [sections 2061 to 2171 of this Appendix] affords to the President an array of authorities to shape defense preparedness programs and to take appropriate steps to maintain and enhance the defense industrial and technological base;

(6) the activities referred to in this subsection are needed in order to—

(A) improve domestic defense industrial base efficiency and responsiveness;

(B) reduce the time required for industrial mobilization in the event of an attack on the United States; or

(C) to respond to actions occurring outside of the United States which could result in the termination or reduction of the availability of strategic and critical materials, including energy, and which could adversely affect the national defense preparedness of the United States;

(7) in order to ensure national defense preparedness, which is essential to national security, it is necessary and appropriate to assure the availability of domestic energy supplies for national defense needs;

(8) to further assure the adequate maintenance of the defense industrial base, to the maximum extent possible, such supplies should be augmented through reliance on renewable fuels, including solar, geothermal, and wind energy and ethanol and its derivatives, and on energy conservation measures;

(9) the domestic defense industrial base is a component part of the core industrial capacity of the Nation;

(10) much of the industrial capacity which is relied upon by the Federal Government for military production and other defense-related purposes is deeply and directly influenced by—

(A) the overall competitiveness of the United States industrial economy; and

(B) the ability of United States industry, in general, to produce internationally competitive products and operate profitably while maintaining adequate research and development to preserve that competitive edge in the future, with respect to military and civilian production;

(11) the domestic defense industrial base is developing a growing dependency on foreign sources for critical components and materials used in manufacturing and assembling major weapons systems for the national defense;

(12) such dependence is threatening the capability of many critical industries to respond rapidly to defense production needs in the event of war or other hostilities or diplomatic confrontation; and

(13) the inability of United States industry, especially smaller subcontractors and suppliers, to provide vital parts and components and other materials would impair our ability to sustain United States Armed Forces in combat for longer than a short period.

(b) Statement of policy

It is the policy of the United States that—

(1) in order to ensure productive capacity in the event of an attack on the United States, the United States should encourage the geographic dispersal of industrial facilities in the United States to discourage the concentration of such productive facilities within limited geographic areas which are vulnerable to attack by an enemy of the United States;

(2) to ensure that essential mobilization requirements are met, consideration should also be given to stockpiling strategic materials to the extent that such stockpiling is economical and feasible;

(3) in the construction of any Government-owned industrial facility, in the rendition of any Government financial assistance for the construction, expansion, or improvement of any industrial facility, and in the production

[1] So in original. The period probably should be a semicolon.

of goods and services, under this or any other Act, each department and agency of the executive branch should apply, under the coordination of the Federal Emergency Management Agency, when practicable and consistent with existing law and the desirability for maintaining a sound economy, the principle of the geographic dispersal of such facilities in the interest of national defense, except that nothing in this paragraph shall preclude the use of existing industrial facilities;

(4) to ensure the adequacy of productive capacity and supply, executive agencies and departments responsible for defense acquisition should continuously assess the capability of the domestic defense industrial base to satisfy peacetime requirements as well as increased mobilization production requirements, specifically evaluating the availability of adequate production sources, including subcontractors and suppliers, materials, skilled labor, and professional and technical personnel;

(5) every effort should be made to foster cooperation between the defense and commercial sectors for research and development and for acquisition of materials, components, and equipment; and

(6) plans and programs to carry out this section shall be undertaken with due consideration for promoting efficiency and competition.

(Sept. 8, 1950, ch. 932, § 2, 64 Stat. 798; June 30, 1953, ch. 171, § 2, 67 Stat. 129; Aug. 9, 1955, ch. 655, § 2, 69 Stat. 580; June 29, 1956, ch. 474, § 4, 70 Stat. 408; Pub. L. 96–294, title I, § 102, June 30, 1980, 94 Stat. 617; Pub. L. 102–558, title I, § 101, Oct. 28, 1992, 106 Stat. 4199.)

REFERENCES IN TEXT

This Act, referred to in subsecs. (a)(5) and (b)(3), means act Sept. 8, 1950, ch. 932, 64 Stat. 798, as amended, known as the Defense Production Act of 1950, which is classified to sections 2061 to 2171 of this Appendix. For complete classification of this Act to the Code, see section 2061 of this Appendix and Tables.

AMENDMENTS

1992—Pub. L. 102–558 amended section generally, substituting provisions relating to findings and statement of policy, for provisions stating that mobilization effort continued to require diversion of materials and facilities from civilian to military use, and to require development of preparedness programs and expansion of productive capacity and supply, in order to reduce time required for full mobilization in case of attack on the United States or to respond to actions occurring outside the United States resulting in termination or reduction of availability of strategic materials, including energy, and provisions stating policy of Congress was to encourage geographical dispersal of industrial facilities, and requiring executive branch departments and agencies to apply principle of geographical dispersal in construction of such facilities.

1980—Pub. L. 96–294 inserted provisions relating to preparedness respecting termination or reduction in availability of strategic and critical materials, including energy, and domestic energy supplies for national defense needs.

1956—Act June 29, 1956, inserted paragraph relating to encouragement of the geographical dispersal of the industrial facilities of the United States.

1955—Act Aug. 9, 1955, provided that mobilization effort requires development of preparedness programs and expansion of productive capacity and supply in order to reduce time required for full mobilization.

1953—Act June 30, 1953, amended section generally to make it conform to the more limited scope of sections 2061 et seq. of this Appendix.

EFFECTIVE DATE OF 1992 AMENDMENT

Section 304 of Pub. L. 102–558 provided that: "This Act [enacting sections 2074, 2077, 2078, 2099a, and 2171 of this Appendix, amending sections 2062, 2091 to 2094, 2097, 2099, 2151 to 2155, 2159 to 2161, 2166, and 2170 of this Appendix, sections 1815, 1817, 1818, 1820, 1834, 1834a, and 3104 of Title 12, Banks and Banking, and section 1143 of Title 30, Mineral Lands and Mining, repealing sections 2162, 2165, 2167, and 2169 of this Appendix, enacting provisions set out as notes under sections 2062, 2099, and 2159 of this Appendix and sections 1815, 1817, 1834, 1834a, and 3104 of Title 12, and repealing provisions set out as notes under sections 1817, 1834, and 1834a of Title 12] and the amendments made by this Act shall be deemed to have become effective on March 1, 1992, except as otherwise specifically provided in this Act."

EFFECTIVE DATE OF 1980 AMENDMENT

Section 107 of Pub. L. 96–294 provided that: "The amendments made by this part [enacting sections 2075, 2076, and 2095 to 2098 of this Appendix, amending sections 2062, 2091 to 2093, 2151, 2161, and 2166 of this Appendix, and enacting a provision set out as a note under section 2061 of this Appendix] shall take effect on the date of the enactment of this part [June 30, 1980]."

EFFECTIVE DATE OF 1955 AMENDMENT

Section 11 of act Aug. 9, 1955, provided that: "The provisions of this Act [amending sections 2062, 2093, 2151, 2158, 2160, 2162, and 2166 of this Appendix and enacting provisions set out as a note under this section] shall take effect as of the close of July 31, 1955."

TERMINATION DATE

For termination of certain provisions of act Sept. 8, 1950, see section 2166 of this Appendix.

REPORTS TO CONGRESS

Pub. L. 104–64, § 4, Dec. 18, 1995, 109 Stat. 689, directed the President to prepare and transmit to Congress an interim report, not later than Jan. 31, 1997, and a final report, not later than Sept. 30, 1997, on proposed legislative modernization of the authorities contained in the Defense Production Act of 1950, section 2061 et seq. of this Appendix.

EVALUATION OF DOMESTIC DEFENSE INDUSTRIAL BASE POLICY

Section 203 of Pub. L. 102–558, established Congressional Commission on the Evaluation of the Defense Industrial Base Policy which was to submit, not later than Mar. 1, 1995, a final report to Congress outlining criteria for maintaining strength of domestic industrial base for purposes of supporting national security strategy of United States, taking into consideration, with respect to each Federal agency and department with any responsibility for maintaining strength of domestic defense industrial base, adequacy of statutory framework, budgets, policies, and programs of such agency or department in maintaining domestic defense industrial base, and whether such elements were being effectively implemented and coordinated within such agency or department, as well as degree to which similar activities in commercial sector were being integrated and implemented by such agency or department, and further provided for membership of Commission, as well as staff, powers, interim reports, appropriations, and termination of Commission 60 days after submission of final report.

TITLE I—PRIORITIES AND ALLOCATIONS

TITLE REFERRED TO IN OTHER SECTIONS

This title is referred to in sections 2157, 2166 of this Appendix.

§ 2071. Priority in contracts and orders

(a) Allocation of materials, services, and facilities

The President is hereby authorized (1) to require that performance under contracts or orders (other than contracts of employment) which he deems necessary or appropriate to promote the national defense shall take priority over performance under any other contract or order, and, for the purpose of assuring such priority, to require acceptance and performance of such contracts or orders in preference to other contracts or orders by any person he finds to be capable of their performance, and (2) to allocate materials, services, and facilities in such manner, upon such conditions, and to such extent as he shall deem necessary or appropriate to promote the national defense.

(b) Critical and strategic materials

The powers granted in this section shall not be used to control the general distribution of any material in the civilian market unless the President finds (1) that such material is a scarce and critical material essential to the national defense, and (2) that the requirements of the national defense for such material cannot otherwise be met without creating a significant dislocation of the normal distribution of such material in the civilian market to such a degree as to create appreciable hardship.

(c) Domestic energy; materials, equipment, and services

(1) Notwithstanding any other provision of this Act [sections 2061 to 2171 of this Appendix], the President may, by rule or order, require the allocation of, or the priority performance under contracts or orders (other than contracts of employment) relating to, materials, equipment, and services in order to maximize domestic energy supplies if he makes the findings required by paragraph (3) of this subsection.

(2) The authority granted by this subsection may not be used to require priority performance of contracts or orders, or to control the distribution of any supplies of materials, services, and facilities in the marketplace, unless the President finds that—

(A) such materials, services, and facilities are scarce, critical, and essential—

(i) to maintain or expand exploration, production, refining, transportation;

(ii) to conserve energy supplies; or

(iii) to construct or maintain energy facilities; and

(B) maintenance or expansion of exploration, production, refining, transportation, or conservation of energy supplies or the construction and maintenance of energy facilities cannot reasonably be accomplished without exercising the authority specified in paragraph (1) of this subsection.

(3) During any period when the authority conferred by this subsection is being exercised, the President shall take such action as may be appropriate to assure that such authority is being exercised in a manner which assures the coordinated administration of such authority with any priorities or allocations established under subsection (a) of this section and in effect during the same period.

(Sept. 8, 1950, ch. 932, title I, § 101, 64 Stat. 799; July 31, 1951, ch. 275, title I, § 101(a), 65 Stat. 132; June 30, 1952, ch. 530, title I, §§ 101, 102, 66 Stat. 296; June 30, 1953, ch. 171, § 3, 67 Stat. 129; Pub. L. 94–163, title I, § 104(a), Dec. 22, 1975, 89 Stat. 878; Pub. L. 102–99, § 6, Aug. 17, 1991, 105 Stat. 490.)

AMENDMENTS

1991—Subsec. (a)(2). Pub. L. 102–99, § 6(1), substituted "materials, services, and facilities" for "materials and facilities".

Subsec. (c)(1). Pub. L. 102–99, § 6(2), substituted "materials, equipment, and services" for "supplies of materials and equipment".

Subsec. (c)(2) to (4). Pub. L. 102–99, § 6(3), (4), added par. (2), redesignated par. (4) as (3), and struck out former pars. (2) and (3) which read as follows:

"(2) The President shall report to the Congress within sixty days after the date of enactment of this subsection on the manner in which the authority contained in paragraph (1) will be administered. This report shall include the manner in which allocations will be made, the procedure for requests and appeals, the criteria for determining priorities as between competing requests, and the office or agency which will administer such authorities.

"(3) The authority granted in this subsection may not be used to require priority performance of contracts or orders, or to control the distribution of any supplies of materials and equipment in the marketplace, unless the President finds that—

"(A) such supplies are scarce, critical, and essential to maintain or further (i) exploration, production, refining, transportation, or (ii) the conservation of energy supplies, or (iii) for the construction and maintenance of energy facilities; and

"(B) maintenance or furtherance of exploration, production, refining, transportation, or conservation of energy supplies or the construction and maintenance of energy facilities cannot reasonably be accomplished without exercising the authority specified in paragraph (1) of this subsection."

1975—Subsec. (c). Pub. L. 94–163 added subsec. (c).

1953—Subsec. (a). Act June 30, 1953, struck out provisions which related to slaughtering of livestock and allocation of meat and meat products.

Subsec. (b). Act June 30, 1953, retained priorities and allocation authority for defense production but generally to discontinue such authority with respect to the civilian market except in the special cases where, because of shortages and demands of the defense effort, there otherwise would be a significant dislocation in the civilian market resulting in appreciable hardship.

1952—Act June 30, 1952, redesignated existing provisions as subsec. (a), inserted provisions relating to meat and meat products, and added subsec. (b).

1951—Act July 31, 1951, inserted provision relating to slaughtering of livestock.

EFFECTIVE DATE OF 1991 AMENDMENT

Section 7 of Pub. L. 102–99 provided that: "This Act [amending this section and sections 2158, 2161, and 2166 of this Appendix, repealing section 2158a of this Appendix, and enacting provisions set out as a note under section 2061 of this Appendix] shall take effect on October 20, 1990."

TERMINATION DATE

Termination of section, see section 2166(a) of this Appendix.

DELEGATION OF FUNCTIONS

Functions of President under act Sept. 8, 1950 [section 2061 et seq. this Appendix], relating to production, conservation, use, control, distribution, and allocation of energy, delegated to Secretary of Energy, see section 4 of Ex. Ord. No. 11790, June 25, 1974, 39 F.R. 23185, set out as a note under section 761 of Title 15, Commerce and Trade.

For delegation of certain authority of President under this section, see sections 201 to 203 of Ex. Ord. No. 12919, June 3, 1994, 59 F.R. 29526, 29527, set out as a note under section 2153 of this Appendix.

PRESIDENTIAL AUTHORITY TO ISSUE ORDERS RELATING TO DOMESTIC ENERGY SUPPLIES

Pub. L. 94–163, title I, §104(b), Dec. 22, 1975, 89 Stat. 879, as amended by Pub. L. 99–58, title I, §101(b), July 2, 1985, 99 Stat. 102; Pub. L. 101–46, §1(2), June 30, 1989, 103 Stat. 132; Pub. L. 101–262, §2(a), Mar. 31, 1990, 104 Stat. 124; Pub. L. 101–360, §2(a), Aug. 10, 1990, 104 Stat. 421; Pub. L. 101–383, §2(1), Sept. 15, 1990, 104 Stat. 727; Pub. L. 105–388, §6, Nov. 13, 1998, 112 Stat. 3479; Pub. L. 106–469, title I, §103(2), Nov. 9, 2000, 114 Stat. 2029, provided that: "The expiration of the Defense Production Act of 1950 [section 2061 et seq. of this Appendix] or any amendment of such Act after the date of enactment of this Act [Dec. 22, 1975] shall not affect the authority of the President under section 101(c) of such Act [subsec. (c) of this section], as amended by subsection (a) of this section and in effect on the date of enactment of this Act, unless Congress by law expressly provides to the contrary."

EXECUTIVE ORDER NO. 10161

Ex. Ord. No. 10161, Sept. 9, 1950, 15 F.R. 6105, as amended by Ex. Ord. No. 10200, Jan. 3, 1951, 16 F.R. 61; Ex. Ord. No. 10233, Apr. 23, 1951, 16 F.R. 3503; Ex. Ord. No. 10281, Aug. 28, 1951, 16 F.R. 8789; Ex. Ord. No. 10301, Nov. 5, 1951, 16 F.R. 11257; Ex. Ord. No. 10324, Feb. 6, 1952, 17 F.R. 1171; Ex. Ord. No. 10359, June 9, 1952, 17 F.R. 5269; Ex. Ord. No. 10373, July 15, 1952, 17 F.R. 6425; Ex. Ord. No. 10377, July 28, 1952, 17 F.R. 6891; Ex. Ord. No. 10390, Sept. 2, 1952, 17 F.R. 7995; and Ex. Ord. No. 10433, Feb. 4, 1953, 18 F.R. 761, which related to delegation of President's functions, was revoked by Ex. Ord. No. 10480, Aug. 18, 1953, 18 F.R. 4939, formerly set out under section 2153 of this Appendix.

ABOLITION OF WAGE STABILIZATION BOARD AND CREATION OF NEW BOARD

Wage Stabilization Board created by Ex. Ord. No. 10161, eff. Sept. 9, 1950, 15 F.R. 6105, as amended, abolished by section 2103(b)(6) of this Appendix. A new Wage Stabilization Board was created by section 2103(b)(1), which terminated according to section 2166 of this Appendix Apr. 30, 1953.

POWERS OF SECRETARY OF COMMERCE UNDER EX. ORD. NO. 10161

The Secretary of Commerce by F.R. Doc. 50–8068, filed Sept. 13, 1950, 15 F.R. 6182, established the National Production Authority in the Department of Commerce to perform the functions and exercise the powers vested in the Secretary of Commerce by Ex. Ord. No. 10161, and established the Advisory Committee on Priorities Administration which was to serve in an advisory capacity with respect to policy matters. The National Production Authority was abolished and its functions merged into the Business and Defense Services Administration by Secretary of Commerce order, dated Oct. 1, 1953, which in turn was abolished by Department Organization Order 40–1A of Sept. 15, 1970 and its functions transferred to the Bureau of Domestic Commerce. All functions of the Bureau of Domestic Commerce were transferred by the Secretary of Commerce to the Domestic and International Business Administration, within the Department of Commerce, eff. Nov. 17, 1972.

SECTION REFERRED TO IN OTHER SECTIONS

This section is referred to in sections 2072, 2095, 2096, 2151, 2157 of this Appendix; title 10 sections 9511, 9512.

§2072. Hoarding of designated scarce materials

In order to prevent hoarding, no person shall accumulate (1) in excess of the reasonable demands of business, personal, or home consumption, or (2) for the purpose of resale at prices in excess of prevailing market prices, materials which have been designated by the President as scarce materials or materials the supply of which would be threatened by such accumulation. The President shall order published in the Federal Register, and in such other manner as he may deem appropriate, every designation of materials the accumulation of which is unlawful and any withdrawal of such designation.

In making such designations the President may prescribe such conditions with respect to the accumulation of materials in excess of the reasonable demands of business, personal, or home consumption as he deems necessary to carry out the objectives of this Act [sections 2061 to 2171 of this Appendix]. This section shall not be construed to limit the authority contained in sections 101 and 704 of this Act [sections 2071 and 2154 of this Appendix].

(Sept. 8, 1950, ch. 932, title I, §102, 64 Stat. 799; July 31, 1951, ch. 275, title I, §101(b), 65 Stat. 132.)

AMENDMENTS

1951—Act July 31, 1951, authorized President to prescribe conditions and exceptions allowing maintenance of substantial inventories of critical materials in certain cases.

TERMINATION DATE

Termination of section, see section 2166(a) of this Appendix.

DELEGATION OF FUNCTIONS

Functions of President under act Sept. 8, 1950 [section 2061 et seq. of this Appendix], relating to production, conservation, use, control, distribution, and allocation of energy, delegated to Secretary of Energy, see section 4 of Ex. Ord. No. 11790, June 25, 1974, 39 F.R. 23185, set out as a note under section 761 of Title 15, Commerce and Trade.

SECTION REFERRED TO IN OTHER SECTIONS

This section is referred to in sections 2157, 2166 of this Appendix.

§2073. Penalties

Any person who willfully performs any act prohibited, or willfully fails to perform any act required, by the provisions of this title [sections 2071 to 2078 of this Appendix] or any rule, regulation, or order thereunder, shall, upon conviction, be fined not more than $10,000 or imprisoned for not more than one year, or both.

(Sept. 8, 1950, ch. 932, title I, §103, 64 Stat. 799.)

TERMINATION DATE

Termination of section, see section 2166(a) of this Appendix.

SECTION REFERRED TO IN OTHER SECTIONS

This section is referred to in section 2157 of this Appendix.

§2074. Limitation on actions without Congressional authorization

(a) Wage or price controls

No provision of this Act [sections 2061 to 2171 of this Appendix] shall be interpreted as providing for the imposition of wage or price controls without the prior authorization of such action by a joint resolution of Congress.

(b) Chemical or biological weapons

No provision of title I of this Act [sections 2071 to 2078 of this Appendix] shall be exercised or interpreted to require action or compliance by any private person to assist in any way in the production of or other involvement in chemical or biological warfare capabilities, unless authorized by the President (or the President's designee who is serving in a position at level I of the Executive Schedule in accordance with section 5312 of title 5, United States Code) without further redelegation.

(Sept. 8, 1950, ch. 932, title I, § 104, as added Pub. L. 102–558, title I, § 112, Oct. 28, 1992, 106 Stat. 4202.)

PRIOR PROVISIONS

A prior section 2074, act Sept. 8, 1950, ch. 932, title I, § 104, as added July 31, 1951, ch. 275, title I, § 101(c), 65 Stat. 132; amended June 30, 1952, ch. 530, § 103, 66 Stat. 297, which related to limitations on imports of fats and oils, terminated at close of June 30, 1953, by terms of section 2166(a) of this Appendix.

EFFECTIVE DATE

Section deemed to have become effective Mar. 1, 1992, see section 304 of Pub. L. 102–558, set out as an Effective Date of 1992 Amendment note under section 2062 of this Appendix.

DELEGATION OF AUTHORITY

Authority of President under subsec. (b) of this section delegated to Secretary of Defense by section 204 of Ex. Ord. No. 12919, June 3, 1994, 59 F.R. 29527, set out as a note under section 2153 of this Appendix.

SECTION REFERRED TO IN OTHER SECTIONS

This section is referred to in section 2166 of this Appendix.

§ 2075. Presidential power to ration gasoline among classes of end-users unaffected

Nothing in this Act [sections 2061 to 2171 of this Appendix] shall be construed to authorize the President to institute, without the approval of the Congress, a program for the rationing of gasoline among classes of end-users.

(Sept. 8, 1950, ch. 932, title I, § 105, as added Pub. L. 96–294, title I, § 103, June 30, 1980, 94 Stat. 617.)

EFFECTIVE DATE

Section effective June 30, 1980, see section 107 of Pub. L. 96–294, set out as an Effective Date of 1980 Amendment note under section 2062 of this Appendix.

TERMINATION DATE

Termination of section, see section 2166(a) of this Appendix.

§ 2076. Designation of energy as a strategic and critical material

For purposes of this Act [sections 2061 to 2171 of this Appendix], "energy" shall be designated as a "strategic and critical material" after the date of the enactment of this section [June 30, 1980]: *Provided*, That no provision of this Act [sections 2061 to 2171 of this Appendix] shall, by virtue of such designation—

(1) grant any new direct or indirect authority to the President for the mandatory allocation or pricing of any fuel or feedstock (including, but not limited to, crude oil, residual fuel oil, any refined petroleum product, natural gas, or coal) or electricity or any other form of energy; or

(2) grant any new direct or indirect authority to the President to engage in the production of energy in any manner whatsoever (such as oil and gas exploration and development, or any energy facility construction), except as expressly provided in sections 305 and 306 [sections 2095 and 2096 of this Appendix] for synthetic fuel production.

(Sept. 8, 1950, ch. 932, title I, § 106, as added Pub. L. 96–294, title I, § 103, June 30, 1980, 94 Stat. 617.)

EFFECTIVE DATE

Section effective June 30, 1980, see section 107 of Pub. L. 96–294, set out as an Effective Date of 1980 Amendment note under section 2062 of this Appendix.

TERMINATION DATE

Termination of section, see section 2166(a) of this Appendix.

§ 2077. Strengthening domestic capability

(a) In general

Utilizing the authority of title III of this Act [sections 2091 to 2099a of this Appendix] or any other provision of law, the President may provide appropriate incentives to develop, maintain, modernize, and expand the productive capacities of domestic sources for critical components, critical technology items, and industrial resources essential for the execution of the national security strategy of the United States.

(b) Critical components and critical technology items

(1) Identification

(A) In general

The President, acting through the Secretary of Defense, shall identify critical components and critical technology items for each item on the Critical Items List of the Commanders-in-Chief of the Unified and Specified Commands and other items within the inventory of weapon systems and defense equipment.

(B) Definition

Any component identified as critical by a National Security Assessment conducted pursuant to section 113(i) of title 10, United States Code, or by a Presidential determination as a result of a petition filed under section 232 of the Trade Expansion Act of 1962 [19 U.S.C. 1862] shall be designated as a critical component for purposes of this Act [sections 2061 to 2171 of this Appendix], unless the President determines that the designation is unwarranted.

(2) Maintenance of reliable sources of supply

The President shall take appropriate actions to assure that critical components or critical technology items are available from reliable sources when needed to meet defense requirements during peacetime, graduated mobilization, and national emergency.

(3) Appropriate action

For purposes of this subsection, appropriate action may include—

(A) restricting contract solicitations to reliable sources;

(B) restricting contract solicitations to domestic sources pursuant to—

(i) section 2304(b)(1)(B) or section 2304(c)(3) of title 10, United States Code;

(ii) section 303(b)(1)(B) or section 303(c)(3) of the Federal Property and Administrative Services Act of 1949 [41 U.S.C. 253(b)(1)(B), (c)(3)]; or

(iii) other statutory authority;

(C) stockpiling critical components; and

(D) developing substitutes for a critical component or a critical technology item.

(Sept. 8, 1950, ch. 932, title I, §107, as added Pub. L. 102–558, title I, §111, Oct. 28, 1992, 106 Stat. 4201.)

EFFECTIVE DATE

Section deemed to have become effective Mar. 1, 1992, see section 304 of Pub. L. 102–558, set out as an Effective Date of 1992 Amendment note under section 2062 of this Appendix.

TERMINATION DATE

Termination of section, see section 2166(a) of this Appendix.

DELEGATION OF FUNCTIONS

Functions of the President under act Sept. 8, 1950 [section 2061 et seq. of this Appendix], relating to the production, conservation, use, control, distribution, and allocation of energy, delegated to the Secretary of Energy, see section 4 of Ex. Ord. No. 11790, eff. June 25, 1974, 39 F.R. 23185, set out as a note under section 761 of Title 15, Commerce and Trade.

§ 2078. Modernization of small business suppliers

(a) In general

In providing any assistance under this Act [sections 2061 to 2171 of this Appendix], the President shall accord a strong preference for small business concerns which are subcontractors or suppliers, and, to the maximum extent practicable, to such small business concerns located in areas of high unemployment or areas that have demonstrated a continuing pattern of economic decline, as identified by the Secretary of Labor.

(b) Modernization of equipment

(1) In general

Funds authorized under title III [sections 2091 to 2099a of this Appendix] may be used to guarantee the purchase or lease of advance manufacturing equipment, and any related services with respect to any such equipment for purposes of this Act [sections 2061 to 2171 of this Appendix].

(2) Small business suppliers

In considering proposals for title III [sections 2091 to 2099a of this Appendix] projects under paragraph (1), the President shall provide a strong preference for proposals submitted by a small business supplier or subcontractor whose proposal—

(A) has the support of the department or agency which will provide the guarantee;

(B) reflects that the small business concern has made arrangements to obtain qualified outside assistance to support the effective utilization of the advanced manufacturing equipment being proposed for installation; and

(C) meets the requirements of section 301, 302, or 303 [section 2091, 2092, or 2093 of this Appendix].

(Sept. 8, 1950, ch. 932, title I, §108, as added Pub. L. 102–558, title I, §111, Oct. 28, 1992, 106 Stat. 4202.)

EFFECTIVE DATE

Section deemed to have become effective Mar. 1, 1992, see section 304 of Pub. L. 102–558, set out as an Effective Date of 1992 Amendment note under section 2062 of this Appendix.

TERMINATION DATE

Termination of section, see section 2166(a) of this Appendix.

DELEGATION OF FUNCTIONS

Functions of the President under act Sept. 8, 1950 [section 2061 et seq. of this Appendix], relating to the production, conservation, use, control, distribution, and allocation of energy, delegated to the Secretary of Energy, see section 4 of Ex. Ord. No. 11790, eff. June 25, 1974, 39 F.R. 23185, set out as a note under section 761 of Title 15, Commerce and Trade.

TITLE II—AUTHORITY TO REQUISITION AND CONDEMN

AMENDMENTS

1951—Act July 31, 1951, ch. 275, title I, §102(a), 65 Stat. 132, in heading inserted "AND CONDEMN".

§ 2081. Omitted

CODIFICATION

Section, acts Sept. 8, 1950, ch. 932, title II, §201, 64 Stat. 799; July 31, 1951, ch. 275, title I, §102 (b), 65 Stat. 132, which related to requisition of property needed for national defense, terminated at close of June 30, 1953, by the terms of section 2166(a) of this Appendix.

TITLE III—EXPANSION OF PRODUCTIVE CAPACITY AND SUPPLY

TITLE REFERRED TO IN OTHER SECTIONS

This title is referred to in sections 2077, 2078, 2161, 2166 of this Appendix.

§ 2091. Loan guarantees

(a) Purpose of loans; guaranteeing agencies; Presidential determinations

(1) In order to expedite production and deliveries or services under Government contracts, the President may authorize, subject to such regulations as he may prescribe, the Department of Defense, the Department of Energy, the Department of Commerce, and such other agencies of the United States engaged in procurement for the national defense as he may designate (hereinafter referred to as "guaranteeing agencies"), without regard to provisions of law relating to the making, performance, amendment, or modification of contracts, to guarantee in whole or in part any public or private financing institution (including any Federal Reserve bank), by commitment to purchase, agreement to share losses, or otherwise, against loss of principal or interest on any loan, discount, or

advance, or on any commitment in connection therewith, which may be made by such financing institution for the purpose of financing any contractor, subcontractor, or other person in connection with the performance of any contract or other operation deemed by the guaranteeing agency to be necessary to expedite or expand production and deliveries or services under Government contracts for the procurement of industrial resources or critical technology items essential to the national defense, or for the purpose of financing any contractor, subcontractor, or other person in connection with or in contemplation of the termination, in the interest of the United States, of any contract made for the national defense; but no small-business concern (as defined in section 714(a)(1) of this Act [former section 2163a(a)(1) of this Appendix]) shall be held ineligible for the issuance of such a guaranty by reason of alternative sources of supply.

(2) Except as provided in section 305 [section 2095 of this Appendix] and section 306 [section 2096 of this Appendix], no authority contained in sections 301, 302, or 303 [sections 2091, 2092, or 2093 of this Appendix] may be used in any manner—

(A) in the development, production, or distribution of synthetic fuel;

(B) for any synthetic fuel project;

(C) to assist any person for the purpose of providing goods or services to a synthetic fuel project; or

(D) to provide any assistance to any person for the purchase of synthetic fuel.

(3) Except during periods of national emergency declared by the Congress or the President, a guarantee may be entered into under this section only if the President determines that—

(A) the guaranteed contract or activity is for industrial resources or a critical technology item which is essential to the national defense;

(B) without the guarantee, United States industry cannot reasonably be expected to provide the needed industrial resources or critical technology item in a timely manner;

(C) the guarantee is the most cost-effective, expedient, and practical alternative for meeting the need involved; and

(D) the combination of the United States national defense demand and foreseeable nondefense demand is not less than the output of domestic industrial capability, as determined by the President, including the output to be established through the guarantee.

(b) Fiscal agents; accountability; reimbursement

Any Federal agency or any Federal Reserve bank, when designated by the President, is authorized to act, on behalf of any guaranteeing agency, as fiscal agent of the United States in the making of such contracts of guarantee and in otherwise carrying out the purposes of this section. All such funds as may be necessary to enable any such fiscal agent to carry out any guarantee made by it on behalf of any guaranteeing agency shall be supplied and disbursed by or under authority from such guaranteeing agency. No such fiscal agent shall have any responsibility or accountability except as agent in taking any action pursuant to or under authority of the provisions of this section. Each such fiscal agent shall be reimbursed by each guaranteeing agency for all expenses and losses incurred by such fiscal agent in acting as agent on behalf of such guaranteeing agency, including among such expenses, notwithstanding any other provision of law, attorneys' fees and expenses of litigation.

(c) Supervision; interest, fees, procedures

All actions and operations of such fiscal agents under authority of or pursuant to this section shall be subject to the supervision of the President, and to such regulations as he may prescribe; and the President is authorized to prescribe, either specifically or by maximum limits or otherwise, rates of interest, guarantee and commitment fees, and other charges which may be made in connection with loans, discounts, advances, or commitments guaranteed by the guaranteeing agencies through such fiscal agents, and to prescribe regulations governing the forms and procedures (which shall be uniform to the extent practicable) to be utilized in connection with such guarantees.

(d) Funds available for guarantees

Each guaranteeing agency is authorized to use for the purposes of this section any funds which have heretofore been appropriated or allocated or which hereafter may be appropriated or allocated to it, or which are or may become available to it, for such purposes or for the purpose of meeting the necessities of the national defense.

(e) Identification of industrial resource shortfall; prevention of personal financial insolvency or bankruptcy

(1)(A) Except as provided in subparagraph (D), a guarantee may be made under this section only if the industrial resource shortfall which such guarantee is intended to correct has been identified in the Budget of the United States, or amendments thereto, submitted to the Congress, accompanied by a statement from the President demonstrating that the budget submission is in accordance with the provisions of subsection (a)(3) of this section.

(B) Any such guarantee may be made only after 60 days have elapsed after such industrial resource shortfall has been identified pursuant to subparagraph (A).

(C) If the making of any guarantee or guarantees to correct an industrial resource shortfall would cause the aggregate outstanding amount of all guarantees for such industrial resource shortfall to exceed $50,000,000, any such guarantee or guarantees may be made only if specifically authorized by law.

(D) The requirements of subparagraphs (A), (B), and (C) may be waived—

(i) during periods of national emergency declared by the Congress or the President; or

(ii) upon a determination by the President, on a nondelegable basis, that a specific guarantee is necessary to avert an industrial resource or critical technology shortfall that would severely impair national defense capability.

(2) The authority conferred by this section shall not be used primarily to prevent the finan-

cial insolvency or bankruptcy of any person, unless

(A) the President certifies that the insolvency or bankruptcy would have a direct and substantially adverse effect upon defense production; and

(B) a copy of such certification, together with a detailed justification thereof, is transmitted to the Congress and to the Committee on Banking, Housing, and Urban Affairs of the Senate and the Committee on Banking, Finance and Urban Affairs of the House of Representatives at least ten days prior to the exercise of that authority for such use.

(Sept. 8, 1950, ch. 932, title III, § 301, 64 Stat. 800; June 30, 1953, ch. 171, § 4, 67 Stat. 129; Pub. L. 91–379, title I, § 104, Aug. 15, 1970, 84 Stat. 799; Pub. L. 96–294, title I, § 104(a), (b), June 30, 1980, 94 Stat. 618; Pub. L. 98–265, §§ 3(a), 4(a), Apr. 17, 1984, 98 Stat. 149, 150; Pub. L. 102–558, title I, §§ 121(a), 141, Oct. 28, 1992, 106 Stat. 4203, 4217.)

AMENDMENTS

1992—Subsec. (a)(1). Pub. L. 102–558, § 121(a)(1), substituted "to expedite or expand production and deliveries or services under Government contracts for the procurement of industrial resources or critical technology items essential to the national defense" for "to expedite production and deliveries or services under Government contracts for the procurement of materials or the performance of services for the national defense,".

Subsec. (a)(3)(A). Pub. L. 102–558, § 121(a)(2), amended subpar. (A) generally. Prior to amendment, subpar. (A) read as follows: "the guaranteed contract or operation is for a material, or the performance of a service, which is essential to the national defense;".

Subsec. (a)(3)(B). Pub. L. 102–558, § 121(a)(3), substituted "without" for "Without" and "the needed industrial resources or critical technology item" for "the capability for the needed material or service".

Subsec. (a)(3)(D). Pub. L. 102–558, § 121(a)(4), amended subpar. (D) generally. Prior to amendment, subpar. (D) read as follows: "the United States national defense demand is equal to, or greater than, the output of domestic industrial capability which the President reasonably determines to be available for national defense, including the output to be established through the guarantee."

Subsec. (e)(1)(A). Pub. L. 102–558, § 121(a)(5), substituted "Except as provided in subparagraph (D)" for "Except during periods of national emergency declared by the Congress or the President".

Subsec. (e)(1)(C). Pub. L. 102–558, § 121(a)(6), substituted "$50,000,000" for "$25,000,000".

Subsec. (e)(1)(D). Pub. L. 102–558, § 121(a)(7), added subpar. (D).

Subsec. (e)(2)(B). Pub. L. 102–558, § 141, substituted "and to the Committee on Banking, Housing, and Urban Affairs of the Senate and the Committee on Banking, Finance and Urban Affairs of the House of Representatives" for "and to the Committees on Banking and Currency of the respective Houses".

1984—Subsec. (a)(3). Pub. L. 98–265, § 3(a), added par. (3).

Subsec. (e)(1). Pub. L. 98–265, § 4(a), substituted provision that a guarantee be made under this section only if the industrial resource shortfall which such guarantee is intended to correct is identified for provision that the maximum obligation under this section not exceed $38,000,000, but if guarantees exceed such amount, Congressional committees be notified and no disapproving resolution be adopted within a 60-day period of continuous session of Congress, with provision for determination of continuity of Congressional session for the purpose of computing such 60-day period.

1980—Subsec. (a). Pub. L. 96–294, § 104(a), designated existing provisions as par. (1), substituted references to Departments of Defense and Energy for references to Departments of Army, Navy, and Air Force, and added par. (2).

Subsec. (e)(1). Pub. L. 96–294, § 104(b), designated existing provisions as subpar. (A), substituted "Except as provided in subparagraph (B)" for "Except with the approval of Congress" and "$38,000,000" for "$20,000,000", and added subpar. (B).

1970—Subsec. (e). Pub. L. 91–379 added subsec. (e).

1953—Subsec. (a). Act June 30, 1953, made it clear that Government guaranties of credit may be made under this section in connection with the termination of Government contracts, and to provide that no small-business concern shall be denied a guaranty merely because an alternative source of supply exists for the item to be procured on the Government contract involved.

CHANGE OF NAME

Committee on Banking, Finance and Urban Affairs of House of Representatives treated as referring to Committee on Banking and Financial Services of House of Representatives by section 1(a) of Pub. L. 104–14, set out as a note preceding section 21 of Title 2, The Congress. Committee on Banking and Financial Services of House of Representatives abolished and replaced by Committee on Financial Services of House of Representatives, and jurisdiction over matters relating to securities and exchanges and insurance generally transferred from Committee on Energy and Commerce of House of Representatives by House Resolution No. 5, One Hundred Seventh Congress, Jan. 3, 2001.

EFFECTIVE DATE OF 1992 AMENDMENT

Amendment by Pub. L. 102–558 deemed to have become effective Mar. 1, 1992, see section 304 of Pub. L. 102–558, set out as a note under section 2062 of this Appendix.

EFFECTIVE DATE OF 1980 AMENDMENT

Amendment by Pub. L. 96–294 effective June 30, 1980, see section 107 of Pub. L. 96–294, set out as a note under section 2062 of this Appendix.

TERMINATION DATE

Termination of section, see section 2166(a) of this Appendix.

TRANSFER OF FUNCTIONS

Act July 30, 1953, ch. 282, title I, § 107(a)(2), (b), 67 Stat. 273, required President to transfer functions, powers, duties, and authority of Reconstruction Finance Corporation under sections 2091 to 2094 of this Appendix within sixty days after July 30, 1953, and provided that all assets, funds, contracts, loans, liabilities, commitments, authorizations, allocations, personnel, and records of Corporation, which Director of Bureau of the Budget [now Office of Management and Budget], determined necessary to performance of such functions were to be transferred to officer or agency of Government to which such functions were transferred.

DELEGATION OF FUNCTIONS

Functions of President under act Sept. 8, 1950 [section 2061 et seq. of this Appendix], relating to production, conservation, use, control, distribution, and allocation of energy, delegated to Secretary of Energy, see section 4 of Ex. Ord. No. 11790, eff. June 25, 1974, 39 F.R. 23185, set out as a note under section 761 of Title 15, Commerce and Trade.

EXECUTIVE ORDER NO. 10223

Ex. Ord. No. 10223, Mar. 12, 1951, 16 F.R. 2247, providing for the performance of certain functions under act Sept. 8, 1950, was revoked by section 404 of Ex. Ord. No. 10281, Aug. 28, 1951, 16 F.R. 8789.

SECTION REFERRED TO IN OTHER SECTIONS

This section is referred to in sections 2078, 2095, 2096 of this Appendix.

§ 2092. Loans to private business enterprises

(a) Purposes

To expedite production and deliveries or services to aid in carrying out Government contracts for the procurement of industrial resources or a critical technology item for the national defense, the President may make provision for loans (including participations in, or guarantees of, loan) to private business enterprises (including research corporations not organized for profit) for the expansion of capacity, the development of technological processes, or the production of essential materials, including the exploration, development, and mining of strategic and critical metals and minerals, and manufacture of newsprint.

(b) Terms and conditions; Presidential determinations

Such loans may be made without regard to the limitations of existing law and on such terms and conditions as the President deems necessary, except that—

(1) financial assistance may be extended only to the extent that it is not otherwise available on reasonable terms; and

(2) except during periods of national emergency declared by the Congress or the President, no such loan may be made unless the President determines that—

(A) the loan is for the expansion of capacity, the development of a technological process, or the production of materials essential to the national defense;

(B) without the loan, United States industry cannot reasonably be expected to provide the needed capacity, technological processes, or materials in a timely manner;

(C) the loan is the most cost-effective, expedient, and practical alternative method for meeting the need; and

(D) the combination of the United States national defense demand and foreseeable nondefense demand is not less than the output of domestic industrial capability, as determined by the President, including the output to be established through the loan.

(c) Identification of industrial resource shortfall

(1) Except as provided in paragraph (4), no loans may be made under this section, unless the industrial resource shortfall which such loan is intended to correct has been identified in the Budget of the United States, or amendments thereto, submitted to the Congress, accompanied by a statement from the President demonstrating that the budget submission is in accordance with the provisions of subsection (b)(2) of this section.

(2) Any such loan may be made only after 60 days have elapsed after such industrial resource shortfall has been identified pursuant to paragraph (1).

(3) If the making of any loan or loans to correct an industrial resource shortfall would cause the aggregate outstanding amount of all loans for such industrial resource shortfall to exceed $50,000,000, any such loan or loans may be made only if specifically authorized by law.

(4) The requirements of paragraphs (1), (2), and (3) may be waived—

(A) during periods of national emergency declared by the Congress or the President; and

(B) upon a determination by the President, on a nondelegable basis, that a specific guarantee is necessary to avert an industrial resource or critical technology shortfall that would severely impair national defense capability.

(Sept. 8, 1950, ch. 932, title III, § 302, 64 Stat. 801; June 30, 1952, ch. 530, title I, § 104, 66 Stat. 298; Pub. L. 93–155, title VIII, § 807(b), Nov. 16, 1973, 87 Stat. 615; Pub. L. 96–294, title I, § 104(c), June 30, 1980, 94 Stat. 618; Pub. L. 98–265, §§ 3(b), 4(b), Apr. 17, 1984, 98 Stat. 149, 151; Pub. L. 102–558, title I, § 121(b), Oct. 28, 1992, 106 Stat. 4204.)

AMENDMENTS

1992—Subsec. (a). Pub. L. 102–558, § 121(b)(1), substituted "for the procurement of industrial resources or a critical technology item for the national defense" for "for the procurement of materials or the performance of services for the national defense".

Subsec. (b)(2)(D). Pub. L. 102–558, § 121(b)(2), amended subpar. (D) generally. Prior to amendment, subpar. (D) read as follows: "the United States national defense demand is equal to, or greater than, domestic industrial capability which the President reasonably determines to be available for national defense, including the output to be established through the loan."

Subsec. (c)(1). Pub. L. 102–558, § 121(b)(3), substituted "Except as provided in paragraph (4), no loans may be made under this section" for "No such loan may be made under this section, except during periods of national emergency declared by the Congress or the President".

Subsec. (c)(3). Pub. L. 102–558, § 121(b)(4), substituted "$50,000,000" for "$25,000,000".

Subsec. (c)(4). Pub. L. 102–558, § 121(b)(5), added par. (4).

1984—Subsec. (a). Pub. L. 98–265, § 3(b), designated existing provision as subsec. (a) and struck out provision that loans be made without regard to limitations of existing law on such terms and conditions as the President deems necessary, except that financial assistance be extended only to the extent not available on reasonable terms, and that with respect to loans in excess of $48,000,000, Congressional committees be notified and no disapproving resolution be adopted within a 60-day period of continuous session of Congress, with provision for determining continuity of Congressional session for the purpose of computing such 60-day period. See subsec. (b).

Subsec. (b). Pub. L. 98–265, § 3(b)(2), added subsec. (b).

Subsec. (c). Pub. L. 98–265, § 4(b), added subsec. (c).

1980—Pub. L. 96–294 substituted "$48,000,000" for "$25,000,000".

1973—Pub. L. 93–155 provided for notification of Congressional Committees with respect to certain proposed loans, Congressional resolution of disapproval, continuity of Congressional sessions, and computation of period.

1952—Act June 30, 1952, brought manufacture of newsprint within its provisions.

EFFECTIVE DATE OF 1992 AMENDMENT

Amendment by Pub. L. 102–558 deemed to have become effective Mar. 1, 1992, see section 304 of Pub. L. 102–558, set out as a note under section 2062 of this Appendix.

EFFECTIVE DATE OF 1980 AMENDMENT

Amendment by Pub. L. 96–294 effective June 30, 1980, see section 107 of Pub. L. 96–294, set out as a note under section 2062 of this Appendix.

TERMINATION DATE

Termination of section, see section 2166(a) of this Appendix.

DELEGATION OF FUNCTIONS

Functions of President under act Sept. 8, 1950 [section 2061 et seq. of this Appendix], relating to production, conservation, use, control, distribution, and allocation of energy, delegated to Secretary of Energy, see section 4 of Ex. Ord. No. 11790, June 25, 1974, 39 F.R. 23185, set out as a note under section 761 of Title 15, Commerce and Trade.

OBLIGATIONS ENTERED INTO BEFORE NOVEMBER 16, 1973

Amendment by Pub. L. 93–155 not affecting the carrying out of any contract, loan, guarantee, commitment, or other obligation entered into prior to Nov. 16, 1973, see section 807(e) of Pub. L. 93–155, set out as a note under section 2307 of Title 10, Armed Forces.

EXECUTIVE ORDER NO. 10634

Ex. Ord. No. 10634, Aug. 31, 1955, 20 F.R. 6433, as amended by Ex. Ord. No. 10773, July 1, 1958, 23 F.R. 5061; Ex. Ord. No. 10782, Sept. 6, 1958, 23 F.R. 6971, which related to loans for facilities destroyed or damaged by major disaster, was revoked by section 5–106 of Ex. Ord. No. 12148, July 20, 1979, 44 F.R. 43243, set out as a note under section 5195 of Title 42, The Public Health and Welfare.

SECTION REFERRED TO IN OTHER SECTIONS

This section is referred to in sections 2078, 2091, 2095, 2096, 2161 of this Appendix.

§2093. Purchase of raw materials and installation of equipment

(a) Presidential provisions

(1) In general

To assist in carrying out the objectives of this Act [sections 2061 to 2171 of this Appendix], the President may make provision—

(A) for purchases of or commitments to purchase an industrial resource or a critical technology item, for Government use or resale; and

(B) for the encouragement of exploration, development, and mining of critical and strategic materials, and other materials.

(2) Treatment of certain agricultural commodities

Purchases for resale under this subsection shall not include that part of the supply of an agricultural commodity which is domestically produced, except to the extent that such domestically produced supply may be purchased for resale for industrial use or stockpiling.

(3) Terms of sales

No commodity purchased under this subsection shall be sold at less than—

(A) the established ceiling price for such commodity, except that minerals, metals, and materials shall not be sold at less than the established ceiling price, or the current domestic market price, whichever is lower; or

(B) if no ceiling price has been established, the higher of—

(i) the current domestic market price for such commodity; or

(ii) the minimum sale price established for agricultural commodities owned or controlled by the Commodity Credit Corporation, as provided in section 407 of the Agricultural Act of 1949 [7 U.S.C. 1427].

(4) Delivery dates

No purchase or commitment to purchase any imported agricultural commodity shall specify a delivery date which is more than 1 year after the expiration of this section.

(5) Presidential determinations

Except as provided in paragraph (7), the President may not execute a contract under this subsection unless the President determines that—

(A) the industrial resource or critical technology item is essential to the national defense;

(B) without Presidential action under the authority provided for in this section, United States industry cannot reasonably be expected to provide the capability for the needed industrial resource or critical technology item in a timely manner;

(C) purchases, purchase commitments, or other action pursuant to this section are the most cost-effective, expedient, and practical alternative method for meeting the need; and

(D) the combination of the United States national defense demand and foreseeable nondefense demand for the industrial resource or critical technology item is not less than the output of domestic industrial capability, as determined by the President, including the output to be established through the purchase, purchase commitment, or other action.

(6) Identification of shortfall

(A) In general

Except as provided in paragraph (7), the President shall take no action under this section unless the industrial resource shortfall which such action is intended to correct has been identified in the Budget of the United States, or amendments thereto, submitted to the Congress and accompanied by a statement from the President demonstrating that the budget submission is in accordance with the provisions of paragraph (5).

(B) Timing of action

Any such action may be taken only after 60 days have elapsed after such industrial resource shortfall has been identified pursuant to subparagraph (A).

(C) Limitation

If the taking of any action or actions under this section to correct an industrial resource shortfall would cause the aggregate outstanding amount of all such actions for such industrial resource shortfall to exceed $50,000,000, any such action or actions may be taken only if specifically authorized by law.

(7) Waiver

The requirements of paragraphs (1) through (6) may be waived—

(A) during periods of national emergency declared by the Congress or the President; or

(B) upon a determination by the President, on a nondelegable basis, that a specific guarantee is necessary to avert an industrial resource or critical technology shortfall that would severely impair national defense capability.

(b) Terms and conditions of purchase

Subject to the limitations in subsection (a) of this section, purchases and commitments to purchase and sales under such subsection may be made without regard to the limitations of existing law, for such quantities, and on such terms and conditions, including advance payments, and for such periods, but not extending beyond a date that is not more than 10 years from the date such purchase, purchase commitment, or sale was initially made, as the President deems necessary, except that purchases or commitments to purchase involving higher than established ceiling prices (or if there be no established ceiling prices, currently prevailing market prices) or anticipated loss on resale shall not be made unless it is determined that supply of the materials could not be effectively increased at lower prices or on terms more favorable to the Government or that such purchases are necessary to assure the availability to the United States of overseas supplies.

(c) Subsidy payments on domestically produced materials; exclusion of agricultural products

If the President finds—

(1) that under generally fair and equitable ceiling prices for any raw or nonprocessed material, there will result a decrease in supplies from high-costs sources of such material, and that the continuation of such supplies is necessary to carry out the objectives of the Act [sections 2061 to 2171 of this Appendix]; or

(2) that an increase in cost of transportation is temporary in character and threatens to impair maximum production or supply in any area at stable prices of any materials;

he may make provision for subsidy payments on any such domestically produced material other than an agricultural commodity in such amounts and in such manner (including purchases of such material and its resale at a loss without regard to the limitations of existing law), and on such terms and conditions, as he determines to be necessary to insure that supplies from such high-cost sources are continued, or that maximum production or supply in such area at stable prices of such materials is maintained, as the case may be.

(d) Transportation, storage, and processing

The procurement power granted to the President by this section shall include the power to transport and store and have processed and refined, any materials procured under this section.

(e) Installation of equipment in industrial facilities

When in his judgment it will aid the national defense, the President is authorized to install additional equipment, facilities, processes or improvements to plants, factories, and other industrial facilities owned by the United States Government, and to install government-owned equipment in plants, factories, and other industrial facilities owned by private persons.

(f) Transfer of excess materials to national stockpile

Notwithstanding any other provision of law to the contrary, metals, minerals, and materials acquired pursuant to the provisions of this section which, in the judgment of the President, are excess to the needs of programs under this Act [sections 2061 to 2171 of this Appendix], shall be transferred to the National Defense Stockpile established by the Strategic and Critical Materials Stock Piling Act (50 U.S.C. 98 et seq.), when the President deems such action to be in the public interest. Transfers made pursuant to this subsection shall be made without charge against or reimbursement from funds appropriated for the purposes of such Act, except that costs incident to such transfer other than acquisition costs shall be paid or reimbursed from such funds, and the acquisition costs of such metals, minerals, and materials transferred shall be deemed to be net losses incurred by the transferring agency and the notes payable issued to the Secretary of the Treasury representing the amounts thereof shall be canceled. Upon the cancellation of any such notes the aggregate amount of borrowing which may be outstanding at any one time under section 304(b)[1] of this Act, as amended [section 2094(b) of this Appendix], shall be reduced in an amount equal to the amount of any notes so canceled.

(g) Development of substitutes for strategic and critical materials

When in his judgment it will aid the national defense, the President may make provision for the development of substitutes for strategic and critical materials, critical components, critical technology items, and other industrial resources.

(Sept. 8, 1950, ch. 932, title III, § 303, 64 Stat. 801; July 31, 1951, ch. 275, title I, § 103(a), 65 Stat. 133; June 30, 1953, ch. 171, §§ 5, 6, 67 Stat. 130; Aug. 9, 1955, ch. 655, § 3, 69 Stat. 580; June 29, 1956, ch. 474, § 2, 70 Stat. 408; Pub. L. 88–343, § 2, June 30, 1964, 78 Stat. 235; Pub. L. 92–325, § 1, June 30, 1972, 86 Stat. 390; Pub. L. 94–273, § 2(29), Apr. 21, 1976, 90 Stat. 376; Pub. L. 96–41, § 3(c), July 30, 1979, 93 Stat. 325; Pub. L. 96–294, title I, § 104(d), June 30, 1980, 94 Stat. 618; Pub. L. 98–265, §§ 3(c), 4(c), Apr. 17, 1984, 98 Stat. 150, 151; Pub. L. 102–558, title I, § 121(c), (d), Oct. 28, 1992, 106 Stat. 4204, 4206.)

REFERENCES IN TEXT

For expiration of this section, referred to in subsec. (a)(4), see section 2166(a) of this Appendix.

The Strategic and Critical Materials Stock Piling Act, referred to in subsec. (f), is act June 7, 1939, ch. 190, as revised generally by Pub. L. 96–41, § 2, July 30, 1979, 93 Stat. 319, which is classified generally to subchapter III (§ 98 et seq.) of chapter 5 of Title 50, War and National Defense. For complete classification of this Act to the Code, see section 98 of Title 50 and Tables.

Section 304(b) of this Act, referred to in subsec. (f), is classified to section 2094(b) of this Appendix, and was repealed and a new subsec. (b) was enacted by Pub. L. 93–426, § 2, Sept. 30, 1974, 88 Stat. 1166, which does not relate to limiting aggregate amount of borrowing which may be outstanding.

AMENDMENTS

1992—Subsec. (a). Pub. L. 102–558, § 121(c)(1), amended subsec. (a) generally, substituting present provisions for provisions relating to purchases for use or resale, development of strategic minerals, metals, and materials, exclusion of certain agricultural commodities, termination of purchase authority, Presidential action, and identification of industrial resource shortfalls.

[1] See References in Text note below.

Subsec. (b). Pub. L. 102–558, § 121(c)(2), substituted "a date that is not more than 10 years from the date such purchase, purchase commitment, or sale was initially made" for "September 30, 1995".

Subsec. (g). Pub. L. 102–558, § 121(d), inserted before period at end ", critical components, critical technology items, and other industrial resources".

1984—Subsec. (a). Pub. L. 98–265, § 3(c), inserted provision requiring President, except during periods of national emergency, to make specific determinations before executing a contract under this subsection.

Pub. L. 98–265, § 4(c), inserted provision requiring President, except during periods of national emergency, to identify industrial resource shortfall before taking any action under this section.

1980—Subsec. (a). Pub. L. 96–294, § 104(d)(1), inserted references to materials after metals wherever appearing.

Subsec. (b). Pub. L. 96–294, § 104(d)(2), substituted "1995" for "1985".

Subsec. (g). Pub. L. 96–294, § 104(d)(3), struck out provisions relating to certifications by Secretaries of Agriculture and Interior regarding short supply of a particular strategic or critical material.

1979—Subsec. (f). Pub. L. 96–41 substituted "the National Defense Stockpile established by the Strategic and Critical Materials Stock Piling Act (50 U.S.C. 98 et seq.)" for "the national stockpile established pursuant to the Act of June 7, 1939, as amended (50 U.S.C. 98–98h)" and "from funds appropriated for the purposes of such Act" for "from funds available under such Act of June 7, 1939, as amended".

1976—Subsec. (b). Pub. L. 94–273 substituted "September" for "June".

1972—Subsec. (b). Pub. L. 92–325 substituted "June 30, 1985" for "June 30, 1975".

1964—Subsec. (b). Pub. L. 88–343 substituted "June 30, 1975" for "June 30, 1965".

1956—Subsec. (b). Act June 29, 1956, substituted "June 30, 1965" for "June 30, 1963".

1955—Subsec. (g). Act Aug. 9, 1955, added subsec. (g).

1953—Subsec. (b). Act June 30, 1953, § 5, substituted "1963" for "1962".

Subsec. (f). Act June 30, 1953, § 6, added subsec. (f).

1951—Act July 31, 1951, amended section generally to broaden authority under this section to include materials generally, to continue prohibition against resale of domestic agricultural commodities except for industrial uses or stockpiling but eliminated it as to imported agricultural commodities, to provide that minerals and metals purchased under subsec. (a) may be sold at less than the established ceiling price, but not less than the current domestic market price, to limit provision barring contracts calling for delivery more than one year after the expiration of this section to imported agricultural commodities, to provide that purchases and commitments to purchase under subsec. (a) may not be made for any period extending beyond June 30, 1952, and to provide for a differential subsidy.

EFFECTIVE DATE OF 1992 AMENDMENT

Amendment by Pub. L. 102–558 deemed to have become effective Mar. 1, 1992, see section 304 of Pub. L. 102–558, set out as a note under section 2062 of this Appendix.

EFFECTIVE DATE OF 1980 AMENDMENT

Amendment by Pub. L. 96–294 effective June 30, 1980, see section 107 of Pub. L. 96–294, set out as a note under section 2062 of this Appendix.

EFFECTIVE DATE OF 1955 AMENDMENT

Amendment by act Aug. 9, 1955, effective as of close of July 31, 1955, see section 11 of act Aug. 9, 1955, set out as a note under section 2062 of this Appendix.

TERMINATION DATE

Termination of section, see section 2166(a) of this Appendix.

DELEGATION OF FUNCTIONS

Functions of President under act Sept. 8, 1950 [section 2061 et seq. of this Appendix], relating to production, conservation, use, control, distribution, and allocation of energy, delegated to Secretary of Energy, see section 4 of Ex. Ord. No. 11790, June 25, 1974, 39 F.R. 23185, set out as a note under section 761 of Title 15, Commerce and Trade.

CLARIFICATION OF STOCKPILE STATUS OF CERTAIN MATERIALS

For provisions that all materials purchased under this section and held in the Defense Production Act inventory as of June 30, 1992, are transferred to the National Defense Stockpile, see section 3315 of Pub. L. 102–484, as amended, set out as a note under section 98c of Title 50, War and National Defense.

EXECUTIVE ORDER NO. 10219

Ex. Ord. No. 10219, Feb. 28, 1951, 16 F.R. 1983, as amended by Ex. Ord. No. 10461, June 17, 1953, 18 F.R. 3513; Ex. Ord. No. 10537, June 22, 1954, 19 F.R. 3807; Ex. Ord. No. 10773, July 1, 1958, 23 F.R. 5061; Ex. Ord. No. 10782, Sept. 6, 1958, 23 F.R. 6971, which related to the responsibilities of Federal agencies with respect to transportation and storage, was superseded by Ex. Ord. No. 11051, Sept. 27, 1962, 27 F.R. 9683, formerly set out as a note under section 2271 of this Appendix.

SECTION REFERRED TO IN OTHER SECTIONS

This section is referred to in sections 2078, 2091, 2094, 2095, 2096, 2161 of this Appendix; title 50 section 98c.

§ 2094. Defense Production Act Fund

(a) Establishment of Fund

There is established in the Treasury of the United States a separate fund to be known as the Defense Production Act Fund (hereafter in this section referred to as "the Fund").

(b) Moneys in Fund

There shall be credited to the Fund—

(1) all moneys appropriated for the Fund, as authorized by section 711(c)[1]; and

(2) all moneys received by the Fund on transactions entered into pursuant to section 303 [section 2093 of this Appendix].

(c) Use of Fund

The Fund shall be available to carry out the provisions and purposes of this title [sections 2091 to 2099a of this Appendix], subject to the limitations set forth in this Act [sections 2061 to 2171 of this Appendix] and in appropriations Acts.

(d) Duration of Fund

Moneys in the Fund shall remain available until expended.

(e) Fund balance

The Fund balance at the close of each fiscal year shall not exceed $400,000,000, excluding any moneys appropriated to the Fund during that fiscal year or obligated funds. If, at the close of any fiscal year, the Fund balance exceeds $400,000,000, the amount in excess of $400,000,000 shall be paid into the general fund of the Treasury.

(f) Fund manager

The President shall designate a Fund manager. The duties of the Fund manager shall include—

[1] See References in Text note below.

(1) determining the liability of the Fund in accordance with subsection (g);

(2) ensuring the visibility and accountability of transactions engaged in through the Fund; and

(3) reporting to the Congress each year regarding activities of the Fund during the previous fiscal year.

(g) Liabilities against Fund

When any agreement entered into pursuant to this title [sections 2091 to 2099a of this Appendix] after December 31, 1991, imposes any contingent liability upon the United States, such liability shall be considered an obligation against the Fund.

(Sept. 8, 1950, ch. 932, title III, § 304, 64 Stat. 802; June 2, 1951, ch. 121, Ch. XI, 65 Stat. 61; July 31, 1951, ch. 275, title I, § 103(b), (c), 65 Stat. 134; Pub. L. 86–560, § 2, June 30, 1960, 74 Stat. 282; Pub. L. 88–343, § 3, June 30, 1964, 78 Stat. 235; Pub. L. 93–426, § 2, Sept. 30, 1974, 88 Stat. 1166; Pub. L. 102–558, title I, § 122, Oct. 28, 1992, 106 Stat. 4206.)

REFERENCES IN TEXT

Section 711(c), referred to in subsec. (b)(1), was classified to section 2161(c) of this Appendix prior to repeal by Pub. L. 104–64, § 3(2), Dec. 18, 1995, 109 Stat. 689.

AMENDMENTS

1992—Pub. L. 102–558 amended section generally. Prior to amendment, section read as follows:

"(a) For the purposes of sections 302 and 303, the President is authorized to utilize such existing departments, agencies, officials, or corporations of the Government as he may deem appropriate, or to create new agencies (other than corporations).

"(b) The Secretary of the Treasury is authorized and directed to cancel the outstanding balance of all unpaid notes issued to the Secretary of the Treasury pursuant to this section, together with interest accrued and unpaid on such notes.

"(c) Any cash balance remaining on June 30, 1974, in the borrowing authority previously authorized by this section, and any funds thereafter received on transactions heretofore or hereafter entered into pursuant to sections 302 and 303 shall be covered into the Treasury as miscellaneous receipts."

1974—Subsec. (b). Pub. L. 93–426 substituted provisions authorizing Secretary of the Treasury to cancel outstanding balance of all unpaid notes issued to Secretary of the Treasury together with interest accrued and unpaid on such notes, for provisions relating to borrowing authority mechanism by which all program operations under the Defense Production Act have been financed since the initiation of the Act in 1950 with an overall limit of $2.1 billion outstanding at any one time and with provisions for payment of interest on the obligations.

Subsec. (c). Pub. L. 93–426 added subsec. (c). Former subsec. (c) was repealed by act July 31, 1951, ch. 275, title I, § 103(c), 65 Stat. 134.

1964—Subsec. (b). Pub. L. 88–343 provided that no new purchases or commitments to purchase shall be made or entered into after June 30, 1964, unless President makes a finding that such new purchases or commitments are essential to national security, and that total of such new purchases or commitments including contingent liabilities, could not exceed $100,000,000.

1960—Subsec. (b). Pub. L. 86–560 substituted "six months" for "quarter".

1951—Subsec. (b). Act July 31, 1951, § 103(b), increased revolving fund from $600,000,000 to $2,100,000,000, and limited contingent liability of the United States.

Act June 2, 1951, increased aggregate of borrowing from $600,000,000 to $1,600,000,000.

Subsec. (c). Act July 31, 1951, § 103(c), repealed subsec. (c) which authorized $1,400,000,000 to be appropriated to carry out sections 2092 and 2093 of this Appendix.

EFFECTIVE DATE OF 1992 AMENDMENT

Amendment by Pub. L. 102–558 deemed to have become effective Mar. 1, 1992, see section 304 of Pub. L. 102–558, set out as a note under section 2062 of this Appendix.

TERMINATION DATE

Termination of section, see section 2166(a) of this Appendix.

DEFENSE PRODUCTION ACT FUND MANAGER

Secretary of Defense designated Defense Production Act Fund Manager in accordance with subsec. (f) of this section, see section 309 of Ex. Ord. No. 12919, June 3, 1994, 59 F.R. 29529, set out as a note under section 2153 of this Appendix.

SECTION REFERRED TO IN OTHER SECTIONS

This section is referred to in section 2093 of this Appendix.

§ 2095. Synthetic fuel production

(a) Immediate Presidential action to meet national defense needs; exercise of authorities; United States Synthetic Fuel Corporation authority unaffected

(1)(A) Subject to subsection (k)(1), in order to encourage and expedite the development of synthetic fuel for use for national defense purposes, the President, utilizing the provisions of this Act [sections 2061 to 2171 of this Appendix] (other than sections 101(a), 101(b), 301, 302, 303, and 306 [sections 2071(a), 2071(b), 2091, 2092, 2093, and 2096 of this Appendix]), and any other applicable provision of law, shall take immediate action to achieve production of synthetic fuel to meet national defense needs.

(B) The President shall exercise the authority granted by this section—

(i) in consultation with the Secretary of Energy;

(ii) through the Department of Defense and any other Federal department or agency designated by the President; and

(iii) consistent with an orderly transition to the separate authorities established pursuant to the United States Synthetic Fuels Corporation Act of 1980 [42 U.S.C. 8701 et seq.].

(2) This section shall not affect the authority of the United States Synthetic Fuels Corporation.

(b) Specific Presidential authorities; requisites, limitations, etc.

(1)(A) To assist in carrying out the objectives of this section, the President, subject to subsections (c) and (d), shall—

(i) contract for purchases of, or commitments to purchase, synthetic fuel for Government use for defense needs;

(ii) subject to paragraph (3), issue guarantees in accordance with the provisions of section 301 [section 2091 of this Appendix], except that the provisions of section 301(e)(1)(B) [section 2091(e)(1)(B) of this Appendix] shall not apply with respect to such guarantees; and

(iii) subject to paragraph (3), make loans in accordance with the provisions of section 302 [section 2092 of this Appendix], except that the provisions of section 302(2) [section 2092(2) of this Appendix] shall not apply with respect to such loans.

(2)(A) Except as provided in subparagraph (B) assistance authorized under this subsection may be provided only to persons who are participating in a synthetic fuel project.

(B) For purposes of fabrication or manufacture of any component of a synthetic fuel project, assistance authorized under paragraph (1)(A)(ii) and paragraph (1)(A)(iii) may be provided to any fabricator or manufacturer of such component.

(3) The President may not utilize the authority under paragraph (1) to provide any loan or guarantee in accordance with the provisions of section 301 [section 2091 of this Appendix] or section 302 [section 2092 of this Appendix] in amounts which exceed the limitations established in such sections unless the President submits to the Congress notification of the proposed loan or guarantee in the manner specified under section 307[1] [section 2097 of this Appendix] and such proposed action is either approved or not disapproved by the Congress under such section. For purposes of section 307[1] [section 2097 of this Appendix], any proposal pertaining to a proposed loan or guarantee, notice of which is transmitted to the Congress under this paragraph, shall be considered to be a synthetic fuel action.

(c) Purchases and commitments to purchase by President; authority; limitations; advance payments prior to construction of synthetic fuel project

(1) Subject to paragraph (2), purchases and commitments to purchase under subsection (b) may be made—

(A) without regard to the limitations of existing law (other than the limitations contained in this Act [sections 2061 to 2171 of this Appendix]) regarding the procurement of goods or services by the Government; and

(B) subject to section 717(a) [section 2166(a) of this Appendix], for such quantities, on such terms and conditions (including advance payments subject to paragraph (3)), and for such periods as the President deems necessary.

(2) Purchases or commitments to purchase under subsection (b) involving higher than established ceiling prices (or if there are no established ceiling prices, currently prevailing market prices as determined by the Secretary of Energy) shall not be made unless it is determined that supplies of synthetic fuel could not be effectively increased at lower prices or on terms more favorable to the Government, or that such commitments or purchases are necessary to assure the availability to the United States of supplies overseas for use for national defense purposes.

(3) Advance payments may not be made under this section unless construction has begun on the synthetic fuel project involved or the President determines that all conditions precedent to construction have been met.

[1] See References in Text note below.

(d) Bidding and contracting procedures and requirements applicable to purchases and commitments to purchase

(1) Except as provided in paragraph (2), any purchase of or commitment to purchase synthetic fuel under subsection (b) shall be made by solicitation of sealed competitive bids.

(2) In any case in which no such bids are submitted to the President or the President determines that no such bids which have been submitted to the President are acceptable, the President may negotiate contracts for such purchases and commitments to purchase.

(3) Any contract for such purchases or commitments to purchase shall provide that the President has the right to refuse delivery of the synthetic fuel involved and to pay the person involved an amount equal to the amount by which the price for such synthetic fuel, as specified in the contract involved, exceeds the market price, as determined by the Secretary of Energy, for such synthetic fuel on the delivery date specified in such contract.

(4)(A)(i) With respect to any person, including any other person who is substantially controlled by such person (as determined by the Secretary of Energy), the President, subject to subparagraph (A)(ii), may not award contracts for the purchase of or commitment to purchase more than 100,000 barrels per day crude oil equivalent of synthetic fuel.

(ii) With respect to any person, including any other person who is substantially controlled by such person (as determined by the Secretary of Energy), the President may not award any contract for the purchase or commitment to purchase of more than 75,000 barrels per day crude oil equivalent of synthetic fuel unless the President submits to the Congress notification of such proposed contract or commitment in the manner specified under section 307[2] [section 2097 of this Appendix] and such proposed action is either approved or not disapproved by the Congress under such section. For purposes of section 307[2] [section 2097 of this Appendix], any proposal pertaining to such a proposed contract or commitment, notice of which is transmitted to the Congress under this subparagraph, shall be considered to be a synthetic fuel action.

(B) A contract for the purchase of or commitment to purchase synthetic fuel may be entered into only for synthetic fuel which is produced in a synthetic fuel project which is located in the United States.

(C) Each contract entered into under this section for the purchase of or commitment to purchase synthetic fuel shall provide that all parties to such contract agree to review and to possibly renegotiate such contract within 10 years after the date of the initial production at the synthetic fuel project involved. At the time of such review, the President shall determine the need for continued financial assistance pursuant to such contract.

(5) In any case in which the President, under the provisions of this section, accepts delivery of any synthetic fuel, such synthetic fuel may be used by an appropriate Federal agency. Such Federal agency shall pay for such synthetic fuel

[2] See References in Text note below.

the prevailing market price for the product which such synthetic fuel is replacing, as determined by the Secretary of Energy, from sums appropriated to such Federal agency for the purchase of fuel, and the President shall pay, from sums appropriated for such purpose pursuant to the authorizations contained in sections 711(a)(2) and 711(a)(3)[3] [section 2161(a)(2) and 2161(a)(3) of this Appendix], an amount equal to the amount by which the contract price for such synthetic fuel as specified in the contract involved exceeds such prevailing market price.

(6) In considering any proposed contract under this section, the President shall take into account the socioeconomic impacts on communities which would be affected by any new or expanded facilities required for the production of the synthetic fuel under such contract.

(e) Scope of Presidential procurement power

The procurement power granted to the President under this section shall include the power to transport and store and have processed and refined any product procured under this section.

(f) Determinations necessary for purchase and sale of synthetic fuel

(1) No authority contained in this section may be exercised to acquire any amount of synthetic fuel unless the President determines that such synthetic fuel is needed to meet national defense needs and that it is not anticipated that such synthetic fuel will be resold by the Government.

(2) In any case in which synthetic fuel is acquired by the Government under this section, such synthetic fuel is no longer needed to meet national defense needs, and such synthetic fuel is not accepted by a Federal agency pursuant to subsection (d)(5), the President shall offer such synthetic fuel to the Secretary of Energy for purposes of meeting the storage requirements of the Strategic Petroleum Reserve.

(3) Any synthetic fuel which is acquired by the Government under this section and which is not used by the Government or accepted by the Secretary of Energy pursuant to paragraph (2) shall be sold in accordance with applicable Federal law.

(g) Maximum liability of Federal Government under contracts; budgetary certifications

(1) Any contract under this section including any amendment or other modification of such contract, shall, subject to the availability of unencumbered appropriations in advance, specify in dollars the maximum liability of the Federal Government under such contract as determined in accordance with paragraph (2).

(2) For the purpose of determining the maximum liability under any contract under paragraph (1)—

(A) loans shall be valued at the initial face value of the loan;

(B) guarantees shall be valued at the initial face value of such guarantee (including any amount of interest which is guaranteed under such guarantee);

(C) purchase agreements shall be valued as of the date of each such contract based upon the President's estimate of the maximum liability under such contract; and

(D) any increase in the liability of the Government pursuant to any amendment or other modification to a contract for a loan, guarantee, or purchase agreement shall be valued in accordance with the applicable preceding subparagraph.

(3) If more than one form of assistance is provided under this section to any synthetic fuel project, then the maximum liability under such contract for purposes of paragraphs (1) and (2) shall be valued at the maximum potential exposure on such project at any time during the life of such project.

(4) Any such contract shall be accompanied by a certification by the Director of the Office of Management and Budget that the necessary appropriations have been made for the purpose of such contract and are available. The remaining available and unencumbered appropriations shall equal the total aggregate appropriations less the aggregate maximum liability of the Federal Government under all contracts pursuant to this section.

(5) Any commitment made under this section which is nullified or voided for any reason shall not be considered in the aggregate maximum liability for the purposes of paragraph (4).

(h) Loan, guarantee, or purchase agreement not to be deemed a major Federal action significantly affecting the quality of the human environment

For purposes of section 102(2)(C) of the National Environmental Policy Act of 1969 (42 U.S.C. 4332(2)(C)), no action in providing any loan, guarantee, or purchase agreement under this section shall be deemed to be a major Federal action significantly affecting the quality of the human environment.

(i) Labor standards; applicability, certifications, etc.

All laborers and mechanics employed for the construction, repair, or alteration of any synthetic fuel project funded, in whole or in part, by a guarantee or loan entered into pursuant to this section shall be paid wages at rates not less than those prevailing on projects of a similar character in the locality as determined by the Secretary of Labor in accordance with the Act entitled "An Act relating to the rate of wages for laborers and mechanics employed on public buildings of the United States and the District of Columbia by contractors and subcontractors, and for other purposes", approved March 3, 1931 (40 U.S.C. 276a et seq.) and commonly known as the Davis-Bacon Act. Guaranteeing agencies shall not extend guarantees and the President shall not make loans for the construction, repair or alteration of any synthetic fuel project unless a certification is provided to the agency or the President, as the case may be, prior to the commencement of construction or at the time of filing an application for a loan or guarantee, if construction has already commenced, that these labor standards will be maintained at the synthetic fuel project. With respect to the labor standards specified in this subsection, the Secretary of Labor shall have the authority and

[3] See References in Text note below.

functions set forth in Reorganization Plan Numbered 14 of 1950 and section 276(c)[4] of title 40 [40 U.S.C. 276c].

(j) Other jurisdictional, etc., authorities relating to water resources and rights unaffected

(1) Nothing in this section shall—

(A) affect the jurisdiction of the States and the United States over waters of any stream or over any ground water resource;

(B) alter, amend, repeal, interpret, modify, or be in conflict with any interstate compact made by any States; or

(C) confer upon any non-Federal entity the ability to exercise any Federal right to the waters of any stream or to any ground water resource.

(2) No synthetic fuel project constructed pursuant to the authorities of this section shall be considered to be a Federal project for purposes of the application for or assignment of water rights.

(k) Termination of contracting or commitment authority of President; renewal or extension of contracts

(1) Subject to paragraph (2), the authority of the President to enter into any new contract or commitment under this section shall cease to be effective on the date on which the President determines that the United States Synthetic Fuels Corporation is established and fully operational consistent with the provisions of the United States Synthetic Fuels Corporation Act of 1980 [42 U.S.C. 8701 et seq.].

(2) Contracts entered into under this section before the date specified in paragraph (1) may be renewed and extended by the President after the date specified in paragraph (1) but only to the extent that Congress has specifically appropriated funds for such renewals and extensions.

(Sept. 8, 1950, ch. 932, title III, § 305, as added Pub. L. 96–294, title I, § 104(e), June 30, 1980, 94 Stat. 619.)

REFERENCES IN TEXT

The United States Synthetic Fuels Corporation Act of 1980, referred to in subsecs. (a)(1)(B)(iii) and (k)(1), is Pub. L. 96–294, title I, pt. B, June 30, 1980, 94 Stat. 633, which was classified generally to chapter 95 (§ 8701 et seq.) of Title 42, The Public Health and Welfare, and was omitted from the Code. For complete classification of this Act to the Code, see Tables.

Section 307, referred to in subsecs. (b)(3) and (d)(4)(A)(ii), is classified to section 2097 of this Appendix and was amended by Pub. L. 102–558, title I, § 151, Oct. 28, 1992, 106 Stat. 4218, and as so amended, provisions relating to congressional approval of synthetic fuel action by the President were struck out.

Section 711, referred to in subsec. (d)(5), is classified to section 2161 of this Appendix and was amended by Pub. L. 102–558, title I, § 152, Oct. 28, 1992, 106 Stat. 4218, repealing subsec. (a)(2) and redesignating subsec. (a)(3) as subsec. (b). Subsec. (b) was subsequently repealed and a new subsec. (b) added by Pub. L. 104–64, § 3(2), Dec. 18, 1995, 109 Stat. 689.

Act approved March 3, 1931 (40 U.S.C. 276a et seq.) and commonly known as the Davis-Bacon Act, referred to in subsec. (i), is act Mar. 3, 1931, ch. 411, 46 Stat. 1494, as amended, which is classified generally to sections 276a to 276a–5 of Title 40, Public Buildings, Property, and Works. For complete classification of this Act to the Code, see Short Title note set out under section 276a of Title 40 and Tables.

Reorganization Plan Numbered 14 of 1950, referred to in subsec. (i), is set out in the Appendix to Title 5, Government Organization and Employees.

Section 276(c) of title 40, referred to in subsec. (i), was repealed by Pub. L. 86–249, § 17(13)–(15), Sept. 9, 1959, 73 Stat. 485. Reference should probably be to section 276c of Title 40, Public Buildings, Property, and Works.

EFFECTIVE DATE

Section effective June 30, 1980, see section 107 of Pub. L. 96–294, set out as an Effective Date of 1980 Amendment note under section 2062 of this Appendix.

TERMINATION DATE

Termination of section, see section 2166(a) of this Appendix.

TERMINATION OF UNITED STATES SYNTHETIC FUELS CORPORATION

United States Synthetic Fuels Corporation terminated by Pub. L. 99–272, title VII, § 7403(b), Apr. 7, 1986, 100 Stat. 144, set out as a note under section 8791 of Title 42, The Public Health and Welfare.

EXECUTIVE ORDER NO. 12242

Ex. Ord. No. 12242, Sept. 30, 1980, 45 F.R. 65175, which related to delegation and exercise of functions relating to synthetic fuels, was revoked, except with respect to any loan guarantee issued under the provisions of that order, by Ex. Ord. No. 12346, § 4, Feb. 8, 1982, 47 F.R. 5993, set out below.

EX. ORD. NO. 12346. TRANSITION OF SYNTHETIC FUEL RESPONSIBILITIES FROM DEPARTMENT OF ENERGY TO UNITED STATES SYNTHETIC FUELS CORPORATION

Ex. Ord. No. 12346, Feb. 8, 1982, 47 F.R. 5993, provided:

By the authority vested in me as President by Section 305(k) of the Defense Production Act of 1950, as amended (50 U.S.C. App. 2095(k)), and having determined that the United States Synthetic Fuels Corporation is established and fully operational consistent with the provisions of the United States Synthetic Fuels Corporation Act of 1980 (Public Law 96–294; 94 Stat. 633 *et seq.*) [42 U.S.C. 8701 et seq.], and to provide for an orderly transition of synthetic fuel responsibilities from the Department of Energy to the United States Synthetic Fuels Corporation, it is hereby ordered as follows:

SECTION 1. No new awards for purchases or commitments for financial assistance shall be made under the provisions of Section 305 of the Defense Production Act of 1950, as amended [this section].

SEC. 2. Synthetic fuels projects or actions initiated by the Department of Energy shall, to the extent provided in the Supplemental Appropriations and Rescissions Act, 1980 (Public Law 96–304; 94 Stat. 880–881) [see 42 U.S.C. 5915 note], transfer to the Corporation upon a majority vote of the Board of Directors of the Corporation, and unexpended balances of the funds obligated for such projects shall be transferred to the Corporation to the extent such projects are transferred to the Corporation.

SEC. 3. The balance of the amounts not committed or not conditionally committed by the Department of Energy which were appropriated by Public Law 96–304 and Public Law 96–126 [see 42 U.S.C. 5915 note] from the Energy Security Reserve to the Department of Energy are available as provided in the Supplemental Appropriations and Rescissions Act, 1981 (Public Law 97–12; 95 Stat. 48) [see 42 U.S.C. 5915 note], to carry out the provisions of Title I of the Energy Security Act (Public Law 96–294; 94 Stat. 616 *et seq.*) [which enacted sections 2075, 2076, and 2095 to 2098 of this Appendix and section 8701 et seq. of Title 42, The Public Health and Welfare, amended sections 2062, 2091 to 2093, 2151, 2161, and 2166 of this Appendix, and enacted provisions set out as

[4] See References in Text note below.

notes under sections 2061 and 2062 of this Appendix and section 8701 of Title 42].

SEC. 4. Executive Order No. 12242 of September 30, 1980 is revoked.

SEC. 5. Notwithstanding the revocation of Executive Order No. 12242, the provisions of that Order shall continue in full force and effect with respect to any loan guarantee issued under the provisions of that Order.

RONALD REAGAN.

SECTION REFERRED TO IN OTHER SECTIONS

This section is referred to in sections 2076, 2091, 2096, 2096a, 2098, 2161 of this Appendix.

§ 2096. Synthetic fuel production subsequent to determinations respecting a national energy supply shortage of defense fuels

(a) Invocation of authorities; judicial review prohibited

(a)(1) At any time after the date of the enactment of this section [June 30, 1980], the President may, subject to paragraph (2), invoke the authorities provided under this section upon making all the following determinations and transmitting a report to the Congress regarding such determinations:

(A) a national energy supply shortage has resulted or is likely to result in a shortfall of petroleum supplies in the United States, and such shortage is expected to persist for a period of time sufficient to seriously threaten the adequacy of defense fuel supplies essential to direct defense and direct defense industrial base programs;

(B) the continued adequacy of such supplies cannot be assured and requires expedited production of synthetic fuel to provide such defense fuel supplies;

(C) the expedited production of synthetic fuel to provide such defense fuel supplies will not be accomplished in a timely manner by the United States Synthetic Fuels Corporation; and

(D) the exercise of the authorities provided under subsection (c) is necessary to provide for the expedited production of synthetic fuel to provide such defense fuel supplies.

(2)(A) Any transmittal under paragraph (1) shall contain a determination by the President regarding the extent of the anticipated shortage of petroleum supplies. If the President determines that such shortage is greater than 25 percent, the authorities invoked by the President under this section shall be effective on the date on which the report required under paragraph (1) is transmitted to the Congress.

(B) If the President determines that such shortage is less than 25 percent, the transmittal under paragraph (1) shall be made in accordance with section 307[1] [section 2097 of this Appendix] and the authorities under this section shall be effective only as provided under such section. For purposes of section 307[1] [section 2097 of this Appendix], any determination to invoke authorities under this section, notice of which is transmitted to the Congress under this subsection, shall be considered to be a synthetic fuel action.

(3) No court shall have the authority to review any determination made by the President under this subsection.

[1] See References in Text note below.

(b) Immediate Presidential action to meet national defense needs; exercise of authorities; United States Synthetic Fuels Corporation authority unaffected

(1)(A) Subject to the requirements of subsection (a), in order to encourage and expedite the development of synthetic fuel for use for national defense purposes, the President, utilizing the provisions of this Act [sections 2061 to 2171 of this Appendix] (other than sections 101(a), 101(b), 301, 302, 303, and 305 [sections 2071(a), 2071(b), 2091, 2092, 2093, and 2095 of this Appendix]), and any other applicable provision of law, shall take immediate action to achieve production of synthetic fuel to meet national defense needs.

(B) The President shall exercise the authority granted by this section—

(i) in consultation with the Secretary of Energy; and

(ii) through the Department of Defense and any other Federal department or agency designated by the President.

(2) This section shall not affect the authority of the United States Synthetic Fuels Corporation.

(c) Specific Presidential authorities; requisites, limitations, etc.

(1)(A) To assist in carrying out the objectives of this section, the President, subject to subsections (d) and (e), shall—

(i) contract for purchases of or commitments to purchase synthetic fuel for Government use for defense needs;

(ii) subject to paragraph (4), issue guarantees in accordance with the provisions of section 301 [section 2091 of this Appendix], except that the provisions of section 301(e)(1)(B) [section 2091(e)(1)(B) of this Appendix] shall not apply with respect to such guarantees;

(iii) subject to paragraph (4), make loans in accordance with the provisions of section 302 [section 2092 of this Appendix], except that the provisions of section 302(2) [section 2092(2) of this Appendix] shall not apply with respect to such loans;

(iv) have the authority to require fuel suppliers to provide synthetic fuel in any case in which the President deems it practicable and necessary to meet the national defense needs of the United States. Nothing in this paragraph shall be intended to provide authority for the President to require fuel suppliers to produce synthetic fuel if such suppliers are not already producing synthetic fuel or do not intend to produce synthetic fuel;

(v) have the authority to install additional equipment, facilities, processes, or improvements to plants, factories, and other industrial facilities owned by the Government, and to install Government-owned equipment in plants, factories, and other industrial facilities owned by private persons; and

(vi) have the authority to undertake Government synthetic fuel projects in accordance with the provisions of paragraph (2).

(B)(i) Except as provided in clause (ii), assistance authorized under this subsection may be provided only to persons who are participating in a synthetic fuel project.

(ii) For purposes of fabrication or manufacture of any component of a synthetic fuel project, assistance authorized under paragraph (1)(A)(ii) and paragraph (1)(A)(iii) may be provided to any fabricator or manufacturer of such component.

(2)(A) The Government, acting through the President, is authorized to own Government synthetic fuel projects. In any case in which the Government owns a Government synthetic fuel project, the Government shall contract for the construction and operation of such project.

(B) The authority of the Government pursuant to subparagraph (A) to own and contract for the construction and operation of any Government synthetic fuel project shall include, among other things, the authority to—

(i) subject to subparagraph (C), take delivery of synthetic fuel from such project; and

(ii) transport and store and have processed and refined such synthetic fuel.

(C) Any synthetic fuel which the Government takes delivery of from a Government synthetic fuel project shall be disposed of in accordance with subsection (g).

(D) To the maximum extent feasible, the President shall utilize the private sector for the activities associated with this paragraph.

(3)(A) Except as provided in subparagraph (B), any contract for the construction or operation of a Government synthetic fuel project shall be made by solicitation of sealed competitive bids.

(B) In any case in which no such bids are submitted to the President or the President determines that no such bids have been submitted which are acceptable to the President, the President may negotiate contracts for such construction and operation.

(4) The President may not utilize the authority under paragraph (1) to provide any loan or guarantee in accordance with the provisions of section 301 [section 2091 of this Appendix] or section 302 [section 2092 of this Appendix] in amounts which exceed the limitations established in such sections unless the President submits to the Congress notification of the proposed loan or guarantee in the manner specified under section 307[2] [section 2097 of this Appendix] and such proposed action is either approved or not disapproved by the Congress under such section. For purposes of section 307[2] [section 2097 of this Appendix], any proposal pertaining to a proposed loan or guarantee, notice of which is transmitted to the Congress under this paragraph, shall be considered to be a synthetic fuel action.

(5) Before the President may utilize any specific authority described under paragraph (1), the President shall transmit to the Congress a statement containing a certification that the determinations made by the President in the transmittal to the Congress under subsection (a)(1) are still valid at the time of the transmittal of such certification.

(6)(A) No authority contained in paragraphs (1)(A)(i) through (1)(A)(iv) may be utilized by the President unless the use of such authority has been authorized by the Congress in an Act hereinafter enacted by the Congress.

[2] See References in Text note below.

(B) The President may not utilize any authority under paragraph (1)(A)(v) or paragraph (1)(A)(vi) unless the proposed exercise of authority has been specifically authorized on a project-by-project basis in an Act hereinafter enacted by the Congress and funds have been specifically appropriated by the Congress for purposes of exercising such authority.

(d) Purchases and commitments to purchase by President; authority; limitations; advance payments prior to construction of synthetic fuel project

(1) Subject to paragraph (2), purchases and commitments to purchase under subsection (c) may be made—

(A) without regard to the limitations of existing law (other than those limitations contained in this Act [sections 2061 to 2171 of this Appendix]) regarding the procurement of goods or services by the Government; and

(B) subject to section 717(a) [section 2166(a) of this Appendix], for such quantities, on such terms and conditions (including advance payments subject to paragraph (3)), and for such periods as the President deems necessary.

(2) Purchases or commitments to purchase under subsection (c) involving higher than established ceiling prices (or if there are no established ceiling prices, currently prevailing market prices as determined by the Secretary of Energy) shall not be made unless it is determined that supplies of synthetic fuel could not be effectively increased at lower prices or on terms more favorable to the Government, or that such commitments or purchases are necessary to assure the availability to the United States of supplies overseas for use for national defense purposes.

(3) Advance payments may not be made under this section unless construction has begun on the synthetic fuel project involved or the President determines that all conditions precedent to construction have been met.

(e) Bidding and contracting procedures and requirements applicable to purchases and commitments to purchase

(1) Except as provided in paragraph (2), any purchase or commitment to purchase synthetic fuel under subsection (c) shall be made by solicitation of sealed competitive bids.

(2) In any case in which no such bids are submitted to the President or the President determines that no such bids which have been submitted to the President are acceptable, the President may negotiate contracts for such purchases and commitments to purchase.

(3) Any contract for such purchases or commitments to purchase shall provide that the President has the right to refuse delivery of the synthetic fuel involved and to pay the person involved an amount equal to the amount by which the price for such synthetic fuel, as specified in the contract involved, exceeds the market price, as determined by the Secretary of Energy, for such synthetic fuel on the delivery date specified in such contract.

(4)(A) With respect to any person, including any other person who is substantially controlled by such person (as determined by the Secretary of Energy), the President, subject to subparagraph (B), may not award contracts for the purchase of or commitment to purchase more than 100,000 barrels per day crude oil equivalent of synthetic fuel.

(B) With respect to any person, including any other person who is substantially controlled by such person (as determined by the Secretary of Energy), the President may not award any contract for the purchase of or commitment to purchase more than 75,000 barrels per day crude oil equivalent of synthetic fuel unless the President submits to the Congress notification of such proposed contract or commitment in the manner specified under section 307[3] [section 2097 of this Appendix] and such proposed action is either approved or not disapproved by the Congress under such section. For purposes of section 307[3] [section 2097 of this Appendix], any proposal pertaining to such a proposed contract or commitment, notice of which is transmitted to the Congress under this subparagraph, shall be considered to be a synthetic fuel action.

(5) A contract for the purchase of or commitment to purchase synthetic fuel may be entered into only for synthetic fuel which is produced in a synthetic fuel project which is located in the United States.

(6) Each contract entered into under this section for the purchase of or commitment to purchase synthetic fuel shall provide that all parties to such contract agree to review and to possibly renegotiate such contract within 10 years after the date of the initial production at the synthetic fuel project involved. At the time of such review, the President shall determine the need for continued financial assistance pursuant to such contract.

(7) In any case in which the President, under the provisions of this section, accepts delivery of any synthetic fuel, such synthetic fuel may be used by an appropriate Federal agency. Such Federal agency shall pay for such synthetic fuel the prevailing market price for the product which such synthetic fuel is replacing, as determined by the Secretary of Energy, from sums appropriated to such Federal agency for the purchase of fuel, and the President shall pay, from sums appropriated for such purpose, an amount equal to the amount by which the contract price for such synthetic fuel as specified in the contract involved exceeds such prevailing market price.

(8) In considering any proposed contract under this section, the President shall take into account the socioeconomic impacts on communities which would be affected by any new or expanded facilities required for the production of the synthetic fuel under such contract.

(f) Scope of Presidential procurement power

The procurement power granted to the President under this section shall include the power to transport and store and have processed and refined any product procured under this section.

(g) Determinations respecting purchase and sale of synthetic fuel

(1) No authority contained in this section may be exercised to acquire any amount of synthetic fuel unless the President determines that such synthetic fuel is needed to meet national defense needs and that it is not anticipated that such synthetic fuel will be resold by the Government.

(2) In any case in which synthetic fuel is acquired by the Government under this section, such synthetic fuel is no longer needed to meet national defense needs, and such synthetic fuel is not accepted by a Federal agency pursuant to subsection (e)(7), the President shall offer such synthetic fuel to the Secretary of Energy for purposes of meeting the storage requirements of the Strategic Petroleum Reserve.

(3) Any synthetic fuel which is acquired by the Government under this section and which is not used by the Government or accepted by the Secretary of Energy pursuant to paragraph (2), shall be sold in accordance with applicable Federal law.

(h) Maximum liability of Federal Government under contracts; budgetary certifications

(1) Any contract under this section, including any amendment or other modification of such contract, shall, subject to the availability of unencumbered appropriations in advance, specify in dollars the maximum liability of the Federal Government under such contract as determined in accordance with paragraph (2).

(2) For the purpose of determining the maximum liability under any contract under paragraph (1)—

(A) loans shall be valued at the initial face value of the loan;

(B) guarantees shall be valued at the initial face value of such guarantee (including any amount of interest which is guaranteed under such guarantee);

(C) purchase agreements shall be valued as of the date of each such contract based upon the President's estimate of the maximum liability under such contract;

(D) contracts for activities under subsection (c)(1)(A)(v) shall be valued at the initial face value of such contract;

(E) Government synthetic fuel projects pursuant to subsection (c)(1)(A)(vi) shall be valued at the current estimated cost to the Government, as determined annually by the President; and

(F) any increase in the liability of the Government pursuant to any amendment or other modification to a contract for a loan, guarantee, purchase agreement, contract for activities under subsection (c)(1)(A)(v), or Government synthetic fuel project pursuant to subsection (c)(1)(A)(vi) shall be valued in accordance with the applicable preceding subparagraph.

(3) If more than one form of assistance is provided under this section to any synthetic fuel project then the maximum liability under such contract for purposes of paragraphs (1) and (2) shall be valued at the maximum potential exposure on such project at any time during the life of such project.

(4) Any such contract shall be accompanied by a certification by the Director of the Office of Management and Budget that the necessary appropriations have been made for the purpose of

[3] See References in Text note below.

such contract and are available. The remaining available and unencumbered appropriations shall equal the total aggregate appropriations less the aggregate maximum liability of the Federal Government under all contracts pursuant to this section.

(5) Any commitment made under this section which is nullified or voided for any reason shall not be considered in the aggregate maximum liability for the purposes of paragraph (4).

(i) Loan, guarantee, or purchase not to be deemed a major Federal action significantly affecting the quality of the human environment

For purposes of section 102(2)(C) of the National Environmental Policy Act of 1969 (42 U.S.C. 4332(2)(C)), no action in providing any loan, guarantee, or purchase agreement under this section, shall be deemed to be a major Federal action significantly affecting the quality of the human environment.

(j) Labor standards; applicability, certifications, etc.

All laborers and mechanics employed for the construction, repair, or alteration of any synthetic fuel project funded, in whole or in part, by a guarantee or loan entered into pursuant to this section shall be paid wages at rates not less than those prevailing on projects of a similar character in the locality as determined by the Secretary of Labor in accordance with the Act entitled "An Act relating to the rate of wages for laborers and mechanics employed on public buildings of the United States and the District of Columbia by contractors and subcontractors and for other purposes", approved March 3, 1931 (40 U.S.C. 276a et seq.) and commonly known as the Davis-Bacon Act. Guaranteeing agencies shall not extend guarantees and the President shall not make loans for the construction, repair or alteration of any synthetic fuel project unless a certification is provided to the agency or the President, as the case may be, prior to the commencement of construction or at the time of filing an application for a loan or guarantee, if construction has already commenced, that these labor standards will be maintained at the synthetic fuel project. With respect to the labor standards specified in this subsection, the Secretary of Labor shall have the authority and functions set forth in Reorganization Plan Numbered 14 of 1950 and section 276(c)[4] of title 40 [40 U.S.C. 276c].

(k) Other jurisdictional, etc., authorities relating to water resources and rights unaffected

(1) Nothing in this section shall—

(A) affect the jurisdiction of the States and the United States over waters of any stream or over any ground water resource;

(B) alter, amend, repeal, interpret, modify, or be in conflict with any interstate compact made by any States; or

(C) confer upon any non-Federal entity the ability to exercise any Federal right to the waters of any stream or to any ground water resource.

(2) No synthetic fuel project constructed pursuant to the authorities of this section shall be considered to be a Federal project for purposes of the application for or assignment of water rights.

(*l*) Renewals and extensions of contracts

Renewals and extensions of contracts entered into under this section shall be made only to the extent that Congress has specifically appropriated funds for such renewals and extensions, unless the President certifies that the determinations under section 306(a)(1) [subsec. (a)(1) of this section] remain in effect for purposes of the use of such authority.

(Sept. 8, 1950, ch. 932, title III, § 306, as added Pub. L. 96–294, title I, § 104(e), June 30, 1980, 94 Stat. 623.)

REFERENCES IN TEXT

Section 307, referred to in subsecs. (a)(2)(B), (c)(4), and (e)(4)(B), is classified to section 2097 of this Appendix and was amended by Pub. L. 102–558, title I, § 151, Oct. 28, 1992, 106 Stat. 4218, and as so amended, provisions relating to congressional approval of synthetic fuel action by the President were struck out.

Act approved March 3, 1931 (40 U.S.C. 276a et seq.) and commonly known as the Davis-Bacon Act, referred to in subsec. (j), is act Mar. 3, 1931, ch. 411, 46 Stat. 1494, as amended, which is classified generally to sections 276a to 276a–5 of Title 40, Public Buildings, Property, and Works. For complete classification of this Act to the Code, see Short Title note set out under section 276a of Title 40 and Tables.

Reorganization Plan Numbered 14 of 1950, referred to in subsec. (j), is set out in the Appendix to Title 5, Government Organization and Employees.

Section 276(c) of title 40, referred to in subsec. (j), was repealed by Pub. L. 86–249, § 17(13) to (15), Sept. 9, 1959, 73 Stat. 485. Reference should probably be to section 276c of Title 40, Public Buildings, Property, and Works.

EFFECTIVE DATE

Section effective June 30, 1980, see section 107 of Pub. L. 96–294, set out as an Effective Date of 1980 Amendment note under section 2062 of this Appendix.

TERMINATION DATE

Termination of section, see section 2166(a) of this Appendix.

TERMINATION OF UNITED STATES SYNTHETIC FUELS CORPORATION

United States Synthetic Fuels Corporation terminated by Pub. L. 99–272, title VII, § 7403(b), Apr. 7, 1986, 100 Stat. 144, set out as a note under section 8791 of Title 42, The Public Health and Welfare.

SECTION REFERRED TO IN OTHER SECTIONS

This section is referred to in sections 2076, 2091, 2095, 2096a, 2098, 2161 of this Appendix.

§ 2096a. Annual reports on synthetic fuel production

Beginning one year after the effective date of this part [June 30, 1980], and annually thereafter, the President shall submit a report to the Congress on actions taken under sections 305 and 306 of the Defense Production Act of 1950 [sections 2095 and 2096 of this Appendix].

(Pub. L. 96–294, title I, § 106, June 30, 1980, 94 Stat. 633.)

CODIFICATION

Section was enacted as part of the Energy Security Act, and not as part of the Defense Production Act of

[4] See References in Text note below.

1950 which comprises sections 2061 to 2171 of this Appendix.

EFFECTIVE DATE

Section effective June 30, 1980, see section 107 of Pub. L. 96–294, set out as an Effective Date of 1980 Amendment note under section 2062 of this Appendix.

§ 2097. Synthetic fuel action

(a) "Synthetic fuel action" defined

For purposes of this section, the term "synthetic fuel action" means any matter required to be transmitted, or submitted to the Congress in accordance with the procedures of this section.

(b) Submission to Congress by President

The President shall transmit any synthetic fuel action (bearing an identification number) to both Houses of the Congress on the same day.

(Sept. 8, 1950, ch. 932, title III, § 307, as added Pub. L. 96–294, title I, § 104(e), June 30, 1980, 94 Stat. 628; amended Pub. L. 102–558, title I, § 151, Oct. 28, 1992, 106 Stat. 4218.)

AMENDMENTS

1992—Subsec. (b). Pub. L. 102–558, § 151(1), struck out after first sentence "If both Houses are not in session on the day on which any synthetic fuel action is received by the appropriate officers of each House, such synthetic fuel action shall be deemed to have been received on the first succeeding day on which both Houses are in session."

Subsecs. (c) to (g). Pub. L. 102–558, § 151(2), struck out subsec. (c) relating to effective date of synthetic fuel action, resolution of disfavor, and earlier effective date; subsec. (d) relating to congressional sessions for purposes of effective date; subsec. (e) relating to later effective date of synthetic fuel action; subsec. (f) relating to construction and applicability of procedures with rules of each House; and subsec. (g) relating to procedures applicable to resolutions of approval and disapproval.

EFFECTIVE DATE OF 1992 AMENDMENT

Amendment by Pub. L. 102–558 deemed to have become effective Mar. 1, 1992, see section 304 of Pub. L. 102–558, set out as a note under section 2062 of this Appendix.

EFFECTIVE DATE

Section effective June 30, 1980, see section 107 of Pub. L. 96–294, set out as an Effective Date of 1980 Amendment note under section 2062 of this Appendix.

TERMINATION DATE

Termination of section, see section 2166(a) of this Appendix.

SECTION REFERRED TO IN OTHER SECTIONS

This section is referred to in sections 2095, 2096 of this Appendix.

§ 2098. Definitions

(a) For purposes of this Act [sections 2061 to 2171 of this Appendix], the term "Government synthetic fuel project" means a synthetic fuel project undertaken in accordance with the provisions of section 306(c) [section 2096(c) of this Appendix].

(b)(1)(A) For purposes of this Act [sections 2061 to 2171 of this Appendix], the term "synthetic fuel" means any solid, liquid, or gas, or combination thereof, which can be used as a substitute for petroleum or natural gas (or any derivatives thereof, including chemical feedstocks) and which is produced by chemical or physical transformation (other than washing, coking, or desulfurizing) of domestic sources of—

(i) coal, including lignite and peat;

(ii) shale;

(iii) tar sands, including those heavy oil resources where—

(I) the cost and the technical and economic risks make extraction and processing of a heavy oil resource uneconomical under applicable pricing and tax policies; and

(II) the costs and risks are comparable to those associated with shale, coal, and tar sand resources (other than heavy oil) qualifying for assistance under section 305 [section 2095 of this Appendix] or section 306 [section 2096 of this Appendix]; and

(iv) water, as a source of hydrogen only through electrolysis.

(B) Such term includes mixtures of coal and combustible liquids, including petroleum.

(C) Such term does not include solids, liquids, or gases, or combinations thereof, derived from biomass, which includes timber, animal and timber waste, municipal and industrial waste, sewage, sludge, oceanic and terrestrial plants, and other organic matter.

(2)(A) For purposes of this Act [sections 2061 to 2171 of this Appendix], the term "synthetic fuel project" means any facility using an integrated process or processes at a specific geographic location in the United States for the purpose of commercial production of synthetic fuel. The project may include only—

(i) the facility, including the equipment, plant, machinery, supplies, and other materials associated with the facility, which converts the domestic resource to synthetic fuel;

(ii) the land and mineral rights required directly for use in connection with the facilities for the production of synthetic fuels;

(iii) any facility or equipment to be used in the extraction of a mineral for use directly and exclusively in such conversion;

(I) which—

(aa) is co-located with the conversion facility or is located in the immediate vicinity of the conversion facility; or

(bb) if not co-located or located in the immediate vicinity, is incidental to the project (except in the event of a coal mine where no other reasonable source of coal is available to the project); and

(II) which is necessary to the project; and

(iv) any transportation facility, electric powerplant, electric transmission line or other facility—

(I) which is for the exclusive use of the project;

(II) which is incidental to the project; and

(III) which is necessary to the project, except that transportation facilities used to transport synthetic fuel away from the project shall be used exclusively to transport synthetic fuel to a storage facility or pipeline connecting to an existing pipeline or processing facility or area within close proximity of the project.

(B)(i) Such term may also include a project which will result in the replacement of a significant amount of oil and is—

(I) used solely for the production of a mixture of coal and combustible liquids, including petroleum, for direct use as a fuel, but shall not include—

(aa) any mineral right; or

(bb) any facility or equipment for extraction of any mineral;

(II) used solely for the commercial production of hydrogen from water through electrolysis; and

(III) a magnetohydrodynamic topping cycle used solely for the commercial production of electricity.

(ii) Such a synthetic fuel project using magnetohydrodynamic technology shall only be eligible for guarantees under section 305 [section 2095 of this Appendix] or section 306 [section 2096 of this Appendix].

(C) For purposes of this paragraph—

(i) the term "exclusive" means for the sole use of the project, except that an incidental by-product might be used for other purposes;

(ii) the term "incidental" means a relatively small portion of the total project cost; and

(iii) the term "necessary" means an integrated part of the project taking into account considerations of economy and efficiency of operation.

(c) For purposes of section 305 [section 2095 of this Appendix] and section 306 [section 2096 of this Appendix], the term "United States" means the several States, the District of Columbia, the Commonwealth of Puerto Rico, Guam, the Virgin Islands, the Northern Mariana Islands, the Trust Territory of the Pacific Islands, and any other territory or possession of the United States.

(Sept. 8, 1950, ch. 932, title III, §308, as added Pub. L. 96–294, title I, §104(e), June 30, 1980, 94 Stat. 631.)

EFFECTIVE DATE

Section effective June 30, 1980, see section 107 of Pub. L. 96–294, set out as an Effective Date of 1980 Amendment note under section 2062 of this Appendix.

TERMINATION DATE

Termination of section, see section 2166(a) of this Appendix.

TERMINATION OF TRUST TERRITORY OF THE PACIFIC ISLANDS

For termination of Trust Territory of the Pacific Islands, see note set out preceding section 1681 of Title 48, Territories and Insular Possessions.

§2099. Annual report on impact of offsets

(a) Annual report on impact of offsets

(1) Report required

Not later than 18 months after April 17, 1984, and annually thereafter, the President shall submit to the Committee on Banking, Finance and Urban Affairs of the House of Representatives and the Committee on Banking, Housing, and Urban Affairs of the Senate, a detailed report on the impact of offsets on the defense preparedness, industrial competitiveness, employment, and trade of the United States.

(2) Duties of the Secretary of Commerce

The Secretary of Commerce (hereafter in this subsection referred to as "the Secretary") shall—

(A) prepare the report required by paragraph (1);

(B) consult with the Secretary of Defense, the Secretary of the Treasury, the Secretary of State, and the United States Trade Representative in connection with the preparation of such report; and

(C) function as the President's Executive Agent for carrying out this section.

(b) Interagency studies and related data

(1) Purpose of report

Each report required under subsection (a) shall identify the cumulative effects of offset agreements on—

(A) the full range of domestic defense productive capability (with special attention paid to the firms serving as lower-tier subcontractors or suppliers); and

(B) the domestic defense technology base as a consequence of the technology transfers associated with such offset agreements.

(2) Use of data

Data developed or compiled by any agency while conducting any interagency study or other independent study or analysis shall be made available to the Secretary to facilitate the execution of the Secretary's responsibilities with respect to trade offset and countertrade policy development.

(c) Notice of offset agreements

(1) In general

If a United States firm enters into a contract for the sale of a weapon system or defense-related item to a foreign country or foreign firm and such contract is subject to an offset agreement exceeding $5,000,000 in value, such firm shall furnish to the official designated in the regulations promulgated pursuant to paragraph (2) information concerning such sale.

(2) Regulations

The information to be furnished under paragraph (1) shall be prescribed in regulations promulgated by the Secretary. Such regulations shall provide protection from public disclosure for such information, unless public disclosure is subsequently specifically authorized by the firm furnishing the information.

(d) Contents of report

(1) In general

Each report under subsection (a) shall include—

(A) a net assessment of the elements of the industrial base and technology base covered by the report;

(B) recommendations for appropriate remedial action under the authority of this Act [sections 2061 to 2171 of this Appendix], or other law or regulations;

(C) a summary of the findings and recommendations of any interagency studies conducted during the reporting period under subsection (b);

(D) a summary of offset arrangements concluded during the reporting period for which information has been furnished pursuant to subsection (c); and

(E) a summary and analysis of any bilateral and multilateral negotiations relating to the use of offsets completed during the reporting period.

(2) Alternative findings or recommendations

Each report required under this section shall include any alternative findings or recommendations offered by any departmental Secretary, agency head, or the United States Trade Representative to the Secretary.

(e) Utilization of annual report in negotiations

The findings and recommendations of the reports required by subsection (a), and any interagency reports and analyses shall be considered by representatives of the United States during bilateral and multilateral negotiations to minimize the adverse effects of offsets.

(Sept. 8, 1950, ch. 932, title III, §309, as added Pub. L. 98–265, §6, Apr. 17, 1984, 98 Stat. 152; amended Pub. L. 99–441, §4, Oct. 3, 1986, 100 Stat. 1117; Pub. L. 102–558, title I, §124, Oct. 28, 1992, 106 Stat. 4207.)

AMENDMENTS

1992—Subsec. (a). Pub. L. 102–558, §124(1), inserted heading, designated existing provisions as par. (1), struck after first sentence "Each such report also shall include a discussion of bilateral and multilateral negotiations on offsets in international procurement and provide information on the types, terms, and magnitude of the offsets.", and added par. (2).

Subsec. (b). Pub. L. 102–558, §124(2), amended subsec. (b) generally, substituting present provisions for provisions delineating the scope and contents of reports based on interagency studies.

Subsecs. (c) to (e). Pub. L. 102–558, §124(3), added subsecs. (c) to (e).

1986—Pub. L. 99–441 designated existing provisions as subsec. (a), inserted subsec. heading, substituted "a detailed report on" for "a report on", and added subsec. (b).

CHANGE OF NAME

Committee on Banking, Finance and Urban Affairs of House of Representatives treated as referring to Committee on Banking and Financial Services of House of Representatives by section 1(a) of Pub. L. 104–14, set out as a note preceding section 21 of Title 2, The Congress. Committee on Banking and Financial Services of House of Representatives abolished and replaced by Committee on Financial Services of House of Representatives, and jurisdiction over matters relating to securities and exchanges and insurance generally transferred from Committee on Energy and Commerce of House of Representatives by House Resolution No. 5, One Hundred Seventh Congress, Jan. 3, 2001.

EFFECTIVE DATE OF 1992 AMENDMENT

Amendment by Pub. L. 102–558 deemed to have become effective Mar. 1, 1992, see section 304 of Pub. L. 102–558, set out as a note under section 2062 of this Appendix.

TERMINATION DATE

Termination of section, see section 2166(a) of this Appendix.

DELEGATION OF FUNCTIONS

Authority of President under this section with respect to offsets delegated to Secretary of Commerce by section 401 of Ex. Ord. No. 12919, June 3, 1994, 59 F.R. 29529, set out as a note under section 2153 of this Appendix.

DEFENSE OFFSETS DISCLOSURE

Pub. L. 106–113, div. B, §1000(a)(7) [div. B, title XII, subtitle D], Nov. 29, 1999, 113 Stat. 1536, 1501A–500, provided that:

"SEC. 1241. SHORT TITLE.

"This subtitle may be cited as the 'Defense Offsets Disclosure Act of 1999'.

"SEC. 1242. FINDINGS AND DECLARATION OF POLICY.

"(a) FINDINGS.—Congress makes the following findings:

"(1) A fair business environment is necessary to advance international trade, economic stability, and development worldwide, is beneficial for American workers and businesses, and is in the United States national interest.

"(2) In some cases, mandated offset requirements can cause economic distortions in international defense trade and undermine fairness and competitiveness, and may cause particular harm to small- and medium-sized businesses.

"(3) The use of offsets may lead to increasing dependence on foreign suppliers for the production of United States weapons systems.

"(4) The offset demands required by some purchasing countries, including some close allies of the United States, equal or exceed the value of the base contract they are intended to offset, mitigating much of the potential economic benefit of the exports.

"(5) Offset demands often unduly distort the prices of defense contracts.

"(6) In some cases, United States contractors are required to provide indirect offsets which can negatively impact nondefense industrial sectors.

"(7) Unilateral efforts by the United States to prohibit offsets may be impractical in the current era of globalization and would severely hinder the competitiveness of the United States defense industry in the global market.

"(8) The development of global standards to manage and restrict demands for offsets would enhance United States efforts to mitigate the negative impact of offsets.

"(b) DECLARATION OF POLICY.—It is the policy of the United States to monitor the use of offsets in international defense trade, to promote fairness in such trade, and to ensure that foreign participation in the production of United States weapons systems does not harm the economy of the United States.

"SEC. 1243. DEFINITIONS.

"In this subtitle:

"(1) APPROPRIATE CONGRESSIONAL COMMITTEES.—The term 'appropriate congressional committees' means—

"(A) the Committee on Foreign Relations of the Senate; and

"(B) the Committee on International Relations of the House of Representatives.

"(2) G–8.—The term 'G–8' means the group consisting of France, Germany, Japan, the United Kingdom, the United States, Canada, Italy, and Russia established to facilitate economic cooperation among the eight major economic powers.

"(3) OFFSET.—The term 'offset' means the entire range of industrial and commercial benefits provided to foreign governments as an inducement or condition to purchase military goods or services, including benefits such as coproduction, licensed production, subcontracting, technology transfer, in-country procurement, marketing and financial assistance, and joint ventures.

"(4) TRANSATLANTIC ECONOMIC PARTNERSHIP.—The term 'Transatlantic Economic Partnership' means the joint commitment made by the United States and the European Union to reinforce their close relationship through an initiative involving the intensification and extension of multilateral and bilateral cooperation and common actions in the areas of trade and investment.

"(5) WASSENAAR ARRANGEMENT.—The term 'Wassenaar Arrangement' means the multilateral export control regime in which the United States participates that seeks to promote transparency and responsibility with regard to transfers of conventional armaments and sensitive dual-use items.

"(6) WORLD TRADE ORGANIZATION.—The term 'World Trade Organization' means the organization established pursuant to the WTO Agreement.

"(7) WTO AGREEMENT.—The term 'WTO Agreement' means the Agreement Establishing the World Trade Organization entered into on April 15, 1994.

"SEC. 1244. SENSE OF CONGRESS.

"It is the sense of Congress that—

"(1) the executive branch should pursue efforts to address trade fairness by establishing reasonable, business-friendly standards for the use of offsets in international business transactions between the United States and its trading partners and competitors;

"(2) the Secretary of Defense, the Secretary of State, the Secretary of Commerce, and the United States Trade Representative, or their designees, should raise with other industrialized nations at every suitable venue the need for transparency and reasonable standards to govern the role of offsets in international defense trade;

"(3) the United States Government should enter into discussions regarding the establishment of multilateral standards for the use of offsets in international defense trade through the appropriate multilateral fora, including such organizations as the Transatlantic Economic Partnership, the Wassenaar Arrangement, the G–8, and the World Trade Organization; and

"(4) the United States Government, in entering into the discussions described in paragraph (3), should take into account the distortions produced by the provision of other benefits and subsidies, such as export financing, by various countries to support defense trade.

"SEC. 1245. REPORTING OF OFFSET AGREEMENTS.

"[Amended section 2776 of title 22.]

"SEC. 1246. EXPANDED PROHIBITION ON INCENTIVE PAYMENTS.

"[Amended section 2779a of title 22.]

"SEC. 1247. ESTABLISHMENT OF REVIEW COMMISSION.

"(a) IN GENERAL.—There is established a National Commission on the Use of Offsets in Defense Trade (in this section referred to as the 'Commission') to address all aspects of the use of offsets in international defense trade.

"(b) COMMISSION MEMBERSHIP.—Not later than 120 days after the date of enactment of this Act [Nov. 29, 1999], the President, with the concurrence of the Majority and Minority Leaders of the Senate and the Speaker and Minority Leader of the House of Representatives, shall appoint 11 individuals to serve as members of the Commission. Commission membership shall include—

"(1) representatives from the private sector, including—

"(A) one each from—

"(i) a labor organization,

"(ii) a United States defense manufacturing company dependent on foreign sales,

"(iii) a United States company dependent on foreign sales that is not a defense manufacturer, and

"(iv) a United States company that specializes in international investment, and

"(B) two members from academia with widely recognized expertise in international economics; and

"(2) five members from the executive branch, including a member from—

"(A) the Office of Management and Budget,

"(B) the Department of Commerce,

"(C) the Department of Defense,

"(D) the Department of State, and

"(E) the Department of Labor.

The member designated from the Office of Management and Budget shall serve as Chairperson of the Commission. The President shall ensure that the Commission is nonpartisan and that the full range of perspectives on the subject of offsets in the defense industry is adequately represented.

"(c) DUTIES.—The Commission shall be responsible for reviewing and reporting on—

"(1) the full range of current practices by foreign governments in requiring offsets in purchasing agreements and the extent and nature of offsets offered by United States and foreign defense industry contractors;

"(2) the impact of the use of offsets on defense subcontractors and nondefense industrial sectors affected by indirect offsets; and

"(3) the role of offsets, both direct and indirect, on domestic industry stability, United States trade competitiveness and national security.

"(d) COMMISSION REPORT.—Not later than 12 months after the Commission is established, the Commission shall submit a report to the appropriate congressional committees. In addition to the items described under subsection (c), the report shall include—

"(1) an analysis of—

"(A) the collateral impact of offsets on industry sectors that may be different than those of the contractor providing the offsets, including estimates of contracts and jobs lost as well as an assessment of damage to industrial sectors;

"(B) the role of offsets with respect to competitiveness of the United States defense industry in international trade and the potential damage to the ability of United States contractors to compete if offsets were prohibited or limited; and

"(C) the impact on United States national security, and upon United States nonproliferation objectives, of the use of coproduction, subcontracting, and technology transfer with foreign governments or companies that results from fulfilling offset requirements, with particular emphasis on the question of dependency upon foreign nations for the supply of critical components or technology;

"(2) proposals for unilateral, bilateral, or multilateral measures aimed at reducing any detrimental effects of offsets; and

"(3) an identification of the appropriate executive branch agencies to be responsible for monitoring the use of offsets in international defense trade.

"(e) PERIOD OF APPOINTMENT; VACANCIES.—Members shall be appointed for the life of the Commission. Any vacancy in the Commission shall not affect its powers, but shall be filled in the same manner as the original appointment.

"(f) INITIAL MEETING.—Not later than 30 days after the date on which all members of the Commission have been appointed, the Commission shall hold its first meeting.

"(g) MEETINGS.—The Commission shall meet at the call of the Chairman.

"(h) COMMISSION PERSONNEL MATTERS.—

"(1) COMPENSATION OF MEMBERS.—Each member of the Commission who is not an officer or employee of the Federal Government shall be compensated at a rate equal to the daily equivalent of the annual rate of basic pay prescribed for level IV of the Executive Schedule under section 5315 of title 5, United States Code, for each day (including travel time) during which such member is engaged in the performance of the duties of the Commission. All members of the Commission who are officers or employees of the United States shall serve without compensation in addition to that received for their services as officers or employees of the United States.

"(2) TRAVEL EXPENSES.—The members of the Commission shall be allowed travel expenses, including per diem in lieu of subsistence, at rates authorized for employees of agencies under subchapter I of chapter 57 of title 5, United States Code, while away from their homes or regular places of business in the performance of services for the Commission.

"(3) STAFF.—

"(A) IN GENERAL.—The Chairman of the Commission may, without regard to the civil service laws and regulations, appoint and terminate an executive director and such other additional personnel as may be necessary to enable the Commission to perform its duties. The employment of an executive director shall be subject to confirmation by the Commission.

"(B) COMPENSATION.—The Chairman of the Commission may fix the compensation of the executive director and other personnel without regard to the provisions of chapter 51 and subchapter III of chapter 53 of title 5, United States Code, relating to classification of positions and General Schedule pay rates, except that the rate of pay for the executive director and other personnel may not exceed the rate payable for level V of the Executive Schedule under section 5316 of such title.

"(4) DETAIL OF GOVERNMENT EMPLOYEES.—Any Federal Government employee may be detailed to the Commission without reimbursement, and such detail shall be without interruption or loss of civil service status or privilege.

"(5) PROCUREMENT OF TEMPORARY AND INTERMITTENT SERVICES.—The Chairman of the Commission may procure temporary and intermittent services under section 3109(b) of title 5, United States Code, at rates for individuals which do not exceed the daily equivalent of the annual rate of basic pay prescribed for level V of the Executive Schedule under section 5316 of such title.

"(i) TERMINATION.—The Commission shall terminate 30 days after the transmission of the report from the President as mandated in section 1248(b).

"SEC. 1248. MULTILATERAL STRATEGY TO ADDRESS OFFSETS.

"(a) IN GENERAL.—The President shall initiate a review to determine the feasibility of establishing, and the most effective means of negotiating, a multilateral treaty on standards for the use of offsets in international defense trade, with a goal of limiting all offset transactions that are considered injurious to the economy of the United States.

"(b) REPORT REQUIRED.—Not later than 90 days after the date on which the Commission submits the report required under section 1247(d), the President shall submit to the appropriate congressional committees a report containing the President's determination pursuant to subsection (a), and, if the President determines a multilateral treaty is feasible or desirable, a strategy for United States negotiation of such a treaty. One year after the date the report is submitted under the preceding sentence, and annually thereafter for 5 years, the President shall submit to the appropriate congressional committees a report detailing the progress toward reaching such a treaty.

"(c) REQUIRED INFORMATION.—The report required by subsection (b) shall include—

"(1) a description of the United States efforts to pursue multilateral negotiations on standards for the use of offsets in international defense trade;

"(2) an evaluation of existing multilateral fora as appropriate venues for establishing such negotiations;

"(3) a description on a country-by-country basis of any United States efforts to engage in negotiations to establish bilateral treaties or agreements with respect to the use of offsets in international defense trade; and

"(4) an evaluation on a country-by-country basis of any foreign government efforts to address the use of offsets in international defense trade.

"(d) COMPTROLLER GENERAL REVIEW.—The Comptroller General of the United States shall monitor and periodically report to Congress on the progress in reaching a multilateral treaty."

DECLARATION OF OFFSET POLICY

Section 123 of Pub. L. 102–558 provided that:

"(a) IN GENERAL.—Recognizing that certain offsets for military exports are economically inefficient and market distorting, and mindful of the need to minimize the adverse effects of offsets in military exports while ensuring that the ability of United States firms to compete for military export sales is not undermined, it is the policy of the Congress that—

"(1) no agency of the United States Government shall encourage, enter directly into, or commit United States firms to any offset arrangement in connection with the sale of defense goods or services to foreign governments;

"(2) United States Government funds shall not be used to finance offsets in security assistance transactions, except in accordance with policies and procedures that were in existence on March 1, 1992;

"(3) nothing in this section shall prevent agencies of the United States Government from fulfilling obligations incurred through international agreements entered into before March 1, 1992; and

"(4) the decision whether to engage in offsets, and the responsibility for negotiating and implementing offset arrangements, reside with the companies involved.

"(b) PRESIDENTIAL APPROVAL OF EXCEPTIONS.—It is the policy of the Congress that the President may approve an exception to the policy stated in subsection (a) after receiving the recommendation of the National Security Council.

"(c) CONSULTATION.—It is the policy of the Congress that the President shall designate the Secretary of Defense to lead, in coordination with the Secretary of State, an interagency team to consult with foreign nations on limiting the adverse effects of offsets in defense procurement. The President shall transmit an annual report on the results of these consultations to the Congress as part of the report required under section 309(a) of the Defense Production Act of 1950 [50 App. U.S.C. 2099(a)]."

EX. ORD. NO. 13177. NATIONAL COMMISSION ON THE USE OF OFFSETS IN DEFENSE TRADE AND PRESIDENT'S COUNCIL ON THE USE OF OFFSETS IN COMMERCIAL TRADE

Ex. Ord. No. 13177, Dec. 4, 2000, 65 F.R. 76558, provided:

By the authority vested in the President by the Constitution and the laws of the United States of America, including Public Law 106–113 [see Tables for classification] and the Federal Advisory Committee Act, as amended (5 U.S.C. App.), and in order to implement section 1247 of Public Law 106–113 (113 Stat. 1501A–502) [set out in a note above] and to create a parallel "President's Council on the Use of Offsets in Commercial Trade," it is hereby ordered as follows:

SECTION 1. *Membership.* Pursuant to Public Law 106–113, the "National Commission on the Use of Offsets in Defense Trade" (Commission) comprises 11 members appointed by the President with the concurrence of the Majority and Minority Leaders of the Senate and the Speaker and the Minority Leader of the House of Representatives. The Commission membership includes: (a) representatives from the private sector, including one each from (i) a labor organization, (ii) a United States defense manufacturing company dependent on foreign sales, (iii) a United States company dependent on foreign sales that is not a defense manufacturer, and (iv) a United States company that specializes in international investment; (b) two members from academia with widely recognized expertise in international economics; and (c) five members from the executive branch, including a member from the: (i) Office of Management and Budget, (ii) Department of Commerce, (iii) Department of Defense, (iv) Department of State, and (v) Department of Labor. The member from the Office of Management and Budget will serve as Chairperson of the Commission and will appoint, and fix the compensation of, the Executive Director of the Commission.

SEC. 2. *Duties.* The Commission will be responsible for reviewing and reporting on: (a) current practices by foreign governments in requiring offsets in purchasing agreements and the extent and nature of offsets offered by United States and foreign defense industry contractors; (b) the impact of the use of offsets on defense subcontractors and nondefense industrial sectors affected by indirect offsets; and (c) the role of offsets, both direct and indirect, on domestic industry stability, United States trade competitiveness, and national security.

SEC. 3. *Commission Report.* Not later than 12 months after the Commission is established, it will report to the appropriate congressional committees. In addition to the items described in section 2 of this order, the report will include: (a) an analysis of (i) the collateral impact of offsets on industry sectors that may be different than those of the contractor paying offsets, including estimates of contracts and jobs lost as well as an assessment of damage to industrial sectors; (ii) the role of offsets with respect to competitiveness of the United States defense industry in international trade and the potential damage to the ability of United States contractors to compete if offsets were prohibited or limited; and (iii) the impact on United States national security, and upon United States nonproliferation objectives, of the use of co-production, subcontracting, and technology transfer with foreign governments or companies, that results from fulfilling offset requirements, with particular emphasis on the question of dependency upon foreign nations for the supply of critical components or technology; (b) proposals for unilateral, bilateral, or multilateral measures aimed at reducing any detrimental effects of offsets; and (c) an identification of the appropriate executive branch agencies to be responsible for monitoring the use of offsets in international defense trade.

SEC. 4. *Administration, Compensation, and Termination.* (a) The Department of Defense will provide administrative support and funding for the Commission and Federal Government employees may be detailed to the Commission without reimbursement.

(b) Members of the Commission who are not officers or employees of the Federal Government will be compensated at a rate of basic pay prescribed for level IV of the Executive Schedule under section 5315 of title 5, United States Code, for each day (including travel time) during which such member is engaged in performance of the duties of the Commission. Members of the Commission who are officers or employees of the Federal Government will serve without compensation in addition to that received for their services as officers or employees of the Federal Government.

(c) Members of the Commission will be allowed travel expenses, including per diem in lieu of subsistence, under subchapter 1 of chapter 57 of title 5, United States Code, while on business in the performance of services for the Commission.

(d) The Commission will terminate 30 days after transmitting the report required in section 1248(b) of Public Law 106–113 (113 Stat. 1501A–505) [set out in a note above].

SEC. 5. *Establishment and Membership.* (a) There is established, pursuant to the Federal Advisory Committee Act, as amended (5 U.S.C. App.), the "President's Council on the Use of Offsets in Commercial Trade" (Council).

(b) The Council shall be composed of the appointed members of the Commission or their designees.

SEC. 6. *Duties and Report of the Council.* The Council shall review and report to the President, through the Director of the Office of Management and Budget, on the use of offsets in commercial trade, including their impact on the United States defense and commercial industrial base. The Council shall consult with and, as appropriate, provide information to the Commission.

SEC. 7. *Administration.* (a) The Department of Defense shall provide administrative support and funding for the Council.

(b) The heads of executive departments and agencies shall, to the extent permitted by law, provide to the Council such information as it may require for the purpose of carrying out its duties.

(c) Members of the Council shall serve without compensation.

SEC. 8. *General.* (a) Notwithstanding any other Executive Order, the functions of the President under the Federal Advisory Committee Act, as amended, except that of reporting to the Congress, that are applicable to the Council, shall be performed by the Department of Defense in accordance with guidelines that have been issued by the Administrator of General Services.

(b) The Council shall terminate on the date of the transmission of the report required by section 1248(b) of Public Law 106–113 (113 Stat. 1501A–505) [set out in a note above].

WILLIAM J. CLINTON.

§2099a. Civil-military integration

An important purpose of this title [sections 2091 to 2099a of this title] is the creation of production capacity that will remain economically viable after guarantees and other assistance provided under this title [said sections] have expired.

(Sept. 8, 1950, ch. 932, title III, §310, as added Pub. L. 102–558, title I, §125, Oct. 28, 1992, 106 Stat. 4208.)

EFFECTIVE DATE

Section deemed to have become effective Mar. 1, 1992, see section 304 of Pub. L. 102–558, set out as an Effective Date of 1992 Amendment note under section 2062 of this Appendix.

TERMINATION DATE

Termination of section, see section 2166(a) of this Appendix.

TITLE IV—PRICE AND WAGE STABILIZATION

§§2101 to 2112. Omitted

CODIFICATION

Section 2101, act Sept. 8, 1950, ch. 932, title IV, §401, 64 Stat. 803, related to purposes of price and wage stabilization and cooperation by government agencies.

Section 2102, acts Sept. 8, 1950, ch. 932, title IV, §402, 64 Stat. 803; July 31, 1951, ch. 275, title I, §104 (a) to (h), 65 Stat. 134; June 30, 1952, ch. 530, title I, §§105 to 111, 66 Stat. 298, related to price and wage controls.

Section 2103, acts Sept. 8, 1950, ch. 932, title IV, §403, 64 Stat. 807; July 31, 1951, ch. 275, title I, §105(a), 65 Stat. 137; June 30, 1952, ch. 530, title I, §112, 66 Stat. 300, authorized an independent agency to administer price and wage controls and rationing, created a Wage Stabilization Board in the Economic Stabilization Agency and prescribed its duties and functions and prescribed the jurisdiction of the Salary Stabilization Board and the Office of Salary Stabilization within the Economic Stabilization Agency. Act Sept. 8, 1950, ch. 932, title IV, §403, 64 Stat. 807, formerly classified to section 2103 of this Appendix, was repealed by Pub. L. 89–554, §8(a), Sept. 6, 1966, 80 Stat. 656.

Section 2104, act Sept. 8, 1950, ch. 932, title IV, §404, 64 Stat. 807, authorized consultation by the President with representatives of persons affected by regulations or orders relating to price and wage controls.

Section 2105, acts Sept. 8, 1950, ch. 932, title IV, 405, 64 Stat. 807; July 31, 1951, ch. 275, title I, §104(i), 65 Stat. 136, related to unlawfulness for violating sections 2101 to 2112 of this appendix or any regulations, orders or requirements issued thereunder.

Section 2106, act Sept. 8, 1950, ch. 932, title IV, §406, 64 Stat. 807, prohibited any construction of sections 2101 to 2112 of this Appendix as requiring any person to sell any material or service, or to perform personal services.

Section 2107, acts Sept. 8, 1950, ch. 932, title IV, §407, 64 Stat. 807; June 30, 1952, ch. 530, title I, §113(a), 66 Stat. 301, related to objections to price and rent control regulations, filing, hearing and determination of protests, procedure, and review.

Section 2108, acts Sept. 8, 1950, ch. 932, title IV, §408, 64 Stat. 808; June 30, 1952, ch. 530, title I, §113(b), 66 Stat. 302, related to determination, by the Emergency Court of Appeals, of validity of price, wage and rent control regulations, procedure, review by the Supreme Court, and stay of civil and criminal proceedings in other courts for determination of such validity.

Section 2109, acts Sept. 8, 1950, ch. 932, title IV, §409, 64 Stat. 811; July 31, 1951, ch. 275, title I, §104(j) to (*l*) 65 Stat. 136, in connection with actions for violations of section 2105 of this Appendix, and regulations or orders, related to injunctions, criminal penalties, recovery of overcharges, and disallowance of fines, penalties, and compromise sums for tax or other purposes.

Section 2110, act Sept. 8, 1950, ch. 932, title IV, §410, 64 Stat. 812, required certain price representations and agreements to be contained in contracts providing for the purchase of processed chickens and turkeys by government agencies.

Section 2111, act Sept. 8, 1950, ch. 932, title IV, §411, as added June 30, 1952, ch. 530, title I, §114, 66 Stat. 304, made it unnecessary to furnish reports on sales or services below ceiling prices if such sales at such prices had been certified to the President.

Section 2112, act Sept. 8, 1950, ch. 932, title IV, §412, as added June 30, 1952, ch. 530, title I, §114, 66 Stat. 304, permitted suspension or termination of price and wage controls over any materials or services, from time to time as economic factors might warrant, and their restoration if deemed necessary.

TERMINATION DATE

Sections 2101 to 2112 terminated at close of Apr. 30, 1953, by the terms of section 2166(a) of this Appendix.

EXECUTIVE ORDER NO. 10160

Ex. Ord. No. 10160, Sept. 9, 1950, 15 F.R. 6103, which related to preservation of records for certain purposes, was revoked by Ex. Ord. No. 10662, Mar. 13, 1956, 21 F.R. 1673.

EX. ORD. NO. 10434. SUSPENSION OF WAGE AND PRICE CONTROLS

Ex. Ord. No. 10434, Feb. 6, 1953, 18 F.R. 809, provided:

1. All regulations and orders issued pursuant to the Defense Production Act of 1950, as amended [see section 2061 of this Appendix], stabilizing wages, salaries, and other compensation, are hereby suspended.

2. The wage, salary, and other compensation adjustments proposed in petitions pending before wage and salary control agencies may now be placed in effect without the approval of such agencies. To the extent that agreements involved in such petitions are conditioned upon approval under Title IV of the Defense Production Act [sections 2101 to 2112 of this Appendix], this order shall be deemed such approval, but such approval shall be subject to paragraph 3 hereof.

3. This order shall not operate to defeat any suit, action, prosecution, or administrative enforcement proceeding, whether heretofore or hereafter commenced, with respect to any right, liability, or offense possessed, incurred, or committed, prior to this date.

DWIGHT D. EISENHOWER.

EXECUTIVE ORDER NO. 10494

Ex. Ord. No. 10494, Oct. 14, 1953, 18 F.R. 6585, as amended by Ex. Ord. No. 10773, July 1, 1958, 23 F.R. 5061; Ex. Ord. No. 10782, Sept. 6, 1958, 23 F.R. 6971, which related to the disposition of remaining functions, was revoked by section 5–103 of Ex. Ord. No. 12148, July 20, 1979, 44 F.R. 43243, set out as a note under section 5195 of Title 42, The Public Health and Welfare.

TITLE V—SETTLEMENT OF LABOR DISPUTES

§§2121 to 2123. Omitted

CODIFICATION

Section 2121, act Sept. 8, 1950, ch. 932, title V, §501, 64 Stat. 812, stated intent of Congress in providing for settlement of labor disputes affecting national defense.

Section 2122, acts Sept. 8, 1950, ch. 932, title V, §502, 64 Stat. 812; July 31, 1951, ch. 275, title I, §105(b), 65 Stat. 137, stated national policy in connection with such settlement, and provided for voluntary conferences.

Section 2123, acts Sept. 8, 1950, ch. 932, title V, §503, 64 Stat. 812; July 31, 1951, ch. 275, title I, §105(c), 65 Stat. 137; June 30, 1952, ch. 530, title I, §115, 66 Stat. 305, provided that, in such settlements, due regard should be given to collective bargaining and other laws, and, as amended by the act of June 30, 1952, requested the President to invoke the Labor-Management Relations Act, 1947, (29 U.S.C. 141 et seq.), with regard to the steel strike then existing.

TERMINATION DATE

Sections 2121 to 2123 terminated at close of Apr. 30, 1953, by the terms of section 2166(a) of this Appendix.

TITLE VI—CONTROL OF REAL ESTATE CREDIT

CODIFICATION

Sections 2132 to 2137 of this Appendix, which comprised this title, terminated on June 30, 1953, by the terms of section 2166(a) of this Appendix. Previous to such termination, act June 30, 1952, ch. 530, title I, §116(a), 66 Stat. 305 amended catchline of title to omit reference to consumer credit control and subtitle heading of this title to read "This title authorizes the regulation of real estate construction credit only."

§2131. Repealed. June 30, 1952, ch. 530, title I, §116(a), 66 Stat. 305

Section, acts Sept. 8, 1950, ch. 932, title VI, §601, 64 Stat. 812; July 31, 1951, ch. 275, title I, §106(a), 65 Stat. 138, related to power to exercise consumer credit controls.

§§2132 to 2137. Omitted

CODIFICATION

Section 2132, act Sept. 8, 1950, ch. 932, title VI, §602, 64 Stat. 813, related to real estate construction credit.

Section 2133, acts Sept. 8, 1950, ch. 932, title VI, §603, 64 Stat. 814; July 31, 1951, ch. 275, title I, §106(b), 65 Stat. 138, prescribed penalties for violating sections 2131, 2132 and 2135 of this Appendix or any regulation or order issued thereunder.

Section 2134, act Sept. 8, 1950, ch. 932, title VI, §604, 64 Stat. 814, related to consumer credit controls.

Section 2135, acts Sept. 8, 1950, ch. 932, title VI, §605, 64 Stat. 814; July 31, 1951, ch. 275, title I, §106(c), 65 Stat. 138; Sept. 1, 1951, ch. 378, title VI, §602(a), 65 Stat. 313, related to real estate loans by government agencies.

Section 2136, act Sept. 8, 1950, ch. 932, title VI, §606, as added Sept. 1, 1951, ch. 378, title VI, §602(b), 65 Stat. 313, related to down-payment requirements on veterans homes.

Section 2137, act Sept. 8, 1950, ch. 932, title VI, §607, as added June 30, 1952, ch. 530, title I, §116(b), 66 Stat. 305, related to credit controls on residential property.

TERMINATION DATE

Sections 2132 to 2137 terminated at close of June 30, 1953, by the terms of section 2166(a) of this Appendix.

TITLE VII—GENERAL PROVISIONS

TITLE REFERRED TO IN OTHER SECTIONS

This title is referred to in section 2166 of this Appendix.

§ 2151. Small business

(a) Participation

Small business concerns shall be given the maximum practicable opportunity to participate as contractors, and subcontractors at various tiers, in all programs to maintain and strengthen the Nation's industrial base and technology base undertaken pursuant to this Act [sections 2061 to 2171 of this Appendix].

(b) Administration of Act

In administering the programs, implementing regulations, policies, and procedures under this Act [sections 2061 to 2171 of this Appendix], requests, applications, or appeals from small business concerns shall, to the maximum extent practicable, be expeditiously handled.

(c) Advisory committee participation

Representatives of small business concerns shall be afforded the maximum opportunity to participate in such advisory committees as may be established pursuant to this Act [sections 2061 to 2171 of this Appendix].

(d) Information

Information about this Act [sections 2061 to 2171 of this Appendix] and activities undertaken in accordance with this Act [said sections] shall be made available to small business concerns.

(e) Allocations under section 101

Whenever the President makes a determination to exercise any authority to allocate any material pursuant to section 101 [section 2071 of this Appendix], small business concerns shall be accorded, to the extent practicable, a fair share of such material, in proportion to the share received by such business concerns under normal conditions, giving such special consideration as may be possible to emerging small business concerns.

(Sept. 8, 1950, ch. 932, title VII, § 701, 64 Stat. 815; July 31, 1951, ch. 275, title I, § 108, 65 Stat. 138; June 30, 1953, ch. 171, § 7, 67 Stat. 130; Aug. 9, 1955, ch. 655, §§ 4, 5, 69 Stat. 580; Pub. L. 96–294, title I, § 105(c), June 30, 1980, 94 Stat. 633; Pub. L. 102–558, title I, § 131, Oct. 28, 1992, 106 Stat. 4209.)

AMENDMENTS

1992—Pub. L. 102–558 amended section generally, substituting present provisions for provisions stating policy to encourage small business enterprises and providing for measures to carry out this policy, for allocation of materials in the civilian market, and for distribution of defense contracts.

1980—Subsec. (d). Pub. L. 96–294 substituted "enactment of the Defense Production Act Amendments of 1980" for "enactment of the Defense Production Act Amendments of 1955".

1955—Subsec. (c). Act Aug. 9, 1955, § 4, struck out specific dates which were the basis for determination of materials in civilian market and inserted provisions requiring that a business receive its fair share based on a representative period before imposition of the allocation.

Subsec. (d). Act Aug. 9, 1955, § 5, added subsec. (d).

1953—Subsec. (c). Act June 30, 1953, amended subsec. (c) generally, the principal change being to provide, in the allocation to business of a fair share of available civilian supply, a new base period for allocating materials not under control on July 1, 1953.

1951—Subsec. (c). Act July 31, 1951, provided that limitations and restrictions on production of specific items shall not exclude new concerns.

EFFECTIVE DATE OF 1992 AMENDMENT

Amendment by Pub. L. 102–558 deemed to have become effective Mar. 1, 1992, see section 304 of Pub. L. 102–558, set out as a note under section 2062 of this Appendix.

EFFECTIVE DATE OF 1980 AMENDMENT

Amendment by Pub. L. 96–294 effective June 30, 1980, see section 107 of Pub. L. 96–294, set out as a note under section 2062 of this Appendix.

EFFECTIVE DATE OF 1955 AMENDMENT

Amendment by act Aug. 9, 1955, effective as of close of July 31, 1955, see section 11 of act Aug. 9, 1955, set out as a note under section 2062 of this Appendix.

TERMINATION DATE

Termination of section, see section 2166(a) of this Appendix.

DELEGATION OF FUNCTIONS

Functions of President under act Sept. 8, 1950 [section 2061 et seq. of this Appendix], relating to production, conservation, use, control, distribution, and allocation of energy, delegated to Secretary of Energy, see section 4 of Ex. Ord. No. 11790, June 25, 1974, 39 F.R. 23185, set out as a note under section 761 of Title 15, Commerce and Trade.

§ 2152. Definitions

For purposes of this Act [sections 2061 to 2171 of this Appendix], the following definitions shall apply:

(1) Critical component

The term "critical component" includes such components, subsystems, systems, and related special tooling and test equipment essential to the production, repair, maintenance, or operation of weapon systems or other items of military equipment identified by the Secretary of Defense as being essential to the execution of the national security strategy of the United States. Components identified as critical by a National Security Assessment conducted pursuant to section 113(i) of title 10, United States Code, or by a Presidential determination as a result of a petition filed under section 232 of the Trade Expansion Act of 1962 [19 U.S.C. 1862] shall be designated as critical components for purposes of this Act [sections 2061 to 2171 of this Appendix], unless the President determines that the designation is unwarranted.

(2) Critical industry for national security

The term "critical industry for national security" means any industry (or industry sector) identified pursuant to section 2503(6)[1] of title 10, United States Code, and such other industries or industry sectors as may be designated by the President as essential to provide industrial resources required for the exe-

[1] See References in Text note below.

cution of the national security strategy of the United States.

(3) Critical technology

The term "critical technology" includes any technology that is included in 1 or more of the plans submitted pursuant to section 6681[2] of title 42, United States Code, or section 2508[2] of title 10, United States Code (unless subsequently deleted), or such other emerging or dual use technology as may be designated by the President.

(4) Critical technology item

The term "critical technology item" means materials directly employing, derived from, or utilizing a critical technology.

(5) Defense contractor

The term "defense contractor" means any person who enters into a contract with the United States—

(A) to furnish materials, industrial resources, or a critical technology for the national defense; or

(B) to perform services for the national defense.

(6) Domestic defense industrial base

The term "domestic defense industrial base" means domestic sources which are providing, or which would be reasonably expected to provide, materials or services to meet national defense requirements during peacetime, graduated mobilization, national emergency, or war.

(7) Domestic source

The term "domestic source" means a business concern—

(A) that performs in the United States or Canada substantially all of the research and development, engineering, manufacturing, and production activities required of such business concern under a contract with the United States relating to a critical component or a critical technology item; and

(B) that procures from business concerns described in subparagraph (A) substantially all of any components and assemblies required under a contract with the United States relating to a critical component or critical technology item.

(8) Essential weapon system

The term "essential weapon system" means a major weapon system and other items of military equipment identified by the Secretary of Defense as being essential to the execution of the national security strategy of the United States.

(9) Facilities

The term "facilities" includes all types of buildings, structures, or other improvements to real property (but excluding farms, churches or other places of worship, and private dwelling houses), and services relating to the use of any such building, structure, or other improvement.

(10) Foreign source

The term "foreign source" means a business entity other than a "domestic source".

(11) Industrial resources

The term "industrial resources" means materials, services, processes, or manufacturing equipment (including the processes, technologies, and ancillary services for the use of such equipment) needed to establish or maintain an efficient and modern national defense industrial capacity.

(12) Materials

The term "materials" includes—

(A) any raw materials (including minerals, metals, and advanced processed materials), commodities, articles, components (including critical components), products, and items of supply; and

(B) any technical information or services ancillary to the use of any such materials, commodities, articles, components, products, or items.

(13) National defense

The term "national defense" means programs for military and energy production or construction, military assistance to any foreign nation, stockpiling, space, and any directly related activity. Such term includes emergency preparedness activities conducted pursuant to title VI of The Robert T. Stafford Disaster Relief and Emergency Assistance Act [42 U.S.C. 5195 et seq.].

(14) Person

The term "person" includes an individual, corporation, partnership, association, or any other organized group of persons, or legal successor or representative thereof, or any State or local government or agency thereof.

(15) Services

The term "services" includes any effort that is needed for or incidental to—

(A) the development, production, processing, distribution, delivery, or use of an industrial resource or a critical technology item; or

(B) the construction of facilities.

(16) Small business concern

The term "small business concern" means a business concern that meets the requirements of section 3(a) of the Small Business Act [15 U.S.C. 632(a)] and the regulations promulgated pursuant to that section, and includes such business concerns owned and controlled by socially and economically disadvantaged individuals or by women.

(17) Small business concern owned and controlled by socially and economically disadvantaged individuals

The term "small business concern owned and controlled by socially and economically disadvantaged individuals" has the same meaning as in section 8(d)(3)(C) of the Small Business Act [15 U.S.C. 637(d)(3)(C)].

(Sept. 8, 1950, ch. 932, title VII, §702, 64 Stat. 815; June 30, 1953, ch. 171, §8, 67 Stat. 130; Pub. L. 91–379, title I, §102, Aug. 15, 1970, 84 Stat. 796; Pub. L. 102–558, title I, §132, Oct. 28, 1992, 106 Stat. 4210; Pub. L. 103–337, div. C, title XXXIV, §3411(b), Oct. 5, 1994, 108 Stat. 3110.)

[2] See References in Text note below.

REFERENCES IN TEXT

Section 2503 of title 10, referred to in par. (2), was repealed and a new section 2503 relating to analysis of the technology and industrial base was enacted by Pub. L. 102–484, div. D, title XLII, §§4202(a), 4213(a), Oct. 23, 1992, 106 Stat. 2659, 2665.

Section 6681 of title 42, referred to in par. (3), was omitted from the Code.

Section 2508 of title 10, referred to in par. (3), was renumbered section 2522 of title 10 by Pub. L. 102–190, div. A, title VIII, §821(b)(1), Dec. 5, 1991, 105 Stat. 1431, and was repealed and a new section relating to defense advanced manufacturing technology partnerships was enacted and renumbered section 2522 by Pub. L. 102–484, div. D, title XLII, §§4202(a), 4232(a), (b), Oct. 23, 1992, 106 Stat. 2659, 2687, and was subsequently repealed.

The Robert T. Stafford Disaster Relief and Emergency Assistance Act, referred to in par. (13), is Pub. L. 93–288, May 22, 1974, 88 Stat. 143, as amended. The Act was renamed the "Robert T. Stafford Disaster Relief and Emergency Assistance Act" by Pub. L. 106–390, title III, §301, Oct. 30, 2000, 1114 Stat. 1572. Title VI of the Act is classified generally to subchapter IV–B (§5195 et seq.) of chapter 68 of Title 42, The Public Health and Welfare. For complete classification of this Act to the Code, see Short Title note set out under section 5121 of Title 42 and Tables.

AMENDMENTS

1994—Par. (13). Pub. L. 103–337 inserted at end "Such term includes emergency preparedness activities conducted pursuant to title VI of The Robert T. Stafford Disaster Relief and Emergency Assistance Act."

1992—Pub. L. 102–558 amended section generally, substituting present provisions for provisions defining terms "person", "materials", "facilities", "national defense", "wages, salaries, and other compensation", and "defense contractor".

1970—Subsec. (d). Pub. L. 91–379, §102(1), inserted reference to space in definition of national defense.

Subsec. (f). Pub. L. 91–379, §102(2), added subsec. (f).

1953—Subsec. (d). Act June 30, 1953, amended subsec. (d) generally which, among other changes, inserted references to construction, military assistance to foreign nations and stockpiling, and struck out specific reference to "operations or activities in connection with the Mutual Defense Assistance Act of 1949, as amended".

EFFECTIVE DATE OF 1992 AMENDMENT

Amendment by Pub. L. 102–558 deemed to have become effective Mar. 1, 1992, see section 304 of Pub. L. 102–558, set out as a note under section 2062 of this Appendix.

TERMINATION DATE

Termination of section, see section 2166(a) of this Appendix.

§2153. Civilian personnel

Any officer or agency head may—

(1) appoint civilian personnel without regard to section 5331(b) of title 5, United States Code, and without regard to the provisions of title 5, United States Code, governing appointments in the competitive service; and

(2) fix the rate of basic pay for such personnel without regard to the provisions of chapter 51 and subchapter III of chapter 53 of title 5, United States Code, relating to classification and General Schedule pay rates,

except that no individual so appointed may receive pay in excess of the annual rate of basic pay payable for GS–18 of the General Schedule, as the President deems appropriate to carry out this Act [sections 2061 to 2171 of this Appendix].

(Sept. 8, 1950, ch. 932, title VII, §703, 64 Stat. 816; July 31, 1951, ch. 275, title I, §109(a), (b), 65 Stat. 138; Pub. L. 102–558, title I, §133, Oct. 28, 1992, 106 Stat. 4212.)

REFERENCES IN TEXT

The provisions of title 5, United States Code, governing appointments in the competitive service, referred to in par. (1), are classified generally to section 3301 et seq. of Title 5, Government Organization and Employees.

AMENDMENTS

1992—Pub. L. 102–558 amended section generally, substituting present provisions for provisions relating to delegation of Presidential authority, creation of new agencies, appointment and compensation of officers and personnel, and State representation in regional offices.

1951—Subsec. (a). Act July 31, 1951, §109(a), provided that executive head of one agency under this act shall be paid at a rate comparable to that paid heads of executive departments.

Subsec. (b). Act July 31, 1951, §109(b), to provide for State representation in regional offices.

EFFECTIVE DATE OF 1992 AMENDMENT

Amendment by Pub. L. 102–558 deemed to have become effective Mar. 1, 1992, see section 304 of Pub. L. 102–558, set out as a note under section 2062 of this Appendix.

TERMINATION DATE

Termination of section, see section 2166(a) of this Appendix.

REFERENCES IN OTHER LAWS TO GS–16, 17, OR 18 PAY RATES

References in laws to the rates of pay for GS–16, 17, or 18, or to maximum rates of pay under the General Schedule, to be considered references to rates payable under specified sections of Title 5, Government Organization and Employees, see section 529 [title I, §101(c)(1)] of Pub. L. 101–509, set out in a note under section 5376 of Title 5.

COMPENSATION OF CERTAIN OFFICIALS IN DOMESTIC AND INTERNATIONAL BUSINESS ADMINISTRATION

Compensation for certain officials in Domestic and International Business Administration fixed at certain prescribed rates by Ex. Ord. No. 11759, Jan. 15, 1974, 39 F.R. 2077, formerly set out as a note under section 1511 of Title 15, Commerce and Trade.

COMPENSATION OF DIRECTOR AND DEPUTY DIRECTOR, BUREAU OF DOMESTIC COMMERCE

Compensation for Director and Deputy Director, Bureau of Domestic Commerce, Department of Commerce, was fixed at certain prescribed rates by Ex. Ord. No. 11567, Nov. 16, 1970, 35 F.R. 17701, which was superseded by Ex. Ord. No. 11759, Jan. 15, 1974, 39 F.R. 2077, formerly set out as a note under section 1511 of Title 15, Commerce and Trade.

EXECUTIVE ORDER NO. 10193

Ex. Ord. No. 10193, Dec. 16, 1950, 15 F.R. 9031, which provided for conduct of mobilization effort of the Government, was revoked by Ex. Ord. No. 10480, Aug. 14, 1953, 18 F.R. 4939, formerly set out below.

EXECUTIVE ORDER NO. 10200

Ex. Ord. No. 10200, Jan. 3, 1951, 16 F.R. 61, as amended by Ex. Ord. No. 10281, Aug. 28, 1951, 16 F.R. 8789; Ex. Ord. No. 10433, Feb. 4, 1953, 18 F.R. 761, which related to establishment of Defense Production Administration, was revoked by Ex. Ord. No. 10480, Aug. 18, 1953, 18 F.R. 4939, formerly set out below.

EXECUTIVE ORDER NO. 10224

Ex. Ord. No. 10224, Mar. 15, 1951, 16 F.R. 2543, as amended by Ex. Ord. No. 10461, June 17, 1953, 18 F.R. 3513, which provided for establishment of the National Advisory Board on Mobilization Policy was revoked by section 7(1) of Ex. Ord. No. 10773, July 1, 1958, 23 F.R. 5061, which was subsequently superseded by Ex. Ord. No. 11051, Sept. 27, 1962, 27 F.R. 9683, formerly set out as a note under section 2271 of this Appendix.

EXECUTIVE ORDER NO. 10281

Ex. Ord. No. 10281, Aug. 28, 1951, 16 F.R. 8789, which related to defense materials procurement and supply, was revoked by Ex. Ord. No. 10480, Aug. 14, 1953, 18 F.R. 4939, formerly set out below.

EXECUTIVE ORDER NO. 10308

Ex. Ord. No. 10308, Dec. 3, 1951, 16 F.R. 12303, creating the Committee on Government Contract Compliance, was revoked and the Committee abolished by Ex. Ord. No. 10479, Aug. 17, 1953, 18 F.R. 4899, which was subsequently revoked by Ex. Ord. No. 10925, Mar. 7, 1961, 26 F.R. 1977.

EXECUTIVE ORDER NO. 10433

Ex. Ord. No. 10433, Feb. 4, 1953, 18 F.R. 761, which provided for merger of Defense Production Administration with the Office of Defense Mobilization, was revoked by Ex. Ord. No. 10480, Aug. 14, 1953, 18 F.R. 4939, formerly set out below.

EXECUTIVE ORDER NO. 10461

Ex. Ord. No. 10461, June 17, 1953, 18 F.R. 3513 which related to transfer of functions effected by Reorganization Plan No. 3 of 1953, was superseded by Ex. Ord. No. 11051, Sept. 27, 1962, 27 F.R. 9683, formerly set out as a note under section 2271 of this Appendix.

EXECUTIVE ORDER NO. 10480

Ex. Ord. No. 10480, Aug. 14, 1953, 18 F.R. 4939, as amended by Ex. Ord. No. 10489, Sept. 26, 1953, 18 F.R. 6201; Ex. Ord. No. 10537, June 22, 1954, 19 F.R. 3807; Ex. Ord. No. 10574, Nov. 8, 1954, 19 F.R. 7249; Ex. Ord. No. 10662, Mar. 14, 1956, 21 F.R. 1673; Ex. Ord. No. 10773, July 1, 1958, 23 F.R. 5061; Ex. Ord. No. 10782, Sept. 6, 1958, 23 F.R. 6971; Ex. Ord. No. 10819, May 11, 1959, 24 F.R. 3779; Ex. Ord. No. 11051, Sept. 27, 1962, 27 F.R. 9683; Ex. Ord. No. 11062, Nov. 19, 1962, 27 F.R. 11447; Ex. Ord. No. 11956, Jan. 13, 1977, 42 F.R. 2947; Ex. Ord. No. 12038, Feb. 3, 1978, 43 F.R. 4957; Ex. Ord. No. 12148, July 20, 1979, 44 F.R. 43239; Ex. Ord. No. 12381, § 4, Sept. 8, 1982, 47 F.R. 39795; Ex. Ord. No. 12521, June 24, 1985, 50 F.R. 26335; Ex. Ord. No. 12649, Aug. 11, 1988, 53 F.R. 30639; Ex. Ord. No. 12773, Sept. 26, 1991, 56 F.R. 49387, which provided for administration of defense mobilization program, was revoked by section 904(a)(3) of Ex. Ord. No. 12919, June 3, 1994, 59 F.R. 29533, set out below.

EXECUTIVE ORDER NO. 10660

Ex. Ord. No. 10660, Feb. 15, 1956, 21 F.R. 1117, as amended by Ex. Ord. No. 10773, July 1, 1958, 23 F.R. 5061; Ex. Ord. No. 10782, Sept. 6, 1958, 23 F.R. 6971; Ex. Ord. No. 11051, Sept. 27, 1962, 27 F.R. 9683, which established a National Defense Executive Reserve, was superseded by Ex. Ord. No. 11179, Sept. 22, 1964, 29 F.R. 13239, formerly set out below.

EXECUTIVE ORDER NO. 11179

Ex. Ord. No. 11179, Sept. 22, 1964, 29 F.R. 13239, as amended by Ex. Ord. No. 12148, July 20, 1979, 44 F.R. 43239, which established National Defense Executive Reserve, was revoked by section 904(a)(5) of Ex. Ord. No. 12919, June 3, 1994, 59 F.R. 29533, set out below.

EX. ORD. NO. 12919. NATIONAL DEFENSE INDUSTRIAL RESOURCES PREPAREDNESS

Ex. Ord. No. 12919, June 3, 1994, 59 F.R. 29525, provided:

By the authority vested in me as President by the Constitution and the laws of the United States of America, including the Defense Production Act of 1950, as amended (64 Stat. 798; 50 U.S.C. App. 2061, *et seq.*), and section 301 of title 3, United States Code, and as Commander in Chief of the Armed Forces of the United States, it is hereby ordered as follows:

PART I—PURPOSE, POLICY AND IMPLEMENTATION

SECTION 101. *Purpose.* This order delegates authorities and addresses national defense industrial resource policies and programs under the Defense Production Act of 1950, as amended ("the Act"), except for the amendments to Title III of the Act [50 App. U.S.C. 2091 et seq.] in the Energy Security Act of 1980 [Pub. L. 96–294] and telecommunication authorities under Executive Order No. 12472 [50 App. U.S.C. 2251 note].

SEC. 102. *Policy.* The United States must have an industrial and technology base capable of meeting national defense requirements, and capable of contributing to the technological superiority of its defense equipment in peacetime and in times of national emergency. The domestic industrial and technological base is the foundation for national defense preparedness. The authorities provided in the Act shall be used to strengthen this base and to ensure it is capable of responding to all threats to the national security of the United States.

SEC. 103. *General Functions.* Federal departments and agencies responsible for defense acquisition (or for industrial resources needed to support defense acquisition) shall:

(a) Identify requirements for the full spectrum of national security emergencies, including military, industrial, and essential civilian demand;

(b) Assess continually the capability of the domestic industrial and technological base to satisfy requirements in peacetime and times of national emergency, specifically evaluating the availability of adequate industrial resource and production sources, including subcontractors and suppliers, materials, skilled labor, and professional and technical personnel;

(c) Be prepared, in the event of a potential threat to the security of the United States, to take actions necessary to ensure the availability of adequate industrial resources and production capability, including services and critical technology for national defense requirements;

(d) Improve the efficiency and responsiveness, to defense requirements, of the domestic industrial base; and

(e) Foster cooperation between the defense and commercial sectors for research and development and for acquisition of materials, components, and equipment to enhance industrial base efficiency and responsiveness.

SEC. 104. *Implementation.* (a) The National Security Council is the principal forum for consideration and resolution of national security resource preparedness policy.

(b) The Director, Federal Emergency Management Agency ("Director, FEMA") shall:

(1) Serve as an advisor to the National Security Council on issues of national security resource preparedness and on the use of the authorities and functions delegated by this order;

(2) Provide for the central coordination of the plans and programs incident to authorities and functions delegated under this order, and provide guidance and procedures approved by the Assistant to the President for National Security Affairs to the Federal departments and agencies under this order;

(3) Establish procedures, in consultation with Federal departments and agencies assigned functions under this order, to resolve in a timely and effective manner conflicts and issues that may arise in implementing the authorities and functions delegated under this order; and

(4) Report to the President periodically concerning all program activities conducted pursuant to this order.

(c) The head of every Federal department and agency assigned functions under this order shall ensure that the performance of these functions is consistent with National Security Council policy and guidelines.

PART II—PRIORITIES AND ALLOCATIONS

SEC. 201. *Delegations of Priorities and Allocations.* (a) The authority of the President conferred by section 101 of the Act [50 App. U.S.C. 2071] to require acceptance and priority performance of contracts or orders (other than contracts of employment) to promote the national defense over performance of any other contracts or orders, and to allocate materials, services, and facilities as deemed necessary or appropriate to promote the national defense, is delegated to the following agency heads:

(1) The Secretary of Agriculture with respect to food resources, food resource facilities, and the domestic distribution of farm equipment and commercial fertilizer;

(2) The Secretary of Energy with respect to all forms of energy;

(3) The Secretary of Health and Human Services with respect to health resources;

(4) The Secretary of Transportation with respect to all forms of civil transportation;

(5) The Secretary of Defense with respect to water resources; and

(6) The Secretary of Commerce for all other materials, services, and facilities, including construction materials.

(b) The Secretary of Commerce, in consultation with the heads of those departments and agencies specified in subsection 201(a) of this order, shall administer the Defense Priorities and Allocations System ("DPAS") regulations that will be used to implement the authority of the President conferred by section 101 of the Act as delegated to the Secretary of Commerce in subsection 201(a)(6) of this order. The Secretary of Commerce will redelegate to the Secretary of Defense, and the heads of other departments and agencies as appropriate, authority for the priority rating of contracts and orders for all materials, services, and facilities needed in support of programs approved under section 202 of this order. The Secretary of Commerce shall act as appropriate upon Special Priorities Assistance requests in a time frame consistent with the urgency of the need at hand.

(c) The Director, FEMA, shall attempt to resolve issues or disagreements on priorities or allocations between Federal departments or agencies in a time frame consistent with the urgency of the issue at hand and, if not resolved, such issues will be referred to the Assistant to the President for National Security Affairs for final determination.

(d) The head of each Federal department or agency assigned functions under subsection 201(a) of this order, when necessary, shall make the finding required under subsection 101(b) of the Act. This finding shall be submitted for the President's approval through the Assistant to the President for National Security Affairs. Upon such approval the head of the Federal department or agency that made the finding may use the authority of subsection 101(a) of the Act to control the general distribution of any material (including applicable services) in the civilian market.

(e) The Assistant to the President for National Security Affairs is hereby delegated the authority under subsection 101(c)(3) of the Act, and will be assisted by the Director, FEMA, in ensuring the coordinated administration of the Act.

SEC. 202. *Determinations.* The authority delegated by section 201 of this order may be used only to support programs that have been determined in writing as necessary or appropriate to promote the national defense:

(a) By the Secretary of Defense with respect to military production and construction, military assistance to foreign nations, stockpiling, outer space, and directly related activities;

(b) By the Secretary of Energy with respect to energy production and construction, distribution and use, and directly related activities; and

(c) By the Director, FEMA, with respect to essential civilian needs supporting national defense, including civil defense and continuity of government and directly related activities.

SEC. 203. *Maximizing Domestic Energy Supplies.* The authority of the President to perform the functions provided by subsection 101(c) of the Act [50 App. U.S.C. 2071(c)] is delegated to the Secretary of Commerce, who shall redelegate to the Secretary of Energy the authority to make the findings described in subsection 101(c)(2)(A) that the materials (including equipment), services, and facilities are critical and essential. The Secretary of Commerce shall make the finding described in subsection 101(c)(2)(A) of the Act that the materials (including equipment), services, or facilities are scarce, and the finding described in subsection 101(c)(2)(B) that it is necessary to use the authority provided by subsection 101(c)(1).

SEC. 204. *Chemical and Biological Warfare.* The authority of the President conferred by subsection 104(b) of the Act [50 App. U.S.C. 2074(b)] is delegated to the Secretary of Defense. This authority may not be further delegated by the Secretary.

PART III—EXPANSION OF PRODUCTIVE CAPACITY AND SUPPLY

SEC. 301. (a) *Financing Institution Guarantees.* To expedite or expand production and deliveries or services under government contracts for the procurement of industrial resources or critical technology items essential to the national defense, the head of each Federal department or agency engaged in procurement for the national defense (referred to as "agency head" in this part) and the President and Chairman of the Export-Import Bank of the United States (in cases involving capacity expansion, technological development, or production in foreign countries) are authorized to guarantee in whole or in part any public or private financing institution, subject to provisions of section 301 of the Act [50 App. U.S.C. 2091]. Guarantees shall be made in consultation with the Department of the Treasury as to the terms and conditions thereof. The Director of the Office of Management and Budget ("OMB") shall be informed when such guarantees are to be made.

(b) *Direct Loan Guarantees.* To expedite or expand production and deliveries or services under government contracts for the procurement of industrial resources or critical technology items essential to the national defense, each agency head is authorized to make direct loan guarantees from funds appropriated to their agency for Title III [50 App. U.S.C. 2091 et seq.].

(c) *Fiscal Agent.* Each Federal Reserve Bank is designated and authorized to act, on behalf of any guaranteeing agency, as fiscal agent in the making of guarantee contracts and in otherwise carrying out the purposes of section 301 of the Act.

(d) *Regulations.* The Board of Governors of the Federal Reserve System is authorized, after consultation with heads of guaranteeing departments and agencies, the Secretary of the Treasury, and the Director, OMB, to prescribe regulations governing procedures, forms, rates of interest, and fees for such guarantee contracts.

SEC. 302. *Loans.* (a) To expedite production and deliveries or services to aid in carrying out government contracts for the procurement of industrial resources or a critical technology item for the national defense, an agency head is authorized, subject to the provisions of section 302 of the Act [50 App. U.S.C. 2092], to submit to the Secretary of the Treasury or the President and Chairman of the Export-Import Bank of the United States (in cases involving capacity expansion, technological development, or production in foreign countries) applications for loans.

(b) To expedite or expand production and deliveries or services under government contracts for the procurement of industrial resources or critical technology items essential to the national defense, each agency head may make direct loans from funds appropriated to their agency for Title III.

(c) After receiving a loan application and determining that financial assistance is not otherwise available on reasonable terms, the Secretary of the Treasury or the President and Chairman of the Export-Import Bank of the United States (in cases involving capacity expansion, technological development, or production in foreign countries) may make loans, subject to provisions of section 302 of the Act.

SEC. 303. *Purchase Commitments.* (a) In order to carry out the objectives of the Act, and subject to the provisions of section 303 [50 App. U.S.C. 2093] thereof, an agency head is authorized to make provision for purchases of, or commitments to purchase, an industrial resource or a critical technology item for government use or resale.

(b) Materials acquired under section 303 of the Act that exceed the needs of the programs under the Act may be transferred to the National Defense Stockpile, if such transfer is determined by the Secretary of Defense as the National Defense Stockpile Manager to be in the public interest.

SEC. 304. *Subsidy Payments.* In order to ensure the supply of raw or non-processed materials from high-cost sources, an agency head is authorized to make subsidy payments, after consultation with the Secretary of the Treasury and the Director, OMB, and subject to the provisions of section 303(c) of the Act [50 App. U.S.C. 2093(c)].

SEC. 305. *Determinations and Findings.* When carrying out the authorities in sections 301 through 303 of this order, an agency head is authorized to make the required determinations, judgments, statements, certifications, and findings, in consultation with the Secretary of Defense, Secretary of Energy or Director, FEMA, as appropriate. The agency head shall provide a copy of the determination, judgment, statement, certification, or finding to the Director, OMB, to the Director, FEMA, and, when appropriate, to the Secretary of the Treasury.

SEC. 306. *Strategic and Critical Materials.* (a) The Secretary of the Interior, in consultation with the Secretary of Defense as the National Defense Stockpile Manager and subject to the provisions of section 303 of the Act [50 App. U.S.C. 2093], is authorized to encourage the exploration, development, and mining of critical and strategic materials and other materials.

(b) An agency head is authorized, pursuant to section 303(g) of the Act, to make provision for the development of substitutes for strategic and critical materials, critical components, critical technology items, and other industrial resources to aid the national defense.

(c) An agency head is authorized, pursuant to section 303(a)(1)(B) of the Act, to make provisions to encourage the exploration, development, and mining of critical and strategic materials and other materials.

SEC. 307. *Government-owned Equipment.* An agency head is authorized, pursuant to section 303(e) of the Act [50 App. U.S.C. 2093(e)], to install additional equipment, facilities, processes, or improvements to facilities owned by the government and to install government-owned equipment in industrial facilities owned by private persons.

SEC. 308. *Identification of Shortfalls.* Except during periods of national emergency or after a Presidential determination in accordance with sections 301(e)(1)(D)(ii), 302(c)(4)(B), or 303(a)(7)(B) of the Act [50 App. U.S.C. 2091(e)(1)(D)(ii), 2092(c)(4)(B), 2093(a)(7)(B)], no guarantee, loan or other action pursuant to sections 301, 302, and 303 of the Act to correct an industrial shortfall shall be taken unless the shortfall has been identified in the Budget of the United States or amendments thereto.

SEC. 309. *Defense Production Act Fund Manager.* The Secretary of Defense is designated the Defense Production Act Fund Manager, in accordance with section 304(f) of the Act [50 App. U.S.C. 2094(f)], and shall carry out the duties specified in that section, in consultation with the agency heads having approved Title III projects and appropriated Title III funds.

SEC. 310. *Critical Items List.* (a) Pursuant to section 107(b)(1)(A) of the Act [50 App. U.S.C. 2077(b)(1)(A)], the Secretary of Defense shall identify critical components and critical technology items for each item on the Critical Items List of the Commanders-in-Chief of the Unified and Specified Commands and other items within the inventory of weapon systems and defense equipment.

(b) Each agency head shall take appropriate action to ensure that critical components or critical technology items are available from reliable sources when needed to meet defense requirements during peacetime, graduated mobilization, and national emergency. "Appropriate action" may include restricting contract solicitations to reliable sources, restricting contract solicitations to domestic sources (pursuant to statutory authority), stockpiling critical components, and developing substitutes for critical components or critical technology items.

SEC. 311. *Strengthening Domestic Capability.* An agency head, in accordance with section 107(a) of the Act [50 App. U.S.C. 2077(a)], may utilize the authority of Title III of the Act [50 App. U.S.C. 2091 et seq.] or any other provision of law, in consultation with the Secretary of Defense, to provide appropriate incentives to develop, maintain, modernize, and expand the productive capacities of domestic sources for critical components, critical technology items, and industrial resources essential for the execution of the national security strategy of the United States.

SEC. 312. *Modernization of Equipment.* An agency head, in accordance with section 108(b) of the Act [50 App. U.S.C. 2078(b)], may utilize the authority of Title III of the Act to guarantee the purchase or lease of advance manufacturing equipment and any related services with respect to any such equipment for purposes of the Act.

PART IV—IMPACT OF OFFSETS

SEC. 401. *Offsets.* (a) The responsibilities and authority conferred upon the President by section 309 of the Act [50 App. U.S.C. 2099] with respect to offsets are delegated to the Secretary of Commerce, who shall function as the President's Executive Agent for carrying out this authority.

(b) The Secretary of Commerce shall prepare the annual report required by section 309(a) of the Act in consultation with the Secretaries of Defense, Treasury, Labor, State, the United States Trade Representative, the Arms Control and Disarmament Agency, the Director of Central Intelligence, and the heads of other departments and agencies as required. The heads of Federal departments and agencies shall provide the Secretary of Commerce with such information as may be necessary for the effective performance of this function.

(c) The offset report shall be subject to the normal interagency clearance process conducted by the Director, OMB, prior to the report's submission by the President to Congress.

PART V—VOLUNTARY AGREEMENTS AND ADVISORY COMMITTEES

SEC. 501. *Appointments.* The authority of the President under sections 708(c) and (d) of the Act [50 App. U.S.C. 2158(c), (d)] is delegated to the heads of each Federal department or agency, except that, insofar as that authority relates to section 101 of the Act [50 App. U.S.C. 2071], it is delegated only to the heads of each Federal department or agency assigned functions under section 201(a) of this order. The authority delegated under this section shall be exercised pursuant to the provisions of section 708 of the Act, and copies and the status of the use of such delegations shall be furnished to the Director, FEMA.

SEC. 502. *Advisory Committees.* The authority of the President under section 708(d) of the Act [50 App. U.S.C. 2158(d)] and delegated in section 501 of this order (relating to establishment of advisory committees) shall be exercised only after consultation with, and in accordance with, guidelines and procedures established by the Administrator of General Services.

PART VI—EMPLOYMENT OF PERSONNEL

SEC. 601. *National Defense Executive Reserve.* (a) In accordance with section 710(e) of the Act [50 App. U.S.C. 2160(e)], there is established in the Executive Branch a National Defense Executive Reserve ("NDER") composed of persons of recognized expertise from various segments of the private sector and from government (except full-time federal employees) for training for employment in executive positions in the Federal Government in the event of an emergency that requires such employment.

(b) The head of any department or agency may establish a unit of the NDER in the department or agency and train members of that unit.

(c) The head of each department or agency with an NDER unit is authorized to exercise the President's authority to employ civilian personnel in accordance with section 703(a) of the Act [50 App. U.S.C. 2153(a)] when activating all or a part of its NDER unit. The exercise of this authority shall be subject to the provisions of subsections 601(d) and (e) of this order and shall not be redelegated.

(d) The head of a department or agency may activate an NDER unit, in whole or in part, upon the written determination that an emergency affecting the national security or defense preparedness of the United States exists and that the activation of the unit is necessary to carry out the emergency program functions of the department or agency.

(e) At least 72 hours prior to activating the NDER unit, the head of the department or agency shall notify, in writing, the Assistant to the President for National Security Affairs of the impending activation and provide a copy of the determination required under subsection 601(d) of this order.

(f) The Director, FEMA, shall coordinate the NDER program activities of departments and agencies in establishing units of the Reserve; provide for appropriate guidance for recruitment, training, and activation; and issue necessary rules and guidance in connection with the program.

(g) This order suspends any delegated authority, regulation, or other requirement or condition with respect to the activation of any NDER unit, in whole or in part, or appointment of any NDER member that is inconsistent with the authorities delegated herein, provided that the aforesaid suspension applies only as long as sections 703(a) and 710(e) of the Act are in effect.

SEC. 602. *Consultants.* The head of each department or agency assigned functions under this order is delegated authority under sections 710(b) and (c) of the Act [50 App. U.S.C. 2160(b), (c)] to employ persons of outstanding experience and ability without compensation and to employ experts, consultants, or organizations. The authority delegated by this section shall not be redelegated.

PART VII—LABOR SUPPLY

SEC. 701. *Secretary of Labor.* The Secretary of Labor, identified in this section as the Secretary, shall:

(a) Collect, analyze, and maintain data needed to make a continuing appraisal of the nation's labor requirements and the supply of workers for purposes of national defense. All agencies of the government shall cooperate with the Secretary in furnishing information necessary for this purpose, to the extent permitted by law;

(b) In response to requests from the head of a Federal department or agency engaged in the procurement for national defense, consult with and advise that department or agency with respect to (1) the effect of contemplated actions on labor supply and utilization, (2) the relation of labor supply to materials and facilities requirements, and (3) such other matters as will assist in making the exercise of priority and allocations functions consistent with effective utilization and distribution of labor;

(c) Formulate plans, programs, and policies for meeting defense and essential civilian labor requirements;

(d) Project skill shortages to facilitate meeting defense and essential civilian needs and establish training programs;

(e) Determine the occupations and skills critical to meeting the labor requirements of defense and essential civilian activities and, with the assistance of the Secretary of Defense, the Director of Selective Service, and such other persons as the Director, FEMA, may designate, develop policies regulating the induction and deferment of personnel for the armed services, except for civilian personnel in the reserves; and

(f) Administer an effective labor-management relations policy to support the activities and programs under this order with the cooperation of other Federal agencies, including the National Labor Relations Board and the Federal Mediation and Conciliation Service.

PART VIII—DEFENSE INDUSTRIAL BASE INFORMATION AND REPORTS

SEC. 801. *Foreign Acquisition of Companies.* The Secretary of the Treasury, in cooperation with the Department of State, the Department of Defense, the Department of Commerce, the Department of Energy, the Department of Agriculture, the Attorney General, and the Director of Central Intelligence, shall complete and furnish a report to the President and then to Congress in accordance with the requirements of section 721(k) of the Act [50 App. U.S.C. 2170(k)] concerning foreign efforts to acquire United States companies involved in research, development, or production of critical technologies and industrial espionage activities directed by foreign governments against private U.S. companies.

SEC. 802. *Defense Industrial Base Information System.* (a) The Secretary of Defense and the heads of other appropriate Federal departments and agencies, as determined by the Secretary of Defense, shall establish an information system on the domestic defense industrial base in accordance with the requirements of section 722 of the Act [50 App. U.S.C. 2171].

(b) In establishing the information system required by subsection (a) of this order, the Secretary of Defense, the Secretary of Commerce, and the heads of other appropriate Federal departments and agencies, as determined by the Secretary of Defense in consultation with the Secretary of Commerce, shall consult with each other for the purposes of performing the duties listed in section 722(d)(1) of the Act.

(c) The Secretary of Defense shall convene a task force consisting of the Secretary of Commerce and the Secretary of each military department and the heads of other appropriate Federal departments and agencies, as determined by the Secretary of Defense in consultation with the Secretary of Commerce, to carry out the duties under section 722(d)(2) of the Act.

(d) The Secretary of Defense shall report to Congress on a strategic plan for developing a cost-effective, comprehensive information system capable of identifying on a timely, ongoing basis vulnerability in critical components and critical technology items. The plans shall include an assessment of the performance and cost-effectiveness of procedures specified in section 722(b) of the Act.

(e) The Secretary of Commerce, acting through the Bureau of the Census, shall consult with the Secretary of Defense and the Director, FEMA, to improve the usefulness of information derived from the Census of Manufacturers in carrying out section 722 of the Act.

(f) The Secretary of Defense shall perform an analysis of the production base for not more than two major weapons systems of each military department in establishing the information system under section 722 of the Act. Each analysis shall identify the critical components of each system.

(g) The Secretary of Defense, in consultation with the Secretary of Commerce, and the heads of other Federal departments and agencies as appropriate, shall issue a biennial report on critical components and technology in accordance with section 722(e) of the Act.

PART IX—GENERAL PROVISIONS

SEC. 901. *Definitions.* In addition to the definitions in section 702 of the Act [50 App. U.S.C. 2152], the following definitions apply throughout this order:

(a) ''Civil transportation'' includes movement of persons and property by all modes of transportation in interstate, intrastate, or foreign commerce within the United States, its territories and possessions, and the District of Columbia, and, without limitation, related public storage and warehousing, ports, services, equipment and facilities, such as transportation carrier shop and repair facilities. However, ''civil transportation'' shall not include transportation owned or controlled by the Department of Defense, use of petroleum and gas pipelines, and coal slurry pipelines used only to supply energy production facilities directly. As applied herein, ''civil transportation'' shall include direction, control, and coordination of civil transportation capacity regardless of ownership.

(b) ''Energy'' means all forms of energy including petroleum, gas (both natural and manufactured), electricity, solid fuels (including all forms of coal, coke, coal chemicals, coal liquification, and coal gasification), and atomic energy, and the production, conservation, use, control, and distribution (including pipelines) of all of these forms of energy.

(c) ''Farm equipment'' means equipment, machinery, and repair parts manufactured for use on farms in connection with the production or preparation for market use of food resources.

(d) ''Fertilizer'' means any product or combination of products that contain one or more of the elements—nitrogen, phosphorus, and potassium—for use as a plant nutrient.

(e) ''Food resources'' means all commodities and products, simple, mixed, or compound, or complements to such commodities or products, that are capable of being ingested by either human beings or animals, irrespective of other uses to which such commodities or products may be put, at all stages of processing from the raw commodity to the products thereof in vendible form for human or animal consumption. ''Food resources'' also means all starches, sugars, vegetable and animal or marine fats and oils, cotton, tobacco, wool, mohair, hemp, flax fiber, and naval stores, but does not mean any such material after it loses its identity as an agricultural commodity or agricultural product.

(f) ''Food resource facilities'' means plants, machinery, vehicles (including on-farm), and other facilities required for the production, processing, distribution, and storage (including cold storage) of food resources, livestock and poultry feed and seed, and for the domestic distribution of farm equipment and fertilizer (excluding transportation thereof).

(g) ''Functions'' include powers, duties, authority, responsibilities, and discretion.

(h) ''Head of each Federal department or agency engaged in procurement for the national defense'' means the heads of the Departments of Defense, Energy, and Commerce, as well as those departments and agencies listed in Executive Order No. 10789 [50 U.S.C. 1431 note].

(i) ''Heads of other appropriate Federal departments and agencies'' as used in part VIII of this order means the heads of such other Federal agencies and departments that acquire information or need information with respect to making any determination to exercise any authority under the Act.

(j) ''Health resources'' means materials, facilities, health supplies, and equipment (including pharmaceutical, blood collecting and dispensing supplies, biological, surgical textiles, and emergency surgical instruments and supplies) required to prevent the impairment of, improve, or restore the physical and mental health conditions of the population.

(k) ''Metals and minerals'' means all raw materials of mineral origin (excluding energy) including their refining, smelting, or processing, but excluding their fabrication.

(*l*) ''Strategic and Critical Materials'' means materials (including energy) that (1) would be needed to supply the military, industrial, and essential civilian needs of the United States during a national security emergency, and (2) are not found or produced in the United States in sufficient quantities to meet such need and are vulnerable to the termination or reduction of the availability of the material.

(m) ''Water resources'' means all usable water, from all sources, within the jurisdiction of the United States, which can be managed, controlled, and allocated to meet emergency requirements.

SEC. 902. *General.* (a) Except as otherwise provided in subsection 902(c) of this order, the authorities vested in the President by title VII of the Act [50 App. U.S.C. 2151 et seq.] may be exercised and performed by the head of each department and agency in carrying out the delegated authorities under the Act and this order.

(b) The authorities which may be exercised and performed pursuant to subsection 902(a) of this order shall include (1) the power to redelegate authorities, and to authorize the successive redelegation of authorities, to departments and agencies, officers, and employees of the government, and (2) the power of subpoena with respect to authorities delegated in parts II, III, and IV of this order, provided that the subpoena power shall be utilized only after the scope and purpose of the investigation, inspection, or inquiry to which the subpoena relates have been defined either by the appropriate officer identified in subsection 902(a) of this order or by such other person or persons as the officer shall designate.

(c) Excluded from the authorities delegated by subsection 902(a) of this order are authorities delegated by parts V, VI, and VIII of this order and the authority with respect to fixing compensation under section 703(a) of the Act [50 App. U.S.C. 2153(a)].

SEC. 903. *Authority.* All previously issued orders, regulations, rulings, certificates, directives, and other actions relating to any function affected by this order shall remain in effect except as they are inconsistent with this order or are subsequently amended or revoked under proper authority. Nothing in this order shall affect the validity or force of anything done under previous delegations or other assignment of authority under the Act.

SEC. 904. *Effect on other Orders.* (a) The following are superseded or revoked:

(1) Section 3, Executive Order No. 8248 of September 8, 1939, (4 FR 3864).

(2) Executive Order No. 10222 of March 8, 1951 (16 FR 2247) [50 App. U.S.C. 2256 note].

(3) Executive Order No. 10480 of August 14, 1953 (18 FR 4939) [formerly set out above].

(4) Executive Order No. 10647 of November 28, 1955 (20 FR 8769) [50 App. U.S.C. 2160 note].

(5) Executive Order No. 11179 of September 22, 1964 (29 FR 13239) [formerly set out above].

(6) Executive Order No. 11355 of May 26, 1967 (32 FR 7803) [50 App. U.S.C. 2160 note].

(7) Sections 7 and 8, Executive Order No. 11912 of April 13, 1976 (41 FR 15825, 15826–27) [42 U.S.C. 6201 note].

(8) Section 3, Executive Order No. 12148 of July 20, 1979 (44 FR 43239, 43241) [42 U.S.C. 5195 note].

(9) Executive Order No. 12521 of June 24, 1985 (50 FR 26335).

(10) Executive Order No. 12649 of August 11, 1988 (53 FR 30639).

(11) Executive Order No. 12773 of September 26, 1991 (56 FR 49387), except that part of the order that amends section 604 of Executive Order [No.] 10480.

(b) Executive Order No. 10789 of November 14, 1958 [50 U.S.C. 1431 note], is amended by deleting ''and in view of the existing national emergency declared by Proclamation No. 2914 of December 16, 1950,'' as it appears in the first sentence.

(c) Executive Order No. 11790 [15 U.S.C. 761 note], as amended, relating to the Federal Energy Administration Act of 1974 [15 U.S.C. 761 et seq.], is amended by deleting ''Executive Order No. 10480'' where it appears in section 4 and substituting this order's number.

(d) Subject to subsection 904(c) of this order, to the extent that any provision of any prior Executive order is inconsistent with the provisions of this order, this order shall control and such prior provision is amended accordingly.

SEC. 905. *Judicial Review*. This order is not intended to create any right or benefit, substantive or procedural, enforceable at law by a party against the United States, its agencies, its officers, or any person.

WILLIAM J. CLINTON.

[For abolition, transfer of functions, and treatment of references to United States Arms Control and Disarmament Agency, see section 6511 et seq. of Title 22, Foreign Relations and Intercourse.]

§2154. Regulations and orders

(a) In general

Subject to section 709 [section 2159 of this Appendix] and subsection (b), the President may prescribe such regulations and issue such orders as the President may determine to be appropriate to carry out this Act [sections 2061 to 2171 of this Appendix].

(b) Procurement regulations

Any procurement regulation, procedure, or form issued pursuant to subsection (a) shall be issued pursuant to section 25 of the Office of Federal Procurement Policy Act [41 U.S.C. 421], and shall conform to any governmentwide procurement policy or regulation issued pursuant to section 6 or 25 of that Act [41 U.S.C. 405, 421].

(Sept. 8, 1950, ch. 932, title VII, §704, 64 Stat. 816; July 31, 1951, ch. 275, title I, §109(c), 65 Stat. 139; Pub. L. 102–558, title I, §134, Oct. 28, 1992, 106 Stat. 4212.)

AMENDMENTS

1992—Pub. L. 102–558 amended section generally, substituting present provisions for provisions authorizing promulgation of rules, regulations, and orders by the President in order to carry out sections 2061 to 2170 of this Appendix.

1951—Act July 31, 1951, limited authority to regulate natural gas where a State agency is handling the matter.

EFFECTIVE DATE OF 1992 AMENDMENT

Amendment by Pub. L. 102–558 deemed to have become effective Mar. 1, 1992, see section 304 of Pub. L. 102–558, set out as a note under section 2062 of this Appendix.

TERMINATION DATE

Termination of section, see section 2166(a) of this Appendix.

DELEGATION OF FUNCTIONS

Functions of President under act Sept. 8, 1950 [section 2061 et seq. of this Appendix], relating to production, conservation, use, control, distribution, and allocation of energy, delegated to Secretary of Energy, see section 4 of Ex. Ord. No. 11790, eff. June 25, 1974, 39 F.R. 23185, set out as a note under section 761 of Title 15, Commerce and Trade.

SECTION REFERRED TO IN OTHER SECTIONS

This section is referred to in section 2072 of this Appendix.

§2155. Investigations; records; reports; subpoenas; right to counsel

(a) The President shall be entitled, while this Act [sections 2061 to 2171 of this Appendix] is in effect and for a period of two years thereafter, by regulation, subpoena, or otherwise, to obtain such information from, require such reports and the keeping of such records by, make such inspection of the books, records, and other writings, premises or property of, and take the sworn testimony of, and administer oaths and affirmations to, any person as may be necessary or appropriate, in his discretion, to the enforcement or the administration of this Act [said sections] and the regulations or orders issued thereunder. The President shall issue regulations insuring that the authority of this subsection will be utilized only after the scope and purpose of the investigation, inspection, or inquiry to be made have been defined by competent authority, and it is assured that no adequate and authoritative data are available from any Federal or other responsible agency. In case of contumacy by, or refusal to obey a subpoena served upon, any person referred to in this subsection, the district court of the United States for any district in which such person is found or resides or transacts business, upon application by the President, shall have jurisdiction to issue an order requiring such person to appear and give testimony or to appear and produce documents, or both; and any failure to obey such order of the court may be punished by such court as a contempt thereof.

(b) The production of a person's books, records, or other documentary evidence shall not be required at any place other than the place where such person usually keeps them, if, prior to the return date specified in the regulations, subpoena, or other document issued with respect thereto, such person furnishes the President with a true copy of such books, records, or other documentary evidence (certified by such person under oath to be a true and correct copy) or enters into a stipulation with the President as to the information contained in such books, records, or other documentary evidence. Witnesses shall be paid the same fees and mileage that are paid witnesses in the courts of the United States.

(c) Any person who willfully performs any act prohibited or willfully fails to perform any act required by the above provisions of this section, or any rule, regulation, or order thereunder, shall upon conviction be fined not more than $10,000 or imprisoned for not more than one year or both.

(d) Information obtained under this section which the President deems confidential or with reference to which a request for confidential treatment is made by the person furnishing such information shall not be published or disclosed unless the President determines that the withholding thereof is contrary to the interest of the national defense, and any person willfully violating this provision shall, upon conviction, be fined not more than $10,000, or imprisoned for not more than one year, or both.

(e) Any person subpoenaed under this section shall have the right to make a record of his testimony and to be represented by counsel.

(Sept. 8, 1950, ch. 932, title VII, §705, 64 Stat. 816; July 31, 1951, ch. 275, title I, §109(d), 65 Stat. 139; June 30, 1952, ch. 530, title I, §117, 66 Stat. 306; June 30, 1953, ch. 171, §9, 67 Stat. 131; Pub. L.

91–452, title II, § 251, Oct. 15, 1970, 84 Stat. 931; Pub. L. 102–558, title I, § 142, Oct. 28, 1992, 106 Stat. 4217.)

AMENDMENTS

1992—Subsec. (a). Pub. L. 102–558, § 142(1), substituted "subpoena" for "subpena" in two places.

Subsec. (b). Pub. L. 102–558, § 142(1), (2), redesignated subsec. (c) as (b) and substituted "subpoena" for "subpena".

Subsec. (c). Pub. L. 102–558, § 142(2), (3), redesignated subsec. (d) as (c) and substituted "$10,000" for "$1,000". Former subsec. (c) redesignated (b).

Subsec. (d). Pub. L. 102–558, § 142(2), (4), redesignated subsec. (e) as (d) and struck out second undesignated par. which read as follows: "All information obtained by the Office of Price Stabilization under this section 705, as amended, and not made public prior to April 30, 1953, shall be deemed confidential and shall not be published or disclosed, either to the public or to another Federal agency except the Congress or any duly authorized committee thereof, and except the Department of Justice for such use as it may deem necessary in the performance of its functions, unless the President determines that the withholding thereof is contrary to the interests of the national defense, and any person willfully violating this provision shall, upon conviction, be fined not more than $10,000 or imprisoned for not more than one year, or both." Former subsec. (d) redesignated (c).

Subsecs. (e), (f). Pub. L. 102–558, § 142(2), (5), redesignated subsec. (f) as (e) and substituted "subpoenaed" for "subpenaed". Former subsec. (e) redesignated (d).

1970—Subsec. (b). Pub. L. 91–452 struck out subsec. (b) which related to immunity from prosecution of any natural person compelled to testify or produce evidence, documentary or otherwise, after claiming his privilege against self-incrimination, and that any such immunity granted would not be construed to vest in any individual any right to priorities assistance, to the allocation of materials, or to any other benefit within the power of the President to grant under sections 2061 to 2166 of this Appendix.

1953—Subsec. (e). Act June 30, 1953, added second par.

1952—Subsec. (f). Act June 30, 1952, added subsec. (f).

1951—Subsec. (a). Act July 31, 1951, made it clear that President has authority to administer oaths and affirmations.

EFFECTIVE DATE OF 1992 AMENDMENT

Amendment by Pub. L. 102–558 deemed to have become effective Mar. 1, 1992, see section 304 of Pub. L. 102–558, set out as a note under section 2062 of this Appendix.

EFFECTIVE DATE OF 1970 AMENDMENT

Amendment by Pub. L. 91–452 effective on sixtieth day following Oct. 15, 1970, and not to affect any immunity to which any individual is entitled under this section by reason of any testimony given before sixtieth day following Oct. 15, 1970, see section 260 of Pub. L. 91–452, set out as an Effective Date; Savings Provision note under section 6001 of Title 18, Crimes and Criminal Procedure.

TERMINATION DATE

Termination of section, see section 2166(a) of this Appendix.

DELEGATION OF FUNCTIONS

Functions of President under act Sept. 8, 1950 [section 2061 et seq. of this Appendix], relating to production, conservation, use, control, distribution, and allocation of energy, delegated to Secretary of Energy, see section 4 of Ex. Ord. No. 11790, June 25, 1974, 39 F.R. 23185, set out as a note under section 761 of Title 15, Commerce and Trade.

§ 2156. Jurisdiction of courts; injunctions; venue; process; effect of termination of provisions

(a) Whenever in the judgment of the President any person has engaged or is about to engage in any acts or practices which constitute or will constitute a violation of any provision of this Act [sections 2061 to 2171 of this Appendix], he may make application to the appropriate court for an order enjoining such acts or practices, or for an order enforcing compliance with such provision, and upon a showing by the President that such person has engaged or is about to engage in any such acts or practices a permanent or temporary injunction, restraining order, or other order, with or without such injunction or restraining order, shall be granted without bond.

(b) The district courts of the United States and the United States courts of any Territory or other place subject to the jurisdiction of the United States shall have jurisdiction of violations of this Act [sections 2061 to 2171 of this Appendix] or any rule, regulation, order, or subpena thereunder, and of all civil actions under this Act [said sections] to enforce any liability or duty created by, or to enjoin any violation of, this Act [said sections] or any rule, regulation, order, or subpena thereunder. Any criminal proceeding on account of any such violation may be brought in any district in which any act, failure to act, or transaction constituting the violation occurred. Any such civil action may be brought in any such district or in the district in which the defendant resides or transacts business. Process in such cases, criminal or civil, may be served in any district wherein the defendant resides or transacts business or wherever the defendant may be found; the subpena for witnesses who are required to attend a court in any district in such case may run into any other district. The termination of the authority granted in any title or section of this Act [said sections], or of any rule, regulation, or order issued thereunder, shall not operate to defeat any suit, action, or prosecution, whether theretofore or thereafter commenced, with respect to any right, liability, or offense incurred or committed prior to the termination date of such title or of such rule, regulation, or order. No costs shall be assessed against the United States in any proceeding under this Act [said sections]. All litigation arising under this Act [said sections] or the regulations promulgated thereunder shall be under the supervision and control of the Attorney General.

(Sept. 8, 1950, ch. 932, title VII, § 706, 64 Stat. 817; July 31, 1951, ch. 275, title I, § 109(e), 65 Stat. 139.)

AMENDMENTS

1951—Subsec. (a). Act July 31, 1951, broadened relief a court may grant when Government seeks to enjoin violations.

TERMINATION DATE

Termination of section, see section 2166(a) of this Appendix.

DELEGATION OF FUNCTIONS

Functions of President under act Sept. 8, 1950 [section 2061 et seq. of this Appendix], relating to production, conservation, use, control, distribution, and allocation of energy, delegated to Secretary of Energy, see section

4 of Ex. Ord. No. 11790, June 25, 1974, 39 F.R. 23185, set out as a note under section 761 of Title 15, Commerce and Trade.

§2157. Liability for compliance with invalid regulations; discrimination against orders or contracts affected by priorities or allocations

No person shall be held liable for damages or penalties for any act or failure to act resulting directly or indirectly from compliance with a rule, regulation, or order issued pursuant to this Act [sections 2061 to 2171 of this Appendix], notwithstanding that any such rule, regulation, or order shall thereafter be declared by judicial or other competent authority to be invalid. No person shall discriminate against orders or contracts to which priority is assigned or for which materials or facilities are allocated under title I of this Act [sections 2071 to 2078 of this Appendix] or under any rule, regulation, or order issued thereunder, by charging higher prices or by imposing different terms and conditions for such orders or contracts than for other generally comparable orders or contracts, or in any other manner.

(Sept. 8, 1950, ch. 932, title VII, §707, 64 Stat. 818; June 30, 1952, ch. 530, title I, §118, 66 Stat. 306.)

AMENDMENTS

1952—Act June 30, 1952, in first sentence struck out "his" before "compliance with".

TERMINATION DATE

Termination of section, see section 2166(a) of this Appendix.

§2158. Voluntary agreements and plans of action for preparedness programs and expansion of production capacity and supply

(a) Immunity from civil and criminal liability or defense to action under antitrust laws; exceptions

Except as specifically provided in subsection (j) of this section, no provision of this Act [sections 2061 to 2171 of this Appendix] shall be deemed to convey to any person any immunity from civil or criminal liability, or to create defenses to actions, under the antitrust laws.

(b) Definitions

For purposes of this Act [sections 2061 to 2171 of this Appendix]—

(1) Antitrust laws

The term "antitrust laws" has the meaning given to such term in subsection (a) of the first section of the Clayton Act [15 U.S.C. 12(a)], except that such term includes section 5 of the Federal Trade Commission Act [15 U.S.C. 45] to the extent that such section 5 applies to unfair methods of competition.

(2) Plan of action

The term "plan of action" means any of 1 or more documented methods adopted by participants in an existing voluntary agreement to implement that agreement.

(c) Prerequisites for agreements and plans of action; delegation of authority to Presidential designees

(1) Upon finding that conditions exist which may pose a direct threat to the national defense or its preparedness programs, the President may consult with representatives of industry, business, financing, agriculture, labor, and other interests in order to provide for the making by such persons, with the approval of the President, of voluntary agreements and plans of action to help provide for the defense of the United States through the development of preparedness programs and the expansion of productive capacity and supply beyond levels needed to meet essential civilian demand in the United States.

(2) The authority granted to the President in paragraph (1) and subsection (d) may be delegated by him (A) to individuals who are appointed by and with the advice and consent of the Senate, or are holding offices to which they have been appointed by and with the advice and consent of the Senate, (B) upon the condition that such individuals consult with the Attorney General and with the Federal Trade Commission not less than ten days before consulting with any persons under paragraph (1), and (C) upon the condition that such individuals obtain the prior approval of the Attorney General, after consultation by the Attorney General with the Federal Trade Commission, to consult under paragraph (1).

(d) Advisory committees; establishment; applicable provisions; membership; notice and participation in meetings; verbatim transcript; availability to public

(1) To achieve the objectives of subsection (c)(1) of this section, the President or any individual designated pursuant to subsection (c)(2) may provide for the establishment of such advisory committees as he determines are necessary. In addition to the requirements specified in this section and except as provided in subsection (n), any such advisory committee shall be subject to the provisions of the Federal Advisory Committee Act, whether or not such Act or any of its provisions expire or terminate during the term of this Act [sections 2061 to 2171 of this Appendix] or of such committees, and in all cases such advisory committees shall be chaired by a Federal employee (other than an individual employed pursuant to section 3109 of title 5, United States Code) and shall include representatives of the public. The Attorney General and the Federal Trade Commission shall have adequate advance notice of any meeting and may have an official representative attend and participate in any such meeting.

(2) A full and complete verbatim transcript shall be kept of such advisory committee meetings, and shall be taken and deposited, together with any agreement resulting therefrom, with the Attorney General and the Federal Trade Commission. Such transcript and agreement shall be made available for public inspection and copying, subject to the provisions of paragraphs (1), (3), and (4) of section 552(b) of title 5, United States Code.

(e) Rules; promulgation by Presidential designees; consultation by Attorney General with Chairman of Federal Trade Commission; approval of Attorney General; procedures; incorporation of standards and procedures for development of agreements and plans of action

(1) The individual or individuals referred to in subsection (c)(2) shall, after approval of the Attorney General, after consultation by the Attorney General with the Chairman of the Federal Trade Commission, promulgate rules, in accordance with section 553 of title 5, United States Code, incorporating standards and procedures by which voluntary agreements and plans of action may be developed and carried out.

(2) In addition to the requirements of section 553 of title 5, United States Code—

(A) general notice of the proposed rulemaking referred to in paragraph (1) shall be published in the Federal Register, and such notice shall include—

(i) a statement of the time, place, and nature of the proposed rulemaking proceedings;

(ii) reference to the legal authority under which the rule is being proposed; and

(iii) either the terms of substance of the proposed rule or a description of the subjects and issues involved;

(B) the required publication of a rule shall be made not less than thirty days before its effective date; and

(C) the individual or individuals referred to in paragraph (1) shall give interested persons the right to petition for the issuance, amendment, or repeal of a rule.

(3) The rules promulgated pursuant to this subsection incorporating standards and procedures by which voluntary agreements may be developed shall provide, among other things, that—

(A) such agreements shall be developed at meetings which include—

(i) the Attorney General or his delegate,

(ii) the Chairman of the Federal Trade Commission or his delegate, and

(iii) an individual designated by the President in subsection (c)(2) or his delegate,

and which are chaired by the individual referred to in clause (iii);

(B) at least seven days prior to any such meeting, notice of the time, place, and nature of the meeting shall be published in the Federal Register;

(C) interested persons may submit written data and views concerning the proposed voluntary agreement, with or without opportunity for oral presentation;

(D) interested persons may attend any such meeting unless the individual designated by the President in subsection (c)(2) finds that the matter or matters to be discussed at such meeting falls within the purview of matters described in section 552b(c) of title 5, United States Code;

(E) a full and verbatim transcript shall be made of any such meeting and shall be transmitted by the chairman of the meeting to the Attorney General and to the Chairman of the Federal Trade Commission;

(F) any voluntary agreement resulting from the meetings shall be transmitted by the chairman of the meetings to the Attorney General, the Chairman of the Federal Trade Commission, and the Congress; and

(G) any transcript referred to in subparagraph (E) and any voluntary agreement referred to in subparagraph (F) shall be available for public inspection and copying, subject to paragraphs (1), (3), and (4) of section 552(b) of title 5, United States Code.

(f) Commencement of agreements and plans of action; expiration date; extensions

(1) A voluntary agreement or plan of action may not become effective unless and until—

(A) the individual referred to in subsection (c)(2) who is to administer the agreement or plan approves it and certifies, in writing, that the agreement or plan is necessary to carry out the purposes of subsection (c)(1) and submits a copy of such agreement or plan to the Congress; and

(B) the Attorney General (after consultation with the Chairman of the Federal Trade Commission) finds, in writing, that such purpose may not reasonably be achieved through a voluntary agreement or plan of action having less anticompetitive effects or without any voluntary agreement or plan of action and publishes such finding in the Federal Register.

(2) Each voluntary agreement or plan of action which becomes effective under paragraph (1) shall expire two years after the date it becomes effective (and at two-year intervals thereafter, as the case may be), unless (immediately prior to such expiration date) the individual referred to in subsection (c)(2) who administers the agreement or plan and the Attorney General (after consultation with the Chairman of the Federal Trade Commission) make the certification or finding, as the case may be, described in paragraph (1) with respect to such voluntary agreement or plan of action and publish such certification or finding in the Federal Register, in which case, the voluntary agreement or plan of action may be extended for an additional period of two years.

(g) Monitoring of agreements and plans of action by Attorney General and Chairman of Federal Trade Commission

The Attorney General and the Chairman of the Federal Trade Commission shall monitor the carrying out of any voluntary agreement or plan of action to assure—

(1) that the agreement or plan is carrying out the purposes of subsection (c)(1);

(2) that the agreement or plan is being carried out under rules promulgated pursuant to subsection (e);

(3) that the participants are acting in accordance with the terms of the agreement or plan; and

(4) the protection and fostering of competition and the prevention of anticompetitive practices and effects.

(h) Required provisions of rules for implementation of agreements and plans of action

The rules promulgated under subsection (e) with respect to the carrying out of voluntary agreements and plans of action shall provide—

(1) for the maintenance, by participants in any voluntary agreement or plan of action, of documents, minutes of meetings, transcripts, records, and other data related to the carrying out of any voluntary agreement or plan of action;

(2) that participants in any voluntary agreement or plan of action agree, in writing, to make available to the individual designated by the President in subsection (c)(2) to administer the voluntary agreement or plan of action, the Attorney General and the Chairman of the Federal Trade Commission for inspection and copying at reasonable times and upon reasonable notice any item maintained pursuant to paragraph (1);

(3) that any item made available to the individual designated by the President in subsection (c)(2) to administer the voluntary agreement or plan of action, the Attorney General, or the Chairman of the Federal Trade Commission pursuant to paragraph (2) shall be available from such individual, the Attorney General, or the Chairman of the Federal Trade Commission, as the case may be, for public inspection and copying, subject to paragraph (1), (3), or (4) of section 552(b) of title 5, United States Code;

(4) that the individual designated by the President in subsection (c)(2) to administer the voluntary agreement or plan of action, the Attorney General, and the Chairman of the Federal Trade Commission, or their delegates, may attend meetings to carry out any voluntary agreement or plan of action;

(5) that a Federal employee (other than an individual employed pursuant to section 3109 of title 5 of the United States Code) shall attend meetings to carry out any voluntary agreement or plan of action;

(6) that participants in any voluntary agreement or plan of action provide the individual designated by the President in subsection (c)(2) to administer the voluntary agreement or plan of action, the Attorney General, and the Chairman of the Federal Trade Commission with adequate prior notice of the time, place, and nature of any meeting to be held to carry out the voluntary agreement or plan of action;

(7) for the attendance by interested persons of any meeting held to carry out any voluntary agreement or plan of action, unless the individual designated by the President in subsection (c)(2) to administer the voluntary agreement or plan of action finds that the matter or matters to be discussed at such meeting falls within the purview of matters described in section 552b(c) of title 5, United States Code;

(8) that the individual designated by the President in subsection (c)(2) to administer the voluntary agreement or plan of action has published in the Federal Register prior notification of the time, place, and nature of any meeting held to carry out any voluntary agreement or plan of action, unless he finds that the matter or matters to be discussed at such meeting falls within the purview of matters described in section 552b(c) of title 5, United States Code, in which case, notification of the time, place, and nature of such meeting shall be published in the Federal Register within ten days of the date of such meeting;

(9) that—

(A) the Attorney General (after consultation with the Chairman of the Federal Trade Commission and the individual designated by the President in subsection (c)(2) to administer a voluntary agreement or plan of action), or

(B) the individual designated by the President in subsection (c)(2), to administer a voluntary agreement or plan of action (after consultation with the Attorney General and the Chairman of the Federal Trade Commission),

may terminate or modify, in writing, the voluntary agreement or plan of action at any time, and that effective, immediately upon such termination or modification, any antitrust immunity conferred upon the participants in the voluntary agreement or plan of action by subsection (j) shall not apply to any act or omission occurring after the time of such termination or modification;

(10) that participants in any voluntary agreement or plan of action be reasonably representative of the appropriate industry or segment of such industry; and

(11) that the individual designated by the President in subsection (c)(2) to administer the voluntary agreement or plan of action shall provide prior written notification of the time, place, and nature of any meeting to carry out a voluntary agreement or plan of action to the Attorney General, the Chairman of the Federal Trade Commission and the Congress.

(i) Rules; promulgation by Attorney General and Chairman of Federal Trade Commission

The Attorney General and the Chairman of the Federal Trade Commission shall each promulgate such rules as each deems necessary or appropriate to carry out his responsibility under this section.

(j) Defenses

(1) In general

Subject to paragraph (4), there shall be available as a defense for any person to any civil or criminal action brought under the antitrust laws (or any similar law of any State) with respect to any action taken to develop or carry out any voluntary agreement or plan of action under this section that—

(A) such action was taken—

(i) in the course of developing a voluntary agreement initiated by the President or a plan of action adopted under any such agreement; or

(ii) to carry out a voluntary agreement initiated by the President and approved in accordance with this section or a plan of action adopted under any such agreement, and

(B) such person—

(i) complied with the requirements of this section and any regulation prescribed under this section; and

(ii) acted in accordance with the terms of the voluntary agreement or plan of action.

(2) Scope of defense

Except in the case of actions taken to develop a voluntary agreement or plan of action, the defense established in paragraph (1) shall be available only if and to the extent that the person asserting the defense demonstrates that the action was specified in, or was within the scope of, an approved voluntary agreement initiated by the President and approved in accordance with this section or a plan of action adopted under any such agreement and approved in accordance with this section. The defense established in paragraph (1) shall not be available unless the President or the President's designee has authorized and actively supervised the voluntary agreement or plan of action.

(3) Burden of persuasion

Any person raising the defense established in paragraph (1) shall have the burden of proof to establish the elements of the defense.

(4) Exception for actions taken to violate the antitrust laws

The defense established in paragraph (1) shall not be available if the person against whom the defense is asserted shows that the action was taken for the purpose of violating the antitrust laws.

(k) Surveys and studies by Attorney General and Federal Trade Commission; content; annual report to Congress and President by Attorney General

The Attorney General and the Federal Trade Commission shall each make surveys for the purpose of determining any factors which may tend to eliminate competition, create or strengthen monopolies, injure small business, or otherwise promote undue concentration of economic power in the course of the administration of this section. Such surveys shall include studies of the voluntary agreements and plans of action authorized by this section. The Attorney General shall (after consultation with the Federal Trade Commission) submit to the Congress and the President at least once every year reports setting forth the results of such studies of voluntary agreements and plans of action.

(*l*) Annual report to Congress and President by Presidential designees; contents

The individual or individuals designated by the President in subsection (c)(2) shall submit to the Congress and the President at least once every year reports describing each voluntary agreement or plan of action in effect and its contribution to achievement of the purpose of subsection (c)(1).

(m) Jurisdiction to enjoin statutory exemption or suspension and order for production of transcripts, etc.; procedures

On complaint, the United States District Court for the District of Columbia shall have jurisdiction to enjoin any exemption or suspension pursuant to subsections (d)(2), (e)(3)(D) and (G), and (h)(3), (7), and (8), and to order the production of transcripts, agreements, items, or other records maintained pursuant to this section by the Attorney General, the Federal Trade Commission or any individual designated under subsection (c)(2), where the court determines that such transcripts, agreements, items, or other records have been improperly withheld from the complainant. In such a case the court shall determine the matter de novo, and may examine the contents of such transcripts, agreements, items, or other records in camera to determine whether such transcripts, agreements, items, or other records or any parts thereof shall be withheld under any of the exemption or suspension provisions referred to in this subsection, and the burden is on the Attorney General, the Federal Trade Commission, or such designated individual, as the case may be, to sustain its action.

(n) Exemption from Advisory Committee Act provisions

Notwithstanding any other provision of law, any activity conducted under a voluntary agreement or plan of action approved pursuant to this section, when conducted in compliance with the requirements of this section, any regulation prescribed under this subsection, and the provisions of the voluntary agreement or plan of action, shall be exempt from the Federal Advisory Committee Act and any other Federal law and any Federal regulation relating to advisory committees.

(*o*) Preemption of contract law in emergencies

In any action in any Federal or State court for breach of contract, there shall be available as a defense that the alleged breach of contract was caused predominantly by action taken during an emergency to carry out a voluntary agreement or plan of action authorized and approved in accordance with this section. Such defense shall not release the party asserting it from any obligation under applicable law to mitigate damages to the greatest extent possible.

(Sept. 8, 1950, ch. 932, title VII, § 708, 64 Stat. 818; June 30, 1952, ch. 530, title I, § 116(c), 66 Stat. 305; Aug. 9, 1955, ch. 655, § 6, 69 Stat. 581; Pub. L. 87–305, § 5(b), Sept. 26, 1961, 75 Stat. 667; Pub. L. 91–151, title I, § 9, Dec. 23, 1969, 83 Stat. 376; Pub. L. 94–152, § 3, Dec. 16, 1975, 89 Stat. 810; Pub. L. 102–99, § 5, Aug. 17, 1991, 105 Stat. 487.)

REFERENCES IN TEXT

The Federal Advisory Committee Act, referred to in subsecs. (d)(1) and (n), is Pub. L. 92–463, Oct. 6, 1972, 86 Stat. 770, as amended, which is set out in the Appendix to Title 5, Government Organization and Employees.

AMENDMENTS

1991—Subsec. (a). Pub. L. 102–99, § 5(1), struck out "and subsection (j) of section 708A" after "subsection (j) of this section".

Subsec. (b). Pub. L. 102–99, § 5(2), added subsec. (b) and struck out former subsec. (b) which read as follows: "As used in this section and section 708A the term 'antitrust laws' means—

"(1) the Act entitled 'An Act to protect trade and commerce against unlawful restraints and monopolies', approved July 2, 1890 (15 U.S.C. 1 et seq.);

"(2) the Act entitled 'An act to supplement existing laws against unlawful restraints and monopolies and for other purposes', approved October 15, 1914 (15 U.S.C. 12 et seq.);

"(3) the Federal Trade Commission Act (15 U.S.C. 41 et seq.);

"(4) sections 73 and 74 of the Act entitled 'An Act to reduce taxation, to provide revenue for the Government, and for other purposes', approved August 27, 1894 (15 U.S.C. 8 and 9);

"(5) the Act of June 19, 1936, chapter 592 (15 U.S.C. 13, 13a, 13b, and 21a); and

"(6) the Act entitled 'An Act to promote export trade and for other purposes', approved April 10, 1918 (15 U.S.C. 61–65)."

Subsec. (c)(1). Pub. L. 102–99, §5(3), inserted "and plans of action" after "voluntary agreements" and substituted "Upon" for "Except as otherwise provided in section 708A(*o*), upon".

Subsec. (c)(2). Pub. L. 102–99, §5(4), struck out at end "For the purpose of carrying out the objectives of title I of this Act, the authority granted in paragraph (1) of this subsection shall not be delegated to more than one individual."

Subsec. (d)(1). Pub. L. 102–99, §5(5), inserted "and except as provided in subsection (n)" after "specified in this section" and struck out ", and the meetings of such committees shall be open to the public" after "representatives of the public".

Subsec. (d)(2). Pub. L. 102–99, §5(6), substituted "paragraphs (1), (3), and (4) of section 552(b)" for "section 552(b)(1) and (b)(3)".

Subsec. (e)(1). Pub. L. 102–99, §5(7), substituted "voluntary agreements and plans of action" for "voluntary agreements".

Subsec. (e)(3)(D). Pub. L. 102–99, §5(8), substituted "section 552b(c)" for "subsection (b)(1) or (b)(3) of section 552".

Subsec. (e)(3)(F). Pub. L. 102–99, §5(9), inserted reference to Congress.

Subsec. (e)(3)(G). Pub. L. 102–99, §5(10), substituted "paragraphs (1), (3), and (4) of section 552(b)" for "subsections (b)(1) and (b)(3) of section 552".

Subsec. (f)(1). Pub. L. 102–99, §5(11)(A), inserted "or plan of action" after "voluntary agreement".

Subsec. (f)(1)(A). Pub. L. 102–99, §5(12), inserted "and submits a copy of such agreement or plan to the Congress" after "subsection (c)(1)".

Pub. L. 102–99, §5(11)(B), inserted "or plan" after "the agreement" wherever appearing.

Subsec. (f)(1)(B). Pub. L. 102–99, §5(13), inserted before period "and publishes such finding in the Federal Register".

Pub. L. 102–99, §5(11)(A), inserted "or plan of action" after "voluntary agreement" wherever appearing.

Subsec. (f)(2). Pub. L. 102–99, §5(14), inserted "and publish such certification or finding in the Federal Register" before ", in which case".

Pub. L. 102–99, §5(11), inserted "or plan" after "the agreement", and "or plan of action" after "voluntary agreement" wherever appearing.

Subsec. (g). Pub. L. 102–99, §5(11)(A), inserted "or plan of action" after "voluntary agreement".

Subsec. (g)(1) to (3). Pub. L. 102–99, §5(11)(B), inserted "or plan" after "the agreement".

Subsec. (h). Pub. L. 102–99, §5(15)(A), inserted "and plans of action" after "voluntary agreements".

Subsec. (h)(1), (2). Pub. L. 102–99, §5(15)(B), inserted "or plan of action" after "voluntary agreement" wherever appearing.

Subsec. (h)(3). Pub. L. 102–99, §5(16), substituted "paragraph (1), (3), or (4) of section 552(b)" for "subsections (b)(1) and (b)(3) of section 552".

Pub. L. 102–99, §5(15)(B), inserted "or plan of action" after "voluntary agreement".

Subsec. (h)(4) to (6). Pub. L. 102–99, §5(15)(B), inserted "or plan of action" after "voluntary agreement" wherever appearing.

Subsec. (h)(7), (8). Pub. L. 102–99, §5(15)(B), (17), inserted "or plan of action" after "voluntary agreement" wherever appearing and substituted "section 552b(c)" for "subsection (b)(1) or (b)(3) of section 552".

Subsec. (h)(9), (10). Pub. L. 102–99, §5(15)(B), inserted "or plan of action" after "voluntary agreement" wherever appearing.

Subsec. (h)(11). Pub. L. 102–99, §5(15)(C)–(E), added par. (11).

Subsec. (j). Pub. L. 102–99, §5(18), added subsec. (j) and struck out former subsec. (j) which read as follows: "There shall be available as a defense for any person to any civil or criminal action brought for violation of the antitrust laws (or any similar law of any State) with respect to any act or omission to act to develop or carry out any voluntary agreement under this section that—

"(1) such act or omission to act was taken in good faith by that person—

"(A) in the course of developing a voluntary agreement under this section, or

"(B) to carry out a voluntary agreement under this section; and

"(2) such person fully complied with this section and the rules promulgated hereunder, and acted in accordance with the terms of the voluntary agreement."

Subsec. (k). Pub. L. 102–99, §5(19), inserted "and plans of action" after "voluntary agreements" wherever appearing.

Subsec. (*l*). Pub. L. 102–99, §5(20), inserted "or plan of action" after "voluntary agreement".

Subsecs. (n), (*o*). Pub. L. 102–99, §5(21), added subsecs. (n) and (*o*).

1975—Subsec. (a). Pub. L. 94–152 substituted provisions relating to immunity from civil and criminal liability under the antitrust laws for provisions authorizing President to approve voluntary programs and agreements under section 2061 et seq. of this Appendix.

Subsec. (b). Pub. L. 94–152 substituted definition of "antitrust laws" for provisions exempting under certain conditions acts or omissions to act pursuant to section 2061 et seq. of this Appendix from the antitrust laws or the Federal Trade Commission Act.

Subsec. (c). Pub. L. 94–152 restructured subsec. (c) into pars. (1) and (2), and, as so restructured, inserted provisions of par. (1) authorizing President to consult with leaders of industry, finance, agriculture and labor with a view to developing voluntary agreements to help provide for the defense of the United States whenever he finds conditions exist which pose a threat to the national defense or preparedness programs and transferred existing provisions to par. (2), and, as transferred, substituted provisions which authorized President to delegate authority granted to him in par. (1) of this subsection and under subsec. (d) of this section, for provisions authorizing delegation of authority of subsec. (b) of this section.

Subsec. (d). Pub. L. 94–152 substituted provisions relating to establishment, membership, meetings, transcripts, etc. of advisory committees, for provisions relating to application of this section to acts or omissions to act after withdrawal of any request or finding under this section or withdrawal of approval of Attorney General.

Subsec. (e). Pub. L. 94–152 substituted provisions relating to promulgation of rules for voluntary agreements, procedures for promulgation and required provisions, for provisions relating to monitoring by Attorney General of agreements in force and reports to President and Congress.

Subsecs. (f) to (m). Pub. L. 94–152 added subsecs. (f) to (m).

1969—Subsec. (b). Pub. L. 91–151, §9(a), struck out provision under which exemption from prohibitions of antitrust laws and application of Federal Trade Commission Act had been limited to only those voluntary agreements covering military equipment purchased by Defense Department.

Subsec. (f). Pub. L. 91–151, §9(b), struck out subsec. (f) which prohibited approval of voluntary credit control agreements under this section after June 30, 1952.

1961—Subsec. (e). Pub. L. 87–305 struck out ", and the reports hereafter required," after "Such surveys" and "within ninety days after the approval of this Act [Sept. 8, 1950], and" after "President" and substituted "studies of voluntary agreements and programs authorized by this section" for "such surveys and including such recommendations as he may deem desirable".

1955—Subsec. (b). Act Aug. 9, 1955, §6(1), inserted proviso.

Subsec. (d). Act Aug. 9, 1955, §6(2), exempted subsequent acts or omissions to act upon withdrawal by Attorney General of his approval of voluntary agreement or program.

Subsec. (e). Act Aug. 9, 1955, §6(3), (4), included studies of voluntary agreements and programs in surveys and reports, and required Attorney General to report to Congress at least once every three months.

1952—Subsec. (f). Act June 30, 1952, added subsec. (f).

EFFECTIVE DATE OF 1991 AMENDMENT

Amendment by Pub. L. 102–99 effective Oct. 20, 1990, see section 7 of Pub. L. 102–99, set out as a note under section 2071 of this Appendix.

EFFECTIVE DATE OF 1975 AMENDMENT

Section 9 of Pub. L. 94–152, as amended by Pub. L. 94–153, Dec. 16, 1975, 89 Stat. 822; Pub. L. 94–220, Feb. 27, 1976, 90 Stat. 195, provided that: "This Act and the amendments made by it [enacting section 2158a of this Appendix, amending sections 2160, 2162, 2166, 2168, and 2169 of this Appendix, and enacting provisions set out as notes under this section and section 2061 of this Appendix] shall take effect at the close of November 30, 1975, except that the amendment made by section 3 [amending this section] shall take effect upon the one hundred and twentieth day beginning after the date of its enactment [Dec. 16, 1975]."

EFFECTIVE DATE OF 1955 AMENDMENT

Amendment by act Aug. 9, 1955, effective as of the close of July 31, 1955, see section 11 of act Aug. 9, 1955, set out as a note under section 2062 of this Appendix.

TERMINATION DATE

Provision for termination of section on June 30, 1972, eliminated in amendment by Pub. L. 92–15, §2, May 18, 1971, 85 Stat. 38, of section 2166(a) of this Appendix.

DELEGATION OF FUNCTIONS

Functions conferred upon President under this section necessary to effect changes in composition of, or to take other action respecting voluntary agreements and programs relating to, small business production pools approved prior to July 31, 1953, delegated to Administrator of Small Business Administration by Ex. Ord. No. 10493, Oct. 14, 1953, 18 F.R. 6583, set out as a note under section 640 of Title 15, Commerce and Trade.

Functions of President under act Sept. 8, 1950 [section 2061 et seq. of this Appendix], relating to production, conservation, use, control, distribution, and allocation of energy, delegated to Secretary of Energy, see section 4 of Ex. Ord. No. 11790, June 25, 1974, 39 F.R. 23185, set out as a note under section 761 of Title 15.

For delegation of authority of President under subsecs. (c) and (d) of this section to heads of each Federal department or agency, see sections 501 and 502 of Ex. Ord. No. 12919, June 3, 1994, 59 F.R. 29525, set out as a note under section 2153 of this Appendix.

CONTINUATION IN EFFECT OF EXISTING VOLUNTARY AGREEMENTS

Section 4 of Pub. L. 94–152 provided that:

"(a) Any voluntary agreement—

"(1) entered into under section 708 of the Defense Production Act of 1950 [this section] prior to the effective date of this Act [see Effective Date of 1975 Amendment note below], and

"(2) in effect immediately prior to such date may continue in effect (except as otherwise provided in section 708A(*o*) of the Defense Production Act of 1950, as amended by this Act) [former section 2158a(*o*) of this Appendix] and shall be carried out in accordance with such section 708, as amended by this Act, and such section 708A.

"(b) No provision of the Defense Production Act of 1950, as amended by this Act [see Short Title of 1975 Amendment note set out under section 2061 of this Appendix] shall be construed as granting immunity for, nor as limiting or in any way affecting any remedy or penalty which may result from any legal action or proceeding arising from, any acts or practices which occurred (1) prior to the date of enactment of this Act [Dec. 16, 1975], (2) outside the scope and purpose or not in compliance with the terms and conditions of the Defense Production Act of 1950 [see section 2061 of this Appendix], or (3) subsequent to the expiration or repeal of the Defense Production Act of 1950.

"(c) Effective on the date of enactment of this Act [Dec. 16, 1975], the immunity conferred by section 708 or 708A of the Defense Production Act of 1950, as amended by this Act [this section and section 2158a of this Appendix], shall not apply to any action taken or authorized to be taken by or under the Emergency Petroleum Allocation Act of 1973 [section 751 et seq. of Title 15, Commerce and Trade]."

TERMINATION OF ADVISORY COMMITTEES

Advisory committees in existence on Jan. 5, 1973, to terminate not later than the expiration of the 2-year period following Jan. 5, 1973, unless, in the case of a committee established by the President or an officer of the Federal Government, such committee is renewed by appropriate action prior to the expiration of such 2-year period, or in the case of a committee established by the Congress, its duration is otherwise provided by law. Advisory committees established after Jan. 5, 1973, to terminate not later than the expiration of the 2-year period beginning on the date of their establishment, unless, in the case of a committee established by the President or an officer of the Federal Government, such committee is renewed by appropriate action prior to the expiration of such 2-year period, or in the case of a committee established by the Congress, its duration is otherwise provided by law. See section 14 of Pub. L. 92–463, Oct. 6, 1972, 86 Stat. 776, set out in the Appendix to Title 5, Government Organization and Employees.

SECTION REFERRED TO IN OTHER SECTIONS

This section is referred to in section 2166 of this Appendix; title 42 section 6272.

§2158a. Repealed. Pub. L. 102–99, §4, Aug. 17, 1991, 105 Stat. 487

Section, act Sept. 8, 1950, ch. 932, title VII, §708A, as added Dec. 16, 1975, Pub. L. 94–152, §3, 89 Stat. 815, related to voluntary agreements and plans of action for international agreements for international allocation of petroleum products and related information systems.

EFFECTIVE DATE OF REPEAL

Repeal effective Oct. 20, 1990, see section 7 of Pub. L. 102–99, set out as an Effective Date of 1991 Amendment note under section 2071 of this Appendix.

§2159. Public participation in rulemaking

(a) Exemption from Administrative Procedure Act

Any regulation issued under this Act [sections 2061 to 2171 of this Appendix] shall not be subject to sections 551 through 559 of title 5, United States Code.

(b) Opportunity for notice and comment

(1) In general

Except as provided in subsection (c), any regulation issued under this Act [sections 2061 to 2171 of this Appendix] shall be published in the Federal Register and opportunity for public comment shall be provided for not less than 30 days, consistent with the requirements of section 553(b) of title 5, United States Code.

(2) Waiver for temporary provisions

The requirements of paragraph (1) may be waived, if—

(A) the officer authorized to issue the regulation finds that urgent and compelling circumstances make compliance with such requirements impracticable;

(B) the regulation is issued on a temporary basis; and

(C) the publication of such temporary regulation is accompanied by the finding made under subparagraph (A) (and a brief statement of the reasons for such finding) and an opportunity for public comment is provided for not less than 30 days before any regulation becomes final.

(3) Consideration of public comments

All comments received during the public comment period specified pursuant to paragraph (1) or (2) shall be considered and the publication of the final regulation shall contain written responses to such comments.

(c) Public comment on procurement regulations

Any procurement policy, regulation, procedure, or form (including any amendment or modification of any such policy, regulation, procedure, or form) issued under this Act [sections 2061 to 2171 of this Appendix] shall be subject to section 22 of the Office of Federal Procurement Policy Act [41 U.S.C. 418b].

(Sept. 8, 1950, ch. 932, title VII, §709, 64 Stat. 819; Pub. L. 102–558, title I, §136(a), Oct. 28, 1992, 106 Stat. 4216.)

REFERENCES IN TEXT

The Administrative Procedure Act, referred to in subsec. (a), was repealed by Pub. L. 89–554, §8(a), Sept. 6, 1966, 80 Stat. 632, and reenacted by the first section thereof principally in subchapter II (§551 et seq.) of chapter 5, and chapter 7 (§701 et seq.), of Title 5, Government Organization and Employees.

AMENDMENTS

1992—Pub. L. 102–558 amended section generally. Prior to amendment, section read as follows: "The functions exercised under this Act shall be excluded from the operation of the Administrative Procedure Act (60 Stat. 237) except as to the requirements of section 3 thereof. Any rule, regulation, or order, or amendment thereto, issued under authority of this Act shall be accompanied by a statement that in the formulation thereof there has been consultation with industry representatives, including trade association representatives, and that consideration has been given to their recommendations, or that special circumstances have rendered such consultation impracticable or contrary to the interest of the national defense, but no such rule, regulation, or order shall be invalid by reason of any subsequent finding by judicial or other authority that such a statement is inaccurate."

EFFECTIVE DATE OF 1992 AMENDMENT

Section 136(b) of Pub. L. 102–558 provided that: "Section 709 of the Defense Production Act of 1950 (50 U.S.C. App. 2159), as amended by subsection (a) of this section, shall not apply to any regulation issued in proposed or final form on or before the date of enactment of this Act [Oct. 28, 1992]."

TERMINATION DATE

Termination of section, see section 2166(a) of this Appendix.

SECTION REFERRED TO IN OTHER SECTIONS

This section is referred to in section 2154 of this Appendix.

§2160. Employment of personnel; appointment policies; nucleus executive reserve; use of confidential information by employees; printing and distribution of reports

(a) Repealed. June 28, 1955, ch. 189, §12(c)(1), 69 Stat. 180.

(b)(1) The President is further authorized, to the extent he deems it necessary and appropriate in order to carry out the provisions of this Act [sections 2061 to 2171 of this Appendix] and subject to such regulations as he may issue, to employ persons of outstanding experience and ability without compensation;

(2) The President shall be guided in the exercise of the authority provided in this subsection by the following policies:

(i) So far as possible, operations under the Act [said sections] shall be carried on by full-time, salaried employees of the Government, and appointments under this authority shall be to advisory or consultative positions only.

(ii) Appointments to positions other than advisory or consultative may be made under this authority only when the requirements of the position are such that the incumbent must personally possess outstanding experience and ability not obtainable on a full-time, salaried basis.

(iii) In the appointment of personnel and in assignment of their duties, the head of the department or agency involved shall take steps to avoid, to as great an extent as possible, any conflict between the governmental duties and the private interests of such personnel.

(3) Appointees under this subsection shall, when policy matters are involved, be limited to advising appropriate full-time salaried Government officials who are responsible for making policy decisions.

(4) Any person employed under this subsection is exempted, with respect to such employment, from the operation of sections 281, 283, 284, 434, and 1914[1] of title 18, United States Code, and section 190[1] of the Revised Statutes (5 U.S.C. 99), except that—

(i) exemption hereunder shall not extend to the negotiation or execution, by such appointee, of Government contracts with the private employer of such appointee or with any corporation, joint stock company, association, firm, partnership, or other entity in the pecuniary profits or contracts of which the appointee has any direct or indirect interest;

(ii) exemption hereunder shall not extend to making any recommendation or taking any action with respect to individual applications to the Government for relief or assistance, on appeal or otherwise, made by the private employer of the appointee or by any corporation, joint stock company, association, firm, part-

[1] See References in Text note below.

nership, or other entity in the pecuniary profits or contracts of which the appointee has any direct or indirect interest;

(iii) exemption hereunder shall not extend to the prosecution by the appointee, or participation by the appointee in any fashion in the prosecution, of any claims against the Government involving any matter concerning which the appointee had any responsibility during his employment under this subsection, during the period of such employment and the further period of two years after the termination of such employment; and

(iv) exemption hereunder shall not extend to the receipt or payment of salary in connection with the appointee's Government service hereunder from any source other than the private employer of the appointee at the time of his appointment hereunder.

(5) Appointments under this subsection shall be supported by written certification by the head of the employing department or agency—

(i) that the appointment is necessary and appropriate in order to carry out the provisions of the Act [sections 2061 to 2171 of this Appendix];

(ii) that the duties of the position to which the appointment is being made require outstanding experience and ability;

(iii) that the appointee has the outstanding experience and ability required by the position; and

(iv) that the department or agency head has been unable to obtain a person with the qualifications necessary for the position on a full-time, salaried basis.

(6) NOTICE AND FINANCIAL DISCLOSURE REQUIREMENTS.—

(A) PUBLIC NOTICE OF APPOINTMENT.—The head of any department or agency who appoints any individual under this subsection shall publish a notice of such appointment in the Federal Register, including the name of the appointee, the employing department or agency, the title of the appointee's position, and the name of the appointee's private employer.

(B) FINANCIAL DISCLOSURE.—Any individual appointed under this subsection who is not required to file a financial disclosure report pursuant to section 101 of the Ethics in Government Act of 1978, shall file a confidential financial disclosure report pursuant to section 107 of that Act with the appointing department or agency.

(7) At least once every three months the Director of the Office of Personnel Management shall survey appointments made under this subsection and shall report his or her findings to the President and make such recommendations as he or she may deem proper.

(8) Persons appointed under the authority of this subsection may be allowed reimbursement for travel, subsistence, and other necessary expenses incurred by them in carrying out the functions for which they were appointed in the same manner as persons employed intermittently in the Federal Government are allowed expenses under section 5703 of title 5, United States Code.

(c) The President is authorized, to the extent he deems it necessary and appropriate in order to carry out the provisions of this Act [sections 2061 to 2171 of this Appendix] to employ experts and consultants or organizations thereof as authorized by section 55a[2] of title 5 of the United States Code [5 U.S.C. 3109]. Individuals so employed may be compensated at rates not in excess of $50 per diem and while away from their homes or regular places of business they may be allowed transportation and not to exceed $15 per diem in lieu of subsistence and other expenses while so employed. The President is authorized to provide by regulation for the exemption of such persons from the operation of sections 281, 283, 284, 434, and 1914[2] of title 18 of the United States Code and section 190[2] of the Revised Statutes (5 U.S.C. 99).

(d) The President may utilize the services of Federal, State, and local agencies and may utilize and establish such regional, local, or other agencies, and utilize such voluntary and uncompensated services, as may from time to time be needed; and he is authorized to provide by regulation for the exemption of persons whose services are utilized under this subsection from the operation of sections 281, 283, 284, 434, and 1914[2] of title 18 of the United States Code and section 190[2] of the Revised Statutes (5 U.S.C. 99).

(e) The President is further authorized to provide for the establishment and training of a nucleus executive reserve for employment in executive positions in Government during periods of emergency. Members of this executive reserve who are not full-time Government employees may be allowed transportation and per diem in lieu of subsistence, in accordance with title 5 of the United States Code (with respect to individuals serving without pay, while away from their homes or regular places of business), for the purpose of participating in the executive reserve training program. The President is authorized to provide by regulation for the exemption of such persons who are not full-time Government employees from the operation of sections 281, 283, 284, 434, and 1914[2] of title 18 of the United States Code and section 190[2] of the Revised Statutes (5 U.S.C. 99).

(f) Whoever, being an officer or employee of the United States or any department or agency thereof (including any Member of the Senate or House of Representatives), receives, by virtue of his office or employment, confidential information, and (1) uses such information in speculating directly or indirectly on any commodity exchange, or (2) discloses such information for the purpose of aiding any other person so to speculate, shall be fined not more than $10,000 or imprisoned not more than one year, or both. As used in this section, the term "speculate" shall not include a legitimate hedging transaction, or a purchase or sale which is accompanied by actual delivery of the commodity.

(g) The President, when he deems such action necessary, may make provision for the printing and distribution of reports, in such number and in such manner as he deems appropriate, concerning the actions taken to carry out the objectives of this Act [sections 2061 to 2171 of this Appendix].

[2] See References in Text note below.

(Sept. 8, 1950, ch. 932, title VII, § 710, 64 Stat. 819; July 31, 1951, ch. 275, title I, § 109(f), 65 Stat. 139; June 28, 1955, ch. 189, § 12(c)(1), 69 Stat. 180; Aug. 9, 1955, ch. 655, §§ 7, 8, 69 Stat. 582, 583; Pub. L. 94–152, § 5, Dec. 16, 1975, 89 Stat. 820; Pub. L. 102–558, title I, § 143, Oct. 28, 1992, 106 Stat. 4217.)

Annual Submission of Reports

Pub. L. 89–348, § 2(11), Nov. 8, 1965, 79 Stat. 1313, modified the provisions of subsection (b)(7) of this section to require annual instead of quarterly submission of the report to the Congress.

References in Text

Sections 281 and 283 of title 18, referred to in subsecs. (b)(4), (c), (d), and (e), were repealed by Pub. L. 87–849, § 2, Oct. 23, 1962, 76 Stat. 1126, except as they may apply to retired officers of the armed forces of the United States, and were supplanted by sections 203 and 205 of Title 18, Crimes and Criminal Procedure. For further details, see Exemptions note set out under section 203 of Title 18.

Sections 284, 434, and 1914 of title 18, referred to in subsecs. (b)(4), (c), (d), and (e), were repealed by Pub. L. 87–849, § 2, Oct. 23, 1962, 76 Stat. 1126, and were supplanted by sections 207, 208, and 209, respectively, of Title 18.

Section 190 of the Revised Statutes (5 U.S.C. 99), referred to in subsecs. (b)(4), (c), (d), and (e), was repealed by Pub. L. 87–849, § 3, Oct. 23, 1962, 76 Stat. 1126. See section 207 of Title 18.

Sections 101 and 107 of the Ethics in Governments Act of 1978, referred to in subsec. (b)(6)(B), are sections 101 and 107 of Pub. L. 95–521, which are set out in the Appendix to Title 5, Government Organization and Employees.

Section 55a of title 5, referred to in subsec. (c), which was based on section 15 of act Aug. 2, 1946, ch. 744, 60 Stat. 810, was repealed by Pub. L. 89–554, § 8(a), Sept. 6, 1966, 80 Stat. 632, and reenacted by the first section thereof as section 3109 of Title 5.

Amendments

1992—Subsec. (b)(6). Pub. L. 102–558, § 143(a), amended par. (6) generally. Prior to amendment, par. (6) read as follows: "The heads of the departments or agencies making appointments under this subsection shall file with the Division of the Federal Register for publication in the Federal Register a statement including the name of the appointee, the employing department or agency, the title of his position, and the name of his private employer, and the appointee shall file with such Division for publication in the Federal Register a statement listing the names of any corporations of which he is an officer or director or within sixty days preceding his appointment has been an officer or director, or in which he owns, or within sixty days preceding his appointment has owned, any stocks, bonds, or other financial interests, and the names of any partnerships in which he is, or was within sixty days preceding his appointment, a partner, and the names of any other businesses in which he owns, or within such sixty-day period has owned, any similar interest. At the end of each succeeding six-month period, the appointee shall file with such Division for publication in the Federal Register a statement showing any changes in such interests during such period."

Subsec. (b)(7). Pub. L. 102–558, § 143(b)(1), substituted "Director of the Office of Personnel Management" for "Chairman of the United States Civil Service Commission" and "his or her findings" for "his findings", struck out "and the Joint Committee on Defense Production" after "to the President", and substituted "he or she may" for "he may".

Subsec. (b)(8). Pub. L. 102–558, § 143(b)(2), substituted "reimbursement for travel, subsistence, and other necessary expenses incurred by them in carrying out the functions for which they were appointed in the same manner as persons employed intermittently in the Federal Government are allowed expenses under section 5703 of title 5, United States Code" for "transportation and not to exceed $15 per diem in lieu of subsistence while away from their homes or regular places of business pursuant to such appointment".

1975—Subsec. (e). Pub. L. 94–152 substituted provisions authorizing per diem in lieu of subsistence in accordance with provisions of title 5 of the United States Code with respect to individuals serving without pay while away from their homes or regular places of business, for provisions authorizing $15 per diem in lieu of subsistence.

1955—Subsec. (a). Act June 28, 1955, repealed subsec. (a) which authorized President to place positions and employ persons temporarily in grades 16, 17, and 18 of the General Schedule established by Classification Act of 1949.

Subsec. (b). Act Aug. 9, 1955, § 7, imposed additional restrictions on employment of persons without compensation by establishing guides to be used by President, requiring written certification, publication of statements, and a survey of appointments.

Subsecs. (e) to (g). Act Aug. 9, 1955, § 8, added subsec. (e) and redesignated former subsecs. (e) and (f) as (f) and (g), respectively.

1951—Subsec. (f). Act July 31, 1951, added subsec. (f).

Effective Date of 1992 Amendment

Amendment by Pub. L. 102–558 deemed to have become effective Mar. 1, 1992, see section 304 of Pub. L. 102–558, set out as a note under section 2062 of this Appendix.

Effective Date of 1975 Amendment

Amendment by Pub. L. 94–152 effective at close of Nov. 30, 1975, see section 9 of Pub. L. 94–152, as amended, set out as a note under section 2158 of this Appendix.

Effective Date of 1955 Amendments

Amendment by act Aug. 9, 1955, effective as of close of July 31, 1955, see section 11 of act Aug. 9, 1955, set out as a note under section 2062 of this Appendix.

Amendment by act June 28, 1955, effective June 28, 1955, see section 13(b) of act June 28, 1955.

Termination Date

Termination of section, see section 2166(a) of this Appendix.

Delegation of Functions

Functions of President under act Sept. 8, 1950 [section 2061 et seq. of this Appendix], relating to production, conservation, use, control, distribution, and allocation of energy, delegated to Secretary of Energy, see section 4 of Ex. Ord. No. 11790, June 25, 1974, 39 F.R. 23185, set out under section 761 of Title 15, Commerce and Trade.

The head of each department or agency assigned functions under Ex. Ord. No. 12919 (relating to national defense industrial resources preparedness) delegated authority under subsecs. (b) and (c) of this section to employ persons of outstanding experience and ability without compensation and to employ experts, consultants, or organizations, with authority so delegated not to be redelegated, pursuant to section 602 of Ex. Ord. No. 12919, June 3, 1994, 59 F.R. 29525, set out as a note under section 2153 of this Appendix.

Executive Order No. 10182

Ex. Ord. No. 10182, Nov. 21, 1950, 15 F.R. 8013, as amended by Ex. Ord. No. 10205, Jan. 16, 1951, 16 F.R. 419, which provided for appointments and exemptions, was revoked by Ex. Ord. No. 10647, Nov. 28, 1955, 20 F.R. 8769, formerly set out below.

Executive Order No. 10647

Ex. Ord. No. 10647, Nov. 28, 1955, 20 F.R. 8769, as amended by Ex. Ord. No. 11355, May 26, 1967, 32 F.R.

7803; Ex. Ord. No. 12107, Dec. 28, 1978, 44 F.R. 1055, which delegated authority to make appointments, was revoked by section 904(a)(4) of Ex. Ord. No. 12919, June 3, 1994, 59 F.R. 29533, set out as a note under section 2153 of this Appendix.

SECTION REFERRED TO IN OTHER SECTIONS

This section is referred to in title 22 sections 2386, 2581.

§ 2161. Authorization of appropriations; availability of funds

(a) Authorization

Except as provided in subsection (b), there are hereby authorized to be appropriated such sums as may be necessary and appropriate for the carrying out of the provisions and purposes of this Act [sections 2061 to 2171 of this Appendix] (including sections 302 and 303 [sections 2092 and 2093 of this Appendix], but excluding sections 305 and 306 [sections 2095 and 2096 of this Appendix]) by the President and such agencies as he may designate or create. Funds made available pursuant to this paragraph for the purposes of this Act [said sections] may be allocated or transferred for any of the purposes of this Act [said sections], with the approval of the Office of Management and Budget, to any agency designated to assist in carrying out this Act [said sections]. Funds so allocated or transferred shall remain available for such period as may be specified in the Acts making such funds available.

(b) Title III authorization

There are authorized to be appropriated for each of fiscal years 1996 through 2001, such sums as may be necessary to carry out title III [sections 2091 to 2099a of this Appendix].

(Sept. 8, 1950, ch. 932, title VII, § 711, 64 Stat. 820; Pub. L. 93–426, § 3, Sept. 30, 1974, 88 Stat. 1167; Pub. L. 96–294, title I, § 105(a), June 30, 1980, 94 Stat. 632; Pub. L. 98–265, § 5, Apr. 17, 1984, 98 Stat. 151; Pub. L. 99–441, § 3, Oct. 3, 1986, 100 Stat. 1117; Pub. L. 101–137, § 9(b), Nov. 3, 1989, 103 Stat. 826; Pub. L. 102–99, § 3, Aug. 17, 1991, 105 Stat. 487; Pub. L. 102–558, title I, §§ 144, 152, 161, Oct. 28, 1992, 106 Stat. 4218, 4219; Pub. L. 104–64, § 3, Dec. 18, 1995, 109 Stat. 689; Pub. L. 105–261, div. A, title X, § 1072(b), Oct. 17, 1998, 112 Stat. 2137; Pub. L. 106–65, div. A, title X, § 1063(b), Oct. 5, 1999, 113 Stat. 769; Pub. L. 106–363, § 2, Oct. 27, 2000, 114 Stat. 1407.)

AMENDMENTS

2000—Subsec. (b). Pub. L. 106–363 substituted "2001" for "2000".

1999—Subsec. (b). Pub. L. 106–65 substituted "fiscal years 1996 through 2000" for "the fiscal years 1996, 1997, 1998, and 1999".

1998—Subsec. (b). Pub. L. 105–261 substituted "1998, and 1999" for "and 1998".

1995—Subsec. (a). Pub. L. 104–64, § 3(1), struck out paragraph designation "(1)" and former par. (1) heading "In general" and in text substituted "Except as provided in subsection (b)," for "Except as provided in subsection (c),,".

Subsecs. (b) to (d). Pub. L. 104–64, § 3(2), added subsec. (b) and struck out former subsec. (b) which authorized appropriations to carry out provisions of section 2095(k)(2) of this Appendix, former subsec. (c) which authorized appropriations for fiscal year 1991 to carry out provisions of sections 2091 to 2093 of this Appendix, and former subsec. (d) which authorized appropriations for fiscal years 1993, 1994, and 1995 to carry out sections 2091 to 2099a of this Appendix.

1992—Subsec. (a). Pub. L. 102–558, § 152(2)(A), inserted heading.

Subsec. (a)(1). Pub. L. 102–558, § 152(2)(A), (B), inserted par. heading, substituted "Except as provided in subsection (c)," for "Except as provided in paragraph (2) and paragraph (4)", and struck out "and for payment of interest under subsection (b) of this section" after "sections 302 and 303".

Pub. L. 102–558, § 144, substituted "Office of Management and Budget" for "Bureau of the Budget".

Subsec. (a)(2). Pub. L. 102–558, § 152(2)(C), struck out par. (2) which read as follows:

"(A) There are hereby authorized to be appropriated without fiscal year limitation not to exceed $3,000,000,000 to carry out the provisions of section 305 until the date on which the authority of the President under such section ceases to be effective in accordance with section 305(k)(1). Subject to subparagraphs (B) and (C), all such funds shall remain available until expended.

"(B) Such funds may be expended to carry out section 305 after such date only if such funds were obligated by the President before such date, or are required to be retained as a reserve against a contingent obligation incurred before such date.

"(C) Any sums appropriated pursuant to this paragraph which have not been expended or obligated pursuant to subparagraph (B) as of the date determined under section 305(k)(1) or are not required to be retained as a reserve against a contingent obligation as specified in subparagraph (B), shall be transferred to the Energy Security Reserve and made available to the Secretary of the Treasury for the United States Synthetic Fuels Corporation pursuant to section 195 of the United States Synthetic Fuels Corporation Act of 1980."

Subsec. (a)(3). Pub. L. 102–558, § 152(2)(D), redesignated par. (3) as subsec. (b). See below.

Subsec. (a)(4). Pub. L. 102–558, § 152(2)(E), redesignated subpar. (A) as subsec. (c) (see below) and struck out subpar. (B) which read as follows: "The aggregate amount of loans, guarantees, purchase agreements, and other actions under sections 301, 302, and 303 during fiscal years 1987, 1988, and 1989 may not exceed $150,000,000."

Subsec. (b). Pub. L. 102–558, § 152(1), (2)(D), redesignated par. (3) of subsec. (a) as subsec. (b), inserted heading, struck out "There are" before "hereby", and struck out former subsec. (b) which read as follows: "Interest shall accrue on (1) the cumulative amount of disbursements to carry out the purposes of sections 302 and 303 (except for storage maintenance, and other operating and administrative expenses), plus any unpaid accrued interest, less the cumulative amount of any funds received on transactions entered into pursuant to sections 302 and 303 and any net losses incurred by an agency in carrying out its functions under sections 302 and 303 when the head of the agency determines that such net losses have occurred; and (2) the current market value of the inventory of materials procured under section 303 as of the first day of each fiscal year commencing with the fiscal year beginning July 1, 1975. At the close of each fiscal year there shall be deposited into the Treasury as miscellaneous receipts, from any amounts appropriated under this section, an amount which the Secretary of the Treasury determines necessary to provide for the payment of any interest accrued and unpaid under this subsection. The rate of interest shall be determined by the Secretary of the Treasury, taking into consideration the average market yield during the month preceding each fiscal year on outstanding marketable obligations of the United States with one year remaining to maturity."

Subsec. (c). Pub. L. 102–558, § 152(2)(E), redesignated subpar. (A) of par. (4) of subsec. (a) as subsec. (c) and inserted heading.

Subsec. (d). Pub. L. 102–558, § 161, added subsec. (d).

1991—Subsec. (a)(4). Pub. L. 102–99 amended par. (4) generally. Prior to amendment, par. (4) read as follows:

"(4)(A) There are authorized to be appropriated for fiscal year 1990, not to exceed $50,000,000 to carry out the provisions of section 303.

"(B) The aggregate amount of loans, guarantees, purchase agreements, and other actions under sections 301, 302, and 303 during fiscal year 1990 may not exceed $50,000,000."

1989—Subsec. (a)(4). Pub. L. 101–137 amended par. (4) generally. Prior to amendment, par. (4) read as follows:

"(A) There are authorized to be appropriated for fiscal years 1987, 1988, and 1989 not to exceed $150,000,000 to carry out the provisions of section 303, except that not more than $30,000,000 is authorized to be appropriated for fiscal year 1987.

"(B) The aggregate amount of loans, guarantees, purchase agreements, and other actions under sections 301, 302, and 303 during fiscal years 1987, 1988, and 1989 may not exceed $150,000,000."

1986—Subsec. (a)(4). Pub. L. 99–441 amended par. (4) generally. Prior to amendment, par. (4) read as follows:

"(A) There are authorized to be appropriated to carry out the provisions of section 303 not to exceed $100,000,000 for fiscal years 1985 and 1986, except that not more than $25,000,000 is authorized to be appropriated for fiscal year 1985.

"(B) The aggregate amount of loans, guarantees, purchase agreements, and other actions under sections 301, 302, and 303 during fiscal years 1985 and 1986 may not exceed $100,000,000."

1984—Subsec. (a)(1), (4). Pub. L. 98–265 inserted "and paragraph (4)" after "paragraph (2)" in par. (1) and added par. (4).

1980—Subsec. (a). Pub. L. 96–294, §105(a), designated existing provisions as par. (1), inserted exclusions of sections 305 and 306, reference to funds made available pursuant to this paragraph, and exception for par. (2), and added pars. (2) and (3).

1974—Pub. L. 93–426 designated existing provisions as subsec. (a), inserted reference to sections 302 and 303 of this Appendix, and added subsec. (b).

EFFECTIVE DATE OF 1992 AMENDMENT

Amendment by Pub. L. 102–558 deemed to have become effective Mar. 1, 1992, see section 304 of Pub. L. 102–558, set out as a note under section 2062 of this Appendix.

EFFECTIVE DATE OF 1991 AMENDMENT

Amendment by Pub. L. 102–99 effective Oct. 20, 1990, see section 7 of Pub. L. 102–99, set out as a note under section 2071 of this Appendix.

EFFECTIVE DATE OF 1980 AMENDMENT

Amendment by Pub. L. 96–294 effective June 30, 1980, see section 107 of Pub. L. 96–294, set out as a note under section 2062 of this Appendix.

TERMINATION DATE

Termination of section, see section 2166(a) of this Appendix.

DELEGATION OF FUNCTIONS

Functions of President under act Sept. 8, 1950 [section 2061 et seq. of this Appendix], relating to production, conservation, use, control, distribution, and allocation of energy, delegated to Secretary of Energy, see section 4 of Ex. Ord. No. 11790, June 25, 1974, 39 F.R. 23185, set out as a note under section 761 of Title 15, Commerce and Trade.

SECTION REFERRED TO IN OTHER SECTIONS

This section is referred to in sections 2094, 2095, 2166 of this Appendix.

§2162. Repealed. Pub. L. 102–558, title I, §153, Oct. 28, 1992, 106 Stat. 4219

Section, acts Sept. 8, 1950, ch. 932, title VII, §712, 64 Stat. 820; June 30, 1952, ch. 530, title I, §119, 66 Stat. 306; Aug. 9, 1955, ch. 655, §9, 69 Stat. 583; June 29, 1956, ch. 474, §§3, 5, 70 Stat. 408, 409; June 30, 1966, Pub. L. 89–482, §2, 80 Stat. 235; July 1, 1968, Pub. L. 90–370, §2, 82 Stat. 279; Dec. 16, 1975, Pub. L. 94–152, §6, 89 Stat. 820, established a Joint Committee on Defense Production.

EFFECTIVE DATE OF REPEAL

Repeal deemed to have become effective Mar. 1, 1992, see section 304 of Pub. L. 102–558, set out as an Effective Date of 1992 Amendment note under section 2062 of this Appendix.

§2163. Territorial application of Act

The provisions of this Act [sections 2061 to 2171 of this Appendix] shall be applicable to the United States, its Territories and possessions, and the District of Columbia.

(Sept. 8, 1950, ch. 932, title VII, §713, 64 Stat. 821.)

TERMINATION DATE

Termination of section, see section 2166(a) of this Appendix.

SECTION REFERRED TO IN OTHER SECTIONS

This section is referred to in section 2166 of this Appendix.

§2163a. Repealed. Pub. L. 89–554, §8(a), Sept. 6, 1966, 80 Stat. 656

Section, act Sept. 8, 1950, ch. 932, title VII, §714, as added July 31, 1951, ch. 275, title I, §110(a) 65 Stat. 139; amended June 30, 1952, ch. 530, title I, §121(a) 66 Stat. 306; June 30, 1953, ch. 171, §10, 67 Stat. 131, created Small Defense Plants Administration, and related generally to encouragement and aid to small-business concerns with respect to defense production. It terminated at close of July 31, 1953, by terms of section 2166(a) of this Appendix. For provisions relating to aid to small business, see section 631 et seq. of Title 15, Commerce and Trade.

REVOLVING FUND CONTINUATION

Act July 16, 1953, ch. 204, §1, 67 Stat. 176, provided in part that the revolving fund established under the Small Defense Plants Administration was to remain available through July 31, 1953, for payment of obligations and direct costs under contracts entered into during fiscal year 1953.

§2164. Separability

If any provision of this Act [sections 2061 to 2171 of this Appendix] or the application of such provision to any person or circumstances shall be held invalid, the remainder of the Act [said sections], and the application of such provision to persons or circumstances other than those as to which it is held invalid, shall not be affected thereby.

(Sept. 8, 1950, ch. 932, title VII, §715, formerly §714, 64 Stat. 821; renumbered §715, July 31, 1951, ch. 275, title I, §110(b), 65 Stat. 144.)

TERMINATION DATE

Termination of section, see section 2166(a) of this Appendix.

§2165. Repealed. Pub. L. 102–558, title I, §154, Oct. 28, 1992, 106 Stat. 4219

Section, acts Sept. 8, 1950, ch. 932, title VII, §716, formerly §715, 64 Stat. 821; renumbered §716, July 31, 1951, ch. 275, title I, §110(b), 65 Stat. 144, related to persons disqualified from employment and penalties.

EFFECTIVE DATE OF REPEAL

Repeal deemed to have become effective Mar. 1, 1992, see section 304 of Pub. L. 102–558, set out as an Effective

Date of 1992 Amendment note under section 2062 of this Appendix.

§ 2166. Termination of Act

(a) Title I [sections 2071 to 2078 of this Appendix] (except section 104),[1] title III [sections 2091 to 2099a of this Appendix], and title VII [sections 2151 to 2171 of this Appendix] (except sections 708 and 721 [sections 2158 and 2170 of this Appendix]), and all authority conferred thereunder, shall terminate at the close of September 30, 2001: *Provided*, That all authority hereby or hereafter extended under title III of this Act [sections 2091 to 2099 of this Appendix] shall be effective for any fiscal year only to such extent or in such amounts as are provided in advance in appropriation Acts. Section 714 of this Act [section 2163a of this Appendix], and all authority conferred thereunder, shall terminate at the close of July 31, 1953. Section 104,[1] and title II [section 2081 of this Appendix], and title VI [sections 2131 to 2137 of this Appendix] of this Act, and all authority conferred thereunder, shall terminate at the close of June 30, 1953. Title IV [sections 2101 to 2112 of this Appendix] and V [sections 2121 to 2123 of this Appendix] of this Act, and all authority conferred thereunder, shall terminate at the close of April 30, 1953.

(b) Notwithstanding the foregoing—

(1) The Congress by concurrent resolution or the President by proclamation may terminate this Act [sections 2061 to 2171 of this Appendix] prior to the termination otherwise provided therefor.

(2) The Congress may also provide by concurrent resolution that any section of this Act [said sections] and all authority conferred thereunder shall terminate prior to the termination otherwise provided therefor.

(3) Any agency created under this Act [said sections] may be continued in existence for purposes of liquidation for not to exceed six months after the termination of the provision authorizing the creation of such agency.

(c) The termination of any section of this Act [sections 2061 to 2171 of this Appendix], or of any agency or corporation utilized under this Act [said sections], shall not affect the disbursement of funds under, or the carrying out of, any contract, guarantee, commitment or other obligation entered into pursuant to this Act [said sections] prior to the date of such termination, or the taking of any action necessary to preserve or protect the interests of the United States in any amounts advanced or paid out in carrying on operations under this Act [said sections], or the taking of any action (including the making of new guarantees) deemed by a guaranteeing agency to be necessary to accomplish the orderly liquidation, adjustment or settlement of any loans guaranteed under this Act [said sections], including actions deemed necessary to avoid undue hardship to borrowers in reconverting to normal civilian production; and all of the authority granted to the President, guaranteeing agencies, and fiscal agents, under section 301 of this Act [section 2091 of this Appendix] shall be applicable to actions taken pursuant to the authority contained in this subsection.

[1] See References in Text note below.

Notwithstanding any other provision of this Act [sections 2061 to 2171 of this Appendix], the termination of title VI [sections 2132 to 2137 of this Appendix] or any section thereof shall not be construed as affecting any obligation, condition, liability, or restriction arising out of any agreement heretofore entered into pursuant to, or under the authority of, section 602 or section 605 of this Act [section 2132 or 2135 of this Appendix], or any issuance thereunder, by any person or corporation and the Federal Government or any agency thereof relating to the provision of housing for defense workers or military personnel in an area designated as a critical defense housing area pursuant to law.

(d) No action for the recovery of any cooperative payment made to a cooperative association by a Market Administrator under an invalid provision of a milk marketing order issued by the Secretary of Agriculture pursuant to the Agricultural Marketing Agreement Act of 1937 [7 U.S.C. 671 et seq.] shall be maintained unless such action is brought by producers specifically named as party plaintiffs to recover their respective share of such payments within ninety days after the date of enactment of the Defense Production Act Amendments of 1952 [June 30, 1952] with respect to any cause of action heretofore accrued and not otherwise barred, or within ninety days after accrual with respect to future payments, and unless each claimant shall allege and prove (1) that he objected at the hearing to the provisions of the order under which such payments were made and (2) that he either refused to accept payments computed with such deduction or accepted them under protest to either the Secretary or the Administrator. The district courts of the United States shall have exclusive original jurisdiction of all such actions regardless of the amount involved. This subsection shall not apply to funds held in escrow pursuant to court order. Notwithstanding any other provision of this Act [sections 2061 to 2171 of this Appendix], no termination date shall be applicable to this subsection.

(Sept. 8, 1950, ch. 932, title VII, § 717, formerly § 716, 64 Stat. 822; June 30, 1951, ch. 198, § 1, 65 Stat. 110; renumbered § 717, July 31, 1951, ch. 275, title I, §§ 110(b), 111, 65 Stat. 144; June 30, 1952, ch. 530, title I, §§ 120, 121(b), 66 Stat. 306; June 30, 1953, ch. 170, § 20, 67 Stat. 126; June 30, 1953, ch. 171, §§ 11, 12, 67 Stat. 131; June 30, 1955, ch. 251, § 5, 69 Stat. 225; Aug. 9, 1955, ch. 655, § 10, 69 Stat. 583; June 29, 1956, ch. 474, § 1, 70 Stat. 408; Pub. L. 85–471, June 28, 1958, 72 Stat. 241; Pub. L. 86–560, § 1, June 30, 1960, 74 Stat. 282; Pub. L. 87–505, June 28, 1962, 76 Stat. 112; Pub. L. 88–343, § 1, June 30, 1964, 78 Stat. 235; Pub. L. 89–482, § 1, June 30, 1966, 80 Stat. 235; Pub. L. 90–370, § 1, July 1, 1968, 82 Stat. 279; Pub. L. 91–300, June 30, 1970, 84 Stat. 367; Pub. L. 91–371, Aug. 1, 1970, 84 Stat. 694; Pub. L. 91–379, title I, § 101, Aug. 15, 1970, 84 Stat. 796; Pub. L. 92–15, § 2, May 18, 1971, 85 Stat. 38; Pub. L. 92–325, § 2, June 30, 1972, 86 Stat. 390; Pub. L. 93–323, June 30, 1974, 88 Stat. 280; Pub. L. 93–367, Aug. 7, 1974, 88 Stat. 419; Pub. L. 93–426, § 4, Sept. 30, 1974, 88 Stat. 1167; Pub. L. 94–42, § 1, June 28, 1975, 89 Stat. 232; Pub. L. 94–100, § 1, Oct. 1, 1975, 89 Stat. 483; Pub. L. 94–152, § 2, Dec. 16, 1975, 89 Stat. 810; Pub. L. 95–37, § 2, June 1, 1977, 91 Stat. 178; Pub. L. 96–77, Sept. 29, 1979, 93 Stat.

588; Pub. L. 96–188, Jan. 28, 1980, 94 Stat. 3; Pub. L. 96–225, Apr. 3, 1980, 94 Stat. 310; Pub. L. 96–250, May 26, 1980, 94 Stat. 371; Pub. L. 96–294, title I, §105(b), June 30, 1980, 94 Stat. 633; Pub. L. 97–47, §1, Sept. 30, 1981, 95 Stat. 954; Pub. L. 97–336, Oct. 15, 1982, 96 Stat. 1630; Pub. L. 98–12, Mar. 29, 1983, 97 Stat. 53; Pub. L. 98–181, title VII, §703, Nov. 30, 1983, 97 Stat. 1267; Pub. L. 98–265, §2, Apr. 17, 1984, 98 Stat. 149; Pub. L. 99–441, §2, Oct. 3, 1986, 100 Stat. 1117; Pub. L. 101–137, §9(a), Nov. 3, 1989, 103 Stat. 826; Pub. L. 101–351, §1, Aug. 9, 1990, 104 Stat. 404; Pub. L. 101–407, §1, Oct. 4, 1990, 104 Stat. 882; Pub. L. 101–411, §1, Oct. 6, 1990, 104 Stat. 893; Pub. L. 102–99, §§2, 8, Aug. 17, 1991, 105 Stat. 487, 490; Pub. L. 102–193, §1, Dec. 6, 1991, 105 Stat. 1593; Pub. L. 102–558, title I, §162, Oct. 28, 1992, 106 Stat. 4219; Pub. L. 104–64, §2, Dec. 18, 1995, 109 Stat. 689; Pub. L. 105–261, div. A, title X, §1072(a), Oct. 17, 1998, 112 Stat. 2137; Pub. L. 106–65, div. A, title X, §1063(a), Oct. 5, 1999, 113 Stat. 769; Pub. L. 106–363, §1, Oct. 27, 2000, 114 Stat. 1407.)

References in Text

Section 104 of this Act, referred to in subsec. (a), was classified to section 2074 of this Appendix and terminated June 30, 1953, by terms of subsec. (a) of this section. A new section 104 was added by act Oct. 28, 1992, Pub. L. 102–558, title I, §112, 106 Stat. 4202, and is classified to section 2074 of this Appendix.

The Agricultural Marketing Agreement Act of 1937, referred to in subsec. (d), is act June 3, 1937, ch. 296, 50 Stat. 246, as amended, which is classified principally to chapter 26A (§671 et seq.) of Title 7, Agriculture. For complete classification of this Act to the Code, see section 674 of Title 7 and Tables.

Amendments

2000—Subsec. (a). Pub. L. 106–363 substituted "September 30, 2001" for "September 30, 2000".

1999—Subsec. (a). Pub. L. 106–65 substituted "September 30, 2000" for "September 30, 1999".

1998—Subsec. (a). Pub. L. 105–261 substituted "September 30, 1999" for "September 30, 1998".

1995—Subsec. (a). Pub. L. 104–64, which directed substitution in first sentence of "Title I (except section 104), title III, and title VII (except sections 708 and 721), and all authority conferred thereunder, shall terminate at the close of September 30, 1998" for "Title I (except section 104), title III, and title VII (except sections 708, 714, 719, and 721) of this Act, and all authority conferred thereunder shall terminate at the close of September 30, 1995" was executed by making the substitution for text which included comma after "thereunder", to reflect the probable intent of Congress.

1992—Subsec. (a). Pub. L. 102–558 substituted "September 30, 1995" for "March 1, 1992".

1991—Subsec. (a). Pub. L. 102–193 substituted "March 1, 1992" for "September 30, 1991".

Pub. L. 102–99 substituted "September 30, 1991" for "October 20, 1990" and "sections 708, 714, 719, and 721" for "sections 708, 714, and 719".

1990—Subsec. (a). Pub. L. 101–411 extended termination date from Oct. 5, 1990, to Oct. 20, 1990.

Pub. L. 101–407 extended termination date from Sept. 30, 1990, to Oct. 5, 1990.

Pub. L. 101–351 extended termination date from Aug. 10, 1990, to Sept. 30, 1990.

1989—Subsec. (a). Pub. L. 101–137 extended termination date from Sept. 30, 1989, to Aug. 10, 1990.

1986—Subsec. (a). Pub. L. 99–441 extended termination date from Sept. 30, 1986, to Sept. 30, 1989.

1984—Subsec. (a). Pub. L. 98–265 extended termination date from Mar. 30, 1984, to Sept. 30, 1986.

1983—Subsec. (a). Pub. L. 98–181 extended termination date from Sept. 30, 1983, to Mar. 30, 1984.

Pub. L. 98–12 extended termination date from Mar. 31, 1983, to Sept. 30, 1983.

1982—Pub. L. 97–336 extended termination date from Sept. 30, 1982, to Mar. 31, 1983.

1981—Subsec. (a). Pub. L. 97–47 extended termination date from Sept. 30, 1981, to Sept. 30, 1982.

1980—Subsec. (a). Pub. L. 96–294 extended termination date from Aug. 27, 1981, to Sept. 30, 1981.

Pub. L. 96–250 extended termination date from May 27, 1980, to Aug. 27, 1980.

Pub. L. 96–225 extended termination date from Mar. 28, 1980, to May 27, 1980.

Pub. L. 96–188 extended termination date from Jan. 28, 1980, to Mar. 28, 1980.

1979—Subsec. (a). Pub. L. 96–77 extended termination date from Sept. 30, 1979, to Jan. 28, 1980.

1977—Subsec. (a). Pub. L. 95–37 extended termination date from Sept. 30, 1977, to Sept. 30, 1979.

1975—Subsec. (a). Pub. L. 94–152 extended termination date from Nov. 30, 1975, to Sept. 30, 1977, and inserted proviso that all authority now or subsequently extended under Title III of this Act [sections 2091 to 2094 of this Appendix] shall be effective for any fiscal year only to such extent and amounts as are provided for in advance in appropriation Acts.

Pub. L. 94–100 extended termination date from Sept. 30, 1975, to Nov. 30, 1975.

Pub. L. 94–42 extended termination date from June 30, 1975, to Sept. 30, 1975.

1974—Subsec. (a). Pub. L. 93–426 extended termination date from June 30, 1974, to June 30, 1975.

Pub. L. 93–367 extended termination date from July 30, 1974, to Sept. 30, 1974.

Pub. L. 93–323 extended termination date from June 30, 1974, to July 30, 1974.

1972—Subsec. (a). Pub. L. 92–325 substituted "June 30, 1974" for "June 30, 1972".

1971—Subsec. (a). Pub. L. 92–15 inserted parenthetical reference to section "708".

1970—Subsec. (a). Pub. L. 91–379 substituted "June 30, 1972" for "August 15, 1970" and "sections 714 and 719" for "section 714".

Pub. L. 91–371 extended termination date from July 30, 1970, to Aug. 15, 1970.

Pub. L. 91–300 extended termination date from June 30, 1970, to July 30, 1970.

1968—Subsec. (a). Pub. L. 90–370 extended termination date from June 30, 1968, to June 30, 1970.

1966—Subsec. (a). Pub. L. 89–482 extended termination date from June 30, 1966, to June 30, 1968.

1964—Subsec. (a). Pub. L. 88–343 extended termination date from June 30, 1964, to June 30, 1966.

1962—Subsec. (a). Pub. L. 87–505 extended termination date from June 30, 1962, to June 30, 1964.

1960—Subsec. (a). Pub. L. 86–560 extended termination date from June 30, 1960, to June 30, 1962.

1958—Subsec. (a). Pub. L. 85–471 extended termination date from June 30, 1958, to June 30, 1960.

1956—Subsec. (a). Act June 29, 1956, extended termination date from June 30, 1956, to June 30, 1958.

1955—Subsec. (a). Act Aug. 9, 1955, extended termination date from July 31, 1955, to June 30, 1956.

Act June 30, 1955, extended termination date from June 30, 1955, to July 31, 1955.

1953—Subsec. (a). Act June 30, 1953, ch. 171, §11, changed termination dates as follows: (1) Title I except section 2074 of this Appendix, from June 30, 1953, to June 30, 1955; (2) Title III, from June 30, 1953, to June 30, 1955; Title VII (except section 2163a of this Appendix), from June 30, 1953 to June 30, 1955.

Subsec. (c). Act June 30, 1953, ch. 171, §12, inserted "or the taking of any action (including the making of new guarantees) deemed by a guaranteeing agency to be necessary to accomplish the orderly liquidation, adjustment or settlement of any loans guaranteed under this Act, including actions deemed necessary to avoid undue hardship to borrowers in reconverting to normal civilian production; and all of the authority granted to the President, guaranteeing agencies, and fiscal agents, under section 301 of this Act shall be applicable to actions taken pursuant to the authority contained in this subsection".

Act June 30, 1953, ch. 170, added second par.

1952—Subsec. (a). Act June 30, 1952, § 121(b), extended termination dates from Apr. 30, 1952, to Apr. 30, 1953, and from June 30, 1952, to June 30, 1953.

Subsec. (d). Act June 30, 1952, § 120, added subsec. (d).

1951—Subsec. (a). Acts July 31, 1951, § 111, and June 30, 1951. Act July 31, 1951, struck out subsec. (a) relating to termination of certain titles of act Sept. 8, 1950, and substituted present subsec. (a). Act June 30, 1951, extended termination date from June 30, 1951, to July 31, 1951.

Subsec. (b). Act July 31, 1951, redesignated subsec. (c) as (b) and struck out former subsec. (b) which related to termination date of certain titles of act Sept. 8, 1950. Former subsec. (b) was amended by act June 30, 1951, to extend termination date from June 30, 1951, to July 31, 1951.

Subsecs. (c), (d). Act July 31, 1951, § 111, redesignated subsec. (d) as (c). Former subsec. (c) redesignated (b).

EFFECTIVE DATE OF 1992 AMENDMENT

Amendment by Pub. L. 102–558 deemed to have become effective Mar. 1, 1992, see section 304 of Pub. L. 102–558, set out as a note under section 2062 of this Appendix.

EFFECTIVE DATE OF 1991 AMENDMENTS

Section 2 of Pub. L. 102–193 provided that: "This Act [amending this section] shall take effect on September 30, 1991."

Amendment by Pub. L. 102–99 effective Oct. 20, 1990, see section 7 of Pub. L. 102–99, set out as a note under section 2071 of this Appendix.

EFFECTIVE DATE OF 1980 AMENDMENT

Amendment by Pub. L. 96–294 effective June 30, 1980, see section 107 of Pub. L. 96–294, set out as a note under section 2062 of this Appendix.

EFFECTIVE DATE OF 1975 AMENDMENT

Amendment by Pub. L. 94–152 effective at close of Nov. 30, 1975, see section 9 of Pub. L. 94–152, as amended, set out as a note under section 2158 of this Appendix.

EFFECTIVE DATE OF 1955 AMENDMENT

Amendment by act Aug. 9, 1955, effective as of close of July 31, 1955, see section 11 of act Aug. 9, 1955, set out as a note under section 2062 of this Appendix.

SECTION REFERRED TO IN OTHER SECTIONS

This section is referred to in sections 2095, 2096 of this Appendix.

§ 2167. Repealed. Pub. L. 102–558, title I, § 155, Oct. 28, 1992, 106 Stat. 4219

Section, act Sept. 8, 1950, ch. 932, title VII, § 718, as added July 1, 1968, Pub. L. 90–370, § 3, 82 Stat. 279, authorized a feasibility study of application of uniform cost accounting standards to defense procurement contracts.

EFFECTIVE DATE OF REPEAL

Repeal deemed to have become effective Mar. 1, 1992, see section 304 of Pub. L. 102–558, set out as an Effective Date of 1992 Amendment note under section 2062 of this Appendix.

§ 2168. Repealed. Pub. L. 100–679, § 5(b), Nov. 17, 1988, 102 Stat. 4063

Section, act Sept. 8, 1950, ch. 932, title VII, § 719, as added Aug. 15, 1970, Pub. L. 91–379, title I, § 103, 84 Stat. 796; amended Dec. 16, 1975, Pub. L. 94–152, § 7, 89 Stat. 820; Nov. 8, 1985, Pub. L. 99–145, title IX, § 934(b), 99 Stat. 700; Nov. 14, 1986, Pub. L. 99–661, div. A, title XIII, § 1342(f), 100 Stat. 3991, related to formation, functions, appointment and compensation of staff, etc., of Cost Accounting Standards Board. See section 422 of Title 41, Public Contracts.

§ 2169. Repealed. Pub. L. 102–558, title I, § 156, Oct. 28, 1992, 106 Stat. 4219

Section, act Sept. 8, 1950, ch. 932, title VII, § 720, as added Sept. 30, 1974, Pub. L. 93–426, § 5, 88 Stat. 1167; amended Mar. 21, 1975, Pub. L. 94–9, 89 Stat. 15; Aug. 5, 1975, Pub. L. 94–72, 89 Stat. 399; Dec. 16, 1975, Pub. L. 94–152, § 8, 89 Stat. 820, established a National Commission on Supplies and Shortages.

EFFECTIVE DATE OF REPEAL

Repeal deemed to have become effective Mar. 1, 1992, see section 304 of Pub. L. 102–558, set out as an Effective Date of 1992 Amendment note under section 2062 of this Appendix.

§ 2170. Authority to review certain mergers, acquisitions, and takeovers

(a) Investigations

The President or the President's designee may make an investigation to determine the effects on national security of mergers, acquisitions, and takeovers proposed or pending on or after the date of enactment of this section [Aug. 23, 1988] by or with foreign persons which could result in foreign control of persons engaged in interstate commerce in the United States. If it is determined that an investigation should be undertaken, it shall commence no later than 30 days after receipt by the President or the President's designee of written notification of the proposed or pending merger, acquisition, or takeover as prescribed by regulations promulgated pursuant to this section. Such investigation shall be completed no later than 45 days after such determination.

(b) Mandatory investigations

The President or the President's designee shall make an investigation, as described in subsection (a), in any instance in which an entity controlled by or acting on behalf of a foreign government seeks to engage in any merger, acquisition, or takeover which could result in control of a person engaged in interstate commerce in the United States that could affect the national security of the United States. Such investigation shall—

(1) commence not later than 30 days after receipt by the President or the President's designee of written notification of the proposed or pending merger, acquisition, or takeover, as prescribed by regulations promulgated pursuant to this section; and

(2) shall be completed not later than 45 days after its commencement.

(c) Confidentiality of information

Any information or documentary material filed with the President or the President's designee pursuant to this section shall be exempt from disclosure under section 552 of title 5, United States Code, and no such information or documentary material may be made public, except as may be relevant to any administrative or judicial action or proceeding. Nothing in this subsection shall be construed to prevent disclosure to either House of Congress or to any duly authorized committee or subcommittee of the Congress.

(d) Action by the President

Subject to subsection (d),[1] the President may take such action for such time as the President considers appropriate to suspend or prohibit any acquisition, merger, or takeover, of a person engaged in interstate commerce in the United States proposed or pending on or after the date of enactment of this section [Aug. 23, 1988] by or with foreign persons so that such control will not threaten to impair the national security. The President shall announce the decision to take action pursuant to this subsection not later than 15 days after the investigation described in subsection (a) is completed. The President may direct the Attorney General to seek appropriate relief, including divestment relief, in the district courts of the United States in order to implement and enforce this section.

(e) Findings of the President

The President may exercise the authority conferred by subsection (c)[1] only if the President finds that—

(1) there is credible evidence that leads the President to believe that the foreign interest exercising control might take action that threatens to impair the national security, and

(2) provisions of law, other than this section and the International Emergency Economic Powers Act (50 U.S.C. 1701–1706), do not in the President's judgment provide adequate and appropriate authority for the President to protect the national security in the matter before the President.

The provisions of subsection (d)[1] of this section shall not be subject to judicial review.

(f) Factors to be considered

For purposes of this section, the President or the President's designee may, taking into account the requirements of national security, consider among other factors—

(1) domestic production needed for projected national defense requirements,

(2) the capability and capacity of domestic industries to meet national defense requirements, including the availability of human resources, products, technology, materials, and other supplies and services,

(3) the control of domestic industries and commercial activity by foreign citizens as it affects the capability and capacity of the United States to meet the requirements of national security,

(4) the potential effects of the proposed or pending transaction on sales of military goods, equipment, or technology to any country—

(A) identified by the Secretary of State—

(i) under section 6(j) of the Export Administration Act of 1979 [section 2405(j) of this Appendix], as a country that supports terrorism;

(ii) under section 6(*l*) of the Export Administration Act of 1979 [section 2405(*l*) of this Appendix], as a country of concern regarding missile proliferation; or

(iii) under section 6(m) of the Export Administration Act of 1979 [section 2405(m) of this Appendix], as a country of concern regarding the proliferation of chemical and biological weapons; or

(B) listed under section 309(c) of the Nuclear Non-Proliferation Act of 1978 [42 U.S.C. 2139a(c)] on the "Nuclear Non-Proliferation-Special Country List" (15 C.F.R. Part 778, Supplement No. 4) or any successor list; and

(5) the potential effects of the proposed or pending transaction on United States international technological leadership in areas affecting United States national security.

(g) Report to the Congress

The President shall immediately transmit to the Secretary of the Senate and the Clerk of the House of Representatives a written report of the President's determination of whether or not to take action under subsection (d), including a detailed explanation of the findings made under subsection (e) and the factors considered under subsection (f). Such report shall be consistent with the requirements of subsection (c) of this Act.[2]

(h) Regulations

The President shall direct the issuance of regulations to carry out this section. Such regulations shall, to the extent possible, minimize paperwork burdens and shall to the extent possible coordinate reporting requirements under this section with reporting requirements under any other provision of Federal law.

(i) Effect on other law

Nothing in this section shall be construed to alter or affect any existing power, process, regulation, investigation, enforcement measure, or review provided by any other provision of law.

(j) Technology risk assessments

In any case in which an assessment of the risk of diversion of defense critical technology is performed by a designee of the President, a copy of such assessment shall be provided to any other designee of the President responsible for reviewing or investigating a merger, acquisition, or takeover under this section.

(k) Quadrennial report

(1) In general

In order to assist the Congress in its oversight responsibilities with respect to this section, the President and such agencies as the President shall designate shall complete and furnish to the Congress, not later than 1 year after the date of enactment of this section[3] and upon the expiration of every 4 years thereafter, a report which—

(A) evaluates whether there is credible evidence of a coordinated strategy by 1 or more countries or companies to acquire United States companies involved in research, development, or production of critical technologies for which the United States is a leading producer; and

(B) evaluates whether there are industrial espionage activities directed or directly as-

[1] See References in Text note below.

[2] So in original. Probably should be "section."

[3] See References in Text note below.

sisted by foreign governments against private United States companies aimed at obtaining commercial secrets related to critical technologies.

(2) "Critical technologies" defined

For the purposes of this subsection, the term "critical technologies" means technologies identified under title VI of the National Science and Technology Policy, Organization, and Priorities Act of 1976 [4] or other critical technology, critical components, or critical technology items essential to national defense identified pursuant to this section.

(3) Release of unclassified study

The report required by this subsection may be classified. An unclassified version of the report shall be made available to the public.

(Sept. 8, 1950, ch. 932, title VII, § 721, as added Pub. L. 100–418, title V, § 5021, Aug. 23, 1988, 102 Stat. 1425; amended Pub. L. 102–484, div. A, title VIII, § 837(a)–(c), (e), Oct. 23, 1992, 106 Stat. 2463–2465; Pub. L. 102–558, title I, § 163, Oct. 28, 1992, 106 Stat. 4219; Pub. L. 103–359, title VIII, § 809(d), Oct. 14, 1994, 108 Stat. 3454.)

REFERENCES IN TEXT

Subsections (c) and (d), referred to in subsecs. (d) and (e), were redesignated subsecs. (d) and (e), respectively, by Pub. L. 102–484. See 1992 Amendment note below.

The International Emergency Economic Powers Act, referred to in subsec. (e)(2), is title II of Pub. L. 95–223, Dec. 28, 1977, 91 Stat. 1626, which is classified generally to chapter 35 (§ 1701 et seq.) of Title 50, War and National Defense. For complete classification of this Act to the Code, see Short Title note set out under section 1701 of Title 50 and Tables.

The date of enactment of this section, referred to in subsec. (k)(1), probably means the date of enactment of Pub. L. 102–558, which enacted subsec. (k) of this section and was approved Oct. 28, 1992.

The National Science and Technology Policy, Organization, and Priorities Act of 1976, referred to in subsec. (k)(2), is Pub. L. 94–282, May 11, 1976, 90 Stat. 459, as amended. Title VI of the Act was classified generally to subchapter VI (§ 6681 et seq.) of chapter 79 of Title 42, The Public Health and Welfare, and was omitted from the Code. For complete classification of this Act to the Code, see Short Title note set out under section 6601 of Title 42 and Tables.

AMENDMENTS

1994—Subsec. (k)(1)(B). Pub. L. 103–359 inserted "or directly assisted" after "directed".

1992—Subsecs. (b) to (e). Pub. L. 102–484, § 837(a), added subsec. (b) and redesignated former subsecs. (b) to (d) as (c) to (e), respectively. Former subsec. (e) redesignated (f).

Subsec. (f). Pub. L. 102–484, § 837(a)(1), (b), redesignated subsec. (e) as (f) and added pars. (4) and (5). Former subsec. (f) redesignated (g).

Subsec. (g). Pub. L. 102–484, § 837(c), amended subsec. (g) generally. Prior to amendment, subsec. (g) read as follows: "If the President determines to take action under subsection (c), the President shall immediately transmit to the Secretary of the Senate and the Clerk of the House of Representatives a written report of the action which the President intends to take, including a detailed explanation of the findings made under subsection (d)."

Pub. L. 102–484, § 837(a)(1), redesignated subsec. (f) as (g). Former subsec. (g) redesignated (h).

Subsecs. (h), (i). Pub. L. 102–484, § 837(a)(1), redesignated subsecs. (g) and (h) as (h) and (i), respectively.

Subsec. (j). Pub. L. 102–484, § 837(e), added subsec. (j).

Subsec. (k). Pub. L. 102–558 added subsec. (k).

EFFECTIVE DATE OF 1992 AMENDMENT

Amendment by Pub. L. 102–558 deemed to have become effective Mar. 1, 1992, see section 304 of Pub. L. 102–558, set out as a note under section 2062 of this Appendix.

INTERIM DIRECTIVE REGARDING DISPOSITION OF CERTAIN MERGERS, ACQUISITIONS, AND TAKEOVERS

Memorandum of the President of the United States, Oct. 26, 1988, 53 F.R. 43999, provided:

Memorandum for the Secretary of the Treasury

By virtue of the authority vested in me by the Constitution and statutes of the United States, including without limitation Section 301 of Title 3 of the United States Code, the Defense Production Act of 1950, as amended (50 U.S.C. App. 2061 *et seq.*), and the Omnibus Trade and Competitiveness Act of 1988 (Pub. L. 100–418, August 23, 1988) (the "Act") [see Tables for classification], it is ordered as follows:

Pending the issuance of an Executive order to implement the Act, the Secretary of the Treasury is hereby designated and empowered to perform the following-described functions of the President: The authority vested in the President by Section 721 of the Defense Production Act of 1950, as amended [this section], relative to mergers, acquisitions, and takeovers proposed or pending on or after the date of enactment of the Act [Aug. 23, 1988] by or with foreign persons which could result in foreign control of persons engaged in interstate commerce in the United States.

The Secretary of the Treasury shall consult with the Committee on Foreign investment in the United States, established pursuant to Executive Order No. 11858 [15 U.S.C. 78b note] and chaired by the representative of the Secretary of the Treasury, to take such actions or make such recommendations as requested by the Secretary of the Treasury.

The delegation provided herein shall terminate, and this interim directive shall be without any further effect, except as may be provided in the Executive order implementing the Act, upon the effective date of such order.

This interim directive shall be published in the Federal Register.

RONALD REAGAN.

SECTION REFERRED TO IN OTHER SECTIONS

This section is referred to in sections 2166, 2170a of this Appendix; title 10 section 2537; title 22 section 3103.

§ 2170a. Prohibition on purchase of United States defense contractors by entities controlled by foreign governments

(a) In general

No entity controlled by a foreign government may merge with, acquire, or take over a company engaged in interstate commerce in the United States that—

(1) is performing a Department of Defense contract, or a Department of Energy contract under a national security program, that cannot be performed satisfactorily unless that company is given access to information in a proscribed category of information; or

(2) during the previous fiscal year, was awarded—

(A) Department of Defense prime contracts in an aggregate amount in excess of $500,000,000; or

(B) Department of Energy prime contracts under national security programs in an aggregate amount in excess of $500,000,000.

[4] See References in Text note below.

(b) Inapplicability to certain cases

The limitation in subsection (a) shall not apply if a merger, acquisition, or takeover is not suspended or prohibited pursuant to section 721 of the Defense Production Act of 1950 (50 U.S.C. App. 2170).

(c) Definitions

In this section:

(1) The term "entity controlled by a foreign government" includes—

(A) any domestic or foreign organization or corporation that is effectively owned or controlled by a foreign government; and

(B) any individual acting on behalf of a foreign government,

as determined by the President.

(2) The term "proscribed category of information" means a category of information that—

(A) with respect to Department of Defense contracts—

(i) includes special access information;

(ii) is determined by the Secretary of Defense to include information the disclosure of which to an entity controlled by a foreign government is not in the national security interests of the United States; and

(iii) is defined in regulations prescribed by the Secretary of Defense for the purposes of this section; and

(B) with respect to Department of Energy contracts—

(i) is determined by the Secretary of Energy to include information described in subparagraph (A)(ii); and

(ii) is defined in regulations prescribed by the Secretary of Energy for the purposes of this section.

(Pub. L. 102–484, div. A, title VIII, §835, Oct. 23, 1992, 106 Stat. 2461.)

CODIFICATION

Section was enacted as part of the National Defense Authorization Act for Fiscal Year 1993, and not as part of the Defense Production Act of 1950 which comprises sections 2061 to 2171 of this Appendix.

§2170b. Reports on foreign industrial espionage

(a) In general

(1) Submission and contents

In order to assist Congress in its oversight functions with respect to this Act and to improve the awareness of United States industry of foreign industrial espionage and the ability of such industry to protect against such espionage, the President shall submit to Congress a report that describes, as of the time of the report, the following:

(A) The respective policy functions and operational roles of the agencies of the executive branch of the Federal Government in identifying and countering threats to United States industry of foreign industrial espionage, including the manner in which such functions and roles are coordinated.

(B) The means by which the Federal Government communicates information on such threats, and on methods to protect against such threats, to United States industry in general and to United States companies known to be targets of foreign industrial espionage.

(C) The specific measures that are being or could be undertaken in order to improve the activities referred to in subparagraphs (A) and (B), including proposals for any modifications of law necessary to facilitate the undertaking of such activities.

(D) The threat to United States industry of foreign industrial espionage and any trends in that threat, including—

(i) the number and identity of the foreign governments conducting foreign industrial espionage;

(ii) the industrial sectors and types of information and technology targeted by such espionage; and

(iii) the methods used to conduct such espionage.

(2) Date of submission

The President shall submit the report required under this subsection not later than six months after the date of the enactment of this Act [Oct. 14, 1994].

(b) Annual update

Not later than one year after the date referred to in paragraph (2) of subsection (a), and on the expiration of each year thereafter, the President shall submit to Congress a report updating the information referred to in paragraph (1)(D) of that subsection.

(c) Form of reports

To the maximum extent practicable, the reports referred to in subsections (a) and (b) shall be submitted in an unclassified form, but may be accompanied by a classified appendix.

(d) Omitted

(e) Definition

For the purposes of this section, "foreign industrial espionage" means industrial espionage conducted by a foreign government or by a foreign company with direct assistance of a foreign government against a private United States company and aimed at obtaining commercial secrets.

(Pub. L. 103–359, title VIII, §809, Oct. 14, 1994, 108 Stat. 3454.)

REFERENCES IN TEXT

This Act, referred to in subsec. (a)(1), is Pub. L. 103–359, Oct. 14, 1994, 108 Stat. 3423, known as the Intelligence Authorization Act for Fiscal Year 1995. For complete classification of this Act to the Code, see Tables.

CODIFICATION

Section is comprised of section 809 of Pub. L. 103–359. Subsec. (d) of section 809 of Pub. L. 103–359 amended section 2170 of this Appendix.

Section was enacted as part of the Counterintelligence and Security Enhancements Act of 1994 and also as part of the Intelligence Authorization Act for Fiscal Year 1995, and not as part of the Defense Production Act of 1950 which comprises sections 2061 to 2171 of this Appendix.

§2171. Defense industrial base information system

(a) Establishment required

(1) In general

The President, acting through the Secretary of Defense and the heads of such other Federal agencies as the President may determine to be appropriate, shall provide for the establishment of an information system on the domestic defense industrial base which—

(A) meets the requirements of this section; and

(B) includes a systematic continuous procedure, to collect and analyze information necessary to evaluate—

(i) the adequacy of domestic industrial capacity to furnish critical components and critical technology items essential to the national security of the United States;

(ii) dependence on foreign sources for critical components and critical technology items essential to defense production; and

(iii) the reliability of foreign sources for critical components and critical technology items.

(2) Incorporation of DINET

The Defense Information Network (or DINET), as established and maintained by the Secretary of Defense on the date of enactment of the Defense Production Act Amendments of 1992 [Oct. 28, 1992], shall be incorporated into the system established pursuant to paragraph (1).

(3) Use of information

Information collected and analyzed under the procedure established pursuant to paragraph (1) shall constitute a basis for making any determination to exercise any authority under this Act [sections 2061 to 2171 of this Appendix] and a procedure for using such information shall be integrated into the decisionmaking process with regard to the exercise of any such authority.

(b) Sources of information

(1) Foreign dependence

(A) Scope of information review

The procedure established to meet the requirement of subsection (a)(1)(B)(ii) shall address defense production with respect to the operations of prime contractors and at least the first 2 tiers of subcontractors, or at lower tiers if a critical component is identified at such lower tier.

(B) Use of existing data collection and review capabilities

To the extent feasible and appropriate, the President shall build upon existing methods of data collection and analysis and shall integrate information available from intelligence agencies with respect to industrial and technological conditions in foreign countries.

(C) Initial emphasis on priority lists

In establishing the procedure referred to in subparagraph (A), the Secretary may place initial emphasis on the production of critical components and critical technology items.

(2) Production base analysis

(A) Comprehensive review

The analysis of the production base for any major system acquisition included in the information system maintained pursuant to subsection (a) shall, in addition to any information and analyses the President may require—

(i) include a review of all subcontractors and suppliers, beginning with any raw material, special alloy, or composite material involved in the production of a completed system;

(ii) identify each contractor and subcontractor (or supplier) at each level of production for such major system acquisition which represents a potential for delaying or preventing the system's production and acquisition, including the identity of each contractor or subcontractor whose contract qualifies as a foreign source or sole source contract and any supplier which is a foreign source or sole source for any item required in the production, including critical components; and

(iii) include information to permit appropriate management of accelerated or surge production.

(B) Initial requirement for study of production bases for not more than 6 major weapon systems

In establishing the information system under subsection (a), the President, acting through the Secretary of Defense, shall require an analysis of the production base for not more than 2 weapons of each military department which are major systems (as defined in section 2302(5) of title 10, United States Code). Each such analysis shall identify the critical components of each system.

(3) Consultation regarding the census of manufacturers

(A) In general

The Secretary of Commerce, acting through the Bureau of the Census, shall consult with the Secretary of Defense and the Director of the Federal Emergency Management Agency to improve the usefulness of information derived from the Census of Manufacturers in carrying out this section.

(B) Issues to be addressed

The consultation required under subparagraph (A) shall address improvements in the level of detail, timeliness, and availability of input and output analyses derived from the Census of Manufacturers necessary to carry out this section.

(c) Strategic plan for developing comprehensive system

(1) Plan required

Not later than December 31, 1993, the President shall provide for the establishment of and report to the Congress on a strategic plan for developing a cost-effective, comprehensive information system capable of identifying on a timely, ongoing basis vulnerability in critical components and critical technology items.

(2) Assessment of certain procedures

In establishing the plan pursuant to paragraph (1), the President shall assess the performance and cost-effectiveness of procedures implemented under subsection (b), and shall seek to build upon such procedures, as appropriate.

(d) Capabilities of system

(1) In general

In connection with the establishment of the information system under subsection (a), the President shall direct the Secretary of Defense, the Secretary of Commerce, and the heads of such other Federal agencies as the President may determine to be appropriate—

(A) to consult with each other and provide such information, assistance, and cooperation as may be necessary to establish and maintain the information system required by this section in a manner which allows the coordinated and efficient entry of information on the domestic defense industrial base into, and the withdrawal, subject to the protection of proprietary data, of information on the domestic defense industrial base from the system on an on-line interactive basis by the Department of Defense;

(B) to assure access to the information on the system, as appropriate, for all participating Federal agencies, including each military department;

(C) to coordinate standards, definitions, and specifications for information on defense production, which is collected by the Department of Defense and the military departments so that such information can be used by any Federal agency or department, as the President determines to be appropriate; and

(D) to assure that the information in the system is updated, as appropriate, with the active assistance of the private sector.

(2) Task force on military-civilian participation

Upon the establishment of the information system under subsection (a), the President shall convene a task force consisting of the Secretary of Defense, the Secretary of Commerce, the Secretary of each military department, and the heads of such other Federal agencies and departments as the President may determine to be appropriate to establish guidelines and procedures to ensure that all Federal agencies and departments which acquire information with respect to the domestic defense industrial base are fully participating in the system, unless the President determines that all appropriate Federal agencies and departments, including each military department, are voluntarily providing information which is necessary for the system to carry out the purposes of this Act [sections 2061 to 2171 of this Appendix] and chapter 148 of title 10, United States Code.

(e) Report on subcontractor and supplier base

(1) Report required

The President shall issue a report (in accordance with paragraph (4)[1] which includes—

(A) a list of critical components, technologies, and technology items for which there is found to be inadequate domestic industrial capacity or capability; and

(B) an assessment of those subsectors of the economy of the United States which—

(i) support production of any component, technology, or technology item listed pursuant to subparagraph (A); or

(ii) have been identified as being critical to the development and production of components required for the production of weapons, weapon systems, and other military equipment essential to the national defense.

(2) Matters to be considered

The assessment made under paragraph (1)(B) shall include consideration of—

(A) the capacity of domestic sources, especially commercial firms, to fulfill peacetime requirements and graduated mobilization requirements for various items of supply and services;

(B) any trend relating to the capabilities of domestic sources to meet such peacetime and mobilization requirements;

(C) the extent to which the production or acquisition of various items of military material is dependent on foreign sources; and

(D) any reason for the decline of the capabilities of selected sectors of the United States economy necessary to meet peacetime and mobilization requirements, including—

(i) stability of defense requirements;

(ii) acquisition policies;

(iii) vertical integration of various segments of the industrial base;

(iv) superiority of foreign technology and production efficiencies;

(v) foreign government support of nondomestic sources; and

(vi) offset arrangements.

(3) Policy recommendations

The report required by paragraph (1) may provide specific policy recommendations to correct deficiencies identified in the assessment, which would help to strengthen domestic sources.

(4) Time for issuance

The report required by paragraph (1) shall be issued not later than July 1 of each even-numbered year which begins after 1992.

(5) Release of unclassified report

The report required by this subsection may be classified. An unclassified version of the report shall be made available to the public.

(Sept. 8, 1950, ch. 932, title VII, §722, as added Pub. L. 102–558, title I, §135, Oct. 28, 1992, 106 Stat. 4212.)

EFFECTIVE DATE

Section deemed to have become effective Mar. 1, 1992, see section 304 of Pub. L. 102–558, set out as an Effective Date of 1992 Amendment note under section 2062 of this Appendix.

TERMINATION DATE

Termination of section, see section 2166(a) of this Appendix.

[1] So in original. Probably should be followed by a closing parenthesis.

DOMESTIC MINERALS PROGRAM EXTENSION

ACT AUG. 7, 1953, CH. 339, 67 STAT. 417

§ 2181. Congressional declaration of policy

It is recognized that the continued dependence on overseas sources of supply for strategic or critical minerals and metals during periods of threatening world conflict or of political instability within those nations controlling the sources of supply of such materials gravely endangers the present and future economy and security of the United States. It is therefore declared to be the policy of the Congress that each department and agency of the Federal Government charged with responsibilities concerning the discovery, development, production, and acquisition of strategic or critical minerals and metals shall undertake to decrease further and to eliminate where possible the dependency of the United States on overseas sources of supply of each such material.

(Aug. 7, 1953, ch. 339, § 2, 67 Stat. 417.)

SHORT TITLE

Section 1 of act Aug. 7, 1953, provided: "That this Act [enacting sections 2181 to 2183 of this Appendix] may be cited as the 'Domestic Minerals Program Extension Act of 1953'."

SECTION REFERRED TO IN OTHER SECTIONS

This section is referred to in section 2182 of this Appendix.

§ 2182. Extension of termination dates of mineral purchase programs

In accordance with the declaration of policy set forth in section 2 of this Act [section 2181 of this Appendix], the termination dates of all purchase programs designed to stimulate the domestic production of tungsten, manganese, chromite, mica, asbestos, beryl, and columbium-tantalum-bearing ores and concentrates and established by regulations issued pursuant to the Defense Production Act of 1950, as amended [sections 2061 to 2171 of this Appendix], shall be extended an additional two years: *Provided*, That this section is not intended and shall not be construed to limit or restrict the regulatory agencies from extending the termination dates of these programs beyond the two-year extension periods provided by this section or from increasing the quantity of materials that may be delivered and accepted under these programs as permitted by existing statutory authority: *Provided further*, That the extended termination date provided by this section for the columbium-tantalum purchase program shall not apply to the purchase of columbium-tantalum-bearing ores and concentrates of foreign origin.

(Aug. 7, 1953, ch. 339, § 3, 67 Stat. 417.)

SECTION REFERRED TO IN OTHER SECTIONS

This section is referred to in section 2183 of this Appendix.

§ 2183. Quarterly ore reports to purchase program producers

In order that those persons who produce or who plan to produce under purchase programs established pursuant to Public Law 774 (Eighty-first Congress) [section 2061 to 2171 of this Appendix] and Public Law 96 (Eighty-second Congress) may be in position to plan their investment and production with due regard to requirements, the responsible agencies controlling such purchase programs are directed to publish at the end of each calendar quarter the amounts of each of the ores and concentrates referred to in section 3 [section 2182 of this Appendix] purchased in that quarter and the total amounts of each which have been purchased under the program.

(Aug. 7, 1953, ch. 339, § 4, 67 Stat. 417.)

REFERENCES IN TEXT

Public Law 774 (Eighty-first Congress), referred to in text, means act Sept. 8, 1950, ch. 932, 64 Stat. 798, as amended, known as the Defense Production Act of 1950, which is classified to sections 2061 et seq. of this Appendix. For complete classification of this Act to the Code, see section 2061 of this Appendix and Tables.

Public Law 96 (Eighty-second Congress), referred to in text, means act July 31, 1951, ch. 275, 65 Stat. 131, known as the Defense Production Act Amendments of 1951, which amended sections 1884, 1892 to 1896, 1898, 1899, 2071, 2072, 2074, 2081, 2093, 2094, 2102, 2103, 2105, 2109, 2122, 2123, 2131, 2133, 2135, 2151, 2153 to 2156, 2160, and 2163a to 2166 of this Appendix, repealed section 694f of former Title 38, Pensions, Bonuses, and Veterans' Relief, and enacted provisions set out as notes under sections 1907 and 2061 of this Appendix. For complete classification of this Act to the Code, see Short Title of 1951 Amendment note set out under section 2061 of this Appendix and Tables.

DOMESTIC TUNGSTEN, ASBESTOS, FLUORSPAR AND COLUMBIUM-TANTALUM PURCHASE PROGRAMS

ACT JULY 19, 1956, CH. 638, 70 STAT. 579

§§ 2191 to 2195. Omitted

CODIFICATION

Sections 2191 to 2195 terminated Dec. 31, 1958, pursuant to section 2194 of this Appendix.

Section 2191, act July 19, 1956, ch. 638, § 2, 70 Stat. 579, related to authorization of certain purchase programs by Department of the Interior.

Section 2192, act July 19, 1956, ch. 638, § 3, 70 Stat. 580, related to availability of materials purchased under sections 2191 to 2195 of this Appendix to the strategic stockpile.

Section 2193, act July 19, 1956, ch. 638, § 4, 70 Stat. 580, related to promulgation of regulations and delegation of certain functions.

Section 2194, act July 19, 1956, ch. 638, § 5, 70 Stat. 580, provided that programs established pursuant to sections 2191 to 2195 of this Appendix were to terminate on Dec. 31, 1958.

Section 2195, act July 19, 1956, ch. 638, § 6, 70 Stat. 580, authorized appropriations for purposes of sections 2191 to 2195 of this Appendix.

DEPENDENTS ASSISTANCE ACT OF 1950

ACT SEPT. 8, 1950, CH. 992, 64 STAT. 794

§§ 2201 to 2209. Omitted

CODIFICATION

Sections 2201 to 2209 terminated July 1, 1973, pursuant to section 2216 of this Appendix.

Section 2201, acts Sept. 8, 1950, ch. 922, § 1, 64 Stat. 794; Sept. 7, 1962, Pub. L. 87–649, § 10, 76 Stat. 496, provided for determination of dependency of parents.

Section 2202, acts Sept. 8, 1950, ch. 922, § 2, 64 Stat. 795; Sept. 7, 1962, Pub. L. 87–649, § 10, 76 Stat. 496, related to dependents of enlisted members in grades E–4 to E–1.

Section 2203, acts Sept. 8, 1950, ch. 922, § 3, 64 Stat. 795; July 10, 1962, Pub. L. 89–731, § 4(1), 76 Stat. 153; Sept. 7, 1962, Pub. L. 87–649, § 10, 76 Stat. 451; Dec. 16, 1967, Pub. L. 90–207, § 4, 81 Stat. 654; Sept. 28, 1971, Pub. L. 92–129, title II, § 206, 85 Stat. 359, related to quarters allowances for enlisted members.

Section 2204, acts Sept. 8, 1950, ch. 922, § 4, 64 Stat. 795; Sept. 7, 1962, Pub. L. 87–649, § 10, 76 Stat. 496; Sept. 28, 1971, Pub. L. 92–129, title II, § 207, 85 Stat. 359, related to quarters allowances and allotments of pay.

Section 2204(a)–(e) was formerly classified to section 252(g)–(k) of former Title 37, Pay and Allowances, prior to the general revision and enactment of Title 37, Pay and Allowances of the Uniformed Services, by Pub. L. 87–649, § 1, Sept. 7, 1962, 76 Stat. 451.

Section 2205, act Sept. 8, 1950, ch. 922, § 5, 64 Stat. 796, provided that quarters allowance shall not be contingent on right to pay.

Section 2206, act Sept. 8, 1950, ch. 922, § 6, 64 Stat. 796, related to allowance and allotment without consent of enlisted member. See sections 553 and 602 of Title 37.

Section 2207, acts Sept. 8, 1950, ch. 922, § 7, 64 Stat. 796; July 10, 1962, Pub. L. 87–531, § 4(2), 76 Stat. 153; Sept. 28, 1971, Pub. L. 92–129, title II, § 208, 85 Stat. 359, provided for enlisted members not affected by act Sept. 8, 1950, ch. 922, as amended.

Section 2208, acts Sept. 8, 1950, ch. 922, § 8, 64 Stat. 796; July 10, 1962, Pub. L. 87–531, § 4(3), 76 Stat. 153, provided for aviation cadets.

Section 2209, act Sept. 8, 1950, ch. 922, § 9, 64 Stat. 796, related to members furnished Government quarters.

SHORT TITLE

Section 17 of act Sept. 8, 1950, ch. 922, 64 Stat. 797, provided that sections 2201 to 2216 of this Appendix were to be cited as the "Dependents Assistance Act of 1950".

REQUIREMENT OF ALLOTMENT OF PAY BY ENLISTED MEMBERS

Act Oct. 12, 1949, ch. 681, title III, § 302(h), 63 Stat. 812, as amended by act July 10, 1962, Pub. L. 87–531, § 3, 76 Stat. 152, provided that the payment of the basic quarters allowance provided for in section 2203 of this Appendix for certain enlisted men with dependents was to be made only for such period as the enlisted men had in effect allotments of pay not less than the sums of the basic allowances for quarters to which the members were entitled plus $40, for the support of the dependent or dependents on whose account the allowances were claimed, provided that such allotments were not to be required in certain cases, that such allotments could be modified in particular instances by regulation of the Secretary of the Department concerned, and that the minimum allotments required for any month were to be based on the lowest rates of basic quarters allowances to which the members were entitled and the lowest pay grades in which the members served during such month.

§§ 2210 to 2212. Repealed. Pub. L. 93–64, title I, § 101, July 9, 1973, 87 Stat. 147

Section 2210, act Sept. 8, 1950, ch. 922, § 10, 64 Stat. 796, authorized regulations and provided for determinations and waivers and delegation of authority.

Section 2211, act Sept. 8, 1950, ch. 922, § 11, 64 Stat. 797, provided for conclusiveness of determinations and waivers, modifications thereof, and waiver of erroneous payments. See section 5584 of Title 5, Government Organization and Employees, section 2774 of Title 10, Armed Forces, and section 716 of Title 32, National Guard.

Section 2212, act Sept. 8, 1950, ch. 922, § 12, 64 Stat. 797, related to allowance of credit by General Accounting Office for accounts of disbursing officers making erroneous payments. See section 5584 of Title 5, Government Organization and Employees, section 2774 of Title 10, Armed Forces, and section 716 of Title 32, National Guard.

EFFECTIVE DATE OF REPEAL

Repeal effective July 1, 1973, see section 206 of Pub. L. 93–64, set out as an Effective Date of 1973 Amendment note under section 401 of Title 37, Pay and Allowances of the Uniformed Services.

§§ 2213 to 2216. Omitted

CODIFICATION

Sections 2213 to 2216 terminated July 1, 1973, pursuant to section 2216 of this Appendix.

Section 2213, act Sept. 8, 1950, ch. 922, § 13, 64 Stat. 797, related to erroneous payments under Servicemen's Dependents Act of 1942.

Section 2213a, act Sept. 8, 1950, ch. 922, § 13a, as added July 24, 1956, ch. 697, 70 Stat. 634, provided penalty for fraudulent acceptance of benefits.

Section 2214, act Sept. 8, 1950, ch. 922, § 14, 64 Stat. 797, provided for discharge for hardship. See section 1173 of Title 10, Armed Forces.

Section 2215, act Sept. 8, 1950, ch. 922, § 15, 64 Stat. 797, related to effective date of act Sept. 8, 1950, ch. 922.

Section 2216, acts Sept. 8, 1950, ch. 922, § 16, 64 Stat. 797; Mar. 23, 1953, ch. 8, 67 Stat. 6; June 30, 1955, ch. 250, title I, § 103, 69 Stat. 224; Mar. 23, 1959, Pub. L. 86–4, § 3, 73 Stat. 13; Mar. 28, 1963, Pub. L. 82–2, § 3, 77 Stat. 4; June 30, 1967, Pub. L. 90–40, § 3, 81 Stat. 105; Sept. 28, 1971, Pub. L. 92–129, title I, § 105, 85 Stat. 355, provided for termination on July 1, 1973, of sections 2201 to 2209 and 2213 to 2216 of this Appendix.

CIVIL DEFENSE

ACT JAN. 12, 1951, CH. 1228, 64 STAT. 1245

TITLE I—GENERAL PROVISIONS

TITLE I—GENERAL PROVISIONS

§§ 2251 to 2264. Repealed. Pub. L. 103–337, div. C, title XXXIV, § 3412(a), (b)(2), Oct. 5, 1994, 108 Stat. 3111

Section 2251, acts Jan. 12, 1951, ch. 1228, § 2, 64 Stat. 1246; Aug. 8, 1958, Pub. L. 85–606, § 2, 72 Stat. 532; July 14, 1976, Pub. L. 94–361, title VIII, § 804(a), 90 Stat. 931; Dec. 1, 1981, Pub. L. 97–86, title VIII, § 803(b), 95 Stat. 1112;

Nov. 30, 1993, Pub. L. 103–160, div. C, title XXXIV, § 3402(a), 107 Stat. 1962, provided that the purpose of sections 2251 to 2303 of this Appendix was to provide a system of civil defense. See section 5195 of Title 42, The Public Health and Welfare.

Section 2252, acts Jan. 12, 1951, ch. 1228, § 3, 64 Stat. 1246; Dec. 1, 1981, Pub. L. 97–86, title VIII, § 803(c), 95 Stat. 1112; Nov. 30, 1993, Pub. L. 103–160, div. C, title XXXIV, § 3402(b), (f)(2), 107 Stat. 1963, 1964, defined terms used in sections 2251 to 2303 of this Appendix. See section 5195a of Title 42.

Section 2253, acts Jan. 12, 1951, ch. 1228, title IV, § 401, 64 Stat. 1254; June 28, 1955, ch. 189, § 12(c)(2), 69 Stat. 180; Aug. 8, 1958, Pub. L. 85–606, § 5, 72 Stat. 534; Aug. 19, 1964, Pub. L. 88–448, title IV, § 402(a)(30), 78 Stat. 494, related to powers and duties of Administrator in carrying out sections 2251 to 2303 of this Appendix. See section 5197 of Title 42.

Section 2254, act Jan. 12, 1951, ch. 1228, title IV, § 402, 64 Stat. 1255, related to exemption from certain employment restrictions.

Section 2255, acts Jan. 12, 1951, ch. 1228, title IV, § 403, 64 Stat. 1255; Mar. 5, 1952, ch. 78, § 1(b), 66 Stat. 13, directed Administrator to establish security restrictions with respect to access to information and property and provided for employee loyalty oaths. See section 5197a of Title 42.

Section 2256, act Jan. 12, 1951, ch. 1228, title IV, § 404, 64 Stat. 1256, related to transfer of functions, property, and personnel of Civil Defense Administration to Administration established by sections 2251 to 2303 of this Appendix.

Section 2257, act Jan. 12, 1951, ch. 1228, title IV, § 405, 64 Stat. 1256, related to utilization by Administrator of existing facilities. See section 5197b of Title 42.

Section 2258, act Jan. 12, 1951, ch. 1228, title IV, § 406, 64 Stat. 1256, directed Administrator to submit annual reports to Congress and the President. See section 5197c of Title 42.

Section 2259, act Jan. 12, 1951, ch. 1228, title IV, § 407, 64 Stat. 1256, related to applicability of sections 2251 to 2303 of this Appendix. See section 5197d of Title 42.

Section 2260, acts Jan. 12, 1951, ch. 1228, title IV, § 408, 64 Stat. 1257; Aug. 8, 1958, Pub. L. 85–606, § 6, 72 Stat. 534; Aug. 2, 1972, Pub. L. 92–360, § 1(2), 86 Stat. 503; July 14, 1976, Pub. L. 94–361, title VIII, § 804(b), 90 Stat. 931; Nov. 9, 1979, Pub. L. 96–107, title VII, § 702, 93 Stat. 810; Dec. 1, 1981, Pub. L. 97–86, title VIII, § 802, 95 Stat. 1111; Oct. 19, 1984, Pub. L. 98–525, title VIII, § 802, 98 Stat. 2572, related to appropriations and transfers of funds. See section 5197e of Title 42.

Section 2261, act Jan. 12, 1951, ch. 1228, title IV, § 409, 64 Stat. 1257, related to loans from Reconstruction Finance Corporation for civil defense projects.

Section 2262, act Jan. 12, 1951, ch. 1228, title IV, § 410, 64 Stat. 1257, related to effect of sections 2251 to 2303 of this Appendix on Atomic Energy Act of 1946. See section 5197f of Title 42.

Section 2263, act Jan. 12, 1951, ch. 1228, title IV, § 411, 64 Stat. 1257, related to investigations of espionage, sabotage, and subversive acts. See section 5197g of Title 42.

Section 2264, act June 2, 1951, ch. 121, Ch. XI, 65 Stat. 61, established a civil defense procurement fund.

SHORT TITLE

Section 1 of act Jan. 12, 1951, which provided that the act of Jan. 12, 1951, enacting sections 2251 to 2297 of this Appendix, was to be cited as the "Federal Civil Defense Act of 1950", prior to repeal by Pub. L. 103–337, div. C, title XXXIV, § 3412(a), Oct. 5, 1994, 108 Stat. 3111.

SEPARABILITY

Section 412 of act Jan. 12, 1951, provided for separability of provisions for act of Jan. 12, 1951, prior to repeal by Pub. L. 103–337, div. C, title XXXIV, § 3412(a), Oct. 5, 1994, 108 Stat. 3111.

APPLICABILITY OF REORGANIZATION PLAN NO. 1 OF 1958

Section 413 of act Jan. 12, 1951, as added by Pub. L. 85–606, § 7, provided that the applicability of Reorg. Plan No. 1 of 1958 (23 F.R. 4991) was to extend to any amendment of act Jan. 12, 1951, prior to repeal by Pub. L. 103–337, div. C, title XXXIV, § 3412(a), Oct. 5, 1994, 108 Stat. 3111.

TITLE II—ORGANIZATION OF ADMINISTRATION

§§ 2271, 2272. Repealed. Pub. L. 103–337, div. C, title XXXIV, § 3412(a), Oct. 5, 1994, 108 Stat. 3111

Section 2271, act Jan. 12, 1951, ch. 1228, title I, § 101, 64 Stat. 1247, related to establishment of Federal Civil Defense Administration.

Section 2272, act Jan. 12, 1951, ch. 1228, title I, § 102, 64 Stat. 1247, created the Civil Defense Advisory Council which was abolished by section 3(a)(3) of Reorg. Plan No. 1 of 1973, eff. July 1, 1973, 38 Stat. 9579, 87 Stat. 1089, set out as a note under section 5195 of Title 42, The Public Health and Welfare.

TITLE III—POWERS AND DUTIES

§§ 2281 to 2284. Repealed. Pub. L. 103–337, div. C, title XXXIV, § 3412(a), Oct. 5, 1994, 108 Stat. 3111

Section 2281, acts Jan. 12, 1951, ch. 1228, title II, § 201, 64 Stat. 1248; Mar. 5, 1952, ch. 78, § 1(a), 66 Stat. 13; June 25, 1952, ch. 461, 66 Stat. 158; Aug. 2, 1956, ch. 888, § 1, 70 Stat. 949; Aug. 8, 1958, Pub. L. 85–606, § 3(a)(1), (2), (b), (c), 72 Stat. 532, 533; Oct. 4, 1961, Pub. L. 87–390, 75 Stat. 820; June 30, 1964, Pub. L. 88–335, 78 Stat. 231; June 10, 1968, Pub. L. 90–336, 82 Stat. 175; Aug. 2, 1972, Pub. L. 92–360, § 1(1), 86 Stat. 503; July 14, 1976, Pub. L. 94–361, title VIII, § 804(c), 90 Stat. 932; Dec. 1, 1981, Pub. L. 97–86, title VIII, § 803(d), 95 Stat. 1113; Nov. 30, 1993, Pub. L. 103–160, div. C, title XXXIV, § 3402(c)(1), 107 Stat. 1964, related to functions and powers of Administrator. See section 5196 of Title 42, The Public Health and Welfare.

Section 2282, act Jan. 12, 1951, ch. 1228, title II, § 202, 64 Stat. 1251, defined "national defense" and "defense" for purposes of former section 2081 of this Appendix. See section 5195a(b) of Title 42.

Section 2283, act Jan. 12, 1951, ch. 1228, title II, § 203, 64 Stat. 1251, related to mutual aid pacts between States and neighboring countries. See section 5196a of Title 42.

Section 2284, act Jan. 12, 1951, ch. 1228, title II, § 204, 64 Stat. 1251, related to insignia, arm bands, and other distinctive articles to be worn or possessed by persons engaged in civil defense activities.

§ 2285. Real property transactions

(a) Reports to the Armed Services Committees

The Director of the Office of Civil and Defense Mobilization, or his designee, may not enter into any of the following listed transactions by or for the use of that agency until after the expiration of thirty days from the date upon which a report of the facts concerning the proposed transaction is submitted to the Committees on Armed Services of the Senate and House of Representatives:

(1) An acquisition of fee title to any real property, if the estimated price is more than $50,000.

(2) A lease of any real property to the United States, if the estimated annual rental is more than $50,000.

(3) A lease of real property owned by the United States, if the estimated annual rental is more than $50,000.

(4) A transfer of real property owned by the United States to another Federal agency or to

a State, if the estimated value is more than $50,000.

(5) A report of excess real property owned by the United States to a disposal agency, if the estimated value is more than $50,000.

If a transaction covered by clause (1) or (2) is part of a project, the report must include a summarization of the general plan for that project, including an estimate of the total cost of the lands to be acquired or leases to be made.

(b) Annual reports to Armed Services Committees

The Director of the Office of Civil and Defense Mobilization shall report annually to the Committees on Armed Services of the Senate and the House of Representatives on transactions described in subsection (a) that involve an estimated value of more than $5,000 but not more than $50,000.

(c) Real property governed by this section

This section applies only to real property in the States of the Union, the District of Columbia, and Puerto Rico. It does not apply to real property for river and harbor projects or flood-control projects, or to leases of Government-owned real property for agricultural or grazing purposes.

(d) Recital of compliance in instrument of conveyance as conclusive

A statement in an instrument of conveyance, including a lease, that the requirements of this section have been met, or that the conveyance is not subject to this section, is conclusive.

(Aug. 10, 1956, ch. 1041, § 43, 70A Stat. 636; Pub. L. 86–70, § 37, June 25, 1959, 73 Stat. 150; Pub. L. 86–500, title V, § 512, June 8, 1960, 74 Stat. 187; Pub. L. 86–624, § 38, June 12, 1960, 74 Stat. 421; Pub. L. 96–470, title II, § 202(c), Oct. 19, 1980, 94 Stat. 2242.)

CODIFICATION

Section was formerly classified to section 171x of Title 5 prior to the general revision and enactment of Title 5, Government Organization and Employees, by Pub. L. 89–554, § 1, Sept. 6, 1966, 80 Stat. 378.

Section was not enacted as a part of the Federal Civil Defense Act of 1950 which formerly comprised sections 2251 to 2303 of this Appendix.

AMENDMENTS

1980—Subsec. (b). Pub. L. 96–470 substituted "annually" for "quarterly".

1960—Subsec. (a). Pub. L. 86–500 substituted "Director of the Office of Civil and Defense Mobilization" for "Administrator of the Federal Civil Defense Administration", prohibited the Director from entering into any of the transactions listed in subsec. (a) until after the expiration of 30 days from the date upon which a report of the facts concerning the proposed transaction is submitted to the Committees on Armed Services of the Senate and House of Representatives, and increased the amounts in cls. (1) to (5) from $25,000 to $50,000.

Subsec. (b). Pub. L. 86–500 substituted "Director of the Office of Civil and Defense Mobilization" for "Administrator" and "$50,000" for "$25,000".

Subsec. (c). Pub. L. 86–624 substituted "States of the Union, the District of Columbia" for "United States, Hawaii."

Pub. L. 86–500 struck out ", Hawaii," after "United States".

Subsec. (d). Pub. L. 86–500 reenacted subsection without change.

1959—Subsec. (c). Pub. L. 86–70 struck out "Alaska," after "United States,".

TERMINATION OF REPORTING REQUIREMENTS

For termination, effective May 15, 2000, of provisions of law requiring submittal to Congress of any annual, semiannual, or other regular periodic report listed in House Document No. 103–7 (in which a report required under subsec. (b) of this section is listed as the 10th item on page 169), see section 3003 of Pub. L. 104–66, as amended, set out as a note under section 1113 of Title 31, Money and Finance.

TRANSFER OF FUNCTIONS

Functions of Federal Civil Defense Administration transferred to President by section 1 of Reorg. Plan No. 1 of 1958, eff. July 1, 1958, 23 F.R. 4991, 72 Stat. 1799, as amended, set out as a note under section 5195 of Title 42, The Public Health and Welfare. The Plan created a new agency in Executive Office of President known as Office of Defense and Civilian Mobilization.

Pub. L. 85–763, Aug. 26, 1958, 72 Stat. 861, amended Reorg. Plan No. 1 of 1958 by redesignating Office of Defense and Civilian Mobilization as Office of Civil and Defense Mobilization.

Pub. L. 87–296, Sept. 22, 1961, 75 Stat. 630, amended Reorg. Plan No. 1 of 1958 by redesignating Office of Civil and Defense Mobilization as Office of Emergency Planning.

Office of Emergency Planning renamed Office of Emergency Preparedness pursuant to section 402 of Pub. L. 90–608, Oct. 21, 1968, 82 Stat. 1194, which provided that references to Office of Emergency Planning after Oct. 21, 1968, should be deemed references to Office of Emergency Preparedness.

Office of Emergency Preparedness, including offices of Director, Deputy Director, Assistant Directors, and Regional Directors, abolished and functions vested by law in Office of Emergency Preparedness or Director of Office of Emergency Preparedness transferred to President by sections 1 and 3(a)(1) of Reorg. Plan No. 1 of 1973, eff. July 1, 1973, 38 F.R. 9579, 87 Stat. 1089, set out as a note under section 5195 of Title 42, The Public Health and Welfare.

Functions vested in Director of Office of Emergency Preparedness as of June 30, 1973, by Executive Order, proclamation, or other directive issued by or on behalf of President or otherwise, with certain exceptions, transferred to Administrator of General Services, effective July 1, 1973, by Ex. Ord. No. 11725, § 3, eff. June 29, 1973, 38 F.R. 17175, formerly set out as a note under section 2271 of this Appendix.

Functions of Administrator of Federal Civil Defense Administration under this section, previously transferred to President, delegated to Director of Federal Emergency Management Agency by section 4–105 of Ex. Ord. No. 12148, July 20, 1979, 44 F.R. 43242, set out as a note under section 5195 of Title 42, The Public Health and Welfare.

§ 2286. Repealed. Pub. L. 103–337, div. C, title XXXIV, § 3412(a), Oct. 5, 1994, 108 Stat. 3111

Section, act Jan. 12, 1951, ch. 1228, title II, § 205, as added Aug. 8, 1958, Pub. L. 85–606, § 4, 72 Stat. 533; amended June 30, 1964, Pub. L. 88–335, 78 Stat. 231; June 10, 1968, Pub. L. 90–336, 82 Stat. 175; Aug. 2, 1972, Pub. L. 92–360, § 1(1), 86 Stat. 503; July 14, 1976, Pub. L. 94–361, title VIII, § 804(d), 90 Stat. 932; Dec. 1, 1981, Pub. L. 97–86, title VIII, § 803(a)(2), (e), 95 Stat. 1112, 1113; Nov. 30, 1993, Pub. L. 103–160, div. C, title XXXIV, § 3402(c)(2), (f)(3), 107 Stat. 1964, 1965, related to financial contributions to States for personnel and administrative expenses. See section 5196b of Title 42, The Public Health and Welfare.

§ 2287. Repealed. Pub. L. 97–214, § 7(8), July 12, 1982, 96 Stat. 173

Section, Pub. L. 89–568, title VI, § 610, Sept. 12, 1966, 80 Stat. 756; Pub. L. 90–110, title VIII, § 807, Oct. 21, 1967, 81

Stat. 308, related to fallout protection. Provisions similar to this section were contained in the Military Construction Authorization Act, 1966, Pub. L. 89–188, title VI, §608, Sept. 16, 1965, 79 Stat. 818.

EFFECTIVE DATE OF REPEAL

Repeal effective Oct. 1, 1982, and applicable to military construction projects, and to construction and acquisition of military family housing, authorized before, on, or after such date, see section 12(a) of Pub. L. 97–214, set out as an Effective Date note under section 2801 of Title 10, Armed Forces.

§§2288, 2289. Repealed. Pub. L. 103–337, div. C, title XXXIV, §3412(a), Oct. 5, 1994, 108 Stat. 3111

Section 2288, act Jan. 12, 1951, ch. 1228, title II, §206, as added Sept. 8, 1980, Pub. L. 96–342, title VII, §703(a)(1), 94 Stat. 1089, related to requirement for State matching funds for construction of emergency operating centers. See section 5196c of Title 42, The Public Health and Welfare.

Section 2289, act Jan. 12, 1951, ch. 1228, title II, §207, as added Dec. 1, 1981, Pub. L. 97–86, title VIII, §803(a)(1), 95 Stat. 1112; amended Nov. 30, 1993, Pub. L. 103–160, div. C, title XXXIV, §3402(d)(1), 107 Stat. 1964, related to use of funds for attack-related civil defense and disaster-related civil defense. See section 5196d of Title 42.

TITLE IV—EMERGENCY AUTHORITY

§§2291 to 2297. Repealed. Pub. L. 103–337, div. C, title XXXIV, §3412(a), Oct. 5, 1994, 108 Stat. 3111

Section 2291, act Jan. 12, 1951, ch. 1228, title III, §301, 64 Stat. 1251, provided that sections 2291 to 2297 of this Appendix applied only during civil defense emergencies and related to proclamation and termination of these emergencies.

Section 2292, act Jan. 12, 1951, ch. 1228, title III, §302, 64 Stat. 1251, related to utilization of Federal departments and agencies during civil defense emergencies.

Section 2293, act Jan. 12, 1951, ch. 1228, title III, §303, 64 Stat. 1252, related to emergency powers of Administrator.

Section 2294, act Jan. 12, 1951, ch. 1228, title III, §304, 64 Stat. 1253, related to governmental immunity from liability for death or injury to employees and to employee benefits.

Section 2295, act Jan. 12, 1951, ch. 1228, title III, §305, 64 Stat. 1253, related to waiver of provisions of Administrative Procedure Act, sections 551 et seq. and 701 et seq. of Title 5, Government Organization and Employees.

Section 2296, act Jan. 12, 1951, ch. 1228, title III, §306, 64 Stat. 1253, related to compensation for acquisition of nongovernmental property, return of the property to the owner, and disposal of surplus property.

Section 2297, acts Jan. 12, 1951, ch. 1228, title III, §307, 64 Stat. 1254; June 3, 1954, ch. 253, 68 Stat. 170; July 11, 1958, Pub. L. 85–514, 72 Stat. 356; June 27, 1962, Pub. L. 87–501, 76 Stat. 111; June 30, 1966, Pub. L. 89–483, 80 Stat. 235; June 30, 1970, Pub. L. 91–299, 84 Stat. 367, provided that sections 2291 to 2297 of this Appendix terminated on June 30, 1974, or on such earlier date as prescribed by concurrent resolution of Congress. Sections 2291 to 2297 terminated June 30, 1974, pursuant to section 2297 of this Appendix.

TITLE V—IMPROVED CIVIL DEFENSE PROGRAM

§§2301 to 2303. Repealed. Pub. L. 103–160, div. C, title XXXIV, §3402(e)(1), Nov. 30, 1993, 107 Stat. 1964

Section 2301, act Jan. 12, 1951, ch. 1228, title V, §501, as added Sept. 8, 1980, Pub. L. 96–342, title VII, §702(a), 94 Stat. 1088, related to sense of Congress concerning improved civil defense program.

Section 2302, act Jan. 12, 1951, ch. 1228, title V, §502, as added Sept. 8, 1980, Pub. L. 96–342, title VII, §702(a), 94 Stat. 1088, listed elements of improved civil defense program.

Section 2303, act Jan. 12, 1951, ch. 1228, title V, §503, as added Sept. 8, 1980, Pub. L. 96–342, title VII, §702(a), 94 Stat. 1089, granted administrative authority to develop and implement improved civil defense program.

EMERGENCY FOOD AID TO INDIA

ACT JUNE 15, 1951, CH. 138, 65 STAT. 69

§§2311 to 2316. Omitted

CODIFICATION

Sections 2311 to 2316 of this Appendix were omitted from the Code in view of the termination of the emergency need which they were enacted to meet.

Section 2311, act June 15, 1951, ch. 138, §2, 65 Stat. 70, related to emergency food relief assistance to India on credit terms including payment by transfer to the United States of materials required by the United States due to deficiencies in its own resources, particularly those found to be strategic and critical.

Section 2312, act June 15, 1951, ch. 138, §3, 65 Stat. 70, related to amount of money available for loan during the period ending June 30, 1952.

Section 2313, act June 15, 1951, ch. 138, §4, 65 Stat. 70, related to permissible use of funds to meet the emergency need arising from the flood, drought, and other conditions existing in India in 1950.

Section 2314, act June 15, 1951, ch. 138, §5, 65 Stat. 70, related to transportation of supplies, to advances by Reconstruction Finance Corporation to Department of Commerce for activation and operation of vessels for such transportation, and to repayment of advances.

Section 2315, act June 15, 1951, ch. 138, §6, 65 Stat. 71, related to payment of charges for ocean freight of relief packages and to funds available for such payment.

Section 2316, act June 15, 1951, ch. 138, §7, 65 Stat. 71, related to establishment of special deposit account in the United States Treasury created by repayments of interest by India on or before Jan. 1, 1957, to uses of funds in the account, and to disbursements from the account.

KOREAN COMBAT PAY

ACT JULY 10, 1952, CH. 630, TITLE VII, 66 STAT. 538

§§2351 to 2356. Repealed. Pub. L. 88–132, §9(b), Oct. 2, 1963, 77 Stat. 216

Section 2351, act July 10, 1952, ch. 630, title VII, §702, 66 Stat. 538, defined terms for purposes of sections 2351 to 2356 of this Appendix.

Section 2352, act July 10, 1952, ch. 630, title VII, §703, 66 Stat. 539, related to conditions governing payment of combat pay to members and former members of the uniformed services.

Section 2353, act July 10, 1952, ch. 630, title VII, §704, 66 Stat. 539, related to members of the uniformed services killed in action, injured in action, and missing in action.

Section 2354, act July 10, 1952, ch. 630, title VII, §705, 66 Stat. 539, related to limitations on combat payments.

Section 2355, act July 10, 1952, ch. 630, title VII, §706, 66 Stat. 539, related to regulations for the administration of sections 2351 to 2356 of this Appendix.

Section 2356, act July 10, 1952, ch. 630, title VII, §707, 66 Stat. 539, related to determinations of fact, conclusiveness of findings, and availability of appropriations.

EFFECTIVE DATE OF REPEAL

Repeal effective Oct. 1, 1963, see section 14 of Pub. L. 88–132, set out as an Effective Date of 1963 Amendment note under section 201 of Title 37, Pay and Allowances of the Uniformed Services.

WORLD WAR II LICENSE AGREEMENTS

ACT AUG. 16, 1950, CH. 716, 64 STAT. 448

§2371. Modification or cancellation of certain license agreements granted Government during World War II

Notwithstanding any other provision of law, the head of any department or other agency in the executive branch of the Government which subsequent to September 9, 1939, entered into any contract or agreement with the holder of any privately owned patent or any right thereunder whereby such holder granted to the United States, without payment of royalty or with reduction or limitation of royalty, any license under such patent or right, is authorized, upon application of the grantor of such license, to enter into such supplemental contract or agreement for the cancellation of the contract or agreement by which such license was granted as the head of such department or agency shall deem to be warranted by equities existing by reason of changes in circumstances occurring since the granting of such license.

(Aug. 16, 1950, ch. 716, 64 Stat. 448.)

CODIFICATION

Section was formerly classified to section 119 of former Title 35, Patents, prior to the general revision and enactment of Title 35, Patents, by act July 19, 1952, ch. 950, §1, 66 Stat. 792.

EMERGENCY SHIP REPAIR PROGRAM

ACT AUG. 20, 1954, CH. 777, 68 STAT. 754

§§2391 to 2394. Repealed. Pub. L. 101–225, title III, §307(16), Dec. 12, 1989, 103 Stat. 1925

Section 2391, act Aug. 20, 1954, ch. 777, §2, 68 Stat. 754, set out purpose of Act as providing for the immediate improvement of merchant vessels in reserve fleet under jurisdiction of Secretary of Commerce, thereby stimulating shipbuilding and ship repair industries of Nation.

Section 2392, act Aug. 20, 1954, ch. 777, §3, 68 Stat. 754, directed Secretary of Commerce, after consultation with Secretary of Defense, to formulate and carry out a modernization program for merchant vessels in national defense reserve under jurisdiction of Secretary of Commerce.

Section 2393, acts Aug. 20, 1954, ch. 777, §4, 68 Stat. 754; Aug. 6, 1956, ch. 1012, 70 Stat. 1067, directed Secretary of Commerce to contract before July 1, 1958, for repair and modernization of vessels after inviting single bids or split bids or both and specified that expenditures not exceed $25,000,000, that contracts be with private shipbuilding or ship repair yards in the United States, and that contracts conform to the Federal Property and Administrative Services Act of 1949, 41 U.S.C. 251 et seq.

Section 2394, act Aug. 20, 1954, ch. 777, §5, 68 Stat. 755, authorized appropriations not in excess of $25,000,000 to carry out this Act.

EXPORT REGULATION

PUB. L. 96–72, SEPT. 29, 1979, 93 STAT. 503

ACT REFERRED TO IN OTHER SECTIONS

This Act is referred to in title 7 sections 1736y, 4001, 5671; title 10 sections 130, 7430; title 15 section 4605; title 16 section 620j; title 22 sections 2304, 2778, 2778a, 2779a, 2780, 2798, 3281, 5472, 5603, 6004, 6445, 7203; title 30 section 185; title 42 section 6212.

§ 2401. Congressional findings

The Congress makes the following findings:

(1) The ability of United States citizens to engage in international commerce is a fundamental concern of United States policy.

(2) Exports contribute significantly to the economic well-being of the United States and the stability of the world economy by increasing employment and production in the United States, and by earning foreign exchange, thereby contributing favorably to the trade balance. The restriction of exports from the United States can have serious adverse effects on the balance of payments and on domestic employment, particularly when restrictions applied by the United States are more extensive than those imposed by other countries.

(3) It is important for the national interest of the United States that both the private sector and the Federal Government place a high priority on exports, consistent with the economic, security, and foreign policy objectives of the United States.

(4) The availability of certain materials at home and abroad varies so that the quantity and composition of United States exports and their distribution among importing countries may affect the welfare of the domestic economy and may have an important bearing upon fulfillment of the foreign policy of the United States.

(5) Exports of goods or technology without regard to whether they make a significant

contribution to the military potential of individual countries or combinations of countries may adversely affect the national security of the United States.

(6) Uncertainty of export control policy can inhibit the efforts of United States business and work to the detriment of the overall attempt to improve the trade balance of the United States.

(7) Unreasonable restrictions on access to world supplies can cause worldwide political and economic instability, interfere with free international trade, and retard the growth and development of nations.

(8) It is important that the administration of export controls imposed for national security purposes give special emphasis to the need to control exports of technology (and goods which contribute significantly to the transfer of such technology) which could make a significant contribution to the military potential of any country or combination of countries which would be detrimental to the national security of the United States.

(9) Minimization of restrictions on exports of agricultural commodities and products is of critical importance to the maintenance of a sound agricultural sector, to a positive contribution to the balance of payments, to reducing the level of Federal expenditures for agricultural support programs, and to United States cooperation in efforts to eliminate malnutrition and world hunger.

(10) It is important that the administration of export controls imposed for foreign policy purposes give special emphasis to the need to control exports of goods and substances hazardous to the public health and the environment which are banned or severely restricted for use in the United States, and which, if exported, could affect the international reputation of the United States as a responsible trading partner.

(11) Availability to controlled countries of goods and technology from foreign sources is a fundamental concern of the United States and should be eliminated through negotiations and other appropriate means whenever possible.

(12) Excessive dependence of the United States, its allies, or countries sharing common strategic objectives with the United States, on energy and other critical resources from potential adversaries can be harmful to the mutual and individual security of all those countries.

(Pub. L. 96–72, §2, Sept. 29, 1979, 93 Stat. 503; Pub. L. 99–64, title I, §102, July 12, 1985, 99 Stat. 120; Pub. L. 103–199, title II, §201(a), Dec. 17, 1993, 107 Stat. 2320.)

PRIOR PROVISIONS

A prior section 2401, Pub. L. 91–184, §2, Dec. 30, 1969, 83 Stat. 841; Pub. L. 92–412, title I, §102, Aug. 29, 1972, 86 Stat. 644; Pub. L. 93–500, §4(a), Oct. 29, 1974, 88 Stat. 1553, setting forth findings of Congress with respect to the Export Administration Act of 1969, expired on Sept. 30, 1979.

AMENDMENTS

1993—Pars. (11) to (13). Pub. L. 103–199 redesignated pars. (12) and (13) as (11) and (12), respectively, and struck out former par. (11) which read as follows: "The acquisition of national security sensitive goods and technology by the Soviet Union and other countries the actions or policies of which run counter to the national security interests of the United States, has led to the significant enhancement of Soviet bloc military-industrial capabilities. This enhancement poses a threat to the security of the United States, its allies, and other friendly nations, and places additional demands on the defense budget of the United States."

1985—Par. (2). Pub. L. 99–64, §102(1), substituted "by earning foreign exchange, thereby contributing favorably to the trade balance" for "by strengthening the trade balance and the value of the United States dollar, thereby reducing inflation".

Par. (3). Pub. L. 99–64, §102(2), substituted "consistent with the economic, security, and foreign policy objectives of the United States" for "which would strengthen the Nation's economy".

Par. (6). Pub. L. 99–64, §102(3), amended par. (6) generally, substituting "inhibit the efforts of United States business and work" for "curtail the efforts of American business".

Par. (9). Pub. L. 99–64, §102(4), substituted "a positive contribution to the balance of payments" for "achievement of a positive balance of payments".

Pars. (10) to (13). Pub. L. 99–64, §102(5), added pars. (10) to (13).

SHORT TITLE OF 1988 AMENDMENT

Pub. L. 100–418, title II, §2441, Aug. 23, 1988, 102 Stat. 1364, provided that: "This part [part II (§§2441–2447) of subtitle D of title II of Pub. L. 100–418, enacting section 2410a of this Appendix, amending sections 2404 and 2413 of this Appendix and section 1864 of Title 19, Customs Duties, and enacting provisions set out as notes under section 2410a of this Appendix] may be cited as the 'Multilateral Export Control Enhancement Amendments Act'."

SHORT TITLE OF 1985 AMENDMENT

Section 1 of Pub. L. 99–64 provided that: "Titles I and II of this Act [enacting sections 4051 to 4053 of Title 15, Commerce and Trade, section 1864 of Title 19, Customs Duties, and section 466c of Title 46, Appendix, Shipping, amending this section and sections 2402, 2403, 2404 to 2406, 2409 to 2411, 2412 to 2417, and 2419 of this Appendix, sections 5314 and 5315 of Title 5, Government Organization and Employees, sections 2304 and 2778 of Title 22, Foreign Relations and Intercourse, and section 185 of Title 30, Mineral Lands and Mining, and enacting provisions set out as notes under sections 2404, 2405, and 2414 of this Appendix and section 5314 of Title 5] may be cited as the 'Export Administration Amendments Act of 1985'."

SHORT TITLE OF 1981 AMENDMENT

Pub. L. 97–145, §1, Dec. 29, 1981, 95 Stat. 1727, provided: "That this Act [amending sections 2405, 2410, 2411, and 2417 of this Appendix and enacting provisions set out as notes under sections 2405, 2410, and 2417 of this Appendix] may be cited as the 'Export Administration Amendments Act of 1981'."

SHORT TITLE

Section 1 of Pub. L. 96–72 provided that: "This Act [enacting this section and sections 2402 to 2420 of this Appendix, amending section 1732 of Title 7, Agriculture, sections 2778 and 3108 of Title 22, Foreign Relations and Intercourse, section 993 of Title 26, Internal Revenue Code, and sections 6212 and 6274 of Title 42, The Public Health and Welfare, and enacting provisions set out as notes under sections 2406 and 2409 of this Appendix and section 3108 of Title 22] may be cited as the 'Export Administration Act of 1979'."

EXECUTIVE ORDER NO. 11753

Ex. Ord. No. 11753, Dec. 20, 1973, 38 F.R. 34983, which established the President's Export Council, was revoked by section 1–402 of Ex. Ord. No. 12131, May 4, 1979, 44 F.R. 26842, set out below.

EX. ORD. NO. 12131. PRESIDENT'S EXPORT COUNCIL

Ex. Ord. No. 12131, May 4, 1979, 44 F.R. 26841, as amended by Ex. Ord. No. 12551, Feb. 21, 1986, 21 F.R. 6509; Ex. Ord. No. 12991, Mar. 6, 1996, 61 F.R. 9587; Ex. Ord. No. 13138, §5, Sept. 30, 1999, 64 F.R. 53880, provided:

By the authority vested in me as President by the Constitution and statutes of the United States of America, and in order to expand the membership of the President's Export Council, in accord with the provisions of the Federal Advisory Committee Act (5 U.S.C. App.), it is hereby ordered as follows:

1–1. ESTABLISHMENT AND MEMBERSHIP

1–101. There is established the President's Export Council.

1–102. The membership of the Council shall be as follows:

(a) The heads of the following Executive agencies or their representatives:

(1) Department of State.

(2) Department of the Treasury.

(3) Department of Agriculture.

(4) Department of Commerce.

(5) Department of Labor.

(6) Office of the Special Representative for Trade Negotiations.

(7) Export-Import Bank of the United States.

(8) Small Business Administration.

(9) Department of Energy.

(b) Five members of the United States Senate, designated by the President of the Senate, and five members of the United States House of Representatives, designated by the Speaker of the House, to serve for a two-year term.

(c) Not to exceed 28 citizens appointed by the President. These individuals shall be selected from those who are not full,time Federal officers or employees. They shall include representatives of business and industry, agriculture, and labor.

1–103. The President shall designate a Chairman and a Vice Chairman from among the members appointed by the President.

1–104. The Secretary of Commerce, with the concurrence of the Chairman, shall appoint an Executive Director.

1–2. FUNCTIONS

1–201. The Council shall serve as a national advisory body on matters relating to United States export trade, including advice on the implementation of the President's National Export Policy, which was announced on September 26, 1978. It shall, through the Secretary of Commerce, report to the President on its activities and on its recommendations for expanding United States exports.

1–202. The Council should survey and evaluate the export expansion activities of the communities represented by the membership. It should identify and examine specific problems which business, industrial, and agricultural practices may cause for export trade, and examine the needs of business, industry, and agriculture to expand their efforts. The Council should recommend specific solutions to these problems and needs.

1–203. The Council may act as liaison among the communities represented by the membership; and, may provide a forum for those communities on current and emerging problems and issues in the field of export expansion. The Council should encourage the business, industrial, and agricultural communities to enter new foreign markets and to expand existing export programs.

1–204. The Council shall provide advice on Federal plans and actions that affect export expansion policies which have an impact on those communities represented by the membership.

1–205. The Council may establish, with the concurrence of the Secretary of Commerce, an executive committee and such other subordinate committees it considers necessary for the performance of its functions. The Chairman of a subordinate committee shall be designated, with the concurrence of the Secretary of Commerce, by the Chairman of the Council from among the membership of the Council. Members of subordinate committees shall be appointed by the Secretary of Commerce.

1–3. ADMINISTRATIVE PROVISIONS

1–301. The Secretary of Commerce shall, to the extent permitted by law, provide the Council, including its executive and subordinate committees, with administrative and staff services, support and facilities as may be necessary for the effective performance of its functions.

1–302. Each member of the Council, including its executive and subordinate committees, who is not otherwise paid a salary by the Federal Government, shall receive no compensation from the United States by virtue of their service on the Council, but all members may receive the transportation and travel expenses, including per diem in lieu of subsistence, authorized by law (5 U.S.C. 5702 and 5703).

1–4. GENERAL PROVISIONS

1–401. Notwithstanding the provisions of any other Executive order, the functions of the President under the Federal Advisory Committee Act (5 U.S.C. App.), except that of reporting annually to the Congress, which are applicable to the Council, shall be performed by the Secretary of Commerce in accordance with guidelines and procedures established by the Administrator of General Services.

1–402. Executive Order No. 11753 is revoked; however, nothing in this Order shall be deemed to require new charters for the Council, including its executive and subordinate committees, which were current immediately prior to the issuance of this Order.

1–403. The Council shall terminate on December 31, 1980, unless sooner extended.

EXTENSION OF TERM OF PRESIDENT'S EXPORT COUNCIL

Term of the President's Export Council extended until Dec. 31, 1982, see section 1–101(*l*) of Ex. Ord. No. 12258, Dec. 31, 1980, 46 F.R. 1251, formerly set out as a note under section 14 of the Federal Advisory Committee Act in the Appendix to Title 5, Government Organization and Employees.

Term of the President's Export Council extended until Sept. 30, 1984, see Ex. Ord. No. 12399, Dec. 31, 1982, 48 F.R. 379, formerly set out as a note under section 14 of the Federal Advisory Committee Act in the Appendix to Title 5.

Term of the President's Export Council extended until Sept. 30, 1985, see Ex. Ord. No. 12489, Sept. 28, 1984, 49 F.R. 38927, formerly set out as a note under section 14 of the Federal Advisory Committee Act in the Appendix to Title 5.

Term of the President's Export Council extended until Sept. 30, 1987, see Ex. Ord. No. 12534, Sept. 30, 1985, 50 F.R. 40319, formerly set out as a note under section 14 of the Federal Advisory Committee Act in the Appendix to Title 5.

Term of the President's Export Council extended until Sept. 30, 1989, see Ex. Ord. No. 12610, Sept. 30, 1987, 52 F.R. 36901, formerly set out as a note under section 14 of the Federal Advisory Committee Act in the Appendix to Title 5.

Term of the President's Export Council extended until Sept. 30, 1991, see Ex. Ord. No. 12692, Sept. 29, 1989, 54 F.R. 40627, formerly set out as a note under section 14 of the Federal Advisory Committee Act in the Appendix to Title 5.

Term of the President's Export Council extended until Sept. 30, 1993, see Ex. Ord. No. 12774, Sept. 27, 1991, 56 F.R. 49835, formerly set out as a note under section 14 of the Federal Advisory Committee Act in the Appendix to Title 5.

Term of the President's Export Council extended until Sept. 30, 1995, see Ex. Ord. No. 12869, Sept. 30, 1993,

58 F.R. 51751, formerly set out as a note under section 14 of the Federal Advisory Committee Act in the Appendix to Title 5.

Term of the President's Export Council extended until Sept. 30, 1997, see Ex. Ord. No. 12974, Sept. 29, 1995, 60 F.R. 51875, formerly set out as a note under section 14 of the Federal Advisory Committee Act in the Appendix to Title 5.

Term of the President's Export Council extended until Sept. 30, 1999, see Ex. Ord. No. 13062, §1(m), Sept. 29, 1997, 62 F.R. 51755, formerly set out as a note under section 14 of the Federal Advisory Committee Act in the Appendix to Title 5.

Term of the President's Export Council extended until Sept. 30, 2001, see Ex. Ord. No. 13138, Sept. 30, 1999, 64 F.R. 53879, set out as a note under section 14 of the Federal Advisory Committee Act in the Appendix to Title 5.

§2402. Congressional declaration of policy

The Congress makes the following declarations:

(1) It is the policy of the United States to minimize uncertainties in export control policy and to encourage trade with all countries with which the United States has diplomatic or trading relations, except those countries with which such trade has been determined by the President to be against the national interest.

(2) It is the policy of the United States to use export controls only after full consideration of the impact on the economy of the United States and only to the extent necessary—

(A) to restrict the export of goods and technology which would make a significant contribution to the military potential of any other country or combination of countries which would prove detrimental to the national security of the United States;

(B) to restrict the export of goods and technology where necessary to further significantly the foreign policy of the United States or to fulfill its declared international obligations; and

(C) to restrict the export of goods where necessary to protect the domestic economy from the excessive drain of scarce materials and to reduce the serious inflationary impact of foreign demand.

(3) It is the policy of the United States (A) to apply any necessary controls to the maximum extent possible in cooperation with all nations, and (B) to encourage observance of a uniform export control policy by all nations with which the United States has defense treaty commitments or common strategic objectives.

(4) It is the policy of the United States to use its economic resources and trade potential to further the sound growth and stability of its economy as well as to further its national security and foreign policy objectives.

(5) It is the policy of the United States—

(A) to oppose restrictive trade practices or boycotts fostered or imposed by foreign countries against other countries friendly to the United States or against any United States person;

(B) to encourage and, in specified cases, require United States persons engaged in the export of goods or technology or other information to refuse to take actions, including furnishing information or entering into or implementing agreements, which have the effect of furthering or supporting the restrictive trade practices or boycotts fostered or imposed by any foreign country against a country friendly to the United States or against any United States person; and

(C) to foster international cooperation and the development of international rules and institutions to assure reasonable access to world supplies.

(6) It is the policy of the United States that the desirability of subjecting, or continuing to subject, particular goods or technology or other information to United States export controls should be subjected to review by and consultation with representatives of appropriate United States Government agencies and private industry.

(7) It is the policy of the United States to use export controls, including license fees, to secure the removal by foreign countries of restrictions on access to supplies where such restrictions have or may have a serious domestic inflationary impact, have caused or may cause a serious domestic shortage, or have been imposed for purposes of influencing the foreign policy of the United States. In effecting this policy, the President shall make reasonable and prompt efforts to secure the removal or reduction of such restrictions, policies, or actions through international cooperation and agreement before imposing export controls. No action taken in fulfillment of the policy set forth in this paragraph shall apply to the export of medicine or medical supplies.

(8) It is the policy of the United States to use export controls to encourage other countries to take immediate steps to prevent the use of their territories or resources to aid, encourage, or give sanctuary to those persons involved in directing, supporting, or participating in acts of international terrorism. To achieve this objective, the President shall make reasonable and prompt efforts to secure the removal or reduction of such assistance to international terrorists through international cooperation and agreement before imposing export controls.

(9) It is the policy of the United States to cooperate with other countries with which the United States has defense treaty commitments or common strategic objectives in restricting the export of goods and technology which would make a significant contribution to the military potential of any country or combination of countries which would prove detrimental to the security of the United States and of those countries with which the United States has defense treaty commitments or common strategic objectives, and to encourage other friendly countries to cooperate in restricting the sale of goods and technology that can harm the security of the United States.

(10) It is the policy of the United States that export trade by United States citizens be given a high priority and not be controlled except when such controls (A) are necessary to

further fundamental national security, foreign policy, or short supply objectives, (B) will clearly further such objectives, and (C) are administered consistent with basic standards of due process.

(11) It is the policy of the United States to minimize restrictions on the export of agricultural commodities and products.

(12) It is the policy of the United States to sustain vigorous scientific enterprise. To do so involves sustaining the ability of scientists and other scholars freely to communicate research findings, in accordance with applicable provisions of law, by means of publication, teaching, conferences, and other forms of scholarly exchange.

(13) It is the policy of the United States to control the export of goods and substances banned or severely restricted for use in the United States in order to foster public health and safety and to prevent injury to the foreign policy of the United States as well as to the credibility of the United States as a responsible trading partner.

(14) It is the policy of the United States to cooperate with countries which are allies of the United States and countries which share common strategic objectives with the United States in minimizing dependence on imports of energy and other critical resources from potential adversaries and in developing alternative supplies of such resources in order to minimize strategic threats posed by excessive hard currency earnings derived from such resource exports by countries with policies adverse to the security interests of the United States.

(Pub. L. 96–72, §3, Sept. 29, 1979, 93 Stat. 504; Pub. L. 99–64, title I, §103, July 12, 1985, 99 Stat. 121; Pub. L. 103–199, title II, §201(b)(2), Dec. 17, 1993, 107 Stat. 2321.)

PRIOR PROVISIONS

A prior section 2402, Pub. L. 91–184, §3, Dec. 30, 1969, 83 Stat. 841; Pub. L. 92–412, title I, §103, Aug. 29, 1972, 86 Stat. 644; Pub. L. 93–500, §§2, 4(b), (c), 11, Oct. 29, 1974, 88 Stat. 1552, 1553, 1556; Pub. L. 95–52, title I, §115, title II, §202, June 22, 1977, 91 Stat. 241, 247, setting forth declaration of policy of Congress with respect to the Export Administration Act of 1969, expired on Sept. 30, 1979.

AMENDMENTS

1993—Par. (15). Pub. L. 103–199 struck out par. (15) which read as follows: "It is the policy of the United States, particularly in light of the Soviet massacre of innocent men, women, and children aboard Korean Air Lines flight 7, to continue to object to exceptions to the International Control List for the Union of Soviet Socialist Republics, subject to periodic review by the President."

1985—Par. (3). Pub. L. 99–64, §103(1), inserted "or common strategic objectives" after "defense treaty commitments".

Par. (7). Pub. L. 99–64, §103(2), substituted "the President shall make reasonable and prompt efforts" for "the President shall make every reasonable effort", and "imposing export controls" for "resorting to the imposition of controls on exports from the United States".

Par. (8). Pub. L. 99–64, §103(3), substituted "the President shall make reasonable and prompt efforts" for "the President shall make every reasonable effort", and "imposing export controls" for "resorting to the imposition of export controls".

Par. (9). Pub. L. 99–64, §103(4), inserted "or common strategic objectives" after "commitments" in two places, and inserted ", and to encourage other friendly countries to cooperate in restricting the sale of goods and technology that can harm the security of the United States".

Pars. (12) to (15). Pub. L. 99–64, §103(5), added pars. (12) to (15).

DELEGATION OF FUNCTIONS

Functions conferred upon President under this section delegated to Secretary of Commerce by Ex. Ord. No. 12214, May 2, 1980, 45 F.R. 29783, set out under section 2403 of this Appendix.

POLICY REGARDING KAL

Section 201(b)(1) of Pub. L. 103–199 provided that: "The Congress finds that—

"(A) President Yeltsin should be commended for meeting personally with representatives of the families of the victims of the shootdown of Korean Airlines (KAL) Flight 7;

"(B) President Yeltsin's Government has met on two separate occasions with United States Government and family members to answer questions associated with the shootdown and has arranged for the families to interview Russians involved in the incident or the search and rescue operations that followed;

"(C) President Yeltsin's Government has also cooperated fully with the International Civil Aviation Organization (ICAO) to allow it to complete its investigation of the incident and has provided numerous materials requested by the ICAO, including radar data and so-called 'black boxes', the digital flight data and cockpit voice recorders from the flight;

"(D) the Export Administration Act of 1979 [sections 2401 to 2420 of this Appendix] continues to state that the United States should continue to object to exceptions to the International Control List for the Union of Soviet Socialist Republics in light of the KAL tragedy, even though the 'no exceptions' policy was rescinded by President Bush in 1990;

"(E) the Government of the United States is seeking compensation from the Russian Government on behalf of the families of the KAL victims, and the Congress expects the Administration to continue to pursue issues related to the shootdown, including that of compensation, with officials at the highest level of the Russian Government; and

"(F) in view of the cooperation provided by President Yeltsin and his government regarding the KAL incident and these other developments, it is appropriate to remove such language from the Export Administration Act of 1979."

POLICY ON MISSILE TECHNOLOGY CONTROL

Pub. L. 101–510, div. A, title XVII, §1701, Nov. 5, 1990, 104 Stat. 1738, provided that: "It should be the policy of the United States to take all appropriate measures—

"(1) to discourage the proliferation, development, and production of the weapons, material, and technology necessary to produce or acquire missiles that can deliver weapons of mass destruction;

"(2) to discourage countries and private persons in other countries from aiding and abetting any states from acquiring such weapons, material, and technology;

"(3) to strengthen United States and existing multilateral export controls to prohibit the flow of materials, equipment, and technology that would assist countries in acquiring the ability to produce or acquire missiles that can deliver weapons of mass destruction, including missiles, warheads and weaponization technology, targeting technology, test and evaluation technology, and range and weapons effect measurement technology; and

"(4) with respect to the Missile Technology Control Regime ('MTCR') and its participating governments—

"(A) to improve enforcement and seek a common and stricter interpretation among MTCR members of MTCR principles;

"(B) to increase the number of countries that adhere to the MTCR; and

"(C) to increase information sharing among United States agencies and among governments on missile technology transfer, including export licensing, and enforcement activities."

SECTION REFERRED TO IN OTHER SECTIONS

This section is referred to in sections 2403, 2404, 2405, 2406, 2407, 2409, 2413 of this Appendix; title 10 section 2410i; title 26 sections 943, 993; title 42 section 6212.

§ 2403. General provisions

(a) Types of licenses

Under such conditions as may be imposed by the Secretary which are consistent with the provisions of this Act [sections 2401 to 2420 of this Appendix], the Secretary may require any of the following types of export licenses:

(1) A validated license, authorizing a specific export, issued pursuant to an application by the exporter.

(2) Validated licenses authorizing multiple exports, issued pursuant to an application by the exporter, in lieu of an individual validated license for each such export, including, but not limited to, the following:

(A) A distribution license, authorizing exports of goods to approved distributors or users of the goods in countries other than controlled countries, except that the Secretary may establish a type of distribution license appropriate for consignees in the People's Republic of China. The Secretary shall grant the distribution license primarily on the basis of the reliability of the applicant and foreign consignees with respect to the prevention of diversion of goods to controlled countries. The Secretary shall have the responsibility of determining, with the assistance of all appropriate agencies, the reliability of applicants and their immediate consignees. The Secretary's determination shall be based on appropriate investigations of each applicant and periodic reviews of licensees and their compliance with the terms of licenses issued under this Act [sections 2401 to 2420 of this Appendix]. Factors such as the applicant's products or volume of business, or the consignees' geographic location, sales distribution area, or degree of foreign ownership, which may be relevant with respect to individual cases, shall not be determinative in creating categories or general criteria for the denial of applications or withdrawal of a distribution license.

(B) A comprehensive operations license, authorizing exports and reexports of technology and related goods, including items from the list of militarily critical technologies developed pursuant to section 5(d) of this Act [section 2404(d) of this Appendix] which are included on the control list in accordance with that section, from a domestic concern to and among its foreign subsidiaries, affiliates, joint venturers, and licensees that have long-term, contractually defined relations with the exporter, are located in countries other than controlled countries (except the People's Republic of China), and are approved by the Secretary. The Secretary shall grant the license to manufacturing, laboratory, or related operations on the basis of approval of the exporter's systems of control, including internal proprietary controls, applicable to the technology and related goods to be exported rather than approval of individual export transactions. The Secretary and the Commissioner of Customs, consistent with their authorities under section 12(a) of this Act [section 2411(a) of this Appendix] and with the assistance of all appropriate agencies, shall periodically, but not less frequently than annually, perform audits of licensing procedures under this subparagraph in order to assure the integrity and effectiveness of those procedures.

(C) A project license, authorizing exports of goods or technology for a specified activity.

(D) A service supply license, authorizing exports of spare or replacement parts for goods previously exported.

(3) A general license, authorizing exports, without application by the exporter.

(4) Such other licenses as may assist in the effective and efficient implementation of this Act [sections 2401 to 2420 of this Appendix].

(b) Control list

The Secretary shall establish and maintain a list (hereinafter in this Act [sections 2401 to 2420 of this Appendix] referred to as the "control list") stating license requirements (other than for general licenses) for exports of goods and technology under this Act [sections 2401 to 2420 of this Appendix].

(c) Foreign availability

In accordance with the provisions of this Act [sections 2401 to 2420 of this Appendix], the President shall not impose export controls for foreign policy or national security purposes on the export from the United States of goods or technology which he determines are available without restriction from sources outside the United States in sufficient quantities and comparable in quality to those produced in the United States so as to render the controls ineffective in achieving their purposes, unless the President determines that adequate evidence has been presented to him demonstrating that the absence of such controls would prove detrimental to the foreign policy or national security of the United States. In complying with the provisions of this subsection, the President shall give strong emphasis to bilateral or multilateral negotiations to eliminate foreign availability. The Secretary and the Secretary of Defense shall cooperate in gathering information relating to foreign availability, including the establishment and maintenance of a jointly operated computer system.

(d) Right of export

No authority or permission to export may be required under this Act [sections 2401 to 2420 of this Appendix], or under regulations issued under this Act [sections 2401 to 2420 of this Appendix], except to carry out the policies set forth in section 3 of this Act [section 2402 of this Appendix].

(e) Delegation of authority

The President may delegate the power, authority, and discretion conferred upon him by this Act [sections 2401 to 2420 of this Appendix] to such departments, agencies, or officials of the Government as he may consider appropriate, except that no authority under this Act [sections 2401 to 2420 of this Appendix] may be delegated to, or exercised by, any official of any department or agency the head of which is not appointed by the President, by and with the advice and consent of the Senate. The President may not delegate or transfer his power, authority, and discretion to overrule or modify any recommendation or decision made by the Secretary, the Secretary of Defense, or the Secretary of State pursuant to the provisions of this Act [sections 2401 to 2420 of this Appendix].

(f) Notification of public; consultation with business

The Secretary shall keep the public fully apprised of changes in export control policy and procedures instituted in conformity with this Act [sections 2401 to 2420 of this Appendix] with a view to encouraging trade. The Secretary shall meet regularly with representatives of a broad spectrum of enterprises, labor organizations, and citizens interested in or affected by export controls, in order to obtain their views on United States export control policy and the foreign availability of goods and technology.

(g) Fees

No fee may be charged in connection with the submission or processing of an export license application.

(Pub. L. 96–72, § 4, Sept. 29, 1979, 93 Stat. 505; Pub. L. 99–64, title I, § 104, July 12, 1985, 99 Stat. 122; Pub. L. 100–418, title II, §§ 2411, 2412, Aug. 23, 1988, 102 Stat. 1347.)

REFERENCES IN TEXT

This Act, referred to in text, is Pub. L. 96–72, Sept. 29, 1979, 93 Stat. 503, as amended, known as the Export Administration Act of 1979, which enacted sections 2401 to 2420 of this Appendix, amended section 1732 of Title 7, Agriculture, sections 2778 and 3108 of Title 22, Foreign Relations and Intercourse, section 993 of Title 26, Internal Revenue Code, and sections 6212 and 6274 of Title 42, The Public Health and Welfare, and enacted provisions set out as notes under sections 2401, 2406, and 2409 of this Appendix and section 3108 of Title 22. For complete classification of this Act to the Code, see Short Title note set out under section 2401 of this Appendix and Tables.

PRIOR PROVISIONS

A prior section 2403, Pub. L. 91–184, § 4, Dec. 30, 1969, 83 Stat. 842; Pub. L. 92–412, title I, § 104(a), (b)(1), Aug. 29, 1972, 86 Stat. 644, 645; Pub. L. 93–500, §§ 3(a), 5(a), 7, 9, 10, 12, Oct. 29, 1974, 88 Stat. 1552–1557; Pub. L. 95–52, title I, §§ 103(a), (b)(1)–(3), (c), 104–110, 113(b), title II, § 201(b), June 22, 1977, 91 Stat. 235–239, 241, 246; Pub. L. 95–223, title III, § 301(a), (b)(1), Dec. 28, 1977, 91 Stat. 1629; Pub. L. 95–384. § 6(d)(2), Sept. 26, 1978, 92 Stat. 731; Pub. L. 95–435, § 5(d), Oct. 10, 1978, 92 Stat. 1052; Pub. L. 96–67, § 2, Sept. 21, 1979, 93 Stat. 415, setting forth provisions relating to authorities to effectuate policies and limitations on exercise of authorities, expired on Sept. 30, 1979.

AMENDMENTS

1988—Subsec. (a)(2)(A). Pub. L. 100–418, § 2412(1), inserted exception authorizing the Secretary to establish a type of distribution license appropriate to consignees in the People's Republic of China.

Subsec. (a)(2)(B). Pub. L. 100–418, § 2412(2), inserted "(except the People's Republic of China)" after "controlled countries".

Subsec. (g). Pub. L. 100–418, § 2411, added subsec. (g).

1985—Subsec. (a)(2). Pub. L. 99–64, § 104(a), amended par. (2) generally, substituting provisions relating to validated licenses authorizing multiple exports including, but not limited to, distribution licenses, comprehensive operations licenses, project licenses, and service supply licenses, for former provisions which read: "A qualified general license, authorizing multiple exports, issued pursuant to an application by the exporter."

Subsec. (b). Pub. L. 99–64, § 104(b), substituted "Control list" for "Commodity control list" in heading and, in text, substituted "control list" for "commodity control list" and "stating license requirements (other than for general licenses) for exports of goods and technology under this Act" for "consisting of any goods or technology subject to export controls under this Act".

Subsec. (c). Pub. L. 99–64, § 104(c), substituted "sufficient" for "significant", inserted "so as to render the controls ineffective in achieving their purposes", and inserted provisions directing that, in complying with the provisions of this subsection, the President shall give strong emphasis to bilateral or multilateral negotiations to eliminate foreign availability, and that the Secretary and the Secretary of Defense shall cooperate in gathering information relating to foreign availability, including the establishment and maintenance of a jointly operated computer system.

Subsec. (f). Pub. L. 99–64, § 104(d), amended subsec. (f) generally, substituting "representatives of a broad spectrum of enterprises, labor organizations, and citizens interested in or affected by export controls, in order to obtain their views on United States export control policy and the foreign availability of goods and technology" for "representatives of the business sector in order to obtain their views on export control policy and the foreign availability of goods and technology".

EXECUTIVE ORDER NO. 11533

Ex. Ord. No. 11533, June 4, 1970, 35 F.R. 8799, as amended by Ex. Ord. No. 11907, Mar. 1, 1976, 41 F.R. 9085, which provided for the administration of the Export Administration Act of 1969, was revoked by Ex. Ord. No. 12002, July 7, 1977, 42 F.R. 35623, set out below.

EXECUTIVE ORDER NO. 11677

Ex. Ord. No. 11677, Aug. 1, 1972, 37 F.R. 15483, formerly set out as a note under this section, which provided for the regulation of exports, was revoked by Ex. Ord. No. 11683, Aug. 29, 1972, 37 F.R. 17813.

EXECUTIVE ORDER NO. 11683

Ex. Ord. No. 11683, Aug. 29, 1972, 37 F.R. 17813, which revoked Ex. Ord. No. 11677, was revoked by Ex. Ord. No. 12002, July 7, 1977, 42 F.R. 35623, set out below.

EXECUTIVE ORDER NO. 11798

Ex. Ord. No. 11798, Aug. 14, 1974, 39 F.R. 29567, which provided for the continuing regulation of exports, was revoked by Ex. Ord. No. 12002, July 7, 1977, 42 F.R. 35623, set out below.

EXECUTIVE ORDER NO. 11818

Ex. Ord. No. 11818, Nov. 5, 1974, 39 F.R. 39429, which provided for the continuing regulation of exports, was revoked by Ex. Ord. No. 12002, July 7, 1977, 42 F.R. 35623, set out below.

EXECUTIVE ORDER NO. 11940

Ex. Ord. No. 11940, Sept. 30, 1976, 41 F.R. 43707, which provided for the continuing regulation of exports, was revoked by Ex. Ord. No. 12002, July 7, 1977, 42 F.R. 35623, set out below.

EX. ORD. NO. 12002. ADMINISTRATION OF EXPORT ADMINISTRATION ACT

Ex. Ord. No. 12002, July 7, 1977, 42 F.R. 35623, as amended by Ex. Ord. No. 12755, Mar. 12, 1991, 56 F.R. 11057, provided:

By virtue of the authority vested in me by the Constitution and statutes of the United States of America, including the Export Administration Act of 1969, as amended (50 U.S.C. App. 2401, et seq.), and as President of the United States of America, it is hereby ordered as follows:

SECTION 1. Except as provided in Section 2, the power, authority, and discretion conferred upon the President by the provisions of the Export Administration Act of 1969, as amended (50 U.S.C. App. 2401, et seq.), hereinafter referred to as the Act, are delegated to the Secretary of Commerce, with the power of successive redelegation.

SEC. 2. (a) The power, authority and discretion conferred upon the President in Sections 4(h) and 4(l) of the Act are retained by the President.

(b) The power, authority and discretion conferred upon the President in Section 3(8) of the Act [section 2402(8) of this Appendix], which directs that every reasonable effort be made to secure the removal or reduction of assistance by foreign countries to international terrorists through cooperation and agreement, are delegated to the Secretary of State, with the power of successive redelegation.

SEC. 3. The Export Administration Review Board, hereinafter referred to as the Board, which was established by Executive Order No. 11533 of June 4, 1970, as amended, is hereby continued. The Board shall continue to have as its members, the Secretary of Commerce, who shall be Chairman of the Board, the Secretary of State, and the Secretary of Defense. The Secretary of Energy and the Director of the United States Arms Control and Disarmament Agency shall be members of the Board, and shall participate in meetings that consider issues involving nonproliferation of armaments and other issues within their respective statutory and policy-making authorities. The Chairman of the Joint Chiefs of Staff and the Director of Central Intelligence shall be non-voting members of the Board. No alternate Board members shall be designated, but the acting head or deputy head of any department or agency may serve in lieu of the head of the concerned department or agency. The Board may invite the heads of other United States Government departments or agencies, other than the agencies represented by the Board members, to participate in the activities of the Board when matters of interest to such departments or agencies are under consideration.

SEC. 4. The Secretary of Commerce may from time to time refer to the Board such particular export license matters, involving questions of national security or other major policy issues, as the Secretary shall select. The Secretary of Commerce shall also refer to the Board any other such export license matter, upon the request of any other member of the Board or of the head of any other United States Government department or agency having any interest in such matter. The Board shall consider the matters so referred to it, giving due consideration to the foreign policy of the United States, the national security, concerns about the nonproliferation of armaments, and the domestic economy, and shall make recommendation thereon to the Secretary of Commerce.

SEC. 5. The President may at any time (a) prescribe rules and regulations applicable to the power, authority, and discretion referred to in this Order, and (b) communicate to the Secretary of Commerce such specific directives applicable thereto as the President shall determine. The Secretary of Commerce shall from time to time report to the President upon the administration of the Act and, as the Secretary deems necessary, may refer to the President recommendations made by the Board under Section 4 of this Order. Neither the provisions of this section nor those of Section 4 shall be construed as limiting the provisions of Section 1 of this Order.

SEC. 6. All delegations, rules, regulations, orders, licenses, and other forms of administrative action made, issued, or otherwise taken under, or continued in existence by, the Executive orders revoked in Section 7 of this Order, and not revoked administratively or legislatively, shall remain in full force and effect under this Order until amended, modified, or terminated by proper authority. The revocations in Section 7 of this Order shall not affect any violation of any rules, regulations, orders, licenses or other forms of administrative action under those Orders during the period those Orders were in effect.

SEC. 7. Executive Order No. 11533 of June 4, 1970, Executive Order No. 11683 of August 29, 1972, Executive Order No. 11798 of August 14, 1974, Executive Order No. 11818 of November 5, 1974, Executive Order No. 11907 of March 1, 1976, and Executive Order No. 11940 of September 30, 1976 are hereby revoked.

[For abolition, transfer of functions, and treatment of references to United States Arms Control and Disarmament Agency, see section 6511 et seq. of Title 22, Foreign Relations and Intercourse.]

EX. ORD. NO. 12214. ADMINISTRATION OF EXPORT ADMINISTRATION ACT

Ex. Ord. No. 12214, May 2, 1980, 45 F.R. 29783, provided:

By the authority vested in me as President of the United States of America by Section 4(e) of the Export Administration Act of 1979 (Public Law 96–72; 50 U.S.C. App. 2403(e)), it is hereby ordered as follows:

1–101. Except as provided in Section 1–102, the functions conferred upon the President by the provisions of the Export Administration Act of 1979, hereinafter referred to as the Act (Public Law 96–72; 50 U.S.C. App. 2401 et seq.), are delegated to the Secretary of Commerce.

1–102. (a) The functions conferred upon the President by Sections 4(e), 5(c), 5(f)(1), 5(h)(6), 6(k), 7(d)(2), 10(g) and 20 of the Act [50 U.S.C. App. 2403(e), 2404(c), 2404(f)(1), 2404(h)(6), 2405(k), 2406(d)(2), 2409(g) and 2419] are reserved to the President.

(b) The functions conferred upon the President by Sections 5(f)(4), 5(i), and 6(g) of the Act [50 U.S.C. App. 2404(f)(4), 2404(i), and 2405(g)] are delegated to the Secretary of State.

1–103. All delegations, rules, regulations, orders, licenses, and other forms of administrative action made, issued or otherwise taken under, or continued in existence by, Section 21 of the Act [50 U.S.C. App. 2420] or Executive Order No. 12002 [set out above], and not revoked administratively or legislatively, shall remain in full force and effect until amended, modified, or terminated by proper authority. This Order does not supersede or otherwise affect Executive Order No. 12002.

1–104. Except to the extent inconsistent with this Order, all actions previously taken pursuant to any function delegated or assigned by this Order shall be deemed to have been taken and authorized by this Order.

JIMMY CARTER.

EXECUTIVE ORDER NO. 12264

Ex. Ord. No. 12264, Jan. 15, 1981, 46 F.R. 4659, which related to the Federal policy regarding the export of banned or significantly restricted substances, was revoked by Ex. Ord. No. 12290, Feb. 17, 1981, 46 F.R. 12943, set out below.

EX. ORD. NO. 12290. IMPLEMENTATION OF EXPORT ADMINISTRATION ACT WITH MINIMUM REGULATORY BURDEN

Ex. Ord. No. 12290, Feb. 17, 1981, 46 F.R. 12943, provided:

By the authority vested in me as President by the Constitution of the United States of America, and in order to ensure that the Export Administration Act of

1979 [sections 2401 to 2420 of this Appendix] is implemented with the minimum regulatory burden, Executive Order No. 12264 of January 15, 1981, entitled "On Federal Policy Regarding the Export of Banned or Significantly Restricted Substances," is hereby revoked.

RONALD REAGAN.

CONTINUATION OF EXPORT CONTROL REGULATIONS

Provisions relating to continued effectiveness of the Export Administration Act of 1979, 50 App. U.S.C. 2401 et seq., and to issuance and continued effectiveness of rules, regulations, orders, licenses, and other forms of administrative action and delegations of authority relating to administration of that Act, were contained in the following:

Ex. Ord. No. 12924, Aug. 19, 1994, 59 F.R. 43437, set out as a note under section 1701 of Title 50, War and National Defense.

Ex. Ord. No. 12923, June 30, 1994, 59 F.R. 34551, formerly set out as a note under section 1701 of Title 50, prior to revocation by Ex. Ord. No. 12924, §4, Aug. 19, 1994, 59 F.R. 43438.

Ex. Ord. No. 12867, Sept. 30, 1993, 58 F.R. 51747, set out as a note under section 1701 of Title 50, War and National Defense.

Ex. Ord. No. 12730, Sept. 30, 1990, 55 F.R. 40373, formerly set out as a note under section 1701 of Title 50, prior to revocation by Ex. Ord. No. 12867, Sept. 30, 1993, 58 F.R. 51747.

Ex. Ord. No. 12525, July 12, 1985, 50 F.R. 28757, set out as a note under section 1701 of Title 50.

Ex. Ord. No. 12470, Mar. 30, 1984, 49 F.R. 13099, formerly set out as a note under section 1701 of Title 50, prior to revocation by Ex. Ord. No. 12525, July 12, 1985, 50 F.R. 28757.

Ex. Ord. No. 12451, Dec. 20, 1983, 48 F.R. 56563, set out as a note under section 1701 of Title 50.

Ex. Ord. No. 12444, Oct. 14, 1983, 48 F.R. 48215, formerly set out as a note under section 1701 of Title 50, prior to revocation by Ex. Ord. No. 12451, Dec. 20, 1983, 48 F.R. 56563.

EX. ORD. NO. 12981. ADMINISTRATION OF EXPORT CONTROLS

Ex. Ord. No. 12981, Dec. 5, 1995, 60 F.R. 62981, as amended by Ex. Ord. No. 13020, Oct. 12, 1996, 61 F.R. 54079; Ex. Ord. No. 13026, §1(b), Nov. 15, 1996, 61 F.R. 58767; Ex. Ord. No. 13117, Mar. 31, 1999, 64 F.R. 16591, provided:

By the authority vested in me as President by the Constitution and the laws of the United States of America, including but not limited to the International Emergency Economic Powers Act (50 U.S.C. 1701 *et. seq.*) ("the Act"), and in order to take additional steps with respect to the national emergency described and declared in Executive Order No. 12924 of August 19, 1994 [50 U.S.C. 1701 note], and continued on August 15, 1995, I, WILLIAM J. CLINTON, President of the United States of America, find that it is necessary for the procedures set forth below to apply to export license applications submitted under the Act and the Export Administration Regulations (15 C.F.R. Part 730 *et. seq.*) ("the Regulations") or under any renewal of, or successor to, the Export Administration Act of 1979, as amended (50 U.S.C. App. 2401 *et. seq.*) ("the Export Administration Act"), and the Regulations. Accordingly, it is hereby ordered as follows:

SECTION 1. *License Review*. To the extent permitted by law and consistent with Executive Order No. 12924 of August 19, 1994, the power, authority, and discretion conferred upon the Secretary of Commerce ("the Secretary") under the Export Administration Act to require, review, and make final determinations with regard to export licenses, documentation, and other forms of information submitted to the Department of Commerce pursuant to the Act and the Regulations or under any renewal of, or successor to, the Export Administration Act and the Regulations, with the power of successive redelegation, shall continue. The Departments of State, Defense, and Energy each shall have the authority to review any export license application submitted to the Department of Commerce pursuant to the Act and the Regulations or under any renewal of, or successor to, the Export Administration Act and the Regulations. The Secretary may refer license applications to other United States Government departments or agencies for review as appropriate. In the event that a department or agency determines that certain types of applications need not be referred to it, such department or agency shall notify the Department of Commerce as to the specific types of such applications that it does not wish to review. All departments or agencies shall promptly respond, on a case-by-case basis, to requests from other departments or agencies for historical information relating to past license applications.

SEC. 2. *Determinations*. (a) All license applications submitted under the Act and the Regulations or any renewal of, or successor to, the Export Administration Act and the Regulations, shall be resolved or referred to the President no later than 90 calendar days after registration of the completed license application.

(b) The following actions related to processing a license application submitted under the Act and the Regulations or any renewal of, or successor to, the Export Administration Act and the Regulations shall not be counted in calculating the time periods prescribed in this order:

(1) *Agreement of the Applicant*. Delays upon which the Secretary and the applicant mutually agree.

(2) *Prelicense Checks*. Prelicense checks through government channels that may be required to establish the identity and reliability of the recipient of items controlled under the Act and the Regulations or any renewal of, or successor to, the Export Administration Act and the Regulations, provided that:

(A) the need for such prelicense check is established by the Secretary, or by another department or agency if the request for prelicense check is made by such department or agency;

(B) the Secretary requests the prelicense check within 5 days of the determination that it is necessary; and

(C) the Secretary completes the analysis of the result of the prelicense check within 5 days.

(3) *Requests for Government-To-Government Assurances*. Requests for government-to-government assurances of suitable end-use of items approved for export under the Act and the Regulations or any renewal of, or successor to, the Export Administration Act and the Regulations, when failure to obtain such assurances would result in rejection of the application, provided that:

(A) the request for such assurances is sent to the Secretary of State within 5 days of the determination that the assurances are required;

(B) the Secretary of State initiates the request of the relevant government within 10 days thereafter; and

(C) the license is issued within 5 days of the Secretary's receipt of the requested assurances. Whenever such prelicense checks and assurances are not requested within the time periods set forth above, they must be accomplished within the time periods established by this section.

(4) *Multilateral Reviews*. Multilateral review of a license application as provided for under the Act and the Regulations or any renewal of, or successor to, the Export Administration Act and the Regulations, as long as multilateral review is required by the relevant multilateral regime.

(5) *Consultations*. Consultation with other governments, if such consultation is provided for by a relevant multilateral regime or bilateral arrangement as a precondition for approving a license.

SEC. 3. *Initial Processing*. Within 9 days of registration of any license application, the Secretary shall, as appropriate:

(a) request additional information from the applicant. The time required for the applicant to supply the additional information shall not be counted in calculating the time periods prescribed in this section.

(b) refer the application and pertinent information to agencies or departments as stipulated in section 1 of this order, and forward to the agencies any relevant information submitted by the applicant that could not be reduced to electronic form.

(c) assure that the stated classification on the application is correct; return the application if a license is not required; and, if referral to other departments or agencies is not required, grant the application or notify the applicant of the Secretary's intention to deny the application.

SEC. 4. *Department or Agency Review.* (a) Each reviewing department or agency shall specify to the Secretary, within 10 days of receipt of a referral as specified in subsection 3(b), any information not in the application that would be required to make a determination, and the Secretary shall promptly request such information from the applicant. If, after receipt of the information so specified or other new information, a reviewing department or agency concludes that additional information would be required to make a determination, it shall promptly specify that additional information to the Secretary, and the Secretary shall promptly request such information from the applicant. The time that may elapse between the date the information is requested by the reviewing department or agency and the date the information is received by the reviewing department or agency shall not be counted in calculating the time periods prescribed in this order. Such information specified by reviewing departments or agencies is in addition to any information that may be requested by the Department of Commerce on its own initiative during the first 9 days after registration of an application.

(b) Within 30 days of receipt of a referral and all required information, a department or agency shall provide the Secretary with a recommendation either to approve or deny the license application. As appropriate, such recommendation may be with the benefit of consultation and discussions in interagency groups established to provide expertise and coordinate interagency consultation. A recommendation that the Secretary deny a license shall include a statement of the reasons for such recommendation that are consistent with the provisions of the Act and the Regulations or any renewal of, or successor to, the Export Administration Act and the Regulations and shall cite both the statutory and the regulatory bases for the recommendation to deny. A department or agency that fails to provide a recommendation within 30 days with a statement of reasons and the statutory and regulatory bases shall be deemed to have no objection to the decision of the Secretary.

SEC. 5. *Interagency Dispute Resolution.* (a) *Committees.* (1)(A) *Export Administration Review Board.* The Export Administration Review Board ("the Board"), which was established by Executive Order No. 11533 of June 4, 1970 [formerly set out above], and continued in Executive Order No. 12002 of July 7, 1977 [set out above], is hereby continued. The Board shall have as its members, the Secretary, who shall be Chair of the Board, the Secretary of State, the Secretary of Defense, and the Secretary of Energy[.] The Chairman of the Joint Chiefs of Staff and the Director of Central Intelligence shall be nonvoting members of the Board. No alternate Board members shall be designated, but the acting head or deputy head of any member department or agency may serve in lieu of the head of the concerned department or agency. The Board may invite the heads of other United States Government departments or agencies, other than the departments or agencies represented by the Board members, to participate in the activities of the Board when matters of interest to such departments or agencies are under consideration.

(B) The Secretary may, from time to time, refer to the Board such particular export license matters, involving questions of national security or other major policy issues, as the Secretary shall select. The Secretary shall also refer to the Board any other such export license matter, upon the request of any other member of the Board or the head of any other United States Government department or agency having any interest in such matter. The Board shall consider the matters so referred to it, giving due consideration to the foreign policy of the United States, the national security, the domestic economy, and concerns about the proliferation of armaments, weapons of mass destruction, missile delivery systems, and advanced conventional weapons and shall make recommendations thereon to the Secretary.

(2) *Advisory Committee on Export Policy.* An Advisory Committee on Export Policy ("ACEP") is established and shall have as its members the Assistant Secretary of Commerce for Export Administration, who shall be Chair of the ACEP, and Assistant Secretary-level representatives of the Departments of State, Defense, and Energy[.] Appropriate representatives of the Joint Chiefs of Staff and of the Nonproliferation Center of the Central Intelligence Agency shall be nonvoting members of the ACEP. Representatives of the departments or agencies shall be the appropriate Assistant Secretary or equivalent (or appropriate acting Assistant Secretary or equivalent in lieu of the Assistant Secretary or equivalent) of the concerned department or agency, or appropriate Deputy Assistant Secretary or equivalent (or the appropriate acting Deputy Assistant Secretary or equivalent in lieu of the Deputy Assistant Secretary or equivalent) of the concerned department or agency. Regardless of the department or agency representative's rank, such representative shall speak and vote at the ACEP on behalf of the appropriate Assistant Secretary or equivalent of such department or agency. The ACEP may invite Assistant Secretary-level representatives of other United States Government departments or agencies, other than the departments and agencies represented by the ACEP members, to participate in the activities of the ACEP when matters of interest to such departments or agencies are under consideration.

(3)(A) *Operating Committee.* An Operating Committee ("OC") of the ACEP is established. The Secretary shall appoint its Chair, who shall also serve as Executive Secretary of the ACEP. Its other members shall be representatives of appropriate agencies in the Departments of Commerce, State, Defense, and Energy[.] The appropriate representatives of the Joint Chiefs of Staff and the Nonproliferation Center of the Central Intelligence Agency shall be nonvoting members of the OC. The OC may invite representatives of other United States Government departments or agencies, other than the departments and agencies represented by the OC members, to participate in the activities of the OC when matters of interest to such departments or agencies are under consideration.

(B) The OC shall review all license applications on which the reviewing departments and agencies are not in agreement. The Chair of the OC shall consider the recommendations of the reviewing departments and agencies and inform them of his or her decision on any such matters within 14 days after the deadline for receiving department and agency recommendations. However, for license applications concerning commercial communication satellites and hot-section technologies for the development, production, and overhaul of commercial aircraft engines that are transferred from the United States Munitions List to the Commerce Control List pursuant to regulations issued by the Departments of Commerce and State after the date of this order, the Chair of the OC shall inform reviewing departments and agencies of the majority vote decision of the OC. As described below, any reviewing department or agency may appeal the decision of the Chair of the OC, or the majority vote decision of the OC in cases concerning the commercial communication satellites and hot-section technologies described above, to the Chair of the ACEP. In the absence of a timely appeal, the Chair's decision (or the majority vote decision in the case of license applications concerning the commercial communication satellites and hot-section technologies described above) will be final.

(b) *Resolution Procedures.* (1) If any department or agency disagrees with a licensing determination of the

Department of Commerce made through the Chair of the OC (or a majority vote decision of the OC in the case of license applications concerning the commercial communication satellites and the hot-section technologies described in section 5(a)(3)(B)), it may appeal the matter to the ACEP for resolution. A department or agency must appeal a matter within 5 days of such a decision. Appeals must be in writing from an official appointed by the President, by and with the advice and consent of the Senate, or an officer properly acting in such capacity, and must cite both the statutory and the regulatory bases for the appeal. The ACEP shall review all departments' and agencies' information and recommendations, and the Chair of the ACEP shall inform the reviewing departments and agencies of the majority vote decision of the ACEP within 11 days from the date of receiving notice of the appeal. Within 5 days of the majority vote decision, any dissenting department or agency may appeal the decision by submitting a letter from the head of the department or agency to the Secretary in his or her capacity as the Chair of the Board. Such letter shall cite both the statutory and the regulatory bases for the appeal. Within the same 5-day period, the Secretary may call a meeting on his or her own initiative to consider a license application. In the absence of a timely appeal, the majority vote decision of the ACEP shall be final.

(2) The Board shall review all departments' and agencies' information and recommendations, and such other export control matters as may be appropriate. The Secretary shall inform the reviewing departments and agencies of the majority vote of the Board within 11 days from the date of receiving notice of appeal. Within 5 days of the decision, any department or agency dissenting from the majority vote decision of the Board may appeal the decision by submitting a letter from the head of the dissenting department or agency to the President. In the absence of a timely appeal, the majority vote decision of the Board shall be final.

SEC. 6. *Encryption Products.* In conducting the license review described in section 1 above, with respect to export controls of encryption products that are or would be, on November 15, 1996, designated as defense articles in Category XIII of the United States Munitions List and regulated by the United States Department of State pursuant to the Arms Export Control Act, 22 U.S.C. 2778 *et seq.*, but that subsequently are placed on the Commerce Control List in the Export Administration Regulations, the Departments of State, Defense, Energy, and Justice shall have the opportunity to review any export license application submitted to the Department of Commerce. The Department of Justice shall, with respect to such encryption products, be a voting member of the Export Administration Review Board described in section 5(a)(1) of this order and of the Advisory Committee on Export Policy described in section 5(a)(2) of this order. The Department of Justice shall be a full member of the Operating Committee of the ACEP described in section 5(a)(3) of this order, and of any other committees and consultation groups reviewing export controls with respect to such encryption products.

SEC. 7. The license review process in this order shall take effect beginning with those license applications registered by the Secretary 60 days after the date of this order and shall continue in effect to the extent not inconsistent with any renewal of the Export Administration Act, or with any successor to that Act.

SEC. 8. *Judicial Review.* This order is intended only to improve the internal management of the executive branch and is not intended to, and does not, create any rights to administrative or judicial review, or any other right or benefit or trust responsibility, substantive or procedural, enforceable by a party against the United States, its agencies or instrumentalities, its officers or employees, or any other person.

WILLIAM J. CLINTON.

[For abolition, transfer of functions, and treatment of references to United States Arms Control and Disarmament Agency, see section 6511 et seq. of Title 22, Foreign Relations and Intercourse.]

EX. ORD. NO. 13026. ADMINISTRATION OF EXPORT CONTROLS ON ENCRYPTION PRODUCTS

Ex. Ord. No. 13026, Nov. 15, 1996, 61 F.R. 58767, provided:

By the authority vested in me as President by the Constitution and the laws of the United States of America, including but not limited to the International Emergency Economic Powers Act (50 U.S.C. 1701 *et seq.*), and in order to take additional steps with respect to the national emergency described and declared in Executive Order 12924 of August 19, 1994 [50 U.S.C. 1701 note], and continued on August 15, 1995, and on August 14, 1996, I, WILLIAM J. CLINTON, President of the United States of America, have decided that the provisions set forth below shall apply to administration of the export control system maintained by the Export Administration Regulations, 15 CFR Part 730 *et seq.* (''the EAR''). Accordingly, it is hereby ordered as follows:

SECTION 1. *Treatment of Encryption Products.* In order to provide for appropriate controls on the export and foreign dissemination of encryption products, export controls of encryption products that are or would be, on this date, designated as defense articles in Category XIII of the United States Munitions List and regulated by the United States Department of State pursuant to the Arms Export Control Act, 22 U.S.C. 2778 *et seq.* (''the AECA''), but that subsequently are placed on the Commerce Control List in the EAR, shall be subject to the following conditions: (a) I have determined that the export of encryption products described in this section could harm national security and foreign policy interests even where comparable products are or appear to be available from sources outside the United States, and that facts and questions concerning the foreign availability of such encryption products cannot be made subject to public disclosure or judicial review without revealing or implicating classified information that could harm United States national security and foreign policy interests. Accordingly, sections 4(c) and 6(h)(2)–(4) of the Export Administration Act of 1979 (''the EAA''), 50 U.S.C. App. 2403(c) and 2405(h)(2)–(4), as amended and as continued in effect by Executive Order 12924 of August 19, 1994, and by notices of August 15, 1995, and August 14, 1996, all other analogous provisions of the EAA relating to foreign availability, and the regulations in the EAR relating to such EAA provisions, shall not be applicable with respect to export controls on such encryption products. Notwithstanding this, the Secretary of Commerce (''Secretary'') may, in his discretion, consider the foreign availability of comparable encryption products in determining whether to issue a license in a particular case or to remove controls on particular products, but is not required to issue licenses in particular cases or to remove controls on particular products based on such consideration;

(b) [Amended Ex. Ord. No. 12981, set out above;]

(c) Because the export of encryption software, like the export of other encryption products described in this section, must be controlled because of such software's functional capacity, rather than because of any possible informational value of such software, such software shall not be considered or treated as ''technology,'' as that term is defined in section 16 of the EAA (50 U.S.C. App. 2415) and in the EAR (61 Fed. Reg. 12714, March 25, 1996);

(d) With respect to encryption products described in this section, the Secretary shall take such actions, including the promulgation of rules, regulations, and amendments thereto, as may be necessary to control the export of assistance (including training) to foreign persons in the same manner and to the same extent as the export of such assistance is controlled under the AECA, as amended by section 151 of Public Law 104–164 [see 22 U.S.C. 2778(b)(1)(A)];

(e) Appropriate controls on the export and foreign dissemination of encryption products described in this section may include, but are not limited to, measures that promote the use of strong encryption products and the development of a key recovery management infrastructure; and

(f) Regulation of encryption products described in this section shall be subject to such further conditions as the President may direct.

SEC. 2. *Effective Date*. The provisions described in section 1 shall take effect as soon as any encryption products described in section 1 are placed on the Commerce Control List in the EAR.

SEC. 3. *Judicial Review*. This order is intended only to improve the internal management of the executive branch and to ensure the implementation of appropriate controls on the export and foreign dissemination of encryption products. It is not intended to, and does not, create any rights to administrative or judicial review, or any other right or benefit or trust responsibility, substantive or procedural, enforceable by a party against the United States, its agencies or instrumentalities, its officers or employees, or any other person.

WILLIAM J. CLINTON.

SECTION REFERRED TO IN OTHER SECTIONS

This section is referred to in sections 2404, 2406, 2409, 2411, 2413, 2414 of this Appendix.

§2403–1. Repealed. Pub. L. 103–199, title II, §203(b), Dec. 17, 1993, 107 Stat. 2322

Section, Pub. L. 93–365, title VII, §709, Aug. 5, 1974, 88 Stat. 408, related to review by Secretary of Defense of applications for export to controlled country of any goods, technology, or industrial techniques developed with Department of Defense funds for purpose of determining whether such export would significantly increase military capability of such country.

§§2403–1a, 2403a. Omitted

CODIFICATION

Section 2403–1a, Pub. L. 91–184, §4A, as added Pub. L. 95–52, title II, §201(a), June 22, 1977, 91 Stat. 244, which set forth provisions prohibiting United States persons from participating in foreign boycotts and administrative enforcement of such prohibitions, expired on Sept. 3, 1979.

Section 2403a, Pub. L. 91–184, §4B, formerly §4A, as added Pub. L. 93–500, §8, Oct. 29, 1974, 88 Stat. 1554, renumbered Pub. L. 95–52, title II, §201(a), June 22, 1977, 91 Stat. 244, which set forth procedures applicable for relief from export controls upon showing of hardship, expired on Sept. 30, 1979.

§2404. National security controls

(a) Authority

(1) In order to carry out the policy set forth in section 3(2)(A) of this Act [section 2402(2)(A) of this Appendix], the President may, in accordance with the provisions of this section, prohibit or curtail the export of any goods or technology subject to the jurisdiction of the United States or exported by any person subject to the jurisdiction of the United States. The authority contained in this subsection includes the authority to prohibit or curtail the transfer of goods or technology within the United States to embassies and affiliates of controlled countries. For purposes of the preceding sentence, the term "affiliates" includes both governmental entities and commercial entities that are controlled in fact by controlled countries. The authority contained in this subsection shall be exercised by the Secretary, in consultation with the Secretary of Defense, and such other departments and agencies as the Secretary considers appropriate, and shall be implemented by means of export licenses described in section 4(a) of this Act [section 2403(a) of this Appendix].

(2) Whenever the Secretary makes any revision with respect to any goods or technology, or with respect to the countries or destinations, affected by export controls imposed under this section, the Secretary shall publish in the Federal Register a notice of such revision and shall specify in such notice that the revision relates to controls imposed under the authority contained in this section.

(3) In issuing regulations to carry out this section, particular attention shall be given to the difficulty of devising effective safeguards to prevent a country that poses a threat to the security of the United States from diverting critical technologies to military use, the difficulty of devising effective safeguards to protect critical goods, and the need to take effective measures to prevent the reexport of critical technologies from other countries to countries that pose a threat to the security of the United States.

(4)(A) No authority or permission may be required under this section to reexport any goods or technology subject to the jurisdiction of the United States to any country which maintains export controls on such goods or technology cooperatively with the United States pursuant to the agreement of the group known as the Coordinating Committee, or pursuant to an agreement described in subsection (k) of this section. The Secretary may require any person reexporting any goods or technology under this subparagraph to notify the Secretary of such reexports.

(B) Notwithstanding subparagraph (A), the Secretary may require authority or permission to reexport the following:

(i) supercomputers;

(ii) goods or technology for sensitive nuclear uses (as defined by the Secretary);

(iii) devices for surreptitious interception of wire or oral communications; and

(iv) goods or technology intended for such end users as the Secretary may specify by regulation.

(5)(A) Except as provided in subparagraph (B), no authority or permission may be required under this section to reexport any goods or technology subject to the jurisdiction of the United States from any country when the goods or technology to be reexported are incorporated in another good and—

(i) the value of the controlled United States content of that other good is 25 percent or less of the total value of the good; or

(ii) the export of the goods or technology to a controlled country would require only notification of the participating governments of the Coordinating Committee.

For purposes of this paragraph, the "controlled United States content" of a good means those goods or technology subject to the jurisdiction of the United States which are incorporated in the good, if the export of those goods or technology from the United States to a country, at the time that the good is exported to that country, would require a validated license.

(B) The Secretary may by regulation provide that subparagraph (A) does not apply to the reexport of a supercomputer which contains goods or technology subject to the jurisdiction of the United States.

(6) Not later than 90 days after the date of the enactment of this paragraph [Aug. 23, 1988], the Secretary shall issue regulations to carry out paragraphs (4) and (5). Such regulations shall define the term "supercomputer" for purposes of those paragraphs.

(b) Policy toward individual countries

(1) In administering export controls for national security purposes under this section, the President shall establish as a list of controlled countries those countries set forth in section 620(f) of the Foreign Assistance Act of 1961 [22 U.S.C. 2370(f)], except that the President may add any country to or remove any country from such list of controlled countries if he determines that the export of goods or technology to such country would or would not (as the case may be) make a significant contribution to the military potential of such country or a combination of countries which would prove detrimental to the national security of the United States. In determining whether a country is added to or removed from the list of controlled countries, the President shall take into account—

(A) the extent to which the country's policies are adverse to the national security interests of the United States;

(B) the country's Communist or non-Communist status;

(C) the present and potential relationship of the country with the United States;

(D) the present and potential relationships of the country with countries friendly or hostile to the United States;

(E) the country's nuclear weapons capability and the country's compliance record with respect to multilateral nuclear weapons agreements to which the United States is a party; and

(F) such other factors as the President considers appropriate.

Nothing in the preceding sentence shall be interpreted to limit the authority of the President provided in this Act [sections 2401 to 2420 of this Appendix] to prohibit or curtail the export of any goods or technology to any country to which exports are controlled for national security purposes other than countries on the list of controlled countries specified in this paragraph. The President shall review not less frequently than every three years in the case of controls maintained cooperatively with other nations, and annually in the case of all other controls, United States policy toward individual countries to determine whether such policy is appropriate in light of the factors set forth in this paragraph.

(2)(A) Except as provided in subparagraph (B), no authority or permission may be required under this section to export goods or technology to a country which maintains export controls on such goods or technology cooperatively with the United States pursuant to the agreement of the group known as the Coordinating Committee or pursuant to an agreement described in subsection (k) of this section, if the export of such goods or technology to the People's Republic of China or a controlled country on the date of the enactment of the Export Enhancement Act of 1988 [Aug. 23, 1988] would require only notification of the participating governments of the Coordinating Committee.

(B)(i) The Secretary may require a license for the export of goods or technology described in subparagraph (A) to such end users as the Secretary may specify by regulation.

(ii) The Secretary may require any person exporting goods or technology under this paragraph to notify the Secretary of those exports.

(C) The Secretary shall, within 3 months after the date of the enactment of the Export Enhancement Act of 1988 [Aug. 23, 1988], determine which countries referred to in subparagraph (A) are implementing an effective export control system consistent with principles agreed to in the Coordinating Committee, including the following:

(i) national laws providing appropriate civil and criminal penalties and statutes of limitations sufficient to deter potential violations;

(ii) a program to evaluate export license applications that includes sufficient technical expertise to assess the licensing status of exports and ensure the reliability of end-users;

(iii) an enforcement mechanism that provides authority for trained enforcement officers to investigate and prevent illegal exports;

(iv) a system of export control documentation to verify the movement of goods and technology; and

(v) procedures for the coordination and exchange of information concerning violations of the agreement of the Coordinating Committee.

The Secretary shall, at least once each year, review the determinations made under the preceding sentence with respect to all countries referred to in subparagraph (A). The Secretary may, as appropriate, add countries to, or remove countries from, the list of countries that are implementing an effective export control system in accordance with this subparagraph. No authority or permission to export may be required for the export of goods or technology to a country on such list.

(3)(A) No authority or permission may be required under this section to export to any country, other than a controlled country, any goods or technology if the export of the goods or technology to controlled countries would require only notification of the participating governments of the Coordinating Committee.

(B) The Secretary may require any person exporting any goods or technology under subparagraph (A) to notify the Secretary of those exports.

(c) Control list

(1) The Secretary shall establish and maintain, as part of the control list, a list of all goods and technology subject to export controls under this section. Such goods and technology shall be clearly identified as being subject to controls under this section.

(2) The Secretary of Defense and other appropriate departments and agencies shall identify goods and technology for inclusion on the list referred to in paragraph (1). Those items which the Secretary and the Secretary of Defense con-

cur shall be subject to export controls under this section shall comprise such list. If the Secretary and the Secretary of Defense are unable to concur on such items, as determined by the Secretary, the Secretary of Defense may, within 20 days after receiving notification of the Secretary's determination, refer the matter to the President for resolution. The Secretary of Defense shall notify the Secretary of any such referral. The President shall, not later than 20 days after such referral, notify the Secretary of his determination with respect to the inclusion of such items on the list. Failure of the Secretary of Defense to notify the President or the Secretary, or failure of the President to notify the Secretary, in accordance with this paragraph, shall be deemed by the Secretary to constitute concurrence in the implementation of the actions proposed by the Secretary regarding the inclusion of such items on the list.

(3) The Secretary shall conduct partial reviews of the list established pursuant to this subsection at least once each calendar quarter in order to carry out the policy set forth in section 3(2)(A) of this Act [section 2402(2)(A) of this Appendix] and the provisions of this section, and shall promptly make such revisions of the list as may be necessary after each such review. Before beginning each quarterly review, the Secretary shall publish notice of that review in the Federal Register. The Secretary shall provide a 30-day period during each review for comment and the submission of data, with or without oral presentation, by interested Government agencies and other affected or potentially affected parties. After consultation with appropriate Government agencies, the Secretary shall make a determination of any revisions in the list within 30 days after the end of the review period. The concurrence or approval of any other department or agency is not required before any such revision is made. The Secretary shall publish in the Federal Register any revisions in the list, with an explanation of the reasons for the revisions. The Secretary shall use the data developed from each review in formulating United States proposals relating to multilateral export controls in the group known as the Coordinating Committee. The Secretary shall further assess, as part of each review, the availability from sources outside the United States of goods and technology comparable to those subject to export controls imposed under this section. All goods and technology on the list shall be reviewed at least once each year. The provisions of this paragraph apply to revisions of the list which consist of removing items from the list or making changes in categories of, or other specifications in, items on the list.

(4) The appropriate technical advisory committee appointed under subsection (h) of this section shall be consulted by the Secretary with respect to changes, pursuant to paragraph (2) or (3), in the list established pursuant to this subsection, and such technical advisory committee may submit recommendations to the Secretary with respect to such changes. The Secretary shall consider the recommendations of the technical advisory committee and shall inform the committee of the disposition of its recommendations.

(5)(A) Not later than 6 months after the date of the enactment of this paragraph [Aug. 23, 1988], the following shall no longer be subject to export controls under this section:

(i) All goods or technology the export of which to controlled countries on the date of the enactment of the Export Enhancement Act of 1988 [Aug. 23, 1988] would require only notification of the participating governments of the Coordinating Committee, except for those goods or technology on which the Coordinating Committee agrees to maintain such notification requirement.

(ii) All medical instruments and equipment, subject to the provisions of subsection (m) of this section.

(B) The Secretary shall submit to the Congress annually a report setting forth the goods and technology from which export controls have been removed under this paragraph.

(6)(A) Notwithstanding subsection (f) or (h)(6) of this section, any export control imposed under this section which is maintained unilaterally by the United States shall expire 6 months after the date of the enactment of this paragraph [Aug. 23, 1988], or 6 months after the export control is imposed, whichever date is later, except that—

(i) any such export controls on those goods or technology for which a determination of the Secretary that there is no foreign availability has been made under subsection (f) or (h)(6) of this section before the end of the applicable 6-month period and is in effect may be renewed for periods of not more than 6 months each, and

(ii) any such export controls on those goods or technology with respect to which the President, by the end of the applicable 6-month period, is actively pursuing negotiations with other countries to achieve multilateral export controls on those goods or technology may be renewed for 2 periods of not more than 6 months each.

(B) Export controls on goods or technology described in clause (i) or (ii) of subparagraph (A) may be renewed only if, before each renewal, the President submits to the Congress a report setting forth all the controls being renewed and stating the specific reasons for such renewal.

(7) Notwithstanding any other provision of this subsection, after 1 year has elapsed since the last review in the Federal Register on any item within a category on the control list the export of which to the People's Republic of China would require only notification of the members of the group known as the Coordinating Committee, an export license applicant may file an allegation with the Secretary that such item has not been so reviewed within such 1-year period. Within 90 days after receipt of such allegation, the Secretary—

(A) shall determine the truth of the allegation;

(B) shall, if the allegation is confirmed, commence and complete the review of the item; and

(C) shall, pursuant to such review, submit a finding for publication in the Federal Register.

In such finding, the Secretary shall identify those goods or technology which shall remain on the control list and those goods or technology which shall be removed from the control list. If such review and submission for publication are not completed within that 90-day period, the goods or technology encompassed by such item shall immediately be removed from the control list.

(d) Militarily critical technologies

(1) The Secretary, in consultation with the Secretary of Defense, shall review and revise the list established pursuant to subsection (c), as prescribed in paragraph (3) of such subsection, for the purpose of insuring that export controls imposed under this section cover and (to the maximum extent consistent with the purposes of this Act [sections 2401 to 2420 of this Appendix]) are limited to militarily critical goods and technologies and the mechanisms through which such goods and technologies may be effectively transferred.

(2) The Secretary of Defense shall bear primary responsibility for developing a list of militarily critical technologies. In developing such list, primary emphasis shall be given to—

(A) arrays of design and manufacturing know-how,

(B) keystone manufacturing, inspection, and test equipment,

(C) goods accompanied by sophisticated operation, application, or maintenance know-how, and

(D) keystone equipment which would reveal or give insight into the design and manufacture of a United States military system,

which are not possessed by, or available in fact from sources outside the United States to, controlled countries and which, if exported, would permit a significant advance in a military system of any such country.

(3) The list referred to in paragraph (2) shall be sufficiently specific to guide the determinations of any official exercising export licensing responsibilities under this Act [sections 2401 to 2420 of this Appendix].

(4) The Secretary and the Secretary of Defense shall integrate items on the list of militarily critical technologies into the control list in accordance with the requirements of subsection (c) of this section. The integration of items on the list of militarily critical technologies into the control list shall proceed with all deliberate speed. Any disagreement between the Secretary and the Secretary of Defense regarding the integration of an item on the list of militarily critical technologies into the control list shall be resolved by the President. Except in the case of a good or technology for which a validated license may be required under subsection (f)(4) or (h)(6) of this section, a good or technology shall be included on the control list only if the Secretary finds that controlled countries do not possess that good or technology, or a functionally equivalent good or technology, and the good or technology or functionally equivalent good or technology is not available in fact to a controlled country from sources outside the United States in sufficient quantity and of comparable quality so that the requirement of a validated license for the export of such good or technology is or would be ineffective in achieving the purpose set forth in subsection (a) of this section. The Secretary and the Secretary of Defense shall jointly submit a report to the Congress, not later than 1 year after the date of the enactment of the Export Administration Amendments Act of 1985 [July 12, 1985], on actions taken to carry out this paragraph. For the purposes of this paragraph, assessment of whether a good or technology is functionally equivalent shall include consideration of the factors described in subsection (f)(3) of this section.

(5) The Secretary of Defense shall establish a procedure for reviewing the goods and technology on the list of militarily critical technologies on an ongoing basis for the purpose of removing from the list of militarily critical technologies any goods or technology that are no longer militarily critical. The Secretary of Defense may add to the list of militarily critical technologies any good or technology that the Secretary of Defense determines is militarily critical, consistent with the provisions of paragraph (2) of this subsection. If the Secretary and the Secretary of Defense disagree as to whether any change in the list of militarily critical technologies by the addition or removal of a good or technology should also be made in the control list, consistent with the provisions of the fourth sentence of paragraph (4) of this subsection, the President shall resolve the disagreement.

(6) The establishment of adequate export controls for militarily critical technology and keystone equipment shall be accompanied by suitable reductions in the controls on the products of that technology and equipment.

(7) The Secretary of Defense shall, not later than 1 year after the date of the enactment of the Export Administration Amendments Act of 1985 [July 12, 1985], report to the Congress on efforts by the Department of Defense to assess the impact that the transfer of goods or technology on the list of militarily critical technologies to controlled countries has had or will have on the military capabilities of those countries.

(e) Export licenses

(1) The Congress finds that the effectiveness and efficiency of the process of making export licensing determinations under this section is severely hampered by the large volume of validated export license applications required to be submitted under this Act [sections 2401 to 2420 of this Appendix]. Accordingly, it is the intent of Congress in this subsection to encourage the use of the multiple validated export licenses described in section 4(a)(2) of this Act [section 2403(a)(2) of this Appendix] in lieu of individual validated licenses.

(2) To the maximum extent practicable, consistent with the national security of the United States, the Secretary shall require a validated license under this section for the export of goods or technology only if—

(A) the export of such goods or technology is restricted pursuant to a multilateral agreement, formal or informal, to which the United States is a party and, under the terms of such multilateral agreement, such export requires the specific approval of the parties to such multilateral agreement;

(B) with respect to such goods or technology, other nations do not possess capabilities comparable to those possessed by the United States; or

(C) the United States is seeking the agreement of other suppliers to apply comparable controls to such goods or technology and, in the judgment of the Secretary, United States export controls on such goods or technology, by means of such license, are necessary pending the conclusion of such agreement.

(3) The Secretary, subject to the provisions of subsection (*l*) of this section, shall not require an individual validated export license for replacement parts which are exported to replace on a one-for-one basis parts that were in a good that has been lawfully exported from the United States.

(4) The Secretary shall periodically review the procedures with respect to the multiple validated export licenses, taking appropriate action to increase their utilization by reducing qualification requirements or lowering minimum thresholds, to combine procedures which overlap, and to eliminate those procedures which appear to be of marginal utility.

(5) The export of goods subject to export controls under this section shall be eligible, at the discretion of the Secretary, for a distribution license and other licenses authorizing multiple exports of goods, in accordance with section 4(a)(2) of this Act [section 2403(a)(2) of this Appendix]. The export of technology and related goods subject to export controls under this section shall be eligible for a comprehensive operations license in accordance with section 4(a)(2)(B) of this Act [section 2403(a)(2)(B) of this Appendix].

(6) Any application for a license for the export to the People's Republic of China of any good on which export controls are in effect under this section, without regard to the technical specifications of the good, for the purpose of demonstration or exhibition at a trade show shall carry a presumption of approval if—

(A) the United States exporter retains title to the good during the entire period in which the good is in the People's Republic of China; and

(B) the exporter removes the good from the People's Republic of China no later than at the conclusion of the trade show.

(f) Foreign availability

(1) Foreign availability to controlled countries

(A) The Secretary, in consultation with the Secretary of Defense and other appropriate Government agencies and with appropriate technical advisory committees established pursuant to subsection (h) of this section, shall review, on a continuing basis, the availability to controlled countries, from sources outside the United States, including countries which participate with the United States in multilateral export controls, of any goods or technology the export of which requires a validated license under this section. In any case in which the Secretary determines, in accordance with procedures and criteria which the Secretary shall by regulation establish, that any such goods or technology are available in fact to controlled countries from such sources in sufficient quantity and of comparable quality so that the requirement of a validated license for the export of such goods or technology is or would be ineffective in achieving the purpose set forth in subsection (a) of this section, the Secretary may not, after the determination is made, require a validated license for the export of such goods or technology during the period of such foreign availability, unless the President determines that the absence of export controls under this section on the goods or technology would prove detrimental to the national security of the United States. In any case in which the President determines under this paragraph that export controls under this section must be maintained notwithstanding foreign availability, the Secretary shall publish that determination, together with a concise statement of its basis and the estimated economic impact of the decision.

(B) The Secretary shall approve any application for a validated license which is required under this section for the export of any goods or technology to a controlled country and which meets all other requirements for such an application, if the Secretary determines that such goods or technology will, if the license is denied, be available in fact to such country from sources outside the United States, including countries which participate with the United States in multilateral export controls, in sufficient quantity and of comparable quality so that denial of the license would be ineffective in achieving the purpose set forth in subsection (a) of this section, unless the President determines that approving the license application would prove detrimental to the national security of the United States. In any case in which the Secretary makes a determination of foreign availability under this subparagraph with respect to any goods or technology, the Secretary shall determine whether a determination of foreign availability under subparagraph (A) with respect to such goods or technology is warranted.

(2) Foreign availability to other than controlled countries

(A) The Secretary shall review, on a continuing basis, the availability to countries other than controlled countries, from sources outside the United States, of any goods or technology the export of which requires a validated license under this section. If the Secretary determines, in accordance with procedures which the Secretary shall establish, that any goods or technology in sufficient quantity and of comparable quality are available in fact from sources outside the United States (other than availability under license from a country which maintains export controls on such goods or technology cooperatively with the United States pursuant to the agreement of the group known as the Coordinating Committee or pursuant to an agreement described in subsection (k) of this section), the Secretary may not, after the determination is made and during the period of such foreign availability, require a validated license for the export of such goods or technology to any country (other than a controlled country) to which the country from which the goods or technology is available does not place controls on the export of such goods or technology. The requirement with respect to a validated license in the preceding sentence shall not apply if the President determines that the absence of export controls under this section on the goods or technology would prove detrimental to the national security of the United States. In any case in which the President determines under this paragraph that export controls under this section must be maintained notwithstanding foreign availability, the Secretary shall publish that determination, together with a concise statement of its basis and the estimated economic impact of the decision.

(B) The Secretary shall approve any application for a validated license which is required under this section for the export of any goods or technology to a country (other than a controlled country) and which meets all other requirements for such an application, if the Secretary determines that such goods or technology are available from foreign sources to that country under the criteria established in subparagraph (A), unless the President determines that approving the license application would prove detrimental to the national security of the United States. In any case in which the Secretary makes a determination of foreign availability under this subparagraph with respect to any goods or technology, the Secretary shall determine whether a determination of foreign availability under subparagraph (A) with respect to such goods or technology is warranted.

(3) Procedures for making determinations

(A) The Secretary shall make a foreign availability determination under paragraph (1) or (2) on the Secretary's own initiative or upon receipt of an allegation from an export license applicant that such availability exists. In making any such determination, the Secretary shall accept the representations of applicants made in writing and supported by reasonable evidence, unless such representations are contradicted by reliable evidence, including scientific or physical examination, expert opinion based upon adequate factual information, or intelligence information. In making determinations of foreign availability, the Secretary may consider such factors as cost, reliability, the availability and reliability of spare parts and the cost and quality thereof, maintenance programs, durability, quality of end products produced by the item proposed for export, and scale of production. For purposes of this subparagraph, "evidence" may include such items as foreign manufacturers' catalogues, brochures, or operations or maintenance manuals, articles from reputable trade publications, photographs, and depositions based upon eyewitness accounts.

(B) In a case in which an allegation is received from an export license applicant, the Secretary shall, upon receipt of the allegation, submit for publication in the Federal Register notice of such receipt. Within 4 months after receipt of the allegation, the Secretary shall determine whether the foreign availability exists, and shall so notify the applicant. If the Secretary has determined that the foreign availability exists, the Secretary shall, upon making such determination, submit the determination for review to other departments and agencies as the Secretary considers appropriate. The Secretary's determination of foreign availability does not require the concurrence or approval of any official, department, or agency to which such a determination is submitted. Not later than 1 month after the Secretary makes the determination, the Secretary shall respond in writing to the applicant and submit for publication in the Federal Register, that—

(i) the foreign availability does exist and—

(I) the requirement of a validated license has been removed,

(II) the President has determined that export controls under this section must be maintained notwithstanding the foreign availability and the applicable steps are being taken under paragraph (4), or

(III) in the case of a foreign availability determination under paragraph (1), the foreign availability determination will be submitted to a multilateral review process in accordance with the agreement of the Coordinating Committee for a period of not more than 4 months beginning on the date of the publication; or

(ii) the foreign availability does not exist.

In any case in which the submission for publication is not made within the time period specified in the preceding sentence, the Secretary may not thereafter require a license for the export of the goods or technology with respect to which the foreign availability allegation was made. In the case of a foreign availability determination under paragraph (1) to which clause (i)(III) applies, no license for such export may be required after the end of the 9-month period beginning on the date on which the allegation is received.

(4) Negotiations to eliminate foreign availability

(A) In any case in which export controls are maintained under this section notwithstanding foreign availability, on account of a determination by the President that the absence of the controls would prove detrimental to the national security of the United States, the President shall actively pursue negotiations with the governments of the appropriate foreign countries for the purpose of eliminating such availability. No later than the commencement of such negotiations, the President shall notify in writing the Committee on Banking, Housing, and Urban Affairs of the Senate and the Committee on Foreign Affairs of the House of Representatives that he has begun such negotiations and why he believes it is important to national security that export controls on the goods or technology involved be maintained.

(B) If, within 6 months after the President's determination that export controls be maintained, the foreign availability has not been eliminated, the Secretary may not, after the end of that 6-month period, require a validated license for the export of the goods or technology involved. The President may extend the 6-month period described in the preceding sentence for an additional period of 12 months if the President certifies to the Congress that the negotiations involved are progressing and that the absence of the export controls involved would prove detrimental to the national security of the United States. Whenever the President has reason to believe that goods or technology subject to export controls for national security purposes by the United States may become available from other countries to controlled countries and that such availability can be prevented or eliminated by means of negotiations with such other countries, the President shall promptly initiate negotiations with the governments of such other countries to prevent such foreign availability.

(C) After an agreement is reached with a country pursuant to negotiations under this paragraph to eliminate or prevent foreign availability of goods or technology, the Secretary may not require a validated license for the export of such goods or technology to that country.

(5) Expedited licenses for items available to countries other than controlled countries

(A) In any case in which the Secretary finds that any goods or technology from foreign sources is of similar quality to goods or technology the export of which requires a validated license under this section and is available to a country other than a controlled country without effective restrictions, the Secretary shall designate such goods or technology as eligible for export to such country under this paragraph.

(B) In the case of goods or technology designated under subparagraph (A), then 20 working days after the date of formal filing with the Secretary of an individual validated license application for the export of those goods or technology to an eligible country, a license for the transaction specified in the application shall become valid and effective and the goods or technology are authorized for export pursuant to such license unless the license has been denied by the Secretary on account of an inappropriate end user. The Secretary may extend the 20-day period provided in the preceding sentence for an additional period of 15 days if the Secretary requires additional time to consider the application and so notifies the applicant.

(C) The Secretary may make a foreign availability determination under subparagraph (A) on the Secretary's own initiative, upon receipt of an allegation from an export license applicant that such availability exists, or upon the submission of a certification by a technical advisory committee of appropriate jurisdiction that such availability exists. Upon receipt of such an allegation or certification, the Secretary shall publish notice of such allegation or certification in the Federal Register and shall make the foreign availability determination within 30 days after such receipt and publish the determination in the Federal Register. In the case of the failure of the Secretary to make and publish such determination within that 30-day period, the goods or technology involved shall be deemed to be designated as eligible for export to the country or countries involved, for purposes of subparagraph (B).

(D) The provisions of paragraphs (1), (2), (3), and (4) do not apply with respect to determinations of foreign availability under this paragraph.

(6) Office of Foreign Availability

The Secretary shall establish in the Department of Commerce an Office of Foreign Availability, which shall be under the direction of the Under Secretary of Commerce for Export Administration. The Office shall be responsible for gathering and analyzing all the necessary information in order for the Secretary to make determinations of foreign availability under this Act [sections 2401 to 2420 of this Appendix]. The Secretary shall make available to the Committee on Foreign Affairs of the House of Representatives and the Committee on Banking, Housing, and Urban Affairs of the Senate at the end of each 6-month period during a fiscal year information on the operations of the Office, and on improvements in the Government's ability to assess foreign availability, during that 6-month period, including information on the training of personnel, the use of computers, and the use of Commercial Service Officers of the United States and Foreign Commercial Service. Such information shall also include a description of representative determinations made under this Act [sections 2401 to 2420 of this Appendix] during that 6-month period that foreign availability did or did not exist (as the case may be), together with an explanation of such determinations.

(7) Sharing of information

Each department or agency of the United States, including any intelligence agency, and all contractors with any such department or agency, shall, upon the request of the Secretary and consistent with the protection of intelligence sources and methods, furnish information to the Office of Foreign Availability concerning foreign availability of goods and technology subject to export controls under this Act [sections 2401 to 2420 of this Appendix]. Each such department or agency shall allow the Office of Foreign Availability access to any information from a laboratory or other facility within such department or agency.

(8) Removal of controls on less sophisticated goods or technology

In any case in which[1] Secretary may not, pursuant to paragraph (1), (2), (3), or (4) of this subsection or paragraph (6) of subsection (h) of this section, require a validated license for the export of goods or technology, then the Secretary may not require a validated license for the export of any similar goods or technology whose function, technological approach, per-

[1] So in original. Probably should be followed by "the".

formance thresholds, and other attributes that form the basis for export controls under this section do not exceed the technical parameters of the goods or technology from which the validated license requirement is removed under the applicable paragraph.

(9) Notice of all foreign availability assessments

Whenever the Secretary undertakes a foreign availability assessment under this subsection or subsection (h)(6), the Secretary shall publish notice of such assessment in the Federal Register.

(10) Availability defined

For purposes of this subsection and subsections (f) and (h), the term "available in fact to controlled countries" includes production or availability of any goods or technology in any country—

(A) from which the goods or technology is not restricted for export to any controlled country; or

(B) in which such export restrictions are determined by the Secretary to be ineffective.

For purposes of subparagraph (B), the mere inclusion of goods or technology on a list of goods or technology subject to bilateral or multilateral national security export controls shall not alone constitute credible evidence that a country provides an effective means of controlling the export of such goods or technology to controlled countries.

(g) Indexing

(1) In order to ensure that requirements for validated licenses and other licenses authorizing multiple exports are periodically removed as goods or technology subject to such requirements becomes obsolete with respect to the national security of the United States, regulations issued by the Secretary may, where appropriate, provide for annual increases in the performance levels of goods or technology subject to any such licensing requirement. The regulations issued by the Secretary shall establish as one criterion for the removal of goods or technology from such license requirements the anticipated needs of the military of controlled countries. Any such goods or technology which no longer meets the performance levels established by the regulations shall be removed from the list established pursuant to subsection (c) of this section unless, under such exceptions and under such procedures as the Secretary shall prescribe, any other department or agency of the United States objects to such removal and the Secretary determines, on the basis of such objection, that the goods or technology shall not be removed from the list. The Secretary shall also consider, where appropriate, removing site visitation requirements for goods and technology which are removed from the list unless objections described in this subsection are raised.

(2)(A) In carrying out this subsection, the Secretary shall conduct annual reviews of the performance levels of goods or technology—

(i) which are eligible for export under a distribution license,

(ii) below which exports to the People's Republic of China require only notification of the governments participating in the group known as the Coordinating Committee, and

(iii) below which no authority or permission to export may be required under subsection (b)(2) or (b)(3) of this section.

The Secretary shall make appropriate adjustments to such performance levels based on these reviews.

(B) In any case in which the Secretary receives a request which—

(i) is to revise the qualification requirements or minimum thresholds of any goods eligible for export under a distribution license, and

(ii) is made by an exporter of such goods, representatives of an industry which produces such goods, or a technical advisory committee established under subsection (h) of this section,

the Secretary, after consulting with other appropriate Government agencies and technical advisory committees established under subsection (h) of this section, shall determine whether to make such revision, or some other appropriate revision, in such qualification requirements or minimum thresholds. In making this determination, the Secretary shall take into account the availability of the goods from sources outside the United States. The Secretary shall make a determination on a request made under this subparagraph within 90 days after the date on which the request is filed. If the Secretary's determination pursuant to such a request is to make a revision, such revision shall be implemented within 120 days after the date on which the request is filed and shall be published in the Federal Register.

(h) Technical advisory committees

(1) Upon written request by representatives of a substantial segment of any industry which produces any goods or technology subject to export controls under this section or being considered for such controls because of their significance to the national security of the United States, the Secretary shall appoint a technical advisory committee for any such goods or technology which the Secretary determines are difficult to evaluate because of questions concerning technical matters, worldwide availability, and actual utilization of production and technology, or licensing procedures. Each such committee shall consist of representatives of United States industry and Government, including the Departments of Commerce, Defense, and State, the intelligence community, and, in the discretion of the Secretary, other Government departments and agencies. No person serving on any such committee who is a representative of industry shall serve on such committee for more than four consecutive years.

(2) Technical advisory committees established under paragraph (1) shall advise and assist the Secretary, the Secretary of Defense, and any other department, agency, or official of the Government of the United States to which the President delegates authority under this Act [sections 2401 to 2420 of this Appendix], with respect to actions designed to carry out the policy set forth in section 3(2)(A) of this Act [section

2402(2)(A) of this Appendix]. Such committees, where they have expertise in such matters, shall be consulted with respect to questions involving (A) technical matters, (B) worldwide availability and actual utilization of production technology, (C) licensing procedures which affect the level of export controls applicable to any goods or technology, (D) revisions of the control list (as provided in subsection (c)(4)), including proposed revisions of multilateral controls in which the United States participates, (E) the issuance of regulations, and (F) any other questions relating to actions designed to carry out the policy set forth in section 3(2)(A) of this Act [section 2402(2)(A) of this Appendix]. Nothing in this subsection shall prevent the Secretary or the Secretary of Defense from consulting, at any time, with any person representing industry or the general public, regardless of whether such person is a member of a technical advisory committee. Members of the public shall be given a reasonable opportunity, pursuant to regulations prescribed by the Secretary, to present evidence to such committees.

(3) Upon request of any member of any such committee, the Secretary may, if the Secretary determines it appropriate, reimburse such member for travel, subsistence, and other necessary expenses incurred by such member in connection with the duties of such member.

(4) Each such committee shall elect a chairman, and shall meet at least every three months at the call of the chairman, unless the chairman determines, in consultation with the other members of the committee, that such a meeting is not necessary to achieve the purposes of this subsection. Each such committee shall be terminated after a period of 2 years, unless extended by the Secretary for additional periods of 2 years. The Secretary shall consult each such committee with respect to such termination or extension of that committee.

(5) To facilitate the work of the technical advisory committees, the Secretary, in conjunction with other departments and agencies participating in the administration of this Act [sections 2401 to 2420 of this Appendix], shall disclose to each such committee adequate information, consistent with national security, pertaining to the reasons for the export controls which are in effect or contemplated for the goods or technology with respect to which that committee furnishes advice.

(6) Whenever a technical advisory committee certifies to the Secretary that goods or technology with respect to which such committee was appointed have become available in fact, to controlled countries, from sources outside the United States, including countries which participate with the United States in multilateral export controls, in sufficient quantity and of comparable quality so that requiring a validated license for the export of such goods or technology would be ineffective in achieving the purpose set forth in subsection (a) of this section, the technical advisory committee shall submit that certification to the Congress at the same time the certification is made to the Secretary, together with the documentation for the certification. The Secretary shall investigate the foreign availability so certified and, not later than 90 days after the certification is made, shall submit a report to the technical advisory committee and the Congress stating that—

(A) the Secretary has removed the requirement of a validated license for the export of the goods or technology, on account of the foreign availability,

(B) the Secretary has recommended to the President that negotiations be conducted to eliminate the foreign availability, or

(C) the Secretary has determined on the basis of the investigation that the foreign availability does not exist.

To the extent necessary, the report may be submitted on a classified basis. In any case in which the Secretary has recommended to the President that negotiations be conducted to eliminate the foreign availability, the President shall actively pursue such negotiations with the governments of the appropriate foreign countries. If, within 6 months after the Secretary submits such report to the Congress, the foreign availability has not been eliminated, the Secretary may not, after the end of that 6-month period, require a validated license for the export of the goods or technology involved. The President may extend the 6-month period described in the preceding sentence for an additional period of 12 months if the President certifies to the Congress that the negotiations involved are progressing and that the absence of the export control involved would prove detrimental to the national security of the United States. After an agreement is reached with a country pursuant to negotiations under this paragraph to eliminate foreign availability of goods or technology, the Secretary may not require a validated license for the export of such goods or technology to that country.

(i) Multilateral export controls

Recognizing the ineffectiveness of unilateral controls and the importance of uniform enforcement measures to the effectiveness of multilateral controls, the President shall enter into negotiations with the governments participating in the group known as the Coordinating Committee (hereinafter in this subsection referred to as the "Committee") with a view toward accomplishing the following objectives:

(1) Enhanced public understanding of the Committee's purpose and procedures, including publication of the list of items controlled for export by agreement of the Committee, together with all notes, understandings, and other aspects of such agreement of the Committee, and all changes thereto.

(2) Periodic meetings of high-level representatives of participating governments for the purpose of coordinating export control policies and issuing policy guidance to the Committee.

(3) Strengthened legal basis for each government's export control system, including, as appropriate, increased penalties and statutes of limitations.

(4) Harmonization of export control documentation by the participating governments to verify the movement of goods and technology subject to controls by the Committee.

(5) Improved procedures for coordination and exchange of information concerning violations of the agreement of the Committee.

(6) Procedures for effective implementation of the agreement through uniform and consistent interpretations of export controls agreed to by the governments participating in the Committee.

(7) Coordination of national licensing and enforcement efforts by governments participating in the Committee, including sufficient technical expertise to assess the licensing status of exports and to ensure end-use verification.

(8) More effective procedures for enforcing export controls, including adequate training, resources, and authority for enforcement officers to investigate and prevent illegal exports.

(9) Agreement to provide adequate resources to enhance the functioning of individual national export control systems and of the Committee.

(10) Improved enforcement and compliance with the agreement through elimination of unnecessary export controls and maintenance of an effective control list.

(11) Agreement to enhance cooperation among members of the Committee in obtaining the agreement of governments outside the Committee to restrict the export of goods and technology on the International Control List, to establish an ongoing mechanism in the Committee to coordinate planning and implementation of export control measures related to such agreements, and to remove items from the International Control List if such items continue to be available to controlled countries or if the control of the items no longer serves the common strategic objectives of the members of the Committee.

For purposes of reviews of the International Control List, the President may include as advisors to the United States delegation to the Committee representatives of industry who are knowledgeable with respect to the items being reviewed.

(j) Commercial agreements with certain countries

(1) Any United States firm, enterprise, or other nongovernmental entity which enters into an agreement with any agency of the government of a controlled country, that calls for the encouragement of technical cooperation and that is intended to result in the export from the United States to the other party of unpublished technical data of United States origin, shall report to the Secretary the agreement with such agency in sufficient detail.

(2) The provisions of paragraph (1) shall not apply to colleges, universities, or other educational institutions.

(k) Negotiations with other countries

The Secretary of State, in consultation with the Secretary of Defense, the Secretary of Commerce, and the heads of other appropriate departments and agencies, shall be responsible for conducting negotiations with other countries, including those countries not participating in the group known as the Coordinating Committee, regarding their cooperation in restricting the export of goods and technology in order to carry out the policy set forth in section 3(9) of this Act [section 2402(9) of this Appendix], as authorized by subsection (a) of this section, including negotiations with respect to which goods and technology should be subject to multilaterally agreed export restrictions and what conditions should apply for exceptions from those restrictions. In cases where such negotiations produce agreements on export restrictions comparable in practice to those maintained by the Coordinating Committee, the Secretary shall treat exports, whether by individual or multiple licenses, to countries party to such agreements in the same manner as exports to members of the Coordinating Committee are treated, including the same manner as exports are treated under subsection (b)(2) of this section and section 10(*o*) of this Act [section 2409(*o*) of this Appendix].

***(l)* Diversion of controlled goods or technology**

(1) Whenever there is reliable evidence, as determined by the Secretary, that goods or technology which were exported subject to national security controls under this section to a controlled country have been diverted to an unauthorized use or consignee in violation of the conditions of an export license, the Secretary for as long as that diversion continues—

(A) shall deny all further exports, to or by the party or parties responsible for that diversion or who conspired in that diversion, of any goods or technology subject to national security controls under this section, regardless of whether such goods or technology are available from sources outside the United States; and

(B) may take such additional actions under this Act [sections 2401 to 2420 of this Appendix] with respect to the party or parties referred to in subparagraph (A) as the Secretary determines are appropriate in the circumstances to deter the further unauthorized use of the previously exported goods or technology.

(2) As used in this subsection, the term "unauthorized use" means the use of United States goods or technology in the design, production, or maintenance of any item on the United States Munitions List, or the military use of any item on the International Control List of the Coordinating Committee.

(m) Goods containing controlled parts and components

Export controls may not be imposed under this section, or under any other provision of law, on a good solely on the basis that the good contains parts or components subject to export controls under this section if such parts or components—

(1) are essential to the functioning of the good,

(2) are customarily included in sales of the good in countries other than controlled countries, and

(3) comprise 25 percent or less of the total value of the good,

unless the good itself, if exported, would by virtue of the functional characteristics of the good as a whole make a significant contribution to the military potential of a controlled country which would prove detrimental to the national security of the United States.

(n) Security measures

The Secretary and the Commissioner of Customs, consistent with their authorities under section 12(a) of this Act [section 2411(a) of this Appendix], and in consultation with the Director of the Federal Bureau of Investigation, shall provide advice and technical assistance to persons engaged in the manufacture or handling of goods or technology subject to export controls under this section to develop security systems to prevent violations or evasions of those export controls.

(*o*) Recordkeeping

The Secretary, the Secretary of Defense, and any other department or agency consulted in connection with a license application under this Act [sections 2401 to 2420 of this Appendix] or a revision of a list of goods or technology subject to export controls under this Act [sections 2401 to 2420 of this Appendix], shall make and keep records of their respective advice, recommendations, or decisions in connection with any such license application or revision, including the factual and analytical basis of the advice, recommendations, or decisions.

(p) National Security Control Office

To assist in carrying out the policy and other authorities and responsibilities of the Secretary of Defense under this section, there is established in the Department of Defense a National Security Control Office under the direction of the Under Secretary of Defense for Policy. The Secretary of Defense may delegate to that office such of those authorities and responsibilities, together with such ancillary functions, as the Secretary of Defense considers appropriate.

(q) Exclusion for agricultural commodities

This section does not authorize export controls on agricultural commodities, including fats, oils, and animal hides and skins.

(Pub. L. 96–72, § 5, Sept. 29, 1979, 93 Stat. 506; Pub. L. 99–64, title I, §§ 105(a)–(c)(1), (d)–(j), 106, 107, July 12, 1985, 99 Stat. 123–129; Pub. L. 100–418, title II, §§ 2413–2418(b), 2419, 2420(a), 2421, 2422, 2446, Aug. 23, 1988, 102 Stat. 1347–1358, 1369.)

PRIOR PROVISIONS

A prior section 2404, Pub. L. 91–184, § 5, Dec. 30, 1969, 83 Stat. 843; Pub. L. 92–412, title I, § 105, Aug. 29, 1972, 86 Stat. 645; Pub. L. 93–500, §§ 3(c), (d), 5(b), (c), 6, Oct. 29, 1974, 88 Stat. 1553, 1554; Pub. L. 95–52, title I, § 111, June 22, 1977, 91 Stat. 240, setting forth determinations, limitations, etc., respecting the control and monitoring of exports, expired on Sept. 30, 1979.

AMENDMENTS

1988—Subsec. (a)(1). Pub. L. 100–418, § 2413, inserted provision defining "affiliates" to include both governmental entities and commercial entities that are controlled in fact by controlled countries.

Subsec. (a)(4) to (6). Pub. L. 100–418, § 2414, added pars. (4) to (6).

Subsec. (b)(2). Pub. L. 100–418, § 2415(a), amended par. (2) generally. Prior to amendment, par. (2) read as follows: "No authority or permission to export may be required under this section before goods or technology are exported in the case of exports to a country which maintains export controls on such goods or technology cooperatively with the United States pursuant to the agreement of the group known as the Coordinating Committee, if the goods or technology is at such a level of performance characteristics that the export of the goods or technology to controlled countries requires only notification of the participating governments of the Coordinating Committee."

Subsec. (b)(3). Pub. L. 100–418, § 2415(b), added par. (3).

Subsec. (c)(2). Pub. L. 100–418, § 2416(a), substituted "If the Secretary and the Secretary of Defense are unable to concur on such items, as determined by the Secretary, the Secretary of Defense may, within 20 days after receiving notification of the Secretary's determination, refer the matter to the President for resolution. The Secretary of Defense shall notify the Secretary of any such referral. The President shall, not later than 20 days after such referral, notify the Secretary of his determination with respect to the inclusion of such items on the list. Failure of the Secretary of Defense to notify the President or the Secretary, or failure of the President to notify the Secretary, in accordance with this paragraph, shall be deemed by the Secretary to constitute concurrence in the implementation of the actions proposed by the Secretary regarding the inclusion of such items on the list." for "If the Secretary and the Secretary of Defense are unable to concur on such items, the matter shall be referred to the President for resolution."

Subsec. (c)(3). Pub. L. 100–418, § 2416(b)(1), amended par. (3) generally. Prior to amendment, par. (3) read as follows: "The Secretary shall review the list established pursuant to this subsection at least once each year in order to carry out the policy set forth in section 3(2)(A) of this Act and the provisions of this section, and shall promptly make such revisions of the list as may be necessary after each such review. Before beginning each annual review, the Secretary shall publish notice of that annual review in the Federal Register. The Secretary shall provide an opportunity during such review for comment and the submission of data, with or without oral presentation, by interested Government agencies and other affected or potentially affected parties. The Secretary shall publish in the Federal Register any revisions in the list, with an explanation of the reasons for the revisions. The Secretary shall further assess, as part of such review, the availability from sources outside the United States of goods and technology comparable to those subject to export controls imposed under this section."

Subsec. (c)(4). Pub. L. 100–418, § 2416(b)(3), added par. (4).

Subsec. (c)(5). Pub. L. 100–418, § 2416(c)(1), added par. (5).

Subsec. (c)(6), (7). Pub. L. 100–418, § 2416(c)(2), (3), added pars. (6) and (7).

Subsec. (d)(5). Pub. L. 100–418, § 2416(b)(2), substituted "on an ongoing basis" for "at least annually".

Subsec. (e)(6). Pub. L. 100–418, § 2417, added par. (6).

Subsec. (f). Pub. L. 100–418, § 2418(a), amended subsec. generally, revising and restating as pars. (1) to (10) provisions of former pars. (1) to (7).

Subsec. (g). Pub. L. 100–418, § 2419, designated existing provisions as par. (1) and added par. (2).

Subsec. (h)(2). Pub. L. 100–418, § 2420(a), added cls. (D) and (E), redesignated former cl. (E) as (F), and struck out former cl. (D) which read as follows: "exports subject to multilateral controls in which the United States participates, including proposed revisions of any such multilateral controls, and".

Subsec. (h)(6). Pub. L. 100–418, § 2418(b), inserted at end "After an agreement is reached with a country pursuant to negotiations under this paragraph to eliminate foreign availability of goods or technology, the Secretary may not require a validated license for the export of such goods or technology to that country."

Subsec. (i). Pub. L. 100–418, § 2421, substituted "Recognizing the ineffectiveness of unilateral controls and the importance of uniform enforcement measures to the effectiveness of multilateral controls, the President" for "The President" and inserted sentence at end authorizing the President, for purposes of reviews of the International Control List, to include as advisors to the United States delegation to the Committee representatives of industry who are knowledgeable with respect to the items being reviewed.

Subsec. (i)(1) to (11). Pub. L. 100–418, § 2446, completely revised and expanded provisions enumerating the objectives of the negotiations, adding pars. (1) to (11) and striking out former pars. (1) to (9).

Subsec. (m). Pub. L. 100–418, § 2422, amended subsec. generally, substituting provision relating to goods containing controlled parts and components for provision relating to goods containing microprocessors.

1985—Subsec. (a)(1). Pub. L. 99–64, § 105(a)(1), inserted sentence providing that the authority contained in this subsection includes the authority to prohibit or curtail the transfer of goods or technology within the United States to embassies and affiliates of controlled countries.

Subsec. (a)(2). Pub. L. 99–64, § 105(a)(2), struck out designation "(A)" before "Whenever the Secretary makes any revision", and struck out subpar. (B) which read as follows: "Whenever the Secretary denies any export license under this section, the Secretary shall specify in the notice to the applicant of the denial of such license that the license was denied under the authority contained in this section. The Secretary shall also include in such notice what, if any, modifications in or restrictions on the goods or technology for which the license was sought would allow such export to be compatible with controls imposed under this section, or the Secretary shall indicate in such notice which officers and employees of the Department of Commerce who are familiar with the application will be made reasonably available to the applicant for consultation with regard to such modifications or restriction, if appropriate."

Subsec. (a)(3). Pub. L. 99–64, § 105(a)(3), struck out "Such regulations shall not be based upon the assumption that such effective safeguards can be devised."

Subsec. (b)(1). Pub. L. 99–64, § 105(b)(1), designated existing provisions as par. (1) and provided that the President shall establish to a list of controlled countries which may be expanded or reduced by the President based upon certain enumerated factors, and struck out provisions which had stated that the policy of the United States toward individual countries should not be determined exclusively on the basis of that country's Communist or non-Communist status but rather on the country's relationships to the United States and countries friendly to the United States.

Pub. L. 99–64, § 105(b)(3), substituted "set forth in this paragraph" for "specified in the preceding sentence" in last sentence.

Subsec. (b)(2). Pub. L. 99–64, § 105(b)(2), added par. (2).

Subsec. (c)(1). Pub. L. 99–64, § 105(c)(1)(A), struck out "commodity" before "control list".

Subsec. (c)(3). Pub. L. 99–64, § 105(c)(1)(B), amended par. (3) generally. Prior to amendment, par. (3) read as follows: "The Secretary shall issue regulations providing for review of the list established pursuant to this subsection not less frequently than every 3 years in the case of controls maintained cooperatively with other countries, and annually in the case of all other controls, in order to carry out the policy set forth in section 3(2)(A) and the provisions of this section, and for the prompt issuance of such revisions of the list as may be necessary. Such regulations shall provide interested Government agencies and other affected or potentially affected parties with an opportunity, during such review, to submit written data, views, or arguments, with or without oral presentation. Such regulations shall further provide that, as part of such review, an assessment be made of the availability from sources outside the United States, or any of its territories or possessions, of goods and technology comparable to those controlled under this section. The Secretary and any agency rendering advice with respect to export controls shall keep adequate records of all decisions made with respect to revision of the list of controlled goods and technology, including the factual and analytical basis for the decision, and, in the case of the Secretary, any dissenting recommendations received from any agency."

Subsec. (d)(2). Pub. L. 99–64, § 106(a)(1), added subpar. (D) and in provisions following subpar. (D) substituted ", or available in fact from sources outside the United States to, controlled countries" for "countries to which exports are controlled under this section".

Subsec. (d)(4) to (7). Pub. L. 99–64, § 106(a)(2), added pars. (4) to (7) and struck out former pars. (4) to (6) which read as follows:

"(4) The initial version of the list referred to in paragraph (2) shall be completed and published in an appropriate form in the Federal Register not later than October 1, 1980.

"(5) The list of militarily critical technologies developed primarily by the Secretary of Defense pursuant to paragraph (2) shall become a part of the commodity control list, subject to the provisions of subsection (c) of this section.

"(6) The Secretary of Defense shall report annually to the Congress on actions taken to carry out this subsection."

Subsec. (e)(1). Pub. L. 99–64, § 105(d)(1), substituted "the multiple validated export licenses described in section 4(a)(2) of this Act in lieu of individual validated licenses" for "a qualified general license in lieu of a validated license".

Subsec. (e)(3) to (5). Pub. L. 99–64, § 105(d)(2), added pars. (3) to (5) and struck out former pars. (3) and (4) which read as follows:

"(3) To the maximum extent practicable, consistent with the national security of the United States, the Secretary shall require a qualified general license, in lieu of a validated license, under this section for the export of goods or technology if the export of such goods or technology is restricted pursuant to a multilateral agreement, formal or informal, to which the United States is a party, but such export does not require the specific approval of the parties to such multilateral agreement.

"(4) Not later than July 1, 1980, the Secretary shall establish procedures for the approval of goods and technology that may be exported pursuant to a qualified general license."

Subsec. (f)(1). Pub. L. 99–64, § 107(a), (i), (j)(1), inserted "the Secretary of Defense and other" after "The Secretary, in consultation with", and substituted "controlled countries" for "such destinations" and "comparable quality" for "sufficient quality".

Subsec. (f)(2). Pub. L. 99–64, § 107(i), substituted "comparable quality" for "sufficient quality".

Subsec. (f)(3). Pub. L. 99–64, § 107(b), amended par. (3) generally. Prior to amendment, par. (3) read as follows: "With respect to export controls imposed under this section, any determination of foreign availability which is the basis of a decision to grant a license for, or to remove a control on, the export of a good or technology, shall be made in writing and shall be supported by reliable evidence, including scientific or physical examination, expert opinion based upon adequate factual information, or intelligence information. In assessing foreign availability with respect to license applications, uncorroborated representations by applicants shall not be deemed sufficient evidence of foreign availability."

Subsec. (f)(4). Pub. L. 99–64, § 107(c), (j)(2), substituted first three sentences for "sentence providing that in any case in which, in accordance with this subsection, export controls are imposed under this section notwithstanding foreign availability, the President shall take steps to initiate negotiations with the governments of the appropriate foreign countries for the purpose of eliminating such availability", and substituted "controlled countries" for "countries to which exports are controlled under this section".

Subsec. (f)(5). Pub. L. 99–64, § 107(d)(1), amended par. (5) generally. Prior to amendment, par. (5) read as follows: "In order to further carry out the policies set forth in this Act, the Secretary shall establish, within the Office of Export Administration of the Department of Commerce, a capability to monitor and gather information with respect to the foreign availability of any goods or technology subject to export controls under this Act.''

Subsec. (f)(6). Pub. L. 99–64, §107(d)(2), substituted ''Office of Foreign Availability'' for ''Office of Export Administration''.

Subsec. (f)(7). Pub. L. 99–64, §107(e), added par. (7).

Subsec. (g). Pub. L. 99–64, §105(e), amended subsec. (g) generally. Prior to amendment, subsec. (g) read as follows: ''In order to ensure that requirements for validated licenses and qualified general licenses are periodically removed as goods or technology subject to such requirements become obsolete with respect to the national security of the United States, regulations issued by the Secretary may, where appropriate, provide for annual increases in the performance levels of goods or technology subject to any such licensing requirement. Any such goods or technology which no longer meet the performance levels established by the latest such increase shall be removed from the list established pursuant to subsection (c) of this section unless, under such exceptions and under such procedures as the Secretary shall prescribe, any other department or agency of the United States objects to such removal and the Secretary determines, on the basis of such objection, that the goods or technology shall not be removed from the list. The Secretary shall also consider, where appropriate, removing site visitation requirements for goods and technology which are removed from the list unless objections described in this subsection are raised.''

Subsec. (h)(1). Pub. L. 99–64, §107(f)(1), inserted reference to the intelligence community.

Subsec. (h)(2)(E). Pub. L. 99–64, §107(f)(2), added cl. (E).

Subsec. (h)(6). Pub. L. 99–64, §107(f)(3), (i), (j)(2), substituted ''controlled countries'' for ''countries to which exports are controlled under this section'', ''comparable quality'' for ''sufficient quality'', and ''the technical advisory committee shall submit that certification to the Congress at the same time the certification is made to the Secretary, together with the documentation for the certification'' for ''and provides adequate documentation for such certification, in accordance with the procedures established pursuant to subsection (f)(1) of this section, the Secretary shall investigate such availability, and if such availability is verified, the Secretary shall remove the requirement of a validated license for the export of the goods or technology, unless the President determines that the absence of export controls under this section would prove detrimental to the national security of the United States'', struck out provision that, in any case in which the President determined that export controls under this section had to be maintained notwithstanding foreign availability, the Secretary had to publish that determination together with a concise statement of its basis and the estimated economic impact of the decision, inserted provisions directing the Secretary to investigate certified foreign availability and, not later than 90 days after the certification is made, submit a report to the technical advisory committee and the Congress, and added subpars. (A) to (C) and concluding provision.

Subsec. (i)(3). Pub. L. 99–64, §105(f)(1), (2), redesignated par. (4) as (3) and substituted ''agreed to by members of the Committee'' for ''agreed to pursuant to paragraph (3)'', and struck out former par. (3) relating to agreement to reduce the scope of the export controls imposed by agreement of the Committee to a level acceptable to and enforceable by all governments participating in the Committee.

Subsec. (i)(4) to (9). Pub. L. 99–64, §105(f)(3), added pars. (4) to (9). Former par. (4) redesignated (3).

Subsec. (j)(1). Pub. L. 99–64, §105(g), amended par. (1) generally. Prior to amendment, par. (1) read as follows: ''Any United States firm, enterprise, or other nongovernmental entity which, for commercial purposes, enters into any agreement with any agency of the government of a country to which exports are restricted for national security purposes, which agreement cites an intergovernmental agreement (to which the United States and such country are parties) calling for the encouragement of technical cooperation and is intended to result in the export from the United States to the other party of unpublished technical data of United States origin, shall report the agreement with such agency to the Secretary.''

Subsec. (k). Pub. L. 99–64, §105(h), inserted '', including those countries not participating in the group known as the Coordinating Committee,'' after ''conducting negotiations with other countries'', and inserted provision that, in cases where such negotiations produce agreements on export restrictions comparable in practice to those maintained by the Coordinating Committee, the Secretary shall treat exports, whether by individual or multiple licenses, to countries party to such agreements in the same manner as exports to members of the Coordinating Committee are treated, including the same manner as exports are treated under subsection (b)(2) of this section and section 10(*o*) of this Act.

Subsec. (*l*). Pub. L. 99–64, §105(i), struck out ''to military use'' after ''Diversion'' in heading, and amended text of subsec. (*l*), generally. Prior to amendment, subsec. (*l*) read as follows:

''(1) Whenever there is reliable evidence that goods or technology, which were exported subject to national security controls under this section to a country to which exports are controlled for national security purposes, have been diverted to significant military use in violation of the conditions of an export license, the Secretary for as long as that diversion to significant military use continues—

''(A) shall deny all further exports to the party responsible for that diversion of any goods or technology subject to national security controls under this section which contribute to that particular military use, regardless of whether such goods or technology are available to that country from sources outside the United States; and

''(B) may take such additional steps under this Act with respect to the party referred to in subparagraph (A) as are feasible to deter the further military use of the previously exported goods or technology.

''(2) As used in this subsection, the terms 'diversion to significant military use' and 'significant military use' means the use of United States goods or technology to design or produce any item on the United States Munitions List.''

Subsecs. (m) to (q). Pub. L. 99–64, §105(j), added subsecs. (m) to (q).

CHANGE OF NAME

Committee on Foreign Affairs of House of Representatives treated as referring to Committee on International Relations of House of Representatives by section 1(a) of Pub. L. 104–14, set out as a note preceding section 21 of Title 2, The Congress.

EFFECTIVE DATE OF 1985 AMENDMENT

Section 105(c)(2) of Pub. L. 99–64 provided that: ''The amendment made by paragraph (1)(B) of this subsection [amending this section] shall take effect on October 1, 1985.''

DELEGATION OF FUNCTIONS

Functions conferred upon President under this section delegated to Secretary of Commerce by Ex. Ord. No. 12214, May 2, 1980, 45 F.R. 29783, set out under section 2403 of this Appendix, with the exception of the functions conferred upon the President under subsecs. (f)(4) and (i) of this section which were delegated to the Secretary of State and the functions conferred upon the President under subsecs. (c), (f)(1), and (h)(6) of this section which were reserved to the President.

REVIEW OF PROPOSED CHANGES TO EXPORT THRESHOLDS FOR COMPUTERS

Pub. L. 106–554, §1(a)(2) [title III, §314], Dec. 21, 2000, 114 Stat. 2763, 2763A–123, provided that: ''Not more than

50 days after the date of the submission of the report referred to in subsection (d) of section 1211 of the National Defense Authorization Act for Fiscal Year 1998 [Pub. L. 105–85] (50 U.S.C. App. 2404 note), the Comptroller General of the United States shall submit an assessment to Congress which contains an analysis of the new computer performance levels being proposed by the President under such section.''

RELEASE OF EXPORT INFORMATION BY DEPARTMENT OF COMMERCE TO OTHER AGENCIES FOR PURPOSE OF NATIONAL SECURITY ASSESSMENT

Pub. L. 105–261, div. A, title XV, § 1522, Oct. 17, 1998, 112 Stat. 2179, provided that:

''(a) RELEASE OF EXPORT INFORMATION.—The Secretary of Commerce shall, upon the written request of an official specified in subsection (c), transmit to that official any information relating to exports that is held by the Department of Commerce and is requested by that official for the purpose of assessing national security risks. The Secretary shall transmit such information within 10 business days after receiving such a request.

''(b) NATURE OF INFORMATION.—The information referred to in subsection (a) includes information concerning—

''(1) export licenses issued by the Department of Commerce;

''(2) exports that were carried out under an export license issued by the Department of Commerce; and

''(3) exports from the United States that were carried out without an export license.

''(c) REQUESTING OFFICIALS.—The officials referred to in subsection (a) are the Secretary of State, the Secretary of Defense, the Secretary of Energy, and the Director of Central Intelligence. Each of those officials may delegate to any other official within their respective departments and agency the authority to request information under subsection (a).''

EXPORT CONTROLS ON HIGH PERFORMANCE COMPUTERS

Pub. L. 105–85, div. A, title XII, subtitle B, Nov. 18, 1997, 111 Stat. 1932, as amended by Pub. L. 105–261, div. A, title XV, § 1524, Oct. 17, 1998, 112 Stat. 2180; Pub. L. 106–65, div. A, title X, § 1067(4), title XIV, § 1407(c), Oct. 5, 1999, 113 Stat. 774, 801; Pub. L. 106–398, § 1 [[div. A], title XII, § 1234(a)], Oct. 30, 2000, 114 Stat. 1654, 1654A–330, provided that:

''SEC. 1211. EXPORT APPROVALS FOR HIGH PERFORMANCE COMPUTERS.

''(a) PRIOR APPROVAL OF EXPORTS AND REEXPORTS.—The President shall require that no digital computer with a composite theoretical performance level of more than 2,000 millions of theoretical operations per second (MTOPS) or with such other composite theoretical performance level as may be established subsequently by the President under subsection (d), may be exported or reexported without a license to a country specified in subsection (b) if the Secretary of Commerce, the Secretary of Defense, the Secretary of Energy, the Secretary of State, or the Director of the Arms Control and Disarmament Agency objects, in writing, to such export or reexport. Any person proposing to export or reexport such a digital computer shall so notify the Secretary of Commerce, who, within 24 hours after receiving the notification, shall transmit the notification to the Secretary of Defense, the Secretary of Energy, the Secretary of State, and the Director of the Arms Control and Disarmament Agency.

''(b) COVERED COUNTRIES.—For purposes of subsection (a), the countries specified in this subsection are the countries listed as 'Computer Tier 3' eligible countries in section 740.7(d) of title 15 of the Code of Federal Regulations, as in effect on June 10, 1997, subject to modification by the President under subsection (e).

''(c) TIME LIMIT.—Written objections under subsection (a) to an export or reexport shall be raised within 10 days after the notification is received under subsection (a). If such a written objection to the export or reexport of a computer is raised, the computer may be exported or reexported only pursuant to a license issued by the Secretary of Commerce under the Export Administration Regulations of the Department of Commerce, without regard to the licensing exceptions otherwise authorized under section 740.7 of title 15 of the Code of Federal Regulations, as in effect on June 10, 1997. If no objection is raised within the 10-day period, the export or reexport is authorized.

''(d) ADJUSTMENT OF COMPOSITE THEORETICAL PERFORMANCE.—The President, in consultation with the Secretary of Commerce, the Secretary of Defense, the Secretary of Energy, the Secretary of State, and the Director of the Arms Control and Disarmament Agency, may establish a new composite theoretical performance level for purposes of subsection (a). Such new level shall not take effect until 60 days after the President submits to the congressional committees designated in section 1215 a report setting forth the new composite theoretical performance level and the justification for such new level. Each report shall, at a minimum—

''(1) address the extent to which high performance computers of a composite theoretical level between the level established in subsection (a) or such level as has been previously adjusted pursuant to this section and the new level, are available from other countries;

''(2) address all potential uses of military significance to which high performance computers at the new level could be applied; and

''(3) assess the impact of such uses on the national security interests of the United States.

''(e) ADJUSTMENT OF COVERED COUNTRIES.—

''(1) IN GENERAL.—The President, in consultation with the Secretary of Commerce, the Secretary of Defense, the Secretary of Energy, the Secretary of State, and the Director of the Arms Control and Disarmament Agency, may add a country to or remove a country from the list of covered countries in subsection (b), except that a country may be removed from the list only in accordance with paragraph (2).

''(2) DELETIONS FROM LIST OF COVERED COUNTRIES.—The removal of a country from the list of covered countries under subsection (b) shall not take effect until 120 days after the President submits to the congressional committees designated in section 1215 a report setting forth the justification for the deletion.

''(3) EXCLUDED COUNTRIES.—A country may not be removed from the list of covered countries under subsection (b) if—

''(A) the country is a 'nuclear-weapon state' (as defined by Article IX of the Treaty on the Non-Proliferation of Nuclear Weapons) and the country is not a member of the North Atlantic Treaty Organization; or

''(B) the country is not a signatory of the Treaty on the Non-Proliferation of Nuclear Weapons and the country is listed on Annex 2 to the Comprehensive Nuclear Test-Ban Treaty.

''(f) CLASSIFICATION.—Each report under subsections (d) and (e) shall be submitted in an unclassified form and may, if necessary, have a classified supplement.

''(g) DELEGATION OF OBJECTION AUTHORITY WITHIN THE DEPARTMENT OF DEFENSE.—For the purposes of the Department of Defense, the authority to issue an objection referred to in subsection (a) shall be executed for the Secretary of Defense by an official at the Assistant Secretary level within the office of the Under Secretary of Defense for Policy. In implementing subsection (a), the Secretary of Defense shall ensure that Department of Defense procedures maximize the ability of the Department of Defense to be able to issue an objection within the 10-day period specified in subsection (c).

''(h) CALCULATION OF 60-DAY PERIOD.—The 60-day period referred to in subsection (d) shall be calculated by excluding the days on which either House of Congress is not in session because of an adjournment of the Congress sine die.

''SEC. 1212. REPORT ON EXPORTS OF HIGH PERFORMANCE COMPUTERS.

''(a) REPORT.—Not later than 60 days after the date of the enactment of this Act [Nov. 18, 1997], the President shall provide to the congressional committees specified in section 1215 a report identifying all exports of digital computers with a composite theoretical performance of more than 2,000 millions of theoretical operations per second (MTOPS) to all countries since January 25, 1996. For each export, the report shall identify—

"(1) whether an export license was applied for and whether one was granted;

"(2) the date of the transfer of the computer;

"(3) the United States manufacturer and exporter of the computer;

"(4) the MTOPS level of the computer; and

"(5) the recipient country and end user.

"(b) ADDITIONAL INFORMATION ON EXPORTS TO CERTAIN COUNTRIES.—In the case of exports to countries specified in subsection (c), the report under subsection (a) shall identify the intended end use for the exported computer and the assessment by the executive branch of whether the end user is a military end user or an end user involved in activities relating to nuclear, chemical, or biological weapons or missile technology. Information provided under this subsection may be submitted in classified form if necessary.

"(c) COVERED COUNTRIES.—For purposes of subsection (b), the countries specified in this subsection are—

"(1) the countries listed as 'Computer Tier 3' eligible countries in section 740.7(d) of title 15 of the Code of Federal Regulations, as in effect on June 10, 1997; and

"(2) the countries listed in section 740.7(e) of title 15 of the Code of Federal Regulations, as in effect on June 10, 1997.

"SEC. 1213. POST-SHIPMENT VERIFICATION OF EXPORT OF HIGH PERFORMANCE COMPUTERS.

"(a) REQUIRED POST-SHIPMENT VERIFICATION.—The Secretary of Commerce shall conduct post-shipment verification of each digital computer with a composite theoretical performance of more than 2,000 millions of theoretical operations per second (MTOPS) that is exported from the United States, on or after the date of the enactment of this Act [Nov. 18, 1998], to a country specified in subsection (b).

"(b) COVERED COUNTRIES.—For purposes of subsection (a), the countries specified in this subsection are the countries listed as 'Computer Tier 3' eligible countries in section 740.7 of title 15 of the Code of Federal Regulations, as in effect on June 10, 1997, subject to modification by the President under section 1211(e).

"(c) ANNUAL REPORT.—The Secretary of Commerce shall submit to the congressional committees specified in section 1215 an annual report on the results of post-shipment verifications conducted under this section during the preceding year. Each such report shall include a list of all such items exported from the United States to such countries during the previous year and, with respect to each such export, the following:

"(1) The destination country.

"(2) The date of export.

"(3) The intended end use and intended end user.

"(4) The results of the post-shipment verification.

"(d) EXPLANATION WHEN VERIFICATION NOT CONDUCTED.—If a post-shipment verification has not been conducted in accordance with subsection (a) with respect to any such export during the period covered by a report, the Secretary shall include in the report for that period a detailed explanation of the reasons why such a post-shipment verification was not conducted.

"(e) ADJUSTMENT OF PERFORMANCE LEVELS.—Whenever a new composite theoretical performance level is established under section 1211(d), that level shall apply for purposes of subsection (a) of this section in lieu of the level set forth in subsection (a).

"SEC. 1214. GAO STUDY ON CERTAIN COMPUTERS; END USER INFORMATION ASSISTANCE.

"(a) IN GENERAL.—The Comptroller General of the United States shall submit to the congressional committees specified in section 1215 a study of the national security risks relating to the sale of computers with a composite theoretical performance of between 2,000 and 7,000 millions of theoretical operations per second (MTOPS) to end users in countries specified in subsection (c). The study shall also analyze any foreign availability of computers described in the preceding sentence and the impact of such sales on United States exporters.

"(b) END USER INFORMATION ASSISTANCE TO EXPORTERS.—The Secretary of Commerce shall establish a procedure by which exporters may seek information on questionable end users in countries specified in subsection (c) who are seeking to obtain computers described in subsection (a).

"(c) COVERED COUNTRIES.—For purposes of subsections (a) and (b), the countries specified in this subsection are the countries listed as 'Computer Tier 3' eligible countries in section 740.7(d) of title 15 of the Code of Federal Regulations, as in effect on June 10, 1997.

"SEC. 1215. CONGRESSIONAL COMMITTEES.

"For purposes of sections 1211(d), 1212(a), 1213(c), and 1214(a) the congressional committees specified in those sections are the following:

"(1) The Committee on Banking, Housing, and Urban Affairs and the Committee on Armed Services of the Senate.

"(2) The Committee on International Relations and the Committee on Armed Services of the House of Representatives."

[Pub. L. 106–398, §1 [[div. A], title XII, §1234(b)], Oct. 30, 2000, 114 Stat. 1654, 1654A–331, provided that: "The amendments made by subsection (a) [amending section 1211 of Pub. L. 105–85, set out above] shall apply to any new composite theoretical performance level established for purposes of section 1211(a) of the National Defense Authorization Act for Fiscal Year 1998 [Pub. L. 105–85] that is submitted by the President pursuant to section 1211(d) of that Act on or after the date of the enactment of this Act [Oct. 30, 2000]."]

[For abolition, transfer of functions, and treatment of references to United States Arms Control and Disarmament Agency, see section 6511 et seq. of Title 22, Foreign Relations and Intercourse.]

REPORTS ON ADVANCED SUPERCOMPUTER SALES TO CERTAIN FOREIGN NATIONS

Pub. L. 105–85, div. C, title XXXI, §3157, Nov. 18, 1997, 111 Stat. 2045, as amended by Pub. L. 106–398, §1 [div. C, title XXXI, §3134], Oct. 30, 2000, 114 Stat. 1654, 1654A–456, provided that:

"(a) REPORTS.—The Secretary of Energy shall require that any company that is a participant in the Accelerated Strategic Computing Initiative (ASCI) program of the Department of Energy report to the Secretary and to the Secretary of Defense each sale by that company to a country designated as a Tier III country of a computer capable of operating at a speed in excess of 2,000 millions theoretical operations per second (MTOPS). The report shall include a description of the following with respect to each such sale:

"(1) The anticipated end-use of the computer sold.

"(2) The software included with the computer.

"(3) Any arrangement under the terms of the sale regarding—

"(A) upgrading the computer;

"(B) servicing the computer; or

"(C) furnishing spare parts for the computer.

"(b) COVERED COUNTRIES.—For purposes of this section, the countries designated as Tier III countries are the countries listed as 'computer tier 3' eligible countries in part 740.7 of title 15 of the Code of Federal Regulations, as in effect on June 10, 1997 (or any successor list).

"(c) QUARTERLY SUBMISSION OF REPORTS.—The Secretary of Energy shall require that reports under subsection (a) be submitted quarterly.

"(d) ANNUAL REPORT.—The Secretary of Energy shall submit to Congress an annual report containing all information received under subsection (a) during the preceding year. The first annual report shall be submitted not later than July 1, 1998.

"(e) ADJUSTMENT OF PERFORMANCE LEVELS.—Whenever a new composite theoretical performance level is established under section 1211(d) [Pub. L. 105–85, set out as a note above], that level shall apply for the purposes of subsection (a) of this section in lieu of the level set forth in subsection (a)."

NATIONAL SECURITY IMPLICATIONS OF UNITED STATES EXPORT CONTROL POLICY

Pub. L. 104–106, div. A, title XIII, § 1322, Feb. 10, 1996, 110 Stat. 478, provided that:

"(a) FINDINGS.—Congress makes the following findings:

"(1) Export controls remain an important element of the national security policy of the United States.

"(2) It is in the national security interest that United States export control policy be effective in preventing the transfer, to potential adversaries or combatants of the United States, of technology that threatens the national security or defense of the United States.

"(3) It is in the national security interest that the United States monitor aggressively the export of militarily critical technology in order to prevent its diversion to potential adversaries or combatants of the United States.

"(4) The Department of Defense relies increasingly on commercial and dual-use technologies, products, and processes to support United States military capabilities and economic strength.

"(5) The maintenance of the military advantage of the United States depends on effective export controls on dual-use items and technologies that are critical to the military capabilities of the Armed Forces.

"(b) SENSE OF CONGRESS.—It is the sense of Congress that—

"(1) the Secretary of Defense should evaluate license applications for the export of militarily critical commodities the export of which is controlled for national security reasons if those commodities are to be exported to certain countries of concern;

"(2) the Secretary of Defense should identify the dual-use items and technologies that are critical to the military capabilities of the Armed Forces, including the military use made of such items and technologies;

"(3) upon identification by the Secretary of Defense of the dual-use items and technologies referred to in paragraph (2), the President should ensure effective export controls or use unilateral export controls on dual-use items and technologies that are critical to the military capabilities of the Armed Forces (regardless of the availability of such items or technologies overseas) with respect to the countries that—

"(A) pose a threat to the national security interests of the United States; and

"(B) are not members in good standing of bilateral or multilateral agreements to which the United States is a party on the use of such items and technologies; and

"(4) the President, upon recommendation of the Secretary of Defense, should ensure effective controls on the re-export by other countries of dual-use items and technologies that are critical to the military capabilities of the Armed Forces.

"(c) ANNUAL REPORT.—(1) Not later than December 1 of each year through 1999, the President shall submit to the committees specified in paragraph (4) a report on the effect of the export control policy of the United States on the national security interests of the United States.

"(2) The report shall include the following:

"(A) A list setting forth each country determined by the Secretary of Defense, the intelligence community, and other appropriate agencies to be a rogue nation or potential adversary or combatant of the United States.

"(B) For each country so listed, a list of—

"(i) the categories of items that the United States currently prohibits for export to the country;

"(ii) the categories of items that may be exported from the United States with an individual license, and in such cases, any licensing conditions normally required and the policy grounds used for approvals and denials; and

"(iii) the categories of items that may be exported under a general license designated 'G-DEST'.

"(C) For each category of items listed under subparagraph (B)—

"(i) a statement whether a prohibition, control, or licensing requirement on a category of items is imposed pursuant to an international multilateral agreement or is unilateral;

"(ii) a statement whether a prohibition, control, or licensing requirement on a category of items is imposed by the other members of an international agreement or is unilateral;

"(iii) when the answer under either clause (i) or clause (ii) is unilateral, a statement concerning the efforts being made to ensure that the prohibition, control, or licensing requirement is made multilateral; and

"(iv) a statement on what impact, if any, a unilateral prohibition is having, or would have, on preventing the rogue nation or potential adversary from attaining the items in question for military purposes.

"(D) A description of United States policy on sharing satellite imagery that has military significance and a discussion of the criteria for determining the imagery that has that significance.

"(E) A description of the relationship between United States policy on the export of space launch vehicle technology and the Missile Technology Control Regime.

"(F) An assessment of United States efforts to support the inclusion of additional countries in the Missile Technology Control Regime.

"(G) An assessment of the ongoing efforts made by potential participant countries in the Missile Technology Control Regime to meet the guidelines established by the Missile Technology Control Regime.

"(H) A discussion of the history of the space launch vehicle programs of other countries, including a discussion of the military origins and purposes of such programs and the current level of military involvement in such programs.

"(3) The President shall submit the report in unclassified form, but may include a classified annex.

"(4) The committees referred to in paragraph (1) are the following:

"(A) The Committee on Armed Services and the Committee on Foreign Relations of the Senate.

"(B) The Committee on National Security [now Committee on Armed Services] and the Committee on International Relations of the House of Representatives.

"(5) For purposes of this subsection, the term 'Missile Technology Control Regime' means the policy statement announced on April 16, 1987, between the United States, the United Kingdom, the Federal Republic of Germany, France, Italy, Canada, and Japan to restrict sensitive missile-relevant transfers based on the Missile Technology Control Regime Annex, and any amendment thereto."

DEPARTMENT OF DEFENSE REVIEW OF EXPORT LICENSES FOR CERTAIN BIOLOGICAL PATHOGENS

Pub. L. 104–106, div. A, title XIII, § 1323, Feb. 10, 1996, 110 Stat. 480, provided that:

"(a) DEPARTMENT OF DEFENSE REVIEW.—Any application to the Secretary of Commerce for a license for the export of a class 2, class 3, or class 4 biological pathogen to a country identified to the Secretary under subsection (c) as a country that is known or suspected to have a biological weapons program shall be referred to the Secretary of Defense for review. The Secretary of

Defense shall notify the Secretary of Commerce within 15 days after receipt of an application under the preceding sentence whether the export of such biological pathogen pursuant to the license would be contrary to the national security interests of the United States.

"(b) DENIAL OF LICENSE IF CONTRARY TO NATIONAL SECURITY INTEREST.—A license described in subsection (a) shall be denied by the Secretary of Commerce if it is determined that the export of such biological pathogen to that country would be contrary to the national security interests of the United States.

"(c) IDENTIFICATION OF COUNTRIES KNOWN OR SUSPECTED TO HAVE A PROGRAM TO DEVELOP OFFENSIVE BIOLOGICAL WEAPONS.—(1) The Secretary of Defense shall determine, for the purposes of this section, those countries that are known or suspected to have a program to develop offensive biological weapons. Upon making such determination, the Secretary shall provide to the Secretary of Commerce a list of those countries.

"(2) The Secretary of Defense shall update the list under paragraph (1) on a regular basis. Whenever a country is added to or deleted from such list, the Secretary shall notify the Secretary of Commerce.

"(3) Determination under this subsection of countries that are known or suspected to have a program to develop offensive biological weapons shall be made in consultation with the Secretary of State and the intelligence community.

"(d) DEFINITION.—For purposes of this section, the term 'class 2, class 3, or class 4 biological pathogen' means any biological pathogen that is characterized by the Centers for Disease Control as a class 2, class 3, or class 4 biological pathogen."

ANNUAL REPORTS ON IMPROVING EXPORT CONTROL MECHANISMS

Pub. L. 104–106, div. A, title XIII, §1324(a), (b), Feb. 10, 1996, 110 Stat. 480, 481, provided that:

"(a) JOINT REPORTS BY SECRETARIES OF STATE AND COMMERCE.—Not later than April 1 of each of 1996 and 1997, the Secretary of State and the Secretary of Commerce shall submit to Congress a joint report, prepared in consultation with the Secretary of Defense, relating to United States export-control mechanisms. Each such report shall set forth measures to be taken to strengthen United States export-control mechanisms, including—

"(1) steps being taken by each Secretary (A) to share on a regular basis the export licensing watchlist of that Secretary's department with the other Secretary, and (B) to incorporate the export licensing watchlist data received from the other Secretary into the watchlist of that Secretary's department;

"(2) steps being taken by each Secretary to incorporate into the watchlist of that Secretary's department similar data from systems maintained by the Department of Defense and the United States Customs Service; and

"(3) a description of such further measures to be taken to strengthen United States export-control mechanisms as the Secretaries consider to be appropriate.

"(b) REPORTS BY INSPECTORS GENERAL.—(1) Not later than April 1 of each of 1996 and 1997, the Inspector General of the Department of State and the Inspector General of the Department of Commerce shall each submit to Congress a report providing that official's evaluation of the effectiveness during the preceding year of the export licensing watchlist screening process of that official's department. The reports shall be submitted in both a classified and unclassified version.

"(2) Each report of an Inspector General under paragraph (1) shall (with respect to that official's department)—

"(A) set forth the number of export licenses granted to parties on the export licensing watchlist;

"(B) set forth the number of end-use checks performed with respect to export licenses granted to parties on the export licensing watchlist the previous year;

"(C) assess the screening process used in granting an export license when an applicant is on the export licensing watchlist; and

"(D) assess the extent to which the export licensing watchlist contains all relevant information and parties required by statute or regulation."

STUDY ON NATIONAL SECURITY EXPORT CONTROLS

Section 2433 of Pub. L. 100–418 directed Secretary of Commerce and Secretary of Defense, not later than 60 days after Aug. 23, 1988, to enter into appropriate arrangements with National Academy of Sciences and National Academy of Engineering to conduct a comprehensive study of adequacy of current export administration system in safeguarding United States national security while maintaining United States international competitiveness and Western technological preeminence, further directed Academies to prepare and submit to President and Congress, not later than 18 months after entering into such arrangements, a report containing a detailed statement of findings and conclusions of Academies pursuant to such study, together with their recommendations for such legislative or regulatory reforms as they considered appropriate, and further provided for an Advisory Panel to aid in such study, as well as executive branch cooperation, and appropriations for such study.

DELEGATION OF AUTHORITY UNDER SECTION 1322(c) OF PUBLIC LAW 104–106

Determination of President of the United States, No. 97–39, Sept. 30, 1997, 62 F.R. 52477, provided:

By the authority vested in me by the Constitution and laws of the United States of America, I hereby delegate to the Secretary of Defense the duties and responsibilities vested in the President by section 1322(c) of the National Defense Authorization Act for Fiscal Year 1996 ("the Act") (Public Law 104–106, 110 Stat. 478–479 (1996)) [set out as a note above].

The reporting requirement delegated by this memorandum may be redelegated not lower than the Under Secretary level. The Department of Defense shall obtain concurrence on the report from the following agencies: the Department of Commerce, the Department of State, the Department of the Treasury, and the Director of Central Intelligence on behalf of the intelligence community prior to submission to the Congress.

Any reference in this memorandum to the provisions of any Act shall be deemed to be a reference to such Act or its provisions as may be amended from time to time.

The Secretary of Defense is authorized and directed to publish this memorandum in the Federal Register.

WILLIAM J. CLINTON.

SECTION REFERRED TO IN OTHER SECTIONS

This section is referred to in sections 5, 2403, 2405, 2410, 2410b, 2411, 2413, 2414, 2415, 2416 of this Appendix; title 12 section 95a; title 19 section 1864; title 22 sections 2797a, 5605, 6004, 6713; title 50 section 1702.

§ 2405. Foreign policy controls

(a) Authority

(1) In order to carry out the policy set forth in paragraph (2)(B), (7), (8), or (13) of section 3 of this Act [section 2402(2)(B), (7), (8), or (13) of this Appendix], the President may prohibit or curtail the exportation of any goods, technology, or other information subject to the jurisdiction of the United States or exported by any person subject to the jurisdiction of the United States, to the extent necessary to further significantly the foreign policy of the United States or to fulfill its declared international obligations. The authority granted by this subsection shall be exercised by the Secretary, in consultation with

the Secretary of State, the Secretary of Defense, the Secretary of Agriculture, the Secretary of the Treasury, the United States Trade Representative, and such other departments and agencies as the Secretary considers appropriate, and shall be implemented by means of export licenses issued by the Secretary.

(2) Any export control imposed under this section shall apply to any transaction or activity undertaken with the intent to evade that export control, even if that export control would not otherwise apply to that transaction or activity.

(3) Export controls maintained for foreign policy purposes shall expire on December 31, 1979, or one year after imposition, whichever is later, unless extended by the President in accordance with subsections (b) and (f). Any such extension and any subsequent extension shall not be for a period of more than one year.

(4) Whenever the Secretary denies any export license under this subsection, the Secretary shall specify in the notice to the applicant of the denial of such license that the license was denied under the authority contained in this subsection, and the reasons for such denial, with reference to the criteria set forth in subsection (b) of this section. The Secretary shall also include in such notice what, if any, modifications in or restrictions on the goods or technology for which the license was sought would allow such export to be compatible with controls implemented under this section, or the Secretary shall indicate in such notice which officers and employees of the Department of Commerce who are familiar with the application will be made reasonably available to the applicant for consultation with regard to such modifications or restrictions, if appropriate.

(5) In accordance with the provisions of section 10 of this Act [section 2409 of this Appendix], the Secretary of State shall have the right to review any export license application under this section which the Secretary of State requests to review.

(6) Before imposing, expanding, or extending export controls under this section on exports to a country which can use goods, technology, or information available from foreign sources and so incur little or no economic costs as a result of the controls, the President should, through diplomatic means, employ alternatives to export controls which offer opportunities of distinguishing the United States from, and expressing the displeasure of the United States with, the specific actions of that country in response to which the controls are proposed. Such alternatives include private discussions with foreign leaders, public statements in situations where private diplomacy is unavailable or not effective, withdrawal of ambassadors, and reduction of the size of the diplomatic staff that the country involved is permitted to have in the United States.

(b) Criteria

(1) Subject to paragraph (2) of this subsection, the President may impose, extend, or expand export controls under this section only if the President determines that—

(A) such controls are likely to achieve the intended foreign policy purpose, in light of other factors, including the availability from other countries of the goods or technology proposed for such controls, and that foreign policy purpose cannot be achieved through negotiations or other alternative means;

(B) the proposed controls are compatible with the foreign policy objectives of the United States and with overall United States policy toward the country to which exports are to be subject to the proposed controls;

(C) the reaction of other countries to the imposition, extension, or expansion of such export controls by the United States is not likely to render the controls ineffective in achieving the intended foreign policy purpose or to be counterproductive to United States foreign policy interests;

(D) the effect of the proposed controls on the export performance of the United States, the competitive position of the United States in the international economy, the international reputation of the United States as a supplier of goods and technology, or on the economic well-being of individual United States companies and their employees and communities does not exceed the benefit to United States foreign policy objectives; and

(E) the United States has the ability to enforce the proposed controls effectively.

(2) With respect to those export controls in effect under this section on the date of the enactment of the Export Administration Amendments Act of 1985 [July 12, 1985], the President, in determining whether to extend those controls, as required by subsection (a)(3) of this section, shall consider the criteria set forth in paragraph (1) of this subsection and shall consider the foreign policy consequences of modifying the export controls.

(c) Consultation with industry

The Secretary in every possible instance shall consult with and seek advice from affected United States industries and appropriate advisory committees established under section 135 of the Trade Act of 1974 [19 U.S.C. 2155] before imposing any export control under this section. Such consultation and advice shall be with respect to the criteria set forth in subsection (b)(1) and such other matters as the Secretary considers appropriate.

(d) Consultation with other countries

When imposing export controls under this section, the President shall, at the earliest appropriate opportunity, consult with the countries with which the United States maintains export controls cooperatively, and with such other countries as the President considers appropriate, with respect to the criteria set forth in subsection (b)(1) and such other matters as the President considers appropriate.

(e) Alternative means

Before resorting to the imposition of export controls under this section, the President shall determine that reasonable efforts have been made to achieve the purposes of the controls through negotiations or other alternative means.

(f) Consultation with Congress

(1) The President may impose or expand export controls under this section, or extend such

controls as required by subsection (a)(3) of this section, only after consultation with the Congress, including the Committee on Foreign Affairs of the House of Representatives and the Committee on Banking, Housing, and Urban Affairs of the Senate.

(2) The President may not impose, expand, or extend export controls under this section until the President has submitted to the Congress a report—

(A) specifying the purpose of the controls;

(B) specifying the determinations of the President (or, in the case of those export controls described in subsection (b)(2), the considerations of the President) with respect to each of the criteria set forth in subsection (b)(1), the bases for such determinations (or considerations), and any possible adverse foreign policy consequences of the controls;

(C) describing the nature, the subjects, and the results of, or the plans for, the consultation with industry pursuant to subsection (c) and with other countries pursuant to subsection (d);

(D) specifying the nature and results of any alternative means attempted under subsection (e), or the reasons for imposing, expanding, or extending the controls without attempting any such alternative means; and

(E) describing the availability from other countries of goods or technology comparable to the goods or technology subject to the proposed export controls, and describing the nature and results of the efforts made pursuant to subsection (h) to secure the cooperation of foreign governments in controlling the foreign availability of such comparable goods or technology.

Such report shall also indicate how such controls will further significantly the foreign policy of the United States or will further its declared international obligations.

(3) To the extent necessary to further the effectiveness of the export controls, portions of a report required by paragraph (2) may be submitted to the Congress on a classified basis, and shall be subject to the provisions of section 12(c) of this Act [section 2411(c) of this Appendix].

(4) In the case of export controls under this section which prohibit or curtail the export of any agricultural commodity, a report submitted pursuant to paragraph (2) shall be deemed to be the report required by section 7(g)(3)(A) of this Act [section 2406(g)(3)(A) of this Appendix].

(5) In addition to any written report required under this section, the Secretary, not less frequently than annually, shall present in oral testimony before the Committee on Banking, Housing, and Urban Affairs of the Senate and the Committee on Foreign Affairs of the House of Representatives a report on policies and actions taken by the Government to carry out the provisions of this section.

(g) Exclusion for medicine and medical supplies and for certain food exports

This section does not authorize export controls on medicine or medical supplies. This section also does not authorize export controls on donations of goods (including, but not limited to, food, educational materials, seeds and hand tools, medicines and medical supplies, water resources equipment, clothing and shelter materials, and basic household supplies) that are intended to meet basic human needs. Before export controls on food are imposed, expanded, or extended under this section, the Secretary shall notify the Secretary of State in the case of export controls applicable with respect to any developed country and shall notify the Administrator of the Agency for International Development in the case of export controls applicable with respect to any developing country. The Secretary of State with respect to developed countries, and the Administrator with respect to developing countries, shall determine whether the proposed export controls on food would cause measurable malnutrition and shall inform the Secretary of that determination. If the Secretary is informed that the proposed export controls on food would cause measurable malnutrition, then those controls may not be imposed, expanded, or extended, as the case may be, unless the President determines that those controls are necessary to protect the national security interests of the United States, or unless the President determines that arrangements are insufficient to ensure that the food will reach those most in need. Each such determination by the Secretary of State or the Administrator of the Agency for International Development, and any such determination by the President, shall be reported to the Congress, together with a statement of the reasons for that determination. It is the intent of Congress that the President not impose export controls under this section on any goods or technology if he determines that the principal effect of the export of such goods or technology would be to help meet basic human needs. This subsection shall not be construed to prohibit the President from imposing restrictions on the export of medicine or medical supplies or of food under the International Emergency Economic Powers Act [50 U.S.C 1701 et seq.]. This subsection shall not apply to any export control on medicine, medical supplies, or food, except for donations, which is in effect on the date of the enactment of the Export Administration Amendments Act of 1985 [July 12, 1985]. Notwithstanding the preceding provisions of this subsection, the President may impose export controls under this section on medicine, medical supplies, food, and donations of goods in order to carry out the policy set forth in paragraph (13) of section 3 of this Act [section 2402(13) of this Appendix].

(h) Foreign availability

(1) In applying export controls under this section, the President shall take all feasible steps to initiate and conclude negotiations with appropriate foreign governments for the purpose of securing the cooperation of such foreign governments in controlling the export to countries and consignees to which the United States export controls apply of any goods or technology comparable to goods or technology controlled under this section.

(2) Before extending any export control pursuant to subsection (a)(3) of this section, the President shall evaluate the results of his actions under paragraph (1) of this subsection and

shall include the results of that evaluation in his report to the Congress pursuant to subsection (f) of this section.

(3) If, within 6 months after the date on which export controls under this section are imposed or expanded, or within 6 months after the date of the enactment of the Export Administration Amendments Act of 1985 [July 12, 1985] in the case of export controls in effect on such date of enactment, the President's efforts under paragraph (1) are not successful in securing the cooperation of foreign governments described in paragraph (1) with respect to those export controls, the Secretary shall thereafter take into account the foreign availability of the goods or technology subject to the export controls. If the Secretary affirmatively determines that a good or technology subject to the export controls is available in sufficient quantity and comparable quality from sources outside the United States to countries subject to the export controls so that denial of an export license would be ineffective in achieving the purposes of the controls, then the Secretary shall, during the period of such foreign availability, approve any license application which is required for the export of the good or technology and which meets all requirements for such a license. The Secretary shall remove the good or technology from the list established pursuant to subsection (*l*) of this section if the Secretary determines that such action is appropriate.

(4) In making a determination of foreign availability under paragraph (3) of this subsection, the Secretary shall follow the procedures set forth in section 5(f)(3) of this Act [section 2404(f)(3) of this Appendix].

(i) International obligations

The provisions of subsections (b), (c), (d), (e), (g), and (h) shall not apply in any case in which the President exercises the authority contained in this section to impose export controls, or to approve or deny export license applications, in order to fulfill obligations of the United States pursuant to treaties to which the United States is a party or pursuant to other international agreements.

(j) Countries supporting international terrorism

(1) A validated license shall be required for the export of goods or technology to a country if the Secretary of State has made the following determinations:

(A) The government of such country has repeatedly provided support for acts of international terrorism.

(B) The export of such goods or technology could make a significant contribution to the military potential of such country, including its military logistics capability, or could enhance the ability of such country to support acts of international terrorism.

(2) The Secretary and the Secretary of State shall notify the Committee on Foreign Affairs of the House of Representatives and the Committee on Banking, Housing, and Urban Affairs and the Committee on Foreign Relations of the Senate at least 30 days before issuing any validated license required by paragraph (1).

(3) Each determination of the Secretary of State under paragraph (1)(A), including each determination in effect on the date of the enactment of the Antiterrorism and Arms Export Amendments Act of 1989 [Dec. 12, 1989], shall be published in the Federal Register.

(4) A determination made by the Secretary of State under paragraph (1)(A) may not be rescinded unless the President submits to the Speaker of the House of Representatives and the chairman of the Committee on Banking, Housing, and Urban Affairs and the chairman of the Committee on Foreign Relations of the Senate—

(A) before the proposed rescission would take effect, a report certifying that—

(i) there has been a fundamental change in the leadership and policies of the government of the country concerned;

(ii) that government is not supporting acts of international terrorism; and

(iii) that government has provided assurances that it will not support acts of international terrorism in the future; or

(B) at least 45 days before the proposed rescission would take effect, a report justifying the rescission and certifying that—

(i) the government concerned has not provided any support for international terrorism during the preceding 6-month period; and

(ii) the government concerned has provided assurances that it will not support acts of international terrorism in the future.

(5) The Secretary and the Secretary of State shall include in the notification required by paragraph (2)—

(A) a detailed description of the goods or services to be offered, including a brief description of the capabilities of any article for which a license to export is sought;

(B) the reasons why the foreign country or international organization to which the export or transfer is proposed to be made needs the goods or services which are the subject of such export or transfer and a description of the manner in which such country or organization intends to use such articles, services, or design and construction services;

(C) the reasons why the proposed export or transfer is in the national interest of the United States;

(D) an analysis of the impact of the proposed export or transfer on the military capabilities of the foreign country or international organization to which such export or transfer would be made;

(E) an analysis of the manner in which the proposed export would affect the relative military strengths of countries in the region to which the goods or services which are the subject of such export would be delivered and whether other countries in the region have comparable kinds and amounts of articles, services, or design and construction services; and

(F) an analysis of the impact of the proposed export or transfer on the United States relations with the countries in the region to which the goods or services which are the subject of such export would be delivered.

(k) Negotiations with other countries

(1) Countries participating in certain agreements

The Secretary of State, in consultation with the Secretary, the Secretary of Defense, and the heads of other appropriate departments and agencies, shall be responsible for conducting negotiations with those countries participating in the groups known as the Coordinating Committee, the Missile Technology Control Regime, the Australia Group, and the Nuclear Suppliers' Group, regarding their cooperation in restricting the export of goods and technology in order to carry out—

(A) the policy set forth in section 3(2)(B) of this Act [section 2402(2)(B) of this Appendix], and

(B) United States policy opposing the proliferation of chemical, biological, nuclear, and other weapons and their delivery systems, and effectively restricting the export of dual use components of such weapons and their delivery systems, in accordance with this subsection and subsections (a) and (*l*).

Such negotiations shall cover, among other issues, which goods and technology should be subject to multilaterally agreed export restrictions, and the implementation of the restrictions consistent with the principles identified in section 5(b)(2)(C) of this Act [section 2404(b)(2)(C) of this Appendix].

(2) Other countries

The Secretary of State, in consultation with the Secretary, the Secretary of Defense, and the heads of other appropriate departments and agencies, shall be responsible for conducting negotiations with countries and groups of countries not referred to in paragraph (1) regarding their cooperation in restricting the export of goods and technology consistent with purposes set forth in paragraph (1). In cases where such negotiations produce agreements on export restrictions that the Secretary, in consultation with the Secretary of State and the Secretary of Defense, determines to be consistent with the principles identified in section 5(b)(2)(C) of this Act [section 2404(b)(2)(C) of this Appendix], the Secretary may treat exports, whether by individual or multiple licenses, to countries party to such agreements in the same manner as exports are treated to countries that are MTCR adherents.

(3) Review of determinations

The Secretary shall annually review any determination under paragraph (2) with respect to a country. For each such country which the Secretary determines is not meeting the requirements of an effective export control system in accordance with section 5(b)(2)(C) [section 2404(b)(2)(C) of this Appendix], the Secretary shall restrict or eliminate any preferential licensing treatment for exports to that country provided under this subsection.

(*l*) Missile technology

(1) Determination of controlled items

The Secretary, in consultation with the Secretary of State, the Secretary of Defense, and the heads of other appropriate departments and agencies—

(A) shall establish and maintain, as part of the control list established under this section, a list of all dual use goods and technology on the MTCR Annex; and

(B) may include, as part of the control list established under this section, goods and technology that would provide a direct and immediate impact on the development of missile delivery systems and are not included in the MTCR Annex but which the United States is proposing to the other MTCR adherents to have included in the MTCR Annex.

(2) Requirement of individual validated licenses

The Secretary shall require an individual validated license for—

(A) any export of goods or technology on the list established under paragraph (1) to any country; and

(B) any export of goods or technology that the exporter knows is destined for a project or facility for the design, development, or manufacture of a missile in a country that is not an MTCR adherent.

(3) Policy of denial of licenses

(A) Licenses under paragraph (2) should in general be denied if the ultimate consignee of the goods or technology is a facility in a country that is not an adherent to the Missile Technology Control Regime and the facility is designed to develop or build missiles.

(B) Licenses under paragraph (2) shall be denied if the ultimate consignee of the goods or technology is a facility in a country the government of which has been determined under subsection (j) to have repeatedly provided support for acts of international terrorism.

(4) Consultation with other departments

(A) A determination of the Secretary to approve an export license under paragraph (2) for the export of goods or technology to a country of concern regarding missile proliferation may be made only after consultation with the Secretary of Defense and the Secretary of State for a period of 20 days. The countries of concern referred to in the preceding sentence shall be maintained on a classified list by the Secretary of State, in consultation with the Secretary and the Secretary of Defense.

(B) Should the Secretary of Defense disagree with the determination of the Secretary to approve an export license to which subparagraph (A) applies, the Secretary of Defense shall so notify the Secretary within the 20 days provided for consultation on the determination. The Secretary of Defense shall at the same time submit the matter to the President for resolution of the dispute. The Secretary shall also submit the Secretary's recommendation to the President on the license application.

(C) The President shall approve or disapprove the export license application within 20 days after receiving the submission of the Secretary of Defense under subparagraph (B).

(D) Should the Secretary of Defense fail to notify the Secretary within the time period prescribed in subparagraph (B), the Secretary may approve the license application without awaiting the notification by the Secretary of Defense. Should the President fail to notify the Secretary of his decision on the export license application within the time period prescribed in subparagraph (C), the Secretary may approve the license application without awaiting the President's decision on the license application.

(E) Within 10 days after an export license is issued under this subsection, the Secretary shall provide to the Secretary of Defense and the Secretary of State the license application and accompanying documents issued to the applicant, to the extent that the relevant Secretary indicates the need to receive such application and documents.

(5) Information sharing

The Secretary shall establish a procedure for information sharing with appropriate officials of the intelligence community, as determined by the Director of Central Intelligence, and other appropriate Government agencies, that will ensure effective monitoring of transfers of MTCR equipment or technology and other missile technology.

(m) Chemical and biological weapons

(1) Establishment of list

The Secretary, in consultation with the Secretary of State, the Secretary of Defense, and the heads of other appropriate departments and agencies, shall establish and maintain, as part of the list maintained under this section, a list of goods and technology that would directly and substantially assist a foreign government or group in acquiring the capability to develop, produce, stockpile, or deliver chemical or biological weapons, the licensing of which would be effective in barring acquisition or enhancement of such capability.

(2) Requirement for validated licenses

The Secretary shall require a validated license for any export of goods or technology on the list established under paragraph (1) to any country of concern.

(3) Countries of concern

For purposes of paragraph (2), the term "country of concern" means any country other than—

(A) a country with whose government the United States has entered into a bilateral or multilateral arrangement for the control of goods or technology on the list established under paragraph (1); and

(B) such other countries as the Secretary of State, in consultation with the Secretary and the Secretary of Defense, shall designate consistent with the purposes of the Chemical and Biological Weapons Control and Warfare Elimination Act of 1991 [22 U.S.C. 5601 et seq.].

(n) Crime control instruments

(1) Crime control and detection instruments and equipment shall be approved for export by the Secretary only pursuant to a validated export license. Notwithstanding any other provision of this Act [sections 2401 to 2420 of this Appendix]—

(A) any determination of the Secretary of what goods or technology shall be included on the list established pursuant to subsection (*l*)[1] of this section as a result of the export restrictions imposed by this subsection shall be made with the concurrence of the Secretary of State, and

(B) any determination of the Secretary to approve or deny an export license application to export crime control or detection instruments or equipment shall be made in concurrence with the recommendations of the Secretary of State submitted to the Secretary with respect to the application pursuant to section 10(e) of this Act [section 2409(e) of this Appendix],

except that, if the Secretary does not agree with the Secretary of State with respect to any determination under subparagraph (A) or (B), the matter shall be referred to the President for resolution.

(2) The provisions of this subsection shall not apply with respect to exports to countries which are members of the North Atlantic Treaty Organization or to Japan, Australia, or New Zealand, or to such other countries as the President shall designate consistent with the purposes of this subsection and section 502B of the Foreign Assistance Act of 1961 [22 U.S.C. 2304].

(*o*) Control list

The Secretary shall establish and maintain, as part of the control list, a list of any goods or technology subject to export controls under this section, and the countries to which such controls apply. The Secretary shall clearly identify on the control list which goods or technology, and which countries or destinations, are subject to which types of controls under this section. Such list shall consist of goods and technology identified by the Secretary of State, with the concurrence of the Secretary. If the Secretary and the Secretary of State are unable to agree on the list, the matter shall be referred to the President. Such list shall be reviewed not less frequently than every three years in the case of controls maintained cooperatively with other countries, and annually in the case of all other controls, for the purpose of making such revisions as are necessary in order to carry out this section. During the course of such review, an assessment shall be made periodically of the availability from sources outside the United States, or any of its territories or possessions, of goods and technology comparable to those controlled for export from the United States under this section.

(p) Effect on existing contracts and licenses

The President may not, under this section, prohibit or curtail the export or reexport of goods, technology, or other information—

(1) in performance of a contract or agreement entered into before the date on which the President reports to the Congress, pursuant to subsection (f) of this section, his intention to impose controls on the export or reex-

[1] See References in Text note below.

port of such goods, technology, or other information, or

(2) under a validated license or other authorization issued under this Act [sections 2401 to 2420 of this Appendix],

unless and until the President determines and certifies to the Congress that—

(A) a breach of the peace poses a serious and direct threat to the strategic interest of the United States,

(B) the prohibition or curtailment of such contracts, agreements, licenses, or authorizations will be instrumental in remedying the situation posing the direct threat, and

(C) the export controls will continue only so long as the direct threat persists.

(q) Extension of certain controls

Those export controls imposed under this section with respect to South Africa which were in effect on February 28, 1982, and ceased to be effective on March 1, 1982, September 15, 1982, or January 20, 1983, shall become effective on the date of the enactment of this subsection [July 12, 1985], and shall remain in effect until 1 year after such date of enactment. At the end of that 1-year period, any of those controls made effective by this subsection may be extended by the President in accordance with subsections (b) and (f) of this section.

(r) Expanded authority to impose controls

(1) In any case in which the President determines that it is necessary to impose controls under this section without any limitation contained in subsection (c), (d), (e), (g), (h), or (m)[2] of this section, the President may impose those controls only if the President submits that determination to the Congress, together with a report pursuant to subsection (f) of this section with respect to the proposed controls, and only if a law is enacted authorizing the imposition of those controls. If a joint resolution authorizing the imposition of those controls is introduced in either House of Congress within 30 days after the Congress receives the determination and report of the President, that joint resolution shall be referred to the Committee on Banking, Housing, and Urban Affairs of the Senate and to the appropriate committee of the House of Representatives. If either such committee has not reported the joint resolution at the end of 30 days after its referral, the committee shall be discharged from further consideration of the joint resolution.

(2) For purposes of this subsection, the term "joint resolution" means a joint resolution the matter after the resolving clause of which is as follows: "That the Congress, having received on   a determination of the President under section 6(*o*)(1)[2] of the Export Administration Act of 1979 with respect to the export controls which are set forth in the report submitted to the Congress with that determination, authorizes the President to impose those export controls.", with the date of the receipt of the determination and report inserted in the blank.

(3) In the computation of the periods of 30 days referred to in paragraph (1), there shall be excluded the days on which either House of Congress is not in session because of an adjournment of more than 3 days to a day certain or because of an adjournment of the Congress sine die.

(s) Spare parts

(1) At the same time as the President imposes or expands export controls under this section, the President shall determine whether such export controls will apply to replacement parts for parts in goods subject to such export controls.

(2) With respect to export controls imposed under this section before the date of the enactment of this subsection [Aug. 23, 1988], an individual validated export license shall not be required for replacement parts which are exported to replace on a one-for-one basis parts that were in a good that was lawfully exported from the United States, unless the President determines that such a license should be required for such parts.

(Pub. L. 96–72, §6, Sept. 29, 1979, 93 Stat. 513; Pub. L. 96–533, title I, §111, Dec. 16, 1980, 94 Stat. 3138; Pub. L. 97–145, §6, Dec. 29, 1981, 95 Stat. 1728; Pub. L. 99–64, title I, §108(a)–(g)(1), (h)–(j)(1), (k), (*l*)(1), July 12, 1985, 99 Stat. 131–136; Pub. L. 99–399, title V, §509(b), Aug. 27, 1986, 100 Stat. 874; Pub. L. 100–418, title II, §2423, Aug. 23, 1988, 102 Stat. 1358; Pub. L. 101–222, §4, Dec. 12, 1989, 103 Stat. 1897; Pub. L. 101–510, div. A, title XVII, §1702(a), Nov. 5, 1990, 104 Stat. 1739; Pub. L. 102–138, title V, §504(b), Oct. 28, 1991, 105 Stat. 724; Pub. L. 102–182, title III, §§304(b), 309(a), Dec. 4, 1991, 105 Stat. 1246, 1258; Pub. L. 103–236, title VII, §736, Apr. 30, 1994, 108 Stat. 506; Pub. L. 104–316, title I, §128(c), Oct. 19, 1996, 110 Stat. 3841; Pub. L. 105–277, div. G, title XIV, §1422(b)(7), Oct. 21, 1998, 112 Stat. 2681–793.)

REFERENCES IN TEXT

The International Emergency Economic Powers Act, referred to in subsec. (g), is title II of Pub. L. 95–223, Dec. 28, 1977, 91 Stat. 1626, which is classified generally to chapter 35 (§1701 et seq.) of Title 50, War and National Defense. For complete classification of this Act to the Code, see Short Title note set out under section 1701 of Title 50 and Tables.

The Chemical and Biological Weapons Control and Warfare Elimination Act of 1991, referred to in subsec. (m)(3)(B), is title III of Pub. L. 102–182, Dec. 4, 1991, 105 Stat. 1245, which is classified principally to chapter 65 (§5601 et seq.) of Title 22, Foreign Relations and Intercourse. For complete classification of this Act to the Code, see Short Title note set out under section 5601 of Title 22 and Tables.

Subsections (*l*) and (m) of this section, referred to in subsecs. (n)(1)(A) and (r)(1), were successively redesignated as subsections (n) and (*o*), respectively, of this section by Pub. L. 101–510, div. A, title XVII, §1702(a)(1), Nov. 5, 1990, 104 Stat. 1739, then as subsections (*o*) and (p), respectively, of this section by Pub. L. 102–182, title III, §304(b), Dec. 4, 1991, 105 Stat. 1246, without corresponding amendments to such references.

Section 6(*o*)(1) of the Export Administration Act of 1979, referred to in subsec. (r)(2), which was classified to subsec. (*o*)(1) of this section, was redesignated successively as section 6(q)(1) by Pub. L. 101–510, div. A, title XVII, §1702(a)(1), Nov. 5, 1990, 104 Stat. 1739, then as section 6(r)(1) by Pub. L. 102–182, title III, §304(b), Dec. 4, 1991, 105 Stat. 1246, without a corresponding amendment to such reference.

PRIOR PROVISIONS

A prior section 2405, Pub. L. 91–184, §6, Dec. 30, 1969, 83 Stat. 844; Pub. L. 95–52, title I, §§103(d), 112, title II,

[2] See References in Text note below.

§ 203(a), June 22, 1977, 91 Stat. 237, 240, 247; Pub. L. 95–223, title III, § 301(b)(2), Dec. 28, 1977, 91 Stat. 1629, setting forth provisions respecting violations and penalties, expired on Sept. 30, 1979.

AMENDMENTS

1998—Subsec. (g). Pub. L. 105–277, which directed amendment of "Section 2405(g) of the Export Administration Act of 1979" by substituting "Administrator of the Agency for International Development" for "Director of the United States International Development Cooperation Agency" in two places and substituting "Administrator" for "Director" in the fourth sentence, was executed to subsec. (g) of this section, which is section 6 of the Export Administration Act of 1979, to reflect the probable intent of Congress.

1996—Subsec. (f)(3). Pub. L. 104–316 struck out after first sentence "Each such report shall, at the same time it is submitted to the Congress, also be submitted to the General Accounting Office for the purpose of assessing the report's full compliance with the intent of this subsection."

1994—Subsec. (j)(5). Pub. L. 103–236 added par. (5).

1991—Subsecs. (m) to (s). Pub. L. 102–182, § 304(b), added subsec. (m) and redesignated former subsecs. (m) to (r) as (n) to (s), respectively.

Pub. L. 102–138, which made an amendment similar to that made by Pub. L. 102–182, § 304(b), by adding a subsec. (m) and redesignating former subsecs. (m) to (r) as (n) to (s), respectively, was repealed by Pub. L. 102–182, § 309(a).

1990—Subsecs. (k) to (r). Pub. L. 101–510 added subsecs. (k) and (*l*) and redesignated former subsecs. (k) to (p) as (m) to (r), respectively.

1989—Subsec. (j). Pub. L. 101–222 amended subsec. (j) generally, substituting pars. (1) to (4) for former pars. (1) and (2).

1988—Subsec. (a)(6). Pub. L. 100–418, § 2423(a), added par. (6).

Subsec. (p). Pub. L. 100–418, § 2423(b), added subsec. (p).

1986—Subsec. (j)(1). Pub. L. 99–399 substituted "$1,000,000" for "$7,000,000".

1985—Subsec. (a)(1). Pub. L. 99–64, § 108(a)(1), substituted "(8), or (13)" for "or (8)", and inserted ", the Secretary of Defense, the Secretary of Agriculture, the Secretary of the Treasury, the United States Trade Representative," after "in consultation with the Secretary of State".

Subsec. (a)(2). Pub. L. 99–64, § 108(a)(3), added par. (2). Former par. (2) redesignated (3).

Subsec. (a)(3). Pub. L. 99–64, § 108(a)(2), (4), redesignated par. (2) as (3) and substituted "subsections (b) and (f)" for "subsections (b) and (e)". Former par. (3) redesignated (4).

Subsec. (a)(4), (5). Pub. L. 99–64, § 108(a)(2), redesignated pars. (3) and (4) as (4) and (5), respectively.

Subsec. (b). Pub. L. 99–64, § 108(b), amended subsec. (b) generally. Prior to amendment, subsec. (b) read as follows: "When imposing, expanding, or extending export controls under this section, the President shall consider—

"(1) the probability that such controls will achieve the intended foreign policy purpose, in light of other factors, including the availability from other countries of the goods or technology proposed for such controls;

"(2) the compatibility of the proposed controls with the foreign policy objectives of the United States, including the effort to counter international terrorism, and with overall United States policy toward the country which is the proposed target of the controls;

"(3) the reaction of other countries to the imposition or expansion of such export controls by the United States;

"(4) the likely effects of the proposed controls on the export performance of the United States, on the competitive position of the United States in the international economy, on the international reputation of the United States as a supplier of goods and technology, and on individual United States companies and their employees and communities, including the effects of the controls on existing contracts;

"(5) the ability of the United States to enforce the proposed controls effectively; and

"(6) the foreign policy consequences of not imposing controls."

Subsec. (c). Pub. L. 99–64, § 108(c), amended subsec. (c) generally. Prior to amendment, subsec. (c) read as follows: "The Secretary, before imposing export controls under this section, shall consult with such affected United States industries as the Secretary considers appropriate, with respect to the criteria set forth in paragraphs (1) and (4) of subsection (b) and such other matters as the Secretary considers appropriate."

Subsec. (d). Pub. L. 99–64, § 108(d)(2), added subsec. (d). Former subsec. (d) redesignated (e).

Subsec. (e). Pub. L. 99–64, § 108(d)(1), redesignated former subsec. (d) as (e). Former subsec. (e) redesignated (f).

Subsec. (f). Pub. L. 99–64, § 108(d)(1), (e), redesignated former subsec. (e) as (f), amended subsec. (f) generally, substituting "Consultation with Congress" for "Notification to Congress" in heading, and in text making consultation with the Congress mandatory and not merely discretionary before the President imposes, expands, or extends export controls. Former subsec. (f) redesignated (g).

Subsec. (g). Pub. L. 99–64, § 108(d)(1), (f), redesignated former subsec. (f) as (g), inserted sentence directing that this section does not authorize export controls on donations of goods that are intended to meet basic human needs, and substituted "This subsection shall not apply to any export control on medicine, medical supplies, or food, except for donations, which is in effect on the date of the enactment of the Export Administration Amendments Act of 1985" for "This subsection shall not apply to any export control on medicine or medical supplies which is in effect on the effective date of this Act or to any export control on food which is in effect on the date of the enactment of the Export Administration Amendments Act of 1981" and inserted: "Notwithstanding the preceding provisions of this subsection, the President may impose export controls under this section on medicine, medical supplies, food, and donations of goods in order to carry out the policy set forth in paragraph (13) of section 3 of this Act."

Subsec. (h). Pub. L. 99–64, § 108(g)(1), designated existing provisions as par. (1) and added pars. (2) to (4).

Pub. L. 99–64, § 108(d)(1), redesignated former subsec. (g) as (h). Former subsec. (h) redesignated (i).

Subsec. (i). Pub. L. 99–64, § 108(d)(1), (h), redesignated former subsec. (h) as (i) and substituted "(e), (g), and (h)" for "(f), and (g)". Former subsec. (i) redesignated (j).

Subsec. (j). Pub. L. 99–64, § 108(d)(1), (i), redesignated former subsec. (i) as (j), amended subsec. (j) generally, designating the existing sentence as par. (1) and former pars. (1) and (2) thereof as subpars. (A) and (B), and adding par. (2). Former subsec. (j) redesignated (k).

Subsec. (k). Pub. L. 99–64, § 108(d)(1), redesignated former subsec. (j) as (k). Former subsec. (k) redesignated (*l*).

Subsec. (k)(1). Pub. L. 99–64, § 108(j)(1), inserted sentence relating to the concurrence of the Secretary of State.

Subsec. (*l*). Pub. L. 99–64, § 108(d)(1), (k), redesignated former subsec. (k) as (*l*), substituted reference to "the control list" for existing reference to "the commodity control list' after "The Secretary shall establish and maintain, as part of", and substituted "The Secretary shall clearly identify on the control list which goods or technology, and which countries or destinations, are subject to which types of controls under this section" for "Such goods or technology shall be clearly identified as subject to controls under this section".

Subsecs. (m) to (*o*). Pub. L. 99–64, § 108(*l*)(1), added subsecs. (m) to (*o*).

1981—Subsec. (f). Pub. L. 97–145 inserted provisions restricting the imposition of export controls on food when such controls would result in measurable malnutrition, unless the President determines that the controls are necessary to protect the United States national security interests or that the food would not reach persons most in need.

1980—Pub. L. 96–533 required notification of certain commercial exports to be given to the Committee on Foreign Relations of the Senate and prescribed that notice be given to the committees at least 30 days before approval of the export license.

CHANGE OF NAME

Committee on Foreign Affairs of House of Representatives treated as referring to Committee on International Relations of House of Representatives by section 1(a) of Pub. L. 104–14, set out as a note preceding section 21 of Title 2, The Congress.

EFFECTIVE DATE OF 1998 AMENDMENT

Amendment by Pub. L. 105–277 effective on earlier of Apr. 1, 1999, or date of abolition of the United States International Development Cooperation Agency pursuant to reorganization plan described in section 6601 of Title 22, Foreign Relations and Intercourse, see section 1401 of Pub. L. 105–277, set out as an Effective Date note under section 6561 of Title 22.

EFFECTIVE DATE OF 1985 AMENDMENT

Section 108(g)(2) of Pub. L. 99–64 provided that: "The amendments made by paragraph (1) of this subsection [amending this section] shall not apply to export controls in effect under subsection (i), (j), or (k) of section 6 of the Export Administration Act of 1979 [subsec. (i), (j), or (k) of this section] (as redesignated by subsection (d) of this section) immediately before the date of the enactment of this Act [July 12, 1985], or to export controls made effective by subsection (i)(2) of this section [there is no section 108(i)(2) of Pub. L. 99–64] or by section 6(n) of the Export Administration Act of 1979 [subsec. (n) of this section] (as added by subsection (*l*)(1) of this section)."

Section 108(j)(2) of Pub. L. 99–64 provided that: "The amendment made by paragraph (1) of this subsection [amending this section] shall apply to determinations of the Secretary of Commerce which are made on or after the date of the enactment of this Act [July 12, 1985]."

Section 108(*l*)(2) of Pub. L. 99–64 provided that: "Subsections (m) and (*o*) of section 6 of the Export Administration Act of 1979 [subsecs. (m) and (*o*) of this section], as added by paragraph (1) of this subsection, shall not apply to export controls in effect immediately before the date of the enactment of this Act [July 12, 1985], or to export controls made effective by subsection (i)(2) of this section [there is no section 108(i)(2) of Pub. L. 99–64] or by section 6(n) of the Export Administration Act of 1979 [subsec. (n) of this section] (as added by paragraph (1) of this subsection)."

DELEGATION OF FUNCTIONS

Functions conferred upon President under this section delegated to Secretary of Commerce by Ex. Ord. No. 12214, May 2, 1980, 45 F.R. 29783, set out under 2403 of this Appendix, with exception of functions conferred upon President under subsec. (g) of this section which were delegated to Secretary of State and functions conferred upon President under subsec. (k) of this section which were reserved to President.

EXERCISE OF STATUTORY AUTHORITIES RESPECTING IMPOSITION OF TOTAL EMBARGO IN EVENT OF SOVIET OR WARSAW PACT MILITARY ACTION IN POLAND

Section 7 of Pub. L. 97–145 provided that: "Notwithstanding any other provision of law, no provision of the Export Administration Act of 1979, as amended by this Act [sections 2401 to 2420 of this Appendix], or of any other Act shall be construed to prohibit the exercise of authorities contained in the Export Administration Act of 1979 to impose a total embargo in the event of Soviet or Warsaw Pact military action against Poland."

ADMINISTRATION OF EXPORT CONTROLS ON ENCRYPTION PRODUCTS

For provision that subsec. (h)(2) to (4) of this section is not applicable with respect to export controls on encryption products, see Ex. Ord. No. 13026, §1(a), set out as a note under section 2403 of this Appendix.

SECTION REFERRED TO IN OTHER SECTIONS

This section is referred to in sections 5, 2170, 2407, 2410, 2410b, 2410c, 2413, 2414, 2416 of this Appendix; title 10 sections 2249a, 2327; title 12 section 95a; title 18 section 2332d; title 19 section 2462; title 22 sections 262p–4q, 2378, 2656f, 2708, 2712, 2797, 2797a, 2797b, 2798, 2799aa–1, 4305, 5605, 6461, 6713, 7205; title 26 section 901; title 28 section 1605; title 50 section 1702.

§ 2406. Short supply controls

(a) Authority

(1) In order to carry out the policy set forth in section 3(2)(C) of this Act [section 2402(2)(C) of this Appendix], the President may prohibit or curtail the export of any goods subject to the jurisdiction of the United States or exported by any person subject to the jurisdiction of the United States. In curtailing exports to carry out the policy set forth in section 3(2)(C) of this Act [section 2402(2)(C) of this Appendix], the President shall allocate a portion of export licenses on the basis of factors other than a prior history of exportation. Such factors shall include the extent to which a country engages in equitable trade practices with respect to United States goods and treats the United States equitably in times of short supply.

(2) Upon imposing quantitative restrictions on exports of any goods to carry out the policy set forth in section 3(2)(C) of this Act [section 2402(2)(C) of this Appendix], the Secretary shall include in a notice published in the Federal Register with respect to such restrictions an invitation to all interested parties to submit written comments within 15 days from the date of publication on the impact of such restrictions and the method of licensing used to implement them.

(3) In imposing export controls under this section, the President's authority shall include, but not be limited to, the imposition of export license fees.

(b) Monitoring

(1) In order to carry out the policy set forth in section 3(2)(C) of this Act [section 2402(2)(C) of this Appendix], the Secretary shall monitor exports, and contracts for exports, of any good (other than a commodity which is subject to the reporting requirements of section 812 [1] of the Agricultural Act of 1970 [7 U.S.C. 612c–3]) when the volume of such exports in relation to domestic supply contributes, or may contribute, to an increase in domestic prices or a domestic shortage, and such price increase or shortage has, or may have, a serious adverse impact on the economy or any sector thereof. Any such monitoring shall commence at a time adequate to assure that the monitoring will result in a data base sufficient to enable policies to be developed, in

[1] See References in Text note below.

accordance with section 3(2)(C) of this Act [section 2402(2)(C) of this Appendix], to mitigate a short supply situation or serious inflationary price rise or, if export controls are needed, to permit imposition of such controls in a timely manner. Information which the Secretary requires to be furnished in effecting such monitoring shall be confidential, except as provided in paragraph (2) of this subsection.

(2) The results of such monitoring shall, to the extent practicable, be aggregated and included in weekly reports setting forth, with respect to each item monitored, actual and anticipated exports, the destination by country, and the domestic and worldwide price, supply, and demand. Such reports may be made monthly if the Secretary determines that there is insufficient information to justify weekly reports.

(3) The Secretary shall consult with the Secretary of Energy to determine whether monitoring or export controls under this section are warranted with respect to exports of facilities, machinery, or equipment normally and principally used, or intended to be used, in the production, conversion, or transportation of fuels and energy (except nuclear energy), including, but not limited to, drilling rigs, platforms, and equipment; petroleum refineries, natural gas processing, liquefaction, and gasification plants; facilities for production of synthetic natural gas or synthetic crude oil; oil and gas pipelines, pumping stations, and associated equipment; and vessels for transporting oil, gas, coal, and other fuels.

(c) Petitions for monitoring or controls

(1)(A) Any entity, including a trade association, firm, or certified or recognized union or group of workers, that is representative of an industry or a substantial segment of an industry that processes metallic materials capable of being recycled may transmit a written petition to the Secretary requesting the monitoring of exports or the imposition of export controls, or both, with respect to any such material, in order to carry out the policy set forth in section 3(2)(C) of this Act [section 2402(2)(C) of this Appendix].

(B) Each petition shall be in such form as the Secretary shall prescribe and shall contain information in support of the action requested. The petition shall include any information reasonably available to the petitioner indicating that each of the criteria set forth in paragraph (3)(A) of this subsection is satisfied.

(2) Within 15 days after receipt of any petition described in paragraph (1), the Secretary shall publish a notice in the Federal Register. The notice shall—

(A) include the name of the material that is the subject of the petition,

(B) include the Schedule B number of the material as set forth in the Statistical Classification of Domestic and Foreign Commodities Exported from the United States,

(C) indicate whether the petitioner is requesting that controls or monitoring, or both, be imposed with respect to the exportation of such material, and

(D) provide that interested persons shall have a period of 30 days beginning on the date of publication of such notice to submit to the Secretary written data, views or arguments, with or without opportunity for oral presentation, with respect to the matter involved.

At the request of the petitioner or any other entity described in paragraph (1)(A) with respect to the material that is the subject of the petition, or at the request of any entity representative of producers or exporters of such material, the Secretary shall conduct public hearings with respect to the subject of the petition, in which case the 30-day period may be extended to 45 days.

(3)(A) Within 45 days after the end of the 30- or 45-day period described in paragraph (2), as the case may be, the Secretary shall determine whether to impose monitoring or controls, or both, on the export of the material that is the subject of the petition, in order to carry out the policy set forth in section 3(2)(C) of this Act [section 2402(2)(C) of this Appendix]. In making such determination, the Secretary shall determine whether—

(i) there has been a significant increase, in relation to a specific period of time, in exports of such material in relation to domestic supply and demand;

(ii) there has been a significant increase in the domestic price of such material or a domestic shortage of such material relative to demand;

(iii) exports of such material are as important as any other cause of a domestic price increase or shortage relative to demand found under clause (ii);

(iv) a domestic price increase or shortage relative to demand found under clause (ii) has significantly adversely affected or may significantly adversely affect the national economy or any sector thereof, including a domestic industry; and

(v) monitoring or controls, or both, are necessary in order to carry out the policy set forth in section 3(2)(C) of this Act [section 2402(2)(C) of this Appendix].

(B) The Secretary shall publish in the Federal Register a detailed statement of the reasons for the Secretary's determination pursuant to subparagraph (A) of whether to impose monitoring or controls, or both, including the findings of fact in support of that determination.

(4) Within 15 days after making a determination under paragraph (3) to impose monitoring or controls on the export of a material, the Secretary shall publish in the Federal Register proposed regulations with respect to such monitoring or controls. Within 30 days after the publication of such proposed regulations, and after considering any public comments on the proposed regulations, the Secretary shall publish and implement final regulations with respect to such monitoring or controls.

(5) For purposes of publishing notices in the Federal Register and scheduling public hearings pursuant to this subsection, the Secretary may consolidate petitions, and responses to such petitions, which involve the same or related materials.

(6) If a petition with respect to a particular material or group of materials has been consid-

ered in accordance with all the procedures prescribed in this subsection, the Secretary may determine, in the absence of significantly changed circumstances, that any other petition with respect to the same material or group of materials which is filed within 6 months after the consideration of the prior petition has been completed does not merit complete consideration under this subsection.

(7) The procedures and time limits set forth in this subsection with respect to a petition filed under this subsection shall take precedence over any review undertaken at the initiative of the Secretary with respect to the same subject as that of the petition.

(8) The Secretary may impose monitoring or controls, on a temporary basis, on the export of a metallic material after a petition is filed under paragraph (1)(A) with respect to that material but before the Secretary makes a determination under paragraph (3) with respect to that material only if—

(A) the failure to take such temporary action would result in irreparable harm to the entity filing the petition, or to the national economy or segment thereof, including a domestic industry, and

(B) the Secretary considers such action to be necessary to carry out the policy set forth in section 3(2)(C) of this Act [section 2402(2)(C) of this Appendix].

(9) The authority under this subsection shall not be construed to affect the authority of the Secretary under any other provision of this Act [sections 2401 to 2420 of this Appendix], except that if the Secretary determines, on the Secretary's own initiative, to impose monitoring or controls, or both, on the export of metallic materials capable of being recycled, under the authority of this section, the Secretary shall publish the reasons for such action in accordance with paragraph (3)(A) and (B) of this subsection.

(10) Nothing contained in this subsection shall be construed to preclude submission on a confidential basis to the Secretary of information relevant to a decision to impose or remove monitoring or controls under the authority of this Act [sections 2401 to 2420 of this Appendix], or to preclude consideration of such information by the Secretary in reaching decisions required under this subsection. The provisions of this paragraph shall not be construed to affect the applicability of section 552(b) of title 5, United States Code.

(d) Domestically produced crude oil

(1) Notwithstanding any other provision of this Act [sections 2401 to 2420 of this Appendix] and notwithstanding subsection (u) of section 28 of the Mineral Leasing Act of 1920 (30 U.S.C. 185), no domestically produced crude oil transported by pipeline over right-of-way granted pursuant to section 203 of the Trans-Alaska Pipeline Authorization Act (43 U.S.C. 1652) (except any such crude oil which (A) is exported to an adjacent foreign country to be refined and consumed therein in exchange for the same quantity of crude oil being exported from that country to the United States; such exchange must result through convenience or increased efficiency of transportation in lower prices for consumers of petroleum products in the United States as described in paragraph (2)(A)(ii) of this subsection, (B) is temporarily exported for convenience or increased efficiency of transportation across parts of an adjacent foreign country and reenters the United States, or (C) is transported to Canada, to be consumed therein, in amounts not to exceed an annual average of 50,000 barrels per day, in addition to exports under subparagraphs (A) and (B), except that any ocean transportation of such oil shall be by vessels documented under section 12106 of title 46, United States Code) may be exported from the United States, or any of its territories and possessions, subject to paragraph (2) of this subsection.

(2) Crude oil subject to the prohibition contained in paragraph (1) may be exported only if—

(A) the President so recommends to the Congress after making and publishing express findings that exports of such crude oil, including exchanges—

(i) will not diminish the total quantity or quality of petroleum refined within, stored within, or legally committed to be transported to and sold within the United States;

(ii) will, within 3 months following the initiation of such exports or exchanges, result in (I) acquisition costs to the refiners which purchase the imported crude oil being lower than the acquisition costs such refiners would have to pay for the domestically produced oil in the absence of such an export or exchange, and (II) not less than 75 percent of such savings in costs being reflected in wholesale and retail prices of products refined from such imported crude oil;

(iii) will be made only pursuant to contracts which may be terminated if the crude oil supplies of the United States are interrupted, threatened, or diminished;

(iv) are clearly necessary to protect the national interest; and

(v) are in accordance with the provisions of this Act [sections 2401 to 2420 of this Appendix]; and

(B) the President includes such findings in his recommendation to the Congress and the Congress, within 60 days after receiving that recommendation, agrees to a joint resolution which approves such exports on the basis of those findings, and which is thereafter enacted into law.

(3) Notwithstanding any other provision of this section or any other provision of law, including subsection (u) of section 28 of the Mineral Leasing Act of 1920 [30 U.S.C. 185(u)], the President may export oil to any country pursuant to a bilateral international oil supply agreement entered into by the United States with such nation before June 25, 1979, or to any country pursuant to the International Emergency Oil Sharing Plan of the International Energy Agency.

(e) Refined petroleum products

(1) In any case in which the President determines that it is necessary to impose export controls on refined petroleum products in order to carry out the policy set forth in section 3(2)(C)

of this Act [section 2402(2)(C) of this Appendix], the President shall notify the Congress of that determination. The President shall also notify the Congress if and when he determines that such export controls are no longer necessary. During any period in which a determination that such export controls are necessary is in effect, no refined petroleum product may be exported except pursuant to an export license specifically authorizing such export. Not later than 5 days after an application for a license to export any refined petroleum product or residual fuel oil is received, the Secretary shall notify the Congress of such application, together with the name of the exporter, the destination of the proposed export, and the amount and price of the proposed export. Such notification shall be made to the chairman of the Committee on Foreign Affairs of the House of Representatives and the chairman of the Committee on Banking, Housing, and Urban Affairs of the Senate.

(2) The Secretary may not grant such license during the 30-day period beginning on the date on which notification to the Congress under paragraph (1) is received, unless the President certifies in writing to the Speaker of the House of Representatives and the President pro tempore of the Senate that the proposed export is vital to the national interest and that a delay in issuing the license would adversely affect that interest.

(3) This subsection shall not apply to (A) any export license application for exports to a country with respect to which historical export quotas established by the Secretary on the basis of past trading relationships apply, or (B) any license application for exports to a country if exports under the license would not result in more than 250,000 barrels of refined petroleum products being exported from the United States to such country in any fiscal year.

(4) For purposes of this subsection, "refined petroleum product" means gasoline, kerosene, distillates, propane or butane gas, diesel fuel, and residual fuel oil refined within the United States or entered for consumption within the United States.

(5) The Secretary may extend any time period prescribed in section 10 of this Act [section 2409 of this Appendix] to the extent necessary to take into account delays in action by the Secretary on a license application on account of the provisions of this subsection.

(f) Certain petroleum products

Petroleum products refined in United States Foreign Trade Zones, or in the United States Territory of Guam, from foreign crude oil shall be excluded from any quantitative restrictions imposed under this section except that, if the Secretary finds that a product is in short supply, the Secretary may issue such regulations as may be necessary to limit exports.

(g) Agricultural commodities

(1) The authority conferred by this section shall not be exercised with respect to any agricultural commodity, including fats and oils or animal hides or skins, without the approval of the Secretary of Agriculture. The Secretary of Agriculture shall not approve the exercise of such authority with respect to any such commodity during any period for which the supply of such commodity is determined by the Secretary of Agriculture to be in excess of the requirements of the domestic economy except to the extent the President determines that such exercise of authority is required to carry out the policies set forth in subparagraph (A) or (B) of paragraph (2) of section 3 of this Act [section 2402(2)(A) or (B) of this Appendix]. The Secretary of Agriculture shall, by exercising the authorities which the Secretary of Agriculture has under other applicable provisions of law, collect data with respect to export sales of animal hides and skins.

(2) Upon approval of the Secretary, in consultation with the Secretary of Agriculture, agricultural commodities purchased by or for use in a foreign country may remain in the United States for export at a later date free from any quantitative limitations on export which may be imposed to carry out the policy set forth in section 3(2)(C) of this Act [section 2402(2)(C) of this Appendix] subsequent to such approval. The Secretary may not grant such approval unless the Secretary receives adequate assurance and, in conjunction with the Secretary of Agriculture, finds (A) that such commodities will eventually be exported, (B) that neither the sale nor export thereof will result in an excessive drain of scarce materials and have a serious domestic inflationary impact, (C) that storage of such commodities in the United States will not unduly limit the space available for storage of domestically owned commodities, and (D) that the purpose of such storage is to establish a reserve of such commodities for later use, not including resale to or use by another country. The Secretary may issue such regulations as may be necessary to implement this paragraph.

(3)(A) If the President imposes export controls on any agricultural commodity in order to carry out the policy set forth in paragraph (2)(B), (2)(C), (7), or (8) of section 3 of this Act [section 2402(2)(B), (2)(C), (7), or (8) of this Appendix], the President shall immediately transmit a report on such action to the Congress, setting forth the reasons for the controls in detail and specifying the period of time, which may not exceed 1 year, that the controls are proposed to be in effect. If the Congress, within 60 days after the date of its receipt of the report, adopts a joint resolution pursuant to paragraph (4) approving the imposition of the export controls, then such controls shall remain in effect for the period specified in the report, or until terminated by the President, whichever occurs first. If the Congress, within 60 days after the date of its receipt of such report, fails to adopt a joint resolution approving such controls, then such controls shall cease to be effective upon the expiration of that 60-day period.

(B) The provisions of subparagraph (A) and paragraph (4) shall not apply to export controls—

(i) which are extended under this Act [sections 2401 to 2420 of this Appendix] if the controls, when imposed, were approved by the Congress under subparagraph (A) and paragraph (4); or

(ii) which are imposed with respect to a country as part of the prohibition or curtailment of all exports to that country.

(4)(A) For purposes of this paragraph, the term "joint resolution" means only a joint resolution the matter after the resolving clause of which is as follows: "That, pursuant to section 7(g)(3) of the Export Administration Act of 1979, the President may impose export controls as specified in the report submitted to the Congress on   .", with the blank space being filled with the appropriate date.

(B) On the day on which a report is submitted to the House of Representatives and the Senate under paragraph (3), a joint resolution with respect to the export controls specified in such report shall be introduced (by request) in the House by the chairman of the Committee on Foreign Affairs, for himself and the ranking minority member of the Committee, or by Members of the House designated by the chairman and ranking minority member; and shall be introduced (by request) in the Senate by the majority leader of the Senate, for himself and the minority leader of the Senate, or by Members of the Senate designated by the majority leader and minority leader of the Senate. If either House is not in session on the day on which such a report is submitted, the joint resolution shall be introduced in that House, as provided in the preceding sentence, on the first day thereafter on which that House is in session.

(C) All joint resolutions introduced in the House of Representatives shall be referred to the appropriate committee and all joint resolutions introduced in the Senate shall be referred to the Committee on Banking, Housing, and Urban Affairs.

(D) If the committee of either House to which a joint resolution has been referred has not reported the joint resolution at the end of 30 days after its referral, the committee shall be discharged from further consideration of the joint resolution or of any other joint resolution introduced with respect to the same matter.

(E) A joint resolution under this paragraph shall be considered in the Senate in accordance with the provisions of section 601(b)(4) of the International Security Assistance and Arms Export Control Act of 1976. For the purpose of expediting the consideration and passage of joint resolutions reported or discharged pursuant to the provisions of this paragraph, it shall be in order for the Committee on Rules of the House of Representatives to present for consideration a resolution of the House of Representatives providing procedures for the immediate consideration of a joint resolution under this paragraph which may be similar, if applicable, to the procedures set forth in section 601(b)(4) of the International Security Assistance and Arms Export Control Act of 1976.

(F) In the case of a joint resolution described in subparagraph (A), if, before the passage by one House of a joint resolution of that House, that House receives a resolution with respect to the same matter from the other House, then—

(i) the procedure in that House shall be the same as if no joint resolution had been received from the other House; but

(ii) the vote on final passage shall be on the joint resolution of the other House.

(5) In the computation of the period of 60 days referred to in paragraph (3) and the period of 30 days referred to in subparagraph (D) of paragraph (4), there shall be excluded the days on which either House of Congress is not in session because of an adjournment of more than 3 days to a day certain or because of an adjournment of the Congress sine die.

(h) Barter agreements

(1) The exportation pursuant to a barter agreement of any goods which may lawfully be exported from the United States, for any goods which may lawfully be imported into the United States, may be exempted, in accordance with paragraph (2) of this subsection, from any quantitative limitation on exports (other than any reporting requirement) imposed to carry out the policy set forth in section 3(2)(C) of this Act [section 2402(2)(C) of this Appendix].

(2) The Secretary shall grant an exemption under paragraph (1) if the Secretary finds, after consultation with the appropriate department or agency of the United States, that—

(A) for the period during which the barter agreement is to be performed—

(i) the average annual quantity of the goods to be exported pursuant to the barter agreement will not be required to satisfy the average amount of such goods estimated to be required annually by the domestic economy and will be surplus thereto; and

(ii) the average annual quantity of the goods to be imported will be less than the average amount of such goods estimated to be required annually to supplement domestic production; and

(B) the parties to such barter agreement have demonstrated adequately that they intend, and have the capacity, to perform such barter agreement.

(3) For purposes of this subsection, the term "barter agreement" means any agreement which is made for the exchange, without monetary consideration, of any goods produced in the United States for any goods produced outside of the United States.

(4) This subsection shall apply only with respect to barter agreements entered into after the effective date of this Act [September 30, 1979].

(i) Unprocessed red cedar

(1) The Secretary shall require a validated license, under the authority contained in subsection (a) of this section, for the export of unprocessed western red cedar (Thuja plicata) logs, harvested from State or Federal lands. The Secretary shall impose quantitative restrictions upon the export of unprocessed western red cedar logs during the 3-year period beginning on the effective date of this Act [September 30, 1979] as follows:

(A) Not more than thirty million board feet scribner of such logs may be exported during the first year of such 3-year period.

(B) Not more than fifteen million board feet scribner of such logs may be exported during the second year of such period.

(C) Not more than five million board feet scribner of such logs may be exported during the third year of such period.

After the end of such 3-year period, no unprocessed western red cedar logs harvested from

State or Federal lands may be exported from the United States.

(2) To the maximum extent practicable, the Secretary shall utilize the multiple validated export licenses described in section 4(a)(2) of this Act [section 2403(a)(2) of this Appendix] in lieu of validated licenses for exports under this subsection.

(3) The Secretary shall allocate export licenses to exporters pursuant to this subsection on the basis of a prior history of exportation by such exporters and such other factors as the Secretary considers necessary and appropriate to minimize any hardship to the producers of western red cedar and to further the foreign policy of the United States.

(4) Unprocessed western red cedar logs shall not be considered to be an agricultural commodity for purposes of subsection (g) of this section.

(5) As used in this subsection, the term "unprocessed western red cedar" means red cedar timber which has not been processed into—

(A) lumber of American Lumber Standards Grades of Number 3 dimension or better, or Pacific Lumber Inspection Bureau Export R-List Grades of Number 3 common or better;

(B) chips, pulp, and pulp products;

(C) veneer and plywood;

(D) poles, posts, or pilings cut or treated with preservative for use as such and not intended to be further processed; or

(E) shakes and shingles.

(j) Effect of controls on existing contracts

The export restrictions contained in subsection (i) of this section and any export controls imposed under this section shall not affect any contract to harvest unprocessed western red cedar from State lands which was entered into before October 1, 1979, and the performance of which would make the red cedar available for export. Any export controls imposed under this section on any agricultural commodity (including fats, oils, and animal hides and skins) or on any forest product or fishery product, shall not affect any contract to export entered into before the date on which such controls are imposed. For purposes of this subsection, the term "contract to export" includes, but is not limited to, an export sales agreement and an agreement to invest in an enterprise which involves the export of goods or technology.

(k) Oil exports for use by United States military facilities

For purposes of subsection (d) of this section, and for purposes of any export controls imposed under this Act [sections 2401 to 2420 of this Appendix], shipments of crude oil, refined petroleum products, or partially refined petroleum products from the United States for use by the Department of Defense or United States-supported installations or facilities shall not be considered to be exports.

(Pub. L. 96–72, §7, Sept. 29, 1979, 93 Stat. 515; Pub. L. 99–64, title I, §§109, 110, July 12, 1985, 99 Stat. 137, 139; Pub. L. 100–180, div. A, title XII, §1246, Dec. 4, 1987, 101 Stat. 1165; Pub. L. 100–418, title II, §2424(a), Aug. 23, 1988, 102 Stat. 1359; Pub. L. 100–449, title III, §305(a), Sept. 28, 1988, 102 Stat. 1876.)

REFERENCES IN TEXT

Section 812 of the Agricultural Act of 1970, referred to in subsec. (b)(1), which was classified to section 612c–3 of Title 7, Agriculture, was repealed by Pub. L. 101–624, title XV, §1578, Nov. 28, 1990, 104 Stat. 3702.

Section 7(g)(3) of the Export Administration Act of 1979, referred to in subsec. (g)(4)(A), is classified to subsec. (g)(3) of this section.

Section 601(b)(4) of the International Security Assistance and Arms Export Control Act of 1976, referred to in subsec. (g)(4)(E), is section 601(b)(4) of Pub. L. 94–329, June 30, 1976, 90 Stat. 729, which made provision for expedited procedures in the Senate, and is not classified to the Code.

PRIOR PROVISIONS

A prior section 2406, Pub. L. 91–184, §7, Dec. 30, 1969, 83 Stat. 845; Pub. L. 95–52, title I, §§113(a), 114, title II, §201(c), June 22, 1977, 91 Stat. 241, 246, setting forth enforcement procedures applicable to the Export Administration Act of 1969, expired on Sept. 30, 1979.

AMENDMENTS

1988—Subsec. (d)(1). Pub. L. 100–449 struck out "or" before "(B)" and inserted ", or (C) is transported to Canada, to be consumed therein, in amounts not to exceed an annual average of 50,000 barrels per day, in addition to exports under subparagraphs (A) and (B), except that any ocean transportation of such oil shall be by vessels documented under section 12106 of title 46, United States Code" after "reenters the United States".

Subsec. (d)(4). Pub. L. 100–418 struck out par. (4) which provided that notwithstanding section 2419 of this Appendix, the provisions of this subsection expire Sept. 30, 1990.

1987—Subsec. (k). Pub. L. 100–180 added subsec. (k).

1985—Subsec. (c). Pub. L. 99–64, §109, amended subsec. (c) generally to require the Secretary to make and publish certain determinations of private petitions as well as on self-initiated motions before imposing monitoring or controls or both on exports of metallic materials capable of being recycled, to require that each petition filed requesting the imposition of monitoring, controls, or both, on metallic materials capable of being recycled indicate that each of the criteria in par. (3)(A) is satisfied, to require the Secretary to publish certain determinations, including findings of fact in support of the determinations, before deciding whether to impose monitoring, controls, or both on exports of such material, including whether there has been a significant increase, in relation to a specific period of time, in exports of such material in relation to domestic supply and demand, and whether exports of such material are as important as any other cause of the domestic price increase or shortage relative to demand, to allow the Secretary to impose monitoring, controls, or both, on a temporary basis after a petition is filed if the Secretary considers such action to be necessary to carry out the policy set forth in section 3(2)(C) of the Act, but before the Secretary makes a determination under par. (3) only if failure to take such temporary action would result in irreparable harm to the entity filing the petition, or to the national economy or segment thereof, including a domestic industry, requires that if the Secretary determines, on his initiative, to monitor, control, or both, the export of such material, the Secretary shall publish the reasons for such determination in accordance with par. (3)(A) and (B), requires that exports of material be as important as any other cause of the increased domestic prices or shortage, and sets a standard under which exports need not be the sole or principal cause of the price rise or domestic shortage in order for exports of the material to be controlled or monitored.

Subsec. (d)(1). Pub. L. 99–64, §110(a)(1), substituted "subject to paragraph (2) of this subsection" for "unless the requirements of paragraph (2) of this subsection are met".

Subsec. (d)(2)(A). Pub. L. 99–64, §110(a)(2), substituted "the President so recommends to the Congress after making and publishing" for "the President makes and publishes" in the provisions preceding cl. (i).

Subsec. (d)(2)(B). Pub. L. 99–64, §110(a)(3), substituted "includes such findings in his recommendation" for "reports such findings" and "after receiving that recommendation, agrees to a joint resolution which approves such exports on the basis of those findings, and which is thereafter enacted into law" for "thereafter, agrees to a concurrent resolution approving such exports on the basis of the findings".

Subsec. (d)(4). Pub. L. 99–64, §110(a)(4), added par. (4).

Subsec. (e)(1). Pub. L. 99–64, §110(b), substituted "In any case in which the President determines that it is necessary to impose export controls on refined petroleum products in order to carry out the policy set forth in section 3(2)(C) of this Act, the President shall notify the Congress of that determination. The President shall also notify the Congress if and when he determines that such export controls are no longer necessary. During any period in which a determination that such export controls are necessary is in effect, no" for "No".

Subsec. (g)(3). Pub. L. 99–64, §110(d), amended par. (3) generally. Prior to amendment, par. (3) read as follows: "If the authority conferred by this section or section 6 is exercised to prohibit or curtail the export of any agricultural commodity in order to carry out the policies set forth in subparagraph (B) or (C) of paragraph (2) of section 3 of this Act, the President shall immediately report such prohibition or curtailment to the Congress, setting forth the reasons therefor in detail. If the Congress, within 30 days after the date of its receipt of such report, adopts a concurrent resolution disapproving such prohibition or curtailment, then such prohibition or curtailment shall cease to be effective with the adoption of such resolution. In the computation of such 30-day period, there shall be excluded the days on which either House is not in session because of an adjournment of more than 3 days to a day certain or because of an adjournment of the Congress sine die."

Subsec. (g)(4), (5). Pub. L. 99–64, §110(d), added pars. (4) and (5).

Subsec. (i)(1). Pub. L. 99–64, §110(c)(1), inserted "harvested from State or Federal lands" after "red cedar logs" in concluding provision.

Subsec. (i)(2). Pub. L. 99–64, §110(c)(3), added par. (2). Former par. (2) redesignated (3).

Subsec. (i)(3), (4). Pub. L. 99–64, §110(c)(2), redesignated former pars. (2) and (3) as (3) and (4), respectively. Former pars. (3) and (4) redesignated (4) and (5), respectively.

Subsec. (i)(5). Pub. L. 99–64, §110(c)(2), redesignated former par. (4) as (5).

Subsec. (i)(5)(A). Pub. L. 99–64, §110(c)(4), amended subpar. (A) generally, substituting "lumber of American Lumber Standards Grades of Number 3 dimension or better, or Pacific Lumber Inspection Bureau Export R-List Grades of Number 3 common or better" for "lumber without wane".

Subsec. (j). Pub. L. 99–64, §110(e), added subsec. (j) and struck out former subsec. (j) which related to the export of horses. See section 466c of Title 46, Appendix, Shipping.

CHANGE OF NAME

Committee on Foreign Affairs of House of Representatives treated as referring to Committee on International Relations of House of Representatives by section 1(a) of Pub. L. 104–14, set out as a note preceding section 21 of Title 2, The Congress.

EFFECTIVE AND TERMINATION DATES OF 1988 AMENDMENT

Amendment by Pub. L. 100–449 effective on the date the United States-Canada Free-Trade Agreement enters into force (Jan. 1, 1989), and to cease to have effect on the date the Agreement ceases to be in force, see section 501(a), (c) of Pub. L. 100–449, set out in a note under section 2112 of Title 19, Customs Duties.

REGULATIONS

Section 19(b)(2) of Pub. L. 96–72 provided that: "Regulations implementing the provisions of section 7(c) of this Act [subsec. (c) of this section] shall be issued and take effect not later than January 1, 1980."

DELEGATION OF FUNCTIONS

Functions conferred upon President under this section delegated to Secretary of Commerce by Ex. Ord. No. 12214, May 2, 1980, 45 F.R. 29783, set out under section 2403 of this Appendix, with exception of functions conferred upon President under subsec. (d)(2) of this section which were reserved to President.

ADEQUACY OF EXISTING STATUTORY RESTRICTIONS ON EXPORT OF CRUDE OIL PRODUCED IN CONTIGUOUS UNITED STATES IN PROTECTING ENERGY AND NATIONAL SECURITY INTEREST AND AMERICAN CONSUMER; STUDY AND REPORT TO CONGRESSIONAL COMMITTEES

Section 2424(b) of Pub. L. 100–418 directed Secretary of Commerce, in consultation with Secretary of Energy, to submit to Congress not later than 12 months after Aug. 23, 1988, a report containing results of a comprehensive review undertaken to assess whether existing statutory restrictions on export of crude oil produced in contiguous United States were adequate to protect energy and national security interests of United States and American consumers, taking into account such things as adequacy of domestic supplies of crude oil and refined petroleum products in meeting national security as well as consumer needs in the United States generally and on West Coast particularly, and further provided for public hearing and comment on this review as well as consultation with other Federal agencies and committees of Congress.

MONITORING OF WOOD EXPORTS

Section 2432 of Pub. L. 100–418 directed Secretary of Commerce, for a period of 2 years beginning on Aug. 23, 1988, to monitor exports of processed and unprocessed wood to all countries of the Pacific Rim, and to include results of such monitoring in monthly reports to Congress, setting forth, with respect to each item monitored, actual exports, destination by country, and domestic and worldwide price, supply, and demand.

UNPROCESSED RED CEDAR EXEMPT FROM EXPORT REGULATIONS

Pub. L. 98–411, title V, §514, Aug. 30, 1984, 98 Stat. 1575, provided that: "None of the funds appropriated or made available by this Act [Pub. L. 98–411] may be used to enforce or give effect to any restriction on the export of unprocessed western red cedar harvested from State lands pursuant to a harvesting contract entered into prior to October 1, 1979."

Pub. L. 96–126, title III, §308, Nov. 27, 1979, 93 Stat. 980, provided that: "Notwithstanding the provisions of any other law, the State of Alaska is exempted from application of the provisions of section 7(i) of the Export Administration Act of 1979 (Public Law 96–72) [subsec. (i) of this section]."

In making continuing appropriations for fiscal year 1981, Pub. L. 96–536, §§101(*o*), 102, Dec. 16, 1980, 94 Stat. 3169, as amended by Pub. L. 97–12, §401, June 5, 1981, 95 Stat. 95, provided in part for the period Dec. 15, 1980, to Sept. 30, 1981: "such amounts as may be necessary for programs, projects, and activities provided for in the Departments of State, Justice, and Commerce, the Judiciary, and Related Agencies Appropriation Act, 1981 (H.R. 7584), to the extent and in the manner provided for in such Act as enacted by the Congress." H.R. 7584, which was enacted by the Congress and vetoed by the President Dec. 13, 1980, contained a section 610 that read: "None of the funds appropriated or made available by this Act may be used to enforce or give effect to the quantitative restrictions required to be imposed by subsection 7(i)(1) of the Export Administration Act of 1979 (Public Law 96–72) [subsec. (i)(1) of this section] in any way which would make such restrictions applicable to the export of: (a) up to ninety million board feet (computed without regard to exports or export authorizations made prior to the effective date of this Act) of unprocessed western red cedar harvested from State or Federal lands pursuant to a harvesting contract entered into prior to October 1, 1979, or any extension thereof; or (b) lumber of American Lumber Standards Grades of Number 3 dimensions or better, of Pacific Lumber Inspection Bureau Export R-List Grades of Number 3 Common or better.''. Continuing appropriations for fiscal year 1982 were made, subject to specified provisions and under the authority and conditions provided in the above cited appropriation Act for fiscal 1981, as follows: For the period Oct. 1, 1981, to Dec. 15, 1981, by Pub. L. 97–51, §§ 101(a)(1), (4), 102, Oct. 1, 1981, 95 Stat. 958, 959, 961, as amended by Pub. L. 97–85, Nov. 23, 1981, 95 Stat. 1098; and for the period Dec. 15, 1981, to Sept. 30, 1982, by Pub. L. 97–92, §§ 101(h), 102, Dec. 15, 1981, 95 Stat. 1190, 1193, as amended by Pub. L. 97–161, Mar. 31, 1982, 96 Stat. 22.

SECTION REFERRED TO IN OTHER SECTIONS

This section is referred to in sections 2405, 2413, 2414 of this Appendix; title 7 section 1736f–1; title 16 sections 620c, 620j; title 26 section 993.

§ 2407. Foreign boycotts

(a) Prohibitions and exceptions

(1) For the purpose of implementing the policies set forth in subparagraph (A) or (B) of paragraph (5) of section 3 of this Act [section 2402(5)(A) or (B) of this Appendix], the President shall issue regulations prohibiting any United States person, with respect to his activities in the interstate or foreign commerce of the United States, from taking or knowingly agreeing to take any of the following actions with intent to comply with, further, or support any boycott fostered or imposed by a foreign country against a country which is friendly to the United States and which is not itself the object of any form of boycott pursuant to United States law or regulation:

(A) Refusing, or requiring any other person to refuse, to do business with or in the boycotted country, with any business concern organized under the laws of the boycotted country, with any national or resident of the boycotted country, or with any other person, pursuant to an agreement with, a requirement of, or a request from or on behalf of the boycotting country. The mere absence of a business relationship with or in the boycotted country with any business concern organized under the laws of the boycotted country, with any national or resident of the boycotted country, or with any other person, does not indicate the existence of the intent required to establish a violation of regulations issued to carry out this subparagraph.

(B) Refusing, or requiring any other person to refuse, to employ or otherwise discriminating against any United States person on the basis of race, religion, sex, or national origin of that person or of any owner, officer, director, or employee of such person.

(C) Furnishing information with respect to the race, religion, sex, or national origin of any United States person or of any owner, officer, director, or employee of such person.

(D) Furnishing information about whether any person has, has had, or proposes to have any business relationship (including a relationship by way of sale, purchase, legal or commercial representation, shipping or other transport, insurance, investment, or supply) with or in the boycotted country, with any business concern organized under the laws of the boycotted country, with any national or resident of the boycotted country, or with any other person which is known or believed to be restricted from having any business relationship with or in the boycotting country. Nothing in this paragraph shall prohibit the furnishing of normal business information in a commercial context as defined by the Secretary.

(E) Furnishing information about whether any person is a member of, has made contributions to, or is otherwise associated with or involved in the activities of any charitable or fraternal organization which supports the boycotted country.

(F) Paying, honoring, confirming, or otherwise implementing a letter of credit which contains any condition or requirement compliance with which is prohibited by regulations issued pursuant to this paragraph, and no United States person shall, as a result of the application of this paragraph, be obligated to pay or otherwise honor or implement such letter of credit.

(2) Regulations issued pursuant to paragraph (1) shall provide exceptions for—

(A) complying or agreeing to comply with requirements (i) prohibiting the import of goods or services from the boycotted country or goods produced or services provided by any business concern organized under the laws of the boycotted country or by nationals or residents of the boycotted country, or (ii) prohibiting the shipment of goods to the boycotting country on a carrier of the boycotted country, or by a route other than that prescribed by the boycotting country or the recipient of the shipment;

(B) complying or agreeing to comply with import and shipping document requirements with respect to the country of origin, the name of the carrier and route of shipment, the name of the supplier of the shipment or the name of the provider of other services, except that no information knowingly furnished or conveyed in response to such requirements may be stated in negative, blacklisting, or similar exclusionary terms, other than with respect to carriers or route of shipment as may be permitted by such regulations in order to comply with precautionary requirements protecting against war risks and confiscation;

(C) complying or agreeing to comply in the normal course of business with the unilateral and specific selection by a boycotting country, or national or resident thereof, of carriers, insurers, suppliers of services to be performed within the boycotting country or specific goods which, in the normal course of business, are identifiable by source when imported into the boycotting country;

(D) complying or agreeing to comply with export requirements of the boycotting country relating to shipments or transshipments of exports to the boycotted country, to any business concern of or organized under the laws of the boycotted country, or to any national or resident of the boycotted country;

(E) compliance by an individual or agreement by an individual to comply with the immigration or passport requirements of any country with respect to such individual or any member of such individual's family or with requests for information regarding requirements of employment of such individual within the boycotting country; and

(F) compliance by a United States person resident in a foreign country or agreement by such person to comply with the laws of that country with respect to his activities exclusively therein, and such regulations may contain exceptions for such resident complying with the laws or regulations of that foreign country governing imports into such country of trademarked, trade named, or similarly specifically identifiable products, or components of products for his own use, including the performance of contractual services within that country, as may be defined by such regulations.

(3) Regulations issued pursuant to paragraphs (2)(C) and (2)(F) shall not provide exceptions from paragraphs (1)(B) and (1)(C).

(4) Nothing in this subsection may be construed to supersede or limit the operation of the antitrust or civil rights laws of the United States.

(5) This section shall apply to any transaction or activity undertaken, by or through a United States person or any other person, with intent to evade the provisions of this section as implemented by the regulations issued pursuant to this subsection, and such regulations shall expressly provide that the exceptions set forth in paragraph (2) shall not permit activities or agreements (expressed or implied by a course of conduct, including a pattern of responses) otherwise prohibited, which are not within the intent of such exceptions.

(b) Foreign policy controls

(1) In addition to the regulations issued pursuant to subsection (a) of this section, regulations issued under section 6 of this Act [section 2405 of this Appendix] shall implement the policies set forth in section 3(5) [section 2402(5) of this Appendix].

(2) Such regulations shall require that any United States person receiving a request for the furnishing of information, the entering into or implementing of agreements, or the taking of any other action referred to in section 3(5) [section 2402(5) of this Appendix] shall report that fact to the Secretary, together with such other information concerning such request as the Secretary may require for such action as the Secretary considers appropriate for carrying out the policies of that section. Such person shall also report to the Secretary whether such person intends to comply and whether such person has complied with such request. Any report filed pursuant to this paragraph shall be made available promptly for public inspection and copying, except that information regarding the quantity, description, and value of any goods or technology to which such report relates may be kept confidential if the Secretary determines that disclosure thereof would place the United States person involved at a competitive disadvantage. The Secretary shall periodically transmit summaries of the information contained in such reports to the Secretary of State for such action as the Secretary of State, in consultation with the Secretary, considers appropriate for carrying out the policies set forth in section 3(5) of this Act [section 2402(5) of this Appendix].

(c) Preemption

The provisions of this section and the regulations issued pursuant thereto shall preempt any law, rule, or regulation of any of the several States or the District of Columbia, or any of the territories or possessions of the United States, or of any governmental subdivision thereof, which law, rule, or regulation pertains to participation in, compliance with, implementation of, or the furnishing of information regarding restrictive trade practices or boycotts fostered or imposed by foreign countries against other countries.

(Pub. L. 96–72, § 8, Sept. 29, 1979, 93 Stat. 521.)

REFERENCES IN TEXT

The antitrust laws of the United States, referred to in subsec. (a)(4), are classified generally to chapter 1 (§ 1 et seq.) of Title 15, Commerce and Trade.

The civil rights laws of the United States, referred to in subsec. (a)(4), are classified generally to chapter 21 (§ 1981 et seq.) of Title 42, The Public Health and Welfare.

PRIOR PROVISIONS

A prior section 2407, Pub. L. 91–184, § 8, Dec. 30, 1969, 83 Stat. 846; Pub. L. 95–52, title II, § 203(b), June 22, 1977, 91 Stat. 247, relating to exemption from administrative procedure and judicial review provisions, expired on Sept. 30, 1979.

DELEGATION OF FUNCTIONS

Functions conferred upon President under this section delegated to Secretary of Commerce by Ex. Ord. No. 12214, May 2, 1980, 45 F.R. 29783, set out under section 2403 of this Appendix.

SECTION REFERRED TO IN OTHER SECTIONS

This section is referred to in sections 2410, 2411, 2412, 2414 of this Appendix; title 19 section 3553; title 22 section 2679c.

§ 2408. Procedures for hardship relief from export controls

(a) Filing of petitions

Any person who, in such person's domestic manufacturing process or other domestic business operation, utilizes a product produced abroad in whole or in part from a good historically obtained from the United States but which has been made subject to export controls, or any person who historically has exported such a good, may transmit a petition of hardship to the Secretary requesting an exemption from such controls in order to alleviate any unique hardship resulting from the imposition of such controls. A petition under this section shall be in such form as the Secretary shall prescribe and shall contain information demonstrating the need for the relief requested.

(b) Decision of Secretary

Not later than 30 days after receipt of any petition under subsection (a), the Secretary shall transmit a written decision to the petitioner granting or denying the requested relief. Such decision shall contain a statement setting forth the Secretary's basis for the grant or denial. Any exemption granted may be subject to such conditions as the Secretary considers appropriate.

(c) Factors to be considered

For purposes of this section, the Secretary's decision with respect to the grant or denial of relief from unique hardship resulting directly or indirectly from the imposition of export controls shall reflect the Secretary's consideration of factors such as the following:

(1) Whether denial would cause a unique hardship to the petitioner which can be alleviated only by granting an exception to the applicable regulations. In determining whether relief shall be granted, the Secretary shall take into account—

(A) ownership of material for which there is no practicable domestic market by virtue of the location or nature of the material;

(B) potential serious financial loss to the applicant if not granted an exception;

(C) inability to obtain, except through import, an item essential for domestic use which is produced abroad from the good under control;

(D) the extent to which denial would conflict, to the particular detriment of the applicant, with other national policies including those reflected in any international agreement to which the United States is a party;

(E) possible adverse effects on the economy (including unemployment) in any locality or region of the United States; and

(F) other relevant factors, including the applicant's lack of an exporting history during any base period that may be established with respect to export quotas for the particular good.

(2) The effect a finding in favor of the applicant would have on attainment of the basic objectives of the short supply control program.

In all cases, the desire to sell at higher prices and thereby obtain greater profits shall not be considered as evidence of a unique hardship, nor will circumstances where the hardship is due to imprudent acts or failure to act on the part of the petitioner.

(Pub. L. 96–72, §9, Sept. 29, 1979, 93 Stat. 524.)

PRIOR PROVISIONS

A prior section 2408, Pub. L. 91–184, §9, Dec. 30, 1969, 83 Stat. 846, relating to providing information to exporters, expired on Sept. 30, 1979.

§2409. Procedures for processing export license applications; other inquiries

(a) Primary responsibility of Secretary

(1) All export license applications required under this Act [sections 2401 to 2420 of this Appendix] shall be submitted by the applicant to the Secretary. All determinations with respect to any such application shall be made by the Secretary, subject to the procedures provided in this section.

(2) It is the intent of the Congress that a determination with respect to any export license application be made to the maximum extent possible by the Secretary without referral of such application to any other department or agency of the Government.

(3) To the extent necessary, the Secretary shall seek information and recommendations from the Government departments and agencies concerned with aspects of United States domestic and foreign policies and operations having an important bearing on exports. Such departments and agencies shall cooperate fully in rendering such information and recommendations.

(b) Initial screening

Within 10 days after the date on which any export license application is submitted pursuant to subsection (a)(1), the Secretary shall—

(1) send the applicant an acknowledgment of the receipt of the application and the date of the receipt;

(2) submit to the applicant a written description of the procedures required by this section, the responsibilities of the Secretary and of other departments and agencies with respect to the application, and the rights of the applicant;

(3) return the application without action if the application is improperly completed or if additional information is required, with sufficient information to permit the application to be properly resubmitted, in which case if such application is resubmitted, it shall be treated as a new application for the purpose of calculating the time periods prescribed in this section;

(4) determine whether it is necessary to refer the application to any other department or agency and, if such referral is determined to be necessary, inform the applicant of any such department or agency to which the application will be referred; and

(5) determine whether it is necessary to submit the application to a multilateral review process, pursuant to a multilateral agreement, formal or informal, to which the United States is a party and, if so, inform the applicant of this requirement.

(c) Action on certain applications

Except as provided in subsection (*o*), in each case in which the Secretary determines that it is not necessary to refer an application to any other department or agency for its information and recommendations, a license shall be formally issued or denied within 60 days after a properly completed application has been submitted pursuant to this section.

(d) Referral to other departments and agencies

Except in the case of exports described in subsection (*o*), in each case in which the Secretary determines that it is necessary to refer an application to any other department or agency for its information and recommendations, the Secretary shall, within 20 days after the submission of a properly completed application—

(1) refer the application, together with all necessary analysis and recommendations of the Department of Commerce, concurrently to all such departments or agencies; and

(2) if the applicant so requests, provide the applicant with an opportunity to review for accuracy any documentation to be referred to any such department or agency with respect to such application for the purpose of describing the export in question in order to determine whether such documentation accurately describes the proposed export.

Notwithstanding the 10-day period set forth in subsection (b), in the case of exports described in subsection (*o*), in each case in which the Secretary determines that it is necessary to refer an application to any other department or agency for its information and recommendations, the Secretary shall, immediately upon receipt of the properly completed application, refer the application to such department or agency for its review. Such review shall be concurrent with that of the Department of Commerce.

(e) Action by other departments and agencies

(1) Any department or agency to which an application is referred pursuant to subsection (d) shall submit to the Secretary the information or recommendations requested with respect to the application. The information or recommendations shall be submitted within 20 days after the department or agency receives the application or, in the case of exports described in subsection (*o*), before the expiration of the time periods permitted by that subsection. Except as provided in paragraph (2), any such department or agency which does not submit its recommendations within the time period prescribed in the preceding sentence shall be deemed by the Secretary to have no objection to the approval of such application.

(2)(A) Except in the case of exports described in subsection (*o*), if the head of any such department or agency notifies the Secretary before the expiration of the time period provided in paragraph (1) for submission of its recommendations that more time is required for review by such department or agency, such department or agency shall have an additional 20-day period to submit its recommendations to the Secretary. If such department or agency does not submit its recommendations within the time period prescribed by the preceding sentence, it shall be deemed by the Secretary to have no objection to the approval of such application.

(B) In the case of exports described in subsection (*o*), if the head of any such department or agency notifies the Secretary, before the expiration of the 15-day period provided in subsection (*o*)(1), that more time is required for review by such department or agency, the Secretary shall notify the applicant, pursuant to subsection (*o*)(1)(C), that additional time is required to consider the application, and such department or agency shall have additional time to consider the application within the limits permitted by subsection (*o*)(2). If such department or agency does not submit its recommendations within the time periods permitted under subsection (*o*), it shall be deemed by the Secretary to have no objection to the approval of such application.

(f) Action by Secretary

(1) Within 60 days after receipt of the recommendations of other departments and agencies with respect to a license application, as provided in subsection (e), the Secretary shall formally issue or deny the license. In deciding whether to issue or deny a license, the Secretary shall take into account any recommendation of a department or agency with respect to the application in question. In cases where the Secretary receives conflicting recommendations, the Secretary shall, within the 60-day period provided for in this subsection, take such action as may be necessary to resolve such conflicting recommendations. The provisions of this paragraph shall not apply in the case of exports described in subsection (*o*).

(2) In cases where the Secretary receives questions or negative considerations or recommendations from any other department or agency with respect to an application, the Secretary shall, to the maximum extent consistent with the national security and foreign policy of the United States, inform the applicant in writing of the specific questions raised and any such negative considerations or recommendations. Before a final determination with respect to the application is made, the applicant shall be entitled—

(A) to respond in writing to such questions, considerations, or recommendations within 30 days after receipt of such information from the Secretary; and

(B) upon the filing of a written request with the Secretary within 15 days after the receipt of such information, to respond in person to the department or agency raising such questions, considerations, or recommendations.

The provisions of this paragraph shall not apply in the case of exports described in subsection (*o*).

(3) In cases where the Secretary has determined that an application should be denied, the applicant shall be informed in writing, within 5 days after such determination is made, of—

(A) the determination,

(B) the statutory basis for the proposed denial,

(C) the policies set forth in section 3 of this Act [section 2402 of this Appendix] which would be furthered by the proposed denial,

(D) what if any modifications in or restrictions on the goods or technology for which the license was sought would allow such export to be compatible with export controls imposed under this Act [sections 2401 to 2420 of this Appendix],

(E) which officers and employees of the Department of Commerce who are familiar with the application will be made reasonably available to the applicant for considerations with regard to such modifications or restrictions, if appropriate,

(F) to the extent consistent with the national security and foreign policy of the United States, the specific considerations which led to the determination to deny the application, and

(G) the availability of appeal procedures.

The Secretary shall allow the applicant at least 30 days to respond to the Secretary's determination before the license application is denied. In the event decisions on license applications are deferred inconsistent with the provisions of this section, the applicant shall be so informed in writing within 5 days after such deferral.

(4) If the Secretary determines that a particular application or set of applications is of exceptional importance and complexity, and that additional time is required for negotiations to modify the application or applications, the Secretary may extend any time period prescribed in this section. The Secretary shall notify the Congress and the applicant of such extension and the reasons therefor. The provisions of this paragraph shall not apply in the case of exports described in subsection (*o*).

(g) Special procedures for Secretary of Defense

(1) Notwithstanding any other provision of this section, the Secretary of Defense is authorized to review any proposed export of any goods or technology to any country to which exports are controlled for national security purposes and, whenever the Secretary of Defense determines that the export of such goods or technology will make a significant contribution, which would prove detrimental to the national security of the United States, to the military potential of any such country, to recommend to the President that such export be disapproved.

(2) Notwithstanding any other provision of law, the Secretary of Defense shall determine, in consultation with the Secretary, and confirm in writing the types and categories of transactions which should be reviewed by the Secretary of Defense in order to make a determination referred to in paragraph (1). Whenever a license or other authority is requested for the export to any country to which exports are controlled for national security purposes of goods or technology within any such type or category, the Secretary shall notify the Secretary of Defense of such request, and the Secretary may not issue any license or other authority pursuant to such request before the expiration of the period within which the President may disapprove such export. The Secretary of Defense shall carefully consider any notification submitted by the Secretary pursuant to this paragraph and, not later than 20 days after notification of the request, shall—

(A) recommend to the President and the Secretary that he disapprove any request for the export of the goods or technology involved to the particular country if the Secretary of Defense determines that the export of such goods or technology will make a significant contribution, which would prove detrimental to the national security of the United States, to the military potential of such country or any other country;

(B) notify the Secretary that he would recommend approval subject to specified conditions; or

(C) recommend to the Secretary that the export of goods or technology be approved.

Whenever the Secretary of Defense makes a recommendation to the President pursuant to paragraph (2)(A), the Secretary shall also submit his recommendation to the President on the request to export if the Secretary differs with the Secretary of Defense. If the President notifies the Secretary, within 20 days after receiving a recommendation from the Secretary of Defense, that he disapproves such export, no license or other authority may be issued for the export of such goods or technology to such country. If the Secretary of Defense fails to make a recommendation or notification under this paragraph within the 20-day period specified in the third sentence, or if the President, within 20 days after receiving a recommendation from the Secretary of Defense with respect to an export, fails to notify the Secretary that he approves or disapproves the export, the Secretary shall approve or deny the request for a license or other authority to export without such recommendation or notification.

(3) The Secretary shall approve or disapprove a license application, and issue or deny a license, in accordance with the provisions of this subsection, and, to the extent applicable, in accordance with the time periods and procedures otherwise set forth in this section.

(h) Multilateral controls

In any case in which an application, which has been finally approved under subsection (c), (f), or (g) of this section, is required to be submitted to a multilateral review process, pursuant to a multilateral agreement, formal or informal, to which the United States is a party, the license shall not be issued as prescribed in such subsections, but the Secretary shall notify the applicant of the approval of the application (and the date of such approval) by the Secretary subject to such multilateral review. The license shall be issued upon approval of the application under such multilateral review. If such multilateral review has not resulted in a determination with respect to the application within 40 days after such date, the Secretary's approval of the license shall be final and the license shall be issued, unless the Secretary determines that issuance of the license would prove detrimental to the national security of the United States. At the time at which the Secretary makes such a determination, the Secretary shall notify the applicant of the determination and shall notify the Congress of the determination, the reasons for the determination, the reasons for which the multilateral review could not be concluded within such 40-day period, and the actions planned or being taken by the United States Government to secure conclusion of the multilateral review. At the end of every 40-day period after such notification to Congress, the Secretary shall advise the applicant and the Congress of the status of the application, and shall report to the Congress in detail on the reasons for the further delay and any further actions being taken by the United States Government to secure conclusion of the multilateral review. In addition, at the time at which the Secretary issues or denies the license upon conclusion of the multilateral review, the Secretary shall notify the Congress of such issuance or denial and of the total time required for the multilateral review.

(i) Records

The Secretary and any department or agency to which any application is referred under this section shall keep accurate records with respect to all applications considered by the Secretary or by any such department or agency, including, in the case of the Secretary, any dissenting recommendations received from any such department or agency.

(j) Appeal and court action

(1) The Secretary shall establish appropriate procedures for any applicant to appeal to the Secretary the denial of an export license application of the applicant.

(2) In any case in which any action prescribed in this section is not taken on a license application within the time periods established by this section (except in the case of a time period extended under subsection (f)(4) of which the applicant is notified), the applicant may file a petition with the Secretary requesting compliance with the requirements of this section. When such petition is filed, the Secretary shall take immediate steps to correct the situation giving rise to the petition and shall immediately notify the applicant of such steps.

(3) If, within 20 days after a petition is filed under paragraph (2), the processing of the application has not been brought into conformity with the requirements of this section, or the application has been brought into conformity with such requirements but the Secretary has not so notified the applicant, the applicant may bring an action in an appropriate United States district court for a restraining order, a temporary or permanent injunction, or other appropriate relief, to require compliance with the requirements of this section. The United States district courts shall have jurisdiction to provide such relief, as appropriate.

(k) Changes in requirements for applications

Except as provided in subsection (b)(3) of this section, in any case in which, after a license application is submitted, the Secretary changes the requirements for such a license application, the Secretary may request appropriate additional information of the applicant, but the Secretary may not return the application to the applicant without action because it fails to meet the changed requirements.

(*l*) Other inquiries

(1) In any case in which the Secretary receives a written request asking for the proper classification of a good or technology on the control list, the Secretary shall, within 10 working days after receipt of the request, inform the person making the request of the proper classification.

(2) In any case in which the Secretary receives a written request for information about the applicability of export license requirements under this Act [sections 2401 to 2420 of this Appendix] to a proposed export transaction or series of transactions, the Secretary shall, within 30 days after receipt of the request, reply with that information to the person making the request.

(m) Small business assistance

Not later than 120 days after the date of the enactment of this subsection [July 12, 1985], the Secretary shall develop and transmit to the Congress a plan to assist small businesses in the export licensing application process under this Act [sections 2401 to 2420 of this Appendix]. The plan shall include, among other things, arrangements for counseling small businesses on filing applications and identifying goods or technology on the control list, proposals for seminars and conferences to educate small businesses on export controls and licensing procedures, and the preparation of informational brochures. The Secretary shall, not later than 120 days after the date of the enactment of the Export Enhancement Act of 1988 [Aug. 23, 1988], report to the Congress on steps taken to implement the plan developed under this subsection to assist small businesses in the export licensing application process.

(n) Reports on license applications

(1) Not later than 180 days after the date of the enactment of this subsection [July 12, 1985], and not later than the end of each 3-month period thereafter, the Secretary shall submit to the Committee on Foreign Affairs of the House of Representatives and to the Committee on Banking, Housing, and Urban Affairs of the Senate a report listing—

(A) all applications on which action was completed during the preceding 3-month period and which required a period longer than the period permitted under subsection (c), (f)(1), or (h) of this section, as the case may be, before notification of a decision to approve or deny the application was sent to the applicant; and

(B) in a separate section, all applications which have been in process for a period longer than the period permitted under subsection (c), (f)(1), or (h) of this section, as the case may be, and upon which final action has not been taken.

(2) With regard to each application, each listing shall identify—

(A) the application case number;

(B) the value of the goods or technology to which the application relates;

(C) the country of destination of the goods or technology;

(D) the date on which the application was received by the Secretary;

(E) the date on which the Secretary approved or denied the application;

(F) the date on which the notification of approval or denial of the application was sent to the applicant; and

(G) the total number of days which elapsed between receipt of the application, in its properly completed form, and the earlier of the last day of the 3-month period to which the report relates, or the date on which notification of approval or denial of the application was sent to the applicant.

(3) With respect to an application which was referred to other departments or agencies, the listing shall also include—

(A) the departments or agencies to which the application was referred;

(B) the date or dates of such referral; and

(C) the date or dates on which recommendations were received from those departments or agencies.

(4) With respect to an application referred to any other department or agency which did not

submit or has not submitted its recommendations on the application within the period permitted under subsection (e) of this section to submit such recommendations, the listing shall also include—

(A) the office responsible for processing the application and the position of the officer responsible for the office; and

(B) the period of time that elapsed before the recommendations were submitted or that has elapsed since referral of the application, as the case may be.

(5) Each report shall also provide an introduction which contains—

(A) a summary of the number of applications described in paragraph (1)(A) and (B) of this subsection, and the value of the goods or technology involved in the applications, grouped according to—

(i) the number of days which elapsed before action on the applications was completed, or which has elapsed without action on the applications being completed, as follows: 61 to 75 days, 76 to 90 days, 91 to 105 days, 106 to 120 days, and more than 120 days; and

(ii) the number of days which elapsed before action on the applications was completed, or which has elapsed without action on the applications being completed, beyond the period permitted under subsection (c), (f)(1), or (h) of this section for the processing of applications, as follows: not more than 15 days, 16 to 30 days, 31 to 45 days, 46 to 60 days, and more than 60 days; and

(B) a summary by country of destination of the number of applications described in paragraph (1)(A) and (B) of this subsection, and the value of the goods or technology involved in the applications, on which action was not completed within 60 days.

(*o*) Exports to members of Coordinating Committee

(1) Fifteen working days after the date of formal filing with the Secretary of an individual validated license application for the export of goods or technology to a country that maintains export controls on such goods or technology pursuant to the agreement of the governments participating in the group known as the Coordinating Committee, a license for the transaction specified in the application shall become valid and effective and the goods or technology are authorized for export pursuant to such license unless—

(A) the application has been otherwise approved by the Secretary, in which case it shall be valid and effective according to the terms of the approval;

(B) the application has been denied by the Secretary pursuant to this section and the applicant has been so informed, or the applicant has been informed, pursuant to subsection (f)(3) of this section, that the application should be denied; or

(C) the Secretary requires additional time to consider the application and the applicant has been so informed.

(2) In the event that the Secretary notifies an applicant pursuant to paragraph (1)(C) that more time is required to consider an individual validated license application, a license for the transaction specified in the application shall become valid and effective and the goods or technology are authorized for export pursuant to such license 30 working days after the date that such license application was formally filed with the Secretary unless—

(A) the application has been otherwise approved by the Secretary, in which case it shall be valid and effective according to the terms of the approval; or

(B) the application has been denied by the Secretary pursuant to this section and the applicant has been so informed, or the applicant has been informed, pursuant to subsection (f)(3) of this section, that the application should be denied.

(3) In reviewing an individual license application subject to this subsection, the Secretary shall evaluate the information set forth in the application and the reliability of the end-user.

(4) Nothing in this subsection shall affect the scope or availability of licenses authorizing multiple exports set forth in section 4(a)(2) of this Act [section 2403(a)(2) of this Appendix].

(5) The provisions of this subsection shall take effect 4 months after the date of the enactment of the Export Administration Amendments Act of 1985 [July 12, 1985].

(Pub. L. 96–72, § 10, Sept. 29, 1979, 93 Stat. 525; Pub. L. 99–64, title I, § 111, July 12, 1985, 99 Stat. 142; Pub. L. 100–418, title II, § 2425(a), (c), Aug. 23, 1988, 102 Stat. 1360, 1361.)

PRIOR PROVISIONS

A prior section 2409, Pub. L. 91–184, § 10, Dec. 30, 1969, 83 Stat. 846; Pub. L. 93–500, § 3(b), Oct. 29, 1974, 88 Stat. 1552; Pub. L. 93–608, § 2(1), Jan. 2, 1975, 88 Stat. 1971; Pub. L. 95–52, title I, § 116(a), (b)(2), June 22, 1977, 91 Stat. 241, 242, setting forth requirements respecting semiannual reports to President and Congress, expired on Sept. 30, 1979.

AMENDMENTS

1988—Subsec. (g)(2). Pub. L. 100–418, § 2425(a)(1)–(3), substituted "President and the Secretary" for "President" in subpar. (A), inserted before last sentence "Whenever the Secretary of Defense makes a recommendation to the President pursuant to paragraph (2)(A), the Secretary shall also submit his recommendation to the President on the request to export if the Secretary differs with the Secretary of Defense.", and inserted at end "If the Secretary of Defense fails to make a recommendation or notification under this paragraph within the 20-day period specified in the third sentence, or if the President, within 20 days after receiving a recommendation from the Secretary of Defense with respect to an export, fails to notify the Secretary that he approves or disapproves the export, the Secretary shall approve or deny the request for a license or other authority to export without such recommendation or notification."

Subsec. (g)(4). Pub. L. 100–418, § 2425(a)(4), struck out par. (4) which read as follows: "Whenever the President exercises his authority under this subsection to modify or overrule a recommendation made by the Secretary of Defense or exercises his authority to modify or overrule any recommendation made by the Secretary of Defense under subsection (c) or (d) of section 5 of this Act with respect to the list of goods and technologies controlled for national security purposes, the President shall promptly transmit to the Congress a statement indicating his decision, together with the recommendation of the Secretary of Defense."

Subsec. (m). Pub. L. 100–418, §2425(c), inserted sentence at end requiring the Secretary, not later than 120 days after Aug. 23, 1988, to report to Congress on steps taken to implement the plan developed to assist small businesses in the export licensing application process.

1985—Pub. L. 99–64, §111(e)(1), inserted "; other inquiries" in section catchline.

Subsec. (c). Pub. L. 99–94, §111(a)(2), (b)(1), substituted "Except as provided in subsection (*o*) of this section, in each case" for "In each case" and "60" for "90".

Subsec. (d). Pub. L. 99–64, §111(a)(3), (b)(2), substituted "Except in the case of exports described in subsection (*o*) of this section, in each case" for "In each case" and "20" for "30" in provisions preceding par. (1), and inserted flush provision following par. (2) relating to exports described in subsec. (*o*) when it becomes necessary to refer an application to another department or agency for information and recommendations.

Subsec. (e)(1). Pub. L. 99–64, §111(b)(3)(A), substituted "Any department or agency to which an application is referred pursuant to subsection (d) shall submit to the Secretary the information or recommendations requested with respect to the application" for "Any department or agency to which an application is referred pursuant to subsection (d) shall submit to the Secretary, within 30 days after its receipt of the application, the information or recommendations requested with respect to such application" and inserted sentence directing that information or recommendations be submitted within 20 days after the department or agency receives the application or, in the case of exports described in subsection (*o*), before the expiration of the time periods permitted by that subsection.

Subsec. (e)(2)(A). Pub. L. 99–64, §111(a)(3), (b)(3)(B)(i), designated existing provisions of par. (2) as subpar. (A) and substituted "Except in the case of exports described in subsection (*o*), if the head" for "If the head" and "20" for "30".

Subsec. (e)(2)(B). Pub. L. 99–64, §111(b)(3)(B)(ii), added subpar. (B).

Subsec. (f)(1). Pub. L. 99–64, §111(a)(2), (b)(4), substituted "60" for "90" in two places and inserted sentence providing that the provisions of this paragraph shall not apply in the case of exports described in subsection (*o*).

Subsec. (f)(2). Pub. L. 99–64, §111(c), inserted "in writing" after "inform the applicant", and substituted provisions describing the steps to which the applicant is entitled before a final determination with respect to the application is made and providing that the provisions of this paragraph shall not apply in the case of exports described in subsection (*o*), for provision that the Secretary accord the applicant an opportunity, before the final determination with respect to the application is made, to respond in writing to such questions, considerations, or recommendations.

Subsec. (f)(3). Pub. L. 99–64, §111(d), inserted two new sentences describing the content of the writing which the applicant is entitled to receive when the Secretary determines that an application should be denied and directing that the Secretary allow the applicant at least 30 days to respond to the Secretary's determination before the license application is denied, and struck out existing sentence which had provided: "In cases where the Secretary has determined that an application should be denied, the applicant shall be informed in writing, within 5 days after such determination is made, of the determination, of the statutory basis for denial, the policies set forth in section 3 of the Act [section 2402 of this Appendix] which would be furthered by denial, and, to the extent consistent with the national security and foreign policy of the United States, the specific considerations which led to the denial, and of the availability of appeal procedures."

Subsec. (f)(4). Pub. L. 99–64, §111(b)(4), inserted sentence providing that provisions of this paragraph shall not apply in the case of exports described in subsec. (*o*).

Subsec. (g)(2). Pub. L. 99–64, §111(a)(3), substituted "20" for "30" in provisions preceding subpar. (A) and in provisions following subpar. (C).

Subsec. (h). Pub. L. 99–64, §111(a)(1), substituted "40" for "60" wherever appearing.

Subsec. (j)(3). Pub. L. 99–64, §111(a)(3), substituted "20" for "30".

Subsecs. (k) to (*o*). Pub. L. 99–64, §111(e)(2), added subsecs. (k) to (*o*).

CHANGE OF NAME

Committee on Foreign Affairs of House of Representatives treated as referring to Committee on International Relations of House of Representatives by section 1(a) of Pub. L. 104–14, set out as a note preceding section 21 of Title 2, The Congress.

REGULATIONS

Section 19(b)(1) of Pub. L. 96–72 provided that: "Regulations implementing the provisions of section 10 of this Act [this section] shall be issued and take effect not later than July 1, 1980."

DELEGATION OF FUNCTIONS

Functions conferred upon President under this section delegated to Secretary of Commerce by Ex. Ord. No. 12214, May 2, 1980, 45 F.R. 29783, set out under section 2403 of this Appendix, with exception of functions conferred upon President under subsec. (g) of this section which were reserved to President.

SECTION REFERRED TO IN OTHER SECTIONS

This section is referred to in sections 2404, 2405, 2406, 2412, 2413, 2416 of this Appendix.

§2410. Violations

(a) In general

Except as provided in subsection (b) of this section, whoever knowingly violates or conspires to or attempts to violate any provision of this Act [sections 2401 to 2420 of this Appendix] or any regulation, order, or license issued thereunder shall be fined not more than five times the value of the exports involved or $50,000, whichever is greater, or imprisoned not more than 5 years, or both.

(b) Willful violations

(1) Whoever willfully violates or conspires to or attempts to violate any provision of this Act [sections 2401 to 2420 of this Appendix] or any regulation, order, or license issued thereunder, with knowledge that the exports involved will be used for the benefit of, or that the destination or intended destination of the goods or technology involved is, any controlled country or any country to which exports are controlled for foreign policy purposes—

(A) except in the case of an individual, shall be fined not more than five times the value of the exports involved or $1,000,000, whichever is greater; and

(B) in the case of an individual, shall be fined not more than $250,000, or imprisoned not more than 10 years, or both.

(2) Any person who is issued a validated license under this Act [sections 2401 to 2420 of this Appendix] for the export of any good or technology to a controlled country and who, with knowledge that such a good or technology is being used by such controlled country for military or intelligence gathering purposes contrary to the conditions under which the license was issued, willfully fails to report such use to the Secretary of Defense—

(A) except in the case of an individual, shall be fined not more than five times the value of the exports involved or $1,000,000, whichever is greater; and

(B) in the case of an individual, shall be fined not more than $250,000, or imprisoned not more than 5 years, or both.

(3) Any person who possesses any goods or technology—

(A) with the intent to export such goods or technology in violation of an export control imposed under section 5 or 6 of this Act [section 2404 or 2405 of this Appendix] or any regulation, order, or license issued with respect to such control, or

(B) knowing or having reason to believe that the goods or technology would be so exported,

shall, in the case of a violation of an export control imposed under section 5 [section 2404 of this Appendix] (or any regulation, order, or license issued with respect to such control), be subject to the penalties set forth in paragraph (1) of this subsection and shall, in the case of a violation of an export control imposed under section 6 [section 2405 of this Appendix] (or any regulation, order, or license issued with respect to such control), be subject to the penalties set forth in subsection (a).

(4) Any person who takes any action with the intent to evade the provisions of this Act [sections 2401 to 2420 of this Appendix] or any regulation, order, or license issued under this Act [sections 2401 to 2420 of this Appendix] shall be subject to the penalties set forth in subsection (a), except that in the case of an evasion of an export control imposed under section 5 or 6 of this Act [section 2404 or 2405 of this Appendix] (or any regulation, order, or license issued with respect to such control), such person shall be subject to the penalties set forth in paragraph (1) of this subsection.

(5) Nothing in this subsection or subsection (a) shall limit the power of the Secretary to define by regulations violations under this Act [sections 2401 to 2420 of this Appendix].

(c) Civil penalties; administrative sanctions

(1) The Secretary (and officers and employees of the Department of Commerce specifically designated by the Secretary) may impose a civil penalty not to exceed $10,000 for each violation of this Act [sections 2401 to 2420 of this Appendix] or any regulation, order, or license issued under this Act [sections 2401 to 2420 of this Appendix], either in addition to or in lieu of any other liability or penalty which may be imposed, except that the civil penalty for each such violation involving national security controls imposed under section 5 of this Act [section 2404 of this Appendix] or controls imposed on the export of defense articles and defense services under section 38 of the Arms Export Control Act [22 U.S.C. 2778] may not exceed $100,000.

(2)(A) The authority under this Act [sections 2401 to 2420 of this Appendix] to suspend or revoke the authority of any United States person to export goods or technology may be used with respect to any violation of the regulations issued pursuant to section 8(a) of this Act [section 2407(a) of this Appendix].

(B) Any administrative sanction (including any civil penalty or any suspension or revocation of authority to export) imposed under this Act [sections 2401 to 2420 of this Appendix] for a violation of the regulations issued pursuant to section 8(a) of this Act [section 2407(a) of this Appendix] may be imposed only after notice and opportunity for an agency hearing on the record in accordance with sections 554 through 557 of title 5, United States Code.

(C) Any charging letter or other document initiating administrative proceedings for the imposition of sanctions for violations of the regulations issued pursuant to section 8(a) of this Act [section 2407(a) of this Appendix] shall be made available for public inspection and copying.

(3) An exception may not be made to any order issued under this Act [sections 2401 to 2420 of this Appendix] which revokes the authority of a United States person to export goods or technology unless the Committee on Foreign Affairs of the House of Representatives and the Committee on Banking, Housing, and Urban Affairs of the Senate are first consulted concerning the exception.

(4) The President may by regulation provide standards for establishing levels of civil penalty provided in this subsection based upon the seriousness of the violation, the culpability of the violator, and the violator's record of cooperation with the Government in disclosing the violation.

(d) Payment of penalties

The payment of any penalty imposed pursuant to subsection (c) may be made a condition, for a period not exceeding one year after the imposition of such penalty, to the granting, restoration, or continuing validity of any export license, permission, or privilege granted or to be granted to the person upon whom such penalty is imposed. In addition, the payment of any penalty imposed under subsection (c) may be deferred or suspended in whole or in part for a period of time no longer than any probation period (which may exceed one year) that may be imposed upon such person. Such a deferral or suspension shall not operate as a bar to the collection of the penalty in the event that the conditions of the suspension, deferral, or probation are not fulfilled.

(e) Refunds

Any amount paid in satisfaction of any penalty imposed pursuant to subsection (c), or any amounts realized from the forfeiture of any property interest or proceeds pursuant to subsection (g), shall be covered into the Treasury as a miscellaneous receipt. The head of the department or agency concerned may, in his discretion, refund any such penalty imposed pursuant to subsection (c), within 2 years after payment, on the ground of a material error of fact or law in the imposition of the penalty. Notwithstanding section 1346(a) of title 28, United States Code, no action for the refund of any such penalty may be maintained in any court.

(f) Actions for recovery of penalties

In the event of the failure of any person to pay a penalty imposed pursuant to subsection (c), a civil action for the recovery thereof may, in the discretion of the head of the department or agency concerned, be brought in the name of the

United States. In any such action, the court shall determine de novo all issues necessary to the establishment of liability. Except as provided in this subsection and in subsection (d), no such liability shall be asserted, claimed, or recovered upon by the United States in any way unless it has previously been reduced to judgment.

(g) Forfeiture of property interest and proceeds

(1) Any person who is convicted under subsection (a) or (b) of a violation of an export control imposed under section 5 of this Act [section 2404 of this Appendix] (or any regulation, order, or license issued with respect to such control) shall, in addition to any other penalty, forfeit to the United States—

(A) any of that person's interest in, security of, claim against, or property or contractual rights of any kind in the goods or tangible items that were the subject of the violation;

(B) any of that person's interest in, security of, claim against, or property or contractual rights of any kind in tangible property that was used in the export or attempt to export that was the subject of the violation; and

(C) any of that person's property constituting, or derived from, any proceeds obtained directly or indirectly as a result of the violation.

(2) The procedures in any forfeiture under this subsection, and the duties and authority of the courts of the United States and the Attorney General with respect to any forfeiture action under this subsection or with respect to any property that may be subject to forfeiture under this subsection, shall be governed by the provisions of section 1963 of title 18, United States Code.

(h) Prior convictions

(1) No person convicted of a violation of this Act [sections 2401 to 2420 of this Appendix] (or any regulation, license, or order issued under this Act [sections 2401 to 2420 of this Appendix]), any regulation, license, or order issued under the International Emergency Economic Powers Act [50 U.S.C. 1701 et seq.], section 793, 794, or 798 of title 18, United States Code, section 4(b) of the Internal Security Act of 1950 (50 U.S.C. 783(b)),[1] or section 38 of the Arms Export Control Act (22 U.S.C. 2778) shall be eligible, at the discretion of the Secretary, to apply for or use any export license under this Act [sections 2401 to 2420 of this Appendix] for a period of up to 10 years from the date of the conviction. The Secretary may revoke any export license under this Act [sections 2401 to 2420 of this Appendix] in which such person has an interest at the time of the conviction.

(2) The Secretary may exercise the authority under paragraph (1) with respect to any person related, through affiliation, ownership, control, or position of responsibility, to any person convicted of any violation of law set forth in paragraph (1), upon a showing of such relationship with the convicted party, and subject to the procedures set forth in section 13(c) of this Act [section 2412(c) of this Appendix].

[1] See References in Text note below.

(i) Other authorities

Nothing in subsection (c), (d), (f), (g), or (h) limits—

(1) the availability of other administrative or judicial remedies with respect to violations of this Act [sections 2401 to 2420 of this Appendix], or any regulation, order, or license issued under this Act [sections 2401 to 2420 of this Appendix];

(2) the authority to compromise and settle administrative proceedings brought with respect to violations of this Act [sections 2401 to 2420 of this Appendix], or any regulation, order, or license issued under this Act [sections 2401 to 2420 of this Appendix]; or

(3) the authority to compromise, remit or mitigate seizures and forfeitures pursuant to section 1(b) of title VI of the Act of June 15, 1917 (22 U.S.C. 401(b)).

(Pub. L. 96–72, §11, Sept. 29, 1979, 93 Stat. 529; Pub. L. 97–145, §4(a)–(c), Dec. 29, 1981, 95 Stat. 1727; Pub. L. 99–64, title I, §112, July 12, 1985, 99 Stat. 146; Pub. L. 100–418, title II, §2426, Aug. 23, 1988, 102 Stat. 1361.)

REFERENCES IN TEXT

The International Emergency Economic Powers Act, referred to in subsec. (h)(1), is title II of Pub. L. 95–223, Dec. 28, 1977, 91 Stat. 1626, which is classified generally to chapter 35 (§1701 et seq.) of Title 50, War and National Defense. For complete classification of this Act to the Code, see Short Title note set out under section 1701 of Title 50 and Tables.

Section 4(b) of the Internal Security Act of 1950 (50 U.S.C. 783(b)), referred to in subsec. (h)(1), was redesignated as section 4(a) of that Act, 50 U.S.C. 783(a), by Pub. L. 103–199, title VIII, §803(2)(B), Dec. 17, 1993, 107 Stat. 2329.

PRIOR PROVISIONS

A prior section 2410, Pub. L. 91–184, §11, Dec. 30, 1969, 83 Stat. 846; Pub. L. 95–52, title II, §204, June 22, 1977, 91 Stat. 247, defining "person" and "United States person" for purposes of the Export Administration Act of 1969, expired on Sept. 30, 1979.

AMENDMENTS

1988—Subsec. (h). Pub. L. 100–418, §2426, designated existing provisions as par. (1), inserted "this Act (or any regulation, license, or order issued under this Act), any regulation, license, or order issued under the International Emergency Economic Powers Act," after "violation of", and added par. (2).

1985—Subsec. (a). Pub. L. 99–64, §112(a), inserted "or conspires to or attempts to violate".

Subsec. (b)(1). Pub. L. 99–64, §112(b)(1), in provisions preceding subpar. (A), substituted "Whoever willfully violates or conspires to or attempts to violate any provision of this Act or any regulation, order, or license issued thereunder, with knowledge that the exports involved will be used for the benefit of, or that the destination or intended destination of the goods or technology involved is, any controlled country or any country to which exports are controlled for foreign policy purposes" for "Whoever willfully exports anything contrary to any provision of this Act or any regulation, order, or license issued thereunder, with knowledge that such exports will be used for the benefit of any country to which exports are restricted for national security or foreign policy purposes".

Subsec. (b)(2). Pub. L. 99–64, §112(b)(2), struck out sentence which provided that for purposes of this paragraph, "controlled country" means any country described in section 620(f) of the Foreign Assistance Act of 1961.

Subsec. (b)(3) to (5). Pub. L. 99–64, §112(b)(3), added pars. (3) to (5).

Subsec. (c)(1). Pub. L. 99–64, §112(c)(1), substituted "Secretary (and officers and employees of the Department of Commerce specifically designated by the Secretary)" for "head of any department or agency exercising any functions under this Act, or any officer or employee of such department or agency specifically designated by the head thereof,".

Subsec. (c)(3), (4). Pub. L. 99–64, §112((c)(2), added pars. (3) and (4).

Subsec. (e). Pub. L. 99–64, §112(d), inserted ", or any amounts realized from the forfeiture of any property interest or proceeds pursuant to subsection (g)," after "Any amount paid in satisfaction of any penalty imposed pursuant to subsection (c)", and inserted "imposed pursuant to subsection (c)" after "refund any such penalty".

Subsecs. (g), (h). Pub. L. 99–64, §112(e)(2), added subsecs. (g) and (h). Former subsec. (g) redesignated (i).

Subsec. (i). Pub. L. 99–64, §112(e)(1), (f), redesignated former subsec. (g) as (i) and substituted "(f), (g), or (h)" for "or (f)" in provisions preceding par. (1).

1981—Subsec. (b)(1). Pub. L. 97–145, §4(a), in penalty provisions, substituted separate penalties for individuals and others in subpars. (A) and (B), for provisions prescribing a fine of not more than five times the value of the exports involved or $100,000, whichever was greater, or imprisonment of not more than 10 years, or both.

Subsec. (b)(2). Pub. L. 97–145, §4(b), in penalty provisions, substituted separate penalties for individuals and others in subpars. (A) and (B), for provisions prescribing a fine of not more than five times the value of the exports involved or $100,000, whichever was greater, or imprisonment for not more than 5 years, or both.

Subsec. (c)(1). Pub. L. 97–145, §3(c), inserted exception that the civil penalty for each violation involving national security controls imposed under section 2404 of this Appendix or controls imposed on the export of defense articles and defense services under section 2778 of title 22 may not exceed $100,000.

CHANGE OF NAME

Committee on Foreign Affairs of House of Representatives treated as referring to Committee on International Relations of House of Representatives by section 1(a) of Pub. L. 104–14, set out as a note preceding section 21 of Title 2, The Congress.

EFFECTIVE DATE OF 1981 AMENDMENT

Section 4(d) of Pub. L. 97–145 provided that: "The amendments made by this section [amending this section] apply with respect to violations occurring after the date of the enactment of this Act [Dec. 29, 1981]."

SECTION REFERRED TO IN OTHER SECTIONS

This section is referred to in sections 2410b, 2411, 2412, 2413 of this Appendix; title 18 sections 951, 1956; title 22 sections 2778, 2779a, 2780; title 50 section 2332.

§ 2410a. Multilateral export control violations

(a) Determination by the President

The President, subject to subsection (c), shall apply sanctions under subsection (b) for a period of not less than 2 years and not more than 5 years, if the President determines that—

(1) a foreign person has violated any regulation issued by a country to control exports for national security purposes pursuant to the agreement of the group known as the Coordinating Committee, and

(2) such violation has resulted in substantial enhancement of Soviet and East bloc capabilities in submarine or antisubmarine warfare, ballistic or antiballistic missile technology, strategic aircraft, command, control, communications and intelligence, or other critical technologies as determined by the President, on the advice of the National Security Council, to represent a serious adverse impact on the strategic balance of forces.

The President shall notify the Congress of each action taken under this section. This section, except subsections (h) and (j), applies only to violations that occur after the date of the enactment of the Export Enhancement Act of 1988 [Aug. 23, 1988].

(b) Sanctions

The sanctions referred to in subsection (a) shall apply to the foreign person committing the violation, as well as to any parent, affiliate, subsidiary, and successor entity of the foreign person, and, except as provided in subsection (c), are as follows:

(1) a prohibition on contracting with, and procurement of products and services from, a sanctioned person, by any department, agency, or instrumentality of the United States Government, and

(2) a prohibition on importation into the United States of all products produced by a sanctioned person.

(c) Exceptions

The President shall not apply sanctions under this section—

(1) in the case of procurement of defense articles or defense services—

(A) under existing contracts or subcontracts, including the exercise of options for production quantities to satisfy United States operational military requirements;

(B) if the President determines that the foreign person or other entity to which the sanctions would otherwise be applied is a sole source supplier of essential defense articles or services and no alternative supplier can be identified; or

(C) if the President determines that such articles or services are essential to the national security under defense coproduction agreements; or

(2) to—

(A) products or services provided under contracts or other binding agreements (as such terms are defined by the President in regulations) entered into before the date on which the President notifies the Congress of the intention to impose the sanctions;

(B) spare parts;

(C) component parts, but not finished products, essential to United States products or production;

(D) routine servicing and maintenance of products; or

(E) information and technology.

(d) Exclusion

The President shall not apply sanctions under this section to a parent, affiliate, subsidiary, and successor entity of a foreign person if the President determines that—

(1) the parent, affiliate, subsidiary, or successor entity (as the case may be) has not knowingly violated the export control regulation violated by the foreign person, and

(2) the government of the country with jurisdiction over the parent, affiliate, subsidiary, or successor entity had in effect, at the time of the violation by the foreign person, an effective export control system consistent with principles agreed to in the Coordinating Committee, including the following:

(A) national laws providing appropriate civil and criminal penalties and statutes of limitations sufficient to deter potential violations;

(B) a program to evaluate export license applications that includes sufficient technical expertise to assess the licensing status of exports and ensure the reliability of end-users;

(C) an enforcement mechanism that provides authority for trained enforcement officers to investigate and prevent illegal exports;

(D) a system of export control documentation to verify the movement of goods and technology; and

(E) procedures for the coordination and exchange of information concerning violations of the agreement of the Coordinating Committee.

(e) Definitions

For purposes of this section—

(1) the term "component part" means any article which is not usable for its intended functions without being imbedded in or integrated into any other product and which, if used in production of a finished product, would be substantially transformed in that process;

(2) the term "finished product" means any article which is usable for its intended functions without being imbedded or integrated into any other product, but in no case shall such term be deemed to include an article produced by a person other than a sanctioned person that contains parts or components of the sanctioned person if the parts or components have been substantially transformed during production of the finished product; and

(3) the term "sanctioned person" means a foreign person, and any parent, affiliate, subsidiary, or successor entity of the foreign person, upon whom sanctions have been imposed under this section.

(f) Subsequent modifications of sanctions

The President may, after consultation with the Congress, limit the scope of sanctions applied to a parent, affiliate, subsidiary, or successor entity of the foreign person determined to have committed the violation on account of which the sanctions were imposed if the President determines that—

(1) the parent, affiliate, subsidiary, or successor entity (as the case may be) has not, on the basis of available evidence, itself violated the export control regulation involved, either directly or through a course of conduct;

(2) the government with jurisdiction over the parent, affiliate, subsidiary, or successor entity has improved its export control system as measured by the criteria set forth in subsection (d)(2);

(3) the parent, affiliate, subsidiary, or successor entity, has instituted improvements in internal controls sufficient to detect and prevent violations of the export control regime implemented under paragraph (2); and

(4) the impact of the sanctions imposed on the parent, affiliate, subsidiary, or successor entity is proportionate to the increased defense expenditures imposed on the United States.

Notwithstanding the preceding sentence, the President may not limit the scope of the sanction referred to in subsection (b)(1) with respect to the parent of the foreign person determined to have committed the violation, until that sanction has been in effect for at least 2 years.

(g) Reports to Congress

The President shall include in the annual report submitted under section 14 [section 2413 of this Appendix], a report on the status of any sanctions imposed under this section, including any exceptions, exclusions, or modifications of sanctions that have been applied under subsection (c), (d), or (f).

(h) Discretionary imposition of sanctions

If the President determines that a foreign person has violated a regulation issued by a country to control exports for national security purposes pursuant to the agreement of the group known as the Coordinating Committee, but in a case in which subsection (a)(2) may not apply, the President may apply the sanctions referred to in subsection (b) against that foreign person for a period of not more than 5 years.

(i) Compensation for diversion of militarily critical technologies to controlled countries

(1) In cases in which sanctions have been applied against a foreign person under subsection (a), the President shall initiate discussions with the foreign person and the government with jurisdiction over that foreign person regarding compensation on the part of the foreign person in an amount proportionate to the costs of research and development and procurement of new defensive systems by the United States and the allies of the United States to counteract the effect of the technological advance achieved by the Soviet Union as a result of the violation by that foreign person.

(2) The President shall, at the time that discussions are initiated under paragraph (1), report to the Congress that such discussions are being undertaken, and shall report to the Congress the outcome of those discussions.

(j) Other actions by the President

Upon making a determination under subsection (a) or (h), the President shall—

(1) initiate consultations with the foreign government with jurisdiction over the foreign person who committed the violation involved, in order to seek prompt remedial action by that government;

(2) initiate discussions with the governments participating in the Coordinating Committee regarding the violation and means to ensure that similar violations do not occur; and

(3) consult with and report to the Congress on the nature of the violation and the actions the President proposes to take, or has taken, to rectify the situation.

(k) Damages for certain violations

(1) In any case in which the President makes a determination under subsection (a), the Secretary of Defense shall determine the costs of restoring the military preparedness of the United States on account of the violation involved. The Secretary of Defense shall notify the Attorney General of his determination, and the Attorney General may bring an action for damages, in any appropriate district court of the United States, to recover such costs against the person who committed the violation, any person that is owned or controlled by the person who committed the violation, and any person who owns and controls the person who committed the violation.

(3)[1] The total amount awarded in any case brought under paragraph (2)[1] shall be determined by the court in light of the facts and circumstances, but shall not exceed the amount of the net loss to the national security of the United States. An action under this subsection shall be commenced not later than 3 years after the violation occurs, or one year after the violation is discovered, whichever is later.

(*l*) Definition

For purposes of this section, the term "foreign person" means any person other than a United States person.

(Pub. L. 96–72, § 11A, as added Pub. L. 100–418, title II, § 2444, Aug. 23, 1988, 102 Stat. 1366.)

PROHIBITION ON PURCHASE OF TOSHIBA PRODUCTS FOR RESALE IN MILITARY EXCHANGE STORES

Pub. L. 101–165, title IX, § 9087, Nov. 21, 1989, 103 Stat. 1148, provided that during period beginning Nov. 21, 1989, and through Dec. 28, 1991, no product manufactured or assembled by Toshiba America, Inc., or Toshiba Corporation (or any of its affiliates or subsidiaries) may be purchased by the Department of Defense for the purpose of resale of such product in a military exchange store or in any other morale, welfare, recreation, or resale activity operated by the Department of Defense (either directly or by concessionaire), with an exception for microwave ovens manufactured or assembled in the United States. Similar provisions were contained in the following prior appropriation acts:

Pub. L. 100–463, title VIII, § 8092, Oct. 1, 1988, 102 Stat. 2270–34.

Pub. L. 100–456, div. A, title III, § 313, Sept. 29, 1988, 102 Stat. 1951.

MANDATORY SANCTIONS AGAINST TOSHIBA AND KONGSBERG

Sections 2442 and 2443 of Pub. L. 100–418 contained congressional statement of findings, directed President to impose, for a period of 3 years, (1) a prohibition on contracting with, and procurement of products and services from, Toshiba Machine Company and Kongsberg Trading Company, and any other foreign person whom President found to have knowingly facilitated the diversion of advanced milling machinery by Toshiba Machine Company and Kongsberg Trading Company to the Soviet Union, by any department, agency, or instrumentality of United States Government, and (2) a prohibition on importation into United States of all products produced by Toshiba Machine Company, Kongsberg Trading Company, and any such foreign person; and directed President to impose, for a period of 3 years, a prohibition on contracting with, and procurement of products and services from, the Toshiba Corporation and Kongsberg Vaapenfabrikk, by any department, agency, or instrumentality of the United States Government, with certain exceptions.

[1] So in original. Subsec. (k) was enacted without a par. (2).

§ 2410b. Missile proliferation control violations

(a) Violations by United States persons

(1) Sanctions

(A) If the President determines that a United States person knowingly—

(i) exports, transfers, or otherwise engages in the trade of any item on the MTCR Annex, in violation of the provisions of section 38 (22 U.S.C. 2778) or chapter 7 of the Arms Export Control Act [22 U.S.C. 2797 et seq.], section 5 or 6 of this Act [section 2404 or 2405 of this Appendix], or any regulations or orders issued under any such provisions,

(ii) conspires to or attempts to engage in such export, transfer, or trade, or

(iii) facilitates such export, transfer, or trade by any other person,

then the President shall impose the applicable sanctions described in subparagraph (B).

(B) The sanctions which apply to a United States person under subparagraph (A) are the following:

(i) If the item on the MTCR Annex involved in the export, transfer, or trade is missile equipment or technology within category II of the MTCR Annex, then the President shall deny to such United States person, for a period of 2 years, licenses for the transfer of missile equipment or technology controlled under this Act [sections 2401 to 2420 of this Appendix].

(ii) If the item on the MTCR Annex involved in the export, transfer, or trade is missile equipment or technology within category I of the MTCR Annex, then the President shall deny to such United States person, for a period of not less than 2 years, all licenses for items the export of which is controlled under this Act [sections 2401 to 2420 of this Appendix].

(2) Discretionary sanctions

In the case of any determination referred to in paragraph (1), the Secretary may pursue any other appropriate penalties under section 11 of this Act [section 2410 of this Appendix].

(3) Waiver

The President may waive the imposition of sanctions under paragraph (1) on a person with respect to a product or service if the President certifies to the Congress that—

(A) the product or service is essential to the national security of the United States; and

(B) such person is a sole source supplier of the product or service, the product or service is not available from any alternative reliable supplier, and the need for the product or service cannot be met in a timely manner by improved manufacturing processes or technological developments.

(b) Transfers of missile equipment or technology by foreign persons

(1) Sanctions

(A) Subject to paragraphs (3) through (7), if the President determines that a foreign person, after the date of the enactment of this section [Nov. 5, 1990], knowingly—

(i) exports, transfers, or otherwise engages in the trade of any MTCR equipment or technology that contributes to the design, development, or production of missiles in a country that is not an MTCR adherent and would be, if it were United States-origin equipment or technology, subject to the jurisdiction of the United States under this Act [sections 2401 to 2420 of this Appendix],

(ii) conspires to or attempts to engage in such export, transfer, or trade, or

(iii) facilitates such export, transfer, or trade by any other person,

or if the President has made a determination with respect to a foreign person under section 73(a) of the Arms Export Control Act [22 U.S.C. 2797b(a)], then the President shall impose on that foreign person the applicable sanctions under subparagraph (B).

(B) The sanctions which apply to a foreign person under subparagraph (A) are the following:

(i) If the item involved in the export, transfer, or trade is within category II of the MTCR Annex, then the President shall deny, for a period of 2 years, licenses for the transfer to such foreign person of missile equipment or technology the export of which is controlled under this Act [sections 2401 to 2420 of this Appendix].

(ii) If the item involved in the export, transfer, or trade is within category I of the MTCR Annex, then the President shall deny, for a period of not less than 2 years, licenses for the transfer to such foreign person of items the export of which is controlled under this Act [sections 2401 to 2420 of this Appendix].

(iii) If, in addition to actions taken under clauses (i) and (ii), the President determines that the export, transfer, or trade has substantially contributed to the design, development, or production of missiles in a country that is not an MTCR adherent, then the President shall prohibit, for a period of not less than 2 years, the importation into the United States of products produced by that foreign person.

(2) Inapplicability with respect to MTCR adherents

Paragraph (1) does not apply with respect to—

(A) any export, transfer, or trading activity that is authorized by the laws of an MTCR adherent, if such authorization is not obtained by misrepresentation or fraud; or

(B) any export, transfer, or trade of an item to an end user in a country that is an MTCR adherent.

(3) Effect of enforcement actions by MTCR adherents

Sanctions set forth in paragraph (1) may not be imposed under this subsection on a person with respect to acts described in such paragraph or, if such sanctions are in effect against a person on account of such acts, such sanctions shall be terminated, if an MTCR adherent is taking judicial or other enforcement action against that person with respect to such acts, or that person has been found by the government of an MTCR adherent to be innocent of wrongdoing with respect to such acts.

(4) Advisory opinions

The Secretary, in consultation with the Secretary of State and the Secretary of Defense, may, upon the request of any person, issue an advisory opinion to that person as to whether a proposed activity by that person would subject that person to sanctions under this subsection. Any person who relies in good faith on such an advisory opinion which states that the proposed activity would not subject a person to such sanctions, and any person who thereafter engages in such activity, may not be made subject to such sanctions on account of such activity.

(5) Waiver and report to Congress

(A) In any case other than one in which an advisory opinion has been issued under paragraph (4) stating that a proposed activity would not subject a person to sanctions under this subsection, the President may waive the application of paragraph (1) to a foreign person if the President determines that such waiver is essential to the national security of the United States.

(B) In the event that the President decides to apply the waiver described in subparagraph (A), the President shall so notify the Congress not less than 20 working days before issuing the waiver. Such notification shall include a report fully articulating the rationale and circumstances which led the President to apply the waiver.

(6) Additional waiver

The President may waive the imposition of sanctions under paragraph (1) on a person with respect to a product or service if the President certifies to the Congress that—

(A) the product or service is essential to the national security of the United States; and

(B) such person is a sole source supplier of the product or service, the product or service is not available from any alternative reliable supplier, and the need for the product or service cannot be met in a timely manner by improved manufacturing processes or technological developments.

(7) Exceptions

The President shall not apply the sanction under this subsection prohibiting the importation of the products of a foreign person—

(A) in the case of procurement of defense articles or defense services—

(i) under existing contracts or subcontracts, including the exercise of options for production quantities to satisfy requirements essential to the national security of the United States;

(ii) if the President determines that the person to which the sanctions would be applied is a sole source supplier of the defense articles and services, that the defense articles or services are essential to the national security of the United States, and that alternative sources are not readily or reasonably available; or

(iii) if the President determines that such articles or services are essential to the national security of the United States under defense coproduction agreements or NATO Programs of Cooperation;

(B) to products or services provided under contracts entered into before the date on which the President publishes his intention to impose the sanctions; or

(C) to—

(i) spare parts,

(ii) component parts, but not finished products, essential to United States products or production,

(iii) routine services and maintenance of products, to the extent that alternative sources are not readily or reasonably available, or

(iv) information and technology essential to United States products or production.

(c) Definitions

For purposes of this section and subsections (k) and (*l*) of section 6 [section 2405(k) and (*l*) of this Appendix]—

(1) the term "missile" means a category I system as defined in the MTCR Annex, and any other unmanned delivery system of similar capability, as well as the specially designed production facilities for these systems;

(2) the term "Missile Technology Control Regime" or "MTCR" means the policy statement, between the United States, the United Kingdom, the Federal Republic of Germany, France, Italy, Canada, and Japan, announced on April 16, 1987, to restrict sensitive missile-relevant transfers based on the MTCR Annex, and any amendments thereto;

(3) the term "MTCR adherent" means a country that participates in the MTCR or that, pursuant to an international understanding to which the United States is a party, controls MTCR equipment or technology in accordance with the criteria and standards set forth in the MTCR;

(4) the term "MTCR Annex" means the Guidelines and Equipment and Technology Annex of the MTCR, and any amendments thereto;

(5) the terms "missile equipment or technology" and "MTCR equipment or technology" mean those items listed in category I or category II of the MTCR Annex;

(6) the term "foreign person" means any person other than a United States person;

(7)(A) the term "person" means a natural person as well as a corporation, business association, partnership, society, trust, any other nongovernmental entity, organization, or group, and any governmental entity operating as a business enterprise, and any successor of any such entity; and

(B) in the case of countries where it may be impossible to identify a specific governmental entity referred to in subparagraph (A), the term "person" means—

(i) all activities of that government relating to the development or production of any missile equipment or technology; and

(ii) all activities of that government affecting the development or production of aircraft, electronics, and space systems or equipment; and

(8) the term "otherwise engaged in the trade of" means, with respect to a particular export or transfer, to be a freight forwarder or designated exporting agent, or a consignee or end user of the item to be exported or transferred.

(Pub. L. 96–72, §11B, as added Pub. L. 101–510, div. A, title XVII, §1702(b), Nov. 5, 1990, 104 Stat. 1741.)

REFERENCES IN TEXT

The Arms Export Control Act, referred to in subsec. (a)(1)(A)(i), is Pub. L. 90–269, Oct. 22, 1968, 82 Stat. 1320, as amended. Chapter 7 of the Act is classified generally to subchapter VII (§2797 et seq.) of chapter 39 of Title 22, Foreign Relations and Intercourse. For complete classification of this Act to the Code, see Short Title note set out under section 2751 of Title 22 and Tables.

DELEGATION OF FUNCTIONS

Functions of President under this section delegated to Secretary of Commerce, with certain exceptions, by section 2(b) of Ex. Ord. No. 12851, June 11, 1993, 58 F.R. 33181, set out as a note under section 2797 of Title 22, Foreign Relations and Intercourse.

SECTION REFERRED TO IN OTHER SECTIONS

This section is referred to in title 22 sections 2375, 2797b.

§2410c. Chemical and biological weapons proliferation sanctions

(a) Imposition of sanctions

(1) Determination by the President

Except as provided in subsection (b)(2), the President shall impose both of the sanctions described in subsection (c) if the President determines that a foreign person, on or after October 28, 1991, has knowingly and materially contributed—

(A) through the export from the United States of any goods or technology that are subject to the jurisdiction of the United States under this Act [sections 2401 to 2420 of this Appendix], or

(B) through the export from any other country of any goods or technology that would be, if they were United States goods or technology, subject to the jurisdiction of the United States under this Act [sections 2401 to 2420 of this Appendix],

to the efforts by any foreign country, project, or entity described in paragraph (2) to use, develop, produce, stockpile, or otherwise acquire chemical or biological weapons.

(2) Countries, projects, or entities receiving assistance

Paragraph (1) applies in the case of—

(A) any foreign country that the President determines has, at any time after January 1, 1980—

(i) used chemical or biological weapons in violation of international law;

(ii) used lethal chemical or biological weapons against its own nationals; or

(iii) made substantial preparations to engage in the activities described in clause (i) or (ii);

(B) any foreign country whose government is determined for purposes of section 6(j) of this Act [section 2405(j) of this Appendix] to be a government that has repeatedly provided support for acts of international terrorism; or

(C) any other foreign country, project, or entity designated by the President for purposes of this section.

(3) Persons against which sanctions are to be imposed

Sanctions shall be imposed pursuant to paragraph (1) on—

(A) the foreign person with respect to which the President makes the determination described in that paragraph;

(B) any successor entity to that foreign person;

(C) any foreign person that is a parent or subsidiary of that foreign person if that parent or subsidiary knowingly assisted in the activities which were the basis of that determination; and

(D) any foreign person that is an affiliate of that foreign person if that affiliate knowingly assisted in the activities which were the basis of that determination and if that affiliate is controlled in fact by that foreign person.

(b) Consultations with and actions by foreign government of jurisdiction

(1) Consultations

If the President makes the determinations described in subsection (a)(1) with respect to a foreign person, the Congress urges the President to initiate consultations immediately with the government with primary jurisdiction over that foreign person with respect to the imposition of sanctions pursuant to this section.

(2) Actions by government of jurisdiction

In order to pursue such consultations with that government, the President may delay imposition of sanctions pursuant to this section for a period of up to 90 days. Following these consultations, the President shall impose sanctions unless the President determines and certifies to the Congress that that government has taken specific and effective actions, including appropriate penalties, to terminate the involvement of the foreign person in the activities described in subsection (a)(1). The President may delay imposition of sanctions for an additional period of up to 90 days if the President determines and certifies to the Congress that that government is in the process of taking the actions described in the preceding sentence.

(3) Report to Congress

The President shall report to the Congress, not later than 90 days after making a determination under subsection (a)(1), on the status of consultations with the appropriate government under this subsection, and the basis for any determination under paragraph (2) of this subsection that such government has taken specific corrective actions.

(c) Sanctions

(1) Description of sanctions

The sanctions to be imposed pursuant to subsection (a)(1) are, except as provided in paragraph (2) of this subsection, the following:

(A) Procurement sanction

The United States Government shall not procure, or enter into any contract for the procurement of, any goods or services from any person described in subsection (a)(3).

(B) Import sanctions

The importation into the United States of products produced by any person described in subsection (a)(3) shall be prohibited.

(2) Exceptions

The President shall not be required to apply or maintain sanctions under this section—

(A) in the case of procurement of defense articles or defense services—

(i) under existing contracts or subcontracts, including the exercise of options for production quantities to satisfy United States operational military requirements;

(ii) if the President determines that the person or other entity to which the sanctions would otherwise be applied is a sole source supplier of the defense articles or services, that the defense articles or services are essential, and that alternative sources are not readily or reasonably available; or

(iii) if the President determines that such articles or services are essential to the national security under defense coproduction agreements;

(B) to products or services provided under contracts entered into before the date on which the President publishes his intention to impose sanctions;

(C) to—

(i) spare parts,

(ii) component parts, but not finished products, essential to United States products or production, or

(iii) routine servicing and maintenance of products, to the extent that alternative sources are not readily or reasonably available;

(D) to information and technology essential to United States products or production; or

(E) to medical or other humanitarian items.

(d) Termination of sanctions

The sanctions imposed pursuant to this section shall apply for a period of at least 12 months following the imposition of sanctions and shall cease to apply thereafter only if the President determines and certifies to the Congress that reliable information indicates that the foreign person with respect to which the determination was made under subsection (a)(1) has ceased to aid or abet any foreign government, project, or entity in its efforts to acquire chemical or biological weapons capability as described in that subsection.

(e) Waiver

(1) Criterion for waiver

The President may waive the application of any sanction imposed on any person pursuant to this section, after the end of the 12-month period beginning on the date on which that sanction was imposed on that person, if the President determines and certifies to the Congress that such waiver is important to the national security interests of the United States.

(2) Notification of and report to Congress

If the President decides to exercise the waiver authority provided in paragraph (1), the President shall so notify the Congress not less than 20 days before the waiver takes effect. Such notification shall include a report fully articulating the rationale and circumstances which led the President to exercise the waiver authority.

(f) Definition of foreign person

For the purposes of this section, the term "foreign person" means—

(1) an individual who is not a citizen of the United States or an alien admitted for permanent residence to the United States; or

(2) a corporation, partnership, or other entity which is created or organized under the laws of a foreign country or which has its principal place of business outside the United States.

(Pub. L. 96–72, § 11C, as added and amended Pub. L. 102–182, title III, §§ 305(a), 309(b)(1), Dec. 4, 1991, 105 Stat. 1247, 1258.)

PRIOR PROVISIONS

A prior section 2410c, Pub. L. 96–72, § 11C, as added Pub. L. 102–138, title V, § 505(a), Oct. 28, 1991, 105 Stat. 724, contained provisions substantially identical to those added by section 305(a) of Pub. L. 102–182, prior to repeal by Pub. L. 102–182, § 309(a).

AMENDMENTS

1991—Subsec. (a)(1). Pub. L. 102–182, § 309(b)(1), substituted "October 28, 1991" for reference to the "date of the enactment of this section" which was enacted Dec. 4, 1991.

DELEGATION OF FUNCTIONS

Functions of President under this section delegated to Secretary of State, with certain exceptions, by section 1(a) of Ex. Ord. No. 12851, June 11, 1993, 58 F.R. 33181, set out as a note under section 2797 of Title 22, Foreign Relations and Intercourse.

SECTION REFERRED TO IN OTHER SECTIONS

This section is referred to in section 2405 of this Appendix.

§ 2411. Enforcement

(a) General authority

(1) To the extent necessary or appropriate to the enforcement of this Act [sections 2401 to 2420 of this Appendix] or to the imposition of any penalty, forfeiture, or liability arising under the Export Control Act of 1949 [former sections 2021 to 2032 of this Appendix] or the Export Administration Act of 1969 [former sections 2401 to 2413 of this Appendix], the head of any department or agency exercising any function thereunder (and officers or employees of such department or agency specifically designated by the head thereof) may make such investigations within the United States, and the Commissioner of Customs (and officers or employees of the United States Customs Service specifically designated by the Commissioner) may make such investigations outside of the United States, and the head of such department or agency (and such officers or employees) may obtain such information from, require such reports or the keeping of such records by, make such inspection of the books, records, and other writings, premises, or property of, and take the sworn testimony of, any person. In addition, such officers or employees may administer oaths or affirmations, and may by subpena require any person to appear and testify or to appear and produce books, records, and other writings, or both, and in the case of contumacy by, or refusal to obey a subpena issued to, any such person, a district court of the United States, after notice to any such person and hearing, shall have jurisdiction to issue an order requiring such person to appear and give testimony or to appear and produce books, records, and other writings, or both, and any failure to obey such order of the court may be punished by such court as a contempt thereof. In addition to the authority conferred by this paragraph, the Secretary (and officers or employees of the Department of Commerce designated by the Secretary) may conduct, outside the United States, pre-license investigations and post-shipment verifications of items licensed for export, and investigations in the enforcement of section 8 of this Act [section 2407 of this Appendix].

(2)(A) Subject to subparagraph (B) of this paragraph, the United States Customs Service is authorized, in the enforcement of this Act [sections 2401 to 2420 of this Appendix], to search, detain (after search), and seize goods or technology at those ports of entry or exit from the United States where officers of the Customs Service are authorized by law to conduct such searches, detentions, and seizures, and at those places outside the United States where the Customs Service, pursuant to agreements or other arrangements with other countries, is authorized to perform enforcement activities.

(B) An officer of the United States Customs Service may do the following in carrying out enforcement authority under this Act [sections 2401 to 2420 of this Appendix]:

(i) Stop, search, and examine a vehicle, vessel, aircraft, or person on which or whom such officer has reasonable cause to suspect there are any goods or technology that has been, is being, or is about to be exported from the United States in violation of this Act [sections 2401 to 2420 of this Appendix].

(ii) Search any package or container in which such officer has reasonable cause to suspect there are any goods or technology that has been, is being, or is about to be exported from the United States in violation of this Act [sections 2401 to 2420 of this Appendix].

(iii) Detain (after search) or seize and secure for trial any goods or technology on or about such vehicle, vessel, aircraft, or person, or in such package or container, if such officer has probable cause to believe the goods or technology has been, is being, or is about to be exported from the United States in violation of this Act [sections 2401 to 2420 of this Appendix].

(iv) Make arrests without warrant for any violation of this Act [sections 2401 to 2420 of this Appendix] committed in his or her presence or view or if the officer has probable cause to believe that the person to be arrested has committed or is committing such a violation.

The arrest authority conferred by clause (iv) of this subparagraph is in addition to any arrest authority under other laws. The Customs Service may not detain for more than 20 days any shipment of goods or technology eligible for export under a general license under section 4(a)(3) [section 2403(a)(3) of this Appendix]. In a case in which such detention is on account of a disagreement between the Secretary and the head of any other department or agency with export license authority under other provisions of law concerning the export license requirements for such goods or technology, such disagreement shall be resolved within that 20-day period. At the end of that 20-day period, the Customs Service shall either release the goods or technology, or seize the goods or technology as authorized by other provisions of law.

(3)(A) Subject to subparagraph (B) of this paragraph, the Secretary shall have the responsibility for the enforcement of section 8 of this Act [section 2407 of this Appendix] and, in the enforcement of the other provisions of this Act [sections 2401 to 2420 of this Appendix], the Secretary is authorized to search, detain (after search), and seize goods or technology at those places within the United States other than those ports specified in paragraph (2)(A) of this subsection. The search, detention (after search), or seizure of goods or technology at those ports and places specified in paragraph (2)(A) may be conducted by officers or employees of the Department of Commerce designated by the Secretary with the concurrence of the Commissioner of Customs or a person designated by the Commissioner.

(B) The Secretary may designate any employee of the Office of Export Enforcement of the Department of Commerce to do the following in carrying out enforcement authority under this Act [sections 2401 to 2420 of this Appendix]:

(i) Execute any warrant or other process issued by a court or officer of competent jurisdiction with respect to the enforcement of the provisions of this Act [sections 2401 to 2420 of this Appendix].

(ii) Make arrests without warrant for any violation of this Act [sections 2401 to 2420 of this Appendix] committed in his or her presence or view, or if the officer or employee has probable cause to believe that the person to be arrested has committed or is committing such a violation.

(iii) Carry firearms in carrying out any activity described in clause (i) or (ii).

(4) The authorities first conferred by the Export Administration Amendments Act of 1985 under paragraph (3) shall be exercised pursuant to guidelines approved by the Attorney General. Such guidelines shall be issued not later than 120 days after the date of the enactment of the Export Administration Amendments Act of 1985 [July 12, 1985].

(5) All cases involving violations of this Act [sections 2401 to 2420 of this Appendix] shall be referred to the Secretary for purposes of determining civil penalties and administrative sanctions under section 11(c) of this Act [section 2410(c) of this Appendix], or to the Attorney General for criminal action in accordance with this Act [sections 2401 to 2420 of this Appendix].

(6) Notwithstanding any other provision of law, the United States Customs Service may expend in the enforcement of export controls under this Act [sections 2401 to 2420 of this Appendix] not more than $12,000,000 in the fiscal year 1985 and not more than $14,000,000 in the fiscal year 1986.

(7) Not later than 90 days after the date of the enactment of the Export Administration Amendments Act of 1985 [July 12, 1985], the Secretary, with the concurrence of the Secretary of the Treasury, shall publish in the Federal Register procedures setting forth, in accordance with this subsection, the responsibilities of the Department of Commerce and the United States Customs Service in the enforcement of this Act [sections 2401 to 2420 of this Appendix]. In addition, the Secretary, with the concurrence of the Secretary of the Treasury, may publish procedures for the sharing of information in accordance with subsection (c)(3) of this section, and procedures for the submission to the appropriate departments and agencies by private persons of information relating to the enforcement of this Act [sections 2401 to 2420 of this Appendix].

(8) For purposes of this section, a reference to the enforcement of this Act [sections 2401 to 2420 of this Appendix] or to a violation of this Act [sections 2401 to 2420 of this Appendix] includes a reference to the enforcement or a violation of any regulation, order, or license issued under this Act [sections 2401 to 2420 of this Appendix].

(b) Immunity

No person shall be excused from complying with any requirements under this section because of his privilege against self-incrimination, but the immunity provisions of section 6002 of title 18, United States Code, shall apply with respect to any individual who specifically claims such privilege.

(c) Confidentiality

(1) Except as otherwise provided by the third sentence of section 8(b)(2) [section 2407(b)(2) of this Appendix] and by section 11(c)(2)(C) of this Act [section 2410(c)(2)(C) of this Appendix], information obtained under this Act [sections 2401 to 2420 of this Appendix] on or before June 30, 1980, which is deemed confidential, including Shippers' Export Declarations, or with reference to which a request for confidential treatment is made by the person furnishing such information, shall be exempt from disclosure under section 552 of title 5, United States Code, and such information shall not be published or disclosed unless the Secretary determines that the withholding thereof is contrary to the national interest. In-

formation obtained under this Act [sections 2401 to 2420 of this Appendix] after June 30, 1980, may be withheld only to the extent permitted by statute, except that information obtained for the purpose of consideration of, or concerning, license applications under this Act [sections 2401 to 2420 of this Appendix] shall be withheld from public disclosure unless the release of such information is determined by the Secretary to be in the national interest. Enactment of this subsection shall not affect any judicial proceeding commenced under section 552 of title 5, United States Code, to obtain access to boycott reports submitted prior to October 31, 1976, which was pending on May 15, 1979; but such proceeding shall be continued as if this Act [sections 2401 to 2420 of this Appendix] had not been enacted.

(2) Nothing in this Act [sections 2401 to 2420 of this Appendix] shall be construed as authorizing the withholding of information from the Congress or from the General Accounting Office. All information obtained at any time under this Act [sections 2401 to 2420 of this Appendix] or previous Acts regarding the control of exports, including any report or license application required under this Act [sections 2401 to 2420 of this Appendix], shall be made available to any committee or subcommittee of Congress of appropriate jurisdiction upon request of the chairman or ranking minority member of such committee or subcommittee. No such committee or subcommittee, or member thereof, shall disclose any information obtained under this Act [sections 2401 to 2420 of this Appendix] or previous Acts regarding the control of exports which is submitted on a confidential basis unless the full committee determines that the withholding of that information is contrary to the national interest. Notwithstanding paragraph (1) of this subsection, information referred to in the second sentence of this paragraph shall, consistent with the protection of intelligence, counterintelligence, and law enforcement sources, methods, and activities, as determined by the agency that originally obtained the information, and consistent with the provisions of section 313 of the Budget and Accounting Act 1921 [31 U.S.C. 716], be made available only by that agency, upon request, to the Comptroller General of the United States or to any officer or employee of the General Accounting Office who is authorized by the Comptroller General to have access to such information. No officer or employee of the General Accounting Office shall disclose, except to the Congress in accordance with this paragraph, any such information which is submitted on a confidential basis and from which any individual can be identified.

(3) Any department or agency which obtains information which is relevant to the enforcement of this Act [sections 2401 to 2420 of this Appendix], including information pertaining to any investigation, shall furnish such information to each department or agency with enforcement responsibilities under this Act [sections 2401 to 2420 of this Appendix] to the extent consistent with the protection of intelligence, counterintelligence, and law enforcement sources, methods, and activities. The provisions of this paragraph shall not apply to information subject to the restrictions set forth in section 9 of title 13, United States Code; and return information, as defined in subsection (b) of section 6103 of the Internal Revenue Code of 1986 [26 U.S.C. 6103(b)], may be disclosed only as authorized by such section. The Secretary and the Commissioner of Customs, upon request, shall exchange any licensing and enforcement information with each other which is necessary to facilitate enforcement efforts and effective license decisions. The Secretary, the Attorney General, and the Commissioner of Customs shall consult on a continuing basis with one another and with the heads of other departments and agencies which obtain information subject to this paragraph, in order to facilitate the exchange of such information.

(d) Reporting requirements

In the administration of this Act [sections 2401 to 2420 of this Appendix], reporting requirements shall be so designed as to reduce the cost of reporting, recordkeeping, and export documentation required under this Act [sections 2401 to 2420 of this Appendix] to the extent feasible consistent with effective enforcement and compilation of useful trade statistics. Reporting, recordkeeping, and export documentation requirements shall be periodically reviewed and revised in the light of developments in the field of information technology.

(e) Simplification of regulations

The Secretary, in consultation with appropriate United States Government departments and agencies and with appropriate technical advisory committees established under section 5(h) [section 2404(h) of this Appendix], shall review the regulations issued under this Act [sections 2401 to 2420 of this Appendix] and the commodity control list in order to determine how compliance with the provisions of this Act [sections 2401 to 2420 of this Appendix] can be facilitated by simplifying such regulations, by simplifying or clarifying such list, or by any other means.

(Pub. L. 96–72, § 12, Sept. 29, 1979, 93 Stat. 530; Pub. L. 97–145, §§ 3, 5, Dec. 29, 1981, 95 Stat. 1727, 1728; Pub. L. 99–64, title I, § 113, July 12, 1985, 99 Stat. 148; Pub. L. 99–514, § 2, Oct. 22, 1986, 100 Stat. 2095; Pub. L. 100–418, title II, § 2427, Aug. 23, 1988, 102 Stat. 1361.)

REFERENCES IN TEXT

The Export Control Act of 1949, referred to in subsec. (a)(1), is act Feb. 26, 1949, ch. 11, 63 Stat. 7, as amended, which was classified to sections 2021 to 2032 of this Appendix, and terminated on Dec. 31, 1969, pursuant to the terms of that Act. For complete classification of this Act to the Code, see Tables.

The Export Administration Act of 1969, referred to in subsec. (a)(1), is Pub. L. 91–184, Dec. 30, 1969, 83 Stat. 841, as amended, which was classified generally to sections 2401 to 2413 of this Appendix, and terminated on Sept. 30, 1979, pursuant to the terms of that Act. For complete classification of this Act to the Code, see Tables.

The Export Administration Amendments Act of 1985, referred to in subsec. (a)(4), is titles I and II of Pub. L. 99–64, July 12, 1985, 99 Stat. 120, which, among other amendments, enacted par. (3) of subsec. (a) of this section. For complete classification of this Act to the Code, see Short Title of 1985 Amendment note set out under section 2401 of this Appendix and Tables.

Section 313 of the Budget and Accounting Act 1921, referred to in subsec. (c)(2), is section 313 of act June 10,

1921, ch. 18, title III, 42 Stat. 26, which was classified to section 54 of former Title 31, and which was repealed by Pub. L. 97–258, §5(b), Sept. 13, 1982, 96 Stat. 1068, and reenacted by the first section thereof as section 716 of Title 31, Money and Finance.

PRIOR PROVISIONS

A prior section 2411, Pub. L. 91–184, §12, Dec. 30, 1969, 83 Stat. 846, relating to the effect on the Act of Feb. 15, 1936 (49 Stat. 1140) and section 414 of the Mutual Security Act of 1934 (22 U.S.C. 1934) provisions of the Export Administration Act of 1969, expired on Sept. 30, 1979.

AMENDMENTS

1988—Subsec. (a)(2)(B). Pub. L. 100–418 inserted at end "The Customs Service may not detain for more than 20 days any shipment of goods or technology eligible for export under a general license under section 4(a)(3). In a case in which such detention is on account of a disagreement between the Secretary and the head of any other department or agency with export license authority under other provisions of law concerning the export license requirements for such goods or technology, such disagreement shall be resolved within that 20-day period. At the end of that 20-day period, the Customs Service shall either release the goods or technology, or seize the goods or technology as authorized by other provisions of law."

1986—Subsec. (c)(3). Pub. L. 99–514 substituted "Internal Revenue Code of 1986" for "Internal Revenue Code of 1954".

1985—Subsec. (a)(1). Pub. L. 99–64, §113(a), designated existing provisions of subsec. (a) as par. (1), substituted "such investigations within the United States, and the Commissioner of Customs (and officers or employees of the United States Customs Service specifically designated by the Commissioner) may make such investigations outside of the United States, and the head of such department or agency (and such officers or employees) may" for "such investigations and", and "a district court of the United States," for "the district court of the United States for any district in which such person is found or resides or transacts business, upon application, and", and inserted sentence providing that in addition to the authority conferred by this paragraph, the Secretary (and officers or employees of the Department of Commerce designated by the Secretary) may conduct, outside the United States, pre-license investigations and post-shipment verifications of items licensed for export, and investigations in the enforcement of section 8 of this Act.

Subsec. (a)(2) to (8). Pub. L. 99–64, §113(a)(5), added pars. (2) to (8).

Subsec. (c)(3). Pub. L. 99–64, §113, substituted "Any department or agency which obtains information which is relevant to the enforcement of this Act, including information pertaining to any investigation, shall furnish such information to each department or agency" for "Departments or agencies which obtain information which is relevant to the enforcement of this Act shall furnish such information to the department or agency", and inserted sentences providing that the Secretary and the Commissioner of Customs, upon request, shall exchange any licensing and enforcement information with each other which is necessary to facilitate enforcement efforts and effective license decisions and that the Secretary, the Attorney General, and the Commissioner of Customs shall consult on a continuing basis with one another and with the heads of other departments and agencies which obtain information subject to this paragraph, in order to facilitate the exchange of such information.

1981—Subsec. (c)(2). Pub. L. 97–145, §5, substantially reenacted existing provisions, inserted provisions that the information may not be withheld from the General Accounting Office, and that the information be made available to the Comptroller General of the United States or to any officer or employee of the General Accounting Office who is authorized to have access to such information which is submitted on a confidential basis and from which any individual can be identified, consistent with the protection of intelligence, counterintelligence, and law enforcement sources, methods, and activities, as determined by the agency that originally obtained the information, and consistent with section 54 of title 31, be made available only by that agency.

Subsec. (c)(3). Pub. L. 97–145, §3, added par. (3).

SECTION REFERRED TO IN OTHER SECTIONS

This section is referred to in sections 2403, 2404, 2405, 2412, 2413 of this Appendix; title 22 sections 2776, 2778, 2779a, 2780, 3281; title 42 section 6274.

§2411a. Omitted

CODIFICATION

A prior section 2411a, Pub. L. 91–184, §13, as added Pub. L. 95–52, title I, §102, June 22, 1977, 91 Stat. 235, authorizing appropriations to carry out purposes of provisions of Export Administration Act of 1969, expired on Sept. 30, 1979.

§2412. Administrative procedure and judicial review

(a) Exemption

Except as provided in section 11(c)(2) [section 2410(c)(2) of this Appendix] and subsection (c) of this section, the functions exercised under this Act [sections 2401 to 2420 of this Appendix] are excluded from the operation of sections 551, 553 through 559, and 701 through 706 of title 5, United States Code.

(b) Public participation

It is the intent of the Congress that, to the extent practicable, all regulations imposing controls on exports under this Act [sections 2401 to 2420 of this Appendix] be issued in proposed form with meaningful opportunity for public comment before taking effect. In cases where a regulation imposing controls under this Act [sections 2401 to 2420 of this Appendix] is issued with immediate effect, it is the intent of the Congress that meaningful opportunity for public comment also be provided and that the regulation be reissued in final form after public comments have been fully considered.

(c) Procedures relating to civil penalties and sanctions

(1) In any case in which a civil penalty or other civil sanction (other than a temporary denial order or a penalty or sanction for a violation of section 8 [section 2407 of this Appendix]) is sought under section 11 of this Act [section 2410 of this Appendix], the charged party is entitled to receive a formal complaint specifying the charges and, at his or her request, to contest the charges in a hearing before an administrative law judge. Subject to the provisions of this subsection, any such hearing shall be conducted in accordance with sections 556 and 557 of title 5, United States Code. With the approval of the administrative law judge, the Government may present evidence in camera in the presence of the charged party or his or her representative. After the hearing, the administrative law judge shall make findings of fact and conclusions of law in a written decision, which shall be referred to the Secretary. The Secretary shall, in a written order, affirm, modify, or vacate the decision

of the administrative law judge within 30 days after receiving the decision. The order of the Secretary shall be final and is not subject to judicial review, except as provided in paragraph (3).

(2) The proceedings described in paragraph (1) shall be concluded within a period of 1 year after the complaint is submitted, unless the administrative law judge extends such period for good cause shown.

(3) The order of the Secretary under paragraph (1) shall be final, except that the charged party may, within 15 days after the order is issued, appeal the order in the United States Court of Appeals for the District of Columbia Circuit, which shall have jurisdiction of the appeal. The court may, while the appeal is pending, stay the order of the Secretary. The court may review only those issues necessary to determine liability for the civil penalty or other sanction involved. In an appeal filed under this paragraph, the court shall set aside any finding of fact for which the court finds there is not substantial evidence on the record and any conclusion of law which the court finds to be arbitrary, capricious, an abuse of discretion, or otherwise not in accordance with law.

(4) An administrative law judge referred to in this subsection shall be appointed by the Secretary from among those considered qualified for selection and appointment under section 3105 of title 5, United States Code. Any person who, for at least 2 of the 10 years immediately preceding the date of the enactment of the Export Administration Amendments Act of 1985 [July 12, 1985], has served as a hearing commissioner of the Department of Commerce shall be included among those considered as qualified for selection and appointment to such position.

(d) Imposition of temporary denial orders

(1) In any case in which it is necessary, in the public interest, to prevent an imminent violation of this Act [sections 2401 to 2420 of this Appendix] or any regulation, order, or license issued under this Act [sections 2401 to 2420 of this Appendix], the Secretary may, without a hearing, issue an order temporarily denying United States export privileges (hereinafter in this subsection referred to as a "temporary denial order") to a person. A temporary denial order may be effective no longer than 180 days unless renewed in writing by the Secretary for additional 180-day periods in order to prevent such an imminent violation, except that a temporary denial order may be renewed only after notice and an opportunity for a hearing is provided.

(2) A temporary denial order shall define the imminent violation and state why the temporary denial order was granted without a hearing. The person or persons subject to the issuance or renewal of a temporary denial order may file an appeal of the issuance or renewal of the temporary denial order with an administrative law judge who shall, within 10 working days after the appeal is filed, recommend that the temporary denial order be affirmed, modified, or vacated. Parties may submit briefs and other material to the judge. The recommendation of the administrative law judge shall be submitted to the Secretary who shall either accept, reject, or modify the recommendation by written order within 5 working days after receiving the recommendation. The written order of the Secretary under the preceding sentence shall be final and is not subject to judicial review, except as provided in paragraph (3). The temporary denial order shall be affirmed only if it is reasonable to believe that the order is required in the public interest to prevent an imminent violation of this Act [sections 2401 to 2420 of this Appendix] or any regulation, order, or license issued under this Act [sections 2401 to 2420 of this Appendix]. All materials submitted to the administrative law judge and the Secretary shall constitute the administrative record for purposes of review by the courts.

(3) An order of the Secretary affirming, in whole or in part, the issuance of a temporary denial order may, within 15 days after the order is issued, be appealed by a person subject to the order to the United States Court of Appeals for the District of Columbia Circuit, which shall have jurisdiction of the appeal. The court may review only those issues necessary to determine whether the standard for issuing the temporary denial order has been met. The court shall vacate the Secretary's order if the court finds that the Secretary's order is arbitrary, capricious, an abuse of discretion, or otherwise not in accordance with law.

(e) Appeals from license denials

A determination of the Secretary, under section 10(f) of this Act [section 2409(f) of this Appendix], to deny a license may be appealed by the applicant to an administrative law judge who shall have the authority to conduct proceedings to determine only whether the item sought to be exported is in fact on the control list. Such proceedings shall be conducted within 90 days after the appeal is filed. Any determination by an administrative law judge under this subsection and all materials filed before such judge in the proceedings shall be reviewed by the Secretary, who shall either affirm or vacate the determination in a written decision within 30 days after receiving the determination. The Secretary's written decision shall be final and is not subject to judicial review. Subject to the limitations provided in section 12(c) of this Act [section 2411(c) of this Appendix], the Secretary's decision shall be published in the Federal Register.

(Pub. L. 96–72, §13, Sept. 29, 1979, 93 Stat. 531; Pub. L. 99–64, title I, §114, July 12, 1985, 99 Stat. 150; Pub. L. 100–418, title II, §2428, Aug. 23, 1988, 102 Stat. 1361.)

PRIOR PROVISIONS

A prior section 2412, Pub. L. 91–184, §14, formerly §13, Dec. 30, 1969, 83 Stat. 847; renumbered §14, Pub. L. 95–52, title I, §102, June 22, 1977, 91 Stat. 235, which set forth the effective date of the Export Administration Act of 1969 as the date upon which the Export Control Act of 1949 expired, Dec. 31, 1969, expired on Sept. 30, 1979.

AMENDMENTS

1988—Subsec. (c)(1). Pub. L. 100–418, §2428(a)(1)(A), inserted ", except as provided in paragraph (3)" before period at end.

Subsec. (c)(3), (4). Pub. L. 100–418, §2428(a)(1)(B), (C), added par. (3) and redesignated former par. (3) as (4).

Subsec. (d)(1). Pub. L. 100–418, §2428(b), substituted "180" for "60" in two places in second sentence.

Subsec. (d)(2). Pub. L. 100–418, §2428(a)(2), inserted ", except as provided in paragraph (3)" after "judicial review" before period at end of fifth sentence and inserted sentence at end that all materials submitted to the administrative law judge and the Secretary constitute the administrative record for purposes of review.

Subsec. (d)(3). Pub. L. 100–418, §2428(a)(2)(B), added par. (3).

1985—Pub. L. 99–64, §114(1), struck out "Exemption from certain provisions relating to" in section catchline.

Subsec. (a). Pub. L. 99–64, §114(2), inserted "and subsection (c) of this section".

Subsecs. (c) to (e). Pub. L. 99–64, §114(3), added subsecs. (c) to (e).

SECTION REFERRED TO IN OTHER SECTIONS

This section is referred to in sections 2410, 2413 of this Appendix.

§2413. Annual report

(a) Contents

Not later than December 31 of each year, the Secretary shall submit to the Congress a report on the administration of this Act [sections 2401 to 2420 of this Appendix] during the preceding fiscal year. All agencies shall cooperate fully with the Secretary in providing information for such report. Such report shall include detailed information with respect to—

(1) the implementation of the policies set forth in section 3 [section 2402 of this Appendix];

(2) general licensing activities under sections 5, 6, and 7 [sections 2404, 2405, and 2406 of this Appendix], and any changes in the exercise of the authorities contained in sections 5(a), 6(a), and 7(a) [sections 2404(a), 2405(a), and 2406(a) of this Appendix];

(3) the results of the review of United States policy toward individual countries pursuant to section 5(b) [section 2404(b) of this Appendix];

(4) the results, in as much detail as may be included consistent with the national security and the need to maintain the confidentiality of proprietary information, of the actions, including reviews and revisions of export controls maintained for national security purposes, required by section 5(c)(3) [section 2404(c)(3) of this Appendix];

(5) actions taken to carry out section 5(d) [section 2404(d) of this Appendix];

(6) changes in categories of items under export control referred to in section 5(e) [section 2404(e) of this Appendix];

(7) determinations of foreign availability made under section 5(f) [section 2404(f) of this Appendix], the criteria used to make such determinations, the removal of any export controls under such section, and any evidence demonstrating a need to impose export controls for national security purposes notwithstanding foreign availability;

(8) actions taken in compliance with section 5(f)(6) [section 2404(f)(6) of this Appendix];

(9) the operation of the indexing system under section 5(g) [section 2404(g) of this Appendix];

(10) consultations with the technical advisory committees established pursuant to section 5(h) [section 2404(h) of this Appendix], the use made of the advice rendered by such committees, and the contributions of such committees toward implementing the policies set forth in this Act [sections 2401 to 2420 of this Appendix];

(11) the effectiveness of export controls imposed under section 6 [section 2405 of this Appendix] in furthering the foreign policy of the United States;

(12) export controls and monitoring under section 7 [section 2406 of this Appendix];

(13) the information contained in the reports required by section 7(b)(2) [section 2406(b)(2) of this Appendix], together with an analysis of—

(A) the impact on the economy and world trade of shortages or increased prices for commodities subject to monitoring under this Act [sections 2401 to 2420 of this Appendix] or section 812[1] of the Agricultural Act of 1970 [7 U.S.C. 612c–3];

(B) the worldwide supply of such commodities; and

(C) actions being taken by other countries in response to such shortages or increased prices;

(14) actions taken by the President and the Secretary to carry out the antiboycott policies set forth in section 3(5) of this Act [section 2402(5) of this Appendix];

(15) organizational and procedural changes undertaken in furtherance of the policies set forth in this Act [sections 2401 to 2420 of this Appendix], including changes to increase the efficiency of the export licensing process and to fulfill the requirements of section 10 [section 2409 of this Appendix], including an accounting of appeals received, court orders issued, and actions taken pursuant thereto under subsection (j) of such section;

(16) delegations of authority by the President as provided in section 4(e) of this Act [section 2403(e) of this Appendix];

(17) efforts to keep the business sector of the Nation informed with respect to policies and procedures adopted under this Act [sections 2401 to 2420 of this Appendix];

(18) any reviews undertaken in furtherance of the policies of this Act, including the results of the review required by section 12(d) [section 2411(d) of this Appendix], and any action taken, on the basis of the review required by section 12(e) [section 2411(e) of this Appendix], to simplify regulations issued under this Act [sections 2401 to 2420 of this Appendix];

(19) violations under section 11 [section 2410 of this Appendix] and enforcement activities under section 12 [section 2411 of this Appendix]; and

(20) the issuance of regulations under the authority of this Act [sections 2401 to 2420 of this Appendix], including an explanation of each case in which regulations were not issued in accordance with the first sentence of section 13(b) [section 2412(b) of this Appendix].

(b) Report on certain export controls

To the extent that the President determines that the policies set forth in section 3 of this

[1] See References in Text note below.

Act [section 2402 of this Appendix] require the control of the export of goods and technology other than those subject to multilateral controls, or require more stringent controls than the multilateral controls, the President shall include in each annual report the reasons for the need to impose, or to continue to impose, such controls and the estimated domestic economic impact on the various industries affected by such controls.

(c) Report on negotiations

The President shall include in each annual report a detailed report on the progress of the negotiations required by section 5(i) [section 2404(i) of this Appendix], until such negotiations are concluded.

(d) Report on exports to controlled countries

The Secretary shall include in each annual report a detailed report which lists every license for exports to controlled countries which was approved under this Act [sections 2401 to 2420 of this Appendix] during the preceding fiscal year. Such report shall specify to whom the license was granted, the type of goods or technology exported, and the country receiving the goods or technology. The information required by this subsection shall be subject to the provisions of section 12(c) of this Act [section 2411(c) of this Appendix].

(e) Report on domestic economic impact of exports to controlled countries

The Secretary shall include in each annual report a detailed description of the extent of injury to United States industry and the extent of job displacement caused by United States exports of goods and technology to controlled countries. The annual report shall also include a full analysis of the consequences of exports of turnkey plants and manufacturing facilities to controlled countries which are used by such countries to produce goods for export to the United States or to compete with United States products in export markets.

(f) Annual report of the President

The President shall submit an annual report to the Congress estimating the additional defense expenditures of the United States arising from illegal technology transfers, focusing on estimated defense costs arising from illegal technology transfers that resulted in a serious adverse impact on the strategic balance of forces. These estimates shall be based on assessment by the intelligence community of any technology transfers that resulted in such serious adverse impact. This report may have a classified annex covering any information of a sensitive nature.

(Pub. L. 96–72, §14, Sept. 29, 1979, 93 Stat. 532; Pub. L. 99–64, title I, §115, July 12, 1985, 99 Stat. 152; Pub. L. 100–418, title II, §§2418(c), 2445, Aug. 23, 1988, 102 Stat. 1357, 1369.)

REFERENCES IN TEXT

Section 812 of the Agricultural Act of 1970, referred to in subsec. (a)(13)(A), which was classified to section 612c–3 of Title 7, Agriculture, was repealed by Pub. L. 101–624, title XV, §1578, Nov. 28, 1990, 104 Stat. 3702.

PRIOR PROVISIONS

A prior section 2413, Pub. L. 91–184, §15, formerly §14, Dec. 30, 1969, 83 Stat. 847; Pub. L. 92–37, June 30, 1971, 85 Stat. 89; Pub. L. 92–150, Oct. 30, 1971, 85 Stat. 416; Pub. L. 92–284, Apr. 29, 1972, 86 Stat. 133; Pub. L. 92–412, title I, §106, Aug. 29, 1972, 86 Stat. 646; Pub. L. 93–327, June 30, 1974, 88 Stat. 287; Pub. L. 93–372, Aug. 14, 1974, 88 Stat. 444; Pub. L. 93–500, §13, Oct. 29, 1974, 88 Stat. 1557; renumbered §15 and amended Pub. L. 95–52, title I, §§101, 102, June 22, 1977, 91 Stat. 235, providing for the termination of authority granted by the Export Administration Act of 1969, expired on Sept. 30, 1979.

AMENDMENTS

1988—Subsec. (a)(8). Pub. L. 100–418, §2418(c), substituted "5(f)(6)" for "5(f)(5)".

Subsec. (f). Pub. L. 100–418, §2445, added subsec. (f).

1985—Subsec. (a)(15). Pub. L. 99–64, §115(a), struck out "an analysis of the time required to process license applications, the number and disposition of export license applications taking more than 30 days to process, and" after "requirements of section 10, including".

Subsecs. (d), (e). Pub. L. 99–64, §115(b), added subsecs. (d) and (e).

DELEGATION OF FUNCTIONS

Functions conferred upon President under this section delegated to Secretary of Commerce by Ex. Ord. No. 12214, May 2, 1980, 45 F.R. 29783, set out under section 2403 of this Appendix.

SECTION REFERRED TO IN OTHER SECTIONS

This section is referred to in section 2410a of this Appendix.

§ 2414. Administrative and regulatory authority

(a) Under Secretary of Commerce

The President shall appoint, by and with the advice and consent of the Senate, an Under Secretary of Commerce for Export Administration who shall carry out all functions of the Secretary under this Act [sections 2401 to 2420 of this Appendix] and such other statutes that relate to national security which were delegated to the office of the Assistant Secretary of Commerce for Trade Administration before the date of the enactment of the Export Administration Amendments Act of 1985 [July 12, 1985], and such other functions under this Act [sections 2401 to 2420 of this Appendix] which were delegated to such office before such date of enactment, as the Secretary may delegate. The President shall appoint, by and with the advice and consent of the Senate, two Assistant Secretaries of Commerce to assist the Under Secretary in carrying out such functions.

(b) Issuance of regulations

The President and the Secretary may issue such regulations as are necessary to carry out the provisions of this Act [sections 2401 to 2420 of this Appendix]. Any such regulations issued to carry out the provisions of section 5(a), 6(a), 7(a), or 8(b) [section 2404(a), 2405(a), 2406(a), or 2407(b) of this Appendix] may apply to the financing, transporting, or other servicing of exports and the participation therein by any person. Any such regulations the purpose of which is to carry out the provisions of section 5 [section 2404 of this Appendix], or of section 4(a) [section 2403(a) of this Appendix] for the purpose of administering the provisions of section 5 [section 2404 of this Appendix], may be issued only after the regulations are submitted for review to the Secretary of Defense, the Secretary of State, such other departments and agencies as the Secretary considers appropriate, and the appropriate technical advisory committee. The preceding sentence does not require the concurrence or approval of any official, department, or agency to which such regulations are submitted.

(c) Amendments to regulations

If the Secretary proposes to amend regulations issued under this Act [sections 2401 to 2420 of this Appendix], the Secretary shall report to the Committee on Banking, Housing, and Urban Affairs of the Senate and the Committee on Foreign Affairs of the House of Representatives on the intent and rationale of such amendments. Such report shall evaluate the cost and burden to United States exporters of the proposed amendments in relation to any enhancement of licensing objectives. The Secretary shall consult with the technical advisory committees authorized under section 5(h) of this Act [section 2404(h) of this Appendix] in formulating or amending regulations issued under this Act [sections 2401 to 2420 of this Appendix]. The procedures defined by regulations in effect on January 1, 1984, with respect to sections 4 and 5 of this Act [sections 2403 and 2404 of this Appendix], shall remain in effect unless the Secretary determines, on the basis of substantial and reliable evidence, that specific change is necessary to enhance the prevention of diversions of exports which would prove detrimental to the national security of the United States or to reduce the licensing and paperwork burden on exporters and their distributors.

(Pub. L. 96–72, §15, Sept. 29, 1979, 93 Stat. 533; Pub. L. 99–64, title I, §116(a), July 12, 1985, 99 Stat. 152; Pub. L. 100–418, title II, §§2420(b), 2429, Aug. 23, 1988, 102 Stat. 1358, 1362.)

AMENDMENTS

1988—Subsec. (a). Pub. L. 100–418, §2429, inserted "and such other statutes that related to national security" after "Secretary under this Act".

Subsec. (b). Pub. L. 100–418, §2420(b), substituted "such other" for "and such other" and inserted ", and the appropriate technical advisory committee" after "appropriate".

1985—Pub. L. 99–64 substituted "Administrative and regulatory authority" for "Regulatory authority" as section catchline, and amended text generally. Prior to amendment, section read as follows: "The President and the Secretary may issue such regulations as are necessary to carry out the provisions of this Act. Any such regulations issued to carry out the provisions of section 5(a), 6(a), 7(a), or 8(b) may apply to the financing, transporting, or other servicing of exports and the participation therein by any person."

CHANGE OF NAME

Committee on Foreign Affairs of House of Representatives treated as referring to Committee on International Relations of House of Representatives by section 1(a) of Pub. L. 104–14, set out as a note preceding section 21 of Title 2, The Congress.

EFFECTIVE DATE OF 1985 AMENDMENT

Subsec. (a) of this section effective Oct. 1, 1987, see section 116(d) of Pub. L. 99–64, set out as a note under section 5314 of Title 5, Government Organization and Employees.

DELEGATION OF FUNCTIONS

Functions conferred upon President under this section delegated to Secretary of Commerce by Ex. Ord. No. 12214, May 2, 1980, 45 F.R. 29783, set out under section 2403 of this Appendix.

SPENDING AUTHORITY UNDER 1985 AMENDMENT

Section 116(e) of Pub. L. 99–64 provided that: "Any new spending authority (within the meaning of section 401 of the Congressional Budget Act of 1974 [2 U.S.C. 651]) which is provided under this section [amending this section and sections 5314 and 5315 of Title 5, Government Organization and Employees] shall be effective for any fiscal year only to the extent or in such amounts as are provided in appropriation Acts."

§2415. Definitions

As used in this Act [sections 2401 to 2420 of this Appendix]—

(1) the term "person" includes the singular and the plural and any individual, partnership, corporation, or other form of association, including any government or agency thereof;

(2) the term "United States person" means any United States resident or national (other than an individual resident outside the United States and employed by other than a United States person), any domestic concern (including any permanent domestic establishment of any foreign concern) and any foreign subsidiary or affiliate (including any permanent foreign establishment) of any domestic concern which is controlled in fact by such domestic concern, as determined under regulations of the President;

(3) the term "good" means any article, natural or manmade substance, material, supply or manufactured product, including inspection and test equipment, and excluding technical data;

(4) the term "technology" means the information and know-how (whether in tangible form, such as models, prototypes, drawings, sketches, diagrams, blueprints, or manuals, or in intangible form, such as training or technical services) that can be used to design, produce, manufacture, utilize, or reconstruct goods, including computer software and technical data, but not the goods themselves;

(5) the term "export" means—

(A) an actual shipment, transfer, or transmission of goods or technology out of the United States;

(B) a transfer of goods or technology in the United States to an embassy or affiliate of a controlled country; or

(C) a transfer to any person of goods or technology either within the United States or outside of the United States with the knowledge or intent that the goods or technology will be shipped, transferred, or transmitted to an unauthorized recipient;

(6) the term "controlled country" means a controlled country under section 5(b)(1) of this Act [section 2404(b)(1) of this Appendix];

(7) the term "United States" means the States of the United States, the District of Columbia, and any commonwealth, territory, dependency, or possession of the United States, and includes the outer Continental Shelf, as defined in section 2(a) of the Outer Continental Shelf Lands Act (43 U.S.C. 1331(a)); and

(8) the term "Secretary" means the Secretary of Commerce.

(Pub. L. 96–72, § 16, Sept. 29, 1979, 93 Stat. 533; Pub. L. 99–64, title I, § 117, July 12, 1985, 99 Stat. 153.)

AMENDMENTS

1985—Par. (3). Pub. L. 99–64, § 117(1), inserted "natural or manmade substance,".

Par. (4). Pub. L. 99–64, § 117(2), amended par. (4) generally, substituting "the term 'technology' means the information and know-how (whether in tangible form, such as models, prototypes, drawings, sketches, diagrams, blueprints, or manuals, or in intangible form, such as training or technical services) that can be used to design, produce, manufacture, utilize, or reconstruct goods, including computer software and technical data, but not the goods themselves;" for "the information and knowhow that can be used to design, produce, manufacture, utilize, or reconstruct goods, including computer software and technical data, but not the goods themselves; and".

Pars. (5) to (8). Pub. L. 99–64, § 117(3), (4), added pars. (5) to (7) and redesignated former par. (5) as (8).

DELEGATION OF FUNCTIONS

Functions conferred upon President under this section delegated to Secretary of Commerce by Ex. Ord. No. 12214, May 2, 1980, 45 F.R. 29783, set out under section 2403 of this Appendix.

SECTION REFERRED TO IN OTHER SECTIONS

This section is referred to in title 22 sections 2679c, 2797c.

§ 2416. Effect on other Acts

(a) In general

Except as otherwise provided in this Act [sections 2401 to 2420 of this Appendix], nothing contained in this Act [sections 2401 to 2420 of this Appendix] shall be construed to modify, repeal, supersede, or otherwise affect the provisions of any other laws authorizing control over exports of any commodity.

(b) Coordination of controls

The authority granted to the President under this Act [sections 2401 to 2420 of this Appendix] shall be exercised in such manner as to achieve effective coordination with the authority exercised under section 38 of the Arms Export Control Act (22 U.S.C. 2778).

(c) Civil aircraft equipment

Notwithstanding any other provision of law, any product (1) which is standard equipment, certified by the Federal Aviation Administration, in civil aircraft and is an integral part of such aircraft, and (2) which is to be exported to a country other than a controlled country, shall be subject to export controls exclusively under this Act [sections 2401 to 2420 of this Appendix]. Any such product shall not be subject to controls under section 38(b)(2) of the Arms Export Control Act [22 U.S.C. 2778(b)(2)].

(d) Nonproliferation controls

(1) Nothing in section 5 or 6 of this Act [section 2404 or 2405 of this Appendix] shall be construed to supersede the procedures published by the President pursuant to section 309(c) of the Nuclear Non-Proliferation Act of 1978 [42 U.S.C. 2139a(c)].

(2) With respect to any export license application which, under the procedures published by the President pursuant to section 309(c) of the Nuclear Non-Proliferation Act of 1978 [42 U.S.C. 2139a(c)], is referred to the Subgroup on Nuclear Export Coordination or other interagency group, the provisions of section 10 of this Act [section 2409 of this Appendix] shall apply with respect to such license application only to the extent that they are consistent with such published procedures, except that if the processing of any such application under such procedures is not completed within 180 days after the receipt of the application by the Secretary, the applicant shall have the rights of appeal and court action provided in section 10(j) of this Act [section 2409(j) of this Appendix].

(e) Termination of other authority

On October 1, 1979, the Mutual Defense Assistance Control Act of 1951 (22 U.S.C. 1611–1613d), is superseded.

(f) Agricultural Act of 1970

Nothing in this Act [sections 2401 to 2420 of this Appendix] shall affect the provisions of the last sentence of section 812[1] of the Agricultural Act of 1970 (7 U.S.C. 612c–3).

(Pub. L. 96–72, § 17, Sept. 29, 1979, 93 Stat. 534; Pub. L. 99–64, title I, § 118, July 12, 1985, 99 Stat. 154.)

REFERENCES IN TEXT

The Mutual Defense Assistance Control Act of 1951, referred to in subsec. (e), is act Oct. 26, 1951, ch. 575, 65 Stat. 644, as amended, which was classified generally to chapter 20A (§ 1611 et seq.) of Title 22, Foreign Relations and Intercourse, prior to its supersedure by subsec. (e) of this section. For complete classification of this Act to the Code, see Tables.

Section 812 of the Agricultural Act of 1970, referred to in subsec. (f), which was classified to section 612c–3 of Title 7, Agriculture, was repealed by Pub. L. 101–624, title XV, § 1578, Nov. 28, 1990, 104 Stat. 3702.

AMENDMENTS

1985—Subsec. (a). Pub. L. 99–64, § 118(a)(1), substituted "Except as otherwise provided in this Act, nothing" for "Nothing".

Subsec. (c). Pub. L. 99–64, § 118(a)(2), struck out sentence which provided that for purposes of this subsection "controlled country" means any country described in section 620(f) of the Foreign Assistance Act of 1961.

Subsec. (f). Pub. L. 99–64, § 118(b), added subsec. (f).

DELEGATION OF FUNCTIONS

Functions conferred upon President under sections 2401 to 2420 of this Appendix delegated to Secretary of Commerce, with certain exceptions, by Ex. Ord. No. 12214, May 2, 1980, 45 F.R. 29783, set out under section 2403 of this Appendix.

§ 2417. Authorization of appropriations

(a) Requirement of authorizing legislation

(1) Notwithstanding any other provision of law, money appropriated to the Department of Commerce for expenses to carry out the purposes of this Act [sections 2401 to 2420 of this Appendix] may be obligated or expended only if—

(A) the appropriation thereof has been previously authorized by law enacted on or after the date of the enactment of the Export Administration Amendments Act of 1985 [July 12, 1985]; or

[1] See References in Text note below.

(B) the amount of all such obligations and expenditures does not exceed an amount previously prescribed by law enacted on or after such date.

(2) To the extent that legislation enacted after the making of an appropriation to carry out the purposes of this Act [sections 2401 to 2420 of this Appendix] authorizes the obligation or expenditure thereof, the limitation contained in paragraph (1) shall have no effect.

(3) The provisions of this subsection shall not be superseded except by a provision of law enacted after the date of the enactment of the Export Administration Amendments Act of 1985 [July 12, 1985] which specifically repeals, modifies, or supersedes the provisions of this subsection.

(b) Authorization

There are authorized to be appropriated to the Department of Commerce to carry out the purposes of this Act [sections 2401 to 2420 of this Appendix]—

(1) $42,813,000 for the fiscal year 1993;

(2) such sums as may be necessary for the fiscal year 1994; and

(3) such additional amounts, for each such fiscal year, as may be necessary for increases in salary, pay, retirement, other employee benefits authorized by law, and other nondiscretionary costs.

(Pub. L. 96–72, § 18, Sept. 29, 1979, 93 Stat. 534; Pub. L. 97–145, § 2(a), Dec. 29, 1981, 95 Stat. 1727; Pub. L. 99–64, title I, § 119, July 12, 1985, 99 Stat. 154; Pub. L. 99–633, § 1, Nov. 7, 1986, 100 Stat. 3522; Pub. L. 100–418, title II, § 2430, Aug. 23, 1988, 102 Stat. 1362; Pub. L. 103–10, § 1, Mar. 27, 1993, 107 Stat. 40.)

AMENDMENTS

1993—Subsec. (b)(1) to (3). Pub. L. 103–10 added pars. (1) to (3) and struck out former pars. (1) to (3) which read as follows:

"(1) $35,935,000 for the fiscal year 1988, of which $12,746,000 shall be available only for enforcement, $2,000,000 shall be available only for foreign availability assessments under subsections (f) and (h)(6) of section 5, and $21,189,000 shall be available for all other activities under this Act;

"(2) $46,913,000 for the fiscal year 1989, of which $15,000,000 shall be available only for enforcement, $5,000,000 shall be available only for foreign availability assessments under subsections (f) and (h)(6) of section 5, $4,000,000 shall be available only for regional export control assistance centers, and $22,913,000 shall be available for all other activities under this Act; and

"(3) such additional amounts for each of the fiscal years 1988 and 1989 as may be necessary for increases in salary, pay, retirement, other employee benefits authorized by law, and other nondiscretionary costs."

1988—Subsec. (b)(1). Pub. L. 100–418, § 2430(1), substituted "the fiscal year 1988" for "each of the fiscal years 1987 and 1988" and struck out "for each such year" after "available" in three places and "and" after semicolon at end.

Subsec. (b)(2), (3). Pub. L. 100–418, § 2430(2), added pars. (2) and (3) and struck out former par. (2) which read as follows: "such additional amounts for each of the fiscal years 1987 and 1988 as may be necessary for increases in salary, pay, retirement, other employee benefits authorized by law, and other nondiscretionary costs."

1986—Subsec. (b). Pub. L. 99–633 amended subsec. (b) generally. Prior to amendment, subsec. (b) read as follows: "There are authorized to be appropriated to the Department of Commerce to carry out the purposes of this Act—

"(1) $24,600,000 for the fiscal year 1985, of which $8,712,000 shall be available only for enforcement, $1,851,000 shall be available only for foreign availability assessments under subsections (f) and (h)(6) of section 5 of this Act, and $14,037,000 shall be available for all other activities under this Act;

"(2) $29,382,000 for the fiscal year 1986, of which $9,243,000 shall be available only for enforcement, $2,000,000 shall be available only for foreign availability assessments under subsections (f) and (h)(6) of section 5 of this Act, and $18,139,000 shall be available for all other activities under this Act; and

"(3) such additional amounts for each of the fiscal years 1985 and 1986 as may be necessary for increases in salary, pay, retirement, other employee benefits authorized by law, and other nondiscretionary costs."

1985—Subsec. (a). Pub. L. 99–64, § 119, amended subsec. (a) generally. Prior to amendment, subsec. (a) read as follows: "Notwithstanding any other provision of law, no appropriation shall be made under any law to the Department of Commerce for expenses to carry out the purposes of this Act unless previously and specifically authorized by law."

Subsec. (b). Pub. L. 99–64, § 119, amended subsec. (b) generally. Prior to amendment, subsec. (b) read as follows: "There are authorized to be appropriated to the Department of Commerce to carry out the purposes of this Act—

"(1) $9,659,000 for each of the fiscal years 1982 and 1983; and

"(2) such additional amounts, for each such fiscal year, as may be necessary for increases in salary, pay, retirement, other employee benefits authorized by law, and other nondiscretionary costs."

1981—Subsec. (b)(1). Pub. L. 97–145 substituted authorization of appropriation of $9,659,000 for each of the fiscal years 1982 and 1983 for authorization of appropriation of $8,000,000 for each of the fiscal years 1980 and 1981, of which $1,250,000 were to be available for each such fiscal year only for purpose of carrying out foreign availability assessments pursuant to section 2404(f)(5) of this Appendix.

EFFECTIVE DATE OF 1981 AMENDMENT

Section 2(b) of Pub. L. 97–145 provided that: "The amendment made by subsection (a) [amending this section] shall be effective as of October 1, 1981."

§ 2418. Effective date

This Act [sections 2401 to 2420 of this Appendix] shall take effect upon the expiration of the Export Administration Act of 1969 [former sections 2401 to 2413 of this Appendix].

(Pub. L. 96–72, § 19(a), Sept. 29, 1979, 93 Stat. 535.)

REFERENCES IN TEXT

The Export Administration Act of 1969, referred to in text, is Pub. L. 91–184, Dec. 30, 1969, 83 Stat. 841, as amended, which was classified generally to sections 2401 to 2413 of this Appendix, and terminated on Sept. 30, 1979, pursuant to the terms of that Act. For complete classification of this Act to the Code, see Tables.

§ 2419. Termination date

The authority granted by this Act [sections 2401 to 2420 of this Appendix] terminates on August 20, 2001.

(Pub. L. 96–72, § 20, Sept. 29, 1979, 93 Stat. 535; Pub. L. 98–108, § 1, Oct. 1, 1983, 97 Stat. 744; Pub. L. 98–207, Dec. 5, 1983, 97 Stat. 1391; Pub. L. 98–222, Feb. 29, 1984, 98 Stat. 36; Pub. L. 99–64, title I, § 120, July 12, 1985, 99 Stat. 155; Pub. L. 100–418, title II, § 2431, Aug. 23, 1988, 102 Stat.

1362; Pub. L. 103–10, § 2, Mar. 27, 1993, 107 Stat. 40; Pub. L. 103–277, July 5, 1994, 108 Stat. 1407; Pub. L. 106–508, Nov. 13, 2000, 114 Stat. 2360.)

AMENDMENTS

2000—Pub. L. 106–508 substituted "August 20, 2001" for "August 20, 1994".

1994—Pub. L. 103–277 substituted "August 20, 1994" for "June 30, 1994".

1993—Pub. L. 103–10 substituted "June 30, 1994" for "September 30, 1990".

1988—Pub. L. 100–418 substituted "1990" for "1989".

1985—Pub. L. 99–64 amended section generally, substituting "September 30, 1989" for "March 30, 1984, or upon any prior date which the President by proclamation may designate."

1984—Pub. L. 98–222 substituted "March 30" for "February 29".

1983—Pub. L. 98–207 substituted "February 29, 1984" for "October 14, 1983".

Pub. L. 98–108 substituted "October 14, 1983" for "September 30, 1983".

DELEGATION OF FUNCTIONS

Functions conferred upon President under sections 2401 to 2420 of this Appendix delegated to Secretary of Commerce with certain exceptions, among them functions conferred upon President under this section, which were reserved to President, see Ex. Ord. No. 12214, May 2, 1980, 45 F.R. 29783, set out under section 2403 of this Appendix.

CONTINUATION OF EXPORT CONTROL REGULATIONS

Provisions relating to continued effectiveness of the Export Administration Act of 1979, 50 App. U.S.C. 2401 et seq., and to issuance and continued effectiveness of rules, regulations, orders, licenses, and other forms of administrative action and delegations of authority relating to administration of that Act, were contained in the following:

Ex. Ord. No. 12924, Aug. 19, 1994, 59 F.R. 43437, set out as a note under section 1701 of Title 50, War and National Defense.

Ex. Ord. No. 12923, June 30, 1994, 59 F.R. 34551, formerly set out as a note under section 1701 of Title 50, prior to revocation by Ex. Ord. No. 12924, § 4, Aug. 19, 1994, 59 F.R. 43438.

Ex. Ord. No. 12867, Sept. 30, 1993, 58 F.R. 51747, set out as a note under section 1701 of Title 50.

Ex. Ord. No. 12730, Sept. 30, 1990, 55 F.R. 40373, formerly set out as a note under section 1701 of Title 50, prior to revocation by Ex. Ord. No. 12867, Sept. 30, 1993, 58 F.R. 51747.

Ex. Ord. No. 12525, July 12, 1985, 50 F.R. 28757, set out as a note under section 1701 of Title 50.

Ex. Ord. No. 12470, Mar. 30, 1984, 49 F.R. 13099, formerly set out as a note under section 1701 of Title 50, prior to revocation by Ex. Ord. No. 12525, July 12, 1985, 50 F.R. 28757.

Ex. Ord. No. 12451, Dec. 20, 1983, 48 F.R. 56563, set out as a note under section 1701 of Title 50.

Ex. Ord. No. 12444, Oct. 14, 1983, 48 F.R. 48215, formerly set out as a note under section 1701 of Title 50, prior to revocation by Ex. Ord. No. 12451, Dec. 20, 1983, 48 F.R. 56563.

§ 2420. Savings provisions

(a) In general

All delegations, rules, regulations, orders, determinations, licenses, or other forms of administrative action which have been made, issued, conducted, or allowed to become effective under the Export Control Act of 1949 [former sections 2021 to 2032 of this Appendix] or the Export Administration Act of 1969 [former sections 2401 to 2413 of this Appendix] and which are in effect at the time this Act takes effect [September 30, 1979] shall continue in effect according to their terms until modified, superseded, set aside, or revoked under this Act [sections 2401 to 2420 of this Appendix].

(b) Administrative proceedings

This Act [sections 2401 to 2420 of this Appendix] shall not apply to any administrative proceedings commenced or any application for a license made, under the Export Administration Act of 1969 [former sections 2401 to 2413 of this Appendix], which is pending at the time this Act takes effect [September 30, 1979].

(Pub. L. 96–72, § 21, Sept. 29, 1979, 93 Stat. 535.)

REFERENCES IN TEXT

The Export Control Act of 1949, referred to in subsec. (a), is act Feb. 26, 1949, ch. 11, 63 Stat. 7, as amended, which was classified to sections 2021 to 2032 of this Appendix, and terminated on Dec. 31, 1969, pursuant to the terms of that Act. For complete classification of this Act to the Code, see Tables.

The Export Administration Act of 1969, referred to in text, is Pub. L. 91–184, Dec. 30, 1969, 83 Stat. 841, as amended, which was classified generally to sections 2401 to 2413 of this Appendix, and terminated on Sept. 30, 1979, pursuant to the terms of that Act. For complete classification of this Act to the Code, see Tables.

ACTS CITED BY POPULAR NAME

The following is an alphabetical list of popular and statutory names of Acts of Congress. The Statutes at Large citation following an entry is to the Act or part of the Act to which the name relates. Not all entries are classified to the United States Code. If an entry is classified mainly to a discrete part of the Code (such as a chapter or subchapter), a Code citation is set out in parentheses. If there is a short title or a short title note in the Code for an entry, a Code citation for the short title or short title note is set out on a separate line. For a complete chronological listing of Acts that have been classified to the Code together with their Code classifications and current status, see Tables II and III in the Tables volumes.

1950 Amendment to Public Law 38
Aug. 5, 1950, ch. 592, 64 Stat. 414

1951 Amendments to the Universal Military Training and Service Act
June 19, 1951, ch. 144, title I, 65 Stat. 75
Short title, see 50 App. U.S.C. 451 note

1955 Amendments to the Universal Military Training and Service Act
June 30, 1955, ch. 250, 69 Stat. 223

1959 Amendment to the Texas City Disaster Relief Act
Pub. L. 86–381, Sept. 25, 1959, 73 Stat. 706

1964 Amendments to the Alaska Omnibus Act
Pub. L. 88–451, Aug. 19, 1964, 78 Stat. 505 (48 U.S.C. note prec. 21)

1979 White House Conference on the Arts Act
Pub. L. 95–272, title I, May 3, 1978, 92 Stat. 222 (20 U.S.C. 951 note)

1979 White House Conference on the Humanities Act
Pub. L. 95–272, title II, May 3, 1978, 92 Stat. 224 (20 U.S.C. 951 note)

1984 Act to Combat International Terrorism
Pub. L. 98–533, Oct. 19, 1984, 98 Stat. 2706 (18 U.S.C. 3071 et seq.)
Short title, see 18 U.S.C. 3071 note

1984 Olympic Commemorative Coin Act
See Olympic Commemorative Coin Act

1988 Olympic Commemorative Coin Act
Pub. L. 100–141, Oct. 28, 1987, 101 Stat. 832 (31 U.S.C. 5112 note)

1992 National Assessment of Chapter 1 Act
Pub. L. 101–305, May 30, 1990, 104 Stat. 253

1992 Olympic Commemorative Coin Act
Pub. L. 101–406, Oct. 3, 1990, 104 Stat. 879 (31 U.S.C. 5112 note)

1992 White House Commemorative Coin Act
Pub. L. 102–281, title I, May 13, 1992, 106 Stat. 133 (31 U.S.C. 5112 note)

1993 White House Conference on Children, Youth, and Families
Pub. L. 101–501, title IX, subtitle B (§981 et seq.), Nov. 3, 1990, 104 Stat. 1280 (42 U.S.C. 12371 et seq.)
Short title, see 42 U.S.C. 12301 note

1997 Emergency Supplemental Appropriations Act for Recovery from Natural Disasters, and for Overseas Peacekeeping Efforts, Including Those in Bosnia
Pub. L. 105–18, June 12, 1997, 111 Stat. 158

1998 Supplemental Appropriations and Rescissions Act
Pub. L. 105–174, May 1, 1998, 112 Stat. 58

1999 Emergency Supplemental Appropriations Act
Pub. L. 106–31, May 21, 1999, 113 Stat. 57

2002 Winter Olympic Commemorative Coin Act
Pub. L. 106–435, Nov. 6, 2000, 114 Stat. 1916 (31 U.S.C. 5112 note)

21st Century Community Learning Centers Act
Pub. L. 89–10, title X, part I (§10901 et seq.), as added Pub. L. 103–382, title I, §101, Oct. 20, 1994, 108 Stat. 3844 (20 U.S.C. 8241 et seq.)
Short title, see 20 U.S.C. 8241

50 States Commemorative Coin Program Act
Pub. L. 104–329, title III, Oct. 20, 1996, 110 Stat. 4012
Pub. L. 105–124, Dec. 1, 1997, 111 Stat. 2534
Short title, see 31 U.S.C. 5101 notes

A.A.A. Farm Relief and Inflation Act
May 12, 1933, ch. 25, 48 Stat. 31

Abaca Production Act of 1950
Aug. 10, 1950, ch. 673, 64 Stat. 435 (50 U.S.C. 541 et seq.)

Abandoned Barge Act of 1992
Pub. L. 102–587, title V, subtitle C (§5301 et seq.), Nov. 4, 1992, 106 Stat. 5081 (46 U.S.C. 4701 et seq.)
Short title, see 46 U.S.C. 4701 note

Abandoned Infants Assistance Act Amendments of 1991
Pub. L. 102–236, Dec. 12, 1991, 105 Stat. 1812
Short title, see 42 U.S.C. 670 note

Abandoned Infants Assistance Act of 1988
Pub. L. 100–505, Oct. 18, 1988, 102 Stat. 2533 (42 U.S.C. 670 note)

Abandoned Mine Reclamation Act of 1990
Pub. L. 101–508, title VI, subtitle A (§6001 et seq.), Nov. 5, 1990, 104 Stat. 1388–289
Short title, see 30 U.S.C. 1201 note

Abandoned Property Collection Act
Mar. 12, 1863, ch. 120, 12 Stat. 820

Abandoned Shipwreck Act of 1987
Pub. L. 100–298, Apr. 28, 1988, 102 Stat. 432 (43 U.S.C. 2101 et seq.)
Short title, see 43 U.S.C. 2101 note

Able Seamen Act
July 8, 1941, ch. 279, 55 Stat. 579

Abolition of Slavery Act (Territories)
June 19, 1862, ch. 111, 12 Stat. 432

Abraham Lincoln Bicentennial Commission Act
Pub. L. 106–173, Feb. 25, 2000, 114 Stat. 14 (36 U.S.C. note prec. 101)

Academic Research Facilities Modernization Act of 1988
Pub. L. 100–570, title II, Oct. 31, 1988, 102 Stat. 2873 (42 U.S.C. 1862a et seq.)
Short title, see 42 U.S.C. 1861 note

Accountable Pipeline Safety and Partnership Act of 1996
Pub. L. 104–304, Oct. 12, 1996, 110 Stat. 3793
Short title, see 49 U.S.C. 60101 note

Accounting and Auditing Act of 1950
Sept. 12, 1950, ch. 946, title I, part II (§110 et seq.), 64 Stat. 834

Acid Precipitation Act of 1980
Pub. L. 96–294, title VII, June 30, 1980, 94 Stat. 770 (42 U.S.C. 8901 et seq.)
Short title, see 42 U.S.C. 8901 note

Acid Transportation Act (Carriage by Sea)
Aug. 2, 1882, ch. 374, §8, 22 Stat. 189

Ackia Battleground National Monument Act
Aug. 27, 1935, ch. 755, 49 Stat. 897 (16 U.S.C. 450r et seq.)

Act for International Development
June 5, 1950, ch. 220, title IV, 64 Stat. 204 (22 U.S.C. 1557 et seq.)

Act for International Development of 1961
Pub. L. 87–195, part I (§101 et seq.), Sept. 4, 1961, 75 Stat. 424 (22 U.S.C. 2151 et seq.)

Act For Reform In Emerging New Democracies and Support and Help for Improved Partnership with Russia, Ukraine, and Other New Independent States
Also known as the FRIENDSHIP Act
Pub. L. 103–199, Dec. 17, 1993, 107 Stat. 2317
Short title, see 22 U.S.C. 5801 note

Act for the Prevention and Punishment of Crimes Against Internationally Protected Persons
Pub. L. 94–467, Oct. 8, 1976, 90 Stat. 1997
Short title, see 18 U.S.C. 112 note

Act for the Prevention and Punishment of the Crime of Hostage-Taking
Pub. L. 98–473, title II, ch. XX, part A (§2001 et seq.), Oct. 12, 1984, 98 Stat. 2186 (18 U.S.C. 1203)
Short title, see 18 U.S.C. 1201 note

Act for the Protection of Foreign Officials and Official Guests of the United States
Pub. L. 92–539, Oct. 24, 1972, 86 Stat. 1070
Short title, see 18 U.S.C. 112 note

Act for the Regulation of Credit Life Insurance and Credit Accident and Health Insurance
Pub. L. 87–686, Sept. 25, 1962, 76 Stat. 580

Act Relating to Children Born Out of Wedlock
Jan. 11, 1951, ch. 1225, 64 Stat. 1240

Act to authorize the United States to participate in chapter II of the Patent Cooperation Treaty
Pub. L. 99–616, Nov. 6, 1986, 100 Stat. 3485
Short title, see 35 U.S.C. 351 note

Act to Prevent Pollution from Ships
Pub. L. 96–478, Oct. 21, 1980, 94 Stat. 2297 (33 U.S.C. 1901 et seq.)
Short title, see 33 U.S.C. 1901 note

Act to Promote the Defense of the United States
Mar. 11, 1941, ch. 11, 55 Stat. 31 (22 U.S.C. 411 et seq.)

ADAMHA Reorganization Act
Pub. L. 102–321, July 10, 1992, 106 Stat. 323
Short title, see 42 U.S.C. 201 note

Adams Act (Agricultural Experiment Stations)
Mar. 16, 1906, ch. 951, 34 Stat. 63

Adams National Historical Park Act of 1998
Pub. L. 105–342, Nov. 2, 1998, 112 Stat. 3200 (16 U.S.C. 410eee et seq.)
Short title, see 16 U.S.C. 410eee note

Adamson Law (Eight Hour Day)
Sept. 3, 5, 1916, ch. 436, 39 Stat. 721 (45 U.S.C. 65 et seq.)
Short title, see 45 U.S.C. 65 note

Additional House Office Building Act of 1955
Apr. 22, 1955, ch. 26, ch. XII–A, 69 Stat. 41 (40 U.S.C. 175 note)

Additional Urgent Deficiency Appropriation Act, 1941
May 24, 1941, ch. 132, 55 Stat. 197

Adjusted Compensation Act
See World War Adjusted Compensation Act

Adjusted Compensation Payment Act, 1936
Jan. 27, 1936, ch. 32, 49 Stat. 1099

Adjustment Act (Irrigation Projects)
May 25, 1926, ch. 383, §§40–46, 48, 50, 44 Stat. 647–650 (43 U.S.C. 423 et seq.)

Adjustment Act (Railroad Land Grants)
Mar. 3, 1887, ch. 376, 24 Stat. 556 (43 U.S.C. 894–899)

Adjustment to Lawful Resident Status of Certain Nationals of Countries for Which Extended Voluntary Departure Has Been Made Available
Pub. L. 100–202, §101(a) [title IX], Dec. 22, 1987, 101 Stat. 1329, 1329–43 (8 U.S.C. 1255a note)

Administrative Conference Act
Pub. L. 88–499, Aug. 30, 1964, 78 Stat. 615

Administrative Dispute Resolution Act
Pub. L. 101–552, Nov. 15, 1990, 104 Stat. 2736 (5 U.S.C. 571 et seq.)
Short title, see 5 U.S.C. 571 note

Administrative Dispute Resolution Act of 1996
Pub. L. 104–320, Oct. 19, 1996, 110 Stat. 3870
Short title, see 5 U.S.C. 571 note

Administrative Expenses Act of 1946
Aug. 2, 1946, ch. 744, 60 Stat. 806

Administrative Office of the United States Courts Personnel Act of 1990
Pub. L. 101–474, Oct. 30, 1990, 104 Stat. 1097

Administrative Orders Review Act
Dec. 29, 1950, ch. 1189, 64 Stat. 1129

Administrative Procedure Act
June 11, 1946, ch. 324, 60 Stat. 237
Short title, see 5 U.S.C. note prec. 551

Administrative Procedure Technical Amendments Act of 1991
Pub. L. 102–354, Aug. 26, 1992, 106 Stat. 944
Short title, see 5 U.S.C. 561 note

Admiral James W. Nance and Meg Donovan Foreign Relations Authorization Act, Fiscal Years 2000 and 2001
Pub. L. 106–113, div. B, §1000(a)(7) [H.R. 3427], Nov. 29, 1999, 113 Stat. 1536, 1501A–405
Short title, see 22 U.S.C. 2651 note

Admiralty Bond Act
Aug. 4, 1790, ch. 35, §67, 1 Stat. 176

Admiralty Island National Monument Land Management Act of 1990
Pub. L. 101–378, title II, Aug. 17, 1990, 104 Stat. 468

Admiralty Jurisdiction Act (Extension)
June 19, 1948, ch. 526, 62 Stat. 496 (46 App. 740)

Adoption and Safe Families Act of 1997
Pub. L. 105–89, Nov. 19, 1997, 111 Stat. 2115
Short title, see 42 U.S.C. 1305 note

Adoption Assistance and Child Welfare Act of 1980
Pub. L. 96–272, June 17, 1980, 94 Stat. 500
Short title, see 42 U.S.C. 1305 note

Adult Education Act
Pub. L. 89–750, title III, as added Pub. L. 100–297, title II, §2102, Apr. 28, 1988, 102 Stat. 302 (20 U.S.C. 1201 et seq.)
Short title, see 20 U.S.C. 1201 note

Adult Education Act of 1966
Renamed the Adult Education Act

Adult Education Amendments of 1988
Pub. L. 100–297, title II, part B (§2101 et seq.), Apr. 28, 1988, 102 Stat. 302
Short title, see 20 U.S.C. 1201 note

Adult Education and Family Literacy Act
Pub. L. 105–220, title II, Aug. 7, 1998, 112 Stat. 1059 (20 U.S.C. 9201 et seq.)
Short title, see 20 U.S.C. 9201 note

Adult Indian Vocational Training Act
Aug. 3, 1956, ch. 930, 70 Stat. 986 (25 U.S.C. 309, 309a)

Adulterated Seeds Act
Aug. 24, 1912, ch. 382, 37 Stat. 506

Advance Pay and Allotment Act of 1961
Pub. L. 87–304, Sept. 26, 1961, 75 Stat. 662

Advancement and Allotment of Pay in Emergency Evacuation Act
See Advance Pay and Allotment Act of 1961

Advertising Act (Public Purchases)
Mar. 2, 1861, ch. 84, §10, 12 Stat. 220; R.S. 3709 (41 U.S.C. 5)

Advisory Commission on Intergovernmental Relations Act of 1959
Pub. L. 86–380, Sept. 24, 1959, 73 Stat. 703 (42 U.S.C. 4271 et seq.)

Advisory Committee on Intergovernmental Relations Act of 1959
See Advisory Commission on Intergovernmental Relations Act of 1959

Advisory Council on California Indian Policy Act of 1992
Pub. L. 102–416, Oct. 14, 1992, 106 Stat. 2131 (25 U.S.C. 651 note)

Advisory Council on California Indian Policy Extension Act of 1998
Pub. L. 105–294, Oct. 27, 1998, 112 Stat. 2818
Short title, see 25 U.S.C. 651 note

Advisory Council on Community Renewal Act
Pub. L. 106–554, §1(a)(7) [title I, subtitle E, part II (§151 et seq.)], Dec. 21, 2000, 114 Stat. 2763, 2763A–622 (26 U.S.C. 1400E note)

Affordable Housing for Seniors and Families Act
Pub. L. 106–569, title VIII, Dec. 27, 2000, 114 Stat. 3018
Short title, see 12 U.S.C. 1701 note

Africa: Seeds of Hope Act of 1998
Pub. L. 105–385, Nov. 13, 1998, 112 Stat. 3460
Short title, see 7 U.S.C. 1691 note

African American History Landmark Theme Study Act
Pub. L. 102–98, Aug. 17, 1991, 105 Stat. 485 (16 U.S.C. 1a–5 note)

African Conflict Resolution Act
Pub. L. 103–381, Oct. 19, 1994, 108 Stat. 3513 (22 U.S.C. 2151 note)

African Development Bank Act
Pub. L. 97–35, title XIII, subtitle B, part 3 (§1331 et seq.), Aug. 13, 1981, 95 Stat. 741 (22 U.S.C. 290i et seq.)
Short title, see 22 U.S.C. 290i note

African Development Foundation Act
Pub. L. 96–533, title V, Dec. 16, 1980, 94 Stat. 3151 (22 U.S.C. 290h et seq.)

African Development Foundation Act—Continued
Short title, see 22 U.S.C. 290h note

African Development Fund Act
Pub. L. 94–302, title II, May 31, 1976, 90 Stat. 593 (22 U.S.C. 290g et seq.)
Short title, see 22 U.S.C. 290g note

African Elephant Conservation Act
Pub. L. 100–478, title II, Oct. 7, 1988, 102 Stat. 2315 (16 U.S.C. 4201 et seq.)
Short title, see 16 U.S.C. 4201 note

African Elephant Conservation Reauthorization Act of 1998
Pub. L. 105–217, Aug. 5, 1998, 112 Stat. 911
Short title, see 16 U.S.C. 4201 note

African Famine Relief and Recovery Act of 1985
Pub. L. 99–8, Apr. 2, 1985, 99 Stat. 21 (22 U.S.C. 2292q, 2292q note)
Short title, see 22 U.S.C. 2151 note

African Growth and Opportunity Act
Pub. L. 106–200, title I, May 18, 2000, 114 Stat. 252 (19 U.S.C. 3701 et seq.)
Short title, see 19 U.S.C. 3701 note

Age Discrimination Act of 1975
Pub. L. 94–135, title III, Nov. 28, 1975, 89 Stat. 728 (42 U.S.C. 6101 et seq.)
Short title, see 42 U.S.C. 6101 note

Age Discrimination Claims Assistance Act of 1988
Pub. L. 100–283, Apr. 7, 1988, 102 Stat. 78 (29 U.S.C. 626 note)

Age Discrimination Claims Assistance Amendments of 1990
Pub. L. 101–504, Nov. 3, 1990, 104 Stat. 1298

Age Discrimination in Employment Act Amendments of 1978
Pub. L. 95–256, Apr. 6, 1978, 92 Stat. 189
Short title, see 29 U.S.C. 621 note

Age Discrimination in Employment Act of 1967
Pub. L. 90–202, Dec. 15, 1967, 81 Stat. 602 (29 U.S.C. 621 et seq.)
Short title, see 29 U.S.C. 621 note

Age Discrimination in Employment Amendments of 1986
Pub. L. 99–592, Oct. 31, 1986, 100 Stat. 3342
Short title, see 29 U.S.C. 621 note

Age Discrimination in Employment Amendments of 1996
Pub. L. 104–208, div. A, title I, §101(a) [title I, §119], Sept. 30, 1996, 110 Stat. 3009, 3009–23
Short title, see 29 U.S.C. 621 note

Agency for Health Care Policy and Research Reauthorization Act of 1992
Pub. L. 102–410, Oct. 13, 1992, 106 Stat. 2094
Short title, see 42 U.S.C. 201 note

Agent Orange Act of 1991
Pub. L. 102–4, Feb. 6, 1991, 105 Stat. 11
Short title, see 38 U.S.C. 101 note

Aging Aircraft Safety Act of 1991
Pub. L. 102–143, title IV, Oct. 28, 1991, 105 Stat. 951

Agricultural Act of 1948
July 3, 1948, ch. 827, 62 Stat. 1247
Short title, see 7 U.S.C. 1281 note

Agricultural Act of 1949
Oct. 31, 1949, ch. 792, 63 Stat. 1051 (7 U.S.C. 1421 et seq.)
Short title, see 7 U.S.C. 1421 note

Agricultural Act of 1954
Aug. 28, 1954, ch. 1041, 68 Stat. 897
Short title, see 7 U.S.C. 1741 note

Agricultural Act of 1956
May 28, 1956, ch. 327, 70 Stat. 188
Short title, see 7 U.S.C. 1281 note

Agricultural Act of 1958
Pub. L. 85–835, Aug. 28, 1958, 72 Stat. 988
Short title, see 7 U.S.C. 1281 note

Agricultural Act of 1961
Pub. L. 87–128, Aug. 8, 1961, 75 Stat. 294
Short title, see 7 U.S.C. 1911 note

Agricultural Act of 1964
Pub. L. 88–297, Apr. 11, 1964, 78 Stat. 173
Short title, see 7 U.S.C. 1281 note

Agricultural Act of 1970
Pub. L. 91–524, Nov. 30, 1970, 84 Stat. 1358
Short title, see 7 U.S.C. 1281 note

Agricultural Act of 1980
Pub. L. 96–494, Dec. 3, 1980, 94 Stat. 2570
Short title, see 7 U.S.C. 4001 note

Agricultural Adjustment Act
May 12, 1933, ch. 25, title I, 48 Stat. 31 (7 U.S.C. 601 et seq.)
Short title, see 7 U.S.C. 601 note

Agricultural Adjustment Act of 1933
See Agricultural Adjustment Act

Agricultural Adjustment Act of 1937
See Agricultural Marketing Agreement Act of 1937June 3, 1937, ch. 296, 50 Stat. 246

Agricultural Adjustment Act of 1938
Feb. 16, 1938, ch. 30, 52 Stat. 31 (7 U.S.C. 1281 et seq.)
Short title, see 7 U.S.C. 1281

Agricultural Adjustment Act of 1980
Pub. L. 96–213, Mar. 18, 1980, 94 Stat. 119
Short title, see 7 U.S.C. 1421 note

Agricultural Aid and Trade Missions Act
Pub. L. 100–202, §§1–16, Dec. 22, 1987, 101 Stat. 1329–445 to 1329–449 (7 U.S.C. 1736bb et seq.)
Short title, see 7 U.S.C. 1691 note

Agricultural Appropriation Act, 1940
June 30, 1939, ch. 253, 53 Stat. 939

Agricultural College Act of 1890
Also known as the Second Morrill Act
Aug. 30, 1890, ch. 841, 26 Stat. 417 (7 U.S.C. 321 et seq.)
Short title, see 7 U.S.C. 321 note

Agricultural Competitiveness and Trade Act of 1988
Pub. L. 100–418, title IV, Aug. 23, 1988, 102 Stat. 1388
Short title, see 7 U.S.C. 5201 note

Agricultural Credit Act of 1978
Pub. L. 95–334, Aug. 4, 1978, 92 Stat. 420
Short title, see 7 U.S.C. 1921 note

Agricultural Credit Act of 1987
Pub. L. 100–233, Jan. 6, 1988, 101 Stat. 1568
Short title, see 12 U.S.C. 2001 note

Agricultural Credit Corporations Act
Mar. 3, 1932, ch. 70, 47 Stat. 60 (12 U.S.C. 1401 et seq.)

Agricultural Credit Improvement Act of 1992
Pub. L. 102–554, Oct. 28, 1992, 106 Stat. 4142
Short title, see 7 U.S.C. 1921 note

Agricultural Credit Technical Corrections Act of 1988
Pub. L. 100–399, Aug. 17, 1988, 102 Stat. 989
Short title, see 12 U.S.C. 2001 note

Agricultural Credits Act of 1923
Mar. 4, 1923, ch. 252, 42 Stat. 1454 (12 U.S.C. 1151 et seq.)

Agricultural Debt Relief Act
See Frazier-Lemke Farm-Mortgage Act

Agricultural Development and Trade Act of 1990
Pub. L. 101–624, title XV, Nov. 28, 1990, 104 Stat. 3632
Short title, see 7 U.S.C. 1691 note

Agricultural Enabling Amendments Act of 1961
Pub. L. 87–128, title I, Aug. 8, 1961, 75 Stat. 295
Short title, see 7 U.S.C. 1911 note

Agricultural Extension Work Act
See Smith-Lever Act

Agricultural Fair Practices Act of 1967
Pub. L. 90–288, Apr. 16, 1968, 82 Stat. 93 (7 U.S.C. 2301 et seq.)
Short title, see 7 U.S.C. 2301 note

Agricultural Foreign Investment Disclosure Act of 1978
Pub. L. 95–460, Oct. 14, 1978, 92 Stat. 1263 (7 U.S.C. 3501 et seq.)
Short title, see 7 U.S.C. 3501 note

Agricultural Market Transition Act
Pub. L. 104–127, title I, Apr. 4, 1996, 110 Stat. 896 (7 U.S.C. 7201 et seq.)
Short title, see 7 U.S.C. 7201(a)

Agricultural Marketing Act
June 15, 1929, ch. 24, 46 Stat. 11 (12 U.S.C. 1141 et seq.)
Short title, see 12 U.S.C. 1141j(f)

Agricultural Marketing Act of 1946
Aug. 14, 1946, ch. 966, title II, 60 Stat. 1087 (7 U.S.C. 1621 et seq.)
Short title, see 7 U.S.C. 1621 note

Agricultural Marketing Agreement Act of 1937
June 3, 1937, ch. 296, 50 Stat. 246

Agricultural Program Reporting and Recordkeeping Improvement Act of 1990
Pub. L. 101–624, title XXV, §2516, Nov. 28, 1990, 104 Stat. 4075 (7 U.S.C. 1421 note)

Agricultural Programs Adjustment Act of 1984
Pub. L. 98–258, Apr. 10, 1984, 98 Stat. 130
Short title, see 7 U.S.C. 1421 note

Agricultural Promotion Programs Act of 1990
Pub. L. 101–624, title XIX, Nov. 28, 1990, 104 Stat. 3838
Short title, see 7 U.S.C. 6001 note

Agricultural Reconciliation Act of 1987
Pub. L. 100–203, title I, Dec. 22, 1987, 101 Stat. 1330
Short title, see 7 U.S.C. 1421 note

Agricultural Reconciliation Act of 1989
Pub. L. 101–239, title I, Dec. 19, 1989, 103 Stat. 2106
Short title, see 7 U.S.C. 1421 note

Agricultural Reconciliation Act of 1990
Pub. L. 101–508, title I, Nov. 5, 1990, 104 Stat. 1388
Short title, see 7 U.S.C. 1421 note

Agricultural Reconciliation Act of 1993
Pub. L. 103–66, title I, Aug. 10, 1993, 107 Stat. 312
Short title, see 7 U.S.C. 1421 note

Agricultural Research Act
Also known as the Bankhead-Jones Act
June 29, 1935, ch. 338, 49 Stat. 436 (7 U.S.C. 427–427j)
Short title, see 7 U.S.C. 427 note

Agricultural Research, Extension, and Education Reform Act of 1998
Pub. L. 105–185, June 23, 1998, 112 Stat. 523
Short title, see 7 U.S.C. 7601 note

Agricultural Risk Protection Act of 2000
Pub. L. 106–224, June 20, 2000, 114 Stat. 358
Short title, see 7 U.S.C. 1501 note

Agricultural Subterminal Facilities Act of 1980
Pub. L. 96–358, Sept. 25, 1980, 94 Stat. 1184 (7 U.S.C. 3701 et seq.)
Short title, see 7 U.S.C. 3701 note

Agricultural Trade Act of 1978
Pub. L. 95–501, Oct. 21, 1978, 92 Stat. 1685 (7 U.S.C. 5601 et seq.)
Short title, see 7 U.S.C. 5601 note

Agricultural Trade and Export Policy Commission Act
Pub. L. 98–412, Aug. 30, 1984, 98 Stat. 1576 (7 U.S.C. 1691 note)

Agricultural Trade Development and Assistance Act of 1954
July 10, 1954, ch. 469, 68 Stat. 454 (7 U.S.C. 1691 et seq.)
Short title, see 7 U.S.C. 1691 note

Agricultural Trade Suspension Adjustment Act of 1980
Pub. L. 96–494, title II, Dec. 3, 1980, 94 Stat. 2570 (7 U.S.C. 4001 et seq.)
Short title, see 7 U.S.C. 4001 note

Agricultural, Rural Development, Food and Drug Administration, and Related Agencies Appropriations Act, 1995
Pub. L. 103–330, Sept. 30, 1994, 108 Stat. 2435

Agriculture and Consumer Protection Act of 1973
Pub. L. 93–86, Aug. 10, 1973, 87 Stat. 221
Short title, see 7 U.S.C. 1281 note

Agriculture and Food Act of 1981
Pub. L. 97–98, Dec. 22, 1981, 95 Stat. 1213
Short title, see 7 U.S.C. 1281 note

Agriculture and Related Agencies Appropriation Act, 1976
Pub. L. 94–122, Oct. 21, 1975, 89 Stat. 641

Agriculture and Related Agencies Appropriation Act, 1977
Pub. L. 94–351, July 12, 1976, 90 Stat. 851

Agriculture and Related Agencies Appropriation Act, 1978
Pub. L. 95–97, Aug. 12, 1977, 91 Stat. 810

Agriculture and Water Policy Coordination Act
Pub. L. 101–624, title XIV, subtitle G (§1481 et seq.), Nov. 28, 1990, 104 Stat. 3622 (7 U.S.C. 5501 et seq.)

Agriculture Export Relief Act of 1998
Pub. L. 105–194, July 14, 1998, 112 Stat. 627
Short title, see 22 U.S.C. 2751 note

Agriculture Regulatory Act
Apr. 4, 1940, ch. 75, 54 Stat. 81 (7 U.S.C. 450c–450g)

Agriculture, Rural Development, and Related Agencies Appropriation Act, 1979
Pub. L. 95–448, Oct. 11, 1978, 92 Stat. 1073

Agriculture, Rural Development, and Related Agencies Appropriation Act, 1980
Pub. L. 96–108, Nov. 9, 1979, 93 Stat. 821

Agriculture, Rural Development, and Related Agencies Appropriation Act, 1981
Pub. L. 96–528, Dec. 15, 1980, 94 Stat. 3095

Agriculture, Rural Development, and Related Agencies Appropriation Act, 1982
Pub. L. 97–103, Dec. 23, 1981, 95 Stat. 1467

Agriculture, Rural Development, and Related Agencies Appropriations Act, 1983
Pub. L. 97–370, Dec. 18, 1982, 96 Stat. 1787

Agriculture, Rural Development, and Related Agencies Appropriations Act, 1986
Pub. L. 99–190, §101(a) [H.R. 3037], Dec. 19, 1985, 99 Stat. 1185; Pub. L. 100–202, §106, Dec. 22, 1987, 101 Stat. 1329–433

Agriculture, Rural Development, and Related Agencies Appropriations Act, 1987
Pub. L. 99–500, §101(a), Oct. 18, 1986, 100 Stat. 1783, and Pub. L. 99–591, §101(a), Oct. 30, 1986, 100 Stat. 3341

Agriculture, Rural Development, Food and Drug Administration, and Related Agencies Appropriations Act, 1992
Pub. L. 102–142, Oct. 28, 1991, 105 Stat. 878

Agriculture, Rural Development, Food and Drug Administration, and Related Agencies Appropriations Act, 1993
Pub. L. 102–341, Aug. 14, 1992, 106 Stat. 873

Agriculture, Rural Development, Food and Drug Administration, and Related Agencies Appropriations Act, 1994
Pub. L. 103–111, Oct. 21, 1993, 107 Stat. 1046

Agriculture, Rural Development, Food and Drug Administration, and Related Agencies Appropriations Act, 1996
Pub. L. 104–37, Oct. 21, 1995, 109 Stat. 299

Agriculture, Rural Development, Food and Drug Administration, and Related Agencies Appropriations Act, 1997
Pub. L. 104–180, Aug. 6, 1996, 110 Stat. 1569

Agriculture, Rural Development, Food and Drug Administration, and Related Agencies Appropriations Act, 1998
Pub. L. 105–86, Nov. 18, 1997, 111 Stat. 2079

Agriculture, Rural Development, Food and Drug Administration, and Related Agencies Appropriations Act, 1999
Pub. L. 105–277, div. A, §101(a), Oct. 21, 1998, 112 Stat. 2681

Agriculture, Rural Development, Food and Drug Administration, and Related Agencies Appropriations Act, 2000
Pub. L. 106–78, Oct. 22, 1999, 113 Stat. 1135

Agriculture, Rural Development, Food and Drug Administration, and Related Agencies Appropriations Act, 2001
Pub. L. 106–387, §1(a) [H.R. 5426], Oct. 28, 2000, 114 Stat. 1549, 1549A–1

Agriculture-Environmental and Consumer Protection Appropriation Act, 1972
Pub. L. 92–73, Aug. 10, 1971, 85 Stat. 183

Agriculture-Environmental and Consumer Protection Appropriation Act, 1973
Pub. L. 92–399, Aug. 22, 1972, 86 Stat. 591

Agriculture-Environmental and Consumer Protection Appropriation Act, 1974
Pub. L. 93–135, Oct. 24, 1973, 87 Stat. 468

Agriculture-Environmental and Consumer Protection Appropriation Act, 1975
Pub. L. 93–563, Dec. 31, 1974, 88 Stat. 1822

Agua Caliente Equalization Act of 1959
Pub. L. 86–339, Sept. 21, 1959, 73 Stat. 602 (25 U.S.C. 951 et seq.)
Short title, see 25 U.S.C. 951 note

Aid to Dependent Children Act
June 14, 1944, ch. 257, 58 Stat. 277

Aid, Trade, and Competitiveness Act of 1992
Pub. L. 102–549, title III, Oct. 28, 1992, 106 Stat. 3658 (22 U.S.C. 2421a et seq.)
Short title, see 22 U.S.C. 2421a note

AIDS Amendments of 1988
Pub. L. 100–607, title II, Nov. 4, 1988, 102 Stat. 3062
Short title, see 42 U.S.C. 201 note

AIDS Housing Opportunity Act
Pub. L. 101–625, title VIII, subtitle D (§851 et seq.), Nov. 28, 1990, 104 Stat. 4375 (42 U.S.C. 12901 et seq.)
Short title, see 42 U.S.C. 12901 note

Aimee's Law
Pub. L. 106–386, div. C, §2001, Oct. 28, 2000, 114 Stat. 1539 (42 U.S.C. 13713)

Air Base Act
See Wilcox Air Base Act

Air Brakes Act (Railroads)
Mar. 2, 1903, ch. 976, §2, 32 Stat. 943

Air Carrier Access Act of 1986
Pub. L. 99–435, Oct. 2, 1986, 100 Stat. 1080

Air Carrier Economic Regulation Act
June 23, 1938, ch. 601, title IV, 52 Stat. 987

Air Commerce Act of 1926
May 20, 1926, ch. 344, 44 Stat. 568

Air Corps Act
July 2, 1926, ch. 721, 44 Stat. 780

Air Engineering Development Center Act of 1949
Oct. 27, 1949, ch. 766, title II, 63 Stat. 937 (50 U.S.C. 521 et seq.)
Short title, see 50 U.S.C. 511 note

Air Engineering Duty Act
June 5, 1935, ch. 175, 49 Stat. 323

Air Force Academy Act
Apr. 1, 1954, ch. 127, 68 Stat. 47

Air Force Headquarters Act
May 12, 1939, ch. 127, 53 Stat. 740

Air Force Organization Act of 1951
Sept. 19, 1951, ch. 407, 65 Stat. 326

Air Mail Act
Feb. 2, 1925, ch. 128, 43 Stat. 805

Air Pollution Control Act
See Clean Air Act

Air Quality Act of 1967
Pub. L. 90–148, Nov. 21, 1967, 81 Stat. 485
Short title, see 42 U.S.C. 7401 note

Air Raid Attack Act
Jan. 27, 1942, ch. 20, 56 Stat. 19

Air Safety Board Act
June 23, 1938, ch. 601, title VII, 52 Stat. 1012

Air Traffic Management System Performance Improvement Act of 1996
Pub. L. 104–264, title II, Oct. 9, 1996, 110 Stat. 3227
Short title, see 49 U.S.C. 40101 note

Air Transport Labor Act
See Railway Labor Act

Air Transportation Security Act of 1974
Pub. L. 93–366, title II, Aug. 5, 1974, 88 Stat. 415

Aircraft Contracts Act
Mar. 5, 1940, ch. 44, 54 Stat. 45

Aircraft Development Act
June 30, 1938, ch. 852, 52 Stat. 1255 (50 U.S.C. 95)

Aircraft Equipment Settlement Leases Act of 1993
Pub. L. 103–7, Mar. 17, 1993, 107 Stat. 36 (11 U.S.C. 1110 note)

Aircraft Parts Secrecy Act
July 13, 1939, ch. 265, 53 Stat. 1000

Aircraft Prize Act
June 24, 1941, ch. 232, 55 Stat. 261

Aircraft Registration Act
June 23, 1938, ch. 601, title V, 52 Stat. 1005

Aircraft Sabotage Act
Pub. L. 98–473, title II, ch. XX, part B (§2011 et seq.), Oct. 12, 1984, 98 Stat. 2187
Short title, see 18 U.S.C. 31 note

Aircraft Safety Act of 2000
Pub. L. 106–181, title V, §506, Apr. 5, 2000, 114 Stat. 136
Short title, see 18 U.S.C. 31 note

Airline Deregulation Act of 1978
Pub. L. 95–504, Oct. 24, 1978, 92 Stat. 1705

Airport and Airway Development Act Amendments of 1976
Pub. L. 94–353, July 12, 1976, 90 Stat. 871

Airport and Airway Development Act of 1970
Pub. L. 91–258, title I, May 21, 1970, 84 Stat. 219

Airport and Airway Improvement Act of 1982
Pub. L. 97–248, title V, Sept. 3, 1982, 96 Stat. 671

Airport and Airway Revenue Act of 1970
Pub. L. 91–258, title II, May 21, 1970, 84 Stat. 236
Short title, see 26 U.S.C. 4041 note

Airport and Airway Revenue Act of 1987
Pub. L. 100–223, title IV, Dec. 30, 1987, 101 Stat. 1532
Short title, see 26 U.S.C. 1 note

Airport and Airway Safety and Capacity Expansion Act of 1987
Pub. L. 100–223, Dec. 30, 1987, 101 Stat. 1486

Airport and Airway Safety, Capacity, Noise Improvement, and Intermodal Transportation Act of 1992
Pub. L. 102–581, Oct. 31, 1992, 106 Stat. 4872

Airport and Airway Trust Fund Tax Reinstatement Act of 1997
Pub. L. 105–2, Feb. 28, 1997, 111 Stat. 4
Short title, see 26 U.S.C. 1 note

Airport Development Acceleration Act of 1973
Pub. L. 93–44, June 18, 1973, 87 Stat. 88

Airport Improvement Program Temporary Extension Act of 1994
Pub. L. 103–260, May 26, 1994, 108 Stat. 698

Airport Noise and Capacity Act of 1990
Pub. L. 101–508, title IX, subtitle D (§9301 et seq.), Nov. 5, 1990, 104 Stat. 1388–378

Airport Revenue Protection Act of 1996
Pub. L. 104–264, title VIII, Oct. 9, 1996, 110 Stat. 3269

Airport Revenue Protection Act of 1996—Continued
Short title, see 49 U.S.C. 40101 note

Airport Security Improvement Act of 2000
Pub. L. 106–528, Nov. 22, 2000, 114 Stat. 2517
Short title, see 49 U.S.C. 40101 note

Airways Modernization Act of 1957
Pub. L. 85–133, Aug. 14, 1957, 71 Stat. 349

Ak-Chin Water Use Amendments Act of 1992
Pub. L. 102–497, §10, Oct. 24, 1992, 106 Stat. 3258

Ak-Chin Water Use Amendments Act of 2000
Pub. L. 106–285, §2, Oct. 10, 2000, 114 Stat. 878

Ala Kahakai National Historic Trail Act
Pub. L. 106–509, Nov. 13, 2000, 114 Stat. 2361
Short title, see 16 U.S.C. 1241 note

Alaska Centennial Act of 1966
Pub. L. 89–375, Mar. 26, 1966, 80 Stat. 82

Alaska Civil Code
June 6, 1900, ch. 786, title III, 31 Stat. 494

Alaska Coal Lands Act
Oct. 20, 1914, ch. 330, 38 Stat. 741

Alaska Communications Disposal Act
Pub. L. 90–135, Nov. 14, 1967, 81 Stat. 441 (40 U.S.C. 771 et seq.)
Short title, see 40 U.S.C. 771 note

Alaska Criminal Code
Mar. 3, 1899, ch. 429, 30 Stat. 1253

Alaska Federal-Civilian Energy Efficiency Swap Act of 1980
Pub. L. 96–571, Dec. 22, 1980, 94 Stat. 3341 (40 U.S.C. 795 et seq.)
Short title, see 40 U.S.C. 795 note

Alaska Fisheries Act
June 6, 1924, ch. 272, 43 Stat. 464

Alaska Five Acre Homestead Act
Mar. 3, 1927, ch. 323, 44 Stat. 1364

Alaska Fur Farming Act
July 3, 1926, ch. 745, 44 Stat. 821

Alaska Game Law
Jan. 13, 1925, ch. 75, as added July 1, 1943, ch. 183, 57 Stat. 301

Alaska Government Act
Aug. 24, 1912, ch. 387, 37 Stat. 512

Alaska Housing Act
Apr. 23, 1949, ch. 89, 63 Stat. 57

Alaska Hydroelectric Power Development Act
Pub. L. 94–587, title II, §203, Oct. 22, 1976, 90 Stat. 2946 (42 U.S.C. 1962d–14a)
Short title, see 42 U.S.C. 1962d–14a(i)

Alaska Industrial School Act
Feb. 25, 1925, ch. 320, 43 Stat. 978

Alaska International Highway Commission Act
May 31, 1938, ch. 299, 52 Stat. 590

Alaska International Rail and Highway Commission Act
Aug. 1, 1956, ch. 840, 70 Stat. 888

Alaska Land Status Technical Corrections Act of 1992
Pub. L. 102–415, Oct. 14, 1992, 106 Stat. 2112
Short title, see 42 U.S.C. 1601 note

Alaska Liquor Repeal Act
Apr. 13, 1934, ch. 119, 48 Stat. 583

Alaska Livestock Grazing Act
Mar. 4, 1927, ch. 513, 44 Stat. 1452 (43 U.S.C. 316 et seq.)
Short title, see 43 U.S.C. 316 note

Alaska Mental Health Enabling Act
July 28, 1956, ch. 772, 70 Stat. 709

Alaska Military Code
Dec. 31, 1941, ch. 644, 55 Stat. 879

Alaska Miner's Labor Lien Act
See Miner's Labor Lien Act

Alaska National Interest Lands Conservation Act
Pub. L. 96–487, Dec. 2, 1980, 94 Stat. 2371 (16 U.S.C. 3101 et seq.)
Short title, see 16 U.S.C. 3101 note

Alaska Native and American Indian Direct Reimbursement Act of 2000
Pub. L. 106–417, Nov. 1, 2000, 114 Stat. 1812
Short title, see 25 U.S.C. 1601 note

Alaska Native Claims Settlement Act
Pub. L. 92–203, Dec. 18, 1971, 85 Stat. 688 (43 U.S.C. 1601 et seq.)
Short title, see 43 U.S.C. 1601 note

Alaska Native Claims Settlement Act Amendments of 1987
Pub. L. 100–241, Feb. 3, 1988, 101 Stat. 1788
Short title, see 43 U.S.C. 1601 note

Alaska Native Culture and Arts Development Act
Pub. L. 103–239, title VII, subtitle C (§721 et seq.), May 4, 1994, 108 Stat. 606
Short title, see 20 U.S.C. 4401 note

Alaska Native Educational Equity, Support and Assistance Act
Pub. L. 89–10, title IX, part C (§9301 et seq.), as added Pub. L. 103–382, title I, §101, Oct. 20, 1994, 108 Stat. 3805 (20 U.S.C. 7931 et seq.)
Short title, see 20 U.S.C. 7931

Alaska Natural Gas Transportation Act of 1976
Pub. L. 94–586, Oct. 22, 1976, 90 Stat. 2903 (15 U.S.C. 719 et seq.)
Short title, see 15 U.S.C. 719 note

Alaska Omnibus Act
Pub. L. 86–70, June 25, 1959, 73 Stat. 141 (48 U.S.C. prec. 21 note)

Alaska Power Administration Asset Sale and Termination Act
Pub. L. 104–58, title I, Nov. 28, 1995, 109 Stat. 557 (42 U.S.C. 7152 note)

Alaska Prohibition Act
Feb. 14, 1917, ch. 53, 39 Stat. 903

Alaska Public Works Act
Aug. 24, 1949, ch. 504, 63 Stat. 627

Alaska Railroad Act
Mar. 12, 1914, ch. 37, 38 Stat. 305 (43 U.S.C. 975–975g)

Alaska Railroad Retirement Act
June 29, 1936, ch. 859, 49 Stat. 2017

Alaska Railroad Transfer Act of 1982
Pub. L. 97–468, title VI, Jan. 14, 1983, 96 Stat. 2556 (45 U.S.C. 1201 et seq.)
Short title, see 45 U.S.C. 1201 note

Alaska Relief of Indigent Act
Mar. 3, 1913, ch. 109, 37 Stat. 728

Alaska Right of Way Act
May 14, 1898, ch. 299, 30 Stat. 409 (43 U.S.C. 942–1 et seq.)
Short title, see 43 U.S.C. 942–1 note

Alaska Road and Trail Act
Jan. 27, 1905, ch. 277, 33 Stat. 616

Alaska Salmon Fisheries Act
Mar. 2, 1889, ch. 415, 25 Stat. 1009

Alaska Special Peace Officers Act
Mar. 3, 1909, ch. 266, 35 Stat. 837

Alaska Statehood Act
Pub. L. 85–508, July 7, 1958, 72 Stat. 339 (48 U.S.C. prec. 21 note)

Alaskan Airports Act
May 28, 1948, ch. 354, 62 Stat. 277

Alaskan Native Townsite Act of 1926
May 25, 1926, ch. 379, 44 Stat. 629

Albert Einstein Distinguished Educator Fellowship Act of 1994
Pub. L. 103–382, title V, part A (§511 et seq.), Oct. 20, 1994, 108 Stat. 4042 (42 U.S.C. 7382 et seq.)
Short title, see 42 U.S.C. 7382 note

Alcohol Abuse, Drug Abuse, and Mental Health Amendments of 1984
Pub. L. 98–509, Oct. 19, 1984, 98 Stat. 2353
Short title, see 42 U.S.C. 201 note

Alcohol and Drug Abuse Amendments of 1983
Pub. L. 98–24, Apr. 26, 1983, 97 Stat. 175
Short title, see 42 U.S.C. 201 note

Alcohol and Drug Abuse Amendments of 1986
Pub. L. 99–570, title IV, subtitle A (§4001 et seq.), Oct. 27, 1986, 100 Stat. 3207–103
Short title, see 42 U.S.C. 201 note

Alcohol and Drug Abuse Education Act
Pub. L. 91–527, Dec. 3, 1970, 84 Stat. 1385 (21 U.S.C. 1001 et seq.)

Alcohol and Drug Abuse Education Act Amendments of 1974
Pub. L. 93–422, Sept. 21, 1974, 88 Stat. 1154

Alcohol and Drug Abuse Education Amendments of 1978
Pub. L. 95–336, Aug. 4, 1978, 92 Stat. 451
Short title, see 20 U.S.C. 1001 note

Alcohol Plants Transfer Act
July 2, 1948, ch. 818, 62 Stat. 1234 (7 U.S.C. 439 et seq.)

Alcoholic and Narcotic Addict Rehabilitation Amendments of 1968
Pub. L. 90–574, title III, Oct. 15, 1968, 82 Stat. 1006

Alcoholic Beverage Labeling Act of 1988
Aug. 29, 1935, ch. 814, title II, as added Pub. L. 100–690, title VIII, §8001(a)(3), Nov. 18, 1988, 102 Stat. 4518 (27 U.S.C. 213 et seq.)
Short title, see 27 U.S.C. 201 note

Alcoholic Rehabilitation Act of 1968
Pub. L. 88–164, title II, part C (§240 et seq.), as added Pub. L. 90–574, title III, §301, Oct. 15, 1968, 82 Stat. 1006

Aldrich Act (Currency)
Mar. 4, 1907, ch. 2913, 34 Stat. 1289

Aldrich-Vreeland Act (National Currency Associations)
May 30, 1908, ch. 229, 35 Stat. 546

Aleutian and Pribilof Islands Restitution Act
Pub. L. 100–383, title II, Aug. 10, 1988, 102 Stat. 911 (50 App. 1989c et seq.)
Short title, see 50 App. 1989c

Aleutian Trade Act of 1990
Pub. L. 101–595, title VI, Nov. 16, 1990, 104 Stat. 2990
Short title, see 46 U.S.C. 2101 note

Aleutian World War II National Historic Areas Act of 1996
Pub. L. 104–333, div. I, title V, §513, Nov. 12, 1996, 110 Stat. 4165 (16 U.S.C. 461 note)

Alien Agency Act
Aug. 7, 1939, ch. 521, 53 Stat. 1244

Alien Contract Labor Law of 1895
Feb. 26, 1885, ch. 164, 23 Stat. 332

Alien Enemy Act
June 25, 1798, ch. 58, 1 Stat. 570

Alien Registration Act, 1940
June 28, 1940, ch. 439, 54 Stat. 670

Alien Species Prevention and Enforcement Act of 1992
Pub. L. 102–393, title VI, §631, Oct. 6, 1992, 106 Stat. 1774
Short title, see 39 U.S.C. 3015 note

Alien Veterans Act
June 21, 1939, ch. 234, 53 Stat. 851

Alien Visa Act
June 20, 1941, ch. 209, 55 Stat. 252

All Writs Act
Mar. 3, 1911, ch. 231, §§234, 261, 262, 36 Stat. 1156, 1162 (see 28 U.S.C. 1651)

Allied Health Professions Personnel Training Act of 1966
Pub. L. 89–751, Nov. 3, 1966, 80 Stat. 1222
Short title, see 42 U.S.C. 201 note

Alpine Lakes Area Management Act of 1976
Pub. L. 94–357, July 12, 1976, 90 Stat. 905 (16 U.S.C. 1132 note)

Alternative Agricultural Research and Commercialization Act of 1990
Pub. L. 101–624, title XVI, subtitle G (§1657 et seq.), Nov. 28, 1990, 104 Stat. 3756 (7 U.S.C. 5901 et seq.)
Short title, see 7 U.S.C. 5901(a)

Alternative Dispute Resolution Act of 1998
Pub. L. 105–315, Oct. 30, 1998, 112 Stat. 2993
Short title, see 28 U.S.C. 1 note

Alternative Mortgage Transaction Parity Act of 1982
Pub. L. 97–320, title VIII, Oct. 15, 1982, 96 Stat. 1545 (12 U.S.C. 3801 et seq.)
Short title, see 12 U.S.C. 3801 note

Alternative Motor Fuels Act of 1988
Pub. L. 100–494, Oct. 14, 1988, 102 Stat. 2441 (42 U.S.C. 6374 et seq.)
Short title, see 42 U.S.C. 6201 note

Alternative Routes to Teacher Certification and Licensure Act of 1992
Pub. L. 89–329, title V, part D, subpt. 2 (§552 et seq.), as added Pub. L. 102–325, title V, §501(a), July 23, 1992, 106 Stat. 698 (20 U.S.C. 1108 et seq.)

Alternative Water Sources Act of 2000
Pub. L. 106–457, title VI, Nov. 7, 2000, 114 Stat. 1975
Short title, see 33 U.S.C. 1251 note

Alzheimer's Disease and Related Dementias Research Act of 1992
Pub. L. 99–660, title IX, Nov. 14, 1986, 100 Stat. 3802 (42 U.S.C. 11201 et seq.)
Short title, see 42 U.S.C. 11201 note

Alzheimer's Disease and Related Dementias Services Research Act of 1986
Renamed the Alzheimer's Disease and Related Dementias Research Act of 1992

Alzheimer's Disease Research, Training, and Education Amendments of 1992
Pub. L. 102–507, Oct. 24, 1992, 106 Stat. 3281
Short title, see 42 U.S.C. 11201 note

Amateur Sports Act of 1978
Pub. L. 95–606, Nov. 8, 1978, 92 Stat. 3045

Amber Hagerman Child Protection Act of 1996
Pub. L. 104–208, div. A, title I, §101(a) [title I, §121[7]], Sept. 30, 1996, 110 Stat. 3009, 3009–26, 3009–31
Short title, see 18 U.S.C. 2241 note

Amendments of 1973 to Federal Law Relating to Explosives
Pub. L. 93–639, Jan. 4, 1975, 88 Stat. 2217
Short title, see 18 U.S.C. 841 note

America the Beautiful Act of 1990
Pub. L. 101–624, title XII, subtitle C (§1261 et seq.), Nov. 28, 1990, 104 Stat. 3553 (16 U.S.C. 2101 note)

America's Law Enforcement and Mental Health Project
Pub. L. 106–515, Nov. 13, 2000, 114 Stat. 2399
Short title, see 42 U.S.C. 3711 note

American Aid to Poland Act of 1988
Pub. L. 100–418, title II, subtitle B, part II (§2221 et seq.), Aug. 23, 1988, 102 Stat. 1336
Short title, see 7 U.S.C. 1421 note

American Antiquities Preservation Act
See National Monument Act (Preservation of Antiquities)

American Arts Gold Medallion Act
Pub. L. 95–630, title IV, Nov. 10, 1978, 92 Stat. 3679 (31 U.S.C. 5111 note)

American Automobile Labeling Act
Pub. L. 92–513, title II, §210, as added Pub. L. 102–388, title III, §355, Oct. 6, 1992, 106 Stat. 1556

American Battlefield Protection Act of 1996
Pub. L. 104–333, div. I, title VI, §604, Nov. 12, 1996, 110 Stat. 4173 (16 U.S.C. 469k)
Short title, see 16 U.S.C. 469k(a)

American Buffalo Coin Commemorative Coin Act of 2000
Also known as the National Museum of the American Indian Commemorative Coin Act of 2000
Pub. L. 106–375, Oct. 27, 2000, 114 Stat. 1435 (31 U.S.C. 5112 note)

American Competitiveness and Workforce Improvement Act of 1998
Pub. L. 105–277, div. C, title IV, Oct. 21, 1998, 112 Stat. 2681–641
Short title, see 8 U.S.C. 1101 note

American Competitiveness in the Twenty-first Century Act of 2000
Pub. L. 106–313, title I, Oct. 17, 2000, 114 Stat. 1251
Short title, see 8 U.S.C. 1101 note

American Conservation and Youth Service Corps Act of 1990
Pub. L. 101–610, title I, subtitle C (§120 et seq.), Nov. 16, 1990, 104 Stat. 3140 (42 U.S.C. 12541 et seq.)
Short title, see 42 U.S.C. 12501 note

American Fire Act
Mar. 3, 1851, ch. 43, §1, 9 Stat. 635 (46 App. U.S.C. 182)

American Fisheries Act
Pub. L. 105–277, div. C, title II, Oct. 21, 1998, 112 Stat. 2681–616
Short title, see 46 U.S.C. 2101 note

American Fisheries Promotion Act
Pub. L. 96–561, title II, Dec. 22, 1980, 94 Stat. 3287
Short title, see 16 U.S.C. 1801 note

American Folklife Preservation Act
Pub. L. 94–201, Jan. 2, 1976, 89 Stat. 1129 (20 U.S.C. 2101 et seq.)
Short title, see 20 U.S.C. 2101 note

American Heart Month Act
Pub. L. 88–254, Dec. 30, 1963, 77 Stat. 843

American Homeownership and Economic Opportunity Act of 2000
Pub. L. 106–569, Dec. 27, 2000, 114 Stat. 2944
Short title, see 12 U.S.C. 1701 note

American Indian Agricultural Resource Management Act
Pub. L. 103–177, Dec. 3, 1993, 107 Stat. 2011 (25 U.S.C. 3701 et seq.)
Short title, see 25 U.S.C. 3701 note

American Indian Education Foundation Act of 2000
Pub. L. 106–568, title XIII, Dec. 27, 2000, 114 Stat. 2936
Short title, see 25 U.S.C. 450 note

American Indian Religious Freedom Act
Pub. L. 95–341, Aug. 11, 1978, 92 Stat. 469 (42 U.S.C. 1996, 1996a)
Short title, see 42 U.S.C. 1996 note

American Indian Religious Freedom Act Amendments of 1994
Pub. L. 103–344, Oct. 6, 1994, 108 Stat. 3125
Short title, see 42 U.S.C. 1996 note

American Indian Trust Fund Management Reform Act of 1994
Pub. L. 103–412, Oct. 25, 1994, 108 Stat. 4239 (25 U.S.C. 4001 et seq.)
Short title, see 25 U.S.C. 4001 note

American Indian, Alaska Native, and Native Hawaiian Culture and Art Development Act
Pub. L. 99–498, title XV, Oct. 17, 1986, 100 Stat. 1600 (20 U.S.C. 4401 et seq.)
Short title, see 20 U.S.C. 4401 note

American Institute in Taiwan Facilities Enhancement Act
Pub. L. 106–212, May 26, 2000, 114 Stat. 332

American Inventors Protection Act of 1999
Pub. L. 106–113, div. B, §1000(a)(9) [title IV], Nov. 29, 1999, 113 Stat. 1536, 1501A–552
Short title, see 35 U.S.C. 1 note

American National Red Cross Act
Jan. 5, 1905, ch. 23, 33 Stat. 599

American National Red Cross Headquarters Act
Feb. 7, 1930, ch. 42, 46 Stat. 66

American Printing House for the Blind Amendments of 1988
Pub. L. 100–630, title IV, Nov. 7, 1988, 102 Stat. 3316
Short title, see 20 U.S.C. 101 note

American Samoa Labor Standards Amendments of 1956
Aug. 8, 1956, ch. 1035, 70 Stat. 1118
Short title, see 29 U.S.C. 201 note

American Society of International Law Headquarters Act
Pub. L. 86–208, Aug. 25, 1959, 73 Stat. 431 (36 U.S.C. 22106 note)

American Society of International Law Incorporation Act
Sept. 20, 1950, ch. 958, 64 Stat. 869

American Technology Preeminence Act of 1991
Pub. L. 102–245, Feb. 14, 1992, 106 Stat. 7
Short title, see 15 U.S.C. 3701 note

American University Incorporation Amendments Act of 1990
Pub. L. 101–480, Oct. 31, 1990, 104 Stat. 1160

American War Mothers Incorporation Act
Feb. 24, 1925, ch. 303, 43 Stat. 966

American-Mexican Boundary Treaty Act of 1972
Pub. L. 92–549, Oct. 25, 1972, 86 Stat. 1161 (22 U.S.C. 277d–34 et seq.)
Short title, see 22 U.S.C. 277d–34 note

American-Mexican Chamizal Convention Act of 1964
Pub. L. 88–300, Apr. 29, 1964, 78 Stat. 184 (22 U.S.C. 277d–17 et seq.)
Short title, see 22 U.S.C. 277d–17 note

American-Mexican Treaty Act of 1950
Sept. 13, 1950, ch. 948, 64 Stat. 846 (22 U.S.C. 277d–1 et seq.)
Short title, see 22 U.S.C. 277d–1 note

Americans with Disabilities Act of 1990
Pub. L. 101–336, July 26, 1990, 104 Stat. 327 (42 U.S.C. 12101 et seq.)
Short title, see 42 U.S.C. 12101 note

Amtrak Authorization and Development Act
Pub. L. 102–533, Oct. 27, 1992, 106 Stat. 3515

Amtrak Improvement Act of 1973
Pub. L. 93–146, Nov. 3, 1973, 87 Stat. 548

Amtrak Improvement Act of 1974
Pub. L. 93–496, Oct. 28, 1974, 88 Stat. 1526

Amtrak Improvement Act of 1975
Pub. L. 94–25, May 26, 1975, 89 Stat. 90

Amtrak Improvement Act of 1976
Pub. L. 94–555, title I, Oct. 19, 1976, 90 Stat. 2613

Amtrak Improvement Act of 1978
Pub. L. 95–421, Oct. 5, 1978, 92 Stat. 923

Amtrak Improvement Act of 1981
Pub. L. 97–35, title XI, subtitle F (§1170 et seq.), Aug. 13, 1981, 95 Stat. 687

Amtrak Reauthorization Act of 1985
Pub. L. 99–272, title IV, subtitle A (§4001 et seq.), Apr. 7, 1986, 100 Stat. 106

Amtrak Reauthorization and Improvement Act of 1990
Pub. L. 101–322, July 6, 1990, 104 Stat. 295

Amtrak Reform and Accountability Act of 1997
Pub. L. 105–134, Dec. 2, 1997, 111 Stat. 2570
Short title, see 49 U.S.C. 20101 note

Amtrak Reorganization Act of 1979
Pub. L. 96–73, title I, Sept. 29, 1979, 93 Stat. 537

Amvets Incorporation Act
July 23, 1947, ch. 298, 61 Stat. 403

Amy Boyer's Law
Pub. L. 106–553, §1(a)(2) [title VI, §635], Dec. 21, 2000, 114 Stat. 2762, 2762A–114
Short title, see 42 U.S.C. 1305 note

Amy Somers Volunteers at Food Banks Act
Pub. L. 105–221, Aug. 7, 1998, 112 Stat. 1248
Short title, see 29 U.S.C. 201 note

Anabolic Steroids Control Act of 1990
Pub. L. 101–647, title XIX, Nov. 29, 1990, 104 Stat. 4851
Short title, see 21 U.S.C. 801 note

Anadromous Fish Conservation Act
Pub. L. 89–304, Oct. 30, 1965, 79 Stat. 1125 (16 U.S.C. 757a et seq.)
Short title, see 16 U.S.C. 757a note

Anchorage Grounds Act
Sept. 15, 1922, ch. 313, 42 Stat. 844 (33 U.S.C. 472)

ANCSA Land Bank Protection Act of 1998
Pub. L. 105–333, Oct. 31, 1998, 112 Stat. 3129
Short title, see 43 U.S.C. 1601 note

Andean Trade Preference Act
Pub. L. 102–182, title II, Dec. 4, 1991, 105 Stat. 1236 (19 U.S.C. 3201 et seq.)
Short title, see 19 U.S.C. 3201 note

Anderson-Price Atomic Energy Damages Act
See Atomic Energy Damages Act

Andrew Johnson Homestead National Monument Act
Aug. 29, 1935, ch. 801, 49 Stat. 958 (16 U.S.C. 450*o* et seq.)

Anglo-Irish Agreement Support Act of 1986
Pub. L. 99–415, Sept. 19, 1986, 100 Stat. 947

Animal Cancer Research Act
Pub. L. 96–469, Oct. 17, 1980, 94 Stat. 2235 (7 U.S.C. 3901 et seq.)
Short title, see 7 U.S.C. 3901 note

Animal Disease Control Cooperation Act of 1947
Feb. 28, 1947, ch. 8, 61 Stat. 7 (21 U.S.C. 114b et seq.)
Short title, see 21 U.S.C. 114b note

Animal Drug Amendments of 1968
Pub. L. 90–399, July 13, 1968, 82 Stat. 342
Short title, see 21 U.S.C. 301 note

Animal Drug Availability Act of 1996
Pub. L. 104–250, Oct. 9, 1996, 110 Stat. 3151
Short title, see 21 U.S.C. 301 note

Animal Enterprise Protection Act of 1992
Pub. L. 102–346, Aug. 26, 1992, 106 Stat. 928
Short title, see 18 U.S.C. 43 note

Animal Industry Act
May 29, 1884, ch. 60, 23 Stat. 31 (7 U.S.C. 391; 21 U.S.C. 112 et seq.)
Short title, see 21 U.S.C. 112 note

Animal Medicinal Drug Use Clarification Act of 1994
Pub. L. 103–396, Oct. 22, 1994, 108 Stat. 4153
Short title, see 21 U.S.C. 301 note

Animal Virus, Serum, Toxin, Antitoxin Act
Mar. 4, 1913, ch. 145, 37 Stat. 828 (21 U.S.C. 151 et seq.)

Animal Welfare Act
Pub. L. 89–544, Aug. 24, 1966, 80 Stat. 350 (7 U.S.C. 2131 et seq.)
Short title, see 7 U.S.C. 2131 note

Animal Welfare Act Amendments of 1976
Pub. L. 94–279, Apr. 22, 1976, 90 Stat. 417
Short title, see 7 U.S.C. 2131 note

Animal Welfare Act of 1970
Pub. L. 91–579, Dec. 24, 1970, 84 Stat. 1560
Short title, see 7 U.S.C. 2131 note

Annual and Sick Leave Act of 1951
Oct. 30, 1951, ch. 631, title II, 65 Stat. 679

Annunzio-Wylie Anti-Money Laundering Act
Pub. L. 102–550, title XV, Oct. 28, 1992, 106 Stat. 4044
Short title, see 12 U.S.C. 1811 note

Antarctic Conservation Act of 1978
Pub. L. 95–541, Oct. 28, 1978, 92 Stat. 2048 (16 U.S.C. 2401 et seq.)
Short title, see 16 U.S.C. 2401 note

Antarctic Marine Living Resources Convention Act of 1984
Pub. L. 98–623, title III, Nov. 8, 1984, 98 Stat. 3398 (16 U.S.C. 2431 et seq.)
Short title, see 16 U.S.C. 2431 note

Antarctic Protection Act of 1990
Pub. L. 101–594, Nov. 16, 1990, 104 Stat. 2975 (16 U.S.C. 2461 et seq.)
Short title, see 16 U.S.C. 2461 note

Antarctic Science, Tourism, and Conservation Act of 1996
Pub. L. 104–227, Oct. 2, 1996, 110 Stat. 3034
Short title, see 16 U.S.C. 2401 note

Anthracite Mine Water Control Act
July 15, 1955, ch. 369, 69 Stat. 352 (30 U.S.C. 571 et seq.)

Anthropological Research Act
Apr. 10, 1928, ch. 335, 45 Stat. 413 (20 U.S.C. 69, 70)

Anti Car Theft Act of 1992
Pub. L. 102–519, Oct. 25, 1992, 106 Stat. 3384
Short title, see 18 U.S.C. 2311 note

Anti-Arson Act of 1982
Pub. L. 97–298, Oct. 12, 1982, 96 Stat. 1319
Short title, see 18 U.S.C. 841 note

Anti-Assignment Act
July 29, 1846, ch. 66, 9 Stat. 41

Anti-Car Theft Improvements Act of 1996
Pub. L. 104–152, July 2, 1996, 110 Stat. 1384
Short title, see 49 U.S.C. 30101 note

Anti-Deficiency Act
Feb. 27, 1906, ch. 510, §3, 34 Stat. 48 (see 31 U.S.C. 1341)

Anti-Drug Abuse Act of 1986
Pub. L. 99–570, Oct. 27, 1986, 100 Stat. 3207
Short title, see 21 U.S.C. 801 note

Anti-Drug Abuse Act of 1988
Pub. L. 100–690, Nov. 18, 1988, 102 Stat. 4181
Short title, see 21 U.S.C. 1501 note

Anti-Drug Abuse Amendments Act of 1988
Pub. L. 100–690, title VI, Nov. 18, 1988, 102 Stat. 4312
Short title, see 21 U.S.C. 801 note

Anti-Dumping Act, 1921
May 27, 1921, ch. 14, title II, 42 Stat. 11 (19 U.S.C. 160 et seq.)

Anti-Economic Discrimination Act of 1994
Pub. L. 103–236, title V, part C (§561 et seq.), Apr. 30, 1994, 108 Stat. 483
Short title, see 22 U.S.C. 2679c note

Anti-Gag Law
Aug. 24, 1912, ch. 389, §6, 37 Stat. 555

Anti-Gambling Act (District of Columbia)
May 16, 1908, ch. 172, §3, 35 Stat. 163

Anti-Heroin Act
June 7, 1924, ch. 352, 43 Stat. 657 (21 U.S.C. 173)

Anti-Immunity Act (Trusts and Interstate Commerce)
June 30, 1906, ch. 3920, 34 Stat. 798

Anti-Injunction Law
Mar. 23, 1932, ch. 90, 47 Stat. 70 (29 U.S.C. 101 et seq.)

Anti-Kickback Act
See Copeland Anti-Kickback Act

Anti-Kickback Act of 1986
Mar. 8, 1946, ch. 80, 60 Stat. 37 (41 U.S.C. 51 et seq.)
Short title, see 41 U.S.C. 51

Anti-Kickback Enforcement Act of 1986
Pub. L. 99–634, Nov. 7, 1986, 100 Stat. 3523
Short title, see 41 U.S.C. 51 note

Anti-Lobbying Act
July 11, 1919, ch. 6, §6, 41 Stat. 68

Anti-Lottery Act
Sept. 19, 1890, ch. 908, 26 Stat. 465

Anti-Merger Act
Dec. 29, 1950, ch. 1184, 64 Stat. 1125

Anti-Moiety Act (Informers)
June 22, 1874, ch. 391, 18 Stat. 186

Anti-Peonage Act
Mar. 2, 1867, ch. 187, 14 Stat. 546 (42 U.S.C. 1994)

Anti-Racketeering Act
June 18, 1934, ch. 569, 48 Stat. 979

Anti-Rebate Act (Railroads)
Feb. 19, 1903, ch. 708, 32 Stat. 847

Anti-Reviver Act (Repeals)
Feb. 25, 1871, ch. 71, §3, 16 Stat. 431

Anti-Secrecy Act (Departmental Information)
Pub. L. 85–619, Aug. 12, 1958, 72 Stat. 547

Anti-Smuggling Act
Aug. 5, 1935, ch. 438, 49 Stat. 517 (19 U.S.C. 1701 et seq.)
Short title, see 19 U.S.C. 1711

Anti-Strike Act
See War Labor Disputes Act

Anti-Strikebreaking Act
June 24, 1936, ch. 746, 49 Stat. 1899

Anti-Subversive Activities Act
Oct. 17, 1940, ch. 897, 54 Stat. 1201

Anti-Terrorism Act of 1987
Pub. L. 100–204, title X, Dec. 22, 1987, 101 Stat. 1406 (22 U.S.C. 5201 et seq.)
Short title, see 22 U.S.C. 5201 note

Anti-Terrorism and Arms Export Amendments Act of 1989
Pub. L. 101–222, Dec. 12, 1989, 103 Stat. 1892
Short title, see 22 U.S.C. 2151 note

Anticounterfeiting Consumer Protection Act of 1996
Pub. L. 104–153, July 2, 1996, 110 Stat. 1386
Short title, see 18 U.S.C. 2311 note

Anticybersquatting Consumer Protection Act
Pub. L. 106–113, div. B, §1000(a)(9) [title III], Nov. 29, 1999, 113 Stat. 1536, 1501A–545
Short title, see 15 U.S.C. 1051 note

Antihijacking Act of 1974
Pub. L. 93–366, title I, Aug. 5, 1974, 88 Stat. 409

Antimicrobial Regulation Technical Corrections Act of 1998
Pub. L. 105–324, Oct. 30, 1998, 112 Stat. 3035
Short title, see 21 U.S.C. 301 note

Antiquities Act of 1906
Also known as the National Monument Act (Preservation of Antiquities)
June 8, 1906, ch. 3060, 34 Stat. 225 (16 U.S.C. 431 et seq.)
Short title, see 16 U.S.C. 431 note

Antiterrorism Act of 1990
Pub. L. 101–519, §132, Nov. 5, 1990, 104 Stat. 2250

Antiterrorism and Effective Death Penalty Act of 1996
Pub. L. 104–132, Apr. 24, 1996, 110 Stat. 1214
Short title, see 18 U.S.C. 1 note

Antitrust Amendments Act of 1990
Pub. L. 101–588, Nov. 16, 1990, 104 Stat. 2879
Short title, see 15 U.S.C. 1 note

Antitrust Civil Process Act
Pub. L. 87–664, Sept. 19, 1962, 76 Stat. 548 (15 U.S.C. 1311 et seq.)
Short title, see 15 U.S.C. 1311 note

Antitrust Procedural Improvements Act of 1980
Pub. L. 96–349, Sept. 12, 1980, 94 Stat. 1154
Short title, see 15 U.S.C. 1311 note

Antitrust Procedures and Penalties Act
Pub. L. 93–528, Dec. 21, 1974, 88 Stat. 1706
Short title, see 15 U.S.C. 1 note

Apex Project, Nevada Land Transfer and Authorization Act of 1989
Pub. L. 101–67, July 31, 1989, 103 Stat. 168

Appalachian Forest Act (Forest Conservation)
See Weeks Law

Appalachian Regional Development Act Amendments of 1967
Pub. L. 90–103, title I, Oct. 11, 1967, 81 Stat. 257

Appalachian Regional Development Act Amendments of 1967—Continued
Short title, see 40 App. 1 note

Appalachian Regional Development Act Amendments of 1969
Pub. L. 91–123, title I, Nov. 25, 1969, 83 Stat. 213
Short title, see 40 App. 1 note

Appalachian Regional Development Act Amendments of 1971
Pub. L. 92–65, title II, Aug. 5, 1971, 85 Stat. 168
Short title, see 40 App. 1 note

Appalachian Regional Development Act Amendments of 1975
Pub. L. 94–188, title I, Dec. 31, 1975, 89 Stat. 1079
Short title, see 40 App. 1 note

Appalachian Regional Development Act of 1965
Pub. L. 89–4, Mar. 9, 1965, 79 Stat. 5 (40 App. 1 et seq.)
Short title, see 40 App. 1

Appalachian Regional Development Reform Act of 1998
Pub. L. 105–393, title II, Nov. 13, 1998, 112 Stat. 3618
Short title, see 40 App. 1 note

Appalachian States Low-Level Radioactive Waste Compact Consent Act
Pub. L. 100–319, May 19, 1988, 102 Stat. 471 (42 U.S.C. 2021d note)

Arbitration Act (Labor Disputes)
June 1, 1898, ch. 370, 30 Stat. 424

Archaeological Resources Protection Act of 1979
Pub. L. 96–95, Oct. 31, 1979, 93 Stat. 721 (16 U.S.C. 470aa et seq.)
Short title, see 16 U.S.C. 470aa note

Arches National Park Act
Pub. L. 92–155, Nov. 12, 1971, 85 Stat. 422 (16 U.S.C. 272 et seq.)

Arches National Park Expansion Act of 1998
Pub. L. 105–329, Oct. 30, 1998, 112 Stat. 3060
Short title, see 16 U.S.C. 272 note

Architect of the Capitol Human Resources Act
Pub. L. 103–283, title III, §312, July 22, 1994, 108 Stat. 1443 (40 U.S.C. 166b–7)
Short title, see 40 U.S.C. 166b–7(a)

Architectural Barriers Act of 1968
Pub. L. 90–480, Aug. 12, 1968, 82 Stat. 718 (42 U.S.C. 4151 et seq.)
Short title, see 42 U.S.C. 4151 note

Architectural Works Copyright Protection Act
Pub. L. 101–650, title VII, Dec. 1, 1990, 104 Stat. 5133
Short title, see 17 U.S.C. 101 note

Arctic Research and Policy Act of 1984
Pub. L. 98–373, title I, July 31, 1984, 98 Stat. 1242 (15 U.S.C. 4101 et seq.)
Short title, see 15 U.S.C. 4101 note

Arctic Tundra Habitat Emergency Conservation Act
Pub. L. 106–108, Nov. 24, 1999, 113 Stat. 1491 (16 U.S.C. 703 note)

Area Redevelopment Act
Pub. L. 87–27, May 1, 1961, 75 Stat. 47 (42 U.S.C. 2501 et seq.)

Arid Land Act
Oct. 2, 1888, ch. 1069, 25 Stat. 526 (43 U.S.C. 662)

Arizona Desert Wilderness Act of 1990
Pub. L. 101–628, titles I–III, Nov. 28, 1990, 104 Stat. 4469–4478
Short title, see 16 U.S.C. 460ddd note

Arizona National Forest Improvement Act of 2000
Pub. L. 106–458, Nov. 7, 2000, 114 Stat. 1983

Arizona Statehood and Enabling Act Amendments of 1999
Pub. L. 106–133, Dec. 7, 1999, 113 Stat. 1682

Arizona Wilderness Act of 1984
Pub. L. 98–406, Aug. 28, 1984, 98 Stat. 1485 (16 U.S.C. 1132 note)

Arizona Wilderness Land Title Resolution Act of 1994
Pub. L. 103–365, Oct. 14, 1994, 108 Stat. 3469

Arizona-Idaho Conservation Act of 1988
Pub. L. 100–696, Nov. 18, 1988, 102 Stat. 4571
Short title, see 16 U.S.C. 460xx note

Arkansas Wild and Scenic Rivers Act of 1992
Pub. L. 102–275, Apr. 22, 1992, 106 Stat. 123
Short title, see 16 U.S.C. 1271 note

Arkansas Wilderness Act of 1984
Also known as the Dale Bumpers Wilderness Resources Protection Act
Pub. L. 98–508, Oct. 19, 1984, 98 Stat. 2349 (16 U.S.C. 1132 notes)

Arkansas-Idaho Land Exchange Act of 1992
Pub. L. 102–584, Nov. 2, 1992, 106 Stat. 4937 (16 U.S.C. 668dd note)

Armament Conference Resolution
See Disarmament Conference Resolution

Armament Retooling and Manufacturing Support Act of 1992
Pub. L. 102–484, div. A, title I, subtitle H (§191 et seq.), Oct. 23, 1992, 106 Stat. 2347 (10 U.S.C. 2501 note)

Armed Career Criminal Act of 1984
Pub. L. 98–473, title II, ch. XVIII (§1801 et seq.), Oct. 12, 1984, 98 Stat. 2185

Armed Forces Absentee Voting Act
See Uniformed and Overseas Citizens Absentee Voting Act

Armed Forces Damages Settlement Act
Jan. 2, 1942, ch. 645, 55 Stat. 880

Armed Forces Enlisted Personnel Bonus Revision Act of 1974
Pub. L. 93–277, May 10, 1974, 88 Stat. 119
Short title, see 37 U.S.C. 101 note

Armed Forces Immigration Adjustment Act of 1991
Pub. L. 102–110, Oct. 1, 1991, 105 Stat. 555
Short title, see 8 U.S.C. 1101 note

Armed Forces Leave Act of 1946
Aug. 9, 1946, ch. 931, 60 Stat. 963

Armed Forces Regular Officer Augmentation Act of 1956
July 20, 1956, ch. 646, 70 Stat. 582

Armed Forces Reserve Act of 1952
July 9, 1952, ch. 608, 66 Stat. 481

Armed Forces Retirement Home Act of 1991
Pub. L. 101–510, div. A, title XV, Nov. 5, 1990, 104 Stat. 1722 (24 U.S.C. 401 et seq.)
Short title, see 24 U.S.C. 401 note

Armed Forces Voluntary Recruitment Act of 1945
Oct. 6, 1945, ch. 393, 59 Stat. 538

Armed Services Procurement Act of 1947
Feb. 19, 1948, ch. 65, 62 Stat. 21

Armistice Day Act
Renamed Veterans Day Act

Armored Car Industry Reciprocity Act of 1993
Pub. L. 103–55, July 28, 1993, 107 Stat. 276 (15 U.S.C. 5901 et seq.)
Short title, see 15 U.S.C. 5901 note

Armored Car Reciprocity Amendments of 1998
Pub. L. 105–287, Oct. 27, 1998, 112 Stat. 2776
Short title, see 15 U.S.C. 5901 note

Arms Control and Disarmament Act
Pub. L. 87–297, Sept. 26, 1961, 75 Stat. 631 (22 U.S.C. 2551 et seq.)
Short title, see 22 U.S.C. 2551 note

Arms Control and Disarmament Act Amendments of 1977
Pub. L. 95–108, Aug. 17, 1977, 91 Stat. 871
Short title, see 22 U.S.C. 2551 note

Arms Control and Disarmament Amendments Act of 1982
Pub. L. 97–339, Oct. 15, 1982, 96 Stat. 1635
Short title, see 22 U.S.C. 2551 note

Arms Control and Disarmament Amendments Act of 1987
Pub. L. 100–213, Dec. 24, 1987, 101 Stat. 1444
Short title, see 22 U.S.C. 2551 note

Arms Control and Disarmament Amendments Act of 1989
Pub. L. 101–216, Dec. 11, 1989, 103 Stat. 1853
Short title, see 22 U.S.C. 2551 note

Arms Control and Nonproliferation Act of 1994
Pub. L. 103–236, title VII, part A (§701 et seq.), Apr. 30, 1994, 108 Stat. 491
Short title, see 22 U.S.C. 2551 note

Arms Control and Nonproliferation Act of 1999
Pub. L. 106–113, div. B, §1000(a)(7) [div. B, title XI], Nov. 29, 1999, 113 Stat. 1536, 1501A–485
Short title, see 22 U.S.C. 2551 note

Arms Control, Nonproliferation, and Security Assistance Act of 1999
Pub. L. 106–113, div. B, §1000(a)(7) [div. B], Nov. 29, 1999, 113 Stat. 1536, 1501A–485
Short title, see 22 U.S.C. 2751 note

Arms Export Control Act
Pub. L. 90–629, Oct. 22, 1968, 82 Stat. 1320 (22 U.S.C. 2751 et seq.)
Short title, see 22 U.S.C. 2751 note

Arms Sale Resolution
May 28, 1934, ch. 365, 48 Stat. 811

Army Air Base Act
Aug. 12, 1935, ch. 511, 49 Stat. 610

Army and Air Force Authorization Act of 1949
July 10, 1950, ch. 454, 64 Stat. 321

Army and Air Force Vitalization and Retirement Equalization Act of 1948
June 29, 1948, ch. 708, 62 Stat. 1081

Army at Polls (Army Appropriation Act)
May 4, 1880, ch. 81, §2, 21 Stat. 113

Army Aviation Cadet Act
June 3, 1941, ch. 165, 55 Stat. 239

Army Clothing-Equipage Act
Feb. 13, 1941, ch. 6, 55 Stat. 7

Army Experimental Test Act
July 15, 1939, ch. 283, 53 Stat. 1042

Army Housing Act
Sept. 24, 1940, ch. 726, 54 Stat. 958

Army Medical Department Act
Apr. 23, 1908, ch. 150, 35 Stat. 66

Army National Guard Combat Readiness Reform Act of 1992
Pub. L. 102–484, div. A, title XI, Oct. 23, 1992, 106 Stat. 2536 (10 U.S.C. 10105 note)

Army Nurse and Medical Specialist Act of 1957
Pub. L. 85–155, title I, Aug. 21, 1957, 71 Stat. 375
Short title, see 10 U.S.C. 3069 note

Army Organization Act of 1950
June 28, 1950, ch. 383, 64 Stat. 263

Army Posts Construction Act
June 29, 1940, ch. 461, 54 Stat. 704

Army Promotion Act
July 31, 1935, ch. 422, 49 Stat. 505

Army Reserve and Retired Personnel Service Law of 1940
Aug. 27, 1940, ch. 689, 54 Stat. 858 (50 App. 401 et seq.)

Army Reserve-National Guard Equity Reimbursement Act
Pub. L. 105–152, Dec. 17, 1997, 111 Stat. 2688

Army-Foreign Service Act
July 15, 1939, ch. 289, 53 Stat. 1045

Army-Navy Medical Services Corps Act of 1947
Aug. 4, 1947, ch. 459, 61 Stat. 734

Army-Navy Nurses Act of 1947
Apr. 16, 1947, ch. 38, 61 Stat. 41

Army-Navy Pay Act
Mar. 7, 1942, ch. 166, 56 Stat. 143

Army-Navy Unification Act
See National Security Act of 1947

Army-Navy-Public Health Service Medical Officer Procurement Act of 1947
Aug. 5, 1947, ch. 494, 61 Stat. 776

Aroostook Band of Micmacs Settlement Act
Pub. L. 102–171, Nov. 26, 1991, 105 Stat. 1143 (25 U.S.C. 1721 note)

Arrest Facilitation Act
Mar. 22, 1934, ch. 73, 48 Stat. 454

Arson Prevention Act of 1994
Pub. L. 103–254, May 19, 1994, 108 Stat. 679
Short title, see 15 U.S.C. 2201 note

Arthritis, Diabetes, and Digestive Disease Amendments of 1976
Pub. L. 94–562, Oct. 19, 1976, 90 Stat. 2645
Short title, see 42 U.S.C. 201 note

Articles for the Government of the Navy
See Uniform Code of Military Justice

Articles of War
See Uniform Code of Military Justice

Articles of War Act (Fugitive Slaves)
Mar. 13, 1862, ch. 40, 12 Stat. 354

Arts and Artifacts Indemnity Act
Pub. L. 94–158, Dec. 20, 1975, 89 Stat. 844 (20 U.S.C. 971 et seq.)
Short title, see 20 U.S.C. 971 note

Arts and Humanities Act of 1980
Pub. L. 96–496, Dec. 4, 1980, 94 Stat. 2583
Short title, see 20 U.S.C. 951 note

Arts in Education Act of 1978
Pub. L. 89–10, title III, part C (§321 et seq,), as added Pub. L. 95–561, title III, §301(a), Nov. 1, 1978, 92 Stat. 2212 (20 U.S.C. 2961–2963)

Arts, Humanities, and Cultural Affairs Act of 1976
Pub. L. 94–462, Oct. 8, 1976, 90 Stat. 1971
Short title, see 20 U.S.C. 951 note

Arts, Humanities, and Museums Amendments of 1985
Pub. L. 99–194, Dec. 20, 1985, 99 Stat. 1332
Short title, see 20 U.S.C. 951 note

Arts, Humanities, and Museums Amendments of 1990
Pub. L. 101–512, title III, §318, Nov. 5, 1990, 104 Stat. 1960
Short title, see 20 U.S.C. 951 note

Asbestos Hazard Emergency Response Act of 1986
Pub. L. 99–519, Oct. 22, 1986, 100 Stat. 2970 (15 U.S.C. 2641 et seq.)
Short title, see 15 U.S.C. 2601 note

Asbestos Information Act of 1988
Pub. L. 100–577, Oct. 31, 1988, 102 Stat. 2901 (15 U.S.C. 2607 note)

Asbestos School Hazard Abatement Act of 1984
Pub. L. 98–377, title V, Aug. 11, 1984, 98 Stat. 1287 (20 U.S.C. 4011 et seq.)
Short title, see 20 U.S.C. 4011 note

Asbestos School Hazard Abatement Reauthorization Act of 1990
Pub. L. 101–637, Nov. 28, 1990, 104 Stat. 4589
Short title, see 20 U.S.C. 4011 note

Asbestos School Hazard Detection and Control Act of 1980
Pub. L. 96–270, June 14, 1980, 94 Stat. 487 (20 U.S.C. 3601 et seq.)
Short title, see 20 U.S.C. 3601 note

Ash Pan Act (Railroads)
May 30, 1908, ch. 225, 35 Stat. 476 (45 U.S.C. 17–21)

Ashurst-Sumners Act
June 6, 1934, ch. 406, 48 Stat. 909

Ashurst-Sumners Act (Shipment in Interstate Commerce of Convict Made Goods)
July 24, 1935, ch. 412, 49 Stat. 494

Asia Foundation Act
Pub. L. 98–164, title IV, Nov. 22, 1983, 97 Stat. 1038 (22 U.S.C. 4401 et seq.)
Short title, see 22 U.S.C. 4401 note

Asian Development Bank Act
Pub. L. 89–369, Mar. 16, 1966, 80 Stat. 71 (22 U.S.C. 285 et seq.)
Short title, see 22 U.S.C. 285 note

Asian Elephant Conservation Act of 1997
Pub. L. 105–96, Nov. 19, 1997, 111 Stat. 2150 (16 U.S.C 4261 et seq.)
Short title, see 16 U.S.C. 4261 note

Assateague Island National Seashore Act
Pub. L. 89–195, Sept. 21, 1965, 79 Stat. 824 (16 U.S.C. 459f et seq.)

Asset Conservation, Lender Liability, and Deposit Insurance Protection Act of 1996
Pub. L. 104–208, div. A, title II, subtitle E (§2501 et seq.), Sept. 30, 1996, 110 Stat. 3009–462
Short title, see 42 U.S.C. 9601 note

Asset Forfeiture Amendments Act of 1988
Pub. L. 100–690, title VI, subtitle B (§6071 et seq.), Nov. 18, 1988, 102 Stat. 4320
Short title, see 21 U.S.C. 801 note

Assets for Independence Act
Pub. L. 105–285, title IV, Oct. 27, 1998, 112 Stat. 2759 (42 U.S.C. 604 note)

Assets for Independence Act Amendments of 2000
Pub. L. 106–554, §1(a)(1) [title VI], Dec. 21, 2000, 114 Stat. 2763, 2763A–74
Short title, see 42 U.S.C. 1305 note

Assignment of Claims Act of 1940
Oct. 9, 1940, ch. 779, 54 Stat. 1029

Assimilative Crimes Statute
June 6, 1940, ch. 241, 54 Stat. 234

Assistance for International Malaria Control Act
Pub. L. 106–570, Dec. 27, 2000, 114 Stat. 3038

Assistance for International Malaria Control Act—Continued
Short title, see 22 U.S.C. 2151 note

Assisted Suicide Funding Restriction Act of 1997
Pub. L. 105–12, Apr. 30, 1997, 111 Stat. 23 (42 U.S.C. 14401 et seq.)
Short title, see 42 U.S.C. 14401 note

Assistive Technology Act of 1998
Pub. L. 105–394, Nov. 13, 1998, 112 Stat. 3627 (29 U.S.C. 3001 et seq.)
Short title, see 29 U.S.C. 3001 note

Assumption Act (State Debts)
Aug. 4, 1790, ch. 34, 1 Stat. 138

Atlantic Coastal Fisheries Act of 2000
Pub. L. 106–555, title I, subtitle B (§121 et seq.), Dec. 21, 2000, 114 Stat. 2766
Short title, see 16 U.S.C. 5101 note

Atlantic Coastal Fisheries Cooperative Management Act
Pub. L. 103–206, title VIII, Dec. 20, 1993, 107 Stat. 2447 (16 U.S.C. 5101 et seq.)
Short title, see 16 U.S.C. 5101 note

Atlantic Fisheries Act
May 4, 1942, ch. 283, 56 Stat. 267

Atlantic Salmon Convention Act of 1982
Pub. L. 97–389, title III, Dec. 29, 1982, 96 Stat. 1951 (16 U.S.C. 3601 et seq.)
Short title, see 16 U.S.C. 3601 note

Atlantic Striped Bass Conservation Act
Pub. L. 98–613, Oct. 31, 1984, 98 Stat. 3187 (16 U.S.C. 5151 et seq.)
Short title, see 16 U.S.C. 5151 note

Atlantic Striped Bass Conservation Act Amendments of 1997
Pub. L. 105–146, Dec. 16, 1997, 111 Stat. 2672
Short title, see 16 U.S.C. 5151 note

Atlantic Tunas Convention Act of 1975
Pub. L. 94–70, Aug. 5, 1975, 89 Stat. 385 (16 U.S.C. 971 et seq.)
Short title, see 16 U.S.C. 971 note

Atlantic Tunas Convention Authorization Act of 1995
Pub. L. 104–43, title III, Nov. 3, 1995, 109 Stat. 382
Short title, see 16 U.S.C. 971 note

ATM Fee Reform Act of 1999
Pub. L. 106–102, title VII, subtitle A (§701 et seq.), Nov. 12, 1999, 113 Stat. 1463
Short title, see 15 U.S.C. 1601 note

Atoka Agreement (Indians)
June 28, 1898, ch. 517, 30 Stat. 495

Atomic Energy Act of 1946
Renamed Atomic Energy Act of 1954

Atomic Energy Act of 1954
Aug. 1, 1946, ch. 724, 60 Stat. 755 (42 U.S.C. 2011 et seq.)
Short title, see 42 U.S.C. 2011 note

Atomic Energy Commission Appropriation Act, 1958
Pub. L. 85–175, Aug. 28, 1957, 71 Stat. 450

Atomic Energy Commission Appropriation Act, 1960
Pub. L. 86–164, Aug. 18, 1959, 73 Stat. 363

Atomic Energy Community Act of 1955
Aug. 4, 1955, ch. 543, 69 Stat. 471 (42 U.S.C. 2301 et seq.)
Short title, see 42 U.S.C. 2301 note

Atomic Energy Damages Act
Also known as the Price-Anderson Act
Aug. 1, 1946, ch. 724, title I, §170, as added Pub. L. 85–256, §4, Sept. 2, 1957, 71 Stat. 576 (42 U.S.C. 2210)
Short title, see 42 U.S.C. 2210 note

Atomic Testing Liability Act
Pub. L. 101–510, div. C, title XXXI, §3141, Nov. 5, 1990, 104 Stat. 1837 (42 U.S.C. 2212)
Short title, see 42 U.S.C. 2212(a)

Atomic Weapons and Special Nuclear Materials Rewards Act
July 15, 1955, ch. 372, 69 Stat. 365 (50 U.S.C. 47a et seq.)
Short title, see 50 U.S.C. 47a note

Atomic Weapons Rewards Act of 1955
Renamed the Atomic Weapons and Special Nuclear Materials Rewards Act

Attendant Allowance Adjustment Act
Pub. L. 101–534, Nov. 7, 1990, 104 Stat. 2352
Short title, see 5 U.S.C. 8101 note

Auburn Indian Restoration Act
Pub. L. 103–434, title II, Oct. 31, 1994, 108 Stat. 4533 (25 U.S.C. 1300l et seq.)
Short title, see 25 U.S.C. 1300l note

Audio Home Recording Act of 1992
Pub. L. 102–563, Oct. 28, 1992, 106 Stat. 4237 (17 U.S.C. 1001 et seq.)
Short title, see 17 U.S.C. 101 note

Augustus F. Hawkins Human Services Reauthorization Act of 1990
Pub. L. 101–501, Nov. 3, 1990, 104 Stat. 1222
Short title, see 42 U.S.C. 9801 note

Augustus F. Hawkins-Robert T. Stafford Elementary and Secondary School Improvement Amendments of 1988
Pub. L. 100–297, Apr. 28, 1988, 102 Stat. 130
Short title, see 20 U.S.C. 6301 note

Authorization for Use of Military Force Against Iraq Resolution
Pub. L. 102–1, Jan. 14, 1991, 105 Stat. 3 (50 U.S.C. 1541 note)

Auto Pricing Law
See Automobile Information Disclosure Act

Automatic Coupler Act (Amendment)
Mar. 2, 1903, ch. 976, 32 Stat. 943

Automatic Coupler Act (Interstate Commerce)
Mar. 2, 1893, ch. 196, 27 Stat. 531

Automobile Dealers' Day in Court Act
Aug. 8, 1956, ch. 1038, 70 Stat. 1125 (15 U.S.C. 1221 et seq.)

Automobile Fuel Efficiency Act of 1980
Pub. L. 96–425, Oct. 10, 1980, 94 Stat. 1821

Automobile Information Disclosure Act
Pub. L. 85–506, July 7, 1958, 72 Stat. 325 (15 U.S.C. 1231 et seq.)
Short title, see 15 U.S.C. 1231 note

Automobile National Heritage Area Act
Pub. L. 105–355, title I, Nov. 6, 1998, 112 Stat. 3247 (16 U.S.C. 461 note)

Automobile Tax Act
June 25, 1940, ch. 419, 54 Stat. 522

Automotive Products Trade Act of 1965
Pub. L. 89–283, Oct. 21, 1965, 79 Stat. 1016 (19 U.S.C. 2001 et seq.)
Short title, see 19 U.S.C. 2001 note

Automotive Propulsion Research and Development Act of 1978
Pub. L. 95–238, title III, Feb. 25, 1978, 92 Stat. 78 (15 U.S.C. 2701 et seq.)
Short title, see 15 U.S.C. 2701 note

Autonomy Act
Aug. 29, 1916, ch. 416, 39 Stat. 545

Aviation Career Incentive Act of 1974
Pub. L. 93–294, May 31, 1974, 88 Stat. 177
Short title, see 37 U.S.C. 101 note

Aviation Day Act
See National Aviation Day Act

Aviation Disaster Family Assistance Act of 1996
Pub. L. 104–264, title VII, Oct. 9, 1996, 110 Stat. 3264
Short title, see 49 U.S.C. 40101 note

Aviation Drug-Trafficking Control Act
Pub. L. 98–499, Oct. 19, 1984, 98 Stat. 2312

Aviation Insurance Reauthorization Act of 1997
Pub. L. 105–137, Dec. 2, 1997, 111 Stat. 2640
Short title, see 49 U.S.C. 40101 note

Aviation Medical Assistance Act of 1998
Pub. L. 105–170, Apr. 24, 1998, 112 Stat. 47 (49 U.S.C. 44701 note)

Aviation Pilots Act
Nov. 5, 1941, ch. 468, 55 Stat. 759

Aviation Safety and Capacity Expansion Act of 1990
Pub. L. 101–508, title IX, subtitle B (§9101 et seq.), Nov. 5, 1990, 104 Stat. 1388–353

Aviation Safety and Noise Abatement Act of 1979
Pub. L. 96–193, Feb. 18, 1980, 94 Stat. 50

Aviation Safety Commission Act of 1986
Pub. L. 99–500, title V, Oct. 18, 1986, 100 Stat. 1783–370, and Pub. L. 99–591, title V, Oct. 30, 1986, 100 Stat. 3341–373 (49 U.S.C. 106 note)

Aviation Safety Research Act of 1988
Pub. L. 100–591, Nov. 3, 1988, 102 Stat. 3011

Aviation Security Improvement Act of 1990
Pub. L. 101–604, Nov. 16, 1990, 104 Stat. 3066

Aviation Service Act
July 18, 1914, ch. 186, 38 Stat. 514

Baby Bonds
See Savings Bond Act

Baby Doe Amendment
Pub. L. 98–457, title I, part B (§121 et seq.), Oct. 9, 1984, 98 Stat. 1752

Baca Location No. 1 Land Acquisition and Study Act of 1990
Pub. L. 101–556, Nov. 15, 1990, 104 Stat. 2762

Bacharach Act
May 29, 1928, ch. 865, 45 Stat. 955

Back Pay Act of 1966
Pub. L. 89–380, Mar. 30, 1966, 80 Stat. 94

Backbone Grant Act (Texas Pacific Railroad)
Mar. 3, 1871, ch. 122, 16 Stat. 573

Bacon-Davis Act
See Davis-Bacon Act

Bad Check Law (District of Columbia)
July 1, 1922, ch. 273, 42 Stat. 820

Bail Reform Act of 1966
Pub. L. 89–465, June 22, 1966, 80 Stat. 214 (18 U.S.C. 3146–3152)
Short title, see 18 U.S.C. 3141 note

Bail Reform Act of 1984
Pub. L. 98–473, title II, ch. I (§202 et seq), Oct. 12, 1984, 98 Stat. 1976
Short title, see 18 U.S.C. 3141 note

Bailey Merchant Marine Act
June 29, 1940, ch. 442, 54 Stat. 684 (46 App. U.S.C. 1242a)

Balanced Budget Act of 1997
Pub. L. 105–33, Aug. 5, 1997, 111 Stat. 251

Balanced Budget and Emergency Deficit Control Act of 1985
Pub. L. 99–177, title II, Dec. 12, 1985, 99 Stat. 1038
Short title, see 2 U.S.C. 900 note

Balanced Budget and Emergency Deficit Control Reaffirmation Act of 1987
Pub. L. 100–119, title I, Sept. 29, 1987, 101 Stat. 754
Short title, see 2 U.S.C. 900 note

Balanced Budget Downpayment Act, I
Pub. L. 104–99, Jan. 26, 1996, 110 Stat. 26

Bald Eagle Protection Act
June 8, 1940, ch. 278, 54 Stat. 250 (16 U.S.C. 668 et seq.)

Baldwin Amendment
Pub. L. 89–139, §4(a), Aug. 28, 1965, 79 Stat. 578

Ball Act (Rents in District of Columbia)
Oct. 22, 1919, ch. 80, title II, 41 Stat. 298

Ballistic Knife Prohibition Act of 1986
Pub. L. 99–570, title X, Oct. 27, 1986, 100 Stat. 3207–166
Short title, see 15 U.S.C. 1241 note

Ballistic Missile Defense Act of 1995
Pub. L. 104–106, div. A, title II, subtitle C (§231 et seq.), Feb. 10, 1996, 110 Stat. 228 (10 U.S.C. 2431 note)

Bandelier National Monument Administrative Improvement and Watershed Protection Act of 1998
Pub. L. 105–376, Nov. 12, 1998, 112 Stat. 3388 (16 U.S.C. 431 note)

Bangladesh Disaster Assistance Act of 1988
Pub. L. 100–576, Oct. 31, 1988, 102 Stat. 2897
Short title, see 7 U.S.C. 1691 note

Bank Bribery Amendments Act of 1985
Pub. L. 99–370, Aug. 4, 1986, 100 Stat. 779
Short title, see 18 U.S.C. 201 note

Bank Conservation Act
Mar. 9, 1933, ch. 1, title II, 48 Stat. 2 (12 U.S.C. 201 et seq.)
Short title, see 12 U.S.C. 201

Bank Deposit Insurance Act
See Federal Deposit Insurance Act

Bank Enterprise Act of 1991
Pub. L. 102–242, title II, subtitle C (§231 et seq.), Dec. 19, 1991, 105 Stat. 2308 (12 U.S.C. 1834 et seq.)
Short title, see 12 U.S.C. 1811 note

Bank Export Services Act
Pub. L. 97–290, title II, Oct. 8, 1982, 96 Stat. 1235
Short title, see 12 U.S.C. 1841 note

Bank for Economic Cooperation and Development in the Middle East and North Africa Act
Pub. L. 104–208, div. A, title I, §101(c) [title VII], Sept. 30, 1996, 110 Stat. 3009–121, 3009–179 (22 U.S.C. 290*o* et seq.)
Short title, see 22 U.S.C. 290*o* note

Bank Holding Company Act Amendments of 1970
Pub. L. 91–607, Dec. 31, 1970, 84 Stat. 1760
Short title, see 12 U.S.C. 1841 note

Bank Holding Company Act of 1956
May 9, 1956, ch. 240, 70 Stat. 133 (12 U.S.C. 1841 et seq.)
Short title, see 12 U.S.C. 1841 note

Bank Holding Company Tax Act of 1976
Pub. L. 94–452, Oct. 2, 1976, 90 Stat. 1503
Short title, see 26 U.S.C. 1 note

Bank Note and Redemption Act
July 12, 1870, ch. 252, 16 Stat. 251

Bank Official Loan Act
June 16, 1933, ch. 89, §12, 48 Stat. 182 (12 U.S.C. 375a)

Bank Protection Act of 1968
Pub. L. 90–389, July 7, 1968, 82 Stat. 294 (12 U.S.C. 1881 et seq.)
Short title, see 12 U.S.C. 1881 note

Bank Robbery Act
May 18, 1934, ch. 304, 48 Stat. 783

Bank Secrecy Act
Pub. L. 91–508, titles I, II, Oct. 26, 1970, 84 Stat. 1114, 1118

Bank Service Company Act
Pub. L. 87–856, Oct. 23, 1962, 76 Stat. 1132 (12 U.S.C. 1861 et seq.)
Short title, see 12 U.S.C. 1861(a)

Bank Service Corporation Act
Renamed the Bank Service Company Act

Bankhead Cotton Act of 1934
See Cotton Control Act

Bankhead Cotton-Control Act
See Cotton Control Act

Bankhead-Jones Act
Also known as the Agricultural Research Act
June 29, 1935, ch. 338, 49 Stat. 436 (7 U.S.C. 427–427j)
Short title, see 7 U.S.C. 427 note

Bankhead-Jones Farm Tenant Act
July 22, 1937, ch. 517, 50 Stat. 522 (7 U.S.C. 1000 et seq.)
Short title, see 7 U.S.C. 1000

Banking Act of 1933
June 16, 1933, ch. 89, 48 Stat. 162
Short title, see 12 U.S.C. 227

Banking Act of 1935
Aug. 23, 1935, ch. 614, 49 Stat. 684
Short title, see 12 U.S.C. 228

Banking Affiliates Act of 1982
Pub. L. 97–320, title IV, §410, Oct. 15, 1982, 96 Stat. 1515
Short title, see 12 U.S.C. 226 note

Banking and Related Programs Authorization Adjustment Act
Pub. L. 97–35, title III, subtitle B (§380 et seq.), Aug. 13, 1981, 95 Stat. 431
Short title, see 12 U.S.C. 635 note

Bankrupt Railroad Service Preservation and Employee Protection Act of 1982
Pub. L. 97–468, title II, Jan. 14, 1983, 96 Stat. 2543

Bankruptcy Act
July 1, 1898, ch. 541, 30 Stat. 544

Bankruptcy Act, Amendments of 1938
See Chandler Act (Bankruptcy Revision)

Bankruptcy Act, Amendments of 1939
See Chandler Rail Bankruptcy Act

Bankruptcy Amendments and Federal Judgeship Act of 1984
Pub. L. 98–353, July 10, 1984, 98 Stat. 333
Short title, see 28 U.S.C. 151 note

Bankruptcy Extension Act
See Municipal Bankruptcy Extension Act

Bankruptcy Judges, United States Trustees, and Family Farmer Bankruptcy Act of 1986
Pub. L. 99–554, Oct. 27, 1986, 100 Stat. 3088
Short title, see 28 U.S.C. 581 note

Bankruptcy Judgeship Act of 1992
Pub. L. 102–361, Aug. 26, 1992, 106 Stat. 965
Short title, see 28 U.S.C. 1 note

Bankruptcy Reform Act of 1978
Pub. L. 95–598, Nov. 6, 1978, 92 Stat. 2549 (11 U.S.C. 101 et seq.)

Bankruptcy Reform Act of 1994
Pub. L. 103–394, Oct. 22, 1994, 108 Stat. 4106

Bankruptcy Reform Act of 1994—Continued
Short title, see 11 U.S.C. 101 note

Bankruptcy Tax Act of 1980
Pub. L. 96–589, Dec. 24, 1980, 94 Stat. 3389
Short title, see 26 U.S.C. 1 note

Barbour Espionage Act
See Espionage Act

Barbour Fight Film Act
June 29, 1940, ch. 443, 54 Stat. 686 (15 U.S.C. 1001)

Barkley-Cole Trust Indenture Act of 1939
See Trust Indenture Act of 1939

Barkley-Norris Resolution (T. V. Authority)
Apr. 4, 1938, ch. 61, 52 Stat. 154

Barrow Gas Field Transfer Act of 1984
Pub. L. 98–366, July 17, 1984, 98 Stat. 468

Barry Goldwater Scholarship and Excellence in Education Act
Pub. L. 99–661, div. A, title XIV, Nov. 14, 1986, 100 Stat. 4007 (20 U.S.C. 4701 et seq.)
Short title, see 20 U.S.C. 4701 note

Bartlett Act (Three Mile Fishery Jurisdiction)
Pub. L. 88–308, May 20, 1964, 78 Stat. 194 (16 U.S.C. 1081 et seq.)

Bartlett Act (Twelve Mile Fishery Jurisdiction)
Pub. L. 89–658, Oct. 14, 1966, 80 Stat. 908 (16 U.S.C. 1091 et seq.)

Base Closure Community Redevelopment and Homeless Assistance Act of 1994
Pub. L. 103–421, Oct. 25, 1994, 108 Stat. 4346
Short title, see 42 U.S.C. 11301 note

Battered Immigrant Women Protection Act of 2000
Pub. L. 106–386, div. B, title V, Oct. 28, 2000, 114 Stat. 1518
Short title, see 8 U.S.C. 1101 note

Battered Women's Testimony Act of 1992
Pub. L. 102–527, Oct. 27, 1992, 106 Stat. 3459 (42 U.S.C. 10702 note)

Battle Act
See Mutual Defense Assistance Control Act of 1951

Battleship Overhaul Act
July 25, 1939, ch. 348, 53 Stat. 1079

Bayh-Dole Act
Also known as the University and Small Business Patent Procedure Act of 1980
Pub. L. 96–517, §6(a), Dec. 12, 1980, 94 Stat. 3018 (35 U.S.C. 200 et seq.)

Beaches Environmental Assessment and Coastal Health Act of 2000
Pub. L. 106–284, Oct. 10, 2000, 114 Stat. 870
Short title, see 33 U.S.C. 1251 note

Beef Promotion and Research Act of 1985
Pub. L. 99–198, title XVI, subtitle A, §1601, Dec. 23, 1985, 99 Stat. 1597
Short title, see 7 U.S.C. 2901 note

Beef Research and Information Act
Pub. L. 94–294, May 28, 1978, 90 Stat. 529 (7 U.S.C. 2901 et seq.)
Short title, see 7 U.S.C. 2901 note

Beer-Wine Revenue Act
Mar. 22, 1933, ch. 4, 48 Stat. 16

Bend Feed Canal Pipeline Project Act of 2000
Pub. L. 106–496, Nov. 9, 2000, 114 Stat. 2218

Bend Pine Nursery Land Conveyance Act
Pub. L. 106–526, Nov. 22, 2000, 114 Stat. 2512

Benjamin Franklin National Memorial Commemorative Medal and Fire Service Bill of Rights Act
Pub. L. 102–406, Oct. 12, 1992, 106 Stat. 1986 (31 U.S.C. 5111 note)

Benning Road Widening Act
May 16, 1908, ch. 172, 35 Stat. 163

Berne Convention Implementation Act of 1988
Pub. L. 100–568, Oct. 31, 1988, 102 Stat. 2853
Short title, see 17 U.S.C. 101 note

Bicentennial of the Constitution Coins Act
Pub. L. 99–582, Oct. 29, 1986, 100 Stat. 3315 (31 U.S.C. 5112 note)

Bicentennial of the United States Capitol Commemorative Coin Act
Pub. L. 103–186, title IV, Dec. 14, 1993, 107 Stat. 2252 (31 U.S.C. 5112 note)

Bicentennial of the United States Congress Commemorative Coin Act
Pub. L. 100–673, Nov. 17, 1988, 102 Stat. 3992 (31 U.S.C. 5112 note)

Big Brothers—Big Sisters of America
Pub. L. 85–870, Sept. 2, 1958, 72 Stat. 1691

Big Cypress National Preserve Addition Act
Pub. L. 100–301, Apr. 29, 1988, 102 Stat. 443 (16 U.S.C. 698m–1 to 698m–4)
Short title, see 16 U.S.C. 698f note

Big South Fork National River and Recreation Area Act
Pub. L. 93–251, title I, §108, Mar. 7, 1974, 88 Stat. 43 (16 U.S.C. 460ee)

Big Thicket National Preserve Addition Act of 1993
Pub. L. 103–46, July 1, 1993, 107 Stat. 229
Short title, see 16 U.S.C. 698 note

Bighorn Canyon National Recreation Area Act
Pub. L. 89–664, Oct. 15, 1966, 80 Stat. 913 (16 U.S.C. 460t et seq.)

Bikini Resettlement and Relocation Act of 2000
Pub. L. 106–188, Apr. 28, 2000, 114 Stat. 228

Bilingual Education Act
Pub. L. 89–10, title VII, pt. A, §7101 et seq., as added Pub. L. 103–382, title I, §101, Oct. 20, 1994, 108 Stat. 3716 (20 U.S.C. 7401 et seq.)
Short title, see 20 U.S.C. 7401

Bill Emerson Good Samaritan Food Donation Act
Pub. L. 89–642, §22, formerly Pub. L. 101–610, title IV, §402, Nov. 16, 1990, 104 Stat. 3183
Short title, see 42 U.S.C. 1791(a)

Bill Emerson Humanitarian Trust Act
Pub. L. 96–494, title III, Dec. 3, 1980, 94 Stat. 2578 (7 U.S.C. 1736f–1)
Short title, see 7 U.S.C. 1736f–1 note

Bill Emerson Humanitarian Trust Act of 1998
Pub. L. 105–385, title II, subtitle B (§211 et seq.), Nov. 13, 1998, 112 Stat. 3465
Short title, see 7 U.S.C. 1691 note

Bill of Abominations (Tariff)
May 19, 1828, ch. 55, 4 Stat. 270

Bill of Lading Act (Interstate and Foreign Commerce)
See Pomerene Bills Of Lading Act

Biological Weapons Anti-Terrorism Act of 1989
Pub. L. 101–298, May 22, 1990, 104 Stat. 201
Short title, see 18 U.S.C. 175 note

Biomass Energy and Alcohol Fuels Act of 1980
Pub. L. 96–294, title II, June 30, 1980, 94 Stat. 683 (42 U.S.C. 8801 et seq.)
Short title, see 42 U.S.C. 8801 note

Biomass Research and Development Act of 2000
Pub. L. 106–224, title III, June 20, 2000, 114 Stat. 428 (7 U.S.C. 7624 note)

Biomaterials Access Assurance Act of 1998
Pub. L. 105–230, Aug. 13, 1998, 112 Stat. 1519 (21 U.S.C. 1601 et seq.)
Short title, see 21 U.S.C. 1601 note

Biomedical Research and Research Training Amendments of 1978
Pub. L. 95–622, title II, Nov. 9, 1978, 92 Stat. 3420
Short title, see 42 U.S.C. 201 note

Biomedical Research Extension Act of 1977
Pub. L. 95–83, title II, Aug. 1, 1977, 91 Stat. 386
Short title, see 42 U.S.C. 201 note

Birth Defects Prevention Act of 1998
Pub. L. 105–168, Apr. 21, 1998, 112 Stat. 43
Short title, see 42 U.S.C. 201 note

Biscayne National Park Act
Pub. L. 96–287, title I, June 28, 1980, 94 Stat. 599 (16 U.S.C. 410gg et seq.)

Bisti/De-Na-Zin Wilderness Expansion and Fossil Forest Protection Act
Pub. L. 104–333, div. I, title X, §1022, Nov. 12, 1996, 110 Stat. 4211

Bituminous Coal Act of 1937
April 26, 1937, ch. 127, 50 Stat. 72 (15 U.S.C. 828 et seq.)

Bituminous Coal Conservation Act of 1935
Aug. 30, 1935, ch. 824, 49 Stat. 991 (15 U.S.C. 801 et seq.)

Black Bass Act
May 20, 1926, ch. 346, 44 Stat. 576 (16 U.S.C. 851 et seq.)

Black Canyon of the Gunnison National Park and Gunnison Gorge National Conservation Area Act of 1999
Pub. L. 106–76, Oct. 21, 1999, 113 Stat. 1126 (16 U.S.C. 410fff et seq.)
Short title, see 16 U.S.C. 410fff note

Black Hills National Forest and Rocky Mountain Research Station Improvement Act
Pub. L. 106–329, Oct. 19, 2000, 114 Stat. 1296

Black Lung Benefits Act
Pub. L. 91–173, title IV, Dec. 30, 1969, 83 Stat. 792 (30 U.S.C. 901 et seq.)
Short title, see 30 U.S.C. 901(b)

Black Lung Benefits Act of 1972
Pub. L. 92–303, May 19, 1972, 86 Stat. 150
Short title, see 30 U.S.C. 801 note

Black Lung Benefits Amendments of 1981
Pub. L. 97–119, title II, Dec. 29, 1981, 95 Stat. 1643
Short title, see 30 U.S.C. 801 note

Black Lung Benefits Reform Act of 1977
Pub. L. 95–239, Mar. 1, 1978, 92 Stat. 95
Short title, see 30 U.S.C. 801 note

Black Lung Benefits Revenue Act of 1977
Pub. L. 95–227, Feb. 10, 1978, 92 Stat. 11
Short title, see 26 U.S.C. 1 note

Black Lung Benefits Revenue Act of 1981
Pub. L. 97–119, title I, subtitle A (§101 et seq.), Dec. 29, 1981, 95 Stat. 1635
Short title, see 26 U.S.C. 1 note

Black Rock Desert-High Rock Canyon Emigrant Trails National Conservation Area Act of 2000
Pub. L. 106–554, §1(a)(4) [title I, §125], Dec. 21, 2000, 114 Stat. 2763, 2763A–229, 2763A–353

Black-Connery Fair Labor Standards Act
See Fair Labor Standards Act of 1938

Black-McKellar Act
June 12, 1934, ch. 466, 48 Stat. 933

Blackstone River Valley National Heritage Corridor Act of 1986
Pub. L. 99–647, Nov. 10, 1986, 100 Stat. 3625 (16 U.S.C. 461 note)

Bland Change of Masters Act
May 31, 1939, ch. 159, 53 Stat. 794

Bland Merchant Marine Act
Aug. 4, 1939, ch. 417, 53 Stat. 1182

Bland Ship Requisitioning Act
See Ship Seizure Bill

Bland War-Risk Insurance Act
See Merchant Marine Act, 1936

Bland-Allison Act (Coinage of Silver)
See Coinage Act (Silver Dollar)

Block Signal Resolution (Railroads)
June 30, 1906, No. 46, 34 Stat. 838 (45 U.S.C. 35)

Blockade of Southern Ports Proclamation (Civil War)
Apr. 19, 1861, No. 4, 12 Stat. 1258

Blood Transfusion Act
Feb. 9, 1927, ch. 91, 44 Stat. 1066 (24 U.S.C. 30)

Bloody Bill Act (Suits against Revenue Officers)
See Force Act (Suits against Revenue Officers)

Blue Star Mothers of America Act
Pub. L. 86–653, July 14, 1960, 74 Stat. 515

Board for International Broadcasting Act of 1973
Pub. L. 93–129, Oct. 19, 1973, 87 Stat. 456 (22 U.S.C. 2871 et seq.)
Short title, see 22 U.S.C. 2871 note

Board for International Broadcasting Authorization Act, Fiscal Years 1980 and 1981
Pub. L. 96–60, title III, Aug. 15, 1979, 93 Stat. 402

Board for International Broadcasting Authorization Act, Fiscal Years 1982 and 1983
Pub. L. 97–241, title IV, Aug. 24, 1982, 96 Stat. 295

Board for International Broadcasting Authorization Act, Fiscal Years 1984 and 1985
Pub. L. 98–164, title III, Nov. 22, 1983, 97 Stat. 1036

Board of Veterans' Appeals Administrative Procedures Improvement Act of 1994
Pub. L. 103–271, July 1, 1994, 108 Stat. 740
Short title, see 38 U.S.C. 301 note

Bodie Protection Act of 1994
Pub. L. 103–433, title X, Oct. 31, 1994, 108 Stat. 4509

Boggs Act
Nov. 2, 1951, ch. 666, 65 Stat. 767 (21 U.S.C. 174)

Boiler Inspection Act of the District of Columbia
July 25, 1936, ch. 802, 49 Stat. 1917

Boise Laboratory Replacement Act of 2000
Pub. L. 106–291, title III, §351, Oct. 11, 2000, 114 Stat. 1004

Bomb Threats Act
Pub. L. 91–452, title XI, §1102(a), Oct. 15, 1970, 84 Stat. 956 (18 U.S.C. 844)

Bond Act (Public Officers)
Mar. 2, 1895, ch. 177, §5, 28 Stat. 807

Bond Limitation Act
See Second Liberty Bond Act

Bond Purchase Clause (Sundry Civil Appropriation Act)
Mar. 3, 1881, ch. 133, §2, 21 Stat. 457

Bonner Act
See Federal Boating Act of 1958

Bonneville Project Act of 1937
Aug. 20, 1937, ch. 720, 50 Stat. 731 (16 U.S.C. 832 et seq.)
Short title, see 16 U.S.C. 832 note

Bonus Act
See World War Adjusted Compensation Act

Bonus Payment Act, 1936
See Adjusted Compensation Payment Act, 1936

Book Postage Act
June 30, 1942, ch. 459, 56 Stat. 462

Booth Act (California School Lands)
Mar. 1, 1877, ch. 81, 19 Stat. 267

Borah Act
Aug. 25, 1937, ch. 777, 50 Stat. 810

Borah Resolution (Armament Conference)
See Disarmament Conference Resolution

Border Smog Reduction Act of 1998
Pub. L. 105–286, Oct. 27, 1998, 112 Stat. 2773
Short title, see 42 U.S.C. 7401 note

Borland Amendment (District of Columbia Improvements)
July 21, 1914, ch. 191, 38 Stat. 524

Bosque Redondo Memorial Act
Pub. L. 106–511, title II, Nov. 13, 2000, 114 Stat. 2369 (16 U.S.C. 431 note)

Boston National Historical Park Act of 1974
Pub. L. 93–431, Oct. 1, 1974, 88 Stat. 1184 (16 U.S.C. 410z et seq.)
Short title, see 16 U.S.C. 410z note

Boulder Canyon Project Act
Dec. 21, 1928, ch. 42, 45 Stat. 1057 (43 U.S.C. 617 et seq.)
Short title, see 43 U.S.C. 617t

Boulder Canyon Project Adjustment Act
July 19, 1940, ch. 643, 54 Stat. 774 (43 U.S.C. 618 et seq.)
Short title, see 43 U.S.C. 618*o*

Boulder City Act of 1958
Pub. L. 85–900, Sept. 2, 1958, 72 Stat. 1726 (43 U.S.C. 617u note)

Bowman Act (Claims)
Mar. 3, 1883, ch. 116, 22 Stat. 485

Boykin Merchant Marine Act
June 6, 1939, ch. 186, 53 Stat. 810

Brady Handgun Violence Prevention Act
Pub. L. 103–159, title I, Nov. 30, 1993, 107 Stat. 1536
Short title, see 18 U.S.C. 921 note

Breast and Cervical Cancer Mortality Prevention Act of 1990
Pub. L. 101–354, Aug. 10, 1990, 104 Stat. 409 (42 U.S.C. 300k et seq.)
Short title, see 42 U.S.C. 201 note

Breast and Cervical Cancer Prevention and Treatment Act of 2000
Pub. L. 106–354, Oct. 24, 2000, 114 Stat. 1381
Short title, see 42 U.S.C. 1305 note

Bretton Woods Agreements Act
July 31, 1945, ch. 339, 59 Stat. 512 (22 U.S.C. 286 et seq.)
Short title, see 22 U.S.C. 286 note

Bretton Woods Agreements Act Amendments of 1978
Pub. L. 95–435, Oct. 10, 1978, 92 Stat. 1051

Bridge Act of 1906
Also known as the General Bridge Act of 1906
Mar. 23, 1906, ch. 1130, 34 Stat. 84 (33 U.S.C. 491 et seq.)
Short title, see 33 U.S.C. 491 note

Bring Them Home Alive Act of 2000
Pub. L. 106–484, Nov. 9, 2000, 114 Stat. 2195 (8 U.S.C. 1157 note)

Brookhart Act
July 3, 1930, ch. 850, 46 Stat. 1003

Brooklyn Bridge Authorization Act
Mar. 3, 1869, ch. 139, 15 Stat. 336

Brooks Act (Architects and Engineers)
See Brooks Architect-Engineers Act

Brooks Act (Data Processing)
See Brooks Automatic Data Processing Act

Brooks Architect-Engineers Act
June 30, 1949, ch. 288, title IX, as added Oct. 27, 1972, Pub. L. 92–582, 86 Stat. 1278 (40 U.S.C. 541 et seq.)
Short title, see 40 U.S.C. 541 note

Brooks Automatic Data Processing Act
June 30, 1949, ch. 288, title I, §111, as added Pub. L. 89–306, Oct. 30, 1965, 79 Stat. 1127 (40 U.S.C. 759)

Brown-Lea Natural Gas Act
See Natural Gas Act

Brown-Lodge Bill
July 7, 1947, ch. 207, 61 Stat. 246

Brown-Stevens Act
May 6, 1910, ch. 202, 36 Stat. 348

Brownsville Wetlands Policy Act of 1994
Pub. L. 103–232, title II, Apr. 11, 1994, 108 Stat. 338

Brush Disposal Act
Aug. 11, 1916, ch. 313, 39 Stat. 462 (16 U.S.C. 490)

Bryson Act
July 19, 1952, ch. 950, 66 Stat. 792 (35 U.S.C. 1 et seq.)

Buck Act
Oct. 9, 1940, ch. 787, 54 Stat. 1059 (see 4 U.S.C. 105–110)

Budget and Accounting Act, 1921
June 10, 1921, ch. 18, 42 Stat. 20

Budget and Accounting Procedures Act of 1950
Sept. 12, 1950, ch. 946, 64 Stat. 832

Budget Enforcement Act of 1990
Pub. L. 101–508, title XIII, Nov. 5, 1990, 104 Stat. 1388–573
Short title, see 2 U.S.C. 900 note

Budget Enforcement Act of 1997
Pub. L. 105–33, title X, Aug. 5, 1997, 111 Stat. 677
Short title, see 2 U.S.C. 900 note

Building Height Act of 1910
June 1, 1910, ch. 263, 36 Stat. 452

Bulgarian Declaration of War
June 5, 1942, ch. 323, 56 Stat. 307

Bull Run Watershed Management Act
Pub. L. 95–200, Nov. 23, 1977, 91 Stat. 1425 (16 U.S.C. 482b note)

Bulletproof Vest Partnership Grant Act of 1998
Pub. L. 105–181, June 16, 1998, 112 Stat. 512 (42 U.S.C 3796*ll* et seq.)
Short title, see 42 U.S.C. 3711 note

Bulletproof Vest Partnership Grant Act of 2000
Pub. L. 106–517, Nov. 13, 2000, 114 Stat. 2407
Short title, see 42 U.S.C. 3711 note

Bureau of Corporations Act
Feb. 14, 1903, ch. 552, §6, 32 Stat. 827

Bureau of Land Management Drug Enforcement Supplemental Authority Act
Pub. L. 99–570, title V, subtitle C (§5061 et seq.), as added Pub. L. 100–690, title VI, §6254(d)(3), Nov. 18, 1988, 102 Stat. 4365 (43 U.S.C. 2 note)

Bureau of Marine Inspection and Navigation Act
May 27, 1936, ch. 463, 49 Stat. 1380

Bureau of Standards Act
See National Institute of Standards and Technology Act

Burke Act (Indians)
May 8, 1906, ch. 2348, 34 Stat. 182 (25 U.S.C. 349)

Burke-Wadsworth Act
See Selective Training and Service Act of 1940

Burnt Timber Act
Mar. 4, 1913, ch. 165, 37 Stat. 1015 (16 U.S.C. 614, 615)

Burton Law (Control and Regulation of Waters of Niagara Falls)
June 29, 1906, ch. 3621, 34 Stat. 626

Burton-Hill Hospital Survey and Construction Act
See Hospital Survey and Construction Act

Bus Regulatory Reform Act of 1982
Pub. L. 97–261, Sept. 20, 1982, 96 Stat. 1102
Short title, see 49 U.S.C. 10101 note

Business Methods Inquiry Act (Executive Departments)
June 25, 1910, ch. 384, 36 Stat. 703

Business Opportunity Development Reform Act of 1988
Pub. L. 100–656, Nov. 15, 1988, 102 Stat. 3853
Short title, see 15 U.S.C. 631 note

Business Opportunity Development Reform Act Technical Corrections Act
Pub. L. 101–37, June 15, 1989, 103 Stat. 70
Short title, see 15 U.S.C. 631 note

Business Records Act
June 20, 1936, ch. 640, 49 Stat. 1561

Butter Standard Act
Mar. 4, 1923, ch. 268, 42 Stat. 1500 (21 U.S.C. 321a)

Buy American Act
Mar. 3, 1933, ch. 212, title III, 47 Stat. 1520 (41 U.S.C. 10a et seq.)
Short title, see 41 U.S.C. 10a note

Buy American Act of 1988
Pub. L. 100–418, title VII, Aug. 23, 1988, 102 Stat. 1545
Short title, see 41 U.S.C. 10a note

Buy Indian Act
June 25, 1910, ch. 431, §23, 36 Stat. 861 (25 U.S.C. 47)

Byrnes Act (Transporting Strikebreakers)
June 24, 1936, ch. 746, 49 Stat. 1899

C.C.C. Act
See Civilian Conservation Corps Act

Cabin User Fee Fairness Act of 2000
Pub. L. 106–291, title VI, Oct. 11, 2000, 114 Stat. 1014 (16 U.S.C. 6201 et seq.)
Short title, see 16 U.S.C. 6201 note

Cable Act (Naturalization and Citizenship of Married Women)
See Married Women's Citizenship Act

Cable Communications Policy Act of 1984
Pub. L. 98–549, Oct. 30, 1984, 98 Stat. 2779 (47 U.S.C. 521 et seq.)
Short title, see 47 U.S.C. 609 note

Cable Television Consumer Protection and Competition Act of 1992
Pub. L. 102–385, Oct. 5, 1992, 106 Stat. 1460
Short title, see 47 U.S.C. 609 note

Cache La Poudre River Corridor Act
Pub. L. 104–323, Oct. 19, 1996, 110 Stat. 3889

Cahaba River National Wildlife Refuge Establishment Act
Pub. L. 106–331, Oct. 19, 2000, 114 Stat. 1303 (16 U.S.C. 668dd note)

Calder Act (Daylight Saving)
Mar. 19, 1918, ch. 24, 40 Stat. 450 (15 U.S.C. 261 et seq.)
Short title, see 15 U.S.C. 261 note

California Bay-Delta Environmental Enhancement and Water Security Act
Pub. L. 104–208, div. E, title I, Sept. 30, 1996, 110 Stat. 3009–748

California Desert Protection Act of 1994
Pub. L. 103–433, §§1, 2, titles I–IX, Oct. 31, 1994, 108 Stat. 4471–4508 (16 U.S.C. 410aaa et seq.)
Short title, see 16 U.S.C. 410aaa note

California Indian Land Transfer Act
Pub. L. 106–568, title IX, Dec. 27, 2000, 114 Stat. 2921

California Military Lands Withdrawal and Overflights Act of 1994
Pub. L. 103–433, title VIII, Oct. 31, 1994, 108 Stat. 4501 (16 U.S.C. 410aaa–82)
Short title, see 16 U.S.C. 410aaa–82 note

California Trail Interpretive Act
Pub. L. 106–577, title I, Dec. 28, 2000, 114 Stat. 3068 (16 U.S.C. 1244 note)

California Wilderness Act of 1984
Pub. L. 98–425, Sept. 28, 1984, 98 Stat. 1619 (16 U.S.C. 543 et seq., 1132 note)

Cambodian Genocide Justice Act
Pub. L. 103–236, title V, part D (§571 et seq.), Apr. 30, 1994, 108 Stat. 486 (22 U.S.C. 2656 note)

Camp W.G. Williams Land Exchange Act of 1989
Pub. L. 101–628, title IX, Nov. 28, 1990, 104 Stat. 4499

Campaign Communications Reform Act
Pub. L. 92–225, title I, Feb. 7, 1972, 86 Stat. 3 (47 U.S.C. 801 et seq.)

Campus Sex Crimes Prevention Act
Pub. L. 106–386, div. B, title VI, §1601, Oct. 28, 2000, 114 Stat. 1537
Short title, see 20 U.S.C. 1001 note

Canada-United States Interparliamentary Group Act
Pub. L. 86–42, June 11, 1959, 73 Stat. 72 (22 U.S.C. 276d–276g)

Canadian Boundary Act
June 13, 1902, ch. 1079, §4, 32 Stat. 373

Canadian Reciprocity Act
July 26, 1911, ch. 3, 37 Stat. 4

Canadian River Project Prepayment Act
Pub. L. 105–316, Oct. 30, 1998, 112 Stat. 2999 (43 U.S.C. 600b note)

Canal Act of 1890
Aug. 30, 1890, ch. 837, §1, 26 Stat. 391 (43 U.S.C. 945)

Canal Tolls Repeal Act
June 15, 1914, ch. 106, 38 Stat. 385

Canal Zone Code
Renamed the Panana Canal Code

Canal Zone Government Act
Apr. 28, 1904, ch. 1758, 33 Stat. 429

Cancer Registries Amendment Act
Pub. L. 102–515, Oct. 24, 1992, 106 Stat. 3372 (42 U.S.C. 280e et seq.)
Short title, see 42 U.S.C. 201 note

Cane River Creole National Historical Park and National Heritage Area Act
Pub. L. 103–449, titles III, IV, Nov. 2, 1994, 108 Stat. 4757, 4760 (16 U.S.C. 410ccc et seq.)
Short title, see 16 U.S.C. 410ccc note

Canola and Rapeseed Research, Promotion, and Consumer Information Act
Pub. L. 104–127, title V, subtitle C (§531 et seq.), Apr. 4, 1996, 110 Stat. 1048 (7 U.S.C. 7441 et seq.)
Short title, see 7 U.S.C. 7401 note

Canyonlands National Park Act
Pub. L. 88–590, Sept. 12, 1964, 78 Stat. 934 (16 U.S.C. 271 et seq.)

Cape Cod National Seashore Act
Pub. L. 87–126, Aug. 7, 1961, 75 Stat. 284 (16 U.S.C. 459b et seq.)

Cape Lookout National Seashore Act
Pub. L. 89–366, Mar. 10, 1966, 80 Stat. 33 (16 U.S.C. 459g et seq.)

Capehart Housing Act
Aug. 11, 1955, ch. 783, title IV, §401, 69 Stat. 646

Capital Markets Efficiency Act of 1996
Pub. L. 104–290, title I, Oct. 11, 1996, 110 Stat. 3417
Short title, see 15 U.S.C. 78a note

Capitol Police Retirement Act
Pub. L. 101–428, Oct. 15, 1990, 104 Stat. 928
Short title, see 5 U.S.C. 8331 note

Capitol Reef National Park Act
Pub. L. 92–207, Dec. 18, 1971, 85 Stat. 739 (16 U.S.C. 273 et seq.)

Capper-Ketcham Act
May 22, 1928, ch. 687, 45 Stat. 711 (7 U.S.C. 343a, 343b)

Capper-Lenroot-Anderson Act (Agricultural Credits)
See Agricultural Credits Act of 1923

Capper-Tincher Act (Grain Futures)
See Commodity Exchange Act

Capper-Volstead Act
See Co-operative Marketing Associations Act

Car Pricing Law
See Automobile Information Disclosure Act

Car Service Act
May 29, 1917, ch. 23, 40 Stat. 101

Carbon Hill National Fish Hatchery Conveyance Act
Pub. L. 104–213, Oct. 1, 1996, 110 Stat. 3016

Cardiac Arrest Survival Act of 2000
Pub. L. 106–505, title IV, subtitle A (§401 et seq.), Nov. 13, 2000, 114 Stat. 2336
Short title, see 42 U.S.C. 201 note

Care for Police Survivors Act of 1998
Pub. L. 105–180, June 16, 1998, 112 Stat. 511
Short title, see 42 U.S.C. 3711 note

Career Compensation Act of 1949
Oct. 12, 1949, ch. 681, 63 Stat. 802

Career Criminals Amendment Act of 1986
Pub. L. 99–570, title I, subtitle I (§1401 et seq.), Oct. 27, 1986, 100 Stat. 3207–39
Short title, see 18 U.S.C. 921 note

Career Education Incentive Act
Pub. L. 95–207, Dec. 13, 1977, 91 Stat. 1464 (20 U.S.C. 2601 et seq.)

Career Incentive Act of 1955
Mar. 31, 1955, ch. 20, 69 Stat. 18

Carey Act (Irrigation)
Aug. 18, 1894, ch. 301, §4, 28 Stat. 422 (43 U.S.C. 641)
Short title, see 43 U.S.C. 641 note

Cargo Preference Act of 1904
See Military Cargo Preference Act of 1904

Caribbean Basin Economic Recovery Act
Pub. L. 98–67, title II, Aug. 5, 1983, 97 Stat. 384 (19 U.S.C. 2701 et seq.)
Short title, see 19 U.S.C. 2701 note

Caribbean Basin Economic Recovery Expansion Act of 1990
Pub. L. 101–382, title II, Aug. 20, 1990, 104 Stat. 655
Short title, see 19 U.S.C. 2701 note

Carjacking Correction Act of 1996
Pub. L. 104–217, Oct. 1, 1996, 110 Stat. 3020
Short title, see 18 U.S.C. 2111 note

Carl D. Perkins Vocational and Applied Technology Education Act
Renamed the Carl D. Perkins Vocational and Technical Education Act of 1998

Carl D. Perkins Vocational and Applied Technology Education Act Amendments of 1990
Pub. L. 101–392, Sept. 25, 1990, 104 Stat. 753
Short title, see 20 U.S.C. 2301 note

Carl D. Perkins Vocational and Applied Technology Education Amendments of 1998
Pub. L. 105–332, Oct. 31, 1998, 112 Stat. 3076
Short title, see 20 U.S.C. 2301 note

Carl D. Perkins Vocational and Technical Education Act of 1998
Pub. L. 88–210, as added Pub. L. 105–332, §1(b), Oct. 31, 1998, 112 Stat. 3076 (20 U.S.C. 2301 et seq.)
Short title, see 20 U.S.C. 2301 note

Carl D. Perkins Vocational Education Act
Renamed Carl D. Perkins Vocational and Technical Education Act of 1998

Carlin Act (Larceny from Interstate Carriers)
Feb. 13, 1913, ch. 50, 37 Stat. 670

Carlisle Act (Internal Revenue)
May 28, 1880, ch. 108, 21 Stat. 148 (19 U.S.C. 468, 469)

Carlisle Act (Spirits Regauging)
Aug. 27, 1894, ch. 349, §50, 28 Stat. 564

Carlsbad Irrigation Project Acquired Land Transfer Act
Pub. L. 106–220, June 20, 2000, 114 Stat. 347

Carmack Amendment to Hepburn Act (Interstate Commerce)
June 29, 1906, ch. 3591, §7 [§20(pars. 11, 12)], 34 Stat. 595

Carriage of Goods by Sea Act
Apr. 16, 1936, ch. 229, 49 Stat. 1207 (46 App. U.S.C. 1300 et seq.)
Short title, see 46 App. U.S.C. 1315

Carriers and Employees Tax Act
Aug. 29, 1935, ch. 813, 49 Stat. 974

Carriers Taxing Act of 1937
June 29, 1937, ch. 405, 50 Stat. 435

Carter Act (Alaska Civil Code)
See Alaska Civil Code

Carter G. Woodson Home National Historic Site Study Act of 2000
Pub. L. 106–349, Oct. 24, 2000, 114 Stat. 1359

Case-Zablocki Act
Pub. L. 92–403, §1, Aug. 22, 1972, 86 Stat. 619 (1 U.S.C. 112b)
Short title, see 1 U.S.C. 112b note

Cash Discount Act
Pub. L. 97–25, July 27, 1981, 95 Stat. 144
Short title, see 15 U.S.C. 1601 note

Cash Management Improvement Act Amendments of 1992
Pub. L. 102–589, Nov. 10, 1992, 106 Stat. 5133
Short title, see 31 U.S.C. 6501 note

Cash Management Improvement Act of 1990
Pub. L. 101–453, Oct. 24, 1990, 104 Stat. 1058
Short title, see 31 U.S.C. 6501 note

Castle Rock Ranch Acquisition Act of 2000
Pub. L. 106–421, Nov. 1, 2000, 114 Stat. 1870

Cat Island National Wildlife Refuge Establishment Act
Pub. L. 106–369, Oct. 27, 2000, 114 Stat. 1417 (16 U.S.C. 668dd note)

Catawba Indian Tribe of South Carolina Land Claims Settlement Act of 1993
Pub. L. 103–116, Oct. 27, 1993, 107 Stat. 1118 (25 U.S.C. 941 et seq.)
Short title, see 25 U.S.C. 941 note

Cattle Contagious Diseases Act of 1903
Feb. 2, 1903, ch. 349, 32 Stat. 791 (21 U.S.C. 112, 120–122)
Short title, see 21 U.S.C. 112 note

Cattle Contagious Diseases Act of 1905
Mar. 3, 1905, ch. 1496, 33 Stat. 1264 (21 U.S.C. 123–127)
Short title, see 21 U.S.C. 123 note

Cattle Inspection Act
Mar. 3, 1891, ch. 555, 26 Stat. 1089

Caustic Poison Act
See Federal Caustic Poison Act

Cave Creek Canyon Protection Act of 1993
Pub. L. 103–56, Aug. 2, 1993, 107 Stat. 278

Cedar River Watershed Land Exchange Act of 1992
Pub. L. 102–453, Oct. 23, 1992, 106 Stat. 2258

Celler Act (Liquor Prescriptions)
Mar. 31, 1933, ch. 18, 48 Stat. 23

Celler Anti-Merger Act
See Anti-Merger Act

Celler-Hennings Act of 1958
Pub. L. 85–752, Aug. 25, 1958, 72 Stat. 845 (28 U.S.C. 334)

Celler-Kefauver Act
See Anti-Merger Act

Census Address List Improvement Act of 1994
Pub. L. 103–430, Oct. 31, 1994, 108 Stat. 4393
Short title, see 13 U.S.C. 1 note

Census of Agriculture Act of 1997
Pub. L. 105–113, Nov. 21, 1997, 111 Stat. 2274
Short title, see 7 U.S.C. 2201 note

Centennial of Flight Commemoration Act
Pub. L. 105–389, Nov. 13, 1998, 112 Stat. 3486 (36 U.S.C. 143 note)

Center for Cultural and Technical Interchange Between East and West Act of 1960
Pub. L. 86–472, ch. VII, May 14, 1960, 74 Stat. 141 (22 U.S.C. 2054 et seq.)
Short title, see 22 U.S.C. 2054 note

Center for Cultural and Technical Interchange Between North and South Act of 1990
Pub. L. 101–513, title II [S. 2364, title II, §206], Nov. 5, 1990, 104 Stat. 1984 (22 U.S.C. 2075)

Central Bering Sea Fisheries Enforcement Act of 1992
Pub. L. 102–582, title III, Nov. 2, 1992, 106 Stat. 4906 (16 U.S.C. 1823 note)

Central Idaho Wilderness Act of 1980
Pub. L. 96–312, July 23, 1980, 94 Stat. 948

Central Intelligence Agency Act of 1949
June 20, 1949, ch. 227, 63 Stat. 208 (50 U.S.C. 403a et seq.)
Short title, see 50 U.S.C. 403a note

Central Intelligence Agency Information Act
Pub. L. 98–477, Oct. 15, 1984, 98 Stat. 2209
Short title, see 50 U.S.C. 401 note

Central Intelligence Agency Retirement Act
Pub. L. 88–643, Oct. 13, 1964, 78 Stat. 1043 (50 U.S.C. 2001 et seq.)
Short title, see 50 U.S.C. 2001 note

Central Intelligence Agency Retirement Act of 1964 for Certain Employees
Renamed the Central Intelligence Agency Retirement Act

Central Intelligence Agency Spouses' Retirement Equity Act of 1982
Pub. L. 97–269, title VI, Sept. 27, 1982, 96 Stat. 1145
Short title, see 50 U.S.C. 2001 note

Central Intelligence Agency Voluntary Separation Pay Act
Pub. L. 103–36, June 8, 1993, 107 Stat. 104
Short title, see 50 U.S.C. 2001 note

Central Midwest Interstate Low-Level Radioactive Waste Compact Amendments Consent Act of 1994
Pub. L. 103–439, Nov. 2, 1994, 108 Stat. 4607

Central Statistical Act
July 25, 1935, ch. 416, 49 Stat. 498

Central Utah Project Completion Act
Pub. L. 102–575, titles II–VI, Oct. 30, 1992, 106 Stat. 4605–4655

Central Valley Project Improvement Act
Pub. L. 102–575, title XXXIV, Oct. 30, 1992, 106 Stat. 4706

Central, Western, and South Pacific Fisheries Development Act
Pub. L. 92–444, Sept. 29, 1972, 86 Stat. 744 (16 U.S.C. 758e et seq.)
Short title, see 16 U.S.C. 758e note

CERCLA
See Comprehensive Environmental Response, Compensation, and Liability Act of 1980

Cerro Grande Fire Assistance Act
Pub. L. 106–246, div. C, title I, July 13, 2000, 114 Stat. 583

Cerro Grande Fire Supplemental
Pub. L. 106–246, div. C, July 13, 2000, 114 Stat. 583

Certified Development Company Program Improvements Act of 2000
Pub. L. 106–554, §1(a)(9) [title III], Dec. 21, 2000, 114 Stat. 2763, 2763A–684
Short title, see 15 U.S.C. 661 note

CETA
See Comprehensive Employment and Training Act

CFTC Reauthorization Act of 1995
Pub. L. 104–9, Apr. 21, 1995, 109 Stat. 154
Short title, see 7 U.S.C. 1 note

Chacoan Outliers Protection Act of 1995
Pub. L. 104–11, May 18, 1995, 109 Stat. 158

Chain Store Act
See Robinson-Patman Antidiscrimination Act

Challenge Grant Amendments of 1983
Pub. L. 98–95, Sept. 26, 1983, 97 Stat. 708
Short title, see 20 U.S.C. 1001 note

Chamberlain-Ferris Act
June 9, 1916, ch. 137, 39 Stat. 218

Chandler Act (Bankruptcy Revision)
June 22, 1938, ch. 575, 52 Stat. 840

Chandler Rail Bankruptcy Act
July 28, 1939, ch. 393, 53 Stat. 1134

Change in Bank Control Act of 1978
Pub. L. 95–630, title VI, Nov. 10, 1978, 92 Stat. 3683
Short title, see 12 U.S.C. 1811 note

Change in Savings and Loan Control Act of 1978
Pub. L. 95–630, title VII, Nov. 10, 1978, 92 Stat. 3687
Short title, see 12 U.S.C. 1701 note

Charitable Assistance and Food Bank Act of 1987
Pub. L. 100–232, Jan. 5, 1988, 101 Stat. 1566
Short title, see 7 U.S.C. 2011 note

Charitable Donation Antitrust Immunity Act of 1997
Pub. L. 105–26, July 3, 1997, 111 Stat. 241
Short title, see 15 U.S.C. 1 note

Charitable Gift Annuity Antitrust Relief Act of 1995
Pub. L. 104–63, Dec. 8, 1995, 109 Stat. 687
Short title, see 15 U.S.C. 1 note

Charity Games Advertising Clarification Act of 1988
Pub. L. 100–625, Nov. 7, 1988, 102 Stat. 3205
Short title, see 18 U.S.C. 1301 note

Charles M. Russell National Wildlife Refuge Enhancement Act of 2000
Pub. L. 106–541, title VIII, Dec. 11, 2000, 114 Stat. 2699

Charter School Expansion Act of 1998
Pub. L. 105–278, Oct. 22, 1998, 112 Stat. 2682 (20 U.S.C. 8065a et seq.)
Short title, see 20 U.S.C. 6301 note

Chattahoochee National Forest Protection Act of 1991
Pub. L. 102–217, Dec. 11, 1991, 105 Stat. 1667 (16 U.S.C. 460ggg et seq.)
Short title, see 16 U.S.C. 460ggg note

Cheaha Wilderness Act
Pub. L. 97–411, Jan. 3, 1983, 96 Stat. 2046 (16 U.S.C. 1132 note)

Chehalis River Basin Fishery Resources Study and Restoration Act of 1990
Pub. L. 101–452, Oct. 24, 1990, 104 Stat. 1054

Chemical and Biological Weapons Control and Warfare Elimination Act of 1991
Pub. L. 102–138, title V, Oct. 28, 1991, 105 Stat. 722 (22 U.S.C. 5601 et seq.)
Pub. L. 102–182, title III, Dec. 4, 1991, 105 Stat. 1245 (22 U.S.C. 5601 et seq.)
Short title, see 22 U.S.C. 5601 note

Chemical Diversion and Trafficking Act of 1988
Pub. L. 100–690, title VI, subtitle A (§6051 et seq.), Nov. 18, 1988, 102 Stat. 4312
Short title, see 21 U.S.C. 801 note

Chemical Safety Information, Site Security and Fuels Regulatory Relief Act
Pub. L. 106–40, Aug. 5, 1999, 113 Stat. 207
Short title, see 42 U.S.C. 7401 note

Chemical Weapons Convention Implementation Act of 1998
Pub. L. 105–277, div. I, Oct. 21, 1998, 112 Stat. 2681–856 (22 U.S.C. 6701 et seq.)
Short title, see 22 U.S.C. 6701 note

Cherokee Agreement Act
July 1, 1902, ch. 1375, 32 Stat. 716

Cherokee Leasing Act
Pub. L. 99–221, Dec. 26, 1985, 99 Stat. 1735
Short title, see 25 U.S.C. 415 note

Chesapeake and Ohio Canal Development Act
Pub. L. 91–664, Jan. 8, 1971, 84 Stat. 1978 (16 U.S.C. 410y et seq.)
Short title, see 16 U.S.C. 410y note

Chesapeake Bay Initiative Act of 1998
Pub. L. 105–312, title V, Oct. 30, 1998, 112 Stat. 2961 (16 U.S.C. 461 note)

Chesapeake Bay Research Coordination Act of 1980
Pub. L. 96–460, Oct. 15, 1980, 94 Stat. 2044 (16 U.S.C. 3001 et seq.)
Short title, see 16 U.S.C. 3001 note

Chesapeake Bay Restoration Act of 2000
Pub. L. 106–457, title II, Nov. 7, 2000, 114 Stat. 1967
Short title, see 33 U.S.C. 1251 note

Cheyenne River Sioux Tribe Equitable Compensation Act
Pub. L. 106–511, title I, Nov. 13, 2000, 114 Stat. 2365

Chief Financial Officers Act of 1990
Pub. L. 101–576, Nov. 15, 1990, 104 Stat. 2838
Short title, see 31 U.S.C. 501 note

Child Abuse Accountability Act
Pub. L. 103–358, Oct. 14, 1994, 108 Stat. 3420
Short title, see 5 U.S.C. 8331 note

Child Abuse Amendments of 1984
Pub. L. 98–457, Oct. 9, 1984, 98 Stat. 1749
Short title, see 42 U.S.C. 5101 note

Child Abuse Prevention and Enforcement Act
Pub. L. 106–177, title I, Mar. 10, 2000, 114 Stat. 35
Short title, see 42 U.S.C. 3711 note

Child Abuse Prevention and Treatment Act
Pub. L. 93–247, Jan. 31, 1974, 88 Stat. 4 (42 U.S.C. 5101 et seq.)
Short title, see 42 U.S.C. 5101 note

Child Abuse Prevention and Treatment Act Amendments of 1996
Pub. L. 104–235, Oct. 3, 1996, 110 Stat. 3063
Short title, see 42 U.S.C. 5101 note

Child Abuse Prevention and Treatment and Adoption Reform Act of 1978
Pub. L. 95–266, Apr. 24, 1978, 92 Stat. 205 (42 U.S.C. 5111 et seq.)
Short title, see 42 U.S.C. 5101 note

Child Abuse Prevention Challenge Grants Reauthorization Act of 1989
Pub. L. 101–126, Oct. 25, 1989, 103 Stat. 764
Short title, see 42 U.S.C. 5101 note

Child Abuse Prevention, Adoption, and Family Services Act of 1988
Pub. L. 100–294, Apr. 25, 1988, 102 Stat. 102
Short title, see 42 U.S.C. 5101 note

Child Abuse Victims' Rights Act of 1986
Pub. L. 99–500, §101(b) [title VII], Oct. 18, 1986, 100 Stat. 1783–39, 1783–74, and Pub. L. 99–591, §101(b) [title VII], Oct. 30, 1986, 100 Stat. 3341–39, 3341–74
Short title, see 18 U.S.C. 2251 note

Child Abuse, Domestic Violence, Adoption and Family Services Act of 1992
Pub. L. 102–295, May 28, 1992, 106 Stat. 187
Short title, see 42 U.S.C. 5101 note

Child Care and Development Block Grant Act of 1990
Pub. L. 97–35, title VI, subtitle A, ch. 8, subch. C (§658A et seq.), as added Pub. L. 101–508, title V, §5082(2), Nov. 5, 1990, 104 Stat. 1388–236 (42 U.S.C. 9858 et seq.)
Short title, see 42 U.S.C. 9801 note

Child Care and Development Block Grant Amendments of 1996
Pub. L. 104–193, title VI, Aug. 22, 1996, 110 Stat. 2278
Short title, see 42 U.S.C. 9801 note

Child Citizenship Act of 2000
Pub. L. 106–395, Oct. 30, 2000, 114 Stat. 1631
Short title, see 8 U.S.C. 1101 note

Child Development Associate Scholarship Assistance Act of 1985
Pub. L. 99–425, title VI, Sept. 30, 1986, 100 Stat. 976 (42 U.S.C. 10901 et seq.)
Short title, see 42 U.S.C. 10901 note

Child Health Act of 1967
Pub. L. 90–248, title III, Jan. 2, 1968, 81 Stat. 921
Short title, see 42 U.S.C. 1305 note

Child Labor Law (District of Columbia)
May 28, 1908, ch. 209, 35 Stat. 420

Child Labor Tax Act
Feb. 24, 1919, ch. 18, title XII, 40 Stat. 1138

Child Nutrition Act of 1966
Pub. L. 89–642, Oct. 11, 1966, 80 Stat. 885 (42 U.S.C. 1771 et seq.)
Short title, see 42 U.S.C. 1771 note

Child Nutrition Amendments of 1978
Pub. L. 95–627, Nov. 10, 1978, 92 Stat. 3603
Short title, see 42 U.S.C. 1751 note

Child Nutrition Amendments of 1986
Pub. L. 99–661, div. D, Nov. 14, 1986, 100 Stat. 4070
Short title, see 42 U.S.C. 1751 note

Child Nutrition Amendments of 1992
Pub. L. 102–342, Aug. 14, 1992, 106 Stat. 911
Short title, see 42 U.S.C. 1751 note

Child Nutrition and WIC Reauthorization Act of 1989
Pub. L. 101–147, Nov. 10, 1989, 103 Stat. 877
Short title, see 42 U.S.C. 1751 note

Child Online Protection Act
Pub. L. 105–277, div. C, title XIV, Oct. 21, 1998, 112 Stat. 2681–736
Short title, see 47 U.S.C. 609 note

Child Pilot Safety Act
Pub. L. 104–264, title VI, Oct. 9, 1996, 110 Stat. 3263 (49 U.S.C. 44724)
Short title, see 49 U.S.C. 40101 note

Child Pornography Prevention Act of 1996
Pub. L. 104–208, div. A, title I, §101(a) [title I, §121], Sept. 30, 1996, 110 Stat. 3009, 3009–26
Short title, see 18 U.S.C. 2251 note

Child Protection Act of 1966
Pub. L. 89–756, Nov. 3, 1966, 80 Stat. 1303
Short title, see 15 U.S.C. 1261 note

Child Protection Act of 1984
Pub. L. 98–292, May 21, 1984, 98 Stat. 204
Short title, see 18 U.S.C. 2251 note

Child Protection and Obscenity Enforcement Act of 1988
Pub. L. 100–690, title VII, subtitle N (§7501 et seq.), Nov. 18, 1988, 102 Stat. 4485
Short title, see 18 U.S.C. 2251 note

Child Protection and Toy Safety Act of 1969
Pub. L. 91–113, Nov. 6, 1969, 83 Stat. 187
Short title, see 15 U.S.C. 1261 note

Child Protection Restoration and Penalties Enhancement Act of 1990
Pub. L. 101–647, title III, Nov. 29, 1990, 104 Stat. 4816
Short title, see 18 U.S.C. 2251 note

Child Safety Protection Act
Pub. L. 103–267, June 16, 1994, 108 Stat. 722
Short title, see 15 U.S.C. 1261 note

Child Sexual Abuse and Pornography Act of 1986
Pub. L. 99–628, Nov. 7, 1986, 100 Stat. 3510
Short title, see 18 U.S.C. 2251 note

Child Support Enforcement Act
Aug. 14, 1935, ch. 531, title IV, part D (§451 et seq.), as added Pub. L. 93–647, §101(a), Jan. 4, 1975, 88 Stat. 2351 (42 U.S.C. 651 et seq.)
Short title, see 42 U.S.C. 651 note

Child Support Enforcement Amendments of 1984
Pub. L. 98–378, Aug. 16, 1984, 98 Stat. 1305
Short title, see 42 U.S.C. 1305 note

Child Support Performance and Incentive Act of 1998
Pub. L. 105–200, July 16, 1998, 112 Stat. 645
Short title, see 42 U.S.C. 1305 note

Child Support Recovery Act of 1992
Pub. L. 102–521, Oct. 25, 1992, 106 Stat. 3403
Short title, see 18 U.S.C. 228 note

Children With Disabilities Temporary Care Reauthorization Act of 1989
Pub. L. 101–127, Oct. 25, 1989, 103 Stat. 770

Children's Bicycle Helmet Safety Act of 1994
Pub. L. 103–267, title II, June 16, 1994, 108 Stat. 726 (15 U.S.C. 6001 et seq.)
Short title, see 15 U.S.C. 6001 note

Children's Bureau Act
Apr. 9, 1912, ch. 73, 37 Stat. 79

Children's Health Act of 2000
Pub. L. 106–310, Oct. 17, 2000, 114 Stat. 1101
Short title, see 42 U.S.C. 201 note

Children's Internet Protection Act
Pub. L. 106–554, §1(a)(4) [div. B, title XVII], Dec. 21, 2000, 114 Stat. 2763, 2763A–335
Short title, see 20 U.S.C. 6301 note

Children's Justice Act
Pub. L. 99–401, title I, Aug. 27, 1986, 100 Stat. 903
Short title, see 42 U.S.C. 5101 note

Children's Justice and Assistance Act of 1986
Pub. L. 99–401, Aug. 27, 1986, 100 Stat. 903
Short title, see 42 U.S.C. 5101 note

Children's Nutrition Assistance Act of 1992
Pub. L. 102–512, Oct. 24, 1992, 106 Stat. 3363
Short title, see 42 U.S.C. 1771 note

Children's Online Privacy Protection Act of 1998
Pub. L. 105–277, div. C, title XIII, Oct. 21, 1998, 112 Stat. 2681–728 (15 U.S.C. 6501 et seq.)
Short title, see 15 U.S.C. 6501 note

Children's Television Act of 1990
Pub. L. 101–437, Oct. 17, 1990, 104 Stat. 996
Short title, see 47 U.S.C. 609 note

Chimpanzee Health Improvement, Maintenance, and Protection Act
Pub. L. 106–551, Dec. 20, 2000, 114 Stat. 2752
Short title, see 42 U.S.C. 201 note

China Aid Act
Feb. 7, 1942, ch. 47, 56 Stat. 82

China Aid Act of 1948
Apr. 3, 1948, ch. 169, title IV, 62 Stat. 158

China Appropriation Act
Feb. 12, 1942, ch. 71, 56 Stat. 89

China Area Aid Act of 1950
June 5, 1950, ch. 220, title II, 64 Stat. 202

China Trade Act (Corporations Act)
June 6, 1932, ch. 209, title I, supp. K (§261 et seq.), 47 Stat. 232

China Trade Act, 1922
Sept. 19, 1922, ch. 346, 42 Stat. 849 (15 U.S.C. 141 et seq.)
Short title, see 15 U.S.C. 141

Chinese Student Protection Act of 1992
Pub. L. 102–404, Oct. 9, 1992, 106 Stat. 1969 (8 U.S.C. 1255 note)

Chippewa Cree Tribe of The Rocky Boy's Reservation Indian Reserved Water Rights Settlement and Water Supply Enhancement Act of 1999
Pub. L. 106–163, Dec. 9, 1999, 113 Stat. 1778

Choctaw-Chickasaw Supplemental Agreement
July 1, 1902, ch. 1362, 32 Stat. 641 (16 U.S.C. 151)

Choctaw-Chickasaw-Cherokee Boundary Dispute Act
Pub. L. 93–195, Dec. 20, 1973, 87 Stat. 769

Choice in Public Housing Management Act of 1992
Sept. 1, 1937, ch. 896, title I, §25, as added Pub. L. 102–550, title I, §121(b), Oct. 28, 1992, 106 Stat. 3701 (42 U.S.C. 1437w)

Christopher Columbus Fellowship Act
Pub. L. 102–281, title IV, subtitle B (§421 et seq.), May 13, 1992, 106 Stat. 142 (20 U.S.C. 5701 et seq.)
Short title, see 20 U.S.C. 5701 note

Christopher Columbus Quincentenary Coin Act
Pub. L. 102–281, title IV, subtitle A (§401 et seq.), May 13, 1992, 106 Stat. 139 (31 U.S.C. 5112 note)

Christopher Columbus Quincentenary Jubilee Act
Pub. L. 98–375, Aug. 7, 1984, 98 Stat. 1257

Chrysler Corporation Loan Guarantee Act of 1979
Pub. L. 96–185, Jan. 7, 1980, 93 Stat. 1324 (15 U.S.C. 1861 et seq.)

Church Arson Prevention Act of 1996
Pub. L. 104–155, July 3, 1996, 110 Stat. 1392
Short title, see 18 U.S.C. 241 note

CIARDS Technical Corrections Act of 1992
Pub. L. 102–496, title VIII, Oct. 24, 1992, 106 Stat. 3196

CIARDS Technical Corrections Act of 1992—Continued
Short title, see 50 U.S.C. 2001 note

Cigarette Safety Act of 1984
Pub. L. 98–567, Oct. 30, 1984, 98 Stat. 2925 (15 U.S.C. 2054 note)

Circuit Court of Appeals Act
Mar. 3, 1891, ch. 517, 26 Stat. 826

Citizens' Rights Act (Foreign States)
July 27, 1868, ch. 249, 15 Stat. 223

Citizenship Act of 1907
Mar. 2, 1907, ch. 2534, 34 Stat. 1228

Citron Flood Compact Act
June 8, 1936, ch. 542, 49 Stat. 1490 (33 U.S.C. 567a)

Civil Activities National Defense Appropriation Act, 1941
June 26, 1940, ch. 430, title I, 54 Stat. 599

Civil Aeronautics Act of 1938
June 23, 1938, ch. 601, 52 Stat. 973

Civil Aeronautics Board Sunset Act of 1984
Pub. L. 98–443, Oct. 4, 1984, 98 Stat. 1703

Civil Asset Forfeiture Reform Act of 2000
Pub. L. 106–185, Apr. 25, 2000, 114 Stat. 202
Short title, see 18 U.S.C. 981 note

Civil Functions Appropriation Act, 1949
June 25, 1948, ch. 655, 62 Stat. 1019

Civil Functions Appropriation Act, 1950
Oct. 13, 1949, ch. 688, 63 Stat. 845

Civil Functions Appropriation Act, 1951
Sept. 6, 1950, ch. 896, Ch. IX, 64 Stat. 724

Civil Functions Appropriation Act, 1952
Oct. 24, 1951, ch. 556, 65 Stat. 616

Civil Functions Appropriation Act, 1955
June 30, 1954, ch. 425, 68 Stat. 330

Civil Functions Appropriations Act, 1953
July 11, 1952, ch. 669, 66 Stat. 579

Civil Functions Appropriations Act, 1954
July 27, 1953, ch. 245, 67 Stat. 197

Civil Justice Reform Act of 1990
Pub. L. 101–650, title I, Dec. 1, 1990, 104 Stat. 5089 (28 U.S.C. 471 et seq.)
Short title, see 28 U.S.C. 1 note

Civil Liberties Act Amendments of 1992
Pub. L. 102–371, Sept. 27, 1992, 106 Stat. 1167
Short title, see 50 App. U.S.C. 1989b note

Civil Liberties Act of 1988
Pub. L. 100–383, title I, Aug. 10, 1988, 102 Stat. 904 (50 App. U.S.C. 1989b et seq.)
Short title, see 50 App. U.S.C. 1989b

Civil Obedience Act of 1968
Pub. L. 90–284, title X, Apr. 11, 1968, 82 Stat. 90 (18 U.S.C. 231 et seq.)
Short title, see 18 U.S.C. 231 note

Civil Relief Act (Soldiers and Sailors)
See the Soldiers' and Sailors' Civil Relief Act of 1918 and the Soldiers' and Sailors' Civil Relief Act of 1940

Civil Rights Act of 1866
Apr. 9, 1866, ch. 31, 14 Stat. 27

Civil Rights Act of 1957
Pub. L. 85–315, Sept. 9, 1957, 71 Stat. 634
Short title, see 42 U.S.C. 1971 note

Civil Rights Act of 1960
Pub. L. 86–449, May 6, 1960, 74 Stat. 86
Short title, see 42 U.S.C. 1971 note

Civil Rights Act of 1964
Pub. L. 88–352, July 2, 1964, 78 Stat. 241
Short title, see 42 U.S.C. 2000a note

Civil Rights Act of 1968
Pub. L. 90–284, Apr. 11, 1968, 82 Stat. 73
Short title, see 42 U.S.C. 3601 note

Civil Rights Act of 1991
Pub. L. 102–166, Nov. 21, 1991, 105 Stat. 1071
Short title, see 42 U.S.C. 1981 note

Civil Rights Attorney's Fees Awards Act of 1976
Pub. L. 94–559, Oct. 19, 1976, 90 Stat. 2641
Short title, see 42 U.S.C. 1988 note

Civil Rights Commission Act of 1978
Pub. L. 95–444, Oct. 10, 1978, 92 Stat. 1067

Civil Rights Commission Act of 1983
Pub. L. 98–183, Nov. 30, 1983, 97 Stat. 1301 (42 U.S.C. 1975 et seq.)
Short title, see 42 U.S.C. 1975 note

Civil Rights Commission Amendments Act of 1994
Pub. L. 103–419, Oct. 25, 1994, 108 Stat. 4338
Short title, see 42 U.S.C. 1975 note

Civil Rights Commission Authorization Act of 1976
Pub. L. 94–292, May 27, 1976, 90 Stat. 524

Civil Rights Commission Authorization Act of 1977
Pub. L. 95–132, Oct. 13, 1977, 91 Stat. 1157

Civil Rights Commission Authorization Act of 1979
Pub. L. 96–81, Oct. 6, 1979, 93 Stat. 642

Civil Rights Commission Authorization Act of 1980
Pub. L. 96–447, Oct. 13, 1980, 94 Stat. 1894

Civil Rights Commission Reauthorization Act of 1989
Pub. L. 101–180, Nov. 28, 1989, 103 Stat. 1325
Short title, see 42 U.S.C. 1975 note

Civil Rights of Institutionalized Persons Act
Pub. L. 96–247, May 23, 1980, 94 Stat. 349 (42 U.S.C. 1997 et seq.)
Short title, see 42 U.S.C. 1997 note

Civil Rights Remedies for Gender-Motivated Violence Act
Pub. L. 103–322, title IV, subtitle C (§40301 et seq.), Sept. 13, 1994, 108 Stat. 1941 (42 U.S.C. 13981)
Short title, see 42 U.S.C. 13701 note

Civil Rights Restoration Act of 1987
Pub. L. 100–259, Mar. 22, 1988, 102 Stat. 28
Short title, see 20 U.S.C. 1681 note

Civil Service Act
Jan. 16, 1883, ch. 27, 22 Stat. 403

Civil Service Due Process Amendments
Pub. L. 101–376, Aug. 17, 1990, 104 Stat. 461
Short title, see 5 U.S.C. 7501 note

Civil Service Examination in State of Domicile Act
July 2, 1909, ch. 2, §7, 36 Stat. 3

Civil Service Miscellaneous Amendments Act of 1983
Pub. L. 98–224, Mar. 2, 1984, 98 Stat. 47
Short title, see 5 U.S.C. 1101 note

Civil Service Reform Act of 1978
Pub. L. 95–454, Oct. 13, 1978, 92 Stat. 1111
Short title, see 5 U.S.C. 1101 note

Civil Service Retirement Act
May 29, 1930, ch. 349, as added July 31, 1956, ch. 804, title IV, §401, 70 Stat. 743

Civil Service Retirement Act Amendments of 1956
July 31, 1956, ch. 804, title IV, §401, 70 Stat. 743

Civil Service Retirement Act Amendments of 1966
Pub. L. 89–504, title V, July 18, 1966, 80 Stat. 300

Civil Service Retirement Amendments of 1969
Pub. L. 91–93, Oct. 20, 1969, 83 Stat. 136
Short title, see 5 U.S.C. 8331 note

Civil Service Retirement Spouse Equity Act of 1984
Pub. L. 98–615, Nov. 8, 1984, 98 Stat. 3195
Short title, see 5 U.S.C. 8331 note

Civil Space Employee Testing Act of 1991
Pub. L. 102–195, §21, Dec. 9, 1991, 105 Stat. 1616 (42 U.S.C. 2473c)
Short title, see 42 U.S.C. 2473c(a)

Civil War Battlefield Commemorative Coin Act of 1992
Pub. L. 102–379, Oct. 5, 1992, 106 Stat. 1362 (31 U.S.C. 5112 note)

Civil War Claims Act
July 4, 1864, ch. 240, 13 Stat. 381

Civil War Sites Study Act of 1990
Pub. L. 101–628, title XII, Nov. 28, 1990, 104 Stat. 4503

Civil Works Administration Act
June 16, 1933, ch. 90, title II, 48 Stat. 200

Civil Works-Emergency Relief Act
Feb. 15, 1934, ch. 13, 48 Stat. 351

Civilian Conservation Corps Act
June 28, 1937, ch. 383, 50 Stat. 319 (16 U.S.C. 584 et seq.)

Civilian Conservation Corps Reforestation Relief Act
Mar. 31, 1933, ch. 17, 48 Stat. 22

Civilian Nautical School Act
June 12, 1940, ch. 337, 54 Stat. 346

Civilian Pilot Training Act of 1939
June 27, 1939, ch. 244, 53 Stat. 855

Claiborne Pell Institute for International Relations and Public Policy Act
Pub. L. 104–319, title III, Oct. 19, 1996, 110 Stat. 3867

Clark Amendment (Angolan Assistance Limitation)
Pub. L. 94–329, title IV, §404, June 30, 1976, 90 Stat. 757

Clarke-McNary Act (Reforestation)
June 7, 1924, ch. 348, 43 Stat. 653

Clarks Fork Wild and Scenic River Designation Act of 1990
Pub. L. 101–628, title XIII, Nov. 28, 1990, 104 Stat. 4509
Short title, see 16 U.S.C. 1271 note

Clason Naturalization Act
July 2, 1940, ch. 512, 54 Stat. 715

Classification Act Amendments of 1962
Pub. L. 87–793, part II, title II, Oct. 11, 1962, 76 Stat. 843

Classification Act of 1923
Mar. 4, 1923, ch. 265, 42 Stat. 1488

Classification Act of 1949
Oct. 28, 1949, ch. 782, 63 Stat. 954

Classified Information Procedures Act
Pub. L. 96–456, Oct. 15, 1980, 94 Stat. 2025 (18 App. U.S.C.)
Short title, see 18 App. U.S.C. 16

Claude Pepper Young Americans Act of 1990
Pub. L. 101–501, title IX, Nov. 3, 1990, 104 Stat. 1262 (42 U.S.C. 12301 et seq.)
Short title, see 42 U.S.C. 12301 note

Clayton Act (Antitrust)
Oct. 15, 1914, ch. 323, 38 Stat. 730 (15 U.S.C. 12 et seq.)
Short title, see 15 U.S.C. 12(b)

Clean Air Act
July 14, 1955, ch. 360, 69 Stat. 322 (42 U.S.C. 7401 et seq.)
Short title, see 42 U.S.C. 7401 note

Clean Air Act Amendments of 1966
Pub. L. 89–675, Oct. 15, 1966, 80 Stat. 954
Short title, see 42 U.S.C. 7401 note

Clean Air Act Amendments of 1977
Pub. L. 95–95, Aug. 7, 1977, 91 Stat. 685
Short title, see 42 U.S.C. 7401 note

Clean Air Act Amendments of 1990
Pub. L. 101–549, Nov. 15, 1990, 104 Stat. 2399
Short title, see 42 U.S.C. 7401 note

Clean Air Amendments of 1970
Pub. L. 91–604, Dec. 31, 1970, 84 Stat. 1676
Short title, see 42 U.S.C. 7401 note

Clean Vessel Act of 1992
Pub. L. 102–587, title V, subtitle F (§5601 et seq.), Nov. 4, 1992, 106 Stat. 5086 (33 U.S.C. 1322 note)

Clean Water Act
See Federal Water Pollution Control Act

Clean Water Act of 1977
Pub. L. 95–217, Dec. 27, 1977, 91 Stat. 1566
Short title, see 33 U.S.C. 1251 note

Clean Water Restoration Act of 1966
Pub. L. 89–753, Nov. 3, 1966, 80 Stat. 1246

Clear Creek County, Colorado, Public Lands Transfer Act of 1993
Pub. L. 103–253, May 19, 1994, 108 Stat. 674

Clear Creek Distribution System Conveyance Act
Pub. L. 106–566, title IV, Dec. 23, 2000, 114 Stat. 2821

Clinger-Cohen Act of 1996
Pub. L. 104–106, divs. D, E, Feb. 10, 1996, 110 Stat. 642, 679 (40 U.S.C. 1401 et seq.)
Short title, see 40 U.S.C. 1401 note; 41 U.S.C. 251 note

Clinical Laboratories Improvement Act of 1967
Pub. L. 90–174, §5, Dec. 5, 1967, 81 Stat. 536 (42 U.S.C. 263a)
Short title, see 42 U.S.C. 201 note

Clinical Laboratory Improvement Amendments of 1988
Pub. L. 100–578, Oct. 31, 1988, 102 Stat. 2903
Short title, see 42 U.S.C. 201 note

Clinical Research Enhancement Act of 2000
Pub. L. 106–505, title II, Nov. 13, 2000, 114 Stat. 2325
Short title, see 42 U.S.C. 201 note

Cooperative Farm Forestry Act
May 18, 1937, ch. 226, 50 Stat. 188 (16 U.S.C. 568b)

Co-operative Marketing Act
July 2, 1926, ch. 725, 44 Stat. 802 (7 U.S.C. 451 et seq.)

Co-operative Marketing Associations Act
Feb. 18, 1922, ch. 57, 42 Stat. 388 (7 U.S.C. 291, 292)

Coal Conservation Act
See Bituminous Coal Conservation Act of 1935

Coal Industry Retiree Health Benefit Act of 1992
Pub. L. 102–486, title XIX, subtitle C (§19141 et seq.), Oct. 24, 1992, 106 Stat. 3036 (26 U.S.C. 9701 et seq.)
Short title, see 26 U.S.C. 1 note

Coal Lands Act
Mar. 3, 1873, ch. 279, 17 Stat. 607

Coal Market Competition Act of 2000
Pub. L. 106–463, Nov. 7, 2000, 114 Stat. 2010
Short title, see 30 U.S.C. 181 note

Coast and Geodetic Survey Commissioned Officers' Act of 1948
June 3, 1948, ch. 390, 62 Stat. 297 (33 U.S.C. 853a et seq.)
Short title, see 33 U.S.C. 853a note

Coast and Geodetic Survey Commissioned Officers' Act of 1961
Pub. L. 87–233, §1, Sept. 14, 1961, 75 Stat. 506

Coast Guard Act
Jan. 28, 1915, ch. 20, 38 Stat. 800

Coast Guard Appropriation Act, 1947
July 12, 1946, ch. 569, 60 Stat. 529

Coast Guard Authorization Act of 1982
Pub. L. 97–322, title I, Oct. 15, 1982, 96 Stat. 1581

Coast Guard Authorization Act of 1984
Pub. L. 98–557, Oct. 30, 1984, 98 Stat. 2860

Coast Guard Authorization Act of 1986
Pub. L. 99–640, Nov. 10, 1986, 100 Stat. 3545

Coast Guard Authorization Act of 1988
Pub. L. 100–448, Sept. 28, 1988, 102 Stat. 1836

Coast Guard Authorization Act of 1989
Pub. L. 101–225, Dec. 12, 1989, 103 Stat. 1908

Coast Guard Authorization Act of 1991
Pub. L. 102–241, Dec. 19, 1991, 105 Stat. 2208

Coast Guard Authorization Act of 1992
Pub. L. 102–587, title V, Nov. 4, 1992, 106 Stat. 5068

Coast Guard Authorization Act of 1993
Pub. L. 103–206, Dec. 20, 1993, 107 Stat. 2419

Coast Guard Authorization Act of 1996
Pub. L. 104–324, Oct. 19, 1996, 110 Stat. 3901

Coast Guard Authorization Act of 1998
Pub. L. 105–383, Nov. 13, 1998, 112 Stat. 3411

Coast Guard Auxiliary and Reserve Act of 1941
Feb. 19, 1941, ch. 8, 55 Stat. 9

Coast Guard Cutter Act
July 15, 1941, ch. 302, 55 Stat. 597

Coast Guard Defense Act
June 2, 1939, ch. 167, 53 Stat. 797

Coast Guard Omnibus Act of 1990
Pub. L. 101–595, title III, Nov. 16, 1990, 104 Stat. 2983

Coast Guard Personnel Act
May 24, 1939, ch. 148, 53 Stat. 756

Coast Guard Regulatory Reform Act of 1996
Pub. L. 104–324, title VI, Oct. 19, 1996, 110 Stat. 3927
Short title, see 46 U.S.C. 2101 note

Coast Guard Reserve Act of 1939
June 23, 1939, ch. 243, 53 Stat. 854

Coast Guard Retirement Act
May 24, 1939, ch. 146, 53 Stat. 755

Coast Survey Ship Act
June 2, 1939, ch. 172, 53 Stat. 803

Coastal Barrier Improvement Act of 1990
Pub. L. 101–591, Nov. 16, 1990, 104 Stat. 2931
Short title, see 16 U.S.C. 3501 note

Coastal Barrier Resources Act
Pub. L. 97–348, Oct. 15, 1982, 96 Stat. 1653 (16 U.S.C. 3501 et seq.)
Short title, see 16 U.S.C. 3501 note

Coastal Barrier Resources Reauthorization Act of 2000
Pub. L. 106–514, Nov. 13, 2000, 114 Stat. 2394
Short title, see 16 U.S.C. 3501 note

Coastal Wetlands Planning, Protection and Restoration Act
Pub. L. 101–646, title III, Nov. 29, 1990, 104 Stat. 4778 (16 U.S.C. 3951 et seq.)
Short title, see 16 U.S.C. 3951 note

Coastal Zone Act Reauthorization Amendments of 1990
Pub. L. 101–508, title VI, subtitle C (§6201 et seq.), Nov. 5, 1990, 104 Stat. 1388–299
Short title, see 16 U.S.C. 1451 note

Coastal Zone Management Act Amendments of 1976
Pub. L. 94–370, July 26, 1976, 90 Stat. 1013
Short title, see 16 U.S.C. 1451 note

Coastal Zone Management Act of 1972
Pub. L. 89–454, title III, as added Pub. L. 92–583, Oct. 27, 1972, 86 Stat. 1280 (16 U.S.C. 1451 et seq.)
Short title, see 16 U.S.C. 1451 note

Coastal Zone Management Improvement Act of 1980
Pub. L. 96–464, Oct. 17, 1980, 94 Stat. 2060
Short title, see 16 U.S.C. 1451 note

Coastal Zone Management Reauthorization Act of 1985
Pub. L. 99–272, title VI, subtitle D (§6041 et seq.), Apr. 7, 1986, 100 Stat. 124
Short title, see 16 U.S.C. 1451 note

Coastal Zone Protection Act of 1996
Pub. L. 104–150, June 3, 1996, 110 Stat. 1380
Short title, see 16 U.S.C. 1451 note

Coastwise Load Line Act, 1935
Aug. 27, 1935, ch. 747, 49 Stat. 888

Coats Human Services Reauthorization Act of 1998
Also known as the Community Opportunities, Accountability, and Training and Educational Services Act of 1998
Pub. L. 105–285, Oct. 27, 1998, 112 Stat. 2702
Short title, see 42 U.S.C. 9801 note

COBRA
See Consolidated Omnibus Budget Reconciliation Act of 1985

Cochran-Hull Act
July 8, 1932, ch. 464, 47 Stat. 649

Cochran-Patterson Act
See Kidnapping Act

Coin Purchase Act
Mar. 17, 1862, ch. 45, 12 Stat. 370

Coinage Act (Silver Dollar)
Feb. 28, 1878, ch. 20, 20 Stat. 25

Coinage Act of 1873
Feb. 12, 1873, ch. 131, 17 Stat. 424

Coinage Act of 1890 (Silver Dollar)
Nov. 1, 1893, ch. 8, 28 Stat. 4

Coinage Act of 1965
Pub. L. 89–81, July 23, 1965, 79 Stat. 254

Collateral Security Act
Mar. 9, 1933, ch. 1, title IV, 48 Stat. 6

Collection of Duties Act (Civil War)
July 13, 1861, ch. 3, 12 Stat. 255

College Housing Amendments of 1955
Aug. 11, 1955, ch. 783, title III, 69 Stat. 644
Short title, see 12 U.S.C. 1701 note

College Scholarship Fraud Prevention Act of 2000
Pub. L. 106–420, Nov. 1, 2000, 114 Stat. 1867
Short title, see 20 U.S.C. 1001 note

Collegiate Initiative To Reduce Binge Drinking and Illegal Alcohol Consumption
Pub. L. 89–329, title I, §119, as added Pub. L. 105–244, title I, §101(a), Oct. 7, 1998, 112 Stat. 1596 (20 U.S.C. 1011h)
Short title, see 20 U.S.C. 1011h(a)

Color Additive Amendments of 1960
Pub. L. 86–618, July 12, 1960, 74 Stat. 397
Short title, see 21 U.S.C. 301 note

Color of Title Act
Dec. 22, 1928, ch. 47, 45 Stat. 1069 (43 U.S.C. 1068, 1068a)

Colorado Canyons National Conservation Area and Black Ridge Canyons Wilderness Act of 2000
Pub. L. 106–353, Oct. 24, 2000, 114 Stat. 1374 (16 U.S.C. 460mmm et seq.)
Short title, see 16 U.S.C. 460mmm note

Colorado River Basin Project Act
Pub. L. 90–537, Sept. 30, 1968, 82 Stat. 885 (43 U.S.C. 1501 et seq.)
Short title, see 43 U.S.C. 1501 note

Colorado River Basin Salinity Control Act
Pub. L. 93–320, June 24, 1974, 88 Stat. 266 (43 U.S.C. 1571 et seq.)
Short title, see 43 U.S.C. 1571 note

Colorado River Floodway Protection Act
Pub. L. 99–450, Oct. 8, 1986, 100 Stat. 1129 (43 U.S.C. 1600 et seq.)
Short title, see 43 U.S.C. 1600 note

Colorado River Storage Project Act
Apr. 11, 1956, ch. 203, 70 Stat. 105 (43 U.S.C. 620 et seq.)
Short title, see 43 U.S.C. 620 note

Colorado Ute Indian Water Rights Settlement Act of 1988
Pub. L. 100–585, Nov. 3, 1988, 102 Stat. 2973

Colorado Ute Settlement Act Amendments of 2000
Pub. L. 106–554, §1(a)(4) [div. B, title III], Dec. 21, 2000, 114 Stat. 2763, 2763A–258

Colorado Wilderness Act of 1993
Pub. L. 103–77, Aug. 13, 1993, 107 Stat. 756 (16 U.S.C. 539i, 539j)
Short title, see 16 U.S.C. 539i note

Columbia Basin Project Act
May 27, 1937, ch. 269, 50 Stat. 208 (16 U.S.C. 835 et seq.)
Short title, see 16 U.S.C. 835 note

Columbia River Gorge National Scenic Area Act
Pub. L. 99–663, Nov. 17, 1986, 100 Stat. 4274 (16 U.S.C. 544 et seq.)
Short title, see 16 U.S.C. 544 note

Colusa Basin Watershed Integrated Resources Management Act
Pub. L. 106–566, title VI, Dec. 23, 2000, 114 Stat. 2823

Comanche, Kiowa, and Apache Tribes Act
June 6, 1900, ch. 813, §6, 31 Stat. 676

Combat Duty Pay Act of 1952
July 10, 1952, ch. 630, title VII, 66 Stat. 538 (50 App. U.S.C. 2351 et seq.)

Combatting Proliferation of Weapons of Mass Destruction Act of 1996
Pub. L. 104–293, title VII, Oct. 11, 1996, 110 Stat. 3470
Short title, see 50 U.S.C. 2301 note

Combined Hydrocarbon Leasing Act of 1981
Pub. L. 97–78, Nov. 16, 1981, 95 Stat. 1070
Short title, see 30 U.S.C. 181 note

Combined Old-Age, Survivors, and Disability Insurance-Income Tax Reporting Amendments of 1975
Pub. L. 94–202, §8, Jan. 2, 1976, 89 Stat. 1137
Short title, see 42 U.S.C. 1305 note

Command of Army Clause
Mar. 2, 1867, ch. 170, §2, 14 Stat. 486

Commemorative Works Act
Pub. L. 99–652, Nov. 14, 1986, 100 Stat. 3650 (40 U.S.C. 1001 et seq.)
Short title, see 40 U.S.C. 1001 note

Commerce and Labor Act
See Department of Commerce and Labor Act

Commerce Court Act
June 18, 1910, ch. 309, 36 Stat. 539

Commerce Under-Secretary Act
June 5, 1939, ch. 180, 53 Stat. 808 (15 U.S.C. 1502, 1503)

Commercial Air Pilots Act
Apr. 29, 1942, ch. 266, 56 Stat. 265

Commercial Fisheries Research and Development Act of 1964
Pub. L. 88–309, May 20, 1964, 78 Stat. 197 (16 U.S.C. 779 et seq.)

Commercial Fishing Industry Vessel Act
Pub. L. 98–364, title IV, July 17, 1984, 98 Stat. 445
Short title, see 46 U.S.C. 2101 note

Commercial Fishing Industry Vessel Anti-Reflagging Act of 1987
Pub. L. 100–239, Jan. 11, 1988, 101 Stat. 1778
Short title, see 46 U.S.C. 2101 note

Commercial Fishing Industry Vessel Safety Act of 1988
Pub. L. 100–424, Sept. 9, 1988, 102 Stat. 1585
Short title, see 46 U.S.C. 2101 note

Commercial Motor Vehicle Safety Act of 1986
Pub. L. 99–570, title XII, Oct. 27, 1986, 100 Stat. 3207–170

Commercial Print Copyright Act
July 31, 1939, ch. 396, 53 Stat. 1142

Commercial Space Act of 1998
Pub. L. 105–303, Oct. 28, 1998, 112 Stat. 2843 (42 U.S.C. 14701 et seq.)
Short title, see 42 U.S.C. 14701 note

Commercial Space Launch Act
Pub. L. 98–575, Oct. 30, 1984, 98 Stat. 3055

Commercial Space Launch Act Amendments of 1988
Pub. L. 100–657, Nov. 15, 1988, 102 Stat. 3900

Commercial Space Transportation Competitiveness Act of 2000
Pub. L. 106–405, Nov. 1, 2000, 114 Stat. 1751
Short title, see 49 U.S.C. 70101 note

Commission on the Advancement of Women and Minorities in Science, Engineering, and Technology Development Act
Pub. L. 105–255, Oct. 14, 1998, 112 Stat. 1889 (42 U.S.C. 1885a note)

Commission on Wartime Relocation and Internment of Civilians Act
Pub. L. 96–317, July 31, 1980, 94 Stat. 964 (50 App. U.S.C. 1981 note)

Commodity Clause of Railroad Rate Act
June 29, 1906, ch. 3591, §1, 34 Stat. 584

Commodity Credit Corporation Act
Mar. 8, 1938, ch. 44, 52 Stat. 107 (15 U.S.C. 713a to 713a–5)

Commodity Credit Corporation Charter Act
June 29, 1948, ch. 704, 62 Stat. 1070 (15 U.S.C. 714 et seq.)
Short title, see 15 U.S.C. 714 note

Commodity Distribution Reform Act and WIC Amendments of 1987
Pub. L. 100–237, Jan. 8, 1988, 101 Stat. 1733 (7 U.S.C. 612c note)

Commodity Exchange Act
Sept. 21, 1922, ch. 369, 42 Stat. 998 (7 U.S.C. 1 et seq.)
Short title, see 7 U.S.C. 1

Commodity Futures Modernization Act of 2000
Pub. L. 106–554, §1(a)(5) [H.R. 5660], Dec. 21, 2000, 114 Stat. 2763, 2763A–365
Short title, see 7 U.S.C. 1 note

Commodity Futures Trading Commission Act of 1974
Pub. L. 93–463, Oct. 23, 1974, 88 Stat. 1389
Short title, see 7 U.S.C. 1 note

Commodity Promotion, Research, and Information Act of 1996
Pub. L. 104–127, title V, subtitle B (§511 et seq.), Apr. 4, 1996, 110 Stat. 1032 (7 U.S.C. 7411 et seq.)
Short title, see 7 U.S.C. 7401 note

Commodore Bill
Apr. 9, 1943, ch. 38, 57 Stat. 59

Communicable Disease Control Amendments Act of 1972
Pub. L. 92–449, Sept. 30, 1972, 86 Stat. 748
Short title, see 42 U.S.C. 201 note

Communicable Disease Control Amendments of 1970
Pub. L. 91–464, Oct. 16, 1970, 84 Stat. 988
Short title, see 42 U.S.C. 201 note

Communications Act Amendments of 1978
Pub. L. 95–234, Feb. 21, 1978, 92 Stat. 33
Short title, see 47 U.S.C. 609 note

Communications Act Amendments, 1952
July 16, 1952, ch. 879, 66 Stat. 711

Communications Act Amendments, 1960
Pub. L. 86–752, Sept. 13, 1960, 74 Stat. 889
Short title, see 47 U.S.C. 609 note

Communications Act of 1934
June 19, 1934, ch. 652, 48 Stat. 1064 (47 U.S.C. 151 et seq.)
Short title, see 47 U.S.C. 609

Communications Amendments Act of 1982
Pub. L. 97–259, title I, Sept. 13, 1982, 96 Stat. 1087
Short title, see 47 U.S.C. 609 note

Communications Assistance for Law Enforcement Act
Pub. L. 103–414, title I, Oct. 25, 1994, 108 Stat. 4279 (47 U.S.C. 1001 et seq.)
Short title, see 47 U.S.C. 1001 note

Communications Decency Act of 1996
Pub. L. 104–104, title V, Feb. 8, 1996, 110 Stat. 133
Short title, see 47 U.S.C. 609 note

Communications Satellite Act of 1962
Pub. L. 87–624, Aug. 31, 1962, 76 Stat. 419 (47 U.S.C. 701 et seq.)
Short title, see 47 U.S.C. 701 note

Communist Control Act of 1954
Aug. 24, 1954, ch. 886, 68 Stat. 775 (50 U.S.C. 841 et seq.)
Short title, see 50 U.S.C. 841 note

Community and Migrant Health Centers Amendments of 1988
Pub. L. 100–386, Aug. 10, 1988, 102 Stat. 919
Short title, see 42 U.S.C. 201 note

Community Broadcasters Protection Act of 1999
Pub. L. 106–113, div. B, §1000(a)(9) [title V, §5008], Nov. 29, 1999, 113 Stat. 1536, 1501A–594
Short title, see 47 U.S.C. 609 note

Community Development Banking and Financial Institutions Act of 1994
Pub. L. 103–325, title I, subtitle A (§101 et seq.), Sept. 23, 1994, 108 Stat. 2163 (12 U.S.C. 4701 et seq.)
Short title, see 12 U.S.C. 4701 note

Community Development Credit Union Revolving Loan Fund Transfer Act
Pub. L. 99–609, Nov. 6, 1986, 100 Stat. 3475 (42 U.S.C. 9822 note)

Community Economic Development Act of 1981
Pub. L. 97–35, title VI, subtitle A, ch. 8, subch. A (§611 et seq.), Aug. 13, 1981, 95 Stat. 489 (42 U.S.C. 9801 et seq.)
Short title, see 42 U.S.C. 9801 note

Community Education Employment Center Act of 1990
Pub. L. 88–210, title III, part G (§361 et seq.), as added Pub. L. 101–392, title III, §310, Sept. 25, 1990, 104 Stat. 794 (20 U.S.C. 2396 et seq.)
Short title, see 20 U.S.C. 2396 note

Community Emergency Drought Relief Act of 1977
Pub. L. 95–31, May 23, 1977, 91 Stat. 169 (42 U.S.C. 5184 note)

Community Environmental Response Facilitation Act
Pub. L. 102–426, Oct. 19, 1992, 106 Stat. 2174
Short title, see 42 U.S.C. 9601 note

Community Forest Restoration Act
Pub. L. 106–393, title VI, Oct. 30, 2000, 114 Stat. 1625

Community Health Services and Facilities Act of 1961
Pub. L. 87–395, Oct. 5, 1961, 75 Stat. 824
Short title, see 42 U.S.C. 201 note

Community Improvement Volunteer Act of 1994
Pub. L. 103–355, title VII, subtitle C (§7301 et seq.), Oct. 13, 1994, 108 Stat. 3382 (40 U.S.C. 276d et seq.)
Short title, see 40 U.S.C. 276d note

Community Investment Corporation Demonstration Act
Pub. L. 102–550, title VIII, §853, Oct. 28, 1992, 106 Stat. 3859 (42 U.S.C. 5305 note)

Community Mental Health Centers Act
Pub. L. 88–164, title II, Oct. 31, 1963, 77 Stat. 290 (42 U.S.C. 2689 et seq.)
Short title, see 42 U.S.C. 2689 note

Community Mental Health Centers Amendments of 1970
Pub. L. 91–211, Mar. 13, 1970, 84 Stat. 54

Community Mental Health Centers Amendments of 1975
Pub. L. 94–63, title III, July 29, 1975, 89 Stat. 308

Community Mental Health Centers Extension Act of 1978
Pub. L. 95–622, title I, Nov. 9, 1978, 92 Stat. 3412

Community Opportunities, Accountability, and Training and Educational Services Act of 1998
Also known as the Coats Human Services Reauthorization Act of 1998
Pub. L. 105–285, Oct. 27, 1998, 112 Stat. 2702
Short title, see 42 U.S.C. 9801 note

Community Outreach Partnership Act of 1992
Pub. L. 102–550, title VIII, §851, Oct. 28, 1992, 106 Stat. 3855 (42 U.S.C. 5307 note)

Community Reinvestment Act of 1977
Pub. L. 95–128, title VIII, Oct. 12, 1977, 91 Stat. 1147 (12 U.S.C. 2901 et seq.)
Short title, see 12 U.S.C. 2901 note

Community Renewal Tax Relief Act of 2000
Pub. L. 106–554, §1(a)(7) [H.R. 5662], Dec. 21, 2000, 114 Stat. 2763, 2763A–587
Short title, see 26 U.S.C. 1 note

Community Scholarship Mobilization Act
Pub. L. 105–244, title VIII, part C (§811 et seq.), Oct. 7, 1998, 112 Stat. 1810 (20 U.S.C. 1070 note)

Community School Partnership Act
Pub. L. 103–382, title V, part B (§521 et seq.), Oct. 20, 1994, 108 Stat. 4045 (20 U.S.C. 1070 note)

Community Schools Act
Pub. L. 93–380, title IV, §405, Aug. 21, 1974, 88 Stat. 549 (20 U.S.C. 1864)

Community Schools and Comprehensive Community Education Act of 1978
Pub. L. 89–10, title VIII, as added Pub. L. 95–561, title VIII, §801(3), Nov. 1, 1978, 92 Stat. 2284 (20 U.S.C. 3281 et seq.)

Community Schools Youth Services and Supervision Grant Program Act of 1994
Pub. L. 103–322, title III, §30401, Sept. 13, 1994, 108 Stat. 1846 (42 U.S.C. 13791)
Short title, see 42 U.S.C. 13791(a)

Community Services Act of 1974
Pub. L. 88–452, titles I–IX, as added Pub. L. 93–644, §§3–12, Jan. 4, 1975, 88 Stat. 2292–2327 (42 U.S.C. 2701 et seq.)
Short title, see 42 U.S.C. 2701 note

Community Services Act Technical Amendments of 1976
Pub. L. 94–341, July 6, 1976, 90 Stat. 803
Short title, see 42 U.S.C. 2701 note

Community Services Block Grant Act
Pub. L. 97–35, title VI, subtitle B (§671 et seq.), as added Pub. L. 105–285, title II, §201, Oct. 27, 1998, 112 Stat. 2728 (42 U.S.C. 9901 et seq.)
Short title, see 42 U.S.C. 9901 note

Community Services Block Grant Amendments of 1994
Pub. L. 103–252, title II, May 18, 1994, 108 Stat. 651
Short title, see 42 U.S.C. 9901 note

Community Health Services Extension Amendments of 1965
Pub. L. 89–109, Aug. 5, 1965, 79 Stat. 435

Commutation Clause of Homestead Act
May 20, 1862, ch. 75, §8, 12 Stat. 393

Compact of Free Association Act of 1985
Pub. L. 99–239, Jan. 14, 1986, 99 Stat. 1770 (48 U.S.C. 1901 et seq., 2001 et seq.)
Short title, see 48 U.S.C. 1901 note

Compensated Emancipation Resolution
Apr. 10, 1862, No. 26, 12 Stat. 617

Competition in Contracting Act of 1984
Pub. L. 98–369, div. B, title VII, July 18, 1984, 98 Stat. 1175
Short title, see 41 U.S.C. 251 note

Competitive Equality Amendments of 1987
Pub. L. 100–86, title I, Aug. 10, 1987, 101 Stat. 554
Short title, see 12 U.S.C. 226 note

Competitive Equality Banking Act of 1987
Pub. L. 100–86, Aug. 10, 1987, 101 Stat. 552
Short title, see 12 U.S.C. 226 note

Competitive, Special, and Facilities Research Grant Act
Pub. L. 89–106, §2, Aug. 4, 1965, 79 Stat. 431 (7 U.S.C. 450i)
Short title, see 7 U.S.C. 450i(a)(2)

Competitiveness Policy Council Act
Pub. L. 100–418, title V, subtitle C (§5201 et seq.), Aug. 23, 1988, 102 Stat. 1454 (15 U.S.C. 4801 et seq.)
Short title, see 15 U.S.C. 4801 note

Comprehensive Alcohol Abuse and Alcoholism Prevention, Treatment, and Rehabilitation Act of 1970
Pub. L. 91–616, Dec. 31, 1970, 84 Stat. 1848 (42 U.S.C. 4501 et seq.)
Short title, see 42 U.S.C. 4541 note

Comprehensive Alcohol Abuse and Alcoholism Prevention, Treatment, and Rehabilitation Act Amendments of 1974
Pub. L. 93–282, title I, May 14, 1974, 88 Stat. 125
Short title, see 42 U.S.C. 4541 note

Comprehensive Alcohol Abuse and Alcoholism Prevention, Treatment, and Rehabilitation Act Amendments of 1976
Pub. L. 94–371, July 26, 1976, 90 Stat. 1035
Short title, see 42 U.S.C. 4541 note

Comprehensive Alcohol Abuse and Alcoholism Prevention, Treatment, and Rehabilitation Act Amendments of 1979
Pub. L. 96–180, Jan. 2, 1980, 93 Stat. 1301
Short title, see 42 U.S.C. 4541 note

Comprehensive Alcohol Abuse, Drug Abuse, and Mental Health Amendments Act of 1988
Pub. L. 100–690, title II, subtitle A (§2011 et seq.), Nov. 18, 1988, 102 Stat. 4193
Short title, see 42 U.S.C. 201 note

Comprehensive Anti-Apartheid Act of 1986
Pub. L. 99–440, Oct. 2, 1986, 100 Stat. 1086 (22 U.S.C. 5001 et seq.)
Short title, see 22 U.S.C. 5001 note

Comprehensive Child Development Act
Pub. L. 97–35, title VI, subtitle A, ch. 8, subch. F, formerly E (§670M et seq.), as added Pub. L. 100–297, title II, §2503, Apr. 28, 1988, 102 Stat. 325 (42 U.S.C. 9881 et seq.)
Short title, see 42 U.S.C. 9801 note

Comprehensive Child Development Centers Act of 1988
Pub. L. 100–297, title II, part E (§2501 et seq.), Apr. 28, 1988, 102 Stat. 325
Short title, see 42 U.S.C. 9801 note

Comprehensive Crime Control Act of 1984
Pub. L. 98–473, title II, Oct. 12, 1984, 98 Stat. 1976
Short title, see 18 U.S.C. 1 note

Comprehensive Drug Abuse Prevention and Control Act of 1970
Pub. L. 91–513, Oct. 27, 1970, 84 Stat. 1236 (21 U.S.C. 801 et seq.)
Short title, see 21 U.S.C. 801 note

Comprehensive Employment and Training Act
Pub. L. 93–203, as added Pub. L. 95–524, §2, Oct. 27, 1978, 92 Stat. 1909 (29 U.S.C. 801 et seq.)

Comprehensive Employment and Training Act Amendments of 1977
Pub. L. 95–44, June 15, 1977, 91 Stat. 220

Comprehensive Employment and Training Act Amendments of 1978
Pub. L. 95–524, Oct. 27, 1978, 92 Stat. 1909

Comprehensive Employment and Training Act of 1973
Renamed Comprehensive Employment and Training Act

Comprehensive Environmental Response, Compensation, and Liability Act of 1980
Pub. L. 96–510, Dec. 11, 1980, 94 Stat. 2767 (42 U.S.C. 9601 et seq.)
Short title, see 42 U.S.C. 9601 note

Comprehensive Forfeiture Act of 1984
Pub. L. 98–473, title II, ch. III (§301 et seq.), Oct. 12, 1984, 98 Stat. 2040
Short title, see 18 U.S.C. 1961 note

Comprehensive Health Manpower Training Act of 1971
Pub. L. 92–157, title I, Nov. 18, 1971, 85 Stat. 431
Short title, see 42 U.S.C. 201 note

Comprehensive Health Planning and Public Health Services Amendments of 1966
Pub. L. 89–749, Nov. 3, 1966, 80 Stat. 1180
Short title, see 42 U.S.C. 201 note

Comprehensive Methamphetamine Control Act of 1996
Pub. L. 104–237, Oct. 3, 1996, 110 Stat. 3099
Short title, see 21 U.S.C. 801 note

Comprehensive Older Americans Act Amendments of 1978
Pub. L. 95–478, Oct. 18, 1978, 92 Stat. 1513
Short title, see 42 U.S.C. 3001 note

Comprehensive Smokeless Tobacco Health Education Act of 1986
Pub. L. 99–252, Feb. 27, 1986, 100 Stat. 30 (15 U.S.C. 4401 et seq.)
Short title, see 15 U.S.C. 4401 note

Comprehensive Smoking Education Act
Pub. L. 98–474, Oct. 12, 1984, 98 Stat. 2200
Short title, see 15 U.S.C. 1331 note

Comprehensive Thrift and Bank Fraud Prosecution and Taxpayer Recovery Act of 1990
Pub. L. 101–647, title XXV, Nov. 29, 1990, 104 Stat. 4859
Short title, see 18 U.S.C. 1001 note

Compromise of 1820 (Missouri)
Mar. 6, 1820, ch. 22, 3 Stat. 545

Compromise of 1850 (California)
Sept. 9, 1850, ch. 50, 9 Stat. 452

Compromise of 1850 (Fugitives from Justice)
Sept. 18, 1850, ch. 55, 9 Stat. 462

Compromise of 1850 (Slave Trade in District of Columbia)
Sept. 20, 1850, ch. 63, 9 Stat. 467

Compromise of 1850 (Texas and New Mexico)
Sept. 9, 1850, ch. 49, 9 Stat. 446

Compromise of 1850 (Utah)
Sept. 9, 1850, ch. 51, 9 Stat. 453

Comptroller General Annuity Adjustment Act of 1978
Pub. L. 95–512, Oct. 25, 1978, 92 Stat. 1799

Compulsory Testimony Act of 1893
Feb. 11, 1893, ch. 83, 27 Stat. 443

Computer Abuse Amendments Act of 1994
Pub. L. 103–322, title XXIX, §290001, Sept. 13, 1994, 108 Stat. 2097
Short title, see 18 U.S.C. 1001 note

Computer Crime Enforcement Act
Pub. L. 106–572, Dec. 28, 2000, 114 Stat. 3058 (42 U.S.C. 3713)
Short title, see 42 U.S.C. 3711 note

Computer Fraud and Abuse Act of 1986
Pub. L. 99–474, Oct. 16, 1986, 100 Stat. 1213
Short title, see 18 U.S.C. 1001 note

Computer Maintenance Competition Assurance Act
Pub. L. 105–304, title III, Oct. 28, 1998, 112 Stat. 2886
Short title, see 17 U.S.C. 101 note

Computer Matching and Privacy Protection Act Amendments of 1989
Pub. L. 101–56, July 19, 1989, 103 Stat. 149
Short title, see 5 U.S.C. 552a note

Computer Matching and Privacy Protection Act of 1988
Pub. L. 100–503, Oct. 18, 1988, 102 Stat. 2507
Short title, see 5 U.S.C. 552a note

Computer Matching and Privacy Protection Amendments of 1990
Pub. L. 101–508, title VII, §7201, Nov. 5, 1990, 104 Stat. 1388–334
Short title, see 5 U.S.C. 552a note

Computer Security Act of 1987
Pub. L. 100–235, Jan. 8, 1988, 101 Stat. 1724

Computer Software Rental Amendments Act of 1990
Pub. L. 101–650, title VIII, Dec. 1, 1990, 104 Stat. 5134
Short title, see 17 U.S.C. 101 note

Comstock Act
Mar. 3, 1873, ch. 258, 17 Stat. 598

Concentration Act
Feb. 17, 1922, ch. 55, 42 Stat. 375

Condemnation Act (Lands for Public Uses)
Aug. 1, 1888, ch. 728, 25 Stat. 357 (40 U.S.C. 257)

Condemned Cannon Act
May 22, 1896, ch. 230, 29 Stat. 133

Condominium and Cooperative Abuse Relief Act of 1980
Pub. L. 96–399, title VI, Oct. 8, 1980, 94 Stat. 1672 (15 U.S.C. 3601 et seq.)
Short title, see 15 U.S.C. 3601 note

Confederated Tribes of the Colville Reservation Grand Coulee Dam Settlement Act
Pub. L. 103–436, Nov. 2, 1994, 108 Stat. 4577

Confiscation Act of 1861
Aug. 6, 1861, ch. 60, 12 Stat. 319

Confiscation Act of 1862
July 17, 1862, ch. 195, 12 Stat. 589

Conformity Act
See Practice Conformity Act

Congaree Swamp National Monument Expansion and Wilderness Act
Pub. L. 100–524, Oct. 24, 1988, 102 Stat. 2606

Congregate Housing Services Act of 1978
Pub. L. 95–557, title IV, Oct. 31, 1978, 92 Stat. 2104 (42 U.S.C. 8001 et seq.)
Short title, see 42 U.S.C. 8001 note

Congressional Accountability Act of 1995
Pub. L. 104–1, Jan. 23, 1995, 109 Stat. 3 (2 U.S.C. 1301 et seq.)
Short title, see 2 U.S.C. 1301 note

Congressional Award Act
Pub. L. 96–114, Nov. 16, 1979, 93 Stat. 851 (2 U.S.C. 801 et seq.)
Short title, see 2 U.S.C. 801 note

Congressional Award Act Amendments of 1988
Pub. L. 100–674, Nov. 17, 1988, 102 Stat. 3996
Short title, see 2 U.S.C. 801 note

Congressional Award Act Amendments of 1992
Pub. L. 102–457, Oct. 23, 1992, 106 Stat. 2265
Short title, see 2 U.S.C. 801 note

Congressional Award Amendments of 1985
Pub. L. 99–161, Nov. 25, 1985, 99 Stat. 934
Short title, see 2 U.S.C. 801 note

Congressional Award Amendments of 1990
Pub. L. 101–525, Nov. 6, 1990, 104 Stat. 2305
Short title, see 2 U.S.C. 801 note

Congressional Budget Act of 1974
Pub. L. 93–344, titles I–IX, July 12, 1974, 88 Stat. 299–330
Short title, see 2 U.S.C. 621 note

Congressional Budget and Impoundment Control Act of 1974
Pub. L. 93–344, July 12, 1974, 88 Stat. 297
Short title, see 2 U.S.C. 621 note

Congressional Merit Scholarships in Mathematics, Science, and Engineering Education
Pub. L. 98–377, title I, part C (§131 et seq.), Aug. 11, 1984, 98 Stat. 1270 (20 U.S.C. 3931 et seq.)

Congressional Operations Appropriation Act, 1978
Pub. L. 95–94, title I, Aug. 5, 1977, 91 Stat. 653

Congressional Operations Appropriation Act, 1979
Pub. L. 95–391, title I, Sept. 30, 1978, 92 Stat. 763

Congressional Operations Appropriation Act, 1980
Pub. L. 96–86, §101(c) [H.R. 4390, title I], Oct. 12, 1979, 93 Stat. 657; Pub. L. 100–202, §106, Dec. 22, 1987, 101 Stat. 1329–433

Congressional Operations Appropriation Act, 1981
Pub. L. 96–536, §101(c) [H.R. 7593, title I], Dec. 16, 1980, 94 Stat. 3167

Congressional Operations Appropriation Act, 1982
Pub. L. 97–51, §101(c) [H.R. 4120, title I], Oct. 1, 1981, 95 Stat. 959

Congressional Operations Appropriation Act, 1983
Pub. L. 97–276, §101(e) [S. 2939, title I], Oct. 2, 1982, 96 Stat. 1189

Congressional Operations Appropriation Act, 1984
Pub. L. 98–51, title I, July 14, 1983, 97 Stat. 263

Congressional Operations Appropriation Act, 1985
Pub. L. 98–367, title I, July 17, 1984, 98 Stat. 472

Congressional Operations Appropriation Act, 1986
Pub. L. 99–151, title I, Nov. 13, 1985, 99 Stat. 792

Congressional Operations Appropriation Act, 1987
Pub. L. 99–500, §101(j) [H.R. 5203, title I], Oct. 18, 1986, 100 Stat. 1783–287, and Pub. L. 99–591, §101(j) [H.R. 5203, title I], Oct. 30, 1986, 100 Stat. 3341–287

Congressional Operations Appropriations Act, 1988
Pub. L. 100–202, §101(i) [title I], Dec. 22, 1987, 101 Stat. 1329–290

Congressional Operations Appropriations Act, 1989
Pub. L. 100–458, title I, Oct. 1, 1988, 102 Stat. 2158

Congressional Operations Appropriations Act, 1990
Pub. L. 101–163, title I, Nov. 21, 1989, 103 Stat. 1041

Congressional Operations Appropriations Act, 1991
Pub. L. 101–520, title I, Nov. 5, 1990, 104 Stat. 2254

Congressional Operations Appropriations Act, 1992
Pub. L. 102–90, title I, Aug. 14, 1991, 105 Stat. 447

Congressional Operations Appropriations Act, 1993
Pub. L. 102–392, title I, Oct. 6, 1992, 106 Stat. 1703

Congressional Operations Appropriations Act, 1994
Pub. L. 103–69, title I, Aug. 11, 1993, 107 Stat. 692

Congressional Operations Appropriations Act, 1995
Pub. L. 103–283, title I, July 22, 1994, 108 Stat. 1423

Congressional Operations Appropriations Act, 1996
Pub. L. 104–53, title I, Nov. 19, 1995, 109 Stat. 514

Congressional Operations Appropriations Act, 1997
Pub. L. 104–197, title I, Sept. 16, 1996, 110 Stat. 2394

Congressional Operations Appropriations Act, 1998
Pub. L. 105–55, title I, Oct. 7, 1997, 111 Stat. 1177

Congressional Operations Appropriations Act, 1999
Pub. L. 105–275, title I, Oct. 21, 1998, 112 Stat. 2430

Congressional Operations Appropriations Act, 2000
Pub. L. 106–57, title I, Sept. 29, 1999, 113 Stat. 408

Congressional Operations Appropriations Act, 2001
Pub. L. 106–554, §1(a)(2) [title I], Dec. 21, 2000, 114 Stat. 2763, 2763A–93

Congressional Recognition for Excellence in Arts Education Act
Pub. L. 96–114, title II, as added Pub. L. 106–533, §1(a), Nov. 22, 2000, 114 Stat. 2545 (2 U.S.C. 811 et seq.)
Short title, see 2 U.S.C. 801 note

Congressional Reports Elimination Act of 1980
Pub. L. 96–470, Oct. 19, 1980, 94 Stat. 2237

Congressional Reports Elimination Act of 1982
Pub. L. 97–375, Dec. 21, 1982, 96 Stat. 1819

Congressional Reports Elimination Act of 1986
Pub. L. 99–386, Aug. 22, 1986, 100 Stat. 821

Connally Hot Oil Act
Also known as the Hot Oil Act
Feb. 22, 1935, ch. 18, 49 Stat. 30 (15 U.S.C. 715 et seq.)
Short title, see 15 U.S.C. 715 note

Connally-Smith Anti-Strike Act
See War Labor Disputes Act

Connecticut Coastal Protection Act of 1990
Pub. L. 101–443, Oct. 19, 1990, 104 Stat. 1028

Conrail Privatization Act
Pub. L. 99–509, title IV, subtitle A (§4001 et seq.), Oct. 21, 1986, 100 Stat. 1892 (45 U.S.C. 1301 et seq.)
Short title, see 45 U.S.C. 1301 note

Conservation Act (Navigable Waters)
See Weeks Law

Conservation of Farmable Wetland Act of 2000
Pub. L. 106–387, §1(a) [title XI], Oct. 28, 2000, 114 Stat. 1549, 1549A–75
Short title, see 16 U.S.C. 3801 note

Conservation Program Improvements Act
Pub. L. 101–624, title XIV, Nov. 28, 1990, 104 Stat. 3568
Short title, see 16 U.S.C. 3801 note

Conservation Service Reform Act of 1986
Pub. L. 99–412, Aug. 28, 1986, 100 Stat. 932
Short title, see 42 U.S.C. 8201 note

Consolidated Appropriations Act, 2001
Pub. L. 106–554, Dec. 21, 2000, 114 Stat. 2763

Consolidated Farm and Rural Development Act
Pub. L. 87–128, title III, Aug. 8, 1961, 75 Stat. 307
Short title, see 7 U.S.C. 1921 note

Consolidated Farmers Home Administration Act of 1961
Renamed the Consolidated Farm and Rural Development Act

Consolidated Federal Funds Report Act of 1982
Pub. L. 97–326, Oct. 15, 1982, 96 Stat. 1607 (31 U.S.C. 6102 note)

Consolidated Federal Funds Report Amendments of 1985
Pub. L. 99–547, Oct. 27, 1986, 100 Stat. 3057
Short title, see 31 U.S.C. 6201 note

Consolidated Omnibus Budget Reconciliation Act of 1985
Pub. L. 99–272, Apr. 7, 1986, 100 Stat. 82

Consolidated Refugee Education Assistance Act
Pub. L. 97–35, title V, subtitle C (§541 et seq.), Aug. 13, 1981, 95 Stat. 458 (8 U.S.C. 1522 note)

Consolidation of Government Bureaus Act
July 3, 1930, ch. 863, 46 Stat. 1016

Conspiracies Act (Civil War)
July 31, 1861, ch. 33, 12 Stat. 284

Conspiracy Act (Offenses Against U.S.)
Mar. 4, 1909, ch. 321, §37, 35 Stat. 1096

Constitution Heritage Act of 1988
Pub. L. 100–433, Sept. 16, 1988, 102 Stat. 1640 (16 U.S.C. 407aa et seq.)
Short title, see 16 U.S.C. 407aa note

Constitutional Amendment Resolution
Mar. 2, 1861, No. 13, 12 Stat. 251

Construction Industry Payment Protection Act of 1999
Pub. L. 106–49, Aug. 17, 1999, 113 Stat. 231
Short title, see 40 U.S.C. 270a note

Consumer Checking Account Equity Act of 1980
Pub. L. 96–221, title III, Mar. 31, 1980, 94 Stat. 145
Short title, see 12 U.S.C. 226 note

Consumer Credit Protection Act
Pub. L. 90–321, May 29, 1968, 82 Stat. 146 (15 U.S.C. 1601 et seq.)
Short title, see 15 U.S.C. 1601 note

Consumer Credit Reporting Reform Act of 1996
Pub. L. 104–208, div. A, title II, subtitle D, ch. 1 (§2401 et seq.), Sept. 30, 1996, 110 Stat. 3009–426
Short title, see 15 U.S.C. 1601 note

Consumer Education Act of 1978
Pub. L. 89–10, title III, part E (§331 et seq.), as added Pub. L. 95–561, title III, §301(a), Nov. 1, 1978, 92 Stat. 2214 (20 U.S.C. 2981 et seq.)

Consumer Goods Pricing Act of 1975
Pub. L. 94–145, Dec. 12, 1975, 89 Stat. 801
Short title, see 15 U.S.C. 1 note

Consumer Home Mortgage Assistance Act of 1974
Pub. L. 93–383, title VII, Aug. 22, 1974, 88 Stat. 714
Short title, see 12 U.S.C. 1464 note

Consumer Leasing Act of 1976
Pub. L. 94–240, Mar. 23, 1976, 90 Stat. 257 (15 U.S.C. 1667 et seq.)
Short title, see 15 U.S.C. 1601 note

Consumer Product Safety Act
Pub. L. 92–573, Oct. 27, 1972, 86 Stat. 1207 (15 U.S.C. 2051 et seq.)
Short title, see 15 U.S.C. 2051 note

Consumer Product Safety Amendments of 1981
Pub. L. 97–35, title XII, subtitle A (§1201 et seq.), Aug. 13, 1981, 95 Stat. 703
Short title, see 15 U.S.C. 2051 note

Consumer Product Safety Commission Improvements Act of 1976
Pub. L. 94–284, May 11, 1976, 90 Stat. 503
Short title, see 15 U.S.C. 2051 note

Consumer Product Safety Improvement Act of 1990
Pub. L. 101–608, Nov. 16, 1990, 104 Stat. 3110
Short title, see 15 U.S.C. 2051 note

Consumer Reporting Employment Clarification Act of 1998
Pub. L. 105–347, Nov. 2, 1998, 112 Stat. 3208
Short title, see 15 U.S.C. 1601 note

Consumer-Patient Radiation Health and Safety Act of 1981
Pub. L. 97–35, title IX, subtitle I (§975 et seq.), Aug. 13, 1981, 95 Stat. 598 (42 U.S.C. 10001 et seq.)
Short title, see 42 U.S.C. 10001 note

Continental Scientific Drilling and Exploration Act
Pub. L. 100–441, Sept. 22, 1988, 102 Stat. 1760 (43 U.S.C. 31 note)

Continued Dumping and Subsidy Offset Act of 2000
Pub. L. 106–387, §1(a) [title X], Oct. 28, 2000, 114 Stat. 1549, 1549A–72
Short title, see 19 U.S.C. 1654 note

Continuing Drug Enterprises Act of 1986
Pub. L. 99–570, title I, subtitle F (§1251 et seq.), Oct. 27, 1986, 100 Stat. 3207–14
Short title, see 21 U.S.C. 801 note

Contraband Seizure Act
Aug. 9, 1939, ch. 618, 53 Stat. 1291

Contract Disputes Act of 1978
Pub. L. 95–563, Nov. 1, 1978, 92 Stat. 2383 (41 U.S.C. 601 et seq.)
Short title, see 41 U.S.C. 601 note

Contract Services for Drug Dependent Federal Offenders Act of 1978
Pub. L. 95–537, Oct. 27, 1978, 92 Stat. 2038

Contract Services for Drug Dependent Federal Offenders Authorization Act of 1983
Pub. L. 98–236, Mar. 20, 1984, 98 Stat. 66

Contract Settlement Act of 1944
July 1, 1944, ch. 358, 58 Stat. 649 (41 U.S.C. 101 et seq.)
Short title, see 41 U.S.C. 101 note

Contract with America Advancement Act of 1996
Pub. L. 104–121, Mar. 29, 1996, 110 Stat. 847
Short title, see 5 U.S.C. 601 note

Contract Work Hours and Safety Standards Act
Pub. L. 87–581, title I, Aug. 13, 1962, 76 Stat. 357 (40 U.S.C. 327 et seq.)
Short title, see 40 U.S.C. 327 note

Contract Work Hours Standards Act
Renamed the Contract Work Hours and Safety Standards Act

Control of Paperwork Amendments of 1978
Pub. L. 95–561, title XII, part B (§1211 et seq.), Nov. 1, 1978, 92 Stat. 2338
Short title, see 20 U.S.C. 1221 note

Controlled Substance Analogue Enforcement Act of 1986
Pub. L. 99–570, title I, subtitle E (§1201 et seq.), Oct. 27, 1986, 100 Stat. 3207–13
Short title, see 21 U.S.C. 801 note

Controlled Substance Registrant Protection Act of 1984
Pub. L. 98–305, May 31, 1984, 98 Stat. 221
Short title, see 18 U.S.C. 2118 note

Controlled Substances Act
Pub. L. 91–513, title II, Oct. 27, 1970, 84 Stat. 1242 (21 U.S.C. 801 et seq.)

Controlled Substances Act—Continued
Short title, see 21 U.S.C. 801 note

Controlled Substances Import and Export Act
Pub. L. 91–513, title III, Oct. 27, 1970, 84 Stat. 1285 (21 U.S.C. 951 et seq.)
Short title, see 21 U.S.C. 951 note

Controlled Substances Import and Export Penalties Enhancement Act of 1986
Pub. L. 99–570, title I, subtitle G (§1301 et seq.), Oct. 27, 1986, 100 Stat. 3207–15
Short title, see 21 U.S.C. 801 note

Controlled Substances Penalties Amendments Act of 1984
Pub. L. 98–473, title II, ch. V (§501 et seq.), Oct. 12, 1984, 98 Stat. 2068
Short title, see 21 U.S.C. 801 note

Controlled Substances Trafficking Prohibition Act
Pub. L. 105–277, div. C, title VIII, subtitle G (§871 et seq.), Oct. 21, 1998, 112 Stat. 2681–707
Short title, see 21 U.S.C. 801 note

Convention on Cultural Property Implementation Act
Pub. L. 97–446, title III, Jan. 12, 1983, 96 Stat. 2350 (19 U.S.C. 2601 et seq.)
Short title, see 19 U.S.C. 2601 note

Convention on the Physical Protection of Nuclear Material Implementation Act of 1982
Pub. L. 97–351, Oct. 15, 1982, 96 Stat. 1663
Short title, see 18 U.S.C. 831 note

Convention on the Settlement of Investment Disputes Act of 1966
Pub. L. 89–532, Aug. 11, 1966, 80 Stat. 344 (22 U.S.C. 1650 et seq.)
Short title, see 22 U.S.C. 1650 note

Conventional Forces in Europe Treaty Implementation Act of 1991
Pub. L. 102–228, Dec. 12, 1991, 105 Stat. 1691
Short title, see 22 U.S.C. 2751 note

Convict-Made Goods Act
Oct. 14, 1940, ch. 872, 54 Stat. 1134

Cooley Tobacco Act
See Agricultural Adjustment Act of 1938

Coolie Trade Prohibition Act
Feb. 19, 1862, ch. 27, 12 Stat. 340

Cooper-Hawes Act (Convict Made Goods)
See Hawes-Cooper Act

Cooperative Forest Management Act
Aug. 25, 1950, ch. 781, 64 Stat. 473
Short title, see 16 U.S.C. 568c note

Cooperative Forestry Assistance Act of 1978
Pub. L. 95–313, July 1, 1978, 92 Stat. 365 (16 U.S.C. 2101 et seq.)
Short title, see 16 U.S.C. 2101 note

Cooperative Research Act
Pub. L. 89–10, title IV, Apr. 11, 1965, 79 Stat. 44 (20 U.S.C. 331–332b)

Cooperative Threat Reduction Act of 1993
Pub. L. 103–160, div. A, title XII, Nov. 30, 1993, 107 Stat. 1777 (22 U.S.C. 5951 et seq.)
Short title, see 22 U.S.C. 5951 note

Coos, Lower Umpqua, and Siuslaw Restoration Act
Pub. L. 98–481, Oct. 17, 1984, 98 Stat. 2250 (25 U.S.C. 714 et seq.)
Short title, see 25 U.S.C. 714 note

Copeland Anti-Kickback Act
June 13, 1934, ch. 482, 48 Stat. 948

Copeland Anti-Racketeering Act
See Anti-Racketeering Act

Copeland Firearms Act
See Federal Firearms Act

Copeland Pure Food and Drugs Act
See Federal Food, Drug and Cosmetic Act

Copeland-Guffey-Gibson Ship Subsidy Act
See Merchant Marine Act, 1936

Copyright Amendments Act of 1992
Pub. L. 102–307, June 26, 1992, 106 Stat. 264
Short title, see 17 U.S.C. 101 note

Copyright Fees and Technical Amendments Act of 1989
Pub. L. 101–318, July 3, 1990, 104 Stat. 287
Short title, see 17 U.S.C. 101 note

Copyright Remedy Clarification Act
Pub. L. 101–553, Nov. 15, 1990, 104 Stat. 2749
Short title, see 17 U.S.C. 101 note

Copyright Renewal Act of 1992
Pub. L. 102–307, title I, June 26, 1992, 106 Stat. 264
Short title, see 17 U.S.C. 101 note

Copyright Royalty Tribunal Reform Act of 1993
Pub. L. 103–198, Dec. 17, 1993, 107 Stat. 2304
Short title, see 17 U.S.C. 101 note

Copyright Royalty Tribunal Reform and Miscellaneous Pay Act of 1989
Pub. L. 101–319, July 3, 1990, 104 Stat. 290
Short title, see 17 U.S.C. 101 note

Coquille Restoration Act
Pub. L. 101–42, June 28, 1989, 103 Stat. 91 (25 U.S.C. 715 et seq.)
Short title, see 25 U.S.C. 715 note

Coral Reef Conservation Act of 2000
Pub. L. 106–562, title II, Dec. 23, 2000, 114 Stat. 2800 (16 U.S.C. 6401 et seq.)
Short title, see 16 U.S.C. 6401 note

Corinth Battlefield Preservation Act of 2000
Pub. L. 106–271, Sept. 22, 2000, 114 Stat. 792 (16 U.S.C. 430f–6 et seq.)
Short title, see 16 U.S.C. 430f–6 note

Corn and Wheat Marketing Quota Act of 1941
May 26, 1941, ch. 133, 55 Stat. 203

Corning National Fish Hatchery Conveyance Act
Pub. L. 104–23, Sept. 6, 1995, 109 Stat. 261

Coronado National Trail Study Act of 1988
Pub. L. 100–559, title II, Oct. 28, 1988, 102 Stat. 2797

Coronado National Trail Study Act of 1988—Continued
Short title, see 16 U.S.C. 1241 note

Corporate Bankruptcy Act
June 7, 1934, ch. 424, 48 Stat. 912

Corporate Reorganization Act
June 22, 1938, ch. 575, 52 Stat. 883

Corporate Surety Act
Aug. 13, 1894, ch. 282, 28 Stat. 279

Corporation for the Promotion of Rifle Practice and Firearms Safety Act
Pub. L. 104–106, div. A, title XVI, Feb. 10, 1996, 110 Stat. 515

Corporation of Foreign Bondholders Act, 1933
May 27, 1933, ch. 38, title II, 48 Stat. 92 (15 U.S.C. 77bb et seq.)
Short title, see 15 U.S.C. 77mm

Corporation Tax Act
Aug. 5, 1909, ch. 6, §38, 36 Stat. 112

Correction Education Demonstration Project Act of 1978
Pub. L. 89–10, title III, part J (§371 et seq.), as added Pub. L. 95–561, title III, §301(a), Nov. 1, 1978, 92 Stat. 2222 (20 U.S.C. §3031 et seq.)

Correction Officers Health and Safety Act of 1998
Pub. L. 105–370, Nov. 12, 1998, 112 Stat. 3374 (18 U.S.C. 4014)
Short title, see 18 U.S.C. 4001 note

Correctional Rehabilitation Study Act of 1965
Pub. L. 89–178, Sept. 10, 1965, 79 Stat. 676

Corrupt Practices Act, 1925
See Federal Corrupt Practices Act, 1925

Cost of Higher Education Review Act of 1997
Pub. L. 105–18, title IV, June 12, 1997, 111 Stat. 207

Cotton Classification Act
Apr. 13, 1937, ch. 75, 50 Stat. 62 (7 U.S.C. 473a et seq.)
Short title, see 7 U.S.C. 473a note

Cotton Control Act
Apr. 21, 1934, ch. 157, 48 Stat. 598 (7 U.S.C. 701 et seq.)

Cotton Futures Act, United States
See United States Cotton Futures Act

Cotton Reports Act
May 27, 1912, ch. 135, §1, 37 Stat. 118 (7 U.S.C. 476)

Cotton Research and Promotion Act
Pub. L. 89–502, July 13, 1966, 80 Stat. 279 (7 U.S.C. 2101 et seq.)
Short title, see 7 U.S.C. 2101 note

Cotton Research and Promotion Act Amendments of 1990
Pub. L. 101–624, title XIX, subtitle G (§1990 et seq.), Nov. 28, 1990, 104 Stat. 3909
Short title, see 7 U.S.C. 2101 note

Cotton Standards Act
See United States Cotton Standards Act

Cotton Statistics and Estimates Act
Mar. 3, 1927, ch. 337, 44 Stat. 1372 (7 U.S.C. 471 et seq.)
Short title, see 7 U.S.C. 471 note

Cotton-Tobacco-Potato Lien Act
Mar. 2, 1936, ch. 112, 49 Stat. 1155

Cotton-Tobacco-Potato Repeal Act
Feb. 10, 1936, ch. 42, 49 Stat. 1106

Coulee Dam Community Act of 1957
Pub. L. 85–240, Aug. 30, 1957, 71 Stat. 524 (16 U.S.C. 835c note)

Council on Wage and Price Stability Act
Pub. L. 93–387, Aug. 24, 1974, 88 Stat. 750 (12 U.S.C. 1901 note)

Council on Wage and Price Stability Act Amendments of 1975
Pub. L. 94–78, Aug. 9, 1975, 89 Stat. 411

Counterfeit Access Device and Computer Fraud and Abuse Act of 1984
Pub. L. 98–473, title II, ch. XXI (§2101 et seq.), Oct. 12, 1984, 98 Stat. 2190
Short title, see 18 U.S.C. 1001 note

Counterfeit Deterrence Act of 1992
Pub. L. 102–550, title XV, subtitle E (§1551 et seq.), Oct. 28, 1992, 106 Stat. 4070
Short title, see 18 U.S.C. 471 note

Counterintelligence and Security Enhancements Act of 1994
Pub. L. 103–359, title VIII, Oct. 14, 1994, 108 Stat. 3434
Short title, see 50 U.S.C. 401 note

Counterintelligence Reform Act of 2000
Pub. L. 106–567, title VI, Dec. 27, 2000, 114 Stat. 2850
Short title, see 50 U.S.C. 1801 note

Court Interpreter Amendments Act of 1988
Pub. L. 100–702, title VII, Nov. 19, 1988, 102 Stat. 4654
Short title, see 28 U.S.C. 1 note

Court Interpreters Act
Pub. L. 95–539, Oct. 28, 1978, 92 Stat. 2040
Short title, see 28 U.S.C. 1 note

Court of Appeals for Veterans Claims Amendments of 1999
Pub. L. 106–117, title X, Nov. 30, 1999, 113 Stat. 1587
Short title, see 38 U.S.C. 101 note

Court of Claims Review Act
May 22, 1939, ch. 140, 53 Stat. 752

Court of Customs Appeals Act
Aug. 5, 1909, ch. 6, §28, 36 Stat. 105

Court of Federal Claims Technical and Procedural Improvements Act of 1992
Pub. L. 102–572, title IX, Oct. 29, 1992, 106 Stat. 4516
Short title, see 28 U.S.C. 1 note

Court of Private Land Claims Act
Mar. 3, 1891, ch. 539, 26 Stat. 854

Court of Veterans Appeals Judges Retirement Act
Pub. L. 101–94, Aug. 16, 1989, 103 Stat. 617
Short title, see 38 U.S.C. 101 note

Court Proctor Act
Aug. 7, 1939, ch. 501, 53 Stat. 1223

Court Reporter Fair Labor Amendments of 1995
Pub. L. 104–26, Sept. 6, 1995, 109 Stat. 264
Short title, see 29 U.S.C. 201 note

Covering-in Act
June 20, 1874, ch. 328, §5, 18 Stat. 110

Cow Creek Band of Umpqua Tribe of Indians Distribution of Judgment Funds Act of 1987
Pub. L. 100–139, Oct. 26, 1987, 101 Stat. 822
Short title, see 25 U.S.C. 712 note

Cow Creek Band of Umpqua Tribe of Indians Recognition Act
Pub. L. 97–391, Dec. 29, 1982, 96 Stat. 1960 (25 U.S.C. 712 et seq.)
Short title, see 25 U.S.C. 712 note

Cranston-Gonzalez National Affordable Housing Act
Pub. L. 101–625, Nov. 28, 1990, 104 Stat. 4079
Short title, see 42 U.S.C. 12701 note

Crawford Amendment (Claims)
See Omnibus Claims Act

Crawford National Fish Hatchery Conveyance Act
Pub. L. 104–215, Oct. 1, 1996, 110 Stat. 3018

Credit Card Fraud Act of 1984
Pub. L. 98–473, title II, ch. XVI (§1601 et seq.), Oct. 12, 1984, 98 Stat. 2183 (18 U.S.C. 1029)
Short title, see 18 U.S.C. 1029 note

Credit Control Act
Pub. L. 91–151, title II, Dec. 23, 1969, 83 Stat. 376 (12 U.S.C. 1901 et seq.)

Credit Repair Organizations Act
Pub. L. 90–321, title IV, as added Pub. L. 104–208, div. A, title II, §2451, Sept. 30, 1996, 110 Stat. 3009–454 (15 U.S.C. 1679 et seq.)
Short title, see 15 U.S.C. 1601 note

Credit Union Act
See Federal Credit Union Act

Credit Union Amendments of 1987
Pub. L. 100–86, title VII, Aug. 10, 1987, 101 Stat. 652
Short title, see 12 U.S.C. 1751 note

Credit Union Membership Access Act
Pub. L. 105–219, Aug. 7, 1998, 112 Stat. 913
Short title, see 12 U.S.C. 1751 note

Creek Original Agreement
Mar. 1, 1901, ch. 676, 31 Stat. 861

Creek Supplemental Agreement
June 30, 1902, ch. 1323, 32 Stat. 500

Crime Awareness and Campus Security Act of 1990
Pub. L. 101–542, title II, Nov. 8, 1990, 104 Stat. 2384
Short title, see 20 U.S.C. 1001 note

Crime Control Act of 1973
Pub. L. 93–83, Aug. 6, 1973, 87 Stat. 197
Short title, see 42 U.S.C. 3711 note

Crime Control Act of 1976
Pub. L. 94–503, Oct. 15, 1976, 90 Stat. 2407
Short title, see 42 U.S.C. 3711 note

Crime Control Act of 1990
Pub. L. 101–647, Nov. 29, 1990, 104 Stat. 4789
Short title, see 18 U.S.C. 1 note

Crime Identification Technology Act of 1998
Pub. L. 105–251, title I, Oct. 9, 1998, 112 Stat. 1871 (42 U.S.C. 14601)
Short title, see 42 U.S.C. 14601 note

Crime Prevention Compact Act
June 6, 1934, ch. 406, 48 Stat. 909

Crime Victims With Disabilities Awareness Act
Pub. L. 105–301, Oct. 27, 1998, 112 Stat. 2838 (42 U.S.C. 3732 note)

Criminal Appeals Act
Mar. 2, 1907, ch. 2564, 34 Stat. 1246

Criminal Code
Mar. 4, 1909, ch. 321, 35 Stat. 1088

Criminal Fine Enforcement Act of 1984
Pub. L. 98–596, Oct. 30, 1984, 98 Stat. 3134

Criminal Fine Improvements Act of 1987
Pub. L. 100–185, Dec. 11, 1987, 101 Stat. 1279
Short title, see 18 U.S.C. 1 note

Criminal Justice Act of 1964
Pub. L. 88–455, Aug. 20, 1964, 78 Stat. 552 (18 U.S.C. 3006A)
Short title, see 18 U.S.C. 3006A note

Criminal Justice Act Revision of 1984
Pub. L. 98–473, title II, ch. XIX, Oct. 12, 1984, 98 Stat. 2185
Short title, see 18 U.S.C. 3006A note

Criminal Justice Act Revision of 1986
Pub. L. 99–651, title I, Nov. 14, 1986, 100 Stat. 3642
Short title, see 18 U.S.C. 3006A note

Criminal Justice Information Services Placement Assistance Act
Pub. L. 103–317, title I, §115, Aug. 26, 1994, 108 Stat. 1736

Criminal Law and Procedure Technical Amendments Act of 1986
Pub. L. 99–646, Nov. 10, 1986, 100 Stat. 3592
Short title, see 18 U.S.C. 1 note

Criminal Victims Protection Act of 1990
Pub. L. 101–581, Nov. 15, 1990, 104 Stat. 2865
Pub. L. 101–647, title XXXI, Nov. 29, 1990, 104 Stat. 4916
Short title, see 11 U.S.C. 101 note

Critical Agricultural Materials Act
Pub. L. 95–592, Nov. 4, 1978, 92 Stat. 2529 (7 U.S.C. 178 et seq.)
Short title, see 7 U.S.C. 178 note

Critical Needs for Tribal Development Act
Pub. L. 102–325, title XIII, part C (§1321 et seq.), July 23, 1992, 106 Stat. 803 (25 U.S.C. 3321 et seq.)

Critical Needs for Tribal Development Act—Continued
Short title, see 25 U.S.C. 3321

Crop Loan Act
Feb. 23, 1934, ch. 23, 48 Stat. 354

Crop Loan and Sugar Appropriation Act
Feb. 4, 1938, ch. 14, 52 Stat. 26

Cross-Border Cooperation and Environmental Safety in Northern Europe Act of 2000
Pub. L. 106–255, Aug. 2, 2000, 114 Stat. 639

Crosser-Wheeler Railroad Unemployment Insurance Act
See Railroad Unemployment Insurance Act

Crow Boundary Settlement Act of 1994
Pub. L. 103–444, Nov. 2, 1994, 108 Stat. 4632 (25 U.S.C. 1776 et seq.)
Short title, see 25 U.S.C. 1776 note

Crow Creek Sioux Tribe Infrastructure Development Trust Fund Act of 1996
Pub. L. 104–223, Oct. 1, 1996, 110 Stat. 3026

Crude Oil Windfall Profit Tax Act of 1980
Pub. L. 96–223, Apr. 2, 1980, 94 Stat. 229
Short title, see 26 U.S.C. 1 note

Cruelty to Animals Act
Also known as the Food and Rest Law, the Live Stock Transportation Act, and the Twenty-Eight Hour Law
June 29, 1906, ch. 3594, 34 Stat. 607
Short title, see 45 U.S.C. 71 note

Cuban Democracy Act of 1992
Pub. L. 102–484, div. A, title XVII, Oct. 23, 1992, 106 Stat. 2575 (22 U.S.C. 6001 et seq.)
Short title, see 22 U.S.C. 6001 note

Cuban Independence Resolution
Apr. 20, 1898, No. 24, 30 Stat. 738

Cuban Liberty and Democratic Solidarity (LIBERTAD) Act of 1996
Pub. L. 104–114, Mar. 12, 1996, 110 Stat. 785 (22 U.S.C. 6021 et seq.)
Short title, see 22 U.S.C. 6021 note

Cuban Political Prisoners and Immigrants
Pub. L. 100–202, §101(a) [title VII], Dec. 22, 1987, 101 Stat. 1329, 1329–39 (8 U.S.C. 1201 note)

Cuban Refugee Adjustment Act
Pub. L. 89–732, Nov. 2, 1966, 80 Stat. 1161 (8 U.S.C. 1255 note)

Cullom Act (Interstate Commerce)
See Interstate Commerce Act

Cumberland Gap National Historical Park Act
June 11, 1940, ch. 304, 54 Stat. 262 (16 U.S.C. 261 et seq.)

Cumberland Island National Seashore Act
Pub. L. 92–536, Oct. 23, 1972, 86 Stat. 1066 (16 U.S.C. 459i et seq.)

Currency Act (Legal Tender Notes)
May 31, 1878, ch. 146, 20 Stat. 87

Currency and Foreign Transactions Reporting Act
Pub. L. 91–508, title II, Oct. 26, 1970, 84 Stat. 1118

Currency Reduction Suspension Act
Feb. 4, 1868, ch. 6, 15 Stat. 34

Current Tax Payment Act of 1943
June 9, 1943, ch. 120, 57 Stat. 126

Curt Flood Act of 1998
Pub. L. 105–297, Oct. 27, 1998, 112 Stat. 2824 (15 U.S.C. 27a)
Short title, see 15 U.S.C. 1 note

Curtis Act (Five Civilized Tribes)
Apr. 26, 1906, ch. 1876, 34 Stat. 137

Curtis Act (Indians in Indian Territory)
June 28, 1898, ch. 517, 30 Stat. 495

Curtis Act (Reclamation and Irrigation)
Feb. 13, 1911, ch. 49, 36 Stat. 902 (43 U.S.C. 468)

Custodial Pay Act
Aug. 1, 1942, ch. 543, 56 Stat. 733

Customs Administration Act of 1890
June 10, 1890, ch. 407, as added Aug. 5, 1909, ch. 6, §28, 36 Stat. 91

Customs Administrative Act of 1938
June 25, 1938, ch. 679, 52 Stat. 1077
Short title, see 19 U.S.C. 1654 note

Customs Administrative Act of 1970
Pub. L. 91–271, titles II, III, June 2, 1970, 84 Stat. 282, 287
Short title, see 19 U.S.C. 1654 note

Customs and Trade Act of 1990
Pub. L. 101–382, Aug. 20, 1990, 104 Stat. 629
Short title, see 19 U.S.C. 2101 note

Customs Bureau Act
Mar. 3, 1927, ch. 348, 44 Stat. 1381

Customs Court Act
See Court of Customs Appeals Act

Customs Courts Act of 1970
Pub. L. 91–271, title I, June 2, 1970, 84 Stat. 274
Short title, see 28 U.S.C. 1 note

Customs Courts Act of 1980
Pub. L. 96–417, Oct. 10, 1980, 94 Stat. 1727
Short title, see 28 U.S.C. 1 note

Customs Employees Salaries Act
May 29, 1928, ch. 865, 45 Stat. 955 (19 U.S.C. 6a–6d)

Customs Enforcement Act of 1986
Pub. L. 99–570, title III, subtitle B (§3101 et seq.), Oct. 27, 1986, 100 Stat. 3207–79
Short title, see 19 U.S.C. 1654 note

Customs Procedural Reform and Simplification Act of 1978
Pub. L. 95–410, Oct. 3, 1978, 92 Stat. 888
Short title, see 19 U.S.C. 1654 note

Customs Reorganization Act
Aug. 24, 1912, ch. 355, §1, 37 Stat. 434 (19 U.S.C. 1)

Customs Simplification Act of 1953
Aug. 8, 1953, ch. 397, 67 Stat. 507
Short title, see 19 U.S.C. 1654 note

Customs Simplification Act of 1954
Sept. 1, 1954, ch. 1213, 68 Stat. 1136
Short title, see 19 U.S.C. 1654 note

Customs Simplification Act of 1956
Aug. 2, 1956, ch. 887, 70 Stat. 943
Short title, see 19 U.S.C. 1654 note

Czechoslovakian Claims Settlement Act of 1981
Pub. L. 97–127, Dec. 29, 1981, 95 Stat. 1675 (22 U.S.C. note prec. 1642)

D'Alesandro Repatriation Act
July 2, 1940, ch. 509, 54 Stat. 715

Dairy and Tobacco Adjustment Act of 1983
Pub. L. 98–180, Nov. 29, 1983, 97 Stat. 1128
Short title, see 7 U.S.C. 1421 note

Dairy Market Enhancement Act of 2000
Pub. L. 106–532, Nov. 22, 2000, 114 Stat. 2541
Short title, see 7 U.S.C. 1621 note

Dairy Production Stabilization Act of 1983
Pub. L. 98–180, title I, Nov. 29, 1983, 97 Stat. 1128 (7 U.S.C. 4501 et seq.)
Short title, see 7 U.S.C. 1421 note

Dakota Water Resources Act of 2000
Pub. L. 106–554, §1(a)(4) [div. B, title VI], Dec. 21, 2000, 114 Stat. 2763, 2763A–281

Dale Bumpers Wilderness Resources Protection Act
Also known as the Arkansas Wilderness Act of 1984
Pub. L. 98–508, Oct. 19, 1984, 98 Stat. 2349 (16 U.S.C. 1132 notes)

Dam Safety Act of 1986
Pub. L. 99–662, title XII, Nov. 17, 1986, 100 Stat. 4260
Short title, see 33 U.S.C. 467 note

Dangerous Cargo Act
R.S. §4472

Dangerous Drug Act of the District of Columbia
July 24, 1956, ch. 676, title II, 70 Stat. 612

Dangerous Drug Control Act for the District of Columbia
July 24, 1956, ch. 676, 70 Stat. 609

Dangerous Drug Diversion Control Act of 1984
Pub. L. 98–473, title II, ch. V, part B (§506 et seq.), Oct. 12, 1984, 98 Stat. 2070
Short title, see 21 U.S.C. 801 note

Danish West Indies Acquisition Act
See Virgin Islands Acquisition Act

Dante B. Fascell North-South Center Act of 1991
Pub. L. 102–138, title II, §208, Oct. 28, 1991, 105 Stat. 694 (22 U.S.C. 2075)
Short title, see 22 U.S.C. 2075(a)

Dante Fascell Biscayne National Park Visitor Center Designation Act
Pub. L. 105–307, Oct. 29, 1998, 112 Stat. 2931 (16 U.S.C. 410gg note)

David L. Boren National Security Education Act of 1991
Pub. L. 102–183, title VIII, Dec. 4, 1991, 105 Stat. 1271 (50 U.S.C. 1901 et seq.)
Short title, see 50 U.S.C. 1901(a)

Davis-Bacon Act
Mar. 3, 1931, ch. 411, 46 Stat. 1494 (40 U.S.C. 276a et seq.)
Short title, see 40 U.S.C. 276a note

Dawes Act (Indians)
See Indian General Allotment Act

Dawes Act (Marriage with Indian Women)
Aug. 9, 1888, ch. 818, 25 Stat. 392 (25 U.S.C. 181 et seq.)

Dayton Aviation Heritage Preservation Act of 1992
Pub. L. 102–419, Oct. 16, 1992, 106 Stat. 2141 (16 U.S.C. 410ww et seq.)
Short title, see 16 U.S.C. 410ww note

Dayton Aviation Heritage Preservation Amendments Act of 2000
Pub. L. 106–356, Oct. 24, 2000, 114 Stat. 1391
Short title, see 16 U.S.C. 410ww note

De Soto Expedition Trail Commission Act of 1990
Pub. L. 101–607, Nov. 16, 1990, 104 Stat. 3105 (16 U.S.C. 1244 note)

De Soto National Memorial Act
Mar. 11, 1948, ch. 109, 62 Stat. 78 (16 U.S.C. 450dd, 450dd–1)

De Soto National Trail Study Act of 1987
Pub. L. 100–187, Dec. 11, 1987, 101 Stat. 1287
Short title, see 16 U.S.C. 1241 note

Deadbeat Parents Punishment Act of 1998
Pub. L. 105–187, June 24, 1998, 112 Stat. 618
Short title, see 18 U.S.C. 228 note

Dealer Reserve Income Adjustment Act of 1960
Pub. L. 86–459, May 13, 1960, 74 Stat. 124 (26 U.S.C. 481 note)

Death in Custody Reporting Act of 2000
Pub. L. 106–297, Oct. 13, 2000, 114 Stat. 1045
Short title, see 42 U.S.C. 13701 note

Death on the High Seas Act
Mar. 30, 1920, ch. 111, 41 Stat. 537 (46 App. U.S.C. 761 et seq.)
Short title, see 46 App. U.S.C. 761 note

Debt Collection Act of 1982
Pub. L. 97–365, Oct. 25, 1982, 96 Stat. 1749
Short title, see 5 U.S.C. 5514 note

Debt Collection Improvement Act of 1996
Pub. L. 104–134, title III, §31001, Apr. 26, 1996, 110 Stat. 1321–358
Short title, see 31 U.S.C. 3701 note

Debt Default Act
See Johnson Debt Default Act

Decennial Census Improvement Act of 1991
Pub. L. 102–135, Oct. 24, 1991, 105 Stat. 635 (13 U.S.C. 141 note)

Deceptive Mail Prevention and Enforcement Act
Pub. L. 106–168, title I, Dec. 12, 1999, 113 Stat. 1806
Short title, see 39 U.S.C. 3001 note

Deceptive Mailings Prevention Act of 1990
Pub. L. 101–524, Nov. 6, 1990, 104 Stat. 2301
Short title, see 39 U.S.C. 3001 note

Declaration of Taking Act
Feb. 26, 1931, ch. 307, 46 Stat. 1421 (40 U.S.C. 258a et seq.)
Short title, see 40 U.S.C. 258a note

Declaration of War against Great Britain
June 18, 1812, ch. 102, 2 Stat. 755

Declaration of War against Spain
Apr. 25, 1898, ch. 189, 30 Stat. 364

Declaration Terminating War with Germany and Austria-Hungary
July 2, 1921, ch. 40, 42 Stat. 105

Declaratory Judgment Act
June 14, 1934, ch. 512, 48 Stat. 955

Deep Seabed Hard Mineral Removal Tax Act of 1979
Pub. L. 96–283, title IV, June 28, 1980, 94 Stat. 582 (26 U.S.C. 4495 et seq.; 30 U.S.C. 1472, 1473)
Short title, see 26 U.S.C. 1 note

Deep Seabed Hard Mineral Resources Act
Pub. L. 96–283, June 28, 1980, 94 Stat. 553 (30 U.S.C. 1401 et seq.)
Short title, see 30 U.S.C. 1401 note

Deep Seabed Hard Mineral Resources Reauthorization Act of 1986
Pub. L. 99–507, Oct. 21, 1986, 100 Stat. 1847
Short title, see 30 U.S.C. 1401 note

Deepwater Port Act Amendments of 1984
Pub. L. 98–419, Sept. 25, 1984, 98 Stat. 1607
Short title, see 33 U.S.C. 1501 note

Deepwater Port Act of 1974
Pub. L. 93–627, Jan. 3, 1975, 88 Stat. 2126 (33 U.S.C. 1501 et seq.)
Short title, see 33 U.S.C. 1501 note

Deepwater Port Modernization Act
Pub. L. 104–324, title V, Oct. 19, 1996, 110 Stat. 3925
Short title, see 33 U.S.C. 1501 note

Defense Acquisition Improvement Act of 1986
Pub. L. 99–500, §101(c) [title X] Oct. 18, 1986, 100 Stat. 1783–82, 1783–130, and Pub. L. 99–591, §101(c) [title X], Oct. 30, 1986, 100 Stat. 3341–82, 3341–130
Pub. L. 99–661, div. A, title IX, formerly title IV, Nov. 14, 1986, 100 Stat. 3910; renumbered title IX, Pub. L. 100–26, §3(5), Apr. 21, 1987, 101 Stat. 273
Short title, see 10 U.S.C. 2302 note

Defense Acquisition Workforce Improvement Act
Pub. L. 101–510, div. A, title XII, Nov. 5, 1990, 104 Stat. 1638 (10 U.S.C. 1701 et seq.)
Short title, see 10 U.S.C. 1701 note

Defense Against Weapons of Mass Destruction Act of 1996
Pub. L. 104–201, div. A, title XIV, Sept. 23, 1996, 110 Stat. 2714 (50 U.S.C. 2301 et seq.)
Short title, see 50 U.S.C. 2301 note

Defense Against Weapons of Mass Destruction Act of 1998
Pub. L. 105–261, div. A, title XIV, Oct. 17, 1998, 112 Stat. 2167 (50 U.S.C. 2301 note)

Defense Aid Appropriation Act, 1945
June 30, 1944, ch. 324, title I, 58 Stat. 628

Defense Aid Appropriation Act, 1946
July 5, 1945, ch. 271, title II, 59 Stat. 429

Defense Aid Supplemental Appropriation Act, 1941
Mar. 27, 1941, ch. 30, 55 Stat. 53

Defense Aid Supplemental Appropriation Act, 1942
Oct. 28, 1941, ch. 460, title I, 55 Stat. 745

Defense Aid Supplemental Appropriation Act, 1943
June 14, 1943, ch. 122, 57 Stat. 151

Defense Appropriation Act, 1951
Sept. 6, 1950, ch. 896, ch. X, 64 Stat. 730

Defense Authorization Amendments and Base Closure and Realignment Act
Pub. L. 100–526, Oct. 24, 1988, 102 Stat. 2623
Short title, see 10 U.S.C. 2687 note

Defense Base Act
Aug. 16, 1941, ch. 357, 55 Stat. 622 (42 U.S.C. 1651 et seq.)
Short title, see 42 U.S.C. 1651 note

Defense Base Closure and Realignment Act of 1990
Pub. L. 101–510, div. B, title XXIX, part A (§2901 et seq.), Nov. 5, 1990, 104 Stat. 1808 (10 U.S.C. 2687 note)

Defense Cataloging and Standardization Act
July 1, 1952, ch. 539, 66 Stat. 318

Defense Contract Bond Act
Apr. 29, 1941, ch. 81, 55 Stat. 147

Defense Conversion, Reinvestment, and Transition Assistance Act of 1992
Pub. L. 102–484, div. D, Oct. 23, 1992, 106 Stat. 2658
Short title, see 10 U.S.C. 2500 note

Defense Conversion, Reinvestment, and Transition Assistance Amendments of 1993
Pub. L. 103–160, div. A, title XIII, Nov. 30, 1993, 107 Stat. 1783
Short title, see 10 U.S.C. 2500 note

Defense Conversion, Reinvestment, and Transition Assistance Amendments of 1994
Pub. L. 103–337, div. A, title XI, Oct. 5, 1994, 108 Stat. 2862
Short title, see 10 U.S.C. 2500 note

Defense Department Overseas Teachers Pay and Personnel Practices Act
Pub. L. 86–91, July 17, 1959, 73 Stat. 213 (20 U.S.C. 901 et seq.)
Short title, see 20 U.S.C. 901 note

Defense Dependents' Education Act of 1978
Pub. L. 95–561, title XIV, Nov. 1, 1978, 92 Stat. 2365 (20 U.S.C. 921 et seq.)
Short title, see 20 U.S.C. 921 note

Defense Drug Interdiction Assistance Act
Pub. L. 99–570, title III, subtitle A (§3051 et seq.), Oct. 27, 1986, 100 Stat. 3207–74
Short title, see 10 U.S.C. 371 note

Defense Economic Adjustment, Diversification, Conversion, and Stabilization Act of 1990
Pub. L. 101–510, div. D, Nov. 5, 1990, 104 Stat. 1848 (10 U.S.C. 2391 note)

Defense Eight-Hour Day Act
Oct. 10, 1940, ch. 838, 54 Stat. 1092

Defense Entry and Departure Act
June 21, 1941, ch. 210, 55 Stat. 252

Defense Highway Act of 1941
Nov. 19, 1941, ch. 474, 55 Stat. 765

Defense Housing Act of 1942
Jan. 21, 1942, ch. 14, 56 Stat. 11

Defense Housing and Community Facilities and Services Act of 1951
Sept. 1, 1951, ch. 378, 65 Stat. 293
Short title, see 42 U.S.C. 1501 note

Defense Housing Appropriation Act
Oct. 14, 1940, ch. 857, 54 Stat. 1115

Defense Industrial Reserve Act
July 2, 1948, ch. 811, 62 Stat. 1225 (50 U.S.C. 451 et seq.)
Short title, see 50 U.S.C. 451 note

Defense of Marriage Act
Pub. L. 104–199, Sept. 21, 1996, 110 Stat. 2419
Short title, see 1 U.S.C. 1 note

Defense Officer Personnel Management Act
Pub. L. 96–513, Dec. 12, 1980, 94 Stat. 2835
Short title, see 10 U.S.C. 101 note

Defense Officer Personnel Management Act Technical Corrections Act
Pub. L. 97–22, July 10, 1981, 95 Stat. 124
Short title, see 10 U.S.C. 101 note

Defense Offsets Disclosure Act of 1999
Pub. L. 106–113, div. B, §1000(a)(7) [div. B, title XII, subtitle D (§1241 et seq.)], Nov. 29, 1999, 113 Stat. 1536, 1501A–500 (50 App. 2099 note)

Defense Patents Act
June 16, 1942, ch. 415, 56 Stat. 370

Defense Procurement Improvement Act of 1985
Pub. L. 99–145, title IX, Nov. 8, 1985, 99 Stat. 682
Short title, see 10 U.S.C. 2302 note

Defense Procurement Reform Act of 1984
Pub. L. 98–525, title XII, Oct. 19, 1984, 98 Stat. 2588
Short title, see 10 U.S.C. 2302 note

Defense Production Act Amendments of 1951
July 31, 1951, ch. 275, 65 Stat. 131
Short title, see 50 App. 2061 note

Defense Production Act Amendments of 1952
June 30, 1952, ch. 530, 66 Stat. 296
Short title, see 50 App. 2061 note

Defense Production Act Amendments of 1953
June 30, 1953, ch. 171, 67 Stat. 129
Short title, see 50 App. 2061 note

Defense Production Act Amendments of 1974
Pub. L. 93–426, Sept. 30, 1974, 88 Stat. 1166
Short title, see 50 App. 2061 note

Defense Production Act Amendments of 1975
Pub. L. 94–152, Dec. 16, 1975, 89 Stat. 810
Short title, see 50 App. 2061 note

Defense Production Act Amendments of 1980
Pub. L. 96–294, title I, part A (§101 et seq.), June 30, 1980, 94 Stat. 617
Short title, see 50 App. 2061 note

Defense Production Act Amendments of 1984
Pub. L. 98–265, Apr. 17, 1984, 98 Stat. 149
Short title, see 50 App. 2061 note

Defense Production Act Amendments of 1986
Pub. L. 99–441, Oct. 3, 1986, 100 Stat. 1117
Short title, see 50 App. 2061 note

Defense Production Act Amendments of 1992
Pub. L. 102–558, Oct. 28, 1992, 106 Stat. 4198
Short title, see 50 App. 2061 note

Defense Production Act Amendments of 1995
Pub. L. 104–64, Dec. 18, 1995, 109 Stat. 689
Short title, see 50 App. 2061 note

Defense Production Act Extension Amendments of 1977
Pub. L. 95–37, June 1, 1977, 91 Stat. 178
Short title, see 50 App. 2061 note

Defense Production Act Extension and Amendments of 1991
Pub. L. 102–99, Aug. 17, 1991, 105 Stat. 487
Short title, see 50 App. 2061 note

Defense Production Act of 1950
Sept. 8, 1950, ch. 932, 64 Stat. 798 (50 App. 2061 et seq.)
Short title, see 50 App. 2061

Defense Productions Act Amendments of 1955
Aug. 9, 1955, ch. 655, 69 Stat. 580

Defense Public Works Act
See Defense Housing Appropriation Act

Defense Technical Corrections Act of 1987
Pub. L. 100–26, Apr. 21, 1987, 101 Stat. 273
Short title, see 10 U.S.C. 101 note

Defense Workers Housing Act
Oct. 1, 1942, ch. 572, 56 Stat. 763

Deficiency Appropriation Act, 1950
June 29, 1950, ch. 405, 64 Stat. 275

Deficiency Appropriation Act, 1964
Pub. L. 88–317, June 9, 1964, 78 Stat. 204

Deficiency Appropriation Act, fiscal year 1934
June 19, 1934, ch. 648, title I, 48 Stat. 1021

Deficit Reduction Act of 1984
Pub. L. 98–369, July 18, 1984, 98 Stat. 494
Short title, see 26 U.S.C. 1 note

DEFRA
See Deficit Reduction Act of 1984

Delaney Amendment
See Food Additives Amendment of 1958

Delaware and Lehigh National Heritage Corridor Act of 1988
Pub. L. 100–692, Nov. 18, 1988, 102 Stat. 4552 (16 U.S.C. 461 note)

Delaware and Lehigh Navigation Canal National Heritage Corridor Act of 1988
Renamed Delaware and Lehigh National Heritage Corridor Act of 1988

Delaware Water Gap National Recreation Area Act
Pub. L. 89–158, Sept. 1, 1965, 79 Stat. 612 (16 U.S.C. 460*o* et seq.)

Delta Development Act
Pub. L. 100–460, title II [S. 2836], Oct. 1, 1988, 102 Stat. 2246 (42 U.S.C. 3121 note)

Delta Regional Authority Act of 2000
Pub. L. 106–554, §1(a)(4) [div. B, title V], Dec. 21, 2000, 114 Stat. 2763, 2763A–268
Short title, see 7 U.S.C. 1921 note

Demonstration Cities and Metropolitan Development Act of 1966
Pub. L. 89–754, Nov. 3, 1966, 80 Stat. 1255 (42 U.S.C. 3301 et seq.)
Short title, see 42 U.S.C. 3331 note

Denali Commission Act of 1998
Pub. L. 105–277, div. C, title III, Oct. 21, 1998, 112 Stat. 2681–637 (42 U.S.C. 3121 note)

Dent Act
Mar. 2, 1919, ch. 94, 40 Stat. 1272

Department of Agriculture Act
May 15, 1862, ch. 72, 12 Stat. 387

Department of Agriculture and Farm Credit Administration Appropriation Act, 1955
June 29, 1954, ch. 409, 68 Stat. 304

Department of Agriculture and Farm Credit Administration Appropriation Act, 1956
May 23, 1955, ch. 43, 69 Stat. 51

Department of Agriculture and Farm Credit Administration Appropriation Act, 1957
June 4, 1956, ch. 355, 70 Stat. 229

Department of Agriculture and Farm Credit Administration Appropriation Act, 1958
Pub. L. 85–118, Aug. 2, 1957, 71 Stat. 329

Department of Agriculture and Farm Credit Administration Appropriation Act, 1959
Pub. L. 85–459, June 13, 1958, 72 Stat. 188

Department of Agriculture and Farm Credit Administration Appropriation Act, 1960
Pub. L. 86–80, July 8, 1959, 73 Stat. 167

Department of Agriculture and Farm Credit Administration Appropriation Act, 1961
Pub. L. 86–532, June 29, 1960, 74 Stat. 232

Department of Agriculture and Related Agencies Appropriation Act, 1962
Pub. L. 87–112, July 26, 1961, 75 Stat. 225

Department of Agriculture and Related Agencies Appropriation Act, 1963
Pub. L. 87–879, Oct. 24, 1962, 76 Stat. 1203

Department of Agriculture and Related Agencies Appropriation Act, 1964
Pub. L. 88–250, Dec. 30, 1963, 77 Stat. 820

Department of Agriculture and Related Agencies Appropriation Act, 1965
Pub. L. 88–573, Sept. 2, 1964, 78 Stat. 862

Department of Agriculture and Related Agencies Appropriation Act, 1966
Pub. L. 89–316, Nov. 2, 1965, 79 Stat. 1165

Department of Agriculture and Related Agencies Appropriation Act, 1967
Pub. L. 89–556, Sept. 7, 1966, 80 Stat. 689

Department of Agriculture and Related Agencies Appropriation Act, 1968
Pub. L. 90–113, Oct. 24, 1967, 81 Stat. 319

Department of Agriculture and Related Agencies Appropriation Act, 1969
Pub. L. 90–463, Aug. 8, 1968, 82 Stat. 639

Department of Agriculture and Related Agencies Appropriation Act, 1970
Pub. L. 91–127, Nov. 26, 1969, 83 Stat. 244

Department of Agriculture and Related Agencies Appropriation Act, 1971
Pub. L. 91–566, Dec. 22, 1970, 84 Stat. 1480

Department of Agriculture Appropriation Act, 1937
June 4, 1936, ch. 489, title I, 49 Stat. 1421

Department of Agriculture Appropriation Act, 1938
June 29, 1937, ch. 404, title I, 50 Stat. 395

Department of Agriculture Appropriation Act, 1939
June 16, 1938, ch. 464, title I, 52 Stat. 711

Department of Agriculture Appropriation Act, 1940
June 30, 1939, ch. 253, title I, 53 Stat. 939

Department of Agriculture Appropriation Act, 1941
June 25, 1940, ch. 421, 54 Stat. 532

Department of Agriculture Appropriation Act, 1942
July 1, 1941, ch. 267, 55 Stat. 408

Department of Agriculture Appropriation Act, 1943
July 22, 1942, ch. 516, 56 Stat. 664

Department of Agriculture Appropriation Act, 1944
July 12, 1943, ch. 215, 57 Stat. 392

Department of Agriculture Appropriation Act, 1945
June 28, 1944, ch. 296, 58 Stat. 425

Department of Agriculture Appropriation Act, 1946
May 5, 1945, ch. 109, 59 Stat. 136

Department of Agriculture Appropriation Act, 1947
June 22, 1946, ch. 445, 60 Stat. 270

Department of Agriculture Appropriation Act, 1948
July 30, 1947, ch. 356, 61 Stat. 523

Department of Agriculture Appropriation Act, 1949
June 19, 1948, ch. 543, 62 Stat. 507

Department of Agriculture Appropriation Act, 1950
June 29, 1949, ch. 280, 63 Stat. 324

Department of Agriculture Appropriation Act, 1951
Sept. 6, 1950, ch. 896, Ch. VI, 64 Stat. 657

Department of Agriculture Appropriation Act, 1952
Aug. 31, 1951, ch. 374, 65 Stat. 225

Department of Agriculture Appropriation Act, 1953
July 5, 1952, ch. 574, 66 Stat. 335

Department of Agriculture Appropriation Act, 1954
July 28, 1953, ch. 251, 67 Stat. 205

Department of Agriculture Organic Act of 1944
Sept. 21, 1944, ch. 412, 58 Stat. 734

Department of Agriculture Organic Act of 1956
Aug. 3, 1956, ch. 950, 70 Stat. 1032
Short title, see 7 U.S.C. 2201 note

Department of Agriculture Reorganization Act of 1994
Pub. L. 103–354, title II, Oct. 13, 1994, 108 Stat. 3209
Short title, see 7 U.S.C. 6901 note

Department of Commerce and Labor Act
Feb. 14, 1903, ch. 552, 32 Stat. 825

Department of Commerce and Related Agencies Appropriation Act, 1956
June 30, 1955, ch. 253, 69 Stat. 226

Department of Commerce and Related Agencies Appropriation Act, 1957
June 20, 1956, ch. 415, 70 Stat. 314

Department of Commerce and Related Agencies Appropriation Act, 1958
Pub. L. 85–52, June 13, 1957, 71 Stat. 70

Department of Commerce and Related Agencies Appropriation Act, 1959
Pub. L. 85–469, June 25, 1958, 72 Stat. 226

Department of Commerce and Related Agencies Appropriation Act, 1960
Pub. L. 86–88, July 13, 1959, 73 Stat. 201

Department of Commerce and Related Agencies Appropriation Act, 1961
Pub. L. 86–451, May 13, 1960, 74 Stat. 93

Department of Commerce and Related Agencies Appropriation Act, 1984
Pub. L. 98–166, title I, Nov. 28, 1983, 97 Stat. 1071

Department of Commerce and Related Agencies Appropriation Act, 1985
Pub. L. 98–411, title I, Aug. 30, 1984, 98 Stat. 1545

Department of Commerce and Related Agencies Appropriations Act, 1996
Pub. L. 104–134, title I, §101[(a)] [title II], Apr. 26, 1996, 110 Stat. 1321, 1321–23

Department of Commerce and Related Agencies Appropriations Act, 1997
Pub. L. 104–208, div. A, title I, §101(a) [title II], Sept. 30, 1996, 110 Stat. 3009, 3009–32

Department of Commerce and Related Agencies Appropriations Act, 1998
Pub. L. 105–119, title II, Nov. 26, 1997, 111 Stat. 2471

Department of Commerce and Related Agencies Appropriations Act, 1999
Pub. L. 105–277, div. A, §101(b) [title II], Oct. 21, 1998, 112 Stat. 2681–50, 2681–77

Department of Commerce and Related Agencies Appropriations Act, 2000
Pub. L. 106–113, div. B, §1000(a)(1) [title II], Nov. 29, 1999, 113 Stat. 1535, 1501A–23

Department of Commerce and Related Agencies Appropriations Act, 2001
Pub. L. 106–553, §1(a)(2) [title II], Dec. 21, 2000, 114 Stat. 2762, 2762A–69

Department of Commerce Appropriation Act, 1940
June 29, 1939, ch. 248, title III, 53 Stat. 907

Department of Commerce Appropriation Act, 1941
May 14, 1940, ch. 189, title II, 54 Stat. 192

Department of Commerce Appropriation Act, 1942
June 28, 1941, ch. 258, title II, 55 Stat. 277

Department of Commerce Appropriation Act, 1943
July 2, 1942, ch. 472, title III, 56 Stat. 489

Department of Commerce Appropriation Act, 1944
July 1, 1943, ch. 182, title III, 57 Stat. 290

Department of Commerce Appropriation Act, 1945
June 28, 1944, ch. 294, title III, 58 Stat. 414

Department of Commerce Appropriation Act, 1946
May 21, 1945, ch. 129, title III, 59 Stat. 187

Department of Commerce Appropriation Act, 1947
July 5, 1946, ch. 541, title III, 60 Stat. 465

Department of Commerce Appropriation Act, 1948
July 9, 1947, ch. 211, title III, 61 Stat. 294

Department of Commerce Appropriation Act, 1949

June 3, 1948, ch. 400, title III, 62 Stat. 321

Department of Commerce Appropriation Act, 1950

July 20, 1949, ch. 354, title III, 63 Stat. 462

Department of Commerce Appropriation Act, 1951

Sept. 6, 1950, ch. 896, Ch. III, title III, 64 Stat. 620

Department of Commerce Appropriation Act, 1952

Oct. 22, 1951, ch. 533, title III, 65 Stat. 586

Department of Commerce Appropriation Act, 1953

July 10, 1952, ch. 651, title III, 66 Stat. 560

Department of Commerce Appropriation Act, 1954

Aug. 5, 1953, ch. 328, title III, 67 Stat. 376

Department of Commerce Appropriation Act, 1955

July 2, 1954, ch. 456, title III, 68 Stat. 422

Department of Commerce Appropriation Act, 1963

Pub. L. 87–843, title III, Oct. 18, 1962, 76 Stat. 1089

Department of Commerce Appropriation Act, 1964

Pub. L. 88–245, title III, Dec. 30, 1963, 77 Stat. 784

Department of Commerce Appropriation Act, 1965

Pub. L. 88–527, title III, Aug. 31, 1964, 78 Stat. 720

Department of Commerce Appropriation Act, 1966

Pub. L. 89–164, title III, Sept. 2, 1965, 79 Stat. 629

Department of Commerce Appropriation Act, 1967

Pub. L. 89–797, title III, Nov. 8, 1966, 80 Stat. 1488

Department of Commerce Appropriation Act, 1968

Pub. L. 90–133, title III, Nov. 8, 1967, 81 Stat. 419

Department of Commerce Appropriation Act, 1969

Pub. L. 90–470, title III, Aug. 9, 1968, 82 Stat. 677

Department of Commerce Appropriation Act, 1970

Pub. L. 91–153, title III, Dec. 24, 1969, 83 Stat. 412

Department of Commerce Appropriation Act, 1971

Pub. L. 91–472, title III, Oct. 21, 1970, 84 Stat. 1048

Department of Commerce Appropriation Act, 1972

Pub. L. 92–77, title III, Aug. 10, 1971, 85 Stat. 254

Department of Commerce Appropriation Act, 1973

Pub. L. 92–544, title III, Oct. 25, 1972, 86 Stat. 1118

Department of Commerce Appropriation Act, 1974

Pub. L. 93–162, title III, Nov. 27, 1973, 87 Stat. 645

Department of Commerce Appropriation Act, 1975

Pub. L. 93–433, title III, Oct. 5, 1974, 88 Stat. 1196

Department of Commerce Appropriation Act, 1976

Pub. L. 94–121, title III, Oct. 21, 1975, 89 Stat. 622

Department of Commerce Appropriation Act, 1977

Pub. L. 94–362, title III, July 14, 1976, 90 Stat. 947

Department of Commerce Appropriation Act, 1978

Pub. L. 95–86, title III, Aug. 2, 1977, 91 Stat. 429

Department of Commerce Appropriation Act, 1979

Pub. L. 95–431, title III, Oct. 10, 1978, 92 Stat. 1030

Department of Commerce Appropriation Act, 1980

Pub. L. 96–68, title III, Sept. 24, 1979, 93 Stat. 423

Department of Commerce Appropriation Act, 1986

Pub. L. 99–180, title I, Dec. 13, 1985, 99 Stat. 1136

Department of Commerce Appropriation Act, 1987

Pub. L. 99–500, §101(b) [title I], Oct. 18, 1986, 100 Stat. 1783–39, and Pub. L. 99–591, §101(b) [title I], Oct. 30, 1986, 100 Stat. 3341–39

Department of Commerce Appropriation Act, 1988

Pub. L. 100–202, §101(a) [title I], Dec. 22, 1987, 101 Stat. 1329–1

Department of Commerce Appropriations Act, 1989

Pub. L. 100–459, title I, Oct. 1, 1988, 102 Stat. 2186

Department of Commerce Appropriations Act, 1990

Pub. L. 101–162, title I, Nov. 21, 1989, 103 Stat. 988

Department of Commerce Appropriations Act, 1991

Pub. L. 101–515, title I, Nov. 5, 1990, 104 Stat. 2101

Department of Commerce Appropriations Act, 1992
Pub. L. 102–140, title II, Oct. 28, 1991, 105 Stat. 799

Department of Commerce Appropriations Act, 1993
Pub. L. 102–395, title II, Oct. 6, 1992, 106 Stat. 1848

Department of Commerce Appropriations Act, 1994
Pub. L. 103–121, title II, Oct. 27, 1993, 107 Stat. 1169

Department of Defense Appropriation Act, 1952
Oct. 18, 1951, ch. 512, 65 Stat. 423

Department of Defense Appropriation Act, 1953
July 10, 1952, ch. 630, 66 Stat. 517

Department of Defense Appropriation Act, 1954
Aug. 1, 1953, ch. 305, 67 Stat. 336

Department of Defense Appropriation Act, 1955
June 30, 1954, ch. 432, 68 Stat. 337

Department of Defense Appropriation Act, 1956
July 13, 1955, ch. 358, 69 Stat. 301

Department of Defense Appropriation Act, 1957
July 2, 1956, ch. 488, 70 Stat. 455

Department of Defense Appropriation Act, 1958
Pub. L. 85–117, Aug. 2, 1957, 71 Stat. 312

Department of Defense Appropriation Act, 1959
Pub. L. 85–724, Aug. 22, 1958, 72 Stat. 711

Department of Defense Appropriation Act, 1960
Pub. L. 86–166, Aug. 18, 1959, 73 Stat. 366

Department of Defense Appropriation Act, 1961
Pub. L. 86–601, July 7, 1960, 74 Stat. 338

Department of Defense Appropriation Act, 1962
Pub. L. 87–144, Aug. 17, 1961, 75 Stat. 365

Department of Defense Appropriation Act, 1963
Pub. L. 87–577, Aug. 9, 1962, 76 Stat. 318

Department of Defense Appropriation Act, 1964
Pub. L. 88–149, Oct. 17, 1963, 77 Stat. 254

Department of Defense Appropriation Act, 1965
Pub. L. 88–446, Aug. 19, 1964, 78 Stat. 465

Department of Defense Appropriation Act, 1966
Pub. L. 89–213, Sept. 29, 1965, 79 Stat. 863

Department of Defense Appropriation Act, 1967
Pub. L. 89–687, Oct. 15, 1966, 80 Stat. 980

Department of Defense Appropriation Act, 1968
Pub. L. 90–96, Sept. 29, 1967, 81 Stat. 231

Department of Defense Appropriation Act, 1969
Pub. L. 90–580, Oct. 17, 1968, 82 Stat. 1120

Department of Defense Appropriation Act, 1970
Pub. L. 91–171, Dec. 29, 1969, 83 Stat. 469

Department of Defense Appropriation Act, 1971
Pub. L. 91–668, Jan. 11, 1971, 84 Stat. 2020

Department of Defense Appropriation Act, 1972
Pub. L. 92–204, Dec. 18, 1971, 85 Stat. 716

Department of Defense Appropriation Act, 1973
Pub. L. 92–570, Oct. 26, 1972, 86 Stat. 1184

Department of Defense Appropriation Act, 1974
Pub. L. 93–238, Jan. 2, 1974, 87 Stat. 1026

Department of Defense Appropriation Act, 1975
Pub. L. 93–437, Oct. 8, 1974, 88 Stat. 1212

Department of Defense Appropriation Act, 1976
Pub. L. 94–212, Feb. 9, 1976, 90 Stat. 153

Department of Defense Appropriation Act, 1977
Pub. L. 94–419, Sept. 22, 1976, 90 Stat. 1279

Department of Defense Appropriation Act, 1978
Pub. L. 95–111, Sept. 21, 1977, 91 Stat. 886

Department of Defense Appropriation Act, 1979
Pub. L. 95–457, Oct. 13, 1978, 92 Stat. 1231

Department of Defense Appropriation Act, 1980
Pub. L. 96–154, Dec. 21, 1979, 93 Stat. 1139

Department of Defense Appropriation Act, 1981
Pub. L. 96–527, Dec. 15, 1980, 94 Stat. 3068

Department of Defense Appropriation Act, 1982
Pub. L. 97–114, Dec. 29, 1981, 95 Stat. 1565

Department of Defense Appropriation Act, 1983
Pub. L. 97–377, title I, § 101(c), Dec. 21, 1982, 96 Stat. 1833

Department of Defense Appropriation Act, 1984
Pub. L. 98–212, Dec. 8, 1983, 97 Stat. 1421

Department of Defense Appropriation Authorization Act, 1974
Pub. L. 93–155, Nov. 16, 1973, 87 Stat. 605

Department of Defense Appropriation Authorization Act, 1975
Pub. L. 93–365, Aug. 5, 1974, 88 Stat. 399

Department of Defense Appropriation Authorization Act, 1976
Pub. L. 94–106, Oct. 7, 1975, 89 Stat. 531

Department of Defense Appropriation Authorization Act, 1977
Pub. L. 94–361, July 14, 1976, 90 Stat. 923

Department of Defense Appropriation Authorization Act, 1978
Pub. L. 95–79, July 30, 1977, 91 Stat. 323

Department of Defense Appropriation Authorization Act, 1979
Pub. L. 95–485, Oct. 20, 1978, 92 Stat. 1611

Department of Defense Appropriations Act, 1985
Pub. L. 98–473, title I, § 101(h), Oct. 12, 1984, 98 Stat. 1904

Department of Defense Appropriations Act, 1986
Pub. L. 99–190, § 101(b), Dec. 19, 1985, 99 Stat. 1185

Department of Defense Appropriations Act, 1987
Pub. L. 99–500, § 101(c), Oct. 18, 1986, 100 Stat. 1783–82, and Pub. L. 99–591, § 101(c), Oct. 30, 1986, 100 Stat. 3341–82

Department of Defense Appropriations Act, 1988
Pub. L. 100–202, § 101(b), Dec. 22, 1987, 101 Stat. 1329–43

Department of Defense Appropriations Act, 1989
Pub. L. 100–463, Oct. 1, 1988, 102 Stat. 2270

Department of Defense Appropriations Act, 1990
Pub. L. 101–165, Nov. 21, 1989, 103 Stat. 1112

Department of Defense Appropriations Act, 1991
Pub. L. 101–511, Nov. 5, 1990, 104 Stat. 1856

Department of Defense Appropriations Act, 1992
Pub. L. 102–172, Nov. 26, 1991, 105 Stat. 1150

Department of Defense Appropriations Act, 1993
Pub. L. 102–396, Oct. 6, 1992, 106 Stat. 1876

Department of Defense Appropriations Act, 1994
Pub. L. 103–139, Nov. 11, 1993, 107 Stat. 1418

Department of Defense Appropriations Act, 1995
Pub. L. 103–335, titles I–VIII, Sept. 30, 1994, 108 Stat. 2599–2616

Department of Defense Appropriations Act, 1996
Pub. L. 104–61, Dec. 1, 1995, 109 Stat. 636

Department of Defense Appropriations Act, 1997
Pub. L. 104–208, div. A, title I, §101(b) [titles I–VIII], Sept. 30, 1996, 110 Stat. 3009–71 to 3009–87

Department of Defense Appropriations Act, 1998
Pub. L. 105–56, Oct. 8, 1997, 111 Stat. 1203

Department of Defense Appropriations Act, 1999
Pub. L. 105–262, Oct. 17, 1998, 112 Stat. 2279

Department of Defense Appropriations Act, 2000
Pub. L. 106–79, Oct. 25, 1999, 113 Stat. 1212

Department of Defense Appropriations Act, 2001
Pub. L. 106–259, Aug. 9, 2000, 114 Stat. 656

Department of Defense Authorization Act, 1980
Pub. L. 96–107, Nov. 9, 1979, 93 Stat. 803

Department of Defense Authorization Act, 1981
Pub. L. 96–342, Sept. 8, 1980, 94 Stat. 1077

Department of Defense Authorization Act, 1982
Pub. L. 97–86, Dec. 1, 1981, 95 Stat. 1099

Department of Defense Authorization Act, 1983
Pub. L. 97–252, Sept. 8, 1982, 96 Stat. 718

Department of Defense Authorization Act, 1984
Pub. L. 98–94, Sept. 24, 1983, 97 Stat. 614

Department of Defense Authorization Act, 1985
Pub. L. 98–525, Oct. 19, 1984, 98 Stat. 2492

Department of Defense Authorization Act, 1986
Pub. L. 99–145, Nov. 8, 1985, 99 Stat. 583

Department of Defense Authorization Act, 1987
Pub. L. 99–661, div. A, Nov. 14, 1986, 100 Stat. 3816

Department of Defense Civilian Intelligence Personnel Policy Act of 1996
Pub. L. 104–201, div. A, title XVI, subtitle B (§1631 et seq.), Sept. 23, 1996, 110 Stat. 2745
Short title, see 10 U.S.C. 1601 note

Department of Defense Reorganization Act of 1958
Pub. L. 85–599, Aug. 6, 1958, 72 Stat. 514

Department of Defense Supplemental Appropriation Authorization Act, 1974
Pub. L. 93–307, June 8, 1974, 88 Stat. 233

Department of Defense Supplemental Appropriation Authorization Act, 1978
Pub. L. 95–184, Nov. 15, 1977, 91 Stat. 1381

Department of Defense Supplemental Appropriation Authorization Act, 1979
Pub. L. 96–29, June 27, 1979, 93 Stat. 78

Department of Defense Supplemental Authorization Act, 1981
Pub. L. 97–39, Aug. 14, 1981, 95 Stat. 939

Department of Education Appropriation Act, 1983
Pub. L. 97–377, title I, §101(e)(1) [title III], Dec. 21, 1982, 96 Stat. 1878, 1895

Department of Education Appropriation Act, 1985
Pub. L. 98–619, title III, Nov. 8, 1984, 98 Stat. 3321

Department of Education Appropriation Act, 1986
Pub. L. 99–178, title III, Dec. 12, 1985, 99 Stat. 1120

Department of Education Appropriations Act, 1987
Pub. L. 99–500, §101(i) [H.R. 5233, title III], Oct. 18, 1986, 100 Stat. 1783–287, and Pub. L. 99–591, §101(i) [H.R. 5233, title III], Oct. 30, 1986, 100 Stat. 3341–287; Pub. L. 100–202, §106, Dec. 22, 1987, 101 Stat. 1329–433

Department of Education Appropriations Act, 1988
Pub. L. 100–202, §101(h) [title III], Dec. 22, 1987, 101 Stat. 1329–256, 1329–275

Department of Education Appropriations Act, 1989
Pub. L. 100–436, title III, Sept. 20, 1988, 102 Stat. 1701

Department of Education Appropriations Act, 1990
Pub. L. 101–166, title III, Nov. 21, 1989, 103 Stat. 1179

Department of Education Appropriations Act, 1991
Pub. L. 101–517, title III, Nov. 5, 1990, 104 Stat. 2210

Department of Education Appropriations Act, 1992
Pub. L. 102–170, title III, Nov. 26, 1991, 105 Stat. 1128

Department of Education Appropriations Act, 1993
Pub. L. 102–394, title III, Oct. 6, 1992, 106 Stat. 1813

Department of Education Appropriations Act, 1994
Pub. L. 103–112, title III, Oct. 21, 1993, 107 Stat. 1100

Department of Education Appropriations Act, 1995

Pub. L. 103–333, title III, Sept. 30, 1994, 108 Stat. 2562

Department of Education Appropriations Act, 1996

Pub. L. 104–134, title I, §101(d) [title III], Apr. 26, 1996, 110 Stat. 1321–211, 1321–229

Department of Education Appropriations Act, 1997

Pub. L. 104–208, div. A, title I, §101(e) [title III], Sept. 30, 1996, 110 Stat. 3009–233, 3009–255

Department of Education Appropriations Act, 1998

Pub. L. 105–78, title III, Nov. 13, 1997, 111 Stat. 1496

Department of Education Appropriations Act, 1999

Pub. L. 105–277, div. A, §101(f) [title III], Oct. 21, 1998, 112 Stat. 2681–337, 2681–363

Department of Education Appropriations Act, 2000

Pub. L. 106–113, div. B, §1000(a)(4) [title III], Nov. 29, 1999, 113 Stat. 1535, 1501A–242

Department of Education Appropriations Act, 2001

Pub. L. 106–554, §1(a)(1) [title III], Dec. 21, 2000, 114 Stat. 2763, 2763A–30

Department of Education Organization Act

Pub. L. 96–88, Oct. 17, 1979, 93 Stat. 668 (20 U.S.C. 3401 et seq.)

Short title, see 20 U.S.C. 3401 note

Department of Energy Act of 1978—Civilian Applications

Pub. L. 95–238, Feb. 25, 1978, 92 Stat. 47

Department of Energy Facilities Safeguards, Security, and Counterintelligence Enhancement Act of 1999

Pub. L. 106–65, div. C, title XXXI, subtitle D (§3141 et seq.), Oct. 5, 1999, 113 Stat. 931 (42 U.S.C. 7383 et seq.)

Short title, see 42 U.S.C. 7383 note

Department of Energy Metal Casting Competitiveness Research Act of 1990

Pub. L. 101–425, Oct. 15, 1990, 104 Stat. 915 (15 U.S.C. 5301 et seq.)

Short title, see 15 U.S.C. 5301 note

Department of Energy National Security and Military Applications of Nuclear Energy Authorization Act of 1979

Pub. L. 95–509, Oct. 24, 1978, 92 Stat. 1775

Department of Energy National Security and Military Applications of Nuclear Energy Authorization Act of 1980

Pub. L. 96–164, Dec. 29, 1979, 93 Stat. 1259

Department of Energy National Security and Military Applications of Nuclear Energy Authorization Act of 1981

Pub. L. 96–540, Dec. 17, 1980, 94 Stat. 3197

Department of Energy National Security and Military Applications of Nuclear Energy Authorization Act of 1982

Pub. L. 97–90, Dec. 4, 1981, 95 Stat. 1163

Department of Energy National Security and Military Applications of Nuclear Energy Authorization Act of 1985

Pub. L. 98–525, title XVI, Oct. 19, 1984, 98 Stat. 2639

Department of Energy National Security and Military Applications of Nuclear Energy Authorization Act of 1986

Pub. L. 99–145, title XV, Nov. 8, 1985, 99 Stat. 766

Department of Energy National Security and Military Applications of Nuclear Energy Authorization Act of 1987

Pub. L. 99–661, div. C, title I, Nov. 14, 1986, 100 Stat. 4055

Department of Energy National Security and Military Applications of Nuclear Energy Authorization Act of 1988

Pub. L. 100–180, div. C, title I, Dec. 4, 1987, 101 Stat. 1231

Department of Energy Organization Act

Pub. L. 95–91, Aug. 4, 1977, 91 Stat. 565 (42 U.S.C. 7101 et seq.)

Short title, see 42 U.S.C. 7101 note

Department of Energy Science Education Enhancement Act

Pub. L. 101–510, div. C, title XXXI, part E (§3161 et seq.), Nov. 5, 1990, 104 Stat. 1840 (42 U.S.C. 7381 et seq.)

Short title, see 42 U.S.C. 7381 note

Department of Energy Standardization Act of 1997

Pub. L. 105–28, July 18, 1997, 111 Stat. 245

Short title, see 42 U.S.C. 7101 note

Department of Health and Human Services Appropriation Act, 1983

Pub. L. 97–377, title I, §101(e)(1) [title II], Dec. 21, 1982, 96 Stat. 1878, 1884

Department of Health and Human Services Appropriation Act, 1985

Pub. L. 98–619, title II, Nov. 8, 1984, 98 Stat. 3311

Department of Health and Human Services Appropriation Act, 1986

Pub. L. 99–178, title II, Dec. 12, 1985, 99 Stat. 1109

Department of Health and Human Services Appropriations Act, 1987

Pub. L. 99–500, §101(i) [H.R. 5233, title II], Oct. 18, 1986, 100 Stat. 1783–287, and Pub. L. 99–591, §101(i) [H.R. 5233, title II], Oct. 30, 1986, 100 Stat. 3341–287; Pub. L. 100–202, §106, Dec. 22, 1987, 101 Stat. 1329–433

Department of Health and Human Services Appropriations Act, 1988

Pub. L. 100–202, §101(h) [title II], Dec. 22, 1987, 101 Stat. 1329–256, 1329–263

Department of Health and Human Services Appropriations Act, 1989
Pub. L. 100–436, title II, Sept. 20, 1988, 102 Stat. 1688

Department of Health and Human Services Appropriations Act, 1990
Pub. L. 101–166, title II, Nov. 21, 1989, 103 Stat. 1166

Department of Health and Human Services Appropriations Act, 1991
Pub. L. 101–517, title II, Nov. 5, 1990, 104 Stat. 2197

Department of Health and Human Services Appropriations Act, 1992
Pub. L. 102–170, title II, Nov. 26, 1991, 105 Stat. 1114

Department of Health and Human Services Appropriations Act, 1993
Pub. L. 102–394, title II, Oct. 6, 1992, 106 Stat. 1799

Department of Health and Human Services Appropriations Act, 1994
Pub. L. 103–112, title II, Oct. 21, 1993, 107 Stat. 1089

Department of Health and Human Services Appropriations Act, 1995
Pub. L. 103–333, title II, Sept. 30, 1994, 108 Stat. 2549

Department of Health and Human Services Appropriations Act, 1996
Pub. L. 104–134, title I, §101(d) [title II], Apr. 26, 1996, 110 Stat. 1321–211, 1321–221

Department of Health and Human Services Appropriations Act, 1997
Pub. L. 104–208, div. A, title I, §101(e) [title II], Sept. 30, 1996, 110 Stat. 3009–233, 3009–242

Department of Health and Human Services Appropriations Act, 1998
Pub. L. 105–78, title II, Nov. 13, 1997, 111 Stat. 1477

Department of Health and Human Services Appropriations Act, 1999
Pub. L. 105–277, div. A, §101(f) [title II], Oct. 21, 1998, 112 Stat. 2681–337, 2681–347

Department of Health and Human Services Appropriations Act, 2000
Pub. L. 106–113, div. B, §1000(a)(4) [title II], Nov. 29, 1999, 113 Stat. 1535, 1501A–225

Department of Health and Human Services Appropriations Act, 2001
Pub. L. 106–554, §1(a)(1) [title II], Dec. 21, 2000, 114 Stat. 2763, 2763A–12

Department of Health, Education, and Welfare Appropriation Act, 1954
July 31, 1953, ch. 296, title II, 67 Stat. 248

Department of Health, Education, and Welfare Appropriation Act, 1955
July 2, 1954, ch. 457, title II, 68 Stat. 437

Department of Health, Education, and Welfare Appropriation Act, 1956
Aug. 1, 1955, ch. 437, title II, 69 Stat. 401

Department of Health, Education, and Welfare Appropriation Act, 1957
June 29, 1956, ch. 477, title II, 70 Stat. 427

Department of Health, Education, and Welfare Appropriation Act, 1958
Pub. L. 85–67, title II, June 29, 1957, 71 Stat. 214

Department of Health, Education, and Welfare Appropriation Act, 1959
Pub. L. 85–580, title II, Aug. 1, 1958, 72 Stat. 461

Department of Health, Education, and Welfare Appropriation Act, 1960
Pub. L. 86–158, title II, Aug. 14, 1959, 73 Stat. 343

Department of Health, Education, and Welfare Appropriation Act, 1961
Pub. L. 86–703, title II, Sept. 2, 1960, 74 Stat. 760

Department of Health, Education, and Welfare Appropriation Act, 1962
Pub. L. 87–290, title II, Sept. 22, 1961, 75 Stat. 594

Department of Health, Education, and Welfare Appropriation Act, 1963
Pub. L. 87–582, title II, Aug. 14, 1962, 76 Stat. 366

Department of Health, Education, and Welfare Appropriation Act, 1964
Pub. L. 88–136, title II, Oct. 11, 1963, 77 Stat. 229

Department of Health, Education, and Welfare Appropriation Act, 1965
Pub. L. 88–605, title II, Sept. 19, 1964, 78 Stat. 963

Department of Health, Education, and Welfare Appropriation Act, 1966
Pub. L. 89–156, title II, Aug. 31, 1965, 79 Stat. 593

Department of Health, Education, and Welfare Appropriation Act, 1967
Pub. L. 89–787, title II, Nov. 7, 1966, 80 Stat. 1382

Department of Health, Education, and Welfare Appropriation Act, 1968
Pub. L. 90–132, title II, Nov. 8, 1967, 81 Stat. 390

Department of Health, Education, and Welfare Appropriation Act, 1969
Pub. L. 90–557, title II, Oct. 11, 1968, 82 Stat. 974

Department of Health, Education, and Welfare Appropriation Act, 1970
Pub. L. 91–204, title II, Mar. 5, 1970, 84 Stat. 27

Department of Health, Education, and Welfare Appropriation Act, 1971
Pub. L. 91–667, title II, Jan. 11, 1971, 84 Stat. 2005

Department of Health, Education, and Welfare Appropriation Act, 1972
Pub. L. 92–80, title II, Aug. 10, 1971, 85 Stat. 289

Department of Health, Education, and Welfare Appropriation Act, 1974
Pub. L. 93–192, title II, Dec. 18, 1973, 87 Stat. 749

Department of Health, Education, and Welfare Appropriation Act, 1979
Pub. L. 95–480, title II, Oct. 18, 1978, 92 Stat. 1571

Department of Housing and Urban Development Act
Pub. L. 89–174, Sept. 9, 1965, 79 Stat. 667 (42 U.S.C. 3531 et seq.)
Short title, see 42 U.S.C. 3531 note

Department of Housing and Urban Development Reform Act of 1989
Pub. L. 101–235, Dec. 15, 1989, 103 Stat. 1987
Short title, see 42 U.S.C. 3531 note

Department of Housing and Urban Development—Independent Agencies Appropriation Act, 1976
Pub. L. 94–116, Oct. 17, 1975, 89 Stat. 581

Department of Housing and Urban Development—Independent Agencies Appropriation Act, 1977
Pub. L. 94–378, Aug. 9, 1976, 90 Stat. 1095

Department of Housing and Urban Development—Independent Agencies Appropriation Act, 1978
Pub. L. 95–119, Oct. 4, 1977, 91 Stat. 1073

Department of Housing and Urban Development—Independent Agencies Appropriation Act, 1979
Pub. L. 95–392, Sept. 30, 1978, 92 Stat. 791

Department of Housing and Urban Development—Independent Agencies Appropriation Act, 1980
Pub. L. 96–103, Nov. 5, 1979, 93 Stat. 771

Department of Housing and Urban Development—Independent Agencies Appropriation Act, 1981
Pub. L. 96–526, Dec. 15, 1980, 94 Stat. 3044

Department of Housing and Urban Development—Independent Agencies Appropriation Act, 1982
Pub. L. 97–101, Dec. 23, 1981, 95 Stat. 1417

Department of Housing and Urban Development—Independent Agencies Appropriation Act, 1983
Pub. L. 97–272, Sept. 30, 1982, 96 Stat. 1160

Department of Housing and Urban Development—Independent Agencies Appropriation Act, 1984
Pub. L. 98–45, July 12, 1983, 97 Stat. 219

Department of Housing and Urban Development—Independent Agencies Appropriation Act, 1985
Pub. L. 98–371, July 18, 1984, 98 Stat. 1213

Department of Housing and Urban Development—Independent Agencies Appropriations Act, 1986
Pub. L. 99–160, Nov. 25, 1985, 99 Stat. 909

Department of Housing and Urban Development—Independent Agencies Appropriations Act, 1987
Pub. L. 99–500, §101(g) [H.R. 5313], Oct. 18, 1986, 100 Stat. 1783–242, and Pub. L. 99–591, §101(g) [H.R. 5313], Oct. 30, 1986, 100 Stat. 3341–242; Pub. L. 100–202, §106, Dec. 22, 1987, 101 Stat. 1329–433

Department of Housing and Urban Development—Independent Agencies Appropriations Act, 1988
Pub. L. 100–202, §101(f), Dec. 22, 1987, 101 Stat. 1329–187

Department of Housing and Urban Development—Independent Agencies Appropriations Act, 1989
Pub. L. 100–404, Aug. 19, 1988, 102 Stat. 1014

Department of Housing and Urban Development; Space, Science, Veterans, and Certain Other Independent Agencies Appropriation Act, 1972
Pub. L. 92–78, Aug. 10, 1971, 85 Stat. 271

Department of Housing and Urban Development; Space, Science, Veterans, and Certain Other Independent Agencies Appropriation Act, 1973
Pub. L. 92–383, Aug. 14, 1972, 86 Stat. 540

Department of Housing and Urban Development; Space, Science, Veterans, and Certain Other Independent Agencies Appropriation Act, 1974
Pub. L. 93–137, Oct. 26, 1973, 87 Stat. 491

Department of Housing and Urban Development; Space, Science, Veterans, and Certain Other Independent Agencies Appropriation Act, 1975
Pub. L. 93–414, Sept. 6, 1974, 88 Stat. 1095

Department of Justice and Related Agencies Appropriation Act, 1984
Pub. L. 98–166, title II, Nov. 28, 1983, 97 Stat. 1080

Department of Justice and Related Agencies Appropriation Act, 1985
Pub. L. 98–411, title II, Aug. 30, 1984, 98 Stat. 1553

Department of Justice and Related Agencies Appropriations Act, 1992
Pub. L. 102–140, title I, Oct. 28, 1991, 105 Stat. 782

Department of Justice and Related Agencies Appropriations Act, 1993
Pub. L. 102–395, title I, Oct. 6, 1992, 106 Stat. 1828

Department of Justice and Related Agencies Appropriations Act, 1994
Pub. L. 103–121, title I, Oct. 27, 1993, 107 Stat. 1153

Department of Justice and Related Agencies Appropriations Act, 1995
Pub. L. 103–317, title I, Aug. 26, 1994, 108 Stat. 1724

Department of Justice Appropriation Act, 1940
June 29, 1939, ch. 248, title II, 53 Stat. 896

Department of Justice Appropriation Act, 1941
May 14, 1940, ch. 189, title III, 54 Stat. 200

Department of Justice Appropriation Act, 1942
June 28, 1941, ch. 258, title III, 55 Stat. 289

Department of Justice Appropriation Act, 1943
July 2, 1942, ch. 472, title II, 56 Stat. 480

Department of Justice Appropriation Act, 1944
July 1, 1943, ch. 182, title II, 57 Stat. 283

Department of Justice Appropriation Act, 1945
June 28, 1944, ch. 294, title II, 58 Stat. 407

Department of Justice Appropriation Act, 1946
May 21, 1945, ch. 129, title II, 59 Stat. 181

Department of Justice Appropriation Act, 1947
July 5, 1946, ch. 541, title II, 60 Stat. 458

Department of Justice Appropriation Act, 1948
July 9, 1947, ch. 211, title II, 61 Stat. 289

Department of Justice Appropriation Act, 1949
June 3, 1948, ch. 400, title II, 62 Stat. 316

Department of Justice Appropriation Act, 1950
July 20, 1949, ch. 354, title II, 63 Stat. 457

Department of Justice Appropriation Act, 1951
Sept. 6, 1950, ch. 896, Ch. III, title II, 64 Stat. 615

Department of Justice Appropriation Act, 1952
Oct. 22, 1951, ch. 533, title II, 65 Stat. 582

Department of Justice Appropriation Act, 1953
July 10, 1952, ch. 651, title II, 66 Stat. 556

Department of Justice Appropriation Act, 1954
Aug. 5, 1953, ch. 328, title II, 67 Stat. 372

Department of Justice Appropriation Act, 1955
July 2, 1954, ch. 456, title II, 68 Stat. 419

Department of Justice Appropriation Act, 1956
July 7, 1955, ch. 279, title II, 69 Stat. 270

Department of Justice Appropriation Act, 1957
June 20, 1956, ch. 414, title II, 70 Stat. 305

Department of Justice Appropriation Act, 1958
Pub. L. 85–49, title II, June 11, 1957, 71 Stat. 60

Department of Justice Appropriation Act, 1959
Pub. L. 85–474, title II, June 30, 1958, 72 Stat. 249

Department of Justice Appropriation Act, 1960
Pub. L. 86–84, title II, July 13, 1959, 73 Stat. 187

Department of Justice Appropriation Act, 1961
Pub. L. 86–678, title II, Aug. 31, 1960, 74 Stat. 561

Department of Justice Appropriation Act, 1962
Pub. L. 87–264, title II, Sept. 21, 1961, 75 Stat. 550

Department of Justice Appropriation Act, 1963
Pub. L. 87–843, title II, Oct. 18, 1962, 76 Stat. 1085

Department of Justice Appropriation Act, 1964
Pub. L. 88–245, title II, Dec. 30, 1963, 77 Stat. 781

Department of Justice Appropriation Act, 1965
Pub. L. 88–527, title II, Aug. 31, 1964, 78 Stat. 716

Department of Justice Appropriation Act, 1966
Pub. L. 89–164, title II, Sept. 2, 1965, 79 Stat. 625

Department of Justice Appropriation Act, 1967
Pub. L. 89–797, title II, Nov. 8, 1966, 80 Stat. 1484

Department of Justice Appropriation Act, 1969
Pub. L. 90–470, title II, Aug. 9, 1968, 82 Stat. 673

Department of Justice Appropriation Act, 1970
Pub. L. 91–153, title II, Dec. 24, 1969, 83 Stat. 408

Department of Justice Appropriation Act, 1971
Pub. L. 91–472, title II, Oct. 21, 1970, 84 Stat. 1045

Department of Justice Appropriation Act, 1972
Pub. L. 92–77, title II, Aug. 10, 1971, 85 Stat. 251

Department of Justice Appropriation Act, 1973
Pub. L. 92–544, title II, Oct. 25, 1972, 86 Stat. 1114

Department of Justice Appropriation Act, 1974
Pub. L. 93–162, title II, Nov. 27, 1973, 87 Stat. 641

Department of Justice Appropriation Act, 1975
Pub. L. 93–433, title II, Oct. 5, 1974, 88 Stat. 1192

Department of Justice Appropriation Act, 1976
Pub. L. 94–121, title II, Oct. 21, 1975, 89 Stat. 617

Department of Justice Appropriation Act, 1977
Pub. L. 94–362, title II, July 14, 1976, 90 Stat. 943

Department of Justice Appropriation Act, 1978
Pub. L. 95–86, title II, Aug. 2, 1977, 91 Stat. 424

Department of Justice Appropriation Act, 1979
Pub. L. 95–431, title II, Oct. 10, 1978, 92 Stat. 1025

Department of Justice Appropriation Act, 1980
Pub. L. 96–68, title II, Sept. 24, 1979, 93 Stat. 419

Department of Justice Appropriation Act, 1986
Pub. L. 99–180, title II, Dec. 13, 1985, 99 Stat. 1141

Department of Justice Appropriation Act, 1987
Pub. L. 99–500, §101(b) [title II], Oct. 18, 1986, 100 Stat. 1783–39, 1783–45, and Pub. L. 99–591, §101(b) [title II], Oct. 30, 1986, 100 Stat. 3341–39, 3341–45

Department of Justice Appropriation Act, 1988
Pub. L. 100–202, §101(a) [title II], Dec. 22, 1987, 101 Stat. 1329, 1329–8

Department of Justice Appropriation Authorization Act, Fiscal Year 1979
Pub. L. 95–624, Nov. 9, 1978, 92 Stat. 3459

Department of Justice Appropriation Authorization Act, Fiscal Year 1980
Pub. L. 96–132, Nov. 30, 1979, 93 Stat. 1040

Department of Justice Appropriations Act, 1989
Pub. L. 100–459, title II, Oct. 1, 1988, 102 Stat. 2192

Department of Justice Appropriations Act, 1990
Pub. L. 101–162, title II, Nov. 21, 1989, 103 Stat. 995

Department of Justice Appropriations Act, 1991
Pub. L. 101–515, title II, Nov. 5, 1990, 104 Stat. 2109

Department of Justice Appropriations Act, 1996
Pub. L. 104–134, title I, §101[(a)] [title I], Apr. 26, 1996, 110 Stat. 1321; renumbered title I, Pub. L. 104–140, §1(a), May 2, 1996, 110 Stat. 1327

Department of Justice Appropriations Act, 1997
Pub. L. 104–208, div. A, title I, §101(a) [title I], Sept. 30, 1996, 110 Stat. 3009

Department of Justice Appropriations Act, 1998
Pub. L. 105–119, title I, Nov. 26, 1997, 111 Stat. 2440

Department of Justice Appropriations Act, 1999
Pub. L. 105–277, div. A, §101(b) [title I], Oct. 21, 1998, 112 Stat. 2681–50

Department of Justice Appropriations Act, 2000
Pub. L. 106–113, div. B, §1000(a)(1) [title I], Nov. 29, 1999, 113 Stat. 1535, 1501A–3

Department of Justice Appropriations Act, 2001
Pub. L. 106–553, §1(a)(2) [title I], Dec. 21, 2000, 114 Stat. 2762, 2762A–51

Department of Justice Assets Forfeiture Fund Amendments Act of 1986
Pub. L. 99–570, title I, subtitle D (§1151 et seq.), Oct. 27, 1986, 100 Stat. 3207–12
Short title, see 28 U.S.C. 1 note

Department of Labor Appropriation Act, 1940
June 29, 1939, ch. 249, 53 Stat. 920

Department of Labor Appropriation Act, 1941
June 26, 1940, ch. 428, title I, 54 Stat. 574

Department of Labor Appropriation Act, 1942
July 1, 1941, ch. 269, title I, 55 Stat. 466

Department of Labor Appropriation Act, 1943
July 2, 1942, ch. 475, title I, 56 Stat. 562

Department of Labor Appropriation Act, 1944
July 12, 1943, ch. 221, title I, 57 Stat. 494

Department of Labor Appropriation Act, 1945
June 28, 1944, ch. 302, title I, 58 Stat. 547

Department of Labor Appropriation Act, 1946
July 3, 1945, ch. 263, title I, 59 Stat. 361

Department of Labor Appropriation Act, 1947
July 26, 1946, ch. 672, title I, 60 Stat. 679

Department of Labor Appropriation Act, 1948
July 8, 1947, ch. 210, title I, 61 Stat. 261

Department of Labor Appropriation Act, 1949
June 14, 1948, ch. 465, title I, 62 Stat. 394

Department of Labor Appropriation Act, 1950
June 29, 1949, ch. 275, title I, 63 Stat. 283

Department of Labor Appropriation Act, 1951
Sept. 6, 1950, ch. 896, Ch. V, title I, 64 Stat. 642

Department of Labor Appropriation Act, 1952
Aug. 31, 1951, ch. 373, title I, 65 Stat. 209

Department of Labor Appropriation Act, 1953
July 5, 1952, ch. 575, title I, 66 Stat. 358

Department of Labor Appropriation Act, 1954
July 31, 1953, ch. 296, title I, 67 Stat. 245

Department of Labor Appropriation Act, 1955
July 2, 1954, ch. 457, title I, 68 Stat. 434

Department of Labor Appropriation Act, 1956
Aug. 1, 1955, ch. 437, title I, 69 Stat. 397

Department of Labor Appropriation Act, 1957
June 29, 1956, ch. 477, title I, 70 Stat. 423

Department of Labor Appropriation Act, 1958
Pub. L. 85–67, title I, June 29, 1957, 71 Stat. 210

Department of Labor Appropriation Act, 1959
Pub. L. 85–580, title I, Aug. 1, 1958, 72 Stat. 457

Department of Labor Appropriation Act, 1960
Pub. L. 86–158, title I, Aug. 14, 1959, 73 Stat. 339

Department of Labor Appropriation Act, 1961
Pub. L. 86–703, title I, Sept. 2, 1960, 74 Stat. 755

Department of Labor Appropriation Act, 1962
Pub. L. 87–290, title I, Sept. 22, 1961, 75 Stat. 589

Department of Labor Appropriation Act, 1963
Pub. L. 87–582, title I, Aug. 14, 1962, 76 Stat. 361

Department of Labor Appropriation Act, 1964
Pub. L. 88–136, title I, Oct. 11, 1963, 77 Stat. 224

Department of Labor Appropriation Act, 1965
Pub. L. 88–605, title I, Sept. 19, 1964, 78 Stat. 959

Department of Labor Appropriation Act, 1966
Pub. L. 89–156, title I, Aug. 31, 1965, 79 Stat. 589

Department of Labor Appropriation Act, 1967
Pub. L. 89–787, title I, Nov. 7, 1966, 80 Stat. 1378

Department of Labor Appropriation Act, 1968
Pub. L. 90–132, title I, Nov. 8, 1967, 81 Stat. 386

Department of Labor Appropriation Act, 1969
Pub. L. 90–557, title I, Oct. 11, 1968, 82 Stat. 970

Department of Labor Appropriation Act, 1970
Pub. L. 91–204, title I, Mar. 5, 1970, 84 Stat. 23

Department of Labor Appropriation Act, 1971
Pub. L. 91–667, title I, Jan. 11, 1971, 84 Stat. 2001

Department of Labor Appropriation Act, 1972
Pub. L. 92–80, title I, Aug. 10, 1971, 85 Stat. 285

Department of Labor Appropriation Act, 1974
Pub. L. 93–192, title I, Dec. 18, 1973, 87 Stat. 747

Department of Labor Appropriation Act, 1976
Pub. L. 94–206, title I, Jan. 28, 1976, 90 Stat. 3

Department of Labor Appropriation Act, 1977
Pub. L. 94–439, title I, Sept. 30, 1976, 90 Stat. 1418

Department of Labor Appropriation Act, 1979
Pub. L. 95–480, title I, Oct. 18, 1978, 92 Stat. 1567

Department of Labor Appropriation Act, 1983
Pub. L. 97–377, title I, §101(e)(1) [title I], Dec. 21, 1982, 96 Stat. 1878

Department of Labor Appropriation Act, 1984
Pub. L. 98–139, title I, Oct. 31, 1983, 97 Stat. 871

Department of Labor Appropriation Act, 1985
Pub. L. 98–619, title I, Nov. 8, 1984, 98 Stat. 3305

Department of Labor Appropriation Act, 1986
Pub. L. 99–178, title I, Dec. 12, 1985, 99 Stat. 1102

Department of Labor Appropriations Act, 1987
Pub. L. 99–500, §101(i) [H.R. 5233, title I], Oct. 18, 1986, 100 Stat. 1783–287, and Pub. L. 99–591, §101(i) [H.R. 5233, title I], Oct. 30, 1986, 100 Stat. 3341–287; Pub. L. 100–202, §106, Dec. 22, 1987, 101 Stat. 1329–433

Department of Labor Appropriations Act, 1988
Pub. L. 100–202, §101(h) [title I], Dec. 22, 1987, 101 Stat. 1329–256

Department of Labor Appropriations Act, 1989
Pub. L. 100–436, title I, Sept. 20, 1988, 102 Stat. 1680

Department of Labor Appropriations Act, 1990
Pub. L. 101–166, title I, Nov. 21, 1989, 103 Stat. 1159

Department of Labor Appropriations Act, 1991
Pub. L. 101–517, title I, Nov. 5, 1990, 104 Stat. 2190

Department of Labor Appropriations Act, 1992
Pub. L. 102–170, title I, Nov. 26, 1991, 105 Stat. 1107

Department of Labor Appropriations Act, 1993
Pub. L. 102–394, title I, Oct. 6, 1992, 106 Stat. 1792

Department of Labor Appropriations Act, 1994
Pub. L. 103–112, title I, Oct. 21, 1993, 107 Stat. 1082

Department of Labor Appropriations Act, 1995
Pub. L. 103–333, title I, Sept. 30, 1994, 108 Stat. 2539

Department of Labor Appropriations Act, 1996
Pub. L. 104–134, title I, §101(d) [title I], Apr. 26, 1996, 110 Stat. 1321–211

Department of Labor Appropriations Act, 1997
Pub. L. 104–208, div. A, title I, §101(e) [title I], Sept. 30, 1996, 110 Stat. 3009–233

Department of Labor Appropriations Act, 1998
Pub. L. 105–78, title I, Nov. 13, 1997, 111 Stat. 1467

Department of Labor Appropriations Act, 1999
Pub. L. 105–277, div. A, §101(f) [title I], Oct. 21, 1998, 112 Stat. 2681–337

Department of Labor Appropriations Act, 2000
Pub. L. 106–113, div. B, §1000(a)(4) [title I], Nov. 29, 1999, 113 Stat. 1535, 1501A–217

Department of Labor Appropriations Act, 2001
Pub. L. 106–554, §1(a)(1) [title I], Dec. 21, 2000, 114 Stat. 2763, 2763A–3

Department of Labor Executive Level Conforming Amendments of 1986
Pub. L. 99–619, Nov. 6, 1986, 100 Stat. 3491
Short title, see 29 U.S.C. 551 note

Departments of Labor, and Health, Education, and Welfare Appropriation Act, 1971
Pub. L. 91–667, Jan. 11, 1971, 84 Stat. 2001

Departments of Labor, and Health, Education, and Welfare, and Related Agencies Appropriation Act, 1970
Pub. L. 91–204, Mar. 5, 1970, 84 Stat. 23

Department of State and Related Agencies Appropriation Act, 1984
Pub. L. 98–166, title III, Nov. 28, 1983, 97 Stat. 1092

Department of State and Related Agencies Appropriation Act, 1985
Pub. L. 98–411, title III, Aug. 30, 1984, 98 Stat. 1564

Department of State and Related Agencies Appropriations Act, 1992
Pub. L. 102–140, title V, Oct. 28, 1991, 105 Stat. 816

Department of State and Related Agencies Appropriations Act, 1993
Pub. L. 102–395, title V, Oct. 6, 1992, 106 Stat. 1864

Department of State and Related Agencies Appropriations Act, 1994
Pub. L. 103–121, title V, Oct. 27, 1993, 107 Stat. 1185

Department of State and Related Agencies Appropriations Act, 1995
Pub. L. 103–317, title V, Aug. 26, 1994, 108 Stat. 1760

Department of State and Related Agencies Appropriations Act, 1996
Pub. L. 104–134, title I, §101[(a)] [title IV], Apr. 26, 1996, 110 Stat. 1321, 1321–36

Department of State and Related Agencies Appropriations Act, 1997
Pub. L. 104–208, div. A, title I, §101(a) [title IV], Sept. 30, 1996, 110 Stat. 3009, 3009–46

Department of State and Related Agencies Appropriations Act, 1998
Pub. L. 105–119, title IV, Nov. 26, 1997, 111 Stat. 2494

Department of State and Related Agencies Appropriations Act, 1999
Pub. L. 105–277, div. A, §101(b) [title IV], Oct. 21, 1998, 112 Stat. 2681–50, 2681–92

Department of State and Related Agency Appropriations Act, 2000
Pub. L. 106–113, div. B, §1000(a)(1) [title IV], Nov. 29, 1999, 113 Stat. 1535, 1501A–38

Department of State and Related Agency Appropriations Act, 2001
Pub. L. 106–553, §1(a)(2) [title IV], Dec. 21, 2000, 114 Stat. 2762, 2762A–90

Department of State Appropriation Act, 1937
May 15, 1936, ch. 405, title I, 49 Stat. 1309

Department of State Appropriation Act, 1940
June 29, 1939, ch. 248, title I, 53 Stat. 885

Department of State Appropriation Act, 1941
May 14, 1940, ch. 189, title I, 54 Stat. 181

Department of State Appropriation Act, 1942
June 28, 1941, ch. 258, title I, 55 Stat. 265

Department of State Appropriation Act, 1943
July 2, 1942, ch. 472, title I, 56 Stat. 468

Department of State Appropriation Act, 1944
July 1, 1943, ch. 182, title I, 57 Stat. 271

Department of State Appropriation Act, 1945
June 28, 1944, ch. 294, title I, 58 Stat. 395

Department of State Appropriation Act, 1946
May 21, 1945, ch. 129, title I, 59 Stat. 169

Department of State Appropriation Act, 1947
July 5, 1946, ch. 541, title I, 60 Stat. 446

Department of State Appropriation Act, 1948
July 9, 1947, ch. 211, title I, 61 Stat. 279

Department of State Appropriation Act, 1949
June 3, 1948, ch. 400, title I, 62 Stat. 305

Department of State Appropriation Act, 1950
July 20, 1949, ch. 354, title I, 63 Stat. 447

Department of State Appropriation Act, 1951
Sept. 6, 1950, ch. 896, Ch. III, title I, 64 Stat. 609

Department of State Appropriation Act, 1952
Oct. 22, 1951, ch. 533, title I, 65 Stat. 575

Department of State Appropriation Act, 1953
July 10, 1952, ch. 651, title I, 66 Stat. 549

Department of State Appropriation Act, 1954
Aug. 5, 1953, ch. 328, title I, 67 Stat. 367

Department of State Appropriation Act, 1955
July 2, 1954, ch. 456, title I, 68 Stat. 413

Department of State Appropriation Act, 1956
July 7, 1955, ch. 279, title I, 69 Stat. 264

Department of State Appropriation Act, 1957
June 20, 1956, ch. 414, title I, 70 Stat. 299

Department of State Appropriation Act, 1958
Pub. L. 85–49, title I, June 11, 1957, 71 Stat. 55

Department of State Appropriation Act, 1959
Pub. L. 85–474, title I, June 30, 1958, 72 Stat. 244

Department of State Appropriation Act, 1960
Pub. L. 86–84, title I, July 13, 1959, 73 Stat. 182

Department of State Appropriation Act, 1961
Pub. L. 86–678, title I, Aug. 31, 1960, 74 Stat. 555

Department of State Appropriation Act, 1962
Pub. L. 87–264, title I, Sept. 21, 1961, 75 Stat. 545

Department of State Appropriation Act, 1963
Pub. L. 87–843, title I, Oct. 18, 1962, 76 Stat. 1080

Department of State Appropriation Act, 1964
Pub. L. 88–245, title I, Dec. 30, 1963, 77 Stat. 776

Department of State Appropriation Act, 1965
Pub. L. 88–527, title I, Aug. 31, 1964, 78 Stat. 711

Department of State Appropriation Act, 1966
Pub. L. 89–164, title I, Sept. 2, 1965, 79 Stat. 620

Department of State Appropriation Act, 1967
Pub. L. 89–797, title I, Nov. 8, 1966, 80 Stat. 1479

Department of State Appropriation Act, 1968
Pub. L. 90–133, title I, Nov. 8, 1967, 81 Stat. 411

Department of State Appropriation Act, 1969
Pub. L. 90–470, title I, Aug. 9, 1968, 82 Stat. 667

Department of State Appropriation Act, 1970
Pub. L. 91–153, title I, Dec. 24, 1969, 83 Stat. 403

Department of State Appropriation Act, 1971
Pub. L. 91–472, title I, Oct. 21, 1970, 84 Stat. 1040

Department of State Appropriation Act, 1972
Pub. L. 92–77, title I, Aug. 10, 1971, 85 Stat. 245

Department of State Appropriation Act, 1973
Pub. L. 92–544, title I, Oct. 25, 1972, 86 Stat. 1109

Department of State Appropriation Act, 1974
Pub. L. 93–162, title I, Nov. 27, 1973, 87 Stat. 636

Department of State Appropriation Act, 1975
Pub. L. 93–433, title I, Oct. 5, 1974, 88 Stat. 1187

Department of State Appropriation Act, 1976
Pub. L. 94–121, title I, Oct. 21, 1975, 89 Stat. 611

Department of State Appropriation Act, 1977
Pub. L. 94–362, title I, July 14, 1976, 90 Stat. 937

Department of State Appropriation Act, 1978
Pub. L. 95–86, title I, Aug. 2, 1977, 91 Stat. 419

Department of State Appropriation Act, 1979
Pub. L. 95–431, title I, Oct. 10, 1978, 92 Stat. 1021

Department of State Appropriation Act, 1980
Pub. L. 96–68, title I, Sept. 24, 1979, 93 Stat. 416

Department of State Appropriation Act, 1986
Pub. L. 99–180, title III, Dec. 13, 1985, 99 Stat. 1149

Department of State Appropriation Act, 1987
Pub. L. 99–500, §101(b) [title III], Oct. 18, 1986, 100 Stat. 1783–39, 1783–57, and Pub. L. 99–591, §101(b) [title III], Oct. 30, 1986, 100 Stat. 3341–39, 3341–57

Department of State Appropriation Act, 1988
Pub. L. 100–202, §101(a) [title III], Dec. 22, 1987, 101 Stat. 1329, 1329–19

Department of State Appropriations Act, 1989
Pub. L. 100–459, title III, Oct. 1, 1988, 102 Stat. 2204

Department of State Appropriations Act, 1990
Pub. L. 101–162, title III, Nov. 21, 1989, 103 Stat. 1006

Department of State Appropriations Act, 1991
Pub. L. 101–515, title III, Nov. 5, 1990, 104 Stat. 2124

Department of State Appropriations Authorization Act of 1973
Pub. L. 93–126, Oct. 18, 1973, 87 Stat. 451
Short title, see 22 U.S.C. 2651 note

Department of State Authorization Act, Fiscal Years 1980 and 1981
Pub. L. 96–60, title I, Aug. 15, 1979, 93 Stat. 395

Department of State Authorization Act, Fiscal Years 1982 and 1983
Pub. L. 97–241, title I, Aug. 24, 1982, 96 Stat. 273

Department of State Authorization Act, Fiscal Years 1984 and 1985
Pub. L. 98–164, title I, title X, Nov. 22, 1983, 97 Stat. 1017, 1051

Department of State Special Agents Retirement Act of 1998
Pub. L. 105–382, Nov. 13, 1998, 112 Stat. 3406
Short title, see 22 U.S.C. 3901 note

Department of the Interior Airports Act
Mar. 18, 1950, ch. 72, 64 Stat. 27

Department of the Interior and Related Agencies Appropriation Act, 1956
June 16, 1955, ch. 147, 69 Stat. 141

Department of the Interior and Related Agencies Appropriation Act, 1957
June 13, 1956, ch. 380, 70 Stat. 257

Department of the Interior and Related Agencies Appropriation Act, 1958
July 1, 1957, Pub. L. 85–77, 71 Stat. 257

Department of the Interior and Related Agencies Appropriation Act, 1959
Pub. L. 85–439, June 4, 1958, 72 Stat. 155

Department of the Interior and Related Agencies Appropriation Act, 1960
Pub. L. 86–60, June 23, 1959, 73 Stat. 92

Department of the Interior and Related Agencies Appropriation Act, 1961
Pub. L. 86–455, May 13, 1960, 74 Stat. 104

Department of the Interior and Related Agencies Appropriation Act, 1962
Pub. L. 87–122, Aug. 3, 1961, 75 Stat. 246

Department of the Interior and Related Agencies Appropriation Act, 1963
Pub. L. 87–578, Aug. 9, 1962, 76 Stat. 335

Department of the Interior and Related Agencies Appropriation Act, 1964
Pub. L. 88–79, July 26, 1963, 77 Stat. 96

Department of the Interior and Related Agencies Appropriation Act, 1965
Pub. L. 88–356, July 7, 1964, 78 Stat. 273

Department of the Interior and Related Agencies Appropriation Act, 1966
Pub. L. 89–52, June 28, 1965, 79 Stat. 174

Department of the Interior and Related Agencies Appropriation Act, 1967
Pub. L. 89–435, May 31, 1966, 80 Stat. 170

Department of the Interior and Related Agencies Appropriation Act, 1968
Pub. L. 90–28, June 24, 1967, 81 Stat. 59

Department of the Interior and Related Agencies Appropriation Act, 1969
Pub. L. 90–425, July 26, 1968, 82 Stat. 425

Department of the Interior and Related Agencies Appropriation Act, 1970
Pub. L. 91–98, Oct. 29, 1969, 83 Stat. 147

Department of the Interior and Related Agencies Appropriation Act, 1971
Pub. L. 91–361, July 31, 1970, 84 Stat. 669

Department of the Interior and Related Agencies Appropriation Act, 1972
Pub. L. 92–76, Aug. 10, 1971, 85 Stat. 229

Department of the Interior and Related Agencies Appropriation Act, 1973
Pub. L. 92–369, Aug. 10, 1972, 86 Stat. 508

Department of the Interior and Related Agencies Appropriation Act, 1974
Pub. L. 93–120, Oct. 4, 1973, 87 Stat. 429

Department of the Interior and Related Agencies Appropriation Act, 1975
Pub. L. 93–404, Aug. 31, 1974, 88 Stat. 803

Department of the Interior and Related Agencies Appropriation Act, 1976, and the period ending September 30, 1976
Pub. L. 94–165, Dec. 23, 1975, 89 Stat. 977

Department of the Interior and Related Agencies Appropriation Act, 1977
Pub. L. 94–373, July 31, 1976, 90 Stat. 1043

Department of the Interior and Related Agencies Appropriation Act, 1978
Pub. L. 95–74, July 26, 1977, 91 Stat. 285

Department of the Interior and Related Agencies Appropriation Act, 1979
Pub. L. 95–465, title I, Oct. 17, 1978, 92 Stat. 1279

Department of the Interior and Related Agencies Appropriation Act, 1980
Pub. L. 96–126, Nov. 27, 1979, 93 Stat. 954

Department of the Interior and Related Agencies Appropriation Act, 1981
Pub. L. 96–514, Dec. 12, 1980, 94 Stat. 2957

Department of the Interior and Related Agencies Appropriation Act, 1982
Pub. L. 97–100, Dec. 23, 1981, 95 Stat. 1391

Department of the Interior and Related Agencies Appropriation Act, 1983
Pub. L. 97–394, Dec. 30, 1982, 96 Stat. 1966

Department of the Interior and Related Agencies Appropriation Act, 1984
Pub. L. 98–146, Nov. 4, 1983, 97 Stat. 919

Department of the Interior and Related Agencies Appropriations Act, 1985
Pub. L. 98–473, title I, §101(c), Oct. 12, 1984, 98 Stat. 1837

Department of the Interior and Related Agencies Appropriations Act, 1986
Pub. L. 99–190, §101(d), Dec. 19, 1985, 99 Stat. 1224

Department of the Interior and Related Agencies Appropriations Act, 1987
Pub. L. 99–500, §101(h), Oct. 18, 1986, 100 Stat. 1783–242, and Pub. L. 99–591, §101(h), Oct. 30, 1986, 100 Stat. 3341–242

Department of the Interior and Related Agencies Appropriations Act, 1988
Pub. L. 100–202, §101(g), Dec. 22, 1987, 101 Stat. 1329–213

Department of the Interior and Related Agencies Appropriations Act, 1989
Pub. L. 100–446, Sept. 27, 1988, 102 Stat. 1774

Department of the Interior and Related Agencies Appropriations Act, 1990
Pub. L. 101–121, Oct. 23, 1989, 103 Stat. 701

Department of the Interior and Related Agencies Appropriations Act, 1991
Pub. L. 101–512, Nov. 5, 1990, 104 Stat. 1915

Department of the Interior and Related Agencies Appropriations Act, 1992
Pub. L. 102–154, Nov. 13, 1991, 105 Stat. 990

Department of the Interior and Related Agencies Appropriations Act, 1993
Pub. L. 102–381, Oct. 5, 1992, 106 Stat. 1374

Department of the Interior and Related Agencies Appropriations Act, 1994
Pub. L. 103–138, Nov. 11, 1993, 107 Stat. 1379

Department of the Interior and Related Agencies Appropriations Act, 1995
Pub. L. 103–332, Sept. 30, 1994, 108 Stat. 2499

Department of the Interior and Related Agencies Appropriations Act, 1996
Pub. L. 104–134, title I, §101(c), Apr. 26, 1996, 110 Stat. 1321–156

Department of the Interior and Related Agencies Appropriations Act, 1997
Pub. L. 104–208, div. A, title I, §101(d), Sept. 30, 1996, 110 Stat. 3009–181

Department of the Interior and Related Agencies Appropriations Act, 1998
Pub. L. 105–83, Nov. 14, 1997, 111 Stat. 1543

Department of the Interior and Related Agencies Appropriations Act, 1999
Pub. L. 105–277, div. A, §101(e), Oct. 21, 1998, 112 Stat. 2681–231

Department of the Interior and Related Agencies Appropriations Act, 2000
Pub. L. 106–113, div. B, §1000(a)(3) [H.R. 3423], Nov. 29, 1999, 113 Stat. 1535, 1501A–135

Department of the Interior and Related Agencies Appropriations Act, 2001
Pub. L. 106–291, Oct. 11, 2000, 114 Stat. 922

Department of the Navy Appropriation Act, 1949
June 24, 1948, ch. 617, 62 Stat. 584

Department of Transportation Act
Pub. L. 89–670, Oct. 15, 1966, 80 Stat. 931

Department of Transportation and Related Agencies Appropriation Act, 1970
Pub. L. 91–168, Dec. 26, 1969, 83 Stat. 454

Department of Transportation and Related Agencies Appropriation Act, 1972
Pub. L. 92–74, Aug. 10, 1971, 85 Stat. 201

Department of Transportation and Related Agencies Appropriation Act, 1973
Pub. L. 92–398, Aug. 22, 1972, 86 Stat. 580

Department of Transportation and Related Agencies Appropriation Act, 1974
Pub. L. 93–98, Aug. 16, 1973, 87 Stat. 329

Department of Transportation and Related Agencies Appropriation Act, 1975
Pub. L. 93–391, Aug. 28, 1974, 88 Stat. 768

Department of Transportation and Related Agencies Appropriation Act, 1976, and the period ending September 30, 1976
Pub. L. 94–134, Nov. 24, 1975, 89 Stat. 695

Department of Transportation and Related Agencies Appropriation Act, 1977
Pub. L. 94–387, Aug. 14, 1976, 90 Stat. 1171

Department of Transportation and Related Agencies Appropriation Act, 1978
Pub. L. 95–85, Aug. 2, 1977, 91 Stat. 402

Department of Transportation and Related Agencies Appropriation Act, 1979
Pub. L. 95–335, Aug. 4, 1978, 92 Stat. 435

Department of Transportation and Related Agencies Appropriation Act, 1980
Pub. L. 96–131, Nov. 30, 1979, 93 Stat. 1023

Department of Transportation and Related Agencies Appropriation Act, 1981
Pub. L. 96–400, Oct. 9, 1980, 94 Stat. 1681

Department of Transportation and Related Agencies Appropriation Act, 1985
Pub. L. 98–473, title I, §101(i), Oct. 12, 1984, 98 Stat. 1944

Department of Transportation and Related Agencies Appropriations Act, 1986
Pub. L. 99–190, §101(e), Dec. 19, 1985, 99 Stat. 1267

Department of Transportation and Related Agencies Appropriation Act, 1982
Pub. L. 97–102, Dec. 23, 1981, 95 Stat. 1442

Department of Transportation and Related Agencies Appropriations Act, 1983
Pub. L. 97–369, Dec. 18, 1982, 96 Stat. 1765

Department of Transportation and Related Agencies Appropriations Act, 1984
Pub. L. 98–78, Aug. 15, 1983, 97 Stat. 453

Department of Transportation and Related Agencies Appropriations Act, 1987
Pub. L. 99–500, §101(*l*) [H.R. 5205], Oct. 18, 1986, 100 Stat. 1783–308, and Pub. L. 99–591, §101(*l*) [H.R. 5205], 100 Stat. 3341–308; Pub. L. 100–202, §106, Dec. 22, 1987, 101 Stat. 1329–433

Department of Transportation and Related Agencies Appropriations Act, 1988
Pub. L. 100–202, §101(*l*), Dec. 22, 1987, 101 Stat. 1329–358

Department of Transportation and Related Agencies Appropriations Act, 1989
Pub. L. 100–457, Sept. 30, 1988, 102 Stat. 2125

Department of Transportation and Related Agencies Appropriations Act, 1990
Pub. L. 101–164, Nov. 21, 1989, 103 Stat. 1069

Department of Transportation and Related Agencies Appropriations Act, 1991
Pub. L. 101–516, Nov. 5, 1990, 104 Stat. 2155

Department of Transportation and Related Agencies Appropriations Act, 1992
Pub. L. 102–143, Oct. 28, 1991, 105 Stat. 917

Department of Transportation and Related Agencies Appropriations Act, 1993
Pub. L. 102–388, Oct. 6, 1992, 106 Stat. 1520

Department of Transportation and Related Agencies Appropriations Act, 1994
Pub. L. 103–122, Oct. 27, 1993, 107 Stat. 1198

Department of Transportation and Related Agencies Appropriations Act, 1995
Pub. L. 103–331, Sept. 30, 1994, 108 Stat. 2471

Department of Transportation and Related Agencies Appropriations Act, 1996
Pub. L. 104–50, Nov. 15, 1995, 109 Stat. 436

Department of Transportation and Related Agencies Appropriations Act, 1997
Pub. L. 104–205, Sept. 30, 1996, 110 Stat. 2951

Department of Transportation and Related Agencies Appropriations Act, 1998
Pub. L. 105–66, Oct. 27, 1997, 111 Stat. 1425

Department of Transportation and Related Agencies Appropriations Act, 1999
Pub. L. 105–277, div. A, §101(g), Oct. 21, 1998, 112 Stat. 2681–439

Department of Transportation and Related Agencies Appropriations Act, 2000
Pub. L. 106–69, Oct. 9, 1999, 113 Stat. 986

Department of Transportation and Related Agencies Appropriations Act, 2001
Pub. L. 106–346, Oct. 23, 2000, 114 Stat. 1356, 1356A–1

Department of Transportation Appropriation Act, 1968
Pub. L. 90–112, Oct. 23, 1967, 81 Stat. 311

Department of Transportation Appropriation Act, 1969
Pub. L. 90–464, Aug. 8, 1968, 82 Stat. 654

Department of Veterans Affairs Act
Pub. L. 100–527, Oct. 25, 1988, 102 Stat. 2635 (38 U.S.C. 301 note)

Department of Veterans Affairs Codification Act
Pub. L. 102–83, Aug. 6, 1991, 105 Stat. 378
Short title, see 38 U.S.C. 101 note

Department of Veterans Affairs Employment Reduction Assistance Act of 1999
Pub. L. 106–117, title XI, Nov. 30, 1999, 113 Stat. 1595 (5 U.S.C. 5597 note)

Department of Veterans Affairs Health Care Personnel Incentive Act of 1998
Pub. L. 105–368, title VIII, Nov. 11, 1998, 112 Stat. 3352 (38 U.S.C. 7671 et seq.)
Short title, see 38 U.S.C. 101 note

Department of Veterans Affairs Health-Care Personnel Act of 1991
Pub. L. 102–40, May 7, 1991, 105 Stat. 187 (38 U.S.C. 7401 et seq.)
Short title, see 38 U.S.C. 101 note

Department of Veterans Affairs Labor Relations Improvement Act of 1991
Pub. L. 102–40, title II, May 7, 1991, 105 Stat. 200 (38 U.S.C. 7421 et seq., 7461 et seq.)
Short title, see 38 U.S.C. 101 note

Department of Veterans Affairs Nurse Pay Act of 1990
Pub. L. 101–366, Aug. 15, 1990, 104 Stat. 430
Short title, see 38 U.S.C. 101 note

Department of Veterans Affairs Physician and Dentist Recruitment and Retention Act of 1991
Pub. L. 102–40, title I, May 7, 1991, 105 Stat. 187 (38 U.S.C. 7431 et seq.)
Short title, see 38 U.S.C. 101 note

Departments of Commerce, Justice, and State, the Judiciary, and Related Agencies Appropriation Act, 1986
Pub. L. 99–180, Dec. 13, 1985, 99 Stat. 1136

Departments of Commerce, Justice, and State, the Judiciary, and Related Agencies Appropriation Act, 1987
Pub. L. 99–500, §101(b), Oct. 18, 1986, 100 Stat. 1783–39, and Pub. L. 99–591, §101(b), Oct. 30, 1986, 100 Stat. 3341–39

Departments of Commerce, Justice, and State, the Judiciary, and Related Agencies Appropriation Act, 1988
Pub. L. 100–202, §101(a), Dec. 22, 1987, 101 Stat. 1329

Departments of Commerce, Justice, and State, the Judiciary, and Related Agencies Appropriations Act, 1984
Pub. L. 98–166, Nov. 28, 1983, 97 Stat. 1071

Departments of Commerce, Justice, and State, the Judiciary, and Related Agencies Appropriation Act, 1985
Pub. L. 98–411, Aug. 30, 1984, 98 Stat. 1545

Departments of Commerce, Justice, and State, the Judiciary, and Related Agencies Appropriations Act, 1989
Pub. L. 100–459, Oct. 1, 1988, 102 Stat. 2186

Departments of Commerce, Justice, and State, the Judiciary, and Related Agencies Appropriations Act, 1990
Pub. L. 101–162, Nov. 21, 1989, 103 Stat. 988

Departments of Commerce, Justice, and State, the Judiciary, and Related Agencies Appropriations Act, 1991
Pub. L. 101–515, Nov. 5, 1990, 104 Stat. 2101

Departments of Commerce, Justice, and State, the Judiciary, and Related Agencies Appropriations Act, 1992
Pub. L. 102–140, Oct. 28, 1991, 105 Stat. 782

Departments of Commerce, Justice, and State, the Judiciary, and Related Agencies Appropriations Act, 1993
Pub. L. 102–395, Oct. 6, 1992, 106 Stat. 1828

Departments of Commerce, Justice, and State, the Judiciary, and Related Agencies Appropriations Act, 1994
Pub. L. 103–121, Oct. 27, 1993, 107 Stat. 1153

Departments of Commerce, Justice, and State, the Judiciary, and Related Agencies Appropriations Act, 1995
Pub. L. 103–317, titles I–VI, Aug. 26, 1994, 108 Stat. 1724–1773

Departments of Commerce, Justice, and State, the Judiciary, and Related Agencies Appropriations Act, 1996
Pub. L. 104–134, title I, §101[(a)], Apr. 26, 1996, 110 Stat. 1321

Departments of Commerce, Justice, and State, the Judiciary, and Related Agencies Appropriations Act, 1997
Pub. L. 104–208, div. A, title I, §101(a), Sept. 30, 1996, 110 Stat. 3009

Departments of Commerce, Justice, and State, the Judiciary, and Related Agencies Appropriations Act, 1998
Pub. L. 105–119, Nov. 26, 1997, 111 Stat. 2440

Departments of Commerce, Justice, and State, the Judiciary, and Related Agencies Appropriations Act, 1999
Pub. L. 105–277, div. A, §101(b), Oct. 21, 1998, 112 Stat. 2681–50

Departments of Commerce, Justice, and State, the Judiciary, and Related Agencies Appropriations Act, 2000
Pub. L. 106–113, div. B, §1000(a)(1) [H.R. 3421], Nov. 29, 1999, 113 Stat. 1535, 1501A–3

Departments of Commerce, Justice, and State, the Judiciary, and Related Agencies Appropriations Act, 2001
Pub. L. 106–553, §1(a)(2) [titles I–VII], Dec. 21, 2000, 114 Stat. 2762, 2762A–51 to 2762A–117

Departments of Labor and Health, Education, and Welfare Appropriation Act, 1976
Pub. L. 94–206, Jan. 28, 1976, 90 Stat. 3

Departments of Labor and Health, Education, and Welfare Appropriation Act, 1977
Pub. L. 94–439, Sept. 30, 1976, 90 Stat. 1418

Departments of Labor and Health, Education, and Welfare Appropriations Act, 1979
Pub. L. 95–480, Oct. 18, 1978, 92 Stat. 1567

Departments of Labor and Health, Education, and Welfare Appropriation Act, 1954
July 31, 1953, ch. 296, 67 Stat. 245

Departments of Labor, and Health, Education, and Welfare Appropriation Act, 1955
July 2, 1954, ch. 457, 68 Stat. 434

Departments of Labor, and Health, Education, and Welfare Appropriation Act, 1957
June 29, 1956, ch. 477, 70 Stat. 423

Departments of Labor, and Health, Education, and Welfare Appropriation Act, 1958
Pub. L. 85–67, June 29, 1957, 71 Stat. 210

Departments of Labor, and Health, Education, and Welfare Appropriation Act, 1959
Pub. L. 85–580, Aug. 1, 1958, 72 Stat. 457

Departments of Labor, and Health, Education, and Welfare Appropriation Act, 1960
Pub. L. 86–158, Aug. 14, 1959, 73 Stat. 339

Departments of Labor, and Health, Education, and Welfare Appropriation Act, 1961
Pub. L. 86–703, Sept. 2, 1960, 74 Stat. 755

Departments of Labor, and Health, Education, and Welfare Appropriation Act, 1962
Pub. L. 87–290, Sept. 22, 1961, 75 Stat. 589

Departments of Labor, and Health, Education, and Welfare Appropriation Act, 1963
Pub. L. 87–582, Aug. 14, 1962, 76 Stat. 361

Departments of Labor, and Health, Education, and Welfare Appropriation Act, 1964
Pub. L. 88–136, Oct. 11, 1963, 77 Stat. 224

Departments of Labor, and Health, Education, and Welfare Appropriation Act, 1965
Pub. L. 88–605, Sept. 19, 1964, 78 Stat. 959

Departments of Labor, and Health, Education, and Welfare Appropriation Act, 1966
Pub. L. 89–156, Aug. 31, 1965, 79 Stat. 589

Departments of Labor, and Health, Education, and Welfare Appropriation Act, 1967
Pub. L. 89–787, Nov. 7, 1966, 80 Stat. 1378

Departments of Labor, and Health, Education, and Welfare Appropriation Act, 1968
Pub. L. 90–132, Nov. 8, 1967, 81 Stat. 386

Departments of Labor, and Health, Education, and Welfare Appropriation Act, 1969
Pub. L. 90–557, Oct. 11, 1968, 82 Stat. 969

Departments of Labor, and Health, Education, and Welfare Appropriation Act, 1971
Pub. L. 91–667, Jan. 11, 1971, 84 Stat. 2001

Departments of Labor, and Health, Education, and Welfare Appropriation Act, 1974
Pub. L. 93–192, Dec. 18, 1973, 87 Stat. 746

Departments of Labor, and Health, Education, and Welfare Supplemental Appropriation Act, 1966
Pub. L. 89–199, Sept. 23, 1965, 79 Stat. 831

Departments of Labor, and Health, Education, and Welfare, and related agencies Appropriation Act, 1956
Aug. 1, 1955, ch. 437, 69 Stat. 397

Departments of Labor, and Health, Education, and Welfare, and Related Agencies Appropriation Act, 1972
Pub. L. 92–80, Aug. 10, 1971, 85 Stat. 285

Departments of Labor, Health and Human Services, and Education and Related Agencies Appropriation Act, 1985
Pub. L. 98–619, Nov. 8, 1984, 98 Stat. 3305

Departments of Labor, Health and Human Services, and Education and Related Agencies Appropriation Act, 1986
Pub. L. 99–178, Dec. 12, 1985, 99 Stat. 1102

Departments of Labor, Health and Human Services, and Education, and Related Agencies Appropriations Act, 1987
Pub. L. 99–500, §101(i) [H.R. 5233], Oct. 18, 1986, 100 Stat. 1783–287, and Pub. L. 99–591, §101(i) [H.R. 5233], Oct. 30, 1986, 100 Stat. 3341–287

Departments of Labor, Health and Human Services, and Education, and Related Agencies Appropriation Act, 1984
Pub. L. 98–139, Oct. 31, 1983, 97 Stat. 871

Departments of Labor, Health and Human Services, and Education and Related Agencies Appropriation Act, 1983
Pub. L. 97–377, title I, §101(e)(1), Dec. 21, 1982, 96 Stat. 1878

Departments of Labor, Health and Human Services, and Education, and Related Agencies Appropriations Act, 1988
Pub. L. 100–202, §101(h), Dec. 22, 1987, 101 Stat. 1329–256

Departments of Labor, Health and Human Services, and Education, and Related Agencies Appropriations Act, 1989
Pub. L. 100–436, Sept. 20, 1988, 102 Stat. 1680

Departments of Labor, Health and Human Services, and Education, and Related Agencies Appropriations Act, 1990
Pub. L. 101–166, Nov. 21, 1989, 103 Stat. 1159

Departments of Labor, Health and Human Services, and Education, and Related Agencies Appropriations Act, 1991
Pub. L. 101–517, Nov. 5, 1990, 104 Stat. 2190

Departments of Labor, Health and Human Services, and Education, and Related Agencies Appropriations Act, 1992
Pub. L. 102–170, Nov. 26, 1991, 105 Stat. 1107

Departments of Labor, Health and Human Services, and Education, and Related Agencies Appropriations Act, 1993
Pub. L. 102–394, Oct. 6, 1992, 106 Stat. 1792

Departments of Labor, Health and Human Services, and Education, and Related Agencies Appropriations Act, 1994
Pub. L. 103–112, Oct. 21, 1993, 107 Stat. 1082

Departments of Labor, Health and Human Services, and Education, and Related Agencies Appropriations Act, 1995
Pub. L. 103–333, Sept. 30, 1994, 108 Stat. 2539

Departments of Labor, Health and Human Services, and Education, and Related Agencies Appropriations Act, 1996
Pub. L. 104–134, title I, §101(d), Apr. 26, 1996, 110 Stat. 1321–211

Departments of Labor, Health and Human Services, and Education, and Related Agencies Appropriations Act, 1997
Pub. L. 104–208, div. A, title I, §101(e), Sept. 30, 1996, 110 Stat. 3009–233

Departments of Labor, Health and Human Services, and Education, and Related Agencies Appropriations Act, 1998
Pub. L. 105–78, Nov. 13, 1997, 111 Stat. 1467

Departments of Labor, Health and Human Services, and Education, and Related Agencies Appropriations Act, 1999
Pub. L. 105–277, div. A, §101(f), Oct. 21, 1998, 112 Stat. 2681–337

Departments of Labor, Health and Human Services, and Education, and Related Agencies Appropriations Act, 2001
Pub. L. 106–554, §1(a)(1) [H.R. 5656], Dec. 21, 2000, 114 Stat. 2763, 2763A–3

Departments of Labor, Health, and Human Services, and Education, and Related Agencies Appropriations Act, 2000
Pub. L. 106–113, div. B, §1000(a)(4) [H.R. 3424], Nov. 29, 1999, 113 Stat. 1535, 1501A–217

Departments of State and Justice, the Judiciary, and related agencies Appropriation Act, 1956
July 7, 1955, ch. 279, 69 Stat. 264

Departments of State and Justice, the Judiciary, and Related Agencies Appropriation Act, 1957
June 20, 1956, ch. 414, 70 Stat. 299

Departments of State and Justice, the Judiciary, and Related Agencies Appropriation Act, 1958
Pub. L. 85–49, June 11, 1957, 71 Stat. 55

Departments of State and Justice, the Judiciary, and Related Agencies Appropriation Act, 1959
Pub. L. 85–474, June 30, 1958, 72 Stat. 244

Departments of State and Justice, the Judiciary, and Related Agencies Appropriation Act, 1960
Pub. L. 86–84, July 13, 1959, 73 Stat. 182

Departments of State and Justice, the Judiciary, and Related Agencies Appropriation Act, 1961
Pub. L. 86–678, Aug. 31, 1960, 74 Stat. 555

Departments of State and Justice, the Judiciary, and Related Agencies Appropriation Act, 1962
Pub. L. 87–264, Sept. 21, 1961, 75 Stat. 545

Departments of State, Justice, and Commerce, the Judiciary, and Related Agencies Appropriation Act, 1973
Pub. L. 92–544, Oct. 25, 1972, 86 Stat. 1109

Departments of State, Justice, and Commerce Appropriation Act, 1944
July 1, 1943, ch. 182, 57 Stat. 271

Departments of State, Justice, and Commerce Appropriation Act, 1945
June 28, 1944, ch. 294, 58 Stat. 395

Departments of State, Justice, and Commerce, the Judiciary, and Related Agencies Appropriation Act, 1963
Pub. L. 87–843, Oct. 18, 1962, 76 Stat. 1080

Departments of State, Justice, and Commerce, the Judiciary, and Related Agencies Appropriation Act, 1964
Pub. L. 88–245, Dec. 30, 1963, 77 Stat. 776

Departments of State, Justice, and Commerce, the Judiciary, and Related Agencies Appropriation Act, 1965
Pub. L. 88–527, Aug. 31, 1964, 78 Stat. 711

Departments of State, Justice, and Commerce, the Judiciary, and related agencies Appropriation Act, 1966
Pub. L. 89–164, Sept. 2, 1965, 79 Stat. 620

Departments of State, Justice, and Commerce, the Judiciary, and related agencies Appropriation Act, 1967
Pub. L. 89–797, Nov. 8, 1966, 80 Stat. 1479

Departments of State, Justice, and Commerce, the Judiciary, and related agencies Appropriation Act, 1968
Pub. L. 90–133, Nov. 8, 1967, 81 Stat. 410

Departments of State, Justice, and Commerce, the Judiciary, and Related Agencies Appropriation Act, 1969
Pub. L. 90–470, Aug. 9, 1968, 82 Stat. 667

Departments of State, Justice, and Commerce, the Judiciary, and Related Agencies Appropriation Act, 1970
Pub. L. 91–153, Dec. 24, 1969, 83 Stat. 403

Departments of State, Justice, and Commerce, the Judiciary, and Related Agencies Appropriation Act, 1971
Pub. L. 91–472, Oct. 21, 1970, 84 Stat. 1040

Departments of State, Justice, and Commerce, the Judiciary, and Related Agencies Appropriation Act, 1972
Pub. L. 92–77, Aug. 10, 1971, 85 Stat. 245

Departments of State, Justice, and Commerce, the Judiciary, and Related Agencies Appropriation Act, 1974
Pub. L. 93–162, Nov. 27, 1973, 87 Stat. 636

Departments of State, Justice, and Commerce, the Judiciary, and Related Agencies Appropriation Act, 1975
Pub. L. 93–433, Oct. 5, 1974, 88 Stat. 1187

Departments of State, Justice, and Commerce, the Judiciary, and Related Agencies Appropriation Act, 1976
Pub. L. 94–121, Oct. 21, 1975, 89 Stat. 611

Departments of State, Justice, and Commerce, the Judiciary, and Related Agencies Appropriation Act, 1977
Pub. L. 94–362, July 14, 1976, 90 Stat. 937

Departments of State, Justice, and Commerce, the Judiciary, and Related Agencies Appropriation Act, 1978
Pub. L. 95–86, Aug. 2, 1977, 91 Stat. 419

Departments of State, Justice, and Commerce, the Judiciary, and Related Agencies Appropriation Act, 1979
Pub. L. 95–431, Oct. 10, 1978, 92 Stat. 1021

Departments of State, Justice, and Commerce, the Judiciary, and Related Agencies Appropriation Act, 1980
Pub. L. 96–68, Sept. 24, 1979, 93 Stat. 416

Departments of State, Justice, Commerce, and the Judiciary Appropriation Act, 1947
July 5, 1946, ch. 541, 60 Stat. 446

Departments of State, Justice and Commerce, and the Judiciary Appropriation Act, 1948
July 9, 1947, ch. 211, 61 Stat. 279

Departments of State, Justice, Commerce, and the Judiciary Appropriation Act, 1949
June 3, 1948, ch. 400, 62 Stat. 305

Departments of State, Justice, Commerce, and the Judiciary Appropriation Act, 1950
July 20, 1949, ch. 354, 63 Stat. 447

Departments of State, Justice, Commerce, and the Judiciary Appropriation Act, 1951
Sept. 6, 1950, ch. 896, Ch. III, 64 Stat. 609

Departments of State, Justice, Commerce, and the Judiciary Appropriation Act, 1952
Oct. 22, 1951, ch. 533, 65 Stat. 575

Departments of State, Justice, Commerce, and The Judiciary Appropriation Act, 1953
July 10, 1952, ch. 651, 66 Stat. 549

Departments of State, Justice, and Commerce Appropriation Act, 1954
Aug. 5, 1953, ch. 328, 67 Stat. 367

Departments of State, Justice, and Commerce and the United States Information Agency Appropriation Act, 1955
July 2, 1954, ch. 456, 68 Stat. 413

Departments of State, Justice, Commerce, the Judiciary, and the Federal Loan Agency Appropriation Act, 1946
May 21, 1945, ch. 129, 59 Stat. 169

Departments of Veterans Affairs and Housing and Urban Development, and Independent Agencies Appropriations Act, 1990
Pub. L. 101–144, Nov. 9, 1989, 103 Stat. 839

Departments of Veterans Affairs and Housing and Urban Development, and Independent Agencies Appropriations Act, 1991
Pub. L. 101–507, Nov. 5, 1990, 104 Stat. 1351

Departments of Veterans Affairs and Housing and Urban Development, and Independent Agencies Appropriations Act, 1992
Pub. L. 102–139, Oct. 28, 1991, 105 Stat. 736

Departments of Veterans Affairs and Housing and Urban Development, and Independent Agencies Appropriations Act, 1993
Pub. L. 102–389, Oct. 6, 1992, 106 Stat. 1571

Departments of Veterans Affairs and Housing and Urban Development, and Independent Agencies Appropriations Act, 1994
Pub. L. 103–124, Oct. 28, 1993, 107 Stat. 1275

Departments of Veterans Affairs and Housing and Urban Development, and Independent Agencies Appropriations Act, 1995
Pub. L. 103–327, Sept. 28, 1994, 108 Stat. 2298

Departments of Veterans Affairs and Housing and Urban Development, and Independent Agencies Appropriations Act, 1996
Pub. L. 104–134, title I, §101(e), Apr. 26, 1996, 110 Stat. 1321–257

Departments of Veterans Affairs and Housing and Urban Development, and Independent Agencies Appropriations Act, 1997
Pub. L. 104–204, Sept. 26, 1996, 110 Stat. 2874

Departments of Veterans Affairs and Housing and Urban Development, and Independent Agencies Appropriations Act, 1998
Pub. L. 105–65, Oct. 27, 1997, 111 Stat. 1344

Departments of Veterans Affairs and Housing and Urban Development, and Independent Agencies Appropriations Act, 1999
Pub. L. 105–276, titles I–IV, VI, Oct. 21, 1998, 112 Stat. 2461–2507, 2670

Departments of Veterans Affairs and Housing and Urban Development, and Independent Agencies Appropriations Act, 2000
Pub. L. 106–74, Oct. 20, 1999, 113 Stat. 1047

Departments of Veterans Affairs and Housing and Urban Development, and Independent Agencies Appropriations Act, 2001
Pub. L. 106–377, §1(a)(1) [titles I–IV], Oct. 27, 2000, 114 Stat. 1441, 1441A–3 to 1441A–52

Dependency and Indemnity Compensation Reform Act of 1992
Pub. L. 102–568, title I, Oct. 29, 1992, 106 Stat. 4321
Short title, see 38 U.S.C. 101 note

Dependent Pension Act
June 27, 1890, ch. 634, 26 Stat. 182

Dependents Assistance Act of 1950
Sept. 8, 1950, ch. 922, 64 Stat. 794 (50 App. U.S.C. 2201 et seq.)
Short title, see 50 App. U.S.C. 2201 note

Dependents' Medical Care Act
June 7, 1956, ch. 374, 70 Stat. 250

Deportation Act
May 10, 1920, ch. 174, 41 Stat. 593

Deposit Insurance Extension Act
Aug. 23, 1935, ch. 614, title I, 49 Stat. 684

Deposit Insurance Flexibility Act
Pub. L. 97–320, title I, Oct. 15, 1982, 96 Stat. 1469
Short title, see 12 U.S.C. 1811 note

Deposit Insurance Funds Act of 1996
Pub. L. 104–208, div. A, title II, subtitle G (§2701 et seq.), Sept. 30, 1996, 110 Stat. 3009–479
Short title, see 12 U.S.C. 1811 note

Depository Institution Management Interlocks Act
Pub. L. 95–630, title II, Nov. 10, 1978, 92 Stat. 3672 (12 U.S.C. 3201 et seq.)
Short title, see 12 U.S.C. 3201 note

Depository Institution-GSE Affiliation Act of 1998
Pub. L. 105–277, div. H, Oct. 21, 1998, 112 Stat. 2681–854
Short title, see 12 U.S.C. 1811 note

Depository Institutions Deregulation Act of 1980
Pub. L. 96–221, title II, Mar. 31, 1980, 94 Stat. 142 (12 U.S.C. 3501 et seq.)

Depository Institutions Deregulation and Monetary Control Act of 1980
Pub. L. 96–221, Mar. 31, 1980, 94 Stat. 132
Short title, see 12 U.S.C. 226 note

Depository Institutions Disaster Relief Act of 1992
Pub. L. 102–485, Oct. 23, 1992, 106 Stat. 2771
Short title, see 12 U.S.C. 1811 note

Depository Institutions Disaster Relief Act of 1993
Pub. L. 103–76, Aug. 12, 1993, 107 Stat. 752
Short title, see 12 U.S.C. 1811 note

Depository Institutions Disaster Relief Act of 1997
Pub. L. 105–18, title V, June 12, 1997, 111 Stat. 211
Short title, see 12 U.S.C. 1811 note

Depository Library Act of 1962
Pub. L. 87–579, Aug. 9, 1962, 76 Stat. 352

Deposits Regulation Act
June 23, 1836, ch. 115, 5 Stat. 52

Depredation Act (Indians)
See Indian Depredation Act

Depredation Act (Timber)
Mar. 3, 1859, ch. 78, 11 Stat. 408

Deputy Chief of Staff Act
July 14, 1939, ch. 269, 53 Stat. 1002

DES Education and Research Amendments of 1992
Pub. L. 102–409, Oct. 13, 1992, 106 Stat. 2092
Short title, see 42 U.S.C. 201 note

Deschutes Resources Conservancy Reauthorization Act of 2000
Pub. L. 106–270, Sept. 22, 2000, 114 Stat. 791

Desertion Act (Navy and Marine Corps)
Aug. 14, 1888, ch. 890, 25 Stat. 442

Destruction of Records Act (Interstate Commerce)
Feb. 25, 1909, ch. 193, 35 Stat. 648

Destruction of War Material Act
Apr. 20, 1918, ch. 59, 40 Stat. 533 (50 U.S.C. 101 et seq.)

Developmental Disabilities Act of 1984
Pub. L. 98–527, Oct. 19, 1984, 98 Stat. 2662 (42 U.S.C. 6000 et seq.)
Short title, see 42 U.S.C. 6000 note

Developmental Disabilities Assistance and Bill of Rights Act
Pub. L. 88–164, title I, as added Pub. L. 98–527, §2, Oct. 19, 1984, 98 Stat. 2662 (42 U.S.C. 6000 et seq.)
Short title, see 42 U.S.C. 6000 note

Developmental Disabilities Assistance and Bill of Rights Act Amendments of 1987
Pub. L. 100–146, Oct. 29, 1987, 101 Stat. 840
Short title, see 42 U.S.C. 6000 note

Developmental Disabilities Assistance and Bill of Rights Act Amendments of 1994
Pub. L. 103–230, Apr. 6, 1994, 108 Stat. 284
Short title, see 42 U.S.C. 6000 note

Developmental Disabilities Assistance and Bill of Rights Act Amendments of 1996
Pub. L. 104–183, Aug. 6, 1996, 110 Stat. 1694
Short title, see 42 U.S.C. 6000 note

Developmental Disabilities Assistance and Bill of Rights Act of 1990
Pub. L. 101–496, Oct. 31, 1990, 104 Stat. 1191
Short title, see 42 U.S.C. 6000 note

Developmental Disabilities Assistance and Bill of Rights Act of 2000
Pub. L. 106–402, Oct. 30, 2000, 114 Stat. 1677 (42 U.S.C. 15001 et seq.)
Short title, see 42 U.S.C. 15001 note

Developmental Disabilities Services and Facilities Construction Act
Renamed Developmental Disabilities Assistance and Bill of Rights Act

Developmental Disabilities Services and Facilities Construction Amendments of 1970
Pub. L. 91–517, Oct. 30, 1970, 84 Stat. 1316

Developmentally Disabled Assistance and Bill of Rights Act
Pub. L. 94–103, Oct. 4, 1975, 89 Stat. 486
Short title, see 42 U.S.C. 6000 note

Dick Act of 1903
See Militia Act of 1903

Dickinson Dam Bascule Gates Settlement Act of 2000
Pub. L. 106–566, title VIII, Dec. 23, 2000, 114 Stat. 2828

Dickstein Alien Officials Act
See Immigration Act of 1924

Dictionary Act
Feb. 25, 1871, ch. 71, 16 Stat. 431

Dietary Supplement Act of 1992
Pub. L. 102–571, title II, Oct. 29, 1992, 106 Stat. 4500
Short title, see 21 U.S.C. 301 note

Dietary Supplement Health and Education Act of 1994
Pub. L. 103–417, Oct. 25, 1994, 108 Stat. 4325
Short title, see 21 U.S.C. 301 note

Digital Millennium Copyright Act
Pub. L. 105–304, Oct. 28, 1998, 112 Stat. 2860
Short title, see 17 U.S.C. 101 note

Digital Performance Right in Sound Recordings Act of 1995
Pub. L. 104–39, Nov. 1, 1995, 109 Stat. 336
Short title, see 17 U.S.C. 101 note

Digital Theft Deterrence and Copyright Damages Improvement Act of 1999
Pub. L. 106–160, Dec. 9, 1999, 113 Stat. 1774
Short title, see 17 U.S.C. 101 note

Dill-Crosser Railway Labor Act
See Railway Labor Act

Dill-Rayburn Communications Act
See Communications Act of 1934

Dingell-Johnson Sport Fish Restoration Act
Aug. 9, 1950, ch. 658, 64 Stat. 430 (16 U.S.C. 777 et seq.)
Short title, see 16 U.S.C. 777 note

Dingley Act (Shipping)
June 26, 1884, ch. 121, 23 Stat. 53

Dingley Act (Tariff)
July 24, 1897, ch. 11, 30 Stat. 151

Diplomatic Relations Act
Pub. L. 95–393, Sept. 30, 1978, 92 Stat. 808
Short title, see 22 U.S.C. 254a note

Diplomatic Security Act
Pub. L. 99–399, titles I–IV, Aug. 27, 1986, 100 Stat. 855–862 (42 U.S.C. 4801 et seq.)
Short title, see 22 U.S.C. 4801 note

Dire Emergency Supplemental Appropriations Act, 1988
Pub. L. 100–393, Aug. 14, 1988, 102 Stat. 969

Dire Emergency Supplemental Appropriations Act, 1992, for Disaster Assistance To Meet Urgent Needs Because of Calamities Such as Those Which Occurred in Los Angeles and Chicago
Pub. L. 102–302, June 22, 1992, 106 Stat. 248

Dire Emergency Supplemental Appropriations Act, 1992, Including Disaster Assistance To Meet the Present Emergencies Arising From the Consequences of Hurricane Andrew, Typhoon Omar, Hurricane Iniki, and Other Natural Disasters, and Additional Assistance to Distressed Communities
Pub. L. 102–368, Sept. 23, 1992, 106 Stat. 1117

Dire Emergency Supplemental Appropriations and Transfers for Relief From the Effects of Natural Disasters, for Other Urgent Needs, and for Incremental Cost of "Operation Desert Shield/Desert Storm" Act of 1992
Pub. L. 102–229, Dec. 12, 1991, 105 Stat. 1701

Dire Emergency Supplemental Appropriations and Transfers, Urgent Supplementals, and Correcting Enrollment Errors Act of 1989
Pub. L. 101–45, June 30, 1989, 103 Stat. 97

Dire Emergency Supplemental Appropriations for Consequences of Operation Desert Shield/Desert Storm, Food Stamps, Unemployment Compensation Administration, Veterans Compensation and Pensions, and Other Urgent Needs Act of 1991
Pub. L. 102–27, Apr. 10, 1991, 105 Stat. 130

Dire Emergency Supplemental Appropriations for Disaster Assistance, Food Stamps, Unemployment Compensation Administration, and Other Urgent Needs, and Transfers, and Reducing Funds Budgeted for Military Spending Act of 1990
Pub. L. 101–302, May 25, 1990, 104 Stat. 213

Dire Emergency Supplemental Appropriations From Contributions of Foreign Governments And/Or Interest for Humanitarian Assistance to Refugees and Displaced Persons In and Around Iraq as a Result of the Recent Invasion of Kuwait and for Peacekeeping Activities and Other Urgent Needs Act of 1991
Pub. L. 102–55, June 13, 1991, 105 Stat. 290

Dire Emergency Supplemental to Meet the Needs of Natural Disasters of National Significance, Fiscal Year 1990
See Fiscal Year 1990 Dire Emergency Supplemental to Meet the Needs of Natural Disasters of National Significance

Direct Loans to Industry Act
Dec. 23, 1913, ch. 6, §13b, as added June 19, 1934, ch. 653, 48 Stat. 1105

Direct Tax Act (Insurrectionary Districts)
June 7, 1862, ch. 98, 12 Stat. 422

Disability Pension Act
June 27, 1890, ch. 634, 26 Stat. 182

Disabled Veterans' and Servicemen's Automobile and Adaptive Equipment Amendments of 1974
Pub. L. 93–538, Dec. 22, 1974, 88 Stat. 1736
Short title, see 38 U.S.C. 101 note

Disabled Veterans' and Servicemen's Automobile Assistance Act of 1970
Pub. L. 91–666, Jan. 11, 1971, 84 Stat. 1998 (38 U.S.C. 3901 et seq.)
Short title, see 38 U.S.C. 101 note

Disadvantaged Minority Health Improvement Act of 1990
Pub. L. 101–527, Nov. 6, 1990, 104 Stat. 2311
Short title, see 42 U.S.C. 201 note

Disarmament Conference Resolution
July 12, 1921, ch. 44, §9, 42 Stat. 141

Disaster Assistance Act of 1988
Pub. L. 100–387, Aug. 11, 1988, 102 Stat. 924
Short title, see 7 U.S.C. 1421 note

Disaster Assistance Act of 1989
Pub. L. 101–82, Aug. 14, 1989, 103 Stat. 564
Short title, see 7 U.S.C. 1421 note

Disaster Loan Act
Apr. 17, 1936, ch. 234, 49 Stat. 1232

Disaster Loan Corporation Act
Feb. 11, 1937, ch. 10, 50 Stat. 19

Disaster Mitigation Act of 2000
Pub. L. 106–390, Oct. 30, 2000, 114 Stat. 1552
Short title, see 42 U.S.C. 5121 note

Disaster Relief Act Amendments of 1980
Pub. L. 96–568, Dec. 22, 1980, 94 Stat. 3334
Short title, see 42 U.S.C. 5121 note

Disaster Relief Act of 1966
Pub. L. 89–769, Nov. 6, 1966, 80 Stat. 1316 (42 U.S.C. 1855aa et seq.)

Disaster Relief Act of 1969
Pub. L. 91–79, Oct. 1, 1969, 83 Stat. 125

Disaster Relief Act of 1970
Pub. L. 91–606, Dec. 31, 1970, 84 Stat. 1744 (42 U.S.C. 4401 et seq.)
Short title, see 42 U.S.C. 4401 note

Disaster Relief Act of 1974
Renamed the Robert T. Stafford Disaster Relief and Emergency Assistance Act

Disaster Relief and Emergency Assistance Amendments of 1988
Pub. L. 100–707, title I, Nov. 23, 1988, 102 Stat. 4689
Short title, see 42 U.S.C. 5121 note

Disbursing Officers' Relief Act
Aug. 1, 1947, ch. 441, 61 Stat. 720

Dischargeability Act
Pub. L. 91–467, Oct. 19, 1970, 84 Stat. 990

Disease Control Amendments of 1976
Pub. L. 94–317, title II, June 23, 1976, 90 Stat. 700
Short title, see 42 U.S.C. 201 note

Disloyal Persons Payments Resolution
Mar. 2, 1867, No. 46, 14 Stat. 571

Displaced Homemakers Self-Sufficiency Assistance Act
Pub. L. 101–554, Nov. 15, 1990, 104 Stat. 2751 (29 U.S.C. 2301 et seq.)
Short title, see 29 U.S.C. 2301 note

Displaced Persons Act of 1948
June 25, 1948, ch. 647, 62 Stat. 1009 (50 App. U.S.C. 1951 et seq.)

Disposition of Affairs Act (Five Civilized Tribes)
Apr. 26, 1906, ch. 1876, 34 Stat. 137

Dispute Resolution Act
Pub. L. 96–190, Feb. 12, 1980, 94 Stat. 17

Distilled Spirits Tax Revision Act of 1979
Pub. L. 96–39, title VIII, subtitle A (§801 et seq.), July 26, 1979, 93 Stat. 273
Short title, see 26 U.S.C. 1 note

Distribution Act of 1841 (Public Lands Proceeds)
Sept. 4, 1841, ch. 16, 5 Stat. 453

Distribution of Judgment Act
See Indian Tribal Judgment Funds Use or Distribution Act

District of Columbia Act for the Regulation of Credit Life Insurance and Credit Accident and Health Insurance
See Act for the Regulation of Credit Life Insurance and Credit Accident and Health Insurance

District of Columbia Administration of Estates Act
Pub. L. 92–88, Aug. 11, 1971, 85 Stat. 313

District of Columbia Administrative Procedure Act
Pub. L. 90–614, Oct. 21, 1968, 82 Stat. 1203

District of Columbia Adoption Improvement Act of 1998
Pub. L. 105–277, div. A, §101(c) [§157], Oct. 21, 1998, 112 Stat. 2681–121, 2681–146

District of Columbia Air Pollution Control Act
Pub. L. 90–440, July 30, 1968, 82 Stat. 458

District of Columbia Alcoholic Beverage Control Act
Jan. 24, 1934, ch. 4, 48 Stat. 319

District of Columbia Alcoholic Rehabilitation Act of 1967
Pub. L. 90–452, Aug. 3, 1968, 82 Stat. 618

District of Columbia Alley Dwelling Act
June 12, 1934, ch. 465, 48 Stat. 930

District of Columbia Anatomical Gift Act
Pub. L. 91–268, §§1–8, May 26, 1970, 84 Stat. 266–270

District of Columbia Appropriation Act of 1950
June 29, 1949, ch. 279, 63 Stat. 303

District of Columbia Appropriation Act of 1952
Aug. 3, 1951, ch. 292, 65 Stat. 155

District of Columbia Appropriation Act of 1974
Pub. L. 93–91, Aug. 14, 1973, 87 Stat. 306

District of Columbia Appropriation Act, 1940
July 15, 1939, ch. 281, 53 Stat. 1004

District of Columbia Appropriation Act, 1941
June 12, 1940, ch. 333, 54 Stat. 307

District of Columbia Appropriation Act, 1942
July 1, 1941, ch. 271, 55 Stat. 499

District of Columbia Appropriation Act, 1943
June 27, 1942, ch. 452, 56 Stat. 424

District of Columbia Appropriation Act, 1944
July 1, 1943, ch. 184, 57 Stat. 312

District of Columbia Appropriation Act, 1945
June 28, 1944, ch. 300, 58 Stat. 509

District of Columbia Appropriation Act, 1946
June 30, 1945, ch. 209, 59 Stat. 271

District of Columbia Appropriation Act, 1947
July 9, 1946, ch. 544, 60 Stat. 501

District of Columbia Appropriation Act, 1948
July 25, 1947, ch. 324, 61 Stat. 425

District of Columbia Appropriation Act, 1949
June 19, 1948, ch. 555, 62 Stat. 537

District of Columbia Appropriation Act of 1951
July 18, 1950, ch. 467, 64 Stat. 347

District of Columbia Appropriation Act, 1953
July 5, 1952, ch. 576, 66 Stat. 374

District of Columbia Appropriation Act, 1954
July 31, 1953, ch. 299, 67 Stat. 278

District of Columbia Appropriation Act, 1955
July 1, 1954, ch. 449, 68 Stat. 378

District of Columbia Appropriation Act, 1956
July 5, 1955, ch. 272, 69 Stat. 246

District of Columbia Appropriation Act, 1957
June 29, 1956, ch. 479, 70 Stat. 439

District of Columbia Appropriation Act, 1958
Pub. L. 85–61, June 27, 1957, 71 Stat. 192

District of Columbia Appropriation Act, 1959
Pub. L. 85–594, Aug. 6, 1958, 72 Stat. 498

District of Columbia Appropriation Act, 1960
Pub. L. 86–104, July 23, 1959, 73 Stat. 225

District of Columbia Appropriation Act, 1961
Pub. L. 86–412, Apr. 8, 1960, 74 Stat. 17

District of Columbia Appropriation Act, 1962
Pub. L. 87–265, Sept. 21, 1961, 75 Stat. 560

District of Columbia Appropriation Act, 1963
Pub. L. 87–867, Oct. 23, 1962, 76 Stat. 1150

District of Columbia Appropriation Act, 1964
Pub. L. 88–252, Dec. 30, 1963, 77 Stat. 835

District of Columbia Appropriation Act, 1965
Pub. L. 88–479, Aug. 22, 1964, 78 Stat. 588

District of Columbia Appropriation Act, 1966
Pub. L. 89–75, July 16, 1965, 79 Stat. 236

District of Columbia Appropriation Act, 1967
Pub. L. 89–743, Nov. 2, 1966, 80 Stat. 1167

District of Columbia Appropriation Act, 1968
Pub. L. 90–134, Nov. 13, 1967, 81 Stat. 435

District of Columbia Appropriation Act, 1969
Pub. L. 90–473, Aug. 10, 1968, 82 Stat. 694

District of Columbia Appropriation Act, 1970
Pub. L. 91–155, Dec. 24, 1969, 83 Stat. 428

District of Columbia Appropriation Act, 1971
Pub. L. 91–337, July 16, 1970, 84 Stat. 432

District of Columbia Appropriation Act, 1972
Pub. L. 92–202, Dec. 18, 1971, 85 Stat. 682

District of Columbia Appropriation Act, 1973
Pub. L. 92–344, July 10, 1972, 86 Stat. 451

District of Columbia Appropriation Act, 1975
Pub. L. 93–405, Aug. 31, 1974, 88 Stat. 822

District of Columbia Appropriation Act, 1976
Pub. L. 94–333, June 30, 1976, 90 Stat. 785

District of Columbia Appropriation Act, 1977
Pub. L. 94–446, title I, Oct. 1, 1976, 90 Stat. 1490

District of Columbia Appropriation Act, 1978
Pub. L. 95–288, June 5, 1978, 92 Stat. 281

District of Columbia Appropriation Act, 1979
Pub. L. 95–373, Sept. 18, 1978, 92 Stat. 699

District of Columbia Appropriation Act, 1980
Pub. L. 96–93, Oct. 30, 1979, 93 Stat. 713

District of Columbia Appropriation Act, 1982
Pub. L. 97–91, Dec. 4, 1981, 95 Stat. 1173

District of Columbia Appropriation Act, 1983
Pub. L. 97–378, Dec. 22, 1982, 96 Stat. 1925

District of Columbia Appropriation Act, 1984
Pub. L. 98–125, Oct. 13, 1983, 97 Stat. 819

District of Columbia Appropriation Act, 1985
Pub. L. 98–473, title I, §101(b) [H.R. 5899], Oct. 12, 1984, 98 Stat. 1837; Pub. L. 100–202, §106, Dec. 22, 1987, 101 Stat. 1329–433

District of Columbia Appropriation Act, 1986
Pub. L. 99–190, §101(c) [H.R. 3067], Dec. 19, 1985, 99 Stat. 1224; Pub. L. 100–202, §106, Dec. 22, 1987, 101 Stat. 1329–433

District of Columbia Appropriations Act, 1987
Pub. L. 99–500, §101(d), Oct. 18, 1986, 100 Stat. 1783–180, and Pub. L. 99–591, §101(d), Oct. 30, 1986, 100 Stat. 3341–180

District of Columbia Appropriations Act, 1988
Pub. L. 100–202, title I, §101(c), Dec. 22, 1987, 101 Stat. 1329–90

District of Columbia Appropriations Act, 1989
Pub. L. 100–462, Oct. 1, 1988, 102 Stat. 2269

District of Columbia Appropriations Act, 1990
Pub. L. 101–168, Nov. 21, 1989, 103 Stat. 1267

District of Columbia Appropriations Act, 1991
Pub. L. 101–518, Nov. 5, 1990, 104 Stat. 2224

District of Columbia Appropriations Act, 1992
Pub. L. 102–111, title I, Oct. 1, 1991, 105 Stat. 559

District of Columbia Appropriations Act, 1993
Pub. L. 102–382, title I, Oct. 5, 1992, 106 Stat. 1422

District of Columbia Appropriations Act, 1994
Pub. L. 103–127, title I, Oct. 29, 1993, 107 Stat. 1336

District of Columbia Appropriations Act, 1995
Pub. L. 103–334, title I, Sept. 30, 1994, 108 Stat. 2576

District of Columbia Appropriations Act, 1996
Pub. L. 104–134, title I, §101(b) [title I], Apr. 26, 1996, 110 Stat. 1321–77

District of Columbia Appropriations Act, 1997
Pub. L. 104–194, Sept. 9, 1996, 110 Stat. 2356

District of Columbia Appropriations Act, 1998
Pub. L. 105–100, title I, Nov. 19, 1997, 111 Stat. 2160

District of Columbia Appropriations Act, 1999
Pub. L. 105–277, div. A, §101(c), Oct. 21, 1998, 112 Stat. 2681–121

District of Columbia Appropriations Act, 2000
Pub. L. 106–113, div. A, title I, Nov. 29, 1999, 113 Stat. 1501

District of Columbia Appropriations Act, 2001
Pub. L. 106–522, Nov. 22, 2000, 114 Stat. 2440

District of Columbia Bail Agency Act
Pub. L. 89–519, July 26, 1966, 80 Stat. 327

District of Columbia Barber Act
June 7, 1938, ch. 322, 52 Stat. 620

District of Columbia Blackout Act
Dec. 26, 1941, ch. 625, 55 Stat. 858

District of Columbia Boiler Inspection Act
See Boiler Inspection Act of the District of Columbia

District of Columbia Bond Financing Improvements Act of 1997
Pub. L. 105–33, title XI, subtitle F (§11501 et seq.), Aug. 5, 1997, 111 Stat. 768

District of Columbia Budgetary Efficiency Act of 1991
Pub. L. 102–102, Aug. 17, 1991, 105 Stat. 495

District of Columbia Business Corporation Act
June 8, 1954, ch. 269, 68 Stat. 177

District of Columbia Campaign Finance Reform and Conflict of Interest Act
Pub. L. 93–376, title I, Aug. 14, 1974, 88 Stat. 447

District of Columbia Certified Public Accountancy Act of 1966
Pub. L. 89–578, Sept. 16, 1966, 80 Stat. 785

District of Columbia Charitable Solicitation Act
Pub. L. 85–87, July 10, 1957, 71 Stat. 278

District of Columbia Civil Contempt Imprisonment Limitation Act of 1989
Pub. L. 101–97, Sept. 23, 1989, 103 Stat. 633

District of Columbia Claims Act
June 16, 1880, ch. 243, 21 Stat. 284

District of Columbia Code
Mar. 3, 1901, ch. 854, 31 Stat. 1189

District of Columbia College Access Act of 1999
Pub. L. 106–98, Nov. 12, 1999, 113 Stat. 1323

District of Columbia Consumer Credit Protection Act of 1971
Pub. L. 92–200, Dec. 17, 1971, 85 Stat. 665

District of Columbia Convention Center and Sports Arena Authorization Act of 1995
Pub. L. 104–28, Sept. 6, 1995, 109 Stat. 267

District of Columbia Cooperative Association Act
June 19, 1940, ch. 397, 54 Stat. 480

District of Columbia Court Reform and Criminal Procedure Act of 1970
Pub. L. 91–358, July 29, 1970, 84 Stat. 473

District of Columbia Court Reorganization Act of 1970
Pub. L. 91–358, title I, July 29, 1970, 84 Stat. 475

District of Columbia Courts and Justice Technical Corrections Act of 1998
Pub. L. 105–274, Oct. 21, 1998, 112 Stat. 2419

District of Columbia Credit Unions Act
June 23, 1932, ch. 272, 47 Stat. 326

District of Columbia Criminal Justice Act
Pub. L. 93–412, Sept. 3, 1974, 88 Stat. 1089

District of Columbia Dangerous Weapons Act
July 8, 1932, ch. 465, 47 Stat. 650

District of Columbia Death Act
Feb. 17, 1885, ch. 126, 23 Stat. 307

District of Columbia Delegate Act
Pub. L. 91–405, title II, Sept. 22, 1970, 84 Stat. 848

District of Columbia Election Act
Aug. 12, 1955, ch. 862, 69 Stat. 699

District of Columbia Emergency Deficit Reduction Act of 1991
Pub. L. 102–106, Aug. 17, 1991, 105 Stat. 539

District of Columbia Emergency Highway Relief Act
Pub. L. 104–21, Aug. 4, 1995, 109 Stat. 257

District of Columbia Emergency Rent Act
Dec. 2, 1941, ch. 553, 55 Stat. 788

District of Columbia Federal Payment Authorization and Borrowing Authority Act of 1967
Pub. L. 90–120, Nov. 3, 1967, 81 Stat. 339

District of Columbia Financial Responsibility and Management Assistance Act of 1995
Pub. L. 104–8, Apr. 17, 1995, 109 Stat. 97

District of Columbia Fire and Casualty Act
See Fire and Casualty Act

District of Columbia Home Rule Act
See District of Columbia Self-Government and Governmental Reorganization Act

District of Columbia Horizontal Property Act
See Horizontal Property Act of the District of Columbia

District of Columbia Hospital Treatment for Drug Addicts Act
See Hospital Treatment for Drug Addicts Act for the District of Columbia

District of Columbia Hospitalization of the Mentally Ill Act
Pub. L. 88–597, Sept. 15, 1964, 78 Stat. 944

District of Columbia Income and Franchise Tax Act of 1947
July 16, 1947, ch. 258, art. I, 61 Stat. 331

District of Columbia Income Tax Act
July 26, 1939, ch. 367, title II, 53 Stat. 1085

District of Columbia Inspector General Improvement Act of 1997
Pub. L. 105–7, Mar. 25, 1997, 111 Stat. 14

District of Columbia Insurance Act
Pub. L. 93–89, Aug. 14, 1973, 87 Stat. 297

District of Columbia Insurance Guaranty Association Act
Pub. L. 93–89, title I, Aug. 14, 1973, 87 Stat. 297

District of Columbia Insurance Placement Act
Pub. L. 90–448, title XII, Aug. 1, 1968, 82 Stat. 567

District of Columbia Judges Retirement Act of 1964
Pub. L. 88–644, Oct. 13, 1964, 78 Stat. 1055

District of Columbia Judicial Efficiency and Improvement Act of 1986
Pub. L. 99–573, Oct. 28, 1986, 100 Stat. 3228

District of Columbia Jury System Act
Pub. L. 99–650, Nov. 14, 1986, 100 Stat. 3635

District of Columbia Justice Reform Act of 1994
Pub. L. 103–303, Aug. 23, 1994, 108 Stat. 1564

District of Columbia Juvenile Fraternal Act
See Juvenile Fraternal Act

District of Columbia Law Enforcement Act of 1953
June 29, 1953, ch. 159, 67 Stat. 90

District of Columbia Legal Aid Act
Pub. L. 86–531, June 27, 1960, 74 Stat. 229

District of Columbia Life Insurance Act
See Life Insurance Act

District of Columbia Management Reform Act of 1997
Pub. L. 105–33, title XI, subtitle B (§11101 et seq.), Aug. 5, 1997, 111 Stat. 731

District of Columbia Management Restoration Act of 1999
Pub. L. 106–1, Mar. 5, 1999, 113 Stat. 3

District of Columbia Materialmen's Act
Feb. 28, 1899, ch. 218, 30 Stat. 906

District of Columbia Medical and Dental Manpower Act of 1970
Pub. L. 91–650, title III, Jan. 5, 1971, 84 Stat. 1934

District of Columbia Medical Facilities Construction Act of 1968
Pub. L. 90–457, Aug. 3, 1968, 82 Stat. 631

District of Columbia Mental Health Program Assistance Act of 1991
Pub. L. 102–150, Oct. 31, 1991, 105 Stat. 980
Short title, see 24 U.S.C. 225 note

District of Columbia Merger Act
Jan. 14, 1933, ch. 10, 47 Stat. 752

District of Columbia Metropolitan Police Relief Association Incorporation Act
Pub. L. 87–523, July 5, 1962, 76 Stat. 135

District of Columbia Minimum Wage Act
Sept. 19, 1918, ch. 174, 40 Stat. 960

District of Columbia minimum-wage law
Renamed District of Columbia Minimum Wage Act

District of Columbia Motor Vehicle Safety Responsibility Act
See Motor Vehicle Safety Responsibility Act of the District of Columbia

District of Columbia Nonprofit Corporation Act
Pub. L. 87–569, Aug. 6, 1962, 76 Stat. 265

District of Columbia Organic Act
June 11, 1878, ch. 180, 20 Stat. 102

District of Columbia Physical Therapists Practice Act
See Physical Therapists Practice Act

District of Columbia Police and Firemen's Salary Act Amendments of 1970
Pub. L. 91–297, titles I, II, June 30, 1970, 84 Stat. 354, 357

District of Columbia Police and Firemen's Salary Act Amendments of 1972
Pub. L. 92–410, title I, Aug. 29, 1972, 86 Stat. 634

District of Columbia Police and Firemen's Salary Act of 1953
June 20, 1953, ch. 146, 67 Stat. 72

District of Columbia Police and Firemen's Salary Act of 1958
Pub. L. 85–584, Aug. 1, 1958, 72 Stat. 480

District of Columbia Police Authorization and Expansion Act of 1989
Pub. L. 101–223, Dec. 12, 1989, 103 Stat. 1901

District of Columbia Policemen and Firemen's Retirement and Disability Act
See Policemen and Firemen's Retirement and Disability Act

District of Columbia Policemen and Firemen's Retirement and Disability Act Amendments of 1957
See Policemen and Firemen's Retirement and Disability Act amendments of 1957

District of Columbia Policemen and Firemen's Retirement and Disability Act Amendments of 1970
See Policemen and Firemen's Retirement and Disability Act Amendments of 1970

District of Columbia Policemen and Firemen's Salary Act Amendments of 1966
Pub. L. 89–810, title I, Nov. 13, 1966, 80 Stat. 1591

District of Columbia Police and Firemen's Salary Act Amendments of 1968
Pub. L. 90–320, May 27, 1968, 82 Stat. 140

District of Columbia Practical Nurses' Licensing Act
Pub. L. 86–708, Sept. 6, 1960, 74 Stat. 802

District of Columbia Practice of Psychology Act
See Practice of Psychology Act

District of Columbia Prohibition Law
Mar. 3, 1917, ch. 165, 39 Stat. 1123

District of Columbia Public Assistance Act of 1962
Pub. L. 87–807, Oct. 15, 1962, 76 Stat. 914

District of Columbia Public Education Act
Pub. L. 89–791, Nov. 7, 1966, 80 Stat. 1426

District of Columbia Public Postsecondary Education Reorganization Act
Pub. L. 93–471, Oct. 26, 1974, 88 Stat. 1423

District of Columbia Public School Food Services Act
Oct. 8, 1951, ch. 448, title I, 65 Stat. 367

District of Columbia Public Space Rental Act
Pub. L. 90–596, Oct. 17, 1968, 82 Stat. 1156

District of Columbia Public Space Utilization Act
Pub. L. 90–598, Oct. 17, 1968, 82 Stat. 1166

District of Columbia Public Utilities Reimbursement Act of 1972
Pub. L. 92–495, Oct. 14, 1972, 86 Stat. 812

District of Columbia Public Utility Act
Mar. 4, 1913, ch. 150, §8, 37 Stat. 974

District of Columbia Public Works Act of 1954
May 18, 1954, ch. 218, 68 Stat. 101

District of Columbia Real Estate Deed Recordation Tax Act
Pub. L. 87–408, title III, Mar. 2, 1962, 76 Stat. 11

District of Columbia Real Property Tax Revision Act of 1974
Pub. L. 93–407, title IV, Sept. 3, 1974, 88 Stat. 1051

District of Columbia Receivership Accountability Act of 2000
Pub. L. 106–397, Oct. 30, 2000, 114 Stat. 1651

District of Columbia Red Light Abatement Act
Feb. 7, 1914, ch. 16, 38 Stat. 280

District of Columbia Redevelopment Act of 1945
Aug. 2, 1946, ch. 736, 60 Stat. 790

District of Columbia Rents and Food Act
See Food Control and the District of Columbia Rents Act

District of Columbia Retirement Protection Act of 1997
Pub. L. 105–33, title XI, subtitle A (§11001 et seq.), Aug. 5, 1997, 111 Stat. 715

District of Columbia Retirement Reform Act
Pub. L. 96–122, Nov. 17, 1979, 93 Stat. 866

District of Columbia Revenue Act of 1937
Aug. 17, 1937, ch. 690, 50 Stat. 673

District of Columbia Revenue Act of 1939
July 26, 1939, ch. 367, 53 Stat. 1085

District of Columbia Revenue Act of 1947
July 16, 1947, ch. 258, 61 Stat. 328

District of Columbia Revenue Act of 1949
May 27, 1949, ch. 146, 63 Stat. 112

District of Columbia Revenue Act of 1956
Mar. 31, 1956, ch. 154, 70 Stat. 68

District of Columbia Revenue Act of 1968
Pub. L. 90–450, Aug. 2, 1968, 82 Stat. 612

District of Columbia Revenue Act of 1969
Pub. L. 91–106, Oct. 31, 1969, 83 Stat. 169

District of Columbia Revenue Act of 1970
Pub. L. 91–650, Jan. 5, 1971, 84 Stat. 1930

District of Columbia Revenue Act of 1971
Pub. L. 92–196, Dec. 15, 1971, 85 Stat. 651

District of Columbia Revenue Bond Act of 1985
Pub. L. 99–216, Dec. 26, 1985, 99 Stat. 1727

District of Columbia Revenue Bond Act of 1988
Pub. L. 100–438, Sept. 20, 1988, 102 Stat. 1718

District of Columbia Revenue Bond Act of 1989
Pub. L. 101–158, Nov. 17, 1989, 103 Stat. 946

District of Columbia Revenue Bond Act of 1990
Pub. L. 101–526, Nov. 6, 1990, 104 Stat. 2309

District of Columbia Sales Tax Act
May 27, 1949, ch. 146, title I, 63 Stat. 112

District of Columbia School Reform Act of 1995
Pub. L. 104–134, title I, §101(b) [title II], Apr. 26, 1996, 110 Stat. 1321–77, 1321–107

District of Columbia Securities Act
Pub. L. 88–503, Aug. 30, 1964, 78 Stat. 620

District of Columbia Self-Government and Governmental Reorganization Act
Pub. L. 93–198, Dec. 24, 1973, 87 Stat. 774

District of Columbia Stadium Act of 1957
Pub. L. 85–300, Sept. 7, 1957, 71 Stat. 619

District of Columbia Street Railway Act
May 23, 1908, ch. 190, 35 Stat. 246

District of Columbia Supplemental Appropriations and Rescissions Act, 1991
Pub. L. 102–111, title II, Oct. 1, 1991, 105 Stat. 571

District of Columbia Supplemental Appropriations and Rescissions Act, 1992
Pub. L. 102–382, title II, Oct. 5, 1992, 106 Stat. 1443

District of Columbia Supplemental Appropriations and Rescissions Act, 1993
Pub. L. 103–127, title II, Oct. 29, 1993, 107 Stat. 1350

District of Columbia Supplemental Appropriations and Rescissions Act, 1994
Pub. L. 103–334, title II, Sept. 30, 1994, 108 Stat. 2595

District of Columbia Tax Act
See District of Columbia Revenue Act of 1939

District of Columbia Teachers' Leave Act of 1949
Oct. 13, 1949, ch. 686, 63 Stat. 842

District of Columbia Teachers' Retirement Act
Jan. 15, 1920, ch. 39, 41 Stat. 387

District of Columbia Teachers' Retirement Amendments of 1970
Pub. L. 91–263, May 22, 1970, 84 Stat. 257

District of Columbia Teachers' Salary Act Amendments of 1966
Pub. L. 89–810, title II, Nov. 13, 1966, 80 Stat. 1594

District of Columbia Teachers' Salary Act Amendments of 1968
Pub. L. 90–319, May 27, 1968, 82 Stat. 132

District of Columbia Teachers' Salary Act Amendments of 1970
Pub. L. 91–297, title III, June 30, 1970, 84 Stat. 358

District of Columbia Teachers' Salary Act Amendments of 1972
Pub. L. 92–518, title I, Oct. 21, 1972, 86 Stat. 1005

District of Columbia Teachers' Salary Act Amendments of 1974
See Teachers' Salary Act Amendments of 1974

District of Columbia Teachers' Salary Act of 1945
July 21, 1945, ch. 321, 59 Stat. 488

District of Columbia Teachers' Salary Act of 1947
July 7, 1947, ch. 208, 61 Stat. 248

District of Columbia Teachers' Salary Act of 1955
Aug. 5, 1955, ch. 569, 69 Stat. 521

District of Columbia Tissue Bank Act
Pub. L. 87–656, Sept. 10, 1962, 76 Stat. 534

District of Columbia Traffic Act, 1925
Mar. 3, 1925, ch. 443, 43 Stat. 1119

District of Columbia Unemployment Compensation Act
Aug. 28, 1935, ch. 794, 49 Stat. 946

District of Columbia Unemployment Compensation Act Amendments of 1971
Pub. L. 92–211, Dec. 22, 1971, 85 Stat. 756

District of Columbia Uniform Act on Fresh Pursuit
See Uniform Act on Fresh Pursuit

District of Columbia Uniform Gifts to Minors Act
Aug. 3, 1956, ch. 947, as added Pub. L. 87–821, §1, Oct. 15, 1962, 76 Stat. 938

District of Columbia Uniform Limited Partnership Act
See Uniform Limited Partnership Act

District of Columbia Uniform Narcotic Drug Act
See Uniform Narcotic Drug Act

District of Columbia Uniform Partnership Act
See Uniform Partnership Act

District of Columbia Use Tax Act
May 27, 1949, ch. 146, title II, 63 Stat. 124

District of Columbia Water and Sewer Authority Act of 1996
Pub. L. 104–184, Aug. 6, 1996, 110 Stat. 1696

District of Columbia Work Release Act
Pub. L. 89–803, Nov. 10, 1966, 80 Stat. 1519

District of Columbia Zoning Act
Mar. 1, 1920, ch. 92, 41 Stat. 500

DNA Analysis Backlog Elimination Act of 2000
Pub. L. 106–546, Dec. 19, 2000, 114 Stat. 2726
Short title, see 42 U.S.C. 13701 note

DNA Identification Act of 1994
Pub. L. 103–322, title XXI, subtitle C (§210301 et seq.), Sept. 13, 1994, 108 Stat. 2065
Short title, see 42 U.S.C. 13701 note

Dockery Act (Accounting)
July 31, 1894, ch. 174, 28 Stat. 205

Doctors Draft Act
Sept. 9, 1950, ch. 939, 64 Stat. 826
Short title, see 50 App. U.S.C. 451 note

Dog and Cat Protection Act of 2000
Pub. L. 106–476, title I, subtitle B, ch. 3 (§1441 et seq.), Nov. 9, 2000, 114 Stat. 2163
Short title, see 19 U.S.C. 1654 note

Dollinger Act (Food and Drugs)
Pub. L. 85–250, Aug. 31, 1957, 71 Stat. 567

Dolphin Protection Consumer Information Act
Pub. L. 101–627, title IX, §901, Nov. 28, 1990, 104 Stat. 4465 (16 U.S.C. 1385)
Short title, see 16 U.S.C. 1385(a)

Domestic and Foreign Investment Improved Disclosure Act of 1977
Pub. L. 95–213, title II, Dec. 19, 1977, 91 Stat. 1498
Short title, see 15 U.S.C. 78a note

Domestic Chemical Diversion Control Act of 1993
Pub. L. 103–200, Dec. 17, 1993, 107 Stat. 2333
Short title, see 21 U.S.C. 801 note

Domestic Housing and International Recovery and Financial Stability Act
Pub. L. 98–181, titles I–XI, Nov. 30, 1983, 97 Stat. 1155–1287
Short title, see 12 U.S.C. 1701 note

Domestic Minerals Program Extension Act of 1953
Aug. 7, 1953, ch. 339, 67 Stat. 417 (50 App. U.S.C. 2181 et seq.)
Short title, see 50 App. U.S.C. 2181 note

Domestic Publication of Foreign Filed Patent Applications Act of 1999
Pub. L. 106–113, div. B, §1000(a)(9) [title IV, subtitle E (§4501 et seq.)], Nov. 29, 1999, 113 Stat. 1536, 1501A–561
Short title, see 35 U.S.C. 1 note

Domestic Relations Tax Reform Act of 1984
Pub. L. 98–369, div. A, title IV, subtitle B (§421 et seq.), July 18, 1984, 98 Stat. 793

Domestic Tungsten, Asbestos, Fluorspar, and Columbium-Tantalum Production and Purchase Act of 1956
July 19, 1956, ch. 638, 70 Stat. 579

Domestic Volunteer Service Act Amendments of 1976
Pub. L. 94–293, May 27, 1976, 90 Stat. 525
Short title, see 42 U.S.C. 4950 note

Domestic Volunteer Service Act Amendments of 1979
Pub. L. 96–143, Dec. 13, 1979, 93 Stat. 1074
Short title, see 42 U.S.C. 4950 note

Domestic Volunteer Service Act Amendments of 1984
Pub. L. 98–288, May 21, 1984, 98 Stat. 189
Short title, see 42 U.S.C. 4950 note

Domestic Volunteer Service Act Amendments of 1986
Pub. L. 99–551, Oct. 27, 1986, 100 Stat. 3071
Short title, see 42 U.S.C. 4950 note

Domestic Volunteer Service Act Amendments of 1989
Pub. L. 101–204, Dec. 7, 1989, 103 Stat. 1806
Short title, see 42 U.S.C. 4950 note

Domestic Volunteer Service Act Amendments of 1993
Pub. L. 103–82, title III, subtitle B (§311 et seq.), Sept. 21, 1993, 107 Stat. 898
Short title, see 42 U.S.C. 4950 note

Domestic Volunteer Service Act of 1973
Pub. L. 93–113, Oct. 1, 1973, 87 Stat. 394 (42 U.S.C. 4950 et seq.)
Short title, see 42 U.S.C. 4950 note

Doug Barnard, Jr.—1996 Atlanta Centennial Olympic Games Commemorative Coin Act
Pub. L. 102–390, title I, Oct. 6, 1992, 106 Stat. 1620 (31 U.S.C. 5112 note)

Doughton Bond Limitation Act
See Second Liberty Bond Act

Doughton Current Tax Payment Act of 1943
See Current Tax Payment Act of 1943

Doughton Unemployment Compensation Act
Apr. 19, 1939, ch. 73, 53 Stat. 581

Driftnet Act Amendments of 1990
Pub. L. 94–265, title II, §206, as added Pub. L. 101–627, title I, §107(a), Nov. 28, 1990, 104 Stat. 4441
Short title, see 16 U.S.C. 1826(a)

Driftnet Impact Monitoring, Assessment, and Control Act of 1987
Pub. L. 100–220, title IV, Dec. 29, 1987, 101 Stat. 1477 (16 U.S.C. 1822 note)

Drive for Teen Employment Act
Pub. L. 105–334, Oct. 31, 1998, 112 Stat. 3137
Short title, see 29 U.S.C. 201 note

Drive-By Shooting Prevention Act of 1994
Pub. L. 103–322, title VI, §60008, Sept. 13, 1994, 108 Stat. 1971 (18 U.S.C. 36)
Short title, see 18 U.S.C. 36 note

Driver's Privacy Protection Act of 1994
Pub. L. 103–322, title XXX, Sept. 13, 1994, 108 Stat. 2099 (18 U.S.C. 2721 et seq.)
Short title, see 18 U.S.C. 2721 note

Dropout Prevention Technical Correction Amendment of 1991
Pub. L. 102–159, Nov. 13, 1991, 105 Stat. 1042

Drug Abuse Control Amendments of 1965
Pub. L. 89–74, July 15, 1965, 79 Stat. 226

Drug Abuse Control Amendments of 1965—Continued
Short title, see 21 U.S.C. 301 note

Drug Abuse Education Act of 1970
Renamed Alcohol and Drug Abuse Education Act

Drug Abuse Office and Treatment Act of 1972
Renamed the Drug Abuse Prevention, Treatment, and Rehabilitation Act

Drug Abuse Prevention and Treatment Amendments of 1978
Pub. L. 95–461, Oct. 14, 1978, 92 Stat. 1268
Short title, see 21 U.S.C. 1101 note

Drug Abuse Prevention, Treatment, and Rehabilitation Act
Pub. L. 92–255, Mar. 21, 1972, 86 Stat. 65 (21 U.S.C. 1101 et seq.)
Short title, see 21 U.S.C. 1101 note

Drug Abuse Prevention, Treatment, and Rehabilitation Amendments of 1979
Pub. L. 96–181, Jan. 2, 1980, 93 Stat. 1309
Short title, see 21 U.S.C. 1101 note

Drug Abuse Treatment Technical Corrections Act of 1989
Pub. L. 101–93, Aug. 16, 1989, 103 Stat. 603
Short title, see 42 U.S.C. 201 note

Drug Abuse Treatment Waiting Period Reduction Amendments of 1990
Pub. L. 101–374, Aug. 15, 1990, 104 Stat. 456
Short title, see 42 U.S.C. 201 note

Drug Addiction Treatment Act of 2000
Pub. L. 106–310, div. B, title XXXV, Oct. 17, 2000, 114 Stat. 1222
Short title, see 21 U.S.C. 801 note

Drug Amendments of 1962
Pub. L. 87–781, Oct. 10, 1962, 76 Stat. 780
Short title, see 21 U.S.C. 301 note

Drug and Alcohol Dependent Offenders Treatment Act of 1986
Pub. L. 99–570, title I, §1861, Oct. 27, 1986, 100 Stat. 3207–53
Short title, see 18 U.S.C. 3661 note

Drug and Alcohol Dependent Offenders Treatment Act of 1989
Pub. L. 101–421, Oct. 12, 1990, 104 Stat. 909
Short title, see 18 U.S.C. 3661 note

Drug and Household Substance Mailing Act of 1990
Pub. L. 101–493, Oct. 31, 1990, 104 Stat. 1184
Short title, see 39 U.S.C. 3001 note

Drug Demand Reduction Act
Pub. L. 105–277, div. D, Oct. 21, 1998, 112 Stat. 2681–751
Short title, see 21 U.S.C. 1801 note

Drug Education and Prevention Relating to Youths
Pub. L. 102–132, Oct. 18, 1991, 105 Stat. 630

Drug Enforcement Enhancement Act of 1986
Pub. L. 99–570, title I, §1451, Oct. 27, 1986, 100 Stat. 3207–40

Drug Export Amendments Act of 1986
Pub. L. 99–660, title I, Nov. 14, 1986, 100 Stat. 3743
Short title, see 21 U.S.C. 301 note

Drug Free Truck Stop Act
Pub. L. 103–322, title XVIII, subtitle B, §180201, Sept. 13, 1994, 108 Stat. 2046
Short title, see 21 U.S.C. 801 note

Drug Listing Act of 1972
Pub. L. 92–387, Aug. 16, 1972, 86 Stat. 559
Short title, see 21 U.S.C. 301 note

Drug Possession Penalty Act of 1986
Pub. L. 99–570, title I, subtitle B (§1051 et seq.), Oct. 27, 1986, 100 Stat. 3207–8
Short title, see 21 U.S.C. 801 note

Drug Price Competition and Patent Term Restoration Act of 1984
Pub. L. 98–417, Sept. 24, 1984, 98 Stat. 1585
Short title, see 21 U.S.C. 301 note

Drug-Free Communities Act of 1997
Pub. L. 105–20, June 27, 1997, 111 Stat. 224
Short title, see 21 U.S.C. 1501 note

Drug-Free Media Campaign Act of 1998
Pub. L. 105–277, div. D, title I, subtitle A (§101 et seq.), Oct. 21, 1998, 112 Stat. 2681–752 (21 U.S.C. 1801 et seq.)
Short title, see 21 U.S.C. 1801 note

Drug-Free Prisons and Jails Act of 1998
Pub. L. 105–277, div. D, title I, subtitle B (§111 et seq.), Oct. 21, 1998, 112 Stat. 2681–753 (42 U.S.C. 3751 note)

Drug-Free Public Housing Act of 1988
Pub. L. 100–690, title V, subtitle C, ch. 3 (§5141 et seq.), Nov. 18, 1988, 102 Stat. 4303 (42 U.S.C. 11921 et seq.)
Short title, see 42 U.S.C. 11901 note

Drug-Free Schools and Communities Act Amendments of 1989
Pub. L. 101–226, Dec. 12, 1989, 103 Stat. 1928
Short title, see 20 U.S.C. 6301 note

Drug-Free Schools and Communities Act of 1986
Pub. L. 89–10, Apr. 11, 1965, title V, as added Pub. L. 100–297, title I, §1001, Apr. 28, 1988, 102 Stat. 252 (20 U.S.C. 3171 et seq.)
Pub. L. 99–570, title IV, subtitle B (§4101 et seq.), Oct. 27, 1986, 100 Stat. 3207–125 (20 U.S.C. 4601 et seq.)
Short title, see 20 U.S.C. 4601 note

Drug-Free Schools Quality Assurance Act
Pub. L. 105–277, div. D, title I, subtitle C (§121 et seq.), Oct. 21, 1998, 112 Stat. 2681–756
Short title, see 20 U.S.C. 6301 note

Drug-Free Workplace Act of 1988
Pub. L. 100–690, title V, subtitle D (§5151 et seq.), Nov. 18, 1988, 102 Stat. 4304 (41 U.S.C. 701 et seq.)
Short title, see 41 U.S.C. 701 note

Drug-Free Workplace Act of 1998
Pub. L. 105–277, div. C, title IX, Oct. 21, 1998, 112 Stat. 2681–707
Short title, see 15 U.S.C. 631 note

Drug-Induced Rape Prevention and Punishment Act of 1996
Pub. L. 104–305, Oct. 13, 1996, 110 Stat. 3807
Short title, see 21 U.S.C. 801 note

Drunk Driving Child Protection Act of 1994
Pub. L. 103–322, title X, Sept. 13, 1994, 108 Stat. 1996
Short title, see 18 U.S.C. 1 note

Drunk Driving Prevention Act of 1988
Pub. L. 100–690, title IX, subtitle A (§9001 et seq.), Nov. 18, 1988, 102 Stat. 4521
Short title, see 23 U.S.C. 401 note

Dual Compensation Act
Pub. L. 88–448, Aug. 19, 1964, 78 Stat. 484

Duchesne City Water Rights Conveyance Act
Pub. L. 106–370, Oct. 27, 2000, 114 Stat. 1421

Duck Stamp Act
Also known as the Migratory Bird Hunting Stamp Act
Mar. 16, 1934, ch. 71, 48 Stat. 451 (16 U.S.C. 718 et seq.)
Short title, see 16 U.S.C. 718 note

Dugger Mountain Wilderness Act of 1999
Pub. L. 106–156, Dec. 9, 1999, 113 Stat. 1741

Dulles International Airport Act
Sept. 7, 1950, ch. 905, 64 Stat. 770

Durham-Humphrey Drug Prescriptions Act
See Humphrey-Durham Drug Prescriptions Act

Dutch John Federal Property Disposition and Assistance Act of 1998
Pub. L. 105–326, Oct. 30, 1998, 112 Stat. 3040 (16 U.S.C. 460v note)

Dwight D. Eisenhower Leadership Development Act of 1992
Pub. L. 89–329, title X, part D (§1081, formerly §1181), as added Pub. L. 102–325, title X, §1004, July 23, 1992, 106 Stat. 783

Dwight D. Eisenhower Mathematics and Science Education Act
Pub. L. 89–10, Apr. 11, 1965, title II, part A (§2001 et seq.), as added Pub. L. 100–297, title I, §1001, Apr. 28, 1988, 102 Stat. 219 (20 U.S.C. 2981 et seq.)

Dwight D. Eisenhower Memorial Bicentennial Civic Center Act
Pub. L. 92–520, Oct. 21, 1972, 86 Stat. 1019 (40 U.S.C. 616)
Short title, see 40 U.S.C. 601 note

Dwight David Eisenhower Commemorative Coin Act of 1988
Pub. L. 100–467, Oct. 3, 1988, 102 Stat. 2275 (31 U.S.C. 5112 note)

Dye and Chemical Control Act, 1921
May 27, 1921, ch. 14, title V, 42 Stat. 18

Dyer Act (Motor Vehicles)
See National Motor Vehicle Theft Act

Early Learning Opportunities Act
Pub. L. 106–554, §1(a)(1) [title VIII], Dec. 21, 2000, 114 Stat. 2763, 2763A–79 (20 U.S.C. 9401 et seq.)
Short title, see 20 U.S.C. 9401 note

Earthquake Hazards Reduction Act of 1977
Pub. L. 95–124, Oct. 7, 1977, 91 Stat. 1098 (42 U.S.C. 7701 et seq.)
Short title, see 42 U.S.C. 7701 note

Earthquake Hazards Reduction Authorization Act of 2000
Pub. L. 106–503, title II, Nov. 13, 2000, 114 Stat. 2304
Short title, see 42 U.S.C. 7701 note

East Fork of the Jemez River and the Pecos River Wild and Scenic Rivers Addition Act of 1989
Pub. L. 101–306, June 6, 1990, 104 Stat. 260
Short title, see 16 U.S.C. 1271 note

Eastern Pacific Tuna Licensing Act of 1984
Pub. L. 98–445, Oct. 4, 1984, 98 Stat. 1715 (16 U.S.C. 972 et seq.)
Short title, see 16 U.S.C. 972 note

Eaton Foreign Service Act
July 19, 1939, ch. 330, 53 Stat. 1067

Economic Cooperation Act of 1948
Apr. 3, 1948, ch. 169, title I, 62 Stat. 137 (22 U.S.C. 1501 et seq.)

Economic Cooperation Act of 1950
June 5, 1950, ch. 220, title I, 64 Stat. 198

Economic Development Administration and Appalachian Regional Development Reform Act of 1998
Pub. L. 105–393, Nov. 13, 1998, 112 Stat. 3596
Short title, see 42 U.S.C. 3121 note

Economic Development Administration Reform Act of 1998
Pub. L. 105–393, title I, Nov. 13, 1998, 112 Stat. 3597
Short title, see 42 U.S.C. 3121 note

Economic Development Plan for the Northwestern Band of the Shoshoni Nation Act
Pub. L. 100–419, Sept. 8, 1988, 102 Stat. 1575

Economic Dislocation and Worker Adjustment Assistance Act
Pub. L. 100–418, title VI, subtitle D (§6301 et seq.), Aug. 23, 1988, 102 Stat. 1524
Short title, see 29 U.S.C. 1501 note

Economic Espionage Act of 1996
Pub. L. 104–294, Oct. 11, 1996, 110 Stat. 3488
Short title, see 18 U.S.C. 1 note

Economic Growth and Regulatory Paperwork Reduction Act of 1996
Pub. L. 104–208, div. A, title II, Sept. 30, 1996, 110 Stat. 3009–394
Short title, see 12 U.S.C. 226 note

Economic Opportunity Act of 1964
Pub. L. 88–452, Aug. 20, 1964, 78 Stat. 508
Short title, see 42 U.S.C. 2701 note

Economic Opportunity Amendments of 1965
Pub. L. 89–253, Oct. 9, 1965, 79 Stat. 973

Economic Opportunity Amendments of 1965—Continued
Short title, see 42 U.S.C. 2701 note

Economic Opportunity Amendments of 1966
Pub. L. 89–794, Nov. 8, 1966, 80 Stat. 1451
Short title, see 42 U.S.C. 2701 note

Economic Opportunity Amendments of 1967
Pub. L. 90–222, Dec. 23, 1967, 81 Stat. 672
Short title, see 42 U.S.C. 2701 note

Economic Opportunity Amendments of 1969
Pub. L. 91–177, Dec. 30, 1969, 83 Stat. 827
Short title, see 42 U.S.C. 2701 note

Economic Opportunity Amendments of 1972
Pub. L. 92–424, Sept. 19, 1972, 86 Stat. 688
Short title, see 42 U.S.C. 2701 note

Economic Opportunity Amendments of 1978
Pub. L. 95–568, Nov. 2, 1978, 92 Stat. 2425
Short title, see 42 U.S.C. 2701 note

Economic Recovery Tax Act of 1981
Pub. L. 97–34, Aug. 13, 1981, 95 Stat. 172
Short title, see 26 U.S.C. 1 note

Economic Stabilization Act Amendments of 1971
Pub. L. 92–210, Dec. 22, 1971, 85 Stat. 743

Economic Stabilization Act Amendments of 1973
Pub. L. 93–28, Apr. 30, 1973, 87 Stat. 27

Economic Stabilization Act of 1970
Pub. L. 91–379, title II, Aug. 15, 1970, 84 Stat. 799 (12 U.S.C. 1901 note)

Economic Stimulus Appropriations Act of 1977
Pub. L. 95–29, May 13, 1977, 91 Stat. 122

Economy Act
June 30, 1932, ch. 314, part II, 47 Stat. 399 (see 31 U.S.C. 1535)

Ecstasy Anti-Proliferation Act of 2000
Pub. L. 106–310, div. B, title XXXVI, subtitle C (§3661 et seq.), Oct. 17, 2000, 114 Stat. 1241
Short title, see 42 U.S.C. 201 note

Edge Act
See Mineral Leasing Act

Edge Act (Federal Reserve Banks)
Dec. 23, 1913, ch. 6, §25A, formerly §25(a), as added Dec. 24, 1919, ch. 18, 41 Stat. 378 (12 U.S.C. 611 et seq.)
Short title, see 12 U.S.C. 611 note

Edible Oil Regulatory Reform Act
Pub. L. 104–55, Nov. 20, 1995, 109 Stat. 546
Short title, see 33 U.S.C. 2701 note

Edmunds Act (Polygamy)
Mar. 22, 1882, ch. 47, 22 Stat. 30

Edmunds-Tucker Act (Polygamy)
Mar. 3, 1887, ch. 397, 24 Stat. 635

Education Amendments of 1972
Pub. L. 92–318, June 23, 1972, 86 Stat. 235
Short title, see 20 U.S.C. 1001 note

Education Amendments of 1974
Pub. L. 93–380, Aug. 21, 1974, 88 Stat. 484
Short title, see 20 U.S.C. 6301 note

Education Amendments of 1976
Pub. L. 94–482, Oct. 12, 1976, 90 Stat. 2081
Short title, see 20 U.S.C. 1001 note

Education Amendments of 1977
Pub. L. 95–112, Sept. 24, 1977, 91 Stat. 911
Short title, see 20 U.S.C. 6301 note

Education Amendments of 1978
Pub. L. 95–561, Nov. 1, 1978, 92 Stat. 2143
Short title, see 20 U.S.C. 6301 note

Education Amendments of 1980
Pub. L. 96–374, Oct. 3, 1980, 94 Stat. 1367
Short title, see 20 U.S.C. 1001 note

Education Amendments of 1984
Pub. L. 98–511, Oct. 19, 1984, 98 Stat. 2366
Short title, see 20 U.S.C. 6301 note

Education and Training for a Competitive America Act of 1988
Pub. L. 100–418, title VI, Aug. 23, 1988, 102 Stat. 1469

Education Consolidation and Improvement Act of 1981
Pub. L. 97–35, title V, subtitle D (§551 et seq.), Aug. 13, 1981, 95 Stat. 463
Short title, see 20 U.S.C. 3801 note

Education Council Act of 1991
Pub. L. 102–62, June 27, 1991, 105 Stat. 305 (20 U.S.C. 1221–1 note)

Education Division and Related Agencies Appropriation Act, 1976
Pub. L. 94–94, Sept. 10, 1975, 89 Stat. 468

Education Flexibility Partnership Act of 1999
Pub. L. 106–25, Apr. 29, 1999, 113 Stat. 41
Short title, see 20 U.S.C. 5801 note

Education Flexibility Partnership Demonstration Act
Pub. L. 103–227, title III, §311(e), Mar. 31, 1994, 108 Stat. 176

Education for All Handicapped Children Act of 1975
Pub. L. 94–142, Nov. 29, 1975, 89 Stat. 773
Short title, see 20 U.S.C. 1400 note

Education for Economic Security Act
Pub. L. 98–377, Aug. 11, 1984, 98 Stat. 1267 (20 U.S.C. 3901 et seq.)
Short title, see 20 U.S.C. 3901 note

Education Infrastructure Act of 1994
Pub. L. 89–10, title XII, as added Pub. L. 103–382, title I, §101, Oct. 20, 1994, 108 Stat. 3870 (20 U.S.C. 8501 et seq.)
Short title, see 20 U.S.C. 8501

Education Land Grant Act
Pub. L. 106–577, title II, Dec. 28, 2000, 114 Stat. 3070 (16 U.S.C. 479a)
Short title, see 16 U.S.C. 479a note

Education of the Deaf Act Amendments of 1992
Pub. L. 102–421, Oct. 16, 1992, 106 Stat. 2151
Short title, see 20 U.S.C. 4301 note

Education of the Deaf Act Amendments of 1993
Pub. L. 103–73, title II, Aug. 11, 1993, 107 Stat. 732

Education of the Deaf Act Amendments of 1993—Continued
Short title, see 20 U.S.C. 4301 note

Education of the Deaf Act of 1986
Pub. L. 99–371, Aug. 4, 1986, 100 Stat. 781 (20 U.S.C. 4301 et seq.)
Short title, see 20 U.S.C. 4301 note

Education of the Deaf Amendments of 1998
Pub. L. 105–244, title IX, part B (§911 et seq.), Oct. 7, 1998, 112 Stat. 1829
Short title, see 20 U.S.C. 4301 note

Education of the Handicapped Act
Renamed Individuals with Disabilities Education Act

Education of the Handicapped Act Amendments of 1983
Pub. L. 98–199, Dec. 2, 1983, 97 Stat. 1357
Short title, see 20 U.S.C. 1400 note

Education of the Handicapped Act Amendments of 1986
Pub. L. 99–457, Oct. 8, 1986, 100 Stat. 1145
Short title, see 20 U.S.C. 1400 note

Education of the Handicapped Act Amendments of 1990
Pub. L. 101–476, Oct. 30, 1990, 104 Stat. 1103
Short title, see 20 U.S.C. 1400 note

Education of the Handicapped Amendments of 1974
Pub. L. 93–380, title VI, Aug. 21, 1974, 88 Stat. 576
Short title, see 20 U.S.C. 1400 note

Education of the Handicapped Amendments of 1977
Pub. L. 95–49, June 17, 1977, 91 Stat. 230
Short title, see 20 U.S.C. 1400 note

Education Professions Development Act
Pub. L. 89–329, title V, Nov. 8, 1965, 79 Stat. 1254
Short title, see 20 U.S.C. 1001 note

Educational Agencies Financial Aid Act
Sept. 30, 1950, ch. 1124, 64 Stat. 1100 (20 U.S.C. 236 et seq.)

Educational Broadcasting Facilities and Telecommunications Demonstration Act of 1976
Pub. L. 94–309, June 5, 1976, 90 Stat. 683
Short title, see 47 U.S.C. 609 note

Educational Mining Act of 1982
Pub. L. 97–406, Jan. 3, 1983, 96 Stat. 2031

Educational Partnerships Act of 1988
Pub. L. 100–418, title VI, subtitle A, ch. 5 (§6041 et seq.), Aug. 23, 1988, 102 Stat. 1483 (20 U.S.C. 5031 et seq.)

Educational Research, Development, Dissemination, and Improvement Act of 1994
Pub. L. 103–227, title IX, Mar. 31, 1994, 108 Stat. 212 (20 U.S.C. 6001 et seq.)
Short title, see 20 U.S.C. 6001

Educational Television Act of 1962
Pub. L. 87–447, May 1, 1962, 76 Stat. 64 (47 U.S.C. 390 et seq.)

Educational Television and Radio Amendments of 1969
Pub. L. 91–97, Oct. 27, 1969, 83 Stat. 146
Short title, see 47 U.S.C. 609 note

Educational, Scientific, and Cultural Materials Importation Act of 1966
Pub. L. 89–651, Oct. 14, 1966, 80 Stat. 897
Short title, see 19 U.S.C. 1654 note

Educational, Scientific, and Cultural Materials Importation Act of 1982
Pub. L. 97–446, title I, subtitle B (§161 et seq.), Jan. 12, 1983, 96 Stat. 2346

EEOC Education, Technical Assistance, and Training Revolving Fund Act of 1992
Pub. L. 102–411, Oct. 14, 1992, 106 Stat. 2102
Short title, see 42 U.S.C. 2000a note

Effigy Mounds National Monument Additions Act
Pub. L. 106–323, Oct. 19, 2000, 114 Stat. 1289 (16 U.S.C. 431 note)

Egg Products Inspection Act
Pub. L. 91–597, Dec. 29, 1970, 84 Stat. 1620 (21 U.S.C. 1031 et seq.)
Short title, see 21 U.S.C. 1031 note

Egg Research and Consumer Information Act
Pub. L. 93–428, Oct. 1, 1974, 88 Stat. 1171 (7 U.S.C. 2701 et seq.)
Short title, see 7 U.S.C. 2701 note

Egg Research and Consumer Information Act Amendments of 1980
Pub. L. 96–276, June 17, 1980, 94 Stat. 541
Short title, see 7 U.S.C. 2701 note

Egg Research and Consumer Information Act Amendments of 1988
Pub. L. 100–575, Oct. 31, 1988, 102 Stat. 2895
Short title, see 7 U.S.C. 2701 note

Egg Research and Consumer Information Act Amendments of 1993
Pub. L. 103–188, Dec. 14, 1993, 107 Stat. 2256
Short title, see 7 U.S.C. 2701 note

Eisenhower Exchange Fellowship Act of 1990
Pub. L. 101–454, Oct. 24, 1990, 104 Stat. 1063 (20 U.S.C. 5201 et seq.)
Short title, see 20 U.S.C. 5201 note

El Camino Real de Tierra Adentro National Historic Trail Act
Pub. L. 106–307, Oct. 13, 2000, 114 Stat. 1074
Short title, see 16 U.S.C. 1241 note

El Camino Real de Tierra Adentro Study Act of 1993
Pub. L. 103–144, Nov. 17, 1993, 107 Stat. 1494
Short title, see 16 U.S.C. 1241 note

El Camino Real Para Los Texas Study Act of 1993
Pub. L. 103–145, Nov. 17, 1993, 107 Stat. 1496
Short title, see 16 U.S.C. 1241 note

El Centro Naval Air Facility Ranges Withdrawal Act
Pub. L. 104–201, div. B, title XXIX, subtitle B (§2921 et seq.), Sept. 23, 1996, 110 Stat. 2813

Election Law
June 10, 1872, ch. 415, 17 Stat. 347, 348

Elective Franchise Act (District of Columbia)
Jan. 8, 1867, ch. 6, 14 Stat. 375

Elective Franchise Act (Territories)
Jan. 25, 1867, ch. 15, 14 Stat. 379

Electoral Commission Act
Jan. 29, 1877, ch. 37, 19 Stat. 227

Electoral Count Act
Feb. 3, 1887, ch. 90, 24 Stat. 373

Electoral Count Resolution
Feb. 8, 1865, No. 12, 13 Stat. 567

Electoral Votes Exclusion Resolution
July 20, 1868, No. 58, 15 Stat. 257

Electric and Hybrid Vehicle Research, Development, and Demonstration Act of 1976
Pub. L. 94–413, Sept. 17, 1976, 90 Stat. 1260 (15 U.S.C. 2501 et seq.)
Short title, see 15 U.S.C. 2501 note

Electric Consumers Protection Act of 1986
Pub. L. 99–495, Oct. 16, 1986, 100 Stat. 1243
Short title, see 16 U.S.C. 791a note

Electric Home and Farm Authority Act
Mar. 31, 1936, ch. 163, 49 Stat. 1186

Electric Utility Companies Act
June 10, 1920, ch. 285, parts II, III, as added Aug. 26, 1935, ch. 687, §213, 49 Stat. 847 (16 U.S.C. 824 et seq., 825 et seq.)

Electronic Benefit Transfer Interoperability and Portability Act of 2000
Pub. L. 106–171, Feb. 11, 2000, 114 Stat. 3
Short title, see 7 U.S.C. 2011 note

Electronic Communications Privacy Act of 1986
Pub. L. 99–508, Oct. 21, 1986, 100 Stat. 1848
Short title, see 18 U.S.C. 2510 note

Electronic Freedom of Information Act Amendments of 1996
Pub. L. 104–231, Oct. 2, 1996, 110 Stat. 3048
Short title, see 5 U.S.C. 552 note

Electronic Fund Transfer Act
Pub. L. 90–321, title IX, as added Pub. L. 95–630, title XX, §2001, Nov. 10, 1978, 92 Stat. 3728 (15 U.S.C. 1693 et seq.)
Short title, see 15 U.S.C. 1601 note

Electronic Signatures in Global and National Commerce Act
Pub. L. 106–229, June 30, 2000, 114 Stat. 464 (15 7001 et seq.)
Short title, see 15 U.S.C. 7001 note

Elementary and Secondary Education Act of 1965
Pub. L. 89–10, as added Pub. L. 103–382, title I, §101, Oct. 20, 1994, 108 Stat. 3519 (20 U.S.C. 6301 et seq.)
Short title, see 20 U.S.C. 6301 note

Elementary and Secondary Education Amendments of 1966
Pub. L. 89–750, Nov. 3, 1966, 80 Stat. 1191
Short title, see 20 U.S.C. 6301 note

Elementary and Secondary Education Amendments of 1967
Pub. L. 90–247, Jan. 2, 1968, 81 Stat. 783
Short title, see 20 U.S.C. 6301 note

Elementary and Secondary Education Amendments of 1969
Pub. L. 91–230, Apr. 13, 1970, 84 Stat. 121

Elementary Mathematics and Science Equipment Act
Pub. L. 89–10, title III, part E (§3501 et seq.), as added Pub. L. 103–382, title I, §101, Oct. 20, 1994, 108 Stat. 3667 (20 U.S.C. 6971 et seq.)
Short title, see 20 U.S.C. 6971

Elkins Act (Interstate Commerce)
Feb. 19, 1903, ch. 708, 32 Stat. 847

Ellender Sugar Act
See Sugar Act of 1937

Elwha River Ecosystem and Fisheries Restoration Act
Pub. L. 102–495, Oct. 24, 1992, 106 Stat. 3173

Emancipation Proclamation
Jan. 1, 1863, No. 17, 12 Stat. 1268

Emergency Adjusted Compensation Act, 1931
Feb. 27, 1931, ch. 318, 46 Stat. 1429

Emergency Agricultural Credit Act of 1984
Pub. L. 98–258, title VI, Apr. 10, 1984, 98 Stat. 138
Short title, see 7 U.S.C. 1921 note

Emergency Agricultural Credit Adjustment Act of 1978
Pub. L. 95–334, title II, Aug. 4, 1978, 92 Stat. 429 (7 U.S.C. note prec. 1961)

Emergency Air Mail Act
Mar. 27, 1934, ch. 100, 48 Stat. 508

Emergency Appropriation Act, 1948
July 3, 1947, ch. 206, 61 Stat. 243

Emergency Appropriation Act, fiscal year 1935
June 19, 1934, ch. 648, title II, 48 Stat. 1055

Emergency Banking Relief Act
Mar. 9, 1933, ch. 1, 48 Stat. 1

Emergency Cargo-Ship Construction Act
Feb. 6, 1941, ch. 5, 55 Stat. 5 (46 App. U.S.C. 1125a)

Emergency Community Facilities Act of 1970
Pub. L. 91–431, Oct. 6, 1970, 84 Stat. 886
Short title, see 42 U.S.C. 3101 note

Emergency Compensation and Special Unemployment Assistance Extension Act of 1975
Pub. L. 94–45, June 30, 1975, 89 Stat. 236
Short title, see 26 U.S.C. 3311 note

Emergency Copyright Act of 1941
Sept. 25, 1941, ch. 421, 55 Stat. 732

Emergency Daylight Saving Time Energy Conservation Act of 1973
Pub. L. 93–182, Dec. 15, 1973, 87 Stat. 707 (15 U.S.C. 260a note)

Emergency Detention Act of 1950
Sept. 23, 1950, ch. 1024, title II, 64 Stat. 1019 (50 U.S.C. 811 et seq.)

Emergency Drought Relief Act of 1996
Pub. L. 104–318, Oct. 19, 1996, 110 Stat. 3862

Emergency Employment Act of 1971
Pub. L. 92–54, July 12, 1971, 85 Stat. 146

Emergency Energy Conservation Act of 1979
Pub. L. 96–102, Nov. 5, 1979, 93 Stat. 749 (42 U.S.C. 8501 et seq.)
Short title, see 42 U.S.C. 8501 note

Emergency Extension Act of 1985
Pub. L. 99–107, Sept. 30, 1985, 99 Stat. 479

Emergency Farm Financial Relief Act
Pub. L. 105–228, Aug. 12, 1998, 112 Stat. 1516
Short title, see 7 U.S.C. 7201 note

Emergency Farm Mortgage Act of 1933
May 12, 1933, ch. 25, title II, 48 Stat. 41

Emergency Food Assistance Act of 1983
Pub. L. 98–8, title II, Mar. 24, 1983, 97 Stat. 35 (7 U.S.C. 612c note)

Emergency Food Stamp Vendor Accountability Act of 1976
Pub. L. 94–339, July 5, 1976, 90 Stat. 799
Short title, see 7 U.S.C. 2011 note

Emergency Health Personnel Act Amendments of 1972
Pub. L. 92–585, Oct. 27, 1972, 86 Stat. 1290
Short title, see 42 U.S.C. 201 note

Emergency Health Personnel Act of 1970
Pub. L. 91–623, Dec. 31, 1970, 84 Stat. 1868
Short title, see 42 U.S.C. 201 note

Emergency Highway Energy Conservation Act
Pub. L. 93–239, Jan. 2, 1974, 87 Stat. 1046 (23 U.S.C. 101 note)

Emergency Home Finance Act of 1970
Pub. L. 91–351, July 24, 1970, 84 Stat. 450
Short title, see 12 U.S.C. 1701 note

Emergency Home Purchase Assistance Act of 1974
Pub. L. 93–449, Oct. 18, 1974, 88 Stat. 1364
Short title, see 12 U.S.C. 1701 note

Emergency Homeowners' Relief Act
Pub. L. 94–50, title I, July 2, 1975, 89 Stat. 249 (12 U.S.C. 2701 et seq.)
Short title, see 12 U.S.C. 2701 note

Emergency Housing Act of 1975
Pub. L. 94–50, July 2, 1975, 89 Stat. 249 (12 U.S.C. 2701 et seq.)
Short title, see 12 U.S.C. 2701 note

Emergency Immigrant Education Act of 1984
Pub. L. 98–511, title VI, Oct. 19, 1984, 98 Stat. 2401
Short title, see 20 U.S.C. 4101 note

Emergency Immigration Act
May 19, 1921, ch. 8, 42 Stat. 5

Emergency Insured Student Loan Act of 1969
Pub. L. 91–95, Oct. 22, 1969, 83 Stat. 141

Emergency Interim Consumer Product Safety Standard Act of 1978
Pub. L. 95–319, July 11, 1978, 92 Stat. 386
Short title, see 15 U.S.C. 2051 note

Emergency Jobs Programs Extension Act of 1976
Pub. L. 94–444, Oct. 1, 1976, 90 Stat. 1476

Emergency Jobs and Unemployment Assistance Act of 1974
Pub. L. 93–567, Dec. 31, 1974, 88 Stat. 1845
Short title, see 42 U.S.C. 3121 note

Emergency Livestock Credit Act of 1974
Pub. L. 93–357, July 25, 1974, 88 Stat. 391 (7 U.S.C. note prec. 1961)

Emergency Livestock Feed Assistance Act of 1988
Oct. 31, 1949, ch. 792, title VI, as added Pub. L. 100–387, title I, §101(a), Aug. 11, 1988, 102 Stat. 925 (7 U.S.C. 1471 et seq.)
Short title, see 7 U.S.C. 1421 note

Emergency Loan Guarantee Act
Pub. L. 92–70, Aug. 9, 1971, 85 Stat. 178 (15 U.S.C. 1841 et seq.)
Short title, see 15 U.S.C. 1841 note

Emergency Low Income Housing Preservation Act of 1987
Renamed Low-Income Housing Preservation and Resident Homeownership Act of 1990

Emergency Medical Services Amendments of 1976
Pub. L. 94–573, Oct. 21, 1976, 90 Stat. 2709
Short title, see 42 U.S.C. 201 note

Emergency Medical Services Systems Act of 1973
Pub. L. 93–154, Nov. 16, 1973, 87 Stat. 594
Short title, see 42 U.S.C. 201 note

Emergency Medical Services Systems Amendments of 1979
Pub. L. 96–142, title I, Dec. 12, 1979, 93 Stat. 1067
Short title, see 42 U.S.C. 201 note

Emergency Natural Gas Act of 1977
Pub. L. 95–2, Feb. 2, 1977, 91 Stat. 4 (15 U.S.C. 717 note)

Emergency Officers' Pay Act
July 15, 1940, ch. 626, 54 Stat. 760

Emergency Officers' Retirement Act
May 24, 1928, ch. 735, 45 Stat. 735

Emergency Oil and Gas Guaranteed Loan Program Act
Pub. L. 106–51, ch. 2, Aug. 17, 1999, 113 Stat. 255 (15 U.S.C. 1841 note)

Emergency Petroleum Allocation Act of 1973
Pub. L. 93–159, Nov. 27, 1973, 87 Stat. 627 (15 U.S.C. 751 et seq.)

Emergency Petroleum Allocation Act of 1975
Pub. L. 94–99, Sept. 29, 1975, 89 Stat. 481

Emergency Planning and Community Right-To-Know Act of 1986
Pub. L. 99–499, title III, Oct. 17, 1986, 100 Stat. 1728 (42 U.S.C. 11001 et seq.)
Short title, see 42 U.S.C. 11001 note

Emergency Powers Continuation Act
July 3, 1952, ch. 570, 66 Stat. 330

Emergency Price Control Act of 1942
Jan. 30, 1942, ch. 26, 56 Stat. 23 (50 App. U.S.C. 901 et seq.)

Emergency Rail Facilities Restoration Act
Pub. L. 92–591, Oct. 27, 1972, 86 Stat. 1304

Emergency Rail Services Act of 1970
Pub. L. 91–663, Jan. 8, 1971, 84 Stat. 1975 (45 U.S.C. 661 et seq.)
Short title, see 45 U.S.C. 661 note

Emergency Railroad Transportation Act, 1933
June 16, 1933, ch. 91, 48 Stat. 211

Emergency Relief Act, 1933
See Federal Emergency Relief Act of 1933

Emergency Relief and Construction Act of 1932
July 21, 1932, ch. 520, 47 Stat. 709

Emergency Relief Appropriation Act of 1935
Apr. 8, 1935, ch. 48, 49 Stat. 115

Emergency Relief Appropriation Act of 1936
June 22, 1936, ch. 689, title II, 49 Stat. 1608

Emergency Relief Appropriation Act of 1937
June 29, 1937, ch. 401, title I, 50 Stat. 352

Emergency Relief Appropriation Act of 1938
June 21, 1938, ch. 554, title I, 52 Stat. 809

Emergency Relief Appropriation Act of 1939
June 30, 1939, ch. 252, 53 Stat. 927

Emergency Relief Appropriation Act, fiscal year 1941
June 26, 1940, ch. 432, 54 Stat. 611

Emergency Relief Appropriation Act, fiscal year 1942
July 1, 1941, ch. 266, 55 Stat. 396

Emergency Relief Appropriation Act, fiscal year 1943
July 2, 1942, ch. 479, 56 Stat. 634

Emergency School Aid Act
Pub. L. 89–10, title VI, as added Pub. L. 95–561, title VI, §601(a), Nov. 1, 1978, 92 Stat. 2252 (20 U.S.C. 3191 et seq.)

Emergency Ship Repair Act of 1954
Aug. 20, 1954, ch. 777, 68 Stat. 754 (50 App. U.S.C. 2391 et seq.)

Emergency Steel Loan Guarantee Act of 1999
Pub. L. 106–51, ch. 1, Aug. 17, 1999, 113 Stat. 252 (15 U.S.C. 1841 note)

Emergency Steel Loan Guarantee and Emergency Oil and Gas Guaranteed Loan Act of 1999
Pub. L. 106–51, Aug. 17, 1999, 113 Stat. 252 (15 U.S.C. 1841 note)

Emergency Student Loan Consolidation Act of 1997
Pub. L. 105–78, title VI, §609, Nov. 13, 1997, 111 Stat. 1522
Short title, see 20 U.S.C. 1001 note

Emergency Supplemental Act, 2000
Pub. L. 106–246, div. B, July 13, 2000, 114 Stat. 525

Emergency Supplemental Appropriation Act, 1940
Feb. 12, 1940, ch. 27, 54 Stat. 22

Emergency Supplemental Appropriations Act of 1994
Pub. L. 103–211, title I, Feb. 12, 1994, 108 Stat. 3

Emergency Supplemental Appropriations and Rescissions for the Department of Defense to Preserve and Enhance Military Readiness Act of 1995
Pub. L. 104–6, Apr. 10, 1995, 109 Stat. 73

Emergency Supplemental Appropriations for Additional Disaster Assistance, for Anti-terrorism Initiatives, for Assistance in the Recovery from the Tragedy that Occurred at Oklahoma City, and Rescissions Act, 1995
Pub. L. 104–19, July 27, 1995, 109 Stat. 194

Emergency Supplemental Appropriations for Relief From the Major, Widespread Flooding in the Midwest Act of 1993
Pub. L. 103–75, Aug. 12, 1993, 107 Stat. 739

Emergency Supplemental Assistance for Israel Act of 1991
Pub. L. 102–21, Mar. 28, 1991, 105 Stat. 70

Emergency Supplemental Persian Gulf Refugee Assistance Act of 1991
Pub. L. 102–45, May 17, 1991, 105 Stat. 247

Emergency Tariff Act
May 27, 1921, ch. 14, title I, 42 Stat. 9

Emergency Technical Provisions Act
Pub. L. 94–43, June 28, 1975, 89 Stat. 233
Short title, see 42 U.S.C. 2701 note

Emergency Technical Provisions Act of 1976
Pub. L. 94–328, June 30, 1976, 90 Stat. 727
Short title, see 20 U.S.C. 1001 note

Emergency Unemployment Compensation Act of 1971
Pub. L. 92–224, title II, Dec. 29, 1971, 85 Stat. 811 (26 U.S.C. 3304 note)

Emergency Unemployment Compensation Act of 1974
Pub. L. 93–572, Dec. 31, 1974, 88 Stat. 1869 (26 U.S.C. 3304 note)

Emergency Unemployment Compensation Act of 1991
Pub. L. 102–164, Nov. 15, 1991, 105 Stat. 1049

Emergency Unemployment Compensation Amendments of 1993
Pub. L. 103–6, Mar. 4, 1993, 107 Stat. 33
Short title, see 26 U.S.C. 1 note

Emergency Unemployment Compensation Extension Act of 1977
Pub. L. 95–19, Apr. 12, 1977, 91 Stat. 39
Short title, see 26 U.S.C. 1 note

Emergency Veterans' Job Training Act of 1983
Renamed Veterans' Job Training Act

Emergency Wetlands Resources Act of 1986
Pub. L. 99–645, Nov. 10, 1986, 100 Stat. 3582 (16 U.S.C. 3901 et seq.)

Emergency Wetlands Resources Act of 1986—Continued
Short title, see 16 U.S.C. 3901 note

Emerging Technologies and Advanced Technology Program Amendments Act of 1991
Pub. L. 102–245, title II, Feb. 14, 1992, 106 Stat. 15
Short title, see 15 U.S.C. 271 note

Employee Commuting Flexibility Act of 1996
Pub. L. 104–188, [title II], §§2101–2103, Aug. 20, 1996, 110 Stat. 1928
Short title, see 29 U.S.C. 251 note

Employee Polygraph Protection Act of 1988
Pub. L. 100–347, June 27, 1988, 102 Stat. 646 (29 U.S.C. 2001 et seq.)
Short title, see 29 U.S.C. 2001 note

Employee Retirement Income Security Act of 1974
Pub. L. 93–406, Sept. 2, 1974, 88 Stat. 829 (29 U.S.C. 1001 et seq.)
Short title, see 29 U.S.C. 1001 note

Employees Vacation Act
See Federal Employees Vacation Act

Employees' Compensation Act
See Federal Employees' Compensation Act (1916)

Employees' Compensation Commission Appropriation Act, 1941
June 26, 1940, ch. 428, title III, 54 Stat. 594

Employees' Compensation Commission Appropriation Act, 1942
July 1, 1941, ch. 269, title III, 55 Stat. 494

Employees' Compensation Commission Appropriation Act, 1943
July 2, 1942, ch. 475, title III, 56 Stat. 588

Employees' Compensation Commission Appropriation Act, 1944
July 12, 1943, ch. 221, title III, 57 Stat. 513

Employees' Compensation Commission Appropriation Act, 1945
June 28, 1944, ch. 302, title III, 58 Stat. 566

Employees' Compensation Commission Appropriation Act, 1946
July 3, 1945, ch. 263, title III, 59 Stat. 377

Employees' Compensation Commission Appropriation Act, 1947
July 26, 1946, ch. 672, title III, 60 Stat. 697

Employers' Liability Act (1906) (Railroads)
June 11, 1906, ch. 3073, 34 Stat. 232

Employers' Liability Act (1908) (Railroads)
Apr. 22, 1908, ch. 149, 35 Stat. 65 (45 U.S.C. 51 et seq.)
Short title, see 45 U.S.C. 51 note

Employment Act of 1946
Feb. 20, 1946, ch. 33, 60 Stat. 23 (15 U.S.C. 1021 et seq.)
Short title, see 15 U.S.C. 1021 note

Employment Opportunities for Disabled Americans Act
Pub. L. 99–643, Nov. 10, 1986, 100 Stat. 3574
Short title, see 42 U.S.C. 1305 note

Employment Opportunities for Handicapped Individuals Act
Renamed Employment Opportunties for Individuals With Disabilities Act

Employment Opportunities for Individuals With Disabilities Act
Pub. L. 93–112, title VI, as added Pub. L. 105–220, title IV, §409, Aug. 7, 1998, 112 Stat. 1210 (29 U.S.C. 795 et seq.)
Short title, see 29 U.S.C. 701 note

Employment Security Act of 1960
Pub. L. 86–778, title V, Sept. 13, 1960, 74 Stat. 970
Short title, see 42 U.S.C. 1305 note

Employment Security Administrative Financing Act of 1954
Aug. 5, 1954, ch. 657, 68 Stat. 668

Employment Security Amendments of 1970
Pub. L. 91–373, Aug. 10, 1970, 84 Stat. 695
Short title, see 26 U.S.C. 3311 note

Employment Stabilization Act of 1931
Feb. 10, 1931, ch. 117, 46 Stat. 1084

Endangered American Wilderness Act of 1978
Pub. L. 95–237, Feb. 24, 1978, 92 Stat. 40 (16 U.S.C. 1132 note)

Endangered Species Act Amendments of 1978
Pub. L. 95–632, Nov. 10, 1978, 92 Stat. 3751
Short title, see 16 U.S.C. 1531 note

Endangered Species Act Amendments of 1982
Pub. L. 97–304, Oct. 13, 1982, 96 Stat. 1411
Short title, see 16 U.S.C. 1531 note

Endangered Species Act of 1973
Pub. L. 93–205, Dec. 28, 1973, 87 Stat. 884 (16 U.S.C. 1531 et seq.)
Short title, see 16 U.S.C. 1531 note

Endangered Species Conservation Act of 1969
Pub. L. 89–669, §§1–3, Oct. 15, 1966, 80 Stat. 926, 927, and Pub. L. 91–135, §§1–5, Dec. 5, 1969, 83 Stat. 275–278 (16 U.S.C. 668aa et seq.)

Energy Act of 2000
Pub. L. 106–469, Nov. 9, 2000, 114 Stat. 2029
Short title, see 42 U.S.C. 6201 note

Energy and Water Development Appropriation Act, 1980
Pub. L. 96–69, Sept. 25, 1979, 93 Stat. 437

Energy and Water Development Appropriation Act, 1981
Pub. L. 96–367, Oct. 1, 1980, 94 Stat. 1331

Energy and Water Development Appropriation Act, 1982
Pub. L. 97–88, Dec. 4, 1981, 95 Stat. 1135

Energy and Water Development Appropriation Act, 1984
Pub. L. 98–50, July 14, 1983, 97 Stat. 247

Energy and Water Development Appropriation Act, 1985
Pub. L. 98–360, July 16, 1984, 98 Stat. 403

Energy and Water Development Appropriation Act, 1986
Pub. L. 99–141, Nov. 1, 1985, 99 Stat. 564

Energy and Water Development Appropriation Act, 1988
Pub. L. 100–202, §101(d), Dec. 22, 1987, 101 Stat. 1329–104

Energy and Water Development Appropriations Act, 1987
Pub. L. 99–500, §101(e), Oct. 18, 1986, 100 Stat. 1783–194, and Pub. L. 99–591, §101(e), Oct. 30, 1986, 100 Stat. 3341–194

Energy and Water Development Appropriations Act, 1989
Pub. L. 100–371, July 19, 1988, 102 Stat. 857

Energy and Water Development Appropriations Act, 1990
Pub. L. 101–101, Sept. 29, 1989, 103 Stat. 641

Energy and Water Development Appropriations Act, 1991
Pub. L. 101–514, Nov. 5, 1990, 104 Stat. 2074

Energy and Water Development Appropriations Act, 1992
Pub. L. 102–104, Aug. 17, 1991, 105 Stat. 510

Energy and Water Development Appropriations Act, 1993
Pub. L. 102–377, Oct. 2, 1992, 106 Stat. 1315

Energy and Water Development Appropriations Act, 1994
Pub. L. 103–126, Oct. 28, 1993, 107 Stat. 1312

Energy and Water Development Appropriations Act, 1995
Pub. L. 103–316, Aug. 26, 1994, 108 Stat. 1707

Energy and Water Development Appropriations Act, 1996
Pub. L. 104–46, Nov. 13, 1995, 109 Stat. 402

Energy and Water Development Appropriations Act, 1997
Pub. L. 104–206, Sept. 30, 1996, 110 Stat. 2984

Energy and Water Development Appropriations Act, 1998
Pub. L. 105–62, Oct. 13, 1997, 111 Stat. 1320

Energy and Water Development Appropriations Act, 1999
Pub. L. 105–245, Oct. 7, 1998, 112 Stat. 1838

Energy and Water Development Appropriations Act, 2000
Pub. L. 106–60, Sept. 29, 1999, 113 Stat. 483

Energy and Water Development Appropriations Act, 2001
Pub. L. 106–377, §1(a)(2) [H.R. 5483], Oct. 27, 2000, 114 Stat. 1441, 1441A–59

Energy Conservation and Production Act
Pub. L. 94–385, Aug. 14, 1976, 90 Stat. 1125 (42 U.S.C. 6801 et seq.)
Short title, see 42 U.S.C. 6801 note

Energy Conservation in Existing Buildings Act of 1976
Pub. L. 94–385, title IV, Aug. 14, 1976, 90 Stat. 1150 (42 U.S.C. 6851 et seq.)
Short title, see 42 U.S.C. 6801 note

Energy Conservation Reauthorization Act of 1998
Pub. L. 105–388, Nov. 13, 1998, 112 Stat. 3477
Short title, see 42 U.S.C. 6201 note

Energy Conservation Standards for New Buildings Act of 1976
Pub. L. 94–385, title III, Aug. 14, 1976, 90 Stat. 1144 (42 U.S.C. 6831 et seq.)
Short title, see 42 U.S.C. 6801 note

Energy Emergency Preparedness Act of 1982
Pub. L. 97–229, Aug. 3, 1982, 96 Stat. 248
Short title, see 42 U.S.C. 6201 note

Energy Employees Occupational Illness Compensation Program Act of 2000
Pub. L. 106–398, §1 [div. C, title XXXVI], Oct. 30, 2000, 114 Stat. 1654, 1654A–494 (42 U.S.C. 7384 et seq.)
Short title, see 42 U.S.C. 7384 note

Energy Policy Act of 1992
Pub. L. 102–486, Oct. 24, 1992, 106 Stat. 2776
Short title, see 42 U.S.C. 13201 note

Energy Policy and Conservation Act
Pub. L. 94–163, Dec. 22, 1975, 89 Stat. 871 (42 U.S.C. 6201 et seq.)
Short title, see 42 U.S.C. 6201 note

Energy Policy and Conservation Act Amendments Act of 1994
Pub. L. 103–406, Oct. 22, 1994, 108 Stat. 4209
Short title, see 42 U.S.C. 6201 note

Energy Policy and Conservation Act Amendments of 1990
Pub. L. 101–383, Sept. 15, 1990, 104 Stat. 727
Short title, see 42 U.S.C. 6201 note

Energy Policy and Conservation Act Amendments of 1994
Pub. L. 103–406, title I, Oct. 22, 1994, 108 Stat. 4209
Short title, see 42 U.S.C. 6201 note

Energy Policy and Conservation Act Amendments of 2000
Pub. L. 106–469, title I, Nov. 9, 2000, 114 Stat. 2029
Short title, see 42 U.S.C. 6201 note

Energy Policy and Conservation Act Extension Amendment of 1990
Pub. L. 101–262, Mar. 31, 1990, 104 Stat. 124
Short title, see 42 U.S.C. 6201 note

Energy Policy and Conservation Act Short-Term Extension Amendment of 1990
Pub. L. 101–360, Aug. 10, 1990, 104 Stat. 421
Short title, see 42 U.S.C. 6201 note

Energy Policy and Conservation Amendments Act of 1985
Pub. L. 99–58, July 2, 1985, 99 Stat. 102

Energy Reorganization Act of 1974
Pub. L. 93–438, Oct. 11, 1974, 88 Stat. 1233 (42 U.S.C. 5801 et seq.)
Short title, see 42 U.S.C. 5801 note

Energy Research and Development Administration Appropriation Authorization Act for Fiscal Year 1977
Pub. L. 95–39, June 3, 1977, 91 Stat. 180

Energy Research and Development Administration Authorization Act of 1977 and 1978—Military Applications
Pub. L. 95–183, Nov. 15, 1977, 91 Stat. 1375

Energy Security Act
Pub. L. 96–294, June 30, 1980, 94 Stat. 611
Short title, see 42 U.S.C. 8801 note

Energy Supply and Environmental Coordination Act of 1974
Pub. L. 93–319, June 22, 1974, 88 Stat. 246 (15 U.S.C. 791 et seq.)
Short title, see 15 U.S.C. 791 note

Energy Tax Act of 1978
Pub. L. 95–618, Nov. 9, 1978, 92 Stat. 3174
Short title, see 26 U.S.C. 1 note

Enforcement Act (Embargo)
Jan. 9, 1809, ch. 5, 2 Stat. 506

Enforcement Act (Tariff)
Mar. 2, 1833, ch. 57, 4 Stat. 632

Engle Act
Pub. L. 85–337, Feb. 28, 1958, 72 Stat. 27

Enhanced Federal Security Act of 2000
Pub. L. 106–547, Dec. 19, 2000, 114 Stat. 2738
Short title, see 18 U.S.C. 700 note

Enlisted Men Status Act
July 14, 1939, ch. 267, 53 Stat. 1001

Enterprise for the Americas Act of 1992
Pub. L. 102–549, title VI, Oct. 28, 1992, 106 Stat. 3664 (22 U.S.C. 2430 et seq.)
Short title, see 22 U.S.C. 2151 note

Enterprise for the Americas Initiative Act of 1992
Pub. L. 102–532, Oct. 27, 1992, 106 Stat. 3509
Short title, see 7 U.S.C. 1691 note

Environmental Education Act
Pub. L. 91–516, Oct. 30, 1970, 84 Stat. 1312 (20 U.S.C. 1531 et seq.)

Environmental Education Act of 1978
Pub. L. 89–10, title III, part H (§351 et seq.), as added Pub. L. 95–561, title III, §301(a), Nov. 1, 1978, 92 Stat. 2217

Environmental Education Amendments of 1974
Pub. L. 93–278, May 10, 1974, 88 Stat. 121

Environmental Export Promotion Act of 1994
Pub. L. 103–392, title IV, Oct. 22, 1994, 108 Stat. 4099
Short title, see 15 U.S.C. 4701 note

Environmental Policy and Conflict Resolution Act of 1998
Pub. L. 105–156, Feb. 11, 1998, 112 Stat. 8
Short title, see 20 U.S.C. 5601 note

Environmental Programs Assistance Act of 1984
Pub. L. 98–313, June 12, 1984, 98 Stat. 235 (42 U.S.C. 4368a)
Short title, see 42 U.S.C. 4368a

Environmental Quality Improvement Act of 1970
Pub. L. 91–224, title II, Apr. 3, 1970, 84 Stat. 114 (42 U.S.C. 4371 et seq.)
Short title, see 42 U.S.C. 4371 note

Environmental Research Geographic Location Information Act
Pub. L. 101–617, Nov. 16, 1990, 104 Stat. 3287 (42 U.S.C. 4366a, 4366a notes)

Environmental Research, Development, and Demonstration Authorization Act of 1976
Pub. L. 94–475, Oct. 11, 1976, 90 Stat. 2069

Environmental Research, Development, and Demonstration Authorization Act of 1978
Pub. L. 95–155, Nov. 8, 1977, 91 Stat. 1257

Environmental Research, Development, and Demonstration Authorization Act of 1979
Pub. L. 95–477, Oct. 18, 1978, 92 Stat. 1507

Environmental Research, Development, and Demonstration Authorization Act of 1980
Pub. L. 96–229, Apr. 7, 1980, 94 Stat. 325

Environmental Research, Development, and Demonstration Authorization Act of 1981
Pub. L. 96–569, Dec. 22, 1980, 94 Stat. 3335

Epidemic Diseases Act
Mar. 27, 1890, ch. 51, 26 Stat. 31

Equal Access Act
Pub. L. 98–377, title VIII, Aug. 11, 1984, 98 Stat. 1302 (20 U.S.C. 4071 et seq.)
Short title, see 20 U.S.C. 4071 note

Equal Access to Justice Act
Pub. L. 96–481, title II, Oct. 21, 1980, 94 Stat. 2325
Short title, see 5 U.S.C. 504 note

Equal Credit Opportunity Act
Pub. L. 90–321, title VII, as added Pub. L. 93–495, title V, §503, Oct. 28, 1974, 88 Stat. 1521 (15 U.S.C. 1691 et seq.)
Short title, see 15 U.S.C. 1601 note

Equal Credit Opportunity Act Amendments of 1976
Pub. L. 94–239, Mar. 23, 1976, 90 Stat. 251
Short title, see 15 U.S.C. 1601 note

Equal Educational Opportunities Act of 1974
Pub. L. 93–380, title II, Aug. 21, 1974, 88 Stat. 514 (20 U.S.C. 1701 et seq.)
Short title, see 20 U.S.C. 1701 note

Equal Employment Opportunity Act of 1972
Pub. L. 92–261, Mar. 24, 1972, 86 Stat. 103
Short title, see 42 U.S.C. 2000a note

Equal Export Opportunity Act
Pub. L. 92–412, title I, Aug. 29, 1972, 86 Stat. 644

Equal Justice for Women in the Courts Act of 1994
Pub. L. 103–322, title IV, subtitle D (§40401 et seq.), Sept. 13, 1994, 108 Stat. 1942
Short title, see 42 U.S.C. 13701 note

Equal Nationality Act
May 24, 1934, ch. 344, 48 Stat. 797

Equal Pay Act of 1963
Pub. L. 88–38, June 10, 1963, 77 Stat. 56
Short title, see 29 U.S.C. 201 note

Equal Rights Act (District of Columbia)
Mar. 18, 1869, ch. 3, 16 Stat. 3

Equal Time Act
June 19, 1934, ch. 652, title III, §315, 48 Stat. 1088 (47 U.S.C. 315)

Equalization Act (Pensions)
June 6, 1874, ch. 219, 18 Stat. 61

Equity in Athletics Disclosure Act
Pub. L. 103–382, title III, §360B, Oct. 20, 1994, 108 Stat. 3969
Short title, see 20 U.S.C. 1001 note

Equity in Educational Land-Grant Status Act of 1994
Pub. L. 103–382, title V, part C (§531 et seq.), Oct. 20, 1994, 108 Stat. 4048 (7 U.S.C. 301 note)

Erdman Act of 1898
June 1, 1898, ch. 370, 30 Stat. 424

Erie Canalway National Heritage Corridor Act
Pub. L. 106–554, §1(a)(4) [div. B, title VIII], Dec. 21, 2000, 114 Stat. 2763, 2763A–295 (16 U.S.C. 461 note)

ERISA
See Employee Retirement Income Security Act

Esch Act (Hours of Service on Railroads)
See Hours of Service Act (Railroads)

Esch Car Service Act
May 29, 1917, ch. 23, 40 Stat. 101

Esch Water Power Act
See Federal Power Act

Esch-Cummings Act (Railroads)
See Transportation Act, 1920

Espionage Act
June 15, 1917, ch. 30, 40 Stat. 217

Espionage and Sabotage Act of 1954
Sept. 3, 1954, ch. 1261, 68 Stat. 1216
Short title, see 18 U.S.C. 2151 note

Estuaries and Clean Waters Act of 2000
Pub. L. 106–457, Nov. 7, 2000, 114 Stat. 1957
Short title, see 33 U.S.C. 2901 note

Estuary Restoration Act of 2000
Pub. L. 106–457, title I, Nov. 7, 2000, 114 Stat. 1958 (33 U.S.C. 2901 et seq.)
Short title, see 33 U.S.C. 2901 note

Ethics in Government Act Amendment of 1990
Pub. L. 101–334, July 16, 1990, 104 Stat. 318
Short title, see 5 App. U.S.C. 101 note

Ethics in Government Act Amendments of 1982
Pub. L. 97–409, Jan. 3, 1983, 96 Stat. 2039
Short title, see 28 U.S.C. 1 note

Ethics in Government Act Amendments of 1985
Pub. L. 99–190, §148, Dec. 19, 1985, 99 Stat. 1324

Ethics in Government Act of 1978
Pub. L. 95–521, Oct. 26, 1978, 92 Stat. 1824 (5 App. U.S.C.)
Short title, see 5 App. U.S.C. 101 note

Ethics Reform Act of 1989
Pub. L. 101–194, Nov. 30, 1989, 103 Stat. 1716
Short title, see 5 App. U.S.C. 101 note

EURATOM Cooperation Act of 1958
Pub. L. 85–846, Aug. 28, 1958, 72 Stat. 1084 (42 U.S.C. 2291 et seq.)
Short title, see 42 U.S.C. 2011 note

European Bank for Reconstruction and Development Act
Pub. L. 101–513, title V, §562(c), Nov. 5, 1990, 104 Stat. 2034 (22 U.S.C. 290*l* et seq.)
Short title, see 22 U.S.C. 290*l* note

European Recovery Program
See Foreign Assistance Act of 1948

European Security Act of 1998
Pub. L. 105–277, div. G, subdiv. B, title XXVII, Oct. 21, 1998, 112 Stat. 2681–839 (22 U.S.C. 1928 note)

Evarts Act (Circuit Courts of Appeals)
See Circuit Court of Appeals Act

Everglades National Park Protection and Expansion Act of 1989
Pub. L. 101–229, Dec. 13, 1989, 103 Stat. 1946 (16 U.S.C. 410r–5 et seq.)
Short title, see 16 U.S.C. 410r–5 note

Ex-Servicemen's Unemployment Compensation Act of 1958
Pub. L. 85–848, Aug. 28, 1958, 72 Stat. 1087

Examination Parity and Year 2000 Readiness for Financial Institutions Act
Pub. L. 105–164, Mar. 20, 1998, 112 Stat. 32
Short title, see 12 U.S.C. 1461 note

Excellence in Education Act
Pub. L. 98–377, title VI, Aug. 11, 1984, 98 Stat. 1295 (20 U.S.C. 4031 et seq.)
Short title, see 20 U.S.C. 4031 note

Excellence in Mathematics, Science and Engineering Education Act of 1990
Pub. L. 101–589, Nov. 16, 1990, 104 Stat. 2881 (20 U.S.C. 5301 et seq.)
Short title, see 20 U.S.C. 5301 note

Excellence in Minority Health Education and Care Act
Pub. L. 100–97, Aug. 18, 1987, 101 Stat. 713
Short title, see 42 U.S.C. 201 note

Excess Profits Tax Act of 1940
Feb. 10, 1939, ch. 2 [Internal Revenue Title, ch. 2, subch. E], as added Oct. 8, 1940, ch. 757, title II, §201, 54 Stat. 975

Excess Profits Tax Act of 1950
Jan. 3, 1951, ch. 1199, 64 Stat. 1137

Excess Profits Tax Amendments of 1941
Mar. 7, 1941, ch. 10, 55 Stat. 17

Exchange Rates and International Economic Policy Coordination Act of 1988
Pub. L. 100–418, title III, subtitle A (§3001 et seq.), Aug. 23, 1988, 102 Stat. 1372 (22 U.S.C. 5301 et seq.)
Short title, see 22 U.S.C. 5301

Excise Tax Act of 1947
Mar. 11, 1947, ch. 17, 61 Stat. 12

Excise Tax Reduction Act of 1954
Mar. 31, 1954, ch. 126, 68 Stat. 37

Excise Tax Reduction Act of 1965
Pub. L. 89–44, June 21, 1965, 79 Stat. 136
Short title, see 26 U.S.C. 1 note

Excise Tax Technical Changes Act of 1958
Pub. L. 85–859, Sept. 2, 1958, 72 Stat. 1275
Short title, see 26 U.S.C. 5001 note

Excise Tax Technical Changes Act of 1959
Pub. L. 86–344, Sept. 21, 1959, 73 Stat. 617

Excise, Estate, and Gift Tax Adjustment Act of 1970
Pub. L. 91–614, Dec. 31, 1970, 84 Stat. 1836
Short title, see 26 U.S.C. 2001 note

Excise-Tax Rate Extension Act of 1964
Pub. L. 88–348, June 30, 1964, 78 Stat. 237
Short title, see 26 U.S.C. 1 note

Executive Exchange Program Voluntary Services Act of 1986
Pub. L. 99–424, Sept. 30, 1986, 100 Stat. 964 (5 U.S.C. 4103 note)

Executive Office Appropriation Act, 1963
Pub. L. 87–575, title III, Aug. 6, 1962, 76 Stat. 315

Executive Office Appropriation Act, 1964
Pub. L. 88–39, title III, June 13, 1963, 77 Stat. 63

Executive Office Appropriation Act, 1965
Pub. L. 88–392, title III, Aug. 1, 1964, 78 Stat. 373

Executive Office Appropriation Act, 1966
Pub. L. 89–57, title III, June 30, 1965, 79 Stat. 201

Executive Office Appropriation Act, 1967
Pub. L. 89–474, title III, June 29, 1966, 80 Stat. 227

Executive Office Appropriation Act, 1968
Pub. L. 90–47, title III, July 7, 1967, 81 Stat. 117

Executive Office Appropriation Act, 1969
Pub. L. 90–350, title III, June 19, 1968, 82 Stat. 194

Executive Office Appropriation Act, 1970
Pub. L. 91–74, title III, Sept. 29, 1969, 83 Stat. 120

Executive Office Appropriation Act, 1971
Pub. L. 91–422, title III, Sept. 26, 1970, 84 Stat. 876

Executive Office Appropriation Act, 1972
Pub. L. 92–49, title III, July 9, 1971, 85 Stat. 110

Executive Office Appropriation Act, 1973
Pub. L. 92–351, title III, July 13, 1972, 86 Stat. 474

Executive Office Appropriation Act, 1974
Pub. L. 93–143, title III, Oct. 30, 1973, 87 Stat. 513

Executive Office Appropriation Act, 1975
Pub. L. 93–381, title III, Aug. 21, 1974, 88 Stat. 617

Executive Office Appropriations Act, 1976
Pub. L. 94–91, title III, Aug. 9, 1975, 89 Stat. 445

Executive Office Appropriations Act, 1977
Pub. L. 94–363, title III, July 14, 1976, 90 Stat. 966

Executive Office Appropriations Act, 1978
Pub. L. 95–81, title III, July 31, 1977, 91 Stat. 344

Executive Office Appropriations Act, 1979
Pub. L. 95–429, title III, Oct. 10, 1978, 92 Stat. 1004

Executive Office Appropriations Act, 1980
Pub. L. 96–74, title III, Sept, 29, 1979, 93 Stat. 563

Executive Office Appropriations Act, 1987
Pub. L. 99–500, §101(m) [title III], Oct. 18, 1986, 100 Stat. 1783–308, 1783–315, and Pub. L. 99–591, §101(m) [title III], Oct. 30, 1986, 100 Stat. 3341–308, 3341–315

Executive Office Appropriations Act, 1988
Pub. L. 100–202, §101(m) [title III], Dec. 22, 1987, 101 Stat. 1329–390, 1329–398

Executive Office Appropriations Act, 1989
Pub. L. 100–440, title III, Sept. 22, 1988, 102 Stat. 1728

Executive Office Appropriations Act, 1990
Pub. L. 101–136, title III, Nov. 3, 1989, 103 Stat. 790

Executive Office Appropriations Act, 1991
Pub. L. 101–509, title III, Nov. 5, 1990, 104 Stat. 1399

Executive Office Appropriations Act, 1992
Pub. L. 102–141, title III, Oct. 28, 1991, 105 Stat. 844

Executive Office Appropriations Act, 1993
Pub. L. 102–393, title III, Oct. 6, 1992, 106 Stat. 1738

Executive Office Appropriations Act, 1994
Pub. L. 103–123, title III, Oct. 28, 1993, 107 Stat. 1235

Executive Office Appropriations Act, 1995
Pub. L. 103–329, title III, Sept. 30, 1994, 108 Stat. 2392

Executive Office Appropriations Act, 1996
Pub. L. 104–52, title III, Nov. 19, 1995, 109 Stat. 477

Executive Office Appropriations Act, 1997
Pub. L. 104–208, div. A, title I, §101(f) [title III], Sept. 30, 1996, 110 Stat. 3009–314, 3009–326

Executive Office Appropriations Act, 1998
Pub. L. 105–61, title III, Oct. 10, 1997, 111 Stat. 1290

Executive Office Appropriations Act, 1999
Pub. L. 105–277, div. A, §101(h) [title III], Oct. 21, 1998, 112 Stat. 2681–480, 2681–492

Executive Office Appropriations Act, 2000
Pub. L. 106–58, title III, Sept. 29, 1999, 113 Stat. 444

Executive Office Appropriations Act, 2001
Pub. L. 106–554, §1(a)(3) [title III], Dec. 21, 2000, 114 Stat. 2763, 2763A–136

Executive Pay Act of 1949
Oct. 15, 1949, ch. 695, 63 Stat. 880

Executive Salary Cost-of-Living Adjustment Act
Pub. L. 94–82, title II, Aug. 9, 1975, 89 Stat. 419
Short title, see 5 U.S.C. 5312 note

Expatriation Act of 1907
Mar. 2, 1907, ch. 2534, 34 Stat. 1228

Expatriation Act of 1954
Sept. 3, 1954, ch. 1256, 68 Stat. 1146
Short title, see 8 U.S.C. 1481 note

Expedited Funds Availability Act
Pub. L. 100–86, title VI, Aug. 10, 1987, 101 Stat. 635 (12 U.S.C. 4001 et seq.)
Short title, see 12 U.S.C. 4001 note

Expediting Act (Trusts and Interstate Commerce)
Feb. 11, 1903, ch. 544, 32 Stat. 823 (15 U.S.C. 28, 29)
Short title, see 15 U.S.C. 29 note

Experimental Air Mail Act
Apr. 15, 1938, ch. 157, 52 Stat. 218

Experimental Program to Stimulate Competitive Research on Space and Aeronautics Act
Pub. L. 102–588, title III, Nov. 4, 1992, 106 Stat. 5119 (42 U.S.C. 2467b, 2467b notes)

Explosives Act
See Federal Explosives Act

Explosives Transportation Act of 1908
May 30, 1908, ch. 234, 35 Stat. 554

Export Administration Act of 1969
Pub. L. 91–184, Dec. 30, 1969, 83 Stat. 841

Export Administration Act of 1979
Pub. L. 96–72, Sept. 29, 1979, 93 Stat. 503 (50 App. U.S.C. 2401 et seq.)
Short title, see 50 App. U.S.C. 2401 note

Export Administration Amendments Act of 1981
Pub. L. 97–145, Dec. 29, 1981, 95 Stat. 1727
Short title, see 50 App. U.S.C. 2401 note

Export Administration Amendments Act of 1985
Pub. L. 99–64, titles I, II, July 12, 1985, 99 Stat. 120, 157
Short title, see 50 App. U.S.C. 2401 note

Export Administration Amendments of 1974
Pub. L. 93–500, Oct. 29, 1974, 88 Stat. 1552

Export Administration Amendments of 1977
Pub. L. 95–52, June 22, 1977, 91 Stat. 235

Export Apple Act
June 10, 1933, ch. 59, 48 Stat. 123 (7 U.S.C. 581 et seq.)
Short title, see 7 U.S.C. 581 note

Export Apple and Pear Act
See Export Apple Act

Export Control Act of 1949
Feb. 26, 1949, ch. 11, 63 Stat. 7 (50 App. U.S.C. 2021 et seq.)

Export Enhancement Act of 1988
Pub. L. 100–418, title II, Aug. 23, 1988, 102 Stat. 1325
Short title, see 15 U.S.C. 4701 note

Export Enhancement Act of 1992
Pub. L. 102–429, Oct. 21, 1992, 106 Stat. 2186
Short title, see 12 U.S.C. 635 note

Export Enhancement Act of 1999
Pub. L. 106–158, Dec. 9, 1999, 113 Stat. 1745
Short title, see 22 U.S.C. 2151 note

Export Enhancement Program Amendments of 1994
Pub. L. 103–465, title IV, §411(a), Dec. 8, 1994, 108 Stat. 4962
Short title, see 7 U.S.C. 5601 note

Export Expansion Finance Act of 1971
Pub. L. 92–126, Aug. 17, 1971, 85 Stat. 345
Short title, see 12 U.S.C. 635 note

Export Grape and Plum Act
Pub. L. 86–687, Sept. 2, 1960, 74 Stat. 734 (7 U.S.C. 591 et seq.)
Short title, see 7 U.S.C. 591 note

Export Trade Act
See Webb-Pomerene Act

Export Trading Company Act Amendments of 1988
Pub. L. 100–418, title III, subtitle E (§3401 et seq.), Aug. 23, 1988, 102 Stat. 1384
Short title, see 12 U.S.C. 1841 note

Export Trading Company Act of 1982
Pub. L. 97–290, title I, Oct. 8, 1982, 96 Stat. 1233 (15 U.S.C. 4001 et seq.)
Short title, see 15 U.S.C. 4001 note

Export-Import Bank Act Amendments of 1978
Pub. L. 95–630, title XIX, Nov. 10, 1978, 92 Stat. 3724
Short title, see 12 U.S.C. 635 note

Export-Import Bank Act Amendments of 1983
Pub. L. 98–181, title VI, Nov. 30, 1983, 97 Stat. 1254
Short title, see 12 U.S.C. 635 note

Export-Import Bank Act Amendments of 1986
Pub. L. 99–472, Oct. 15, 1986, 100 Stat. 1200
Short title, see 12 U.S.C. 635 note

Export-Import Bank Act of 1945
July 31, 1945, ch. 341, 59 Stat. 526 (12 U.S.C. 635 et seq.)

Export-Import Bank Act of 1945—Continued
Short title, see 12 U.S.C. 635 note

Export-Import Bank Amendments of 1974
Pub. L. 93–646, Jan. 4, 1975, 88 Stat. 2333
Short title, see 12 U.S.C. 635 note

Export-Import Bank and Reconstruction Finance Corporation Appropriation Act, 1950
June 30, 1949, ch. 286, title III, 63 Stat. 374

Export-Import Bank and Tied Aid Credit Amendments of 1988
Pub. L. 100–418, title III, subtitle D (§3301 et seq.), Aug. 23, 1988, 102 Stat. 1383
Short title, see 12 U.S.C. 635 note

Export-Import Bank Extension Act
Mar. 4, 1939, ch. 5, 53 Stat. 510

Export-Import Bank of Washington Appropriation Act, 1952
Aug. 11, 1951, ch. 301, title III, 65 Stat. 188

Export-Import Bank of Washington Appropriation Act, 1953
June 30, 1952, ch. 523, title III, 66 Stat. 293

Export-Import Bank of Washington, and Reconstruction Finance Corporation Appropriation Act, 1955
May 28, 1954, ch. 242, title III, 68 Stat. 149

Export-Import Bank Reauthorization Act of 1997
Pub. L. 105–121, Nov. 26, 1997, 111 Stat. 2528
Short title, see 12 U.S.C. 635 note

Extra Long Staple Cotton Act of 1983
Pub. L. 98–88, Aug. 26, 1983, 97 Stat. 494
Short title, see 7 U.S.C. 1421 note

Extradition Act (1869)
Mar. 3, 1869, ch. 141, 15 Stat. 337

Extradition Treaties Interpretation Act of 1998
Pub. L. 105–323, title II, Oct. 30, 1998, 112 Stat. 3033 (18 U.S.C. 3181 note)

FAA Civil Penalty Administrative Assessment Act of 1992
Pub. L. 102–345, Aug. 26, 1992, 106 Stat. 923

FAA Research, Engineering, and Development Authorization Act of 1998
Pub. L. 105–155, Feb. 11, 1998, 112 Stat. 5
Short title, see 49 U.S.C. 40101 note

FAA Research, Engineering, and Development Management Reform Act of 1996
Pub. L. 104–264, title XI, Oct. 9, 1996, 110 Stat. 3278
Short title, see 49 U.S.C. 40101 note

Fact Finders' Act
Dec. 5, 1924, ch. 4, §4, 43 Stat. 701
Short title, see 43 U.S.C. 371 note

Faddis Machine Tool Act
Oct. 10, 1940, ch. 836, 54 Stat. 1090 (50 App. U.S.C. 711 et seq.)

Fair Credit and Charge Card Disclosure Act of 1988
Pub. L. 100–583, Nov. 3, 1988, 102 Stat. 2960
Short title, see 15 U.S.C. 1601 note

Fair Credit Billing Act
Pub. L. 93–495, title III, Oct. 28, 1974, 88 Stat. 1511
Short title, see 15 U.S.C. 1601 note

Fair Credit Reporting Act
Pub. L. 90–321, title VI, as added Pub. L. 91–508, title VI, §601, Oct. 26, 1970, 84 Stat. 1127 (15 U.S.C. 1681 et seq.)
Short title, see 15 U.S.C. 1601 note

Fair Debt Collection Practices Act
Pub. L. 90–321, title VIII, as added Pub. L. 95–109, Sept. 20, 1977, 91 Stat. 874 (15 U.S.C. 1692 et seq.)
Short title, see 15 U.S.C. 1601 note

Fair Housing Act
Pub. L. 90–284, title VIII, Apr. 11, 1968, 82 Stat. 81 (42 U.S.C. 3601 et seq.)
Short title, see 42 U.S.C. 3601 note

Fair Housing Act of 1968
See Fair Housing Act

Fair Housing Amendments Act of 1988
Pub. L. 100–430, Sept. 13, 1988, 102 Stat. 1619
Short title, see 42 U.S.C. 3601 note

Fair Labor Standards Act of 1938
June 25, 1938, ch. 676, 52 Stat. 1060 (29 U.S.C. 201 et seq.)
Short title, see 29 U.S.C. 201

Fair Labor Standards Amendments of 1949
Oct. 26, 1949, ch. 736, 63 Stat. 910
Short title, see 29 U.S.C. 201 note

Fair Labor Standards Amendments of 1955
Aug. 12, 1955, ch. 867, 69 Stat. 711
Short title, see 29 U.S.C. 201 note

Fair Labor Standards Amendments of 1961
Pub. L. 87–30, May 5, 1961, 75 Stat. 65
Short title, see 29 U.S.C. 201 note

Fair Labor Standards Amendments of 1966
Pub. L. 89–601, Sept. 23, 1966, 80 Stat. 830
Short title, see 29 U.S.C. 201 note

Fair Labor Standards Amendments of 1974
Pub. L. 93–259, Apr. 8, 1974, 88 Stat. 55
Short title, see 29 U.S.C. 201 note

Fair Labor Standards Amendments of 1977
Pub. L. 95–151, Nov. 1, 1977, 91 Stat. 1245
Short title, see 29 U.S.C. 201 note

Fair Labor Standards Amendments of 1985
Pub. L. 99–150, Nov. 13, 1985, 99 Stat. 787
Short title, see 29 U.S.C. 201 note

Fair Labor Standards Amendments of 1989
Pub. L. 101–157, Nov. 17, 1989, 103 Stat. 938
Short title, see 29 U.S.C. 201 note

Fair Packaging and Labeling Act
Pub. L. 89–755, Nov. 3, 1966, 80 Stat. 1296 (15 U.S.C. 1451 et seq.)
Short title, see 15 U.S.C. 1451 note

Fair Share Refugee Act
Pub. L. 86–648, July 14, 1960, 74 Stat. 504

Fair Trade Act
Aug. 17, 1937, ch. 690, title VIII, 50 Stat. 693

Fair Trade in Auto Parts Act of 1988
Pub. L. 100–418, title II, subtitle A, part II (§2121 et seq.), Aug. 23, 1988, 102 Stat. 1325 (15 U.S.C. 4701 et seq.)
Short title, see 15 U.S.C. 4701 note

Fair Trade in Automotive Parts Act of 1998
Pub. L. 105–261, div. C, title XXXVIII, Oct. 17, 1998, 112 Stat. 2275 (15 U.S.C. 4705 et seq.)
Short title, see 15 U.S.C. 4701 note

Fairness in Music Licensing Act of 1998
Pub. L. 105–298, title II, Oct. 27, 1998, 112 Stat. 2830
Short title, see 17 U.S.C. 101 note

Fall River Water Users District Rural Water System Act of 1998
Pub. L. 105–352, Nov. 3, 1998, 112 Stat. 3222

Fallen Timbers Battlefield and Fort Miamis National Historic Site Act of 1999
Pub. L. 106–164, Dec. 9, 1999, 113 Stat. 1792

Fallon Paiute Shoshone Indian Tribes Water Rights Settlement Act of 1990
Pub. L. 101–618, Nov. 16, 1990, 104 Stat. 3289

False Branding or Marking Act
July 1, 1902, ch. 1357, 32 Stat. 632 (21 U.S.C. 16, 17)

False Claims Act
Mar. 2, 1863, ch. 67, 12 Stat. 696

False Claims Amendments Act of 1986
Pub. L. 99–562, Oct. 27, 1986, 100 Stat. 3153
Short title, see 31 U.S.C. 3701 note

False Identification Crime Control Act of 1982
Pub. L. 97–398, Dec. 31, 1982, 96 Stat. 2009
Short title, see 18 U.S.C. 1001 note

False Statements Accountability Act of 1996
Pub. L. 104–292, Oct. 11, 1996, 110 Stat. 3459
Short title, see 18 U.S.C. 1001 note

Families of Children With Disabilities Support Act of 1994
Pub. L. 91–230, title VI, part I (§701 et seq.), as added Pub. L. 103–382, title III, §315, Oct. 20, 1994, 108 Stat. 3937

Families of Children With Disabilities Support Act of 2000
Pub. L. 106–402, title II, Oct. 30, 2000, 114 Stat. 1728 (42 U.S.C. 15091 et seq.)
Short title, see 42 U.S.C. 15001 note

Family and Community Endeavor Schools Act
Pub. L. 103–322, title III, §30402, Sept. 13, 1994, 108 Stat. 1852

Family and Medical Leave Act of 1993
Pub. L. 103–3, Feb. 5, 1993, 107 Stat. 6 (5 U.S.C. 6381 et seq.; 29 U.S.C. 2601 et seq.)
Short title, see 29 U.S.C. 2601 note

Family Educational Rights and Privacy Act of 1974
Pub. L. 93–380, title V, §513, Aug. 21, 1974, 88 Stat. 571 (20 U.S.C. 1232g)
Short title, see 20 U.S.C. 1221 note

Family Planning and Population Research Act of 1975
Pub. L. 94–63, title II, July 29, 1975, 89 Stat. 306
Short title, see 42 U.S.C. 201 note

Family Planning Services and Population Research Act of 1970
Pub. L. 91–572, Dec. 24, 1970, 84 Stat. 1504
Short title, see 42 U.S.C. 201 note

Family Practice of Medicine Act
Pub. L. 91–696, Dec. 25, 1970, 84 Stat. 2080–1

Family Resource Act
Pub. L. 101–501, title IX, subtitle A, ch. 3 (§955 et seq.), Nov. 3, 1990, 104 Stat. 1278 (42 U.S.C. 12351 et seq.)
Short title, see 42 U.S.C. 12301 note

Family Support Act of 1988
Pub. L. 100–485, Oct. 13, 1988, 102 Stat. 2343
Short title, see 42 U.S.C. 1305 note

Family Unity Demonstration Project Act
Pub. L. 103–322, title III, subtitle S (§31901 et seq.), Sept. 13, 1994, 108 Stat. 1892 (42 U.S.C. 13881 et seq.)
Short title, see 42 U.S.C. 13701 note

Family Violence Prevention and Services Act
Pub. L. 98–457, title III, Oct. 9, 1984, 98 Stat. 1757 (42 U.S.C. 10401 et seq.)
Short title, see 42 U.S.C. 10401 note

Famine Prevention and Freedom From Hunger Improvement Act of 2000
Pub. L. 106–373, Oct. 27, 2000, 114 Stat. 1427
Short title, see 22 U.S.C. 2151 note

Far Eastern Economic Assistance Act of 1950
Feb. 14, 1950, ch. 16, 64 Stat. 5

Farm Bankruptcy Act
See Frazier-Lemke Farm Mortgage Act

Farm Bill of 1938
See Agricultural Adjustment Act of 1938

Farm Credit Act Amendments of 1980
Pub. L. 96–592, Dec. 24, 1980, 94 Stat. 3437
Short title, see 12 U.S.C. 2001 note

Farm Credit Act Amendments of 1986
Pub. L. 99–509, title I, subtitle D (§1031 et seq.), Oct. 21, 1986, 100 Stat. 1877
Short title, see 12 U.S.C. 2001 note

Farm Credit Act of 1933
June 16, 1933, ch. 98, 48 Stat. 257 (12 U.S.C. 1131 et seq.)

Farm Credit Act of 1937
Aug. 19, 1937, ch. 704, 50 Stat. 703

Farm Credit Act of 1953
Aug. 6, 1953, ch. 335, 67 Stat. 390

Farm Credit Act of 1955
Aug. 11, 1955, ch. 785, 69 Stat. 655

Farm Credit Act of 1956
July 26, 1956, ch. 741, 70 Stat. 659

Farm Credit Act of 1959
Pub. L. 86–168, Aug. 18, 1959, 73 Stat. 384

Farm Credit Act of 1971
Pub. L. 92–181, Dec. 10, 1971, 85 Stat. 583 (12 U.S.C. 2001 et seq.)
Short title, see 12 U.S.C. 2001 note

Farm Credit Administration Appropriation Act of 1938
June 29, 1937, ch. 404, title II, 50 Stat. 433

Farm Credit Administration Appropriation Act of 1939
June 16, 1938, ch. 464, title II, 52 Stat. 750

Farm Credit Administration Appropriation Act of 1940
June 30, 1939, ch. 253, title II, 53 Stat. 978

Farm Credit Amendments Act of 1985
Pub. L. 99–205, Dec. 23, 1985, 99 Stat. 1678
Short title, see 12 U.S.C. 2001 note

Farm Credit Banks and Associations Safety and Soundness Act of 1992
Pub. L. 102–552, Oct. 28, 1992, 106 Stat. 4102
Short title, see 12 U.S.C. 2001 note

Farm Credit System Agricultural Export and Risk Management Act
Pub. L. 103–376, Oct. 19, 1994, 108 Stat. 3497
Short title, see 12 U.S.C. 2001 note

Farm Credit System Reform Act of 1996
Pub. L. 104–105, Feb. 10, 1996, 110 Stat. 162
Short title, see 12 U.S.C. 2001 note

Farm Credits Act
See Agricultural Credits Act of 1923

Farm Disaster Assistance Act of 1987
Pub. L. 100–45, May 27, 1987, 101 Stat. 318
Short title, see 7 U.S.C. 1421 note

Farm Interest Act
June 16, 1938, ch. 462, 52 Stat. 709

Farm Labor Contractor Registration Act Amendments of 1974
Pub. L. 93–518, Dec. 7, 1974, 88 Stat. 1652
Short title, see 7 U.S.C. 2041 note

Farm Labor Contractor Registration Act of 1963
Pub. L. 88–582, Sept. 7, 1964, 78 Stat. 920 (7 U.S.C. 2041 et seq.)
Short title, see 7 U.S.C. 2041 note

Farm Labor Supply Appropriation Act, 1944
Feb. 14, 1944, ch. 16, title I, 58 Stat. 11 (50 App. U.S.C. 1351 et seq.)

Farm Mortgage Act
See Frazier-Lemke Farm Mortgage Act

Farm Mortgage Foreclosure Act
June 11, 1934, ch. 446, 48 Stat. 929

Farm Poundage Quota Revisions Act of 1990
Pub. L. 101–577, Nov. 15, 1990, 104 Stat. 2856
Short title, see 7 U.S.C. 1281 note

Farm Research Act
See Agricultural Research Act; Bankhead-Jones Act

Farm Tenant Act
See Bankhead-Jones Farm Tenant Act

Farmer-to-Consumer Direct Marketing Act of 1976
Pub. L. 94–463, Oct. 8, 1976, 90 Stat. 1982 (7 U.S.C. 3001 et seq.)
Short title, see 7 U.S.C. 3001 note

Farmers Home Administration Improvement Act of 1994
Pub. L. 103–248, May 11, 1994, 108 Stat. 619
Short title, see 7 U.S.C. 1921 note

Farmers' Home Administration Act of 1946
Aug. 14, 1946, ch. 964, 60 Stat. 1062
Short title, see 7 U.S.C. 1001 note

Farmington Wild and Scenic River Act
Pub. L. 103–313, Aug. 26, 1994, 108 Stat. 1699
Short title, see 16 U.S.C. 1271 note

Farmington Wild and Scenic River Study Act
Pub. L. 99–590, title II, Oct. 30, 1986, 100 Stat. 3332
Short title, see 16 U.S.C. 1271 note

Farmland Protection Policy Act
Pub. L. 97–98, title XV, subtitle I (§1539 et seq.), Dec. 22, 1981, 95 Stat. 1341 (7 U.S.C. 4201 et seq.)
Short title, see 7 U.S.C. 4201 note

Farms for the Future Act of 1990
Pub. L. 101–624, title XIV, subtitle E, ch. 2 (§1465 et seq.), Nov. 28, 1990, 104 Stat. 3616 (7 U.S.C. 4201 note)

Fascell Fellowship Act
Pub. L. 99–399, title X, Aug. 27, 1986, 100 Stat. 893 (22 U.S.C. 4901 et seq.)
Short title, see 22 U.S.C. 4901 note

Fascell Fellowship Amendments Act of 1990
Pub. L. 101–454, §9, Oct. 24, 1990, 104 Stat. 1065
Short title, see 22 U.S.C. 4901 note

Fastener Quality Act
Pub. L. 101–592, Nov. 16, 1990, 104 Stat. 2943 (15 U.S.C. 5401 et seq.)
Short title, see 15 U.S.C. 5401 note

Fastener Quality Act Amendments Act of 1999
Pub. L. 106–34, June 8, 1999, 113 Stat. 118
Short title, see 15 U.S.C. 5401 note

Father Aull Site Transfer Act of 1996
Pub. L. 104–208, div. A, title I, §101(d) [title I, §122], Sept. 30, 1996, 110 Stat. 3009–181, 3009–203

Father Theodore M. Hesburgh Congressional Gold Medal Act
Pub. L. 106–153, Dec. 9, 1999, 113 Stat. 1733 (31 U.S.C. 5111 note)

Father's Day Act
Pub. L. 92–278, Apr. 24, 1972, 86 Stat. 124

FBI Files Act
See Jencks Act

FDA Export Reform and Enhancement Act of 1996
Pub. L. 104–134, title II, ch. 1A (§2101 et seq.), Apr. 26, 1996, 110 Stat. 1321–313
Short title, see 21 U.S.C. 301 note

FDIC Assessment Rate Act of 1990
Pub. L. 101–508, title II, subtitle A (§2001 et seq.), Nov. 5, 1990, 104 Stat. 1388–14
Short title, see 12 U.S.C. 1811 note

Federal Acquisition Reform Act of 1996
Renamed Clinger-Cohen Act of 1996

Federal Acquisition Streamlining Act of 1994
Pub. L. 103–355, Oct. 13, 1994, 108 Stat. 3243
Short title, see 41 U.S.C. 251 note

Federal Activities Inventory Reform Act of 1998
Pub. L. 105–270, Oct. 19, 1998, 112 Stat. 2382 (31 U.S.C. 501 note)

Federal Advisory Committee Act
Pub. L. 92–463, Oct. 6, 1972, 86 Stat. 770 (5 App. U.S.C.)
Short title, see 5 App. U.S.C. 1

Federal Advisory Committee Act Amendments of 1997
Pub. L. 105–153, Dec. 17, 1997, 111 Stat. 2689
Short title, see 5 App. U.S.C. 1 note

Federal Agriculture Improvement and Reform Act of 1996
Pub. L. 104–127, Apr. 4, 1996, 110 Stat. 888
Short title, see 7 U.S.C. 7201 note

Federal Aid Highway Act
July 11, 1916, ch. 241, 39 Stat. 355

Federal Aid Highway Act of 1938
June 8, 1938, ch. 328, 52 Stat. 633

Federal-Aid Highway Act of 1981
Pub. L. 97–134, Dec. 29, 1981, 95 Stat. 1699
Short title, see 23 U.S.C. 101 note

Federal Aid in Fish Restoration Act
See Dingell-Johnson Sport Fish Restoration Act

Federal Aid in Wildlife Restoration Act
See Pittman-Robertson Wildlife Restoration Act

Federal Aid in Wildlife Restoration Act Amendments of 1970
Pub. L. 91–503, title I, Oct. 23, 1970, 84 Stat. 1097
Short title, see 16 U.S.C. 669 note

Federal-Aid Road Act
July 11, 1916, ch. 241, 39 Stat. 355

Federal Airport Act
May 13, 1946, ch. 251, 60 Stat. 170

Federal Alcohol Administration Act
Aug. 29, 1935, ch. 814, 49 Stat. 977 (27 U.S.C. 201 et seq.)
Short title, see 27 U.S.C. 201

Federal Anti-Injunction Act
See Norris-LaGuardia Act

Federal Anti-Tampering Act
Pub. L. 98–127, Oct. 13, 1983, 97 Stat. 831 (18 U.S.C. 1365; 35 U.S.C. 155A)
Short title, see 18 U.S.C. 1365 note

Federal Arbitration Act
See United States Arbitration Act

Federal Aviation Act of 1958
Pub. L. 85–726, Aug. 23, 1958, 72 Stat. 731

Federal Aviation Administration Authorization Act of 1994
Pub. L. 103–305, Aug. 23, 1994, 108 Stat. 1569
Short title, see 49 U.S.C. 40101 note

Federal Aviation Administration Drug Enforcement Assistance Act of 1988
Pub. L. 100–690, title VII, subtitle E (§7201 et seq.), Nov. 18, 1988, 102 Stat. 4424

Federal Aviation Administration Research, Engineering, and Development Authorization Act of 1990
Pub. L. 101–508, title IX, subtitle C (§9201 et seq.), Nov. 5, 1990, 104 Stat. 1388–372

Federal Aviation Administration Research, Engineering, and Development Authorization Act of 1992
Pub. L. 102–581, title III, Oct. 31, 1992, 106 Stat. 4895

Federal Aviation Administration Research, Engineering, and Development Authorization Act of 1994
Pub. L. 103–305, title III, Aug. 23, 1994, 108 Stat. 1589
Short title, see 49 U.S.C. 40101 note

Federal Aviation Reauthorization Act of 1996
Pub. L. 104–264, Oct. 9, 1996, 110 Stat. 3213
Short title, see 49 U.S.C. 40101 note

Federal Banking Agency Audit Act
Pub. L. 95–320, July 21, 1978, 92 Stat. 391

Federal Boat Safety Act of 1971
Pub. L. 92–75, Aug. 10, 1971, 85 Stat. 213

Federal Boating Act of 1958
Pub. L. 85–911, Sept. 2, 1958, 72 Stat. 1754

Federal Capital Investment Program Information Act of 1984
Pub. L. 98–501, title II, Oct. 19, 1984, 98 Stat. 2324
Short title, see 31 U.S.C. 1101 note

Federal Caustic Poison Act
Mar. 4, 1927, ch. 489, 44 Stat. 1406 (15 U.S.C. 401 et seq.)

Federal Cave Resources Protection Act of 1988
Pub. L. 100–691, Nov. 18, 1988, 102 Stat. 4546 (16 U.S.C. 4301 et seq.)
Short title, see 16 U.S.C. 4301 note

Federal Child Support Enforcement Act
See Child Support Enforcement Act

Federal Cigarette Labeling and Advertising Act
Pub. L. 89–92, July 27, 1965, 79 Stat. 282 (15 U.S.C. 1331 et seq.)
Short title, see 15 U.S.C. 1331 note

Federal Civil Defense Act of 1950
Jan. 12, 1951, ch. 1228, 64 Stat. 1245 (50 App. U.S.C. 2251 et seq.)
Short title, see 50 App. U.S.C. 2251 note

Federal Civil Penalties Inflation Adjustment Act of 1990
Pub. L. 101–410, Oct. 5, 1990, 104 Stat. 890 (28 U.S.C. 2461 note)

Federal Civilian Employee and Contractor Travel Expenses Act of 1985
Pub. L. 99–234, Jan. 2, 1986, 99 Stat. 1756
Short title, see 5 U.S.C. 5701 note

Federal Claims Collection Act of 1966
Pub. L. 89–508, July 19, 1966, 80 Stat. 308

Federal Coal Leasing Amendments Act of 1975
Renamed Federal Coal Leasing Amendments Act of 1976

Federal Coal Leasing Amendments Act of 1976
Pub. L. 94–377, Aug. 4, 1976, 90 Stat. 1083
Short title, see 30 U.S.C. 181 note

Federal Coal Mine Health and Safety Act of 1969
Renamed Federal Mine Safety and Health Act of 1977

Federal Coal Mine Safety Act
May 7, 1941, ch. 87, 55 Stat. 177 (30 U.S.C. 451 et seq.)

Federal Coal Mine Safety Act Amendments of 1965
Pub. L. 89–376, Mar. 26, 1966, 80 Stat. 84

Federal Columbia River Transmission System Act
Pub. L. 93–454, Oct. 18, 1974, 88 Stat. 1376 (16 U.S.C. 838 et seq.)
Short title, see 16 U.S.C. 838 note

Federal Communications Commission Authorization Act of 1983
Pub. L. 98–214, Dec. 8, 1983, 97 Stat. 1467
Short title, see 47 U.S.C. 609 note

Federal Communications Commission Authorization Act of 1988
Pub. L. 100–594, Nov. 3, 1988, 102 Stat. 3021
Short title, see 47 U.S.C. 609 note

Federal Communications Commission Authorization Act of 1990
Pub. L. 101–396, Sept. 28, 1990, 104 Stat. 848
Short title, see 47 U.S.C. 609 note

Federal Contested Election Act
Pub. L. 91–138, Dec. 5, 1969, 83 Stat. 284 (2 U.S.C. 381 et seq.)
Short title, see 2 U.S.C. 381 note

Federal Control Act (Transportation System)
Mar. 21, 1918, ch. 25, 40 Stat. 451

Federal Corrupt Practices Act, 1925
Feb. 28, 1925, ch. 368, title III, 43 Stat. 1070 (2 U.S.C. 241 et seq.)

Federal Courts Administration Act of 1992
Pub. L. 102–572, Oct. 29, 1992, 106 Stat. 4506
Short title, see 28 U.S.C. 1 note

Federal Courts Improvement Act of 1982
Pub. L. 97–164, Apr. 2, 1982, 96 Stat. 25
Short title, see 28 U.S.C. 1 note

Federal Courts Improvement Act of 1996
Pub. L. 104–317, Oct. 19, 1996, 110 Stat. 3847
Short title, see 28 U.S.C. 1 note

Federal Courts Improvement Act of 2000
Pub. L. 106–518, Nov. 13, 2000, 114 Stat. 2410
Short title, see 28 U.S.C. 1 note

Federal Courts Study Act
Pub. L. 100–702, title I, Nov. 19, 1988, 102 Stat. 4644 (28 U.S.C. 331 note)

Federal Courts Study Committee Implementation Act of 1990
Pub. L. 101–650, title III, Dec. 1, 1990, 104 Stat. 5104
Short title, see 28 U.S.C. 1 note

Federal Credit Reform Act of 1990
Pub. L. 93–344, title V, as added Pub. L. 101–508, title XIII, §13201(a), Nov. 5, 1990, 104 Stat. 1388–609 (2 U.S.C. 661 et seq.)
Short title, see 2 U.S.C. 621 note

Federal Credit Union Act
June 26, 1934, ch. 750, 48 Stat. 1216 (12 U.S.C. 1751 et seq.)
Short title, see 12 U.S.C. 1751

Federal Crop Insurance Act
Feb. 16, 1938, ch. 30, title V, 52 Stat. 72 (7 U.S.C. 1501 et seq.)
Short title, see 7 U.S.C. 1501

Federal Crop Insurance Act of 1980
Pub. L. 96–365, Sept. 26, 1980, 94 Stat. 1312
Short title, see 7 U.S.C. 1501 note

Federal Crop Insurance Commission Act of 1988
Pub. L. 100–546, Oct. 28, 1988, 102 Stat. 2730 (7 U.S.C. 1508 note)

Federal Crop Insurance Reform Act of 1994
Pub. L. 103–354, title I, Oct. 13, 1994, 108 Stat. 3179
Short title, see 7 U.S.C. 1501 note

Federal Crop Insurance Reform and Department of Agriculture Reorganization Act of 1994
Pub. L. 103–354, Oct. 13, 1994, 108 Stat. 3178
Short title, see 7 U.S.C. 6901 note

Federal Death Penalty Act of 1994
Pub. L. 103–322, title VI, Sept. 13, 1994, 108 Stat. 1959
Short title, see 18 U.S.C. 3591 note

Federal Debt Collection Procedures Act of 1990
Pub. L. 101–647, title XXXVI, Nov. 29, 1990, 104 Stat. 4933
Short title, see 28 U.S.C. 1 note

Federal Debt Recovery Act
Pub. L. 99–578, Oct. 28, 1986, 100 Stat. 3305

Federal Deposit Insurance Act
Sept. 21, 1950, ch. 967, §§1, 2, 64 Stat. 873 (12 U.S.C. 1811 et seq.)
Short title, see 12 U.S.C. 1811 note

Federal Deposit Insurance Corporation Act
See Federal Deposit Insurance Act

Federal Deposit Insurance Corporation Improvement Act of 1991
Pub. L. 102–242, Dec. 19, 1991, 105 Stat. 2236
Short title, see 12 U.S.C. 1811 note

Federal District Court Organization Act of 1978
Pub. L. 95–408, Oct. 2, 1978, 92 Stat. 883

Federal District Court Organization Act of 1978—Continued
Short title, see 28 U.S.C. 1 note

Federal District Court Organization Act of 1980
Pub. L. 96–462, Oct. 15, 1980, 94 Stat. 2053
Short title, see 28 U.S.C. 1 note

Federal District Court Organization Act of 1984
Pub. L. 98–620, title IV, subtitle B (§404 et seq.), Nov. 8, 1984, 98 Stat. 3361
Short title, see 28 U.S.C. 1 note

Federal Drivers Act
Pub. L. 87–258, Sept. 21, 1961, 75 Stat. 539

Federal Drug Law Enforcement Agent Protection Act of 1986
Pub. L. 99–570, title I, subtitle U (§1991 et seq.), Oct. 27, 1986, 100 Stat. 3207–59
Short title, see 21 U.S.C. 801 note

Federal Election Campaign Act Amendments of 1974
Pub. L. 93–443, Oct. 15, 1974, 88 Stat. 1263
Short title, see 2 U.S.C. 431 note

Federal Election Campaign Act Amendments of 1976
Pub. L. 94–283, May 11, 1976, 90 Stat. 475
Short title, see 2 U.S.C. 431 note

Federal Election Campaign Act Amendments of 1979
Pub. L. 96–187, Jan. 8, 1980, 93 Stat. 1339
Short title, see 2 U.S.C. 431 note

Federal Election Campaign Act of 1971
Pub. L. 92–225, Feb. 7, 1972, 86 Stat. 3 (2 U.S.C. 431 et seq.)
Short title, see 2 U.S.C. 431 note

Federal Emergency Relief Act of 1933
May 12, 1933, ch. 30, 48 Stat. 55

Federal Employee Representation Improvement Act of 1996
Pub. L. 104–177, Aug. 6, 1996, 110 Stat. 1563
Short title, see 18 U.S.C. 201 note

Federal Employee Substance Abuse Education and Treatment Act of 1986
Pub. L. 99–570, title VI, Oct. 27, 1986, 100 Stat. 3207–157
Short title, see 5 U.S.C. 7301 note

Federal Employee Travel Reform Act of 1996
Pub. L. 104–201, div. A, title XVII, Sept. 23, 1996, 110 Stat. 2752
Short title, see 5 U.S.C. 5701 note

Federal Employees Benefits Improvement Act of 1986
Pub. L. 99–251, Feb. 27, 1986, 100 Stat. 14
Short title, see 5 U.S.C. 8901 note

Federal Employees Clean Air Incentives Act
Pub. L. 103–172, Dec. 2, 1993, 107 Stat. 1995
Short title, see 5 U.S.C. 7901 note

Federal Employees Family Friendly Leave Act
Pub. L. 103–388, Oct. 22, 1994, 108 Stat. 4079
Short title, see 5 U.S.C. 6301 note

Federal Employees Flexible and Compressed Work Schedules Act of 1978
Pub. L. 95–390, Sept. 29, 1978, 92 Stat. 755 (5 U.S.C. 5550a, 6101 note)

Federal Employees Flexible and Compressed Work Schedules Act of 1982
Pub. L. 97–221, July 23, 1982, 96 Stat. 227 (5 U.S.C. 6120 et seq.)
Short title, see 5 U.S.C. 6101 note

Federal Employees Health Benefits Act of 1959
Pub. L. 86–382, Sept. 28, 1959, 73 Stat. 708

Federal Employees Health Benefits Amendments Act of 1988
Pub. L. 100–654, Nov. 14, 1988, 102 Stat. 3837
Short title, see 5 U.S.C. 8901 note

Federal Employees Health Benefits Children's Equity Act of 2000
Pub. L. 106–394, Oct. 30, 2000, 114 Stat. 1629
Short title, see 5 U.S.C. 8901 note

Federal Employees Health Care Protection Act of 1998
Pub. L. 105–266, Oct. 19, 1998, 112 Stat. 2363
Short title, see 5 U.S.C. 8901 note

Federal Employees International Organization Service Act
Pub. L. 85–795, Aug. 28, 1958, 72 Stat. 959

Federal Employees Leave Sharing Act of 1988
Pub. L. 100–566, Oct. 31, 1988, 102 Stat. 2834 (5 U.S.C. 6331 et seq., 6361 et seq.)
Short title, see 5 U.S.C. 6301 note

Federal Employees Leave Sharing Amendments Act of 1993
Pub. L. 103–103, Oct. 8, 1993, 107 Stat. 1022
Short title, see 5 U.S.C. 6301 note

Federal Employees Liability Reform and Tort Compensation Act of 1988
Pub. L. 100–694, Nov. 18, 1988, 102 Stat. 4563
Short title, see 28 U.S.C. 1 note

Federal Employees Life Insurance Improvement Act
Pub. L. 105–311, Oct. 30, 1998, 112 Stat. 2950
Short title, see 5 U.S.C. 8701 note

Federal Employees Part-Time Career Employment Act of 1978
Pub. L. 95–437, Oct. 10, 1978, 92 Stat. 1055 (5 U.S.C. 3401 et seq.)
Short title, see 5 U.S.C. 3401 note

Federal Employees Pay Act Amendments of 1954
Sept. 1, 1954, ch. 1208, title II, 68 Stat. 1109

Federal Employees Pay Act of 1945
June 30, 1945, ch. 212, 59 Stat. 295

Federal Employees Pay Act of 1946
May 24, 1946, ch. 270, 60 Stat. 216

Federal Employees Pay Comparability Act of 1990
Pub. L. 101–509, title V, §529 [§§1–412], Nov. 5, 1990, 104 Stat. 1427
Short title, see 5 U.S.C. 5301 note

Federal Employees Salary Act of 1964
Pub. L. 88–426, title I, Aug. 14, 1964, 78 Stat. 400

Federal Employees Salary Act of 1965
Pub. L. 89–301, Oct. 29, 1965, 79 Stat. 1111

Federal Employees Salary Act of 1966
Pub. L. 89–504, title I, July 18, 1966, 80 Stat. 288

Federal Employees Salary Act of 1970
Pub. L. 91–231, Apr. 15, 1970, 84 Stat. 195 (5 U.S.C. 5332 note)

Federal Employees Salary Increase Act of 1955
June 28, 1955, ch. 189, 69 Stat. 172

Federal Employees Salary Increase Act of 1958
Pub. L. 85–462, June 20, 1958, 72 Stat. 203

Federal Employees Salary Increase Act of 1960
Pub. L. 86–568, title I, part B (§111 et seq.), July 1, 1960, 74 Stat. 298

Federal Employees Unemployment Compensation Act
Aug. 14, 1935, ch. 531, title XV, as added Sept. 1, 1954, ch. 1212, §4(a), 68 Stat. 1130

Federal Employees Uniform Allowance Act
Sept. 1, 1954, ch. 1208, title IV, 68 Stat. 1114

Federal Employees Vacation Act
Mar. 14, 1936, ch. 140, 49 Stat. 1161

Federal Employees' Compensation Act (1908)
May 30, 1908, ch. 236, 35 Stat. 556

Federal Employees' Compensation Act (1916)
Sept. 7, 1916, ch. 458, 39 Stat. 742

Federal Employees' Compensation Act Amendments of 1949
Oct. 14, 1949, ch. 691, 63 Stat. 854

Federal Employees' Compensation Act Amendments of 1960
Pub. L. 86–767, Sept. 13, 1960, 74 Stat. 906

Federal Employees' Compensation Act Amendments of 1966
Pub. L. 89–488, July 4, 1966, 80 Stat. 252

Federal Employees' Group Life Insurance Act of 1954
Aug. 17, 1954, ch. 752, 68 Stat. 736

Federal Employees' Group Life Insurance Act of 1980
Pub. L. 96–427, Oct. 10, 1980, 94 Stat. 1831
Short title, see 5 U.S.C. 8701 note

Federal Employees' Retirement Contribution Temporary Adjustment Act of 1983
Pub. L. 98–168, title II, Nov. 29, 1983, 97 Stat. 1106 (5 U.S.C. 8331 note)

Federal Employees' Retirement System Act of 1986
Pub. L. 99–335, June 6, 1986, 100 Stat. 514
Short title, see 5 U.S.C. 8401 note

Federal Employees' Retirement System Open Enrollment Act of 1997
Pub. L. 105–61, title VI, §642, Oct. 10, 1997, 111 Stat. 1318 (5 U.S.C. 8331 note)

Federal Employees' Retirement System Technical Corrections Act of 1986
Pub. L. 99–556, Oct. 27, 1986, 100 Stat. 3131
Short title, see 5 U.S.C. 8401 note

Federal Employers' Liability Act (Railroads)
See Employers' Liability Act (1908) (Railroads)

Federal Employment Service Act
See Wagner-Peyser Act

Federal Energy Administration Act Amendments of 1976
Pub. L. 94–385, title I, Aug. 14, 1976, 90 Stat. 1127
Short title, see 15 U.S.C. 761 note

Federal Energy Administration Act of 1974
Pub. L. 93–275, May 7, 1974, 88 Stat. 96 (15 U.S.C. 761 et seq.)
Short title, see 15 U.S.C. 761 note

Federal Energy Administration Authorization Act of 1977
Pub. L. 95–70, July 21, 1977, 91 Stat. 275
Short title, see 15 U.S.C. 761 note

Federal Energy Management Improvement Act of 1988
Pub. L. 100–615, Nov. 5, 1988, 102 Stat. 3185
Short title, see 42 U.S.C. 8201 note

Federal Energy Regulatory Commission Member Term Act of 1990
Pub. L. 101–271, Apr. 11, 1990, 104 Stat. 135
Short title, see 42 U.S.C. 7101 note

Federal Environmental Pesticide Control Act of 1972
Pub. L. 92–516, Oct. 21, 1972, 86 Stat. 973 (7 U.S.C. 136 et seq.)
Short title, see 7 U.S.C. 136 note

Federal Erroneous Retirement Coverage Corrections Act
Pub. L. 106–265, title II, Sept. 19, 2000, 114 Stat. 770 (5 U.S.C. 8331 note)

Federal Escape Act
May 14, 1930, ch. 274, §§9, 11, 46 Stat. 327

Federal Executive Pay Act of 1956
July 31, 1956, ch. 804, title I, 70 Stat. 736

Federal Executive Salary Act of 1964
Pub. L. 88–426, title III, Aug. 14, 1964, 78 Stat. 415

Federal Explosives Act
Oct. 6, 1917, ch. 83, 40 Stat. 385 (50 U.S.C. 121 et seq.)

Federal Facility Compliance Act of 1992
Pub. L. 102–386, title I, Oct. 6, 1992, 106 Stat. 1505
Short title, see 42 U.S.C. 6901 note

Federal Farm Board Act
See Agricultural Marketing Act

Federal Farm Loan Act
July 17, 1916, ch. 245, 39 Stat. 360

Federal Farm Mortgage Corporation Act
Jan. 31, 1934, ch. 7, 48 Stat. 344 (12 U.S.C. 1020 et seq.)

Federal Financial Assistance Management Improvement Act of 1999
Pub. L. 106–107, Nov. 20, 1999, 113 Stat. 1486 (31 U.S.C. 6101 note)

Federal Financial Institutions Examination Council Act of 1978
Pub. L. 95–630, title X, Nov. 10, 1978, 92 Stat. 3694 (12 U.S.C. 3301 et seq.)
Short title, see 12 U.S.C. 3301 note

Federal Financial Management Act of 1994
Pub. L. 103–356, title IV, Oct. 13, 1994, 108 Stat. 3412
Short title, see 31 U.S.C. 3301 note

Federal Financial Management Improvement Act of 1996
Pub. L. 104–208, div. A, title I, §101(f) [title VIII], Sept. 30, 1996, 110 Stat. 3009–314, 3009–389 (31 U.S.C. 3512 note)

Federal Financing Bank Act of 1973
Pub. L. 93–224, Dec. 29, 1973, 87 Stat. 937 (12 U.S.C. 2281 et seq.)
Short title, see 12 U.S.C. 2281 note

Federal Fire Prevention and Control Act of 1974
Pub. L. 93–498, Oct. 29, 1974, 88 Stat. 1535 (15 U.S.C. 2201 et seq.)
Short title, see 15 U.S.C. 2201 note

Federal Firearms Act
June 30, 1938, ch. 850, 52 Stat. 1250 (15 U.S.C. 901 et seq.)

Federal Firearms License Reform Act of 1993
Pub. L. 103–159, title III, Nov. 30, 1993, 107 Stat. 1545
Short title, see 18 U.S.C. 921 note

Federal Flood Insurance Act of 1956
Aug. 7, 1956, ch. 1025, 70 Stat. 1078 (42 U.S.C. 2401 et seq.)

Federal Food and Drugs Act of 1906
June 30, 1906, ch. 3915, 34 Stat. 768

Federal Food, Drug, and Cosmetic Act
June 25, 1938, ch. 675, 52 Stat. 1040 (21 U.S.C. 301 et seq.)
Short title, see 21 U.S.C. 301

Federal Grant and Cooperative Agreement Act of 1977
Pub. L. 95–224, Feb. 3, 1978, 92 Stat. 3

Federal Gun Control Act
See Gun Control Act of 1968

Federal Hazardous Substances Act
Pub. L. 86–613, July 12, 1960, 74 Stat. 372 (15 U.S.C. 1261 et seq.)
Short title, see 15 U.S.C. 1261 note

Federal Highway Act
Nov. 9, 1921, ch. 119, 42 Stat. 212

Federal Highway Act of 1940
Sept. 5, 1940, ch. 715, 54 Stat. 867

Federal Highway Act of 1960
Pub. L. 86–657, July 14, 1960, 74 Stat. 522
Short title, see 23 U.S.C. 101 note

Federal Home Loan Bank Act
July 22, 1932, ch. 522, 47 Stat. 725 (12 U.S.C. 1421 et seq.)
Short title, see 12 U.S.C. 1421

Federal Home Loan Bank System Modernization Act of 1999
Pub. L. 106–102, title VI, Nov. 12, 1999, 113 Stat. 1450
Short title, see 12 U.S.C. 1421 note

Federal Home Loan Mortgage Corporation Act
Pub. L. 91–351, title III, July 24, 1970, 84 Stat. 451 (12 U.S.C. 1451 et seq.)
Short title, see 12 U.S.C. 1451 note

Federal Housing Act
See National Housing Act

Federal Housing Enterprises Financial Safety and Soundness Act of 1992
Pub. L. 102–550, title XIII, Oct. 28, 1992, 106 Stat. 3941 (12 U.S.C. 4501 et seq.)
Short title, see 12 U.S.C. 4501 note

Federal Impoundment and Information Act
Pub. L. 92–599, title IV, Oct. 27, 1972, 86 Stat. 1325

Federal Information Centers Act
Pub. L. 95–491, Oct. 20, 1978, 92 Stat. 1641 (40 U.S.C. 760)
Short title, see 40 U.S.C. 760 note

Federal Insecticide, Fungicide, and Rodenticide Act
June 25, 1947, ch. 125, as added Pub. L. 92–516, §2, Oct. 21, 1972, 86 Stat. 973 (7 U.S.C. 136 et seq.)
Short title, see 7 U.S.C. 136 note

Federal Insecticide, Fungicide, and Rodenticide Act Amendments of 1988
Pub. L. 100–532, Oct. 25, 1988, 102 Stat. 2654
Short title, see 7 U.S.C. 136 note

Federal Insurance Contributions Act
Aug. 16, 1954, ch. 736, §1(d) [Internal Revenue Title, chapter 21], 68A Stat. 415 (26 U.S.C. 3101 et seq.)
Short title, see 26 U.S.C. 3128

Federal Interpleader Act
May 8, 1926, ch. 273, 44 Stat. 416

Federal Interpleader Act of 1936
Jan. 20, 1936, ch. 13, 49 Stat. 1096

Federal Judgeship Act of 1990
Pub. L. 101–650, title II, Dec. 1, 1990, 104 Stat. 5098
Short title, see 28 U.S.C. 1 note

Federal Judicial Salary Act of 1964
Pub. L. 88–426, title IV, Aug. 14, 1964, 78 Stat. 433
Short title, see 28 U.S.C. 1 note

Federal Judicial Salary Act of 1966
Pub. L. 89–504, title II, July 18, 1966, 80 Stat. 293
Short title, see 28 U.S.C. 1 note

Federal Juvenile Delinquency Act
June 16, 1938, ch. 486, 52 Stat. 764

Federal Kidnapping Act
See Kidnapping Act

Federal Laboratory Animal Welfare Act
See Animal Welfare Act

Federal Land Exchange Facilitation Act of 1988
Pub. L. 100–409, Aug. 20, 1988, 102 Stat. 1086
Short title, see 43 U.S.C. 1701 note

Federal Land Policy and Management Act of 1976
Pub. L. 94–579, Oct. 21, 1976, 90 Stat. 2744 (43 U.S.C. 1701 et seq.)
Short title, see 43 U.S.C. 1701 note

Federal Land Transaction Facilitation Act
Pub. L. 106–248, title II, July 25, 2000, 114 Stat. 613 (43 U.S.C. 2301 et seq.)
Short title, see 43 U.S.C. 2301 note

Federal Lands Cleanup Act of 1985
Pub. L. 99–402, Aug. 27, 1986, 100 Stat. 910

Federal Law Enforcement Animal Protection Act of 2000
Pub. L. 106–254, Aug. 2, 2000, 114 Stat. 638 (18 U.S.C. 1368)
Short title, see 18 U.S.C. 1368 note

Federal Law Enforcement Dependents Assistance Act of 1996
Pub. L. 104–238, Oct. 3, 1996, 110 Stat. 3114 (42 U.S.C. 3796d et seq.)
Short title, see 42 U.S.C. 3711 note

Federal Law Enforcement Pay Reform Act of 1990
Pub. L. 101–509, title V, §529 [title IV], Nov. 5, 1990, 104 Stat. 1427, 1465 (5 U.S.C. 5305 note)

Federal Legislative Salary Act of 1964
Pub. L. 88–426, title II, Aug. 14, 1964, 78 Stat. 413
Short title, see 2 U.S.C. 31 note

Federal Legislative Salary Act of 1966
Pub. L. 89–504, title III, July 18, 1966, 80 Stat. 294

Federal Loan Agency Appropriation Act, 1946
May 21, 1945, ch. 129, title V, 59 Stat. 200

Federal Magistrate Act of 1979
Pub. L. 96–82, Oct. 10, 1979, 93 Stat. 643
Short title, see 28 U.S.C. 631 note

Federal Magistrates Act
Pub. L. 90–578, Oct. 17, 1968, 82 Stat. 1107
Short title, see 28 U.S.C. 631 note

Federal Managers' Financial Integrity Act of 1982
Pub. L. 97–255, Sept. 8, 1982, 96 Stat. 814

Federal Maritime Commission Authorization Act of 1990
Pub. L. 101–595, Nov. 16, 1990, 104 Stat. 2979

Federal Maritime Commission Authorization Act of 1991
Pub. L. 102–100, Aug. 17, 1991, 105 Stat. 491

Federal Marshals Act
June 15, 1935, ch. 259, 49 Stat. 377

Federal Mass Transportation Act of 1987
Pub. L. 100–17, title III, Apr. 2, 1987, 101 Stat. 223

Federal Meat Inspection Act
Act Mar. 4, 1907, ch. 2907, titles I to IV, 34 Stat. 1260 (21 U.S.C. 601 et seq.)
Short title, see 21 U.S.C. 601 note

Federal Medical Care Recovery Act
Pub. L. 87–693, Sept. 25, 1962, 76 Stat. 593 (42 U.S.C. 2651 et seq.)

Federal Metal and Nonmetallic Mine Safety Act
Pub. L. 89–577, Sept. 16, 1966, 80 Stat. 772 (30 U.S.C. 721 et seq.)

Federal Mine Safety and Health Act of 1977
Pub. L. 91–173, Dec. 30, 1969, 83 Stat. 742 (30 U.S.C. 801 et seq.)
Short title, see 30 U.S.C. 801 note

Federal Mine Safety and Health Amendments Act of 1977
Pub. L. 95–164, Nov. 9, 1977, 91 Stat. 1290
Short title, see 30 U.S.C. 801 note

Federal National Mortgage Association Charter Act
June 27, 1934, ch. 847, title III, as added Aug. 2, 1954, ch. 649, title II, §201, 68 Stat. 612 (12 U.S.C. 1716 et seq.)
Short title, see 12 U.S.C. 1716 note

Federal Nonnuclear Energy Research and Development Act of 1974
Pub. L. 93–577, Dec. 31, 1974, 88 Stat. 1878 (42 U.S.C. 5901 et seq.)
Short title, see 42 U.S.C. 5901 note

Federal Noxious Weed Act of 1974
Pub. L. 93–629, Jan. 3, 1975, 88 Stat. 2148 (7 U.S.C. 2801 et seq.)
Short title, see 7 U.S.C. 2801 note

Federal Oil and Gas Royalty Management Act of 1982
Pub. L. 97–451, Jan. 12, 1983, 96 Stat. 2447 (30 U.S.C. 1701 et seq.)
Short title, see 30 U.S.C. 1701 note

Federal Oil and Gas Royalty Simplification and Fairness Act of 1996
Pub. L. 104–185, Aug. 13, 1996, 110 Stat. 1700
Short title, see 30 U.S.C. 1701 note

Federal Onshore Oil and Gas Leasing Reform Act of 1987
Pub. L. 100–203, title V, subtitle B (§5101 et seq.), Dec. 22, 1987, 101 Stat. 1330–256
Short title, see 30 U.S.C. 181 note

Federal Pay Comparability Act of 1970
Pub. L. 91–656, Jan. 8, 1971, 84 Stat. 1946
Short title, see 5 U.S.C. 5301 note

Federal Payment Reauthorization Act of 1994
Pub. L. 103–373, Oct. 19, 1994, 108 Stat. 3488

Federal Pesticide Act of 1978
Pub. L. 95–396, Sept. 30, 1978, 92 Stat. 819
Short title, see 7 U.S.C. 136 note

Federal Photovoltaic Utilization Act
Pub. L. 95–619, title V, part 4 (§561 et seq.), Nov. 9, 1978, 92 Stat. 3280 (42 U.S.C. 8271 et seq.)
Short title, see 42 U.S.C. 8201 note

Federal Physicians Comparability Allowance Act of 1978
Pub. L. 95–603, Nov. 6, 1978, 92 Stat. 3018 (5 U.S.C. 5948)
Short title, see 5 U.S.C. 5948 note

Federal Physicians Comparability Allowance Amendments of 1979
Pub. L. 96–166, Dec. 29, 1979, 93 Stat. 1273
Short title, see 5 U.S.C. 5948 note

Federal Physicians Comparability Allowance Amendments of 1981
Pub. L. 97–141, Dec. 29, 1981, 95 Stat. 1719
Short title, see 5 U.S.C. 5948 note

Federal Physicians Comparability Allowance Amendments of 1983
Pub. L. 98–168, title I, Nov. 29, 1983, 97 Stat. 1105
Short title, see 5 U.S.C. 5948 note

Federal Physicians Comparability Allowance Amendments of 2000
Pub. L. 106–571, Dec. 28, 2000, 114 Stat. 3054
Short title, see 5 U.S.C. 5948 note

Federal Plant Pest Act
Pub. L. 85–36, title I, May 23, 1957, 71 Stat. 31 (7 U.S.C. 150aa et seq.)
Short title, see 7 U.S.C. 150aa note

Federal Possession and Control Act (Railroads in War)
Aug. 29, 1916, ch. 418, 39 Stat. 645

Federal Power Act
June 10, 1920, ch. 285, 41 Stat. 1063 (16 U.S.C. 791a et seq.)
Short title, see 16 U.S.C. 791a

Federal Prison Industries, Incorporated, and The Institute of Inter-American Affairs Appropriation Act, 1951
Sept. 6, 1950, ch. 896, Ch. III, title V, 64 Stat. 633

Federal Prison Industries, Incorporated, and The Institute of Inter-American Affairs Appropriation Act, 1950
July 20, 1949, ch. 354, title V, 63 Stat. 474

Federal Prisoner Health Care Copayment Act of 2000
Pub. L. 106–294, Oct. 12, 2000, 114 Stat. 1038
Short title, see 18 U.S.C. 4001 note

Federal Program Information Act
Pub. L. 95–220, Dec. 28, 1977, 91 Stat. 1615

Federal Property and Administrative Services Act of 1949
June 30, 1949, ch. 288, 63 Stat. 377 (40 U.S.C. 471 et seq.)
Short title, see 40 U.S.C. 471 note

Federal Property Management Improvement Act of 1988
Pub. L. 100–612, Nov. 5, 1988, 102 Stat. 3180
Short title, see 40 U.S.C. 471 note

Federal Public Buildings Appropriation Act of 1938
June 21, 1938, ch. 554, title III, 52 Stat. 818

Federal Public Transportation Act of 1978
Pub. L. 95–599, title III, Nov. 6, 1978, 92 Stat. 2735

Federal Public Transportation Act of 1982
Pub. L. 97–424, title III, Jan. 6, 1983, 96 Stat. 2140

Federal Question Jurisdictional Amendments Act of 1980
Pub. L. 96–486, Dec. 1, 1980, 94 Stat. 2369
Short title, see 28 U.S.C. 1 note

Federal Railroad Safety Act of 1970
Pub. L. 91–458, title II, Oct. 16, 1970, 84 Stat. 971

Federal Railroad Safety Authorization Act of 1973
Pub. L. 93–90, Aug. 14, 1973, 87 Stat. 305

Federal Railroad Safety Authorization Act of 1975
Pub. L. 94–56, July 19, 1975, 89 Stat. 263

Federal Railroad Safety Authorization Act of 1976
Pub. L. 94–348, July 8, 1976, 90 Stat. 817

Federal Railroad Safety Authorization Act of 1978
Pub. L. 95–574, Nov. 2, 1978, 92 Stat. 2459

Federal Railroad Safety Authorization Act of 1980
Pub. L. 96–423, Oct. 10, 1980, 94 Stat. 1811

Federal Railroad Safety Authorization Act of 1982
Pub. L. 97–468, title VII, Jan. 14, 1983, 96 Stat. 2579

Federal Railroad Safety Authorization Act of 1994
Pub. L. 103–440, title II, Nov. 2, 1994, 108 Stat. 4619
Short title, see 49 U.S.C. 20101 note

Federal Records Act of 1950
June 30, 1949, ch. 288, title V, as added Sept. 5, 1950, ch. 849, §6(d), 64 Stat. 583

Federal Records Management Amendments of 1976
Pub. L. 94–575, Oct. 21, 1976, 90 Stat. 2723
Short title, see 44 U.S.C. 101 note

Federal Register Act
July 26, 1935, ch. 417, 49 Stat. 500

Federal Regulation of Lobbying Act
Aug. 2, 1946, ch. 753, title III, 60 Stat. 839 (2 U.S.C. 261 et seq.)
Short title, see 2 U.S.C. 261 note

Federal Reporting Act of 2000
Pub. L. 106–569, title XI, Dec. 27, 2000, 114 Stat. 3029

Federal Reports Act of 1942
Dec. 24, 1942, ch. 811, 56 Stat. 1078

Federal Reports Elimination Act of 1998
Pub. L. 105–362, Nov. 10, 1998, 112 Stat. 3280

Federal Reports Elimination and Sunset Act of 1995
Pub. L. 104–66, Dec. 21, 1995, 109 Stat. 707

Federal Reserve Act
Dec. 23, 1913, ch. 6, 38 Stat. 251 (12 U.S.C. 221 et seq.)
Short title, see 12 U.S.C. 226

Federal Reserve Bank Branch Modernization Act
Pub. L. 102–491, Oct. 24, 1992, 106 Stat. 3144
Short title, see 12 U.S.C. 226 note

Federal Reserve Board Retirement Portability Act
Pub. L. 106–168, title II, Dec. 12, 1999, 113 Stat. 1817
Short title, see 5 U.S.C. 8401 note

Federal Reserve Note Security Act
Mar. 6, 1934, ch. 47, 48 Stat. 398

Federal Reserve Reform Act of 1977
Pub. L. 95–188, title II, Nov. 16, 1977, 91 Stat. 1387
Short title, see 12 U.S.C. 226 note

Federal Revenue Sharing Act
See State and Local Fiscal Assistance Act of 1972

Federal Revenue Sharing Act (National Forest Revenues for National Forest Road and Trail Expenditures)
Mar. 4, 1913, ch. 145, 37 Stat. 843 (16 U.S.C. 501)

Federal Revenue Sharing Act (National Forest Revenues for Public School and Road Expenditures)
May 23, 1908, ch. 192, 35 Stat. 260 (16 U.S.C. 500)

Federal Rules of Civil Procedure Amendments Act of 1982
Pub. L. 97–462, Jan. 12, 1983, 96 Stat. 2527
Short title, see 28 U.S.C. 2071 note

Federal Rules of Criminal Procedure Amendments Act of 1975
Pub. L. 94–64, July 31, 1975, 89 Stat. 370
Short title, see 18 App. U.S.C. Rule 60 note

Federal Salary Act Amendments of 1977
Pub. L. 95–19, title IV, Apr. 12, 1977, 91 Stat. 45

Federal Salary Act of 1967
Pub. L. 90–206, title II, Dec. 16, 1967, 81 Stat. 624
Short title, see 5 U.S.C. 5332 note

Federal Salary and Fringe Benefits Act of 1966
Pub. L. 89–504, July 18, 1966, 80 Stat. 288

Federal Salary Reform Act of 1962
Pub. L. 87–793, part II (§501 et seq.), Oct. 11, 1962, 76 Stat. 841

Federal Savings and Loan Insurance Corporation Recapitalization Act of 1987
Pub. L. 100–86, title III, Aug. 10, 1987, 101 Stat. 585
Short title, see 12 U.S.C. 226 note

Federal Security Agency Appropriation Act, 1941
June 26, 1940, ch. 428, title II, 54 Stat. 580

Federal Security Agency Appropriation Act, 1942
July 1, 1941, ch. 269, title II, 55 Stat. 471

Federal Security Agency Appropriation Act, 1943
July 2, 1942, ch. 475, title II, 56 Stat. 567

Federal Security Agency Appropriation Act, 1944
July 12, 1943, ch. 221, title II, 57 Stat. 498

Federal Security Agency Appropriation Act, 1945
June 28, 1944, ch. 302, title II, 58 Stat. 552

Federal Security Agency Appropriation Act, 1946
July 3, 1945, ch. 263, title II, 59 Stat. 365

Federal Security Agency Appropriation Act, 1947
July 26, 1946, ch. 672, title II, 60 Stat. 687

Federal Security Agency Appropriation Act, 1948
July 8, 1947, ch. 210, title II, 61 Stat. 264

Federal Security Agency Appropriation Act, 1949
June 14, 1948, ch. 465, title II, 62 Stat. 396

Federal Security Agency Appropriation Act, 1950
June 29, 1949, ch. 275, title II, 63 Stat. 284

Federal Security Agency Appropriation Act, 1951
Sept. 6, 1950, ch. 896, ch. V, title II, 64 Stat. 645

Federal Security Agency Appropriation Act, 1952
Aug. 31, 1951, ch. 373, title II, 65 Stat. 212

Federal Security Agency Appropriation Act, 1953
July 5, 1952, ch. 575, title II, 66 Stat. 361

Federal Seed Act
Aug. 9, 1939, ch. 615, 53 Stat. 1275 (7 U.S.C. 1551 et seq.)
Short title, see 7 U.S.C. 1551

Federal Seed Act Amendments of 1982
Pub. L. 97–439, Jan. 8, 1983, 96 Stat. 2287
Short title, see 7 U.S.C. 1551 note

Federal Ship Financing Act of 1972
Pub. L. 92–507, Oct. 19, 1972, 86 Stat. 909
Short title, see 46 App. U.S.C. 1245 note

Federal Ship Mortgage Insurance Act
June 29, 1936, title XI, as added June 23, 1938, ch. 600, §46, 52 Stat. 969

Federal Sick Leave Act
Mar. 14, 1936, ch. 141, 49 Stat. 1162

Federal Supplemental Compensation Act of 1982
Pub. L. 97–248, title VI, subtitle A (§601 et seq.), Sept. 3, 1982, 96 Stat. 702 (26 U.S.C. 3304 note)

Federal Supplemental Compensation Amendments of 1983
Pub. L. 98–135, Oct. 24, 1983, 97 Stat. 857

Federal Tax Lien Act of 1966
Pub. L. 89–719, Nov. 2, 1966, 80 Stat. 1125
Short title, see 26 U.S.C. 6321 note

Federal Tea Tasters Repeal Act of 1996
Pub. L. 104–128, Apr. 9, 1996, 110 Stat. 1198
Short title, see 21 U.S.C. 41 note

Federal Technology Transfer Act of 1986
Pub. L. 99–502, Oct. 20, 1986, 100 Stat. 1785
Short title, see 15 U.S.C. 3701 note

Federal Timber Contract Payment Modification Act
Pub. L. 98–478, Oct. 16, 1984, 98 Stat. 2213 (16 U.S.C. 539f, 618, 619)
Short title, see 16 U.S.C. 618 note

Federal Tort Claims Act
Aug. 2, 1946, ch. 753, title IV, 60 Stat. 842

Federal Trade Commission Act
Sept. 26, 1914, ch. 311, 38 Stat. 717 (15 U.S.C. 41 et seq.)
Short title, see 15 U.S.C. 58

Federal Trade Commission Act Amendments of 1994
Pub. L. 103–312, Aug. 26, 1994, 108 Stat. 1691
Short title, see 15 U.S.C. 58 note

Federal Trade Commission Improvements Act of 1980
Pub. L. 96–252, May 28, 1980, 94 Stat. 374
Short title, see 15 U.S.C. 58 note

Federal Trade Commission Reauthorization Act of 1996
Pub. L. 104–216, Oct. 1, 1996, 110 Stat. 3019
Short title, see 15 U.S.C. 58 note

Federal Trademark Dilution Act of 1995
Pub. L. 104–98, Jan. 16, 1996, 109 Stat. 985
Short title, see 15 U.S.C. 1051 note

Federal Transit Act
Pub. L. 88–365, July 9, 1964, 78 Stat. 302

Federal Transit Act Amendments of 1991
Pub. L. 102–240, title III, Dec. 18, 1991, 105 Stat. 2087

Federal Transit Act of 1998
Pub. L. 105–178, title III, June 9, 1998, 112 Stat. 338
Short title, see 49 U.S.C. 5101 note

Federal Triangle Development Act
Pub. L. 100–113, Aug. 21, 1987, 101 Stat. 735 (40 U.S.C. 1101 et seq.)
Short title, see 40 U.S.C. 1101 note

Federal Unemployment Tax Act
Aug. 16, 1954, ch. 736, §1(d) [Internal Revenue Title, chapter 23], 68A Stat. 439 (26 U.S.C. 3301 et seq.)
Short title, see 26 U.S.C. 3311

Federal Urban Land-Use Act
June 30, 1949, ch. 288, title VIII, as added Oct. 16, 1968, Pub. L. 90–577, title V, §501, 82 Stat. 1104 (40 U.S.C. 531 et seq.)
Short title, see 40 U.S.C. 531 note

Federal Vacancies Reform Act of 1998
Pub. L. 105–277, div. C, title I, §151, Oct. 21, 1998, 112 Stat. 2681–611 (5 U.S.C. 3345 et seq.)
Short title, see 5 U.S.C. 3301 note

Federal Voting Assistance Act of 1955
Aug. 9, 1955, ch. 656, 69 Stat. 584 (42 U.S.C. 1973cc et seq.)
Short title, see 42 U.S.C. 1971 note

Federal Water Pollution Control Act
June 30, 1948, ch. 758, as added Oct. 18, 1972, Pub. L. 92–500, §2, 86 Stat. 816 (33 U.S.C. 1251 et seq.)
Short title, see 33 U.S.C. 1251 note

Federal Water Pollution Control Act Amendments of 1961
Pub. L. 87–88, July 20, 1961, 75 Stat. 204
Short title, see 43 U.S.C. 390b note

Federal Water Pollution Control Act Amendments of 1972
Pub. L. 92–500, Oct. 18, 1972, 86 Stat. 816
Short title, see 33 U.S.C. 1251 note

Federal Water Power Act
Renamed Federal Power Act

Federal Water Project Recreation Act
Pub. L. 89–72, July 9, 1965, 79 Stat. 213 (16 U.S.C. 460*l*–12 et seq.)
Short title, see 16 U.S.C. 460*l*–12 note

Federal Workforce Restructuring Act of 1994
Pub. L. 103–226, Mar. 30, 1994, 108 Stat. 111
Short title, see 5 U.S.C. 2101 note

Federal Youth Corrections Act
Title 18, chapter 402

Federal-Aid Highway Act of 1944
Dec. 20, 1944, ch. 626, 58 Stat. 838

Federal-Aid Highway Act of 1948
June 29, 1948, ch. 732, 62 Stat. 1105

Federal-Aid Highway Act of 1950
Sept. 7, 1950, ch. 912, 64 Stat. 785

Federal-Aid Highway Act of 1952
June 25, 1952, ch. 462, 66 Stat. 158

Federal-Aid Highway Act of 1954
May 6, 1954, ch. 181, 68 Stat. 70

Federal-Aid Highway Act of 1956
June 29, 1956, ch. 462, title I, 70 Stat. 374

Federal-Aid Highway Act of 1958
Pub. L. 85–381, Apr. 16, 1958, 72 Stat. 89

Federal-Aid Highway Act of 1959
Pub. L. 86–342, Sept. 21, 1959, 73 Stat. 611
Short title, see 23 U.S.C. 101 note

Federal-Aid Highway Act of 1961
Pub. L. 87–61, June 29, 1961, 75 Stat. 122
Short title, see 23 U.S.C. 101 note

Federal-Aid Highway Act of 1962
Pub. L. 87–866, Oct. 23, 1962, 76 Stat. 1145
Short title, see 23 U.S.C. 101 note

Federal-Aid Highway Act of 1964
Pub. L. 88–423, Aug. 13, 1964, 78 Stat. 397
Short title, see 23 U.S.C. 101 note

Federal-Aid Highway Act of 1966
Pub. L. 89–574, Sept. 13, 1966, 80 Stat. 766
Short title, see 23 U.S.C. 101 note

Federal-Aid Highway Act of 1968
Pub. L. 90–495, Aug. 23, 1968, 82 Stat. 815
Short title, see 23 U.S.C. 101 note

Federal-Aid Highway Act of 1970
Pub. L. 91–605, title I, Dec. 31, 1970, 84 Stat. 1713
Short title, see 23 U.S.C. 101 note

Federal-Aid Highway Act of 1973
Pub. L. 93–87, title I, Aug. 13, 1973, 87 Stat. 250
Short title, see 23 U.S.C. 101 note

Federal-Aid Highway Act of 1976
Pub. L. 94–280, title I, May 5, 1976, 90 Stat. 425
Short title, see 23 U.S.C. 101 note

Federal-Aid Highway Act of 1978
Pub. L. 95–599, title I, Nov. 6, 1978, 92 Stat. 2689
Short title, see 23 U.S.C. 101 note

Federal-Aid Highway Act of 1982
Pub. L. 97–327, Oct. 15, 1982, 96 Stat. 1611
Short title, see 23 U.S.C. 101 note

Federal-Aid Highway Act of 1987
Pub. L. 100–17, title I, Apr. 2, 1987, 101 Stat. 134
Short title, see 23 U.S.C. 101 note

Federal-Aid Highway Amendments Act of 1963
Pub. L. 88–157, Oct. 24, 1963, 77 Stat. 276
Short title, see 23 U.S.C. 101 note

Federal-Aid Highway Amendments of 1974
Pub. L. 93–643, Jan. 4, 1975, 88 Stat. 2281
Short title, see 23 U.S.C. 101 note

Federal-State Communications Joint Board Act
Pub. L. 92–131, Sept. 30, 1971, 85 Stat. 363
Short title, see 47 U.S.C. 609 note

Federal-State Extended Unemployment Compensation Act of 1970
Pub. L. 91–373, title II, Aug. 10, 1970, 84 Stat. 708 (26 U.S.C. 3304 note)

Federal-State Tax Collection Act of 1972
Pub. L. 92–512, title II, Oct. 20, 1972, 86 Stat. 936
Short title, see 26 U.S.C. 1 note

Federally Recognized Indian Tribe List Act of 1994
Pub. L. 103–454, title I, Nov. 2, 1994, 108 Stat. 4791 (25 U.S.C. 479a et seq.)
Short title, see 25 U.S.C. 479a note

Federally Supported Health Centers Assistance Act of 1992
Pub. L. 102–501, Oct. 24, 1992, 106 Stat. 3268
Short title, see 42 U.S.C. 201 note

Federally Supported Health Centers Assistance Act of 1995
Pub. L. 104–73, Dec. 26, 1995, 109 Stat. 777
Short title, see 42 U.S.C. 201 note

Feed Grain Act of 1963
Pub. L. 88–26, May 20, 1963, 77 Stat. 44
Short title, see 7 U.S.C. 1339a note

FEGLI Living Benefits Act
Pub. L. 103–409, Oct. 25, 1994, 108 Stat. 4230
Short title, see 5 U.S.C. 8701 note

Fencing Act (Public Lands)
Feb. 25, 1885, ch. 149, 23 Stat. 321 (43 U.S.C. 1061 et seq.)

Fertility Clinic Success Rate and Certification Act of 1992
Pub. L. 102–493, Oct. 24, 1992, 106 Stat. 3146 (42 U.S.C. 263a–1 et seq.)
Short title, see 42 U.S.C. 201 note

Fess-Kenyon Act
See the Vocational Rehabilitation Act

Fetal Alcohol Syndrome and Fetal Alcohol Effect Prevention and Services Act
Pub. L. 105–392, title IV, §419, Nov. 13, 1998, 112 Stat. 3591
Short title, see 42 U.S.C. 201 note

FHA Downpayment Simplification Extension Act of 2000
Pub. L. 106–281, Oct. 6, 2000, 114 Stat. 865
Short title, see 12 U.S.C. 1701 note

Fifth Circuit Court of Appeals Reorganization Act of 1980
Pub. L. 96–452, Oct. 14, 1980, 94 Stat. 1994
Short title, see 28 U.S.C. 1 note

Fifth Supplemental National Defense Appropriation Act, 1941
Apr. 5, 1941, ch. 41, 55 Stat. 123

Fifth Supplemental National Defense Appropriation Act, 1942
Mar. 5, 1942, ch. 141, 56 Stat. 128

Filled Cheese Act
June 6, 1896, ch. 337, 29 Stat. 253

Filled Milk Act
Mar. 4, 1923, ch. 262, 42 Stat. 1486 (21 U.S.C. 61 et seq.)
Short title, see 21 U.S.C. 61 note

Financial Institutions Anti-Fraud Enforcement Act of 1990
Pub. L. 101–647, title XXV, subtitle H (§2560 et seq.), Nov. 29, 1990, 104 Stat. 4893 (12 U.S.C. 4201 et seq.)
Short title, see 12 U.S.C. 4201 note

Financial Institutions Emergency Acquisitions Amendments of 1987
Pub. L. 100–86, title V, Aug. 10, 1987, 101 Stat. 623
Short title, see 12 U.S.C. 1811 note

Financial Institutions Reform, Recovery, and Enforcement Act of 1989
Pub. L. 101–73, Aug. 9, 1989, 103 Stat. 183
Short title, see 12 U.S.C. 1811 note

Financial Institutions Regulatory and Interest Rate Control Act of 1978
Pub. L. 95–630, Nov. 10, 1978, 92 Stat. 3641
Short title, see 12 U.S.C. 226 note

Financial Institutions Supervisory Act of 1966
Pub. L. 89–695, Oct. 16, 1966, 80 Stat. 1028
Short title, see 12 U.S.C. 1464 note

Financial Regulation Simplification Act of 1980
Pub. L. 96–221, title VIII, Mar. 31, 1980, 94 Stat. 191 (12 U.S.C. 3521 et seq.)

Financial Regulatory Relief and Economic Efficiency Act of 2000
Pub. L. 106–569, title XII, Dec. 27, 2000, 114 Stat. 3032
Short title, see 12 U.S.C. 1811 note

Financial Reports Act of 1988
Pub. L. 100–418, title III, subtitle G (§3601 et seq.), Aug. 23, 1988, 102 Stat. 1387 (22 U.S.C. 5351 et seq.)
Short title, see 22 U.S.C. 5351

Fine Arts Commission Act
May 17, 1910, ch. 243, 36 Stat. 371 (40 U.S.C. 104, 106)

Finland War Debt Act
June 15, 1940, ch. 371, 54 Stat. 398

Finnish Loan Act
Mar. 2, 1940, ch. 34, 54 Stat. 38

Fire Administration Authorization Act of 1992
Pub. L. 102–522, Oct. 26, 1992, 106 Stat. 3410

Fire Administration Authorization Act of 2000
Pub. L. 106–503, title I, Nov. 13, 2000, 114 Stat. 2298
Short title, see 15 U.S.C. 2201 note

Fire and Casualty Act
Oct. 9, 1940, ch. 792, 54 Stat. 1063

Fire Island National Seashore Act
Pub. L. 88–587, Sept. 11, 1964, 78 Stat. 928 (16 U.S.C. 459e et seq.)

Fire Island National Seashore Amendments Act of 1984
Pub. L. 98–482, Oct. 17, 1984, 98 Stat. 2255
Short title, see 16 U.S.C. 459e note

Fire Research and Safety Act of 1968
Pub. L. 90–259, Mar. 1, 1968, 82 Stat. 34

Fire Safe Cigarette Act of 1990
Pub. L. 101–352, Aug. 10, 1990, 104 Stat. 405 (15 U.S.C. 2054 note)

Firearms Owners' Protection Act
Pub. L. 99–308, May 19, 1986, 100 Stat. 449
Short title, see 18 U.S.C. 921 note

Firefighters' Safety Study Act
Pub. L. 101–446, Oct. 22, 1990, 104 Stat. 1045 (15 U.S.C. 2223a et seq.)
Short title, see 15 U.S.C. 2223a note

First Decontrol Act of 1947
Mar. 31, 1947, ch. 29, 61 Stat. 34

First Deficiency Act, fiscal year 1926
Mar. 3, 1926, ch. 44, 44 Stat. 161

First Deficiency Act, fiscal year 1928
Dec. 22, 1927, ch. 5, 45 Stat. 2

First Deficiency Appropriation Act, 1940
Apr. 6, 1940, ch. 77, 54 Stat. 82

First Deficiency Appropriation Act, 1941
Apr. 1, 1941, ch. 32, 55 Stat. 62

First Deficiency Appropriation Act, 1942
Feb. 21, 1942, ch. 108, 56 Stat. 98

First Deficiency Appropriation Act, 1943
Mar. 18, 1943, ch. 17, 57 Stat. 21

First Deficiency Appropriation Act, 1945
Apr. 25, 1945, ch. 95, 59 Stat. 77

First Deficiency Appropriation Act, 1946
Dec. 28, 1945, ch. 589, 59 Stat. 632

First Deficiency Appropriation Act, 1947
May 1, 1947, ch. 49, 61 Stat. 58

First Deficiency Appropriation Act, 1948
May 10, 1948, ch. 270, 62 Stat. 213

First Deficiency Appropriation Act, 1949
May 24, 1949, ch. 138, 63 Stat. 76

First Deficiency Appropriation Act, fiscal year 1939
Mar. 15, 1939, ch. 10, 53 Stat. 512

First Deficiency Appropriations Act, fiscal year 1936
June 22, 1936, ch. 689, 49 Stat. 1597

First Inventor Defense Act of 1999
Pub. L. 106–113, div. B, §1000(a)(9) [title IV, subtitle C (§4301 et seq.)], Nov. 29, 1999, 113 Stat. 1536, 1501A–555
Short title, see 35 U.S.C. 1 note

First Ladies National Historic Site Act of 2000
Pub. L. 106–291, title I, §145, Oct. 11, 2000, 114 Stat. 950 (16 U.S.C. 461 note)

First Liberty Bond Act
Apr. 24, 1917, ch. 4, 40 Stat. 35

First Liberty Loan Act
See First Liberty Bond Act

First Morrill Act
Also known as the Morrill ActJuly 2, 1862, ch. 130, 12 Stat. 503 (7 U.S.C. 301 et seq.)
Short title, see 7 U.S.C. 301 note

First Supplemental Appropriation Act, 1945
Dec. 22, 1944, ch. 660, 58 Stat. 853

First Supplemental Appropriation Act, 1947
Aug. 8, 1946, ch. 870, 60 Stat. 910

First Supplemental Civil Functions Appropriation Act, 1941
Oct. 9, 1940, ch. 780, 54 Stat. 1030

First Supplemental National Defense Appropriation Act, 1941
June 26, 1940, ch. 430, 54 Stat. 599

First Supplemental National Defense Appropriation Act, 1942
Aug. 25, 1941, ch. 409, 55 Stat. 669

First Supplemental National Defense Appropriation Act, 1943
July 25, 1942, ch. 524, 56 Stat. 704

First Supplemental National Defense Appropriation Act, 1944
Dec. 23, 1943, ch. 380, 57 Stat. 611

First Supplemental Surplus Appropriation Rescission Act, 1946
Feb. 18, 1946, ch. 30, 60 Stat. 6

First War Powers Act, 1941
Dec. 18, 1941, ch. 593, 55 Stat. 838 (50 App. U.S.C. 601 et seq.)

Fiscal Year 1981 Airport Development Authorization Act
Pub. L. 97–35, title XI, subtitle A, part 1 (§1101 et seq.), Aug. 13, 1981, 95 Stat. 622

Fiscal Year 1990 Dire Emergency Supplemental to Meet the Needs of Natural Disasters of National Significance
Pub. L. 101–100, §108, as added Pub. L. 101–130, Oct. 26, 1989, 103 Stat. 775

Fiscal Year Adjustment Act
Pub. L. 94–273, Apr. 21, 1976, 90 Stat. 375

Fiscal Year Transition Act
Pub. L. 94–274, Apr. 21, 1976, 90 Stat. 383

Fish and Game Sanctuary Act
Mar. 10, 1934, ch. 54, 48 Stat. 400 (16 U.S.C. 694 et seq.)

Fish and Seafood Promotion Act of 1986
Pub. L. 99–659, title II, Nov. 14, 1986, 100 Stat. 3715 (16 U.S.C. 4001 et seq.)
Short title, see 16 U.S.C. 4001 note

Fish and Wildlife Act of 1956
Aug. 8, 1956, ch. 1036, 70 Stat. 1119 (16 U.S.C. 742a et seq.)
Short title, see 16 U.S.C. 742a note

Fish and Wildlife Conservation Act of 1980
Pub. L. 96–366, Sept. 29, 1980, 94 Stat. 1322 (16 U.S.C. 2901 et seq.)
Short title, see 16 U.S.C. 2901 note

Fish and Wildlife Coordination Act
Mar. 10, 1934, ch. 55, 48 Stat. 401 (16 U.S.C. 661 et seq.)
Short title, see 16 U.S.C. 661 note

Fish and Wildlife Improvement Act of 1978
Pub. L. 95–616, Nov. 8, 1978, 92 Stat. 3110
Short title, see 16 U.S.C. 742a note

Fish and Wildlife Programs Improvement and National Wildlife Refuge System Centennial Act of 2000
Pub. L. 106–408, Nov. 1, 2000, 114 Stat. 1762
Short title, see 16 U.S.C. 669 note

Fish and Wildlife Revenue Enhancement Act of 1998
Pub. L. 105–328, Oct. 30, 1998, 112 Stat. 3057
Short title, see 16 U.S.C. 742a note

Fish Restoration and Management Projects Act
See Dingell-Johnson Sport Fish Restoration Act

Fisheries Act of 1995
Pub. L. 104–43, Nov. 3, 1995, 109 Stat. 366 (16 U.S.C. 5501 et seq.)
Short title, see 16 U.S.C. 5501 note

Fisheries Amendments of 1982
Pub. L. 97–389, Dec. 29, 1982, 96 Stat. 1949
Short title, see 16 U.S.C. 3601 note

Fisheries Financing Act
Pub. L. 104–297, title III, Oct. 11, 1996, 110 Stat. 3615
Short title, see 46 App. U.S.C. 1245 note

Fisheries Restoration and Irrigation Mitigation Act of 2000
Pub. L. 106–502, Nov. 13, 2000, 114 Stat. 2294 (16 U.S.C. 777 note)

Fisheries Survey Vessel Authorization Act of 2000
Pub. L. 106–450, title III, Nov. 7, 2000, 114 Stat. 1945 (33 U.S.C. 891b note)

Fishermen's Protective Act Amendments of 2000
Pub. L. 106–450, title I, Nov. 7, 2000, 114 Stat. 1941
Short title, see 22 U.S.C. 1971 note

Fishermen's Protective Act of 1967
Aug. 27, 1954, ch. 1018, 68 Stat. 883 (22 U.S.C. 1971 et seq.)
Short title, see 22 U.S.C. 1971 note

Fishery Conservation Amendments of 1990
Pub. L. 101–627, Nov. 28, 1990, 104 Stat. 4436
Short title, see 16 U.S.C. 1801 note

Fishery Conservation and Management Act of 1976
Renamed Magnuson-Stevens Fishery Conservation and Management Act

Fishery Conservation Zone Transition Act
Pub. L. 95–6, Feb. 21, 1977, 91 Stat. 14
Short title, see 16 U.S.C. 1801 note

Fishlake National Forest Enlargement Act
Pub. L. 102–292, May 26, 1992, 106 Stat. 181

Fitzgerald Act (Apprentice Labor)
See National Apprenticeship Act

Fitzgerald-Tyson Act
See Emergency Officers' Retirement Act

Five Civilized Tribes Act (Disposition of Affairs)
Apr. 26, 1906, ch. 1876, 34 Stat. 137

Five-Year School Building Program Act
Feb. 26, 1925, ch. 342, 43 Stat. 986

Flag Protection Act of 1989
Pub. L. 101–131, Oct. 28, 1989, 103 Stat. 777
Short title, see 18 U.S.C. 700 note

Flammable Fabrics Act
June 30, 1953, ch. 164, 67 Stat. 111 (15 U.S.C. 1191 et seq.)
Short title, see 15 U.S.C. 1191 note

Fletcher-Rayburn Securities Act of 1933
See Securities Act of 1933

Flexible Tariff Act
June 17, 1930, ch. 497, title III, §336, 46 Stat. 701 (19 U.S.C. 1336)

Flight Officer Act
July 8, 1942, ch. 493, 56 Stat. 649

Flood Control Act of 1917
Mar. 1, 1917, ch. 144, 39 Stat. 948

Flood Control Act of 1928
May 15, 1928, ch. 569, 45 Stat. 534 (33 U.S.C. 702a et seq.)

Flood Control Act of 1936
June 22, 1936, ch. 688, 49 Stat. 1570

Flood Control Act of 1937
Aug. 28, 1937, ch. 877, 50 Stat. 876

Flood Control Act of 1938
June 28, 1938, ch. 795, 52 Stat. 1215

Flood Control Act of 1939
Aug. 11, 1939, ch. 699, 53 Stat. 1414

Flood Control Act of 1941
Aug. 18, 1941, ch. 377, 55 Stat. 638

Flood Control Act of 1944
Dec. 22, 1944, ch. 665, 58 Stat. 887

Flood Control Act of 1946
July 24, 1946, ch. 596, 60 Stat. 641

Flood Control Act of 1948
June 30, 1948, ch. 771, title II, 62 Stat. 1175

Flood Control Act of 1950
May 17, 1950, ch. 188, title II, 64 Stat. 170

Flood Control Act of 1954
Sept. 3, 1954, ch. 1264, title II, 68 Stat. 1256

Flood Control Act of 1958
Pub. L. 85–500, title II, July 3, 1958, 72 Stat. 305

Flood Control Act of 1960
Pub. L. 86–645, title II, July 14, 1960, 74 Stat. 488

Flood Control Act of 1962
Pub. L. 87–874, title II, Oct. 23, 1962, 76 Stat. 1180

Flood Control Act of 1965
Pub. L. 89–298, title II, Oct. 27, 1965, 79 Stat. 1073

Flood Control Act of 1966
Pub. L. 89–789, title II, Nov. 7, 1966, 80 Stat. 1418

Flood Control Act of 1968
Pub. L. 90–483, title II, Aug. 13, 1968, 82 Stat. 739

Flood Control Act of 1970
Pub. L. 91–611, title II, Dec. 31, 1970, 84 Stat. 1824

Flood Disaster Protection Act of 1973
Pub. L. 93–234, Dec. 31, 1973, 87 Stat. 975
Short title, see 42 U.S.C. 4001 note

Flood Rehabilitation Act, 1952
Oct. 24, 1951, ch. 555, 65 Stat. 615

Floral Research and Consumer Information Act
Pub. L. 97–98, title XVII, Dec. 22, 1981, 95 Stat. 1348 (7 U.S.C. 4301 et seq.)
Short title, see 7 U.S.C. 4301 note

Florida Canal-Pipe Line Act
July 23, 1942, ch. 520, 56 Stat. 703 (15 U.S.C. note prec. 715)

Florida Indian Land Claims Settlement Act of 1982
Pub. L. 97–399, Dec. 31, 1982, 96 Stat. 2012 (25 U.S.C. 1741 et seq.)
Short title, see 25 U.S.C. 1741 note

Florida Keys National Marine Sanctuary and Protection Act
Pub. L. 101–605, Nov. 16, 1990, 104 Stat. 3089 (16 U.S.C. 1433 note)

Florida Wilderness Act of 1983
Pub. L. 98–430, Sept. 28, 1984, 98 Stat. 1665 (16 U.S.C. 1132 note)

Floyd D. Spence National Defense Authorization Act for Fiscal Year 2001
Pub. L. 106–398, §1 [H.R. 5408], Oct. 30, 2000, 114 Stat. 1654, 1654A–1

Fluid Milk Promotion Act of 1990
Pub. L. 101–624, title XIX, subtitle H (§1999A et seq.), Nov. 28, 1990, 104 Stat. 3914 (7 U.S.C. 6401 et seq.)
Short title, see 7 U.S.C. 6401 note

Fluid Milk Promotion Amendments Act of 1993
Pub. L. 103–72, Aug. 11, 1993, 107 Stat. 717
Short title, see 7 U.S.C. 6401 note

Follow Through Act
Pub. L. 97–35, title VI, subtitle A, ch. 8, subch. D, formerly subch. C (§661 et seq.), Aug. 13, 1981, 95 Stat. 508 (42 U.S.C. 9861 et seq.)
Short title, see 42 U.S.C. 9801 note

Food Additives Amendment of 1958
Pub. L. 85–929, Sept. 6, 1958, 72 Stat. 1784
Short title, see 21 U.S.C. 301 note

Food Additives Transitional Provisions Amendment of 1961
Pub. L. 87–19, Apr. 7, 1961, 75 Stat. 42

Food Additives Transitional Provisions Amendment of 1964
Pub. L. 88–625, Oct. 3, 1964, 78 Stat. 1002
Short title, see 21 U.S.C. 342 note

Food and Agriculture Act of 1962
Pub. L. 87–703, Sept. 27, 1962, 76 Stat. 605
Short title, see 7 U.S.C. 1281 note

Food and Agriculture Act of 1965
Pub. L. 89–321, Nov. 3, 1965, 79 Stat. 1187
Short title, see 7 U.S.C. 608c note

Food and Agriculture Act of 1977
Pub. L. 95–113, Sept. 29, 1977, 91 Stat. 913
Short title, see 7 U.S.C. 1281 note

Food and Drug Act of 1906
See Federal Food and Drugs Act of 1906

Food and Drug Administration Act of 1988
Pub. L. 100–607, title V, Nov. 4, 1988, 102 Stat. 3120
Short title, see 21 U.S.C. 301 note

Food and Drug Administration Modernization Act of 1997
Pub. L. 105–115, Nov. 21, 1997, 111 Stat. 2296
Short title, see 21 U.S.C. 301

Food and Drug Administration Revitalization Act
Pub. L. 101–635, Nov. 28, 1990, 104 Stat. 4583
Short title, see 21 U.S.C. 301 note

Food and Forage Act
Mar. 2, 1861, ch. 84, §10, 12 Stat. 220; R.S. 3732 (41 U.S.C. 11)

Food and Rest Law (Transportation of Animals)
Also known as the Cruelty to Animals Act, the Live Stock Transportation Act, and the Twenty-Eight Hour Law
June 29, 1906, ch. 3594, 34 Stat. 607
Short title, see 45 U.S.C. 71 note

Food Control and the District of Columbia Rents Act
Oct. 22, 1919, ch. 80, 41 Stat. 297

Food for Peace Act of 1966
Pub. L. 89–808, Nov. 11, 1966, 80 Stat. 1526
Short title, see 7 U.S.C. 1691 note

Food for Progress Act of 1985
Pub. L. 99–198, title XI, §1110, Dec. 23, 1985, 99 Stat. 1472 (7 U.S.C. 1736*o*)
Short title, see 7 U.S.C. 1736*o*(a)

Food Production Stimulation Act
Nov. 21, 1918, ch. 212, 40 Stat. 1045

Food Quality Protection Act of 1996
Pub. L. 104–170, Aug. 3, 1996, 110 Stat. 1489
Short title, see 7 U.S.C. 136 note

Food Security Act of 1985
Pub. L. 99–198, Dec. 23, 1985, 99 Stat. 1354
Short title, see 7 U.S.C. 1281 note

Food Security Commodity Reserve Act of 1996
Renamed Bill Emerson Humanitarian Trust Act

Food Security Improvements Act of 1986
Pub. L. 99–260, Mar. 20, 1986, 100 Stat. 45
Short title, see 7 U.S.C. 1281 note

Food Security Wheat Reserve Act of 1980
Renamed Bill Emerson Humanitarian Trust Act

Food Stamp Act Amendments of 1980
Pub. L. 96–249, May 26, 1980, 94 Stat. 357
Short title, see 7 U.S.C. 2011 note

Food Stamp Act Amendments of 1982
Pub. L. 97–253, title I, subtitle E (§140 et seq.), Sept. 8, 1982, 96 Stat. 772
Short title, see 7 U.S.C. 2011 note

Food Stamp Act of 1964
Renamed Food Stamp Act of 1977

Food Stamp Act of 1977
Pub. L. 88–525, Aug. 31, 1964, 78 Stat. 703 (7 U.S.C. 2011 et seq.)
Short title, see 7 U.S.C. 2011 note

Food Stamp and Commodity Distribution Amendments of 1981
Pub. L. 97–98, title XIII, Dec. 22, 1981, 95 Stat. 1282
Short title, see 7 U.S.C. 2011 note

Food Stamp Program Improvements Act of 1994
Pub. L. 103–225, Mar. 25, 1994, 108 Stat. 106

Food, Agriculture, Conservation, and Trade Act Amendments of 1991
Pub. L. 102–237, Dec. 13, 1991, 105 Stat. 1818
Short title, see 7 U.S.C. 1421 note

Food, Agriculture, Conservation, and Trade Act of 1990
Pub. L. 101–624, Nov. 28, 1990, 104 Stat. 3359
Short title, see 7 U.S.C. 1421 note

Food, Drug, and Cosmetic Act
See Federal Food, Drug, and Cosmetic Act

Foot-and-Mouth Disease Act (Mexico)
See Animal Disease Control Cooperation Act of 1947

Foraker Act (Puerto Rico)
Also known as the Puerto Rico Civil Code
Apr. 12, 1900, ch. 191, 31 Stat. 77

Force Act (Suits against Revenue Officers)
Mar. 2, 1833, ch. 57, §3, 4 Stat. 633

Force Act of 1870
May 31, 1870, ch. 114, 16 Stat. 140

Fordney-McCumber Act
See Tariff Act of 1922

Foreign Affairs Agencies Consolidation Act of 1998
Pub. L. 105–277, div. G, subdiv. A (§1101 et seq.), Oct. 21, 1998, 112 Stat. 2681–765 (22 U.S.C. 6501 et seq.)
Short title, see 22 U.S.C. 6501 note

Foreign Affairs Reform and Restructuring Act of 1998
Pub. L. 105–277, div. G, Oct. 21, 1998, 112 Stat. 2681–761
Short title, see 22 U.S.C. 6501 note

Foreign Agents Registration Act of 1938
June 8, 1938, ch. 327, 52 Stat. 631 (22 U.S.C. 611 et seq.)
Short title, see 22 U.S.C. 611 note

Foreign Aid Act of 1947
Dec. 17, 1947, ch. 520, 61 Stat. 934

Foreign Aid and Related Agencies Appropriation Act, 1963
Pub. L. 87–872, Oct. 23, 1962, 76 Stat. 1163

Foreign Aid and Related Agencies Appropriation Act, 1964
Pub. L. 88–258, Jan. 6, 1964, 77 Stat. 857

Foreign Aid Appropriation Act, 1950
Oct. 6, 1949, ch. 621, 63 Stat. 709

Foreign Aid Appropriation Act, 1951
Sept. 6, 1950, ch. 896, Ch. XI, 64 Stat. 757

Foreign Assistance Act of 1948
Apr. 3, 1948, ch. 169, 62 Stat. 137

Foreign Assistance Act of 1961
Pub. L. 87–195, Sept. 4, 1961, 75 Stat. 424 (22 U.S.C. 2151 et seq.)
Short title, see 22 U.S.C. 2151 note

Foreign Assistance Act of 1962
Pub. L. 87–565, Aug. 1, 1962, 76 Stat. 255
Short title, see 22 U.S.C. 2151 note

Foreign Assistance Act of 1963
Pub. L. 88–205, Dec. 16, 1963, 77 Stat. 379
Short title, see 22 U.S.C. 2151 note

Foreign Assistance Act of 1964
Pub. L. 88–633, Oct. 7, 1964, 78 Stat. 1009
Short title, see 22 U.S.C. 2151 note

Foreign Assistance Act of 1965
Pub. L. 89–171, Sept. 6, 1965, 79 Stat. 653
Short title, see 22 U.S.C. 2151 note

Foreign Assistance Act of 1966
Pub. L. 89–583, Sept. 19, 1966, 80 Stat. 795
Short title, see 22 U.S.C. 2151 note

Foreign Assistance Act of 1967
Pub. L. 90–137, Nov. 14, 1967, 81 Stat. 445
Short title, see 22 U.S.C. 2151 note

Foreign Assistance Act of 1968
Pub. L. 90–554, Oct. 8, 1968, 82 Stat. 960
Short title, see 22 U.S.C. 2151 note

Foreign Assistance Act of 1969
Pub. L. 91–175, Dec. 30, 1969, 83 Stat. 805
Short title, see 22 U.S.C. 2151 note

Foreign Assistance Act of 1971
Pub. L. 92–226, Feb. 7, 1972, 86 Stat. 20
Short title, see 22 U.S.C. 2151 note

Foreign Assistance Act of 1973
Pub. L. 93–189, Dec. 17, 1973, 87 Stat. 714
Short title, see 22 U.S.C. 2151 note

Foreign Assistance Act of 1974
Pub. L. 93–559, Dec. 30, 1974, 88 Stat. 1795
Short title, see 22 U.S.C. 2151 note

Foreign Assistance and Related Agencies Appropriation Act, 1962
Pub. L. 87–329, Sept. 30, 1961, 75 Stat. 717

Foreign Assistance and Related Agencies Appropriation Act, 1965
Pub. L. 88–634, Oct. 7, 1964, 78 Stat. 1015

Foreign Assistance and Related Agencies Appropriation Act, 1966
Pub. L. 89–273, Oct. 20, 1965, 79 Stat. 1002

Foreign Assistance and Related Agencies Appropriation Act, 1967
Pub. L. 89–691, Oct. 15, 1966, 80 Stat. 1018

Foreign Assistance and Related Agencies Appropriation Act, 1968
Pub. L. 90–249, Jan. 2, 1968, 81 Stat. 936

Foreign Assistance and Related Agencies Appropriation Act, 1969
Pub. L. 90–581, Oct. 17, 1968, 82 Stat. 1137

Foreign Assistance and Related Programs Appropriation Act, 1970
Pub. L. 91–194, Feb. 9, 1970, 84 Stat. 5

Foreign Assistance and Related Programs Appropriation Act, 1971
Pub. L. 91–619, Dec. 31, 1970, 84 Stat. 1856

Foreign Assistance and Related Programs Appropriation Act, 1972
Pub. L. 92–242, Mar. 8, 1972, 86 Stat. 48

Foreign Assistance and Related Programs Appropriation Act, 1974
Pub. L. 93–240, Jan. 2, 1974, 87 Stat. 1049

Foreign Assistance and Related Programs Appropriations Act, 1975
Pub. L. 94–11, Mar. 26, 1975, 89 Stat. 17

Foreign Assistance and Related Programs Appropriations Act, 1976, and the period ending September 30, 1976
Pub. L. 94–330, June 30, 1976, 90 Stat. 771

Foreign Assistance and Related Programs Appropriations Act, 1978
Pub. L. 95–148, Oct. 31, 1977, 91 Stat. 1230

Foreign Assistance and Related Programs Appropriations Act, 1979
Pub. L. 95–481, Oct. 18, 1978, 92 Stat. 1591

Foreign Assistance and Related Programs Appropriations Act, 1982
Pub. L. 97–121, Dec. 29, 1981, 95 Stat. 1647

Foreign Assistance and Related Programs Appropriations Act, 1983
Pub. L. 97–377, §101(b)(1), Dec. 21, 1982, 96 Stat. 1831

Foreign Assistance and Related Programs Appropriations Act, 1984
Pub. L. 98–151, §101(b)(1), Nov. 14, 1983, 97 Stat. 964

Foreign Assistance and Related Programs Appropriations Act, 1985
Pub. L. 98–473, title I, §101(1), Oct. 12, 1984, 98 Stat. 1884

Foreign Assistance and Related Programs Appropriations Act, 1986
Pub. L. 99–190, §101(i), Dec. 19, 1985, 99 Stat. 1291

Foreign Assistance and Related Programs Appropriations Act, 1987
Pub. L. 99–500, §101(f), Oct. 18, 1986, 100 Stat. 1783–213, and Pub. L. 99–591, §101(f), Oct. 30, 1986, 100 Stat. 3341–214

Foreign Bank Secrecy Act of 1970
See Currency and Foreign Transactions Reporting Act

Foreign Bank Supervision Enhancement Act of 1991
Pub. L. 102–242, title II, subtitle A (§201 et seq.), Dec. 19, 1991, 105 Stat. 2286
Short title, see 12 U.S.C. 3101 note

Foreign Claims Act
Jan. 2, 1942, ch. 645, as added Apr. 22, 1943, ch. 67, 57 Stat. 66

Foreign Corrupt Practices Act Amendments of 1988
Pub. L. 100–418, title V, subtitle A, part I (§5001 et seq.), Aug. 23, 1988, 102 Stat. 1415
Short title, see 15 U.S.C. 78a note

Foreign Corrupt Practices Act of 1977
Pub. L. 95–213, title I, Dec. 19, 1977, 91 Stat. 1494
Short title, see 15 U.S.C. 78a note

Foreign Debt Reserving Act of 1989
Pub. L. 101–240, title IV, Dec. 19, 1989, 103 Stat. 2501
Short title, see 12 U.S.C. 3901 note

Foreign Direct Investment and International Financial Data Improvements Act of 1990
Pub. L. 101–533, Nov. 7, 1990, 104 Stat. 2344
Short title, see 22 U.S.C. 3141 note

Foreign Disaster Assistance Act of 1974
Pub. L. 93–333, July 8, 1974, 88 Stat. 290
Short title, see 22 U.S.C. 2151 note

Foreign Earned Income Act of 1978
Pub. L. 95–615, §§201–210, Nov. 8, 1978, 92 Stat. 3098
Short title, see 26 U.S.C. 1 note

Foreign Economic Administration Appropriation Act, 1945
June 30, 1944, ch. 324, title III, 58 Stat. 630

Foreign Economic Assistance Act of 1950
June 5, 1950, ch. 220, 64 Stat. 198

Foreign Gifts and Decorations Act of 1966
Pub. L. 89–673, Oct. 15, 1966, 80 Stat. 952 (22 U.S.C. 2621 et seq.)
Short title, see 22 U.S.C. 2621 note

Foreign Intelligence Surveillance Act of 1978
Pub. L. 95–511, Oct. 25, 1978, 92 Stat. 1783 (50 U.S.C. 1801 et seq.)
Short title, see 50 U.S.C. 1801 note

Foreign Investment in Real Property Tax Act of 1980
Pub. L. 96–499, title XI, subtitle C (§1121 et seq.), Dec. 5, 1980, 94 Stat. 2682
Short title, see 26 U.S.C. 1 note

Foreign Investment Study Act of 1974
Pub. L. 93–479, Oct. 26, 1974, 88 Stat. 1450 (15 U.S.C. 78b note)

Foreign Investors Tax Act of 1966
Pub. L. 89–809, title I, Nov. 13, 1966, 80 Stat. 1541
Short title, see 26 U.S.C. 861 note

Foreign Language Assistance Act of 1988
Pub. L. 89–10, title II, part B (§2101 et seq.), as added Pub. L. 100–297, title I, §1001, Apr. 28, 1988, 102 Stat. 228 (20 U.S.C. 3001 et seq.)
Pub. L. 100–418, title VI, subtitle A, ch. 3, subch. A (§6021 et seq.), Aug. 23, 1988, 102 Stat. 1476 (20 U.S.C. 5011 et seq.)

Foreign Language Assistance Act of 1994
Pub. L. 89–10, title VII, part B (§7201 et seq.), as added Pub. L. 103–382, title I, §101, Oct. 20, 1994, 108 Stat. 3737 (20 U.S.C. 7511 et seq.)
Short title, see 20 U.S.C. 7511

Foreign Military Sales Act
Renamed Arms Export Control Act

Foreign Missions Act
Pub. L. 97–241, title II, Aug. 24, 1982, 96 Stat. 282 (22 U.S.C. 4301 et seq.)
Short title, see 22 U.S.C. 4301 note

Foreign Missions Amendments Act of 1983
Pub. L. 98–164, title VI, Nov. 22, 1983, 97 Stat. 1042
Short title, see 22 U.S.C. 4301 note

Foreign Narcotics Kingpin Designation Act
Pub. L. 106–120, title VIII, Dec. 3, 1999, 113 Stat. 1626 (21 U.S.C. 1901 et seq.)
Short title, see 21 U.S.C. 1901 note

Foreign Operations, Export Financing, and Related Programs Appropriations Act, 1988
Pub. L. 100–202, §101(e), Dec. 22, 1987, 101 Stat. 1329–131

Foreign Operations, Export Financing, and Related Programs Appropriations Act, 1989
Pub. L. 100–461, Oct. 1, 1988, 102 Stat. 2268

Foreign Operations, Export Financing, and Related Programs Appropriations Act, 1990
Pub. L. 101–167, Nov. 21, 1989, 103 Stat. 1195

Foreign Operations, Export Financing, and Related Programs Appropriations Act, 1991
Pub. L. 101–513, Nov. 5, 1990, 104 Stat. 1979

Foreign Operations, Export Financing, and Related Programs Appropriations Act, 1993
Pub. L. 102–391, Oct. 6, 1992, 106 Stat. 1633

Foreign Operations, Export Financing, and Related Programs Appropriations Act, 1994
Pub. L. 103–87, titles I–V, Sept. 30, 1993, 107 Stat. 931–945

Foreign Operations, Export Financing, and Related Programs Appropriations Act, 1995
Pub. L. 103–306, titles I–V, Aug. 23, 1994, 108 Stat. 1608–1624

Foreign Operations, Export Financing, and Related Programs Appropriations Act, 1996
Pub. L. 104–107, Feb. 12, 1996, 110 Stat. 704

Foreign Operations, Export Financing, and Related Programs Appropriations Act, 1997
Pub. L. 104–208, div. A, title I, §101(c) [titles I–V], Sept. 30, 1996, 110 Stat. 3009–121 to 3009–139

Foreign Operations, Export Financing, and Related Programs Appropriations Act, 1998
Pub. L. 105–118, Nov. 26, 1997, 111 Stat. 2386

Foreign Operations, Export Financing, and Related Programs Appropriations Act, 1999
Pub. L. 105–277, div. A, §101(d), Oct. 21, 1998, 112 Stat. 2681–150

Foreign Operations, Export Financing, and Related Programs Appropriations Act, 2000
Pub. L. 106–113, div. B, §1000(a)(2) [H.R. 3422], Nov. 29, 1999, 113 Stat. 1535, 1501A–63

Foreign Operations, Export Financing, and Related Programs Appropriations Act, 2001
Pub. L. 106–429, §101(a) [H.R. 5526], Nov. 6, 2000, 114 Stat. 1900, 1900A–3

Foreign Operations, Export Financing, and Related Programs Supplemental Appropriations Act, 1994
Pub. L. 103–306, title VI, Aug. 23, 1994, 108 Stat. 1656

Foreign Relations Authorization Act of 1972
Pub. L. 92–352, July 13, 1972, 86 Stat. 489
Short title, see 22 U.S.C. 2651 note

Foreign Relations Authorization Act, Fiscal Year 1976
Pub. L. 94–141, Nov. 29, 1975, 89 Stat. 756
Short title, see 22 U.S.C. 2651 note

Foreign Relations Authorization Act, Fiscal Year 1977
Pub. L. 94–350, July 12, 1976, 90 Stat. 823
Short title, see 22 U.S.C. 2651 note

Foreign Relations Authorization Act, Fiscal Year 1978
Pub. L. 95–105, Aug. 17, 1977, 91 Stat. 844

Foreign Relations Authorization Act, Fiscal Year 1979
Pub. L. 95–426, Oct. 7, 1978, 92 Stat. 963

Foreign Relations Authorization Act, Fiscal Years 1986 and 1987
Pub. L. 99–93, Aug. 16, 1985, 99 Stat. 405
Short title, see 22 U.S.C. 2651 note

Foreign Relations Authorization Act, Fiscal Years 1988 and 1989
Pub. L. 100–204, Dec. 22, 1987, 101 Stat. 1331
Short title, see 22 U.S.C. 2651 note

Foreign Relations Authorization Act, Fiscal Years 1990 and 1991
Pub. L. 101–246, Feb. 16, 1990, 104 Stat. 15
Short title, see 22 U.S.C. 2651 note

Foreign Relations Authorization Act, Fiscal Years 1992 and 1993
Pub. L. 102–138, Oct. 28, 1991, 105 Stat. 647
Short title, see 22 U.S.C. 2651 note

Foreign Relations Authorization Act, Fiscal Years 1994 and 1995
Pub. L. 103–236, Apr. 30, 1994, 108 Stat. 382
Short title, see 22 U.S.C. 2651 note

Foreign Relations Authorization Act, Fiscal Years 1998 and 1999
Pub. L. 105–277, div. G, subdiv. B (§2001 et seq.), Oct. 21, 1998, 112 Stat. 2681–801
Short title, see 22 U.S.C. 2651 note

Foreign Relations Authorization Act, Fiscal Years 2000 and 2001
See Admiral James W. Nance and Meg Donovan Foreign Relations Authorization Act, Fiscal Years 2000 and 2001

Foreign Relations Persian Gulf Conflict Emergency Supplemental Authorization Act, Fiscal Year 1991
Pub. L. 102–20, Mar. 27, 1991, 105 Stat. 68

Foreign Securities Act
Apr. 13, 1934, ch. 112, 48 Stat. 574 (see 18 U.S.C. 955)

Foreign Service Act
May 24, 1924, ch. 182, 43 Stat. 140

Foreign Service Act Amendments of 1955
Apr. 5, 1955, ch. 23, 69 Stat. 24

Foreign Service Act Amendments of 1956
July 28, 1956, ch. 770, 70 Stat. 704

Foreign Service Act Amendments of 1960
Pub. L. 86–723, Sept. 8, 1960, 74 Stat. 831

Foreign Service Act Amendments of 1969
Pub. L. 91–201, Feb. 28, 1970, 84 Stat. 17

Foreign Service Act of 1946
Aug. 13, 1946, ch. 957, titles I–X, 60 Stat. 999–1030 (22 U.S.C. 801 et seq.)

Foreign Service Act of 1980
Pub. L. 96–465, Oct. 17, 1980, 94 Stat. 2071 (22 U.S.C. 3901 et seq.)
Short title, see 22 U.S.C. 3901 note

Foreign Service Annuity Adjustment Act of 1965
Pub. L. 89–308, Oct. 31, 1965, 79 Stat. 1129
Short title, see 22 U.S.C. 801 note

Foreign Service Buildings Act, 1926
May 7, 1926, ch. 250, 44 Stat. 403 (22 U.S.C. 292 et seq.)
Short title, see 22 U.S.C. 299

Foreign Service Pension System Act of 1986
Pub. L. 99–335, title IV, June 6, 1986, 100 Stat. 609
Short title, see 22 U.S.C. 3901 note

Foreign Service Personnel Act
Apr. 24, 1939, ch. 84, 53 Stat. 583

Foreign Service Retirement Amendments of 1976
Pub. L. 94–350, title V, July 12, 1976, 90 Stat. 834

Foreign Service Salary Reform Act of 1962
Pub. L. 87–793, title V, Oct. 11, 1962, 76 Stat. 861

Foreign Shipping Practices Act of 1988
Pub. L. 100–418, title X, subtitle A (§10001 et seq.), Aug. 23, 1988, 102 Stat. 1570
Short title, see 46 App. U.S.C. 1701 note

Foreign Sovereign Immunities Act of 1976
Pub. L. 94–583, Oct. 21, 1976, 90 Stat. 2891 (28 U.S.C. 1602 et seq.)
Short title, see 28 U.S.C. 1 note

Foreign Stations Act
May 29, 1934, ch. 370, 48 Stat. 815

Foreign Trade Antitrust Improvements Act of 1982
Pub. L. 97–290, title IV, Oct. 8, 1982, 96 Stat. 1246
Short title, see 15 U.S.C. 1 note

Foreign Trade Zones Act
June 18, 1934, ch. 590, 48 Stat. 998 (19 U.S.C. 81a et seq.)
Short title, see 19 U.S.C. 81a note

Forest and Rangeland Renewable Resources Planning Act of 1974
Pub. L. 93–378, Aug. 17, 1974, 88 Stat. 476 (16 U.S.C. 1600 et seq.)
Short title, see 16 U.S.C. 1600 note

Forest and Rangeland Renewable Resources Research Act of 1978
Pub. L. 95–307, June 30, 1978, 92 Stat. 353
Short title, see 16 U.S.C. 1600 note

Forest Ecosystems and Atmospheric Pollution Research Act of 1988
Pub. L. 100–521, Oct. 24, 1988, 102 Stat. 2601
Short title, see 16 U.S.C. 1600 note

Forest Exchange Act
Mar. 20, 1922, ch. 105, 42 Stat. 465 (16 U.S.C. 485, 486)

Forest Pest Control Act
June 25, 1947, ch. 141, 61 Stat. 177 (16 U.S.C. 594–1 et seq.)
Short title, see 16 U.S.C. 594–1 note

Forest Products Act
May 22, 1928, ch. 678, 45 Stat. 699 (16 U.S.C. 581 et seq.)

Forest Reserve Act (California)
Oct. 1, 1890, ch. 1263, 26 Stat. 650

Forest Reserve Homestead Act
June 11, 1906, ch. 3074, 34 Stat. 233

Forest Resources Conservation and Shortage Relief Act of 1990
Pub. L. 101–382, title IV, Aug. 20, 1990, 104 Stat. 714 (16 U.S.C. 620 et seq.)
Short title, see 16 U.S.C. 620 note

Forest Resources Conservation and Shortage Relief Act of 1997
Pub. L. 105–83, title VI, Nov. 14, 1997, 111 Stat. 1617
Short title, see 16 U.S.C. 620 note

Forest Resources Conservation and Shortage Relief Amendments Act of 1993
Pub. L. 103–45, July 1, 1993, 107 Stat. 223
Short title, see 16 U.S.C. 620 note

Forest Stewardship Act of 1990
Pub. L. 101–624, title XII, Nov. 28, 1990, 104 Stat. 3521
Short title, see 16 U.S.C. 2101 note

Forest Transfer Act
Feb. 1, 1905, ch. 288, 33 Stat. 628

Forest Wildfire Emergency Pay Equity Act of 1988
Pub. L. 100–523, Oct. 24, 1988, 102 Stat. 2605
Short title, see 5 U.S.C. 5547 note

Forfeiture Act (Railroad Land Grants)
See Railroad Land Grant Forfeiture Act

Former Presidents Act of 1958
Pub. L. 85–745, Aug. 25, 1958, 72 Stat. 838 (3 U.S.C. 102 note)

Former Prisoner of War Benefits Act of 1981
Pub. L. 97–37, Aug. 14, 1981, 95 Stat. 935
Short title, see 38 U.S.C. 101 note

Former Soviet Union Demilitarization Act of 1992
Pub. L. 102–484, div. A, title XIV, Oct. 23, 1992, 106 Stat. 2563 (22 U.S.C. 5901 et seq.)
Short title, see 22 U.S.C. 5901 note

Fort Carson-Pinon Canyon Military Lands Withdrawal Act
Pub. L. 104–201, div. B, title XXIX, subtitle A (§2901 et seq.), Sept. 23, 1996, 110 Stat. 2807

Fort Donelson National Battlefield Act
Pub. L. 86–738, Sept. 8, 1960, 74 Stat. 875 (16 U.S.C. 428k et seq.)

Fort Hall Indian Reservation Act
June 6, 1900, ch. 813, 31 Stat. 672

Fort Hall Indian Water Rights Act of 1990
Pub. L. 101–602, Nov. 16, 1990, 104 Stat. 3059

Fort McDowell Indian Community Water Rights Settlement Act of 1990
Pub. L. 101–628, title IV, Nov. 28, 1990, 104 Stat. 4480

Fort Peck Reservation Rural Water System Act of 2000
Pub. L. 106–382, Oct. 27, 2000, 114 Stat. 1451

Fort Peck Rural County Water Supply System Act of 1996
Pub. L. 104–300, Oct. 11, 1996, 110 Stat. 3646

Fort Vancouver National Historic Site Act
June 19, 1948, ch. 546, 62 Stat. 532 (16 U.S.C. 450ff et seq.)

Foster Care Independence Act of 1999
Pub. L. 106–169, Dec. 14, 1999, 113 Stat. 1822
Short title, see 42 U.S.C. 1305 note

Foundation for the Advancement of Military Medicine Act of 1983
Pub. L. 98–36, May 27, 1983, 97 Stat. 200
Short title, see 10 U.S.C. 171 note

Four Corners Interpretive Center Act
Pub. L. 106–143, Dec. 7, 1999, 113 Stat. 1703

Fourteenth Census Act
Mar. 3, 1919, ch. 97, 40 Stat. 1291

Fourth Liberty Bond Act
July 9, 1918, ch. 142, 40 Stat. 844

Fourth Liberty Loan Act
See Fourth Liberty Bond Act

Fourth Supplemental Appropriation Act, 1961
Pub. L. 87–74, June 30, 1961, 75 Stat. 195

Fourth Supplemental National Defense Appropriation Act, 1941
Mar. 17, 1941, ch. 16, 55 Stat. 34

Frank Annunzio Act
Pub. L. 102–281, title IV, May 13, 1992, 106 Stat. 139 (20 U.S.C. 5701 et seq.; 31 U.S.C. 5112 note)
Short title, see 20 U.S.C. 5701 note

Fraudulent Advertising Act (D.C.)
May 29, 1916, ch. 130, 39 Stat. 165

Frazier-Lemke Farm-Mortgage Act
June 28, 1934, ch. 869, 48 Stat. 1289

Fredericksburg and Spotsylvania County Battlefields Memorial National Military Park Expansion Act of 1989
Pub. L. 101–214, Dec. 11, 1989, 103 Stat. 1849 (16 U.S.C. 425k et seq.)
Short title, see 16 U.S.C. 425k note

Free Coinage of Gold Act
See Specie Payment Resumption Act

Free Homestead Act
May 17, 1900, ch. 479, 31 Stat. 179 (43 U.S.C. 179)

Free Trade Zone Act
See Foreign Trade Zones Act

Freedmen's Bureau Records Preservation Act of 2000
Pub. L. 106–444, Nov. 6, 2000, 114 Stat. 1929 (44 U.S.C. 2910)
Short title, see 44 U.S.C. 101 note

Freedom for Russia and Emerging Eurasion Democracies and Open Markets Support Act of 1992
Also known as the FREEDOM Support Act
Pub. L. 102–511, Oct. 24, 1992, 106 Stat. 3320 (22 U.S.C. 5801 et seq.)
Short title, see 22 U.S.C. 5801 note

Freedom of Access to Clinic Entrances Act of 1994
Pub. L. 103–259, May 26, 1994, 108 Stat. 694 (18 U.S.C. 248)
Short title, see 18 U.S.C. 248 note

Freedom of Information Act
Title 5, section 552
Short title, see 5 U.S.C. 552 note

Freedom of Information Reform Act of 1986
Pub. L. 99–570, title I, subtitle N (§1801 et seq.), Oct. 27, 1986, 100 Stat. 3207–48
Short title, see 5 U.S.C. 552 note

FREEDOM Support Act
Also known as the Freedom for Russia and Emerging Eurasion Democracies and Open Markets Support Act of 1992
Pub. L. 102–511, Oct. 24, 1992, 106 Stat. 3320 (22 U.S.C. 5801 et seq.)
Short title, see 22 U.S.C. 5801 note

Freedom to E-File Act
Pub. L. 106–222, June 20, 2000, 114 Stat. 353 (7 U.S.C. 7031 et seq.)
Short title, see 7 U.S.C. 6901 note

French Spoliation Claims Act
Jan. 20, 1885, ch. 25, 23 Stat. 283

Fresh Cut Flowers and Fresh Cut Greens Promotion and Information Act of 1993
Pub. L. 103–190, Dec. 14, 1993, 107 Stat. 2266 (7 U.S.C. 6801 et seq.)
Short title, see 7 U.S.C. 6801 note

FRIENDSHIP Act
Also known as the Act For Reform In Emerging New Democracies and Support and Help for Improved Partnership with Russia, Ukraine, and Other New Independent States
Pub. L. 103–199, Dec. 17, 1993, 107 Stat. 2317
Short title, see 22 U.S.C. 5801 note

FSC Repeal and Extraterritorial Income Exclusion Act of 2000
Pub. L. 106–519, Nov. 15, 2000, 114 Stat. 2423
Short title, see 26 U.S.C. 1 note

Fuel Distribution Act
Sept. 22, 1922, ch. 413, 42 Stat. 1025

Fugitive Felon Act
May 18, 1934, ch. 302, 48 Stat. 782 (see 18 U.S.C. 1073)

Fugitive Slave Act of 1793
Feb. 12, 1793, ch. 7, 1 Stat. 302

Fugitive Slave Act of 1850
Sept. 18, 1850, ch. 60, 9 Stat. 462

Full Employment and Balanced Growth Act of 1978
Pub. L. 95–523, Oct. 27, 1978, 92 Stat. 1887 (15 U.S.C. 3101 et seq.)
Short title, see 15 U.S.C. 3101 note

Full Faith and Credit for Child Support Orders Act
Pub. L. 103–383, Oct. 20, 1994, 108 Stat. 4063 (28 U.S.C. 1738B)
Short title, see 28 U.S.C. 1 note

Fuller Act (Pensions, Civil War, War with Mexico)
May 1, 1920, ch. 165, 41 Stat. 585

Fund for the Improvement and Reform of Schools and Teaching Act
Pub. L. 100–297, title III, part B (§3201 et seq.), Apr. 28, 1988, 102 Stat. 338 (20 U.S.C. 4801 et seq.)
Short title, see 20 U.S.C. 4801 note

Funding Act of 1790
Aug. 4, 1790, ch. 34, 1 Stat. 138

Funding Act of 1866
Apr. 12, 1866, ch. 39, 14 Stat. 31

Funeral Transportation and Living Expense Benefits Act of 1974
Pub. L. 93–257, Mar. 29, 1974, 88 Stat. 53 (37 U.S.C. 406 note)

Fur Products Labeling Act
Aug. 8, 1951, ch. 298, 65 Stat. 175 (15 U.S.C. 69 et seq.)
Short title, see 15 U.S.C. 69 note

Fur Seal Act Amendments of 1983
Pub. L. 98–129, Oct. 14, 1983, 97 Stat. 835
Short title, see 16 U.S.C. 1151 note

Fur Seal Act of 1966
Pub. L. 89–702, Nov. 2, 1966, 80 Stat. 1091 (16 U.S.C. 1151 et seq.)
Short title, see 16 U.S.C. 1151 note

Future Trading Act
Aug. 24, 1921, ch. 86, 42 Stat. 187

Futures Trading Act of 1978
Pub. L. 95–405, Sept. 30, 1978, 92 Stat. 865
Short title, see 7 U.S.C. 1 note

Futures Trading Act of 1982
Pub. L. 97–444, Jan. 11, 1983, 96 Stat. 2294
Short title, see 7 U.S.C. 1 note

Futures Trading Act of 1986
Pub. L. 99–641, Nov. 10, 1986, 100 Stat. 3556
Short title, see 7 U.S.C. 1 note

Futures Trading Practices Act of 1992
Pub. L. 102–546, Oct. 28, 1992, 106 Stat. 3590
Short title, see 7 U.S.C. 1 note

G. I. Bill of Rights
See Servicemen's Readjustment Act of 1944

Gallatin Land Consolidation Act of 1998
Pub. L. 105–267, Oct. 19, 1998, 112 Stat. 2371

Gallatin Range Consolidation and Protection Act of 1993
Pub. L. 103–91, Oct. 1, 1993, 107 Stat. 987

Gambling Devices Act of 1962
Pub. L. 87–840, Oct. 18, 1962, 76 Stat. 1075
Short title, see 15 U.S.C. 1171 note

Gambling Devices Transportation Act
Jan. 2, 1951, ch. 1194, 64 Stat. 1134 (15 U.S.C. 1171 et seq.)
Short title, see 15 U.S.C. 1171 note

Game and Wildlife Act
June 15, 1935, ch. 261, 49 Stat. 378

Garfield Act (Compulsory Railway Connection)
June 15, 1866, ch. 124, 14 Stat. 66; R.S. §5258 (45 U.S.C. 84)

Garn-St Germain Depository Institutions Act of 1982
Pub. L. 97–320, Oct. 15, 1982, 96 Stat. 1469
Short title, see 12 U.S.C. 226 note

Garrison Diversion Unit Reformulation Act of 1986
Pub. L. 99–294, May 12, 1986, 100 Stat. 418

Gas Related Activities Act of 1990
Pub. L. 101–572, Nov. 15, 1990, 104 Stat. 2810 (15 U.S.C. 79k note)

Gasohol Competition Act of 1980
Pub. L. 96–493, Dec. 2, 1980, 94 Stat. 2568 (15 U.S.C. 26a)
Short title, see 15 U.S.C. 1

Gasoline Tax and Postage Rate Act
June 16, 1933, ch. 96, 48 Stat. 254

Gasque Spanish War Pensions Act
May 24, 1938, ch. 268, 52 Stat. 440

Gateway National Recreation Area Act
Pub. L. 92–592, Oct. 27, 1972, 86 Stat. 1308 (16 U.S.C. 460cc et seq.)

Gateway Visitor Center Authorization Act of 1999
Pub. L. 106–131, Dec. 7, 1999, 113 Stat. 1678 (16 U.S.C. 407m note)

Gay Act (Public Lands in Louisiana)
Mar. 2, 1889, ch. 395, 25 Stat. 877

Gearhart Armistice Day Act
See Armistice Day Act

Geary Act (Chinese Exclusion)
May 5, 1892, ch. 60, 27 Stat. 25

General Accounting Act of 1974
Pub. L. 93–604, Jan. 2, 1975, 88 Stat. 1959

General Accounting Office Act of 1980
Pub. L. 96–226, Apr. 3, 1980, 94 Stat. 311

General Accounting Office Act of 1996
Pub. L. 104–316, Oct. 19, 1996, 110 Stat. 3826
Short title, see 31 U.S.C. 701 note

General Accounting Office Personnel Act of 1980
Pub. L. 96–191, Feb. 15, 1980, 94 Stat. 27

General Accounting Office Personnel Amendments Act of 1988
Pub. L. 100–426, Sept. 9, 1988, 102 Stat. 1598
Short title, see 31 U.S.C. 701 note

General Allotment Act (Indians)
See Indian General Allotment Act

General Appropriation Act, 1951
Sept. 6, 1950, ch. 896, 64 Stat. 595

General Aviation Revitalization Act of 1994
Pub. L. 103–298, Aug. 17, 1994, 108 Stat. 1552 (49 U.S.C. 40101 note)

General Bridge Act of 1906
Also known as Bridge Act of 1906
Mar. 23, 1906, ch. 1130, 34 Stat. 84 (33 U.S.C. 491 et seq.)
Short title, see 33 U.S.C. 491 note

General Bridge Act of 1946
Aug. 2, 1946, ch. 753, title V, 60 Stat. 847 (33 U.S.C. 525 et seq.)
Short title, see 33 U.S.C. 525 note

General Education Provisions Act
Pub. L. 90–247, title IV, Jan. 2, 1968, 81 Stat. 814 (20 U.S.C. 1221 et seq.)
Short title, see 20 U.S.C. 1221(a)

General Government Matters Appropriation Act, 1956
June 29, 1955, ch. 226, 69 Stat. 192

General Government Matters Appropriation Act, 1957
June 13, 1956, ch. 385, 70 Stat. 276

General Government Matters Appropriation Act, 1958
Pub. L. 85–48, June 5, 1957, 71 Stat. 49

General Government Matters Appropriation Act, 1959
Pub. L. 85–468, June 25, 1958, 72 Stat. 220

General Government Matters Appropriation Act, 1960
Pub. L. 86–79, July 8, 1959, 73 Stat. 161

General Government Matters Appropriation Act, 1961
Pub. L. 86–642, July 12, 1960, 74 Stat. 473

General Government Matters, Department of Commerce, and Related Agencies Appropriation Act, 1962
Pub. L. 87–125, Aug. 3, 1961, 75 Stat. 268

General Land Office Act
Apr. 25, 1812, ch. 68, 2 Stat. 716

General Leasing Act
See Mineral Leasing Act

General Mining Act of 1872
May 10, 1872, ch. 152, 17 Stat. 91; R.S. §§2319–2328, 2331, 2333–2338, 2344
Short title, see 30 U.S.C. 22 note

Generalized System of Preferences Renewal Act of 1984
Pub. L. 98–573, title V, Oct. 30, 1984, 98 Stat. 3018
Short title, see 19 U.S.C. 2101 note

Generic Animal Drug and Patent Term Restoration Act
Pub. L. 100–670, Nov. 16, 1988, 102 Stat. 3971

Generic Animal Drug and Patent Term Restoration Act—Continued
Short title, see 21 U.S.C. 301 note

Generic Drug Enforcement Act of 1992
Pub. L. 102–282, May 13, 1992, 106 Stat. 149 (21 U.S.C. 335a–335c)
Short title, see 21 U.S.C. 301 note

Genesee River Protection Act of 1989
Pub. L. 101–175, Nov. 27, 1989, 103 Stat. 1294 (16 U.S.C. 1276 note)

Genocide Convention Implementation Act of 1987 (the Proxmire Act)
Pub. L. 100–606, Nov. 4, 1988, 102 Stat. 3045 (18 U.S.C. 1091 et seq.)
Short title, see 18 U.S.C. 1091 note

George Bill
Feb. 24, 1945, ch. 4, 59 Stat. 5 (12 U.S.C. 1801 et seq.)

George Bush School of Government and Public Service Act
Pub. L. 104–319, title IV, Oct. 19, 1996, 110 Stat. 3867

George Rogers Clark National Historical Park Act
Pub. L. 89–517, July 23, 1966, 80 Stat. 325 (16 U.S.C. 291 et seq.)

George Washington Commemorative Coin Act
Pub. L. 97–104, Dec. 23, 1981, 95 Stat. 1491

George Washington National Forest Mount Pleasant Scenic Area Act
Renamed Mount Pleasant National Scenic Area Act

George-Barden Act
See Vocational Education Act of 1946

George-Deen Vocational Education Act
See Vocational Education Act of 1946

George-Murray Contract Settlement Act of 1944
See Contract Settlement Act of 1944

Georgia Wilderness Act of 1986
Pub. L. 99–555, Oct. 27, 1986, 100 Stat. 3129 (16 U.S.C. 1132 note)

Geothermal Energy Act of 1980
Pub. L. 96–294, title VI, June 30, 1980, 94 Stat. 763 (30 U.S.C. 1501 et seq.)
Short title, see 30 U.S.C. 1501 note

Geothermal Energy Research, Development, and Demonstration Act of 1974
Pub. L. 93–410, Sept. 3, 1974, 88 Stat. 1079 (30 U.S.C. 1101 et seq.)
Short title, see 30 U.S.C. 1101 note

Geothermal Steam Act Amendments of 1988
Pub. L. 100–443, Sept. 22, 1988, 102 Stat. 1766
Short title, see 30 U.S.C. 1001 note

Geothermal Steam Act of 1970
Pub. L. 91–581, Dec. 24, 1970, 84 Stat. 1566 (30 U.S.C. 1001 et seq.)
Short title, see 30 U.S.C. 1001 note

Gerry Act (Corrupt Practices)
Oct. 16, 1918, ch. 187, 40 Stat. 1013

GI Bill Improvement Act of 1977
Pub. L. 95–202, Nov. 23, 1977, 91 Stat. 1433
Short title, see 38 U.S.C. 101 note

GI Fiancées Act
June 29, 1946, ch. 520, 60 Stat. 339 (50 App. U.S.C. 1851 et seq.)

Gifted and Talented Children's Education Act of 1978
Pub. L. 89–10, title IX, as added Pub. L. 95–561, title VIII, §802, Nov. 1, 1978, 92 Stat. 2292

Gillespie-Tillman Resolution (Transportation of Coal and Oil)
Mar. 7, 1906, No. 8, 34 Stat. 823

Glacier Bay National Park Boundary Adjustment Act of 1998
Pub. L. 105–317, Oct. 30, 1998, 112 Stat. 3002 (16 U.S.C. 410hh–1 note)

Glacier Bay National Park Resource Management Act of 2000
Pub. L. 106–455, Nov. 7, 2000, 114 Stat. 1953 (16 U.S.C. 410hh–4 note)

Glacier National Park Act
Aug. 22, 1914, ch. 264, 38 Stat. 699 (16 U.S.C. 163, 168–177)

Glass Bank Official Loan Act
See Bank Official Loan Act

Glass Ceiling Act of 1991
Pub. L. 102–166, title II, Nov. 21, 1991, 105 Stat. 1081 (42 U.S.C. 2000e note)

Glass Federal Reserve Note Act
June 30, 1939, ch. 256, 53 Stat. 991 (12 U.S.C. 412)

Glass R.F.C. Recovery Loan Act
See Reconstruction Finance Corporation Act

Glass Reserve Note Act
See Federal Reserve Act

Glass-Steagall Act, 1932
Feb. 27, 1932, ch. 58, 47 Stat. 56 (12 U.S.C. 347a, 347b, 412)
Short title, see 12 U.S.C. 226 note

Glass-Steagall Act, 1933
See Banking Act of 1933

Glen Canyon National Recreation Area Act
Pub. L. 92–593, Oct. 27, 1972, 86 Stat. 1311 (16 U.S.C. 460dd et seq.)

Global AIDS and Tuberculosis Relief Act of 2000
Pub. L. 106–264, Aug. 19, 2000, 114 Stat. 748
Short title, see 22 U.S.C. 6801 note

Global AIDS Research and Relief Act of 2000
Pub. L. 106–264, title I, Aug. 19, 2000, 114 Stat. 749 (22 U.S.C. 6801 et seq.)
Short title, see 22 U.S.C. 6801 note

Global Change Research Act of 1990
Pub. L. 101–606, Nov. 16, 1990, 104 Stat. 3096 (15 U.S.C. 2921 et seq.)
Short title, see 15 U.S.C. 2921 note

Global Climate Change Prevention Act of 1990
Pub. L. 101–624, title XXIV, Nov. 28, 1990, 104 Stat. 4058 (7 U.S.C. 6701 et seq.)
Short title, see 7 U.S.C. 6701 note

Global Climate Protection Act of 1987
Pub. L. 100–204, title XI, Dec. 22, 1987, 101 Stat. 1407 (15 U.S.C. 2901 note)

Global Environmental Protection Assistance Act of 1989
Pub. L. 101–240, title VII, Dec. 19, 1989, 103 Stat. 2521 (22 U.S.C. 2281 et seq.)
Short title, see 22 U.S.C. 2151 note

Goals 2000: Educate America Act
Pub. L. 103–227, titles I–IV, VI–VIII, X, Mar. 31, 1994, 108 Stat. 125–191, 200–211, 265–280 (20 U.S.C. 5801 et seq.)
Short title, see 20 U.S.C. 5801 note

Gold Bullion Coin Act of 1985
Pub. L. 99–185, Dec. 17, 1985, 99 Stat. 1177
Short title, see 31 U.S.C. 5112 note

Gold Clause Act
Aug. 27, 1935, ch. 780, 49 Stat. 938

Gold Hoarding Act
Mar. 9, 1933, ch. 1, title I, §3, 48 Stat. 2

Gold Labeling Act of 1976
Pub. L. 94–450, Oct. 1, 1976, 90 Stat. 1501
Short title, see 15 U.S.C. 294 note

Gold Repeal Joint Resolution
June 5, 1933, ch. 48, 48 Stat. 112

Gold Reserve Act of 1934
Jan. 30, 1934, ch. 6, 48 Stat. 337

Gold Standard Act
Mar. 14, 1900, ch. 41, 31 Stat. 45

Gold Star Mothers Act
Aug. 16, 1937, ch. 659, 50 Stat. 660

Golden Eagle Protection Act
Pub. L. 87–884, Oct. 24, 1962, 76 Stat. 1246

Golden Gate National Recreation Area Act
Pub. L. 92–589, Oct. 27, 1972, 86 Stat. 1299 (16 U.S.C. 460bb et seq.)

Golden Gate National Recreation Area Addition Act of 1992
Pub. L. 102–299, June 9, 1992, 106 Stat. 236
Short title, see 16 U.S.C. 460bb note

Golden Gate National Recreation Area Boundary Adjustment Act of 2000
Pub. L. 106–350, Oct. 24, 2000, 114 Stat. 1361
Short title, see 16 U.S.C. 460bb note

Golden Nematode Act
June 15, 1948, ch. 471, 62 Stat. 442 (7 U.S.C. 150 et seq.)
Short title, see 7 U.S.C. 150 note

Goldwater-Nichols Department of Defense Reorganization Act of 1986
Pub. L. 99–433, Oct. 1, 1986, 100 Stat. 992
Short title, see 10 U.S.C. 111 note

Good Neighbor Environmental Act of 1992
Pub. L. 102–532, §2, Oct. 27, 1992, 106 Stat. 3509 (7 U.S.C. 1738*o* et seq.)
Short title, see 7 U.S.C. 1691 note

Good Roads Act
See Federal-Aid Road Act

Good Samaritan Food Donation Act
Renamed Bill Emerson Good Samaritan Food Donation Act

Good-McCormick Act (Budget)
See Budget and Accounting Act, 1921

Gould Amendment (Food and Drugs)
Mar. 3, 1913, ch. 117, 37 Stat. 732

Government Corporation Control Act
Dec. 6, 1945, ch. 557, 59 Stat. 597

Government Corporations Appropriations Act, 1947
July 20, 1946, ch. 589, 60 Stat. 586

Government Corporations Appropriation Act, 1948
July 30, 1947, ch. 358, 61 Stat. 574

Government Corporations Appropriation Act, 1949
June 30, 1948, ch. 773, 62 Stat. 1183

Government Employee Rights Act of 1991
Pub. L. 102–166, title III, Nov. 21, 1991, 105 Stat. 1088 (42 U.S.C. 2000e–16a et seq.)
Short title, see 42 U.S.C. 2000e–16a(a)

Government Employees Incentive Awards Act
Sept. 1, 1954, ch. 1208, title III, 68 Stat. 1112

Government Employees Salary Reform Act of 1964
Pub. L. 88–426, Aug. 14, 1964, 78 Stat. 400

Government Employees Training Act
Pub. L. 85–507, July 7, 1958, 72 Stat. 327

Government Employees' Compensation Act
See Federal Employees' Compensation Act (1916)

Government Employers' Liability Act
See Federal Employees' Compensation Act (1908)

Government in the Sunshine Act
Pub. L. 94–409, Sept. 13, 1976, 90 Stat. 1241
Short title, see 5 U.S.C. 552b note

Government Losses in Shipment Act
July 8, 1937, ch. 444, 50 Stat. 479
Short title, see 40 U.S.C. 721 note

Government Management Reform Act of 1994
Pub. L. 103–356, Oct. 13, 1994, 108 Stat. 3410
Short title, see 31 U.S.C. 3301 note

Government Paperwork Elimination Act
Pub. L. 105–277, div. C, title XVII, Oct. 21, 1998, 112 Stat. 2681–749 (44 U.S.C. 3504 note)

Government Performance and Results Act of 1993
Pub. L. 103–62, Aug. 3, 1993, 107 Stat. 285
Short title, see 31 U.S.C. 1101 note

Government Printing Office Electronic Information Access Enhancement Act of 1993
Pub. L. 103–40, June 8, 1993, 107 Stat. 112 (44 U.S.C. 4101 et seq.)

Government Printing Office Electronic Information Access Enhancement Act of 1993—Continued
Short title, see 44 U.S.C. 101 note

Government Printing Office Inspector General Act of 1988
Pub. L. 100–504, title II, Oct. 18, 1988, 102 Stat. 2530 (44 U.S.C. 3901 et seq.)
Short title, see 44 U.S.C. 101 note

Government Reorganization Act
See Reorganization Act of 1939

Government Securities Act Amendments of 1993
Pub. L. 103–202, Dec. 17, 1993, 107 Stat. 2344
Short title, see 15 U.S.C. 78a note

Government Securities Act of 1986
Pub. L. 99–571, Oct. 28, 1986, 100 Stat. 3208
Short title, see 15 U.S.C. 78a note

Government Surplus Airports and Equipment Act
July 30, 1947, ch. 404, 61 Stat. 678

Government-Aided Railroad and Telegraph Act
Aug. 7, 1888, ch. 772, 25 Stat. 382 (47 U.S.C. 9–15)

Governor's Appointment Proclamation (Alabama)
June 21, 1865, No. 43, 13 Stat. 767

Governor's Appointment Proclamation (Florida)
July 13, 1865, No. 47, 13 Stat. 771

Governor's Appointment Proclamation (Georgia)
June 17, 1865, No. 41, 13 Stat. 764

Governor's Appointment Proclamation (Mississippi)
June 13, 1865, No. 39, 13 Stat. 761

Governor's Appointment Proclamation (North Carolina)
May 29, 1865, No. 38, 13 Stat. 760

Governor's Appointment Proclamation (South Carolina)
June 30, 1865, No. 46, 13 Stat. 769

Governor's Appointment Proclamation (Texas)
June 17, 1865, No. 42, 13 Stat. 765

Graduate Public Health Training Amendments of 1964
Pub. L. 88–497, Aug. 27, 1964, 78 Stat. 613
Short title, see 42 U.S.C. 201 note

Graduation Act of 1854 (Public Lands)
Aug. 4, 1854, ch. 244, 10 Stat. 574

Grain Futures Act
Renamed the Commodity Exchange Act

Grain Inspection Act
See United States Grain Standards Act

Grain Quality Improvement Act of 1986
Pub. L. 99–641, title III, Nov. 10, 1986, 100 Stat. 3564
Short title, see 7 U.S.C. 71 note

Grain Quality Incentives Act of 1990
Pub. L. 101–624, title XX, Nov. 28, 1990, 104 Stat. 3928
Short title, see 7 U.S.C. 71 note

Grain Standards Act
See United States Grain Standards Act

Grain Standards and Warehouse Improvement Act of 2000
Pub. L. 106–472, Nov. 9, 2000, 114 Stat. 2058
Short title, see 7 U.S.C. 71 note

Gramm-Leach-Bliley Act
Pub. L. 106–102, Nov. 12, 1999, 113 Stat. 1338
Short title, see 12 U.S.C. 1811 note

Gramm-Rudman-Hollings Act
See Balanced Budget and Emergency Deficit Control Act of 1985

Grand Canyon National Park Enlargement Act
Pub. L. 93–620, Jan. 3, 1975, 88 Stat. 2089 (16 U.S.C. 228a et seq.)
Short title, see 16 U.S.C. 221 note

Grand Canyon Protection Act of 1992
Pub. L. 102–575, title XVIII, Oct. 30, 1992, 106 Stat. 4669

Grand Ronde Restoration Act
Pub. L. 98–165, Nov. 22, 1983, 97 Stat. 1064 (25 U.S.C. 713 et seq.)
Short title, see 25 U.S.C. 713 note

Granite Watershed Enhancement and Protection Act of 1998
Pub. L. 105–281, Oct. 26, 1998, 112 Stat. 2695

Grant-Kohrs Ranch National Historic Site Boundary Adjustment Act of 1998
Pub. L. 105–365, Nov. 10, 1998, 112 Stat. 3301

Graton Rancheria Restoration Act
Pub. L. 106–568, title XIV, Dec. 27, 2000, 114 Stat. 2939 (25 U.S.C. 1300n et seq.)
Short title, see 25 U.S.C. 1300n note

Great Ape Conservation Act of 2000
Pub. L. 106–411, Nov. 1, 2000, 114 Stat. 1789 (16 U.S.C. 6301 et seq.)
Short title, see 16 U.S.C. 6301 note

Great Basin National Park Act of 1986
Pub. L. 99–565, Oct. 27, 1986, 100 Stat. 3181 (16 U.S.C. 410mm et seq.)
Short title, see 16 U.S.C. 410mm note

Great Lakes Coastal Barrier Act of 1988
Pub. L. 100–707, title II, §204, Nov. 23, 1988, 102 Stat. 4713
Short title, see 16 U.S.C. 3501 note

Great Lakes Critical Programs Act of 1990
Pub. L. 101–596, Nov. 16, 1990, 104 Stat. 3000
Short title, see 33 U.S.C. 1251 note

Great Lakes Fish and Wildlife Restoration Act of 1990
Pub. L. 101–537, title I, Nov. 8, 1990, 104 Stat. 2370 (16 U.S.C. 941 et seq.)
Pub. L. 101–646, title II, Nov. 29, 1990, 104 Stat. 4773 (16 U.S.C. 941 et seq.)
Short title, see 16 U.S.C. 941 note

Great Lakes Fish and Wildlife Restoration Act of 1998
Pub. L. 105–265, Oct. 19, 1998, 112 Stat. 2358
Short title, see 16 U.S.C. 941 note

Great Lakes Fish and Wildlife Tissue Bank Act
Pub. L. 102–440, title II, Oct. 23, 1992, 106 Stat. 2233 (16 U.S.C. 943 et seq.)
Short title, see 16 U.S.C. 943 note

Great Lakes Fishery Act of 1956
June 4, 1956, ch. 358, 70 Stat. 242 (16 U.S.C. 931 et seq.)
Short title, see 16 U.S.C. 931 note

Great Lakes Oil Pollution Research and Development Act
Pub. L. 101–537, title II, Nov. 8, 1990, 104 Stat. 2375
Pub. L. 101–646, title IV, Nov. 29, 1990, 104 Stat. 4788
Short title, see 33 U.S.C. 2701 note

Great Lakes Pilotage Act of 1960
Pub. L. 86–555, June 30, 1960, 74 Stat. 259

Great Lakes Planning Assistance Act of 1988
Pub. L. 100–707, title II, Nov. 23, 1988, 102 Stat. 4711
Short title, see 33 U.S.C. 426p note

Great Lakes Shoreline Mapping Act of 1987
Pub. L. 100–220, title III, subtitle B (§3201 et seq.), Dec. 29, 1987, 101 Stat. 1475 (33 U.S.C. 883a note)

Great Sand Dunes National Park and Preserve Act of 2000
Pub. L. 106–530, Nov. 22, 2000, 114 Stat. 2527 (16 U.S.C. 410hhh et seq.)
Short title, see 16 U.S.C. 410hhh note

Greek Loan of 1929 Settlement Act
Pub. L. 89–766, Nov. 5, 1966, 80 Stat. 1314

Greek-Turkish Assistance Act of 1948
Apr. 3, 1948, ch. 169, title III, 62 Stat. 157

Greens Creek Land Exchange Act of 1995
Pub. L. 104–123, Apr. 1, 1996, 110 Stat. 879

Greer Spring Acquisition and Protection Act of 1991
Pub. L. 102–220, Dec. 11, 1991, 105 Stat. 1674 (16 U.S.C. 539h, 539h note)

Griffin-Landrum Act
See Labor-Management Reporting and Disclosure Act of 1959

Griffith Project Prepayment and Conveyance Act
Pub. L. 106–249, July 26, 2000, 114 Stat. 619

GSP Renewal Act of 1996
Pub. L. 104–188, title I, subtitle J (§1951 et seq.), Aug. 20, 1996, 110 Stat. 1917
Short title, see 19 U.S.C. 2101 note

Guam Development Fund Act of 1968
Pub. L. 90–601, Oct. 17, 1968, 82 Stat. 1172 (48 U.S.C. 1428 et seq.)
Short title, see 48 U.S.C. 1421 note

Guam Elective Governor Act
Pub. L. 90–497, Sept. 11, 1968, 82 Stat. 842
Short title, see 48 U.S.C. 1421 note

Guam Excess Lands Act
Pub. L. 103–339, Oct. 6, 1994, 108 Stat. 3116

Guam Organic Act Amendments of 1998
Pub. L. 105–291, Oct. 27, 1998, 112 Stat. 2785
Short title, see 48 U.S.C. 1421 note

Guard and Reserve Forces Facilities Authorization Act, 1976
Pub. L. 94–107, title VII, Oct. 7, 1975, 89 Stat. 568

Guard and Reserves Forces Facilities Authorization Act, 1977
Pub. L. 94–431, title VII, Sept. 30, 1976, 90 Stat. 1368

Guatemala Relief and Rehabilitation Act of 1976
Pub. L. 94–276, Apr. 21, 1976, 90 Stat. 397 (22 U.S.C. 2292g)

Guayule Rubber Act
Mar. 5, 1942, ch. 140, 56 Stat. 126 (7 U.S.C. 171 et seq.)

Guffey-Snyder Coal Act
See Bituminous Coal Conservation Act of 1935

Guffey-Vinson Act
See Bituminous Coal Act of 1937

Gulf Islands National Seashore Act
Pub. L. 91–660, Jan. 8, 1971, 84 Stat. 1967 (16 U.S.C. 459h et seq.)

Gun Control Act of 1968
Pub. L. 90–618, Oct. 22, 1968, 82 Stat. 1213
Short title, see 18 U.S.C. 921 note

Gun-Free School Zones Act of 1990
Pub. L. 101–647, title XVII, §1702, Nov. 29, 1990, 104 Stat. 4844
Short title, see 18 U.S.C. 921 note

Gun-Free Schools Act of 1994
Pub. L. 103–227, title X, part B (§1031 et seq.), Mar. 31, 1994, 108 Stat. 270
Pub. L. 89–10, title XIV, §14601, as added Pub. L. 103–382, title I, §101, Oct. 20, 1994, 108 Stat. 3907 (20 U.S.C. 8921)
Short title, see 20 U.S.C. 6301 note, 8921(a)

Gwynne Act
See Portal-to-Portal Act of 1947

Habeas Corpus Act (Civil War)
Mar. 3, 1863, ch. 81, 12 Stat. 755

Haida Land Exchange Act of 1986
Pub. L. 99–664, Nov. 17, 1986, 100 Stat. 4303

Haitian Refugee Immigration Fairness Act of 1998
Pub. L. 105–277, div. A, §101(h) [title IX], Oct. 21, 1998, 112 Stat. 2681–480, 2681–538 (8 U.S.C. 1377, 1378)
Short title, see 8 U.S.C. 1101 note

Haleakalā National Park Act
Pub. L. 86–744, Sept. 13, 1960, 74 Stat. 881 (16 U.S.C. 396b)

Hall-Mark Act
Feb. 21, 1905, ch. 720, 33 Stat. 732 (15 U.S.C. 291 et seq.)

Hall-Mark Act (Gold and Silver Articles)
See Jewelers' Liability Act (Gold and Silver Articles)

Halogeton Glomeratus Control Act
July 14, 1952, ch. 721, 66 Stat. 597 (7 U.S.C. 1651 et seq.)
Short title, see 7 U.S.C. 1651 note

Handicapped Children's Early Education Assistance Act
Pub. L. 90–538, Sept. 30, 1968, 82 Stat. 901 (20 U.S.C. 621 et seq.)

Handicapped Children's Protection Act of 1986
Pub. L. 99–372, Aug. 5, 1986, 100 Stat. 796
Short title, see 20 U.S.C. 1400 note

Handicapped Programs Technical Amendments Act of 1988
Pub. L. 100–630, Nov. 7, 1988, 102 Stat. 3289
Short title, see 20 U.S.C. 1400 note

Harbor Development and Navigation Improvement Act of 1986
Pub. L. 99–662, title II, Nov. 17, 1986, 100 Stat. 4089 (33 U.S.C. 2231 et seq.)
Short title, see 33 U.S.C. 2201 note

Harbor Maintenance Revenue Act of 1986
Pub. L. 99–662, title XIV, Nov. 17, 1986, 100 Stat. 4266
Short title, see 26 U.S.C. 1 note

Hare-Hawes-Cutting Act
Jan. 17, 1933, ch. 11, 47 Stat. 761

Harmful Algal Bloom and Hypoxia Research and Control Act of 1998
Pub. L. 105–383, title VI, Nov. 13, 1998, 112 Stat. 3447 (16 U.S.C. 1451 note)

Harriet Tubman Special Resource Study Act
Pub. L. 106–516, Nov. 13, 2000, 114 Stat. 2404

Harrison Act (Restrictions on Territories)
See Special Laws Prohibition Act (Territories)

Harrison Act of 1914
Dec. 17, 1914, ch. 1, 38 Stat. 785

Harrison Naval Stores Act
See Naval Stores Act

Harry S Truman Memorial Scholarship Act
Pub. L. 93–642, Jan. 4, 1975, 88 Stat. 2276 (20 U.S.C. 2001 et seq.)
Short title, see 20 U.S.C. 2001 note

Hart-Scott-Rodino Antitrust Improvements Act of 1976
Pub. L. 94–435, Sept. 30, 1976, 90 Stat. 1383
Short title, see 15 U.S.C. 1 note

Harter Act (Carriage of Goods by Sea)
Feb. 13, 1893, ch. 105, 27 Stat. 445 (46 App. U.S.C. 190 et seq.)
Short title, see 46 App. U.S.C. 181 note, 190 note

Haskell Indian Nations University and Southwestern Indian Polytechnic Institute Administrative Systems Act of 1998
Pub. L. 105–337, Oct. 31, 1998, 112 Stat. 3171 (25 U.S.C. 3731 note)

Hass Avocado Promotion, Research, and Information Act of 2000
Pub. L. 106–387, §1(a) [title XII], Oct. 28, 2000, 114 Stat. 1549, 1549A–79 (7 U.S.C. 7801 et seq.)
Short title, see 7 U.S.C. 7801 note

Hastings Amendment
June 30, 1919, ch. 4, 41 Stat. 4

Hatch Act of 1887
Mar. 2, 1887, ch. 314, 24 Stat. 440 (7 U.S.C. 361a et seq.)
Short title, see 7 U.S.C. 361a note

Hatch Act Reform Amendments of 1993
Pub. L. 103–94, Oct. 6, 1993, 107 Stat. 1001
Short title, see 5 U.S.C. 7301 note

Hatch Political Activity Act
Aug. 2, 1939, ch. 410, 53 Stat. 1147

Hatch-Sumners Act (Additional Judgeships)
May 31, 1938, ch. 290, 52 Stat. 584

Hate Crime Statistics Act
Pub. L. 101–275, Apr. 23, 1990, 104 Stat. 140 (28 U.S.C. 534 note)

Hatfield-Keller Railroad Retirement Act
See Railroad Retirement Act

Hawaii Omnibus Act
Pub. L. 86–624, July 12, 1960, 74 Stat. 411 (48 U.S.C. note prec. 491)

Hawaii Prohibition Act
May 23, 1918, ch. 84, 40 Stat. 560

Hawaii Statehood Admissions Act
Pub. L. 86–3, Mar. 18, 1959, 73 Stat. 4 (48 U.S.C. note prec 491)

Hawaii Territorial Act
See Hawaiian Organic Act

Hawaii Tropical Forest Recovery Act
Pub. L. 102–574, Oct. 29, 1992, 106 Stat. 4593 (16 U.S.C. 4502a, 4503a et seq.)
Short title, see 16 U.S.C. 4501 note

Hawaii Volcanoes National Park Adjustment Act of 1998
Renamed Hawai`i Volcanoes National Park Adjustment Act of 1998

Hawai'i Volcanoes National Park Adjustment Act of 1998
Pub. L. 105–380, Nov. 12, 1998, 112 Stat. 3401
Short title, see 16 U.S.C. 391 note

Hawaii Volcanoes National Park Adjustment Act of 2000
Pub. L. 106–510, Nov. 13, 2000, 114 Stat. 2363
Short title, see 16 U.S.C. 1 note

Hawaii Water Resources Act of 2000
Pub. L. 106–566, title I, Dec. 23, 2000, 114 Stat. 2818
Short title, see 43 U.S.C. 390h note

Hawaiian Annexation Resolution
July 7, 1898, Res. No. 55, 30 Stat. 750

Hawaiian Home Lands Recovery Act
Pub. L. 104–42, title II, Nov. 2, 1995, 109 Stat. 357 (48 U.S.C. note prec. 491)

Hawaiian Homelands Homeownership Act of 2000
Pub. L. 106–568, title II, Dec. 27, 2000, 114 Stat. 2872 (25 U.S.C. 4221 et seq.)
Pub. L. 106–569, title V, subtitle B (§511 et seq.), Dec. 27, 2000, 114 Stat. 2966 (25 U.S.C. 4221 et seq.)
Short title, see 25 U.S.C. 4101 notes

Hawaiian Homes Commission Act, 1920
July 9, 1921, ch. 42, 42 Stat. 108

Hawaiian Islands National Marine Sanctuary Act
Pub. L. 102–587, title II, subtitle C (§2301 et seq.), Nov. 4, 1992, 106 Stat. 5055 (16 U.S.C. 1433 note)

Hawaiian Organic Act
Apr. 30, 1900, ch. 339, 31 Stat. 141

Hawes-Cooper Act
Jan. 19, 1929, ch. 79, 45 Stat. 1084

Hawley Act (Settlement of Claims against Germany)
June 5, 1930, ch. 402, 46 Stat. 500

Hawley-Smoot Tariff Act
See Tariff Act of 1930

Hayden-Cartwright Act
June 16, 1936, ch. 582, 49 Stat. 1519

Hayden-Cartwright Federal Highway Act of 1938
See Federal Aid Highway Act of 1938

Hazard Mitigation and Relocation Assistance Act of 1993
Pub. L. 103–181, Dec. 3, 1993, 107 Stat. 2054
Short title, see 42 U.S.C. 5121 note

Hazardous and Solid Waste Amendments of 1984
Pub. L. 98–616, Nov. 8, 1984, 98 Stat. 3221
Short title, see 42 U.S.C. 6901 note

Hazardous Liquid Pipeline Safety Act of 1979
Pub. L. 96–129, title II, Nov. 30, 1979, 93 Stat. 1003

Hazardous Materials Transportation Act
Pub. L. 93–633, title I, Jan. 3, 1975, 88 Stat. 2156

Hazardous Materials Transportation Act Amendments of 1976
Pub. L. 94–474, Oct. 11, 1976, 90 Stat. 2068

Hazardous Materials Transportation Authorization Act of 1994
Pub. L. 103–311, title I, Aug. 26, 1994, 108 Stat. 1673
Short title, see 49 U.S.C. 5101 note

Hazardous Materials Transportation Control Act of 1970
Pub. L. 91–458, title III, Oct. 16, 1970, 84 Stat. 977

Hazardous Materials Transportation Uniform Safety Act of 1990
Pub. L. 101–615, Nov. 16, 1990, 104 Stat. 3244

Hazardous Substance Response Revenue Act of 1980
Pub. L. 96–510, title II, Dec. 11, 1980, 94 Stat. 2796
Short title, see 26 U.S.C. 1 note

Head Start Act
Pub. L. 97–35, title VI, subtitle A, ch. 8, subch. B (§635 et seq.), Aug. 13, 1981, 95 Stat. 499 (42 U.S.C. 9831 et seq.)
Short title, see 42 U.S.C. 9801 note

Head Start Act Amendments of 1994
Pub. L. 103–252, title I, May 18, 1994, 108 Stat. 624
Short title, see 42 U.S.C. 9801 note

Head Start Amendments of 1998
Pub. L. 105–285, title I, Oct. 27, 1998, 112 Stat. 2703
Short title, see 42 U.S.C. 9801 note

Head Start Expansion and Quality Improvement Act
Pub. L. 101–501, title I, subtitle A (§101 et seq.), Nov. 3, 1990, 104 Stat. 1224
Short title, see 42 U.S.C. 9801 note

Head Start Improvement Act of 1992
Pub. L. 102–401, Oct. 7, 1992, 106 Stat. 1956
Short title, see 42 U.S.C. 9801 note

Head Start Supplemental Authorization Act of 1989
Pub. L. 101–120, Oct. 23, 1989, 103 Stat. 700
Short title, see 42 U.S.C. 9801 note

Head Start Transition Project Act
Pub. L. 101–501, title I, subtitle B (§131 et seq.), Nov. 3, 1990, 104 Stat. 1238 (42 U.S.C. 9855 et seq.)
Short title, see 42 U.S.C. 9801 note

Headstart, Economic Opportunity, and Community Partnership Act of 1974
Pub. L. 93–644, Jan. 4, 1975, 88 Stat. 2291
Short title, see 42 U.S.C. 2701 note

Headstart-Follow Through Act
Pub. L. 88–452, title V, as added Pub. L. 93–644, §8(a), Jan. 4, 1975, 88 Stat. 2300 (42 U.S.C. 2921 et seq.)

Health Amendments Act of 1956
Aug. 2, 1956, ch. 871, 70 Stat. 923

Health Care Quality Improvement Act of 1986
Pub. L. 99–660, title IV, Nov. 14, 1986, 100 Stat. 3784 (42 U.S.C. 11101 et seq.)
Short title, see 42 U.S.C. 11101 note

Health Care Research and Quality Act of 1999
See Healthcare Research and Quality Act of 1999

Health Care Services in the Home Act of 1987
Pub. L. 100–175, title VI, Nov. 29, 1987, 101 Stat. 979 (42 U.S.C. 280c et seq.)
Short title, see 42 U.S.C. 201 note

Health Centers Consolidation Act of 1996
Pub. L. 104–299, Oct. 11, 1996, 110 Stat. 3626
Short title, see 42 U.S.C. 201 note

Health Education Act of 1978
Pub. L. 89–10, title III, part I (§361 et seq.), as added Pub. L. 95–561, title III, §301(a), Nov. 1, 1978, 92 Stat. 2221 (20 U.S.C. 3021 et seq.)

Health Information, Health Promotion, and Vaccine Injury Compensation Amendments of 1991
Pub. L. 102–168, Nov. 26, 1991, 105 Stat. 1102

Health Information, Health Promotion, and Vaccine Injury Compensation Amendments of 1991—Continued
Short title, see 42 U.S.C. 201 note

Health Insurance for the Aged Act
Pub. L. 89–97, title I, July 30, 1965, 79 Stat. 290
Short title, see 42 U.S.C. 1305 note

Health Insurance Portability and Accountability Act of 1996
Pub. L. 104–191, Aug. 21, 1996, 110 Stat. 1936
Short title, see 42 U.S.C. 201 note

Health Maintenance Organization Act of 1973
Pub. L. 93–222, Dec. 29, 1973, 87 Stat. 914 (42 U.S.C. 300e et seq.)
Short title, see 42 U.S.C. 201 note

Health Maintenance Organization Amendments of 1976
Pub. L. 94–460, Oct. 8, 1976, 90 Stat. 1945
Short title, see 42 U.S.C. 201 note

Health Maintenance Organization Amendments of 1978
Pub. L. 95–559, Nov. 1, 1978, 92 Stat. 2131
Short title, see 42 U.S.C. 201 note

Health Maintenance Organization Amendments of 1981
Pub. L. 97–35, title IX, subtitle F (§940 et seq.), Aug. 13, 1981, 95 Stat. 572
Short title, see 42 U.S.C. 201 note

Health Maintenance Organization Amendments of 1986
Pub. L. 99–660, title VIII, Nov. 14, 1986, 100 Stat. 3799
Short title, see 42 U.S.C. 201 note

Health Maintenance Organization Amendments of 1988
Pub. L. 100–517, Oct. 24, 1988, 102 Stat. 2578
Short title, see 42 U.S.C. 201 note

Health Manpower Act of 1968
Pub. L. 90–490, Aug. 16, 1968, 82 Stat. 773
Short title, see 42 U.S.C. 201 note

Health Omnibus Programs Extension of 1988
Pub. L. 100–607, Nov. 4, 1988, 102 Stat. 3048
Short title, see 42 U.S.C. 201 note

Health Planning and Health Services Research and Statistics Extension Act of 1977
Pub. L. 95–83, title I, Aug. 1, 1977, 91 Stat. 383
Short title, see 42 U.S.C. 201 note

Health Planning and Resources Development Amendments of 1979
Pub. L. 96–79, Oct. 4, 1979, 93 Stat. 592
Short title, see 42 U.S.C. 201 note

Health Professions Education Extension Amendments of 1992
Pub. L. 102–408, Oct. 13, 1992, 106 Stat. 1992
Short title, see 42 U.S.C. 201 note

Health Professions Education Partnerships Act of 1998
Pub. L. 105–392, Nov. 13, 1998, 112 Stat. 3524
Short title, see 42 U.S.C. 201 note

Health Professions Educational Assistance Act of 1963
Pub. L. 88–129, Sept. 24, 1963, 77 Stat. 164
Short title, see 42 U.S.C. 201 note

Health Professions Educational Assistance Act of 1976
Pub. L. 94–484, Oct. 12, 1976, 90 Stat. 2243
Short title, see 42 U.S.C. 201 note

Health Professions Educational Assistance Amendments of 1965
Pub. L. 89–290, Oct. 22, 1965, 79 Stat. 1052
Short title, see 42 U.S.C. 201 note

Health Professions Reauthorization Act of 1988
Pub. L. 100–607, title VI, Nov. 4, 1988, 102 Stat. 3122
Short title, see 42 U.S.C. 201 note

Health Professions Training Assistance Act of 1985
Pub. L. 99–129, Oct. 22, 1985, 99 Stat. 523
Short title, see 42 U.S.C. 201 note

Health Programs Extension Act of 1973
Pub. L. 93–45, June 18, 1973, 87 Stat. 91
Short title, see 42 U.S.C. 201 note

Health Programs Extension Act of 1980
Pub. L. 96–538, Dec. 17, 1980, 94 Stat. 3183
Short title, see 42 U.S.C. 201 note

Health Promotion and Disease Prevention Amendments of 1984
Pub. L. 98–551, Oct. 30, 1984, 98 Stat. 2815
Short title, see 42 U.S.C. 201 note

Health Research and Health Services Amendments of 1976
Pub. L. 94–278, Apr. 22, 1976, 90 Stat. 401

Health Research Extension Act of 1985
Pub. L. 99–158, Nov. 20, 1985, 99 Stat. 820
Short title, see 42 U.S.C. 201 note

Health Research Facilities Act of 1956
July 30, 1956, ch. 779, 70 Stat. 717

Health Research Facilities Amendments of 1965
Pub. L. 89–115, Aug. 9, 1965, 79 Stat. 448
Short title, see 42 U.S.C. 201 note

Health Services Amendments Act of 1986
Pub. L. 99–280, Apr. 24, 1986, 100 Stat. 399
Short title, see 42 U.S.C. 201 note

Health Services Amendments of 1985
Pub. L. 99–117, Oct. 7, 1985, 99 Stat. 491
Short title, see 42 U.S.C. 201 note

Health Services and Centers Amendments of 1978
Pub. L. 95–626, Nov. 10, 1978, 92 Stat. 3551
Short title, see 42 U.S.C. 201 note

Health Services Extension Act of 1977
Pub. L. 95–83, title III, Aug. 1, 1977, 91 Stat. 387
Short title, see 42 U.S.C. 201 note

Health Services Extension Act of 1978
Pub. L. 95–626, title II, Nov. 10, 1978, 92 Stat. 3570
Short title, see 42 U.S.C. 201 note

Health Services Research and Evaluation and Health Statistics Act of 1974
Pub. L. 93–353, title I, July 23, 1974, 88 Stat. 362
Short title, see 42 U.S.C. 201 note

Health Services Research, Health Statistics, and Health Care Technology Act of 1978
Pub. L. 95–623, Nov. 9, 1978, 92 Stat. 3443
Short title, see 42 U.S.C. 201 note

Health Services Research, Health Statistics, and Medical Libraries Act of 1974
Pub. L. 93–353, July 23, 1974, 88 Stat. 362
Short title, see 42 U.S.C. 201 note

Health Training Improvement Act of 1970
Pub. L. 91–519, Nov. 2, 1970, 84 Stat. 1342
Short title, see 42 U.S.C. 201 note

Healthcare Research and Quality Act of 1999
Pub. L. 106–129, Dec. 6, 1999, 113 Stat. 1653
Short title, see 42 U.S.C. 201 note

Healthy Meals for Children Act
Pub. L. 104–149, May 29, 1996, 110 Stat. 1379
Short title, see 42 U.S.C. 1751 note

Healthy Meals for Healthy Americans Act of 1994
Pub. L. 103–448, Nov. 2, 1994, 108 Stat. 4699
Short title, see 42 U.S.C. 1751 note

Heard Act
Aug. 13, 1894, ch. 280, 28 Stat. 278

Hearing Aid Compatibility Act of 1988
Pub. L. 100–394, Aug. 16, 1988, 102 Stat. 976
Short title, see 47 U.S.C. 609 note

Heart Disease, Cancer, and Stroke Amendments of 1965
Pub. L. 89–239, Oct. 6, 1965, 79 Stat. 926
Short title, see 42 U.S.C. 201 note

Heart Disease, Cancer, Stroke, and Kidney Disease Amendments of 1970
Pub. L. 91–515, title I, Oct. 30, 1970, 84 Stat. 1297
Short title, see 42 U.S.C. 201 note

Helen Keller National Center Act
Pub. L. 98–221, title II, Feb. 22, 1984, 98 Stat. 32 (29 U.S.C. 1901 et seq.)
Short title, see 29 U.S.C. 1901 noted

Helium Act
Mar. 3, 1925, ch. 426, as added Pub. L. 86–777, §2, Sept. 13, 1960, 74 Stat. 918 (50 U.S.C. 167 et seq.)
Short title, see 50 U.S.C. 167 note

Helium Act Amendments of 1960
Pub. L. 86–777, Sept. 13, 1960, 74 Stat. 918
Short title, see 50 U.S.C. 167 note

Helium Gas Act
Sept. 1, 1937, ch. 895, 50 Stat. 885

Helium Privatization Act of 1996
Pub. L. 104–273, Oct. 9, 1996, 110 Stat. 3315
Short title, see 50 U.S.C. 167 note

Hells Canyon National Recreation Area Act
Pub. L. 94–199, Dec. 31, 1975, 89 Stat. 1117 (16 U.S.C. 460gg et seq.)

Hepburn Act (Interstate Commerce)
June 29, 1906, ch. 3591, 34 Stat. 584

Herger-Feinstein Quincy Library Group Forest Recovery Act
Pub. L. 105–277, div. A, §101(e) [title IV, §401], Oct. 21, 1998, 112 Stat. 2681–231, 2681–305 (16 U.S.C. 2104 note)

Heyburn Act (Pure Food and Drugs)
See Federal Food and Drugs Act of 1906

Hickenlooper Amendment
Pub. L. 88–633, part III, §301(d)(4), Oct. 7, 1964, 78 Stat. 1013 (22 U.S.C. 2370(e)(2))

High Plains States Groundwater Demonstration Program Act of 1983
Pub. L. 98–434, Sept. 28, 1984, 98 Stat. 1675 (43 U.S.C. 390g et seq.)
Short title, see 43 U.S.C. 390g note

High Seas Driftnet Fisheries Enforcement Act
Pub. L. 102–582, Nov. 2, 1992, 106 Stat. 4900
Short title, see 16 U.S.C. 1801 note

High Seas Driftnet Fishing Moratorium Protection Act
Pub. L. 104–43, title VI, Nov. 3, 1995, 109 Stat. 391 (16 U.S.C. 1826d et seq.)
Short title, see 16 U.S.C. 1801 note

High Seas Fishing Compliance Act of 1995
Pub. L. 104–43, title I, Nov. 3, 1995, 109 Stat. 367 (16 U.S.C. 5501 et seq.)
Short title, see 16 U.S.C. 5501 note

High-Performance Computing Act of 1991
Pub. L. 102–194, Dec. 9, 1991, 105 Stat. 1594 (15 U.S.C. 5501 et seq.)
Short title, see 15 U.S.C. 5501 note

High-Speed Ground Transportation Act
Pub. L. 89–220, Sept. 30, 1965, 79 Stat. 893

Higher Education Act of 1965
Pub. L. 89–329, Nov. 8, 1965, 79 Stat. 1219 (20 U.S.C. 1001 et seq.)
Short title, see 20 U.S.C. 1001 note

Higher Education Amendments of 1966
Pub. L. 89–752, Nov. 3, 1966, 80 Stat. 1240
Short title, see 20 U.S.C. 1001 note

Higher Education Amendments of 1968
Pub. L. 90–575, Oct. 16, 1968, 82 Stat. 1014
Short title, see 20 U.S.C. 1001 note

Higher Education Amendments of 1986
Pub. L. 99–498, Oct. 17, 1986, 100 Stat. 1268
Short title, see 20 U.S.C. 1001 note

Higher Education Amendments of 1992
Pub. L. 102–325, July 23, 1992, 106 Stat. 448
Short title, see 20 U.S.C. 1001 note

Higher Education Amendments of 1998
Pub. L. 105–244, Oct. 7, 1998, 112 Stat. 1581
Short title, see 20 U.S.C. 1001 note

Higher Education Facilities Act of 1963
Pub. L. 88–204, Dec. 16, 1963, 77 Stat. 363 (20 U.S.C. 701 et seq.)

Higher Education Facilities Act of 1992
Pub. L. 89–329, title VII, part A (§711 et seq.), as added Pub. L. 102–325, title VII, §703,

Higher Education Facilities Act of 1992—Continued
July 23, 1992, 106 Stat. 738 (20 U.S.C. 1132b et seq.)

Higher Education Technical Amendments Act of 1987
Pub. L. 100–50, June 3, 1987, 101 Stat. 335
Short title, see 20 U.S.C. 1001 note

Higher Education Technical Amendments of 1979
Pub. L. 96–49, Aug. 13, 1979, 93 Stat. 351
Short title, see 20 U.S.C. 1001 note

Higher Education Technical Amendments of 1991
Pub. L. 102–26, Apr. 9, 1991, 105 Stat. 123
Short title, see 20 U.S.C. 1001 note

Higher Education Technical Amendments of 1993
Pub. L. 103–208, Dec. 20, 1993, 107 Stat. 2457
Short title, see 20 U.S.C. 1001 note

Higher Education Tribal Grant Authorization Act
Pub. L. 102–325, title XIII, part B (§1311 et seq.), July 23, 1992, 106 Stat. 798 (25 U.S.C. 3301 et seq.)
Short title, see 25 U.S.C. 3301

Highway Beautification Act of 1965
Pub. L. 89–285, Oct. 22, 1965, 79 Stat. 1028
Short title, see 23 U.S.C. 101 note

Highway Improvement Act of 1982
Pub. L. 97–424, title I, Jan. 6, 1983, 96 Stat. 2097
Short title, see 23 U.S.C. 101 note

Highway Post Office Service Act of 1955
Aug. 1, 1956, ch. 813, 70 Stat. 781

Highway Revenue Act of 1956
June 29, 1956, ch. 462, title II, 70 Stat. 387
Short title, see 26 U.S.C. 4041 note

Highway Revenue Act of 1978
Pub. L. 95–599, title V, Nov. 6, 1978, 92 Stat. 2756
Short title, see 23 U.S.C. 101 note

Highway Revenue Act of 1982
Pub. L. 97–424, title V, Jan. 6, 1983, 96 Stat. 2168
Short title, see 26 U.S.C. 1 note

Highway Revenue Act of 1987
Pub. L. 100–17, title V, Apr. 2, 1987, 101 Stat. 256
Short title, see 26 U.S.C. 1 note

Highway Safety Act of 1966
Pub. L. 89–564, Sept. 9, 1966, 80 Stat. 731 (23 U.S.C. 401 et seq.)
Short title, see 23 U.S.C. 401 note

Highway Safety Act of 1970
Pub. L. 91–605, title II, Dec. 31, 1970, 84 Stat. 1739
Short title, see 23 U.S.C. 401 note

Highway Safety Act of 1973
Pub. L. 93–87, title II, Aug. 13, 1973, 87 Stat. 282
Short title, see 23 U.S.C. 401 note

Highway Safety Act of 1976
Pub. L. 94–280, title II, May 5, 1976, 90 Stat. 451
Short title, see 23 U.S.C. 401 note

Highway Safety Act of 1978
Pub. L. 95–599, title II, Nov. 6, 1978, 92 Stat. 2727
Short title, see 23 U.S.C. 401 note

Highway Safety Act of 1982
Pub. L. 97–424, title II, Jan. 6, 1983, 96 Stat. 2137
Short title, see 23 U.S.C. 401 note

Highway Safety Act of 1987
Pub. L. 100–17, title II, Apr. 2, 1987, 101 Stat. 218
Short title, see 23 U.S.C. 401 note

Highway Safety Act of 1991
Pub. L. 102–240, title II, part A (§2001 et seq.), Dec. 18, 1991, 105 Stat. 2070
Short title, see 23 U.S.C. 401 note

Hill-Burton Act
See Hospital Survey and Construction Act

Hillory J. Farias and Samantha Reid Date-Rape Drug Prohibition Act of 2000
Pub. L. 106–172, Feb. 18, 2000, 114 Stat. 7
Short title, see 21 U.S.C. 801 note

Hispanic Cultural Center Act of 1997
Pub. L. 105–127, Dec. 1, 1997, 111 Stat. 2543

Hiss Act (Pensions)
Sept. 1, 1954, ch. 1214, 68 Stat. 1142

Historic Sites Act of 1935
Also known as the Historic Sites, Buildings and Antiquities Act
Aug. 21, 1935, ch. 593, 49 Stat. 666 (16 U.S.C. 461 et seq.)
Short title, see 16 U.S.C. 461 note

Historic Sites, Buildings and Antiquities Act
Also known as the Historic Sites Act of 1935
Aug. 21, 1935, ch. 593, 49 Stat. 666 (16 U.S.C. 461 et seq.)
Short title, see 16 U.S.C. 461 note

History of the House Awareness and Preservation Act
Pub. L. 106–99, Nov. 12, 1999, 113 Stat. 1330 (2 U.S.C. 183 et seq.)
Short title, see 2 U.S.C. 183 note

Hmong Veterans' Naturalization Act of 2000
Pub. L. 106–207, May 26, 2000, 114 Stat. 316 (8 U.S.C. 1423 note)

Hobbs Administrative Orders Review Act of 1950
See Administrative Orders Review Act

Hobbs Act (Anti-Racketeering)
July 3, 1946, ch. 537, 60 Stat. 420 (see 18 U.S.C. 1951)
Short title, see 18 U.S.C. 1951 note

Hobbs Bridge Act
Also known as the Truman-Hobbs Act
June 21, 1940, ch. 409, 54 Stat. 497 (33 U.S.C. 511 et seq.)
Short title, see 33 U.S.C. 511 note

Hobby Protection Act
Pub. L. 93–167, Nov. 29, 1973, 87 Stat. 686 (15 U.S.C. 2101 et seq.)
Short title, see 15 U.S.C. 2101 note

Hoch-Smith Resolution
Jan. 30, 1925, ch. 120, 43 Stat. 801

Holding Company Regulation Act
See Public Utility Holding Company Act of 1935

Holiday Pay Act
June 29, 1938, ch. 818, 52 Stat. 1246

Holocaust Victims Redress Act
Pub. L. 105–158, Feb. 13, 1998, 112 Stat. 15

Home Energy Assistance Act of 1980
Pub. L. 96–223, title III, Apr. 2, 1980, 94 Stat. 288 (42 U.S.C. 8601 et seq.)
Short title, see 42 U.S.C. 8601 note

Home Equity Loan Consumer Protection Act of 1988
Pub. L. 100–709, Nov. 23, 1988, 102 Stat. 4725
Short title, see 15 U.S.C. 1601 note

Home Health Care and Alzheimer's Disease Amendments of 1990
Pub. L. 101–557, Nov. 15, 1990, 104 Stat. 2766
Short title, see 42 U.S.C. 201 note

HOME Investment Partnerships Act
Pub. L. 101–625, title II, Nov. 28, 1990, 104 Stat. 4094 (42 U.S.C. 12721 et seq.)
Short title, see 42 U.S.C. 12701 note

Home Mortgage Disclosure Act of 1975
Pub. L. 94–200, title III, Dec. 31, 1975, 89 Stat. 1125 (12 U.S.C. 2801 et seq.)
Short title, see 12 U.S.C. 2801 note

Home Mortgage Relief Act
May 28, 1935, ch. 150, 49 Stat. 293

Home Owners' Loan Act
June 13, 1933, ch. 64, 48 Stat. 128 (12 U.S.C. 1461 et seq.)
Short title, see 12 U.S.C. 1461

Home Owners' Loan Act of 1933
Renamed Home Owners' Loan Act

Home Ownership and Equity Protection Act of 1994
Pub. L. 103–325, title I, subtitle B (§151 et seq.), Sept. 23, 1994, 108 Stat. 2190
Short title, see 15 U.S.C. 1601 note

Home Port Act
Feb. 16, 1925, ch. 235, 43 Stat. 947

Homeless Children's Assistance Act of 1992
Pub. L. 102–512, title I, Oct. 24, 1992, 106 Stat. 3363
Short title, see 42 U.S.C. 1771 note

Homeless Eligibility Clarification Act
Pub. L. 99–570, title XI, Oct. 27, 1986, 100 Stat. 3207–167
Short title, see 7 U.S.C. 2011 note

Homeless Housing Act of 1986
Pub. L. 99–500, §101(g) [H.R. 5313, title V], Oct. 18, 1986, 100 Stat. 1783–242, and Pub. L. 99–591, §101(g) [H.R. 5313, title V], Oct. 30, 1986, 100 Stat. 3341–242 (42 U.S.C. 11361 note); Pub. L. 100–202, §106, Dec. 22, 1987, 101 Stat. 1329–433

Homeless Veterans Comprehensive Service Programs Act of 1992
Pub. L. 102–590, Nov. 10, 1992, 106 Stat. 5136
Short title, see 38 U.S.C. 101 note

Homeowners Protection Act of 1998
Pub. L. 105–216, July 29, 1998, 112 Stat. 897 (12 U.S.C. 4901 et seq.)
Short title, see 12 U.S.C. 4901 note

Homeownership and Opportunity Through HOPE Act
Pub. L. 101–625, title IV, Nov. 28, 1990, 104 Stat. 4148
Short title, see 42 U.S.C. 1437aaa note

Homeownership Opportunity Act of 1979
Pub. L. 96–153, title III, §311, Dec. 21, 1979, 93 Stat. 1115
Short title, see 12 U.S.C. 1701 note

Homestead Act
May 20, 1862, ch. 75, 12 Stat. 392

Homesteaders' Relief Act
May 21, 1934, ch. 320, 48 Stat. 787 (43 U.S.C. 237b)

Honey Research, Promotion, and Consumer Information Act
Pub. L. 98–590, Oct. 30, 1984, 98 Stat. 3115 (7 U.S.C. 4601 et seq.)
Short title, see 7 U.S.C. 4601 note

Honey Research, Promotion, and Consumer Information Act Amendments of 1990
Pub. L. 101–624, title XIX, subtitle F, ch. 1 (§1981 et seq.), Nov. 28, 1990, 104 Stat. 3904
Short title, see 7 U.S.C. 4601 note

Honeybee Act
Aug. 31, 1922, ch. 301, 42 Stat. 833 (7 U.S.C. 281 et seq.)
Short title, see 7 U.S.C. 281 note

Hood Bay Land Exchange Act of 1997
Pub. L. 105–60, Oct. 10, 1997, 111 Stat. 1269

Hoopa Valley Reservation South Boundary Adjustment Act
Pub. L. 105–79, Nov. 13, 1997, 111 Stat. 1527 (25 U.S.C. 1300i–1 note)

Hoopa-Yurok Settlement Act
Pub. L. 100–580, Oct. 31, 1988, 102 Stat. 2924 (25 U.S.C. 1300i et seq.)
Short title, see 25 U.S.C. 1300i(a)

Hoover Dam Miscellaneous Sales Act
Pub. L. 106–461, Nov. 7, 2000, 114 Stat. 1989 (43 U.S.C. 619 note)

Hoover Power Plant Act of 1984
Pub. L. 98–381, Aug. 17, 1984, 98 Stat. 1333 (43 U.S.C. 619 et seq.)
Short title, see 43 U.S.C. 619 note

Hop Marketing Act
See Agricultural Adjustment Act

Horizontal Property Act of the District of Columbia
Pub. L. 88–218, Dec. 21, 1963, 77 Stat. 449

Horn of Africa Recovery and Food Security Act
Pub. L. 102–274, Apr. 21, 1992, 106 Stat. 115 (22 U.S.C. 2151 note)

Horse Protection Act
Pub. L. 91–540, Dec. 9, 1970, 84 Stat. 1404 (15 U.S.C. 1821 et seq.)
Short title, see 15 U.S.C. 1821 note

Horse Protection Act Amendments of 1976
Pub. L. 94–360, July 13, 1976, 90 Stat. 915
Short title, see 15 U.S.C. 1821 note

Horse Protection Act of 1970
Renamed Horse Protection Act

Hospital and Medical Facilities Amendments of 1964
Pub. L. 88–443, Aug. 18, 1964, 78 Stat. 447 (42 U.S.C. 291 et seq.)
Short title, see 42 U.S.C. 201 note

Hospital and Medical Facilities Construction and Modernization Assistance Amendments of 1968
Pub. L. 90–574, title IV, Oct. 15, 1968, 82 Stat. 1011
Short title, see 42 U.S.C. 201 note

Hospital Survey and Construction Act
Aug. 13, 1946, ch. 958, 60 Stat. 1040

Hospital Survey and Construction Amendments of 1949
Oct. 25, 1949, ch. 722, 63 Stat. 898

Hospital Treatment for Drug Addicts Act for the District of Columbia
June 24, 1953, ch. 149, as added July 24, 1956, ch. 676, title I, §101, 70 Stat. 609

Hospitalization Act
Mar. 3, 1919, ch. 98, 40 Stat. 1302

Hostage Relief Act of 1980
Pub. L. 96–449, Oct. 14, 1980, 94 Stat. 1967 (5 U.S.C. 5561 note)

Hot Oil Act
Also known as the Connally Hot Oil Act
Feb. 22, 1935, ch. 18, 49 Stat. 30 (15 U.S.C. 715 et seq.)
Short title, see 15 U.S.C. 715 note

Hot Oil Extension Act
June 29, 1939, ch. 250, 53 Stat. 927

Hotel and Motel Fire Safety Act of 1990
Pub. L. 101–391, Sept. 25, 1990, 104 Stat. 747
Short title, see 15 U.S.C. 2201 note

Houlton Band of Maliseet Indians Supplementary Claims Settlement Act of 1986
Pub. L. 99–566, Oct. 27, 1986, 100 Stat. 3184 (25 U.S.C. 1724 note)

Hours of Service Act (Public Works)
June 25, 1868, ch. 72, 15 Stat. 77

Hours of Service Act (Railroads)
Mar. 4, 1907, ch. 2939, 34 Stat. 1415
Short title, see 45 U.S.C. 61 note

House Employees Position Classification Act
Pub. L. 88–652, Oct. 13, 1964, 78 Stat. 1079 (2 U.S.C. 291 et seq.)
Short title, see 2 U.S.C. 291 note

House of Representatives Administrative Reform Technical Corrections Act
Pub. L. 104–186, Aug. 20, 1996, 110 Stat. 1718
Short title, see 2 U.S.C. 31 note

Household Goods Transportation Act of 1980
Pub. L. 96–454, Oct. 15, 1980, 94 Stat. 2011
Short title, see 49 U.S.C. 10101 note

Housing Act
May 16, 1918, ch. 74, 40 Stat. 550

Housing Act of 1948
Aug. 10, 1948, ch. 832, 62 Stat. 1268
Short title, see 12 U.S.C. 1701 note

Housing Act of 1949
July 15, 1949, ch. 338, 63 Stat. 413
Short title, see 42 U.S.C. 1441 note

Housing Act of 1950
Apr. 20, 1950, ch. 94, 64 Stat. 48
Short title, see 12 U.S.C. 1701 note

Housing Act of 1952
July 14, 1952, ch. 723, 66 Stat. 601
Short title, see 12 U.S.C. 1701 note

Housing Act of 1954
Aug. 2, 1954, ch. 649, 68 Stat. 590
Short title, see 12 U.S.C. 1701 note

Housing Act of 1956
Aug. 7, 1956, ch. 1029, 70 Stat. 1091
Short title, see 12 U.S.C. 1701 note

Housing Act of 1957
Pub. L. 85–104, July 12, 1957, 71 Stat. 294

Housing Act of 1959
Pub. L. 86–372, Sept. 23, 1959, 73 Stat. 654
Short title, see 12 U.S.C. 1701 note

Housing Act of 1961
Pub. L. 87–70, June 30, 1961, 75 Stat. 149
Short title, see 12 U.S.C. 1701 note

Housing Act of 1964
Pub. L. 88–560, Sept. 2, 1964, 78 Stat. 769
Short title, see 12 U.S.C. 1701 note

Housing Affordability Barrier Removal Act of 2000
Pub. L. 106–569, title I, Dec. 27, 2000, 114 Stat. 2946
Short title, see 42 U.S.C. 12701 note

Housing Amendments of 1953
June 30, 1953, ch. 170, 67 Stat. 121
Short title, see 12 U.S.C. 1701 note

Housing Amendments of 1955
Aug. 11, 1955, ch. 783, 69 Stat. 635
Short title, see 12 U.S.C. 1701 note

Housing and Community Development Act of 1974
Pub. L. 93–383, Aug. 22, 1974, 88 Stat. 633 (42 U.S.C. 5301 et seq.)
Short title, see 42 U.S.C. 5301 note

Housing and Community Development Act of 1977
Pub. L. 95–128, Oct. 12, 1977, 91 Stat. 1111
Short title, see 42 U.S.C. 5301 note

Housing and Community Development Act of 1980
Pub. L. 96–399, Oct. 8, 1980, 94 Stat. 1614
Short title, see 42 U.S.C. 5301 note

Housing and Community Development Act of 1987
Pub. L. 100–242, Feb. 5, 1988, 101 Stat. 1815
Short title, see 42 U.S.C. 5301 note

Housing and Community Development Act of 1992
Pub. L. 102–550, Oct. 28, 1992, 106 Stat. 3672
Short title, see 42 U.S.C. 5301 note

Housing and Community Development Amendments of 1978
Pub. L. 95–557, Oct. 31, 1978, 92 Stat. 2080
Short title, see 42 U.S.C. 5301 note

Housing and Community Development Amendments of 1979
Pub. L. 96–153, Dec. 21, 1979, 93 Stat. 1101
Short title, see 42 U.S.C. 5301 note

Housing and Community Development Amendments of 1981
Pub. L. 97–35, title III, subtitle A (§300 et seq.), Aug. 13, 1981, 95 Stat. 384
Short title, see 42 U.S.C. 5301 note

Housing and Community Development Reconciliation Amendments of 1985
Pub. L. 99–272, title III, Apr. 7, 1986, 100 Stat. 101
Short title, see 42 U.S.C. 5301 note

Housing and Community Development Technical Amendments Act of 1984
Pub. L. 98–479, Oct. 17, 1984, 98 Stat. 2218
Short title, see 42 U.S.C. 5301 note

Housing and Rent Act of 1947
June 30, 1947, ch. 163, 61 Stat. 193 (50 App. U.S.C. 1881 et seq.)

Housing and Rent Act of 1948
Mar. 30, 1948, ch. 161, 62 Stat. 93

Housing and Rent Act of 1949
Mar. 30, 1949, ch. 42, 63 Stat. 18

Housing and Rent Act of 1950
June 23, 1950, ch. 354, 64 Stat. 255

Housing and Rent Act of 1953
Apr. 30, 1953, ch. 31, 67 Stat. 23

Housing and Urban Development Act of 1965
Pub. L. 89–117, Aug. 10, 1965, 79 Stat. 451
Short title, see 12 U.S.C. 1701 note

Housing and Urban Development Act of 1968
Pub. L. 90–448, Aug. 1, 1968, 82 Stat. 476
Short title, see 12 U.S.C. 1701 note

Housing and Urban Development Act of 1969
Pub. L. 91–152, Dec. 24, 1969, 83 Stat. 379
Short title, see 12 U.S.C. 1701 note

Housing and Urban Development Act of 1970
Pub. L. 91–609, Dec. 31, 1970, 84 Stat. 1770
Short title, see 12 U.S.C. 1701 note

Housing and Urban-Rural Recovery Act of 1983
Pub. L. 98–181, titles I–V, Nov. 30, 1983, 97 Stat. 1159–1240
Short title, see 12 U.S.C. 1701 note

Housing Authorization Act of 1976
Pub. L. 94–375, Aug. 3, 1976, 90 Stat. 1067
Short title, see 12 U.S.C. 1701 note

Housing Deficiency Act
Mar. 4, 1939, ch. 6, 53 Stat. 511

Housing for Older Persons Act of 1995
Pub. L. 104–76, Dec. 28, 1995, 109 Stat. 787
Short title, see 42 U.S.C. 3601 note

Housing Opportunity Program Extension Act of 1996
Pub. L. 104–120, Mar. 28, 1996, 110 Stat. 834
Short title, see 12 U.S.C. 1701 note

Hovering Vessels
Aug. 5, 1935, ch. 438, titles II, IV, 49 Stat. 521, 529

Howard M. Metzenbaum Multiethnic Placement Act of 1994
Pub. L. 103–382, title V, part E, subpart 1 (§551 et seq.), Oct. 20, 1994, 108 Stat. 4056
Short title, see 42 U.S.C. 1305 note

Howard University Endowment Act
Pub. L. 98–480, title II, Oct. 17, 1984, 98 Stat. 2245 (20 U.S.C. 130aa et seq.)
Short title, see 20 U.S.C. 130aa note

Hubert H. Humphrey Institute of Public Affairs and the Everett McKinley Dirksen Congressional Leadership Research Center Assistance Act
Pub. L. 95–270, Apr. 27, 1978, 92 Stat. 220 (20 U.S.C. 2566–2569)
Short title, see 20 U.S.C. 2566 note

HUBZone Act of 1997
Pub. L. 105–135, title VI, Dec. 2, 1997, 111 Stat. 2627
Short title, see 15 U.S.C. 631 note

HUBZones in Native America Act of 2000
Pub. L. 106–554, §1(a)(9) [title VI, subtitle A (§601 et seq.)], Dec. 21, 2000, 114 Stat. 2763, 2763A–697
Short title, see 15 U.S.C. 631 note

HUD Demonstration Act of 1993
Pub. L. 103–120, Oct. 27, 1993, 107 Stat. 1144
Short title, see 42 U.S.C. 11301 note

Hudson River Valley National Heritage Area Act of 1996
Pub. L. 104–333, div. II, title IX, Nov. 12, 1996, 110 Stat. 4275

Human Rights, Refugee, and Other Foreign Relations Provisions Act of 1996
Pub. L. 104–319, Oct. 19, 1996, 110 Stat. 3864
Short title, see 22 U.S.C. 2151 note

Human Services Amendments of 1994
Pub. L. 103–252, May 18, 1994, 108 Stat. 623
Short title, see 42 U.S.C. 9801 note

Human Services Reauthorization Act
Pub. L. 98–558, Oct. 30, 1984, 98 Stat. 2878
Short title, see 42 U.S.C. 9801 note

Human Services Reauthorization Act of 1986
Pub. L. 99–425, Sept. 30, 1986, 100 Stat. 966

Human Services Reauthorization Act of 1986—Continued
Short title, see 42 U.S.C. 9801 note

Humane Methods of Slaughter Act of 1958
Pub. L. 85–765, Aug. 27, 1958, 72 Stat. 862 (7 U.S.C. 1901 et seq.)

Humane Methods of Slaughter Act of 1978
Pub. L. 95–445, Oct. 10, 1978, 92 Stat. 1069
Short title, see 21 U.S.C. 601 note

Hump Law
Pub. L. 86–155, Aug. 11, 1959, 73 Stat. 333

Humphrey-Durham Act
See Humphrey-Durham Drug Prescriptions Act

Humphrey-Durham Drug Prescriptions Act
Oct. 26, 1951, ch. 578, 65 Stat. 648

Humphrey-Hawkins Act
See Full Employment and Balanced Growth Act of 1978

Humphrey-Thye-Blatnik-Andresen Act
June 22, 1956, ch. 425, 70 Stat. 326
Short title, see 16 U.S.C. 577d–1

Hungarian Declaration of War
June 5, 1942, ch. 324, 56 Stat. 307

Hunger Prevention Act of 1988
Pub. L. 100–435, Sept. 19, 1988, 102 Stat. 1645
Short title, see 7 U.S.C. 2011

Hyde Amendment (Abortion)
Pub. L. 94–439, title II, §209, Sept. 30, 1976, 90 Stat. 1434

Hydrogen Future Act of 1996
Pub. L. 104–271, Oct. 9, 1996, 110 Stat. 3304
Short title, see 42 U.S.C. 12401 note

Hydrographic Services Improvement Act of 1998
Pub. L. 105–384, title III, Nov. 13, 1998, 112 Stat. 3454 (33 U.S.C. 892 et seq.)
Short title, see 33 U.S.C. 851 note

I Am An American Day Act
May 3, 1940, ch. 183, 54 Stat. 178

I.R.C.
Renamed Internal Revenue Code of 1939

ICC Termination Act of 1995
Pub. L. 104–88, Dec. 29, 1995, 109 Stat. 803
Short title, see 49 U.S.C. 101 note

ICCVAM Authorization Act of 2000
Pub. L. 106–545, Dec. 19, 2000, 114 Stat. 2721 (42 U.S.C. 285*l*–2 et seq.)
Short title, see 42 U.S.C. 201 note

Idaho Admission Act
July 3, 1890, ch. 656, 26 Stat. 215

Idaho Land Exchange Act of 1993
Pub. L. 103–17, Apr. 12, 1993, 107 Stat. 50

Identity Theft and Assumption Deterrence Act of 1998
Pub. L. 105–318, Oct. 30, 1998, 112 Stat. 3007
Short title, see 18 U.S.C. 1001 note

Illegal Immigration Reform and Immigrant Responsibility Act of 1996
Pub. L. 104–208, div. C, Sept. 30, 1996, 110 Stat. 3009–546
Short title, see 8 U.S.C. 1101 note

Illinois and Michigan Canal National Heritage Corridor Act of 1984
Pub. L. 98–398, title I, Aug. 24, 1984, 98 Stat. 1456

Illinois Land Conservation Act of 1995
Pub. L. 104–106, div. B, title XXIX, Feb. 10, 1996, 110 Stat. 594 (16 U.S.C. 1609 note)

Illinois Wilderness Act of 1990
Pub. L. 101–633, Nov. 28, 1990, 104 Stat. 4577

Immediate Transportation Act
June 10, 1880, ch. 190, 21 Stat. 173

Immigrant Fund Act
Aug. 3, 1882, ch. 376, 22 Stat. 214

Immigration Act of 1917
Feb. 5, 1917, ch. 29, 39 Stat. 874

Immigration Act of 1921
May 19, 1921, ch. 8, 42 Stat. 5

Immigration Act of 1924
May 26, 1924, ch. 190, 43 Stat. 153

Immigration Act of 1990
Pub. L. 101–649, Nov. 29, 1990, 104 Stat. 4978
Short title, see 8 U.S.C. 1101 note

Immigration Amendments of 1988
Pub. L. 100–658, Nov. 15, 1988, 102 Stat. 3908
Short title, see 8 U.S.C. 1101 note

Immigration and Nationality Act
June 27, 1952, ch. 477, 66 Stat. 163 (8 U.S.C. 1101 et seq.)
Short title, see 8 U.S.C. 1101 note

Immigration and Nationality Act Amendments of 1976
Pub. L. 94–571, Oct. 20, 1976, 90 Stat. 2703
Short title, see 8 U.S.C. 1101 note

Immigration and Nationality Act Amendments of 1981
Pub. L. 97–116, Dec. 29, 1981, 95 Stat. 1611
Short title, see 8 U.S.C. 1101 note

Immigration and Nationality Act Amendments of 1986
Pub. L. 99–653, Nov. 14, 1986, 100 Stat. 3655
Short title, see 8 U.S.C. 1101 note

Immigration and Nationality Technical Corrections Act of 1994
Pub. L. 103–416, Oct. 25, 1994, 108 Stat. 4305
Short title, see 8 U.S.C. 1101 note

Immigration and Naturalization Service Data Management Improvement Act of 2000
Pub. L. 106–215, June 15, 2000, 114 Stat. 337
Short title, see 8 U.S.C. 1101 note

Immigration Marriage Fraud Amendments of 1986
Pub. L. 99–639, Nov. 10, 1986, 100 Stat. 3537
Short title, see 8 U.S.C. 1101 note

Immigration Nursing Relief Act of 1989
Pub. L. 101–238, Dec. 18, 1989, 103 Stat. 2099
Short title, see 8 U.S.C. 1101 note

Immigration Reform and Control Act of 1986
Pub. L. 99–603, Nov. 6, 1986, 100 Stat. 3359
Short title, see 8 U.S.C. 1101 note

Immigration Services and Infrastructure Improvements Act of 2000
Pub. L. 106–313, title II, Oct. 17, 2000, 114 Stat. 1262 (8 U.S.C. 1571 et seq.)
Short title, see 8 U.S.C. 1551 note

Immigration Technical Corrections Act of 1988
Pub. L. 100–525, Oct. 24, 1988, 102 Stat. 2609
Short title, see 8 U.S.C. 1101 note

Immigration Technical Corrections Act of 1991
Pub. L. 102–232, title III, Dec. 12, 1991, 105 Stat. 1742
Short title, see 8 U.S.C. 1101 note

Immunity Act of 1954
Aug. 20, 1954, ch. 769, 68 Stat. 745

Immunity of Witnesses Act
Pub. L. 91–452, title II, §201(a), Oct. 15, 1970, 84 Stat. 926 (18 U.S.C. 6001 et seq.)

Impact Aid Act
See Educational Agencies Financial Aid Act

Impact Aid Reauthorization Act of 1988
Pub. L. 100–297, title II, part A (§2001 et seq.), Apr. 28, 1988, 102 Stat. 293 (20 U.S.C. 236 et seq.)

Impact Aid Reauthorization Act of 2000
Pub. L. 106–398, §1 [[div. A], title XVIII], Oct. 30, 2000, 114 Stat. 1654, 1654A–368
Short title, see 20 U.S.C. 6301 note

Import Milk Act
Feb. 15, 1927, ch. 155, 44 Stat. 1101 (21 U.S.C. 141 et seq.)
Short title, see 21 U.S.C. 141 note

Imported Cigarette Compliance Act of 2000
Pub. L. 106–476, title IV, Nov. 9, 2000, 114 Stat. 2176
Short title, see 26 U.S.C. 1 note

Imported Vehicle Safety Compliance Act of 1988
Pub. L. 100–562, Oct. 31, 1988, 102 Stat. 2818

Impoundment Control Act of 1974
Pub. L. 93–344, title X, Parts A (§1001 et seq.) and B (§1011 et seq.), July 12, 1974, 88 Stat. 332 (2 U.S.C. 681 et seq.)
Short title, see 2 U.S.C. 621 note

Improved Penalty Administration and Compliance Tax Act
Pub. L. 101–239, title VII, subtitle G (§7701 et seq.), Dec. 19, 1989, 103 Stat. 2388
Short title, see 26 U.S.C. 1 note

Improving America's Schools Act of 1994
Pub. L. 103–382, Oct. 20, 1994, 108 Stat. 3518
Short title, see 20 U.S.C. 6301 note

Incarcerated Witness Fees Act of 1991
Pub. L. 102–417, Oct. 14, 1992, 106 Stat. 2138
Short title, see 28 U.S.C. 1 note

Incentive Grants for Local Delinquency Prevention Programs Act
Pub. L. 93–415, title V, as added Pub. L. 102–586, §5(a), Nov. 4, 1992, 106 Stat. 5027 (42 U.S.C. 5781 et seq.)
Short title, see 42 U.S.C. 5601 note

Income Tax Amendment Resolution
July 31, 1909, No. 40, 36 Stat. 184

Income Tax Return Act
Apr. 10, 1936, ch. 189, 49 Stat. 1199

Indemnity Act (American Forces Abroad)
Apr. 18, 1918, ch. 57, 40 Stat. 532

Indemnity Act (President's Orders and Proclamations, Civil War)
Mar. 2, 1867, ch. 155, 14 Stat. 432

Indemnity Act (State War Expenses, Civil War)
July 27, 1861, ch. 21, 12 Stat. 276

Independent Agencies Appropriation Act, 1972
Pub. L. 92–49, title IV, July 9, 1971, 85 Stat. 113

Independent Agencies Appropriation Act, 1973
Pub. L. 92–351, title IV, July 13, 1972, 86 Stat. 478

Independent Agencies Appropriations Act, 1975
Pub. L. 93–381, title IV, Aug. 21, 1974, 88 Stat. 619

Independent Agencies Appropriations Act, 1976
Pub. L. 94–91, title IV, Aug. 9, 1975, 89 Stat. 448

Independent Agencies Appropriations Act, 1977
Pub. L. 94–363, title IV, July 14, 1976, 90 Stat. 968

Independent Agencies Appropriations Act, 1978
Pub. L. 95–81, title IV, July 31, 1977, 91 Stat. 346

Independent Agencies Appropriations Act, 1979
Pub. L. 95–429, title IV, Oct. 10, 1978, 92 Stat. 1006

Independent Agencies Appropriations Act, 1980
Pub. L. 96–74, title IV, Sept. 29, 1979, 93 Stat. 565

Independent Agencies Appropriations Act, 1987
Pub. L. 99–500, §101(m) [title IV], Oct. 18, 1986, 100 Stat. 1783–308, 1783–317, and Pub. L. 99–591, §101(m) [title IV], Oct. 30, 1986, 100 Stat. 3341–308, 3341–317

Independent Agencies Appropriations Act, 1988
Pub. L. 100–202, §101(m) [title IV], Dec. 22, 1987, 101 Stat. 1329–390, 1329–401

Independent Agencies Appropriations Act, 1989
Pub. L. 100–440, title IV, Sept. 22, 1988, 102 Stat. 1731

Independent Agencies Appropriations Act, 1990
Pub. L. 101–136, title IV, Nov. 3, 1989, 103 Stat. 794

Independent Agencies Appropriations Act, 1991
Pub. L. 101–509, title IV, Nov. 5, 1990, 104 Stat. 1403

Independent Agencies Appropriations Act, 1992
Pub. L. 102–141, title IV, Oct. 28, 1991, 105 Stat. 848

Independent Agencies Appropriations Act, 1993
Pub. L. 102–393, title IV, Oct. 6, 1992, 106 Stat. 1742

Independent Agencies Appropriations Act, 1994
Pub. L. 103–123, title IV, Oct. 28, 1993, 107 Stat. 1238

Independent Agencies Appropriations Act, 1995
Pub. L. 103–329, title IV, Sept. 30, 1994, 108 Stat. 2396

Independent Agencies Appropriations Act, 1996
Pub. L. 104–52, title IV, Nov. 19, 1995, 109 Stat. 480

Independent Agencies Appropriations Act, 1997
Pub. L. 104–208, div. A, title I, §101(f) [title IV], Sept. 30, 1996, 110 Stat. 3009–314, 3009–330

Independent Agencies Appropriations Act, 1998
Pub. L. 105–61, title IV, Oct. 10, 1997, 111 Stat. 1295

Independent Agencies Appropriations Act, 1999
Pub. L. 105–277, div. A, §101(h) [title IV], Oct. 21, 1998, 112 Stat. 2681–480, 2681–498

Independent Agencies Appropriations Act, 2000
Pub. L. 106–58, title IV, Sept. 29, 1999, 113 Stat. 449

Independent Agencies Appropriations Act, 2001
Pub. L. 106–554, §1(a)(3) [title IV], Dec. 21, 2000, 114 Stat. 2763, 2763A–140

Independent Counsel Reauthorization Act of 1987
Pub. L. 100–191, Dec. 15, 1987, 101 Stat. 1293
Short title, see 28 U.S.C. 1 note

Independent Counsel Reauthorization Act of 1994
Pub. L. 103–270, June 30, 1994, 108 Stat. 732
Short title, see 28 U.S.C. 1 note

Independent Offices Act, 1928
Feb. 11, 1927, ch. 104, 44 Stat. 1069

Independent Offices Act, 1929
May 16, 1928, ch. 580, 45 Stat. 573

Independent Offices and Department of Housing and Urban Development Appropriation Act, 1968
Pub. L. 90–121, Nov. 3, 1967, 81 Stat. 341

Independent Offices and Department of Housing and Urban Development Appropriation Act, 1969
Pub. L. 90–550, Oct. 4, 1968, 82 Stat. 937

Independent Offices and Department of Housing and Urban Development Appropriation Act, 1970
Pub. L. 91–126, Nov. 26, 1969, 83 Stat. 221

Independent Offices and Department of Housing and Urban Development Appropriation Act, 1971
Pub. L. 91–556, Dec. 17, 1970, 84 Stat. 1442

Independent Offices Act, 1931
Apr. 19, 1930, ch. 201, 46 Stat. 229

Independent Offices Appropriation Act, 1932
Feb. 23, 1931, ch. 281, 46 Stat. 1355

Independent Offices Appropriation Act, 1933
June 30, 1932, ch. 330, 47 Stat. 452

Independent Offices Appropriation Act, 1934
June 16, 1933, ch. 101, 48 Stat. 283

Independent Offices Appropriation Act, 1935
Mar. 28, 1934, ch. 102, 48 Stat. 509

Independent Offices Appropriation Act, 1936
Feb. 2, 1935, ch. 3, 49 Stat. 6

Independent Offices Appropriation Act, 1937
Mar. 19, 1936, ch. 156, 49 Stat. 1167

Independent Offices Appropriation Act, 1938
June 28, 1937, ch. 396, 50 Stat. 329

Independent Offices Appropriation Act, 1939
May 23, 1938, ch. 259, 52 Stat. 410

Independent Offices Appropriation Act, 1940
Mar. 16, 1939, ch. 11, 53 Stat. 524

Independent Offices Appropriation Act, 1941
Apr. 18, 1940, ch. 107, 54 Stat. 111

Independent Offices Appropriation Act, 1942
Apr. 5, 1941, ch. 40, 55 Stat. 92

Independent Offices Appropriation Act, 1943
June 27, 1942, ch. 450, 56 Stat. 392

Independent Offices Appropriation Act, 1944
June 26, 1943, ch. 145, 57 Stat. 169

Independent Offices Appropriation Act, 1945
June 27, 1944, ch. 286, 58 Stat. 361

Independent Offices Appropriation Act, 1946
May 3, 1945, ch. 106, 59 Stat. 106

Independent Offices Appropriation Act, 1947
Mar. 28, 1946, ch. 113, 60 Stat. 60

Independent Offices Appropriation Act, 1948
July 30, 1947, ch. 359, 61 Stat. 585

Independent Offices Appropriation Act, 1949
Apr. 20, 1948, ch. 219, 62 Stat. 176

Independent Offices Appropriation Act, 1950
Aug. 24, 1949, ch. 506, 63 Stat. 631

Independent Offices Appropriation Act, 1951
Sept. 6, 1950, ch. 896, ch. VIII, 64 Stat. 697

Independent Offices Appropriation Act, 1952
Aug. 31, 1951, ch. 376, 65 Stat. 268

Independent Offices Appropriation Act, 1953
July 5, 1952, ch. 578, 66 Stat. 393

Independent Offices Appropriation Act, 1955
June 24, 1954, ch. 359, 68 Stat. 272

Independent Offices Appropriation Act, 1956
June 30, 1955, ch. 244, 69 Stat. 199

Independent Offices Appropriation Act, 1957
June 27, 1956, ch. 452, 70 Stat. 339

Independent Offices Appropriation Act, 1958
Pub. L. 85–69, June 29, 1957, 71 Stat. 227

Independent Offices Appropriation Act, 1959
Pub. L. 85–844, Aug. 28, 1958, 72 Stat. 1063

Independent Offices Appropriation Act, 1960
Pub. L. 86–255, Sept. 14, 1959, 73 Stat. 500

Independent Offices Appropriation Act, 1961
Pub. L. 86–626, July 12, 1960, 74 Stat. 425

Independent Offices Appropriation Act, 1962
Pub. L. 87–141, Aug. 17, 1961, 75 Stat. 342

Independent Offices Appropriation Act, 1963
Pub. L. 87–741, Oct. 3, 1962, 76 Stat. 716

Independent Offices Appropriation Act, 1964
Pub. L. 88–215, Dec. 19, 1963, 77 Stat. 425

Independent Offices Appropriation Act, 1965
Pub. L. 88–507, Aug. 30, 1964, 78 Stat. 640

Independent Offices Appropriation Act, 1966
Pub. L. 89–128, Aug. 16, 1965, 79 Stat. 520

Independent Offices Appropriation Act, 1967
Pub. L. 89–555, Sept. 6, 1966, 80 Stat. 663

Independent Safety Board Act Amendment of 1978
Pub. L. 95–363, Sept. 11, 1978, 92 Stat. 597

Independent Safety Board Act Amendments of 1981
Pub. L. 97–74, Nov. 3, 1981, 95 Stat. 1065

Independent Safety Board Act Amendments of 1988
Pub. L. 100–372, July 19, 1988, 102 Stat. 876

Independent Safety Board Act Amendments of 1990
Pub. L. 101–641, Nov. 28, 1990, 104 Stat. 4654

Independent Safety Board Act Amendments of 1994
Pub. L. 103–411, Oct. 25, 1994, 108 Stat. 4236
Short title, see 49 U.S.C. 101 note

Independent Safety Board Act of 1974
Pub. L. 93–633, title III, Jan. 3, 1975, 88 Stat. 2166

Independent Treasury Act of 1840
July 4, 1840, ch. 41, 5 Stat. 385

Independent Treasury Act of 1846
Aug. 6, 1846, ch. 90, 9 Stat. 59

India Emergency Food Aid Act of 1951
June 15, 1951, ch. 138, 65 Stat. 69 (50 App. U.S.C. 2311 et seq.)

India-Pakistan Relief Act of 1998
Pub. L. 105–277, div. A, §101(a) [title IX], Oct. 21, 1998, 112 Stat. 2681, 2681–40 (22 U.S.C. 2799aa–1 note)

Indian Affairs Administration Act
Aug. 8, 1946, ch. 907, 60 Stat. 939 (25 U.S.C. 1a)

Indian Alcohol and Substance Abuse Prevention and Treatment Act of 1986
Pub. L. 99–570, title IV, subtitle C (§4201 et seq.), Oct. 27, 1986, 100 Stat. 3207–137 (25 U.S.C. 2401 et seq.)
Short title, see 25 U.S.C. 2401 note

Indian Arts and Crafts Act
Aug. 27, 1935, ch. 748, 49 Stat. 891 (25 U.S.C. 305 et seq.)

Indian Arts and Crafts Act of 1990
Pub. L. 101–644, title I, Nov. 29, 1990, 104 Stat. 4662 (25 U.S.C. 305d, 305e)
Short title, see 25 U.S.C. 305 note

Indian Arts and Crafts Enforcement Act of 2000
Pub. L. 106–497, Nov. 9, 2000, 114 Stat. 2219
Short title, see 25 U.S.C. 305 note

Indian Child Protection and Family Violence Prevention Act
Pub. L. 101–630, title IV, Nov. 28, 1990, 104 Stat. 4544 (25 U.S.C. 3201 et seq.)
Short title, see 25 U.S.C. 3201 note

Indian Child Welfare Act of 1978
Pub. L. 95–608, Nov. 8, 1978, 92 Stat. 3069 (25 U.S.C. 1901 et seq.)
Short title, see 25 U.S.C. 1901 note

Indian Civil Rights Act of 1968
Pub. L. 90–284, title II, Apr. 11, 1968, 82 Stat. 77 (25 U.S.C. 1301 et seq.)
Short title, see 25 U.S.C. 1301 note

Indian Claims Commission Act
Aug. 13, 1946, ch. 959, 60 Stat. 1049 (25 U.S.C. 70 et seq.)

Indian Claims Limitation Act of 1982
Pub. L. 97–394, title I, §§2–6, Dec. 30, 1982, 96 Stat. 1976–1978
Short title, see 28 U.S.C. 2415 note

Indian Crimes Act of 1976
Pub. L. 94–297, May 29, 1976, 90 Stat. 585
Short title, see 18 U.S.C. 1151 note

Indian Dams Safety Act of 1994
Pub. L. 103–302, Aug. 23, 1994, 108 Stat. 1560 (25 U.S.C. 3801 et seq.)
Short title, see 25 U.S.C. 3801 note

Indian Depredation Act
Mar. 3, 1891, ch. 538, 26 Stat. 851

Indian Education Act
Pub. L. 92–318, title IV, June 23, 1972, 86 Stat. 334

Indian Education Act of 1988
Pub. L. 100–297, title V, part C (§5301 et seq.), Apr. 28, 1988, 102 Stat. 395 (25 U.S.C. 2601 et seq.)
Short title, see 25 U.S.C. 2601 note

Indian Education Amendments of 1984
Pub. L. 98–511, title V, Oct. 19, 1984, 98 Stat. 2391
Short title, see 25 U.S.C. 2001 note

Indian Education Amendments of 1988
Pub. L. 100–297, title V, part A (§5101 et seq.), Apr. 28, 1988, 102 Stat. 363
Short title, see 25 U.S.C. 2001 note

Indian Education Assistance Act
Pub. L. 93–638, title II, Jan. 4, 1975, 88 Stat. 2213 (25 U.S.C. 455 et seq.)
Short title, see 25 U.S.C. 450 note

Indian Education Technical Amendments Act of 1985
Pub. L. 99–89, Aug. 15, 1985, 99 Stat. 379
Short title, see 25 U.S.C. 2001 note

Indian Elementary and Secondary School Assistance Act
Sept. 30, 1950, ch. 1124, title III, as added Pub. L. 92–318, title IV, §411(a), June 23, 1972, 86 Stat. 334

Indian Employment, Training and Related Services Demonstration Act of 1992
Pub. L. 102–477, Oct. 23, 1992, 106 Stat. 2302 (25 U.S.C. 3401 et seq.)
Short title, see 25 U.S.C. 3401 note

Indian Employment, Training, and Related Services Demonstration Act Amendments of 2000
Pub. L. 106–568, title XI, Dec. 27, 2000, 114 Stat. 2930
Short title, see 25 U.S.C. 3401 note

Indian Environmental General Assistance Program Act of 1992
Pub. L. 95–134, title V, §502, as added Pub. L. 102–497, §11, Oct. 24, 1992, 106 Stat. 3258 (42 U.S.C. 4368b)
Short title, see 42 U.S.C. 4368b(a)

Indian Environmental Regulatory Enhancement Act of 1990
Pub. L. 101–408, Oct. 4, 1990, 104 Stat. 883
Short title, see 42 U.S.C. 2991 note

Indian Financing Act Amendments of 1984
Pub. L. 98–449, Oct. 4, 1984, 98 Stat. 1725
Short title, see 25 U.S.C. 1451 note

Indian Financing Act of 1974
Pub. L. 93–262, Apr. 12, 1974, 88 Stat. 77 (25 U.S.C. 1451 et seq.)
Short title, see 25 U.S.C. 1451 note

Indian Gaming Regulatory Act
Pub. L. 100–497, Oct. 17, 1988, 102 Stat. 2467 (18 U.S.C. 1866–1868; 25 U.S.C. 2701 et seq.)
Short title, see 25 U.S.C. 2701 note

Indian General Allotment Act
Feb. 8, 1887, ch. 119, 24 Stat. 388
Short title, see 25 U.S.C. 331 note

Indian Health Amendments of 1992
Pub. L. 102–573, Oct. 29, 1992, 106 Stat. 4526
Short title, see 25 U.S.C. 1601 note

Indian Health Care Amendments of 1980
Pub. L. 96–537, Dec. 17, 1980, 94 Stat. 3173
Short title, see 25 U.S.C. 1601 note

Indian Health Care Amendments of 1988
Pub. L. 100–713, Nov. 23, 1988, 102 Stat. 4784
Short title, see 25 U.S.C. 1601 note

Indian Health Care Amendments of 1990
Pub. L. 101–630, title V, Nov. 28, 1990, 104 Stat. 4556
Short title, see 25 U.S.C. 1601 note

Indian Health Care Improvement Act
Pub. L. 94–437, Sept. 30, 1976, 90 Stat. 1400 (25 U.S.C. 1601 et seq.)
Short title, see 25 U.S.C. 1601 note

Indian Health Care Improvement Technical Corrections Act of 1996
Pub. L. 104–313, Oct. 19, 1996, 110 Stat. 3820
Short title, see 25 U.S.C. 1601 note

Indian Housing Act of 1988
Pub. L. 100–358, June 29, 1988, 102 Stat. 676 (42 U.S.C. 1437aa et seq.)
Short title, see 42 U.S.C. 1437 note

Indian Land Consolidation Act
Pub. L. 97–459, title II, Jan. 12, 1983, 96 Stat. 2517 (25 U.S.C. 2201 et seq.)
Short title, see 25 U.S.C. 2201 note

Indian Land Consolidation Act Amendments of 2000
Pub. L. 106–462, Nov. 7, 2000, 114 Stat. 1991
Short title, see 25 U.S.C. 2201 note

Indian Lands Open Dump Cleanup Act of 1994
Pub. L. 103–399, Oct. 22, 1994, 108 Stat. 4164 (25 U.S.C. 3901 et seq.)
Short title, see 25 U.S.C. 3901 note

Indian Law Enforcement Reform Act
Pub. L. 101–379, Aug. 18, 1990, 104 Stat. 473 (25 U.S.C. 2801 et seq.)
Short title, see 25 U.S.C. 2801 note

Indian Law Technical Amendments of 1987
Pub. L. 100–153, Nov. 5, 1987, 101 Stat. 886
Short title, see 25 U.S.C. 331 note

Indian Long-Term Leasing Act
Aug. 9, 1955, ch. 615, 69 Stat. 539 (25 U.S.C. 415 et seq.)

Indian Major Crimes Act
Mar. 3, 1885, ch. 341, 23 Stat. 385 (see 18 U.S.C. 1153)

Indian Mineral Development Act of 1982
Pub. L. 97–382, Dec. 22, 1982, 96 Stat. 1938 (25 U.S.C. 2101 et seq.)
Short title, see 25 U.S.C. 2101 note

Indian Omnibus Law
May 29, 1908, ch. 216, 35 Stat. 444 (25 U.S.C. 404)

Indian Peaks Wilderness Area, the Arapaho National Recreation Area and the Oregon Islands Wilderness Area Act
Pub. L. 95–450, Oct. 11, 1978, 92 Stat. 1095 (16 U.S.C. 460jj et seq.)
Short title, see 16 U.S.C. 460jj note

Indian Reorganization Act
June 18, 1934, ch. 576, 48 Stat. 984 (25 U.S.C. 461 et seq.)
Short title, see 25 U.S.C. 461 note

Indian Self-Determination Act
Pub. L. 93–638, title I, Jan. 4, 1975, 88 Stat. 2206 (25 U.S.C. 450f et seq.)
Short title, see 25 U.S.C. 450 note

Indian Self-Determination Act Amendments of 1994
Pub. L. 103–413, Oct. 25, 1994, 108 Stat. 4250
Short title, see 25 U.S.C. 450 note

Indian Self-Determination and Education Assistance Act
Pub. L. 93–638, Jan. 4, 1975, 88 Stat. 2203 (25 U.S.C. 450 et seq.)
Short title, see 25 U.S.C. 450 note

Indian Self-Determination and Education Assistance Act Amendments of 1988
Pub. L. 100–472, Oct. 5, 1988, 102 Stat. 2285
Short title, see 25 U.S.C. 450 note

Indian Self-Determination and Education Assistance Act Amendments of 1990
Pub. L. 101–644, title II, Nov. 29, 1990, 104 Stat. 4665
Short title, see 25 U.S.C. 450 note

Indian Self-Determination Contract Reform Act of 1994
Pub. L. 103–413, title I, Oct. 25, 1994, 108 Stat. 4250
Short title, see 25 U.S.C. 450 note

Indian Tribal Economic Development and Contract Encouragement Act of 2000
Pub. L. 106–179, Mar. 14, 2000, 114 Stat. 46
Short title, see 25 U.S.C. 71 note

Indian Tribal Governmental Tax Status Act of 1982
Pub. L. 97–473, title II, Jan. 14, 1983, 96 Stat. 2607
Short title, see 26 U.S.C. 1 note

Indian Tribal Judgment Funds Use or Distribution Act
Pub. L. 93–134, Oct. 19, 1973, 87 Stat. 466 (25 U.S.C. 1401 et seq.)
Short title, see 25 U.S.C. 1401(c)

Indian Tribal Justice Act
Pub. L. 103–176, Dec. 3, 1993, 107 Stat. 2004 (25 U.S.C. 3601 et seq.)
Short title, see 25 U.S.C. 3601 note

Indian Tribal Justice Technical and Legal Assistance Act of 2000
Pub. L. 106–559, Dec. 21, 2000, 114 Stat. 2778 (25 U.S.C. 3651 et seq.)
Short title, see 25 U.S.C. 3651 note

Indian Tribal Regulatory Reform and Business Development Act of 2000
Pub. L. 106–447, Nov. 6, 2000, 114 Stat. 1934 (25 U.S.C. 4301 note)

Indian Tribal Tort Claims and Risk Management Act of 1998
Pub. L. 105–277, div. A, §101(e) [title VII], Oct. 21, 1998, 112 Stat. 2681–231, 2681–335 (25 U.S.C. 450f note)

Indian Vocational Training Act
See Adult Indian Vocational Training Act

Indiana Dunes National Lakeshore Access and Enhancement Act
Pub. L. 102–430, Oct. 23, 1992, 106 Stat. 2208
Short title, see 16 U.S.C. 460u note

Indiana Dunes National Lakeshore Act
Pub. L. 89–761, Nov. 5, 1966, 80 Stat. 1309 (16 U.S.C. 460u et seq.)

Individual Income Tax Act of 1944
May 29, 1944, ch. 210, 58 Stat. 231

Individuals with Disabilities Education Act
Pub. L. 91–230, title VI, as added Pub. L. 105–17, title I, §101, June 4, 1997, 111 Stat. 37 (20 U.S.C. 1400 et seq.)
Short title, see 20 U.S.C. 1400(a)

Individuals with Disabilities Education Act Amendments of 1991
Pub. L. 102–119, Oct. 7, 1991, 105 Stat. 587
Short title, see 20 U.S.C. 1400 note

Individuals with Disabilities Education Act Amendments of 1997
Pub. L. 105–17, June 4, 1997, 111 Stat. 37
Short title, see 20 U.S.C. 1400 note

Indochina Migration and Refugee Assistance Act of 1975
Pub. L. 94–23, May 23, 1975, 89 Stat. 87 (22 U.S.C. 2601 note)

Indochina Refugee Children Assistance Act of 1976
Pub. L. 94–405, Sept. 10, 1976, 90 Stat. 1225

Indochinese Refugee Resettlement and Protection Act of 1987
Pub. L. 100–202, §101(a) [title VIII], Dec. 22, 1987, 101 Stat. 1329, 1329–40

Industrial Control and Public Works Act
June 16, 1933, ch. 90, title II, 48 Stat. 200 (40 U.S.C. 401 et seq.)

Industrial Loans Act
See Reconstruction Finance Corporation Act

Industrial Productivity and Labor Costs Act
June 7, 1940, ch. 267, 54 Stat. 249 (29 U.S.C. 2b)

Industrial Relations Commission Act
Aug. 23, 1912, ch. 351, 37 Stat. 415

Infant Formula Act of 1980
Pub. L. 96–359, Sept. 26, 1980, 94 Stat. 1190
Short title, see 21 U.S.C. 301 note

Inflation Act
See Thomas Amendment

Information Technology Management Reform Act of 1996
Renamed Clinger-Cohen Act of 1996

Informer's Act
See False Claims Act

Injury Compensation Act
See Federal Employees' Compensation Act (1916)

Injury Control Act of 1990
Pub. L. 101–558, Nov. 15, 1990, 104 Stat. 2772
Short title, see 42 U.S.C. 201 note

Injury Prevention Act of 1986
Pub. L. 99–649, Nov. 10, 1986, 100 Stat. 3633 (42 U.S.C. 280b et seq.)
Short title, see 42 U.S.C. 280b note

Inland Navigational Rules Act of 1980
Pub. L. 96–591, Dec. 24, 1980, 94 Stat. 3415 (33 U.S.C. 2001 et seq.)
Short title, see 33 U.S.C. 2001 note

Inland Waterways Revenue Act of 1978
Pub. L. 95–502, title II, Oct. 21, 1978, 92 Stat. 1696
Short title, see 26 U.S.C. 1 note

Insanity Defense Reform Act of 1984
Pub. L. 98–473, title II, ch. IV (§401 et seq.), Oct. 12, 1984, 98 Stat. 2057 (18 U.S.C. 4241 et seq.)
Short title, see 18 U.S.C. 4241 note

Insect Control Act
Apr. 6, 1937, ch. 69, as added May 9, 1938, ch. 192, 52 Stat. 344 (7 U.S.C. 148 et seq.)

Insect Pest Act
March 3, 1905, ch. 1501, 33 Stat. 1269 (7 U.S.C. 141 et seq.)

Insecticide Act of 1910
Apr. 26, 1910, ch. 191, 36 Stat. 331 (7 U.S.C. 121 et seq.)

Insider Trading and Securities Fraud Enforcement Act of 1988
Pub. L. 100–704, Nov. 19, 1988, 102 Stat. 4677
Short title, see 15 U.S.C. 78a note

Insider Trading Sanctions Act of 1984
Pub. L. 98–376, Aug. 10, 1984, 98 Stat. 1264
Short title, see 15 U.S.C. 78a note

Inspector General Act Amendments of 1988
Pub. L. 100–504, title I, Oct. 18, 1988, 102 Stat. 2515
Short title, see 5 App. U.S.C. 1 note

Inspector General Act of 1978
Pub. L. 95–452, Oct. 12, 1978, 92 Stat. 1101 (5 App. U.S.C.)
Short title, see 5 App. U.S.C. 1

Installment Sales Revision Act of 1980
Pub. L. 96–471, Oct. 19, 1980, 94 Stat. 2247
Short title, see 26 U.S.C. 1 note

Installment Tax Correction Act of 2000
Pub. L. 106–573, Dec. 28, 2000, 114 Stat. 3061
Short title, see 26 U.S.C. 1 note

Institute of Inter-American Affairs Act
Aug. 5, 1947, ch. 498, 61 Stat. 780 (22 U.S.C. 281 et seq.)

Insular Areas Drug Abuse Amendments of 1988
Pub. L. 100–690, title IX, subtitle D (§9301 et seq.), Nov. 18, 1988, 102 Stat. 4535
Short title, see 48 U.S.C. 1494 note

Insular Liquor Repeal Act
Mar. 2, 1934, ch. 37, 48 Stat. 361

Insurance Act of 1946
Aug. 1, 1946, ch. 728, 60 Stat. 781

Insurance Act of 1951
Apr. 25, 1951, ch. 39, part II (§10 et seq.), 65 Stat. 36

Insurance Company Loan Act
June 10, 1933, ch. 55, 48 Stat. 119

Insurance Moratorium Act
See McCarran-Ferguson Act

Insurance Regulation Act
See McCarran-Ferguson Act

Insurrection Ended Proclamation
Apr. 2, 1866, No. 1, 14 Stat. 811

Intellectual Property and Communications Omnibus Reform Act of 1999
Pub. L. 106–113, div. B, §1000(a)(9) [S. 1948], Nov. 29, 1999, 113 Stat. 1536, 1501A–521
Short title, see 35 U.S.C. 1 note

Intelligence and Intelligence-Related Activities Authorization Act for Fiscal Year 1979
Pub. L. 95–370, Sept. 17, 1978, 92 Stat. 626

Intelligence and Intelligence-Related Activities Authorization Act for Fiscal Year 1980
Pub. L. 96–100, Nov. 2, 1979, 93 Stat. 733

Intelligence Authorization Act for Fiscal Year 1981
Pub. L. 96–450, Oct. 14, 1980, 94 Stat. 1975

Intelligence Authorization Act for Fiscal Year 1982
Pub. L. 97–89, Dec. 4, 1981, 95 Stat. 1150

Intelligence Authorization Act for Fiscal Year 1983
Pub. L. 97–269, titles I–V, VII, Sept. 27, 1982, 96 Stat. 1142–1144, 1155

Intelligence Authorization Act for Fiscal Year 1984
Pub. L. 98–215, Dec. 9, 1983, 97 Stat. 1473

Intelligence Authorization Act for fiscal year 1985
Pub. L. 98–618, Nov. 8, 1984, 98 Stat. 3298

Intelligence Authorization Act for Fiscal Year 1986
Pub. L. 99–169, Dec. 4, 1985, 99 Stat. 1002

Intelligence Authorization Act for Fiscal Year 1987
Pub. L. 99–569, Oct. 27, 1986, 100 Stat. 3190

Intelligence Authorization Act for Fiscal Year 1993
Pub. L. 102–496, Oct. 24, 1992, 106 Stat. 3180

Intelligence Authorization Act for Fiscal Year 1994
Pub. L. 103–178, Dec. 3, 1993, 107 Stat. 2024

Intelligence Authorization Act for Fiscal Year 1995
Pub. L. 103–359, Oct. 14, 1994, 108 Stat. 3423

Intelligence Authorization Act for Fiscal Year 1996
Pub. L. 104–93, Jan. 6, 1996, 109 Stat. 961

Intelligence Authorization Act for Fiscal Year 1997
Pub. L. 104–293, Oct. 11, 1996, 110 Stat. 3461

Intelligence Authorization Act for Fiscal Year 1998
Pub. L. 105–107, Nov. 20, 1997, 111 Stat. 2248

Intelligence Authorization Act for Fiscal Year 1999
Pub. L. 105–272, Oct. 20, 1998, 112 Stat. 2396

Intelligence Authorization Act for Fiscal Year 2000
Pub. L. 106–120, Dec. 3, 1999, 113 Stat. 1606

Intelligence Authorization Act for Fiscal Year 2001
Pub. L. 106–567, Dec. 27, 2000, 114 Stat. 2831

Intelligence Authorization Act, Fiscal Year 1988
Pub. L. 100–178, Dec. 2, 1987, 101 Stat. 1009

Intelligence Authorization Act, Fiscal Year 1989
Pub. L. 100–453, Sept. 29, 1988, 102 Stat. 1904

Intelligence Authorization Act, Fiscal Year 1990
Pub. L. 101–193, Nov. 30, 1989, 103 Stat. 1701

Intelligence Authorization Act, Fiscal Year 1991
Pub. L. 102–88, Aug. 14, 1991, 105 Stat. 429

Intelligence Authorization Act, Fiscal Year 1992
Pub. L. 102–183, Dec. 4, 1991, 105 Stat. 1260

Intelligence Community Whistleblower Protection Act of 1998
Pub. L. 105–272, title VII, Oct. 20, 1998, 112 Stat. 2413
Short title, see 5 App. U.S.C. 1 note

Intelligence Identities Protection Act of 1982
Pub. L. 97–200, June 23, 1982, 96 Stat. 122 (50 U.S.C. 421 et seq.)
Short title, see 50 U.S.C. 401 note

Intelligence Organization Act of 1992
Pub. L. 102–496, title VII, Oct. 24, 1992, 106 Stat. 3188
Short title, see 50 U.S.C. 401 note

Intelligence Renewal and Reform Act of 1996
Pub. L. 104–293, title VIII, Oct. 11, 1996, 110 Stat. 3474
Short title, see 50 U.S.C. 401 note

Intelligent Transportation Systems Act of 1998
Pub. L. 105–178, title V, subtitle C (§5201 et seq.), June 9, 1998, 112 Stat. 452 (23 U.S.C. 502 note)

Intelligent Vehicle-Highway Systems Act of 1991
Pub. L. 102–240, title VI, part B (§6051 et seq.), Dec. 18, 1991, 105 Stat. 2189 (23 U.S.C. 307 note)

Inter-American Coffee Agreement Act
Apr. 11, 1941, ch. 59, 55 Stat. 133 (19 U.S.C. 1355, 1356)

Inter-American Development Bank Act
Pub. L. 86–147, Aug. 7, 1959, 73 Stat. 299 (22 U.S.C. 283 et seq.)
Short title, see 22 U.S.C. 283 note

Inter-American Foundation Act
Pub. L. 91–175, part IV, Dec. 30, 1969, 83 Stat. 821 (22 U.S.C. 290f)
Short title, see 22 U.S.C. 290f note

Inter-American Investment Corporation Act
Pub. L. 98–473, title I, §101(1) [S. 2416, title II], Oct. 12, 1984, 98 Stat. 1884, 1885 (22 U.S.C. 283aa et seq.)
Short title, see 22 U.S.C. 283aa note

Inter-American Statistical Institute Act
Jan. 27, 1942, ch. 22, 56 Stat. 20 (22 U.S.C. 269d)

Intercoastal Shipping Act, 1933
Mar. 3, 1933, ch. 199, 47 Stat. 1425

Intercountry Adoption Act of 2000
Pub. L. 106–279, Oct. 6, 2000, 114 Stat. 825 (42 U.S.C. 14901 et seq.)
Short title, see 42 U.S.C. 14901 note

Intercourse Act (Indian Tribes)
June 30, 1834, ch. 161, 4 Stat. 729

Intercourse Act (Insurrectionary States)
July 2, 1864, ch. 225, 13 Stat. 375

Interest and Dividend Tax Compliance Act of 1983
Pub. L. 98–67, title I, Aug. 5, 1983, 97 Stat. 369
Short title, see 26 U.S.C. 1 note

Interest Equalization Tax Act
Pub. L. 88–563, Sept. 2, 1964, 78 Stat. 809
Short title, see 26 U.S.C. 263 note

Interest Equalization Tax Extension Act of 1965
Pub. L. 89–243, Oct. 9, 1965, 79 Stat. 954
Short title, see 26 U.S.C. 263 note

Interest Equalization Tax Extension Act of 1967
Pub. L. 90–59, July 31, 1967, 81 Stat. 145
Short title, see 26 U.S.C. 6011 note

Interest Equalization Tax Extension Act of 1969
Pub. L. 91–128, Nov. 26, 1969, 83 Stat. 261
Short title, see 26 U.S.C. 4182 note

Interest Equalization Tax Extension Act of 1971
Pub. L. 92–9, Apr. 1, 1971, 85 Stat. 13
Short title, see 26 U.S.C. 861 note

Interest Equalization Tax Extension Act of 1973
Pub. L. 93–17, Apr. 10, 1973, 87 Stat. 12
Short title, see 26 U.S.C. 2104

Intergovernmental Anti-recession Assistance Act of 1977
Pub. L. 95–30, title VI, May 23, 1977, 91 Stat. 164

Intergovernmental Cooperation Act of 1968
Pub. L. 90–577, Oct. 16, 1968, 82 Stat. 1098
Short title, see 42 U.S.C. 4201 note

Intergovernmental Personnel Act of 1970
Pub. L. 91–648, Jan. 5, 1971, 84 Stat. 1909 (42 U.S.C. 4701 et seq.)
Short title, see 42 U.S.C. 4701 note

Interim Federal Aviation Administration Authorization Act
Pub. L. 106–6, Mar. 31, 1999, 113 Stat. 10
Short title, see 49 U.S.C. 40101 note

Interior Department Appropriation Act, 1938
Aug. 9, 1937, ch. 570, 50 Stat. 564

Interior Department Appropriation Act, 1939
May 9, 1938, ch. 187, 52 Stat. 291

Interior Department Appropriation Act, 1940
May 10, 1939, ch. 119, 53 Stat. 685

Interior Department Appropriation Act, 1941
June 18, 1940, ch. 395, 54 Stat. 406

Interior Department Appropriation Act, 1942
June 28, 1941, ch. 259, 55 Stat. 303

Interior Department Appropriation Act, 1943
July 2, 1942, ch. 473, 56 Stat. 506

Interior Department Appropriation Act, 1944
July 12, 1943, ch. 219, 57 Stat. 451

Interior Department Appropriation Act, 1945
June 28, 1944, ch. 298, 58 Stat. 463

Interior Department Appropriation Act, 1946
July 3, 1945, ch. 262, 59 Stat. 318

Interior Department Appropriation Act, 1947
July 1, 1946, ch. 529, 60 Stat. 348

Interior Department Appropriation Act, 1948
July 25, 1947, ch. 337, 61 Stat. 460

Interior Department Appropriation Act, 1949
June 29, 1948, ch. 754, 62 Stat. 1112

Interior Department Appropriation Act, 1950
Oct. 12, 1949, ch. 680, 63 Stat. 765

Interior Department Appropriation Act, 1951
Sept. 6, 1950, ch. 896, ch. VII, 64 Stat. 679

Interior Department Appropriation Act, 1952
Aug. 31, 1951, ch. 375, 65 Stat. 248

Interior Department Appropriation Act, 1953
July 9, 1952, ch. 597, 66 Stat. 445

Interior Department Appropriation Act, 1954
July 31, 1953, ch. 298, 67 Stat. 261

Interior Department Appropriation Act, 1955
July 1, 1954, ch. 446, 68 Stat. 361

Interjurisdictional Fisheries Act of 1986
Pub. L. 99–659, title III, Nov. 14, 1986, 100 Stat. 3731 (16 U.S.C. 4101 et seq.)
Short title, see 16 U.S.C. 4101 note

Intermodal Safe Container Transportation Act of 1992
Pub. L. 102–548, Oct. 28, 1992, 106 Stat. 3646
Short title, see 49 U.S.C. 501 note

Intermodal Safe Container Transportation Amendments Act of 1996
Pub. L. 104–291, title II, Oct. 11, 1996, 110 Stat. 3453
Short title, see 49 U.S.C. 5101 note

Intermodal Surface Transportation Efficiency Act of 1991
Pub. L. 102–240, Dec. 18, 1991, 105 Stat. 1914
Short title, see 49 U.S.C. 101 note

Internal Revenue Code
Renamed Internal Revenue Code of 1939

Internal Revenue Code of 1939
Feb. 10, 1939, ch. 2, 53 Stat. 1
Short title, see 26 U.S.C. note prec. 1

Internal Revenue Code of 1954
Renamed Internal Revenue Code of 1986

Internal Revenue Code of 1986
Aug. 16, 1954, ch. 736, §1(d) [Internal Revenue Title], 68A Stat. 3 (Title 26, §1 et seq.)
Short title, see 26 U.S.C. note prec. 1

Internal Revenue Service Restructuring and Reform Act of 1998
Pub. L. 105–206, July 22, 1998, 112 Stat. 685
Short title, see 26 U.S.C. 1 note

Internal Security Act of 1950
Sept. 23, 1950, ch. 1024, 64 Stat. 987
Short title, see 50 U.S.C. 781 note

International Academic Opportunity Act of 2000
Pub. L. 106–309, title III, Oct. 17, 2000, 114 Stat. 1094 (22 U.S.C. 2462 note)

International Air Transportation Competition Act of 1979
Pub. L. 96–192, Feb. 15, 1980, 94 Stat. 35

International Air Transportation Fair Competitive Practices Act of 1974
Pub. L. 93–623, Jan. 3, 1975, 88 Stat. 2102

International Anti-Bribery and Fair Competition Act of 1998
Pub. L. 105–366, Nov. 10, 1998, 112 Stat. 3302
Short title, see 15 U.S.C. 78a note

International Anti-Corruption and Good Governance Act of 2000
Pub. L. 106–309, title II, Oct. 17, 2000, 114 Stat. 1090
Short title, see 22 U.S.C. 2151 note

International Antitrust Enforcement Assistance Act of 1994
Pub. L. 103–438, Nov. 2, 1994, 108 Stat. 4597 (15 U.S.C. 6201 et seq.)
Short title, see 15 U.S.C. 6201 note

International Arms Sales Code of Conduct Act of 1999
Pub. L. 106–113, div. B, §1000(a)(7) [div. B, title XII, subtitle F (§1261 et seq.)], Nov. 29, 1999, 113 Stat. 1536, 1501A–508 (22 U.S.C. 2551 note)

International Atomic Energy Agency Participation Act of 1957
Pub. L. 85–177, Aug. 28, 1957, 71 Stat. 453 (22 U.S.C. 2021 et seq.)
Short title, see 22 U.S.C. 2021 note

International Aviation Facilities Act
June 16, 1948, ch. 473, 62 Stat. 450

International Banking Act of 1978
Pub. L. 95–369, Sept. 17, 1978, 92 Stat. 607 (12 U.S.C. 3101 et seq.)
Short title, see 12 U.S.C. 3101 note

International Banking Facility Deposit Insurance Act
Pub. L. 97–110, title I, Dec. 26, 1981, 95 Stat. 1513
Short title, see 12 U.S.C. 1811 note

International Bridge Act of 1972
Pub. L. 92–434, Sept. 26, 1972, 86 Stat. 731 (33 U.S.C. 535 et seq.)
Short title, see 33 U.S.C. 535 note

International Carriage of Perishable Foodstuffs Act
Pub. L. 97–325, Oct. 15, 1982, 96 Stat. 1603 (7 U.S.C. 4401 et seq.)
Short title, see 7 U.S.C. 4401 note

International Center Act
Pub. L. 90–553, Oct. 8, 1968, 82 Stat. 958

International Child Abduction Remedies Act
Pub. L. 100–300, Apr. 29, 1988, 102 Stat. 437 (42 U.S.C. 11601 et seq.)
Short title, see 42 U.S.C. 11601 note

International Children's Emergency Fund Assistance Act of 1948
Apr. 3, 1948, ch. 169, title II, 62 Stat. 157 (22 U.S.C. 1531 et seq.)

International Claims Settlement Act of 1949
Mar. 10, 1950, ch. 54, 64 Stat. 12 (22 U.S.C. 1621 et seq.)
Short title, see 22 U.S.C. 1621 note

International Coffee Agreement Act of 1965
Pub. L. 89–23, May 22, 1965, 79 Stat. 112 (19 U.S.C. 1356a–1356e)

International Coffee Agreement Act of 1968
Pub.L. 90–634, title III, Oct. 24, 1968, 82 Stat. 1348 (19 U.S.C. 1396f–1396j)

International Coffee Agreement Act of 1980
Pub. L. 96–599, Dec. 24, 1980, 94 Stat. 3491 (19 U.S.C. 1356k et seq.)
Short title, see 19 U.S.C. 1356k note

International Communication Agency Authorization Act, Fiscal Years 1980 and 1981
Pub. L. 96–60, title II, Aug. 15, 1979, 93 Stat. 398

International Cooperation in Global Change Research Act of 1990
Pub. L. 101–606, title II, Nov. 16, 1990, 104 Stat. 3102 (15 U.S.C. 2951 et seq.)
Short title, see 15 U.S.C. 2921 note

International Cultural Exchange and Trade Fair Participation Act of 1956
Aug. 1, 1956, ch. 811, 70 Stat. 778 (22 U.S.C. 1991 et seq.)

International Debt Management Act of 1988
Pub. L. 100–418, title III, subtitle B (§3101 et seq.), Aug. 23, 1988, 102 Stat. 1375 (22 U.S.C. 5321 et seq.)
Short title, see 22 U.S.C. 5321

International Development and Finance Act of 1989
Pub. L. 101–240, Dec. 19, 1989, 103 Stat. 2492
Short title, see 22 U.S.C. 2151 note

International Development and Food Assistance Act of 1975
Pub. L. 94–161, Dec. 20, 1975, 89 Stat. 849
Short title, see 22 U.S.C. 2151 note

International Development and Food Assistance Act of 1977
Pub. L. 95–88, Aug. 3, 1977, 91 Stat. 533
Short title, see 22 U.S.C. 2151 note

International Development and Food Assistance Act of 1978
Pub. L. 95–424, Oct. 6, 1978, 92 Stat. 937
Short title, see 22 U.S.C. 2151 note

International Development Association Act
Pub. L. 86–565, June 30, 1960, 74 Stat. 293 (22 U.S.C. 284 et seq.)
Short title, see 22 U.S.C. 284 note

International Development Cooperation Act of 1979
Pub. L. 96–53, Aug. 14, 1979, 93 Stat. 359
Short title, see 22 U.S.C. 2151 note

International Dolphin Conservation Act of 1992
Pub. L. 102–523, Oct. 26, 1992, 106 Stat. 3425
Short title, see 16 U.S.C. 1361 note

International Dolphin Conservation Program Act
Pub. L. 105–42, Aug. 15, 1997, 111 Stat. 1122
Short title, see 16 U.S.C. 1361 note

International Economic Policy Act of 1972
Pub. L. 92–412, title II, Aug. 29, 1972, 86 Stat. 646 (22 U.S.C. 2841 et seq.)

International Education Act of 1966
Pub. L. 89–698, Oct. 29, 1966, 80 Stat. 1066 (20 U.S.C. 1171 et seq.)

International Emergency Economic Powers Act
Pub. L. 95–223, title II, Dec. 28, 1977, 91 Stat. 1626 (50 U.S.C. 1701 et seq.)
Short title, see 50 U.S.C. 1701 note

International Environment Protection Act of 1983
Pub. L. 98–164, title VII, Nov. 22, 1983, 97 Stat. 1045
Short title, see 22 U.S.C. 2151 note

International Finance Corporation Act
Aug. 11, 1955, ch. 788, 69 Stat. 669 (22 U.S.C. 282 et seq.)
Short title, see 22 U.S.C. 282 note

International Financial Institutions Act
Pub. L. 95–118, Oct. 3, 1977, 91 Stat. 1067
Short title, see 22 U.S.C. 261 note

International Forestry Cooperation Act of 1990
Pub. L. 101–513, title VI, Nov. 5, 1990, 104 Stat. 2070 (16 U.S.C. 4501 et seq.)
Short title, see 16 U.S.C. 4501 note

International Health Research Act of 1960
Pub. L. 86–610, July 12, 1960, 74 Stat. 364 (22 U.S.C. 2101 et seq.)
Short title, see 22 U.S.C. 2101 note

International Investment and Trade in Services Survey Act
Pub. L. 94–472, Oct. 11, 1976, 90 Stat. 2059 (22 U.S.C. 3101 et seq.)
Short title, see 22 U.S.C. 3101 note

International Investment Survey Act of 1976
Renamed the International Investment and Trade in Services Survey Act

International Lending Supervision Act of 1983
Pub. L. 98–181, title IX, Nov. 30, 1983, 97 Stat. 1278 (12 U.S.C. 3901 et seq.)
Short title, see 12 U.S.C. 3901 note

International Malaria Control Act of 2000
Pub. L. 106–570, title I, Dec. 27, 2000, 114 Stat. 3039 (22 U.S.C. 2151b–1)
Short title, see 22 U.S.C. 2151 note

International Maritime and Port Security Act
Pub. L. 99–399, title IX, Aug. 27, 1986, 100 Stat. 889 (46 App. U.S.C. 1801 et seq.)
Short title, see 46 App. U.S.C. 1801 note

International Maritime Satellite Telecommunications Act
Pub. L. 87–624, title V, as added Pub. L. 95–564, Nov. 1, 1978, 92 Stat. 2392 (47 U.S.C. 751 et seq.)
Short title, see 47 U.S.C. 701 note

International Narcotics Control Act of 1985
Pub. L. 99–83, title VI, Aug. 8, 1985, 99 Stat. 228
Short title, see 22 U.S.C. 2151 note

International Narcotics Control Act of 1986
Pub. L. 99–570, title II, Oct. 27, 1986, 100 Stat. 3207–60
Short title, see 22 U.S.C. 2151 note

International Narcotics Control Act of 1988
Pub. L. 100–690, title IV, Nov. 18, 1988, 102 Stat. 4261
Short title, see 22 U.S.C. 2151 note

International Narcotics Control Act of 1989
Pub. L. 101–231, Dec. 13, 1989, 103 Stat. 1954
Short title, see 22 U.S.C. 2151 note

International Narcotics Control Act of 1990
Pub. L. 101–623, Nov. 21, 1990, 104 Stat. 3350
Short title, see 22 U.S.C. 2151 note

International Narcotics Control Act of 1992
Pub. L. 102–583, Nov. 2, 1992, 106 Stat. 4914
Short title, see 22 U.S.C. 2151 note

International Narcotics Control Corrections Act of 1994
Pub. L. 103–447, Nov. 2, 1994, 108 Stat. 4691
Short title, see 22 U.S.C. 2151 note

International Navigational Rules Act of 1977
Pub. L. 95–75, July 27, 1977, 91 Stat. 308 (33 U.S.C. 1601 et seq.)
Short title, see 33 U.S.C. 1601 note

International Organizations Immunities Act
Dec. 29, 1945, ch. 652, title I, 59 Stat. 669 (22 U.S.C. 288 et seq.)
Short title, see 22 U.S.C. 288 note

International Organizations Procurement Act of 1947
Aug. 4, 1947, ch. 479, 61 Stat. 752

International Parental Kidnapping Crime Act of 1993
Pub. L. 103–173, Dec. 2, 1993, 107 Stat. 1998 (18 U.S.C. 1204)
Short title, see 18 U.S.C. 1201 note

International Patient Act of 2000
Pub. L. 106–406, Nov. 1, 2000, 114 Stat. 1755
Short title, see 8 U.S.C. 1101 note

International Peacekeeping Act of 1992
Pub. L. 102–311, July 2, 1992, 106 Stat. 277

International Religious Freedom Act of 1998
Pub. L. 105–292, Oct. 27, 1998, 112 Stat. 2787 (22 U.S.C. 6401 et seq.)
Short title, see 22 U.S.C. 6401 note

International Safe Container Act
Pub. L. 95–208, Dec. 13, 1977, 91 Stat. 1475 (46 App. U.S.C. 1501 et seq.)
Short title, see 46 App. U.S.C. 1501 note

International Securities Enforcement Cooperation Act of 1990
Pub. L. 101–550, title II, Nov. 15, 1990, 104 Stat. 2714
Short title, see 15 U.S.C. 78a note

International Security and Development Assistance Authorizations Act of 1983
Pub. L. 98–151, §101(b)(2), Nov. 14, 1983, 97 Stat. 968

International Security and Development Cooperation Act of 1980
Pub. L. 96–533, Dec. 16, 1980, 94 Stat. 3131
Short title, see 22 U.S.C. 2151 note

International Security and Development Cooperation Act of 1981
Pub. L. 97–113, Dec. 29, 1981, 95 Stat. 1519
Short title, see 22 U.S.C. 2151 note

International Security and Development Cooperation Act of 1985
Pub. L. 99–83, Aug. 8, 1985, 99 Stat. 190
Short title, see 22 U.S.C. 2151 note

International Security Assistance Act of 1977
Pub. L. 95–92, Aug. 4, 1977, 91 Stat. 614
Short title, see 22 U.S.C. 2151 note

International Security Assistance Act of 1978
Pub. L. 95–384, Sept. 26, 1978, 92 Stat. 730
Short title, see 22 U.S.C. 2151 note

International Security Assistance Act of 1979
Pub. L. 96–92, Oct. 29, 1979, 93 Stat. 701
Short title, see 22 U.S.C. 2151 note

International Security Assistance and Arms Export Control Act of 1976
Pub. L. 94–329, June 30, 1976, 90 Stat. 729
Short title, see 22 U.S.C. 2151 note

International Trade and Investment Act
Pub. L. 98–573, title III, Oct. 30, 1984, 98 Stat. 3000
Short title, see 19 U.S.C. 2101 note

International Travel Act of 1961
Pub. L. 87–63, June 29, 1961, 75 Stat. 129 (22 U.S.C. 2121 et seq.)
Short title, see 22 U.S.C. 2121 note

International Tuberculosis Control Act of 2000
Pub. L. 106–264, title II, Aug. 19, 2000, 114 Stat. 758
Short title, see 22 U.S.C. 2151 note

International Understanding Act
Pub. L. 89–10, title III, part N (§393 et seq.), as added Pub. L. 96–374, title VI, §601(b), Oct. 3, 1980, 94 Stat. 1470 (20 U.S.C. 3063 et seq.)

International Voyage Load Line Act of 1973
Pub. L. 93–115, Oct. 1, 1973, 87 Stat. 418

International Waterways Act
June 13, 1902, ch. 1079, 32 Stat. 373

International Wheat Agreement Act of 1949
Oct. 27, 1949, ch. 772, 63 Stat. 945 (7 U.S.C. 1641 et seq.)
Short title, see 7 U.S.C. 1641 note

Internet False Identification Prevention Act of 2000
Pub. L. 106–578, Dec. 28, 2000, 114 Stat. 3075
Short title, see 18 U.S.C. 1001 note

Internet Tax Freedom Act
Pub. L. 105–277, div. C, title XI, Oct. 21, 1998, 112 Stat. 2681–719 (47 U.S.C. 151 note)

Interpleader Act
See Federal Interpleader Act

Interstate 90 Land Exchange Act of 1998
Pub. L. 105–277, div. A, §101(e) [title VI], Oct. 21, 1998, 112 Stat. 2681–231, 2681–326 (16 U.S.C. 539k note)

Interstate 90 Land Exchange Amendment
Pub. L. 106–113, div. B, §1000(a)(3) [title III, §346], Nov. 29, 1999, 113 Stat. 1535, 1501A–204

Interstate Agreement on Detainers Act
Pub. L. 91–538, Dec. 9, 1970, 84 Stat. 1397 (18 App. U.S.C.)
Short title, see 18 App. U.S.C. 1

Interstate Commerce Act
Feb. 4, 1887, ch. 104, 24 Stat. 379

Interstate Commerce Commission Dangerous Article Act
See Dangerous Cargo Act

Interstate Compact on Mental Health Act
Pub. L. 92–280, Apr. 26, 1972, 86 Stat. 126

Interstate Horseracing Act of 1978
Pub. L. 95–515, Oct. 25, 1978, 92 Stat. 1811 (15 U.S.C. 3001 et seq.)
Short title, see 15 U.S.C. 3001 note

Interstate Land Sales Full Disclosure Act
Pub. L. 90–448, title XIV, Aug. 1, 1968, 82 Stat. 590 (15 U.S.C. 1701 et seq.)
Short title, see 15 U.S.C. 1701 note

Interstate Meat Packing Law
June 10, 1942, ch. 403, 56 Stat. 351

Interstate Transportation of Dangerous Criminals Act of 2000
Also known as Jeanna's Act
Pub. L. 106–560, Dec. 21, 2000, 114 Stat. 2784 (42 U.S.C. 13726 et seq.)
Short title, see 42 U.S.C. 13701 note

Intervention on the High Seas Act
Pub. L. 93–248, Feb. 5, 1974, 88 Stat. 8 (33 U.S.C. 1471 et seq.)
Short title, see 33 U.S.C. 1471 note

Invalid Pension Act
June 27, 1890, ch. 634, 26 Stat. 182

Invention Secrecy Act of 1951
Feb. 1, 1952, ch. 4, 66 Stat. 3

Inventors' Rights Act of 1999
Pub. L. 106–113, div. B, §1000(a)(9) [title IV, subtitle A (§4101 et seq.)], Nov. 29, 1999, 113 Stat. 1536, 1501A–552
Short title, see 35 U.S.C. 1 note

Investment Advisers Act of 1940
Aug. 22, 1940, ch. 686, title II, 54 Stat. 847 (15 U.S.C. 80b–1 et seq.)
Short title, see 15 U.S.C. 80b–20

Investment Advisers Supervision Coordination Act
Pub. L. 104–290, title III, Oct. 11, 1996, 110 Stat. 3436
Short title, see 15 U.S.C. 80b–20 note

Investment Company Act Amendments of 1996
Pub. L. 104–290, title II, Oct. 11, 1996, 110 Stat. 3426
Short title, see 15 U.S.C. 80a–51 note

Investment Company Act of 1940
Aug. 22, 1940, ch. 686, title I, 54 Stat. 789 (15 U.S.C. 80a–1 et seq.)
Short title, see 15 U.S.C. 80a–51

Investment Company Amendments Act of 1970
Pub. L. 91–547, Dec. 14, 1970, 84 Stat. 1413
Short title, see 15 U.S.C. 80a–51 note

Iran and Libya Sanctions Act of 1996
Pub. L. 104–172, Aug. 5, 1996, 110 Stat. 1541 (50 U.S.C. 1701 note)

Iran Nonproliferation Act of 2000
Pub. L. 106–178, Mar. 14, 2000, 114 Stat. 38 (50 U.S.C. 1701 note)

Iran-Iraq Arms Non-Proliferation Act of 1992
Pub. L. 102–484, div. A, title XVI, Oct. 23, 1992, 106 Stat. 2571 (50 U.S.C. 1701 note)

Iraq Liberation Act of 1998
Pub. L. 105–338, Oct. 31, 1998, 112 Stat. 3178 (22 U.S.C. 2151 note)

Iraq Sanctions Act of 1990
Pub. L. 101–513, title V, §§586–586J, Nov. 5, 1990, 104 Stat. 2047–2054 (50 U.S.C. 1701 note)

Irish Peace Process Cultural and Training Program Act of 1998
Pub. L. 105–319, Oct. 30, 1998, 112 Stat. 3013 (8 U.S.C. 1101 note)

Irish Wilderness Act of 1984
Pub. L. 98–289, May 21, 1984, 98 Stat. 199 (16 U.S.C. 1132 note)

Irrigation Investigation Act
See Arid Land Act

Irrigation Project Contract Extension Act of 1996
Pub. L. 104–326, Oct. 19, 1996, 110 Stat. 4000

Irrigation Project Contract Extension Act of 1998
Pub. L. 105–293, Oct. 27, 1998, 112 Stat. 2816

Isolated Tract Act
Mar. 28, 1912, ch. 67, 37 Stat. 77

ISTEA
See Intermodal Surface Transportation Efficiency Act of 1991

Isthmian Canal Act
June 28, 1902, ch. 1302, 32 Stat. 481

Ivanpah Valley Airport Public Lands Transfer Act
Pub. L. 106–362, Oct. 27, 2000, 114 Stat. 1404

Jackson Multi-Agency Campus Act of 2000
Pub. L. 106–272, Sept. 22, 2000, 114 Stat. 797

Jackson-Vanik Amendment
Pub. L. 93–618, title I, §§152, 153, title IV, §§402, 407, 409, Jan. 3, 1975, 88 Stat. 2004, 2006, 2056, 2063, 2064

Jacob K. Javits Gifted and Talented Students Education Act of 1988
Pub. L. 89–10, title IV, part B (§4101 et seq.), as added Pub. L. 100–297, title I, §1001, Apr. 28, 1988, 102 Stat. 237 (20 U.S.C. 3061 et seq.)

Jacob K. Javits Gifted and Talented Students Education Act of 1994
Pub. L. 89–10, title X, part B (§10201 et seq.), as added Pub. L. 103–382, title I, §101, Oct. 20, 1994, 108 Stat. 3820 (20 U.S.C. 8031 et seq.)
Short title, see 20 U.S.C. 8031

Jadwin Act
See Flood Control Act of 1928

James Madison Commemoration Commission Act
Pub. L. 106–550, Dec. 19, 2000, 114 Stat. 2745 (36 U.S.C. note prec. 101)

James Madison Memorial Fellowship Act
Pub. L. 99–500, §101(b) [title VIII], Oct. 18, 1986, 100 Stat. 1783–39, 1783–76, and Pub. L. 99–591, §101(b) [title VIII], Oct. 30, 1986, 100 Stat. 3341–39, 3341–76 (20 U.S.C. 4501 et seq.)
Short title, see 20 U.S.C. 4501 note

James Madison—Bill of Rights Commemorative Coin Act
Pub. L. 102–281, title V, May 13, 1992, 106 Stat. 145 (31 U.S.C. 5112 note)

Jamestown 400th Commemoration Commission Act of 2000
Pub. L. 106–554, §1(a)(4) [div. B, title I, §127 [S. 2885]], Dec. 21, 2000, 114 Stat. 2763, 2763A–229, 2763A–359 (16 U.S.C. 81 note)
Pub. L. 106–565, Dec. 23, 2000, 114 Stat. 2812 (16 U.S.C. 81 note)

Japan-United States Friendship Act
Pub. L. 94–118, Oct. 20, 1975, 89 Stat. 603 (22 U.S.C. 2901 et seq.)
Short title, see 22 U.S.C. 2901 note

Japanese American National Historic Landmark Theme Study Act
Pub. L. 102–248, title II, Mar. 3, 1992, 106 Stat. 42

Japanese Imperial Government Disclosure Act of 2000
Pub. L. 106–567, title VIII, Dec. 27, 2000, 114 Stat. 2864 (5 U.S.C. 552 note)

Japanese Technical Literature Act of 1986
Pub. L. 99–382, Aug. 14, 1986, 100 Stat. 811
Short title, see 15 U.S.C. 3701 note

Japanese-American Evacuation Claims Act of 1948
July 2, 1948, ch. 814, 62 Stat. 1231 (50 App. U.S.C. 1981 et seq.)

Javits-Wagner-O'Day Act
June 25, 1938, ch. 697, 52 Stat. 1196 (41 U.S.C. 46 et seq.)
Short title, see 41 U.S.C. 46 note

Jeanna's Act
Also known as Interstate Transportation of Dangerous Criminals Act of 2000
Pub. L. 106–560, Dec. 21, 2000, 114 Stat. 2784 (42 U.S.C. 13726 et seq.)
Short title, see 42 U.S.C. 13701 note

Jeanne Clery Disclosure of Campus Security Policy and Campus Crime Statistics Act
Pub. L. 89–329, title IV, §485(f), as added Pub. L. 101–542, title II, §204(a), Nov. 8, 1990, 104 Stat. 2385 (20 U.S.C. 1092(f))
Short title, see 20 U.S.C. 1092(f)(15)

Jefferson Commemorative Coin Act of 1993
Pub. L. 103–186, title I, Dec. 14, 1993, 107 Stat. 2245 (31 U.S.C. 5112 note)

Jefferson National Expansion Memorial Act
May 17, 1954, ch. 204, 68 Stat. 98 (16 U.S.C. 450jj et seq.)

Jefferson National Expansion Memorial Amendments Act of 1984
Pub. L. 98–398, title II, Aug. 24, 1984, 98 Stat. 1472 (16 U.S.C. 450jj–3 et seq.)
Short title, see 16 U.S.C. 450jj note

Jencks Act
Pub. L. 85–269, Sept. 2, 1957, 71 Stat. 595 (18 U.S.C. 3500)

Jennifer's Law
Pub. L. 106–177, title II, Mar. 10, 2000, 114 Stat. 36 (42 U.S.C. 14661 et seq.)
Short title, see 42 U.S.C. 14661 note

Jerusalem Embassy Act of 1995
Pub. L. 104–45, Nov. 8, 1995, 109 Stat. 398

Jewelers' Liability Act (Gold and Silver Articles)
Also known as the National Gold and Silver Stamping Act of 1906
June 13, 1906, ch. 3289, 34 Stat. 260 (15 U.S.C. 294 et seq.)
Short title, see 15 U.S.C. 294 note

Jicarilla Apache Tribe Water Rights Settlement Act
Pub. L. 102–441, Oct. 23, 1992, 106 Stat. 2237

Job Evaluation Policy Act of 1970
Pub. L. 91–216, Mar. 17, 1970, 84 Stat. 72 (5 U.S.C. 5104 note)

Job Training Partnership Act
Pub. L. 97–300, Oct. 13, 1982, 96 Stat. 1322 (29 U.S.C. 1501 et seq.)
Short title, see 29 U.S.C. 1501 note

Job Training Partnership Act Amendments of 1986
Pub. L. 99–496, Oct. 16, 1986, 100 Stat. 1261
Short title, see 29 U.S.C. 1501 note

Job Training Reform Amendments of 1992
Pub. L. 102–367, Sept. 7, 1992, 106 Stat. 1021
Short title, see 29 U.S.C. 1501 note

Jobs for Employable Dependent Individuals Act
Pub. L. 100–628, title VII, subtitle B (§711 et seq.), Nov. 7, 1988, 102 Stat. 3248 (29 U.S.C. 1791 et seq.)
Short title, see 29 U.S.C. 1501 note

Jobs Through Exports Act of 1992
Pub. L. 102–549, Oct. 28, 1992, 106 Stat. 3651
Short title, see 22 U.S.C. 2151 note

Jobs Through Trade Expansion Act of 1994
Pub. L. 103–392, Oct. 22, 1994, 108 Stat. 4098
Short title, see 22 U.S.C. 2151 note

John C. Stennis Center for Public Service Training and Development Act
Pub. L. 100–458, title I, subtitle B (§111 et seq.), Oct. 1, 1988, 102 Stat. 2172 (2 U.S.C. 1101 et seq.)
Short title, see 2 U.S.C. 1101 note

John F. Kennedy Center Act
Pub. L. 85–874, Sept. 2, 1958, 72 Stat. 1698 (20 U.S.C. 76h et seq.)
Short title, see 20 U.S.C. 76h note

John F. Kennedy Center Act Amendments of 1984
Pub. L. 98–473, title I, §101(c) [part], Oct. 12, 1984, 98 Stat. 1837, 1876
Short title, see 20 U.S.C. 76h note

John F. Kennedy Center Act Amendments of 1994
Pub. L. 103–279, July 21, 1994, 108 Stat. 1409
Short title, see 20 U.S.C. 76h note

John F. Kennedy Center for the Performing Arts Authorization Act of 1998
Pub. L. 105–226, Aug. 12, 1998, 112 Stat. 1513
Short title, see 20 U.S.C. 76h note

John F. Kennedy Center Parking Improvement Act of 1997
Pub. L. 105–95, Nov. 19, 1997, 111 Stat. 2148
Short title, see 20 U.S.C. 76h note

John H. Chafee Coastal Barrier Resources System Act
Pub. L. 106–167, Dec. 9, 1999, 113 Stat. 1803
Short title, see 16 U.S.C. 3501 note

John William Rolen Act
Pub. L. 106–117, title V, §501, Nov. 30, 1999, 113 Stat. 1573
Short title, see 38 U.S.C. 101 note

Johnson Act (Gambling)
See Gambling Devices Transportation Act

Johnson Act (Immigration)
See Immigration Act of 1921

Johnson Act (Injunctions Affecting Utility Rates)
May 14, 1934, ch. 283, 48 Stat. 775

Johnson Act (Maritime Workers' Compensation)
Oct. 6, 1917, ch. 97, 40 Stat. 395

Johnson Amendment
See Corporation of Foreign Bondholders Act, 1933

Johnson Debt Default Act
See Foreign Securities Act

Johnson Fish Restoration Act
See Dingell-Johnson Sport Fish Restoration Act

Johnson-O'Malley Act
Apr. 16, 1934, ch. 147, 48 Stat. 596 (25 U.S.C. 452 et seq.)
Short title, see 25 U.S.C. 452 note

Johnson-Reed Act (Immigration)
See Immigration Act of 1924

Joint Funding Simplification Act of 1974
Pub. L. 93–510, Dec. 5, 1974, 88 Stat. 1604
Short title, see 42 U.S.C. 4251 note

Joint Service Pay Act
See Pay Readjustment Act of 1922

Jones Act (Intoxicating Liquors)
Mar. 2, 1929, ch. 473, 45 Stat. 1446

Jones Act (Merchant Marine)
See Merchant Marine Act, 1920

Jones Act (Philippine Government)
See Autonomy Act

Jones Act (Puerto Rico)
See Puerto Rican Federal Relations Act

Jones Agricultural Adjustment Act of 1938
See Agricultural Adjustment Act of 1938

Jones Amendment (Liquor Advertisements)
Mar. 3, 1917, ch. 162, §5, 39 Stat. 1069

Jones Farm Loan Act
See Emergency Farm Mortgage Act of 1933

Jones-Connally Farm-Relief Act
Apr. 7, 1934, ch. 103, 48 Stat. 528

Jones-Costigan Sugar Act
See Sugar Control Act

Jones-McCormack Act (Saturday Half Holidays)
Mar. 3, 1931, ch. 396, 46 Stat. 1482

Jones-Miller Act (Narcotics Import and Export)
May 26, 1922, ch. 202, 42 Stat. 596

Jones-Reid Act
See Flood Control Act of 1928

Jones-White Act
See Merchant Marine Act, 1928

Jordan Supplemental Economic Assistance Authorization Act of 1985
Pub. L. 99–88, title IV, Aug. 15, 1985, 99 Stat. 376

Joshua Tree National Monument Act
Sept. 25, 1950, ch. 1030, 64 Stat. 1033 (16 U.S.C. 450ii et seq.)

JTPA
See Job Training Partnership Act

Juan Bautista de Anza National Historic Trail Act
Pub. L. 101–365, Aug. 15, 1990, 104 Stat. 429
Short title, see 16 U.S.C. 1241 note

Judicial Amendments Act of 1994
Pub. L. 103–420, Oct. 25, 1994, 108 Stat. 4343
Short title, see 28 U.S.C. 1 note

Judicial Code
Mar. 3, 1911, ch. 231, 36 Stat. 1087

Judicial Councils Reform and Judicial Conduct and Disability Act of 1980
Pub. L. 96–458, Oct. 15, 1980, 94 Stat. 2035
Short title, see 28 U.S.C. 1 note

Judicial Discipline and Removal Reform Act of 1990
Pub. L. 101–650, title IV, Dec. 1, 1990, 104 Stat. 5122
Short title, see 28 U.S.C. 1 note

Judicial Housekeeping Act of 1986
Pub. L. 99–657, Nov. 14, 1986, 100 Stat. 3670
Short title, see 28 U.S.C. 1 note

Judicial Improvements Act of 1985
Pub. L. 99–336, June 19, 1986, 100 Stat. 633
Short title, see 28 U.S.C. 1 note

Judicial Improvements Act of 1990
Pub. L. 101–650, Dec. 1, 1990, 104 Stat. 5089
Short title, see 28 U.S.C. 1 note

Judicial Improvements and Access to Justice Act
Pub. L. 100–702, Nov. 19, 1988, 102 Stat. 4642
Short title, see 28 U.S.C. 1 note

Judicial Naturalization Ceremonies Amendments of 1991
Pub. L. 102–232, title I, Dec. 12, 1991, 105 Stat. 1733
Short title, see 8 U.S.C. 1101 note

Judicial Survivors Annuity Act
Aug. 3, 1956, ch. 944, §2, 70 Stat. 1021 (28 U.S.C. 376)

Judicial Survivors' Annuities Reform Act
Pub. L. 94–554, Oct. 19, 1976, 90 Stat. 2603
Short title, see 28 U.S.C. 1 note

Judiciary Act of 1789
Sept. 24, 1789, ch. 20, 1 Stat. 73

Judiciary Appropriation Act, 1941
May 14, 1940, ch. 189, title IV, 54 Stat. 207

Judiciary Appropriation Act, 1942
June 28, 1941, ch. 258, title IV, 55 Stat. 298

Judiciary Appropriation Act, 1944
June 28, 1943, ch. 173, title II, 57 Stat. 239

Judiciary Appropriation Act, 1945
June 26, 1944, ch. 277, title II, 58 Stat. 354

Judiciary Appropriation Act, 1946
May 21, 1945, ch. 129, title IV, 59 Stat. 196

Judiciary Appropriation Act, 1947
July 5, 1946, ch. 541, title IV, 60 Stat. 475

Judiciary Appropriation Act, 1948
July 9, 1947, ch. 211, title IV, 61 Stat. 302

Judiciary Appropriation Act 1949
June 3, 1948, ch. 400, title IV, 62 Stat. 329

Judiciary Appropriation Act, 1950
July 20, 1949, ch. 354, title IV, 63 Stat. 470

Judiciary Appropriation Act, 1951
Sept. 6, 1950, ch. 896, Ch. III, title IV, 64 Stat. 629

Judiciary Appropriation Act, 1952
Oct. 22, 1951, ch. 533, title IV, 65 Stat. 594

Judiciary Appropriation Act, 1953
July 10, 1952, ch. 651, title IV, 66 Stat. 567

Judiciary Appropriation Act, 1954
Aug. 1, 1953, ch. 304, title II, 67 Stat. 332

Judiciary Appropriation Act, 1955
July 2, 1954, ch. 455, title II, 68 Stat. 409

Judiciary Appropriation Act, 1956
July 7, 1955, ch. 279, title III, 69 Stat. 274

Judiciary Appropriation Act, 1957
June 20, 1956, ch. 414, title III, 70 Stat. 308

Judiciary Appropriation Act, 1958
Pub. L. 85–49, title III, June 11, 1957, 71 Stat. 64

Judiciary Appropriation Act, 1959
Pub. L. 85–474, title III, June 30, 1958, 72 Stat. 253

Judiciary Appropriation Act, 1960
Pub. L. 86–84, title III, July 13, 1959, 73 Stat. 190

Judiciary Appropriation Act, 1961
Pub. L. 86–678, title III, Aug. 31, 1960, 74 Stat. 565

Judiciary Appropriation Act, 1962
Pub. L. 87–264, title III, Sept. 21, 1961, 75 Stat. 554

Judiciary Appropriation Act, 1963
Pub. L. 87–843, title IV, Oct. 18, 1962, 76 Stat. 1097

Judiciary Appropriation Act, 1964
Pub. L. 88–245, title IV, Dec. 30, 1963, 77 Stat. 793

Judiciary Appropriation Act, 1965
Pub. L. 88–527, title IV, Aug. 31, 1964, 78 Stat. 728

Judiciary Appropriation Act, 1966
Pub. L. 89–164, title IV, Sept. 2, 1965, 79 Stat. 636

Judiciary Appropriation Act, 1967
Pub. L. 89–797, title IV, Nov. 8, 1966, 80 Stat. 1497

Judiciary Appropriation Act, 1968
Pub. L. 90–133, title IV, Nov. 8, 1967, 81 Stat. 426

Judiciary Appropriation Act, 1969
Pub. L. 90–470, title IV, Aug. 9, 1968, 82 Stat. 683

Judiciary Appropriation Act, 1970
Pub. L. 91–153, title IV, Dec. 24, 1969, 83 Stat. 418

Judiciary Appropriation Act, 1971
Pub. L. 91–472, title IV, Oct. 21, 1970, 84 Stat. 1055

Judiciary Appropriation Act, 1972
Pub. L. 92–77, title IV, Aug. 10, 1971, 85 Stat. 261

Judiciary Appropriation Act, 1973
Pub. L. 92–544, title IV, Oct. 25, 1972, 86 Stat. 1124

Judiciary Appropriation Act, 1974
Pub. L. 93–162, title IV, Nov. 27, 1973, 87 Stat. 650

Judiciary Appropriation Act, 1975
Pub. L. 93–433, title IV, Oct. 5, 1974, 88 Stat. 1200

Judiciary Appropriation Act, 1976
Pub. L. 94–121, title IV, Oct. 21, 1975, 89 Stat. 629

Judiciary Appropriation Act, 1977
Pub. L. 94–362, title IV, July 14, 1976, 90 Stat. 952

Judiciary Appropriation Act, 1978
Pub. L. 95–86, title IV, Aug. 2, 1977, 91 Stat. 434

Judiciary Appropriation Act, 1979
Pub. L. 95–431, title IV, Oct. 10, 1978, 92 Stat. 1035

Judiciary Appropriation Act, 1980
Pub. L. 96–68, title IV, Sept. 24, 1979, 93 Stat. 427

Judiciary Appropriation Act, 1984
Pub. L. 98–166, title IV, Nov. 28, 1983, 97 Stat. 1098

Judiciary Appropriation Act, 1985
Pub. L. 98–411, title IV, Aug. 30, 1984, 98 Stat. 1570

Judiciary Appropriation Act, 1986
Pub. L. 99–180, title IV, Dec. 13, 1985, 99 Stat. 1153

Judiciary Appropriation Act, 1987
Pub. L. 99–500, §101(b) [title IV], Oct. 18, 1986, 100 Stat. 1783–39, 1783–61, and Pub. L. 99–591, §101(b) [title IV], Oct. 30, 1986, 100 Stat. 3341–39, 3341–61

Judiciary Appropriation Act, 1988
Pub. L. 100–202, §101(a) [title IV], Dec. 22, 1987, 101 Stat. 1329, 1329–24

Judiciary Appropriations Act, 1989
Pub. L. 100–459, title IV, Oct. 1, 1988, 102 Stat. 2209

Judiciary Appropriations Act, 1990
Pub. L. 101–162, title IV, Nov. 21, 1989, 103 Stat. 1010

Judiciary Appropriations Act, 1991
Pub. L. 101–515, title IV, Nov. 5, 1990, 104 Stat. 2129

Judiciary Appropriations Act, 1992
Pub. L. 102–140, title III, Oct. 28, 1991, 105 Stat. 807

Judiciary Appropriations Act, 1993
Pub. L. 102–395, title III, Oct. 6, 1992, 106 Stat. 1856

Judiciary Appropriations Act, 1994
Pub. L. 103–121, title III, Oct. 27, 1993, 107 Stat. 1177

Judiciary Appropriations Act, 1995
Pub. L. 103–317, title III, Aug. 26, 1994, 108 Stat. 1749

Judiciary Appropriations Act, 1996
Pub. L. 104–134, title I, §101[(a)] [title III], Apr. 26, 1996, 110 Stat. 1321, 1321–32

Judiciary Appropriations Act, 1997
Pub. L. 104–208, div. A, title I, §101(a) [title III], Sept. 30, 1996, 110 Stat. 3009, 3009–42

Judiciary Appropriations Act, 1998
Pub. L. 105–119, title III, Nov. 26, 1997, 111 Stat. 2488

Judiciary Appropriations Act, 1999
Pub. L. 105–277, div. A, §101(b) [title III], Oct. 21, 1998, 112 Stat. 2681–50, 2681–89

Judiciary Appropriations Act, 2000
Pub. L. 106–113, div. B, §1000(a)(1) [title III], Nov. 29, 1999, 113 Stat. 1535, 1501A–33

Judiciary Appropriations Act, 2001
Pub. L. 106–553, §1(a)(2) [title III], Dec. 21, 2000, 114 Stat. 2762, 2762A–80

Judiciary Establishment Appropriation Act, 1943
July 2, 1942, ch. 472, title IV, 56 Stat. 501

Judiciary Office Building Development Act
Pub. L. 100–480, Oct. 7, 1988, 102 Stat. 2328 (40 U.S.C. 1201 et seq.)
Short title, see 40 U.S.C. 1201 note

June Act (Pensions)
June 27, 1890, ch. 634, 26 Stat. 182

Junior Duck Stamp Conservation and Design Program Act of 1994
Pub. L. 103–340, Oct. 6, 1994, 108 Stat. 3119 (16 U.S.C. 719 et seq.)
Short title, see 16 U.S.C. 719 note

Juniper Butte Range Withdrawal Act
Pub. L. 105–261, div. B, title XXIX, Oct. 17, 1998, 112 Stat. 2226

Jury Selection and Service Act of 1968
Pub. L. 90–274, Mar. 27, 1968, 82 Stat. 53
Short title, see 28 U.S.C. 1861 note

Jury System Improvements Act of 1978
Pub. L. 95–572, Nov. 2, 1978, 92 Stat. 2453
Short title, see 28 U.S.C. 1861 note

Justice Assistance Act of 1984
Pub. L. 98–473, title II, ch. VI, div. I (§601 et seq.), Oct. 12, 1984, 98 Stat. 2077
Short title, see 42 U.S.C. 3711 note

Justice Department Organized Crime and Drug Enforcement Enhancement Act of 1988
Pub. L. 100–690, title I, subtitle B (§1051 et seq.), Nov. 18, 1988, 102 Stat. 4189 (28 U.S.C. 509 note)

Justice for Victims of Terrorism Act of 1996
Pub. L. 104–132, title II, subtitle C (§231 et seq.), Apr. 24, 1996, 110 Stat. 1243
Short title, see 42 U.S.C. 10601 note

Justice System Improvement Act of 1979
Pub. L. 96–157, Dec. 27, 1979, 93 Stat. 1167
Short title, see 42 U.S.C. 3711 note

Juvenile Court Act of the District of Columbia
Mar. 19, 1906, ch. 960, 34 Stat. 73

Juvenile Delinquency and Youth Offenses Control Act of 1961
Pub. L. 87–274, Sept. 22, 1961, 75 Stat. 572 (42 U.S.C. 2541 et seq.)

Juvenile Delinquency Prevention Act
Pub. L. 90–445, as added Pub. L. 92–381, §1, Aug. 14, 1972, 86 Stat. 532 (42 U.S.C. 3801 et seq.)

Juvenile Delinquency Prevention and Control Act Amendments of 1971
Pub. L. 92–31, June 30, 1971, 85 Stat. 84

Juvenile Delinquency Prevention and Control Act of 1968
Renamed Juvenile Delinquency Prevention Act

Juvenile Drug Trafficking Act of 1986
Pub. L. 99–570, title I, subtitle C (§1101 et seq.), Oct. 27, 1986, 100 Stat. 3207–10
Short title, see 21 U.S.C. 801 note

Juvenile Fraternal Act
May 29, 1928, ch. 862, 45 Stat. 953

Juvenile Justice Amendments of 1977
Pub. L. 95–115, Oct. 3, 1977, 91 Stat. 1048
Short title, see 42 U.S.C. 5601 note

Juvenile Justice Amendments of 1980
Pub. L. 96–509, Dec. 8, 1980, 94 Stat. 2750
Short title, see 42 U.S.C. 5601 note

Juvenile Justice and Delinquency Prevention Act of 1974
Pub. L. 93–415, Sept. 7, 1974, 88 Stat. 1109 (42 U.S.C. 5601 et seq.)
Short title, see 42 U.S.C. 5601 note

Juvenile Justice and Delinquency Prevention Amendments of 1988
Pub. L. 100–690, title VII, subtitle F (§7250 et seq.), Nov. 18, 1988, 102 Stat. 4434
Short title, see 42 U.S.C. 5601 note

Juvenile Justice, Runaway Youth, and Missing Children's Act Amendments of 1984
Pub. L. 98–473, title II, ch. VI, div. II (§610 et seq.), Oct. 12, 1984, 98 Stat. 2107
Short title, see 42 U.S.C. 5601 note

Kake Tribal Corporation Land Transfer Act
Pub. L. 106–283, Oct. 6, 2000, 114 Stat. 867
Short title, see 43 U.S.C. 1601 note

Kansas-Nebraska Act
May 30, 1854, ch. 59, 10 Stat. 277

Kaw Act (Indians)
July 1, 1902, ch. 1361, 32 Stat. 636

Keating-Owen Act (Child Labor)
Sept. 1, 1916, ch. 432, 39 Stat. 675

Kellogg Act (Advances for Agricultural Purposes)
Aug. 24, 1921, ch. 80, 42 Stat. 181

Kellogg Act (Cable Companies)
May 27, 1921, ch. 12, 42 Stat. 8 (47 U.S.C. 34 et seq.)

Kenai Natives Association Equity Act Amendments of 1996
Pub. L. 104–333, div. I, title III, §311, Nov. 12, 1996, 110 Stat. 4139 (43 U.S.C. 1784 note)

Kentucky National Forest Land Transfer Act of 2000
Pub. L. 106–429, §101(a) [title V, §595(a) [S. 3140]], Nov. 6, 2000, 114 Stat. 1900, 1900A–60, 1900A–71

Kentucky Wilderness Act of 1985
Pub. L. 99–197, Dec. 23, 1985, 99 Stat. 1351 (16 U.S.C. 1132 note)

Keogh-Smathers Act
See Self-Employed Individuals Tax Retirement Act of 1962

Kern-McGillicuddy Act
See Federal Employees' Compensation Act (1916)

Kerr-Mills Social Security Act
See Social Security Amendments of 1960

Kerr-Smith Tobacco Control Act
June 28, 1934, ch. 866, 48 Stat. 1275

"Kick-Back" Racket Act
See Copeland Anti-Kickback Act

Kidnapping Act
June 22, 1932, ch. 271, as added May 18, 1934, ch. 301, 48 Stat. 781

Kids 2000 Act
Pub. L. 106–313, title I, §112, Oct. 17, 2000, 114 Stat. 1260 (42 U.S.C. 13751 note)

Kilday Bill
Pub. L. 85–422, May 20, 1958, 72 Stat. 122

King Holiday and Service Act of 1994
Pub. L. 103–304, Aug. 23, 1994, 108 Stat. 1565
Short title, see 42 U.S.C. 12501 note

Kinkaid Act (Homestead Entries in Nebraska)
Apr. 28, 1904, ch. 1801, 33 Stat. 547 (43 U.S.C. 224)

Klamath Basin Water Supply Enhancement Act of 2000
Pub. L. 106–498, Nov. 9, 2000, 114 Stat. 2221

Klamath Indian Termination Act
See Klamath Termination Act

Klamath Indian Tribe Restoration Act
Pub. L. 99–398, Aug. 27, 1986, 100 Stat. 849 (25 U.S.C. 566 et seq.)
Short title, see 25 U.S.C. 566 note

Klamath River Basin Fishery Resources Restoration Act
Pub. L. 99–552, Oct. 27, 1986, 100 Stat. 3080 (16 U.S.C. 460ss et seq.)
Short title, see 16 U.S.C. 460ss note

Klamath Termination Act
Aug. 13, 1954, ch. 732, 68 Stat. 718 (25 U.S.C. 564 et seq.)

Klamath Welfare Act
Mar. 29, 1948, ch. 160, 62 Stat. 92 (25 U.S.C. 544, 545)
Short title, see 25 U.S.C. 544 note

Knutson-Vandenberg Act
June 9, 1930, ch. 416, 46 Stat. 527 (16 U.S.C. 576 et seq.)
Short title, see 16 U.S.C. 576 note

Koniag Lands Conveyance Amendments of 1991
Pub. L. 102–489, Oct. 24, 1992, 106 Stat. 3138

Korean War Veterans Memorial Thirty-Eighth Anniversary Commemorative Coin Act
Pub. L. 101–495, Oct. 31, 1990, 104 Stat. 1187 (31 U.S.C. 5112 note)

Kramer Patent Act
Aug. 5, 1939, ch. 450, 53 Stat. 1212

Kristen's Act
Pub. L. 106–468, Nov. 9, 2000, 114 Stat. 2027 (42 U.S.C. 14665)
Short title, see 42 U.S.C. 14661 note

Ku Klux Act
Apr. 20, 1871, ch. 22, 17 Stat. 13

Ku Klux Klan Act
See Ku Klux Act

La Follette Act (Seamen)
See Seamen's Act

La Follette Hours of Labor Act (Railroads)
See Hours of Service Act (Railroads)

La Follette-Barden Vocational Rehabilitation Act
See Vocational Rehabilitation Act Amendments of 1943

La Follette-Bulwinkle Act (Venereal Diseases)
May 24, 1938, ch. 267, 52 Stat. 439

La Guardia-McKeown Act
Mar. 3, 1933, ch. 204, 47 Stat. 1467

Labor Day Act
June 28, 1894, ch. 118, 28 Stat. 96

Labor Disputes Act
See Norris-La Guardia Act

Labor Law (Eight-Hour Law)
See Contract Work Hours and Safety Standards Act

Labor Management Cooperation Act of 1978
Pub. L. 95–524, §6, Oct. 27, 1978, 92 Stat. 2020
Short title, see 29 U.S.C. 141 note

Labor Relations Act
See National Labor Relations Act

Labor-Disputes Joint Resolution
June 19, 1934, ch. 677, 48 Stat. 1183

Labor-Federal Security Appropriation Act, 1941
June 26, 1940, ch. 428, 54 Stat. 574

Labor-Federal Security Appropriation Act, 1942
July 1, 1941, ch. 269, 55 Stat. 466

Labor-Federal Security Appropriation Act, 1943
July 2, 1942, ch. 475, 56 Stat. 562

Labor-Federal Security Appropriation Act, 1944
July 12, 1943, ch. 221, 57 Stat. 494

Labor-Federal Security Appropriation Act, 1945
June 28, 1944, ch. 302, 58 Stat. 547

Labor-Federal Security Appropriation Act, 1946
July 3, 1945, ch. 263, 59 Stat. 361

Labor-Federal Security Appropriation Act, 1947
July 26, 1946, ch. 672, 60 Stat. 679

Labor-Federal Security Appropriation Act, 1948
July 8, 1947, ch. 210, 61 Stat. 260

Labor-Federal Security Appropriation Act, 1949
June 14, 1948, ch. 465, 62 Stat. 394

Labor-Federal Security Appropriation Act, 1950
June 29, 1949, ch. 275, 63 Stat. 283

Labor-Federal Security Appropriation Act, 1951
Sept. 6, 1950, ch. 896, Ch. V, 64 Stat. 642

Labor-Federal Security Appropriation Act, 1952
Aug. 31, 1951, ch. 373, 65 Stat. 209

Labor-Federal Security Appropriation Act, 1953
July 5, 1952, ch. 575, 66 Stat. 358

Labor-Management Relations Act, 1947
June 23, 1947, ch. 120, 61 Stat. 136 (29 U.S.C. 141 et seq.)
Short title, see 29 U.S.C. 141(a)

Labor-Management Reporting and Disclosure Act of 1959
Pub. L. 86–257, Sept. 14, 1959, 73 Stat. 519 (29 U.S.C. 401 et seq.)
Short title, see 29 U.S.C. 401 note

Laboratory Animal Act of 1966
See Animal Welfare Act

Lac Vieux Desert Band of Lake Superior Chippewa Indians Act
Pub. L. 100–420, Sept. 8, 1988, 102 Stat. 1577 (25 U.S.C. 1300h et seq.)
Short title, see 25 U.S.C. 1300h note

Lacey Act (Game)
May 25, 1900, ch. 553, 31 Stat. 187

Lacey Act Amendments of 1981
Pub. L. 97–79, Nov. 16, 1981, 95 Stat. 1073 (16 U.S.C. 3371 et seq.)
Short title, see 16 U.S.C. 3371 note

Lackawanna Valley National Heritage Area Act of 2000
Pub. L. 106–278, title I, Oct. 6, 2000, 114 Stat. 814 (16 U.S.C. 461 note)

Lake Andes-Wagner/Marty II Act of 1992
Pub. L. 102–575, title XX, Oct. 30, 1992, 106 Stat. 4677

Lake Champlain Special Designation Act of 1990
Pub. L. 101–596, title III, Nov. 16, 1990, 104 Stat. 3006
Short title, see 33 U.S.C. 1251 note

Lake Erie and Ohio River Ship Canal Act
June 30, 1906, ch. 3933, 34 Stat. 809

Lake Oconee Land Exchange Act
Pub. L. 106–41, Aug. 5, 1999, 113 Stat. 215

Lake Ontario Protection Act of 1976
Pub. L. 94–587, §180, Oct. 22, 1976, 90 Stat. 2939 (33 U.S.C. 426*l*)
Short title, see 33 U.S.C. 426*l*(d)

Lake Pontchartrain Basin Restoration Act of 2000
Pub. L. 106–457, title V, Nov. 7, 2000, 114 Stat. 1973
Short title, see 33 U.S.C. 1251 note

Lake Tahoe Restoration Act
Pub. L. 106–506, Nov. 13, 2000, 114 Stat. 2351

Lamprey River Study Act of 1991
Pub. L. 102–214, Dec. 11, 1991, 105 Stat. 1663
Short title, see 16 U.S.C. 1271 note

Lamprey Wild and Scenic River Extension Act
Pub. L. 106–192, May 2, 2000, 114 Stat. 233
Short title, see 16 U.S.C. 1271 note

Land Acquisition Policy Act of 1960
Pub. L. 86–645, title III, July 14, 1960, 74 Stat. 502 (33 U.S.C. 596, 597)
Short title, see 33 U.S.C. 597 note

Land and Water Conservation Fund Act of 1965
Pub. L. 88–578, Sept. 3, 1964, 78 Stat. 897 (16 U.S.C. 460*l*–4 et seq.)
Short title, see 16 U.S.C. 460*l*–4 note

Land Between the Lakes Protection Act of 1998
Pub. L. 105–277, div. A, §101(e) [title V], Oct. 21, 1998, 112 Stat. 2681–231, 2681–310 (16 U.S.C. 460*lll* et seq.)
Short title, see 16 U.S.C. 460*lll* note

Land Disposal Program Flexibility Act of 1996
Pub. L. 104–119, Mar. 26, 1996, 110 Stat. 830
Short title, see 42 U.S.C. 6901 note

Land Grant Act (Northern Pacific)
July 2, 1864, ch. 217, 13 Stat. 365

Land Grant Adjustment Act
See Adjustment Act (Railroad Land Grants)

Land Remote Sensing Policy Act of 1992
Pub. L. 102–555, Oct. 28, 1992, 106 Stat. 4163 (15 U.S.C. 5601 et seq.)
Short title, see 15 U.S.C. 5601 note

Land Remote-Sensing Commercialization Act Amendments of 1987
Pub. L. 100–147, title III, Oct. 30, 1987, 101 Stat. 876

Land Remote-Sensing Commercialization Act of 1984
Pub. L. 98–365, July 17, 1984, 98 Stat. 451 (15 U.S.C. 4201 et seq.)
Short title, see 15 U.S.C. 4201 note

Landrum-Griffin Act
See Labor-Management Reporting and Disclosure Act of 1959

Lanham Act
Also known as the Trademark Act of 1946
July 5, 1946, ch. 540, 60 Stat. 427 (15 U.S.C. 1051 et seq.)
Short title, see 15 U.S.C. 1051 note

Lanham Patent Act
Aug. 5, 1939, ch. 451, 53 Stat. 1212

Lanham Public War Housing Act
Oct. 14, 1940, ch. 862, 54 Stat. 1125 (42 U.S.C. 1521 et seq.)
Short title, see 42 U.S.C. 1501 note

Latin American Development Act
Pub. L. 86–735, Sept. 8, 1960, 74 Stat. 869 (22 U.S.C. 1942 et seq.)
Short title, see 22 U.S.C. 1942 note

Launch Services Purchase Act of 1990
Pub. L. 101–611, title II, Nov. 16, 1990, 104 Stat. 3205 (42 U.S.C. 2465b et seq.)
Short title, see 42 U.S.C. 2451 note

Launching Our Communities' Access to Local Television Act of 2000
Pub. L. 106–553, §1(a)(2) [title X], Dec. 21, 2000, 114 Stat. 2762, 2762A–128 (47 U.S.C. 1101 et seq.)
Short title, see 47 U.S.C. 1101 note

Law Enforcement Assistance Act of 1965
Pub. L. 89–197, Sept. 22, 1965, 79 Stat. 828 (18 U.S.C. prec. 201 note)

Law Enforcement Availability Pay Act of 1994
Pub. L. 103–329, title VI, §633, Sept. 30, 1994, 108 Stat. 2425
Short title, see 5 U.S.C. 5541 note

Law Enforcement Pay Equity Act of 2000
Pub. L. 106–554, §1(a)(4) [div. B, title IX], Dec. 21, 2000, 114 Stat. 2763, 2763A–303
Short title, see 5 U.S.C. 5301 note

Law Enforcement Scholarships and Recruitment Act
Pub. L. 103–322, title XX, subtitle B (§200201 et seq.), Sept. 13, 1994, 108 Stat. 2057 (42 U.S.C. 14111 et seq.)
Short title, see 42 U.S.C. 13701 note

Law Enforcement Technology Advertisement Clarification Act of 1997
Pub. L. 105–112, Nov. 21, 1997, 111 Stat. 2273
Short title, see 18 U.S.C. 2510 note

Law-Related Education Act of 1978
Pub. L. 89–10, title III, part G (§346 et seq.), as added Pub. L. 95–561, title III, §301(a), Nov. 1, 1978, 92 Stat. 2216 (20 U.S.C. 3001 et seq.)

Lea Act (Radio-Coercive Practices)
Apr. 16, 1946, ch. 138, 60 Stat. 89 (Title 47, §506)

Lea-Brown Act (Natural Gas)
See Natural Gas Act

Lea-Wagner Act
See Investment Advisers Act of 1940; Investment Company Act of 1940

Lea-Wheeler Transportation Act
See Transportation Act of 1940

Lead Contamination Control Act of 1988
Pub. L. 100–572, Oct. 31, 1988, 102 Stat. 2884 (42 U.S.C. 300j–21 et seq.)
Short title, see 42 U.S.C. 201 note

Lead-Based Paint Exposure Reduction Act
Pub. L. 102–550, title X, subtitle B (§1021), Oct. 28, 1992, 106 Stat. 3912 (15 U.S.C. 2681 et seq.)
Short title, see 15 U.S.C. 2601 note

Lead-Based Paint Poisoning Prevention Act
Pub. L. 91–695, Jan. 13, 1971, 84 Stat. 2078 (42 U.S.C. 4801 et seq.)
Short title, see 42 U.S.C. 4801 note

Lead-Zinc Small Producers Stabilization Act of October 3, 1961
Pub. L. 87–347, Oct. 3, 1961, 75 Stat. 766 (30 U.S.C. 681 et seq.)

Leadership in Educational Administration Development Act of 1984
Pub. L. 98–558, title IX, Oct. 30, 1984, 98 Stat. 2902 (20 U.S.C. 4201 et seq.)

Lease-Lend Act
See Act to Promote the Defense of the United States

Leasehold Management Bankruptcy Amendments Act of 1983
Pub. L. 98–353, title III, subtitle C (§361 et seq.), July 10, 1984, 98 Stat. 361
Short title, see 11 U.S.C. 101 note

Leave Act of the United States
Mar. 14, 1936, ch. 140, 49 Stat. 1161

Leavitt Act (Indians)
July 1, 1932, ch. 369, 47 Stat. 564 (25 U.S.C. 386a)

Lebanon Emergency Assistance Act of 1983
Pub. L. 98–43, June 27, 1983, 97 Stat. 214

Lechuguilla Cave Protection Act of 1993
Pub. L. 103–169, Dec. 2, 1993, 107 Stat. 1983 (16 U.S.C. 4301 note)

Lee Metcalf Wilderness and Management Act of 1983
Pub. L. 98–140, Oct. 31, 1983, 97 Stat. 901 (16 U.S.C. 1132 note)

Lee-Caraway-Gearhart Act (Cotton and Tobacco)
See Agricultural Adjustment Act of 1938

Legal Certainty for Bank Products Act of 2000
Pub. L. 106–554, §1(a)(5) [title IV], Dec. 21, 2000, 114 Stat. 2763, 2763A–457 (7 U.S.C. 27 et seq.)
Short title, see 7 U.S.C. 1 note

Legal Immigration Family Equity Act
Also known as the LIFE Act
Pub. L. 106–553, §1(a)(2) [title XI], Dec. 21, 2000, 114 Stat. 2762, 2762A–142
Short title, see 8 U.S.C. 1101 note

Legal Services Corporation Act
Pub. L. 88–452, title X, as added Pub. L. 93–355, §2, July 25, 1974, 88 Stat. 378 (42 U.S.C. 2996 et seq.)
Short title, see 42 U.S.C. 2701 note

Legal Services Corporation Act Amendments of 1977
Pub. L. 95–222, Dec. 28, 1977, 91 Stat. 1619
Short title, see 42 U.S.C. 2701 note

Legal Services Corporation Act of 1974
Pub. L. 93–355, July 25, 1974, 88 Stat. 378 (42 U.S.C. 2996 et seq.)
Short title, see 42 U.S.C. 2701 note

Legislative Appropriation Act, 1954
Aug. 1, 1953, ch. 304, title I, 67 Stat. 318

Legislative Appropriation Act, 1955
July 2, 1954, ch. 455, title I, 68 Stat. 396

Legislative Appropriation Act, 1956
Aug. 5, 1955, ch. 568, 69 Stat. 499

Legislative Branch Appropriation Act, 1936
July 8, 1935, ch. 374, 49 Stat. 459

Legislative Branch Appropriation Act, 1938
May 18, 1937, ch. 223, 50 Stat. 169

Legislative Branch Appropriation Act, 1939
May 17, 1938, ch. 236, 52 Stat. 381

Legislative Branch Appropriation Act, 1940
June 16, 1939, ch. 208, 53 Stat. 822

Legislative Branch Appropriation Act, 1941
June 18, 1940, ch. 396, 54 Stat. 462

Legislative Branch Appropriation Act, 1942
July 1, 1941, ch. 268, 55 Stat. 446

Legislative Branch Appropriation Act, 1943
June 8, 1942, ch. 396, 56 Stat. 330

Legislative Branch Appropriation Act, 1944
June 28, 1943, ch. 173, title I, 57 Stat. 220

Legislative Branch Appropriation Act, 1945
June 26, 1944, ch. 277, title I, 58 Stat. 334

Legislative Branch Appropriation Act, 1946
June 13, 1945, ch. 189, 59 Stat. 238

Legislative Branch Appropriation Act, 1947
July 1, 1946, ch. 530, 60 Stat. 386

Legislative Branch Appropriation Act, 1948
July 17, 1947, ch. 262, 61 Stat. 361

Legislative Branch Appropriation Act, 1949
June 14, 1948, ch. 467, 62 Stat. 423

Legislative Branch Appropriation Act, 1950
June 22, 1949, ch. 235, 63 Stat. 216

Legislative Branch Appropriation Act, 1951
Sept. 6, 1950, ch. 896, Ch. II, 64 Stat. 595

Legislative Branch Appropriation Act, 1952
Oct. 11, 1951, ch. 485, 65 Stat. 387

Legislative Branch Appropriation Act, 1953
July 9, 1952, ch. 598, 66 Stat. 464

Legislative Branch Appropriation Act, 1954
See Legislative Appropriation Act, 1954

Legislative Branch Appropriation Act, 1955
See Legislative Appropriation Act, 1955

Legislative Branch Appropriation Act, 1956
See Legislative Appropriation Act, 1956

Legislative Branch Appropriation Act, 1957
June 27, 1956, ch. 453, 70 Stat. 356

Legislative Branch Appropriation Act, 1958
Pub. L. 85–75, July 1, 1957, 71 Stat. 244

Legislative Branch Appropriation Act, 1959
Pub. L. 85–570, July 31, 1958, 72 Stat. 439

Legislative Branch Appropriation Act, 1960
Pub. L. 86–176, Aug. 21, 1959, 73 Stat. 398

Legislative Branch Appropriation Act, 1961
Pub. L. 86–628, July 12, 1960, 74 Stat. 446

Legislative Branch Appropriation Act, 1962
Pub. L. 87–130, Aug. 10, 1961, 75 Stat. 320

Legislative Branch Appropriation Act, 1963
Pub. L. 87–730, Oct. 2, 1962, 76 Stat. 680

Legislative Branch Appropriation Act, 1964
Pub. L. 88–248, Dec. 30, 1963, 77 Stat. 803

Legislative Branch Appropriation Act, 1965
Pub. L. 88–454, Aug. 20, 1964, 78 Stat. 535

Legislative Branch Appropriation Act, 1966
Pub. L. 89–90, July 27, 1965, 79 Stat. 265

Legislative Branch Appropriation Act, 1967
Pub. L. 89–545, Aug. 27, 1966, 80 Stat. 354

Legislative Branch Appropriation Act, 1968
Pub. L. 90–57, July 28, 1967, 81 Stat. 127

Legislative Branch Appropriation Act, 1969
Pub. L. 90–417, July 23, 1968, 82 Stat. 398

Legislative Branch Appropriation Act, 1970
Pub. L. 91–145, Dec. 12, 1969, 83 Stat. 338

Legislative Branch Appropriation Act, 1971
Pub. L. 91–382, Aug. 18, 1970, 84 Stat. 807

Legislative Branch Appropriation Act, 1972
Pub. L. 92–51, July 9, 1971, 85 Stat. 125

Legislative Branch Appropriation Act, 1973
Pub. L. 92–342, July 10, 1972, 86 Stat. 432

Legislative Branch Appropriation Act, 1974
Pub. L. 93–145, Nov. 1, 1973, 87 Stat. 527

Legislative Branch Appropriation Act, 1975
Pub. L. 93–371, Aug. 13, 1974, 88 Stat. 424

Legislative Branch Appropriation Act, 1976
Pub. L. 94–59, July 25, 1975, 89 Stat. 269

Legislative Branch Appropriation Act, 1977
Pub. L. 94–440, Oct. 1, 1976, 90 Stat. 1439

Legislative Branch Appropriation Act, 1978
Pub. L. 95–94, Aug. 5, 1977, 91 Stat. 653

Legislative Branch Appropriation Act, 1979
Pub. L. 95–391, Sept. 30, 1978, 92 Stat. 763

Legislative Branch Appropriation Act, 1980
Pub. L. 96–86, §101(c) [H.R. 4390], Oct. 12, 1979, 93 Stat. 657; Pub. L. 100–202, §106, Dec. 22, 1987, 101 Stat. 1329–433

Legislative Branch Appropriation Act, 1981
Pub. L. 96–536, §101(c) [H.R. 7593], Dec. 16, 1980, 94 Stat. 3167

Legislative Branch Appropriation Act, 1982
Pub. L. 97–51, §101(c) [H.R. 4120], Oct. 1, 1981, 95 Stat. 959

Legislative Branch Appropriation Act, 1983
Pub. L. 97–276, §101(e) [S. 2939], Oct. 2, 1982, 96 Stat. 1189

Legislative Branch Appropriation Act, 1984
Pub. L. 98–51, July 14, 1983, 97 Stat. 263

Legislative Branch Appropriations Act, 1985
Pub. L. 98–367, July 17, 1984, 98 Stat. 472

Legislative Branch Appropriations Act, 1986
Pub. L. 99–151, Nov. 13, 1985, 99 Stat. 792

Legislative Branch Appropriations Act, 1987
Pub. L. 99–500, §101(j) [H.R. 5203], Oct. 18, 1986, 100 Stat. 1783–287, and Pub. L. 99–591, §101(j) [H.R. 5203], Oct. 30, 1986, 100 Stat. 3341–287

Legislative Branch Appropriations Act, 1988
Pub. L. 100–202, §101(i), Dec. 22, 1987, 101 Stat. 1329–290

Legislative Branch Appropriations Act, 1989
Pub. L. 100–458, Oct. 1, 1988, 102 Stat. 2158

Legislative Branch Appropriations Act, 1990
Pub. L. 101–163, Nov. 21, 1989, 103 Stat. 1041

Legislative Branch Appropriations Act, 1991
Pub. L. 101–520, Nov. 5, 1990, 104 Stat. 2254

Legislative Branch Appropriations Act, 1992
Pub. L. 102–90, Aug. 14, 1991, 105 Stat. 447

Legislative Branch Appropriations Act, 1993
Pub. L. 102–392, Oct. 6, 1992, 106 Stat. 1703

Legislative Branch Appropriations Act, 1994
Pub. L. 103–69, Aug. 11, 1993, 107 Stat. 692

Legislative Branch Appropriations Act, 1995
Pub. L. 103–283, July 22, 1994, 108 Stat. 1423

Legislative Branch Appropriations Act, 1996
Pub. L. 104–53, Nov. 19, 1995, 109 Stat. 514

Legislative Branch Appropriations Act, 1997
Pub. L. 104–197, Sept. 16, 1996, 110 Stat. 2394

Legislative Branch Appropriations Act, 1998
Pub. L. 105–55, Oct. 7, 1997, 111 Stat. 1177

Legislative Branch Appropriations Act, 1999
Pub. L. 105–275, Oct. 21, 1998, 112 Stat. 2430

Legislative Branch Appropriations Act, 2000
Pub. L. 106–57, Sept. 29, 1999, 113 Stat. 408

Legislative Branch Appropriations Act, 2001
Pub. L. 106–554, §1(a)(2) [H.R. 5657], Dec. 21, 2000, 114 Stat. 2763, 2763A–93

Legislative Branch Supplemental Appropriations Act, 1999
Pub. L. 106–57, title IV, Sept. 29, 1999, 113 Stat. 428

Legislative Pay Act of 1929
June 20, 1929, ch. 33, 46 Stat. 32

Legislative Reorganization Act of 1946
Aug. 2, 1946, ch. 753, 60 Stat. 812
Short title, see 2 U.S.C. 72a note

Legislative Reorganization Act of 1970
Pub. L. 91–510, Oct. 26, 1970, 84 Stat. 1140
Short title, see 2 U.S.C. 72a note

Legislative and Judiciary Appropriation Act, 1944
June 28, 1943, ch. 173, 57 Stat. 220

Legislative and Judiciary Appropriation Act, 1945
June 26, 1944, ch. 277, 58 Stat. 334

Legislative-Judiciary Appropriation Act, 1954
Aug. 1, 1953, ch. 304, 67 Stat. 318

Legislative-Judiciary Appropriation Act, 1955
July 2, 1954, ch. 455, 68 Stat. 396

Leif Ericson Millennium Commemorative Coin Act
Pub. L. 106–126, title I, Dec. 6, 1999, 113 Stat. 1643 (31 U.S.C. 5112 note)

Lemon Law
See Magnuson-Moss Warranty—Federal Trade Commission Improvement Act

Lend-Lease Act
See Act to Promote the Defense of the United States

Leprosy Act
Mar. 3, 1905, ch. 1443, 33 Stat. 1009

Lesinski Pension Increase Act
June 6, 1940, ch. 246, 54 Stat. 237

Lever Act (Food and Fuel Control)
Aug. 10, 1917, ch. 53, 40 Stat. 276

Lewis and Clark Expedition Bicentennial Commemorative Coin Act
Pub. L. 106–126, title III, Dec. 6, 1999, 113 Stat. 1647 (31 U.S.C. 5112 note)

Lewis and Clark Rural Water System Act of 2000
Pub. L. 106–246, div. B, title IV, July 13, 2000, 114 Stat. 579

Liability Risk Retention Act of 1986
Pub. L. 97–45, Sept. 25, 1981, 95 Stat. 949 (15 U.S.C. 3901 et seq.)
Short title, see 15 U.S.C. 3901 note

Liberty Coin Act
Pub. L. 99–61, title II, July 9, 1985, 99 Stat. 115
Short title, see 31 U.S.C. 5112 note

Liberty Memorial Act of 1993
Pub. L. 103–206, title IX, Dec. 20, 1993, 107 Stat. 2454

Library of Congress Bicentennial Commemorative Coin Act of 1998
Pub. L. 105–268, Oct. 19, 1998, 112 Stat. 2378 (31 U.S.C. 5112 note)

Library of Congress Fiscal Operations Improvement Act of 2000
Pub. L. 106–481, Nov. 9, 2000, 114 Stat. 2187
Short title, see 2 U.S.C. 182a note

Library of Congress Police Act
Aug. 4, 1950, ch. 561, 64 Stat. 411

Library of Congress Trust Fund Board Act
Mar. 3, 1925, ch. 423, 43 Stat. 1107 (2 U.S.C. 154 et seq.)
Short title, see 2 U.S.C. 154 note

Library Services Act
Renamed Library Services and Construction Act

Library Services and Construction Act
June 19, 1956, ch. 407, 70 Stat. 293 (20 U.S.C. 351 et seq.)
Short title, see 20 U.S.C. 351 note

Library Services and Construction Act Amendments of 1966
Pub. L. 89–511, July 19, 1966, 80 Stat. 313

Library Services and Construction Act Amendments of 1977
Pub. L. 95–123, Oct. 7, 1977, 91 Stat. 1095

Library Services and Construction Act Amendments of 1984
Pub. L. 98–480, title I, Oct. 17, 1984, 98 Stat. 2236

Library Services and Construction Act Amendments of 1990
Pub. L. 101–254, Mar. 15, 1990, 104 Stat. 101

Library Services and Construction Amendments of 1970
Pub. L. 91–600, Dec. 30, 1970, 84 Stat. 1660

Library Services and Technology Act
Pub. L. 94–462, title II, subtitle B (§211 et seq.), as added Pub. L. 104–208, div. A, title I, §101(e) [title VII, §702], Sept. 30, 1996, 110 Stat. 3009–233, 3009–295 (20 U.S.C. 9121 et seq.)
Short title, see 20 U.S.C. 9101 note

Liens on Vessels Act
June 23, 1910, ch. 373, 36 Stat. 604.

Lieu Lands Act (Forest Reservations)
June 4, 1897, ch. 2, 30 Stat. 36

Lieu Lands Act (Indian Reservations)
Apr. 21, 1904, ch. 1402, 33 Stat. 211

Lieu Lands Act (Northern Pacific Railroad)
July 1, 1898, ch. 546, 30 Stat. 620

Lieutenant General Act
Aug. 5, 1939, ch. 454, 53 Stat. 1214

LIFE Act
Also known as the Legal Immigration Family Equity Act
Pub. L. 106–553, §1(a)(2) [title XI], Dec. 21, 2000, 114 Stat. 2762, 2762A–142
Short title, see 8 U.S.C. 1101 note

LIFE Act Amendments of 2000
Pub. L. 106–554, §1(a)(4) [div. B, title XV], Dec. 21, 2000, 114 Stat. 2763, 2763A–324
Short title, see 8 U.S.C. 1101 note

Life Insurance Act
June 19, 1934, ch. 672, 48 Stat. 1125

Life Insurance Company Income Tax Act of 1959
Pub. L. 86–69, June 25, 1959, 73 Stat. 112
Short title, see 26 U.S.C. 1 note

Life Insurance Company Tax Act for 1955
Mar. 13, 1956, ch. 83, 70 Stat. 36
Short title, see 26 U.S.C. 1 note

Life-Saving Service Act
Mar. 26, 1908, ch. 99, 35 Stat. 46

Lime Research, Promotion, and Consumer Information Act of 1990
Pub. L. 101–624, title XIX, subtitle D (§1951 et seq.), Nov. 28, 1990, 104 Stat. 3870 (7 U.S.C. 6201 et seq.)
Short title, see 7 U.S.C. 6201 note

Lime Research, Promotion, and Consumer Information Improvement Act
Pub. L. 103–194, Dec. 14, 1993, 107 Stat. 2294
Short title, see 7 U.S.C. 6201 note

Limitation of Armament Resolution
See Disarmament Conference Resolution

Limited Partnership Rollup Reform Act of 1993
Pub. L. 103–202, title III, Dec. 17, 1993, 107 Stat. 2359
Short title, see 15 U.S.C. 78a note

Lincoln County Land Act of 2000
Pub. L. 106–298, Oct. 13, 2000, 114 Stat. 1046

Lincoln County, Montana, Lands Transfer Act of 1994
Pub. L. 103–398, Oct. 22, 1994, 108 Stat. 4162

Lincoln Highway Study Act of 2000
Pub. L. 106–563, Dec. 23, 2000, 114 Stat. 2809

Lindbergh Kidnapping Act
See Kidnapping Act

Line Item Veto Act
Pub. L. 104–130, Apr. 9, 1996, 110 Stat. 1200
Short title, see 2 U.S.C. 681 note

Line Item Veto Act of 1996
Pub. L. 93–344, title X, Part C (§1021 et seq.), as added Pub. L. 104–130, §2, Apr. 9, 1996, 110 Stat. 1200 (2 U.S.C. 691 et seq.)
Short title, see 2 U.S.C. 621 note

Linthicum-Moses Act
See Foreign Service Act

Liquor Administration Act
See Federal Alcohol Administration Act

Liquor Enforcement Act of 1936
June 25, 1936, ch. 815, 49 Stat. 1928 (27 U.S.C. 221 et seq.)

Liquor Law Repeal and Enforcement Act
Aug. 27, 1935, ch. 740, 49 Stat. 872 (27 U.S.C. 122)

Liquor Tax Administration Act
June 26, 1936, ch. 830, 49 Stat. 1939

Liquor Taxing Act of 1934
Jan. 11, 1934, ch. 1, 48 Stat. 313

Literacy Involves Families Together Act
Pub. L. 106–554, §1(a)(4) [div. B, title XVI], Dec. 21, 2000, 114 Stat. 2763, 2763A–328
Short title, see 20 U.S.C. 6301 note

Little Cigar Act of 1973
Pub. L. 93–109, Sept. 21, 1973, 87 Stat. 352
Short title, see 15 U.S.C. 1331 note

Little River Canyon National Preserve Act of 1992
Pub. L. 102–427, Oct. 21, 1992, 106 Stat. 2179 (16 U.S.C. 698q et seq.)
Short title, see 16 U.S.C. 698q note

Little Traverse Bay Bands of Odawa Indians and the Little River Band of Ottawa Indians Act
Pub. L. 103–324, Sept. 21, 1994, 108 Stat. 2156 (25 U.S.C. 1300k et seq.)
Short title, see 25 U.S.C. 1300k note

Livable Cities Act of 1978
Pub. L. 95–557, title VIII, Oct. 31, 1978, 92 Stat. 2122 (42 U.S.C. 8141 et seq.)
Short title, see 42 U.S.C. 8101 note

Live-Stock Bankruptcy Act
May 15, 1935, ch. 114, 49 Stat. 246

Livestock Fraud Protection Act
Pub. L. 98–473, title II, ch. XI, part I (§1110 et seq.), Oct. 12, 1984, 98 Stat. 2148
Short title, see 18 U.S.C. 641 note

Livestock Mandatory Reporting Act of 1999
Pub. L. 106–78, title IX, Oct. 22, 1999, 113 Stat. 1188 (7 U.S.C. 1635 note)

Live Stock Transportation Act
Also known as the Cruelty to Animals Act, the Food and Rest Law, and the Twenty-Eight Hour Law
June 29, 1906, ch. 3594, 34 Stat. 607
Short title, see 45 U.S.C. 71 note

Lloyd-La Follette Act
Aug. 24, 1912, ch. 389, §6, 37 Stat. 555

Load Line Act
Mar. 2, 1929, ch. 508, 45 Stat. 1492

Lobbying Disclosure Act of 1995
Pub. L. 104–65, Dec. 19, 1995, 109 Stat. 691 (2 U.S.C. 1601 et seq.)
Short title, see 2 U.S.C. 1601 note

Lobbying Disclosure Technical Amendments Act of 1998
Pub. L. 105–166, Apr. 6, 1998, 112 Stat. 38
Short title, see 2 U.S.C. 1601 note

Local Government Antitrust Act of 1984
Pub. L. 98–544, Oct. 24, 1984, 98 Stat. 2750 (15 U.S.C. 34 et seq.)
Short title, see 15 U.S.C. 1 note

Local Government Fiscal Assistance Amendments of 1983
Pub. L. 98–185, Nov. 30, 1983, 97 Stat. 1309

Local Public Works Capital Development and Investment Act of 1976
Pub. L. 94–369, title I, July 22, 1976, 90 Stat. 999 (42 U.S.C. 6701 et seq.)
Short title, see 42 U.S.C. 6701 note

Local Rail Service Assistance Act of 1978
Pub. L. 95–607, title I, Nov. 8, 1978, 92 Stat. 3059

Local Rail Service Reauthorizing Act
Pub. L. 101–213, Dec. 11, 1989, 103 Stat. 1843

Locomotive Inspection Act
Feb. 17, 1911, ch. 103, 36 Stat. 913

Lodge Act (Consular Reorganization)
Apr. 5, 1906, ch. 1366, 34 Stat. 99

Lodge Act (Philippine Organic Act)
See Philippine Organic Act of 1902

Logan Act (Foreign Relations)
Jan. 30, 1799, ch. 1, 1 Stat. 613

Long Island Sound Improvement Act of 1990
Pub. L. 101–596, title II, Nov. 16, 1990, 104 Stat. 3004

Long Island Sound Improvement Act of 1990—Continued
Short title, see 33 U.S.C. 1251 note

Long Island Sound Restoration Act
Pub. L. 106–457, title IV, Nov. 7, 2000, 114 Stat. 1973
Short title, see 33 U.S.C. 1251 note

Long-Term Care Security Act
Pub. L. 106–265, title I, Sept. 19, 2000, 114 Stat. 762 (5 U.S.C. 9001 et seq.)
Short title, see 5 U.S.C. 9001 note

Longevity Pay Act
Mar. 3, 1883, ch. 97, 22 Stat. 472, 473

Longshore and Harbor Workers' Compensation Act
Mar. 4, 1927, ch. 509, 44 Stat. 1424 (33 U.S.C. 901 et seq.)
Short title, see 33 U.S.C. 901

Longshore and Harbor Workers' Compensation Act Amendments of 1984
Pub. L. 98–426, Sept. 28, 1984, 98 Stat. 1639
Short title, see 33 U.S.C. 901 note

Longshoremen's and Harbor Workers' Compensation Act Amendments of 1972
Pub. L. 92–576, Oct. 27, 1972, 86 Stat. 1251
Short title, see 33 U.S.C. 901 note

Lorton Technical Corrections Act of 1998
Pub. L. 105–277, div. C, title I, §141, Oct. 21, 1998, 112 Stat. 2681–600

Los Padres Condor Range and River Protection Act
Pub. L. 102–301, June 19, 1992, 106 Stat. 242

Lost Bond Act
Apr. 9, 1934, ch. 105, 48 Stat. 571

Lost Property Act (Military Service)
Mar. 3, 1885, ch. 335, 23 Stat. 350

Low-Income Home Energy Assistance Act of 1981
Pub. L. 97–35, title XXVI, Aug. 13, 1981, 95 Stat. 893 (42 U.S.C. 8621 et seq.)
Short title, see 42 U.S.C. 8621 note

Low-Income Home Energy Assistance Amendments of 1994
Pub. L. 103–252, title III, May 18, 1994, 108 Stat. 657
Short title, see 42 U.S.C. 8621 note

Low-Income Home Energy Assistance Amendments of 1998
Pub. L. 105–285, title III, Oct. 27, 1998, 112 Stat. 2756
Short title, see 42 U.S.C. 8621 note

Low-Income Housing Preservation and Resident Homeownership Act of 1990
Pub. L. 100–242, title II, Feb. 5, 1988, 101 Stat. 1877 (12 U.S.C. 4101 et seq.)
Short title, see 12 U.S.C. 4101 note

Low-Level Radioactive Waste Policy Act
Pub. L. 96–573, as added Pub. L. 99–240, title I, §102, Jan. 15, 1986, 99 Stat. 1842 (42 U.S.C. 2021b et seq.)
Short title, see 42 U.S.C. 2021b note

Low-Level Radioactive Waste Policy Amendments Act of 1985
Pub. L. 99–240, title I, Jan. 15, 1986, 99 Stat. 1842 (42 U.S.C. 2021b et seq.)
Short title, see 42 U.S.C. 2021b note

Low-Rent Housing Act
See United States Housing Act of 1937

Lowden Act (Purchase of Embassy Buildings, etc.)
Feb. 17, 1911, ch. 105, 36 Stat. 917 (22 U.S.C. 133)

Lower Brule Sioux Tribe Infrastructure Development Trust Fund Act
Pub. L. 105–132, Dec. 2, 1997, 111 Stat. 2563

Lower Colorado River Basin Project Act
See Colorado River Basin Project Act

Lower Colorado Water Supply Act
Pub. L. 99–655, Nov. 14, 1986, 100 Stat. 3665

Lower Delaware Wild and Scenic Rivers Act
Pub. L. 106–418, Nov. 1, 2000, 114 Stat. 1817
Short title, see 16 U.S.C. 1271 note

Lower Mississippi Delta Development Act
Pub. L. 100–460, title II [H.R. 5378], Oct. 1, 1988, 102 Stat. 2246 (42 U.S.C. 3121 note)

Lower Rio Grande Valley Water Resources Conservation and Improvement Act of 2000
Pub. L. 106–576, Dec. 28, 2000, 114 Stat. 3065

Lower Saint Croix River Act of 1972
Pub. L. 92–560, Oct. 25, 1972, 86 Stat. 1174
Short title, see 16 U.S.C. 1271 note

Lucas Act
Aug. 7, 1946, ch. 864, 60 Stat. 902 (41 U.S.C. 106 note)

Luce Patent Act
Aug. 9, 1939, ch. 619, 53 Stat. 1293

Lupus Research and Care Amendments of 2000
Pub. L. 106–505, title V, Nov. 13, 2000, 114 Stat. 2342
Short title, see 42 U.S.C. 201 note

Macon's Law
May 1, 1810, ch. 39, 2 Stat. 605

Magistrates' Retirement Parity Act of 1987
Pub. L. 100–53, June 18, 1987, 101 Stat. 367
Short title, see 5 U.S.C. 8331 note

Magnetic Fusion Energy Engineering Act of 1980
Pub. L. 96–386, Oct. 7, 1980, 94 Stat. 1539 (42 U.S.C. 9301 et seq.)
Short title, see 42 U.S.C. 9301 note

Magnuson Fishery Conservation and Management Act
Renamed Magnuson-Stevens Fishery Conservation and Management Act

Magnuson-Moss Warranty—Federal Trade Commission Improvement Act
Pub. L. 93–637, Jan. 4, 1975, 88 Stat. 2183 (15 U.S.C. 2301 et seq.)
Short title, see 15 U.S.C. 2301 note

Magnuson-Stevens Fishery Conservation and Management Act
Pub. L. 94–265, Apr. 13, 1976, 90 Stat. 331 (16 U.S.C. 1801 et seq.)
Short title, see 16 U.S.C. 1801 note

Mahaffie Act
Apr. 9, 1948, ch. 180, 62 Stat. 162

Mail Fraud Act
Mar. 4, 1909, ch. 321, §§215, 216, 35 Stat. 1130, 1131 (See 18 U.S.C. 1341, 1342)

Mail Order Consumer Protection Amendments of 1983
Pub. L. 98–186, Nov. 30, 1983, 97 Stat. 1315
Short title, see 39 U.S.C. 3001 note

Mail Order Drug Paraphernalia Control Act
Pub. L. 99–570, title I, subtitle O (§1821 et seq.), Oct. 27, 1986, 100 Stat. 3207–51
Short title, see 21 U.S.C. 801 note

Maine Acadian Culture Preservation Act
Pub. L. 101–543, Nov. 8, 1990, 104 Stat. 2389 (16 U.S.C. 461 note)

Maine Indian Claims Settlement Act of 1980
Pub. L. 96–420, Oct. 10, 1980, 94 Stat. 1785 (25 U.S.C. 1721 et seq.)
Short title, see 25 U.S.C. 1721 note

Maine Wilderness Act of 1990
Pub. L. 101–401, Sept. 28, 1990, 104 Stat. 863

Major Crimes Act (Indians)
See Indian Major Crimes Act

Major Fraud Act Amendments of 1989
Pub. L. 101–123, Oct. 23, 1989, 103 Stat. 759
Short title, see 18 U.S.C. 1001 note

Major Fraud Act of 1988
Pub. L. 100–700, Nov. 19, 1988, 102 Stat. 4631
Short title, see 18 U.S.C. 1001 note

Malcolm Baldrige National Quality Improvement Act of 1987
Pub. L. 100–107, Aug. 20, 1987, 101 Stat. 724
Short title, see 15 U.S.C. 3701 note

Mammography Quality Standards Act of 1992
Pub. L. 102–539, Oct. 27, 1992, 106 Stat. 3547
Short title, see 42 U.S.C. 201 note

Mammography Quality Standards Reauthorization Act of 1998
Pub. L. 105–248, Oct. 9, 1998, 112 Stat. 1864
Short title, see 42 U.S.C. 201 note

Man-Power Act
Aug. 31, 1918, ch. 166, 40 Stat. 955

Management Interlocks Revision Act of 1988
Pub. L. 100–650, Nov. 10, 1988, 102 Stat. 3819
Short title, see 12 U.S.C. 3201 note

Manassas National Battlefield Park Amendments of 1980
Pub. L. 96–442, Oct. 13, 1980, 94 Stat. 1885
Short title, see 16 U.S.C. 429b note

Manassas National Battlefield Park Amendments of 1988
Pub. L. 100–647, title X, Nov. 10, 1988, 102 Stat. 3810
Short title, see 16 U.S.C. 429b note

Mancos Project Private Power Development Authorization Act of 1994
Pub. L. 103–434, title XI, Oct. 31, 1994, 108 Stat. 4549

Mandamus Act
Pub. L. 87–748, §1(a), Oct. 5, 1962, 76 Stat. 744 (28 U.S.C. 1361)

Mandatory Detention for Offenders Convicted of Serious Crimes Act
Pub. L. 101–647, title IX, Nov. 29, 1990, 104 Stat. 4826
Short title, see 18 U.S.C. 3141 note

Mandatory Victims Restitution Act of 1996
Pub. L. 104–132, title II, subtitle A (§201 et seq.), Apr. 24, 1996, 110 Stat. 1227
Short title, see 18 U.S.C. 3551 note

Manderson Act (Printing and Binding)
Jan. 12, 1895, ch. 23, 28 Stat. 601

Mann Act
See White-slave Traffic Act

Mann-Elkins Act
June 18, 1910, ch. 309, 36 Stat. 539

Manpower Act of 1965
Pub. L. 89–15, Apr. 26, 1965, 79 Stat. 75

Manpower Development and Training Act of 1962
Pub. L. 87–415, Mar. 15, 1962, 76 Stat. 23 (42 U.S.C. 2571 et seq.)

Manpower Development and Training Amendments of 1966
Pub. L. 89–792, Nov. 7, 1966, 80 Stat. 1434

Manufactured Housing Improvement Act of 2000
Pub. L. 106–569, title VI, Dec. 27, 2000, 114 Stat. 2997
Short title, see 42 U.S.C. 5401 note

Marihuana and Health Reporting Act
Pub. L. 91–296, title V, June 30, 1970, 84 Stat. 352 (42 U.S.C. 242 note)

Marihuana Tax Act of 1937
Aug. 2, 1937, ch. 553, 50 Stat. 551

Marine Corps Personnel Act
May 29, 1934, ch. 367, 48 Stat. 811

Marine Insurance Act (District of Columbia)
Mar. 4, 1922, ch. 93, 42 Stat. 401

Marine Mammal Health and Stranding Response Act
Pub. L. 102–587, title III, Nov. 4, 1992, 106 Stat. 5059
Short title, see 16 U.S.C. 1361 note

Marine Mammal Protection Act Amendments of 1988
Pub. L. 100–711, Nov. 23, 1988, 102 Stat. 4755
Short title, see 16 U.S.C. 1361 note

Marine Mammal Protection Act Amendments of 1994
Pub. L. 103–238, Apr. 30, 1994, 108 Stat. 532
Short title, see 16 U.S.C. 1361 note

Marine Mammal Protection Act of 1972
Pub. L. 92–522, Oct. 21, 1972, 86 Stat. 1027 (16 U.S.C. 1361 et seq.)
Short title, see 16 U.S.C. 1361 note

Marine Mammal Rescue Assistance Act of 2000
Pub. L. 106–555, title II, Dec. 21, 2000, 114 Stat. 2767
Short title, see 16 U.S.C. 1361 note

Marine Mineral Resources Research Act of 1996
Pub. L. 104–325, Oct. 19, 1996, 110 Stat. 3994 (30 U.S.C. 1901 et seq.)
Short title, see 30 U.S.C. 1901 note

Marine Plastic Pollution Research and Control Act of 1987
Pub. L. 100–220, title II, Dec. 29, 1987, 101 Stat. 1460
Short title, see 33 U.S.C. 1901 note

Marine Protection, Research, and Sanctuaries Act of 1972
Pub. L. 92–532, Oct. 23, 1972, 86 Stat. 1052 (16 U.S.C. 1431 et seq., 1447 et seq.; 33 U.S.C. 1401 et seq., 2801 et seq.)
Short title, see 33 U.S.C. 1401 note

Marine Resources and Engineering Development Act of 1966
Pub. L. 89–454, title I, June 17, 1966, 80 Stat. 203 (33 U.S.C. 1101 et seq.)
Short title, see 33 U.S.C. 1101 note

Marine Sanctuaries Amendments of 1984
Pub. L. 98–498, Oct. 19, 1984, 98 Stat. 2296
Short title, see 16 U.S.C. 1431 note

Marine Science, Technology, and Policy Development Act of 1987
Pub. L. 100–220, title III, Dec. 29, 1987, 101 Stat. 1469
Short title, see 33 U.S.C. 1121 note

Marine War-Risk Insurance Act
See Merchant Marine Act, 1936

Marion National Fish Hatchery and Claude Harris National Aquacultural Research Center Conveyance Act
Pub. L. 105–239, Sept. 23, 1998, 112 Stat. 1564

Maritime Academy Act of 1958
Pub. L. 85–672, Aug. 18, 1958, 72 Stat. 622

Maritime Act of 1981
Pub. L. 97–31, Aug. 6, 1981, 95 Stat. 151
Short title, see 46 App. U.S.C. 1601 note

Maritime Administration Authorization Act for Fiscal Year 2000
Pub. L. 106–65, div. C, title XXXVI, Oct. 5, 1999, 113 Stat. 975
Short title, see 46 App. U.S.C. 1245 note

Maritime Appropriation Authorization Act for Fiscal Year 1978
Pub. L. 95–173, Nov. 12, 1977, 91 Stat. 1359

Maritime Appropriation Authorization Act for Fiscal Year 1979
Pub. L. 95–298, June 26, 1978, 92 Stat. 339

Maritime Appropriation Authorization Act for Fiscal Year 1981
Pub. L. 96–459, Oct. 15, 1980, 94 Stat. 2042

Maritime Appropriation Authorization Act for Fiscal Year 1985
Pub. L. 98–556, Oct. 30, 1984, 98 Stat. 2858

Maritime Appropriation Authorization Act of 1975
Pub. L. 94–127, Nov. 13, 1975, 89 Stat. 680

Maritime Appropriation Authorization Act of Fiscal Year 1977
Pub. L. 94–404, Sept. 10, 1976, 90 Stat. 1224

Maritime Drug Law Enforcement Act
Pub. L. 96–350, Sept. 15, 1980, 94 Stat. 1159 (46 App. U.S.C. 1901 et seq.)
Short title, see 46 App. U.S.C. 1901

Maritime Drug Law Enforcement Prosecution Improvements Act of 1986
Pub. L. 99–570, title III, subtitle C (§3201 et seq.), Oct. 27, 1986, 100 Stat. 3207–95
Short title, see 46 App. U.S.C. 1901 note

Maritime Education and Training Act of 1980
Pub. L. 96–453, Oct. 15, 1980, 94 Stat. 1997
Short title, see 46 App. U.S.C. 1295 note

Maritime Labor Agreements Act of 1980
Pub. L. 96–325, Aug. 8, 1980, 94 Stat. 1021
Short title, see 46 App. U.S.C. 842 note

Maritime Safety Act of 1984
Pub. L. 98–498, title II, subtitle A (§210 et seq.), Oct. 19, 1984, 98 Stat. 2303
Short title, see 46 U.S.C. 3301 note

Maritime Security Act of 1996
Pub. L. 104–239, Oct. 8, 1996, 110 Stat. 3118
Short title, see 46 App. U.S.C. 1245 note

Marjory Stoneman Douglas Wilderness and Ernest F. Coe Visitor Center Designation Act
Pub. L. 105–82, Nov. 13, 1997, 111 Stat. 1540
Short title, see 16 U.S.C. 410r–5 note

Market Reform Act of 1990
Pub. L. 101–432, Oct. 16, 1990, 104 Stat. 963
Short title, see 15 U.S.C. 78a note

Marketing Quotas Act
See Agricultural Adjustment Act of 1938

Married Women's Citizenship Act
Sept. 22, 1922, ch. 411, 42 Stat. 1021

Married Women's Rights Act (District of Columbia)
June 1, 1896, ch. 303, 29 Stat. 193

Marsh-Billings National Historical Park Establishment Act
Renamed the Marsh-Billings-Rockefeller National Historical Park Establishment Act

Marsh-Billings-Rockefeller National Historical Park Establishment Act
Pub. L. 102–350, Aug. 26, 1992, 106 Stat. 934 (16 U.S.C. 410vv et seq.)
Short title, see 16 U.S.C. 410vv note

Marshall Plan
See Foreign Assistance Act of 1948

Martin Luther King, Jr., Federal Holiday Commission Extension Act
Pub. L. 101–30, May 17, 1989, 103 Stat. 60

Mashantucket Pequot Indian Claims Settlement Act
Pub. L. 98–134, Oct. 18, 1983, 97 Stat. 851 (25 U.S.C. 1751 et seq.)
Short title, see 25 U.S.C. 1751 note

Massachusetts Bay Protection Act of 1988
Pub. L. 100–653, title X, Nov. 14, 1988, 102 Stat. 3835
Short title, see 33 U.S.C. 1251 note

Materials Act of 1947
July 31, 1947, ch. 406, 61 Stat. 681 (30 U.S.C. 601 et seq.)
Short title, see 30 U.S.C. 601 note

Maternal and Child Health and Mental Retardation Planning Amendments of 1963
Pub. L. 88–156, Oct. 24, 1963, 77 Stat. 273
Short title, see 42 U.S.C. 1305 note

Maternal and Child Health Services Block Grant Act
Pub. L. 97–35, title XXI, subtitle D (§2191 et seq.), Aug. 13, 1981, 95 Stat. 818
Short title, see 42 U.S.C. 1305 note

Maternity Act
Nov. 23, 1921, ch. 135, 42 Stat. 224

May Army Officer Strength Act
Apr. 13, 1938, ch. 146, 52 Stat. 216

May Defense Expediting Act
June 28, 1940, ch. 440, 54 Stat. 676

Mayfield Act
Mar. 4, 1927, ch. 510, 44 Stat. 1446

McCarran Act
See Internal Security Act of 1950

McCarran Amendment (Department of Justice Appropriation Act, 1953)
July 10, 1952, ch. 651, title II, §208(a)–(c), 66 Stat. 560 (43 U.S.C. 666)

McCarran-Ferguson Act
Mar. 9, 1945, ch. 20, 59 Stat. 33 (15 U.S.C. 1011 et seq.)
Short title, see 15 U.S.C. 1011 note

McCarran-Lea Civil Aeronautics Authority Act
See Civil Aeronautics Act of 1938

McCarran-Walter Act
See Immigration and Nationality Act

McCormick Act (Budget)
See Budget and Accounting Act, 1921

McCreary Act (Chinese Exclusion)
Nov. 3, 1893, ch. 14, 28 Stat. 7

McCumber Act (Pensions)
Feb. 6, 1907, ch. 468, 34 Stat. 879

McCumber Act (Transportation)
Apr. 28, 1904, ch. 1766, 33 Stat. 518

McDuffie-Tydings Act of 1934
See Philippine Independence Act

McFadden Act (Branch Banks)
Feb. 25, 1927, ch. 191, 44 Stat. 1224

McFadden-Pepper Act
See McFadden Act (Branch Banks)

McGillicuddy Act
See Federal Employees' Compensation Act (1916)

McGregor Act
See Lanham Public War Housing Act

McGuire Bill
July 14, 1952, ch. 745, 66 Stat. 631

McIntire-Stennis Act of 1962
Also known as the McIntire-Stennis Cooperative Forestry Act
Pub. L. 87–788, Oct. 10, 1962, 76 Stat. 806 (16 U.S.C. 582a et seq.)
Short title, see 16 U.S.C. 582a note

McIntire-Stennis Cooperative Forestry Act
Also known as the McIntire-Stennis Act of 1962
Pub. L. 87–788, Oct. 10, 1962, 76 Stat. 806 (16 U.S.C. 582a et seq.)
Short title, see 16 U.S.C. 582a note

McKellar-Mead 40-Hour Mail Act
Aug. 14, 1935, ch. 535, 49 Stat. 650

McKeown Act (Corporate Bankruptcy)
June 7, 1934, ch. 424, 48 Stat. 911

McKinley Act (Tariff)
Oct. 1, 1890, ch. 1244, 26 Stat. 567

McKinney Act
See McKinney-Vento Homeless Assistance Act

McKinney-Vento Homeless Assistance Act
Pub. L. 100–77, July 22, 1987, 101 Stat. 482 (42 U.S.C. 11301 et seq.)
Short title, see 42 U.S.C. 11301 note

McMahon Atomic Energy Act
See Atomic Energy Act of 1954

McNamara-O'Hara Service Contract Act
See Service Contract Act of 1965

McNary-Mapes Amendment (Pure Foods)
July 8, 1930, ch. 874, 46 Stat. 1019

McSweeney-McNary Act
See Forest Products Act

Mead Air Mail Extension Act
Jan. 14, 1938, ch. 9, 52 Stat. 6

Mead Two-Cent Postal Rate Act
June 24, 1940, ch. 414, 54 Stat. 505

Meat Import Act of 1979
Pub. L. 88–482, §2, Aug. 22, 1964, 78 Stat. 594 (19 U.S.C. 2253 note)

Meat Inspection Act
See Federal Meat Inspection Act

Medals of Honor Act (Railroads and Motor Vehicles)
Feb. 23, 1905, ch. 744, 33 Stat. 743

Medicaid Act
Aug. 14, 1935, ch. 531, title XIX, as added Pub. L. 89–97, title I, §121(a), July 30, 1965, 79 Stat. 343

Medicaid Voluntary Contribution and Provider-Specific Tax Amendments of 1991
Pub. L. 102–234, Dec. 12, 1991, 105 Stat. 1793
Short title, see 42 U.S.C. 1305 note

Medical Care Expense Recovery Act
See Federal Medical Care Recovery Act

Medical Care Recovery Act
See Federal Medical Care Recovery Act

Medical Device Amendments of 1976
Pub. L. 94–295, May 28, 1976, 90 Stat. 539
Short title, see 21 U.S.C. 301 note

Medical Device Amendments of 1992
Pub. L. 102–300, June 16, 1992, 106 Stat. 238
Short title, see 21 U.S.C. 301 note

Medical Facilities Construction and Modernization Amendments of 1970
Pub. L. 91–296, June 30, 1970, 84 Stat. 336
Short title, see 42 U.S.C. 201 note

Medical Facilities Survey and Construction Act of 1954
July 12, 1954, ch. 471, 68 Stat. 461

Medical Library Assistance Act of 1965
Pub. L. 89–291, Oct. 22, 1965, 79 Stat. 1059
Short title, see 42 U.S.C. 201 note

Medical Library Assistance Extension Act of 1970
Pub. L. 91–212, Mar. 13, 1970, 84 Stat. 63
Short title, see 42 U.S.C. 201 note

Medical Malpractice Immunity Act
Pub. L. 94–464, Oct. 8, 1976, 90 Stat. 1985

Medical Waste Tracking Act of 1988
Pub. L. 100–582, Nov. 1, 1988, 102 Stat. 2950
Short title, see 42 U.S.C. 6901 note

Medicare Act
Aug. 14, 1935, ch. 531, title XVIII, as added Pub. L. 89–97, title I, §102(a), July 30, 1965, 79 Stat. 291

Medicare and Medicaid Amendments of 1980
Pub. L. 96–499, title IX, Dec. 5, 1980, 94 Stat. 2609
Short title, see 42 U.S.C. 1305 note

Medicare and Medicaid Amendments of 1981
Pub. L. 97–35, title XXI, Aug. 13, 1981, 95 Stat. 783
Short title, see 42 U.S.C. 1305 note

Medicare and Medicaid Budget Reconciliation Amendments of 1984
Pub. L. 98–369, div. B, title III, July 18, 1984, 98 Stat. 1061
Short title, see 42 U.S.C. 1305 note

Medicare and Medicaid Budget Reconciliation Amendments of 1985
Pub. L. 99–272, title IX, Apr. 7, 1986, 100 Stat. 151
Short title, see 42 U.S.C. 1305 note

Medicare and Medicaid Patient and Program Protection Act of 1987
Pub. L. 100–93, Aug. 18, 1987, 101 Stat. 680
Short title, see 42 U.S.C. 1305 note

Medicare Catastrophic Coverage Act of 1988
Pub. L. 100–360, July 1, 1988, 102 Stat. 683
Short title, see 42 U.S.C. 1305 note

Medicare Catastrophic Coverage Repeal Act of 1989
Pub. L. 101–234, Dec. 13, 1989, 103 Stat. 1979
Short title, see 42 U.S.C. 1305 note

Medicare, Medicaid, and SCHIP Balanced Budget Refinement Act of 1999
Pub. L. 106–113, div. B, §1000(a)(6) [H.R. 3426], Nov. 29, 1999, 113 Stat. 1536, 1501A–321
Short title, see 42 U.S.C. 1305 note

Medicare, Medicaid, and SCHIP Benefits Improvement and Protection Act of 2000
Pub. L. 106–554, §1(a)(6) [H.R. 5661], Dec. 21, 2000, 114 Stat. 2763, 2763A–463
Short title, see 42 U.S.C. 1305 note

Medicare-Medicaid Anti-Fraud and Abuse Amendments
Pub. L. 95–142, Oct. 25, 1977, 91 Stat. 1175
Short title, see 42 U.S.C. 1305 note

Medicine Equity and Drug Safety Act of 2000
Pub. L. 106–387, §1(a) [title VII, §745], Oct. 28, 2000, 114 Stat. 1549, 1549A–35
Short title, see 21 U.S.C. 301 note

Megan's Law
Pub. L. 104–145, May 17, 1996, 110 Stat. 1345
Short title, see 42 U.S.C. 13701 note

Mellon Art Gallery Act
Mar. 24, 1937, ch. 50, 50 Stat. 51 (20 U.S.C. 71 et seq.)

Membrane Processes Research Act of 1992
Pub. L. 102–490, Oct. 24, 1992, 106 Stat. 3142 (42 U.S.C. 10341 et seq.)
Short title, see 42 U.S.C. 10341 note

Menominee Restoration Act
Pub. L. 93–197, Dec. 22, 1973, 87 Stat. 770 (25 U.S.C. 903 et seq.)
Short title, see 25 U.S.C. 903 note

Mental Health Amendments of 1967
Pub. L. 90–31, June 24, 1967, 81 Stat. 79
Short title, see 42 U.S.C. 201 note

Mental Health Amendments of 1990
Pub. L. 101–639, Nov. 28, 1990, 104 Stat. 4600
Short title, see 42 U.S.C. 201 note

Mental Health Parity Act of 1996
Pub. L. 104–204, title VII, Sept. 26, 1996, 110 Stat. 2944
Short title, see 42 U.S.C. 201 note

Mental Health Study Act of 1955
July 28, 1955, ch. 417, 69 Stat. 381
Short title, see 42 U.S.C. 201 note

Mental Health Systems Act
Pub. L. 96–398, Oct. 7, 1980, 94 Stat. 1564 (42 U.S.C. 9401 et seq.)
Short title, see 42 U.S.C. 9401 note

Mental Retardation Amendments of 1967
Pub. L. 90–170, Dec. 4, 1967, 81 Stat. 527

Mental Retardation Facilities and Community Mental Health Centers Construction Act Amendments of 1965
Pub. L. 89–105, Aug. 4, 1965, 79 Stat. 427

Mental Retardation Facilities Construction Act
Pub. L. 88–164, title I, Oct. 31, 1963, 77 Stat. 282

Merchant Marine Act of 1970
Pub. L. 91–469, Oct. 21, 1970, 84 Stat. 1018
Short title, see 46 App. U.S.C. 1245 note

Merchant Marine Act, 1920
June 5, 1920, ch. 250, 41 Stat. 988

Merchant Marine Act, 1928
May 22, 1928, ch. 675, 45 Stat. 689

Merchant Marine Act, 1936
June 29, 1936, ch. 858, 49 Stat. 1985 (46 App. U.S.C. 1101 et seq.)
Short title, see 46 App. U.S.C. 1245

Merchant Marine Decorations and Medals Act
Pub. L. 100–324, May 30, 1988, 102 Stat. 576 (46 App. U.S.C. 2001 et seq.)
Short title, see 46 App. U.S.C. 2001 note

Merchant Marine Emergency Act
Oct. 10, 1940, ch. 839, 54 Stat. 1092

Merchant Mariner Memorial Act of 1990
Pub. L. 101–595, title VII, §709, Nov. 16, 1990, 104 Stat. 2996

Merchant Ship Priorities Act
July 14, 1941, ch. 297, 55 Stat. 591 (50 App. U.S.C. 1281 et seq.)

Merchant Ship Sales Act of 1946
Mar. 8, 1946, ch. 82, 60 Stat. 41 (50 App. U.S.C. 1735 et seq.)
Short title, see 50 App. U.S.C. 1735 note

Mercury-Containing and Rechargeable Battery Management Act
Pub. L. 104–142, May 13, 1996, 110 Stat. 1329 (42 U.S.C. 14301 et seq.)
Short title, see 42 U.S.C. 14301 note

Mercury-Containing Battery Management Act
Pub. L. 104–142, title II, May 13, 1996, 110 Stat. 1336 (42 U.S.C. 14331 et seq.)
Short title, see 42 U.S.C. 14301 note

Merrimack River Study Act of 1990
Pub. L. 101–356, Aug. 10, 1990, 104 Stat. 417
Short title, see 16 U.S.C. 1271 note

Mesquite Lands Act of 1988
Pub. L. 99–548, Oct. 27, 1986, 100 Stat. 3061

Methamphetamine Anti-Proliferation Act of 2000
Pub. L. 106–310, div. B, title XXXVI, Oct. 17, 2000, 114 Stat. 1227
Short title, see 21 U.S.C. 801 note

Methamphetamine Trafficking Penalty Enhancement Act of 1998
Pub. L. 105–277, div. E, Oct. 21, 1998, 112 Stat. 2681–759
Short title, see 21 U.S.C. 801 note

Methane Hydrate Research and Development Act of 2000
Pub. L. 106–193, May 2, 2000, 114 Stat. 234 (30 U.S.C. 1902 note)

Methane Transportation Research, Development, and Demonstration Act of 1980
Pub. L. 96–512, Dec. 12, 1980, 94 Stat. 2827 (15 U.S.C. 3801 et seq.)
Short title, see 15 U.S.C. 3801 note

Metlakatla Indian Community Enrollment Act of 1980
Pub. L. 96–505, Dec. 5, 1980, 94 Stat. 2743

Metric Conversion Act of 1975
Pub. L. 94–168, Dec. 23, 1975, 89 Stat. 1007 (15 U.S.C. 205a et seq.)
Short title, see 15 U.S.C. 205a note

Metric Education Act of 1978
Pub. L. 89–10, title III, part B (§311 et seq.), as added Pub. L. 95–561, title III, §301(a), Nov. 1, 1978, 92 Stat. 2211

Metric System Act
July 28, 1866, ch. 301, 14 Stat. 339

Metropolitan Washington Airports Act Amendments of 1991
Pub. L. 102–240, title VII, Dec. 18, 1991, 105 Stat. 2197

Metropolitan Washington Airports Act of 1986
Pub. L. 99–500, title VI, Oct. 18, 1986, 100 Stat. 1783–373, and Pub. L. 99–591, title VI, Oct. 30, 1986, 100 Stat. 3341–376

Metropolitan Washington Airports Amendments Act of 1996
Pub. L. 104–264, title IX, Oct. 9, 1996, 110 Stat. 3274

Metropolitan Washington Waste Management Study Act
Pub. L. 102–386, title II, Oct. 6, 1992, 106 Stat. 1517

Mexican Agricultural Workers Importation Act
July 12, 1951, ch. 223, 65 Stat. 119

Mexican Border Act
Jan. 31, 1942, ch. 31, 56 Stat. 40 (7 U.S.C. 149)

Mexican Debt Disclosure Act of 1995
Pub. L. 104–6, title IV, Apr. 10, 1995, 109 Stat. 89 (31 U.S.C. 5302 note)

Mexican War Act
May 13, 1846, ch. 16, 9 Stat. 9

Mexico-United States Interparliamentary Group Act
Pub. L. 86–420, Apr. 9, 1960, 74 Stat. 40 (22 U.S.C. 276h et seq.)

Miccosukee Reserved Area Act
Pub. L. 105–313, Oct. 30, 1998, 112 Stat. 2964 (16 U.S.C. 410 note)

Miccosukee Settlement Act of 1997
Pub. L. 105–83, title VII, Nov. 14, 1997, 111 Stat. 1624 (25 U.S.C. 1750 et seq.)
Short title, see 25 U.S.C. 1750 note

Michigan Indian Land Claims Settlement Act
Pub. L. 105–143, Dec. 15, 1997, 111 Stat. 2652

Michigan Public Lands Improvement Act of 1988
Pub. L. 100–537, Oct. 28, 1988, 102 Stat. 2711

Michigan Public Lands Improvement Act of 1990
Pub. L. 101–442, title II, §209, Oct. 18, 1990, 104 Stat. 1026

Michigan Scenic Rivers Act of 1991
Pub. L. 102–249, Mar. 3, 1992, 106 Stat. 45
Short title, see 16 U.S.C. 1271 note

Michigan Wilderness Act of 1987
Pub. L. 100–184, Dec. 8, 1987, 101 Stat. 1274 (16 U.S.C. 1132 note)

Mickey Leland Childhood Hunger Relief Act
Pub. L. 103–66, title XIII, ch. 3 (§13901 et seq.), Aug. 10, 1993, 107 Stat. 672
Short title, see 7 U.S.C. 2011 note

Mickey Leland Food for Peace Act
Pub. L. 101–624, title XV, subtitle A (§1511 et seq.), Nov. 28, 1990, 104 Stat. 3633
Short title, see 7 U.S.C. 1691 note

Mickey Leland Memorial Domestic Hunger Relief Act
Pub. L. 101–624, title XVII, Nov. 28, 1990, 104 Stat. 3783
Short title, see 7 U.S.C. 2011 note

Microenterprise for Self-Reliance Act of 2000
Pub. L. 106–309, title I, Oct. 17, 2000, 114 Stat. 1079
Short title, see 22 U.S.C. 2151 note

Microenterprise for Self-Reliance and International Anti-Corruption Act of 2000
Pub. L. 106–309, Oct. 17, 2000, 114 Stat. 1078
Short title, see 22 U.S.C. 2151 note

Microlending Expansion Act of 1992
Pub. L. 102–366, title I, subtitle B (§111 et seq.), Sept. 4, 1992, 106 Stat. 989
Short title, see 15 U.S.C. 631 note

Microloan Program Technical Corrections Act of 1999
Pub. L. 106–22, Apr. 27, 1999, 113 Stat. 36
Short title, see 15 U.S.C. 631 note

Micronesian Claims Act of 1971
Pub. L. 92–39, July 1, 1971, 85 Stat. 92 (50 App. U.S.C. 2018 et seq.)

Mid-Dakota Rural Water System Act of 1992
Pub. L. 102–575, title XIX, Oct. 30, 1992, 106 Stat. 4673

Middle East Peace and Stability Act
Pub. L. 85–7, Mar. 9, 1957, 71 Stat. 5 (22 U.S.C. 1961 et seq.)

Middle East Peace Facilitation Act of 1993
Pub. L. 103–125, Oct. 28, 1993, 107 Stat. 1309

Middle East Peace Facilitation Act of 1994
Pub. L. 103–236, title V, part E (§581 et seq.), Apr. 30, 1994, 108 Stat. 488

Middle East Peace Facilitation Act of 1995
Pub. L. 104–107, title VI, Feb. 12, 1996, 110 Stat. 755

Middle Income Student Assistance Act
Pub. L. 95–566, Nov. 1, 1978, 92 Stat. 2402
Short title, see 20 U.S.C. 1001 note

Midnight Basketball League Training and Partnership Act
Pub. L. 103–227, title X, part D (§1051 et seq.), Mar. 31, 1994, 108 Stat. 274
Short title, see 42 U.S.C. 11901 note

Midshipmen Increase Act
Sept. 4, 1940, ch. 706, 54 Stat. 867

Migrant and Community Health Centers Amendments of 1978
Pub. L. 95–626, title I, part A (§101 et seq.), Nov. 10, 1978, 92 Stat. 3551
Short title, see 42 U.S.C. 201 note

Migrant and Seasonal Agricultural Worker Protection Act
Pub. L. 97–470, Jan. 14, 1983, 96 Stat. 2583 (29 U.S.C. 1801 et seq.)
Short title, see 29 U.S.C. 1801 note

Migrant Health Act
July 1, 1944, ch. 373, title III, §329, formerly §310, as added Pub. L. 87–692, Sept. 25, 1962, 76 Stat. 592
Short title, see 42 U.S.C. 201 note

Migration and Refugee Assistance Act of 1962
Pub. L. 87–510, June 28, 1962, 76 Stat. 121 (22 U.S.C. 2601 et seq.)
Short title, see 22 U.S.C. 2601 note

Migratory Bird Conservation Act
Feb. 18, 1929, ch. 257, 45 Stat. 1222 (16 U.S.C. 715 et seq.)
Short title, see 16 U.S.C. 715

Migratory Bird Hunting and Conservation Stamp Promotion Act
Pub. L. 105–269, Oct. 19, 1998, 112 Stat. 2381
Short title, see 16 U.S.C. 718 note

Migratory Bird Hunting Stamp Act
Also known as the Duck Stamp Act
Mar. 16, 1934, ch. 71, 48 Stat. 451 (16 U.S.C. 718 et seq.)
Short title, see 16 U.S.C. 718 note

Migratory Bird Treaty Act
July 3, 1918, ch. 128, 40 Stat. 755 (16 U.S.C. 703 et seq.)
Short title, see 16 U.S.C. 710

Migratory Bird Treaty Reform Act of 1998
Pub. L. 105–312, title I, Oct. 30, 1998, 112 Stat. 2956
Short title, see 16 U.S.C. 710 note

Mike Mansfield Fellowship Act
Pub. L. 103–236, title II, part C (§251 et seq.), Apr. 30, 1994, 108 Stat. 428 (22 U.S.C. 6101 et seq.)
Short title, see 22 U.S.C. 6101 note

Miles Land Exchange Act of 1998
Pub. L. 105–288, Oct. 27, 1998, 112 Stat. 2778

Military Appropriation Act, 1938
July 1, 1937, ch. 423, 50 Stat. 442

Military Appropriation Act, 1939
June 11, 1938, ch. 347, 52 Stat. 642

Military Appropriation Act, 1940
Apr. 26, 1939, ch. 88, 53 Stat. 592

Military Appropriation Act, 1941
June 13, 1940, ch. 343, 54 Stat. 350

Military Appropriation Act, 1942
June 30, 1941, ch. 262, 55 Stat. 366

Military Appropriation Act, 1943
July 2, 1942, ch. 477, 56 Stat. 611

Military Appropriation Act, 1944
July 1, 1943, ch. 185, 57 Stat. 347

Military Appropriation Act, 1945
June 28, 1944, ch. 303, 58 Stat. 573

Military Appropriation Act, 1946
July 3, 1945, ch. 265, 59 Stat. 384

Military Appropriation Act, 1947
July 16, 1946, ch. 583, 60 Stat. 541

Military Appropriation Act, 1948
July 30, 1947, ch. 357, 61 Stat. 551

Military Cargo Preference Act of 1904
Apr. 28, 1904, ch. 1766, 33 Stat. 518 (see 10 U.S.C. 2631)

Military Child Care Act of 1989
Pub. L. 101–189, div. A, title XV (§1501 et seq.), Nov. 29, 1989, 103 Stat. 1589

Military Construction Act of 1958
Pub. L. 85–685, titles I–V, Aug. 20, 1958, 72 Stat. 636–664

Military Construction Act of 1959
Pub. L. 86–149, titles I–III, Aug. 10, 1959, 73 Stat. 302–318

Military Construction Act of 1960
Pub. L. 86–500, titles I–V, June 8, 1960, 74 Stat. 166–188

Military Construction Act of 1961
Pub. L. 87–57, titles I–VI, June 27, 1961, 75 Stat. 96–112

Military Construction Appropriation Act of 1959
Pub. L. 85–852, Aug. 28, 1958, 72 Stat. 1096

Military Construction Appropriation Act, 1960
Pub. L. 86–275, Sept. 16, 1959, 73 Stat. 558

Military Construction Appropriation Act, 1961
Pub. L. 86–630, July 12, 1960, 74 Stat. 463

Military Construction Appropriation Act, 1962
Pub. L. 87–302, Sept. 26, 1961, 75 Stat. 658

Military Construction Appropriation Act, 1963
Pub. L. 87–684, Sept. 25, 1962, 76 Stat. 576

Military Construction Appropriation Act, 1964
Pub. L. 88–220, Dec. 21, 1963, 77 Stat. 463

Military Construction Appropriation Act, 1965
Pub. L. 88–576, Sept. 2, 1964, 78 Stat. 887

Military Construction Appropriation Act, 1966
Pub. L. 89–202, Sept. 25, 1965, 79 Stat. 835

Military Construction Appropriation Act, 1967
Pub. L. 89–744, Nov. 2, 1966, 80 Stat. 1174

Military Construction Appropriation Act, 1968
Pub. L. 90–180, Dec. 8, 1967, 81 Stat. 550

Military Construction Appropriation Act, 1969
Pub. L. 90–513, Sept. 26, 1968, 82 Stat. 864

Military Construction Appropriation Act, 1970
Pub. L. 91–170, Dec. 29, 1969, 83 Stat. 465

Military Construction Appropriation Act, 1971
Pub. L. 91–544, Dec. 11, 1970, 84 Stat. 1409

Military Construction Appropriation Act, 1972
Pub. L. 92–160, Nov. 18, 1971, 85 Stat. 482

Military Construction Appropriation Act, 1973
Pub. L. 92–547, Oct. 25, 1972, 86 Stat. 1156

Military Construction Appropriation Act, 1974
Pub. L. 93–194, Dec. 20, 1973, 87 Stat. 766

Military Construction Appropriation Act, 1975
Pub. L. 93–636, Jan. 3, 1975, 88 Stat. 2179

Military Construction Appropriation Act, 1976
Pub. L. 94–138, Nov. 28, 1975, 89 Stat. 745

Military Construction Appropriation Act, 1977
Pub. L. 94–367, July 16, 1976, 90 Stat. 993

Military Construction Appropriation Act, 1978
Pub. L. 95–101, Aug. 15, 1977, 91 Stat. 837

Military Construction Appropriation Act, 1979
Pub. L. 95–374, Sept. 18, 1978, 92 Stat. 707

Military Construction Appropriation Act, 1980
Pub. L. 96–130, Nov. 30, 1979, 93 Stat. 1017

Military Construction Appropriation Act, 1981
Pub. L. 96–436, Oct. 13, 1980, 94 Stat. 1863

Military Construction Appropriation Act, 1982
Pub. L. 97–106, Dec. 23, 1981, 95 Stat. 1503

Military Construction Appropriation Act, 1983
Pub. L. 97–323, Oct. 15, 1982, 96 Stat. 1591

Military Construction Appropriations Act, 1984
Pub. L. 98–116, Oct. 11, 1983, 97 Stat. 795

Military Construction Appropriations Act, 1985
Pub. L. 98–473, title I, §101(e), Oct. 12, 1984, 98 Stat. 1877

Military Construction Appropriations Act, 1986
Pub. L. 99–173, Dec. 10, 1985, 99 Stat. 1024

Military Construction Appropriations Act, 1987
Pub. L. 99–500, §101(k) [title I], Oct. 18, 1986, 100 Stat. 1783–287, and Pub. L. 99–591, §101(k) [title I], Oct. 30, 1986, 100 Stat. 3341–287

Military Construction Appropriations Act, 1988
Pub. L. 100–202, §101(j), Dec. 22, 1987, 101 Stat. 1329–311

Military Construction Appropriations Act, 1989
Pub. L. 100–447, Sept. 27, 1988, 102 Stat. 1829

Military Construction Appropriations Act, 1990
Pub. L. 101–148, Nov. 10, 1989, 103 Stat. 920

Military Construction Appropriations Act, 1991
Pub. L. 101–519, Nov. 5, 1990, 104 Stat. 2240

Military Construction Appropriations Act, 1992
Pub. L. 102–136, Oct. 25, 1991, 105 Stat. 637

Military Construction Appropriations Act, 1993
Pub. L. 102–380, Oct. 5, 1992, 106 Stat. 1366

Military Construction Authorization Act, 1982
Pub. L. 97–99, Dec. 23, 1981, 95 Stat. 1359

Military Construction Authorization Act, 1983
Pub. L. 97–321, Oct. 15, 1982, 96 Stat. 1549

Military Construction Authorization Act, 1984
Pub. L. 98–115, Oct. 11, 1983, 97 Stat. 757

Military Construction Authorization Act, 1985
Pub. L. 98–407, Aug. 28, 1984, 98 Stat. 1495

Military Construction Authorization Act, 1986
Pub. L. 99–167, Dec. 3, 1985, 99 Stat. 961

Military Construction Authorization Act, 1987
Pub. L. 99–661, div. B, Nov. 14, 1986, 100 Stat. 4012

Military Construction Authorization Act, 1988 and 1989
Pub. L. 100–180, div. B, Dec. 4, 1987, 101 Stat. 1179

Military Construction Authorization Act, 1989
Pub. L. 100–456, div. B, Sept. 29, 1988, 102 Stat. 2087

Military Construction Codification Act
Pub. L. 97–214, July 12, 1982, 96 Stat. 153
Short title, see 10 U.S.C. 2801 note

Military Extraterritorial Jurisdiction Act of 2000
Pub. L. 106–523, Nov. 22, 2000, 114 Stat. 2488 (18 U.S.C. 3261 et seq.)
Short title, see 18 U.S.C. 3261 note

Military Family Act of 1985
Pub. L. 99–145, title VIII, Nov. 8, 1985, 99 Stat. 678 (10 U.S.C. 113 note)

Military Force Structure Review Act of 1996
Pub. L. 104–201, div. A, title IX, subtitle B (§921 et seq.), Sept. 23, 1996, 110 Stat. 2623–2628 (10 U.S.C. 111 note)

Military Functions Appropriation Act, 1949
June 24, 1948, ch. 632, 62 Stat. 647

Military Health Care Amendments of 1987
Pub. L. 100–180, div. A, title VII, Dec. 4, 1987, 101 Stat. 1108
Short title, see 10 U.S.C. 1071 note

Military Housing Assistance Act of 1995
Pub. L. 104–106, div. B, title XXVIII, §2822, Feb. 10, 1996, 110 Stat. 556
Short title, see 38 U.S.C. 101 note

Military Justice Act of 1968
Pub. L. 90–632, Oct. 24, 1968, 82 Stat. 1335
Short title, see 10 U.S.C. 801 note

Military Justice Act of 1983
Pub. L. 98–209, Dec. 6, 1983, 97 Stat. 1393
Short title, see 10 U.S.C. 801 note

Military Justice Amendments of 1981
Pub. L. 97–81, Nov. 20, 1981, 95 Stat. 1085
Short title, see 10 U.S.C. 801 note

Military Justice Amendments of 1986
Pub. L. 99–661, div. A, title VIII, Nov. 14, 1986, 100 Stat. 3905
Short title, see 10 U.S.C. 801 note

Military Justice Amendments of 1995
Pub. L. 104–106, div. A, title XI, Feb. 10, 1996, 110 Stat. 461
Short title, see 10 U.S.C. 801 note

Military Lands Withdrawal Act of 1986
Pub. L. 99–606, §§1–15, Nov. 6, 1986, 100 Stat. 3457–3468

Military Lands Withdrawal Act of 1999
Pub. L. 106–65, div. B, title XXX, Oct. 5, 1999, 113 Stat. 885

Military Medical Benefits Amendments of 1966
Pub. L. 89–614, Sept. 30, 1966, 80 Stat. 862
Short title, see 10 U.S.C. 1071 note

Military Pay and Allowances Benefits Act of 1980
Pub. L. 96–579, Dec. 23, 1980, 94 Stat. 3359
Short title, see 37 U.S.C. 101 note

Military Personnel and Civilian Employees' Claims Act of 1964
Pub. L. 88–558, Aug. 31, 1964, 78 Stat. 767

Military Personnel and Compensation Amendments of 1980
Pub. L. 96–343, Sept. 8, 1980, 94 Stat. 1123
Short title, see 37 U.S.C. 101 note

Military Personnel Claims Act of 1945
May 29, 1945, ch. 135, 59 Stat. 225

Military Reservation Act
July 26, 1939, ch. 373, 53 Stat. 1123

Military Retirement Reform Act of 1986
Pub. L. 99–348, July 1, 1986, 100 Stat. 682
Short title, see 10 U.S.C. 1401 note

Military Secretary Act
Mar. 28, 1939, ch. 19, 53 Stat. 551

Military Selective Service Act
June 24, 1948, ch. 625, title I, 62 Stat. 604 (50 App. U.S.C. 451 et seq.)
Short title, see 50 App. U.S.C. 451(a)

Military Selective Service Act of 1967
Renamed Military Selective Service Act

Military Survivor Benefits Improvement Act of 1989
Pub. L. 101–189, div. A, title XIV, Nov. 29, 1989, 103 Stat. 1577
Short title, see 10 U.S.C. 1447 note

Militia Act of 1903
Jan. 21, 1903, ch. 196, 32 Stat. 775

Milk Importation Act
See Import Milk Act

Miller Act
Aug. 24, 1935, ch. 642, 49 Stat. 793 (40 U.S.C. 270a et seq.)
Short title, see 40 U.S.C. 270a note

Miller-Tydings Fair Trade Act
See Fair Trade Act

Mills Act (Customs Reorganization)
Mar. 4, 1923, ch. 251, 42 Stat. 1453

Millspaugh Act (D.C. Banks)
Apr. 26, 1922, ch. 147, 42 Stat. 500

Milwaukee Railroad Restructuring Act
Pub. L. 96–101, Nov. 4, 1979, 93 Stat. 736 (45 U.S.C. 901 et seq.)
Short title, see 45 U.S.C. 901 note

Mine Dewatering Act
See Anthracite Mine Water Control Act

Miner's Labor Lien Act (Alaska)
June 25, 1910, ch. 422, 36 Stat. 848

Mineral Land Free Timber Act
June 3, 1878, ch. 150, 20 Stat. 88 (16 U.S.C. 604 et seq.)

Mineral Lands Leasing Act
See Mineral Leasing Act

Mineral Leasing Act
Feb. 25, 1920, ch. 85, 41 Stat. 437 (30 U.S.C. 181 et seq.)
Short title, see 30 U.S.C. 181 note

Mineral Leasing Act for Acquired Lands
Aug. 7, 1947, ch. 513, 61 Stat. 913 (30 U.S.C. 351 et seq.)
Short title, see 30 U.S.C. 351 note

Mineral Leasing Act of 1920
See Mineral Leasing Act

Mineral Leasing Act Revision of 1960
Pub. L. 86–705, Sept. 2, 1960, 74 Stat. 781 (30 U.S.C. 181 et seq.)
Short title, see 30 U.S.C. 181 note

Mineral Revenue Payments Clarification Act of 2000
Pub. L. 106–393, title V, Oct. 30, 2000, 114 Stat. 1624
Short title, see 30 U.S.C. 181 note

Minimum Wage and Hour Act
See Fair Labor Standards Act of 1938

Minimum Wage Increase Act of 1996
Pub. L. 104–188, [title II], §2104, Aug. 20, 1996, 110 Stat. 1928
Short title, see 29 U.S.C. 201 note

Minimum Wage Law (District of Columbia)
See District of Columbia Minimum Wage Act

Mining and Mineral Resources Institutes Act
Pub. L. 98–409, Aug. 29, 1984, 98 Stat. 1536 (30 U.S.C. 1221 et seq.)
Short title, see 30 U.S.C. 1201 note

Mining and Mineral Resources Research Institute Act of 1984
Renamed Mining and Mineral Resources Institutes Act

Mining and Mineral Resources Research Institute Amendments of 1988
Pub. L. 100–483, Oct. 12, 1988, 102 Stat. 2339
Short title, see 30 U.S.C. 1201 note

Mining and Minerals Policy Act of 1970
Pub. L. 91–631, Dec. 31, 1970, 84 Stat. 1876 (30 U.S.C. 21a)
Short title, see 30 U.S.C. 21a note

Mining Claims Rights Restoration Act of 1955
Aug. 11, 1955, ch. 797, 69 Stat. 681 (30 U.S.C. 621 et seq.)
Short title, see 30 U.S.C. 621 note

Mining in the Parks Act
Pub. L. 94–429, Sept. 28, 1976, 90 Stat. 1342 (16 U.S.C. 1901 et seq.)
Short title, see 16 U.S.C. 1901 note

Minnesota Public Lands Improvement Act of 1990
Pub. L. 101–442, title II, Oct. 18, 1990, 104 Stat. 1020

Minnesota Valley National Wildlife Refuge Act
Pub. L. 94–466, Oct. 8, 1976, 90 Stat. 1992 (16 U.S.C. 668kk et seq.)

Minor and Technical Criminal Law Amendments Act of 1988
Pub. L. 100–690, title VII, subtitle B (§7011 et seq.), Nov. 18, 1988, 102 Stat. 4395
Short title, see 18 U.S.C. 1 note

Minority Health and Health Disparities Research and Education Act of 2000
Pub. L. 106–525, Nov. 22, 2000, 114 Stat. 2495
Short title, see 42 U.S.C. 201 note

Minority-Focused Civics Education Act of 1994
Pub. L. 103–227, title VIII, Mar. 31, 1994, 108 Stat. 209 (20 U.S.C. 5981 et seq.)
Short title, see 20 U.S.C. 5981

Minute Man National Historical Park Amendments of 1991
Pub. L. 102–488, Oct. 24, 1992, 106 Stat. 3135
Short title, see 16 U.S.C. 410s note

Minuteman Missile National Historic Site Establishment Act of 1999
Pub. L. 106–115, Nov. 29, 1999, 113 Stat. 1540 (16 U.S.C. 461 note)

Miscellaneous and Technical Immigration and Naturalization Amendments of 1991
Pub. L. 102–232, Dec. 12, 1991, 105 Stat. 1733
Short title, see 8 U.S.C. 1101 note

Miscellaneous and Technical Social Security Act Amendments of 1989
Pub. L. 101–239, title X, Dec. 19, 1989, 103 Stat. 2470
Short title, see 42 U.S.C. 1305 note

Miscellaneous Appropriations Act, 2001
Pub. L. 106–554, §1(a)(4) [H.R. 5666], Dec. 21, 2000, 114 Stat. 2763, 2763A–171

Miscellaneous International Affairs Authorizations Act of 1988
Pub. L. 100–461, title V, §555 [S. 2757], Oct. 1, 1988, 102 Stat. 2268–36

Miscellaneous Revenue Act of 1980
Pub. L. 96–605, Dec. 28, 1980, 94 Stat. 3521
Short title, see 26 U.S.C. 1 note

Miscellaneous Revenue Act of 1982
Pub. L. 97–362, Oct. 25, 1982, 96 Stat. 1726
Short title, see 26 U.S.C. 1 note

Miscellaneous Trade and Technical Corrections Act of 1996
Pub. L. 104–295, Oct. 11, 1996, 110 Stat. 3514
Short title, see 19 U.S.C. 1654 note

Miscellaneous Trade and Technical Corrections Act of 1999
Pub. L. 106–36, June 25, 1999, 113 Stat. 127
Short title, see 19 U.S.C. 1654 note

Missile Defense Act of 1991
Pub. L. 102–190, div. A, title II, part C (§231 et seq.), Dec. 5, 1991, 105 Stat. 1321–1326 (10 U.S.C. 2431 note)

Missing Children Act
Pub. L. 97–292, Oct. 12, 1982, 96 Stat. 1259
Short title, see 28 U.S.C. 1 note

Missing Children's Assistance Act
Pub. L. 93–415, title IV, as added Pub. L. 98–473, title II, §660, Oct. 12, 1984, 98 Stat. 2125
Short title, see 42 U.S.C. 5601 note

Missing Persons Act
Mar. 7, 1942, ch. 166, 56 Stat. 143

Missing, Exploited, and Runaway Children Protection Act
Pub. L. 106–71, Oct. 12, 1999, 113 Stat. 1032
Short title, see 42 U.S.C. 5601 note

Mission Indian Relief Act of 1891
Jan. 12, 1891, ch. 65, 26 Stat. 712

Mississippi National Forest Improvement Act of 1999
Pub. L. 106–113, div. B, §1000(a)(3) [title IV], Nov. 29, 1999, 113 Stat. 1535, 1501A–210
Short title, see 7 U.S.C. 1281 note

Mississippi National Forest Wilderness Act of 1984
Pub. L. 98–515, Oct. 19, 1984, 98 Stat. 2420 (16 U.S.C. 1132 note)

Mississippi River Corridor Study Commission Act of 1989
Pub. L. 101–398, Sept. 28, 1990, 104 Stat. 855

Mississippi River Flood Control Act
See Flood Control Act of 1928

Mississippi Sioux Tribes Judgment Fund Distribution Act of 1998
Pub. L. 105–387, Nov. 13, 1998, 112 Stat. 3471 (25 U.S.C. 1300d–21 et seq.)
Short title, see 25 U.S.C. 1300d note

Missouri Compromise
Mar. 6, 1820, ch. 22, 3 Stat. 545

Missouri Enabling Act
See Missouri Compromise

Missouri River Protection and Improvement Act of 2000
Pub. L. 106–541, title VII, Dec. 11, 2000, 114 Stat. 2694

Missouri River Restoration Act of 2000
Pub. L. 106–541, title IX, Dec. 11, 2000, 114 Stat. 2707

Mitchell Act (Columbia River Basin Fishery Development)
May 11, 1938, ch. 193, 52 Stat. 345 (16 U.S.C. 755 et seq.)

Miwaleta Park Expansion Act
Pub. L. 106–432, Nov. 6, 2000, 114 Stat. 1908

Mixed Flour Act
June 13, 1898, ch. 448, §§35–49, 30 Stat. 467–470

Mni Wiconi Act Amendments of 1994
Pub. L. 103–434, title VIII, Oct. 31, 1994, 108 Stat. 4539

Mni Wiconi Project Act of 1988
Pub. L. 100–516, §§1–12, Oct. 24, 1988, 102 Stat. 2566–2572

Mobile Telecommunications Sourcing Act
Pub. L. 106–252, July 28, 2000, 114 Stat. 626
Short title, see 4 U.S.C. 1 note

Model Secondary School for the Deaf Act
Pub. L. 89–694, Oct. 15, 1966, 80 Stat. 1027 (20 U.S.C. 693 et seq.)
Short title, see 20 U.S.C. 693 note

Mohegan Nation of Connecticut Land Claims Settlement Act of 1994
Pub. L. 103–377, Oct. 19, 1994, 108 Stat. 3501 (25 U.S.C. 1775 et seq.)
Short title, see 25 U.S.C. 1775 note

Moiety Act (Informers)
See Anti-Moiety Act (Informers)

Mollie Beattie Wilderness Area Act
Pub. L. 104–167, July 29, 1996, 110 Stat. 1451 (16 U.S.C. 1132 note)

Monetary Act
July 6, 1939, ch. 260, 53 Stat. 998

Monetary Control Act of 1980
Pub. L. 96–221, title I, Mar. 31, 1980, 94 Stat. 132
Short title, see 12 U.S.C. 226 note

Money Laundering and Financial Crimes Strategy Act of 1998
Pub. L. 105–310, Oct. 30, 1998, 112 Stat. 2941 (31 U.S.C. 5340 et seq.)
Short title, see 31 U.S.C. 5301 note

Money Laundering Control Act of 1986
Pub. L. 99–570, title I, subtitle H (§1351 et seq.), Oct. 27, 1986, 100 Stat. 3207–18
Short title, see 18 U.S.C. 981 note

Money Laundering Prosecution Improvements Act of 1988
Pub. L. 100–690, title VI, subtitle E (§6181 et seq.), Nov. 18, 1988, 102 Stat. 4354
Short title, see 18 U.S.C. 981 note

Money Laundering Suppression Act of 1994
Pub. L. 103–325, title IV, Sept. 23, 1994, 108 Stat. 2243
Short title, see 31 U.S.C. 5301 note

Monopoly Appropriation Act
Apr. 26, 1939, ch. 104, 53 Stat. 624

Monroe Doctrine Act
Apr. 10, 1941, ch. 49, 55 Stat. 133 (22 U.S.C. 504)

Montana Wilderness Study Act of 1977
Pub. L. 95–150, Nov. 1, 1977, 91 Stat. 1243

Montgomery GI Bill Act of 1984
Pub. L. 98–525, title VII, Oct. 19, 1984, 98 Stat. 2553
Short title, see 38 U.S.C. 101 note

Moratorium Act
See Soldiers' and Sailors' Civil Relief Acts of 1918 and 1940

Morgan P. Hardiman Task Force on Missing and Exploited Children Act
Pub. L. 103–322, title XVII, subtitle C (§170301 et seq.), Sept. 13, 1994, 108 Stat. 2043
Short title, see 42 U.S.C. 5601 note

Morrill Act (Agricultural and Mechanical Colleges)
Also known as the First Morrill Act
July 2, 1862, ch. 130, 12 Stat. 503 (7 U.S.C. 301 et seq.)
Short title, see 7 U.S.C. 301 note

Morrill Act (Tariff)
Mar. 2, 1861, ch. 68, 12 Stat. 178

Morris Act (Chippewa Indians of Minnesota)
June 27, 1902, ch. 1157, 32 Stat. 400 (25 U.S.C. 197 note)

Morris K. Udall Parkinson's Disease Research Act of 1997
Pub. L. 105–78, title VI, §603, Nov. 13, 1997, 111 Stat. 1519
Short title, see 42 U.S.C. 201 note

Morris K. Udall Scholarship and Excellence in National Environmental and Native American Public Policy Act of 1992
Pub. L. 102–259, Mar. 19, 1992, 106 Stat. 78 (20 U.S.C. 5601 et seq.)
Short title, see 20 U.S.C. 5601 note

Morrison Act (Tariff)
Mar. 3, 1883, ch. 121, 22 Stat. 488

Mortgage Purchase Amendments of 1981
Pub. L. 97–110, title II, Dec. 26, 1981, 95 Stat. 1514
Short title, see 12 U.S.C. 1451 note

Mortgage Subsidy Bond Tax Act of 1980
Pub. L. 96–499, title XI, subtitle A (§1101 et seq.), Dec. 5, 1980, 94 Stat. 2660
Short title, see 26 U.S.C. 1 note

Moses Agreement (Indian Land Patents)
July 4, 1884, ch. 180, 23 Stat. 79, 80

Mosquito Craft Base Act
June 24, 1941, ch. 234, 55 Stat. 262

Mother's Day Act
May 8, 1914, No. 13, 38 Stat. 770

Motor Boat Regulations Act
June 9, 1910, ch. 268, 36 Stat. 462

Motor Carrier Act of 1980
Pub. L. 96–296, July 1, 1980, 94 Stat. 793
Short title, see 49 U.S.C. 10101 note

Motor Carrier Act of 1991
Pub. L. 102–240, title IV, Dec. 18, 1991, 105 Stat. 2140

Motor Carrier Act, 1935
Renamed part II of the Interstate Commerce Act

Motor Carrier Safety Act of 1984
Pub. L. 98–554, title II, Oct. 30, 1984, 98 Stat. 2832

Motor Carrier Safety Act of 1990
Pub. L. 101–500, §15, Nov. 3, 1990, 104 Stat. 1218

Motor Carrier Safety Improvement Act of 1999
Pub. L. 106–159, Dec. 9, 1999, 113 Stat. 1748
Short title, see 49 U.S.C. 101 note

Motor Vehicle Air Pollution Control Act
Renamed National Emission Standards Act

Motor Vehicle and Schoolbus Safety Amendments of 1974
Pub. L. 93–492, Oct. 27, 1974, 88 Stat. 1470

Motor Vehicle Information and Cost Savings Act
Pub. L. 92–513, Oct. 20, 1972, 86 Stat. 947
Short title, see 15 U.S.C. 1901 note

Motor Vehicle Information and Cost Savings Act Amendments of 1976
Pub. L. 94–364, July 14, 1976, 90 Stat. 981

Motor Vehicle Safety and Cost Savings Authorization Act of 1982
Pub. L. 97–331, Oct. 15, 1982, 96 Stat. 1619

Motor Vehicle Safety Responsibility Act of the District of Columbia
May 25, 1954, ch. 222, 68 Stat. 120

Motor Vehicle Theft Law Enforcement Act of 1984
Pub. L. 98–547, Oct. 25, 1984, 98 Stat. 2754
Short title, see 18 U.S.C. 2311 note

Motor Vehicle Theft Prevention Act
Pub. L. 103–322, title XXII, Sept. 13, 1994, 108 Stat. 2074 (42 U.S.C. 14171 et seq.)
Short title, see 42 U.S.C. 13701 note

Motorboat Act of 1940
Apr. 25, 1940, ch. 155, 54 Stat. 163

Mount Pleasant National Scenic Area Act
Pub. L. 103–314, Aug. 26, 1994, 108 Stat. 1703 (16 U.S.C. 545 et seq.)
Short title, see 16 U.S.C. 545 note

Mount Rogers National Recreation Area Act
Pub. L. 89–438, May 31, 1966, 80 Stat. 190 (16 U.S.C. 460r et seq.)

Mount Rushmore Commemorative Coin Act
Pub. L. 101–332, July 16, 1990, 104 Stat. 313 (31 U.S.C. 5112 note)

Mount Rushmore Memorial Act of 1938
June 15, 1938, ch. 402, 52 Stat. 694

Mount St. Helens National Volcanic Monument Completion Act
Pub. L. 105–279, Oct. 23, 1998, 112 Stat. 2690

Mountain Park Project Act of 1994
Pub. L. 103–434, title IV, Oct. 31, 1994, 108 Stat. 4536

Mrs. Murphy (Civil Rights Act) Exemption
Pub. L. 90–284, title VIII, §803(b)(2), Apr. 11, 1968, 82 Stat. 82 (42 U.S.C. 3603(b)(2))

Muhammad Ali Boxing Reform Act
Pub. L. 106–210, May 26, 2000, 114 Stat. 321
Short title, see 15 U.S.C. 6301 note

Multiemployer Pension Plan Amendments Act of 1980
Pub. L. 96–364, Sept. 26, 1980, 94 Stat. 1208
Short title, see 29 U.S.C. 1001 note

Multifamily Assisted Housing Reform and Affordability Act of 1997
Pub. L. 105–65, title V, Oct. 27, 1997, 111 Stat. 1384
Short title, see 12 U.S.C. 1701 note

Multifamily Housing Finance Improvement Act
Pub. L. 102–550, title V, subtitle C (§541 et seq.), Oct. 28, 1992, 106 Stat. 3794–3801 (12 U.S.C. 1715z–22, 1715z–22a)
Short title, see 12 U.S.C. 1701 note

Multifamily Housing Property Disposition Reform Act of 1994
Pub. L. 103–233, Apr. 11, 1994, 108 Stat. 342
Short title, see 12 U.S.C. 1701 note

Multifamily Mortgage Foreclosure Act of 1981
Pub. L. 97–35, title III, subtitle A, part 6 (§361 et seq.), Aug. 13, 1981, 95 Stat. 422 (12 U.S.C. 3701 et seq.)
Short title, see 12 U.S.C. 3701 note

Multilateral Development Banks Procurement Act of 1988
Pub. L. 100–418, title III, subtitle C (§3201 et seq.), Aug. 23, 1988, 102 Stat. 1382
Short title, see 22 U.S.C. 262s note

Multilateral Export Control Enhancement Amendments Act
Pub. L. 100–418, title II, subtitle D, part II (§2441 et seq.), Aug. 23, 1988, 102 Stat. 1364
Short title, see 50 App. U.S.C. 2401 note

Multilateral Investment Guarantee Agency Act
Pub. L. 100–202, §101(e) [title I [H.R. 3750, title IV]], Dec. 22, 1987, 101 Stat. 1329–131, 1329–134
Short title, see 22 U.S.C. 290k note

Multinational Force and Observers Participation Resolution
Pub. L. 97–132, Dec. 29, 1981, 95 Stat. 1693 (22 U.S.C. 3421 et seq.)
Short title, see 22 U.S.C. 3401 note

Multinational Force in Lebanon Resolution
Pub. L. 98–119, Oct. 12, 1983, 97 Stat. 805 (50 U.S.C. 1541 note)

Multiple Mineral Development Act
Aug. 13, 1954, ch. 730, 68 Stat. 708 (30 U.S.C. 521 et seq.)

Multiple Use Law
See Multiple Mineral Development Act

Multiple-Use Sustained-Yield Act of 1960
Pub. L. 86–517, June 12, 1960, 74 Stat. 215 (16 U.S.C. 528 et seq.)
Short title, see 16 U.S.C. 528 note

Municipal Bankruptcy Act
May 24, 1934, ch. 345, 48 Stat. 798

Municipal Bankruptcy Extension Act
Apr. 10, 1936, ch. 186, 49 Stat. 1198

Municipal Wastewater Treatment Construction Grant Amendments of 1981
Pub. L. 97–117, Dec. 29, 1981, 95 Stat. 1623
Short title, see 33 U.S.C. 1251 note

Munition Manufacturer's Tax Act of 1916
Sept. 8, 1916, ch. 463, title III, 39 Stat. 780

Muscle Shoals Act
See Tennessee Valley Authority Act of 1933

Museum and Library Services Act
Pub. L. 94–462, title II, as added Pub. L. 104–208, div. A, title I, §101(e) [title VII, §702], Sept. 30, 1996, 110 Stat. 3009–233, 3009–293 (20 U.S.C. 9101 et seq.)
Short title, see 20 U.S.C. 9101 note

Museum and Library Services Act of 1996
Pub. L. 104–208, div. A, title I, §101(e) [title VII], Sept. 30, 1996, 110 Stat. 3009–233, 3009–293
Short title, see 20 U.S.C. 9101 note

Museum and Library Services Technical and Conforming Amendments of 1997
Pub. L. 105–128, Dec. 1, 1997, 111 Stat. 2548
Short title, see 20 U.S.C. 9101 note

Museum Services Act
Renamed Museum and Library Services Act

Mushroom Promotion, Research, and Consumer Information Act of 1990
Pub. L. 101–624, title XIX, subtitle B (§1921 et seq.), Nov. 28, 1990, 104 Stat. 3854 (7 U.S.C. 6101 et seq.)
Short title, see 7 U.S.C. 6101 note

Mustering-Out Payment Act of 1944
Feb. 3, 1944, ch. 9, 58 Stat. 8

Mutual Defense Assistance Act
Oct. 6, 1949, ch. 626, 63 Stat. 714 (22 U.S.C. 1571 et seq.)

Mutual Defense Assistance Control Act of 1951
Oct. 26, 1951, ch. 575, 65 Stat. 644 (22 U.S.C. 1611 et seq.)
Short title, see 22 U.S.C. 1611 note

Mutual Educational and Cultural Exchange Act of 1961
Pub. L. 87–256, Sept. 21, 1961, 75 Stat. 527 (22 U.S.C. 2451 et seq.)
Short title, see 22 U.S.C. 2451 note

Mutual Security Act of 1951
Oct. 10, 1951, ch. 479, 65 Stat. 373

Mutual Security Act of 1952
June 20, 1952, ch. 449, 66 Stat. 141

Mutual Security Act of 1953
July 16, 1953, ch. 195, 67 Stat. 152

Mutual Security Act of 1954
Aug. 26, 1954, ch. 937, 68 Stat. 832 (22 U.S.C. 1750 et seq.)
Short title, see 22 U.S.C. 1754 note

Mutual Security Act of 1955
July 8, 1955, ch. 301, 69 Stat. 283

Mutual Security Act of 1956
July 18, 1956, ch. 627, 70 Stat. 555

Mutual Security Act of 1957
Pub. L. 85–141, Aug. 14, 1957, 71 Stat. 355

Mutual Security Act of 1958
Pub. L. 85–477, June 30, 1958, 72 Stat. 261

Mutual Security Act of 1959
Pub. L. 86–108, July 24, 1959, 73 Stat. 246

Mutual Security Act of 1960
Pub. L. 86–472, May 14, 1960, 74 Stat. 134

Mutual Security and Related Agencies Appropriation Act, 1961
Pub. L. 86–704, Sept. 2, 1960, 74 Stat. 776

Mutual Security Appropriation Act, 1952
Oct. 31, 1951, ch. 656, 65 Stat. 730

Mutual Security Appropriation Act, 1953
July 15, 1952, ch. 758, Ch. XI, 66 Stat. 649

Mutual Security Appropriation Act, 1954
Aug. 7, 1953, ch. 351, 67 Stat. 478

Mutual Security Appropriation Act, 1955
Sept. 3, 1954, ch. 1262, 68 Stat. 1219

Mutual Security Appropriation Act, 1956
Aug. 2, 1955, ch. 491, 69 Stat. 435

Mutual Security Appropriation Act, 1957
July 31, 1956, ch. 803, 70 Stat. 733

Mutual Security Appropriation Act, 1958
Pub. L. 85–279, Sept. 3, 1957, 71 Stat. 601

Mutual Security Appropriation Act, 1959
Pub. L. 85–853, Aug. 28, 1958, 72 Stat. 1100

Mutual Security Appropriation Act, 1960
Pub. L. 86–383, Sept. 28, 1959, 73 Stat. 717

Myers Patent Act
Aug. 5, 1939, ch. 452, 53 Stat. 1213

NAFTA Worker Security Act
Pub. L. 103–182, title V, subtitle A (§501 et seq.), Dec. 8, 1993, 107 Stat. 2149
Short title, see 19 U.S.C. 2101 note

Nampa and Meridian Conveyance Act
Pub. L. 106–466, Nov. 7, 2000, 114 Stat. 2024

Narcotic Addict Rehabilitation Act of 1966
Pub. L. 89–793, titles I–IV, Nov. 8, 1966, 80 Stat. 1438–1448
Short title, see 42 U.S.C. 3401 note

Narcotic Addict Rehabilitation Amendments of 1971
Pub. L. 92–420, Sept. 16, 1972, 86 Stat. 677
Short title, see 42 U.S.C. 3401 note

Narcotic Addict Treatment Act of 1974
Pub. L. 93–281, May 14, 1974, 88 Stat. 124
Short title, see 21 U.S.C. 801 note

Narcotic Control Act of 1956
July 18, 1956, ch. 629, 70 Stat. 567

Narcotic Drugs Import and Export Act
Feb. 9, 1909, ch. 100, 35 Stat. 614

Narcotics Control Trade Act
Pub. L. 93–618, title VIII, as added Pub. L. 99–570, title IX, §9001, Oct. 27, 1986, 100 Stat. 3207–164 (19 U.S.C. 2491 et seq.)
Short title, see 19 U.S.C. 2491

Narcotics Manufacturing Act of 1960
Pub. L. 86–429, Apr. 22, 1960, 74 Stat. 55 (21 U.S.C. 501 et seq.)

Narcotics Penalties and Enforcement Act of 1986
Pub. L. 99–570, title I, subtitle A (§1001 et seq.), Oct. 27, 1986, 100 Stat. 3207–2
Short title, see 21 U.S.C. 801 note

Nation's Capital Bicentennial Designation Act
Pub. L. 105–100, title I, §147, Nov. 19, 1997, 111 Stat. 2180

Nation's Capital Religious Liberty and Academic Freedom Act
Pub. L. 101–168, §141, Nov. 21, 1989, 103 Stat. 1284

National Advisory Committee on Oceans and Atmosphere Act of 1977
Pub. L. 95–63, July 5, 1977, 91 Stat. 265 (33 U.S.C. 857–13 et seq.)
Short title, see 33 U.S.C. 851 note

National Advisory Committee on Semiconductor Research and Development Act of 1988
Pub. L. 100–418, title V, §5142, Aug. 23, 1988, 102 Stat. 1444 (15 U.S.C. 4632)
Short title, see 15 U.S.C. 4632(a)

National Advisory Council on the Public Service Act of 1990
Pub. L. 101–363, Aug. 14, 1990, 104 Stat. 424 (5 U.S.C. 3301 note)

National Aeronautics and Space Act of 1958
Pub. L. 85–568, July 29, 1958, 72 Stat. 426 (42 U.S.C. 2451 et seq.)
Short title, see 42 U.S.C. 2451 note

National Aeronautics and Space Administration Authorization Act of 1966
Pub. L. 89–53, June 28, 1965, 79 Stat. 192

National Aeronautics and Space Administration Authorization Act of 1986
Pub. L. 99–170, Dec. 5, 1985, 99 Stat. 1012

National Aeronautics and Space Administration Authorization Act of 1988
Pub. L. 100–147, Oct. 30, 1987, 101 Stat. 860

National Aeronautics and Space Administration Authorization Act of 2000
Pub. L. 106–391, Oct. 30, 2000, 114 Stat. 1577

National Aeronautics and Space Administration Authorization Act, 1961
Pub. L. 86–481, June 1, 1960, 74 Stat. 151

National Aeronautics and Space Administration Authorization Act, 1962
Pub. L. 87–98, July 21, 1961, 75 Stat. 216

National Aeronautics and Space Administration Authorization Act for the fiscal year 1963
Pub. L. 87–584, Aug. 14, 1962, 76 Stat. 382

National Aeronautics and Space Administration Authorization Act, 1964
Pub. L. 88–113, Sept. 6, 1963, 77 Stat. 141

National Aeronautics and Space Administration Authorization Act, 1965
Pub. L. 88–369, July 11, 1964, 78 Stat. 310

National Aeronautics and Space Administration Authorization Act, 1967
Pub. L. 89–528, Aug. 5, 1966, 80 Stat. 336

National Aeronautics and Space Administration Authorization Act, 1968
Pub. L. 90–67, Aug. 21, 1967, 81 Stat. 168

National Aeronautics and Space Administration Authorization Act, 1969
Pub. L. 90–373, July 3, 1968, 82 Stat. 280

National Aeronautics and Space Administration Authorization Act, 1970
Pub. L. 91–119, Nov. 18, 1969, 83 Stat. 196

National Aeronautics and Space Administration Authorization Act, 1971
Pub. L. 91–303, July 2, 1970, 84 Stat. 368

National Aeronautics and Space Administration Authorization Act, 1972
Pub. L. 92–68, Aug. 6, 1971, 85 Stat. 174

National Aeronautics and Space Administration Authorization Act, 1973
Pub. L. 92–304, May 19, 1972, 86 Stat. 157

National Aeronautics and Space Administration Authorization Act, 1974
Pub. L. 93–74, July 23, 1973, 87 Stat. 171

National Aeronautics and Space Administration Authorization Act, 1975
Pub. L. 93–316, June 22, 1974, 88 Stat. 240

National Aeronautics and Space Administration Authorization Act, 1976
Pub. L. 94–39, June 19, 1975, 89 Stat. 218

National Aeronautics and Space Administration Authorization Act, 1977
Pub. L. 94–307, June 4, 1976, 90 Stat. 677

National Aeronautics and Space Administration Authorization Act, 1978
Pub. L. 95–76, July 30, 1977, 91 Stat. 312

National Aeronautics and Space Administration Authorization Act, 1979
Pub. L. 95–401, Sept. 30, 1978, 92 Stat. 857

National Aeronautics and Space Administration Authorization Act, 1980
Pub. L. 96–48, Aug. 8, 1979, 93 Stat. 345

National Aeronautics and Space Administration Authorization Act, 1981
Pub. L. 96–316, July 30, 1980, 94 Stat. 960

National Aeronautics and Space Administration Authorization Act, 1982
Pub. L. 97–96, Dec. 21, 1981, 95 Stat. 1207

National Aeronautics and Space Administration Authorization Act, 1983
Pub. L. 97–324, Oct. 15, 1982, 96 Stat. 1597

National Aeronautics and Space Administration Authorization Act, 1984
Pub. L. 98–52, July 15, 1983, 97 Stat. 281

National Aeronautics and Space Administration Authorization Act, 1985
Pub. L. 98–361, July 16, 1984, 98 Stat. 422

National Aeronautics and Space Administration Authorization Act, Fiscal Year 1989
Pub. L. 100–685, Nov. 17, 1988, 102 Stat. 4083

National Aeronautics and Space Administration Authorization Act, Fiscal Year 1991
Pub. L. 101–611, Nov. 16, 1990, 104 Stat. 3188

National Aeronautics and Space Administration Authorization Act, Fiscal Year 1992
Pub. L. 102–195, Dec. 9, 1991, 105 Stat. 1605

National Aeronautics and Space Administration Authorization Act, Fiscal Year 1993
Pub. L. 102–588, Nov. 4, 1992, 106 Stat. 5107

National Aeronautics and Space Administration Federal Employment Reduction Assistance Act of 1996
Pub. L. 104–204, title IV, §432, Sept. 26, 1996, 110 Stat. 2931 (5 U.S.C. 5597 note)

National Agricultural Policy Commission Act of 1985
Renamed National Commission on Agriculture and Rural Development Policy Act of 1985

National Agricultural Research, Extension, and Teaching Policy Act Amendments of 1981
Pub. L. 97–98, title XIV, Dec. 22, 1981, 95 Stat. 1294
Short title, see 7 U.S.C. 3101 note

National Agricultural Research, Extension, and Teaching Policy Act Amendments of 1985
Pub. L. 99–198, title XIV, Dec. 23, 1985, 99 Stat. 1542
Short title, see 7 U.S.C. 3101 note

National Agricultural Research, Extension, and Teaching Policy Act of 1977
Pub. L. 95–113, title XIV, Sept. 29, 1977, 91 Stat. 981 (7 U.S.C. 3101 et seq.)
Short title, see 7 U.S.C. 3101 note

National Agricultural Weather Information System Act of 1990
Pub. L. 101–624, title XVI, subtitle D (§1637 et seq.), Nov. 28, 1990, 104 Stat. 3747 (7 U.S.C. 5851 et seq.)
Short title, see 7 U.S.C. 5851(a)

National Air Museum Amendments Act of 1965
Pub. L. 89–509, July 19, 1966, 80 Stat. 310
Short title, see 20 U.S.C. 77 note

National and Community Service Act
Pub. L. 101–610, title I, subtitle D (§140 et seq.), Nov. 16, 1990, 104 Stat. 3150
Short title, see 42 U.S.C. 12501 note

National and Community Service Act of 1990
Pub. L. 101–610, Nov. 16, 1990, 104 Stat. 3127 (42 U.S.C. 12501 et seq.)
Short title, see 42 U.S.C. 12501 note

National and Community Service Technical Amendment Act of 1992
Pub. L. 102–384, Oct. 5, 1992, 106 Stat. 1455
Short title, see 42 U.S.C. 12501 note

National and Community Service Technical Amendments Act of 1991
Pub. L. 102–10, Mar. 12, 1991, 105 Stat. 29
Short title, see 42 U.S.C. 12501 note

National and Community Service Trust Act of 1993
Pub. L. 103–82, Sept. 21, 1993, 107 Stat. 785
Short title, see 42 U.S.C. 12501 note

National Antidrug Reorganization and Coordination Act
Pub. L. 99–570, title VII , Oct. 27, 1986, 100 Stat. 3207–160

National Appliance Energy Conservation Act of 1987
Pub. L. 100–12, Mar. 17, 1987, 101 Stat. 103
Short title, see 42 U.S.C. 6201 note

National Appliance Energy Conservation Amendments of 1988
Pub. L. 100–357, June 28, 1988, 102 Stat. 671
Short title, see 42 U.S.C. 6201 note

National Apprenticeship Act
Aug. 16, 1937, ch. 663, 50 Stat. 664 (29 U.S.C. 50 et seq.)
Short title, see 29 U.S.C. 50 note

National Aquaculture Act of 1980
Pub. L. 96–362, Sept. 26, 1980, 94 Stat. 1198 (16 U.S.C. 2801 et seq.)
Short title, see 16 U.S.C. 2801 note

National Aquaculture Improvement Act of 1985
Pub. L. 99–198, title XVII, subtitle C [D] (§1731 et seq.), Dec. 23, 1985, 99 Stat. 1641
Short title, see 16 U.S.C. 2801 note

National Archives Act
June 19, 1934, ch. 668, 48 Stat. 1122

National Archives and Records Administration Act of 1984
Pub. L. 98–497, Oct. 19, 1984, 98 Stat. 2280
Short title, see 44 U.S.C. 101 note

National Archives Trust Fund Board Act
July 9, 1941, ch. 284, 55 Stat. 581

National Arthritis Act of 1974
Pub. L. 93–640, Jan. 4, 1975, 88 Stat. 2217
Short title, see 42 U.S.C. 201 note

National Arthritis Act Technical Amendments of 1976
Pub. L. 94–278, title VI, Apr. 22, 1976, 90 Stat. 413
Short title, see 42 U.S.C. 201 note

National Arts and Cultural Development Act of 1964
Pub. L. 88–579, Sept. 3, 1964, 78 Stat. 905 (20 U.S.C. 781 et seq.)

National Assessment of Educational Progress Improvement Act
Pub. L. 100–297, title III, part C (§3401 et seq.), Apr. 28, 1988, 102 Stat. 344
Short title, see 20 U.S.C. 1221 note

National Aviation Day Act
May 11, 1939, ch. 123, 53 Stat. 739

National Bank Act
June 3, 1864, ch. 106, 13 Stat. 99
Short title, see 12 U.S.C. 38

National Bank Consolidation and Merger Act
Nov. 7, 1918, ch. 209, as added Pub. L. 86–230, §20, Sept. 8, 1959, 73 Stat. 460 (12 U.S.C. 215 et seq.)
Short title, see 12 U.S.C. 215 note

National Bank Receivership Act
June 30, 1876, ch. 156, 19 Stat. 63
Short title, see 12 U.S.C. 191 note

National Bank Tax Act
Mar. 4, 1923, ch. 267, 42 Stat. 1499 (12 U.S.C. 548)

National Bankruptcy Review Commission Act
Pub. L. 103–394, title VI, Oct. 22, 1994, 108 Stat. 4147 (11 U.S.C. note prec. 101)

National Banks Extension Act
July 12, 1882, ch. 290, 22 Stat. 162

National Bone Marrow Registry Reauthorization Act of 1998
Pub. L. 105–196, July 16, 1998, 112 Stat. 631
Short title, see 42 U.S.C. 201 note

National Bureau of Standards Act
Renamed National Institute of Standards and Technology Act

National Bureau of Standards Authorization Act for Fiscal Year 1983
Pub. L. 97–286, Oct. 6, 1982, 96 Stat. 1222

National Bureau of Standards Authorization Act for Fiscal Year 1986
Pub. L. 99–73, July 29, 1985, 99 Stat. 171

National Bureau of Standards Authorization Act for Fiscal Year 1987
Pub. L. 99–574, Oct. 28, 1986, 100 Stat. 3236

National Bureau of Standards Authorization Act for Fiscal Years 1981 and 1982
Pub. L. 96–461, Oct. 15, 1980, 94 Stat. 2049

National Cancer Act Amendments of 1974
Pub. L. 93–352, July 23, 1974, 88 Stat. 358
Short title, see 42 U.S.C. 201 note

National Cancer Act of 1971
Pub. L. 92–218, Dec. 23, 1971, 85 Stat. 778
Short title, see 42 U.S.C. 201 note

National Cancer Institute Act
Aug. 5, 1937, ch. 565, 50 Stat. 559

National Capital Area Interest Arbitration Standards Act of 1995
Pub. L. 104–50, title IV, Nov. 15, 1995, 109 Stat. 463 (40 U.S.C. 1301 et seq.)
Short title, see 40 U.S.C. 1301 note

National Capital Area Transit Act of 1972
Pub. L. 92–517, Oct. 21, 1972, 86 Stat. 999

National Capital Planning Act of 1952
July 19, 1952, ch. 949, 66 Stat. 781
Short title, see 40 U.S.C. 71 note

National Capital Revitalization and Self-Government Improvement Act of 1997
Pub. L. 105–33, title XI, Aug. 5, 1997, 111 Stat. 712

National Capital Transportation Act of 1960
Pub. L. 86–669, July 14, 1960, 74 Stat. 537 (40 U.S.C. 651 et seq.)

National Capital Transportation Act of 1965
Pub. L. 89–173, Sept. 8, 1965, 79 Stat. 663 (40 U.S.C. 681 et seq.)

National Capital Transportation Act of 1969
Pub. L. 91–143, Dec. 9, 1969, 83 Stat. 320

National Capital Transportation Act of 1972
Pub. L. 92–349, July 13, 1972, 86 Stat. 464

National Capital Transportation Amendments of 1979
Pub. L. 96–184, Jan. 3, 1980, 93 Stat. 1320

National Capital Transportation Amendments of 1990
Pub. L. 101–551, Nov. 15, 1990, 104 Stat. 2733

National Cattle Theft Act
Aug. 18, 1941, ch. 366, 55 Stat. 631

National Cave and Karst Research Institute Act of 1998
Pub. L. 105–325, Oct. 30, 1998, 112 Stat. 3038 (16 U.S.C. 4310 note)

National Cemeteries Act of 1973
Pub. L. 93–43, June 18, 1973, 87 Stat. 75
Short title, see 38 U.S.C. 101 note

National Center for the Study of Afro-American History and Culture Act
Pub. L. 96–430, title II, Oct. 10, 1980, 94 Stat. 1846 (20 U.S.C. 3701 et seq.)
Short title, see 20 U.S.C. 3701 note

National Child Protection Act of 1993
Pub. L. 103–209, Dec. 20, 1993, 107 Stat. 2490 (42 U.S.C. 5119 et seq.)
Short title, see 42 U.S.C. 5101 note

National Childhood Vaccine Injury Act of 1986
Pub. L. 99–660, title III, Nov. 14, 1986, 100 Stat. 3755
Short title, see 42 U.S.C. 201 note

National Children's Island Act of 1995
Pub. L. 104–163, July 19, 1996, 110 Stat. 1416

National Climate Program Act
Pub. L. 95–367, Sept. 17, 1978, 92 Stat. 601 (15 U.S.C. 2901 et seq.)
Short title, see 15 U.S.C. 2901 note

National Coal Heritage Area Act of 1996
Pub. L. 104–333, div. II, title I, Nov. 12, 1996, 110 Stat. 4243 (16 U.S.C. 461 note)

National Coal Imports Reporting Act of 1985
Pub. L. 99–58, title II, July 2, 1985, 99 Stat. 107
Short title, see 42 U.S.C. 7277 note

National Coastal Monitoring Act
Pub. L. 92–532, title V, as added Pub. L. 102–567, title V, §501, Oct. 29, 1992, 106 Stat. 4293 (33 U.S.C. 2801 et seq.)
Short title, see 33 U.S.C. 2801 note

National Commission on Acquired Immune Deficiency Syndrome Act
Pub. L. 100–607, title II, subtitle D (§241 et seq.), Nov. 4, 1988, 102 Stat. 3104 (42 U.S.C. 300cc note)

National Commission on Agriculture and Rural Development Policy Act of 1985
Pub. L. 99–198, title XVII, subtitle C (§1721 et seq.), Dec. 23, 1985, 99 Stat. 1637 (7 U.S.C. 5001 et seq.)
Short title, see 7 U.S.C. 5001 note

National Commission on Judicial Discipline and Removal Act
Pub. L. 101–650, title IV, subtitle II (§408 et seq.), Dec. 1, 1990, 104 Stat. 5124 (28 U.S.C. 372 note)

National Commission on Libraries and Information Science Act
Pub. L. 91–345, July 20, 1970, 84 Stat. 440 (20 U.S.C. 1501 et seq.)
Short title, see 20 U.S.C. 1501 note

National Commission on Libraries and Information Science Act Amendments of 1991
Pub. L. 102–95, Aug. 14, 1991, 105 Stat. 479
Short title, see 20 U.S.C. 1501 note

National Commission on Measured Responses to Achieve a Drug-Free America by 1995 Authorization Act
Pub. L. 100–690, title VII, §7604, Nov. 18, 1988, 102 Stat. 4508

National Commission on Product Safety Act
Pub. L. 90–146, Nov. 20, 1967, 81 Stat. 466 (15 U.S.C. 1262 note)

National Commission on Supplies and Shortages Act of 1974
Sept. 8, 1950, ch. 932, title VII, §720, as added Pub. L. 93–426, §5, Sept. 30, 1974, 88 Stat. 1167 (50 App. U.S.C. 2169)

National Commission to Prevent Infant Mortality Act of 1986
Pub. L. 99–660, title II, Nov. 14, 1986, 100 Stat. 3752 (42 U.S.C. 285g note)

National Commission to Support Law Enforcement Act
Pub. L. 101–515, title II, §211(B), Nov. 5, 1990, 104 Stat. 2122 (42 U.S.C. 3721 note)

National Community Economic Partnership Act of 1994
Pub. L. 103–322, title III, subtitle K (§31101 et seq.), Sept. 13, 1994, 108 Stat. 1882 (42 U.S.C. 13821 et seq.)
Short title, see 42 U.S.C. 13701 note

National Competitiveness Technology Transfer Act of 1989
Pub. L. 101–189, div. C, title XXXI, part C (§3131 et seq.), Nov. 29, 1989, 103 Stat. 1674
Short title, see 15 U.S.C. 3701 note

National Consumer Cooperative Bank Act
Pub. L. 95–351, Aug. 20, 1978, 92 Stat. 499 (12 U.S.C. 3001 et seq.)
Short title, see 12 U.S.C. 3001 note

National Consumer Cooperative Bank Act Amendments of 1981
Pub. L. 97–35, title III, subtitle C (§390 et seq.), Aug. 13, 1981, 95 Stat. 433
Short title, see 12 U.S.C. 3001 note

National Consumer Cooperative Bank Amendments of 1989
Pub. L. 101–206, Dec. 7, 1989, 103 Stat. 1832
Short title, see 12 U.S.C. 3001 note

National Consumer Health Information and Health Promotion Act of 1976
Pub. L. 94–317, title I, June 23, 1976, 90 Stat. 695
Short title, see 42 U.S.C. 201 note

National Contaminated Sediment Assessment and Management Act
Pub. L. 102–580, title V, Oct. 31, 1992, 106 Stat. 4864

National Cooley's Anemia Control Act
Pub. L. 92–414, Aug. 29, 1972, 86 Stat. 650

National Cooperative Production Amendments of 1993
Pub. L. 103–42, June 10, 1993, 107 Stat. 117
Short title, see 15 U.S.C. 4301 note

National Cooperative Research Act of 1984
Renamed National Cooperative Research and Production Act of 1993

National Cooperative Research and Production Act of 1993
Pub. L. 98–462, Oct. 11, 1984, 98 Stat. 1815 (15 U.S.C. 4301 et seq.)
Short title, see 15 U.S.C. 4301 note

National Council on Education Standards and Testing Act
Pub. L. 102–62, title IV, June 27, 1991, 105 Stat. 314 (20 U.S.C. 1221–1 note)

National Credit Union Central Liquidity Facility Act
Pub. L. 95–630, title XVIII, Nov. 10, 1978, 92 Stat. 3719
Short title, see 12 U.S.C. 1751 note

National Crime Prevention and Privacy Compact Act of 1998
Pub. L. 105–251, title II, subtitle A (§211 et seq.), Oct. 9, 1998, 112 Stat. 1874 (42 U.S.C. 14611 et seq.)
Short title, see 42 U.S.C. 14601 note

National Criminal History Access and Child Protection Act
Pub. L. 105–251, title II, Oct. 9, 1998, 112 Stat. 1874
Short title, see 42 U.S.C. 14601 note

National Critical Materials Act of 1984
Pub. L. 98–373, July 31, 1984, 98 Stat. 1248 (30 U.S.C. 1801 et seq.)
Short title, see 30 U.S.C. 1801 note

National Cultural Center Act
Renamed John F. Kennedy Center Act

National Cultural Center Amendments of 1963
Pub. L. 88–100, Aug. 19, 1963, 77 Stat. 128

National Dam Safety Program Act
Pub. L. 92–367, Aug. 8, 1972, 86 Stat. 506 (33 U.S.C. 467 et seq.)
Short title, see 33 U.S.C. 467 note

National Deafness and Other Communication Disorders Act of 1988
Pub. L. 100–553, Oct. 28, 1988, 102 Stat. 2769
Short title, see 42 U.S.C. 201 note

National Defense Act of 1916
June 3, 1916, ch. 134, 39 Stat. 166

National Defense Authorization Act for Fiscal Year 1987
Pub. L. 99–661, Nov. 14, 1986, 100 Stat. 3816

National Defense Authorization Act for Fiscal Year 1991
Pub. L. 101–510, Nov. 5, 1990, 104 Stat. 1485

National Defense Authorization Act for Fiscal Year 1993
Pub. L. 102–484, Oct. 23, 1992, 106 Stat. 2315

National Defense Authorization Act for Fiscal Year 1994
Pub. L. 103–160, Nov. 30, 1993, 107 Stat. 1547

National Defense Authorization Act for Fiscal Year 1995
Pub. L. 103–337, Oct. 5, 1994, 108 Stat. 2663

National Defense Authorization Act for Fiscal Year 1996
Pub. L. 104–106, Feb. 10, 1996, 110 Stat. 186

National Defense Authorization Act for Fiscal Year 1997
Pub. L. 104–201, Sept. 23, 1996, 110 Stat. 2422

National Defense Authorization Act for Fiscal Year 1998
Pub. L. 105–85, Nov. 18, 1997, 111 Stat. 1629

National Defense Authorization Act for Fiscal Year 1999
See Strom Thurmond National Defense Authorization Act for Fiscal Year 1999

National Defense Authorization Act for Fiscal Year 2000
Pub. L. 106–65, Oct. 5, 1999, 113 Stat. 512

National Defense Authorization Act for Fiscal Years 1988 and 1989
Pub. L. 100–180, Dec. 4, 1987, 101 Stat. 1019

National Defense Authorization Act for Fiscal Years 1990 and 1991
Pub. L. 101–189, Nov. 29, 1989, 103 Stat. 1352

National Defense Authorization Act for Fiscal Years 1992 and 1993
Pub. L. 102–190, Dec. 5, 1991, 105 Stat. 1290

National Defense Authorization Act, Fiscal Year 1989
Pub. L. 100–456, Sept. 29, 1988, 102 Stat. 1918

National Defense Education Act Amendments, 1964
Pub. L. 88–665, Oct. 16, 1964, 78 Stat. 1100

National Defense Education Act of 1958
Pub. L. 85–864, Sept. 2, 1958, 72 Stat. 1580 (20 U.S.C. 401 et seq.)

National Defense Emergency Appropriation Act
Dec. 23, 1941, ch. 621, 55 Stat. 855

National Defense Facilities Act of 1950
Sept. 11, 1950, ch. 945, 64 Stat. 829

National Defense Housing Act
See Lanham Public War Housing Act

National Defense Patents Act
Aug. 21, 1941, ch. 393, 55 Stat. 657

National Defense Ship Radio Act
Dec. 17, 1941, ch. 588, 55 Stat. 808

National Defense Stockpile Amendments of 1987
Pub. L. 100–180, div. C, title II, Dec. 4, 1987, 101 Stat. 1245
Short title, see 50 U.S.C. 98 note

National Dental Research Act
June 24, 1948, ch. 621, 62 Stat. 598
Short title, see 42 U.S.C. 201 note

National Diabetes Mellitus Research and Education Act
Pub. L. 93–354, July 23, 1974, 88 Stat. 373
Short title, see 42 U.S.C. 201 note

National Driver Register Act of 1982
Pub. L. 97–364, title II, Oct. 25, 1982, 96 Stat. 1740 (23 U.S.C. 401 note)

National Dropout Prevention Act of 1991
Pub. L. 102–103, title I, Aug. 17, 1991, 105 Stat. 497
Short title, see 20 U.S.C. 6301 note

National Drought Policy Act of 1998
Pub. L. 105–199, July 16, 1998, 112 Stat. 641 (42 U.S.C. 5121 note)

National Drug Interdiction Improvement Act of 1986
Pub. L. 99–570, title III, Oct. 27, 1986, 100 Stat. 3207–73

National Earthquake Hazards Reduction Program Reauthorization Act
Pub. L. 101–614, Nov. 16, 1990, 104 Stat. 3231
Short title, see 42 U.S.C. 7701 note

National Education Commission on Time and Learning Act
Pub. L. 102–62, title I, June 27, 1991, 105 Stat. 305 (20 U.S.C. 1221–1 note)

National Education Statistics Act of 1994
Pub. L. 103–382, title IV, Oct. 20, 1994, 108 Stat. 4029 (20 U.S.C. 9001 et seq.)
Short title, see 20 U.S.C. 9001 note

National Emergencies Act
Pub. L. 94–412, Sept. 14, 1976, 90 Stat. 1255 (50 U.S.C. 1601 et seq.)
Short title, see 50 U.S.C. 1601 note

National Emission Standards Act
July 14, 1955, ch. 360, title II, as added Pub. L. 89–272, title I, §101(8), Oct. 20, 1965, 79 Stat. 992
Short title, see 42 U.S.C. 7401 note

National Employment Service Act
See Wagner-Peyser Act

National Endowment for Children's Educational Television Act of 1990
Pub. L. 101–437, title II, Oct. 17, 1990, 104 Stat. 997
Short title, see 47 U.S.C. 609 note

National Endowment for Democracy Act
Pub. L. 98–164, title V, Nov. 22, 1983, 97 Stat. 1039 (22 U.S.C. 4411 et seq.)
Short title, see 22 U.S.C. 4411 note

National Energy Conservation Policy Act
Pub. L. 95–619, Nov. 9, 1978, 92 Stat. 3206 (42 U.S.C. 8201 et seq.)
Short title, see 42 U.S.C. 8201 note

National Energy Extension Service Act
Pub. L. 95–39, title V, June 3, 1977, 91 Stat. 191 (42 U.S.C. 7001 et seq.)
Short title, see 42 U.S.C. 7001 note

National Environmental Education Act
Pub. L. 101–619, Nov. 16, 1990, 104 Stat. 3325 (20 U.S.C. 5501 et seq.)
Short title, see 20 U.S.C. 5501 note

National Environmental Policy Act of 1969
Pub. L. 91–190, Jan. 1, 1970, 83 Stat. 852 (42 U.S.C. 4321 et seq.)
Short title, see 42 U.S.C. 4321 note

National Fallen Firefighters Foundation Act
Pub. L. 102–522, title II, Oct. 26, 1992, 106 Stat. 3417

National Family Caregiver Support Act
Pub. L. 89–73, title III, part E, as added Pub. L. 106–501, title III, §316(2), Nov. 13, 2000, 114 Stat. 2253
Short title, see 42 U.S.C. 3001 note

National Film Preservation Act of 1988
Pub. L. 100–446, title I, §§1–13, Sept. 27, 1988, 102 Stat. 1782–1788 (2 U.S.C. 178 et seq.)
Short title, see 2 U.S.C. 178 note

National Film Preservation Act of 1992
Pub. L. 102–307, title II, June 26, 1992, 106 Stat. 267 (2 U.S.C. 179 et seq.)
Short title, see 2 U.S.C. 179 note

National Film Preservation Act of 1996
Pub. L. 104 285, title I, Oct. 11, 1996, 110 Stat. 3377 (2 U.S.C. 179*l* et seq.)
Short title, see 2 U.S.C. 179*l* note

National Film Preservation Foundation Act
Pub. L. 104–285, title II, Oct. 11, 1996, 110 Stat. 3382

National Firearms Act
Aug. 16, 1954, ch. 736, §1(d) [Internal Revenue Title, chapter 53], as added Pub. L. 90–618, title II, §201, Oct. 22, 1968, 82 Stat. 1227 (Title 26, §5801 et seq.)
Short title, see 26 U.S.C. 5849

National Firearms Act Amendments of 1968
Pub. L. 90–618, title II, §201, Oct. 22, 1968, 82 Stat. 1227
Short title, see 26 U.S.C. 5849 note

National Fish and Wildlife Foundation Establishment Act
Pub. L. 98–244, Mar. 26, 1984, 98 Stat. 107 (16 U.S.C. 3701 et seq.)

National Fish and Wildlife Foundation Establishment Act—Continued
Short title, see 16 U.S.C. 3701 note

National Fish and Wildlife Foundation Establishment Act Amendments of 1990
Pub. L. 101–593, title I, §110, Nov. 16, 1990, 104 Stat. 2959
Short title, see 16 U.S.C. 3701 note

National Fish and Wildlife Foundation Establishment Act Amendments of 2000
Pub. L. 106–408, title II, Nov. 1, 2000, 114 Stat. 1777
Short title, see 16 U.S.C. 3701 note

National Fish and Wildlife Foundation Improvement Act of 1994
Pub. L. 103–232, title I, Apr. 11, 1994, 108 Stat. 336
Short title, see 16 U.S.C. 3701 note

National Fishing Enhancement Act of 1984
Pub. L. 98–623, title II, Nov. 8, 1984, 98 Stat. 3394 (33 U.S.C. 2101 et seq.)
Short title, see 33 U.S.C. 2101 note

National Flag Week Act
Pub. L. 89–443, June 9, 1966, 80 Stat. 194

National Flood Insurance Act of 1968
Pub. L. 90–448, title XIII, Aug. 1, 1968, 82 Stat. 572 (42 U.S.C. 4001 et seq.)
Short title, see 42 U.S.C. 4001 note

National Flood Insurance Reform Act of 1994
Pub. L. 103–325, title V, Sept. 23, 1994, 108 Stat. 2255
Short title, see 42 U.S.C. 4001 note

National Forest Foundation Act
Pub. L. 101–593, title IV, Nov. 16, 1990, 104 Stat. 2969 (16 U.S.C. 583j et seq.)
Short title, see 16 U.S.C. 583j note

National Forest Foundation Act Amendment Act of 1993
Pub. L. 103–106, Oct. 12, 1993, 107 Stat. 1031
Short title, see 16 U.S.C. 583j note

National Forest Management Act of 1976
Pub. L. 94–588, Oct. 22, 1976, 90 Stat. 2949
Short title, see 16 U.S.C. 1600 note

National Forest Ski Area Permit Act of 1986
Pub. L. 99–522, Oct. 22, 1986, 100 Stat. 3000 (16 U.S.C. 497b)
Short title, see 16 U.S.C. 497b note

National Forest System Drug Control Act of 1986
Pub. L. 99–570, title XV, Oct. 27, 1986, 100 Stat. 3207–191 (16 U.S.C. 559b et seq.)
Short title, see 16 U.S.C. 559b note

National Forest-Dependent Rural Communities Economic Diversification Act of 1990
Pub. L. 101–624, title XXIII, subtitle G, ch. 2 (§2372 et seq.), Nov. 28, 1990, 104 Stat. 4046 (7 U.S.C. 6611 et seq.)
Short title, see 7 U.S.C. 6601 note

National Foundation on the Arts and the Humanities Act Amendments of 1983
Pub. L. 98–306, May 31, 1984, 98 Stat. 223
Short title, see 20 U.S.C. 951 note

National Foundation on the Arts and the Humanities Act of 1965
Pub. L. 89–209, Sept. 29, 1965, 79 Stat. 845 (20 U.S.C. 951 et seq.)
Short title, see 20 U.S.C. 951 note

National Foundation on the Arts and the Humanities Amendments of 1970
Pub. L. 91–346, July 20, 1970, 84 Stat. 443
Short title, see 20 U.S.C. 951 note

National Foundation on the Arts and the Humanities Amendments of 1973
Pub. L. 93–133, Oct. 19, 1973, 87 Stat. 461
Short title, see 20 U.S.C. 951 note

National Gallery of Art Act
Mar. 24, 1937, ch. 50, 50 Stat. 51 (20 U.S.C. 71 et seq.)

National Gambling Impact Study Commission Act
Pub. L. 104–169, Aug. 3, 1996, 110 Stat. 1482 (18 U.S.C. 1955 note)

National Geography Studies Centers Act
Pub. L. 100–569, title II, Oct. 31, 1988, 102 Stat. 2862
Short title, see 20 U.S.C. 6301 note

National Geologic Mapping Act of 1992
Pub. L. 102–285, May 18, 1992, 106 Stat. 166 (43 U.S.C. 31a et seq.)
Short title, see 43 U.S.C. 31a note

National Geologic Mapping Reauthorization Act of 1997
Pub. L. 105–36, Aug. 5, 1997, 111 Stat. 1107
Short title, see 43 U.S.C. 31a note

National Geologic Mapping Reauthorization Act of 1999
Pub. L. 106–148, Dec. 9, 1999, 113 Stat. 1719
Short title, see 43 U.S.C. 31a note

National Gold and Silver Stamping Act of 1906
Also known as the Jewelers' Liability Act (Gold and Silver Articles)
June 13, 1906, ch. 3289, 34 Stat. 260 (15 U.S.C. 294 et seq.)
Short title, see 15 U.S.C. 294 note

National Guard Act of 1933
June 15, 1933, ch. 87, 48 Stat. 153

National Guard Mobilization Act of 1940
Army Reserve and Retired Personnel Service Law of 1940

National Guard Officers' Act
June 19, 1935, ch. 277, 49 Stat. 391

National Guard Technicians Act of 1968
Pub. L. 90–486, Aug. 13, 1968, 82 Stat. 755
Short title, see 32 U.S.C. 709 note

National Health Museum Development Act
Pub. L. 105–78, title VII, Nov. 13, 1997, 111 Stat. 1524 (20 U.S.C. 50 note)

National Health Planning and Resources Development Act of 1974
Pub. L. 93–641, Jan. 4, 1975, 88 Stat. 2225
Short title, see 42 U.S.C. 201 note

National Health Service Corps Revitalization Amendments of 1990
Pub. L. 101–597, Nov. 16, 1990, 104 Stat. 3013
Short title, see 42 U.S.C. 201 note

National Health Survey Act
July 3, 1956, ch. 510, 70 Stat. 489
Short title, see 42 U.S.C. 201 note

National Heart Act
June 16, 1948, ch. 481, 62 Stat. 464
Short title, see 42 U.S.C. 201 note

National Heart, Blood Vessel, Lung, and Blood Act of 1972
Pub. L. 92–423, Sept. 19, 1972, 86 Stat. 679
Short title, see 42 U.S.C. 201 note

National Highway System Designation Act of 1995
Pub. L. 104–59, Nov. 28, 1995, 109 Stat. 568
Short title, see 23 U.S.C. 101 note

National Highway Traffic Safety Administration Authorization Act of 1991
Pub. L. 102–240, title II, part B (§2500 et seq.), Dec. 18, 1991, 105 Stat. 2081 (49 U.S.C. 30101 note)

National Highway Traffic Safety Administration Reauthorization Act of 1998
Pub. L. 105–178, title VII, subtitle A (§7101 et seq.), June 9, 1998, 112 Stat. 465
Short title, see 49 U.S.C. 30101 note

National Historic Lighthouse Preservation Act of 2000
Pub. L. 106–355, Oct. 24, 2000, 114 Stat. 1385
Short title, see 16 U.S.C. 470 note

National Historic Preservation Act
Pub. L. 89–665, Oct. 15, 1966, 80 Stat. 915 (16 U.S.C. 470 et seq.)
Short title, see 16 U.S.C. 470(a)

National Historic Preservation Act Amendments of 1980
Pub. L. 96–515, Dec. 12, 1980, 94 Stat. 2987
Short title, see 16 U.S.C. 470 note

National Historic Preservation Act Amendments of 1992
Pub. L. 102–575, title XL, Oct. 30, 1992, 106 Stat. 4753
Short title, see 16 U.S.C. 470 note

National Historic Preservation Act Amendments of 2000
Pub. L. 106–208, May 26, 2000, 114 Stat. 318
Short title, see 16 U.S.C. 470 note

National Historical Publications and Records Commission Amendments of 1988
Pub. L. 100–365, July 13, 1988, 102 Stat. 823
Short title, see 44 U.S.C. 101 note

National Homeownership Trust Act
Pub. L. 101–625, title III, subtitle A (§301 et seq.), Nov. 28, 1990, 104 Stat. 4129 (42 U.S.C. 12851 et seq.)
Short title, see 42 U.S.C. 12701 note

National Housing Act
June 27, 1934, ch. 847, 48 Stat. 1246 (12 U.S.C. 1701 et seq.)
Short title, see 12 U.S.C. 1701

National Housing Act Amendments of 1938
Feb. 3, 1938, ch. 13, 52 Stat. 8
Short title, see 12 U.S.C. 1701a

National Housing Census Act
Aug. 11, 1939, ch. 688, 53 Stat. 1406

National Imagery and Mapping Agency Act of 1996
Pub. L. 104–201, div. A, title XI, Sept. 23, 1996, 110 Stat. 2675
Short title, see 10 U.S.C. 441 note

National Independent Colleges and Universities Discovery Act
Pub. L. 102–325, title XIV, part B (§1421 et seq.), July 23, 1992, 106 Stat. 824 (20 U.S.C. 1221–1 note)

National Indian Forest Resources Management Act
Pub. L. 101–630, title III, Nov. 28, 1990, 104 Stat. 4532 (25 U.S.C. 3101 et seq.)
Short title, see 25 U.S.C. 3101 note

National Industrial Recovery Act
June 16, 1933, ch. 90, 48 Stat. 195

National Industrial Recovery Extension Act
June 14, 1935, ch. 246, 49 Stat. 375

National Industrial Reserve Act of 1948
Renamed Defense Industrial Reserve Act

National Institute of Standards and Technology Act
Mar. 3, 1901, ch. 872, 31 Stat. 1449 (15 U.S.C. 271 et seq.)
Short title, see 15 U.S.C. 271 note

National Institute of Standards and Technology Authorization Act for Fiscal Year 1989
Pub. L. 100–519, title I, Oct. 24, 1988, 102 Stat. 2589

National Institute on Deafness and Other Communication Disorders and Health Research Extension Act of 1988
Pub. L. 100–607, title I, Nov. 4, 1988, 102 Stat. 3048
Short title, see 42 U.S.C. 201 note

National Institutes of Health Amendments of 1990
Pub. L. 101–613, Nov. 16, 1990, 104 Stat. 3224
Short title, see 42 U.S.C. 201 note

National Institutes of Health Revitalization Act of 1993
Pub. L. 103–43, June 10, 1993, 107 Stat. 122
Short title, see 42 U.S.C. 201 note

National Insurance Development Act of 1975
Pub. L. 94–13, Apr. 8, 1975, 89 Stat. 68
Short title, see 12 U.S.C. 1701 note

National Invasive Species Act of 1996
Pub. L. 104–332, Oct. 26, 1996, 110 Stat. 4073
Short title, see 16 U.S.C. 4701 note

National Irrigation Act of 1902
Also known as the Reclamation Act
June 17, 1902, ch. 1093, 32 Stat. 388
Short title, see 43 U.S.C. 371 note

National Kiwifruit Research, Promotion, and Consumer Information Act
Pub. L. 104–127, title V, subtitle D (§551 et seq.), Apr. 4, 1996, 110 Stat. 1064 (7 U.S.C. 7461 et seq.)
Short title, see 7 U.S.C. 7401 note

National Labor Relations Act
July 5, 1935, ch. 372, 49 Stat. 449 (29 U.S.C. 151 et seq.)

National Labor Relations Board Appropriation Act, 1941
June 26, 1940, ch. 428, title IV, 54 Stat. 595

National Labor Relations Board Appropriation Act, 1942
July 1, 1941, ch. 269, title IV, 55 Stat. 495

National Labor Relations Board Appropriation Act, 1943
July 2, 1942, ch. 475, title IV, 56 Stat. 590

National Labor Relations Board Appropriation Act, 1944
July 12, 1943, ch. 221, title IV, 57 Stat. 515

National Labor Relations Board Appropriation Act, 1945
June 28, 1944, ch. 302, title IV, 58 Stat. 567

National Labor Relations Board Appropriation Act, 1946
July 3, 1945, ch. 263, title IV, 59 Stat. 377

National Labor Relations Board Appropriation Act, 1947
July 26, 1946, ch. 672, title IV, 60 Stat. 698

National Labor Relations Board Appropriation Act, 1948
July 8, 1947, ch. 210, title III, 61 Stat. 276

National Labor Relations Board Appropriation Act, 1949
June 14, 1948, ch. 465, title III, 62 Stat. 404

National Labor Relations Board Appropriation Act, 1951
Sept. 6, 1950, ch. 896, Ch. V, title III, 64 Stat. 655

National Labor Relations Board Appropriation Act, 1952
Aug. 31, 1951, ch. 373, title III, 65 Stat. 221

National Labor Relations Board Appropriation Act, 1953
July 5, 1952, ch. 575, title III, 66 Stat. 370

National Law Enforcement Cooperation Act of 1990
Pub. L. 101–647, title VI, subtitle B (§611 et seq.), Nov. 29, 1990, 104 Stat. 4823 (28 U.S.C. 534 note)

National Law Enforcement Museum Act
Pub. L. 106–492, Nov. 9, 2000, 114 Stat. 2210

National Library of Medicine Act
Aug. 3, 1956, ch. 907, 70 Stat. 960
Short title, see 42 U.S.C. 201 note

National Literacy Act of 1991
Pub. L. 102–73, July 25, 1991, 105 Stat. 333
Short title, see 20 U.S.C. 1201 note

National Manufactured Housing Construction and Safety Standards Act of 1974
Pub. L. 93–383, title VI, Aug. 22, 1974, 88 Stat. 700 (42 U.S.C. 5401 et seq.)
Short title, see 42 U.S.C. 5401 note

National Marine Sanctuaries Act
Pub. L. 92–532, title III, Oct. 23, 1972, 86 Stat. 1061 (16 U.S.C. 1431 et seq.)
Short title, see 16 U.S.C. 1431 note

National Marine Sanctuaries Amendments Act of 2000
Pub. L. 106–513, Nov. 13, 2000, 114 Stat. 2381
Short title, see 16 U.S.C. 1431 note

National Marine Sanctuaries Preservation Act
Pub. L. 104–283, Oct. 11, 1996, 110 Stat. 3363
Short title, see 16 U.S.C. 1431 note

National Marine Sanctuaries Program Amendments Act of 1992
Pub. L. 102–587, title II, Nov. 4, 1992, 106 Stat. 5039
Short title, see 16 U.S.C. 1431 note

National Maritime Heritage Act of 1994
Pub. L. 103–451, Nov. 2, 1994, 108 Stat. 4769 (16 U.S.C. 5401 et seq.)
Short title, see 16 U.S.C. 5401 note

National Mass Transportation Assistance Act of 1974
Pub. L. 93–503, Nov. 26, 1974, 88 Stat. 1565

National Materials and Minerals Policy, Research and Development Act of 1980
Pub. L. 96–479, Oct. 21, 1980, 94 Stat. 2305 (30 U.S.C. 1601 et seq.)
Short title, see 30 U.S.C. 1601 note

National Materials Policy Act of 1970
Pub. L. 91–512, title II, Oct. 26, 1970, 84 Stat. 1234 (42 U.S.C. 6901 note)

National Medal of Honor Memorial Act
Pub. L. 106–83, Oct. 28, 1999, 113 Stat. 1293 (16 U.S.C. 431 note)

National Mediation Board Appropriation Act, 1941
June 26, 1940, ch. 428, title V, 54 Stat. 595

National Mediation Board Appropriation Act, 1942
July 1, 1941, ch. 269, title V, 55 Stat. 495

National Mediation Board Appropriation Act, 1943
July 2, 1942, ch. 475, title V, 56 Stat. 590

National Mediation Board Appropriation Act, 1944
July 12, 1943, ch. 221, title V, 57 Stat. 515

National Mediation Board Appropriation Act, 1945
June 28, 1944, ch. 302, title V, 58 Stat. 568

National Mediation Board Appropriation Act, 1946
July 3, 1945, ch. 263, title V, 59 Stat. 378

National Mediation Board Appropriation Act, 1947
July 26, 1946, ch. 672, title V, 60 Stat. 699

National Mediation Board Appropriation Act, 1948
July 8, 1947, ch. 210, title IV, 61 Stat. 277

National Mediation Board Appropriation Act, 1949
June 14, 1948, ch. 465, title IV, 62 Stat. 405

National Mediation Board Appropriation Act, 1950
June 29, 1949, ch. 275, title III, 63 Stat. 296

National Mediation Board Appropriation Act, 1951
Sept. 6, 1950, ch. 896, Ch. V, title IV, 64 Stat. 655

National Mediation Board Appropriation Act, 1952
Aug. 31, 1951, ch. 373, title IV, 65 Stat. 221

National Mediation Board Appropriation Act, 1953
July 5, 1952, ch. 575, title IV, 66 Stat. 370

National Mental Health Act
July 3, 1946, ch. 538, 60 Stat. 421
Short title, see 42 U.S.C. 201 note

National Military Establishment Appropriation Act, 1950
Oct. 29, 1949, ch. 787, 63 Stat. 987

National Military Establishment Lands Act of 1950
July 11, 1950, ch. 456, 64 Stat. 325

National Mimbres Culture Study Act of 1988
Pub. L. 100–559, title III, Oct. 28, 1988, 102 Stat. 2798

National Missile Defense Act of 1999
Pub. L. 106–38, July 22, 1999, 113 Stat. 205
Short title, see 10 U.S.C. 101 note

National Mobile Home Construction and Safety Standards Act of 1974
Renamed National Manufactured Housing Construction and Safety Standards Act of 1974

National Moment of Remembrance Act
Pub. L. 106–579, Dec. 28, 2000, 114 Stat. 3078 (36 U.S.C. 116 note)

National Monument Act (Preservation of Antiquities)
Also known as the Antiquities Act of 1906
June 8, 1906, ch. 3060, 34 Stat. 225 (16 U.S.C. 431 et seq.)
Short title, see 16 U.S.C. 431 note

National Motor Vehicle Theft Act
Oct. 29, 1919, ch. 89, 41 Stat. 324

National Museum Act of 1966
Pub. L. 89–674, Oct. 15, 1966, 80 Stat. 953
Short title, see 20 U.S.C. 41 note

National Museum of the American Indian Act
Pub. L. 101–185, Nov. 28, 1989, 103 Stat. 1336 (20 U.S.C. 80q et seq.)
Short title, see 20 U.S.C. 80q note

National Museum of the American Indian Act Amendments of 1996
Pub. L. 104–278, Oct. 9, 1996, 110 Stat. 3355
Short title, see 20 U.S.C. 80q note

National Museum of the American Indian Commemorative Coin Act of 2000
Also known as the American Buffalo Coin Commemorative Coin Act of 2000
Pub. L. 106–375, Oct. 27, 2000, 114 Stat. 1435 (31 U.S.C. 5112 note)

National Narcotics Act of 1984
Pub. L. 98–473, title II, ch. XIII (§1301 et seq.), Oct. 12, 1984, 98 Stat. 2168 (21 U.S.C. 1201 et seq.)

National Narcotics Leadership Act of 1988
Pub. L. 100–690, title I, subtitle A (§1001 et seq.), Nov. 18, 1988, 102 Stat. 4181
Short title, see 21 U.S.C. 1501 note

National Natural Resources Conservation Foundation Act
Pub. L. 104–127, title III, subtitle F (§351 et seq.), Apr. 4, 1996, 110 Stat. 1010 (16 U.S.C. 5801 et seq.)
Short title, see 16 U.S.C. 5801 note

National Neighborhood Policy Act
Pub. L. 95–24, title II, Apr. 30, 1977, 91 Stat. 56 (42 U.S.C. 1441 note)

National Nuclear Security Administration Act
Pub. L. 106–65, div. C, title XXXII, Oct. 5, 1999, 113 Stat. 953 (50 U.S.C. 2401 et seq.)
Short title, see 50 U.S.C. 2401 note

National Nutrition Monitoring and Related Research Act of 1990
Pub. L. 101–445, Oct. 22, 1990, 104 Stat. 1034 (7 U.S.C. 5301 et seq.)
Short title, see 7 U.S.C. 5301 note

National Ocean Pollution Planning Act of 1978
Pub. L. 95–273, May 8, 1978, 92 Stat. 228 (33 U.S.C. 1701 et seq.)
Short title, see 33 U.S.C. 1701 note

National Ocean Pollution Research and Development and Monitoring Planning Act of 1978
Renamed National Ocean Pollution Planning Act of 1978

National Oceanic and Atmospheric Administration Authorization Act of 1992
Pub. L. 102–567, Oct. 29, 1992, 106 Stat. 4270

National Oceanic and Atmospheric Administration Marine Fisheries Program Authorization Act
Pub. L. 98–210, Dec. 6, 1983, 97 Stat. 1409

National Oceanic and Atmospheric Administration Ocean and Coastal Programs Authorization Act of 1989
Pub. L. 101–224, Dec. 12, 1989, 103 Stat. 1905

National Oilheat Research Alliance Act of 2000
Pub. L. 106–469, title VII, Nov. 9, 2000, 114 Stat. 2043 (42 U.S.C. 6201 note)

National Organ Transplant Act
Pub. L. 98–507, Oct. 19, 1984, 98 Stat. 2339
Short title, see 42 U.S.C. 201 note

National Park Foundation Act
Pub. L. 90–209, Dec. 18, 1967, 81 Stat. 656 (16 U.S.C. 19e et seq.)

National Park Foundation Act—Continued
Short title, see 16 U.S.C. 19e note

National Park Police Drug Enforcement Supplemental Authority Act
Pub. L. 99–570, title V, subtitle B (§5051 et seq.), Oct. 27, 1986, 100 Stat. 3207–156 (16 U.S.C. 1 note)

National Park Service Concessions Management Improvement Act of 1998
Pub. L. 105–391, title IV, Nov. 13, 1998, 112 Stat. 3503 (16 U.S.C. 5951 et seq.)
Short title, see 16 U.S.C. 5901 note

National Park Service Concessions Policy Act
See National Park System Concessions Policy Act

National Park Service Organic Act
Aug. 25, 1916, ch. 408, 39 Stat. 535 (16 U.S.C. 1 et seq.)
Short title, see 16 U.S.C. 1 note

National Park Service Studies Act of 1999
Pub. L. 106–113, div. B, §1000(a)(3) [title III, §326], Nov. 29, 1999, 113 Stat. 1535, 1501A–194 (16 U.S.C. 1a–5 note)

National Park System Concessions Policy Act
Pub. L. 89–249, Oct. 9, 1965, 79 Stat. 969 (16 U.S.C. 20 et seq.)

National Park System General Authorities Act
Pub. L. 91–383, Aug. 18, 1970, 84 Stat. 825 (16 U.S.C. 1a—1 et seq.)
Short title, see 16 U.S.C. 1 note

National Park System New Areas Studies Act
Pub. L. 105–391, title III, Nov. 13, 1998, 112 Stat. 3501
Short title, see 16 U.S.C. 1 note

National Park System Visitor Facilities Fund Act
Pub. L. 97–433, Jan. 8, 1983, 96 Stat. 2277 (16 U.S.C. 19aa et seq.)
Short title, see 16 U.S.C. 19aa note

National Parks Air Tour Management Act of 2000
Pub. L. 106–181, title VIII, Apr. 5, 2000, 114 Stat. 185
Short title, see 49 U.S.C. 40128 note

National Parks and Recreation Act of 1978
Pub. L. 95–625, Nov. 10, 1978, 92 Stat. 3467
Short title, see 16 U.S.C. 1 note

National Parks Omnibus Management Act of 1998
Pub. L. 105–391, Nov. 13, 1998, 112 Stat. 3497 (16 U.S.C. 5901 et seq.)
Short title, see 16 U.S.C. 5901 note

National Police Athletic League Youth Enrichment Act of 2000
Pub. L. 106–367, Oct. 27, 2000, 114 Stat. 1412 (42 U.S.C. 13751 note)

National Portrait Gallery Act
Pub. L. 87–443, Apr. 27, 1962, 76 Stat. 62 (20 U.S.C. 75a et seq.)
Short title, see 20 U.S.C. 75a note

National Productivity and Quality of Working Life Act of 1975
Pub. L. 94–136, Nov. 28, 1975, 89 Stat. 733 (15 U.S.C. 2401 et seq.)
Short title, see 15 U.S.C. 2401 note

National Prohibition Act
Oct. 28, 1919, ch. 85, 41 Stat. 305

National Recording Preservation Act of 2000
Pub. L. 106–474, Nov. 9, 2000, 114 Stat. 2085
Short title, see 2 U.S.C. 1701 note

National Research Act
Pub. L. 93–348, July 12, 1974, 88 Stat. 342
Short title, see 42 U.S.C. 201 note

National Research Service Award Act of 1974
Pub. L. 93–348, title I, July 12, 1974, 88 Stat. 342
Short title, see 42 U.S.C. 201 note

National School Lunch Act
Renamed Richard B. Russell National School Lunch Act

National School Lunch Act and Child Nutrition Act of 1966 Amendments of 1975
Pub. L. 94–105, Oct. 7, 1975, 89 Stat. 511
Short title, see 42 U.S.C. 1751 note

National School Lunch Act and Child Nutrition Amendments of 1977
Pub. L. 95–166, Nov. 10, 1977, 91 Stat. 1325
Short title, see 42 U.S.C. 1751 note

National School Lunch and Child Nutrition Act Amendments of 1973
Pub. L. 93–150, Nov. 7, 1973, 87 Stat. 560
Short title, see 42 U.S.C. 1751 note

National School Lunch and Child Nutrition Act Amendments of 1974
Pub. L. 93–326, June 30, 1974, 88 Stat. 286
Short title, see 42 U.S.C. 1751 note

National Science and Technology Policy, Organization, and Priorities Act of 1976
Pub. L. 94–282, May 11, 1976, 90 Stat. 459 (42 U.S.C. 6601 et seq.)
Short title, see 42 U.S.C. 6601 note

National Science Foundation Act of 1950
May 10, 1950, ch. 171, 64 Stat. 149 (42 U.S.C. 1861 et seq.)
Short title, see 42 U.S.C. 1861 note

National Science Foundation Authorization Act for Fiscal Year 1979
Pub. L. 95–434, Oct. 10, 1978, 92 Stat. 1049

National Science Foundation Authorization Act for Fiscal Year 1980
Pub. L. 96–44, Aug. 2, 1979, 93 Stat. 333

National Science Foundation Authorization Act for Fiscal Year 1986
Pub. L. 99–159, title I, Nov. 22, 1985, 99 Stat. 887
Short title, see 42 U.S.C. 1861 note

National Science Foundation Authorization Act for Fiscal Year 1987
Pub. L. 99–383, Aug. 21, 1986, 100 Stat. 813
Short title, see 42 U.S.C. 1861 note

National Science Foundation Authorization Act of 1971
Pub. L. 91–356, July 24, 1970, 84 Stat. 471

National Science Foundation Authorization Act of 1972
Pub. L. 92–86, Aug. 11, 1971, 85 Stat. 308

National Science Foundation Authorization Act of 1973
Pub. L. 92–372, Aug. 10, 1972, 86 Stat. 526

National Science Foundation Authorization Act of 1988
Pub. L. 100–570, Oct. 31, 1988, 102 Stat. 2865
Short title, see 42 U.S.C. 1861 note

National Science Foundation Authorization Act of 1998
Pub. L. 105–207, July 29, 1998, 112 Stat. 869
Short title, see 42 U.S.C. 1861 note

National Science Foundation Authorization Act, 1970
Pub. L. 91–120, Nov. 18, 1969, 83 Stat. 203

National Science Foundation Authorization Act, 1974
Pub. L. 93–96, Aug. 16, 1973, 87 Stat. 315

National Science Foundation Authorization Act, 1975
Pub. L. 93–413, Sept. 4, 1974, 88 Stat. 1093

National Science Foundation Authorization Act, 1976
Pub. L. 94–86, Aug. 9, 1975, 89 Stat. 427

National Science Foundation Authorization Act, 1977
Pub. L. 94–471, Oct. 11, 1976, 90 Stat. 2053
Short title, see 42 U.S.C. 1861 note

National Science Foundation Authorization Act, Fiscal Year 1978
Pub. L. 95–99, Aug. 15, 1977, 91 Stat. 831
Short title, see 42 U.S.C. 1861 note

National Science Foundation Authorization and Science and Engineering Equal Opportunities Act
Pub. L. 96–516, Dec. 12, 1980, 94 Stat. 3007
Short title, see 42 U.S.C. 1861 note

National Science Foundation Authorization and Science and Technology Equal Opportunities Act
Renamed National Science Foundation Authorization and Science and Engineering Equal Opportunities Act

National Science Foundation University Infrastructure Act of 1988
Pub. L. 100–418, title VI, subtitle E (§6401 et seq.), Aug. 23, 1988, 102 Stat. 1542
Short title, see 42 U.S.C. 1861 note

National Science, Engineering, and Mathematics Authorization Act of 1986
Pub. L. 99–159, Nov. 22, 1985, 99 Stat. 887
Short title, see 20 U.S.C. 3901 note

National Sea Grant College and Program Act of 1966
Renamed National Sea Grant College Program Act

National Sea Grant College Program Act
Pub. L. 89–454, title II, as added Pub. L. 89–688, §1, Oct. 15, 1966, 80 Stat. 998 (33 U.S.C. 1121 et seq.)
Short title, see 33 U.S.C. 1121 note

National Sea Grant College Program Authorization Act of 1987
Pub. L. 100–220, title III, subtitle A (§3101 et seq.), Dec. 29, 1987, 101 Stat. 1469
Short title, see 33 U.S.C. 1121 note

National Sea Grant College Program Authorization Act of 1991
Pub. L. 102–186, Dec. 4, 1991, 105 Stat. 1282
Short title, see 33 U.S.C. 1121 note

National Sea Grant College Program Reauthorization Act of 1998
Pub. L. 105–160, Mar. 6, 1998, 112 Stat. 21
Short title, see 33 U.S.C. 1121 note

National Securities Markets Improvement Act of 1996
Pub. L. 104–290, Oct. 11, 1996, 110 Stat. 3416
Short title, see 15 U.S.C. 78a note

National Security Act Amendments of 1949
Aug. 10, 1949, ch. 412, 63 Stat. 578
Short title, see 50 U.S.C. 401 note

National Security Act of 1947
July 26, 1947, ch. 343, 61 Stat. 495 (50 U.S.C. 401 et seq.)
Short title, see 50 U.S.C. 401 note

National Security Agency Act of 1959
Pub. L. 86–36, May 29, 1959, 73 Stat. 63 (50 U.S.C. 402 note)

National Security Agency Voluntary Separation Act
July 26, 1947, ch. 343, title III, §301, as added Pub. L. 106–567, title III, §304(a), Dec. 27, 2000, 114 Stat. 2836 (50 U.S.C. 409a)

National Security and Corporate Fairness under the Biological Weapons Convention Act
Pub. L. 106–113, div. B, §1000(a)(7) [div. B, title XI, subtitle A, ch. 2 (§1121 et seq.)], Nov. 29, 1999, 113 Stat. 1536, 1501A–490 (22 U.S.C. 5601 note)

National Security Education Act of 1991
Renamed David L. Boren National Security Education Act of 1991

National Service Life Insurance Act of 1940
Oct. 8, 1940, ch. 757, title VI, part I (§601 et seq.), 54 Stat. 1008

National Shipbuilding and Shipyard Conversion Act of 1993
Pub. L. 103–160, div. A, title XIII, subtitle D (§1351 et seq.), Nov. 30, 1993, 107 Stat. 1809 (10 U.S.C. 2501 note)

National Sickle Cell Anemia Control Act
Pub. L. 92–294, May 16, 1972, 86 Stat. 136

National Sickle Cell Anemia, Cooley's Anemia, Tay-Sachs, and Genetic Diseases Act
Pub. L. 94–278, title IV, Apr. 22, 1976, 90 Stat. 407
Short title, see 42 U.S.C. 201 note

National Skill Standards Act of 1994
Pub. L. 103–227, title V, Mar. 31, 1994, 108 Stat. 191 (20 U.S.C. 5931 et seq.)
Short title, see 20 U.S.C. 5931

National Space Council Authorization Act of 1990
Pub. L. 101–328, July 8, 1990, 104 Stat. 308

National Space Grant College and Fellowship Act
Pub. L. 100–147, title II, Oct. 30, 1987, 101 Stat. 869 (42 U.S.C. 2486 et seq.)
Short title, see 42 U.S.C. 2486 note

National Stolen Property Act
May 22, 1934, ch. 333, 48 Stat. 794

National Summit Conference on Education Act of 1984
Pub. L. 98–524, §5, Oct. 19, 1984, 98 Stat. 2489

National Superconductivity and Competitiveness Act of 1988
Pub. L. 100–697, Nov. 19, 1988, 102 Stat. 4613 (15 U.S.C. 5201 et seq.)
Short title, see 15 U.S.C. 5201 note

National Swine Flu Immunization Program of 1976
Pub. L. 94–380, Aug. 12, 1976, 90 Stat. 1113
Short title, see 42 U.S.C. 201 note

National Teacher Training Project Act of 1994
Pub. L. 89–10, title II, §2103, as added Pub. L. 103–382, title I, §101, Oct. 20, 1994, 108 Stat. 3617 (20 U.S.C. 6623)
Short title, see 20 U.S.C. 6623(a)

National Technical Information Act of 1988
Pub. L. 100–519, title II, subtitle B (§211 et seq.), Oct. 24, 1988, 102 Stat. 2594 (15 U.S.C. 3704b)
Short title, see 15 U.S.C. 3701 note

National Technical Institute for the Deaf Act
Pub. L. 89–36, June 8, 1965, 79 Stat. 125 (20 U.S.C. 681 et seq.)
Short title, see 20 U.S.C. 681 note

National Technology Transfer and Advancement Act of 1995
Pub. L. 104–113, Mar. 7, 1996, 110 Stat. 775
Short title, see 15 U.S.C. 3701 note

National Telecommunications and Information Administration Organization Act
Pub. L. 102–538, title I, Oct. 27, 1992, 106 Stat. 3533 (47 U.S.C. 901 et seq.)
Short title, see 47 U.S.C. 901 note

National Tourism Policy Act
Pub. L. 97–63, Oct. 16, 1981, 95 Stat. 1011
Short title, see 22 U.S.C. 2121 note

National Traffic and Motor Vehicle Safety Act Amendments of 1972
Pub. L. 92–548, Oct. 25, 1972, 86 Stat. 1159

National Traffic and Motor Vehicle Safety Act of 1966
Pub. L. 89–563, Sept. 9, 1966, 80 Stat. 718
Short title, see 15 U.S.C. 1381 note

National Trails System Act
Pub. L. 90–543, Oct. 2, 1968, 82 Stat. 919 (16 U.S.C. 1241 et seq.)
Short title, see 16 U.S.C. 1241 note

National Trails System Act Amendments of 1983
Pub. L. 98–11, title II, Mar. 28, 1983, 97 Stat. 42
Short title, see 16 U.S.C. 1241 note

National Trails System Improvements Act of 1988
Pub. L. 100–470, Oct. 4, 1988, 102 Stat. 2281
Short title, see 16 U.S.C. 1241 note

National Transportation Policy
See Transportation Act of 1940

National Transportation Safety Board Amendments Act of 2000
Pub. L. 106–424, Nov. 1, 2000, 114 Stat. 1883
Short title, see 49 U.S.C. 1101 note

National Transportation Safety Board Amendments of 1996
Pub. L. 104–291, title I, Oct. 11, 1996, 110 Stat. 3452
Short title, see 49 U.S.C. 1101 note

National Underground Railroad Freedom Center Act
Pub. L. 106–291, title I, §150, Oct. 11, 2000, 114 Stat. 956
Short title, see 16 U.S.C. 461 note

National Underground Railroad Network to Freedom Act of 1998
Pub. L. 105–203, July 21, 1998, 112 Stat. 678 (16 U.S.C. 469*l*, 469*l*–1)
Short title, see 16 U.S.C. 461 note

National Urban Policy and New Community Development Act of 1970
Pub. L. 91–609, title VII, Dec. 31, 1970, 84 Stat. 1791 (42 U.S.C. 4501 et seq.)
Short title, see 42 U.S.C. 4501 note

National Venereal Disease Prevention and Control Act
Pub. L. 92–449, title II, Sept. 30, 1972, 86 Stat. 750
Short title, see 42 U.S.C. 201 note

National Visitor Center Emergency Repair Act of 1980
Pub. L. 96–610, Dec. 28, 1980, 94 Stat. 3564
Short title, see 40 U.S.C. 801 note

National Visitor Center Facilities Act of 1968
Pub. L. 90–264, Mar. 12, 1968, 82 Stat. 43 (40 U.S.C. 801 et seq.)
Short title, see 40 U.S.C. 801 note

National Vocational Student Loan Insurance Act of 1965
Pub. L. 89–287, Oct. 22, 1965, 79 Stat. 1037 (20 U.S.C. 981 et seq.)

National Voter Registration Act of 1993
Pub. L. 103–31, May 20, 1993, 107 Stat. 77 (42 U.S.C. 1973gg et seq.)
Short title, see 42 U.S.C. 1973gg note

National War Agencies Appropriation Act, 1944
July 12, 1943, ch. 228, 57 Stat. 522

National War Agencies Appropriation Act, 1945
June 28, 1944, ch. 301, 58 Stat. 533

National War Agencies Appropriation Act, 1946
July 17, 1945, ch. 319, 59 Stat. 473

National Water Commission Act
Pub. L. 90–515, Sept. 26, 1968, 82 Stat. 868 (42 U.S.C. 1962a note)

National Weather Modification Policy Act of 1976
Pub. L. 94–490, Oct. 13, 1976, 90 Stat. 2359 (15 U.S.C. 330 note)

National Whale Conservation Fund Act of 1998
Pub. L. 105–277, div. A, §101(b) [title IX], Oct. 21, 1998, 112 Stat. 2681–50, 2681–119
Short title, see 16 U.S.C. 3701 note

National Wildlife Refuge System Administration Act Amendments of 1974
Pub. L. 93–509, Dec. 3, 1974, 88 Stat. 1603
Short title, see 16 U.S.C. 668dd note

National Wildlife Refuge System Administration Act of 1966
Pub. L. 89–669, §§4, 5, Oct. 15, 1966, 80 Stat. 927–929 (16 U.S.C. 668dd, 668ee)
Short title, see 16 U.S.C. 668dd note

National Wildlife Refuge System Centennial Act
Pub. L. 106–408, title III, Nov. 1, 2000, 114 Stat. 1782 (16 668dd note)

National Wildlife Refuge System Improvement Act of 1997
Pub. L. 105–57, Oct. 9, 1997, 111 Stat. 1252
Short title, see 16 U.S.C. 668dd note

National Wildlife Refuge System Improvement Act of 1998
Pub. L. 105–312, title II, Oct. 30, 1998, 112 Stat. 2957
Short title, see 16 U.S.C. 668dd note

National Wildlife Refuge System Volunteer and Community Partnership Enhancement Act of 1998
Pub. L. 105–242, Oct. 5, 1998, 112 Stat. 1574
Short title, see 16 U.S.C. 742a note

National Women's Business Council Reauthorization Act of 2000
Pub. L. 106–554, §1(a)(9) [title VII], Dec. 21, 2000, 114 Stat. 2763, 2763A–701
Short title, see 15 U.S.C. 631 note

National Wool Act of 1954
Aug. 28, 1954, ch. 1041, title VII, 68 Stat. 910 (7 U.S.C. 1781 et seq.)
Short title, see 7 U.S.C. 1781 note

National Youth Administration Appropriation Act, 1941
June 26, 1940, ch. 428, title II, pars. 1–21, 54 Stat. 590–594

National Youth Administration Appropriation Act, 1942
July 1, 1941, ch. 269, title II, pars. 1–23, 55 Stat. 487–491

National Youth Administration Appropriation Act, 1943
July 2, 1942, ch. 475, title II, pars. 1–26, 56 Stat. 571–575

National-bank act
See National Bank Act

Nationality Act of 1940
Oct. 14, 1940, ch. 876, 54 Stat. 1137 (8 U.S.C. 501 et seq.)

Native American Business Development, Trade Promotion, and Tourism Act of 2000
Pub. L. 106–464, Nov. 7, 2000, 114 Stat. 2012 (25 U.S.C. 4301 et seq.)
Short title, see 25 U.S.C. 4301 note

Native American Graves Protection and Repatriation Act
Pub. L. 101–601, Nov. 16, 1990, 104 Stat. 3048 (25 U.S.C. 3001 et seq.)
Short title, see 25 U.S.C. 3001 note

Native American Housing Assistance and Self-Determination Act of 1996
Pub. L. 104–330, Oct. 26, 1996, 110 Stat. 4016 (25 U.S.C. 4101 et seq.)
Short title, see 25 U.S.C. 4101 note

Native American Languages Act
Pub. L. 101–477, title I, Oct. 30, 1990, 104 Stat. 1153 (25 U.S.C. 2901 et seq.)
Short title, see 25 U.S.C. 2901 note

Native American Languages Act of 1992
Pub. L. 102–524, §§1–3, Oct. 26, 1992, 106 Stat. 3434–3437
Short title, see 42 U.S.C. 2991 note

Native American Laws Technical Corrections Act of 2000
Pub. L. 106–568, title VIII, Dec. 27, 2000, 114 Stat. 2916
Short title, see 25 U.S.C. 450 note

Native American Programs Act Amendments of 1984
Pub. L. 98–558, title X, Oct. 30, 1984, 98 Stat. 2905
Short title, see 42 U.S.C. 2991 note

Native American Programs Act Amendments of 1987
Pub. L. 100–175, title V, Nov. 29, 1987, 101 Stat. 973
Short title, see 42 U.S.C. 2991 note

Native American Programs Act Amendments of 1992
Pub. L. 102–375, title VIII, subtitle C (§821 et seq.), Sept. 30, 1992, 106 Stat. 1295
Short title, see 42 U.S.C. 2991 note

Native American Programs Act Amendments of 1998
Pub. L. 105–361, Nov. 10, 1998, 112 Stat. 3278
Short title, see 42 U.S.C. 2991 note

Native American Programs Act of 1974
Pub. L. 88–452, title VIII, as added Pub. L. 93–644, §11, Jan. 4, 1975, 88 Stat. 2323 (42 U.S.C. 2991 et seq.)
Short title, see 42 U.S.C. 2991

Native American Veterans' Memorial Establishment Act of 1994
Pub. L. 103–384, Oct. 22, 1994, 108 Stat. 4067 (20 U.S.C. 80q–5 note)

Native Americans Educational Assistance Act
Pub. L. 102–524, §4, Oct. 26, 1992, 106 Stat. 3437 (25 U.S.C. 2001 note)

Native Hawaiian Education Act
Pub. L. 89–10, title IX, part B (§9201 et seq.), as added Pub. L. 103–382, title I, §101, Oct. 20, 1994, 108 Stat. 3794 (20 U.S.C. 7901 et seq.)
Short title, see 20 U.S.C. 7901

Native Hawaiian Health Care Act of 1988
Renamed Native Hawaiian Health Care Improvement Act

Native Hawaiian Health Care Improvement Act
Pub. L. 100–579, Oct. 31, 1988, 102 Stat. 2916 (42 U.S.C. 11701 et seq.)
Pub. L. 100–690, title II, subtitle D (§2301 et seq.), Nov. 18, 1988, 102 Stat. 4222 (42 U.S.C. 11701 et seq.)
Short title, see 42 U.S.C. 11701 note

Native Latex Commercialization and Economic Development Act of 1978
Renamed the Critical Agricultural Materials Act

Native Townsite Act of 1926
See Alaskan Native Townsite Act of 1926

NATO Enlargement Facilitation Act of 1996
Pub. L. 104–208, div. A, title I, §101(c) [title VI], Sept. 30, 1996, 110 Stat. 3009–121, 3009–173 (22 U.S.C. 1928 note)

NATO Participation Act of 1994
Pub. L. 103–447, title II, Nov. 2, 1994, 108 Stat. 4695 (28 U.S.C. 1928 note)

Natural Gas Act
June 21, 1938, ch. 556, 52 Stat. 821 (15 U.S.C. 717 et seq.)
Short title, see 15 U.S.C. 717w

Natural Gas Pipeline Safety Act Amendments of 1974
Pub. L. 93–403, Aug. 30, 1974, 88 Stat. 802

Natural Gas Pipeline Safety Act Amendments of 1976
Pub. L. 94–477, Oct. 11, 1976, 90 Stat. 2073

Natural Gas Pipeline Safety Act of 1968
Pub. L. 90–481, Aug. 12, 1968, 82 Stat. 720

Natural Gas Policy Act of 1978
Pub. L. 95–621, Nov. 9, 1978, 92 Stat. 3350 (15 U.S.C. 3301 et seq.)
Short title, see 15 U.S.C. 3301 note

Natural Gas Wellhead Decontrol Act of 1989
Pub. L. 101–60, July 26, 1989, 103 Stat. 157
Short title, see 15 U.S.C. 3301 note

Nautical Education Act
Aug. 4, 1939, ch. 416, 53 Stat. 1181

Navajo and Hopi Indian Relocation Amendments Act of 1980
Pub. L. 96–305, July 8, 1980, 94 Stat. 929
Short title, see 25 U.S.C. 640d note

Navajo and Hopi Indian Relocation Amendments of 1988
Pub. L. 100–666, Nov. 16, 1988, 102 Stat. 3929
Short title, see 25 U.S.C. 640d note

Navajo Community College Act
Pub. L. 92–189, Dec. 15, 1971, 85 Stat. 646 (25 U.S.C. 640a et seq.)
Short title, see 25 U.S.C. 640a note

Navajo Community College Assistance Act of 1978
Pub. L. 95–471, title II, Oct. 17, 1978, 92 Stat. 1329
Short title, see 25 U.S.C. 640a note

Navajo Nation Trust Land Leasing Act of 2000
Pub. L. 106–568, title XII, Dec. 27, 2000, 114 Stat. 2933
Short title, see 25 U.S.C. 415 note

Navajo-Hopi Land Dispute Settlement Act of 1996
Pub. L. 104–301, Oct. 11, 1996, 110 Stat. 3649 (25 U.S.C. 640d note)

Navajo-Hopi Land Settlement Act of 1974
Pub. L. 93–531, Dec. 22, 1974, 88 Stat. 1712 (25 U.S.C. 640d et seq.)

Navajo-Hopi Rehabilitation Act
Apr. 19, 1950, ch. 92, 64 Stat. 44 (25 U.S.C. 631 et seq.)

Navajo-Hopi Relocation Housing Program Reauthorization Act of 1991
Pub. L. 102–180, Dec. 2, 1991, 105 Stat. 1230
Short title, see 25 U.S.C. 640d note

Naval Academy Act
June 3, 1941, ch. 162, 55 Stat. 238

Naval Academy Age Limit Act
Sept. 24, 1940, ch. 729, 54 Stat. 959

Naval Air Base Act
Apr. 25, 1939, ch. 87, 53 Stat. 590

Naval Air Station Act
Aug. 16, 1941, ch. 359, 55 Stat. 624

Naval Aircraft-Public Works Act
June 15, 1940, ch. 375, 54 Stat. 400

Naval Appropriation Act, 1942
May 6, 1941, ch. 86, 55 Stat. 151

Naval Appropriation Act, 1943
Feb. 7, 1942, ch. 46, title I, 56 Stat. 54

Naval Appropriation Act, 1944
June 26, 1943, ch. 147, title I, 57 Stat. 197

Naval Appropriation Act, 1945
June 22, 1944, ch. 269, title I, 58 Stat. 301

Naval Appropriation Act, 1946
May 29, 1945, ch. 130, 59 Stat. 201

Naval Appropriation Act, 1947
July 8, 1946, ch. 543, title I, 60 Stat. 481

Naval Aviation Cadet Act
Apr. 15, 1935, ch. 71, 49 Stat. 156

Naval Aviation Cadet Act of 1942
Aug. 4, 1942, ch. 547, 56 Stat. 737

Naval Aviation Personnel Act of 1940
Aug. 27, 1940, ch. 694, 54 Stat. 864

Naval Aviation Reserve Act of 1939
June 13, 1939, ch. 205, 53 Stat. 819

Naval Drydock Act
Sept. 18, 1940, ch. 723, 54 Stat. 956

Naval Facilities Act
July 29, 1941, ch. 328, 55 Stat. 608

Naval Line-Officer Act
July 22, 1935, ch. 402, 49 Stat. 487

Naval Militia Act
Feb. 16, 1914, ch. 21, 38 Stat. 283

Naval Parity Act
Mar. 27, 1934, ch. 95, 48 Stat. 503

Naval Petroleum Reserves Production Act of 1976
Pub. L. 94–258, Apr. 5, 1976, 90 Stat. 303
Short title, see 42 U.S.C. 6501 note

Naval Plant-Protection Force Act
Aug. 11, 1941, ch. 352, 55 Stat. 616

Naval Public Works Act
June 2, 1939, ch. 169, 53 Stat. 798

Naval R.O.T.C. Act
Sept. 11, 1940, ch. 718, 54 Stat. 884

Naval Reserve Act of 1938
June 25, 1938, ch. 690, 52 Stat. 1175

Naval Service Appropriations Act, 1922
July 12, 1921, ch. 44, 42 Stat. 122

Naval Ship Alteration Act
Jan. 29, 1941, ch. 1, 55 Stat. 3

Naval Special Duty Act
July 17, 1941, ch. 304, 55 Stat. 598

Naval Staff Corps Act
Aug. 5, 1935, ch. 439, 49 Stat. 530

Naval Stores Act
Mar. 3, 1923, ch. 217, 42 Stat. 1435 (7 U.S.C. 91 et seq.)
Short title, see 7 U.S.C. 91

Navy and Marine Corps Officer Augmentation Act of 1955
Aug. 9, 1955, ch. 668, 69 Stat. 606

Navy Construction Act
May 17, 1938, ch. 243, 52 Stat. 401

Navy Department Appropriation Act, 1948
July 18, 1947, ch. 268, 61 Stat. 382

Navy Department Reorganization Act
June 20, 1940, ch. 400, 54 Stat. 492

Navy Enlisted Strength Act
Apr. 22, 1941, ch. 74, 55 Stat. 145

Navy Local Defense Ship Act
Nov. 21, 1941, ch. 502, 55 Stat. 782

Navy Ordnance Act
Mar. 17, 1942, ch. 187, 56 Stat. 172

Navy Personnel Act
Mar. 3, 1899, ch. 413, 30 Stat. 1004

Navy Promotion Act
May 29, 1934, ch. 368, 48 Stat. 814

Navy Shipbuilding and Repair Act
Jan. 29, 1942, ch. 25, 56 Stat. 23

Navy Shipbuilding Facilities Act
Jan. 31, 1941, ch. 4, 55 Stat. 5

Navy Shipbuilding Program Act
Feb. 6, 1942, ch. 45, 56 Stat. 53

Navy-Marine Advancement Act
Feb. 23, 1942, ch. 110, 56 Stat. 120

Navy-Marine Corps Enlisted Strength Act
Jan. 12, 1942, ch. 1, 56 Stat. 3

Navy-Yard Tracks Act
May 27, 1908, ch. 203, 35 Stat. 397

Nazi War Crimes Disclosure Act
Pub. L. 105–246, Oct. 8, 1998, 112 Stat. 1859 (5 U.S.C. 552 note)

Nebraska Wilderness Act of 1985
Pub. L. 99–504, Oct. 20, 1986, 100 Stat. 1802 (16 U.S.C. 460rr et seq., 1132 note)

Nebraska-Kansas Act
See Kansas-Nebraska Act

Need-Based Educational Aid Antitrust Protection Act of 1997
Pub. L. 105–43, Sept. 17, 1997, 111 Stat. 1140
Short title, see 15 U.S.C. 1 note

Needlestick Safety and Prevention Act
Pub. L. 106–430, Nov. 6, 2000, 114 Stat. 1901

Negotiated Rates Act of 1993
Pub. L. 103–180, Dec. 3, 1993, 107 Stat. 2044

Negotiated Rulemaking Act of 1990
Pub. L. 101–648, Nov. 29, 1990, 104 Stat. 4969 (5 U.S.C. 561 et seq.)
Short title, see 5 U.S.C. 561 note

Negotiated Shipbuilding Contracting Act of 1976
Pub. L. 94–372, July 31, 1976, 90 Stat. 1042
Short title, see 46 App. U.S.C. 1245 note

Neighborhood Children's Internet Protection Act
Pub. L. 106–554, §1(a)(4) [div. B, title XVII, subtitle C (§1731 et seq.)], Dec. 21, 2000, 114 Stat. 2763, 2763A–350
Short title, see 47 U.S.C. 609 note

Neighborhood Reinvestment Corporation Act
Pub. L. 95–557, title VI, Oct. 31, 1978, 92 Stat. 2115 (42 U.S.C. 8101 et seq.)
Short title, see 42 U.S.C. 8101 note

Neighborhood Self-Help Development Act of 1978
Pub. L. 95–557, title VII, Oct. 31, 1978, 92 Stat. 2119 (42 U.S.C. 8121 et seq.)
Short title, see 42 U.S.C. 8101 note

Nelson Act (Alaska Roads, Schools, and Insane)
Jan. 27, 1905, ch. 277, 33 Stat. 616

Nelson Act (Bankruptcy Act of 1898)
See Bankruptcy Act

Nelson Act (Chippewa Indians of Minnesota)
Jan. 14, 1889, ch. 24, 25 Stat. 642

Nelson Act (Criminal Appeals)
See Criminal Appeals Act

Nelson Act (Department of Commerce and Labor)
See Department of Commerce and Labor Act

Nelson Amendment (Agricultural Colleges)
Mar. 4, 1907, ch. 2907, [part], 34 Stat. 1256, 1281

Nelson Bill
Pub. L. 91–405, title II, §§204(a)–(e), 206(b), Sept. 22, 1970, 84 Stat. 852, 853, 855

Nematocide, Plant Regulator, Defoliant, and Desiccant Amendment of 1959
Pub. L. 86–139, Aug. 7, 1959, 73 Stat. 286

Neotropical Migratory Bird Conservation Act
Pub. L. 106–247, July 20, 2000, 114 Stat. 593 (16 U.S.C. 6101 et seq.)
Short title, see 16 U.S.C. 6101 note

Net Worth Certificate Act
Pub. L. 97–320, title II, Oct. 15, 1982, 96 Stat. 1489
Short title, see 12 U.S.C. 1811 note

Neutrality Act of 1939
Nov. 4, 1939, ch. 2, 54 Stat. 4 (22 U.S.C. 441 et seq.)
Short title, see 22 U.S.C. 441 note

Nevada Wilderness Protection Act of 1989
Pub. L. 101–195, Dec. 5, 1989, 103 Stat. 1784 (16 U.S.C. 1132 note)

Nevada-Florida Land Exchange Authorization Act of 1988
Pub. L. 100–275, Mar. 31, 1988, 102 Stat. 52

New Communities Act of 1968
Pub. L. 90–448, title IV, Aug. 1, 1968, 82 Stat. 513 (42 U.S.C. 3901 et seq.)
Short title, see 42 U.S.C. 3901 note

New England Fishery Resources Restoration Act of 1990
Pub. L. 101–593, title I, §111, Nov. 16, 1990, 104 Stat. 2960 (16 U.S.C. 777e–1)
Short title, see 16 U.S.C. 777e–1(a)

New GI Bill Continuation Act
Pub. L. 100–48, June 1, 1987, 101 Stat. 331
Short title, see 38 U.S.C. 101 note

New Hampshire Forest Management Initiatives Act of 1988
Pub. L. 100–446, title II, §§1–6, Sept. 27, 1988, 102 Stat. 1805, 1806

New Hampshire Wilderness Act of 1984
Pub. L. 98–323, June 19, 1984, 98 Stat. 259 (16 U.S.C. 1132 note)

New Markets Venture Capital Program Act of 2000
Pub. L. 106–554, §1(a)(8) [§1] Dec. 21, 2000, 114 Stat. 2763, 2763A–653
Short title, see 15 U.S.C. 661 note

New Mexico Statehood and Enabling Act Amendments of 1997
Pub. L. 105–37, Aug. 7, 1997, 111 Stat. 1113

New Orleans Jazz National Historical Park Act of 1994
Pub. L. 103–433, title XXII, Oct. 31, 1994, 108 Stat. 4519 (16 U.S.C. 410bbb et seq.)
Short title, see 16 U.S.C. 410bbb note

New York City Loan Guarantee Act of 1978
Pub. L. 95–339, Aug. 8, 1978, 92 Stat. 460

New York City Seasonal Financing Act of 1975
Pub. L. 94–143, Dec. 9, 1975, 89 Stat. 797

Newborns' and Mothers' Health Protection Act of 1996
Pub. L. 104–204, title VI, Sept. 26, 1996, 110 Stat. 2935
Short title, see 42 U.S.C. 201 note

Newlands Act (Irrigation)
See Reclamation Act; National Irrigation Act of 1902

Newlands Act (Railroad Mediation)
July 15, 1913, ch. 6, 38 Stat. 103

Newlands Resolution (Annexation of Hawaii)
July 7, 1898, No. 55, 30 Stat. 750

Newspaper Preservation Act
Pub. L. 91–353, July 24, 1970, 84 Stat. 466 (15 U.S.C. 1801 et seq.)
Short title, see 15 U.S.C. 1801 note

Newton Amendment to the Carmack Amendment
Apr. 23, 1930, ch. 208, 46 Stat. 251

Next Generation Internet Research Act of 1998
Pub. L. 105–305, Oct. 28, 1998, 112 Stat. 2919
Short title, see 15 U.S.C. 5501 note

Nez Perce National Historical Park Act
Pub. L. 89–19, May 15, 1965, 79 Stat. 110 (16 U.S.C. 281 et seq.)

Nez Perce National Historical Park Additions Act of 1991
Pub. L. 102–576, Oct. 30, 1992, 106 Stat. 4770 (16 U.S.C. 281 et seq.)
Short title, see 16 U.S.C. 281 note

Niagara Power Project Act
Pub. L. 85–159, Aug. 21, 1957, 71 Stat. 401 (16 U.S.C. 836 et seq.)

Nicaraguan Adjustment and Central American Relief Act
Pub. L. 105–100, title II, Nov. 19, 1997, 111 Stat. 2193
Short title, see 8 U.S.C. 1101 note

Nine Hour Law (Railroads)
See Hours of Service Act (Railroads)

Nineteenth Amendment
June 5, 1919, 41 Stat. 362

Niobrara Scenic River Designation Act of 1991
Pub. L. 102–50, May 24, 1991, 105 Stat. 254
Short title, see 16 U.S.C. 1271 note

No Electronic Theft (NET) Act
Pub. L. 105–147, Dec. 16, 1997, 111 Stat. 2678
Short title, see 18 U.S.C. 2311 note

No Net Cost Tobacco Program Act of 1982
Pub. L. 97–218, July 20, 1982, 96 Stat. 197
Short title, see 7 U.S.C. 1281 note

NOAA Fleet Modernization Act
Pub. L. 102–567, title VI, Oct. 29, 1992, 106 Stat. 4299 (33 U.S.C. 891 et seq.)

NOAA Fleet Modernization Act—Continued
Short title, see 33 U.S.C. 851 note

Noise Control Act of 1972
Pub. L. 92–574, Oct. 27, 1972, 86 Stat. 1234 (42 U.S.C. 4901 et seq.)
Short title, see 42 U.S.C. 4901 note

Noise Pollution and Abatement Act of 1970
July 14, 1955, ch. 360, title IV, as added Pub. L. 91–604, §14, Dec. 31, 1970, 84 Stat. 1709 (42 U.S.C. 7641 et seq.)
Short title, see 42 U.S.C. 7401 note

Noise Reduction Reimbursement Act of 1989
Pub. L. 101–71, Aug. 4, 1989, 103 Stat. 181

Nolan Act (Patents)
Mar. 3, 1921, ch. 126, 41 Stat. 1313

Nolan Minimum Wage Law (District of Columbia)
See District of Columbia Minimum Wage Act

Non-Intercourse Act (Foreign Relations)
Mar. 1, 1809, ch. 24, 2 Stat. 528

Non-Vessel-Operating Common Carrier Act of 1991
Pub. L. 102–251, title II, §201, Mar. 9, 1992, 106 Stat. 60
Short title, see 46 App. U.S.C. 1701 note

Non-Vessel-Operating Common Carrier Amendments of 1990
Pub. L. 101–595, title VII, §710, Nov. 16, 1990, 104 Stat. 2996
Short title, see 46 App. U.S.C. 1701 note

Nonappropriated Fund Instrumentalities Employees' Retirement Credit Act of 1986
Pub. L. 99–638, §2, Nov. 10, 1986, 100 Stat. 3535
Short title, see 5 U.S.C. 8331 note

Noncitizen Benefit Clarification and Other Technical Amendments Act of 1998
Pub. L. 105–306, Oct. 28, 1998, 112 Stat. 2926
Short title, see 42 U.S.C. 1305 note

Nonindigenous Aquatic Nuisance Prevention and Control Act of 1990
Pub. L. 101–646, title I, Nov. 29, 1990, 104 Stat. 4761 (16 U.S.C. 4701 et seq.)
Short title, see 16 U.S.C. 4701 note

Nonprofit Institutions Act
May 26, 1938, ch. 283, 52 Stat. 446 (15 U.S.C. 13c)

Nonsale Disposals Act of 1878
See Mineral Land Free Timber Act

Nontraditional Employment for Women Act
Pub. L. 102–235, Dec. 12, 1991, 105 Stat. 1806
Short title, see 29 U.S.C. 1501 note

Norris Act (Conveyances by Union Pacific Ry. Co.)
June 24, 1912, ch. 181, 37 Stat. 138

Norris Muscle Shoals Act
See Tennessee Valley Authority Act of 1933

Norris-LaGuardia Act (Labor Disputes)
Mar. 23, 1932, ch. 90, 47 Stat. 70 (29 U.S.C. 101 et seq.)
Short title, see 29 U.S.C. 101 note

Norris-Rayburn Rural Electrification Act
See Rural Electrification Act of 1936

North American Free Trade Agreement Implementation Act
Pub. L. 103–182, Dec. 8, 1993, 107 Stat. 2057
Short title, see 19 U.S.C. 3301 note

North American Wetlands Conservation Act
Pub. L. 101–233, Dec. 13, 1989, 103 Stat. 1968 (16 U.S.C. 4401 et seq.)
Short title, see 16 U.S.C. 4401 note

North American Wetlands Conservation Act Amendments of 1994
Pub. L. 103–375, Oct. 19, 1994, 108 Stat. 3494
Short title, see 16 U.S.C. 4401 note

North Atlantic Treaty Organization Mutual Support Act of 1979
Pub. L. 96–323, Aug. 4, 1980, 94 Stat. 1016 (10 U.S.C. 2341 et seq.)
Short title, see 10 U.S.C. 2341 note

North Carolina Wilderness Act of 1984
Pub. L. 98–324, June 19, 1984, 98 Stat. 263 (16 U.S.C. 1132 note)

North Korea Threat Reduction Act of 1999
Pub. L. 106–113, div. B, §1000(a)(7) [div. A, title VIII, subtitle B (§821 et seq.)], Nov. 29, 1999, 113 Stat. 1536, 1501A–472

North Pacific Anadromous Stocks Act of 1992
Pub. L. 102–567, title VIII, Oct. 29, 1992, 106 Stat. 4309 (16 U.S.C. 5001 et seq.)
Short title, see 16 U.S.C. 5001 note

North Pacific Anadromous Stocks Convention Act of 1992
Pub. L. 102–587, title VIII, Nov. 4, 1992, 106 Stat. 5098 (16 U.S.C. 5001 et seq.)
Short title, see 16 U.S.C. 5001 note

North Pacific Fisheries Act of 1954
Aug. 12, 1954, ch. 669, 68 Stat. 698 (16 U.S.C. 1021 et seq.)
Short title, see 16 U.S.C. 1021 note

North-South Center Act of 1991
Renamed Dante B. Fascell North-South Center Act of 1991

Northeast Rail Service Act of 1981
Pub. L. 97–35, title XI, subtitle E (§1131 et seq.), Aug. 13, 1981, 95 Stat. 643
Short title, see 45 U.S.C. 1101 note

Northern Cheyenne Indian Reserved Water Rights Settlement Act of 1992
Pub. L. 102–374, Sept. 30, 1992, 106 Stat. 1186

Northern Great Plains Rural Development Act
Pub. L. 103–318, Aug. 26, 1994, 108 Stat. 1781 (7 U.S.C. 2661 note)

Northern Pacific Halibut Act
June 7, 1924, ch. 345, 43 Stat. 648

Northern Pacific Halibut Act of 1937
June 28, 1937, ch. 392, 50 Stat. 325 (16 U.S.C. 772 et seq.)

Northern Pacific Halibut Act of 1982
Pub. L. 97–176, May 17, 1982, 96 Stat. 78 (16 U.S.C. 773 et seq.)

Northern Pacific Halibut Act of 1982—Continued
Short title, see 16 U.S.C. 773 note

Northwest Atlantic Fisheries Act of 1950
Sept. 27, 1950, ch. 1054, 64 Stat. 1067 (16 U.S.C. 981 et seq.)

Northwest Atlantic Fisheries Convention Act of 1995
Pub. L. 104–43, title II, Nov. 3, 1995, 109 Stat. 377 (16 U.S.C. 5601 et seq.)
Short title, see 16 U.S.C. 5601 note

Northwest Power Act
See Pacific Northwest Electric Power Planning and Conservation Act

Northwest Straits Marine Conservation Initiative Act
Pub. L. 105–384, title IV, Nov. 13, 1998, 112 Stat. 3458

Northwest Territory Ordinance of 1787
July 13, 1787, 1 Stat. 51

Notaries Public Expense Act of 1955
July 11, 1956, ch. 554, 70 Stat. 519

Notice to Lessees Numbered 5 Gas Royalty Act of 1987
Pub. L. 100–234, Jan. 6, 1988, 101 Stat. 1719

Nuclear Career Incentive Act of 1975
Pub. L. 94–356, July 12, 1976, 90 Stat. 901
Short title, see 37 U.S.C. 101 note

Nuclear Non-Proliferation Act of 1978
Pub. L. 95–242, Mar. 10, 1978, 92 Stat. 120 (22 U.S.C. 3201 et seq.)
Short title, see 22 U.S.C. 3201 note

Nuclear Proliferation Prevention Act of 1994
Pub. L. 103–236, title VIII, Apr. 30, 1994, 108 Stat. 507 (22 U.S.C. 6301 et seq.)
Short title, see 22 U.S.C. 6301 note

Nuclear Safety Research, Development, and Demonstration Act of 1980
Pub. L. 96–567, Dec. 22, 1980, 94 Stat. 3329 (42 U.S.C. 9701 et seq.)
Short title, see 42 U.S.C. 9701 note

Nuclear Waste Policy Act of 1982
Pub. L. 97–425, Jan. 7, 1983, 96 Stat. 2201 (42 U.S.C. 10101 et seq.)
Short title, see 42 U.S.C. 10101 note

Nuclear Waste Policy Amendments Act of 1987
Pub. L. 100–202, Sec. 101(d) [title III [H.R. 3545, title V, subtitle A]], Dec. 22, 1987, 101 Stat. 1329–104, 1329–121
Pub. L. 100–203, title V, subtitle A (§5001 et seq.), Dec. 22, 1987, 101 Stat. 1330–227
Short title, see 42 U.S.C. 10101 note

Nuisance Tax Extension Act
June 29, 1937, ch. 402, 50 Stat. 358

Nurse Education Amendments of 1985
Pub. L. 99–92, Aug. 16, 1985, 99 Stat. 393
Short title, see 42 U.S.C. 201 note

Nurse Education and Practice Improvement Amendments of 1992
Pub. L. 102–408, title II, Oct. 13, 1992, 106 Stat. 2069
Short title, see 42 U.S.C. 201 note

Nurse Training Act of 1964
Pub. L. 88–581, Sept. 4, 1964, 78 Stat. 908
Short title, see 42 U.S.C. 201 note

Nurse Training Act of 1971
Pub. L. 92–158, Nov. 18, 1971, 85 Stat. 465
Short title, see 42 U.S.C. 201 note

Nurse Training Act of 1975
Pub. L. 94–63, title IX, July 29, 1975, 89 Stat. 354
Short title, see 42 U.S.C. 201 note

Nurse Training Amendments of 1979
Pub. L. 96–76, title I, Sept. 29, 1979, 93 Stat. 579
Short title, see 42 U.S.C. 201 note

Nursery Stock Quarantine Act
See Plant Quarantine Act

Nurses Training Act
June 15, 1943, ch. 126, 57 Stat. 153

Nursing Education and Practice Improvement Act of 1998
Pub. L. 105–392, title I, subtitle B (§121 et seq.), Nov. 13, 1998, 112 Stat. 3562
Short title, see 42 U.S.C. 201 note

Nursing Home Resident Protection Amendments of 1999
Pub. L. 106–4, Mar. 25, 1999, 113 Stat. 7
Short title, see 42 U.S.C. 1305 note

Nursing Relief for Disadvantaged Areas Act of 1999
Pub. L. 106–95, Nov. 12, 1999, 113 Stat. 1312
Short title, see 8 U.S.C. 1101 note

Nursing Shortage Reduction and Education Extension Act of 1988
Pub. L. 100–607, title VII, Nov. 4, 1988, 102 Stat. 3153
Short title, see 42 U.S.C. 201 note

Nutrition Labeling and Education Act Amendments of 1993
Pub. L. 103–80, Aug. 13, 1993, 107 Stat. 773
Short title, see 21 U.S.C. 301 note

Nutrition Labeling and Education Act of 1990
Pub. L. 101–535, Nov. 8, 1990, 104 Stat. 2353
Short title, see 21 U.S.C. 301 note

O and P Nonimmigrant Amendments of 1991
Pub. L. 102–232, title II, Dec. 12, 1991, 105 Stat. 1736
Short title, see 8 U.S.C. 1101 note

O'Mahoney-Hatch Act
Aug. 8, 1946, ch. 916, 60 Stat. 950

O'Mahoney-Ramspeck Act (Civil Service Extension To Postmasters)
June 25, 1938, ch. 678, 52 Stat. 1076

OBRA
See Omnibus Budget Reconciliation Acts

Obstruction of Interstate Commerce Act
Aug. 10, 1917, ch. 51, 40 Stat. 272

Occupational Safety and Health Act of 1970
Pub. L. 91–596, Dec. 29, 1970, 84 Stat. 1590 (29 U.S.C. 651 et seq.)
Short title, see 29 U.S.C. 651 note

Occupational Safety and Health Administration Compliance Assistance Authorization Act of 1998
Pub. L. 105–197, July 16, 1998, 112 Stat. 638
Short title, see 29 U.S.C. 651 note

Ocean Dumping Act
Pub. L. 92–532, title I, Oct. 23, 1972, 86 Stat. 1053 (33 U.S.C. 1411 et seq.)

Ocean Dumping Ban Act of 1988
Pub. L. 100–688, title I, Nov. 18, 1988, 102 Stat. 4139
Short title, see 33 U.S.C. 1401 note

Ocean Mail Act of 1891
Mar. 3, 1891, ch. 519, 26 Stat. 830

Ocean Pollution Reduction Act
Pub. L. 103–431, Oct. 31, 1994, 108 Stat. 4396
Short title, see 33 U.S.C. 1251 note

Ocean Shipping Act of 1978
Pub. L. 95–483, Oct. 18, 1978, 92 Stat. 1607
Short title, see 46 App. U.S.C. 842 note

Ocean Shipping Reform Act of 1998
Pub. L. 105–258, Oct. 14, 1998, 112 Stat. 1902
Short title, see 46 App. U.S.C. 1701 note

Ocean Thermal Energy Conversion Act of 1980
Pub. L. 96–320, Aug. 3, 1980, 94 Stat. 974 (42 U.S.C. 9101 et seq.)
Short title, see 42 U.S.C. 9101 note

Ocean Thermal Energy Conversion Research, Development, and Demonstration Act
Pub. L. 96–310, July 17, 1980, 94 Stat. 941 (42 U.S.C. 9001 et seq.)
Short title, see 42 U.S.C. 9001 note

Oceans Act of 1992
Pub. L. 102–587, Nov. 4, 1992, 106 Stat. 5039
Short title, see 16 U.S.C. 1431 note

Oceans Act of 2000
Pub. L. 106–256, Aug. 7, 2000, 114 Stat. 644 (33 U.S.C. 857–19 note)

OCS Paperwork and Reporting Act
Pub. L. 99–367, July 31, 1986, 100 Stat. 774
Short title, see 43 U.S.C. 1301 note

Odometer Disclosure Act
Pub. L. 92–513, title IV, Oct. 20, 1972, 86 Stat. 961

Office of Correctional Education Act of 1990
Pub. L. 101–392, title VI, Sept. 25, 1990, 104 Stat. 840
Short title, see 20 U.S.C. 3401 note

Office of Education and Related Agencies Appropriation Act, 1972
Pub. L. 92–48, July 9, 1971, 85 Stat. 103

Office of Education Appropriation Act, 1971
Pub. L. 91–380, Aug. 18, 1970, 84 Stat. 800

Office of Federal Procurement Policy Act
Pub. L. 93–400, Aug. 30, 1974, 88 Stat. 796 (41 U.S.C. 401 et seq.)
Short title, see 41 U.S.C. 401 note

Office of Federal Procurement Policy Act Amendments of 1979
Pub. L. 96–83, Oct. 10, 1979, 93 Stat. 648
Short title, see 41 U.S.C. 401 note

Office of Federal Procurement Policy Act Amendments of 1983
Pub. L. 98–191, Dec. 1, 1983, 97 Stat. 1325
Short title, see 41 U.S.C. 401 note

Office of Federal Procurement Policy Act Amendments of 1988
Pub. L. 100–679, Nov. 17, 1988, 102 Stat. 4055
Short title, see 41 U.S.C. 401 note

Office of Government Ethics Amendment of 1992
Pub. L. 102–506, Oct. 24, 1992, 106 Stat. 3280
Short title, see 5 App. U.S.C. 101 note

Office of Government Ethics Authorization Act of 1996
Pub. L. 104–179, Aug. 6, 1996, 110 Stat. 1566
Short title, see 5 App. U.S.C. 101 note

Office of Government Reports Act
June 9, 1941, ch. 189, 55 Stat. 247

Office of National Drug Control Policy Reauthorization Act of 1998
Pub. L. 105–277, div. C, title VII, Oct. 21, 1998, 112 Stat. 2681–670 (21 U.S.C. 1701 et seq.)
Short title, see 21 U.S.C. 1701 note

Officer Grade Limitation Act of 1954
May 5, 1954, ch. 180, 68 Stat. 65

Officer Personnel Act of 1947
Aug. 7, 1947, ch. 512, 61 Stat. 795

Officers' Competency Certificates Act
July 17, 1939, ch. 316, 53 Stat. 1049

Offshore Shrimp Fisheries Act Amendments of 1975
Pub. L. 94–58, July 24, 1975, 89 Stat. 266

Offshore Shrimp Fisheries Act of 1973
Pub. L. 93–242, Jan. 2, 1974, 87 Stat. 1061 (16 U.S.C. 1100b et seq.)

Oh! Grab Me Act (Embargo 1807)
Dec. 22, 1807, ch. 5, 2 Stat. 451

Ohio & Erie Canal National Heritage Corridor Act of 1996
Pub. L. 104–333, div. II, title VIII, Nov. 12, 1996, 110 Stat. 4267 (16 U.S.C. 461 note)

Oil and Gas Prospecting Act
Aug. 21, 1935, ch. 599, 49 Stat. 674

Oil Lands Leasing Act
See Mineral Leasing Act

Oil Pipe Line Act
May 21, 1896, ch. 212, 29 Stat. 127 (43 U.S.C. 962 et seq.)
Short title, see 43 U.S.C. 962 note

Oil Pollution Act Amendments of 1973
Pub. L. 93–119, Oct. 4, 1973, 87 Stat. 424
Short title, see 33 U.S.C. 1001 note

Oil Pollution Act of 1990
Pub. L. 101–380, Aug. 18, 1990, 104 Stat. 484 (33 U.S.C. 2701 et seq.)

Oil Pollution Act of 1990—Continued
Short title, see 33 U.S.C. 2701 note

Oil Pollution Act, 1924
June 7, 1924, ch. 316, 43 Stat. 604 (33 U.S.C. 431 et seq.)

Oil Pollution Act, 1961, as amended
Pub. L. 87–167, Aug. 30, 1961, 75 Stat. 402 (33 U.S.C. 1001 et seq.)
Short title, see 33 U.S.C. 1001 note

Oil Terminal and Oil Tanker Environmental Oversight and Monitoring Act of 1990
Pub. L. 101–380, title V, §5002, Aug. 18, 1990, 104 Stat. 544 (33 U.S.C. 2732)
Short title, see 33 U.S.C. 2732(a)(1)

Oklahoma City National Memorial Act of 1997
Pub. L. 105–58, Oct. 9, 1997, 111 Stat. 1261
Short title, see 16 U.S.C. 450ss note

Oklahoma Indian Welfare ActI12Also known as the Oklahoma Welfare Act
June 26, 1936, ch. 831, 49 Stat. 1967 (25 U.S.C. 501 et seq.)
Short title, see 25 U.S.C. 501 note

Oklahoma Welfare Act
Also known as the Oklahoma Indian Welfare Act
June 26, 1936, ch. 831, 49 Stat. 1967 (25 U.S.C. 501 et seq.)
Short title, see 25 U.S.C. 501 note

Old Age Assistance Claims Settlement Act
Pub. L. 98–500, Oct. 19, 1984, 98 Stat. 2317 (25 U.S.C. 2301 et seq.)
Short title, see 25 U.S.C. 2301 note

Old Age Pension Act
See Social Security Act

Old Series Currency Adjustment Act
Pub. L. 87–66, June 30, 1961, 75 Stat. 146

Old-Age, Survivors, and Disability Insurance Amendments of 1965
Pub. L. 89–97, title III, July 30, 1965, 79 Stat. 361
Short title, see 42 U.S.C. 1305 note

Older American Community Service Employment Act
Pub. L. 89–73, title V, as added Pub. L. 106–501, title V, §501, Nov. 13, 2000, 114 Stat. 2267
Short title, see 42 U.S.C. 3001 note

Older Americans Act Amendments of 1967
Pub. L. 90–42, July 1, 1967, 81 Stat. 106
Short title, see 42 U.S.C. 3001 note

Older Americans Act Amendments of 1969
Pub. L. 91–69, Sept. 17, 1969, 83 Stat. 108

Older Americans Act Amendments of 1981
Pub. L. 97–115, Dec. 29, 1981, 95 Stat. 1595
Short title, see 42 U.S.C. 3001 note

Older Americans Act Amendments of 1984
Pub. L. 98–459, Oct. 9, 1984, 98 Stat. 1767
Short title, see 42 U.S.C. 3001 note

Older Americans Act Amendments of 1986
Pub. L. 99–269, Apr. 1, 1986, 100 Stat. 78
Short title, see 42 U.S.C. 3001 note

Older Americans Act Amendments of 1987
Pub. L. 100–175, Nov. 29, 1987, 101 Stat. 926
Short title, see 42 U.S.C. 3001 note

Older Americans Act Amendments of 1992
Pub. L. 102–375, Sept. 30, 1992, 106 Stat. 1195
Short title, see 42 U.S.C. 3001 note

Older Americans Act Amendments of 2000
Pub. L. 106–501, Nov. 13, 2000, 114 Stat. 2226
Short title, see 42 U.S.C. 3001 note

Older Americans Act of 1965
Pub. L. 89–73, July 14, 1965, 79 Stat. 218 (42 U.S.C. 3001 et seq.)
Short title, see 42 U.S.C. 3001 note

Older Americans Act Technical Amendments of 1993
Pub. L. 103–171, Dec. 2, 1993, 107 Stat. 1988
Short title, see 42 U.S.C. 3001 note

Older Americans Amendments of 1975
Pub. L. 94–135, Nov. 28, 1975, 89 Stat. 713
Short title, see 42 U.S.C. 3001 note

Older Americans Comprehensive Services Amendments of 1973
Pub. L. 93–29, May 3, 1973, 87 Stat. 30
Short title, see 42 U.S.C. 3001 note

Older Americans Personal Health Education and Training Act
Pub. L. 89–73, title VII, as added Pub. L. 98–459, title VII, §701, Oct. 9, 1984, 98 Stat. 1788

Older Workers Benefit Protection Act
Pub. L. 101–433, Oct. 16, 1990, 104 Stat. 978
Short title, see 29 U.S.C. 621 note

Oleomargarine Act of 1886
Aug. 2, 1886, ch. 840, 24 Stat. 209

Olympic and Amateur Sports Act Amendments of 1998
Pub. L. 105–277, div. C, title I, §142, Oct. 21, 1998, 112 Stat. 2681–603
Short title, see 36 U.S.C. 101 note

Olympic Commemorative Coin Act
Pub. L. 97–220, July 22, 1982, 96 Stat. 222 (31 U.S.C. 5112 note)

Olympic Winter Games Authorization Act of 1976
Pub. L. 94–427, Sept. 28, 1976, 90 Stat. 1336

Omnibus Adjustment Act of May 25, 1926
May 25, 1926, ch. 383, 44 Stat. 636

Omnibus Budget Reconciliation Act of 1981
Pub. L. 97–35, Aug. 13, 1981, 95 Stat. 357

Omnibus Budget Reconciliation Act of 1982
Pub. L. 97–253, Sept. 8, 1982, 96 Stat. 763

Omnibus Budget Reconciliation Act of 1983
Pub. L. 98–270, Apr. 18, 1984, 98 Stat. 157

Omnibus Budget Reconciliation Act of 1986
Pub. L. 99–509, Oct. 21, 1986, 100 Stat. 1874

Omnibus Budget Reconciliation Act of 1987
Pub. L. 100–203, Dec. 22, 1987, 101 Stat. 1330

Omnibus Budget Reconciliation Act of 1989
Pub. L. 101–239, Dec. 19, 1989, 103 Stat. 2106

Omnibus Budget Reconciliation Act of 1990
Pub. L. 101–508, Nov. 5, 1990, 104 Stat. 1388

Omnibus Budget Reconciliation Act of 1993
Pub. L. 103–66, Aug. 10, 1993, 107 Stat. 312

Omnibus Claims Act
Mar. 4, 1915, ch. 140, §5, 38 Stat. 996

Omnibus Consolidated and Emergency Supplemental Appropriations Act, 1999
Pub. L. 105–277, Oct. 21, 1998, 112 Stat. 2681

Omnibus Consolidated Appropriations Act, 1997
Pub. L. 104–208, Sept. 30, 1996, 110 Stat. 3009

Omnibus Consolidated Rescissions and Appropriations Act of 1996
Pub. L. 104–134, Apr. 26, 1996, 110 Stat. 1321

Omnibus Crime Control Act of 1970
Pub. L. 91–644, Jan. 2, 1971, 84 Stat. 1880
Short title, see 42 U.S.C. 3711 note

Omnibus Crime Control and Safe Streets Act of 1968
Pub. L. 90–351, June 19, 1968, 82 Stat. 197
Short title, see 42 U.S.C. 3711 note

Omnibus Diplomatic Security and Antiterrorism Act of 1986
Pub. L. 99–399, Aug. 27, 1986, 100 Stat. 853
Short title, see 22 U.S.C. 4801 note

Omnibus Drug Supplemental Appropriations Act of 1987
Pub. L. 99–500, title II, Oct. 18, 1986, 100 Stat. 1783–353, and Pub. L. 99–591, title II, Oct. 30, 1986, 100 Stat. 3341–356

Omnibus Education Reconciliation Act of 1981
Pub. L. 97–35, title V, Aug. 13, 1981, 95 Stat. 441
Short title, see 20 U.S.C. 3489 note

Omnibus Flood Control Act
Aug. 11, 1939, ch. 699, 53 Stat. 1414

Omnibus Indian Advancement Act
Pub. L. 106–568, Dec. 27, 2000, 114 Stat. 2868
Short title, see 25 U.S.C. 4101 note

Omnibus Insular Areas Act of 1992
Pub. L. 102–247, Feb. 24, 1992, 106 Stat. 33
Short title, see 16 U.S.C. 410tt note

Omnibus Judgeship Act
Aug. 28, 1935, ch. 793, 49 Stat. 945

Omnibus Low-Level Radioactive Waste Interstate Compact Consent Act
Pub. L. 99–240, title II, Jan. 15, 1986, 99 Stat. 1859 (42 U.S.C. 2021d note)

Omnibus Oregon Wild and Scenic Rivers Act of 1988
Pub. L. 100–557, title I, Oct. 28, 1988, 102 Stat. 2782
Short title, see 16 U.S.C. 1271 note

Omnibus Parks and Public Lands Management Act of 1996
Pub. L. 104–333, Nov. 12, 1996, 110 Stat. 4093
Short title, see 16 U.S.C. 1 note

Omnibus Parks Technical Corrections Act of 2000
Pub. L. 106–176, Mar. 10, 2000, 114 Stat. 23
Short title, see 16 U.S.C. 1 note

Omnibus Public Lands and National Forests Adjustments Act of 1988
Pub. L. 100–699, Nov. 19, 1988, 102 Stat. 4624

Omnibus Reconciliation Act of 1980
Pub. L. 96–499, Dec. 5, 1980, 94 Stat. 2599

Omnibus Small Business Capital Formation Act of 1980
Pub. L. 96–477, title V, Oct. 21, 1980, 94 Stat. 2291 (15 U.S.C. 80c et seq.)
Short title, see 15 U.S.C. 80c note

Omnibus Taxpayer Bill of Rights
Pub. L. 100–647, title VI, subtitle J (§6226 et seq.), Nov. 10, 1988, 102 Stat. 3730
Short title, see 26 U.S.C. 1 note

Omnibus Territories Act of 1977
Pub. L. 95–134, Oct. 15, 1977, 91 Stat. 1159

Omnibus Trade and Competitiveness Act of 1988
Pub. L. 100–418, Aug. 23, 1988, 102 Stat. 1107
Short title, see 19 U.S.C. 2901 note

Omnibus Transportation Employee Testing Act of 1991
Pub. L. 102–143, title V, Oct. 28, 1991, 105 Stat. 952

One-Hundred-and-Sixty Acre Homestead Act
See Homestead Act

Onion Futures Act
Pub. L. 85–839, Aug. 28, 1958, 72 Stat. 1013 (7 U.S.C. 13–1)

Online Copyright Infringement Liability Limitation Act
Pub. L. 105–304, title II, Oct. 28, 1998, 112 Stat. 2877
Short title, see 17 U.S.C. 101 note

Opal Creek Wilderness and Opal Creek Scenic Recreation Area Act of 1996
Pub. L. 104–208, div. B, title I, Sept. 30, 1996, 110 Stat. 3009–523
Short title, see 16 U.S.C. 545b note

Open Meetings, Government in the Sunshine Act
See Government in the Sunshine Act

Open-market Reorganization for the Betterment of International Telecommunications Act
Also known as the ORBIT Act
Pub. L. 106–180, Mar. 17, 2000, 114 Stat. 48
Short title, see 47 U.S.C. 701 note

Operation Desert Shield/Desert Storm Supplemental Appropriations Act, 1991
Pub. L. 102–28, Apr. 10, 1991, 105 Stat. 161

Opium Poppy Control Act of 1942
Dec. 11, 1942, ch. 720, 56 Stat. 1045 (21 U.S.C. 188 et seq.)

Optional Inter Partes Reexamination Procedure Act of 1999
Pub. L. 106–113, div. B, §1000(a)(9) [title IV, subtitle F (§4601 et seq.)], Nov. 29, 1999, 113 Stat. 1536, 1501A–567 (35 U.S.C. 311 et seq.)

Optional Inter Partes Reexamination Procedure Act of 1999—Continued
Short title, see 35 U.S.C. 1 note

Options Pilot Program Act of 1990
Pub. L. 101–624, title XI, subtitle E (§1151 et seq.), Nov. 28, 1990, 104 Stat. 3518 (7 U.S.C. 1421 note)

ORBIT Act
Also known as the Open-market Reorganization for the Betterment of International Telecommunications Act
Pub. L. 106–180, Mar. 17, 2000, 114 Stat. 48
Short title, see 47 U.S.C. 701 note

Ordnance Tool Act
May 11, 1939, ch. 122, 53 Stat. 739

Oregon Land Exchange Act of 2000
Pub. L. 106–257, Aug. 8, 2000, 114 Stat. 650

Oregon Public Lands Transfer and Protection Act of 1998
Pub. L. 105–321, Oct. 30, 1998, 112 Stat. 3020
Short title, see 43 U.S.C. 390h note

Oregon Resource Conservation Act of 1996
Pub. L. 104–208, div. B, Sept. 30, 1996, 110 Stat. 3009–523

Oregon Wilderness Act of 1984
Pub. L. 98–328, June 26, 1984, 98 Stat. 272 (16 U.S.C. 460*oo*, 1132 note)

Organ Donor Leave Act
Pub. L. 106–56, Sept. 24, 1999, 113 Stat. 407
Short title, see 5 U.S.C. 6301 note

Organ Procurement Organization Certification Act of 2000
Pub. L. 106–505, title VII, §701, Nov. 13, 2000, 114 Stat. 2346
Short title, see 42 U.S.C. 201 note

Organ Transplant Amendments Act of 1988
Pub. L. 100–607, title IV, Nov. 4, 1988, 102 Stat. 3114
Short title, see 42 U.S.C. 201 note

Organic Act of Alaska
Aug. 24, 1912, ch. 387, 37 Stat. 512

Organic Act of Guam
Aug. 1, 1950, ch. 512, 64 Stat. 384 (48 U.S.C. 1421 et seq.)
Short title, see 48 U.S.C. 1421 note

Organic Act of Puerto Rico
Mar. 2, 1917, ch. 145, 39 Stat. 951 (48 U.S.C. 731 et seq.)

Organic Act of the Virgin Islands of the United States
June 22, 1936, ch. 699, 49 Stat. 1807 (48 U.S.C. 1405 et seq.)
Short title, see 48 U.S.C. 1406m

Organic Foods Production Act of 1990
Pub. L. 101–624, title XXI, Nov. 28, 1990, 104 Stat. 3935 (7 U.S.C. 6501 et seq.)
Short title, see 7 U.S.C. 6501 note

Organized Crime Control Act of 1970
Pub. L. 91–452, Oct. 15, 1970, 84 Stat. 922
Short title, see 18 U.S.C. 1961 note

Organotin Antifouling Paint Control Act of 1988
Pub. L. 100–333, June 16, 1988, 102 Stat. 605 (33 U.S.C. 2401 et seq.)
Short title, see 33 U.S.C. 2401 note

Original Packages Act (Intoxicating Liquors)
Also known as the Wilson Act
Aug. 8, 1890, ch. 728, 26 Stat. 313 (27 U.S.C. 121)
Short title, see 27 U.S.C. 121 note

Oroville-Tonasket Claim Settlement and Conveyance Act
Pub. L. 105–9, Apr. 14, 1997, 111 Stat. 16

Orphan Drug Act
Pub. L. 97–414, Jan. 4, 1983, 96 Stat. 2049
Short title, see 21 U.S.C. 301 note

Orphan Drug Amendments of 1985
Pub. L. 99–91, Aug. 15, 1985, 99 Stat. 387
Short title, see 21 U.S.C. 301 note

Orphan Drug Amendments of 1988
Pub. L. 100–290, Apr. 18, 1988, 102 Stat. 90
Short title, see 21 U.S.C. 301 note

Osage Act (Indians)
June 28, 1906, ch. 3572, 34 Stat. 539

Osage Tribe of Indians Technical Corrections Act of 1984
Pub. L. 98–605, Oct. 30, 1984, 98 Stat. 3163

Otay Mountain Wilderness Act of 1999
Pub. L. 106–145, Dec. 9, 1999, 113 Stat. 1711

Outdoor Recreation Resources Review Act
Pub. L. 85–470, June 28, 1958, 72 Stat. 238 (16 U.S.C. 17k note)

Outer Banks Protection Act
Pub. L. 101–380, title VI, §6003, Aug. 18, 1990, 104 Stat. 555 (33 U.S.C. 2753)

Outer Continental Shelf Deep Water Royalty Relief Act
Pub. L. 104–58, title III, Nov. 28, 1995, 109 Stat. 563
Short title, see 43 U.S.C. 1301 note

Outer Continental Shelf Lands Act
Aug. 7, 1953, ch. 345, 67 Stat. 462 (43 U.S.C. 1331 et seq.)
Short title, see 43 U.S.C. 1301 note

Outer Continental Shelf Lands Act Amendments of 1978
Pub. L. 95–372, Sept. 18, 1978, 92 Stat. 629
Short title, see 43 U.S.C. 1801 note

Outer Continental Shelf Lands Act Amendments of 1985
Pub. L. 99–272, title VIII, Apr. 7, 1986, 100 Stat. 147
Short title, see 43 U.S.C. 1301 note

Outer Continental Shelf Operations Indemnification Clarification Act of 1988
Pub. L. 100–610, title I, Nov. 5, 1988, 102 Stat. 3176
Short title, see 43 U.S.C. 1801 note

Over-the-Counter Market Act
June 25, 1938, ch. 677, 52 Stat. 1070

Overman Act
May 20, 1918, ch. 78, 40 Stat. 556

Overseas Citizens Voting Rights Act of 1975
Pub. L. 94–203, Jan. 2, 1976, 89 Stat. 1142 (42 U.S.C. 1973dd et seq.)
Short title, see 42 U.S.C. 1971 note

Overseas Differentials and Allowances Act
Pub. L. 86–707, Sept. 6, 1960, 74 Stat. 792

Overseas Private Investment Corporation Amendments Act of 1974
Pub. L. 93–390, Aug. 27, 1974, 88 Stat. 763
Short title, see 22 U.S.C. 2151 note

Overseas Private Investment Corporation Amendments Act of 1978
Pub. L. 95–268, Apr. 24, 1978, 92 Stat. 213
Short title, see 22 U.S.C. 2151 note

Overseas Private Investment Corporation Amendments Act of 1981
Pub. L. 97–65, Oct. 16, 1981, 95 Stat. 1021
Short title, see 22 U.S.C. 2151 note

Overseas Private Investment Corporation Amendments Act of 1985
Pub. L. 99–204, Dec. 23, 1985, 99 Stat. 1669
Short title, see 22 U.S.C. 2151 note

Overseas Private Investment Corporation Amendments Act of 1988
Pub. L. 100–461, title V, §555 [H.R. 5263, title I, and S. 2757, title I], Oct. 1, 1988, 102 Stat. 2268–36
Short title, see 22 U.S.C. 2151 note

Ozark National Scenic Riverways Act
Pub. L. 88–492, Aug. 27, 1964, 78 Stat. 608 (16 U.S.C. 460m et seq.)

Pacific Charter Commission Act of 2000
Pub. L. 106–570, title IV, Dec. 27, 2000, 114 Stat. 3047 (22 U.S.C. 2656 note)

Pacific Northwest Electric Power Planning and Conservation Act
Pub. L. 96–501, Dec. 5, 1980, 94 Stat. 2697 (16 U.S.C. 839 et seq.)
Short title, see 16 U.S.C. 839 note

Pacific Salmon Treaty Act of 1985
Pub. L. 99–5, Mar. 15, 1985, 99 Stat. 7 (16 U.S.C. 3631 et seq.)
Short title, see 16 U.S.C. 3631 note

Pacific Yew Act
Pub. L. 102–335, Aug. 7, 1992, 106 Stat. 859 (16 U.S.C. 4801 et seq.)
Short title, see 16 U.S.C. 4801 note

Packers and Stockyards Act, 1921
Aug. 15, 1921, ch. 64, 42 Stat. 159 (7 U.S.C. 181 et seq.)
Short title, see 7 U.S.C. 181

Paddy Creek Wilderness Act of 1981
Pub. L. 97–407, Jan. 3, 1983, 96 Stat. 2033 (16 U.S.C. 1132 note)

Padre Island National Seashore Act
Pub. L. 87–712, Sept. 28, 1962, 76 Stat. 650 (16 U.S.C. 459d et seq.)

Paiute Indian Tribe of Utah Restoration Act
Pub. L. 96–227, Apr. 3, 1980, 94 Stat. 317 (25 U.S.C. 761 et seq.)
Short title, see 25 U.S.C. 761 note

Palace of the Governors Annex Act
Pub. L. 106–291, title I, §147, Oct. 11, 2000, 114 Stat. 953

Palmetto Bend Conveyance Act
Pub. L. 106–512, Nov. 13, 2000, 114 Stat. 2378

Palo Alto Battlefield National Historic Site Act of 1991
Pub. L. 102–304, June 23, 1992, 106 Stat. 256 (16 U.S.C. 461 note)

Pam Lychner Sexual Offender Tracking and Identification Act of 1996
Pub. L. 104–236, Oct. 3, 1996, 110 Stat. 3093
Short title, see 42 U.S.C. 13701 note

Pan-American Naval Academy Act
July 14, 1941, ch. 292, 55 Stat. 589

Panama and Isthmian Canal Act
Mar. 2, 1931, ch. 375, 46 Stat. 1471

Panama Canal Act
Aug. 24, 1912, ch. 390, 37 Stat. 560

Panama Canal Act Amendments of 1996
Pub. L. 104–201, div. C, title XXXV, subtitle B (§3521 et seq.), Sept. 23, 1996, 110 Stat. 2860
Short title, see 22 U.S.C. 3601 note

Panama Canal Act of 1979
Pub. L. 96–70, Sept. 27, 1979, 93 Stat. 452 (22 U.S.C. 3601 et seq.)
Short title, see 22 U.S.C. 3601 note

Panama Canal Amendments Act of 1985
Pub. L. 99–209, Dec. 23, 1985, 99 Stat. 1716
Short title, see 22 U.S.C. 3601 note

Panama Canal Amendments Act of 1995
Pub. L. 104–106, div. C, title XXXV, subtitle B (§3521 et seq.), Feb. 10, 1996, 110 Stat. 638
Short title, see 22 U.S.C. 3601 note

Panama Canal Code
Pub. L. 87–845, Oct. 18, 1962, 76A Stat. 1

Panama Canal Commission Authorization Act for Fiscal Year 1991
Pub. L. 101–510, div. C, title XXXV, Nov. 5, 1990, 104 Stat. 1845

Panama Canal Commission Authorization Act for Fiscal Year 1992
Pub. L. 102–190, div. C, title XXXV, Dec. 5, 1991, 105 Stat. 1586

Panama Canal Commission Authorization Act for Fiscal Year 1993
Pub. L. 102–484, div. C, title XXXV, Oct. 23, 1992, 106 Stat. 2655

Panama Canal Commission Authorization Act for Fiscal Year 1994
Pub. L. 103–160, div. C, title XXXV, Nov. 30, 1993, 107 Stat. 1965

Panama Canal Commission Authorization Act for Fiscal Year 1995
Pub. L. 103–337, div. C, title XXXVI, Oct. 5, 1994, 108 Stat. 3111

Panama Canal Commission Authorization Act for Fiscal Year 1996
Pub. L. 104–106, div. C, title XXXV, subtitle A (§3501 et seq.), Feb. 10, 1996, 110 Stat. 637

Panama Canal Commission Authorization Act for Fiscal Year 1997
Pub. L. 104–201, div. C, title XXXV, subtitle A (§3501 et seq.), Sept. 23, 1996, 110 Stat. 2859

Panama Canal Commission Authorization Act for Fiscal Year 1998
Pub. L. 105–85, div. C, title XXXV, subtitle A (§3501 et seq.), Nov. 18, 1997, 111 Stat. 2062

Panama Canal Commission Authorization Act for Fiscal Year 1999
Pub. L. 105–261, div. C, title XXXV, Oct. 17, 1998, 112 Stat. 2267

Panama Canal Commission Authorization Act for Fiscal Year 2000
Pub. L. 106–65, div. C, title XXXV, Oct. 5, 1999, 113 Stat. 974
Short title, see 22 U.S.C. 3601 note

Panama Canal Commission Authorization Act, Fiscal Year 1986
Pub. L. 99–223, Dec. 28, 1985, 99 Stat. 1738

Panama Canal Commission Authorization Act, Fiscal Year 1987
Pub. L. 99–368, Aug. 1, 1986, 100 Stat. 775

Panama Canal Commission Authorization Act, Fiscal Year 1990
Pub. L. 101–189, div. C, title XXXV, Nov. 29, 1989, 103 Stat. 1688

Panama Canal Commission Compensation Fund Act of 1988
Pub. L. 100–705, Nov. 19, 1988, 102 Stat. 4685
Short title, see 22 U.S.C. 3601 note

Panama Canal Revolving Fund Act
Pub. L. 100–203, title V, subtitle E, part 2 (§5421 et seq.), Dec. 22, 1987, 101 Stat. 1330–271
Short title, see 22 U.S.C. 3601 note

Panama Canal Transition Facilitation Act of 1997
Pub. L. 105–85, div. C, title XXXV, subtitle B (§3511 et seq.), Nov. 18, 1997, 111 Stat. 2062
Short title, see 22 U.S.C. 3601 note

Panama Defense Road Act
July 20, 1939, ch. 335, 53 Stat. 1071

Pandering Law
Pub. L. 90–206, title III, §301(a), Dec. 16, 1967, 81 Stat. 645

Paperwork Reduction Act
Title 44, chapter 35 (44 U.S.C. 3501 et seq.)
Short title, see 44 U.S.C. 3501 note

Paperwork Reduction Act of 1980
Pub. L. 96–511, Dec. 11, 1980, 94 Stat. 2812
Short title, see 44 U.S.C. 101 note

Paperwork Reduction Act of 1995
Pub. L. 104–13, May 22, 1995, 109 Stat. 163
Short title, see 44 U.S.C. 101 note

Paperwork Reduction Reauthorization Act of 1986
Pub. L. 99–500, §101(m) [title VIII], Oct. 18, 1986, 100 Stat. 1783–308, 1783–335, and Pub. L. 99–591, §101(m) [title VIII], Oct. 30, 1986, 100 Stat. 3341–308, 3341–335
Short title, see 44 U.S.C. 101 note

Par Value Modification Act
Pub. L. 92–268, Mar. 31, 1972, 86 Stat. 116

Parental Kidnaping Prevention Act of 1980
Pub. L. 96–611, §§6–10, Dec. 28, 1980, 94 Stat. 3568–3573
Short title, see 42 U.S.C. 1305 note

Parimutuel Licensing Simplification Act of 1988
Pub. L. 100–413, Aug. 22, 1988, 102 Stat. 1101 (28 U.S.C. 534 note)

Parity Act
See Soil Conservation and Domestic Allotment Act

Parker-Watson Act
See Railway Labor Act

Parole Act
June 25, 1910, ch. 387, 36 Stat. 819

Parole Commission and Reorganization Act
Pub. L. 94–233, Mar. 15, 1976, 90 Stat. 219

Parole Commission Phaseout Act of 1996
Pub. L. 104–232, Oct. 2, 1996, 110 Stat. 3055 (18 U.S.C. 4201 note)

Part I of the Interstate Commerce Act
Feb. 4, 1887, ch. 104, part I, 24 Stat. 379

Part II of the Interstate Commerce Act
Feb. 4, 1887, ch. 104, part II, as added Aug. 9, 1935, ch. 498, 49 Stat. 543

Part III of the Interstate Commerce Act
Feb. 4, 1887, ch. 104, part III, as added Sept. 18, 1940, ch. 722, title II, §201, 54 Stat. 929

Part IV of the Interstate Commerce Act
Feb. 4, 1887, ch. 104, part IV, as added May 16, 1942, ch. 318, §1, 56 Stat. 284

Partial Payments Act (Railroads)
Feb. 26, 1921, ch. 72, 41 Stat. 1145

Participation Sales Act of 1966
Pub. L. 89–429, May 24, 1966, 80 Stat. 164
Short title, see 12 U.S.C. 1701 note

Partnership for Health Amendments of 1967
Pub. L. 90–174, Dec. 5, 1967, 81 Stat. 533
Short title, see 42 U.S.C. 201 note

Partnerships for Wildlife Act
Pub. L. 102–587, title VII, Nov. 4, 1992, 106 Stat. 5094 (16 U.S.C. 3741 et seq.)
Short title, see 16 U.S.C. 3741 note

Partnerships in Education for Mathematics, Science, and Engineering Act
Pub. L. 98–377, title III, part A (§301 et seq.), formerly title III, Aug. 11, 1984, 98 Stat. 1283 (20 U.S.C. 3981 et seq.)

Partnerships in Education for Mathematics, Science, and Engineering Act—Continued
Short title, see 20 U.S.C. 3981 note

Paskenta Band Restoration Act
Pub. L. 103–454, title III, Nov. 2, 1994, 108 Stat. 4793 (25 U.S.C. 1300m et seq.)
Short title, see 25 U.S.C. 1300m note

Passenger act, eighteen hundred and eight-two
Aug. 2, 1882, ch. 374, 22 Stat. 186

Passenger Railroad Rebuilding Act of 1980
Pub. L. 96–254, title II, May 30, 1980, 94 Stat. 410

Passenger Vessel Safety Act of 1993
Pub. L. 103–206, title V, Dec. 20, 1993, 107 Stat. 2439
Short title, see 46 U.S.C. 2101 note

Patent and Plant Variety Protection Remedy Clarification Act
Pub. L. 102–560, Oct. 28, 1992, 106 Stat. 4230
Short title, see 7 U.S.C. 2321 note

Patent and Trademark Fee Fairness Act of 1999
Pub. L. 106–113, div. B, §1000(a)(9) [title IV, subtitle B (§4201 et seq.)], Nov. 29, 1999, 113 Stat. 1536, 1501A–554
Short title, see 35 U.S.C. 1 note

Patent and Trademark Office Authorization Act of 1991
Pub. L. 102–204, Dec. 10, 1991, 105 Stat. 1636

Patent and Trademark Office Authorization Act of 1993
Pub. L. 103–179, Dec. 3, 1993, 107 Stat. 2040

Patent and Trademark Office Efficiency Act
Pub. L. 106–113, div. B, §1000(a)(9) [title IV, subtitle G (§4701 et seq.)], Nov. 29, 1999, 113 Stat. 1536, 1501A–572
Short title, see 35 U.S.C. 1 note

Patent Fee Integrity and Innovation Protection Act of 1999
Pub. L. 106–42, Aug. 5, 1999, 113 Stat. 217

Patent Law Amendments Act of 1984
Pub. L. 98–622, Nov. 8, 1984, 98 Stat. 3383
Short title, see 35 U.S.C. 1 note

Patent Law Foreign Filing Amendments Act of 1988
Pub. L. 100–418, title IX, §9101, Aug. 23, 1988, 102 Stat. 1567
Short title, see 35 U.S.C. 1 note

Patent Term Guarantee Act of 1999
Pub. L. 106–113, div. B, §1000(a)(9) [title IV, subtitle D (§4401 et seq.)], Nov. 29, 1999, 113 Stat. 1536, 1501A–557
Short title, see 35 U.S.C. 1 note

Patterson Act
See Kidnapping Act

Paul Coverdell National Forensic Sciences Improvement Act of 2000
Pub. L. 106–561, Dec. 21, 2000, 114 Stat. 2787
Short title, see 42 U.S.C. 3711 note

Paul D. Coverdell Fellows Program Act of 2000
Pub. L. 106–309, title IV, §408, Oct. 17, 2000, 114 Stat. 1100 (22 U.S.C. 2517 note)

Paul D. Coverdell World Wise Schools Act of 2000
Pub. L. 106–570, title VI, Dec. 27, 2000, 114 Stat. 3051 (22 U.S.C. 2517 note)

Pay Readjustment Act of 1922
June 10, 1922, ch. 212, 42 Stat. 625

Pay Readjustment Act of 1942
June 16, 1942, ch. 413, 56 Stat. 359

Pay Saving Act
June 18, 1956, ch. 402, 70 Stat. 291

Pay-as-you-go Tax Act
See Current Tax Payment Act of 1943

Payment in Lieu of Taxes Act
Pub. L. 94–565, Oct. 20, 1976, 90 Stat. 2662

Payment-in-Kind Tax Treatment Act of 1983
Pub. L. 98–4, Mar. 11, 1983, 97 Stat. 7 (26 U.S.C. 61 note)

Payments in Lieu of Taxes Act
Pub. L. 103–397, Oct. 22, 1994, 108 Stat. 4156
Short title, see 31 U.S.C. 6901 note

Payne-Aldrich Act (Tariff)
Aug. 5, 1909, ch. 6, 36 Stat. 11

Peace Corps Act
Pub. L. 87–293, Sept. 22, 1961, 75 Stat. 612 (22 U.S.C. 2501 et seq.)
Short title, see 22 U.S.C. 2501 note

Peace Corps Act Amendments of 1978
Pub. L. 95–331, Aug. 2, 1978, 92 Stat. 414
Short title, see 22 U.S.C. 2501 note

Pecan Promotion and Research Act of 1990
Pub. L. 101–624, title XIX, subtitle A (§1905 et seq.), Nov. 28, 1990, 104 Stat. 3838 (7 U.S.C. 6001 et seq.)
Short title, see 7 U.S.C. 6001 note

Pecos National Historical Park Expansion Act of 1990
Pub. L. 101–536, Nov. 8, 1990, 104 Stat. 2368 (16 U.S.C. 410rr–7)
Short title, see 16 U.S.C. 410rr note

Peer Review Improvement Act of 1982
Pub. L. 97–248, title I, subtitle C (§141 et seq.), Sept. 3, 1982, 96 Stat. 381
Short title, see 42 U.S.C. 1305 note

Pelagic Sealing Act
Aug. 24, 1912, ch. 373, 37 Stat. 499

Pemigewasset River Study Act of 1989
Pub. L. 101–357, Aug. 10, 1990, 104 Stat. 418
Short title, see 16 U.S.C. 1271 note

Penalty Mail Act of 1948
June 25, 1948, ch. 658, title III, 62 Stat. 1048

Pendleton Act (Civil Service)
See Civil Service Act

Penitentiary Act
Mar. 2, 1831, ch. 37, 4 Stat. 448

Pennsylvania Avenue Development Corporation Act of 1972
Pub. L. 92–578, Oct. 27, 1972, 86 Stat. 1266 (40 U.S.C. 871 et seq.)
Short title, see 40 U.S.C. 871 note

Pennsylvania Battlefields Protection Act of 1999
Pub. L. 106–86, Oct. 31, 1999, 113 Stat. 1298
Short title, see 16 U.S.C. 410aa note

Pennsylvania Wilderness Act of 1984
Pub. L. 98–585, Oct. 30, 1984, 98 Stat. 3100

Penny Stock Reform Act of 1990
Pub. L. 101–429, title V, Oct. 15, 1990, 104 Stat. 951
Short title, see 15 U.S.C. 78a note

Pension Annuitants Protection Act of 1994
Pub. L. 103–401, Oct. 22, 1994, 108 Stat. 4172
Short title, see 29 U.S.C. 1001 note

Pension Policy Commission Act
Pub. L. 96–14, May 24, 1979, 93 Stat. 29 (29 U.S.C. 1001 note)

Pension Protection Act
Pub. L. 100–203, title IX, subtitle D, part II (§9302 et seq.), Dec. 22, 1987, 101 Stat. 1330–333
Short title, see 26 U.S.C. 1 note

Peonage Abolition Act
Mar. 2, 1867, ch. 187, 14 Stat. 546

Per Capita Act
Pub. L. 98–64, Aug. 2, 1983, 97 Stat. 365 (25 U.S.C. 117a et seq.)
Short title, see 25 U.S.C. 117a note

Performance Management and Recognition System Amendments of 1991
Pub. L. 102–22, Mar. 28, 1991, 105 Stat. 71

Performance Management and Recognition System Reauthorization Act of 1989
Pub. L. 101–103, Sept. 30, 1989, 103 Stat. 670

Performance Management and Recognition System Termination Act
Pub. L. 103–89, Sept. 30, 1993, 107 Stat. 981
Short title, see 5 U.S.C. 5301 note

Performance Rating Act of 1950
Sept. 30, 1950, ch. 1123, 64 Stat. 1098

Perishable Agricultural Commodities Act Amendments of 1995
Pub. L. 104–48, Nov. 15, 1995, 109 Stat. 424
Short title, see 7 U.S.C. 499a note

Perishable Agricultural Commodities Act, 1930
June 10, 1930, ch. 436, 46 Stat. 531 (7 U.S.C. 499a et seq.)
Short title, see 7 U.S.C. 499a(a)

Perkins County Rural Water System Act of 1999
Pub. L. 106–136, Dec. 7, 1999, 113 Stat. 1688

Permanent Appropriation Repeal Act, 1934
June 26, 1934, ch. 756, 48 Stat. 1224

Persian Gulf Conflict Higher Education Assistance Act
Pub. L. 102–25, title III, part E (§371 et seq.), Apr. 6, 1991, 105 Stat. 93 (20 U.S.C. 1070 note)

Persian Gulf Conflict Supplemental Authorization and Personnel Benefits Act of 1991
Pub. L. 102–25, Apr. 6, 1991, 105 Stat. 75
Short title, see 10 U.S.C. 101 note

Persian Gulf War Veterans Act of 1998
Pub. L. 105–277, div. C, title XVI, Oct. 21, 1998, 112 Stat. 2681–742
Short title, see 38 U.S.C. 101 note

Persian Gulf War Veterans' Benefits Act
Pub. L. 103–446, title I, Nov. 2, 1994, 108 Stat. 4647
Short title, see 38 U.S.C. 101 note

Persian Gulf War Veterans' Benefits Act of 1991
Pub. L. 102–25, title III, part C (§331 et seq.), Apr. 6, 1991, 105 Stat. 88
Short title, see 38 U.S.C. 101 note

Persian Gulf War Veterans' Health Status Act
Pub. L. 102–585, title VII, Nov. 4, 1992, 106 Stat. 4975 (38 U.S.C. 527 note)

Personal Responsibility and Work Opportunity Reconciliation Act of 1996
Pub. L. 104–193, Aug. 22, 1996, 110 Stat. 2105
Short title, see 42 U.S.C. 1305 note

Pesticide Monitoring Improvements Act of 1988
Pub. L. 100–418, title IV, subtitle G (§4701 et seq.), Aug. 23, 1988, 102 Stat. 1411 (21 U.S.C. 1401 et seq.)
Short title, see 21 U.S.C. 1401 note

Pesticides Research Act
Pub. L. 85–582, Aug. 1, 1958, 72 Stat. 479 (16 U.S.C. 742d–1, 742d–1 note)

Petersburg National Battlefield Act
Pub. L. 87–603, Aug. 24, 1962, 76 Stat. 403 (16 U.S.C. 423h–1 et seq.)

Petrillo Bill
See Communications Act of 1934

Petroglyph National Monument Boundary Adjustment Act
Pub. L. 105–174, title III, §3005, May 1, 1998, 112 Stat. 82

Petroglyph National Monument Establishment Act of 1990
Pub. L. 101–313, title I, June 27, 1990, 104 Stat. 272 (16 U.S.C. 431 note)

Petroleum Act
See Hot Oil Act

Petroleum Marketing Practices Act
Pub. L. 95–297, June 19, 1978, 92 Stat. 322 (15 U.S.C. 2801 et seq.)
Short title, see 15 U.S.C. 2801 note

Petroleum Marketing Practices Act Amendments of 1994
Pub. L. 103–371, Oct. 19, 1994, 108 Stat. 3484
Short title, see 15 U.S.C. 2801 note

Petroleum Overcharge Distribution and Restitution Act of 1986
Pub. L. 99–509, title III, subtitle A (§3001 et seq.), Oct. 21, 1986, 100 Stat. 1881 (15 U.S.C. 4501 et seq.)
Short title, see 15 U.S.C. 4501 note

Petroleum Pipe Line Act
July 30, 1941, ch. 333, 55 Stat. 610 (15 U.S.C. note prec. 715)

Philanthropy Protection Act of 1995
Pub. L. 104–62, Dec. 8, 1995, 109 Stat. 682
Short title, see 15 U.S.C. 80a–51 note

Philippine Army, Scouts, and Guerilla Veterans of World War II Naturalization Act of 1997
Pub. L. 105–119, title I, §112, Nov. 26, 1997, 111 Stat. 2459
Short title, see 8 U.S.C. 1101 note

Philippine Currency Reserve Act
June 16, 1934, ch. 655, 48 Stat. 1115

Philippine Independence Act
Mar. 24, 1934, ch. 84, 48 Stat. 456

Philippine Organic Act of 1902
July 1, 1902, ch. 1369, 32 Stat. 691

Philippine Property Act of 1946
July 3, 1946, ch. 536, 60 Stat. 418 (22 U.S.C. 1381 et seq.)
Short title, see 22 U.S.C. 1381 note

Philippine Rehabilitation Act of 1946
Apr. 30, 1946, ch. 243, 60 Stat. 128

Philippine tariff revision law of nineteen hundred and five
Mar. 3, 1905, ch. 1408, 33 Stat. 928

Philippine Trade Act of 1946
Apr. 30, 1946, ch. 244, 60 Stat. 141 (22 U.S.C. 1251 et seq.)
Short title, see 22 U.S.C. 1354 note

Philippine Trade Agreement Revision Act of 1955
Aug. 1, 1955, ch. 438, 69 Stat. 413 (22 U.S.C. 1373 et seq.)
Short title, see 22 U.S.C. 1373 note

Philippine Travel Pay Act
May 2, 1940, ch. 182, 54 Stat. 176

Phipps Law
May 9, 1924, ch. 150, 43 Stat. 116 (43 U.S.C. 384)

Physical Education for Progress Act
Pub. L. 89–10, title X, part L, as added Pub. L. 106–554, §1(a)(1) [title VII, §701], Dec. 21, 2000, 114 Stat. 2763, 2763A–76
Short title, see 20 U.S.C. 6301 note

Physical Therapists Practice Act
Pub. L. 87–280, Sept. 22, 1961, 75 Stat. 578

Physical Valuation of Property Act
See Valuation Act (Interstate Commerce)

Pickett Act
June 25, 1910, ch. 421, 36 Stat. 847 (43 U.S.C. 141 et seq.)

Pictured Rocks National Lakeshore Act
Pub. L. 89–668, Oct. 15, 1966, 80 Stat. 922 (16 U.S.C. 460s et seq.)

Pilot Records Improvement Act of 1996
Pub. L. 104–264, title V, Oct. 9, 1996, 110 Stat. 3259
Short title, see 49 U.S.C. 40101 note

Pipeline Safety Act of 1979
Pub. L. 96–129, Nov. 30, 1979, 93 Stat. 989

Pipeline Safety Act of 1992
Pub. L. 102–508, Oct. 24, 1992, 106 Stat. 3289

Pipeline Safety Reauthorization Act of 1988
Pub. L. 100–561, Oct. 31, 1988, 102 Stat. 2805

Piracy and Counterfeiting Amendments Act of 1982
Pub. L. 97–180, May 24, 1982, 96 Stat. 91
Short title, see 18 U.S.C. 2311 note

Piscataway Park Expansion Act of 1994
Pub. L. 103–350, Oct. 6, 1994, 108 Stat. 3146

Pitman-Bloom Act
See Neutrality Act of 1939

Pittman Act
Apr. 23, 1918, ch. 63, 40 Stat. 535

Pittman Embassy Picketing Act
Feb. 15, 1938, ch. 29, 52 Stat. 30 (22 U.S.C. 255a, 255b)

Pittman Underground Water Act
Oct. 22, 1919, ch. 77, 41 Stat. 293

Pittman-Robertson Wildlife Restoration Act
Act Sept. 2, 1937, ch. 899, 50 Stat. 917 (16 U.S.C. 669 et seq.)
Short title, see 16 U.S.C. 669 note

Plant Patent Amendments Act of 1998
Pub. L. 105–289, Oct. 27, 1998, 112 Stat. 2780
Short title, see 35 U.S.C. 1 note

Plant Protection Act
Pub. L. 106–224, title IV, June 20, 2000, 114 Stat. 438 (7 U.S.C. 7701 et seq.)
Short title, see 7 U.S.C. 7701 note

Plant Quarantine Act
Aug. 20, 1912, ch. 308, 37 Stat. 315 (7 U.S.C. 151 et seq.)

Plant Variety Protection Act
Pub. L. 91–577, Dec. 24, 1970, 84 Stat. 1542 (7 U.S.C. 2321 et seq.)
Short title, see 7 U.S.C. 2321 note

Plant Variety Protection Act Amendments of 1994
Pub. L. 103–349, Oct. 6, 1994, 108 Stat. 3136
Short title, see 7 U.S.C. 2321 note

Platt Amendment (Cuba)
Mar. 2, 1901, ch. 803, 31 Stat. 897

PLO Commitments Compliance Act of 1989
Pub. L. 101–246, title VIII, Feb. 16, 1990, 104 Stat. 76

Point Reyes National Seashore Act
Pub. L. 87–657, Sept. 13, 1962, 76 Stat. 538 (16 U.S.C. 459c et seq.)

Points of Light Foundation Act
Pub. L. 101–610, title III, Nov. 16, 1990, 104 Stat. 3180 (42 U.S.C. 12661 et seq.)
Short title, see 42 U.S.C. 12501 note

Poison Control Center Enhancement and Awareness Act
Pub. L. 106–174, Feb. 25, 2000, 114 Stat. 18 (42 U.S.C. 14801 et seq.)
Short title, see 42 U.S.C. 14801 note

Poison Prevention Packaging Act of 1970
Pub. L. 91–601, Dec. 30, 1970, 84 Stat. 1670 (15 U.S.C. 1471 et seq.)
Short title, see 15 U.S.C. 1471 note

Police Corps Act
Pub. L. 103–322, title XX, subtitle A (§200101 et seq.), Sept. 13, 1994, 108 Stat. 2049 (42 U.S.C. 14091 et seq.)
Short title, see 42 U.S.C. 13701 note

Police, Fire, and Emergency Officers Educational Assistance Act of 1998
Pub. L. 105–390, Nov. 13, 1998, 112 Stat. 3495
Short title, see 42 U.S.C. 3711 note

Policemen and Firemen's Retirement and Disability Act
Sept. 1, 1916, ch. 433, §12, as added Pub. L. 85–157, §3, Aug. 21, 1957, 71 Stat. 391

Policemen and Firemen's Retirement and Disability Act amendments of 1957
Pub. L. 85–157, Aug. 21, 1957, 71 Stat. 391

Policemen and Firemen's Retirement and Disability Act Amendments of 1970
Pub. L. 91–509, Oct. 26, 1970, 84 Stat. 1136

Poliomyelitis Vaccination Assistance Act of 1955
Aug. 12, 1955, ch. 863, 69 Stat. 704 (42 U.S.C. 246 note)

Political Disabilities Removal Act
May 22, 1872, ch. 193, 17 Stat. 142

Pollution Prevention Act of 1990
Pub. L. 101–508, title VI, subtitle F (§6501 et seq.), Nov. 5, 1990, 104 Stat. 1388–320 (42 U.S.C. 13101 et seq.)
Short title, see 42 U.S.C. 13101 note

Pollution Prosecution Act of 1990
Pub. L. 101–593, title II, Nov. 16, 1990, 104 Stat. 2962 (42 U.S.C. 4321 note)

Pomerene Bills of Lading Act (Interstate Commerce)
Aug. 29, 1916, ch. 415, 39 Stat. 538

Ponca Restoration Act
Pub. L. 101–484, Oct. 31, 1990, 104 Stat. 1167 (25 U.S.C. 983 et seq.)
Short title, see 25 U.S.C. 983 note

Popcorn Promotion, Research, and Consumer Information Act
Pub. L. 104–127, title V, subtitle E (§571 et seq.), Apr. 4, 1996, 110 Stat. 1074 (7 U.S.C. 7481 et seq.)
Short title, see 7 U.S.C. 7401 note

Pope John Paul II Congressional Gold Medal Act
Pub. L. 106–250, July 27, 2000, 114 Stat. 622 (31 U.S.C. 5111 note)

Population Education Act
Pub. L. 89–10, Apr. 11, 1965, title III, part M (§391 et seq.), as added Pub. L. 95–561, title III, §301(a), Nov. 1, 1978, 92 Stat. 2227

Pork Promotion, Research, and Consumer Information Act of 1985
Pub. L. 99–198, title XVI, subtitle B (§1611 et seq.), Dec. 23, 1985, 99 Stat. 1606 (7 U.S.C. 4801 et seq.)
Short title, see 7 U.S.C. 4801 note

Port and Tanker Safety Act of 1978
Pub. L. 95–474, Oct. 17, 1978, 92 Stat. 1471
Short title, see 33 U.S.C. 1221 note

Port Chicago National Memorial Act of 1992
Pub. L. 102–562, title II, Oct. 28, 1992, 106 Stat. 4235 (16 U.S.C. 431 note)

Portability of Benefits for Nonappropriated Fund Employees Act of 1990
Pub. L. 101–508, title VII, §7202, Nov. 5, 1990, 104 Stat. 1388–335
Short title, see 5 U.S.C. 2101 note

Portal-to-Portal Act of 1947
May 14, 1947, ch. 52, 61 Stat. 84 (29 U.S.C. 251 et seq.)
Short title, see 29 U.S.C. 251 note

Porter Act
See Foreign Service Buildings Act, 1926

Porter Resolution (Narcotic Drugs)
Mar. 2, 1923, ch. 190, 42 Stat. 1431

Ports and Waterways Safety Act
Pub. L. 92–340, July 10, 1972, 86 Stat. 424 (33 U.S.C. 1221 et seq.)
Short title, see 33 U.S.C. 1221 note

Posse Comitatus Act (Use of Army)
June 18, 1878, ch. 263, §15, 20 Stat. 152

Post Office Department Appropriation Act, 1937
June 23, 1936, ch. 725, title II, 49 Stat. 1846

Post Office Department Appropriation Act, 1938
May 14, 1937, ch. 180, title II, 50 Stat. 155

Post Office Department Appropriation Act, 1939
Mar. 28, 1938, ch. 55, title II, 52 Stat. 140

Post Office Department Appropriation Act, 1940
May 6, 1939, ch. 115, title II, 53 Stat. 675

Post Office Department Appropriation Act, 1941
Mar. 25, 1940, ch. 71, title II, 54 Stat. 70

Post Office Department Appropriation Act, 1942
May 31, 1941, ch. 156, title II, 55 Stat. 227

Post Office Department Appropriation Act, 1943
Mar. 10, 1942, ch. 178, title II, 56 Stat. 162

Post Office Department Appropriation Act, 1944
June 30, 1943, ch. 179, title II, 57 Stat. 263

Post Office Department Appropriation Act, 1945
Apr. 22, 1944, ch. 175, title II, 58 Stat. 207

Post Office Department Appropriation Act, 1946
Apr. 24, 1945, ch. 92, title II, 59 Stat. 68

Post Office Department Appropriation Act, 1947
July 20, 1946, ch. 588, title II, 60 Stat. 580

Post Office Department Appropriation Act, 1948
July 1, 1947, ch. 186, title II, 61 Stat. 228

Post Office Department Appropriation Act, 1949
June 14, 1948, ch. 466, title II, 62 Stat. 416

Post Office Department Appropriation Act, 1950
June 30, 1949, ch. 286, title II, 63 Stat. 367

Post Office Department Appropriation Act, 1951
Sept. 6, 1950, ch. 896, Ch. IV, title II, 64 Stat. 640

Post Office Department Appropriation Act, 1952
Aug. 11, 1951, ch. 301, title II, 65 Stat. 186

Post Office Department Appropriation Act, 1953
June 30, 1952, ch. 523, title II, 66 Stat. 292

Post Office Department Appropriation Act, 1954
June 18, 1953, ch. 132, title II, 67 Stat. 70

Post Office Department Appropriation Act, 1955
May 28, 1954, ch. 242, title II, 68 Stat. 147

Post Office Department Appropriation Act, 1960
Pub. L. 86–39, title II, June 11, 1959, 73 Stat. 68

Post Office Department Appropriation Act, 1961
Pub. L. 86–561, title II, June 30, 1960, 74 Stat. 287

Post Office Department Appropriation Act, 1962
Pub. L. 87–159, title II, Aug. 21, 1961, 75 Stat. 396

Post Office Department Appropriation Act, 1963
Pub. L. 87–575, title II, Aug. 6, 1962, 76 Stat. 313

Post Office Department Appropriation Act, 1964
Pub. L. 88–39, title II, June 13, 1963, 77 Stat. 61

Post Office Department Appropriation Act, 1965
Pub. L. 88–392, title II, Aug. 1, 1964, 78 Stat. 371

Post Office Department Appropriation Act, 1966
Pub. L. 89–57, title II, June 30, 1965, 79 Stat. 199

Post Office Department Appropriation Act, 1967
Pub. L. 89–474, title II, June 29, 1966, 80 Stat. 225

Post Office Department Appropriation Act, 1968
Pub. L. 90–47, title II, July 7, 1967, 81 Stat. 115

Post Office Department Appropriation Act, 1969
Pub. L. 90–350, title II, June 19, 1968, 82 Stat. 192

Post Office Department Appropriation Act, 1970
Pub. L. 91–74, title II, Sept. 29, 1969, 83 Stat. 118

Post Office Department Appropriation Act, 1971
Pub. L. 91–422, title II, Sept. 26, 1970, 84 Stat. 874

Post Office Department Financial Control Act of 1950
Aug. 17, 1950, ch. 735, 64 Stat. 460

Post Office Department Property Act of 1954
July 22, 1954, ch. 560, title II, 68 Stat. 521

Post-Vietnam Era Veterans' Educational Assistance Act of 1977
Pub. L. 94–502, title IV, Oct. 15, 1976, 90 Stat. 2392
Short title, see 38 U.S.C. 101 note

Postal Employees Hours Act
See McKellar-Mead 40-Hour Mail Act

Postal Employees Safety Enhancement Act
Pub. L. 105–241, Sept. 28, 1998, 112 Stat. 1572
Short title, see 39 U.S.C. 101 note

Postal Employees Salary Adjustment Act of 1962
Pub. L. 87–793, part II, title III (§701 et seq.), Oct. 11, 1962, 76 Stat. 850

Postal Employees Salary Increase Act of 1960
Pub. L. 86–568, title I, part A (§101 et seq.), July 1, 1960, 74 Stat. 296

Postal Field Service Classification Act of 1955
See Postal Field Service Compensation Act of 1955

Postal Field Service Compensation Act of 1955
June 10, 1955, ch. 137, 69 Stat. 88

Postal Pay Act of 1945
July 6, 1945, ch. 274, 59 Stat. 435

Postal Policy Act of 1958
Pub. L. 85–426, title I, May 27, 1958, 72 Stat. 134

Postal Rate Increase Act, 1958
Pub. L. 85–426, title II, May 27, 1958, 72 Stat. 138

Postal Rate Revision and Federal Employees Salary Act of 1948
July 3, 1948, ch. 830, 62 Stat. 1260

Postal Reorganization Act
Pub. L. 91–375, Aug. 12, 1970, 84 Stat. 719 (39 U.S.C. 101 et seq.)
Short title, see 39 U.S.C. 101 note

Postal Reorganization Act Amendments of 1976
Pub. L. 94–421, Sept. 24, 1976, 90 Stat. 1303
Short title, see 39 U.S.C. 101 note

Postal Revenue and Federal Salary Act of 1967
Pub. L. 90–206, Dec. 16, 1967, 81 Stat. 613
Short title, see 5 U.S.C. 5332 note

Postal Salary Act of 1945
July 6, 1945, ch. 274, 59 Stat. 435

Postal Salary Classification Act of 1925
See Reclassification Act of 1925

Postal Savings Depositories Act
June 25, 1910, ch. 386, 36 Stat. 814

Postal Savings System Statute of Limitations Act
Pub. L. 98–359, July 13, 1984, 98 Stat. 402
Short title, see 31 U.S.C. 1301 note

Postal Service and Federal Employees Salary Act of 1962
Pub. L. 87–793, Oct. 11, 1962, 76 Stat. 832

Postal Service Appropriation Act, 1972
Pub. L. 92–49, title II, July 9, 1971, 85 Stat. 110

Postal Service Appropriation Act, 1973
Pub. L. 92–351, title II, July 13, 1972, 86 Stat. 474

Postal Service Appropriation Act, 1974
Pub. L. 93–143, title II, Oct. 30, 1973, 87 Stat. 513

Postal Service Appropriation Act, 1975
Pub. L. 93–381, title II, Aug. 21, 1974, 88 Stat. 616

Postal Service Appropriation Act, 1976
Pub. L. 94–91, title II, Aug. 9, 1975, 89 Stat. 444

Postal Service Appropriation Act, 1977
Pub. L. 94–363, title II, July 14, 1976, 90 Stat. 965

Postal Service Appropriation Act, 1978
Pub. L. 95–81, title II, July 31, 1977, 91 Stat. 343

Postal Service Appropriation Act, 1979
Pub. L. 95–429, title II, Oct. 10, 1978, 92 Stat. 1004

Postal Service Appropriation Act, 1980
Pub. L. 96–74, title II, Sept. 29, 1979, 93 Stat. 562

Postal Service Appropriations Act, 1987
Pub. L. 99–500, §101(m) [title II], Oct. 18, 1986, 100 Stat. 1783–308, 1783–314, and Pub. L. 99–591, §101(m) [title II], Oct. 30, 1986, 100 Stat. 3341–308, 3341–314

Postal Service Appropriation Act, 1988
Pub. L. 100–202, §101(m) [title II], Dec. 22, 1987, 101 Stat. 1329–390, 1329–397

Postal Service Appropriation Act, 1989
Pub. L. 100–440, title II, Sept. 22, 1988, 102 Stat. 1727

Postal Service Appropriations Act, 1990
Pub. L. 101–136, title II, Nov. 3, 1989, 103 Stat. 790

Postal Service Appropriations Act, 1991
Pub. L. 101–509, title II, Nov. 5, 1990, 104 Stat. 1396

Postal Service Appropriations Act, 1992
Pub. L. 102–141, title II, Oct. 28, 1991, 105 Stat. 842

Postal Service Appropriations Act, 1993
Pub. L. 102–393, title II, Oct. 6, 1992, 106 Stat. 1737

Postal Service Appropriations Act, 1994
Pub. L. 103–123, title II, Oct. 28, 1993, 107 Stat. 1234

Postal Service Appropriations Act, 1995
Pub. L. 103–329, title II, Sept. 30, 1994, 108 Stat. 2392

Postal Service Appropriations Act, 1996
Pub. L. 104–52, title II, Nov. 19, 1995, 109 Stat. 476

Postal Service Appropriations Act, 1998
Pub. L. 105–61, title II, Oct. 10, 1997, 111 Stat. 1290

Postal Service Appropriations Act, 1999
Pub. L. 105–277, div. A, §101(h) [title II], Oct. 21, 1998, 112 Stat. 2681–480, 2681–492

Postal Service Appropriations Act, 2000
Pub. L. 106–58, title II, Sept. 29, 1999, 113 Stat. 444

Postal Service Appropriations Act, 2001
Pub. L. 106–554, §1(a)(3) [title II], Dec. 21, 2000, 114 Stat. 2763, 2763A–135

Posthumous Citizenship for Active Duty Service Act of 1989
Pub. L. 101–249, Mar. 6, 1990, 104 Stat. 94
Short title, see 8 U.S.C. 1101 note

Postsecondary Student Assistance Amendments of 1981
Pub. L. 97–35, title V, subtitle B (§531 et seq.), Aug. 13, 1981, 95 Stat. 450
Short title, see 20 U.S.C. 1001 note

Potato Act of 1935
Aug. 24, 1935, ch. 641, title II, 49 Stat. 782 (7 U.S.C. 801 et seq.)

Potato Research and Promotion Act
Pub. L. 91–670, title III, Jan. 11, 1971, 84 Stat. 2041 (7 U.S.C. 2611 et seq.)
Short title, see 7 U.S.C. 2611 note

Potato Research and Promotion Act Amendments of 1982
Pub. L. 97–244, Aug. 26, 1982, 96 Stat. 310
Short title, see 7 U.S.C. 2611 note

Potato Research and Promotion Act Amendments of 1990
Pub. L. 101–624, title XIX, subtitle C (§1935 et seq.), Nov. 28, 1990, 104 Stat. 3865
Short title, see 7 U.S.C. 2611 note

Poultry Producers Financial Protection Act of 1987
Pub. L. 100–173, Nov. 23, 1987, 101 Stat. 917
Short title, see 7 U.S.C. 181 note

Poultry Products Inspection Act
Pub. L. 85–172, Aug. 28, 1957, 71 Stat. 441 (21 U.S.C. 451 et seq.)
Short title, see 21 U.S.C. 451 note

Poultry Racket Act
Aug. 15, 1921, ch. 64, title V, as added Aug. 14, 1935, ch. 532, 49 Stat. 648

Power or Train Brakes Safety Appliance Act of 1958
Pub. L. 85–375, Apr. 11, 1958, 72 Stat. 86

Powerplant and Industrial Fuel Use Act of 1978
Pub. L. 95–620, Nov. 9, 1978, 92 Stat. 3289 (42 U.S.C. 8301 et seq.)
Short title, see 42 U.S.C. 8301 note

Powers of Appointment Act of 1951
June 28, 1951, ch. 165, 65 Stat. 91

Practical Nurse Training Extension Act of 1961
Pub. L. 87–22, Apr. 24, 1961, 75 Stat. 44
Short title, see 20 U.S.C. 11 note

Practice Conformity Act
June 1, 1872, ch. 255, 17 Stat. 196

Practice of Psychology Act
Pub. L. 91–657, Jan. 8, 1971, 84 Stat. 1955

Preferred Surety Bond Guarantee Program Act of 1988
Pub. L. 100–590, title II, Nov. 3, 1988, 102 Stat. 3007
Short title, see 15 U.S.C. 661 note

Pregnancy Discrimination Act
Pub. L. 95–555, Oct. 31, 1978, 92 Stat. 2076 (42 U.S.C. 2000e(k))

Prescription Drug Amendments of 1992
Pub. L. 102–353, Aug. 26, 1992, 106 Stat. 941
Short title, see 21 U.S.C. 301 note

Prescription Drug Import Fairness Act of 2000
Pub. L. 106–387, §1(a) [title VII, §746], Oct. 28, 2000, 114 Stat. 1549, 1549A–40
Short title, see 21 U.S.C. 301 note

Prescription Drug Marketing Act of 1987
Pub. L. 100–293, Apr. 22, 1988, 102 Stat. 95
Short title, see 21 U.S.C. 301 note

Prescription Drug User Fee Act of 1992
Pub. L. 102–571, title I, Oct. 29, 1992, 106 Stat. 4491
Short title, see 21 U.S.C. 301 note

Preserving Affordable Housing for Senior Citizens and Families into the 21st Century Act
Pub. L. 106–74, title V, Oct. 20, 1999, 113 Stat. 1100
Short title, see 12 U.S.C. 1701 note

President John F. Kennedy Assassination Records Collection Act of 1992
Pub. L. 102–526, Oct. 26, 1992, 106 Stat. 3443 (44 U.S.C. 2107 note)

President John F. Kennedy Assassination Records Collection Extension Act of 1994
Pub. L. 103–345, Oct. 6, 1994, 108 Stat. 3128
Short title, see 44 U.S.C. 2107 note

President's Emergency Food Assistance Act of 1984
Pub. L. 98–473, title III, Oct. 12, 1984, 98 Stat. 2194 (7 U.S.C. 1728 et seq.)
Short title, see 7 U.S.C. 1728 note

President's Media Commission on Alcohol and Drug Abuse Prevention Act
Pub. L. 99–570, title VIII, Oct. 27, 1986, 100 Stat. 3207–161 (21 U.S.C. 1301 et seq.)
Short title, see 21 U.S.C. 1301 note

Presidential and Executive Office Accountability Act
Pub. L. 104–331, Oct. 26, 1996, 110 Stat. 4053
Short title, see 3 U.S.C. 1 note

Presidential Election Campaign Fund Act
Title 26, chapter 95 (26 U.S.C. 9001 et seq.)
Short title, see 26 U.S.C. 9001

Presidential Election Campaign Fund Act of 1966
Pub. L. 89–809, title III, Nov. 13, 1966, 80 Stat. 1587
Short title, see 26 U.S.C. 6096 note

Presidential Inaugural Ceremonies Act
Aug. 6, 1956, ch. 974, 70 Stat. 1049

Presidential Libraries Act
Aug. 12, 1955, ch. 859, 69 Stat. 695

Presidential Libraries Act of 1986
Pub. L. 99–323, May 27, 1986, 100 Stat. 495
Short title, see 44 U.S.C. 101 note

Presidential Primary Matching Payment Account Act
Title 26, chapter 96 (26 U.S.C. 9031 et seq.)
Short title, see 26 U.S.C. 9031

Presidential Protection Assistance Act of 1976
Pub. L. 94–524, Oct. 17, 1976, 90 Stat. 2475 (18 U.S.C. 3056 note)

Presidential Recordings and Materials Preservation Act
Pub. L. 93–526, Dec. 19, 1974, 88 Stat. 1695 (44 U.S.C. 2111 note, 3315–3324)

Presidential Records Act of 1978
Pub. L. 95–591, Nov. 4, 1978, 92 Stat. 2523 (44 U.S.C. 2201 et seq.)
Short title, see 44 U.S.C. 101 note

Presidential Science and Technology Advisory Organization Act of 1976
Pub. L. 94–282, title II, May 11, 1976, 90 Stat. 463 (42 U.S.C. 6611 et seq.)
Short title, see 42 U.S.C. 6601 note

Presidential Succession Act
Jan. 19, 1886, ch. 4, 24 Stat. 1

Presidential Threat Protection Act of 2000
Pub. L. 106–544, Dec. 19, 2000, 114 Stat. 2715
Short title, see 18 U.S.C. 871 note

Presidential Transition Act of 1963
Pub. L. 88–277, Mar. 7, 1964, 78 Stat. 153 (3 U.S.C. 102 note)

Presidential Transition Act of 2000
Pub. L. 106–293, Oct. 12, 2000, 114 Stat. 1035
Short title, see 3 U.S.C. 101 note

Presidential Transitions Effectiveness Act
Pub. L. 100–398, Aug. 17, 1988, 102 Stat. 985
Short title, see 3 U.S.C. 1 note

Pretrial Services Act of 1982
Pub. L. 97–267, Sept. 27, 1982, 96 Stat. 1136
Short title, see 18 U.S.C. 3141 note

Prevailing Rate Equalization Adjustment Act of 1972
Pub. L. 92–298, May 17, 1972, 86 Stat. 146 (5 U.S.C. 5343 note)

Preventive Health Amendments of 1984
Pub. L. 98–555, Oct. 30, 1984, 98 Stat. 2854
Short title, see 42 U.S.C. 201 note

Preventive Health Amendments of 1992
Pub. L. 102–531, Oct. 27, 1992, 106 Stat. 3469
Short title, see 42 U.S.C. 201 note

Preventive Health Amendments of 1993
Pub. L. 103–183, Dec. 14, 1993, 107 Stat. 2226
Short title, see 42 U.S.C. 201 note

Pribilof Islands Transition Act
Pub. L. 106–562, title I, Dec. 23, 2000, 114 Stat. 2794
Short title, see 16 U.S.C. 1151 note

Price Adjustment Act of 1938
June 21, 1938, ch. 554, title V, 52 Stat. 819

Price Control Act of 1942
See Emergency Price Control Act of 1942

Price Control Extension Act of 1946
July 25, 1946, ch. 671, 60 Stat. 664

Price Discrimination Act
See Robinson-Patman Antidiscrimination Act

Price-Anderson Act
See, also the Atomic Energy Damages Act
Aug. 1, 1946, ch. 724, title I, §170, as added Pub. L. 85–256, §4, Sept. 2, 1957, 71 Stat. 576 (42 U.S.C. 2210)
Short title, see 42 U.S.C. 2210 note

Price-Anderson Amendments Act of 1988
Pub. L. 100–408, Aug. 20, 1988, 102 Stat. 1066
Short title, see 42 U.S.C. 2011 note

Primary Dealers Act of 1988
Pub. L. 100–418, title III, subtitle F (§3501 et seq.), Aug. 23, 1988, 102 Stat. 1386 (22 U.S.C. 5341 et seq.)
Short title, see 22 U.S.C. 5341

Primary Health Care Act of 1978
Pub. L. 95–626, title I, part B (§111 et seq.), Nov. 10, 1978, 92 Stat. 3562
Short title, see 42 U.S.C. 201 note

PRIME Act
Also known as the Program for Investment in Microentrepreneurs Act of 1999
Pub. L. 103–325, title I, subtitle C (§171 et seq.), as added Pub. L. 106–102, title VII, §725, Nov. 12, 1999, 113 Stat. 1471 (15 U.S.C. 6901 et seq.)
Short title, see 15 U.S.C. 6901 note

Printing Act
Jan. 12, 1895, ch. 23, 28 Stat. 601

Priorities and Allocations Act
June 28, 1940, ch. 440, 54 Stat. 676 (42 U.S.C 1501 et seq.; 50 App. U.S.C. 1151 et seq.)

Priority of Shipments Act (Railroads)
Aug. 10, 1917, ch. 51, 40 Stat. 272

Prison Escape Act
Aug. 3, 1935, ch. 432, 49 Stat. 513

Prison Litigation Reform Act of 1995
Pub. L. 104–134, title I, §101[(a)] [title VIII], Apr. 26, 1996, 110 Stat. 1321, 1321–66
Short title, see 18 U.S.C. 3601 note

Prison Testing Act of 1988
Pub. L. 100–607, title IX, Nov. 4, 1988, 102 Stat. 3171
Short title, see 42 U.S.C. 300ff–48 note

Privacy Act
Title 5, section 552a

Privacy Act of 1974
Pub. L. 93–579, Dec. 31, 1974, 88 Stat. 1896
Short title, see 5 U.S.C. 552a note

Privacy Protection Act of 1980
Pub. L. 96–440, Oct. 13, 1980, 94 Stat. 1879 (42 U.S.C. 2000aa et seq.)
Short title, see 42 U.S.C. 2000aa note

Privacy Protection for Rape Victims Act of 1978
Pub. L. 95–540, Oct. 28, 1978, 92 Stat. 2046 (28 App. U.S.C. Rule 412)
Short title, see 28 App. U.S.C. Rule 1103 note

Private Mortgage Insurance Technical Corrections and Clarification Act
Pub. L. 106–569, title IV, Dec. 27, 2000, 114 Stat. 2956
Short title, see 12 U.S.C. 4901 note

Private Ownership of Special Nuclear Materials Act
Pub. L. 88–489, Aug. 26, 1964, 78 Stat. 602
Short title, see 42 U.S.C. 2011 note

Private Securities Litigation Reform Act of 1995
Pub. L. 104–67, Dec. 22, 1995, 109 Stat. 737
Short title, see 15 U.S.C. 78a note

Pro-Children Act of 1994
Pub. L. 103–227, title X, part C (§1041 et seq.), Mar. 31, 1994, 108 Stat. 271 (20 U.S.C. 6081 et seq.)
Short title, see 20 U.S.C. 6081

Probation Act
Mar. 4, 1925, ch. 521, 43 Stat. 1259

Process Act
May 8, 1792, ch. 36, 1 Stat. 275; R.S. §§601, 679, 799, 857, 911, 913, 947, 974, 975, 1004

Process Patent Amendments Act of 1988
Pub. L. 100–418, title IX, subtitle A (§9001 et seq.), Aug. 23, 1988, 102 Stat. 1563
Short title, see 35 U.S.C. 1 note

Processed Products Inspection Improvement Act of 1986
Pub. L. 99–641, title IV, Nov. 10, 1986, 100 Stat. 3567
Short title, see 21 U.S.C. 601 note

Produce Agency Act
Mar. 3, 1927, ch. 309, 44 Stat. 1355 (7 U.S.C. 491 et seq.)

Product Development and Testing Act of 2000
Pub. L. 106–476, title I, subtitle B, ch. 2 (§1431 et seq.), Nov. 9, 2000, 114 Stat. 2161

Product Liability Risk Retention Act of 1981
Renamed Liability Risk Retention Act of 1986

Professional and Amateur Sports Protection Act
Pub. L. 102–559, Oct. 28, 1992, 106 Stat. 4227 (28 U.S.C. 3701 et seq.)
Short title, see 28 U.S.C. 1 note

Professional Boxing Safety Act of 1996
Pub. L. 104–272, Oct. 9, 1996, 110 Stat. 3309 (15 U.S.C. 6301 et seq.)
Short title, see 15 U.S.C. 6301 note

Professional Engineers' Registration Act
Sept. 19, 1950, ch. 953, 64 Stat. 854

Program for Investment in Microentrepreneurs Act of 1999
Also known as the PRIME Act
Pub. L. 103–325, title I, subtitle C (§171 et seq.), as added Pub. L. 106–102, title VII, §725, Nov. 12, 1999, 113 Stat. 1471 (15 U.S.C. 6901 et seq.)

Program for Investment in Microentrepreneurs Act of 1999—Continued
Short title, see 15 U.S.C. 6901 note

Program Fraud Civil Remedies Act of 1986
Pub. L. 99–509, title VI, subtitle B (§6101 et seq.), Oct. 21, 1986, 100 Stat. 1934 (31 U.S.C. 3801 et seq.)
Short title, see 31 U.S.C. 3801 note

Prohibition of Cigarette Sales to Minors in Federal Buildings and Lands Act
Pub. L. 104–52, title VI, §636, Nov. 19, 1995, 109 Stat. 507 (40 U.S.C. 486 note)

Prohibition Reorganization Act of 1930
May 27, 1930, ch. 342, 46 Stat. 427 (27 U.S.C. 101 et seq.)

Prohibition Repeal Act
See Liquor Law Repeal and Enforcement Act

Proliferation Prevention Enhancement Act of 1999
Pub. L. 106–113, div. B, §1000(a)(7) [div. B, title XII, subtitle E (§1251 et seq.)], Nov. 29, 1999, 113 Stat. 1536, 1501A–505
Short title, see 13 U.S.C. 1 note

Prompt Payment Act
Pub. L. 97–177, May 21, 1982, 96 Stat. 85

Prompt Payment Act Amendments of 1988
Pub. L. 100–496, Oct. 17, 1988, 102 Stat. 2455
Short title, see 31 U.S.C. 3901 note

Propaganda Agency Act
See Foreign Agents Registration Act of 1938

Propane Education and Research Act of 1996
Pub. L. 104–284, Oct. 11, 1996, 110 Stat. 3370 (15 U.S.C. 6401 et seq.)
Short title, see 15 U.S.C. 6401 note

Property Claims Act of 1943
Oct. 27, 1943, ch. 287, 57 Stat. 582

Property Requisitioning Act
Oct. 16, 1941, ch. 445, 55 Stat. 742 (50 App. U.S.C. 721 et seq.)

Prostate Cancer Research and Prevention Act
Pub. L. 106–505, title VI, Nov. 13, 2000, 114 Stat. 2345
Short title, see 42 U.S.C. 201 note

Protecting Seniors From Fraud Act
Pub. L. 106–534, Nov. 22, 2000, 114 Stat. 2555
Short title, see 15 U.S.C. 6101 note

Protection and Advocacy for Individuals with Mental Illness Act
Pub. L. 99–319, May 23, 1986, 100 Stat. 478 (42 U.S.C. 10801 et seq.)
Short title, see 42 U.S.C. 10801 note

Protection and Advocacy for Mentally Ill Individuals Act of 1986
Renamed Protection and Advocacy for Individuals with Mental Illness Act

Protection and Advocacy for Mentally Ill Individuals Amendments Act of 1988
Pub. L. 100–509, Oct. 20, 1988, 102 Stat. 2543
Short title, see 42 U.S.C. 10801 note

Protection and Advocacy for Mentally Ill Individuals Amendments Act of 1991
Pub. L. 102–173, Nov. 27, 1991, 105 Stat. 1217
Short title, see 42 U.S.C. 10801 note

Protection and Reduction of Government Secrecy Act
Pub. L. 103–236, title IX, Apr. 30, 1994, 108 Stat. 525 (50 U.S.C. 435 note)

Protection Island National Wildlife Refuge Act
Pub. L. 97–333, Oct. 15, 1982, 96 Stat. 1623 (16 U.S.C. 668dd note)

Protection of Children Against Sexual Exploitation Act of 1977
Pub. L. 95–225, Feb. 6, 1978, 92 Stat. 7 (18 U.S.C. 2251 et seq.)
Short title, see 18 U.S.C. 2251 note

Protection of Children From Sexual Predators Act of 1998
Pub. L. 105–314, Oct. 30, 1998, 112 Stat. 2974
Short title, see 18 U.S.C. 1 note

Protection of Foreign Officials and Official Guests of the United States Act
See Act for the Protection of Foreign Officials and Official Guests of the United States

Protection of Public Property Act
June 1, 1948, ch. 359, 62 Stat. 281 (40 U.S.C. 318 et seq.)
Short title, see 40 U.S.C. 318 note

Provisional Governments Resolution (Virginia, Texas, Mississippi)
Feb. 18, 1869, No. 8, 15 Stat. 344

Psychotropic Substances Act of 1978
Pub. L. 95–633, Nov. 10, 1978, 92 Stat. 3768
Short title, see 21 U.S.C. 801 note

Public and Assisted Housing Drug Elimination Act of 1990
Pub. L. 100–690, title V, subtitle C, ch. 2 (§5121 et seq.), Nov. 18, 1988, 102 Stat. 4301 (42 U.S.C. 11901 et seq.)
Short title, see 42 U.S.C. 11901 note

Public and Assisted Housing Drug Elimination Program Amendments of 1998
Pub. L. 105–276, title V, subtitle G, §586, Oct. 21, 1998, 112 Stat. 2646
Short title, see 42 U.S.C. 11901 note

Public Broadcasting Act of 1967
Pub. L. 90–129, Nov. 7, 1967, 81 Stat. 365
Short title, see 47 U.S.C. 609 note

Public Broadcasting Amendments Act of 1981
Pub. L. 97–35, title XII, subtitle B, ch. 1 (§1221 et seq.), Aug. 13, 1981, 95 Stat. 725
Short title, see 47 U.S.C. 609 note

Public Broadcasting Financing Act of 1970
Pub. L. 91–437, Oct. 7, 1970, 84 Stat. 888
Short title, see 47 U.S.C. 609 note

Public Broadcasting Financing Act of 1975
Pub. L. 94–192, Dec. 31, 1975, 89 Stat. 1099
Short title, see 47 U.S.C. 609 note

Public Buildings Act of 1926
May 25, 1926, ch. 380, 44 Stat. 630 (40 U.S.C. 341 et seq.)

Public Buildings Act of 1949
June 16, 1949, ch. 218, 63 Stat. 176

Public Buildings Act of 1959
Pub. L. 86–249, Sept. 9, 1959, 73 Stat. 479 (40 U.S.C. 601 et seq.)
Short title, see 40 U.S.C. 601 note

Public Buildings Amendments of 1972
Pub. L. 92–313, June 16, 1972, 86 Stat. 216
Short title, see 40 U.S.C. 601 note

Public Buildings Amendments of 1988
Pub. L. 100–678, Nov. 17, 1988, 102 Stat. 4049
Short title, see 40 U.S.C. 601 note

Public Buildings Cooperative Use Act of 1976
Pub. L. 94–541, title I, Oct. 18, 1976, 90 Stat. 2505
Short title, see 40 U.S.C. 601 note

Public Buildings Purchase Contract Act of 1954
July 22, 1954, ch. 560, title I, 68 Stat. 518
Short title, see 40 U.S.C. 356 note

Public Contracts Act
See Walsh-Healey Act

Public Credit Act
Mar. 18, 1869, ch. 1, 16 Stat. 1

Public Debt Act of 1939
July 20, 1939, ch. 336, 53 Stat. 1071

Public Debt Act of 1941
Feb. 19, 1941, ch. 7, 55 Stat. 7

Public Debt Act of 1942
Mar. 28, 1942, ch. 205, 56 Stat. 189

Public Debt Act of 1943
Apr. 11, 1943, ch. 52, 57 Stat. 63

Public Debt Act of 1944
June 9, 1944, ch. 240, 58 Stat. 272

Public Debt Act of 1945
Apr. 3, 1945, ch. 51, 59 Stat. 47

Public Debt Act of 1946
June 26, 1946, ch. 501, 60 Stat. 316

Public Debt Act of 1959
Pub. L. 86–74, June 30, 1959, 73 Stat. 156

Public Debt and Tax Rate Extension Act of 1960
Pub. L. 86–564, June 30, 1960, 74 Stat. 290

Public Documents Act
Pub. L. 93–526, title II, Dec. 19, 1974, 88 Stat. 1698
Short title, see 44 U.S.C. 101 note

Public Health and Marine-Hospital Service Act
July 1, 1902, ch. 1370, 32 Stat. 712

Public Health Cigarette Smoking Act of 1969
Pub. L. 91–222, Apr. 1, 1970, 84 Stat. 87
Short title, see 15 U.S.C. 1331 note

Public Health Improvement Act
Pub. L. 106–505, Nov. 13, 2000, 114 Stat. 2314
Short title, see 42 U.S.C. 201 note

Public Health Service Act
July 1, 1944, ch. 373, 58 Stat. 682 (42 U.S.C. 201 et seq.)
Short title, see 42 U.S.C. 201 note

Public Health Service Act Technical Amendments Act
Pub. L. 102–352, Aug. 26, 1992, 106 Stat. 938
Short title, see 42 U.S.C. 201 note

Public Health Service Administrative Amendments of 1979
Pub. L. 96–76, title III, Sept. 29, 1979, 93 Stat. 584
Short title, see 42 U.S.C. 201 note

Public Health Service Amendments of 1987
Pub. L. 100–177, Dec. 1, 1987, 101 Stat. 986
Short title, see 42 U.S.C. 201 note

Public Health Service Commissioned Corps Personnel Act of 1960
Pub. L. 86–415, Apr. 8, 1960, 74 Stat. 32
Short title, see 42 U.S.C. 201 note

Public Health Threats and Emergencies Act
Pub. L. 106–505, title I, Nov. 13, 2000, 114 Stat. 2315
Short title, see 42 U.S.C. 201 note

Public Housing Anti-Crime Amendments of 1980
Pub. L. 96–399, title II, §209, Oct. 8, 1980, 94 Stat. 1635 (12 U.S.C. 1701z–6 note)

Public Housing Drug Elimination Act of 1988
Renamed Public and Assisted Housing Drug Elimination Act of 1990

Public Housing Security Demonstration Act of 1978
Pub. L. 95–557, title II, §207, Oct. 31, 1978, 92 Stat. 2093 (12 U.S.C. 1701z–6 note)

Public Interest Declassification Act of 2000
Pub. L. 106–567, title VII, Dec. 27, 2000, 114 Stat. 2856 (50 U.S.C. 435 note)

Public Land Administration Act
Pub. L. 86–649, July 14, 1960, 74 Stat. 506 (43 U.S.C. 1361 et seq.)

Public Lands and National Parks Act of 1983
Pub. L. 98–141, Oct. 31, 1983, 97 Stat. 909
Short title, see 16 U.S.C. 1 note

Public Lands Corps Act of 1993
Pub. L. 91–378, title II, as added Pub. L. 103–82, title I, §105(6), Sept. 21, 1993, 107 Stat. 848 (16 U.S.C. 1721 et seq.)
Short title, see 16 U.S.C. 1701 note

Public Rangelands Improvement Act of 1978
Pub. L. 95–514, Oct. 25, 1978, 92 Stat. 1803 (43 U.S.C. 1901 et seq.)
Short title, see 43 U.S.C. 1901 note

Public Safety and Recreational Firearms Use Protection Act
Pub. L. 103–322, title XI, subtitle A (§110101 et seq.), Sept. 13, 1994, 108 Stat. 1996
Short title, see 18 U.S.C. 921 note

Public Safety Officers' Benefits Act of 1976
Pub. L. 94–430, Sept. 29, 1976, 90 Stat. 1346
Short title, see 42 U.S.C. 3711 note

Public Safety Partnership and Community Policing Act of 1994
Pub. L. 103–322, title I, Sept. 13, 1994, 108 Stat. 1807
Short title, see 42 U.S.C. 3711 note

Public Salary Tax Act of 1939
Apr. 12, 1939, ch. 59, 53 Stat. 574

Public Telecommunications Act of 1988
Pub. L. 100–626, Nov. 7, 1988, 102 Stat. 3207
Short title, see 47 U.S.C. 609 note

Public Telecommunications Act of 1992
Pub. L. 102–356, Aug. 26, 1992, 106 Stat. 949
Short title, see 47 U.S.C. 609 note

Public Telecommunications Financing Act of 1978
Pub. L. 95–567, Nov. 2, 1978, 92 Stat. 2405
Short title, see 47 U.S.C. 609 note

Public Utilities Review Act
May 14, 1934, ch. 283, 48 Stat. 775

Public Utility Act of 1935
Aug. 26, 1935, ch. 687, 49 Stat. 803

Public Utility Holding Company Act of 1935
Aug. 26, 1935, ch. 687, title I, 49 Stat. 803 (15 U.S.C. 79 et seq.)
Short title, see 15 U.S.C. 79

Public Utility Regulatory Policies Act of 1978
Pub. L. 95–617, Nov. 9, 1978, 92 Stat. 3117 (16 U.S.C. 2601 et seq.)
Short title, see 16 U.S.C. 2601 note

Public Vessels Act
Mar. 3, 1925, ch. 428, 43 Stat. 1112 (46 App. U.S.C. 781 et seq.)
Short title, see 46 App. U.S.C. 781 note

Public Welfare Amendments of 1962
Pub. L. 87–543, July 25, 1962, 76 Stat. 172
Short title, see 42 U.S.C. 1305 note

Public Works Acceleration Act
Pub. L. 87–658, Sept. 14, 1962, 76 Stat. 541 (42 U.S.C. 2641 et seq.)
Short title, see 42 U.S.C. 2641 note

Public Works Act (Bonds of Contractors)
See Miller Act

Public Works Administration Act
June 16, 1933, ch. 90, title II, 48 Stat. 200 (40 U.S.C. 401 et seq.)

Public Works Administration Appropriation Act of 1938
June 21, 1938, ch. 554, title II, 52 Stat. 816

Public Works Administration Extension Act of 1937
June 29, 1937, ch. 401, title II, 50 Stat. 357

Public Works and Atomic Energy Commission Appropriation Act, 1968
Pub. L. 90–147, Nov. 20, 1967, 81 Stat. 471

Public Works and Economic Development Act Amendments of 1971
Pub. L. 92–65, title I, Aug. 5, 1971, 85 Stat. 166
Short title, see 42 U.S.C. 3121 note

Public Works and Economic Development Act Amendments of 1976
Pub. L. 94–487, Oct. 12, 1976, 90 Stat. 2331
Short title, see 42 U.S.C. 3121 note

Public Works and Economic Development Act of 1965
Pub. L. 89–136, Aug. 26, 1965, 79 Stat. 552 (42 U.S.C. 3121 et seq.)
Short title, see 42 U.S.C. 3121 note

Public Works Appropriation Act, 1956
July 15, 1955, ch. 370, 69 Stat. 354

Public Works Appropriation Act, 1957
July 2, 1956, ch. 490, 70 Stat. 474

Public Works Appropriation Act, 1958
Pub. L. 85–167, Aug. 26, 1957, 71 Stat. 416

Public Works Appropriation Act, 1959
Pub. L. 85–863, Sept. 2, 1958, 72 Stat. 1572

Public Works Appropriation Act, 1960
Pub. L. 86–254, Sept. 10, 1959, 73 Stat. 491

Public Works Appropriation Act, 1961
Pub. L. 86–700, Sept. 2, 1960, 74 Stat. 743

Public Works Appropriation Act, 1962
Pub. L. 87–330, Sept. 30, 1961, 75 Stat. 722

Public Works Appropriation Act, 1963
Pub. L. 87–880, Oct. 24, 1962, 76 Stat. 1216

Public Works Appropriation Act, 1964
Pub. L. 88–257, Dec. 31, 1963, 77 Stat. 844

Public Works Appropriation Act, 1965
Pub. L. 88–511, Aug. 30, 1964, 78 Stat. 682

Public Works Appropriation Act, 1966
Pub. L. 89–299, Oct. 28, 1965, 79 Stat. 1096

Public Works Appropriation Act, 1967
Pub. L. 89–689, Oct. 15, 1966, 80 Stat. 1002

Public Works Employment Act of 1976
Pub. L. 94–369, July 22, 1976, 90 Stat. 999 (42 U.S.C. 6701 et seq.)
Short title, see 42 U.S.C. 6701 note

Public Works Employment Act of 1977
Pub. L. 95–28, title I, May 13, 1977, 91 Stat. 116
Short title, see 42 U.S.C. 6701 note

Public Works Employment Appropriations Act
Pub. L. 94–447, Oct. 1, 1976, 90 Stat. 1497

Public Works for Water and Power Development and Atomic Energy Commission Appropriation Act, 1973
Pub. L. 92–405, Aug. 25, 1972, 86 Stat. 621

Public Works for Water and Power Development and Atomic Energy Commission Appropriation Act, 1974
Pub. L. 93–97, Aug. 16, 1973, 87 Stat. 318

Public Works for Water and Power Development and Atomic Energy Commission Appropriation Act, 1975
Pub. L. 93–393, Aug. 28, 1974, 88 Stat. 782

Public Works for Water and Power Development and Energy Research Appropriation Act, 1976
Pub. L. 94–180, Dec. 26, 1975, 89 Stat. 1035

Public Works for Water and Power Development and Energy Research Appropriation Act, 1977
Pub. L. 94–355, July 12, 1976, 90 Stat. 889

Public Works for Water and Power Development and Energy Research Appropriation Act, 1978
Pub. L. 95–96, Aug. 7, 1977, 91 Stat. 797

Public Works for Water and Power Resources Development and Atomic Energy Commission Appropriation Act, 1969
Pub. L. 90–479, Aug. 12, 1968, 82 Stat. 705

Public Works for Water, Pollution Control, and Power Development and Atomic Energy Commission Appropriation Act, 1970
Pub. L. 91–144, Dec. 11, 1969, 83 Stat. 323

Public Works for Water, Pollution Control, and Power Development and Atomic Energy Commission Appropriation Act, 1971
Pub. L. 91–439, Oct. 7, 1970, 84 Stat. 890

Public Works Improvement Act of 1984
Pub. L. 98–501, title I, Oct. 19, 1984, 98 Stat. 2320 (42 U.S.C. 3121 note)

Publicity in Taking Evidence Act (Anti-Trust)
Mar. 3, 1913, ch. 114, 37 Stat. 731 (15 U.S.C. 30)

Publicity of Political Contributions Act
June 25, 1910, ch. 392, 36 Stat. 822

Pueblo Lands Act of 1924
June 7, 1924, ch. 331, 43 Stat. 636 (25 U.S.C. 331 note)

Puerto Rican Federal Relations Act
Mar. 2, 1917, ch. 145, 39 Stat. 951 (48 U.S.C. 731 et seq.)
Short title, see 48 U.S.C. 731 note

Puerto Rican Rehabilitation Act
Feb. 11, 1936, ch. 51, 49 Stat. 1135

Puerto Rico Civil Code
Also known as the Foraker Act
Apr. 12, 1900, ch. 191, 31 Stat. 77

Pure Food and Drugs Act
See Federal Food and Drugs Act of 1906

Purnell Act of 1925
Feb. 24, 1925, ch. 308, 43 Stat. 970

Purnell Act (Corn Borer Eradication)
Feb. 9, 1927, ch. 90, 44 Stat. 1065 (7 U.S.C. 146)

Puyallup Tribe of Indians Settlement Act of 1989
Pub. L. 101–41, June 21, 1989, 103 Stat. 83 (25 U.S.C. 1773 et seq.)
Short title, see 25 U.S.C. 1773 note

Qualified Thrift Lender Reform Act of 1991
Pub. L. 102–242, title IV, subtitle G (§436 et seq.), Dec. 19, 1991, 105 Stat. 2381
Short title, see 12 U.S.C. 1461 note

Quality Housing and Work Responsibility Act of 1998
Pub. L. 105–276, title V, Oct. 21, 1998, 112 Stat. 2518
Short title, see 42 U.S.C. 1437 note

Quiet Communities Act of 1978
Pub. L. 95–609, Nov. 8, 1978, 92 Stat. 3079
Short title, see 42 U.S.C. 4901 note

Quinebaug and Shetucket Rivers Valley National Heritage Corridor Act of 1994
Pub. L. 103–449, title I, Nov. 2, 1994, 108 Stat. 4752 (16 U.S.C. 461 note)

Quinebaug and Shetucket Rivers Valley National Heritage Corridor Reauthorization Act of 1999
Pub. L. 106–149, Dec. 9, 1999, 113 Stat. 1726

R.F.C. Relief Obligations Act
See Steagall R.F.C. Relief Obligations Act

R.M.S. Titanic Maritime Memorial Act of 1986
Pub. L. 99–513, Oct. 21, 1986, 100 Stat. 2082 (16 U.S.C. 450rr et seq.)
Short title, see 16 U.S.C. 450rr note

Racketeer Influenced and Corrupt Organizations Act (RICO)
Pub. L. 91–452, title IX, §901(a), Oct. 15, 1970, 84 Stat. 941 (18 U.S.C. 1961 et seq.)

Radiation Control for Health and Safety Act of 1968
Pub. L. 90–602, Oct. 18, 1968, 82 Stat. 1173
Short title, see 21 U.S.C. 301 note

Radiation Exposure Compensation Act
Pub. L. 101–426, Oct. 15, 1990, 104 Stat. 920 (42 U.S.C. 2210 note)

Radiation Exposure Compensation Act Amendments of 2000
Pub. L. 106–245, July 10, 2000, 114 Stat. 501
Short title, see 42 U.S.C. 2011 note

Radiation-Exposed Veterans Compensation Act of 1988
Pub. L. 100–321, May 20, 1988, 102 Stat. 485
Short title, see 38 U.S.C. 101 note

Radio Act of 1927
Feb. 23, 1927, ch. 169, 44 Stat. 1162 (47 U.S.C. 81 et seq.)

Radio Broadcasting to Cuba Act
Pub. L. 98–111, Oct. 4, 1983, 97 Stat. 749 (22 U.S.C. 1465 et seq.)
Short title, see 22 U.S.C. 1465 note

Radio Free Asia Act of 1998
Pub. L. 105–261, div. C, title XXXIX, Oct. 17, 1998, 112 Stat. 2277

Radon Gas and Indoor Air Quality Research Act of 1986
Pub. L. 99–499, title IV, Oct. 17, 1986, 100 Stat. 1758 (42 U.S.C. 7401 note)

Rail Amendments of 1976
Pub. L. 94–555, title II, Oct. 19, 1976, 90 Stat. 2616
Short title, see 45 U.S.C. 701 note

Rail Passenger Service Act
Pub. L. 91–518, Oct. 30, 1970, 84 Stat. 1327
Short title, see 45 U.S.C. 501 note

Rail Passenger Service Act of 1970
See Rail Passenger Service Act

Rail Safety and Service Improvement Act of 1982
Pub. L. 97–468, titles II–VII, Jan. 14, 1983, 96 Stat. 2543–2579

Rail Safety Enforcement and Review Act
Pub. L. 102–365, Sept. 3, 1992, 106 Stat. 972

Rail Safety Improvement Act of 1974
Pub. L. 93–633, title II, Jan. 3, 1975, 88 Stat. 2164

Rail Safety Improvement Act of 1988
Pub. L. 100–342, June 22, 1988, 102 Stat. 624

Rail Transportation Improvement Act
Pub. L. 94–555, Oct. 19, 1976, 90 Stat. 2613

Railroad Act (Alaska)
See Alaska Railroad Act

Railroad and Telegraph Seizure Act (Civil War)
Jan. 31, 1862, ch. 15, 12 Stat. 334

Railroad Assessment Act
June 13, 1934, ch. 498, 48 Stat. 954

Railroad Control Act
Mar. 21, 1918, ch. 25, 40 Stat. 451

Railroad Land Grant Forfeiture Act
Sept. 29, 1890, ch. 1040, 26 Stat. 496 (43 U.S.C. 904 et seq.)

Railroad Motive Power and Equipment Act
Nov. 19, 1919, ch. 116, 41 Stat. 359

Railroad Rate Act
See Interstate Commerce Act

Railroad Rate Adjustment Act of 1973
Pub. L. 93–69, title II, July 10, 1973, 87 Stat. 166

Railroad Retirement Act
June 27, 1934, ch. 868, 48 Stat. 1283 (Title 45, §201 et seq.)

Railroad Retirement Act of 1935
Aug. 29, 1935, ch. 812, 49 Stat. 967 (45 U.S.C. 215 et seq.)

Railroad Retirement Act of 1937
Aug. 29, 1935, ch. 812, as added June 24, 1937, ch. 382, part I, 50 Stat. 307 (45 U.S.C. 228a et seq.)

Railroad Retirement Act of 1974
Pub. L. 93–445, title I, Oct. 16, 1974, 88 Stat. 1305 (45 U.S.C. 231 et seq.)

Railroad Retirement Amendments of 1973
Pub. L. 93–69, title I, July 10, 1973, 87 Stat. 162
Short title, see 26 U.S.C. 1 note

Railroad Retirement Board Appropriation Act, 1941
June 26, 1940, ch. 428, title VI, 54 Stat. 596

Railroad Retirement Board Appropriation Act, 1942
July 1, 1941, ch. 269, title VI, 55 Stat. 496

Railroad Retirement Board Appropriation Act, 1943
July 2, 1942, ch. 475, title VI, 56 Stat. 591

Railroad Retirement Board Appropriation Act, 1944
July 12, 1943, ch. 221, title VI, 57 Stat. 516

Railroad Retirement Board Appropriation Act, 1945
June 28, 1944, ch. 302, title VI, 58 Stat. 569

Railroad Retirement Board Appropriation Act, 1946
July 3, 1945, ch. 263, title VI, 59 Stat. 379

Railroad Retirement Board Appropriation Act, 1947
July 26, 1946, ch. 672, title VI, 60 Stat. 699

Railroad Retirement Board Appropriation Act, 1948
July 8, 1947, ch. 210, title V, 61 Stat. 277

Railroad Retirement Board Appropriation Act, 1949
June 14, 1948, ch. 465, title V, 62 Stat. 405

Railroad Retirement Board Appropriation Act, 1950
June 29, 1949, ch. 275, title IV, 63 Stat. 297

Railroad Retirement Board Appropriation Act, 1951
Sept. 6, 1950, ch. 896, Ch. V, title V, 64 Stat. 656

Railroad Retirement Board Appropriation Act, 1952
Aug. 31, 1951, ch. 373, title V, 65 Stat. 222

Railroad Retirement Board Appropriation Act, 1953
July 5, 1952, ch. 575, title V, 66 Stat. 371

Railroad Retirement Board Appropriation Act, 1954
July 31, 1953, ch. 296, title V, 67 Stat. 258

Railroad Retirement Board Appropriation Act, 1955
July 2, 1954, ch. 457, title V, 68 Stat. 446

Railroad Retirement Revenue Act of 1983
Pub. L. 98–76, title II, Aug. 12, 1983, 97 Stat. 419
Short title, see 26 U.S.C. 1 note

Railroad Retirement Solvency Act of 1983
Pub. L. 98–76, Aug. 12, 1983, 97 Stat. 411
Short title, see 45 U.S.C. 231t note

Railroad Retirement Tax Act
Aug. 16, 1954, ch. 736, 68A Stat. 431 (26 U.S.C. 3201 et seq.)
Short title, see 26 U.S.C. 3233

Railroad Revitalization and Regulatory Reform Act of 1976
Pub. L. 94–210, Feb. 5, 1976, 90 Stat. 31 (45 U.S.C. 801 et seq.)
Short title, see 45 U.S.C. 801 note

Railroad Unemployment Insurance Act
June 25, 1938, ch. 680, 52 Stat. 1094 (45 U.S.C. 351 et seq.)
Short title, see 45 U.S.C. 367

Railroad Unemployment Insurance Amendments Act of 1996
Pub. L. 104–251, Oct. 9, 1996, 110 Stat. 3161
Short title, see 45 U.S.C. 367 note

Railroad Unemployment Insurance and Retirement Improvement Act of 1988
Pub. L. 100–647, title VII, Nov. 10, 1988, 102 Stat. 3757
Short title, see 45 U.S.C. 367 note

Rails to Resources Act of 2000
Pub. L. 106–570, title III, Dec. 27, 2000, 114 Stat. 3043 (49 U.S.C. note prec. 28101)

Railway Labor Act
May 20, 1926, ch. 347, 44 Stat. 577 (45 U.S.C. 151 et seq.)
Short title, see 45 U.S.C. 151

Railway Mail Service Pay Act
July 28, 1916, ch. 261, 39 Stat. 412

Raker Act
Dec. 19, 1913, ch. 4, 38 Stat. 242

Raker Act (Reclamation and Irrigation)
May 15, 1922, ch. 190, 42 Stat. 541 (43 U.S.C. 511 et seq.)

Ramspeck Act
Nov. 26, 1940, ch. 919, title I, 54 Stat. 1211

Ramspeck-Mead Act
Aug. 1, 1941, ch. 346, 55 Stat. 613

Randolph-Sheppard Act
Also known as Randolph-Sheppard Vending Stand Act
June 20, 1936, ch. 638, 49 Stat. 1559 (20 U.S.C. 107 et seq.)
Short title, see 20 U.S.C. 107 note

Randolph-Sheppard Act Amendments of 1974
Pub. L. 93–516, title II, Dec. 7, 1974, 88 Stat. 1622
Short title, see 20 U.S.C. 107 note

Randolph-Sheppard Vending Stand Act
Also known as Randolph-Sheppard Act
June 20, 1936, ch. 638, 49 Stat. 1559 (20 U.S.C. 107 et seq.)
Short title, see 20 U.S.C. 107 note

Rankin Act
See Gold Star Mothers Act

Rankin Veterans Act
May 3, 1939, ch. 109, 53 Stat. 652

Rankin Veterans Pension Act
June 10, 1942, ch. 402, 56 Stat. 350

Rankin World War Widows Act
May 13, 1938, ch. 214, 52 Stat. 352

Ransdell Act
May 26, 1930, ch. 320, 46 Stat. 379

Rate Act
See Interstate Commerce Act

Rattlesnake National Recreation Area and Wilderness Act of 1980
Pub. L. 96–476, Oct. 19, 1980, 94 Stat. 2271 (16 U.S.C. 460*ll* et seq.)
Short title, see 16 U.S.C. 460*ll* note

Reading Excellence Act
Pub. L. 105–277, div. A, §101(f) [title VIII], Oct. 21, 1998, 112 Stat. 2681–337, 2681–391

Ready to Learn Act
Pub. L. 102–545, Oct. 27, 1992, 106 Stat. 3586
Short title, see 20 U.S.C. 6301 note

Real Estate Settlement Procedures Act Amendments of 1975
Pub. L. 94–205, Jan. 2, 1976, 89 Stat. 1157
Short title, see 12 U.S.C. 2601 note

Real Estate Settlement Procedures Act of 1974
Pub. L. 93–533, Dec. 22, 1974, 88 Stat. 1724 (12 U.S.C. 2601 et seq.)
Short title, see 12 U.S.C. 2601 note

Reapportionment Act of 1901
Jan. 16, 1901, ch. 93, 31 Stat. 733

Reapportionment Act of 1911
Aug. 8, 1911, ch. 5, 37 Stat. 13

Reapportionment Act of 1929
June 18, 1929, ch. 28, 46 Stat. 21

Rebel Correspondence Act (Civil War)
Feb. 25, 1863, ch. 60, 12 Stat. 696

Rechargeable Battery Recycling Act
Pub. L. 104–142, title I, May 13, 1996, 110 Stat. 1332 (42 U.S.C. 14321 et seq.)
Short title, see 42 U.S.C. 14301 note

Reciprocal Tariff Act
June 12, 1934, ch. 474, 48 Stat. 943 (19 U.S.C. 1351 et seq.)

Reciprocal Trade Relations Act
July 26, 1911, ch. 3, 37 Stat. 4

Reclamation Act
Also known as the National Irrigation Act of 1902
June 17, 1902, ch. 1093, 32 Stat. 388
Short title, see 43 U.S.C. 371 note

Reclamation Authorization Act of 1975
Pub. L. 94–228, Mar. 11, 1976, 90 Stat. 205

Reclamation Authorizations Act of 1976
Pub. L. 94–423, Sept. 28, 1976, 90 Stat. 1324

Reclamation Development Act of 1974
Pub. L. 93–493, Oct. 27, 1974, 88 Stat. 1486

Reclamation Fund Act
June 25, 1910, ch. 407, 36 Stat. 835

Reclamation Project Act of 1939
Aug. 4, 1939, ch. 418, 53 Stat. 1187 (43 U.S.C. 485 et seq.)
Short title, see 43 U.S.C. 485k

Reclamation Project Authorization Act of 1972
Pub. L. 92–514, Oct. 20, 1972, 86 Stat. 964

Reclamation Projects Authorization and Adjustment Act of 1992
Pub. L. 102–575, Oct. 30, 1992, 106 Stat. 4600
Short title, see 43 U.S.C. 371 note

Reclamation Recreation Management Act of 1992
Pub. L. 102–575, title XXVIII, Oct. 30, 1992, 106 Stat. 4690 (16 U.S.C. 460*l*–31 et seq.)
Short title, see 16 U.S.C. 460*l*–31 note

Reclamation Recycling and Water Conservation Act of 1996
Pub. L. 104–266, Oct. 9, 1996, 110 Stat. 3290
Short title, see 43 U.S.C. 390h note

Reclamation Reform Act of 1982
Pub. L. 97–293, title II, Oct. 12, 1982, 96 Stat. 1263 (43 U.S.C. 390aa et seq.)
Short title, see 43 U.S.C. 390aa

Reclamation Safety of Dams Act Amendments of 1984
Pub. L. 98–404, Aug. 28, 1984, 98 Stat. 1481
Short title, see 43 U.S.C. 506 note

Reclamation Safety of Dams Act of 1978
Pub. L. 95–578, Nov. 2, 1978, 92 Stat. 2471 (43 U.S.C. 506 et seq.)
Short title, see 43 U.S.C. 506 note

Reclamation States Drought Assistance Act of 1988
Pub. L. 100–387, title IV, subtitle B, part I (§411 et seq.), Aug. 11, 1988, 102 Stat. 957 (43 U.S.C. 502 note)

Reclamation States Emergency Drought Relief Act of 1991
Pub. L. 102–250, Mar. 5, 1992, 106 Stat. 53 (43 U.S.C. 2201 et seq.)
Short title, see 43 U.S.C. 2201 note

Reclamation Wastewater and Groundwater Study and Facilities Act
Pub. L. 102–575, title XVI, Oct. 30, 1992, 106 Stat. 4663 (43 U.S.C. 390h et seq.)
Short title, see 43 U.S.C. 390h note

Reclassification Act of 1923 (District of Columbia salaries)
See Classification Act of 1923

Reclassification Act of 1925 (Postal Salaries)
Feb. 28, 1925, ch. 368, title I, 43 Stat. 1053

Reconstruction Finance Corporation Act
Jan. 22, 1932, ch. 8, 47 Stat. 5 (15 U.S.C. 601 et seq.)

Reconstruction Finance Corporation Appropriation Act, 1952
Nov. 1, 1951, ch. 664, Ch. IV, title III, 65 Stat. 740

Reconstruction Finance Corporation Disaster Loan Act
Apr. 13, 1934, ch. 121, 48 Stat. 589

Reconstruction Finance Corporation Exports Resolution
Mar. 26, 1934, ch. 90, 48 Stat. 500

Reconstruction Finance Corporation Liquidation Act
July 30, 1953, ch. 282, title I, 67 Stat. 230
Short title, see 15 U.S.C. note prec. 601

Reconstruction Finance Corporation Tax Exemption Act
Mar. 20, 1936, ch. 160, 49 Stat. 1185 (12 U.S.C. 51e et seq.)

Record Carrier Competition Act of 1981
Pub. L. 97–130, Dec. 29, 1981, 95 Stat. 1687
Short title, see 47 U.S.C. 609 note

Record Rental Amendment of 1984
Pub. L. 98–450, Oct. 4, 1984, 98 Stat. 1727
Short title, see 17 U.S.C. 101 note

Recording Act of 1955
Aug. 5, 1955, ch. 573, 69 Stat. 534

Recreation and Public Purposes Act
June 14, 1926, ch. 578, 44 Stat. 741 (43 U.S.C. 869 et seq.)
Short title, see 43 U.S.C. 869 note

Recreation and Public Purposes Amendment Act of 1988
Pub. L. 100–648, Nov. 10, 1988, 102 Stat. 3813
Short title, see 43 U.S.C. 869 note

Recreational Boating Fund Act of 1980
Pub. L. 96–451, title II, Oct. 14, 1980, 94 Stat. 1987

Recreational Boating Safety Act of 1986
Pub. L. 99–626, Nov. 7, 1986, 100 Stat. 3504
Short title, see 46 U.S.C. 13101 note

Recreational Boating Safety and Facilities Improvement Act of 1980
Pub. L. 96–451, title I, Oct. 14, 1980, 94 Stat. 1983

Recreational Hunting Safety and Preservation Act of 1994
Pub. L. 103–322, title XXXII, subtitle H (§320801 et seq.), Sept. 13, 1994, 108 Stat. 2121 (16 U.S.C. 5201 et seq.)
Short title, see 16 U.S.C. 5201 note

Red Cross Act
See American National Red Cross Act

Red Light Abatement Act (District of Columbia)
Feb. 7, 1914, ch. 16, 38 Stat. 280

Red River Designation Act of 1993
Pub. L. 103–170, Dec. 2, 1993, 107 Stat. 1986
Short title, see 16 U.S.C. 1271 note

Red River National Wildlife Refuge Act
Pub. L. 106–300, Oct. 13, 2000, 114 Stat. 1055 (16 U.S.C. 668dd note)

Red Rock Canyon National Conservation Area Establishment Act of 1990
Pub. L. 101–621, Nov. 16, 1990, 104 Stat. 3342 (16 U.S.C. 460ccc et seq.)
Short title, see 16 U.S.C. 460ccc note

Redemption and Bank Note Act
See Bank Note and Redemption Act

Reed Amendment
Mar. 3, 1917, ch. 162, §5, 39 Stat. 1069

Reed-Bulwinkle Act
June 17, 1948, ch. 491, 62 Stat. 472

Reed-Jenkins Act
May 29, 1928, ch. 864, 45 Stat. 954

Reed-Johnson Act
See World War Veterans' Act, 1924

Reemployment of Merchant Marine Members
June 23, 1943, ch. 142, 57 Stat. 162 (50 App. U.S.C. 1471 et seq.)

Referees Salary and Expense Fund Act of 1984
Pub. L. 98–353, title III, subtitle E (§381 et seq.), July 10, 1984, 98 Stat. 364

Referees' Salary Act (Bankruptcy)
June 28, 1946, ch. 512, 60 Stat. 323

Reforestation Relief Act
Mar. 31, 1933, ch. 17, 48 Stat. 22

Refuge Recreation Act
Pub. L. 87–714, Sept. 28, 1962, 76 Stat. 653 (16 U.S.C. 460k et seq.)
Short title, see 16 U.S.C. 460k note

Refuge Revenue Sharing Act
June 15, 1935, ch. 261, title IV, §401, 49 Stat. 383 (16 U.S.C. 715s)

Refugee Act of 1980
Pub. L. 96–212, Mar. 17, 1980, 94 Stat. 102
Short title, see 8 U.S.C. 1101 note

Refugee Assistance Amendments of 1982
Pub. L. 97–363, Oct. 15, 1982, 96 Stat. 1734
Short title, see 8 U.S.C. 1101 note

Refugee Assistance Extension Act of 1986
Pub. L. 99–605, Nov. 6, 1986, 100 Stat. 3449
Short title, see 8 U.S.C. 1101 note

Refugee Education Assistance Act of 1980
Pub. L. 96–422, Oct. 10, 1980, 94 Stat. 1799 (8 U.S.C. 1522 note)

Refugee Relief Act of 1953
Aug. 7, 1953, ch. 336, 67 Stat. 400 (50 App. U.S.C. 1971 et seq.)

Refuse Act of 1899
Mar. 3, 1899, ch. 425, §13, 30 Stat. 1152 (33 U.S.C. 407)
Short title, see 33 U.S.C. 407 note

Regional Action Planning Commission Amendments of 1969
Pub. L. 91–123, title II, Nov. 25, 1969, 83 Stat. 216
Short title, see 42 U.S.C. 3121 note

Regional Action Planning Commission Improvement Act of 1975
Pub. L. 94–188, title II, Dec. 31, 1975, 89 Stat. 1087
Short title, see 42 U.S.C. 3121 note

Regional Development Act of 1975
Pub. L. 94–188, Dec. 31, 1975, 89 Stat. 1079
Short title, see 42 U.S.C. 3121 note

Regional Rail Reorganization Act Amendments of 1975
Pub. L. 94–5, Feb. 28, 1975, 89 Stat. 7
Short title, see 45 U.S.C. 701 note

Regional Rail Reorganization Act of 1973
Pub. L. 93–236, Jan. 2, 1974, 87 Stat. 985 (45 U.S.C. 701 et seq.)
Short title, see 45 U.S.C. 701 note

Register Act
See Federal Register Act

Regulatory Fairness Act
Pub. L. 100–473, Oct. 6, 1988, 102 Stat. 2299
Short title, see 16 U.S.C. 791a note

Regulatory Flexibility Act
Pub. L. 96–354, Sept. 19, 1980, 94 Stat. 1164 (5 U.S.C. 601 et seq.)
Short title, see 5 U.S.C. 601 note

Rehabilitation Act Amendments of 1974
Pub. L. 93–516, title I, Dec. 7, 1974, 88 Stat. 1617
Short title, see 29 U.S.C. 701 note

Rehabilitation Act Amendments of 1986
Pub. L. 99–506, Oct. 21, 1986, 100 Stat. 1807
Short title, see 29 U.S.C. 701 note

Rehabilitation Act Amendments of 1991
Pub. L. 102–52, June 6, 1991, 105 Stat. 260
Short title, see 29 U.S.C. 701 note

Rehabilitation Act Amendments of 1992
Pub. L. 102–569, Oct. 29, 1992, 106 Stat. 4344
Short title, see 29 U.S.C. 701 note

Rehabilitation Act Amendments of 1993
Pub. L. 103–73, Aug. 11, 1993, 107 Stat. 718
Short title, see 29 U.S.C. 701 note

Rehabilitation Act Amendments of 1998
Pub. L. 105–220, title IV, Aug. 7, 1998, 112 Stat. 1092
Short title, see 29 U.S.C. 701 note

Rehabilitation Act Extension of 1976
Pub. L. 94–230, Mar. 15, 1976, 90 Stat. 211
Short title, see 29 U.S.C. 701 note

Rehabilitation Act of 1973
Pub. L. 93–112, Sept. 26, 1973, 87 Stat. 355 (29 U.S.C. 701 et seq.)
Short title, see 29 U.S.C. 701 note

Rehabilitation Amendments of 1984
Pub. L. 98–221, Feb. 22, 1984, 98 Stat. 17
Short title, see 29 U.S.C. 701 note

Rehabilitation and Betterment Act of 1949
Oct. 7, 1949, ch. 650, 63 Stat. 724 (43 U.S.C. 504)
Short title, see 43 U.S.C. 504 note

Rehabilitation, Comprehensive Services, and Developmental Disabilities Amendments of 1978
Pub. L. 95–602, Nov. 6, 1978, 92 Stat. 2955
Short title, see 29 U.S.C. 701 note

Reindeer Industry Act of 1937
Sept. 1, 1937, ch. 897, 50 Stat. 900 (25 U.S.C. 500 et seq.)
Short title, see 25 U.S.C. 500 note

Relief Aid for War-Devastated Countries
May 31, 1947, ch. 90, 61 Stat. 125

Relief-Recovery Act of 1938
See Work Relief and Public Works Appropriation Act of 1938

Religious Freedom Restoration Act of 1993
Pub. L. 103–141, Nov. 16, 1993, 107 Stat. 1488 (42 U.S.C. 2000bb et seq.)
Short title, see 42 U.S.C. 2000bb note

Religious Land Use and Institutionalized Persons Act of 2000
Pub. L. 106–274, Sept. 22, 2000, 114 Stat. 803 (42 U.S.C. 2000cc et seq.)
Short title, see 42 U.S.C. 2000cc note

Religious Liberty and Charitable Donation Protection Act of 1998
Pub. L. 105–183, June 19, 1998, 112 Stat. 517
Short title, see 11 U.S.C. 101 note

Religious Workers Act of 2000
Pub. L. 106–409, Nov. 1, 2000, 114 Stat. 1787
Short title, see 8 U.S.C. 1101 note

Removal of Causes Act
Mar. 3, 1875, ch. 137, 18 Stat. 470

Removal of Regulatory Barriers to Affordable Housing Act of 1992
Pub. L. 102–550, title XII, Oct. 28, 1992, 106 Stat. 3938 (42 U.S.C. 12705a et seq.)
Short title, see 42 U.S.C. 12705a note

Removal of Restrictions on Service Act
Dec. 13, 1941, ch. 571, 55 Stat. 799

Renegotiation Act
Apr. 28, 1942, ch. 247, title IV, §403, 56 Stat. 245 (50 App. U.S.C. 1191)

Renegotiation Act of 1948
May 21, 1948, ch. 333, §3, 62 Stat. 259 (50 App. U.S.C. 1193)

Renegotiation Act of 1951
Mar. 23, 1951, ch. 15, 65 Stat. 7 (50 App. U.S.C. 1211 et seq.)

Renegotiation Amendments Act of 1956
Aug. 1, 1956, ch. 821, 70 Stat. 786

Renegotiation Amendments Act of 1968
Pub. L. 90–634, title I, Oct. 24, 1968, 82 Stat. 1345

Renewable Energy and Energy Efficiency Technology Competitiveness Act of 1989
Pub. L. 101–218, Dec. 11, 1989, 103 Stat. 1859 (42 U.S.C. 12001 et seq.)
Short title, see 42 U.S.C. 12001 note

Renewable Energy Industry Development Act of 1983
Pub. L. 98–370, July 18, 1984, 98 Stat. 1211
Short title, see 42 U.S.C. 6201 note

Renewable Energy Resources Act of 1980
Pub. L. 96–294, title IV, June 30, 1980, 94 Stat. 715 (42 U.S.C. 7371 et seq.)
Short title, see 42 U.S.C. 7371 note

Renewable Resources Extension Act Amendments of 1987
Pub. L. 100–231, Jan. 5, 1988, 101 Stat. 1565
Short title, see 16 U.S.C. 1600 note

Renewable Resources Extension Act of 1978
Pub. L. 95–306, June 30, 1978, 92 Stat. 349 (16 U.S.C. 1671 et seq.)
Short title, see 16 U.S.C. 1600 note

Reorganization Act Amendments of 1984
Pub. L. 98–614, Nov. 8, 1984, 98 Stat. 3192
Short title, see 5 U.S.C. 901 note

Reorganization Act of 1939
Apr. 3, 1939, ch. 36, 53 Stat. 561

Reorganization Act of 1945
Dec. 20, 1945, ch. 582, 59 Stat. 613

Reorganization Act of 1949
June 20, 1949, ch. 226, 63 Stat. 203

Reorganization Act of 1977
Pub. L. 95–17, Apr. 6, 1977, 91 Stat. 29
Short title, see 5 U.S.C. 901 note

Repatriation Act
Oct. 5, 1917, ch. 68, 40 Stat. 340

Reports Consolidation Act of 2000
Pub. L. 106–531, Nov. 22, 2000, 114 Stat. 2537
Short title, see 31 U.S.C. 3501 note

Representatives Election Act
July 14, 1862, ch. 170, 12 Stat. 572

Republic of the Philippines Military Assistance Act
June 26, 1946, ch. 500, 60 Stat. 315

Research and Training for Eastern Europe and the Independent States of the Former Soviet Union Act of 1983
Pub. L. 98–164, title VIII, Nov. 22, 1983, 97 Stat. 1047 (22 U.S.C. 4501 et seq.)
Short title, see 22 U.S.C. 4501 note

Research Facilities Act
Pub. L. 88–74, as added Pub. L. 104–127, title VIII, §884(a), Apr. 4, 1996, 110 Stat. 1176 (7 U.S.C. 390 et seq.)
Short title, see 7 U.S.C. 390 note

Research on Aging Act of 1974
Pub. L. 93–296, May 31, 1974, 88 Stat. 184
Short title, see 42 U.S.C. 201 note

Reserve Corps Compensation Act
July 15, 1939, ch. 284, 53 Stat. 1042

Reserve Forces Act of 1955
Aug. 9, 1955, ch. 665, 69 Stat. 598

Reserve Forces Bill of Rights and Vitalization Act
Pub. L. 90–168, Dec. 1, 1967, 81 Stat. 521
Short title, see 10 U.S.C. 138 note

Reserve Forces Facilities Act of 1958
Pub. L. 85–685, title VI, Aug. 20, 1958, 72 Stat. 664

Reserve Forces Facilities Act of 1959
Pub. L. 86–149, title V, Aug. 10, 1959, 73 Stat. 324

Reserve Forces Facilities Act of 1960
Pub. L. 86–500, title VI, June 8, 1960, 74 Stat. 188

Reserve Forces Facilities Act of 1961
Pub. L. 87–57, title VII, June 27, 1961, 75 Stat. 112

Reserve Forces Facilities Authorization Act, 1964
Pub. L. 88–174, title VII, Nov. 7, 1963, 77 Stat. 329

Reserve Forces Facilities Authorization Act, 1965
Pub. L. 88–390, title VII, Aug. 1, 1964, 78 Stat. 365

Reserve Forces Facilities Authorization Act, 1966
Pub. L. 89–188, title VII, Sept. 16, 1965, 79 Stat. 819

Reserve Forces Facilities Authorization Act, 1967
Pub. L. 89–568, title VII, Sept. 12, 1966, 80 Stat. 757

Reserve Forces Facilities Authorization Act, 1968
Pub. L. 90–110, title IX, Oct. 21, 1967, 81 Stat. 309

Reserve Forces Facilities Authorization Act, 1969
Pub. L. 90–408, title IX, July 21, 1968, 82 Stat. 392

Reserve Forces Facilities Authorization Act, 1970
Pub. L. 91–142, title VIII, Dec. 5, 1969, 83 Stat. 318

Reserve Forces Facilities Authorization Act, 1971
Pub. L. 91–511, title VII, Oct. 26, 1970, 84 Stat. 1227

Reserve Forces Facilities Authorization Act, 1972
Pub. L. 92–145, title VIII, Oct. 27, 1971, 85 Stat. 414

Reserve Forces Facilities Authorization Act, 1973
Pub. L. 92–545, title VIII, Oct. 25, 1972, 86 Stat. 1154

Reserve Forces Facilities Authorization Act, 1974
Pub. L. 93–166, title VII, Nov. 29, 1973, 87 Stat. 685

Reserve Forces Facilities Authorization Act, 1975
Pub. L. 93–552, title VII, Dec. 27, 1974, 88 Stat. 1770

Reserve Forces Revitalization Act of 1996
Pub. L. 104–201, div. A, title XII, Sept. 23, 1996, 110 Stat. 2688
Short title, see 10 U.S.C. 10001 note

Reserve Officer Personnel Act of 1954
Sept. 3, 1954, ch. 1257, 68 Stat. 1147

Reserve Officer Personnel Management Act
Pub. L. 103–337, div. A, title XVI, Oct. 5, 1994, 108 Stat. 2921
Short title, see 10 U.S.C. 10001 note

Reserve Officers' Training Corps Vitalization Act of 1964
Pub. L. 88–647, Oct. 13, 1964, 78 Stat. 1063
Short title, see 10 U.S.C. 2031 note

Residential Lead-Based Paint Hazard Reduction Act of 1992
Pub. L. 102–550, title X, Oct. 28, 1992, 106 Stat. 3897 (42 U.S.C. 4851 et seq.)
Short title, see 42 U.S.C. 4851 note

Resolution Trust Corporation Completion Act
Pub. L. 103–204, Dec. 17, 1993, 107 Stat. 2369
Short title, see 12 U.S.C. 1421 note

Resolution Trust Corporation Funding Act of 1991
Pub. L. 102–18, Mar. 23, 1991, 105 Stat. 58
Short title, see 12 U.S.C. 1421 note

Resolution Trust Corporation Refinancing, Restructuring, and Improvement Act of 1991
Pub. L. 102–233, Dec. 12, 1991, 105 Stat. 1761
Short title, see 12 U.S.C. 1421 note

Resolution Trust Corporation Thrift Depositor Protection Reform Act of 1991
Pub. L. 102–233, title III, Dec. 12, 1991, 105 Stat. 1767
Short title, see 12 U.S.C. 1421 note

Resource Conservation and Recovery Act of 1976
Pub. L. 94–580, Oct. 21, 1976, 90 Stat. 2795 (42 U.S.C. 6901 et seq.)
Short title, see 42 U.S.C. 6901 note

Resource Recovery Act of 1970
Pub. L. 91–512, Oct. 26, 1970, 84 Stat. 1227

Restrictions Removal Act (Oklahoma)
May 27, 1908, ch. 199, 35 Stat. 312

Resumption Act (Currency)
See Specie Payment Resumption Act

Retired Federal Employees Health Benefits Act
Pub. L. 86–724, Sept. 8, 1960, 74 Stat. 849

Retiree Benefits Bankruptcy Protection Act of 1988
Pub. L. 100–334, June 16, 1988, 102 Stat. 610
Short title, see 11 U.S.C. 101 note

Retirement and Survivors' Annuities for Bankruptcy Judges and Magistrates Act of 1988
Pub. L. 100–659, Nov. 15, 1988, 102 Stat. 3910
Short title, see 28 U.S.C. 1 note

Retirement Equity Act of 1984
Pub. L. 98–397, Aug. 23, 1984, 98 Stat. 1426
Short title, see 29 U.S.C. 1001 note

Retirement Protection Act of 1994
Pub. L. 103–465, title VII, subtitle F (§750 et seq.), Dec. 8, 1994, 108 Stat. 5012
Short title, see 26 U.S.C. 1 note

Retirement-Straight Line Adjustment Act of 1958
Pub. L. 85–866, title I, §94, Sept. 2, 1958, 72 Stat. 1669 (26 U.S.C. 1016 note)

Revenue Act of 1916
Sept. 8, 1916, ch. 463, 39 Stat. 756

Revenue Act of 1917
Oct. 3, 1917, ch. 63, 40 Stat. 300

Revenue Act of 1918
Feb. 24, 1919, ch. 18, 40 Stat. 1057

Revenue Act of 1921
Nov. 23, 1921, ch. 136, 42 Stat. 227

Revenue Act of 1924
June 2, 1924, ch. 234, 43 Stat. 253

Revenue Act of 1926
Feb. 26, 1926, ch. 27, 44 Stat. 9

Revenue Act of 1928
May 29, 1928, ch. 852, 45 Stat. 791

Revenue Act of 1932
June 6, 1932, ch. 209, 47 Stat. 169

Revenue Act of 1934
May 10, 1934, ch. 277, 48 Stat. 680

Revenue Act of 1935
Aug. 30, 1935, ch. 829, 49 Stat. 1014

Revenue Act of 1936
June 22, 1936, ch. 690, 49 Stat. 1648

Revenue Act of 1937
Aug. 26, 1937, ch. 815, 50 Stat. 813

Revenue Act of 1938
May 28, 1938, ch. 289, 52 Stat. 447

Revenue Act of 1939
June 29, 1939, ch. 247, 53 Stat. 862

Revenue Act of 1940
June 25, 1940, ch. 419, 54 Stat. 516

Revenue Act of 1942
Oct. 21, 1942, ch. 619, 56 Stat. 798

Revenue Act of 1943
Feb. 25, 1944, ch. 63, 58 Stat. 21

Revenue Act of 1945
Nov. 8, 1945, ch. 453, 59 Stat. 556

Revenue Act of 1948
Apr. 2, 1948, ch. 168, 62 Stat. 110

Revenue Act of 1950
Sept. 23, 1950, ch. 994, 64 Stat. 906

Revenue Act of 1951
Oct. 20, 1951, ch. 521, 65 Stat. 452

Revenue Act of 1962
Pub. L. 87–834, Oct. 16, 1962, 76 Stat. 960
Short title, see 26 U.S.C. 1 note

Revenue Act of 1964
Pub. L. 88–272, Feb. 26, 1964, 78 Stat. 19
Short title, see 26 U.S.C. 1 note

Revenue Act of 1971
Pub. L. 92–178, Dec. 10, 1971, 85 Stat. 497
Short title, see 26 U.S.C. 1 note

Revenue Act of 1978
Pub. L. 95–600, Nov. 6, 1978, 92 Stat. 2763
Short title, see 26 U.S.C. 1 note

Revenue Act of 1987
Pub. L. 100–203, title X, Dec. 22, 1987, 101 Stat. 1330–382
Short title, see 26 U.S.C. 1 note

Revenue Adjustment Act of 1975
Pub. L. 94–164, Dec. 23, 1975, 89 Stat. 970
Short title, see 26 U.S.C. 1 note

Revenue Adjustments Act of 1980
Pub. L. 96–499, title XI, Dec. 5, 1980, 94 Stat. 2660

Revenue and Expenditure Control Act of 1968
Pub. L. 90–364, June 28, 1968, 82 Stat. 251
Short title, see 26 U.S.C. 1 note

Revenue Forgone Reform Act
Pub. L. 103–123, title VII, Oct. 28, 1993, 107 Stat. 1267
Short title, see 39 U.S.C. 101 note

Revenue Reconciliation Act of 1989
Pub. L. 101–239, title VII, Dec. 19, 1989, 103 Stat. 2301
Short title, see 26 U.S.C. 1 note

Revenue Reconciliation Act of 1990
Pub. L. 101–508, title XI, Nov. 5, 1990, 104 Stat. 1388–400
Short title, see 26 U.S.C. 1 note

Revenue Reconciliation Act of 1993
Pub. L. 103–66, title XIII, ch. 1 (§13001 et seq.), Aug. 10, 1993, 107 Stat. 416
Short title, see 26 U.S.C. 1 note

Revised Organic Act of the Virgin Islands
July 22, 1954, ch. 558, 68 Stat. 497 (48 U.S.C. 1541 et seq.)
Short title, see 48 U.S.C. 1541 note

Revolutionary War and War of 1812 Historic Preservation Study Act of 1996
Pub. L. 104–333, div. I, title VI, §603, Nov. 12, 1996, 110 Stat. 4172 (16 U.S.C. 1a–5 note)

Reynolds Aviation Training Act
See Army Aviation Cadet Act

Rhinoceros and Tiger Conservation Act of 1994
Pub. L. 103–391, Oct. 22, 1994, 108 Stat. 4094 (16 U.S.C. 5301 et seq.)
Short title, see 16 U.S.C. 5301 note

Rhinoceros and Tiger Conservation Act of 1998
Pub. L. 105–312, title IV, Oct. 30, 1998, 112 Stat. 2959
Short title, see 16 U.S.C. 5301 note

Rhode Island Indian Claims Settlement Act
Pub. L. 95–395, Sept. 30, 1978, 92 Stat. 813 (25 U.S.C. 1701 et seq.)
Short title, see 25 U.S.C. 1701 note

Rice Production Act of 1975
Pub. L. 94–214, Feb. 16, 1976, 90 Stat. 181
Short title, see 7 U.S.C. 428c note

Richard B. Russell National School Lunch Act
June 4, 1946, ch. 281, 60 Stat. 230 (42 U.S.C. 1751 et seq.)
Short title, see 42 U.S.C. 1751 note

Richmond National Battlefield Park Act of 2000
Pub. L. 106–511, title V, Nov. 13, 2000, 114 Stat. 2373 (16 U.S.C. 423*l*–1 et seq.)

Ricky Ray Hemophilia Relief Fund Act of 1998
Pub. L. 105–369, Nov. 12, 1998, 112 Stat. 3368 (42 U.S.C. 300c–22 note)

RICO
See Racketeer Influenced and Corrupt Organizations Act (RICO)

Riegle Community Development and Regulatory Improvement Act of 1994
Pub. L. 103–325, Sept. 23, 1994, 108 Stat. 2160
Short title, see 12 U.S.C. 4701 note

Riegle-Neal Amendments Act of 1997
Pub. L. 105–24, July 3, 1997, 111 Stat. 238
Short title, see 12 U.S.C. 1811 note

Riegle-Neal Interstate Banking and Branching Efficiency Act of 1994
Pub. L. 103–328, Sept. 29, 1994, 108 Stat. 2338
Short title, see 12 U.S.C. 1811 note

Right of Way Act of 1891
Mar. 3, 1891, ch. 561, §18, 26 Stat. 1101

Right to Financial Privacy Act of 1978
Pub. L. 95–630, title XI, Nov. 10, 1978, 92 Stat. 3697 (12 U.S.C. 3401 et seq.)
Short title, see 12 U.S.C. 3401 note

Right to Work Law
July 5, 1935, ch. 372, §14, 49 Stat. 457 (29 U.S.C. 164)

Rio Grande American Canal Extension Act of 1990
Pub. L. 101–438, Oct. 18, 1990, 104 Stat. 1001

Rio Grande Designation Act of 1994
Pub. L. 103–242, May 4, 1994, 108 Stat. 611
Short title, see 16 U.S.C. 1271 note

Rio Grande Pollution Correction Act of 1987
Pub. L. 100–465, Oct. 3, 1988, 102 Stat. 2272 (22 U.S.C. 277g et seq.)
Short title, see 22 U.S.C. 277g note

Risk Retention Amendments of 1986
Pub. L. 99–563, Oct. 27, 1986, 100 Stat. 3170
Short title, see 15 U.S.C. 3901 note

River and Harbor Act of 1899
See Rivers and Harbors Appropriation Act of 1899

River and Harbor Act of 1910
June 25, 1910, ch. 382, 36 Stat. 630

River and Harbor Act of 1911
Feb. 27, 1911, ch. 166, 36 Stat. 933

River and Harbor Act of 1912
July 25, 1912, ch. 253, 37 Stat. 201

River and Harbor Act of 1913
Mar. 4, 1913, ch. 144, 37 Stat. 801

River and Harbor Act of 1914
Oct. 2, 1914, ch. 313, 38 Stat. 725

River and Harbor Act of 1915
Mar. 4, 1915, ch. 142, 38 Stat. 1049

River and Harbor Act of 1916
July 27, 1916, ch. 260, 39 Stat. 391

River and Harbor Act of 1917
Aug. 8, 1917, ch. 49, 40 Stat. 250

River and Harbor Act of 1918
July 18, 1918, ch. 155, 40 Stat. 904

River and Harbor Act of 1919
Mar. 2, 1919, ch. 95, 40 Stat. 1275

River and Harbor Act of 1920
June 5, 1920, ch. 252, 41 Stat. 1009

River and Harbor Act of 1922
Sept. 22, 1922, ch. 427, 42 Stat. 1038

River and Harbor Act of 1930
July 3, 1930, ch. 847, 46 Stat. 918

River and Harbor Act of 1945
Mar. 2, 1945, ch. 19, 59 Stat. 10

River and Harbor Act of 1948
June 30, 1948, ch. 771, title I, 62 Stat. 1172

River and Harbor Act of 1950
May 17, 1950, ch. 188, title I, 64 Stat. 163

River and Harbor Act of 1954
Sept. 3, 1954, ch. 1264, title I, 68 Stat. 1248

River and Harbor Act of 1958
Pub. L. 85–500, title I, July 3, 1958, 72 Stat. 297

River and Harbor Act of 1960
Pub. L. 86–645, title I, July 14, 1960, 74 Stat. 480

River and Harbor Act of 1962
Pub. L. 87–874, title I, Oct. 23, 1962, 76 Stat. 1173

River and Harbor Act of 1965
Pub. L. 89–298, title III, Oct. 27, 1965, 79 Stat. 1089

River and Harbor Act of 1966
Pub. L. 89–789, title I, Nov. 7, 1966, 80 Stat. 1405

River and Harbor Act of 1968
Pub. L. 90–483, title I, Aug. 13, 1968, 82 Stat. 731

River and Harbor Act of 1970
Pub. L. 91–611, title I, Dec. 31, 1970, 84 Stat. 1818

River Basin Monetary Authorization Act of 1967
Pub. L. 90–17, May 12, 1967, 81 Stat. 15

River Basin Monetary Authorization Act of 1968
Pub. L. 90–483, title III, Aug. 13, 1968, 82 Stat. 750

River Basin Monetary Authorization Act of 1971
Pub. L. 92–222, Dec. 23, 1971, 85 Stat. 798

River Basin Monetary Authorization Act of 1974
Pub. L. 93–251, title II, Mar. 7, 1974, 88 Stat. 49

Rivers and Harbors Appropriation Act of 1899
Mar. 3, 1899, ch. 425, 30 Stat. 1121

Rivers of Steel National Heritage Area Act
See Steel Industry American Heritage Area Act of 1996

Roads Employment Act
June 18, 1934, ch. 586, 48 Stat. 993

Robert A. Taft Institute Assistance Act
Pub. L. 96–374, title XIII, part H, subpart 1 (§1371 et seq.), Oct. 3, 1980, 94 Stat. 1502

Robert T. Stafford Disaster Relief and Emergency Assistance Act
Pub. L. 93–288, May 22, 1974, 88 Stat. 143 (42 U.S.C. 5121 et seq.)
Short title, see 42 U.S.C. 5121 note

Roberts Act
Pub. L. 88–515, Aug. 30, 1964, 78 Stat. 696 (40 U.S.C. 701 et seq.)
Short title, see 40 U.S.C. 701 note

Robertson-Pittman Wildlife Restoration Act
See Pittman-Robertson Wildlife Restoration Act

Robinson-Patman Act
Also known as the Robinson-Patman Antidiscrimination Act and as the Robinson-Patman Price Discrimination Act
June 19, 1936, ch. 592, 49 Stat. 1526 (15 U.S.C. 13–13b, 21a)
Short title, see 15 U.S.C. 13 note

Robinson-Patman Antidiscrimination Act
Also known as the Robinson-Patman Act and as the Robinson-Patman Price Discrimination Act
June 19, 1936, ch. 592, 49 Stat. 1526 (15 U.S.C. 13–13b, 21a)
Short title, see 15 U.S.C. 13 note

Robinson-Patman Price Discrimination Act
Also known as the Robinson-Patman Act and as the Robinson-Patman Antidiscrimination Act

Robinson-Patman Price Discrimination Act—Continued
June 19, 1936, ch. 592, 49 Stat. 1526 (15 U.S.C. 13–13b, 21a)
Short title, see 15 U.S.C. 13 note

Rock Island Railroad Transition and Employee Assistance Act
Pub. L. 96–254, title I, May 30, 1980, 94 Stat. 399 (45 U.S.C. 1001 et seq.)
Short title, see 45 U.S.C. 1001 note

Rocky Mountain Arsenal National Wildlife Refuge Act of 1992
Pub. L. 102–402, Oct. 9, 1992, 106 Stat. 1961 (16 U.S.C. 668dd note)

Rocky Mountain National Park Act
Jan. 26, 1915, ch. 19, 38 Stat. 798 (16 U.S.C. 191, 193 et seq.)

Roger's Act (Foreign Service)
See Foreign Service Act

Roosevelt Campobello International Park Act
Pub. L. 88–363, July 7, 1964, 78 Stat. 299 (16 U.S.C. 1101 et seq.)
Short title, see 16 U.S.C. 1101 note

Roosevelt Library Act
July 18, 1939, ch. 324, 53 Stat. 1062

Rosie the Riveter/World War II Home Front National Historical Park Establishment Act of 2000
Pub. L. 106–352, Oct. 24, 2000, 114 Stat. 1370 (16 U.S.C. 410ggg et seq.)
Short title, see 16 U.S.C. 410ggg note

Route 66 Study Act of 1990
Pub. L. 101–400, Sept. 28, 1990, 104 Stat. 861

Royalty Adjustment Act of 1942
Oct. 31, 1942, ch. 634, 56 Stat. 1013

Rubber Act of 1948
Mar. 31, 1948, ch. 166, 62 Stat. 101 (50 App. U.S.C. 1921 et seq.)

Rubber Producing Facilities Disposal Act of 1953
Aug. 7, 1953, ch. 338, 67 Stat. 408 (50 App. U.S.C. 1941 et seq.)
Short title, see 50 App. U.S.C. 1941 note

Rules Enabling Act
Pub. L. 100–702, title IV, Nov. 19, 1988, 102 Stat. 4648 (28 U.S.C. 2071 et seq.)

Rules of Decision Act
June 25, 1948, ch. 646, 62 Stat. 944 (28 U.S.C. 1652)

Rumanian Declaration of War
June 5, 1942, ch. 325, 56 Stat. 307

Runaway and Homeless Youth Act
Pub. L. 93–415, title III, Sept. 7, 1974, 88 Stat. 1129 (42 U.S.C. 5701 et seq.)
Short title, see 42 U.S.C. 5601 note

Rural Access to Emergency Devices Act
Also known as the Rural AED Act
Pub. L. 106–505, title IV, subtitle B (§411 et seq.), Nov. 13, 2000, 114 Stat. 2340 (42 U.S.C. 254c note)

Rural AED Act
Also known as the Rural Access to Emergency Devices Act
Pub. L. 106–505, title IV, subtitle B (§411 et seq.), Nov. 13, 2000, 114 Stat. 2340 (42 U.S.C. 254c note)

Rural Air Service Survival Act
Pub. L. 104–264, title II, §278, Oct. 9, 1996, 110 Stat. 3249
Short title, see 49 U.S.C. 40101 note

Rural Crisis Recovery Program Act of 1987
Pub. L. 100–219, Dec. 29, 1987, 101 Stat. 1456
Short title, see 7 U.S.C. 2661 note

Rural Development Act of 1972
Pub. L. 92–419, Aug. 30, 1972, 86 Stat. 657
Short title, see 7 U.S.C. 1921 note

Rural Development Policy Act of 1980
Pub. L. 96–355, Sept. 24, 1980, 94 Stat. 1171
Short title, see 7 U.S.C. 2201 note

Rural Development, Agriculture, and Related Agencies Appropriations Act, 1988
Pub. L. 100 202, §101(k), Dec. 22, 1987, 101 Stat. 1329–322

Rural Development, Agriculture, and Related Agencies Appropriations Act, 1989
Pub. L. 100–460, Oct. 1, 1988, 102 Stat. 2229

Rural Development, Agriculture, and Related Agencies Appropriations Act, 1990
Pub. L. 101–161, Nov. 21, 1989, 103 Stat. 951

Rural Development, Agriculture, and Related Agencies Appropriations Act, 1991
Pub. L. 101–506, Nov. 5, 1990, 104 Stat. 1315

Rural Economic Development Act of 1990
Pub. L. 101–624, title XXIII, Nov. 28, 1990, 104 Stat. 3979
Short title, see 7 U.S.C. 1921 note

Rural Education Achievement Program
Pub. L. 89–10, title X, part J, subpart 2, as added Pub. L. 106–554, §1(a)(9) [title IX, §901], Dec. 21, 2000, 114 Stat. 2763, 2763A–89
Short title, see 20 U.S.C. 6301 note

Rural Electrification Act of 1936
May 20, 1936, ch. 432, 49 Stat. 1363 (7 U.S.C. 901 et seq.)
Short title, see 7 U.S.C. 901

Rural Electrification Act of 1938
June 21, 1938, ch. 554, title IV, 52 Stat. 818

Rural Electrification Administration Improvement Act of 1992
Pub. L. 102–428, Oct. 21, 1992, 106 Stat. 2183
Short title, see 7 U.S.C. 901 note

Rural Electrification Administration Technical Amendments Act of 1976
Pub. L. 94–570, Oct. 20, 1976, 90 Stat. 2701
Short title, see 7 U.S.C. 901 note

Rural Electrification Loan Restructuring Act of 1993
Pub. L. 103–129, Nov. 1, 1993, 107 Stat. 1356
Short title, see 7 U.S.C. 901 note

Rural Health and Safety Education Act of 1990
Pub. L. 101–624, title XXIII, §2390, Nov. 28, 1990, 104 Stat. 4055
Short title, see 7 U.S.C. 2661 note

Rural Health Clinics Act of 1983
Pub. L. 98–194, Dec. 1, 1983, 97 Stat. 1345
Short title, see 42 U.S.C. 201 note

Rural Housing Amendments of 1983
Pub. L. 98–181, title V, Nov. 30, 1983, 97 Stat. 1240
Short title, see 42 U.S.C. 1441 note

Rural Industrial Assistance Act of 1986
Pub. L. 99–409, Aug. 28, 1986, 100 Stat. 923
Short title, see 7 U.S.C. 1921 note

Rural Local Broadcast Signal Act
Pub. L. 106–113, div. B, §1000(a)(9) [title II], Nov. 29, 1999, 113 Stat. 1536, 1501A–544 (47 U.S.C. 338 note)

Rural Post-Roads Act
See Federal-Aid Road Act

Rural Rehabilitation Corporation Trust Liquidation Act
May 3, 1950, ch. 152, 64 Stat. 98

Rural Small Business Enhancement Act of 1990
Pub. L. 101–574, title III, Nov. 15, 1990, 104 Stat. 2827
Short title, see 15 U.S.C. 631 note

Rural Telecommunications Improvements Act of 1990
Pub. L. 101–624, title XXIII, subtitle F (§2351 et seq.), Nov. 28, 1990, 104 Stat. 4038
Short title, see 7 U.S.C. 901 note

Rural Telephone Cooperative Associations ERISA Amendments Act of 1991
Pub. L. 102–89, Aug. 14, 1991, 105 Stat. 446
Short title, see 29 U.S.C. 1001 note

Russell Amendment
June 27, 1944, ch. 286, title II, §213, 58 Stat. 387

Russell-Overton Amendment
Sept. 16, 1940, ch. 720, §9, 54 Stat. 892

Ryan White CARE Act Amendments of 1996
Pub. L. 104–146, May 20, 1996, 110 Stat. 1346
Short title, see 42 U.S.C. 201 note

Ryan White CARE Act Amendments of 2000
Pub. L. 106–345, Oct. 20, 2000, 114 Stat. 1319
Short title, see 42 U.S.C. 201 note

Ryan White Comprehensive AIDS Resources Emergency Act of 1990
Pub. L. 101–381, Aug. 18, 1990, 104 Stat. 576
Short title, see 42 U.S.C. 201 note

Sabbatino Amendment
See Hickenlooper Amendment

Saccharin Study and Labeling Act
Pub. L. 95–203, Nov. 23, 1977, 91 Stat. 1451
Short title, see 21 U.S.C. 301 note

Saccharin Study and Labeling Act Amendment of 1983
Pub. L. 98–22, Apr. 22, 1983, 97 Stat. 173
Short title, see 21 U.S.C. 301 note

Saccharin Study and Labeling Act Amendment of 1981
Pub. L. 97–42, Aug. 14, 1981, 95 Stat. 946
Short title, see 21 U.S.C. 301 note

Saddleback Mountain-Arizona Settlement Act of 1995
Pub. L. 104–102, Feb. 6, 1996, 110 Stat. 50

Safe and Drug-Free Schools and Communities Act of 1994
Pub. L. 89–10, title IV, as added Pub. L. 103–382, title I, §101, Oct. 20, 1994, 108 Stat. 3672 (20 U.S.C. 7101 et seq.)
Short title, see 20 U.S.C. 7101

Safe Drinking Water Act
July 1, 1944, ch. 373, title XIV, as added Pub. L. 104–182, title V, §501(e), Aug. 6, 1996, 110 Stat. 1691 (42 U.S.C. 300f et seq.)
Short title, see 42 U.S.C. 201 note

Safe Drinking Water Act Amendments of 1986
Pub. L. 99–339, June 19, 1986, 100 Stat. 642
Short title, see 42 U.S.C. 201 note

Safe Drinking Water Act Amendments of 1996
Pub. L. 104–182, Aug. 6, 1996, 110 Stat. 1613
Short title, see 42 U.S.C. 201 note

Safe Drinking Water Act of 1974
Pub. L. 93–523, Dec. 16, 1974, 88 Stat. 1660
Short title, see 42 U.S.C. 201 note

Safe Drinking Water Amendments of 1977
Pub. L. 95–190, Nov. 16, 1977, 91 Stat. 1393
Short title, see 42 U.S.C. 201 note

Safe Homes for Women Act of 1994
Pub. L. 103–322, title IV, subtitle B (§40201 et seq.), Sept. 13, 1994, 108 Stat. 1925
Short title, see 42 U.S.C. 13701 note

Safe Medical Devices Act of 1990
Pub. L. 101–629, Nov. 28, 1990, 104 Stat. 4511
Short title, see 21 U.S.C. 301 note

Safe Schools Act of 1994
Pub. L. 103–227, title VII, Mar. 31, 1994, 108 Stat. 204 (20 U.S.C. 5961 et seq.)
Short title, see 20 U.S.C. 5961(a)

Safe Streets for Women Act of 1994
Pub. L. 103–322, title IV, subtitle A (§40101 et seq.), Sept. 13, 1994, 108 Stat. 1903
Short title, see 42 U.S.C. 13701 note

Safe Streets Law of 1968
See Gun Control Act of 1968

Safer Streets and Neighborhoods Act of 1994
Pub. L. 103–322, title XXXII, subtitle G (§320701 et seq.), Sept. 13, 1994, 108 Stat. 2121
Short title, see 42 U.S.C. 3711 note

Saginaw Chippewa Indian Tribe of Michigan Distribution of Judgment Funds Act
Pub. L. 99–346, June 30, 1986, 100 Stat. 674

Saguaro National Monument Expansion Act of 1991
Pub. L. 102–61, June 19, 1991, 105 Stat. 303

Saguaro National Park Establishment Act of 1994
Pub. L. 103–364, Oct. 14, 1994, 108 Stat. 3467 (16 U.S.C. 410zz et seq.)
Short title, see 16 U.S.C. 410zz note

Sailing School Vessels Act of 1982
Pub. L. 97–322, title II, Oct. 15, 1982, 96 Stat. 1588
Short title, see 46 App. U.S.C. 446 note

Saint Croix Island Heritage Act
Pub. L. 106–529, Nov. 22, 2000, 114 Stat. 2524 (16 U.S.C. 450hh note)

Saint Elizabeths Hospital and District of Columbia Mental Health Services Act
Pub. L. 98–621, Nov. 8, 1984, 98 Stat. 3369
Short title, see 24 U.S.C. 225 note

Saint Helena Island National Scenic Area Act
Pub. L. 106–431, Nov. 6, 2000, 114 Stat. 1905 (16 U.S.C. 546 et seq.)
Short title, see 16 U.S.C. 546 note

Saint Lawrence Seaway Act
May 13, 1954, ch. 201, 68 Stat. 92 (33 U.S.C. 981 et seq.)

Salary Grab Act
Mar. 3, 1873, ch. 226, 17 Stat. 485

Saline Act (Public Lands)
Jan. 31, 1901, ch. 186, 31 Stat. 745 (30 U.S.C. 162)

Saline Water Conversion Act
July 3, 1952, ch. 568, 66 Stat. 328 (42 U.S.C. 1951 et seq.)

Saline Water Conversion Act of 1971
Pub. L. 92–60, July 29, 1971, 85 Stat. 159 (42 U.S.C. 1959 et seq.)
Short title, see 42 U.S.C. 1959 note

Saline Water Demonstration Act
Pub. L. 85–883, Sept. 2, 1958, 72 Stat. 1706 (42 U.S.C. 1958a et seq.)

Salmon and Steelhead Conservation and Enhancement Act of 1980
Pub. L. 96–561, title I, Dec. 22, 1980, 94 Stat. 3275 (16 U.S.C. 3301 et seq.)
Short title, see 16 U.S.C. 3301 note

Salmon Fisheries Act
See Alaska Salmon Fisheries Act

Salt Lake City Watershed Improvement Act of 1990
Pub. L. 101–634, Nov. 28, 1990, 104 Stat. 4580

Salt River Bay National Historical Park and Ecological Preserve at St. Croix, Virgin Islands, Act of 1992
Pub. L. 102–247, title I, Feb. 24, 1992, 106 Stat. 33 (16 U.S.C. 410tt et seq.)
Short title, see 16 U.S.C. 410tt note

Salt River Pima-Maricopa Indian Community Water Rights Settlement Act of 1988
Pub. L. 100–512, Oct. 20, 1988, 102 Stat. 2549

Salton Sea Reclamation Act of 1998
Pub. L. 105–372, Nov. 12, 1998, 112 Stat. 3377

Saltonstall-Kennedy Act
Aug. 11, 1939, ch. 696, §2, 53 Stat. 1412 (15 U.S.C. 713c–3)
Short title, see 15 U.S.C. 713c–3 note

Salvage Act
Aug. 1, 1912, ch. 268, 37 Stat. 242

San Antonio Missions National Historical Park
Pub. L. 95–629, title II, Nov. 10, 1978, 92 Stat. 3636 (16 U.S.C. 410ee)

San Carlos Act
June 7, 1924, ch. 288, 43 Stat. 475

San Carlos Apache Tribe Water Rights Settlement Act of 1992
Pub. L. 102–575, title XXXVII, Oct. 30, 1992, 106 Stat. 4740

San Carlos Indian Irrigation Project Divestiture Act of 1991
Pub. L. 102–231, Dec. 12, 1991, 105 Stat. 1722

San Carlos Mineral Strip Act of 1990
Pub. L. 101–447, Oct. 22, 1990, 104 Stat. 1047

San Domingo Resolution
Jan. 12, 1871, No. 7, 16 Stat. 591

San Francisco Maritime National Historical Park Act of 1988
Pub. L. 100–348, June 27, 1988, 102 Stat. 654 (16 U.S.C. 410nn et seq.)
Short title, see 16 U.S.C. 410nn note

San Juan Basin Wilderness Protection Act of 1984
Pub. L. 98–603, Oct. 30, 1984, 98 Stat. 3155 (16 U.S.C. 1132 note)

San Juan Island National Historical Park Act
Pub. L. 89–565, Sept. 9, 1966, 80 Stat. 737 (16 U.S.C. 282 et seq.)

San Luis Rey Indian Water Rights Settlement Act
Pub. L. 100–675, title I, Nov. 17, 1988, 102 Stat. 4000

Sand Creek Massacre National Historic Site Establishment Act of 2000
Pub. L. 106–465, Nov. 7, 2000, 114 Stat. 2019 (16 U.S.C. 461 note)

Sand Creek Massacre National Historic Site Study Act of 1998
Pub. L. 105–243, Oct. 6, 1998, 112 Stat. 1579

Sanitary Food Transportation Act of 1990
Pub. L. 101–500, Nov. 3, 1990, 104 Stat. 1213

Santa Fe Indian School Act
Pub. L. 106–568, title VIII, subtitle B (§821 et seq.), Dec. 27, 2000, 114 Stat. 2919

Santa Rosa and San Jacinto Mountains National Monument Act of 2000
Pub. L. 106–351, Oct. 24, 2000, 114 Stat. 1362 (16 U.S.C. 431 note)

Santini-Burton Act
Pub. L. 96–586, Dec. 23, 1980, 94 Stat. 3381

Santo Domingo Pueblo Claims Settlement Act of 2000
Pub. L. 106–425, Nov. 1, 2000, 114 Stat. 1890 (25 U.S.C. 1777 et seq.)
Short title, see 25 U.S.C. 1777 note

SARA
See Superfund Amendments and Reauthorization Act of 1986

Saratoga National Historical Park Act
June 1, 1938, ch. 316, 52 Stat. 608 (16 U.S.C. 159 et seq.)

Satellite Home Viewer Act of 1988
Pub. L. 100–667, title II, Nov. 16, 1988, 102 Stat. 3949
Short title, see 17 U.S.C. 101 note

Satellite Home Viewer Act of 1994
Pub. L. 103–369, Oct. 18, 1994, 108 Stat. 3477
Short title, see 17 U.S.C. 101 note

Satellite Home Viewer Improvement Act of 1999
Pub. L. 106–113, div. B, §1000(a)(9) [title I], Nov. 29, 1999, 113 Stat. 1536, 1501A–523
Short title, see 17 U.S.C. 101 note

Saulsbury Resolution (District of Columbia Rents)
May 31, 1918, ch. 90, 40 Stat. 593

Save Your Vision Week Act
Pub. L. 88–242, Dec. 30, 1963, 77 Stat. 629

Savings and Loan Holding Company Amendments of 1967
Pub. L. 90–255, Feb. 14, 1968, 82 Stat. 5
Short title, see 12 U.S.C. 1701 note

Savings Are Vital to Everyone's Retirement Act of 1997
Pub. L. 105–92, Nov. 19, 1997, 111 Stat. 2139
Short title, see 29 U.S.C. 1001 note

Savings Bond Act
Feb. 4, 1935, ch. 5, 49 Stat. 20

Savings in Construction Act of 1996
Pub. L. 104–289, Oct. 11, 1996, 110 Stat. 3411
Short title, see 15 U.S.C. 205a note

Sawtooth National Recreation Area Act
Pub. L. 92–400, Aug. 22, 1972, 86 Stat. 612 (16 U.S.C. 460aa et seq.)

School Dropout Assistance Act
Pub. L. 89–10, title V, part C (§5301 et seq.), as added Pub. L. 103–382, title I, §101, Oct. 20, 1994, 108 Stat. 3701 (20 U.S.C. 7261 et seq.)
Short title, see 20 U.S.C. 7261

School Dropout Demonstration Assistance Act of 1988
Pub. L. 89–10, title VI, part A (§6001 et seq.), as added Pub. L. 100–297, title I, §1001, Apr. 28, 1988, 102 Stat. 265 (20 U.S.C. 3241 et seq.)

School Dropout Prevention and Basic Skills Improvement Act of 1990
Pub. L. 101–600, Nov. 16, 1990, 104 Stat. 3042
Short title, see 20 U.S.C. 6301 note

School Facilities Construction Act
Pub. L. 85–620, title I, §101, Aug. 12, 1958, 72 Stat. 548

School Lunch and Child Nutrition Amendments of 1986
Pub. L. 99–500, title III, Oct. 18, 1986, 100 Stat. 1783–359, and Pub. L. 99–591, title III, Oct. 30, 1986, 100 Stat. 3341–362
Short title, see 42 U.S.C. 1751 note

School-to-Work Opportunities Act of 1994
Pub. L. 103–239, May 4, 1994, 108 Stat. 568 (20 U.S.C. 6101 et seq.)
Short title, see 20 U.S.C. 6101 note

Schuylkill River Valley National Heritage Area Act
Pub. L. 106–278, title II, Oct. 6, 2000, 114 Stat. 819 (16 U.S.C. 461 note)

Science and Engineering Equal Opportunities Act
Pub. L. 96–516, part B (§31 et seq.), Dec. 12, 1980, 94 Stat. 3010 (42 U.S.C. 1885 et seq.)
Short title, see 42 U.S.C. 1861 note

Scientific and Advanced-Technology Act of 1992
Pub. L. 102–476, Oct. 23, 1992, 106 Stat. 2297
Short title, see 42 U.S.C. 1861 note

Scrapping of Naval Vessels Act
July 1, 1922, ch. 263, 42 Stat. 814

Sea Food Inspection Act
Aug. 27, 1935, ch. 739, 49 Stat. 871

Sea Grant Program Improvement Act of 1976
Pub. L. 94–461, Oct. 8, 1976, 90 Stat. 1961
Short title, see 33 U.S.C. 1121 note

Sea of Okhotsk Fisheries Enforcement Act of 1995
Pub. L. 104–43, title V, Nov. 3, 1995, 109 Stat. 391
Short title, see 16 U.S.C. 1823 note

Seal Fisheries Act
Apr. 21, 1910, ch. 183, 36 Stat. 326

Seamen Discharge Act
Mar. 24, 1937, ch. 49, 50 Stat. 49

Seamen's Act
Mar. 4, 1915, ch. 153, 38 Stat. 1164

Seamen's Service Act
Pub. L. 91–603, Dec. 31, 1970, 84 Stat. 1674
Short title, see 10 U.S.C. 2604 note

Search Warrant Act
June 15, 1917, ch. 30, title XI, 40 Stat. 228

Second Decontrol Act of 1947
July 15, 1947, ch. 248, 61 Stat. 321 (50 App. U.S.C. 645 note)

Second Defense Aid Supplemental Appropriation Act, 1942
Mar. 5, 1942, ch. 141, title III, 56 Stat. 130

Second Deficiency Act, fiscal year, 1928
May 29, 1928, ch. 853, 45 Stat. 883

Second Deficiency Appropriation Act, 1940
June 27, 1940, ch. 437, 54 Stat. 628

Second Deficiency Appropriation Act, 1941
July 3, 1941, ch. 273, 55 Stat. 541

Second Deficiency Appropriation Act, 1942
July 2, 1942, ch. 476, 56 Stat. 593

Second Deficiency Appropriation Act, 1943
July 12, 1943, ch. 229, 57 Stat. 537

Second Deficiency Appropriation Act, 1944
June 28, 1944, ch. 304, 58 Stat. 597

Second Deficiency Appropriation Act, 1945
July 5, 1945, ch. 271, 59 Stat. 412

Second Deficiency Appropriation Act, 1946
May 18, 1946, ch. 263, 60 Stat. 183

Second Deficiency Appropriation Act, 1947
May 26, 1947, ch. 82, 61 Stat. 106

Second Deficiency Appropriation Act, 1948
June 25, 1948, ch. 658, 62 Stat. 1027

Second Deficiency Appropriation Act, 1949
June 23, 1949, ch. 236, 63 Stat. 231

Second Deficiency Appropriation Act, fiscal year 1920
Mar. 6, 1920, ch. 94, 41 Stat. 503

Second Deficiency Appropriation Act, Fiscal Year 1924
Dec. 5, 1924, ch. 4, 43 Stat. 672

Second Deficiency Appropriation Act, fiscal year 1938
June 25, 1938, ch. 681, 52 Stat. 1114

Second Deficiency Appropriation Act, fiscal year 1939
May 2, 1939, ch. 107, 53 Stat. 626

Second Independent Offices Appropriation Act, 1954
July 27, 1953, ch. 241, 67 Stat. 187

Second Liberty Bond Act
Sept. 24, 1917, ch. 56, 40 Stat. 288

Second Liberty Loan Act
See Second Liberty Bond Act

Second Morrill Act
Also known as the Agricultural College Act of 1890
Aug. 30, 1890, ch. 841, 26 Stat. 417 (7 U.S.C. 321 et seq.)
Short title, see 7 U.S.C. 321 note

Second Revenue Act of 1940
Oct. 8, 1940, ch. 757, 54 Stat. 974

Second Supplemental Appropriation Act, 1950
Oct. 28, 1949, ch. 783, 63 Stat. 973

Second Supplemental Appropriation Act, 1948
July 31, 1947, ch. 414, 61 Stat. 695

Second Supplemental Appropriation Act, 1951
Jan. 6, 1951, ch. 1213, 64 Stat. 1223

Second Supplemental Appropriation Act, 1952
Nov. 1, 1951, ch. 665, 65 Stat. 760

Second Supplemental Appropriation Act, 1953
Mar. 28, 1953, ch. 12, 67 Stat. 8

Second Supplemental Appropriation Act, 1955
Apr. 22, 1955, ch. 26, 69 Stat. 28

Second Supplemental Appropriation Act, 1956
May 19, 1956, ch. 313, 70 Stat. 161

Second Supplemental Appropriation Act, 1957
July 31, 1956, ch. 805, 70 Stat. 763

Second Supplemental Appropriation Act, 1958
Pub. L. 85–352, Mar. 28, 1958, 72 Stat. 50

Second Supplemental Appropriation Act, 1959
Pub. L. 86–30, May 20, 1959, 73 Stat. 33

Second Supplemental Appropriation Act, 1960
Pub. L. 86–424, Apr. 13, 1960, 74 Stat. 42

Second Supplemental Appropriation Act, 1961
Pub. L. 86–722, Sept. 8, 1960, 74 Stat. 821

Second Supplemental Appropriation Act, 1962
Pub. L. 87–545, July 25, 1962, 76 Stat. 209

Second Supplemental Appropriation Act, 1965
Pub. L. 89–16, Apr. 30, 1965, 79 Stat. 81

Second Supplemental Appropriation Act, 1966
Pub. L. 89–426, May 13, 1966, 80 Stat. 141

Second Supplemental Appropriation Act, 1967
Pub. L. 90–21, May 29, 1967, 81 Stat. 30

Second Supplemental Appropriation Act, 1968
Pub. L. 90–392, July 9, 1968, 82 Stat. 307

Second Supplemental Appropriations Act, 1969
Pub. L. 91–47, July 22, 1969, 83 Stat. 49

Second Supplemental Appropriations Act, 1970
Pub. L. 91–305, July 6, 1970, 84 Stat. 376

Second Supplemental Appropriations Act, 1971
Pub. L. 92–18, May 25, 1971, 85 Stat. 40

Second Supplemental Appropriations Act, 1972
Pub. L. 92–306, May 27, 1972, 86 Stat. 163

Second Supplemental Appropriations Act, 1973
Pub. L. 93–50, July 1, 1973, 87 Stat. 99

Second Supplemental Appropriations Act, 1974
Pub. L. 93–305, June 8, 1974, 88 Stat. 195

Second Supplemental Appropriations Act, 1975
Pub. L. 94–32, June 12, 1975, 89 Stat. 173

Second Supplemental Appropriations Act, 1976
Pub. L. 94–303, June 1, 1976, 90 Stat. 597

Second Supplemental Appropriations Act, 1978
Pub. L. 95–355, Sept. 8, 1978, 92 Stat. 523

Second Supplemental Appropriations Act, 1984
Pub. L. 98–396, Aug. 22, 1984, 98 Stat. 1369

Second Supplemental National Defense Appropriation Act, 1941
Sept. 9, 1940, ch. 717, title III, 54 Stat. 884

Second Supplemental National Defense Appropriation Act, 1942
Oct. 28, 1941, ch. 460, 55 Stat. 745

Second Supplemental National Defense Appropriation Act, 1943
Oct. 26, 1942, ch. 629, 56 Stat. 990

Second Supplemental Surplus Appropriation Rescission Act, 1946
May 27, 1946, ch. 271, 60 Stat. 221

Second Urgent Deficiency Appropriation Act, 1946
Mar. 28, 1946, ch. 114, 60 Stat. 82

Second Urgent Deficiency Appropriation Act, 1947
June 27, 1947, ch. 156, 61 Stat. 183

Second Urgent Deficiency Appropriation Act, 1955
May 27, 1955, ch. 107, 69 Stat. 68

Second Urgent Deficiency Appropriation Act, 1957
Pub. L. 85–15, Apr. 16, 1957, 71 Stat. 11

Second War Powers Act, 1942
Mar. 27, 1942, ch. 199, 56 Stat. 176 (50 App. U.S.C. 631 et seq.)

Second Washington Airport Act
See Dulles International Airport Act

Secondary Mortgage Market Enhancement Act of 1984
Pub. L. 98–440, Oct. 3, 1984, 98 Stat. 1689
Short title, see 12 U.S.C. 1701 note

Secondary Schools Basic Skills Demonstration Assistance Act of 1988
Pub. L. 89–10, title VI, part B (§6101 et seq.), as added Pub. L. 100–297, title I, §1001, Apr. 28, 1988, 102 Stat. 270 (20 U.S.C. 3261 et seq.)
Pub. L. 100–418, title VI, subtitle A, ch. 7, subch. B (§6071 et seq.), Aug. 23, 1988, 102 Stat. 1496 (20 U.S.C. 5061 et seq.)

Secrecy of Military Information Act
Jan. 26, 1942, ch. 19, 56 Stat. 19

Secure Embassy Construction and Counterterrorism Act of 1999
Pub. L. 106–113, div. B, §1000(a)(7) [div. A, title VI], Nov. 29, 1999, 113 Stat. 1536, 1501A–451
Short title, see 22 U.S.C. 4801 note

Secure Rural Schools and Community Self-Determination Act of 2000
Pub. L. 106–393, Oct. 30, 2000, 114 Stat. 1607
Short title, see 16 U.S.C. 500 note

Securities Act Amendments of 1964
Pub. L. 88–467, Aug. 20, 1964, 78 Stat. 565
Short title, see 15 U.S.C. 78a note

Securities Act of 1933
May 27, 1933, ch. 38, title I, 48 Stat. 74 (15 U.S.C. 77a et seq.)
Short title, see 15 U.S.C. 77a

Securities Acts Amendments of 1975
Pub. L. 94–29, June 4, 1975, 89 Stat. 97
Short title, see 15 U.S.C. 78a note

Securities Acts Amendments of 1990
Pub. L. 101–550, Nov. 15, 1990, 104 Stat. 2713
Short title, see 15 U.S.C. 78a note

Securities and Exchange Commission Authorization Act of 1987
Pub. L. 100–181, Dec. 4, 1987, 101 Stat. 1249
Short title, see 15 U.S.C. 78a note

Securities and Exchange Commission Authorization Act of 1990
Pub. L. 101–550, title I, Nov. 15, 1990, 104 Stat. 2713
Short title, see 15 U.S.C. 78a note

Securities and Exchange Commission Authorization Act of 1996
Pub. L. 104–290, title IV, Oct. 11, 1996, 110 Stat. 3441
Short title, see 15 U.S.C. 78a note

Securities Enforcement Remedies and Penny Stock Reform Act of 1990
Pub. L. 101–429, Oct. 15, 1990, 104 Stat. 931
Short title, see 15 U.S.C. 78a note

Securities Exchange Act of 1934
June 6, 1934, ch. 404, 48 Stat. 881 (15 U.S.C. 78a et seq.)
Short title, see 15 U.S.C. 78a

Securities Investor Protection Act Amendments of 1978
Pub. L. 95–283, May 21, 1978, 92 Stat. 249
Short title, see 15 U.S.C. 78aaa note

Securities Investor Protection Act of 1970
Pub. L. 91–598, Dec. 30, 1970, 84 Stat. 1636 (15 U.S.C. 78aaa et seq.)
Short title, see 15 U.S.C. 78aaa note

Securities Litigation Uniform Standards Act of 1998
Pub. L. 105–353, Nov. 3, 1998, 112 Stat. 3227
Short title, see 15 U.S.C. 78a note

Security Assistance Act of 1999
Pub. L. 106–113, div. B, §1000(a)(7) [div. B, title XII], Nov. 29, 1999, 113 Stat. 1536, 1501A–497
Short title, see 22 U.S.C. 2151 note

Security Assistance Act of 2000
Pub. L. 106–280, Oct. 6, 2000, 114 Stat. 845
Short title, see 22 U.S.C. 2151 note

Sedition Act
July 14, 1798, ch. 74, 1 Stat. 596

Seed and Feed Loan Act
Apr. 26, 1924, ch. 132, 43 Stat. 110

Seed Grain Loan Act
Mar. 20, 1922, ch. 109, 42 Stat. 467

"Seeing-Eye" Dogs on Railroads Act
July 5, 1937, ch. 432, 50 Stat. 475

Selective Draft Act
May 18, 1917, ch. 15, 40 Stat. 76

Selective Service Act of 1948
Renamed Military Selective Service Act

Selective Service Amendment Act of 1969
Pub. L. 91–124, Nov. 26, 1969, 83 Stat. 220
Short title, see 50 App. U.S.C. 451 note

Selective Service Extension Act of 1950
June 30, 1950, ch. 445, 64 Stat. 318
Short title, see 50 App. U.S.C. 451 note

Selective Training and Service Act of 1940
Sept. 16, 1940, ch. 720, 54 Stat. 885 (50 App. U.S.C. 301 et seq.)

Self-Employed Individuals Tax Retirement Act of 1962
Pub. L. 87–792, Oct. 10, 1962, 76 Stat. 809
Short title, see 26 U.S.C. 401 note

Self-Employment Contributions Act of 1954
Aug. 16, 1954, ch. 736, 68A Stat. 353 (26 U.S.C. 1401 et seq.)
Short title, see 26 U.S.C. 1403(a)

Selma to Montgomery National Trail Study Act of 1989
Pub. L. 101–321, July 3, 1990, 104 Stat. 293
Short title, see 16 U.S.C. 1241 note

Semiconductor Chip Protection Act of 1984
Pub. L. 98–620, title III, Nov. 8, 1984, 98 Stat. 3347 (17 U.S.C. 901 et seq.)
Short title, see 17 U.S.C. 101 note

Semiconductor International Protection Extension Act of 1991
Pub. L. 102–64, June 28, 1991, 105 Stat. 320
Short title, see 17 U.S.C. 101 note

Seminole Indian Land Claims Settlement Act of 1987
Pub. L. 100–228, Dec. 31, 1987, 101 Stat. 1556 (25 U.S.C. 1772 et seq.)
Short title, see 25 U.S.C. 1772 note

Seminole Original Agreement
July 1, 1898, ch. 542, 30 Stat. 567

Seminole Supplemental Agreement
June 2, 1900, ch. 610, 31 Stat. 250

Semipostal Authorization Act
Pub. L. 106–253, July 28, 2000, 114 Stat. 634
Short title, see 39 U.S.C. 101 note

Senators' Election Act
July 25, 1866, ch. 245, 14 Stat. 243; R.S. §§14–19 (2 U.S.C. 1a et seq.)

Seneca Nation Settlement Act of 1990
Pub. L. 101–503, Nov. 3, 1990, 104 Stat. 1292 (25 U.S.C. 1774 et seq.)
Short title, see 25 U.S.C. 1774 note

Senior Citizens Against Marketing Scams Act of 1994
Pub. L. 103–322, title XXV, Sept. 13, 1994, 108 Stat. 2081 (18 U.S.C. 2325 et seq.)
Short title, see 18 U.S.C. 2325 note

Senior Citizens Housing Act of 1962
Pub. L. 87–723, Sept. 28, 1962, 76 Stat. 670
Short title, see 12 U.S.C. 1701 note

Senior Citizens' Freedom to Work Act of 2000
Pub. L. 106–182, Apr. 7, 2000, 114 Stat. 198
Short title, see 42 U.S.C. 1305 note

Senior Citizens' Right to Work Act of 1996
Pub. L. 104–121, title I, Mar. 29, 1996, 110 Stat. 847
Short title, see 42 U.S.C. 1305 note

Senior Executive Service Improvements Act
Pub. L. 102–175, Dec. 2, 1991, 105 Stat. 1222
Short title, see 5 U.S.C. 3301 note

Seniority Act for Rural Mail Carriers
May 18, 1948, ch. 298, 62 Stat. 236

Sentencing Act of 1987
Pub. L. 100–182, Dec. 7, 1987, 101 Stat. 1266
Short title, see 18 U.S.C. 3551 note

Sentencing Guidelines Act of 1986
Pub. L. 99–363, July 11, 1986, 100 Stat. 770
Short title, see 28 U.S.C. 1 note

Sentencing Reform Act of 1984
Pub. L. 98–473, title II, ch. II (§211 et seq.), Oct. 12, 1984, 98 Stat. 1987
Short title, see 18 U.S.C. 3551 note

Sentencing Reform Amendments Act of 1985
Pub. L. 99–217, Dec. 26, 1985, 99 Stat. 1728
Short title, see 18 U.S.C. 3551 note

Serve-America: The Community Service, Schools and Service-Learning Act of 1990
Pub. L. 101–610, title I, subtitle B (§110 et seq.), Nov. 16, 1990, 104 Stat. 3132 (42 U.S.C. 12521 et seq.)
Short title, see 42 U.S.C. 12501 note

Service Contract Act of 1965
Pub. L. 89–286, Oct. 22, 1965, 79 Stat. 1034 (41 U.S.C. 351 et seq.)
Short title, see 41 U.S.C. 351 note

Service Extension Act of 1941
Aug. 18, 1941, ch. 362, 55 Stat. 626

Service Flag and Button
Oct. 17, 1942, ch. 615, 56 Stat. 796

Service Members Occupational Conversion and Training Act of 1992
Pub. L. 102–484, div. D, title XLIV, subtitle G (§4481 et seq.), Oct. 23, 1992, 106 Stat. 2757 (10 U.S.C. 1143 note)

Servicemen's and Veterans' Survivor Benefits Act
Aug. 1, 1956, ch. 837, 70 Stat. 857

Servicemen's Dependents Allowance Act of 1942
June 23, 1942, ch. 443, 56 Stat. 381

Servicemen's Indemnity Act of 1951
Apr. 25, 1951, ch. 39, part I (§1 et seq.), 65 Stat. 33

Servicemen's Readjustment Act of 1944
June 22, 1944, ch. 268, 58 Stat. 284

Settlement of Mexican Claims Act Amendments of 1945
Apr. 3, 1945, ch. 52, 59 Stat. 49

Settlement of Mexican Claims Act of 1942
Dec. 18, 1942, ch. 766, 56 Stat. 1058

Settlement of War Claims Act of 1928
Mar. 10, 1928, ch. 167, 45 Stat. 254

Seven Crimes Act
Mar. 3, 1885, ch. 341, §9, 23 Stat. 385

Seventh Supplemental National Defense Appropriation Act, 1942
June 23, 1942, ch. 444, 56 Stat. 387

Sex Crimes Against Children Prevention Act of 1995
Pub. L. 104–71, Dec. 23, 1995, 109 Stat. 774 (28 U.S.C. 994 note)

Sexual Abuse Act of 1986
Pub. L. 99–646, §87, Nov. 10, 1986, 100 Stat. 3620, and Pub. L. 99–654, Nov. 14, 1986, 100 Stat. 3660 (18 U.S.C. 2241 et seq.)
Short title, see 18 U.S.C. 2241 note

Shackleford Act
July 11, 1916, ch. 241, 39 Stat. 355

Shareholder Communications Act of 1985
Pub. L. 99–222, Dec. 28, 1985, 99 Stat. 1737
Short title, see 15 U.S.C. 78a note

Shareholder Communications Improvement Act of 1990
Pub. L. 101–550, title III, Nov. 15, 1990, 104 Stat. 2721
Short title, see 15 U.S.C. 78a note

Shark Finning Prohibition Act
Pub. L. 106–557, Dec. 21, 2000, 114 Stat. 2772 (16 U.S.C. 1822 note)

Shawnee Tribe Status Act of 2000
Pub. L. 106–568, title VII, Dec. 27, 2000, 114 Stat. 2913 (25 U.S.C. 1041 et seq.)
Short title, see 25 U.S.C. 1041 note

Sheep Promotion, Research, and Information Act of 1994
Pub. L. 103–407, Oct. 22, 1994, 108 Stat. 4210 (7 U.S.C. 7101 et seq.)
Short title, see 7 U.S.C. 7101 note

Shenandoah National Park Act
May 22, 1926, ch. 363, 44 Stat. 616 (16 U.S.C. 403 et seq.)

Shenandoah Valley Battlefields National Historic District and Commission Act of 1996
Pub. L. 104–333, div. I, title VI, §606, Nov. 12, 1996, 110 Stat. 4174 (16 U.S.C. 461 note)

Sheppard Air Corps Cadet Act
See Army Aviation Cadet Act

Sheppard Bone-Dry Law in District of Columbia
Mar. 3, 1917, ch. 165, 39 Stat. 1123

Sheppard-Towner Act (Maternity Hygiene)
See Maternity Act

Sherley Amendment (Food and Drugs)
Aug. 23, 1912, ch. 352, 37 Stat. 416

Sherman Act
July 2, 1890, ch. 647, 26 Stat. 209 (15 U.S.C. 1 et seq.)
Short title, see 15 U.S.C. 1 note

Sherman Purchase of Silver Act of July 14, 1890
July 14, 1890, ch. 708, 26 Stat. 289

Sherwood Act (Mexican, Civil War Pensions)
May 11, 1912, ch. 123, 37 Stat. 112

Ship Load Line Act
See Coastwise Load Line Act, 1935

Ship Mortgage Act, 1920
June 5, 1920, ch. 250, §30, 41 Stat. 1000

Ship Seizure Bill
June 6, 1941, ch. 174, 55 Stat. 242 (50 App. 1271 et seq.)

Ship Subsidies Act
See Merchant Marine Act, 1936

Shipbuilding Act
May 10, 1892, ch. 63, 27 Stat. 27

Shipping Act Amendments of 1979
Pub. L. 96–25, June 19, 1979, 93 Stat. 71
Short title, see 46 App. U.S.C. 842 note

Shipping Act of 1984
Pub. L. 98–237, Mar. 20, 1984, 98 Stat. 67 (46 App. U.S.C. 1701 et seq.)
Short title, see 46 App. U.S.C. 1701 note

Shipping Act, 1916
Sept. 7, 1916, ch. 451, 39 Stat. 728 (46 App. U.S.C. 801 et seq.)
Short title, see 46 App. U.S.C. 842

Shipstead-Nolan Act
July 10, 1930, ch. 881, 46 Stat. 1020 (16 U.S.C. 577 et seq.)
Short title, see 16 U.S.C. 577 note

Shirley Temple Act (Child Labor)
June 25, 1938, ch. 676, §13(c), 52 Stat. 1068 (29 U.S.C. 213(c))

Shivwits Band of the Paiute Indian Tribe of Utah Water Rights Settlement Act
Pub. L. 106–263, Aug. 18, 2000, 114 Stat. 737

Shoalwater Bay Indian Tribe—Dexter-by-the-Sea Claim Settlement Act
Pub. L. 98–432, Sept. 28, 1984, 98 Stat. 1671

Shore Line Erosion Protection Act (Public Property)
Pub. L. 89–298, title III, §310(b), Oct. 27, 1965, 79 Stat. 1095

Shore Protection Act of 1988
Pub. L. 100–688, title IV, Nov. 18, 1988, 102 Stat. 4154 (33 U.S.C. 2601 et seq.)
Short title, see 33 U.S.C. 2601 note

Shoreline Erosion Control Demonstration Act of 1974
Pub. L. 93–251, title I, §54, Mar. 7, 1974, 88 Stat. 26 (42 U.S.C. 1962d–5 note)

Sick Leave Act
See Federal Sick Leave Act

Signal Inspection Act (Railroads)
Feb. 4, 1887, ch. 104, part I, §25, formerly §26, as added Feb. 28, 1920, ch. 91, title IV, §441, 41 Stat. 498

Sikes Act
Pub. L. 86–797, Sept. 15, 1960, 74 Stat. 1052 (16 U.S.C. 670 et seq.)
Short title, see 16 U.S.C. 670 note

Sikes Act Amendments of 1978
Pub. L. 95–420, Oct. 5, 1978, 92 Stat. 921
Short title, see 16 U.S.C. 670 note

Sikes Act Improvement Act of 1997
Pub. L. 105–85, div. B, title XXIX, Nov. 18, 1997, 111 Stat. 2016
Short title, see 16 U.S.C. 670 note

Siletz Indian Tribe Restoration Act
Pub. L. 95–195, Nov. 18, 1977, 91 Stat. 1415 (25 U.S.C. 711 et seq.)
Short title, see 25 U.S.C. 711 note

Silk Road Strategy Act of 1999
Pub. L. 106–113, div. B, §1000(a)(2) [title V, §596], Nov. 29, 1999, 113 Stat. 1535, 1501A–123
Short title, see 22 U.S.C. 2151 note

Sills Act (Pensions, Spanish War, Philippine Insurrection, China Relief Expedition)
June 5, 1920, ch. 245, 41 Stat. 982

Silver Coin Issue Resolution
July 22, 1876, No. 17, 19 Stat. 215

Silver Coin Proof Sets Act
Pub. L. 101–585, Nov. 15, 1990, 104 Stat. 2874
Short title, see 31 U.S.C. 5101 note

Silver Purchase Act of 1934
June 19, 1934, ch. 674, 48 Stat. 1178

Silvio O. Conte National Fish and Wildlife Refuge Act
Pub. L. 102–212, Dec. 11, 1991, 105 Stat. 1655 (16 U.S.C. 668dd note)

Single Audit Act Amendments of 1996
Pub. L. 104–156, July 5, 1996, 110 Stat. 1396
Short title, see 31 U.S.C. 7501 note

Single Audit Act of 1984
Pub. L. 98–502, Oct. 19, 1984, 98 Stat. 2327 (31 U.S.C. 7501 et seq.)
Short title, see 31 U.S.C. 7501 note

Single Family Mortgage Foreclosure Act of 1994
Pub. L. 103–327, title II [S. 2881, title VIII], Sept. 28, 1994, 108 Stat. 2316 (12 U.S.C. 3751 et seq.)
Short title, see 12 U.S.C. 3751 note

Single-Employer Pension Plan Amendments Act of 1986
Pub. L. 99–272, title XI, Apr. 7, 1986, 100 Stat. 237
Short title, see 29 U.S.C. 1001 note

Sipsey Wild and Scenic River and Alabama Addition Act of 1988
Pub. L. 100–547, Oct. 28, 1988, 102 Stat. 2736
Short title, see 16 U.S.C. 1271 note

Sitka National Cemetery Transfer Act of 1983
Pub. L. 98–63, title I, §§1–3, July 30, 1983, 97 Stat. 322, 323

Sixteen Hour Law (Railroads)
See Hours of Service Act (Railroads)

Sixth Supplemental National Defense Appropriation Act, 1942
Apr. 28, 1942, ch. 247, 56 Stat. 226

Slave Trade Abolishment Act (District of Columbia)
Sept. 20, 1850, ch. 63, 9 Stat. 467

Slave Trade Prohibition Act
Mar. 2, 1807, ch. 22, 2 Stat. 426

Small Business Access to Surety Bonding Survey Act of 1992
Pub. L. 102–366, title III, subtitle A (§301 et seq.), Sept. 4, 1992, 106 Stat. 1002 (15 U.S.C. 694b note)

Small Business Act
Pub. L. 85–536, July 18, 1958, 72 Stat. 384 (15 U.S.C. 631 et seq.)
Short title, see 15 U.S.C. 631 note

Small Business Act Amendments of 1961
Pub. L. 87–305, Sept. 26, 1961, 75 Stat. 666
Short title, see 15 U.S.C. 631 note

Small Business Act Amendments of 1967
Pub. L. 90–104, title I, Oct. 11, 1967, 81 Stat. 268
Short title, see 15 U.S.C. 631 note

Small Business Administration Reauthorization and Amendment Act of 1988
Pub. L. 100–590, Nov. 3, 1988, 102 Stat. 2989
Short title, see 15 U.S.C. 631 note

Small Business Administration Reauthorization and Amendments Act of 1990
Pub. L. 101–574, Nov. 15, 1990, 104 Stat. 2814
Short title, see 15 U.S.C. 631 note

Small Business Administration Reauthorization and Amendments Act of 1994
Pub. L. 103–403, Oct. 22, 1994, 108 Stat. 4175
Short title, see 15 U.S.C. 631 note

Small Business Amendments of 1974
Pub. L. 93–386, Aug. 23, 1974, 88 Stat. 742
Short title, see 15 U.S.C. 631 note

Small Business and Federal Procurement Competition Enhancement Act of 1984
Pub. L. 98–577, Oct. 30, 1984, 98 Stat. 3066
Short title, see 41 U.S.C. 251 note

Small Business Budget Reconciliation and Loan Consolidation/Improvement Act of 1981
Pub. L. 97–35, title XIX, Aug. 13, 1981, 95 Stat. 767
Short title, see 15 U.S.C. 631 note

Small Business Competitiveness Demonstration Program Act of 1988
Pub. L. 100–656, title VII, Nov. 15, 1988, 102 Stat. 3889 (15 U.S.C. 644 note)

Small Business Computer Security and Education Act of 1984
Pub. L. 98–362, July 16, 1984, 98 Stat. 431
Short title, see 15 U.S.C. 631 note

Small Business Credit and Business Opportunity Enhancement Act of 1992
Pub. L. 102–366, Sept. 4, 1992, 106 Stat. 986
Short title, see 15 U.S.C. 631 note

Small Business Credit Crunch Relief Act of 1992
Pub. L. 102–366, title I, subtitle A (§101 et seq.), Sept. 4, 1992, 106 Stat. 987
Short title, see 15 U.S.C. 631 note

Small Business Development Center Act of 1980
Pub. L. 96–302, title II, July 2, 1980, 94 Stat. 843
Short title, see 15 U.S.C. 631 note

Small Business Development Center Improvement Act of 1984
Pub. L. 98–395, Aug. 21, 1984, 98 Stat. 1366
Short title, see 15 U.S.C. 631 note

Small Business Economic Policy Act of 1980
Pub. L. 96–302, title III, July 2, 1980, 94 Stat. 848
Short title, see 15 U.S.C. 631 note

Small Business Emergency Relief Act
Pub. L. 94–190, Dec. 31, 1975, 89 Stat. 1095 (41 U.S.C. 252 note)

Small Business Employee Ownership Act of 1980
Pub. L. 96–302, title V, July 2, 1980, 94 Stat. 850
Short title, see 15 U.S.C. 631 note

Small Business Energy Loan Act
Pub. L. 95–315, July 4, 1978, 92 Stat. 377
Short title, see 15 U.S.C. 631 note

Small Business Equity Enhancement Act of 1992
Pub. L. 102–366, title IV, Sept. 4, 1992, 106 Stat. 1007
Short title, see 15 U.S.C. 661 note

Small Business Export Expansion Act of 1980
Pub. L. 96–481, title I, part B (§110 et seq.), Oct. 21, 1980, 94 Stat. 2323
Short title, see 15 U.S.C. 631 note

Small Business Guaranteed Credit Enhancement Act of 1993
Pub. L. 103–81, Aug. 13, 1993, 107 Stat. 780
Short title, see 15 U.S.C. 631 note

Small Business Innovation Development Act of 1982
Pub. L. 97–219, July 22, 1982, 96 Stat. 217
Short title, see 15 U.S.C. 631 note

Small Business Innovation Research Program Reauthorization Act of 1992
Pub. L. 102–564, title I, Oct. 28, 1992, 106 Stat. 4249
Short title, see 15 U.S.C. 631 note

Small Business Innovation Research Program Reauthorization Act of 2000
Pub. L. 106–554, §1(a)(9) [title I], Dec. 21, 2000, 114 Stat. 2763, 2763A–668
Short title, see 15 U.S.C. 631 note

Small Business International Trade and Competitiveness Act
Pub. L. 100–418, title VIII, Aug. 23, 1988, 102 Stat. 1553
Short title, see 15 U.S.C. 631 note

Small Business Investment Act Amendments of 1960
Pub. L. 86–502, June 11, 1960, 74 Stat. 196
Short title, see 15 U.S.C. 661 note

Small Business Investment Act Amendments of 1961
Pub. L. 87–341, Oct. 3, 1961, 75 Stat. 752
Short title, see 15 U.S.C. 661 note

Small Business Investment Act Amendments of 1963
Pub. L. 88–273, Feb. 28, 1964, 78 Stat. 146
Short title, see 15 U.S.C. 661 note

Small Business Investment Act Amendments of 1966
Pub. L. 89–779, Nov. 6, 1966, 80 Stat. 1359
Short title, see 15 U.S.C. 661 note

Small Business Investment Act Amendments of 1967
Pub. L. 90–104, title II, Oct. 11, 1967, 81 Stat. 269
Short title, see 15 U.S.C. 661 note

Small Business Investment Act Amendments of 1972
Pub. L. 92–595, Oct. 27, 1972, 86 Stat. 1314
Short title, see 15 U.S.C. 661 note

Small Business Investment Act of 1958
Pub. L. 85–699, Aug. 21, 1958, 72 Stat. 689 (15 U.S.C. 661 et seq.)
Short title, see 15 U.S.C. 661 note

Small Business Investment Corrections Act of 2000
Pub. L. 106–554, §1(a)(9) [title IV], Dec. 21, 2000, 114 Stat. 2763, 2763A–690
Short title, see 15 U.S.C. 661 note

Small Business Investment Improvement Act of 1999
Pub. L. 106–9, Apr. 5, 1999, 113 Stat. 17
Short title, see 15 U.S.C. 661 note

Small Business Investment Incentive Act of 1980
Pub. L. 96–477, Oct. 21, 1980, 94 Stat. 2275
Short title, see 15 U.S.C. 80a–51 note

Small Business Issuers' Simplification Act of 1980
Pub. L. 96–477, title VI, Oct. 21, 1980, 94 Stat. 2294
Short title, see 15 U.S.C. 77a note

Small Business Job Protection Act of 1996
Pub. L. 104–188, Aug. 20, 1996, 110 Stat. 1755
Short title, see 26 U.S.C. 1 note

Small Business Lending Enhancement Act of 1995
Pub. L. 104–36, Oct. 12, 1995, 109 Stat. 295
Short title, see 15 U.S.C. 631 note

Small Business Loan Improvement Act of 2000
Pub. L. 106–554, §1(a)(9) [title II], Dec. 21, 2000, 114 Stat. 2763, 2763A–681
Short title, see 15 U.S.C. 631 note

Small Business Loan Securitization and Secondary Market Enhancement Act of 1994
Pub. L. 103–325, title II, subtitle A (§201 et seq.), Sept. 23, 1994, 108 Stat. 2198
Short title, see 15 U.S.C. 78a note

Small Business Mobilization Law
June 11, 1942, ch. 404, 56 Stat. 351

Small Business Prepayment Penalty Relief Act of 1994
Pub. L. 103–403, title V, Oct. 22, 1994, 108 Stat. 4198
Short title, see 15 U.S.C. 661 note

Small Business Programs Improvement Act of 1996
Pub. L. 104–208, div. D, Sept. 30, 1996, 110 Stat. 3009–724
Short title, see 15 U.S.C. 631 note

Small Business Programs Reauthorization Act of 2000
Pub. L. 106–554, §1(a)(9) [title V], Dec. 21, 2000, 114 Stat. 2763, 2763A–691
Short title, see 15 U.S.C. 631 note

Small Business Protection Act of 1967
Pub. L. 90–104, title III, Oct. 11, 1967, 81 Stat. 272 (15 U.S.C. 634 note)

Small Business Reauthorization Act of 1997
Pub. L. 105–135, Dec. 2, 1997, 111 Stat. 2592
Short title, see 15 U.S.C. 631 note

Small Business Reauthorization Act of 2000
Pub. L. 106–554, §1(a)(9), Dec. 21, 2000, 114 Stat. 2763, 2763A–667
Short title, see 15 U.S.C. 631 note

Small Business Regulatory Enforcement Fairness Act of 1996
Pub. L. 104–121, title II, Mar. 29, 1996, 110 Stat. 857 (5 U.S.C. 601 note)

Small Business Research and Development Enhancement Act of 1992
Pub. L. 102–564, Oct. 28, 1992, 106 Stat. 4249
Short title, see 15 U.S.C. 631 note

Small Business Secondary Market Improvements Act of 1984
Pub. L. 98–352, July 10, 1984, 98 Stat. 329
Short title, see 15 U.S.C. 631 note

Small Business Tax Revision Act of 1958
Pub. L. 85–866, title II, Sept. 2, 1958, 72 Stat. 1676
Short title, see 26 U.S.C. 1 note

Small Business Technology Transfer Act of 1992
Pub. L. 102–564, title II, Oct. 28, 1992, 106 Stat. 4256
Short title, see 15 U.S.C. 631 note

Small Business Year 2000 Readiness Act
Pub. L. 106–8, Apr. 2, 1999, 113 Stat. 13
Short title, see 15 U.S.C. 631 note

Small Reclamation Projects Act of 1956
Aug. 6, 1956, ch. 972, 70 Stat. 1044 (43 U.S.C. 422a et seq.)
Short title, see 43 U.S.C. 422k

Small Tract Act of 1938
June 1, 1938, ch. 317, 52 Stat. 609 (43 U.S.C. 682a et seq.)

Small Tract Act of 1983
See Small Tracts Act

Small Tracts Act
Pub. L. 97–465, Jan. 12, 1983, 96 Stat. 2535 (16 U.S.C. 521c et seq.)

Smaller War Plants Corporation
June 11, 1942, ch. 404, §4, 56 Stat. 353

Smith Act (Reclamation and Irrigation)
Aug. 11, 1916, ch. 319, 39 Stat. 506 (43 U.S.C. 621 et seq.)

Smith Act of 1940
June 28, 1940, ch. 439, title I, 54 Stat. 670

Smith River National Recreation Area Act
Pub. L. 101–612, §§1–14, Nov. 16, 1990, 104 Stat. 3209–3222 (16 U.S.C. 460bbb et seq.)
Short title, see 16 U.S.C. 460bbb note

Smith-Connally Anti-Strike Act
See War Labor Disputes Act

Smith-Hughes Vocational Education Act
Feb. 23, 1917, ch. 114, 39 Stat. 929 (20 U.S.C. 11 et seq.)
Short title, see 20 U.S.C. 11 note

Smith-Lever Act
May 8, 1914, ch. 79, 38 Stat. 372 (7 U.S.C. 341 et seq.)
Short title, see 7 U.S.C. 341 note

Smith-Sears Act
June 27, 1918, ch. 107, 40 Stat. 617

Smithsonian Institution Sesquicentennial Commemorative Coin Act of 1995
Pub. L. 104–96, Jan. 10, 1996, 109 Stat. 981 (31 U.S.C. 5112 note)

Smoot-Burton Act (British War Debt)
Feb. 28, 1923, ch. 146, 42 Stat. 1325

Smoot-Hawley Act
See Tariff Act of 1930

Snoqualmie National Forest Boundary Adjustment Act of 1996
Pub. L. 104–208, div. A, title I, §101(d) [title III, §325], Sept. 30, 1996, 110 Stat. 3009–181, 3009–226

Snyder Act (Indian Affairs Bureau)
Nov. 2, 1921, ch. 115, 42 Stat. 208 (25 U.S.C. 13)
Short title, see 25 U.S.C. 13 note

Social Security Act
Aug. 14, 1935, ch. 531, 49 Stat. 620 (42 U.S.C. 301 et seq.)
Short title, see 42 U.S.C. 1305

Social Security Act Amendments of 1939
Aug. 10, 1939, ch. 666, 53 Stat. 1360

Social Security Act Amendments of 1946
Aug. 10, 1946, ch. 951, 60 Stat. 978

Social Security Act Amendments of 1947
Aug. 6, 1947, ch. 510, 61 Stat. 793

Social Security Act Amendments of 1950
Aug. 28, 1950, ch. 809, 64 Stat. 477
Short title, see 42 U.S.C. 1305 note

Social Security Act Amendments of 1952
July 18, 1952, ch. 945, 66 Stat. 767
Short title, see 42 U.S.C. 1305 note

Social Security Act Amendments of 1994
Pub. L. 103–432, Oct. 31, 1994, 108 Stat. 4398
Short title, see 42 U.S.C. 1305 note

Social Security Amendments of 1954
Sept. 1, 1954, ch. 1206, 68 Stat. 1052

Social Security Amendments of 1956
Aug. 1, 1956, ch. 836, 70 Stat. 807
Short title, see 42 U.S.C. 1305 note

Social Security Amendments of 1958
Pub. L. 85–840, Aug. 28, 1958, 72 Stat. 1013
Short title, see 42 U.S.C. 1305 note

Social Security Amendments of 1960
Pub. L. 86–778, Sept. 13, 1960, 74 Stat. 924

Social Security Amendments of 1960—Continued
Short title, see 42 U.S.C. 1305 note

Social Security Amendments of 1961
Pub. L. 87–64, June 30, 1961, 75 Stat. 131
Short title, see 42 U.S.C. 1305 note

Social Security Amendments of 1965
Pub. L. 89–97, July 30, 1965, 79 Stat. 286
Short title, see 42 U.S.C. 1305 note

Social Security Amendments of 1967
Pub. L. 90–248, Jan. 2, 1968, 81 Stat. 821
Short title, see 42 U.S.C. 1305 note

Social Security Amendments of 1969
Pub. L. 91–172, title X, Dec. 30, 1969, 83 Stat. 737
Short title, see 42 U.S.C. 1305 note

Social Security Amendments of 1972
Pub. L. 92–603, Oct. 30, 1972, 86 Stat. 1329
Short title, see 42 U.S.C. 1305 note

Social Security Amendments of 1974
See Social Services Amendments of 1974

Social Security Amendments of 1977
Pub. L. 95–216, Dec. 20, 1977, 91 Stat. 1509
Short title, see 42 U.S.C. 1305 note

Social Security Amendments of 1983
Pub. L. 98–21, Apr. 20, 1983, 97 Stat. 65
Short title, see 42 U.S.C. 1305 note

Social Security Disability Amendments of 1980
Pub. L. 96–265, June 9, 1980, 94 Stat. 441
Short title, see 42 U.S.C. 1305 note

Social Security Disability Benefits Reform Act of 1984
Pub. L. 98–460, Oct. 9, 1984, 98 Stat. 1794
Short title, see 42 U.S.C. 1305 note

Social Security Domestic Employment Reform Act of 1994
Pub. L. 103–387, Oct. 22, 1994, 108 Stat. 4071
Short title, see 26 U.S.C. 1 note

Social Security Independence and Program Improvements Act of 1994
Pub. L. 103–296, Aug. 15, 1994, 108 Stat. 1464
Short title, see 42 U.S.C. 1305 note

Social Security Number Confidentiality Act of 2000
Pub. L. 106–433, Nov. 6, 2000, 114 Stat. 1910
Short title, see 31 U.S.C. 3301 note

Social Services Amendments of 1974
Pub. L. 93–647, Jan. 4, 1975, 88 Stat. 2337
Short title, see 42 U.S.C. 1305 note

Social Services Block Grant Act
Pub. L. 97–35, title XXIII, subtitle C (§2351 et seq.), Aug. 13, 1981, 95 Stat. 867
Short title, see 42 U.S.C. 1305 note

Sockeye Salmon or Pink Salmon Fishing Act of 1947
July 29, 1947, ch. 345, 61 Stat. 511 (16 U.S.C. 776 et seq.)
Short title, see 16 U.S.C. 776 note

Sodbuster Law
Pub. L. 99–198, title XII, subtitles A–E (§§1201–1245), Dec. 23, 1985, 99 Stat. 1504–1516 (16 U.S.C. 3801 et seq.)
Short title, see 16 U.S.C. 3801 note

Soft Drink Interbrand Competition Act
Pub. L. 96–308, July 9, 1980, 94 Stat. 939 (15 U.S.C. 3501 et seq.)
Short title, see 15 U.S.C. 3501 note

Soil and Water Resources Conservation Act of 1977
Pub. L. 95–192, Nov. 18, 1977, 91 Stat. 1407 (16 U.S.C. 2001 et seq.)
Short title, see 16 U.S.C. 2001 note

Soil Bank Act
May 28, 1956, ch. 327, title I, 70 Stat. 188 (7 U.S.C. 1801 et seq.)

Soil Conservation and Domestic Allotment Act
Apr. 27, 1935, ch. 85, 49 Stat. 163 (16 U.S.C. 590a et seq.)
Short title, see 16 U.S.C. 590q(b)

Soil Erosion Act
See Soil Conservation and Domestic Allotment Act

Solar Energy and Energy Conservation Act of 1980
Pub. L. 96–294, title V, June 30, 1980, 94 Stat. 719
Short title, see 12 U.S.C. 3601 note

Solar Energy and Energy Conservation Bank Act
Pub. L. 96–294, title V, subtitle A (§502 et seq.), June 30, 1980, 94 Stat. 719 (12 U.S.C. 3601 et seq.)
Short title, see 12 U.S.C. 3601 note

Solar Energy Research, Development, and Demonstration Act of 1974
Pub. L. 93–473, Oct. 26, 1974, 88 Stat. 1431 (42 U.S.C. 5551 et seq.)
Short title, see 42 U.S.C. 5501 note

Solar Heating and Cooling Demonstration Act of 1974
Pub. L. 93–409, Sept. 3, 1974, 88 Stat. 1069 (42 U.S.C. 5501 et seq.)
Short title, see 42 U.S.C. 5501 note

Solar Photovoltaic Energy Research, Development, and Demonstration Act of 1978
Pub. L. 95–590, Nov. 4, 1978, 92 Stat. 2513 (42 U.S.C. 5581 et seq.)
Short title, see 42 U.S.C. 5501 note

Solar, Wind, Waste, and Geothermal Power Production Incentives Act of 1990
Pub. L. 101–575, Nov. 15, 1990, 104 Stat. 2834
Short title, see 16 U.S.C. 791a note

Soldier's Vote Act
Sept. 16, 1942, ch. 561, 56 Stat. 753 (50 U.S.C. 301 et seq.)

Soldiers' and Sailors' Civil Relief Act Amendments of 1942
Oct. 6, 1942, ch. 581, 56 Stat. 769
Short title, see 50 App. U.S.C. 501 note

Soldiers' and Sailors' Civil Relief Act Amendments of 1991
Pub. L. 102–12, Mar. 18, 1991, 105 Stat. 34
Short title, see 50 App. U.S.C. 501 note

Soldiers' and Sailors' Civil Relief Act of 1918
Mar. 8, 1918, ch. 20, 40 Stat. 440 (50 App. U.S.C. 101 et seq.)

Soldiers' and Sailors' Civil Relief Act of 1940
Oct. 17, 1940, ch. 888, 54 Stat. 1178 (50 App. U.S.C. 501 et seq.)
Short title, see 50 App. U.S.C. 501

Soldiers' and Sailors' Homestead Act
Apr. 4, 1872, ch. 85, 17 Stat. 49

Soldiers' Bonus Act
See World War Adjusted Compensation Act

Soldiers' Families Freedom Resolution
Mar. 3, 1865, No. 29, 13 Stat. 571

Solid Waste Disposal Act
Pub. L. 89–272, title II, Oct. 20, 1965, 79 Stat. 997 (42 U.S.C. 6901 et seq.)
Short title, see 42 U.S.C. 6901 note

Solid Waste Disposal Act Amendments of 1980
Pub. L. 96–482, Oct. 21, 1980, 94 Stat. 2334
Short title, see 42 U.S.C. 6901 note

Sonny Bono Copyright Term Extension Act
Pub. L. 105–298, title I, Oct. 27, 1998, 112 Stat. 2827
Short title, see 17 U.S.C. 101 note

South African Democratic Transition Support Act of 1993
Pub. L. 103–149, Nov. 23, 1993, 107 Stat. 1503 (22 U.S.C. 5001 note)

South Carolina National Heritage Corridor Act of 1996
Pub. L. 104–333, div. II, title VI, Nov. 12, 1996, 110 Stat. 4260 (16 U.S.C. 461 note)

South Pacific Tuna Act of 1988
Pub. L. 100–330, June 7, 1988, 102 Stat. 591 (16 U.S.C. 973 et seq.)
Short title, see 16 U.S.C. 973 note

South Platte River Compact
Mar. 8, 1926, ch. 46, 44 Stat. 195

Southeast Federal Center Public-Private Development Act of 2000
Pub. L. 106–407, Nov. 1, 2000, 114 Stat. 1758

Southeast Interstate Low-Level Radioactive Waste Compact Amendments Consent Act of 1989
Pub. L. 101–171, Nov. 22, 1989, 103 Stat. 1289

Southern Arizona Water Rights Settlement Act of 1982
Pub. L. 97–293, title III, Oct. 12, 1982, 96 Stat. 1274

Southern Arizona Water Rights Settlement Technical Amendments Act of 1992
Pub. L. 102–497, §8, Oct. 24, 1992, 106 Stat. 3256

Southern California Indian Land Transfer Act
Pub. L. 100–581, title VII, Nov. 1, 1988, 102 Stat. 2946

Southern Nevada Project Act
Pub. L. 89–292, Oct. 22, 1965, 79 Stat. 1068 (43 U.S.C. 616ggg et seq.)

Southern Nevada Public Land Management Act of 1998
Pub. L. 105–263, Oct. 19, 1998, 112 Stat. 2343
Short title, see 31 U.S.C. 6901 note

Southwestern Low-Level Radioactive Waste Disposal Compact Consent Act
Pub. L. 100–712, Nov. 23, 1988, 102 Stat. 4773 (42 U.S.C. 2021d note)

Soviet Nuclear Threat Reduction Act of 1991
Pub. L. 102–228, title II, Dec. 12, 1991, 105 Stat. 1693 (22 U.S.C. 2551 note)

Soviet Scientists Immigration Act of 1992
Pub. L. 102–509, Oct. 24, 1992, 106 Stat. 3316 (8 U.S.C. 1153 note)

Soviet-Eastern European Research and Training Act of 1983
Renamed Research and Training for Eastern Europe and the Independent States of the Former Soviet Union Act of 1983

Soybean Promotion, Research, and Consumer Information Act
Pub. L. 101–624, title XIX, subtitle E (§1965 et seq.), Nov. 28, 1990, 104 Stat. 3881 (7 U.S.C. 6301 et seq.)
Short title, see 7 U.S.C. 6301 note

Space Basis Act (Carriage of Mail by Railroads)
July 28, 1916, ch. 261, 39 Stat. 425

Spanish Colonization Commemorative Act of 1988
Pub. L. 100–559, title IV, Oct. 28, 1988, 102 Stat. 2798

Spanish Peaks Wilderness Act of 2000
Pub. L. 106–456, Nov. 7, 2000, 114 Stat. 1955

Spanish War Claims Act
Mar. 2, 1901, ch. 800, 31 Stat. 877

Spanish War Tax Act (Reduction)
Mar. 2, 1901, ch. 806, 31 Stat. 938

Spanish-American Peace Treaty Proclamation
Dec. 10, 1898, 30 Stat. 1754

Spark M. Matsunaga Hydrogen Research, Development, and Demonstration Act of 1990
Pub. L. 101–566, Nov. 15, 1990, 104 Stat. 2797 (42 U.S.C. 12401 et seq.)
Short title, see 42 U.S.C. 12401 note

"SPARS" Act
Feb. 19, 1941, ch. 8, title IV, as added Nov. 23, 1942, ch. 639, §1, 56 Stat. 1020

Special Central American Assistance Act of 1979
Pub. L. 96–257, May 31, 1980, 94 Stat. 422
Short title, see 22 U.S.C. 2151 note

Special Drawing Rights Act
Pub. L. 90–349, June 19, 1968, 82 Stat. 188 (22 U.S.C. 286n et seq.)
Short title, see 22 U.S.C. 286n note

Special Energy Research and Development Appropriation Act, 1975
Pub. L. 93–322, June 30, 1974, 88 Stat. 276

Special Foreign Assistance Act of 1971
Pub. L. 91–652, Jan. 5, 1971, 84 Stat. 1942
Short title, see 22 U.S.C. 2151 note

Special Foreign Assistance Act of 1986
Pub. L. 99–529, Oct. 24, 1986, 100 Stat. 3010
Short title, see 22 U.S.C. 2151 note

Special Health Revenue Sharing Act of 1975
Pub. L. 94–63, title I, July 29, 1975, 89 Stat. 304
Short title, see 42 U.S.C. 201 note

Special International Security Assistance Act of 1979
Pub. L. 96–35, July 20, 1979, 93 Stat. 89 (22 U.S.C. 3401 et seq.)
Short title, see 22 U.S.C. 3401 note

Special Laws Prohibition Act (Territories)
July 30, 1886, ch. 818, 24 Stat. 170 (48 U.S.C. 1471 et seq.)

Special Projects Act
July 26, 1954, ch. 576, as added Pub. L. 93–380, title IV, §402(a)(1), Aug. 21, 1974, 88 Stat. 544 (20 U.S.C. 1851 et seq.)

Specie Payment Resumption Act
Jan. 14, 1875, ch. 15, 18 Stat. 296

Speedy Trial Act Amendments Act of 1979
Pub. L. 96–43, Aug. 2, 1979, 93 Stat. 327
Short title, see 18 U.S.C. 3161 note

Speedy Trial Act of 1974
Pub. L. 93–619, Jan. 3, 1975, 88 Stat. 2076 (18 U.S.C. 3161 et seq.)
Short title, see 18 U.S.C. 3161 note

Spence Act (Savings and Loan Holding Companies)
Pub. L. 86–374, Sept. 23, 1959, 73 Stat. 691

Spending Reduction Act of 1984
Pub. L. 98–369, div. B, July 18, 1984, 98 Stat. 1057

Spoils of War Act of 1994
Pub. L. 103–236, title V, part B (§551 et seq.), Apr. 30, 1994, 108 Stat. 482 (50 U.S.C. 2201 et seq.)
Short title, see 50 U.S.C. 2201 note

Sponge Act
Aug. 15, 1914, ch. 253, 38 Stat. 692 (16 U.S.C. 781 et seq.)

Spooner Act (Panama Canal)
June 28, 1902, ch. 1302, 32 Stat. 481

Sportfishing and Boating Safety Act of 1998
Pub. L. 105–178, title VII, subtitle D (§7401 et seq.), June 9, 1998, 112 Stat. 482
Short title, see 16 U.S.C. 777 note

Spring Mountains National Recreation Area Act
Pub. L. 103–63, Aug. 4, 1993, 107 Stat. 297 (16 U.S.C. 460hhh et seq.)
Short title, see 16 U.S.C. 460hhh note

Springer Act
See Special Laws Prohibition Act (Territories)

Spruce Knob-Seneca Rocks National Recreation Area Act
Pub. L. 89–207, Sept. 28, 1965, 79 Stat. 843 (16 U.S.C. 460p et seq.)

Stabilization Act of 1942
Oct. 2, 1942, ch. 578, 56 Stat. 765 (50 App. U.S.C. 961 et seq.)

Stabilization Extension Act of 1944
June 30, 1944, ch. 325, 58 Stat. 632

Stabilization Fund-Dollar Devaluation Act
See Gold Reserve Act of 1934

Stagecoach Reservoir Project Act of 1994
Pub. L. 103–434, title X, Oct. 31, 1994, 108 Stat. 4547

Staggers Rail Act of 1980
Pub. L. 96–448, Oct. 14, 1980, 94 Stat. 1895
Short title, see 49 U.S.C. 10101 note

Stamp Out Breast Cancer Act
Pub. L. 105–41, Aug. 13, 1997, 111 Stat. 1119
Short title, see 39 U.S.C. 101 note

Stamp Payments Act
July 17, 1862, ch. 196, 12 Stat. 592; R.S. §3583

Standard Barrel Act (Apple Barrels)
Aug. 3, 1912, ch. 273, 37 Stat. 250

Standard Barrel Act (Fruits, Vegetables, etc.)
Mar. 4, 1915, ch. 158, 38 Stat. 1186 (15 U.S.C. 234 et seq.)

Standard Barrel Act (Lime Barrels)
Aug. 23, 1916, ch. 396, 39 Stat. 530 (15 U.S.C. 237 et seq.)

Standard Baskets Act
Aug. 31, 1916, ch. 426, 39 Stat. 673 (15 U.S.C. 251 et seq.)

Standard Reference Data Act
Pub. L. 90–396, July 11, 1968, 82 Stat. 339 (15 U.S.C. 290 et seq.)
Short title, see 15 U.S.C. 290 note

Star Schools Act
Pub. L. 89–10, title III, part B (§3201 et seq.), as added Pub. L. 103–382, title I, §101, Oct. 20, 1994, 108 Stat. 3654 (20 U.S.C. 6891 et seq.)
Short title, see 20 U.S.C. 6891

Star Schools Program Assistance Act
Pub. L. 98–377, title IX, as added Pub. L. 100–297, title II, §2302, Apr. 28, 1988, 102 Stat. 320 (20 U.S.C. 4081 et seq.)
Short title, see 20 U.S.C. 4081 note

Star-Spangled Banner National Historic Trail Study Act of 1999
Pub. L. 106–135, Dec. 7, 1999, 113 Stat. 1685
Short title, see 16 U.S.C. 1241 note

State and Local Fiscal Assistance Act Amendments of 1980
Pub. L. 96–604, Dec. 28, 1980, 94 Stat. 3516

State and Local Fiscal Assistance Act of 1972
Pub. L. 92–512, title I, Oct. 20, 1972, 86 Stat. 919

State and Local Fiscal Assistance Amendments of 1976
Pub. L. 94–488, Oct. 13, 1976, 90 Stat. 2341

State and Local Government Cost Estimate Act of 1981
Pub. L. 97–108, Dec. 23, 1981, 95 Stat. 1510
Short title, see 2 U.S.C. 621 note

State and Local Law Enforcement Assistance Act of 1986
Pub. L. 99–570, title I, subtitle K (§1551 et seq.), Oct. 27, 1986, 100 Stat. 3207–41
Short title, see 42 U.S.C. 3711 note

State Bank Aid Act
Mar. 24, 1933, ch. 8, 48 Stat. 20

State Comprehensive Mental Health Services Plan Act of 1986
Pub. L. 99–660, title V, Nov. 14, 1986, 100 Stat. 3794
Short title, see 42 U.S.C. 201 note

State Constitutions Act (Virginia, Texas, Mississippi)
Apr. 10, 1869, ch. 17, 16 Stat. 40

State Department Basic Authorities Act of 1956
Aug. 1, 1956, ch. 841, 70 Stat. 890
Short title, see 22 U.S.C. 2651 note

State Department/USIA Authorization Act, Fiscal Year 1975
Pub. L. 93–475, Oct. 26, 1974, 88 Stat. 1439
Short title, see 22 U.S.C. 2651 note

State Dependent Care Development Grants Act
Pub. L. 97–35, title VI, ch. 8, subch. D (§670A et seq.), as added Pub. L. 98–558, title I, §109, Oct. 30, 1984, 98 Stat. 2880 (42 U.S.C. 9871 et seq.)
Short title, see 42 U.S.C. 9801 note

State Energy Efficiency Programs Improvement Act of 1990
Pub. L. 101–440, Oct. 18, 1990, 104 Stat. 1006
Short title, see 42 U.S.C. 6201 note

State Flexibility Clarification Act
Pub. L. 106–141, Dec. 7, 1999, 113 Stat. 1699
Short title, see 2 U.S.C. 621 note

State Forest Aid Act
Aug. 29, 1935, ch. 808, 49 Stat. 963 (16 U.S.C. 567a et seq.)

State Justice Institute Act of 1984
Pub. L. 98–620, title II, Nov. 8, 1984, 98 Stat. 3336 (42 U.S.C. 10701 et seq.)
Short title, see 42 U.S.C. 10701 note

State Taxation of Depositories Act
Pub. L. 93–100, §7, Aug. 16, 1973, 87 Stat. 347 (12 U.S.C. 548 note)

State Technical Services Act of 1965
Pub. L. 89–182, Sept. 14, 1965, 79 Stat. 679 (15 U.S.C. 1351 et seq.)
Short title, see 15 U.S.C. 1351 note

State Veterans' Home Assistance Improvement Act of 1977
Pub. L. 95–62, July 5, 1977, 91 Stat. 262
Short title, see 38 U.S.C. 101 note

Statehood Act (Arizona and New Mexico)
June 20, 1910, ch. 310, 36 Stat. 557–579

Statue of Liberty-Ellis Island Commemorative Coin Act
Pub. L. 99–61, July 9, 1985, 99 Stat. 113 (31 U.S.C. 5112 note)

Statutes of Limitations Act (Fraud During WWII)
Aug. 24, 1942, ch. 555, 56 Stat. 747

Steagall Commodity Credit Act
July 1, 1941, ch. 270, 55 Stat. 498

Steagall National Housing Act of 1938
See National Housing Act Amendments of 1938

Steagall National Housing Act of 1939
June 3, 1939, ch. 175, 53 Stat. 804

Steagall R. F. C. Relief Obligations Act
Feb. 24, 1938, ch. 32, 52 Stat. 79

Steagall Stock Liability Act
See Federal Reserve Act

Steagall-Wagner National Housing Act of 1938
See National Housing Act Amendments of 1938

Steamboat Inspection Act
May 27, 1936, ch. 463, 49 Stat. 1380

Steamtown National Historic Site Act of 1986
Pub. L. 99–500, §101(h) [title I, §§1–5], Oct. 18, 1986, 100 Stat. 1783–242, 1783–248, and Pub. L. 99–591, §101(h) [title I, §§1–5], Oct. 30, 1986, 100 Stat. 3341–242, 3341–248 (16 U.S.C. 461 note)

Steel and Aluminum Energy Conservation and Technology Competitiveness Act of 1988
Pub. L. 100–680, Nov. 17, 1988, 102 Stat. 4073 (15 U.S.C. 5101 et seq.)
Short title, see 15 U.S.C. 5101 note

Steel Import Stabilization Act
Pub. L. 98–573, title VIII, Oct. 30, 1984, 98 Stat. 3043 (19 U.S.C. 2253 note)

Steel Industry American Heritage Area Act of 1996
Pub. L. 104–333, div. II, title IV, Nov. 12, 1996, 110 Stat. 4252 (16 U.S.C. 461 note)

Steel Industry Compliance Extension Act of 1981
Pub. L. 97–23, July 17, 1981, 95 Stat. 139
Short title, see 42 U.S.C. 7401 note

Steel Trade Liberalization Program Implementation Act
Pub. L. 101–221, Dec. 12, 1989, 103 Stat. 1886
Short title, see 19 U.S.C. 2101 note

Steens Mountain Cooperative Management and Protection Act of 2000
Pub. L. 106–399, Oct. 30, 2000, 114 Stat. 1655 (16 U.S.C. 460nnn et seq.)
Short title, see 16 U.S.C. 460nnn note

Sterling Act (Employers' Liability)
See Employers' Liability Act (1908) (Railroads)

Sterling-Lehlbach Act (Classification, Federal Employees)
See Classification Act of 1923

Stevenson-Wydler Technology Innovation Act of 1980
Pub. L. 96–480, Oct. 21, 1980, 94 Stat. 2311 (15 U.S.C. 3701 et seq.)
Short title, see 15 U.S.C. 3701 note

Stewart B. McKinney Homeless Assistance Act
Renamed McKinney-Vento Homeless Assistance Act

Stewart B. McKinney Homeless Assistance Amendments Act of 1988
Pub. L. 100–628, Nov. 7, 1988, 102 Stat. 3224
Short title, see 42 U.S.C. 11301 note

Stewart B. McKinney Homeless Assistance Amendments Act of 1990
Pub. L. 101–645, Nov. 29, 1990, 104 Stat. 4673
Pub. L. 101–645, title VI, Nov. 29, 1990, 104 Stat. 4734
Short title, see 42 U.S.C. 11301 notes

Stewart B. McKinney Homeless Housing Assistance Amendments Act of 1992
Pub. L. 102–550, title XIV, Oct. 28, 1992, 106 Stat. 4012
Short title, see 42 U.S.C. 11301 note

Stewart B. McKinney National Wildlife Refuge Designation Act of 1987
Pub. L. 100–38, May 13, 1987, 101 Stat. 306

Stobb Act (National Prohibition)
Jan. 15, 1931, ch. 29, 46 Stat. 1036

Stock Reservoir Act
Jan. 13, 1897, ch. 11, 29 Stat. 484 (43 U.S.C. 952 et seq.)

Stock-Raising Homestead Act
Dec. 29, 1916, ch. 9, 39 Stat. 862 (43 U.S.C. 291 et seq.)

Stockholders' Liability Act
See Federal Reserve Act

Stone Act
Aug. 4, 1892, ch. 375, 27 Stat. 348 (30 U.S.C. 161)

Strategic and Critical Materials Stock Piling Act
June 7, 1939, ch. 190, 53 Stat. 811 (50 U.S.C. 98 et seq.)
Short title, see 50 U.S.C. 98 note

Strategic and Critical Materials Stock Piling Revision Act of 1979
Pub. L. 96–41, July 30, 1979, 93 Stat. 319
Short title, see 50 U.S.C. 98 note

Strategic and Critical Materials Transaction Authorization Act of 1979
Pub. L. 96–175, Dec. 29, 1979, 93 Stat. 1289

Strategic and Critical Minerals Act of 1990
Pub. L. 101–498, Nov. 2, 1990, 104 Stat. 1207
Short title, see 30 U.S.C. 1201 note

Strategic Material Loan Act
See Reconstruction Finance Corporation Act

Strategic Petroleum Reserve Amendments Act of 1981
Pub. L. 97–35, title X, subtitle C (§1031 et seq.), Aug. 13, 1981, 95 Stat. 618
Short title, see 42 U.S.C. 6201 note

Strategic War Materials Act
See Strategic and Critical Materials Stock Piling Act

Streambank Erosion Control Evaluation and Demonstration Act of 1974
Pub. L. 93–251, title I, §32, Mar. 7, 1974, 88 Stat. 21 (42 U.S.C. 1962d–5 note)

Street Railway Merger Act (District of Columbia)
Jan. 14, 1933, ch. 10. 47 Stat. 752

Strengthening Abuse and Neglect Courts Act of 2000
Pub. L. 106–314, Oct. 17, 2000, 114 Stat. 1266 (42 U.S.C. 670 note)

Strikebreaker Act
June 24, 1936, ch. 746, 49 Stat. 1899

Striped Bass Act of 1991
Pub. L. 102–130, Oct. 17, 1991, 105 Stat. 626
Short title, see 16 U.S.C. 757a note

Striped Bass Conservation, Atlantic Coastal Fisheries Management, and Marine Mammal Rescue Assistance Act of 2000
Pub. L. 106–555, Dec. 21, 2000, 114 Stat. 2765
Short title, see 16 U.S.C. 1361 note

Strom Thurmond National Defense Authorization Act for Fiscal Year 1999
Pub. L. 105–261, Oct. 17, 1998, 112 Stat. 1920

Student Financial Assistance Amendments of 1985
Pub. L. 99–272, title XVI, Apr. 7, 1986, 100 Stat. 339
Short title, see 20 U.S.C. 1001 note

Student Financial Assistance Technical Amendments Act of 1982
Pub. L. 97–301, Oct. 13, 1982, 96 Stat. 1400
Short title, see 20 U.S.C. 1001 note

Student Financial Assistance Technical Corrections Act of 1986
Pub. L. 99–320, May 23, 1986, 100 Stat. 491
Short title, see 20 U.S.C. 1001 note

Student Loan Consolidation and Technical Amendments Act of 1983
Pub. L. 98–79, Aug. 15, 1983, 97 Stat. 476
Short title, see 20 U.S.C. 1001 note

Student Loan Default Prevention Initiative Act of 1990
Pub. L. 101–508, title III, subtitle A (§3001 et seq.), Nov. 5, 1990, 104 Stat. 1388–25
Short title, see 20 U.S.C. 1001 note

Student Loan Marketing Association Reorganization Act of 1996
Pub. L. 104–208, div. A, title I, §101(e) [title VI], Sept. 30, 1996, 110 Stat. 3009–233, 3009–275
Short title, see 20 U.S.C. 1001 note

Student Loan Reconciliation Amendments of 1989
Pub. L. 101–239, title II, subtitle A (§2001 et seq.), Dec. 19, 1989, 103 Stat. 2111
Short title, see 20 U.S.C. 1001 note

Student Loan Reform Act of 1993
Pub. L. 103–66, title IV, subtitle A (§4011 et seq.), Aug. 10, 1993, 107 Stat. 341
Short title, see 20 U.S.C. 1001 note

Student Right-To-Know Act
Pub. L. 101–542, title I, Nov. 8, 1990, 104 Stat. 2381
Short title, see 20 U.S.C. 1001 note

Student Right-To-Know and Campus Security Act
Pub. L. 101–542, Nov. 8, 1990, 104 Stat. 2381
Short title, see 20 U.S.C. 1001 note

Subchapter S Revision Act of 1982
Pub. L. 97–354, Oct. 19, 1982, 96 Stat. 1669
Short title, see 26 U.S.C. 1 note

Subcontractors' Gratuities and Kick-Backs Act (Public Contracts)
See Anti-Kickback Act of 1986

Submarine Cable Act
Feb. 29, 1888, ch. 17, 25 Stat. 41 (47 U.S.C. 21 et seq.)
Short title, see 47 U.S.C. 21 note

Submerged Lands Act
May 22, 1953, ch. 65, 67 Stat. 29 (43 U.S.C. 1301 et seq.)
Short title, see 43 U.S.C. 1301 note

Subsistence Expense Act of 1926
June 3, 1926, ch. 457, 44 Stat. 688

Subversive Activities Control Act of 1950
Sept. 23, 1950, ch. 1024, title I, 64 Stat. 987 (50 U.S.C. 781 et seq.)
Short title, see 50 U.S.C. 781 note

Subversive Activities Control Board Tenure Act
Aug. 5, 1955, ch. 580, 69 Stat. 539

Sudbury, Assabet, and Concord Wild and Scenic River Act
Pub. L. 106–20, Apr. 9, 1999, 113 Stat. 30
Short title, see 16 U.S.C. 1271 note

Sudbury, Assabet, and Concord Wild and Scenic River Study Act
Pub. L. 101–628, title VII, Nov. 28, 1990, 104 Stat. 4497
Short title, see 16 U.S.C. 1271 note

Sudden Infant Death Syndrome Act of 1974
Pub. L. 93–270, Apr. 22, 1974, 88 Stat. 90
Short title, see 42 U.S.C. 201 note

Sudden Infant Death Syndrome Amendments of 1979
Pub. L. 96–142, title II, Dec. 12, 1979, 93 Stat. 1070
Short title, see 42 U.S.C. 201 note

Suffrage Amendment
Aug. 26, 1920, 41 Stat. 1823

Sugar Act Amendments of 1962
Pub. L. 87–535, July 13, 1962, 76 Stat. 156

Sugar Act Amendments of 1965
Pub. L. 89–331, Nov. 8, 1965, 79 Stat. 1271

Sugar Act Amendments of 1971
Pub. L. 92–138, Oct. 14, 1971, 85 Stat. 379

Sugar Act of 1937
Sept. 1, 1937, ch. 898, 50 Stat. 903

Sugar Act of 1948
Aug. 8, 1947, ch. 519, 61 Stat. 922 (7 U.S.C. 1100 et seq.)

Sugar Control Act
May 9, 1934, ch. 263, 48 Stat. 670

Sugar Control Extension Act of 1947
Mar. 31, 1947, ch. 30, 61 Stat. 35

Sugar Pine Dam and Reservoir Conveyance Act
Pub. L. 106–566, title V, Dec. 23, 2000, 114 Stat. 2822

Sugarbush Land Exchange Act of 1996
Pub. L. 104–208, div. A, §101(d) [title III, §326], Sept. 30, 1996, 110 Stat. 3009–181, 3009–226

Suits in Admiralty Act
Mar. 9, 1920, ch. 95, 41 Stat. 525 (46 App. U.S.C. 741 et seq.)
Short title, see 46 App. U.S.C. 741 note

Sulloway Act (Pensions)
See Widows' Pension Act

Summary Courts-Martial Act
June 18, 1898, ch. 469, 30 Stat. 483

Sumners Courts Act
June 29, 1940, ch. 445, 54 Stat. 688

Sumners-Amherst Act
Oct. 14, 1940, ch. 872, 54 Stat. 1134

Sumners-McCarran Act
Mar. 1, 1937, ch. 21, 50 Stat. 24

Sunshine Act
See Government in the Sunshine Act

Superfund Act
See Comprehensive Environmental Response, Compensation, and Liability Act of 1980

Superfund Amendments and Reauthorization Act of 1986
Pub. L. 99–499, Oct. 17, 1986, 100 Stat. 1613
Short title, see 42 U.S.C. 9601 note

Superfund Revenue Act of 1986
Pub. L. 99–499, title V, Oct. 17, 1986, 100 Stat. 1760
Short title, see 26 U.S.C. 1 note

Supplement to Second Liberty Bond Act
Sept. 24, 1918, ch. 176, 40 Stat. 965

Supplemental Appropriation Act, 1948
July 30, 1947, ch. 361, 61 Stat. 610

Supplemental Appropriation Act, 1949
Aug. 13, 1948, ch. 835, 62 Stat. 1289

Supplemental Appropriation Act, 1950
Oct. 14, 1949, ch. 694, 63 Stat. 869

Supplemental Appropriation Act, 1951
Sept. 27, 1950, ch. 1052, 64 Stat. 1044

Supplemental Appropriation Act, 1952
Nov. 1, 1951, ch. 664, 65 Stat. 736

Supplemental Appropriation Act, 1953
July 15, 1952, ch. 758, 66 Stat. 637

Supplemental Appropriation Act, 1954
Aug. 7, 1953, ch. 340, 67 Stat. 418

Supplemental Appropriation Act, 1955
Aug. 26, 1954, ch. 935, 68 Stat. 800

Supplemental Appropriation Act, 1956
Aug. 4, 1955, ch. 541, 69 Stat. 450

Supplemental Appropriation Act, 1957
July 27, 1956, ch. 748, 70 Stat. 678

Supplemental Appropriation Act, 1958
Pub. L. 85–170, Aug. 28, 1957, 71 Stat. 426

Supplemental Appropriation Act, 1959
Pub. L. 85–766, Aug. 27, 1958, 72 Stat. 864

Supplemental Appropriation Act, 1960
Pub. L. 86–213, Sept. 1, 1959, 73 Stat. 437

Supplemental Appropriation Act, 1961
Pub. L. 86–651, July 14, 1960, 74 Stat. 509

Supplemental Appropriation Act, 1962
Pub. L. 87–332, Sept. 30, 1961, 75 Stat. 733

Supplemental Appropriation Act, 1963
Pub. L. 88–25, May 17, 1963, 77 Stat. 20

Supplemental Appropriation Act, 1965
Pub. L. 88–635, Oct. 7, 1964, 78 Stat. 1023

Supplemental Appropriation Act, 1966
Pub. L. 89–309, Oct. 31, 1965, 79 Stat. 1133

Supplemental Appropriation Act, 1967
Pub. L. 89–697, Oct. 27, 1966, 80 Stat. 1057

Supplemental Appropriation Act, 1968
Pub. L. 90–239, Jan. 2, 1968, 81 Stat. 773

Supplemental Appropriation Act, 1969
Pub. L. 90–608, Oct. 21, 1968, 82 Stat. 1190

Supplemental Appropriation Act, 1970
Pub. L. 91–166, Dec. 26, 1969, 83 Stat. 447

Supplemental Appropriation Act, 1971
Pub. L. 91–665, Jan. 8, 1971, 84 Stat. 1981

Supplemental Appropriations Act of 1993
Pub. L. 103–50, July 2, 1993, 107 Stat. 241

Supplemental Appropriations Act of 1996
Pub. L. 104–134, title II, Apr. 26, 1996, 110 Stat. 1321–311

Supplemental Appropriations Act, 1972
Pub. L. 92–184, Dec. 15, 1971, 85 Stat. 627

Supplemental Appropriations Act, 1973
Pub. L. 92–607, Oct. 31, 1972, 86 Stat. 1498

Supplemental Appropriations Act, 1974
Pub. L. 93–245, Jan. 3, 1974, 87 Stat. 1071

Supplemental Appropriations Act, 1975
Pub. L. 93–554, Dec. 27, 1974, 88 Stat. 1771

Supplemental Appropriations Act, 1976
Pub. L. 94–157, Dec. 18, 1975, 89 Stat. 826

Supplemental Appropriations Act, 1977
Pub. L. 95–26, May 4, 1977, 91 Stat. 61

Supplemental Appropriations Act, 1978
Pub. L. 95–240, Mar. 7, 1978, 92 Stat. 107

Supplemental Appropriations Act, 1979
Pub. L. 96–38, July 25, 1979, 93 Stat. 97

Supplemental Appropriations Act, 1982
Pub. L. 97–257, Sept. 10, 1982, 96 Stat. 818

Supplemental Appropriations Act, 1983
Pub. L. 98–63, July 30, 1983, 97 Stat. 301

Supplemental Appropriations Act, 1984
Pub. L. 98–181, Nov. 30, 1983, 97 Stat. 1153

Supplemental Appropriations Act, 1985
Pub. L. 99–88, Aug. 15, 1985, 99 Stat. 293

Supplemental Appropriations Act, 1987
Pub. L. 100–71, July 11, 1987, 101 Stat. 391

Supplemental Appropriations and Rescission Act, 1980
Pub. L. 96–304, July 8, 1980, 94 Stat. 857

Supplemental Appropriations and Rescission Act, 1981
Pub. L. 97–12, June 5, 1981, 95 Stat. 14

Supplemental Appropriations for the New Independent States of the Former Soviet Union Act, 1993
Pub. L. 103–87, title VI, Sept. 30, 1993, 107 Stat. 974

Supplemental Defense Appropriation Act, 1958
Pub. L. 85–322, Feb. 11, 1958, 72 Stat. 6

Supplemental Defense Appropriation Act, 1966
Pub. L. 89–374, Mar. 25, 1966, 80 Stat. 79

Supplemental Defense Appropriation Act, 1967
Pub. L. 90–8, Apr. 4, 1967, 81 Stat. 8

Supplemental Federal Security Agency Appropriation Act, 1949
June 16, 1948, ch. 472, 62 Stat. 443

Supplemental Government Corporations Appropriation Act, 1948
July 29, 1947, ch. 346, 61 Stat. 514

Supplemental Housing Authorization Act of 1977
Pub. L. 95–24, Apr. 30, 1977, 91 Stat. 55
Short title, see 12 U.S.C. 1701 note

Supplemental Independent Offices Appropriation Act, 1949
June 30, 1948, ch. 775, 62 Stat. 1196

Supplemental Labor Department Appropriation Act, 1960
Pub. L. 86–535, June 29, 1960, 74 Stat. 250

Supplemental Military Appropriation Act, 1940
July 1, 1939, ch. 258, 53 Stat. 992

Supplemental National Defense Appropriation Act, 1948
May 21, 1948, ch. 333, 62 Stat. 258

Supplemental Naval Appropriation Act, 1943
Mar. 31, 1943, ch. 30, 57 Stat. 52

Supplemental Post Office Department Appropriation Act, 1949
June 19, 1948, ch. 558, title II, 62 Stat. 564

Supplemental Treasury and Post Office Departments Appropriation Act, 1949
June 19, 1948, ch. 558, 62 Stat. 560

Supplemental Treasury Department Appropriation Act, 1949
June 19, 1948, ch. 558, title I, 62 Stat. 561

Supplemental Veterans Administration Appropriation Act, 1962
Pub. L. 87–404, Feb. 13, 1962, 76 Stat. 8

Support for East European Democracy (SEED) Act of 1989
Pub. L. 101–179, Nov. 28, 1989, 103 Stat. 1298 (22 U.S.C. 5401 et seq.)
Short title, see 22 U.S.C. 5401 note

Support for Overseas Cooperative Development Act
Pub. L. 106–309, title IV, §401, Oct. 17, 2000, 114 Stat. 1096
Short title, see 22 U.S.C. 2151 note

Surety Companies Act
See Corporate Surety Act

Surface Freight Forwarder Deregulation Act of 1986
Pub. L. 99–521, Oct. 22, 1986, 100 Stat. 2993
Short title, see 49 U.S.C. 10101 note

Surface Mining Control and Reclamation Act of 1977
Pub. L. 95–87, Aug. 3, 1977, 91 Stat. 445 (30 U.S.C. 1201 et seq.)
Short title, see 30 U.S.C. 1201 note

Surface Transportation and Uniform Relocation Assistance Act of 1987
Pub. L. 100–17, Apr. 2, 1987, 101 Stat. 132
Short title, see 23 U.S.C. 101 note

Surface Transportation Assistance Act of 1978
Pub. L. 95–599, Nov. 6, 1978, 92 Stat. 2689
Short title, see 23 U.S.C. 101 note

Surface Transportation Assistance Act of 1982
Pub. L. 97–424, Jan. 6, 1983, 96 Stat. 2097
Short title, see 23 U.S.C. 101 note

Surface Transportation Extension Act of 1997
Pub. L. 105–130, Dec. 1, 1997, 111 Stat. 2552
Short title, see 23 U.S.C. 101 note

Surface Transportation Revenue Act of 1991
Pub. L. 102–240, title VIII, Dec. 18, 1991, 105 Stat. 2203
Short title, see 26 U.S.C. 1 note

Surface Transportation Revenue Act of 1998
Pub. L. 105–178, title IX, June 9, 1998, 112 Stat. 499
Short title, see 26 U.S.C. 1 note

Surplus Agricultural Commodities Disposal Act of 1982
Pub. L. 97–358, Oct. 21, 1982, 96 Stat. 1714
Short title, see 7 U.S.C. 1421 note

Surplus Commodities Corporation Act
June 27, 1942, ch. 454, 56 Stat. 461

Surplus Fund-Certified Claims Act of 1949
July 6, 1949, ch. 299, 63 Stat. 407

Surplus Property Act of 1944
Oct. 3, 1944, ch. 479, 58 Stat. 765 (50 App. U.S.C. 1611 et seq.)

Survey Manual Legalization Act (Public Lands)
Oct. 1, 1890, ch. 1262, 26 Stat. 650

Survivor Benefit Plan Amendments of 1985
Pub. L. 99–145, title VII, Nov. 8, 1985, 99 Stat. 666
Short title, see 10 U.S.C. 1447 note

Susan B. Anthony Dollar Coin Act of 1978
Pub. L. 95–447, Oct. 10, 1978, 92 Stat. 1072

Sustainable Fisheries Act
Pub. L. 104–297, Oct. 11, 1996, 110 Stat. 3559
Short title, see 16 U.S.C. 1801 note

Swamp Land Act of 1850
Sept. 28, 1850, ch. 84, 9 Stat. 519

Sweet Act (War Risk Insurance Amendment)
Dec. 24, 1919, ch. 16, 41 Stat. 371

Swift Rail Development Act of 1994
Pub. L. 103–440, title I, Nov. 2, 1994, 108 Stat. 4615 (49 U.S.C. 26101 et seq.)
Short title, see 49 U.S.C. 20101 note

Swine Health Protection Act
Pub. L. 96–468, Oct. 17, 1980, 94 Stat. 2229 (7 U.S.C. 3801 et seq.)
Short title, see 7 U.S.C. 3801 note

Symms National Recreational Trails Act of 1991
Pub. L. 102–240, title I, part B (§1301 et seq.), Dec. 18, 1991, 105 Stat. 2064 (16 U.S.C. 1261 et seq.)
Short title, see 16 U.S.C. 1261 note

Synthetic Fuels Corporation Act of 1985
Pub. L. 99–272, title VII, subtitle E (§7401 et seq.), Apr. 7, 1986, 100 Stat. 143–145 (42 U.S.C. 8791 note)

Synthetic Liquid Fuels Act
Apr. 5, 1944, ch. 172, 58 Stat. 190 (30 U.S.C. 321 et seq.)

Taconic Mountains Protection Act of 1991
Pub. L. 102–59, June 18, 1991, 105 Stat. 300

Taft-Hartley Act
See Labor-Management Relations Act, 1947

Taiwan Relations Act
Pub. L. 96–8, Apr. 10, 1979, 93 Stat. 14 (22 U.S.C. 3301 et seq.)
Short title, see 22 U.S.C. 3301 note

Take Pride in America Act
Pub. L. 101–628, title XI, Nov. 28, 1990, 104 Stat. 4502 (16 U.S.C. 4601 et seq.)
Short title, see 16 U.S.C. 4601 note

Tallgrass Prairie National Preserve Act of 1996
Pub. L. 104–333, div. I, title X, subtitle A (§1001 et seq.), Nov. 12, 1996, 110 Stat. 4204 (16 U.S.C. 698u et seq.)
Short title, see 16 U.S.C. 698u note

Talmadge-Aiken Act
Pub. L. 87–718, Sept. 28, 1962, 76 Stat. 663 (7 U.S.C. 450)

Tandem Truck Safety Act of 1984
Pub. L. 98–554, title I, Oct. 30, 1984, 98 Stat. 2829

Tank Vessel Act
June 23, 1936, ch. 729, 49 Stat. 1889

Tariff Act of 1922
Sept. 21, 1922, ch. 356, 42 Stat. 858

Tariff Act of 1930
June 17, 1930, ch. 497, 46 Stat. 590
Short title, see 19 U.S.C. 1654

Tariff Board Act
Aug. 5, 1909, ch. 6, §2, 36 Stat. 82

Tariff Classification Act of 1962
Pub. L. 87–456, May 24, 1962, 76 Stat. 72
Short title, see 19 U.S.C. 1654 note

Tariff Commission of 1882
May 15, 1882, ch. 145, 22 Stat. 64

Tariff of 1894
Aug. 27, 1894, ch. 349, 28 Stat. 509

Tariff of 1913
Oct. 3, 1913, ch. 16, 38 Stat. 114

Tariff Suspension and Trade Act of 2000
Pub. L. 106–476, Nov. 9, 2000, 114 Stat. 2101
Short title, see 19 U.S.C. 1654 note

Tarsney Act (Erection of Public Buildings)
Feb. 20, 1893, ch. 146, 27 Stat. 468

Taunton River Wild and Scenic River Study Act of 2000
Pub. L. 106–318, Oct. 19, 2000, 114 Stat. 1278
Short title, see 16 U.S.C. 1271 note

Tax Adjustment Act of 1945
July 31, 1945, ch. 340, 59 Stat. 517

Tax Adjustment Act of 1966
Pub. L. 89–368, Mar. 15, 1966, 80 Stat. 38
Short title, see 26 U.S.C. 3401 note

Tax and Trade Relief Extension Act of 1998
Pub. L. 105–277, div. J, Oct. 21, 1998, 112 Stat. 2681–886
Short title, see 26 U.S.C. 1 note

Tax Equity and Fiscal Responsibility Act of 1982
Pub. L. 97–248, Sept. 3, 1982, 96 Stat. 324
Short title, see 26 U.S.C. 1 note

Tax Extension Act of 1991
Pub. L. 102–227, Dec. 11, 1991, 105 Stat. 1686
Short title, see 26 U.S.C. 1 note

Tax Loophole Act of 1937
See Revenue Act of 1937

Tax Rate Extension Act of 1955
Mar. 30, 1955, ch. 18, 69 Stat. 14
Short title, see 26 U.S.C. 4041 note

Tax Rate Extension Act of 1956
Mar. 29, 1956, ch. 115, 70 Stat. 66
Short title, see 26 U.S.C. 4041 note

Tax Rate Extension Act of 1957
Pub. L. 85–12, Mar. 29, 1957, 71 Stat. 9
Short title, see 26 U.S.C. 1 note

Tax Rate Extension Act of 1958
Pub. L. 85–475, June 30, 1958, 72 Stat. 259
Short title, see 26 U.S.C. 1 note

Tax Rate Extension Act of 1959
Pub. L. 86–75, June 30, 1959, 73 Stat. 157
Short title, see 26 U.S.C. 1 note

Tax Rate Extension Act of 1961
Pub. L. 87–72, June 30, 1961, 75 Stat. 193
Short title, see 26 U.S.C. 1 note

Tax Rate Extension Act of 1962
Pub. L. 87–508, June 28, 1962, 76 Stat. 114
Short title, see 26 U.S.C. 1 note

Tax Rate Extension Act of 1963
Pub. L. 88–52, June 29, 1963, 77 Stat. 72
Short title, see 26 U.S.C. 1 note

Tax Reduction Act of 1975
Pub. L. 94–12, Mar. 29, 1975, 89 Stat. 26
Short title, see 26 U.S.C. 1 note

Tax Reduction and Simplification Act of 1977
Pub. L. 95–30, May 23, 1977, 91 Stat. 126
Short title, see 26 U.S.C. 1 note

Tax Reform Act of 1969
Pub. L. 91–172, Dec. 30, 1969, 83 Stat. 487
Short title, see 26 U.S.C. 1 note

Tax Reform Act of 1976
Pub. L. 94–455, Oct. 4, 1976, 90 Stat. 1520
Short title, see 26 U.S.C. 1 note

Tax Reform Act of 1984
Pub. L. 98–369, div. A, July 18, 1984, 98 Stat. 494
Short title, see 26 U.S.C. 1 note

Tax Reform Act of 1986
Pub. L. 99–514, Oct. 22, 1986, 100 Stat. 2085
Short title, see 26 U.S.C. 1 note

Tax Relief Extension Act of 1999
Pub. L. 106–170, title V, Dec. 17, 1999, 113 Stat. 1918
Short title, see 26 U.S.C. 1 note

Tax Simplification Act
See Individual Income Tax Act of 1944

Tax Technical Corrections Act of 1998
Pub. L. 105–206, title VI, July 22, 1998, 112 Stat. 790
Short title, see 26 U.S.C. 1 note

Tax Treatment Extension Act of 1977
Pub. L. 95–615, §§1–8, Nov. 8, 1978, 92 Stat. 3097
Short title, see 26 U.S.C. 1 note

Tax Treatment of Partnership Items Act of 1982
Pub. L. 97–248, title IV, Sept. 3, 1982, 96 Stat. 648
Short title, see 26 U.S.C. 1 note

Taxpayer Bill of Rights 2
Pub. L. 104–168, July 30, 1996, 110 Stat. 1452
Short title, see 26 U.S.C. 1 note

Taxpayer Bill of Rights 3
Pub. L. 105–206, title III, July 22, 1998, 112 Stat. 726
Short title, see 26 U.S.C. 1 note

Taxpayer Browsing Protection Act
Pub. L. 105–35, Aug. 5, 1997, 111 Stat. 1104
Short title, see 26 U.S.C. 1 note

Taxpayer Relief Act of 1997
Pub. L. 105–34, Aug. 5, 1997, 111 Stat. 788
Short title, see 26 U.S.C. 1 note

Taylor Grazing Act
June 28, 1934, ch. 865, 48 Stat. 1269 (43 U.S.C. 315 et seq.)
Short title, see 43 U.S.C. 315 note

Taylor T. V. A. Act
July 16, 1941, ch. 303, 55 Stat. 597

TEA 21 Restoration Act
Pub. L. 105–206, title IX, July 22, 1998, 112 Stat. 834
Short title, see 23 U.S.C. 101 note

Tea Importation Act
Mar. 2, 1897, ch. 358, 29 Stat. 604 (21 U.S.C. 41 et seq.)
Short title, see 21 U.S.C. 41 note

Teachers' Retirement Law (District of Columbia)
Jan. 15, 1920, ch. 39, 41 Stat. 387

Teachers' Salary Act Amendments of 1974
Pub. L. 93–407, title II, Sept. 3, 1974, 88 Stat. 1042

Tech-Prep Education Act
Pub. L. 88–210, title II, as added Pub. L. 105–332, §1(b), Oct. 31, 1998, 112 Stat. 3117 (20 U.S.C. 2371 et seq.)
Short title, see 20 U.S.C. 2301 note

Technical Amendments Act of 1958
Pub. L. 85–866, title I, Sept. 2, 1958, 72 Stat. 1606
Short title, see 26 U.S.C. 1 note

Technical Amendments to the Federal Courts Improvement Act of 1984
Pub. L. 98–620, title IV, subtitle C (§412 et seq.), Nov. 8, 1984, 98 Stat. 3362

Technical Amendments to Various Indian Laws Act of 1991
Pub. L. 102–238, Dec. 17, 1991, 105 Stat. 1908
Short title, see 25 U.S.C. 2201 note

Technical and Miscellaneous Civil Service Amendments Act of 1992
Pub. L. 102–378, Oct. 2, 1992, 106 Stat. 1346
Short title, see 5 U.S.C. 1101 note

Technical and Miscellaneous Revenue Act of 1988
Pub. L. 100–647, Nov. 10, 1988, 102 Stat. 3342
Short title, see 26 U.S.C. 1 note

Technical Changes Act of 1953
Aug. 15, 1953, ch. 512, 67 Stat. 615

Technical Corrections Act of 1979
Pub. L. 96–222, Apr. 1, 1980, 94 Stat. 194
Short title, see 26 U.S.C. 1 note

Technical Corrections Act of 1982
Pub. L. 97–448, Jan. 12, 1983, 96 Stat. 2365
Short title, see 26 U.S.C. 1 note

Technology Administration Act of 1998
Pub. L. 105–309, Oct. 30, 1998, 112 Stat. 2935
Short title, see 15 U.S.C. 271 note

Technology Administration Authorization Act of 1991
Pub. L. 102–245, title I, Feb. 14, 1992, 106 Stat. 7
Short title, see 15 U.S.C. 3701 note

Technology Assessment Act of 1972
Pub. L. 92–484, Oct. 13, 1972, 86 Stat. 797 (2 U.S.C. 471 et seq.)
Short title, see 2 U.S.C. 471 note

Technology Competitiveness Act
Pub. L. 100–418, title V, subtitle B, part I (§5101 et seq.), Aug. 23, 1988, 102 Stat. 1426
Short title, see 15 U.S.C. 271 note

Technology for Education Act of 1994
Pub. L. 89–10, title III, as added Pub. L. 103–382, title I, §101, Oct. 20, 1994, 108 Stat. 3636 (20 U.S.C. 6801 et seq.)
Short title, see 20 U.S.C. 6801

Technology Transfer Commercialization Act of 2000
Pub. L. 106–404, Nov. 1, 2000, 114 Stat. 1742
Short title, see 15 U.S.C. 3701 note

Technology-Related Assistance for Individuals With Disabilities Act Amendments of 1994
Pub. L. 103–218, Mar. 9, 1994, 108 Stat. 50

Technology-Related Assistance for Individuals With Disabilities Act of 1988
Pub. L. 100–407, Aug. 19, 1988, 102 Stat. 1044 (29 U.S.C. 2201 et seq.)
Short title, see 29 U.S.C. 2201 note

Ted Stevens Olympic and Amateur Sports Act
Title 36, chapter 2205 (§220501 et seq.)
Short title, see 36 U.S.C. 220501(a)

Ted Weiss Child Support Enforcement Act of 1992
Pub. L. 102–537, Oct. 27, 1992, 106 Stat. 3531
Short title, see 15 U.S.C. 1601 note

Teen Suicide Prevention Act of 2000
Pub. L. 106–386, div. B, title VI, §1602, Oct. 28, 2000, 114 Stat. 1538 (42 U.S.C. 290bb–36 note)

Teenage Draft Act
Nov. 13, 1942, ch. 638, 56 Stat. 1018

TEFRA
See Tax Equity and Fiscal Responsibility Act of 1982

Telecommunications Accessibility Enhancement Act of 1988
Pub. L. 100–542, Oct. 28, 1988, 102 Stat. 2721 (40 U.S.C. 762 et seq.)
Short title, see 40 U.S.C. 762 note

Telecommunications Act of 1996
Pub. L. 104–104, Feb. 8, 1996, 110 Stat. 56
Short title, see 47 U.S.C. 609 note

Telecommunications Authorization Act of 1992
Pub. L. 102–538, Oct. 27, 1992, 106 Stat. 3533

Telecommunications for the Disabled Act of 1982
Pub. L. 97–410, Jan. 3, 1983, 96 Stat. 2043
Short title, see 47 U.S.C. 609 note

Telecommunications Trade Act of 1988
Pub. L. 100–418, title I, subtitle C, part 4 (§1371 et seq.), Aug. 23, 1988, 102 Stat. 1216 (19 U.S.C. 3101 et seq.)
Short title, see 19 U.S.C. 3101 note

Telegraph Company Merger Act
See Communications Act of 1934

Telemarketing and Consumer Fraud and Abuse Prevention Act
Pub. L. 103–297, Aug. 16, 1994, 108 Stat. 1545 (15 U.S.C. 6101 et seq.)
Short title, see 15 U.S.C. 6101 note

Telemarketing Fraud Prevention Act of 1998
Pub. L. 105–184, June 23, 1998, 112 Stat. 520
Short title, see 18 U.S.C. 1 note

Telephone Consumer Protection Act of 1991
Pub. L. 102–243, Dec. 20, 1991, 105 Stat. 2394
Short title, see 47 U.S.C. 609 note

Telephone Disclosure and Dispute Resolution Act
Pub. L. 102–556, Oct. 28, 1992, 106 Stat. 4181 (15 U.S.C. 5701 et seq.)
Short title, see 15 U.S.C. 5701(a)

Telephone Operator Consumer Services Improvement Act of 1990
Pub. L. 101–435, Oct. 17, 1990, 104 Stat. 986
Short title, see 47 U.S.C. 609 note

Television Broadcasting to Cuba Act
Pub. L. 101–246, title II, part D (§241 et seq.), Feb. 16, 1990, 104 Stat. 58 (22 U.S.C. 1465aa et seq.)
Short title, see 22 U.S.C. 1465aa note

Television Decoder Circuitry Act of 1990
Pub. L. 101–431, Oct. 15, 1990, 104 Stat. 960
Short title, see 47 U.S.C. 609 note

Television Program Improvement Act of 1990
Pub. L. 101–650, title V, §501, Dec. 1, 1990, 104 Stat. 5127 (47 U.S.C. 303c)
Short title, see 47 U.S.C. 303c(a)

Teller Act (Omnibus Statehood Act)
Feb. 22, 1889, ch. 180, 25 Stat. 676

Teller Resolution (Cuba)
Apr. 20, 1898, No. 24, 30 Stat. 738

Temple Act (Topographical Survey)
Feb. 27, 1925, ch. 360, 43 Stat. 1011

Temporary Child Care for Children With Disabilities and Crisis Nurseries Act Amendments of 1992
Pub. L. 102–295, title II, May 28, 1992, 106 Stat. 200

Temporary Child Care for Children With Disabilities and Crisis Nurseries Act of 1986
Pub. L. 99–401, title II, Aug. 27, 1986, 100 Stat. 907 (42 U.S.C. 5117 et seq.)
Short title, see 42 U.S.C. 5117 note

Temporary Child Care for Handicapped Children and Crisis Nurseries Act of 1986
See Temporary Child Care for Children With Disabilities and Crisis Nurseries Act of 1986

Temporary Emergency Food Assistance Act of 1983
Renamed Emergency Food Assistance Act of 1983

Temporary Emergency Wildfire Suppression Act
Pub. L. 100–428, Sept. 9, 1988, 102 Stat. 1615 (42 U.S.C. 1856m et seq.)
Short title, see 42 U.S.C. 1856m note

Temporary Extended Railroad Unemployment Insurance Benefits Act of 1961
Pub. L. 87–7, Mar. 24, 1961, 75 Stat. 16 (45 U.S.C. 401 et seq.)
Short title, see 45 U.S.C. 401 note

Temporary Extended Unemployment Compensation Act of 1961
Pub. L. 87–6, Mar. 24, 1961, 75 Stat. 8

Temporary Unemployment Compensation Act of 1958
Pub. L. 85–441, June 4, 1958, 72 Stat. 171 (42 U.S.C. 1400 et seq.)

Tennessee Restoration Resolution
July 24, 1866, No. 73, 14 Stat. 364

Tennessee Valley Authority Act of 1933
May 18, 1933, ch. 32, 48 Stat. 58 (16 U.S.C. 831 et seq.)
Short title, see 16 U.S.C. 831

Tennessee Valley Authority Bond Limitation Act
Pub. L. 89–537, Aug. 12, 1966, 80 Stat. 346

Tennessee Valley Authority Bridge Act
Nov. 21, 1941, ch. 480, 55 Stat. 773 (16 U.S.C. 831c–1)

Tennessee Wilderness Act of 1984
Pub. L. 98–578, Oct. 30, 1984, 98 Stat. 3088 (16 U.S.C. 1132 note)

Tennessee Wilderness Act of 1986
Pub. L. 99–490, Oct. 16, 1986, 100 Stat. 1235 (16 U.S.C. 1132 note)

Terminal Inspection Act
Mar. 4, 1915, ch. 144, 38 Stat. 1113 (7 U.S.C. 7760)
Short title, see 7 U.S.C. 7760 note

Territorial Enabling Act of 1950
July 18, 1950, ch. 466, 64 Stat. 344

Territorial Practice Act
Apr. 7, 1874, ch. 80, 18 Stat. 27

Terry Beirn Community Based AIDS Research Initiative Act of 1991
Pub. L. 102–96, Aug. 14, 1991, 105 Stat. 481
Short title, see 42 U.S.C. 201 note

Terry Peak Land Transfer Act of 1999
Pub. L. 106–138, Dec. 7, 1999, 113 Stat. 1693

Texas Annexation Resolution
Mar. 1, 1845, No. 8, 5 Stat. 797

Texas Band of Kickapoo Act
Pub. L. 97–429, Jan. 8, 1983, 96 Stat. 2269 (25 U.S.C. 1300b–11 et seq.)
Short title, see 25 U.S.C. 1300b–11 note

Texas Low-Level Radioactive Waste Disposal Compact Consent Act
Pub. L. 105–236, Sept. 20, 1998, 112 Stat. 1542 (42 U.S.C. 2021d note)

Texas National Forests Improvement Act of 2000
Pub. L. 106–330, Oct. 19, 2000, 114 Stat. 1299

Texas Volunteer Pensions Act
May 30, 1908, ch. 230, 35 Stat. 553

Texas Wilderness Act of 1984
Pub. L. 98–574, Oct. 30, 1984, 98 Stat. 3051 (16 U.S.C. 1132 note)

Textile Fiber Products Identification Act
Pub. L. 85–897, Sept. 2, 1958, 72 Stat. 1717 (15 U.S.C. 70 et seq.)
Short title, see 15 U.S.C. 70 note

Thanksgiving Day Act
Dec. 26, 1941, ch. 631, 55 Stat. 862

Third Deficiency Appropriation Act, 1946
July 23, 1946, ch. 591, 60 Stat. 600

Third Deficiency Appropriation Act, 1949
Oct. 10, 1949, ch. 662, 63 Stat. 738

Third Deficiency Appropriation Act, fiscal year 1939
Aug. 9, 1939, ch. 633, 53 Stat. 1301

Third Liberty Bond Act
Apr. 4, 1918, ch. 44, 40 Stat. 502

Third Liberty Loan Act
See Third Liberty Bond Act

Third Supplemental Appropriation Act, 1948
Dec. 23, 1947, ch. 524, 61 Stat. 941

Third Supplemental Appropriation Act, 1951
June 2, 1951, ch. 121, 65 Stat. 52

Third Supplemental Appropriation Act, 1952
June 5, 1952, ch. 369, 66 Stat. 101

Third Supplemental Appropriation Act, 1954
May 11, 1954, ch. 200, 68 Stat. 81

Third Supplemental Appropriation Act, 1957
Pub. L. 85–58, June 21, 1957, 71 Stat. 176

Third Supplemental Appropriation Act, 1961
Pub. L. 87–14, Mar. 31, 1961, 75 Stat. 20

Third Supplemental National Defense Appropriation Act, 1941
Oct. 8, 1940, ch. 756, 54 Stat. 965

Third Supplemental National Defense Appropriation Act, 1942
Dec. 17, 1941, ch. 591, 55 Stat. 810

Third Supplemental Surplus Appropriation Rescission Act, 1946
July 23, 1946, ch. 591, title II, 60 Stat. 624

Third Urgent Deficiency Appropriation Act, 1946
June 21, 1946, ch. 425, 60 Stat. 262

Thomas Alva Edison Commemorative Coin Act
Pub. L. 105–331, Oct. 31, 1998, 112 Stat. 3073 (31 U.S.C. 5112 note)

Thomas Amendment
May 12, 1933, ch. 25, title III, 48 Stat. 51

Thomas Cole National Historic Site Act
Pub. L. 106–146, Dec. 9, 1999, 113 Stat. 1714

Thomas Jefferson Commemoration Commission Act
Pub. L. 102–343, Aug. 17, 1992, 106 Stat. 915

Threatening Communication Act
May 15, 1939, ch. 133, 53 Stat. 742

Three Affiliated Tribes and Standing Rock Sioux Tribe Equitable Compensation Act
Pub. L. 102–575, title XXXV, Oct. 30, 1992, 106 Stat. 4731

Three Million Dollar Act
Mar. 3, 1847, ch. 50, 9 Stat. 174

Three Per Cent Act (Immigration)
May 19, 1921, ch. 8, 42 Stat. 5

Thrift Industry Recovery Act
Pub. L. 100–86, title IV, Aug. 10, 1987, 101 Stat. 604
Short title, see 12 U.S.C. 226 note

Thrift Institutions Restructuring Act
Pub. L. 97–320, title III, Oct. 15, 1982, 96 Stat. 1496
Short title, see 12 U.S.C. 1461 note

Thrift Savings Fund Investment Act of 1987
Pub. L. 100–43, May 22, 1987, 101 Stat. 315
Short title, see 5 U.S.C. 8401 note

Thrift Savings Investment Funds Act of 1996
Pub. L. 104–208, div. A, title I, §101(f) [title VI, §659 [title I]], Sept. 30, 1996, 110 Stat. 3009–314, 3009–372
Short title, see 5 U.S.C. 8401 note

Thrift Savings Plan Act of 1996
Pub. L. 104–208, div. A, title I, §101(f) [title VI, §659 [title II]], Sept. 30, 1996, 110 Stat. 3009–314, 3009–372, 3009–374
Short title, see 5 U.S.C. 8401 note

Thrift Savings Plan Technical Amendments Act of 1990
Pub. L. 101–335, July 17, 1990, 104 Stat. 319
Short title, see 5 U.S.C. 8401 note

Thurman Act (Pacific Railroads)
May 7, 1878, ch. 96, 20 Stat. 56

Ticket to Work and Work Incentives Improvement Act of 1999
Pub. L. 106–170, Dec. 17, 1999, 113 Stat. 1860
Short title, see 42 U.S.C. 1305 note

Tidelands
See Submerged Lands Act

Tijuana River Valley Estuary and Beach Sewage Cleanup Act of 2000
Pub. L. 106–457, title VIII, Nov. 7, 2000, 114 Stat. 1977 (22 U.S.C. 277d–43 et seq.)
Short title, see 22 U.S.C. 277d–43 note

Tillman-Gillespie Resolution (Transportation of Coal and Oil)
Mar. 7, 1906, ch. 8, 34 Stat. 823

Timber and Stone Act
June 3, 1878, ch. 151, 20 Stat. 89 (43 U.S.C. 311 et seq.)

Timber Culture Repeal Act
Mar. 3, 1891, ch. 561, 26 Stat. 1095

Timbisha Shoshone Homeland Act
Pub. L. 106–423, Nov. 1, 2000, 114 Stat. 1875 (16 U.S.C. 410aaa note)

Tin Protection Act
Feb. 15, 1936, ch. 74, 49 Stat. 1140 (50 U.S.C. 86 et seq.)

Tincher-Capper Act (Grain Futures)
See Commodity Exchange Act

Title I of the Elementary and Secondary Education Act of 1965
Sept. 30, 1950, ch. 1124, title II, as added Pub. L. 89–10, title I, §2, Apr. 11, 1965, 79 Stat. 27

Title II, Military Appropriation act, 1941
June 26, 1940, ch. 430, title II, 54 Stat. 601

Title II, Military Appropriation Act, 1942
Aug. 25, 1941, ch. 409, title I, 55 Stat. 669

Title II, Naval Appropriation Act, 1942
July 3, 1941, ch. 273, title I [part], 55 Stat. 557–559

Title II, Naval Appropriation Act, 1943
June 23, 1942, ch. 444[part], 56 Stat. 387

Title III of the Naval Appropriation Act for the Fiscal Year 1941
June 26, 1940, ch. 430, title III, 54 Stat. 604

Title III, Military Appropriation Act, 1941
Sept. 9, 1940, ch. 717, title I, 54 Stat. 872

Title III, Military Appropriation Act, 1942
Dec. 17, 1941, ch. 591, title I, 55 Stat. 810

Title III, Naval Appropriation Act for the fiscal year 1942
Aug. 25, 1941, ch. 409, title II, 55 Stat. 670

Title III, Naval Appropriation Act, 1943
Oct. 26, 1942, ch. 629, title I, 56 Stat. 990

Title IV of the Naval Appropriation Act for the fiscal year 1941
Sept. 9, 1940, ch. 717, title II, 54 Stat. 875

Title IV, Naval Appropriation Act, 1942
Oct. 28, 1941, ch. 460, title II [part], 55 Stat. 753

Title to Movable Property Act
July 29, 1954, ch. 616, 68 Stat. 580 (43 U.S.C. 499a)
Short title, see 43 U.S.C. 499a note

Title V, Military Appropriation Act, 1942
Mar. 5, 1942, ch. 141, title I, 56 Stat. 128

Title V, Naval Appropriation Act, 1942
Dec. 17, 1941, ch. 591, title II, 55 Stat. 814

Title V, Naval Appropriation Act, 1943
June 26, 1943, ch. 147, title II, 57 Stat. 218

Title VI, Military Appropriation Act, 1941
Apr. 5, 1941, ch. 41, title I, 55 Stat. 123

Title VI, Military Appropriation Act, 1942
Apr. 28, 1942, ch. 247, title I, 56 Stat. 226

Title VI, Naval Appropriation Act, 1942
Feb. 7, 1942, ch. 46, title II, 56 Stat. 78

Title VII, Naval Appropriation Act for the fiscal year 1941
Apr. 5, 1941, ch. 41, title II, 55 Stat. 128

Title VII, Naval Appropriation Act, 1942
Apr. 28, 1942, ch. 247, title II, 56 Stat. 229

Title VIII, Naval Appropriation Act for the fiscal year 1941
July 3, 1941, ch. 273, title I [part], 55 Stat. 556

Title VIII, Naval Appropriation Act, 1942
June 23, 1942, ch. 444 [part], 56 Stat. 387

Tiwa Indians Act
Pub. L. 90–287, Apr. 12, 1968, 82 Stat. 93

Tlingit and Haida Status Clarification Act
Pub. L. 103–454, title II, Nov. 2, 1994, 108 Stat. 4792 (25 U.S.C. 1212 et seq.)
Short title, see 25 U.S.C. 1212 note

Tobacco Adjustment Act of 1983
Pub. L. 98–180, title II, Nov. 29, 1983, 97 Stat. 1143
Short title, see 7 U.S.C. 1421 note

Tobacco Control Act
Apr. 25, 1936, ch. 249, 49 Stat. 1239 (7 U.S.C. 515 et seq.)
Short title, see 7 U.S.C. 515 note

Tobacco Inspection Act
Aug. 23, 1935, ch. 623, 49 Stat. 731 (7 U.S.C. 511 et seq.)
Short title, see 7 U.S.C. 511q

Tobacco Statistics Act
Apr. 30, 1912, ch. 102, 37 Stat. 106

Tohono O'odham Tat Momolikot Dam Settlement Act
Pub. L. 99–469, Oct. 14, 1986, 100 Stat. 1195

Tokyo Exposition Act
May 22, 1908, ch. 185, 35 Stat. 183

Tongass Timber Reform Act
Pub. L. 101–626, Nov. 28, 1990, 104 Stat. 4426
Short title, see 16 U.S.C. 539d note

Tonnage Measurement Simplification Act
Pub. L. 96–594, title II, Dec. 24, 1980, 94 Stat. 3461

Torres-Martinez Desert Cahuilla Indians Claims Settlement Act
Pub. L. 106–568, title VI, Dec. 27, 2000, 114 Stat. 2906 (25 U.S.C. 1778 et seq.)
Short title, see 25 U.S.C. 1778 note

Torture Victim Protection Act of 1991
Pub. L. 102–256, Mar. 12, 1992, 106 Stat. 73 (28 U.S.C. 1350 note)

Torture Victims Relief Act of 1998
Pub. L. 105–320, Oct. 30, 1998, 112 Stat. 3016 (22 U.S.C. 2152 note)

Torture Victims Relief Reauthorization Act of 1999
Pub. L. 106–87, Nov. 3, 1999, 113 Stat. 1301
Short title, see 22 U.S.C. 2151 note

Tourism Policy and Export Promotion Act of 1992
Pub. L. 102–372, Sept. 30, 1992, 106 Stat. 1170
Short title, see 22 U.S.C. 2121 note

Towner-Sheppard Act (Maternity Hygiene)
See Maternity Act

Toxic Substances Control Act
Pub. L. 94–469, Oct. 11, 1976, 90 Stat. 2003 (15 U.S.C. 2601 et seq.)
Short title, see 15 U.S.C. 2601 note

Toy Safety Act of 1984
Pub. L. 98–491, Oct. 17, 1984, 98 Stat. 2269
Short title, see 15 U.S.C. 1261 note

Trade Act of 1974
Pub. L. 93–618, Jan. 3, 1975, 88 Stat. 1978 (19 U.S.C. 2101 et seq.)
Short title, see 19 U.S.C. 2101

Trade Adjustment Assistance Reform and Extension Act of 1986
Pub. L. 99–272, title XIII, subtitle A, part 1 (§13001 et seq.), Apr. 7, 1986, 100 Stat. 300
Short title, see 19 U.S.C. 2101 note

Trade Agreements Act
June 12, 1934, ch. 474, 48 Stat. 943 (19 U.S.C. 1351 et seq.)

Trade Agreements Act of 1979
Pub. L. 96–39, July 26, 1979, 93 Stat. 144 (19 U.S.C. 2501 et seq.)
Short title, see 19 U.S.C. 2501

Trade Agreements Extension Act of 1948
June 26, 1948, ch. 678, 62 Stat. 1053

Trade Agreements Extension Act of 1949
Sept. 26, 1949, ch. 585, 63 Stat. 697
Short title, see 19 U.S.C. 1654 note

Trade Agreements Extension Act of 1951
June 16, 1951, ch. 141, 65 Stat. 72
Short title, see 19 U.S.C. 1654 note

Trade Agreements Extension Act of 1953
Aug. 7, 1953, ch. 348, 67 Stat. 472
Short title, see 19 U.S.C. 1654 note

Trade Agreements Extension Act of 1955
June 21, 1955, ch. 169, 69 Stat. 162
Short title, see 19 U.S.C. 1654 note

Trade Agreements Extension Act of 1958
Pub. L. 85–686, Aug. 20, 1958, 72 Stat. 673
Short title, see 19 U.S.C. 1654 note

Trade and Development Act of 2000
Pub. L. 106–200, May 18, 2000, 114 Stat. 251
Short title, see 19 U.S.C. 3701 note

Trade and Development Enhancement Act of 1983
Pub. L. 98–181, title VI, part C (§641 et seq.), Nov. 30, 1983, 97 Stat. 1263 (12 U.S.C. 635*o* et seq.)
Short title, see 12 U.S.C. 635*o* note

Trade and Intercourse Act of 1790 (Indians)
July 22, 1790, ch. 33, 1 Stat. 137

Trade and Intercourse Act of 1834
See Intercourse Act (Indian Tribes)

Trade and Tariff Act of 1984
Pub. L. 98–573, Oct. 30, 1984, 98 Stat. 2948
Short title, see 19 U.S.C. 1654 note

Trade Commission Act
See Federal Trade Commission Act

Trade Deficit Review Commission Act
Pub. L. 105–277, div. A, §127, Oct. 21, 1998, 112 Stat. 2681–547 (19 U.S.C. 2213 note)

Trade Dollar Retirement Act
Mar. 3, 1887, ch. 396, 24 Stat. 634

Trade Expansion Act of 1962
Pub. L. 87–794, Oct. 11, 1962, 76 Stat. 872 (19 U.S.C. 1801 et seq.)
Short title, see 19 U.S.C. 1801 note

Trade Fair Act of 1959
Pub. L. 86–14, Apr. 22, 1959, 73 Stat. 18 (19 U.S.C. 1751 et seq.)
Short title, see 19 U.S.C. 1751 note

Trade Sanctions Reform and Export Enhancement Act of 2000
Pub. L. 106–387, §1(a) [title IX], Oct. 28, 2000, 114 Stat. 1549, 1549A–67 (22 U.S.C. 7201 et seq.)
Short title, see 22 U.S.C. 7201 note

Trademark Act of 1946
Also known as the Lanham Act
July 5, 1946, ch. 540, 60 Stat. 427 (15 U.S.C. 1051 et seq.)
Short title, see 15 U.S.C. 1051 note

Trademark Amendments Act of 1999
Pub. L. 106–43, Aug. 5, 1999, 113 Stat. 218
Short title, see 15 U.S.C. 1051 note

Trademark Clarification Act of 1984
Pub. L. 98–620, title I, Nov. 8, 1984, 98 Stat. 3335
Short title, see 15 U.S.C. 1051 note

Trademark Counterfeiting Act of 1984
Pub. L. 98–473, title II, ch. XV (§1501 et seq.), Oct. 12, 1984, 98 Stat. 2178
Short title, see 18 U.S.C. 2311 note

Trademark Law Revision Act of 1988
Pub. L. 100–667, title I, Nov. 16, 1988, 102 Stat. 3935
Short title, see 15 U.S.C. 1051 note

Trademark Law Treaty Implementation Act
Pub. L. 105–330, title I, Oct. 30, 1998, 112 Stat. 3064
Short title, see 15 U.S.C. 1051 note

Trademark Remedy Clarification Act
Pub. L. 102–542, Oct. 27, 1992, 106 Stat. 3567
Short title, see 15 U.S.C. 1051 note

Trades Unions Act
June 29, 1886, ch. 567, 24 Stat. 86

Trading with the enemy Act
Oct. 6, 1917, ch. 106, 40 Stat. 411 (50 App. U.S.C. 1 et seq.)

Trading with the enemy Act—Continued
Short title, see 50 App. U.S.C. 1

Trafficking Victims Protection Act of 2000
Pub. L. 106–386, div. A, Oct. 28, 2000, 114 Stat. 1466 (22 U.S.C. 7101 et seq.)
Short title, see 22 U.S.C. 7101 note

Trail Act (Alaska)
See Alaska Road and Trail Act

Training Technology Transfer Act of 1988
Pub. L. 100–418, title VI, subtitle B (§6101 et seq.), Aug. 23, 1988, 102 Stat. 1500 (20 U.S.C. 5091 et seq.)
Short title, see 20 U.S.C. 5091

Tramroad Act
Jan. 21, 1895, ch. 37, 28 Stat. 635 (43 U.S.C. 956)

Trans-Alaska Pipeline Authorization Act
Pub. L. 93–153, title II, Nov. 16, 1973, 87 Stat. 584 (43 U.S.C. 1651 et seq.)
Short title, see 43 U.S.C. 1651 note

Trans-Alaska Pipeline System Reform Act of 1990
Pub. L. 101–380, title VIII, Aug. 18, 1990, 104 Stat. 564
Short title, see 43 U.S.C. 1651 note

Transplant Amendments Act of 1990
Pub. L. 101–616, Nov. 16, 1990, 104 Stat. 3279
Short title, see 42 U.S.C. 201 note

Transportation Act, 1920
Feb. 28, 1920, ch. 91, 41 Stat. 456

Transportation Act of 1940
Sept. 18, 1940, ch. 722, 54 Stat. 898

Transportation Act of 1958
Pub. L. 85–625, Aug. 12, 1958, 72 Stat. 568

Transportation Equity Act for the 21st Century
Pub. L. 105–178, June 9, 1998, 112 Stat. 107
Short title, see 23 U.S.C. 101 note

Transportation Infrastructure Finance and Innovation Act of 1998
Pub. L. 105–178, title I, subtitle E, ch. 1 (§1501 et seq.), June 9, 1998, 112 Stat. 241 (23 U.S.C. 181 et seq.)
Short title, see 23 U.S.C. 101 note

Transportation of Foreign Mail by Aircraft Act
Aug. 27, 1940, ch. 693, 54 Stat. 862

Transportation Payment Act of 1972
Pub. L. 92–550, Oct. 25, 1972, 86 Stat. 1163

Transportation Recall Enhancement, Accountability, and Documentation (TREAD) Act
Pub. L. 106–414, Nov. 1, 2000, 114 Stat. 1800
Short title, see 49 U.S.C. 30101 note

Transportation Safety Act of 1974
Pub. L. 93–633, Jan. 3, 1975, 88 Stat. 2156

Trauma Care Systems Planning and Development Act of 1990
Pub. L. 101–590, Nov. 16, 1990, 104 Stat. 2915
Short title, see 42 U.S.C. 201 note

Travel and Transportation Reform Act of 1998
Pub. L. 105–264, Oct. 19, 1998, 112 Stat. 2350
Short title, see 5 U.S.C. 5701 note

Travel Expense Act of 1949
June 9, 1949, ch. 185, 63 Stat. 166

Travel Expense Amendments Act of 1975
Pub. L. 94–22, May 19, 1975, 89 Stat. 84
Short title, see 5 U.S.C. 5701 note

TREAD Act
See Transportation Recall Enhancement, Accountability, and Documentation (TREAD) Act

Treasury and General Government Appropriations Act, 1998
Pub. L. 105–61, Oct. 10, 1997, 111 Stat. 1272

Treasury and General Government Appropriations Act, 1999
Pub. L. 105–277, div. A, §101(h), Oct. 21, 1998, 112 Stat. 2681–480

Treasury and General Government Appropriations Act, 2000
Pub. L. 106–58, Sept. 29, 1999, 113 Stat. 430

Treasury and General Government Appropriations Act, 2001
Pub. L. 106–554, §1(a)(3), Dec. 21, 2000, 114 Stat. 2763, 2763A–125

Treasury and Post Office Departments Appropriation Act, 1941
Mar. 25, 1940, ch. 71, 54 Stat. 55

Treasury and Post Office Departments Appropriation Act, 1942
May 31, 1941, ch. 156, 55 Stat. 212

Treasury and Post Office Departments Appropriation Act, 1943
Mar. 10, 1942, ch. 178, 56 Stat. 150

Treasury and Post Office Departments Appropriation Act, 1944
June 30, 1943, ch. 179, 57 Stat. 250

Treasury and Post Office Departments Appropriation Act, 1945
Apr. 22, 1944, ch. 175, 58 Stat. 195

Treasury and Post Office Departments Appropriation Act, 1946
Apr. 24, 1945, ch. 92, 59 Stat. 56

Treasury and Post Office Departments Appropriation Act, 1947
July 20, 1946, ch. 588, 60 Stat. 568

Treasury and Post Office Departments Appropriation Act, 1948
July 1, 1947, ch. 186, 61 Stat. 216

Treasury and Post Office Departments Appropriation Act, 1949
June 14, 1948, ch. 466, 62 Stat. 408

Treasury and Post Office Departments Appropriation Act, 1950
June 30, 1949, ch. 286, 63 Stat. 356

Treasury and Post Office Departments Appropriation Act, 1952
Aug. 11, 1951, ch. 301, 65 Stat. 182

Treasury and Post Office Departments Appropriation Act, 1953
June 30, 1952, ch. 523, 66 Stat. 289

Treasury and Post Office Departments Appropriation Act, 1954
June 18, 1953, ch. 132, 67 Stat. 67

Treasury Department Appropriation Act, 1937
June 23, 1936, ch. 725, title I, 49 Stat. 1827

Treasury Department Appropriation Act, 1938
May 14, 1937, ch. 180, title I, 50 Stat. 137

Treasury Department Appropriation Act, 1939
Mar. 28, 1938, ch. 55, title I, 52 Stat. 120

Treasury Department Appropriation Act 1940
May 6, 1939, ch. 115, title I, 53 Stat. 654

Treasury Department Appropriation Act 1941
Mar. 25, 1940, ch. 71, title I, 54 Stat. 55

Treasury Department Appropriation Act, 1942
May 31, 1941, ch. 156, title I, 55 Stat. 212

Treasury Department Appropriation Act, 1943
Mar. 10, 1942, ch. 178, title I, 56 Stat. 150

Treasury Department Appropriation Act, 1944
June 30, 1943, ch. 179, title I, 57 Stat. 250

Treasury Department Appropriation Act, 1945
Apr. 22, 1944, ch. 175, title I, 58 Stat. 195

Treasury Department Appropriation Act, 1946
Apr. 24, 1945, ch. 92, title I, 59 Stat. 56

Treasury Department Appropriation Act, 1947
July 20, 1946, ch. 588, title I, 60 Stat. 568

Treasury Department Appropriation Act, 1948
July 1, 1947, ch. 186, title I, 61 Stat. 216

Treasury Department Appropriation Act, 1949
June 14, 1948, ch. 466, title I, 62 Stat. 408

Treasury Department Appropriation Act, 1950
June 30, 1949, ch. 286, title I, 63 Stat. 356

Treasury Department Appropriation Act, 1951
Sept. 6, 1950, ch. 896, Ch. IV, title I, 64 Stat. 634

Treasury Department Appropriation Act, 1952
Aug. 11, 1951, ch. 301, title I, 65 Stat. 182

Treasury Department Appropriation Act, 1953
June 30, 1952, ch. 523, title I, 66 Stat. 289

Treasury Department Appropriation Act, 1954
June 18, 1953, ch. 132, title I, 67 Stat. 67

Treasury Department Appropriation Act, 1955
May 28, 1954, ch. 242, title I, 68 Stat. 144

Treasury Department Appropriation Act, 1960
Pub. L. 86–39, title I, June 11, 1959, 73 Stat. 65

Treasury Department Appropriation Act, 1961
Pub. L. 86–561, title I, June 30, 1960, 74 Stat. 283

Treasury Department Appropriation Act, 1962
Pub. L. 87–159, title I, Aug. 21, 1961, 75 Stat. 393

Treasury Department Appropriation Act, 1963
Pub. L. 87–575, title I, Aug. 6, 1962, 76 Stat. 310

Treasury Department Appropriation Act, 1964
Pub. L. 88–39, title I, June 13, 1963, 77 Stat. 58

Treasury Department Appropriation Act, 1965
Pub. L. 88–392, title I, Aug. 1, 1964, 78 Stat. 367

Treasury Department Appropriation Act, 1966
Pub. L. 89–57, title I, June 30, 1965, 79 Stat. 196

Treasury Department Appropriation Act, 1968
Pub. L. 90–47, title I, July 7, 1967, 81 Stat. 113

Treasury Department Appropriation Act, 1969
Pub. L. 90–350, title I, June 19, 1968, 82 Stat. 190

Treasury Department Appropriation Act, 1970
Pub. L. 91–74, title I, Sept. 29, 1969, 83 Stat. 116

Treasury Department Appropriation Act, 1971
Pub. L. 91–422, title I, Sept. 26, 1970, 84 Stat. 872

Treasury Department Appropriation Act, 1973
Pub. L. 92–351, title I, July 13, 1972, 86 Stat. 471

Treasury Department Appropriation Act, 1974
Pub. L. 93–143, title I, Oct. 30, 1973, 87 Stat. 511

Treasury Department Appropriation Act, 1967
Pub. L. 89–474, title I, June 29, 1966, 80 Stat. 222

Treasury Department Appropriation Act, 1972
Pub. L. 92–49, title I, July 9, 1971, 85 Stat. 108

Treasury Department Appropriations Act, 1975
Pub. L. 93–381, title I, Aug. 21, 1974, 88 Stat. 613

Treasury Department Appropriations Act, 1976
Pub. L. 94–91, title I, Aug. 9, 1975, 89 Stat. 441

Treasury Department Appropriations Act, 1977
Pub. L. 94–363, title I, July 14, 1976, 90 Stat. 963

Treasury Department Appropriations Act, 1978
Pub. L. 95–81, title I, July 31, 1977, 91 Stat. 341

Treasury Department Appropriations Act, 1979
Pub. L. 95–429, title I, Oct. 10, 1978, 92 Stat. 1001

Treasury Department Appropriations Act, 1980
Pub. L. 96–74, title I, Sept. 29, 1979, 93 Stat. 559

Treasury Department Appropriations Act, 1987
Pub. L. 99–500, §101(m) [title I], Oct. 18, 1986, 100 Stat. 1783–308, and Pub. L. 99–591, §101(m) [title I], Oct. 30, 1986, 100 Stat. 3341–308

Treasury Department Appropriations Act, 1988
Pub. L. 100–202, §101(m) [title I], Dec. 22, 1987, 101 Stat. 1329–390

Treasury Department Appropriations Act, 1989
Pub. L. 100–440, title I, Sept. 22, 1988, 102 Stat. 1721

Treasury Department Appropriations Act, 1990
Pub. L. 101–136, title I, Nov. 3, 1989, 103 Stat. 783

Treasury Department Appropriations Act, 1991
Pub. L. 101–509, title I, Nov. 5, 1990, 104 Stat. 1389

Treasury Department Appropriations Act, 1992
Pub. L. 102–141, title I, Oct. 28, 1991, 105 Stat. 834

Treasury Department Appropriations Act, 1993
Pub. L. 102–393, title I, Oct. 6, 1992, 106 Stat. 1729

Treasury Department Appropriations Act, 1994
Pub. L. 103–123, title I, Oct. 28, 1993, 107 Stat. 1226

Treasury Department Appropriations Act, 1995
Pub. L. 103–329, title I, Sept. 30, 1994, 108 Stat. 2382

Treasury Department Appropriations Act, 1996
Pub. L. 104–52, title I, Nov. 19, 1995, 109 Stat. 468

Treasury Department Appropriations Act, 1997
Pub. L. 104–208, div. A, title I, §101(f) [title I], Sept. 30, 1996, 110 Stat. 3009–314

Treasury Department Appropriations Act, 1998
Pub. L. 105–61, title I, Oct. 10, 1997, 111 Stat. 1272

Treasury Department Appropriations Act, 1999
Pub. L. 105–277, div. A, §101(h) [title I], Oct. 21, 1998, 112 Stat. 2681–480

Treasury Department Appropriations Act, 2000
Pub. L. 106–58, title I, Sept. 29, 1999, 113 Stat. 430

Treasury Department Appropriations Act, 2001
Pub. L. 106–554, §1(a)(3) [title I], Dec. 21, 2000, 114 Stat. 2763, 2763A–125

Treasury Forfeiture Fund Act of 1992
Pub. L. 102–393, title VI, §638, Oct. 6, 1992, 106 Stat. 1779
Short title, see 31 U.S.C. 9701 note

Treasury, Post Office, and Executive Office Appropriation Act, 1964
Pub. L. 88–39, June 13, 1963, 77 Stat. 58

Treasury, Post Office, and Executive Office Appropriation Act, 1965
Pub. L. 88–392, Aug. 1, 1964, 78 Stat. 367

Treasury, Post Office, and Executive Office Appropriation Act, 1966
Pub. L. 89–57, June 30, 1965, 79 Stat. 196

Treasury, Post Office, and Executive Office Appropriation Act, 1967
Pub. L. 89–474, June 29, 1966, 80 Stat. 222

Treasury, Post Office, and Executive Office Appropriation Act, 1968
Pub. L. 90–47, July 7, 1967, 81 Stat. 113

Treasury, Post Office, and Executive Office Appropriation Act, 1969
Pub. L. 90–350, June 19, 1968, 82 Stat. 190

Treasury, Post Office, and Executive Office Appropriation Act, 1970
Pub. L. 91–74, Sept. 29, 1969, 83 Stat. 116

Treasury, Post Office, and Executive Office Appropriation Act, 1971
Pub. L. 91–422, Sept. 26, 1970, 84 Stat. 872

Treasury, Postal Service and General Government Appropriations Act, 1988
Pub. L. 100–202, §101(m), Dec. 22, 1987, 101 Stat. 1329–390

Treasury, Postal Service and General Government Appropriations Act, 1989
Pub. L. 100–440, Sept. 22, 1988, 102 Stat. 1721

Treasury, Postal Service and General Government Appropriations Act, 1990
Pub. L. 101–136, Nov. 3, 1989, 103 Stat. 783

Treasury, Postal Service and General Government Appropriations Act, 1991
Pub. L. 101–509, Nov. 5, 1990, 104 Stat. 1389

Treasury, Postal Service and General Government Appropriations Act, 1992
Pub. L. 102–141, Oct. 28, 1991, 105 Stat. 834

Treasury, Postal Service and General Government Appropriations Act, 1995
Pub. L. 103–329, Sept. 30, 1994, 108 Stat. 2382

Treasury, Postal Service, and General Government Appropriation Act, 1972
Pub. L. 92–49, July 9, 1971, 85 Stat. 108

Treasury, Postal Service, and General Government Appropriation Act, 1973
Pub. L. 92–351, July 13, 1972, 86 Stat. 471

Treasury, Postal Service, and General Government Appropriation Act, 1974
Pub. L. 93–143, Oct. 30, 1973, 87 Stat. 510

Treasury, Postal Service, and General Government Appropriation Act, 1975
Pub. L. 93–381, Aug. 21, 1974, 88 Stat. 613

Treasury, Postal Service, and General Government Appropriation Act, 1976
Pub. L. 94–91, Aug. 9, 1975, 89 Stat. 441

Treasury, Postal Service, and General Government Appropriation Act, 1977
Pub. L. 94–363, July 14, 1976, 90 Stat. 963

Treasury, Postal Service, and General Government Appropriation Act, 1978
Pub. L. 95–81, July 31, 1977, 91 Stat. 341

Treasury, Postal Service, and General Government Appropriation Act, 1984
Pub. L. 98–151, §101(f) [H.R. 4139, S. 1646], Nov. 14, 1983, 97 Stat. 973; Pub. L. 100–202, §106, Dec. 22, 1987, 101 Stat. 1329–433

Treasury, Postal Service, and General Government Appropriations Act, 1979
Pub. L. 95–429, Oct. 10, 1978, 92 Stat. 1001

Treasury, Postal Service, and General Government Appropriations Act, 1980
Pub. L. 96–74, Sept. 29, 1979, 93 Stat. 559

Treasury, Postal Service, and General Government Appropriations Act, 1993
Pub. L. 102–393, Oct. 6, 1992, 106 Stat. 1729

Treasury, Postal Service, and General Government Appropriations Act, 1994
Pub. L. 103–123, Oct. 28, 1993, 107 Stat. 1226

Treasury, Postal Service, and General Government Appropriations Act, 1996
Pub. L. 104–52, Nov. 19, 1995, 109 Stat. 468

Treasury, Postal Service, and General Government Appropriations Act, 1997
Pub. L. 104–208, div. A, title I, §101(f), Sept. 30, 1996, 110 Stat. 3009–314

Treasury-Post Office Appropriation Act, 1938
May 14, 1937, ch. 180, 50 Stat. 137

Treasury-Post Office Appropriation Act, 1939
Mar. 28, 1938, ch. 55, 52 Stat. 120

Treasury-Post Office Appropriation Act, 1940
May 6, 1939, ch. 115, 53 Stat. 654

Treasury-Post Office Appropriation Act, 1956
June 1, 1955, ch. 113, 69 Stat. 72

Treasury-Post Office Appropriation Act, 1957
Apr. 2, 1956, ch. 161, 70 Stat. 92

Treasury-Post Office Appropriation Act, 1958
Pub. L. 85–37, May 27, 1957, 71 Stat. 35

Treasury-Post Office Appropriation Act, 1959
Pub. L. 85–354, Mar. 28, 1958, 72 Stat. 61

Treasury-Post Office Appropriation Act, 1960
Pub. L. 86–39, June 11, 1959, 73 Stat. 65

Treasury-Post Office Appropriation Act, 1961
Pub. L. 86–561, June 30, 1960, 74 Stat. 283

Treasury-Post Office Appropriation Act, 1962
Pub. L. 87–159, Aug. 21, 1961, 75 Stat. 393

Treasury-Post Office Departments and Executive Office Appropriation Act, 1963
Pub. L. 87–575, Aug. 6, 1962, 76 Stat. 310

Treasury-Post Office Departments Appropriation Act, 1951
Sept. 6, 1950, ch. 896, Ch. IV, 64 Stat. 634

Tribal Development Student Assistance Act
Pub. L. 102–325, title XIII, part E (§1341 et seq.), July 23, 1992, 106 Stat. 809 (25 U.S.C. 3331 et seq.)
Short title, see 25 U.S.C. 3331

Tribal Economic Development and Technology Related Education Assistance Act of 1990
Pub. L. 95–471, title IV, as added Pub. L. 101–392, title III, §312, Sept. 25, 1990, 104 Stat. 804
Short title, see 25 U.S.C. 1801 note

Tribal Self-Governance Act of 1994
Pub. L. 103–413, title II, Oct. 25, 1994, 108 Stat. 4270
Short title, see 25 U.S.C. 450 note

Tribal Self-Governance Amendments of 2000
Pub. L. 106–260, Aug. 18, 2000, 114 Stat. 711
Short title, see 25 U.S.C. 450 note

Tribal Self-Governance Demonstration Project Act
Pub. L. 102–184, Dec. 4, 1991, 105 Stat. 1278
Short title, see 25 U.S.C. 450f note

Tribally Controlled College or University Assistance Act of 1978
Pub. L. 95–471, Oct. 17, 1978, 92 Stat. 1325 (25 U.S.C. 1801 et seq.)
Short title, see 25 U.S.C. 1801 note

Tribally Controlled Community College Assistance Act of 1978
Renamed Tribally Controlled College or University Assistance Act of 1978

Tribally Controlled Community College Assistance Amendments of 1986
Pub. L. 99–428, Sept. 30, 1986, 100 Stat. 982
Short title, see 25 U.S.C. 1801 note

Tribally Controlled Schools Act of 1988
Pub. L. 100–297, title V, part B (§5201 et seq.), Apr. 28, 1988, 102 Stat. 385 (25 U.S.C. 2501 et seq.)
Short title, see 25 U.S.C. 2501 note

Tribally Controlled Vocational Institutions Support Act of 1990
Pub. L. 88–210, title III, part H (§381 et seq.), as added Pub. L. 101–392, title III, §311, Sept. 25, 1990, 104 Stat. 799
Short title, see 20 U.S.C. 2397 note

Trinity River Basin Fish and Wildlife Management Act of 1984
Pub. L. 98–541, Oct. 24, 1984, 98 Stat. 2721

Trinity River Basin Fish and Wildlife Management Reauthorization Act of 1995
Pub. L. 104–143, May 15, 1996, 110 Stat. 1338

Troops-to-Teachers Program Act of 1999
Pub. L. 106–65, div. A, title XVII, Oct. 5, 1999, 113 Stat. 817 (20 U.S.C. 9301 et seq.)
Short title, see 20 U.S.C. 9301

Tropical Forest Conservation Act of 1998
Pub. L. 87–195, part V, as added Pub. L. 105–214, §1, July 29, 1998, 112 Stat. 885 (22 U.S.C. 2431 et seq.)
Short title, see 22 U.S.C. 2151 note

Truck and Bus Safety and Regulatory Reform Act of 1988
Pub. L. 100–690, title IX, subtitle B (§9101 et seq.), Nov. 18, 1988, 102 Stat. 4527

Truckee-Carson-Pyramid Lake Water Rights Settlement Act
Pub. L. 101–618, title II, Nov. 16, 1990, 104 Stat. 3294

Trucking Industry Regulatory Reform Act of 1994
Pub. L. 103–311, title II, Aug. 26, 1994, 108 Stat. 1683

Truman-Hobbs Act
Also known as the Hobbs Bridge Act
June 21, 1940, ch. 409, 54 Stat. 497 (33 U.S.C. 511 et seq.)
Short title, see 33 U.S.C. 511 note

Trust Fund Code of 1981
Aug. 16, 1954, ch. 736, subtitle I, as added Dec. 29, 1981, Pub. L. 97–119, title I, §103(a), 95 Stat. 1636
Short title, see 26 U.S.C. 9500

Trust Indenture Act of 1939
May 27, 1933, ch. 38, title III, as added Aug. 3, 1939, ch. 411, 53 Stat. 1149 (15 U.S.C. 77aaa et seq.)
Short title, see 15 U.S.C. 77aaa

Trust Indenture Reform Act of 1990
Pub. L. 101–550, title IV, Nov. 15, 1990, 104 Stat. 2721
Short title, see 15 U.S.C. 77aaa note

Truth in Lending Act
Pub. L. 90–321, title I, May 29, 1968, 82 Stat. 146 (15 U.S.C. 1601 et seq.)
Short title, see 15 U.S.C. 1601 note

Truth in Lending Act Amendments of 1995
Pub. L. 104–29, Sept. 30, 1995, 109 Stat. 271
Short title, see 15 U.S.C. 1601 note

Truth in Lending Class Action Relief Act of 1995
Pub. L. 104–12, May 18, 1995, 109 Stat. 161
Short title, see 15 U.S.C. 1601 note

Truth in Lending Simplification and Reform Act
Pub. L. 96–221, title VI, Mar. 31, 1980, 94 Stat. 168
Short title, see 15 U.S.C. 1601 note

Truth in Mileage Act of 1986
Pub. L. 99–579, Oct. 28, 1986, 100 Stat. 3309

Truth in Negotiations Act
Pub. L. 87–653, Sept. 10, 1962, 76 Stat. 528

Truth in Regulating Act of 2000
Pub. L. 106–312, Oct. 17, 2000, 114 Stat. 1248 (5 U.S.C. 801 note)

Truth in Savings Act
Pub. L. 102–242, title II, subtitle F (§261 et seq.), Dec. 19, 1991, 105 Stat. 2334 (12 U.S.C. 4301 et seq.)
Short title, see 12 U.S.C. 4301 note

Truth in Securities Act
See Securities Act of 1933

Tuberculosis Prevention Amendments of 1990
Pub. L. 101–368, Aug. 15, 1990, 104 Stat. 446
Short title, see 42 U.S.C. 201 note

Tuberculosis Registration Act (District of Columbia)
May 13, 1908, ch. 165, 35 Stat. 126

Tucker Act (Admiralty-Limitations)
June 30, 1932, ch. 315, 47 Stat. 420

Tucker Act (Claims)
Mar. 3, 1887, ch. 359, 24 Stat. 505

Tuna Conventions Act of 1950
Sept. 7, 1950, ch. 907, 64 Stat. 777 (16 U.S.C. 951 et seq.)
Short title, see 16 U.S.C. 951 note

Tunnel Site Act
R.S. §2323 (30 U.S.C. 27)
Short title, see 30 U.S.C. 27 note

Twentieth Amendment Adjustment Act
June 5, 1934, ch. 390, 48 Stat. 879

Twenty-Eight Hour Law (Transportation of Animals)
Also known as the Cruelty to Animals Act, the Food and Rest Law, and the Live Stock Transportation Act
June 29, 1906, ch. 3594, 34 Stat. 607
Short title, see 45 U.S.C. 71 note

Twenty-First Century Research Laboratories Act
Pub. L. 106–505, title III, Nov. 13, 2000, 114 Stat. 2330
Short title, see 42 U.S.C. 201 note

Twenty-First Century Workforce Commission Act
Pub. L. 105–220, title III, subtitle C (§331 et seq.), Aug. 7, 1998, 112 Stat. 1087 (29 U.S.C. 2701 note)

Twin Falls County Landfill Act of 1994
Pub. L. 103–281, July 22, 1994, 108 Stat. 1420

Tydings Amendment
Nov. 13, 1942, ch. 638, 56 Stat. 1018

Tydings-McDuffie Act of 1934
See Philippine Independence Act

Tyson-Fitzgerald Act
See Emergency Officers' Retirement Act

U.S. Holocaust Assets Commission Act of 1998
Pub. L. 105–186, June 23, 1998, 112 Stat. 611 (22 U.S.C. 1621 note)

U.S. Holocaust Assets Commission Extension Act of 1999
Pub. L. 106–155, Dec. 9, 1999, 113 Stat. 1740
Short title, see 22 U.S.C. 1621 note

U.S.-China Relations Act of 2000
Pub. L. 106–286, div. B, Oct. 10, 2000, 114 Stat. 891 (22 U.S.C. 6901 et seq.)
Short Title, see 22 U.S.C. 6901 note

Uintah and Ouray Reservation Termination Act of 1954
Aug. 27, 1954, ch. 1009, 68 Stat. 868 (25 U.S.C. 677 et seq.)

Umatilla Basin Project Act
Pub. L. 100–557, title II, Oct. 28, 1988, 102 Stat. 2791

Underwood Tariff Act
Oct. 3, 1913, ch. 16, 38 Stat. 114

Undetectable Firearms Act of 1988
Pub. L. 100–649, Nov. 10, 1988, 102 Stat. 3816
Short title, see 18 U.S.C. 921 note

Unemployment Compensation Amendments of 1976
Pub. L. 94–566, Oct. 20, 1976, 90 Stat. 2667
Short title, see 26 U.S.C. 3311 note

Unemployment Compensation Amendments of 1992
Pub. L. 102–318, July 3, 1992, 106 Stat. 290
Short title, see 26 U.S.C. 1 note

Unemployment Compensation Amendments of 1993
Pub. L. 103–152, Nov. 24, 1993, 107 Stat. 1516

Unemployment Compensation Amendments of 1993—Continued
Short title, see 26 U.S.C. 1 note

Unemployment Relief Act
Mar. 31, 1933, ch. 17, 48 Stat. 22

Unfair Competition Act
Sept. 8, 1916, ch. 463, title VIII, 39 Stat. 798 (15 U.S.C. 71 et seq.)

Unfunded Mandates Reform Act of 1995
Pub. L. 104–4, Mar. 22, 1995, 109 Stat. 48 (2 U.S.C. 1501 et seq.)
Short title, see 2 U.S.C. 1501 note

Uniform Act on Fresh Pursuit
July 26, 1939, ch. 375, 53 Stat. 1124

Uniform Code of Military Justice
May 5, 1950, ch. 169, 64 Stat. 108 (See 10 U.S.C. 801 et seq.)

Uniform Cotton Classing Fees Act of 1987
Pub. L. 100–108, Aug. 20, 1987, 101 Stat. 728
Short title, see 7 U.S.C. 471 note

Uniform Federal Crime Reporting Act of 1988
Pub. L. 100–690, title VII, §7332, Nov. 18, 1988, 102 Stat. 4468 (28 U.S.C. 534 note)

Uniform Fiduciaries Act
May 14, 1928, ch. 545, 45 Stat. 509

Uniform Limited Partnership Act
Pub. L. 87–716, Sept. 28, 1962, 76 Stat. 655

Uniform Narcotic Drug Act
June 20, 1938, ch. 532, 52 Stat. 785

Uniform Partnership Act
Pub. L. 87–709, Sept. 27, 1962, 76 Stat. 636

Uniform Regulatory Jurisdiction Act of 1988
Pub. L. 100–474, Oct. 6, 1988, 102 Stat. 2302
Short title, see 15 U.S.C. 717w note

Uniform Relocation Act Amendments of 1987
Pub. L. 100–17, title IV, Apr. 2, 1987, 101 Stat. 246

Uniform Relocation Assistance and Real Property Acquisition Policies Act of 1970
Pub. L. 91–646, Jan. 2, 1971, 84 Stat. 1894 (42 U.S.C. 4601 et seq.)
Short title, see 42 U.S.C. 4601 note

Uniform Retirement Date Act
Apr. 23, 1930, ch. 209, 46 Stat. 253

Uniform Time Act of 1966
Pub. L. 89–387, Apr. 13, 1966, 80 Stat. 107
Short title, see 15 U.S.C. 260 note

Uniformed and Overseas Citizens Absentee Voting Act
Pub. L. 99–410, Aug. 28, 1986, 100 Stat. 924 (42 U.S.C. 1973ff et seq.)
Short title, see 42 U.S.C. 1971 note, 1973ff note

Uniformed Services Contingency Option Act of 1953
Aug. 8, 1953, ch. 393, 67 Stat. 501

Uniformed Services Employment and Reemployment Rights Act of 1994
Pub. L. 103–353, Oct. 13, 1994, 108 Stat. 3149
Short title, see 38 U.S.C. 101 note

Uniformed Services Former Spouses' Protection Act
Pub. L. 97–252, title X, Sept. 8, 1982, 96 Stat. 730
Short title, see 10 U.S.C. 1401 note

Uniformed Services Health Professions Revitalization Act of 1972
Pub. L. 92–426, Sept. 21, 1972, 86 Stat. 713 (10 U.S.C. 2112 et seq., 2120 et seq.)
Short title, see 10 U.S.C. 2112 note

Uniformed Services Health Professionals Special Pay Act of 1980
Pub. L. 96–284, June 28, 1980, 94 Stat. 587

Uniformed Services Pay Act of 1963
Pub. L. 88–132, Oct. 2, 1963, 77 Stat. 210
Short title, see 37 U.S.C. 101 note

Uniformed Services Pay Act of 1981
Pub. L. 97–60, Oct. 14, 1981, 95 Stat. 989
Short title, see 37 U.S.C. 101 note

Uniformed Services Survivor Benefits Amendments of 1980
Pub. L. 96–402, Oct. 9, 1980, 94 Stat. 1705
Short title, see 10 U.S.C. 1447 note

Uniformed Services Survivors' Benefits Amendments of 1978
Pub. L. 95–397, Sept. 30, 1978, 92 Stat. 843
Short title, see 10 U.S.C. 1431 note

Union Pacific Railroad Charter
July 1, 1862, ch. 120, 12 Stat. 489

Union Station Redevelopment Act of 1981
Pub. L. 97–125, Dec. 29, 1981, 95 Stat. 1667
Short title, see 40 U.S.C. 801 note

Union Station Tracks Act
May 23, 1908, ch. 190, 35 Stat. 246

Unitary Wind Tunnel Plan Act of 1949
Oct. 27, 1949, ch. 766, title I, 63 Stat. 936 (50 U.S.C. 511 et seq.)
Short title, see 50 U.S.C. 511 note

United Nations Environment Program Participation Act of 1973
Pub. L. 93–188, Dec. 15, 1973, 87 Stat. 713 (22 U.S.C. 287 note)

United Nations Headquarters Agreement Act
Aug. 4, 1947, ch. 482, 61 Stat. 756 (22 U.S.C. 287 note)

United Nations Palestine Refugee Aid Act of 1950
June 5, 1950, ch. 220, title III, 64 Stat. 203 (22 U.S.C. 1556 et seq.)

United Nations Participation Act of 1945
Dec. 20, 1945, ch. 583, 59 Stat. 619 (22 U.S.C. 287 et seq.)
Short title, see 22 U.S.C. 287 note

United Nations Reform Act of 1999
Pub. L. 106–113, div. B, §1000(a)(7) [div. A, title IX], Nov. 29, 1999, 113 Stat. 1536, 1501A–475

United Nations Relief and Rehabilitation Administration Participation Act, 1946
Dec. 14, 1945, ch. 577, 59 Stat. 609

United Nations Relief and Rehabilitation Administration Participation Appropriation Act, 1945
June 30, 1944, ch. 324, title II, 58 Stat. 629

United Services Organization's 50th Anniversary Commemorative Coin Act
Pub. L. 101–404, Oct. 2, 1990, 104 Stat. 875 (31 U.S.C. 5112 note)

United States $1 Coin Act of 1997
Pub. L. 105–124, §4, Dec. 1, 1997, 111 Stat. 2536
Short title, see 31 U.S.C. 5101 note

United States Arbitration Act
Feb. 12, 1925, ch. 213, 43 Stat. 883

United States Capitol Visitor Center Commemorative Coin Act of 1999
Pub. L. 106–126, title II, Dec. 6, 1999, 113 Stat. 1644 (31 U.S.C. 5112 note)

United States Coast Guard Bicentennial Medal Act
Pub. L. 101–260, Mar. 30, 1990, 104 Stat. 122 (31 U.S.C. 5111 note)

United States Commemorative Coin Act of 1996
Pub. L. 104–329, Oct. 20, 1996, 110 Stat. 4005
Short title, see 31 U.S.C. 5101 note

United States Commission on Civil Rights Act of 1983
Renamed Civil Rights Commission Act of 1983

United States Commission on Civil Rights Authorization Act of 1992
Pub. L. 102–400, Oct. 7, 1992, 106 Stat. 1955
Short title, see 42 U.S.C. 1975 note

United States Commission on Civil Rights Reauthorization Act of 1991
Pub. L. 102–167, Nov. 26, 1991, 105 Stat. 1101
Short title, see 42 U.S.C. 1975 note

United States Commissioners Act
May 28, 1896, ch. 252, §§19–21, 29 Stat. 184

United States Cotton Futures Act
Pub. L. 94–455, title XIX, §1952, Oct. 4, 1976, 90 Stat. 1841 (7 U.S.C. 15b)
Short title, see 7 U.S.C. 15b(a)

United States cotton futures Act
Aug. 18, 1914, ch. 255, 38 Stat. 693
Aug. 11, 1916, ch. 313, pt. A, §§1–22, 39 Stat. 476–482

United States Cotton Standards Act
Mar. 4, 1923, ch. 288, 42 Stat. 1517 (7 U.S.C. 51 et seq.)
Short title, see 7 U.S.C. 51

United States Fire Administration Authorization Act for Fiscal Years 1998 and 1999
Pub. L. 105–108, Nov. 20, 1997, 111 Stat. 2264
Short title, see 15 U.S.C. 2201 note

United States Fishing Fleet Improvement Act
Pub. L. 86–516, June 12, 1960, 74 Stat. 212

United States Grain Standards Act
Aug. 11, 1916, ch. 313, part B (§1 et seq.), 39 Stat. 482 (7 U.S.C. 71 et seq.)
Short title, see 7 U.S.C. 71

United States Grain Standards Act Amendments of 1988
Pub. L. 100–518, Oct. 24, 1988, 102 Stat. 2584
Short title, see 7 U.S.C. 71 note

United States Grain Standards Act Amendments of 1993
Pub. L. 103–156, Nov. 24, 1993, 107 Stat. 1525
Short title, see 7 U.S.C. 71 note

United States Grain Standards Act of 1976
Pub. L. 94–582, Oct. 21, 1976, 90 Stat. 2867
Short title, see 7 U.S.C. 71 note

United States Holocaust Assets Commission Act of 1998
See U.S. Holocaust Assets Commission Act of 1998

United States Housing Act Amendments of 1938
June 21, 1938, ch. 554, title VI, 52 Stat. 820

United States Housing Act of 1937
Sept. 1, 1937, ch. 896, 50 Stat. 888 (42 U.S.C. 1437 et seq.)
Short title, see 42 U.S.C. 1437 note

United States Information Agency Appropriations Authorization Act of 1973
Pub. L. 93–168, Nov. 29, 1973, 87 Stat. 688
Short title, see 22 U.S.C. 1431 note

United States Information Agency Authorization Act, Fiscal Year 1976
Pub. L. 94–272, Apr. 21, 1976, 90 Stat. 374

United States Information Agency Authorization Act, Fiscal Years 1982 and 1983
Pub. L. 97–241, title III, Aug. 24, 1982, 96 Stat. 291

United States Information Agency Authorization Act, Fiscal Years 1984 and 1985
Pub. L. 98–164, title II, Nov. 22, 1983, 97 Stat. 1030

United States Information and Educational Exchange Act of 1948
Jan. 27, 1948, ch. 36, 62 Stat. 6 (22 U.S.C. 1431 et seq.)
Short title, see 22 U.S.C. 1431 note

United States Institute of Peace Act
Pub. L. 98–525, title XVII, Oct. 19, 1984, 98 Stat. 2649 (22 U.S.C. 4601 et seq.)
Short title, see 22 U.S.C. 4601 note

United States Insular Areas Drug Abuse Act of 1986
Pub. L. 99–570, title V, subtitle A (§5001 et seq.), Oct. 27, 1986, 100 Stat. 3207–154 (48 U.S.C. 1494 et seq.)
Short title, see 48 U.S.C. 1494 note

United States International Broadcasting Act of 1994
Pub. L. 103–236, title III, Apr. 30, 1994, 108 Stat. 432 (22 U.S.C. 6201 et seq.)
Short title, see 22 U.S.C. 6201 note

United States Mint Numismatic Coin Clarification Act of 2000
Pub. L. 106–445, Nov. 6, 2000, 114 Stat. 1931
Short title, see 31 U.S.C. 5101 note

United States Mint Reauthorization and Reform Act of 1992
Pub. L. 102–390, title II, Oct. 6, 1992, 106 Stat. 1624
Short title, see 31 U.S.C. 5101 note

United States National Tourism Organization Act of 1996
Pub. L. 104–288, Oct. 11, 1996, 110 Stat. 3402 (22 U.S.C. 2141 et seq.)
Short title, see 22 U.S.C. 2121 note

United States Patent and Trademark Office Reauthorization Act, Fiscal Year 1999
Pub. L. 105–358, Nov. 10, 1998, 112 Stat. 3272
Short title, see 35 U.S.C. 1 note

United States Public Vessel Medical Waste Anti-Dumping Act of 1988
Pub. L. 100–688, title III, subtitle A (§3101 et seq.), Nov. 18, 1988, 102 Stat. 4152 (33 U.S.C. 2501 et seq.)
Short title, see 33 U.S.C. 2501 note

United States Railway Association Amendments Act of 1978
Pub. L. 95–565, Nov. 1, 1978, 92 Stat. 2397
Short title, see 45 U.S.C. 701 note

United States Synthetic Fuels Corporation Act of 1980
Pub. L. 96–294, title I, part B (§111 et seq.), June 30, 1980, 94 Stat. 633 (42 U.S.C. 8702 et seq.)

United States Veterans Commemorative Coin Act of 1993
Pub. L. 103–186, title II, Dec. 14, 1993, 107 Stat. 2247 (31 U.S.C. 5112 note)

United States Veterans' Bureau Act
Aug. 9, 1921, ch. 57, title I, 42 Stat. 147

United States Warehouse Act
Aug. 11, 1916, ch. 313, part C (§1 et seq.), as added Pub. L. 106–472, title II, §201, Nov. 9, 2000, 114 Stat. 2061 (7 U.S.C. 241 et seq.)
Short title, see 7 U.S.C. 241 note

United States-Canada Free-Trade Agreement Implementation Act of 1988
Pub. L. 100–449, Sept. 28, 1988, 102 Stat. 1851 (19 U.S.C. 2112 note)

United States-Caribbean Basin Trade Partnership Act
Pub. L. 106–200, title II, May 18, 2000, 114 Stat. 275
Short title, see 19 U.S.C. 2701 note

United States-Hong Kong Policy Act of 1992
Pub. L. 102–383, Oct. 5, 1992, 106 Stat. 1448 (22 U.S.C. 5701 et seq.)
Short title, see 22 U.S.C. 5701 note

United States-India Fund for Cultural, Educational, and Scientific Cooperation Act
Pub. L. 98–164, title IX, Nov. 22, 1983, 97 Stat. 1051 (22 U.S.C. 290j et seq.)
Short title, see 22 U.S.C. 290j note

United States-Israel Free Trade Area Implementation Act of 1985
Pub. L. 99–47, June 11, 1985, 99 Stat. 82 (19 U.S.C. 2112 note)

United States-Japan Fishery Agreement Approval Act of 1987
Pub. L. 100–220, Dec. 29, 1987, 101 Stat. 1458
Short title, see 16 U.S.C. 1801 note

United States-Macau Policy Act of 2000
Pub. L. 106–570, title II, Dec. 27, 2000, 114 Stat. 3040 (22 U.S.C. 6901 note)

United States-Mexico Border Health Commission Act
Pub. L. 103–400, Oct. 22, 1994, 108 Stat. 4169 (22 U.S.C. 290n et seq.)
Short title, see 22 U.S.C. 290n note

Universal Military Training and Service Act
Renamed Military Selective Service Act

University and Small Business Patent Procedure Act of 1980
Also known as the Bayh Dole Act
Pub. L. 96–517, §6(a), Dec. 12, 1980, 94 Stat. 3018 (35 U.S.C. 200 et seq.)

Unjust Conviction Law
May 24, 1938, ch. 266, 52 Stat. 438

Unlisted Securities Trading Act
May 27, 1936, ch. 462, 49 Stat. 1375
Short title, see 15 U.S.C. 78a note

Unlisted Trading Privileges Act of 1994
Pub. L. 103–389, Oct. 22, 1994, 108 Stat. 4081
Short title, see 15 U.S.C. 78a note

Upper Colorado Act
See Colorado River Storage Project Act

Upper Delaware Scenic and Recreational River Mongaup Visitor Center Act of 1999
Pub. L. 106–119, Dec. 3, 1999, 113 Stat. 1604 (16 U.S.C. 1274 note)

Upper Housatonic National Heritage Area Study Act of 2000
Pub. L. 106–470, Nov. 9, 2000, 114 Stat. 2055

Upper Mississippi River Management Act of 1986
Pub. L. 99–662, title XI, §1103, Nov. 17, 1986, 100 Stat. 4225 (33 U.S.C. 652)
Short title, see 33 U.S.C. 652(a)

Upper Mississippi River National Wildlife and Fish Refuge Act
June 7, 1924, ch. 346, 43 Stat. 650 (16 U.S.C. 721 et seq.)
Short title, see 16 U.S.C. 721

Uranium Mill Tailings Radiation Control Act of 1978
Pub. L. 95–604, Nov. 8, 1978, 92 Stat. 3021 (42 U.S.C. 7901 et seq.)
Short title, see 42 U.S.C. 7901 note

Uranium Mill Tailings Remedial Action Amendments Act of 1988
Pub. L. 100–616, Nov. 5, 1988, 102 Stat. 3192
Short title, see 42 U.S.C. 7901 note

Urban Growth and New Community Development Act of 1970
Renamed National Urban Policy and New Community Development Act of 1970

Urban Mass Transportation Act of 1964
Renamed Federal Transit Act

Urban Mass Transportation Assistance Act of 1970
Pub. L. 91–453, Oct. 15, 1970, 84 Stat. 962

Urban Park and Recreation Recovery Act of 1978
Pub. L. 95–625, title X, Nov. 10, 1978, 92 Stat. 3538 (16 U.S.C. 2501 et seq.)
Short title, see 16 U.S.C. 2501 note

Urban Property Protection and Reinsurance Act of 1968
Pub. L. 90–448, title XI, Aug. 1, 1968, 82 Stat. 555
Short title, see 12 U.S.C. 1701 note

Urgent Assistance for Democracy in Panama Act of 1990
Pub. L. 101–243, Feb. 14, 1990, 104 Stat. 7

Urgent Deficiency and Supplemental Appropriation Act, fiscal years 1939 and 1940
June 30, 1939, ch. 254, 53 Stat. 980

Urgent Deficiency Appropriation Act, 1940
Feb. 12, 1940, ch. 28, 54 Stat. 35

Urgent Deficiency Appropriation Act, 1943
July 12, 1943, ch. 218, 57 Stat. 431

Urgent Deficiency Appropriation Act, 1947
Mar. 22, 1947, ch. 20, 61 Stat. 14

Urgent Deficiency Appropriation Act, 1948
Mar. 3, 1948, ch. 91, 62 Stat. 59

Urgent Deficiency Appropriation Act, 1950
Mar. 27, 1950, ch. 77, 64 Stat. 37

Urgent Deficiency Appropriation Act, 1952
June 30, 1952, ch. 532, 66 Stat. 309

Urgent Deficiency Appropriation Act, 1955
Jan. 25, 1955, ch. 3, 69 Stat. 4

Urgent Deficiency Appropriation Act, 1956
Feb. 14, 1956, ch. 34, 70 Stat. 12

Urgent Deficiency Appropriation Act, 1958
Pub. L. 85–400, May 14, 1958, 72 Stat. 108

Urgent Relief for the Homeless Supplemental Appropriations Act of 1987
Pub. L. 100–71, title IV, July 11, 1987, 101 Stat. 466

Urgent Supplemental Appropriations Act of 1989 to Meet the Dire Emergency Created by the Crisis of Drug Abuse
Pub. L. 100–690, title X, Nov. 18, 1988, 102 Stat. 4539

Urgent Supplemental Appropriations Act, 1982
Pub. L. 97–216, July 18, 1982, 96 Stat. 180

Urgent Supplemental Appropriations Act, 1986
Pub. L. 99–349, July 2, 1986, 100 Stat. 710

Uruguay Round Agreements Act
Pub. L. 103–465, Dec. 8, 1994, 108 Stat. 4809
Short title, see 19 U.S.C. 3501 note

Use of Assisted Housing by Aliens Act of 1996
Pub. L. 104–208, div. C, title V, subtitle E (§571 et seq.), Sept. 30, 1996, 110 Stat. 3009–684
Short title, see 42 U.S.C. 1436a note

USEC Privatization Act
Pub. L. 104–134, title III, ch. 1, subch. A (§3101 et seq.), Apr. 26, 1996, 110 Stat. 1321–335 (42 U.S.C. 2297h et seq.)
Short title, see 42 U.S.C. 2011 note

Used Oil Recycling Act of 1980
Pub. L. 96–463, Oct. 15, 1980, 94 Stat. 2055
Short title, see 42 U.S.C. 6901 note

Utah Schools and Lands Exchange Act of 1998
Pub. L. 105–335, Oct. 31, 1998, 112 Stat. 3139

Utah Schools and Lands Improvement Act of 1993
Pub. L. 103–93, Oct. 1, 1993, 107 Stat. 995

Utah West Desert Land Exchange Act of 2000
Pub. L. 106–301, Oct. 13, 2000, 114 Stat. 1059

Utah Wilderness Act of 1984
Pub. L. 98–428, Sept. 28, 1984, 98 Stat. 1657 (16 U.S.C. 1132 notes)

Utility Holding Company Act
See Public Utility Holding Company Act of 1935

Vaccination Assistance Act of 1962
Pub. L. 87–868, Oct. 23, 1962, 76 Stat. 1155
Short title, see 42 U.S.C. 201 note

Vaccine and Immunization Amendments of 1990
Pub. L. 101–502, Nov. 3, 1990, 104 Stat. 1285
Short title, see 42 U.S.C. 201 note

Vaccine Compensation Amendments of 1987
Pub. L. 100–203, title IV, subtitle D (§4301 et seq.), Dec. 22, 1987, 101 Stat. 1330–221
Short title, see 42 U.S.C. 201 note

Vaccine Injury Compensation Program Modification Act
Pub. L. 105–277, div. C, title XV, Oct. 21, 1998, 112 Stat. 2681–741
Short title, see 26 U.S.C. 1 note

Valles Caldera Preservation Act
Pub. L. 106–248, title I, July 25, 2000, 114 Stat. 598 (16 U.S.C. 698v et seq.)
Short title, see 16 U.S.C. 698v note

Valley Forge National Historical Park Act
Pub. L. 94–337, July 4, 1976, 90 Stat. 796 (16 U.S.C. 410aa et seq.)

Valuation Act
Mar. 1, 1913, ch. 92, 37 Stat. 701

Van Nuys Anti-Trust Act
Oct. 10, 1942, ch. 589, 56 Stat. 781 (15 U.S.C. 16 note)

Van Zandt Patent Act
Aug. 7, 1939, ch. 568, 53 Stat. 1264

Vegetable Ink Printing Act of 1994
Pub. L. 103–348, Oct. 6, 1994, 108 Stat. 3133 (44 U.S.C. 501 note)

Vermont Wilderness Act of 1984
Pub. L. 98–322, June 19, 1984, 98 Stat. 253 (16 U.S.C. 460nn et seq., 1132 note)

Vessel Bridge-to-Bridge Radiotelephone Act
Pub. L. 92–63, Aug. 4, 1971, 85 Stat. 164 (33 U.S.C. 1201 et seq.)
Short title, see 33 U.S.C. 1201 note

Vessel Documentation Act
Pub. L. 96–594, title I, Dec. 24, 1980, 94 Stat. 3453

Vessel Hull Design Protection Act
Pub. L. 105–304, title V, Oct. 28, 1998, 112 Stat. 2905 (17 U.S.C. 1301 et seq.)
Short title, see 17 U.S.C. 101 note

Veterans Adjusted Compensation Act, 1936
See Adjusted Compensation Payment Act, 1936

Veterans and Survivors Pension Adjustment Act of 1974
Pub. L. 93–527, Dec. 21, 1974, 88 Stat. 1702
Short title, see 38 U.S.C. 101 note

Veterans and Survivors Pension Adjustment Act of 1976
Pub. L. 94–432, Sept. 30, 1976, 90 Stat. 1369
Short title, see 38 U.S.C. 101 note

Veterans and Survivors Pension Adjustment Act of 1977
Pub. L. 95–204, Dec. 2, 1977, 91 Stat. 1455
Short title, see 38 U.S.C. 101 note

Veterans and Survivors Pension Interim Adjustment Act of 1975
Pub. L. 94–169, Dec. 23, 1975, 89 Stat. 1013
Short title, see 38 U.S.C. 101 note

Veterans Benefits Act of 1998
Pub. L. 105–178, title VIII, subtitle B (§8201 et seq.), June 9, 1998, 112 Stat. 492
Short title, see 38 U.S.C. 101 note

Veterans Benefits and Health Care Improvement Act of 2000
Pub. L. 106–419, Nov. 1, 2000, 114 Stat. 1822
Short title, see 38 U.S.C. 101 note

Veterans Claims Assistance Act of 2000
Pub. L. 106–475, Nov. 9, 2000, 114 Stat. 2096
Short title, see 38 U.S.C. 101 note

Veterans Compensation Cost-of-Living Adjustment Act of 1994
Pub. L. 103–418, Oct. 25, 1994, 108 Stat. 4336
Short title, see 38 U.S.C. 101 note

Veterans Day Act
May 13, 1938, ch. 210, 52 Stat. 351

Veterans Disability Compensation and Survivor Benefits Act of 1974
Pub. L. 93–295, May 31, 1974, 88 Stat. 180
Short title, see 38 U.S.C. 101 note

Veterans Disability Compensation and Survivor Benefits Act of 1975
Pub. L. 94–71, Aug. 5, 1975, 89 Stat. 395
Short title, see 38 U.S.C. 101 note

Veterans Disability Compensation and Survivor Benefits Act of 1976
Pub. L. 94–433, Sept. 30, 1976, 90 Stat. 1374
Short title, see 38 U.S.C. 101 note

Veterans Disability Compensation and Survivor Benefits Act of 1977
Pub. L. 95–117, Oct. 3, 1977, 91 Stat. 1063
Short title, see 38 U.S.C. 101 note

Veterans Education and Employment Amendments of 1989
Pub. L. 101–237, title IV, Dec. 18, 1989, 103 Stat. 2078
Short title, see 38 U.S.C. 101 note

Veterans Employment Opportunities Act of 1998
Pub. L. 105–339, Oct. 31, 1998, 112 Stat. 3182
Short title, see 5 U.S.C. 2101 note

Veterans Entrepreneurship and Small Business Development Act of 1999
Pub. L. 106–50, Aug. 17, 1999, 113 Stat. 233
Short title, see 15 U.S.C. 631 note

Veterans Flag Act
July 11, 1939, ch. 263, 53 Stat. 999

Veterans Health Care Act of 1992
Pub. L. 102–585, Nov. 4, 1992, 106 Stat. 4943
Short title, see 38 U.S.C. 101 note

Veterans Health Care Expansion Act of 1973
Pub. L. 93–82, Aug. 2, 1973, 87 Stat. 179
Short title, see 38 U.S.C. 101 note

Veterans Health Programs Extension Act of 1994
Pub. L. 103–452, Nov. 2, 1994, 108 Stat. 4783
Short title, see 38 U.S.C. 101 note

Veterans Health Programs Extension and Improvement Act of 1979
Pub. L. 96–151, Dec. 20, 1979, 93 Stat. 1092
Short title, see 38 U.S.C. 101 note

Veterans Home Loan Indemnity and Restructuring Act of 1989
Pub. L. 101–237, title III, Dec. 18, 1989, 103 Stat. 2069
Short title, see 38 U.S.C. 101 note

Veterans Home Loan Program Amendments of 1992
Pub. L. 102–547, Oct. 28, 1992, 106 Stat. 3633
Short title, see 38 U.S.C. 101 note

Veterans Hospitalization and Medical Services Modernization Amendments of 1966
Pub. L. 89–785, Nov. 7, 1966, 80 Stat. 1368
Short title, see 38 U.S.C. 101 note

Veterans Housing Act of 1974
Pub. L. 93–569, Dec. 31, 1974, 88 Stat. 1863
Short title, see 38 U.S.C. 101 note

Veterans Housing Amendments Act of 1976
Pub. L. 94–324, June 30, 1976, 90 Stat. 720
Short title, see 38 U.S.C. 101 note

Veterans Medical Technical and Conforming Amendments of 1976
Pub. L. 94–581, title II, Oct. 21, 1976, 90 Stat. 2855
Short title, see 38 U.S.C. 101 note

Veterans Millennium Health Care and Benefits Act
Pub. L. 106–117, Nov. 30, 1999, 113 Stat. 1545
Short title, see 38 U.S.C. 101 note

Veterans Omnibus Health Care Act of 1976
Pub. L. 94–581, Oct. 21, 1976, 90 Stat. 2842
Short title, see 38 U.S.C. 101 note

Veterans' Pension and Readjustment Assistance Act of 1967
Pub. L. 90–77, Aug. 31, 1967, 81 Stat. 178
Short title, see 38 U.S.C. 101 note

Veterans Programs Enhancement Act of 1998
Pub. L. 105–368, Nov. 11, 1998, 112 Stat. 3315
Short title, see 38 U.S.C. 101 note

Veterans Reconciliation Act of 1993
Pub. L. 103–66, title XII, Aug. 10, 1993, 107 Stat. 413
Short title, see 38 U.S.C. 101 note

Veterans Reconciliation Act of 1997
Pub. L. 105–33, title VIII, Aug. 5, 1997, 111 Stat. 663
Short title, see 38 U.S.C. 101 note

Veterans' Administration and Department of Defense Health Resources Sharing and Emergency Operations Act
Pub. L. 97–174, May 4, 1982, 96 Stat. 70
Short title, see 38 U.S.C. 101 note

Veterans' Administration Health-Care Amendments of 1980
Pub. L. 96–330, Aug. 26, 1980, 94 Stat. 1030
Short title, see 38 U.S.C. 101 note

Veterans' Administration Health-Care Amendments of 1985
Pub. L. 99–166, Dec. 3, 1985, 99 Stat. 941
Short title, see 38 U.S.C. 101 note

Veterans' Administration Health-Care Programs Improvement and Extension Act of 1982
Pub. L. 97–251, Sept. 8, 1982, 96 Stat. 711
Short title, see 38 U.S.C. 101 note

Veterans' Administration Medical School Assistance and Health Manpower Training Act of 1972
Pub. L. 92–541, Oct. 24, 1972, 86 Stat. 1100
Short title, see 38 U.S.C. 101 note

Veterans' Administration Physician and Dentist Pay Comparability Act of 1975
Pub. L. 94–123, Oct. 22, 1975, 89 Stat. 669
Short title, see 38 U.S.C. 101 note

Veterans' Administration Physician and Dentist Pay Comparability Amendments of 1977
Pub. L. 95–201, Nov. 23, 1977, 91 Stat. 1429
Short title, see 38 U.S.C. 101 note

Veterans' Administration Programs Extension Act of 1978
Pub. L. 95–520, Oct. 26, 1978, 92 Stat. 1820
Short title, see 38 U.S.C. 101 note

Veterans' and Survivors' Pension Improvement Act of 1978
Pub. L. 95–588, Nov. 4, 1978, 92 Stat. 2497
Short title, see 38 U.S.C. 101 note

Veterans' Benefits Act of 1957
Pub. L. 85–56, June 17, 1957, 71 Stat. 83

Veterans' Benefits Act of 1992
Pub. L. 102–568, Oct. 29, 1992, 106 Stat. 4320
Short title, see 38 U.S.C. 101 note

Veterans' Benefits Act of 1997
Pub. L. 105–114, Nov. 21, 1997, 111 Stat. 2277
Short title, see 38 U.S.C. 101 note

Veterans' Benefits Amendments of 1989
Pub. L. 101–237, Dec. 18, 1989, 103 Stat. 2062
Short title, see 38 U.S.C. 101 note

Veterans' Benefits and Programs Improvement Act of 1988
Pub. L. 100–689, Nov. 18, 1988, 102 Stat. 4161
Short title, see 38 U.S.C. 101 note

Veterans' Benefits and Services Act of 1988
Pub. L. 100–322, May 20, 1988, 102 Stat. 487
Short title, see 38 U.S.C. 101 note

Veterans' Benefits Improvement Act of 1984
Pub. L. 98–543, Oct. 24, 1984, 98 Stat. 2735
Short title, see 38 U.S.C. 101 note

Veterans' Benefits Improvement Act of 1988
Pub. L. 100–687, div. B, Nov. 18, 1988, 102 Stat. 4122
Short title, see 38 U.S.C. 101 note

Veterans' Benefits Improvement and Health-Care Authorization Act of 1986
Pub. L. 99–576, Oct. 28, 1986, 100 Stat. 3248
Short title, see 38 U.S.C. 101 note

Veterans' Benefits Improvements Act of 1994
Pub. L. 103–446, Nov. 2, 1994, 108 Stat. 4645
Short title, see 38 U.S.C. 101 note

Veterans' Benefits Improvements Act of 1996
Pub. L. 104–275, Oct. 9, 1996, 110 Stat. 3322
Short title, see 38 U.S.C. 101 note

Veterans' Benefits Programs Improvement Act of 1991
Pub. L. 102–86, Aug. 14, 1991, 105 Stat. 414
Short title, see 38 U.S.C. 101 note

Veterans' Cemetery Protection Act of 1997
Pub. L. 105–101, Nov. 19, 1997, 111 Stat. 2202 (28 U.S.C. 994 note)

Veterans' Compensation Amendments of 1991
Pub. L. 102–3, Feb. 6, 1991, 105 Stat. 7
Short title, see 38 U.S.C. 101 note

Veterans' Compensation and Program Improvements Amendments of 1984
Pub. L. 98–223, Mar. 2, 1984, 98 Stat. 37
Short title, see 38 U.S.C. 101 note

Veterans' Compensation and Relief Act of 1972
Pub. L. 92–328, June 30, 1972, 86 Stat. 393
Short title, see 38 U.S.C. 101 note

Veterans' Compensation Cost-of-Living Adjustment Act of 1987
Pub. L. 100–227, Dec. 31, 1987, 101 Stat. 1552
Short title, see 38 U.S.C. 101 note

Veterans' Compensation Cost-of-Living Adjustment Act of 1992
Pub. L. 102–510, Oct. 24, 1992, 106 Stat. 3318
Short title, see 38 U.S.C. 101 note

Veterans' Compensation Cost-of-Living Adjustment Act of 1995
Pub. L. 104–57, Nov. 22, 1995, 109 Stat. 555
Short title, see 38 U.S.C. 101 note

Veterans' Compensation Cost-of-Living Adjustment Act of 1996
Pub. L. 104–263, Oct. 9, 1996, 110 Stat. 3212
Short title, see 38 U.S.C. 101 note

Veterans' Compensation Cost-of-Living Adjustment Act of 1999
Pub. L. 106–118, Nov. 30, 1999, 113 Stat. 1601
Short title, see 38 U.S.C. 101 note

Veterans' Compensation Cost-of-Living Adjustment Act of 2000
Pub. L. 106–413, Nov. 1, 2000, 114 Stat. 1798
Short title, see 38 U.S.C. 101 note

Veterans' Compensation Rate Amendments of 1991
Pub. L. 102–152, Nov. 12, 1991, 105 Stat. 985
Short title, see 38 U.S.C. 101 note

Veterans' Compensation Rate Amendments of 1997
Pub. L. 105–98, Nov. 19, 1997, 111 Stat. 2155
Short title, see 38 U.S.C. 101 note

Veterans' Compensation Rate Increase and Job Training Amendments of 1985
Pub. L. 99–238, Jan. 13, 1986, 99 Stat. 1765
Short title, see 38 U.S.C. 101 note

Veterans' Compensation Rates Amendments of 1993
Pub. L. 103–140, Nov. 11, 1993, 107 Stat. 1485
Short title, see 38 U.S.C. 101 note

Veterans' Compensation, Education, and Employment Amendments of 1982
Pub. L. 97–306, Oct. 14, 1982, 96 Stat. 1429
Short title, see 38 U.S.C. 101 note

Veterans' Dioxin and Radiation Exposure Compensation Standards Act
Pub. L. 98–542, Oct. 24, 1984, 98 Stat. 2725

Veterans' Disability Compensation and Housing Benefits Amendments of 1980
Pub. L. 96–385, Oct. 7, 1980, 94 Stat. 1528
Short title, see 38 U.S.C. 101 note

Veterans' Disability Compensation and Survivors' Benefits Act of 1978
Pub. L. 95–479, Oct. 18, 1978, 92 Stat. 1560
Short title, see 38 U.S.C. 101 note

Veterans' Disability Compensation and Survivors' Benefits Amendments of 1979
Pub. L. 96–128, Nov. 28, 1979, 93 Stat. 982
Short title, see 38 U.S.C. 101 note

Veterans' Disability Compensation, Housing, and Memorial Benefits Amendments of 1981
Pub. L. 97–66, Oct. 17, 1981, 95 Stat. 1026
Short title, see 38 U.S.C. 101 note

Veterans' Education and Employment Assistance Act of 1976
Pub. L. 94–502, Oct. 15, 1976, 90 Stat. 2383
Short title, see 38 U.S.C. 101 note

Veterans' Education and Rehabilitation Equalization Amendments Act of 1974
Pub. L. 93–602, title II, Jan. 2, 1975, 88 Stat. 1958
Short title, see 38 U.S.C. 101 note

Veterans Education and Training Amendments Act of 1970
Pub. L. 91–219, Mar. 26, 1970, 84 Stat. 76
Short title, see 38 U.S.C. 101 note

Veterans' Education and Training Amendments of 1950
July 13, 1950, ch. 461, 64 Stat. 336

Veterans' Educational Assistance Act of 1984
Renamed the Montgomery GI Bill Act of 1984

Veterans' Educational Assistance Amendments of 1991
Pub. L. 102–127, Oct. 10, 1991, 105 Stat. 619
Short title, see 38 U.S.C. 101 note

Veterans' Emergency Housing Act of 1946
May 22, 1946, ch. 268, 60 Stat. 207 (50 App. U.S.C. 1821 et seq.)

Veterans' Employment and Readjustment Act of 1972
Pub. L. 92–540, title V, Oct. 24, 1972, 86 Stat. 1094
Short title, see 38 U.S.C. 101 note

Veterans' Employment, Training, and Counseling Amendments of 1988
Pub. L. 100–323, May 20, 1988, 102 Stat. 556
Short title, see 38 U.S.C. 101 note

Veterans' Health Care Act of 1984
Pub. L. 98–528, Oct. 19, 1984, 98 Stat. 2686
Short title, see 38 U.S.C. 101 note

Veterans' Health Care Amendments of 1979
Pub. L. 96–22, June 13, 1979, 93 Stat. 47
Short title, see 38 U.S.C. 101 note

Veterans' Health Care Amendments of 1983
Pub. L. 98–160, Nov. 21, 1983, 97 Stat. 993
Short title, see 38 U.S.C. 101 note

Veterans' Health Care Eligibility Reform Act of 1996
Pub. L. 104–262, Oct. 9, 1996, 110 Stat. 3177
Short title, see 38 U.S.C. 101 note

Veterans' Health Care, Training, and Small Business Loan Act of 1981
Pub. L. 97–72, Nov. 3, 1981, 95 Stat. 1047
Short title, see 38 U.S.C. 101 note

Veterans' Health-Care Amendments of 1986
Pub. L. 99–272, title XIX, Apr. 7, 1986, 100 Stat. 372
Short title, see 38 U.S.C. 101 note

Veterans' Home Loan Program Emergency Amendments of 1988
Pub. L. 100–253, Feb. 29, 1988, 102 Stat. 20
Short title, see 38 U.S.C. 101 note

Veterans' Home Loan Program Improvements and Property Rehabilitation Act of 1987
Pub. L. 100–198, Dec. 21, 1987, 101 Stat. 1315
Short title, see 38 U.S.C. 101 note

Veterans' Housing Act of 1970
Pub. L. 91–506, Oct. 23, 1970, 84 Stat. 1108
Short title, see 38 U.S.C. 101 note

Veterans' Housing Benefits Act of 1978
Pub. L. 95–476, Oct. 18, 1978, 92 Stat. 1497
Short title, see 38 U.S.C. 101 note

Veterans' Insurance Act of 1974
Pub. L. 93–289, May 24, 1974, 88 Stat. 165
Short title, see 38 U.S.C. 101 note

Veterans' Insurance Reform Act of 1996
Pub. L. 104–275, title IV, Oct. 9, 1996, 110 Stat. 3337
Short title, see 38 U.S.C. 101

Veterans' Job Training Act
Pub. L. 98–77, Aug. 15, 1983, 97 Stat. 443 (29 U.S.C. 2913 note)

Veterans' Judicial Review Act
Pub. L. 100–687, div. A, Nov. 18, 1988, 102 Stat. 4105
Short title, see 38 U.S.C. 101 note

Veterans' Medical Programs Amendments of 1992
Pub. L. 102–405, Oct. 9, 1992, 106 Stat. 1972
Short title, see 38 U.S.C. 101 note

Veterans' Oral History Project Act
Pub. L. 106–380, Oct. 27, 2000, 114 Stat. 1447 (20 U.S.C. 2141 et seq.)
Short title, see 20 U.S.C. 2101 note

Veterans' Paralysis Act
July 19, 1939, ch. 329, 53 Stat. 1067

Veterans' Pension Act of 1959
Pub. L. 86–211, Aug. 29, 1959, 73 Stat. 432
Short title, see 38 U.S.C. 101 note

Veterans' Preference Act of 1944
June 27, 1944, ch. 287, 58 Stat. 387

Veterans' Radiation Exposure Amendments of 1992
Pub. L. 102–578, Oct. 30, 1992, 106 Stat. 4774
Short title, see 38 U.S.C. 101 note

Veterans' Readjustment Assistance Act of 1952
July 16, 1952, ch. 875, 66 Stat. 663

Veterans' Readjustment Benefits Act of 1966
Pub. L. 89–358, Mar. 3, 1966, 80 Stat. 12
Short title, see 38 U.S.C. 101 note

Veterans' Rehabilitation and Education Amendments of 1980
Pub. L. 96–466, Oct. 17, 1980, 94 Stat. 2171
Short title, see 38 U.S.C. 101 note

Veterans' Small Business Loan Act of 1981
Pub. L. 97–72, title III, Nov. 3, 1981, 95 Stat. 1055
Short title, see 38 U.S.C. 101 note

Veterinary Medical Education Act of 1966
Pub. L. 89–709, Nov. 2, 1966, 80 Stat. 1103
Short title, see 42 U.S.C. 201 note

Vicksburg Campaign Trail Battlefields Preservation Act of 2000
Pub. L. 106–487, Nov. 9, 2000, 114 Stat. 2202

Victim and Witness Protection Act of 1982
Pub. L. 97–291, Oct. 12, 1982, 96 Stat. 1248
Short title, see 18 U.S.C. 1501 note

Victim Rights Clarification Act of 1997
Pub. L. 105–6, Mar. 19, 1997, 111 Stat. 12
Short title, see 18 U.S.C. 3481 note

Victims of Child Abuse Act of 1990
Pub. L. 101–647, title II, Nov. 29, 1990, 104 Stat. 4792 (42 U.S.C. 13001 et seq.)
Short title, see 42 U.S.C. 13001 note

Victims of Crime Act of 1984
Pub. L. 98–473, title II, ch. XIV (§1401 et seq.), Oct. 12, 1984, 98 Stat. 2170 (42 U.S.C. 10601 et seq.)
Short title, see 42 U.S.C. 10601 note

Victims of Terrorism Compensation Act
Pub. L. 99–399, title VIII, Aug. 27, 1986, 100 Stat. 879
Short title, see 5 U.S.C. 5569 note

Victims of Trafficking and Violence Protection Act of 2000
Pub. L. 106–386, Oct. 28, 2000, 114 Stat. 1464
Short title, see 22 U.S.C. 7101 note

Victims' Rights and Restitution Act of 1990
Pub. L. 101–647, title V, Nov. 29, 1990, 104 Stat. 4820
Short title, see 42 U.S.C. 10601 note

Victory Liberty Loan Act
Mar. 3, 1919, ch. 100, 40 Stat. 1309

Video Privacy Protection Act of 1988
Pub. L. 100–618, Nov. 5, 1988, 102 Stat. 3195
Short title, see 18 U.S.C. 2701 note

Vietnam Education Foundation Act of 2000
Pub. L. 106–554, §1(a)(4) [div. B, title II], Dec. 21, 2000, 114 Stat. 2763, 2763A–254 (22 U.S.C. 2452 et seq.)

Vietnam Era Veterans' Readjustment Assistance Act of 1972
Pub. L. 92–540, Oct. 24, 1972, 86 Stat. 1074
Short title, see 38 U.S.C. 101 note

Vietnam Era Veterans' Readjustment Assistance Act of 1974
Pub. L. 93–508, Dec. 3, 1974, 88 Stat. 1578
Short title, see 38 U.S.C. 101 note

Vietnam Veterans National Medal Act
Pub. L. 98–566, Oct. 30, 1984, 98 Stat. 2923

Vinson Naval Parity Act
See Naval Parity Act

Vinson-Patman-McCormack Act
See Adjusted Compensation Payment Act, 1936

Vinson-Trammell Parity Act
See Naval Parity Act

Violence Against Women Act of 1994
Pub. L. 103–322, title IV, Sept. 13, 1994, 108 Stat. 1902
Short title, see 42 U.S.C. 13701 note

Violence Against Women Act of 2000
Pub. L. 106–386, div. B, Oct. 28, 2000, 114 Stat. 1491
Short title, see 42 U.S.C. 13701 note

Violent Crime Control and Law Enforcement Act of 1994
Pub. L. 103–322, Sept. 13, 1994, 108 Stat. 1796
Short title, see 42 U.S.C. 13701 note

Violent Crime Control Appropriations Act, 1995
Pub. L. 103–317, title VIII, Aug. 26, 1994, 108 Stat. 1777

Virgin Islands Acquisition Act
Mar. 3, 1917, ch. 171, 39 Stat. 1132 (48 U.S.C. 1391 et seq.)

Virgin Islands Corporation Act
June 30, 1949, ch. 285, 63 Stat. 350 (48 U.S.C. 1407 et seq.)
Short title, see 48 U.S.C. 1407 note

Virgin Islands Elective Governor Act
Pub. L. 90–496, Aug. 23, 1968, 82 Stat. 837
Short title, see 48 U.S.C. 1541 note

Virgin Islands Nonimmigrant Alien Adjustment Act of 1982
Pub. L. 97–271, Sept. 30, 1982, 96 Stat. 1157 (8 U.S.C. 1255 note)

Virgin Islands Organic Act Amendments of 1959
Pub. L. 86–289, Sept. 16, 1959, 73 Stat. 568
Short title, see 48 U.S.C. 1541 note

Virgin Islands Permanent Government Act
See Organic Act of the Virgin Islands of the United States

Virginia Wilderness Act of 1984
Pub. L. 98–586, Oct. 30, 1984, 98 Stat. 3105 (16 U.S.C. 1132 note)

Virus-Serum-Toxin Act
Mar. 4, 1913, ch. 145, §1 [part], 37 Stat. 832, 833 (21 U.S.C. 151 et seq.)
Short title, see 21 U.S.C. 151 note

Visa Waiver Permanent Program Act
Pub. L. 106–396, Oct. 30, 2000, 114 Stat. 1637
Short title, see 8 U.S.C. 1101 note

Visual Artists Rights Act of 1990
Pub. L. 101–650, title VI, Dec. 1, 1990, 104 Stat. 5128
Short title, see 17 U.S.C. 101 note

Vocational Education Act of 1917
See Smith-Hughes Vocational Education Act

Vocational Education Act of 1936
See Vocational Education Act of 1946

Vocational Education Act of 1946
June 8, 1936, ch. 541, as added Aug. 1, 1946, ch. 725, 60 Stat. 775 (20 U.S.C. 15h et seq.)
Short title, see 20 U.S.C. 11 note

Vocational Education Act of 1963
Pub. L. 88–210, title I, as added Pub. L. 94–482, title II, §202(a), Oct. 12, 1976, 90 Stat. 2169 (20 U.S.C. 2301 et seq.)

Vocational Education Amendments of 1968
Pub. L. 90–576, Oct. 16, 1968, 82 Stat. 1064
Short title, see 20 U.S.C. 2301 note

Vocational Educational Act of 1934
May 21, 1934, ch. 324, 48 Stat. 792

Vocational Rehabilitation Act
June 2, 1920, ch. 219, as added July 6, 1943, ch. 190, §1, 57 Stat. 374 (29 U.S.C. 31 et seq.)

Vocational Rehabilitation Act Amendments of 1943
July 6, 1943, ch. 190, 57 Stat. 374

Vocational Rehabilitation Act Amendments of 1965
Pub. L. 89–333, Nov. 8, 1965, 79 Stat. 1282

Vocational Rehabilitation Amendments of 1954
Aug. 3, 1954, ch. 655, 68 Stat. 652
Short title, see 20 U.S.C. 107 note

Vocational Rehabilitation Amendments of 1967
Pub. L. 90–99, Oct. 3, 1967, 81 Stat. 250

Vocational Rehabilitation Amendments of 1968
Pub. L. 90–391, July 7, 1968, 82 Stat. 297

Volstead Act
See National Prohibition Act

Volstead Act (Drainage under State Laws)
May 20, 1908, ch. 181, 35 Stat. 169 (43 U.S.C. 1021 et seq.)

Voluntary Home Mortgage Credit Act
Aug. 2, 1954, ch. 649, title VI, 68 Stat. 637 (12 U.S.C. 1750aa et seq.)

Voluntary Service Act
R.S. §3679

Volunteer Army Act
Apr. 22, 1898, ch. 187, 30 Stat. 361

Volunteer Employment Act (Civil War)
July 22, 1861, ch. 9, 12 Stat. 268

Volunteer Protection Act of 1997
Pub. L. 105–19, June 18, 1997, 111 Stat. 218 (42 U.S.C. 14501 et seq.)
Short title, see 42 U.S.C. 14501 note

Volunteers for Children Act
Pub. L. 105–251, title II, subtitle B (§221 et seq.), Oct. 9, 1998, 112 Stat. 1885
Short title, see 42 U.S.C. 5101 note

Volunteers in the National Forests Act of 1972
Pub. L. 92–300, May 18, 1972, 86 Stat. 147 (16 U.S.C. 558a et seq.)
Short title, see 16 U.S.C. 558a note

Volunteers in the Parks Act of 1969
Pub. L. 91–357, July 29, 1970, 84 Stat. 472 (16 U.S.C. 18g et seq.)
Short title, see 16 U.S.C. 18g note

Voorhis Anti-Propaganda Act
Oct. 17, 1940, ch. 897, 54 Stat. 1201

Voting Accessibility for the Elderly and Handicapped Act
Pub. L. 98–435, Sept. 28, 1984, 98 Stat. 1678 (42 U.S.C. 1973ee et seq.)
Short title, see 42 U.S.C. 1971 note, 1973ee note

Voting Rights Act Amendments of 1970
Pub. L. 91–285, June 22, 1970, 84 Stat. 314
Short title, see 42 U.S.C. 1971 note, 1973 note

War Department Civil Appropriation Act, 1945
June 26, 1944, ch. 275, 58 Stat. 327

War Department Civil Appropriation Act, 1946
Mar. 31, 1945, ch. 45, 59 Stat. 39

War Department Civil Appropriation Act, 1947
May 2, 1946, ch. 247, 60 Stat. 160

War Department Civil Appropriation Act, 1948
July 31, 1947, ch. 411, 61 Stat. 686

War Finance Corporation Act
Apr. 5, 1918, ch. 45, 40 Stat. 506 (15 U.S.C. 331 et seq.)

War Hazards Compensation Act
Dec. 2, 1942, ch. 668, titles I, II, 56 Stat. 1028, 1033 (42 U.S.C. 1701 et seq.)
Short title, see 42 U.S.C. 1701 note

War Housing Appropriation Act
July 2, 1942, ch. 478, 56 Stat. 633

War Labor Disputes Act
June 25, 1943, ch. 144, 57 Stat. 163 (50 App. U.S.C. 1501 et seq.)

War Manpower Commission Appropriation Act, 1944
July 12, 1943, ch. 221, title VII, 57 Stat. 517

War Manpower Commission Appropriation Act, 1945
June 28, 1944, ch. 302, title VII, 58 Stat. 570

War Manpower Commission Appropriation Act, 1946
July 3, 1945, ch. 263, title VII, 59 Stat. 380

War Minerals Relief Act
Mar. 2, 1919, ch. 94, §5, 40 Stat. 1274

War Mobilization and Reconversion Act of 1944
Oct. 3, 1944, ch. 480, 58 Stat. 785 (50 App. U.S.C. 1651 et seq.)
Short title, see 50 App. U.S.C. 1651 note

War Orphans' Educational Assistance Act of 1956
June 29, 1956, ch. 476, 70 Stat. 411

War Overtime Pay Act of 1943
May 7, 1943, ch. 93, 57 Stat. 75 (50 U.S.C. 1401 et seq.)

War Pay and Allowances Act of 1942
See Missing Persons Act

War Powers Resolution
Pub. L. 93–148, Nov. 7, 1973, 87 Stat. 555 (50 U.S.C. 1541 et seq.)
Short title, see 50 U.S.C. 1541 note

War Risk Insurance Act
Sept. 2, 1914, ch. 293, 38 Stat. 711

War Time Act
Jan. 20, 1942, ch. 7, 56 Stat. 9

War Time Passport Act
May 22, 1918, ch. 81, 40 Stat. 559 (22 U.S.C. 223 et seq.)

War Time Prohibition Act
Nov. 21, 1918, ch. 212, 40 Stat. 1045

War-Risk Insurance Fund Act
June 5, 1942, ch. 332, 56 Stat. 310

Warehouse Act
See United States Warehouse Act

Warehouse Receipts Act (District of Columbia)
Apr. 15, 1910, ch. 167, 36 Stat. 301

Warm Springs Study Act of 1988
Pub. L. 100–559, title VIII, Oct. 28, 1988, 102 Stat. 2801

Warner Canyon Ski Hill Land Exchange Act of 1997
Pub. L. 105–40, Aug. 11, 1997, 111 Stat. 1117

Warrant Officer Act of 1954
May 29, 1954, ch. 249, 68 Stat. 157

Warrant Officer Management Act
Pub. L. 102–190, div. A, title XI, Dec. 5, 1991, 105 Stat. 1491 (10 U.S.C. 571 et seq.)
Short title, see 10 U.S.C. 571 note

Warren Act (Reclamation)
Feb. 21, 1911, ch. 141, 36 Stat. 925 (43 U.S.C. 523 et seq.)
Short title, see 43 U.S.C. 523 note

Warsaw Convention (International Air Transportation)
Oct. 12, 1929, 49 Stat. 3000, TS 876 (49 U.S.C. 40105 note)

Wartime Violation of Italian American Civil Liberties Act
Pub. L. 106–451, Nov. 7, 2000, 114 Stat. 1947
Short title, see 50 App. U.S.C. 1981 note

Washington Conference for Limitation of Armaments
See Disarmament Conference Resolution

Washington Metropolitan Region Development Act
Pub. L. 86–527, June 27, 1960, 74 Stat. 223 (40 U.S.C. 131 et seq.)
Short title, see 40 U.S.C. 131 note

Washington National Airport Act
June 29, 1940, ch. 444, 54 Stat. 686

Washington Park Wilderness Act of 1988
Pub. L. 100–668, Nov. 16, 1988, 102 Stat. 3961
Short title, see 16 U.S.C. 90 note

Washington State Wilderness Act of 1984
Pub. L. 98–339, July 3, 1984, 98 Stat. 299

Washington-Rochambeau Revolutionary Route National Heritage Act of 2000
Pub. L. 106–473, Nov. 9, 2000, 114 Stat. 2083

Waste Isolation Pilot Plant Land Withdrawal Act
Pub. L. 102–579, Oct. 30, 1992, 106 Stat. 4777

Waste Isolation Pilot Plant Land Withdrawal Amendment Act
Pub. L. 104–201, div. C, title XXXI, subtitle F (§3181 et seq.), Sept. 23, 1996, 110 Stat. 2851

Water Bank Act
Pub. L. 91–559, Dec. 19, 1970, 84 Stat. 1468 (16 U.S.C. 1301 et seq.)
Short title, see 16 U.S.C. 1301 note

Water Bank Extension Act of 1994
Pub. L. 103–393, Oct. 22, 1994, 108 Stat. 4105 (16 U.S.C. 1305 note)

Water Desalination Act of 1996
Pub. L. 104–298, Oct. 11, 1996, 110 Stat. 3622 (42 U.S.C. 10301 note)

Water Facilities Act
Aug. 28, 1937, ch. 870, 50 Stat. 869 (16 U.S.C. 590r et seq.)

Water Pollution Control Act
Renamed Federal Water Pollution Control Act

Water Pollution Control Act Amendments of 1956
July 9, 1956, ch. 518, 70 Stat. 498

Water Power Act
See Federal Power Act

Water Quality Act of 1965
Pub. L. 89–234, Oct. 2, 1965, 79 Stat. 903

Water Quality Act of 1987
Pub. L. 100–4, Feb. 4, 1987, 101 Stat. 7
Short title, see 33 U.S.C. 1251 note

Water Quality Improvement Act of 1970
Pub. L. 91–224, title I, Apr. 3, 1970, 84 Stat. 91

Water Research and Development Act of 1978
Pub. L. 95–467, Oct. 17, 1978, 92 Stat. 1305 (42 U.S.C. 7801 et seq.)
Short title, see 42 U.S.C. 7801 note

Water Resources Development Act of 1974
Pub. L. 93–251, title I, Mar. 7, 1974, 88 Stat. 12
Short title, see 42 U.S.C. 1962 note

Water Resources Development Act of 1976
Pub. L. 94–587, Oct. 22, 1976, 90 Stat. 2917

Water Resources Development Act of 1986
Pub. L. 99–662, Nov. 17, 1986, 100 Stat. 4082 (33 U.S.C. 2201 et seq.)
Short title, see 33 U.S.C. 2201 note

Water Resources Development Act of 1988
Pub. L. 100–676, Nov. 17, 1988, 102 Stat. 4012
Short title, see 33 U.S.C. 2201 note

Water Resources Development Act of 1990
Pub. L. 101–640, Nov. 28, 1990, 104 Stat. 4604
Short title, see 33 U.S.C. 2201 note

Water Resources Development Act of 1992
Pub. L. 102–580, Oct. 31, 1992, 106 Stat. 4797
Short title, see 33 U.S.C. 2201 note

Water Resources Development Act of 1996
Pub. L. 104–303, Oct. 12, 1996, 110 Stat. 3658
Short title, see 33 U.S.C. 2201 note

Water Resources Development Act of 1999
Pub. L. 106–53, Aug. 17, 1999, 113 Stat. 269
Short title, see 33 U.S.C. 2201 note

Water Resources Development Act of 2000
Pub. L. 106–541, Dec. 11, 2000, 114 Stat. 2572
Short title, see 33 U.S.C. 2201 note

Water Resources Planning Act
Pub. L. 89–80, July 22, 1965, 79 Stat. 244 (42 U.S.C. 1962 et seq.)
Short title, see 42 U.S.C. 1962 note

Water Resources Research Act of 1964
Pub. L. 88–379, July 17, 1964, 78 Stat. 329 (42 U.S.C. 1961 et seq.)
Short title, see 42 U.S.C. 1961 note

Water Resources Research Act of 1984
Pub. L. 98–242, Mar. 22, 1984, 98 Stat. 97 (42 U.S.C. 10301 et seq.)
Short title, see 42 U.S.C. 10301 note

Water Supply Act of 1958
Pub. L. 85–500, title III, July 3, 1958, 72 Stat. 319
Short title, see 43 U.S.C. 390b note

Watermelon Research and Promotion Act
Pub. L. 99–198, title XVI, subtitle C (§1641 et seq.), Dec. 23, 1985, 99 Stat. 1622 (7 U.S.C. 4901 et seq.)
Short title, see 7 U.S.C. 4901 note

Watermelon Research and Promotion Improvement Act of 1993
Pub. L. 103–189, Dec. 14, 1993, 107 Stat. 2259
Short title, see 7 U.S.C. 4901 note

Watershed Protection and Flood Prevention Act
Aug. 4, 1954, ch. 656, 68 Stat. 666 (16 U.S.C. 1001 et seq.)
Short title, see 16 U.S.C. 1001 note

Ways and Means Act (Civil War)
Mar. 3, 1863, ch. 73, 12 Stat. 709

Weapons of Mass Destruction Control Act of 1992
Pub. L. 102–484, div. A, title XV, Oct. 23, 1992, 106 Stat. 2567

Weather Modification Reporting Act of 1972
Pub. L. 92–205, Dec. 18, 1971, 85 Stat. 735 (15 U.S.C. 330 et seq.)
Short title, see 15 U.S.C. 330 note

Weather Service Modernization Act
Pub. L. 102–567, title VII, Oct. 29, 1992, 106 Stat. 4303 (15 U.S.C. 313 note)

Web-Based Education Commission Act
Pub. L. 105–244, title VIII, part J (§851 et seq.), Oct. 7, 1998, 112 Stat. 1822

Webb Exporter Combination Act
See Webb-Pomerene Act

Webb-Kenyon Act
Mar. 1, 1913, ch. 90, 37 Stat. 699
Short title, see 27 U.S.C. 122 note

Webb-Pomerene Act (Export Trade)
Apr. 10, 1918, ch. 50, 40 Stat. 516 (15 U.S.C. 61 et seq.)
Short title, see 15 U.S.C. 66

Weeks Law
Mar. 1, 1911, ch. 186, 36 Stat. 961
Short title, see 16 U.S.C. 552 note

Wei Jingsheng Freedom of Conscience Act
Private Law 106–14, Nov. 22, 2000

Weights and Measures Act (District of Columbia)
Mar. 3, 1921, ch. 118, 41 Stat. 1217

Weir Farm National Historic Site Establishment Act of 1990
Pub. L. 101–485, Oct. 31, 1990, 104 Stat. 1171 (16 U.S.C. 461 note)

Weir Farm National Historic Site Expansion Act of 1994
Pub. L. 103–449, title II, Nov. 2, 1994, 108 Stat. 4756

Wekiva Wild and Scenic River Act of 2000
Pub. L. 106–299, Oct. 13, 2000, 114 Stat. 1050
Short title, see 16 U.S.C. 1271 note

Welch Act
May 28, 1928, ch. 814, 45 Stat. 776

Welfare and Pension Plans Disclosure Act
Pub. L. 85–836, Aug. 28, 1958, 72 Stat. 997 (29 U.S.C. 301 et seq.)

Welfare and Pension Plans Disclosure Act Amendments of 1962
Pub. L. 87–420, Mar. 20, 1962, 76 Stat. 35
Short title, see 18 U.S.C. 664 note

Wellton-Mohawk Transfer Act
Pub. L. 106–221, June 20, 2000, 114 Stat. 351

Wendell H. Ford Aviation Investment and Reform Act for the 21st Century
Pub. L. 106–181, Apr. 5, 2000, 114 Stat. 61
Short title, see 49 U.S.C. 40101 note

West Point Act
Oct. 1, 1942, ch. 573, 56 Stat. 763

West Point Cadet Act
June 7, 1935, ch. 201, 49 Stat. 332

West Valley Demonstration Project Act
Pub. L. 96–368, Oct. 1, 1980, 94 Stat. 1347 (42 U.S.C. 2021a note)

West Virginia Admission Act
Dec. 31, 1862, ch. 6, 12 Stat. 633

West Virginia National Interest River Conservation Act of 1987
Pub. L. 100–534, Oct. 26, 1988, 102 Stat. 2699
Short title, see 16 U.S.C. 460m–15 note

Western Hemisphere Drug Elimination Act
Pub. L. 105–277, div. C, title VIII, Oct. 21, 1998, 112 Stat. 2681–693
Short title, see 21 U.S.C. 801 note

Western Hemisphere Drug Elimination Technical Corrections Act
Pub. L. 106–35, June 15, 1999, 113 Stat. 126

Western Water Policy Review Act of 1992
Pub. L. 102–575, title XXX, Oct. 30, 1992, 106 Stat. 4693 (43 U.S.C. 371 note)

Wetlands Act of 1961
See Wetlands Loan Act

Wetlands and Wildlife Enhancement Act of 1998
Pub. L. 105–312, title III, Oct. 30, 1998, 112 Stat. 2958
Short title, see 16 U.S.C. 4401 note

Wetlands Loan Act
Pub. L. 87–383, Oct. 4, 1961, 75 Stat. 813 (16 U.S.C. 715k–3 et seq.)
Short title, see 16 U.S.C. 715k–3 note

Wetlands Loan Extension Act of 1976
Pub. L. 94–215, Feb. 17, 1976, 90 Stat. 189
Short title, see 16 U.S.C. 715 note

Whale Conservation and Protection Study Act
Pub. L. 94–532, Oct. 17, 1976, 90 Stat. 2491 (16 U.S.C. 917 et seq.)
Short title, see 16 U.S.C. 917 note

Whaling Convention Act of 1949
Aug. 9, 1950, ch. 653, 64 Stat. 421 (16 U.S.C. 916 et seq.)
Short title, see 16 U.S.C. 916 note

Whaling Treaty Act
May 1, 1936, ch. 251, 49 Stat. 1246 (16 U.S.C. 901 et seq.)

Wheat Acreage Act
See Agricultural Adjustment Act of 1938

Wheat and Wheat Foods Research and Nutrition Education Act
Pub. L. 95–113, title XVII, Sept. 29, 1977, 91 Stat. 1031 (7 U.S.C. 3401 et seq.)
Short title, see 7 U.S.C. 3401 note

Wheat Research and Promotion Act
Pub. L. 91–430, Sept. 26, 1970, 84 Stat. 885 (7 U.S.C. 1292 note)

Wheeler Coal-Miners Act
See Railroad Retirement Act of 1937

Wheeler-Case Act
July 16, 1943, ch. 242, 57 Stat. 566

Wheeler-Howard Act
See Indian Reorganization Act

Wheeler-Lea Act
Mar. 21, 1938, ch. 49, 52 Stat. 111

Wheeler-Lea Transportation Act
See Transportation Act of 1940

Wheeling National Heritage Area Act of 2000
Pub. L. 106–291, title I, §157, Oct. 11, 2000, 114 Stat. 963 (16 U.S.C. 461 note)

Wherry Act (Housing Near Military Establishments)
June 27, 1934, ch. 847, title VIII, as added Aug. 8, 1949, ch. 403, §1, 63 Stat. 570

Whistleblower Protection Act of 1989
Pub. L. 101–12, Apr. 10, 1989, 103 Stat. 16
Short title, see 5 U.S.C. 1201 note

White Act (Collisions on Great Lakes)
Feb. 8, 1895, ch. 64, 28 Stat. 645 (33 U.S.C. 241 et seq.)

White Cane Safety Day Act
Pub. L. 88–628, Oct. 6, 1964, 78 Stat. 1003

White Charger Act
Pub. L. 86–616, §10, July 12, 1960, 74 Stat. 395

White Clay Creek Study Act
Pub. L. 102–215, Dec. 11, 1991, 105 Stat. 1664
Short title, see 16 U.S.C. 1271 note

White Clay Creek Wild and Scenic Rivers System Act
Pub. L. 106–357, Oct. 24, 2000, 114 Stat. 1393
Short title, see 16 U.S.C. 1271 note

White Earth Reservation Land Settlement Act of 1985
Pub. L. 99–264, Mar. 24, 1986, 100 Stat. 61 (25 U.S.C. 331 note)

White House Conference for a Drug Free America
Pub. L. 99–570, title I, subtitle S (§1931 et seq.), Oct. 27, 1986, 100 Stat. 3207–56 (20 U.S.C. 4601 note)

White House Conference on Handicapped Individuals Act
Pub. L. 93–516, title III, Dec. 7, 1974, 88 Stat. 1631

White House Conference on Productivity Act
Pub. L. 97–367, Oct. 25, 1982, 96 Stat. 1761 (15 U.S.C. 2401 note)

White House Conference on Small Business Authorization Act (1984)
Pub. L. 98–276, May 8, 1984, 98 Stat. 169 (15 U.S.C. 631 note)

White House Conference on Small Business Authorization Act (1990)
Pub. L. 101–409, Oct. 5, 1990, 104 Stat. 885 (15 U.S.C. 631 note)

White House Police Act
Apr. 22, 1940, ch. 133, 54 Stat. 156

White Phosphorous Matches Act
Apr. 9, 1912, ch. 75, 37 Stat. 81

White Pine Blister Rust Protection Act
Apr. 26, 1940, ch. 159, 54 Stat. 168 (16 U.S.C. 594a)

White Russian Act
June 8, 1934, ch. 429, 48 Stat. 926

White-slave traffic Act
June 25, 1910, ch. 395, 36 Stat. 825

Whitman Mission National Historic Site
Pub. L. 87–471, May 31, 1962, 76 Stat. 90 (16 U.S.C. 433n)

Wholesome Meat Act
Pub. L. 90–201, Dec. 15, 1967, 81 Stat. 584
Short title, see 21 U.S.C. 601 note

Wholesome Poultry Products Act
Pub. L. 90–492, Aug. 18, 1968, 82 Stat. 791
Short title, see 21 U.S.C. 451 note

WIC Farmers' Market Nutrition Act of 1992
Pub. L. 102–314, July 2, 1992, 106 Stat. 280
Short title, see 42 U.S.C. 1771 note

WIC Infant Formula Procurement Act of 1992
Pub. L. 102–512, title II, Oct. 24, 1992, 106 Stat. 3364
Short title, see 42 U.S.C. 1771 note

Widows' Pension Act
Apr. 19, 1908, ch. 147, 35 Stat. 64

Wilcox Air Base Act
Aug. 12, 1935, ch. 511, 49 Stat. 610

Wild and Scenic Rivers Act
Pub. L. 90–542, Oct. 2, 1968, 82 Stat. 906 (16 U.S.C. 1271 et seq.)
Short title, see 16 U.S.C. 1271 note

Wild Bird Conservation Act of 1992
Pub. L. 102–440, title I, Oct. 23, 1992, 106 Stat. 2224 (16 U.S.C. 4901 et seq.)
Short title, see 16 U.S.C. 4901 note

Wild Free-Roaming Horses and Burros Act
Pub. L. 92–195, Dec. 15, 1971, 85 Stat. 649 (16 U.S.C. 1331 et seq.)
Short title, see 16 U.S.C. 1331 note

Wild Horse Annie Act
Pub. L. 86–234, Sept. 8, 1959, 73 Stat. 470 (18 U.S.C. 47)

Wild Horses' Act
See Wild Free-Roaming Horses and Burros Act

Wilderness Act
Pub. L. 88–577, Sept. 3, 1964, 78 Stat. 890 (16 U.S.C. 1131 et seq.)
Short title, see 16 U.S.C. 1131 note

Wildfire Disaster Recovery Act of 1989
Pub. L. 101–286, May 9, 1990, 104 Stat. 171
Short title, see 16 U.S.C. 551 note

Wildfire Suppression Aircraft Transfer Act of 1996
Pub. L. 104–307, Oct. 14, 1996, 110 Stat. 3811 (10 U.S.C. 2576 note)

Wildfire Suppression Assistance Act
Pub. L. 101–11, Apr. 7, 1989, 103 Stat. 15
Short title, see 42 U.S.C. 1856m note

Wildlife and Sport Fish Restoration Programs Improvement Act of 2000
Pub. L. 106–408, title I, Nov. 1, 2000, 114 Stat. 1763
Short title, see 16 U.S.C. 669 note

Wildlife Conservation Act
See Fish and Wildlife Coordination Act

Wildlife Refuge Revenue Sharing Act
See Refuge Revenue Sharing Act

Wildlife Restoration Act
See Pittman-Robertson Wildlife Restoration Act

Wiley Act (Food and Drugs)
See Federal Food and Drugs Act of 1906

Wiley Act (Homestead Lands, Alabama)
Mar. 3, 1903, ch. 1013, 32 Stat. 1222

William F. Goodling Child Nutrition Reauthorization Act of 1998
Pub. L. 105–336, Oct. 31, 1998, 112 Stat. 3143
Short title, see 42 U.S.C. 1751 note

William Levi Dawson Chair of Public Affairs Act
Pub. L. 96–374, title XIII, part H, subpart 3 (§1381 et seq.), Oct. 3, 1980, 94 Stat. 1503

Williams Act
Pub. L. 90–439, July 29, 1968, 82 Stat. 454

Williams-Steiger Occupational Safety and Health Act of 1970
See Occupational Safety and Health Act of 1970

Williamson Act (Veterans' Administration)
July 3, 1930, ch. 863, 46 Stat. 1016

Willis-Campbell Act
Nov. 23, 1921, ch. 134, 42 Stat. 222

Wilmot Proviso (Slavery in Territories)
June 19, 1862, ch. 111, 12 Stat. 432

Wilson Act (Northern Pacific Railroad)
July 1, 1898, ch. 546 [part], 30 Stat. 597, 620

Wilson Act
Also known as the Original Packages Act
Aug. 8, 1890, ch. 728, 26 Stat. 313 (27 U.S.C. 121)
Short title, see 27 U.S.C. 121 note

Wilson Tariff Act
Aug. 27, 1894, ch. 349, §73 et seq., 28 Stat. 570 (15 U.S.C. 8 et seq.)
Short title, see 15 U.S.C. 8 note

WIN Demonstration Program Extension Act of 1988
Pub. L. 100–364, July 11, 1988, 102 Stat. 822
Short title, see 42 U.S.C. 1305 note

Wind Energy Systems Act of 1980
Pub. L. 96–345, Sept. 8, 1980, 94 Stat. 1139 (42 U.S.C. 9201 et seq.)
Short title, see 42 U.S.C. 9201 note

Windfall Tax Extension Act
Mar. 13, 1937, ch. 40, 50 Stat. 29

Winding Stair Mountain National Recreation and Wilderness Area Act
Pub. L. 100–499, Oct. 18, 1988, 102 Stat. 2491 (16 U.S.C. 460vv et seq.)
Short title, see 16 U.S.C. 460vv note

Wine Equity and Export Expansion Act of 1984
Pub. L. 98–573, title IX, Oct. 30, 1984, 98 Stat. 3047 (19 U.S.C. 2801 et seq.)
Short title, see 19 U.S.C. 2801 note

Winslow Act
Mar. 4, 1923, ch. 285, 42 Stat. 1511

Winslow Partial Payment Act (Railroads)
See Partial Payments Act (Railroads)

Winter Run Chinook Salmon Captive Broodstock Act of 1993
Pub. L. 103–292, Aug. 11, 1994, 108 Stat. 1458

WIPO Copyright and Performances and Phonograms Treaties Implementation Act of 1998
Pub. L. 105–304, title I, Oct. 28, 1998, 112 Stat. 2861
Short title, see 17 U.S.C. 101 note

Wireless Communications and Public Safety Act of 1999
Pub. L. 106–81, Oct. 26, 1999, 113 Stat. 1286
Short title, see 47 U.S.C. 609 note

Wireless Telephone Protection Act
Pub. L. 105–172, Apr. 24, 1998, 112 Stat. 53
Short title, see 18 U.S.C. 1001 note

Wisconsin Wilderness Act of 1984
Pub. L. 98–321, June 19, 1984, 98 Stat. 250 (16 U.S.C. 1132 note)

Witness Security Reform Act of 1984
Pub. L. 98–473, title II, ch. XI, pt. F, subpt. A (§1207 et seq.), Oct. 12, 1984, 98 Stat. 2153 (18 U.S.C. 3521 et seq.)
Short title, see 18 U.S.C. 3521 note

Wolf Trap Farm Park Act
Pub. L. 89–671, Oct. 15, 1966, 80 Stat. 950 (16 U.S.C. 284 et seq.)
Short title, see 16 U.S.C. 284 note

Women in Apprenticeship and Nontraditional Occupations Act
Pub. L. 102–530, Oct. 27, 1992, 106 Stat. 3465 (29 U.S.C. 2501 et seq.)
Short title, see 29 U.S.C. 2501 note

Women Veterans Health Programs Act of 1992
Pub. L. 102–585, title I, Nov. 4, 1992, 106 Stat. 4944
Short title, see 38 U.S.C. 101 note

Women's Armed Services Integration Act of 1948
June 12, 1948, ch. 449, 62 Stat. 356

Women's Business Center Amendments Act of 1999
Pub. L. 106–17, Apr. 6, 1999, 113 Stat. 27
Short title, see 15 U.S.C. 631 note

Women's Business Centers Sustainability Act of 1999
Pub. L. 106–165, Dec. 9, 1999, 113 Stat. 1795
Short title, see 15 U.S.C. 631 note

Women's Business Development Act of 1991
Pub. L. 102–191, Dec. 5, 1991, 105 Stat. 1589
Short title, see 15 U.S.C. 631 note

Women's Business Ownership Act of 1988
Pub. L. 100–533, Oct. 25, 1988, 102 Stat. 2689
Short title, see 15 U.S.C. 631 note

Women's Educational Equity Act
Pub. L. 89–10, title IV, part A (§4001 et seq.), as added Pub. L. 100–297, title I, §1001, Apr. 28, 1988, 102 Stat. 234 (20 U.S.C. 3041 et seq.)

Women's Educational Equity Act of 1974
Pub. L. 93–380, title IV, §408, Aug. 21, 1974, 88 Stat. 554 (20 U.S.C. 1866)

Women's Educational Equity Act of 1978
Pub. L. 89–10, Apr. 11, 1965, title IX, part C (§931 et seq.), as added Pub. L. 95–561, title VIII, §802, Nov. 1, 1978, 92 Stat. 2298 (20 U.S.C. 3341 et seq.)

Women's Educational Equity Act of 1994
Pub. L. 89–10, title V, part B (§5201 et seq.), as added Pub. L. 103–382, title I, §101, Oct. 20, 1994, 108 Stat. 3695 (20 U.S.C. 7231 et seq.)
Short title, see 20 U.S.C. 7231(a)

Women's Educational Equity Amendments of 1984
Pub. L. 98–511, title IV, Oct. 19, 1984, 98 Stat. 2389
Short title, see 20 U.S.C. 6301 note

Women's Health and Cancer Rights Act of 1998
Pub. L. 105–277, div. A, §101(f) [title IX], Oct. 21, 1998, 112 Stat. 2681–337, 2681–436
Short title, see 42 U.S.C. 201 note

Women's Health Research and Prevention Amendments of 1998
Pub. L. 105–340, Oct. 31, 1998, 112 Stat. 3191
Short title, see 42 U.S.C. 201 note

Women's Naval Reserve Act
July 30, 1942, ch. 538, 56 Stat. 730

Women's Progress Commemoration Act
Pub. L. 105–341, Oct. 31, 1998, 112 Stat. 3196 (16 U.S.C. 470a note)

Wood Residue Utilization Act of 1980
Pub. L. 96–554, Dec. 19, 1980, 94 Stat. 3257 (16 U.S.C. 1681 et seq.)
Short title, see 16 U.S.C. 1600 note

Woodrow Wilson Memorial Act of 1968
Pub. L. 90–637, Oct. 24, 1968, 82 Stat. 1356 (20 U.S.C. 80e et seq.)
Short title, see 20 U.S.C. 80e note

Woodrow Wilson Memorial Bridge Authority Act of 1995
Pub. L. 104–59, title IV, Nov. 28, 1995, 109 Stat. 627

Wool and Woolens Act (Tariff)
Mar. 2, 1867, ch. 197, 14 Stat. 559; R.S. §§2504, 2912, 2916

Wool Products Labeling Act of 1939
Oct. 14, 1940, ch. 871, 54 Stat. 1128 (15 U.S.C. 68 et seq.)
Short title, see 15 U.S.C. 68 note

Work Hours and Safety Act of 1962
Pub. L. 87–581, Aug. 13, 1962, 76 Stat. 357 (40 U.S.C. 327 et seq.)
Short title, see 40 U.S.C. 327 note

Work Made For Hire and Copyright Corrections Act of 2000
Pub. L. 106–379, Oct. 27, 2000, 114 Stat. 1444
Short title, see 17 U.S.C. 101 note

Work Relief and Public Works Appropriation Act of 1938
June 21, 1938, ch. 554, 52 Stat. 809

Worker Adjustment and Retraining Notification Act
Pub. L. 100–379, Aug. 4, 1988, 102 Stat. 890 (29 U.S.C. 2101 et seq.)
Short title, see 29 U.S.C. 2101 note

Worker Economic Opportunity Act
Pub. L. 106–202, May 18, 2000, 114 Stat. 308
Short title, see 29 U.S.C. 201 note

Workers Technology Skill Development Act
Pub. L. 103–382, title V, part D (§541 et seq.), Oct. 20, 1994, 108 Stat. 4051 (29 U.S.C. 2701 et seq.)
Short title, see 29 U.S.C. 2701 note

Workers' Family Protection Act
Pub. L. 102–522, title II, §209, Oct. 26, 1992, 106 Stat. 3420 (29 U.S.C. 671a)
Short title, see 29 U.S.C. 671a(a)

Workforce Investment Act of 1998
Pub. L. 105–220, Aug. 7, 1998, 112 Stat. 936
Short title, see 20 U.S.C. 9201 note

World Cup USA 1994 Commemorative Coin Act
Pub. L. 102–281, title II, May 13, 1992, 106 Stat. 135 (31 U.S.C. 5112 note)

World War Adjusted Compensation Act
May 19, 1924, ch. 157, 43 Stat. 121

World War II 50th Anniversary Commemorative Coin Act
Pub. L. 102–414, Oct. 14, 1992, 106 Stat. 2106 (31 U.S.C. 5112 note)

World War Veterans' Act, 1924
June 7, 1924, ch. 320, 43 Stat. 607

World's Fair Act
Apr. 29, 1939, ch. 106, 53 Stat. 625

Wright Brothers Day Act
Pub. L. 88–209, Dec. 17, 1963, 77 Stat. 402

Wunderlich Act
May 11, 1954, ch. 199, 68 Stat. 81 (41 U.S.C. 321 et seq.)

Wyoming Land Act
May 29, 1908, ch. 220, 35 Stat. 465

Wyoming Wilderness Act of 1984
Pub. L. 98–550, Oct. 30, 1984, 98 Stat. 2807 (16 U.S.C. 1132 notes)

Y2K Act
Pub. L. 106–37, July 20, 1999, 113 Stat. 185 (15 U.S.C. 6601 et seq.)
Short title, see 15 U.S.C. 6601 note

Yavapai-Prescott Indian Tribe Water Rights Settlement Act of 1994
Pub. L. 103–434, title I, Oct. 31, 1994, 108 Stat. 4526

Year 2000 Health Objectives Planning Act
Pub. L. 101–582, Nov. 15, 1990, 104 Stat. 2867 (42 U.S.C. 246 note)

Year 2000 Information and Readiness Disclosure Act
Pub. L. 105–271, Oct. 19, 1998, 112 Stat. 2386 (15 U.S.C. 1 note)

Yellowstone National Park Protection Act
May 7, 1894, ch. 72, 28 Stat. 73 (16 U.S.C. 24 et seq.)

Young Astronaut Program Medal Act
Pub. L. 99–295, May 12, 1986, 100 Stat. 427 (31 U.S.C. 5111 note)

Youth Conservation Corps Act of 1970
Pub. L. 91–378, title I, Aug. 13, 1970, 84 Stat. 794 (16 U.S.C. 1701 et seq.)
Short title, see 16 U.S.C. 1701 note

Youth Drug and Mental Health Services Act
Pub. L. 106–310, div. B, Oct. 17, 2000, 114 Stat. 1168
Short title, see 42 U.S.C. 201 note

Youth Employment and Demonstration Projects Act of 1977
Pub. L. 95–93, Aug. 5, 1977, 91 Stat. 627

Youth Employment Demonstration Amendments of 1981
Pub. L. 97–14, June 16, 1981, 95 Stat. 98

Ysleta del Sur Pueblo and Alabama and Coushatta Indian Tribes of Texas Restoration Act
Pub. L. 100–89, Aug. 18, 1987, 101 Stat. 666 (25 U.S.C. 731 et seq., 1300g et seq.)
Short title, see 25 U.S.C. 731 note

Yugoslav Emergency Relief Assistance Act of 1950
Dec. 29, 1950, ch. 1182, 64 Stat. 1122

Yukon River Salmon Act of 1995
Pub. L. 104–43, title VII, Nov. 3, 1995, 109 Stat. 392 (16 U.S.C. 5701 et seq.)
Short title, see 16 U.S.C. 5701 note

Yukon River Salmon Act of 2000
Pub. L. 106–450, title II, Nov. 7, 2000, 114 Stat. 1941 (16 U.S.C. 5721 et seq.)
Short title, see 16 U.S.C. 5701 note

Yuma Crossing National Heritage Area Act of 2000
Pub. L. 106–319, Oct. 19, 2000, 114 Stat. 1280 (16 U.S.C. 461 note)

Zuni Land Conservation Act of 1990
Pub. L. 101–486, Oct. 31, 1990, 104 Stat. 1174

Zuni River Watershed Act of 1992
Pub. L. 102–338, Aug. 11, 1992, 106 Stat. 866

Zuni-Cibola National Historical Park Establishment Act of 1988
Pub. L. 100–567, Oct. 31, 1988, 102 Stat. 2847 (16 U.S.C. 410pp et seq.)
Short title, see 16 U.S.C. 410pp note

TABLES

TABLE I—REVISED TITLES

The following tables represent those titles of the United States Code that have been revised and renumbered since adoption of the Code in 1926. These tables show where former sections of the revised titles have been incorporated in this edition of the Code.

Abbreviations

Rep.—Repealed. Where "Rep." appears in the new sections column, the former section was repealed prior to, or at the time of, the enactment of the revised Title, and was not restated in the revised Title.
Elim.—Eliminated. Where "Elim." appears in the new sections column, the former section was not restated in the revised Title and was not repealed.

TITLE 1—GENERAL PROVISIONS

[This title was enacted into law by act July 30, 1947, ch. 388, §1, 61 Stat. 633. This table shows where sections of former Title 1 were incorporated in revised Title 1.]

Title 1 Former Sections	Title 1 New Sections
1	1
2	2
3	3
4	4
5	5
6	6
21	101
22	102
23	103
24	104
25	105
26	106
27	107
28	108
29	109
29a	110
29b	111
30	112
30a	113
31	114
51a	201
52	202
53	203
54	204
54a	205
54b	206
54c	207
54d	208
55	209
56	210
57	211
58	212
59	213
60	Rep.

TITLE 3—THE PRESIDENT

[This title was enacted into law by act June 25, 1948, ch. 644, §1, 62 Stat. 672. This table shows where sections of former Title 3 were incorporated in revised Title 3.]

Title 3 Former Sections	Title 3 New Sections
1	1
2	3
3	4
4	2
5	7
5a	7
6	5
7	6
7a	6
8	8
9	9
9a	9
10	10
11	11
11a	11
11b	12
11c	13
12	11, 12
13	13
14	11
15	11
16	14
17	15
18	18
19	17
20	16
21	19
22	19
23	20
24	19
41	101
42	102
43	103
44	104
45	105
45a	106
46	107
47	108
48	109
49	110
50	109
51	109
52	109
53	201
54	Elim.
61	202
62	203
62a	205
62b	206
63	204
64	207
65	Rep.
66	Rep.
67	208

TITLE 4—FLAG AND SEAL, SEAT OF GOVERNMENT, AND THE STATES

[This title was enacted into law by act July 30, 1947, ch. 389, §1, 61 Stat. 641. This table shows where sections of former Title 4 were incorporated in revised Title 4.]

Title 4 Former Sections	Title 4 New Sections
1	1
2	2
3	3
4	41
5	42
6	71
7	72
8	73
9	101
10	102
11	103
12	104
13	105
14	106
15	107
16	108
17	109
18	110

TITLE 5—GOVERNMENT ORGANIZATION AND EMPLOYEES

[This title was enacted into law by Pub. L. 89–554, § 1, Sept. 6, 1966, 80 Stat. 378. This table shows where sections of former Title 5 were incorporated in revised Title 5.]

Title 5 Former Sections	*Title 5 New Sections*
1, 2	101
3	Rep.
4	3345
5	3346
6	3347
7	3348
8	3349
9	5535
10	2901
11, 12	2902
13–14a, 15	Rep.
16	3331
16a	2903, 2904
17, 17a	Rep.
17b, 17c	2905
18	2903
19	Rep.
20	2904
21	2906
21a	3332
21b	5507
22	301
22–1 (less 3d–5th provisos)	7532
22–1 (3d proviso)	3571, 5594
22–1 (4th and 5th provisos)	7312
22–2	7533
22–3	7531
22a	302
23–26c	Rep.
27	6106
28	6105
29, 29a, 30 to 30b–1, 30c to 30e–1, 30f–30m.	Rep.
30n	6322
30n–1	T. 28 § 1823
30*o*	5537
30p	5515
30q	6321
30r(a)	6323
30r(b)	3551
30r(c)	502, 5534
30r(d)	2105
31–31b, 32	Rep.
33	7154
34–35a, 36–37a	Rep.
38	3341
39, 40	3342
41	T. 14 § 632
42, 42a	Rep.
43	3101
43a	3102
44	T. 31 § 492–1 (See Rev. T. 31 Table)
45	Rep.
46	3103
46a	5511
46b	5513
46c	T. 31 § 699a (See Rev. T. 31 Table)
46d, 46e	5514
47	3103; T. 18 § 1916
47a	8301; T. 10 § 1221
48	T. 28 § 514
49	3106
50	5501; T. 18 § 1916
51	5536
52	5502
53	3108
54	3107
55	Rep.
55a	3109
56	5503
57–59c	Rep.
60	T. 2 § 162
61	D.C. Code, § 31–1009
61a	5552
61a–1(a), (f)	5534a
61a–1(b)–(e)	Rep.
61b (1st, 2d sentences)	5551
61b (3d–5th sentences)	6306
61b (6th sentence)	5551
61c–61e	Rep.
61f	5582
61g	5581
61h	5583
61i	5581
61j	5582
61k	5581
62–64a	Rep.
65	T. 2 § 162
66	T. 18 § 1914
67	T. 7 § 2220
68	T. 8 § 1353c
69	5535, 5536
70	5536
70a, 70b	5945
70c	5942
71	5536
72	5535
73, 73a	Rep.
73b	5731
73b–1(a), (b)	5724
73b–1(c)	5730
73b–1(d)	5725
73b–1(e)	5726
73b–1(f)	5727
73b–2	5703
73b–3(a) (less 3d–6th provisos)	5722
73b–3(a) (3d, 4th provisos)	5728
73b–3(a) (5th, 6th provisos)	5729
73b–3 (less (a))	5723
73b–4	T. 41 § 5a
73b–4a, 73b–4b	5724a
73b–4c	5726
73b–4d	5724
73b–4e	5724a
73b–4f	5724
73b–5	5732
73c	5727
73c–1, 73c–2, 73d	Rep.
73e	5731
73f, 74–75a	Rep.
75a–1	Elim.
75b–75d, 76	Rep.
76a	T. 20 § 244a
77, 77a	Rep.
78, 78a, 78a–1, 79, 80	T. 31 §§ 638a–638e (See Rev. T. 31 Table)
81, 81a	Rep.
82	5512
83	5946
84	5505
84a	T. 4 § 111
84b, 84c	5517
84d	5518
85	5502
86	Rep.
86a	6104
87–87c	6103
88	T. 31 § 554 (See Rev. T. 31 Table)
89	Rep.
90	T. 28 § 414
91	T. 28 § 520
92	Rep.
92a	2903
93	303
93a	Rep.
94	304
95, 95a	503
96	304
97, 98	Rep.
99, 100	Rep. See T. 18 § 207.
101	501
102	Rep.
103	5741
103a, 103b	5742
104	T. 31 § 492–2 (See Rev. T. 31 Table)
104a, 105	Rep.
105a	2954
106	2952
107	Rep.
108	T. 44 § 121 (See Rev. T. 44 Table)
109	Rep.
110	T. 40 § 484–1
111, 112	Rep.
113	7351
114	7341
114a	7342 note
115, 115a	7341
116	Elim.
116a, 117	Rep.
118	T. 31 § 686–2 (See Rev. T. 31 Table)
118a	5912
118b	T. 31 § 530a (See Rev. T. 31 Table)
118c	5943
118c–1 to 118e	Rep.
118f	5944
118g	7903
118h	5941
118i(a) (1st 4 sentences)	7324
118i(a) (5th sentence)	7327
118i(b) (less last proviso, and less last sentence).	7325
118i(b) (last proviso, last sentence).	Elim.
118i(c)	1308
118j, 118j–1	Rep.

Title 5 Former Sections	*Title 5 New Sections*
118k(a)	1501, 1502
118k(b)	1504, 1505, 1506
118k(c)	1508
118k(d)	1302, 1507
118k(e), (f)	1501
118k–1	1501, 7324
118k–2	1501
118k–3	7324
118*l*	1501, 7324
118m	7327
118n	1503, 7326
118*o*	7323
118p	7311
118q	3333
118r	T. 18 §1918
119–123	Elim.
124–131a, 132–133r	Rep.
133s, 133t	Elim.
133u, 133v	Rep.
133w	Elim.
133x to 133y–16	Rep.
133z	901
133z–1	903
133z–2	904
133z–3	905
133z–4	906
133z–5, 133z–6	902
133z–7, 133z–8	907
133z–9	906
133z–10	908
133z–11 to 133z–15	909–913
134	T. 40 §721
134a	T. 40 §722
134b	T. 40 §723
134b–1	T. 40 §724
134b–2	T. 40 §725
134c	T. 40 §726
134d	T. 40 §727
134e	T. 40 §728
134f	T. 40 §729
134g, 134h	T. 40 §721 note
135–138j	Rep.
139–139f	T. 44 §§421–427 (See Rev. T. 44 Table)
140, 140a	T. 31 §§483a, 483b (See Rev. T. 31 Table)
141–149	Rep.
150	7901
150e–150i	T. 10 §2575
150j	T. 10 §§4712, 9712
150j–1 to 150j–3	T. 10 §§4713, 9713
150k	2105
150k–1(a)	8171
150k–1(b)	8172
150k–1(c)	8173
150m–150*o*	T. 10 §2541
150p	T. 10 §2572
150q–150t	T. 10 §2601
151	T. 22 §2651
151a	T. 22 §2652
151b	T. 22 §2653
151c	T. 22 §2658
151d to 152–1	Rep.
152a	T. 22 §2654
152b	T. 22 §2655
152c, 152d, 153	Rep.
153a	T. 22 §2663
154	T. 22 §2664
154a	Rep.
155	T. 22 §2665
156	T. 22 §2656
157	Rep.
158	T. 22 §2657
159, 160	Rep.
161	T. 22 §2659
162–164	Rep.
165	T. 22 §2660
166–168d	Rep.
169	T. 22 §2661
170	T. 22 §2668
170a	T. 22 §2681
170b	T. 22 §2682
170c	T. 22 §2683
170d	Rep.
170e	T. 22 §2666
170e–1	T. 22 §2667
170f	T. 22 §2662
170g	T. 22 §2669
170h	T. 22 §2670
170i	T. 22 §2671
170j	T. 22 §2672
170k	T. 22 §2673
170*l*	T. 22 §2674
170m	T. 22 §2675
170n	T. 22 §2676
170*o*	T. 22 §2677
170p	T. 22 §2678
170q	T. 22 §2679
170r, 170s	Rep.
170t	T. 22 §2680
170u	T. 22 §2684
171	T. 10 §§131, 133
171–1	T. 50 §408
171–2	T. 50 §409
171a(a), (b)	T. 10 §133
171a(c)	T. 10 §§125, 136, 141, 3010, 3012, 5011, 5031, 8010, 8012
171a(d)	T. 10 §133
171a(e)	T. 10 §132
171a(f)	T. 10 §133
171a(g)–(i)	Elim.
171a(j)	T. 10 §124
171a–1	T. 10 §133
171b	Rep.
171c	T. 10 §§134–136, 718, 2358
171c–1, 171c–2, 171d to 171d–2	Rep.
171e	T. 10 §171
171f	T. 10 §§141, 142
171g	T. 10 §143
171h, 171i	Rep.
171j	T. 10 §173
171j–1 to 171*l*	Rep.
171m	T. 50 §411
171m–1	T. 10 §2211
171n	T. 50 §410
171*o*	Rep.
171p, 171q	T. 10 §1581
171r	T. 10 §1582
171s	T. 10 §§3230, 5416, 8230
171s–1	T. 31 §700 (See Rev. T. 31 Table)
171t	T. 10 §2571
171u	Rep.
171v	T. 10 §1583
171w	T. 10 §2385
171x, 171y	Rep.
171y–1	T. 10 §§3205, 5417, 8205
171z	T. 10 §2661
171z–1	T. 10 §2681
171z–2	T. 31 §700a (See Rev. T. 31 Table)
171z–3 to 171z–5	T. 10 §§2673–2675
172	T. 10 §136
172a	T. 10 §§3014, 5061, 8014
172b, 172c	T. 10 §§2203, 2204
172d	T. 10 §2208
172d–1	T. 10 §2210
172e	T. 10 §2209
172f	T. 10 §126
172g, 172h	T. 10 §§2205, 2206
172i	T. 10 §2701
172j	T. 50 §412
173	T. 10 §2451
173a	Rep.
173b	T. 10 §2451
173c–173e	T. 10 §§2452–2454
173f–173h	T. 10 §2455
173i	T. 10 §2456
174	T. 31 §650a (See Rev. T. 31 Table)
174a	T. 37 §412
174b	T. 10 §2666
174c	Elim.
174d	T. 10 §2207
174e	T. 10 §2387
174f	Elim.
174g	T. 31 §638f (See Rev. T. 31 Table)
174h	Elim.
174i	T. 31 §700b (See Rev. T. 31 Table)
181	T. 10 §3012
181–1(a)	T. 10 §3012
181–1(b)	Elim.
181–1(c)	T. 10 §101(5); T. 50 §409(a)
181–1(d)	T. 10 §3011
181–1(e)	T. 10 §3062
181–2	T. 10 §3012
181–3	T. 10 §3001
181–4	T. 10 §§3012, 4532
181–5	T. 10 §§3013, 3017
181a, 182, 182a, 183, 184	Rep.
185–187	T. 10 §3016
187a, 188, 189	Rep.
189a	T. 10 §§4025, 9025
189b	Rep.
189c	T. 10 §2632
189d	Rep.
190	T. 10 §3012
191	T. 10 §4831
191a	T. 10 §1552
192, 192a, 193–194a, 195–197	Rep.
198	T. 10 §4714
199	T. 10 §§3693, 8693
200	T. 10 §1551
201	Rep.
202	T. 10 §§4565, 9565
203–207i, 208–213	Rep.
214	Elim.
215–216a, 217	Rep.
218	T. 10 §2381
219–219b, 220	Rep.
221	T. 10 §§4540, 9540
222	T. 31 §649a (See Rev. T. 31 Table)
223	Rep.
224	T. 22 §276aa
225	T. 22 §276bb

Title 5 Former Sections	Title 5 New Sections
226	T. 22 §276cc
227	T. 22 §276dd
228	T. 22 §276ee
229–232	Rep.
233–233c	(See former 150q–150t)
234–234f	Rep.
235	T. 10 §4531
235a	T. 10 §4503
235b	T. 10 §174
235c	T. 10 §1584
235d	T. 10 §2352
235e	T. 10 §§2353, 2357
235f, 235g	T. 10 §§2354, 2355
235h	T. 10 §§174, 2356
241–245	T. 31 §§1001–1005 (See Rev. T. 31 Table)
245a	Rep. and Elim.
246	T. 31 §1006 (See Rev. T. 31 Table)
246a	Rep.
247–248a	T. 31 §§1007–1009 (See Rev. T. 31 Table)
248b	Rep.
248c–248e	T. 31 §§1010, 1011, 1013 (See Rev. T. 31 Table)
249, 249a	Rep.
249b, 250	T. 31 §§1014, 1015 (See Rev. T. 31 Table)
251	Rep.
252–258a, 259–265	T. 31 §§1016–1030 (See Rev. T. 31 Table)
266–269	Rep.
270, 271	Elim.
272–274	Rep.
275	T. 10 §1552
276	Rep.
277	T. 31 §1031 (See Rev. T. 31 Table)
281	T. 19 §2071
281a	T. 19 §2072
281b	T. 19 §2073
281c	T. 21 §163
281d, 281e	Rep.
281f	T. 19 §2072
281g	T. 19 §2074
282	T. 21 §161
282a	T. 21 §162
282b	T. 21 §164
282c	T. 21 §165
291	T. 28 §§501, 503
292	T. 28 §502
293	T. 28 §505
293a	Rep.
294	T. 28 §504
295, 295–1	T. 28 §506
295a	Rep.
295b	Rep. and Elim.
296	Rep.
297	Rep. and Elim.
297a	Rep.
298	T. 28 §543
298a	5108
299	T. 28 §533
300	T. 28 §§533, 534
300a	T. 18 §§3052, 3107
300b	T. 31 §224b (See Rev. T. 31 Table)
300c, 300c–1	Rep.
300d	T. 28 §536
300e–302	Rep.
303, 304	T. 28 §§511, 512
305	T. 28 §521; T. 44 §296a (See Rev. T. 44 Table)
306	T. 28 §516
306a	Rep.
307	T. 28 §513
308	Rep.
309	T. 28 §518
310	T. 28 §515
311	Rep.
311a	T. 28 §535
312	T. 28 §§543, 547, 548
313	T. 28 §514
314	3106
315	T. 28 §515
316	T. 28 §517
317	T. 28 §§547, 569
318	T. 28 §§549, 569
319	T. 28 §523
320, 321	Rep.
322	T. 31 §1010 (See Rev. T. 31 Table)
323, 324	T. 28 §547
325	T. 31 §1012 (See Rev. T. 31 Table)
326	T. 31 §1011 (See Rev. T. 31 Table)
327	T. 28 §547
328	T. 31 §1013 (See Rev. T. 31 Table)
329	T. 28 §§547, 569
330, 331	T. 28 §547
332	Rep. See Fed. Rules Civ. Proc. rule 2.
333	T. 28 §522
334–339	Rep.
340	T. 28 §534
341	T. 28 §524
341a	T. 28 §568
341b	T. 28 §526
341c	T. 28 §§536, 537
341d	T. 8 §1555
341e	T. 28 §525
341f	T. 18 §4010
341g	T. 18 §4011
341h	T. 42 §250a
342	T. 8 §1551
342a	Elim.
342b	T. 8 §1552
342b–1	T. 8 §1553
342c	T. 8 §1353a
342d	T. 8 §1353b
342e	T. 8 §1353d
342f	Rep.
342g	T. 8 §1554
342h–342k	Elim.
342*l*	T. 8 §1557
361	Rep. See T. 39 §§201, 203.
362	Rep. See T. 39 §207.
363, 363a, 364	Rep. See T. 39 §204.
364–1(a)	Rep. See T. 39 §§204, 401.
364–1(b), 364a, 364b	Rep.
365	Rep. See T. 39 §1011.
366	Rep. See T. 39 §401.
367	Rep. See T. 39 §2201.
368	Rep.
369	Rep. See T. 39 §§202, 401, 403, 404.
370	Rep. See T. 39 §§1001, 1006.
371	Rep.
372, 373	Rep. See T. 39 §407.
374	Rep. See T. 39 §2202.
375	Rep. See T. 39 §407.
376	Rep.
377	Rep. See T. 39 §401.
378–382	Rep.
383, 384	Rep. See T. 39 §2601.
385–388	Rep.
389	Rep. See T. 39 §5213.
390, 391	Rep.
392	Rep. See T. 39 §2603.
393	Rep. See T. 39 §401.
411	T. 10 §5031
411a(a)	T. 10 §101(5); T. 50 §409(b)
411a(b)	T. 10 §5012
411a(c)	T. 10 §§5013, 5402
411b, 412	T. 10 §5031
412a	T. 10 §§6952, 7202–7211, 7214, 7215, 7218, 7301, 7472, 7478, 7571, 7572, 7576, 7578, 7579
412b	T. 10 §2381
413	T. 10 §5031
414, 415, 415a	Rep.
415b	T. 10 §7473
415c	T. 10 §7472
415d	T. 10 §2632
415e, 416, 417	Rep.
418	T. 10 §7216
419	T. 10 §7221
419a	T. 10 §7220
419b	T. 10 §7222
419c	T. 10 §7202
420, 420a, 421	T. 10 §5034
421a	Rep.
421a–1	T. 10 §§5034, 5036
421b	T. 10 §§5033, 5036
421c	T. 10 §7211
421d	T. 10 §7204
421e	T. 10 §§7203, 7205
421f	T. 10 §§7207–7209
421g	T. 10 §§6081, 7204, 7205, 7211, 7214, 7218, 7571, 7572, 7576, 7579
422, 422a, 423	Rep.
423a	T. 10 §§5081, 5082, 5111
423b	T. 10 §5081
423c–423f	T. 10 §§5085–5088
423g, 423h	T. 10 §§5111, 5112
423i	T. 10 §5082
423j	T. 10 §5036
423k	T. 10 §§5085, 5086, 5088, 5111
424	T. 10 §5081
425	Rep.
425a	T. 10 §§5083, 5133, 5148, 5201
426, 426a	Rep.
427	T. 10 §5081
427a	T. 10 §5084
428	T. 10 §5148
429	T. 10 §§5131, 5132
430	T. 10 §5132
430a	T. 10 §7303
430b	T. 10 §5132
431	T. 10 §5132
432	T. 10 §§5137, 5141, 5146, 5147
432a	T. 10 §5135
433	T. 10 §5147
434	T. 10 §§5141, 5144
435	T. 10 §5145
436	Rep.

Title 5 Former Sections	*Title 5 New Sections*
437	T. 10 §5146
438	T. 10 §5137
439	T. 10 §§5133, 5136
440	T. 10 §§5137, 5146
441	T. 10 §§5133, 5148
441a	T. 10 §5133
442, 443	Rep.
444	T. 10 §5149
445	T. 10 §§5135, 5147
446	T. 10 §§5135, 5141
447	T. 10 §§5135, 5144
448	T. 10 §5145
448a	T. 10 §5135
448b	T. 10 §5145
449	T. 10 §§5135, 5146
450	Rep.
451	T. 10 §5137
452	T. 10 §§5134–5136
453	T. 10 §5149
454	Rep.
455	T. 10 §5132
456	Rep.
456a	T. 10 §1552
456b, 456c	T. 10 §5138
456d	T. 10 §6029
457	T. 10 §7391
457a, 457b	Rep.
458	T. 10 §§7392, 7394
458a	T. 10 §7393
459	T. 10 §7394
460, 460a	Rep.
461	T. 10 §7395
462	Rep.
463	T. 10 §7395
464	T. 10 §7396
465	Rep.
466	T. 10 §7217
467, 468, 468a, 469, 470	Rep.
471	T. 10 §§5063, 5064
475	T. 10 §§5150, 5151
475a, 475b	T. 10 §5150
475c	T. 10 §5153
475d	T. 10 §§5151, 5152
475e	T. 10 §7522
475f	Rep.
475g	T. 10 §174
475h	T. 10 §1584
475i	T. 10 §2352
475j	T. 10 §§2353, 2357
475k, 475*l*	T. 10 §§2354, 2355
475m	T. 10 §§174, 2356
476, 476a, 476b	T. 10 §§1581, 1582
477–477c	(See former 150q–150t)
481	T. 43 §1451
481a	T. 43 §1452
482	T. 43 §1453
482a	Rep.
483	T. 43 §1454
483–1	Rep. and Elim.
483–2	Rep.
483a	T. 43 §1455
484	T. 43 §1456
485	T. 43 §1457
486	T. 43 §1458
487	T. 43 §1459
488	T. 43 §1460
489	T. 43 §1461
490	Rep. See T. 28 §1733
491	T. 43 §1462
492	T. 43 §1463
493	T. 43 §1464
494	Rep.
495	T. 43 §1465
496, 496a, 497	Rep.
498	T. 43 §1466
499, 500	Rep.
501	Elim.
502	T. 43 §1467
503	T. 43 §1468
511	T. 7 §2201
512	T. 7 §2202
513	T. 7 §2203
514	T. 7 §2204
514a	T. 7 §2210
514b	T. 7 §2211
514c	Rep.
514d (1st, 3d pars.)	Rep.
514d (2d par.)	3101
515	T. 7 §2205
516	T. 7 §2206
516a	T. 7 §450c
516b (less 3d sentence)	T. 7 §450d
516b (3d sentence)	5109
516c	T. 7 §450e
516d	T. 7 §450f
516e	T. 7 §450g
517	T. 7 §2212
517a	Rep.
517b	T. 7 §2213
517c	Rep.
518	Elim.
518a	T. 7 §2214
519	T. 7 §2215
520	T. 7 §2216
520a	T. 7 §2232
521	T. 7 §2217
522	T. 7 §2218
523–527	Rep.
528	T. 7 §2219
529	Rep.
530	T. 7 §2221
531	T. 7 §2222
532	T. 7 §2223
533	T. 7 §2224
534–537	Rep.
538	T. 7 §2227
539–541b	Rep.
541c	T. 7 §2233
541d	T. 7 §2228
541e	T. 7 §2229
542	T. 7 §2234
542–1	T. 7 §2235
542–2	T. 7 §2236
542a	T. 7 §2237
542b	T. 7 §2238
542c	T. 7 §2239
543	T. 7 §2240
543a	T. 7 §2230
543b	T. 7 §2231
544–548	Rep.
549	T. 7 §2241
550	Rep.
551	T. 7 §2242
552	T. 7 §2243
552a	T. 7 §2244
553	T. 7 §2245
554	T. 7 §2246
555	T. 7 §2247
556, 556a	Rep.
556b	T. 7 §2248
557	T. 7 §2207
557a	T. 7 §2208
558	T. 7 §2209
558a, 559–562	Rep.
563	T. 7 §450b
564	T. 7 §2220
564a	T. 7 §2249
565	Rep.
565a	T. 7 §2250
565b	T. 7 §2250a
566	T. 7 §2251
567	T. 7 §2253
568	Rep.
568a	T. 7 §2254
568b	Rep.
569	T. 7 §2252
570	T. 7 §2255
571	T. 7 §2256
572	T. 7 §2257
573	T. 7 §2258
574	T. 7 §2225
574a	T. 7 §2226
575	T. 7 §2259
576	T. 7 §2260
577	T. 7 §2261
578	T. 7 §2262
579	T. 7 §2263
591	T. 15 §1501
591a	T. 15 §1502
591b	T. 15 §1503
592	T. 15 §1504
592a	T. 15 §1505
592a–1, 592a–2	Rep.
592a–3	T. 15 §1506
592a–4	T. 15 §1507
592b	T. 15 §1508
592c, 592d, 593	Rep.
593a	T. 15 §1509
594	T. 15 §1510
595	Rep.
596	T. 15 §1512
596a	T. 15 §1514
597	T. 15 §1511
597a, 597a–1, 597b–597d	Rep.
598	T. 15 §1515
599	T. 15 §1513
600–600b	Rep.
601	T. 15 §1516
601a–601d	T. 15 §§189, 189a, 192, 192a
602	T. 15 §1517
603	T. 15 §1518
604	T. 15 §1519
605	Rep.
606	T. 15 §1520
606a	Rep.
607	T. 15 §1521
608	Rep.
608a	T. 15 §1522
608b	T. 15 §1523
608c	T. 15 §1524
611	T. 29 §551
611a	T. 29 §552
611b	T. 29 §553
611c	Rep. and Elim.
612, 613	Rep.
613a	T. 29 §554

Title 5 Former Sections	*Title 5 New Sections*
613b	T. 29 § 555
614	Rep.
615	T. 29 § 556
616	T. 29 § 557
617	T. 29 § 558
618	T. 29 § 559
619	Rep.
620	T. 29 § 560
621	T. 29 § 561
622	T. 29 § 562
622a	T. 29 § 563
623	T. 42 § 3501
623a	T. 42 § 3508
623b	T. 42 § 3503
623c	T. 42 § 3504
623d	T. 42 § 3505
623e	T. 42 § 3507
623f	T. 42 § 3506
623g	T. 42 § 3502
623h	T. 42 § 3501a
623i	Elim.
624	T. 42 § 3531
624a	T. 42 § 3532
624b	T. 42 § 3533
624c	T. 42 § 3534
624d	T. 42 § 3535
624e	T. 42 § 3536
624f	T. 42 § 3537
626(a)	T. 10 § 8012
626(b)	Rep.
626(c)	T. 10 § 101(5); T. 50 § 409(c)
626(d)	T. 10 § 8013
626(e)	T. 10 § 8012
626(f)	T. 10 § 8033
626(g)	T. 10 § 8011
626–1	T. 10 § 8013, 8017
626–2	T. 10 §§ 8012, 9532
626a	T. 10 § 8012
626b	T. 10 § 8013
626c(a), (f)	T. 10 § 8062
626c(b)	T. 10 § 743
626c(c)–(e), 626c–1 to 626c–3, 626d, 626e.	Rep.
626f	(See former 150p)
626g–626j	(See former 150q–150t)
626k	Rep.
626*l*, 626m	T. 10 § 9441
626n	T. 10 § 2632
626*o*	Rep.
626p	T. 10 § 9774
626q, 626r	T. 10 § 9301
626s to 626s–2	T. 10 § 2481
626s–3	T. 10 § 2667
626s–4, 626s–5	Rep.
626s–6	T. 10 § 2667
626t, 626u	T. 10 § 1581
626v–626y, 627	Rep.
627a	T. 10 §§ 8208, 8215
627b	T. 10 §§ 8071, 8208, 8297, 8299, 8305, 8504, 8685, 8888, 8915, 8916, 8927, 8962, 8991
627c	Rep.
627d	T. 10 § 8256
627e	T. 10 § 8685
627f	T. 10 §§ 8549, 8580, 8818
627g–627*l*	Rep.
628	T. 10 § 9531
628a	T. 10 § 9503
628b	T. 10 § 174
628c	T. 10 § 1584
628d	T. 10 § 2352
628e	T. 10 §§ 2353, 2357
628f, 628g	T. 10 §§ 2354, 2355
628h	T. 10 §§ 174, 2356
630	T. 40 § 751
630a	T. 40 § 752
630b	T. 40 § 753
630c	Rep.
630d	T. 40 § 754
630e	T. 40 § 755
630f	Rep.
630g	T. 40 § 756
630g–1	T. 40 § 757
630g–2	T. 40 § 759
630h	T. 40 § 758
630i	Elim.
630j	Rep.
631	3301, 7301
631a, 631b(a)	Elim.
631b(b), (c)	3304
632 (1st par.)	1101
632 (2d–4th pars.)	1102
632 (5th par.)	1103
633(1)	1301, 3302
633(2)1	3304
633(2)2	3318
633(2)3	3306
633(2)4	3321
633(2)5	7321
633(2)6	7152, 7322
633(2)7	1302, 3304
633(2)8	2951, 3302
633(2)9	7153

Title 5 Former Sections	*Title 5 New Sections*
633(3)	1302, 1307
633(4)	1303
633(5)	1308
633a–633e	Rep.
634	1306
635 (1st 5 sentences)	1104, 1105
635 (6th sentence)	1105, 3305
635 (7th sentence)	3304
636	Rep.
637	T. 18 § 1917
638	2102, 3304, 3361
638a	Rep.
638b	3307, 3322
639	Rep.
640	7352
641	3319
642	3303
642a	2953
643–645b	Rep.
645c–645e	Elim.
646–651b	Rep.
652(a)	7501
652(b)	5591–5593
652(c)	7101
652(d)	7102
652a–652c	5596
653, 654	Rep.
655–657	1304
658	Elim.
659	3327
661–663b, 664–669a, 670–672c, 673–673b.	Rep.
673c (1st par., less provisos)	Rep.
673c (1st proviso)	6102
673c (2d, 3d provisos)	5541
673c (2d par.), 674–678b	Rep.
679	Elim.
680–684, 691, 691a, 692–692d, 693 to 693–2, 693a–693d, 694, 649a, 695, 695a, 696, 696a, 697, 697a, 698–698b, 699, 699a, 700, 700a, 701, 701a, 702, 702a, 703, 703a, 704, 704a, 705, 705a, 706, 706a, 707, 707a, 708, 708a, 709–615.	Rep.
715a	3323
715b–715d, 716–718a, 719, 719–1, 719a, 719b, 720–729a, 730–736c, 737–739b, 740, 740a.	Rep.
740b–740i	(See former 2281–2288)
745–745r	Rep.
751	8102
752	8117
753	8105
754	8106
755(a), (b)	8107
755(c)	8108
755(d)	8109
756(a)	8110
756(b)	8111
756(c)	8112
756(d)	8113
756a	Rep.
757	8116
758	8118
759(a)	8103
759(b)	8104
759(c)	3315a
760(A)	8133
760(B)	8101, 8133
760(C)–(G)	8133
760(H)	8101
760(I)–(K)	8133
760(L)	T. 18 § 1921
760(M)	8101
761	8134
762	8114
763	8115
764	8135
765–767	8119
768, 769	8121
770	8122
771, 772, 773(a)	8123
773(b)	8127; T. 18 § 292
773(c)	8125
774(a)	8120
774(b)	T. 18 § 1922
775	8130
776	8131
777	8132
778	8145
779	8120
780	8126
781	8145
782	Rep.
783	8145, 8149
784(a)	8148
784(b), (c)	7902
785	8147
786	8124
787	8128
788	8129
789	T. 18 § 1920
790	8101

Title 5 Former Sections	Title 5 New Sections
791	8131
791–1 to 791–3, 791–4(a)	Rep.
791–4(b)	8150
791a	Rep.
791b	Elim.
792	Rep.
793 (1st par.)	8146
793 (2d par., 1st sentence)	8146
793 (2d par., 2d sentence)	8138
793 (2d par., 3d, 4th sentences)	8146
793 (3d par.)	8146
793 (4th par., 1st sentence)	8138
793 (4th par., 2d sentence)	8136
793 (5th par., 1st through 6th sentences).	8137
793 (5th par., 7th sentence)	8128
793 (5th par., 8th sentence)	8137
793a(a), (b)	8146a
793a(c)	8101
794	8101, 8139
795–797a, 798–801	Rep.
802	8140
803(a)–(c)	8141
803(d)	Rep.
803a	8150
821–823	Rep.
823a	(See former 73c)
824–834	Rep.
835	5701
836	5702
837	5704
838	5705
839	5706
840	5707
841, 842	5708
851	1302, 2108
852 (1st 2 sentences)	3309, 3310
852 (less 1st 2 sentences)	Elim.
853	3311
854	3308, 3312, 3351, 3363, 3504
855	3306, 3319
856	3313
857	3317, 3318, 3364
858	3320
859	3305
860	1302
861	3501–3503
862	3316
863	3315, 7512, 7701
864	3315, 3318
865	3314
866, 867	Rep.
868	1302, 7701
869	3320
901(a)	5541
901(b)	Rep.
901(c)	T. 2 §60e–2. Rep. in part.
901(d), (e)	5541
902	5541; T. 2 §60e–2
911	5542
912	5543
912a, 912b	5542
913	5544
914	5506
921	5545
921a	5546
922	5546
926	5545
931	T. 2 §60e–3
932	T. 2 §60e–4
932a	T. 2 §60e–5
932b	T. 2 §60e–6
932c(a)–(c)	T. 2 §60e–7
932c(d)	8331
932d(a)–(c)	T. 2 §60e–8
932d(d)	8331
932d(e)	Rep.
932d(f)	T. 2 §60e–8
932e(a)–(e)	T. 2 §60e–9
932e(f)	8331
932f(a)–(d)	T. 2 §60e–10
932f(e)	8331
932f(f)	T. 2 §60e–10
932f(g)	Rep.
932g(a)–(c)	T. 2 §60e–11
932g(d)	8331
932g(e)	T. 2 §60e–11
932h(a), (b)	T. 2 §60e–12
932h(c)	8331
932h(d)	T. 2 §60e–12
932i(a), (b)	T. 2 §60e–13
932i(c)	8331
932i(d), (e)	T. 2 §60e–13
933	5544; T. 2 §60e–2b
933a	T. 31 §46a (See Rev. T. 31 Table)
934, 935	Rep.
941	5549
942–942b	Rep.
943	5547
943a	Rep.
944(a)	6101
944(b), (c)	5504
944(d)	5504, 6101
945	5504, 5548, 6101
946	5342
947–954	Rep.
955	T. 2 §60e–4a
956–958	Rep.
1001	551
1002	552
1003	553
1004	554
1005	555
1006	556
1007	557
1008	558
1009	701–706
1010 (1st sentence)	3105
1010 (2d sentence)	7521
1010 (3d sentence)	4301, 5335, 5362
1010 (4th sentence)	3344
1010 (5th sentence)	1305
1011	559
1012–1014	500
1031–1040	T. 28 §§2341–2350
1041	T. 28 §2352
1042	T. 28 §2351
1045(a)–(d)	Elim.
1045(e)	571
1045a	572
1045b	573
1045c	574
1045d	575
1045e	576
1051	5352, 5353
1052	5351
1053	8144
1054	8331, 8332
1055	5354
1056	Rep.
1057	5355
1058	5356
1071	5101
1072, 1072a	5115
1073	Rep.
1074	7154
1075	Rep.
1076	Elim.
1081	5102
1082	5102, 5341, 5342
1083	5103
1084(a)	T. 2 §60e–2a
1084(b), (c)	5102, 5103
1085	305
1091	5102
1092, 1093	5106
1094	5105
1101	5112
1102	5107, 5110
1103	5110
1104	5111
1105(a)–(*l*)	3324, 5108
1105(m)	Rep.
1105a	5114
1105b	Elim.
1106	5113
1107	5337
1111, 1112	5104
1113	5332
1114–1116	Rep.
1117	5595
1121	5335
1122	5336
1123	5335, 5336
1124, 1125	Rep.
1131	5333
1132	5334
1133	5333
1134	5545
1141, 1142	Rep.
1151	305
1152, 1153	Rep.
1161	3104, 3325, 5361
1162(a)	3325
1162(b)	5361
1162(c)	3104
1163	3104
1171	5301
1172	5302
1173	5303
1174	5304
1181	5343
1182(a)	5344, 5581
1182(b)	8331
1182(c)	5344
1183	8704
1184	Rep.
2001	4301
2002	4302
2003	4307
2004	4303
2005	4304
2006	4305
2007(a)	4308
2007(b)–(d)	4306
2061	5508, 6301, 6305

Title 5 Former Sections	Title 5 New Sections
2061a	5551, 6302
2062(a), (b)	6303
2062(c), (d)	6304
2062(e)	6303
2062(f)	6305
2062(g)	6310
2062(h)	6302
2062(i)	6303
2062a, 2062b	Rep.
2063	6307
2064(a)–(c)	6302
2064(d)	6309
2064(e)	6308
2065	6311
2066(a)	6304
2066(b)–(d)	Rep.
2067	6301
2068–2070	Rep.
2071	6324
2091(a)	8701, 8716
2091(b)	8701
2091(c)	8706
2091(d)	8701, 8716
2092(a)–(c)	8704
2092(d)	Rep.
2093	8705
2094(a) (1st par.)	8707
2094(a) (2d par.)	8702
2094(b)	8708
2094(c), (d)	8714. Elim. in part.
2095	8706
2096	8709, 8710
2097	8711, 8712
2098	8703
2099	Elim.
2100	8716. Elim. in part.
2101	8713. Elim. in part.
2102	1308. Elim. in part.
2103	8715. Elim. in part.
2121	1308, 4506
2122	4501
2123(a)	4503
2123(b)	4504
2123(c)	4505
2123(d), (e)	4502
2123(f)	3362
2123(g)	4502
2131	5901
2132	5901, 8331
2133	5901
2134	5902
2151	T. 10 §1481
2152, 2153	T. 10 §§1481, 1482
2154	T. 10 §1481
2155–2160	T. 10 §§1483–1488
2161, 2162	T. 10 §1482
2163	Rep.
2171	T. 42 §1973cc–1
2172	T. 42 §1973cc–2
2173	T. 42 §1973cc–3
2181	T. 42 §1973cc–11
2182	T. 42 §1973cc–12
2183	T. 42 §1973cc–13
2184	T. 42 §1973cc–14
2185	T. 42 §1973cc–15
2191	T. 42 §1973cc–21
2192	T. 42 §1973cc–22
2193	T. 42 §1973cc–23
2194	T. 42 §1973cc–24
2195	T. 42 §1973cc–25
2196	T. 42 §1973cc–26
2201–2209	Rep.
2210	5311
2211(a)	5312
2211(b)(1)–(14)	5313
2211(b)(15) (less proviso)	Elim.
2211(b)(15) (proviso)	5314
2211(b)(16)–(19)	5313
2211(c)(1)–(38)	5314
2211(c)(39) (less proviso)	Elim.
2211(c)(39) (proviso)	5315
2211(c)(40)–(45)	5314
2211(c)(46) (less proviso)	Elim.
2211(c)(46) (proviso)	5315
2211(c)(47)	5314
2211(d)	5315
2211(e)	5316
2211(f)	5317
2211(g)	5315, 5316
2212	5363
2213	5364
2251(a)–(g)	8331
2251(h)–(j)	8341
2251(k)–(t)	8331
2252(a)–(d)	8331
2252(e)	8347
2252(f)	8331, 8347
2252(g)	8331, 8332
2252(h)	8331, 8332, 8347
2253(a)–(e)	8332
2253(f), (g)	8333
2253(h)–(j)	8332
2254	8334

Title 5 Former Sections	Title 5 New Sections
2255	8335
2256(a)–(e)	8336
2256(f)	8333, 8336
2257	8337
2258	8338
2259	8339
2260	8341
2261	8342
2262	8343
2263(a)	3323
2263(b), (c)	8344
2264	8345
2265	8346
2266(a)–(e)	8347
2266(f)	1308
2266(g)	8347
2267	8348
2268	8340
2281	8311
2282	8312
2283(a)	8314
2283(b), (c)	8315
2283a	8313
2284(a), (b)	8316
2284(c), (d)	8317
2284a(a)	8317
2284a(b)	8316
2285(a), (b)	8318
2285(c)	8320
2286	8321
2287	8319
2288	8322
2301(1)–(3)	Elim.
2301(4)	4117
2302	4101
2303	4102
2304	4113
2305	4118
2306	4103
2307	4104
2308	4105
2309	4109
2310	4108
2311	4106
2312, 2313	4107
2314	4114
2315	4115
2316	4116
2317(a)	4113
2317(b), (c)	1308
2318(a)	4111
2318(b)	4110
2318(c)	4111
2318(d)	4107
2318(e)	4117
2319	4112
2331	3343, 3581
2332	3343
2333	3582, 3583
2334	3584
2351–2356	T. 20 §§901–906
2357	5334
2358(a)	5541, 6301
2358(b)	T. 20 §907
2358(c)	8331, 8701
2371–2379	T. 42 §§4271–4279
3001	8901
3002(a)–(f)	8901, 8905, 8913
3002(g)	Rep.
3003	8903
3004	8904
3005	8902
3006	8906
3007	8909
3008(a)	Rep.
3008(b)	8909
3009(a), (b)	8913
3009(c)	8908
3009(d)	8907
3010	8910
3011	1308
3012	8911
3013(a)	1104, 5109
3013(b)	Rep.
3014	8912
3031	Elim.
3032	5921
3033–3035	5922
3036	5923
3037	5924
3038	5925
3039	5913
3051–3060	Elim.
3071	5521
3072	5522
3073	5523
3074	5524
3075	5525
3076	5527
3077	Rep.
3078	5526
3101	3326, 3501, 5531, 6303. Elim. in part.

Title 5 Former Sections	Title 5 New Sections
3102(a)–(e)	5532
3102(f)–(h)	Elim.
3103	3326
3104	Elim.
3105(a)–(d)	5533
3105(e)	Elim.
3105(f)	5533
3121–3127	5911

TITLE 6—OFFICIAL AND PENAL BONDS

[This title was enacted into law by act July 30, 1947, ch. 390, §1, 61 Stat. 646. This table shows where sections of former Title 6 were incorporated in revised Title 6. Title 6 was repealed by act Sept. 13, 1982, Pub. L. 97–258, §5(b), 96 Stat. 1068, 1085.]

Title 6 Former Sections	Title 6 New Sections
1	1
2	2
3	3
4	4
5	5
6	6
7	7
8	8
9	9
10	10
11	11
12	12
13	13
14	14
15	15

TITLE 9—ARBITRATION

[This title was enacted into law by act July 30, 1947, ch. 392, §1, 61 Stat. 669. This table shows where sections of former Title 9 were incorporated in revised Title 9.]

Title 9 Former Sections	Title 9 New Sections
1	1
2	2
3	3
4	4
5	5
6	6
7	7
8	8
9	9
10	10
11	11
12	12
13	13
14	Rep.
15	14

TITLE 10—ARMED FORCES

[This title was enacted into law by act Aug. 10, 1956, ch. 1041, §1, 70A Stat. 1, replacing former Title 10, Army and Air Force, and Title 34, Navy. Tables for both former titles are set out.]

A. TITLE 10, U.S.C.

[Showing disposition of all sections of former Title 10, Army and Air Force.]

Title 10 *Former Sections*	*Title 10* *New Sections*
1	Rep.
1a(a)	3001
1a(b)	101
1a(c), (d)	Rep.
1b	3062
1c	3075
1d, 1e	3074
1f	Rep.
1g(a)	3063
1g(b)	3064
1g(c)–(f)	3065
2–10	Rep.
11	3536
12–14	Rep.
15	T. 18 §1385
15a	4711, 9711
16	3061, 8061
16a	3492, 8492
17, 17a	Rep.
18	T. 37 §31a (See Rev. T. 37 Table)
19	1031
19a	4833
20	3062, 8062
20a	4503, 4531, 9503, 9531
20b	122
20c	Rep.
20i	3062
20j(a)	3201
20j(b)	3205, 3213
20j(c)	3225
20j(d)	3222, 3223
20r	8062
20s(a)	8201
20s(b)	8205, 8213
20s(c)	8225
20s(d)	8222, 8223
20t	8062
21	Rep.
21a	3031
21b	3034
21c	3035
21d	3034
21e	3032
21f	3036
21g	3039
21h	3037, 3040
22, 22a	Rep.
23, 23a	Rep.
24–32a	Rep.
33, 33a	Rep.
34–37	Rep.
38	3033, 3034, 8033, 8034
41, 42	Rep.
51	Rep.
52	4024
53	Rep.
61	Rep.
61–1	3072, 3209, 3210
61a	3037
62	3037, 8072
62a	3037
63, 64	Rep.
65	3292
66–70c	Rep.
71, 72	Rep.
72a	(See former 1195a)
73	(See former 1377)
74	Elim.
75	(See former 1259d)
76	(See former 1259e)
77	Elim.
81, 81a	Rep.
81–1	3067–3070
81–2	3311, 3685, 3818, 8067, 8685, 8818
82	3579, 8579
83	Rep.
91	Rep.
91a (less (c)–(f))	3294, 8294
91a(c)	3294 nt.
91a(d)	3444, 8444
91a(e)	3452, 8452
91a(f)	5652a
91b	Rep.
92, 92a	Rep.
93	3289, 8289
94	Rep.
95	(See former 82)
96	3546, 8546
97–100	Rep.
101–103	3302, 8302
104	Rep.
105, 106	3539
107, 108	4022, 9022
121	Rep.
121a (less (c)–(f))	3294, 8294
121a(c)	3294 nt.
121a(d)	3444, 8444
121a(e)	3452, 8452
121a(f)	5652a
121b	Rep.
122–124	Rep.
125	3303
126–131	Rep.
141	Rep.
142	Rep. in part. Elim. in part.
143	Rep.
143a	3302, 8302
144, 145	Rep.
145a, 145a–1	Rep.
146	Rep.
151	Rep.
152	Rep. in part. Elim. in part.
153–156	Rep.
156a	3068, 3209
156b	3068
156c	3504, 3962, 3991
156d	3068
156e	3287, 3290
156f–156i	Rep.
161–165	Rep.
166(a)	3069, 3206, 8206
166(b)	3069
166(c)	3291, 8291
166(d)	Rep. See 3291(c)
166a(a)	3070, 3207, 8207
166a(b)	3070
166a(c)	3291, 8291
166a(d)	Rep. See 3291(c)
166b to 166b–2	Rep.
166b–3	8067, 8209, 8296, 8579, 8683, 8963
166c to 166d–1	Rep.
166e(a)	3574, 3579, 8574, 8579
166e(b), (c)	Rep.
166f	3206, 3207, 3212, 3304, 8206, 8207, 8212, 8304
166g(a), (b)	3504, 3881, 3882, 3887, 3912, 3928, 3962, 3991, 8881, 8882, 8887, 8912, 8928, 8891
166g(c)	Rep.
166h	Rep.
166i	3683, 8683
166j	3818, 8818
166k	3205
166*l*	Rep.
171–177	Rep.
181	3036, 3040, 3074, 3209, 3216
181a	3040, 3209, 3493; T. 33 §583a
181b	3038
181c	3535
181d	3535 nt.
182–186	Rep.
187	Elim.
188	Rep.
189 (1st sent.)	Elim.
189 (less 1st sent.)	3534
190	3534
190a	T. 33 §§575, 701b–9
190b	T. 33 §§576, 701b–10
191–196	Rep.
197, 197a	Elim.
198	T. 50 §64a
199	(See former 190a)
211, 212	Rep.
213	Elim.
214, 215	Rep.
221, 222	Rep.
223	Elim.
231	Rep.
231a	3073
232	3293, 8293

Title 10 Former Sections	*Title 10 New Sections*
233	Rep. in part. Elim. in part.
234	Rep.
235	3581, 8581
236, 237	Rep.
238, 239	3547, 8547
240	Rep.
251–253	Rep.
261, 262	Rep.
271–277	Rep.
281–283	Rep.
291–291b	Rep.
291c, 291c–1	3691, 8691
291d	3692, 8692
291e	3691, 8691
291f, 291f–1	Rep.
291f–2	8257
291g	Rep.
292	Rep.
292–1, 292a	Rep.
292a–1, 292a–3	Rep.
292b to 292b–3	Rep.
292c	8537
292c–1	9305
292d, 293	Rep.
294	8577
295	Rep.
296, 296a	9303
297	Rep.
297a	8257
298, 298a	Rep.
298a–1	9304
298b	4656, 9656
298c	4628, 9628
299	8257, 8356, 8817
299a–299d	Rep.
299e	8356
300	Rep.
300a–300c	Elim.
301, 302	Rep.
303	Rep.
304	Rep. See T. 37 §402(a)–(c)
304a	Rep.
304b	Rep. See T. 37 §402(a)–(c)
305, 306	Rep.
307	Elim.
308, 308a	Rep.
309	Elim.
310(a), (b)	2271
310(c)	2272
310(d)	2273
310(e)	2271, 2272
310(f), (g)	2272
310(h)	2271
310(i)	2273
310(j)	2272, 2279
310(k)	2274
310(*l*), (m)	2276
310(n)	2272
310(*o*)	2277
310(p)	2276
310(q)	Rep.
310(r)	Elim.
310(s)	2271
310(t)	2275
311	2382
312	2278
313	Rep.
316, 316–1	3071
316a	3209, 3215
316b	3071, 3504, 3962, 3991
316c(a)	3311
316c(b)	Rep.
316c(c)	3211
316d	3580
316e	3685
321	Rep. See 3063 nt.
321a	Elim.
322–332	Rep.
333	Elim.
334, 335	Rep.
336	Elim.
337–343	Rep.
351–353	Rep.
354	3355, 8355
355, 355a	Rep.
356–359a	Rep.
360, 361	Rep.
361a	Rep.
361b	Rep.
362, 362a	Rep.
363–365	Rep.
366	Rep.
367	Elim.
367a, 368	Rep.
369, 369a	Rep.
369b	684
370	Rep.
371	Rep. See T. 5 §§3551, 6323(a), (b)
371a	Rep. See T. 5 §6323(a), (b)
371b	Rep. See T. 5 §§502, 5534
371c	Elim.
372–375	Rep.
376	3357

Title 10 Former Sections	*Title 10 New Sections*
377, 378	Rep.
381, 382	4382, 9382
383, 384	4383, 9383
385	4384, 9384
385a	4387, 9387
385b	4387
386	3540, 8540
386a	4387, 9387
387, 387a	4387, 9387
388	Rep.
389	4386, 9386. Rep. in part.
390	4386, 9386
391	Elim.
421–424	Rep.
425	(See former 628–1)
426, 427	Rep.
441	4385, 9385
442	4411–4414, 9411–9414
443	4385, 9385
444	(See former 387a)
445	Rep.
451–455	Rep.
455a–455c	3722, 8722
455d	Rep.
455e	3723, 8723; T. 32 §320
455f	Rep.
456	3687, 3688, 3721, 8687, 8688, 8721
456–1	3687 nt.
456–2	Rep.
456a, 457	Rep.
481	3205
481a	Rep.
481b	Rep.
482–482c	Rep.
483, 484	Rep.
484a	3814, 8814
485, 486	Rep.
486a	4353, 9353. Rep. in part. See 4353 nt.
487, 487a	Rep.
488, 489	Rep.
490, 491	3302, 8302
491a–491c	1521
491c–1	1521 nt.
491d	1523
492–494	Rep.
495	3544, 8544
496	Rep.
497	3545, 8545
498	3543, 8543
498a	Rep.
499	3446, 8446
499a, 499b	Rep.
500	3681, 8681
501	Elim.
502–504	Rep.
505–505e	Rep.
506(a)	3281, 3284, 8281, 8284
506(b)	3282, 3283
506(c)	3283, 3533
506(d)	3209, 8209
506(e), (f)	Rep.
506a(a)	3210, 8210
506a(b), (c)	3573, 8573
506b(a)	Rep.
506b(b)	3066, 3531, 8066, 8531
506b(c)	711. Rep. in part. See T. 37 §414
506b(d)	3962, 3991, 8962, 8991. Rep. in part. See 3962 nt.
506c(a)	3284, 8284
506c(b)	3285, 8285
506c(c)	3287, 8287
506c(d)	3288, 3295, 8288, 8295
506c(e)	3286, 8286
506c(f)	3212, 3287, 3574, 4353, 8212, 8287, 8574, 9353
506c(g)	Rep.
506c–1	Rep.
506c–2(a)	Rep. See 3284
506c–2(b)	3285
506c–3	3286
506c–4(a)	3287. Rep. in part. See 3287 nt.
506c–4(b)	3287
506c–4(c)	3212, 3287, 3574, 4353
506c–5	3288, 3295
506c–6	3888, 3927
506c–7	3285–3288, 3295, 3314. Rep. in part. See 3287 nt.
506c–8	Rep.
506c–9	3314
506c–10	Rep. See 3287 nt.
506d(a), (b)	3442, 8442
506d(c)	3442, 3572, 8442, 8572
506d(d)	3443, 8443
506d(e)	3444, 8444
506d(f)	3447, 8447
506d(g)	Rep.
506d(h)	3491, 8491
506d(i)	3441, 8441
506d–1 to 506d–3	3202
506d–4	686
507	3578, 8578
507a	3576, 5954, 8576

Title 10 Former Sections	Title 10 New Sections
511	3571, 8571
512, 512a	Rep.
513	3395, 3445, 3447, 8395, 8445, 8447
514	Rep.
515	744
516	Rep.
517	741
521–528	Rep.
531–534	Rep.
535, 535a	4301
536–539	Rep.
540	712
541	Elim.
551, 551a	Rep.
552–552c	Rep.
553–553b	Rep.
554, 555	Rep.
555a	3302, 3309, 8302, 8309
556	3309, 8309
556a	3302, 3309, 8302, 8309
557	Rep.
558	3312, 3394, 3451, 8312, 8394, 8451
559(a)	3296, 8296
559(b)	3211, 3212, 8211, 8212
559(c)	3296, 8296
559(d)	3296, 3574, 8296, 8574
559(e)	Rep.
559a(a)	3297, 3308, 8297, 8308
559a(b)	3313, 8313
559a(c)	3297, 8297
559a(d)	Rep.
559b	3212, 3298, 8212, 8298
559c(a)–(d)	3299, 8299
559c(e)	3300, 8300
559c(f)	3299, 8299
559c(g)	3303, 8303
559c(h)	3303, 3913, 8303, 8913
559c(i)	3913, 8913
559c(j)	3299, 8299
559c(k)	3212, 3299, 8212, 8299
559c(*l*)	8301
559c(m)	Rep.
559c–1	3299
559d	3305, 8305
559e	3306, 8306
559f	3307, 8307
559g	3036, 3212
559h, 559i	Rep.
559j	3296
559k	3818
559*l*–559*o*	Rep.
571–575	Rep.
576	3544, 8544
576a	Rep.
577	3544, 8544
578, 579	Rep.
580	3784, 8784
581	3781, 8781
582	3782, 8782
583	3782–3784, 3786, 8782–8784, 8786
584	3785, 8785
585	3786, 8786
586	Elim.
587	Rep.
591	3310, 8310
591–1	3311, 3818
591a	3448, 8448
592	Rep.
593	3548, 3575, 8548, 8575
593a	Rep.
594	3964, 3992, 8964, 8992
595	Elim.
596, 597	Rep.
598	(See former 631a)
599	Rep.
600(a), (b)	101
600(c)	564
600(d)	564, 1166, 1167, 1255, 1263, 1293, 1305. Rep. in part. See 1164 nt.
600a	555, 597, 745, 3445, 3448, 8445, 8448
600b	Rep.
600c	555, 556, 597, 3448, 8448
600d	515, 1165
600e	557, 598, 3449, 8449
600f	558
600g	559, 561
600h	560, 562
600i	562, 563
600j	557
600k	564
600*l*(a)	1293
600*l*(b)	1255, 1263, 1305. Rep. in part. See 1164 nt.
600*l*(c)	1164
600*l*(d)	1371, 1401
600*l*(e)	564, 1164, 1166, 1255, 1263, 1305
600*l*(f)	1371, 1401
600*l*(g)	Elim.
600m	515, 1166
600n	1167
600*o*	Rep.
600p	565, 599, 3450, 8450
600q	Rep.
600r	564, 1164, 1255, 1263, 1305
602	Rep.
603–604a	Rep.
605–607	Rep.
608	3639, 8639
609	3635, 8635
610	3690, 8690
611	Rep.
612	1522
621	3256, 8256
621a	Rep.
621b	3256, 3818
621c, 621d	Elim.
622–625	3253, 8253
626, 626a	Rep.
627	3256, 8256
628	3256, 3815, 3816, 8256, 8815, 8816
628–1	3256, 8256
628a	3262, 8262
628b	3263, 8263
629	3638, 8638
629a	972
630, 631	Rep.
631a	3258, 3684, 8258, 8684
632, 633	Rep.
634	3254, 3812, 8254, 8812
635	3255, 8255
636	3256, 8256
636a	Rep.
637	Elim.
641–642a	Rep.
643, 644	Rep.
645	Elim.
651	Rep.
652	3813, 8813
652a	3811, 8811
653, 653a	Rep.
654, 654a	Rep.
654b, 655	Elim.
656	Rep.
657	Elim.
658	Rep.
661	Elim.
662	Rep.
663	4023, 9023
664, 665	Rep.
671	Elim.
671a	Rep.
672, 673	Elim.
681, 682	Elim.
683, 683a	Rep.
684	T. 37 §4c (See Rev. T. 37 Table)
685	Elim.
686	Rep.
691, 692	Rep.
693	Elim.
694	T. 37 §235a (See Rev. T. 37 Table)
695–699	Rep.
711–716	Elim.
716a	Rep.
716b	4561, 9561
717–722	Rep.
723	4593, 9593
724–726	4561, 9561
727	Elim.
728	4775, 9775
729	Rep.
741	Elim.
742–748a	Rep.
749	4743, 9743
757	Elim.
758–760	Rep.
771, 772	Rep.
781	Elim.
782–786	Rep.
787	Elim.
801–811	Rep.
821–823	Rep.
824	T. 5 §73c (See Rev. T. 5 Table)
825	4748, 9748
831	4562, 9562
832	Elim.
833	Rep.
834	4563, 9563
835	Rep.
841, 842	Rep.
843	4306, 9306
844, 845	Rep.
846	Rep.
847	Rep.
847a	3632, 8632
847b	Rep.
847c, 847d	3632, 8632
848	Rep.
849	3633, 8633
850–852	Rep.
861, 861a	Rep.
862	T. 37 §310b (See Rev. T. 37 Table)
862a	T. 31 §493b
862b	Rep.
863–866j	Rep.

Title 10 Former Sections	*Title 10 New Sections*
867	Rep.
868	2771
869	T. 31 §492d
870	Rep.
871, 872	4837, 9837
873, 874	Rep.
875–875c	4837, 9837
876	3636, 8636
877	2772
878	4840, 9840
891–894	3689, 8689
895	Elim.
902, 902a	Rep.
903, 903a	3688, 8688
904	4621, 9621
904a–904d	Rep.
905	3634, 8634
906–906a	Rep.
907, 908	Rep.
908a–908c	1035
909	Elim.
910	Rep.
911	Elim.
912–914	Rep.
914a	Elim.
915–916d	Rep.
917	Rep.
918	Elim.
919	Rep.
920	1584 nt.
921	3532
931–938	Rep.
938a	(See former 984)
939–940a	Rep.
941	Rep.
941a(a)	3883, 3885, 3886, 3961, 3991, 8883, 8885, 8886, 8961, 8991
941a(b)	3888, 3927, 8888, 8927
941a(c)	3919, 8919
941a(d)	3211, 3913, 3915, 3916, 3921–3923, 8211, 8913, 8916, 8921–8923
941a(e)	3303, 3888, 3913, 3927, 3961, 3991, 8303, 8888, 8913, 8927, 8961, 8991
941a(f)	3313, 8313
942	3924, 8924
943	3918, 8918
943a	3911, 8911
944–946	Rep.
947	3917, 3925, 8917, 8925
947a	3917, 3961, 8917, 8961
948	3914, 3991, 8914, 8991
948a	3914, 8914
951	3887, 3926, 3928, 8887, 8926, 8928
951a	3926, 8926
951b	3887, 3926, 3928, 8887, 8926, 8928
952	Elim.
953	Rep.
953a	3926, 8926
954, 955	Rep.
956	3914 nt.
957	Rep.
958	3925, 8925
961–966	Rep.
970	Rep.
971	3991, 8991
971a	Rep.
971b	3911, 3991, 8911, 8991. Elim. in part.
971c	3963 nt.
972–973a	Rep.
974–979	Rep.
980	3991, 8991
981–982a	Rep.
983–985h	Rep.
986	Rep.
990–996	Rep.
997	3504
998	T. 32 §314
999	3503, 8503
1001	3966, 8966
1002, 1003	3963, 3991, 8963, 8991
1004	3964, 3992, 8964, 8992
1005	Elim.
1006	3965, 8965
1007	Rep.
1011–1013	Rep.
1014	1375
1015	Rep.
1021, 1022	Rep.
1023	772, 3681, 8681
1024	3582, 8582
1025	3961, 8961
1026	3961, 3962, 3991
1026a	Rep.
1026b	T. 33 §642a
1026b–1, 1026c	Rep.
1027–1028a	Rep.
1028b	772
1028c	Elim.
1028d	Rep.
1028e	Elim.
1029–1035	Rep.
1036	3966, 8966
1036a	676, 1331, 1332. Rep. in part. See 1331
1036b	1333, 1401
1036c	1001, 1334
1036d	1331, 1336
1036e	101, 1332, 1333
1036f	Rep.
1036g	1334, 1335
1036h	1337
1036i	Rep.
1041	4334
1042	4334, 9334
1043, 1044	4349, 9349
1051–1052a	Rep.
1053–1054a	Rep.
1055–1060	4355, 9355
1061	4331, 9331
1061a	4332, 9332
1062, 1063	4333, 9333
1064	4333
1065	4334
1066	Rep.
1067	4340
1068–1070	Rep.
1071	4331
1072	Rep.
1073	4331
1074–1076	Rep.
1077, 1077a	4331
1078	Rep.
1078a	4331
1079	4334, 9334
1079a(a)	4336, 9336
1079a(b)	3962, 3991, 8962, 8991
1079a(c)	3886, 3920, 8886, 8920
1080–1082	Rep.
1083	4337, 9337
1084, 1085	Rep.
1086	4338
1087	4331, 4332, 9331, 9332
1088	4331
1089	4331, 4335, 9331, 9335
1091	Rep.
1091–1	4347, 9347
1091a–1091e	Rep.
1092	Rep.
1092a	4342, 9342
1092b	4342, 4346, 4351, 9342, 9346, 9351
1092c	4348, 9348
1092c–1	541
1092d	4343, 9343
1093	4345, 9345
1093a, 1093b	Rep.
1093c	4344, 9344
1093d	T. 20 §221a
1094	Rep.
1095, 1096	4346, 9346
1097	Rep.
1098	4342, 9342
1099	4346
1100, 1101	Rep.
1102	4349, 9349
1103, 1104	4351, 9351
1105	4349, 9349
1106	4350, 9350
1111, 1112	Rep.
1121, 1121a	Elim.
1122–1124	Rep.
1125	4354
1126	4354, 9354
1127	Rep.
1131–1136	Rep.
1137	4337, 9337
1138, 1139	4339
1140–1143	Rep.
1144	4341, 9341
1145	Elim.
1146–1149	Rep.
1149a	4350, 9350
1150	T. 37 §308a (See Rev. T. 37 Table)
1151	Rep.
1161	Rep.
1161a	4333 nt.
1162	T. 44 §87 (See Rev. T. 44 Table)
1163	4352, 9352
1171	Rep.
1172	4302, 9302
1173, 1174	Rep.
1175	Elim.
1176	4302, 9302
1177–1178a	Rep.
1179	4627, 4629, 9627, 9629
1180	4651, 9651
1180a, 1180b	Rep.
1181	3540, 8540
1182	4654, 9654
1182a	Rep.
1183	4653, 9653
1184	Rep.
1185	4652, 9652
1186–1186b	Rep.
1191, 1192	Rep.

Title 10 Former Sections	*Title 10 New Sections*
1192a	4506, 9506
1193–1195	Rep.
1195a	4533, 4561
1196	4621, 9621
1197	4535, 9535
1198	4534, 9534
1199, 1199a	Rep.
1200–1203	Rep.
1204	Elim.
1205, 1206	Rep.
1206a	4539
1207	2384
1208	Rep.
1209, 1210	4538
1210a	Rep.
1211	Elim.
1212	Rep.
1213, 1214	2421
1221–1225	Rep.
1231	Rep.
1232	4622, 9622
1233–1235	4621, 9621
1236	4624, 9624
1237, 1238	4621, 9621
1239	4623, 9623
1240	Rep.
1241	4621, 9621
1251, 1252	Rep.
1253	4621, 9621
1254	4624, 9624
1255, 1256	2542
1257	Rep.
1257a	T. 5 §150p (See Rev. T. 5 Table)
1257b	2573
1258	Rep.
1259	4682, 9682
1259a–1259c	Rep.
1259d, 1259e	4564, 0504
1261	Rep.
1262	4681, 9681
1262a	Rep.
1262b	2574
1263–1267	Rep.
1268	Elim.
1269–1269b	2481
1270	2667
1270a–1270c	Rep.
1270d	2667
1271, 1271a	Rep.
1272–1274	Rep.
1281–1286	Rep.
1287	4591, 9591
1288	Rep.
1289	Rep.
1301	4832, 9832
1302	4838, 9838
1303	4839, 9839. See T. 18 §702
1304	4835
1305	9835
1311	Rep.
1312	4834. Rep. in part.
1313	4834
1314	Rep.
1315	3631, 8631
1316, 1317	4836, 9836
1318	Rep.
1319	4592, 9592
1320	Rep.
1331	Rep.
1332	4779, 9779
1333	Rep.
1334	4536, 9536
1335	4779, 9779
1336, 1336a	Rep.
1337	Rep.
1337a	4774, 9774
1337b	4774
1337c	Elim.
1337d	Rep.
1337e	Elim.
1338	Rep.
1339	4774, 9774
1340	Rep.
1341	4772, 9772
1342	4771, 9771
1343	Rep.
1343a–1343c	9773
1343d	9774
1344	4771, 9771
1345	4779, 9779
1346	4778, 9778
1347	T. 36 §12
1348	4777, 9777
1349	Rep.
1350	Elim.
1351	2669
1352–1354	Rep.
1361	4742, 9742
1362	T. 49 §6
1363	4741, 9741
1364	Rep.
1365	2631
1366	Rep.
1367	4745
1368	4747
1369, 1370	4744
1371	4744, 4747
1371a	4746, 9746
1372–1375b	Rep.
1376	Rep.
1377	4749
1391	3611, 8611
1392	Rep.
1393	771–774, 3612, 6297, 8612
1394	Rep.
1395	4621, 4629, 9621, 9629
1401, 1402	Rep.
1403	3741, 8741
1404, 1405	Rep.
1406	3742, 8742
1407	3743, 8743
1408, 1408a	Rep.
1408b	1121, 1122
1409	3744, 3752, 8744, 8752
1410	3745, 8745
1411	3744, 8744
1412	3746, 8746
1413, 1413a	Elim.
1414, 1414a	Elim.
1415	Elim.
1415a	3751, 3752, 8751, 8752. Rep. in part. See 3751 nt.
1415b, 1415c	3751, 8751. Rep. in part. See 3751 nt.
1416	3747, 8747
1417–1421	Rep.
1422, 1423	Elim.
1423a, 1423b	Rep.
1423c	Elim.
1424	3748, 8748
1425	Rep. See T. 18 §704
1426	Elim.
1427	1123
1428	3750, 8750
1429	3749, 3752, 8749, 8752
1430–1430b	Rep.
1430c–1430h	Elim.
1431	807 nt.
1432	3637, 8637
1433	Rep.
1434–1443	Elim.
1451	3661
1452	Rep.
1453–1455	3661
1456	3662, 8662
1457–1457b	3663, 8663
1458, 1459	3661
1460	858 nt.
1461	Elim.
1471–1578	Rep.
1579	(See former 629)
1580	(See former 652a)
1581–1583	Rep.
1584–1584c	T. 5 §150j to 150j–3 (See Rev. T. 5 Table)
1585	(See former 15a)
1586–1590	Rep.
1591	(See former 507)
1592	(See former 507a)
1593, 1593a	Rep.
1594–1594b	Rep.
1595–1597a	Rep.
1598–1605	Rep.
1701–1710	Rep.
1711	Elim.
1712–1719	Rep.
1801 (less (b))	Rep.
1801(b)	101
1802–1804	Rep.
1805	9833
1806	Rep.
1811	8031
1812	8034
1813	8035
1814	8034
1815	8032
1831	8062
1832	8075
1833	8076
1834	Rep.
1835	101, 8078; T. 32 §101
1836	Rep.
1837	8067, 8211, 8296, 8574
1838, 1839	8074
1840	8072. Elim. in part.
1843–1849	8202
1850	686
1850a	8285, 8287. Rep. in part. See 8284
1850b	8286
1850c(a)	8287, 8888, 8927
1850c(b)	8287
1850c(c)	8287, 8888, 8927
1850c(d)	8287
1850c(e)	8212, 8287, 8574, 9353. Rep. in part. See 8212 nt.
1850d	8288, 8295

Title 10 Former Sections	Title 10 New Sections
1850e	Rep.
1850f	8314
1850g (less (c))	Rep.
1850g(c)	Rep. See 8299 nt.
1850h	Rep. See 8287 nt.
1850i	Rep. See 8287 nt., 8299 nt.
1850j	8285–8288, 8295, 8314
1850k	8285
1851	9331
1852(a)	Rep.
1852(b)	Elim.
1853	9331 nt.
1854	9331
1855	Elim.
1856	541
1857	9331 nt.
1861	4802, 4806, 9802, 9806
1862	4803, 4806, 9803, 9806
1863	4804, 9804
1864, 1865	4805, 9805
1866	4802, 4803, 9802, 9803

B. Title 34, U.S.C.

[Showing disposition of all sections of former Title 34, Navy.]

Title 34 Former Sections	Title 10 New Sections
1	5501
2	5403, 5405
3	5404
3a(a), (b)	5447, 5448
3a(c)	5701 nt.
3a(d)	6387
3a(e)	5701 nt.
3b(a), (b)	5449
3b(c)	5701 nt.
3b(d)	6388
3b(e)	5701 nt.
3c(a)	5442–5444, 5446, 5596, 5652–5661, 5663, 5711, 5786, 6386. Rep. in part.
3c(b)	5442–5444, 5666, 5786, 6371–6380, 6382, 6383, 6385
3c(c)	5596
3c(d)	5784, 5788
3c(e)	5596, 5784, 6326
3c(f)	See T. 37 §415
3c(g)	5596
3c(h)	5596, 5784, 5786, 5788
3c(i)	Rep.
3c(j)	6381, 6383, 6400
3d	5445, 5546, 5596, 5662, 5711, 5784, 5785, 6386
3e	5234, 5451, 5662, 5711, 5785, 6386
3f	5442 nt.
4(a)	5447, 5448
4(b–e)	5447
4(f)	5447, 5448, 5455
4(g)	5454
5	5449, 5454, 5455
5a(a)–(e)	5442
5a(f)	5444
5a(g)	5442, 5443
5a(h)	5444
5a(i)	5442–5444, 5447–5449
5a(j)	5454, 5507
5a(k)	5442–5444
5a–1	5451
5a–2	686
5b	5591–5594
6–10	Rep.
10a	5501. Rep. in part.
11	5572
12	5572, 5573
13, 14	5572, 5582
15	Rep.
16	Elim.
17	5573a
17a–17c	Rep.
21	5599
21a	Rep.
21b	5574
21c(c)	3294 nt.
21c(d)	3444, 8444
21c(e)	5787a
21c(f)	5652a
21c (less (c)–(f))	5572, 5574
21d	5574
21e	5446, 5574, 5578, 5579, 5581, 5663, 5702, 5707, 5708, 5710, 5711, 5753, 5762, 5766, 5773, 5776, 6033, 6393
22, 23	5574
24, 25	Rep.
26	5987
30a	5404, 6027, 6028. Rep. in part.
30a–1	5139
30b, 30c	Rep.
30d	Elim.
30e	5579
30f	5572
30g	6392
30h	5579, 5945
30i	Rep.
30j	5579
30k–30m	5579 nt.
31	Rep.
32	Rep.
33	Rep.
34	5412, 6013, 6014
34a	6014
35–37	Rep.
41, 42	Rep.
43	5572, 6027. Rep. in part.
43a	5140
43b	Rep.
43b–1	Elim.
43c	5580, 6392
43c–1	5601
43d	5945, 6030
43e, 43f	Rep.
43g(a)	6396
43g(b)	5140
43g(c)	6151
43g(d)	6325, 6396
43g(e)	Rep.
43g(f)	6151, 6325, 6396
43g(g)	6151, 6329, 6404
43g(h)	6324, 6396
43g(i)	772
43h(a) (provisos)	6033, 6086, 7577
43h (less provisos of (a))	Rep.
43i	6393
43j	Elim.
43k–43*o*	Rep.
51	5578, 6027
51a	Rep.
51b(c)	3294 nt.
51b(d)	3444, 8444
51b(e)	5787a
51b(f)	5652a
51b (less (c)–(f))	5572, 5578
51c	5578, 5787a
52	5578
53, 54	T. 5 §§456b, 456c (See Rev. T. 5 Table)
55	T. 5 §456d (See Rev. T. 5 Table)
61	5575
61a–63	Rep.
64–66	6026
67	6113
71	5587
71a, 71b	Rep.
72	5406
73	5587
74, 74a	Rep.
75, 76	Rep.
77	5572, 5587
78	5407, 5587
79	Rep.
81	Rep.
82–86	Rep.
91	5576
92, 93	Rep.
93a	5572, 5576
94	Rep.
95, 96	6031
97	5142
101	Elim.
102	Rep.
105	5532–5534, 5572, 5590
105a (proviso)	Rep.
105a (less proviso)	5410
105b (1st sent.)	Rep.
105b (less 1st sent.)	5452–5455
105c	5590
105d	5143
105e (proviso)	Rep.
105e (less proviso)	5777
105f	Rep.
105g	6015
105h	6033
105i	6294, 6393
105j	5446, 5504, 5596, 5663, 5704–5707, 5710, 5711, 5784
105k	5446, 5504, 5590, 5663, 5664, 5711, 5753, 5763, 5774

Title 34 Former Sections	Title 10 New Sections
111, 112	Rep.
121–132a	Rep.
133, 134	Rep.
135(a), (b)	101
135(c)	564
135(d)	564, 1166, 1167, 1255, 1263, 1293, 1305. Rep. in part. See 1164 nt.
135a	555, 597, 5503, 5596–5593, 5787; T. 14 §§435–438
135b	Rep.
135c	555, 556, 597, 5596–5598, 5787; T. 14 §§435–438
135d	515, 1165
135e, 135f	Rep.
135g	T. 14 §§435–438
141–146	Rep.
151	5401
152	Rep.
153	5401, 5402
161	5532, 5533
161a	(See former 206)
162	5535
163	5532
171–175	Rep.
176	6013
177	Rep.
181	5533, 5534, 5538, 6293
181a	5538
182	5534
183, 183a	5536
183b	972
184	5539
185	5537
186	5538
187	5531. Rep in part. See T. 14 §350
188	5534. Rep. in part. See T. 14 §351
189	Rep. See T. 14 §§350, 351
191	5401, 5410, 5412, 6296
192, 193	6291
194	Rep.
195	6295
196	Rep.
197	6297
197a, 198	Rep.
199	6298
200	Rep.
201–201b	5540
202	Rep.
203	6293
204	Rep.
205, 206	Elim.
211	6019
211a(a) (1st proviso of 2d sent.)	Rep.
211a(a) (less 1st proviso of 2d sent.).	5504, 5786
211a(b)–(d)	Rep.
211a(e) (words before 2d proviso).	Rep.
211a(e) (less words before 2d proviso).	Elim.
211a(f)–(h)	Rep.
211a(i) (less 1st proviso)	5504
211a(j)	Rep.
211a(k) (1st, 2d, 4th, 5th provisos).	Elim.
211a(k) (less 1st, 2d, 4th, 5th provisos).	Rep.
211a(*l*), (m)	Rep.
211a(n)	5597, 5787
211a(*o*)	5504, 5505, 5786
211a(p)	Rep.
211a(q)	5780–5782
211a(r)	6371
211a(s)	Rep.
211a(t)	Elim.
211b	5408, 5587
211b–1 to 211b–5	Elim.
211c(a)	5572, 5589
211c(e)–(g)	5409
211c(h)	Rep.
211c (less (e)–(h))	5589
211d	5231, 5501
211e	5450
212, 212a	Rep.
213–215	Rep.
216	5981
217	5948
217a, 217a–1	Rep.
217a–2	1031
217b	7476
218	5950
219	6143
220	5949
221	Rep.
222	6018
223, 224	Rep.
225	5133
226	6405
227	Rep.
228	6406
228a	Elim.
228b, 229	Rep.
230	T. 37 §4c–1 (See Rev. T. 37 Table)
231, 232	Rep.
233	5862
234, 235	Rep.
241, 241a	741
242–244a	Rep.
245	Rep.
246	5946
247, 248	5953
249–251	Rep.
251a	744
252	Rep.
253	5945
254, 255	Rep.
256	5577
257	Rep.
258	5504
259	Rep.
259a	745
260–263	Rep.
264	5951
265	5947
266	6031
271, 272	5861
272a	Elim.
273	Rep.
274, 275	5862
276–279	5863
280	5866
281, 282	5863
283	5865
284, 285	5862
285a	5442, 5444, 5447, 5449, 5452
285b–285d	1521
285e	1522
285e–1	1521 nt.
285f	1523
286 to 286h–2	Rep.
286i–294a	Rep.
295–297b	Rep.
298–303	Rep.
304–304g	5701 nt.
305–305g	5701 nt.
306	5701–5703
306a	5705
306b(a)(1)	6371
306b(a)(2)	6378
306b(a)(3)	5751, 5754
306b(a)(4), (5)	5751
306b(b)(1)	6378
306b(b)(2)	5753, 5754
306b(b)(3)	5753
306c(a)(1)	5706
306c(a)(2)	5756
306c(a)(3)	5757
306c(a)(4), (5)	5758, 5759
306c(a)(6), (7)	5758
306c(a)(8)	6371
306c(a)(9)	5707
306c(a)(10)–(12)	5764, 5765
306c(a)(13), (14)	5768
306c(b)(1)	5706
306c(b)(2)–(8)	5762
306c(b)(9)	5761
306c(b)(10)	5707
306c(b)(11), (12)	5766
306c(c)	5755, 6407
306d(a)	5707, 5776. Rep. in part.
306d(b)	5707, 5776
306d(c)(1)	5707
306d(c)(2)	5708, 6384
306e	5708, 5710
306f(a)(1)	5769, 5771
306f(a)(2)	5769, 5771, 5775
306f(a)(3)	5770
306f(b)(1), (2)	5773, 5775
306f(b)(3)	5772, 5775
306f(c)(1)	5777
306f(c)(2)	5780, 5791
306f(c)(3)	5781, 5791
306f(c)(4)	5782, 5791
306f(c)(5), (6)	5783
306f(d)(1)	Rep.
306f(d)(2)	5508
306f(d)(3)	5652, 5652b
306f(d)(4)	5653
306f(d)(5)	5655
306f(d)(6)	5654
306f(d)(7)	5656
306f(d)(8)	5657
306f(d)(9)	5658
306f(d)(10)	5659
306f(d)(11)	5660
306f(d)(12)	5661
306f(d)(13)	5651
306f(d)(14)	5507
306g	5788
306h	5596, 5779, 5784
306i–306k	Rep.
306*l*	5862
306m	Rep.
306n	Elim.
306*o*	5788
306p	5861, 5862

Title 34 Former Sections	Title 10 New Sections
306q	5751, 6371, 6376, 6377
306r	Rep.
306s	5767
306t	Rep.
307(a)	5704, 5754, 5755, 5771
307(b)	5787b, 5788
307(c)	5704
307(d)	5752, 5754
307(e)	5664
307(f)	5753
307(g), (h)	5707
307(i)	5760. Rep. in part. See 6401 nt.
307(j)	5707, 5760, 5771, 5775
307(k)	5707, 5763. Rep. in part. See 6401 nt.
307(*l*)	5707, 5708
307(m)	5710
307(n)	5775
307(*o*)	5774, 5775
307(p) (1st sent.)	5403–5405, 5447–5449
307(p) (less 1st sent.)	Rep.
307(q)	5770
307(r)	Rep.
311–313a	Rep.
314	5788
321–324	Rep.
330	557, 598, 5596–5598, 5787; T. 14 §§ 435–438
330a	558
330b	559, 561
330c	560, 562
330d	562, 563
330e	557
330f	564
330g	565, 599
331–331b	Rep.
332–332c	Rep.
333–335b	Rep.
336, 337	Rep.
338	5572, 5586
338a (provisos)	Rep.
338a (less provisos)	5586
338b	5586
338c (proviso)	Rep.
338c (less proviso)	5504
338d	5586
338e	Rep.
338f (proviso)	5586
338f (less proviso)	Rep.
338g	5504, 5586
339(a), (b)	5586
339(c)	Elim.
341–343	5790
344	Rep.
345–347	5789
348–348u	Rep.
349–349k	Rep.
350, 350a	5597, 5787; T. 14 §§ 435–438
350b	5787; T. 14 §§ 435–438
350c(a)	5597, 5787; T. 14 §§ 435–438
350c(b)	Rep.
350d	5597, 5787, 6395; T. 14 §§ 435–438
350e	5501, 5597, 5787; T. 14 §§ 435–438
350f(a) (1st, 3d, 4th provisos)	Rep.
350f(a) (less 1st, 3d, 4th provisos).	5597, 5787, 6326; T. 14 §§ 435–438
350f(b)	Rep. See T. 37 § 414
350g	Rep.
350h	5442–5444, 5447–5449; T. 14 §§ 758a, 759a
350i(a)	5597, 5787, 6488; T. 14 §§ 435–438, 758a, 759a
350i(b)(1)	Rep.
350i(b)(2)	6151. Rep. in part. See T. 42 § 212(g)
350i(c)	Rep.
350i(d)	6488
350i(e)	6161, 6326
350j	5597, 5787. Rep. in part. See T. 14 § 351; T. 42 § 212(g)
350k	5597, 5787. Rep. in part. See T. 42 § 212(g)
351–353	Rep.
354	6241
355	6243
356	6242
356a	6244
356b	6246
357	Rep.
358	6247
358a	6255
359	6253, 6254
360	6248
361	Elim.
362	6249
363	6250
364	6245, 6247, 6249–6252
364a	T. 14 § 492a. Rep. in part. See T. 14 §§ 494, 497
364b	Rep.
365	T. 38 §§ 391–394 (See Rev. T. 38 Table)
366	Elim.

Title 34 Former Sections	Title 10 New Sections
367	7218
371	1123
372–375	(See former 371)
381	6321
382	Rep.
383	6322
384	Rep.
385	6329
386	5864
387–388a	Rep.
389	772, 6016, 6325, 6381, 6383, 6394, 6400
390–393	Rep.
394	1375
395–396a	Rep.
397	Rep.
399 to 399c–1	Rep.
399d	772
399e	Elim.
399f	Rep.
399g	(See former 399c–1)
399h	Rep.
400	Rep.
401	5955
402, 402a	Rep.
403–405	Rep.
405a	6392
406–410	Rep.
410a	6394
410b, 410b–1	6323
410c	6151, 6325, 6328, 6404
410d	6390, 6404
410e	Rep.
410f–410i	5701 nt.
410j(a)	6376–6384
410j(b)	6376–6378
410j(c)	6379
410j(d)	6383
410j(e)	6380
410j(f)	6383
410j(g)	6381, 6383, 6400, 6404
410j(h)	6382–6384, 6404
410j(i)	Rep.
410j(j)	5865
410j(k)	6381
410j(*l*)	Elim.
410j(m)	6382–6384. Elim. in part.
410k	Elim.
410*l*(a)	6371, 6381
410*l*(b)	5709, 5710, 6372, 6381
410*l*(c)	6381
410*l*(d)–(k)	Rep.
410m	6325, 6326, 6381
410n	6150, 6483
410*o* (last proviso)	Elim.
410*o* (less last proviso)	5233
410p(a)	6390
410p(b)	Rep.
410q	6149
410r(a)	5776, 6151, 6380, 6382, 6400
410r(b)	5143, 6398
410r(c)	6399
410r(d)	5143
410r(e)	5143, 6398, 6399
410r(f)	Rep.
410r(g)	5143, 6151, 6325
410r(h)	5143, 6151, 6328, 6404
410r(i)	6400
410r(j)	6401, 6402, 6404. Rep. in part. See 6401 nt.
410r(k)	5143, 6398, 6399
410s–418	Rep.
419–419b	6394
421–423	6481
423a	Rep.
424–426	5982
427	Rep.
428	5507, 6487. Rep. in part. See T. 42 § 212(g)
429 (proviso)	Rep.
429 (less proviso)	5507
430(a)	1293
430(b)(1)	1255
430(b)(2)	1305
430(b)(3)	Rep. See 1164 nt.
430(b) (less (1)–(3))	1263
430(c)	1164
430(d)	1371, 1401
430(e)	564, 1164, 1166, 1255, 1263, 1305
430(f)	1371, 1401, 6325
430(g)	Elim.
430a	515, 1166
430b	1167
430c	564, 1164, 1255, 1263, 1305
430d	565, 599, 6409
431, 432	6326
433	6482
434	6484
435–440a	Rep.
440h	6017
440h–1	6323. Rep. in part.
440i	676, 1331, 1332
440j	1333, 1401

Title 34 Former Sections	*Title 10 New Sections*
440k	1001, 1334
440*l*	1331, 1336
440m	101, 1332, 1333
440n	6034
440*o*	1334, 1335
440p	1337
440q, 441	Rep.
441a	712
442–448	Rep.
448a, 448b	Elim.
449	6114
450	Rep.
450a, 450b	Elim.
450b–1	Rep.
450c	Elim.
451	5941
452	7293
453	Rep.
461–463	7292
471–473	Rep.
474	7224
481–486a	Rep.
487	Rep.
488	7301
489	Elim.
490	7297
491	7304
492	7305
493, 493a	Rep.
493a–1	7307
493b	7306
493c	7298
494	Elim.
495 (2d proviso of 1st par.)	Rep.
495 (1st par., less 2d proviso)	Elim.
495 (less 1st par.)	7342, 7343
495a	7342
496	2382, 7300
496a	Rep.
496b	Elim.
407	Rep.
498 to 498–5	Elim.
498a to 498a–2	Elim.
498a–3, 498a–4	Rep.
498a–5	Elim.
498b	(See former 749b)
498c to 498c–3	Elim.
498c–4	Rep.
498c–5, 498c–6	Elim.
498c–7 to 498c–13	Rep.
498c–14, 498c–15	Elim.
498d	Rep.
498d–1	7296
498d–2	Elim.
498e	Rep.
498f to 498f–2	Elim.
498g	Rep.
498g–1	7295
498h	7294, 7344
498i	Rep.
498j	7302
498k	Rep.
498*l*	7299
498m (2d sent. of 3d par.)	7296
498m (less 2d sent of 3d par.)	Elim.
498n–498q	Elim.
501	5943
502–504	Rep.
505	7474
506–508	Rep.
509	7475
510–514	Rep.
520	T. 33 §733; T. 40 §255; T. 50 §175
520a	Rep.
521	7219
522	Rep.
522a	2667
522b–522d	Rep.
522e	2667
523	7223
524 (1st par.)	7421–7423, 7426, 7430
524 (2d par.)	7426, 7430
524 (3d par.)	7430, 7432
524 (4th par.)	7424, 7431
524 (5th par.)	7425, 7432, 7434
524 (6th par.)	7428, 7429
524 (7th par.)	Rep.
524 (8th par.)	7435
524 (9th par.)	7436
524 (10th par.)	7433
524 (11th par.)	7437, 7438
524a	7421
525	Rep.
526	Elim.
527	7580
528	2631
528a	Rep.
529–531a	Rep.
532–532a	Rep.
533, 533a	7601
534	Rep.
535	Rep. See T. 14 §§144, 145
536	7603
537	6155
538	7602
539	4621, 9621
540	4625, 9625
540a	Rep.
541	4564, 9564
542	7604
543, 544	Rep.
544a	T. 31 §495a
545	2574
546	T. 5 §150p (See Rev. T. 5 Table)
546a	Rep.
546b	7541
546c	Rep.
546d	7542
546e	7307. Rep. in part.
546f	7308
546g	7545
546h	7545, 7546
546i	7544
546j	Elim.
546k	7308, 7545
546*l*–546n	Rep.
547, 548	Rep.
549, 550	2542
551–551a	Rep.
551b	2573
552	7605
553	Rep.
553a–553c	2481
554, 555	Rep.
555a, 555b	2421
555c	Elim.
555d, 555e	7227
555f	7228
556	7212
557	7213
558	7575
559	7206
560–567	Rep.
568	2383
569–579	Rep.
580	7229
580a	Elim.
581	Rep.
582	7521
583	2384
584	7210
591	6011
592, 593	Rep.
593a	5792
594	Rep.
595	6202
596	6221, 6224
597	1551
598, 599	Rep.
600	7625
600a	7623
600b	7624
600c, 600d	7623
601–603	Rep.
604	T. 37 §31a (See Rev. T. 37 Table)
605	7215
606	7214
607	Rep.
608	6156
609	122
610	Rep.
621	5201
622	5201, 5502
623	Rep.
623a	5202
623b	5232, 5233, 5502
623c	5952
624–625b	Rep.
625c	5588, 5707
625d	5588
625e, 625f	5204
625g	6020
625h(a)	5405, 5448, 5453–5455, 5532–5534, 5572, 5590, 5596, 5704–5708, 5711, 5752, 5755, 5760, 5771, 5775, 5777, 5784, 5787b, 5788, 6015, 6033, 6151, 6325, 6328, 6380, 6382, 6398–6402, 6404
625h(b) (proviso)	Rep.
625h(b) (less proviso)	5410
625h(c) (proviso)	Rep.
625h(c) (less proviso)	5411
625h(d)	5206, 5453, 5787b
625h(f)	Rep. See 5760
625h(g)	Rep. See 6401, 6402, 6404
626(a)	5405, 5448, 5454, 5455, 6387
626(b)–(d)	5448
626(e)–(n)	5701 nt.
626(*o*), (p)	5448
626(q)–(y)	5701 nt.
626	5405, 5448, 5454, 5455, 6387.
626–1(a)	5443, 5445, 5454, 5504, 5505, 5703, 5705, 5707, 5708, 5711, 5751, 5755, 5756, 5765, 5768, 5769, 5775, 5777, 5780, 5783, 5785, 5786, 5788, 5791, 5862, 5865, 6321, 6322, 6325, 6329, 6376, 6377, 6379–6384, 6386

Title 34 Former Sections	Title 10 New Sections
626–1(b)–(d)	5443
626–1(e)	5770
626–1(f)	5703, 5707
626–1(g)	5703
626–1(h)	5751, 5769, 5775
626–1(i)	5765
626–1(j)	741
626–1(k)	5703, 5709
626–1(*l*)	5709, 5710, 6373, 6381
626–1(m)	5709, 6373
626–1(n)	6374, 6381
626–1(*o*)	5443, 5703, 5707, 5708, 5757, 5765, 5769, 5775, 6383
626–1(p)	5703, 5707, 5708, 5759, 5765, 5769, 5775, 6377, 6378
626–1(q)	5709, 5710, 6375, 6381
626–1(r)	5709, 6375
626–1(s)	5706, 6378
626–1(t)	5707
626–1(u)	Rep.
626–1(v)	Elim.
626–1(w)	(See former 626–1(t))
626–1(x)	(See former 626–1(u))
626–1(y)	Rep.
626a, 626b	Rep.
627, 627a	Rep.
628	Rep.
629	5502
630–632a	Rep.
632b (1st par.)	Rep.
632b (less 1st par.)	5203
632c	Rep.
632d	5588
633	Rep.
634	5583, 5585
635	5595
636	Rep.
637	5584
638	Rep.
639	5504, 5572, 5584
639a–646	Rep.
651	741, 5502
651a–654	Rep.
661–662c	Rep.
663, 664	Rep.
665, 666	5861
667–667f	Rep.
668–669b	Rep.
670, 671	5790
671a	5443, 5448, 5453
672	5789
681–685	Rep.
685a	5201
685b	5205
686–688	Rep.
691, 691–1	Rep.
691a	Rep.
691b	Elim.
691c, 691d	Rep.
692	5533, 5534, 5538, 6293
692a	5538
693	5531
694	Rep.
695	6158
696, 697	Elim.
701	6222, 6224
701–1 to 701–5	6222 nt.
701a	Rep.
702	6223
711, 712	Rep.
713	5944
714	6012
715–718	Rep.
721–723	Rep.
724	7581
725	6032
731	Rep.
732, 732a	6021
733, 734	Rep.
735 (par. 1)	6023
735 (par. 2)	6025
735 (par. 3)	6024
735 (pars. 4, 5)	5942
735 (par. 6)	Rep.
735 (par. 7)	5942
735 (par. 8)	Rep.
735a	Rep.
735b	6911
736	6022
737, 737a	6914
738 (last sent.)	6914
738 (less last sent.)	Rep.
741–748	Rep.
749 (2d proviso of par. 7)	7341
749 (less 2d proviso of par. 7)	Rep.
749a to 749c–1	Rep.
749d, 749e	7341
749f	Rep.
751, 751a	Rep.
752–770	Rep.
771, 772	6115
773, 774	Rep.
781–783b	Rep.
784–790	Rep.
801–805	Rep.
811	Rep.
821(a), (b)	6901
821(c), (d)	Rep.
822	6901
831	Rep.
841	Rep.
841a–841e	6915; T. 14 §§758a, 759a
841f	Rep.
841g	T. 14 §§758a, 759a
841h	6915; T. 14 §§758a, 759a
842–843a	Rep.
844 to 849d–1	Rep.
849e–849i	Rep.
850	Rep.
850a, 850b	6911
850c	6912. Rep. in part. See T. 37 §402(a)–(c)
850d	Rep.
850e	6912
850f, 850g	6913
850h	5788
850i, 850j	Rep.
850k to 850k–2	Elim.
850*l*, 850m	Rep.
851 to 853a–1	Rep.
835b to 853c–1	Rep.
853c–2 to 853c–2a	6902
853c–3	6902
853c–4 (proviso)	6902
853c–4 (less proviso)	Rep.
853c–5	Rep.
853c–6	Elim.
853d, 853e	Rep.
853e–1	684
853f to 853g–1	Rep.
853h–853j	Rep.
854 (proviso)	Rep.
854 (less proviso)	6330
854a	6330, 6332
854b	Elim.
854c	6330, 6331. Rep. in part.
854c–1 to 854c–5	6330 nt.
854d	6485, 6486. Rep. in part.
854e (2d, 4th provisos)	6331
854e (3d, 5th provisos)	Elim.
854e (less 3d–5th provisos)	6485
854f	6201
854g	Rep.
855–855b	Rep.
855c(a)	6148
855c (less (a))	Elim.
855c–1	6148
855c–2	Rep.
855c–3	8687 nt.
855c–4	Rep.
855d to 855i–1	Rep.
855j–855s	Rep.
856 to 857c–1	Rep.
857d–857g	Rep.
858–858c	Rep.
861–861f	(See former 842, 843, 844–848)
862, 863	6141
864	Rep.
864a	5701 nt.
864b	5507
865	Rep.
865a	T. 37 §257 (See Rev. T. 37 Table)
865b	5062
866–869	Rep.
870	5788
870a	Elim.
871–875	Rep.
875a	T. 37 §310c (See Rev. T. 37 Table)
875b	T. 37 §310d (See Rev. T. 37 Table)
876–877a	Rep.
878	Rep.
879	6321, 6322, 6326
879a	Elim.
879b, 880	Rep.
881	6406
882	Rep.
882a	6111
882b	Rep.
882c, 882d	6111
883	6112
884	Rep.
885	6152
886, 887	Rep.
887a–889	Rep.
890	2772
891	6154
892–894a	Rep.
895–895a	Rep.
896–896b	Rep.
897	Rep.
898	6157; T. 14 §471a
899	Rep.
899a	7523
900	Rep.

Title 34 Former Sections	Title 10 New Sections
900a	6292
900b, 901	Rep.
901a	6081, 6086
902	Rep.
902a–902c	6082
902d	6083
903–907	Rep.
908	6084
909	6085
911	7571
911a	7571, 7572
911b–911d	7574
911e	Rep.
912–914	Rep.
915	7572
915a	7576
915b	6087, 7578, 7579
915c	Elim.
916, 916a	Rep.
917, 919	Rep.
921	Rep.
921a, 921b	6203
922–929	Rep.
931	6146
932	6142
933, 933a	Rep.
935–936	Rep.
937–939	1035
941	Rep.
941a	2771
942	6522
943, 944	6521
945	Elim.
951	T. 37 §243 (See Rev. T. 37 Table)
952	T. 37 §244 (See Rev. T. 37 Table)
953	6145
954	6144
961	6147
962	Rep.
963	6117
971–977	Rep.
981–984a	Rep.
985–989	Rep.
991–993d	Rep.
993e	Elim.
994–995a	Rep.
996–1001	Rep.
1011	Rep.
1012–1017	Elim.
1020, 1020a	6903
1020b, 1020c	6904–6906
1020d	6023, 6906
1020e(a)	6904, 6906
1020e(b)	6909
1020e(c)	6904, 6909
1020e(d) (1st sent.)	5504, 6904, 6906, 6909
1020e(d) (less 1st sent.)	Rep.
1020f	6907, 6909
1020g, 1020h	6907–6909
1020i	6910
1020j	6913
1020k	Rep.
1020*l*	6901
1020m	Rep.
1021	6951
1031	Rep.
1032	6954, 6958
1032–1	6955
1032a, 1033	Rep.
1033a, 1034	6954
1035	Rep.
1035a	6954
1036 to 1036–2	6957
1036a–1039	6954
1040, 1041	6956
1042, 1043	6958
1044–1045a	Rep.
1046	Rep.
1047	6956, 6958
1048	6959
1049	6956
1051, 1052	Rep.
1052a	6960
1053	6963
1054	6966
1055	Rep.
1056	6966
1057 (Proviso of 3d sent.)	Rep.
1057 (3d sent. less proviso)	5504
1057 (less 3d sent.)	5573
1057–1	541
1057a (last sent.)	Rep. See 4353 nt., 6967 nt.; T. 46 §1126a–1 nt.
1057a (less last sent.)	6976
1057a–1	(See former 1076f)
1057b	Rep.
1061	Rep.
1062	6961
1062a	6962
1063–1067	6964
1068	6965
1071	6952, 7478
1072	Rep.
1073	7082
1073a	7083
1073b	7084
1073c	7081
1073c–1	7081, 7085
1073c–2	7086
1073c–3	7087
1073d	7081
1073e	7088
1073f	Rep. See 7085 nt.
1074	7043, 7081
1076	7041
1076a	7042
1076b	7044, 7081
1076c	7043
1076d	7046
1076e	7045
1076f	7047
1081, 1082	Rep.
1083–1088	6968
1091	Rep.
1091a	6969
1101–1103	6970
1104	Elim.
1105	Rep.
1106	6971
1107, 1108	Rep.
1108a	Elim.
1108b (last proviso)	Elim.
1108b (less last proviso)	6971
1109	Rep.
1109a	Elim.
1110	Rep.
1111	6972
1115–1115c	6973
1116	Rep.
1117	Elim.
1118–1120	6974
1121	T. 46 §1335
1122	T. 46 §1336
1123	5985. Rep. in part. See T. 46 §1337
1123a	T. 46 §1337
1123b	T. 46 §1338
1123c	T. 46 §1339
1123d	T. 46 §1340
1123e	T. 46 §1341
1123f–1125	Rep.
1126	5986
1127	Rep.
1128	7547
1129, 1130	5984
1131, 1132	7651
1133	7657
1134	7658
1135	7659
1136	7656
1137	7655, 7676
1138	7660, 7661
1139	7662
1140	7663
1141	7653, 7654
1142	7664
1143	7665
1144	7666
1145	7667
1146	7680
1147	7679
1148	7669
1149	7670
1150	7670, 7671
1151	7668
1152	7677
1153	7673
1154, 1155	7676
1156	7675
1157	7674
1158	7651, 7672
1158a	Rep.
1159	7651, 7652
1160	7653
1161	7652
1162	7663
1163	7655, 7676
1164 (1st sent.)	Rep.
1164 (less 1st sent.)	7652
1165	7681
1166	7652
1167	7678
1200, 1201	Rep.

TITLE 11—BANKRUPTCY

[This title was enacted into law by Pub. L. 95–598, title I, § 101, Nov. 6, 1978, 92 Stat. 2549. This Table lists the sections of former Title 11, and indicates the sections of revised Title 11 which cover similar and related subject matter.]

Title 11 Former Sections	Title 11 New Sections
1(1)–(3)	Rep.
1(4)	101(12)
1(5)–(7)	Rep.
1(8)	101(8)
1(9), (10)	Rep.
1(11)	101(9)
1(12), (13)	Rep.
1(14)	101(11)
1(15), (16)	Rep.
1(17)	101(17), (18)
1(18)	Rep.
1(19)	101(26)
1(20)–(22)	Rep.
1(23)	101(30)
1(24)	101(31)
1(25), (26)	Rep.
1(27)	101(34)
1(28), (29)	Rep.
1(29a)	101(38)
1(30)	101(40)
1(31)	Rep.
1(32)	101(24)
1(33), (34)	Rep.
1(35)	102(7)
11(a)(1)	109(a)
11(a)(2)	502(j)
11(a)(2A)	505(a), (b)
11(a)(3), (4)	Rep.
11(a)(5)	721
11(a)(6)	Rep.
11(a)(7)	363
11(a)(8)	350
11(a)(9)–(14)	Rep.
11(a)(15)	105
11(a)(16)	Rep.
11(a)(17)	324
11(a)(18)	303(i)
11(a)(19), (20)	Rep.
11(a)(21)	543(b), (c)
11(a)(22)	305(a)(2)
11(b)	Rep.
21	303(h)
22	109(b)
22(a)	301
22(b)	303(a)
23(a)	Rep.
23(b)	303(b)
23(c)–(f)	Rep.
23(g)	723
23(h)–(k)	Rep.
24	522
25(a)(1)	343, 521(4)
25(a)(2)	Rep.
25(a)(3)	521(2)
25(a)(4)	521(3)
25(a)(5)	521(3)
25(a)(6)	521(2)
25(a)(7)	521(2)
25(a)(8), (9)	521(1)
25(a)(10)	343, 344
25(a)(11)	521(3)
25(b)	Rep.
26	541(a)
27, 28	Rep.
29(a)	362
29(b)–(d)	Rep.
29(e)	108(a), (b)
29(f)	108(c)
30, 31	(See former 501–1103)
32(a)	727(a)(10), 1141(d)(4)
32(b)	727(c)
32(c)(1)	727(a)(2), (4)
32(c)(2)	727(a)(3)
32(c)(3)	727(a)(4)
32(c)(4)	727(a)(2)
32(c)(5)	727(a)(8), (9)
32(c)(6)	727(a)(6)
32(c)(7)	727(a)(5)
32(c)(8)	Rep.
32(d), (e)	Rep.
32(f)	524(a)
32(g), (h)	Rep.
33	727(d), (e), 1328(e)
34	524(e)
35(a)(1)	523(a)(1)
35(a)(2)	523(a)(2)
35(a)(3)	523(a)(3)
35(a)(4)	523(a)(4)
35(a)(5), (6)	Rep.
35(a)(7)	523(a)(5)
35(a)(8)	523(a)(6)
35(b)	523(b), 349(a)
35(c)	523(c)
35(c)(4)	362
41(a)	Rep.
41(b)	303(d)
41(c)–(e)	Rep.
41(f)	301
42	T. 28 § 1480
43	Rep.
44(a)	343
44(b)–(f)	Rep.
44(g)	549(c)
44(h)–(*l*)	Rep.
45–51	Rep.
52, 53	Rep.
54	Rep.
55	T. 28 § 1475
61–71	Rep.
72(a)	702
72(b)	705
72(c)	327(c)
73	321
74	325, 703(a)
75(a)(1)	704(1)
75(a)(2)	345
75(a)(3)	704(2)
75(a)(4)	Rep.
75(a)(5)	704(2)
75(a)(6)	Rep.
75(a)(7)	704(3)
75(a)(8)	704(4)
75(a)(9)	704(5)
75(a)(10)	704(6)
75(a)(11), (12)	Rep.
75(a)(13)	704(8)
75(a)(14)	Rep.
75(b), (c)	Rep.
76(a), (b)	Rep.
76(c)	326(a), 330
76(d)	Rep.
76(e)	326(d)
76(f), (g)	Rep.
76a	330
77	107
78(a)	Rep.
78(b)	322(a)
78(c)	322(b)(1)
78(d)	322(b)(2)
78(e)	Rep.
78(f), (g)	322(b)(2)
78(h)	Rep.
78(i)	322(c)
78(j)–(*l*)	Rep.
78(m)	322(d)
78(n)	Rep.
79–82	Rep.
91, 92	341
93(a)–(c)	Rep.
93(d)	502(a), (c)
93(e)	Rep.
93(f)	502(b)
93(g)	502(d)
93(h)	506(a), (b)
93(i)	501(b), 509
93(j)	724(a)
93(k)	502(j)
93(*l*), (m)	Rep.
93(n)	501(a), 726(a)(3)
93a	Rep.
94	342
95(a)	301
95(b)	303(b)
95(c), (d)	Rep.
95(e)	303(b)
95(f)	303(c)
95(g)	303(j), 707
95(h)	Rep.
96	547
96(a)(4)	547(e)(1)(B)
96(b)	550, 551
96(c)	547(c)(4), 553
96(d)	329
96(e)(1)	741
96(e)(2)	745, 751, 752
96(e)(3)	753
96(e)(5)	749
101	345
101a	Rep.
102(a)(1)	503(b)(2)
102(a)(2)–(4)	Rep.
102(b)	Rep.
102(c)	504
102(d)	Rep.
103	101(4)
103(a)(9)	502(b)(7)

Title 11 Former Sections	Title 11 New Sections
103(c)	365
103a	Rep.
104(a)	507
104(a)(1)	503(b)
104(a)(2)	507(a)(3)
104(a)(4)	502(b)(4), 505(a), (b)
104(b)	Rep.
105(a)–(c)	Rep.
105(d)	508
105(e)	Rep.
106(a)	347(a)
106(b)	Rep.
107(a)	349(b), 547(b), (d), 551
107(b), (c)	545
107(c)(1)(A)	545(1)
107(c)(1)(B)	545(2), 546(b)
107(c)(1)(C)	545(3), (4)
107(c)(2)	551
107(c)(3)	724(b)
107(d)(1)(a)–(c)	Rep.
107(d)(1)(d)	101(26)
107(d)(1)(e)	Rep.
107(d)(2)	548(a)
107(d)(3)	550
107(d)(4)	548(b)
107(d)(5)	548(d)(1)
107(d)(6)	548(c), 550, 551
107(d)(7)	Rep.
107(e), (f)	Rep.
108	502(b)(3), 553
109(a)	303(e)
109(b)	303(i)
109(c)	Rep.
109(d)	303(g), 543(b), (c)
110(a)	541(a)
110(a)(3)	541(b)
110(a)(5)	522(d)(7), (8)
110(b)	365
110(c)	541(e), 544(a)
110(d)(1)	549(a)
110(d)(2), (3)	542(c)
110(d)(4), (5)	Rep.
110(e)	544(b)
110(f)	363
110(g)–(i)	Rep.
111, 112	Rep.
201, 202	(See former 501–1103)
202a–204	Rep.
205(a)	Rep.
205(b)	1171(b), 1172
205(c)(1)	1163
205(c)(2)	1166
205(c)(3)–(5)	Rep.
205(c)(6)	1169
205(c)(7)–(13)	Rep.
205(d)	Rep.
205(e)	1173
205(f)–(i)	Rep.
205(j)	1168
205(k), (*l*)	Rep.
205(m)	101(33)
205(n)	1167, 1171(a)
205(*o*)	1170
205(p)–(s)	Rep.
205a	Rep.
206, 207	(See former 501–1103)
208	Rep.
301–303	Rep.
401(1)	101(4)
401(2)	Rep.
401(3)	101(9)
401(4)	Rep.
401(5)	101(11)
401(6)	101(28)
401(7)	101(30)
401(8)	101(12)
401(9)	Rep.
401(10)	902(2)
401(11)	903(3)
402(a)	Rep.
402(b)(1), (2)	901
402(b)(3)	Rep.
402(c)	904
402(d)	921(b)
403	903
404	101(29), 109(c)
405(a)	921(a), (c)–(f)
405(b)	901, 924
405(c)	Rep.
405(d)	923
405(e)	901
405(e)(1)	922(a)
405(f), (g)	Rep.
405(h)	901, 926
406, 407	Rep.
408(a)	925
408(b)	901
408(c)	Rep.
409	901
410(a)	941, 942
410(b)	942
411, 412	901
413	901, 943(a)
414(a)	901
414(b)(1)	943(b)(5), (6)
414(b)(2)	943(b)(2)
414(b)(3)	Rep.
414(b)(4)	943(b)(3)
414(b)(5)	Rep.
414(b)(6)	943(b)(4)
415(a)	944(a)
415(b)(1)	944(b)
415(b)(2)	944(c)
416(a)	Rep.
416(b)	901
416(c)	Rep.
416(d)	347(b), 901
416(e)	945(a)
416(f)	Rep.
417	946
418	927
501, 502	Rep.
506(1)	101(4)
506(2), (3)	Rep.
506(4)	101(9)
506(5)	101(12)
506(6)	101(11)
506(7)	Rep.
506(8)	101(23)
506(9)	101(31)
506(10)	Rep.
506(11)	101(35)
506(12), (13)	Rep.
507	1124
511, 512	Rep.
513	362
514, 515	Rep.
516(1)	365
516(2)	364
516(3)	363
516(4)	362
516(5), (6)	1110
517–521	Rep.
526	303(b)
527	Rep.
528	T. 28 §1472
529–533	Rep.
536, 537	303(d)
541–549	Rep.
556	1104(a)
557	327
558	101(13)
559	1105
560	324, 1104(c)
561, 562	Rep.
563	1107(a)
564	1106(a)(2)
565	Rep.
566	107
567(1)	1106(a)(3)
567(2)	Rep.
567(3)	1106(a)(4)(A)
567(4)	Rep.
567(5)	1106(a)(4)
567(6)	Rep.
568	1104(b), 1106(b)
569	1106(a)(5)
570	1121
571–574	Rep.
575	1125(d)
576	1125(b)
577, 578	Rep.
579	1126, 1128(a)
580	1128(b)
586	541(a)
587	1106
588	1107(a)
589	1108
590	Rep.
591	327
596	501(a), 1111
597	1122
598	501(a)
599	1126(a)
600, 601	Rep.
602	502(b)(7)
603	1126(e)
604	1143
605	347(b)
606	1109(b)
607	1109
608	1109(a)
609–613	Rep.
616(1)	1123(b)(1)
616(2)	1123(a)(5), (b)(4)
616(3)	Rep.
616(4)	1123(b)(2)
616(5)	1123(a)(3)
616(6)	1123(a)(2)
616(7)–(9)	Rep.
616(10)	1123(a)(5)
616(11)	1123(a)(7)
616(12)(a)	1123(a)(6)
616(12)(b)	Rep.
616(13)	1123(b)(3)
616(14)	1123(b)(5)

Title 11 Former Sections	*Title 11 New Sections*
621(1)	1129(a)(1)
621(2)	1129(a)(7), (11)
621(3)	1129(a)(3)
621(4)	1129(a)(4)
621(5)	1129(a)(5)
622	1127
623	1127(d)
624(1)	1141(a)
624(2)	1129(a)(6), 1142(a)
624(3), (4)	Rep.
625	Rep.
626	1141(c)
627	1142(b)
628(1)	1141(d)(1)–(3)
628(2)–(4)	Rep.
629(a)	1101(2)
629(b)	Rep.
629(c)	1127(b)
636	1112(b)
637	Rep.
638	348
641(1), (2)	Rep.
641(3), (4)	330
641(5)	503(b)(4)
642(1)	503(b)(3), (5)
642(2)	Rep.
642(3)	503(b)(4)
643	503(b)(3), (4)
644(1)	330
644(2)	503(b)(4)
644(3)	330
644(4)	503(b)(3), (4)
645–650	Rep.
656–659	Rep.
661	108(c)
662	Rep.
663	362
664(a)	1145(a)
664(b)	1145(b)
665, 666	Rep.
667	1146(c)
668	346(j)(1)
669	1129(d)
670	346(j)(5)
671, 672	Rep.
676	Rep.
701, 702	Rep.
706(1), (2)	Rep.
706(3)	101(12), 109(d)
706(4)	Rep.
706(5)	101(31)
707(1)	101(9)
707(2)	101(4), (11)
708	1124
711, 712	Rep.
713(1)	365
713(2)	363
713(3)	Rep.
714	362
715, 716	Rep.
721–728	Rep.
731–733	Rep.
734	341
735	341
735(3)	1128(a)
736	341
736(2)	501(a)
736(3)	343
737(1)	Rep.
737(2)	1129(a)(9)
737(3)	1128(a)
738	1102
739(1)(a)	1103(c)(2)
739(1)(b)–(e)	1103(c)(3)
739(1)(f)	1104(c)(5)
739(2)	503(b)(4), 1103(a)
741	Rep.
742	1107(a)
743	1108
744	364
751	1122
752	Rep.
753	502(b)(7)
754, 755	Rep.
755a	501(a)
756	Rep.
757(1)	Rep.
757(2)	1123(b)(2)
757(3)–(7)	Rep.
757(8)	1123(b)(5)
761	1129(a)(3)
762	Rep.
763	1127
764	1127(d)
765	1127(c)
766(1)	1129(a)(1)
766(2)	1129(a)(7), (11)
766(3)	1129(a)(2)
766(4)	1129(a)(3)
767(1)	1141(a)
767(2)–(4)	Rep.
768–770	Rep.
771	1141(d)(1)–(3)

Title 11 Former Sections	*Title 11 New Sections*
772	Rep.
776, 777	1112(b)
778	348
779–781	Rep.
786	1144
787(1)	1127(b)
787(2)	1127(c)
787(3)	1127(d)
787(4)	Rep.
791	108(c)
792	Rep.
793(a)	1145(a)
793(b)	1145(b)
794	Rep.
795	346(j)(1)
796	346(j)(5)
797	Rep.
799	Rep.
801, 802	Rep.
806(1)	Rep.
806(2)	101(4)
806(3), (4)	Rep.
806(5)	101(9)
806(6)	101(12), 109(d)
806(7)	101(11)
806(8)	101(23)
806(9)	101(31)
807	1124
811, 812	Rep.
813(1)	365
813(2)	363
813(3)	Rep.
814	362
815, 816	Rep.
821–827	Rep.
828	362
831	Rep.
832	1104(a)
833	Rep.
834	341
835	341, 1128(a)
836	341
836(2)	501(a)
836(3)	343
837(1)	1104(a)
837(2)	Rep.
837(3)	1128(a)
841	Rep.
842	1106
843	348
844	1107(a)
845	1108
846	364
851	501(a), 1111
852	1122
853	Rep.
854	501(a)
855–857	Rep.
858	502(b)(7)
859	Rep.
861(1)–(3)	Rep.
861(4)	1123(b)(2)
861(5), (6)	Rep.
861(7)	1123(b)(4)
861(8)	Rep.
861(9)	1123(a)(3)
861(10)	1123(a)(2)
861(11)	Rep.
861(12)	1123(a)(5)
861(13)	1123(b)(5)
866	Rep.
867	1129(a)(3)
868	Rep.
869	1127(a), (b)
870	1127(d)
871	1127(c)
872(1)	1129(a)(1)
872(2)	1129(a)(7), (11)
872(3)	1129(a)(2)
872(4)	1129(a)(3)
872(5)	1129(a)(4)
873(1)	1141(a)
873(2)	1142(a)
873(3)	Rep.
874	1141(c)
875	1142(b)
876	1141(d)(1)–(3)
877	Rep.
881, 882	1112(b)
883	348
884–886	Rep.
891(1)	Rep.
891(2), (3)	330
892(1)	503(b)(3)
892(2)	Rep.
892(3)	503(b)(4)
893(1)	Rep.
893(2)	503(b)(4)
893(3)	330
893(4)	503(b)(4)
894–898	Rep.
906–909	Rep.
911	1144

Title 11 Former Sections	Title 11 New Sections
916	108(c)
917	362
918(a)	1145(a)
918(b)	1145(b)
919	Rep.
920	346(j)(1)
921	1129(d)
922	346(j)(5)
923	Rep.
926	Rep.
1001, 1002	Rep.
1006(1)	101(4)
1006(2)	101(9)
1006(3)	101(12), 109(e)
1006(4)	101(11)
1006(5)	Rep.
1006(6)	101(31)
1006(7)	Rep.
1006(8)	101(24), 109(e)
1007	Rep.
1011, 1012	Rep.
1013(1)	365
1013(2)	Rep.
1014	362
1015, 1016	Rep.
1021–1026	Rep.
1031	Rep.
1032, 1033	341
1033(1)	343, 501(a)
1033(2)	1321
1033(5)	1324
1036	1303
1037	Rep.
1041–1044	Rep.
1046(1)	1322(b)(1)
1046(2)	1322(b)(2)
1046(3)	1322(a)(2)
1046(4)	1322(a)(1)
1046(5)	1329(a)
1046(6)	1322(b)(7)
1046(7)	1322(b)(10)
1051	1325(a)(3)
1052	Rep.
1053	1323(a)
1054	1323(c)
1055	Rep.
1056(a)(1)	1325(a)(1)
1056(a)(2)	1325(a)(6)
1056(a)(3)	Rep.
1056(a)(4)	1325(a)(3)
1056(b)	502(b)
1057	1327(a)
1058	Rep.
1059	1326(a)
1060	1328(a), (c), (d)
1061	1328(b)
1062	Rep.
1066	348, 1307
1067	348
1068, 1069	Rep.
1071	1330
1076	108(c)
1077–1079	Rep.
1080	1305(a)(1)
1086	Rep.
1101–1103	Rep.
1200–1255	Rep.

TITLE 13—CENSUS

[This title was enacted into law by act Aug. 31, 1954, ch. 1158, 68 Stat. 1012. This table shows where sections of former Title 13 have been incorporated in revised Title 13.]

Title 13 Former Sections	Title 13 New Sections
1	2
2	21
3, 4	Rep.
5	22
6	22
7–9	Rep.
21–41	Rep.
41a	Rep.
42–55	Rep.
61–69	Rep.
71	41
72	42
72a	42
73	9, 214
74	43, 224, 241
75	44
76	45
77	Rep.
81	61
82	5
83	9, 214
84	224, 241
85	62
86	63
91–98	Rep.
101	T. 42 §244a
106	Rep.
106 note	Rep.
107	Rep.
111	5, 24, 101, 102, 103, 225
112	Rep.
113	101
114	Rep.
121	131, 181
122	6, 9, 24, 25, 211, 212, 213, 214, 221, 222, 223, 224, 225
123	5, 132
201	141
202	143
203	23, 24
204	5, 144
205	25
206	145
207	211
208	9, 212, 213
209	221, 222, 223
210	224
211	9
212	Rep.
213	7
214	10
215	6
216	5, 23, 146
217	Rep.
218	8
219, 220	Rep.
251	5, 161, 163
252	6, 9, 24, 162, 211, 212, 213, 214
253	Rep.

TITLE 14—COAST GUARD

[This title was enacted into law by act Aug. 4, 1949, ch. 393, §1, 63 Stat. 495. This table shows where former sections of Title 14 have been incorporated in revised Title 14.]

Title 14 Former Sections	*Title 14 New Sections*
1	1, 3, 4(a), (b)
2	467
2a	Elim.
3	3, 571
3a	481, 465, 488, 576
4	Rep.
5	41
5a–6	Rep.
6a	42
6b	47, 222, 462
6c	225
6d	224(c)
6e, 6f	433(a), (b)
7	4(c)
8	Rep.
9	41, 43
10	Rep.
10a	224(c), 226
10b–10f	Rep.
10g	432(a)
10h	432(b)
10i	Rep.
11	44, 45
11a	47, 48
12	47, 48
12a	Rep.
13	485(b)
14	Rep.
15	182, 183
15a	184
15a–1	182, 185
15b	187, 188
15c	187, 189
15d	186
15e	191
15f	190
15g	193
15h	194
15i	192
15j	Rep.
15k	476
16	223
16a, 16b	Rep.
16c	223
17	223
18	223, 224
19, 19a, 20	Rep.
20a	228, 461
20a–1	228
20a–2	301
20b	Rep.
20c	228
21	41, 225
21a	228, 301
21b	433(c)
22	632
23	352
24	Rep.
25	182
26	636
27	636
28	92(b), 144(a), 145(a)
29	88, 92(c), 93(b)
30	485(a)
31	144(b), 145(b)
31a	144(c)
31b	93(k)
31c	151
32, 33	(See former 131, 132)
34	632
34–1	T. 34 §450b–1
34a	Rep.
35	351, 365, 367
35a	351, 367
35b	366
35c	367
35d	433(d)
36	651
37	651
38	Rep.
39	484
40, 40a	Rep.
41	505
41a	504
42	145(a)
43	(See former 127)
43a	641(a)
44	Rep.
45	89(a)
46	89(b)
47	89(c)
48	634(a)
48a	91
49	148
50	432(c)
50a	Rep. in part, elim. in part
50b	640
50c	643
50d	T. 37 §31a
50e	433(e).
50f–50j	T. 5 §§150p–150t
50k	90(a)
50*l*	90(b)
50m	81
50n	82
50*o*	81
51	89, 92(i)
52	89, 93(a)
53	88, 93(a)
54	93(c)
55	88, 93, (d)
56	Rep.
57	145(a)
58	632
59	Rep.
60	88
61	88(a)
62	88
63	88
64	638
65	Rep.
66	89
67	89
68	637
69	92(d), 93(h)
70	Rep.
71	646
72–74	Rep.
91	93(d), 632
92	633
93	92(c), 93(b)
94	92(c), 93(h)
95	92(a), 93(b)
96	92(f)
97	93(b), (c)
98	Rep.
98a	92(c), 93(b)
99	632
100–102	Rep.
103	632
104	88(a), 89(b)
105–107	Rep.
108	93(h), (i)
109	92(d), 93(h), (i)
110	93(m)
111	93(e)
112	93(b), (c)
121	461
121a–121c	Rep.
121d	433(h)
122–127	Rep.
127a	Elim.
128	Rep.
129	464
130, 130a	Elim.
131	92(i)
132	479
132a, 133	Rep.
133a	475
134	478(b)
135	478
136	Rep.
136a	466
137	Rep.
138	472
141	562
142	561
143	563, 564, 566, 567
144	569(a)
145	569(b)
146	570
147	575, 644
148	482
161	46
161a	49
162	49
162a	230, 232, 243, 303, 313, 423
162b	T. 34 §428
163	Rep.
164, 165	240, 310
165a	241, 311
165b	240, 241, 310, 311
166	Rep.
167	423
167a	T. 37 §26a
167b	Rep.
167b–1	Elim.
167b–2	483
167b–3	Elim.
167c	T. 34 §399c–1

Title 14 Former Sections	Title 14 New Sections
168	246, 315, 364
169	233, 241, 306, 311, 356
170	425, 635
171	234
172	233, 245, 306, 314, 356, 363
173	230, 303, 353
174	421(b)
174a	239, 309
175	231, 304, 354, 424
175a	238, 244
175b	235
175c	423
175d–175f	Rep.
176, 177	Rep.
178	431(a)
178a	431(b)
178b	431(c)
179	Rep.
180	432(d)
181	432(e)
182	433(f)
183	433(g)
185	357(a)
185a	355
185b	358
185c	359, 360
185d	357(a), (c), 423
185e	633
186	755(e)
191	Rep.
192	93(m)
193–196	500
201	226
202	Rep.
203	226(a)
204	226(a), 227
205	Rep.
206	302, 351
207, 208	Rep.
251–259	Rep.
260	821
261	822
262	823
263	821
264	825
265	826
266	827
266a	828
266b	829
267	830
268	831
269	Rep.
270	832
271	893
301	751
302	752
303	754
304	751
305	753, 754
306	755
307	756
308	757
309	758
310	759
311	755(c)
312	760
313	761
314, 315	Rep.
351	753, 823
352	891, 892
353	Rep.
354	894
381–388	Rep.

TITLE 17—COPYRIGHTS

[This title was enacted into law by act July 30, 1947, ch. 391, 61 Stat. 652, and was revised in its entirety by Pub. L. 94–553, title I, §101, Oct. 19, 1976, 90 Stat. 2541, effective Jan. 1, 1978. Table I following shows where the sections of Title 17 prior to 1947 were incorporated into the 1947 revision. Table II shows where the subject matter of sections of Title 17 as revised in 1947 was incorporated in the 1976 revision.]

TABLE I

Title 17 Former Sections	*Title 17 1947 Revision Sections*
1	1
2	2
3	3
4	4
5	5
6	7
7	8
8	9
9	10
10	11
11	12
12	13
13	14
14	15
15	16
16	17
17	18
18	19
19	20
20	21
21	22
22	23
23	24
24	Rep.
25	101
26	102
27	103
28	104
29	105
30	106
31	107
32	108
33	109
34	110
35	111
36	112
37	113
38	114
39	115
40	116
41	27
42	28
43	29
44	30
45	31
46	32
47	201
48	202
49	203
50	204
51	205
52	206
53	207
54	208
55	209
56	210
57	211
58	212
59	213
60	214
61	215
62	26
63	6
64	6
65	25

TABLE II

Title 17 1947 Revision Sections	*Title 17 New Sections*
1	106, 116
2	301
3	102, 103
4	102
5	102
6	102
7	103
8	104, 105, 303
9	104
10	401
11	410
12	408
13	407, 411
14	407
15	407
16	601
17	407
18	407, 506
19	401
20	401, 402
21	405
22	601
23	601
24	203, 301 et seq.
25	301 et seq.
26	101
27	109, 202
28	201, 204
29	204
30	205
31	205
32	201
101	412, 501–504
102	Rep. See T. 28 §1338
103	Rep. See F.R. Civ. Proc.
104	110, 506
105	506
106	602
107	602
108	603
109	603
110	Rep. See T. 28 §1338
111	Rep. See T. 28 §1400
112	502
113	502
114	502
115	507
116	505
201	701(a)
202	701(a)
203	708(c)
204	Rep.
205	701(c)
206	701(b)
207	702
208	705
209	407, 410
210	707
211	707
212	705
213	704
214	704
215	708(a), (b)
216	703

TITLE 18—CRIMES AND CRIMINAL PROCEDURE

[This title was enacted into law by act June 25, 1948, ch. 645, §1, 62 Stat. 683. This table shows where sections of former Title 18 have been incorporated in revised Title 18.]

Title 18 Former Sections	*Title 18 New Sections*
1, 2	2381
3	2382
4	2383
5	953
6	2384
7	2389
8	2390
9	2387
10	2385
11	2385, 2387
12	Rep. See Cr. Proc. R. 41(c).
13	2385, 2387
14–17	2386
21	958
22	959
23	962
24	961
25	960
26	T. 22 §461
27	T. 22 §462
28	T. 22 §463
29	T. 22 §464
30	959
31	967
32	963
33	964
34	965
35	966
36	963, 964, 965, 966, 967
37	756, 3058
38	T. 22 §465
39	5, 3241
51	241
52	242
53	Rep.
53a	2236
54	372
55	592
56–58	593
59	592, 593
61	594
61a	595
61b	600
61c	601
61d	604
61e	605
61f	598
61g	594, 595, 598, 600, 601, 604, 605
61h	T. 5 §118i (See Rev. T. 5 Table)
61i	T. 5 §118j (See Rev. T. 5 Table)
61j, 61k	Rep.
61*l*	T. 5 §118k (See Rev. T. 5 Table)
61m	608
61m–1	611
61n	595
61*o*	T. 5 §118*l* (See Rev. T. 5 Table)
61p	T. 5 §118m (See Rev. T. 5 Table)
61q	Rep.
61r	T. 5 §118n (See Rev. T. 5 Table)
61s	595
61t	610
61u	595
61v–61x	Elim.
62–62b	612
71	497
72	494
73	495
74	1002
75	1016
76	912
76a, 76b	701
76c	707, 916
76d	707
76e	705
77	Rep.
77a	913
78	914
79	1003
80	287, 1001
81	289
82	641, 1361
83	286
84	1022
85	1023
86	1024
87	641
88	371
89	871
90	T. 34 §1167 (See Rev. T. 34 Table)
91	201
92	285
93	434
94	1381
95	1232
96	2152
97	1382
97a	1383
97b	757
98	11, 957
99	2112
100	641
101	641, 3435
102	Rep.
103	1852
103a, 103b	1851
104	1853
105	1854
106	1855
107	1856
107a	1863
108	3613
109	1862
110	1857
111	1858
112	1859
113	1860
114	1861
115	T. 25 §202
116	1362
117	2074
118	111
119	496
120	551
121	2231, 2232, 2233
122	T. 19 §70
123	912
124	211
125	543
126	541
127	1019
128	2233
129	507
130	1017
131	506
132	499
133	5
134, 135	Rep.
136	498
137–143	Rep.
144	2194
145	41
146	508
147	509
148	3056
149	210
150	211
151	210, 211
171	872
172	652
173	653
174	650
175	648
176	643
177, 178	649
178a	371
179	3497
180	3487
181	6514
182	641
183	654
184	435
185	646
186	645
187	647
188	2075
189	2073
190, 191	Rep.
192	1901
193	291
194	1091
195	1018
196	1912
198, 198a	283
199	205
200	204
201	1913
202	216
203	281
204	431
205	432
206	433
207	202
208	602
209	603
210	606
211	607
212	602, 603, 606, 607
213	T. 5 §118*o* (See Rev. T. 5 Table)
214	1902

Title 18 Former Sections	*Title 18 New Sections*
215	2072
216	1905
231	1621
232	1622
233	1506
234, 235	2071
236	505
237	206
238	207
239	208
240	210
241	1503
241a	1505
242	Rep.
243	1504
244	755
245	1501
246	752, 1071
247	752
248	753
249	754
250	873
251	4
252	752, 1792
253	1114, 2231
254	111, 2231
261	8
262	471
263	Rep.
264	474
265	472
266	476
267	477
268	473
269	642
270	478
271	479
272	482
273	483
274	480
275	481
276	484
277	485
278	490
279	331
280	332
281	486
282, 282a	491
283	487
284	488
285	489
286	492
287	Rep. See Cr. Proc. R. 41(a), (b), (f).
288	11
289	335
290	Rep.
291	333
292	475
293	336
294	371
301	12
302	1729
303	1693
304	1696
305	1697
306	1696
307	1694
308	1695
309	1696
310	1730
311	1731
312	1706
313	1707
314	1704
315	2115
316	2116
317	1702, 1708
318	1703, 1709
319	1703, 1710
320	2114
321	1705, 1708
321a	1725
322	1700
323	1698
324, 325	1701
326	1724
327	1699
328	1720
329	1712
330	1726
331	1721
332	1727
333	1713
334	1461
335	1463, 1718
336	1302
337	1303
338	1341
338a	876, 3239
338b	877, 3239
338c	1714
338d	Rep.
339	1342
340	1716
341, 342	Rep.
343–345	1717
346	5, 1717
347	500
348	501
349	11, 502
349a	503
350	504
351	1723
352	1732
353	1722
354	288
355	1711, 3497
356	440
357	1719
358	1728
359	1692
360	12
361	1715
381	5, 1364
382	831, 832
383	835
384	833
385	832, 833, 834, 835
386	832, 833, 834, 835
387	1301
388	1264
389	1265
390	1263
391	42
392	43
393	44
393a	43, 44, 3054, 3112
394	42, 43, 44
395	T. 16 § 667e
396	1462
396a, 396b	1761
396c–396e	1762
397, 398	2421
399	2422
400	2423
401	2421
402(1)	T. 8 § 1557
402(2), (3)	2424
403	Rep.
404	2421
405–407	Rep.
407a	1231
408	10, 2311, 2312, 2313
408a	1201
408b	10
408c	1201
408c–1	1202
408d	875, 3239
408e	1073
409	659, 660, 2117
410, 411	659
412	660
412a	1992
413	Rep.
414(a)	10
414(b), (c)	2311
415	2314
416	2315
417	2311
418, 418a, 419	Rep.
419a(a)	2311
419a(b)	10
419b	2316
419c	2317
419d	Rep.
420	T. 4 § 112
420a to 420e–1	1951
420f–420h	1821
421, 422	1585
423	1584
424	1582
425	1585
426	1587
427	1586
428	1588
429–442	T. 46 §§ 1351–1364 (See Rev. T. 46 Table)
443	1583
444, 445	1581
446	1584
451	7
452	1111
453	1112
454	1111, 1112
455	113
456	1113
457	2031
458	2032
459	2198
460	2198, 3286, 3614
461	1115
462	114
463	2111
464	81, 1363
465	81, 1363

Title 18 Former Sections	*Title 18 New Sections*
466	661
467	662, 3435
467a	1025
468	13
469–474	2199
481	1651
482	2191
483	2192
484	2193
485	1655
486	2195
487	2271
488	1658
489	1659
490	2276
491	2272
492	2273
493	1661
494	1654
495	1652
496	1653
497	1656
498	1657
499, 500	969
501	9
502	5, 2275
503, 504	2277
505	1081
506	1082
507	1083
508, 511–518	Rep.
518a	1384
519–521	Rep.
522	1991
523	244
532–535	Rep.
536	T. 50 §42
541	1
542	3566
543	3567
544	3563
545	3564
546, 547	3231
548	1151, 1153, 3242
549	1151, 1153
550	2
551	3
552	1660
553	3236
554	Rep. See Cr. Proc. R. 6(f).
554a	Rep. See Cr. Proc. R. 6.
555	Rep. See Cr. Proc. R. 7(a).
556	Rep. See Cr. Proc. R. 6(d), 52(a).
556a	3288, 3289
556b	Rep.
557	Rep. See Cr. Proc. R. 8, 13, 14.
558	Rep. See Cr. Proc. R. 7.
559	Rep. See Cr. Proc. R. 7.
560	Rep. See Cr. Proc. R. 7.
561	Rep. See Cr. Proc. R. 12(b)(5).
562	3432
562a	Rep. See Cr. Proc. R. 10.
563	3005
564	Rep. See Cr. Proc. R. 11, 12(b)(3).
565	Rep. See Cr. Proc. R. 31(c).
566	Rep. See Cr. Proc. R. 31(a), (b).
567	1111
568	3570
569	3565
570	3612
571–573	Rep.
574	3241
575	3059
576	3401
576a	3402
576b–576d	3401
581	Rep.
581a, 581b	3281
582	3282
583	3290
584	3283
585	T. 26 [I.R.C. 1939] §3748(a) (See T. 26 [I.R.C. 1986] §6531)
586	T. 26 [I.R.C. 1939] §3748(b) (See T. 26 [I.R.C. 1986] §6531)
587	3288
588	3289
589	3288, 3289
590	Rep.
590a	3287
591	3041
592	Rep.
593	Rep. See Cr. Proc. R. 5(a).
594	3045
595	Rep. See Cr. Proc. R. 4, 5.
596, 597	3141
598	3144
599	3142
600	3143
601	Rep. See Cr. Proc. R. 46(f)(1), (2).
602	3047
603	4084
604	3049
605	3012
611–616	Rep. See Cr. Proc. R. 41.
617	3105
618, 619	3109
620–626	Rep. See Cr. Proc. R. 41.
627	Rep.
628	2231
629	1621
630	2235
631	2234
632	5
633	Rep.
641	3569
642, 643	T. 46 §§7, 8 (See Rev. T. 46 Table)
644	T. 28 §1822
645	3611
646	3617
647	3616
651	3184
652	3185
653	3186
654	3188
655	3190
656	3191
657	3189
658	3181
659	3192
660	3051, 3193
661	752, 1502
662	3182, 3195
662a	5001
662b	3042
662c	752, 3183, 3195
662d	3187, 3195
662e	755
663	3194
664	Rep.
665	755
666, 667	Rep.
668	3195, 3498
669–676	D.C. Code, §§23–701, 23–702, 23–705
681	Rep. See Cr. Proc. R. 37.
682	3731
683	Rep.
687	3771
688	3772
689	3771, 3772
691	Rep.
692	4086
693–700	Rep.
701	4007
702	Rep.
703	4006
704	D.C. Code, §24–424
704a	D.C. Code, §24–423
705–707	Rep.
708, 709	436
709a	3568
710, 710a	4161
711	4166
712, 712a	Rep.
713	4163, 4165
714	4202
715	Rep.
716	4203, 4204
716a	4203
716b	4164
717	4205
718	4206
719	4207
720	Rep.
721	4281
722	Rep.
723	3570
723a	4201
723b	Rep.
723c	4205
724	3651
725	3653
726	3654
726–1, 726a	T. 28 §604
727	3655
728	3656
729	T. 28 §§1495, 2513
730–732	T. 28 §2513
733–733b	4085
741	4001
742–744	Rep.
744a	4122
744b	4125
744c	4122, 4123
744d–744f	4126
744g	4124
744h	4162
744h–1	Rep.
744i, 744j	4121
744k	4122
744*l*	4126
744m	4127
744n	4128

Title 18 Former Sections	Title 18 New Sections
744o–744r	Elim.
745	Rep.
746	4281
746a	4282
746b	4283
747–749	Rep.
750	T. 5 §678b (See Rev. T. 5 Table)
751, 752	4005
753	4041
753a	4042
753b	4002, 4042
753c	4003
753d	4009
753e	4001
753f	4082, 4083
753g	4008
753h	751
753i	752, 1072
753j	1791
753k	3050
754	4004
761	Rep.
762	4083
763–776, 791–801, 811–815	Rep.
816	4321
817–819, 831–840	Rep.
851	4125
852	Rep.
853–855	4125
871–875	Rep.
876	4241
877	4242
878	4243
879, 880, 901–906	Rep.
907	4081
908	1791
909	751
910	752, 1072
911, 912	Rep.
921	5031
922	5032, 5033
923	5033
924	5034
925	5035
926	5036
927	5037
928	Elim.
929	Rep.

TITLE 23—HIGHWAYS

[This title was enacted into law by Pub. L. 85–767, § 1, Aug. 27, 1958, 72 Stat. 885. This table shows where sections of former Title 23 have been incorporated in revised Title 23.]

Title 23 Former Sections	Title 23 New Sections
1	Rep.
2	101
2a	101(a)
2b	101(a)
3	Rep.
3a	Rep.
3b	Rep.
4	Rep.
5	Rep.
6	103(b), (e), 105(c), 121(c)
6–1	103(c)
6a	103(d)
6a–1	105(d)
6a–2	310
6b	Rep.
6c	Rep.
7	110(a)
8	109(a)
8a	109(a), 112(a)
9	301
9a	129(a)
9a–1	Rep.
9b	129(a)
10	109(a)
10a	Rep.
10b	Rep.
10c	Rep.
11	Rep.
12	105(a), 106(a), (c), 121(d)
12a	121(c)
12b	Rep.
13	114(a)
13–1	112(b), (c)
13a	Rep.
13b	103(d)
14	121(a), (b), (e)
14a	Elim.
15	Rep.
16	Rep.
17	316
18	317(a)–(c)
19	315
20	Rep.
20a	Rep.
21	104(a), (b)(1)
21–1	307(a), (b)
21a	104(b), 105(a), 106(a), 114(a), 118(a), (c)
21a–1	Rep.
21a–2	Elim.
21b	Rep.
21c	311
21d	Rep.
21e	122
22	104(e)
23	101(a), 202(b), 204(a)–(c), 205(a)–(c)
23a	Rep.
23b	Rep.
23b–1	Rep.
23c	205(c)
24	Rep.
24a	109(e)
25	Rep.
26	Rep.
41	101(a), 105(e)
41a	101(a), 103(b)
41b	101(a), 103(b)
42	Rep.
43	Rep.
44	Rep.
45	Elim.
46	See T. 18 § 1020
47–53	Rep.
54	Elim.
54a	Rep.
54b	Elim.
55	126
55a	Rep.
55b	126(b)
56	Rep.
57	314
58	Elim.
59	Elim.
59a	Rep.
60	103(d)
61	307(c)
62	318
63	109(d)
64	320(a)
65	320(b)
66	320(c)
67	320(d)
68	320(e)
69	320(f)
70	313
71	303(a)
72	303 note
73	303(a)
101	Rep.
101a	Rep.
102	Rep.
103	Rep.
104	Rep.
105	Rep.
106	210(a), (b)
107	Rep.
108	Rep.
109	Rep.
110	Rep.
111	Rep.
112	Rep.
113	Rep.
114	210(e)
115	308(a)
116	Rep.
117	312
151(a)	104 note
151(b), (c)	104(c), 117(a)–(c), 118(b)
152	204(f), 205(d)
153	206(a), 207(a), 208(a), (b)
154	209(a)
155	203
156	101(b), 103(f), 104(b)(1), 116(d), 119(a), (b), 120(h)
157	103(d)
158(a)	101(b)
158(b)	101 note
158(c)	104(b)(4)
158(d)	104(b)(5)
158(d)	104 note
158(e)	120(c)
158(f), (g)	118(c)
158(h)	115
158(i)	109(b)
158(j)	127
158(k)	307 note
159	107
160	108
161	124
162	123
163	111
164	129(b)–(d)
165	Elim.
166	113
167	101(b), 128(a), (b), 304
168	Elim.
169 (less last proviso)	Rep.
169 (last proviso)	Elim.
170	305
171	306
172	Rep.
173	120 note
174	307 note
175	Elim.

TITLE 26—INTERNAL REVENUE CODE OF 1986

[The Internal Revenue Code of 1954 (redesignated the Internal Revenue Code of 1986 by Pub. L. 99–514, §2, Oct. 22, 1986, 100 Stat. 2095) was enacted by act Aug. 16, 1954, ch. 736, §1, 68A Stat. 1, superseding the Internal Revenue Code of 1939. Section numbers of the Internal Revenue Code of 1986 are identical to those of Title 26. This table shows where sections of former Title 26, Internal Revenue Code of 1939, were incorporated in revised Title 26, Internal Revenue Code of 1986.]

Title 26 Former Sections	*Title 26 New Sections*
1	Omitted
2	7806(a)
3, 4	Omitted
11	1
12(a), (b)(1), (2)	Omitted
12(b)(3), (c)	1
12(d)	2
12(e)	Omitted
12(f)	1
12(g), 13(a)	Omitted
13(b)	11
13(c)–(f), 14	Omitted
15(a), (b)	11
15(c)	1551
21	63
22(a)	61
22(b)(1)	101
22(b)(2)(A)	72
22(b)(2)(B)	72, 403
22(b)(2)(C)	72
22(b)(3)–(5)	102–104
22(b)(6)	107
22(b)(7)	894
22(b)(8)	115, 526, 892, 893, 911, 912, 933, 943
22(b)(9), (10)	108
22(b)(11)–(14)	109, 111–113
22(b)(15)	621
22(b)(16), (17)	114, 121
22(c)	471
22(d)(1)–(5)	472
22(d)(6)	1321, 6155(a)
22(e)	301(a)
22(f)	1001
22(g)	861, 862, 863, 864
22(h)	Chapter 1, Subchapter G, Part III
22(i)	Omitted
22(j)	76
22(k)	71
22(*l*)	691
22(m)	73, 6201(c)
22(n)	62
22(*o*)	75
23	161, 211
23(a)(1)(A), (B)	162
23(a)(1)(C)	263
23(a)(2)	212
23(b)	163, 265
23(c)(1)	164
23(c)(2)	Omitted
23(c)(3), (d)	164
23(e)–(i)	165
23(j)	1091
23(k)(1)	166, 593
23(k)(2)	165(g)(1), 166(e), 582
23(k)(3)	165(g)(2)
23(k)(4), (5)	166
23(k)(6)	166, 271
23(*l*)	167
23(m)	611
23(n)	167
23(*o*)	170
23(p)	404
23(q)	170
23(r)	591
23(s)	172
23(t)	168, 169
23(u)	215
23(v)	171
23(w)	691
23(x)	213
23(y)	Omitted
23(z)	216
23(aa)(1)	141
23(aa)(2)	36
23(aa)(3)	144
23(aa)(4)	4, 142
23(aa)(5)–(7)	142–144
23(bb)	173
23(cc)	616
23(dd)	592
23(ee)	1202
23(ff)	615
24(a)	261
24(a)(1)	262
24(a)(2), (3)	263
24(a)(4), (5)	264, 265
24(a)(6)	264
24(a)(7)	266
24(b), (c)	267
24(d)	273
24(e)	1451
24(f)	268
25(a)	35
25(b)(1)	151
25(b)(2)	153
25(b)(3)	152
26	241
26(a)	242
26(b)(1)–(3)	243–245
26(b)	246
26(c)	545, 556
26(d)	535, 545, 601
26(e)	Omitted
26(f)	561, 562, 564
26(g)	565
26(h)	247
26(i)	922
27(a)	561
27(b)	535, 562
27(c)–(i)	562, 564
28	565
31	33
32	32
33	6401
34	Omitted
35	31
41	441, 446
42(a)	451
42(b)–(d)	454
43	461
44	453, 7101
45	482
46	442
47	443, 6011(a)
48	441, 7701
51	6001, 6011(a)
51(a)	6001, 6012(a), 6065(b)
51(b)	6012(b)(1), 6013(a), 6014(b)
51(c)	6012(b)
51(d)	Omitted. See 6064.
51(e)	6065(a)
51(f)	6014(a), (b), 6151(a), (b), 6155(a)
51(g)	6012(b), 6013(b), 6653(a), 6659
52	6012(a), (b), 6062
53	6072, 6081, 6091
54(a)–(b)	6001
54(c)–(e)	Omitted
54(f)	6033(a), 6065(b)
55	6103, 7213(a)
56(a)	6151(a)
56(b)	6152, 6601(c)(2)
56(c)	6161(a), 6162(a), 6165, 7101
56(d)–(f)	Omitted
56(g)	6313
56(h)	Omitted
56(i)	6151(b)
56(j), 57	Omitted
58	6012(b), 6015, 6064, 6065, 6073(a), (c), 6081(a), 6091(b), 6103, 6161(a)
59(a)–(c)	6153
59(d)	6201(b), 6315, 6601(g)
60	6015(g), 6073(b), (d), (e), 6091(b), 6153(b), (d), (e)
61	Omitted
62	7805
63	6108
64	7701
101(1)–(11), (13)–(19)	501
101(12)	521, 522
101	502
102(a)	531, 532
102(b), (c)	533
102(d), (e)	535, 541
102(f)	536
103	891
104(a)	581
104(b)	11
105	632
106	1347
107(a), (b)	1301, 1302
107(c)	1304(a)
107(d)	1303
107(e)	1304(b)
108	21
109	921
110	594
111	1001
112(a)	1002

Title 26 Former Sections	Title 26 New Sections
112(b)(1)	1031
112(b)(2)	1036
112(b)(3)	354, 355
112(b)(4)	361
112(b)(5)	351
112(b)(6)	332
112(b)(6)(D)	7101
112(b)(7)	333
112(b)(8)	1081
112(b)(9)	373
112(b)(10)	371
112(b)(11)	355
112(c)	351, 356, 371, 1031
112(d)	361, 371
112(e)	351, 356, 361, 371, 1031
112(f)	1033
112(g), (h)	368
112(i)	367
112(j)	Omitted
112(k)	357, 371
112(*l*)	371
112(m)	1071
112(n)	1034
113(a)	1012
113(a)(1)	1013
113(a)(2)–(4)	1015
113(a)(5)	1014
113(a)(6)	358, 1031
113(a)(7), (8)	362
113(a)(9)	1033
113(a)(10)	1091
113(a)(11), (12)	1051, 1052
113(a)(13)	723, 732
113(a)(14)	1053
113(a)(15)	334
113(a)(16)	1052
113(a)(17)	1082
113(a)(18)	334
113(a)(19)	307
113(a)(20), (21)	373
113(a)(22)	372
113(a)(23)	358
113(b)	1011
113(b)(1), (2)	1016
113(b)(3), (4)	1017, 1018
113(c), (d)	1019, 1020
113(e)	1022
114(a)	167(f)
114(b)(1)	612
114(b)(2)	Omitted
114(b)(3)	613(b)(3)
114(b)(4)	613(b)(4)
115(a)	301, 316
115(b)	301, 316
115(c)	302, 312, 331, 342
115(d), (e)	301
115(f)	305
115(g)(1)	302
115(g)(2)	304
115(g)(3)	303
115(h)	312
115(i)	302, 346
115(j)	301
115(k)	Omitted
115(*l*), (m)	312
116(a)	911
116(b)	Omitted
116(c)	892
116(d), (e)	115
116(f)	943
116(g)	526
116(h)	893
116(i)	121(a)(17)
116(j), (k)	912
116(*l*)	933
117(a)	1221, 1222
117(b)	1202
117(c)	1201
117(d)	1211
117(e)(1)	1212
117(e)(2)	Omitted
117(f)	1232
117(g)(1), (2)	1233, 1234
117(g)(3)	1238
117(h)	1223
117(i)	582
117(j)	1231
117(k)	631
117(*l*)	1233
117(m)	341
117(n)	1236
117(*o*), (p)	1239, 1240
118	1091
119(a), (b)	861
119(c), (d)	862
119(e)	861, 862, 863
119(f)	864
120	170
121	583
122	172
123	77
124	Omitted
124A, 124B	168, 169
125	171
126	691
127(a), (b)	Omitted
127(c)(1)–(5)	1331–1335
127(d)	1336
127(e), (f)	1337
128	1346
129, 130	269, 270
130A	421
131(a)	901
131(b)	904
131(c)	905, 6155(a), 7101
131(d), (e)	905
131(f)	902
131(g)	901(c)
131(h)	903
131(i)	905
141	1501–1505, 6071, 6081(a), 6091(b)(2), 6503(a)(2)
142	6012(a), (b), 6065(a)
143(a)	1451
143(b)	1441
143(c)	1461, 6011(a), 6072(a), 6091(b), 6151(a)
143(d), (e)	1462, 1463
143(f)	1464, 6414
143(g)	1461
143(h)	1443, 6151
144	1442, 6151(a)
145	7201, 7202, 7203, 7343
146	443, 6155(a), 6601(a), 6658, 6851, 7101
147	6041(b), (c), 6071, 6081(a), 6091(a)
148	6042, 6043, 6044, 6065(a), 6071, 6081(a), 6091(a)
149	6045, 6065(a), 6071, 6081(a), 6091(a)
150	6071, 6081(a), 6091(a), 7001(a), 7231
151	Omitted
153(a)	6033(b), 6071, 6081(a), 6091(a)
153(b)	6034, 6071, 6081(b), 6091(a)
153(c)	6104
153(d)	7201, 7203
154	692
161	641
162(a)	642(c)
162(b)	651, 652, 661, 662
162(c)	661
162(d)	643, 663
162(e), (f)	642
162(g)	681
163(a)(1), (2), (b)	642
163(c)	642(a)(1)
164	652, 662
165(a)	401, 501(a)
165(b)–(d)	402
166, 167	676, 677
168	642
169(a)–(c)	584, 6065
169(d)(1)–(4), (e)	584
169(f)	6032, 6065(a)
169(g)	584
170	584, 642
171	682
172	642
181, 182	701, 702
183(a), (b)	702, 703
183(c)	702
183(d)	703(a)
184, 186	702
187	6031, 6063, 6065(a)
188	706
189	702, 703
190	Omitted
191	704
201(a)(1)	802
201(a)(2), (3)	807
201(b)	801
201(c)(1)–(7)	803(a)–(g)
201(d)–(f)	803(h)–(j)
201(g), 202(a)	Omitted
202(b)	804(a)
202(c)	806
203	Omitted
203A	805
204(a)(1)	831(a)
204(a)(2)	831(b), 832
204(a)(3)	831(b)
204(b)(1)	832(b)(1)
204(b)(2)	832(a)
204(b)(3)–(7)	832(b)(2)–(6)
204(c)–(e)	832(c)–(e)
204(f)	832(c)(12)
205, 206	841, 842
207(a)(1), (2)	821(a)
207(a)(3), (4)	821(b), (c)
207(a)(5)	822(e)
207(a)(6)	821(d)
207(b)(1)	822(a), (b)
207(b)(2), (3)	823(1), (2)
207(b)(4)	822(a)
207(b)(4)(A)–(F)	822(c)
207(c), (d)	822(d)(1), (2)
207(e)	822(e)

Title 26 Former Sections	Title 26 New Sections
207(f)	822(d)(3)
207(g), 208	Omitted
211, 212	871, 872
213(a)–(c)	873
213(d)	142(b)(1)
214	873
215	874, 6011(a), 6065(b)
216	874
217	6011(a), 6012(a), 6072(c)
218(a)	6151(a)
219	875
220	876
221	877
231(a)	881
231(b), (c)	882(a), (b)
231(d)	883
232(a), (b)	882
233	882, 6065(a)
234	882
235(a)	882, 6011(a), 6072(c)
235(b)	6012(a)
236(a)	6151(a)
236(b)	884(1)
237	884(3)
238	884(4)
251	931, 6011(a)
252	932
261	11
262	941
263	942
265	943
271	6211, 6653(c)(1)
272(a)	6212(a), (b)(2), 6213(a)
272(b)	6155(a), 6215(a)
272(c)	6155(a), 6213(c)
272(d)	6213(d)
272(e)	6214(a)
272(f)	6212(c), 6213(b)(1)
272(g), (h)	6214(b), (c)
272(i)	6152(c), 6601(c)(2)
272(j)	6161(b), 6165, 7101
272(k)	6212(b)
273(a)–(i), (k)	6155, 6861, 6863(a), (b), 7101
273(j)	6404(b)
274	6036, 6155(a), 6161(c), 6503(b), 6871, 6872, 6873
275	6501
276	6501(c), 6502(a)
277	6503(a)
291	6651(a), 6659
292	6155(a), 6601
293	6653(a), (b), 6659
294	6601, 6651(c), 6654(a)
295–298	6601
299	6658
311, 312	6901, 6903
313	Omitted
321	6403
322(a)(1)–(3)	6401, 6402
322(a)(4)	31
322(b)(1)–(3)	6511
322(b)(4)	6151(c), 6513(a), 6611(d)
322(b)(5), (6)	6511(d)
322(c)	6512(a)
322(d)	6512(b)
322(e)	6151(c), 6513(b), 6611(d)
322(f)	Omitted
322(g)	6511(d)
331–334	552–555
335, 336(a)–(c)	556
336(d)	557
337	551
338	6035(a)
339	6035(b)
340	7201, 7203
361	851
362	852, 855
371–373	1081–1083
391–393, 394(a)–(c)	Omitted
394(d)	312
394(e), (f), 395, 396	Omitted
400	3
401, 402	4
403	36
404	4
421(a), (b)	501, 511
421(c), (d)	512
422(a)	512
422(b), 423, 424	513, 514, 515
480, 481	1401, 1402
482	1403, 6017
500–503	541–544
504(a), (b)	545
504(c)	562, 563
504(d)	Omitted
504(e)	545
505(a)–(c)	545
505(d)	Omitted
505(e)	546
506(a)–(h)	547
506(i), (j), 507(a)	Omitted
507(b)	543
508	Omitted
509	531
510	Chapter 1, Subchapter G, Part III
511	6103, 7213(a)
650, 651	1471
722(g)	6105
800	2001, 2101
801, 802	Omitted
810	2001(a), 2011(a), (b)
811	2031(a)
811(a), (b)	2033, 2034
811(c)	2035, 2036, 2037
811(d)(1)	2038(a)(1)
811(d)(2)	2038(a)(2)
811(d)(3)	2038(b)
811(d)(4)	Omitted
811(e)–(g)	2040–2042
811(h)	2044
811(i)	2043(a)
811(j)	2032
811(k), (*l*)	2031(b), 2035
811(m)	Omitted
812	2051
812(a)	Omitted
812(b)	2043(b), 2053, 2054
812(c)	2013
812(d), (e)	Omitted. See 2055, 2056.
813(a)(1)	Omitted
813(a)(2)	2012
813(b)	2011
813(c)	2014
820	6036, 6091(a)
821(a)	6018, 6065(a)
821(b)	6071, 6075(a), 6081(a)
821(c)	6091(b)
821(d)	6001
821(e)	Omitted
822(a)(1)	6151(a)
822(a)(2)	6161(a)(2), 6165, 6503(d), 7101
822(b)	2002
823	6314(b)
824	Omitted
825	2204
826(a)	7404
826(b)–(d)	2205–2207
827(a)	6324(a)(1), 6325(a)(1)
827(b), (c)	6324(a)(2), (3)
828, 840, 841	Omitted
850	2202
851	Omitted
860	2101
861	2102, 2103, 2106
862, 863	2104, 2105
864(a)	6018, 6065(a)
864(b)	6071, 6075(a), 6081(a)
864(c)	6091(b)
865	Omitted
870	6211(a), 6653(c)(1)
871(a)	6212(a), 6213(a)
871(b)	6155(a), 6215(a)
871(c)	6155(a), 6213(c)
871(d), (e)	6213(d), 6214(a)
871(f)	6212(c), 6213(b)
871(g)	6214(c)
871(h)	6161(b)(2), 6165, 6503(d), 7101
871(i)	6155(a), 6653(b), 6659(a)
872(a)	6155(a), 6861(a)
872(b)–(e)	6861(b)–(e)
872(f)	6863(a), (b)(2), 7101
872(g)	6155(a), 6863(b)(1)
872(h)	6863(a), (b)(2)
872(i)	6155(a), 6861(f)
872(j)	6861(g)
873	6404(b)
874(a)	6501(a)
874(b)(1)	6501(c)(1), (3)
874(b)(2)	6502(a)
874(b)(3)	2016, 6071, 6081, 6091, 6155
875	6503(a)(1)
876	Omitted
890	6601(a), (b), (f)(1)
891	6155(a), 6601(a), (d), (f)(1)
892	6601(a), (c)(3)
893	6601(a), (c), (f)
894(a)	6651(a), 6653(a)
894(b)	7201, 7202, 7203, 7207, 7269, 7343
900(a)	6901(a), (b)
900(b), (c)	6901(c), (f)
900(d)	6904, 7421(b)
900(e)	6901(h)
901(a), (b)	6903(a)
901(c)	6903(b)
901(d)	6212(b)
910, 911, 912	6511, 6512(a), (b)
913, 920, 921	Omitted
925	6163(a), 6601(a), (b)
926	6163(a), 7101
927	2015
930(a)	2203
930(b)–(d), 931	Omitted
935	2001, 2052, 2101
936(a)	Omitted
936(b), (c)	2012, 2014

Title 26 Former Sections	Title 26 New Sections
937	6018(a), 7203
938	6103
939	2201
1000(a)	2501
1000(b)	2511(a)
1000(c)	2514
1000(d), (e)	Omitted
1000(f)	2513
1000(g)	Omitted
1001(a), (b)	2502(a), (c)
1001(c)	Omitted
1002	2512(b)
1003	2503
1004(a)(1)–(3)	2521–2523
1004(b), (c)	2522, 2524
1005	2512(a)
1006(a)	6019(a), 6065(a)
1006(b)	6075(b), 6091(b)(1)
1007	6001
1008(a)	2502(d), 6151(a)
1008(b)	6161(a)(1)
1008(c)	Omitted
1008(d)	6313
1008(e)	6314(a)
1009	6324(b), 6325(a)(1)
1010	Omitted
1011	6211(a), 6653(c)(1)
1012(a)	6212(a), 6213(a)
1012(b)	6155(a), 6215(a)
1012(c)	6155(a), 6213(c)
1012(d)	6213(d)
1012(e)	6214(a)
1012(f)	6212(c), 6213(b)
1012(g), (h)	6214(b), (c)
1012(i)	6161(b)(1), 6165, 7101
1012(j)	6212(b)
1013(a)	6155(a), 6861(a)
1013(b)–(e)	6861(b)–(e)
1013(f)	6863(a), (b)(2), 7101
1013(g)	6155(a), 6863(b)(1)
1013(h)	6863(a), (b)(2)
1013(i)	6155(a), 6861(f)
1013(j)	6861(g)
1014	6404(b)
1015(a)	6871
1015(b)	6155(a), 6161(c), 6503(b), 6873(a)
1016	6501, 6502(a)
1017	6503(a)(1)
1018	Omitted
1019	6653, 6659(b)
1020	6601(a), (f)(1)
1021	6155(a), 6601(a), (d), (f)(1)
1022	6601(a), (c)(3)
1023	6601(a), (c)(1), (f)(1)
1024(a)	7201, 7203
1024(b)	7201
1025(a)	6901(a), (b)
1025(b)–(d)	6901(c), (e), (f)
1025(e)	6904, 7421(b)
1025(f)	6901(h)
1025(g)	6901(g)
1026(a)	6903(a)
1026(b)	6903
1026(c)	6903(b)
1027(a)	6402(a)
1027(b)	6511(a), (b)
1027(c), (d)	6512(a), (b)
1028	Omitted
1029	7805(a)
1030(a)	2502(b)
1030(b)	2511(b)
1031	6103
1100, 1101	7441, 7442
1102(a)–(g)	7443(a)–(g)
1103(a)–(d)	7444(a)–(d)
1104–1106	7445–7447
1110, 111	7451, 7453
1112, 1113	7454(a), 7455
1114(a), (b)	7456(a), (c)
1115(a), (b)	7457(a), (b)
1116	7458
1117(a)–(f)	7459(a)–(f)
1117(g)	6155(a), 6659, 6673
1117(h)	Omitted
1118	7460
1119, 1120, 1121	6902, 7461, 7462
1130–1133	7471–7474
1140–1143	7481–7484
1144	Omitted
1145	7101, 7485(a)
1146	7486
1250–1252	1491–1493
1253	1494, 6071, 6081(a), 6091(a), 6151(a)
1400	3101
1401(a), (b)	3102(a), (b)
1401(c)	6205(a), 6413(a)(1)
1401(d)(1), (2)	Omitted
1401(d)(3), (4)	6413(c)(1), (2)
1402	3502
1403	6051(a)
1410	3111
1411	6205(a), 6413(a)
1412	3112
1420(a)	3501
1420(b)	6601(a), (f)(1)
1420(c)	6011(a), 6071, 6081(a), 6091(a), 6302(b)
1420(d)	6313
1420(e)	3122
1421	6205(b), 6413(b)
1422	3503
1423(a)	6802(1)
1423(b), (c)	6803(a)(1), (2)
1424	7509
1425(a)	7209
1425(b)	7208(1)
1426(a)–(e)	3121(a)–(e)
1426(f)	7701(a)(1)
1426(g)–(*l*)	3121(f)–(k)
1427, 1428	3123, 3124
1429	7805(a), (c)
1430, 1431	Omitted
1432	3125
1500	3201
1501(a), (b)	3202(a), (b)
1501(c)	6205(a)(1), 6413(a)(1)
1502	6205(b), 6413(b)
1503	3502(a)
1510, 1511, 1512	3211, 3212, 3502
1520	3221
1521	6205(a)(1), 6413(a)(1)
1522	6205(b), 6413(b)
1530(a)	3501
1530(b)	6011(a), 6071, 6081(a), 6091(a), 6151(a)
1530(c)	6601(a), (f)(1)
1530(d)	6313
1531	3503
1532(a)–(e)	3231(a)–(e)
1532(f)	7701(a)(9)
1532(g), (h)	3231(f), (g)
1532(i)	7701(a)(1)
1534	3232
1535	7805(a), (c)
1536, 1537	Omitted
1538	3233
1600	3301
1601(a)–(c)	3302
1601(d)	6413(d)
1602	3303
1603	3304
1604(a)	6011(a), 6065, 6071, 6091(b)(1), (2)
1604(b)	6081(a)
1604(c)	6106
1605(a)	3501
1605(b)	6601(a), (f)(1)
1605(c)	6152(a)(3), (b), 6155(a), 6601(c)(2)
1605(d)	6161(a)(1)
1605(e)	6313
1606	3305
1607(a)–(j)	3306(a)–(j)
1607(k)	7701(a)(1)
1607(*l*)–(*o*)	3306(k)–(n)
1608	3307
1609	7805(a), (c)
1610	Omitted
1611	3308
1621	3401
1622(a), (b)	3402(a), (b)
1622(c)(1)(A)	Omitted
1622(c)(1)(B), (2)–(5)	3402(c)
1622(d)	3402(d)
1622(e)	3502(b)
1622(f)(1)	6414
1622(f)(2)	6401, 6402
1622(g)–(k)	3402(e)–(i)
1623	3403
1624	3404, 6011(a)
1625(c)	6081(a)
1626(a)	7204
1626(b)	6674
1626(d)	7205
1627	Omitted
1631	6651(a)
1632	3504
1633(a), (b)	6051(a)–(d)
1633(c)	6081(a)
1634(a)	7204
1634(b)	6659, 6674
1635(a)	6501(a)
1635(b)	6501(c)(1), (3)
1635(c)	6501(c)(2)
1635(d)	6502(a)
1635(e)	6501(b)(2)
1635(f), (g)	Omitted
1636(a)(1)	6511(a), (b)(1)
1636(a)(2)	6511(b)(2)
1636(b)	Omitted
1636(c)	6513(c)
1636(d), (e)	Omitted
1650	4001, 4011, 4021, 4471
1651	4031
1652–1655	Omitted
1656(a), (b), (c)	5063(a), (b), (c)
1657–1659	Omitted
1700	4231, 4232, 6011(a)

Title 26 Former Sections	Title 26 New Sections
1701	4233
1702, 1703	4234
1704	4232
1710	4241
1711	4243
1712	4242
1715(a)	4291
1715(b), (c)	6151(a)
1715(d)	6415(b), (c), (d), 6416(a)
1716(a)	6011(a), 6065(a)
1716(b)	6071, 6081(a)
1716(c)	6091(b)(1), (2)
1717	6601(a), (f)(1)
1718(a)	7201, 7203
1718(b)	7201, 7202
1718(c)	6659, 6671(a), 6672
1718(d)	6671(b), 7343
1719	6302(b)
1720	6001
1721–1723	Omitted
1800	4301, 4311, 4321
1801	4311, 4312, 4314, 4315, 4381
1802	4301, 4302, 4304, 4321, 4322, 4323, 4341, 4342, 4343, 4344, 4351, 4352, 4353, 4381
1804	4371, 4372, 4373
1805	4891, 4892, 4894, 4895, 4896, 7701(a)(1)
1807	4451
1808	4303, 4373, 4382
1809	4383, 4454, 4893, 6201(a)(2), 6801(a), (b)
1815	6804
1816	Omitted
1817(a)–(c)	6802(1)–(3)
1818(a)	6803(b)(1), 7101
1818(b)	6803(b)(2)
1819	Omitted
1820	7271(2), (3)
1821(a)(1)	7201, 7203
1821(a)(2)	7201, 7202
1821(a)(3)	6653(e), 6659, 6671(a), 6672
1821(a)(4)	6671(b), 7343
1821(b)(3)	4374, 7270
1821(b)(4)	7201
1822	7208(3), 7271(1)
1823	7303(1)
1823(a)–(c)	7208(2)–(4)
1830	4453
1831	4452, 4455, 7272
1832	4456
1835	6001
1836–1838	Omitted
1850	4286
1851	4291
1852(a)	6011(a), 6065(a), 6071
1852(b)	6091(b)(1), (2)
1853(a), (b)	6151(a)
1853(c)	6601(a), (f)(1)
1854	6415(a), (b), (d)
1855, 1856	Omitted
1857	4287
1858, 1859	Omitted
1900, 1901, 1902	4881, 4883, 4884
1902(a)(1)	6011(a), 6065(a), 6071
1902(a)(2)	6091(b)(1), (2)
1902(a)(3), (b)	6151(a)
1903	4885
1904	Omitted
1905, 1906	4882, 4883
1907	Omitted
1920(a), (b)	4851(a), (b)
1920(c)	4871, 6804
1921	4861
1922	4863
1923	4864
1924	4865
1925	4853, 7492
1926	4854
1927	4862
1928	4872, 6001
1929(a)	7233(1), (2)
1929(b)	7263(b)
1929(c)	7263(a)
1930	4874, 7493
1931	4852, 7701(a)(1)
1932	4873
1933	4876
1934	Omitted
1935	4875
2000(a), (b)	5701(a)
2000(c)(1), (2)	5701(b), (c)
2000(d)	5701(d), (e)
2000(g)(1)–(3)	5707(a)–(c)
2001(a)	5703(a)
2002(b)	5703(d)
2002(c)	5703(a)
2010	5702(b)
2012	5712
2013	5711(a), (b)
2014	5713(a), (b)
2017	5721
2018	5741
2019	5722
2030	5702(e)
2032	5712
2033	5711(a), (b)
2036	5721
2037	5741
2038	5722
2039(a)	5711(a), (b)
2039(b)	5722, 5741
2040	5704(c)
2050	5702(b)(1)
2052	5712
2053	5711(a), (b)
2054	5713(a), (b)
2055	Omitted
2056	5741
2057	Omitted
2058	5732
2059, 2060	5731
2070–2075	Omitted
2100(a), (b)	5723(a)
2100(c)(1)	5723(d)
2100(c)(2)	5723(a)
2100(d)	5723(b), (c)
2100(e)	5723(a)
2101	5704(c)
2102	5723(a)
2103(a)(1)	5723(a)
2103(e)	5752
2104(a)	5751(a)
2110(a), (b)	5702(c), (d)
2111(a)(1), (2)	5723(a)
2111(a)(3)	5723(d)
2111(b)	5723(a)
2111(c)	5723(b), (c)
2111(d), (e)(1)	5723(a)
2111(e)(2)	5723(d)
2111(f)	5704(a), 5723(d)
2112(a)(1)	5723(a)
2112(e)	5752
2113	5751(a)
2130(a), (b)	5723(a), 5762(a)(4), (6)
2130(c)	5723(a), 5762
2130(d)	5704(d)
2135(a)(1), (2)	5704(b), (c)
2135(a)(3)	5704(b)
2136(a)	5706
2137	5705(a)
2150	Omitted
2151	5762(a)(5)
2152–2154	Omitted
2155(a)	5762(a)(4), (5)
2155(b)	5763(a)
2156(a)	5762(a)(2), (3)
2156(b)	5762(a)(3)
2156(c)	5761(b)
2160(a)	5762(a)(4)
2160(b)–(d)	5762(a)(5)
2160(e)	5762(a)(6)
2160(g)(1), (2)	5762(a)(8), (9)
2160(g)(3)	5762(a)(6)
2160(h)	5763(a)
2160(i)	5762(a)(9), (10)
2161(a)	5762(a)(1)
2161(b)	5763(c)
2161(c)	5762(a)(1)
2161(e)–(g)	5762(a)(2)
2161(h)	5763(b)
2161(i)(1)	5763(b)
2161(j)(1)	5763(b)
2161(*l*)(1)	5763(b)
2161(m)(1)	5761(a)
2161(m)(2)	5763(b)
2162(a)(2)	5762(a)(1)
2162(a)(3)–(5)	5762(a)(2)
2162(b)(1)	5762(a)(4), (5)
2163	Omitted
2170(a)(2)	5751(a), 5762(a)(5)
2170(a)(4)	5762(a)(6)
2170(b)	5762(a)(5), 5763(a)
2171(a)	5763(a)
2171(b)(1)	5762(a)(4)
2171(b)(2)	5762(a)(4), (5)
2172(a)	5762(a)(8)
2172(b)	5762(a)(6)
2172(c)	5762(a)(9)
2172(d)	5762(a)(6)
2172(e), (f)	5762(a)(9)
2173(a), 2174	5762(a)(5)
2175	5763(a)
2176(a)(2)	5762(a)(10)
2176(a)(3)	5762(a)(8)
2180(a)	5762(a)(1)
2180(b)	5763(c)
2180(d)–(f)	5762(a)(2)
2180(g)(1)	5763(b)
2180(h)	5763(b)
2180(i)(1)	5763(b)
2180(k)(1)	5763(b)
2180(*l*)(1)	5761(a)
2180(*l*)(2)	5763(b)
2181	Omitted
2190	5753

Title 26 Former Sections	Title 26 New Sections
2191–2193	Omitted
2194	5703(a), 5722, 5741
2197(b)	5704(b)
2198	5705(a)
2300	4592, 4593
2302	4594, 4596, 6001, 7101, 7641
2303	4595, 4597, 6001
2304	4595
2305	4813
2306	4591, 4812
2307	4593, 4816
2308(a)	7234(a)
2308(b)	7265(a)(1)
2308(c)	7234(b)
2308(d)	7234(d)(4)
2308(e)	7265(b)
2308(f)	Omitted
2308(g)	7234(d)(2)
2308(h), (i)	7234(c), (d)
2308(j)	7265(c)
2309	7303(2), (3), (5)
2310	Omitted
2311	4591, 4818
2312–2314	Omitted
2320	4826
2321	4811, 4813
2322	4814, 4826, 6001, 7101, 7641
2323	4815, 4826
2324	4815, 6001
2325	4817
2326(a)	7235(a), 7265(a)
2326(b), (c)	7235(b), (c)
2327	4812, 4813, 4816, 4818, 7235(e), 7265(b), (c)
2350	4846
2351	4831, 4832, 6201(a)(2)(A)
2352	4833, 4846, 6001, 7101, 7641
2353, 2354	4834, 4846
2355	4832
2356	4831, 4832
2357	7236, 7266(b)–(f)
2358	7303(2), (4), (5)
2359	Omitted
2360	4835
2361	4832
2362	Omitted
2400	4001, 4003
2401	4011, 4012
2402	4021, 4022
2403(a)	6011(a), 6065(a), 6071, 6081(a), 6091(b)(1), (2)
2403(b)	6151(a), 6601(a), (f)(1)
2403(c)	4051
2404, 2405	4052, 4053
2406	4055, 4056
2407	6416(a), (b)
2408	Omitted
2409	7261
2410, 2411	Omitted
2412	4002, 4003, 4012, 4013
2413	4054
2450	4041
2451(a)	6011(a), 6071, 6081(a), 6091(b)(1), (2), 6151(a)
2451(b)	6151(a), 6601(a), (f)(1)
2452(a)	6416(b)(2)(D)
2452(b)	6416(a)
2453	4055, 6416(b)(2)(A)
2454, 2455	Omitted
2456	4222
2470	4511, 4513
2471	6011(a), 6065(a), 6071, 6081(a), 6091(b)(1), (2)
2472	6151(a)
2473	6417(a)
2474	4513, 6417(b), 7101
2475	6601(a), (f)(1)
2477	4512
2478, 2479	Omitted
2480	7809(a)
2481, 2482	Omitted
2483	7654
2490	4561, 4571, 4581
2491	4561, 4562, 4571, 4572, 4581, 4582
2492	4582, 4602
2493	4601
2494	Omitted
2550	4701, 4771
2550(c)	6302(b)
2551	4702
2552	4703, 4771
2553	4704, 4723
2554	4705
2555	4732, 6001
2555(a)	6065(a)
2555(b)	6071
2555(c)	6065(a), 6071
2555(c)(1)	6081(a), 6091(a)
2556	4773
2557(a)	7237(b)
2557(b)(1)	7237(a)
2557(b)(2)	7201, 7203
2557(b)(3)	7201, 7202
2557(b)(4)	6671(a), 6672
2557(b)(8)	6671(b), 7343
2558	4706, 4733, 7301(a)
2559, 2560	Omitted
2561	4734
2562	4736
2563	4774
2564	4735
2565	Omitted
2567	4711, 4712
2568, 2569	4712, 4713
2569(b)	7101
2569(d)	6001
2569(d)(4)	7641
2570	7238
2571	4714, 7301(a)
2590	4741, 4771
2591	4742
2592	4743, 4771
2593	4744
2594(a)	6001
2595	4773
2596	7237(a)
2597	7491
2598	4745, 7301(a)
2599, 2600	Omitted
2601	4756
2602	4774
2603	4762
2604, 2606	Omitted
2650	4802
2651	4801, 4803
2651(c)(2)	6201(a)(2)(A)
2652(a)	6801(a)
2653	4804
2653(b)	6001, 7641
2653(d)	7101
2654, 2655	4805
2656	7274
2656(a)	7206(4)
2656(b)	7239(a)
2656(c)	7271(1), 7303(6)(B)
2656(d)	7239(b)
2656(f)	7201
2656(g)	7272
2656(h)	7267(d)
2656(i)	7267(c)
2656(j), (k)	7267(a), (b)
2657(a), (b)	7303(6)(B)
2657(c)	7303(6)(A)
2657(d)	7328
2657(e)	7301(c)
2657(f)	7303(6)(B)
2658	Omitted
2659	4803
2660	Omitted
2700	4181, 4182, 4224, 5831
2701	6011(a), 6065(a), 6071, 6081(a), 6091(b)(1), (2)
2702	6151(a)
2703(a)	6416(f)
2704	4216
2705	4225, 6416(e)
2706	6601(a), (f)(1)
2707(a)	6671(a), 6672
2707(b)	7201, 7203
2707(c)	7201, 7202
2707(d)	6671(b), 7343
2708	6302(b)
2709	6001
2710–2712	Omitted
2720–2723	5811–5814
2724	5842, 6001(a)
2725	5843
2726(a)–(c)	5851–5853
2727, 2728	5844, 5845
2729	5861
2730(a), (b)	5862(a), (b)
2731–2733	5846–5848
2733(a)	7701(a)(1)
2734	5821
2734(e)	6071, 6091(a)
2800(a)	5001(a)(9) (Rev. See 5001(a)(8))
2800(a)(1)	5001(a)(1), 5005(a), 5006(a)
2800(a)(1)(A)	5026(a)(1), 5007(a)
2800(a)(1)(B)	5689
2800(a)(2)	5001(a)(2)
2800(a)(3)	5001(a)(3), 5007(b)(2)
2800(a)(4)	5001(a)(4) (Rev. See 5001(a)(10)), 5007(c) (Rev. See 7652, 7805)
2800(a)(5)	5021(a), 5025(b)
2800(a)(6)	5001(a)(5) (Rev. See 5001(a)(4))
2800(b)(2)	5006(c)
2800(c)	5001(b)
2800(d)	5005(b)
2800(e)(1)	5004(a)(1)
2800(e)(2)	5004(a)(2) (Rev. See 5004(b)(2))
2800(e)(3)	5004(a)(3) (Rev. See 5004(b)(3))
2800(e)(4)	5004(a)(4) (Rev. See 5004(b)(4))
2800(f)	5006(d), 5007(b)(1)
2801(b)	5021(b) (Rev. Omitted)
2801(c)(1)	5391
2801(c)(2)	5025(e) (Rev. See 5025(f))

Title 26 Former Sections	*Title 26 New Sections*
2801(d)	5281 (Rev. See 5201(a))
2801(e)	5025
2801(e)(1)	5272(a) (Rev. See 5173(a), (d)), 5281(a) (Rev. See 5201(a))
2801(e)(2)	5273(a) (Rev. See 5178(a)), 5627 (Rev. See 5687))
2801(e)(3)	5386(b), 5391
2801(e)(4)	5386(a)
2801(e)(5)	5023 (Rev. See 5687)
2801(f)	5628 (Rev. See 5601(a)(10), 5687)
2802(a)	5009(a) (Rev. See 5205(c)(1), (f), 5206(c)), 5010(a) (Rev. See 5205(e))
2802(b)	5010(b) (Rev. See 5205(f))
2802(c)	5027(a) (Rev. See 5061, 5205)
2803(a)	5008(b)(1)(E) (Rev. See 5205(c)(2))
2803(b)	5008(b)(3) (Rev. See 5205(g))
2803(c)	5008(b)(4)
2803(d)	5008(b)(2) (Rev. See 5205(g))
2803(e)	5008(b)(5)
2803(f)	5640 (Rev. See 5613(b))
2803(g)	5642 (Rev. See 5604(a)(1), (4)–(6), (10), (12)–(15), (b))
2804	5211 (Rev. See 5311)
2805(a)	5688(a)
2805(b)	5688(b)
2806(a)(1), (2)	5634 (Rev. See 5601(a)(13), 5615(7))
2806(b)(1)	5645 (Rev. See 7214)
2806(c)	5625 (Rev. See 5612(a))
2806(d)	5639 (Rev. See 5613(a))
2806(e)	5646 (Rev. See Subtitle F)
2806(f)	5626 (Rev. See 5602, 5615(3))
2806(g)	5687 (See 7301, 7302)
2807	5622 (Rev. See 5610)
2808(a)	5212(a) (Rev. See 5204(b))
2809(a)	5002(a) (Rev. See 5002(a)(5))
2809(b)(1)	5002(b)(1) (Rev. See 5002(a)(6)(A))
2809(b)(2)	5002(b)(2) (Rev. See 5002(a)(6)(B))
2809(c)	5002(c) (Rev. See 5002(a)(7))
2809(d)	5002(d) (Rev. See 5002(a)(8))
2810(a)	5174(a) (Rev. See 5179(a), 5505(d)), 5601 (Rev. See 5505(i), 5601(a)(1), 5615(1))
2811	5213(a), 5609
2812(a)	5175(a) (Rev. See 5171(a), 5172), 5271 (Rev. See 5171(a), (c), 5172, 5178(a)(1)(A), (4)(B)–(D)), 5603 (Rev. See 5601(a)(2), (3))
2813(a)	5282 (Rev. See 5201(a), 5202(a), 5204(a), (c), 5205(d), 5206(c), 5251)
2814(a)(1)	5176(a), (c) (Rev. See 5173(a), (b), 5176(a)), 5177(c) (Rev. See 5173(b)(1), 5551(c)), 5604 (Rev. See 5601(a)(4), (5), 5615(3))
2814(a)(2)	5176(d) (Rev. See 5173(b))
2815(a)	5177(a), 5605 (Rev. See 7214)
2815(b)(1)(A)	5177(b)(1) (Rev. See 5173(b)(1)(A))
2815(b)(1)(B)	5177(b)(2) (Rev. See 5173(b)(1)(B))
2815(b)(1)(C)	5177(b)(3) (Rev. See 5173(b)(1)(C))
2815(b)(1)(D)	5177(b)(4) (Rev. See 5173(b)(3))
2815(c)–(e)	5551(a), (b)(1), (c)
2816(a)	5178 (Rev. See 5171(a), 5172)
2817(a)	5179(a) (Rev. Omitted)
2817(b)	5179(b) (Rev. Omitted)
2818(a)	5105(a)
2818(b)	5602 (Rev. See 5615(2), 5687)
2819	5171 (Rev. See 5178(a)(1)(B), (b), (c)(2), 5505(b), 5601(a)(6)), 5607 (Rev. See 5505(i), 5601(a)(6))
2820(a)	5173(b) (Rev. See 5178(a)(2)(B), 5202(b)), 5192(b) (Rev. See 5202(b)), 5193(a) (Rev. See 5201(a), 5202(f), 5204(a), 5205(b), 5206(a), (c), 5211)
2821	5682
2822(a)	5173(a) (Rev. See 5178(a)(1)(A), (2)(C)), 5618 (Rev. See 5687)
2823(a)	5173(c) (Rev. See 5173(a)(2)(C))
2824	Omitted
2825	5215 (Rev. See 5201(c), 5312(a), (c), 5373(a), 5562)
2826(a)	5196(a) (Rev. See 5203(a)), 5617 (Rev. See 5687)
2827(a)	5196(b) (Rev. See 5203(b)), 5616 (Rev. See 5687)
2828(a)	5196(c) (Rev. See 5203(c)), 5283 (Rev. See 5203(c), (d)), 5615 (Rev. See 5203(c), (e), 5687)
2829(a)	5552 (See 5503, 5505(e))
2830(a)	5196(d) (Rev. See 5203(d)), 5283 (Rev. See 5203(c), (d))
2831	5116(a) (Rev. See 5115), 5180(a), 5274(a) (Rev. See 5180), 5681
2832	5172 (Rev. See 5171(a), 5172, 5173(a), 5178(a)(1)(A), 5601(a)(2), (4))
2833(a)	5606 (Rev. See 5601(a)(4), 5602, 5615(3))
2834	5216(a) (Rev. See 5222(a)(1), (2)(D), 5501, 5502(a), 5503, 5504(a), (b), 5505(a), (c), 5601(a)(7), (8), (9)(A)), 5608(a), (b) (Rev. See 5601(a)(7), (8), (9)(A), (12), 5615(4))
2835	Omitted
2836	5195(a) (Rev. See 5201(c)), 5613 (Rev. See 5687)
2837	Omitted
2838	5192(c) (Rev. See 5202(a), (b)), 5612 (Rev. See 5687)
2839(a)	5196(e) (Rev. See 5203(b), (c)), 5619 (Rev. See 5687)
2840	Omitted
2841(a)	5197(a)(1)(A) (Rev. See 5207(a), (d))
2841(b)	5197(a)(1)(B) (Rev. See 5207(a), (d))
2841(c)	5620 (Rev. See 5603, 5615(5))
2842	5611 (Rev. See 5603)
2843	5610 (Rev. See 5603)
2844(a)	5197(b) (Rev. See 5207(c))
2845	Omitted
2846(a)	5007(e)(1) (Rev. See 5004(b)(1), 5006(a)(3))
2847(a)	5007(e)(2) (Rev. Omitted)
2848	Omitted
2849	5191(a) (Rev. See 5221(a))
2850(a)	5191(a) (Rev. See 5221(a)), 5650 (Rev. See 5601(a)(14), 5615(3))
2851	5682
2852	5624 (Rev. See 5611)
2853(a)	5623 (Rev. See 5609)
2854	5649 (Rev. See 5614)
2855(a)	5285(a) (Rev. See 5207(b))
2856	5629 (Rev. See 5610(a)(10), (11))
2857(a)	5114(a) (Rev. See 5114(a)(1), 5146(a)), 5285(b) (Rev. See 5207(c)), 5621 (Rev. See 5603)
2858	5114(b)
2859	5197(a)(2) (Rev. See 5207(a)), 5621 (Rev. See 5603)
2860	Omitted
2861(a)	5282(b) (Rev. See 5202(a), 5204(a), (c), 5205(d), 5206(c))
2862(a)	5282(c) (Rev. See 5205(d))
2863(a)	5115(a) (Rev. See 5205(d))
2865(a)	5630 (Rev. See 5687)
2866	5010(c) (Rev. See 5205(g)), 5636 (Rev. See 5604(a)(2), (3), (7)–(9), (17), 7301)
2867	5635 (Rev. See 5604(a)(17))
2868	5637 (Rev. See 5604(a)(18))
2869	5638 (Rev. See 5604(a)(19), 5613, 7301, 7302)
2870	5195(b) (Rev. See 5201(c)), 5614 (Rev. See 5687, 7301)
2871	5214(a) (Rev. See 5301(a)), 5641 (Rev. See 5606, 5613, 7301, 7302, 7321–7323)
2872	5231 (Rev. See 5171(a), 5172, 5173(a), 5178(a)(1)(A), (B), (3)(A), (B)), 5241(b) (Rev. See 5202(a), (c), (d))
2873	5231 (Rev. See 5171(a), 5172, 5173(a), 5178(a)(1)(A), (B), (3)(A), (B)), 5241(a) (Rev. See 5201(a), 5202(a), (c))
2874(a)	5252 (Rev. See 5236)
2875	5231 (Rev. See 5171(a), 5172, 5173(a), 5178(a)(1)(A), (B), (3)(A), (B)), 5246(a) (Rev. See 5212)
2876	5631 (Rev. See 5601(a)(12), 5615(6), 5687)
2877(a)	5192(d) (Rev. See 7803; T. 5 §301)
2878(a)	5193(a) (Rev. See 5201(a), 5202(f), 5204(a), 5205(b), 5206(a), (c), 5211)
2878(b)	5009(c), 5193(b) (Rev. See 5206(a), 5214(a)(4))
2878(c)	5193(c) (Rev. See 5206(b))
2878(d)	5193(d) (Rev. See 5204(c))
2879(a)	5242(a) (Rev. See 5211, 5231(a))
2879(b)	5006(a) (Rev. See 5006(a)(1), (2), 5008(c))
2879(c)	5232(a) (Rev. See 5005(c)(1), 5006(a)(2), 5173(a), (c)(1))
2879(d)	5232(a), (c) (Rev. See 5005(c)(1), 5006(a)(2), 5173(a), (c)(1), 5176(a), (b))
2880(a)	5006(b)
2881(a)	5245 (Rev. See 5204(a))
2882(a)	5244 (Rev. See 5213)
2883(a)	5194(a) (Rev. See 5211(a), 5212, 5213)
2883(b)	5194(d) (Rev. See 5214(a))
2883(c)	5194(c) (Rev. See 5241)
2883(d)	5194(e)(1) (Rev. See 5212, 5213)
2883(e)	5025(d), 5194(f) (Rev. See 5005(c)(1), 5212, 5223(a), (d))
2883(f)	5194(g) (Rev. See 5201(a), 5204(a), 5212)

Title 26 Former Sections	Title 26 New Sections
2883(g)	5194(h) (Rev. Omitted)
2884(a)	5250(a) (Rev. See 5205(b))
2885(a)	5247(a) (Rev. See 5175(a), 5206(a), 5214(a)(4))
2885(b)	5009(b) (Rev. See 5205(i)(4), 5247(b)
2885(d)	5648 (Rev. See 5608)
2886(a)	5247(c)
2887	5012(a) (Rev. See 5009)
2888(a)	5247(d) (Rev. See 5206(a))
2889, 2890	Omitted
2891(a)	5522(a) (Rev. See 5214(a))
2891(b)	5011(a) (Rev. See 5008(a))
2900	5006(a) (Rev. See 5006(a)(1), (2), 5008(c))
2901(a)(1)	5011(a)(1)(A) (Rev. See 5008(a)(1)(A))
2901(a)(2)	5011(a)(1)(B) (Rev. See 5008(a)(1)(B)), 5011(b) (Rev. See 5008(b)(1))
2901(b)	5011(a)(1)(B), (2) (Rev. See 5008(a)(1)(B), (2))
2901(c)	5011(a)(3) (Rev. See 5008(a)(3), (4))
2901(d)	5011(a)(4) (Rev. See 5008(a)(4))
2903(a)	5243(a) (Rev. See 5171, 5172, 5178(a)(3), (4)(A), 5233(a), (b))
2903(b)	5008(a)(1) (Rev. See 5205(a)(1), (3))
2903(c)	5008(a)(2) (Rev. See 5205(a)(3))
2903(d)	5008(a)(3)
2903(e)	5008(a)(4)
2903(f)	5243(d) (Rev. See 5206(c))
2903(g)	5243(c) (Rev. See 5233(c))
2904(a)	5243(a), (b) (Rev. See 5171, 5172, 5178(a)(3), (4)(A), 5202(g), 5233(a), (b))
2905	5243(e) (Rev. See 5175, 5206(c), 5214(a)(4))
2908	5643 (Rev. See 5601(a)(12), 5604(a)(11), (12), (16), 5615(6), 5687)
2909	5644 (Rev. See 5604(a)(4), (5), (10))
2910(a)	5243(b) (Rev. See 5202(g), 5233(b))
2911	5243(f) (Rev. See T. 27 §121)
2912, 2913	5632 (Rev. See 5601(a)(12), 5615(6))
2914(a)	5633 (Rev. See 7214)
2915(a)	5241(c) (Rev. See 7803; T. 5 §301)
2916(a)	5194(b)
3030(a)	5001(a)(9) (Rev. See 5001(a)(8))
3030(a)(1)	5001(a)(5), (9) (Rev. See 5001(a)(4), (8)), 5041(a), 5041(b), 5042(a)(2), 5362, 5368(b)
3030(a)(2)	5022, 5041(b)(4)
3030(b)	5043(b)
3031(a)	5354, 5362, 5373(b)(1), 5373(b)(3), 5391
3032(a)	5373(a), 5382(b)(2)
3033(a)	5373(b)(1)
3034(a), 3035	5366
3036	5025(f) (Rev. See 5025(g)), 5373(a), 5381, 5382(a), (b)(1), (2), 5383(a), (b)(3), (4), 5392
3037(a)	5362, 5373(b)(4)
3038(a)	5362
3039(a)	5370(a)(1)
3040(a)	5351, 5354, 5356, 5368(a), (b), 5369
3041(a)	5043(b), 5368(a)
3042(a)	5192(a) (Rev. See 5202(a)), 5366
3043(a)	5661(a) (See Chapter 68), (b), 5385(b)
3044	5381, 5382, 5383, 5392
3045	5381, 5382, 5384, 5392
3070(a)	5331(a) (Rev. See 5171(a), 5172, 5173(a), (c), 5178(a)(5), 5202(e), 5207(a), (c), (d), 5214(a), 5241, 5242, 5273(b)(1), (2), (d), 5275)
3070(b)	5331(b), (c) (Rev. See 5214(a), 5273(a), (b)(1), (2), (d))
3072	5647 (Rev. See 5273(b)(1), (2), (d), 5601(a)(12), 5607, 5615(6))
3073(a)	5332 (Rev. See 5273(c))
3074(a)	5333 (Rev. See 5243)
3100(a)	5301 (See 5171(a), (b)(1), 5172, 5173(a), (b))
3101(a)	5302 (Rev. See 5171(a), (b)(1), 5172, 5173(a), (c), 5178(a)(3)(A), (B), 5201(a), 5206(a))
3102	5303 (Rev. See 5171(a), (b)(1), 5172, 5173(a), (c), 5178(a)(5), 5241, 5242, 5273(b)(1), (2), (d))
3103	5306 (Rev. See 5025(d), (e)(1), 5103, 5113(a), 5173(c), 5201(a), (c), 5204(c), 5243(a)(1)(A), 5306), 5312(c)
3104(a)	5309 (Rev. See 5222(b)), 5412 (Rev. See 5222(b), 5412)
3105(a)	5305 (Rev. See 5171, 5172, 5173(a), 5178(a)(1)(A), (5), 5201(a), (b), 5207(a), (c), (d), 5211, 5223(a), 5235, 5273(b)(1), (2), (d), 5275, 5312(b))
3106(a)	5307 (Rev. See 5178(a)(2)(A), 5201(a))
3107	5308 (Rev. See 5212, 5223(a))
3108(a)	5310(a) (Rev. See 5214(a), 5241, 5242, 5273(b)(1), (2), (d))
3108(b)	5310(b) (Rev. See 5214(a), 5313)
3108(c)	5310(c) (Rev. See 5214(a))
3108(d)	5310(d) (Rev. See 5272(b))
3109	5310(a) (Rev. See 5214(a), 5241, 5242, 5273(b)(1), (2), (d))
3110	5502 (Rev. Omitted)
3111	5001(a)(6)
3112(a)	5004(b) (Rev. See 5004(a)(1), (b)(1)), 5005(c) (Rev. See 5005(a), (b)(1), (c)(1))
3112(b)	5007(d) (Rev. See 5007(a)(1)), 5689
3113(a)	5011(c)
3114(a)	5304(a) (Rev. See 5171(b)(1), 5271(a), (b), (c), (e)(1), (f), 5272(a))
3114(b)	5304(b) (Rev. See 5271(e))
3114(c)	5304(c) (Rev. See 5271(e))
3114(d)	5304(d)
3115(a)	5686(a) (Rev. See 5687)
3116	5686(b) (Rev. See 5505(i), 5686(a)), 7302
3117(a)	5314 (Rev. See 5557)
3118	5688(d)
3119	5315
3120	5316
3121(a), (c)	5313(a), (b) (Rev. See 5275)
3121(d)	5317(b) (Rev. See 5274)
3122	5317(a)
3123	5318 (Rev. See 5314(a)(2))
3124(a)	5119 (Rev. See 5002(a))
3125(a)	5001(a)(8) (Rev. See 5001(a)(9)), 5007(d) (Rev See 5007(a)(1)), 5311 (Rev. See 5232)
3125(b)	5310(b) (Rev. See 5214(a), 5313)
3126	Omitted
3150(a)	5051(a)
3150(b)(1)	5054 (Rev. See 5054(a)(1))
3150(b)(2)	5055 (Rev. See 5054(a)(1), (2), (c), (d))
3150(b)(3)	5689
3150(c)	5051(b)
3152	Omitted
3153(b)	5053(a), 5401(b)
3153(c)	5053(b)
3155(a), (b)	5401(a), (b)
3155(c)	5415(a)
3155(f)	5412, 5413, 5675
3156	Omitted
3157(a)	5055 (Rev. See 5054(a)(1), (2), (c), (d))
3158	5402(a), 5411
3159(a)–(c)	5671, 5672, 5673, 5674
3159(e)–(i)	5676(1)–(5)
3159(j)	5674
3160	5052(b)
3170	Omitted
3171(a)	5367, 5555(a) (Rev. See 5207(b)–(d))
3172(a)	5061(b)
3173(a)	5683
3173(b)(1)–(3)	5684 (Rev. See 5687 and Subtitle F)
3173(b)(4)	5690
3173(c)	5685
3173(d)	5688(c)
3174	5064 (Rev. See 5065)
3175	5557 (Rev. See 5560)
3176(a)	5556 (Rev. See 5505(h))
3177(a)	5521(a)
3177(b)	5521(c)(1), (2)
3177(c)	5521(b)
3177(d)(1), (2)	5521(d)(1), (2)
3178	5523
3179(a), (b)	5062(a), (b)
3180	Omitted
3182(a)	5511
3182(b)	5001(a)(7)
3183(a)	5217(a) (Rev. See 5005(c)(1), (2), 5025(d), (e)(2), 5212, 5223(a), 5234(b))
3183(b)	5217(b) (Rev. See 5561)
3183(c)	5217(c) (Rev. Omitted)
3190–3195	Omitted
3206	4821
3207	7235(d), 7264
3208	4822, 4826
3210	4841
3211	7266(a)
3212	4842
3220	4721, 6001, 6151(a)
3221	4722
3222	4772
3223	Omitted
3224	4724
3225	7237(a)
3226	4775
3227	4725
3228	4731, 7343, 7701(a)

Title 26 Former Sections	*Title 26 New Sections*
3230	4751, 4752, 6151(a)
3231	4753
3232	4772
3233	4754, 6001, 6065(a), 6071, 6081(a), 6091(a)
3234	4755
3235	7237(a)
3236	4775
3237	4756
3238	4761, 7701(a)
3239	Omitted
3250(a)(1)	5111(a)(1) (Rev. See 5111(a))
3250(a)(3)	5111(a)(2) (Rev. See 5112(b))
3250(a)(4)	5113(a)
3250(b)(1)	5121(a)(1) (Rev. See 5121(a))
3250(b)(2)	5122(c) (Rev. See 5121(a)(2))
3250(b)(4)	5121(a)(2) (Rev. See 5122(a), (b))
3250(c)(1)	5091
3250(d)(1)	5111(b)(1) (Rev. See 5111(b))
3250(d)(2)	5111(b)(2) (Rev. See 5112(c))
3250(d)(3)	5091, 5113(b) (Rev. See 5113(a))
3250(e)(1)	5121(b)(1) (Rev. See 5122(b))
3250(e)(2)	5121(b)(2) (Rev. See 5122(b))
3250(e)(3)	5121(c) (Rev. See 5121(c), 5122(c))
3250(e)(4)	5123(a) (Rev. See 5113(a))
3250(f)(1)	5081
3250(g)	5113(c) (Rev. See 5113(a))
3250(h)	5025(g) (Rev. See 5025(h))
3250(i)	5025(h) (Rev. See 5025(i))
3250(j)(1)	5101
3250(j)(3)	5106 (Rev. See 5106(b))
3250(*l*)(1), (2)	5131(a), (b)
3250(*l*)(3)–(5)	5132–5134
3251(a)	5113(d)(1) (Rev. See 5113(c)(1))
3251(b)	5113(d)(2) (Rev. See 5113(c)(2))
3251(c)	5123(c) (Rev. See 5113(e))
3252(a)	5124(a)
3252(b)	5124(b) (Rev. See 5146(a))
3252(c)	5124(c) (Rev. See 5146(a))
3252(d)	5692 (Rev. See 5603)
3253	5691 (Rev. See 5607, 5613, 5615, 5661(a), 5671, 5673, 5676(4), 5683, 7301, 7301(a), 7302)
3254(b)	5112(a) (Rev. See 5111(a), 5112(b))
3254(c)(1)	5122(a) (Rev. See 5121(a)(1), 5122(a))
3254(c)(2)	5111 (Rev. See 5111(a), (b), 5112(b), (c))
3254(d)	5052(a), 5092, 5402(a)
3254(e)	5112(b) (Rev. See 5112(c))
3254(f)	5122(b)
3254(g)	5025(c), 5082, 5387(c)
3254(h)	5102
3255(a)	5123(b)(1)
3255(b)	5123(b)(2) (Rev. See 5123(b)(2)(A))
3255(c)	5123(b)(3) (Rev. See 5113(d)(1), (2))
3260	5801(a)
3261(a)	5802
3261(b)	5841
3262	5803
3263(a)	5854(a)
3263(b)	5854(a), (b)
3267	4461, 4462, 4463
3268	4471, 4472, 4473
3270(a)	5141, 7011(a)
3271	4901
3271(a)	5142(a)
3271(b)	5142(b), 6151(a)
3271(c)(1)	5104, 5142(c)
3272(a)	5143(a) (Rev. See Subtitle F), 6011(a), 6065(a), 6071, 6081(a), 6091(b), 6151(a)
3273(a)	5145 (Rev. See 5144), 6801(a)
3273(b)	5146 (Rev. See 6806(a), 7273(a)), 6806(a)
3274	5693 (Rev. See 5692), 7273(a)
3275	5147 (Rev. See 6107), 6107
3276	4906, 5148 (Rev. See 5145)
3277	4902, 5144(a) (Rev. See 5143(a))
3278	4903, 5144(c) (Rev. See 5113(a), 5143(c)(1)–(3))
3279	4904, 5144(b) (Rev. See 5143(b))
3280(a)	4905, 5144 (Rev. See 5113(a) 5143), 7011(b)
3281	6302(b)
3282	5149 (Rev. See 5147), 6302(b)
3283	4907, 5144(e) (Rev. See 5143(e))
3285	4401, 4402, 4404, 4421
3286	6419
3287	4403
3290	4411
3291	4412, 6091(b)
3292	4413, 4903, 4907, 6107
3293	6806(c)
3294	7262, 7273(b)
3297	4422
3298	4423
3300(a)	6801(a)
3300(b)	7208
3300(c)	6808
3301(a)	6801(b), 6804
3301(b)	6808
3303	Omitted
3304(a)–(d)	6805(a)–(d)
3304(e), 3305	Omitted
3310	6331(a)
3310(a)	6011(a), 6071, 6601(c)(4), 6659
3310(b)	6011(a), 6601(c)(4), 6659
3310(c)	6601(a), (f)(1), 6659
3310(d)	6155(a), 6601(f)(1), 6659
3310(e)	6659
3310(f)(1)	6011(a), 6071, 6081(a)
3310(f)(2)	5703(c), 6302(c)
3311	6155(a), 6201(a)(2)(A), 6601(c)(4), 6659
3312(a)	6501(a)
3312(b)	6501(c)(1), (3)
3312(c)	6501(c)(2)
3312(d)	6502(a)
3313	5705(a), 6511(a), (b)(1), (2)
3314	Omitted
3320(a)	7268
3320(b)	Omitted
3321	7206(4)
3321(b)	7301
3321(c)	Omitted
3322	7301(d)
3323(a)(1), (2)	7271(4)
3323(a)(3)	7208(5)
3323(b)	7303(7)
3324(a)–(c)	7341(a)–(c)
3325	7211
3326	7304
3330	6065(a)
3331	5704(b), 7510
3332–3335	Omitted
3350(a), (b)	7652(b)(1), (2)
3351(a)	7653(a)(2)
3351(b), (c)	7653(b), (c)
3360(a)	7652(a)(1)
3360(b)	7101, 7652(a)(2), 7803(c)
3360(c)	7652(a)(3)
3361(a)	7653(a)(1)
3361(b), (c)	7653(b), (c)
3400(a), (c)	4071, 4072, 4073
3400(b), 3401	Omitted
3403	4061, 4062, 4063
3403(e)	6416(c)
3404	4141, 4142, 4143, 4151, 4152
3405	4111, 4112, 4113
3406(a)(1)	4161
3406(a)(2)	Omitted
3406(a)(3)	4121
3406(a)(4)	4171, 4172, 4173
3406(a)(5)	Omitted
3406(a)(6)	4191, 4192
3406(a)(7)–(9)	Omitted
3406(a)(10)	4131
3406(b)	4221
3406(c)	Omitted
3407	4181, 4182, 4224, 5831
3408	4201, 4221
3408(b)	6416(d)
3409(a)	4211
3409(b)	Omitted
3412(a)–(f)	4081, 4082, 4083, 4101, 4102, 7101, 7232
3412(g)	6412(b)
3413	4091, 4092, 4093, 7101
3414, 3415, 3416	Omitted
3420	4521, 4531, 4541, 4551
3422	4521
3423	4531, 4532
3424	4551, 4552, 4553
3425	4541, 4542
3430	4601
3431	Omitted
3440	4217
3441	4216
3442	4220, 4224
3443	6416, 6611
3444, 3445, 3446	4218, 4219, 4223
3447	Omitted
3448(a)	6011(a), 6065(a), 6071, 6081(a), 6091(b), 6151(a)
3448(b)	6151(a), 6601(a), (f)(1)
3449, 3450	Omitted
3451	4222
3453	Omitted
3460	4281, 4282, 4283
3461	6011(a), 6065(a), 6071, 6081, 6091(b), 6151(a)
3462	Omitted
3465	4251, 4252, 4253, 4254
3466	4253, 4292
3467	4291, 6011(a), 6065(a), 6071, 6081(a), 6091(b), 6151(a), 6161(a)
3468	Omitted
3469(a), (b), (c)	4261, 4262
3469(d)	4291, 6011(a), 6065(a), 6071, 6091(b), 6151(a)
3469(e)	6081(a), 6161(a)
3469(f)	4262, 4292
3470	6151(a), 6601(a), (f)
3471	6415, 6416(f)

Title 26 Former Sections	*Title 26 New Sections*
3472–3474	Omitted
3475(a)	4271, 4272
3475(b)	4272, 4292
3475(c)	4271, 4291, 6011(a), 6065(a), 6071, 6091(b), 6151(a)
3475(d)	6081(a), 6161(a)
3475(e)	4273, 7272
3480	4331, 4361
3481	4331, 4332, 4341, 4342, 4343, 4344, 4351–4353
3482	4361, 4362
3483	4382
3490	4501, 4503
3491	4501, 6011(a), 6071, 6091(b), 6151(a)
3492	4502
3493(a)	6418(b)
3493(b)	6511(e)(2)
3494(a)	6418(a)
3494(b)	6511(e)(1)
3495	6601(a), (f)
3496–3498	Omitted
3500, 3501	4501, 4504
3506	7240
3507	4502, 7701(a)
3508	4501, 6412(d)
3600	7601(a)
3601(a)(1), (2)	7606(a), (b)
3601(b)	7342
3601(c)	7212(a), (b)
3602	Omitted
3603	6001
3604(a)	6046(a), 6071, 6091(a)
3604(b)	6046(b), (c), 6065(a)
3604(c)	7201, 7203
3611(a)(1)	6011(a), 6065(a), 6081(a), 6091(a), (b)(1), (2)
3611(a)(2)	6020(a), 6065(a)
3611(b)	6071
3611(c)	6065(a), 6071, 6001(a), (b)(1), (2)
3612(a), (c)	6020(b)
3612(d)(1)	6651(a)
3612(d)(2)	6653(b)
3612(e)	Omitted
3612(f)	6201(a)(1)
3613	6021
3614	7602, 7605(a)
3615	7605(a)
3615(a)–(c)	7602
3615(d)	7603
3615(e)	7604(b)
3616(a)	7207
3616(b)	7210
3616(c), 3617	Omitted
3630	6101
3631	7605(b)
3632(a)	7622(a)
3632(a)(1)	7602
3632(b)	7622(b)
3633	7402(b)
3633(a)	7604(a)
3633(b)	Omitted
3634	6081(a)
3640	6201(a)
3641	6203
3642	6204
3643	Omitted
3644	6202
3645, 3646	Omitted
3647	6201(a)
3650	7621
3651(a)(1)	6301
3651(a)(2), (b)	Omitted
3652	6302(a)
3653(a), (b)	7421(a), (b)
3654	Omitted
3655(a)	6303(a), 6659
3655(b)	6601(a), (f)(1), 6659
3656(a)(1)	6311(a)
3656(a)(2)(A), (B)	6311(b)(1), (2)
3656(b)(1)	6311(a)
3656(b)(2)	6311(b)(1)
3657	6312(a)
3658	6313
3659(a)	6314(a)
3659(b)	Omitted
3660	6331(a)
3660(a)	6155(a), 6862
3660(b)	6863(a), 7101
3661	7501
3662, 3663	Omitted
3670	6321
3671	6322
3672	7207
3672(a), (b)	6323(a), (d)
3673(a), (b)	6325(a)(1), (2)
3674(a), (b)	6325(b)(1), (2)
3675	6325(c)
3676	7102
3677	Omitted
3678	7403
3679(a)	7424(a)
3679(b)	Omitted
3679(c), (d)	7424(b), (c)
3680	Omitted
3690	6331(a), (b)
3691	6334
3692	6331(a), (b), 6334(c)
3693	6335(e)(2)(E)
3693(a)–(c)	6335(a), (b), (d)
3693(d)	6335(e)(2)(F)
3694	6342(a)
3695(a)	6335(e)(1), (2)(A)
3695(b)	6335(e)(2), 7505(a)
3695(c)	7505(b)
3696	6337(a)
3697(a)–(d)	6339(a)(1)–(4)
3698	Omitted
3700	6331(a), (b)
3701	6335(e)(2)(E)
3701(a)–(c)	6335(a), (b), (d)
3701(d)	6335(e)(1), (2)(A), (B)
3701(e)	6335(e)(1)
3701(f)	6335(e)(2)(D), (F), (3)
3702(a)	6337(a)
3702(b)(1), (2)	6337(b)(1), (2)
3702(c)	6337(c)
3703(a)	6338(c)
3703(b)	6338(a)
3704(a)	6338(c)
3704(b)	6338(b)
3704(c)(1), (2)	6339(b)(1), (2)
3705	Omitted
3706(a), (b)	6340(a)
3706(c)–(e)	Omitted
3706(f)	6340(b)
3707	Omitted
3710(a), (b)	6332(a), (b)
3710(c)	6332(c), 7343
3711	6333
3712	6335(c), 6342(b)
3713, 3714(a)	Omitted
3714(b)	6502(b)
3715	6331(c)
3716	6341
3717	Omitted
3720(a)(1)–(3)	7301(a)–(c)
3720(b)	7321
3720(c)	Omitted
3721, 3722	7322, 7324
3722(a), (b)	7324(1), (2)
3722(c)	7101, 7324(3)
3722(d)	7324(4)
3723(a)–(c)	7323(a)–(c)
3723(d)	Omitted
3724	7101, 7325
3725	6807
3726	7327
3727	Omitted
3740	7401
3742, 3743, 3745	Omitted
3746(a)	7405(a)
3746(b)	6532(b), 7405(b)
3746(c)	Omitted
3746(d)	6602
3747	7406
3748	6531
3760, 3761	7121, 7122
3762	7206(5)
3770(a)(1)	6402(a), 6404(a)
3770(a)(2)	6401(a)
3770(a)(3)	6407
3770(a)(4)	6402(a)
3770(a)(5)	6402(a), 6404(a)
3770(b)	7423
3770(b)(1), (2)	7423(1), (2)
3770(c)	6401(c)
3771(a)	6611(a)
3771(b)(1)	6611(b)(1)
3771(b)(2)	6611(b)(2), (e)
3771(c)	6611(c)
3771(d)	Omitted
3771(e)	6611(f)
3771(f), (g)	Omitted
3772(a)(1)	7422(a)
3772(a)(2), (3)	6532(a)(1), (4)
3772(b)	7422(b)
3772(c)	Omitted
3772(d), (e)	7422(c), (d)
3773	Omitted
3774	6514(a)
3774(b)	6532(a)(2)
3775	6514(b)
3777(a)–(c)	6405(a)–(c)
3778	Omitted
3779(a)	6091(a), 6164(a)
3779(b)	6065(a), 6071, 6081(a), 6164(b)
3779(c)–(g)	6164(c)–(g)
3779(h)	6155(a), 6164(h)
3779(i)	6601(a), (e), (f)(1)
3780(a)	6065(a), (b), 6071, 6091(a), 6411(a)
3780(b)	6411(b)
3780(c)	6213(b)(2)
3781	6164(i), 6411(c)
3790	6406, 6611(g)
3791(a)	6071, 6081(a), 6091(a), (b)(1), (2), 7805(a)

Title 26 Former Sections	Title 26 New Sections
3791(b)	7805(b)
3792	7623
3793	7206(3)
3793(a)(2)	7303(8)
3793(b)	7206(2), 7207
3793(b)(2)	7343
3794	6601(a)
3795(a)–(d)	7506(a)–(d)
3797(a)(1)–(11)	7701(a)(1)–(11)
3797(a)(12)	7701(a)(13)
3797(a)(13)	Omitted
3797(a)(14)–(20)	1465, 7701(a)(14)–(20)
3797(b), (c)	7701(b), (c)
3798	7507
3799	76
3800	7402(a)
3801	1311–1314
3802	7511
3803	7852(a)
3804(a)	7508(a)
3804(b), (c)	Omitted
3804(d)	7508(b)
3804(e)	Omitted
3804(f)	7508(a)
3805	6072(e)
3806	1481
3808	Omitted
3809(a)	7206(1)
3809(b)	6061, 6064
3809(c)	6065(a)
3810	Omitted
3811	7651
3812	6521
3813, 3814	503, 504
3900	7802
3901(a)	6801(a), 7805(c)
3901(b)	7803(b)(2)
3905, 3906, 3910, 3911, 3915, 3916	Omitted
3920, 3921	7803(a)
3930(a)	7801(b)
3930(b)	Omitted
3931, 3932	7801(b), (c)
3940–3942	Omitted
3943	7101, 7803(c)
3944, 3950–3955, 3960–3967	Omitted
3970	7808
3971(a), (b)	7809(a), (b)
3971(b)(1)–(3)	7809(b)(1)–(3)
3975–3978	7803(d)
3990, 3991	Omitted
3992	7101, 7402(d), 7803(c)
3993, 3994	Omitted
3995(c)	7402(d)
3996, 3997	Omitted
4000	7803(a)
4001–4003	Omitted
4010	7101, 7803(c)
4011, 4012	Omitted
4013(a)	5241
4013(b)–(d)	Omitted
4014–4022, 4030–4033	Omitted
4040	7803(b)(1)
4041(a)	7803(a)
4041(b)	Omitted
4042	7402(c)
4043–4046	Omitted
4047(a)(1)	7213(b)
4047(b)	7214(b)
4047(c), (d)	Omitted
4047(e)	7214(a)
4048	7344
5000–5004	8001–8005
5010–5012	8021–8023

TITLE 28—JUDICIARY AND JUDICIAL PROCEDURE

[This title was enacted into law by act June 25, 1948, ch. 646, §1, 62 Stat. 869. This table shows where sections of former Title 28 were incorporated in revised Title 28.]

Title 28 Former Sections	Title 28 New Sections
1–4bb	132–134
1 nt	133
5	135
5a	T. 48 §1392a
5b	Elim.
6, 7	751
8	751, 954
9	604, 755
9a	1915
9a(a)	753, 1920
9a(b)	753
9a(c)	550, 604, 753, 1915
9a(d)	753
9a(e)	1915
9b	Rep. See Civ. Proc. R. 75.
10	457
11, 12	Rep. See Civ. Proc. R. 6(c), Cr. Proc. R. 45(c).
13	452
14	Rep. See Cr. Proc. R. 45(c).
15	141
16	140, 296
17	291, 292, 295, 296
18	296
19	Rep.
20	295
21	292
22	291, 296
23	296
24	455
25	144
26	143
27	137
41(1)	1331, 1332, 1341, 1342, 1345, 1354, 1359
41(2)	Rep.
41(3)	1333, 1356
41(4)	Rep.
41(5)	1340
41(6)	1339
41(7)	1338
41(8)	1337
41(9)	1355
41(10)	Rep.
41(11)	1357
41(12–14)	1343
41(15)	1344
41(16)	1348
41(17)	1350
41(18)	1351
41(19)	1334
41(20)	1346, 2401, 2402
41(21)	Rep.
41(22)	Rep.
41(23)	1337
41(24)	1353
41(25)	1357, 1399
41(26)	1335, 1397, 2361
41(27), (28)	1336
42	1349
43	1398
44	2321
45	Rep.
45a	2323
46	2324
47	1253, 2101, 2284, 2325
47a	1253, 2101, 2284
48	2322
49–51	Rep.
52	Elim.
53	T. 15 §146a
71	1441, 1445, 1447
72	1446, 1447
73	Rep.
74	1443, 1446, 1447
75	1446
76	1442, 1446, 1447
77	1442
78	1449
79	1450
80	1359, 1447, 1919
81	1447
82	Rep.
83	1447, 1448
101	T. 18 §3235
102	T. 18 §3238
103	T. 18 §3237
104	1395
105	1396
106–108	1395
109	1400, 1694
110	1394
111	1391
112	1391, 1401, 1693, 1695
113	1392
114	1393, 1441
115	Rep. See Civ. Proc. R. 4(f).
116	1392
117	754, 1692
118	1655
119	1404
120	Rep.
121	1405; T. 18 §3240
122	1656
123	Rep.
124	959; T. 18 §1911
124a	960
125	959
126	458
127	957
128	604, 752
141	Rep.
142	81
143	82
144	83
145	84
146	85, 140
147	86
148	87
149	89
149a, 149b	Rep.
150	90
150a	Rep.
151	92
152	93
153	94
154, 155	Rep.
156, 156a	95
157	96
158	97
159	98
160	99
161	Rep.
162	Rep.
163	1404
164	Rep. See Civ. Proc. R. 77.
165	Rep.
166	100
167	101
168	102
169	103
170	104
171	105
172	106
173	107
174	108
175	109
176	110
177	111
178, 178a	112
179	113
179a	Elim.
180	114
181	115, 1865
182	116, 138
182a	116
183	117
184	118
184a	Elim.
185	120
186	121
186a	Elim.
187	122
188	123
189	124
189a	Elim.
190	125
191	126
192, 192a	127
193	128
194	129
195	130
196	131
211	41
211a	Rep.
212	43, 46
213	44
213a–213h	Elim.
214	Rep.
215	42
216	45, 47, 292
216a	45
217	Rep.
218	231, 456
219	2071
220	547
221	711, 956
222	711, 954
222a	604, 712
223	48

Title 28 Former Sections	*Title 28 New Sections*
224	Rep.
225(a)	1291, 1293
225(b)	1292
225(c)	Rep.
225(d)	1294
225(e), (f)	Rep.
226	Rep.
227	1292
227a	1292, 2107
228, 228a	Rep. See Civ. Proc. R. 73.
229	Rep.
230	2107
231	2108
241	171, 173, 453
242	Rep.
243	174, 175
244	791, 795, 956
245	604
246	952
247	Rep.
248	415, 791
249	T. 18 §282
250(1)	1491, 1501
250(2)	1503, 2501
250(3)	1496
250a	1497, 2501
250b	Rep.
251	Rep.
252	2508
253	2512
254	1493, 2510
255	2510
256	Rep.
257	1492, 2509
258	2412
259	1502
259a	T. 25 §70w (Rep. See T. 28 §1505).
260	1500
261	2502
262	2501
263	792, 2071
264	459, 953
265	Rep. See Ct. Claims R. 1, 10, 16 et seq.[1]
266	Rep. See Ct. Claims R. 10.[1]
267, 268	Rep.
268a	604, 793
269	792, 2503
270	456, 792, 794
271	Rep.
272	2507
273	Rep.
274	2504
275, 275a	2505
276	2503
277	Rep. See Ct. Claims R. 40 et seq.[1]
278	2503
278a	604, 793
279, 280	2514
281, 282	2515
283	2520
283a	791, 2520
284	2516
285	2517
286	2519
287	1494, 2511
288	1255
289	791
290, 291	Rep.
292	2506
293	Rep.
296	251–254, 456, 1581, 2071, 2639, 2640
296a	456
297	2636
301	211–213, 215, 293, 296
301a	213
301b	(See former 301a)
302	214, 452, 456, 604
303	604, 832
304	604, 831, 956, 957, 1926
305	604, 831, 833, 834, 956
306	604, 834
307	211, 2071
308	1256, 1541
309	Rep.
309a	1542
310	2601
311	Rep.
312	216
321	1
322	4
323	3
324	5
325	671–673
326	671, 1737
327	671, 954
328	675
329	6
330	1911
331	672
332, 333	673
334	411
335	412
336	Elim.
337	413
338	2
339, 340	Rep.
341	1251
342	1651
343	1872
344	1257, 2103, 2106
345	Rep.
346, 347	1254
348, 349	Rep.
349a	1252, 2101
350	2101
351	2102
352	Rep. See Sup. Ct. R. 32.
353	Rep.
354	676
371(1)	Rep.
371(2)	1355
371(3)	1333
371(4)	1333, 1356
371(5)	1338
371(6)	1334
371(7)	1251
371(8)	1251, 1351
372	453
373	454
374	456
374a	Elim.
374b	604
374c, 374d	752
375	136, 294, 371
375a	294, 371
375b–375d	372
375e	Rep.
375f	294
375g, 375h	373
376, 377	1651
377a–377c	D.C. Code, §§16-3501 to 16-3503
378	Rep.
379	2283
380	1253, 2101, 2281, 2284
380a	1253, 2101, 2282, 2284
381	Rep. See Civ. Proc. R. 65.
382	Rep. See Civ. Proc. R. 65(c).
383	Rep. See Civ. Proc. R. 65(d).
384	Rep.
385	459; T. 18 §401
386	T. 18 §§402, 3691
387	T. 18 §402
388	Rep.
389	T. 18 §§402, 3691
390	T. 18 §3285
390a	T. 18 §402
391	Rep. See Civ. Proc. R. 59, 61; Cr. Proc. R. 33, 52.
392	T. 18 §3043
393	T. 22 §258a
394	1654
395	556, 955
396	556, 955
397, 398	Rep.
399	1653
400	2201, 2202
401	2403
402	374
411	1861
412, 412a	1864
413	1865
414	Rep.
415	1861, 1863
416	1867, 1868
417	1866, 1868
417a	Rep. See Cr. Proc. R. 24(c).
418	1866
419	T. 18 §3321
420	Rep. See Cr. Proc. R. 6(c).
421	Rep. See Cr. Proc. R. 6(a), (g).
422	Rep. See Cr. Proc. R. 6(g).
423	1869
424	1870
425	Rep. See Cr. Proc. R. 24(b).
426	Rep.
430, 430a	Rep.
431–432a	Rep.
433, 434	Rep.
441–443	Rep.
444	601, 603, 606, 608
445	602, 603, 607
446	604, 609
447	604, 605
448	332
449	333, 456
450	333, 604, 610
451–453	2241
454	2242
455–461	2243
462	2252
463(a)	2253
463(b)–(d)	Rep.
464	Rep. See Civ. Proc. R. 73–75, 81(a)(2).

Title 28 Former Sections	*Title 28 New Sections*
465	2251
466	2253
481	501
481a	Elim.
482	504
483	502
484	550
485–489	547
490	541
490a	Elim.
491	541
492, 493	542
494	543
495	548
496–498	564
499	564, 1737
500–502	564
503	547
504	549
504a	T. 18 §3053
505	550
506	546
507	554
508	555
509, 510	Rep.
511	506, 544, 545
512	951
513, 514	952, 1737
515–517	952
518, 519	Rep.
520	Rep. See Civ. Proc. R. 81(b).
521	Rep.
522	T. 18 §2076
523	953
523a, 523b	457
524	505, 541, 751
525	636, 953
526	631
527	631, 958
528	638
528a	638, 639
529	Rep. See Cr. Proc. R. 55.
530	413, 414
530a	Elim.
531	T. 18 §1910
541, 542	671
543	1913
544	604, 711, 961, 962
545	604
546	711
547	604, 713
548	Rep.
549	1914
550, 551	Rep.
552	1917
553	1914
554	Rep.
555	1914
556	Rep.
557	604, 751
558	604
559	Rep.
560	604, 962
561, 561a	604
562	604, 962
563	604, 961
564	Rep.
565, 566	604
567–569	751
570	Rep.
571, 572	1923
572a	T. 18 §155
573	Rep.
574	553, 1921
575	Rep.
576	553
577	551, 1929
578	1923
578a	551
578b, 578c	Rep.
579	508, 552
580	508
581	Rep.
582, 583	552, 553
584, 584a, 585	553
586	509, 550
586a	Rep.
587	509, 553
588, 589	Rep.
590	T. 18 §203
591	Rep.
592	509
593	510
594	502
595, 596	604, 755
597–597c	635
598–599a	636
600–600b	1871
600c	1821, 1825
600d	Rep.
601	Elim.
602	1824
603–604a	1823

Title 28 Former Sections	*Title 28 New Sections*
605	Rep.
606, 607	T. 44 §§325, 326 (See Rev. T. 44 Table)
608	1825, 1871
609	Rep.
631	Rep. See Civ. Proc. R. 43.
632	T. 18 §3481
633	Rep.
634	T. 18 §3486
635	Rep. See Civ. Proc. R. 43(a).
636	Rep. See Civ. Proc. R. 34, 55.
637	2072, 2073
638	1731
639–641	Note prec. 1781
642	Rep. See Civ. Proc. R. 28.
643, 644	Rep. See Civ. Proc. R. 26 et seq.
645	Rep. See Civ. Proc. R. 27(a)(4).
646	Rep. See Civ. Proc. R. 26 et seq.
647	Rep. See Civ. Proc. R. 45; Cr. Proc. R. 17.
648	Rep. See Civ. Proc. R. 45(d); Cr. Proc. R. 17(f).
649–652	1782
653	1781, 1782
654	Rep. See Civ. Proc. R. 45(e)(1); Cr. Proc. R. 17(e).
655	Rep. See Civ. Proc. R. 45; Cr. Proc. R. 17.
656	Rep. See Cr. Proc. R. 17(b).
657	Rep. See Cr. Proc. R. 46(b).
658	Rep.
659	Rep. See Cr. Proc. R. 46(b).
660	Rep.
661–667	1733
668	T. 18 §3497
669	Rep.
670	1743
671	1733
672	Rep.
673	1744
674	1745
675	Rep.
676	1736
677	1740
678–680	Rep.
681–684	1734
685, 686	1735
687	1738
688	1739
689	1742
690	T. 30 §53
695	1732
695a	T. 18 §3491
695b	T. 18 §3492
695c	T. 18 §3493
695d	T. 18 §3494
695e	1741
695e–1	T. 22 §4222
695f	T. 18 §3495
695g	T. 18 §3496
695h	Rep.
701	1782
702	1785
703, 704	1782
711–713	1783
714–718	1784
721	1691
722	Rep. See Civ. Proc. R. 4.
723	2071, 2073
723a	T. 18 §3772
723a–1	T. 18 §3771
723b, 723c	2072
724	Rep.
725	1652
726	Rep. See Civ. Proc. R. 64.
727	Rep. See Civ. Proc. R. 69.
728	Rep.
729	T. 42 §1988
730	2072, 2073
731	2071
732–734	Rep.
735	Rep. See Civ. Proc. R. 4; Cr. Proc. R. 4, 9; Adm. R. 1.[2]
736	Rep.
737	See 2710
738	See 2711
739	See 2712
740	See 2713
741	See 2714
742	See 2715
743	See 2716
744	See 2717
745	Rep.
746	Rep. See Civ. Proc. R. 64.
747	2463
748–750	2405
751, 752	Rep.
753	Adm. R. 6–8, 10, 12[2]
754	2464
755–757	Rep.
758	636
759, 760	Rep.
761	2071, 2072

Title 28 Former Sections	*Title 28 New Sections*
762	1402
763	Rep. See Civ. Proc. R. 4(d), 12(a), 55(e).
764	Rep. See Civ. Proc. R. 52, 75.
765	2411
766	2409
767	Rep. See Civ. Proc. R. 4(h).
768	Rep. See Sup. Ct. R. 20.
769	Rep. See Civ. Proc. R. 40.
770	1873
771	Adm. R. 46½[2]
772	Rep. See Civ. Proc. R. 39(c), 48.
773	Rep. See Civ. Proc. R. 38 et seq.
774	2406
775	Rep.
776	Rep. See Civ. Proc. R. 46, 63, 75.
777	Rep. See Civ. Proc. R. 1, 15, 61.
778–780	Rep. See Civ. Proc. R. 25, 81.
780a	2404
781	2407
782	Rep. See Civ. Proc. R. 12(a).
783	Rep.
784	T. 19 §579
785	1874
786	Rep.
787	T. 19 §580
788	See 2718
789	Rep.
790	Rep. See Civ. Proc. R. 75; Adm. R. 49.[2]
791	2462
792	2284
811	1961
811a	Rep.
812	1962
813	Rep.
814	1962
815	Rep. See Civ. Proc. R. 41(d), 42(a), 54(d), 68.
816	Rep.
817	Elim.
818	2465
819	Rep.
820	Rep.
821	1928
822	1918
823, 824	Rep.
825	Rep. See Civ. Proc. R. 42(a).
826	Rep.
827	2465
828	1922
829	1927
830	1920
831	1924
832–836	1915
837	1916
838	Rep. See Civ. Proc. R. 4.
839	2413
840	Rep. See Civ. Proc. R. 59, 62.
841	Rep. See Civ. Proc. R. 62(f).
842	2006
843–845	2007
846	2005
847	2001
848	2004
849	2002
850	2003
851	2041
852	2042
861	Rep.
861a	Rep.
861b	Elim.
862	Rep.
863	Rep. See Civ. Proc. R. 75; Adm. R. 49.[2]
864	Rep. See Civ. Proc. R. 75(k).
865–867	Rep.
868	Rep. See Sup. Ct. R. 10, 36.
869	Rep.
870	2408
871	2104
872	Rep. See Civ. Proc. R. 73.
873	Rep.
874	Rep. See Civ. Proc. R. 62(d), 73(d); Sup. Ct. R. 36.
875	Rep. See Civ. Proc. R. 46, 52, 73, 75.
876, 877	2106
878	1912
879	2105
880	Rep.
901, 902	2410
903	1444
904, 905	2410
906	Rep.
921	2672
922	2673
931(a)	1346, 1402, 2402, 2411, 2412, 2674
931(b)	2675, 2676
932	1346, 2411
933(a)(1)	1291
933(a)(2)	1504, 2110
933(b)	Rep.
934	2677
941	2671
942	2401
943	2680
944	2678
945	2679
946	Elim.

[1] Court of Claims Rules were replaced by U.S. Claims Court Rules effective Oct. 1, 1982.

[2] Admiralty Rules were superseded July 1, 1966, by Supplemental Rules for Certain Admiralty and Maritime Claims.

TITLE 31—MONEY AND FINANCE

[This title was enacted into law by Pub. L. 97–258, §1, Sept. 13, 1982, 96 Stat. 877. This table shows where sections of former Title 31 were incorporated in revised Title 31.]

Title 31 Former Sections	Title 31 New Sections
1	Rep.
2	701, 1101
11(a)	1105
11(b), (c)	1106
11(d)–(f)	1105
11(g) (1st–3d sentences)	1106
11(g) (last sentence)–(i) (1st sentence).	1105
11(i) (last sentence), (j)	1108
11(k)(1)	1105
11(k)(2)	1113
11 note	1105
11a	1109
11b	T. 2 §661
11c	1110
11d	1104
12	Rep.
13	1105
14	1107
15	1108
16 (1st sentence)	501
16 (2d, 3d sentences)	502
16 (last sentence related to preparation of budgets and appropriations).	1104
16 (last sentence related to appropriations request).	1108
16a	502
16b	Rep.
16c	502
17(a) (related to employees)	521
17(a) (related to expenses)	522
17(b), (c)	Rep.
18, 18a	1111
18b	1104
18c	1112
19	1105
20	1113
21	1104
22–24	1108
25	1105
26	Rep.
27	1103
28	1114
41	702
42(a) (1st sentence words before comma).	702
42(a) (1st sentence words after comma, last sentence), (b).	703
42a	703
43 (1st par.)	703
43 (2d par. 1st, 2d, 4th, last sentences).	772
43 (2d par. 3d sentence)	779
43 (3d par.)	772
43 (last par.)	775
43a	703
43b(a)–(c)	773
43b(d), (e)	774
43b(f)	776
43b(g)	771
43b(h)	778
43b(i), (j) (less last 13 words before colon).	775
43b(j) (last 13 words before colon).	776
43b(k)	775
43b(*l*), (m)	770
43b(n), (*o*)	774
43b(p)	771
43b(q)	773
43b(r)	779
43c	777
44 (1st sentence)	711, 731, 3301, 3323, 3324, 3521, 3522, 3526, 3529, 3531, 3541, 3702, (See §2(b) of Pub. L. 97–258)
44 (2d, last sentences)	3526
45	Rep.
46	704
46a to 48	Rep.
49	3511
49a	5120
50, 51	Rep.
51–1	702
51a, 52(a), (b)	731
52(c), (d)	711
52–1 (related to appointment, pay and assignment).	731
52–1 (related to direct)	711
52–2	732
52–3(a)–(d)	751
52–3(e)–(g)	752
52–3(h)	753
52–3(i)	754
52–3(j), (k)	753
52–3(*l*)	755
52–3(m)	753
52–4(a)	733
52–4(b)	731
52–5	732
52–6	735
52–7	736
52a	Rep.
52b, 52c	731
53(a) (1st sentence words before 5th comma).	712
53(a) (1st sentence words after 5th comma, last sentence).	719
53(b)	712
53(c)–(e)	719
53(f)	718
54	716
55	Rep.
56	731
57, 58	Rep.
59, 60 (1st sentence)	712
60 (last sentence)	719
61	715
65(a)–(e)	Rep.
65(f)	3511
65a	3501
65b	3521
66(a)	3511
66(b) (less Treasury Department).	3512
66(b) (related to Treasury Department).	3513
66(c)	3512
66a	3512
66b	3513
66c	3326
66d	3514
67(a)–(c)	3523
67(d)(1)–(3)	713
67(d)(4)	719
67(e)(1)–(5), (7)	714
67(e)(6)(A)	719
67(e)(6)(B)	718
67(f)	3524
68	9501
68a	9503
68b	9504
68c, 68d	9502
71 (related to accounts)	3526
71 (related to claims)	3702
71a	3702
72, 73	Rep.
74 (1st, 2d pars., last par. words after 4th comma).	3526
74 (last par. words before 4th comma).	3529
75	3521
76 (1st, last sentences)	3324
76 (2d, 3d sentences)	3323
77	3323
78	3522
79	Rep.
80–80c	3522
81	3522
82	3521
82a	3325
82a–1, 82a–2	3527
82b	3325
82b–1	3521
82c	3528
82d (words before semicolon)	3541
82d (words after semicolon)	3529
82e (related to 31:82b)	3325
82e (related to 31:82c)	3528
82e (related to 31:82d)	3529
82f (related to disbursing officers).	3325
82f (related to certifying officers).	3528
82g (related to disbursing officers).	3322
82g (related to certifying officers).	3528
82h	T. 7 §1032a
82i	3526
82j to 82p	Rep.
83, 84	Rep.
85	T. 48 §1469–1
86	3702
87, 88	Rep.
89–92	3531
93, 94	Rep.
95	T. 10 §4842
95a	3527
95b (related to Army, Navy, Air Force).	T. 10 §2777

Title 31 *Former Sections*	*Title 31* *New Sections*
95b (related to State Department).	T. 22 §2668
96–102	Rep.
103	T. 10 §2778
103a	T. 10 §2773
103b	T. 10 §2773
104	T. 10 §7861
105	Rep.
106	T. 10 §7862
107	3526
107a	Rep.
108	T. 10 §7231
109–116	Rep.
117	711
118–121	Rep.
122	3702
123 (words before 1st proviso)	3329
123 (provisos)	3330
124 (1st par.)	3329
124 (last par.)	3330
125 (1st par.)	3329
125 (last par.)	3330
126	3329
127	321
128	3329
129–131	3712
132	3328
133	Rep.
134	3328
135	3525
141	301
142–146	Rep.
147 (less disbursement)	3301
147 (related to disbursement)	3323
148–154	Rep.
155	(See former 1003)
156	3333
157	327
161, 162	Rep.
163	329
164–166	Rep.
171	303
172, 173	Rep.
174	5144
175	5155
176	Rep.
177	5114
178, 179	Rep.
180	5141
181	5143
181 note	5142
181a	5142
181b, 181c	5141
181d, 181e	Rep.
191, 192	3713
193	9309
194	Rep.
195	3715
196–199	Rep.
200(a)	1501
200(b), (c)	1108
200(d)	1502
200(e)	1501
201, 202	Rep.
203	3727
204–206	Rep.
207	3714
208–214	Rep.
215	3723
215a	Rep.
216, 217	3723
218–224	Rep.
224a, 224a note	3725
224b, 224b note	3724
224c to 226	Rep.
227	3728
228	Rep.
229	T. 2 §190*l*
230	T. 2 §190m
231	3729
232(A)–(E)	3730
232(F)	3731
233	3730
234	Rep.
235	3731
236, 237	3702
237a	3712
238, 238 note	3722
239	3727
240(1), (2), (4)	3701
240(3)	3721
241(a)–(d)	3721
241(e)	Rep.
241(f)	3721
242–243a	3721
243a note	3721
244	3726
251 (1st sentence words after 1st comma).	5131
251 (less 1st sentence words after 1st comma).	304
252	Rep.
253	5132
254	Rep.
261	5131
262	Rep.
263	5131
264–271	Rep.
272	5111
273 (1st, 2d sentences)	5132
273 (last sentence)	5122
274	5121
275	5111
276	5112
277	5121
278, 279	5131
280	Rep.
281	5131
282	Rep.
283 (1st sentence)	5131
283 (2d, last sentences)	5133
284–286	Rep.
287	5131
291	Rep.
292	5131
293, 294	Rep.
301–304	Rep.
311–315a	Rep.
315b	5118
316–316d	Rep.
317(a), (b)	5112
317(c)	Rep.
317a, 317b	Rep.
317c	5120
317d to 317e–1	Rep.
317f	321
318–320	Rep.
321	5112
322	5111
323	Rep.
324	5112
324a	5114
324b to 324c	5112
324d, 324e	Rep.
324f	5131
324g	Rep.
324h	5111
324i	Rep.
325	5121
326	Rep.
327–330	5121
331, 332	5122
333	Rep.
334	5122
335	5116
336–339	Rep.
340	5111
341	Rep.
342	5111
343, 344	5121
345	5111
346	5112
347	5121
348, 349	Rep.
350, 351	5113
352	Rep.
353	5111
354–356	5133
357, 358	5122
359	Rep.
360	5121
361 (1st sentence words before 1st comma).	5131
361 (1st sentence words after 1st comma, last sentence).	5132
362	5121
363	Rep.
364	5102
365	5133
366	Rep.
367, 368	5111
369	5132
370	Rep.
371	5101
372	5151
373–388*o*	Rep.
391(a)	5111
391(b)–(d)	5112
392	5103
393(a)	5111
393(b)	Rep.
394	5116
395, 396	5111
397	321
398(1)–(4), (6)	5112
398(5)	5113
399	5112
401, 402	5115
403	Rep.
404	5119
405, 405a	Rep.
405a–1	5116
405a–2, 405a–3	5119
405b	5117
406–408	Rep.
408a (last proviso)	5117

Title 31 Former Sections	*Title 31 New Sections*
408a (less last proviso)	5119
408b to 412	Rep.
413–416	5114
417	Rep.
418, 418a	5114
419	5114
420	5119
421, 422	5120
423	Rep.
424	5153
425, 426	5154
427	321
428–430	Rep.
440	Rep.
441	5117
442, 443	Rep.
444 (1st sentence words between 2d and 3d semicolons).	5119
444 (less 1st sentence words between 2d and 3d semicolons).	Rep.
445, 446	Rep.
448–448e	Rep.
449	Rep.
449a	5152
449b, 449c	Rep.
451–455	Rep.
456	5103
457–462	Rep.
463, 463 note	5118
471	Rep.
472	302
473	3303
474–483	Rep.
483a	9701
483b	T. 10 §1042
484	3302
485	Rep.
486	321
486a to 488	Rep.
488a	T. 16 §580*o*–2
488b to 488b–2	Rep.
488b–3	T. 16 §580*o*
488b–4	T. 16 §580*o*–1
488b–5	T. 16 §580*o*–3
488b–6	T. 16 §580*o*–4
489	T. 40 §485a
489a	T. 10 §2636
490	3302
491	Rep.
492(a)	3322
492(b)–(d)	3332
492 note	3332
492–1	3321
492–2	Rep.
492a–492c	3342
492d	Rep.
493	T. 10 §4841
493a	T. 10 §2776
493b, 494	Rep.
495	3302
495a	Rep.
496, 497	3522
497a	3532
498	3522
499–504b	Rep.
505	3545
506, 507	3541
508	3542
509	Rep.
510–513	3542
514	3541
516	3541
517–519	3543
520	3544
521	3302
522	3304
523, 524	Rep.
525	3302
526	3327
527	3328
528(a)–(c)	3331
528(d)	321
528(e)	Rep.
528(f), (g)	3331
528(h)	Rep.
529	3324
529a	Rep.
529b	T. 19 §2076
529c	T. 19 §2077
529d	T. 19 §2078
529e	T. 19 §2079
529f	T. 19 §2080
529g, 529h	Rep.
529i, 529j	T. 10 §2395
530	Rep.
530a, 530b	3324
531	T. 15 §196
532	T. 28 §571
533	Rep.
534	T. 16 §556d
535	T. 22 §268b
536, 537	T. 10 §2777
538	3526
539, 540	T. 10 §2777
541	3526
542, 543	Rep.
544	3341
545	3302
546	Rep.
547	T. 22 §2668a
547a	9702
548	3305
549	Rep.
550	T. 33 §877
551, 552	1345
553	T. 42 §3514
554	Rep.
555	T. 26 §4986 note
561–563a	3343
564	321
571	Rep.
581	1104
581 note	1303
581a	1104
581b	1108
581c	1531
581c–1	Rep.
581d	3530
582–622	Rep.
623	1104
624–626	Rep.
627, 628	1301
628–1	1532
628–2, 628–3	T. 10 §2779
628a	1534
629–638	Rep.
638a(a)–(c)(1)	1343
638a(c)(2) (1st, last sentences)	1344
638a(c)(2) (2d sentence)	1349
638a(d)	Rep.
638a(e)	1343
638a–1	1343
638b	T. 33 §576a
638c	1343 note
638d, 638e	1343
638f	Elim.
639–649	Rep.
649a	T. 10 §956 note
649b	Rep.
649c	T. 10 §2394
650	Rep.
650a	T. 37 §406
650b to 660	Rep.
661	T. 33 §878
662	T. 16 §754a
663, 663a	Rep.
664	Rep.
665(a)	1341
665(b)	1342
665(c) (less (1) (last sentence))	1512
665(c)(1) (last sentence)	1511
665(d)(1), (2) (1st–4th sentences, 6th sentence 1st–22d words).	1513
665(d)(2) (5th sentence, 6th sentence less 1st–22d words).	1511
665(d)(2) (last sentence related to spending and obligations).	1341
665(d)(2) (last sentence related to voluntary services).	1342
665(d)(2) (last sentence related to price supports).	1511
665(e)	1515
665(f)(1)	1516
665(f)(2)	1511
665(g) (1st sentence)	1513
665(g) (less 1st sentence)	1514
665(h)	1517
665(i)(1) (words before semicolon related to (a), (b)).	1549
665(i)(1) (words after semicolon related to (a), (b)).	1550
665(i)(1) (words before semicolon related to (h)).	1518
665(i)(1) (words after semicolon related to (h)).	1519
665(i)(2) (related to (a), (b))	1351
665(i)(2) (related to (h))	1517
665a	1515
665b	1502
666	T. 10 §4541
667	Rep.
668	T. 41 §11a
668a	1308
669 (words before semicolon)	1513
669 (words after semicolon)	1341
670	1302
671	T. 2 §§68–2, 95a
671a	Rep.
672, 673	1346
674–678	Rep.
679–680a	1348
681	Rep.
682	1307
683–685	Rep.
685a	1537

Title 31 Former Sections	*Title 31 New Sections*
686(a)	1535
686(b)	1536
686(c)	1535
686–1	1535
686–2	3324
686a	Rep.
686b(a), (b), (c) (related to 31:686, 686b).	1535
686b(c) (related to 31:686)	1536
686c to 688	Rep.
689	T. 40 §166a–1
690	Rep.
691	1346
692	T. 43 §1470
693	T. 43 §1471
693a	T. 28 §524
694, 695	Rep.
696	1347
697	1533
698	T. 32 §107
698a	T. 37 §1012
699	T. 42 §2459a
699a	1309
699b	T. 5 §3101 note
700	T. 10 §1584 note
700a, 700b	Elim.
700c	Rep.
700d	T. 38 §203
701(a), (b)	1552
701(c) (1st sentence)	1551
701(c) (last sentence), (d)	1552
702	1553
703(a)	1554
703(b)	1556
704	Rep.
705	1552
706	1555
707	1551
708	1557
711(1)–(3)	1305
711(4)–(11)	Rep.
711(11a)–(23)	1305
712	Rep.
712a	1502
712b to 716	Rep.
717, 718	1301
719, 720	Rep.
721	1310
722	T. 2 §30
723, 723a	T. 10 §2661a
724	1306
724a (1st sentence)	1304
724a (last sentence)	T. 39 §409
725	Rep.
725a to 725d	Elim.
725e	Rep.
725f	Elim.
725g	Rep.
725h	T. 24 §21b
725i to 725k	Rep.
725*l*, 725m	Elim.
725n, 725*o*	Rep.
725p(a) (last sentence)	331
725p (less (a) (last sentence))	Rep.
725p note	1322
725p–1	1322
725q(a) (last sentence)	331
725q (less (a) (last sentence))	Rep.
725q–1	1322
725q–1a	1324
725q–2	T. 18 §3150a
725r	1323
725s (less (a) (last sentence last proviso)).	1321
725s(a) (last sentence last proviso).	1322
725s–1	T. 25 §385a
725s–2	T. 25 §385b
725s–3	T. 25 §385c
725s–4	T. 18 §4043
725t, 725u	Rep.
725v(a)	Rep.
725v(b) (related to marshals)	T. 28 §572a
725v(b) (related to clerks)	T. 28 §2043
725w	1503
725x to 725z	Rep.
731–733 (words before semicolon).	3123
733 (words after semicolon), 734.	5116
734a to 738	Rep.
738a	3125
739	3121
740	3127
741	Rep.
741a	324
742, 742a	3124
743–751	Rep.
752 (1st–4th pars. less 2d par. form of bonds).	3102
752 (2d par. related to form of bonds).	3121
752 (last par.)	3107
752a	Rep.
753(a) (less form of notes, certificates of indebtedness, and Treasury bills).	3103
753(a) (related to form of notes, certificates of indebtedness, and Treasury bills).	3121
753(b)	Rep.
753(c)	3103
753(d) (1st sentence)	3108
753(d) (2d sentence)	3123
753(d) (last sentence related to 31:771).	3122
753(d) (last sentence less related to 31:771).	3129
754(a) (less form of certificates of indebtedness and Treasury bills, finality).	3104
754(a) (related to form of certificates of indebtedness and Treasury bills, finality).	3121
754(b)	Rep.
754(c)	T. 12 §221
754(d)	Rep.
754a	3111
754b	3121
755–757	Rep.
757a	(See former 405b)
757b, 757b–1	3101
757b–2	Rep.
757c(a)–(d) (1st sentence)	3105
757c(d) (last sentence)	3108
757c(e)	3129
757c(f), (g)	Rep.
757c(h)	3105
757c(i) (1st–6th sentences)	3126
757c(i) (last sentence)	331
757c(j)	3105
757c–1	Rep.
757c–2(a)–(c) (1st sentence)	3106
757c–2(c) (last sentence)	3108
757c–2(d)	3106
757c–3	3109
757c–4, 757c–5	3121
757d	3128
757e	3113
757f	331
758	3108
759–761	3129
761a to 765	Rep.
766	3123
767	3112
767a	Rep.
767b	3112
768 (words before semicolon)	3123
768 (words after semicolon)	3121
769, 770	Rep.
771, 772	3122
772a	3121
773	Rep.
773a–773d	5118
774	Rep.
801–804	3110
804a to 809	Rep.
821	5301
822	5304
822a(a)–(c)	5302
822a(d)	325
822b	5117, 5119, 5304
823, 824	Rep.
841	Rep.
846	9101
847, 848	9103
849	9104
850	9105
851	9106
852	9109
856	9101
857	9105
858	9106
859	1105
866	9105
867	9107
868 (less (d) (1st sentence related to 31:867)).	9108
868(d) (1st sentence related to 31:867).	9107
869(a)	9102
869(b)	Rep.
870	9107
871	Rep. See T. 40 §33a
901–904	3113
911	5119
912, 913	Rep.
914–917	5119
931–937	Rep.
938	5303
951	3701
952(a)–(d)(3)	3711
952(d)(4)	3701
952(e)(1) (1st to 3d sentences)	3717
952(e)(1) (last sentence)	3701
952(e)(2)–(7)	3717

Title 31 Former Sections	Title 31 New Sections
952(e)(8)	3701
952(f)	3718
952 note	3711
953	3711 note
954(a)–(d)	3716
954(e)	3701
955	3719
971–973	Rep.
1001	301
1002 (less words between 4th and 5th semicolons).	321
1002 (words between 4th and 5th semicolons).	331
1003	329
1004–1005a	301
1006, 1007	301
1008	Rep.
1009	301
1010 (related to seal)	301
1010 (related to books, papers, and records).	Rep.
1011	321
1012, 1013	Rep.
1014	328
1015	Rep.
1016	309
1017	321
1018	329
1019	Rep.
1020	1102
1020–1, 1020a	Rep.
1021, 1022	Rep.
1023(a)	321
1023(b)	3302
1023(c)	T. 18 §3059
1024	321
1025	Rep.
1026	330
1027	331
1028	Rep.
1029, 1030	331
1031, 1032	326
1033	322
1034	T. 21 §967
1035	T. 21 §968
1036	T. 21 §969
1037	T. 26 §7802
1038	323
1051	5311
1052(a)–(i)	5312
1052(j)	5319
1052(k)	Rep.
1052(*l*)	5312
1053	321
1054(a), (b) (1st sentence)	5318
1054(b) (last sentence related to civil penalties).	5321
1054(b) (last sentence related to criminal penalties).	5322
1055	5318
1056	5321
1057	5320
1058, 1059	5322
1060	Rep.
1061	5319
1062	Rep.
1081–1083	5313
1101	5316
1102	5317
1103, 1104	5321
1105	5317
1121, 1122	5314
1141, 1142	5315
1143(a)	5321
1143(b) (words before last comma).	5320
1143(b) (words after last comma).	5321
1151, 1152(a), (b)	1112
1152(c)–(f)	1113
1153(a)–(c)	1113
1153(d)	1112
1154(a)–(c)	717
1154(d) (1st sentence)	702
1154(d) (last sentence)	731
1154(e)	719
1155(a)	702
1155(b)	719
1156	Rep.
1157	717, 719, 720, 1112
1171–1174	719
1175(a)	734
1175(b)	719
1175(c)	734
1176	720
1201	9302
1202	3530
1203, 1204	Rep.
1221	6702
1222, 1223	Rep.
1224(a)(1), (2) (related to trustee).	6703
1224(a)(2) (related to report)	6724
1224(b)	Rep.
1224(c), (d), (e)	6703
1225(a), (b)	6707
1225(c)	Rep.
1226(a)(1)(A)	6705
1226(a)(1)(B)	6707
1226(a)(2)	6705
1226(b)	6706
1226(c)	Rep.
1227(a), (b)(1)	6708
1227(b)(2), (3)	6709
1227(b)(4)	6708
1227(b)(5)	6709
1227(b)(6), (7)	6712
1227(c)	6711
1227(d)	6701
1227(e)	6710
1228(a)(1)	6713
1228(a)(2)	6707
1228(a)(3)	6701
1228(a)(4)	6707
1228(a)(5)	6702
1228(a)(6)	6712
1228(a)(7)	6713
1228(b)	6707
1228(c)(1)	6707
1228(c)(2)(A)	6701
1228(c)(2)(B)	6707
1228(d)	6708
1228(e)	6709
1228(f)(1)	6707
1228(f)(2)	6708
1228(f)(3), (last sentence)	6709
1228(g)	6707
1228(h)	6713
1241(a)	6724
1241(b), (c)	6714
1241(d)	6724
1241(e)	6714, 6724
1241(f)	6724
1241(g)	6714
1242(a)	6716
1242(b)(1)–(3)(B) (1st sentence)	6717
1242(b)(3)(B) (2d sentence)	6718
1242(b)(3)(B) (last sentence)	6717
1242(b)(3)(C)	6718
1242(b)(3)(D), (E)	6717
1242(c)(1)	6701
1242(c)(2), (3) (related to proceedings).	6717
1242(c)(3) (related to suspensions and terminations).	6718
1242(c)(4)	6701
1242(d)	6719
1242(e), (f)	6718
1242(g)	6720
1242(h)	6716
1243(a), (b)	6704
1243(c)	6723
1243(d)	6715
1243 note	7301–7305
1244	6721
1245	6723
1261(a)	6703, 6724
1261(b)(1)–(7)	Rep.
1261(b)(8)	6701
1261(c)	6701
1262(a)	321
1262(b)	Rep.
1263	6722
1264	6713
1265	Rep.
1301	T. 2 §621
1302	T. 2 §622
1303	T. 2 §623
1321	T. 2 §631
1322	T. 2 §632
1323	T. 2 §633
1324	T. 2 §634
1325	T. 2 §635
1326	T. 2 §636
1327	T. 2 §637
1328	T. 2 §638
1329	T. 2 §639
1330	T. 2 §640
1331	T. 2 §641
1332	T. 2 §642
1351	T. 2 §651
1352	T. 2 §652
1353	T. 2 §653
1400	T. 2 §681
1401	T. 2 §682
1402	T. 2 §683
1403	T. 2 §684
1404	T. 2 §685
1405	T. 2 §686
1406	T. 2 §687
1407	T. 2 §688
1501–1510	Rep.
1521–1531	Elim.
1601	6902
1602	6903
1603	6904

Title 31 *Former Sections*	*Title 31* *New Sections*
1604	6903
1605	6902
1606	6901
1607	6906
1701	6101
1702	Rep.
1703	6102
1704(a)–(c)	6103
1704(d), (e)	6102
1705	6104
1706	Rep.
1707	6105
1801(a)(1)	3902
1801(a)(2)	3903
1801(b)–(d)	3902
1802	3904
1803	3906
1804	3905
1805–1806	3901

TITLE 32—NATIONAL GUARD

[This title was enacted into law by act Aug. 10, 1956, ch. 1041, §2, 70A Stat. 596. This table shows where sections of former Title 32 are incorporated in revised Title 32.]

Title 32 Former Sections	*Title 32 New Sections*
1	T. 10 §311
2	101; T. 10 §101
3	T. 10 §312
4	305, 313
4a	Rep.
4b	101; T. 10 §101
4c (1st 33 words)	101; T. 10 §101
4c (less 1st 33 words)	Rep.
5, 6	104
7	Rep.
8	104
9	103
10 (proviso)	104
10 (less proviso)	T. 10 §§3542, 8542
11–14	314
15	105
16	104
17	110
18–20	Rep.
21	106
22	107
23	Rep.
24	108
25	Rep.
26	Elim.
31	701
32	Rep.
33	702
34	Rep.
35	702
36	Rep.
37	Elim.
38	Rep.
39, 39a	703
40	Rep.
42, 42a	709
43	Rep.
44	Elim.
45	712
46	711
47	710
47–1, 47a	Elim.
47b, 48	Rep.
49, 50	708
51	Elim.
61	501
62	502
63	503
64	504
65	505
66, 67	506
68, 69	315
70	Rep.
71	507
72	317
73	Rep.
74	707
75	Rep. See T. 5 §§502, 3551, 5534, 6323(a), (b)
76	Rep. See T. 5 §6323(a), (b)
81	Rep.
81a	T. 10 §§3500, 8500
81b	T. 10 §§3501, 8501
81c	Rep.
82	T. 10 §§3499, 8499
83	T. 10 §§3502, 8502
84	Rep.
85, 86	Elim.
91	326
92	327
93	328
94	329
95	330
96	331
97	332, 333
111	305, 307
112	312
113	307
113a	Rep.
114	324
115	323; T. 10 §§3820, 8820
121, 122	Rep.
123	304
124	302
125	322
131	Rep.
132, 133	303
134	Rep.
141, 142	Elim.
142a–143a	Rep.
144–148	Rep.
149–152	Elim.
153	Rep.
154 (last proviso of 2d par.)	710
154 (2d par., less last proviso)	T. 31 §698a
154 (last par.)	303, 322, 323
154 (less 2d and last pars.)	Rep. See T. 37 §§206(a), (b), 402(b)
155	Rep.
156	705; T. 10 §§4621, 9621
157	Rep.
158	503
159, 160	Rep.
160a	318, 321; T. 10 §§3687, 3688, 3721, 8687, 8688, 8721
160b	3687 nt.
160c–164	Rep.
164a, 164b	319
164c	Rep.
164d	320; T. 10 §§3723, 8723
164e	Rep.
171	Rep.
172, 173	T. 10 §3015
174	T. 10 §§3541, 8541
175	T. 10 §§3496, 8496
176	T. 31 §698
181	T. 10 §4308
181a	T. 10 §4312
181b	T. 10 §§4312, 4313
181c	T. 10 §4308
181d, 181e	Elim.
182	T. 10 §4307
183	316; T. 10 §4310
184	T. 10 §4310
185	Rep.
186	T. 10 §4309
191	Rep.
192, 193	104 nt.
194(b)	109. Rep. in part.
194 (less (b))	109
195	Rep.
196	713

TITLE 34—NAVY

[This title was superseded by Title 10, Armed Forces. See Parallel Table B under Title 10]

TITLE 35—PATENTS

[This title was enacted into law by act July 19, 1952, ch. 950, §1, 66 Stat. 792. This table shows where sections of former Title 35 were incorporated in revised Title 35.]

Title 35 Former Sections	Title 35 New Sections
1	1
2	3
3	2
4	4
5	5
6	6
7	7
10	8
11	31, 32
11a	33
12	22
13	11
14	10
14a	(See former §78)
15	12
16	11(a) 1
17–19	Rep.
20	14
21	21
22	Rep.
23	Rep.
31	101, 102, 161
32	102(d), 119, 172
32a, 32b	Rep.
33	111, 112, 162
34	113, 114
35	115
36	131
37	133, 267
38	Rep.
39	153
40	154
40a–40d	Rep.
41	151
42–42f	Rep.
43	Rep.
44	152
45	266
46	147
47	261
48	Rep.
49	287
50	292
51	132, 135
52	135
53	23
54–56	24
56a	164
57	134
58, 59	Rep.
59a	141; T. 28 §1542
60	142
61	143
62	144
63	145, 146
64	251, 252
65	253
66	291
67	281, 284
68	T. 28 §1498
69	102(g), 282
70	283–286, 290
71	288
72	102, 104
72a	146, 291
73	171
74, 75	289
76	114
77	173
78	12, 13, 41
79	42
80–87	Rep.
88	254
89–96	Elim.
101–108	Elim.
109	104
110–118a	Elim.
119	T. 50 App. §2371
151	181
152	182
153	183
154	184
155	185
156	186
157	187
158	188
159	Rep.

TITLE 36—PATRIOTIC AND NATIONAL OBSERVANCES, CEREMONIES, AND ORGANIZATIONS

[This title was enacted into law by Pub. L. 105–225, §1, Aug. 12, 1998, 112 Stat. 1253. This table shows where sections of former Title 36 were incorporated in revised Title 36.]

Title 36 Former Sections	Title 36 New Sections
1, 1a, 2 (1st sentence words before 2d comma).	300101
2 (1st sentence words between 2d comma and 3d semicolon).	300105
2 (1st sentence words between 3d and 4th semicolons).	300106
2 (1st sentence words after 4th semicolon).	300105
2 (last sentence)	300106
3	300102
4	Rep.
4a	300103
5 (matter before (a)), (a), (b), (c) (1st–5th pars.).	300104
5(c) (6th par.)	300107
5(c) (last par.)	300104
6, 7	300110
8	300111
9	300109
10–12	Rep.
13	300108
14	Rep.
15	300108
16	Rep.
17, 17a, 17b	Rep.
18 (words before "for patriotic").	153101
18 (words beginning with "for patriotic").	153102
18a (1st sentence)	153103
18a (last sentence)	153105
18b (1st sentence)	153107
18b (last sentence)	153106
18c	153104
20 (1st sentence words before "for the promotion").	21301
20 (1st sentence words beginning with "for the promotion").	21302
20 (2d sentence)	21303
20 (3d sentence words before 2d comma).	21305
20 (3d sentence words after 2d comma).	21304
20 (4th, 5th sentences)	21307
20 (last sentence)	21306
20a	153301
20b	153302
20c	153303
20d	153304
20e, 20f	153301
20g	10102
21, 22 (words before 2d comma)	30901
22 (words after 2d comma)	30904
23	30902
24 (words before semicolon)	30904
24 (words after semicolon)	30906
25 (1st–5th sentences)	30903
25 (6th sentence)	30904
25 (7th, 8th sentences)	30903
25 (last sentence)	30904
26	30907
27	30905
28	30908
29	10102
31, 32 (words before 2d comma)	80301
32 (words after 2d comma)	80304
33 (words before 19th comma)	80302
33 (words after 19th comma)	80306
34 (1st–7th sentences)	80303
34 (last sentence)	80304
35	80303
36	80305
37	80307
38	80304
38a	10102
39	80307
41, 42	21701
43	21702
44 (words before 4th semicolon less perpetual succession).	21704
44 (words before 4th semicolon related to perpetual succession).	21701
44 (words between 4th and 5th semicolons).	21705
44 (words after 5th semicolon)	21704
45	21703
46	21706
47	21704
48	21705
49	21708
50	21707
51	10102
56–56h	Elim.
57	140101
57a	140102
57b(a)	140101
57b(b)–(j)	140103
58	140104
59	10102
61–66	Rep.
67, 67a	22701
67b(1)–(10)	22702
67b(11)	22707
67c (less perpetual succession)	22705
67c (related to perpetual succession).	22701
67d(1), (2)	22707
67d(3)	22704
67d(4)	22708
67e (words before 3d comma, words after 3d comma related to discrimination in membership).	22703
67e (words after 3d comma related to discrimination in holding office).	22704
67f(1) (1st sentence)	22703
67f(1) (last sentence), (2)	22704
67g	22705
67h	22712
67i(1)	22701
67i(2)–(5)	22705
67j	22711
67k	22710
67*l*	22704
67m	22709
67n, 67*o*	22707
67p	22706
67q	22710
67r	22705
67s	10102
71–77	Elim.
78, 78a	130101
78b	130102
78c(1)	130101
78c(2)–(10)	130105
78d	130103
78e, 78f	130104
78g(a)	130108
78g(b)	130110
78h, 78i	130107
78j	130111
78k	130107
78*l*	130109
78m	Rep.
78n	130112
78*o*	130106
78p	130113
78q	10102
81–88	Rep.
90a, 90b	50301
90c	50302
90d (less perpetual succession)	50304
90d (related to perpetual succession).	50301
90e	50303
90f	50306
90g	50304
90h	50305
90i	50308
90j	50307
90k	10102
91, 92	22501
93	22502
94	22508
95 (words before colon)	22504
95 (words between colon and 1st comma).	22501
95 (words after 1st comma)	22504
96 (1st sentence)	22507
96 (last sentence)	22506
97	22503
98	22506
99	22504
100	22505
101	22510
102	22509
103	22501
104	10102
105	22501
111, 112	230101
113	230102
114 (words before 4th semicolon less perpetual succession).	230104
114 (words before 4th semicolon related to perpetual succession).	230101

Title 36 Former Sections	Title 36 New Sections
114 (words between 4th and 5th semicolons).	230105
114 (words after 5th semicolon)	230104
115	230103
116	230104
117	230105
118	230107
119	230106
120	10102
121 (1st, 2d pars.)	2101
121 (3d par.)	2102
121 (last par.)	2101
121a	Rep.
121b	2102
122	2101
122a	2102
122b	2104
123	2105
123 note	2112
124	2105
125	2106
125a	2107
125b	2108
126	Rep.
127	2111
128	2103
129, 130	Rep.
131	2103
132	2111
133	2103
134, 135	Rep.
135a	(Previously transferred to T. 41 §6v and subsequently repealed)
136–138	2103
138a	Rep.
138b (1st–3d pars.)	2103
138b (4th par.)	2110
138b (last par.)	2103
138c, 138c note	2109
138d	2103
139 (words before "for patriotic, historical, and educational purposes").	153901
139 (words beginning with "for patriotic, historical, and educational purposes").	153902
139a	153903
139b	153904
140	154301
140 note	10102
140a	154302
140b(a)	154301
140b(b)–(j)	154303
140c	154304
141, 142	117
142a	109
142b	125
142c, 142c–1	134
143	105
144	(See former 170)
145	128
146	107
147, 148	111
149	141
150	103
151	118
151a	134
152	Rep.
153	106
154	T. 8 §1448a
155	121
155a	2502
155b	2501
156	124
157	110
157a	122
157b	112
158	140
159	108
160	120
161	131
162	115
163	123
164	113
165	130
166	133
167(1), (2)	136
167(3), (4) (related to Police Week).	137
167(4) (related to Peace Officers Memorial Day).	136
168	132
169	143
169a	138
169b	101
169c	114
169d	142
169e	139
169f	126
169g	116
169h	119
169i	104
169i note	701
169i–1(a)(1)	703
169i–1(a)(2)	702
169i–1(b)	704
169i–1(c)	Rep.
169j—169j–10	Rep.
169k	102
169*l*	129
169m	127
170, 171	301
172–178	T. 4 §§4–10
179–182	901
182a–184	Rep.
185	(See former 169h)
186	302
187	303
188	304
189, 189 note	902
189a	902
201	40301
202	40302
203	40303
204	40305
205 (less perpetual succession)	40304
205 (related to perpetual succession).	40301
206	40306
207	40307
208	10102
221, 222	190101
223	190102
224 (less perpetual succession)	190105
224 (related to perpetual succession).	190101
225	190103
226, 227(a)–(d)	190104
227(e)	190103
228	190105
229, 230, 231 (words before 2d comma).	190107
231 (words after 2d comma)	190112
232	190111
233	190109
234	190107
235	Rep.
236 (1st sentence)	190108
236 (2d, last sentences), 237	190110
238	190106
239	10102
251	150301
252	150302
253 (words before 1st comma)	150304
253 (words after 1st comma)	150303
254	150302
254 note	10102
271, 272	70901
273	70902
274	70906
275 (1st sentence)	70910
275 (2d, last sentences)	70912
276	70903
277	70905
278	70904
279, 280	70908
281	70913
282	70908
283	70911
284	Rep.
285	70914
286	70907
287	70912
288	70909
289	70906
290	70901
291	10102
311, 312	140301
313	140302
314(a)	140301
314(b)–(k), 315	140303
316	140304
317	140305
341	22101
342 (1st sentence)	22102
342 (2d, last sentences)	22105
343	22103
344	22106
345 (less perpetual succession)	22104
345 (related to perpetual succession).	22101
346 (1st sentence)	22109
346 (last sentence)	22108
347	22105
348	22107
349	Rep.
350	22101
351	22104
352	10102
371 (1st sentence)	220502
371 (last sentence)	220508
372	220502
373	220501
374	220503
375(a) (words before cl. (1) less perpetual succession).	220505

Title 36 Former Sections	Title 36 New Sections
375(a) (words before cl. (1) related to perpetual succession).	220502
375(a)(1)–(16), (b)	220505
376	220504
377, 378	220507
379	220505
380	220506
381	220510
382	10102
382a(a)	220511
382a(b)	Rep.
382b	220509
383	220502
384	Rep.
391(a)	220521
391(b), (c)	220522
391(d)	220521
392(a)(1)–(3)	220524
392(a)(4)	220525
392(a)(5)–(9)	220524
392(b)	220525
393, 393 note	220523
394	220521
395(a)	220527
395(b)(1)–(4)	220528
395(b)(5)	220521
395(c)	220529
396	220526
401	150502
402	150503
403	150506
404(a)	150509
404(b)	150511
405	150504
406, 407	150505
408	150506
409–411	150508
412	150512
413	150510
414, 415	150508
416	Rep.
417	150513
418	150507
419	150511
420	150501
421	10102
426	Rep.
431, 432	150701
433	150702
434	150706
435(a)	150709
435(b)	150711
436	150703
437	150704
438	150705
439, 440	150708
441	150712
442	150708
443	150710
444	Rep.
445	150713
446	150707
447	10102
461, 462	152501
463	152502
464	152505
465(a)	152508
465(b)	152510
466	152503
467–469	152504
470, 471	152507
472	152511
473	152507
474	152509
475	Rep.
476	152512
477	152506
478	152505
479	10102
491	Rep.
492	Rep.
493	Elim.
501, 502	30701
503	30702
504	30705
505 (1st sentence)	30708
505 (2d, 3d sentences)	30710
505 (last sentence)	30708
506	30703
507, 508	30704
509, 510	30707
511	30711
512	30707
513	30709
514	Rep.
515	30712
516	30706
517	30710
518	10102
531, 532	200301
533	200302
534(1)	200301
534(2)–(10)	200305
535	200303
536–538	200304
539(a)	200308
539(b)	200310
540, 541	200307
542	200311
543	200307
544	200309
545	Rep.
546	200312
547	200306
548	200305
549	200313
550	10102
571, 572	70501
573	70502
574	70505
575(a)	70508
575(b)	70510
576	70503
577, 578	70504
579, 580	70507
581	70511
582	70507
583	70509
584	Rep.
585	70512
586	70503
587	70506
588	70505
589	10102
601, 602	151901
603	151902
604(1)	151901
604(2)–(9)	151905
605(a)	151907
605(b)	151909
606	151903
607, 608	151904
609, 610	151906
611	151910
612	151906
613	151908
614	Rep.
615	151911
616	151905
617	10102
631, 632	130301
633	130302
634(1)	130301
634(2)–(9)	130305
635(a)	130307
635(b)	130309
636	130303
637, 638	130304
639, 640	130306
641	130310
642	130306
643	130308
644	Rep.
645	130311
646	130305
647	10102
648	130301
661, 662	152301
663	152302
664	152305
665 (1st sentence)	152308
665 (2d, 3d sentences)	152310
665 (last sentence)	152308
666	152303
667, 668	152304
669, 670	152307
671	152311
672	152307
673	152309
674	Rep.
675	152312
676	152306
677	152310
678	152305
679	152301
680	10102
691, 692	31101
693	31102
694(1)	31101
694(2)–(9)	31105
695(a)	31107
695(b)	31109
696	31103
697, 698	31104
699, 700	31106
701	31110
702	31106
703	31108
704	Rep.
705	31111
706	31105
707	10102
721(a)	Rep.
721(b)	501
722(a), (b)	502

Title 36 Former Sections	*Title 36 New Sections*
723	510
724	503
725 (1st–3d sentences)	504
725 (4th sentence)	508
725 (last sentence)	504
726	Rep.
727	505
728 (1st, 2d sentences)	506
728 (3d, last sentences)	509
729	507
730	501–505, 508, 510
741–747	Rep.
748	Rep.
749	Rep.
761, 762	230301
763	230302
764(1)	230301
764(2)–(10)	230305
765	230303
766(a)	230304
766(b)	230303
767, 768	230304
769(a)	230308
769(b)	230310
770, 771	230307
772	230311
773	230307
774	230309
775	Rep.
776	230312
777	230306
778	230305
779	230313
780	10102
791, 792	40501
793	40502
794	40505
795(a)	40507
795(b)	40509
796	40503
797, 798	40504
799(a) (1st sentence words before last comma).	40506
799(a) (1st sentence words after last comma).	40510
799(a) (last sentence), (b), 800	40506
801	40510
802	40506
803	40508
804	Rep.
805	40511
806	40505
807	10102
821, 822	140501
823	140502
824(1)	140501
824(2)–(9)	140505
825(a)	140507
825(b)	140510
826	140503
827, 828	140504
829, 830	140506
831	140509
832	140506
833	140508
834	Rep.
835	140511
836	140505
837	10102
851, 852	30301
853(1)–(3), (4) (less words between 1st comma and semicolon).	30302
853(4) (words between 1st comma and semicolon).	30307
854	30305
855(a)	30308
855(b)	30310
856	30303
857, 858	30304
859, 860	30307
861	30311
862	30307
863	30309
864	Rep.
865	30312
866	30305
867	30306
868	10102
881, 882	30101
883	30102
884(1)	30101
884(2)–(9)	30105
885(a)	30108
885(b)	30110
886	30103
887, 888	30104
889, 890	30107
891	30111
892	30107
893	30109
894	Rep.
895	30106
896	30105
897	30112
898	10102
911, 912	110301
913	110302
914(a)	110301
914(b)–(h)	110304
915(a)	110306
915(b)	110308
916, 917	110303
918, 919	110305
920	110309
921	110305
922	110307
923	Rep.
924	110310
925	110304
926	10102
941, 942	30502
943	30503
944(1)	30502
944(2)–(10)	30506
945 (1st sentence)	30504
945 (last sentence)	30501
946, 947	30505
948 (1st sentence 1st–14th words).	30509
948 (1st sentence 15th–last words, 2d, last sentences).	30511
949, 950	30508
951	30512
952	30508
953	30510
954	Rep.
955	30513
956	30507
957	30514
958	10102
971, 972	20101
973(A) (1st sentence words before proviso).	20102
973(A) (1st sentence proviso)	20106
973(A) (last sentence), (B)–(G)	20102
974(1)	20101
974(2)–(9)	20105
975(a)	20107
975(b)	20109
976	20103
977, 978	20104
979, 980	20106
981	20110
982	20106
983	20108
984	Rep.
985	20111
986	20101
987	20105
988	10102
1001, 1002	153701
1003	153702
1004(1)	153701
1004(2)–(8)	153705
1005	153703
1006–1008	153704
1009(a)	153708
1009(b)	153710
1010, 1011	153707
1012	153711
1013	153707
1014	153709
1015	Rep.
1016	153712
1017	153706
1018	153705
1019	153713
1020	10102
1041	154101
1042	154102
1043	154105
1044(1)	154101
1044(2)–(9)	154105
1045(a)	154108
1045(b)	154110
1046	154103
1047, 1048	154104
1049, 1050	154107
1051	154111
1052	154107
1053	154109
1054	Rep.
1055	154113
1056	154106
1057	154105
1058	154112
1059	10102
1071, 1072	130501
1073	130502
1074	130505
1075(a)	130508
1075(b)	130511
1076	130503
1077, 1078	130504
1079, 1080	130507

Title 36 Former Sections	Title 36 New Sections
1081	130512
1082	130507
1083	130509
1084 (less (b) (2d sentence cl. (2))).	10101
1084(b) (2d sentence cl. (2))	130510
1085	130513
1086	130506
1087	130505
1088	10102
1101(1)–(76), (77) (related to Fleet Reserve Association), (79), (80).	10101
1101(77) (related to NNRCF)	Rep.
1102, 1103	10101
1151, 1152	170101
1153	170102
1154 (less perpetual succession).	170104
1154 (related to perpetual succession).	170101
1155, 1156	170106
1157	170103
1158	170107
1159	170111
1160	170105
1161	170108
1162	170109
1163	170104
1164	170106
1165	170110
1166	10101
1167	10102
1201, 1202	220301
1203	220302
1204	220305
1205(a)	220310
1205(b)	220312
1206	220303
1207, 1208	220304
1209	220308
1210	220313
1211	220308
1212	220311
1213(a)	10101
1213(b)	220314
1214	220315
1215	220306
1216 (1st sentence)	220305
1216 (last sentence)	220309
1217	220314
1218	10102
1219	220307
1301	220101
1302	220102
1303	220105
1304(a), (b)	220108
1304(c)	220114
1304(d), (e)	220108
1305(a)	220103
1305(b)–(d)	220104
1306 (1st sentence)	220105
1306 (last sentence)	220109
1307	220106
1308	220107
1309(a)	220110
1309(b), (c)	220112
1309(d)	220111
1309(e), (f)	220113
1309(g)	(See 36:1101)
1309(h)	10102
1401	2301
1402, 1403	2302
1404	2307
1404 (notes)	2302, 2307
1405	2303
1406	2305
1407	2304
1408	2309
1409	2308
1410	2306
1411	Rep.
1501	152702
1502	152706
1503	152703
1504	152710
1505	152704
1506, 1507	152705
1508	152707
1509	152711
1510	152709
1511	152712
1512	10102
1513	152701
1514 (1st sentence)	152708
1514 (last sentence)	152702
1601	80502
1602	80506
1603 (less discrimination)	80503
1603 (related to discrimination in membership).	80504
1603 (related to discrimination in holding office).	80505
1604	80510
1605	80504
1606, 1607	80505
1608	80507
1609	80511
1610	80509
1611	80512
1612	10102
1613	80501
1614 (1st sentence)	80508
1614 (last sentence)	80502
1701	100102
1702	100106
1703	100103
1704	100110
1705	100104
1706, 1707	100105
1708	100107
1709	100111
1710	100109
1711	100112
1712	10102
1713	100101
1714 (1st sentence)	100108
1714 (last sentence), 1715	100102
1801	220702
1802	220706
1803	220703
1804	220710
1805	220704
1806, 1807	220705
1808	220707
1809	220711
1810	220709
1811	220712
1812	10102
1813	220701
1814 (1st sentence)	220708
1814 (last sentence), 1815	220702
1901	20702
1902	20706
1903	20703
1904	20710
1905	20704
1906, 1907	20705
1908	20707
1909	20711
1910	20709
1911	20712
1912	10102
1913	20701
1914	20708
2001	151502
2002	151506
2003	151503
2004	151510
2005	151504
2006, 2007	151505
2008(a)–(e)	151507
2008(f)	151508
2009	151511
2010	151509
2011	151512
2012	10102
2013	151501
2014 (1st sentence)	151508
2014 (last sentence), 2015	151502
2101	20902
2102	20906
2103	20903
2104	20911
2105	20904
2106, 2107	20905
2108(a)–(e)	20908
2108(f)	20909
2109	20912
2110	20910
2111	20913
2112	10102
2113	20901
2114 (1st sentence)	20909
2114 (last sentence)	20902
2115	20907
2116	20902
2201	70302
2202	70306
2203	70303
2204	70310
2205	70304
2206, 2207	70305
2208	70307
2209	70311
2210	70309
2211	70312
2212	10102
2213	70301
2214 (1st sentence)	70308
2214 (last sentence), 2215	70302
2301	150102
2302	150107
2303	150103
2304	150111
2305	150105

Title 36 Former Sections	*Title 36 New Sections*
2306, 2307	150106
2308(a)–(e)	150108
2308(f)	150109
2309	150112
2310	150110
2311	150113
2312	10102
2313	150101
2314 (1st sentence)	150109
2314 (last sentence), 2315	150102
2316	150104
2401	21102
2402	21106
2403	21103
2404	21110
2405 (words before 3d comma, words after 3d comma related to discrimination in membership).	21104
2405 (words after 3d comma related to discrimination in holding office), 2406, 2407.	21105
2408(a)–(d)	21107
2408(e)	21108
2409	21111
2410	21109
2411	21112
2412	10102
2413	21101
2414 (1st sentence)	21108
2414 (last sentence), 2415	21102
2501	170502
2502	170506
2503	170503
2504	170510
2505 (words before 3d comma, words after 3d comma related to discrimination in membership).	170504
2505 (words after 3d comma related to discrimination in holding office), 2506, 2507.	170505
2508	170507
2509	170511
2510	170509
2511	170512
2512	10102
2513	170501
2514 (1st sentence)	170508
2514 (last sentence), 2515	170502
2601	40102
2602	40106
2603	40103
2604	40110
2605	40104
2606, 2607	40105
2608	40107
2609	40111
2610	40109
2611	40112
2612	10102
2613	40101
2614 (1st sentence)	40108
2614 (last sentence), 2615	40102
2701(a)	110102
2701(b)	110108
2702	110106
2703	110103
2704	110110
2705	110104
2706, 2707	110105
2708	110107
2709	110111
2710	110109
2711	110112
2712	10102
2713	110101
2714 (1st sentence)	110108
2714 (last sentence), 2715	110102
2801	154502
2802	154506
2803	154503
2804	154510
2805	154504
2806, 2807	154505
2808(a)–(e)	154507
2808(f)	154508
2809	154511
2810	154509
2811	154512
2812	10102
2813	154501
2814 (1st sentence)	154508
2814 (last sentence), 2815	154502
2901	152902
2902	152906
2903	152903
2904	152911
2905 (words before 3d comma, words after 3d comma related to discrimination in membership).	152904
2905 (words after 3d comma related to discrimination in holding office), 2906, 2907.	152905
2908(a)–(e)	152908
2908(f)	152909
2909	152907
2910	152912
2911	152910
2912	152913
2913	10102
2914	152901
2915 (1st sentence)	152909
2915 (last sentence), 2916	152902
3001	210302
3002	210306
3003	210303
3004	210311
3005 (words before 3d comma, words after 3d comma related to discrimination in membership).	210304
3005 (words after 3d comma related to discrimination in holding office), 3006, 3007.	210305
3008	210308
3009	210312
3010	210310
3011	210313
3012	10102
3013	210301
3014 (1st sentence)	210309
3014 (last sentence)	210302
3015	210307
3016	210302
3101	240102
3102	240106
3103	240103
3104	240110
3105	240104
3106, 3107	240105
3108	240107
3109	240111
3110	240109
3111	240112
3112	10102
3113	240101
3114 (1st sentence)	240108
3114 (last sentence), 3115	240102
3201	20501
3202	20502
3203 (1st sentence)	20503
3203 (last sentence)	20505
3204	20504
3205	20503
3206	Rep.
3207	20501
3208	20506
3209	10102
3301	21901
3302 (1st sentence)	21905
3302 (last sentence)	21902
3303 (less perpetual succession).	21903
3303 (related to perpetual succession).	21901
3304	21905
3305	21904
3306	21906
3307	21903
3308	21908
3309	21907
3310	10102
3401, 3402	22301
3403	22302
3404(1)	22301
3404(2)–(9)	22305
3405(a)	22308
3405(b)	22310
3406	22303
3407, 3408	22304
3409, 3410	22307
3411	22311
3412	22307
3413	22309
3414	Rep.
3415	22312
3416	22306
3417	22305
3418	10102
3501(a)	80101
3501(b)	80102
3501(c)	80106
3502	80104
3503 (1st sentence)	80103
3503 (last sentence), 3504	80105
3601	170302
3602	170306
3603	170303
3604	170311
3605 (words before 1st comma, words after 1st comma related to discrimination in membership).	170304
3605 (words after 1st comma related to discrimination in holding office), 3606, 3607.	170305

Title 36 Former Sections	Title 36 New Sections
3608	170308
3609	170312
3610	170310
3611	170313
3612	10102
3613	170301
3614	170309
3615	170307
3616	170302
3701	50102
3702	50106
3703	50103
3704	50110
3705	50104
3706, 3707	50105
3708	50107
3709	50111
3710	50109
3711	50112
3712	10102
3713	50101
3714	50108
3715	50102
3801	230502
3802	230506
3803	230503
3804	230511
3805	230504
3806, 3807, 3808 (related to directors and officers).	230505
3808 (related to membership)	230504
3809	230508
3810	230512
3811	230510
3812	230513
3813	10102
3814	230501
3815	230509
3816	230507
3817	230502
3901	22902
3902	22906
3903	22903
3904	22910
3905	22904
3906, 3907	22905
3908(a)–(e)	22907
3908(f)	22908
3909	22911
3910	22909
3911	22912
3912	10102
3913	22901
3914 (1st sentence)	22908
3914 (last sentence), 3915	22902
4001	154702
4002	154706
4003	154703
4004	154711
4005	154704
4006, 4007, 4008 (related to directors and officers).	154705
4008 (related to membership)	154704
4009	154708
4010	154712
4011	154710
4012	154713
4013	10102
4014	154701
4015 (1st sentence)	154709
4015 (last sentence)	154702
4016	154707
4017	154702
4101	152102
4102	152106
4103	152103
4104	152104
4105, 4106	152105
4107(a)–(e)	152107
4107(f)	152108
4108	152111
4109	152110
4110	152109
4111	152112
4112	10102
4113	152101
4114	152108
4115	152102
4201	20301
4202	20302
4203 (words before 1st comma)	20303
4203 (words after 1st comma)	20304
4204 (related to meeting)	20305
4204 (related to report)	20306
4205	20304
4206	10102
4301, 4302	23101
4303(1) (1st sentence words before 8th comma).	23102
4303(1) (1st sentence words after 8th comma).	23106
4303(1) (last sentence), (2)–(7)	23102
4304(1)	23101
4304(2)–(9)	23105
4305(a)	23107
4305(b)	23110
4306	23103
4307–4309	23104
4310, 4311	23106
4312	23111
4313	23106
4314	23108
4315 (less (b) (2d sentence cl. (2))).	10101
4315(b) (2d sentence cl. (2))	23109
4316	23112
4317	23105
4318	10102
4401 (words before "for the following objects and purposes").	70701
4401 (words beginning with "for the following objects and purposes").	70702
4402 (words before last semicolon).	70704
4402 (words after last semicolon).	70705
4403	70701
4404 (1st–3d sentences)	70703
4404 (4th sentence related to adopting and altering seal).	70704
4404 (4th sentence less adopting and altering seal).	70703
4404 (5th sentence related to establishing bylaws).	70704
4404 (5th sentence less establishing bylaws).	70703
4404 (last sentence related to employment authority).	70704
4404 (last sentence less employment authority).	70703
4405	70707
4406	70705
4407	70706
4408	10102
4501	150901
4502	150905
4503	150902
4504	150905
4505(a)	150907
4505(b)	150910
4506	150903
4507, 4508	150904
4509, 4510	150906
4511	150911
4512	150906
4513	150908
4514 (less (b) (2d sentence cl. (2))).	10101
4514(b) (2d sentence cl. (2))	150909
4515	150912
4516	150905
4517	10102
4601, 4602	153501
4603	153502
4604	153505
4605, 4606	153504
4607(a)	153508
4607(b)	153511
4608	153503
4609	153512
4610 (less (b) (2d sentence cl. (2))).	10101
4610(b) (2d sentence cl. (2))	153510
4611	153509
4612, 4613	153507
4614	153513
4615	153507
4616	153506
4617	10102
4701, 4702 (words before 2d comma).	210101
4702 (words after 2d comma)	210105
4703	210102
4704 (1st par.)	210104
4704 (last par. related to regulations for membership).	210103
4704 (last par. less regulations for membership).	210104
4705	210106
4706	10102
4707	210105
4801	60102
4802	60106
4803	60103
4804	60110
4805(a), (b) (related to discrimination in membership).	60104
4805(b) (related to discrimination in holding office), 4806, 4807.	60105
4808	60107
4809	60111
4810	60109
4811	60112

Title 36 Former Sections	Title 36 New Sections
4812	10102
4813	60101
4814	60108
4815	60102
4901	21501
4902	21504
4903 (words before 8th comma less "gratuitously or otherwise").	21502
4903 ("gratuitously or otherwise" and words after 8th comma).	21505
4904 (1st sentence)	21503
4904 (last sentence)	21506
4905–4908	21503
4909	21501
4910	10102
5001	140702
5002	140706
5003	140703
5004	140710
5005	140704
5006, 5007, 5008 (related to directors and officers).	140705
5008 (related to membership)	140704
5009	140707
5010	140711
5011	140709
5012	140712
5013	10102
5014 (1st sentence)	140708
5014 (last sentence), 5015	140702
5016	140701
5101	190302
5102	190306
5103	190303
5104	190311
5105	190304
5106, 5107, 5108 (related to directors and officers).	190305
5108 (related to membership)	190304
5109	190308
5110	190312
5111	190310
5112	190313
5113	10102
5114 (1st sentence)	190309
5114 (last sentence)	190302
5115	190307
5116	190302
5117	190301
5201(a)	151301
5201(b)	151302
5202(a)–(f)	151303
5202(g)(1)(A)	151304
5202(g)(1)(B), (C)	151305
5202(g)(2), (h)	151304
5203(a)(1)	151301
5203(a)(2), (3)	151306
5203(a)(4)	151308
5203(b), (c)(1), (2) (words before 2d comma).	151305
5203(c)(2) (words after 2d comma).	151303
5203(c)(3)–(5)	151305
5204, 5205	151307
5206(a)	10101
5206(b)	151311
5206(c)	151309
5207	151310
5301	151101
5302 (1st sentence)	151102
5302 (last sentence)	151104
5303	151105
5304	151106
5305	151103
5306	151104
5307	Rep.
5308	151107
5309	151105
5310	151101
5311	10102
5401 (1st sentence words before "for the education of the general public").	200101
5401 (1st sentence words beginning with "for the education of the general public").	200102
5401 (2d sentence words before proviso).	200103
5401 (2d sentence proviso, 3d sentence).	200104
5401 (last sentence words before proviso).	200105
5401 (last sentence proviso)	200104
5402	10102
5501(a) (less "nonprofit")	40701
5501(a) (related to nonprofit)	40704
5501(b)(1)	40701
5501(b)(2)	40705
5501(c)(1)–(4)	40702
5501(c)(5)	Elim.
5501(d)	40702

Title 36 Former Sections	Title 36 New Sections
5502(a) (words before cl. (1))	40721
5502(a) (less words before cl. (1)).	40722
5502(b)	40724
5502(c)	40730
5502(d)	Rep.
5503	40723
5504(a)	40731
5504(b), (c)	40732
5504(d)	40731
5504(e)(1)	40732
5504(e)(2)	40733
5505	40728
5506(a)	40729
5506(b), (c)	40728
5506(d)	40729
5507	40727
5508(a)(1), (2)	40703
5508(a)(3)	40704
5508(b)–(e)	40703
5509	40706
5521	Rep.
5522	Elim.
5523	Rep.
5601	70102
5602	70106
5603	70103
5604	70110
5605	70104
5606, 5607	70105
5608(a)–(d)	70107
5608(e)	70108
5608(f)	70103
5608(g) (related to membership).	70104
5608(g) (related to directors and officers).	70105
5609	70111
5610	70109
5611	70112
5612	10102
5613 (related to termination of charter).	70102
5613 (related to duty to maintain status).	70108
5614	70102
5615	70101
5701(a)	151701
5701(b)	151702
5702(a)–(f)	151703
5702(g)(1)(A)	151704
5702(g)(1)(B), (C)	151705
5702(g)(2)(A) (1st, 2d sentences, last sentence related to employees).	151704
5702(g)(2)(A) (last sentence related to board of directors).	151703
5702(g)(2)(B), (C)	151704
5703(a)(1)	151701
5703(a)(2), (3)	151706
5703(a)(4), (a) (last par.)	151708
5703(b), (c)(1)–(4), (5) (words before 2d comma).	151705
5703(c)(5) (words after 2d comma).	151703
5703(c)(6), (7), (last par.)	151705
5704, 5705	151707
5706(a)	10101
5706(b)	151712
5706(c)	151709
5707	151710
5708	151711
5801	20202
5802	20206
5803	20203
5804	20210
5805	20204
5806, 5807	20205
5808(a)–(d)	20207
5808(e)	20208
5808(f)	20203
5808(g) (related to directors and officers).	20205
5808(g) (related to membership).	20204
5809	20211
5810	20209
5811	20212
5812	10102
5813 (related to termination of charter).	20202
5813 (related to duty to maintain status).	20208
5814	20202
5815	20201
5901	21002
5902	21006
5903	21003
5904	21010
5905	21004
5906, 5907	21005
5908(a)–(d)	21007
5908(e)	21008

Title 36 Former Sections	Title 36 New Sections
5908(f)	21003
5908(g) (related to membership).	21004
5908(g) (related to directors and officers).	21005
5909	21011
5910	21009
5911	21012
5912	10102
5913 (related to termination of charter).	21002
5913 (related to duty to maintain status).	21008
5914	21002
5915	21001

TITLE 37—PAY AND ALLOWANCES OF THE UNIFORMED SERVICES

[This title was enacted into law by Pub. L. 87–649, §1, Sept. 7, 1962, 76 Stat. 451. This table shows where sections of former Title 37 were incorporated in revised Title 37.]

Title 37 Former Sections	*Title 37 New Sections*
1–3	Rep.
3a	Elim.
4–4b	Rep.
4c	T. 10 §§3682, 8682
4c–1	T. 10 §6116
5–8a	Rep.
9, 9a	Rep.
10, 10a	Rep.
11–13a	Rep.
14, 14a	Rep.
15–16a	Rep.
17, 17a	Rep.
18, 18a	Rep.
19, 19a	Rep.
20, 20a	Rep.
21, 21a	Rep.
22–26a	Rep.
27–29b	Rep.
30, 31	Rep.
31a (less proviso of (b))	T. 10 §§701–704
31a(b) (proviso)	501
32(b), (d), (e), (g), (h)	501
32(c)	Rep.
32(f)	101, 502; T. 10 §§702–704
32 (less (b)–(e), (g), (h))	101
33(a)	Rep.
33(b)	502, 503
33(c), (d)	501
33(e)	T. 10 §704
33a–37	Rep.
38	504; T. 10 §702
39	501–503. Rep. in part. See T. 33 §857a
101–101b	Rep.
102–103b	Rep.
104–111	Rep.
111a	403
111b	Elim.
112	Rep.
112a	Elim.
112b	Rep.
112c	T. 10 §7477
112d–112i	Rep.
113, 114	Rep.
115	Elim.
115a to 117a–1	Rep.
117b, 118	Rep.
118a	Elim.
118a–1	301
118b–120	Rep.
201–208a	Rep.
209–221	Rep.
231(g)	401, 420
231 (less (g))	101
232(a)	203
232(c) (last sent.)	T. 10 §517
232(d)	204
232 (less (a), last sent. of (c), (d)).	201
233 (less proviso of (d))	205
233(d) (proviso)	Elim.
234	302, 303
234a	Rep.
234b	Elim.
235	301
235a	901
236	304
237	305
238	Elim.
239	308
240	307
241	306
242	Rep.
243	902
244	Rep.
251, 251a	402
252(a)–(f)	403
252 (less (a)–(f))	Rep. See T. 50 App. §§2201–2204
253(a)	404
253(b)	405
253(c)	406, 407, 409, 411
253(d)	404
253(e)	410
253(f)–(h)	411
253a	Rep.
254	414
255	415–417
256	415
256a	419
257	414
271	T. 10 §§1204, 1362; T. 33 §857a; T. 42 §213a
272(a), (b)	T. 10 §§1201–1203; T. 33 §857a; T. 42 §213a
272(c)	T. 10 §§1204–1206; T. 33 §857a; T. 42 §213a
272(d)	T. 10 §§1210, 1372, 1373, 1401, 1402; T. 33 §857a; T. 42 §213a
272(e)	T. 10 §§1210, 1401; T. 33 §857a; T. 42 §213a
272(f)	T. 10 §§1201, 1204, 1210; T. 33 §857a; T. 42 §213a
272(g)	T. 10 §1209; T. 33 §857a; T. 42 §213a
272(h)	T. 10 §1403; T. 33 §857a; T. 42 §213a
272(i)	T. 10 §1215; T. 33 §857a; T. 42 §213a
273	T. 10 §1212; T. 33 §857a; T. 42 §213a
274	T. 10 §1210; T. 33 §857a; T. 42 §213a
275–277	T. 10 §1211; T. 33 §857a; T. 42 §213a
278	T. 10 §1207; T. 33 §857a; T. 42 §213a
279	T. 10 §§1372, 1373; T. 33 §857a; T. 42 §213a
280	T. 10 §1213; T. 33 §857a; T. 42 §213a
281	Rep.
282	T. 10 §1208. Rep. in part. See T. 10 §1208 nt.; T. 42 §212(g)
283	T. 10 §1214, 1216; T. 33 §857a; T. 42 §213a
284	T. 10 §1216; T. 33 §857a; T. 42 §213a
285	Rep.
301(a)	206, 402
301(b)	206, 1002
301(c)	309
301(d)	301
301(e)	206, 301, 309, 402, 1002
301(f)	Rep.
302	T. 33 §853*o*–1
303	423
304	201, 421
305	418
306	T. 10 §6153; T. 14 §510
307	Elim.
308	201, 422
308a	204
309	1003
310	1004
310a	Rep.
310b	1005
310c, 310c–1	1006
310d	1006
311	Elim. See T. 10 §568 nt.
312	Rep.
313	Elim.
314	903
315	Rep.
316	T. 10 §1402; T. 33 §857a; T. 42 §213a
317	Elim.
318, 319	Rep.
320	403
321	Rep.
321a	Elim.
322, 322a	Rep.
323	801
324	1001
351	601
352	602
353	602, 603
354	604
361–363	T. 10 §2771; T. 32 §714; T. 33 §857a; T. 42 §213a
364, 365	T. 10 §2771; T. 32 §714; T. 33 §857a; T. 42 §213a. Rep. in part. See T. 10 §2771 nt.
371(e), (f)	T. 10 §1435; T. 33 §857a; T. 42 §213a
371 (less (e), (f))	T. 10 §1431; T. 33 §857a; T. 42 §213a
372(a)	T. 10 §§1431, 1432; T. 33 §857a; T. 42 §213a
372(b)	T. 10 §1431; T. 33 §857a; T. 42 §213a
372 (less (a), (b))	T. 10 §1433; T. 33 §857a; T. 42 §213a
372a–372c	Rep.
373(c)	T. 10 §1436; T. 33 §857a; T. 42 §213a
373(d)	T. 10 §1439; T. 33 §857a; T. 42 §213a
373 (less (c), (d))	T. 10 §1434; T. 33 §857a; T. 42 §213a
374	T. 10 §1438; T. 33 §857a; T. 42 §213a

Title 37 Former Sections	Title 37 New Sections
375	T. 10 §1444; T. 33 §857a; T. 42 §213a
376	T. 10 §1442; T. 33 §857a; T. 42 §213a
377	T. 10 §§1443, 1444; T. 33 §857a; T. 42 §213a
378	T. 10 §1440; T. 33 §857a; T. 42 §213a
379	T. 10 §1437; T. 33 §857a; T. 42 §213a
380	T. 10 §1441; T. 33 §857a; T. 42 §213a
381	Rep.
401	T. 10 §1071
402(a)	T. 10 §§1072, 1074, 1076, 1079
402 (less (a))	T. 10 §1073

Title 37 Former Sections	Title 37 New Sections
403(a), (b)	T. 10 §1076
403(c)–(e)	T. 10 §1078
403 (less (a)–(e))	T. 10 §1077
404	T. 10 §1084
405	Rep.
411(c)	T. 10 §1080
411 (less (c))	T. 10 §1079
412	T. 10 §1081
413	T. 10 §1082
414	T. 10 §1079
421(c)	T. 10 §1076
421(d)	T. 10 §1085
421 (less (c), (d))	T. 10 §1074
422	T. 10 §1075
423	T. 10 §1083

TITLE 38—VETERANS' BENEFITS

[This title was enacted into law by Pub. L. 85–857, §1, Sept. 2, 1958, 72 Stat. 1105. Table I shows where sections of former Title 38 were incorporated in revised Title 38. Table II shows the disposition of sections of Title 38 by 1991 renumbering.]

TABLE I

Title 38 Former Sections	Title 38 New Sections
1–3	Rep.
4	(See former 11e)
5 to 11a–3	Rep.
11b to 11c–1	Rep.
11d, 11d–1	Rep.
11e to 11*l*	Rep.
12, 12a	Rep.
13–13g	Rep.
14–14e	Rep.
15–15n	Rep.
16–16j	Rep.
17–17j	Rep.
21	Rep.
23–26c	Rep.
27–32a	Rep.
33–39a	Rep.
41–49a	Rep.
50–61	Rep.
71–72a	Rep.
73–77	Rep.
91–97	Rep.
101–104	Rep.
111–116	Rep.
121–125	Rep.
126	T. 18 §289
127–129	Rep.
130	T. 18 §290
131–134	Rep.
151–155a	Rep.
156–168b	Rep.
169–179	Rep.
191–206	Rep.
221–230	Rep.
231	(See former 179)
232	Rep.
238–238e	Rep.
241–252e	Rep.
253, 254	Rep.
261, 262	Rep.
264–277	Rep.
281–285	Rep.
286	(See former 325a)
287–291b	Rep.
291c	(See former 326b)
291d–294	Rep.
311, 311a	Rep.
312–314	Rep.
321–321c	Rep.
322–324a	Rep.
325, 325a	Rep.
326–326c	Rep.
327–332	Rep.
341	(See former 33)
341a	(See former 274)
341b	(See former 275)
341c	(See former 291b)
341d	(See former 321c)
341e	(See former 326c)
341f	Rep.
351, 351a	Rep.
352–357b	Rep.
358 to 364q–1	Rep.
364h, 364j	Rep.
365 to 365b–1	Rep.
365c–365h	Rep.
366–370*l*	Rep.
371–374a	Rep.
375–379	Rep.
381 to 381–2	Rep.
381a–381f	Rep.
391–394	Rep.
421–423	Rep.
424	753
424a–438m	Rep.
439–441	Rep.
442	756
443	755
444	Rep.
445	784(a)–(h)
445a	Rep.
445b	784(i)
445c	Rep.
445d	784(b), (h)
446	Rep.
447	754
448–452	Rep.
453	3102
454, 454a	Rep.
455–459f	Rep.
460	Rep.
461	Elim.

TABLE I—Continued

Title 38 Former Sections	Title 38 New Sections
462	(See former 557)
471 to 471a–5	Rep.
472 to 472b–1	Rep.
472c–472e	Rep.
473, 473a	Rep.
474–483a	Rep.
484–488a	Rep.
489 to 501a–1	Rep.
501b–505a	Rep.
506–507b	Rep.
508	Rep.
509, 509a	Rep.
510	Rep.
511	741, 743, 757(a), 782
511a	Rep.
512	742, 743, 744(a), (b), 745, 749–752
512a	Rep.
512b	748
512b–1	744(c)
512c	758
512d	757(c)
513	757(b)
514	Rep.
515	759(a)
516–516b	Rep.
517	760
518	747
531–539	Rep.
551–555a	Rep.
556, 556a	Rep.
557	Rep.
571–576	Rep.
581–582c	Rep.
583	Rep.
591, 592	Rep.
601–603	Rep.
611–613a	Rep.
614–618e	Rep.
619–623	Rep.
631, 632	Rep.
641–647a	Rep.
648–650	Rep.
661–670	Rep.
681–683	Rep.
686–686c	Rep.
687–687c	Rep.
688–688b	Rep.
691–691g	Rep.
693–693g	Rep.
693h	T. 10 §1553
693i	T. 10 §1554
694(a)	1801(a), 1802(a), (b), 1803(a)(1), (b)
694(b)	1803(b)–(d)
694(c)	1802(c)
694(d)	1802(d), (f)
694(e)	1802(d)
694(f)	1802(e)
694(g)	1803(a)(2)
694a	1810
694b	1812
694c	1813
694c–1	1822
694d	212(a), 1804(a)–(c)
694e	T. 7 §1001(b)(2)
694f	Rep.
694g	1816, 1817
694h	1814
694i	1815
694j	1820(a)–(c)
694k	1821
694*l*	1810(a), (b), 1811(a)–(j)
694m	1811(k), 1823
694n	1804(d)
694*o*, 694p	Rep.
695	2010
695a	2011
695b	2012
695c	2013
695d	Rep.
695e	2014
695f	Rep.
696 to 696f–1	Rep.
696g–696m	Rep.
697(a)	Rep.
697(b)	616
697a, 697b	Rep.
697c	101(2)
697d, 697e	Rep.
697f	109(b)
697g	1510, 1824
700, 701	Rep.

TABLE I—Continued

Title 38 Former Sections	*Title 38 New Sections*
701a	1502(a), (c)(2), (3), (d)
702–703c	Rep.
704, 704a	Rep.
705–706c	Rep.
707–715a	Rep.
716–729b	Rep.
730–750	Rep.
Vet. Reg. No. 1(a), Pts. I–VI, VIII, IX.	Rep.
Pt. VII	217, 351, 1501–1508, 3013, 3107(c)
Vet. Reg. Nos. 2–12	Rep.
801(a)	Rep.
801(b)	101
801(c)	Rep.
801(d)–(f)	701
802(a)	703
802(b), (c)(1)	Rep.
802(c)(2)	719(b)
802(d)	Rep.
802(e)	702
802(f)	704–707
802(g)	701(3), 716(b), 717(a)
802(h)	716(a), (b)
802(i)	716(d)
802(j), (k)	716(e)
802(*l*)	716(f)
802(m)(1)	708
802(m)(2)	Rep.
802(n)	712
802(*o*)	Rep.
802(p)	709
802(q)	703
802(r)	713
802(s)	Rep.
802(t)	717(b), (c)
802(u)	717(d)
802(v)(1)	715, 719(b)
802(v)(2)	721(d)
802(w)	710
802(x)	783
802(y)	Rep.
802(z)	714
803	703, 741
804	719(a)
805	720
805a	786
806	782
807	721(a)–(c)
808	210–212, 785
809	3102
810	108
811	Rep.
812	711
813	787(b)
814	3502(b)
815	787(a)
816	718
817	784(a)–(h)
818–820	Rep.
821	722(a)
822	723(a), (c)
823	724
824	781
851–858	Rep.
901	1601(c)
911	1601(a)
916	1610
917	1612
918	1613
919	1611
926	1620
927	1621
928	1622
929	1623(a), (b)
930	1624
931	1623(c)
932	1625
933	1626
941	1631
942	1632
943	1633
944	1634
951	1641
952	1642
953	1643
954	1644
955	1645
961	1651
962	1652
963	1653
964	1654
965	1655
966	1656
971(a)	1661(a)
971(b)	213
971(c)	111, 1661(b)
972	1662(a)
973	1663
974	1664
975	1665

TABLE I—Continued

Title 38 Former Sections	*Title 38 New Sections*
975a	Rep.
976	1666
977	1667
978	1668
979–981	Rep.
982	1669
983, 984	Rep.
991	2001
992	2002
993	2003
994	2004
995	2005
996	2006
997	2007
998	2008
999	2009
1011	2101
1012	2102
1013	2104
1014	2103
1015	2105
1016	Rep.
1031	1701(d)
1032	1701(a)–(c)
1033(a)	1761(a)
1033(b)	213
1033(c)	111, 1761(b)
1033(d)	1662(b)
1033(e)	1761(c)
1033(f)	1761(d)
1034	1762
1035	1763
1036	1764
1037	1765
1038	1766
1039	1767
1040	1768
1041–1045	Rep.
1051	1710
1052	1711
1053	1712
1054	1713
1055	1714
1061	1720
1062	1721
1063	1722
1064	1723
1065	1724
1066	1725
1067	1726
1068	1731
1069	1732
1070	1733
1071	1734
1072	1735
1073	1736
1074	1737
1081	1740
1082	1741
1083	1742
1084	1743
1101(1)	101(1)
1101(2)(A)–(C)	Rep.
1101(2)(D)	403
1101(2)(E)	Rep.
1101(3)	101(27)
1101(4)	101(21)
1101(5)	101(22)
1101(6)(A)	101(23)
1101(6)(B)	106(d)
1101(6)(C)	101(22), (23)
1101(7)	101(4), (5)
1101(8)	101(3), 404
1101(9)	101(25)
1101(10)(A)	401(1)
1101(10)(B)	403
1101(11)(A)	402(a)
1101(11)(B)	402(b)
1101(11)(C)	402(c)(2)
1101(11)(D)	421(b)
1101(11)(E)	402(c)(1)
1101(11)(F)	421(a)
1101(12)	106(c)
1102	3005
1103(a)	412
1103(b)–(d)	422
1111	410(a)
1112	411
1113	413
1114	414
1115	415
1116	416
1117	410(a)
1118	417(b)
1119(a), (b)	Rep.
1119(c)	410(b)
1119(d)	3104(b)(2)
1119(e)	101(3)
1120	Rep.
1131, 1132	Rep.

TABLE I—Continued

Title 38 Former Sections	Title 38 New Sections
1133(a)	Rep.
1133(b)	423
1133(c)–(e)	Rep.
1134	Rep.
2101(1)–(9)	101(1)–(9)
2101(10)	501(1)
2101(11)	Rep.
2101(12)–(18)	101(11)–(17)
2102	102(a)
2103	103(a), (b)
2104	104
2105	105
2106	101(18)
2107	102(b)
2121	111
2122	108
2123	3303
2124(a)	101(21)(D)
2124(b)	106(a)
2125	107
2126	3109
2127	109(a)
2128	110
2141–2150	Rep.
2201	201
2202	202
2210	210
2211	211, 785
2212	212
2213	214
2214	215
2215	216
2216	3304
2230	230
2231	231
2232	232
2233	233
2234	234
2235	Rep.
2301	301
2302	302
2310	310
2311	106(b)
2312	311
2313	312
2314	313
2315	314
2316	315
2321	321
2322	322
2331	331
2332	106(b)
2333	332
2334	333
2335	334
2336	335
2337	336
2341	341
2342	342
2343	343
2351	351
2352	352
2353	353
2354	354
2355	355
2356	356
2357	357
2358	358
2401	501
2402	502
2403	503
2404	504
2405	505
2410	510
2411	511
2412	512
2421	521
2422	522
2423	523
2431	531
2432(a)–(d)	532
2432(e)	501(3)
2433	533
2434	534
2435	535
2436	536
2437	537
2441	541
2442	542
2443	543
2444	544
2445	545
2460	560
2461	561
2462	562
2501	601
2502	602
2510	610
2511	611
2512	612
2513	613
2514	614
2515	615
2521	621
2522	622
2523	623
2524	624
2525	625
2526	626
2527	627
2531	631
2532	632
2533	633
2534	634
2601	801
2602	802
2603	803
2604	804
2605	805
2701	1901
2702	1902
2703	1903
2704(a)	1904
2704(b)	Rep.
2705	1905
2801	901
2802	902
2803	903
2804	904
2805	905
2901	3001
2902	3002
2903	3003
2904	3004
2910	3010
2911	3011
2912	3012
2920	3020
2921	3021
2922	3022
3001	753, 3101
3002	3102
3003	3103
3004	3104
3005	3105
3006	3106
3007	3107(a), (b)
3008	3108
3101	3501
3102	3502
3103	3503
3104	3504
3201	3301
3202	3302
3211	3311
3212	3312
3213	3313
3301	4001
3302	4002
3303	4003
3304	4004
3305	4005
3306	4006
3307	4007
3308	4008
3401	4101
3402	4102
3403	4103
3404	4104
3405	4105
3406	4106
3407	4107
3408	4108
3409	4109
3410	4110
3411	4111
3412	4112
3413(a)	4113
3413(b), (c)	Rep.
3414	4114
3415	4115
3501	3201
3502	3202
3503	3203
3504	3204
3601	3401
3602	3402
3603	3403
3604	3404
3605	3405
3701	5001
3702	5002
3703	5003
3704	5004
3705	5005
3711	5011
3712	5012
3713	5013
3714	5006
3715	5014

TABLE I—Continued

Title 38 Former Sections	Title 38 New Sections
3716	213
3801	5101
3802	5102
3803	5103
3804	5104
3805	5105
3901	5201
3902	5202
3903	5203
3904	5204
3905	5205
3906	5206
3907	5207
3908	5208
3909	5209
3910	5210
3920	5220
3921	5221
3922	5222
3923	5223
3924	5224
3925	5225
3926	5226
3927	5227
3928	5228
4001	4201
4002	4202
4003	4203
4004	4204
4005	4205
4006	4206
4007	4207
4008	4208

TABLE II

Title 38 Former Sections	Title 38 Renumbered Sections
201	Rep. See 301(b)
202	Rep. See 302
203	Rep. See 313
210(a)	Rep.
210(b)(1)	Rep. See 303
210(b)(1), (2)	Rep. See 510
210(b)(3)	Rep. See 711
210(c)(1)	Rep. See 501(a), (b)
210(c)(2), (3)	Rep. See 503
210(d)	Rep. See 304
211(a)	Rep. See 511
211(b)	Rep. See 505
212	Rep. See 512
213	Rep. See 513
214	Rep. See 529
215	Rep. See 525
216	Rep. See 521
217	Rep. See 522
218(a)	Rep. See 901
218(b)	Rep. See 902
218(c)	Rep. See 903
218(d)	Rep. See 904
218(e)	Rep. See 905
219	Rep. See 527
220	Rep. See 523
221	Rep. See 541
222	Rep. See 542
223(a), (b)	Rep. See 501(c), (d)
223(c)	Rep. See 502
224	Rep. See 515(a)
230(a), (b)	Rep. See 314, 315
230(c)	Rep. See 316
231	Rep. See 701
232	Rep.
233	Rep. See 703
234	Rep. See 705
235	Rep. See 707
236	Rep. See 515(b)
240	Rep. See 7721
241	Rep. See 7722
242	Rep. See 7723
243	Rep. See 7724
244	Rep. See 7725
245	Rep. See 7726
246	Rep.
301	1101
302	1102
310	1110
311	1111
312	1112
313	1113
314	1114
315	1115
316	1116
321	1121
322	1122
331	1131
332	1132
333	1133
334	1134

TABLE II—Continued

Title 38 Former Sections	Title 38 Renumbered Sections
335	1135
336	Rep.
337	1137
341	1141
342	1142
343	Rep.
351	1151
352	1152
353	1153
354	1154
355	1155
356	Rep.
357	1157
358	1158
359	1159
360	1160
361	1161
362	1162
363	1163
401	1301
402	1302
403	Rep.
404	1304
410	1310
411	1311
412	1312
413	1313
414	1314
415	1315
416	1316
417	1317
418	1318
421	1321
422	1322
423	1323
501	1501
502	1502
503	1503
504	1504
505	1505
506	1506
507	1507
508	1508
510	Rep.
511	1511
512	1512
521	1521
522	1522
523	1523
524	1524
525	1525
531	Rep.
532	1532
533	1533
534	1534
535	1535
536	1536
537	1537
541	1541
542	1542
543	1543
544	Rep.
560	1560
561	1561
562	1562
601	1701
602	1702
603	1703
610	1710
611	1711
612	1712
612A	1712A
612B	1712B
613	1713
614	1714
615	1715
616	1716
617	1717
618	1718
619	1719
620	1720
620A	1720A
620B	1720B
620C	1720C
621	1721
622	1722
622A	1722A
623	1723
624	1724
625	Rep.
626	1726
627	1727
628	1728
629	1729
630	1730
631	1731
632	1732
633	1733
634	1734
635	1735

TABLE II—Continued

Title 38 Former Sections	Title 38 Renumbered Sections
641	1741
642	1742
643	1743
644	Rep.
651	1751
652	1752
653	1753
654	1754
661	1761
662	1762
663	1763
664	1764
701	1901
702	1902
703	1903
704	1904
705	1905
706	1906
707	1907
708	1908
709	1909
710	1910
711	1911
712	1912
713	1913
714	1914
715	1915
716	1916
717	1917
718	1918
719	1919
720	1920
721	1921
722	1922
723	1923
724	1924
725	1925
726	1926
727	1927
728	1928
729	1929
740	1940
741	1941
742	1942
743	1943
744	1944
745	1945
746	1946
747	1947
748	1948
749	1949
750	1950
751	1951
752	1952
753	1953
754	1954
755	1955
756	1956
757	1957
758	1958
759	1959
760	1960
761	1961
762	1962
763	1963
765	1965
766	1966
767	1967
768	1968
769	1969
770	1970
771	1971
772	1972
773	1973
774	1974
775	1975
776	1976
777	1977
778	1978
779	1979
781	1981
782	1982
783	1983
784	1984
785	1985
786	1986
787	1987
788	1988
801	2101
802	2102
803	2103
804	2104
805	2105
806	2106
901	2301
902	2302
903	2303
904	2304
905	2305
906	2306

TABLE II—Continued

Title 38 Former Sections	Title 38 Renumbered Sections
907	2307
908	2308
1000	2400
1001	2401
1002	2402
1003	2403
1004	2404
1005	2405
1006	2406
1007	2407
1008	2408
1009	2409
1010	2410
1401	3001
1402	3002
1411	3011
1412	3012
1413	3013
1414	3014
1415	3015
1416	3016
1417	3017
1418	3018
1418A	3018A
1419	3019
1421	3021
1422	3022
1423	3023
1431	3031
1432	3032
1433	3033
1434	3034
1435	3035
1436	3036
1500	3100
1501	3101
1502	3102
1503	3103
1504	3104
1505	3105
1506	3106
1507	3107
1508	3108
1509	3109
1510	3110
1511	3111
1512	3112
1513	3113
1514	3114
1515	3115
1516	3116
1517	3117
1518	3118
1519	3119
1520	3120
1521	3121
1601	3201
1602	3202
1621	3221
1622	3222
1623	3223
1624	3224
1625	3225
1631	3231
1632	3232
1633	3233
1634	3234
1641	3241
1642	Rep.
1643	3243
1651	3451
1652	3452
1661	3461
1662	3462
1663	Rep.
1670	3470
1671	3471
1672	Rep.
1673	3473
1674	3474
1675	Rep.
1676	3476
1677, 1678	Rep.
1681	3481
1682	3482
1682A	Rep.
1683	3483
1684	3484
1685	3485
1686, 1687	Rep.
1690	3490
1691	3491
1692	3492
1693	3493
1695–1698	Rep.
1700	3500
1701	3501
1710	3510
1711	3511
1712	3512

TABLE II—Continued

Title 38 Former Sections	Title 38 Renumbered Sections
1713	3513
1714	3514
1720	3520
1721	3521
1722	Rep.
1723	3523
1724	3524
1725, 1726	Rep.
1731	3531
1732	3532
1733	3533
1734	3534
1735	3535
1736	3536
1737	3537
1738	Rep.
1740	3540
1741	3541
1742	3542
1743	3543
1761	3561
1762	3562
1763	3563
1764	Rep.
1765	3565
1766	3566
1770	3670
1771	3671
1772	3672
1773	3673
1774	3674
1774A	3674A
1775	3675
1776	3676
1777	3677
1778	3678
1779	3679
1780	3680
1781	3681
1782	3682
1783	3683
1784	3684
1784A	3684A
1785	3685
1786	3686
1787	3687
1788	3688
1789	3689
1790	3690
1791	3691
1792	3692
1793	3693
1794	3694
1795	3695
1796	3696
1797	3697
1797A	3697A
1798	3698
1799	3699
1801	3701
1802	3702
1803	3703
1804	3704
1805	3705
1806	3706
1807	Rep.
1810	3710
1811	3711
1812	3712
1813	3713
1814	3714
1815–1817A	Elim.
1818	Rep.
1819	Elim.
1820	3720
1821	3721
1822	Rep.
1823	3723
1824	3724
1825	3725
1826	3726
1827	3727
1828	3728
1829	3729
1830	3730
1831	3731
1832	3732
1833	3733
1834	3734
1835	3735
1841	3741
1842	3742
1843	3743
1844	3744
1845	3745
1846	3746
1847	3747
1848	3748
1849	3749
1850	3750

TABLE II—Continued

Title 38 Former Sections	Title 38 Renumbered Sections
1851	3751
1901	3901
1902	3902
1903	3903
1904	3904
2000	4100
2001	4101
2002	4102
2002A	4102A
2003	4103
2003A	4103A
2004	4104
2004A	4104A
2005	4105
2006	4106
2007	4107
2008	4108
2009	4109
2010	4110
2010A	4110A
2011	4211
2012	4212
2013	4213
2014	4214
2021	4301
2022	4302
2023	4303
2024	4304
2025	4305
2026	4306
2027	4307
3001	5101
3002	5102
3003	5103
3004	5104
3005	5105
3006	5106
3007	5107
3008	5108
3009	5109
3010	5110
3011	5111
3012	5112
3013	5113
3020	5120
3021	5121
3022	5122
3023	5123
3101	5301
3102	5302
3103	5303
3103A	5303A
3104	5304
3105	5305
3106	5306
3107	5307
3108	5308
3109	5309
3110	5310
3111	5311
3112	5312
3113	5313
3114	5314
3115	5315
3116	5316
3117	5317
3118	5318
3201	5501
3202	5502
3203	5503
3204	5504
3205	5505
3301	5701
3302	5702
3303	5703
3304	5704
3305	5705
3311	5711
3312	5712
3313	5713
3401	5901
3402	5902
3403	5903
3404	5904
3405	5905
3501	6101
3502	6102
3503	6103
3504	6104
3505	6105
4001	7101
4002	7102
4003	7103
4004	7104
4005	7105
4005A	7105A
4006	7106
4007	7107
4008	7108
4009	7109

TABLE II—Continued

Title 38 Former Sections	Title 38 Renumbered Sections
4010	7110
4051	7251
4052	7252
4053	7253
4054	7254
4055	7255
4056	7256
4061	7261
4062	7262
4063	7263
4064	7264
4065	7265
4066	7266
4067	7267
4068	7268
4069	7269
4081	7281
4082	7282
4083	7283
4084	7284
4085	7285
4091	7291
4092	7292
4096	7296
4097	7297
4098	7298
4101(a)	Rep. See 7301
4101(b)	Rep. See 7302
4101(c)(1), (2), (4)	Rep. See 7303
4101(c)(3)	Rep. See 7317
4101(e)	Rep. See 7425(a)
4101(f)(1), (3), (4)	Rep. See 7314
4101(f)(2)	Rep. See 7315
4102	Rep. See 7305
4103	Rep. See 7306
4104	Rep. See 7401
4105	Rep. See 7402(a)–(d)
4106	Rep. See 7403
4107(a)–(d)	Rep. See 7404
4107(e)	Rep. See 7453
4107(f)	Rep. See 7454
4107(g)	Rep. See 7455
4107(h)	Rep. See 7456
4107(i)	Rep. See 7426(c)
4107(j)	Rep. See 7457
4108(a) (partial)	Rep. See 7421
4108(a)	Rep. See 7423(a)–(c)
4108(b)	Rep. See 7402(e)
4108(c)	Rep. See 7423(d)
4108(d)	Rep. See 7424(b)
4109	Rep. See 7426(a)
4110	Rep. See 7464
4111	Rep. See 7408
4112(a)	Rep. See 7312
4112(b), (c)	Rep. See 7313
4113	Rep. See 7424(a)
4114(a)	Rep. See 7405
4114(b)	Rep. See 7406
4114(c)–(g)	Rep. See 7407
4115	Rep. See 7304
4116	Rep. See 7316
4117	Rep. See 7409
4118	Rep. See 7431–7440
4119	Rep. See 7425(b)
4120	Rep. See 7458
4121	Rep. See 7471
4122	Rep. See 7472
4123	Rep. See 7473
4124	Rep. See 7474
4131	7331
4132	7332
4133	7333
4134	7334
4141	7451
4142	7452
4143–4146	Rep.
4151	Rep. See 7311(a)–(e)
4152	Rep. See 7311(f), (g)
4161	7361
4162	7362
4163	7363
4164	7364
4165	7365
4166	7366
4167	7367
4168	7368
4201	7801
4202	7802
4203	7803
4204	7804
4205	7805
4206	7806
4207	7807
4208	7808
4209	7809
4210	7810
4301	7601
4302	7602
4303	7603
4304	7604
4311	7611
4312	7612
4313	7613
4314	7614
4315	7615
4316	7616
4317	7617
4318	7618
4321	7621
4322	7622
4323	7623
4324	7624
4325	7625
4331	7631
4332	7632
4333	7633
4334	7634
4335	7635
4336	7636
4351	7651
4352	7652
4353	7653
4354	7654
4355	7655
5001	8101
5002	8102
5003	8103
5004	8104
5005	8105
5006	8106
5007	8107
5008	8108
5009	8109
5010	8110
5011	8111
5011A	8111A
5012	8112
5013	8113
5014	8114
5015	8115
5016	8116
5021	8121
5022	8122
5023	8123
5024	8124
5025	8125
5031	8131
5032	8132
5033	8133
5034	8134
5035	8135
5036	8136
5037	8137
5051	8151
5052	8152
5053	8153
5054	8154
5055	8155
5056	8156
5057	Rep.
5070	8201
5071	8211
5072	8212
5073	8213
5074	8214
5081	8221
5082	8222
5083	8223
5091	8231
5092	8232
5093	8233
5096	8241
5101	8301
5102	8302
5103	8303
5104	8304
5105	8305
5201	8501
5202	8502
5203	8503
5204	8504
5205	8505
5206	8506
5207	8507
5208	8508
5209	8509
5210	8510
5220	8520
5221	8521
5222	8522
5223	8523
5224	8524
5225	8525
5226	8526
5227	8527
5228	8528

TITLE 39—POSTAL SERVICE

[This title was first enacted into law by Pub. L. 86–682, §1, Sept. 2, 1960, 74 Stat. 578. It was again revised by Pub. L. 91–375, §2, Aug. 12, 1970, 84 Stat. 719, as part of the creation of the United States Postal Service as an independent establishment of the executive branch. Table I following shows where the sections of Title 39 prior to 1960 were incorporated into the 1960 revision. Table II shows where the subject matter of sections of Title 39 as revised in 1960 was incorporated in the 1976 revision.]

TABLE I

Title 39 Former Sections	*Title 39 1960 Revision Sections*
1–3	701
4, 5	707
6	710
7	709
8	1, 510
9	509
10, 11	2102
11a	Rep.
12	2102
13	Rep.
14	2102
31	3311
31a	3311, 3314
31b	3311, 3312
31c	Rep.
31d	3313
32	3312
33	Rep.
34	502
35	Rep.
36	502
37	2405
38	2209, 3315
39	3315
39a	3315, 3317
40	2406
41	Rep.
42, 43	2208
44	2404
45	2208–2210
46, 47	2209
48	Rep.
49, 49a	2403
50, 51	Rep.
52	2008, 6420
53–54a, 55	Rep.
56, 56a	711
57–57c	Rep.
57d	711
58–60a, 61–68	Rep.
69, 70	704
81	Rep.
82	703
83–103a	Rep.
103b	3334
104–108	Rep.
109	3555
110–112d, 113–120	Rep.
121	3555
122	Rep.
123	3556
124–127	Rep.
128	3332
129–131	Rep.
132	502
133	Rep.
133a	3336
134–136	Rep.
136a	3335
137–139a, 140	Rep.
141–145	712
151	6106
152	6001
153, 153a	6002
153b	Rep.
154	3116
155, 156	6003
157	502
158	705, 6004
159–160a	705
161	705, 2011
162	6002, 6005
163	Rep.
164	2004
165	2501, 6006
166	Rep.
167	2009, 6006, 6007
168	Rep.
169, 169a	6007
170	Rep.
171	501
172	Rep.
173, 174	3115
175, 176	Rep.
191	6005
192	Rep.
192a	3339
193	Rep.
194, 195	3113
196	3114
197, 197a, 198	Rep.
199	3543
200–207a, 208–211	Rep.
212	6009
213–215	3337
216–219	3338
221	4251, 4451, 4551
221a	4251, 4451
222	4251
223	4252
224	4351
225	4058, 4365
226	4354
226a	4352, 4357
226b	Rep.
227	4353
228	4366
229	4355
230	4356
231	4368; T. 18 §1733
232	4352
233	4369
234	4367; T. 18 §1734
235	4451, 4555
236–238	4451
239	4060
240	4002, 4551, 4555
240a, 240b	4552
241	Rep.
242	2001
243	4001, 4002, 4058
244	5006, 5007
245, 245a	Rep.
245a–1	5006
245a–2	5010
245b	Rep.
245b–1	5007
245c	5009
245d	Rep.
245d–1	5007
246 to 246a–1	Rep.
246b	507
246c	5007, 5008
246c–1	5008
246d, 246e	Rep.
246f	507
247	Elim.
248	4059
249	4365, 4453, 4555
250	4058, 4251
251	4058
252, 253	Rep.
254	6438
255	4003
256	4001, 4057
257	4004
258	4001, 4003
259	4005, 4057
259a	4006
259b, 259c	4007
260	Rep.
260a	507, 5012
261	4105
270	2301
270a	2302
270b	2303
270c	2304
270d	2305
270e	2306
271	4051, 4052
272	Rep.
272a	4109, 4110
273	4052, 4053
273a	4052
274	Rep.
275	2501, 2505
276	Rep.
276a	2501

TABLE I—Continued

Title 39 Former Sections	*Title 39 1960 Revision Sections*
276b, 276c	Rep.
276d	6006
277, 278	Rep.
278a	4101, 4102, 4103, 4105
278b	4106
279	708
280	4054, 4251, 4253
281	Rep.
282	4052
283	4358, 4359, 4363, 4364
284	4361
285	4052
286	4358
287–289	Rep.
289a	2302, 4352, 4358, 4359, 4360, 4362, 4452
290	4652
290a	4052, 4452
290a–1	4052, 4451, 4452
291	Rep.
291a	4052
291b	4421, 4422
292	4553
292a	4052, 4554, 6008
293–293b	Rep.
293c	4653
294, 294a	Rep.
295	4052, 4364
296–299	Rep.
300	4055
301, 302	Rep.
302a	4651
303	4253, 4254, 4303
321	4152, 4153
321–1	4152
321a	5003
321b–321h	Rep.
321i	2302, 4155, 4156
321j	4157
321k	4158
321*l*	4152, 4158, 4159
321m	4160
321n	4154
321*o*	2302, 4166
321p	2302, 4156, 5004
321q	2302, 4156
321r	4156, 4165, 4167
322	Rep.
323	4152
324	Rep.
325	4163
325a	Elim.
326	4162
327	4161
328	Rep.
329	4164
330	4152
331	4451, 4653, 4654
332–334	Rep.
335	4165
336	4167
337	Rep.
338	4152
351	2501
352	2004
353	Rep.
354	2503, 2510
355	2004
355a	2204
356	2503, 4251
357	2503
358	2502
358a	4251
359	Rep.
360	2504
361	Rep.
362	2503
363, 364	Rep.
365	2507
366	Rep.
367	2507
368	2508
368a	2508, 2509
369	Rep.
370	2507
371	2506
381	5001
381a	5005, 5011
382, 383	Rep.
383a	2204
384	Rep.
384a	5001
385	5002
386	Rep.
387	5001, 5005
338	Rep.
388a	5010
401–405	Rep.
406	4101, 4108
407	Rep.

TABLE I—Continued

Title 39 Former Sections	*Title 39 1960 Revision Sections*
408	4107, 4108
409	4103
410	4102
411	4105
421, 422	Rep.
422a	6412
422b	6413
423	Rep.
423a, 423b	6427
423c	6428
424	6402, 6405
425	6402, 6417
425a	6401, 6420
426	6402, 6418, 6419
427	6419
428	6417
429	6402, 6411
430	6402
431	Rep.
432	6421
433	6402, 6437
434	6401, 6402, 6407, 6414, 6415, 6416, 6422, 6423, 6424, 6425
435	6402, 6426
436	6402, 6405
437	6413
438	Rep.
439	6439
440	6424
441	Rep.
442	6424
443	6434
444, 445	6429
446	6430
447	6431, 6436
448	6432
449	6405, 6408
450	6410
451	6402
461	Rep.
462	4301, 4302
462a	4301, 4304
463	Rep.
463a	4303
464	Rep.
465	6301
465a–465f, 466–468	Rep.
469	4301
469a–469s	Rep.
470	6303
471, 472	Rep.
473, 474	6402
475	4301, 4302, 4303, 4305, 6301
476	2102
481	6101, 6105
482	6101, 6106, 6402
483	6101, 6106
484, 485	6101
486	6101, 6402
487	6101
487a	6408
488	4304, 6102
488a	4304, 6302
488b	6302
489	6440
490, 491	Rep.
492	6166
493	6402
494	902
495	4056
496	902
497	905
498	904
499	906
500	901
501	6107
502–506	Rep.
507	6433
508	Rep.
521	Rep.
522	4159
523	6203
524	Rep.
525	6203
526–528	Rep.
529	6203
530–536	Rep.
537, 538	6204
539	6203, 6207
540	6202
541	6203
541–1	Rep.
541a	6202, 6214
542, 543	6208
544–547	6209
548	Elim.
549	6208
550	Rep.
551	6209
552	Rep.

TABLE I—Continued

Title 39 Former Sections	Title 39 1960 Revision Sections
553	6209
554	Elim.
555	6210
556	6206
557	Elim.
558	6210
559	6211
560, 561	6203
562	6214
563	6207
564	6205
565	6215
566	6206
567, 568	6207
569	Rep.
570	6207, 6208
571	6215
572	Rep.
573	6203
574, 575	Rep.
576	6212
577	2102
578	6401, 6403, 6423
579	6403
601, 601a, 602, 602a, 603–607a, 608–618a, 619–623.	Rep.
624	3333
625	3556
626	Rep.
627	3555
628, 629	Rep.
630	3582
631	3111
632, 632a	3333
633–637	Rep.
638	3116
639	4370
640	Rep.
651	6101, 6402
652	6101, 6402
653	6101
654	6101, 6409
655	6304, 6435
656	6106, 6406
657–666	Rep.
667	6403, 6404
668	Rep.
669	6103
670, 671	Rep.
672	706
673, 674	Rep.
691–693a, 694, 695	Rep.
696	502
697–699	Rep.
700	903
701	3555
702	Rep.
703	3556
704	3112
711	5101, 5102
712	506
713	2209, 5102, 5103
714	2209, 3316
715	2005
716	Rep.
716a	5102
717–719	Rep.
720	5102
721, 722	Rep.
723	5103, 5104
724	5102
725, 726	Rep.
727	5103
727a	2204
728	5103
728a	2202, 5103
729	5103
730, 731	Rep.
732	4005, 4057
733–738	Rep.
738a	5105
739	Rep.
751	5203, 5204, 5205
752	Rep.
753	5206
754	5210
755	5207, 5208
756	5211, 5213
756a	5223
757	5213
758	5213, 5217, 5219, 5220
759	5203, 5214, 5215, 5216, 5217, 5218, 5219, 5221
760, 761	Rep.
762	5212
763–765	Rep.
766	5201
767	5222
768	5206, 5208
769	5203

TABLE I—Continued

Title 39 Former Sections	Title 39 1960 Revision Sections
770	5209
771	5224
781	Rep.
782	1
783	1, 2209
784	1
785	708
786	2201
787, 788	Rep.
789	2408
790	2410
791	1, 2407
792, 793	Rep.
794	2207, 2208, 2401, 2402
794a	2202
794b	2211
794c	2206
794d	2302
794e	Rep.
794f	509, 2101, 2102
794g	Rep.
795	2212
801	Rep.
802	2006
803, 804	2004
805	508
806–808	Rep.
809	2004
809a–811	Rep.
812	3104
813–819	Rep.
820	3331
821–823a, 824–824e, 825	Rep.
826	2331
827, 828	Rep.
829	2007
829a, 829b	2203
830	6305
831–833	Rep.
834	3302
835, 836	Rep.
837	See T. 28 §2710
838	See T. 28 §2711
839	See T. 28 §2712
840	See T. 28 §2713
841	See T. 28 §2714
842	See T. 28 §2715
843	See T. 28 §2716
844	See T. 28 §2717
845	Rep.
846	See T. 28 §2718
847, 847a	504
848, 848a	Rep.
848b	2202
851–856b, 857–861b, 862–862c	Rep.
862d	3557
863–867a, 868–876c, 877–878b, 879–890.	Rep.
901	2115
902	2104–2108, 2110
903	2103
904	2110
905	2113
906	2111
907	2111, 2112, 2114
908	2109
909	2116
951	1, 3101
952	Rep.
961	3301, 3501
962	3502
963	3333, 3511–3531, 3582
964	3335
965	Rep.
971	3333, 3542
972	3543
973	702, 3544
974	3541
975	Rep.
981	3333, 3552, 3556, 3557
982	3553
983	Rep.
984	3558
991	3551
992	3559
993	3554
994	3555
995	Rep.
1001	3333, 3541
1002	3571
1003	3573
1004	3574
1005	3575
1006	3302, 3572
1007	3101, 3333, 3581
1007a	3576
1008	2008, 3542
1009	3543
1010	3544
1021	Rep.

TABLE I—Continued

Title 39 Former Sections	Title 39 1960 Revision Sections
1031	702
1032	3105
1033–1038	Rep.
1051	6351
1052	6352
1053	6106, 6352
1054	6353
1055	6354
1056	6355
1071	2231
1072	2232
1073	2233
1074	2234
1075	2332

TABLE II

Title 39 1960 Revision Sections	Title 39 New Sections
1	See 102, 2001
2	See 403
301	See 201
302	See 203
303	See 207
304	See 203
305	See 204
306	See 206
307	See 204
308	Rep.
308a	See 204
309	See 402
501	See 202, 401, 403, 404
502	Elim.
503	See 2002
504	See 403
505	See 407
506	See 408
507	See 404, 3622
508	See 401
509	See 404
510	See 401
701	See 403, 404
702	See 403
703, 704	Elim.
705	See 404, 406
706	Elim.
707–710	See 404
711	Rep.
712	See 406, 2601
901	601
902	602
903	603
904	604
905	605
906	606
2001–2006	See 401
2007–2009	See 404
2010	2201
2011	See 404
2101, 2102	See 401
2103	See 401, 2002
2104–2106	See 401
2107	Elim.
2108	See 401
2109	Elim.
2110–2112	See 401
2113	See 2002
2114	See 401, 410
2115	See 401, 2002
2116	See 2402
2201	See 2002, 2004, 2401
2202	See 2003
2203	See 2401
2204	See 2603
2205	Elim.
2206	See 2008
2207, 2208	See 401, 2008
2209	See 1001
2210	See 2601
2211	See 401, 2008
2212	See 2601
2231–2234	See 2003, 2010
2301	See 101
2302	See 101, 403, 3621–3623, 3641, 3661
2303	See 2009, 3401, 3403, 3621–3623, 3627, 3641, 3661
2304	See 2402, 3601, 3621–3628, 3641, 3661
2305	Elim.
2306	See 1005, 3621
2331	See 2402
2332	Rep.
2401	See 2601
2402	2602
2403, 2404	See 2601
2405, 2406	Elim.
2407	See 404
2408	2605

TABLE II—Continued

Title 39 1960 Revision Sections	Title 39 New Sections
2409	See 2603
2410	2604
2411, 2501–2505	See 404
2506	405
2507–2510	See 404
3101	Elim.
3103	1011
3104	1009
3105	See 1001, 1006
3106	See 1003
3107	Elim.
3108	See 1001
3111	Elim.
3112	See 1010
3113, 3114	See 1001
3115	See 1008
3116, 3301–3303, 3311, 3312	See 1001
3313, 3314	Elim.
3315	See 1001
3316, 3317	Elim.
3331	See 1001
3332	Elim.
3333	See 1001, 1006
3334	See 1005
3335	See 1001
3336	Elim.
3337	See 1007
3338, 3339	Elim.
3501	See 1003
3502, 3511–3531, 3541–3544	Elim.
3551	See 1001
3552–3557	Elim.
3558	Rep.
3559, 3560	Elim.
3571	See 1001
3572–3577, 3581, 3582	Elim.
4001, 4002	See 3001
4003	3003
4004	3004
4005	3005
4006	3006
4007	3007
4008	Elim.
4009	3008
4010	3002
4051, 4052	See 404
4053, 4054	Elim.
4055	See 3681
4056	Elim.
4057	See 404, 3623
4058–4060	Elim.
4101–4103	See 404
4104	See 407
4105	See 404
4106	Elim.
4107	See 404
4108	Elim.
4109	See 404
4110	Elim.
4151	3201
4152	3202
4153	3203
4154	3204
4155	3205
4156	3206
4157	Rep.
4158	See 3207
4159	3208
4160	3209
4161	See 3210
4162	See 3211
4163	3212
4164	3213
4165	3214
4166	3215
4167	See 3216
4168	3217
4169	See 3401
4170	See 3402
4171	3218
4251	See 3623
4252	See 3682
4253, 4254, 4301, 4302	Elim.
4303	See 3401
4304	Elim.
4305	See 3682
4351–4357	Elim.
4358	See 3626, 3627
4359	See 3626, 3627
4360, 4361	Rep.
4362–4368	Elim.
4369	See 3685
4370	Elim.
4421	See 3626, 3627
4422	See 3626, 3627
4451	Elim.
4452	See 3626, 3627
4453, 4551	Elim.
4552	See 3682
4553	Elim.

TABLE II—Continued

Title 39 1960 Revision Sections	Title 39 New Sections
4554	See 3626, 3627, 3682, 3683
4555–4559	Elim.
4560	See 3401
4651	Elim.
4652	Rep.
4653	See 3403
4654	3404
4655	3405
5001–5013, 5101–5105, 5201–5229	Elim.
6001, 6002	See 404
6003, 6004	Elim.
6005	See 101
6006–6009	Elim.
6101	See 5001
6102	Elim.
6103	See 5002
6104	See 5005
6105	5003
6106	See 5004
6107	See 101
6201	See 5201
6202	See 5202, 5210
6203	See 5007, 5203
6204	See 5203, 5204
6205	See 5204
6206	See 5205
6207	See 5206
6208	See 5207
6209	See 5208
6210	See 5209
6211	Elim.
6212	See 3662

TABLE II—Continued

Title 39 1960 Revision Sections	Title 39 New Sections
6213	See 5210
6214	See 5211
6215	See 5212
6216	See 5213
6301	See 5401
6302, 6303	See 5402
6304	See 5403
6305, 6351–6355	Elim.
6401	See 5201
6402	See 5005, 5215
6402a	See 5214
6403	See 5005
6404	5601
6405	See 5605
6406	5602
6407	See 5005
6408	See 5605
6409	Elim.
6410	5603
6411, 6412	See 5005
6413	See 5005, 5605
6414, 6415	Elim.
6416	See 5005
6417–6421	Elim.
6422, 6423	See 5005
6424–6431	Elim.
6432	5006
6433	See 5007
6434	Elim.
6435	5604
6436–6440	Elim.

TITLE 44—PUBLIC PRINTING AND DOCUMENTS

[This title was enacted into law by Pub. L. 90–620, §1, Oct. 22, 1968, 82 Stat. 1238. This table shows where sections of former Title 44 were incorporated in revised Title 44.]

Title 44 Former Sections	*Title 44 New Sections*
1	101
2	102
4	103
5	509
6	510
7	511
8	512
9	513
10	514
11	515
12	516
13	517
14	504
15, 16	Rep.
31	301
32	304
33–35	Rep.
36	508
37, 38	Rep.
39	302
39a	303
40	305
41	306
42	307
43–46	Rep.
47	316
48	Elim.
49	313
50, 51	Rep.
51a	Elim.
52	Elim.
52a	308
53	T. 18 §442
54–57	Rep.
58	505
59	312
60	Rep.
61	315
62	314
63	309
63a	309
64	311
71	1702
72	1705
72a	1708
73	308, 1702
74	1703
75	1704
76	1710
77	1711
78	1720
79	1707
80	1713
81	1712
81a	1901
81b	1902
81c	1914
82	1905
83	1904
84	1910
84a	1912
85	1903, 1906
85a	1913
86	1909
87	1907
87a	Rep.
88	1908
89	Elim.
90	Rep.
91	1717
91a	1716
92	1119, 1911
93	1721
94	1709
95	1701
96	1722
111	501
111a	502
111b	503
111c	Elim.
112, 113	Rep.
114	1706
115	506, 507
116	501, 1123
117	1103
118	1104
119	1120
120	Elim.
121	1111
131	701
132	702
133	703
134	702
135	705
136	714
137	704
138	715
139	1718
139a	1719
140	716
141	718
142	719
143	738
144	717
145	Elim.
146	734
147	713
148	720
149	721
150	722
151	723
152	724
153	725
154	726
155	727
156	1326
157	730
158	731
159	732
160	735
161	736
162	733
163	908
164	Rep.
165	739
166	740
167	741
168	737
169	Elim.
170	1333
181	901
182	902
182a	903
182b	904
182c	905
183	906
184	Rep.
185	907
186	Rep.
187	909
188	910
189	706
189a	707
190	708
191	709
191a	710
192	711
193	712
194–196	Rep.
196a	728
197	729
211	1101
212 (1st sent.)	1115
212 (2d sent.)	1114
213 (1st par.)	1102
213 (2d par., 1st sent.)	1116
213 (2d par., 2d sent., 1st cl.)	1302
213 (2d par., 2d, 3d sents.)	1308–1310, 1336
213 (3d par.)	1116
213a	1117
214	1107
215	1110
215a	1714
216	1105
217	1715
218	1106
219	1102, 1113
219a	1118
220	1108
221	Rep.
222	1112
223	Rep.
224	1109
225	1121
226	Rep.
227	1122
228, 229	Elim.
230	310
241	1301
242	Rep.
243	1303
244	Rep.
245	1304
246	1307
247	Rep.
248	1306
249	1328
250	1317
251, 252	Rep.
253	1313

Title 44 Former Sections	Title 44 New Sections
254	1314
255, 256	Rep.
257	Elim.
258	1315
259	1316
260	1318
261	1319
262	1320
263	1312
265	1321
266	1322
267	Elim.
268	Rep.
269	1323
270	1324
271	1325
272	1327
273	1329
274	Rep.
275	1331
275a	Rep.
275b	1332
276	Rep.
276a	1333
277	Rep.
278	1334
279	1335
279a	Rep.
280, 280a	Rep.
281, 282	Rep.
283	1337
283a	Rep.
284	1338
285	1339
286, 287	Rep.
288	1340
289	1341
290	1342
291	1343
292	Elim.
293, 294	Rep.
295	1344
296	Rep.
296a	1305
297	1311
298	1330
300–300f	Rep.
300f–1	Rep.
300g, 300h	Rep.
300h–1	Rep.
300i–300k	Rep.
300aa	Rep.
300bb	2301
300cc	2305
300dd	2306
300ee	2307
300ff	2303
300gg	2308
300hh	2302
300ii	2304
300jj	Rep.
301	1502
302	1503
303	1504
304	1501
305	1505
306	1506
307	1507
308	1508
309	1509
310, 310a	Rep.
311	1510
311a	Rep.
312	1511
313, 314	Rep.

Title 44 Former Sections	Title 44 New Sections
321	3701
322	3703
323	Rep.
324	3702
325	3703
326	Rep.
351–365	Rep.
366	3301
367	3302
368	3303
369	3304
370	3305
371	3306
372	3307
373	3308
374	3309
375	3310
376	3311
377	Rep.
378	3312
379	3313
380	3314
391	1506, 2108, 2301, 2501, 2902
392	2903
393(a)	2501
393(b)	2502
393(c)	2503
393(d)	2504
393(e)	2505
393(f)	2504 nt.
393(g)	2506
393(h)	2507
394	2701
395(a)	2904
395(b)	2905
395(c)	2906
395(d)	2907
395(e)	2908
395(f)	2909
396(a)	3101
396(b)	3102
396(c)	3103
396(d)	3104
396(e)	3105
396(f)	3106
396(g)	3107
396a	2910
397(a)	2103
397(b)	2104
397(c)	2105
397(d)	2106
397(e)	2107
397(f)	2108
397(g)	Rep.
397(h)	2109
397(i)	2110
397(j)	2101
398	2111
399	2112
400	2113
401	2901
402	2114
421	3501
422(a)	3503
422(b)	3504
422(c)	3505
422(d)	3506
422(e)	3507
423	3508
424	3509
425	3510
426	3502
427	3511

TITLE 46—SHIPPING

[This title was enacted into law by Pub. L. 98–89, §1, Aug. 26, 1983, 97 Stat. 500; Pub. L. 99–509, title V, subtitle B, §5101, Oct. 21, 1986, 100 Stat. 1913; Pub. L. 100–424, §6, Sept. 9, 1988, 102 Stat. 1591; and Pub. L. 100–710, Nov. 23, 1988, 102 Stat. 4735. This table shows where sections of former Title 46 were incorporated in revised Title 46.]

Title 46 Former Sections	Title 46 New Sections
1	Rep.
2	2103
3	Rep.
4	2105
5, 6	Rep.
7	2107
8	2108
9 (less (c))	3316
9(c)	46 App.
11, 12	Rep.
13, 14	46 App.
15–41	Rep.
42	46 App.
43–56	Rep.
57	46 App.
58	Rep.
59	46 App.
60–63	Rep.
65(1)	2101(10)
65(2)	2101(11)
65(3)	2101(34)
65a	12113
65b	12102
65c	12114
65d	12115
65e	12103
65f	12116
65g	12104
65h	12105
65i	12106
65j	12107
65k	12108
65*l*	12109
65m	12110
65n	12122
65o	12111
65p	12112
65q	12117
65r	12118
65s	12119
65t	12120
65u	2107, 12122(a)
65v(1)	2104
65v(2)	12121
65w	12101
71	12102, 14102, 14104, 14501, 14502, 14504, 14511, 14521, 14522
72	14503
73, 74	Rep.
75	14512
76	Rep.
77	14502, 14512
78, 79	Rep.
80	(See former 660–1)
81	14306
82	3101
83	14502, 14513
83a–83g	14513
83h	14102
83i	14702
83j	14701
83k	2107
85–85g	Rep.
86	5114, 5115
86a	5101
86b	5102
86c	5102, 5103, 5104, 5106
86d	5107
86e	5108
86f	5109
86g	5112
86h	5113
86i	5116
88	5102
88a	5104, 5108
88b	5103, 5107
88c	5112
88d	5109
88e	5112
88f	5113
88g	5116
88h, 88i	Rep.
91	46 App.
91a–96	Rep.
97, 98	46 App.
99	Rep.
100	46 App.
101, 102	Rep.
103	Rep.
104	46 App.
105–110	Rep.
111	46 App.
112, 113	Rep.
121–125	46 App.
126, 127	Rep.
128, 129	46 App.
130, 131	Rep.
132–135	46 App.
141–146	46 App.
151–162	Rep.
163	46 App.
170	3306(a)(5). Rep. in part.
170(14)	2106
170a, 170b	Rep.
171–175	Rep.
178, 179	Rep.
181–183	46 App.
183a	Rep.
183b–196	46 App.
201	11301
202	11302
203	11303
211	8501(a)
212	8501(b)
213	8501(c), (e)
214	7101
214(c)	7106
215	8501(d), 8502
216(a)	9301(2)
216(b)	2101(34)
216(c)	9301(3)
216(d)	9301(1)
216(e), (f)	Rep.
216a	9302(a), (b), (d)
216b(a)–(c)	9303
216b(d)	9305
216b(e)	9304
216c	9303
216d	9305
216e(a)–(c)	9308
216e(d)	2107
216e(e)	2106
216f	9302(c)
216g	9306
216h	9307
216i	Rep.
221	8103
222	8101
223	8301
224	7101, 8101
224a	8303, 8304
224a(2)	7111
225	7106, 7109, 7113
226	7101, 7106, 7703
227	Rep.
228	7101, 7106, 7703
229	7101, 7106, 7703
229a	7101, 7103
229b	7101, 7103
229c	7106, 7108, 7318
229d	Rep.
229e	7105
229f	7110
229g	7103, 7318
229h	Rep.
230	7112
231	7105
232	7110
233	7109
234	3315
235	8104
236	8103
237, 238	Rep.
239	6101, 6301, 7703
239(d)	6303
239(e)	6304, 7705
239(f)	6304
239(g)	6305, 7701
239(i)	6306
239(j)	6301, 6307
239(k)	6305
239a(a)	7503(a), 7704(a)
239a(b)	2101(34)
239a(c)	7302
239b(a)	7503(b)
239b(b)	7704(b), (c)
240	7703
241	8304
242	7101, 7102, 8302(a)–(d)
243	7101, 7104, 7107, 7108
244	7101, 7105
245	8302(g), (h)
246(a)	8302(a)–(d)
246(b)	Rep.

Title 46 Former Sections	Title 46 New Sections
246(c)	7703
247	7101
248	8302
249–249c	Rep.
251–251b	46 App.
252–261	Rep.
262	46 App.
263–276	Rep.
277	46 App.
278–288	Rep.
289–292b	46 App.
293–293b	Rep.
294–315	Rep.
316	46 App.
317, 318	Rep.
319–324	46 App.
325	Rep.
326–328	46 App.
329, 330	Rep.
331	2110
332–335	Rep.
336	46 App.
351–353	Rep.
354, 355	46 App.
361	2101(16), (37)
362	2109, 3301(9), 3314
362(a)	3303
362(b)	3504
362(c)	3505
363	2109
364	8502
365	Rep.
366	3306
367	2101(16), (33), 2303, 3301(7), 3302
369	3305, 3306, 3316
369(b)	3503
369(e)	3318
371	Rep.
372	2103
373–374a	Rep.
375	3306
376–382a–1	Rep.
382b	2104, 2111, 2112
382b–1	3317(b)
382c–385	Rep.
390	3302, 3304
390(a)	2101(21)(B)
390(b)	2101(35)
390(d)	2101(34)
390(e)	2101(13)
390(f)	2101(27)
390(g)	2101(30)
390(h)	2101(28)
390(i)	2101(29)
390a	3301(4), (5), (8), 3305
390a(a)	3307(2)
390a(b)	3317(a), 7114
390b	3306, 8901, 8902
390c	3303(a), 3309, 3311
390c(b), (c)	3313
390d	2106, 3318(a), 8906
390e–390g	Rep.
391	3301(1), (4), (9), 3304, 3305
391(b)	3307(3)
391(c)	2101(22), 3307(1)
391(e)	3302
391a	3301(10), 3702, 8502
391a(2)(A)	2101(9)
391a(2)(B)	2101(12)
391a(2)(C)	2101(14)
391a(2)(D)	2101(15)
391a(2)(E)	2101(20)
391a(2)(F)	3701(4)
391a(2)(G)	2101(24)
391a(2)(H)	2101(5)
391a(2)(I)	2101(34)
391a(2)(J)	3701(5)
391a(2)(K)	3701(6)
391a(2)(L)	2101(46)
391a(2)(M)	2101(38)
391a(2)(N)	2101(8)
391a(2)(O)	2101(23)
391a(2)(P)	3701(2)
391a(2)(Q)	3701(3)
391a(2)(R)	3701(1)
391a(2)(S)	2101(7)
391a(3)	2101(39), 2301, 3303, 3702(a)
391a(4)	2109
391a(4)(B)	8703(c)
391a(5)	3702
391a(6)	3703
391a(7)	3704–3709
391a(8)	3309, 3313
391a(8)(A)	3710, 3712
391a(8)(B)	3711, 3712
391a(8)(C)	3711
391a(8)(D)	3710
391a(8)(E)	3710, 3711
391a(9)	9102
391a(10)(A)	8703(a)
391a(10)(B)	9101(b)
391a(10)(C)	7317, 8703(b)
391a(10)(D)	Rep. See 7701 et seq.
391a(11)	9101(a)
391a(12)	3703
391a(13)	3713
391a(14)	2107, 3718
391a(14)(C)	2106
391a(15)	3714
391a(16)	3717
391a(17)	3715
391a(18)	3716
391b	Rep.
392	3304–3306
392(b)	3307(3)
393, 394	Rep.
395	3301(6), 3305, 3311
395(d)	3309
395(e)	2101(32)
396, 397	Rep.
398	3318
399	3309, 3311, 3314
400	3312
401, 402	Rep.
403	3318
404	2101(13), (16), (17), 3301(1), 3302, 3306, 3307
404–1	3301(3), 3305, 3501
404–1(1)	2101(19)
404–1(4)	2101(21)(C)
404–1(6)	3307(2), (3)
404–1(8)	8301
404a	Rep.
405	2101(40), 3301(9), 3305
405(b)	8104
405(b)(1)(A)	2101(34)
405(b)(2)	8904
405(b)(3)	8905(b)
406	3305
407	3305, 3318
408	3305, 3306, 3318
409	Rep.
410	3318
411, 412	3306
413	3318
414	3310, 7502
415	Rep.
416	2104, 3306
417	(See former 416)
418, 419	Rep.
420	3302, 3306
431–434	Rep.
435	3308, 3313
436	2106, 3318
437–440	Rep.
441	46 App.
441(1)	2101(18)
441(2)	2101(31)
442	3302
443	46 App.
444	8701
444	46 App.
445	2113, 3306
446–446c	46 App.
446d	8101
451	3501
452	3501(b), (c)
453	2113
454–457	T. 33 §§1233–1236
458	Rep.
459	3306
460, 460a, 461	3502
462	2106, 3501, 3502
463, 463a, 464	Rep.
465	(See former 170)
466	Rep.
466a	3901
466b	3902
467–469	Rep.
470, 471	8102
472	Rep.
473	3306
474–476	Rep.
477–479	3306
480	2301
481	2106, 3306
481(a)	2101(34)
481(c)	2106
481(d)	3318
482, 483	3306
484–488	Rep.
489	3306
490	Rep.
491	46 App.
492	3506
493–496	Rep.
497	2106, 3318, 8502
498	Rep.
511–522	Rep.
526	2101(43)
526a–526d	Rep.
526e	4102(b)
526f	Rep.
526g	4102(a)
526h	4103
526i	4102(c)

Title 46 Former Sections	Title 46 New Sections
526j	4102(d)
526k–526n	Rep.
526*o*	2106, 2107, 4106
526p	2107, 3306, 4104
526q–526t	Rep.
526u	4101
527–527h	Rep.
531	10601
532	Rep. See 11501
533, 534	10602
541–542a	Rep.
543	2104
544, 545	Rep.
546	10102
547–549	Rep.
561, 562	Rep.
563	11110
564	10301, 10302
565	10305
566	10301
567, 568	10321
569	10309
570	10308
571	10321
572, 573	Rep.
574	10301, 10501, 10502
575	10508
576	10509
577	10307
578	11107
579	Rep.
591	10313(a)
592	10313(b)
593	10313(b)
594	10313(c)
595	10313(d)
596	10313(e)–(i), 10504
597	2101(12), 10313(e)–(i), 10504
598	10313(e), 10504(a), (d), 10505(d)
599	2101(12), 10314, 10315, 10505, 10506
599(g)	10316
600	10317
601	11108, 11109
602	11111
603–608, 611	Rep.
621	10701, 10702
622	10703
623	10711
624	10704, 10705
625	10706
626	10707
627	10709
628	10708, 10710
641, 642	10310
643	8701, 8702, 10102(c), 10311, 10503
643(a)	7302, 7303, 7318
643(b)	7304
643(c)	7302, 10306
643(e)	10311
643(f)	7319, 7502
643(h)	7501
643(*l*)	7316, 10103
643a	8701
643b	Rep.
644	10312(a), (b), (d)–(f)
645, 646, 651	Rep.
652	10312(c)
653	10901, 10902(a), 10907
654	10901, 10903(a), (b)
655	10901, 10904
656	10901, 10905
657	10905
658	10901, 10906, 10908
659	10903(c)
660	10903(d)
660–1	11101
660a	3305, 3308
660b	3308
661	10321
662	10902(b)
663	Rep.
664	10907
665	10321, 11106(b)–(d)
666	11102(a)
667	11102(b)
668, 669	Rep.
670, 671	11103
672	8701, 8702
672(a)	2101(34)
672(b)	7306
672(b)(1)	7307
672(b)(2)	7308
672(b)(3)	7309, 7310
672(b)(4)	7311
672(c)	7301, 7315
672(d)	8702(d)
672(e)	8702(b), (c)
672(f)	7312
672(g)	7313, 7314
672(h)	8103
672(i)	7302
672(j)	2106, 8702(e)
672–1, 672–2	Rep.
672a	8103
672b, 672b–1, 672c	Rep.
673	8104
674–677	Rep.
678	11104(a)
679	11104(b)–(d)
680, 681	Rep.
682	10318, 10507
683	10318, 10507
684	11105
685	11106(a)
686, 687	Rep.
688	46 App.
689	2103, 2104
690	8103
691	Sec. 2(f) of Pub. L. 98–89
692	Rep.
701	11501
702	11502
703	11503
704	T. 18 § 2196
705	11504
706	11505
707	10319
708	T. 18 § 2279
709	Rep.
710	11506
710a	Rep.
710b	(See former 239a)
710c	(See former 239b)
711	Rep.
712	11507
713	10101, 10303, 10304
721–727	46 App.
728	2304
729–731	46 App.
732–735	Rep.
738, 738a	46 App.
738b	Rep.
738c	46 App.
738d	Rep.
740–752	46 App.
761, 762	46 App.
763	Rep.
763a–768	46 App.
781–790	46 App.
791–799	Rep.
801–803	46 App.
804	Rep.
804a	46 App.
805–807	Rep.
808	46 App.
808 (4th par.)	31328
809–810a	Rep.
811	46 App.
812–817c	Rep.
817d, 817e	46 App.
818–832	Rep.
833	46 App.
833a	Rep.
834–837	46 App.
838	31306
839	46 App.
840–841c	Rep.
842	46 App.
843–848	Rep.
861	46 App.
862–864	Rep.
864, 864b	46 App.
865–869	46 App.
870–870d	Rep.
871, 872	46 App.
873, 874	Rep.
875–877	46 App.
878–880	Rep.
881	3305, 3316, 12119
882	3304
883–885	46 App.
886	Rep.
887–889	46 App.
891	46 App.
891a	Rep.
891b, 891c	46 App.
891d–891r	Rep.
891s, 891t	Rep.
891u–891x	46 App.
891y	Rep.
911(1), (2)	30101(1)
911(3)	Rep.
911(4)	30101(1)
911(5)	31301(3)
921	31321(a)(1), (e)
922(a), (b)	31322(a)(1)
922(b)	31301(6)(A)
922(c), (d)	Rep.
922(e), (f)	31322(c)
923	31324
924	31323(a), (b)
925	31343
925(b)	31321(f), (h)
926(a), (b)	31321(b)
926(c)	Rep.
926(d)	31322(b)

Title 46 Former Sections	Title 46 New Sections
927	31302(1), (2)
941(a)	Rep.
941(b) (1st sentence)	31330(a), (c)
941(b) (last sentence)	31323(c)
941(c)	31304
951 (1st par.)	31325(a), (b)(1), (c), (d)
951 (2d par. less proviso)	31301(6)(B)
951 (2d par. proviso)	31326(b)(2)
952 (1st, 2d sentences)	31325(e)
952 (last sentence)	31308
953(a)	31301(5)
953(b)	31326(a), (b)(1)
954(a)	31325(b)(2)
954(b)	31303
961(a)	Rep.
961(b)	31327
961(c)	31326(a)
961(d), (e)	31328
961(f)	31329
971	31342
972	31341
973	31341(a)
974	31305
975	31307
981–984	Rep.
1011	Rep.
1012	31321(a)(2)
1013, 1014	Rep.
1101	46 App.
1111–1111a	46 App.
1111b, 1111c	Rep.
1112	46 App.
1113	Rep.
1114–1119	46 App.
1119a, 1119b	Rep.
1120–1125a	46 App.
1126	Rep.
1126–1	46 App.
1126a, 1126a–1	Rep.
1126b, 1126b–1	Rep.
1126c, 1126d	Rep.
1127–1128h	Rep.
1131	46 App.
1132	8103
1132(a)	7102
1132(g)	8302
1141–1144	Rep.
1145	Rep.
1151–1155	46 App.
1155a	Rep.
1156–1161	46 App.
1171–1181	46 App.
1182	Rep.
1183–1185	46 App.
1191–1205	46 App.
1206	Rep.
1211–1213	46 App.
1214	Rep.
1221	Rep.
1222, 1223	46 App.
1224, 1225	Rep.
1226–1228	46 App.
1241–1242	46 App.
1242–1	Rep.
1242a	46 App.
1243	Rep.
1244, 1245	46 App.
1246	Rep.
1247, 1248	46 App.
1251–1262	Rep.
1271–1275	46 App.
1276–1279	Rep.
1279a	46 App.
1279b	Rep.
1279c–1295e	46 App.
1295f(a), (b)	46 App.
1295f(c)	2101(17), 3301(2), 3306, 3307(1)
1295f(d)(1)	46 App.
1295f(d)(2), (3)	3318(g)
1295g(a)–(d)	46 App.
1295g(e)(1)	2101(17)
1295g(e)(2)–(5)	Rep.
1300–1315	46 App.
1331–1341	Rep.
1351–1364	Rep.
1381–1388	Rep.
1401–1413	Rep.
1451	Rep.
1452(1)(A), (B)	2101(25)
1452(1)(C)	2101(42)
1452(2)	2101(45)
1452(3)	2101(41)
1452(5)	2101(21)(D)
1452(7)	2101(26)
1452(8)	2101(1)
1452(9)	2101(34)
1452(10)	2102(2)
1452(11)	2102(1)
1452(12)	2102(4)
1452(13)	2102(5)
1452(14)	2102(3)
1453	4105, 4301
1454, 1455	4302
1456	4302(a)(3)
1457	4303
1458	4305
1459	4306
1460	4304, 4306
1461(a)	4307(a)
1461(b)	4311(f)
1461(c)	4307(b)
1461(d)	2302(a), (b)
1461(e)	8903
1461(f)	8903, 8905(a)
1462	4308
1463	4309
1464	4310
1464(g)	4302
1465	2303
1466	12301
1467	12302
1468	12303
1469	12304
1470	12305
1471	12306
1472	12307
1473	12308
1474	13101
1475	13102
1476	13103
1477	13104
1478	13105
1479	13106
1479a	13107
1480	13108
1481	13109
1482	13110
1483	2302(b), 4311(a), 12309(a)
1484(a)	4311(b)
1484(b)	2106, 2302(a), (c), 4311(c), 12309(b)
1484(c)	2107
1484(d)	4311(d), 12309(c)
1485	2305, 4311(e)
1486	6101, 6102
1487	Rep.
1488	4302
1489	4311(g)
1501–1507	46 App.
1508	Rep.
1601–1605	46 App.
1606	Rep.
1607–1610	46 App.
1707a	Rep.
1717	Rep.
1720, 1721	Rep.

TITLE 49—TRANSPORTATION

[This title was enacted into law by Pub. L. 95–473, §1, Oct. 17, 1978, 92 Stat. 1337; Pub. L. 97–449, §1, Jan. 12, 1983, 96 Stat. 2413; and Pub. L. 103–272, §1, July 5, 1994, 108 Stat. 745. This table shows where sections of former Title 49 were incorporated in revised Title 49.]

Title 49 Former Sections	*Title 49 New Sections*
1(1), (2)	10501
1(3)	10102
1(4) (related to standards)	10701
1(4) (2d sentence last cl.)	10702
1(4) (1st sentence related to through routes and 2d sentence less last cl.).	10703
1(4) (1st sentence 14th–23d words).	11101
1(5)(a)	10701
1(5)(b) (7th and 8th sentences)	10709
1(5)(b) (less 7th and 8th sentences).	10701
1(5)(c)(i)	10709
1(5)(c)(ii)	10102
1(5)(d)	Rep.
1(5½)	10749
1(6) (last sentence)	10750
1(6) (less last sentence)	10702 (See also 10701(a))
1(7) (1st sentence, 32 words before 8th semicolon–9th semicolon).	10721
1(7) (1st sentence words before 2d semicolon, words between 5th semicolon and 21st word after 7th semicolon, 1st–18th words after 9th semicolon, 1st proviso (words before semicolon), 2d, and 3d provisos).	10722
1(7) (1st sentence 1st–4th and 13th–20th words after 2d semicolon and words between 3d and 5th semicolons).	10723
1(7) (1st sentence 5th–12th and 21st–29th words after 2d semicolon and last 11 words before 1st proviso).	10723
1(7) (1st sentence 1st proviso, words between semicolon and colon).	10724
1(7) (less 1st sentence)	11905
1(8)	10746
1(9)	11104
1(10)	10102
1(11)	11121
1(12) (3d sentence)	11902
1(12) (less 3d sentence)	11126
1(13)	11121
1(14)(a)	11122
1(14)(b)	11121
1(14)(c)	11105
1(15) (related to car service less last sentence).	11123
1(15) (last sentence)	11128
1(15) (related to service less last sentence).	11127
1(16) (related to traffic less (b)).	11124
1(16) (related to service less (b)).	11127
1(16)(b)	11125
1(17)(a) (1st sentence)	11121
1(17)(a) (last sentence less proviso).	11901
1(17)(a) (last sentence proviso)	10501
1(17)(b)	11907
1(18)(a), (b)	10901
1(18)(c)	10902
1(18)(d)	10907
1(18)(e) (related to action by the Attorney General).	11703
1(18)(e) (related to Commission action).	11702
1(18)(e)	11901
1(18)(e) (related to State enforcement).	11505
1(19)–(22)	Rep.
1 note	10711
1a(1) (1st sentence)	10903
1a(1) (less 1st and last sentences).	10904
1a(1) (last sentence)	10907
1a(2), (3)	10904
1a(4)	10903
1a(5)	10904
1a(6), (7)	10905
1a(8)	Rep.
1a(9) (related to Commission action).	11702
1a(9) (related to action by the Attorney General).	11703
1a(9) (last sentence)	11901
1a(9) (related to State enforcement).	11505
1a(10)	10906
1a(11)	10905
2	10741
3(1)	10741
3(1a)	Rep.
3(2) (1st sentence)	10743
3(2) (less 1st sentence)	10744
3(3)	10744
3(4) (1st sentence 2d cl., 2d sentence related to standards).	10701
3(4) (less 1st sentence 2d cl., and 2d sentence related to facilities).	10742
3(5)	11103
4	10726
5(1) (words between semicolon and 1st colon).	11914
5(1) (less words between semicolon and 1st colon).	11342
5(2)(a)	11343
5(2)(b)–(e)	11344
5(2)(f)	11347
5(2)(g), (h)	11345
5(3)(a)–(e)	11346
5(3)(f) (last sentence)	11346
5(3)(f) (less last sentence)	11350
5(3)(g)	11346
5(4)	11348
5(5)–(7)	11343
5(8) (last sentence)	11912
5(8) (less last sentence)	11701
5(9)	11702
5(10)	11351
5(11)	11343
5(12)	11341
5(13)	Rep.
5(14)	11343
5(15) (words after semicolon)	11914
5(15) (less words after semicolon).	11321
5(16), (17)	11321
5a	Rep.
5b, 5c	10706
6(1)	10762
6(2)	10765
6(3), (4)	10762
6(5)	10764
6(6)	10762
6(7)	10761
6(8)	11128
6(9)	10762
6(10)	11901
6(11)	10503
6(12)	10765
7	10745
8, 9	11705
10(1)	11914
10(2)–(4)	11904
11	10301
12(1)(a) (less 2d sentence words after semicolon and last sentence words after 1st semicolon and before last semicolon).	10321
12(1)(a) (words after semicolon in 2d sentence).	10311
12(1)(a) (last sentence less words before 1st semicolon and after last semicolon).	11703
12(1)(b)	10505
12(2)–(7)	10321
13(1)	11701
13(2) (last sentence)	11502
13(2) (less last sentence)	11701
13(3)	11502
13(4), (5)	11501
13(6)	10326
13a(1)	10908
13a(2)	10909
14(1), (2)	10310
14(3) (last sentence)	10311
14(3) (less last sentence)	10310
15(1)	10704
15(2)	10324
15(3), (4)	10705
15(5)	10748
15(6)	10705
15(7)	10708
15(8)	10707
15(9)	10709

Title 49 Former Sections	Title 49 New Sections
15(10)	10763
15(11)	11710
15(12)	10763
15(13), (14)	11910
15(15)	10747
15(16)	10321
15(17)	10727
15(18)	10728
15(19)	10729
15a(1)–(5)	10704
15a(6), 15b	Rep.
16(1), (2)	11705
16(3)(c), (g)	11705
16(3)(h)	Rep.
16(3) (less (c), (g), and (h))	11706
16(4)	11705
16(5)	10329
16(6)	10324
16(7)	11914
16(8)–(10)	11901
16(11)	10301
16(12) (related to Commission action).	11702
16(12) (related to action by the Attorney General).	11703
16(12) (related to action by private person).	11705
16(12) (enforcement of money award).	11705
16(13)	10303
16a	Rep.
17(1)	10302
17(2) (1st sentence 80th–98th words and 2d sentence).	10304
17(2) (less 80th–90th words in 1st sentence, less 2d sentence).	10305
17(3) (less 2d sentence and last 42 words of 3d sentence).	10306
17(3) (2d sentence)	10301
17(3) (last 42 words of 3d sentence).	10321
17(4) (1st and 3d sentences)	10305
17(4) (2d sentence)	10303
17(5)	10322
17(6), (7)	10323
17(8)	10324
17(9)(j)	10310
17(9) (less (j))	10327
17(10)	10325
17(11)	10305, 10306
17(12)	10328
17(13)	10308
17(14)(a)	11701
17(14)(b)	Rep.
17(15)	10309
17 note	10306
18(1) (1st and 3d sentences)	10301
18(1) (2d sentence)	10303
18(1) (4th sentence)	10307
18(1) (last sentence)	10321
18(2)	10301
19	10307
19a(a) (1st and last sentences)	10781
19a(a) (2d and 3d sentences)	10301
19a(b)	10782
19a(c)	10781
19a(d)	Rep.
19a(e)	10783
19a(f), (g)	10784
19a(h)–(j)	10785
19a(k) (1st sentence)	10786
19a(k) (less 1st sentence)	11901
19a*(l)*	11703
20(1), (2)	11145
20(3) (less (e))	11142
20(3)(e)	Rep.
20(4)	11143
20(5)	11144
20(6) (2d sentence, 1st cl.)	11144
20(6) (2d sentence, 2d cl.)	11145
20(6) (less 2d sentence)	11144
20(7)(a)	11901
20(7)(b) (proviso)	11144
20(7)(b) (less proviso)	11909
20(7)(c)–(e)	11901
20(7)(f)	11910
20(8)	11141
20(9)	11703
20(10)	10301
20(11) (2d sentence, 1st proviso).	10103
20(11) (less 1st sentence 2d proviso related to released value, 2d sentence less words before 2d proviso).	11707
20(11) (1st sentence 2d proviso related to released value), 2d sentence (less 1st–5th provisos).	10730
20(12)	11707
20a(1)–(10)	11301
20a(11) (2d and 3d sentences)	11709

Title 49 Former Sections	Title 49 New Sections
20a(11) (less 2d, 3d, and 4th sentences).	11301
20a(11) (last sentence)	11911
20a(12) (last sentence)	11911
20a(12) (less last sentence)	11322
20b(1)	11361
20b(2) (1st–3d sentences, 4th sentence less words between 8th comma and period, 9th sentence).	11362
20b(2) (4th sentence, words between 8th comma and period, 8th comma and period, 8th sentence).	11363
20b(2) (5th and 7th sentences)	11364
20b(2) (less 1st–9th sentences)	11365
20b(3) (1st and last sentences)	11362
20b(3) (less 1st and last sentences).	11363
20b(4)	11365
20b(5)	11361
20b(6)	11366
20b(7)	Rep.
20b(8)	11362
20b(9)	11367
20b(10)	10321
20b(11)	11367
20b(12)	Rep.
20b(13)	11361
20c	11303
21	10311
22(1) (1st sentence 1st 26th and 62d–76th words).	10721
22(1) (1st sentence 77th–86th words and 2d proviso, 2d–4th sentences).	10722
22(1) (1st sentence words between 2d and 4th semicolons).	10722
22(1) (1st sentence words between 4th and 5th semicolons).	10722
22(1) (1st sentence 27th–61st words and words between 1st and 2d semicolons).	10723
22(1) (1st sentence words between 6th semicolon and 1st proviso).	10723
22(1) (last 2 sentences)	10724
22(1) (1st sentence words between 5th and 6th semicolons).	10103
22(1) (1st proviso 1st sentence)	Rep.
22(2) (less 1st sentence proviso).	10721
22(2) (1st sentence proviso)	Rep.
23	11703
25	Rep.
26(a)	20102
26(b)	20502
26(c)	20503
26(d)	20504
26(e)	20502
26(f) (words before last semicolon).	20505
26(f) (words after last semicolon).	20902
26(g)	501
26(h) (1st sentence words before last comma).	21302
26(h) (1st sentence words after last comma).	21304
26(h) (2d, 3d sentences, 4th sentence words before last comma).	21302
26(h) (4th sentence words after last comma, 5th sentence).	21304
26(h) (last sentence)	21302
26a	11504
26b	10381–10388
26c	11503
27	Rep.
41(1) (1st sentence)	11915
41(1) (less 1st sentence)	11903
41(2) (related to corporate violations).	11903
41(2) (related to corporate violations).	11915
41(2) (last sentence)	11916
41(3)	11902
42	Rep.
43	11703
44, 45	T. 15 §§28, 29
46	11913
47, 48	Rep.
49	Elim.
50 (related to notice)	10329
50 (related to process)	10330
51 (related to ownership)	11321
51 (related to 49:6(11))	10503
52	10783
53	Elim.
54–59	Rep.

Title 49 Former Sections	Title 49 New Sections
60	11507
61–64	Rep.
65, 65a	10721
66	T. 31 §3726
67	Elim.
71–79	Rep.
80	T. 40 §316
81	80102
82, 83	80103
84, 85	80112
86, 87	80103
88, 89	80110
90–92	80111
93	80108
94	80114
95	80107
96–99	80110
100–102	80113
103	80115
104	Rep.
105	80109
106	80111
107, 108	80104
109 (1st sentence)	80106
109 (last sentence)	80103
110	80104
111	80105
112, 113	80106
114–116	80107
117, 118	80104
119, 120	80105
121	80116
122	80101
123, 124	Rep.
141	Rep.
142	303a
143	Rep.
151–157	Rep.
171–173a, 174–184	Rep.
201	Rep.
211–213	T. 43 §§1441–1443
214	Rep.
231	Rep.
241–246	T. 50 §§151–154, 156, 157
250–268	Rep.
301	Rep.
302(a), (b)(1)	10521
302(b) (less (1))	11506
302(c)	10523
303(a)(1)	10102
303(a)(2)	10342
303(a)(3)	Rep.
303(a)(4)	10341
303(a)(5)–(7)	Rep.
303(a)(8), (9)	10102
303(a)(10) (proviso)	10522
303(a)(10) (less proviso)	10521
303(a)(11)	10521, 10927
303(a)(12), (13)	10102
303(a)(14) (words before 2d comma).	10102
303(a)(14) (words after 2d comma).	10502
303(a)(15)–(19)	10102
303(a)(20), (21)	Rep.
303(a)(22), (23)	31501
303(b)	10526
303(c) (words between 6th and 7th commas).	10521
303(c) (words before "nor", less words between 6th and 7th commas).	10921
303(c) (less words before "nor").	10524
304(a) (matter preceding (1))	10321
304(a)(1) (related to service)	11101
304(a)(1) (related to accounts)	11142
304(a)(1)–(2) (related to qualifications, hours of service, and safety).	31502
304(a)(2) (less "qualifications" through period).	11142
304(a)(3) (1st sentence)	31502
304(a)(3) (last sentence) (related to "Secs. 304(c), 305, 320, 321, 322(a), (b), (d), (f), (g)").	502–507, 522, 523, 525, 526
304(a)(3) (last sentence) (related to "Sec. 305(d) (related to liability)").	525
304(a)(3) (last sentence) (related to "Sec. 324").	31504
304(a)(3a) (last sentence) (related to "Secs. 304(c), 305, 320, 321, 322(a), (b), (d), (f), (g)").	502–507, 522, 523, 525, 526
304(a)(3a) (1st sentence)	31502
304(a)(3a) (last sentence) (related to "Sec. 305(d) (related to liability)").	525
304(a)(3a) (last sentence) (related to "Sec. 324").	31504
304(a)(4)	11142
304(a)(4a)	10525
304(a)(5)	31503
304(a)(6)	10321
304(a)(7) (words after semicolon).	10311
304(a)(7) (less words after semicolon).	10321
304(b)	11102
304(c)	11701
304(d) (related to administration matters).	10303
304(d) (related to reports)	10310
304(d)	10311
304(e)	11107
304(f)	11101
304a(1)–(4)	11706
304a(5), (6)	11705
304a(7)	Rep.
304a(8)	11706
305(a) (1st and 2d sentences)	10341
305(a) (3d sentence less proviso).	10342
305(a) (3d sentence proviso)	10344
305(a) (less 1st–3d sentences)	10343
305(b) (2d sentence, 1st 12 words).	10344
305(b) (1st, 3d, 5th, and 12th sentences).	10342
305(b) (2d sentence 13th–37th words).	10341
305(b) (4th and 6th sentences)	10342
305(b) (7th–9th sentences)	10343
305(b) (10th sentence)	10342
305(b) (11th sentence)	10344
305(b) (less 1st–12th sentences)	10342
305(c) (related to the Commission).	10307
305(c) (related to joint boards)	10344
305(d) (related to Commission and employee board subpena power).	10321
305(d) (related to joint boards)	10344
305(d) (related to liability)	11913
305(e)	10328
305(f) (4th sentence)	10344
305(f) (less 4th sentence)	11502
305(g) (proviso)	Rep.
305(g) (less proviso)	11705, 11706
305(h)	10301–10306, 10308, 10309, 10321–10325, 10328
305(i) (related to members of Commission).	10301
305(i) (related to joint board)	10344
305(i) (related to examiner)	10306
305(j)	10301
305a	10344 note
306(a)(1) (word before proviso)	10921
306(a)(1) (words after colon)	Rep.
306(a)(2)	10932
306(a)(3)–(5)	Rep.
306(a)(6)	10931
306(a)(7)	10932
306(b), 307	10922
308(a), (b)	10922
308(c), (d)	10932
309(a)(1) (words before 1st proviso).	10921
309(a)(1) (words between 1st and last colons).	Rep.
309(a)(1) (last proviso)	10526
309(a)(2)	10932
309(a)(3)–(5)	Rep.
309(b) (last proviso)	10932
309(b) (less last proviso)	10923
310	10930
310a(a)	10928
310a(b)	11349
310a(c)	10928
310a(c)	11349
311(a) (words before 1st proviso).	10921
311(a) (words after 1st colon)	10924
311(b), (c) (words before 2d comma).	10924
311(c) (words after 2d comma)	10927
311(d)	11144
312(a)	10925
312(b)	10926
312(c)	Rep.
313	11304
314 (related to securities)	11302
314 (related to penalties)	11911
315	10927
316 (related to standards)	10701
316(a) (1st–24th, 45th–59th words).	10703
316(a) (60th–143d words)	10702
316(a) (25th–44th words)	11101
316(b) (related to standards)	10701
316(b) (16th–33d words)	11101
316(b) (less 16th–33d words)	10702
316(c) (less 2d sentence)	10703
316(c) (2d sentence)	10702
316(d) (1st sentence)	10701

Title 49 Former Sections	*Title 49 New Sections*
316(d) (less 1st sentence)	10741
316(e) (2d sentence 2d cl.)	10705
316(e) (2d sentence less 2d cl. and less proviso).	10704
316(e) (proviso)	10521
316(e) (less 2d sentence)	11701
316(f)	10705
316(g) (less proviso)	10708
316(g) (proviso)	Rep.
316(h)	10701
316(i)	10704
316(j)	10103
317(a)	10762
317(b) (proviso)	10103, 10721–10724
317(b) (less proviso)	10761
317(c)	10762
317(d)	10761
318(a) (1st sentence related to standards).	10701
318(a) (1st and 4th sentences, and 7th sentence proviso related to relief).	10702
318(a) (2d, 5th, and 6th sentences, and 7th sentence proviso related to general requirements).	10762
318(a) (3d sentence, 7th sentence less proviso, and 7th sentence proviso related to relief).	10761
318(b)	10704
318(c) (proviso)	Rep.
318(c) (less proviso)	10708
319	10730, 11707
320(a) (1st and 2d sentences)	11145
320(a) (less 1st and 2d sentences).	10764
320(b)	11145
320(c)	11143
320(d)	11144
320(e)	11141
320(f)	504
320(g)	11144
321(a)	10329
321(b)	10324
321(c)	10330
321(d) (related to orders)	10324
321(d) (related to notice)	10329
321(d) (related to process)	10330
322(a)	11914
322(b)(1)	11702
322(b) (less (1))	11708
322(c) (related to rate violations).	11904
322(c) (related to evasion of regulation).	11906
322(d)–(f)	11910
322(g)	11909
322(h)	11901
323 (1st sentence)	10743
323 (less 1st sentence)	10744
324	11106
324a	10747
325	31503
325a	11504
326, 327	Rep.
401–403	Rep.
421–422a	Rep.
422b	Elim.
423–427	Rep.
451–460	Rep.
461	Elim.
481–496	Rep.
521–524	Rep.
551–560	Rep.
581, 582	Rep.
601–603	Rep.
621–623	Rep.
641–649	Rep.
671–685	Rep.
701–705	Rep.
711–722	Rep.
751–758	Rep.
781	80302
782	80303
783 (1st sentence)	80304
783 (last sentence)	80303
784 (proviso)	80304
784 (less proviso)	80306
785	80305
786	80306
787(a)–(c)	80301
787(d)–(g)	80302
788, 789	80304
901	Rep.
902(a)	10102
902(b)	Rep.
902(c), (d) (less exception)	10102
902(d) (words after 1st comma)	10502
902(e) (1st and 2d sentences)	10102
902(e) (3d–5th sentences)	10544
902(f)–(h)	10102
902(i)	10541

Title 49 Former Sections	*Title 49 New Sections*
902(j)–(m)	10102
903(a)	10541
903(b)–(d)	10542
903(e)(1)	10544
903(e)(2) (last sentence)	Rep.
903(e)(2) (less last sentence)	10544
903(e)(3)	10544
903(f)	10543
903(g), (h)	10544
903(i)	10721
903(j), (k)	10541
903*(l)*	10929
904(a)	10321
904(b) (words after last semicolon).	10311
904(b) (less words after last semicolon).	10321
904(c)	11102
904(d)	11108
904(e)	11701
905(a) (1st sentence related to standards and 2d sentence).	10701
905(a) (1st sentence 1st cl.)	11101
905(a) (less 1st sentence 1st cl. and last sentence).	10702
905(b) (4th sentence)	10701, 10702
905(b) (less 4th sentence)	10703
905(c)	10741
905(d) (1st sentence 2d cl., 2d sentence related to facilities).	10701
905(d) (less 1st sentence 2d cl., 2d sentence related to standards).	10742
906(a), (b)	10762
906(c) (proviso)	10103, 10721–10724
906(c) (less proviso)	10761
906(d) (1st sentence)	10761
906(d) (less 1st sentence)	10762
906(e) (1st sentence related to standards).	10701
906(e) (1st sentence and 7th sentence proviso related to relief).	10702
906(e) (2d, 4th, 5th, and 6th sentences, and 7th sentence provision, related to general requirements).	10762
906(e) (3d sentence, and 7th sentence less proviso, and 7th sentence proviso related to relief).	10761
907(a)	11701
907(b)	10704
907(c)	10701
907(d), (e)	10705
907(f)	10704
907(g) (proviso)	Rep.
907(g) (less proviso)	10708
907(h)	10704
907(i) (proviso)	Rep.
907(i) (less proviso)	10708
908(a)–(e), (f)(4)	11705
908(f) (less (4))	11706
908(g)	11705
909(a) (words before 1st proviso).	10921
909(a) (words after 1st colon)	Rep.
909(b)–(e)	10922
909(f) (words before 1st proviso).	10921
909(f) (words after 1st colon)	Rep.
909(g)	10923
910	10930
911(a)	10928
911(b)	11349
912	10926
912a	10925
913(a)	11145
913(b)	10764
913(c)	11142
913(d)	11143
913(e)–(g)	11144
913 (less (a)–(g))	11141
914	10747
915(a)	10329
915(b)	11701
915(c), (d)	10324
915(e)	11914
916(a)	10301–10306, 10308, 10309, 10321–10325, 10328, 11703, 11913
916(b) (related to Commission action).	11702
916(b) (related to action by the Attorney General).	11703
916(b) (related to action by private person).	11705
916(c)	10310
916(d)	10303
917(a)	11914
917(b), (c)	11904
917(d)	11909
917(e)	11910

Title 49 Former Sections	*Title 49 New Sections*
917(f) (1st and 2d sentences)	11910
917 (less (a)–(e) and (f) (1st and 2d sentences)).	11910
918 (1st sentence)	10743
918 (less 1st sentence)	10744
919	10301
920–922	Rep.
922a	11303
922b	11504
923	Rep.
1001	Rep.
1002(a)(2)	Rep.
1002(a)(1), (3), (4), (5), (8)	10102
1002(a)(6), (7)	10561
1002(b), (c)	10562
1003(a)	10321
1003(b)	11101
1003(c), (d)	10927
1003(e) (words after last semicolon).	10311
1003(e) (less words after last semicolon).	10321
1003(f)	11701
1004(a) (1st cl.)	11101
1004(a) (related to standards)	10701
1004(a) (related to carrier authority).	10702
1004(b), (c)	10741
1004(d)	10766
1005(a), (b)	10762
1005(c) (proviso)	10103, 10721–10724
1005(c) (less proviso)	10761
1005(d)	10762
1005(e)	10761
1006(a)	11701
1006(b)	10704
1006(c)	10701
1006(d)	10704
1006(e) (proviso)	Rep.
1006(e) (less proviso)	10708
1006(f) (2d and 3d sentences)	10502
1006(f) (less 2d last sentences)	11502
1006(f) (4th and last sentences)	11501
1006a(5), (6)	11705
1006a (less (5), (6), (7))	11706
1006a(7)	Rep.
1007, 1008	10725
1009	10766
1010(a)(1) (words before semicolon).	10921
1010(a) (less words before semicolon in par. (1)).	Rep.
1010(b)	10923
1010(c) (less 2d sentence, words before semicolon).	10923
1010(c) (2d sentence, words before semicolon).	10930
1010(d), (e)	10923
1010(f)	10925
1010(g)	10926
1010(h)	10930
1010(i) (1st sentence)	10933
1010(i) (less 1st sentence and 2d sentence words before semicolon).	11908
1010(i) (related to Commission action).	11702
1010(i) (related to enforcement by the United States).	11703
1010(i) (related to private enforcement).	11704
1010(i) (related to State enforcement).	11505
1011(a)	11323
1011(b) (last proviso)	Rep.
1011(b) (less last proviso)	10930
1011(c)	11323
1011(d)	11701
1011(e)	11702
1011(f)	11701
1011(g)	11323
1012(a) (1st and 2d sentences)	11145
1012(a) (3d sentence)	11142
1012(a) (last sentence)	10764
1012(b)	11145
1012(c)–(e)	11144
1012(f)	11141
1013 (1st sentence related to released value).	10730
1013	11707
1014	10743
1015	10747
1016(a)	10329
1016(b), (c)	10324
1016(d)	11914
1017(a)	10301–10306, 10308, 10309, 10311, 10321–10325, 10328, 11703, 11705, 11913
1017(b)(1) (related to Commission action).	11702
1017(b)(1) (related to action by the Attorney General).	11703
1017(b)(1) (related to action by private person).	11705
1017(b) (less (1))	11708
1017(c)	10310
1017(d)	10303
1018	10749
1019	Rep.
1020 (related to service)	11127
1020 (related to penalties)	11901
1021(a)	11914
1021(b), (c)	11904
1021(d)	11909
1021(e), (f)	11910
1021 (less (a)–(f))	11703
1022	Rep.
1101–1103	Rep.
1103a	Elim.
1104–1120	Rep.
1151	47301
1152	47302
1153	47303
1154	47302
1155–1157(b)	47304
1157(c)	Rep.
1158	47304
1159(a) (1st sentence)	47305
1159(a) (last sentence)	47306
1159(b)–(d)	47305
1159a, 1159b	41310
1160	47305
1181–1185	Rep.
1201–1203	80504
1211–1215	Rep.
1231–1240	Rep.
1301(1)	Rep.
1301(2), (3) (less proviso)	40102
1301(3) (proviso)	40109
1301(4)–(12)	40102
1301(13)	Rep.
1301(14) (related to certificate)	41101
1301(14) (less certificate)–(37)	40102
1301(38)	46501
1301(39)–(41)	40102
1302, 1303	40101
1303 note	44111, 44713, 45302, 46301, 46306, 46315
1304	40103
1305(a), (b)(1)	41713
1305(b)(2)	40102
1305(c), (d) (related to (a), (b)(1)).	41713
1305(d) (related to (b)(2))	40102
1305(d) (related to (c))	41713
1306–1308	Rep.
1321–1323	Rep.
1324(a)	40113
1324(b), (c)	41711
1324(d)	40114
1325	Rep.
1341(a), (b)	106
1341(c)	Rep.
1342	106
1343(a)(1), (2) (related to cooperative agreements).	324
1343(a)(2) (related to Deputy Administrator).	106
1343(b)	329
1343(c)	40107
1343(d)	323
1343(e)	Rep.
1343(f), (g) (1st sentence 33d–43d words).	323
1343(g) (less 1st sentence 33d–43d words).	325
1343(h)	Rep.
1343(i)	322
1344(a)–(d)	40110
1344(a)	322
1344(b)	331
1344(c)(1)	326
1344(d) (less words after semicolon).	322
1344(d) (words after semicolon)	(See former section 1348(b).)
1344(e)	322, 40111
1344(f)	40112
1344(g)	40110
1344(h)	47124
1345	40107
1346, 1346a	40104
1347	40101
1348(a)	40103
1348(b) (1st sentence cl. (3))	44721
1348(b) (1st sentence less cl. (3), 2d sentence).	44502
1348(b) (3d, last sentences)	44721
1348(c), (d)	40103
1348(e)	40109
1348(f)	40106
1348 notes	44506, 44514, 44719
1348a	44506
1349(a) (1st, 2d sentences)	44502
1349(a) (3d, last sentences)	40103
1349(b), 1350	44502
1351	44720
1352	329

Title 49 Former Sections	*Title 49 New Sections*
1353(a)	44501
1353(b)	44504
1353(c)	44505
1353(d)	44501
1353(e)	44507
1353(f)	44508
1353(g)	44511
1353(h)	44512
1353(i)	44513
1353 notes	44506, 48102
1354(a)	40113
1354(b)	40114
1354(c) (related to this chapter).	46104
1354(c) (related to Airport and Airway Improvement Act of 1982).	47122
1354(c) (related to Federal Airport Act and Airport and Airway Development Act of 1970).	Rep.
1354(d)	40108
1354(e)	308(b), 40113
1354(f)	45302
1354 note	44515, 48110
1354a (1st sentence)	44510
1354a (2d sentence)	48106
1354a (3d, last sentences)	44510
1355 (less (a) (last sentence related to fees)).	44702
1355(a) (last sentence related to fees).	45303
1356(a) (1st, 2d sentences)	44901
1356(a) (3d sentence 1st–18th words).	44938
1356(a) (3d sentence 19th–last words).	44901
1356(a) (last sentence), (b)	44938
1356(c)	44901
1356a	Rep.
1356b	44903
1357(a), (b)	44903
1357(c)	44935
1357(d)(1), (2)	40119
1357(d)(3)–(8)	44912
1357(d)(9)	48107
1357(e)(1)	40119, 44937
1357(e)(2), (3), (f), (g)	44903
1357(g)	44936
1357(h)–(j)	44935
1357(k)(1)–(3)	44906
1357(k)(4)	44938
1357 notes	44904, 44906, 44914, 44936, 44938
1358	44915
1358a	44932
1358b(a)	44933
1358b(b)	44934
1358b(c)	Rep.
1358c	44913
1358d	44905
1358d note	44910
1359	Rep.
1371(a)	41101
1371(b), (c)	41108
1371(d)(1)–(3)	41102
1371(d)(4)(A)(i), (ii) (related to joint services).	41101
1371(d)(4)(A)(ii) (related to joint rates, fares), (B).	41503
1371(d)(5)–(7)	Rep.
1371(d)(8) (1st sentence)	41102
1371(d)(8) (last sentence)	41110
1371(d)(9)	41108
1371(e)(1)–(4)	41109
1371(e)(5)–(7)(A)	Rep.
1371(e)(7)(B)	41109
1371(e)(7)(C)	Rep.
1371(f), (g)	41110
1371(h)	41105
1371(i)	41101
1371(j)	41312
1371(k)	42112
1371(*l*)	41903
1371(m)	41107
1371(n)(1)	Rep.
1371(n)(2)–(6)	41104
1371(*o*)	41106
1371(p)	41111
1371(q)	41112
1371(r)	41110
1371a (related to certificate)	41110
1371a (related to permit)	41304
1372(a)	41301
1372(b)	41302
1372(c), (d)	41305
1372(e) (related to duration of permits).	41304
1372(e) (related to terms, conditions, or limitations of permits).	41305
1372(f)	41304
1372(g)	41303
1372(h)	41306

Title 49 Former Sections	*Title 49 New Sections*
1373(a)	41504
1373(b)(1) (1st sentence)	41510
1373(b)(1) (2d–last sentences)	41511
1373(b)(2)	41510
1373(c)(1), (2)	41504
1373(c)(3)	41509
1373(d)	41506
1374(a)(1)	41702
1374(a)(2)	41501
1374(b)	41310
1374(c)	41705
1374(d)(1)	41706
1374(d)(2)	46301
1374 note	41706
1375(a)	Rep.
1375(b)	41902
1375(c), (d)	41903
1375(e)(1)	41912
1375(e)(2)	41904
1375(f)(1) (1st sentence)	41905
1375(f)(1) (2d–last sentences), (2).	41908
1375(g)	41911
1375(h)	41906
1375(i)	Rep.
1375(j)	T. 39 §5007
1376(a)–(e)	41901
1376(f)	41910
1376(g)	Rep.
1376(h)(1)	41907
1376(h)(2)	41909
1376(h)(3)	41907
1376a, 1376b	Rep.
1377(a)	41708
1377(b), (c)	Rep.
1377(d), (e) (1st–3d sentences)	41700
1377(e) (last sentence)	41708
1378, 1379	Rep.
1380, 1380 note	44909
1381(a)	41712
1381(b)	41707
1382(a), (b)	41309
1382(c)	42111
1383	40102
1384	41308
1385	41711
1386(a)	41701
1386(b)	40109
1387, 1388(a)(1)–(3)	Rep.
1388(a)(4)	41103
1388(b)(1)(A)	Rep.
1388(b)(1)(B), (2)	41103
1388(b)(3)	Rep.
1388(b)(4)	41110
1388(c), (d)	41103
1389(a)	41731
1389(b)(1)	41733
1389(b)(2)	41734
1389(b)(3), (4)	41733
1389(b)(5)–(8)	41734
1389(b)(9)	41733
1389(c)	41735
1389(d)	41736
1389(e)(1)	41738
1389(e)(2)–(g)	41737
1389(h)	41741
1389(i)	41739
1389(j)	41740
1389(k)(1)	41732
1389(k)(2)–(5)	41731
1389(*l*)	41737
1389(m)	41742
1401(a)	44101
1401(b)	44102
1401(c), (d)	44103
1401(e)(1)	44105
1401(e)(2)(A)–(C)	44106
1401(e)(2)(D), (E)	44103
1401(e)(2)(F)	44106
1401(f), (g)	44103
1401(h)	44111
1401 note	44111, 44703, 44713
1402	44104
1403(a), (b)	44107
1403(c), (d)	44108
1403(e), (f)	44107
1403(g)	44110
1403(h)	44704
1404	44112
1405 (1st sentence)	44104
1405 (2d sentence)	44103
1405 (last sentence)	46301
1406, 1406 note	44108
1421(a), (b) (1st sentence related to standards, rules, and regulations).	44701
1421(b) (1st sentence related to issuing certificates).	44702
1421(b) (2d sentence)	44702
1421(b) (last sentence), (c)	44701
1421(d)	44712
1421(e)	44714
1421(f)	44716

Title 49 Former Sections	*Title 49 New Sections*
1421 notes	44716, 44717, 44722
1422(a) (1st–10th words)	44702
1422(a) (11th–last words), (b)(1), (2)(A), (B).	44703
1422(b)(2)(C)	44710
1422(c), (d)	44703
1423(a)(1) (related to issuing certificates).	44702
1423(a)(1) (related to regulations for appliances), (2).	44704
1423(b) (related to issuing certificates).	44702
1423(b) (related to basis for issuing, and contents of, certificates).	44704
1423(c) (related to issuing certificates).	44702
1423(c) (related to basis for issuing, and contents of, certificates).	44704
1424(a) (related to issuing certificates).	44702
1424(a) (related to standards)	44701
1424(b)	44705
1425	44713
1426 (1st sentence)	44708
1426 (last sentence)	44702
1427 (1st sentence)	44707
1427 (last sentence), 1428	44702
1429(a) (1st–7th sentences)	44709
1429(a) (8th–last sentences related to Administrator under subchapter VII).	1153
1429(a) (8th–last sentences less Administrator under subchapter VII), (b).	44709
1429(c)	44710
1430	44711
1431(a)–(d)	44715
1431(e)	44709
1432(a) (related to issuing certificates).	44702
1432(a) (related to standards)	44701
1432(b), (c)	44706
1432(d)	44914
1433(a), (b)	40103 note
1433(c)	Rep.
1434(a)	45102
1434(b)	45103
1434(c)	45105
1434(d)	45104
1434(e)	45106
1434(f)	45101
1441(a)(1), (2)	1132
1441(a)(3)	1116
1441(a)(4)	1131
1441(a)(5)	1116
1441(b)	1113
1441(c) (1st sentence)	1132
1441(c) (2d, last sentences), (d)	1134
1441(e)	1154
1441(f)	1131
1441(g), 1442	1132
1443	1112
1461(a)	41307
1461(b)	41509
1462	40105
1463	44720
1471(a)(1) (related to subchapter VII).	1155
1471(a)(1) (less subchapter VII), (2) (related to subchapter III, V, VI, or XII, §1501, 1514, or 1515(e)(2)(B), and Postal Service).	46301
1471(a)(2) (related to 1471(c))	46302
1471(a)(2) (related to 1471(d))	46303
1471(a)(2) (related to subchapter VII).	1155
1471(a)(3) (less (D)(v) (related to Administrator under subchapter VII)).	46301
1471(a)(3)(D)(v) (related to Administrator under subchapter VII).	1153
1471(b)	46304
1471(c)	46302
1471(d)	46303
1472(a)	46316
1472(b)	46306
1472(c)	46308
1472(d)	46309
1472(e)	46310
1472(f)	46311
1472(g)	46313
1472(h)(1)	40113
1472(h)(2)	46312
1472(h)(3)	40113
1472(i)	46502
1472(j)	46504
1472(k)	46506
1472(*l*)	46505
1472(m)	46507

Title 49 Former Sections	*Title 49 New Sections*
1472(n)(1)	46502
1472(n)(2)	46501
1472(n)(3)	46502
1472(n)(4)	46501
1472(*o*)	T. 28 §538
1472(p)	1155
1472(q)	46315
1472(r)	46314
1473(a)	Rep.
1473(b)(1)	1155, 46305
1473(b)(2), (3)	46304
1473(b)(4)	1155, 46305
1473(c)	46503
1474	T. 19 §1644a
1475	Rep.
1481	46102
1482(a)–(c)	46101
1482(d), (e)	Rep.
1482(f)	41507
1482(g)	Rep.
1482(h)	41508
1482(i)	Rep.
1482(j)(1)–(7)	41509
1482(j)(8)	Rep.
1482(j)(9), (10)	41509
1482(k)	Rep.
1482a	41505
1483(a)	Rep.
1483(b)	41502
1483(c)–(e)	Rep.
1484	46104
1485(a)	46105
1485(b), (c)	46103
1485(d)–(f)	46105
1486 (related to CAB)	1153, 46110
1486 (related to Secretary)	46110
1487(a) (related to CAB)	1151, 46106
1487(a) (related to Attorney General).	46107
1487(a) (related to party in interest).	46108
1487(a) (related to Secretary)	46106
1487(b) (related to CAB)	1151, 46107
1487(b) (related to Secretary)	46107
1488 (related to CAB)	1151, 46107
1488 (related to Secretary)	46107
1489	1152, 46109
1490	41710
1501	44718
1502(a)	40105
1502(b)	40101
1502(c), (d)	40105
1503	40114
1504	40115
1505	40113
1506	40120
1507	44502
1508(a)	40103
1508(b)	41703
1509(a)	40120
1509(b)–(e)	T. 19 §1644a
1509(f), 1509 note	44109
1510	40120
1511	44902
1512, 1513(a), (b)	40116
1513(c)	Rep.
1513(d)	40116
1513(e)	40117
1513(f)	40116
1514	40106
1515	44907
1515 note	44910
1515a	44908
1516	41704
1517, 1518	40118
1519	44721
1521, 1522	40103
1523	46307
1531	44301
1532(a)	44302
1532(b), (c)	44306
1533	44303
1534	44305
1535	44304
1536(a)–(d)	44307
1536(e)	Rep.
1536(f)	44307
1537(a) (1st sentence)	44308
1537(a) (last sentence words between 2d and 3d commas).	44302
1537(a) (last sentence less words between 2d and 3d commas).	44306
1537(b)–(d)	44308
1537(e)	Rep.
1537(f)	44308
1538, 1539	Rep.
1540	44309
1541	44302
1542	44310
1551(a)(1)(A)	41102
1551(a)(1)(B)	41102, 41110
1551(a)(1)(C)	41109

Title 49 *Former Sections*	*Title 49* *New Sections*
1551(a)(1)(D)	41312
1551(a)(1)(E) (related to 49:1371(n)(1)).	Rep.
1551(a)(1)(E) (related to 49:1371(n)(4)).	41104
1551(a)(1)(F), (G), (2), (3)	Rep.
1551(a)(4)(A) (related to 49:1371(*l*)).	41903
1551(a)(4)(A) (related to 49:1371(m)).	41107
1551(a)(4)(A) (related to 49:1375(b)).	41902
1551(a)(4)(A) (related to 49:1375(c), (d)).	41903
1551(a)(4)(B) (related to 49:1373(a)).	41504
1551(a)(4)(B) (related to 49:1373(b)).	41510, 41511
1551(a)(4)(B) (related to 49:1373(c)(1), (2)).	41504
1551(a)(4)(B) (related to 49:1373(c)(3)).	41509
1551(a)(4)(B) (related to 49:1373(d)).	41506
1551(a)(4)(C) (related to 49:1374(a)(1)).	41702
1551(a)(4)(C) (related to 49:1374(a)(2)).	Rep.
1551(a)(4)(C) (related to 49:1374(b)).	41310
1551(a)(5)(A)–(C), (D) (related to 49:1482(d), (e), (g)).	Rep.
1551(a)(5)(D) (related to 49:1482(h)).	41508
1551(a)(5)(D) (related to 49:1482(i)).	Rep.
1551(a)(6) (related to 49:1382)	41309
1551(a)(6) (related to 49:1384)	41308
1551(a)(7)	Rep.
1551(a)(8)	41107, 41901–41903
1551(b)(1)(A)	Rep.
1551(b)(1)(B)	40105
1551(b)(1)(C) (related to 49:1378, 1379).	Rep.
1551(b)(1)(C) (related to 49:1382(a), (b)).	41309
1551(b)(1)(C) (related to 49:1382(c)).	42111
1551(b)(1)(C) (related to 49:1384)	41308
1551(b)(1)(D)	41901; T. 39 §5402
1551(b)(1)(E)	10526, 10749, 40101–40103, 40105, 40106, 40109, 40113, 40114, 40118, 41102–41112, 41302–41307, 41312, 41502–41511, 41701, 41703, 41704, 41708–41713, 41901–41903, 41907, 41910, 44712, 46101–46107, 46109, 46110, 46301–46305, 46309, 46311, 46313, 46316, 47501; T. 18 §6001; T. 39 §5007
1551(b)(2)	Rep.
1551(b)(3)	41107, 41901–41903
1551(c)–(e)	Rep.
1552(a)(1) (1st sentence)	42102
1552(a)(1) (last sentence)	42101
1552(a)(2)–(c)	42102
1552(d)(1), (2) (1st–3d sentences).	42103
1552(d)(2)(4th sentence)	42102
1552(d)(2) (last sentence), (3)	42103
1552(e)	42102
1552(f)	42104
1552(g)	42105
1552(h)	42101
1552(i)	42101–42103
1552(j)	42106
1553(a)(1)–(5)	Rep.
1553(a)(6)	T. 42 §6362
1553(a)(7)	T. 2 §451
1553(a)(8)–(10), (b)	Rep.
1553(c)	41901
1554–1557	Rep.
1601–1601b	5301
1601c	308(e)
1602(a)(1), (2)(A), (B)	5309
1602(a)(2)(C)	5323
1602(a)(3)–(5)	5309
1602(a)(6)–(8)	5328
1602(b), (c)	5309
1602(d)–(g)	5323
1602(h)	5337
1602(i)–(*l*)	5309
1602(m) (1st sentence)	5338
1602(m) (2d–last sentences)	5318
1602(n), 1602 note	5309
1602–1	Rep.
1602a	5323
1603(a)	5309
1603(b)(1)	5335
1603(b)(2)	Rep.
1603(c) (1st sentence)	5312
1603(c) (last sentence)	5338
1603(d)	5309
1604, 1604a	Rep.
1604b	5310
1605(a)	5312
1605(b), (c)	Rep.
1605(d)	5312
1606(a)	5324
1606(b)	Rep.
1607(a) (1st sentence)	5301
1607(a) (2d–last sentences), (b)–(g).	5303
1607(h)	5304
1607(i), (j)	5305
1607(k)	5334
1607(*l*)	5305
1607(m)	5306
1607(n)	5303
1607(*o*)	5306
1607(p)	5303
1607(q)	5323
1607a(a)–(d)	5336
1607a(e)(1)	5307, 5336
1607a(e)(2)–(k)(1)	5307
1607a(k)(2)	5336
1607a(k)(3), (*l*)	Rep.
1607a(m)(1)	5307
1607a(m)(2)–(*o*)	5336
1607a(p)	5307
1607a(q)	5336
1607a(r)	5307
1607a(s), (t)	5336
1607a note	5307
1607a–1	Rep.
1607a–2(a), (b)	5308
1607a–2(c)	5338
1607b, 1607c(a)	5312
1607c(b)(1)–(8)(B)(ii)	5317
1607c(b)(8)(B)(iii)	5338
1607c(b)(8)(B)(iv)–(10)(B)	5317
1607c(b)(10)(C)	5338
1607c(b)(10)(D)–(12)	5317
1607c(b)(13)	5338
1607c(b)(14), (15)	5317
1607c(c)(1)–(5)	5316
1607c(c)(6)	5338
1607c(c)(7)	5316
1608(a)	5334
1608(b)	5325
1608(c)	5302
1608(d)	5324
1608(e)	5323
1608(f)	10531
1608(g), (h)(1)	5323
1608(h)(2)	5302
1608(i)	5334
1608(j)	5323
1608(k)	5334
1608(*l*)	5326
1608(m)	5323
1608 notes	5302, 5318
1608 note (related to authority and functions reserved to Secretary of Housing and Urban Development).	5334
1609	5333
1610(a) (1st sentence)	5301
1610(a) (last sentence)–(c)	5324
1611(a), (b)	5335
1611(c)	Rep.
1612(a)	5301
1612(b) (1st sentence)	5310
1612(b) (last sentence)	5338
1612(c)	5310
1612(d)	5338
1612(e), (f)	5310
1613	Rep.
1614(a) (1st, 2d sentences)	5311
1614(a) (last sentence)	5338
1614(b)–(f)	5311
1614(g) (related to 1612(b))	5310
1614(g) (related to this section)–(i).	5311
1615(a)[no (b)]	5332
1616	5322
1617	5338
1618	5329
1618a	5331
1619	5327
1620	5321
1621	5319
1622(a)	5313
1622(b)(1)–(8) (related to this subsection).	5314
1622(b)(8) (related to subsection (a)(1)).	5313
1622(c)	5320
1623	5335
1624	5330
1625(a)–(c)	5315
1625(d)	5338
1631–1633	Elim.
1634	329
1635–1641	Elim.
1642, 1643	Rep.
1651(a), (b)(1)	101

Title 49 Former Sections	*Title 49 New Sections*
1651(b)(2)	303
1652(a)–(d)	102
1652(e) (related to FAA)	106
1652(e)(1) (related to FHWA)	104
1652(e)(1) (related to FRA)	103
1652(e)(3) (related to USCG)	108
1652(e)(3) (related to FHWA)	104
1652(e)(3) (related to FRA)	103
1652(e)(4) (related to FHWA)	104
1652(e)(4) (related to FRA)	103
1652(f)	Rep.
1652a	103
1652b	44931
1652b note	337
1653(a)	301
1653(b)	302
1653(c)	351
1653(d)	352
1653(e)	307
1653(f)	303
1653(g)	304
1653(h)	Rep.
1653(i)(1)	5562
1653(i)(2)	5563
1653(i)(3)	5564
1653(i)(4)	5562
1653(i)(5)	5565
1653(i)(6)	Rep.
1653(i)(7)	5567
1653(i)(8)	5566
1653(i)(9)	5568
1653(i)(10)	5561
1653(i)(11)	5562
1653 note	335
1653a	Rep.
1654(a)–(e)	333
1654(a)	22102
1654(b), (c)	22101
1654(d)	22106
1654(e)	22105
1654(f)	22103
1654(g)	22104
1654(h)	22108
1654(i)	22106
1654(j)	22105
1654(k)–(m)	22107
1654(n)–(p)	22101
1654(q)	22108
1654a	308(d)
1655(a)(1)(A)	Rep.
1655(a)(1)(B), (C)	(See §2 of Pub. L. 97–449.)
1655(a)(1)(D)	Rep.
1655(a)(1)(E)–(M)	(See §2 of Pub. L. 97–449.)
1655(a)(2)(A) (related to 49:1634).	329
1655(a)(2), (3)	Rep.
1655(a)(4)	(See §2 of Pub. L. 97–449.)
1655(a)(5)	Rep.
1655(a)(6)(A)	30102
1655(a)(6)(B)	(See §2 of Pub. L. 97–449.)
1655(b)(1), (2)	108
1655(b)(3)	Rep.
1655(c)(1) (1st sentence proviso, 2d, last sentences).	106
1655(c)(1)	1116, 1131, 1132, 1153, 40101–40109, 40113, 40114, 44103–44105, 44107, 44110, 44501, 44502, 44504, 44505, 44701–44705, 44707–44709, 44711, 44713, 44720, 44721, 45303, 46101–46107, 46110, 46301, 46304, 46308, 46311, 46313, 46316, 47151–47153, 47302–47306
1655(c)(2)	Rep.
1655(d) (1st sentence)	1112, 1113, 1116, 1131, 1132, 1134, 1151–1155
1655(d) (last sentence)	1153
1655(e)(1)(A)	20302, 21302
1655(e)(1)(B)	20302
1655(e)(1)(C)	20302, 21302
1655(e)(1)(D)	Rep.
1655(e)(1)(E), (F)	20701–20703, 21302
1655(e)(1)(G)	20702, 20703, 21302
1655(e)(1)(H)	Rep.
1655(e)(1)(I)	20305, 20504
1655(e)(1)(J)	20305
1655(e)(1)(K)	20901, 20902, 21302
1655(e)(2)	Rep.
1655(e)(3)	80504
1655(e)(4)	Rep.
1655(e)(5)	(See §2 of Pub. L. 97–449.)
1655(e)(6)(A)	20502–20505, 21302
1655(e)(6)(B)	3103
1655(e)(6)(C)	3102, 3103
1655(e)(6)(D) (related to "Sec. 321(a), (c)").	503
1655(e)(6)(D) (related to "Sec. 324").	3104
1655(f)(1)	Rep.
1655(f)(2)	501, 502, 504–507, 521–526
1655(f)(3)(A), (C) (related to FRA).	103
1655(f)(3)(B), (C) (related to FHWA).	104
1655(g)(1)–(3), (4)(A), (B), (E), (5), (6).	(See §2 of Pub. L. 97–449.)
1655(h), (i)	Rep.
1656(less (a) next-to-last par.)	305
1656(a) (next-to-last par.)	(See T. 42 §1962a–2(a).)
1657(a), (b)	323
1657(c), (d)	324
1657(e)–(g)	322
1657(h), (i)	Rep.
1657(j)	327
1657(k)	102
1657(*l*)	331
1657(m)	326
1657(n)	329
1657(*o*)	325
1657(p)	324
1657(q)(1)–(3)	330
1657(q)(4)	Rep.
1657(r)	328
1657–1	353
1657a	332
1658	308(a)
1659	Rep.
1660	335
1671(1)–(4) (1st–32d words)	60101
1671(4) (33d–last words)	60104
1671(5), (6)	60101
1671(7)	60115
1671(8)–(17)	60101
1671 note	60101
1672(a)(1) (1st–5th sentences)	60102
1672(a)(1) (6th sentence)	60104
1672(a)(1) (7th, 8th sentences)	60102
1672(a)(1) (9th, last sentences)	60104
1672(a)(2), (3), (b)	60102
1672(c)	60104
1672(d)	60118
1672(e)–(g)	60102
1672(h)	60108
1672(i)	60109
1672(j)	60110
1672(k)	60113
1673	60115
1674(a)	60105
1674(b), (c) (related to agreement).	60106
1674(c) (related to certification).	60105
1674(d)	60107
1674(e)	60105
1674(f)	60106
1674a	60103
1674b(a)	Rep.
1674b(b)(1)–(3)	60111
1674b(b)(4)	60119
1674b(c)	60111
1675	60119
1676(a)	60104
1676(b)	60117
1677(a), (b)(1)	60118
1677(b)(2), (c)	60120
1678, 1679	Rep.
1679a(a), (b)	60122
1679a(c)	60123
1679a(d)	60122
1679b(a)	60120
1679b(b)	60112
1680	60108
1681(a)–(e)	60117
1681(f)	60120
1682	60117
1682 note	60117
1682a	60301
1683	60124
1684(a)	60125
1684(b)	Rep.
1684(c)–(e)	60125
1684(f)	Rep.
1685(a)	60116
1685(b)	60113
1686	60121
1687(a)–(e)	60114
1687(f)	60125
1687(g)	60123
1687(h)	60114
1688	60101
1701–1703	Rep.
1704	44503
1711–1713	Rep.
1713a	47127
1714–1730	Rep.
1731	47106
1741	80503
1742	Rep.
1743	44502
1761, 1762	Rep.
1801	5101
1802	5102
1803, 1804(a)(1)–(3)	5103
1804(a)(4), (5)	5125
1804(b)(1)–(3)	5112
1804(b)(4)	5125
1804(b)(5)–(9), (c)	5112

Title 49 Former Sections	*Title 49 New Sections*
1804(d)	5120
1804(e), (f)	5104
1804(g)	5110
1805(a)	5106
1805(b)	5107
1805(c)	5108
1805(d)	5109
1805(e), (f)	Rep.
1805 note	5109
1806	5117
1807	5114
1808(a) (1st sentence, last sentence words before semicolon).	5121
1808(a) (last sentence words after semicolon).	5122
1808(b)–(e)	5121
1809(a)	5123
1809(b)	5124
1810	5122
1811(a)–(e)	5125
1811(f)	5126
1812	5127
1813	5105
1813 note	5105, 5118
1814	5113
1815(a)–(f)	5116
1815(g)(1)–(6)	5115
1815(g)(7)	5116
1815(g)(8)	5115
1815(g)(9)	5116
1815(h)(1)–(5)	5108
1815(h)(6)	5116
1815(i)	5127
1816(a)–(c)	5107
1816(d)	5127
1817	5111
1818	5126
1819(a)–(g)	5119
1819(h)	5127
1901	Rep.
1902	1111
1903(a)(1)(A)	1112, 1113, 1116, 1131, 1132, 1134, 1151, 1152, 1154, 1155
1903(a)(1)(B)–(2)	1131
1903(a)(3)–(8)	1116
1903(a)(9)	1133
1903(b)(1)	1113
1903(b)(2)	1134
1903(b)(3), (4)	1113
1903(b)(5)	1134
1903(b)(6)–(9)	1113
1903(b)(10)	1115
1903(b)(11)	1114
1903(b)(12)	1113
1903(c)	1154
1903(d)	1153
1904	1117
1905(a)–(c)(2)	1114
1905(c)(3)	1114, 1154
1905(d)	1154
1906	1135
1907	1118
2001(1)–(4) (1st–27th words)	60101
2001(4) (28th–last words)	60104
2001(5)–(9)	60101
2001(10)	60115
2001(11)	60101
2001 note	60101
2002(a)–(c) (4th sentence)	60102
2002(c) (last sentence), (d)	60104
2002(e), (f)	60102
2002(g)	60104
2002(h)	60118
2002(i)–(k)	60102
2002(*l*)	60108
2002(m)	60109
2002(n)	60102
2003	60115
2004(a)	60105
2004(b), (c) (related to agreement).	60106
2004(c) (related to certification).	60105
2004(d)	60107
2004(e), (f)	60105
2004(g)	60106
2005	60119
2006(a), (b)(1)	60118
2006(b)(2), (c)	60120
2007(a), (b)	60122
2007(c)	60123
2007(d)	60122
2008(a)	60120
2008(b)	60112
2009(a), (b)	60108
2009(c)	Rep.
2009(d)	60108
2010(a)–(e)	60117
2010(f)	60120
2011	60117
2012	60124
2013(a)	60125
2013(b)	Rep.
2014	60121
2015, 2015 note	60102
2016	60101
2101	47501
2102	47502
2103(a)	47503
2103(b)	47505
2104(a)–(d)	47504
2104(e), 2105	Rep.
2106	47507
2107	47506
2108	Rep.
2121	Rep.
2122(a)	47508
2122(b)–2124	Rep.
2125	47510
2151	47521
2152	47523
2153(a)–(g)	47524
2153(h)	47533
2154	47525
2155	47527
2156	47526
2157(a)–(c)	47528
2157(d)	47530
2157(e)	47531
2157(f)	47532
2157(g)	47528
2157(h)	47522
2157(i)	47528
2158	47529
2201	47101
2202(a)(1)–(5)	47102
2202(a)(6)	47107
2202(a)(7)	47102
2202(a)(8)	47102, 47106
2202(a)(9), (10)	47102
2202(a)(11)	47117
2202(a)(12)–(19)	47102
2202(a)(20)	47101
2202(a)(21)–(23)	47102
2202(a)(24)	47104, 47107, 48101–48104, 48108
2202(a)(25)	Rep.
2202(b)	47102
2203(a)	47103
2203(b)	44501
2203(c), (d)(1)	47103
2203(d)(2)	Rep.
2204(a) (1st sentence)	47104
2204(a) (2d sentence)	48103
2204(a) (last sentence)	Rep.
2204(b)(1)	47104
2204(b)(2)	47107
2204(c)	Rep.
2204(d)	47113
2204 note	47104
2205(a)(1), (2)	48101
2205(a)(3)	44502
2205(b)(1)	44509
2205(b)(2)–(5)	48102
2205(c)	48104
2205(d)	48105
2205(e)(1)–(3)	48108
2205(e)(4)	47117
2205(e)(5)	48108
2205(f)	48109
2205 note	44502
2206(a), (b)(1)–(5)(C)	47114
2206(b)(5)(D)	47117
2206(b)(5)(E), (F), (6), (7)	47114
2206(c)	47115
2206(d)	47116
2206(e), (f)	47114
2206 note	47115
2207(a)–(e)(2)	47117
2207(e)(3)	Rep.
2207(f)	47118
2208(a)(1)	47105
2208(a)(2)	Rep.
2208(a)(3)	47105
2208(b)(1)(A)–(D)	47106
2208(b)(1)(E)	47107
2208(b)(2)–(4)	47106
2208(b)(5) (1st sentence, last sentence words before 11th comma).	47101
2208(b)(5) (last sentence words after 11th comma)–(8).	47106
2208(b)(9)	47120
2208(c)–(e)	47105
2209	47109
2210(a), (b)	47107
2210(c)	47105
2210(d)–(h)	47107
2210 note	47107
2211	47108
2212(a), (b)(1)	47110
2212(b)(2)–(4)	47119
2212(b)(5)	47109
2212(b)(6), (c), (d)	47110
2213	47111
2214	47112

Title 49 Former Sections	Title 49 New Sections
2215	47125
2216	47126
2217	47121
2218(a)	47122
2218(b) (related to application)	47106
2218(b) (related to payment)	47111
2219	47123
2220	47129
2221	Rep.
2222, 2222 note	47124
2223	Rep.
2224	44514
2225	44913
2226	49104
2226a	49101
2226b	49105
2226c	49102
2226d	49103
2227	47128
2301	31101
2302	31102
2302 notes	31104, 31307
2303	31103
2304, 2304 note	31104
2305	31105
2306	31106
2307	31107
2311(a)–(i)	31111
2311(j)	31112
2312	31114
2313	31115
2314, 2315	Rep.
2316	31113
2401–2407	Elim.
2421–2433	Elim.
2451–2461	49101–49109
2501	31131
2501 notes	5113, 31161
2502	31131
2503	31132
2504	31135
2505	31136
2505 note	31137
2506	31140
2507	31141
2508	31134
2509	31142
2510	31133
2511	31143
2511a	31162
2512	31144
2513–2517(a)	Rep.
2517(b)	31145
2518	31146
2519	31147
2520	Rep.
2521	31137
2601, 2602	70101
2603	70102
2604(a)(1)	70103
2604(a)(2)	70116
2604(b)	70103
2605(a), (b)	70104
2605(c)	70117
2606 (1st sentence)	70105
2606 (last sentence)	70107
2607, 2608(a), (b)	70105
2608(c)	70114
2609	70107
2610	70108
2611	70110
2612	Rep.
2613	70106
2614(a), (b)(1)–(3)	70111
2614(b)(4)	70109
2614(c)	70112
2614(d)	70111
2615(a)	70112
2615(b)	70113
2615(c)	70112
2616–2618	70115
2619	70116
2620	70117
2621, 2622	Rep.
2623 (last sentence)	70118
2623 (less last sentence)	70119
2701	31302
2702	31303
2703	31304
2704(a), (b)	31305
2704(c)–(e)	31312
2705	31308
2706, 2706 note	31309
2707	31310
2708	31311
2709	31313
2710	31314
2711	31315
2712, 2713	Rep.
2714	31316
2715	31317
2716	31301
2717	31306
2718	31310
2801	5701
2801 note	5713
2802	5702
2803	5703
2804	5704
2805	5705
2806	5706
2807	5707
2808	5708
2809	5710
2810	5711
2811	5712
2812	5714

TABLE II—REVISED STATUTES 1878

Showing where sections of the Revised Statutes of the United States of 1878 will be found in this edition of the United States Code.

Abbreviations

Rep.—Repealed. Where "Rep." appears in the status column following a U.S.C. reference, an explanation of the repeal can be found under such U.S.C. title and section. Where no U.S.C. reference appears, the Rev. St. section was repealed prior to the adoption of the United States Code (1926) or for other reasons was not included in the Code but was subsequently repealed.

Rev. T.—Revised Title. Where "Rev. T." appears in the status column, the U.S.C. reference is to title and section where the Rev. St. section was originally allocated in the U.S.C. To locate the Rev. St. section in the U.S.C. new title, see Table I.

Elim.—Eliminated. Where "Elim." appears in the status column following a U.S.C. reference, the reason for the elimination of the text can be found under such U.S.C. title and section.

I.R.C. '39—Internal Revenue Code of 1939. Where I.R.C. '39 appears in the status column, it is an indication that the provision was repealed or otherwise superseded by the Internal Revenue Code of 1939.

R.S. Sec.	U.S.C.		Status
	Title	Section	
1–6	1	1–5, 31	Rev. T.
7–11	1	21–25	Rev. T.
12, 13	1	28, 29	Rev. T.
14–17			Rep.
18, 19	2	1a, 1b	
20, 21			Rep.
22	2	6	
23, 24			Rep.
25–27	2	7–9	
28, 29	2	21, 22	
30	2	25	
31–33	2	26	
34	2	27	
35			Rep.
36	2	32	
37			Rep.
38, 39	2	34, 35	
40, 41	2	39, 40	
42			Rep.
43	2	41	Rep.
44	2	42	Rep.
45			Rep.
46	2	47	
47, 48	2	48	
49, 50	2	38	Rep.
51–53			Rep.
54	2	74	Elim.
	2	84a	
55, 56	2	60c, 64	Elim.
57, 58	2	65, 75	Rep.
59	2	65, 75	Rep.
60, 61	2	102	Rep.
62, 63	2	103, 104	Elim.
64	2	105	
65, 66	2	106	
67–69	2	107–109	
70, 71	2	113, 114	
72	2	116	Rep.
73	2	63, 76	Rep.
74–78			Rep.
79	44	321	Rev. T.
80–82	2	131–132a	
83, 84	2	134, 135	
85–93			Rep.
94	2	137a	Elim.
95	2	137	
96, 97	2	144, 145	
98	2	146	
99, 100	2	151, 152	
101–104	2	191–194	
105–129	2	201–225	Rep.
130			Rep.
131–134	3	1–4	Rev. T.
135, 136			Rep.
137–141	3	8–11, 13	Rev. T.
142			Rep.
143–145	3	14–16	Rev. T.
146–150			Rep.
151	3	23	Rev. T.
152–154	3	41, 42, 44	Rev. T.
155–157			Rep.
158–160	5	1–3	Rev. T.
161, 162	5	22, 26	Rev. T.
163, 164			Rep.
165, 166	5	33, 38	Rev. T.
167, 168			Rep.
169, 170	5	43, 51	Rev. T.
171, 172			Rep.
173–175	5	23–25	Rev. T.
176	31	492–1	Rev. T.
177–182	5	4–9	Rev. T.
183–186	5	93–96	Rev. T.
187, 188	5	48, 91	Rev. T.
189, 190	5	49, 99	Rev. T.
191			Rep.
192	5	102	Rev. T.
193	31	492–2	Rev. T.
194			Rep.
195, 196	5	106, 107	Rev. T.
197	5	109	Rev. T.
198			Rep.
199	22	2651	
200	5	152	Rev. T.
201			Rep.
202, 203	22	2656, 2657	
204, 205	5	159, 160	Rev. T.
206	22	2659	
207	46	579	Rev. T.
208, 209	5	163, 164	Rev. T.
210 (part)	22	2660	
210 (part)	44	191a	Rev. T.
211	15	188	
212			Rep.
213, 214	5	166, 181	Rev. T.
215	5	185, 186	Rev. T.
216, 217	5	190, 191	Rev. T.
218	5	198	Rev. T.
219, 220	10	1192, 1363	Rev. T.
221–223			Rep.
224	5	199	Rev. T.
225	10	1302, 1303	Rev. T.
226	5	201	Rev. T.
227			Rep.
228–230	5	215–217	Rev. T.
231, 232			Rep.
233, 234	31	1001, 1006	Rev. T.
235			Rep.
236, 237	31	71, 1020	Rev. T.
238			Rep.
239	31	1024	Rev. T.
240, 241	31	1022, 1025	Rev. T.
242			Rep.

R.S. Sec.	U.S.C.		Status
	Title	Section	
243	31	163, 1003	Rev. T.
244	31	1018	Rev. T.
245, 246	31	1007, 1008	Rev. T.
247			Rep.
248	31	1002	Rev. T.
249	19	3	
250			Rep.
251	15	185	Rep.
	19	66	
			I.R.C. '39
	31	427	Rev. T.
252, 253			Rep.
254	31	428, 429	Rev. T.
255, 256			Rep.
257	31	1027	Rev. T.
258	19	67	Rep.
259	15	183	
260	5	268	Rev. T.
261	31	1024	Rev. T.
262	5	269	Rev. T.
263	15	184	Rep.
264	33	888	Elim.
265	15	187	Rep.
266, 267	5	270, 271	Rev. T.
268–273			Rep.
274	31	48	Rev. T.
275, 276			Rep.
277, 278	31	73, 95	Rev. T.
279			Rep.
280, 281	31	94, 96	Rev. T.
282, 283	31	101, 103	Rev. T.
284, 285	31	104	Rev. T.
286, 287	34	953, 954	Rev. T.
288–290			Rep.
291, 292	31	107, 109	Rev. T.
293, 294	31	111, 112	Rev. T.
295–298	31	115–118	Rev. T.
299			Rep.
300	31	119	Rev. T.
300A, 300B			Rep.
301–304	31	141–144	Rev. T.
305	31	147	Rev. T.
306–310	31	149–153	Rev. T.
311			Rep.
312	31	161	Rev. T.
313			Rep.
314, 315	31	164, 165	Rev. T.
316, 317			Rep.
318	31	50	Rev. T.
319			I.R.C. '39
320			Rep.
321			I.R.C. '39
322, 323			Rep.
324	12	1	
325	12	2	
326	12	3	
327	12	4	
327A	12	4a	
328	12	8	
329	12	11	
330	12	12	
331	12	13	
332			Rep.
333	12	14	
334			Rep.
335	15	176	
336, 337	15	173, 174	Rep.
338	15	186	Rep.
339–341	15	179–181	Rep.
342	15	182	
343–345	31	251–253	Rev. T.
346, 347	5	291, 293	Rev. T.
348	5	295	Rev. T.
349, 350	5	297	Rev. T.
351, 352			Rep.
353, 354	5	292, 303	Rev. T.
355	40	255	
356	5	304	Rev. T.
357–359	5	307–309	Rev. T.
360	5	311	Rev. T.
361, 362	5	306, 317	Rev. T.
363–367	5	312–316	Rev. T.
368, 369	5	318, 319	Rev. T.
370, 371	5	302, 320	Rev. T.
372	31	1010	Rev. T.
373, 374	5	323, 324	Rev. T.
375	31	1012	Rev. T.
376	31	1011	Rev. T.
377	5	327	Rev. T.
378	31	1013	Rev. T.
379–382	5	329–332	Rev. T.
383	44	296a	Rev. T.
384, 385	5	333, 336	Rev. T.
386, 387	5	338, 339	Rev. T.
388	5	361	Rev. T.
389, 390	5	363, 364	Rev. T.
391, 392	5	365	Rev. T.
393, 394			Rep.
395, 396	5	362, 369	Rev. T.
397–403	5	371–377	Rev. T.
404	39	431	Rev. T.
405–408	5	378–381	Rev. T.
409	5	383	Rev. T.
410, 411	5	385, 386	Rev. T.
412			Rep.
413	5	387	Rev. T.
414			Rep.
415	5	411	Rev. T.
416			Rep.
417, 418	5	412, 413	Rev. T.
419, 420	5	429, 430	Rev. T.
421	5	432	Rev. T.
422	5	433, 434	Rev. T.
423–426	5	435–438	Rev. T.
427			
428, 429	5	418, 466	Rev. T.
430	5	431	Rev. T.
431, 432	5	457, 458	Rev. T.
433			Rep.
434	5	462	Rev. T.
435			Rep.
436	5	463	Rev. T.
437	43	1451	
438	43	1453	
439	43	1454	
440			Rep.
441	20	4361	
441	43	1457	
442	43	1458	
443			Rep.
444	43	1459	
445			Rep.
446, 447	43	1, 5	Rep.
448, 449			Rep.
450, 451	43	8, 9	Rep.
452	43	11	
453, 454	43	2, 12	
455	43	17	
456	43	14	
457	43	835	Rep.
458	43	15	Rep.
459, 460	43	6, 18	
461	43	21	Rep.
462, 463	25	1, 2	
464, 465	25	8, 9	
466			Rep.
467	25	266	Rep.
468, 469			Rep.
470, 471	38	1, 2	Rev. T.
471	43	784	Rep.
472	38	3	Rev. T.
473	43	785	Elim.
474	38	121	Rev. T.
475, 476	35	1, 2	Rev. T.
477			Rep.
478, 479	35	3, 5	Rev. T.
480–482	35	4, 6, 7	Rev. T.
483	35	6	Rev. T.
484, 485			Rep.
486–489	35	10–13	Rev. T.
490–492			Rep.
493	35	78	Rev. T.
494	35	20	Rev. T.
495, 496	35	17, 19	Rev. T.
497–500			Rep.
501, 502	44	82, 83	Rev. T.
503			Rep.
504	44	91a	Rev. T.
505			Rep.
506	44	90	Rev. T.
507–511			Rep.
512–515	41	1–4	Rep.
516	20	1	
517	20	2	
518, 519	20	4, 5	Rep.
520	7	2201	
521, 522			Rep.
523	7	2215	
524	7	2216	Rep.
525	7	2206	
526	7	2204	
527	7	415	
528, 529	7	2207	
530–564			Rep.
565	34	1147	Rev. T.
566	28	770	Rev. T.
567–595			Rep.
596	28	21	Rev. T.
597–647			Rep.
648, 649	28	770, 773	Rev. T.
650–697			Rep.
698	28	863	Rev. T.
699			Rep.
700, 701	28	875, 876	Rev. T.
702–710			Rep.
711	28	371	Rev. T.
712–714			Rep.
715	28	9, 595	Rev. T.
716–720			Rep.
721	28	725	Rev. T.
722	42	1988	
723			Rep.
724	28	636	Rev. T.
725–749			Rep.

R.S. Sec.	U.S.C.		Status
	Title	Section	
750	28	790	Rev. T.
751–762	28	451–462	Rev. T.
763, 764			Rep.
765, 766	28	464, 465	Rev. T.
767	28	481	Rev. T.
768			Rep.
769	28	482	Rev. T.
770			Rep.
771	28	485	Rev. T.
772, 773	28	487	Rev. T.
774–776	28	488	Rev. T.
777, 778			Rep.
779, 780	28	491, 493	Rev. T.
781			Rep.
782	28	494	Rev. T.
783	28	496, 499	Rev. T.
784–788	28	500–504	Rev. T.
789, 790	28	506, 507	Rev. T.
791–795	28	509–513	Rev. T.
796–798	28	517–519	Rev. T.
799	28	523	Rev. T.
800–822			Rep.
823	28	548, 571, 574, 600, 600c, 601	Rev. T.
824	28	572	Rev. T.
825–827			Rep.
828	28	555, 556	Rev. T.
829	28	574	Rev. T.
830, 831			Rep.
832	28	573	Rev. T.
833	28	567, 586	Rev. T.
834	28	586	Rev. T.
835–837			Rep.
838	28	486	Rev. T.
839–845			Rep.
846	28	577	Rev. T.
847			Rep.
848	28	600c, 601	Rev. T.
849–851	28	603–605	Rev. T.
852	28	600	Rev. T.
853, 854	44	325, 326	Rev. T.
855	28	608	Rev. T.
856			Rep.
857	28	609	Rev. T.
858, 859	28	631, 634	Rev. T.
860			Rep.
861, 862	28	635, 637	Rev. T.
863–865	28	nt prec. 1781	
866–881	28	664–659	Rev. T.
882–886	28	661–665	Rev. T.
887, 888	28	668, 669	Rev. T.
889	28	671	Rev. T.
890	28	670	Rev. T.
891–898	28	672–679	Rev. T.
899–907	28	681–689	Rev. T.
908	1	30a	Rev. T.
909			Rep.
910	30	53	
911–914	28	721–724	Rev. T.
915, 916	28	726, 727	Rev. T.
917–923	28	730–736	Rev. T.
924–932	39	837–845	Rev. T.
933–947	28	746–760	Rev. T.
948–950	28	767–769	Rev. T.
951–956	28	774–779	Rev. T.
957–959	28	781–783	Rev. T.
960	19	579	Rep.
961, 962	28	785, 786	Rev. T.
963	19	580	
964	39	846	Rev. T.
965, 966	28	780, 811	Rev. T.
967, 968	28	814, 815	Rev. T.
969–979	28	817–827	Rev. T.
980			Rep.
981–984	28	828–831	Rev. T.
985–993	28	838–846	Rev. T.
994–996	28	850–852	Rev. T.
997	28	862	Rev. T.
998–1001	28	867–870	Rev. T.
1002			Rep.
1003–1005	28	871–873	Rev. T.
1006	34	1146	Rev. T.
1007	28	874	Rev. T.
1008, 1009			Rep.
1010–1012	28	878–880	Rev. T.
1013	28	864	Rev. T.
1014	18	591	Rev. T.
1015–1020	18	596–601	Rev. T.
1021, 1022	18	554, 555	Rev. T.
1023	18	560	Rev. T.
1024	18	557	Rev. T.
1025, 1026	18	556, 561	Rev. T.
1027–1030	18	602–605	Rev. T.
1031	28	425	Rev. T.
1032	18	564	Rev. T.
1033, 1034	18	562, 563	Rev. T.
1035, 1036	18	565, 566	Rev. T.
1037–1040			Rep.
1041, 1042	18	569, 641	Rev. T.
1043–1046	18	581–584	Rev. T.

R.S. Sec.	U.S.C.		Status
	Title	Section	
1047	28	791	Rev. T.
1048–1074			Rep.
1075	28	268a	Rev. T.
1076–1084			Rep.
1085	28	278a	Rev. T.
1086–1088			Rep.
1089	31	225	Rev. T.
1090–1095			Rep.
1096–1098	10	498	Rev. T.
1099–1103			Rep.
1104, 1105	10	252, 253	Rev. T.
1106, 1107			Rep.
1108	10	282	Rev. T.
1109, 1110			Rep.
1111	10	1140, 1161	Rev. T.
1112	10	611	Rev. T.
1113–1115			Rep.
1116	10	621	Rev. T.
1117			Rep.
1118	10	622	Rev. T.
1119–1121			Rep.
1122	10	523	Rev. T.
1123, 1124			Rep.
1125	10	238	Rev. T.
1126			Rep.
1127	10	239	Rev. T.
1128–1131			Rep.
1132	10	7	Rev. T.
1133, 1134			Rep.
1135	10	1259e	Rev. T.
	34	541	Rev. T.
1136	10	1339	Rev. T.
1137			Rep.
1138	10	1315	Rev. T.
1139, 1140			Rep.
1141	10	1195a	Rev. T.
1142			Rep.
1143	10	1259d	Rev. T.
	34	541	Rev. T.
1144	10	875c, 1237, 1315	Rev. T.
1145	10	1232	Rev. T.
1146–1148			Rep.
1149, 1150	10	1239, 1315	Rev. T.
1151, 1152			Rep.
1153	10	185	Rev. T.
1154, 1155			Rep.
1156, 1157	10	182, 184	Rev. T.
1158	10	183	Rev. T.
1159–1163			Rep.
1164–1167	10	192–196	Rev. T.
1168			Rep.
1169	10	82	Rev. T.
1170–1173			Rep.
1174, 1175	10	104, 726	Rev. T.
1176–1178	38	247–249	Rev. T.
1179–1182			Rep.
1183	10	176	Rev. T.
1184–1188			Rep.
1189	37	310b	Rev. T.
1190			Rep.
1191, 1192	10	1312, 1314	Rev. T.
1193–1198			Rep.
1199	10	62	Rev. T.
1200			Rep.
1201	10	63	Rev. T.
1202–1208			Rep.
1209, 1210	10	521, 522	Rev. T.
1211, 1212	10	524, 528	Rev. T.
1213–1221			Rep.
1222, 1223	10	576, 577	Rev. T.
1224, 1225	10	495, 1182a	Rev. T.
	34	1229	Rev. T.
1226	10	516, 1392	Rev. T.
1227	10	1426	Rev. T.
1228	10	579	Rev. T.
1229	10	572, 575	Rev. T.
1230, 1231	10	573, 1172	Rev. T.
1232	10	608	Rev. T.
1233			Rep.
1234	10	497	Rev. T.
1235, 1236			Rep.
1237	10	610	Rev. T.
1238–1240			Rep.
1241, 1242	10	1261, 1317	Rev. T.
1243	10	941, 943	Rev. T.
1244	10	944	Rev. T.
1245	10	931	Rev. T.
1246–1250	10	961–965	Rev. T.
1251, 1252	10	933, 934	Rev. T.
1253, 1254	10	966, 1025	Rev. T.
1255	10	1024	Rev. T.
1256	10	1023	Rev. T.
1257, 1258	10	557, 1021	Rev. T.
1259	10	990, 996	Rev. T.
1260	10	1178	Rev. T.
1261	10	671a, 692	Rev. T.
1262, 1263			Rep.
1264	10	691	Rev. T.
1265, 1266	10	841, 849	Rev. T.
1267			Rep.
1268	10	861	Rev. T.

R.S. Sec.	U.S.C.		Status
	Title	Section	
1269			Rep.
1270	10	806	Rev. T.
1271–1273			Rep.
1274, 1275	10	971, 984	Rev. T.
1276	10	786	Rev. T.
1277–1284			Rep.
1285	10	695	Rev. T.
1286, 1287			Rep.
1288	37	242	Rev. T.
1289, 1290			Rep.
1291	10	893	Rev. T.
1292			Rep.
1293, 1294	10	716b, 729	Rev. T.
1295			Rep.
1296	10	831, 1391	Rev. T.
1297			Rep.
1298, 1299	10	834, 875c	Rev. T.
1300, 1301	10	875, 875b	Rev. T.
1302	10	874	Rev. T.
1303, 1304	10	871, 872	Rev. T.
1305–1307	10	906–908	Rev. T.
1308	10	835	Rev. T.
1309, 1310	10	1061, 1066	Rev. T.
1311, 1312	10	1042, 1065	Rev. T.
1313	10	1063	Rev. T.
1314	10	1062, 1081	Rev. T.
1315, 1316			Rep.
1317	10	1098	Rev. T.
1318	10	1094, 1100	Rev. T.
1319, 1320	10	1096, 1099	Rev. T.
1321, 1322	10	1101, 1105	Rev. T.
1323	10	1102	Rev. T.
1324, 1325	10	1044, 1104	Rev. T.
1326, 1327			Rep.
1327, 1328	10	1051, 1053	Rev. T.
1329			Rep.
1330	10	1144	Rev. T.
1331	10	1041	Rev. T.
1332			Rep.
1333	10	1080	Rev. T.
1334–1336	10	1131–1133	Rev. T.
1337	10	1135	Rev. T.
1338	10	1085	Rev. T.
1339, 1340			Rep.
1341	10	1142	Rev. T.
1342, 1343			Rep.
1344–1361	10	1451–1458	Rev. T.
1362	34	1	Rev. T.
1363–1366			Rep.
1367	34	111	Rev. T.
1368			Rep.
1369	34	11, 21	Rev. T.
1370	34	23	Rev. T.
1371, 1372			Rep.
1373, 1374	34	24, 25	Rev. T.
1375	5	451	Rev. T.
1376, 1377			Rep.
1378, 1379	34	11, 61	Rev. T.
1380	34	323	Rev. T.
1381–1385	34	62–66	Rev. T.
1386–1388			Rep.
1389	34	67	Rev. T.
1390–1392			Rep.
1393	34	76	Rev. T.
1394			Rep.
1395, 1396	34	11, 91	Rev. T.
1397, 1398	34	95, 96	Rev. T.
1399, 1400			Rep.
1401	34	102	Rev. T.
1402, 1403	34	11, 81	Rev. T.
1404	34	223	Rev. T.
1405	34	122	Rev. T.
1406	34	121	Rev. T.
1407	34	134, 351	Rev. T.
1408, 1409	34	174, 198	Rev. T.
1410	34	146	Rev. T.
1411	34	21	Rev. T.
1412			Rep.
1413	34	11, 79, 141	Rev. T.
1414, 1415	34	142, 143	Rev. T.
1416			Rep.
1417, 1418	34	133, 182	Rev. T.
1419	34	161	Rev. T.
1420	34	161, 163	Rev. T.
1421, 1422	34	177, 201	Rev. T.
1423–1425			Rep.
1426, 1427	34	192, 193	Rev. T.
1428	34	211	Rev. T.
1429	34	194	Rev. T.
1430, 1431	34	219, 220	Rev. T.
1432	34	218	Rev. T.
1433	34	217	Rev. T.
1434	34	216	Rev. T.
1435, 1436	34	221, 225	Rev. T.
1437	10	1366	Rev. T.
	34	447	Rev. T.
1438, 1439	34	144, 145	Rev. T.
1440–1442	34	226–228	Rev. T.
1443, 1444	34	381, 384	Rev. T.
1445	34	382	Rev. T.
1446, 1447			Rep.
1448	34	411	Rev. T.
1449–1454	34	413–418	Rev. T.
1455	34	412	Rev. T.
1456, 1457	34	385, 389	Rev. T.
1458, 1459	34	400, 401	Rev. T.
1460, 1461			Rep.
1462	34	421	Rev. T.
1463–1465	34	424–426	Rev. T.
1466, 1467	34	241, 242	Rev. T.
1468–1470	34	246–248	Rev. T.
1471	5	440	Rev. T.
1472			Rep.
1473	5	442	Rev. T.
1474, 1475	34	251	Rev. T.
1476			Rep.
1477	34	251	Rev. T.
1478, 1479			Rep.
1480	34	395	Rev. T.
1481, 1482	34	252, 397	Rev. T.
1483	34	258	Rev. T.
1484			Rep.
1485, 1486	34	244, 245	Rev. T.
1487	34	913	Rev. T.
1488	34	253	Rev. T.
1489, 1490	34	249, 250	Rev. T.
1491, 1492			Rep.
1493	34	271	Rev. T.
1494	34	272, 666	Rev. T.
1495, 1496	34	273, 274	Rev. T.
1497			Rep.
1498–1502	34	275–279	Rev. T.
1503–1505	34	281–283	Rev. T.
1506, 1507	34	341, 342	Rev. T.
1508–1510	34	345–347	Rev. T.
1511, 1512	34	1021, 1031	Rev. T.
1513, 1514			Rep.
1515–1518	34	1043–1046	Rev. T.
1519, 1520	34	1053, 1054	Rev. T.
1521	34	1057	Rev. T.
1522–1525			Rep.
1526, 1527	34	1056, 1101	Rev. T.
1528	34	1072	Rev. T.
1529–1531			Rep.
1532, 1533	34	462, 463	Rev. T.
1534, 1535	34	452, 453	Rev. T.
1536	14	53	Rev. T.
	34	471	Rev. T.
1537–1539	34	483–485	Rev. T.
1540, 1541			Rep.
1542, 1543	34	501, 502	Rev. T.
1544	34	507	Rev. T.
1545			Rep.
1546	34	510	Rev. T.
1547, 1548	34	591, 592	Rev. T.
1549	34	529	Rev. T.
1550, 1551	34	594, 595	Rev. T.
1552, 1553			Rep.
1554, 1555	5	418	Rev. T.
1556			Rep.
1557	34	881	Rev. T.
1558, 1559			Rep.
1560	34	862	Rev. T.
1561, 1562			Rep.
1563, 1564	34	875, 876	Rev. T.
1565–1570			Rep.
1571	34	224	Rev. T.
1572, 1573			Rep.
1574, 1575	37	243, 244	Rev. T.
1576	34	932	Rev. T.
1577–1579			Rep.
1580–1583	34	902–905	Rev. T.
1584			Rep.
1585	34	907	Rev. T.
1586, 1587	34	921, 922	Rev. T.
1588	34	991	Rev. T.
1589, 1590			Rep.
1591, 1592	34	993, 994	Rev. T.
1593	34	998	Rev. T.
1594–1599			Rep.
1600	34	653	Rev. T.
1601, 1602			Rep.
1603, 1604	34	651, 652	Rev. T.
1605–1607	34	670–672	Rev. T.
1608			Rep.
1609, 1610	34	694, 695	Rev. T.
1611	34	717	Rev. T.
1612, 1613	34	971, 972	Rev. T.
1614	24	3	Rep.
1615			Rep.
1616, 1617	34	711, 713	Rev. T.
1618			Rep.
1619	34	712	Rev. T.
1620, 1621	34	714, 715	Rev. T.
1622, 1623	34	681	Rev. T.
1624	34	1200	Rev. T.
1625–1663			Rep.
1664	10	1312	Rev. T.
1665	50	53	Rep.
1666	50	55	Rep. See T. 10 §4532(b).
1667, 1668			Rep.
1669	50	56	Rep.
1670			Rep.

R.S. Sec.	U.S.C. Title	U.S.C. Section	Status
1671	50	57	Rep.
1672, 1673			Rep.
1674	22	40, 51	Rep.
1675	22	32	Rep.
1676–1684			Rep.
1685, 1686	22	20, 36	Rep.
1687			Rep.
1688	22	39	Rep.
1689	22	4191	
1690–1692			Rep.
1693	22	168	Rep.
1694			Rep.
1695	22	51a, 55	Rep.
1696	22	58	Rep.
1697, 1698	22	11	Rep.
1699–1701	22	106–108	Rep.
1702–1705			Rep.
1706	22	109	Rep.
1707	22	4193	
1708	22	4194	
1709	22	4195	Rep.
1710	22	4196	
1711	22	4197	
1712, 1713	22	80, 82	Rep.
1714	22	71	Rep.
1715	22	4200	
1716	22	4202	
1717	22	4204	
1718	22	4205	
1719	22	4207	
1720, 1721			Rep.
1722	22	4208	
1723	22	4209	
1724	22	4210	
1725	22	4211	
1726	22	4212	Rep.
1727	22	4212, 4213	Rep.
1728	22	4214	Rep.
1729, 1730			Rep.
1731	22	4216	
1732, 1733			Rep.
1734	22	4217	
1735, 1736	22	1199	Rep.
1737	22	4218	
1738	22	105	Rep.
1739			Rep.
1740	22	121	Rep.
1741			Rep.
1742, 1743	22	123, 125	Rep.
1744	22	33	Rep.
1745	22	4219	
1746	22	4220	
1747			Rep.
1748, 1749	22	129, 130	Rep.
1750	22	4221	
			I.R.C. '39
1751			Rep.
1752	22	132	Rep.
1753	5	631	Rev. T.
1754	5	35	Rev. T.
1755			
1756			Rep.
1757–1759	5	16, 18, 21	Rev. T.
1760, 1761	5	52, 56	Rev. T.
1762			Rep.
1763–1766	5	58, 69, 70, 82	Rev. T.
1767–1772			Rep.
1773–1775	5	10, 13, 14	Rev. T.
1776	31	554	
1777–1779	5	89, 92, 102	Rev. T.
1780–1783			Rep.
1784	5	113	Rev. T.
1785			Rep.
1786	5	14a	Rev. T.
1787–1789			Rep.
1790	19	49	Rep.
1791	4	1	Rev. T.
1792	4	1, 2	Rev. T.
1793–1796	4	4–7	Rev. T.
1797	40	19	
1798	40	8	Rep.
1799			Rep.
1800	40	45	
1801	40	48	
1802	40	54	
1803	40	56	
1804	40	57	Elim.
1805	40	55	
1806	40	58	Elim.
1807	40	46	
1808	40	47	
1809	40	49	
1810	40	51	
1811	40	52	
1812	40	20	Rep.
	40	50	
1813	40	65	Elim.
1814	40	187	
1815	40	189	
1816	40	166, 170	
1817			Rep.
1818	40	66	
1819	40	192	Elim.
1820	40	193	
1821	40	206	
1822	40	207	
1823	40	208	
1824	40	210	
1825	40	211	
1826	40	215	
1827	40	216	
1828	18	702	Rev. T.
1829	3	49	Rev. T.
1830	40	102	
1831	40	188	
1832	3	50	Rev. T.
	40	218	Rep.
1833	3	51	Rev. T.
	40	219	Rep.
1834	3	52	Rev. T.
	40	220	Rep.
1835	40	221	Elim.
1836–1838	4	9–11	Rev. T.
1839	48	1451	
1840	48	1452	
1841	48	1453	Rep.
1842			Rep.
1843, 1844	48	1454, 1455	Rep.
1845–1853			Rep.
1854	48	1460a	Rep.
1855	48	1457	Rep.
1856			Rep.
1857, 1858	48	1458, 1459	Rep.
1859			Rep.
1860	48	1460	Rep.
1861–1863			Rep.
1864	48	1463a	Rep.
1865–1867			Rep.
1868	48	1463	Rep.
1869–1872			Rep.
1873	48	1453a	Rep.
1874–1877			Rep.
1878	48	1465	Rep.
1879–1882			Rep.
1883, 1884	48	1467, 1468	Rep.
1885			Rep.
1886	48	1469	Rep.
1887			Rep.
1888	48	1470	Rep.
1889			Rep.
1890	48	1480	Rep.
1891			Rep.
1892–1895	48	1482–1485	Rep.
1896–1955			Rep.
1956	16	644	
1957	16	645	Elim.
1958			Rep.
1959	16	646	
1960	16	647	
1961	16	649	
1962–1972			Rep.
1973	16	655	
1974	16	657	Rep.
1975	16	655	
1976	16	656	
1977	42	1981	
1977A	42	1981a	
1978	42	1982	
1979	42	1983	
1980	42	1985	
1981	42	1986	
1982	42	1987	
1983	42	1989	
1984	42	1989	
1985	42	1990	
1986	8	52	Rep.
1987	42	1991	
1988	42	1992	
1989	42	1993	Rep.
1990	42	1994	
1991			Rep.
1992, 1993	8	1, 6	Rep.
1994			Rep.
1995	8	2	Elim.
1996, 1997	8	12	Rep.
1998	8	11	Rep. See T. 10 §§3253, 8253.
	10	624	Rev. T.
1999	8	1481 nt	
2000, 2001	22	1731, 1732	
2002			Rep.
2003	42	1972	
2004	42	1971	
2005–2031			Rep.
2032, 2033	8	61, 62	Elim.
2034–2036			Rep.
2037	8	65	Elim.
2038	24	261	Elim.
2039	25	21	Rep.
2040			
2041			Rep.
2042	25	24	Elim.
2043, 2044			Rep.

R.S. Sec.	U.S.C. Title	U.S.C. Section	Status
2045–2051	....	....	Rep.
2052	25	26	Rep.
2053	25	64	
2054, 2055	....	....	Rep.
2056–2058	25	28, 29, 31	Rep.
2059	25	62	
2060, 2061	25	30, 38	Rep.
2062	25	27	Elim.
2063	25	39	Rep.
2064	25	35	Rep.
2065	....	....	Rep.
2066, 2067	25	40, 41	
2068	25	42	Rep.
2069	25	45	
2070	....	....	Rep.
2071	25	271	
2072	25	48	
2073	25	65	
2074, 2075	25	50, 51	Rep.
2076	25	60	
2077, 2078	25	54, 68	Rep.
2079, 2080	25	71, 72	
2081, 2082	25	114, 115	
2083, 2084	25	91, 92	Elim.
2085	25	98	
2086	25	111	
2087	25	130	
2088	25	112	
2089	25	113	
2090	25	132	
2091	....	....	Rep.
2092	25	131	
2093	25	152	
2094	25	153	
2095, 2096	25	157, 158	
2097	25	122	
2098	25	126	Elim.
2099	....	....	Rep.
2100	25	127	
2101	25	138	
2102	....	....	Rep.
2103, 2104	25	81, 82	
2105, 2106	25	83, 84	Rep.
2107	....	....	Rep.
2108	25	159	
2109	25	146	
2110	25	141	Elim.
2111–2113	25	171–173	Rep.
2114	25	174	
2115, 2116	25	176, 177	
2117, 2118	25	179, 180	
2119	25	185	
2120	25	186	Rep.
2121	25	187	Elim.
2122, 2123	25	188, 189	Rep.
2124	25	201	
2125, 2126	25	193, 194	
2127	25	192	
2128–2131	....	....	Rep.
2132, 2133	25	263, 264	
2134	25	219	Rep.
2135, 2136	25	265, 266	Rep.
2137	25	216	Rep.
2138	25	214	Rep.
2139, 2140	25	241, 246	Rep.
2141	25	251	
2142	25	213	Rep.
2143, 2144	25	212, 215	Rep.
2145, 2146	25	217, 218	Rep.
2147–2155	25	220–228	Rep.
2156, 2157	25	229, 230	
2158–2163	8	331–335, 337	Rep.
2164	8	135	Rep.
2165–2168	....	....	Rep.
2169	8	359	Elim.
2170	8	361	Rep.
2171	....	....	Rep.
2172	8	7	Rep.
2173–2217	....	....	Rep.
2218	43	54	
2219	43	53	
2220, 2221	43	55, 56	
2222	43	77	Rep.
2223	43	52	
2224, 2225	43	57, 58	
2226, 2227	....	....	Rep.
2228	43	74	Elim.
2229	43	59	
2230–2232	43	61–63	Rep.
2233	....	....	Rep.
2234–2236	43	72, 78, 79	Rep.
2237–2239	43	80a, 82, 84	Rep.
2240	43	80a	Rep.
2241	....	....	Rep.
2242	43	88	Rep.
2243	43	81	Rep.
2244	43	76	Rep.
2245	43	89	
2246	43	75	
2247	43	107	
2248	43	122	
2249	43	123	
2250, 2251	43	125, 126	
2252	43	121	
2253–2255	43	127–129	
2256–2274	....	....	Rep.
2275, 2276	43	851, 852	
2277–2285	....	....	Rep.
2286	43	858	
2287	....	....	Rep.
2288	43	174	Rep.
2289–2293	43	161, 162, 164, 171, 255	Rep.
2294	43	254	Rep.
2295, 2296	43	163, 175	Rep.
2297, 2298	43	169, 211	Rep.
2299	....	....	Rep.
2300	43	183	Rep.
2301	43	173	Rep.
2302	43	184, 201	Rep.
2303	....	....	Rep.
2304–2307	43	271, 272, 274, 278	Rep.
2308, 2309	43	239, 277	Rep.
2310, 2311	43	191	Rep.
2312–2317	....	....	Rep.
2318–2321	30	21–24	
2322–2326	30	26–30	
2327	30	34	
2328	30	33	
2329, 2330	30	35, 36	
2331	30	35	
2332	30	38	
2333	30	37	
2334–2338	30	39–43	
2339	30	51	
	43	661	
2340	30	52	
	43	661	
2341–2345	30	44–48	Elim.
2346	30	50	
2347–2352	30	71–76	
2353–2355	43	672–674	Rep.
2356, 2357	43	677, 678	Rep.
2358, 2359	43	684, 685	Rep.
2360–2363	43	687–690	Rep.
2364	43	683	Rep.
2365, 2366	43	676, 692	Rep.
2367	....	....	Rep.
2368	43	691	Rep.
2369–2371	43	693–695	Rep.
2372	43	697	Rep.
2373	....	....	Rep.
2374	43	696	Rep.
2375, 2376	43	698, 699	Rep.
2377	43	867	Elim.
2378, 2379	43	857	
2380–2385	43	711–716	Rep.
2386–2389	43	717–720	Rep.
2390	....	....	Rep.
2391–2394	43	721–724	Rep.
2395–2397	43	751–753	
2398, 2399	43	754, 755	Rep.
2400	43	756	Rep.
2401	43	759	
2402	43	760	
2403	43	762	
2404, 2405	43	764, 765	Rep.
2406	43	766	
2407–2409	43	767–769	Rep.
2410	43	770	
2411	43	771	Rep.
2412	....	....	Rep.
2413	43	774	
2414	43	821	Rep.
2415–2417	43	823–825	Rep.
2418–2422	43	791–795	Rep.
2423	43	827	Rep.
2424	43	796	Rep.
2425–2427	43	800–802	Rep.
2428–2430	43	797–799	Rep.
2431–2435	43	803–807	Rep.
2436, 2437	43	822, 826	Rep.
2438	43	808	Rep.
2439, 2440	43	828, 830	Rep.
2441	43	829	Rep.
2442	43	782	Rep.
2443–2446	43	831–834	Rep.
2447, 2448	43	1151, 1152	Rep.
2449	43	859	
2450	43	1161	
2451	43	1162	
2452–2454	....	....	Rep.
2455	43	1171	Rep.
2456	43	1163	
2457	43	1164	
2458, 2459	16	591, 592	Rep.
2460	16	593	
2461–2463	16	595–597	Rep.
2464–2468	....	....	Rep.
2469, 2470	43	19, 20	Rep.
2471–2473	43	1191–1193	Rep.

R.S. Sec.	U.S.C. Title	U.S.C. Section	Status
2474	16	21	
2475	16	22	
2476	43	931	
2477	43	932	Rep.
2478	43	1201	
2479	43	982	
2480	43	983	
2481	43	984	
2482	43	981	
2483	43	985	Elim.
2484	43	986	
2485	43	865	
2486	43	865	
2487	43	865	
2488	43	987	
2489			Rep.
2490	43	988	
2491–2579			Rep.
2580	19	61	Rep.
2581–2610			Rep.
2611, 2612	19	26, 379	Rep.
2613, 2614	19	5, 22	Rep.
2615	19	23, 376	Rep.
2616, 2617	19	21, 24	Rep.
2618			Rep.
2619	19	31	Rep.
2620	19	31, 32	Rep.
2621–2623	19	33–35	Rep.
2624			Rep.
2625	19	9	Rep.
2626–2628	19	39–41	Rep.
2629, 2630	19	8, 10	Rep.
2631	19	10 nt	Rep.
2632, 2633	19	11, 37	Rep.
2634			Rep.
2635	19	59	Rep.
2636	19	60	
2637, 2638			Rep.
2639–2641	19	42–44	Rep.
2642			Rep.
2643–2645	19	45–47	Rep.
2646–2648	19	54, 55, 57	Rep.
2649	19	12	Rep.
2650			Rep.
2651	19	14	Rep.
2652, 2653			Rep.
2654	19	58	Rep.
2655–2686			Rep.
2687	5	57	Rev. T.
	19	53	Rep.
2688–2746			Rep.
2747, 2748	14	52, 69	Rev. T.
2749	14	58	Rev. T.
2750			Rep.
2751	14	16	Rev. T.
2752–2755			Rep.
2756	14	33, 131	Rev. T.
2757			Rep.
2758, 2759	14	51, 60	Rev. T.
2760, 2761	14	66, 70	Rev. T.
2762	14	67	Rev. T.
2763	19	541	Rep.
2764, 2765	14	64, 68	Rev. T.
2766	19	231	Elim.
2767	19	232	
2768	19	231	Elim.
2769	19	233	
2770–2791			Rep.
2792	19	289	Rep.
	46	110, 112	Rev. T.
	46 App.	124	
2793	19	288	
	46 App.	111, 123	
2794–2803			Rep.
2804	19	192	Rep.
2805–2854			Rep.
2855	19	338	
2856–2860			Rep.
2861	19	339	
2862	19	340	
2863	19	341	
2864–2884			Rep.
2885, 2886	19	273, 274	Rep.
2887–2903			Rep.
2904	19	240	
2905–2917			Rep.
2918	19	390	Rep.
2919	19	391	
2920–2933			Rep.
2934	19	134	Rep.
2935–2937			Rep.
2938	19	378	Rep.
2939			Rep.
2940–2942	19	16–18	Rep.
2943			Rep.
2944	19	56	Rep.
2945–2950			Rep.
2951	19	420	Rep.
2952–2998			Rep.
2999	19	15	Rep.
3000–3008			Rep.
3009	19	197	

R.S. Sec.	U.S.C. Title	U.S.C. Section	Status
3010			Rep.
3011, 3012, 3012½, 3013			Rep.
3014	19	199	
3015–3026			Rep.
3027	19	129	
3028–3047			Rep.
3048	31	711	Rev. T.
3049–3060			Rep.
3061	19	482	
3062	19	483	Rep.
3063–3067			Rep.
3068	19	70	
3069, 3070			Rep.
3071	19	507	
3072	19	506	Rep.
3073	19	508	
3074–3086			Rep.
3087	19	528	
3088			Rep.
3089	19	526	Rep.
3090			Rep.
3091–3093	19	1595 nt	
3094	19	574	
3095–3110			Rep.
3111	19	282	Rep.
3112			Rep.
3113	19	283	
3114, 3115	19	257, 258	Rep.
3116–3119	19	284–287	Rep.
3120, 3121			Rep.
3122	19	290	Rep.
3123			Rep.
3124, 3125	19	291, 292	Rep.
3126, 3127	19	293, 294	
3128, 3129			Rep.
3140–3143			I.R.C. '39
3144			Rep.
3145			Rep.
3146, 3147			I.R.C. '39
3148			Rep.
3149, 3150			I.R.C. '39
3151			Rep.
3152–3156			I.R.C. '39
3157			Rep.
3158			I.R.C. '39
3159, 3160			Rep.
3161–3166			I.R.C. '39
3167	18	216	Rev. T.
			I.R.C. '39
3168–3177			I.R.C. '39
3178			Rep.
3179–3221			I.R.C. '39
3222			Rep.
3223, 3224			I.R.C. '39
3225			Rep.
3226			I.R.C. '39
3227			Rep.
3228–3244			I.R.C. '39
3245			Rep.
3246–3296			I.R.C. '39
3297			Rep.
3298–3320			I.R.C. '39
3321			Rep.
3322			I.R.C. '39
3323			Rep. in part.
			I.R.C. '39
3324–3327			I.R.C. '39
3328			Rep.
3329–3360			I.R.C. '39
3361			Rep.
3362–3364			I.R.C. '39
3365			Rep.
3366–3377			I.R.C. '39
3378–3380			Rep.
3381–3400			I.R.C. '39
3401			Rep.
3402–3409			I.R.C. '39
3410			Rep.
3411			I.R.C. '39
3412, 3413			Rep.
3414–3417			I.R.C. '39
3418–3432			Rep.
3433, 3434			I.R.C. '39
3435, 3436			Rep.
3437			I.R.C. '39
3437 (Sched. A)			Rep.
3438–3442			Rep.
3443–3464			I.R.C. '39
3465			Rep.
3466–3472	31	191–197	Rev. T.
3473	19	197	Rep.
	31	198	Rev. T.
3474	31	199	Rev. T.
3475–3488	31	201–214	Rev. T.
3489			Rep.
3490–3494	31	231–235	Rev. T.
3495	31	261	Rev. T.
3496–3498	31	263–265	Rev. T.
3499–3501	31	268–270	Rev. T.
3502	31	254, 271	Rep.
3503	31	272	Rep.
3504	31	266, 272	Rep.

R.S. Sec.	U.S.C.		Status
	Title	Section	
3505	31	318	Rep.
3506, 3507	31	273, 277	Rep.
3508–3510	31	274–276	Rep.
3511	31	314, 315	Rev. T.
3512	31	319	Rev. T.
3513, 3514	31	316, 321	Rev. T.
3515, 3516	31	317, 322	Rev. T.
3517, 3518	31	324, 325	Rev. T.
3519–3524	31	327–332	Rev. T.
3525–3527	31	334–336	Rev. T.
3528, 3529	31	340, 341	Rev. T.
3530–3545	31	343–358	Rev. T.
3546	31	360	Rev. T.
3547–3550	31	363–366	Rev. T.
3551, 3552	31	368, 369	Rev. T.
3553, 3554	31	278, 279	Rev. T.
3555	31	281	Rev. T.
3556	31	280	Rev. T.
3557–3562	31	282–287	Rev. T.
3563	31	371	Rev. T.
3564, 3565			Rep.
3566–3568	31	373–375	Rev. T.
3569	15	204	
3570	15	205	
3571	31	401	Rev. T.
3572–3575			Rep.
3576	31	413	Rev. T.
3577, 3578	31	416, 417	Rev. T.
3579			Rep.
3580, 3581	31	420, 421	Rev. T.
3582, 3583			Rep.
3584, 3585	31	456, 457	Rev. T.
3586			Rep.
3587	31	460	Rev. T.
3588–3590	31	452–454	Rev. T.
3591	31	472	Rev. T.
3592			Rep.
3593	31	474	Rev. T.
3594–3599			Rep.
3600	31	475	Rev. T.
3601–3612			Rep.
3613–3617	31	480–484	Rev. T.
3618, 3619	31	487, 490	Rev. T.
3620, 3621	31	492, 495	Rev. T.
3622, 3623	31	496, 498	Rev. T.
3624–3633	31	505–514	Rev. T.
3634–3646	31	516–528	Rev. T.
3647, 3648	31	119, 529	Rev. T.
3649, 3650	31	548, 549	Rev. T.
3651–3653	31	543–545	Rev. T.
3654–3658			Rep.
3659, 3660	31	547a, 585	Rev. T.
3661	31	589	Rev. T.
3662, 3663	31	591, 594	Rev. T.
3664, 3665	31	597, 598	Rev. T.
3666			Rep.
3667, 3668	31	583, 610	Rev. T.
3669			Rep.
3670	31	624	Rev. T.
3671, 3672	31	583, 625	Rev. T.
3673, 3674	31	631, 632	Rev. T.
3675, 3676	31	77, 634	Rev. T.
3677	7	2208	
3678, 3679	31	628, 665	Rev. T.
3680			Rep.
3681	31	672	Rev. T.
3682, 3683	31	674, 675	Rev. T.
3684, 3685	31	681, 685	Rev. T.
3686	44	265	Rev. T.
3687, 3688			Rep.
3689, 3690	31	711, 712	Rev. T.
3691, 3692	31	715, 720	Rev. T.
3693	31	731	Rev. T.
3694–3697			Rep.
3698–3700	31	732–734	Rev. T.
3701	31	742	
3702–3707	31	735–740	Rev. T.
3708			Rep.
3709	41	5	
3710	41	8	
3711–3713	40	109	Rep.
3714	10	1191	Rev. T.
	34	560	Rev. T.
3715, 3716	10	1198, 1202	Rev. T.
3717	41	9	Rep.
3718–3720	34	561–563	Rev. T.
3721	34	569, 570	Rev. T.
3722–3724	34	572–574	Rev. T.
3725–3727	34	576–578	Rev. T.
3728	34	580	Rev. T.
3729	34	579	Rev. T.
	41	25	Rep.
3730	34	581	Rev. T.
3731	10	1207	Rev. T.
	34	583	Rev. T.
3732	41	11	
3733	41	12	
3734	40	259, 267	
3735	41	13	
3736	41	14	
3737	41	15	
3738–3740			Rep.
3741	41	22	
3742			Rep.
3743	41	20	Rep.
3744–3747	41	16–19	Rep.
3748	10	1316	Rev. T.
3749	40	301	
	40	302	Rep.
3750	40	301	
3751	40	306	
3752	40	305	
3753	40	308	
3754	40	309	
3755	40	310	
3756–3804			Rep.
3805, 3806	44	192, 193	Rev. T.
3807–3809			Rep.
3810	44	212, 285	Rev. T.
3811			Rep.
3812	15	187	Rep.
3813–3827			Rep.
3828	44	324	Rev. T.
3829	39	1	Rev. T.
3830–3832			Rep.
3833	39	825	Rev. T.
3834	39	34	Rev. T.
3835	39	36, 37	Rev. T.
3836	39	38	Rev. T.
3837			Rep.
3838	39	40	Rev. T.
3839–3841	39	4, 6, 7	Rev. T.
3842–3845	39	41–44	Rev. T.
3846–3848	39	46–48	Rev. T.
3849, 3850	39	51, 52	Rev. T.
3851			Rep.
3852–3856			Rep.
3857, 3858	39	62, 812	Rev. T.
3859			Rep.
3860–3862	39	64–66	Rev. T.
3863	39	133	Rev. T.
3864	39	2	Rev. T.
3865, 3866			Rep.
3867, 3868	39	154, 155	Rev. T.
3869			Rep.
3870, 3871	39	157, 158	Rev. T.
3872			Rep.
3873, 3874	39	162, 163	Rev. T.
3875–3878			Rep.
3879, 3880	39	240, 810	Rev. T.
3881			Rep.
3882, 3883	39	251, 252	Rev. T.
3884			Rep.
3885	39	253	Rev. T.
3886, 3887			Rep.
3888, 3889	39	254, 639	Rev. T.
3890–3894			Rep.
3895, 3896	39	258, 271	Rev. T.
3897			Rep.
3898	39	274	Rev. T.
3899			Rep.
3900, 3901	39	272, 279	Rev. T.
3902–3910			Rep.
3911–3913	39	296–298	Rev. T.
3914, 3915	39	351, 354	Rev. T.
3916, 3917	39	356, 360	Rev. T.
3918, 3919	39	361, 363	Rev. T.
3920	18	331	Rev. T.
	39	364	Rev. T.
3921	39	365, 366	Rev. T.
3922–3925			Rep.
3926, 3927	39	381, 384	Rev. T.
3928, 3929	39	386, 389	Rev. T.
3930	39	251	Rev. T.
3931, 3932	39	402, 405	Rev. T.
3933	39	383	Rev. T.
3934–3939	39	404–409	Rev. T.
3940, 3941	39	400, 421	Rev. T.
3942, 3943	39	411, 449	Rev. T.
3944	39	445	Rev. T.
3945, 3946	39	426, 427	Rev. T.
3947			Rep.
3948, 3949	39	428, 429	Rev. T.
3950, 3951	39	422, 434	Rev. T.
3952–3954			Rep.
3955–3959	39	435–439	Rev. T.
3960, 3961	39	430, 441	Rev. T.
3962, 3963	39	443, 444	Rev. T.
3964	39	481	Rev. T.
3965–3969	39	483–487	Rev. T.
3970			Rep.
3971–3975	39	489–493	Rev. T.
3976, 3977			Rep.
3978	39	494	Rev. T.
3979			Rep.
3980	39	495	Rev. T.
3981–3986			Rep.
3987	39	496	Rev. T.
3988			Rep.
3989–3991	39	497–499	Rev. T.
3992			Rep.
3993, 3994	39	500, 501	Rev. T.
3995–3998			Rep.
3999	39	521	Rev. T.

R.S. Sec.	U.S.C. Title	U.S.C. Section	Status
4000–4005			Rep.
4006–4011	39	651–656	Rev. T.
4012	39	669	Rev. T.
4013			Rep.
4014, 4015	39	670, 671	Rev. T.
4016			Rep.
4017	39	41, 497–499, 691, 695–697, 700, 787	Rev. T.
4018	39	696	Rev. T.
4019, 4020	39	695, 697	Rev. T.
4021–4023	39	672–674	Rev. T.
4024, 4025			Rep.
4026	39	700	Rev. T.
4027–4029	39	711–713	Rev. T.
4030			Rep.
4031	39	714	Rev. T.
4032			Rep.
4033, 4034	39	719, 720	Rev. T.
4035, 4036			Rep.
4037, 4038	39	723, 725	Rev. T.
4039, 4040	39	728, 729	Rev. T.
4041–4046	39	732–737	Rev. T.
4047, 4048			Rep.
4049–4051	39	781–783	Rev. T.
4052	39	785	Rev. T.
4053			Rep.
4054–4060	39	786–792	Rev. T.
4061	39	411	Rev. T.
4062	22	251, 255	Rep.
4063–4065	22	252–254	Rep.
4066	22	254	Rep.
4067	50	21	
4068	50	22	
4069	50	23	
4070	50	24	
4071–4074	28	701–704	Rev. T.
4075	22	211	Rep.
4976	22	212	
4077	22	218	
4078	22	219	Rep.
4079	22	256	
4080	22	257	
4081	22	258	
4082	22	4192	Rep.
4083–4085	22	141–143	Rep.
4086, 4087	22	145, 149	Rep.
4088	22	180	Rep.
4089	22	151	Rep.
4090	22	166, 167	Rep.
4091	22	165	Rep.
4092–4096			Rep.
4097, 4098	22	154, 161	Rep.
4099, 4100	22	160, 162	Rep.
4101, 4102	22	155, 156	Rep.
4103	22	158	Rep.
4104	22	157	Rep.
4105, 4106	22	150, 152	Rep.
4107, 4108	22	153, 163	Rep.
4109, 4110	22	164, 179	Rep.
4111–4116	22	168–173	Rep.
4117–4119	22	146–148	Rep.
4120	22	159	Rep.
4121, 4122	22	174	Rep.
4123, 4124			Rep.
4125	22	141, 181	Rep.
4126	22	141, 183	Rep.
4127	22	141, 177	Rep.
4128–4130	22	176–178	Rep.
4131	46	221	Rev. T.
4132	46	11	Rev. T.
4133–4135			Rep.
4136	46 App.	14	
4137–4139	46	15, 16, 20	Rev. T.
4140			Rep.
4141, 4142	46	17, 19	Rev. T.
4143–4145	46	21, 22, 25	Rev. T.
4146–4149	46	23, 24, 71, 72	Rev. T.
4150–4154	46	74–77, 81	Rev. T.
4155–4164	46	25–34	Rev. T.
4165			Rep.
4166–4172	46	35–41	Rev. T.
4173	46 App.	42	
4174	46	43	Rev. T.
4175			Rep.
4176–4178	46	44–46	Rev. T.
4179–4181	46	50, 54, 73	Rev. T.
4182, 4183	46	55, 56	Rev. T.
4184	46 App.	57	
4185, 4186			Rep.
4187	46	58	Rev. T.
4188	46 App.	59	
4189–4191	46	60–62	Rev. T.
4192–4196			Rep.
4197	46 App.	91	
4198	46	94	Rev. T.
4199	46	93	Rev. T.
4200, 4201	46	92, 96	Rev. T.
4202	46 App.	97	
4203			Rep.
4204	46 App.	98	
4205	46	99	Rev. T.
4206	46 App.	100	
4207		Rep.	
4208	46	102	Rev. T.
4209–4212			Rep.
4213–4215	46	101, 103, 109	Rev. T.
4216			Rep.
4217, 4218	46	105, 106	Rev. T.
4219	46 App.	121	
4220	46 App.	122	
4221	46	113	Rev. T.
4221	46 App.	125	
4222	46	126	Rev. T.
4223, 4224			Rep.
4225	46 App.	128	
4226	46 App.	129	
4227	46 App.	135	
4228	46 App.	141	
4229–4232			Rep.
4233	33	301, 302, 311–323, 331, 341–352	Rep.
4233A–4233C	33	353–355	Rep.
4234			Rep.
4235–4237	46	211–213	Rev. T.
4238	46 App.	721	
4239	46 App.	722	
4240	46 App.	723	
4241	46 App.	724	
4242–4244			Rep.
4245	14	94	Rev. T.
4246–4248			Rep.
4249	14	98a	Rev. T.
4250, 4251	46	227, 611	Rev. T.
4252–4277			Rep.
4278–4280	46	172–174	Rev. T.
4281	46 App.	181	
4282	46 App.	182	
4283	46 App.	183	
4283A	46 App.	183b	
4283B	46 App.	183c	
4284	46 App.	184	
4285	46 App.	185	
4286	46 App.	186	
4287	46 App.	187	
4288	46	175	Rev. T.
4289	46 App.	188	
4290–4292	46	201–203	Rev. T.
4293	33	381	
4294	33	382	
4295	33	383	
4296	33	384	
4297	33	385	
4298	33	386	
4299	33	387	
4300	33	391	
4301	33	392	
4302	33	393	
4303	28	424	Rev. T.
	33	394	
4304	33	395	
4305	33	396	
4306–4308	46	351–353	Rev. T.
4309	46 App.	354	
4310	46 App.	355	
4311	46 App.	251	
4312–4319	46	252–259	Rev. T.
4320	46 App.	262	
4321–4332	46	263–274	Rev. T.
4333, 4334	46	275, 287	Rev. T.
4335	46	276	Rev. T.
4336	46 App.	277	
4337–4345	46	278–286	Rev. T.
4346, 4347			Rep.
4348–4358	46	293–301, 305, 306	Rev. T.
4359–4369	46	303, 304, 307–315	Rev. T.
4370	46 App.	316	
4371, 4372	46	317, 318	Rev. T.
4373	46 App.	321	
4374	46 App.	322	
4375	46 App.	323	
4376	46 App.	324	
4377	46	325	Rev. T.
4378	46 App.	326	
4379	46 App.	327	
4380	46 App.	328	
4381, 4382	46	329, 330	Rev. T.
4383–4385	46	333–335	Rev. T.
4386–4390			Rep.
4391–4394	46	531–544	Rev. T.
4395	16	741	Rep.
4396	16	744	
4397	16	744	
4398	16	745	
4399–4401	46	361, 362, 364	Rev. T.

R.S. Sec.	U.S.C. Title	U.S.C. Section	Status
4402, 4403	46	371, 372	Rev. T.
4404	46	373, 374	Rev. T.
4405–4409	46	375–379	Rev. T.
4410	46	439	Rev. T.
4411	46	380	Rev. T.
4412, 4413	46	381	Rev. T.
4414–4416	46	382, 384, 385	Rev. T.
4417, 4417a	46	391, 391a	Rev. T.
4418–4420	46	392–394	Rev. T.
4421, 4422	46	399, 401	Rev. T.
4423	46	400	Rev. T.
4424–4426	46	402–404	Rev. T.
4426a	46	404–1	Rev. T.
4427–4434	46	405–412	Rev. T.
4435, 4436			Rep.
4437	46	413	Rev. T.
4438, 4438a	46	224, 224a	Rev. T.
4439	46	226	Rev. T.
4440, 4441	46	228, 229	Rev. T.
4442, 4443	46	214, 230	Rev. T.
4444	46	215	Rev. T.
4445–4448	46	231–234	Rev. T.
4449	46	240	Rev. T.
4450, 4451	46	239, 440	Rev. T.
4452			Rep.
4453–4456	46	435–438	Rev. T.
4457	46	414	Rev. T.
4458, 4459			Rep.
4460	46	415	Rev. T.
4461			Rep.
4462	46	416	Rev. T.
4463	46	222	Rev. T.
4464–4466	46	451–453	Rev. T.
4467–4471	46	460–464	Rev. T.
4472	46	170	Rev. T.
4473–4488	46	466–481	Rev. T.
4489	46		Rep.
4490	46	482	Rev. T.
4491, 4492	46	489, 490	Rev. T.
4493	46 App.	491	
4494–4500	46	492–498	Rev. T.
4501–4503	46	541–543	Rev. T.
4504–4507	46	546–549	Rev. T.
4508	46	545	Rev. T.
4509, 4510	46	561, 562	Rev. T.
4511–4518	46	564–571	Rev. T.
4519	46	577	Rev. T.
4520–4522	46	574–576	Rev. T.
4523	46	578	Rev. T.
4524–4530	46	591–597	Rev. T.
4531–4534			Rep.
4535	46	600	Rev. T.
4536			Rep.
4537	46	602	Rev. T.
4538–4545	46	621–628	Rev. T.
4546–4548	46	603–605	Rev. T.
4549–4553	46	641–645	Rev. T.
4554–4572	46	651–669	Rev. T.
4573–4578	46	674–679	Rev. T.
4579–4583	46	681–685	Rev. T.
4584–4587			Rep.
4588	46	686	Rev. T.
4589, 4590			Rep.
4591	46	687	Rev. T.
4592–4594			Rep.
4595	46	542a	Rev. T.
4596, 4597	46	701, 702	Rev. T.
4598, 4599			Rep.
4600	46	703	Rev. T.
4601			Rep.
4602	46	704	T. 18 §2196.
4603–4605	46	705–707	Rev. T.
4606	46	708	See T. 18 §2279.
4607, 4608	46	709, 710	Rev. T.
4609			Rep.
4610–4612	46	711–713	Rev. T.
4613–4615	34	1131–1133	Rev. T.
4616			Rep.
4617–4619	34	1134–1136	Rev. T.
4620			Rep.
4621–4629	34	1137–1145	Rev. T.
4630	34	1151	Rev. T.
4631–4635			Rep.
4636–4641	34	1146–1151	Rev. T.
4642, 4643			Rep.
4644–4647	34	1152–1155	Rev. T.
4648, 4649			Rep.
4650–4652	34	1156–1158	Rev. T.
4653–4660			Rep.
4661, 4662	33	727, 728	
4663–4667			Rep.
4668	33	739	Rep. See T. 14 §81.
4669–4672			Rep.
4673	33	745	Rep.
4674	33	742	Rep.
4675			Rep.
4676	33	736	Rep. See T. 14 §86.
4677	33	735	
4678	33	734	Rep. See T. 14 §87.
4679	33	719	Elim.
4680	33	725	
4681–4683	33	881–883	Rep.
4684	33	883	Rep.
4685	33	884	
4686–4688	33	885–887	Rep.
4689			Rep.
4690	33	888	Rep.
4691			Rep.
4692, 4693	38	151, 152	Rev. T.
4694	38	155	Rev. T.
4695, 4696	38	153, 154	Rev. T.
4697, 4698	38	155a, 156	Rev. T.
4698½, 4699	38	58, 177	Rev. T.
4700, 4701	38	30, 31	Rev. T.
4702, 4703	38	191, 193	Rev. T.
4704	38	202	Rev. T.
4705, 4706	38	198, 200	Rev. T.
4707	38	203, 204	Rev. T.
4708	38	205	Rev. T.
4709, 4710			Rep.
4711	38	116	Rev. T.
4712, 4713	38	21, 95	Rev. T.
4714			Rep.
4715	38	25	Rev. T.
4716–4718			Rep.
4719	38	53	Rev. T.
4720	38	28	Rev. T.
4721			Rep.
4722	38	23	Rev. T.
4723			Rep.
4724	38	26a	Rev. T.
4725–4727			Rep.
4728, 4729	38	221, 223	Rev. T.
4730–4733			Rep.
4734, 4735	38	55, 201	Rev. T.
4736–4740			Rep.
4741	14	177	Rev. T.
4742	38	329	Rev. T.
4743			Rep.
4744	38	121	Rev. T.
	43	781	Rep.
4745	38	129	Rev. T.
4746	18	81	Rev. T.
	38	126	Rev. T.
	43	787	Rep. See T. 18 §289.
4747	38	54	Rev. T.
4748	38	41	Rev. T.
	43	785, 786	Rep.
4749	10	1433	Rev. T.
4750	38	224	Rev. T.
4751			Rep.
4752	34	1151	Rev. T.
	38	225	Rev. T.
4753–4755	38	226–228	Rev. T.
4756, 4757	38	229, 230	Rev. T.
4758–4765			Rep.
4766	38	44–47, 49, 75, 126, 192	Rev. T.
4767–4775			Rep.
4776	38	74	Rev. T.
4777–4782			Rep.
4783	38	127	Rev. T.
4784			Rep.
4785	38	111	Rev. T.
	43	842	Rep.
4786	38	114	Rev. T.
	43	844	Rep.
4787, 4788	38	242, 243	Rev. T.
4789			Rep.
4790, 4791	38	243, 246	Rev. T.
4792	42	97	
4793–4796	42	88–91	
4797	42	112	
4798	4	8	Rev. T.
4799, 4800	42	113, 114	Rep.
4801	24	2	Rep.
4802	42	4, 11	Rep.
4803	24	26a	Rep.
4804	24	12	Rep.
4805	24	11a	Rep.
4806	24	7	Rep.
4807	24	15	
4808, 4809	24	3, 4	Rep.
4810	24	14	
4811	24	17	
4812	24	16	
4813	24	6	
4814	24	49	Rep.
4815, 4816	24	41, 43	Rep.
4817			Rep.
4818–4820	24	44, 45, 51	Rep.
4821–4824	24	49, 50, 53, 54	Rep.
4825–4827	24	71, 73, 74	Rep.
4828			Rep.
4829	24	91	Rep.
4830, 4831	24	77, 111	Rep.
4832			Rep.
4833	24	133	Rep.

R.S. Sec.	U.S.C. Title	U.S.C. Section	Status
4834, 4835	24	76, 137	Rep.
4836, 4837	....	....	Rep.
4838, 4839	24	161, 165	Rep.
4840–4844	24	162–164, 191, 201	Rep.
4845–4848	....	....	Rep.
4849–4852	24	205, 206, 211, 211a	Rep.
4853, 4854	24	204	Rep.
4855–4857	24	211b, 221, 222	Rep.
4858	24	170	Rep.
4859	24	231	Elim.
4860–4863	24	233–236	Elim.
4864	....	....	Rep.
4865	24	242	Elim.
4866–4868	24	245–247	Elim.
4869	24	249	Elim.
4870–4875	24	271–276	Rep.
4876	....	....	Rep.
4877, 4878	24	279, 281	Rep.
4879, 4880	24	283, 284	Elim.
4881, 4882	24	286, 287	Rep.
4883–4885	35	39–41	Rev. T.
4886–4888	35	31–33	Rev. T.
4889–4891	35	34	Rev. T.
4892–4894	35	35–37	Rev. T.
4895, 4896	35	44, 46	Rev. T.
4897–4901	35	38, 47–50	Rev. T.
4902	....	....	Rep.
4903–4911	35	51–58, 59a	Rev. T.
4912–4919	35	60–67	Rev. T.
4920–4923	35	69–72	Rev. T.
4924–4928	....	....	Rep.
4929–4931	35	73, 76, 77	Rev. T.
4932	....	....	Rep.
4933, 4934	35	73, 78	Rev. T.
4935, 4936	35	79	Rev. T.
4937–4952	....	....	Rep.
4953	17	24	Rev. T.
4954–5132	....	....	Rep.
5133	12	21	
5134	12	22	
5135	12	23	
5136	12	24	
5136A	12	24a	
5136B	12	25a	
5137	12	29	
5138	12	51	Rep.
5139	12	52	
5140	12	53	
5141	12	54	Rep.
5142	12	57	
5143	12	59	
5144	12	61	
5145	12	71	
5146	12	72	
5147	12	73	
5148	12	74	
5149	12	75	
5150	12	76	
5151	12	63	Rep.
5152	12	66	
5153	12	90	
5154	12	35	
5155	12	36	
5156	12	39	
5156A	12	215c	
5157	12	37	
5158	12	102	Rep.
5159	12	101a	Rep.
5160–5167	12	168–175	Rep.
5168	12	26	
5169	12	27	
5170	12	28	Rep.
5171	....	....	Rep.
5172–5174	12	104, 107, 108	Rep.
5175–5181	....	....	Rep.
5182–5187	12	109, 110, 124, 151, 152, 581	Rep.
5188, 5189	....	....	Rep.
5190	12	81	
5191	12	141–143	
5192	12	144	
5193, 5194	....	....	Rep.
5195	12	123	Rep.
5196	12	89	Rep.
5197	12	85	
5198	12	86, 94	
5199	12	60	
5200	12	84	
5201	12	83	
5202, 5203	12	82, 87	Rep.
5204	12	56	
5205	12	55	
5206	12	88	Rep.
5207	12	582	
5208	12	501	
5208, 5209	12	591, 592	Rep.
5210	12	62	
5211	12	161	
5212	12	163	Rep.
5213	12	164	
5214	12	541	
5215–5218	12	544–547	Elim.
5219	12	548	
5220	12	181	
5221	12	182	
5222–5225	12	183–186	Rep.
5226–5231	12	131–134, 137, 138	Rep.
5232, 5233	12	135, 136	Rep.
5234	12	192	
5235	12	193	
5236	12	194	
5237	12	195	Rep.
5238	12	196	
5239	12	93	
5239A	12	93a	
5240	12	481–485	
5241	12	165	Elim.
5242	12	91	
5243	12	583	Rep.
5244	12	43	
5244	33	8	
5245	....	....	Rep.
5246	33	9	
5247	33	6	
5248	33	31	
5249	....	....	Rep.
5250	33	501	Elim.
5251	33	10	
5252	33	4	
5253	33	543	
5254	33	420	
5255	....	....	Rep.
5256–5262	45	81, 82, 84–88	Rep.
5263–5265	47	1, 2, 6	Rep.
5266–5269	47	3–5, 8	Rep.
5270	18	651, 652	Rev. T.
5271	18	655	Rev. T.
5272, 5273	18	653, 654	Rev. T.
5274–5279	18	658–663	Rev. T.
5280–5293	....	....	Rep.
5294	46	7	Rev. T.
5295	18	644	Rev. T.
5296	18	641	Rev. T.
5297–5300	50	201–204	Rep. See T. 10 §§331–334.
5301	50	205	
5302	50	206	
5303	50	207	
5304	50	208	
5305	50	209	Rep.
5306	50	210	
5307	50	211	
5308	50	212	
5309	50	213	
5310	50	214	Rep. See T. 10 §7651.
5311	50	215	
5312	50	216	
5313	50	217	
5314	50	218	Rep.
5315	50	219	
5316	50	220	
5317	50	221	
5318	19	540	
	50	222	Elim.
5319	50	223	
5320	50	224	
5321	50	225	
5322	50	226	
5323–5395	....	....	Rep.
5396, 5397	18	558, 559	Rev. T.
5398–5484	....	....	Rep.
5485	38	112	Rev. T.
	43	843	Rep.
5486	38	127	Rev. T.
5487–5516	....	....	Rep.
5517	42	1990	
5518–5535	....	....	Rep.
5536	18	701	Rev. T.
5537–5542	18	691–695	Rev. T.
5543	18	713	Rev. T.
5544	18	712, 712a, 713	Rev. T.
5545	18	703	Rev. T.
5546	18	696–698	Rev. T.
5547	18	699	Rev. T.
5548–5550	18	705–707	Rev. T.
5551–5567	....	....	Rep. See T. 46, §§1351–1354.
5568, 5569	....	....	Rep.
5570	48	1411	
5571	48	1412	
5572	48	1413	
5573	48	1414	
5574	48	1415	
5575	48	1416	
5576	48	1417	

R.S. Sec.	U.S.C.		Status
	Title	Section	
5577	48	1418	
5578	48	1419	
5579	20	41	
5580	20	42	
5581	20	43	
5582	20	44	
5583	20	46	
5584	20	48	
5585	20	45	
5586	20	50	
5587	20	51	
5588	20	52	
5589	20	53	
5590	20	54	
5591	20	55	
5592	20	56	
5593	20	57	
5594	20	67	
5595, 5596			
5597, 5598			Rep.
5599	1	29a	Rev. T.
5600, 5601			

TABLE III—STATUTES AT LARGE

(1789–1899 contained in this volume)

Showing where the Acts of Congress will be found in the United States Code

Abbreviations

Rep.—Repealed. Where "Rep." appears in the status column following a U.S.C. reference, an explanation of the repeal can be found under such U.S.C. title and section.

Rev. T.—Revised Title. Where "Rev. T." appears in the status column, the U.S.C. reference is to title and section where the section of the Act of Congress was originally allocated in the U.S.C. To locate the section of the Act in the U.S.C. revised title, see Table I.

Elim.—Eliminated. Where "Elim." appears in the status column following a U.S.C. reference, the reason for the elimination of the text can be found under such U.S.C. title and section. Where "Elim." appears in the status column and the U.S.C. column is blank, the text had at one time appeared as a note to a prior section of the Code.

I.R.C. '39.—Internal Revenue Code of 1939. Where I.R.C. '39 appears in the status column, it is an indication that the provision was repealed or otherwise superseded by the Internal Revenue Code of 1939.

R.S.—Revised Statutes of 1878. Where "R.S." followed by a § number appears in the status column, the provision was restated in the cited section of the Revised Statutes of 1878. See Table II showing where sections of the Revised Statutes of 1878 will be found in the United States Code.

1st Cong.					U.S.C.		
1 Stat.		Chapter	Section	Page	Title	Section	Status
1789—June	1	1	2	23			R.S. §28
			2	23			R.S. §29
			2	23			R.S. §30
			3	23			R.S. §1836
			3	23			R.S. §1837
July	27	4	1	28			R.S. §161
			1	28			R.S. §199
			1	28			R.S. §202
			2	29			R.S. §203
			4	29			R.S. §203
Aug.	7	7	1	49			R.S. §161
			1	49			R.S. §214
			1	49			R.S. §216
			2	50			R.S. §217
			4	50			R.S. §217
		9	4	54			R.S. §4235
Sept.	2	12	1	65			R.S. §161
			1	65			R.S. §233
			1	65			R.S. §257
			1	65			R.S. §268
			1	65			R.S. §276
			1	65			R.S. §301
			1	65			R.S. §312
			2	65			R.S. §248
			2	65			R.S. §3669
			3	66			R.S. §269
			4	66			R.S. §302
			4	66			R.S. §305
			4	66			R.S. §311
			6	67			R.S. §313
			6	67			R.S. §3675
			8	67			R.S. §243
			8	67			R.S. §1788
			8	67			R.S. §1789
	15	14	1	68			R.S. §161
			1	68			R.S. §199
			1	68			R.S. §202
			2	68			R.S. §204
			3	68			R.S. §1793
			4	68			R.S. §1794
			5	69			R.S. §882
			6	69			R.S. §71
			6	69			R.S. §213
			7	69			R.S. §203

1st Cong.				U.S.C.		
1 Stat.	Chapter	Section	Page	Title	Section	Status
1789—Sept. 23	Pub. R. 3		97			R.S. §206
24	19		72			R.S. §153
	20	1	73			R.S. §530
		1	73			R.S. §674
		1	73			R.S. §675
		2	73			R.S. §531
		3	73			R.S. §551
		3	73			R.S. §552
		3	73			R.S. §562
		3	73			R.S. §581
		3	74			R.S. §572
		4	74			R.S. §604
		4	74			R.S. §608
		4	74			R.S. §614
		5	75			R.S. §658
		5	75			R.S. §661
		6	76			R.S. §583
		6	76			R.S. §602
		6	76			R.S. §671
		7	76			R.S. §555
		7	76			R.S. §619
		7	76			R.S. §677
		7	76			R.S. §782
		7	76			R.S. §794
		7	76			R.S. §795
		8	76			R.S. §712
		9	76			R.S. §563
		9	76			R.S. §566
		9	76			R.S. §629
		9	76			R.S. §711
		9	76			R.S. §734
		10	77			R.S. §1002
		11	78			R.S. §629
		11	78			R.S. §711
		11	79			R.S. §739
		12	79			R.S. §639
		12	79			R.S. §646
		12	79			R.S. §647
		12	79			R.S. §648
		13	80			R.S. §687
		13	80			R.S. §688
		13	80			R.S. §689
		13	80			R.S. §690
		13	80			R.S. §711
		14	81			R.S. §716
		14	81			R.S. §751
		14	81			R.S. §752
		14	81			R.S. §753
		15	82			R.S. §724
		16	82			R.S. §723
		17	83			R.S. §725
		17	83			R.S. §726
		18	83			R.S. §987
		20	83			R.S. §968
		21	83			R.S. §631
		22	84			R.S. §633
		22	84			R.S. §691
		22	84			R.S. §700
		22	84			R.S. §997
		22	84			R.S. §998
		22	84			R.S. §999
		22	84			R.S. §1000
		22	84			R.S. §1011
		23	85			R.S. §1007
		23	85			R.S. §1010
		24	85			R.S. §701
		25	85			R.S. §709
		25	85			R.S. §710
		25	85			R.S. §1003
		25	85			R.S. §1010
		25	85			R.S. §1017
		26	87			R.S. §961
		27	87			R.S. §680
		27	87			R.S. §776
		27	87			R.S. §779
		27	87			R.S. §780
		27	87			R.S. §782
		27	87			R.S. §783
		27	87			R.S. §787
		28	87			R.S. §789
		28	87			R.S. §790
		28	87			R.S. §922
		29	88			R.S. §729
		29	88			R.S. §802
		29	88			R.S. §803
		29	88			R.S. §804
		29	88			R.S. §810

1st Cong.					U.S.C.		
1 Stat.		Chapter	Section	Page	Title	Section	Status
1789—Sept.	24	20	30	88			R.S. §861
			30	88			R.S. §863
			30	88			R.S. §864
			30	88			R.S. §865
			30	88			R.S. §866
			31	90			R.S. §955
			31	90			R.S. §956
			32	91			R.S. §954
			33	91			R.S. §727
			33	91			R.S. §879
			33	91			R.S. §1014
			33	91			R.S. §1015
			33	91			R.S. §1016
			34	92			R.S. §721
			35	92			R.S. §346
			35	92			R.S. §354
			35	92			R.S. §359
			35	92			R.S. §747
			35	92			R.S. §767
			35	92			R.S. §769
			35	92			R.S. §771
	29	21	2	93			R.S. §913
1790—Apr.	30	9	1	112			R.S. §5331
			2	112			R.S. §5333
			3	113			R.S. §5339
			4	113			R.S. §5340
			5	113			R.S. §5402
			6	113			R.S. §5390
			7	113			R.S. §5041
			7	113			R.S. §5343
			8	113			R.S. §730
			8	113			R.S. §5360
			8	113			R.S. §5369
			8	113			R.S. §5372
			8	113			R.S. §5383
			9	114			R.S. §5373
			10	114			R.S. §5323
			11	114			R.S. §5324
			11	114			R.S. §5533
			12	115			R.S. §5359
			12	115			R.S. §5384
			13	115			R.S. §5348
			15	115			R.S. §5394
			16	116			R.S. §5356
			17	116			R.S. §5357
			18	116			R.S. §5392
			18	116			R.S. §5393
			19	116			R.S. §5396
			20	116			R.S. §5397
			21	117			R.S. §5449
			21	117			R.S. §5499
			22	117			R.S. §5398
			22	117			R.S. §5446
			23	117			R.S. §5400
			23	117			R.S. §5401
			24	117			R.S. §5326
			25	117			R.S. §4063
			26	117			R.S. §4064
			27	117			R.S. §4065
			27	117			R.S. §4066
			28	118			R.S. §4062
			29	118			R.S. §1033
			29	118			R.S. §1034
			30	119			R.S. §1032
			31	119			R.S. §5329
			32	119			R.S. §1043
			32	119			R.S. §1044
			32	119			R.S. §1045
			33	119			R.S. §5325
May	26	11		122			R.S. §905
June	4	17	1	126			R.S. §531
			1	126			R.S. §608
			1	126			R.S. §767
			1	126			R.S. §776
			2	126			R.S. §551
	23	21	1	128			R.S. §608
			2	128			R.S. §531
			2	128			R.S. §551
July	16	28	1	130			R.S. §1795
			6	130			R.S. §1796
	20	29	1	131			R.S. §4520
			1	131			R.S. §4521
			2	131			R.S. §4522
			3	132			R.S. §4556
			3	132			R.S. §4557
			3	132			R.S. §4558

1st Cong.					U.S.C.		
1 Stat.		Chapter	Section	Page	Title	Section	Status
1790—July	20	29	4	133			R.S. §4537
			4	133			R.S. §4601
			6	133			R.S. §4529
			6	133			R.S. §4530
			6	133			R.S. §4546
			6	133			R.S. §4547
			7	134			R.S. §4598
			9	135			R.S. §4564
				135			R.S. §4219
Aug.	4	35	67	176			R.S. §919
			67	176			R.S. §923
			67	176			R.S. §938
			67	176			R.S. §940
			67	176			R.S. §941
			68	177			R.S. §939
1791—Mar.	2	12	1	197			R.S. §767
			1	197			R.S. §776
			2	197			R.S. §531
			2	197			R.S. §551
			3	197			R.S. §608
	8	18		215			R.S. §244
2d Cong.							
1 Stat.							
1792—Mar.	1	8	1	239			R.S. §131
			1	239			R.S. §132
			2	239			R.S. §135
			2	239			R.S. §138
			2	239			R.S. §139
			2	239			R.S. §140
			3	240			R.S. §136
			3	240			R.S. §138
			4	240			R.S. §141
			5	240			R.S. §142
			6	240			R.S. §143
			7	240			R.S. §144
			8	240			R.S. §145
			9	240			R.S. §146
			10	240			R.S. §147
			10	240			R.S. §148
			10	240			R.S. §149
			10	240			R.S. §150
			11	241			R.S. §151
			12	241			R.S. §152
Apr.	2	16	20	250			R.S. §8563
	12	20		252			R.S. §73
	13	21	2	253			R.S. §658
	14	24	2	255			R.S. §1707
			2	255			R.S. §1709
			2	255			R.S. §1710
			2	255			R.S. §3689
			3	255			R.S. §4238
			6	256			R.S. §1698
			9	257			R.S. §1714
May	8	33	1	271			R.S. §1625
			1	271			R.S. §1626
			1	271			R.S. §1627
			1	271			R.S. §1628
			2	272			R.S. §1629
			3	272			R.S. §1630
			3	272			R.S. §1631
			4	272			R.S. §1632
			5	273			R.S. §1633
			6	273			R.S. §1634
			6	273			R.S. §1635
			8	273			R.S. §1638
			9	273			R.S. §1639
			10	273			R.S. §1640
			11	274			R.S. §1641
		36	1	275			R.S. §911
			2	276			R.S. §913
			5	277			R.S. §974
			5	277			R.S. §975
			6	278			R.S. §857
			9	278			R.S. §1004
			10	278			R.S. §799
			10	278			R.S. §947
			11	278			R.S. §601
			12	279			R.S. §679
		37	4	280			R.S. §1291
			6	280			R.S. §249
			9	281			R.S. §248
			12	281			R.S. §244
			12	281			R.S. §1788
			12	281			R.S. §1789

2d Cong.

1 Stat.	Chapter	Section	Page	U.S.C.		Status
				Title	Section	
1792—Dec. 31	1	1	287			R.S. §4131
		2	288			R.S. §4132
		2	288			R.S. §4133
		3	288			R.S. §4141
		3	288			R.S. §4178
		4	289			R.S. §4142
		4	289			R.S. §4143
		4	289			R.S. §4144
		6	290			R.S. §4148
		6	290			R.S. §4149
		7	290			R.S. §4145
		7	290			R.S. §4146
		7	290			R.S. §4174
		8	290			R.S. §4147
		9	291			R.S. §4155
		9	291			R.S. §4156
		10	292			R.S. §4158
		11	293			R.S. §4143
		11	293			R.S. §4144
		11	293			R.S. §4159
		11	293			R.S. §4160
		12	293			R.S. §4144
		12	293			R.S. §4161
		12	293			R.S. §4162
		12	293			R.S. §4163
		13	294			R.S. §4167
		13	294			R.S. §4168
		14	294			R.S. §4169
		14	294			R.S. §4170
		15	295			R.S. §4171
		16	295			R.S. §4172
		17	295			R.S. §4173
		18	296			R.S. §4175
		19	296			R.S. §4176
		20	296			R.S. §4180
		21	296			R.S. §4181
		22	296			R.S. §4182
		23	297			R.S. §4183
		24	297			R.S. §4184
		25	297			R.S. §4185
		26	298			R.S. §4187
		26	298			R.S. §4188
		27	298			R.S. §4189
		28	298			R.S. §4375
		29	298			R.S. §919
		29	298			R.S. §923
		29	298			R.S. §938
		29	298			R.S. §939
		29	298			R.S. §940
		29	298			R.S. §941
		29	298			R.S. §4305
1793—Feb. 9	4	2	300			R.S. §291
	5	3	301			R.S. §3566
12	7	1	302			R.S. §5278
		2	302			R.S. §5279
18	8	1	305			R.S. §4311
		2	305			R.S. §4312
		2	305			R.S. §4319
		3	306			R.S. §4322
		3	306			R.S. §4323
		4	306			R.S. §4320
		4	306			R.S. §4321
		5	307			R.S. §4324
		5	307			R.S. §4377
		6	307			R.S. §4371
		6	308			R.S. §4372
		7	308			R.S. §4333
		8	308			R.S. §4337
		8	308			R.S. §4338
		9	308			R.S. §4325
		9	308			R.S. §4326
		10	309			R.S. §4327
		11	309			R.S. §4334
		12	309			R.S. §4335
		13	309			R.S. §4336
		14	309			R.S. §4349
		14	309			R.S. §4350
		15	310			R.S. §4351
		15	310			R.S. §4352
		16	311			R.S. §4353
		16	311			R.S. §4354
		17	311			R.S. §4355
		17	311			R.S. §4356
		18	312			R.S. §4359
		18	312			R.S. §4360
		19	313			R.S. §4362
		19	313			R.S. §4363

2d Cong.					U.S.C.		
1 Stat.		Chapter	Section	Page	Title	Section	Status
1793—Feb.	18	8	20	313			R.S. §4361
			21	313			R.S. §4364
			21	313			R.S. §4365
			22	314			R.S. §4366
			24	314			R.S. §4367
			24	314			R.S. §4368
			24	314			R.S. §4369
			25	315			R.S. §4332
			26	315			R.S. §4331
			28	315			R.S. §4379
			29	315			R.S. §4373
			29	315			R.S. §4374
			30	316			R.S. §4375
			31	316			R.S. §4376
			32	316			R.S. §4377
			33	316			R.S. §4378
			34	316			R.S. §4381
			34	316			R.S. §4383
			35	317			R.S. §919
			35	317			R.S. §923
			35	317			R.S. §938
			35	317			R.S. §939
			35	317			R.S. §940
			35	317			R.S. §941
			35	317			R.S. §4380
			37	317			R.S. §4385
		9		318			R.S. §153
Mar.	2	22	3	334			R.S. §662
			4	334			R.S. §627
			4	334			R.S. §727
			4	334			R.S. §1014
			4	334			R.S. §1015
			4	334			R.S. §1016
			5	334			R.S. §716
			5	334			R.S. §717
			5	334			R.S. §719
			5	334			R.S. §720
			6	335			R.S. §876
			7	335			R.S. §918
			8	335			R.S. §993
3d Cong.							
1 Stat.							
1794—Jan.	13	1		341			R.S. §1791
Mar.	22	11	1	347			R.S. §563
			1	347			R.S. §629
			1	347			R.S. §5551
			2	349			R.S. §5552
			3	349			R.S. §5564
			4	349			R.S. §5554
Apr.	2	14	2	352			R.S. §1662
			5	352			R.S. §1665
	3	17		353			R.S. §34
May	8	23	3	357			R.S. §388
	19	32		369			R.S. §671
June	9	64	1	404			R.S. §570
			1	408			R.S. §938
			2	408			R.S. §572
Dec.	12	3		409			R.S. §1000
1795—Jan.	2	9	2	424			R.S. §1653
			3	424			R.S. §1651
			6	424			R.S. §1655
Feb.	28	36	1	424			R.S. §1642
			1	424			R.S. §1654
			1	424			R.S. §5297
			4	424			R.S. §1644
			5	424			R.S. §1649
			6	424			R.S. §1658
			7	424			R.S. §1659
			8	425			R.S. §1660
			9	425			R.S. §788
Mar.	2	40	1	426			R.S. §4662
			2	426			R.S. §4662
		41		426			R.S. §4357
4th Cong.							
1 Stat.							
1796—May	18	29	1	464			R.S. §2223
			2	465			R.S. §2395
			9	468			R.S. §2476
	28	36	4	477			R.S. §4588
			4	477			R.S. §4589

4th Cong.					U.S.C.		
1 Stat.		Chapter	Section	Page	Title	Section	Status
1796—May	28	36	6	478			R.S. §4590
			7	478			R.S. §4591
June	1	45	1	489			R.S. §4306
			2	489			R.S. §4306
			4	490			R.S. §4307
1797—Jan.	31	2	2	496			R.S. §552
Mar.	2	7		498			R.S. §4164
				498			R.S. §4329
	3	9	5	503			R.S. §4206
		13		506			R.S. §5292
		20	1	512			R.S. §886
			1	512			R.S. §887
			1	512			R.S. §3624
			3	514			R.S. §951
			3	514			R.S. §957
			5	515			R.S. §3466
			6	515			R.S. §986
		27		517			R.S. §658
5th Cong.							
1 Stat.							
1797—June	27	5		523			R.S. §4165
July	1	7	4	523			R.S. §1616
			6	524			R.S. §1615
1798—Apr.	30	35	1	553			R.S. §161
			1	553			R.S. §415
			1	553			R.S. §417
			3	554			R.S. §418
May	3	36		554			R.S. §101
June	6	49	1	561			R.S. §3471
			3	562			R.S. §3471
July	6	66	1	577			R.S. §4067
			1	577			R.S. §4068
			2	577			R.S. §4069
			3	578			R.S. §4070
	11	72	1	594			R.S. §1611
			1	594			R.S. §1616
			2	595			R.S. §1615
			3	595			R.S. §1616
			4	595			R.S. §1609
			4	595			R.S. §1621
			5	595			R.S. §1610
			6	596			R.S. §1619
	16	77	1	605			R.S. §3689
			4	606			R.S. §4801
		83		609			R.S. §727
		85	3	610			R.S. §3714
			6	610			R.S. §3743
1799—Jan.	30	1		613			R.S. §5335
Feb.	25	12	1	619			R.S. §4792
			1	619			R.S. §4796
			2	619			R.S. §4793
			2	619			R.S. §4795
			3	620			R.S. §4794
			4	620			R.S. §4797
			5	620			R.S. §4800
			6	620			R.S. §4798
			7	621			R.S. §4799
	28	19	1	625			R.S. §781
			2	625			R.S. §782
			8	626			R.S. §976
Mar.	2	22	1	627			R.S. §2522
			1	627			R.S. §2523
			2	627			R.S. §2517
			2	627			R.S. §2527
			2	628			R.S. §2529
			2	629			R.S. §2518
			2	629			R.S. §2519
			3	629			R.S. §2531
			3	630			R.S. §2532
			3	630			R.S. §2533
			4	630			R.S. §2533
			4	630			R.S. §2534
			5	631			R.S. §2535
			5	631			R.S. §2536
			6	631			R.S. §2525
			6	631			R.S. §2526
			7	632			R.S. §2541
			7	632			R.S. §2542
			8	632			R.S. §2543
			8	632			R.S. §2544
			9	633			R.S. §2546
			9	633			R.S. §2547
			10	634			R.S. §2548
			10	634			R.S. §2549

5th Cong.

1 Stat.	Chapter	Section	Page	U.S.C. Title	U.S.C. Section	Status
1799—Mar. 2	22	10	634			R.S. §2550
		10	634			R.S. §2551
		11	635			R.S. §2552
		11	635			R.S. §2553
		13	636			R.S. §2557
		13	636			R.S. §2558
		14	636			R.S. §2559
		14	636			R.S. §2560
		14	637			R.S. §2561
		17	638			R.S. §2599
		17	638			R.S. §2600
		17	638			R.S. §2603
		17	638			R.S. §2604
		17	639			R.S. §2568
		18	639			R.S. §2770
		18	639			R.S. §2771
		19	640			R.S. §2772
		19	640			R.S. §2834
		20	641			R.S. §2616
		20	641			R.S. §2617
		20	641			R.S. §2618
		21	642			R.S. §2621
		21	642			R.S. §2622
		21	642			R.S. §2623
		21	642			R.S. §2624
		21	642			R.S. §2626
		21	642			R.S. §2627
		21	642			R.S. §2628
		21	643			R.S. §2640
		22	644			R.S. §2625
		22	644			R.S. §2629
		22	644			R.S. §2630
		22	644			R.S. §2632
		23	644			R.S. §2806
		23	644			R.S. §2807
		23	644			R.S. §2808
		24	646			R.S. §2809
		24	646			R.S. §2810
		25	646			R.S. §2811
		25	646			R.S. §2812
		25	646			R.S. §2813
		26	647			R.S. §2814
		26	647			R.S. §2815
		27	648			R.S. §2867
		28	648			R.S. §2868
		29	648			R.S. §2773
		30	649			R.S. §2774
		30	649			R.S. §2775
		31	651			R.S. §2791
		32	651			R.S. §2776
		32	651			R.S. §2777
		32	651			R.S. §2778
		33	652			R.S. §2779
		34	652			R.S. §2780
		34	652			R.S. §2781
		34	652			R.S. §2782
		34	652			R.S. §2783
		34	652			R.S. §2784
		36	655			R.S. §2785
		36	655			R.S. §2786
		36	655			R.S. §2787
		36	655			R.S. §2788
		36	655			R.S. §2789
		37	658			R.S. §2794
		37	658			R.S. §2883
		38	658			R.S. §2884
		39	659			R.S. §2885
		44	660			R.S. §2886
		45	661			R.S. §2795
		45	661			R.S. §2796
		45	661			R.S. §2797
		46	661			R.S. §2799
		46	661			R.S. §2800
		46	661			R.S. §2801
		46	661			R.S. §2802
		49	664			R.S. §2805
		49	664			R.S. §2869
		49	664			R.S. §2870
		50	665			R.S. §2872
		50	665			R.S. §2873
		50	665			R.S. §2874
		51	665			R.S. §2882
		52	665			R.S. §2926
		52	665			R.S. §2927
		53	667			R.S. §2875
		53	667			R.S. §2876

5th Cong.				U.S.C.		
1 Stat.	Chapter	Section	Page	Title	Section	Status
1799—Mar. 2	22	53	667			R.S. §2877
		53	667			R.S. §2878
		54	668			R.S. §3067
		54	668			R.S. §3069
		54	668			R.S. §3070
		55	668			R.S. §2888
		55	668			R.S. §2889
		56	669			R.S. §2969
		56	670			R.S. §2879
		56	670			R.S. §2880
		56	670			R.S. §2881
		56	670			R.S. §3689
		57	671			R.S. §2887
		60	672			R.S. §2891
		60	672			R.S. §2892
		60	672			R.S. §2893
		60	672			R.S. §2894
		61	673			R.S. §2903
		62	675			R.S. §3058
		63	675			R.S. §2790
		64	675			R.S. §4154
		65	676			R.S. §942
		65	676			R.S. §960
		65	676			R.S. §963
		65	676			R.S. §3466
		65	676			R.S. §3467
		65	676			R.S. §3468
		66	677			R.S. §2839
		66	677			R.S. §2840
		68	678			R.S. §3066
		69	678			R.S. §3082
		70	678			R.S. §909
		70	678			R.S. §923
		70	678			R.S. §3072
		71	678			R.S. §909
		71	678			R.S. §971
		71	678			R.S. §3068
		71	678			R.S. §3073
		72	678			R.S. §2890
		73	680			R.S. §2635
		73	680			R.S. §2636
		73	680			R.S. §2637
		75	680			R.S. §3015
		75	680			R.S. §3016
		75	680			R.S. §3028
		75	680			R.S. §3029
		76	682			R.S. §3035
		80	687			R.S. §563
		80	687			R.S. §629
		80	687			R.S. §965
		80	687			R.S. §3038
		80	687			R.S. §3041
		80	687			R.S. §3042
		80	688			R.S. §959
		80	688			R.S. §3040
		80	689			R.S. §3039
		81	689			R.S. §3043
		81	689			R.S. §3044
		81	689			R.S. §3045
		81	689			R.S. §3046
		81	689			R.S. §3047
		82	692			R.S. §3049
		84	694			R.S. §3050
		84	694			R.S. §3051
		85	694			R.S. §2896
		86	695			R.S. §2638
		87	695			R.S. §1788
		87	695			R.S. §1789
		89	695			R.S. §919
		89	695			R.S. §923
		89	695			R.S. §938
		89	695			R.S. §940
		89	695			R.S. §941
		89	695			R.S. §970
		89	695			R.S. §1047
		89	695			R.S. §3087
		90	696			R.S. §939
		91	697			R.S. §3089
		91	697			R.S. §3090
		92	697			R.S. §3095
		93	698			R.S. §4197
		93	698			R.S. §4198
		93	698			R.S. §4199
		93	698			R.S. §4201
		93	698			R.S. §4202
		93	698			R.S. §4206

5th Cong.					U.S.C.		
1 Stat.		Chapter	Section	Page	Title	Section	Status
1799—Mar.	2	22	97	699			R.S. §2747
			98	699			R.S. §1492
			98	699			R.S. §2756
			98	699			R.S. §2757
			99	700			R.S. §2760
			99	700			R.S. §2761
			99	700			R.S. §2762
			100	700			R.S. §2747
			100	700			R.S. §2748
			101	700			R.S. §2763
			102	700			R.S. §2764
			102	700			R.S. §2765
			105	702			R.S. §2515
			105	702			R.S. §3096
			106	702			R.S. §3097
			110	703			R.S. §3094
			111	704			R.S. §2769
		23	1	705			R.S. §2619
			2	706			R.S. §2654
			2	706			R.S. §2655
			2	706			R.S. §2656
			2	706			R.S. §2657
			2	706			R.S. §2659
			2	706			R.S. §2660
			2	706			R.S. §2733
			2	706			R.S. §4186
			2	707			R.S. §2642
			2	708			R.S. §2639
			2	708			R.S. §2706
			4	709			R.S. §2686
		32	1	727			R.S. §943
			3	727			R.S. §944
		36	1	729			R.S. §3689
			2	729			R.S. §1614
			2	729			R.S. §3689
			2	729			R.S. §4808
		38		729			R.S. §276
		41	2	731			R.S. §207
	3	48	8	752			R.S. §1114
			9	752			R.S. §1094
6th Cong.							
2 Stat.							
1800—Jan.	6	4	1	4			R.S. §992
			2	5			R.S. §991
Feb.	11	6		7			R.S. §5292
Apr.	23	33		47			R.S. §1624
	24	37	5	56			R.S. §82
May	7	45	3	61			R.S. §790
			3	61			R.S. §994
		46	2	61			R.S. §1668
			3	61			R.S. §1669
			4	62			R.S. §1629
			4	68			R.S. §1671
	10	49	1	68			R.S. §2517
			1	68			R.S. §2518
			1	68			R.S. §2619
			2	68			R.S. §2520
			3	68			R.S. §2533
			4	68			R.S. §2552
			4	68			R.S. §2553
			4	68			R.S. §2772
		51	1	70			R.S. §563
			1	70			R.S. §629
			1	70			R.S. §5556
			2	70			R.S. §5381
			3	71			R.S. §5382
			4	71			R.S. §5553
			4	71			R.S. §5557
			4	71			R.S. §5558
			4	71			R.S. §5560
			5	71			R.S. §563
			5	71			R.S. §629
			7	71			R.S. §5565
		54	1	72			R.S. §2660
			1	72			R.S. §2706
			2	72			R.S. §2659
		55	1	73			R.S. §2236
			3	73			R.S. §2395
			6	75			R.S. §2236
		58		79			R.S. §257
				80			R.S. §3669
	13	61		82			R.S. §801
		64	2	82			R.S. §3027
1801—Feb.	25	7	1	101			R.S. §2531

6th Cong. 2 Stat.	Chapter	Section	Page	U.S.C. Title	U.S.C. Section	Status
1801—Feb. 25	7	1	102			R.S. §2532
		3	102			R.S. §2522
		3	102			R.S. §2524
27	15	7	106			R.S. §680
		8	106			R.S. §705
Mar. 3	25		116			R.S. §2836
	28	2	121			R.S. §2838
7th Cong.						
2 Stat.						
1802—Jan. 26	2	1	128			R.S. §80
		2	129			R.S. §85
		3	129			R.S. §88
		3	129			R.S. §89
		4	129			R.S. §92
		4	129			R.S. §93
Feb. 6	4	6	129			R.S. §82
Mar. 16	9	4	134			R.S. §1239
		5	134			R.S. §1240
		5	134			R.S. §1277
		5	134			R.S. §1295
		6	134			R.S. §1146
		11	134			R.S. §1116
		13	135			R.S. §1189
		16	135			R.S. §1186
		23	136			R.S. §1237
		27	137			R.S. §1323
		28	137			R.S. §1309
		28	137			R.S. §1311
Apr. 14	28	1	153			R.S. §2165
		1	153			R.S. §2171
		3	155			R.S. §2165
		4	155			R.S. §2172
		4	155			R.S. §1993
29	31	1	156			R.S. §685
		1	156			R.S. §686
		5	158			R.S. §614
		6	159			R.S. §651
		6	159			R.S. §652
		6	159			R.S. §697
		7	162			R.S. §531
		7	162			R.S. §551
		15	165			R.S. §572
		19	165			R.S. §776
		19	165			R.S. §781
		20	165			R.S. §767
		27	166			R.S. §572
		29	167			R.S. §807
		29	167			R.S. §818
		29	167			R.S. §880
		30	167			R.S. §805
May 1	45	9	182			R.S. §2550
		9	182			R.S. §2551
3	51	1	192			R.S. §3689
		5	193			R.S. §4805
1803—Feb. 19	7	2	201			R.S. §551
		4	202			R.S. §767
		5	202			R.S. §776
		5	202			R.S. §781
28	9	1	203			R.S. §4576
		2	203			R.S. §4309
		2	203			R.S. §4310
		2	203			R.S. §4573
		3	203			R.S. §4582
		3	203			R.S. §4584
		4	204			R.S. §4577
		4	204			R.S. §4578
		7	204			R.S. §1737
	13	2	206			R.S. §1313
Mar. 2	15	1	207			R.S. §232
		1	207			R.S. §1636
		2	207			R.S. §1627
		2	207			R.S. §1628
		2	207			R.S. §1632
		3	207			R.S. §1631
	16		208			R.S. §4308
	18	1	209			R.S. §4191
		3	210			R.S. §4166
		4	210			R.S. §5292
3	26	2	228			R.S. §2531
		2	228			R.S. §2548
		3	229			R.S. §2535
		4	229			R.S. §2517
		4	229			R.S. §2518
	27	17	235			R.S. §2476

7th Cong.

2 Stat.	Chapter	Section	Page	U.S.C. Title	U.S.C. Section	Status
1803—Mar. 3	40	2	244			R.S. §631
		2	244			R.S. §691
		2	244			R.S. §692
		2	244			R.S. §695
		2	244			R.S. §698
		2	244			R.S. §700
		2	244			R.S. §701
		2	244			R.S. §968
		2	244			R.S. §1010
		2	244			R.S. §1011
		2	244			R.S. §1012

8th Cong.

2 Stat.	Chapter	Section	Page	U.S.C. Title	U.S.C. Section	Status
1804—Feb. 24	13	4	252			R.S. §2568
		4	252			R.S. §2569
		7	253			R.S. §2570
		9	254			R.S. §2707
		11	254			R.S. §2564
		11	254			R.S. §2565
		11	254			R.S. §2661
Mar. 23	31	4	273			R.S. §572
26	40	1	290			R.S. §5366
		2	290			R.S. §5365
		3	290			R.S. §1046
		3	290			R.S. §1047
	44		291			R.S. §583
	47	2	293			R.S. §2168
	50		295			R.S. §137
			295			R.S. §138
			295			R.S. §139
			295			R.S. §140
27	52	1	296			R.S. §4134
		2	297			R.S. §4165
	56	1	298			R.S. §906
		2	299			R.S. §905
		2	299			R.S. §906
	57	6	300			R.S. §4225
	58	1	300			R.S. §2660
		2	301			R.S. §2659
1805—Jan. 11	6		310			R.S. §2527
Feb. 11	14	2	313			R.S. §2396
14	15		314			R.S. §2895
22	18	2	316			R.S. §2776
Mar. 3	34	1	336			R.S. §2535
		1	336			R.S. §2536
		2	336			R.S. §2535
		2	336			R.S. §2536
		3	336			R.S. §2603
		3	336			R.S. §2604
		4	336			R.S. §2604
	40		339			R.S. §4226

9th Cong.

2 Stat.	Chapter	Section	Page	U.S.C. Title	U.S.C. Section	Status
1806—Jan. 22	4	3	349			R.S. §2527
Apr. 10	20	1	359			R.S. §1342
		1	367			R.S. §1158
		2	371			R.S. §1343
	21	1	372			R.S. §783
		2	373			R.S. §784
		3	374			R.S. §785
		4	374			R.S. §786
21	35	2	390			R.S. §1534
		3	390			R.S. §1369
		3	390			R.S. §1395
		3	390			R.S. §1405
		3	390			R.S. §1535
	41	6	397			R.S. §1776
	45	1	399			R.S. §2542
		2	399			R.S. §2559
		2	399			R.S. §2560
	47	3	402			R.S. §1540
1807—Feb. 10	8	1	413			R.S. §4681
		2	413			R.S. §4682
		3	414			R.S. §4686
13	13		418			R.S. §719
24	16	2	420			R.S. §608
	17	4	421			R.S. §781
	19		422			R.S. §970
Mar. 2	22	2	426			R.S. §563
		7	428			R.S. §563
		7	428			R.S. §629
		7	428			R.S. §5380

2 Stat.	Chapter	Section	Page	U.S.C. Title	U.S.C. Section	Status
9th Cong.						
2 Stat.						
1807—Mar. 2	22	7	428			R.S. §5555
		7	428			R.S. §5557
		7	428			R.S. §5558
3	39		443			R.S. §5297
10th Cong.						
2 Stat.						
1807—Dec. 15	3		451			R.S. §2517
			451			R.S. §2518
			451			R.S. §2660
1808—Feb. 25	22		468			R.S. §781
Mar. 31	40		479			R.S. §2358
Apr. 12	43	5	483			R.S. §1237
21	48	1	484			R.S. §3739
		2	484			R.S. §3740
		3	484			R.S. §3741
		4	484			R.S. §3742
23	55	1	490			R.S. §1661
		2	490			R.S. §1662
		3	490			R.S. §1667
25	61	2	497			R.S. §2548
		2	497			R.S. §2549
1809—Mar. 2	27	1	534			R.S. §587
		1	534			R.S. §637
		2	535			R.S. §588
		2	535			R.S. §589
		3	535			R.S. §590
3	28	1	535			R.S. §3623
		1	535			R.S. §3675
		1	535			R.S. §3678
		2	536			R.S. §271
		5	536			R.S. §229
		5	536			R.S. §257
11th Cong.						
2 Stat.						
1810—Feb. 24	11		556			R.S. §2355
Mar. 26	19		568			R.S. §4190
Apr. 30	37	33	603			R.S. §1629
May 1	44	2	608			R.S. §1684
	50		612			R.S. §94
1811—Feb. 26	26	1	650			R.S. §1614
		1	650			R.S. §4807
		1	650			R.S. §4808
		2	650			R.S. §4809
		3	650			R.S. §4810
		4	650			R.S. §4811
		5	650			R.S. §4812
		5	650			R.S. §4813
28	28		651			R.S. §4579
Mar. 2	31	1	655			R.S. §2535
		2	655			R.S. §2535
		2	655			R.S. §2536
		4	656			R.S. §2525
	33	2	657			R.S. §2603
		2	657			R.S. §2604
		3	657			R.S. §2535
		4	657			R.S. §2535
		7	658			R.S. §2568
		7	658			R.S. §2569
		8	658			R.S. §2552
		8	658			R.S. §2553
3	46	12	666			R.S. §5251
12th Cong.						
2 Stat.						
1811—Nov. 28	2		667			R.S. §572
1812—Jan. 11	14	16	673			R.S. §1342
		21	674			R.S. §1237
		22	674			R.S. §1289
		22	674			R.S. §1290
23	17	2	676			R.S. §584
Feb. 6	20		676			R.S. §572
20	25	1	679			R.S. §627
		1	679			R.S. §945
		3	682			R.S. §861
		3	682			R.S. §867
Mar. 2	Pub. R. 1		786			R.S. §94
12	40	1	694			R.S. §4316
		2	694			R.S. §4317
26	45		696			R.S. §658

12th Cong.

2 Stat.	Chapter	Section	Page	U.S.C. Title	U.S.C. Section	Status
1812—Mar. 28	46	3	696			R.S. §1133
		5	697			R.S. §1133
30	47	6	699			R.S. §1378
		6	699			R.S. §1383
Apr. 8	50	4	703			R.S. §781
25	68	1	716			R.S. §440
		1	716			R.S. §453
		4	717			R.S. §454
		4	717			R.S. §891
		5	717			R.S. §454
		6	717			R.S. §455
		7	717			R.S. §457
		8	717			R.S. §458
		8	717			R.S. §459
		9	717			R.S. §456
		10	717			R.S. §452
		11	717			R.S. §446
29	71		719			R.S. §551
	72	2	720			R.S. §1309
		2	720			R.S. §1313
		2	720			R.S. §1337
		3	721			R.S. §1319
		3	721			R.S. §1321
		3	721			R.S. §1322
		4	721			R.S. §1213
		4	721			R.S. §1214
		4	721			R.S. §1215
May 22	92		742			R.S. §1138
June 26	107	17	763			R.S. §4759
July 6	130		781			R.S. §4068
	137	4	785			R.S. §1209
		4	785			R.S. §1604
Dec. 18	5		788			R.S. §551
			788			R.S. §552
			788			R.S. §713
1813—Jan. 29	16	12	796			R.S. §1342
		13	796			R.S. §1342
		15	796			R.S. §1289
		15	796			R.S. §1290
Feb. 2	18	1	797			R.S. §1659
		2	797			R.S. §1660
	22	1	799			R.S. §4760
		2	799			R.S. §4761
		3	800			R.S. §4762
		4	800			R.S. §4763
27	35		806			R.S. §1875
			806			R.S. §1876
			806			R.S. §1880
			806			R.S. §1881
			806			R.S. §1882
Mar. 3	42	3	809			R.S. §4574
		12	811			R.S. §2170
	45	3	815			R.S. §572
	48	5	817			R.S. §219
	50		818			R.S. §4157
	52	4	819			R.S. §1205

13th Cong.

3 Stat.	Chapter	Section	Page	U.S.C. Title	U.S.C. Section	Status
1813—June 19	2	1	2			R.S. §4391
		1	2			R.S. §4392
		2	2			R.S. §4393
		2	2			R.S. §4394
July 22	14	1	19			R.S. §977
		2	20			R.S. §978
		2	21			R.S. §979
		3	21			R.S. §921
		3	21			R.S. §982
	18		35			R.S. §2564
30	36		53			R.S. §2171
Aug. 2	58		86			R.S. §4761
Dec. 27	Pub. R. 1		140			R.S. §98
			140			R.S. §503
			140			R.S. §3798
1814—Mar. 30	37	12	114			R.S. §1204
		14	115			R.S. §1288
Apr. 9	49	1	120			R.S. §541
		2	120			R.S. §551
		3	121			R.S. §608
16	58	3	124			R.S. §1604
		5	125			R.S. §1369
		5	125			R.S. §1395
18	65		127			R.S. §4741
	78		133			R.S. §218
			133			R.S. §428

13th Cong.					U.S.C.		
3 Stat.		Chapter	Section	Page	Title	Section	Status
1814—Apr.	18	78		133			R.S. §1554
				133			R.S. §1555
		80		134			R.S. §1631
		84		136			R.S. §1569
Oct.	21	Pub. R. 3		246			R.S. §80
Dec.	1	Pub. R. 7		248	44	88	Rev. T.
	15	13	1	151			R.S. §1135
			1	151			R.S. §1143
			2	151			R.S. §1135
1815—Jan.	30	27		195			R.S. §80
Feb.	8	38	4	203			R.S. §1163
			5	203			R.S. §1166
			7	204			R.S. §1220
			7	204			R.S. §1303
			7	204			R.S. §1342
			8	204			R.S. §1164
			8	204			R.S. §1167
			9	204			R.S. §1165
			11	204			R.S. §1293
			11	204			R.S. §1297
	22	51		212			R.S. §57
				212			R.S. §58
				212			R.S. §59
Mar.	3	79	7	224			R.S. §1116
			7	224			R.S. §1237
		95		235			R.S. §767
				235			R.S. §776
		101	4	245			R.S. §563
			4	245			R.S. §629
		Pub. R. 11		249			R.S. §65
				249			R.S. §66
				249			R.S. §67
				249			R.S. §68
14th Cong.							
3 Stat.							
1816—Mar.	22	31	1	258			R.S. §658
			1	258			R.S. §572
			4	258			R.S. §658
		32	2	259			R.S. §2165
Apr.	2	39	1	261			R.S. §705
			2	261			R.S. §706
	16	46	3	284			R.S. §94
	20	64		295			R.S. §1631
	24	69	3	297			R.S. §1190
			4	298			R.S. §1188
			6	298			R.S. §1191
			7	298			R.S. §1296
			7	298			R.S. §1302
			8	298			R.S. §1302
			9	298			R.S. §1205
			12	299			R.S. §1272
		71		299			R.S. §2771
	26	81		302			R.S. §2568
				302			R.S. §2571
		95		306			R.S. §2657
				306			R.S. §2733
	27	107	6	314			R.S. §4219
			6	314			R.S. §4227
		127	1	317			R.S. §2439
			2	317			R.S. §2440
		Pub. R. 6	1	342			R.S. §198
			1	342			R.S. §510
			1	342			R.S. §3800
			2	342			R.S. §510
			3	342			R.S. §511
	29	135		320			R.S. §1661
		151		325			R.S. §2223
1817—Jan.	14	3		344			R.S. §4219
				344			R.S. §4227
Feb.	8	10		345			R.S. §101
Mar.	1	22		347			R.S. §2458
				347			R.S. §2459
		24	1	350			R.S. §1383
		30	1	350			R.S. §627
			1	350			R.S. §863
			1	350			R.S. §945
		31	2	351			R.S. §2497
			2	351			R.S. §2498
			4	351			R.S. §4347
			6	352			R.S. §4219
	3	40	1	362			R.S. §4209
			1	362			R.S. §4210
			2	362			R.S. §4211

14th Cong. 3 Stat.	Chapter	Section	Page	U.S.C. Title	U.S.C. Section	Status
1817—Mar. 3	42		363			R.S. §1862
			363			R.S. §1863
	45	2	366			R.S. §236
		3	366			R.S. §268
		3	366			R.S. §276
		4	366			R.S. §277
		5	367			R.S. §283
		5	367			R.S. §3673
		6	367			R.S. §260
		6	367			R.S. §283
		8	367			R.S. §269
		8	367			R.S. §318
		9	367			R.S. §273
		9	367			R.S. §3673
		10	367			R.S. §269
		11	367			R.S. §886
		12	368			R.S. §297
		13	368			R.S. §250
		13	368			R.S. §272
		15	368			R.S. §276
	49	2	368			R.S. §2659
	50		369			R.S. §4219
	100	2	390			R.S. §531
		2	390			R.S. §551
		3	390			R.S. §4208
		4	391			R.S. §767
		5	391			R.S. §776
		5	391			R.S. §781
	109	4	397			R.S. §3128
		7	397			R.S. §2616
		7	397			R.S. §2630
	114		399			R.S. §3472
15th Cong.						
3 Stat.						
1818—Jan. 22	5	3	404			R.S. §46
		3	404			R.S. §47
Mar. 9	14		408			R.S. §2559
			408			R.S. §2560
Apr. 3	29	2	413			R.S. §552
		4	413			R.S. §767
		5	413			R.S. §776
		5	413			R.S. §781
	32	1	414			R.S. §599
		3	414			R.S. §541
		6	415			R.S. §657
4	34	1	415			R.S. §1791
		2	415			R.S. §1792
11	51		425			R.S. §2603
			425			R.S. §2604
14	58		425			R.S. §4686
	61	2	426			R.S. §1309
		7	427			R.S. §1141
		7	427			R.S. §3715
		9	427			R.S. §1150
16	64	1	427			R.S. §1211
		2	427			R.S. §1209
		2	427			R.S. §1604
18	75		433			R.S. §2536
	76		433			R.S. §2535
20	80	2	439			R.S. §205
		4	439			R.S. §3808
	83	8	443			R.S. §935
		9	443			R.S. §936
		10	444			R.S. §937
	84		444			R.S. §1654
	88	1	447			R.S. §5281
		2	448			R.S. §5282
		2	448			R.S. §5291
		3	448			R.S. §5283
		4	448			R.S. §730
		4	448			R.S. §5284
		5	448			R.S. §5285
		6	449			R.S. §5286
		8	449			R.S. §5287
		9	449			R.S. §5288
		10	449			R.S. §5289
		11	450			R.S. §5290
		13	450			R.S. §5291
	91	1	450			R.S. §629
		2	451			R.S. §629
		2	451			R.S. §5551
		3	451			R.S. §5378
		4	451			R.S. §629
		4	451			R.S. §5379
		4	451			R.S. §5553

3 Stat.		Chapter	Section	Page	U.S.C. Title	U.S.C. Section	Status
15th Cong.							
1818—Apr.	20	91	6	452			R.S. §5377
			7	452			R.S. §629
			9	452			R.S. §1046
			9	452			R.S. §1047
		108	1	462			R.S. §545
			1	462			R.S. §572
			1	462			R.S. §579
			2	462			R.S. §551
			3	462			R.S. §551
			4	462			R.S. §608
			4	462			R.S. §658
			5	463			R.S. §767
			5	463			R.S. §776
		110	2	464			R.S. §2517
		113	2	465			R.S. §2518
		123		466			R.S. §2237
				466			R.S. §2238
				466			R.S. §2240
1819—Feb.	4	12	1	478			R.S. §531
			1	478			R.S. §767
			1	478			R.S. §770
			1	478			R.S. §776
			2	479			R.S. §571
			2	479			R.S. §1002
			3	479			R.S. §767
			3	479			R.S. §770
			3	479			R.S. §776
			4	479			R.S. §781
	20	36		486			R.S. §3050
Mar.	2	48	1	492			R.S. §4348
			1	492			R.S. §4351
			1	492			R.S. §4355
			1	492			R.S. §4359
			2	493			R.S. §4349
	3	70	2	502			R.S. §551
			4	503			R.S. §767
			5	503			R.S. §776
			5	503			R.S. §781
		77	1	510			R.S. §4293
			2	512			R.S. §4294
			3	513			R.S. §4295
			4	513			R.S. §4296
			5	513			R.S. §5368
		85		516			R.S. §2071
		98		526			R.S. §2369
		101	1	532			R.S. §629
			1	532			R.S. §5557
			1	532			R.S. §5558
			1	532			R.S. §5559
			1	532			R.S. §5560
			2	533			R.S. §5561
			3	533			R.S. §5562
			5	534			R.S. §5563
		107		538			R.S. §1531
				538			R.S. §1532
16th Cong.							
3 Stat.							
1820—Feb.	10	11	1	541			R.S. §263
			1	541			R.S. §336
			4	541			R.S. §336
			7	542			R.S. §337
			11	542			R.S. §4200
			12	543			R.S. §337
			14	543			R.S. §251
			15	543			R.S. §251
Mar.	6	22	6	547			R.S. §3689
	30	27		554			R.S. §604
Apr.	21	47	2	564			R.S. §552
			6	565			R.S. §767
			7	565			R.S. §776
	24	51	1	566			R.S. §2353
			1	566			R.S. §2397
			2	566			R.S. §2356
			3	566			R.S. §2357
			5	567			R.S. §2238
			5	567			R.S. §2360
			6	567			R.S. §2365
May	1	52	2	567			R.S. §228
			2	567			R.S. §429
			7	568			R.S. §3736
			8	568			R.S. §3670
	12	97		577			R.S. §1637
	15	102	1	582			R.S. §769
			1	582			R.S. §2244

16th Cong.					U.S.C.		
3 Stat.		Chapter	Section	Page	Title	Section	Status
1820—May	15	102	1	582			R.S. §2613
			2	582			R.S. §769
			3	582			R.S. §1191
			4	582			R.S. §238
		107	2	592			R.S. §3625
			2	592			R.S. §3626
			2	592			R.S. §3627
			2	592			R.S. §3628
			2	592			R.S. §3629
			2	592			R.S. §3630
			2	592			R.S. §3631
			2	592			R.S. §3632
			3	594			R.S. §3633
			3	594			R.S. §3634
			3	594			R.S. §3635
			4	595			R.S. §3636
			4	595			R.S. §3637
			5	595			R.S. §3636
			6	595			R.S. §3637
			8	596			R.S. §791
			8	596			R.S. §797
			9	596			R.S. §3638
		111	1	598			R.S. §572
			4	598			R.S. §781
		112		598			R.S. §4661
		113	1	600			R.S. §563
			2	600			R.S. §5368
			3	600			R.S. §730
			3	600			R.S. §5370
			3	600			R.S. §5371
			4	600			R.S. §730
			4	600			R.S. §5376
			5	600			R.S. §730
			5	601			R.S. §5375
		136		607			R.S. §2458
1821—Mar.	2	13	2	615			R.S. §1101
			8	615			R.S. §1134
			11	615			R.S. §1293
		14		616			R.S. §3098
				616			R.S. §3099
		16		617			R.S. §2566
				617			R.S. §2567
				617			R.S. §2662
	3	48		642			R.S. §2603
		51		643			R.S. §601
				643			R.S. §637
		52	3	644			R.S. §4661
		Pub. R. 2		646			R.S. §5536
				646			R.S. §5537
				646			R.S. §5538
17th Cong.							
3 Stat.							
1822—Feb.	23	9		651			R.S. §2460
Mar.	16	12	2	653			R.S. §551
			4	653			R.S. §767
			5	653			R.S. §776
			5	653			R.S. §781
Apr.	17	24		662			R.S. §2543
		25		662			R.S. §2531
May	6	56	4	681			R.S. §4208
	7	62	2	684			R.S. §2562
			2	684			R.S. §2563
			3	684			R.S. §2562
			3	684			R.S. §2563
			4	684			R.S. §2562
			4	684			R.S. §2563
			5	684			R.S. §2562
			5	684			R.S. §2563
			6	684			R.S. §2562
			7	684			R.S. §2562
			7	684			R.S. §2563
			8	684			R.S. §2619
			8	684			R.S. §2663
			11	685			R.S. §4348
		90	3	689			R.S. §273
			3	689			R.S. §313
			3	689			R.S. §3673
		96	3	692	40	307	Elim.
		107	1	693			R.S. §2535
			2	693			R.S. §2548
			2	693			R.S. §2549
			2	693			R.S. §2552
			2	693			R.S. §2619
			2	693			R.S. §2771

17th Cong. 3 Stat.	Chapter	Section	Page	U.S.C. Title	U.S.C. Section	Status
1822—May 7	107	5	694			R.S. §2518
		7	694			R.S. §2659
		8	694			R.S. §2660
		8	694			R.S. §2674
		9	695			R.S. §2690
		9	695			R.S. §2719
		10	695			R.S. §2391
		10	695			R.S. §2720
		11	695			R.S. §2691
		12	695			R.S. §2641
		13	695			R.S. §2643
		15	695			R.S. §2634
		15	695			R.S. §2723
		16	696			R.S. §2693
	118	1	697			R.S. §2215
		2	697			R.S. §2217
		3	697			R.S. §2216
1823—Jan. 23	6		721			R.S. §460
30	7		721			R.S. §563
			721			R.S. §4293
			721			R.S. §4294
			721			R.S. §4295
			721			R.S. §4296
			721			R.S. §5368
3	9		723			R.S. §1563
			723			R.S. §3648
Feb. 21	11		726			R.S. §531
			726			R.S. §546
			726			R.S. §552
			726			R.S. §571
			726			R.S. §572
			726			R.S. §817
Mar. 1	21	3	730			R.S. §2963
		4	730			R.S. §2841
		6	733			R.S. §2842
		7	733			R.S. §2843
		7	733			R.S. §2844
		8	733			R.S. §2845
		9	734			R.S. §2846
		10	734			R.S. §2847
		10	734			R.S. §2848
		11	734			R.S. §2849
		12	734			R.S. §2850
		16	735			R.S. §2529
		16	735			R.S. §2544
		16	735			R.S. §2549
		16	735			R.S. §2558
		16	735			R.S. §2560
		16	735			R.S. §2569
		16	735			R.S. §2609
		16	735			R.S. §2614
		16	735			R.S. §2947
		17	736			R.S. §2724
		17	736			R.S. §2725
		19	736			R.S. §2610
		19	736			R.S. §2945
		21	736			R.S. §2928
		22	737			R.S. §2851
		23	737			R.S. §2852
		24	737			R.S. §5417
		28	737			R.S. §3036
		29	738			R.S. §3034
		32	738			R.S. §3030
		32	738			R.S. §3031
	Pub. R. 1		789			R.S. §61
3	29	7	755			R.S. §2207
		7	755			R.S. §2208
		7	756			R.S. §2211
	38	1	771			R.S. §5421
		2	772			R.S. §5422
	41		773			R.S. §658
	45		776			R.S. §572
	53		779			R.S. §2366
	58	1	781			R.S. §3099
		4	782			R.S. §2799
	72		789			R.S. §563
18th Cong.						
4 Stat.						
1824—Jan. 7	3		1			R.S. §991
Mar. 10	28	2	9			R.S. §552
		8	10			R.S. §767
		9	10			R.S. §584
Apr. 22	39	1	19			R.S. §991
		2	20			R.S. §991

18th Cong.

4 Stat.	Chapter	Section	Page	U.S.C. Title	U.S.C. Section	Status
1824—May 24	138		31			R.S. §2372
	141		34			R.S. §2407
25	145	1	34			R.S. §658
		3	35			R.S. §817
26	158	2	43			R.S. §2562
	161		44			R.S. §2554
	167	1	48			R.S. §531
		1	48			R.S. §767
		1	48			R.S. §770
		1	48			R.S. §776
		1	48			R.S. §781
		3	49			R.S. §584
	169		50			R.S. §2286
	170		50			R.S. §545
			50			R.S. §551
			50			R.S. §579
	172	2	51			R.S. §3470
	186	1	69			R.S. §2167
		4	69			R.S. §2165
1825—Jan. 12	4		79			R.S. §2918
	5		80			R.S. §2362
			80			R.S. §3689
Feb. 25	13	3	91			R.S. §3689
Mar. 3	45		95			R.S. §3037
	64	38	113			R.S. §889
		38	113			R.S. §958
	65	1	115			R.S. §5385
		2	115			R.S. §5386
		3	115			R.S. §5391
		4	115			R.S. §5339
		4	115			R.S. §5345
		5	115			R.S. §730
		6	116			R.S. §5361
		7	116			R.S. §5362
		8	116			R.S. §5357
		9	116			R.S. §5358
		10	117			R.S. §5363
		11	117			R.S. §5387
		12	118			R.S. §5481
		13	118			R.S. §5392
		13	118			R.S. §5393
		14	118			R.S. §730
		14	118			R.S. §1032
		15	118			R.S. §5542
		17	119			R.S. §5416
		18	120			R.S. §5435
		18	120			R.S. §5436
		19	120			R.S. §5423
		22	121			R.S. §5346
		23	122			R.S. §5364
		26	122			R.S. §5328
	78		124			R.S. §658
	93	1	127			R.S. §1241
		2	127			R.S. §1241
	96	1	127			R.S. §2535
		1	127			R.S. §2603
		2	127			R.S. §2517
	99	1	129			R.S. §4313
		2	129			R.S. §4137
		3	129			R.S. §4138
		3	129			R.S. §4315
		4	129			R.S. §4139
		4	129			R.S. §4314
		5	129			R.S. §4139
	107	1	132			R.S. §4240
		2	133			R.S. §4239

19th Cong.

4 Stat.

4 Stat.	Chapter	Section	Page	U.S.C. Title	U.S.C. Section	Status
1826—Apr. 5	23		153			R.S. §572
May 4	37	2	160			R.S. §658
18	74	1	173			R.S. §1133
		1	173			R.S. §1139
		2	174			R.S. §1221
		3	174			R.S. §1304
20	83		179			R.S. §2276
	124		184			R.S. §985
	136		188			R.S. §810
22	154	2	194			R.S. §1829
1827—Jan. 24	4	1	197			R.S. §861
		1	197			R.S. §868
		1	197			R.S. §870
		2	199			R.S. §861
		2	199			R.S. §869
		2	199			R.S. §870
Feb. 22	21		206			R.S. §2771

				U.S.C.		
4 Stat.	**Chapter**	**Section**	**Page**	**Title**	**Section**	**Status**
19th Cong.						
1827—Mar. 2	41		226			R.S. §572
	58		237			R.S. §2527
			237			R.S. §2535
3	94	3	242			R.S. §2458
20th Cong.						
4 Stat.						
1828—Jan. 25	2		246			R.S. §1766
Mar. 10	16		254			R.S. §572
Apr. 28	41	2	264			R.S. §1838
		3	264			R.S. §3752
May 2	45	4	266			R.S. §1801
		4	266			R.S. §1810
		4	266			R.S. §1819
19	55	10	274			R.S. §252
		10	274			R.S. §257
	68	1	278			R.S. §913
		1	278			R.S. §992
		2	281			R.S. §988
23	71	7	287			R.S. §2361
	75	7	290			R.S. §5244
24	96		301			R.S. §2370
	111	1	308			R.S. §4228
		2	308			R.S. §4229
		4	309			R.S. §4230
	116	2	310			R.S. §2165
	119		312			R.S. §4321
	121	1	313			R.S. §1370
		1	313			R.S. §1371
		2	313			R.S. §1373
		2	313			R.S. §1374
		2	313			R.S. §1382
		3	313			R.S. §1369
1829—Jan. 6	5		330			R.S. §781
21	8		331			R.S. §658
	9		331			R.S. §781
	10	1	331			R.S. §2562
		1	331			R.S. §2619
		2	331			R.S. §2562
	12	1	332			R.S. §685
		1	332			R.S. §686
		2	332			R.S. §685
Feb. 24	19		335			R.S. §658
Mar. 2	41		359			R.S. §5280
3	51	3	363			R.S. §1812
21st Cong.						
4 Stat.						
1830—Jan. 13	Pub. R. 2		429			R.S. §94
Feb. 11	14	1	372			R.S. §4344
		2	373			R.S. §4346
Mar. 23	35		382			R.S. §2835
31	48	4	392			R.S. §2373
		5	392			R.S. §2374
		5	392			R.S. §2375
		5	392			R.S. §2376
	49		392			R.S. §2568
	50		392			R.S. §2542
May 5	87	1	399			R.S. §776
		2	399			R.S. §781
	89		399			R.S. §572
28	147	2	409			R.S. §2529
		2	409			R.S. §2544
		2	409			R.S. §2615
		2	409			R.S. §2929
		4	410			R.S. §2899
		5	410			R.S. §3032
		5	410			R.S. §3033
		6	411			R.S. §2530
		6	411			R.S. §2545
		8	411			R.S. §2925
	148	7	412			R.S. §2114
		8	412			R.S. §2114
	152		414			R.S. §2554
29	153	1	414			R.S. §349
		1	414			R.S. §3625
		1	414			R.S. §3626
		1	414			R.S. §3633
		1	414			R.S. §3750
		2	414			R.S. §372
		2	414			R.S. §791
		2	414			R.S. §797
		3	414			R.S. §373
		3	414			R.S. §374
		3	414			R.S. §375

21st Cong.

4 Stat.	Chapter	Section	Page	U.S.C. Title	U.S.C. Section	Status
1830—May 29	153	3	414			R.S. §773
		4	415			R.S. §772
		4	415			R.S. §3083
		5	415			R.S. §379
		6	415			R.S. §378
		7	415			R.S. §377
	163	1	417			R.S. §2412
		2	417			R.S. §2413
	179	1	417			R.S. §1342
		2	417			R.S. §1342
	183		418			R.S. §1342
	213	1	422			R.S. §572
		2	422			R.S. §658
31	219	1	425			R.S. §4219
		2	425			R.S. §4228
1831—Jan. 27	10		434			R.S. §572
Feb. 12	20		441			R.S. §4306
	24		442			R.S. §3036
Mar. 2	66	1	472			R.S. §2461
		2	472			R.S. §2462
		3	472			R.S. §4751
	76	1	475			R.S. §2568
		1	475			R.S. §2574
		2	476			R.S. §2575
		2	476			R.S. §3055
		3	476			R.S. §2546
		4	476			R.S. §2562
		4	476			R.S. §2563
		4	476			R.S. §2619
		4	476			R.S. §2664
		5	476			R.S. §2517
	87	1	480			R.S. §2544
		1	480			R.S. §2568
		1	480			R.S. §2619
		1	480			R.S. §2708
		1	480			R.S. §2822
		1	480			R.S. §2823
		1	480			R.S. §2825
		2	481			R.S. §2826
		2	481			R.S. §2827
		3	481			R.S. §2828
		3	481			R.S. §2829
		3	481			R.S. §2830
		4	481			R.S. §2831
		5	481			R.S. §2544
		5	481			R.S. §2708
		5	482			R.S. §2619
	91		482			R.S. §781
	99	1	487			R.S. §725
		2	488			R.S. §5399
3	116	1	492			R.S. §2207
		1	492			R.S. §2223
		4	493			R.S. §2230
		4	493			R.S. §2233
		5	493			R.S. §2208
		5	493			R.S. §2225

22d Cong.

4 Stat.	Chapter	Section	Page	U.S.C. Title	U.S.C. Section	Status
1832—Feb. 10	15		497			R.S. §658
Apr. 5	65		503			R.S. §2354
			503			R.S. §2397
	66		503			R.S. §940
	67	2	504			R.S. §1109
		2	504			R.S. §1110
May 31	109	2	520			R.S. §2063
July 9	174	1	564			R.S. §462
		1	564			R.S. §463
		3	564			R.S. §464
		4	564			R.S. §2139
		5	564			R.S. §2073
10	191	1	570			R.S. §4681
		2	571			R.S. §4685
	194	1	572			R.S. §4750
		1	572			R.S. §4758
		5	573			R.S. §4807
		5	573			R.S. §4809
		5	573			R.S. §4810
13	201	2	577			R.S. §2562
		2	577			R.S. §2563
		8	577			R.S. §2563
	207	8	579			R.S. §4228
14	221	1	579			R.S. §81
		2	579			R.S. §95

22d Cong.				U.S.C.		
4 Stat.	Chapter	Section	Page	Title	Section	Status
1832—July 14	221	3	579			R.S. §83
		4	579			R.S. §84
	224	4	582			R.S. §1188
	227	5	591			R.S. §2885
		9	592			R.S. §2949
		13	593			R.S. §2911
	233		597			R.S. §5293
	Pub. R. 11		608			R.S. §198
			608			R.S. §510
1833—Feb. 5	16		611			R.S. §2517
Mar. 2	54		619			R.S. §470
			619			R.S. §471
	55	3	630			R.S. §3009
	57	1	632			R.S. §3465
		2	632			R.S. §620
		2	632			R.S. §934
		3	633			R.S. §543
		3	633			R.S. §646
		4	634			R.S. §645
		6	634			R.S. §5537
		6	634			R.S. §5538
		7	634			R.S. §751
		7	634			R.S. §752
		7	634			R.S. §753
	67	8	647			R.S. §2463
		8	647			R.S. §4205
	68	6	647			R.S. §1118
		6	647			R.S. §1342
	74	1	651			R.S. §2527
		1	651			R.S. §2529
		2	651			R.S. §2527
		2	651			R.S. §2529
23d Cong.						
4 Stat.						
1834—June 28	102		702			R.S. §2359
30	132	2	713			R.S. §1342
		2	713			R.S. §1621
		3	713			R.S. §1610
		4	713			R.S. §1603
		4	713			R.S. §1617
		5	713			R.S. §1612
		6	713			R.S. §1598
		8	713			R.S. §1620
		9	713			R.S. §1604
	133		714			R.S. §1172
	135	1	715			R.S. §2566
		1	715			R.S. §2567
		1	715			R.S. §2568
		1	715			R.S. §2666
		2	715			R.S. §2832
		3	715			R.S. §2833
		4	715			R.S. §2527
		5	715			R.S. §2543
		9	716			R.S. §2541
		10	716			R.S. §2542
		10	716			R.S. §2619
		10	716			R.S. §2667
		11	716			R.S. §2517
		11	716			R.S. §2518
	161	2	729			R.S. §2129
		2	729			R.S. §2131
		3	729			R.S. §2130
		3	729			R.S. §2132
		4	729			R.S. §2133
		6	730			R.S. §2134
		7	730			R.S. §2135
		8	730			R.S. §2137
		9	730			R.S. §2117
		10	730			R.S. §2147
		11	730			R.S. §2118
		12	730			R.S. §2116
		13	731			R.S. §2111
		14	731			R.S. §2112
		15	731			R.S. §2113
		16	731			R.S. §2154
		16	731			R.S. §2155
		17	731			R.S. §2156
		18	732			R.S. §2157
		19	732			R.S. §2152
		21	732			R.S. §2141
		21	732			R.S. §2150
		22	733			R.S. §2126
		23	733			R.S. §2150
		23	733			R.S. §2151

23d Cong.				U.S.C.		
4 Stat.	Chapter	Section	Page	Title	Section	Status
1834—June 30	161	24	733			R.S. §533
		25	733			R.S. §2145
		27	733			R.S. §2124
		28	734			R.S. §2125
	162	3	735			R.S. §2050
		4	735			R.S. §2059
		4	735			R.S. §2060
		4	735			R.S. §2062
		5	736			R.S. §2065
		7	736			R.S. §2058
		7	736			R.S. §2066
		8	737			R.S. §2075
		9	737			R.S. §2068
		9	737			R.S. §2069
		9	737			R.S. §2072
		10	737			R.S. §2074
		10	737			R.S. §2076
		10	737			R.S. §2077
		11	737			R.S. §2086
		12	737			R.S. §2062
		12	737			R.S. §2082
		13	737			R.S. §2083
		13	737			R.S. §2088
		13	737			R.S. §2091
		14	738			R.S. §2078
		16	738			R.S. §2110
		17	738			R.S. §465
	163		739			R.S. §5539
1835—Feb. 24	23		753			R.S. §781
Mar. 8	27	1	756			R.S. §1557
		1	757			R.S. §1372
		1	757			R.S. §1442
		1	757			R.S. §1593
		2	757			R.S. §1566
	33		773			R.S. §5442
	34		773			R.S. §572
	40	1	775			R.S. §5360
		2	776			R.S. §5359
		3	776			R.S. §4347
		4	777			R.S. §1031
		4	777			R.S. §1032
		5	777			R.S. §5536
		5	777			R.S. §5548
	46	1	779			R.S. §470
		2	779			R.S. §470
		2	779			R.S. §471
		3	779			R.S. §470
	49		780			R.S. §1141
			780			R.S. §1150
			780			R.S. §3715
24th Cong.						
5 Stat.						
1836—Mar. 19	44	1	7			R.S. §1650
		2	7			R.S. §1653
		3	7			R.S. §1652
		4	7			R.S. §1657
		5	7			R.S. §1656
Apr. 20	54	10	14			R.S. §1881
		10	14			R.S. §1882
	55		16			R.S. §4377
May 9	59	2	25			R.S. §209
20	76		31			R.S. §2448
	77		31			R.S. §1766
			31			R.S. §4734
June 15	100	4	51			R.S. §533
		4	51			R.S. §551
		4	51			R.S. §572
		4	51			R.S. §581
		6	51			R.S. §767
		7	51			R.S. §776
		7	51			R.S. §781
23	119	2	57			R.S. §5245
	121	5	60			R.S. §3689
July 1	234	2	62			R.S. §551
		4	62			R.S. §767
		5	62			R.S. §776
		5	62			R.S. §781
2	270	8	81			R.S. §276
		15	82			R.S. §889
		15	82			R.S. §952
		15	82			R.S. §958
		15	82			R.S. §964
		16	83			R.S. §775
		16	83			R.S. §792

24th Cong.

5 Stat.	Chapter	Section	Page	U.S.C. Title	U.S.C. Section	Status
1836—July 2	270	38	88			R.S. §5535
		44	89			R.S. §276
4	352	1	107			R.S. §440
		1	107			R.S. §446
		1	107			R.S. §453
		2	109			R.S. §448
		2	109			R.S. §891
		3	110			R.S. §449
		4	111			R.S. §447
		4	111			R.S. §459
		6	111			R.S. §450
		7	111			R.S. §460
		7	111			R.S. §891
		7	111			R.S. §2469
		9	111			R.S. §2245
		12	112			R.S. §162
		13	112			R.S. §2247
		14	112			R.S. §452
	356	6	117			R.S. §64
1837—Jan. 9	1	1	135			R.S. §2093
		2	135			R.S. §2094
		3	135			R.S. §2095
		4	135			R.S. §2096
Feb. 13	13		146			R.S. §2660
			146			R.S. §2771
Mar. 2	21		153			R.S. §1418
			153			R.S. §1419
			153			R.S. §4236
3	33	1	163, 164			R.S. §447
	34	2	177			R.S. §608
		2	177			R.S. §658
		3	177			R.S. §571
		3	177			R.S. §608
		3	177			R.S. §1002
	43	1	187			R.S. §470
		2	187			R.S. §471

25th Cong.

5 Stat.	Chapter	Section	Page	U.S.C. Title	U.S.C. Section	Status
1837—Oct. 12	3	2	204			R.S. §826
16	10	2	207			R.S. §3689
Dec. 22	1		208			R.S. §1536
1838—Feb. 22	12		210			R.S. §658
Mar. 10	33		215			R.S. §572
			215			R.S. §658
28	46		215			R.S. §571
			215			R.S. §1002
June 18	115	1	247			R.S. §539
		1	247			R.S. §572
		1	247			R.S. §608
		1	247			R.S. §658
		2	247			R.S. §552
		2	247			R.S. §572
		6	248			R.S. §767
		6	248			R.S. §776
		7	248			R.S. §781
	118	1	249			R.S. §547
		1	249			R.S. §781
		3	250			R.S. §552
		7	250			R.S. §584
		8	250			R.S. §586
		10	250			R.S. §776
		11	250			R.S. §767
July 5	162	7	257			R.S. §1130
		10	257			R.S. §1137
		17	258			R.S. §1146
		17	258			R.S. §1148
		17	258			R.S. §1294
		18	259			R.S. §1124
		19	259			R.S. §1309
		19	259			R.S. §1337
		20	259			R.S. §1190
		25	259			R.S. §1184
		25	259			R.S. §1185
		25	259			R.S. §1188
		27	260			R.S. §1153
		28	260			R.S. §1321
		30	260			R.S. §1116
		31	260			R.S. §1224
7	169	8	267			R.S. §2566
		8	267			R.S. §2567
		8	267			R.S. §2619
		8	267			R.S. §2668
	175		287			R.S. §2566
			287			R.S. §2832

25th Cong.

5 Stat.	Chapter	Section	Page	U.S.C. Title	U.S.C. Section	Status
1838—July 7	178		288			R.S. §2798
	185		297			R.S. §5437
	187		302			R.S. §204
	193		308			R.S. §658
	194		308			R.S. §1121
			308			R.S. §1153
1839—Jan. 18	3	1	313			R.S. §547
		1	313			R.S. §552
		1	313			R.S. §586
		1	313			R.S. §608
		1	313			R.S. §767
		1	313			R.S. §776
		1	313			R.S. §781
		9	314			R.S. §672
Feb. 6	20	2	315			R.S. §552
		2	315			R.S. §581
		7	316			R.S. §767
		7	316			R.S. §776
		10	316			R.S. §584
16	27	1	317			R.S. §571
		1	317			R.S. §608
		1	317			R.S. §658
		2	317			R.S. §608
		2	317			R.S. §658
		3	317			R.S. §1002
28	35		321			R.S. §942
			321			R.S. §990
	36	1	321			R.S. §737
		3	322			R.S. §732
		4	322			R.S. §1047
		5	322			R.S. §5327
		6	322			R.S. §1020
		8	322			R.S. §615
		8	322			R.S. §616
Mar. 3	81	5	337			R.S. §572
	82	2	348			R.S. §3010
	83	3	349			R.S. §1765
		3	349			R.S. §1779

26th Cong.

5 Stat.	Chapter	Section	Page	U.S.C. Title	U.S.C. Section	Status
1840—Mar. 4	4	1	369			R.S. §470
		2	369			R.S. §470
		2	369			R.S. §471
		3	369			R.S. §470
		4	370			R.S. §470
		4	370			R.S. §471
Apr. 4	6	1	370			R.S. §4339
		2	370			R.S. §4573
May 8	23		380			R.S. §572
27	27		381			R.S. §2528
June 12	35		384			R.S. §2246
	36	1	384			R.S. §2218
		2	385			R.S. §2248
July 4	43	1	392			R.S. §672
		2	393			R.S. §669
		2	393			R.S. §670
		3	393			R.S. §691
		4	393			R.S. §967
20	47		394			R.S. §800
			394			R.S. §801
	48		395			R.S. §4523
			395			R.S. §4583
			395			R.S. §4584
			396			R.S. §4559
			396			R.S. §4560
			396			R.S. §4561
			396			R.S. §4562
			397			R.S. §1736
			397			R.S. §4563
			397			R.S. §4575
	50	3	398			R.S. §1309
		3	398			R.S. §1337
	Pub. R. 5		409			R.S. §98
			409			R.S. §503
			409			R.S. §3799
1841—Jan. 14	2		410			R.S. §942
			410			R.S. §990
Mar. 3	26	2	417			R.S. §458
	35	1	427			R.S. §770
		5	432			R.S. §2647
		5	432			R.S. §2688
		5	432			R.S. §2689
		5	432			R.S. §2690
		5	432			R.S. §2704
		5	432			R.S. §2719

5 Stat.	Chapter	Section	Page	U.S.C. Title	U.S.C. Section	Status
26th Cong.						
1841—Mar. 3	35	5	432			R.S. §2720
		6	432			R.S. §2956
27th Cong.						
1841—Aug. 16	8	2	440			R.S. §4724
Sept. 4	16	7	455			R.S. §2249
		8	455			R.S. §2378
		8	455			R.S. §2379
		10	455			R.S. §2258
		10	455			R.S. §2259
		10	455			R.S. §2260
		10	455			R.S. §2261
		11	456			R.S. §2273
		12	456			R.S. §2238
		12	456			R.S. §2263
		13	456			R.S. §2262
		14	457			R.S. §2282
		15	457			R.S. §2264
11	25	2	465			R.S. §3659
	Pub. R. 6		468			R.S. §355
1842—May 18	29		480			R.S. §1888
June 4	38		489			R.S. §2534
July 27	68		496			R.S. §572
Aug. 1	109		499			R.S. §913
			499			R.S. §992
3	120	1	499			R.S. §2533
		2	499			R.S. §2531
		3	499			R.S. §2533
		3	500			R.S. §2534
		3	500			R.S. §2669
4	121		500			R.S. §1395
			500			R.S. §1405
	123		504			R.S. §1002
9	126		504			R.S. §2527
16	179		507			R.S. §2603
			507			R.S. §2604
	180		507			R.S. §658
	181		507			R.S. §208
23	183	2	510			R.S. §1765
	186	2	512			R.S. §1191
		2	512			R.S. §1663
		2	512			R.S. §1664
		3	513			R.S. §1133
		6	513			R.S. §1311
	188	1	516			R.S. §727
		1	516			R.S. §1014
		1	517			R.S. §563
		1	517			R.S. §4546
		1	517			R.S. §4547
		2	517			R.S. §879
		3	517			R.S. §563
		3	517			R.S. §578
		3	517			R.S. §4211
		4	517			R.S. §5356
		5	517			R.S. §574
		5	517			R.S. §638
		6	518			R.S. §862
		6	518			R.S. §917
		6	518			R.S. §918
		8	518			R.S. §966
26	202	2	524			R.S. §677
		11	525			R.S. §60
		11	525			R.S. §194
		11	525			R.S. §195
		12	525			R.S. §1764
		13	525			R.S. §173
		13	525			R.S. §174
		13	525			R.S. §175
		14	525			R.S. §3660
		15	526			R.S. §171
		15	526			R.S. §172
		16	526			R.S. §192
		19	527			R.S. §3683
		20	527			R.S. §60
		20	527			R.S. §62
		20	527			R.S. §193
		25	533			R.S. §3681
	205		534			R.S. §2271
	206	1	535			R.S. §1624
		2	535			R.S. §1549
		4	535			R.S. §1384
		6	536			R.S. §1389
	207	1	536			R.S. §237
		1	536			R.S. §257

27th Cong.

5 Stat.		Chapter	Section	Page	U.S.C. Title	U.S.C. Section	Status
1842—Aug.	26	207	2	537			R.S. §11
			2	537			R.S. §237
	29	257		539			R.S. §751
				539			R.S. §752
				539			R.S. §753
				539			R.S. §762
				539			R.S. §763
				539			R.S. §764
				539			R.S. §765
				539			R.S. §766
		259	2	541			R.S. §1844
			2	541			R.S. §1886
		264		545			R.S. §677
				545			R.S. §681
				545			R.S. §682
				545			R.S. §683
	30	270	15	563			R.S. §3017
			15	563			R.S. §3027
			16	563			R.S. §2902
			16	563			R.S. §2905
			17	564			R.S. §2909
			17	564			R.S. §2922
			17	564			R.S. §2923
			17	564			R.S. §2924
			17	564			R.S. §2930
			19	565			R.S. §2865
			20	565			R.S. §2499
			21	565			R.S. §2901
			21	565			R.S. §2921
			22	566			R.S. §2946
			23	566			R.S. §2949
			24	566			R.S. §2652
	31	279	6	577			R.S. §1391
			6	577			R.S. §1394
			7	577			R.S. §1552
		286	2	579			R.S. §419
			8	580			R.S. §420
1843—Jan.	20	4	1	597			R.S. §470
			2	597			R.S. §471
Feb.	15	82	1	600			R.S. §658
			2	600			R.S. §572
	24	44		601			R.S. §658
Mar.	1	49		602			R.S. §3689
		52	2	606			R.S. §1315
	3	71		609			R.S. §2517
		72		609			R.S. §2507
		74	2	610			R.S. §582
		78	1	611			R.S. §2122
			2	611			R.S. §2123
		83		617			R.S. §429
				617			R.S. §3718
				617			R.S. §3720
		86	2	620			R.S. §2269
			4	620			R.S. §2261
			5	620			R.S. §2265
			6	620			R.S. §2270
			9	621			R.S. §2272
		95	1	627			R.S. §891
			1	627			R.S. §2470
			2	628			R.S. §891
		97		628			R.S. §658
		100		637			R.S. §2214
				640			R.S. §4683
				640			R.S. §4684
		Pub. R. 7		650			R.S. §2443

28th Cong.

5 Stat.		Chapter	Section	Page	U.S.C. Title	U.S.C. Section	Status
1844—Apr.	2	8	1	653			R.S. §3074
			1	653			R.S. §3075
			1	653			R.S. §3076
			1	653			R.S. §3077
			2	653			R.S. §3689
			3	654			R.S. §3079
	12	12	3	655			R.S. §658
	30	15		657			R.S. §4724
				657			R.S. §4735
		Pub. R. 5		717			R.S. §3798
May	31	31		658			R.S. §699
June	3	37		660			R.S. §4691
	4	38		660			R.S. §572
		39		661			R.S. §2619
	12	47		663			R.S. §2897
	15	51	1	664			R.S. §2527
			1	664			R.S. §2548

28th Cong. 5 Stat.	Chapter	Section	Page	U.S.C. Title	U.S.C. Section	Status
1844—June 15	51	1	664			R.S. §2549
		1	664			R.S. §2552
		1	664			R.S. §2553
		1	664			R.S. §2559
		1	664			R.S. §2560
		2	664			R.S. §2566
		3	664			R.S. §2568
	69	1	670			R.S. §1849
		2	671			R.S. §1856
	Pub. R. 16		719			R.S. §259
			719			R.S. §334
			719			R.S. §335
17	103		680			R.S. §533
	105	1	681			R.S. §69
		1	681			R.S. §170
		1	681			R.S. §4687
		2	693			R.S. §3663
		2	693			R.S. §3664
		5	696			R.S. §267
		6	696			R.S. §266
	107	1	700			R.S. §1414
		1	700			R.S. §1415
		1	700			R.S. §1438
		1	700			R.S. §1439
		1	700			R.S. §1567
		1	700			R.S. §1568
		4	703			R.S. §1550
		5	703			R.S. §3730
1845—Jan. 23	1		721			R.S. §131
			721			R.S. §133
			721			R.S. §134
Feb. 20	17	2	725			R.S. §1433
26	20		726			R.S. §566
			726			R.S. §576
	22		727			R.S. §3011
Mar. 1	39		731			R.S. §658
3	43	20	739			R.S. §563
		20	739			R.S. §629
	70	1	750			R.S. §3002
		7	751			R.S. §3056
		9	752			R.S. §3008
		10	752			R.S. §3017
		11	752			R.S. §3057
	71	2	763			R.S. §3680
	75	1	788			R.S. §3689
		3	788			R.S. §534
		3	788			R.S. §551
		4	788			R.S. §581
		7	788			R.S. §767
		7	788			R.S. §770
		8	788			R.S. §776
		8	788			R.S. §781
	76	2	789			R.S. §551
		4	789			R.S. §767
		4	789			R.S. §770
		5	789			R.S. §776
		5	789			R.S. §781
		6	790			R.S. §3689
	77	2	794			R.S. §1404
		3	794			R.S. §3721
		6	794			R.S. §1442
		6	794			R.S. §1557
		7	794			R.S. §1391
	78		795			R.S. §2747
	Pub. R. 15		801			R.S. §2576
29th Cong.						
9 Stat.						
1845—Dec. 29	1	2	1			R.S. §551
		3	1			R.S. §767
		3	1			R.S. §770
		3	1			R.S. §776
		3	2			R.S. §781
31	2	1	2			R.S. §2578
		1	2			R.S. §2579
		2	2			R.S. §2578
		2	2			R.S. §2579
		3	2			R.S. §2578
		3	2			R.S. §2579
		3	2			R.S. §2709
1846—Jan. 7	Pub. R. 2		108			R.S. §3669
14	4		3			R.S. §470
Feb. 11	7	1	3			R.S. §2687
		2	3			R.S. §2645
		3	3			R.S. §2948

29th Cong.				U.S.C.		
9 Stat.	Chapter	Section	Page	Title	Section	Status
1846—May 13	16	7	10			R.S. §4730
15	21	1	12			R.S. §1154
		4	13			R.S. §1156
		4	13			R.S. §1157
		5	13			R.S. §1152
June 17	28	2	17			R.S. §1191
18	29	6	18			R.S. §1130
		7	18			R.S. §1205
		11	18			R.S. §1162
27	34		20			R.S. §2092
July 15	38		38			R.S. §658
16	56	1	38			R.S. §2601
		7	38			R.S. §2602
20	60		38			R.S. §3689
			38			R.S. §4251
			38			R.S. §4585
			38			R.S. §4587
29	66		41			R.S. §3477
30	74	4	43			R.S. §2920
		9	44			R.S. §2616
		9	44			R.S. §2617
		10	44			R.S. §1624
Aug. 3	78	1	51			R.S. §2450
		1	51			R.S. §2451
		2	51			R.S. §2452
		3	51			R.S. §2453
		4	51			R.S. §2454
		5	51			R.S. §2455
6	84	1	53			R.S. §2964
		1	53			R.S. §2973
		1	53			R.S. §2974
		1	53			R.S. §2975
		1	53			R.S. §2979
		1	53			R.S. §2980
		1	53			R.S. §3009
		3	54			R.S. §2985
		3	55			R.S. §2986
		3	55			R.S. §2987
		4	55			R.S. §2988
		5	55			R.S. §251
		5	55			R.S. §2989
	89	4	57			R.S. §551
		5	57			R.S. §767
		5	57			R.S. §770
		5	57			R.S. §776
		5	58			R.S. §781
	90	1	59			R.S. §3591
		1	59			R.S. §3593
		3	59			R.S. §3598
		3	59			R.S. §3599
		4	59			R.S. §3598
		4	59			R.S. §3599
		5	60			R.S. §3595
		5	60			R.S. §3600
		6	60			R.S. §3639
		7	60			R.S. §3600
		9	61			R.S. §3615
		10	61			R.S. §3640
		10	61			R.S. §3642
		10	61			R.S. §3644
		11	62			R.S. §3649
		12	62			R.S. §3650
		13	62			R.S. §3653
		15	62			R.S. §3616
		16	63			R.S. §887
		16	63			R.S. §3643
		16	63			R.S. §5490
		16	63			R.S. §5491
		16	63			R.S. §5492
		16	63			R.S. §5493
		16	63			R.S. §5494
		16	63			R.S. §5495
		16	63			R.S. §5496
		18	64			R.S. §3473
		20	64			R.S. §3651
		21	65			R.S. §3645
		21	65			R.S. §3652
		22	65			R.S. §3596
		22	65			R.S. §3597
8	96	2	71			R.S. §1327
		2	71			R.S. §1328
		2	71			R.S. §1329
		3	71			R.S. §1309
	98	1	72			R.S. §658
		2	72			R.S. §1037
		3	72			R.S. §810
		3	72			R.S. §813

29th Cong.				U.S.C.		
9 Stat.	Chapter	Section	Page	Title	Section	Status
1846—Aug. 8	98	3	72			R.S. §1038
		3	72			R.S. §1039
		4	73			R.S. §1018
		5	73			R.S. §5383
		6	73			R.S. §1019
		7	73			R.S. §879
		7	73			R.S. §881
		11	74			R.S. §878
	100	1	75			R.S. §1777
		2	76			R.S. §908
	102		77			R.S. §3053
	103	3	78			R.S. §5246
	104		78			R.S. §1002
	105		78			R.S. §728
	106	2	79			R.S. §2231
		2	79			R.S. §2232
	107	1	80			R.S. §895
		2	80			R.S. §71
	110		82			R.S. §3074
10	176	1	98			R.S. §1416
		6	101			R.S. §3719
	178	1	102			R.S. §5579
		2	102			R.S. §3689
		2	102			R.S. §5590
		3	103			R.S. §5580
		3	103			R.S. §5581
		3	103			R.S. §5582
		3	103			R.S. §5593
		4	104			R.S. §5588
		5	104			R.S. §5589
		6	105			R.S. §5586
		7	105			R.S. §5583
		7	105			R.S. §5584
		8	105			R.S. §5585
		8	105			R.S. §5587
		9	105			R.S. §5592
		11	106			R.S. §5594
	180	2	107			R.S. §3707
1847—Feb. 9	7		123			R.S. §3689
			123			R.S. §3698
11	8	8	125			R.S. §1169
		9	126			R.S. §2418
		9	126			R.S. §2419
15	9		126			R.S. §658
20	13	2	127			R.S. §4781
22	17		128			R.S. §567
			128			R.S. §568
			128			R.S. §569
			128			R.S. §704
23	20	1	131			R.S. §534
		1	131			R.S. §551
		1	131			R.S. §553
		2	131			R.S. §572
		2	131			R.S. §575
		2	131			R.S. §581
		2	131			R.S. §658
		3	131			R.S. §4241
		5	131			R.S. §767
		5	131			R.S. §770
		6	131			R.S. §776
		6	131			R.S. §781
		8	132			R.S. §534
Mar. 2	40	3	154			R.S. §1598
		3	154			R.S. §1602
3	48	1	171			R.S. §1549
		1	171			R.S. §3618
		1	171			R.S. §3692
		1	172			R.S. §1405
		2	172			R.S. §3721
		3	172			R.S. §1414
		3	172			R.S. §1415
		3	172			R.S. §1438
		3	172			R.S. §1568
		4	173			R.S. §1569
		6	173			R.S. §284
	51		175			R.S. §730
			175			R.S. §5374
	53	3	179			R.S. §3689
	55		181			R.S. §941
	57	1	182			R.S. §2578
		1	182			R.S. §2579
		2	182			R.S. §2578
		2	182			R.S. §2579
		3	182			R.S. §2578
		3	182			R.S. §2579
		3	182			R.S. §2710

29th Cong.					U.S.C.		
9 Stat.		Chapter	Section	Page	Title	Section	Status
1847—Mar.	3	57	4	183			R.S. §2578
			4	183			R.S. §2579
		60	1	183			R.S. §2517
			2	183			R.S. §2517
			2	183			R.S. §2518
			3	183			R.S. §2517
			3	183			R.S. §2518
		61	2	184			R.S. §1130
			12	185			R.S. §1187
			13	185			R.S. §1183
			17	186			R.S. §1214
			17	186			R.S. §1216
			17	186			R.S. §1285
			17	186			R.S. §1286
			18	186			R.S. §1101
			22	187			R.S. §1187
		66	1	203			R.S. §2066
			3	203			R.S. §2086
			3	203			R.S. §2087
30th Cong.							
9 Stat.							
1848—Jan.	26	4		209			R.S. §451
		5		209			R.S. §2535
				209			R.S. §4345
				210			R.S. §2536
				210			R.S. §2537
				210			R.S. §2540
Feb.	22	12	2	212			R.S. §567
			2	212			R.S. §568
			2	212			R.S. §569
			2	212			R.S. §704
Mar.	14	18		213			R.S. §933
May	9	40		220			R.S. §2566
				220			R.S. §2567
				220			R.S. §2616
	27	48	1	232			R.S. §3126
			2	232			R.S. §3127
	29	50	4	234			R.S. §576
			4	234			R.S. §581
June	26	70	1	237			R.S. §2933
			2	238			R.S. §2934
			3	238			R.S. §2935
			4	238			R.S. §2936
			4	238			R.S. §2937
			5	238			R.S. §2529
			5	238			R.S. §2544
			5	238			R.S. §2549
			5	238			R.S. §2558
			5	238			R.S. §2569
			5	238			R.S. §2612
			5	238			R.S. §2743
			6	239			R.S. §2611
			6	239			R.S. §2616
			6	239			R.S. §2617
		73		240			R.S. §86
				240			R.S. §87
July	1	Pub. R. 13		336			R.S. §4743
	19	104	3	247			R.S. §1130
			3	247			R.S. §1187
	29	118	2	264			R.S. §2099
			4	264			R.S. §3689
Aug.	3	121	11	272			R.S. §3721
			12	272			R.S. §1399
			12	272			R.S. §1400
			12	272			R.S. §1401
			13	272			R.S. §1551
	7	141	2	274			R.S. §4214
			3	274			R.S. §4215
		143	1	274			R.S. §532
			1	274			R.S. §552
			1	274			R.S. §572
			2	274			R.S. §572
		144		275			R.S. §2527
		145		275			R.S. §2601
	11	151	1	280			R.S. §535
			1	280			R.S. §572
			2	280			R.S. §552
			2	280			R.S. §572
			4	280			R.S. §608
			4	280			R.S. §658
			5	280			R.S. §608
			5	280			R.S. §658
			7	281			R.S. §767
			7	281			R.S. §776

30th Cong.				U.S.C.		
9 Stat.	**Chapter**	**Section**	**Page**	**Title**	**Section**	**Status**
1848—Aug. 11	151	7	281			R.S. §777
		8	281			R.S. §571
		8	281			R.S. §608
		8	281			R.S. §658
		9	281			R.S. §1002
		10	281			R.S. §584
	154		282			R.S. §658
	155	1	282			R.S. §4729
		2	283			R.S. §4728
		2	283			R.S. §4729
		3	283			R.S. §4728
		3	283			R.S. §4729
	Pub. R. 26		340			R.S. §94
12	166		292			R.S. §828
	167	1	302			R.S. §5270
		2	302			R.S. §5271
		3	302			R.S. §5272
		4	303			R.S. §5273
		5	303			R.S. §5274
	169		303			R.S. §572
			303			R.S. §658
14	177	10	327			R.S. §1881
		10	327			R.S. §1882
1849—Jan. 19	20		341			R.S. §470
Feb. 22	61	1	346			R.S. §907
		2	347			R.S. §372
		2	347			R.S. §883
		3	347			R.S. §882
Mar. 2	80	3	350			R.S. §1187
		3	350			R.S. §1192
	82		350			R.S. §907
	83	3	351			R.S. §1121
		4	351			R.S. §1130
3	103		377			R.S. §1618
	108	1	395			R.S. §161
		1	395			R.S. §277
		1	395			R.S. §437
		1	395			R.S. §440
		2	395			R.S. §444
		3	395			R.S. §248
		3	395			R.S. §441
		5	395			R.S. §441
		6	395			R.S. §441
		7	395			R.S. §441
		7	395			R.S. §443
		8	395			R.S. §441
		9	395			R.S. §441
		12	396			R.S. §269
		12	396			R.S. §316
		12	396			R.S. §317
		12	396			R.S. §318
		12	396			R.S. §2639
		13	396			R.S. §234
		13	396			R.S. §245
		13	396			R.S. §2204
	110	1	398			R.S. §3617
		2	398			R.S. §3048
		2	398			R.S. §3689
		5	399			R.S. §2978
		6	399			R.S. §258
	112	1	400			R.S. §2582
		2	400			R.S. §2582
		3	400			R.S. §2582
	118		403			R.S. §800
			403			R.S. §801
	122	1	409			R.S. §2578
		1	409			R.S. §2579
		7	410			R.S. §4342
	124	1	410			R.S. §586
		1	410			R.S. §744
		1	411			R.S. §584
		3	411			R.S. §744
		4	412			R.S. §560
		5	412			R.S. §768
		5	412			R.S. §778
	125		412			R.S. §2517
	127	2	414			R.S. §2549
		2	414			R.S. §4343
	129	1	414			R.S. §3482
		2	415			R.S. §3483
		2	415			R.S. §3689
		3	415			R.S. §277
		5	415			R.S. §3486
		6	416			R.S. §3487
		6	416			R.S. §3689
		7	416			R.S. §3485

30th Cong.					U.S.C.	
9 Stat.	**Chapter**	**Section**	**Page**	**Title**	**Section**	**Status**
1849—Mar. 3	Pub. R. 17		419			R.S. § 285
31st Cong.						
9 Stat.						
1850—Feb. 14	Pub. R. 4	1	560			R.S. § 2954
May 23	11	1	428			R.S. § 2176
		2	428			R.S. § 2177
		3	428			R.S. § 2178
		4	428			R.S. § 2179
		5	429			R.S. § 2185
		5	429			R.S. § 2186
		5	429			R.S. § 2194
		6	429			R.S. § 2180
		7	429			R.S. § 2189
		8	429			R.S. § 2197
		9	430			R.S. § 2181
		10	430			R.S. § 2187
		11	430			R.S. § 2192
		12	430			R.S. § 2198
		13	430			R.S. § 2199
		14	431			R.S. § 2180
		14	431			R.S. § 2182
		14	431			R.S. § 2193
		14	431			R.S. § 2202
		15	431			R.S. § 2191
		16	431			R.S. § 2203
		18	431			R.S. § 2190
		19	431			R.S. § 2183
		19	431			R.S. § 2196
		19	431			R.S. § 2204
		21	432			R.S. § 2201
		22	432			R.S. § 2206
		23	432			R.S. § 2175
		25	432			R.S. § 21
		27	433			R.S. § 2184
June 5	16	2	437			R.S. § 2046
		4	437			R.S. § 2058
July 29	27	1	440			R.S. § 4192
		1	440			R.S. § 4193
		3	440			R.S. § 4194
		4	441			R.S. § 4195
		5	441			R.S. § 4142
		5	441			R.S. § 4155
		5	441			R.S. § 4196
		5	441			R.S. § 4319
		6	441			R.S. § 4559
		7	441			R.S. § 5367
	29		442			R.S. § 2531
	30	1	442			R.S. § 587
		1	442			R.S. § 591
		1	442			R.S. § 596
		2	443			R.S. § 593
		3	443			R.S. § 595
		4	443			R.S. § 594
Aug. 30	43	2	445			R.S. § 2188
Sept. 9	49	2	447			R.S. § 1839
		2	447			R.S. § 1840
		2	447			R.S. § 1896
		3	447			R.S. § 1841
		3	447			R.S. § 1842
		4	448			R.S. § 1843
		4	448			R.S. § 1844
		5	448			R.S. § 1847
		5	448			R.S. § 1848
		5	448			R.S. § 1849
		5	448			R.S. § 1922
		6	448			R.S. § 1846
		6	448			R.S. § 1859
		6	448			R.S. § 1860
		7	449			R.S. § 1850
		7	449			R.S. § 1851
		8	449			R.S. § 1857
		9	449			R.S. § 1854
		10	449			R.S. § 702
		10	449			R.S. § 1864
		10	449			R.S. § 1865
		10	449			R.S. § 1866
		10	449			R.S. § 1867
		10	449			R.S. § 1868
		10	449			R.S. § 1869
		10	449			R.S. § 1870
		10	449			R.S. § 1871
		10	449			R.S. § 1872
		10	449			R.S. § 1883
		10	449			R.S. § 1907
		10	449			R.S. § 1909

31st Cong. 9 Stat.	Chapter	Section	Page	U.S.C. Title	U.S.C. Section	Status
1850—Sept. 9	49	10	449			R.S. §1910
		10	449			R.S. §1912
		10	449			R.S. §1926
		11	450			R.S. §1875
		11	450			R.S. §1876
		11	450			R.S. §1881
		11	450			R.S. §1882
		12	450			R.S. §1877
		12	450			R.S. §1878
		12	450			R.S. §1935
		12	450			R.S. §1939
		12	450			R.S. §1942
		13	451			R.S. §1885
		13	451			R.S. §1944
		14	451			R.S. §1862
		14	451			R.S. §1863
		15	452			R.S. §1946
		16	452			R.S. §1873
		16	452			R.S. §1913
		16	452			R.S. §1918
		17	452			R.S. §1891
	51	1	453			R.S. §1839
		1	453			R.S. §1840
		1	453			R.S. §1897
		2	453			R.S. §1841
		2	453			R.S. §1842
		3	453			R.S. §1843
		3	453			R.S. §1844
		4	454			R.S. §1846
		4	454			R.S. §1847
		4	454			R.S. §1848
		4	454			R.S. §1849
		4	454			R.S. §1922
		5	454			R.S. §1859
		5	454			R.S. §1860
		6	454			R.S. §1850
		6	454			R.S. §1851
		7	455			R.S. §1857
		8	455			R.S. §1854
		9	455			R.S. §702
		9	455			R.S. §1864
		9	455			R.S. §1865
		9	455			R.S. §1866
		9	455			R.S. §1867
		9	455			R.S. §1868
		9	455			R.S. §1869
		9	455			R.S. §1870
		9	455			R.S. §1871
		9	455			R.S. §1872
		9	455			R.S. §1883
		9	455			R.S. §1907
		9	455			R.S. §1909
		9	455			R.S. §1910
		9	455			R.S. §1912
		9	455			R.S. §1926
		10	456			R.S. §1875
		10	456			R.S. §1876
		10	456			R.S. §1881
		10	456			R.S. §1882
		11	456			R.S. §1877
		11	456			R.S. §1878
		11	456			R.S. §1935
		11	456			R.S. §1939
		11	456			R.S. §1942
		12	457			R.S. §1885
		12	457			R.S. §1944
		13	457			R.S. §1862
		13	457			R.S. §1863
		14	457			R.S. §1953
		15	457			R.S. §1946
		16	458			R.S. §1873
		16	458			R.S. §1913
		17	458			R.S. §1891
16	52	1	458			R.S. §782
		1	458			R.S. §1772
		2	458			R.S. §782
	55	1	459			R.S. §263
		2	459			R.S. §263
26	69		469			R.S. §3129
27	76	1	496			R.S. §2207
		2	496			R.S. §2209
		2	496			R.S. §2211
		3	496			R.S. §2409
28	77	6	504			R.S. §4678
		7	504			R.S. §4672
	78	3	507			R.S. §3617

31st Cong. 9 Stat.		Chapter	Section	Page	U.S.C. Title	U.S.C. Section	Status
1850—Sept.	28	79	1	508			R.S. §2582
			1	508			R.S. §2583
			2	508			R.S. §2583
			4	509			R.S. §5293
			5	509			R.S. §2597
			5	509			R.S. §2601
			6	509			R.S. §2598
			7	510			R.S. §2598
			8	510			R.S. §2595
			8	510			R.S. §2596
			9	510			R.S. §2596
			10	510			R.S. §2967
			11	510			R.S. §2568
			11	510			R.S. §2823
			12	511			R.S. §2603
			12	511			R.S. §2604
			13	511			R.S. §2527
			13	511			R.S. §2529
			14	511			R.S. §2568
			14	511			R.S. §2708
			14	511			R.S. §2823
			17	512			R.S. §2978
			18	512			R.S. §3054
			19	512			R.S. §2822
			20	512			R.S. §2576
			21	512			R.S. §2569
		80		512			R.S. §435
				513			R.S. §3718
				515			R.S. §3728
				515			R.S. §4611
				515	34	868	Rev. T.
		84	1	519			R.S. §2479
			1	519			R.S. §2490
			2	519			R.S. §2480
			3	519			R.S. §2481
			4	520			R.S. §2479
		85	1	520			R.S. §2418
			1	520			R.S. §2421
			1	520			R.S. §2438
			2	520			R.S. §2422
			3	520			R.S. §2423
			3	520			R.S. §2424
			4	521			R.S. §2436
			4	521			R.S. §2437
		86	3	522			R.S. §581
			6	522			R.S. §584
			6	522			R.S. §586
			8	522			R.S. §770
			9	522			R.S. §781
	30	90		523			R.S. §48
1851—Feb.	14	8	1	567			R.S. §2586
			1	567			R.S. §2587
			2	567			R.S. §2670
			3	567			R.S. §2586
			3	567			R.S. §2711
	19	11	1	568			R.S. §105
			2	568			R.S. §106
			3	568			R.S. §110
			3	568			R.S. §111
			4	569			R.S. §114
			4	569			R.S. §115
			5	569			R.S. §116
			6	569			R.S. §108
			7	569			R.S. §120
			7	569			R.S. §122
			7	569			R.S. §125
			8	569			R.S. §123
			9	569			R.S. §121
			9	569			R.S. §126
			10	570			R.S. §112
			11	570			R.S. §128
			11	570			R.S. §129
	27	14	2	586			R.S. §2046
			2	586			R.S. §2050
			5	587			R.S. §2058
			6	587			R.S. §2048
			6	587			R.S. §2049
			6	587			R.S. §2056
			6	587			R.S. §2057
			8	587			R.S. §2070
Mar.	3	22		594			R.S. §1309
				594			R.S. §1335
		24	1	594			R.S. §533
			1	594			R.S. §608
			2	594			R.S. §572
			2	594			R.S. §581
			3	595			R.S. §571

31st Cong.

9 Stat.	Chapter	Section	Page	U.S.C. Title	U.S.C. Section	Status
1851—Mar. 3	24	3	595			R.S. §608
		3	595			R.S. §1002
		4	595			R.S. §556
		4	595			R.S. §767
		4	595			R.S. §770
		4	595			R.S. §776
		4	595			R.S. §781
	25	1	595			R.S. §4814
		2	595			R.S. §4815
		3	595			R.S. §4816
		4	596			R.S. §4821
		5	596			R.S. §4820
		5	596			R.S. §4823
		6	596			R.S. §4822
		7	596			R.S. §3689
		7	596			R.S. §4818
		7	596			R.S. §4819
		8	597			R.S. §4817
	32		600			R.S. §198
			600			R.S. §510
			600			R.S. §511
	33		618			R.S. §1204
	34		621			R.S. §1578
			621			R.S. §1579
			621			R.S. §1583
	37	2	628			R.S. §4663
		3	628			R.S. §4663
		4	629			R.S. §4063
		9	629			R.S. §4664
	38	2	630			R.S. §2950
		3	630			R.S. §2608
		3	630			R.S. §2727
		3	630			R.S. §2930
	40		631			R.S. §658
	43	1	635			R.S. §4282
		3	635			R.S. §4283
		4	635			R.S. §4284
		4	635			R.S. §4285
		5	636			R.S. §4286
		6	636			R.S. §4287
		7	636			R.S. §4288
		7	636			R.S. §4289
	44		636			R.S. §581

32d Cong.

10 Stat.	Chapter	Section	Page	U.S.C. Title	U.S.C. Section	Status
1852—Mar. 22	19	1	3			R.S. §2277
		1	3			R.S. §2414
		1	3			R.S. §2415
		2	4			R.S. §2238
		3	4			R.S. §2240
		3	4			R.S. §2242
		4	4			R.S. §2420
		5	4			R.S. §2433
Apr. 2	20		5			R.S. §587
			5			R.S. §592
			5			R.S. §593
			5			R.S. §594
			5			R.S. §595
May 4	25	1	5			R.S. §572
		2	5			R.S. §532
10	33		5			R.S. §572
			5			R.S. §658
June 15	49		10			R.S. §1884
July 3	54	7	12			R.S. §3639
21	66		16			R.S. §849
			21			R.S. §2406
	68	2	25			R.S. §2673
30	74	2	25			R.S. §2195
Aug. 6	81	1	29			R.S. §1309
		2	29			R.S. §1337
26	91	2	30			R.S. §3758
		2	30			R.S. §3759
		10	34			R.S. §3764
		12	34			R.S. §3756
		12	34			R.S. §3757
		12	35			R.S. §3793
30	96	1	37			R.S. §3002
		2	37			R.S. §3003
		3	38			R.S. §2580
		3	38			R.S. §2734
		4	38			R.S. §3008
	103	3	56			R.S. §2086
	106	37	74			R.S. §5482
31	108	2	97			R.S. §3474

32d Cong.				U.S.C.		
10 Stat.	Chapter	Section	Page	Title	Section	Status
1852—Aug. 31	108	6	98			R.S. §2577
		6	98			R.S. §2740
		8	98			R.S. §3788
		18	100			R.S. §1763
	112	5	113			R.S. §4663
		6	118			R.S. §4663
		7	118			R.S. §4663
		8	119			R.S. §4653
		8	119			R.S. §4656
		8	119			R.S. §4657
		8	119			R.S. §4658
		9	119			R.S. §4654
		9	119			R.S. §4655
		10	119			R.S. §4656
		10	119			R.S. §4658
		12	119			R.S. §4670
		12	119			R.S. §4671
		13	120			R.S. §4669
		14	120			R.S. §4665
		14	120			R.S. §4666
		16	120			R.S. §4659
		17	120			R.S. §4679
		17	120			R.S. §4680
	115	1	143			R.S. §2823
		2	144			R.S. §2568
		2	144			R.S. §2708
		2	144			R.S. §2823
		3	144			R.S. §2535
		3	144			R.S. §2540
		3	144			R.S. §4345
Dec. 23	4		149			R.S. §4136
1853—Jan. 22	24	1	152			R.S. §2219
		2	152			R.S. §2220
		3	152			R.S. §2221
Feb. 14	69	4	158			R.S. §2209
26	80	1	161			R.S. §823
		1	161			R.S. §1883
		1	162			R.S. §824
		1	162			R.S. §920
		1	162			R.S. §980
		1	162			R.S. §982
		1	162			R.S. §1024
		1	162			R.S. §1027
		1	162			R.S. §1028
		1	162			R.S. §1029
		1	163			R.S. §632
		1	163			R.S. §698
		1	163			R.S. §750
		1	163			R.S. §828
		1	163			R.S. §840
		1	164			R.S. §829
		1	165			R.S. §715
		2	165			R.S. §830
		3	165			R.S. §833
		3	166			R.S. §835
		3	166			R.S. §839
		3	166			R.S. §841
		3	166			R.S. §843
		3	166			R.S. §844
		3	166			R.S. §845
		3	167			R.S. §831
		3	167			R.S. §847
		3	167			R.S. §848
		3	167			R.S. §850
		3	168			R.S. §851
		3	168			R.S. §853
		3	168			R.S. §854
		3	168			R.S. §855
		3	168			R.S. §856
		3	168			R.S. §863
		3	168			R.S. §983
		3	169			R.S. §877
		3	169			R.S. §984
		3	169			R.S. §1030
	81	1	170			R.S. §3477
		2	170			R.S. §5498
		4	170			R.S. §5403
		5	170			R.S. §5408
		6	171			R.S. §5450
		6	171			R.S. §5451
		6	171			R.S. §5500
		6	171			R.S. §5501
		6	171			R.S. §5502
Mar. 2	89		172			R.S. §3655
			172			R.S. §3656
	90	1	172			R.S. §1839

32d Cong. 10 Stat.	Chapter	Section	Page	U.S.C. Title	U.S.C. Section	Status
1853—Mar. 2	90	1	172			R.S. §1840
		1	172			R.S. §1898
		2	173			R.S. §1841
		3	173			R.S. §1843
		3	173			R.S. §1844
		4	173			R.S. §1846
		4	173			R.S. §1847
		4	173			R.S. §1848
		4	173			R.S. §1849
		4	173			R.S. §1922
		4	173			R.S. §1923
		5	174			R.S. §1859
		5	174			R.S. §1860
		6	175			R.S. §1850
		6	175			R.S. §1851
		6	175			R.S. §1924
		7	175			R.S. §1857
		8	175			R.S. §1854
		9	175			R.S. §702
		9	175			R.S. §1864
		9	175			R.S. §1865
		9	175			R.S. §1866
		9	175			R.S. §1867
		9	175			R.S. §1868
		9	175			R.S. §1869
		9	175			R.S. §1870
		9	175			R.S. §1871
		9	175			R.S. §1872
		9	175			R.S. §1883
		9	175			R.S. §1907
		9	175			R.S. §1909
		9	175			R.S. §1910
		9	175			R.S. §1911
		9	175			R.S. §1912
		9	175			R.S. §1926
		10	176			R.S. §1875
		10	176			R.S. §1876
		10	176			R.S. §1881
		10	176			R.S. §1882
		11	176			R.S. §1877
		11	176			R.S. §1878
		11	176			R.S. §1938
		11	176			R.S. §1940
		11	176			R.S. §1941
		12	177			R.S. §1952
		13	177			R.S. §1885
		13	177			R.S. §1944
		14	178			R.S. §1862
		14	178			R.S. §1863
		14	178			R.S. §1906
		17	179			R.S. §1953
		18	179			R.S. §1873
		18	179			R.S. §1913
		18	179			R.S. §1918
		19	179			R.S. §1951
		20	179			R.S. §1947
		21	179			R.S. §1950
8	96		183			R.S. §3763
	97	1	189			R.S. §440
		1	189			R.S. §2250
		1	190			R.S. §3782
		1	204			R.S. §2241
		1	204			R.S. §2251
		1	207			R.S. §1830
		2	209			R.S. §4689
		3	209			R.S. §163
		3	209			R.S. §164
		3	209			R.S. §170
		3	209			R.S. §176
		3	209			R.S. §264
		3	211			R.S. §166
		3	211			R.S. §167
		3	211			R.S. §215
		3	211			R.S. §235
		3	211			R.S. §351
		6	212			R.S. §200
	98	1	214			R.S. §1666
		1	214			R.S. §4690
		6	214			R.S. §3596
		9	219			R.S. §1207
	104	4	239			R.S. §5483
	143		244			R.S. §2279
			244			R.S. §2280
	144		244			R.S. §2251
	145	1	244			R.S. §2207
		1	244			R.S. §2210

32d Cong. 10 Stat.	Chapter	Section	Page	U.S.C. Title	U.S.C. Section	Status
1853—Mar. 8	145	1	244			R.S. §2211
		2	245			R.S. §2224
		3	245			R.S. §2223
		4	245			R.S. §2409
		4	245			R.S. §2410
		5	245			R.S. §2236
		8	247			R.S. §2411
		10	247			R.S. §2222
		10	247			R.S. §2223
		10	247			R.S. §2230
		11	248			R.S. §2209
		11	248			R.S. §2224
	147	1	256			R.S. §2446
		2	257			R.S. §2371
	152	1	258			R.S. §2450
		2	258			R.S. §2456
33d Cong.						
10 Stat.						
1854—Feb. 2	9		266			R.S. §2568
			266			R.S. §2708
			266			R.S. §2823
10	11	1	267			R.S. §46
			267			R.S. §56
		2	267			R.S. §57
		2	267			R.S. §59
Mar. 27	25		269			R.S. §2281
	26	1	269			R.S. §533
		3	270			R.S. §2145
		3	270			R.S. §2146
		4	270			R.S. §2143
		5	270			R.S. §2142
28	30	1	270			R.S. §2960
		1	270			R.S. §2962
		1	271			R.S. §2958
		2	271			R.S. §2965
		2	271			R.S. §2976
		3	271			R.S. §2961
		4	272			R.S. §2971
		4	271			R.S. §2983
		5	272			R.S. §2999
		5	272			R.S. §3000
		6	272			R.S. §3001
		7	272			R.S. §2953
		7	272			R.S. §2955
		7	272			R.S. §2957
		8	273			R.S. §2984
		8	273			R.S. §3689
		9	273			R.S. §2989
Apr. 22	52	1	276			R.S. §167
		1	276			R.S. §168
		3	276			R.S. §2204
May 10	59	11	281			R.S. §1881
		11	281			R.S. §1882
31	60	2	297			R.S. §6
		2	297			R.S. §882
July 17	84	6	306			R.S. §2242
		7	306			R.S. §2207
		7	306			R.S. §2209
20	99	1	307			R.S. §572
		1	307			R.S. §579
		2	307			R.S. §658
22	103	1	308			R.S. §2207
		1	308			R.S. §2210
		10	309			R.S. §2207
27	105		310			R.S. §2535
			311			R.S. §2536
29	159	1	315			R.S. §1778
		2	315			R.S. §863
Aug. 2	189	1	333			R.S. §2568
		1	333			R.S. §2572
		2	334			R.S. §2573
	191		334			R.S. §2568
			334			R.S. §2708
			334			R.S. §2823
	192	2	334			R.S. §2568
		2	334			R.S. §2823
	193	1	335			R.S. §2578
		2	335			R.S. §2578
		2	335			R.S. §2579
		2	335			R.S. §2671
3	196		344			R.S. §2966
	198		345			R.S. §2568
			345			R.S. §2823
	201		346			R.S. §2449

33d Cong. 10 Stat.	Chapter	Section	Page	U.S.C. Title	U.S.C. Section	Status
1854—Aug. 3	202	1	346			R.S. §2562
		1	346			R.S. §2563
		1	346			R.S. §2818
		1	346			R.S. §2819
		2	346			R.S. §2568
		2	346			R.S. §2708
		2	346			R.S. §2823
4	242	8	572			R.S. §495
		11	573			R.S. §3603
		12	573			R.S. §55
		14	573			R.S. §3614
		15	573			R.S. §1797
		15	573			R.S. §1798
		15	573			R.S. §1812
		15	573			R.S. §1828
		15	573			R.S. §3669
	247	2	575			R.S. §1282
		2	575			R.S. §1284
		3	575			R.S. §1285
		3	575			R.S. §1286
		5	575			R.S. §1214
		5	575			R.S. §1215
5	267		578			R.S. §1662
	268	1	585			R.S. §3718
		1	586			R.S. §1612
		1	586			R.S. §1613
		4	587			R.S. §1488
Dec. 14	1	1	597			R.S. §4242
		2	597			R.S. §4243
		3	597			R.S. §4246
		4	597			R.S. §4245
22	10		599			R.S. §2447
1855—Feb. 10	71	1	604			R.S. §1993
		2	604			R.S. §1994
	73	1	604			R.S. §544
		2	604			R.S. §608
		2	605			R.S. §579
		7	605			R.S. §551
		8	605			R.S. §767
		8	605			R.S. §770
		8	605			R.S. §776
		8	605			R.S. §781
13	96	1	606			R.S. §536
		2	606			R.S. §572
		2	606			R.S. §608
		2	606			R.S. §658
		7	607			R.S. §551
		8	607			R.S. §781
		9	607			R.S. §767
		9	607			R.S. §776
21	117		611			R.S. §2207
			611			R.S. §2210
	118	3	612			R.S. §670
24	122	1	612			R.S. §1049
		1	612			R.S. §1059
		1	612			R.S. §1072
		3	613			R.S. §1070
		3	613			R.S. §1075
		3	613			R.S. §1081
		3	613			R.S. §1082
		3	613			R.S. §1084
		3	613			R.S. §1085
		4	613			R.S. §1077
		5	613			R.S. §1083
		9	614			R.S. §1087
		10	614			R.S. §1051
		10	614			R.S. §1052
		11	614			R.S. §1053
		11	614			R.S. §1054
		11	614			R.S. §1076
	123		614			R.S. §5280
	124	3	615			R.S. §2243
	125		615			R.S. §598
28	127	2	616			R.S. §1593
		3	617			R.S. §1442
Mar. 2	136	1	627			R.S. §1426
		1	627			R.S. §1427
		1	627			R.S. §1429
		2	627			R.S. §1573
		3	627			R.S. §1431
		4	627			R.S. §1624
		5	627			R.S. §1624
		6	627			R.S. §1624
		7	627			R.S. §1624
		8	627			R.S. §1624
		9	627			R.S. §1624
	140		630			R.S. §746

33d Cong. 10 Stat.	Chapter	Section	Page	U.S.C. Title	U.S.C. Section	Status
1855—Mar. 2	141	2	630			R.S. §2752
	147	1	634			R.S. §2483
		2	634			R.S. §2482
		2	634			R.S. §3689
3	169	7	639			R.S. §1667
		7	639			R.S. §1671
	175	1	651			R.S. §3763
		1	656			R.S. §3596
		4	669			R.S. §163
		4	669			R.S. §164
		4	669			R.S. §176
		4	669			R.S. §201
		8	670			R.S. §3662
		8	670			R.S. §3663
		8	670			R.S. §3664
		12	670			R.S. §823
		12	671			R.S. §1883
		13	671			R.S. §2578
		22	673			R.S. §2051
		26	674			R.S. §2209
	198	2	680			R.S. §2712
	199	1	682			R.S. §4838
		2	682			R.S. §4840
		2	682			R.S. §4841
		2	682			R.S. §4842
		3	682			R.S. §4839
		5	683			R.S. §4844
		6	683			R.S. §4853
		7	683			R.S. §4858
	204	8	700			R.S. §2144
		10	701			R.S. §2064
	207	1	701			R.S. §2425
		1	701			R.S. §2426
		1	701			R.S. §2438
		2	702			R.S. §2428
		2	702			R.S. §2429
		2	702			R.S. §2430
		3	702			R.S. §2425
		3	702			R.S. §2427
		3	702			R.S. §2431
		7	702			R.S. §2434
		8	702			R.S. §2426
		9	702			R.S. §2427
		10	702			R.S. §2426
		11	702			R.S. §2427
	213	1	715			R.S. §4252
		1	715			R.S. §4253
		1	715			R.S. §4254
		2	716			R.S. §4255
		3	716			R.S. §4256
		4	717			R.S. §4257
		5	717			R.S. §4258
		6	717			R.S. §4260
		6	717			R.S. §4262
		6	718			R.S. §4261
		7	718			R.S. §4263
		8	718			R.S. §4259
		9	718			R.S. §4264
		11	719			R.S. §4265
		12	719			R.S. §4266
		13	719			R.S. §4267
		14	719			R.S. §4268
		14	719			R.S. §4269
		15	720			R.S. §629
		15	720			R.S. §4270
		16	720			R.S. §4271
		17	720			R.S. §4272
34th Cong.						
11 Stat.						
1856—Feb. 20	1		1			R.S. §473
Mar. 19	8		1			R.S. §547
28	9		2			R.S. §5540
Apr. 23	18		4			R.S. §572
			4			R.S. §658
	19	2	5			R.S. §1340
		2	5			R.S. §1341
		3	5			R.S. §1332
	20		5			R.S. §71
May 14	26	1	8			R.S. §2432
		2	8			R.S. §2435
		3	8			R.S. §2431
		4	8			R.S. §2426
		5	9			R.S. §2426
		7	9			R.S. §2433

34th Cong.				U.S.C.		
11 Stat.	Chapter	Section	Page	Title	Section	Status
1856—May 14	Pub. R. 9		144			R.S. § 251
			144			R.S. § 338
June 14	45		22			R.S. § 572
			22			R.S. § 658
26	47		22			R.S. § 2450
			22			R.S. § 2457
	48	2	23			R.S. § 658
Aug. 6	81	1	30			R.S. § 1052
		3	30			R.S. § 1055
		3	30			R.S. § 1056
16	119	1	43			R.S. § 571
		1	43			R.S. § 572
		2	43			R.S. § 817
		3	43			R.S. § 571
	123	2	48			R.S. § 36
		5	49			R.S. § 42
		6	49			R.S. § 40
	124	1	49			R.S. § 846
		2	49			R.S. § 846
		3	49			R.S. § 981
		5	49			R.S. § 1915
		7	50			R.S. § 810
		7	50			R.S. § 811
		8	50			R.S. § 849
		10	50			R.S. § 1871
		12	50			R.S. § 299
		13	50			R.S. § 628
	125	2	51			R.S. § 1179
18	127	1	52			R.S. § 1675
		1	52			R.S. § 1676
		2	52			R.S. § 1680
		3	52			R.S. § 1690
		4	55			R.S. § 1730
		5	55			R.S. § 1699
		5	55			R.S. § 1701
		6	55			R.S. § 1692
		8	55			R.S. § 1740
		9	56			R.S. § 1686
		10	56			R.S. § 1685
		11	56			R.S. § 1739
		12	56			R.S. § 1738
		13	56			R.S. § 1697
		14	57			R.S. § 1695
		15	57			R.S. § 1700
		15	57			R.S. § 1703
		16	57			R.S. § 208
		16	57			R.S. § 1731
		16	57			R.S. § 1745
		16	57			R.S. § 4207
		17	58			R.S. § 1723
		17	58			R.S. § 1726
		18	58			R.S. § 208
		18	58			R.S. § 1687
		18	58			R.S. § 1724
		18	58			R.S. § 1725
		18	58			R.S. § 1727
		18	58			R.S. § 1728
		18	58			R.S. § 1747
		18	59			R.S. § 4213
		19	59			R.S. § 1741
		19	59			R.S. § 1751
		20	59			R.S. § 1719
		20	59			R.S. § 1743
		21	60			R.S. § 1744
		22	60			R.S. § 208
		22	60			R.S. § 211
		22	60			R.S. § 1706
		22	60			R.S. § 1748
		22	60			R.S. § 1752
		24	61			R.S. § 1750
		26	62			R.S. § 4580
		26	62			R.S. § 4581
		26	62			R.S. § 4583
		26	62			R.S. § 4584
		27	62			R.S. § 1708
		27	62			R.S. § 1713
		27	62			R.S. § 1715
		28	63			R.S. § 1711
		28	63			R.S. § 1718
		30	63			R.S. § 1746
		31	64			R.S. § 1674
		31	64			R.S. § 1689
		32	64			R.S. § 1735
	128	2	80			R.S. § 2148
	129	17	92			R.S. § 2583
		17	92			R.S. § 2744
	160	5	101			R.S. § 4663

34th Cong.				U.S.C.		
11 Stat.	Chapter	Section	Page	Title	Section	Status
1856—Aug. 18	162	5	118			R.S. §1613
	164	1	119			R.S. §5570
		1	119			R.S. §5571
		2	119			R.S. §5573
		2	119			R.S. §5574
		3	120			R.S. §5575
		4	120			R.S. §5578
		5	120			R.S. §5577
		6	120			R.S. §5576
	170	2	139			R.S. §208
		2	139			R.S. §1712
	Pub. R. 18		145			R.S. §167
1857—Jan. 16	12	1	154			R.S. §1593
		3	154			R.S. §1594
		4	154			R.S. §1457
		4	154			R.S. §1461
24	19	1	155			R.S. §102
		2	156			R.S. §859
		3	156			R.S. §104
28	Pub. R. 5	2	253			R.S. §3798
		3	253			R.S. §501
		5	253			R.S. §97
Feb. 7	36	1	157			R.S. §4857
		3	157			R.S. §4848
		4	157			R.S. §4850
		5	158			R.S. §4851
		6	158			R.S. §4852
		7	158			R.S. §4855
		8	158			R.S. §4854
		9	158			R.S. §4856
16	45	1	161			R.S. §1309
		3	161			R.S. §1338
	46	1	161			R.S. §4859
		2	161			R.S. §4862
		3	162			R.S. §4866
		4	162			R.S. §4864
		4	162			R.S. §4869
		6	162			R.S. §4868
21	56	1	163			R.S. §2366
		1	163			R.S. §3567
		2	163			R.S. §3474
		2	163			R.S. §3566
		2	163			R.S. §3568
		3	163			R.S. §3474
		3	163			R.S. §3584
	57	1	164			R.S. §548
		2	164			R.S. §572
		2	164			R.S. §579
		2	164			R.S. §658
		5	165			R.S. §551
		6	165			R.S. §767
		6	165			R.S. §770
		6	165			R.S. §776
		6	165			R.S. §781
26	60	5	167			R.S. §3689
Mar. 2	62		168			R.S. §2559
			168			R.S. §2560
			168			R.S. §2817
	63		168			R.S. §2491
3	90	1	169			R.S. §2089
		3	185			R.S. §2046
	100	1	197			R.S. §540
		2	197			R.S. §572
		7	198			R.S. §551
		8	198			R.S. §767
		8	198			R.S. §776
		8	198			R.S. §781
		9	198			R.S. §767
		9	198			R.S. §776
		10	198			R.S. §608
	102		199			R.S. §2564
			199			R.S. §2565
			199			R.S. §2708
			199			R.S. §2713
			199			R.S. §2820
	105		200			R.S. §2562
			200			R.S. §2563
			200			R.S. §2619
			200			R.S. §2664
	106	2	203			R.S. §1191
		3	203			R.S. §1663
	107	1	212			R.S. §2207
		1	212			R.S. §2213
		5	220			R.S. §234
		10	221			R.S. §2578
	108	2	228			R.S. §155

34th Cong.					U.S.C.		
11 Stat.		Chapter	Section	Page	Title	Section	Status
1857—Mar.	3	108	2	228			R.S. §156
			8	229			R.S. §2647
		111	3	246			R.S. §436
		114	2	249			R.S. §3639
			2	249			R.S. §5489
			3	249			R.S. §3621
			3	249			R.S. §5492
		116	1	250			R.S. §5341
			2	250			R.S. §5342
			3	250			R.S. §5343
		117		251			R.S. §2484
		Pub. R. 14		255			R.S. §55
35th Cong.							
11 Stat.							
1857—Dec.	23	1	6	258			R.S. §3473
			11	259			R.S. §3578
1858—Jan.	27	3		260			R.S. §2565
				260			R.S. §2713
				260			R.S. §2820
Feb.	10	5	1	260			R.S. §572
			2	260			R.S. §658
May	4	27	1	272			R.S. §739
			1	272			R.S. §740
			1	272			R.S. §741
			2	272			R.S. §739
			2	272			R.S. §742
		28		272			R.S. §572
				272			R.S. §658
	11	31	3	285			R.S. §531
			3	285			R.S. §551
			3	285			R.S. §767
			3	285			R.S. §770
			3	285			R.S. §776
			3	285			R.S. §781
	18	39	1	289			R.S. §2229
			3	290			R.S. §5411
			4	290			R.S. §5412
		40	1	290			R.S. §2471
			2	291			R.S. §2472
			3	291			R.S. §2473
June	2	82	2	308			R.S. §3665
	3	84	1	308			R.S. §2444
			2	309			R.S. §2414
		85		309			R.S. §4725
				309			R.S. §4726
				309			R.S. §4727
	11	147		314			R.S. §572
				314			R.S. §658
	12	153	5	319			R.S. §1530
			5	319			R.S. §1531
			5	319			R.S. §1532
		154	1	319			R.S. §4688
			5	326			R.S. §3680
			10	326			R.S. §2273
			17	327			R.S. §3657
			18	328			R.S. §703
		155	2	332			R.S. §2149
		156		333			R.S. §1309
				333			R.S. §1310
				333			R.S. §1312
				333			R.S. §1313
				333			R.S. §1334
				333			R.S. §1337
	14	160	4	337			R.S. §253
		163	3	363			R.S. §2153
		166		366			R.S. §1874
1859—Feb.	2	19		378			R.S. §2240
	5	22	1	379			R.S. §441
			1	379			R.S. §497
			1	379			R.S. §3808
			1	379			R.S. §3813
			2	379			R.S. §74
			3	380			R.S. §445
			3	380			R.S. §499
			4	380			R.S. §500
			5	380			R.S. §497
			5	380			R.S. §501
			7	380			R.S. §497
			10	381			R.S. §506
			11	381			R.S. §96
		23		381			R.S. §5420
	14	33	4	384			R.S. §3689
	26	58		385			R.S. §2275
				385			R.S. §2276

35th Cong.					U.S.C.		
11 Stat.		Chapter	Section	Page	Title	Section	Status
1859—Feb.	28	64	1	387			R.S. §2362
			1	387			R.S. §3689
			2	388			R.S. §2363
		65		388			R.S. §3689
		66	8	401			R.S. §2156
Mar.	3	74		402			R.S. §572
		76	2	407			R.S. §1488
			2	407			R.S. §1590
		78		408			R.S. §5388
		80	3	422			R.S. §3792
			3	422			R.S. §3794
		81	2	424			R.S. §4668
			3	424			R.S. §4674
			6	424			R.S. §4663
		83	1	432			R.S. §1136
			4	434			R.S. §4815
			5	434			R.S. §4814
			5	434			R.S. §4821
			6	434			R.S. §4820
			7	434			R.S. §4814
			7	434			R.S. §4819
			7	434			R.S. §4824
		84	1	435			R.S. §1800
			1	435			R.S. §1801
			1	435			R.S. §1802
			1	435			R.S. §1807
			1	435			R.S. §1808
			1	435			R.S. §1809
			1	435			R.S. §1810
			1	435			R.S. §1811
			1	435			R.S. §1812
			5	436			R.S. §1803
			5	436			R.S. §1804
			6	436			R.S. §1805
			7	436			R.S. §1806
		85	2	437			R.S. §531
			2	437			R.S. §551
			3	437			R.S. §767
			3	437			R.S. §770
			3	437			R.S. §776
			3	437			R.S. §781
			5	437			R.S. §537
			5	437			R.S. §560
			5	437			R.S. §572
			5	437			R.S. §768
			5	437			R.S. §778
			6	438			R.S. §537
			6	438			R.S. §572
			7	438			R.S. §537
			7	438			R.S. §572
			8	438			R.S. §560
			8	438			R.S. §768
			8	438			R.S. §778
		Pub. R. 14	1	442			R.S. §49
			1	442			R.S. §50
36th Cong.							
12 Stat.							
1860—Mar.	12	5	1	3			R.S. §2479
			1	3			R.S. §2490
			2	3			R.S. §2490
	24	8	1	3			R.S. §5349
			2	3			R.S. §4275
			2	3			R.S. §4276
			3	4			R.S. §4277
			4	4			R.S. §5350
			5	4			R.S. §5351
May	5	37		14			R.S. §2205
June	1	66		23			R.S. §4843
		67	1	24			R.S. §1397
			1	24			R.S. §1398
			3	27			R.S. §1571
			4	27			R.S. §1442
			4	27			R.S. §1557
			5	27			R.S. §1592
	9	85	1	28			R.S. §572
			3	29			R.S. §581
	13	120	2	30			R.S. §4860
	16	134	1	39			R.S. §2578
			1	39			R.S. §2579
			2	39			R.S. §2578
			2	39			R.S. §2579
			3	39			R.S. §2578
			3	40			R.S. §2579
			4	40			R.S. §2581
		135		40			R.S. §1675

36th Cong. 12 Stat.		Chapter	Section	Page	U.S.C. Title	U.S.C. Section	Status
1860—June	16	136	1	40			R.S. §5566
			2	41			R.S. §5567
	21	163	1	66			R.S. §1195
			4	68			R.S. §1146
		164		69			R.S. §5409
				69			R.S. §5410
	22	179	1	72			R.S. §4083
			2	72			R.S. §4084
			3	73			R.S. §4085
			4	73			R.S. §4086
			5	73			R.S. §4117
			5	73			R.S. §4118
			6	73			R.S. §4119
			7	74			R.S. §4087
			8	74			R.S. §4104
			8	74			R.S. §4105
			9	74			R.S. §4089
			10	74			R.S. §4106
			11	74			R.S. §4107
			12	75			R.S. §4097
			13	75			R.S. §4091
			14	75			R.S. §4101
			15	75			R.S. §4102
			15	75			R.S. §4103
			17	75			R.S. §4120
			18	76			R.S. §4099
			19	76			R.S. §4098
			20	76			R.S. §4100
			21	76			R.S. §4125
			22	76			R.S. §4128
			22	76			R.S. §4130
			23	76			R.S. §4110
			24	77			R.S. §4090
			25	77			R.S. §4111
			25	77			R.S. §4112
			25	77			R.S. §4113
			25	77			R.S. §4114
			25	77			R.S. §4115
			25	77			R.S. §4116
			26	77			R.S. §4121
			27	78			R.S. §4108
			27	78			R.S. §4109
			28	78			R.S. §4126
			29	78			R.S. §4127
			30	78			R.S. §4088
			31	79			R.S. §4082
		181	1	81			R.S. §3666
			3	83			R.S. §1378
			3	83			R.S. §1383
			3	83			R.S. §1389
			3	83			R.S. §1583
		184		84			R.S. §5271
	23	203	1	90			R.S. §2441
			2	91			R.S. §2442
		205		93			R.S. §3762
				93			R.S. §3763
		Pub. R. 25	2	117			R.S. §3760
			2	117			R.S. §3761
			2	117			R.S. §3763
			2	117			R.S. §3783
			2	117			R.S. §3819
			2	117			R.S. §3821
			3	118			R.S. §3760
			3	118			R.S. §3815
			3	118			R.S. §3816
			3	118			R.S. §3817
			4	118			R.S. §3783
			5	118			R.S. §3785
			5	118			R.S. §3786
			6	118			R.S. §3760
			7	118			R.S. §3820
			8	119			R.S. §3779
			9	119			R.S. §3814
			9	119			R.S. §3821
			10	119			R.S. §3765
			11	120			R.S. §3784
	25	211		106			R.S. §1800
				106			R.S. §1801
				106			R.S. §1812
1861—Jan.	29	20	4	128			R.S. §531
			4	128			R.S. §551
			4	128			R.S. §767
			4	128			R.S. §770
			4	128			R.S. §776
			4	128			R.S. §781
			5	128			R.S. §572
			5	128			R.S. §658

36th Cong. 12 Stat.	Chapter	Section	Page	U.S.C. Title	U.S.C. Section	Status
1861—Feb. 8	30		130			R.S. §2046
18	38	1	131			R.S. §2239
		1	131			R.S. §2240
		1	131			R.S. §2241
		2	131			R.S. §2255
		3	131			R.S. §2239
		3	131			R.S. §2240
		3	131			R.S. §2241
20	44		135			R.S. §3821
			135			R.S. §3822
21	49	1	147			R.S. §1538
		1	147			R.S. §1539
		7	150			R.S. §3686
28	58		171			R.S. §1690
	59	1	172			R.S. §1839
		1	172			R.S. §1840
		1	172			R.S. §1847
		1	172			R.S. §1848
		1	172			R.S. §1849
		1	172			R.S. §1899
		2	172			R.S. §1841
		3	172			R.S. §1843
		3	172			R.S. §1844
		4	173			R.S. §1846
		4	173			R.S. §1922
		5	173			R.S. §1859
		5	173			R.S. §1860
		6	174			R.S. §1851
		6	174			R.S. §1925
		7	174			R.S. §1857
		8	174			R.S. §1854
		9	174			R.S. §1864
		9	174			R.S. §1865
		9	174			R.S. §1866
		9	174			R.S. §1867
		9	174			R.S. §1868
		9	174			R.S. §1869
		9	174			R.S. §1870
		9	174			R.S. §1871
		9	174			R.S. §1872
		9	174			R.S. §1883
		9	174			R.S. §1907
		9	174			R.S. §1909
		9	174			R.S. §1910
		9	174			R.S. §1912
		10	175			R.S. §1875
		10	175			R.S. §1876
		10	175			R.S. §1881
		10	175			R.S. §1882
		11	175			R.S. §1877
		11	175			R.S. §1878
		11	175			R.S. §1935
		11	175			R.S. §1939
		12	176			R.S. §1885
		12	176			R.S. §1944
		13	176			R.S. §1862
		13	176			R.S. §1863
		14	176			R.S. §1946
		15	176			R.S. §1873
		15	176			R.S. §1913
		15	176			R.S. §1918
		15	176			R.S. §1919
		16	176			R.S. §1891
		17	176			R.S. §2207
		17	176			R.S. §2210
	60	1	177			R.S. §4845
		1	177			R.S. §4846
		1	177			R.S. §4847
		2	177			R.S. §4849
Mar. 2	68	9	182			R.S. §2504
		10	183			R.S. §2504
		12	183			R.S. §2504
		15	186			R.S. §2504
		19	187			R.S. §2504
		20	189			R.S. §2504
		21	190			R.S. §2504
		22	191			R.S. §2504
		23	193			R.S. §2505
		24	196			R.S. §2516
		26	196			R.S. §2951
		27	197			R.S. §3021
		28	197			R.S. §2904
		29	197			R.S. §336
		32	197			R.S. §2910
		32	197			R.S. §2952
	81		209			R.S. §2880

36th Cong.				U.S.C.		
12 Stat.	Chapter	Section	Page	Title	Section	Status
1861—Mar. 2	83	17	214			R.S. §2207
		17	214			R.S. §2210
	84	1	219			R.S. §841
		10	220			R.S. §3709
		10	220			R.S. §3715
		10	220			R.S. §3732
	86	1	239			R.S. §1839
		1	239			R.S. §1840
		1	239			R.S. §1900
		2	239			R.S. §1841
		3	240			R.S. §1843
		3	240			R.S. §1844
		4	240			R.S. §1846
		4	240			R.S. §1847
		4	240			R.S. §1848
		4	240			R.S. §1849
		4	240			R.S. §1922
		5	241			R.S. §1859
		5	241			R.S. §1860
		6	241			R.S. §1851
		6	241			R.S. §1925
		7	241			R.S. §1857
		8	241			R.S. §1854
		9	241			R.S. §702
		9	241			R.S. §1864
		9	241			R.S. §1865
		9	241			R.S. §1866
		9	241			R.S. §1867
		9	241			R.S. §1868
		9	241			R.S. §1869
		9	241			R.S. §1870
		9	241			R.S. §1871
		9	241			R.S. §1872
		9	241			R.S. §1883
		9	241			R.S. §1907
		9	241			R.S. §1909
		9	241			R.S. §1910
		9	241			R.S. §1912
		9	241			R.S. §1926
		10	242			R.S. §1875
		10	242			R.S. §1876
		10	242			R.S. §1881
		10	242			R.S. §1882
		11	242			R.S. §1877
		11	242			R.S. §1878
		11	242			R.S. §1935
		11	242			R.S. §1939
		11	242			R.S. §1942
		12	243			R.S. §1885
		12	243			R.S. §1944
		13	243			R.S. §1862
		13	243			R.S. §1863
		14	243			R.S. §1946
		15	243			R.S. §1873
		15	243			R.S. §1913
		15	243			R.S. §1918
		15	243			R.S. §1919
		16	244			R.S. §1891
		17	244			R.S. §2207
		17	244			R.S. §2208
	87	1	244			R.S. §501
		2	245			R.S. §502
		4	245			R.S. §510
		4	245			R.S. §3800
		6	245			R.S. §683
37th Cong.						
12 Stat.						
1861—July 13	3	1	255			R.S. §5314
		2	256			R.S. §5315
		3	256			R.S. §5316
		4	256			R.S. §564
		4	256			R.S. §734
		4	256			R.S. §5317
		5	257			R.S. §564
		5	257			R.S. §734
		5	257			R.S. §1342
		5	257			R.S. §5301
		5	257			R.S. §5304
		5	257			R.S. §5305
		7	257			R.S. §5318
		7	257			R.S. §5319
		8	257			R.S. §5292
		9	258			R.S. §564
		9	258			R.S. §734
17	4	1	258			R.S. §1378

37th Cong.				U.S.C.		
12 Stat.	Chapter	Section	Page	Title	Section	Status
1861—July 17	4	2	258			R.S. §1379
		4	258			R.S. §1381
		4	258			R.S. §1432
		4	258			R.S. §1564
		5	258			R.S. §1380
		5	258			R.S. §1383
	5		259			R.S. §3473
			259			R.S. §3589
18	7	1	264			R.S. §1580
		2	265			R.S. §1581
		3	265			R.S. §1581
		4	265			R.S. §1581
		4	265			R.S. §1582
		7	265			R.S. §3726
	8	3	268			R.S. §1537
22	9	2	269			R.S. §1646
		3	269			R.S. §1647
25	19	1	275			R.S. §1596
		2	275			R.S. §1597
		3	275			R.S. §1599
	20	2	275			R.S. §2749
		3	275			R.S. §2758
29	24	1	279			R.S. §1100
		1	280			R.S. §1099
		2	280			R.S. §1099
		2	280			R.S. §1111
		3	280			R.S. §1098
	25	1	281			R.S. §5298
		2	282			R.S. §5300
		3	282			R.S. §1342
		3	282			R.S. §1644
		3	282			R.S. §1650
		4	282			R.S. §1649
		5	282			R.S. §1658
		6	282			R.S. §1659
		6	282			R.S. §1660
		7	282			R.S. §788
31	32		284			R.S. §1342
			284			R.S. §5301
	33		284			R.S. §1980
			284			R.S. §5336
			284			R.S. §5518
Aug. 2	36		285			R.S. §1542
	37	1	285			R.S. §350
		1	285			R.S. §362
		2	285			R.S. §363
3	42	4	287			R.S. §1152
		4	287			R.S. §1154
		4	287			R.S. §1155
		4	287			R.S. §1156
		4	287			R.S. §1157
		6	288			R.S. §1238
		6	288			R.S. §1277
		8	288			R.S. §1320
		8	288			R.S. §1325
		11	289			R.S. §1342
		12	289			R.S. §1102
		14	289			R.S. §1175
		15	289			R.S. §1243
		15	289			R.S. §1622
		16	289			R.S. §1245
		16	289			R.S. §1255
		16	289			R.S. §1257
		16	289			R.S. §1258
		16	289			R.S. §1622
		17	289			R.S. §1246
		17	289			R.S. §1622
		17	289			R.S. §1623
		17	290			R.S. §1247
		17	290			R.S. §1248
		17	290			R.S. §1249
		17	290			R.S. §1250
		17	290			R.S. §1251
		17	290			R.S. §1252
		17	290			R.S. §1253
		17	290			R.S. §1275
		17	290			R.S. §1449
		18	290			R.S. §1256
		20	290			R.S. §1265
		21	290			R.S. §1443
		22	290			R.S. §1457
		22	290			R.S. §1458
		22	290			R.S. §1459
		22	290			R.S. §1590
		23	291			R.S. §1448
		23	291			R.S. §1450

37th Cong. 12 Stat.		Chapter	Section	Page	U.S.C. Title	U.S.C. Section	Status
1861—Aug.	3	42	23	291			R.S. §1451
			23	291			R.S. §1452
			23	291			R.S. §1453
			23	291			R.S. §1454
			23	291			R.S. §1455
			23	291			R.S. §1457
			23	291			R.S. §1593
			24	291			R.S. §1457
	5	45	1	292			R.S. §2504
			2	292			R.S. §2504
			4	293			R.S. §3019
		46	5	313			R.S. §3473
		48	1	314			R.S. §4296
			1	314			R.S. §4297
			2	315			R.S. §4298
			3	315			R.S. §4299
		49		315			R.S. §1720
		51	2	316			R.S. §1533
		54	2	316			R.S. §1342
			2	316			R.S. §1624
			3	317			R.S. §1342
	6	55		317			R.S. §770
				317			R.S. §836
		56	1	317			R.S. §5337
			2	317			R.S. §5338
		57	2	317			R.S. §1152
			2	317			R.S. §1154
			2	317			R.S. §1156
			2	317			R.S. §1157
			5	318			R.S. §1662
			5	318			R.S. §1663
		59		318			R.S. §602
				318			R.S. §603
		60	1	319			R.S. §5308
			2	319			R.S. §563
			2	319			R.S. §629
			2	319			R.S. §711
			2	319			R.S. §734
			2	319			R.S. §735
			2	319			R.S. §5309
			3	319			R.S. §5311
		61		319			R.S. §1013
		64	2	326			R.S. §1758
		65		327			R.S. §350
Dec.	21	1	1	329			R.S. §1444
			8	329			R.S. §1459
			8	329			R.S. §1463
			8	329			R.S. §1465
			4	329			R.S. §1434
			4	329			R.S. §1459
			4	329			R.S. §1464
			6	330			R.S. §1458
	24	3		330			R.S. §1342
1862—Jan.	24	11		333			R.S. §103
				333			R.S. §859
	31	15	4	334			R.S. §220
Feb.	4	17		336			R.S. §1690
				336			R.S. §1700
	12	20		338			R.S. §3473
				338			R.S. §3589
		21		338			R.S. §1437
	13	25	2	339			R.S. §1116
			4	340			R.S. §1343
			4	340			R.S. §1624
			5	340			R.S. §1342
	19	27	1	340			R.S. §2158
			1	340			R.S. §2159
			2	340			R.S. §2160
			3	340			R.S. §2161
			4	341			R.S. §2162
			5	341			R.S. §4274
			6	341			R.S. §2163
	25	33	1	345			R.S. §3473
			1	345			R.S. §3571
			1	345			R.S. §3579
			1	345			R.S. §3588
			1	345			R.S. §3589
			1	345			R.S. §3651
			2	346			R.S. §3701
			5	346			R.S. §3009
			5	346			R.S. §3473
			5	346			R.S. §3689
			5	346			R.S. §3694
Mar.	6	37	1	353			R.S. §3603
			1	353			R.S. §3604
			2	353			R.S. §3602

37th Cong.				U.S.C.		
12 Stat.	Chapter	Section	Page	Title	Section	Status
1862—Mar. 13	40		354			R.S. §1624
14	41	6	369			R.S. §438
		6	369			R.S. §439
17	45	1	370			R.S. §3700
		2	370			R.S. §3589
		4	370			R.S. §3580
		4	370			R.S. §3581
19	48		373			R.S. §3601
Apr. 2	53		376			R.S. §4742
16	Pub. R. 28		617			R.S. §1816
17	57	4	381			R.S. §1581
21	59	5	382			R.S. §3639
		5	383			R.S. §3592
		5	383			R.S. §3594
May 15	71	1	386			R.S. §572
		1	386			R.S. §658
		2	386			R.S. §584
		2	386			R.S. §585
		2	386			R.S. §665
		2	386			R.S. §670
		3	386			R.S. §815
		4	386			R.S. §579
		4	386			R.S. §580
		4	386			R.S. §581
		6	386			R.S. §577
		7	387			R.S. §557
		7	387			R.S. §620
		8	387			R.S. §727
		9	387			R.S. §745
		10	387			R.S. §946
	72	2	387			R.S. §520
		2	387			R.S. §521
		3	387			R.S. §525
		3	387			R.S. §526
		3	387			R.S. §528
		3	388			R.S. §3677
		4	388			R.S. §522
		4	388			R.S. §523
		4	388			R.S. §524
20	75	1	392			R.S. §2289
		2	392			R.S. §2290
		3	393			R.S. §2295
		4	393			R.S. §2296
		5	393			R.S. §2297
		6	393			R.S. §2238
		6	393			R.S. §2240
		6	393			R.S. §2298
		6	393			R.S. §2299
		6	393			R.S. §2300
		8	393			R.S. §2301
	76	2	394			R.S. §3607
	81	1	404			R.S. §5320
		2	404			R.S. §5321
		3	404			R.S. §5312
		4	405			R.S. §5292
30	86	1	409			R.S. §2398
		2	409			R.S. §2399
		3	409			R.S. §2400
		5	409			R.S. §2252
		6	409			R.S. §2237
		6	409			R.S. §2238
		6	409			R.S. §2240
		7	410			R.S. §2266
		8	410			R.S. §2228
		9	410			R.S. §2209
		9	410			R.S. §2210
		10	410			R.S. §2401
		10	410			R.S. §3689
June 2	92	1	411			R.S. §2583
		1	411			R.S. §2735
		2	411			R.S. §2672
		2	411			R.S. §2703
		2	411			R.S. §2714
	93	1	411			R.S. §3744
		2	411			R.S. §3745
		3	411			R.S. §3746
		4	412			R.S. §512
		4	412			R.S. §513
		4	412			R.S. §514
		4	412			R.S. §515
		4	412			R.S. §888
		5	412			R.S. §3747
	94		413			R.S. §2257
5	96		421			R.S. §1683
14	101	1	427			R.S. §2119
		2	427			R.S. §2120
		3	427			R.S. §2121

37th Cong. 12 Stat.	Chapter	Section	Page	U.S.C. Title	U.S.C. Section	Status
1862—June 17	103	1	430			R.S. §800
		1	430			R.S. §801
		1	430			R.S. §820
		2	430			R.S. §821
18	Pub. R. 36		620			R.S. §1802
20	116		432			R.S. §2559
			432			R.S. §2560
21	Pub. R. 37		620			R.S. §1116
			620			R.S. §1120
July 1	119	1	432			R.S. §319
		2	433			R.S. §3141
		2	433			R.S. §3142
		116	488			R.S. §3689
	120	5	492			R.S. §3689
		15	496			R.S. §5257
	126	1	501			R.S. §5352
		3	501			R.S. §1890
2	127	3	502			R.S. §1646
	128		502			R.S. §1756
			502			R.S. §1759
	130	1	503	7	301	
		2	503	7	302	
		3	504	7	303	
		4	504	7	304	
		5	504	7	305	
		6	505	7	306	Rep.
		7	505			R.S. §2238
		7	505			R.S. §2240
		7	505	7	307	
		8	505	7	308	
5	133	2	500			R.S. §3689
		2	508			R.S. §4818
		3	508			R.S. §1162
		3	508			R.S. §1293
		3	508			R.S. §1297
		10	510			R.S. §1147
	134	1	510			R.S. §416
		1	510			R.S. §419
		1	510			R.S. §421
		1	510			R.S. §422
		1	510			R.S. §423
		1	510			R.S. §424
		1	510			R.S. §425
		1	510			R.S. §426
		2	510			R.S. §421
		2	510			R.S. §1542
		4	511			R.S. §419
		4	511			R.S. §420
		5	511			R.S. §430
		5	511			R.S. §3676
	135	1	528			R.S. §2080
		5	529			R.S. §2084
		6	529			R.S. §2108
11	142	1	532			R.S. §3473
		1	532			R.S. §3571
		1	532			R.S. §3579
		1	532			R.S. §3588
		1	532			R.S. §3651
		2	532			R.S. §3577
	145		536			R.S. §536
	150		537			R.S. §2552
			537			R.S. §2553
12	Pub. R. 54		624			R.S. §51
14	163	5	546			R.S. §2504
		6	549			R.S. §2504
		7	550			R.S. §2504
		8	550			R.S. §2504
		11	554			R.S. §3725
		12	555			R.S. §2504
		13	555			R.S. §2504
		15	558			R.S. §4219
		15	558			R.S. §4227
		16	558			R.S. §2898
		18	559			R.S. §2863
		20	559			R.S. §3001
		21	559			R.S. §2971
		21	559			R.S. §3018
		21	560			R.S. §2977
		21	560			R.S. §3017
		21	560			R.S. §3025
		22	560			R.S. §2982
	164	1	564			R.S. §1545
		3	565			R.S. §1386
		4	565			R.S. §1580
		4	565			R.S. §1624
		5	565			R.S. §1547

70-027 D 38 : QL 3

37th Cong.				U.S.C.		
12 Stat.	**Chapter**	**Section**	**Page**	**Title**	**Section**	**Status**
1862—July 14	164	7	565			R.S. §1396
		9	565			R.S. §1517
	169	2	572			R.S. §2648
		4	572			R.S. §2658
	174		575			R.S. §572
	175		575			R.S. §1383
15	178	1	576			R.S. §572
		1	576			R.S. §658
		2	576			R.S. §608
16	180		577			R.S. §1781
	182	3	582			R.S. §2204
	183	1	583			R.S. §1362
		1	583			R.S. §1467
		1	583			R.S. §1492
		3	583			R.S. §1529
		3	584			R.S. §1435
		4	584			R.S. §1504
		7	584			R.S. §1365
		7	584			R.S. §1366
		7	584			R.S. §1497
		8	584			R.S. §1444
		8	584			R.S. §1446
		9	584			R.S. §1364
		9	584			R.S. §1508
		9	584			R.S. §1597
		9	584			R.S. §1607
		11	585			R.S. §1441
		11	585			R.S. §1492
		11	585			R.S. §1514
		11	585			R.S. §1515
		11	585			R.S. §1516
		11	585			R.S. §1517
		11	585			R.S. §1519
		13	585			R.S. §1466
		14	585			R.S. §1460
		15	586			R.S. §1339
		15	586			R.S. §1556
		18	587			R.S. §1375
		19	587			R.S. §1578
		20	587			R.S. §1559
		20	587			R.S. §1590
		20	587			R.S. §1594
		20	587			R.S. §1595
	184		587	34	505	Rev. T.
	189	1	588			R.S. §858
		2	589			R.S. §729
	190	1	589			R.S. §1342
		4	589			R.S. §1342
17	195	1	589			R.S. §5332
		2	590			R.S. §5334
		3	590			R.S. §5332
	196	2	592			R.S. §3583
	197	1	592			R.S. §5568
		2	593			R.S. §5569
	199		593			R.S. §3622
			593			R.S. §5491
	200	1	594			R.S. §1272
		2	594			R.S. §1271
		5	594			R.S. §1646
		6	594			R.S. §1647
		7	595			R.S. §1566
		8	595			R.S. §1123
		11	595			R.S. §1342
		12	596			R.S. §1244
		12	596			R.S. §1255
		12	596			R.S. §1622
		14	596			R.S. §3737
		15	596			R.S. §3731
		18	596			R.S. §4878
		21	597			R.S. §1116
		21	597			R.S. §2166
		22	597			R.S. §1129
	201	1	597			R.S. §1625
		1	597			R.S. §1643
		1	597			R.S. §1648
		2	598			R.S. §1645
		5	598			R.S. §1342
		6	598			R.S. §1200
		6	598			R.S. §1342
		7	598			R.S. §1342
		11	599			R.S. §1102
		11	599			R.S. §1103
		16	600			R.S. §1191
	204	1	600			R.S. §1624
		1	604			R.S. §1023
		5	607			R.S. §1624

37th Cong. 12 Stat.	Chapter	Section	Page	U.S.C. Title	U.S.C. Section	Status
1862—July 17	204	7	607			R.S. §1624
		8	607			R.S. §1624
		11	607			R.S. §4752
		14	609			R.S. §1574
		14	609			R.S. §1624
		15	609			R.S. §1575
		16	609			R.S. §1624
		17	610			R.S. §1422
		17	610			R.S. §1423
		17	610			R.S. §1424
		17	610			R.S. §1425
		17	610			R.S. §1572
		18	610			R.S. §1410
		19	610			R.S. §1548
	205	1	610			R.S. §3478
		2	610			R.S. §3479
	Pub. R. 68	2	628			R.S. §41
	Pub. R. 70		629			R.S. §4781
1863—Jan. 6	7		634			R.S. §1102
			634			R.S. §1103
	Pub. R. 2	1	822			R.S. §3781
13	9		634			R.S. §658
17	Pub. R. 9		822			R.S. §3571
			822			R.S. §3588
30	14	2	637			R.S. §3811
Feb. 4	20	1	639			R.S. §2751
		2	639			R.S. §2750
		3	640			R.S. §2754
		4	640			R.S. §1492
9	25	2	646			R.S. §1760
		2	040			R.S. §1761
	27		648			R.S. §1917
20	44	1	656			R.S. §314
		2	656			R.S. §315
	46		656			R.S. §5330
	47		657			R.S. §572
			657			R.S. §658
21	49		657			R.S. §572
			657			R.S. §658
	50		657			R.S. §1000
	50		657			R.S. §1001
	52		658			R.S. §2535
			658			R.S. §2536
			658			R.S. §2695
24	54	1	660			R.S. §538
		2	661			R.S. §572
		2	661			R.S. §579
		2	661			R.S. §608
		2	661			R.S. §658
		7	661			R.S. §551
		8	661			R.S. §767
		8	661			R.S. §770
		8	661			R.S. §776
		8	662			R.S. §781
		9	662			R.S. §740
	56	1	664			R.S. §1839
		1	664			R.S. §1840
		1	664			R.S. §1901
		2	665			R.S. §702
		2	665			R.S. §1841
		2	665			R.S. §1842
		2	665			R.S. §1843
		2	665			R.S. §1844
		2	665			R.S. §1846
		2	665			R.S. §1847
		2	665			R.S. §1848
		2	665			R.S. §1849
		2	665			R.S. §1850
		2	665			R.S. §1851
		2	665			R.S. §1854
		2	665			R.S. §1857
		2	665			R.S. §1859
		2	665			R.S. §1860
		2	665			R.S. §1862
		2	665			R.S. §1863
		2	665			R.S. §1864
		2	665			R.S. §1865
		2	665			R.S. §1866
		2	665			R.S. §1867
		2	665			R.S. §1868
		2	665			R.S. §1869
		2	665			R.S. §1870
		2	665			R.S. §1871
		2	665			R.S. §1872
		2	665			R.S. §1873
		2	665			R.S. §1875

37th Cong.

12 Stat.	Chapter	Section	Page	U.S.C. Title	U.S.C. Section	Status
1863—Feb. 24	56	2	665			R.S. §1876
		2	665			R.S. §1877
		2	665			R.S. §1878
		2	665			R.S. §1881
		2	665			R.S. §1882
		2	665			R.S. §1883
		2	665			R.S. §1885
		2	665			R.S. §1891
		2	665			R.S. §1908
		2	665			R.S. §1909
		2	665			R.S. §1910
		2	665			R.S. §1913
		2	665			R.S. §1918
		2	665			R.S. §1922
		2	665			R.S. §1935
		2	665			R.S. §1939
		2	665			R.S. §1942
		2	665			R.S. §1944
		2	665			R.S. §1946
25	58	55	680			R.S. §380
		57	680			R.S. §5415
	59	3	696			R.S. §2204
	61		696			R.S. §1781
Mar. 2	67	1	696			R.S. §1342
		1	696			R.S. §1624
		1	696			R.S. §5438
		1	696			R.S. §5439
		2	697			R.S. §1624
		3	698			R.S. §3490
		3	698			R.S. §5438
		3	698			R.S. §5439
		4	698			R.S. §563
		4	698			R.S. §3491
		5	698			R.S. §3492
		6	698			R.S. §3493
		7	698			R.S. §3494
		8	698			R.S. §1783
	69	2	699			R.S. §572
		2	699			R.S. §658
	70	1	700			R.S. §1842
		2	700			R.S. §1842
		3	700			R.S. §1883
		3	700			R.S. §1927
		3	700			R.S. §1929
		3	700			R.S. §1930
		4	701			R.S. §1842
3	73	1	710			R.S. §3701
		2	710			R.S. §3476
		2	710			R.S. §3590
		3	710			R.S. §3473
		3	710			R.S. §3571
		3	710			R.S. §3579
		3	710			R.S. §3651
		3	711			R.S. §3588
		4	711			R.S. §3574
		4	711			R.S. §3575
		5	711			R.S. §254
		5	711			R.S. §3473
		6	711			R.S. §3578
	74	19	725			R.S. §322
		19	725			R.S. §323
	75	2	731			R.S. §1342
		21	735			R.S. §1342
		23	735			R.S. §1242
		23	735			R.S. §3748
		24	735			R.S. §5455
		27	736			R.S. §1342
		28	736			R.S. §1203
		29	736			R.S. §1342
		30	736			R.S. §1342
		31	736			R.S. §1265
		32	736			R.S. §1342
		35	736			R.S. §1236
		37	737			R.S. §1102
		37	737			R.S. §1103
		38	737			R.S. §1343
		38	737			R.S. §1624
	76	1	737			R.S. §2853
		1	737			R.S. §2854
		1	738			R.S. §2855
		1	738			R.S. §2857
		1	738			R.S. §2860
		1	738			R.S. §2864
		1	739			R.S. §2858
		1	739			R.S. §2859
		2	739			R.S. §376

37th Cong. 12 Stat.	Chapter	Section	Page	U.S.C. Title	U.S.C. Section	Status
1863—Mar. 3	76	3	739			R.S. §5445
		4	739			R.S. §5444
		5	740			R.S. §3081
		6	740			R.S. §5451
		6	740			R.S. §5452
		6	740			R.S. §5501
		8	740			R.S. §5443
		9	740			R.S. §3749
		10	740			R.S. §3469
		11	741			R.S. §825
		11	741			R.S. §834
		11	741			R.S. §835
		12	741			R.S. §827
		12	741			R.S. §834
		13	741			R.S. §989
		13	741			R.S. §771
		13	741			R.S. §773
		14	741			R.S. §1047
	77	7	742			R.S. §2504
		7	742			R.S. §3026
	78	1	743			R.S. §1157
		1	743			R.S. §4663
		3	743			R.S. §1206
		3	743			R.S. §1207
		4	743			R.S. §1160
		4	743			R.S. §1207
		4	743			R.S. §1208
		5	743			R.S. §3483
		5	743			R.S. §3689
		6	743			R.S. §280
		8	744			R.S. §1174
		8	744			R.S. §1234
		9	744			R.S. §1233
		11	744			R.S. §1146
	79	12	752			R.S. §3605
		16	753			R.S. §2536
		16	753			R.S. §2694
		24	754			R.S. §1694
		25	754			R.S. §1202
		25	754			R.S. §1342
	80	1	754			R.S. §2380
		2	754			R.S. §2381
	81	5	756			R.S. §641
		5	756			R.S. §642
		5	756			R.S. §646
	82		758			R.S. §1264
	87	1	760			R.S. §2644
		2	761			R.S. §2535
		2	761			R.S. §2536
		4	761			R.S. §2599
		4	761			R.S. §2600
	88	1	761			R.S. §2578
		1	761			R.S. §2579
		2	761			R.S. §1928
	89		761			R.S. §303
			761			R.S. §304
	90		762			R.S. §5322
	91	2	763			R.S. §706
		3	763			R.S. §4845
		11	764			R.S. §705
		11	764			R.S. §706
	92	1	765			R.S. §1049
		2	765			R.S. §1060
		3	765			R.S. §1059
		3	765			R.S. §1061
		4	765			R.S. §94
		4	765			R.S. §1053
		4	765			R.S. §1054
		4	765			R.S. §1058
		4	765			R.S. §1070
		4	765			R.S. §1071
		4	765			R.S. §1075
		4	766			R.S. §1050
		5	766			R.S. §707
		5	766			R.S. §708
		7	766			R.S. §1089
		7	766			R.S. §1090
		7	766			R.S. §1091
		7	766			R.S. §1092
		7	766			R.S. §1093
		8	766			R.S. §1079
		8	766			R.S. §1080
		9	767			R.S. §1066
		10	767			R.S. §1069
		11	767			R.S. §707
		11	767			R.S. §708

37th Cong.				U.S.C.		
12 Stat.	Chapter	Section	Page	Title	Section	Status
1863—Mar. 3	92	11	767			R.S. §1086
		12	767			R.S. §1072
		12	767			R.S. §1073
		13	768			R.S. §1052
	93	1	768			R.S. §617
		2	768			R.S. §615
		2	768			R.S. §616
		2	768			R.S. §618
		2	768			R.S. §793
		2	768			R.S. §795
		3	768			R.S. §618
	95	1	769			R.S. §4071
		2	769			R.S. §4073
		3	769			R.S. §4074
		4	770			R.S. §875
	96	5	770			R.S. §3592
		5	770			R.S. §3594
		5	770			R.S. §3639
	99		792			R.S. §2067
	100	1	794			R.S. §664
		2	794			R.S. §608
	108		804			R.S. §31
	111	1–3	806	36	251–253	Rev. T.
	117	1	808			R.S. §1839
		1	808			R.S. §1840
		1	808			R.S. §1902
		2	809			R.S. §1841
		3	809			R.S. §1843
		3	809			R.S. §1844
		4	809			R.S. §1846
		4	809			R.S. §1847
		4	809			R.S. §1848
		4	809			R.S. §1849
		4	809			R.S. §1922
		4	809			R.S. §1923
		5	810			R.S. §1859
		5	810			R.S. §1860
		6	810			R.S. §1842
		6	810			R.S. §1851
		7	811			R.S. §1857
		8	811			R.S. §1854
		9	811			R.S. §702
		9	811			R.S. §1864
		9	811			R.S. §1865
		9	811			R.S. §1866
		9	811			R.S. §1867
		9	811			R.S. §1868
		9	811			R.S. §1869
		9	811			R.S. §1870
		9	811			R.S. §1871
		9	811			R.S. §1872
		9	811			R.S. §1883
		9	811			R.S. §1907
		9	811			R.S. §1909
		9	811			R.S. §1910
		9	811			R.S. §1912
		9	811			R.S. §1926
		10	812			R.S. §1875
		10	812			R.S. §1876
		10	812			R.S. §1881
		10	812			R.S. §1882
		11	812			R.S. §1877
		11	812			R.S. §1878
		11	812			R.S. §1935
		11	812			R.S. §1939
		11	812			R.S. §1940
		11	812			R.S. §1941
		11	812			R.S. §1943
		12	813			R.S. §1885
		12	813			R.S. §1945
		13	813			R.S. §1862
		13	813			R.S. §1863
		13	813			R.S. §1891
		13	813			R.S. §1906
		14	814			R.S. §1946
		15	814			R.S. §1873
		16	814			R.S. §1951
		19	814			R.S. §1949
	118	4	818			R.S. §3727
		5	818			R.S. §1388
	120	3	820			R.S. §1059
		3	820			R.S. §3689
	Pub. R. 25		825	34	869	Rev. T.
	Pub. R. 27	3	826			R.S. §265
		3	826			R.S. §3798
		3	826			R.S. §3812

37th Cong. 12 Stat.	Chapter	Section	Page	U.S.C. Title	U.S.C. Section	Status
1863—Mar. 3	Pub. R. 32	2	828			R.S. §3722
38th Cong.						
13 Stat.						
1864—Jan. 26	5	2	2			R.S. §581
		2	2			R.S. §666
		2	2			R.S. §670
Feb. 3	Pub. R. 11		402			R.S. §3791
19	11	1	4			R.S. §658
		3	4			R.S. §664
		3	4			R.S. §670
		6	5			R.S. §840
		8	5			R.S. §572
Mar. 3	17		13			R.S. §3701
11	28		22			R.S. §2568
			22			R.S. §2708
			22			R.S. §2823
14	30	1	22			R.S. §76
		1	25			R.S. §3789
		1	25			R.S. §3821
		3	26			R.S. §234
		3	26			R.S. §245
		7	28			R.S. §314
15	33		29			R.S. §2139
			29			R.S. §2140
17	Pub. R. 20		404			R.S. §3699
21	36	10	32			R.S. §3689
	38	2	35			R.S. §2238
		2	35			R.S. §2290
		3	35			R.S. §2294
		4	35			R.S. §2238
		4	35			R.S. §2293
		5	35			R.S. §2268
		6	36			R.S. §2238
		6	36			R.S. §2240
25	40	1	36			R.S. §4203
		2	36			R.S. §4212
Apr. 1	45	3	39			R.S. §1339
	47	2	39			R.S. §1517
8	48	1	39			R.S. §2046
		4	40			R.S. §2056
		6	41			R.S. §2115
		7	41			R.S. §2061
9	53	1	46			R.S. §1121
		1	46			R.S. §1122
		1	46			R.S. §1271
		3	46			R.S. §1126
		3	46			R.S. §1127
		4	46			R.S. §1125
	54		46			R.S. §2518
21	63	1	53			R.S. §1496
		1	53			R.S. §1497
		1	53			R.S. §1499
		2	53			R.S. §1498
		3	53			R.S. §1500
		3	53			R.S. §1501
		3	53			R.S. §1502
		3	53			R.S. §1503
		4	53			R.S. §1447
		4	53			R.S. §1493
		4	53			R.S. §1494
		4	53			R.S. §1504
		6	54			R.S. §1506
		6	54			R.S. §1605
		7	54			R.S. §1382
		7	54			R.S. §1393
		7	54			R.S. §1467
		7	54			R.S. §1590
	65		54			R.S. §2543
			54			R.S. §2544
22	66	2	55			R.S. §5462
		5	55			R.S. §5462
29	69		58			R.S. §4233
	70		61			R.S. §4586
	71		61			R.S. §2737
May 5	78	2	64			R.S. §4179
6	83	1	69			R.S. §4148
		1	69			R.S. §4331
		2	69			R.S. §4150
		3	70			R.S. §4153
		4	72			R.S. §4186
		5	72			R.S. §4152
12	85	1	74			R.S. §829
		1	74			R.S. §830
		1	74			R.S. §5546
		2	75			R.S. §5547

38th Cong.				U.S.C.		
13 Stat.	Chapter	Section	Page	Title	Section	Status
1864—May 12	85	3	75			R.S. §830
		3	75			R.S. §5545
16	86	2	75			R.S. §1624
17	87	11	78			R.S. §889
	89	3	79			R.S. §1407
		3	79			R.S. §1408
		3	79			R.S. §1409
21	93	1	84			R.S. §1518
		3	85			R.S. §1528
		4	85			R.S. §1511
26	95	1	85			R.S. §1839
		1	85			R.S. §1840
		1	85			R.S. §1903
		2	86			R.S. §1841
		3	86			R.S. §1843
		3	86			R.S. §1844
		4	87			R.S. §1846
		4	87			R.S. §1847
		4	87			R.S. §1848
		4	87			R.S. §1849
		4	87			R.S. §1922
		4	87			R.S. §1923
		5	87			R.S. §1859
		5	87			R.S. §1860
		6	88			R.S. §1842
		6	88			R.S. §1851
		7	88			R.S. §1857
		8	88			R.S. §1854
		9	88			R.S. §702
		9	88			R.S. §1864
		9	88			R.S. §1865
		9	88			R.S. §1866
		9	88			R.S. §1867
		9	88			R.S. §1868
		9	88			R.S. §1869
		9	88			R.S. §1870
		9	88			R.S. §1871
		9	88			R.S. §1872
		9	88			R.S. §1883
		9	88			R.S. §1907
		9	88			R.S. §1909
		9	88			R.S. §1910
		9	88			R.S. §1912
		9	88			R.S. §1926
		10	89			R.S. §1875
		10	89			R.S. §1876
		10	89			R.S. §1881
		10	89			R.S. §1882
		11	90			R.S. §1877
		11	90			R.S. §1878
		11	90			R.S. §1935
		11	90			R.S. §1939
		11	90			R.S. §1940
		11	90			R.S. §1941
		11	90			R.S. §1943
		12	91			R.S. §1885
		12	91			R.S. §1945
		13	91			R.S. §1862
		13	91			R.S. §1863
		13	91			R.S. §1891
		13	91			R.S. §1906
		14	91			R.S. §1946
		15	91			R.S. §1873
		16	91			R.S. §1951
		17	91			R.S. §1949
	96		92			R.S. §1386
			92			R.S. §1387
28	98	4	94			R.S. §4232
June 3	106	1	99			R.S. §324
		1	99			R.S. §325
		1	99			R.S. §326
		1	99			R.S. §327
		1	100			R.S. §328
		1	100			R.S. §329
		2	100			R.S. §330
		2	100			R.S. §884
		3	100			R.S. §331
		4	100			R.S. §5158
		5	100			R.S. §5133
		6	101			R.S. §885
		6	101			R.S. §5134
		6	101			R.S. §5135
		7	101			R.S. §5138
		8	101			R.S. §5136
		8	101			R.S. §5190
		9	102			R.S. §5145

38th Cong. 13 Stat.	Chapter	Section	Page	U.S.C. Title	U.S.C. Section	Status
1864—June 3	106	9	102			R.S. §5146
		9	102			R.S. §5147
		9	102			R.S. §5149
		9	102			R.S. §5150
		10	102			R.S. §5145
		10	102			R.S. §5146
		10	102			R.S. §5148
		11	102			R.S. §5144
		12	102			R.S. §5139
		12	102			R.S. §5151
		12	102			R.S. §5169
		13	103			R.S. §5142
		13	103			R.S. §5143
		14	103			R.S. §5140
		15	103			R.S. §5141
		16	104			R.S. §5159
		16	104			R.S. §5160
		16	104			R.S. §5161
		17	104			R.S. §5168
		18	104			R.S. §5169
		18	104			R.S. §5170
		19	105			R.S. §5162
		19	105			R.S. §5163
		19	105			R.S. §5164
		20	105			R.S. §5163
		20	105			R.S. §5165
		22	105			R.S. §5172
		22	105			R.S. §5175
		22	105			R.S. §5177
		23	106			R.S. §3473
		23	106			R.S. §3475
		23	106			R.S. §3651
		23	106			R.S. §5182
		23	106			R.S. §5183
		23	106			R.S. §5184
		25	106			R.S. §5166
		26	107			R.S. §5167
		27	107			R.S. §5187
		28	107			R.S. §5137
		29	108			R.S. §5200
		30	108			R.S. §5197
		30	108			R.S. §5198
		31	108			R.S. §5191
		31	108			R.S. §5192
		32	109			R.S. §5195
		32	109			R.S. §5196
		33	109			R.S. §5199
		34	109			R.S. §5211
		35	110			R.S. §5201
		36	110			R.S. §5202
		37	110			R.S. §5203
		38	110			R.S. §5204
		39	111			R.S. §5206
		40	111			R.S. §5210
		41	111			R.S. §5173
		41	111			R.S. §5214
		41	111			R.S. §5215
		41	111			R.S. §5216
		41	111			R.S. §5217
		41	111			R.S. §5219
		42	112			R.S. §5220
		42	112			R.S. §5221
		42	112			R.S. §5222
		42	112			R.S. §5224
		43	112			R.S. §5222
		43	112			R.S. §5225
		44	112			R.S. §5154
		45	113			R.S. §5153
		46	113			R.S. §5226
		46	113			R.S. §5228
		47	114			R.S. §5227
		47	114			R.S. §5229
		47	114			R.S. §5230
		47	114			R.S. §5232
		47	114			R.S. §5233
		48	114			R.S. §5230
		49	114			R.S. §5231
		50	114			R.S. §5234
		50	114			R.S. §5235
		50	114			R.S. §5236
		50	114			R.S. §5237
		50	115			R.S. §629
		50	115			R.S. §736
		51	115			R.S. §5238
		52	115			R.S. §5242
		53	116			R.S. §5239

38th Cong. 13 Stat.	Chapter	Section	Page	U.S.C. Title	U.S.C. Section	Status
1864—June 3	106	54	116			R.S. §5240
		54	116			R.S. §5241
		55	116			R.S. §5209
		56	116			R.S. §380
		57	116			R.S. §563
		57	116			R.S. §629
		57	116			R.S. §736
		58	117			R.S. §5189
		59	117			R.S. §5415
		61	117			R.S. §333
		62	118			R.S. §5156
		62	118			R.S. §5177
		63	118			R.S. §5152
	107		118			R.S. §3789
	109		119			R.S. §2535
			119			R.S. §2536
7	111		120			R.S. §1417
			120			R.S. §1426
			120			R.S. §1427
			120			R.S. §1573
8	114		120			R.S. §5461
11	116	1	121			R.S. §4079
		2	121			R.S. §4080
		2	121			R.S. §4081
	117		122			R.S. §3753
			122			R.S. §3754
	118		123			R.S. §1048
	119		123			R.S. §1782
	120		124			R.S. §531
			124			R.S. §551
			124			R.S. §571
			124			R.S. §572
			124			R.S. §608
			124			R.S. §658
			124			R.S. §767
			124			R.S. §770
			124			R.S. §776
			124			R.S. §781
			124			R.S. §1002
	121	2	124			R.S. §4300
		3	125			R.S. §4301
		4	125			R.S. §4301
		5	125			R.S. §4304
		6	125			R.S. §4302
		7	125			R.S. §4303
	122		125			R.S. §2586
17	130	1	134			R.S. §4318
		2	134			R.S. §2675
		3	134			R.S. §2654
		3	134			R.S. §2657
		4	134			R.S. §2597
		5	134			R.S. §2620
	131		135			R.S. §1842
20	136	1	138			R.S. §1674
		1	138			R.S. §1690
		2	139			R.S. §1704
		2	139			R.S. §1705
		3	140			R.S. §1721
	143		143			R.S. §538
	145	1	144			R.S. §1111
		1	144			R.S. §1181
		1	144			R.S. §1278
		4	144			R.S. §1154
		8	145			R.S. §1289
		8	145			R.S. §1290
		10	145			R.S. §1190
		11	145			R.S. §1265
25	147	1	148			R.S. §80
		1	155			R.S. §527
		2	159			R.S. §235
		2	159			R.S. §303
		6	160			R.S. §3488
		7	161			R.S. §3609
	150		182			R.S. §3484
	152		183			R.S. §1444
	155	1	184			R.S. §75
		1	184			R.S. §196
		1	184			R.S. §3798
		3	185			R.S. §196
		4	185			R.S. §3798
		4	185			R.S. §3810
		5	185			R.S. §3798
		6	185			R.S. §3797
		7	185			R.S. §3807
		9	186			R.S. §3780
		10	186			R.S. §3809

38th Cong.				U.S.C.		
13 Stat.	Chapter	Section	Page	Title	Section	Status
1864—June 25	155	10	186			R.S. §3818
		12	186			R.S. §3790
27	163	1	195			R.S. §832
		2	196			R.S. §834
		2	196			R.S. §835
		2	196			R.S. §841
		4	196			R.S. §832
	164	1	197			R.S. §3100
		1	197			R.S. §3101
		2	197			R.S. §3102
		3	197			R.S. §3103
		4	197			R.S. §3104
		5	198			R.S. §3105
		5	198			R.S. §3106
		7	198			R.S. §2605
		8	198			R.S. §5293
	165	2	199			R.S. §897
		4	199			R.S. §897
28	170		201			R.S. §1428
			201			R.S. §4219
30	171	1	202			R.S. §2504
		1	202			R.S. §2914
		2	202			R.S. §2504
		3	203			R.S. §2504
		6	208			R.S. §2504
		7	209			R.S. §2504
		8	210			R.S. §2504
		9	210			R.S. §2504
		10	211			R.S. §2504
		11	211			R.S. §2504
		12	213			R.S. §2504
		13	213			R.S. §2504
		14	214			R.S. §2931
		15	215			R.S. §2932
		16	215			R.S. §3012½
		16	215			R.S. §3689
		17	215			R.S. §2502
		19	216			R.S. §2962
		19	216			R.S. §2975
		27	217			R.S. §2837
		28	218			R.S. §5305
		29	218			R.S. §2803
	172	1	218			R.S. §3701
		2	218			R.S. §3473
		2	218			R.S. §3476
		2	218			R.S. §3590
		5	220			R.S. §3572
		5	220			R.S. §3574
		5	220			R.S. §3575
		7	220			R.S. §3706
		8	221			R.S. §251
		9	221			R.S. §3578
		10	221			R.S. §5414
		10	221			R.S. §5431
		11	221			R.S. §5430
		13	222			R.S. §5413
	173	1	223			R.S. §319
		1	223			R.S. §321
		1	223			R.S. §3465
		2	223			R.S. §277
		3	224			R.S. §322
		3	224			R.S. §323
		7	224			R.S. §3141
		7	224			R.S. §3142
		9	225			R.S. §3143
		10	225			R.S. §3148
		11	225			R.S. §3173
		12	225			R.S. §3172
		13	226			R.S. §3173
		14	226			R.S. §3174
		14	226			R.S. §3175
		14	226			R.S. §3176
		15	226			R.S. §3179
		16	227			R.S. §3180
		17	228			R.S. §3317
		18	228			R.S. §3181
		20	229			R.S. §3182
		25	231			R.S. §3145
		26	232			R.S. §3147
		32	236			R.S. §3209
		33	236			R.S. §3211
		33	236			R.S. §3212
		35	237			R.S. §3217
		36	238			R.S. §3167
		36	238			R.S. §3183
		37	238			R.S. §3177

38th Cong.				U.S.C.		
13 Stat.	Chapter	Section	Page	Title	Section	Status
1864—June 30	173	38	238			R.S. §3167
		38	238			R.S. §3177
		39	238			R.S. §3149
		40	239			R.S. §3149
		41	239			R.S. §563
		41	239			R.S. §629
		41	239			R.S. §732
		41	239			R.S. §3183
		42	239			R.S. §3158
		43	239			R.S. §239
		43	239			R.S. §261
		44	239			R.S. §3689
		45	240			R.S. §3194
		48	240			R.S. §734
		48	240			R.S. §3452
		48	240			R.S. §3453
		48	240			R.S. §3458
		48	241			R.S. §3459
		52	242			R.S. §3165
		58	244			R.S. §3151
		79	251			R.S. §3407
		82	258			R.S. §1
		92	263			R.S. §3366
		92	263			R.S. §3367
		92	263			R.S. §3404
		92	263			R.S. §3405
		110	277			R.S. §3408
		110	277			R.S. §3409
		110	278			R.S. §3414
		110	278			R.S. §3415
		110	278			R.S. §3417
		124	285			R.S. §3438
		126	287			R.S. §1
		133	288			R.S. §3439
		151	291			R.S. §3418
		154	292			R.S. §3420
		155	292			R.S. §3423
		155	292			R.S. §3429
		156	293			R.S. §3423
		157	293			R.S. §3424
		158	293			R.S. §3422
		161	294			R.S. §3425
		161	294			R.S. §3426
		161	294			R.S. §3689
		163	295			R.S. §3421
		165	296			R.S. §3423
		165	296			R.S. §3430
		166	296			R.S. §3431
		167	296			R.S. §3432
		168	296			R.S. §3419
		168	296			R.S. §3433
		169	297			R.S. §3435
		170	297			R.S. §3427
		170	298			R.S. §3428
		170	301			R.S. §3437
		171	302			R.S. §3441
		171	302			R.S. §3442
		172	303			R.S. §3443
		179	305			R.S. §563
		179	305			R.S. §629
		179	305			R.S. §732
		180	306			R.S. §3454
		182	306			R.S. §3140
	174	1	306			R.S. §4615
		2	307			R.S. §4616
		3	307			R.S. §4617
		4	307			R.S. §4618
		4	307			R.S. §4619
		5	307			R.S. §4621
		6	308			R.S. §4622
		7	308			R.S. §4623
		8	308			R.S. §4627
		8	308			R.S. §4628
		9	309			R.S. §4634
		10	309			R.S. §4630
		10	309			R.S. §4631
		10	309			R.S. §4632
		10	309			R.S. §4633
		11	310			R.S. §4635
		11	310			R.S. §4642
		12	310			R.S. §1430
		12	310			R.S. §1576
		12	310			R.S. §4643
		13	310			R.S. §565
		13	310			R.S. §631
		13	310			R.S. §692

38th Cong.				U.S.C.		
13 Stat.	Chapter	Section	Page	Title	Section	Status
1864—June 30	174	13	310			R.S. §695
		13	310			R.S. §696
		13	310			R.S. §698
		13	310			R.S. §701
		13	310			R.S. §1009
		13	310			R.S. §1012
		13	310			R.S. §4637
		14	311			R.S. §4639
		14	311			R.S. §4640
		15	311			R.S. §4638
		16	311			R.S. §3689
		16	311			R.S. §4641
		17	312			R.S. §4644
		18	312			R.S. §4645
		19	312			R.S. §835
		19	312			R.S. §836
		19	312			R.S. §842
		20	312			R.S. §4646
		21	312			R.S. §4647
		22	313			R.S. §4650
		23	313			R.S. §4620
		23	313			R.S. §4648
		24	313			R.S. §4649
		25	313			R.S. §4651
		26	313			R.S. §4626
		27	314			R.S. §4624
		28	314			R.S. §4625
		29	314			R.S. §4652
		30	315			R.S. §4629
		31	315			R.S. §5441
		32	315			R.S. §4614
		33	315			R.S. §4613
	183		325			R.S. §4781
	184	1, 2	325	16	48	
	Pub. R. 56		412			R.S. §1818
July 1	196		335			R.S. §2238
			335			R.S. §2240
	201	1	342			R.S. §1421
		4	342			R.S. §1569
	202		342			R.S. §2568
			342			R.S. §2708
			342			R.S. §2823
	204		343			R.S. §1553
			343			R.S. §5455
	205	2	343			R.S. §2382
		3	344			R.S. §2383
		4	344			R.S. §2384
	Pub. R. 60		414			R.S. §2402
			414			R.S. §3689
	Pub. R. 62		414			R.S. §4753
2	210	2	347			R.S. §1814
		2	348			R.S. §1551
		3	351			R.S. §858
		3	351			R.S. §1078
		8	352			R.S. §2212
	215		356			R.S. §1342
	216	3	357	43	942–3	
		7	359			R.S. §3689
		8	359			R.S. §3689
		15	362	45	83	Rep.
	219	1	373			R.S. §1491
		2	373			R.S. §1406
		4	373			R.S. §416
	221		374			R.S. §2364
	224		375			R.S. §461
	225	2	375			R.S. §1059
		3	376			R.S. §1059
		4	376			R.S. §5303
		5	376			R.S. §5302
		7	377			R.S. §5310
		9	377			R.S. §5304
		10	377			R.S. §5306
		10	377			R.S. §5307
		10	377			R.S. §5313
	226	1	378			R.S. §2416
		2	379			R.S. §2417
	Pub. R. 67		416			R.S. §1330
	Pub. R. 68		416			R.S. §1111
4	237	5	380			R.S. §1118
		5	380			R.S. §1342
	242	5	383			R.S. §3639
	245	1	385			R.S. §572
		1	385			R.S. §581
		2	385			R.S. §658
		2	385			R.S. §806
	247		387			R.S. §4773

38th Cong. 13 Stat.		Chapter	Section	Page	U.S.C. Title	U.S.C. Section	Status
1864—July	4	248	1	389			R.S. §286
			2	390			R.S. §287
			2	390			R.S. §288
			2	390			R.S. §3689
			3	390			R.S. §274
			3	390			R.S. §289
			3	390			R.S. §3689
		249	1	390			R.S. §4252
			2	390			R.S. §4265
			9	392			R.S. §4273
			10	392			R.S. §4204
		252	1	393			R.S. §1522
			2	393			R.S. §1394
			2	393			R.S. §1403
			3	393			R.S. §1523
			4	393			R.S. §1523
			4	393			R.S. §1525
			5	393			R.S. §1524
			5	393			R.S. §1556
			7	394			R.S. §3724
		Pub. R. 75		416			R.S. §1277
Dec.	21	6	1	420			R.S. §1362
			1	420			R.S. §1466
			2	420			R.S. §1367
			3	420			R.S. §1444
	22	9		420			R.S. §2971
1865—Jan.	10	11		420			R.S. §5580
	24	19	1	424			R.S. §1467
			1	424			R.S. §1506
			1	424			R.S. §1605
			2	424			R.S. §1507
			2	424			R.S. §1508
			2	424			R.S. §1597
			2	424			R.S. §1606
			2	424			R.S. §1607
	28	22		425			R.S. §3701
	30	Pub. R. 10		567			R.S. §2346
Feb.	13	32		427			R.S. §3613
	14	Pub. R. 15		568			R.S. §77
				568			R.S. §3801
	20	42		431			R.S. §2543
	23	47	1	432			R.S. §924
			1	432			R.S. §933
			2	433			R.S. §925
			2	433			R.S. §926
			3	433			R.S. §927
			4	433			R.S. §928
			5	434			R.S. §929
			6	434			R.S. §930
			7	434			R.S. §931
			9	434			R.S. §932
			9	434			R.S. §933
		50	1	436			R.S. §4859
			2	436			R.S. §3689
			2	436			R.S. §4869
	25	52	1	437			R.S. §2002
			1	437			R.S. §2003
			1	437			R.S. §5528
			1	437			R.S. §5530
			1	437			R.S. §5532
			2	438			R.S. §5529
			2	438			R.S. §5531
			2	438			R.S. §5532
		54	1	438			R.S. §541
			1	438			R.S. §551
			1	438			R.S. §572
			1	438			R.S. §608
			1	438			R.S. §658
			1	438			R.S. §767
			1	438			R.S. §770
			1	438			R.S. §776
			2	438			R.S. §542
			3	438			R.S. §599
			3	438			R.S. §600
		55		438			R.S. §4340
	27	64	1	440			R.S. §531
			1	440			R.S. §551
			1	440			R.S. §572
			1	440			R.S. §767
			1	440			R.S. §776
			2	440			R.S. §608
			2	440			R.S. §658
			2	440			R.S. §664
			6	440			R.S. §837
			7	440			R.S. §670
			7	440			R.S. §840
			9	441			R.S. §910

38th Cong.				U.S.C.		
13 Stat.	**Chapter**	**Section**	**Page**	**Title**	**Section**	**Status**
1865—Feb. 28	67	2	442			R.S. §3066
		2	442			R.S. §5295
		3	442			R.S. §3107
		3	442			R.S. §3108
		4	442			R.S. §3074
		4	442			R.S. §3075
	69		444			R.S. §4328
	70		444			R.S. §4151
	71	2	445			R.S. §2716
		3	445			R.S. §2715
	72	2	445			R.S. §2601
Mar. 2	73		445			R.S. §527
	74	7	467			R.S. §3721
		7	467			R.S. §3729
	76		468			R.S. §349
3	77	2	469			R.S. §3701
	78	1	469			R.S. §3145
		1	471			R.S. §3149
		1	471			R.S. §3165
		1	471			R.S. §3167
		1	482			R.S. §3432
		1	482			R.S. §3433
		1	482			R.S. §3441
		1	483			R.S. §563
		1	483			R.S. §629
		3	483			R.S. §3210
		4	483			R.S. §3144
		6	484			R.S. §3412
		6	484			R.S. §3413
		7	484			R.S. §5155
		14	486			R.S. §3410
		14	486			R.S. §3411
		14	486			R.S. §3416
		15	486			R.S. §3161
		15	486			R.S. §3162
	79	9	488			R.S. §1264
		12	489			R.S. §1230
		12	489			R.S. §1624
		18	490			R.S. §1118
		18	490			R.S. §1342
		18	490			R.S. §1419
		18	490			R.S. §1420
		18	490			R.S. §1624
		21	490			R.S. §1996
		21	490			R.S. §1998
		25	491			R.S. §225
	80	1	491			R.S. §2504
		2	492			R.S. §2504
		3	493			R.S. §2504
		4	493			R.S. §4219
		7	493			R.S. §2900
		7	493			R.S. §2906
		12	494			R.S. §962
		12	494			R.S. §3014
		13	495			R.S. §2984
		13	495			R.S. §3689
	81	5	497			R.S. §1145
		5	497			R.S. §1299
		6	497			R.S. §1149
		6	497			R.S. §1150
		6	497			R.S. §1301
	82		498			R.S. §5171
			498			R.S. §5178
	86	1	500			R.S. §804
		1	500			R.S. §808
		1	500			R.S. §809
		1	500			R.S. §1021
		2	500			R.S. §1031
		3	500			R.S. §5536
		3	500			R.S. §5541
		4	501			R.S. §648
		4	501			R.S. §649
		4	501			R.S. §700
		4	501			R.S. §987
	87	7	502			R.S. §3689
	98		516			R.S. §351
	101		518			R.S. §4193
	107	2	530			R.S. §2385
		2	530			R.S. §2386
	111		532			R.S. §2862
	113		533			R.S. §858
	114		533			R.S. §434
	117		535			R.S. §4391
	121	1	538			R.S. §5549
		2	538			R.S. §5550
	124	1	539			R.S. §1556
		2	539			R.S. §1569

38th Cong.					U.S.C.		
13 Stat.		Chapter	Section	Page	Title	Section	Status
1865—Mar.	3	124	3	539			R.S. §1408
			3	539			R.S. §1409
			6	539			R.S. §1411
		127	3	561			R.S. §2081
			4	562			R.S. §2310
			4	562			R.S. §2311
			4	562			R.S. §2312
			8	563			R.S. §2138
			9	563			R.S. §2127
		Pub. R. 27	1	571			R.S. §1754
			2	571			R.S. §1755
		Pub. R. 29		571			R.S. §2037
		Pub. R. 32		572			R.S. §3821
39th Cong.							
14 Stat.							
1866—Jan.	12	Pub. R. 2	1	347			R.S. §3759
Feb.	10	8		3			R.S. §4135
Mar.	6	12	1	3			R.S. §2493
			2	4			R.S. §2494
			2	4			R.S. §2495
	10	15	3	5			R.S. §3178
			4	5			R.S. §3178
		Pub. R. 12		350			R.S. §531
	14	17	1	8			R.S. §2970
			2	8			R.S. §3052
	16	18		9			R.S. §2508
	17	19	2	9			R.S. §1052
			3	9			R.S. §1057
	21	21	1	10			R.S. §4825
			2	10			R.S. §4827
			3	10			R.S. §4826
			3	10			R.S. §4828
			4	10			R.S. §4830
			5	10			R.S. §3689
			5	10			R.S. §4831
			6	11			R.S. §4829
			7	11			R.S. §4832
			8	11			R.S. §4834
			9	11			R.S. §4835
			10	11			R.S. §4833
			13	11			R.S. §4836
Apr.	5	24	1	12			R.S. §5418
			2	13			R.S. §5391
		25	1	13			R.S. §99
			2	13			R.S. §100
			3	13			R.S. §94
		26		14			R.S. §572
	6	27		14			R.S. §290
	7	28	12	25			R.S. §3576
			14	26			R.S. §3595
			14	26			R.S. §3596
			14	26			R.S. §3600
	9	31	1	27			R.S. §699
			1	27			R.S. §1978
			1	27			R.S. §1992
			3	27			R.S. §563
			3	27			R.S. §629
			3	27			R.S. §641
			3	27			R.S. §642
			3	27			R.S. §646
			3	27			R.S. §699
			3	27			R.S. §722
			4	28			R.S. §1982
			4	28			R.S. §1983
			5	28			R.S. §1984
			5	28			R.S. §1985
			7	29			R.S. §1986
			7	29			R.S. §1987
			8	29			R.S. §1988
			9	29			R.S. §1989
			10	29			R.S. §699
	12	39		31			R.S. §3582
	13	44	1	32			R.S. §2599
			1	32			R.S. §2600
			1	32			R.S. §2675
			2	33			R.S. §2593
			2	33			R.S. §2594
			2	33			R.S. §2675
			3	33			R.S. §2517
	17	45	4	38			R.S. §3718
			5	38			R.S. §1515
			5	38			R.S. §1516
	20	63	1	40			R.S. §3618
			1	40			R.S. §3689

39th Cong. 14 Stat.		Chapter	Section	Page	U.S.C. Title	U.S.C. Section	Status
1866—Apr.	20	63	1	40			R.S. §3692
			1	40			R.S. §4806
			2	40			R.S. §2748
			2	40			R.S. §3618
			2	40			R.S. §3692
	26	68		41			R.S. §3762
				41			R.S. §3763
May	2	70	1	41			R.S. §306
			2	41			R.S. §307
			3	42			R.S. §308
			4	42			R.S. §306
			5	42			R.S. §309
			6	42			R.S. §310
	3	72	1	43			R.S. §1378
			1	43			R.S. §1380
			2	43			R.S. §1383
	9	75	1	44			R.S. §1059
			2	44			R.S. §1062
	11	80	3	46			R.S. §641
			3	46			R.S. §642
			3	46			R.S. §646
			5	46			R.S. §641
			5	46			R.S. §642
			5	46			R.S. §646
	16	81	3	47			R.S. §3573
			4	47			R.S. §5462
		83		48			R.S. §572
		84		48			R.S. §1367
	18	85	4	49			R.S. §3669
	21	86	1	50			R.S. §5525
			2	50			R.S. §5524
		88		51			R.S. §681
				51			R.S. §682
	30	102		54			R.S. §4075
				54			R.S. §4076
				54			R.S. §4077
				54			R.S. §4078
June	1	105		56			R.S. §2509
	8	110	2	59			R.S. §1316
			2	59			R.S. §1320
	14	122	1	64			R.S. §3620
			2	64			R.S. §5488
			3	65			R.S. §5497
	15	123	2	65			R.S. §2034
		124	1	66			R.S. §5258
			2	66			R.S. §5258
	16	Pub. R. 49	1	359			R.S. §1317
			1	359			R.S. §1318
			1	359			R.S. §1319
	21	127	1	66			R.S. §2302
			1	66			R.S. §2303
			2	67			R.S. §2290
			2	67			R.S. §2291
			2	67			R.S. §2292
		129	1	69			R.S. §431
			2	69			R.S. §432
			3	69			R.S. §433
	23	138	1	73			R.S. §5247
			8	73			R.S. §230
			8	73			R.S. §3717
	27	142		76			R.S. §4806
	29	156		77			R.S. §2207
				77			R.S. §2210
				77			R.S. §2213
July	3	162	1	81			R.S. §4278
			1	81			R.S. §5353
			2	81			R.S. §5354
			3	81			R.S. §5355
			3	82			R.S. §4279
			5	82			R.S. §4280
	4	166	4	85			R.S. §2207
			4	85			R.S. §2210
			5	86			R.S. §2318
			5	86			R.S. §2408
	13	176	4	92			R.S. §3716
			5	92			R.S. §1229
			5	92			R.S. §1342
			5	92			R.S. §1624
			6	92			R.S. §1313
			6	92			R.S. §1314
			6	92			R.S. §1322
			6	92			R.S. §1331
			7	93			R.S. §1235
			7	93			R.S. §1287
		177		93			R.S. §4237

39th Cong.					U.S.C.		
14 Stat.		Chapter	Section	Page	Title	Section	Status
1866—July	13	179	1	93			R.S. §4843
			2	94			R.S. §4843
		180		94			R.S. §2535
				94			R.S. §2536
		184	9	101			R.S. §3173
			9	101			R.S. §3174
			9	101			R.S. §3175
			9	101			R.S. §3176
			9	103			R.S. §3182
			9	106			R.S. §3145
			9	106			R.S. §3146
			9	106			R.S. §3147
			9	106			R.S. §3184
			9	106			R.S. §3193
			9	107			R.S. §3186
			9	107			R.S. §3187
			9	107			R.S. §3188
			9	107			R.S. §3189
			9	107			R.S. §3190
			9	107			R.S. §3194
			9	108			R.S. §3191
			9	108			R.S. §3192
			9	108			R.S. §3195
			9	108			R.S. §3196
			9	108			R.S. §3204
			9	108			R.S. §3206
			9	109			R.S. §3197
			9	109			R.S. §3198
			9	109			R.S. §3199
			9	109			R.S. §3201
			9	109			R.S. §3202
			9	110			R.S. §2
			9	110			R.S. §3183
			9	110			R.S. §3200
			9	110			R.S. §3203
			9	110			R.S. §3205
			9	110			R.S. §3213
			9	110			R.S. §3218
			9	110			R.S. §3219
			9	111			R.S. §563
			9	111			R.S. §629
			9	111			R.S. §711
			9	111			R.S. §732
			9	111			R.S. §733
			9	111			R.S. §734
			9	111			R.S. §919
			9	111			R.S. §969
			9	111			R.S. §3214
			9	111			R.S. §3216
			9	111			R.S. §3220
			9	111			R.S. §3225
			9	111			R.S. §3453
			9	112			R.S. §3452
			9	112			R.S. §3458
			9	112			R.S. §3459
			9	113			R.S. §3232
			9	113			R.S. §3233
			9	113			R.S. §3235
			9	113			R.S. §3237
			9	114			R.S. §3236
			9	114			R.S. §3241
			9	115			R.S. §3234
			9	115			R.S. §3407
			9	117			R.S. §3244
			9	122			R.S. §3243
			9	122			R.S. §3246
			9	126			R.S. §3366
			9	126			R.S. §3367
			9	126			R.S. §3404
			9	126			R.S. §3405
			9	137			R.S. §3408
			9	140			R.S. §3438
			9	141			R.S. §3420
			9	141			R.S. §3423
			9	141			R.S. §3429
			9	142			R.S. §3422
			9	143			R.S. §3421
			9	144			R.S. §3430
			9	144			R.S. §3435
			9	145			R.S. §3437
			9	146			R.S. §3419
			9	146			R.S. §5484
			9 [bis]	146			R.S. §3409
			9	146			R.S. §3410
			9	146			R.S. §3411
			9	146			R.S. §3412
			9	146			R.S. §3413

39th Cong. 14 Stat.	Chapter	Section	Page	U.S.C. Title	U.S.C. Section	Status
1866—July 13	184	9	146			R.S. §3416
		9	146			R.S. §3417
		9	147			R.S. §3414
		9	147			R.S. §3415
		11	150			R.S. §3185
		13	151			R.S. §3436
		14	151			R.S. §3450
		14	151			R.S. §3457
		15	152			R.S. §3462
		16	152			R.S. §3455
		19	152			R.S. §563
		19	152			R.S. §629
		19	152			R.S. §3226
		20	153			R.S. §3161
		20	153			R.S. §3162
		25	154			R.S. §3266
		28	155			R.S. §3434
		29	155			R.S. §3151
		29	155			R.S. §3449
		38	160			R.S. §3290
		38	160			R.S. §3325
		41	161			R.S. §3161
		43	162			R.S. §3288
		44	163			R.S. §1
		46	163			R.S. §3335
		47	164			R.S. §3336
		48	164			R.S. §3339
		49	164			R.S. §3337
		50	165			R.S. §3338
		51	165			R.S. §3340
		52	165			R.S. §3341
		53	166			R.S. §3342
		54	166			R.S. §3343
		54	166			R.S. §3344
		54	166			R.S. §3345
		54	166			R.S. §3346
		54	166			R.S. §3347
		54	166			R.S. §3348
		55	167			R.S. §3349
		56	167			R.S. §3353
		57	167			R.S. §3352
		58	167			R.S. §3354
		59	167			R.S. §3168
		60	168			R.S. §3158
		62	168			R.S. §5451
		62	168			R.S. §5501
		63	169			R.S. §3460
		63	169			R.S. §3461
		64	170			R.S. §322
		64	170			R.S. §323
		64	170			R.S. §334
		64	170			R.S. §349
		67	171			R.S. §629
		67	171			R.S. §643
		67	171			R.S. §646
		67	171			R.S. §5446
		67	172			R.S. §934
		67	172			R.S. §3171
		69	172			R.S. §710
		69	172			R.S. §1017
18	201	1	178			R.S. §3
		1	178			R.S. §4
		2	178			R.S. §3059
		2	178			R.S. §3060
		3	178			R.S. §3061
		3	178			R.S. §3062
		3	178			R.S. §3064
		3	179			R.S. §3063
		4	179			R.S. §3082
		5	179			R.S. §3065
		6	179			R.S. §5447
		7	179			R.S. §3084
		7	179			R.S. §3085
		8	180			R.S. §3088
		9	180			R.S. §3098
		9	180			R.S. §3099
		10	180			R.S. §3071
		11	180			R.S. §3074
		11	180			R.S. §3075
		12	181			R.S. §3076
		12	181			R.S. §3077
		13	181			R.S. §3078
		14	181			R.S. §3079
		15	181			R.S. §3080
		16	182			R.S. §5293
		19	182			R.S. §2859

39th Cong. 14 Stat.	Chapter	Section	Page	U.S.C. Title	U.S.C. Section	Status
1866—July 18	201	20	182			R.S. §3110
		21	183			R.S. §4370
		22	183			R.S. §3111
		22	183			R.S. §3112
		22	183			R.S. §3113
		23	183			R.S. §3114
		23	184			R.S. §3115
		23	184			R.S. §4330
		24	184			R.S. §4189
		25	184			R.S. §2806
		25	184			R.S. §2811
		26	184			R.S. §3120
		28	184			R.S. §4224
		28	184			R.S. §4384
		29	185			R.S. §2633
		29	185			R.S. §2653
		30	185			R.S. §1790
		31	186			R.S. §3086
		33	186			R.S. §2692
		34	186			R.S. §2687
		35	186			R.S. §5451
		35	186			R.S. §5501
		36	187			R.S. §3012
		37	187			R.S. §2959
		38	187			R.S. §2919
		40	187			R.S. §2647
		40	187			R.S. §3619
		41	188			R.S. §3109
		42	188			R.S. §1780
		43	188			R.S. §4327
23	208	1	191			R.S. §681
		1	191			R.S. §682
		1	191			R.S. §683
		1	199			R.S. §527
		1	202			R.S. §3601
		2	206			R.S. §301
		4	206			R.S. §155
		4	206			R.S. §156
		4	206			R.S. §157
		5	207			R.S. §349
		5	207			R.S. §351
		6	207			R.S. §167
		8	207			R.S. §416
		9	208			R.S. §2737
		12	208			R.S. §3689
	209		208	7	305	
	210	1	209			R.S. §684
		1	209			R.S. §686
		2	209			R.S. §604
		2	209			R.S. §658
	213		212			R.S. §4136
	219	1	218			R.S. §2485
		2	219			R.S. §2486
		3	219			R.S. §2487
		4	219			R.S. §2488
		5	220			R.S. §2489
24	230	1	221			R.S. §5263
		1	221			R.S. §5264
		2	221			R.S. §5266
		3	221			R.S. §5265
		3	221			R.S. §5267
		4	222			R.S. §5268
25	231	1	222			R.S. §1362
		1	222			R.S. §1363
		1	222			R.S. §1364
		1	222			R.S. §1460
		1	222			R.S. §1466
		1	222			R.S. §1508
		2	222			R.S. §1364
		5	223			R.S. §1435
		6	223			R.S. §1367
		7	223			R.S. §1391
		7	223			R.S. §1402
	232	1	223			R.S. §1094
		1	223			R.S. §1095
		2	223			R.S. §1096
		2	223			R.S. §1097
	233	1	225			R.S. §1674
		1	225			R.S. §1683
		1	225			R.S. §1690
		2	226			R.S. §200
		3	226			R.S. §1729
		3	226			R.S. §1732
	242	9	241			R.S. §5
	245	1	243			R.S. §14
		1	243			R.S. §15

39th Cong.					U.S.C.		
14 Stat.		**Chapter**	**Section**	**Page**	**Title**	**Section**	**Status**
1866—July	25	245	2	243			R.S. §16
			2	243			R.S. §17
			3	244			R.S. §18
			3	244			R.S. §19
		252		250			R.S. §2586
				250			R.S. §2587
		255		251			R.S. §2521
				251			R.S. §2718
		Pub. R. 77		365			R.S. §80
		262	5	252			R.S. §2338
			7	252			R.S. §2343
			8	253			R.S. §2477
			9	253			R.S. §2339
			10	253			R.S. §2341
			11	253			R.S. §2342
		266	2	280			R.S. §2097
			4	280			R.S. §2128
		268	4	288			R.S. §1933
		269	4	289			R.S. §3024
		Pub. R. 80		366			R.S. §427
		278	21	299			R.S. §5259
		280		300			R.S. §531
				300			R.S. §551
				300			R.S. §572
				300			R.S. §579
				300			R.S. §608
				300			R.S. §658
				300			R.S. §767
				300			R.S. §776
				300			R.S. §781
		281		301			R.S. §3880
		284	1	302			R.S. §2536
			1	302			R.S. §2614
			1	302			R.S. §2939
			2	302			R.S. §2536
			2	302			R.S. §2615
			3	302			R.S. §2938
			3	302			R.S. §2943
			4	303			R.S. §2538
			4	303			R.S. §2539
			4	303			R.S. §2745
			4	303			R.S. §2940
			5	303			R.S. §2941
			6	303			R.S. §2729
			6	303			R.S. §2731
			7	303			R.S. §2729
			8	303			R.S. §2942
			9	303			R.S. §2944
			10	304			R.S. §2738
		286	1	304			R.S. §4608
			2	304			R.S. §4608
		287	2	305			R.S. §3798
			3	305			R.S. §429
			4	305			R.S. §3766
			4	305			R.S. §3767
			4	305			R.S. §3768
			4	305			R.S. §3769
			4	305			R.S. §3770
			4	305			R.S. §3771
			4	305			R.S. §3772
			4	305			R.S. §3821
			5	306			R.S. §3773
			5	306			R.S. §3774
			5	306			R.S. §3775
			5	306			R.S. §3776
			5	306			R.S. §3777
			5	306			R.S. §3778
		288		306			R.S. §639
				306			R.S. §640
				306			R.S. §646
		Pub. R. 90		369			R.S. §608
				369			R.S. §658
	28	293	1	308			R.S. §2676
			1	308			R.S. §2677
			1	308			R.S. §2678
			2	308			R.S. §2578
			2	308			R.S. §2579
			3	308			R.S. §2578
			3	308			R.S. §2579
			4	308			R.S. §2697
			4	308			R.S. §2705
			4	308			R.S. §2721
			4	308			R.S. §2722
			4	308			R.S. §2728
			4	308			R.S. §2739
			4	308			R.S. §2746

39th Cong. 14 Stat.		Chapter	Section	Page	U.S.C. Title	U.S.C. Section	Status
1866—July	28	293	5	309			R.S. §2646
			6	309			R.S. §3074
		296	8	322			R.S. §1577
			8	322			R.S. §1579
			11	322			R.S. §4083
			12	322			R.S. §3689
			17	323			R.S. §47
			17	323	2	43	Elim.
		297	8	327			R.S. §277
		298	1	328			R.S. §2504
			1	328			R.S. §2804
			3	328			R.S. §336
			3	328			R.S. §5574
			5	328			R.S. §336
			5	328			R.S. §3005
			6	329			R.S. §336
			6	329			R.S. §3006
			7	329			R.S. §3013
			9	330			R.S. §2907
			9	330			R.S. §2908
			10	330			R.S. §2972
			12	330			R.S. §2500
			13	330			R.S. §334
			13	330			R.S. §336
			13	330			R.S. §339
			13	330			R.S. §340
			13	330			R.S. §341
			13	330			R.S. §342
			13	331			R.S. §263
			13	331			R.S. §4177
		299	1	332			R.S. §1094
			2	332			R.S. §1099
			2	332			R.S. §1100
			3	332			R.S. §1102
			3	332			R.S. §1103
			3	332			R.S. §1104
			3	332			R.S. §1105
			4	332			R.S. §1108
			6	333			R.S. §1106
			6	333			R.S. §1107
			6	333			R.S. §1112
			6	333			R.S. §1276
			7	333			R.S. §1109
			7	333			R.S. §1111
			7	333			R.S. §1121
			7	333			R.S. §1122
			7	333			R.S. §1179
			9	333			R.S. §1097
			9	333			R.S. §1098
			10	333			R.S. §1128
			11	334			R.S. §1131
			12	334			R.S. §1198
			12	334			R.S. §1199
			12	334			R.S. §1200
			12	334			R.S. §1201
			12	334			R.S. §1342
			13	334			R.S. §1132
			14	334			R.S. §1132
			16	334			R.S. §1140
			17	334			R.S. §1168
			17	334			R.S. §1171
			17	334			R.S. §1191
			17	335			R.S. §1180
			18	335			R.S. §1182
			18	335			R.S. §1187
			19	335			R.S. §1151
			20	335			R.S. §1152
			20	335			R.S. §1154
			20	335			R.S. §1156
			21	335			R.S. §1159
			21	335			R.S. §1161
			21	335			R.S. §1162
			22	335			R.S. §1195
			22	335			R.S. §1196
			22	335			R.S. §1197
			23	336			R.S. §1193
			25	336			R.S. §1144
			25	336			R.S. §1150
			25	336			R.S. §1299
			25	336			R.S. §1300
			25	336			R.S. §3618
			25	336			R.S. §3692
			26	336			R.S. §1225
			27	336			R.S. §1231
			28	336			R.S. §1218
			30	337			R.S. §1121

39th Cong.				U.S.C.		
14 Stat.	Chapter	Section	Page	Title	Section	Status
1866—July 28	299	30	337			R.S. §1122
		30	337			R.S. §1124
		31	337			R.S. §1217
		34	337			R.S. §1226
	301	1	339			R.S. §3569
		2	340			R.S. §3570
	302		341			R.S. §3658
	304		342			R.S. §572
			342			R.S. §579
	305		342			R.S. §4791
	311		344			R.S. §2207
			344			R.S. §2213
	312	1	344			R.S. §1493
		1	344			R.S. §1494
		1	344			R.S. §1504
		2	345			R.S. §1593
1867—Jan. 25	15		379			R.S. §1860
Feb. 5	26	1	383			R.S. §5434
		2	383			R.S. §3708
		2	383			R.S. §5188
		3	383			R.S. §3708
		4	383			R.S. §5432
		5	384			R.S. §5433
		6	384			R.S. §5453
		7	384			R.S. §5454
	27		385			R.S. §642
			385			R.S. §646
	28	1	385			R.S. §751
		1	385			R.S. §752
		1	385			R.S. §753
		1	385			R.S. §754
		1	385			R.S. §755
		1	385			R.S. §756
		1	385			R.S. §757
		1	385			R.S. §758
		1	385			R.S. §759
		1	385			R.S. §760
		1	385			R.S. §761
		1	385			R.S. §763
		1	385			R.S. §765
		1	385			R.S. §766
		2	386			R.S. §709
		2	386			R.S. §710
		2	386			R.S. §997
		2	386			R.S. §998
		2	386			R.S. §999
		2	386			R.S. §1003
		2	386			R.S. §1010
		2	386			R.S. §1017
	32		391			R.S. §4778
			391			R.S. §4779
			391			R.S. §4780
	34	1	391			R.S. §5591
		2	391			R.S. §5590
	Pub. R. 11	1	565			R.S. §3254
21	56	1	397			R.S. §31
		2	397			R.S. §32
		2	397			R.S. §33
	59	1	398			R.S. §3758
		1	398			R.S. §3759
		2	398			R.S. §3758
		2	398			R.S. §3759
		2	398			R.S. §3760
22	60		399			R.S. §658
	61	1	399			R.S. §4877
		2	399			R.S. §4873
		2	399			R.S. §4876
		3	400			R.S. §4881
		4	400			R.S. §4870
		5	400			R.S. §4871
		6	400			R.S. §4872
25	78		410			R.S. §4370
	79		410			R.S. §1200
	81	1	410			R.S. §2680
		2	410			R.S. §2548
		2	410			R.S. §2549
		2	410			R.S. §2552
		2	410			R.S. §2679
	82	1	411			R.S. §2555
		1	411			R.S. §2772
		2	411			R.S. §2555
	Pub. R. 28	4	568			R.S. §3689
28	99		412			R.S. §1690
	100	2	416			R.S. §1577
		2	416			R.S. §1579
		3	416			R.S. §1309

39th Cong. 14 Stat.	Chapter	Section	Page	U.S.C. Title	U.S.C. Section	Status
1867—Feb. 28	100	3	416			R.S. §1337
		3	416			R.S. §1339
	101	1	416			R.S. §2753
		2	416			R.S. §2755
	103	1	417			R.S. §2541
		1	417			R.S. §2543
		1	417			R.S. §2544
		1	417			R.S. §2696
		2	417			R.S. §4341
	Pub. R. 30	2	569			R.S. §170
Mar. 2	144	2	421			R.S. §5247
	145	5	423			R.S. §1170
		6	423			R.S. §1625
		7	423			R.S. §1121
		7	423			R.S. §1122
		7	423			R.S. §1132
		7	423			R.S. §1159
		7	423			R.S. §1161
		7	423			R.S. §1261
	146		424			R.S. §5543
	149	1	425			R.S. §4667
		4	425			R.S. §4673
	150	1	426			R.S. §1889
		2	426			R.S. §1932
		4	426			R.S. §1914
	151		427			R.S. §1914
	154	1	430			R.S. §1767
		1	430			R.S. §4778
		2	430			R.S. §1768
		2	430			R.S. §4778
		3	430			R.S. §1769
		4	431			R.S. §1770
		5	431			R.S. §1771
		6	431			R.S. §1772
		6	431			R.S. §1773
		7	431			R.S. §1775
		8	431			R.S. §1774
		9	431			R.S. §1762
	156	1	433			R.S. §606
		2	433			R.S. §677
		2	433			R.S. §680
		2	433			R.S. §715
		2	433			R.S. §832
		2	433			R.S. §4799
	158	1	434			R.S. §440
		1	434			R.S. §516
		2	434			R.S. §517
		3	434			R.S. §518
		4	434			R.S. §519
	159	1	434			R.S. §1219
		1	434			R.S. §1342
		2	435			R.S. §1292
	162	8	439	20	123	
	163		439			R.S. §246
			439			R.S. §247
	166	1	440			R.S. §527
		1	440			R.S. §529
		1	445			R.S. §3145
		2	457			R.S. §1078
	167	1	464			R.S. §80
		1	464			R.S. §4865
		2	466			R.S. §519
		2	466			R.S. §1797
		2	466			R.S. §1800
		2	466			R.S. §1821
		4	466			R.S. §4660
		4	466			R.S. §4672
		5	466			R.S. §2726
		5	466			R.S. §2732
		7	466			R.S. §3823
		7	466			R.S. §3824
		10	467			R.S. §3786
		10	467			R.S. §3826
		12	467			R.S. §1663
	168	3	470			R.S. §3023
		4	470			R.S. §2741
		7	470			R.S. §2721
		9	470			R.S. §554
		10	471			R.S. §681
		10	471			R.S. §682
		10	471			R.S. §3689
	169	1	471			R.S. §3172
		1	471			R.S. §3173
		3	471			R.S. §773
		3	472			R.S. §774
		3	472			R.S. §3215

39th Cong. 14 Stat.	Chapter	Section	Page	U.S.C. Title	U.S.C. Section	Status
1867—Mar. 2	169	4	472			R.S. §3208
		4	472			R.S. §3750
		4	472			R.S. §3751
		5	472			R.S. §3437
		7	473			R.S. §3152
		7	473			R.S. §3463
		8	473			R.S. §3184
		8	473			R.S. §3185
		8	473			R.S. §3187
		9	473			R.S. §3145
		9	473			R.S. §3149
		9	473			R.S. §3242
		10	475			R.S. §563
		10	475			R.S. §629
		10	475			R.S. §3224
		10	475			R.S. §3339
		13	480			R.S. §3689
		14	481			R.S. §3253
		17	481			R.S. §3151
		19	482			R.S. §3166
		25	483			R.S. §563
		25	483			R.S. §629
		25	483			R.S. §711
		25	483			R.S. §734
		26	483			R.S. §3170
		28	484			R.S. §5448
		30	484			R.S. §731
		30	484			R.S. §5440
		32	484			R.S. §3406
		33	484			R.S. §4223
	170	7	487			R.S. §3689
	172	1	490			R.S. §1413
		3	492			R.S. §1546
	173	2	515			R.S. §2100
		3	515			R.S. §468
	174	1	516			R.S. §1362
		1	516			R.S. §1367
		1	516			R.S. §1466
		2	516			R.S. §1523
		3	516			R.S. §1412
		3	516			R.S. §1600
		4	516			R.S. §1527
		5	516			R.S. §1624
		6	516			R.S. §4756
		6	516			R.S. §4757
		7	517			R.S. §1596
		7	517			R.S. §1601
		8	517			R.S. §1513
		9	517			R.S. §1461
		9	517			R.S. §1591
		9	517			R.S. §1592
	176	1	517			R.S. §563
		1	517			R.S. §711
		1	517			R.S. §4972
		1	517			R.S. §4973
		1	517			R.S. §4974
		1	517			R.S. §4975
		2	518			R.S. §630
		2	518			R.S. §4979
		2	518			R.S. §4986
		2	518			R.S. §5057
		3	518			R.S. §4993
		3	518			R.S. §4994
		3	518			R.S. §4995
		4	519			R.S. §4996
		4	519			R.S. §4998
		4	519			R.S. §4999
		4	519			R.S. §5000
		4	519			R.S. §5007
		4	519			R.S. §5008
		4	519			R.S. §5009
		5	519			R.S. §4997
		5	519			R.S. §5001
		5	519			R.S. §5002
		5	519			R.S. §5004
		5	519			R.S. §5125
		6	520			R.S. §5010
		6	520			R.S. §5011
		7	520			R.S. §5005
		7	520			R.S. §5006
		8	520			R.S. §630
		8	520			R.S. §4980
		8	520			R.S. §4981
		8	520			R.S. §4982
		8	520			R.S. §4983
		9	520			R.S. §4989

39th Cong. 14 Stat.	Chapter	Section	Page	U.S.C. Title	U.S.C. Section	Status
1867—Mar. 2	176	10	521			R.S. §4990
		11	521			R.S. §5014
		11	521			R.S. §5015
		11	521			R.S. §5016
		11	521			R.S. §5017
		11	521			R.S. §5018
		11	521			R.S. §5019
		11	521			R.S. §5032
		12	522			R.S. §5033
		12	522			R.S. §5090
		13	522			R.S. §5034
		13	522			R.S. §5036
		14	522			R.S. §5044
		14	522			R.S. §5045
		14	522			R.S. §5047
		14	522			R.S. §5049
		14	522			R.S. §5050
		14	522			R.S. §5051
		14	522			R.S. §5052
		14	522			R.S. §5053
		14	522			R.S. §5054
		14	522			R.S. §5056
		14	522			R.S. §5066
		14	523			R.S. §5046
		15	524			R.S. §5055
		15	524			R.S. §5058
		15	524			R.S. §5062
		16	524			R.S. §5047
		16	524			R.S. §5048
		17	524			R.S. §5059
		17	524			R.S. §5060
		17	524			R.S. §5061
		17	524			R.S. §5094
		18	525			R.S. §5035
		18	525			R.S. §5037
		18	525			R.S. §5038
		18	525			R.S. §5039
		18	525			R.S. §5040
		18	525			R.S. §5041
		18	525			R.S. §5042
		18	525			R.S. §5043
		19	525			R.S. §5067
		19	525			R.S. §5068
		19	525			R.S. §5069
		19	525			R.S. §5070
		19	525			R.S. §5071
		19	525			R.S. §5072
		20	526			R.S. §5073
		20	526			R.S. §5075
		21	526			R.S. §5074
		21	526			R.S. §5105
		21	526			R.S. §5106
		22	527			R.S. §5076
		22	527			R.S. §5077
		22	527			R.S. §5078
		22	527			R.S. §5079
		22	527			R.S. §5080
		22	527			R.S. §5081
		23	528			R.S. §5083
		23	528			R.S. §5084
		23	528			R.S. §5085
		23	528			R.S. §5095
		24	528			R.S. §4984
		24	528			R.S. §4985
		24	528			R.S. §5082
		25	528			R.S. §5063
		25	528			R.S. §5065
		26	529			R.S. §5020
		26	529			R.S. §5086
		26	529			R.S. §5087
		26	529			R.S. §5088
		26	529			R.S. §5089
		26	529			R.S. §5104
		26	529			R.S. §5107
		27	529			R.S. §5091
		27	529			R.S. §5092
		27	529			R.S. §5102
		28	530			R.S. §5064
		28	530			R.S. §5093
		28	530			R.S. §5096
		28	530			R.S. §5097
		28	530			R.S. §5098
		28	530			R.S. §5099
		28	530			R.S. §5100
		28	530			R.S. §5101
		29	531			R.S. §5108

39th Cong. 14 Stat.	Chapter	Section	Page	U.S.C. Title	U.S.C. Section	Status
1867—Mar. 2	176	29	531			R.S. §5109
		29	531			R.S. §5110
		29	531			R.S. §5113
		30	532			R.S. §5116
		31	532			R.S. §5111
		32	532			R.S. §5114
		32	532			R.S. §5115
		33	533			R.S. §5117
		33	533			R.S. §5118
		34	533			R.S. §5119
		34	533			R.S. §5120
		35	534			R.S. §5128
		35	534			R.S. §5129
		35	534			R.S. §5130
		35	534			R.S. §5131
		36	534			R.S. §5121
		37	535			R.S. §5122
		38	535			R.S. §4991
		38	535			R.S. §4992
		38	535			R.S. §5003
		39	536			R.S. §5021
		39	536			R.S. §5023
		39	536			R.S. §5128
		39	536			R.S. §5129
		40	536			R.S. §5024
		40	536			R.S. §5025
		41	537			R.S. §5026
		41	537			R.S. §5027
		42	537			R.S. §5026
		42	537			R.S. §5028
		42	537			R.S. §5029
		42	537			R.S. §5030
		42	537			R.S. §5031
		43	538			R.S. §5103
		44	539			R.S. §5132
		45	539			R.S. §5012
		46	539			R.S. §5419
		47	540			R.S. §5124
		47	540			R.S. §5126
		47	540			R.S. §5127
		48	540			R.S. §5013
		49	541			R.S. §4977
		49	541			R.S. §4978
		49	541			R.S. §4988
	177		541			R.S. §2387
			541			R.S. §2388
			541			R.S. §2389
			541			R.S. §2391
			541			R.S. §2392
			541			R.S. §2393
	178	1	542			R.S. §2535
		1	542			R.S. §2536
		1	542			R.S. §2619
		1	542			R.S. §2717
		1	542			R.S. §2816
		2	542			R.S. §2816
		3	542			R.S. §2968
	179		542			R.S. §2207
			542			R.S. §2210
	180		543			R.S. §990
			543			R.S. §991
	185	2	545			R.S. §614
	186	1	545			R.S. §2035
		2	545			R.S. §2036
	187	1	546			R.S. §1990
		1	546			R.S. §5526
		2	546			R.S. §1991
		2	546			R.S. §5527
	188	1	546			R.S. §3090
		1	546			R.S. §3689
		2	547			R.S. §3091
		2	547			R.S. §3092
		2	547			R.S. §3093
		3	547			R.S. §2981
	193		557			R.S. §5456
	196		558			R.S. §639
			558			R.S. §646
	197	1	559			R.S. §2504
		1	559			R.S. §2912
		1	559			R.S. §2916
		2	561			R.S. §2504
	Pub. R. 46		571			R.S. §3480
	Pub. R. 47	2	571			R.S. §2510
	Pub. R. 48		571			R.S. §3622
			571			R.S. §5491
	Pub. R. 49		572			R.S. §5218

40th Cong. 15 Stat.	Chapter	Section	Page	U.S.C. Title	U.S.C. Section	Status
1867—Mar. 12	1		1			R.S. §4826
			1			R.S. §4828
22	Pub. R. 8		21			R.S. §2504
25	7	1	5			R.S. §531
		1	5			R.S. §551
		1	5			R.S. §767
		1	5			R.S. §776
		2	5			R.S. §572
		2	5			R.S. §604
		2	5			R.S. §608
		4	5			R.S. §554
	Pub. R. 11		22			R.S. §2504
26	8	2	6			R.S. §3412
		2	6			R.S. §3413
		2	6			R.S. §3414
27	Pub. R. 15		23			R.S. §1688
29	13	2	7			R.S. §3823
		2	7			R.S. §3824
		2	7			R.S. §3826
		3	8			R.S. §3825
	16		10			R.S. §2543
	Pub. R. 18		24			R.S. §39
	Pub. R. 19		24			R.S. §2504
	Pub. R. 22		25			R.S. §278
	Pub. R. 27		28			R.S. §5253
30	20	1	11			R.S. §1822
		1	11			R.S. §1824
		2	12			R.S. §1820
		3	12			R.S. §1800
		3	12			R.S. §1801
		3	12			R.S. §1802
	24	2	13			R.S. §1816
July 19	28		14			R.S. §1997
			14			R.S. §4749
1868—Jan. 31	Pub. R. 8		246			R.S. §3710
			246			R.S. §3735
Feb. 3	5		34			R.S. §2505
4	6		34			R.S. §3582
10	7		34			R.S. §5219
12	8	1	35			R.S. §43
		2	36			R.S. §3678
25	13		37			R.S. §860
Mar. 2	Pub. R. 16	1	249			R.S. §4676
9	22	1	40			R.S. §210
		1	40			R.S. §3803
		2	40			R.S. §3805
		4	40			R.S. §3804
		4	40			R.S. §3806
12	Pub. R. 19		250			R.S. §1298
16	29		42			R.S. §281
	30		42			R.S. §1327
19	31	4	44			R.S. §275
		4	44			R.S. §279
27	34	1	44			R.S. §699
		2	44			R.S. §763
30	36		54			R.S. §191
	38	1	57			R.S. §1690
		1	57			R.S. §1702
		1	57			R.S. §1733
		2	58			R.S. §1223
		2	58			R.S. §1440
31	41	5	59			R.S. §3257
		7	60			R.S. §3230
June 5	50		63			R.S. §2517
			63			R.S. §2578
8	53		67			R.S. §2392
			67			R.S. §2394
	Pub. R. 32		253			R.S. §4837
17	61	1	69			R.S. §1413
		1	69			R.S. §1543
		2	72			R.S. §1417
25	71	1	75			R.S. §707
		1	75			R.S. §708
		2	75			R.S. §1088
		3	75			R.S. §1074
		4	75			R.S. §1078
		4	75			R.S. §1079
		4	75			R.S. §1080
		5	75			R.S. §351
		5	75			R.S. §359
		6	76			R.S. §188
		7	76			R.S. §1063
		7	76			R.S. §1064
		7	76			R.S. §1065
		8	77			R.S. §1067
		9	77			R.S. §1057
	72		77			R.S. §3738

40th Cong. 15 Stat.	Chapter	Section	Page	U.S.C. Title	U.S.C. Section	Status
1868—June 25	74	1	78			R.S. §2599
		2	78			R.S. §2599
		3	78			R.S. §2599
	75		78			R.S. §2543
	79		80			R.S. §572
			80			R.S. §608
			80			R.S. §658
	81		80			R.S. §675
July 3	118		82			R.S. §572
11	139		85			R.S. §1757
13	Pub. R. 55		257			R.S. §5248
			257			R.S. §5250
16	175		91			R.S. §2207
			91			R.S. §2210
20	176	1	92			R.S. §441
		1	92			R.S. §516
		1	92			R.S. §517
		1	94			R.S. §1825
		1	95			R.S. §3763
		1	96			R.S. §155
		1	99			R.S. §334
		1	106			R.S. §277
		1	109			R.S. §770
		2	110			R.S. §3826
		4	110			R.S. §3826
		6	110			R.S. §1815
	177		110			R.S. §257
			111			R.S. §3786
			111			R.S. §3787
			112			R.S. §2747
			115			R.S. §1816
	179		121			R.S. §3596
	185		125			R.S. §1228
	186	1	125			R.S. §3244
		1	125			R.S. §3251
		2	125			R.S. §3244
		2	125			R.S. §3249
		2	125			R.S. §3250
		2	125			R.S. §3255
		4	126			R.S. §3248
		4	126			R.S. §3251
		4	126			R.S. §3282
		5	126			R.S. §3258
		6	126			R.S. §3259
		7	127			R.S. §3260
		8	127			R.S. §3262
		9	128			R.S. §3263
		11	130			R.S. §3244
		11	130			R.S. §3280
		12	130			R.S. §3266
		14	130			R.S. §3265
		15	130			R.S. §3271
		16	131			R.S. §3267
		17	131			R.S. §3261
		17	131			R.S. §3269
		18	132			R.S. §3275
		18	132			R.S. §3279
		19	132			R.S. §3303
		19	133			R.S. §3285
		19	133			R.S. §3304
		19	133			R.S. §3305
		19	133			R.S. §3307
		20	133			R.S. §3309
		21	134			R.S. §3273
		21	134			R.S. §3284
		21	134			R.S. §3302
		22	134			R.S. §3310
		23	135			R.S. §3287
		23	135			R.S. §3293
		24	136			R.S. §3294
		25	136			R.S. §3295
		25	136			R.S. §3320
		25	137			R.S. §3321
		25	137			R.S. §3322
		26	137			R.S. §3238
		26	137			R.S. §3312
		27	137			R.S. §3313
		28	138			R.S. §3314
		29	138			R.S. §3316
		30	138			R.S. §3311
		31	139			R.S. §3286
		32	139			R.S. §3276
		33	139			R.S. §3277
		34	140			R.S. §3278
		35	140			R.S. §3283
		36	140			R.S. §3296
		36	140			R.S. §3299

40th Cong.				U.S.C.		
15 Stat.	Chapter	Section	Page	Title	Section	Status
1868—July 20	186	36	140			R.S. §3333
		37	141			R.S. §3327
		38	141			R.S. §3252
		39	141			R.S. §3256
		39	141			R.S. §3326
		40	141			R.S. §3268
		40	141			R.S. §3306
		41	141			R.S. §3298
		42	142			R.S. §3331
		42	142			R.S. §3332
		43	142			R.S. §3324
		43	142			R.S. §3445
		44	142			R.S. §3242
		44	142			R.S. §3281
		45	143			R.S. §3318
		46	144			R.S. §3319
		47	144			R.S. §3323
		48	144			R.S. §3328
		49	144			R.S. §3159
		49	144			R.S. §3160
		49	144			R.S. §3163
		50	145			R.S. §3151
		50	145			R.S. §3152
		51	145			R.S. §3163
		51	145			R.S. §3166
		52	145			R.S. §3153
		52	146			R.S. §3154
		52	146			R.S. §3155
		52	146			R.S. §3273
		52	146			R.S. §3274
		52	147			R.S. §3300
		52	147			R.S. §3301
		53	147			R.S. §3156
		53	147			R.S. §3157
		53	147			R.S. §3291
		53	147			R.S. §3292
		54	147			R.S. §3329
		55	148			R.S. §3330
		56	149			R.S. §3272
		57	149			R.S. §3320
		57	149			R.S. §3321
		57	150			R.S. §3289
		58	150			R.S. §3334
		59	151			R.S. §3243
		59	151			R.S. §3244
		59	151			R.S. §3247
		59	151			R.S. §3308
		59	151			R.S. §3317
		60	152			R.S. §3244
		60	152			R.S. §3371
		61	152			R.S. §3368
		62	153			R.S. §3362
		63	153			R.S. §3244
		63	153			R.S. §3355
		64	154			R.S. §3356
		65	154			R.S. §3357
		66	155			R.S. §3358
		66	155			R.S. §3359
		67	155			R.S. §3369
		68	156			R.S. §3364
		69	156			R.S. §3372
		70	156			R.S. §3373
		71	156			R.S. §3366
		71	156			R.S. §3374
		71	156			R.S. §3375
		72	156			R.S. §3376
		72	156			R.S. §3406
		73	157			R.S. §3385
		74	157			R.S. §3386
		75	158			R.S. §3370
		76	158			R.S. §3360
		77	158			R.S. §3377
		78	159			R.S. §3363
		78	159			R.S. §3378
		79	159			R.S. §3380
		81	160			R.S. §3394
		81	160			R.S. §3396
		82	160			R.S. §3387
		83	160			R.S. §3388
		84	161			R.S. §3389
		85	161			R.S. §3392
		86	161			R.S. §3390
		86	162			R.S. §3391
		87	162			R.S. §3395
		88	162			R.S. §3393
		89	162			R.S. §3397

40th Cong.				U.S.C.		
15 Stat.	Chapter	Section	Page	Title	Section	Status
1868—July 20	186	89	162			R.S. §3404
		89	162			R.S. §3406
		90	163			R.S. §3398
		91	163			R.S. §3399
		92	163			R.S. §3400
		93	163			R.S. §3402
		94	164			R.S. §3403
		95	164			R.S. §3401
		96	164			R.S. §3456
		97	164			R.S. §3168
		98	165			R.S. §3169
		99	165			R.S. §3451
		100	165			R.S. §3444
		101	165			R.S. §3238
		101	165			R.S. §3446
		102	166			R.S. §3229
		102	166			R.S. §3231
		103	166			R.S. §3447
		104	166			R.S. §1
		106	167			R.S. §563
		106	167			R.S. §629
		106	167			R.S. §3207
		107	167			R.S. §3448
	Pub. R. 64		260			R.S. §4222
23	227	1	168			R.S. §177
		2	168			R.S. §178
		2	168			R.S. §181
		3	168			R.S. §179
		3	168			R.S. §180
		3	168			R.S. §182
	229	2	170			R.S. §4754
		2	170			R.S. §4755
25	233	3	177			R.S. §3733
		3	177			R.S. §5503
	235	1	178			R.S. §1839
		1	178			R.S. §1840
		1	178			R.S. §1904
		2	178			R.S. §1841
		3	179			R.S. §1843
		3	179			R.S. §1844
		4	179			R.S. §1846
		4	179			R.S. §1847
		4	179			R.S. §1848
		4	179			R.S. §1849
		4	179			R.S. §1922
		5	179			R.S. §1859
		5	179			R.S. §1860
		6	180			R.S. §1842
		6	180			R.S. §1851
		6	180			R.S. §1925
		7	180			R.S. §1857
		8	180			R.S. §1854
		9	180			R.S. §702
		9	180			R.S. §1864
		9	180			R.S. §1865
		9	180			R.S. §1866
		9	180			R.S. §1867
		9	180			R.S. §1868
		9	180			R.S. §1869
		9	180			R.S. §1870
		9	180			R.S. §1871
		9	180			R.S. §1872
		9	180			R.S. §1883
		9	180			R.S. §1907
		9	180			R.S. §1909
		9	180			R.S. §1910
		9	180			R.S. §1912
		9	180			R.S. §1926
		10	181			R.S. §1875
		10	181			R.S. §1876
		10	181			R.S. §1881
		10	181			R.S. §1882
		11	181			R.S. §1877
		11	181			R.S. §1878
		11	181			R.S. §1935
		11	181			R.S. §1939
		12	182			R.S. §1885
		12	182			R.S. §1944
		13	182			R.S. §1862
		13	182			R.S. §1863
		14	183			R.S. §1946
		15	183			R.S. §1873
		15	183			R.S. §1913
		15	183			R.S. §1918
		15	183			R.S. §1919

40th Cong.				U.S.C.		
15 Stat.	Chapter	Section	Page	Title	Section	Status
1868—July 25	235	16	183			R.S. § 1891
		17	183			R.S. § 1948
	236		183			R.S. § 1047
	Pub. R. 72		260			R.S. § 3792
			260			R.S. § 3796
	Pub. R. 73		261			R.S. § 1227
27	246	18	197			R.S. § 889
		19	197			R.S. § 890
	249	1	223			R.S. § 1999
		2	224			R.S. § 2000
		3	224			R.S. § 2001
	254		226			R.S. § 2856
	255	1	226			R.S. § 1000
		1	226			R.S. § 1001
		2	227			R.S. § 640
		2	227			R.S. § 646
	256		227			R.S. § 2377
	257		227			R.S. § 2555
	258	1	227			R.S. § 5112
		3	228			R.S. § 5076
		3	228			R.S. § 5079
	259		228			R.S. § 463
	262	2	232			R.S. § 4863
		3	233			R.S. § 4861
		4	233			R.S. § 4864
		7	234			R.S. § 4867
	264	14	237			R.S. § 4787
	270		239			R.S. § 572
			239			R.S. § 658
	272	1	239			R.S. § 1842
		2	240			R.S. § 1920
		2	240			R.S. § 1921
	273	1	240			R.S. § 1954
		2	240			R.S. § 2591
		2	240			R.S. § 2592
		2	240			R.S. § 2681
		3	240			R.S. § 2633
		3	240			R.S. § 4140
		4	241			R.S. § 1955
		5	241			R.S. § 4358
		6	241			R.S. § 1956
		7	241			R.S. § 1957
		8	242			R.S. § 1958
		8	242			R.S. § 5293
		9	242			R.S. § 5293
	275		242			R.S. § 1916
	276	2	243			R.S. § 1068
		3	243			R.S. § 1059
	Pub. R. 76		262			R.S. § 231
Dec. 15	Pub. R. 1		343			R.S. § 525
1869—Jan. 8	7		266			R.S. § 896
23	15		267			R.S. § 110
Feb. 9	24		269			R.S. § 2158
			269			R.S. § 2159
19	32		270			R.S. § 5207
	33	4	271			R.S. § 3592
		4	271			R.S. § 3594
		4	271			R.S. § 3639
	34		271			R.S. § 608
	35		271			R.S. § 2511
22	42	1	273			R.S. § 2517
		1	273			R.S. § 2518
		2	273			R.S. § 2682
		3	273			R.S. § 2541
	43		274			R.S. § 572
			274			R.S. § 658
24	45		274			R.S. § 2504
25	47	2	275			R.S. § 3689
Mar. 1	48	2	280			R.S. § 1570
	52	2	281			R.S. § 1209
		2	281			R.S. § 1210
		2	281			R.S. § 1604
	54		282			R.S. § 4231
	57		282			R.S. § 3150
3	121		283			R.S. § 363
			283			R.S. § 508
			284			R.S. § 1816
			290			R.S. § 3671
			292			R.S. § 507
			292			R.S. § 509
			300			R.S. § 1846
	122		301			R.S. § 226
			301			R.S. § 255
			301			R.S. § 4675
	123		311			R.S. § 235
			311			R.S. § 240

40th Cong.

15 Stat.	Chapter	Section	Page	U.S.C. Title	U.S.C. Section	Status
1869—Mar. 3	123		311			R.S. §241
			311			R.S. §262
			311			R.S. §3654
	124	2	318			R.S. §1094
		2	318			R.S. §1108
		4	318			R.S. §1119
		5	318			R.S. §1094
		5	318			R.S. §1099
		5	318			R.S. §1102
		5	318			R.S. §1106
		5	318			R.S. §1111
		5	318			R.S. §1279
		6	318			R.S. §1128
		6	318			R.S. §1129
		6	318			R.S. §1131
		6	318			R.S. §1151
		6	318			R.S. §1159
		6	318			R.S. §1168
		6	318			R.S. §1194
		6	318			R.S. §1208
		7	318			R.S. §1211
		7	318			R.S. §1604
	125	2	321			R.S. §1742
		3	321			R.S. §1716
		3	321			R.S. §1722
		3	322			R.S. §4221
		5	322			R.S. §1734
		6	322			R.S. §1690
		6	322			R.S. §1696
		7	322			R.S. §1690
		7	322			R.S. §1693
		7	322			R.S. §4121
	128	1	324			R.S. §871
		2	325			R.S. §872
		3	325			R.S. §873
		4	325			R.S. §874
	130	1	326			R.S. §5211
		1, 2	326			R.S. §5213
		2	327			R.S. §5212
	135		335			R.S. §5208
	138		336			R.S. §2445
	141	1	337			R.S. §5275
		2	338			R.S. §5276
		3	338			R.S. §5277
	142		338			R.S. §1040
	Pub. R. 22		348			R.S. §1959

41st Cong.

16 Stat.	Chapter	Section	Page	U.S.C. Title	U.S.C. Section	Status
1869—Mar. 18	1		1			R.S. §3693
29	Pub. R. 5		52			R.S. §3153
Apr. 3	9		6			R.S. §1096
5	10	1	6			R.S. §1767
		1	6			R.S. §4778
		2	7			R.S. §1768
		2	7			R.S. §4778
		3	7			R.S. §1769
6	11		7			R.S. §5209
10	16	2	39			R.S. §2090
		2	39			R.S. §2101
		4	40			R.S. §2039
	18	1	41			R.S. §3244
		1	41			R.S. §3262
		1	42			R.S. §3309
		1	43			R.S. §3393
		2	43			R.S. §3429
		3	43			R.S. §3379
		3	44			R.S. §3365
	20		44			R.S. §1200
	22	1	44			R.S. §673
		1	44			R.S. §719
		2	44			R.S. §582
		2	44			R.S. §587
		2	44			R.S. §590
		2	44			R.S. §591
		2	44			R.S. §592
		2	44			R.S. §593
		2	44			R.S. §594
		2	44			R.S. §607
		2	44			R.S. §609
		2	44			R.S. §611
		2	44			R.S. §612
		2	44			R.S. §616
		2	44			R.S. §662
		2	44			R.S. §664

41st Cong.				U.S.C.		
16 Stat.	Chapter	Section	Page	Title	Section	Status
1869—Apr. 10	22	2	44			R.S. §671
		2	44			R.S. §717
		2	44			R.S. §727
		2	44			R.S. §751
		2	44			R.S. §752
		2	44			R.S. §1015
		2	44			R.S. §1016
		2	44			R.S. §3637
		2	45			R.S. §555
		2	45			R.S. §619
		3	45			R.S. §557
		3	45			R.S. §620
		4	45			R.S. §610
		5	45			R.S. §714
	25		46			R.S. §363
			46			R.S. §385
	28		47			R.S. §2599
			47			R.S. §2600
	Pub. R. 11		53			R.S. §1129
	Pub. R. 15		55			R.S. §183
1870—Jan. 20	7		61			R.S. §5246
21	9	1	62			R.S. §1622
		2	62			R.S. §1259
Feb. 1	11		63			R.S. §1784
3	Pub. R. 8		368			R.S. §212
5	14	2	65			R.S. §2207
		2	65			R.S. §2210
9	Pub. R. 12		369			R.S. §221
21	18		67			R.S. §1327
			67			R.S. §1328
			67			R.S. §1329
Mar. 7	23		75			R.S. §183
23	29	5	77			R.S. §1867
		5	77			R.S. §1927
25	30		77			R.S. §3481
Apr. 6	Pub. R. 32		372			R.S. §1259
May 4	73		96			R.S. §1930
			96			R.S. §1931
	Pub. R. 40		373			R.S. §1225
	Pub. R. 42		374			R.S. §282
6	87	1	118			R.S. §2194
		2	118			R.S. §2191
		3	118			R.S. §2200
	92		121			R.S. §5248
12	102	1	122			R.S. §2649
		2	122			R.S. §2650
		2	122			R.S. §2651
		3	123			R.S. §2651
15	Pub. R. 62	3	377			R.S. §2102
27	Pub. R. 66	1	378			R.S. §349
31	114	1	140			R.S. §629
		1	140			R.S. §2004
		2	140			R.S. §629
		2	140			R.S. §2005
		2	140			R.S. §2006
		3	140			R.S. §629
		3	140			R.S. §2007
		3	140			R.S. §2008
		4	141			R.S. §629
		4	141			R.S. §2009
		4	141			R.S. §5506
		5	141			R.S. §5507
		6	141			R.S. §5508
		7	141			R.S. §5509
		8	142			R.S. §629
		8	142			R.S. §1022
		9	142			R.S. §1982
		9	142			R.S. §1983
		10	142			R.S. §1984
		10	142			R.S. §1985
		10	142			R.S. §5517
		11	142			R.S. §5516
		12	143			R.S. §1986
		12	143			R.S. §1987
		13	143			R.S. §1989
		14	143			R.S. §563
		14	143			R.S. §629
		14	143			R.S. §1786
		15	143			R.S. §1787
		16	144			R.S. §563
		16	144			R.S. §629
		16	144			R.S. §641
		16	144			R.S. §699
		16	144			R.S. §1977
		16	144			R.S. §2164
		17	144			R.S. §5510

41st Cong. 16 Stat.	Chapter	Section	Page	U.S.C. Title	U.S.C. Section	Status
1870—May 31	114	18	144			R.S. §563
		18	144			R.S. §629
		18	144			R.S. §641
		18	144			R.S. §699
		18	144			R.S. §722
		19	144			R.S. §5511
		20	145			R.S. §5512
		21	145			R.S. §5514
		22	145			R.S. §5515
		23	146			R.S. §563
		23	146			R.S. §629
		23	146			R.S. §2010
June 7	124		148			R.S. §1054
14	127	1	150			R.S. §2586
		1	150			R.S. §2587
		2	151			R.S. §2588
		3	151			R.S. §2589
		4	151			R.S. §2590
	128		151			R.S. §5544
15	129	1	152			R.S. §3595
		1	152			R.S. §3600
		2	152			R.S. §3598
		2	152			R.S. §3599
		4	152			R.S. §3596
		5	152			R.S. §3606
17	130		152			R.S. §1879
	132	1	153			R.S. §4787
		1	153			R.S. §4788
		2	153			R.S. §4789
		3	153			R.S. §4790
	133	5	154			R.S. §2173
21	Pub. R. 75		380			R.S. §3755
22	150	1	162			R.S. §346
		2	162			R.S. §179
		2	162			R.S. §347
		2	162			R.S. §348
		3	162			R.S. §349
		3	162			R.S. §350
		3	162			R.S. §351
		4	162			R.S. §358
		5	162			R.S. §359
		5	162			R.S. §367
		5	162			R.S. §370
		6	163			R.S. §356
		6	163			R.S. §357
		8	163			R.S. §161
		9	163			R.S. §349
		10	163			R.S. §349
		10	163			R.S. §351
		11	163			R.S. §371
		12	164			R.S. §196
		12	164			R.S. §384
		13	164			R.S. §352
		14	164			R.S. §360
		14	164			R.S. §361
		15	164			R.S. §368
		15	164			R.S. §369
		15	164			R.S. §830
		15	164			R.S. §832
		15	164			R.S. §833
		15	164			R.S. §835
		15	164			R.S. §836
		15	164			R.S. §839
		15	164			R.S. §840
		15	164			R.S. §841
		15	164			R.S. §844
		15	164			R.S. §845
		15	164			R.S. §4647
		16	164			R.S. §362
		16	164			R.S. §363
		17	164			R.S. §189
		17	164			R.S. §362
		17	164			R.S. §365
		17	164			R.S. §366
		18	165			R.S. §383
29	169	1	169			R.S. §4585
		2	169			R.S. §4587
		3	170			R.S. §4803
		4	170			R.S. §4803
		5	170			R.S. §3689
		5	170			R.S. §4803
		6	170			R.S. §3689
		6	170			R.S. §4802
		7	170			R.S. §3
	170	1	170			R.S. §4214
		2	170			R.S. §4216

41st Cong. 16 Stat.	Chapter	Section	Page	U.S.C. Title	U.S.C. Section	Status
1870—June 29	170	3	170			R.S. §4217
		4	171			R.S. §4218
	171		171			R.S. §2253
	175	1	171			R.S. §550
		1	171			R.S. §576
		1	171			R.S. §608
		2	171			R.S. §572
		2	171			R.S. §608
		2	171			R.S. §658
		3	171			R.S. §550
		3	171			R.S. §572
		3	171			R.S. §576
		3	171			R.S. §608
		3	171			R.S. §658
		4	171			R.S. §581
		4	171			R.S. §668
		4	171			R.S. §670
		8	172			R.S. §551
		8	172			R.S. §554
		8	172			R.S. §767
		8	172			R.S. §770
		8	172			R.S. §776
		9	172			R.S. §623
30	177	1	172			R.S. §4978
		1	173			R.S. §4987
		2	174			R.S. §4976
	178	1	174			R.S. §537
		1	174			R.S. §560
		1	174			R.S. §744
		1	174			R.S. §768
		1	174			R.S. §778
		2	174			R.S. §572
		3	174			R.S. §560
		3	174			R.S. §744
		3	174			R.S. §768
		3	174			R.S. §778
	179		174			R.S. §4787
	180	1	175			R.S. §559
		1	175			R.S. §572
		1	175			R.S. §625
		1	175			R.S. §658
		2	175			R.S. §584
		2	175			R.S. §585
		2	175			R.S. §665
		2	175			R.S. §670
		3	175			R.S. §815
		4	175			R.S. §581
		5	175			R.S. §579
		5	175			R.S. §580
		6	175			R.S. §577
		7	175			R.S. §559
		7	175			R.S. §560
		7	175			R.S. §625
		7	175			R.S. §794
		7	175			R.S. §796
	181		176			R.S. §949
July 1	185	1	176			R.S. §3116
		1	176			R.S. §3117
		1	176			R.S. §3118
		1	177			R.S. §3119
		1	177			R.S. §3121
		2	177			R.S. §3122
		3	177			R.S. §3123
		4	177			R.S. §3124
		5	177			R.S. §3125
		7	177			R.S. §4381
		7	178			R.S. §4382
		9	179			R.S. §5293
	187		179			R.S. §3150
	188		180			R.S. §572
	189	1	180			R.S. §1960
		2	180			R.S. §1961
		3	180			R.S. §1962
		4	180			R.S. §1963
		4	180			R.S. §1964
		4	180			R.S. §1971
		5	181			R.S. §1963
		5	181			R.S. §1965
		5	181			R.S. §1966
		5	181			R.S. §1967
		5	181			R.S. §1968
		6	181			R.S. §1963
		6	181			R.S. §1969
		6	182			R.S. §1970
		7	182			R.S. §1957

41st Cong.				U.S.C.		
16 Stat.	Chapter	Section	Page	Title	Section	Status
1870—July 1	189	7	182			R.S. §5293
		8	182			R.S. §1972
	190	1	182			R.S. §2582
		1	182			R.S. §2824
		2	182			R.S. §2584
	193		183			R.S. §2390
	194	1	183			R.S. §4083
		1	183			R.S. §4129
		2	183			R.S. §4128
		2	183			R.S. §4130
		3	184			R.S. §4095
		4	184			R.S. §4092
		5	184			R.S. §4093
		6	184			R.S. §4094
		7	184			R.S. §4096
		9	184			R.S. §4122
		10	184			R.S. §4123
	196		186			R.S. §2278
	200		188			R.S. §4882
	Pub. R. 96	1	384			R.S. §1509
		1	384			R.S. §1510
	Pub. R. 97		384			R.S. §2680
	202[1]	3	646			R.S. §3689
7	210	4	190			R.S. §5249
	211		190			R.S. §2568
			190			R.S. §2708
			190			R.S. §2823
	214		192			R.S. §572
			192			R.S. §658
8	225	1	193			R.S. §4764
		2	194			R.S. §4765
		4	194			R.S. §4766
		4	194			R.S. §4782
		4	194			R.S. §5487
		5	194			R.S. §4767
		6	194			R.S. §4784
		7	194			R.S. §4786
		9	195			R.S. §4768
		10	195			R.S. §4769
	226		195			R.S. §5209
	230	1	198			R.S. §440
		1	198			R.S. §441
		1	198			R.S. §475
		2	198			R.S. §476
		4	199			R.S. §477
		6	199			R.S. §479
		7	199			R.S. §481
		9	199			R.S. §494
		10	199			R.S. §482
		12	200			R.S. §478
		13	200			R.S. §484
		14	200			R.S. §485
		15	200			R.S. §486
		16	200			R.S. §480
		17	200			R.S. §487
		18	200			R.S. §488
		19	200			R.S. §483
		20	200			R.S. §489
		21	200			R.S. §4883
		22	201			R.S. §4884
		23	201			R.S. §4885
		24	201			R.S. §4886
		25	201			R.S. §4887
		26	201			R.S. §4888
		27	201			R.S. §4889
		28	201			R.S. §4890
		29	201			R.S. §4891
		30	202			R.S. §4892
		31	202			R.S. §4893
		32	202			R.S. §4894
		33	202			R.S. §4895
		34	202			R.S. §4896
		35	202			R.S. §4897
		36	203			R.S. §4898
		37	203			R.S. §4899
		38	203			R.S. §4900
		39	203			R.S. §4901
		40	203			R.S. §4902
		41	204			R.S. §4903
		42	204			R.S. §4904
		43	204			R.S. §4905
		44	204			R.S. §4906
		44	204			R.S. §4908

[1] Private Law.

41st Cong.				U.S.C.		
16 Stat.	Chapter	Section	Page	Title	Section	Status
1870—July 8	230	45	204			R.S. §4906
		45	204			R.S. §4907
		45	204			R.S. §4908
		46	204			R.S. §4909
		47	205			R.S. §4910
		48	205			R.S. §4911
		49	205			R.S. §4912
		50	205			R.S. §4914
		51	205			R.S. §4913
		52	205			R.S. §4915
		53	205			R.S. §4916
		54	206			R.S. §4917
		55	206			R.S. §629
		55	206			R.S. §711
		55	206			R.S. §4921
		56	207			R.S. §699
		56	207			R.S. §711
		57	207			R.S. §892
		57	207			R.S. §893
		58	207			R.S. §711
		58	207			R.S. §4918
		59	207			R.S. §4919
		60	207			R.S. §973
		60	207			R.S. §4922
		61	208			R.S. §4920
		62	208			R.S. §4923
		63	208			R.S. §4924
		64	208			R.S. §4925
		65	208			R.S. §4926
		66	209			R.S. §4927
		67	209			R.S. §4928
		68	209			R.S. §4934
		69	209			R.S. §496
		69	209			R.S. §4935
		70	209			R.S. §4936
		71	209			R.S. §4929
		72	210			R.S. §4930
		73	210			R.S. §4931
		74	210			R.S. §4932
		75	210			R.S. §4934
		76	210			R.S. §4933
		77	210			R.S. §4937
		77	210			R.S. §4938
		78	211			R.S. §4941
		78	211			R.S. §4946
		79	211			R.S. §4939
		79	211			R.S. §4942
		80	211			R.S. §4940
		81	211			R.S. §4947
		82	212			R.S. §4944
		83	212			R.S. §4945
		84	212			R.S. §4943
		85	212			R.S. §90
		85	212			R.S. §4948
		85	212			R.S. §4949
		85	212			R.S. §4950
		85	212			R.S. §4951
		86	212			R.S. §4952
		87	212			R.S. §4953
		88	212			R.S. §4954
		89	213			R.S. §4955
		90	213			R.S. §4956
		91	213			R.S. §4957
		92	213			R.S. §4958
		93	213			R.S. §4959
		94	213			R.S. §4960
		96	214			R.S. §4961
		97	214			R.S. §4962
		98	214			R.S. §4963
		99	214			R.S. §4964
		100	214			R.S. §4965
		101	214			R.S. §4966
		102	215			R.S. §4967
		103	215			R.S. §4971
		104	215			R.S. §4968
		105	215			R.S. §4969
		106	215			R.S. §629
		106	215			R.S. §711
		106	215			R.S. §4970
		107	215			R.S. §699
		108	215			R.S. §972
		111	216			R.S. §3616
9	235	12	217			R.S. §2329
		12	217			R.S. §2330
		13	217			R.S. §2332
		16	218			R.S. §2406

41st Cong.				U.S.C.		
16 Stat.	Chapter	Section	Page	Title	Section	Status
1870—July 9	235	17	218			R.S. §2340
		17	218			R.S. §2344
11	238		222			R.S. §3667
			222			R.S. §4755
	243	1	229			R.S. §3711
		2	229			R.S. §3712
		2	229			R.S. §3713
	244		229			R.S. §2568
			229			R.S. §2708
			229			R.S. §2823
	246		230			R.S. §2207
			230			R.S. §2210
	Pub. R. 106		387			R.S. §1608
12	251	1	230			R.S. §242
		1	230			R.S. §3141
		1	230			R.S. §3153
		1	230			R.S. §3795
		2	230			R.S. §165
		3	230			R.S. §167
		3	250			R.S. §1054
		3	250			R.S. §3682
		4	250			R.S. §1835
		5	251			R.S. §3690
		6	251			R.S. §3691
		7	251			R.S. §3679
		8	251			R.S. §2704
		8	251			R.S. §2719
		8	251			R.S. §2720
	252	1	251			R.S. §5176
		1	251			R.S. §5177
		1	251			R.S. §5178
		3	252			R.S. §5185
		3	252			R.S. §5186
		4	253			R.S. §5186
		5	253			R.S. §5186
		5	253			R.S. §5196
		6	253			R.S. §5179
		6	253			R.S. §5180
		7	254			R.S. §5181
14	254	1	254			R.S. §5395
		2	254			R.S. §5424
		2	254			R.S. §5425
		2	254			R.S. §5426
		2	254			R.S. §5427
		3	254			R.S. §5428
		4	255			R.S. §5429
		7	256			R.S. §2169
	255	1	256			R.S. §3244
		1	256			R.S. §3319
		3	256			R.S. §3438
		3	256			R.S. §3439
		4	257			R.S. §3423
		4	257			R.S. §3425
		4	257			R.S. §3430
		5	257			R.S. §3422
		18	261			R.S. §3142
		21	262			R.S. §2504
		22	265			R.S. §2505
		24	269			R.S. §3026
		25	269			R.S. §4220
		25	269			R.S. §4223
		27	269			R.S. §3438
		27	269			R.S. §3439
		29	270			R.S. §2990
		29	270			R.S. §2991
		30	270			R.S. §2992
		31	270			R.S. §2993
		33	271			R.S. §2995
		33	271			R.S. §2996
		34	271			R.S. §251
		34	271			R.S. §2614
		34	271			R.S. §2615
		35	271			R.S. §2532
		35	271			R.S. §2536
		35	271			R.S. §2544
		35	271			R.S. §2553
		35	271			R.S. §2565
		35	271			R.S. §2569
		35	271			R.S. §2598
		35	271			R.S. §2600
		35	271			R.S. §2602
		35	271			R.S. §2604
		35	271			R.S. §2997
		36	271			R.S. §2532
		36	271			R.S. §2536
		36	271			R.S. §2544

41st Cong.				U.S.C.		
16 Stat.	Chapter	Section	Page	Title	Section	Status
1870—July 14	255	36	271			R.S. §2553
		36	271			R.S. §2565
		36	271			R.S. §2569
		36	271			R.S. §2587
		36	271			R.S. §2598
		36	271			R.S. §2600
		36	271			R.S. §2602
		36	271			R.S. §2604
		36	271			R.S. §2606
		36	271			R.S. §2614
		36	271			R.S. §2615
		36	271			R.S. §2730
		37	271			R.S. §2998
	256	1	272			R.S. §3701
		2	272			R.S. §3689
		4	273			R.S. §3697
		6	273			R.S. §3688
		6	273			R.S. §3695
		6	273			R.S. §3696
	257		274			R.S. §5222
			274			R.S. §5223
	259		275			R.S. §3430
	262		276			R.S. §5113
	264		277	36	252	Rev. T.
	268		278			R.S. §2568
			278			R.S. §2708
			278			R.S. §2823
	269		278			R.S. §2578
			278			R.S. §2579
			278			R.S. §2821
	271		279			R.S. §1930
	272	2	279			R.S. §2267
		2	279			R.S. §2281
15	292	1	291			R.S. §683
		1	294			R.S. §4865
		1	296			R.S. §3734
		1	304			R.S. §2367
		1	305			R.S. §2404
		1	305	43	881	
		2	308			R.S. §3828
		3	309			R.S. §2759
		3	309			R.S. §4677
		11	310			R.S. §3689
	293	1	311	40	32	Rep.
	294	2	317			R.S. §1107
		2	317			R.S. §1115
		2	317			R.S. §1155
		4	317			R.S. §1243
		4	317			R.S. §1622
		5	317			R.S. §1243
		5	317			R.S. §1258
		6	318			R.S. §1094
		7	318			R.S. §1094
		8	318			R.S. §1094
		9	318			R.S. §1102
		10	318			R.S. §1099
		10	318			R.S. §1100
		10	318			R.S. §1102
		10	318			R.S. §1103
		10	318			R.S. §1106
		10	318			R.S. §1107
		12	318			R.S. §1121
		12	318			R.S. §1122
		13	319			R.S. §1333
		14	319			R.S. §1232
		16	319			R.S. §1212
		16	319			R.S. §1604
		17	319			R.S. §1229
		17	319			R.S. §1266
		18	319			R.S. §1222
		20	319	10	16	Rev. T.
		21	319			R.S. §1324
		21	319			R.S. §1526
		22	319			R.S. §1113
		23	320			R.S. §1260
		24	320			R.S. §1261
		24	320			R.S. §1262
		24	320			R.S. §1263
		24	320			R.S. §1265
		24	320			R.S. §1267
		24	320			R.S. §1268
		24	320			R.S. §1269
		24	320			R.S. §1270
		24	320			R.S. §1271
		24	320			R.S. §1273

41st Cong.					U.S.C.		
16 Stat.		Chapter	Section	Page	Title	Section	Status
1870—July	15	294	24	320			R.S. §1274
			25	320			R.S. §2238
		295	1	321			R.S. §1556
			3	330			R.S. §1556
			4	332			R.S. §1558
			4	332			R.S. §1566
			4	332			R.S. §1585
			5	333			R.S. §1588
			5	333			R.S. §1590
			5	333			R.S. §1591
			5	333			R.S. §1624
			6	333			R.S. §1445
			6	333			R.S. §1456
			6	333			R.S. §1624
			7	333			R.S. §1560
			7	333			R.S. §1561
			7	333			R.S. §1562
			7	333			R.S. §1624
			8	333			R.S. §1505
			9	333			R.S. §1363
			10	333			R.S. §1363
			10	334			R.S. §1490
			11	334			R.S. §1376
			11	334			R.S. §1377
			12	334			R.S. §1512
			12	334			R.S. §1513
			12	334			R.S. §1521
			12	334			R.S. §1556
			13	334			R.S. §1411
			14	334			R.S. §1624
			15	334			R.S. §3622
			15	334			R.S. §5491
			17	334			R.S. §1586
			17	334			R.S. §1587
		296	2	360			R.S. §2085
			2	360			R.S. §2086
			3	360			R.S. §2039
			3	360			R.S. §2040
			3	360			R.S. §2041
			3	360			R.S. §2086
			4	360			R.S. §2098
			6	360			R.S. §2054
		298	1	363			R.S. §852
			2	363			R.S. §812
			3	363			R.S. §800
			3	363			R.S. §801
		300	1	364			R.S. §197
			2	364			R.S. §1883
			3	364			R.S. §1834
		302	1	365			R.S. §70
			2	365			R.S. §72
		Pub. R. 131		391			R.S. §1826
Dec.	22	6		397			R.S. §2504
				397			R.S. §2915
		Pub. R. 2		589			R.S. §800
				589			R.S. §801
1871—Jan.	10	15	1	398			R.S. §1892
			2	398			R.S. §1893
			2	398			R.S. §1894
			3	398			R.S. §1895
	11	Pub. R. 5		590			R.S. §490
				590			R.S. §491
				590			R.S. §492
				590			R.S. §894
	20	23		399			R.S. §3689
Feb.	3	35	1	403			R.S. §549
			2	403			R.S. §572
			2	403			R.S. §608
			3	403			R.S. §549
			3	403			R.S. §572
			3	403			R.S. §608
			3	403			R.S. §658
			4	403			R.S. §581
			4	403			R.S. §668
			4	403			R.S. §670
			8	404			R.S. §551
			8	404			R.S. §554
			8	404			R.S. §767
			8	404			R.S. §776
			9	404			R.S. §622
	8	39		407			R.S. §2562
				407			R.S. §2563
	9	Pub. R. 22	1	594			R.S. §4395
			2	594			R.S. §4396
			3	594			R.S. §4397
			4	594			R.S. §4398

41st Cong. 16 Stat.	Chapter	Section	Page	U.S.C. Title	U.S.C. Section	Status
1871—Feb. 10	45		408			R.S. §3111
			408			R.S. §3112
			409			R.S. §3113
	Pub. R. 27	1	595			R.S. §4585
		1	595			R.S. §4587
		1	595			R.S. §4804
		2	595			R.S. §2793
		2	595			R.S. §4382
14	50	1	411			R.S. §4732
		1	411			R.S. §4736
		1	411			R.S. §4738
		2	411			R.S. §4737
		3	411			R.S. §4739
		3	411			R.S. §4740
	51	1	412			R.S. §184
		1	412			R.S. §185
		1	412			R.S. §186
		3	412			R.S. §187
		3	412			R.S. §364
15	53		412			R.S. §1757
17	Pub. R. 36		597			R.S. §505
21	61		417			R.S. §1681
	62	1	419			R.S. §906
		41	428			R.S. §1819
	63		429			R.S. §572
			429			R.S. §658
	Pub. R. 40		598			R.S. §5252
25	71	1	431			R.S. §7
		1	431			R.S. §8
		1	431			R.S. §9
		1	431			R.S. §10
		2	431			R.S. §1
		3	431			R.S. §12
		4	432			R.S. §13
	72		432			R.S. §348
28	99	1	433			R.S. §5512
		1	433			R.S. §5513
		2	433			R.S. §2011
		3	434			R.S. §2014
		4	434			R.S. §2016
		5	434			R.S. §2017
		5	434			R.S. §2018
		6	435			R.S. §2019
		7	435			R.S. §2020
		8	436			R.S. §2021
		8	436			R.S. §2022
		9	436			R.S. §2023
		10	436			R.S. §5522
		10	436			R.S. §5523
		11	437			R.S. §5521
		12	437			R.S. §2024
		13	437			R.S. §2025
		13	437			R.S. §2026
		13	437			R.S. §2027
		14	438			R.S. §3689
		15	438			R.S. §629
		16	438			R.S. §643
		16	438			R.S. §646
		17	439			R.S. §645
		17	439			R.S. §950
		19	440			R.S. §27
	100	1	440			R.S. §4399
		1	440			R.S. §4498
		1	440			R.S. §4499
		2	440			R.S. §4470
		3	440			R.S. §4471
		4	441			R.S. §4472
		4	441			R.S. §4473
		4	442			R.S. §4474
		5	442			R.S. §4475
		5	442			R.S. §4476
		6	442			R.S. §4477
		6	442			R.S. §4478
		6	442			R.S. §4479
		7	442			R.S. §4481
		8	443			R.S. §4482
		8	443			R.S. §4483
		9	443			R.S. §4484
		9	443			R.S. §4485
		9	443			R.S. §4486
		10	443			R.S. §4480
		11	443			R.S. §4415
		11	443			R.S. §4417
		11	443			R.S. §4418
		11	443			R.S. §4419
		11	443			R.S. §4421
		11	445			R.S. §4491

41st Cong. 16 Stat.	Chapter	Section	Page	U.S.C. Title	U.S.C. Section	Status
1871—Feb. 28	100	12	445			R.S. §4422
		13	445			R.S. §4457
		14	446			R.S. §4438
		14	446			R.S. §4463
		15	446			R.S. §4439
		16	446			R.S. §4440
		17	446			R.S. §4441
		18	447			R.S. §4442
		18	447			R.S. §4443
		18	447			R.S. §4446
		19	447			R.S. §4450
		19	447			R.S. §4451
		20	447			R.S. §4452
		21	448			R.S. §4453
		21	448			R.S. §4454
		21	448			R.S. §4455
		22	448			R.S. §4456
		23	448			R.S. §4404
		23	449			R.S. §4405
		24	449			R.S. §4406
		25	449			R.S. §4407
		26	449			R.S. §4408
		27	449			R.S. §4409
		28	449			R.S. §4410
		28	449			R.S. §4411
		29	450			R.S. §4412
		29	450			R.S. §4413
		30	450			R.S. §4496
		30	450			R.S. §4497
		31	450			R.S. §4423
		31	450			R.S. §4424
		32	450			R.S. §4425
		33	451			R.S. §4416
		35	451			R.S. §4428
		35	451			R.S. §4429
		36	451			R.S. §4430
		37	451			R.S. §4431
		38	452			R.S. §4432
		39	452			R.S. §4433
		39	452			R.S. §4434
		39	452			R.S. §4435
		39	452			R.S. §4436
		40	452			R.S. §4437
		41	453			R.S. §4400
		42	453			R.S. §4487
		43	453			R.S. §4494
		44	453			R.S. §4495
		45	453			R.S. §4179
		46	453			R.S. §4492
		47	454			R.S. §4233
		48	454			R.S. §4464
		48	454			R.S. §4465
		48	454			R.S. §4466
		49	454			R.S. §4467
		49	454			R.S. §4468
		49	454			R.S. §4469
		50	455			R.S. §4494
		50	455			R.S. §4495
		51	455			R.S. §4401
		51	455			R.S. §4444
		52	455			R.S. §4488
		52	455			R.S. §4489
		53	455			R.S. §4490
		54	456			R.S. §4448
		55	456			R.S. §4449
		56	456			R.S. §4445
		56	456			R.S. §4447
		57	456			R.S. §563
		57	456			R.S. §629
		57	456			R.S. §5344
		58	456			R.S. §4426
		58	456			R.S. §4427
		60	457			R.S. §4458
		61	457			R.S. §4457
		62	457			R.S. §4404
		62	457			R.S. §4414
		63	458			R.S. §4402
		63	458			R.S. §4403
		64	458			R.S. §5294
		65	458			R.S. §4460
		65	458			R.S. §4461
		65	458			R.S. §4462
		66	458			R.S. §3689
		67	458			R.S. §4459
		68	458			R.S. §4500

41st Cong. 16 Stat.	Chapter	Section	Page	U.S.C. Title	U.S.C. Section	Status
1871—Feb. 28	100	69	458			R.S. §4281
		70	459			R.S. §4234
	Pub. R. 45		599			R.S. §4832
Mar. 3	106	1	471			R.S. §572
		2	472			R.S. §814
		4	472			R.S. §556
		5	472			R.S. §533
		5	472			R.S. §554
		5	472			R.S. §572
		5	472			R.S. §608
	108		473			R.S. §559
			473			R.S. §625
			473			R.S. §743
	111	1	474			R.S. §899
		2	475			R.S. §900
		3	475			R.S. §901
	113	1	477			R.S. §1822
		1	478			R.S. §3809
		1	479			R.S. §1799
		1	483			R.S. §242
		1	485			R.S. §3594
		3	492			R.S. §416
		3	494			R.S. §596
		3	494			R.S. §607
		4	495			R.S. §607
	114	1	500			R.S. §1816
		1	506			R.S. §2038
		4	514			R.S. §3689
		9	514			R.S. §1753
	115	1	517			R.S. §3789
		2	521			R.S. §3687
	116	5	525			R.S. §3689
		6	525			R.S. §3689
	117	3	535			R.S. §3723
		5	535			R.S. §1368
		5	535			R.S. §1474
		5	535			R.S. §1556
		5	536			R.S. §1370
		6	536			R.S. §1376
		6	536			R.S. §1385
		6	536			R.S. §1475
		6	536			R.S. §1556
		7	536			R.S. §1390
		7	536			R.S. §1476
		8	536			R.S. §1392
		9	536			R.S. §1402
		9	536			R.S. §1477
		9	536			R.S. §1478
		9	536			R.S. §1479
		10	537			R.S. §421
		10	537			R.S. §1436
		10	537			R.S. §1485
		10	537			R.S. §1486
		10	537			R.S. §1487
		11	537			R.S. §1481
		11	537			R.S. §1482
		12	537			R.S. §1468
		12	537			R.S. §1469
		12	537			R.S. §1470
		12	537			R.S. §1471
		12	537			R.S. §1472
		12	537			R.S. §1473
		12	537			R.S. §1489
		12	537			R.S. §1565
	120	1	566			R.S. §2079
		1	568			R.S. §2107
		3	570			R.S. §2103
		3	570			R.S. §2105
	125		580			R.S. §2496
	127		581			R.S. §2403
	130	1	583			R.S. §2582
		1	583			R.S. §2583
		1	583			R.S. §2698
		2	583			R.S. §2585
		3	583			R.S. §2583
		3	583			R.S. §2698
		3	583			R.S. §2824
	132		583			R.S. §4895
	136		584			R.S. §91
	Pub. R. 49		600			R.S. §3704
			600			R.S. §3705
	Pub. R. 52		601			R.S. §2267
	Pub. R. 53		601			R.S. §3282

41st Cong.				U.S.C.		
16 Stat.	**Chapter**	**Section**	**Page**	**Title**	**Section**	**Status**
1870—July 1	202[1]	3	646			R.S. §3689
42d Cong.						
17 Stat.						
1871—Mar. 20	1		1			R.S. §5579
			1			R.S. §5580
24	2	1	1			R.S. §995
		1	1			R.S. §5504
		2	1			R.S. §996
		3	2			R.S. §798
		4	2			R.S. §5504
		5	2			R.S. §5505
	5	1	2			R.S. §492
		2	3			R.S. §493
		2	3			R.S. §4934
30	7		3			R.S. §2518
Apr. 12	12[1]	1	641			R.S. §3689
		2	642			R.S. §3689
19	16		4			R.S. §4770
	17	1	4			R.S. §2552
		2	4			R.S. §2553
		2	4			R.S. §2699
		3	5			R.S. §2552
20	21	15	10			R.S. §2600
		15	10			R.S. §2990
		16	10			R.S. §2287
		27	12			R.S. §4243
		27	12			R.S. §4244
	22	1	13			R.S. §563
		1	13			R.S. §629
		1	13			R.S. §699
		1	13			R.S. §1979
		2	13			R.S. §563
		2	13			R.S. §629
		2	13			R.S. §699
		2	13			R.S. §1980
		2	13			R.S. §5336
		2	13			R.S. §5406
		2	13			R.S. §5407
		2	13			R.S. §5518
		2	13			R.S. §5519
		2	13			R.S. §5520
		3	14			R.S. §5299
		5	15			R.S. §800
		5	15			R.S. §801
		5	15			R.S. §822
		6	15			R.S. §629
		6	15			R.S. §1981
	24		16			R.S. §2683
1872—Feb. 1	10		27			R.S. §572
			27			R.S. §658
2	11	1	28			R.S. §20
		2	28			R.S. §23
		3	28			R.S. §25
		4	28			R.S. §26
		6	29			R.S. §22
	12	1	29			R.S. §300
		1	29			R.S. §3646
		2	29			R.S. §300
		2	29			R.S. §3647
Mar. 1	22		32			R.S. §5191
	24	1	32			R.S. §2474
		2	33			R.S. §2475
	25		33			R.S. §2568
			33			R.S. §2569
			33			R.S. §2700
5	29		35			R.S. §2512
	30	1	35			R.S. §5543
		1	35			R.S. §5545
		1	35			R.S. §5546
		1	35			R.S. §5547
		1	35			R.S. §5549
		1	35			R.S. §5550
		2	35			R.S. §353
	31	1	35			R.S. §1973
		1	35			R.S. §1974
		1	35			R.S. §1975
		3	35			R.S. §1976
	33		36			R.S. §3419
	34		36			R.S. §2990
			36			R.S. §2997
	35		36			R.S. §597

[1] Private Law.

[1] Private Law.

42d Cong. 17 Stat.	Chapter	Section	Page	U.S.C. Title	U.S.C. Section	Status
1872—Mar. 12	47		40			R.S. §1168
18	56	1	40			R.S. §902
		2	41			R.S. §903
		3	41			R.S. §904
	57		41			R.S. §2997
30	72		44			R.S. §644
Apr. 2	79	3	47			R.S. §54
	80		47			R.S. §2543
	81		48			R.S. §5572
			48			R.S. §5574
5	86		50			R.S. §2994
	88	2	51			R.S. §3689
9	90		51			R.S. §4250
13	99		52			R.S. §572
			52			R.S. §658
17	103		53			R.S. §2578
22	114		55			R.S. §3689
30	129		58			R.S. §3004
May 1	131		59			R.S. §2505
			59			R.S. §2775
			59			R.S. §2785
			59			R.S. §3689
3	139		61			R.S. §237
8	140	1	64			R.S. §63
		1	64			R.S. §3761
		1	65			R.S. §1799
		1	66			R.S. §79
		1	68			R.S. §256
		1	70			R.S. §3601
		1	71			R.S. §3608
		1	73			R.S. §1887
		1	73			R.S. §1939
		1	76			R.S. §2207
		1	76			R.S. §2208
		1	76			R.S. §2209
		1	76			R.S. §2210
		1	82			R.S. §1054
		2	82			R.S. §3661
		3	83			R.S. §3762
		3	83			R.S. §3802
		3	83			R.S. §3821
		5	83			R.S. §313
		5	83			R.S. §3618
		5	83			R.S. §3672
		5	83			R.S. §3692
		13	85			R.S. §312
		13	85			R.S. §1049
9	143		88			R.S. §572
			88			R.S. §658
	145	2	89			R.S. §3689
	146		89			R.S. §863
			89			R.S. §864
			89			R.S. §866
	147		90			R.S. §1905
	149	1	90			R.S. §2283
		3	90			R.S. §2284
		3	90			R.S. §2285
10	152	1	91			R.S. §2319
		2	91			R.S. §2320
		3	91			R.S. §2322
		4	92			R.S. §2323
		5	92			R.S. §2324
		6	92			R.S. §2325
		7	94			R.S. §2321
		7	94			R.S. §2326
		8	94			R.S. §2327
		9	94			R.S. §2328
		10	94			R.S. §2331
		11	94			R.S. §2333
		12	95			R.S. §2238
		12	95			R.S. §2334
		13	95			R.S. §2335
		14	96			R.S. §2336
		15	96			R.S. §2337
		16	96			R.S. §2344
15	160	1	116			R.S. §1280
		2	116			R.S. §1281
		3	116			R.S. §1282
		4	117			R.S. §1283
		4	117			R.S. §1284
	161	1	117			R.S. §1305
		2	117			R.S. §1306
		3	117			R.S. §1302
		4	117			R.S. §1307
		5	117			R.S. §1308
	162	1	117			R.S. §1117
		2	117			R.S. §1342

42d Cong. 17 Stat.	Chapter	Section	Page	U.S.C. Title	U.S.C. Section	Status
1872—May 17	169		120			R.S. §1690
18	172	1	127			R.S. §268
		2	134			R.S. §3689
		3	134			R.S. §1995
	173	1	135			R.S. §4874
		2	135			R.S. §4875
21	176		135			R.S. §658
	177	1	136			R.S. §2103
		2	136			R.S. §2103
		2	136			R.S. §2104
		2	136			R.S. §2106
	178		137	31	100	Rev. T.
			137	38	130	Rev. T.
			137	43	841	Rep.
22	194		142			R.S. §201
			142			R.S. §1682
			144			R.S. §504
			144			R.S. §1690
23	195	1	146			R.S. §1544
		1	151			R.S. §1584
		1	153			R.S. §1483
		2	154			R.S. §1541
	197		156			R.S. §3689
	199	1	157			R.S. §2595
		1	157			R.S. §2596
		1	157			R.S. §2675
		2	157			R.S. §2595
		2	157			R.S. §2596
	201		157			R.S. §572
	202		158			R.S. §1026
27	218	1	162			R.S. §3221
		2	162			R.S. §3222
		2	162			R.S. §3223
28	228	1	164			R.S. §1176
		1	164	38	250	Rev. T.
		2	164			R.S. §1177
		3	164			R.S. §1178
29	233	1	186			R.S. §2042
		7	190			R.S. §445
		7	190			R.S. §466
30	239		192			R.S. §23
			192			R.S. §27
31	240		192			R.S. §1399
			192			R.S. §1480
	241		192			R.S. §2254
June 1	254	1	196			R.S. §3702
		2	196			R.S. §3703
	255	1	196			R.S. §650
		1	196			R.S. §651
		1	196			R.S. §652
		1	196			R.S. §693
		2	196			R.S. §631
		2	196			R.S. §635
		2	196			R.S. §636
		2	196			R.S. §701
		2	196			R.S. §1008
		3	197			R.S. §948
		3	197			R.S. §1005
		4	197			R.S. §912
		4	197			R.S. §953
		5	197			R.S. §914
		6	197			R.S. §915
		6	197			R.S. §916
		7	197			R.S. §718
		7	197			R.S. §719
		8	198			R.S. §1025
		9	198			R.S. §1035
		10	198			R.S. §1036
		11	198			R.S. §1007
		12	198			R.S. §1041
		13	198			R.S. §738
		13	198			R.S. §739
		14	198			R.S. §1042
		14	198			R.S. §5296
		16	199			R.S. §847
	256	2	201			R.S. §4029
		5	202			R.S. §190
	257		202			R.S. §4878
3	279		214			R.S. §1132
4	280	1	214			R.S. §2792
		2	215			R.S. §3007
	282	1	215			R.S. §543
		2	215			R.S. §572
		2	215			R.S. §658
		3	215			R.S. §543
		4	215			R.S. §581
		4	215			R.S. §667

42d Cong. 17 Stat.	Chapter	Section	Page	U.S.C. Title	U.S.C. Section	Status
1872—June 4	282	4	215			R.S. §670
		4	215			R.S. §816
		7	217			R.S. §767
		8	217			R.S. §551
		8	217			R.S. §554
		9	217			R.S. §621
		10	217			R.S. §898
	284	1	218			R.S. §571
		1	218			R.S. §608
		3	218			R.S. §572
		3	218			R.S. §658
	286		218			R.S. §1182
	287		220			R.S. §1832
5	306		226			R.S. §1561
	307		226			R.S. §1589
6	315	1	230			R.S. §2504
		3	232			R.S. §2501
		3	232			R.S. §2503
		4	232			R.S. §2504
		5	233			R.S. §2505
		6	237			R.S. §2917
		9	238			R.S. §3020
		10	238			R.S. §2513
		10	238			R.S. §2514
		11	238			R.S. §3022
		11	238			R.S. §3689
		12	238			R.S. §3245
		12	238			R.S. §3251
		12	239			R.S. §3244
		12	239			R.S. §3249
		12	239			R.S. §3260
		12	239			R.S. §3264
		12	239			R.S. §3266
		12	239			R.S. §3267
		12	239			R.S. §3270
		12	239			R.S. §3271
		12	239			R.S. §3280
		12	240			R.S. §3242
		12	240			R.S. §3281
		12	240			R.S. §3293
		12	240			R.S. §3305
		12	240			R.S. §3307
		12	240			R.S. §3310
		12	240			R.S. §3313
		12	240			R.S. §3314
		12	240			R.S. §3323
		12	240			R.S. §3328
		12	240			R.S. §3332
		12	240			R.S. §3445
		12	241			R.S. §3152
		12	241			R.S. §3154
		12	241			R.S. §3159
		12	241			R.S. §3160
		12	241			R.S. §3163
		12	241			R.S. §3329
		12	242			R.S. §3330
		12	243			R.S. §3289
		12	243			R.S. §3320
		12	243			R.S. §3321
		13	243			R.S. §3262
		13	243			R.S. §3309
		13	244			R.S. §3244
		13	244			R.S. §3308
		13	244			R.S. §3317
		14	244			R.S. §3153
		14	244			R.S. §3157
		15	245			R.S. §3315
		16	245			R.S. §3335
		17	245			R.S. §3244
		17	245			R.S. §3336
		18	245			R.S. §3339
		19	245			R.S. §3337
		20	246			R.S. §3338
		21	246			R.S. §3340
		22	246			R.S. §3341
		23	247			R.S. §3342
		24	247			R.S. §3343
		24	247			R.S. §3344
		24	247			R.S. §3346
		24	247			R.S. §3347
		24	248			R.S. §3345
		24	248			R.S. §3348
		25	248			R.S. §3349
		26	249			R.S. §3350
		27	249			R.S. §3351
		28	249			R.S. §3352

42d Cong.				U.S.C.		
17 Stat.	Chapter	Section	Page	Title	Section	Status
1872—June 6	315	29	249			R.S. §3353
		30	249			R.S. §3354
		31	250			R.S. §3361
		31	250			R.S. §3368
		31	251			R.S. §3244
		31	251			R.S. §3381
		31	251			R.S. §3382
		31	252			R.S. §3237
		31	252			R.S. §3362
		31	252			R.S. §3371
		31	252			R.S. §3383
		31	252			R.S. §3384
		31	252			R.S. §3437
		31	253			R.S. §3355
		31	253			R.S. §3369
		31	253			R.S. §3372
		31	253			R.S. §3374
		31	253			R.S. §3376
		31	254			R.S. §3385
		31	254			R.S. §3386
		31	255			R.S. §3397
		31	255			R.S. §3444
		32	255			R.S. §3242
		33	255			R.S. §3406
		34	255			R.S. §3435
		36	256			R.S. §3418
		37	256			R.S. §3408
		37	256			R.S. §3409
		37	256			R.S. §3414
		40	257			R.S. §3460
		40	257			R.S. §3461
		41	257			R.S. §3689
		44	257			R.S. §3226
		44	257			R.S. §3227
		44	257			R.S. §3228
	316	1	261			R.S. §1672
		1	261			R.S. §1673
		2	261			R.S. §1342
		2	261			R.S. §1624
7	322	1	262			R.S. §4501
		2	262			R.S. §4502
		3	262			R.S. §4502
		3	262			R.S. §4505
		3	262			R.S. §4506
		4	263			R.S. §4507
		4	263			R.S. §4508
		5	263			R.S. §4592
		6	263			R.S. §4593
		7	263			R.S. §4595
		8	263			R.S. §4503
		8	263			R.S. §4504
		9	263			R.S. §4509
		9	263			R.S. §4592
		10	264			R.S. §4510
		11	264			R.S. §4609
		12	264			R.S. §4504
		12	264			R.S. §4511
		12	264			R.S. §4513
		12	264			R.S. §4520
		13	265			R.S. §4512
		14	265			R.S. §4514
		14	265			R.S. §4515
		14	265			R.S. §4516
		15	265			R.S. §4517
		15	265			R.S. §4518
		15	265			R.S. §4523
		16	266			R.S. §4531
		17	266			R.S. §4532
		18	266			R.S. §4533
		19	266			R.S. §4534
		20	266			R.S. §4519
		21	266			R.S. §4527
		22	266			R.S. §4549
		23	267			R.S. §4550
		24	267			R.S. §4551
		25	267			R.S. §4554
		26	267			R.S. §4555
		27	267			R.S. §4552
		28	268			R.S. §4553
		29	268			R.S. §2174
		30	268			R.S. §4524
		31	268			R.S. §4535
		32	268			R.S. §4525
		33	269			R.S. §4526
		34	269			R.S. §4528
		35	269			R.S. §4529

42d Cong.				U.S.C.		
17 Stat.	Chapter	Section	Page	Title	Section	Status
1872—June 7	322	36	269			R.S. §4565
		37	269			R.S. §4566
		38	269			R.S. §4567
		39	270			R.S. §4568
		40	270			R.S. §4569
		41	270			R.S. §4570
		42	270			R.S. §4571
		42	270			R.S. §4572
		43	271			R.S. §4538
		44	271			R.S. §4539
		45	271			R.S. §4540
		46	272			R.S. §4541
		47	272			R.S. §4542
		48	272			R.S. §4543
		49	272			R.S. §4544
		50	273			R.S. §4545
		51	273			R.S. §4596
		52	274			R.S. §4597
		53	274			R.S. §4599
		54	274			R.S. §4602
		55	275			R.S. §4604
		56	275			R.S. §4600
		56	275			R.S. §4603
		57	275			R.S. §4605
		58	275			R.S. §4290
		59	276			R.S. §4291
		60	276			R.S. §4292
		61	276			R.S. §4536
		62	276			R.S. §4606
		63	276			R.S. §4607
		64	276			R.S. §4610
		65	277			R.S. §4612
		66	277			R.S. §4594
		68	277			R.S. §4612
8	332		282			R.S. §1690
	333	2	282			R.S. §819
	334	1	282			R.S. §608
		1	282			R.S. §658
		2	283			R.S. §658
		3	283			R.S. §663
	335	1	283			R.S. §161
		1	283			R.S. §388
		2	283			R.S. §388
		2	284			R.S. §389
		3	284			R.S. §390
		3	284			R.S. §393
		4	284			R.S. §393
		5	285			R.S. §395
		6	285			R.S. §396
		8	285			R.S. §413
		9	286			R.S. §3668
		10	286			R.S. §397
		12	286			R.S. §412
		13	287			R.S. §403
		14	287			R.S. §3858
		15	287			R.S. §391
		15	287			R.S. §392
		16	287			R.S. §3832
		17	287			R.S. §5266
		18	287			R.S. §402
		19	287			R.S. §414
		20	287			R.S. §210
		20	287			R.S. §399
		21	287			R.S. §276
		21	287			R.S. §292
		22	287			R.S. §277
		22	287			R.S. §313
		24	288			R.S. §297
		24	288			R.S. §298
		25	288			R.S. §270
		26	288			R.S. §235
		28	289			R.S. §3836
		29	289			R.S. §405
		30	289			R.S. §400
		31	289			R.S. §4017
		32	289			R.S. §4017
		33	289			R.S. §4018
		34	289			R.S. §4019
		35	289			R.S. §4020
		36	289			R.S. §4021
		37	289			R.S. §4022
		38	290			R.S. §4023
		39	290			R.S. §4024
		40	290			R.S. §4025
		41	290			R.S. §4049
		42	290			R.S. §4050

42d Cong. 17 Stat.	Chapter	Section	Page	U.S.C. Title	U.S.C. Section	Status
1872—June 8	335	43	290			R.S. §4051
		44	290			R.S. §4052
		45	291			R.S. §4053
		46	291			R.S. §4054
		47	291			R.S. §3674
		48	291			R.S. §4055
		49	291			R.S. §4056
		50	291			R.S. §4057
		51	291			R.S. §4058
		52	291			R.S. §294
		53	292			R.S. §406
		54	292			R.S. §407
		55	292			R.S. §408
		56	292			R.S. §3641
		57	292			R.S. §4059
		58	292			R.S. §4060
		59	292			R.S. §4061
		60	292			R.S. §3835
		61	292			R.S. §3829
		62	292			R.S. §3829
		63	292			R.S. §3830
		64	293			R.S. §3831
		65	293			R.S. §3834
		66	293			R.S. §3837
		67	293			R.S. §3838
		68	293			R.S. §3839
		69	293			R.S. §3840
		70	293			R.S. §3841
		71	293			R.S. §3842
		72	293			R.S. §3843
		73	293			R.S. §3844
		74	293			R.S. §3845
		75	293			R.S. §3846
		76	294			R.S. §3848
		77	294			R.S. §3849
		78	294			R.S. §3850
		79	294			R.S. §3851
		80	294			R.S. §3852
		81	294			R.S. §3853
		82	294			R.S. §3854
		83	294			R.S. §3855
		84	294			R.S. §3856
		85	294			R.S. §3857
		86	295			R.S. §3859
		87	295			R.S. §3860
		88	295			R.S. §3861
		89	295			R.S. §3862
		90	296			R.S. §3863
		91	296			R.S. §3864
		92	296			R.S. §3865
		93	296			R.S. §3866
		94	296			R.S. §3867
		95	296			R.S. §3868
		96	296			R.S. §3869
		97	296			R.S. §3870
		98	296			R.S. §3871
		99	296			R.S. §3872
		100	296			R.S. §3873
		101	296			R.S. §3874
		102	297			R.S. §4027
		103	297			R.S. §4028
		104	297			R.S. §4029
		105	297			R.S. §4030
		106	297			R.S. §4031
		107	298			R.S. §4032
		108	298			R.S. §4033
		109	298			R.S. §4034
		110	298			R.S. §4035
		111	298			R.S. §4036
		112	298			R.S. §4037
		113	298			R.S. §4038
		114	298			R.S. §4039
		115	298			R.S. §4040
		116	298			R.S. §5463
		117	299			R.S. §4042
		118	299			R.S. §4042
		118	299			R.S. §4043
		119	299			R.S. §4044
		120	299			R.S. §293
		121	299			R.S. §4045
		122	299			R.S. §4046
		123	300			R.S. §4047
		124	300			R.S. §4048
		126	300			R.S. §3926
		127	300			R.S. §3927
		128	300			R.S. §3928

42d Cong. 17 Stat.	Chapter	Section	Page	U.S.C. Title	U.S.C. Section	Status
1872—June 8	335	129	300			R.S. §3926
		130	300			R.S. §3875
		131	300			R.S. §3876
		132	300			R.S. §3877
		133	300			R.S. §3878
		134	300			R.S. §3879
		135	301			R.S. §3880
		136	301			R.S. §3881
		137	301			R.S. §3882
		138	301			R.S. §3883
		139	301			R.S. §3884
		140	301			R.S. §3885
		141	301			R.S. §3886
		142	301			R.S. §3887
		143	301			R.S. §3888
		144	301			R.S. §3889
		145	301			R.S. §3890
		146	302			R.S. §3891
		147	302			R.S. §3892
		148	302			R.S. §3893
		148	302			R.S. §3894
		149	302			R.S. §3893
		149	302			R.S. §3894
		150	302			R.S. §3896
		151	302			R.S. §3898
		152	302			R.S. §3898
		153	303			R.S. §3900
		154	303			R.S. §3901
		155	303			R.S. §3902
		156	303			R.S. §3903
		157	303			R.S. §3904
		158	303			R.S. §3905
		159	303			R.S. §3906
		160	303			R.S. §3907
		161	303			R.S. §3908
		162	303			R.S. §3909
		163	304			R.S. §3910
		164	304			R.S. §3911
		165	304			R.S. §3912
		166	304			R.S. §3913
		167	304			R.S. §398
		168	304			R.S. §3914
		169	304			R.S. §3915
		170	304			R.S. §3916
		171	304			R.S. §3917
		172	304			R.S. §3918
		173	305			R.S. §3919
		174	305			R.S. §3920
		175	305			R.S. §3921
		176	305			R.S. §3922
		177	305			R.S. §3923
		178	305			R.S. §5464
		179	306			R.S. §5465
		188	307			R.S. §3930
		189	307			R.S. §3931
		190	307			R.S. §3932
		191	308			R.S. §3933
		192	308			R.S. §3934
		193	308			R.S. §3935
		194	308			R.S. §3936
		195	308			R.S. §3937
		196	308			R.S. §3938
		197	308			R.S. §401
		198	308			R.S. §3939
		199	308			R.S. §3940
		200	308			R.S. §3964
		205	309			R.S. §3964
		206	309			R.S. §3972
		207	309			R.S. §3973
		208	309			R.S. §3974
		209	309			R.S. §3975
		210	309			R.S. §3997
		211	309			R.S. §3998
		212	309			R.S. §3999
		213	309			R.S. §4000
		214	309			R.S. §4001
		215	309			R.S. §3965
		216	309			R.S. §3966
		217	310			R.S. §3967
		218	310			R.S. §3968
		219	310			R.S. §3969
		220	310			R.S. §3970
		221	310			R.S. §3971
		222	310			R.S. §3976
		223	310			R.S. §3977
		224	310			R.S. §3978

42d Cong.				U.S.C.		
17 Stat.	**Chapter**	**Section**	**Page**	**Title**	**Section**	**Status**
1872—June 8	335	225	310			R.S. §3979
		226	310			R.S. §3980
		227	311			R.S. §3981
		228	311			R.S. §3982
		229	311			R.S. §3983
		230	311			R.S. §3984
		231	311			R.S. §3985
		232	311			R.S. §3986
		233	311			R.S. §3987
		234	311			R.S. §3988
		235	312			R.S. §3989
		236	312			R.S. §3990
		237	312			R.S. §3991
		238	312			R.S. §3992
		239	312			R.S. §3993
		240	312			R.S. §3994
		241	312			R.S. §3995
		242	313			R.S. §3996
		243	313			R.S. §3941
		244	313			R.S. §3944
		245	313			R.S. §3945
		246	313			R.S. §3946
		247	313			R.S. §3947
		248	313			R.S. §3948
		249	313			R.S. §3949
		250	313			R.S. §3950
		251	313			R.S. §3951
		252	313			R.S. §3952
		253	313			R.S. §3953
		254	315			R.S. §3954
		255	315			R.S. §3955
		256	315			R.S. §3956
		257	315			R.S. §3957
		258	315			R.S. §3958
		259	315			R.S. §3959
		260	315			R.S. §3960
		261	315			R.S. §3961
		262	315			R.S. §404
		263	315			R.S. §4006
		264	316			R.S. §3943
		265	316			R.S. §3942
		266	316			R.S. §3962
		267	316			R.S. §4007
		268	316			R.S. §4008
		269	316			R.S. §4009
		270	316			R.S. §4010
		271	316			R.S. §3963
		272	316			R.S. §4011
		273	316			R.S. §4012
		274	317			R.S. §4013
		275	317			R.S. §4014
		276	317			R.S. §4015
		277	317			R.S. §4016
		278	318			R.S. §5466
		279	318			R.S. §5467
		280	318			R.S. §5468
		281	318			R.S. §5469
		283	319			R.S. §5470
		284	320			R.S. §5471
		285	320			R.S. §5472
		286	320			R.S. §5534
		287	320			R.S. §5473
		288	320			R.S. §5474
		290	320			R.S. §5475
		291	321			R.S. §5476
		292	321			R.S. §5477
		293	321			R.S. §5478
		294	321			R.S. §5479
		296	322			R.S. §3899
		297	322			R.S. §3924
		298	322			R.S. §3925
		299	322			R.S. §4026
		300	322			R.S. §3929
		300	323			R.S. §4041
		301	323			R.S. §5480
		302	323			R.S. §3895
		303	323			R.S. §919
		305	323			R.S. §3833
		309	324			R.S. §381
		309	324			R.S. §775
		310	324			R.S. §382
		311	324			R.S. §296
		314	324			R.S. §410
		314	324			R.S. §411
		315	325			R.S. §295

42d Cong.				U.S.C.		
17 Stat.	Chapter	Section	Page	Title	Section	Status
1872—June 8	335	316	325			R.S. §409
		317	325			R.S. §4059
	336		330			R.S. §558
			330			R.S. §559
			330			R.S. §560
			330			R.S. §561
			330			R.S. §624
			330			R.S. §626
			330			R.S. §678
			330			R.S. §840
	337	9	332			R.S. §3689
	338	1	333			R.S. §2304
		1	333			R.S. §2305
		2	333			R.S. §2306
		3	333			R.S. §2307
		4	333			R.S. §2308
		5	334			R.S. §2309
	339		334			R.S. §5045
	340		334			R.S. §2368
			334			R.S. §4979
			334			R.S. §4986
	341		334			R.S. §572
			334			R.S. §658
	344		335			R.S. §1858
	346	1	336			R.S. §5193
		2	336			R.S. §5193
		3	336			R.S. §5194
	347		336			R.S. §2688
	348		337			R.S. §3618
			337			R.S. §3692
	350		337			R.S. §770
			337			R.S. §781
	357		340			R.S. §2368
	368		345			R.S. §4877
10	415	1	347			R.S. §2031
		1	348			R.S. §2011
		1	348			R.S. §2012
		1	348			R.S. §2013
		1	349			R.S. §2015
		1	349			R.S. §2028
		1	349			R.S. §2029
		1	349			R.S. §2030
		1	349			R.S. §2009
		1	352			R.S. §3684
		1	355			R.S. §3685
		1	358			R.S. §2405
		1	362			R.S. §1831
		1	366			R.S. §222
		1	366			R.S. §2032
		1	366			R.S. §2033
		1	366			R.S. §2038
		1	366			R.S. §5266
		1	367			R.S. §5269
		7	369			R.S. §3689
	419		378			R.S. §1254
			378			R.S. §1622
	420		378			R.S. §5404
			378			R.S. §5405
	424	2	381			R.S. §2313
		2	381			R.S. §2314
		3	381			R.S. §2315
		4	381			R.S. §2316
	425		381			R.S. §3689
	426		382			R.S. §1151
			382			R.S. §1194
	434		390			R.S. §1889
Dec. 17	4	9	400			R.S. §4420
24	13	1	401			R.S. §3163
		1	401			R.S. §3172
		1	401			R.S. §3173
		1	401			R.S. §3174
		1	401			R.S. §3175
		1	401			R.S. §3178
		1	401			R.S. §3180
		1	401			R.S. §3185
		1	401			R.S. §3220
		1	401			R.S. §3225
		1	401			R.S. §3233
		1	401			R.S. §3244
		1	401			R.S. §3258
		1	401			R.S. §3259
		1	401			R.S. §3260
		1	401			R.S. §3261
		1	401			R.S. §3262
		1	401			R.S. §3263
		1	401			R.S. §3264

42d Cong. 17 Stat.		Chapter	Section	Page	U.S.C. Title	U.S.C. Section	Status
1872—Dec.	24	13	1	401			R.S. §3265
			1	401			R.S. §3267
			1	401			R.S. §3275
			1	401			R.S. §3291
			1	401			R.S. §3301
			1	401			R.S. §3310
			1	401			R.S. §3311
			1	401			R.S. §3317
			1	401			R.S. §3357
			1	401			R.S. §3383
			2	402			R.S. §3176
			2	402			R.S. §3182
			2	402			R.S. §3184
			2	402			R.S. §3185
			2	402			R.S. §3191
			2	402			R.S. §3218
			2	402			R.S. §3253
			2	402			R.S. §3258
			2	402			R.S. §3415
			2	402			R.S. §3438
			2	402			R.S. §3439
			2	402			R.S. §3440
			3	402			R.S. §3238
			3	402			R.S. §3239
			3	402			R.S. §3312
			4	403			R.S. §3240
			4	403			R.S. §3244
			5	403			R.S. §3414
			6	403			R.S. §3307
			6	403			R.S. §3314
			6	403			R.S. §3383
			7	403			R.S. §3437
			9	403			R.S. §320
		14		404			R.S. §1934
1873—Jan.	8	18		406			R.S. §1813
	9	21		406			R.S. §3878
				407			R.S. §3897
	10	24	1	408			R.S. §107
			1	408			R.S. §108
			1	408			R.S. §109
			2	408			R.S. §117
			3	408			R.S. §108
			3	408			R.S. §113
			3	408			R.S. §118
			3	408			R.S. §119
			3	408			R.S. §124
			3	408			R.S. §125
			4	409			R.S. §127
	11	34		410			R.S. §4247
				410			R.S. §4248
	15	35		410			R.S. §4504
				410			R.S. §4511
	16	36	1	411			R.S. §748
			2	411			R.S. §749
	17	39		411			R.S. §2742
	20	43		412			R.S. §332
	23	48	1	416			R.S. §1852
			2	416			R.S. §1853
			2	416			R.S. §1861
			3	416			R.S. §1845
			4	416			R.S. §1855
		51		417			R.S. §3689
				417			R.S. §4825
				417			R.S. §4826
				417			R.S. §4827
				417			R.S. §4828
				417			R.S. §4829
				417			R.S. §4830
				417			R.S. §4831
				417			R.S. §4832
				417			R.S. §4833
				417			R.S. §4834
				417			R.S. §4835
				417			R.S. §4836
				417			R.S. §4837
	24	62		418			R.S. §1362
		63		418			R.S. §1936
				418			R.S. §1937
		64		419			R.S. §684
	31	82		421			R.S. §44
Feb.	1	88		422			R.S. §1287
	7	120	1	422			R.S. §658
			2	422			R.S. §613
			2	422			R.S. §658
			2	423			R.S. §659
	12	131	1	424			R.S. §343

42d Cong.				U.S.C.		
17 Stat.	Chapter	Section	Page	Title	Section	Status
1873—Feb. 12	131	2	424			R.S. §345
		3	424			R.S. §3496
		4	424			R.S. §3503
		4	424			R.S. §3504
		4	424			R.S. §3506
		5	425			R.S. §3507
		6	425			R.S. §3508
		7	425			R.S. §3509
		8	425			R.S. §3510
		9	425			R.S. §3502
		10	425			R.S. §3500
		11	425			R.S. §3501
		12	426			R.S. §344
		12	426			R.S. §3498
		12	426			R.S. §3499
		13	426			R.S. §3514
		14	426			R.S. §3505
		14	426			R.S. §3511
		14	426			R.S. §3512
		14	426			R.S. §3585
		15	427			R.S. §3513
		15	427			R.S. §3586
		16	427			R.S. §3515
		16	427			R.S. §3587
		17	427			R.S. §3516
		18	427			R.S. §3517
		19	427			R.S. §3518
		20	427			R.S. §3519
		21	427			R.S. §3520
		22	428			R.S. §3521
		23	428			R.S. §3522
		24	428			R.S. §3523
		25	428			R.S. §3524
		26	428			R.S. §3525
		27	428			R.S. §3526
		28	428			R.S. §3527
		29	429			R.S. §3528
		30	429			R.S. §3529
		31	429			R.S. §3530
		32	429			R.S. §3531
		33	429			R.S. §3533
		34	429			R.S. §3534
		35	429			R.S. §3532
		36	430			R.S. §3535
		37	430			R.S. §3536
		38	430			R.S. §3537
		39	430			R.S. §3538
		40	430			R.S. §3539
		41	430			R.S. §3540
		42	431			R.S. §3541
		43	431			R.S. §3542
		44	431			R.S. §3543
		45	431			R.S. §3544
		46	431			R.S. §3546
		47	431			R.S. §3545
		48	432			R.S. §3547
		49	432			R.S. §3548
		50	432			R.S. §3549
		51	432			R.S. §3550
		52	432			R.S. §3551
		53	432			R.S. §3552
		54	433			R.S. §3553
		54	433			R.S. §3554
		55	433			R.S. §3555
		56	433			R.S. §3556
		56	433			R.S. §3557
		57	433			R.S. §3558
		57	433			R.S. §3559
		57	433			R.S. §3560
		58	433			R.S. §3560
		58	433			R.S. §3561
		60	434			R.S. §3562
		61	434			R.S. §5457
		62	434			R.S. §5458
		63	434			R.S. §5459
		64	434			R.S. §5460
		65	434			R.S. §3497
		65	435			R.S. §3592
		65	435			R.S. §3594
		65	435			R.S. §3595
		65	435			R.S. §3596
		65	435			R.S. §3600
		65	435			R.S. §3615
		66	435			R.S. §3495
		66	435			R.S. §3592
		66	435			R.S. §3594

42d Cong. 17 Stat.	Chapter	Section	Page	U.S.C. Title	U.S.C. Section	Status
1873—Feb. 13	135		436			R.S. §5123
14	137		437			R.S. §3680
	138	1	437			R.S. §2046
		1	437			R.S. §2052
		1	437			R.S. §2070
		1	438			R.S. §2053
		1	438			R.S. §2055
		1	457			R.S. §467
		1	459			R.S. §2136
		6	463			R.S. §2043
		6	463			R.S. §2044
		6	463			R.S. §2045
		6	463			R.S. §2047
		7	463			R.S. §469
		7	463			R.S. §2109
18	159		465			R.S. §2345
19	166		466			R.S. §333
21	173		468			R.S. §3297
22	184	1	471			R.S. §1675
		1	472			R.S. §1677
		1	472			R.S. §1678
		1	472			R.S. §1679
		1	473			R.S. §1690
		1	473			R.S. §1706
		2	474			R.S. §1749
		3	474			R.S. §1717
		3	474			R.S. §2861
	187		475			R.S. §208
25	198	1	475			R.S. §2568
		1	475			R.S. §2569
		2	476			R.S. §2568
		2	476			R.S. §2569
		2	476			R.S. §2665
	200	1	476			R.S. §608
		1	476			R.S. §653
		2	476			R.S. §654
		3	476			R.S. §655
		4	476			R.S. §656
		5	477			R.S. §572
28	210		479			R.S. §1336
Mar. 1	213	1	482			R.S. §2506
		3	482			R.S. §2866
		4	483			R.S. §4347
	215		484			R.S. §572
	217		484			R.S. §442
3	223	2	484			R.S. §608
		2	484			R.S. §694
		4	485			R.S. §608
		4	485			R.S. §634
	224		485			R.S. §1142
	225	1	485			R.S. §2544
		2	485			R.S. §2736
	226	1	485			R.S. §130
		1	485			R.S. §176
		1	486			R.S. §35
		1	486			R.S. §37
		1	486			R.S. §45
		1	486			R.S. §52
		1	486			R.S. §53
		1	486			R.S. §153
		1	486			R.S. §154
		1	486			R.S. §160
		1	486			R.S. §200
		1	486			R.S. §234
		1	486	2	43	Rep.
		1	486			R.S. §237
		1	486			R.S. §438
		1	486			R.S. §676
		1	488			R.S. §38
		1	488			R.S. §1821
		1	488			R.S. §1823
		1	491			R.S. §1817
		1	491			R.S. §1827
		1	492			R.S. §235
		1	494			R.S. §3145
		1	495			R.S. §3601
		1	495			R.S. §3603
		1	496			R.S. §3605
		1	496			R.S. §3606
		1	496			R.S. §3607
		1	496			R.S. §3608
		1	496			R.S. §3609
		1	496			R.S. §3610
		1	496			R.S. §3611
		1	496			R.S. §3612
		2	508			R.S. §5260
		2	508			R.S. §5261

42d Cong. 17 Stat.	Chapter	Section	Page	U.S.C. Title	U.S.C. Section	Status
1873—Mar. 3	226	3	508			R.S. §201
		3	508			R.S. §276
		3	508			R.S. §316
		3	508			R.S. §349
		3	508			R.S. §389
		3	508			R.S. §393
		3	508			R.S. §446
		3	508			R.S. §470
		3	508			R.S. §521
		4	509			R.S. §5256
		4	509			R.S. §5262
	227		510			R.S. §78
			510			R.S. §227
			511			R.S. §223
	228	5	543			R.S. §3595
		5	543			R.S. §3600
		8	543			R.S. §3596
		9	543			R.S. §3611
		9	543			R.S. §3612
	229		545			R.S. §4877
			546			R.S. §1173
	230	1	547			R.S. §1462
		1	547			R.S. §1463
		1	555			R.S. §1484
		1	555			R.S. §1495
		1	555			R.S. §1520
		1	555			R.S. §1524
		1	555			R.S. §1556
		1	555			R.S. §1588
		1	555			R.S. §1589
		1	556			R.S. §1444
		2	556			R.S. §1006
		2	556			R.S. §1009
		2	556			R.S. §4636
	231	1	557			R.S. §394
		1	557			R.S. §3827
		1	557			R.S. §3865
		1	558			R.S. §4002
		1	558			R.S. §4003
		1	558			R.S. §4004
		1	558			R.S. §4005
		3	559	7	305	
	232	4	559			R.S. §2913
		5	559			R.S. §3330
	233		563			R.S. §5255
	234	1	566			R.S. §4692
		1	566			R.S. §4693
		1	567			R.S. §4694
		2	567			R.S. §4695
		2	567			R.S. §4696
		3	568			R.S. §4697
		4	569			R.S. §4698
		4	569			R.S. §4698½
		5	569			R.S. §4699
		6	569			R.S. §4700
		7	569			R.S. §4701
		8	569			R.S. §4702
		8	570			R.S. §4722
		9	570			R.S. §4703
		10	570			R.S. §4704
		11	570			R.S. §4705
		12	570			R.S. §4706
		13	571			R.S. §4707
		14	571			R.S. §4708
		15	572			R.S. §4709
		16	572			R.S. §4710
		17	572			R.S. §4711
		18	572			R.S. §4712
		18	572			R.S. §4731
		19	573			R.S. §4713
		20	573			R.S. §4715
		21	573			R.S. §4714
		22	573			R.S. §4748
		23	573			R.S. §4716
		24	573			R.S. §4717
		25	574			R.S. §4718
		26	574			R.S. §4719
		27	574			R.S. §4720
		28	574			R.S. §4721
		29	575			R.S. §472
		30	575			R.S. §474
		30	575			R.S. §4744
		31	575			R.S. §4783
		31	575			R.S. §4785
		31	575			R.S. §5485
		31	575			R.S. §5486

42d Cong. 17 Stat.	Chapter	Section	Page	U.S.C. Title	U.S.C. Section	Status
1873—Mar. 3	234	32	575			R.S. §4745
		33	575			R.S. §4746
		33	575			R.S. §4747
		34	576			R.S. §4771
		34	576			R.S. §4772
		35	576			R.S. §4777
		36	576			R.S. §4774
		37	576			R.S. §4775
		38	577			R.S. §4776
	235		577			R.S. §5045
	238	1	578			R.S. §384
		2	578			R.S. §386
		2	578			R.S. §498
		3	578			R.S. §387
	239		578			R.S. §24
	240		579			R.S. §2871
	243		580			R.S. §4580
	244		580			R.S. §3084
			580			R.S. §3164
			581			R.S. §838
			581			R.S. §3085
	245	1	581			R.S. §4071
		2	581			R.S. §4072
	248		582			R.S. §224
	249	1	582			R.S. §1344
		2	582			R.S. §1345
		2	582			R.S. §4124
		3	583			R.S. §1346
		4	583			R.S. §1347
		5	583			R.S. §1348
		6	583			R.S. §1349
		6	583			R.S. §1350
		6	583			R.S. §1351
		6	583			R.S. §1352
		6	583			R.S. §1353
		6	583			R.S. §1354
		6	583			R.S. §1355
		7	584			R.S. §1356
		8	584			R.S. §1357
		9	584			R.S. §1358
		10	584			R.S. §1359
		11	584			R.S. §1360
		12	584			R.S. §1361
	251		584			R.S. §2568
			584			R.S. §2718
	252	1	584			R.S. §4386
		1	585			R.S. §4387
		1	585			R.S. §4388
		2	585			R.S. §4389
		3	585			R.S. §4390
	253	1	585			R.S. §2582
		1	585			R.S. §2583
		1	585			R.S. §2607
		1	585			R.S. §2684
		2	586			R.S. §2582
		2	586			R.S. §2583
		2	586			R.S. §2607
		2	586			R.S. §2735
	254		586			R.S. §3339
	258	1	598			R.S. §2491
		1	598			R.S. §5389
		2	599			R.S. §3893
		3	599			R.S. §2491
		4	599			R.S. §1785
		5	599			R.S. §2492
	259		600			R.S. §4414
	262		601			R.S. §4723
	263		601			R.S. §572
	264	1	601			R.S. §2586
		1	601			R.S. §2587
		2	601			R.S. §2586
		2	601			R.S. §2587
		3	601			R.S. §2685
		3	602			R.S. §2702
	265		602			R.S. §4548
	266		602			R.S. §2288
	267		602			R.S. §4879
			602			R.S. §4880
	268	1	602			R.S. §3564
		2	603			R.S. §3565
	269	1	603			R.S. §5205
		3	603			R.S. §5243
		4	603			R.S. §5174
	270		604			R.S. §1326
	271		604			R.S. §2631

42d Cong. 17 Stat.		Chapter	Section	Page	U.S.C. Title	U.S.C. Section	Status
1873—Mar.	3	272		604			R.S. §3847
				604			R.S. §4046
		273		604			R.S. §2701
		276		605			R.S. §4878
		277	1	605			R.S. §2464
			2	606			R.S. §2465
			2	606			R.S. §2466
			3	606			R.S. §2467
			4	606			R.S. §2317
			5	606			R.S. §2468
			6	606			R.S. §2238
		278		606			R.S. §5254
		279	1	607			R.S. §2347
			2	607			R.S. §2348
			3	607			R.S. §2349
			4	607			R.S. §2350
			5	607			R.S. §2351
			6	607			R.S. §2352
		282		608			R.S. §1670
		283		609			R.S. §2274
		307		619			R.S. §4249
1871—Apr.	12	12[1]	1	641			R.S. §3689
			2	642			R.S. §3689
43d Cong.							
18 Stat.							
1874—Jan.	8	7		2	26	1226	I.R.C. '39
	20	11		4	2	38	Rep.
				4	2	43	Elim.
				4	2	48	
	22	14		5			Rep.
	29	19		6	31	367	Rev. T.
Feb.	4	22		14	40	28	Elim.
Mar.	4	44		19	5	187	Rev. T.
	5	46		19	5	365	Rev. T.
	7	50		20	40	29	Elim.
	23	62	1	23	22	182	Elim.
	24	Pub. R. 6		286	39	809	Rev. T.
				286	41	13a	Rep.
Apr.	7	80	1	27	48	1464	Rep.
	17	106		30	46	270	Rev. T.
	18	110		31	46 App.	336	
	20	117	1	33	10	174, 175	Rev. T.
May	8	154		43	10	842	Rev. T.
	9	163		43			Rep.
	12	168		45	31	261	Rev. T.
June	1	200		50	28	728	Rev. T.
	6	219		61	38	28 nt	Rev. T.
		223	1, 2	62	43	1153, 1154	Rep.
	9	259	1, 2	64			I.R.C. '39
		260		64	46	544	Rev. T.
	11	275	1, 4	67, 70	22	37, 122	Rep.
	17	294		77	22	124, 126	Rep.
	18	298	1	78	38	157	Rev. T.
		299		78			Rep.
		301	1, 3	78, 79	17	18, 63	Rev. T.
		305		80	43	862, 914	Elim.
	20	328	1	85	2	62	
			1	87	2	77	
			1	88	22	2660	
			1	88	5	373	Rev. T.
			1	88	40	28	Elim.
			1	88	44	191a, 193	Rev. T.
			1	90	5	152	Rev. T.
			1	90	22	2664	
			1	90	44	321	Rev. T.
			1	96	31	265, 268	Rev. T.
			1	97	31	261	Rev. T.
			1	99	48	1456	Rep.
			1	101	10	642a	Rev. T.
			1	109	5	334	Rev. T.
			2	109	28	524	Rev. T.
			3	109	5	71	Rev. T.
			4, 5	109, 110	31	583, 711, 713	Rev. T.
		330		111	43	867	Elim.
		331		111	45	83	Rep.
		333	2	113			Elim.
		337	2	116	40	65	Elim.
		343	1	123	12	38	
			3	123	12	121, 123, 131	Rep.
			4	124	12	176	Rep.
			5	124	12	105	Rep.
			6	124	31	402	Rev. T.

[1] Private Law.

43d Cong. 18 Stat.		Chapter	Section	Page	U.S.C. Title	U.S.C. Section	Status
1874—June	20	343	6	124	31	402	Rev. T.
			8	125	12	126	Rep.
		344	6, 7	127	14	192, 193	Rev. T.
			8, 9	127	14	92, 108	Rev. T.
			10–13	128	33	361–364	Rep.
	22	388		135	48	1487	Rep.
		389	1	147	25	64	
			10	177	25	87	Rep.
		391	5	187	19	535	
			8	188	19	537	
			13	188	19	494	Rep.
		392	2	192	34	1200	Rev. T.
		400		194	43	888	
		414		200	45	89	Rep.
		419		202	31	370	Rev. T.
	23	453		203	34	1066, 1067	Rev. T.
		455		206	12	124	Rep.
				206	31	422	Rev. T.
				216	31	721	Rev. T.
				220	33	740b	Rep.
				223	24	261	Elim.
		456	1	231	39	354	Rev. T.
			5	232	39	283	Rev. T.
			6	233	39	282, 285	Rev. T.
			9	233	39	231	Rev. T.
			12	235	39	426, 427, 434	Rev. T.
			13	237	39	290	Rev. T.
		458	2	244	10	62	Rev. T.
		465	1–3	251, 252	24	212–214	Rep.
		468		252	28	243	Rev. T.
		476	1	275	31	682	Rev. T.
			2	276	40	254	Rep.
		486		282	50	52, 53	Rep.
Dec.	28	9	2	294	1	106a	Rev. T.
			2	294	5	159	Rev. T.
1875—Jan.	14	15	1	296	31	417	Rev. T.
			2, 3	296	31	332, 333, 402	Rev. T.
	19	19		302	12	151	Rep.
	22	22		303	19	530	Elim.
Feb.	8	36	11	309	19	24, 26, 27	Rep.
			12	309			Rep.
			13, 16, 17	310, 311			I.R.C. '39
			19	311	12	562	Rep.
			19	311			I.R.C. '39
			20, 21	311	12	563, 564	Rep.
			21	311			I.R.C. '39
			23 (pt)	312	19	64	
			23–25	312			I.R.C. '39
	11	41		315	30	28	
	16	77	1, 2	315	28	771, 772	Rev. T.
	18	80	1	316	2	106	
			1	316	2	107	
			1	317	31	1024	Rev. T.
			1	317	12	12	
			1	317	12	14	
			1	317	31	104	Rev. T.
			1	317	43	2	
			1	317	44	321	Rev. T.
			1	318	8	359	Rep.
			1	318	25	218	Rep.
			1	318	28	577, 874, 879	Rev. T.
			1	319	12	569	Rep.
			1	319			I.R.C. '39
			1	319	31	286	Rev. T.
			1	319	39	501	Rev. T.
			1	320	12	94	
			1	320	12	110, 133, 185	Rep.
			1	320	39	723	Rev. T.
			1	320	46 App.	188	
			1	320	46	227, 304	Rev. T.
	19	89		329	12	481	
				329	12	482	
				329	12	483	
				329	12	484	
				329	12	485	
	22	95	2	333	28	497, 515	Rev. T.
			3–6	333, 334	28	514, 520–522	Rev. T.
	23	99		334	43	989	
Mar.	1	114	3, 4	336	8	44, 45	Rep.
			5	337	42	1984	Elim.
		115		337	10	16	Rev. T.
	2	119	1	338	2	223	Rep.
			2	338	2	203	Rep.
	3	128	1	340	39	54	Rev. T.
			4	343	31	113	Rev. T.

43d Cong.

18 Stat.	Chapter	Section	Page	U.S.C. Title	U.S.C. Section	Status
1875—Mar. 3	128	4	343	39	781	Rev. T.
		5, 7	343	39	325, 329	Rev. T.
	129	1	344	2	62	
		1	345	40	209	
		1	346	2	77	
		1	349	5	153	Rev. T.
		1	352	15	178	
		1	352	15	179	Rep.
		1	359	24	111, 122	Rep.
		1	359	31	711	Rev. T.
		3	370	31	624	Rev. T.
	130		372	12	106	Rep.
			372	14	96	Rev. T.
			372	33	730a	
			374	38	123	Rev. T.
			376	40	189	
			376	40	190	
			377	42	10	Rep.
			388	50	64a	Rep.
			389	2	34	
		2	397	31	109	Rev. T.
		3	399	12	127	Rep.
		6	400	2	7	
		8	401	2	118	
	131	5	418	31	713a	Rev. T.
		12	419			I.R.C. '39
		14	420	5	11	Rev. T.
		15	420	43	189	Rep.
	132	1	421	25	64	
		1	424	25	129	
		2	449	25	128	
		3	449	25	137	
		4	449	25	133	
		5	449			Rep.
		6	450	25	135	
		7	450	25	96	Rep.
		9	450	25	95	Rep.
		10	450	25	37	Rep.
	133	1	452	5	73	Rev. T.
		1	453	10	1376	Rev. T.
		1	455	50	84	Rep.
		2	455	41	10	Elim.
	135		467	10	1084, 1136	Rev. T.
	141	1, 2, 4	477	8	336, 338, 339	Rep.
	144	1, 2	479	18	100, 101	Rev. T.
	145	1	479	18	713	Rev. T.
		2	480	18	700	Rev. T.
	149		481	31	227	Rev. T.
	151	2, 3	481, 482	18	110	Rev. T.
	152	1	482	43	934	
		2	482	43	935	
		3	482	43	936	
		4	483	43	937	
		5	483	43	938	
		6	483	43	939	
	153		483	22	32	Rep.
	154		484			I.R.C. '39
	155		484	34	201	Rev. T.
	156	3–5	485, 486	24	1, 7, 193	Rep.
		6	486	24	11, 11a	Rep.

44th Cong.

19 Stat.	Chapter	Section	Page	U.S.C. Title	U.S.C. Section	Status
1876—Feb. 1	6		2	22	178	Rep.
Apr. 13	56		32	18	582	Rev. T.
18	66	1	34	2	23	
		2	34	2	24	
21	72	1	35	43	890	
		2	35	43	891	
		3	36	43	892	
27	84		38	43	762	
29	86		41	40	214	
May 1	88	1	41	2	195	
		1	43	48	1466	Rep.
5	91		52	30	49	
8	Pub. R. 10		213			I.R.C. '39
13	95		53			I.R.C. '39
23	103		54	2	51	
June 10	122		58	25	160	
26	146		61	10	1312	Rev. T.
	147	1, 4	61, 62	28	481, 490	Rev. T.
30	156	1		12	191 nt	
		2	63	12	191	
		3	63	12	197	

44th Cong.					U.S.C.		
19 Stat.		Chapter	Section	Page	Title	Section	Status
1876—June	30	156	4	64	12	55	
			5	64	31	424	Rev. T.
		159		66, 69	34	133, 509	Rev. T.
July	5	167		74	34	1129	Rev. T.
	12	179	4	80	31	114	Rev. T.
			6, 11, 14	80, 82	39	31, 82, 362	Rev. T.
			15	82	39	248	Rev. T.
		183		88	18	696–698	Rev. T.
		185		90	46	302	Rev. T.
	22	Pub. R. 17	1	215	31	407, 417	Rev. T.
	24	226	1	99	24	278	Rep.
	29	239		102	10	842	Rev. T.
	31	246		105	31	589	Rev. T.
				105	44	321	Rev. T.
				115	40	27	Elim.
				121	43	757	
				121	43	881	
Aug.	7	255		126	10	1067	Rev. T.
	11	260		129	39	427, 434	Rev. T.
	12	263		131	10	611, 915	Rev. T.
	15	287	1	145	2	49	
			1	147	40	162	
			1	147	40	163	
			1	147	40	187	
			1	147	40	192	Elim.
			1	152	19	13 nt	Elim.
			1	152			I.R.C. '39
			3, 5, 6	169	5	37, 45, 118o	Rev. T.
		289	3	199	25	97	
			4	200	31	613	Rev. T.
			5	200	25	261	
		300	1	203	38	241	Rev. T.
			2	204	38	245	Rev. T.
		304		206	28	642	Rev. T.
1877—Jan.	12	18	2	221	43	686	Rep.
	19	27		223	38	4, 11e	Rev. T.
Feb.	27	69	1	241	5	109, 185, 186, 303	Rev. T.
			1	241	10	1302	Rev. T.
			1	241	15	176	
			1	241	15	183	
			1	242	10	7, 195, 196, 622, 1339	Rev. T.
			1	243	10	104, 495, 806, 996, 1178, 1312	Rev. T.
			1	244	5	451 nt	Rev. T.
			1	244	10	1135	Rev. T.
			1	244	25	65	
			1	244	25	241	Rep.
			1	244	43	1161	
			1	244	43	1162	
			1	245	19	31	Rep.
			1	247	19	197	
			1	248			I.R.C. '39
			1	249	10	1191	Rev. T.
			1	249			I.R.C. '39
			1	249	31	198, 286, 349, 375, 487, 492, 496, 506, 594, 625, 720	Rev. T.
			1	249	34	560	Rev. T.
			1	249	41	20	Rep.
			1	249	41	22	
			1	250	46 App.	121	
			1	251	46	79, 201, 228, 255, 258, 259, 329, 379, 384, 394, 399	Rev. T.
			1	251	46 App.	184	
			1	251	46 App.	262	
			1	252	12	108	Rep.
			1	252	12	161	
			1	252	12	186	Rep.
			1	252	46	170, 229, 460, 482, 566, 576, 676, 707	Rev. T.
			1	252	47	8	Rep.
			1	253	20	41	
			1	253	50	213	
	28	73		264	38	123 nt., 155a nt., 164	Rev. T.
Mar.	2	82	4	269			Elim.
	3	101	1	291	25	100	Rep.
		102	1	298	40	163	
			1	315	43	130	
		103	2, 3	335	39	35, 430	Rev. T.
			5, 6	335	39	321	Rev. T.
		105		347	24	202	Elim.
				348	40	167	
				353	31	415	Rev. T.
				359	40	27	Elim.
		106	1	370	40	34	
		107	1	377	43	321	
			2	377	43	322	

44th Cong.					U.S.C.		
19 Stat.		Chapter	Section	Page	Title	Section	Status
1877—Mar.	3	107	3	377	43	322	
			3	377	43	323	
			4		43	327	
			5		43	328	
			7		43	329	
			8		43	323	
			8		43	325	
		113	1, 3, 4	392	43	725–727	Rep.
		114	1, 2, 4–11	393			I.R.C. '39
		116		395	43	990	
		120		403			Rep.
		121		403	38	222	Rev. T.
45th Cong.							
20 Stat.							
1877—Dec.	10	6		5	44	161	Rev. T.
1878—Feb.	28	20	1	25	31	316, 458	Rev. T.
			3	26	31	405	Rev. T.
Mar.	9	26	20	27			Elim.
	16	37		30	28	632	Rev. T.
		Pub. R. 16		249			I.R.C. '39
Apr.	10	58		36	5	218	Rev. T.
		66	1, 5	37, 38	42	86, 92a	Rep.
	30	76	2	46	16	601	
			2	46	16	602	
May	4	91		50	34	112	Rev. T.
	17	107	2, 3, 5	62	39	445, 446, 449	Rev. T.
	31	146		87	31	404	Rev. T.
June	3	150	1	88	16	604	
			2	88	16	605	
			3	89	16	606	
		151	1–3	89, 90	43	311–313	Rep.
			4	90	18	103	Rev. T.
			5	90	16	603	Elim.
		152		91	43	253	Rep.
	7	160		99	2	206, 225	Rep.
	8	170		102	31	283, 430	Rev. T.
	11	180	2 (pt), 5	103, 107	10	189, 190	Rev. T.
	14	Pub. R. 30		253	34	565	Rev. T.
		191	4	130	31	714	Rev. T.
		193		131	22	141, 177	Rep.
	17	259	1, 2	141, 143	39	45, 806	Rev. T.
		260		143	34	341	Rev. T.
		261		144	38	159	Rev. T.
	18	263	2, 5, 8	149, 150	10	500, 664, 801	Rev. T.
			9	151	10	728	Rev. T.
			15	152	10	15	Rev. T.
		265	3	163	14	109	Rev. T.
			4	163	14	104	Rev. T.
			7–9	164	14	91, 99, 111	Rev. T.
			10, 12	165	14	110, 194	Rev. T.
		267	1, 2	165	34	276	Rev. T.
		268		166	38	153	Rev. T.
	19	311	1, 2	167	5	272, 273	Rev. T.
		312	1–3	167, 168	31	539–541	Rev. T.
		317		171	18	102	Rev. T.
		324		175	46 App.	725	
		329	1	183	43	8, 9	Rep.
			1	191	31	358, 359, 361, 362	Rev. T.
			1	193	48	75	Elim.
			1	193	48	1462	Rep.
			1	201	43	130	
			1	203	31	677	Rev. T.
			1	205	5	297	Rev. T.
			1	205	31	711	Rev. T.
	20	359	1	216	44	322	Rev. T.
			1	220	40	103	
			1	223	50	76	Rep.
			1	240	39	367	Rev. T.
Dec.	16	5		258	16	361	
1879—Jan.	25	23	1, 4	265	38	91, 116	Rev. T.
	27	28	1	273	22	81	Rep.
	28	30	1–4	274–275	43	1155	Rep.
	31	39	1–3	277	28	684–686	Rev. T.
Feb.	3	40	1	278	2	190*l*	
			2	279	2	190m	
		44		281	24	280	Rep.
	4	45		281	39	37	Rev. T.
	14	68		286	44	279a	Rev. T.
				288	31	640	Rev. T.
	15	83	2	295	34	21	Rev. T.
	21	95	4	317	39	103a, 108	Rev. T.
		97	8	320	28	481, 490	Rev. T.
	26	105		322	34	1126	Rev. T.
Mar.	1	125	1, 2	327			I.R.C. '39

45th Cong.				U.S.C.		
20 Stat.	**Chapter**	**Section**	**Page**	**Title**	**Section**	**Status**
1879—Mar. 1	125	2	327	28	518	Rev. T.
		2–6, 8	328–341			I.R.C. '39
		9	341	18	593	Rev. T.
		10	342			I.R.C. '39
		11	342	19	467	
		12	342	19	468	
		13	343	19	469	
		14–16, 18, 20, 21	343–351			I.R.C. '39
		22	351	12	570	Rep.
		22	351			I.R.C. '39
3	170		352	43	762	
	173		353	38	250	Rev. T.
	180	1	357	31	611	Rev. T.
		1	357	39	638	Rev. T.
		6	358	5	389	Rev. T.
		7–9	358	39	221, 222, 280	Rev. T.
		12, 14–16, 17–19, 21, 24–26, 29, 30.	359–362	39	225–228, 236, 237, 239, 243, 250, 275, 286, 384, 435	Rev. T.
		31	362	39	63	Rev. T.
	182	1	383	31	359	Rev. T.
		1	383	40	303a	Rep.
		1	388	40	30	Elim.
		1	389	10	1459	Rev. T.
		1	390	24	80	Rep.
		1	391	40	165	Rep.
		1	391	40	189	
		1	394	43	1457	
		1	394	20	59	
		1	394	43	31	
		1	394	43	41	
		1	395	24	203	Elim.
		1	397	20	61	Rep.
		1	400	2	226	Rep.
		2	402	8	63	Elim.
	183		412	50	61	Rep.
		1	419	2	69	
		1	420	45	90	Rep.
	186	1, 2	468	20	101	
		3	468	20	102	
		4	469	20	104	
	187	2	470	38	91–93	Rev. T.
	189	1, 2	470, 471	16	598, 599	Rep.
	191		472	43	204	Rep.
	192		472	43	251	Rep.
	200		484	38	159	Rev. T.
46th Cong.						
21 Stat.						
1879—May 12	5		3	34	133, 161, 182	Rev. T.
June 9	12	1–3	7, 8	31	337, 338, 456	Rev. T.
14	23		20			I.R.C. '39
	Pub. R. 6		50	42	98	
21	34	3	30	31	407	Rev. T.
		3	30	38	57	Rev. T.
23	35	1	31	10	722	Rev. T.
		1	31	47	7	Elim.
		4	34	10	1071, 1133	Rev. T.
		7	35	25	273	
		8	35	10	1332	Rev. T.
28	43	1	37	33	641	
		2	37	33	642	
		2	37	33	643	Elim.
		3–5	37, 38	33	647	
		6	38	33	644	
		8		33	646	
30	52	3	44	5	335	Rev. T.
	54		44	46	332	Rev. T.
July 1	60		46	43	205	Rep.
	62		47	40	307	Elim.
	63	1	48	43	235	Rep.
Dec. 20	1	1	59			I.R.C. '39
22	2		59	31	174	Rev. T.
1880—Jan. 22	9	1	61	30	29	
		2	61	30	28	
Feb. 14	25		66	12	153	Rep.
Apr. 1	41		70	25	161	
7	48	2	72	39	441	Rev. T.
16	56		74	48	1488	Rep.
20	58		76	28	146	Rev. T.
May 3	73		86	34	903	Rev. T.
11	85	1	131	25	104	
14	89	1	140	43	202	Rep.
		2	141	43	82, 185	Rep.
		3	141	43	166, 223	Rep.
28	108	1–8, 10, 11	145–148			I.R.C. '39

46th Cong.					U.S.C.		
21 Stat.		Chapter	Section	Page	Title	Section	Status
1880—May	28	108	12	148	19	468	
			13	148	19	469	
			14, 15	148			I.R.C. '39
			18	149			I.R.C. '39
	31	113		151	16	746	
June	1	115		153	10	1074	Rev. T.
	4	121	1	156	24	179	Rep.
	7	Pub. R. 44		308			Elim.
	8	129		164	5	428	Rev. T.
	8	136		166	43	172	Rep.
	9	161	1	167			I.R.C. '39
	11	206	1	177, 179	39	41, 357, 497–499, 692, 695–697, 700, 787	Rev. T.
	15	227	3, 4	238	43	679, 680	Rep.
	16	235		263	33	755	Rep.
				271	15	189	Elim.
				274	43	33	Rep.
				277	48	1481	Rep.
		236	1	281	38	158	Rev. T.
		244	1–4	287	43	263	Rep.
		246	3	289	16	361	
Dec.	17	2		311	43	82	Rep.
1881—Jan.	13	19		315	43	893	
	21	25	1	317	44	323	Rev. T.
	31	32	2, 3	604	5	114, 115	Rev. T.
Feb.	1	33	1	322	31	261	Rev. T.
	23	73	2	338	34	161, 182	Rev. T.
	26	80	2	350	24	138	Rep.
		82		352	12	162	Rep.
Mar.	1	95		374	31	332	Rev. T.
		96	1	374	39	421, 601, 691	Rev. T.
	3	130	1	388	40	167	
			1	391	15	189	Elim.
			1	412	5	112	Rev. T.
		133	2	457	31	741	Rev. T.
		134	1 (pt)	460	10	189	Rev. T.
		136		474	33	647 nt	
		140		505	30	32	
		144	7	507	28	481, 490	Rev. T.
		150		510	34	245	Rev. T.
		153		511	43	169	Rep.
		Pub. R. 26		521	15	201	
47th Cong.							
22 Stat.							
1882—Mar.	17	41	1, 2	29, 30	39	49, 49a	Rev. T.
	22	47	8	31	48	1461	Rep.
Apr.	25	87	1, 3	47	28	481, 490	Rev. T.
	26	106	1	49	30	31	
			2	49	30	25	
May	1	112		52	33	420	
			1	53	39	447	Rev. T.
		116	1	54	39	50	Rev. T.
		117	2–5, 7	56, 57	14	93, 97, 101, 103, 107	Rev. T.
			8	57	14	106	Rev. T.
			10	58	14	104	Rev. T.
		126	1, 3	59	8	263, 264, 280	Rep.
			6, 8–13, 15	60, 61	8	265–269, 271–273	Rep.
			16		8	274	Rep.
	17	163	1	70	25	23	Elim.
			1	86	25	55	Rep.
			1	87	25	28	Rep.
			6	88	25	46	
			6	88	25	63	
			7	88	25	3	
	26	190		97	31	326	Rev. T.
June	22	236		108	31	148	Rev. T.
	30	254	1	118	10	578, 801, 873, 942, 945, 970	Rev. T.
			1	121	24	18	
			3	122	10	873	Rev. T.
		255		123	10	1068	Rev. T.
July	1	258	1–11	126, 127	40	194–204	Rep.
		262		133	31	603	Rev. T.
	12	290	4	163	12	94a	Rep.
			8, 9	164	12	177, 178	Rep.
			12	165	12	146	Rep.
			12	165	31	429	Rev. T.
			13	166	12	591	Rep.
	20	312	3	172	28	481, 490	Rev. T.
	25	349	2	175	38	121	Rev. T.
			2	175	43	781	Rep.
			3	175	38	124	Rev. T.
			4	175	38	71	Rev. T.
			5	176	38	29	Rev. T.
	31	360		179	25	264	

47th Cong.				U.S.C.		
22 Stat.	Chapter	Section	Page	Title	Section	Status
1882—July 31	361	1	180	39	495, 638, 639	Rev. T.
	363		181	25	276	
Aug. 2	373	2	185	39	103a, 108	Rev. T.
	374	1–7	186–189	46	151–157	Rev. T.
		8	189	46	156a, 171	Rev. T.
		9–13	189–191	46	158–162	Rev. T.
		14	191	46	151 nt	Rep.
	378	1, 2	215	18	657, 667	Rev. T.
		3, 4	215, 216	18	656, 668	Rev. T.
		5	216	18	655	Rev. T.
	379	2	216	39	434	Rev. T.
	Pub. R. 63		391	44	297	Rev. T.
5	389	1	228	5	112	Rev. T.
		1	229	5	40	Rev. T.
		1	229			I.R.C. '39
		1	238	5	183	Rev. T.
		1	241	40	35	
		1	243	40	69	Elim.
		1	253	5	391	Rev. T.
		1	254	28	333	Rev. T.
		4	255	5	39, 45, 46, 50	Rev. T.
		5	256	31	583	Rev. T.
	390	1	270	2	61	
	391	1	285, 286	34	81, 386, 395, 402, 892, 1031, 1055, 1057	Rev. T.
		2	296	34	491, 544	Rev. T.
	395		299	50	51	Elim.
	398	1, 2	300	46	77, 81	Rev. T.
7	433	1	305	40	263	Rep.
		1	309	33	494 nt	
		1	310	46	407	Rev. T.
		1	312	31	339, 545	Rev. T.
		1	322	24	138	Rep.
		1	327	43	763	
		1	330	24	172, 195, 212	Rep.
		1	336	5	90	Rev. T.
		1	337	2	117	
		1	432	24	138	Rep.
	438	1, 2	345	38	191, 199	Rev. T.
	441	1	346	46	362	Rev. T.
8	468		373			I.R.C. '39
	469		373, 374	38	44–47, 49, 75, 192	Rev. T.
1883—Jan. 9	16		401			I.R.C. '39
	17		402	19	193	Rep.
16	27	1–3	403, 404	5	632, 633, 635	Rev. T.
		4	405	40	42	
		5	405	5	637	Rev. T.
		6	405			Rep.
		7–10	406	5	638, 640–642	Rev. T.
		11		5	642a	Rev. T.
Feb. 28	58	2	432	38	129	Rev. T.
Mar. 3	91		453	38	165, 169, 170	Rev. T.
	93	1	456	10	747	Rev. T.
		1	457	10	525	Rev. T.
	97	1	472	34	1, 112, 241	Rev. T.
		1	472	38	151	Rev. T.
		1	473	34	231	Rev. T.
		2	481	34	222	Rev. T.
	101	2	484	43	87	Rep.
	102		484	7	304	
	118		487	30	171	
	120		487	5	218	Rev. T.
	121	1	488	12	541	
		1	488	12	544, 545	Elim.
		1	488	12	566, 567, 569, 570	Rep.
		5	489			I.R.C. '39
	123	2–5	527, 528	39	715–718	Rev. T.
	128	1	552	31	595	Rev. T.
		1	553	40	9	Rep.
		2	563	39	322	Rev. T.
	130	1, 2	564	24	59, 60	Rep.
		3	564	24	57	Rep.
		4–6	564, 565	24	52, 55, 56	Rep.
		7	565	10	996	Rev. T.
		7–9	565	24	43, 46, 48	Rep.
		10	565	24	41	Rep.
	133	1	566	46	103	Rev. T.
	134		567	48	1460	Rep.
	141	2	590	25	155	
		2	592	2	133	
		5	599	34	492	Rev. T.
	142	1–3	600–602	39	54, 57, 61	Rev. T.
		4	602	39	54, 54a	Rev. T.
	143		615	40	59	Rep.
			616	31	485	Rev. T.
			621	40	173	
			625	35	45	Rev. T.

47th Cong.					U.S.C.		
22 Stat.		**Chapter**	**Section**	**Page**	**Title**	**Section**	**Status**
1883—Mar.	3	143		627	16	23	
				629	20	64	Rep.
				631	28	542	Rev. T.
				632	2	33	Rep.
48th Cong.							
23 Stat.							
1884—Feb.	1	Pub. R. 4		266	38	8	Rev. T.
Mar.	1	9		3	39	482	Rev. T.
May	13	44		21	20	47	
		46	2, 3	22	5	16	Rev. T.
	17	53	8	26	25	280a	Elim.
	29	60	1	31	7	391	
			2	31	21	119	
			3	32	21	114	
			4	32	21	112	
			4	32	21	120	
			5	32	21	113	
			5	32	21	120	
			6	32	21	115	
			7	32	21	117	
			8	33	21	130	
			9	33	21	118	
			11		21	114a	
			12		21	113a	
			13		21	114a–1	
					21	116	
June	9	73		40	39	287	Rev. T.
	20	107		50	36	254	Rev. T.
	26	121	1	53	46	221	Rev. T.
			2	54	46	682	Rev. T.
			3	54	46	685	Rev. T.
			4	54	46	658	Rev. T.
			5, 6	54, 55	46	684, 703	Rev. T.
			7	55	46	683	Rev. T.
			9	55	46	679	Rev. T.
			10, 11	55, 56	46	599, 670	Rev. T.
			12	56	22	4206	
			13	56	46	101	Rev. T.
			14	57	46 App.	121	
			15	57	24	26a	Rep.
			16	57	19	145	Rep.
			18	57	46 App.	189	
			19, 20	58	46	572, 573	Rev. T.
			21	58	46	47	Rev. T.
			26	59	46	8	Rev. T.
			27	59	46	541	Rev. T.
		122		60	34	1	Rev. T.
		123		60	2	191	
	27	126		60	39	127, 842	Rev. T.
		127		60	29	1, 3	
July	4	180	1	94	25	195, 249	Rep.
			1	96	43	190	Rep.
			6	97	25	46	
			6	97	25	63	
			8	97	25	88	
			9	98	25	221	Elim.
			10	98	25	154	
		181	3	99	38	111, 193	Rev. T.
			3	99	43	842	Rep.
			4	99	38	114	Rev. T.
			4	99	43	844	Rep.
			5	101	43	1464	
			6	101	38	115	Rev. T.
	5	214	1–3	103	43	1071–1073	Rep.
			5	104	43	1074	Rep.
			6	104	10	1348	Rev. T.
			6	104	43	933	Rep.
		217		108	10	1238	Rev. T.
				108	34	1129	Rev. T.
				109–111	10	1200, 1347, 1364, 1377	Rev. T.
				112	10	96	Rev. T.
				113	31	499	Rev. T.
		220		115–118	8	263–266, 268, 269, 271–274	Rep.
		221	1	118	46	1	Rev. T.
			2	118, 119	46	2, 28, 39, 40, 43, 44, 55, 56, 265, 275	Rev. T.
			3	119	46 App.	3	
			4, 6	119	46	4, 5	Rev. T.
			8 (less (c))		46	9	Rev. T.
			8(c)		46 App.	9	
		225	1	122	18	585	Rev. T.
		228	1	132	46	329	Rev. T.
			2, 3	132, 133	46	330	Rev. T.
		229	4	147	33	5	

48th Cong. 23 Stat.		Chapter	Section	Page	U.S.C. Title	U.S.C. Section	Status
1884—July	5	234	1, 3	156, 158	39	50, 321, 321a, 384	Rev. T.
		235	1	122	18	584	Rev. T.
	7	332		198	33	722	Rep.
				199	14	65	Rev. T.
				204	41	24	
				209	40	163a	
				212	43	34	
				213	24	194	Rep.
				214	20	65	Rep.
		334	1	254	5	266	Rev. T.
			1, 3	254, 258	31	622, 714, 1026	Rev. T.
1885—Jan.	6	Pub. R. 5		516	5	86	Rev. T.
	30	43	1	291	34	901	Rev. T.
			3	295	5	467	Rev. T.
Feb.	11	55		298	46	412	Rev. T.
	14	67		305	10	947a	Rev. T.
	16	123		306	31	528	Rev. T.
	25	149	1	321	43	1061	
			2	321	43	1062	
			3	322	43	1063	
			4	322	43	1064	
			5	322	43	1065	
			6	322	43	1066	
		150		324	15	190	
	26	164	2	332	8	141	Rep.
Mar.	3	335	1	350	31	218	Rev. T.
			2–5b		31	219–222b	Rev. T.
		338	2	356	7	2209	
		340		362	38	24	Rev. T.
		342	1	385	39	128	Rev. T.
			1	386	39	10, 280, 424	Rev. T.
			1	387	39	283	Rev. T.
			3, 5, 6	387, 388	39	165, 169, 170	Rev. T.
		360	1(1)	494	16	743	Rep.
			1(2)		16	743a	
				497	43	1453	
				499	43	758	
				502	50	77	Rep.
				510	24	76	Rep.
				512	2	98	Rep.
49th Cong.							
24 Stat.							
1886—Jan.	19	4	1, 2	1, 2	3	21, 22	Rev. T.
			3	2	3	1	Rev. T.
Mar.	19	22	1, 2	5	38	195, 196	Rev. T.
	29	28	1	8	12	198	
			2	8	12	199	
			3	8	12	200	
	31	41		9	31	144	Rev. T.
Apr.	29	64		15			I.R.C. '39
May	1	73	1	18	12	58	Rep.
			2	18	12	30	
			3	19	12	31	
			4	19	12	32	
	6	88		22	43	206	Rep.
	17	338		50	10	486	Rev. T.
	20	362	1	69	20	111	
			2	69	20	112	
			3	69	20	113	
June	19	421	1	79	46	329, 330, 331, 440, 541, 542a	Rev. T.
			2	80	46	563, 646	Rev. T.
			3	80	46	599	Rev. T.
			4	80	46 App.	188	
			5	81	46	77	Rev. T.
			6	81	46	45	Rev. T.
			7	81	46 App.	319	
			8	81	46 App.	289	
			9	81	46 App.	320	
			13	82	46	671	Rev. T.
			14	82	46	392, 393	Rev. T.
			15	82	19	145	Rep.
			17	82	46 App.	142	
			18	83	46	679	Rev. T.
	28	Pub. R. 15		342	2	93	Elim.
	29	567	1–5	86	29	21–25	Rep.
July	9	755	1, 2	129	46	458, 459	Rev. T.
			3	129	46	483	Rev. T.
		756	2	129	24	117	Rep.
	10	764	1	143	43	882	
			2	143	43	883	
			3	143	43	884	
			4	143	43	885	
	26	781	1	151	50	59	Rep.
			2	157	31	713, 716	Rev. T.
	30	818	1, 2	170, 171	48	1471, 1475	Rep.

49th Cong.

24 Stat.	Chapter	Section	Page	U.S.C. Title	U.S.C. Section	Status
1886—July 30	818	3	171	48	1473	Rep.
		4, 6, 7	171	48	1472, 1478, 1479	Rep.
Aug. 2	840	1–8, 10–20	209–212			I.R.C. '39
	849	2	215	34	481	Rev. T.
4	896	1	218			I.R.C. '39
	899		220	38	166	Rev. T.
	901	1–5	220, 221	39	165, 167, 171–173	Rev. T.
	902	1	227	31	176	Rev. T.
		1	245, 246	31	607	Rev. T.
		1	255	31	590	Rev. T.
	903	1	268	34	1082	Rev. T.
5	929	2	329	33	407a	
		8	335	33	552	Rep.
Dec. 20	2		351	37	308a	Rev. T.
23	9		353	38	229, 230	Rev. T.
1887—Jan. 3	12		354	46	382	Rev. T.
	13	1	355	39	151	Rev. T.
29	70	1, 2	371	38	261, 262	Rev. T.
	72	7	372	10	1171	Rev. T.
Feb. 3	90	1–7	373–375	3	5–7, 17–20	Rev. T.
4	104			49	27 nt	Rep.
		1	379	49	1	Rev. T.
		1a		49	1a	Rev. T.
		2	379	49	2	Rev. T.
		3–5	380	49	3–5	Rev. T.
		5a		49	5b	Rev. T.
		5b		49	5c	Rev. T.
		6–10	380	49	6–10	Rev. T.
		11–13	383	49	11–13	Rev. T.
		13a		49	13a	Rev. T.
		14, 15	384	49	14, 15	Rev. T.
		15a		49	15a	Rev. T.
		16	384	49	16	Rev. T.
		16a		49	16a	Rev. T.
		17	385	49	17	Rev. T.
		18, 19	386	49	18, 19	Rev. T.
		19a		49	19a	Rev. T.
		20	386	49	20	Rev. T.
		20a–20c		49	20a–20c	Rev. T.
		21, 22	387	49	21, 22	Rev. T.
		23		49	23	Rev. T.
		24		49	11, 18	Rev. T.
		25		49	25, 26	Rev. T.
		26–28		49	26a, 26c	Rev. T.
		29		49	27	Rev. T.
		201–204		49	301–304	Rev. T.
		204a		49	304a	Rev. T.
		205–210		49	305–310	Rev. T.
		210a		49	310a	Rev. T.
		211–213		49	311–313	Rev. T.
		214		15	77c	Rev. T.
		214		49	314	Rev. T.
		215–224		49	315–324	Rev. T.
		225		49	324a	Rev. T.
		226		49	325	Rev. T.
		226A		49	325a	Rev. T.
		227, 228		49	326, 327	Rev. T.
		301–312		49	901–912	Rev. T.
		312a		49	912a	Rev. T.
		313–320		49	913–920	Rev. T.
		320		49	153, 153 nt	Rev. T.
		321, 322		49	921, 922	Rev. T.
		323, 324		49	922a, 922b	Rev. T.
		325		49	923	Rev. T.
		401–406		49	1001–1006	Rev. T.
		406a		49	1006a	Rev. T.
		407–422		49	1007–1022	Rev. T.
		501–509		49	1231–1239	Rev. T.
		510		49	1239a	Rev. T.
		511		49	1240	Rev. T.
	105	1, 2	387, 388	35	74, 75	Rev. T.
8	119	1–3	388, 389	25	331–333	Rep.
		4	389	25	334	
		5	389	25	348	
		6	390	8	3	Elim.
		6	390	25	349	
		7	390	25	381	
		8	391	25	339	
		10	391	25	341	
		11	391	25	342	
				25	354	
12	129	3	402	32	32	Rev. T.
23	210	1–3	409	21	191–193	Rep.
	213	1, 2	411	18	708, 709	Rev. T.
	Pub. R. 6		644			Rep.
Mar. 2	314	1	440	7	361a	

49th Cong. 24 Stat.		Chapter	Section	Page	U.S.C. Title	U.S.C. Section	Status
1887—Mar.	2	314	2	440	7	361b	
			3	441	7	361c	
			4	441	7	361d	
			5	441	7	361e	
			6	441	7	361f	
			7	441	7	361g	
			8	441	7	361h	
			9	442	7	361i	
			10		7	361a nt	
		318		445	2	223	Rep.
		320	1	463	25	155	
			1	465	25	299	Rep.
	3	339		475	46 App.	143	
		340	1	476	48	1501	
			2	477	48	1502	
			3	477	48	1503	
			4	477	48	1504	
			5		48	1505	
			6		48	1506	
			7		48	1507	
		345	4, 5	491, 492	45	94, 95	Rep.
		346		492	39	578	Rev. T.
		359	4–7, 10	506, 507	28	761–765	Rev. T.
		362		512	31	601	Rev. T.
				512	40	273, 278	Rep.
				515	31	405	Rev. T.
				523	16	744	
				526	43	85	Elim.
				527	31	612	Rev. T.
				539	24	76, 120	Rep.
		376	1	556	43	894	
			2	556	43	895	
			3	557	43	896	
			4	557	43	897	
			5	557	43	898	
			7	558	43	899	
		388	1	569	39	156	Rev. T.
		392	1	596	2	112	
		396	3	635	31	328, 332, 336	Rev. T.
		397	1, 2	635	28	633, 660	Rev. T.
			26	641	48	1480a	Rep.
50th Cong.							
25 Stat.							
1888—Jan.	20	1		1	16	741	Elim.
		2	1	1	39	249	Rev. T.
Feb.	1	4	1	9	8	63	Elim.
	18	15		40	35	39	Rev. T.
	29	17	1	41	47	21	
			2	41	47	22	
			3	41	47	23	
			4	41	47	24	
			5	42	47	25	
			6	42	47	26	
			7	42	47	27	
			8	42	47	28	
			9	42	47	29	
			10	42	47	30	
			11	42	47	31	
			12	42	47	32	
			13	42	47	33	
Mar.	9	30		45	8	82	Elim.
	30	47	1	57	44	43	Rev. T.
Apr.	2	54		76	43	21	Rep.
	4	61	1	80	46 App.	121	
			2	80	46	331, 440	Rev. T.
	24	194		94	33	591	
May	1	212		112	10	1127	Rev. T.
	9	231	1, 2	135	39	49, 49a	Rev. T.
June	1	338		165	10	671a	Rev. T.
	7	369		173	38	91, 94	Rev. T.
		373		176	7	372	Rep.
	13	389	1	182	29	1	
			2	182	29	3	
			7	183	29	4	
			8	183	29	6	
	18	393		186	22	80, 82	Rep.
	29	496	1	209	33	441	
			2	209	33	442	
			3	209	33	443	
			3	209	33	444	
			3	209	33	445	
			3	209	33	446	
			3	209	33	447	
			3	209	33	448	

50th Cong.				U.S.C.		
25 Stat.	Chapter	Section	Page	Title	Section	Status
1888—June 29	496	4	210	33	449	
		4	210	33	450	
		5	210	33	451	
		6	210	33	451a	
		7		33	451b	
July 11	615	1	258	40	168	
		1	262	2	138	
19	679	2	336	48	1474	Rep.
24	702	1	336, 346	39	11a, 13	Rev. T.
Aug. 1	727		355	42	106	Rep.
	728	1	357	40	257	
		2	357	40	258	Elim.
7	772	1	382	47	9	
		2	383	47	10	
		3	383	47	11	
		4	383	47	12	
		5	384	47	13	
		6	384	47	14	
		7	385	47	15	
8	786		387	5	12	Rev. T.
	787	1, 2	387	6	4, 5	Rev. T.
9	818	1	392	25	181	
		2	392	25	182	
		3	392	25	183	
11	860	1	419	33	601	
		1	420	33	604	
		1	421	33	605	
		1	422	33	602	
		2	423	33	500	
		3	423	33	622	
		3	423	33	623	Rep.
		4	424	33	602	
		6	424	33	4	
		7	424	33	604	
		7	424	33	605	
		8	424	33	556	
		11	425	33	608	
14	890	1–5	443	34	1012, 1016	Rev. T.
27	913		449	38	171, 173	Rev. T.
	914	1	450	24	134	Rep.
Sept. 13	1015	5–11, 13, 14	477–479	8	275–283	Rep.
22	1028	1, 6	489, 490	50	11, 15	Rep.
26	1037		491	10	1182a	Rev. T.
			491	34	1129	Rev. T.
Oct. 1	1064	1	504	8	275	Rep.
2	1069		511	14	37	Rev. T.
			526, 527	43	662	
			529	20	49	Elim.
			530	49	56	Rev. T.
			543	31	719	Rev. T.
			546	2	68	
			546	2	95	
12	1098		557	43	21	Rep.
18	1194		560			I.R.C. '39
	1197		564	46	467	Rev. T.
19	1210	1	506	8	140	Rep.
		1	587	2	105	
		3	600	5	417	Rev. T.
	1214	2	612	25	350	
	1216	1, 2	613	3	11, 12, 13	Rev. T.
1889—Jan. 4	19	1, 2	639	42	12, 13	Rep.
	20		640	36	20	Rev. T.
16	50		650	39	165	Rev. T.
30	100	1	654	39	712	Rev. T.
Feb. 6	113	6	656	18	681	Rev. T.
8	115		657	34	199	Rev. T.
	116		657	50	66	Rep.
9	119	2, 3	658	34	934, 935	Rev. T.
	122	1	659	5	109	Rev. T.
		1	659	7	2202	
		1	659	7	2208	
		1	659	7	2215	
		1	659	21	119	
		1, 4	659	22	80, 82	Rep.
			659			I.R.C. '39
		1	659	39	329	Rev. T.
		2	659	7	2212	Rep.
		3	659			Rep.
		4	659	7	2202	
		4	659	7	2208	
		4	659	7	2215	
12	132		659	38	163	Rev. T.
16	171		672	5	112	Rev. T.
	172		673	25	196	
22	180		676	48	1460a	Rep.
		21	682	28	481, 490	Rev. T.

50th Cong.

25 Stat.	Chapter	Section	Page	U.S.C. Title	U.S.C. Section	Status
1889—Mar. 1	331		781	34	916	Rev. T.
	332		782	38	59	Rev. T.
2	371		817	5	454	Rev. T.
			818	34	525	Rev. T.
	373		840	7	2205	
			840	7	364	Rep.
	374	1	841, 844	39	86, 88, 164	Rev. T.
	381	1	854	43	700	Rep.
		3, 4	854	43	234, 681	Rep.
		6, 7	854, 855	43	214, 252	Rep.
	382	1	855	10	1362	Rev. T.
		1–10	855–862	49	6, 10, 12, 14, 16–18, 20–23	Rev. T.
	390	2–9	869–871	10	1435–1442	Rev. T.
	393	3–5	873, 874	39	255–257	Rev. T.
	396	2	879	34	1045	Rev. T.
	410	1	907	31	600	Rev. T.
	411	1	941	40	256, 260, 268	Rep.
		1	944	5	363	Rev. T.
		1	945	31	414	Rev. T.
		1	954	49	57	Rev. T.
		1	955	31	353	Rev. T.
		1	971	5	194a	Rev. T.
		1	975	24	134	Rep.
	412	10	1003	25	272	
	418	1	1012	46	481	Rev. T.
	422	1	1013	25	340	

51st Cong.

26 Stat.	Chapter	Section	Page	U.S.C. Title	U.S.C. Section	Status
1890—Feb. 7	8		6	34	598	Rev. T.
27	20	1, 2	13	10	526, 527	Rev. T.
		3	14	10	523	Rev. T.
Mar. 4	25		16	38	174	Rev. T.
5	26		17	5	182	Rev. T.
27	51	1–3	31	42	95, 107, 108	Rep.
Apr. 4	63	1	40	38	4	Rev. T.
9	73	3	50			Elim.
14	80		55	5	200	Rev. T.
			55	34	597	Rev. T.
16	85		56	39	601	Rev. T.
26	161		67	28	180	Rev. T.
30	173	2	78	20	81	
		3	78	20	82	
May 2	182	18, 20–22	90, 91	43	1091–1094	Rep.
		23	92	43	1095	
		24, 27	92, 93	43	1096, 1097	Rep.
14	207	1–7	109, 110	43	1111–1117	Rep.
24	292		120	46 App.	725	
26	355		121	43	254	Rep.
June 10	407	12	136	19	1518	Elim.
		12	136	28	296, 297	Rev. T.
		30	142	5	296	Rev. T.
		31	136	28	296	Rev. T.
13	423		152	10	1334	Rev. T.
16	426	4	158	10	651	Rev. T.
18	431		161			I.R.C. '39
	432		162			I.R.C. '39
25	616		180	46	365	Rev. T.
27	634	1–4	182, 183	38	203, 205, 266, 281, 324, 328	Rev. T.
30	639	1	187	38	96 nt	Rev. T.
	640		194	34	543	Rev. T.
			197	31	640	Rev. T.
			197	34	561	Rev. T.
			205	31	641	Rev. T.
July 1	646		209	31	99	Rev. T.
2	647	1	209	15	1	
		2	209	15	2	
		3	209	15	3	
		4	209	15	4	
		5	210	15	5	
		6	210	15	6	
		7		15	6a	
		8	210	15	7	
3	656	16	217	28	481, 490	Rev. T.
10	664	16	225	28	481, 490	Rev. T.
11	667	1	235	5	643	Rev. T.
		1	236	31	1006	Rev. T.
		1	242	15	202	
		1	254	5	420	Rev. T.
		1	257	43	3	Rep.
		1	259	44	283a	Rev. T.
		1	265	5	295	Rev. T.
		2	268	31	592	Rev. T.
14	707		288	7	2205	
			288	7	368	Elim.
			288	7	391	

51st Cong.

26 Stat.	Chapter	Section	Page	U.S.C. Title	U.S.C. Section	Status
1890—July 14	707		288	21	119	
			288	22	80	Rep.
	708	2	289	12	145	Rep.
		2	289	31	408, 410, 453	Rev. T.
		3	289	31	412	Rev. T.
		6	289	12	122	Rep.
26	721		292	46	382	Rev. T.
Aug. 8	728		313	27	121	
18	797	1	316	50	171	Rep.
		1	316	50	174	Elim.
		2	320	50	54	Rep.
19	801		320	46	563	Rev. T.
	802	1	320	33	61, 62, 301	Rep.
		1		33	142	Rep.
		1	321–328	33	63, 71–84, 91, 92, 101–113, 121, 131, 141	Rep.
	806	1–11	333–336	16	424	
		12		16	424–1	
28	812	1, 2	362	19	63	Rep.
	Pub. R. 41		678	2	137b	Elim.
29	819		369	43	889	
	820	1	371	5	19, 20	Rev. T.
30	837	1	382	33	887	Rep.
		1	391	43	212	Rep.
		1	391	43	321	
		1	391	43	662	
		1	391	43	945	
		1	394, 399	31	601, 651	Rev. T.
		1	400	10	861a	Rev. T.
		1	401	16	446	
		3	412	40	120	Elim.
		4	413	31	497	Rev. T.
	839	4	415	21	18	
		5	415	19	181	
		6	416	21	104	
		7	416	21	102	
		8	416	21	103	
		9	416	21	101	
		10	417	21	105	
	841	1	417	7	322	
		1	418	7	323	
		2	418	7	324	
		3	418	7	325	
		4	419	7	321	
		4	419	7	326	
		5		7	326a	
		5	419	7	327	Rep.
		6	419	7	328	
Sept. 1	Pub. R. 43		679	31	99	Rev. T.
4	875	1, 2	425	33	367, 368	Rep.
		3	425	33	367 nt	Rep.
19	907	2	452	33	625	Rep.
		11	455	33	413 nt	
		13	455	33	606	
		15	456	10	742	Rev. T.
	908	2, 3	466	39	259, 732	Rev. T.
25	926	1	478	16	41	
		2	478	16	43	
	Pub. R. 50		681	10	1427	Rev. T.
			681	34	371	Rev. T.
26	944		484	31	276	Rev. T.
	945	1, 2	485	31	315, 317, 323, 324, 348, 350	Rev. T.
27	1001	1, 7	492, 495	40	83, 84	Elim.
29	1040	1	496	43	904	
		2	496	43	905	
		3	496	43	906	
		6	498	43	907	
30	1121		502	43	729	Rep.
	1125		504	10	947a	Rev. T.
	1126	1	511	31	1028	Rev. T.
		1	511	19	30	Rep.
		1	537	31	226	Rev. T.
	Pub. R. 59		684	43	261	
Oct. 1	1241	1	562	34	661	Rev. T.
		2, 3	562	10	492, 556, 932	Rev. T.
	1244	10, 26, 28, 29, 31, 33–35, 42, 43, 45, 53.	614, 618–622, 624			I.R.C. '39
	1256	1	645	2	78	
		2	645	2	79	
		3	645	2	80	
		4, 5	645, 646	2	82	Rep.
		6	646	2	83	
		7	646	2	84	Rep.
		9	646	31	1020	Rev. T.
	1260		648	39	823	Rev. T.
	1262		650	43	755	Rep.

51st Cong.					U.S.C.		
26 Stat.		Chapter	Section	Page	Title	Section	Status
1890—Oct.	1	1263	1	650	16	471c	
			2	651	16	55	
			2	651	16	61	
			3	651	16	471d	
		1266	1	653	15	311	Elim.
			2	653	10	212, 214	Rev. T.
			3	653	15	313	
			4	653	15	312	
			9	654	10	215	Rev. T.
			9	654	15	317	
Dec.	18	22		690	19	62	Rep.
	22	26		692	46	404	Rev. T.
	24	Pub. R. 7	1	1113	10	189	Rev. T.
1891—Jan.	13	70		716	34	1129	Rev. T.
	16	74		718	24	47	Rep.
Feb.	6	113		733	5	7	Rev. T.
	10	122	2	737	10	695	Rev. T.
		127	4	742	18	286	Rev. T.
		128		743	49	12	Rev. T.
		130		748	38	127	Rev. T.
	16	238		763	10	1021, 1022	Rev. T.
	18	244		764	43	905	
				764	43	906	
	21	250	1, 2	765, 766	46	46, 48	Rev. T.
		252	1, 2	766	33	554	
	24	283		769	50	12	Rep.
		284		773	10	52	Rev. T.
				779	31	651	Rev. T.
	28	383	1	794	25	331	Rep.
			3	795	25	397	
			4	795	25	336	
			5	795	25	371	
		384		796	43	851	
				797	43	852	
Mar.	2	494		807	31	641	Rev. T.
		498		824	10	1435	Rev. T.
	3	517	2, 9, 10	826, 829	28	543, 544, 547, 877	Rev. T.
			11	829	28	228, 228a, 230	Rev. T.
		519	1–9	830–832	39	657–665	Rev. T.
		521	1, 2	833	46	466a, 466b	Rev. T.
			3		46 App.	466c	
		529	1, 4	839	18	741	Rev. T.
			2	839	18	744	Rev. T.
			5	839	18	743	Rev. T.
			7	840	18	746–748	Rev. T.
			8	840	18	713	Rev. T.
			9	840	18	742, 745	Rev. T.
		533	1	842	16	362	
			3	843	16	363	
			4	843	16	364	
			5	844	16	365	
			6	844	16	366	
			7	844	16	367	
			8	844	16	368	
		540		868	40	67	Elim.
		541	1	914	2	99	Rep.
			1	923	42	15	Rep.
			1	934	5	421	Rev. T.
			1	940	35	14	Rev. T.
			1	944, 945			Rep.
			3	948	31	326	Rev. T.
		542		968	19	13 nt	Elim.
				978	16	424	
				979	38	26	Rev. T.
		543	16	1026	43	1098	Rep.
			37	1043	43	1099	
		548	1	1082	38	114, 244	Rev. T.
			3	1083	38	122	Rev. T.
		551	7	1085	8	1552	
		559		1093	16	607	
				1093	43	1166	
		561	1	1095	43	893	
			1	1095	43	1181	
			2	1096	43	321	
			2	1096	43	327	
			2	1096	43	328	
			2	1097	43	329	
			2	1097	43	323	
			2	1097	43	325	
			3	1097	43	174	Rep.
			4	1097	30	35	
			4	1097	30	36	
			4	1097	30	48	
			4	1097	30	52	
			4	1097	30	44, 45	Elim.
			4	1097	43	174, 185, 202, 718	Rep.
			4	1097	43	893	

51st Cong.					U.S.C.		
26 Stat.		Chapter	Section	Page	Title	Section	Status
1891—Mar.	3	561	4	1097	43	989	
			5	1097	43	161, 162	Rep.
			6	1098	43	173	Rep.
			7	1098	43	165	Elim.
			7	1098	43	1165	
			8	1099	16	607	
			8	1099	16	608	
			8	1099	16	609	
			8	1099	16	610	
			8	1099	16	611	
			8	1099	16	611a	
			8	1099	43	1166	
			9	1099	43	671	Rep.
			10	1099	43	1197	
			11	1099	43	732	Rep.
			13	1100	43	687a–6	Rep.
			15	1101	25	495	
			16	1101	43	728	Rep.
			17	1101	43	212	Rep.
			17	1101	43	663	
			18	1101	43	946	
			19	1102	43	947	
			20	1102	43	948	
			21	1102	43	949	
			24	1103	16	471	Rep.
		562		1103	38	241, 242	Rev. T.
		568		1418	38	289	Rev. T.
52d Cong.							
27 Stat.							
1892—Mar.	9	14		7	28	643	Rev. T.
Apr.	11	40		15	24	91	Rep.
		41	1	16	46	481	Rev. T.
	12	Pub. R. 8		395	20	91	
May	5	60	1–8	25	8	263, 281, 282, 284–288	Rep.
	9	62		27	5	192	Rev. T.
June	25	133		59	43	906	
July	6	154		87	31	172	Rev. T.
	13	158	5	111	33	628	
		164	1	120, 143	25	27, 284	Elim.
		165	5	148	39	522	Rev. T.
	14	169		149	38	175	Rev. T.
	16	195		177	10	877	Rev. T.
				177	34	890	Rev. T.
				178	10	715b, 1335	Rev. T.
		196	1	194	31	97	Rev. T.
			1	197	15	177	Rep.
			1	199	31	595	Rev. T.
			1	200			I.R.C. '39
	19	206		243, 245	5	429, 437, 440, 467	Rev. T.
				243	34	561	Rev. T.
				245	5	454	Rev. T.
				245	31	640	Rev. T.
				245	34	222	Rev. T.
	20	209	1–5	252	28	832–836	Rev. T.
	23	234		260	25	241, 243	Rep.
		237	6	263	10	1125	Rev. T.
	26	248	1	267	46 App.	144	
			2	268	46 App.	145	
		249	1	268	39	422	Rev. T.
		251		270	43	82	Rep.
				270	43	185	
		255	1, 2	272	38	42, 43	Rev. T.
		256	1	272	25	4	
			2	273	25	5	
			3	273	25	6	
			4	273	25	7	
	27	267		275	5	193	Rev. T.
		270	1	276	10	1312	Rev. T.
			3	277	10	94	Rev. T.
		273		278	10	1442	Rev. T.
		277	1, 2	281, 282	38	371	Rev. T.
			3	282	38	379	Rev. T.
			5	282	38	378	Rev. T.
	28	315		321	34	661, 662	Rev. T.
		316		321	40	303	Rep.
		317		322	12	125	Rep.
	29	320	15	325	40	101	
	30	328	1–4	336	10	502–504, 504 nt	Rev. T.
Aug.	1	352	1, 2	340	40	321, 322	Rep.
			3	340	40	323	Elim.
	3	360		345	12	197	
	4	375	1	348	30	161	
			2	348	18	103	Rev. T.

52d Cong. 27 Stat.		Chapter	Section	Page	U.S.C. Title	U.S.C. Section	Status
1892—Aug.	4	375	2	348	43	311	Rep.
			3	348	30	161	
	5	379	1, 2	348, 349	38	311, 311a	Rev. T.
		380	1	351	40	277	Rep.
			1	362	31	619	Rev. T.
			1	368	43	124	
			1	384	24	123	Rep.
		390	1	384	24	123	Elim.
Dec.	13	Pub. R. 1		752	31	166	Rev. T.
1893—Jan.	5	18		413	38	264	Rev. T.
	23	41		421	39	156	Rev. T.
	31	54		427	43	906	
Feb.	3	58		429	38	377	Rev. T.
	9	74	9	436	35	59, 60, 63	Rev. T.
	11	83		443	49	46	Rev. T.
	13	103		444	16	607	
		105	1	445	46 App.	190	
			2	445	46 App.	191	
			3	445	46 App.	192	
			4	445	46 App.	193	
			5	446	46 App.	194	
			6	446	46 App.	196	
			7	446	46 App.	195	
			8	446	46 App.	190 nt	
	15	114	1–5	449–451	42	81, 82, 92–94	Rep.
			6, 7	452	42	84, 111	Rep.
			8	452	42	100	Rep.
			9	452	42	98	Rep.
			10		42	102	Rep.
			11, 12		42	83, 99	Rep.
			13–15		42	82a, 94a, 94c	Rep.
			16, 17		42	94b, 94d	Rep.
	18	136		461	50	14	Rep.
	27	168		479	31	493b	Rev. T.
				480	10	719	Rev. T.
				484	10	1336, 1340	Rev. T.
				485	10	1203	Rev. T.
				485	41	6	Rep.
Mar.	1	183	1	507	33	661	
			2	507	33	662	
			3	507	33	663	
			4	507	33	664	
			5	507	33	665	
			6	508	33	666	
			7	508	33	667	
			8	508	33	668	
			9	508	33	669	
			10	508	33	670	
			11	508	33	671	
			12	508	33	672	
			13	508	33	673	
			14	509	33	674	
			15	509	33	675	
			16	509	33	676	
			17	509	33	677	
			18	509	33	678	
			19	510	33	679	
			20	510	33	680	
			21	510	33	681	Rep.
			22	510	33	682	
			23	510	33	683	
			24	511	33	684	
			25	511	33	685	
		186		515, 520	10	1076, 1124	Rev. T.
	2	196	1–6, 8	531, 532	45	1–7	Rep.
	3	199	1	553	2	30	
		202		557	33	316	Rep.
		206	8	570	8	172	Rep.
		208		585	16	654	Elim.
				591	5	53	Rev. T.
				592	43	861	
				593	43	202, 254, 275	Rep.
				593	43	1076	Rep.
				593	43	1181	
				595	20	121 nt	
		209	1	614	25	67	Rep.
			1	628	25	283	
			1	631	25	175	
			1	631	25	178	
			1	635	25	283	
		210	1	653	24	118	Rep.
		211	1	683	46 App.	725	
			1	689	15	177	Rep.
			3	715	40	286	
			4, 5	715	5	28–30	Rev. T.
		212		716	5	435	Rev. T.

Date	Chapter	Section	Page	U.S.C. Title	U.S.C. Section	Status
52d Cong.						
27 Stat.						
1893—Mar. 3	212		716	31	639	Rev. T.
			717	5	446	Rev. T.
			717, 724, 732	34	196, 561, 566	Rev. T.
	213	1	733	39	354	Rev. T.
	220		745	28	481, 490	Rev. T.
	221	1	746	15	206	
		2	746	15	207	
		3	746	15	208	
	225	1–3	751	28	847–849	Rev. T.
	226		751	28	465	Rev. T.
53d Cong.						
28 Stat.						
1893—Sept. 1	Pub. R. 4		11	43	1118	Rep.
Oct. 31	Pub. R. 13		13	46 App.	726	
Nov. 1	8		4	31	311	Rev. T.
			5	1	26	Rev. T.
	13		7	34	1129	Rev. T.
	14	1, 2	7, 8	8	287, 289	Rep.
Dec. 12	1		15	43	906	
21	3		18	38	56	Rev. T.
	6		21	39	35	Rev. T.
	Pub. R. 21		757	2	74	Elim.
1894—Jan. 11	10	1	26	43	100	
		2	26	43	101	
22	16		28	46	408	Rev. T.
	17		28	5	380	Rev. T.
27	J. Res. No. 9		577	2	137c	
	21	3, 4	31, 32	39	716–718	Rev. T.
		6	32	39	728	Rev. T.
		7, 8	32	39	719, 735	Rev. T.
		9–11	33	39	720, 721, 729	Rev. T.
		12	33	39	722	Rev. T.
Mar. 12	36		41	20	41	
			41	20	42	
			41	20	55	
17	Art. III		1211	8	298	Elim.
29	49	1–4	47	31	89–92	Rev. T.
Apr. 4	63	1	40	38	11e	Rev. T.
May 5	Pub. R. 24		582	31	542	Rev. T.
7	72	1	73	16	24	
		3	73	16	25	Rep.
		4	73	16	26	
		5–7	73	16	27–29	Rep.
		8	75	16	13	Rep.
		9	75	16	30	
		10	75	16	24 nt	
		10	75	16	30a	
11	Pub. R. 26		583	10	1427	Rev. T.
			583	34	374	Rev. T.
28	83		82	33	77, 79, 106, 141	Rep.
30	87		84	43	1156	Rep.
June 28	118		96	5	87	Rev. T.
July 12	131	1, 2	101, 102	15	221, 222	Rep.
16	137	2, 4	106, 107	39	359, 730	Rev. T.
	138	14, 16	110, 111	28	481, 490	Rev. T.
18	141		113	38	73	Rev. T.
23	Pub. R. 37		587	22	267a	
26	165		132	5	449	Rev. T.
	167		151	10	1064	Rev. T.
31	174	1	179	42	15	Rep.
		1	197	43	32	
		2	205	5	62	Rev. T.
		3	205	25	96	Rep.
		4	205			Rep.
		4	205	46	679	Rev. T.
		4	206	31	93, 506, 514	Rev. T.
		5	206	22	4211	
		7	206	25	96	Rep.
		7	206	31	72	Rev. T.
		7	207	43	14	
		8, 10	207	31	74, 1019	Rev. T.
		10	208	31	162	Rev. T.
		11	209	31	76, 147	Rev. T.
		12	209	5	267	Rev. T.
		12	209	31	78, 496	Rev. T.
		13	210	5	321	Rev. T.
		13, 14	210	31	84, 86	Rev. T.
		15	210	31	1029	Rev. T.
		16	210	31	150	Rev. T.
		17	210	28	666	Rev. T.
		18	210	41	20	Rep.
		19	210	19	42	Rep.
		20	210	31	87	Rev. T.

53d Cong. 28 Stat.		Chapter	Section	Page	U.S.C. Title	U.S.C. Section	Status
1894—July	31	174	22	210	31	1019	Rev. T.
			22	210	19	42	Rep.
			22	210	28	667	Rev. T.
			22	210	31	75	Rev. T.
			22	211	41	21	Rep.
			23	211	31	88	Rev. T.
Aug.	1	179	2	216	10	623, 625	Rev. T.
	3	198		222	16	32	
	4	213		229	24	8	Rep.
		228		236	31	650	Rev. T.
				237	10	750	Rev. T.
		232	1	246	10	190	Rev. T.
	8	236	1	263	43	941	
			2	263	43	942	Elim.
		238		272	7	2203	
				273	15	314	Elim.
	13	280		278	40	270	Rep.
		281	1	278	31	425	Rev. T.
			2	278	31	426	Rev. T.
		282	1–8	279, 280	6	6–13	Rev. T.
	15	288		285	43	755	Rep.
		290	1	305	25	345	
			1	305	25	402	
			1	311	25	281	
			4	312	25	99	
			10	313	25	44	
			11	313	25	286	
	18	299	1	356	33	31	
			2	360	33	452	
			3	360	33	443	
			3	360	33	444	
			3	361	33	445	
			3	361	33	446	
			3	362	33	447	
			3	362	33	448	
			4	362	33	1	
			5	362	33	499	
		300		372	42	82	Rep.
		301	1	383	15	203	
			1	384	20	83	Elim.
			1	390	5	342j	Rev. T.
			1	391	8	107	Rep.
			1	391	48	212	Elim.
			1	394	43	863	
			1	397	43	276	Rep.
			1	403	5	193	Rev. T.
			1	405	16	417	Elim.
			1	411	24	119	Rep.
			1	412	24	75, 84, 93, 94, 112	Rep.
			1	412	39	321	Rev. T.
			1	416	18	595	Rev. T.
			1	416	28	575, 576	Rev. T.
			1	418	22	264	Elim.
			4	422	43	641	
	20	302	1	423	43	759	
			2	423	43	762	
	23	307	1	447	44	151	Rev. T.
		314	1, 2	491	43	1077, 1078	Rep.
			3		43	1081	Rep.
		316	1	492	24	133	Rep.
		319		499	38	60	Rev. T.
	27	349	25	552	31	372	Rev. T.
			26	552	19	192	Rep.
			33	557			Rep.
			34	557	18	216	Rev. T.
			34, 40, 43, 46–52, 54–60, 62, 63.	558–567			I.R.C. '39
			64, 65	567			Rep.
			66, 69	567, 568			I.R.C. '39
			73	570	15	8	
			74	570	15	9	
			75	570	15	10	
			76	570	15	11	
			77	570	15	15 nt	Elim.
			78		15	8 nt	
Dec.	13	3		594	43	783	Rep.
	15	7		595	46	7	Rev. T.
	27	12		597	16	430f	
	29	14		599	43	234	Rep.
1895—Jan.	12	23		601	43	1457	
			1	601	44	1	Rev. T.
			2	601	44	4, 133, 134, 137, 140, 144, 146, 154, 160	Rev. T.
			3–12	601, 602	44	5–14	Rev. T.
			13, 14	603	44	181–182b	Rev. T.
			15, 16	603	44	15, 16	Rev. T.

53d Cong. 28 Stat.	Chapter	Section	Page	U.S.C. Title	U.S.C. Section	Status
1895—Jan. 12	23	17	603	15	187	Rep.
		17	603	31	589	Rev. T.
		17–21	603, 604	44	31, 33, 34, 49, 56	Rev. T.
		22	604	44	35	Rev. T.
		23	604			Rep.
		24	604	44	184	Rev. T.
		25	604	44	112	Rev. T.
		26, 27	604	44	36, 37	Rev. T.
		29	605	44	57	Rev. T.
		30, 31	605	44	51, 60	Rev. T.
		32	605	44	54	Rev. T.
		33, 34	605	44	38, 53	Rev. T.
		36, 37	606	44	32, 162, 185	Rev. T.
		38	607	44	55	Rev. T.
		39, 40	607	44	40, 150, 188	Rev. T.
		41, 42	607	44	113, 114	Rev. T.
		43	607	44	48	Rev. T.
		44	607			Rep.
		45, 46	607	44	41, 44	Rev. T.
		47	607	44	42	Rev. T.
		48	608			Rep.
		49–51	608	44	40, 216	Rev. T.
		52, 53	608	44	58, 83, 135	Rev. T.
		54	608	44	131	Rev. T.
		55, 56	609	44	189, 191–193	Rev. T.
		57	609	44	147	Rev. T.
		58	610	44	217	Rev. T.
		60	610	44	165	Rev. T.
		61	610	44	71, 83	Rev. T.
		62	610	44	76	Rev. T.
		63	611	44	167	Rev. T.
		64	611			Rep.
		65	611	39	323	Rev. T.
		66	611	44	74	Rev. T.
		67	611	44	78	Rev. T.
		68	612	44	157	Rev. T.
		69–71	612	44	77, 86, 166	Rev. T.
		72	612	44	158	Rev. T.
		73	612	44	132, 241	Rev. T.
		73	613	44	244, 250, 254, 256, 279, 296	Rev. T.
		73	613	44	247	Rev. T.
		73	614	44	195	Rev. T.
		73	614	44	248, 253, 258–260, 263, 269, 271	Rev. T.
		73	615	1	30	Rev. T.
		73	615	44	196, 196a, 212, 285	Rev. T.
		73	616	44	151, 223, 243, 245, 249, 274, 275, 289, 291, 293, 295	Rev. T.
		73	617	44	148, 149, 183	Rev. T.
		73	618	44	81, 288	Rev. T.
		73	619	44	280, 283	Rev. T.
		73	620	44	218, 283, 284	Rev. T.
		74	620	44	92	Rev. T.
		75, 76	620	44	91, 246	Rev. T.
		77	621	5	458	Rev. T.
		78	621	44	265	Rev. T.
		79	621	44	261	Rev. T.
		80	621	44	115	Rev. T.
		82	622	44	190	Rev. T.
		83, 84	622	44	155, 294	Rev. T.
		85	622	39	326	Rev. T.
		86	622	44	116	Rev. T.
		87	622	44	111	Rev. T.
		88, 89	622	44	80, 211, 213	Rev. T.
		90, 91	623	44	215, 222	Rev. T.
		92–94	623	44	96, 117, 219	Rev. T.
		95	623	44	93	Rev. T.
		97	624	44	119	Rev. T.
		98	624	10	1162	Rev. T.
		98	624	44	87	Rev. T.
				44	215a	Rev. T.
16	24	1	624	46	25, 259, 331	Rev. T.
		2	624	46	23	Rev. T.
		3	625	46 App.	262	
		4, 5	625	46	103, 107, 108	Rev. T.
	29		630	10	1075	Rev. T.
21	37	1	635	43	956	
		2		43	957	
26	50		641	25	343	
Feb. 8	61		643	49	22	Rev. T.
	64	1	645	33	241, 242	Rep.
		1	645	33	301	Rep.
		1	645–647	33	251–262	Rep.
		1	647, 648	33	271, 272	Rep.
		1	648, 649	33	281–295	Rep.

53d Cong. 28 Stat.		Chapter	Section	Page	U.S.C. Title	U.S.C. Section	Status
1895—Feb.	8	64	2	649	33	244	Rep.
			3	649	33	243	Rep.
	11	79		650	40	55	
				650	40	57, 58	Elim.
		80		651	16	430g	
	12	83		658	10	1197	Rev. T.
	15	92	1	664	43	1077, 1080	Rep.
		Pub. R. 13		970	38	290	Rev. T.
	18	97		667	46	563	Rev. T.
	19	102		672	33	61	Rep.
			1	672	33	301–303, 311–323, 331, 341–352	Rep.
			2	672	33	151	
			3	672	33	303	Rep.
	20	105	1–3	673	31	262–264, 283, 284	Rev. T.
	26	133		687	43	1171	Rep.
	28	139	1	690	46	412	Rev. T.
Mar.	1	145	8	697	25	241a	Rep.
		146	1, 2	699	46	362, 382	Rev. T.
	2	161		704	38	176	Rev. T.
		169		737	15	315	
		172	1	740	33	473	Elim.
			2	741	33	473	Rep.
		173	1, 2, 4	741, 743	46	77–79	Rev. T.
		174	1–3	744	43	176	Elim.
		177	1	766	2	67	
			1	768	2	97	Rep.
			1	769	1	26	Rev. T.
			1	771	2	101	
			1	780	5	342h	Rev. T.
			1	780	8	1552	
			1	780	8	1554	
			1	780	42	15a	Rep.
			1	787, 788	5	197, 216	Rev. T.
			1	803	39	804	Rev. T.
			1	805	29	5	
			1	805	44	270	Rev. T.
			3	807	43	16	
			4	807	31	78	Rev. T.
			5	807	7	2216	Rep.
			5(1)	807	19	27	Rep.
			5(2–4)	807	6	1–3	Rev. T.
			6	808	40	109	Rep.
			7	808	31	593	Rev. T.
			10	809	28	666	Rev. T.
		181		814	10	1442	Rev. T.
		182		814	16	600	Rep.
		186		826	34	1127	Rev. T.
				828	34	1061	Rev. T.
				843	46	382	Rev. T.
		187	1	844	31	1016	Rev. T.
		188	1	899	43	856	
			1	906	25	286	
		189	1	914	40	274	Rep.
			1	933	5	112	Rev. T.
			1	937	43	886	
			1	956	28	570	Rev. T.
			1	957	18	762–765	Rev. T.
			1	958	44	153, 168	Rev. T.
			1	959	40	190a	Elim.
			1	960	44	260	Rev. T.
			1	961	44	37, 162, 185	Rev. T.
			1	962	44	2	Rev. T.
		191	4	964	39	259	Rev. T.
		193		964	38	96	Rev. T.
54th Cong.							
29 Stat.							
1895—Dec.	18	Pub. R. 1		459	44	298	Rev. T.
1896—Jan.	23	8		4	43	906	
Feb.	7	Pub. R. 14		463	44	138	Rev. T.
	12	18		6	43	897	
	18	22		8	10	1061, 1083, 1137	Rev. T.
	20	23	1–3	8, 9	36	18–18b	Rev. T.
			4		36	18c	Rev. T.
	26	33		21	16	424	
				25	31	110	Rev. T.
	27	34		32	22	2668a	
Mar.	2	37		39	46	7	Rev. T.
		39	1	42	43	900	
			2	43	43	901	
			3	43	43	902	
	6	46		45	38	323	Rev. T.
		49	1–3	54, 55	33	474	
	13	54		57	38	32	Rev. T.

54th Cong.					U.S.C.		
29 Stat.		Chapter	Section	Page	Title	Section	Status
1896—Mar.	13	Pub. R. 23		466	44	213	Rev. T.
	16	59		60	10	862b	Rev. T.
	19	Pub. R. 31		468	44	183	Rev. T.
	28	73		75	5	11	Rev. T.
Apr.	1	87		85	45	6	Rep.
	20	Pub. R. 46		471	44	247	Rev. T.
	25	140		106	7	415	
				108	15	318	
May	2	Pub. R. 51		473	10	1405	Rev. T.
	11	168	1, 2	116, 117	43	1119	Rep.
	14	179		120	43	957	
	15	182	1	120	16	411	
			2	121	16	412	
	18	195		122	19	194	Rep.
	19	204		124	35	78	Rev. T.
		208	1–4	126, 127	33	461–464	Rep.
	21	212	1	127	43	962	
			2	127	43	963	
			3	127	43	964	
			4	127	43	965	
	22	231		133	5	150p	Rev. T.
				133	10	1257a	Rev. T.
	25	239		136	34	564	Rev. T.
	28	252	1	143	40	213	Rep.
			1	148	31	670	Rev. T.
			1	171	20	3	Rep.
			1	176	39	807	Rev. T.
			3, 4	179	5	38, 267	Rev. T.
			5	179	31	495	Rev. T.
			6	179	8	52	Rep.
			6	179	28	571, 574, 578, 578a, 578b	Rev. T.
			6	179	34	1152, 1153, 1155	Rev. T.
			6	179	46	440	Rev. T.
			8	181	28	483, 524, 580	Rev. T.
			10	182	28	493, 582	Rev. T.
			11	182	28	492, 583	Rev. T.
			12	183	28	524, 584	Rev. T.
			13	183	28	577, 586, 598	Rev. T.
			14	183	28	587	Rev. T.
			15–18	183	28	484, 588–590	Rev. T.
			19	184	5	92	Rev. T.
			19	184	8	45	Rep.
			19	184	18	591, 594, 595, 641	Rev. T.
			19	184	22	257	
			19	184			I.R.C. '39
			19–21	184	28	525–527, 597, 642, 828, 844	Rev. T.
			19	184	46	603, 604	Rev. T.
			19	184	49	12	Rev. T.
			21	185	28	529	Rev. T.
			23	185	5	337	Rev. T.
			24	186	28	578, 578a, 580, 581, 582–584, 586, 587, 589, 590, 597	Rev. T.
		255	1	188	46	221	Rev. T.
			2	188	46	214, 225, 229	Rev. T.
			3	189	46	221	Rev. T.
June	3	312	2	197	43	173	Rep.
		314	3	234	33	606	
			7	235	5	63	Rev. T.
			7	235	33	544	Rep.
	5	331		251	5	428	Rev. T.
		337	2–18	253–256			I.R.C. '39
	8	370		262	39	240, 334	Rev. T.
		371	1–4	263	19	472–475	Rep.
		373		268	40	485a	
				275	31	173	Rev. T.
	9	386		313	39	3, 160	Rev. T.
				316	31	610a	Rev. T.
	10	398	1	336	25	117	Rep.
			1	348	25	287	
		399	1	361	34	232, 883, 931	Rev. T.
			1	370	34	569, 570	Rev. T.
			1	372	34	526	Rev. T.
		400	1	380	18	761, 762, 766	Rev. T.
		401	1	381	33	91	Rep.
	11	420	1	413	48	37	Elim.
			1	414	31	261	Rev. T.
			1	421	14	129	Rev. T.
			1	434	43	642	
			1	435	43	38	
			1	445	24	82	Rep.
			1	453	44	45, 260	Rev. T.
			1	454	44	183	Rev. T.
		424		458	39	49	Rev. T.
		Pub. R. 62		476	34	192	Rev. T.
Dec.	22	3		481	28	494	Rev. T.
1897—Jan.	7	3	1	90	25	197	
	13	11	1	484	43	952	

54th Cong.

29 Stat.		Chapter	Section	Page	U.S.C. Title	U.S.C. Section	Status
1897—Jan.	13	11	2	484	43	953	
			3	484	43	954	
			4	484	43	955	
	18	61	1	489	46	404, 520	Rev. T.
		62	1–3, 7	490, 491	43	1131–1134	Rep.
	20	67		491, 492	46	46, 48	Rev. T.
	21	83		494	14	196	Rev. T.
	26	92		497	10	1421	Rev. T.
Feb.	4	146		511			Rep.
	9	205		517	24	91	Rep.
	10	214		519	10	1112	Rev. T.
	11	216		526	30	101	Elim.
	13	221		526	34	322	Rev. T.
	15	231		530	46	382	Rev. T.
	17	Pub. R. 12		700	44	183	Rev. T.
		248		805	38	289	Rev. T.
	18	250		535	43	906	
		Pub. R. 13	1	701	43	42	
			2	701	43	43	
	19	263		536	28	543	Rev. T.
		265	1	544	2	136	
			1	545	2	131	
			1	545	2	140	
			1	546	2	131	
			1	546	2	136	
			1	546	2	139	Elim.
			1	554	42	19	Rep.
			1, 3	577, 578	28	591, 852	Rev. T.
	20	268		590	39	321	Rev. T.
	26	335		599	43	664	
	27	340		599	39	381	Rev. T.
Mar.	2	354		600	12	197	
		358	1–10, 13	604–607	21	41–50	Rep.
		363		618	48	1501	
				618	48	1502	
				618	48	1503	
				618	48	1504	
				619	48	1505	
				619	48	1506	
				619	48	1507	
	3	372	1	621	16	413	
			2	621	16	414	
			3	621	16	415	Rep.
			4	622	16	416	
			5	622	16	413, 414, 416	
			5	622	16	415	Rep.
		375		624	40	86	Elim.
		376	1	624	31	312	Rev. T.
		378		625	24	281	Rep.
		379	1–8	626–628			I.R.C. '39
		385		647	5	387	Rev. T.
				648	31	583	Rev. T.
				648	39	695, 730	Rev. T.
		386		663	45	91	Rep.
		389	1	687	46	549	Rev. T.
			2, 3	688	46	660–1, 677	Rev. T.
			4	689	46	624	Rev. T.
			5	689	33	320	Rep.
			6, 7	689	46	625, 628	Rev. T.
			8	689	46	563	Rev. T.
			9	689	46	330	Rev. T.
			11	690	33	364	Rep.
			12	690	33	323, 331, 341, 342	Rep.
			13	690	33	350, 351	Rep.
			14	690	46	366	Rev. T.
			19	691	46	564	Rev. T.
		391	1, 2	692	35	31, 69	Rev. T.
			3–5	693	35	32, 37, 47	Rev. T.
			6	694	35	70	Rev. T.
			7	694	35	43	Rev. T.

55th Cong.

30 Stat.		Chapter	Section	Page	U.S.C. Title	U.S.C. Section	Status
1897—June	4	2	1	18	31	171–173	Rev. T.
			1	18	39	715	Rev. T.
			1	27	31	342	Rev. T.
			1	29	48	240	Rep.
			1	34	16	473	
			1	34	16	474	
			1	34	16	475	
			1	35	16	476	Rep.
			1	35	16	477	
			1	35	16	551	
			1	36	16	473	
			1	36	16	478	

55th Cong.

30 Stat.	Chapter	Section	Page	U.S.C. Title	U.S.C. Section	Status
1897—June 4	2	1	36	16	479	
		1	36	16	480	
		1	36	16	481	
		1	36	16	482	
		1	39	5	460	Rev. T.
		1	43	16	424	
		1	44	16	430g	
		1	48	31	178, 583, 604	Rev. T.
		1	54	24	58	Rep.
		1	61	44	260, 270	Rev. T.
		1	62	44	159	Rev. T.
7	3	1	79	25	278	Elim.
		1	83	25	274	
		1	86	5	103	Rev. T.
		1	90	25	58	
		1	90	25	184	
		1	90	25	197	
	4	1	96–102	33	154–156, 171–183, 191, 192, 201–213, 221, 222, 231, 232	Rep.
		2–4	102, 103	33	157–159	Rep.
		5	103	46	381	Rev. T.
23	8		105	43	1131	Rep.
July 19	9	1	121	24	78	Rep.
		1	121	38	11d–1	Rev. T.
		1	136	2	105	
24	11	9, 10	206			I.R.C. '39
		14	207	19	145	Rep.
	13		214	46 App.	141	
1898—Jan. 27	10		234	43	72	Rep.
Feb. 17	26	1	248	46 App.	290	Elim.
		2	248	46 App.	289	
		3	248	46 App.	291	
Mar. 4	35	1	252	48	1476	Rep.
11	57		274	31	206	Rev. T.
14	60		276	38	44	Rev. T.
15	68	1	286	19	29	Rep.
		3	316	31	678	Rev. T.
		4	316	44	195, 196	Rev. T.
		6	316	40	109	Rep.
		7	316	5	29, 30, 32	Rev. T.
		8	317	28	541	Rev. T.
		9	317	5	370	Rev. T.
	69		326	10	1208	Rev. T.
23	86		340	46	228	Rev. T.
Apr. 11	Pub. R. 21		737	50	178	Rep.
21	184		360	46	382	Rev. T.
22	187	1, 3	361	10	1, 3	Rev. T.
26	191	6	365	10	1432	Rev. T.
		7	365	37	235a	Rev. T.
29	229	3, 4	368	43	991	
May 4	234		373, 374	5	447, 457	Rev. T.
			377	24	6	
			380	34	21, 23	Rev. T.
			390	34	461	Rev. T.
	Pub. R. 30		741	34	352	Rev. T.
11	292	1	404	43	956	
		2	404	43	951	
14	299	1	409	43	270	Rep.
		2	409	43	942–1	
		3	410	43	942–2	
		4	410	43	942–3	
		4	410	43	942–4	
		5	410	43	942–5	
		6	411	43	942–6	
		7	412	43	942–7	
		8	412	43	942–8	
		9	413	43	942–9	
		10	413	43	270–4, 687a, 687a–2 to 687a–5	Rep.
		11	414	16	607a	
		11	414	16	615a	
		13	415	48	392	Elim.
17	339	1, 2	416	29	766	Rep.
	340		417	18	749	Rev. T.
18	344	1, 2	418	43	311, 675	Rep.
19	347		419	39	358a	Rev. T.
21	348		420	31	261	Rev. T.
26	363		420	10	864	Rev. T.
June 1	369		423	10	864	Rev. T.
6	389		432	5	15	Rev. T.
10	423	1, 2	440	35	6 nt	Rev. T.
13	446	1	441, 443	39	126, 285	Rev. T.
		2	444	39	428	Rev. T.
		3	444	39	132	Rev. T.
		4	444	39	276, 278	Rev. T.
	448	1	448			I.R.C. '39

55th Cong.					U.S.C.		
30 Stat.		Chapter	Section	Page	Title	Section	Status
1898—June	13	448	31	466			I.R.C. '39
			32	466	31	756	Rev. T.
			34	467	31	412	Rev. T.
			35–42, 44–48	467–470			I.R.C. '39
	16	458		473	43	240	Rep.
	17	463	1	474	34	31, 35, 121	Rev. T.
			2, 4	475	34	33, 887a	Rev. T.
		468	1	474	34	35	Rev. T.
	24	495	1	487	28	481, 482, 490, 491	Rev. T.
			2	487	28	511	Rev. T.
July	1	541	1	544	11	1	Rev. T.
			2	545	11	11	Rev. T.
			3	546	11	21	Rev. T.
			4, 5	547	11	22, 23	Rev. T.
			6, 7	548	11	24, 25	Rev. T.
			8–12	549	11	26–30	Rev. T.
			13–17	550	11	31–35	Rev. T.
			18–20	551	11	41–43	Rev. T.
			21–23	552	11	44–46	Rev. T.
			24–27	553	11	47–50	Rev. T.
			28–32	554	11	51–55	Rev. T.
			33–38	555	11	61–66	Rev. T.
			38	555	2	206	Rep.
			39	555	11	67	Rev. T.
			40–42	556	11	68–70	Rev. T.
			43–48	557	11	71–76	Rev. T.
			49–51	558	11	77–79	Rev. T.
			52–55	559	11	80–82, 91	Rev. T.
			56, 57	560	11	92, 93	Rev. T.
			58, 59	561	11	94, 95	Rev. T.
			60	562	11	96	Rev. T.
			61–63	562	11	101–103	Rev. T.
			64, 65	563	11	104, 105	Rev. T.
			66, 67	564	11	106, 107	Rev. T.
			68–70	565	11	108–110	Rev. T.
			71, 72		11	111, 112	Rev. T.
			73–77		11	201–205	Rev. T.
			77A, 77B		11	206, 207	Rev. T.
			78–80		11	301–303	Rev. T.
			81–98		11	401–418	Rev. T.
			101, 102		11	501, 502	Rev. T.
			106, 107		11	506, 507	Rev. T.
			111–121		11	511–521	Rev. T.
			126–133		11	526–533	Rev. T.
			136, 137		11	536, 537	Rev. T.
			141–149		11	541–549	Rev. T.
			156–180		11	556–580	Rev. T.
			186–191		11	586–591	Rev. T.
			196–213		11	596–613	Rev. T.
			216		11	616	Rev. T.
			221–227		11	621–627	Rev. T.
			228		11	628, 629	Rev. T.
			236–238		11	636–638	Rev. T.
			241–250		11	641–650	Rev. T.
			256–259		11	656–659	Rev. T.
			261–272		11	661–672	Rev. T.
			276		11	676	Rev. T.
			301, 302		11	701, 702	Rev. T.
			306–308		11	706–708	Rev. T.
			311–316		11	711–716	Rev. T.
			321–328		11	721–728	Rev. T.
			331–339		11	731–739	Rev. T.
			341–344		11	741–744	Rev. T.
			351–353		11	751–753	Rev. T.
			354		11	754, 755	Rev. T.
			355		11	755a	Rev. T.
			356, 357		11	756, 757	Rev. T.
			361–372		11	761–772	Rev. T.
			376–381		11	776–781	Rev. T.
			386, 387		11	786, 787	Rev. T.
			391–397		11	791–797	Rev. T.
			399		11	799	Rev. T.
			401, 402		11	801, 802	Rev. T.
			406, 407		11	806, 807	Rev. T.
			411–416		11	811–816	Rev. T.
			421–428		11	821–828	Rev. T.
			431–437		11	831–837	Rev. T.
			441–446		11	841–846	Rev. T.
			451–459		11	851–859	Rev. T.
			461–477		11	861–877	Rev. T.
			481–486		11	881–886	Rev. T.
			491–498		11	891–898	Rev. T.
			506–509		11	906–909	Rev. T.
			511		11	911	Rev. T.
			516–523		11	916–923	Rev. T.
			526		11	926	Rev. T.

55th Cong.					U.S.C.		
30 Stat.		Chapter	Section	Page	Title	Section	Status
1898—July	1	541	601, 602		11	1001, 1002	Rev. T.
			606, 607		11	1006, 1007	Rev. T.
			611–616		11	1011–1016	Rev. T.
			621–626		11	1021–1026	Rev. T.
			631–633		11	1031–1033	Rev. T.
			636, 637		11	1036, 1037	Rev. T.
			641–644		11	1041–1044	Rev. T.
			646		11	1046	Rev. T.
			651, 652		11	1051, 1052	Rev. T.
			654–662		11	1054–1062	Rev. T.
			666–669		11	1066–1069	Rev. T.
			671		11	1071	Rev. T.
			676–680		11	1076–1080	Rev. T.
			686		11	1086	Rev. T.
			700–703		11	1100–1103	Rev. T.
			705, 706		11	1205, 1206	Rev. T.
			710–715		11	1210–1215	Rev. T.
			720–722		11	1220–1222	Rev. T.
			725–729		11	1225–1229	Rev. T.
			735–738		11	1235–1238	Rev. T.
			740		11	1240	Rev. T.
			745, 746		11	1245, 1246	Rev. T.
			750		11	1250	Rev. T.
			755		11	1255	Rev. T.
		543	1, 2	570	40	60, 75	Elim.
			3, 4	570	40	67, 78	Elim.
			5	570	40	79	
			6	571	40	80	Elim.
		545	1	573	25	27	Elim.
			1	595	25	23	Elim.
			6	596	25	191	Rep.
			7	596	25	136	
		546		604	8	63	Elim.
			1	604	14	13, 19	Rev. T.
			1	614	40	285	
			1	618	16	607	
			1	618	16	611	
			1	624	20	121	
			1	631	33	686	
			1	640	24	81	Rep.
			1	644	5	85	Rev. T.
	7	571	1	653	5	30	Rev. T.
			1	661	31	361	Rev. T.
			1	672	40	164	Elim.
			1	673	16	554a	
			1	674	43	1111, 1112, 1115–1117	Rep.
			1	676	25	100	Rep.
		578		718	18	81	Rev. T.
				718	38	126	Rev. T.
				718	43	787	Rep.
		582		720	43	33	Elim.
		584		721	10	864	Rev. T.
		Pub. R. 55	1	750	48	661	Elim.
			1	751	8	293	Rep.
			1	751	48	499	Elim.
	8	636		722	10	1126	Rev. T.
		Pub. R. 57		752	15	312	
Dec.	21	28	1–6	755, 756	46	569, 576, 593, 596, 597, 604	Rev. T.
			7–11	757, 758	46	653–656, 658	Rev. T.
			12–15	758, 759	46	661, 663, 665, 669	Rev. T.
			16–18	759, 760	46	683–685	Rev. T.
			19–21	760, 761	46	701–703	Rev. T.
			22, 23	761, 762	46	712, 713	Rev. T.
			24, 25	763, 764	46	599, 683	Rev. T.
			26	764	46	569, 576, 593, 596, 597, 599, 604, 653–656, 658, 663, 665, 669, 713	Rev. T.
		29	1	764, 765	46	224, 226, 228, 391	Rev. T.
		36	1, 2	770, 771	22	11	Rep.
			3	771	22	4217	
1899—Jan.	12	46	2	784	10	878	Rev. T.
	28	Pub. R. 12		1388	44	139	Rev. T.
	31	78	7	811	24	207	Elim.
Feb.	8	121		822	28	780	Rev. T.
	14	154		836	2	9	
	21	176		841	16	430h	
		177		843			I.R.C. '39
	24	187	1	864	5	27	Rev. T.
			1	884	39	176	Rev. T.
			4	890	5	30, 98	Rev. T.
	27	205		892	43	887	
	28	221	1	908	16	495	
			2	908	16	496	
		227		915	35	46	Rev. T.
Mar.	1	324	1	927	25	36	
			8	947	25	116	

55th Cong.					U.S.C.		
30 Stat.		Chapter	Section	Page	Title	Section	Status
1899—Mar.	1	325		957	41	6	Rep.
		327	4, 5	966	39	332, 723, 725, 726	Rev. T.
		328		966	43	1131	Rep.
	2	352	1	977	10	1312	Rev. T.
			4	978	10	621	Rev. T.
			7	979	10	232	Rev. T.
			16	981	10	894	Rev. T.
		362		984	39	238	Rev. T.
		374	1	990	25	312	
			2	990	25	313	
			3	991	25	314	
			4	991	25	315	
			6	992	25	316	
			7	992	25	317	
			8	992	25	318	
		377	1	993	16	91	
			2	994	16	92	
			3	994	16	93	
	3	413	1	1004	34	395	Rev. T.
			4	1005	34	274	Rev. T.
			7	1005	34	1, 252, 314	Rev. T.
			7	1006	5	432	Rev. T.
			7	1006	34	21, 245, 253, 395	Rev. T.
			8	1006	34	387	Rev. T.
			10	1006	34	324	Rev. T.
			11	1007	34	391	Rev. T.
			12	1007	34	121, 259, 260, 331, 332, 332a	Rev. T.
			13	1007	34	865, 880, 1137, 1140, 1147, 1151, 1152, 1158, 1158a	Rev. T.
			14	1007	34	124, 125	Rev. T.
			15	1008	34	126, 127, 259	Rev. T.
			17	1008	34	431, 432	Rev. T.
			19	1008	34	634	Rev. T.
			20	1009	34	637, 664	Rev. T.
			25	1009	34	593	Rev. T.
		421		1024	34	866	Rev. T.
				1027	24	6	
		423		1073	50	66	Rep.
		424	1	1085	20	58	Elim.
			1	1090			I.R.C. '39
			1	1097	16	488	
			1	1098	43	751a	
			1	1101	20	122	
			1	1101	24	250	Elim.
		425	1	1148	33	686	
			1	1148	33	687	
			7	1150	33	549	Rep.
			9	1151	33	401	
			10	1151	33	403	
			11	1151	33	404	
			12	1151	33	406	
			13	1152	33	407	
			14	1152	33	408	
			15	1152	33	409	
			16	1153	33	411	
			16	1153	33	412	
			17	1153	33	413	
			18	1153	33	502	
			19	1154	33	414	
			20	1154	33	415	
			20(a)	1154	33	418	
			20(a)	1155	33	416	
		427	1	1233	16	525	
			1	1233	43	665	
			1	1233	43	958	
			1	1237	28	508	Rev. T.
		429	363	1325	10	15	Rev. T.
			459	1336	48	111	Elim.
		435	1, 2	1349			I.R.C. '39
		441		1354	28	754	Rev. T.
		454		1372	19	195	Rep.
		458	1	1377	40	107	Elim.
			2	1378	40	89	
			2	1378	40	108	Elim.
		460		1379, 1380	38	44–47, 49, 75, 192	Rev. T.

Title 26 Former Sections	*Title 26 New Sections*
937	6018(a), 7203
938	6103
939	2201
1000(a)	2501
1000(b)	2511(a)
1000(c)	2514
1000(d), (e)	Omitted
1000(f)	2513
1000(g)	Omitted
1001(a), (b)	2502(a), (c)
1001(c)	Omitted
1002	2512(b)
1003	2503
1004(a)(1)–(3)	2521–2523
1004(b), (c)	2522, 2524
1005	2512(a)
1006(a)	6019(a), 6065(a)
1006(b)	6075(b), 6091(b)(1)
1007	6001
1008(a)	2502(d), 6151(a)
1008(b)	6161(a)(1)
1008(c)	Omitted
1008(d)	6313
1008(e)	6314(a)
1009	6324(b), 6325(a)(1)
1010	Omitted
1011	6211(a), 6653(c)(1)
1012(a)	6212(a), 6213(a)
1012(b)	6155(a), 6215(a)
1012(c)	6155(a), 6213(c)
1012(d)	6213(d)
1012(e)	6214(a)
1012(f)	6212(c), 6213(b)
1012(g), (h)	6214(b), (c)
1012(i)	6161(b)(1), 6165, 7101
1012(j)	6212(b)
1013(a)	6155(a), 6861(a)
1013(b)–(e)	6861(b)–(e)
1013(f)	6863(a), (b)(2), 7101
1013(g)	6155(a), 6863(b)(1)
1013(h)	6863(a), (b)(2)
1013(i)	6155(a), 6861(f)
1013(j)	6861(g)
1014	6404(b)
1015(a)	6871
1015(b)	6155(a), 6161(c), 6503(b), 6873(a)
1016	6501, 6502(a)
1017	6503(a)(1)
1018	Omitted
1019	6653, 6659(b)
1020	6601(a), (f)(1)
1021	6155(a), 6601(a), (d), (f)(1)
1022	6601(a), (c)(3)
1023	6601(a), (c)(1), (f)(1)
1024(a)	7201, 7203
1024(b)	7201
1025(a)	6901(a), (b)
1025(b)–(d)	6901(c), (e), (f)
1025(e)	6904, 7421(b)
1025(f)	6901(h)
1025(g)	6901(g)
1026(a)	6903(a)
1026(b)	6903
1026(c)	6903(b)
1027(a)	6402(a)
1027(b)	6511(a), (b)
1027(c), (d)	6512(a), (b)
1028	Omitted
1029	7805(a)
1030(a)	2502(b)
1030(b)	2511(b)
1031	6103
1100, 1101	7441, 7442
1102(a)–(g)	7443(a)–(g)
1103(a)–(d)	7444(a)–(d)
1104–1106	7445–7447
1110, 111	7451, 7453
1112, 1113	7454(a), 7455
1114(a), (b)	7456(a), (c)
1115(a), (b)	7457(a), (b)
1116	7458
1117(a)–(f)	7459(a)–(f)
1117(g)	6155(a), 6659, 6673
1117(h)	Omitted
1118	7460
1119, 1120, 1121	6902, 7461, 7462
1130–1133	7471–7474
1140–1143	7481–7484
1144	Omitted
1145	7101, 7485(a)
1146	7486
1250–1252	1491–1493
1253	1494, 6071, 6081(a), 6091(a), 6151(a)
1400	3101
1401(a), (b)	3102(a), (b)
1401(c)	6205(a), 6413(a)(1)
1401(d)(1), (2)	Omitted
1401(d)(3), (4)	6413(c)(1), (2)
1402	3502
1403	6051(a)
1410	3111
1411	6205(a), 6413(a)
1412	3112
1420(a)	3501
1420(b)	6601(a), (f)(1)
1420(c)	6011(a), 6071, 6081(a), 6091(a), 6302(b)
1420(d)	6313
1420(e)	3122
1421	6205(b), 6413(b)
1422	3503
1423(a)	6802(1)
1423(b), (c)	6803(a)(1), (2)
1424	7509
1425(a)	7209
1425(b)	7208(1)
1426(a)–(e)	3121(a)–(e)
1426(f)	7701(a)(1)
1426(g)–(*l*)	3121(f)–(k)
1427, 1428	3123, 3124
1429	7805(a), (c)
1430, 1431	Omitted
1432	3125
1500	3201
1501(a), (b)	3202(a), (b)
1501(c)	6205(a)(1), 6413(a)(1)
1502	6205(b), 6413(b)
1503	3502(a)
1510, 1511, 1512	3211, 3212, 3502
1520	3221
1521	6205(a)(1), 6413(a)(1)
1522	6205(b), 6413(b)
1530(a)	3501
1530(b)	6011(a), 6071, 6081(a), 6091(a), 6151(a)
1530(c)	6601(a), (f)(1)
1530(d)	6313
1531	3503
1532(a)–(e)	3231(a)–(e)
1532(f)	7701(a)(9)
1532(g), (h)	3231(f), (g)
1532(i)	7701(a)(1)
1534	3232
1535	7805(a), (c)
1536, 1537	Omitted
1538	3233
1600	3301
1601(a)–(c)	3302
1601(d)	6413(d)
1602	3303
1603	3304
1604(a)	6011(a), 6065, 6071, 6091(b)(1), (2)
1604(b)	6081(a)
1604(c)	6106
1605(a)	3501
1605(b)	6601(a), (f)(1)
1605(c)	6152(a)(3), (b), 6155(a), 6601(c)(2)
1605(d)	6161(a)(1)
1605(e)	6313
1606	3305
1607(a)–(j)	3306(a)–(j)
1607(k)	7701(a)(1)
1607(*l*)–(*o*)	3306(k)–(n)
1608	3307
1609	7805(a), (c)
1610	Omitted
1611	3308
1621	3401
1622(a), (b)	3402(a), (b)
1622(c)(1)(A)	Omitted
1622(c)(1)(B), (2)–(5)	3402(c)
1622(d)	3402(d)
1622(e)	3502(b)
1622(f)(1)	6414
1622(f)(2)	6401, 6402
1622(g)–(k)	3402(e)–(i)
1623	3403
1624	3404, 6011(a)
1625(c)	6081(a)
1626(a)	7204
1626(b)	6674
1626(d)	7205
1627	Omitted
1631	6651(a)
1632	3504
1633(a), (b)	6051(a)–(d)
1633(c)	6081(a)
1634(a)	7204
1634(b)	6659, 6674
1635(a)	6501(a)
1635(b)	6501(c)(1), (3)
1635(c)	6501(c)(2)
1635(d)	6502(a)
1635(e)	6501(b)(2)
1635(f), (g)	Omitted
1636(a)(1)	6511(a), (b)(1)
1636(a)(2)	6511(b)(2)
1636(b)	Omitted
1636(c)	6513(c)
1636(d), (e)	Omitted
1650	4001, 4011, 4021, 4471
1651	4031
1652–1655	Omitted
1656(a), (b), (c)	5063(a), (b), (c)
1657–1659	Omitted
1700	4231, 4232, 6011(a)